P RESENTED

TO

_____

BY

_____

ON

_____

"You will seek me and find me

when you seek me with all your heart."

JEREMIAH 29:13

■

the
JOURNEY

A BIBLE FOR SEEKING GOD
& UNDERSTANDING LIFE

new international version

ZondervanPublishingHouse
Grand Rapids, Michigan

A Division of HarperCollinsPublishers

The Journey: A Bible for Seeking God and Understanding Life
Copyright © 1996 by Willow Creek Association

Requests for information should be addressed to
The Zondervan Corporation
Grand Rapids, Michigan, 49530

Notes, book introductions, Five Alive Reading Plan, introductory articles, and subject
index © 1996 by Willow Creek Association. NIV Dictionary/Concordance © 1994,
Where to Find It © 1986 by Zondervan Publishing House.

The Holy Bible, New International Version
Copyright © 1973, 1978, 1984 by International Bible Society
All rights reserved

Library of Congress Catalog Card Number 95-62351

Published by Willow Creek Association
67 East Algonquin Road
South Barrington, Illinois, 60010, U.S.A.
http://www.willowcreek.com

and

Zondervan Publishing House
Grand Rapids, Michigan, 49530, U.S.A.
http://www.zondervan.com

Printed in the United States of America
All rights reserved

Notes written and edited by
Judson Poling, Willow Creek Church
Bill Perkins
Mark Mittelberg, Willow Creek Association
Michael Vander Klipp, Zondervan Publishing House

Interior design by Sharon Wright
Cover design by Jager Associates, Inc.

97 98 99 00 01 7 6 5 4 3 2 1

RRD

A portion of the purchase price of this NIV Bible has been provided to International Bible Society to support the
work of helping people around the world!

CONTENTS

THE OLD TESTAMENT

THE NEW TESTAMENT

ALPHABETICAL ORDER OF THE BOOKS OF THE BIBLE

The books of the New Testament are indicated by *italics*.

READ THIS FIRST

This is not a Bible for formal religious settings. It's for people in the real world. It's the kind of Bible you take to McDonald's on a Saturday morning. After you've read the sports section in your favorite paper, get a second cup of coffee and spend some time in this book. It'll help you see the "standings" of a much more important league.

This is a Bible for people who work hard—sometimes too hard—and who aren't afraid to look at things in new ways. It's for street-smart types who know how to size up quickly what's a waste of time, and move on. It's for regular folks, those of us who are down-to-earth enough to interrupt with an honest question and discerning enough to detect a phony answer. It's designed to capture the interest of those more familiar with channel surfing than church hopping. It's for people who know some problems don't have tidy, sewn-up solutions but are willing to work to discover the best answers to those problems.

In short, it's written for "seekers."

Now, you may have never labeled yourself a seeker, but it's not a bad title. It shows you're willing to put out some effort to find truth. It means you're a risk-taker, because seeking can lead to finding, and finding can lead to changing. While change doesn't come easy for most of us, a seeker will be willing to change if it means finally coming to terms with truth and where it can be found.

This Bible is guaranteed not to spontaneously burst into flames if it's read by those who don't yet believe it's God's book. Feel free to set it aside and go for long walks to mull over what you just read. Hopefully, this Bible will show up often in the midst of small gatherings of people anxious to talk about the possibility that God is real. A healthy, spirited discussion of its contents would make this book break into a cover-to-cover grin—if books could smile.

There aren't any pages in this Bible to write out your family tree, or to record weddings or funerals. Pick another book for flower pressing. But if you'll read it, ponder it, and put it to the test, this Bible will do something amazing. It will point to answers to some of your most fundamental questions. No, it won't answer them all. But it might direct you to some deeply satisfying conclusions.

Be advised that as you read you may find the tables being turned. This Bible will begin asking some hard questions about *you*. If you're really a seeker, you'll be ready for that. Finding the truth you're looking for is a distinct possibility—and you'll welcome it. Let other people question for questioning's sake. You live in a world where you have to face the facts, even if at first you don't like what you see. *Reality* is the true seeker's bottom line, including reality about oneself.

So, welcome to *The Journey*. And congratulations for taking the time to examine firsthand this version of the all-time best-seller that claims to be a message from God. You're among a minority who have the integrity to check something out before writing it off.

Of course, we don't think you'll write it off. We think you'll find what we have found. You see, according to this book, every true seeker can *know* how much he or she matters to God. The Bible makes it clear: God is fervently seeking to have a relationship with you. We're confident you'll soon discover that for yourself.

Judson Poling, general editor and writer
Bill Perkins, writer
Mark Mittelberg, contributing editor, Willow Creek Association
Michael Vander Klipp, editor, Zondervan Publishing House

WHAT'S A "SPIRITUAL SEEKER"?

If you've picked up this Bible, you may very well be a "spiritual seeker"—someone who is looking for truth. If someone gave this book to you, apparently that person thinks you're a seeker, or hopes you'll soon become one. To be a seeker in the spiritual realm is to seriously consider—or reconsider—what God means to you.

Maybe the success you've enjoyed in your life isn't as satisfying as you thought it would be. Maybe the fun is starting to feel routine. Maybe things you used to deal with are starting to deal with you. Maybe you just want your "good" life to be good at a deeper, more meaningful level. Whatever the case, if you're trying to discover spiritual truth, you're qualified to be called a "seeker."

As a seeker, you're open to the possibility that God might be real and able to make a definite difference. Things in your life don't have to be really rotten to make you become a seeker—you don't have to be desperate. But you're looking for something more, and you've stopped pretending to have it all together. You know you don't know—but you want to know.

So here you are, a seeker, and here is this book, the Bible. Given the time it was written and the cultural differences between then and now, how are you going to understand its message? Fewer and fewer people have been exposed to the Bible through formal education. Yet seekers want to know what's in these pages—not only because the Bible has sold more copies than any other book in history, but because so many people claim they've met God as they've read its pages and embraced its message. In light of the Bible's enduring reputation, can a person be open-minded and not give it at least some consideration?

Several features make this book "user-friendly" for those trying to comprehend the Bible for the first time. To begin with, it contains an accurate and easily understandable translation of the Bible called the *New International Version*—one of the most widely read English-language translations in print today. Paired with that excellent translation are informational notes that highlight passages of special interest to seekers. These notes fall into the following six categories:

Discovering God

Reasons to Believe

Addressing Questions

Knowing Yourself

Strengthening Relationships

Managing Resources

Be careful not to confuse the comments of our writers and editors with the actual text of the Bible. In these notes we hoped to address those areas of life most often questioned by people engaged in a spiritual search. If you want to further explore specific themes, see the index to subjects at the back of this book (page 1663).

Bible book introductions summarize the central ideas and give general information about the various books, and introductory articles use everyday illustrations to help the reader who is unfamiliar with the Bible "dig in" to the text. In the back you'll find a reference tool called a "dictionary concordance," designed to define any unfamiliar terms or ideas that you find as you study (page 1669). And don't miss the feature called "Where to Find It," which lists locations of the Biblical events that are most familiar to people who have had some exposure to the Bible (page 1699). Finally, there's some fairly helpful information in the beginning of the Bible—this article, for example!

So what's the best way to begin? Do you just start reading at page 1? Do you indiscriminately flip pages hoping God will mystically talk to you? Because the Bible is actually a collection of individual books, we suggest that you first get an overview by reading from a few books, then go back and read the rest of the Bible. For this purpose we've developed a reading plan that focuses on five key Bible books: Genesis (page 2), Deuteronomy (page 212), John (page 1380), Acts (page 1422) and Romans (page 1466). By reading them, you will get a fairly comprehensive view of the main themes of the whole Bible. (See page xix for more information on the "Five Alive" reading plan.)

If you'd like an even quicker summary, we suggest that you begin by reading the Gospel of John (it begins on page 1380). There you'll find out about Jesus, the One who's at the center of everything else that's written in the Bible.

Finally, for people who are anxious to read the Bible's message in brief, we've prepared a summary of the Bible's message using actual quotes from various books. This brief synopsis isn't a substitute for reading the Bible, but it's a great way to catch a glimpse of the big picture. You can read it beginning on page xv.

A word of caution: Be careful not to read into the Bible things it doesn't really say. Opening the Bible and pointing to a verse for inspiration—sort of a "flip-and-sip" method of studying the Bible—can lead to deceptive interpretations. Always take into account a verse's context. Study themes within the Bible, not just unrelated statements here and there. Determine that when you don't understand something, you'll use some of the helps in this Bible to get at the meaning. Also, talk to somebody who is familiar with the Bible's teaching. It's O.K. to ask questions—that's what a seeker is supposed to do!

Understand that you hold in your hands an entire library that offers the potential for a lifetime of learning. While you may eventually "graduate" to a more detailed study version (such as *The Student Bible, The Quest Study Bible* or *The NIV Study Bible*), the Bible you have here is an excellent beginning point. It's designed to set you on a course we hope you'll continue on for the rest of your life.

That, in a nutshell, is what *The Journey* is all about. We sincerely hope you'll understand and benefit from it.

There is one other thing we should tell you up front: You're not the only seeker in this process. No, we're not talking about all the other spiritual inquirers out there. We're talking about someone who is seeking *you.*

You see, Jesus Christ is the ultimate "seeker." He once said his whole purpose was "to seek and to save what was lost" (Luke chapter 19, verse 10 [page 1369]). So as you read, remember: *The Bible isn't so much a book about people's search for God as it is a record of God's search for us.* It's the story of God's repeated refusal to allow humanity to wander away from him unchallenged. In this book, you'll see how God made possible "life in the opposite direction"—a life he offers you.

As a seeker, we think you'll end up finding what you're looking for! Jesus went so far as to promise you actually would (see Matthew chapter 7, verses 7 and 8 [page 1267]). If you're ot willing to let that happen, reconsider before you get in too deep! This is not a "safe" ook—its message is a life-changing one. And it's fine if you don't yet believe that message. od's promise to you today is simply this: "You will seek me and find me when you seek me ith all your heart" (Jeremiah chapter 29, verse 13 [page 1032]).

HOW TO SEEK GOD

Are you a seeker? If so, we offer you some good news and some bad news. The good news is that God is not lost in the woods. The bad new is, *you are.*
This realization can be painful. It involves facing your own finite nature and recog nizing that some of your life choices have been less than "enlightened." It's O.K. to admit th you're not sure of God, but if you're a true seeker, you'll admit that you're not so sure of you self, either. Rest assured that you don't have to go it alone—God wants to help you find the right path through the forest of your life.

Becoming a genuine seeker means you've begun to open yourself up to a different way of living—one that includes God in the loop. That thought contains great possibilities, and some potentially frightening implications. Clearly, if you become convinced that God exists and you choose to follow him, you'll never be the same again. And change is hard for most us.

So what are you supposed to do as a seeker? How can you go about this all-important task of pursuing God and his truth? Well, the outline below doesn't claim to be the final and authoritative word on the subject. But with a humble recognition that the stakes are sky-high—and believing you are very precious to God—here are four questions to help you in you search. They aren't the map to your ultimate destination, but they may keep you from getting waylaid while you make your journey.

1. Why do you want to know God—what do you hope to get from him?

People seek God for a variety of reasons. Some think their search will lead to a more ful filling life or a greater sense of purpose. Others are looking for relief from their pain. Still oth ers are curious and just want to find out what's true. What is your reason? You should be aware of your aspirations and motivations, because you may be looking for the wrong thing.

Perhaps you're a seeker, for example, because you want to find greater happiness. Wha if you do find God, but your life circumstances lead to *less* happiness? Will you feel cheated? Believers often report that God gives them greater joy, meaning and purpose in life. But nearly every believer will also admit to experiencing periods of difficulty.

So this is a good question to ask yourself: What am I looking for? And, conversely, Wha does God offer me? As you read this Bible you'll discover how much he's already given. But he may not give you exactly what you've anticipated. So expect the unexpected, and make it your goal to find God, no matter what the outcome or perks. The bottom line is that a true seeker seeks the Giver of life, not just his gifts.

2. Are you placing limitations on what God can ask from you?

Two people who have fallen deeply in love don't go into a marriage with the intention o ignoring each other's wishes after the wedding ceremony. Such a commitment involves adjusting personal priorities in the interest of building the relationship. When they establish their residence, for example, a couple will usually discuss at length the furnishings, wall hangings, and other touches that will make their house (or apartment) a home. In the same way, it would be absurd for a seeker to open up to God but give no thought to the possibility that God may want to rearrange a few pieces of furniture when he moves in.

Of course, some people are fearful that God wants to throw out all the furniture and condemn their house as uninhabitable. They think that God is just waiting to stifle their ever pleasure and ridicule their every action. But nothing could be further from the truth! God cre ated us to be in relationship with him and with each other. Through creation, through the ole, and through Jesus Christ, God tells us that he wants us to enjoy this life in a way that's line with his purpose for us.

But the question remains: Do you realize that God wants to be a powerful presence in ur life, not just an idea in your head? Following him means following his *leadership*. So let's honest—accepting that leadership will affect your lifestyle.

Here is where many seekers' searches find the ditch. They declare intellectual reasons dismissing the claims of the Bible, but in truth they are not willing to give up some activity ey know is offensive to God. If that's you, you need to know that God will take you as you e, but he doesn't want to leave you as you are. He wants you to let him make you into what wants you to be.

What do you think about Jesus?

A spiritual seeker may think the proper order of inquiry is to first decide if there's a God philosophical question) and then figure out who Jesus is (a historical question). But other and possibly even more exciting way would be to reverse the order, or at least work ough the questions in tandem.

Many seekers discover that when they deal with the person of Jesus, at the same time ey find answers to many of their other questions.

■ Is there a God? (Yes, and he came to earth in human form in the person of Jesus Christ. See John chapter 16, verse 28 [page 1410].)
■ Does God love me? (Yes! Look at what he did to show that love. See John chapter 3, verses 16–17 [page 1387].)
■ What religion is the right one? (Reconsider that question in light of the fact that God wants a relationship with *you*, not your religious affiliation. See Galatians chapter 3, verses 26–28 [page 1527].)
■ What do I have to do to live forever? (Accept Jesus as your forgiver and your leader. See John chapter 3, verse 36 [page 1387].)
■ How can I experience meaning and purpose in life? (By following Jesus and by culti- vating your relationships with God and with other people. See Matthew chapter 22, verses 37–40 [page 1290].)

According to the Bible, until a seeker comes to terms with Jesus, he or she hasn't dealt ith the issue that's most important in starting a relationship with God.

Consider this reality: Jesus is the most influential person in history. This poor itinerant eacher, the son of a carpenter but also the Son of God, changed the entire course of world story. How can any serious spiritual search overlook him? For example, look at any calen- ar. Today's date is based on a reckoning that hinges on Jesus' life. Because of him, people ere moved to split world history into two eras—"before him" and "after him" (B.C. and A.D.).

How will you respond to Jesus?

It's not enough to intellectually agree with Jesus' claims. If you read through this book d recognize Jesus as the true Son of God, a man who walked the earth, lived a perfect life, ed, and rose again from the dead, you must choose to cross the line of faith and receive m. This is a once-for-all decision—a "crisis." A "process" follows, but you have to start by viting him into your life and accepting that he paid the debt you owe for your sin but could ever pay yourself.

Salvation in Jesus is a totally free gift, and receiving it is as easy as saying, "Jesus, I cknowledge my sin and your payment for it on the cross. I now ask you to be my forgiver nd leader." But you must respond personally and deliberately or the gift will remain nopened and unenjoyed.

ome Practical Helps

Keeping in mind the above questions, here are some practical ideas to guide you in your piritual search:

■ Ask God to reveal himself to you if you're not sure he's there.

- Read what is contained within these pages, especially the summary "Five Alive" bo (Genesis, Deuteronomy, John, Acts, Romans).
- Talk to people who display a genuine relationship with God; those who obviously lo him and who live their lives by a different set of principles.
- Spend time in nature, observing and experiencing God's creation.
- Listen to older people who have walked with God for a long time.
- Question things everybody seems to take for granted—be a lover of truth.
- Ask God-followers *why* they believe what they believe and how they know their beliefs are true.
- Recognize that following God must make sense: Truth may go beyond reason, but against it.
- Read what other believers say about Christianity—spend time scouring the shelves a Christian bookstore or church library for credible authors, or ask your Christian friends for a list of authors who have inspired them in their walk with God.
- Write down your questions, especially about what you read in the Bible, and take them to a knowledgeable Christian who respects your seeking process.
- Expect ongoing questions and some doubts along the way.
- Know your presuppositions—the things you already believe—and try not to let them interfere with your quest for the truth.
- Stay open to actually finding what you're looking for—fear of commitment and chan can keep you from finding the truth.
- Keep a journal of your thoughts and feelings during your search.
- Know your personal issues—your past will profoundly influence your present ability be objective.
- Remember that you don't have to know everything to know something.
- Determine to seek for a specific period of time, and continually evaluate your progress. Then try to reach an appropriate conclusion.
- *Act* on what you decide.

"Ask and it will be given to you; seek and you will find; knock and the door will be opened you. For everyone who asks receives; he who seeks finds; and to him who knocks, the door will be opened."

—Jesus (Matthew chapter 7, verses 7–

A SUMMARY OF THE BIBLE

— In Its Own Words

In the beginning God created the heavens and the earth. Then God said, "Let us make man in our image, in our likeness, and let them rule over the fish of the sea and the birds of the air, over the livestock, over all the earth, and over all the creatures that ⸺e along the ground." So God created man in his own image, in the image of God he cre⸺ ⸺ him; male and female he created them. God saw all that he had made, and it was very ⸺d.

God made mankind upright, but men have gone in search of many schemes.

The LORD saw how great man's wickedness on the earth had become, and that every ⸺nation of the thoughts of his heart was only evil all the time. The LORD was grieved that ⸺ad made man on the earth, and his heart was filled with pain.

After this, the word of the LORD came to Abram in a vision: "Do not be afraid, Abram. I ⸺ your shield, your very great reward." He took him outside and said, "Look up at the heav⸺ and count the stars—if indeed you can count them." Then he said to him, "So shall your ⸺pring be." Abram believed the LORD, and he credited it to him as righteousness.

When Abram was ninety-nine years old, the LORD appeared to him and said, "I am God ⸺ighty; walk before me and be blameless. I will confirm my covenant between me and you ⸺ will greatly increase your numbers." Abram fell face down, and God said to him, "As for ⸺ this is my covenant with you: You will be the father of many nations. No longer will you ⸺ called Abram; your name will be Abraham, for I have made you a father of many nations. I ⸺ make you very fruitful; I will make nations of you, and kings will come from you.

Hear, O heavens! Listen, O earth! For the LORD has spoken: "I reared children and ⸺ught them up, but they have rebelled against me. The ox knows his master, the donkey ⸺ owner's manger, but Israel does not know, my people do not understand. Ah, sinful ⸺on, a people loaded with guilt, a brood of evildoers, children given to corruption! They ⸺e forsaken the LORD; they have spurned the Holy One of Israel and turned their backs on ⸺. The multitude of your sacrifices—what are they to me?" says the LORD. "I have more than ⸺ough of burnt offerings, of rams and the fat of fattened animals; I have no pleasure in the ⸺od of bulls and lambs and goats. Come now, let us reason together," says the LORD. ⸺ough your sins are like scarlet, they shall be as white as snow; though they are red as ⸺nson, they shall be like wool."

Nevertheless, there will be no more gloom for those who were in distress. In the future ⸺ will honor Galilee of the Gentiles, by the way of the sea, along the Jordan—The people ⸺lking in darkness have seen a great light; on those living in the land of the shadow of ⸺th a light has dawned. For to us a child is born, to us a son is given, and the government ⸺ be on his shoulders. And he will be called Wonderful Counselor, Mighty God, Everlasting ⸺her, Prince of Peace. Of the increase of his government and peace there will be no end. ⸺ will reign on David's throne and over his kingdom, establishing and upholding it with jus⸺e and righteousness from that time on and forever. The zeal of the LORD Almighty will ⸺complish this.

He grew up before him like a tender shoot, and like a root out of dry ground. He had no ⸺auty or majesty to attract us to him, nothing in his appearance that we should desire him. ⸺ was despised and rejected by men, a man of sorrows, and familiar with suffering. Like ⸺e from whom men hide their faces he was despised, and we esteemed him not. Surely he ⸺k up our infirmities and carried our sorrows, yet we considered him stricken by God, smit⸺ by him, and afflicted. But he was pierced for our transgressions, he was crushed for our iniquities; the punishment that brought us peace was upon him, and by his wounds we are healed. We all, like sheep, have gone astray, each of us has turned to his own way; and the LORD has laid on him the iniquity of us all. He was assigned a grave with the wicked, and with the rich in his death, though he had done no violence, nor was any deceit in his mouth. Yet it was the LORD's will to crush him and cause him to suffer, and though the LORD makes his life a guilt offering, he will see his offspring and prolong his days, and the will of the LORD will prosper in his hand. After the suffering of his soul, he will see the light of life and be satisfied; by his knowledge my righteous servant will justify many, and he will bear their iniquities.

In the past God spoke to our forefathers through the prophets at many times and in various ways, but in these last days he has spoken to us by his Son, whom he appointed heir of all things, and through whom he made the universe. The Son is the radiance of God's glory and the exact representation of his being, sustaining all things by his powerful word. He was with God in the beginning. In him was life, and that life was the light of men.

There came a man who was sent from God; his name was John. He came as a witness to testify concerning that light, so that through him all men might believe. He himself was not the light; he came only as a witness to the light. The true light that gives light to every man was coming into the world. He was in the world, and though the world was made through him, the world did not recognize him. He came to that which was his own, but his own did not receive him. Yet to all who received him, to those who believed in his name, he gave the right to become children of God.

The Word became flesh and made his dwelling among us. We have seen his glory, the glory of the One and Only, who came from the Father, full of grace and truth. For the law was given through Moses; grace and truth came through Jesus Christ. He is the image of the invisible God, the firstborn over all creation. For by him all things were created: things in heaven and on earth, visible and invisible, whether thrones or powers or rulers or authorities; all things were created by him and for him. He is before all things, and in him all things hold together. And he is the head of the body, the church; he is the beginning and the firstborn from among the dead, so that in everything he might have the supremacy. For God was pleased to have all his fullness dwell in him, and through him to reconcile to himself all things, whether things on earth or things in heaven, by making peace through his blood, shed on the cross. For in Christ all the fullness of the Deity lives in bodily form.

And there were shepherds living out in the fields nearby, keeping watch over their flocks at night. An angel of the Lord appeared to them, and the glory of the Lord shone around them, and they were terrified. But the angel said to them, "Do not be afraid. I bring you good news of great joy that will be for all the people. Today in the town of David a Savior has been born to you; he is Christ the Lord."

And Jesus grew in wisdom and stature, and in favor with God and men.

Now Jesus himself was about thirty years old when he began his ministry. He went to Nazareth, where he had been brought up, and on the Sabbath day he went into the synagogue, as was his custom. And he stood up to read. The scroll of the prophet Isaiah was handed to him. Unrolling it, he found the place where it is written: "The Spirit of the Lord is on me, because he has anointed me to preach good news to the poor. He has sent me to proclaim freedom for the prisoners and recovery of sight for the blind, to release the oppressed, to proclaim the year of the Lord's favor." Then he rolled up the scroll, gave it back to the attendant and sat down. The eyes of everyone in the synagogue were fastened on him, and he began by saying to them, "Today this scripture is fulfilled in your hearing."

"I tell you the truth, if anyone keeps my word, he will never see death." At this the Jews exclaimed, "Now we know that you are demon-possessed! Abraham died and so did the prophets, yet you say that if anyone keeps your word, he will never taste death. Are you greater than our father Abraham? He died, and so did the prophets. Who do you think you are?" Jesus replied, "If I glorify myself, my glory means nothing. My Father, whom you claim as your God, is the one who glorifies me. Though you do not know him, I know him. If I said

not, I would be a liar like you, but I do know him and keep his word. Your father Abra-
m rejoiced at the thought of seeing my day; he saw it and was glad." "You are not yet fifty
ars old," the Jews said to him, "and you have seen Abraham!" "I tell you the truth," Jesus
swered, "before Abraham was born, I am!"

When Jesus came to the region of Caesarea Philippi, he asked his disciples, "Who do
ople say the Son of Man is?" They replied, "Some say John the Baptist; others say Elijah;
d still others, Jeremiah or one of the prophets." "But what about you?" he asked. "Who do
u say I am?" Simon Peter answered, "You are the Christ, the Son of the living God." Jesus
plied, "Blessed are you, Simon son of Jonah, for this was not revealed to you by man, but
my Father in heaven."

Now the Passover and the Feast of Unleavened Bread were only two days away, and the
ief priests and the teachers of the law were looking for some sly way to arrest Jesus and
him. "But not during the Feast," they said, "or the people may riot." Then Judas Iscariot,
e of the Twelve, went to the chief priests to betray Jesus to them. They were delighted to
ar this and promised to give him money. So he watched for an opportunity to hand him
er.

Now the betrayer had arranged a signal with them: "The one I kiss is the man; arrest
m and lead him away under guard." Going at once to Jesus, Judas said, "Rabbi!" and
ssed him. The men seized Jesus and arrested him. The chief priests and the whole San-
drin were looking for evidence against Jesus so that they could put him to death, but they
d not find any. Many testified falsely against him, but their statements did not agree. Then
e high priest stood up before them and asked Jesus, "Are you not going to answer? What
this testimony that these men are bringing against you?" But Jesus remained silent and
ve no answer. Again the high priest asked him, "Are you the Christ, the Son of the Blessed
e?" "I am," said Jesus. "And you will see the Son of Man sitting at the right hand of the
ghty One and coming on the clouds of heaven." The high priest tore his clothes. "Why do
need any more witnesses?" he asked. "You have heard the blasphemy. What do you
nk?" They all condemned him as worthy of death.

They brought Jesus to the place called Golgotha (which means The Place of the Skull).
d they crucified him. Dividing up his clothes, they cast lots to see what each would get. It
as the third hour when they crucified him. The written notice of the charge against him
ad: THE KING OF THE JEWS. And at the ninth hour Jesus cried out in a loud voice, *"Eloi, Eloi,*
ma sabachthani?"–which means, "My God, my God, why have you forsaken me?" With a
ud cry, Jesus breathed his last. The curtain of the temple was torn in two from top to bot-
m. And when the centurion, who stood there in front of Jesus, heard his cry and saw how
died, he said, "Surely this man was the Son of God!"

When the Sabbath was over, Mary Magdalene, Mary the mother of James, and Salome
ught spices so that they might go to anoint Jesus' body. Very early on the first day of the
eek, just after sunrise, they were on their way to the tomb and they asked each other, "Who
ll roll the stone away from the entrance of the tomb?" But when they looked up, they saw
at the stone, which was very large, had been rolled away. As they entered the tomb, they
w a young man dressed in a white robe sitting on the right side, and they were alarmed.
on't be alarmed," he said. "You are looking for Jesus the Nazarene, who was crucified. He
as risen! He is not here."

Suddenly Jesus met them. "Greetings," he said. They came to him, clasped his feet and
orshiped him. Then Jesus said to them, "Do not be afraid. Go and tell my brothers to go to
alilee; there they will see me."

Now Thomas (called Didymus), one of the Twelve, was not with the disciples when
sus came. So the other disciples told him, "We have seen the Lord!" But he said to them,
nless I see the nail marks in his hands and put my finger where the nails were, and put my
and into his side, I will not believe it." A week later his disciples were in the house again,
d Thomas was with them. Though the doors were locked, Jesus came and stood among

them and said, "Peace be with you!" Then he said to Thomas, "Put your finger here; see my hands. Reach out your hand and put it into my side. Stop doubting and believe." Thomas s to him, "My Lord and my God!"

If you confess with your mouth, "Jesus is Lord," and believe in your heart that God raised him from the dead, you will be saved. For it is with your heart that you believe and a justified, and it is with your mouth that you confess and are saved. As the Scripture says, "Anyone who trusts in him will never be put to shame." For there is no difference between Jew and Gentile —the same Lord is Lord of all and richly blesses all who call on him, for, "Everyone who calls on the name of the Lord will be saved." Salvation is found in no one el for there is no other name under heaven given to men by which we must be saved.

You know the message God sent to the people of Israel, telling the good news of pea through Jesus Christ, who is Lord of all. You know what has happened throughout Judea, beginning in Galilee after the baptism that John preached—how God anointed Jesus of Nazareth with the Holy Spirit and power, and how he went around doing good and healing all who were under the power of the devil, because God was with him. We are witnesses o everything he did in the country of the Jews and in Jerusalem. They killed him by hanging him on a tree, but God raised him from the dead on the third day and caused him to be se

Jesus did many other miraculous signs in the presence of his disciples, which are not recorded in this book. But these are written that you may believe that Jesus is the Christ, th Son of God, and that by believing you may have life in his name.

Gen. 1:1, Gen. 1:26, Gen. 1:27, Gen. 1:31, Eccl. 7:29, Gen. 6:5, Gen. 6:6, Gen. 15:1, Gen. 15:5, Gen. 15:6, Gen. 17 Gen. 17:2, Gen. 17:3, Gen. 17:4, Gen. 17:5, Gen. 17:6, Isa. 1:2, Isa. 1:3, Isa. 1:4, Isa. 1:11, Isa. 1:18, Isa. 9:1, Isa. 9 Isa. 9:6, Isa. 9:7, Isa. 53:2, Isa. 53:3, Isa. 53:4, Isa. 53:5, Isa. 53:6, Isa. 53:9, Isa. 53:10, Isa. 53:11, Hebr. 1:1, Hebr. 1:2, Hebr. 1:3, John 1:2, John 1:4, John 1:6, John 1:7, John 1:8, John 1:9, John 1:10, John 1:11, John 1:12, John 1:14, John 1:17, Col. 1:15, Col. 1:16, Col. 1:17, Col. 1:18, Col. 1:19, Col. 1:20, Col. 2:9, Luke 2:8, Luke 2:9, Luke 2:10, Luke 2:11, Luke 2:52, Luke 3:23, Luke 4:16, Luke 4:17, Luke 4:18, Luke 4:19, Luke 4:20, Luke 4:21, John 8:51, John 8:52, John 8:53, John 8:54, John 8:55, John 8:56, John 8:57, John 8:58, Matt. 16:13, Matt. 16:14, Mat 16:15, Matt. 16:16, Matt. 16:17, Mark 14:1, Mark 14:2, Mark 14:10, Mark 14:11, Mark 14:44, Mark 14:45, Mark 14:46, Mark 14:55, Mark 14:56, Mark 14:60, Mark 14:61, Mark 14:62, Mark 14:63, Mark 14:64, Mark 15:22, Mar 15:24, Mark 15:25, Mark 15:26, Mark 15:34, Mark 15:37, Mark 15:38, Mark 15:39, Mark 16:1, Mark 16:2, Mark 16:3, Mark 16:4, Mark 16:5, Mark 16:6, Matt. 28:9, Matt. 28:10, John 20:24, John 20:25, John 20:26, John 20:27 John 20:28, Rom. 10:9, Rom. 10:10, Rom. 10:11, Rom. 10:12, Rom. 10:13, Acts 4:12, Acts 10:36, Acts 10:37, Acts 10:38, Acts 10:39, Acts 10:40, John 20:30, John 20:31.

FIVE ALIVE

A One-Month Reading Plan Covering Five Books that Contain the Essential Teachings of the Bible

---

READING PLAN

(age xx for book summaries and main themes.)

1 *Genesis 1—4*
d creates a perfect world, but humanity falls into sin.

2 *Genesis 5—9*
d destroys the evil world with a flood but spares Noah
d his family. The rainbow is the sign of God's promise
recreate instead of obliterate humanity.

3 *Genesis 10—14*
umanity rebels against God again at the tower of
bel; God calls Abram to start a "new community."

4 *Genesis 15—19*
d pledges to bless the whole world through Abram;
destroys Sodom and Gomorrah, showing his resolve
restrain human sin.

5 *Genesis 20—24*
aac, the son of God's promise, is born. God provides
m with a family, and so expands his covenant people.

6 *Genesis 25—28*
cob deceives his twin brother Esau and his father Isaac,
t experiences God's kindness in spite of his scheming.

7 *Genesis 29—36*
e story of Jacob's family life and reconciliation with Esau.

8 *Genesis 37—41*
seph earns his brothers' envy and is betrayed. Through
fascinating series of events, Joseph goes from being a
ave and prisoner to being second in command under
ypt's Pharaoh.

9 *Genesis 42—45*
seph's brothers come to Egypt looking for food,
d discover that God has turned their treachery into
umph for Joseph.

10 *Genesis 46—50*
cob's entire family moves to Egypt, and the nation of
rael flourishes.

11 *Deuteronomy 1—6*
oses, God's chosen leader over Israel, prepares God's
eople to enter the promised land by reviewing God's
mmands (including the Ten Commandments).

12 *Deuteronomy 7—10*
oses makes predictions of prosperity for an obedient
rael and gives them warnings from their past.

13 *Deuteronomy 11—15*
oses gives the people God's rules for worship, cleanli-
ss and respect for each other in the promised land.

14 *Deuteronomy 16—20*
e Israelites hear God's rules about worship festivals, es-
blishing a government and legal system, and going to war.

15 *Deuteronomy 21—25*
ese chapters contain instructions for keeping the peo-
le of Israel from evil influences.

16 *Deuteronomy 26—30*
od gives Israel a choice: "Obey me and live, or disobey
d be destroyed."

17 *Deuteronomy 31—34*
oses appoints a successor, blesses the tribes of
rael, and gets a final look at God's promised land
efore he dies.

Day 18 *John 1—5*
After waiting many centuries, Israel gets its first look at
its Messiah, Jesus, who shows his divinity through various miracles.

Day 19 *John 6—11*
Jesus affirms his identity as the Messiah and performs
convincing miracles. The Jewish leaders refuse to accept
Jesus' claims and plot to have him killed.

Day 20 *John 12—16*
Jesus enters Jerusalem in triumph and predicts his coming suffering and death. He promises that the Holy Spirit
will come to take his place when he returns to heaven.

Day 21 *John 17—21*
Jesus prays for all his followers throughout all time and
resolutely faces his execution. Three days later he
appears again alive—victorious forever over the power of
death!

Day 22 *Acts 1—5*
Christ ascends to heaven and, as promised, the Holy
Spirit comes. The church grows by leaps and bounds,
and Jewish opposition heats up.

Day 23 *Acts 6—10*
Persecution scatters believers so that Christ's message is
heard in non-Jewish regions. Saul's conversion and
Peter's vision serve to sharpen the new church's focus
on reaching all people everywhere.

Day 24 *Acts 11—15*
Church leaders in Jerusalem debate Jewish custom as it
relates to non-Jewish believers. Meanwhile, the apostles
continue their bold stand for Christ in faraway cities.

Day 25 *Acts 16—20*
Paul and the apostles travel to various cities where they
preach and experience opposition, persecution, prison,
and even a riot. Still, the church grows in each city.

Day 26 *Acts 21—28*
This is the action-packed account of Paul's arrest and
journey to stand trial in Rome; eventually he carries the
word of Christ's resurrection to the leaders of this leading capital city of the ancient world.

Day 27 *Romans 1—4*
Paul begins this letter by emphasizing the "bad news"
that all have sinned, but then shares the "good
news" that reconciliation with God is available through
faith in Jesus Christ.

Day 28 *Romans 5—8*
Paul tells us that even though sin is pervasive and powerful, we can have the assurance that all of our sin is
covered by Christ's death and resurrection. A new life is
available through a relationship with Jesus Christ.

Day 29 *Romans 9—11*
Paul explains that God, in his grace, chooses disobedient
people to become his followers—just as he did with the
Israelites of long ago. Only because of God's work can
anyone be rescued from sin.

Day 30 *Romans 12—16*
Paul gives guidelines for living the kind of life that
pleases God day by day.

FIVE ALIVE
Book Summaries and Main Themes

GENESIS

What It's About

This book, written by the prophet Moses, outlines the "beginnings" of God's work in this world. It describes the perfect creation—including humans—that God made out of nothing. Unfortunately, the relationship between the first people and God was broken by rebellion. God refused to give up, and the rest of the book outlines how God reached out to various individuals, promising to be their God if they in turn would promise to serve him exclusively. These people—Noah, Abraham, Isaac, Jacob and Joseph—were the ancestors of the Jews. Out of this family line, God eventually brought Jesus Christ into the world—the one who would repair the brokenness between us and God forever.

What To Look For

- One God, who is a person and who created the universe.
- Humanity's rejection of God—the "fall."
- God's kindness in reaching out to people and promising to be their God.
- How God works out his purposes even through imperfect people.

DEUTERONOMY

What It's About

This book represents Moses' last words to the people of Israel. Throughout its pages Moses summarizes God's laws for his people's lives. He also encourages Israel to follow these laws because of the benefits such obedience will bring. God's love for his people shines through this book, and many of the principles that govern that relationship apply across the board every generation. Although we will encounter trials and struggles throughout our lives (as the Israelites), God promises to remain faithful because of his everlasting love.

What To Look For

- God's love and concern for his people.
- God's rules, which reveal his holy character.
- The common sense contained in God's laws.
- The call to remain true to God, no matter what.

JOHN

What It's About

In this book, John looks deeply into the meaning behind Jesus' life on this earth. He introduces Jesus Christ as the miracle-working Son of God, the Savior who was promised to Abraham, Isaac, and Jacob. This truth is laid out in the very first paragraph of the book, where John declares that Jesus Christ—the "word"—participated in creating the universe. Even though some of these ideas are complex, John brings them all together in chapter 3, verse 16, where he provides the Bible's most concise explanation of the plan of salvation. Later the book John sums up his goals for his work: "These are written that you may believe that Jesus is the Christ, the Son of God, and that by believing you may have life in his name" (chapter 20, verse 31).

To Look For

- Evidence that Jesus Christ is God's unique Son, and that he was present with his heavenly Father even at creation.
- The details of John's eyewitness account, which focus on the significance of Jesus' miracles and teaching.
- Jesus' work in the world described by images of life, light, water, bread and fruit.
- The direct way that John explains Jesus' mission on earth.

S

It's About

exciting book was written by Luke, the author of one of the four Biblical books about s' life. This book's main focus is the story of how the good news of Jesus' victory over n spread like wildfire throughout the Mediterranean region. Luke's readers follow the of the disciples as they perform amazing miracles and preach to multitudes of people. also meet Paul, a missionary who once persecuted Jesus' followers. The account of s conversion—including a flash of light from the sky and Christ's own voice—is one of most dramatic stories in the book. Acts follows the apostles on a whirlwind tour of many where the word of Christ's resurrection was first heard and believed, even in the midst rsecution. The last few chapters tell the story of Paul's trip to Rome—delayed by a fierce n and a violent shipwreck—to stand trial before Caesar himself. Each of the apostles rienced trouble and danger as they spoke to others about their faith. But Christ never em, for he was at work in them through the Spirit—exactly as he is in his followers to-

To Look For

- The amazing power of the Holy Spirit to change the lives of individuals.
- The spread of the church and the incredible numbers of new believers in Jesus.
- How the apostles responded to Christ's directives, even though they suffered for their faithfulness.
- The strong message that Jesus and the new life he offers is for all people.

MANS

It's About

l, nobody's perfect." This common phrase has been true since the beginning of human ry. The third chapter of this book picks up that theme as it sums up this letter from Paul e church in Rome (perhaps before you jump into the reading plan you'd like to skim this ter first). In it Paul explains that we all disobey God and our conscience, no matter how ll we think we are. That's what it means to be a "sinner." The good news of Romans is God has provided a way that we can be forgiven and experience a new quality of life. In pter 8, one of the Bible's most powerful passages, Paul tells us that the only life worth liv- s the one that has been "captured" by God's Spirit and is being led by him. Paul suffered air share of persecution, but God's goodness carried him through every hardship. Paul ts us to know, "If a guy like me can do it, so can you."

To Look For

- The clear message that we're forgiven—"saved"—by trust in God, not by our own efforts.
- Paul's response when faced with challenges and his admission that he's no super-man.
- Paul's frank discussion of his own inner struggles.
- The power that we can tap into when we live our lives with the help of the Spirit.

GENESIS

Introduction

THE BOTTOM LINE

This book answers some of life's deepest questions, such as "Where did everything come from?" and "Why are we here?" In it you'll find out about your maker, the powerful being we call "God." You'll also find out why our world is in such a mess today—because of sin, committed by people who were remarkably like us. As you read through this book, you discover the good news that God hasn't given up on us. Long ago he began a plan that unfolds throughout the rest of the Bible—and continues today—to restore what was lost the beginning.

CENTRAL IDEAS

- God created the universe and is its only rightful ruler.
- People—not God—have spoiled the perfect creation that God made.
- God worked through his chosen people (e.g., Noah, Abraham) to spread the news of his desire to close the gap between himself and people.
- God uses ordinary people to accomplish his purposes in this world.

OUTLINE

1 Creation history (1:1–11:26)
 A Adam and Eve (2:4–25)
 B Sin enters the world (ch. 3)
 C Sin's progress (4:1–16)
 D Genealogies (4:17–5:32)
 E The great flood (6:1–9:29)
 F Spread of the nations (10:1–11:26)
2 Human history (11:27–50:26)
 A Abraham (11:27–25:18)
 B Jacob (25:19–35:29)
 C Esau (36:1–37:1)
 D Joseph (37:2–50:26)

TITLE

Genesis means "beginnings"—the beginning of the universe, of human history, and of God's dealings with humankind.

AUTHOR AND READERS

Moses, leader of the Israelites in the ancient world, wrote this book. Although it gives an account of our human ancestors, the truths it contains are for every person on earth.

On my eighth birthday my parents gave me a BB gun. Its cold steel barrel and carved wooden stock made it a thing of beauty. The gun and I formed a deadly partnership. Cans, bottles, road signs—nothing was safe from us.

Well, almost nothing. One afternoon I raised my gun and aimed at a bird perched in the willow tree in our backyard. Just as I was about to squeeze the trigger, my older sister, Patsy, ran into the yard waving her arms and yelling. As the bird fluttered away, Patsy looked at me and smiled. She said nothing, but her smug face taunted, "See, I have more power than you!"

In that moment something inside of me took control. I lowered the barrel and aimed at my sister. A look of horror replaced her smug confidence, and she took off at a full run. I aimed at the part of her I considered most heavily padded and thought, "Sit on this!" as I pulled the trigger. The BB found its mark, and she grabbed her posterior and yelped. She darted into the house screaming, "I've been shot! I've been shot!" For a brief moment I wondered what had made me do something so cruel—then I realized how much I enjoyed it.

lowered the barrel and aimed at my sister.

After my dad disciplined me, he confiscated my gun. But while he had the power to take away the tools I used for evil, he wasn't able to take away that dark part of my personality that enjoyed doing wrong.

All of us have areas in our lives in which we have, at best, mixed motives. We know to do the right thing, yet we end up doing what is wrong. The particulars of our inner battles may be different, but we all struggle with duplicity. We all have enjoyed doing what we know we shouldn't. We've all groveled before some authority, justifying our excesses, promising reform, and pleading for mercy. And we've all gone right out and done the same thing over again.

The Bible is the only book in the world that adequately explains the source of this universal phenomenon. It doesn't shy away from describing a wide assortment of human failures, and it contains ample illustrations of sinful people in action. This first book, Genesis, makes it clear that after God made the world good, something happened that spoiled it. Humans are the original "moral polluters" (and over the years we've added other forms of pollution as well!). But God has this "thing" for people. He has this thing for *you*.

Want to find out how it all began? That's what Genesis means—"Beginnings." Turn to page 7 and read chapter 3 to find out how our problems with God and with each other started. Maybe you'll see something of yourself in the behavior of humankind's "first couple." It's not a pretty picture. But don't despair. Even though this book contains a lot of bad news, Genesis chapter 3, verse 15 (page 7) promises that there's great news coming!

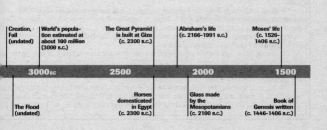

Creation, Fall (undated)	World's population estimated at about 100 million (3000 B.C.)	The Great Pyramid is built at Giza (c. 2300 B.C.)	Abraham's life (c. 2166–1991 B.C.)	Moses' life (c. 1526–1406 B.C.)
3000 BC	**2500**	**2000**	**1500**	
The Flood (undated)		Horses domesticated in Egypt (c. 2300 B.C.)	Glass made by the Mesopotamians (c. 2100 B.C.)	Book of Genesis written (c. 1446–1406 B.C.)

GENESIS

The Beginning

1 In the beginning God created the heavens and the earth. [2]Now the eawas*a* formless and empty, darkness was over the surface of the deep, the Spirit of God was hovering over the waters.

[3]And God said, "Let there be light," and there was light. [4]God saw that the light good, and he separated the light from the darkness. [5]God called the light "dand the darkness he called "night." And there was evening, and there was mcing—the first day.

[6]And God said, "Let there be an expanse between the waters to separate water fwater." [7]So God made the expanse and separated the water under the expafrom the water above it. And it was so. [8]God called the expanse "sky." And thwas evening, and there was morning—the second day.

[9]And God said, "Let the water under the sky be gathered to one place, and letground appear." And it was so. [10]God called the dry ground "land," and the gaered waters he called "seas." And God saw that it was good.

a2 Or possibly become

◻ :::::::::::::::::::::::::::::: **DISCOVERING GOD** ::::::::::::::::::::::::::::::

1:1
The God Who Is There

The Bible opens with the assumption that God exists. He is the all-knowing and all-powerful being who created everything from nothing. While we humans have the capability to imagine thingthat don't exist, we can't *create* something from nothing. We can only create something from something, combining different elements into things that never existed before. God is vastly differenfrom us in that he literally spoke into being the basic elements of the universe—space, time anmatter—and then fashioned everything that exists.

Can we prove God's existence? Throughout history, many individuals have expended mucenergy developing "arguments for the existence of God." Such arguments help some people, whileaving other people unconvinced. The Bible never tries to *prove* God's existence. It simply affirmthat God exists. And it assumes that anyone who seeks God will find him, because he is the Orwho is always there, eager to meet any who look for him (see Hebrews chapter 11, verse 6 [pag1596]).

Enough evidence is available, however, to draw a reasonable conclusion about God's exitence. For example, could something as ordered as the universe come into being by chance? Thatlike a car coming together (with a full tank of gas and the key in the ignition) as a result of aearthquake in Detroit! Likewise, how can we explain mere matter becoming self-aware without apre-existing intelligent and conscious cause?

Universal order and human intelligence are two of many phenomena that point to an aknowing and all-powerful Creator. The very fact that the universe exists and that we human creatures exist points to the source of those realities; that is, to God. Whether or not those argumenare persuasive is an issue each of us may want to debate.

In the end, however, the Bible simply invites its readers to take an honest and careful loat God and at Jesus, the one who claims that he is the way to God (see John chapter 14, verse[page 1407]). We are challenged to find out for ourselves whether Jesus is who he claims to b

¹¹Then God said, "Let the land produce vegetation: seed-bearing plants and trees on the land that bear fruit with seed in it, according to their various kinds." And it was so. ¹²The land produced vegetation: plants bearing seed according to their kinds and trees bearing fruit with seed in it according to their kinds. And God saw that it was good. ¹³And there was evening, and there was morning—the third day.

¹⁴And God said, "Let there be lights in the expanse of the sky to separate the day from the night, and let them serve as signs to mark seasons and days and years, ¹⁵and let them be lights in the expanse of the sky to give light on the earth." And it was so. ¹⁶God made two great lights—the greater light to govern the day and the lesser light to govern the night. He also made the stars. ¹⁷God set them in the expanse of the sky to give light on the earth, ¹⁸to govern the day and the night, and to separate light from darkness. And God saw that it was good. ¹⁹And there was evening, and there was morning—the fourth day.

²⁰And God said, "Let the water teem with living creatures, and let birds fly above the earth across the expanse of the sky." ²¹So God created the great creatures of the sea and every living and moving thing with which the water teems, according to their kinds, and every winged bird according to its kind. And God saw that it was good. ²²God blessed them and said, "Be fruitful and increase in number and fill the water in the seas, and let the birds increase on the earth." ²³And there was evening, and there was morning—the fifth day.

²⁴And God said, "Let the land produce living creatures according to their kinds: livestock, creatures that move along the ground, and wild animals, each according to its kind." And it was so. ²⁵God made the wild animals according to their kinds, the livestock according to their kinds, and all the creatures that move along the ground according to their kinds. And God saw that it was good.

²⁶Then God said, "Let us make man in our image, in our likeness, and let them rule over the fish of the sea and the birds of the air, over the livestock, over all the earth,ᵃ and over all the creatures that move along the ground."

≡≡≡≡≡≡≡ KNOWING YOURSELF ≡≡≡≡≡≡≡
1:27–31 **A New Identity** God created both woman and man in his image and appointed them as equal caretakers over the earth. Notice that the first human couple were created in God's *image*. God blessed them and gave them special responsibilities. As you reflect on your own worth, consider the fact that God made you in his image—capable of reasoning, relating and ruling. These gifts are meant to be affirmed and expressed throughout your life. Note also that according to the Bible, sexism—or any other form of discrimination—did not originate with God but with people. *All* individuals, whatever our gender or race, are made in his image. God's intention for us is that we respect his imprint in every human being we meet.

²⁷So God created man in
    his own image,
in the image of God he created him;
    male and female he created them.

²⁸God blessed them and said to them, "Be fruitful and increase in number; fill the earth and subdue it. Rule over the fish of the sea and the birds of the air and over every living creature that moves on the ground."

²⁹Then God said, "I give you every seed-bearing plant on the face of the whole earth and every tree that has fruit with seed in it. They will be yours for food. ³⁰And to all the beasts of the earth and all the birds of the air and all the creatures

ᵃ Hebrew; Syriac all the wild animals

that move on the ground—everything that has the breath of life in it—I give eve
green plant for food." And it was so.

³¹God saw all that he had made, and it was very good. And there was evenir
and there was morning—the sixth day.

2 Thus the heavens and the earth were completed in all their vast array.

²By the seventh day God had finished the work he had been doing; so on the seven
day he rested^a from all his work. ³And God blessed the seventh day and made
holy, because on it he rested from all the work of creating that he had done.

Adam and Eve

⁴This is the account of the heavens and the earth when they were created.

When the Lᴏʀᴅ God made the earth and the heavens— ⁵and no shrub of the field h
yet appeared on the earth^b and no plant of the field had yet sprung up, for the Lᴏʀᴅ G
had not sent rain on the earth^b and there was no man to work the ground, ⁶b

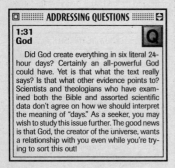

> **◻ ▦ ADDRESSING QUESTIONS ▦ ⊟**
>
> **1:31**
> **God** **Q**
>
> Did God create everything in six literal 24-
> hour days? Certainly an all-powerful God
> could have. Yet is that what the text really
> says? Is that what other evidence points to?
> Scientists and theologians who have exam-
> ined both the Bible and assorted scientific
> data don't agree on how we should interpret
> the meaning of "days." As a seeker, you may
> wish to study this issue further. The good news
> is that God, the creator of the universe, wants
> a relationship with you even while you're try-
> ing to sort this out!

streams^c came up from the earth and w
tered the whole surface of the groun
⁷the Lᴏʀᴅ God formed the man^d from t
dust of the ground and breathed into I
nostrils the breath of life, and the man b
came a living being.

⁸Now the Lᴏʀᴅ God had planted a gard
in the east, in Eden; and there he put I
man he had formed. ⁹And the Lᴏʀᴅ G
made all kinds of trees grow out of t
ground—trees that were pleasing to I
eye and good for food. In the middle
the garden were the tree of life and I
tree of the knowledge of good and evil.

¹⁰A river watering the garden flow
from Eden; from there it was separated i
four headwaters. ¹¹The name of the first
the Pishon; it winds through the ent
land of Havilah, where there is gold. ¹²(T

gold of that land is good; aromatic resin^e and onyx are also there.) ¹³The name of I
second river is the Gihon; it winds through the entire land of Cush.^f ¹⁴The name of I
third river is the Tigris; it runs along the east side of Asshur. And the fourth river
the Euphrates.

¹⁵The Lᴏʀᴅ God took the man and put him in the Garden of Eden to work it and ta
care of it. ¹⁶And the Lᴏʀᴅ God commanded the man, "You are free to eat from any tree
the garden; ¹⁷but you must not eat from the tree of the knowledge of good and evil,
when you eat of it you will surely die."

¹⁸The Lᴏʀᴅ God said, "It is not good for the man to be alone. I will make a help
suitable for him."

¹⁹Now the Lᴏʀᴅ God had formed out of the ground all the beasts of the field and all
birds of the air. He brought them to the man to see what he would name them; a
whatever the man called each living creature, that was its name. ²⁰So the man ga
names to all the livestock, the birds of the air and all the beasts of the field.

But for Adam^g no suitable helper was found. ²¹So the Lᴏʀᴅ God caused the man to

---

^a2 Or ceased; also in verse 3   ^b5 Or land; also in verse 6   ^c6 Or mist   ^d7 The Hebrew for man (adam) sounds
like and may be related to the Hebrew for ground (adamah); it is also the name Adam (see Gen. 2:20).   ^e12 Or good; pearl
^f13 Possibly southeast Mesopotamia   ^g20 Or the man

o a deep sleep; and while he was sleeping, he took one of the man's ribs*a* and closed the place with flesh. **22**Then the LORD God made a woman from the rib*b* he had taken of the man, and he brought her to the man.

3The man said,

This is now bone of my bones
　and flesh of my flesh;
he shall be called 'woman,*c*'
　for she was taken out of
　　man."

or this reason a man will leave his fa-
r and mother and be united to his wife,
i they will become one flesh.

5The man and his wife were both na-
l, and they felt no shame.

e Fall of Humanity

Now the serpent was more crafty than any of the wild an-
ls the LORD God had made. He said to woman, "Did God really say, 'You must eat from any tree in the garden'?"

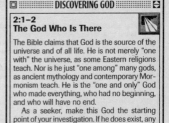
The woman said to the serpent, "We may eat fruit from the trees in the garden, **3**but
i did say, 'You must not eat fruit from the tree that is in the middle of the garden, and
must not touch it, or you will die.'"

"You will not surely die," the serpent said to the woman. **5**"For God knows that when
eat of it your eyes will be opened, and you will be like God, knowing good and evil."
When the woman saw that the fruit of the tree was good for food and pleasing to the
, and also desirable for gaining wisdom, she took some and ate it. She also gave some
her husband, who was with her, and he ate it. **7**Then the eyes of both of them were
ned, and they realized they were naked; so they sewed fig leaves together and made
erings for themselves.

Then the man and his wife heard the sound of the LORD God as he was walking in the
den in the cool of the day, and they hid from the LORD God among the trees of the
den. **9**But the LORD God called to the man, "Where are you?"

0He answered, "I heard you in the garden, and I was afraid because I was naked; so
d."

1And he said, "Who told you that you were naked? Have you eaten from the tree that
mmanded you not to eat from?"

2The man said, "The woman you put here with me—she gave me some fruit from the
, and I ate it."

3Then the LORD God said to the woman, "What is this you have done?"
he woman said, "The serpent deceived me, and I ate."

4So the LORD God said to the serpent, "Because you have done this,

　　"Cursed are you above all the livestock
　　　and all the wild animals!
　　You will crawl on your belly
　　　and you will eat dust
　　　all the days of your life.
　　15And I will put enmity
　　　between you and the woman,

a Or took part of the man's side　　*b 22 Or part*　　*c 23 The Hebrew for woman sounds like the Hebrew for man.*

3:1–21
Sin

The account of Adam and Eve in the garden of Eden is bursting with insight into human and spir itual realities. Setting aside all the scientific questions of creation versus evolution for a momen this simple story is actually a multilayered drama unparalleled in ancient literature. Compared t other ancient creation stories, this narrative is surprisingly free of mythological elements. And th universal nature of the main characters might make you think it was written yesterday.

In this chapter we discover the origins of human suffering. Here we find two people living an ideal environment unscarred by hatred or conflict. They enjoy an open relationship with Go and with each other. Yet that's not the way real life is for any of us. So what happened to mak the world the way it is today?

The story revolves around one simple request that God made to the first couple: Eat all yo want from anywhere you want, but don't eat from this one certain tree (chapter 2, verses 16–1 [page 6]). Not that the fruit of that tree was bad; on the contrary, like everything God made, it wa undoubtedly good. But the Creator gave Adam and Eve freedom to choose—even if that mea they could choose what was wrong. The command about the fruit served as a test of their wi ingness to obey God.

Enter the talking serpent, later identified as the devil. The Bible describes the devil as a re being. He was originally a good angel who, along with many other angels, rejected God and wa banished from heaven and sent to earth (see Revelation chapter 12, verses 7–9 [page 1644]). Th earthly form he took in this instance may well have been snake-like.

Why did he go after these two people? Because corrupting the highest achievement of God creation was the best way for the devil to continue his rebellion against God. And this crafty fa llen angel knew exactly how to break down Adam and Eve's resistance.

First, the devil called into question the accuracy of what God had said (verse 1). By misquo ing God's instructions, he planted a seed of doubt in Eve's mind. Second, he maligned God's cha acter (verse 4), questioning God's goodness and convincing Eve that God was keeping somethin beneficial from her. Finally, he promised that something wonderful would occur if she would sir ply take a bite (verse 5). This final step painted a distorted picture of sinful actions, as if they co tained only pleasure with no undesirable side effects. This is the same "one-two-three punch" th Satan often uses to break down people today.

The strategy worked. The more Eve looked at the fruit, the more appealing it became. Sh took a bite, and then she urged Adam to try it. Shame, guilt, and fear followed. Instead of havir a close relationship with God and with each other, Adam and Eve were reduced to hiding an blaming.

Make no mistake about it: The Bible says that we are spiritual as well as physical being which means that both natural and supernatural forces affect our experience. In that first act disobedience, Adam and Eve set a corrupted pattern that we all follow. At virtually every stage life, we all "miss the mark" and know firsthand the pain of guilt and shame.

Fortunately, this story also holds a pledge from God that the damage done will not last fo ever. God predicts the serpent's eventual destruction (verse 15). He does so with a curious phras assuring the serpent that an offspring of Eve—though wounded temporarily by the serpent—w ultimately crush his head.

This first promise of the devil's eventual overthrow comes into clearer focus as the Bibl message unfolds. Much later, in an obscure village in Palestine, a descendant of Eve—Jesus hir self—was born as the Savior of the world. When Jesus died by crucifixion, the devil gloated ove his apparent victory. But Jesus arose from the dead! He shrugged off his temporary wounds ar delivered a fatal blow to the serpent's head. Jesus' conquering act assures us that the devil's plar are doomed to fail.

and between your offspring*a* and hers;
he will crush*b* your head,
    and you will strike his heel."

¹⁶To the woman he said,

"I will greatly increase your pains in childbearing;
    with pain you will give birth to children.
Your desire will be for your husband,
    and he will rule over you."

¹⁷To Adam he said, "Because you listened to your wife and ate from the tree about ʻhich I commanded you, 'You must not eat of it,'

"Cursed is the ground because of you;
    through painful toil you will eat of it
    all the days of your life.
¹⁸It will produce thorns and thistles for you,
    and you will eat the plants of the field.

5 Or seed   *b 15* Or strike

ADDRESSING QUESTIONS

3:24
Human Experience

Q

Why did God create Adam and Eve when he knew they were going to sin? This is an often-asked question with deep emotional undertones. Was this some kind of setup? Did God enjoy the prospect of creating people he could later condemn?

First, let's address the emotional side of this question. Whatever answer we come up with, be assured that everything else the Bible teaches about God leads us to believe in his goodness and wisdom. The very fact that he works hard to win back the people he has created *must* mean that he doesn't want people to separate themselves from him (see Ezekiel chapter 18, verse 23 [page 1104]). If, as a seeker, you're afraid you'll find a cruel and judgmental God at the end of your search, you need to explore the multitude of biblical references that clearly reveal his kindness (see, for example, Psalm 16 [page 664], Jeremiah chapter 29, verses 11 and 12 [page 1032] and John chapter 3, verse 16 [page 1387]).

So why did God make people if he knew they would sin? As we answer this question keep in mind an important distinction: God didn't make people who *would* reject him, he made people who *could* reject him. There's a difference.

Maybe an analogy will help. A couple who decides to have a child doesn't do so because they believe that child will be perfect. They have the child so that they can give her their love and be loved in return. Even though they know their child will invariably disappoint them, they still desire that relationship.

In other words, *the potential for love exists only alongside the potential for rejection.* If you take away the freedom to refuse love, you take away love itself. In the same way, God knew in advance that some people would reject him. He also knew that some people would accept his love. And the value of having a relationship with those who would turn to him far outweighed the loss of those who wouldn't.

A relationship of love is possible because God gave us the dignity of choice, in spite of how we would abuse it. What a relief it is to know that our foolish preference for distance from God is not greater than his relentless pursuit of us.

Don't miss an important detail as you consider how this story answers the question of why God created us. Note that after Adam and Eve sinned, they became "seekers." What they were seeking, however, was distance from God! In contrast, God, the original seeker, came looking and calling for them (verse 9). Adam and Eve could have ignored God's initiative and stayed in the woods. Instead, they responded to God's call. After that, God initiated their restoration.

God still seeks to bring wandering people to himself today. How will you respond?

¹⁹By the sweat of your brow
    you will eat your food
until you return to the ground,
    since from it you were taken;
for dust you are
    and to dust you will return."

²⁰Adam^a named his wife Eve,^b because she would become the mother of all th living.

²¹The LORD God made garments of skin for Adam and his wife and clothed them. ²²An the LORD God said, "The man has now become like one of us, knowing good and evil. I must not be allowed to reach out his hand and take also from the tree of life and eat, an live forever." ²³So the LORD God banished him from the Garden of Eden to work the grou from which he had been taken. ²⁴After he drove the man out, he placed on the ea side^c of the Garden of Eden cherubim and a flaming sword flashing back and forth guard the way to the tree of life.

Cain and Abel

4 Adam^a lay with his wife Eve, and she became pregnant and gave birth Cain.^d She said, "With the help of the LORD I have brought forth^e a mar ²Later she gave birth to his brother Abel.

Now Abel kept flocks, and Cain worked the soil. ³In the course of time Cain broug some of the fruits of the soil as an offering to the LORD. ⁴But Abel brought fat portions fro some of the firstborn of his flock. The LORD looked with favor on Abel and his offering, ⁵b on Cain and his offering he did not look with favor. So Cain was very angry, and his fa was downcast.

⁶Then the LORD said to Cain, "Why are you angry? Why is your face downcast? ⁷If y do what is right, will you not be accepted? But if you do not do what is right, sin crouching at your door; it desires to have you, but you must master it."

⁸Now Cain said to his brother Abel, "Let's go out to the field."^f And while they were the field, Cain attacked his brother Abel and killed him.

⁹Then the LORD said to Cain, "Where is your brother Abel?"

"I don't know," he replied. "Am I my brother's keeper?"

¹⁰The LORD said, "What have you done? Listen! Your brother's blood cries out to me fro the ground. ¹¹Now you are under a curse and driven from the ground, which opened mouth to receive your brother's blood from your hand. ¹²When you work the ground, will no longer yield its crops for you. You will be a restless wanderer on the earth."

¹³Cain said to the LORD, "My punishment is more than I can bear. ¹⁴Today you a driving me from the land, and I will be hidden from your presence; I will be a restle wanderer on the earth, and whoever finds me will kill me."

¹⁵But the LORD said to him, "Not so^g; if anyone kills Cain, he will suffer vengean seven times over." Then the LORD put a mark on Cain so that no one who found him wou kill him. ¹⁶So Cain went out from the LORD's presence and lived in the land of Nod,^h ea of Eden.

¹⁷Cain lay with his wife, and she became pregnant and gave birth to Enoch. Cain w then building a city, and he named it after his son Enoch. ¹⁸To Enoch was born Irad, a Irad was the father of Mehujael, and Mehujael was the father of Methushael, and Meth shael was the father of Lamech.

¹⁹Lamech married two women, one named Adah and the other Zillah. ²⁰Adah ga birth to Jabal; he was the father of those who live in tents and raise livestock. ²¹F

^a20,1 Or *The man*   ^b20 *Eve* probably means *living.*   ^c24 Or *placed in front*   ^d1 *Cain* sounds like the Hebrew for *brought forth* or *acquired.*   ^e1 Or *have acquired*   ^f8 Samaritan Pentateuch, Septuagint, Vulgate and Syriac; Masoretic Text does not have *"Let's go out to the field."*   ^g15 Septuagint, Vulgate and Syriac; Hebrew *Very well*   ^h16 *Nod* means *wandering* (see verses 12 and 14).

rother's name was Jubal; he was the father of all who play the harp and flute. ²²Zillah
lso had a son, Tubal-Cain, who forged all kinds of tools out of*a* bronze and iron.
ubal-Cain's sister was Naamah.
²³Lamech said to his wives,

> "Adah and Zillah, listen to me;
>> wives of Lamech, hear my words.
> I have killed*b* a man for wounding me,
>> a young man for injuring me.
> ²⁴If Cain is avenged seven times,
>> then Lamech seventy-seven times."

²⁵Adam lay with his wife again, and she gave birth to a son and named him Seth,*c*
aying, "God has granted me another child in place of Abel, since Cain killed him." ²⁶Seth
lso had a son, and he named him Enosh.
At that time men began to call on*d* the name of the LORD.

rom Adam to Noah

5   This is the written account of Adam's line.

When God created man, he made him in the likeness of God. ²He created them male
nd female and blessed them. And when they were created, he called them "man.*e*"

³When Adam had lived 130 years, he
ad a son in his own likeness, in his own
mage; and he named him Seth. ⁴After Seth
vas born, Adam lived 800 years and had
ther sons and daughters. ⁵Altogether,
dam lived 930 years, and then he died.

⁶When Seth had lived 105 years, he be-
ame the father*f* of Enosh. ⁷And after he
ecame the father of Enosh, Seth lived 807
ears and had other sons and daughters.
Altogether, Seth lived 912 years, and then
e died.

⁹When Enosh had lived 90 years, he be-
ame the father of Kenan. ¹⁰And after he
ecame the father of Kenan, Enosh lived
15 years and had other sons and daugh-
ers. ¹¹Altogether, Enosh lived 905 years,
nd then he died.

¹²When Kenan had lived 70 years, he
ecame the father of Mahalalel. ¹³And after
e became the father of Mahalalel, Kenan
ved 840 years and had other sons and
aughters. ¹⁴Altogether, Kenan lived 910
ears, and then he died.

¹⁵When Mahalalel had lived 65 years, he
ecame the father of Jared. ¹⁶And after he
ecame the father of Jared, Mahalalel lived

▣ ▥▥▥▥▥ KNOWING YOURSELF ▥▥▥▥▥ ▤

4:4–5
Sin

This passage shows us that it's possible to be
the wrong kind of seeker. Both Cain and Abel
approached God, but he only accepted one of
them. Why?

The key is found in verse 5. The problem
wasn't just the offering; it was the person making the offering. The verses that follow show
the murderous results of Cain's anger. Clearly,
Cain's offering wasn't presented in the right
spirit; he had a "spiritual dysfunction."

Throughout the Bible we discover that God
looks beyond our actions and considers our
motives. A person can't just go through the
motions with God. God knows what's inside
each of us and is unimpressed by rituals that
have no sincerity or substance behind them.

As you continue to seek God, know that he
cannot be fooled. Honestly face your spiritual
"shadows," and come to God admitting that
they exist. In that way you'll not only be seeking the God who is real, you'll seek him by being real.

---

30 years and had other sons and daughters. ¹⁷Altogether, Mahalalel lived 895 years,
nd then he died.

¹⁸When Jared had lived 162 years, he became the father of Enoch. ¹⁹And after he

---

22 Or *who instructed all who work in*   *b23* Or *I will kill*   *c25 Seth* probably means *granted.*   *d26* Or *to proclaim*
e Hebrew *adam*   *f6 Father* may mean *ancestor;* also in verses 7-26.

became the father of Enoch, Jared lived 800 years and had other sons and daughters
²⁰Altogether, Jared lived 962 years, and then he died.

²¹When Enoch had lived 65 years, he became the father of Methuselah. ²²And after he
became the father of Methuselah, Enoch walked with God 300 years and had other sons
and daughters. ²³Altogether, Enoch lived 365 years. ²⁴Enoch walked with God; then he
was no more, because God took him away.

²⁵When Methuselah had lived 187 years, he became the father of Lamech. ²⁶And after
he became the father of Lamech, Methuselah lived 782 years and had other sons and
daughters. ²⁷Altogether, Methuselah lived 969 years, and then he died.

²⁸When Lamech had lived 182 years, he had a son. ²⁹He named him Noah^a and said,
"He will comfort us in the labor and painful toil of our hands caused by the ground the
LORD has cursed." ³⁰After Noah was born, Lamech lived 595 years and had other sons and
daughters. ³¹Altogether, Lamech lived 777 years, and then he died.

³²After Noah was 500 years old, he became the father of Shem, Ham and Japheth.

The Flood

6 When men began to increase in number on the earth and daughters were
born to them, ²the sons of God saw that the daughters of men were beautiful, and they married any of them they chose. ³Then the LORD said, "My Spirit will not
contend with^b man forever, for he is mor-
tal^c; his days will be a hundred and twenty years."

⁴The Nephilim were on the earth in
those days—and also afterward—when the
sons of God went to the daughters of men
and had children by them. They were the
heroes of old, men of renown.

⁵The LORD saw how great man's wickedness on the earth had become, and that
every inclination of the thoughts of his
heart was only evil all the time. ⁶The LORD
was grieved that he had made man on the
earth, and his heart was filled with pain.
⁷So the LORD said, "I will wipe mankind,
whom I have created, from the face of the
earth—men and animals, and creatures
that move along the ground, and birds of
the air—for I am grieved that I have made
them." ⁸But Noah found favor in the eyes of
the LORD.

⁹This is the account of Noah.

Noah was a righteous man, blameless
among the people of his time, and he
walked with God. ¹⁰Noah had three sons:
Shem, Ham and Japheth.

¹¹Now the earth was corrupt in God's
sight and was full of violence. ¹²God saw
how corrupt the earth had become, for all the people on earth had corrupted their ways.
¹³So God said to Noah, "I am going to put an end to all people, for the earth is filled with
violence because of them. I am surely going to destroy both them and the earth. ¹⁴S

DISCOVERING GOD

6:3
Life with God

Before you conclude from this passage that
God decided to wipe out humanity while in a
fit of rage, note that before the flood people
were described as *exceptionally* evil, yet God
was patient. God allowed Noah to build the
ark, during which time Noah must have
warned his neighbors and others of the destruction to come. Apparently, nobody responded.

Both this passage and history as a whole
are full of the tension between God's love for
his creatures and his grief over how sin corrupts them. Basically, our sin is like a heavy
ball and chain that each of us carries with us
throughout our lives. God hates sin, and offers to forgive us and release us from its
weight in our lives. However, if we ignore that
call and refuse to be set free, God will honor
our decision and allow us to carry our sin all
alone. If we choose to "go swimming" with that
weight, what happens next is our responsibility, not God's.

What's the alternative? Seek God as Noah
did and walk daily in God's presence (verse 9).

---

a 29 Noah sounds like the Hebrew for *comfort.*   *b 3* Or *My spirit will not remain in*   *c 3* Or *corrupt*

make yourself an ark of cypress[a] wood; make rooms in it and coat it with pitch inside and out. [15]This is how you are to build it: The ark is to be 450 feet long, 75 feet wide and 45 feet high.[b] [16]Make a roof for it and finish[c] the ark to within 18 inches[d] of the top. Put a door in the side of the ark and make lower, middle and upper decks. [17]I am going to bring floodwaters on the earth to destroy all life under the heavens, every creature that has the breath of life in it. Everything on earth will perish. [18]But I will establish my covenant with you, and you will enter the ark—you and your sons and your wife and your sons' wives with you. [19]You are to bring into the ark two of all living creatures, male and female, to keep them alive with you. [20]Two of every kind of bird, of every kind of animal and of every kind of creature that moves along the ground will come to you to be kept alive. [21]You are to take every kind of food that is to be eaten and store it away as food for you and for them."

[22]Noah did everything just as God commanded him.

7 The LORD then said to Noah, "Go into the ark, you and your whole family, because I have found you righteous in this generation. [2]Take with you seven[e] of every kind of clean animal, a male and its mate, and two of every kind of unclean animal, a male and its mate, [3]and also seven of every kind of bird, male and female, to keep their various kinds alive throughout the earth. [4]Seven days from now I will send rain on the earth for forty days and forty nights, and I will wipe from the face of the earth every living creature I have made."

[5]And Noah did all that the LORD commanded him.

[6]Noah was six hundred years old when the floodwaters came on the earth. [7]And Noah and his sons and his wife and his sons' wives entered the ark to escape the waters of the flood. [8]Pairs of clean and unclean animals, of birds and of all creatures that move along the ground, [9]male and female, came to Noah and entered the ark, as God had commanded Noah. [10]And after the seven days the floodwaters came on the earth.

[11]In the six hundredth year of Noah's life, on the seventeenth day of the second month—on that day all the springs of the great deep burst forth, and the floodgates of the heavens were opened. [12]And rain fell on the earth forty days and forty nights.

[13]On that very day Noah and his sons, Shem, Ham and Japheth, together with his wife and the wives of his three sons, entered the ark. [14]They had with them every wild animal according to its kind, all livestock according to their kinds, every creature that moves along the ground according to its kind and every bird according to its kind, everything with wings. [15]Pairs of all creatures that have the breath of life in them came to Noah and entered the ark. [16]The animals going in were male and female of every living thing, as God had commanded Noah. Then the LORD shut him in.

[17]For forty days the flood kept coming on the earth, and as the waters increased they lifted the ark high above the earth. [18]The waters rose and increased greatly on the earth, and the ark floated on the surface of the water. [19]They rose greatly on the earth, and all the high mountains under the entire heavens were covered. [20]The waters rose and covered the mountains to a depth of more than twenty feet.[f,g] [21]Every living thing that moved on the earth perished—birds, livestock, wild animals, all the creatures that swarm over the earth, and all mankind. [22]Everything on dry land that had the breath of life in its nostrils died. [23]Every living thing on the face of the earth was wiped out; men and animals and the creatures that move along the ground and the birds of the air were wiped from the earth. Only Noah was left, and those with him in the ark.

[24]The waters flooded the earth for a hundred and fifty days.

The meaning of the Hebrew for this word is uncertain.   [b]15 Hebrew *300 cubits long, 50 cubits wide and 30 cubits* (about 140 meters long, 23 meters wide and 13.5 meters high)   [c]16 Or *Make an opening for light by finishing* Hebrew *a cubit* (about 0.5 meter)   [e]2 Or *seven pairs;* also in verse 3   [f]20 Hebrew *fifteen cubits* (about 6.9 meters) Or *rose more than twenty feet, and the mountains were covered*

8 But God remembered Noah and all the wild animals and the livestock that were with him in the ark, and he sent a wind over the earth, and the waters receded. ²Now the springs of the deep and the floodgates of the heavens had been closed, and the rain had stopped falling from the sky. ³The water receded steadily from the earth. At the end of the hundred and fifty days the water had gone down, ⁴and on the seventeenth day of the seventh month the ark came to rest on the mountains of Ararat. ⁵The waters continued to recede until the tenth month, and on the first day of the tenth month the tops of the mountains became visible.

⁶After forty days Noah opened the window he had made in the ark ⁷and sent out a raven, and it kept flying back and forth until the water had dried up from the earth. ⁸Then he sent out a dove to see if the water had receded from the surface of the ground. ⁹But the dove could find no place to set its feet because there was water over all the surface of the earth; so it returned to Noah in the ark. He reached out his hand and took the dove and brought it back to himself in the ark. ¹⁰He waited seven more days and again sent out the dove from the ark. ¹¹When the dove returned to him in the evening, there in its beak was a freshly plucked olive leaf! Then Noah knew that the water had receded from the earth. ¹²He waited seven more days and sent the dove out again, but this time it did not return to him.

¹³By the first day of the first month Noah's six hundred and first year, the water had dried up from the earth. Noah then removed the covering from the ark and saw that the surface of the ground was dry. ¹⁴By the twenty-seventh day of the second month the earth was completely dry.

¹⁵Then God said to Noah, ¹⁶"Come out of the ark, you and your wife and your sons and their wives. ¹⁷Bring out every kind of living creature that is with you—the birds, the animals, and all the creatures that move along the ground—so they can multiply on the earth and be fruitful and increase in numbers upon it."

¹⁸So Noah came out, together with his sons and his wife and his sons' wives. ¹⁹All the animals and all the creatures that move along the ground and all the birds—everything that moves on the earth—came out of the ark, one kind after another.

²⁰Then Noah built an altar to the LORD and, taking some of all the clean animals and clean birds, he sacrificed burnt offerings on it. ²¹The LORD smelled the pleasing aroma and said in his heart: "Never again will I curse the ground because of man, even though[a] every inclination of his heart is evil from childhood. And never again will I destroy all living creatures, as I have done.

²²"As long as the earth endures,
    seedtime and harvest,

> cold and heat,
> summer and winter,
> day and night
> will never cease."

d's Covenant With Noah

Then God blessed Noah and his sons, saying to them, "Be fruitful and increase in number and fill the earth. ²The fear and dread of you will fall upon
the beasts of the earth and all the birds of the air, upon every creature that moves
ng the ground, and upon all the fish of the sea; they are given into your hands.
erything that lives and moves will be food for you. Just as I gave you the green plants,
w give you everything.

"But you must not eat meat that has its lifeblood still in it. ⁵And for your lifeblood I will
ely demand an accounting. I will demand an accounting from every animal. And from
n man, too, I will demand an accounting for the life of his fellow man.

> ⁶"Whoever sheds the blood of man,
>   by man shall his blood be shed;
>   for in the image of God
>   has God made man.

for you, be fruitful and increase in
ber; multiply on the earth and in-
se upon it."

hen God said to Noah and to his sons
n him: ⁹"I now establish my covenant
you and with your descendants after
¹⁰and with every living creature that
with you—the birds, the livestock
all the wild animals, all those that
e out of the ark with you—every living
ture on earth. ¹¹I establish my
enant with you: Never again will all
be cut off by the waters of a flood;
er again will there be a flood to
roy the earth."

And God said, "This is the sign of the
enant I am making between me and
and every living creature with you, a
enant for all generations to come: 13]
e set my rainbow in the clouds, and it
be the sign of the covenant between
and the earth. ¹⁴Whenever I bring
ds over the earth and the rainbow
ears in the clouds, ¹⁵I will remember
covenant between me and you and all
ng creatures of every kind. Never again
the waters become a flood to destroy

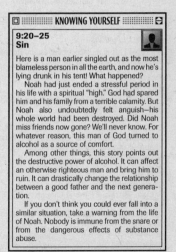

▣ ▓▓▓▓▓▓ KNOWING YOURSELF ▓▓▓▓▓▓ ⊟

9:20–25
Sin

Here is a man earlier singled out as the most
blameless person in all the earth, and now he's
lying drunk in his tent! What happened?

Noah had just ended a stressful period in
his life with a spiritual "high." God had spared
him and his family from a terrible calamity. But
Noah also undoubtedly felt anguish—his
whole world had been destroyed. Did Noah
miss friends now gone? We'll never know. For
whatever reason, this man of God turned to
alcohol as a source of comfort.

Among other things, this story points out
the destructive power of alcohol. It can affect
an otherwise righteous man and bring him to
ruin. It can drastically change the relationship
between a good father and the next generation.

If you don't think you could ever fall into a
similar situation, take a warning from the life
of Noah. Nobody is immune from the snare or
from the dangerous effects of substance
abuse.

ife. ¹⁶Whenever the rainbow appears in the clouds, I will see it and remember the
rlasting covenant between God and all living creatures of every kind on the earth."

So God said to Noah, "This is the sign of the covenant I have established between me
all life on the earth."

Sons of Noah

The sons of Noah who came out of the ark were Shem, Ham and Japheth. (Ham was the father of Canaan.) ¹⁹These were the three sons of Noah, and from them came people who were scattered over the earth.

²⁰Noah, a man of the soil, proceeded*ᵃ* to plant a vineyard. ²¹When he drank some of its wine, he became drunk and lay uncovered inside his tent. ²²Ham, the father of Canaan, saw his father's nakedness and told his two brothers outside. ²³But Shem and Japheth took a garment and laid it across their shoulders; then they walked in backward and covered their father's nakedness. Their faces were turned the other way so that they would not see their father's nakedness.

²⁴When Noah awoke from his wine and found out what his youngest son had done to him, ²⁵he said,

> "Cursed be Canaan!
> The lowest of slaves
> will he be to his brothers."

²⁶He also said,

> "Blessed be the Lᴏʀᴅ, the God of Shem!
> May Canaan be the slave of Shem.*ᵇ*
> ²⁷May God extend the territory of Japheth*ᶜ*;
> may Japheth live in the tents of Shem,
> and may Canaan be his*ᵈ* slave."

²⁸After the flood Noah lived 350 years. ²⁹Altogether, Noah lived 950 years, and then he died.

The Table of Nations

10 This is the account of Shem, Ham and Japheth, Noah's sons, who themselves had sons after the flood.

The Japhethites

²The sons*ᵉ* of Japheth:
> Gomer, Magog, Madai, Javan, Tubal, Meshech and Tiras.
³The sons of Gomer:
> Ashkenaz, Riphath and Togarmah.
⁴The sons of Javan:
> Elishah, Tarshish, the Kittim and the Rodanim.*ᶠ* ⁵(From these the maritime peoples spread out into their territories by their clans within their nations, each with their own language.)

The Hamites

⁶The sons of Ham:
> Cush, Mizraim,*ᵍ* Put and Canaan.
⁷The sons of Cush:
> Seba, Havilah, Sabtah, Raamah and Sabteca.
> The sons of Raamah:
> Sheba and Dedan.

⁸Cush was the father*ʰ* of Nimrod, who grew to be a mighty warrior on the earth. ⁹He was a mighty hunter before the Lᴏʀᴅ; that is why it is said, "Like Nimrod, a mighty hunter before the Lᴏʀᴅ." ¹⁰The first centers of his kingdom were Babylon, Erech, Akkad and Calneh, in*ⁱ* Shinar.*ʲ* ¹¹From that land he went to Assyria, where he built Nineveh,

---

ᵃ20 Or soil, was the first   *ᵇ26 Or be his slave*   *ᶜ27 Japheth sounds like the Hebrew for extend.*   *ᵈ27 Or their*
ᵉ2 Sons may mean descendants or successors or nations; also in verses 3, 4, 6, 7, 20–23, 29 and 31.   *ᶠ4 Some manuscripts of the Masoretic Text and Samaritan Pentateuch (see also Septuagint and 1 Chron. 1:7); most manuscripts of the Masoretic Text Dodanim*   *ᵍ6 That is, Egypt; also in verse 13*   *ʰ8 Father may mean ancestor or predecessor or founder; also in verses 13, 15, 24 and 26.*   *ⁱ10 Or Erech and Akkad—all of them in*   *ʲ10 That is, Babylonia*

both Ir,^a Calah ¹²and Resen, which is between Nineveh and Calah; that is the great

zraim was the father of
the Ludites, Anamites, Lehabites, Naphtuhites, ¹⁴Pathrusites, Casluhites (from whom the Philistines came) and Caphtorites.

naan was the father of
Sidon his firstborn,^b and of the Hittites, ¹⁶Jebusites, Amorites, Girgashites, ¹⁷Hivites, Arkites, Sinites, ¹⁸Arvadites, Zemarites and Hamathites.

er the Canaanite clans scattered ¹⁹and the borders of Canaan reached from Sidon rd Gerar as far as Gaza, and then toward Sodom, Gomorrah, Admah and Zeboiim, as ; Lasha.

hese are the sons of Ham by their clans and languages, in their territories and ns.

emites

ons were also born to Shem, whose older brother was^c Japheth; Shem was the stor of all the sons of Eber.

ne sons of Shem:
Elam, Asshur, Arphaxad, Lud and Aram.

ne sons of Aram:
Uz, Hul, Gether and Meshech.^d

phaxad was the father of^e Shelah,
and Shelah the father of Eber.

vo sons were born to Eber:
One was named Peleg,^f because in his time the earth was divided; his brother was named Joktan.

ktan was the father of
Almodad, Sheleph, Hazarmaveth, Jerah, ²⁷Hadoram, Uzal, Diklah, ²⁸Obal, Abimael, Sheba, ²⁹Ophir, Havilah and Jobab. All these were sons of Joktan.

e region where they lived stretched from Mesha toward Sephar, in the eastern hill ry.

hese are the sons of Shem by their clans and languages, in their territories and ns.

hese are the clans of Noah's sons, according to their lines of descent, within their ns. From these the nations spread out over the earth after the flood.

Tower of Babel

Now the whole world had one language and a common speech. ²As men moved eastward,^g they found a plain in Shinar^h and settled there.

ney said to each other, "Come, let's make bricks and bake them thoroughly." They brick instead of stone, and tar for mortar. ⁴Then they said, "Come, let us build elves a city, with a tower that reaches to the heavens, so that we may make a name urselves and not be scattered over the face of the whole earth."

t the LORD came down to see the city and the tower that the men were building. LORD said, "If as one people speaking the same language they have begun to do this, nothing they plan to do will be impossible for them. ⁷Come, let us go down and se their language so they will not understand each other."

the LORD scattered them from there over all the earth, and they stopped building the

Nineveh with its city squares   ^b15 Or of the Sidonians, the foremost   ^c21 Or Shem, the older brother of
Septuagint and 1 Chron. 1:17; Hebrew Mash   ^e24 Hebrew; Septuagint father of Cainan, and Cainan was the father
t25 Peleg means division.   ^g2 Or from the east; or in the east   ^h2 That is, Babylonia

city. [9]That is why it was called Babel[a]—because there the LORD confused the langua[...]
the whole world. From there the LORD scattered them over the face of the whole e[...]

From Shem to Abram

[10]This is the account of Shem.

Two years after the flood, when Shem was 100 years old, he became the fath[...]
Arphaxad. [11]And after he became the father of Arphaxad, Shem lived 500 years an[...]
other sons and daughters.

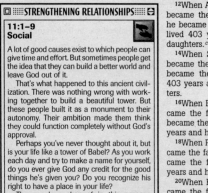

STRENGTHENING RELATIONSHIPS

11:1–9
Social

A lot of good causes exist to which people can give time and effort. But sometimes people get the idea that they can build a better world and leave God out of it.

That's what happened to this ancient civilization. There was nothing wrong with working together to build a beautiful tower. But these people built it as a monument to their autonomy. Their ambition made them think they could function completely without God's approval.

Perhaps you've never thought about it, but is your life like a tower of Babel? As you work each day and try to make a name for yourself, do you ever give God any credit for the good things he's given you? Do you recognize his right to have a place in your life?

The people spoken of in this passage didn't. To be sure, they became famous—but not in the way they had planned. Without God they became "Babel" (from which we get our word "babble"). Their dreams were left unfinished; their ambitions went unfulfilled.

[12]When Arphaxad had lived 35 year[...] became the father of Shelah. [13]And [...] he became the father of Shelah, Arph[...] lived 403 years and had other sons [...] daughters.[c]

[14]When Shelah had lived 30 year[...] became the father of Eber. [15]And afte[...] became the father of Eber, Shelah [...] 403 years and had other sons and da[...]ters.

[16]When Eber had lived 34 years, he[...] came the father of Peleg. [17]And afte[...] became the father of Peleg, Eber lived[...] years and had other sons and daughte[...]

[18]When Peleg had lived 30 years, h[...] came the father of Reu. [19]And after h[...] came the father of Reu, Peleg lived[...] years and had other sons and daughte[...]

[20]When Reu had lived 32 years, he[...] came the father of Serug. [21]And afte[...] became the father of Serug, Reu lived[...] years and had other sons and daughte[...]

[22]When Serug had lived 30 years, h[...] came the father of Nahor. [23]And afte[...] became the father of Nahor, Serug [...] 200 years and had other sons and da[...]ters.

[24]When Nahor had lived 29 years, he became the father of Terah. [25]And aft[...] became the father of Terah, Nahor lived 119 years and had other sons and daug[...]

[26]After Terah had lived 70 years, he became the father of Abram, Nahor and Hara[...]

[27]This is the account of Terah.

Terah became the father of Abram, Nahor and Haran. And Haran became the fat[...] Lot. [28]While his father Terah was still alive, Haran died in Ur of the Chaldeans, [...] land of his birth. [29]Abram and Nahor both married. The name of Abram's wife was [...] and the name of Nahor's wife was Milcah; she was the daughter of Haran, the fat[...] both Milcah and Iscah. [30]Now Sarai was barren; she had no children.

[31]Terah took his son Abram, his grandson Lot son of Haran, and his daughter-i[...]

[a]9 That is, Babylon; *Babel* sounds like the Hebrew for *confused.*   [b]10 *Father* may mean *ancestor;* also in verses 11–25[...] [c]12,13 Hebrew; Septuagint (see also Luke 3:35, 36 and note at Gen. 10:24) *35 years, he became the father of Cainan.* [13]An[...] *after he became the father of Cainan, Arphaxad lived 430 years and had other sons and daughters, and then he died. When [...] Cainan had lived 130 years, he became the father of Shelah. And after he became the father of Shelah, Cainan lived 330 ye[...] and had other sons and daughters*

ai, the wife of his son Abram, and together they set out from Ur of the Chaldeans to go
anaan. But when they came to Haran, they settled there.
Terah lived 205 years, and he died in Haran.

Call of Abram

The LORD had said to Abram,
"Leave your country, your peo-
and your father's household and go to
land I will show you.

> 2"I will make you into a
>   great nation
>   and I will bless you;
> I will make your name
>   great,
>   and you will be a
>   blessing.
> 3I will bless those who
>   bless you,
>   and whoever curses
>   you I will curse;
> and all peoples on
>   earth
>   will be blessed
>   through you."

So Abram left, as the LORD had told him;
Lot went with him. Abram was seven-
ve years old when he set out from Ha-
5He took his wife Sarai, his nephew
all the possessions they had accumu-
d and the people they had acquired in Haran, and they set out for the land of Canaan,
they arrived there.
Abram traveled through the land as far as the site of the great tree of Moreh at
chem. At that time the Canaanites were in the land. 7The LORD appeared to Abram and
, "To your offspring^a I will give this land." So he built an altar there to the LORD, who
appeared to him.
rom there he went on toward the hills east of Bethel and pitched his tent, with
nel on the west and Ai on the east. There he built an altar to the LORD and called on
name of the LORD. 9Then Abram set out and continued toward the Negev.

am in Egypt

Now there was a famine in the land, and Abram went down to Egypt to live there for
hile because the famine was severe. 11As he was about to enter Egypt, he said to his
Sarai, "I know what a beautiful woman you are. 12When the Egyptians see you, they
say, 'This is his wife.' Then they will kill me but will let you live. 13Say you are my
er, so that I will be treated well for your sake and my life will be spared because of
"
When Abram came to Egypt, the Egyptians saw that she was a very beautiful wom-
15And when Pharaoh's officials saw her, they praised her to Pharaoh, and she was
n into his palace. 16He treated Abram well for her sake, and Abram acquired sheep
cattle, male and female donkeys, menservants and maidservants, and camels.
But the LORD inflicted serious diseases on Pharaoh and his household because of

---

DISCOVERING GOD

12:1–20
Life with God

This chapter marks a significant step in God's
dealings with the human race. With God's call
to this man Abram (whose name God later
changed to "Abraham"), God began to build
a new community of people who would reach
the rest of the world with God's love.

Note that God's intent was not just to make
a nation out of Abraham's family but to be a
blessing to all the people on earth (verse 3).
Abraham's descendants, the Hebrew people,
were to fill this role in the ancient world.

The high point of this plan was to take place
many years in the future, when the most famous Hebrew in all history would give up his
life—not just for one nation, but for all the
world's people. That well-known descendant
of Abraham was Jesus of Nazareth, whom we
read about in the second part of the Bible.

From this point on, God identifies a growing group of individuals as his people. In that
sense, this chapter marks the end of the beginning and the dawn of a new era.

---

seed

Abram's wife Sarai. ¹⁸So Pharaoh summoned Abram. "What have you done to me?" he said. "Why didn't you tell me she was your wife? ¹⁹Why did you say, 'She is my sister,' so that I took her to be my wife? Now then, here is your wife. Take her and go!" ²⁰Then Pharaoh gave orders about Abram to his men, and they sent him on his way, with his wife and everything he had.

Abram and Lot Separate

13 So Abram went up from Egypt to the Negev, with his wife and everything he had, and Lot went with him. ²Abram had become very wealthy in livestock and in silver and gold.

³From the Negev he went from place to place until he came to Bethel, to the place between Bethel and Ai where his tent had been earlier ⁴and where he had first built an altar. There Abram called on the name of the Lord.

⁵Now Lot, who was moving about with Abram, also had flocks and herds and tents. ⁶But the land could not support them while they stayed together, for their possessions were so great that they were not able to stay together. ⁷And quarreling arose between Abram's herdsmen and the herdsmen of Lot. The Canaanites and Perizzites were also living in the land at that time.

⁸So Abram said to Lot, "Let's not have any quarreling between you and me, or between your herdsmen and mine, for we are brothers. ⁹Is not the whole land before you? Let's part company. If you go to the left, I'll go to the right; if you go to the right, I'll go to the left."

¹⁰Lot looked up and saw that the whole plain of the Jordan was well watered, like the garden of the Lord, like the land of Egypt, toward Zoar. (This was before the Lord destroyed Sodom and Gomorrah.) ¹¹So Lot chose for himself the whole plain of the Jordan and set out toward the east. The two men parted company: ¹²Abram lived in the land of Canaan, while Lot lived among the cities of the plain and pitched his tents near Sodom. ¹³Now the men of Sodom were wicked and were sinning greatly against the Lord.

¹⁴The Lord said to Abram after Lot had parted from him, "Lift up your eyes from where you are and look north and south, east and west. ¹⁵All the land that you see I will give to you and your offspring*a* forever. ¹⁶I will make your offspring like the dust of the earth, so that if anyone could count the dust, then your offspring could be counted. ¹⁷Go, walk through the length and breadth of the land, for I am giving it to you."

¹⁸So Abram moved his tents and went to live near the great trees of Mamre at Hebron, where he built an altar to the Lord.

Abram Rescues Lot

14 At this time Amraphel king of Shinar,*b* Arioch king of Ellasar, Kedorlaomer king of Elam and Tidal king of Goiim ²went to war against Bera king of Sodom, Birsha king of Gomorrah, Shinab king of Admah, Shemeber king of Zeboiim, and the king of Bela (that is, Zoar). ³All these latter kings joined forces in the Valley of Siddim (the Salt Sea*c*). ⁴For twelve years they had been subject to Kedorlaomer, but in the thirteenth year they rebelled.

⁵In the fourteenth year, Kedorlaomer and the kings allied with him went out and defeated the Rephaites in Ashteroth Karnaim, the Zuzites in Ham, the Emites in Shaveh Kiriathaim ⁶and the Horites in the hill country of Seir, as far as El Paran near the desert. ⁷Then they turned back and went to En Mishpat (that is, Kadesh), and they conquered the whole territory of the Amalekites, as well as the Amorites who were living in Hazazon Tamar.

⁸Then the king of Sodom, the king of Gomorrah, the king of Admah, the king of Zeboiim and the king of Bela (that is, Zoar) marched out and drew up their battle lines in the Valley of Siddim ⁹against Kedorlaomer king of Elam, Tidal king of Goiim, Amraphel

---

a 15 Or *seed*; also in verse 16   *b 1* That is, Babylonia; also in verse 9   *c 3* That is, the Dead Sea

hinar and Arioch king of Ellasar—four kings against five. ¹⁰Now the Valley of Siddim
full of tar pits, and when the kings of Sodom and Gomorrah fled, some of the men
into them and the rest fled to the hills. ¹¹The four kings seized all the goods of Sodom
Gomorrah and all their food; then they went away. ¹²They also carried off Abram's
hew Lot and his possessions, since he was living in Sodom.
One who had escaped came and reported this to Abram the Hebrew. Now Abram
living near the great trees of Mamre the Amorite, a brother *a* of Eshcol and Aner, all
whom were allied with Abram. ¹⁴When Abram heard that his relative had been taken
ive, he called out the 318 trained men born in his household and went in pursuit as
as Dan. ¹⁵During the night Abram divided his men to attack them and he routed them,
uing them as far as Hobah, north of Damascus. ¹⁶He recovered all the goods and
ght back his relative Lot and his possessions, together with the women and the
er people.
After Abram returned from defeating Kedorlaomer and the kings allied with him, the
of Sodom came out to meet him in the Valley of Shaveh (that is, the King's Valley).
Then Melchizedek king of Salem *b* brought out bread and wine. He was priest of God
t High, ¹⁹and he blessed Abram, saying,

> "Blessed be Abram by God Most High,
>   Creator *c* of heaven and earth.
> ²⁰And blessed be *d* God Most High,
>   who delivered your enemies into your hand."

n Abram gave him a tenth of everything.
The king of Sodom said to Abram, "Give me the people and keep the goods for
rself."
But Abram said to the king of Sodom, "I have raised my hand to the LORD, God Most
1, Creator of heaven and earth, and have taken an oath ²³that I will accept nothing
nging to you, not even a thread or the thong of a sandal, so that you will never be
e to say, 'I made Abram rich.' ²⁴I will accept nothing but what my men have eaten and
share that belongs to the men who went with me—to Aner, Eshcol and Mamre. Let
have their share."

s Covenant With Abram

5 After this, the word of the LORD came to Abram in a vision:

> "Do not be afraid, Abram.
> I am your shield, *e*
> your very great reward. *f*"

ut Abram said, "O Sovereign LORD, what can you give me since I remain childless and
one who will inherit *g* my estate is Eliezer of Damascus?" ³And Abram said, "You
given me no children; so a servant in my household will be my heir."
hen the word of the LORD came to him: "This man will not be your heir, but a son
ing from your own body will be your heir." ⁵He took him outside and said, "Look up
he heavens and count the stars—if indeed you can count them." Then he said to him,
shall your offspring be."
Abram believed the LORD, and he credited it to him as righteousness.
He also said to him, "I am the LORD, who brought you out of Ur of the Chaldeans to give
this land to take possession of it."
ut Abram said, "O Sovereign LORD, how can I know that I will gain possession of it?"

---

r a relative; or an ally   *b* 18 That is, Jerusalem   *c* 19 Or Possessor; also in verse 22   *d* 20 Or And praise be
e 1 Or sovereign   *f* 1 Or shield; / your reward will be very great   *g* 2 The meaning of the Hebrew for this
is uncertain.

⁹So the LORD said to him, "Bring me a heifer, a goat and a ram, each three years along with a dove and a young pigeon."

¹⁰Abram brought all these to him, cut them in two and arranged the halves opp each other; the birds, however, he did not cut in half. ¹¹Then birds of prey came down the carcasses, but Abram drove them away.

¹²As the sun was setting, Abram fell into a deep sleep, and a thick and drea darkness came over him. ¹³Then the LORD said to him, "Know for certain that your dese dants will be strangers in a country their own, and they will be enslaved mistreated four hundred years. ¹⁴But I punish the nation they serve as slaves, afterward they will come out with g possessions. ¹⁵You, however, will g your fathers in peace and be buried good old age. ¹⁶In the fourth genera your descendants will come back here the sin of the Amorites has not yet read its full measure."

¹⁷When the sun had set and dark had fallen, a smoking firepot with a bla torch appeared and passed between pieces. ¹⁸On that day the LORD made a enant with Abram and said, "To descendants I give this land, from the er ᵃ of Egypt to the great river, the Eup tes— ¹⁹the land of the Kenites, Keniz Kadmonites, ²⁰Hittites, Perizzites, R aites, ²¹Amorites, Canaanites, Girgas and Jebusites."

▣ ▦ DISCOVERING GOD ▦ ⊟

15:5–6
Life with God

When Abram looked up at the night sky, he remembered and believed God's promise to bless him with as many descendants as the stars he saw. Abram and Sarai had no children, and they were quite old. Abram could only base his assurance on God's ability to do the miraculous.

That's a good definition of faith. It's trusting in God's promises even though they may look impossible. It's not belief *in spite of* the facts; it's belief that must go *beyond* the facts.

And notice God's response. Abram wasn't a perfect man (see chapter 12, verses 10–20 [page 19] for an example); he needed forgiveness and a right standing with God, just as each one of us do. Abram's faith—his trust in God—gave him that standing.

The same is true for you today. As you seek God, you'll do well to follow Abram's example and trust God as best you can to lead you step by step. In the end you'll find that his promises are trustworthy, and that true faith has definite rewards.

Hagar and Ishmael

16 Now Sarai, Abram's wife, borne him no children. But had an Egyptian maidservant named gar; ²so she said to Abram, "The LORD kept me from having children. Go, sleep with my maidservant; perhaps I can bu family through her."

Abram agreed to what Sarai said. ³So after Abram had been living in Canaan ten ye Sarai his wife took her Egyptian maidservant Hagar and gave her to her husband t his wife. ⁴He slept with Hagar, and she conceived.

When she knew she was pregnant, she began to despise her mistress. ⁵Then S said to Abram, "You are responsible for the wrong I am suffering. I put my servant in arms, and now that she knows she is pregnant, she despises me. May the LORD ju between you and me."

⁶"Your servant is in your hands," Abram said. "Do with her whatever you think b Then Sarai mistreated Hagar; so she fled from her.

⁷The angel of the LORD found Hagar near a spring in the desert; it was the spring th beside the road to Shur. ⁸And he said, "Hagar, servant of Sarai, where have you c from, and where are you going?"

"I'm running away from my mistress Sarai," she answered.

⁹Then the angel of the LORD told her, "Go back to your mistress and submit to

ᵃ 18 Or *Wadi*

e angel added, "I will so increase your descendants that they will be too numerous to
t."

The angel of the LORD also said to her:

> "You are now with child
>   and you will have a son.
> You shall name him Ishmael,ᵃ
>   for the LORD has heard of your misery.
> ¹²He will be a wild donkey of a man;
>   his hand will be against everyone
>   and everyone's hand against him,
> and he will live in hostility
>   towardᵇ all his brothers."

She gave this name to the LORD who spoke to her: "You are the God who sees me," for
said, "I have now seenᶜ the One who sees me." ¹⁴That is why the well was called
Lahai Roiᵈ; it is still there, between Kadesh and Bered.

So Hagar bore Abram a son, and Abram gave the name Ishmael to the son she had
e. ¹⁶Abram was eighty-six years old when Hagar bore him Ishmael.

Covenant of Circumcision

When Abram was ninety-nine years old, the LORD appeared to him and said,
"I am God Almightyᵉ; walk before me and be blameless. ²I will confirm my
nant between me and you and will greatly increase your numbers."

bram fell facedown, and God said to him, ⁴"As for me, this is my covenant with you:
will be the father of many nations. ⁵No longer will you be called Abramᶠ; your name
be Abraham,ᵍ for I have made you a father of many nations. ⁶I will make you very
ıl; I will make nations of you, and kings will come from you. ⁷I will establish my
nant as an everlasting covenant between me and you and your descendants after
for the generations to come, to be your God and the God of your descendants after
⁸The whole land of Canaan, where you are now an alien, I will give as an everlast-
ossession to you and your descendants after you; and I will be their God."

hen God said to Abraham, "As for you, you must keep my covenant, you and your
endants after you for the generations to come. ¹⁰This is my covenant with you and
descendants after you, the covenant you are to keep: Every male among you shall
circumcised. ¹¹You are to undergo circumcision, and it will be the sign of the covenant
een me and you. ¹²For the generations to come every male among you who is eight
old must be circumcised, including those born in your household or bought with
ey from a foreigner—those who are not your offspring. ¹³Whether born in your
ehold or bought with your money, they must be circumcised. My covenant in your
is to be an everlasting covenant. ¹⁴Any uncircumcised male, who has not been
mcised in the flesh, will be cut off from his people; he has broken my covenant."

iod also said to Abraham, "As for Sarai your wife, you are no longer to call her Sarai;
aame will be Sarah. ¹⁶I will bless her and will surely give you a son by her. I will
her so that she will be the mother of nations; kings of peoples will come from her."
Abraham fell facedown; he laughed and said to himself, "Will a son be born to a man
ndred years old? Will Sarah bear a child at the age of ninety?" ¹⁸And Abraham said
d, "If only Ishmael might live under your blessing!"

hen God said, "Yes, but your wife Sarah will bear you a son, and you will call him
.ʰ I will establish my covenant with him as an everlasting covenant for his descen-
s after him. ²⁰And as for Ishmael, I have heard you: I will surely bless him; I will

---

ɪmael means God hears.   ᵇ12 Or live to the east / of   ᶜ13 Or seen the back of   ᵈ14 Beer Lahai Roi means
the Living One who sees me.   ᵉ1 Hebrew El-Shaddai   ᶠ5 Abram means exalted father.   ᵍ5 Abraham
ather of many.   ʰ19 Isaac means he laughs.

make him fruitful and will greatly increase his numbers. He will be the father of tv
rulers, and I will make him into a great nation. ²¹But my covenant I will establish
Isaac, whom Sarah will bear to you by this time next year." ²²When he had fini
speaking with Abraham, God went up from him.

²³On that very day Abraham took his son Ishmael and all those born in his house
or bought with his money, every male in his household, and circumcised them, as
told him. ²⁴Abraham was ninety-nine years old when he was circumcised, ²⁵and hi
Ishmael was thirteen; ²⁶Abraham and his son Ishmael were both circumcised or
same day. ²⁷And every male in Abraham's household, including those born in his h
hold or bought from a foreigner, was circumcised with him.

The Three Visitors

18 The LORD appeared to Abraham near the great trees of Mamre while he
sitting at the entrance to his tent in the heat of the day. ²Abraham looke
and saw three men standing nearby. When he saw them, he hurried from the entrar
his tent to meet them and bowed low to the ground.

³He said, "If I have found favor in your eyes, my lord,ᵃ do not pass your servar
⁴Let a little water be brought, and then you may all wash your feet and rest unde
tree. ⁵Let me get you something to eat, so you can be refreshed and then go on
way—now that you have come to your servant."

"Very well," they answered, "do as you say."

⁶So Abraham hurried into the tent to Sarah. "Quick," he said, "get three seahsᵇ c
flour and knead it and bake some bread."

⁷Then he ran to the herd and selected a choice, tender calf and gave it to a ser
who hurried to prepare it. ⁸He then brought some curds and milk and the calf tha
been prepared, and set these before them. While they ate, he stood near them un
tree.

⁹"Where is your wife Sarah?" they asked him.

"There, in the tent," he said.

¹⁰Then the LORDᶜ said, "I will surely return to you about this time next year, and
your wife will have a son."

Now Sarah was listening at the entrance to the tent, which was behind him. ¹¹
ham and Sarah were already old and well advanced in years, and Sarah was pas
age of childbearing. ¹²So Sarah laughed to herself as she thought, "After I am wor
and my masterᵈ is old, will I now have this pleasure?"

¹³Then the LORD said to Abraham, "Why did Sarah laugh and say, 'Will I really h
child, now that I am old?' ¹⁴Is anything too hard for the LORD? I will return to you
appointed time next year and Sarah will have a son."

¹⁵Sarah was afraid, so she lied and said, "I did not laugh."

But he said, "Yes, you did laugh."

Abraham Pleads for Sodom

¹⁶When the men got up to leave, they looked down toward Sodom, and Abr
walked along with them to see them on their way. ¹⁷Then the LORD said, "Shall
from Abraham what I am about to do? ¹⁸Abraham will surely become a great and pe
ful nation, and all nations on earth will be blessed through him. ¹⁹For I have choser
so that he will direct his children and his household after him to keep the way of the
by doing what is right and just, so that the LORD will bring about for Abraham what h
promised him."

²⁰Then the LORD said, "The outcry against Sodom and Gomorrah is so great and the
so grievous ²¹that I will go down and see if what they have done is as bad as the c
that has reached me. If not, I will know."

ᵃ3 Or O Lord   ᵇ6 That is, probably about 20 quarts (about 22 liters)   ᶜ10 Hebrew Then he   ᵈ12 Or husban

The men turned away and went to-
d Sodom, but Abraham remained
ding before the Lord.ª ²³Then Abra-
approached him and said: "Will you
eep away the righteous with the wick-
²⁴What if there are fifty righteous peo-
in the city? Will you really sweep it
y and not spareᵇ the place for the
e of the fifty righteous people in it?
r be it from you to do such a thing—to
the righteous with the wicked, treating
righteous and the wicked alike. Far be
om you! Will not the Judgeᶜ of all the
h do right?"

ᵗThe Lord said, "If I find fifty righteous
ple in the city of Sodom, I will spare the
le place for their sake."

ᵗThen Abraham spoke up again: "Now
I have been so bold as to speak to the
l, though I am nothing but dust and
es, ²⁸what if the number of the righ-
us is five less than fifty? Will you de-
y the whole city because of five peo-
?"

ᶠ I find forty-five there," he said, "I will
destroy it."

ᵗOnce again he spoke to him, "What if
y forty are found there?"

e said, "For the sake of forty, I will not
t."

▢ ▦▦▦▦▦ ADDRESSING QUESTIONS ▦▦▦▦▦ ↵

18:13–15
God

This unusual meeting between Abraham and
three men is actually a divine encounter in
which God takes on human form. On rare occasions in the Old Testament, God appears in
some physical way to get his point across.
(This kind of communication culminated 2000
years later when Jesus of Nazareth was born;
one of his titles was "Immanuel," which means
"God with us.")

Perhaps you're thinking that you'd have no
problem believing in God if he were to appear
to you miraculously. But neither Abraham nor
Sarah viewed this encounter as a summit
meeting with God. As a matter of fact, Sarah
was quick with a doubter's laugh (as Abraham had been; see Genesis 17, verse 17 [page
23]) and even lied right to God's face.

Be cautious of the unusual or bizarre in the
spiritual realm. Faith that is built primarily on
such infrequent "happenings" doesn't have a
very solid foundation. God certainly can and
sometimes will do unexpected things that will
affect you personally. But as you seek out
God's direction in your life, you'll also discover
him at work in the everyday occurrences. And
it's the perception of God's hand in everything
you do that provides the firmest foundation
for building up your faith.

ᵗThen he said, "May the Lord not be an-
but let me speak. What if only thirty can be found there?"
e answered, "I will not do it if I find thirty there."
Abraham said, "Now that I have been so bold as to speak to the Lord, what if only
nty can be found there?"
e said, "For the sake of twenty, I will not destroy it."
ᵗThen he said, "May the Lord not be angry, but let me speak just once more. What if
y ten can be found there?"
e answered, "For the sake of ten, I will not destroy it."
When the Lord had finished speaking with Abraham, he left, and Abraham returned
e.

lom and Gomorrah Destroyed

9 The two angels arrived at Sodom in the evening, and Lot was sitting in the
gateway of the city. When he saw them, he got up to meet them and bowed
n with his face to the ground. ²"My lords," he said, "please turn aside to your ser-
's house. You can wash your feet and spend the night and then go on your way early
e morning."
lo," they answered, "we will spend the night in the square."
sut he insisted so strongly that they did go with him and entered his house. He

Masoretic Text; an ancient Hebrew scribal tradition *but the Lord remained standing before Abraham*   ᵇ24 *Or forgive;*
ª verse 26   ᶜ25 *Or Ruler*

prepared a meal for them, baking bread without yeast, and they ate. ⁴Before they
gone to bed, all the men from every part of the city of Sodom—both young and old—
rounded the house. ⁵They called to Lot, "Where are the men who came to you toni
Bring them out to us so that we can have sex with them."

⁶Lot went outside to meet them and shut the door behind him ⁷and said, "No,
friends. Don't do this wicked thing. ⁸Look, I have two daughters who have never s
with a man. Let me bring them out to you, and you can do what you like with them.
don't do anything to these men, for they have come under the protection of my roof."

⁹"Get out of our way," they replied. And they said, "This fellow came here as an a
and now he wants to play the judge! We'll treat you worse than them." They
bringing pressure on Lot and moved forward to break down the door.

¹⁰But the men inside reached out and pulled Lot back into the house and shut the d
¹¹Then they struck the men who were at the door of the house, young and old,
blindness so that they could not find the door.

¹²The two men said to Lot, "Do you have anyone else here—sons-in-law, son
daughters, or anyone else in the city who belongs to you? Get them out of here, ¹

cause we are going to destroy this pl
The outcry to the LORD against its peop
so great that he has sent us to destroy

¹⁴So Lot went out and spoke to his s
in-law, who were pledged to marryᵃ
daughters. He said, "Hurry and get ou
this place, because the LORD is about to
stroy the city!" But his sons-in-law tho
he was joking.

¹⁵With the coming of dawn, the an
urged Lot, saying, "Hurry! Take your
and your two daughters who are here
you will be swept away when the ci
punished."

¹⁶When he hesitated, the men gras
his hand and the hands of his wife ar
his two daughters and led them safely
of the city, for the LORD was mercifu
them. ¹⁷As soon as they had brought t
out, one of them said, "Flee for your l
Don't look back, and don't stop anyw
in the plain! Flee to the mountains or
will be swept away!"

¹⁸But Lot said to them, "No, my lo
please! ¹⁹Yourᶜ servant has found fav
yourᶜ eyes, and youᶜ have shown g
kindness to me in sparing my life. But I can't flee to the mountains; this disaster
overtake me, and I'll die. ²⁰Look, here is a town near enough to run to, and it is smal
me flee to it—it is very small. Then my life will be spared."

²¹He said to him, "Very well, I will grant this request too; I will not overthrow the
you speak of. ²²But flee there quickly, because I cannot do anything until you reac
(That is why the town was called Zoar.ᵈ)

²³By the time Lot reached Zoar, the sun had risen over the land. ²⁴Then the LORD ra
down burning sulfur on Sodom and Gomorrah—from the LORD out of the heavens. ²⁵
he overthrew those cities and the entire plain, including all those living in the cities—

▣ STRENGTHENING RELATIONSHIPS ⊟

19:4–8
Social

Most people who've heard about Sodom and
Gomorrah associate those places with unre-
strained lust. In this part of the story, the men
of Sodom intended to commit homosexual
rape. Truly this passage demonstrates humanity at its worst, with unbridled appetites directing human behavior.

Note how this wickedness affected Lot and
his family. With such overt displays of immorality, their moral sensibilities had dulled. Was
Lot all that much better for offering his daughters to these men in place of the human-like
angels who were visiting? His behavior is rep-
rehensible—a telling story of how Lot slowly
conformed to the company he kept. In the end,
it's hard for readers to tell who "the good guy"
is in this story.

What's the lesson in this passage? Choose
your associates carefully. You could easily become like them.

ᵃ14 Or were married to   ᵇ18 Or No, Lord; or No, my lord   ᶜ19 The Hebrew is singular.   ᵈ22 Zoar means sma

the vegetation in the land. ²⁶But Lot's wife looked back, and she became a pillar of

Early the next morning Abraham got up and returned to the place where he had
od before the LORD. ²⁸He looked down toward Sodom and Gomorrah, toward all the
d of the plain, and he saw dense smoke rising from the land, like smoke from a
ace.
So when God destroyed the cities of the plain, he remembered Abraham, and he
ught Lot out of the catastrophe that overthrew the cities where Lot had lived.

and His Daughters

Lot and his two daughters left Zoar and settled in the mountains, for he was afraid to
y in Zoar. He and his two daughters lived in a cave. ³¹One day the older daughter said
he younger, "Our father is old, and there is no man around here to lie with us, as is
custom all over the earth. ³²Let's get our father to drink wine and then lie with him
preserve our family line through our father."
That night they got their father to drink wine, and the older daughter went in and
with him. He was not aware of it when she lay down or when she got up.
The next day the older daughter said to the younger, "Last night I lay with my father.
's get him to drink wine again tonight, and you go in and lie with him so we can
serve our family line through our father." ³⁵So they got their father to drink wine that
ht also, and the younger daughter went and lay with him. Again he was not aware of
hen she lay down or when she got up.
So both of Lot's daughters became pregnant by their father. ³⁷The older daughter had
on, and she named him Moab[a]; he is the father of the Moabites of today. ³⁸The
nger daughter also had a son, and she named him Ben-Ammi[b]; he is the father of
Ammonites of today.

raham and Abimelech

20 Now Abraham moved on from there into the region of the Negev and lived
between Kadesh and Shur. For a while he stayed in Gerar, ²and there Abra-
n said of his wife Sarah, "She is my sister." Then Abimelech king of Gerar sent for
ah and took her.
But God came to Abimelech in a dream one night and said to him, "You are as good as
d because of the woman you have taken; she is a married woman."
Now Abimelech had not gone near her, so he said, "Lord, will you destroy an innocent
ion? ⁵Did he not say to me, 'She is my sister,' and didn't she also say, 'He is my
ther'? I have done this with a clear conscience and clean hands."
Then God said to him in the dream, "Yes, I know you did this with a clear conscience,
I so I have kept you from sinning against me. That is why I did not let you touch her.
w return the man's wife, for he is a prophet, and he will pray for you and you will
. But if you do not return her, you may be sure that you and all yours will die."
Early the next morning Abimelech summoned all his officials, and when he told them
that had happened, they were very much afraid. ⁹Then Abimelech called Abraham in
I said, "What have you done to us? How have I wronged you that you have brought
h great guilt upon me and my kingdom? You have done things to me that should not
done." ¹⁰And Abimelech asked Abraham, "What was your reason for doing this?"
¹¹Abraham replied, "I said to myself, 'There is surely no fear of God in this place, and
y will kill me because of my wife.' ¹²Besides, she really is my sister, the daughter of
father though not of my mother; and she became my wife. ¹³And when God had me
nder from my father's household, I said to her, 'This is how you can show your love to
Everywhere we go, say of me, "He is my brother." ' "
Then Abimelech brought sheep and cattle and male and female slaves and gave

---

Moab sounds like the Hebrew for *from father*.   b 38 Ben-Ammi means *son of my people*.

them to Abraham, and he returned Sarah his wife to him. ¹⁵And Abimelech said, "My l
is before you; live wherever you like."

¹⁶To Sarah he said, "I am giving your brother a thousand shekels*a* of silver. This i
cover the offense against you before all who are with you; you are completely vir
cated."

¹⁷Then Abraham prayed to God, and God healed Abimelech, his wife and his slave ʛ
so they could have children again, ¹⁸for the LORD had closed up every womb in Abin
lech's household because of Abraham's wife Sarah.

The Birth of Isaac

21 Now the LORD was gracious to Sarah as he had said, and the LORD did
Sarah what he had promised. ²Sarah became pregnant and bore a sor
Abraham in his old age, at the very time God had promised him. ³Abraham gave
name Isaac*b* to the son Sarah bore him. ⁴When his son Isaac was eight days
Abraham circumcised him, as God commanded him. ⁵Abraham was a hundred years
when his son Isaac was born to him.

⁶Sarah said, "God has brought me laughter, and everyone who hears about this
laugh with me." ⁷And she added, "Who would have said to Abraham that Sarah wc
nurse children? Yet I have borne him a son in his old age."

Hagar and Ishmael Sent Away

⁸The child grew and was weaned, and on the day Isaac was weaned Abraham hel
great feast. ⁹But Sarah saw that the son whom Hagar the Egyptian had borne to Abrah
was mocking, ¹⁰and she said to Abraham, "Get rid of that slave woman and her son,
that slave woman's son will never share in the inheritance with my son Isaac."

¹¹The matter distressed Abraham greatly because it concerned his son. ¹²But God s
to him, "Do not be so distressed about the boy and your maidservant. Listen to whate
Sarah tells you, because it is through Isaac that your offspring*c* will be reckoned. ¹³I
make the son of the maidservant into a nation also, because he is your offspring."

¹⁴Early the next morning Abraham took some food and a skin of water and gave th
to Hagar. He set them on her shoulders and then sent her off with the boy. She went
her way and wandered in the desert of Beersheba.

¹⁵When the water in the skin was gone, she put the boy under one of the bush
¹⁶Then she went off and sat down nearby, about a bowshot away, for she thought
cannot watch the boy die." And as she sat there nearby, she*d* began to sob.

¹⁷God heard the boy crying, and the angel of God called to Hagar from heaven and s
to her, "What is the matter, Hagar? Do not be afraid; God has heard the boy crying as
lies there. ¹⁸Lift the boy up and take him by the hand, for I will make him into a gi
nation."

¹⁹Then God opened her eyes and she saw a well of water. So she went and filled
skin with water and gave the boy a drink.

²⁰God was with the boy as he grew up. He lived in the desert and became an arcr
²¹While he was living in the Desert of Paran, his mother got a wife for him from Eg

The Treaty at Beersheba

²²At that time Abimelech and Phicol the commander of his forces said to Abrah
"God is with you in everything you do. ²³Now swear to me here before God that you
not deal falsely with me or my children or my descendants. Show to me and the cou
where you are living as an alien the same kindness I have shown to you."

²⁴Abraham said, "I swear it."

²⁵Then Abraham complained to Abimelech about a well of water that Abimele

a16 That is, about 25 pounds (about 11.5 kilograms)   *b3* *Isaac* means *he laughs.*   *c12* Or *seed*   *d16* Hebrew;
Septuagint *the child*

vants had seized. ²⁶But Abimelech said, "I don't know who has done this. You did not
me, and I heard about it only today."

²⁷So Abraham brought sheep and cattle and gave them to Abimelech, and the two men
de a treaty. ²⁸Abraham set apart seven ewe lambs from the flock, ²⁹and Abimelech
ed Abraham, "What is the meaning of these seven ewe lambs you have set apart by
mselves?"

³⁰He replied, "Accept these seven lambs from my hand as a witness that I dug this
ll."

³¹So that place was called Beersheba,ᵃ because the two men swore an oath there.

³²After the treaty had been made at Beersheba, Abimelech and Phicol the commander
his forces returned to the land of the Philistines. ³³Abraham planted a tamarisk tree in
ersheba, and there he called upon the name of the LORD, the Eternal God. ³⁴And
aham stayed in the land of the Philistines for a long time.

raham Tested

2 Some time later God tested Abraham. He said to him, "Abraham!"
"Here I am," he replied.

²Then God said, "Take your son, your only son, Isaac, whom you love, and go to the
ion of Moriah. Sacrifice him there as a burnt offering on one of the mountains I will tell
ı about."

³Early the next morning Abraham got up and saddled his donkey. He took with him
o of his servants and his son Isaac. When he had cut enough wood for the burnt
ering, he set out for the place God had told him about. ⁴On the third day Abraham
ked up and saw the place in the distance. ⁵He said to his servants, "Stay here with the

Beersheba can mean well of seven or well of the oath.

:: DISCOVERING GOD ::

22:1–2, 12–18
Life with God

What is going on here? Why would God make Abraham wait years for his promised son, only to
ı urn around and make this heart-wrenching request?

If all we knew of God was from a quick reading of these few verses, we'd be left with more
questions than answers. But some important points emerge after closer examination that can help
you understand who God is and what he wants to do in your life if you respond to him.

First, Abraham needed to be reminded that his son Isaac was a gift from God. Ultimately,
everything we have belongs to God and must be held before him with an open hand.

Second, Abraham had God's promise that Isaac would have descendants. The current situation, however, appeared to contradict that assurance. So Abraham could either trust God in the
midst of confusion or reject God because of unanswered questions. After decades of knowing
God's character, of observing his love and kindness, and of being delivered from difficult situations, Abraham knew he could trust God with these new questions based on God's previous trustworthiness. The same holds true for us.

Third, much more was going on here than meets the eye. Had Abraham looked only at the
short term, he might have taken Isaac and run away. But by obeying God, he gave us a picture of
a time when another "only Son" would walk up a hill and lie down to die. That's what Jesus did
for us. In that case, however, God didn't spare him—the knife fell, so to speak, when Jesus was
crucified. Because of that sacrifice, we all can have new life.

Finally, as Abraham took his son back with him, he gave us a picture of Jesus' resurrection.
In both instances a situation of death led to unexpected life.

It's not easy to embark on a life where God gets to be God. Times of testing will come. But
et Abraham's example be yours. You can say as he did in verse 8, "God himself will provide."

donkey while I and the boy go over there. We will worship and then we will come b
to you."

⁶Abraham took the wood for the burnt offering and placed it on his son Isaac, and
himself carried the fire and the knife. As the two of them went on together, ⁷Isaac sp
up and said to his father Abraham, "Father?"

"Yes, my son?" Abraham replied.

"The fire and wood are here," Isaac said, "but where is the lamb for the burnt offerin

⁸Abraham answered, "God himself will provide the lamb for the burnt offering,
son." And the two of them went on together.

⁹When they reached the place God had told him about, Abraham built an altar th
and arranged the wood on it. He bound his son Isaac and laid him on the altar, on to
the wood. ¹⁰Then he reached out his hand and took the knife to slay his son. ¹¹But
angel of the Lord called out to him from heaven, "Abraham! Abraham!"

"Here I am," he replied.

¹²"Do not lay a hand on the boy," he said. "Do not do anything to him. Now I know
you fear God, because you have not withheld from me your son, your only son."

¹³Abraham looked up and there in a thicket he saw a ramᵃ caught by its horns.
went over and took the ram and sacrificed it as a burnt offering instead of his son.
Abraham called that place The Lord Will Provide. And to this day it is said, "On
mountain of the Lord it will be provided."

¹⁵The angel of the Lord called to Abraham from heaven a second time ¹⁶and said
swear by myself, declares the Lord, that because you have done this and have
withheld your son, your only son, ¹⁷I will surely bless you and make your descendants
numerous as the stars in the sky and as the sand on the seashore. Your descendants
take possession of the cities of their enemies, ¹⁸and through your offspringᵇ all nati
on earth will be blessed, because you have obeyed me."

¹⁹Then Abraham returned to his servants, and they set off together for Beersheba.
Abraham stayed in Beersheba.

Nahor's Sons

²⁰Some time later Abraham was told, "Milcah is also a mother; she has borne sons
your brother Nahor: ²¹Uz the firstborn, Buz his brother, Kemuel (the father of Ara
²²Kesed, Hazo, Pildash, Jidlaph and Bethuel." ²³Bethuel became the father of Rebel
Milcah bore these eight sons to Abraham's brother Nahor. ²⁴His concubine, whose na
was Reumah, also had sons: Tebah, Gaham, Tahash and Maacah.

The Death of Sarah

23 Sarah lived to be a hundred and twenty-seven years old. ²She died at K
ath Arba (that is, Hebron) in the land of Canaan, and Abraham went
mourn for Sarah and to weep over her.

³Then Abraham rose from beside his dead wife and spoke to the Hittites.ᶜ He said,
am an alien and a stranger among you. Sell me some property for a burial site here
can bury my dead."

⁵The Hittites replied to Abraham, ⁶"Sir, listen to us. You are a mighty prince among
Bury your dead in the choicest of our tombs. None of us will refuse you his tomb
burying your dead."

⁷Then Abraham rose and bowed down before the people of the land, the Hittites.
said to them, "If you are willing to let me bury my dead, then listen to me and interce
with Ephron son of Zohar on my behalf ⁹so he will sell me the cave of Machpelah, wh
belongs to him and is at the end of his field. Ask him to sell it to me for the full price
a burial site among you."

ᵃ13 Many manuscripts of the Masoretic Text, Samaritan Pentateuch, Septuagint and Syriac; most manuscripts of the Masoretic T
a ram behind ,him;   ᵇ18 Or seed   ᶜ3 Or the sons of Heth; also in verses 5, 7, 10, 16, 18 and 20

⁰Ephron the Hittite was sitting among his people and he replied to Abraham in the aring of all the Hittites who had come to the gate of his city. ¹¹"No, my lord," he said. sten to me; I give*a* you the field, and I give*a* you the cave that is in it. I give*a* it to in the presence of my people. Bury your dead."

²Again Abraham bowed down before the people of the land ¹³and he said to Ephron their hearing, "Listen to me, if you will. I will pay the price of the field. Accept it from so I can bury my dead there."

⁴Ephron answered Abraham, ¹⁵"Listen to me, my lord; the land is worth four hundred ekels*b* of silver, but what is that between me and you? Bury your dead."

⁶Abraham agreed to Ephron's terms and weighed out for him the price he had named the hearing of the Hittites: four hundred shekels of silver, according to the weight rent among the merchants.

⁷So Ephron's field in Machpelah near Mamre—both the field and the cave in it, and all trees within the borders of the field—was deeded ¹⁸to Abraham as his property in the sence of all the Hittites who had come to the gate of the city. ¹⁹Afterward Abraham ied his wife Sarah in the cave in the field of Machpelah near Mamre (which is at oron) in the land of Canaan. ²⁰So the field and the cave in it were deeded to Abraham the Hittites as a burial site.

ac and Rebekah

4 Abraham was now old and well advanced in years, and the LORD had blessed him in every way. ²He said to the chief*c* servant in his household, the one charge of all that he had, "Put your hand under my thigh. ³I want you to swear by the ᴅ, the God of heaven and the God of rth, that you will not get a wife for my n from the daughters of the Canaanites, ong whom I am living, ⁴but will go to country and my own relatives and get a fe for my son Isaac."

ᵗThe servant asked him, "What if the man is unwilling to come back with me this land? Shall I then take your son ck to the country you came from?"

⁶"Make sure that you do not take my son ck there," Abraham said. ⁷"The LORD, the d of heaven, who brought me out of my her's household and my native land and o spoke to me and promised me on th, saying, 'To your offspring*d* I will give s land'—he will send his angel before 1 so that you can get a wife for my son m there. ⁸If the woman is unwilling to me back with you, then you will be re-sed from this oath of mine. Only do not ke my son back there." ⁹So the servant t his hand under the thigh of his master raham and swore an oath to him con-ning this matter.

¹⁰Then the servant took ten of his mas-'s camels and left, taking with him all ads of good things from his master. He

STRENGTHENING RELATIONSHIPS

24:3-4
Marriage

The Bible doesn't endorse any one approach to finding a mate, but it does set forth a clear prerequisite—shared spiritual viewpoints. God's people are advised against marrying others who don't have the same desire to put God first in every area of life. When two people are first committed to following God's plan for their lives, they will experience the oneness and fulfillment God intended for the lifelong union of marriage.

If you're married but are having difficulties, could it be that some of them come from not sharing a common spiritual foundation? If you're contemplating marriage, realize that there may be heartache ahead if the two of you don't agree on what will be the final authority in your marriage before you say "I do."

God's purpose isn't to limit your choices—he wants to extend your joys. The best marriage counseling advice you can get is this: Work together to build your relationship on the solid ground of God and the teaching of the Bible.

Or sell   *b 15 That is, about 10 pounds (about 4.5 kilograms)*   *c 2 Or oldest*   *d 7 Or seed*

set out for Aram Naharaim*a* and made his way to the town of Nahor. ¹¹He had camels kneel down near the well outside the town; it was toward evening, the time women go out to draw water.

¹²Then he prayed, "O LORD, God of my master Abraham, give me success today, a show kindness to my master Abraham. ¹³See, I am standing beside this spring, and daughters of the townspeople are coming out to draw water. ¹⁴May it be that when I to a girl, 'Please let down your jar that I may have a drink,' and she says, 'Drink, and water your camels too'—let her be the one you have chosen for your servant Isaac. this I will know that you have shown kindness to my master."

¹⁵Before he had finished praying, Rebekah came out with her jar on her shoulder. S was the daughter of Bethuel son of Milcah, who was the wife of Abraham's brot Nahor. ¹⁶The girl was very beautiful, a virgin; no man had ever lain with her. She w down to the spring, filled her jar and came up again.

¹⁷The servant hurried to meet her and said, "Please give me a little water from y jar."

¹⁸"Drink, my lord," she said, and quickly lowered the jar to her hands and gave hi drink.

¹⁹After she had given him a drink, she said, "I'll draw water for your camels too, u they have finished drinking." ²⁰So she quickly emptied her jar into the trough, ran bac the well to draw more water, and drew enough for all his camels. ²¹Without sayin word, the man watched her closely to learn whether or not the LORD had made journey successful.

²²When the camels had finished drinking, the man took out a gold nose ring weigh a beka*b* and two gold bracelets weighing ten shekels.*c* ²³Then he asked, "Wh daughter are you? Please tell me, is there room in your father's house for us to spend night?"

²⁴She answered him, "I am the daughter of Bethuel, the son that Milcah bore to Nah ²⁵And she added, "We have plenty of straw and fodder, as well as room for you to sp the night."

²⁶Then the man bowed down and worshiped the LORD, ²⁷saying, "Praise be to the L the God of my master Abraham, who has not abandoned his kindness and faithfulnes my master. As for me, the LORD has led me on the journey to the house of my mast relatives."

²⁸The girl ran and told her mother's household about these things. ²⁹Now Rebekah a brother named Laban, and he hurried out to the man at the spring. ³⁰As soon as he seen the nose ring, and the bracelets on his sister's arms, and had heard Rebekah what the man said to her, he went out to the man and found him standing by the cam near the spring. ³¹"Come, you who are blessed by the LORD," he said. "Why are standing out here? I have prepared the house and a place for the camels."

³²So the man went to the house, and the camels were unloaded. Straw and food were brought for the camels, and water for him and his men to wash their feet. ³³T food was set before him, but he said, "I will not eat until I have told you what I have say."

"Then tell us," ⌊Laban⌋ said.

³⁴So he said, "I am Abraham's servant. ³⁵The LORD has blessed my master abundan and he has become wealthy. He has given him sheep and cattle, silver and gold, mens vants and maidservants, and camels and donkeys. ³⁶My master's wife Sarah has bo him a son in her*d* old age, and he has given him everything he owns. ³⁷And my ma made me swear an oath, and said, 'You must not get a wife for my son from the dau ters of the Canaanites, in whose land I live, ³⁸but go to my father's family and to my c clan, and get a wife for my son.'

a 10 That is, Northwest Mesopotamia (about 110 grams)   *b 22* That is, about 1/5 ounce (about 5.5 grams)   *c 22* That is, about 4 ounces   *d 36* Or *his*

³⁹"Then I asked my master, 'What if the woman will not come back with me?'

⁴⁰"He replied, 'The Lord, before whom I have walked, will send his angel with you and ake your journey a success, so that you can get a wife for my son from my own clan ad from my father's family. ⁴¹Then, when you go to my clan, you will be released from y oath even if they refuse to give her to you—you will be released from my oath.'

⁴²"When I came to the spring today, I said, 'O Lord, God of my master Abraham, if you ill, please grant success to the journey on which I have come. ⁴³See, I am standing ⋅side this spring; if a maiden comes out to draw water and I say to her, "Please let me ink a little water from your jar," ⁴⁴and if she says to me, "Drink, and I'll draw water for ur camels too," let her be the one the Lord has chosen for my master's son.'

⁴⁵"Before I finished praying in my heart, Rebekah came out, with her jar on her shoul- ⋅r. She went down to the spring and drew water, and I said to her, 'Please give me a ink.'

⁴⁶"She quickly lowered her jar from her shoulder and said, 'Drink, and I'll water your mels too.' So I drank, and she watered the camels also.

⁴⁷"I asked her, 'Whose daughter are you?'

"She said, 'The daughter of Bethuel son of Nahor, whom Milcah bore to him.'

"Then I put the ring in her nose and the bracelets on her arms, ⁴⁸and I bowed down nd worshiped the Lord. I praised the Lord, the God of my master Abraham, who had led ⋅e on the right road to get the granddaughter of my master's brother for his son. ⁴⁹Now you will show kindness and faithfulness to my master, tell me; and if not, tell me, so I ⋅ay know which way to turn."

⁵⁰Laban and Bethuel answered, "This is from the Lord; we can say nothing to you one ⋅ay or the other. ⁵¹Here is Rebekah; take her and go, and let her become the wife of ⋅ur master's son, as the Lord has directed."

⁵²When Abraham's servant heard what they said, he bowed down to the ground ⋅efore the Lord. ⁵³Then the servant brought out gold and silver jewelry and articles of ⋅othing and gave them to Rebekah; he also gave costly gifts to her brother and to her ⋅other. ⁵⁴Then he and the men who were with him ate and drank and spent the night ⋅ere.

When they got up the next morning, he said, "Send me on my way to my master."

⁵⁵But her brother and her mother replied, "Let the girl remain with us ten days or so; ⋅en you[a] may go."

⁵⁶But he said to them, "Do not detain me, now that the Lord has granted success to my ⋅urney. Send me on my way so I may go to my master."

⁵⁷Then they said, "Let's call the girl and ask her about it." ⁵⁸So they called Rebekah ⋅nd asked her, "Will you go with this man?"

"I will go," she said.

⁵⁹So they sent their sister Rebekah on her way, along with her nurse and Abraham's ⋅rvant and his men. ⁶⁰And they blessed Rebekah and said to her,

> "Our sister, may you increase
>   to thousands upon thousands;
> may your offspring possess
>   the gates of their enemies."

⁶¹Then Rebekah and her maids got ready and mounted their camels and went back ⋅ith the man. So the servant took Rebekah and left.

⁶²Now Isaac had come from Beer Lahai Roi, for he was living in the Negev. ⁶³He went ⋅ut to the field one evening to meditate,[b] and as he looked up, he saw camels ap- ⋅roaching. ⁶⁴Rebekah also looked up and saw Isaac. She got down from her camel ⁶⁵and ⋅sked the servant, "Who is that man in the field coming to meet us?"

"He is my master," the servant answered. So she took her veil and covered herself.

⁵5 Or she   b 63 The meaning of the Hebrew for this word is uncertain.

⁶⁶Then the servant told Isaac all he had done. ⁶⁷Isaac brought her into the tent of ▮ mother Sarah, and he married Rebekah. So she became his wife, and he loved her; a Isaac was comforted after his mother's death.

The Death of Abraham

25 Abraham took[a] another wife, whose name was Keturah. ²She bore h Zimran, Jokshan, Medan, Midian, Ishbak and Shuah. ³Jokshan was the fath of Sheba and Dedan; the descendants of Dedan were the Asshurites, the Letushites a the Leummites. ⁴The sons of Midian were Ephah, Epher, Hanoch, Abida and Eldaah. these were descendants of Keturah.

⁵Abraham left everything he owned to Isaac. ⁶But while he was still living, he ga gifts to the sons of his concubines and sent them away from his son Isaac to the land the east.

⁷Altogether, Abraham lived a hundred and seventy-five years. ⁸Then Abraha breathed his last and died at a good c age, an old man and full of years; and was gathered to his people. ⁹His sons Isa and Ishmael buried him in the cave Machpelah near Mamre, in the field Ephron son of Zohar the Hittite, ¹⁰the fie Abraham had bought from the Hittites There Abraham was buried with his w Sarah. ¹¹After Abraham's death, G blessed his son Isaac, who then lived ne Beer Lahai Roi.

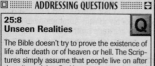

⬛ ▦▦▦▦ ADDRESSING QUESTIONS ▦▦▦▦ ⬓

25:8
Unseen Realities   **Q**

The Bible doesn't try to prove the existence of life after death or of heaven or hell. The Scriptures simply assume that people live on after they die and that God has some sort of reward and punishment system.

The details of life after death unfold as the Scriptures unfold. But even here in the first book of the Bible we find a phrase that hints at this reality by telling us that Abraham was "gathered to his people." Physically, he was a long way off from the burial sites of his ancestors, so surely this cannot refer to actually laying his body among those of his extended family. The phrase "gathered to his people," however, does point to some sort of existence beyond this life. As you continue to look through this book, you may want to search out more clues to what the afterlife will be like.

Ishmael's Sons

¹²This is the account of Abraham's s Ishmael, whom Sarah's maidservant, Hag the Egyptian, bore to Abraham.

¹³These are the names of the sons of Is mael, listed in the order of their birth: N baioth the firstborn of Ishmael, Kedar, A beel, Mibsam, ¹⁴Mishma, Dumah, Mass ¹⁵Hadad, Tema, Jetur, Naphish and Ked mah. ¹⁶These were the sons of Ishma and these are the names of the twelve tr al rulers according to their settlements a camps. ¹⁷Altogether, Ishmael lived a hundred and thirty-seven years. He breathed ▮ last and died, and he was gathered to his people. ¹⁸His descendants settled in the ar from Havilah to Shur, near the border of Egypt, as you go toward Asshur. And they liv in hostility toward[c] all their brothers.

Jacob and Esau

¹⁹This is the account of Abraham's son Isaac.

Abraham became the father of Isaac, ²⁰and Isaac was forty years old when he marri Rebekah daughter of Bethuel the Aramean from Paddan Aram[d] and sister of Laban t Aramean.

²¹Isaac prayed to the LORD on behalf of his wife, because she was barren. The Lo answered his prayer, and his wife Rebekah became pregnant. ²²The babies jostled ea

---

a1 Or had taken   *b10 Or the sons of Heth*   *c18 Or lived to the east of*   *d20 That is, Northwest Mesopotamia*

her within her, and she said, "Why is this happening to me?" So she went to inquire of
e LORD.

²³The LORD said to her,

> "Two nations are in your womb,
>   and two peoples from within you will be separated;
> one people will be stronger than the other,
>   and the older will serve the younger."

²⁴When the time came for her to give birth, there were twin boys in her womb. ²⁵The
st to come out was red, and his whole body was like a hairy garment; so they named
m Esau.ᵃ ²⁶After this, his brother came out, with his hand grasping Esau's heel; so he
as named Jacob.ᵇ Isaac was sixty years old when Rebekah gave birth to them.

²⁷The boys grew up, and Esau became a skillful hunter, a man of the open country,
hile Jacob was a quiet man, staying among the tents. ²⁸Isaac, who had a taste for wild
ame, loved Esau, but Rebekah loved Jacob.

²⁹Once when Jacob was cooking some stew, Esau came in from the open country,
mished. ³⁰He said to Jacob, "Quick, let me have some of that red stew! I'm famished!"
hat is why he was also called Edom.ᶜ)

³¹Jacob replied, "First sell me your birthright."

³²"Look, I am about to die," Esau said. "What good is the birthright to me?"

³³But Jacob said, "Swear to me first." So he swore an oath to him, selling his birthright
Jacob.

³⁴Then Jacob gave Esau some bread and some lentil stew. He ate and drank, and then
ot up and left.

So Esau despised his birthright.

saac and Abimelech

26 Now there was a famine in the land—besides the earlier famine of Abraham's time—and Isaac went to Abimelech king of the Philistines in Gerar.
The LORD appeared to Isaac and said, "Do not go down to Egypt; live in the land where
tell you to live. ³Stay in this land for a while, and I will be with you and will bless you.
or to you and your descendants I will give all these lands and will confirm the oath I
wore to your father Abraham. ⁴I will make your descendants as numerous as the stars in
he sky and will give them all these lands, and through your offspringᵈ all nations on
arth will be blessed, ⁵because Abraham obeyed me and kept my requirements, my
ommands, my decrees and my laws." ⁶So Isaac stayed in Gerar.

⁷When the men of that place asked him about his wife, he said, "She is my sister,"
ecause he was afraid to say, "She is my wife." He thought, "The men of this place might
ll me on account of Rebekah, because she is beautiful."

⁸When Isaac had been there a long time, Abimelech king of the Philistines looked
own from a window and saw Isaac caressing his wife Rebekah. ⁹So Abimelech sum-
oned Isaac and said, "She is really your wife! Why did you say, 'She is my sister'?"

Isaac answered him, "Because I thought I might lose my life on account of her."

¹⁰Then Abimelech said, "What is this you have done to us? One of the men might well
ave slept with your wife, and you would have brought guilt upon us."

¹¹So Abimelech gave orders to all the people: "Anyone who molests this man or his
ife shall surely be put to death."

¹²Isaac planted crops in that land and the same year reaped a hundredfold, because
e LORD blessed him. ¹³The man became rich, and his wealth continued to grow until he
ecame very wealthy. ¹⁴He had so many flocks and herds and servants that the Philis-

ᵃ5 *Esau may mean* hairy; *he was also called* Edom, *which means* red.   ᵇ26 *Jacob means* he grasps the heel *(figuratively,*
deceives).   ᶜ30 *Edom means* red.   ᵈ4 *Or* seed

tines envied him. [15]So all the wells that his father's servants had dug in the time of [h]
father Abraham, the Philistines stopped up, filling them with earth.

[16]Then Abimelech said to Isaac, "Move away from us; you have become too power[ful]
for us."

[17]So Isaac moved away from there and encamped in the Valley of Gerar and settl[ed]
there. [18]Isaac reopened the wells that had been dug in the time of his father Abraha[m]
which the Philistines had stopped up after Abraham died, and he gave them the sam[e]
names his father had given them.

[19]Isaac's servants dug in the valley and discovered a well of fresh water there. [20]B[ut]
the herdsmen of Gerar quarreled with Isaac's herdsmen and said, "The water is ours!"
he named the well Esek,[a] because they disputed with him. [21]Then they dug anoth[er]
well, but they quarreled over that one also; so he named it Sitnah.[b] [22]He moved on fro[m]
there and dug another well, and no one quarreled over it. He named it Rehobot[h]
saying, "Now the LORD has given us room and we will flourish in the land."

[23]From there he went up to Beersheba. [24]That night the LORD appeared to him and sa[id,]
"I am the God of your father Abraham. Do not be afraid, for I am with you; I will bless y[ou]
and will increase the number of your descendants for the sake of my servant Abraham[."]

[25]Isaac built an altar there and called on the name of the LORD. There he pitched h[is]
tent, and there his servants dug a well.

[26]Meanwhile, Abimelech had come to him from Gerar, with Ahuzzath his person[al]
adviser and Phicol the commander of his forces. [27]Isaac asked them, "Why have you com[e]
to me, since you were hostile to me and sent me away?"

[28]They answered, "We saw clearly that the LORD was with you; so we said, 'The[re]
ought to be a sworn agreement between us'—between us and you. Let us make a trea[ty]
with you [29]that you will do us no harm, just as we did not molest you but always treate[d]
you well and sent you away in peace. And now you are blessed by the LORD."

[30]Isaac then made a feast for them, and they ate and drank. [31]Early the next mornin[g]
the men swore an oath to each other. Then Isaac sent them on their way, and they le[ft]
him in peace.

[32]That day Isaac's servants came and told him about the well they had dug. They sai[d,]
"We've found water!" [33]He called it Shibah,[d] and to this day the name of the town h[as]
been Beersheba.[e]

[34]When Esau was forty years old, he married Judith daughter of Beeri the Hittite, an[d]
also Basemath daughter of Elon the Hittite. [35]They were a source of grief to Isaac an[d]
Rebekah.

Jacob Gets Isaac's Blessing

27 When Isaac was old and his eyes were so weak that he could no longer se[e,]
he called for Esau his older son and said to him, "My son."

"Here I am," he answered.

[2]Isaac said, "I am now an old man and don't know the day of my death. [3]Now then, g[et]
your weapons—your quiver and bow—and go out to the open country to hunt some wi[ld]
game for me. [4]Prepare me the kind of tasty food I like and bring it to me to eat, so tha[t I]
may give you my blessing before I die."

[5]Now Rebekah was listening as Isaac spoke to his son Esau. When Esau left for th[e]
open country to hunt game and bring it back, [6]Rebekah said to her son Jacob, "Look[, I]
overheard your father say to your brother Esau, [7]'Bring me some game and prepare m[e]
some tasty food to eat, so that I may give you my blessing in the presence of the Lo[rd]
before I die.' [8]Now, my son, listen carefully and do what I tell you: [9]Go out to the flo[ck]
and bring me two choice young goats, so I can prepare some tasty food for your fathe[r]

---

[a]20 *Esek* means dispute.   [b]21 *Sitnah* means opposition.   [c]22 *Rehoboth* means room.   [d]33 *Shibah* can mean
oath or seven.   [e]33 *Beersheba* can mean well of the oath or well of seven.

ust the way he likes it. ¹⁰Then take it to your father to eat, so that he may give you his
blessing before he dies."

¹¹Jacob said to Rebekah his mother, "But my brother Esau is a hairy man, and I'm a
man with smooth skin. ¹²What if my father touches me? I would appear to be tricking
him and would bring down a curse on myself rather than a blessing."

¹³His mother said to him, "My son, let the curse fall on me. Just do what I say; go and
get them for me."

¹⁴So he went and got them and brought them to his mother, and she prepared some
tasty food, just the way his father liked it. ¹⁵Then Rebekah took the best clothes of Esau
her older son, which she had in the house, and put them on her younger son Jacob.
¹⁶She also covered his hands and the smooth part of his neck with the goatskins. ¹⁷Then
she handed to her son Jacob the tasty food and the bread she had made.

¹⁸He went to his father and said, "My father."

"Yes, my son," he answered. "Who is it?"

¹⁹Jacob said to his father, "I am Esau your firstborn. I have done as you told me. Please
sit up and eat some of my game so that you may give me your blessing."

²⁰Isaac asked his son, "How did you find it so quickly, my son?"

"The LORD your God gave me success," he replied.

²¹Then Isaac said to Jacob, "Come near so I can touch you, my son, to know whether
you really are my son Esau or not."

²²Jacob went close to his father Isaac, who touched him and said, "The voice is the
voice of Jacob, but the hands are the hands of Esau." ²³He did not recognize him, for his
hands were hairy like those of his brother Esau; so he blessed him. ²⁴"Are you really my
son Esau?" he asked.

"I am," he replied.

²⁵Then he said, "My son, bring me some of your game to eat, so that I may give you my
blessing."

Jacob brought it to him and he ate; and he brought some wine and he drank. ²⁶Then
his father Isaac said to him, "Come here, my son, and kiss me."

²⁷So he went to him and kissed him. When Isaac caught the smell of his clothes, he
blessed him and said,

> "Ah, the smell of my son
>   is like the smell of a field
>   that the LORD has blessed.
> ²⁸May God give you of heaven's dew
>   and of earth's richness—
>   an abundance of grain and new wine.
> ²⁹May nations serve you
>   and peoples bow down to you.
> Be lord over your brothers,
>   and may the sons of your mother bow down to you.
> May those who curse you be cursed
>   and those who bless you be blessed."

³⁰After Isaac finished blessing him and Jacob had scarcely left his father's presence, his
brother Esau came in from hunting. ³¹He too prepared some tasty food and brought it to
his father. Then he said to him, "My father, sit up and eat some of my game, so that you
may give me your blessing."

³²His father Isaac asked him, "Who are you?"

"I am your son," he answered, "your firstborn, Esau."

³³Isaac trembled violently and said, "Who was it, then, that hunted game and brought
it to me? I ate it just before you came and I blessed him—and indeed he will be blessed!"

³⁴When Esau heard his father's words, he burst out with a loud and bitter cry and sa to his father, "Bless me—me too, my father!"

³⁵But he said, "Your brother came deceitfully and took your blessing."

³⁶Esau said, "Isn't he rightly named Jacob*ª*? He has deceived me these two times: H took my birthright, and now he's taken my blessing!" Then he asked, "Haven't yc reserved any blessing for me?"

³⁷Isaac answered Esau, "I have made him lord over you and have made all his relative his servants, and I have sustained him with grain and new wine. So what can I possibl do for you, my son?"

³⁸Esau said to his father, "Do you have only one blessing, my father? Bless me too, m father!" Then Esau wept aloud.

³⁹His father Isaac answered him,

> "Your dwelling will be
>   away from the earth's richness,
>   away from the dew of heaven above.
> ⁴⁰You will live by the sword
>   and you will serve your brother.
> But when you grow restless,
>   you will throw his yoke
>   from off your neck."

Jacob Flees to Laban

⁴¹Esau held a grudge against Jacob because of the blessing his father had given hir He said to himself, "The days of mourning for my father are near; then I will kill m brother Jacob."

⁴²When Rebekah was told what her older son Esau had said, she sent for her younge son Jacob and said to him, "Your brother Esau is consoling himself with the thought c killing you. ⁴³Now then, my son, do what I say: Flee at once to my brother Laban i Haran. ⁴⁴Stay with him for a while until your brother's fury subsides. ⁴⁵When your broth er is no longer angry with you and forgets what you did to him, I'll send word for you t come back from there. Why should I lose both of you in one day?"

⁴⁶Then Rebekah said to Isaac, "I'm disgusted with living because of these Hittite wom en. If Jacob takes a wife from among the women of this land, from Hittite women lik these, my life will not be worth living."

28 So Isaac called for Jacob and blessed*ᵇ* him and commanded him: "Do nc marry a Canaanite woman. ²Go at once to Paddan Aram,*ᶜ* to the house c your mother's father Bethuel. Take a wife for yourself there, from among the daughters c Laban, your mother's brother. ³May God Almighty*ᵈ* bless you and make you fruitful an increase your numbers until you become a community of peoples. ⁴May he give you an your descendants the blessing given to Abraham, so that you may take possession of th land where you now live as an alien, the land God gave to Abraham." ⁵Then Isaac ser Jacob on his way, and he went to Paddan Aram, to Laban son of Bethuel the Aramean the brother of Rebekah, who was the mother of Jacob and Esau.

⁶Now Esau learned that Isaac had blessed Jacob and had sent him to Paddan Aram 1 take a wife from there, and that when he blessed him he commanded him, "Do not marr a Canaanite woman," ⁷and that Jacob had obeyed his father and mother and had gone 1 Paddan Aram. ⁸Esau then realized how displeasing the Canaanite women were to hi father Isaac; ⁹so he went to Ishmael and married Mahalath, the sister of Nebaioth an daughter of Ishmael son of Abraham, in addition to the wives he already had.

ª36 Jacob means he grasps the heel (figuratively, he deceives).
also in verses 5, 6 and 7   *ᵇ1 Or greeted*   *ᶜ2 That is, Northwest Mesopotamia;*
ᵈ3 Hebrew El-Shaddai

Jacob's Dream at Bethel

¹⁰Jacob left Beersheba and set out for Haran. ¹¹When he reached a certain place, he stopped for the night because the sun had set. Taking one of the stones there, he put it under his head and lay down to sleep. ¹²He had a dream in which he saw a stairwayᵃ resting on the earth, with its top reaching to heaven, and the angels of God were ascending and descending on it. ¹³There above itᵇ stood the LORD, and he said: "I am the LORD, the God of your father Abraham and the God of Isaac. I will give you and your descendants the land on which you are lying. ¹⁴Your descendants will be like the dust of the earth, and you will spread out to the west and to the east, to the north and to the south. All peoples on earth will be blessed through you and your offspring. ¹⁵I am with you and will watch over you wherever you go, and I will bring you back to this land. I will not leave you until I have done what I have promised you."

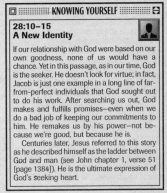

▣ ⬚⬚⬚⬚⬚⬚ **KNOWING YOURSELF** ⬚⬚⬚⬚⬚⬚ ⬀

28:10–15
A New Identity

If our relationship with God were based on our own goodness, none of us would have a chance. Yet in this passage, as in our time, God is the seeker. He doesn't look for virtue; in fact, Jacob is just one example in a long line of far-from-perfect individuals that God sought out to do his work. After searching us out, God makes and fulfills promises—even when we do a bad job of keeping our commitments to him. He remakes us by his power—not because we're good, but because he is.

Centuries later, Jesus referred to this story as he described himself as the ladder between God and man (see John chapter 1, verse 51 [page 1384]). He is the ultimate expression of God's seeking heart.

¹⁶When Jacob awoke from his sleep, he thought, "Surely the LORD is in this place, and I was not aware of it." ¹⁷He was afraid and said, "How awesome is this place! This is none other than the house of God; this is the gate of heaven."

¹⁸Early the next morning Jacob took the stone he had placed under his head and set it up as a pillar and poured oil on top of it. ¹⁹He called that place Bethel,ᶜ though the city used to be called Luz.

²⁰Then Jacob made a vow, saying, "If God will be with me and will watch over me on this journey I am taking and will give me food to eat and clothes to wear ²¹so that I return safely to my father's house, then the LORDᵈ will be my God ²²andᵉ this stone that I have set up as a pillar will be God's house, and of all that you give me I will give you a tenth."

Jacob Arrives in Paddan Aram

29 Then Jacob continued on his journey and came to the land of the eastern peoples. ²There he saw a well in the field, with three flocks of sheep lying near it because the flocks were watered from that well. The stone over the mouth of the well was large. ³When all the flocks were gathered there, the shepherds would roll the stone away from the well's mouth and water the sheep. Then they would return the stone to its place over the mouth of the well.

⁴Jacob asked the shepherds, "My brothers, where are you from?"

"We're from Haran," they replied.

⁵He said to them, "Do you know Laban, Nahor's grandson?"

"Yes, we know him," they answered.

⁶Then Jacob asked them, "Is he well?"

"Yes, he is," they said, "and here comes his daughter Rachel with the sheep."

⁷"Look," he said, "the sun is still high; it is not time for the flocks to be gathered. Water the sheep and take them back to pasture."

ᵃ12 Or ladder   ᵇ13 Or There beside him   ᶜ19 Bethel means house of God.   ᵈ20,21 Or Since God . . . father's house, the LORD   ᵉ21,22 Or house, and the LORD will be my God, ²²then

⁸"We can't," they replied, "until all the flocks are gathered and the stone has been rolled away from the mouth of the well. Then we will water the sheep."

⁹While he was still talking with them, Rachel came with her father's sheep, for she was a shepherdess. ¹⁰When Jacob saw Rachel daughter of Laban, his mother's brother, and Laban's sheep, he went over and rolled the stone away from the mouth of the well and watered his uncle's sheep. ¹¹Then Jacob kissed Rachel and began to weep aloud. ¹²He had told Rachel that he was a relative of her father and a son of Rebekah. So she ran and told her father.

¹³As soon as Laban heard the news about Jacob, his sister's son, he hurried to meet him. He embraced him and kissed him and brought him to his home, and there Jacob told him all these things. ¹⁴Then Laban said to him, "You are my own flesh and blood."

Jacob Marries Leah and Rachel

After Jacob had stayed with him for a whole month, ¹⁵Laban said to him, "Just because you are a relative of mine, should you work for me for nothing? Tell me what your wages should be."

¹⁶Now Laban had two daughters; the name of the older was Leah, and the name of the younger was Rachel. ¹⁷Leah had weak*ᵃ* eyes, but Rachel was lovely in form, and beautiful. ¹⁸Jacob was in love with Rachel and said, "I'll work for you seven years in return for your younger daughter Rachel."

¹⁹Laban said, "It's better that I give her to you than to some other man. Stay here with me." ²⁰So Jacob served seven years to get Rachel, but they seemed like only a few days to him because of his love for her.

²¹Then Jacob said to Laban, "Give me my wife. My time is completed, and I want to lie with her."

²²So Laban brought together all the people of the place and gave a feast. ²³But when evening came, he took his daughter Leah and gave her to Jacob, and Jacob lay with her. ²⁴And Laban gave his servant girl Zilpah to his daughter as her maidservant.

²⁵When morning came, there was Leah! So Jacob said to Laban, "What is this you have done to me? I served you for Rachel, didn't I? Why have you deceived me?"

²⁶Laban replied, "It is not our custom here to give the younger daughter in marriage before the older one. ²⁷Finish this daughter's bridal week; then we will give you the younger one also, in return for another seven years of work."

²⁸And Jacob did so. He finished the week with Leah, and then Laban gave him his daughter Rachel to be his wife. ²⁹Laban gave his servant girl Bilhah to his daughter Rachel as her maidservant. ³⁰Jacob lay with Rachel also, and he loved Rachel more than Leah. And he worked for Laban another seven years.

Jacob's Children

³¹When the LORD saw that Leah was not loved, he opened her womb, but Rachel was barren. ³²Leah became pregnant and gave birth to a son. She named him Reuben,*ᵇ* for she said, "It is because the LORD has seen my misery. Surely my husband will love me now."

³³She conceived again, and when she gave birth to a son she said, "Because the LORD heard that I am not loved, he gave me this one too." So she named him Simeon.*ᶜ*

³⁴Again she conceived, and when she gave birth to a son she said, "Now at last my husband will become attached to me, because I have borne him three sons." So he was named Levi.*ᵈ*

³⁵She conceived again, and when she gave birth to a son she said, "This time I will praise the LORD." So she named him Judah.*ᵉ* Then she stopped having children.

ᵃ17 Or *delicate*   *ᵇ32 Reuben* sounds like the Hebrew for *he has seen my misery;* the name means *see, a son.*
ᶜ33 Simeon probably means *one who hears.*   *ᵈ34 Levi* sounds like and may be derived from the Hebrew for *attached.*
ᵉ35 Judah sounds like and may be derived from the Hebrew for *praise.*

30 When Rachel saw that she was not bearing Jacob any children, she became jealous of her sister. So she said to Jacob, "Give me children, or I'll die!"

²Jacob became angry with her and said, "Am I in the place of God, who has kept you from having children?"

³Then she said, "Here is Bilhah, my maidservant. Sleep with her so that she can bear children for me and that through her I too can build a family."

⁴So she gave him her servant Bilhah as a wife. Jacob slept with her, ⁵and she became pregnant and bore him a son. ⁶Then Rachel said, "God has vindicated me; he has listened to my plea and given me a son." Because of this she named him Dan.ᵃ

⁷Rachel's servant Bilhah conceived again and bore Jacob a second son. ⁸Then Rachel said, "I have had a great struggle with my sister, and I have won." So she named him Naphtali.ᵇ

⁹When Leah saw that she had stopped having children, she took her maidservant Zilpah and gave her to Jacob as a wife. ¹⁰Leah's servant Zilpah bore Jacob a son. ¹¹Then Leah said, "What good fortune!"ᶜ So she named him Gad.ᵈ

¹²Leah's servant Zilpah bore Jacob a second son. ¹³Then Leah said, "How happy I am! The women will call me happy." So she named him Asher.ᵉ

¹⁴During wheat harvest, Reuben went out into the fields and found some mandrake plants, which he brought to his mother Leah. Rachel said to Leah, "Please give me some of your son's mandrakes."

¹⁵But she said to her, "Wasn't it enough that you took away my husband? Will you take my son's mandrakes too?"

"Very well," Rachel said, "he can sleep with you tonight in return for your son's mandrakes."

¹⁶So when Jacob came in from the fields that evening, Leah went out to meet him. "You must sleep with me," she said. "I have hired you with my son's mandrakes." So he slept with her that night.

¹⁷God listened to Leah, and she became pregnant and bore Jacob a fifth son. ¹⁸Then Leah said, "God has rewarded me for giving my maidservant to my husband." So she named him Issachar.ᶠ

¹⁹Leah conceived again and bore Jacob a sixth son. ²⁰Then Leah said, "God has presented me with a precious gift. This time my husband will treat me with honor, because I have borne him six sons." So she named him Zebulun.ᵍ

²¹Some time later she gave birth to a daughter and named her Dinah.

²²Then God remembered Rachel; he listened to her and opened her womb. ²³She became pregnant and gave birth to a son and said, "God has taken away my disgrace." ²⁴She named him Joseph,ʰ and said, "May the Lᴏʀᴅ add to me another son."

Jacob's Flocks Increase

²⁵After Rachel gave birth to Joseph, Jacob said to Laban, "Send me on my way so I can go back to my own homeland. ²⁶Give me my wives and children, for whom I have served you, and I will be on my way. You know how much work I've done for you."

²⁷But Laban said to him, "If I have found favor in your eyes, please stay. I have learned by divination thatⁱ the Lᴏʀᴅ has blessed me because of you." ²⁸He added, "Name your wages, and I will pay them."

²⁹Jacob said to him, "You know how I have worked for you and how your livestock has fared under my care. ³⁰The little you had before I came has increased greatly, and the Lᴏʀᴅ has blessed you wherever I have been. But now, when may I do something for my own household?"

³¹"What shall I give you?" he asked.

ᵃ6 *Dan* here means *he has vindicated*.   ᵇ8 *Naphtali* means *my struggle*.   ᶜ11 Or *"A troop is coming!"*   ᵈ11 *Gad* can mean *good fortune* or *a troop*.   ᵉ13 *Asher* means *happy*.   ᶠ18 *Issachar* sounds like the Hebrew for *reward*. ᵍ20 *Zebulun* probably means *honor*.   ʰ24 *Joseph* means *may he add*.   ⁱ27. Or possibly *have become rich and*

"Don't give me anything," Jacob replied. "But if you will do this one thing for me, I will go on tending your flocks and watching over them: ³²Let me go through all your flocks today and remove from them every speckled or spotted sheep, every dark-colored lamb and every spotted or speckled goat. They will be my wages. ³³And my honesty will testify for me in the future, whenever you check on the wages you have paid me. Any goat in my possession that is not speckled or spotted, or any lamb that is not dark-colored, will be considered stolen."

³⁴"Agreed," said Laban. "Let it be as you have said." ³⁵That same day he removed all the male goats that were streaked or spotted, and all the speckled or spotted female goats (all that had white on them) and all the dark-colored lambs, and he placed them in the care of his sons. ³⁶Then he put a three-day journey between himself and Jacob, while Jacob continued to tend the rest of Laban's flocks.

³⁷Jacob, however, took fresh-cut branches from poplar, almond and plane trees and made white stripes on them by peeling the bark and exposing the white inner wood of the branches. ³⁸Then he placed the peeled branches in all the watering troughs, so that they would be directly in front of the flocks when they came to drink. When the flocks were in heat and came to drink, ³⁹they mated in front of the branches. And they bore young that were streaked or speckled or spotted. ⁴⁰Jacob set apart the young of the flock by themselves, but made the rest face the streaked and dark-colored animals that belonged to Laban. Thus he made separate flocks for himself and did not put them with Laban's animals. ⁴¹Whenever the stronger females were in heat, Jacob would place the branches in the troughs in front of the animals so they would mate near the branches, ⁴²but if the animals were weak, he would not place them there. So the weak animals went to Laban and the strong ones to Jacob. ⁴³In this way the man grew exceedingly prosperous and came to own large flocks, and maidservants and menservants, and camels and donkeys.

Jacob Flees From Laban

31 Jacob heard that Laban's sons were saying, "Jacob has taken everything our father owned and has gained all this wealth from what belonged to our father." ²And Jacob noticed that Laban's attitude toward him was not what it had been.

³Then the Lᴏʀᴅ said to Jacob, "Go back to the land of your fathers and to your relatives, and I will be with you."

⁴So Jacob sent word to Rachel and Leah to come out to the fields where his flocks were. ⁵He said to them, "I see that your father's attitude toward me is not what it was before, but the God of my father has been with me. ⁶You know that I've worked for your father with all my strength, ⁷yet your father has cheated me by changing my wages ten times. However, God has not allowed him to harm me. ⁸If he said, 'The speckled ones will be your wages,' then all the flocks gave birth to speckled young; and if he said, 'The streaked ones will be your wages,' then all the flocks bore streaked young. ⁹So God has taken away your father's livestock and has given them to me.

¹⁰"In breeding season I once had a dream in which I looked up and saw that the male goats mating with the flock were streaked, speckled or spotted. ¹¹The angel of God said to me in the dream, 'Jacob.' I answered, 'Here I am.' ¹²And he said, 'Look up and see that all the male goats mating with the flock are streaked, speckled or spotted, for I have seen all that Laban has been doing to you. ¹³I am the God of Bethel, where you anointed a pillar and where you made a vow to me. Now leave this land at once and go back to your native land.'"

¹⁴Then Rachel and Leah replied, "Do we still have any share in the inheritance of our father's estate? ¹⁵Does he not regard us as foreigners? Not only has he sold us, but he has used up what was paid for us. ¹⁶Surely all the wealth that God took away from our father belongs to us and our children. So do whatever God has told you."

¹⁷Then Jacob put his children and his wives on camels, ¹⁸and he drove all his livestock

ahead of him, along with all the goods he had accumulated in Paddan Aram,[a] to go to his father Isaac in the land of Canaan.

[19]When Laban had gone to shear his sheep, Rachel stole her father's household gods. [20]Moreover, Jacob deceived Laban the Aramean by not telling him he was running away. [21]So he fled with all he had, and crossing the River,[b] he headed for the hill country of Gilead.

Laban Pursues Jacob

[22]On the third day Laban was told that Jacob had fled. [23]Taking his relatives with him, he pursued Jacob for seven days and caught up with him in the hill country of Gilead. [24]Then God came to Laban the Aramean in a dream at night and said to him, "Be careful not to say anything to Jacob, either good or bad."

[25]Jacob had pitched his tent in the hill country of Gilead when Laban overtook him, and Laban and his relatives camped there too. [26]Then Laban said to Jacob, "What have you done? You've deceived me, and you've carried off my daughters like captives in war. [27]Why did you run off secretly and deceive me? Why didn't you tell me, so I could send you away with joy and singing to the music of tambourines and harps? [28]You didn't even let me kiss my grandchildren and my daughters good-by. You have done a foolish thing. [29]I have the power to harm you; but last night the God of your father said to me, 'Be careful not to say anything to Jacob, either good or bad.' [30]Now you have gone off because you longed to return to your father's house. But why did you steal my gods?"

[31]Jacob answered Laban, "I was afraid, because I thought you would take your daughters away from me by force. [32]But if you find anyone who has your gods, he shall not live. In the presence of our relatives, see for yourself whether there is anything of yours here with me; and if so, take it." Now Jacob did not know that Rachel had stolen the gods.

[33]So Laban went into Jacob's tent and into Leah's tent and into the tent of the two maidservants, but he found nothing. After he came out of Leah's tent, he entered Rachel's tent. [34]Now Rachel had taken the household gods and put them inside her camel's saddle and was sitting on them. Laban searched through everything in the tent but found nothing.

[35]Rachel said to her father, "Don't be angry, my lord, that I cannot stand up in your presence; I'm having my period." So he searched but could not find the household gods.

[36]Jacob was angry and took Laban to task. "What is my crime?" he asked Laban. "What sin have I committed that you hunt me down? [37]Now that you have searched through all my goods, what have you found that belongs to your household? Put it here in front of your relatives and mine, and let them judge between the two of us.

[38]"I have been with you for twenty years now. Your sheep and goats have not miscarried, nor have I eaten rams from your flocks. [39]I did not bring you animals torn by wild beasts; I bore the loss myself. And you demanded payment from me for whatever was stolen by day or night. [40]This was my situation: The heat consumed me in the daytime and the cold at night, and sleep fled from my eyes. [41]It was like this for the twenty years I was in your household. I worked for

DISCOVERING GOD

31:34
Spiritual Fraud

Superstition ran rampant among the people of Canaan. Its influence was such that even some of God's people who lived in Canaan clung to the local idols. Even today it's not uncommon to find people who believe in God but still rely on other spiritually deceptive practices (such as horoscopes) for daily advice.

What about you? Do you fear certain days or numbers? Do you treat certain inanimate objects as if they had power? If you hold to God, you hold to the greatest power in the universe. All other so-called powers are pretenders. As you search out God's ways, you'll find that he deserves your loyalty. And if you put your trust in him, he will be faithful to you.

---

[a]19 That is, Northwest Mesopotamia   [b]21 That is, the Euphrates

you fourteen years for your two daughters and six years for your flocks, and you changed my wages ten times. ⁴²If the God of my father, the God of Abraham and the Fear of Isaac, had not been with me, you would surely have sent me away empty-handed. But God has seen my hardship and the toil of my hands, and last night he rebuked you."

⁴³Laban answered Jacob, "The women are my daughters, the children are my children, and the flocks are my flocks. All you see is mine. Yet what can I do today about these daughters of mine, or about the children they have borne? ⁴⁴Come now, let's make a covenant, you and I, and let it serve as a witness between us."

⁴⁵So Jacob took a stone and set it up as a pillar. ⁴⁶He said to his relatives, "Gather some stones." So they took stones and piled them in a heap, and they ate there by the heap. ⁴⁷Laban called it Jegar Sahadutha,ᵃ and Jacob called it Galeed.ᵇ

⁴⁸Laban said, "This heap is a witness between you and me today." That is why it was called Galeed. ⁴⁹It was also called Mizpah,ᶜ because he said, "May the Lᴏʀᴅ keep watch between you and me when we are away from each other. ⁵⁰If you mistreat my daughters or if you take any wives besides my daughters, even though no one is with us, remember that God is a witness between you and me."

⁵¹Laban also said to Jacob, "Here is this heap, and here is this pillar I have set up between you and me. ⁵²This heap is a witness, and this pillar is a witness, that I will not go past this heap to your side to harm you and that you will not go past this heap and pillar to my side to harm me. ⁵³May the God of Abraham and the God of Nahor, the God of their father, judge between us."

So Jacob took an oath in the name of the Fear of his father Isaac. ⁵⁴He offered a sacrifice there in the hill country and invited his relatives to a meal. After they had eaten, they spent the night there.

⁵⁵Early the next morning Laban kissed his grandchildren and his daughters and blessed them. Then he left and returned home.

Jacob Prepares to Meet Esau

32 Jacob also went on his way, and the angels of God met him. ²When Jacob saw them, he said, "This is the camp of God!" So he named that place Mahanaim.ᵈ

³Jacob sent messengers ahead of him to his brother Esau in the land of Seir, the country of Edom. ⁴He instructed them: "This is what you are to say to my master Esau: 'Your servant Jacob says, I have been staying with Laban and have remained there till now. ⁵I have cattle and donkeys, sheep and goats, menservants and maidservants. Now I am sending this message to my lord, that I may find favor in your eyes.'"

⁶When the messengers returned to Jacob, they said, "We went to your brother Esau, and now he is coming to meet you, and four hundred men are with him."

⁷In great fear and distress Jacob divided the people who were with him into two groups,ᵉ and the flocks and herds and camels as well. ⁸He thought, "If Esau comes and attacks one group,ᶠ the groupᶠ that is left may escape."

⁹Then Jacob prayed, "O God of my father Abraham, God of my father Isaac, O Lᴏʀᴅ, who said to me, 'Go back to your country and your relatives, and I will make you prosper,' ¹⁰I am unworthy of all the kindness and faithfulness you have shown your servant. I had only my staff when I crossed this Jordan, but now I have become two groups. ¹¹Save me, I pray, from the hand of my brother Esau, for I am afraid he will come and attack me, and also the mothers with their children. ¹²But you have said, 'I will surely make you prosper and will make your descendants like the sand of the sea, which cannot be counted.'"

¹³He spent the night there, and from what he had with him he selected a gift for his brother Esau: ¹⁴two hundred female goats and twenty male goats, two hundred ewes and twenty rams, ¹⁵thirty female camels with their young, forty cows and ten bulls, and

---

ᵃ 47 The Aramaic *Jegar Sahadutha* means *witness heap.*   ᵇ 47 The Hebrew *Galeed* means *witness heap.*   ᶜ 49 *Mizpah* means *watchtower.*   ᵈ 2 *Mahanaim* means *two camps.*   ᵉ 7 Or *camps*; also in verse 10   ᶠ 8 Or *camp*

twenty female donkeys and ten male donkeys. ¹⁶He put them in the care of his servants, each herd by itself, and said to his servants, "Go ahead of me, and keep some space between the herds."

¹⁷He instructed the one in the lead: "When my brother Esau meets you and asks, 'To whom do you belong, and where are you going, and who owns all these animals in front of you?' ¹⁸then you are to say, 'They belong to your servant Jacob. They are a gift sent to my lord Esau, and he is coming behind us.'"

¹⁹He also instructed the second, the third and all the others who followed the herds: "You are to say the same thing to Esau when you meet him. ²⁰And be sure to say, 'Your servant Jacob is coming behind us.'" For he thought, "I will pacify him with these gifts I am sending on ahead; later, when I see him, perhaps he will receive me." ²¹So Jacob's gifts went on ahead of him, but he himself spent the night in the camp.

Jacob Wrestles With God

²²That night Jacob got up and took his two wives, his two maidservants and his eleven sons and crossed the ford of the Jabbok. ²³After he had sent them across the stream, he sent over all his possessions. ²⁴So Jacob was left alone, and a man wrestled with him till daybreak. ²⁵When the man saw that he could not overpower him, he touched the socket of Jacob's hip so that his hip was wrenched as he wrestled with the man. ²⁶Then the man said, "Let me go, for it is daybreak."

But Jacob replied, "I will not let you go unless you bless me."

²⁷The man asked him, "What is your name?"

"Jacob," he answered.

²⁸Then the man said, "Your name will no longer be Jacob, but Israel,^a because you have struggled with God and with men and have overcome."

²⁹Jacob said, "Please tell me your name."

But he replied, "Why do you ask my name?" Then he blessed him there.

³⁰So Jacob called the place Peniel,^b saying, "It is because I saw God face to face, and yet my life was spared."

³¹The sun rose above him as he passed Peniel,^c and he was limping because of his hip. ³²Therefore to this day the Israelites do not eat the tendon attached to the socket of the hip, because the socket of Jacob's hip was touched near the tendon.

Jacob Meets Esau

33 Jacob looked up and there was Esau, coming with his four hundred men; so he divided the children among Leah, Rachel and the two maidservants. ²He put the maidservants and their children in front, Leah and her children next, and Rachel and Joseph in the rear. ³He himself went on ahead and bowed down to the ground seven times as he approached his brother.

⁴But Esau ran to meet Jacob and embraced him; he threw his arms around his neck and kissed him. And they wept. ⁵Then Esau looked up and saw the women and children. "Who are these with you?" he asked.

Jacob answered, "They are the children God has graciously given your servant."

⁶Then the maidservants and their children approached and bowed down. ⁷Next, Leah and her children came and bowed down. Last of all came Joseph and Rachel, and they too bowed down.

⁸Esau asked, "What do you mean by all these droves I met?"

"To find favor in your eyes, my lord," he said.

⁹But Esau said, "I already have plenty, my brother. Keep what you have for yourself."

¹⁰"No, please!" said Jacob. "If I have found favor in your eyes, accept this gift from me. For to see your face is like seeing the face of God, now that you have received me

---

^a28 *Israel means he struggles with God.*   ^b30 *Peniel means face of God.*   ^c31 *Hebrew Penuel, a variant of Peniel*

favorably. ¹¹Please accept the present that was brought to you, for God has been gracious to me and I have all I need." And because Jacob insisted, Esau accepted it.

¹²Then Esau said, "Let us be on our way; I'll accompany you."

¹³But Jacob said to him, "My lord knows that the children are tender and that I must care for the ewes and cows that are nursing their young. If they are driven hard just one day, all the animals will die. ¹⁴So let my lord go on ahead of his servant, while I move along slowly at the pace of the droves before me and that of the children, until I come to my lord in Seir."

¹⁵Esau said, "Then let me leave some of my men with you."

"But why do that?" Jacob asked. "Just let me find favor in the eyes of my lord."

¹⁶So that day Esau started on his way back to Seir. ¹⁷Jacob, however, went to Succoth, where he built a place for himself and made shelters for his livestock. That is why the place is called Succoth.ᵃ

¹⁸After Jacob came from Paddan Aram,ᵇ he arrived safely at theᶜ city of Shechem in Canaan and camped within sight of the city. ¹⁹For a hundred pieces of silver,ᵈ he bought from the sons of Hamor, the father of Shechem, the plot of ground where he pitched his tent. ²⁰There he set up an altar and called it El Elohe Israel.ᵉ

Dinah and the Shechemites

34 Now Dinah, the daughter Leah had borne to Jacob, went out to visit the women of the land. ²When Shechem son of Hamor the Hivite, the ruler of that area, saw her, he took her and violated her. ³His heart was drawn to Dinah daughter of Jacob, and he loved the girl and spoke tenderly to her. ⁴And Shechem said to his father Hamor, "Get me this girl as my wife."

⁵When Jacob heard that his daughter Dinah had been defiled, his sons were in the fields with his livestock; so he kept quiet about it until they came home.

⁶Then Shechem's father Hamor went out to talk with Jacob. ⁷Now Jacob's sons had come in from the fields as soon as they heard what had happened. They were filled with grief and fury, because Shechem had done a disgraceful thing inᶠ Israel by lying with Jacob's daughter—a thing that should not be done.

⁸But Hamor said to them, "My son Shechem has his heart set on your daughter. Please give her to him as his wife. ⁹Intermarry with us; give us your daughters and take our daughters for yourselves. ¹⁰You can settle among us; the land is open to you. Live in it, tradeᵍ in it, and acquire property in it."

¹¹Then Shechem said to Dinah's father and brothers, "Let me find favor in your eyes, and I will give you whatever you ask. ¹²Make the price for the bride and the gift I am to bring as great as you like, and I'll pay whatever you ask me. Only give me the girl as my wife."

¹³Because their sister Dinah had been defiled, Jacob's sons replied deceitfully as they spoke to Shechem and his father Hamor. ¹⁴They said to them, "We can't do such a thing; we can't give our sister to a man who is not circumcised. That would be a disgrace to us. ¹⁵We will give our consent to you on one condition only: that you become like us by circumcising all your males. ¹⁶Then we will give you our daughters and take your daughters for ourselves. We'll settle among you and become one people with you. ¹⁷But if you will not agree to be circumcised, we'll take our sisterʰ and go."

¹⁸Their proposal seemed good to Hamor and his son Shechem. ¹⁹The young man, who was the most honored of all his father's household, lost no time in doing what they said, because he was delighted with Jacob's daughter. ²⁰So Hamor and his son Shechem went to the gate of their city to speak to their fellow townsmen. ²¹"These men are friendly toward us," they said. "Let them live in our land and trade in it; the land has plenty of

---

ᵃ17 Succoth means shelters.   ᵇ18 That is, Northwest Mesopotamia   ᶜ18 Or arrived at Shalem, a   ᵈ19 Hebrew hundred kesitahs; a kesitah was a unit of money of unknown weight and value.   ᵉ20 El Elohe Israel can mean God, the God of Israel or mighty is the God of Israel.   ᶠ7 Or against   ᵍ10 Or move about freely; also in verse 21   ʰ17 Hebrew daughter

room for them. We can marry their daughters and they can marry ours. ²²But the men will consent to live with us as one people only on the condition that our males be circumcised, as they themselves are. ²³Won't their livestock, their property and all their other animals become ours? So let us give our consent to them, and they will settle among us."

²⁴All the men who went out of the city gate agreed with Hamor and his son Shechem, and every male in the city was circumcised.

²⁵Three days later, while all of them were still in pain, two of Jacob's sons, Simeon and Levi, Dinah's brothers, took their swords and attacked the unsuspecting city, killing every male. ²⁶They put Hamor and his son Shechem to the sword and took Dinah from Shechem's house and left. ²⁷The sons of Jacob came upon the dead bodies and looted the city where*a* their sister had been defiled. ²⁸They seized their flocks and herds and donkeys and everything else of theirs in the city and out in the fields. ²⁹They carried off all their wealth and all their women and children, taking as plunder everything in the houses.

³⁰Then Jacob said to Simeon and Levi, "You have brought trouble on me by making me a stench to the Canaanites and Perizzites, the people living in this land. We are few in number, and if they join forces against me and attack me, I and my household will be destroyed."

³¹But they replied, "Should he have treated our sister like a prostitute?"

Jacob Returns to Bethel

35 Then God said to Jacob, "Go up to Bethel and settle there, and build an altar there to God, who appeared to you when you were fleeing from your brother Esau."

²So Jacob said to his household and to all who were with him, "Get rid of the foreign gods you have with you, and purify yourselves and change your clothes. ³Then come, let us go up to Bethel, where I will build an altar to God, who answered me in the day of my distress and who has been with me wherever I have gone." ⁴So they gave Jacob all the foreign gods they had and the rings in their ears, and Jacob buried them under the oak at Shechem. ⁵Then they set out, and the terror of God fell upon the towns all around them so that no one pursued them.

⁶Jacob and all the people with him came to Luz (that is, Bethel) in the land of Canaan. ⁷There he built an altar, and he called the place El Bethel,*b* because it was there that God revealed himself to him when he was fleeing from his brother.

⁸Now Deborah, Rebekah's nurse, died and was buried under the oak below Bethel. So it was named Allon Bacuth.*c*

⁹After Jacob returned from Paddan Aram,*d* God appeared to him again and blessed him. ¹⁰God said to him, "Your name is Jacob,*e* but you will no longer be called Jacob; your name will be Israel.*f*" So he named him Israel.

¹¹And God said to him, "I am God Almighty*g*; be fruitful and increase in number. A nation and a community of nations will come from you, and kings will come from your body. ¹²The land I gave to Abraham and Isaac I also give to you, and I will give this land to your descendants after you." ¹³Then God went up from him at the place where he had talked with him.

¹⁴Jacob set up a stone pillar at the place where God had talked with him, and he poured out a drink offering on it; he also poured oil on it. ¹⁵Jacob called the place where God had talked with him Bethel.*h*

---

a 27 Or *because*   *b 7 El Bethel* means *God of Bethel.*   *c 8 Allon Bacuth* means *oak of weeping.*   *d 9* That is, Northwest Mesopotamia; also in verse 26   *e 10 Jacob* means *he grasps the heel* (figuratively, *he deceives*).   *f 10 Israel* means *he struggles with God.*   *g 11* Hebrew *El-Shaddai*   *h 15 Bethel* means *house of God.*

The Deaths of Rachel and Isaac

¹⁶Then they moved on from Bethel. While they were still some distance from Ephrath, Rachel began to give birth and had great difficulty. ¹⁷And as she was having great difficulty in childbirth, the midwife said to her, "Don't be afraid, for you have another son." ¹⁸As she breathed her last—for she was dying—she named her son Ben-Oni.ᵃ But his father named him Benjamin.ᵇ

¹⁹So Rachel died and was buried on the way to Ephrath (that is, Bethlehem). ²⁰Over her tomb Jacob set up a pillar, and to this day that pillar marks Rachel's tomb.

²¹Israel moved on again and pitched his tent beyond Migdal Eder. ²²While Israel was living in that region, Reuben went in and slept with his father's concubine Bilhah, and Israel heard of it.

□ :::::::::: **KNOWING YOURSELF** :::::::::: ⮂

35:10
A New Identity

Throughout the Bible God renamed key individuals. For example, God changed the name of Abram (meaning "exalted father") to Abraham ("father of many"; see chapter 17, verse 5 [page 23]). Here God changed the name of Jacob (meaning "he deceives") to Israel ("he struggles with God").

In biblical times, a person's name often reflected that person's character. A change in a name meant that the person had changed—either internally or in relationship with another person. Today, when a person decides to put his or her complete trust in Christ, God sees that person in a new light. In a sense, God changes that person's "name" to reflect the change in the relationship between himself and that person.

As he did with Abram and Jacob, he's ready to offer you a new spiritual identity.

Jacob had twelve sons:

²³The sons of Leah:

Reuben the firstborn of Jacob, Simeon, Levi, Judah, Issachar and Zebulun.

²⁴The sons of Rachel:

Joseph and Benjamin.

²⁵The sons of Rachel's maidservant Bilhah:

Dan and Naphtali.

²⁶The sons of Leah's maidservant Zilpah:

Gad and Asher.

These were the sons of Jacob, who were born to him in Paddan Aram.

²⁷Jacob came home to his father Isaac in Mamre, near Kiriath Arba (that is, Hebron), where Abraham and Isaac had stayed. ²⁸Isaac lived a hundred and eighty years. ²⁹Then he breathed his last and died and was gathered to his people, old and full of years. And his sons Esau and Jacob buried him.

Esau's Descendants

36 This is the account of Esau (that is, Edom).

²Esau took his wives from the women of Canaan: Adah daughter of Elon the Hittite, and Oholibamah daughter of Anah and granddaughter of Zibeon the Hivite—³also Basemath daughter of Ishmael and sister of Nebaioth.

⁴Adah bore Eliphaz to Esau, Basemath bore Reuel, ⁵and Oholibamah bore Jeush, Jalam and Korah. These were the sons of Esau, who were born to him in Canaan.

⁶Esau took his wives and sons and daughters and all the members of his household, as well as his livestock and all his other animals and all the goods he had acquired in Canaan, and moved to a land some distance from his brother Jacob. ⁷Their possessions were too great for them to remain together; the land where they were staying could not support them both because of their livestock. ⁸So Esau (that is, Edom) settled in the hill country of Seir.

⁹This is the account of Esau the father of the Edomites in the hill country of Seir.

ᵃ 18 Ben-Oni means son of my trouble.   ᵇ 18 Benjamin means son of my right hand.

¹⁰These are the names of Esau's sons:

Eliphaz, the son of Esau's wife Adah, and Reuel, the son of Esau's wife Basemath.

¹¹The sons of Eliphaz:

Teman, Omar, Zepho, Gatam and Kenaz.

¹²Esau's son Eliphaz also had a concubine named Timna, who bore him Amalek. These were grandsons of Esau's wife Adah.

¹³The sons of Reuel:

Nahath, Zerah, Shammah and Mizzah. These were grandsons of Esau's wife Basemath.

¹⁴The sons of Esau's wife Oholibamah daughter of Anah and granddaughter of Zibeon, whom she bore to Esau:

Jeush, Jalam and Korah.

¹⁵These were the chiefs among Esau's descendants:

The sons of Eliphaz the firstborn of Esau:

Chiefs Teman, Omar, Zepho, Kenaz, ¹⁶Korah,ᵃ Gatam and Amalek. These were the chiefs descended from Eliphaz in Edom; they were grandsons of Adah.

¹⁷The sons of Esau's son Reuel:

Chiefs Nahath, Zerah, Shammah and Mizzah. These were the chiefs descended from Reuel in Edom; they were grandsons of Esau's wife Basemath.

¹⁸The sons of Esau's wife Oholibamah:

Chiefs Jeush, Jalam and Korah. These were the chiefs descended from Esau's wife Oholibamah daughter of Anah.

¹⁹These were the sons of Esau (that is, Edom), and these were their chiefs.

²⁰These were the sons of Seir the Horite, who were living in the region:

Lotan, Shobal, Zibeon, Anah, ²¹Dishon, Ezer and Dishan. These sons of Seir in Edom were Horite chiefs.

²²The sons of Lotan:

Hori and Homam.ᵇ Timna was Lotan's sister.

²³The sons of Shobal:

Alvan, Manahath, Ebal, Shepho and Onam.

²⁴The sons of Zibeon:

Aiah and Anah. This is the Anah who discovered the hot springsᶜ in the desert while he was grazing the donkeys of his father Zibeon.

²⁵The children of Anah:

Dishon and Oholibamah daughter of Anah.

²⁶The sons of Dishon:ᵈ

Hemdan, Eshban, Ithran and Keran.

²⁷The sons of Ezer:

Bilhan, Zaavan and Akan.

²⁸The sons of Dishan:

Uz and Aran.

²⁹These were the Horite chiefs:

Lotan, Shobal, Zibeon, Anah, ³⁰Dishon, Ezer and Dishan. These were the Horite chiefs, according to their divisions, in the land of Seir.

The Rulers of Edom

³¹These were the kings who reigned in Edom before any Israelite king reignedᵉ:
³²Bela son of Beor became king of Edom. His city was named Dinhabah.
³³When Bela died, Jobab son of Zerah from Bozrah succeeded him as king.

ᵃ16 Masoretic Text; Samaritan Pentateuch (see also Gen. 36:11 and 1 Chron. 1:36) does not have *Korah.*   ᵇ22 Hebrew *Hemam,* a variant of *Homam* (see 1 Chron. 1:39)   ᶜ24 Vulgate; Syriac *discovered water;* the meaning of the Hebrew for this word is uncertain.   ᵈ26 Hebrew *Dishan,* a variant of *Dishon*   ᵉ31 Or *before an Israelite king reigned over them*

³⁴When Jobab died, Husham from the land of the Temanites succeeded him as king. ³⁵When Husham died, Hadad son of Bedad, who defeated Midian in the country of Moab, succeeded him as king. His city was named Avith. ³⁶When Hadad died, Samlah from Masrekah succeeded him as king. ³⁷When Samlah died, Shaul from Rehoboth on the river*a* succeeded him as king. ³⁸When Shaul died, Baal-Hanan son of Acbor succeeded him as king. ³⁹When Baal-Hanan son of Acbor died, Hadad*b* succeeded him as king. His city was named Pau, and his wife's name was Mehetabel daughter of Matred, the daughter of Me-Zahab.

⁴⁰These were the chiefs descended from Esau, by name, according to their clans and regions:

Timna, Alvah, Jetheth, ⁴¹Oholibamah, Elah, Pinon, ⁴²Kenaz, Teman, Mibzar, ⁴³Magdiel and Iram. These were the chiefs of Edom, according to their settlements in the land they occupied.

This was Esau the father of the Edomites.

Joseph's Dreams

37 Jacob lived in the land where his father had stayed, the land of Canaan.

²This is the account of Jacob.

Joseph, a young man of seventeen, was tending the flocks with his brothers, the sons of Bilhah and the sons of Zilpah, his father's wives, and he brought their father a bad report about them.

▣ STRENGTHENING RELATIONSHIPS ↩

37:3
Parenting

Playing favorites with your children is dangerous. One of the keys to successful parenting is to affirm the unique character in each of your children without being preferential to one in particular.

While Jacob was growing up, his mother favored him while his father favored his twin brother, Esau (see chapter 25, verse 28 [page 35]). Their favoritism led to all kinds of competition and trouble. In this passage Jacob (called Israel) favors Joseph, his youngest son. And the sibling rivalry that this favoritism inspires will soon break Jacob's heart.

³Now Israel loved Joseph more than any of his other sons, because he had been born to him in his old age; and he made a richly ornamented*c* robe for him. ⁴When his brothers saw that their father loved him more than any of them, they hated him and could not speak a kind word to him.

⁵Joseph had a dream, and when he told it to his brothers, they hated him all the more. ⁶He said to them, "Listen to this dream I had: ⁷We were binding sheaves of grain out in the field when suddenly my sheaf rose and stood upright, while your sheaves gathered around mine and bowed down to it."

⁸His brothers said to him, "Do you intend to reign over us? Will you actually rule us?" And they hated him all the more because of his dream and what he had said.

⁹Then he had another dream, and he told it to his brothers. "Listen," he said, "I had another dream, and this time the sun and moon and eleven stars were bowing down to me."

¹⁰When he told his father as well as his brothers, his father rebuked him and said, "What is this dream you had? Will your mother and I and your brothers actually come and bow down to the ground before you?" ¹¹His brothers were jealous of him, but his father kept the matter in mind.

---

a 37 Possibly the Euphrates   *b 39.* Many manuscripts of the Masoretic Text, Samaritan Pentateuch and Syriac (see also 1 Chron. 1:50); most manuscripts of the Masoretic Text *Hadar*   *c 3* The meaning of the Hebrew for *richly ornamented* is uncertain; also in verses 23 and 32.

eph Sold by His Brothers

Now his brothers had gone to graze their father's flocks near Shechem, ¹³and Israel
to Joseph, "As you know, your brothers are grazing the flocks near Shechem. Come,
going to send you to them."

"ery well," he replied.

So he said to him, "Go and see if all is well with your brothers and with the flocks,
bring word back to me." Then he sent him off from the Valley of Hebron.

hen Joseph arrived at Shechem, ¹⁵a man found him wandering around in the fields
asked him, "What are you looking for?"

He replied, "I'm looking for my brothers. Can you tell me where they are grazing their
s?"

"They have moved on from here," the man answered. "I heard them say, 'Let's go to
an.'"

Joseph went after his brothers and found them near Dothan. ¹⁸But they saw him in
distance, and before he reached them, they plotted to kill him.

"Here comes that dreamer!" they said to each other. ²⁰"Come now, let's kill him and
w him into one of these cisterns and say that a ferocious animal devoured him. Then
l see what comes of his dreams."

When Reuben heard this, he tried to rescue him from their hands. "Let's not take his
" he said. ²²"Don't shed any blood. Throw him into this cistern here in the desert, but
t lay a hand on him." Reuben said this to rescue him from them and take him back to
father.

So when Joseph came to his brothers, they stripped him of his robe—the richly
mented robe he was wearing— ²⁴and they took him and threw him into the cistern.
the cistern was empty; there was no water in it.

As they sat down to eat their meal, they looked up and saw a caravan of Ishmaelites
ng from Gilead. Their camels were loaded with spices, balm and myrrh, and they
e on their way to take them down to Egypt.

Judah said to his brothers, "What will we gain if we kill our brother and cover up his
d? ²⁷Come, let's sell him to the Ishmaelites and not lay our hands on him; after all, he
r brother, our own flesh and blood." His brothers agreed.

So when the Midianite merchants came by, his brothers pulled Joseph up out of the
ern and sold him for twenty shekels ᵃ of silver to the Ishmaelites, who took him to
ot.

When Reuben returned to the cistern and saw that Joseph was not there, he tore his
nes. ³⁰He went back to his brothers and said, "The boy isn't there! Where can I turn
?"

Then they got Joseph's robe, slaughtered a goat and dipped the robe in the blood.
ey took the ornamented robe back to their father and said, "We found this. Examine
see whether it is your son's robe."

He recognized it and said, "It is my son's robe! Some ferocious animal has devoured
Joseph has surely been torn to pieces."

Then Jacob tore his clothes, put on sackcloth and mourned for his son many days.
his sons and daughters came to comfort him, but he refused to be comforted. "No,"
aid, "in mourning will I go down to the grave ᵇ to my son." So his father wept for

Meanwhile, the Midianites ᶜ sold Joseph in Egypt to Potiphar, one of Pharaoh's
ials, the captain of the guard.

ᵃhat is, about 8 ounces (about 0.2 kilogram)   ᵇ35 Hebrew Sheol   ᶜ36 Samaritan Pentateuch, Septuagint, Vulgate
riac (see also verse 28); Masoretic Text Medanites

Judah and Tamar

38 At that time, Judah left his brothers and went down to stay with a m[an] Adullam named Hirah. ²There Judah met the daughter of a Canaanite named Shua. He married her and lay with her; ³she became pregnant and gave bir[th] a son, who was named Er. ⁴She conceived again and gave birth to a son and named [him] Onan. ⁵She gave birth to still another son and named him Shelah. It was at Kezib tha[t she] gave birth to him.

⁶Judah got a wife for Er, his firstborn, and her name was Tamar. ⁷But Er, Jud[ah's] firstborn, was wicked in the LORD's sight; so the LORD put him to death.

⁸Then Judah said to Onan, "Lie with your brother's wife and fulfill your duty to h[er as] a brother-in-law to produce offspring for your brother." ⁹But Onan knew that the [off-] spring would not be his; so whenever [he] lay with his brother's wife, he spilled [his] semen on the ground to keep from pro[duc-]ing offspring for his brother. ¹⁰What he [did] was wicked in the LORD's sight; so he [put] him to death also.

¹¹Judah then said to his daughter-in-[law] Tamar, "Live as a widow in your fat[her's] house until my son Shelah grows up." [For] he thought, "He may die too, just lik[e his] brothers." So Tamar went to live in he[r fa-]ther's house.

¹²After a long time Judah's wife, [the] daughter of Shua, died. When Judah [had] recovered from his grief, he went u[p to] Timnah, to the men who were shearin[g his] sheep, and his friend Hirah the Adulla[mite] went with him.

¹³When Tamar was told, "Your fathe[r-in-] law is on his way to Timnah to shea[r his] sheep," ¹⁴she took off her widow's clo[thes,] covered herself with a veil to disguise [her-]self, and then sat down at the entran[ce to] Enaim, which is on the road to Timnah[. For] she saw that, though Shelah had [now] grown up, she had not been given to [him] as his wife.

¹⁵When Judah saw her, he thought she was a prostitute, for she had covered her [face.] ¹⁶Not realizing that she was his daughter-in-law, he went over to her by the road and said, "Come now, let me sleep with you."

"And what will you give me to sleep with you?" she asked.

¹⁷"I'll send you a young goat from my flock," he said.

"Will you give me something as a pledge until you send it?" she asked.

¹⁸He said, "What pledge should I give you?"

"Your seal and its cord, and the staff in your hand," she answered. So he gave [them to] her and slept with her, and she became pregnant by him. ¹⁹After she left, she took of[f her] veil and put on her widow's clothes again.

²⁰Meanwhile Judah sent the young goat by his friend the Adullamite in order to ge[t his] pledge back from the woman, but he did not find her. ²¹He asked the men who [lived] there, "Where is the shrine prostitute who was beside the road at Enaim?"

"There hasn't been any shrine prostitute here," they said.

So he went back to Judah and said, "I didn't find her. Besides, the men who lived
e said, 'There hasn't been any shrine prostitute here.'"

Then Judah said, "Let her keep what she has, or we will become a laughingstock.
' all, I did send her this young goat, but you didn't find her."

About three months later Judah was told, "Your daughter-in-law Tamar is guilty of
titution, and as a result she is now pregnant."

dah said, "Bring her out and have her burned to death!"

As she was being brought out, she sent a message to her father-in-law. "I am
nant by the man who owns these," she said. And she added, "See if you recognize
se seal and cord and staff these are."

Judah recognized them and said, "She is more righteous than I, since I wouldn't give
to my son Shelah." And he did not sleep with her again.

When the time came for her to give birth, there were twin boys in her womb. 28As
was giving birth, one of them put out his hand; so the midwife took a scarlet thread
tied it on his wrist and said, "This one came out first." 29But when he drew back his
d, his brother came out, and she said, "So this is how you have broken out!" And he
named Perez.a 30Then his brother, who had the scarlet thread on his wrist, came
and he was given the name Zerah.b

eph and Potiphar's Wife

9 Now Joseph had been taken
down to Egypt. Potiphar, an
otian who was one of Pharaoh's offi-
, the captain of the guard, bought him
the Ishmaelites who had taken him
e.

he LORD was with Joseph and he pros-
ed, and he lived in the house of his
ptian master. 3When his master saw
the LORD was with him and that the
gave him success in everything he did,
eph found favor in his eyes and be-
e his attendant. Potiphar put him in
ge of his household, and he entrusted
ts care everything he owned. 5From the
he put him in charge of his household
of all that he owned, the LORD blessed
household of the Egyptian because of
ph. The blessing of the LORD was on ev-
hing Potiphar had, both in the house
in the field. 6So he left in Joseph's
ything he had; with Joseph in charge,
did not concern himself with anything
pt the food he ate.

ow Joseph was well-built and hand-
e, 7and after a while his master's wife
notice of Joseph and said, "Come to bed with me!"

ut he refused. "With me in charge," he told her, "my master does not concern himself
anything in the house; everything he owns he has entrusted to my care. 9No one is
ater in this house than I am. My master has withheld nothing from me except you,
ause you are his wife. How then could I do such a wicked thing and sin against God?"

---

a Perez means breaking out.   *b 30* Zerah can mean scarlet or brightness.

¹⁰And though she spoke to Joseph day after day, he refused to go to bed with her or be with her.

¹¹One day he went into the house to attend to his duties, and none of the house servants was inside. ¹²She caught him by his cloak and said, "Come to bed with me!" he left his cloak in her hand and ran out of the house.

¹³When she saw that he had left his cloak in her hand and had run out of the h ¹⁴she called her household servants. "Look," she said to them, "this Hebrew has brought to us to make sport of us! He came in here to sleep with me, but I screa ¹⁵When he heard me scream for help, he left his cloak beside me and ran out o house."

¹⁶She kept his cloak beside her until his master came home. ¹⁷Then she told him story: "That Hebrew slave you brought us came to me to make sport of me. ¹⁸But as as I screamed for help, he left his cloak beside me and ran out of the house."

¹⁹When his master heard the story his wife told him, saying, "This is how your treated me," he burned with anger. ²⁰Joseph's master took him and put him in prison place where the king's prisoners were confined.

But while Joseph was there in the prison, ²¹the LORD was with him; he showed kindness and granted him favor in the eyes of the prison warden. ²²So the warde Joseph in charge of all those held in the prison, and he was made responsible for al was done there. ²³The warden paid no attention to anything under Joseph's care cause the LORD was with Joseph and gave him success in whatever he did.

The Cupbearer and the Baker

40 Some time later, the cupbearer and the baker of the king of Egypt offe their master, the king of Egypt. ²Pharaoh was angry with his two offi the chief cupbearer and the chief baker, ³and put them in custody in the house c captain of the guard, in the same prison where Joseph was confined. ⁴The captain c guard assigned them to Joseph, and he attended them.

After they had been in custody for some time, ⁵each of the two men—the cupb and the baker of the king of Egypt, who were being held in prison—had a drear same night, and each dream had a meaning of its own.

⁶When Joseph came to them the next morning, he saw that they were dejected. ⁷S asked Pharaoh's officials who were in custody with him in his master's house, "Wh your faces so sad today?"

⁸"We both had dreams," they answered, "but there is no one to interpret them."

Then Joseph said to them, "Do not interpretations belong to God? Tell me dreams."

⁹So the chief cupbearer told Joseph his dream. He said to him, "In my dream I s vine in front of me, ¹⁰and on the vine were three branches. As soon as it budd blossomed, and its clusters ripened into grapes. ¹¹Pharaoh's cup was in my hand, took the grapes, squeezed them into Pharaoh's cup and put the cup in his hand."

¹²"This is what it means," Joseph said to him. "The three branches are three ¹³Within three days Pharaoh will lift up your head and restore you to your position you will put Pharaoh's cup in his hand, just as you used to do when you were cupbearer. ¹⁴But when all goes well with you, remember me and show me kind mention me to Pharaoh and get me out of this prison. ¹⁵For I was forcibly carried off the land of the Hebrews, and even here I have done nothing to deserve being put dungeon."

¹⁶When the chief baker saw that Joseph had given a favorable interpretation, he to Joseph, "I too had a dream: On my head were three baskets of bread.ᵃ ¹⁷In th basket were all kinds of baked goods for Pharaoh, but the birds were eating them c the basket on my head."

ᵃ16 Or three wicker baskets

This is what it means," Joseph said. "The three baskets are three days. ¹⁹Within days Pharaoh will lift off your head and hang you on a tree.ᵃ And the birds will eat your flesh."

ow the third day was Pharaoh's birthday, and he gave a feast for all his officials. He up the heads of the chief cupbearer and the chief baker in the presence of his als: ²¹He restored the chief cupbearer to his position, so that he once again put the nto Pharaoh's hand, ²²but he hangedᵇ the chief baker, just as Joseph had said to in his interpretation.

he chief cupbearer, however, did not remember Joseph; he forgot him.

aoh's Dreams

When two full years had passed, Pharaoh had a dream: He was standing by the Nile, ²when out of the river there came up seven cows, sleek and fat, and grazed among the reeds. ³After them, seven other cows, ugly and gaunt, came up f the Nile and stood beside those on the riverbank. ⁴And the cows that were ugly gaunt ate up the seven sleek, fat cows. Then Pharaoh woke up.

e fell asleep again and had a second dream: Seven heads of grain, healthy and , were growing on a single stalk. ⁶After them, seven other heads of grain sprouted— and scorched by the east wind. ⁷The thin heads of grain swallowed up the seven hy, full heads. Then Pharaoh woke up; it had been a dream.

the morning his mind was troubled, so he sent for all the magicians and wise men ypt. Pharaoh told them his dreams, but no one could interpret them for him.

nen the chief cupbearer said to Pharaoh, "Today I am reminded of my shortcomings. araoh was once angry with his servants, and he imprisoned me and the chief baker e house of the captain of the guard. ¹¹Each of us had a dream the same night, and dream had a meaning of its own. ¹²Now a young Hebrew was there with us, a int of the captain of the guard. We told him our dreams, and he interpreted them for iving each man the interpretation of his dream. ¹³And things turned out exactly as nterpreted them to us: I was restored to my position, and the other man was ed.ᵇ"

o Pharaoh sent for Joseph, and he was quickly brought from the dungeon. When he shaved and changed his clothes, he came before Pharaoh.

haraoh said to Joseph, "I had a dream, and no one can interpret it. But I have heard d of you that when you hear a dream you can interpret it."

I cannot do it," Joseph replied to Pharaoh, "but God will give Pharaoh the answer he es."

hen Pharaoh said to Joseph, "In my dream I was standing on the bank of the Nile, en out of the river there came up seven cows, fat and sleek, and they grazed among eeds. ¹⁹After them, seven other cows came up—scrawny and very ugly and lean. I lever seen such ugly cows in all the land of Egypt. ²⁰The lean, ugly cows ate up the n fat cows that came up first. ²¹But even after they ate them, no one could tell that had done so; they looked just as ugly as before. Then I woke up.

In my dreams I also saw seven heads of grain, full and good, growing on a single ²³After them, seven other heads sprouted—withered and thin and scorched by the wind. ²⁴The thin heads of grain swallowed up the seven good heads. I told this to nagicians, but none could explain it to me."

hen Joseph said to Pharaoh, "The dreams of Pharaoh are one and the same. God has aled to Pharaoh what he is about to do. ²⁶The seven good cows are seven years, and even good heads of grain are seven years; it is one and the same dream. ²⁷The n lean, ugly cows that came up afterward are seven years, and so are the seven hless heads of grain scorched by the east wind: They are seven years of famine.

ᵃ and impale you on a pole   ᵇ 22,13 Or impaled

²⁸"It is just as I said to Pharaoh: God has shown Pharaoh what he is about ²⁹Seven years of great abundance are coming throughout the land of Egypt, ³⁰but years of famine will follow them. Then all the abundance in Egypt will be forgotten the famine will ravage the land. ³¹The abundance in the land will not be remem because the famine that follows it will be so severe. ³²The reason the dream was gi Pharaoh in two forms is that the matter has been firmly decided by God, and God v it soon.

³³"And now let Pharaoh look for a discerning and wise man and put him in cha the land of Egypt. ³⁴Let Pharaoh appoint commissioners over the land to take a fifth harvest of Egypt during the seven years of abundance. ³⁵They should collect all th of these good years that are coming and store up the grain under the autho Pharaoh, to be kept in the cities for food. ³⁶This food should be held in reserve f country, to be used during the seven years of famine that will come upon Egypt, s the country may not be ruined by the famine."

³⁷The plan seemed good to Pharaoh and to all his officials. ³⁸So Pharaoh asked "Can we find anyone like this man, one in whom is the spirit of God ᵃ?"

³⁹Then Pharaoh said to Joseph, "Since God has made all this known to you, there one so discerning and wise as you. ⁴⁰You shall be in charge of my palace, and people are to submit to your orders. Only with respect to the throne will I be greate you."

Joseph in Charge of Egypt

⁴¹So Pharaoh said to Joseph, "I hereby put you in charge of the whole land of E ⁴²Then Pharaoh took his signet ring from his finger and put it on Joseph's fing dressed him in robes of fine linen and put a gold chain around his neck. ⁴³He ha ride in a chariot as his second-in-command,ᵇ and men shouted before him, wayᶜ!" Thus he put him in charge of the whole land of Egypt.

⁴⁴Then Pharaoh said to Joseph, "I am Pharaoh, but without your word no one v hand or foot in all Egypt." ⁴⁵Pharaoh gave Joseph the name Zaphenath-Paneah and

ᵃ38 Or of the gods   ᵇ43 Or in the chariot of his second-in-command; or in his second chariot   ᶜ43 Or Bow dow

---

▣ ⬛ ░░░░░░░░░░░░░░░ **ADDRESSING QUESTIONS** ░░░░░░░░░░░░░░░

41:16
Unseen Realities

Joseph made it clear to Pharaoh that he wasn't psychic. The Bible actually condemns the p tices of fortune-telling and divination (see Deuteronomy chapter 18, verses 10–13 [page 2 Joseph claimed that he was merely relaying a message from God—as a prophet, rather than a tune-teller.

The Bible does not teach that all dreams foretell future events. Current research indic that dreams are the mind's way of processing strong feelings and experiences. The Bible c teach, however, that a dream may have significance beyond our immediate personal experie The difficulty is knowing when any particular dream has divine origins.

If you sense that God is leading you in some unusual way, the Bible recommends taki variety of steps:

- Carefully research the issue (Proverbs chapter 14, verse 15 [page 821]).
- Ask God for wisdom (James chapter 1, verse 5 [page 1602]).
- Seek out the counsel of advisors (Proverbs chapter 15, verse 22 [page 824]).
- Make sure that what you propose doesn't violate a scriptural command (Joshua cha 22, verse 5 [page 286]).
- Make sure your plans include God (Psalm 127, verse 1 [page 781]; Proverbs chapte verses 5–6 [page 805]).

n Asenath daughter of Potiphera, priest of On,*a* to be his wife. And Joseph went oughout the land of Egypt.

⁴⁶Joseph was thirty years old when he entered the service of Pharaoh king of Egypt. d Joseph went out from Pharaoh's presence and traveled throughout Egypt. ⁴⁷During e seven years of abundance the land produced plentifully. ⁴⁸Joseph collected all the d produced in those seven years of abundance in Egypt and stored it in the cities. In ch city he put the food grown in the fields surrounding it. ⁴⁹Joseph stored up huge antities of grain, like the sand of the sea; it was so much that he stopped keeping ords because it was beyond measure.

⁵⁰Before the years of famine came, two sons were born to Joseph by Asenath daughter Potiphera, priest of On. ⁵¹Joseph named his firstborn Manasseh*b* and said, "It is cause God has made me forget all my trouble and all my father's household." ⁵²The cond son he named Ephraim*c* and said, "It is because God has made me fruitful in the d of my suffering."

⁵³The seven years of abundance in Egypt came to an end, ⁵⁴and the seven years of nine began, just as Joseph had said. There was famine in all the other lands, but in the ole land of Egypt there was food. ⁵⁵When all Egypt began to feel the famine, the ople cried to Pharaoh for food. Then Pharaoh told all the Egyptians, "Go to Joseph and what he tells you."

⁵⁶When the famine had spread over the whole country, Joseph opened the storehouses d sold grain to the Egyptians, for the famine was severe throughout Egypt. ⁵⁷And all e countries came to Egypt to buy grain from Joseph, because the famine was severe in the world.

seph's Brothers Go to Egypt

2 When Jacob learned that there was grain in Egypt, he said to his sons, "Why do you just keep looking at each other?" ²He continued, "I have heard that re is grain in Egypt. Go down there and buy some for us, so that we may live and not ."

³Then ten of Joseph's brothers went down to buy grain from Egypt. ⁴But Jacob did not d Benjamin, Joseph's brother, with the others, because he was afraid that harm might me to him. ⁵So Israel's sons were among those who went to buy grain, for the famine s in the land of Canaan also.

⁶Now Joseph was the governor of the land, the one who sold grain to all its people. So en Joseph's brothers arrived, they bowed down to him with their faces to the ground. s soon as Joseph saw his brothers, he recognized them, but he pretended to be a anger and spoke harshly to them. "Where do you come from?" he asked.

"From the land of Canaan," they replied, "to buy food."

⁸Although Joseph recognized his brothers, they did not recognize him. ⁹Then he re- embered his dreams about them and said to them, "You are spies! You have come to see ere our land is unprotected."

¹⁰"No, my lord," they answered. "Your servants have come to buy food. ¹¹We are all the ns of one man. Your servants are honest men, not spies."

¹²"No!" he said to them. "You have come to see where our land is unprotected."

¹³But they replied, "Your servants were twelve brothers, the sons of one man, who es in the land of Canaan. The youngest is now with our father, and one is no more."

¹⁴Joseph said to them, "It is just as I told you: You are spies! ¹⁵And this is how you will tested: As surely as Pharaoh lives, you will not leave this place unless your youngest ther comes here. ¹⁶Send one of your number to get your brother; the rest of you will kept in prison, so that your words may be tested to see if you are telling the truth. If

That is, Heliopolis; also in verse 50   b 51 Manasseh sounds like and may be derived from the Hebrew for forget. Ephraim sounds like the Hebrew for twice fruitful.

you are not, then as surely as Pharaoh lives, you are spies!" ¹⁷And he put them al
custody for three days.

¹⁸On the third day, Joseph said to them, "Do this and you will live, for I fear God:
you are honest men, let one of your brothers stay here in prison, while the rest of you
and take grain back for your starving households. ²⁰But you must bring your youn₍
brother to me, so that your words may be verified and that you may not die." This ₍
proceeded to do.

²¹They said to one another, "Surely we are being punished because of our brother.
saw how distressed he was when he pleaded with us for his life, but we would
listen; that's why this distress has come upon us."

²²Reuben replied, "Didn't I tell you not to sin against the boy? But you wouldn't lis₍
Now we must give an accounting for his blood." ²³They did not realize that Joseph c₍
understand them, since he was using an interpreter.

²⁴He turned away from them and began to weep, but then turned back and spok₍
them again. He had Simeon taken from them and bound before their eyes.

²⁵Joseph gave orders to fill their bags with grain, to put each man's silver back in
sack, and to give them provisions for their journey. After this was done for them, ²⁶t₍
loaded their grain on their donkeys and left.

²⁷At the place where they stopped for the night one of them opened his sack to
feed for his donkey, and he saw his silver in the mouth of his sack. ²⁸"My silver has b₍
returned," he said to his brothers. "Here it is in my sack."

Their hearts sank and they turned to each other trembling and said, "What is this ₍
God has done to us?"

²⁹When they came to their father Jacob in the land of Canaan, they told him all ₍
had happened to them. They said, ³⁰"The man who is lord over the land spoke harshl₍
us and treated us as though we were spying on the land. ³¹But we said to him, 'We
honest men; we are not spies. ³²We were twelve brothers, sons of one father. One is
more, and the youngest is with our father in Canaan.'

³³"Then the man who is lord over the land said to us, 'This is how I will know whe₍
you are honest men: Leave one of your brothers here with me, and take food for y₍
starving households and go. ³⁴But bring your youngest brother to me so I will know ₍
you are not spies but honest men. Then I will give your brother back to you, and you
trade*ᵃ* in the land.'"

a 34 Or move about freely

ADDRESSING QUESTIONS

42:21–22
Human Experience

Like Joseph's brothers, people who carry guilt feelings often see adverse circumstances as som₍
kind of payback for the wrong they've done. But the Bible does not endorse this simplistic, cause₍
and-effect rationale. Sometimes innocent people suffer while guilty people get away with evil—₍
least for the time being. In the future, this will change. When Jesus returns, all deeds will be see₍
for what they are. Only at that future time will faithfulness be completely rewarded and evil b₍
thoroughly punished (see Revelation chapter 20, verses 11–13 [page 1653] for an illustration ₍
this principle.)

However, the Bible does teach that we experience consequences in a general sense. Even₍
tually bad actions *do* produce bad results in our lives. For example, the body can only take s₍
many years of alcohol abuse; eventually the internal organs will begin to malfunction. High
integrity living often gives one peace of mind and other tangible benefits.

But don't look to the successes or failures in your life as a barometer of God's level of ap₍
proval. If you want to follow him, you'll need to obey what is commanded in Scripture even if short₍
term benefits are lacking. In the end, you'll find that all your efforts to do right were worthwhile.

⁵As they were emptying their sacks, there in each man's sack was his pouch of silver! ₋en they and their father saw the money pouches, they were frightened. ³⁶Their father ₋ob said to them, "You have deprived me of my children. Joseph is no more and Simeon ₋o more, and now you want to take Benjamin. Everything is against me!"

⁷Then Reuben said to his father, "You may put both of my sons to death if I do not ₋g him back to you. Entrust him to my care, and I will bring him back."

⁸But Jacob said, "My son will not go down there with you; his brother is dead and he ₋he only one left. If harm comes to him on the journey you are taking, you will bring my ₋y head down to the grave*ᵃ* in sorrow."

₋e Second Journey to Egypt

3 Now the famine was still severe in the land. ²So when they had eaten all the grain they had brought from Egypt, their father said to them, "Go back and ₋ us a little more food."

³But Judah said to him, "The man warned us solemnly, 'You will not see my face again ₋ess your brother is with you.' ⁴If you will send our brother along with us, we will go ₋wn and buy food for you. ⁵But if you will not send him, we will not go down, because ₋ man said to us, 'You will not see my face again unless your brother is with you.'"

⁶Israel asked, "Why did you bring this trouble on me by telling the man you had ₋ther brother?"

⁷They replied, "The man questioned us closely about ourselves and our family. 'Is your ₋er still living?' he asked us. 'Do you have another brother?' We simply answered his ₋estions. How were we to know he would say, 'Bring your brother down here'?"

⁸Then Judah said to Israel his father, "Send the boy along with me and we will go at ₋ce, so that we and you and our children may live and not die. ⁹I myself will guarantee ₋ safety; you can hold me personally responsible for him. If I do not bring him back to ₋ and set him here before you, I will bear the blame before you all my life. ¹⁰As it is, if ₋ had not delayed, we could have gone and returned twice."

¹¹Then their father Israel said to them, "If it must be, then do this: Put some of the best ₋ducts of the land in your bags and take them down to the man as a gift—a little balm ₋d a little honey, some spices and myrrh, some pistachio nuts and almonds. ¹²Take ₋ble the amount of silver with you, for you must return the silver that was put back ₋o the mouths of your sacks. Perhaps it was a mistake. ¹³Take your brother also and go ₋ck to the man at once. ¹⁴And may God Almighty*ᵇ* grant you mercy before the man so ₋ he will let your other brother and Benjamin come back with you. As for me, if I am ₋reaved, I am bereaved."

¹⁵So the men took the gifts and double the amount of silver, and Benjamin also. They ₋rried down to Egypt and presented themselves to Joseph. ¹⁶When Joseph saw Benja-₋n with them, he said to the steward of his house, "Take these men to my house, ₋ughter an animal and prepare dinner; they are to eat with me at noon."

¹⁷The man did as Joseph told him and took the men to Joseph's house. ¹⁸Now the men ₋re frightened when they were taken to his house. They thought, "We were brought ₋re because of the silver that was put back into our sacks the first time. He wants to ₋ack us and overpower us and seize us as slaves and take our donkeys."

¹⁹So they went up to Joseph's steward and spoke to him at the entrance to the house. ₋Please, sir," they said, "we came down here the first time to buy food. ²¹But at the ₋ce where we stopped for the night we opened our sacks and each of us found his ₋ver—the exact weight—in the mouth of his sack. So we have brought it back with us. ₋Ve have also brought additional silver with us to buy food. We don't know who put our ₋ver in our sacks."

²³"It's all right," he said. "Don't be afraid. Your God, the God of your father, has given ₋ treasure in your sacks; I received your silver." Then he brought Simeon out to them.

Hebrew *Sheol*   *ᵇ14* Hebrew *El-Shaddai*

²⁴The steward took the men into Joseph's house, gave them water to wash their and provided fodder for their donkeys. ²⁵They prepared their gifts for Joseph's arriva noon, because they had heard that they were to eat there.

²⁶When Joseph came home, they presented to him the gifts they had brought into house, and they bowed down before him to the ground. ²⁷He asked them how they w and then he said, "How is your aged father you told me about? Is he still living?"

²⁸They replied, "Your servant our father is still alive and well." And they bowed lov pay him honor.

²⁹As he looked about and saw his brother Benjamin, his own mother's son, he ask "Is this your youngest brother, the one you told me about?" And he said, "God be graci to you, my son." ³⁰Deeply moved at the sight of his brother, Joseph hurried out looked for a place to weep. He went into his private room and wept there.

³¹After he had washed his face, he came out and, controlling himself, said, "Serve food."

³²They served him by himself, the brothers by themselves, and the Egyptians who with him by themselves, because Egyptians could not eat with Hebrews, for tha detestable to Egyptians. ³³The men had been seated before him in the order of th ages, from the firstborn to the youngest; and they looked at each other in astonishme ³⁴When portions were served to them from Joseph's table, Benjamin's portion was times as much as anyone else's. So they feasted and drank freely with him.

A Silver Cup in a Sack

44 Now Joseph gave these instructions to the steward of his house: "Fill men's sacks with as much food as they can carry, and put each man's si in the mouth of his sack. ²Then put my cup, the silver one, in the mouth of the young one's sack, along with the silver for his grain." And he did as Joseph said.

³As morning dawned, the men were sent on their way with their donkeys. ⁴They not gone far from the city when Joseph said to his steward, "Go after those men at or and when you catch up with them, say to them, 'Why have you repaid good with e ⁵Isn't this the cup my master drinks from and also uses for divination? This is a wic thing you have done.'"

⁶When he caught up with them, he repeated these words to them. ⁷But they said him, "Why does my lord say such things? Far be it from your servants to do anything that! ⁸We even brought back to you from the land of Canaan the silver we found ins the mouths of our sacks. So why would we steal silver or gold from your master's hou ⁹If any of your servants is found to have it, he will die; and the rest of us will become lord's slaves."

¹⁰"Very well, then," he said, "let it be as you say. Whoever is found to have it become my slave; the rest of you will be free from blame."

¹¹Each of them quickly lowered his sack to the ground and opened it. ¹²Then steward proceeded to search, beginning with the oldest and ending with the young And the cup was found in Benjamin's sack. ¹³At this, they tore their clothes. Then they loaded their donkeys and returned to the city.

¹⁴Joseph was still in the house when Judah and his brothers came in, and they th themselves to the ground before him. ¹⁵Joseph said to them, "What is this you h done? Don't you know that a man like me can find things out by divination?"

¹⁶"What can we say to my lord?" Judah replied. "What can we say? How can we pr our innocence? God has uncovered your servants' guilt. We are now my lord's slaves— ourselves and the one who was found to have the cup."

¹⁷But Joseph said, "Far be it from me to do such a thing! Only the man who was fo to have the cup will become my slave. The rest of you, go back to your father in pea

¹⁸Then Judah went up to him and said: "Please, my lord, let your servant speak a w to my lord. Do not be angry with your servant, though you are equal to Pharaoh hims

ly lord asked his servants, 'Do you have a father or a brother?' ²⁰And we answered, 'we have an aged father, and there is a young son born to him in his old age. His brother is dead, and he is the only one of his mother's sons left, and his father loves him.'

²¹"Then you said to your servants, 'Bring him down to me so I can see him for myself.' ²²And we said to my lord, 'The boy cannot leave his father; if he leaves him, his father will die.' ²³But you told your servants, 'Unless your youngest brother comes down with you, you will not see my face again.' ²⁴When we went back to your servant my father, we told him what my lord had said.

²⁵"Then our father said, 'Go back and buy a little more food.' ²⁶But we said, 'We cannot go down. Only if our youngest brother is with us will we go. We cannot see the man's face unless our youngest brother is with us.'

²⁷"Your servant my father said to us, 'You know that my wife bore me two sons. ²⁸One of them went away from me, and I said, "He has surely been torn to pieces." And I have not seen him since. ²⁹If you take this one from me too and harm comes to him, you will bring my gray head down to the grave^a in misery.'

³⁰"So now, if the boy is not with us when I go back to your servant my father and if my father, whose life is closely bound up with the boy's life, ³¹sees that the boy isn't there, he will die. Your servants will bring the gray head of our father down to the grave in sorrow. ³²Your servant guaranteed the boy's safety to my father. I said, 'If I do not bring him back to you, I will bear the blame before you, my father, all my life!'

³³"Now then, please let your servant remain here as my lord's slave in place of the boy, and let the boy return with his brothers. ³⁴How can I go back to my father if the boy is not with me? No! Do not let me see the misery that would come upon my father."

Joseph Makes Himself Known

45 Then Joseph could no longer control himself before all his attendants, and he cried out, "Have everyone leave my presence!" So there was no one with Joseph when he made himself known to his brothers. ²And he wept so loudly that the Egyptians heard him, and Pharaoh's household heard about it.

³Joseph said to his brothers, "I am Joseph! Is my father still living?" But his brothers were not able to answer him, because they were terrified at his presence.

⁴Then Joseph said to his brothers, "Come close to me." When they had done so, he said, "I am your brother Joseph, the one you sold into Egypt! ⁵And now, do not be distressed and do not be angry with yourselves for selling me here, because it was to save lives that God sent me ahead of you. ⁶For two years now there has been famine in the land, and for the next five years there will not be plowing and reaping. ⁷But God sent me ahead of you to preserve for you a remnant on earth and to save your lives by a great deliverance.^b

⁸"So then, it was not you who sent me here, but God. He made me father to Pharaoh, lord of his entire household and ruler of all Egypt. ⁹Now hurry back to my father and say to him, 'This is what your son Joseph says: God has made me lord of all Egypt. Come down to me; don't delay. ¹⁰You shall live in the region of Goshen and be near me—you, your children and grandchildren, your flocks and herds, and all you have. ¹¹I will provide for you there, because five years of famine are still to come. Otherwise you and your household and all who belong to you will become destitute.'

¹²"You can see for yourselves, and so can my brother Benjamin, that it is really I who am speaking to you. ¹³Tell my father about all the honor accorded me in Egypt and about everything you have seen. And bring my father down here quickly."

¹⁴Then he threw his arms around his brother Benjamin and wept, and Benjamin embraced him, weeping. ¹⁵And he kissed all his brothers and wept over them. Afterward his brothers talked with him.

¹⁶When the news reached Pharaoh's palace that Joseph's brothers had come, Pharaoh

^a Hebrew *Sheol*; also in verse 31   ^b 7 Or *save you as a great band of survivors*

and all his officials were pleased. [17]Pharaoh said to Joseph, "Tell your brothers, 'Do th
Load your animals and return to the land of Canaan, [18]and bring your father and y
families back to me. I will give you the best of the land of Egypt and you can enjoy the
of the land.'

[19]"You are also directed to tell them, 'Do this: Take some carts from Egypt for y
children and your wives, and get your father and come. [20]Never mind about your belo
ings, because the best of all Egypt will be yours.'"

[21]So the sons of Israel did this. Joseph gave them carts, as Pharaoh had command
and he also gave them provisions for their journey. [22]To each of them he gave r
clothing, but to Benjamin he gave th
hundred shekels[a] of silver and five set
clothes. [23]And this is what he sent to
father: ten donkeys loaded with the b
things of Egypt, and ten female donk
loaded with grain and bread and ot
provisions for his journey. [24]Then he s
his brothers away, and as they were le
ing he said to them, "Don't quarrel on
way!"

[25]So they went up out of Egypt and ca
to their father Jacob in the land of Cana
[26]They told him, "Joseph is still alive
fact, he is ruler of all Egypt." Jacob v
stunned; he did not believe them. [27]
when they told him everything Joseph l
said to them, and when he saw the ca
Joseph had sent to carry him back,
spirit of their father Jacob revived. [28]/
Israel said, "I'm convinced! My son Jos
is still alive. I will go and see him befo
die."

DISCOVERING GOD

45:8
The God Who Is There

Joseph saw God at work even in the evil plot
of his brothers from years before. While the
brothers were responsible for their wrongdoing, God did his work through those events.
Through Joseph, God preserved a whole nation and the surrounding regions from a great
famine (compare Joseph's words in chapter
50, verses 19–20 [page 69]).

One of the benefits of a relationship with
God is that he has promised to work in every
circumstance to bring eventual good out of it
(see Romans 8, verse 28 [page 1479]).
That doesn't mean that everything that happens to you will be good (see the note on
Genesis chapter 42, verses 21–22 [page 58]),
but you can be confident in God's power to
reclaim whatever happens for a better purpose.

Jacob Goes to Egypt

46 So Israel set out with all
was his, and when he reac
Beersheba, he offered sacrifices to the God of his father Isaac.

[2]And God spoke to Israel in a vision at night and said, "Jacob! Jacob!"

"Here I am," he replied.

[3]"I am God, the God of your father," he said. "Do not be afraid to go down to Egypt,
I will make you into a great nation there. [4]I will go down to Egypt with you, and I
surely bring you back again. And Joseph's own hand will close your eyes."

[5]Then Jacob left Beersheba, and Israel's sons took their father Jacob and their child
and their wives in the carts that Pharaoh had sent to transport him. [6]They also took v
them their livestock and the possessions they had acquired in Canaan, and Jacob and
his offspring went to Egypt. [7]He took with him to Egypt his sons and grandsons and
daughters and granddaughters—all his offspring.

[8]These are the names of the sons of Israel (Jacob and his descendants) who wen
Egypt:

Reuben the firstborn of Jacob.

[9]The sons of Reuben:
Hanoch, Pallu, Hezron and Carmi.

[a]22 That is, about 7 1/2 pounds (about 3.5 kilograms)

¹⁰The sons of Simeon:

Jemuel, Jamin, Ohad, Jakin, Zohar and Shaul the son of a Canaanite woman.

¹¹The sons of Levi:

Gershon, Kohath and Merari.

¹²The sons of Judah:

Er, Onan, Shelah, Perez and Zerah (but Er and Onan had died in the land of Canaan).

The sons of Perez:

Hezron and Hamul.

¹³The sons of Issachar:

Tola, Puah,ᵃ Jashubᵇ and Shimron.

¹⁴The sons of Zebulun:

Sered, Elon and Jahleel.

¹⁵These were the sons Leah bore to Jacob in Paddan Aram,ᶜ besides his daughter Dinah. These sons and daughters of his were thirty-three in all.

¹⁶The sons of Gad:

Zephon,ᵈ Haggi, Shuni, Ezbon, Eri, Arodi and Areli.

¹⁷The sons of Asher:

Imnah, Ishvah, Ishvi and Beriah.

Their sister was Serah.

The sons of Beriah:

Heber and Malkiel.

¹⁸These were the children born to Jacob by Zilpah, whom Laban had given to his daughter Leah—sixteen in all.

¹⁹The sons of Jacob's wife Rachel:

Joseph and Benjamin. ²⁰In Egypt, Manasseh and Ephraim were born to Joseph by Asenath daughter of Potiphera, priest of On.ᵉ

²¹The sons of Benjamin:

Bela, Beker, Ashbel, Gera, Naaman, Ehi, Rosh, Muppim, Huppim and Ard.

²²These were the sons of Rachel who were born to Jacob—fourteen in all.

²³The son of Dan:

Hushim.

²⁴The sons of Naphtali:

Jahziel, Guni, Jezer and Shillem.

²⁵These were the sons born to Jacob by Bilhah, whom Laban had given to his daughter Rachel—seven in all.

²⁶All those who went to Egypt with Jacob—those who were his direct descendants, not counting his sons' wives—numbered sixty-six persons. ²⁷With the two sonsᶠ who had been born to Joseph in Egypt, the members of Jacob's family, which went to Egypt, were seventyᵍ in all.

²⁸Now Jacob sent Judah ahead of him to Joseph to get directions to Goshen. When they arrived in the region of Goshen, ²⁹Joseph had his chariot made ready and went to Goshen to meet his father Israel. As soon as Joseph appeared before him, he threw his arms around his fatherʰ and wept for a long time.

³⁰Israel said to Joseph, "Now I am ready to die, since I have seen for myself that you are still alive."

a 3 Samaritan Pentateuch and Syriac (see also 1 Chron. 7:1); Masoretic Text Puvah   b 13 Samaritan Pentateuch and some Septuagint manuscripts (see also Num. 26:24 and 1 Chron. 7:1); Masoretic Text Iob   c 15 That is, Northwest Mesopotamia   d 6 Samaritan Pentateuch and Septuagint (see also Num. 26:15); Masoretic Text Ziphion   e 20 That is, Heliopolis   f 7 Hebrew; Septuagint the nine children   g 27 Hebrew (see also Exodus 1:5 and footnote); Septuagint (see also Acts 7:14) seventy-five   h 29 Hebrew around him

³¹Then Joseph said to his brothers and to his father's household, "I will go up and speak to Pharaoh and will say to him, 'My brothers and my father's household, who we living in the land of Canaan, have come to me. ³²The men are shepherds; they ten livestock, and they have brought along their flocks and herds and everything they own ³³When Pharaoh calls you in and asks, 'What is your occupation?' ³⁴you should answe 'Your servants have tended livestock from our boyhood on, just as our fathers did.' The you will be allowed to settle in the region of Goshen, for all shepherds are detestable the Egyptians."

47 Joseph went and told Pharaoh, "My father and brothers, with their floc and herds and everything they own, have come from the land of Canaan an are now in Goshen." ²He chose five of his brothers and presented them before Pharaoh ³Pharaoh asked the brothers, "What is your occupation?"

"Your servants are shepherds," they replied to Pharaoh, "just as our fathers were ⁴They also said to him, "We have come to live here awhile, because the famine is seve in Canaan and your servants' flocks have no pasture. So now, please let your servan settle in Goshen."

⁵Pharaoh said to Joseph, "Your father and your brothers have come to you, ⁶and th land of Egypt is before you; settle your father and your brothers in the best part of th land. Let them live in Goshen. And if you know of any among them with special abiliti put them in charge of my own livestock."

⁷Then Joseph brought his father Jacob in and presented him before Pharaoh. Aft Jacob blessed ᵃ Pharaoh, ⁸Pharaoh asked him, "How old are you?"

⁹And Jacob said to Pharaoh, "The years of my pilgrimage are a hundred and thirty. M years have been few and difficult, and they do not equal the years of the pilgrimage my fathers." ¹⁰Then Jacob blessed ᵇ Pharaoh and went out from his presence.

¹¹So Joseph settled his father and his brothers in Egypt and gave them property in th best part of the land, the district of Rameses, as Pharaoh directed. ¹²Joseph also provide his father and his brothers and all his father's household with food, according to th number of their children.

Joseph and the Famine

¹³There was no food, however, in the whole region because the famine was seve both Egypt and Canaan wasted away because of the famine. ¹⁴Joseph collected all th money that was to be found in Egypt and Canaan in payment for the grain they we buying, and he brought it to Pharaoh's palace. ¹⁵When the money of the people of Egy and Canaan was gone, all Egypt came to Joseph and said, "Give us food. Why should v die before your eyes? Our money is used up."

¹⁶"Then bring your livestock," said Joseph. "I will sell you food in exchange for yo livestock, since your money is gone." ¹⁷So they brought their livestock to Joseph, and gave them food in exchange for their horses, their sheep and goats, their cattle an donkeys. And he brought them through that year with food in exchange for all the livestock.

¹⁸When that year was over, they came to him the following year and said, "We cann hide from our lord the fact that since our money is gone and our livestock belongs to yo there is nothing left for our lord except our bodies and our land. ¹⁹Why should we peri before your eyes—we and our land as well? Buy us and our land in exchange for foc and we with our land will be in bondage to Pharaoh. Give us seed so that we may li and not die, and that the land may not become desolate."

²⁰So Joseph bought all the land in Egypt for Pharaoh. The Egyptians, one and all, sc their fields, because the famine was too severe for them. The land became Pharaoh ²¹and Joseph reduced the people to servitude,ᶜ from one end of Egypt to the oth

ᵃ7 Or greeted   ᵇ10 Or said farewell to   ᶜ21 Samaritan Pentateuch and Septuagint (see also Vulgate); Masoretic Text
and he moved the people into the cities

²²However, he did not buy the land of the priests, because they received a regular allotment from Pharaoh and had food enough from the allotment Pharaoh gave them. That is why they did not sell their land.

²³Joseph said to the people, "Now that I have bought you and your land today for Pharaoh, here is seed for you so you can plant the ground. ²⁴But when the crop comes in, give a fifth of it to Pharaoh. The other four-fifths you may keep as seed for the fields and as food for yourselves and your households and your children."

²⁵"You have saved our lives," they said. "May we find favor in the eyes of our lord; we will be in bondage to Pharaoh."

²⁶So Joseph established it as a law concerning land in Egypt—still in force today—that a fifth of the produce belongs to Pharaoh. It was only the land of the priests that did not become Pharaoh's.

²⁷Now the Israelites settled in Egypt in the region of Goshen. They acquired property there and were fruitful and increased greatly in number.

²⁸Jacob lived in Egypt seventeen years, and the years of his life were a hundred and forty-seven. ²⁹When the time drew near for Israel to die, he called for his son Joseph and said to him, "If I have found favor in your eyes, put your hand under my thigh and promise that you will show me kindness and faithfulness. Do not bury me in Egypt, ³⁰but when I rest with my fathers, carry me out of Egypt and bury me where they are buried."

"I will do as you say," he said.

³¹"Swear to me," he said. Then Joseph swore to him, and Israel worshiped as he leaned on the top of his staff.ᵃ

Manasseh and Ephraim

48 Some time later Joseph was told, "Your father is ill." So he took his two sons Manasseh and Ephraim along with him. ²When Jacob was told, "Your son Joseph has come to you," Israel rallied his strength and sat up on the bed.

³Jacob said to Joseph, "God Almightyᵇ appeared to me at Luz in the land of Canaan, and there he blessed me ⁴and said to me, 'I am going to make you fruitful and will increase your numbers. I will make you a community of peoples, and I will give this land as an everlasting possession to your descendants after you.'

⁵"Now then, your two sons born to you in Egypt before I came to you here will be reckoned as mine; Ephraim and Manasseh will be mine, just as Reuben and Simeon are mine. ⁶Any children born to you after them will be yours; in the territory they inherit they will be reckoned under the names of their brothers. ⁷As I was returning from Paddan,ᶜ to my sorrow Rachel died in the land of Canaan while we were still on the way, a little distance from Ephrath. So I buried her there beside the road to Ephrath" (that is, Bethlehem).

⁸When Israel saw the sons of Joseph, he asked, "Who are these?"

⁹"They are the sons God has given me here," Joseph said to his father.

Then Israel said, "Bring them to me so I may bless them."

¹⁰Now Israel's eyes were failing because of old age, and he could hardly see. So Joseph brought his sons close to him, and his father kissed them and embraced them.

¹¹Israel said to Joseph, "I never expected to see your face again, and now God has allowed me to see your children too."

¹²Then Joseph removed them from Israel's knees and bowed down with his face to the ground. ¹³And Joseph took both of them, Ephraim on his right toward Israel's left hand and Manasseh on his left toward Israel's right hand, and brought them close to him. ¹⁴But Israel reached out his right hand and put it on Ephraim's head, though he was the younger, and crossing his arms, he put his left hand on Manasseh's head, even though Manasseh was the firstborn.

---

31 Or *Israel bowed down at the head of his bed*   ᵇ3 Hebrew *El-Shaddai*   ᶜ7 That is, Northwest Mesopotamia

¹⁵Then he blessed Joseph and said,

> "May the God before whom my fathers
>   Abraham and Isaac walked,
> the God who has been my shepherd
>   all my life to this day,
> ¹⁶the Angel who has delivered me from all harm
>   —may he bless these boys.
> May they be called by my name
>   and the names of my fathers Abraham and Isaac,
> and may they increase greatly
>   upon the earth."

¹⁷When Joseph saw his father placing his right hand on Ephraim's head he wa displeased; so he took hold of his father's hand to move it from Ephraim's head Manasseh's head. ¹⁸Joseph said to him, "No, my father, this one is the firstborn; put yo right hand on his head."

¹⁹But his father refused and said, know, my son, I know. He too will becom a people, and he too will become grea Nevertheless, his younger brother will b greater than he, and his descendants wi become a group of nations." ²⁰He blesse them that day and said,

> "In yourᵃ name will Israel
>   pronounce this blessing:
> 'May God make you like
>   Ephraim and Manasseh.'"

So he put Ephraim ahead of Manasseh.

²¹Then Israel said to Joseph, "I am abou to die, but God will be with youᵇ and tak youᵇ back to the land of yourᵇ father ²²And to you, as one who is over you brothers, I give the ridge of landᶜ I too from the Amorites with my sword and m bow."

Jacob Blesses His Sons

49 Then Jacob called for his son and said: "Gather around so can tell you what will happen to you i days to come.

> ²"Assemble and listen, sons of
>   Jacob;
>   listen to your father Israel.

> ³"Reuben, you are my firstborn,
>   my might, the first sign of my strength,
>   excelling in honor, excelling in power.
> ⁴Turbulent as the waters, you will no longer excel,

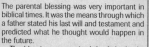

┌─────────────────────────────────────┐
│ ▣ **STRENGTHENING RELATIONSHIPS** ⤢ │
│   │
│ **48:19-20**   │
│ **Parenting**   │
│   │
│ The parental blessing was very important in │
│ biblical times. It was the means through which │
│ a father stated his last will and testament and │
│ predicted what he thought would happen in │
│ the future. │
│   The blessing summarized the father's ob- │
│ servations concerning his children. He didn't │
│ just tell them what he would give them—he │
│ told them *who they were*. Thus the blessing │
│ helped the children understand their place in │
│ the world. │
│   It's important in every culture for parents │
│ to discover how their children have been │
│ uniquely gifted and to affirm their design. One │
│ of the sad commentaries on many parents to- │
│ day is that they fail to give their children "the │
│ blessing"—the sense that they recognize and │
│ approve of their child's unique, God-given │
│ identity. │
│   If you're a parent, don't fail to be your chil- │
│ dren's greatest student. Observe them; learn │
│ about them; affirm who they are. The blessing │
│ you give—or withhold—will profoundly shape │
│ their future. │
└─────────────────────────────────────┘

ᵃ20 The Hebrew is singular.   *ᵇ21 The Hebrew is plural.*   *ᶜ22 Or And to you I give one portion more than to your brothers—the portion*

for you went up onto your father's bed,
onto my couch and defiled it.

5"Simeon and Levi are brothers—
their swords*a* are weapons of violence.
6Let me not enter their council,
let me not join their assembly,
for they have killed men in their anger
and hamstrung oxen as they pleased.
7Cursed be their anger, so fierce,
and their fury, so cruel!
I will scatter them in Jacob
and disperse them in Israel.

8"Judah,*b* your brothers will praise you;
your hand will be on the neck of your enemies;
your father's sons will bow down to you.
9You are a lion's cub, O Judah;
you return from the prey, my son.
Like a lion he crouches and lies down,
like a lioness—who dares to rouse him?
10The scepter will not depart from Judah,
nor the ruler's staff from between his feet,
until he comes to whom it belongs*c*
and the obedience of the nations is his.
11He will tether his donkey to a vine,
his colt to the choicest branch;
he will wash his garments in wine,
his robes in the blood of grapes.
12His eyes will be darker than wine,
his teeth whiter than milk.*d*

13"Zebulun will live by the seashore
and become a haven for ships;
his border will extend toward Sidon.

14"Issachar is a rawboned*e* donkey
lying down between two saddlebags.*f*
15When he sees how good is his resting place
and how pleasant is his land,
he will bend his shoulder to the burden
and submit to forced labor.

16"Dan*g* will provide justice for his people
as one of the tribes of Israel.
17Dan will be a serpent by the roadside,
a viper along the path,
that bites the horse's heels
so that its rider tumbles backward.

18"I look for your deliverance, O LORD.

---

5 The meaning of the Hebrew for this word is uncertain.   *b8* Judah sounds like and may be derived from the Hebrew for
raise.   *c10* Or until Shiloh comes; or until he comes to whom tribute belongs   *d12* Or will be dull from wine, / his
*teeth white from milk   *e14* Or strong   *f14* Or campfires   *g16* Dan here means he provides justice.*

19"Gad^a will be attacked by a band of raiders,
   but he will attack them at their heels.

20"Asher's food will be rich;
   he will provide delicacies fit for a king.

21"Naphtali is a doe set free
   that bears beautiful fawns.^b

22"Joseph is a fruitful vine,
   a fruitful vine near a spring,
   whose branches climb over a wall.^c
23With bitterness archers attacked him;
   they shot at him with hostility.
24But his bow remained steady,
   his strong arms stayed^d limber,
because of the hand of the Mighty One of Jacob,
   because of the Shepherd, the Rock of Israel,
25because of your father's God, who helps you,
   because of the Almighty,^e who blesses you
with blessings of the heavens above,
   blessings of the deep that lies below,
   blessings of the breast and womb.
26Your father's blessings are greater
   than the blessings of the ancient mountains,
   than^f the bounty of the age-old hills.
Let all these rest on the head of Joseph,
   on the brow of the prince among^g his brothers.

27"Benjamin is a ravenous wolf;
   in the morning he devours the prey,
   in the evening he divides the plunder."

28All these are the twelve tribes of Israel, and this is what their father said to them when he blessed them, giving each the blessing appropriate to him.

The Death of Jacob

29Then he gave them these instructions: "I am about to be gathered to my people. Bury me with my fathers in the cave in the field of Ephron the Hittite, 30the cave in the field Machpelah, near Mamre in Canaan, which Abraham bought as a burial place from Ephron the Hittite, along with the field. 31There Abraham and his wife Sarah were buried, there Isaac and his wife Rebekah were buried, and there I buried Leah. 32The field and the cave in it were bought from the Hittites.^h"

33When Jacob had finished giving instructions to his sons, he drew his feet up into the bed, breathed his last and was gathered to his people.

50 Joseph threw himself upon his father and wept over him and kissed him. 2Then Joseph directed the physicians in his service to embalm his father Israel. So the physicians embalmed him, 3taking a full forty days, for that was the time required for embalming. And the Egyptians mourned for him seventy days.

4When the days of mourning had passed, Joseph said to Pharaoh's court, "If I have found favor in your eyes, speak to Pharaoh for me. Tell him, 5'My father made me swear

a19 Gad can mean attack and band of raiders.   b21 Or free; / he utters beautiful words   c22 Or Joseph is a wild colt, / a wild colt near a spring, / a wild donkey on a terraced hill   d23,24 Or archers will attack . . . will shoot . . . will remain . . . will stay   e25 Hebrew Shaddai   f26 Or of my progenitors, / as great as   g26 Or the one separated from   h32 Or the sons of Heth

an oath and said, "I am about to die; bury me in the tomb I dug for myself in the land of Canaan." Now let me go up and bury my father; then I will return.' "

⁶Pharaoh said, "Go up and bury your father, as he made you swear to do."

⁷So Joseph went up to bury his father. All Pharaoh's officials accompanied him—the dignitaries of his court and all the dignitaries of Egypt— ⁸besides all the members of Joseph's household and his brothers and those belonging to his father's household. Only their children and their flocks and herds were left in Goshen. ⁹Chariots and horsemenᵃ also went up with him. It was a very large company.

¹⁰When they reached the threshing floor of Atad, near the Jordan, they lamented loudly and bitterly; and there Joseph observed a seven-day period of mourning for his father. ¹¹When the Canaanites who lived there saw the mourning at the threshing floor of Atad, they said, "The Egyptians are holding a solemn ceremony of mourning." That is why that place near the Jordan is called Abel Mizraim.ᵇ

¹²So Jacob's sons did as he had commanded them: ¹³They carried him to the land of Canaan and buried him in the cave in the field of Machpelah, near Mamre, which Abraham had bought as a burial place from Ephron the Hittite, along with the field. ¹⁴After burying his father, Joseph returned to Egypt, together with his brothers and all the others who had gone with him to bury his father.

Joseph Reassures His Brothers

¹⁵When Joseph's brothers saw that their father was dead, they said, "What if Joseph holds a grudge against us and pays us back for all the wrongs we did to him?" ¹⁶So they sent word to Joseph, saying, "Your father left these instructions before he died: ¹⁷'This is what you are to say to Joseph: I ask you to forgive your brothers the sins and the wrongs they committed in treating you so badly.' Now please forgive the sins of the servants of the God of your father." When their message came to him, Joseph wept.

¹⁸His brothers then came and threw themselves down before him. "We are your slaves," they said.

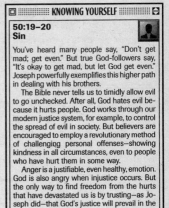

╔══════════════════════════════════════╗
║ ▦ ░░░░░ **KNOWING YOURSELF** ░░░░░ ▤ ║

50:19–20
Sin

You've heard many people say, "Don't get mad; get even." But true God-followers say, "It's okay to get mad, but let God get even." Joseph powerfully exemplifies this higher path in dealing with his brothers.

The Bible never tells us to timidly allow evil to go unchecked. After all, God hates evil because it hurts people. God works through our modern justice system, for example, to control the spread of evil in society. But believers are encouraged to employ a revolutionary method of challenging personal offenses—showing kindness in all circumstances, even to people who have hurt them in some way.

Anger is a justifiable, even healthy, emotion. God is also angry when injustice occurs. But the only way to find freedom from the hurts that have devastated us is by trusting—as Joseph did—that God's justice will prevail in the end.

¹⁹But Joseph said to them, "Don't be afraid. Am I in the place of God? ²⁰You intended to harm me, but God intended it for good to accomplish what is now being done, the saving of many lives. ²¹So then, don't be afraid. I will provide for you and your children." And he reassured them and spoke kindly to them.

The Death of Joseph

²²Joseph stayed in Egypt, along with all his father's family. He lived a hundred and ten years ²³and saw the third generation of Ephraim's children. Also the children of Makir son of Manasseh were placed at birth on Joseph's knees.ᶜ

²⁴Then Joseph said to his brothers, "I am about to die. But God will surely come to your aid and take you up out of this land to the land he promised on oath to Abraham, Isaac

---

ᵃ9 Or charioteers   ᵇ11 *Abel Mizraim* means *mourning of the Egyptians.*   ᶜ23 That is, were counted as his

and Jacob." ²⁵And Joseph made the sons of Israel swear an oath and said, "God wi
surely come to your aid, and then you must carry my bones up from this place."

²⁶So Joseph died at the age of a hundred and ten. And after they embalmed him, h
was placed in a coffin in Egypt.

🔲 ::::::::::::::::::::::::::::::::::: **EPILOGUE** ::::::::::::::::::::::::::::::::::: 🔄

This is the first book of the Bible, and it sets the stage for all that follows. It is also the first book
in the "Five Alive" series. *The Journey* focuses on this book and four others to summarize the central message of the Bible.

In these pages you have read about the God who made everything, the people who ruined
that good creation, and the first steps God took to get his wayward human family back.

One of God's most crucial interventions was to identify Abraham as the "seed" of the Hebrew people. Abraham's offspring would eventually grow into a great nation, and that nation would
be a light to the whole world.

To read the story of how God established this nation in the land he had promised, turn to the
book called "Deuteronomy" (page 212). There you'll meet Moses, the great leader who fulfilled
God's promise, spoken through Joseph, to deliver Israel from Egypt (chapter 50, verses 24–25
[page 69]). Notice the theme that is beginning to emerge—God is a deliverer, a rescuer. He fulfills
this role throughout the Bible.

People who seek God will find that the barrier between us and him is not just lack of information, but our spiritually self-destructive tendency to sin. To remove that barrier, we need more
than just information or education—we need to claim God's promise to free us from our sin and
accept the salvation that he offers. God is the only being who can provide that freedom, and he
will if we will just ask.

I couldn't believe it: I had recently left my wife for this woman, and now she wanted me to go to church! It didn't matter what we were doing just before church or just after, or how we lived the rest of the week. She had to be in church every Sunday. Other than this idiosyncrasy, she seemed perfect. So I went with her.

Her church was small and traditional, and the minister preached on why Christians in his particular denomination had a leg up on everyone else. I left telling my girlfriend that the message was baloney. "Fine," she said angrily, "You pick the church next week."

I was stumped. I couldn't go back to her church—that would be admitting I was wrong, and I didn't ever do that. The only church that popped into my mind was one my assistant had been telling me about for four years. "I've heard about this unusual church . . ." I began.

When my girlfriend and I pulled up the following Sunday, I noticed that the grounds were immaculate. "There's somebody around here who cares," I thought. As a middle-management businessman, I paid attention to those kind of things. I was even more intrigued by the auditorium. It was theater style—there were no stained-glass windows and no statues of the saints. There wasn't even a crucifix. "Is this really a church?" I wondered. Then the music started—I actually liked it! It was the kind of music I listened to, except that the content was different.

The announcements raised my eyebrows even more: The church didn't want my money. "How do they pay for this place?" I wondered. Now they really had my attention.

During the message, the pastor did something I'd never heard a pastor do: He used himself as an example in his message, which was on being patient. He told us about how he had run home from church to catch a football game, scrambled to the local convenience store at half-time to get a newspaper, and then got frustrated when he was caught behind someone who was slowly ordering a sandwich. That was me! Not only was I impatient, but I was also a liar and a thief. I had lost a job because of stealing. I thought that if people really knew me they would run in the opposite direction. God, I had surmised, was the same.

But then I heard the pastor say that I mattered to God. No matter what. No matter where I was in life. A glimmer of hope slipped into my mind: Could this possibly be true? The answer to that question was going to change my family and me forever.

"That was the most sacrilegious place I've ever been to," my girlfriend said as we left the church that Sunday. I didn't tell her how I was feeling, but my inner turmoil wouldn't go away. What was that experience all about? Was it a fluke? If there was a God, could I possibly matter to him? In search of an answer, I decided to go to church by myself. Something I'd never done before: I decided to go to church by myself. "Impress me again," I half-prayed. "I dare you."

The second Sunday was similar to the first. Again I heard the message that I mattered to God—and to this church. I walked out feeling challenged but encouraged—so much so that I came back the third week. This time the message was on different kinds of faithfulness—marital, relational and spiritual. It didn't take much soul-searching to realize that I had none of the qualities the pastor was speaking about.

What I did next went against everything I had done only months earlier. I broke it off with my girlfriend and called my estranged wife to ask if she would go to church with me the next Sunday. She was shocked and skeptical at my request, but she agreed to go to church with me.

It was a cool ride to the church—and not because of the temperature! We didn't even speak until afterward.

"Well, what did you think?" I asked. She gave me a puzzled look. "I really liked it. It was like coming home."

Several weeks passed. I asked my wife if she was willing to take me back. After some thought she said yes, and we went to counseling. We also met some people who presented the plan of salvation to us. After hearing it we both decided to thoroughly investigate Christianity. People at the church seemed confident we would find the claims of Christ to be true.

Six months later, a weekend message forced me to choose: Was Jesus a liar? Or was he crazy? The only alternative was to accept his claims to be the Son of God and Savior of the world. I had come to the point where I was ready to acknowledge that as the truth. With tears streaming down my face, I asked Jesus to forgive me of my sins and to lead my life. I felt as if a two-ton weight had been removed from my shoulders. My wife accepted Christ a few months later. Now, with God as the center of our lives, our marriage has begun the healing process and is growing stronger and stronger.

EXODUS

Introduction

THE BOTTOM LINE

he book of Exodus is filled with all the elements of a great feature film: an unlikely and flawed hero; a tyrant who opposes what's right; intrigue; murder; a suspenseful chase scene; and plenty of awesome "special effects." But this isn't a movie—this is actual history. God supernaturally rescued his people from slavery in Egypt. Even though those early Israelites were often a cranky, disobedient lot, God led them to a new life in the land he had promised to give them. He does the same thing spiritually for every person who listens to his call today.

CENTRAL IDEAS

- God is concerned about human suffering and listens when people cry out to him.
- God uses even hesitant people to do great things for him.
- This book contains rules for living that came directly from God's hand to Moses.
- Pain and suffering are a part of life, and are only made worse by disobeying God.

OUTLINE

1. God prepares to deliver his people from slavery in Egypt (1:1–12:28)
2. The exodus from Egypt (12:29–18:27)
3. God's promises to his people (chs. 19–24)
4. Instructions on relating to God (chs. 25–40)

TITLE

Exodus means "leaving" or "migration"; it tells the story of the nation of Israel leaving slavery in Egypt and finding a land of their own.

AUTHOR AND READERS

Moses wrote this book as a lasting memorial of God's goodness to the people of Israel.

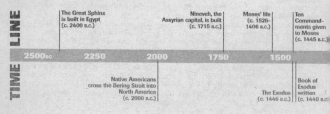

TIME LINE

	The Great Sphinx is built in Egypt (c. 2400 B.C.)		Nineveh, the Assyrian capital, is built (c. 1715 B.C.)	Moses' life (c. 1526-1406 B.C.)	Ten Commandments given to Moses (c. 1445 B.C.)
2500BC	**2250**	**2000**	**1750**	**1500**	
		Native Americans cross the Bering Strait into North America (c. 2000 B.C.)		The Exodus (c. 1446 B.C.)	Book of Exodus written (c. 1440 B.C.)

People who live in California are used to earthquakes. It's not at all uncommon for them to be awakened in the middle of the night to the sound of their dishes rattling and the rumble of some subterranean shift. Usually such activity doesn't disrupt "business as usual." But when a severe tremor hits, life can be reduced to its bare essentials.

That's what happened to many San Fernando Valley residents caught in the nightmarish aftermath of a violent earthquake some time ago. Homes were leveled in a matter of seconds. All of their worldly belongings were buried in rubble.

Ironically, people of wealth were instant paupers, now consumed with simple survival—and even that became difficult. Families stood in line for as long as five hours to get water. Some waited even longer only to have the truck run dry before they could get any. What had been available a few hours before by simply opening a spigot now was more scarce than gold—and in the hot sun, just as precious.

Homes were leveled in a matter of seconds.

While you may never have lived through an earthquake, you've probably experienced a crisis that shook your world apart—a lost job, a broken relationship, the death of a loved one, or something equally devastating. At such times you may have wondered how you could go on. When life is reduced to its basics, so are you. Your true colors come out against the backdrop of life's darkest moments.

God's people, the Israelites, experienced this phenomenon. After God delivered them from slavery in Egypt, he led them into the wilderness. Two-and-a-half-million people found themselves in a barren land without adequate food or water.

It's easy to follow God when he parts the Red Sea for you. But what do you do when the path isn't clear? The Israelites did what we all tend to do—they whined. The voices that had formerly sung God's praises now griped about his apparently evil intentions. Turn to chapter 16, verse 1–chapter 17, verse 7 (page 91) to read about some of their reactions and God's miraculous care for them. God, as always, was faithful. He kept on providing—daily. He may not have made them wealthy; he may not have given them all that they wanted; but he did give them what they needed. That was true of God then, and it's true of God now.

As you consider what life might be like if you choose to follow God, understand one thing—doing so doesn't mean that you'll never experience hard times. But you can count on God's provision even when you're wandering in an emotional or spiritual desert. That's a promise he has given all of his followers for all time. And you don't even have to whine for it!

EXODUS

The Israelites Oppressed

1 These are the names of the sons of Israel who went to Egypt with Jacob, each with his family: **2**Reuben, Simeon, Levi and Judah; **3**Issachar, Zebulun and Benjamin; **4**Dan and Naphtali; Gad and Asher. **5**The descendants of Jacob numbered seventy*a* in all; Joseph was already in Egypt.

6Now Joseph and all his brothers and all that generation died, **7**but the Israelites were fruitful and multiplied greatly and became exceedingly numerous, so that the land was filled with them.

8Then a new king, who did not know about Joseph, came to power in Egypt. **9**"Look," he said to his people, "the Israelites have become much too numerous for us. **10**Come, we must deal shrewdly with them or they will become even more numerous and, if war breaks out, will join our enemies, fight against us and leave the country."

11So they put slave masters over them to oppress them with forced labor, and they built Pithom and Rameses as store cities for Pharaoh. **12**But the more they were oppressed, the more they multiplied and spread; so the Egyptians came to dread the Israelites **13**and worked them ruthlessly. **14**They made their lives bitter with hard labor in brick and mortar and with all kinds of work in the fields; in all their hard labor the Egyptians used them ruthlessly.

15The king of Egypt said to the Hebrew midwives, whose names were Shiphrah and Puah, **16**"When you help the Hebrew women in childbirth and observe them on the delivery stool, if it is a boy, kill him; but if it is a girl, let her live." **17**The midwives, however, feared God and did not do what the king of Egypt had told them to do; they let the boys live. **18**Then the king of Egypt summoned the midwives and asked them, "Why have you done this? Why have you let the boys live?"

19The midwives answered Pharaoh, "Hebrew women are not like Egyptian women; they are vigorous and give birth before the midwives arrive."

20So God was kind to the midwives and the people increased and became even more numerous. **21**And because the midwives feared God, he gave them families of their own.

22Then Pharaoh gave this order to all his people: "Every boy that is born*b* you must throw into the Nile, but let every girl live."

The Birth of Moses

2 Now a man of the house of Levi married a Levite woman, **2**and she became pregnant and gave birth to a son. When she saw that he was a fine child, she hid him for three months. **3**But when she could hide him no longer, she got a papyrus basket for him and coated it with tar and pitch. Then she placed the child in it and put it among the reeds along the bank of the Nile. **4**His sister stood at a distance to see what would happen to him.

5Then Pharaoh's daughter went down to the Nile to bathe, and her attendants were walking along the river bank. She saw the basket among the reeds and sent her slave girl to get it. **6**She opened it and saw the baby. He was crying, and she felt sorry for him. "This is one of the Hebrew babies," she said.

---

a 5 Masoretic Text (see also Gen. 46:27); Dead Sea Scrolls and Septuagint (see also Acts 7:14 and note at Gen. 46:27) *seventy-five*   *b 22* Masoretic Text; Samaritan Pentateuch, Septuagint and Targums *born to the Hebrews*

⁷Then his sister asked Pharaoh's daughter, "Shall I go and get one of the Hebrew women to nurse the baby for you?"

⁸"Yes, go," she answered. And the girl went and got the baby's mother. ⁹Pharaoh's daughter said to her, "Take this baby and nurse him for me, and I will pay you." So the woman took the baby and nursed him. ¹⁰When the child grew older, she took him to Pharaoh's daughter and he became her son. She named him Moses,^a saying, "I drew him out of the water."

Moses Flees to Midian

¹¹One day, after Moses had grown up, he went out to where his own people were and watched them at their hard labor. He saw an Egyptian beating a Hebrew, one of his own people. ¹²Glancing this way and that and seeing no one, he killed the Egyptian and hid him in the sand. ¹³The next day he went out and saw two Hebrews fighting. He asked the one in the wrong, "Why are you hitting your fellow Hebrew?"

¹⁴The man said, "Who made you ruler and judge over us? Are you thinking of killing me as you killed the Egyptian?" Then Moses was afraid and thought, "What I did must have become known."

¹⁵When Pharaoh heard of this, he tried to kill Moses, but Moses fled from Pharaoh and went to live in Midian, where he sat down by a well. ¹⁶Now a priest of Midian had seven daughters, and they came to draw water and fill the troughs to water their father's flock. ¹⁷Some shepherds came along and drove them away, but Moses got up and came to their rescue and watered their flock.

¹⁸When the girls returned to Reuel their father, he asked them, "Why have you returned so early today?"

¹⁹They answered, "An Egyptian rescued us from the shepherds. He even drew water for us and watered the flock."

²⁰"And where is he?" he asked his daughters. "Why did you leave him? Invite him to have something to eat."

²¹Moses agreed to stay with the man, who gave his daughter Zipporah to Moses in marriage. ²²Zipporah gave birth to a son, and Moses named him Gershom,^b saying, "I have become an alien in a foreign land."

²³During that long period, the king of Egypt died. The Israelites groaned in their slavery and cried out, and their cry for help because of their slavery went up to God. ²⁴God heard their groaning and he remembered his covenant with Abraham, with Isaac and with Jacob. ²⁵So God looked on the Israelites and was concerned about them.

Moses and the Burning Bush

3 Now Moses was tending the flock of Jethro his father-in-law, the priest of Midian, and he led the flock to the far side of the desert and came to Horeb, the mountain of God. ²There the angel of the LORD appeared to him in flames of fire from within a bush. Moses saw that though the bush was on fire it did not burn up. ³So Moses thought, "I will go over and see this strange sight—why the bush does not burn up."

⁴When the LORD saw that he had gone over to look, God called to him from within the bush, "Moses! Moses!"

And Moses said, "Here I am."

⁵"Do not come any closer," God said. "Take off your sandals, for the place where you are standing is holy ground." ⁶Then he said, "I am the God of your father, the God of Abraham, the God of Isaac and the God of Jacob." At this, Moses hid his face, because he was afraid to look at God.

⁷The LORD said, "I have indeed seen the misery of my people in Egypt. I have heard them crying out because of their slave drivers, and I am concerned about their suffering. So I have come down to rescue them from the hand of the Egyptians and to bring them

^a10 Moses sounds like the Hebrew for draw out.   ^b22 Gershom sounds like the Hebrew for an alien there.

up out of that land into a good and spacious land, a land flowing with milk and honey
the home of the Canaanites, Hittites, Amorites, Perizzites, Hivites and Jebusites. 9And no
the cry of the Israelites has reached me, and I have seen the way the Egyptians a
oppressing them. 10So now, go. I am sending you to Pharaoh to bring my people th
Israelites out of Egypt."

11But Moses said to God, "Who am I, that I should go to Pharaoh and bring the Israelite
out of Egypt?"

12And God said, "I will be with you. And this will be the sign to you that it is I wh
have sent you: When you have brought the people out of Egypt, you*a* will worship Go
on this mountain."

13Moses said to God, "Suppose I go to the Israelites and say to them, 'The God of yo
fathers has sent me to you,' and they ask me, 'What is his name?' Then what shall I te
them?"

14God said to Moses, "I AM WHO I AM.*b* Th
is what you are to say to the Israelites: 'I A
has sent me to you.'"

15God also said to Moses, "Say to the Is
raelites, 'The LORD,*c* the God of your fa
thers—the God of Abraham, the God
Isaac and the God of Jacob—has sent me
you.' This is my name forever, the name l
which I am to be remembered from gene
ation to generation.

16"Go, assemble the elders of Israel ar
say to them, 'The LORD, the God of your fa
thers—the God of Abraham, Isaac and Ja
cob—appeared to me and said: I hav
watched over you and have seen what ha
been done to you in Egypt. 17And I hav
promised to bring you up out of your miser
in Egypt into the land of the Canaanite
Hittites, Amorites, Perizzites, Hivites an
Jebusites—a land flowing with milk and
honey.'

18"The elders of Israel will listen to yo
Then you and the elders are to go to th
king of Egypt and say to him, 'The LORD, th
God of the Hebrews, has met with us. Le
us take a three-day journey into the dese
to offer sacrifices to the LORD our God.' 19B
I know that the king of Egypt will not le
you go unless a mighty hand compels hin
20So I will stretch out my hand and strik
the Egyptians with all the wonders that
will perform among them. After that, h
will let you go.

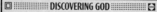

DISCOVERING GOD

3:14–15
The God Who Is There

The God of the Bible is a personal God. That means he is not just a force, not just some*thing*, but some*one*. The Bible makes this clear by the titles it uses to describe him. Here God reveals himself to Moses and says that he should be identified as "I AM WHO I AM," or simply "I AM." This name emphasizes God's timelessness—he's the one who always has been and always will be.

In the next verse God uses a proper name, translated "LORD." The letters that form this word in the original Hebrew language are YHWH. The word "I AM" in Hebrew is very similar to the letters YHWH; it's clear God wanted Moses to understand the close relation of these names in sound and meaning.

Throughout the Bible, God uses many words and phrases to refer to himself as he tries to help us grasp his multifaceted nature. And when we come to the second part of the Bible—the New Testament—and read about Jesus, we find out something astounding. Jesus refers back to this incident and says that *he is the "I AM" who talked to Moses* (John chapter 8, verses 56–59 [page 1397])! In Jesus Christ, the rescuing God of Moses' day actually came down in the form of a man and delivered humanity once and for all.

21"And I will make the Egyptians favorably disposed toward this people, so that whe
you leave you will not go empty-handed. 22Every woman is to ask her neighbor and an
woman living in her house for articles of silver and gold and for clothing, which you wil
put on your sons and daughters. And so you will plunder the Egyptians."

a12 The Hebrew is plural.   *b14* Or *I WILL BE WHAT I WILL BE*   *c15* The Hebrew for LORD sounds like and may be derived
from the Hebrew for *I AM* in verse 14.

⌐ns for Moses

Moses answered, "What if they do not believe me or listen to me and say, 'The LORD did not appear to you'?"

²Then the LORD said to him, "What is that in your hand?"

"A staff," he replied.

³The LORD said, "Throw it on the ground."

Moses threw it on the ground and it became a snake, and he ran from it. ⁴Then the LORD ⌐d to him, "Reach out your hand and take it by the tail." So Moses reached out and took ⌐ld of the snake and it turned back into a staff in his hand. ⁵"This," said the LORD, "is so ⌐at they may believe that the LORD, the God of their fathers—the God of Abraham, the ⌐d of Isaac and the God of Jacob—has appeared to you."

⌐Then the LORD said, "Put your hand inside your cloak." So Moses put his hand into his ⌐ak, and when he took it out, it was leprous,ᵃ like snow.

⁷"Now put it back into your cloak," he said. So Moses put his hand back into his cloak, ⌐d when he took it out, it was restored, like the rest of his flesh.

⁸Then the LORD said, "If they do not believe you or pay attention to the first miraculous ⌐n, they may believe the second. ⁹But if they do not believe these two signs or listen to ⌐u, take some water from the Nile and pour it on the dry ground. The water you take ⌐m the river will become blood on the ground."

¹⁰Moses said to the LORD, "O Lord, I have never been eloquent, neither in the past nor ⌐ce you have spoken to your servant. I am slow of speech and tongue."

¹¹The LORD said to him, "Who gave man his mouth? Who makes him deaf or mute? Who ⌐ves him sight or makes him blind? Is it not I, the LORD? ¹²Now go; I will help you speak ⌐d will teach you what to say."

¹³But Moses said, "O Lord, please send someone else to do it."

¹⁴Then the LORD's anger burned against Moses and he said, "What about your brother, ⌐ron the Levite? I know he can speak well. He is already on his way to meet you, and ⌐s heart will be glad when he sees you. ¹⁵You shall speak to him and put words in his ⌐outh; I will help both of you speak and will teach you what to do. ¹⁶He will speak to the ⌐ople for you, and it will be as if he were your mouth and as if you were God to him. ⌐But take this staff in your hand so you can perform miraculous signs with it."

⌐oses Returns to Egypt

¹⁸Then Moses went back to Jethro his father-in-law and said to him, "Let me go back ⌐ my own people in Egypt to see if any of them are still alive."

Jethro said, "Go, and I wish you well."

¹⁹Now the LORD had said to Moses in Midian, "Go back to Egypt, for all the men who ⌐anted to kill you are dead." ²⁰So Moses took his wife and sons, put them on a donkey ⌐d started back to Egypt. And he took the staff of God in his hand.

²¹The LORD said to Moses, "When you return to Egypt, see that you perform before ⌐araoh all the wonders I have given you the power to do. But I will harden his heart so ⌐at he will not let the people go. ²²Then say to Pharaoh, 'This is what the LORD says: ⌐rael is my firstborn son, ²³and I told you, "Let my son go, so he may worship me." But ⌐u refused to let him go; so I will kill your firstborn son.'"

²⁴At a lodging place on the way, the LORD met ⌐Moses,ᵇ and was about to kill him. ⌐But Zipporah took a flint knife, cut off her son's foreskin and touched ⌐Moses'⌐ feet with ⌐ᶜ "Surely you are a bridegroom of blood to me," she said. ²⁶So the LORD let him alone. ⌐t that time she said "bridegroom of blood," referring to circumcision.)

²⁷The LORD said to Aaron, "Go into the desert to meet Moses." So he met Moses at the ⌐ountain of God and kissed him. ²⁸Then Moses told Aaron everything the LORD had sent ⌐m to say, and also about all the miraculous signs he had commanded him to perform.

The Hebrew word was used for various diseases affecting the skin—not necessarily leprosy.   ᵇ24 Or ⌐Moses' son;⌐
⌐rew him   ᶜ25 Or and drew near ⌐Moses', feet

29Moses and Aaron brought together all the elders of the Israelites, 30and Aaron
them everything the LORD had said to Moses. He also performed the signs before
people, 31and they believed. And when they heard that the LORD was concerned ab
them and had seen their misery, they bowed down and worshiped.

Bricks Without Straw

5 Afterward Moses and Aaron went to Pharaoh and said, "This is what
LORD, the God of Israel, says: 'Let my people go, so that they may hol
festival to me in the desert.'"
2Pharaoh said, "Who is the LORD, that I should obey him and let Israel go? I do not kn
the LORD and I will not let Israel go."
3Then they said, "The God of the Hebrews has met with us. Now let us take a thr
day journey into the desert to offer sacrifices to the LORD our God, or he may strike us w
plagues or with the sword."
4But the king of Egypt said, "Moses and Aaron, why are you taking the people aw
from their labor? Get back to your work!" 5Then Pharaoh said, "Look, the people of
land are now numerous, and you are stopping them from working."
6That same day Pharaoh gave this order to the slave drivers and foremen in charge
the people: 7"You are no longer to supply the people with straw for making bricks;
them go and gather their own straw. 8But require them to make the same number
bricks as before; don't reduce the quota. They are lazy; that is why they are crying
'Let us go and sacrifice to our God.' 9Make the work harder for the men so that they k
working and pay no attention to lies."
10Then the slave drivers and the foremen went out and said to the people, "This
what Pharaoh says: 'I will not give you any more straw. 11Go and get your own str
wherever you can find it, but your work will not be reduced at all.'" 12So the peo
scattered all over Egypt to gather stubble to use for straw. 13The slave drivers k
pressing them, saying, "Complete the work required of you for each day, just as wh
you had straw." 14The Israelite foremen appointed by Pharaoh's slave drivers were be
en and were asked, "Why didn't you meet your quota of bricks yesterday or today,
before?"
15Then the Israelite foremen went and appealed to Pharaoh: "Why have you trea
your servants this way? 16Your servants are given no straw, yet we are told, 'Ma
bricks!' Your servants are being beaten, but the fault is with your own people."
17Pharaoh said, "Lazy, that's what you are—lazy! That is why you keep saying, 'Let
go and sacrifice to the LORD.' 18Now get to work. You will not be given any straw, yet y
must produce your full quota of bricks."
19The Israelite foremen realized they were in trouble when they were told, "You
not to reduce the number of bricks required of you for each day." 20When they l
Pharaoh, they found Moses and Aaron waiting to meet them, 21and they said, "May
LORD look upon you and judge you! You have made us a stench to Pharaoh and his offici
and have put a sword in their hand to kill us."

God Promises Deliverance

22Moses returned to the LORD and said, "O Lord, why have you brought trouble upon t
people? Is this why you sent me? 23Ever since I went to Pharaoh to speak in your nar
he has brought trouble upon this people, and you have not rescued your people at a
6 Then the LORD said to Moses, "Now you will see what I will do to Phara
Because of my mighty hand he will let them go; because of my mighty ha
he will drive them out of his country."
2God also said to Moses, "I am the LORD. 3I appeared to Abraham, to Isaac and to Jac

s God Almighty,[a] but by my name the LORD[b] I did not make myself known to them.[c] [4]I lso established my covenant with them to give them the land of Canaan, where they ived as aliens. [5]Moreover, I have heard the groaning of the Israelites, whom the Egyp- ians are enslaving, and I have remembered my covenant.

[6]"Therefore, say to the Israelites: 'I am the LORD, and I will bring you out from under the voke of the Egyptians. I will free you from being slaves to them, and I will redeem you vith an outstretched arm and with mighty acts of judgment. [7]I will take you as my own beople, and I will be your God. Then you will know that I am the LORD your God, who brought you out from under the yoke of the Egyptians. [8]And I will bring you to the land swore with uplifted hand to give to Abraham, to Isaac and to Jacob. I will give it to you is a possession. I am the LORD.'"

[9]Moses reported this to the Israelites, but they did not listen to him because of their discouragement and cruel bondage.

[10]Then the LORD said to Moses, [11]"Go, tell Pharaoh king of Egypt to let the Israelites go put of his country."

[12]But Moses said to the LORD, "If the Isra- elites will not listen to me, why would Pharaoh listen to me, since I speak with altering lips[d]?"

Family Record of Moses and Aaron

[13]Now the LORD spoke to Moses and Aar- on about the Israelites and Pharaoh king of Egypt, and he commanded them to bring the Israelites out of Egypt.

[14]These were the heads of their fami- lies[e]:

The sons of Reuben the firstborn son of Israel were Hanoch and Pallu, Hez- ron and Carmi. These were the clans of Reuben.

[15]The sons of Simeon were Jemuel, Jamin, Ohad, Jakin, Zohar and Shaul the son of a Canaanite woman. These were the clans of Simeon.

[16]These were the names of the sons of Levi according to their records: Ger- shon, Kohath and Merari. Levi lived 137 years.

[17]The sons of Gershon, by clans, were Libni and Shimei.

[18]The sons of Kohath were Amram, Izhar, Hebron and Uzziel. Kohath lived 133 years.

[19]The sons of Merari were Mahli and Mushi.

These were the clans of Levi according to their records.

[20]Amram married his father's sister Jochebed, who bore him Aaron and Moses. Amram lived 137 years.

[21]The sons of Izhar were Korah, Nepheg and Zicri.

[22]The sons of Uzziel were Mishael, Elzaphan and Sithri.

[23]Aaron married Elisheba, daughter of Amminadab and sister of Nahshon, and she bore him Nadab and Abihu, Eleazar and Ithamar.

▣ STRENGTHENING RELATIONSHIPS ⬌

5:19–23
Leadership

Good leaders know that bad situations some- times need to get worse before they get bet- ter. Even though God had confirmed Moses' mission, he cried out to God because his lead- ership had only made the nation's situation harder—and the people were not exactly grateful.

If you're a leader, you can almost count on opposition to your vision for change. Even if it's for the better, the going may get tough. Moses provides an excellent example for deal- ing with such opposition: Talk to God about your concerns; and make sure that what you're proposing really is the right course to take. Once you're sure of that, keep at it—a new day will eventually come, as it did for Mo- ses and the Israelites.

---

3 Hebrew El-Shaddai   *b3 See note at Exodus 3:15.*   *c3 Or Almighty, and by my name the LORD did I not let myself be known to them?*   *d12 Hebrew I am uncircumcised of lips; also in verse 30*   *e14 The Hebrew for families here and in verse 25 refers to units larger than clans.*

²⁴The sons of Korah were Assir, Elkanah and Abiasaph. These were the Korahite clans.

²⁵Eleazar son of Aaron married one of the daughters of Putiel, and she bore him Phinehas.

These were the heads of the Levite families, clan by clan.

²⁶It was this same Aaron and Moses to whom the LORD said, "Bring the Israelites out Egypt by their divisions." ²⁷They were the ones who spoke to Pharaoh king of Egy about bringing the Israelites out of Egypt. It was the same Moses and Aaron.

Aaron to Speak for Moses

²⁸Now when the LORD spoke to Moses in Egypt, ²⁹he said to him, "I am the LORD. Te Pharaoh king of Egypt everything I tell you."

³⁰But Moses said to the LORD, "Since I speak with faltering lips, why would Pharac listen to me?"

7 Then the LORD said to Moses, "See, I have made you like God to Pharaoh, ar your brother Aaron will be your prophet. ²You are to say everything I con mand you, and your brother Aaron is to tell Pharaoh to let the Israelites go out of h country. ³But I will harden Pharaoh's heart, and though I multiply my miraculous sig and wonders in Egypt, ⁴he will not listen to you. Then I will lay my hand on Egypt ar with mighty acts of judgment I will bring out my divisions, my people the Israelites. ⁵An the Egyptians will know that I am the LORD when I stretch out my hand against Egypt ar bring the Israelites out of it."

⁶Moses and Aaron did just as the LORD commanded them. ⁷Moses was eighty years ol and Aaron eighty-three when they spoke to Pharaoh.

Aaron's Staff Becomes a Snake

⁸The LORD said to Moses and Aaron, ⁹"When Pharaoh says to you, 'Perform a miracle then say to Aaron, 'Take your staff and throw it down before Pharaoh,' and it will becon a snake."

¹⁰So Moses and Aaron went to Pharaoh and did just as the LORD commanded. Aaro threw his staff down in front of Pharaoh and his officials, and it became a snake. ¹¹Pha aoh then summoned wise men and sorcerers, and the Egyptian magicians also did th same things by their secret arts: ¹²Each one threw down his staff and it became a snak But Aaron's staff swallowed up their staffs. ¹³Yet Pharaoh's heart became hard and h would not listen to them, just as the LORD had said.

The Plague of Blood

¹⁴Then the LORD said to Moses, "Pharaoh's heart is unyielding; he refuses to let th people go. ¹⁵Go to Pharaoh in the morning as he goes out to the water. Wait on the bar of the Nile to meet him, and take in your hand the staff that was changed into a snak ¹⁶Then say to him, 'The LORD, the God of the Hebrews, has sent me to say to you: Let m people go, so that they may worship me in the desert. But until now you ne listened. ¹⁷This is what the LORD says: By this you will know that I am the LORD: With th staff that is in my hand I will strike the water of the Nile, and it will be changed int blood. ¹⁸The fish in the Nile will die, and the river will stink; the Egyptians will not l able to drink its water.'"

¹⁹The LORD said to Moses, "Tell Aaron, 'Take your staff and stretch out your hand ove the waters of Egypt—over the streams and canals, over the ponds and all the reservoirs' and they will turn to blood. Blood will be everywhere in Egypt, even in the woode buckets and stone jars."

²⁰Moses and Aaron did just as the LORD had commanded. He raised his staff in th presence of Pharaoh and his officials and struck the water of the Nile, and all the wate

vas changed into blood. ²¹The fish in the Nile died, and the river smelled so bad that the
.gyptians could not drink its water. Blood was everywhere in Egypt.

²²But the Egyptian magicians did the same things by their secret arts, and Pharaoh's
1eart became hard; he would not listen to Moses and Aaron, just as the LORD had said.
²³Instead, he turned and went into his palace, and did not take even this to heart. ²⁴And
1ll the Egyptians dug along the Nile to get drinking water, because they could not drink
:he water of the river.

The Plague of Frogs

8 ²⁵Seven days passed after the LORD struck the Nile. ¹Then the LORD said to Moses,
"Go to Pharaoh and say to him, 'This is what the LORD says: Let my people go, so
:hat they may worship me. ²If you refuse to let them go, I will plague your whole country
with frogs. ³The Nile will teem with frogs. They will come up into your palace and your
sedroom and onto your bed, into the houses of your officials and on your people, and into
your ovens and kneading troughs. ⁴The frogs will go up on you and your people and all
your officials.' "

⁵Then the LORD said to Moses, "Tell Aaron, 'Stretch out your hand with your staff over
:he streams and canals and ponds, and make frogs come up on the land of Egypt.' "

⁶So Aaron stretched out his hand over the waters of Egypt, and the frogs came up and
covered the land. ⁷But the magicians did the same things by their secret arts; they also
made frogs come up on the land of Egypt.

⁸Pharaoh summoned Moses and Aaron and said, "Pray to the LORD to take the frogs
away from me and my people, and I will let your people go to offer sacrifices to the LORD."

⁹Moses said to Pharaoh, "I leave to you the honor of setting the time for me to pray for
you and your officials and your people that you and your houses may be rid of the frogs,
except for those that remain in the Nile."

¹⁰"Tomorrow," Pharaoh said.

Moses replied, "It will be as you say, so that you may know there is no one like the LORD
our God. ¹¹The frogs will leave you and your houses, your officials and your people; they
will remain only in the Nile."

¹²After Moses and Aaron left Pharaoh, Moses cried out to the LORD about the frogs he
had brought on Pharaoh. ¹³And the LORD did what Moses asked. The frogs died in the
houses, in the courtyards and in the fields. ¹⁴They were piled into heaps, and the land
reeked of them. ¹⁵But when Pharaoh saw that there was relief, he hardened his heart
and would not listen to Moses and Aaron, just as the LORD had said.

The Plague of Gnats

¹⁶Then the LORD said to Moses, "Tell Aaron, 'Stretch out your staff and strike the dust of
the ground,' and throughout the land of Egypt the dust will become gnats." ¹⁷They did
this, and when Aaron stretched out his hand with the staff and struck the dust of the
ground, gnats came upon men and animals. All the dust throughout the land of Egypt
became gnats. ¹⁸But when the magicians tried to produce gnats by their secret arts, they
could not. And the gnats were on men and animals.

¹⁹The magicians said to Pharaoh, "This is the finger of God." But Pharaoh's heart was
hard and he would not listen, just as the LORD had said.

The Plague of Flies

²⁰Then the LORD said to Moses, "Get up early in the morning and confront Pharaoh as he
goes to the water and say to him, 'This is what the LORD says: Let my people go, so that
they may worship me. ²¹If you do not let my people go, I will send swarms of flies on you
and your officials, on your people and into your houses. The houses of the Egyptians will
be full of flies, and even the ground where they are.

²²"'But on that day I will deal differently with the land of Goshen, where my people

live; no swarms of flies will be there, so that you will know that I, the LORD, am in this land. 23I will make a distinction[a] between my people and your people. This miraculous sign will occur tomorrow.'"

24And the LORD did this. Dense swarms of flies poured into Pharaoh's palace and into the houses of his officials, and throughout Egypt the land was ruined by the flies.

25Then Pharaoh summoned Moses and Aaron and said, "Go, sacrifice to your God here in the land."

26But Moses said, "That would not be right. The sacrifices we offer the LORD our God would be detestable to the Egyptians. And if we offer sacrifices that are detestable in their eyes, will they not stone us? 27We must take a three-day journey into the desert to offer sacrifices to the LORD our God, as he commands us."

28Pharaoh said, "I will let you go to offer sacrifices to the LORD your God in the desert, but you must not go very far. Now pray for me."

29Moses answered, "As soon as I leave you, I will pray to the LORD, and tomorrow the flies will leave Pharaoh and his officials and his people. Only be sure that Pharaoh does not act deceitfully again by not letting the people go to offer sacrifices to the LORD."

30Then Moses left Pharaoh and prayed to the LORD, 31and the LORD did what Moses asked: The flies left Pharaoh and his officials and his people; not a fly remained. 32But this time also Pharaoh hardened his heart and would not let the people go.

The Plague on Livestock

9 Then the LORD said to Moses, "Go to Pharaoh and say to him, 'This is what the LORD, the God of the Hebrews, says: "Let my people go, so that they may worship me." 2If you refuse to let them go and continue to hold them back, 3the hand of the LORD will bring a terrible plague on your livestock in the field—on your horses and donkeys and camels and on your cattle and sheep and goats. 4But the LORD will make a distinction between the livestock of Israel and that of Egypt, so that no animal belonging to the Israelites will die.'"

5The LORD set a time and said, "Tomorrow the LORD will do this in the land." 6And the next day the LORD did it: All the livestock of the Egyptians died, but not one animal belonging to the Israelites died. 7Pharaoh sent men to investigate and found that not even one of the animals of the Israelites had died. Yet his heart was unyielding and he would not let the people go.

The Plague of Boils

8Then the LORD said to Moses and Aaron, "Take handfuls of soot from a furnace and have Moses toss it into the air in the presence of Pharaoh. 9It will become fine dust over the whole land of Egypt, and festering boils will break out on men and animals throughout the land."

10So they took soot from a furnace and stood before Pharaoh. Moses tossed it into the air, and festering boils broke out on men and animals. 11The magicians could not stand before Moses because of the boils that were on them and on all the Egyptians. 12But the LORD hardened Pharaoh's heart and he would not listen to Moses and Aaron, just as the LORD had said to Moses.

The Plague of Hail

13Then the LORD said to Moses, "Get up early in the morning, confront Pharaoh and say to him, 'This is what the LORD, the God of the Hebrews, says: Let my people go, so that they may worship me, 14or this time I will send the full force of my plagues against you and against your officials and your people, so you may know that there is no one like me in all the earth. 15For by now I could have stretched out my hand and struck you and your

[a] 23 Septuagint and Vulgate; Hebrew *will put a deliverance*

ople with a plague that would have wiped you off the earth. ¹⁶But I have raised you
ᵃ for this very purpose, that I might show you my power and that my name might be
oclaimed in all the earth. ¹⁷You still set yourself against my people and will not let
em go. ¹⁸Therefore, at this time tomorrow I will send the worst hailstorm that has ever
len on Egypt, from the day it was founded till now. ¹⁹Give an order now to bring your
estock and everything you have in the field to a place of shelter, because the hail will
ll on every man and animal that has not been brought in and is still out in the field, and
ey will die.'"

²⁰Those officials of Pharaoh who feared the word of the LORD hurried to bring their
aves and their livestock inside. ²¹But those who ignored the word of the LORD left their
aves and livestock in the field.

²²Then the LORD said to Moses, "Stretch out your hand toward the sky so that hail will
ll all over Egypt—on men and animals and on everything growing in the fields of
ypt." ²³When Moses stretched out his staff toward the sky, the LORD sent thunder and
il, and lightning flashed down to the
ound. So the LORD rained hail on the land

Egypt; ²⁴hail fell and lightning flashed
ack and forth. It was the worst storm in all
e land of Egypt since it had become a
ation. ²⁵Throughout Egypt hail struck ev-
ything in the fields—both men and ani-
als; it beat down everything growing in
e fields and stripped every tree. ²⁶The
ly place it did not hail was the land of
oshen, where the Israelites were.

²⁷Then Pharaoh summoned Moses and
aron. "This time I have sinned," he said to
em. "The LORD is in the right, and I and
y people are in the wrong. ²⁸Pray to the
ORD, for we have had enough thunder and
ail. I will let you go; you don't have to
ay any longer."

²⁹Moses replied, "When I have gone out
f the city, I will spread out my hands in
rayer to the LORD. The thunder will stop
nd there will be no more hail, so you may
now that the earth is the LORD's. ³⁰But I
now that you and your officials still do not
ear the LORD God."

³¹(The flax and barley were destroyed,
nce the barley had headed and the flax
vas in bloom. ³²The wheat and spelt, however, were not destroyed, because they ripen
ter.)

³³Then Moses left Pharaoh and went out of the city. He spread out his hands toward
e LORD; the thunder and hail stopped, and the rain no longer poured down on the land.
⁴When Pharaoh saw that the rain and hail and thunder had stopped, he sinned again:
e and his officials hardened their hearts. ³⁵So Pharaoh's heart was hard and he would
ot let the Israelites go, just as the LORD had said through Moses.

ADDRESSING QUESTIONS

9:12
Human Experience

Are we programmed by God, or can we make our own choices in life?

A quick read of this verse might make one think that God "rigged" Pharaoh's attitudes. If that were the case, Pharaoh would have had no choice but to ignore Moses. But that interpretation doesn't fit other verses that say that Pharaoh hardened *his own* heart (see verse 7, and also chapter 8, verses 15 and 19 [page 81]).

The Bible is clear about the fact that we are responsible for the choices we make. God may work through negative events of history and turn them around for good, but we are still accountable for what we do.

In Pharaoh's case, God *amplified* Pharaoh's hard-heartedness so that it would be more dramatic. But Pharaoh made his own choice to enslave and exploit the Hebrews. And, like all of us, he was accountable for the results of that choice.

6 Or have spared you

The Plague of Locusts

10 Then the LORD said to Moses, "Go to Pharaoh, for I have hardened his hea and the hearts of his officials so that I may perform these miraculous signs mine among them ²that you may tell your children and grandchildren how I dealt harsh with the Egyptians and how I performed my signs among them, and that you may kno that I am the LORD."

³So Moses and Aaron went to Pharaoh and said to him, "This is what the LORD, the Go of the Hebrews, says: 'How long will you refuse to humble yourself before me? Let m people go, so that they may worship me. ⁴If you refuse to let them go, I will bring locus into your country tomorrow. ⁵They will cover the face of the ground so that it cannot k seen. They will devour what little you have left after the hail, including every tree that growing in your fields. ⁶They will fill your houses and those of all your officials and a the Egyptians—something neither your fathers nor your forefathers have ever seen fro the day they settled in this land till now.'" Then Moses turned and left Pharaoh.

⁷Pharaoh's officials said to him, "How long will this man be a snare to us? Let th people go, so that they may worship the LORD their God. Do you not yet realize that Egy is ruined?"

⁸Then Moses and Aaron were brought back to Pharaoh. "Go, worship the LORD yo God," he said. "But just who will be going?"

⁹Moses answered, "We will go with our young and old, with our sons and daughter and with our flocks and herds, because we are to celebrate a festival to the LORD."

¹⁰Pharaoh said, "The LORD be with you—if I let you go, along with your women an children! Clearly you are bent on evil.ᵃ ¹¹No! Have only the men go; and worship th LORD, since that's what you have been asking for." Then Moses and Aaron were driven ou of Pharaoh's presence.

¹²And the LORD said to Moses, "Stretch out your hand over Egypt so that locusts w swarm over the land and devour everything growing in the fields, everything left by th hail."

¹³So Moses stretched out his staff over Egypt, and the LORD made an east wind blow across the land all that day and all that night. By morning the wind had brought th locusts; ¹⁴they invaded all Egypt and settled down in every area of the country in grea numbers. Never before had there been such a plague of locusts, nor will there ever b again. ¹⁵They covered all the ground until it was black. They devoured all that was le after the hail—everything growing in the fields and the fruit on the trees. Nothing gree remained on tree or plant in all the land of Egypt.

¹⁶Pharaoh quickly summoned Moses and Aaron and said, "I have sinned against th LORD your God and against you. ¹⁷Now forgive my sin once more and pray to the LORD you God to take this deadly plague away from me."

¹⁸Moses then left Pharaoh and prayed to the LORD. ¹⁹And the LORD changed the wind t a very strong west wind, which caught up the locusts and carried them into the Re Sea.ᵇ Not a locust was left anywhere in Egypt. ²⁰But the LORD hardened Pharaoh's hea and he would not let the Israelites go.

The Plague of Darkness

²¹Then the LORD said to Moses, "Stretch out your hand toward the sky so that darknes will spread over Egypt—darkness that can be felt." ²²So Moses stretched out his han toward the sky, and total darkness covered all Egypt for three days. ²³No one could se anyone else or leave his place for three days. Yet all the Israelites had light in the place where they lived.

²⁴Then Pharaoh summoned Moses and said, "Go, worship the LORD. Even your wome and children may go with you; only leave your flocks and herds behind."

ᵃ 10 Or Be careful, trouble is in store for you!   ᵇ 19 Hebrew Yam Suph; that is, Sea of Reeds

²⁵But Moses said, "You must allow us to have sacrifices and burnt offerings to present to the LORD our God. ²⁶Our livestock too must go with us; not a hoof is to be left behind. We have to use some of them in worshiping the LORD our God, and until we get there we will not know what we are to use to worship the LORD."

²⁷But the LORD hardened Pharaoh's heart, and he was not willing to let them go. ²⁸Pharaoh said to Moses, "Get out of my sight! Make sure you do not appear before me again! The day you see my face you will die."

²⁹"Just as you say," Moses replied, "I will never appear before you again."

The Plague on the Firstborn

11 Now the LORD had said to Moses, "I will bring one more plague on Pharaoh and on Egypt. After that, he will let you go from here, and when he does, he will drive you out completely. ²Tell the people that men and women alike are to ask their neighbors for articles of silver and gold." ³(The LORD made the Egyptians favorably disposed toward the people, and Moses himself was highly regarded in Egypt by Pharaoh's officials and by the people.)

⁴So Moses said, "This is what the LORD says: 'About midnight I will go throughout Egypt. ⁵Every firstborn son in Egypt will die, from the firstborn son of Pharaoh, who sits on the throne, to the firstborn son of the slave girl, who is at her hand mill, and all the firstborn of the cattle as well. ⁶There will be loud wailing throughout Egypt—worse than there has ever been or ever will be again. ⁷But among the Israelites not a dog will bark at any man or animal.' Then you will know that the LORD makes a distinction between Egypt and Israel. ⁸All these officials of yours will come to me, bowing down before me and saying, 'Go, you and all the people who follow you!' After that I will leave." Then Moses, hot with anger, left Pharaoh.

⁹The LORD had said to Moses, "Pharaoh will refuse to listen to you—so that my wonders may be multiplied in Egypt." ¹⁰Moses and Aaron performed all these wonders before Pharaoh, but the LORD hardened Pharaoh's heart, and he would not let the Israelites go out of his country.

The Passover

12 The LORD said to Moses and Aaron in Egypt, ²"This month is to be for you the first month, the first month of your year. ³Tell the whole community of Israel that on the tenth day of this month each man is to take a lamb*a* for his family, one for each household. ⁴If any household is too small for a whole lamb, they must share one with their nearest neighbor, having taken into account the number of people there are. You are to determine the amount of lamb needed in accordance with what each person will eat. ⁵The animals you choose must be year-old males without defect, and you may take them from the sheep or the goats. ⁶Take care of them until the fourteenth day of the month, when all the people of the community of Israel must slaughter them at twilight. ⁷Then they are to take some of the blood and put it on the sides and tops of the doorframes of the houses where they eat the lambs. ⁸That same night they are to eat the meat roasted over the fire, along with bitter herbs, and bread made without yeast. ⁹Do not eat the meat raw or cooked in water, but roast it over the fire—head, legs and inner parts. ¹⁰Do not leave any of it till morning; if some is left till morning, you must burn it. ¹¹This is how you are to eat it: with your cloak tucked into your belt, your sandals on your feet and your staff in your hand. Eat it in haste; it is the LORD's Passover.

¹²"On that same night I will pass through Egypt and strike down every firstborn—both men and animals—and I will bring judgment on all the gods of Egypt. I am the LORD. ¹³The blood will be a sign for you on the houses where you are; and when I see the blood, I will pass over you. No destructive plague will touch you when I strike Egypt.

¹⁴"This is a day you are to commemorate; for the generations to come you shall cele-

a3 The Hebrew word can mean lamb or kid; also in verse 4.

brate it as a festival to the LORD—a lasting ordinance. ¹⁵For seven days you are to eat bread made without yeast. On the first day remove the yeast from your houses, for whoever eats anything with yeast in it from the first day through the seventh must be cut off from Israel. ¹⁶On the first day hold a sacred assembly, and another one on the seventh day. Do no work at all on these days, except to prepare food for everyone to eat—that is all you may do.

¹⁷"Celebrate the Feast of Unleavened Bread, because it was on this very day that I brought your divisions out of Egypt. Celebrate this day as a lasting ordinance for the generations to come. ¹⁸In the first month you are to eat bread made without yeast, from the evening of the fourteenth day until the evening of the twenty-first day. ¹⁹For seven days no yeast is to be found in your houses. And whoever eats anything with yeast in it must be cut off from the community of Israel, whether he is an alien or native-born. ²⁰Eat nothing made with yeast. Wherever you live, you must eat unleavened bread."

²¹Then Moses summoned all the elders of Israel and said to them, "Go at once and select the animals for your families and slaughter the Passover lamb. ²²Take a bunch of hyssop, dip it into the blood in the basin and put some of the blood on the top and on both sides of the doorframe. Not one of you shall go out the door of his house until morning. ²³When the LORD goes through the land to strike down the Egyptians, he will see the blood on the top and sides of the doorframe and will pass over that doorway, and he will not permit the destroyer to enter your houses and strike you down.

²⁴"Obey these instructions as a lasting ordinance for you and your descendants. ²⁵When you enter the land that the LORD will give you as he promised, observe this ceremony. ²⁶And when your children ask you, 'What does this ceremony mean to you?' ²⁷then tell them, 'It is the Passover sacrifice to the LORD, who passed over the houses of the Israelites in Egypt and spared our homes when he struck down the Egyptians.'" Then the people bowed down and worshiped. ²⁸The Israelites did just what the LORD commanded Moses and Aaron.

ADDRESSING QUESTIONS

12:21–23
Unseen Realities   **Q**

This passage powerfully and clearly expresses an important theme found throughout the Bible—the spiritual law of *substitution*.

Before God delivered his people from slavery in Egypt, he required that they take certain steps to avoid the experience of his judgment on the Egyptians. Israelite families were to mark their homes with the blood of a year-old lamb as an act of faith. When they did so, God spared their lives. In a sense, God exchanged that lamb's life for the lives of those who were "covered" by its blood. This principle was also demonstrated in the sacrificial religious rituals of the Jewish people. Temple worship dictated that people cover their sins by offering an innocent animal in their place.

The most compelling and dramatic example of this substitution principle is Jesus Christ. He claimed that when he died, he gave his life to cover the sins of a multitude of people (see Mark chapter 10, verse 45 [page 1322]). Like the blood of the Passover Lamb, Jesus (who was called the "Lamb of God" [see John chapter 1, verse 29 (page 1383)]) "covers" those who become his followers so that they don't experience God's judgment for their wrongdoing.

God has provided his once-and-for-all sacrifice for each one of us in Jesus Christ. But we must personally receive what God has done, or it will be of no benefit. We cannot deliver ourselves from the future day of judgment, but God has done it for us by giving us a perfect and complete "substitute"—Jesus' blood, shed for us on the cross.

Receiving the forgiveness for which Jesus paid isn't difficult. If you decide to accept this free gift of God, simply tell God that you need his mercy and that you want him to lead you from now on. Like the Israelites, you'll be set free from slavery and led to a new life with God.

29At midnight the LORD struck down all the firstborn in Egypt, from the firstborn of Pharaoh, who sat on the throne, to the firstborn of the prisoner, who was in the dungeon, and the firstborn of all the livestock as well. 30Pharaoh and all his officials and all the Egyptians got up during the night, and there was loud wailing in Egypt, for there was not a house without someone dead.

The Exodus

31During the night Pharaoh summoned Moses and Aaron and said, "Up! Leave my people, you and the Israelites! Go, worship the LORD as you have requested. 32Take your flocks and herds, as you have said, and go. And also bless me."

33The Egyptians urged the people to hurry and leave the country. "For otherwise," they said, "we will all die!" 34So the people took their dough before the yeast was added, and carried it on their shoulders in kneading troughs wrapped in clothing. 35The Israelites did as Moses instructed and asked the Egyptians for articles of silver and gold and for clothing. 36The LORD had made the Egyptians favorably disposed toward the people, and they gave them what they asked for; so they plundered the Egyptians.

37The Israelites journeyed from Rameses to Succoth. There were about six hundred thousand men on foot, besides women and children. 38Many other people went up with them, as well as large droves of livestock, both flocks and herds. 39With the dough they had brought from Egypt, they baked cakes of unleavened bread. The dough was without yeast because they had been driven out of Egypt and did not have time to prepare food for themselves.

40Now the length of time the Israelite people lived in Egypt*a* was 430 years. 41At the end of the 430 years, to the very day, all the LORD's divisions left Egypt. 42Because the LORD kept vigil that night to bring them out of Egypt, on this night all the Israelites are to keep vigil to honor the LORD for the generations to come.

Passover Restrictions

43The LORD said to Moses and Aaron, "These are the regulations for the Passover:

"No foreigner is to eat of it. 44Any slave you have bought may eat of it after you have circumcised him, 45but a temporary resident and a hired worker may not eat of it.

46"It must be eaten inside one house; take none of the meat outside the house. Do not break any of the bones. 47The whole community of Israel must celebrate it.

48"An alien living among you who wants to celebrate the LORD's Passover must have all the males in his household circumcised; then he may take part like one born in the land. No uncircumcised male may eat of it. 49The same law applies to the native-born and to the alien living among you."

50All the Israelites did just what the LORD had commanded Moses and Aaron. 51And on that very day the LORD brought the Israelites out of Egypt by their divisions.

Consecration of the Firstborn

13 The LORD said to Moses, 2"Consecrate to me every firstborn male. The first offspring of every womb among the Israelites belongs to me, whether man or animal."

3Then Moses said to the people, "Commemorate this day, the day you came out of Egypt, out of the land of slavery, because the LORD brought you out of it with a mighty hand. Eat nothing containing yeast. 4Today, in the month of Abib, you are leaving. 5When the LORD brings you into the land of the Canaanites, Hittites, Amorites, Hivites and Jebusites—the land he swore to your forefathers to give you, a land flowing with milk and honey—you are to observe this ceremony in this month: 6For seven days eat bread made without yeast and on the seventh day hold a festival to the LORD. 7Eat unleavened bread

40 Masoretic Text; Samaritan Pentateuch and Septuagint Egypt and Canaan

during those seven days; nothing with yeast in it is to be seen among you, nor shall a yeast be seen anywhere within your borders. ⁸On that day tell your son, 'I do it because of what the LORD did for me when I came out of Egypt.' ⁹This observance will for you like a sign on your hand and a reminder on your forehead that the law of the L is to be on your lips. For the LORD brought you out of Egypt with his mighty hand. ¹⁰Y must keep this ordinance at the appointed time year after year.

¹¹"After the LORD brings you into the land of the Canaanites and gives it to you, as promised on oath to you and your forefathers, ¹²you are to give over to the LORD the fi offspring of every womb. All the firstborn males of your livestock belong to the Lo ¹³Redeem with a lamb every firstborn donkey, but if you do not redeem it, break its ne Redeem every firstborn among your sons.

¹⁴"In days to come, when your son asks you, 'What does this mean?' say to him, 'W a mighty hand the LORD brought us out of Egypt, out of the land of slavery. ¹⁵Wh Pharaoh stubbornly refused to let us go, the LORD killed every firstborn in Egypt, both m and animal. This is why I sacrifice to the LORD the first male offspring of every womb a redeem each of my firstborn sons.' ¹⁶And it will be like a sign on your hand and a symb on your forehead that the LORD brought us out of Egypt with his mighty hand."

Crossing the Sea

¹⁷When Pharaoh let the people go, God did not lead them on the road through t Philistine country, though that was shorter. For God said, "If they face war, they mig change their minds and return to Egypt." ¹⁸So God led the people around by the des road toward the Red Sea.ᵃ The Israelites went up out of Egypt armed for battle.

¹⁹Moses took the bones of Joseph with him because Joseph had made the sons of Isra swear an oath. He had said, "God will surely come to your aid, and then you must car my bones up with you from this place."ᵇ

²⁰After leaving Succoth they camped at Etham on the edge of the desert. ²¹By day t LORD went ahead of them in a pillar of cloud to guide them on their way and by night a pillar of fire to give them light, so that they could travel by day or night. ²²Neither t pillar of cloud by day nor the pillar of fire by night left its place in front of the peopl

14 Then the LORD said to Moses, ²"Tell the Israelites to turn back and encam near Pi Hahiroth, between Migdol and the sea. They are to encamp by th sea, directly opposite Baal Zephon. ³Pharaoh will think, 'The Israelites are wanderi around the land in confusion, hemmed in by the desert.' ⁴And I will harden Pharaoh heart, and he will pursue them. But I will gain glory for myself through Pharaoh and his army, and the Egyptians will know that I am the LORD." So the Israelites did this.

⁵When the king of Egypt was told that the people had fled, Pharaoh and his official changed their minds about them and said, "What have we done? We have let the Israe ites go and have lost their services!" ⁶So he had his chariot made ready and took h army with him. ⁷He took six hundred of the best chariots, along with all the oth chariots of Egypt, with officers over all of them. ⁸The LORD hardened the heart of Pharac king of Egypt, so that he pursued the Israelites, who were marching out boldly. ⁹Th Egyptians—all Pharaoh's horses and chariots, horsemenᶜ and troops—pursued the Isr elites and overtook them as they camped by the sea near Pi Hahiroth, opposite Ba Zephon.

¹⁰As Pharaoh approached, the Israelites looked up, and there were the Egyptian marching after them. They were terrified and cried out to the LORD. ¹¹They said to Mose "Was it because there were no graves in Egypt that you brought us to the desert to di What have you done to us by bringing us out of Egypt? ¹²Didn't we say to you in Egyp 'Leave us alone; let us serve the Egyptians'? It would have been better for us to serve th Egyptians than to die in the desert!"

ᵃ18 Hebrew *Yam Suph*; that is, Sea of Reeds   ᵇ19 See Gen. 50:25.   ᶜ9 Or *charioteers*; also in verses 17, 18, 23, 26 and 28

¹³Moses answered the people, "Do not be afraid. Stand firm and you will see the deliverance the LORD will bring you today. The Egyptians you see today you will never see again. ¹⁴The LORD will fight for you; you need only to be still."

¹⁵Then the LORD said to Moses, "Why are you crying out to me? Tell the Israelites to move on. ¹⁶Raise your staff and stretch out your hand over the sea to divide the water so that the Israelites can go through the sea on dry ground. ¹⁷I will harden the hearts of the Egyptians so that they will go in after them. And I will gain glory through Pharaoh and all his army, through his chariots and his horsemen. ¹⁸The Egyptians will know that I am the LORD when I gain glory through Pharaoh, his chariots and his horsemen."

¹⁹Then the angel of God, who had been traveling in front of Israel's army, withdrew and went behind them. The pillar of cloud also moved from in front and stood behind them, ²⁰coming between the armies of Egypt and Israel. Throughout the night the cloud brought darkness to the one side and light to the other side; so neither went near the other all night long.

²¹Then Moses stretched out his hand over the sea, and all that night the LORD drove the sea back with a strong east wind and turned it into dry land. The waters were divided, ²²and the Israelites went through the sea on dry ground, with a wall of water on their right and on their left.

²³The Egyptians pursued them, and all Pharaoh's horses and chariots and horsemen followed them into the sea. ²⁴During the last watch of the night the LORD looked down from the pillar of fire and cloud at the Egyptian army and threw it into confusion. ²⁵He made the wheels of their chariots come off*ᵃ* so that they had difficulty driving. And the Egyptians said, "Let's get away from the Israelites! The LORD is fighting for them against Egypt."

²⁶Then the LORD said to Moses, "Stretch out your hand over the sea so that the waters may flow back over the Egyptians and their chariots and horsemen." ²⁷Moses stretched out his hand over the sea, and at daybreak the sea went back to its place. The Egyptians were fleeing toward*ᵇ* it, and the LORD swept them into the sea. ²⁸The water flowed back and covered the chariots and horsemen—the entire army of Pharaoh that had followed the Israelites into the sea. Not one of them survived.

²⁹But the Israelites went through the sea on dry ground, with a wall of water on their right and on their left. ³⁰That day the LORD saved Israel from the hands of the

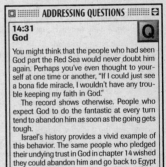

ADDRESSING QUESTIONS

14:31
God

Q

You might think that the people who had seen God part the Red Sea would never doubt him again. Perhaps you've even thought to yourself at one time or another, "If I could just see a bona fide miracle, I wouldn't have any trouble keeping my faith in God."

The record shows otherwise. People who expect God to do the fantastic at every turn tend to abandon him as soon as the going gets tough.

Israel's history provides a vivid example of this behavior. The same people who pledged their undying trust in God in chapter 14 wished they could abandon him and go back to Egypt by the beginning of chapter 16 (page 91)!

Egyptians, and Israel saw the Egyptians lying dead on the shore. ³¹And when the Israelites saw the great power the LORD displayed against the Egyptians, the people feared the LORD and put their trust in him and in Moses his servant.

The Song of Moses and Miriam

15   Then Moses and the Israelites sang this song to the LORD:

> "I will sing to the LORD,
>   for he is highly exalted.
> The horse and its rider

ᵃ25 Or He jammed the wheels of their chariots (see Samaritan Pentateuch, Septuagint and Syriac)   *ᵇ27 Or from*

he has hurled into the sea.
²The LORD is my strength and my song;
he has become my salvation.
He is my God, and I will praise him,
my father's God, and I will exalt him.
³The LORD is a warrior;
the LORD is his name.
⁴Pharaoh's chariots and his army
he has hurled into the sea.
The best of Pharaoh's officers
are drowned in the Red Sea.ᵃ
⁵The deep waters have covered them;
they sank to the depths like a stone.

⁶"Your right hand, O LORD,
was majestic in power.
Your right hand, O LORD,
shattered the enemy.
⁷In the greatness of your majesty
you threw down those who opposed you.
You unleashed your burning anger;
it consumed them like stubble.
⁸By the blast of your nostrils
the waters piled up.
The surging waters stood firm like a wall;
the deep waters congealed in the heart of the sea.

⁹"The enemy boasted,
'I will pursue, I will overtake them.
I will divide the spoils;
I will gorge myself on them.
I will draw my sword
and my hand will destroy them.'
¹⁰But you blew with your breath,
and the sea covered them.
They sank like lead
in the mighty waters.

¹¹"Who among the gods is like you, O LORD?
Who is like you—
majestic in holiness,
awesome in glory,
working wonders?
¹²You stretched out your right hand
and the earth swallowed them.

¹³"In your unfailing love you will lead
the people you have redeemed.
In your strength you will guide them
to your holy dwelling.
¹⁴The nations will hear and tremble;
anguish will grip the people of Philistia.
¹⁵The chiefs of Edom will be terrified,
the leaders of Moab will be seized with trembling,

ᵃ4 Hebrew *Yam Suph*; that is, Sea of Reeds; also in verse 22

the people*a* of Canaan will melt away;
16 terror and dread will fall upon them.
By the power of your arm
    they will be as still as a stone—
until your people pass by, O LORD,
    until the people you bought*b* pass by.
17You will bring them in and plant them
    on the mountain of your inheritance—
the place, O LORD, you made for your dwelling,
    the sanctuary, O Lord, your hands established.
18The LORD will reign
    for ever and ever."

19When Pharaoh's horses, chariots and horsemen*c* went into the sea, the LORD brought
[th]e waters of the sea back over them, but the Israelites walked through the sea on dry
[gr]ound. 20Then Miriam the prophetess, Aaron's sister, took a tambourine in her hand, and
[al]l the women followed her, with tambourines and dancing. 21Miriam sang to them:

"Sing to the LORD,
    for he is highly exalted.
The horse and its rider
    he has hurled into the sea."

[Th]e Waters of Marah and Elim

22Then Moses led Israel from the Red Sea and they went into the Desert of Shur. For
[thr]ee days they traveled in the desert without finding water. 23When they came to
[M]arah, they could not drink its water because it was bitter. (That is why the place is
[ca]lled Marah.*d*) 24So the people grumbled against Moses, saying, "What are we to
[dr]ink?"

25Then Moses cried out to the LORD, and the LORD showed him a piece of wood. He threw
[it] into the water, and the water became sweet.

There the LORD made a decree and a law for them, and there he tested them. 26He said,
["If] you listen carefully to the voice of the LORD your God and do what is right in his eyes,
[if] you pay attention to his commands and keep all his decrees, I will not bring on you any
[of] the diseases I brought on the Egyptians, for I am the LORD, who heals you."

27Then they came to Elim, where there were twelve springs and seventy palm trees,
[an]d they camped there near the water.

[M]anna and Quail

16 The whole Israelite community set out from Elim and came to the Desert of
Sin, which is between Elim and Sinai, on the fifteenth day of the second
[m]onth after they had come out of Egypt. 2In the desert the whole community grumbled
[ag]ainst Moses and Aaron. 3The Israelites said to them, "If only we had died by the LORD's
[h]and in Egypt! There we sat around pots of meat and ate all the food we wanted, but you
[h]ave brought us out into this desert to starve this entire assembly to death."

4Then the LORD said to Moses, "I will rain down bread from heaven for you. The people
[ar]e to go out each day and gather enough for that day. In this way I will test them and
[se]e whether they will follow my instructions. 5On the sixth day they are to prepare what
[th]ey bring in, and that is to be twice as much as they gather on the other days."

6So Moses and Aaron said to all the Israelites, "In the evening you will know that it
[w]as the LORD who brought you out of Egypt, 7and in the morning you will see the glory of
[th]e LORD, because he has heard your grumbling against him. Who are we, that you should
[gr]umble against us?" 8Moses also said, "You will know that it was the LORD when he gives

a 5 Or rulers   b 16 Or created   c 19 Or charioteers   d 23 Marah means bitter.

you meat to eat in the evening and all the bread you want in the morning, because h
has heard your grumbling against him. Who are we? You are not grumbling against u
but against the LORD."

⁹Then Moses told Aaron, "Say to the entire Israelite community, 'Come before the LOR
for he has heard your grumbling.'"

¹⁰While Aaron was speaking to the whole Israelite community, they looked toward th
desert, and there was the glory of the LORD appearing in the cloud.

¹¹The LORD said to Moses, ¹²"I have heard the grumbling of the Israelites. Tell ther
'At twilight you will eat meat, and in th
morning you will be filled with bread. The
you will know that I am the LORD yo
God.'"

¹³That evening quail came and covere
the camp, and in the morning there was
layer of dew around the camp. ¹⁴When th
dew was gone, thin flakes like frost on th
ground appeared on the desert floo
¹⁵When the Israelites saw it, they said ᵗ
each other, "What is it?" For they did n
know what it was.

Moses said to them, "It is the bread th
LORD has given you to eat. ¹⁶This is wh
the LORD has commanded: 'Each one is ᵗ
gather as much as he needs. Take a
omerᵃ for each person you have in yo
tent.'"

¹⁷The Israelites did as they were tol
some gathered much, some little. ¹⁸Ar
when they measured it by the omer, h
who gathered much did not have too mucl
and he who gathered little did not have tc
little. Each one gathered as much as h
needed.

¹⁹Then Moses said to them, "No one is ᵗ
keep any of it until morning."

²⁰However, some of them paid no atter
tion to Moses; they kept part of it unt
morning, but it was full of maggots and be
gan to smell. So Moses was angry wit
them.

²¹Each morning everyone gathered a
much as he needed, and when the su
grew hot, it melted away. ²²On the sixt

KNOWING YOURSELF

16:3–4
Character

The situation looked hopeless. These two-and-a-half-million Israelites desperately needed food and water. When God didn't provide for the Israelites in the way they expected, they became angry and accused him of taking them into the wilderness to starve them to death. But they failed to recognize that God saw their predicament and had plans to take care of them.

God supplied them with "manna." Literally, the word means, "What is it?" and recalls the people's first reaction when they saw it on the ground (verse 15). God's provision was unusual, but that shouldn't have come as a big surprise. After all, these were the same people who had miraculously walked through the Red Sea.

Why did God meet their need in this way? Like everything that God does, this "deed" was meant to lead people back to the "deed-doer." God wanted the people to depend on him completely.

This passage shows us that God will do whatever is necessary to provide for his followers so they can accomplish his purposes. While he may not meet their needs in predictable ways or supply every single need, he will make sure they have enough.

God has reasons for his methods—often higher purposes and plans that we can't see. Like Moses, we need to trust in God and wait for his provision in our lives.

---

day, they gathered twice as much—tw
omersᵇ for each person—and the leaders of the community came and reported this ᵗ
Moses. ²³He said to them, "This is what the LORD commanded: 'Tomorrow is to be a day ᵒ
rest, a holy Sabbath to the LORD. So bake what you want to bake and boil what you war
to boil. Save whatever is left and keep it until morning.'"

²⁴So they saved it until morning, as Moses commanded, and it did not stink or g
maggots in it. ²⁵"Eat it today," Moses said, "because today is a Sabbath to the LORD. Yo

---

ᵃ16 That is, probably about 2 quarts (about 2 liters); also in verses 18, 32, 33 and 36   ᵇ22 That is, probably about 4 quarts
(about 4.5 liters)

'l not find any of it on the ground today. ²⁶Six days you are to gather it, but on the
·enth day, the Sabbath, there will not be any."

²⁷Nevertheless, some of the people went out on the seventh day to gather it, but they
nd none. ²⁸Then the LORD said to Moses, "How long will youᵃ refuse to keep my
mmands and my instructions? ²⁹Bear in mind that the LORD has given you the Sabbath;
at is why on the sixth day he gives you bread for two days. Everyone is to stay where
is on the seventh day; no one is to go out." ³⁰So the people rested on the seventh day.
³¹The people of Israel called the bread manna.ᵇ It was white like coriander seed and
·ted like wafers made with honey. ³²Moses said, "This is what the LORD has command-
: 'Take an omer of manna and keep it for the generations to come, so they can see the
·ad I gave you to eat in the desert when I brought you out of Egypt.'"

³³So Moses said to Aaron, "Take a jar and put an omer of manna in it. Then place it
·ore the LORD to be kept for the generations to come."

³⁴As the LORD commanded Moses, Aaron put the manna in front of the Testimony, that
might be kept. ³⁵The Israelites ate manna forty years, until they came to a land that
·s settled; they ate manna until they reached the border of Canaan.
³⁶(An omer is one tenth of an ephah.)

·ater From the Rock

7 The whole Israelite community set out from the Desert of Sin, traveling from
place to place as the LORD commanded. They camped at Rephidim, but there
·s no water for the people to drink. ²So they quarreled with Moses and said, "Give us
·ter to drink."

Moses replied, "Why do you quarrel with me? Why do you put the LORD to the test?"
³But the people were thirsty for water there, and they grumbled against Moses. They

· The Hebrew is plural.   b31 Manna means What is it? (see verse 15).

Chapters 16 and 17
Life with God

After Moses led them through the Red Sea, the Israelites probably thought life would be easy.
Four hundred years of slavery had come to an end. God was working miracles that Cecil B. De
Mille would have trouble duplicating. With all the strings God was pulling, surely paradise on earth
couldn't be far off.

Were they ever wrong!

Their newfound freedom didn't bring luxury; it brought hunger and thirst and fear. Under-
standably, the people were angry. "Look at the mess we're in now, Moses!" they said through
clenched teeth. They even accused God of taking them into the wilderness to starve them to death.
But the Israelites failed to realize the complexity of God's unfolding plans.

It's easy to think we've got God figured out, especially when things seem to be going our
way. But the God who created the universe may have plans that go beyond our limited agenda.

In this passage, for instance, God attempted to teach the people how to live by faith. These
former slaves, who were accustomed to doing whatever their human masters told them, needed
some tutoring before they could become a nation that listened carefully to God and functioned as
a light to the whole world.

As you read through chapters 16 and 17, note the lessons God tried to teach them. They're
the same lessons he wants all of us to learn today:
- God met the Israelites' needs—not their wants.
- God provided for *daily* needs—no more.
- God remained faithful even though the Israelites complained.
- Whenever God leads he provides.

said, "Why did you bring us up out of Egypt to make us and our children and livestock d
of thirst?"

⁴Then Moses cried out to the LORD, "What am I to do with these people? They are almo
ready to stone me."

⁵The LORD answered Moses, "Walk on ahead of the people. Take with you some of th
elders of Israel and take in your hand the staff with which you struck the Nile, and go.
will stand there before you by the rock at Horeb. Strike the rock, and water will come o
of it for the people to drink." So Moses did this in the sight of the elders of Israel. ⁷And h
called the place Massah*ᵃ* and Meribah*ᵇ* because the Israelites quarreled and becau
they tested the LORD saying, "Is the LORD among us or not?"

The Amalekites Defeated

⁸The Amalekites came and attacked the Israelites at Rephidim. ⁹Moses said to Joshu
"Choose some of our men and go out to fight the Amalekites. Tomorrow I will stand o
top of the hill with the staff of God in my hands."

¹⁰So Joshua fought the Amalekites as Moses had ordered, and Moses, Aaron and H
went to the top of the hill. ¹¹As long as Moses held up his hands, the Israelites we
winning, but whenever he lowered his hands, the Amalekites were winning. ¹²Whe
Moses' hands grew tired, they took a stone and put it under him and he sat on it. Aaro
and Hur held his hands up—one on one side, one on the other—so that his han
remained steady till sunset. ¹³So Joshua overcame the Amalekite army with the swor

¹⁴Then the LORD said to Moses, "Write this on a scroll as something to be remembere
and make sure that Joshua hears it, because I will completely blot out the memory
Amalek from under heaven."

¹⁵Moses built an altar and called it The LORD is my Banner. ¹⁶He said, "For hands we
lifted up to the throne of the LORD. The*ᶜ* LORD will be at war against the Amalekites fro
generation to generation."

Jethro Visits Moses

18 Now Jethro, the priest of Midian and father-in-law of Moses, heard of ever
thing God had done for Moses and for his people Israel, and how the Lo
had brought Israel out of Egypt.

²After Moses had sent away his wife Zipporah, his father-in-law Jethro received h
³and her two sons. One son was named Gershom,*ᵈ* for Moses said, "I have become
alien in a foreign land"; ⁴and the other was named Eliezer,*ᵉ* for he said, "My father's Go
was my helper; he saved me from the sword of Pharaoh."

⁵Jethro, Moses' father-in-law, together with Moses' sons and wife, came to him in th
desert, where he was camped near the mountain of God. ⁶Jethro had sent word to hi
"I, your father-in-law Jethro, am coming to you with your wife and her two sons."

⁷So Moses went out to meet his father-in-law and bowed down and kissed him. Th
greeted each other and then went into the tent. ⁸Moses told his father-in-law abo
everything the LORD had done to Pharaoh and the Egyptians for Israel's sake and about
the hardships they had met along the way and how the LORD had saved them.

⁹Jethro was delighted to hear about all the good things the LORD had done for Israel
rescuing them from the hand of the Egyptians. ¹⁰He said, "Praise be to the LORD, w
rescued you from the hand of the Egyptians and of Pharaoh, and who rescued the peop
from the hand of the Egyptians. ¹¹Now I know that the LORD is greater than all other go
for he did this to those who had treated Israel arrogantly." ¹²Then Jethro, Moses' fathe
in-law, brought a burnt offering and other sacrifices to God, and Aaron came with all t
elders of Israel to eat bread with Moses' father-in-law in the presence of God.

¹³The next day Moses took his seat to serve as judge for the people, and they sto

---

ᵃ7 Massah means testing.   *ᵇ7* Meribah means quarreling.   *ᶜ16* Or "Because a hand was against the throne of the
LORD, the   *ᵈ3* Gershom sounds like the Hebrew for an alien there.   *ᵉ4* Eliezer means my God is helper.

round him from morning till evening. ¹⁴When his father-in-law saw all that Moses was doing for the people, he said, "What is this you are doing for the people? Why do you one sit as judge, while all these people stand around you from morning till evening?"

¹⁵Moses answered him, "Because the people come to me to seek God's will. ¹⁶Whenever they have a dispute, it is brought to me, and I decide between the parties and inform them of God's decrees and laws."

¹⁷Moses' father-in-law replied, "What you are doing is not good. ¹⁸You and these people who come to you will only wear yourselves out. The work is too heavy for you; you cannot handle it alone. ¹⁹Listen now to me and I will give you some advice, and may God be with you. You must be the people's representative before God and bring their disputes to him. ²⁰Teach them the decrees and laws, and show them the way to live and the duties they are to perform. ²¹But select capable men from all the people—men who fear God, trustworthy men who hate dishonest gain—and appoint them as officials over thousands, hundreds, fifties and tens. ²²Have them serve as judges for the people at all times, but have them bring every difficult case to you; the simple cases they can decide themselves. That will make your load lighter, because they will share it with you. ²³If you do this and God so commands, you will be able to stand the strain, and all these people will go home satisfied."

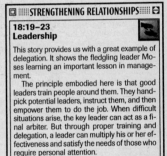

STRENGTHENING RELATIONSHIPS

18:19–23
Leadership

This story provides us with a great example of delegation. It shows the fledgling leader Moses learning an important lesson in management.

The principle embodied here is that good leaders train people around them. They hand-pick potential leaders, instruct them, and then empower them to do the job. When difficult situations arise, the key leader can act as a final arbiter. But through proper training and delegation, a leader can multiply his or her effectiveness and satisfy the needs of those who require personal attention.

²⁴Moses listened to his father-in-law and did everything he said. ²⁵He chose capable men from all Israel and made them leaders of the people, officials over thousands, hundreds, fifties and tens. ²⁶They served as judges for the people at all times. The difficult cases they brought to Moses, but the simple ones they decided themselves.

²⁷Then Moses sent his father-in-law on his way, and Jethro returned to his own country.

At Mount Sinai

19 In the third month after the Israelites left Egypt—on the very day—they came to the Desert of Sinai. ²After they set out from Rephidim, they entered the Desert of Sinai, and Israel camped there in the desert in front of the mountain.

³Then Moses went up to God, and the LORD called to him from the mountain and said, "This is what you are to say to the house of Jacob and what you are to tell the people of Israel: ⁴'You yourselves have seen what I did to Egypt, and how I carried you on eagles' wings and brought you to myself. ⁵Now if you obey me fully and keep my covenant, then out of all nations you will be my treasured possession. Although the whole earth is mine, ⁶you* will be for me a kingdom of priests and a holy nation.' These are the words you are to speak to the Israelites."

⁷So Moses went back and summoned the elders of the people and set before them all the words the LORD had commanded him to speak. ⁸The people all responded together, "We will do everything the LORD has said." So Moses brought their answer back to the LORD.

⁹The LORD said to Moses, "I am going to come to you in a dense cloud, so that the people

*5,6 Or possession, for the whole earth is mine. ⁶You

will hear me speaking with you and will always put their trust in you." Then Moses to the LORD what the people had said.

¹⁰And the LORD said to Moses, "Go to the people and consecrate them today and tomo row. Have them wash their clothes ¹¹and be ready by the third day, because on that d the LORD will come down on Mount Sinai in the sight of all the people. ¹²Put limits for t people around the mountain and tell them, 'Be careful that you do not go up the mou tain or touch the foot of it. Whoever touches the mountain shall surely be put to deat ¹³He shall surely be stoned or shot with arrows; not a hand is to be laid on him. Wheth man or animal, he shall not be permitted to live.' Only when the ram's horn sounds long blast may they go up to the mountain."

¹⁴After Moses had gone down the mountain to the people, he consecrated them, ar they washed their clothes. ¹⁵Then he said to the people, "Prepare yourselves for the thi day. Abstain from sexual relations."

¹⁶On the morning of the third day there was thunder and lightning, with a thick clou over the mountain, and a very loud trumpet blast. Everyone in the camp trembled. ¹⁷The Moses led the people out of the camp to meet with God, and they stood at the foot of th mountain. ¹⁸Mount Sinai was covered with smoke, because the LORD descended on it i fire. The smoke billowed up from it like smoke from a furnace, the whole mountain trembled violently, ¹⁹and the sound of the trumpet grew louder and louder. Then Mose spoke and the voice of God answered him.ᵇ

²⁰The LORD descended to the top of Mount Sinai and called Moses to the top of th mountain. So Moses went up ²¹and the LORD said to him, "Go down and warn the peop so they do not force their way through see the LORD and many of them peris ²²Even the priests, who approach the LOR must consecrate themselves, or the LOR will break out against them."

²³Moses said to the LORD, "The peop cannot come up Mount Sinai, because yc yourself warned us, 'Put limits around th mountain and set it apart as holy.'"

²⁴The LORD replied, "Go down and brin Aaron up with you. But the priests and th people must not force their way through t come up to the LORD, or he will break ov against them."

²⁵So Moses went down to the people an told them.

REASONS TO BELIEVE

20:1–17
The Amazing Bible

These "Ten Commandments" form the core of God's moral standards for humankind. The first five address our relationship with God and our parents; the last five address how we treat our neighbors. Together they form a brief yet comprehensive summary of the behavior that should exemplify God's people.

Unfortunately, not one of us can live up to these rules by ourselves. We need a faith-based relationship with God, because a performance-based relationship is hopeless. In our own strength, we will always fall short of God's perfect standard for our lives.

The Ten Commandments are the perfect tool to help us understand our spiritual condition. They show us what we cannot do—obey God's commands perfectly by ourselves—so that we come to God for what only he can do—forgive us through the power of Jesus Christ.

The Ten Commandments

20 And God spoke all thes words:

²"I am the LORD your God, who brought you out of Egypt, out of the land of slavery.

³"You shall have no other gods be-foreᶜ me.

⁴"You shall not make for yourself an idol in the form of anything in heaven above or on the earth beneath or in the waters below. ⁵You shall not bow down to them or worship them; for I, the LORD your God, am a jealous God, punishing the

ᵃ18 Most Hebrew manuscripts; a few Hebrew manuscripts and Septuagint *all the people*   ᵇ19 Or *and God answered him with thunder*   ᶜ3 Or *besides*

children for the sin of the fathers to the third and fourth generation of those who hate me, ⁶but showing love to a thousand ⌐generations⌐ of those who love me and keep my commandments.

⁷"You shall not misuse the name of the LORD your God, for the LORD will not hold anyone guiltless who misuses his name.

⁸"Remember the Sabbath day by keeping it holy. ⁹Six days you shall labor and do all your work, ¹⁰but the seventh day is a Sabbath to the LORD your God. On it you shall not do any work, neither you, nor your son or daughter, nor your manservant or maidservant, nor your animals, nor the alien within your gates. ¹¹For in six days the LORD made the heavens and the earth, the sea, and all that is in them, but he rested on the seventh day. Therefore the LORD blessed the Sabbath day and made it holy.

¹²"Honor your father and your mother, so that you may live long in the land the LORD your God is giving you.

¹³"You shall not murder.

¹⁴"You shall not commit adultery.

¹⁵"You shall not steal.

¹⁶"You shall not give false testimony against your neighbor.

¹⁷"You shall not covet your neighbor's house. You shall not covet your neighbor's wife, or his manservant or maidservant, his ox or donkey, or anything that belongs to your neighbor."

¹⁸When the people saw the thunder and lightning and heard the trumpet and saw the mountain in smoke, they trembled with fear. They stayed at a distance ¹⁹and said to Moses, "Speak to us yourself and we will listen. But do not have God speak to us or we will die."

²⁰Moses said to the people, "Do not be afraid. God has come to test you, so that the fear of God will be with you to keep you from sinning."

²¹The people remained at a distance, while Moses approached the thick darkness where God was.

Idols and Altars

²²Then the LORD said to Moses, "Tell the Israelites this: 'You have seen for yourselves that I have spoken to you from heaven: ²³Do not make any gods to be alongside me; do not make for yourselves gods of silver or gods of gold.

²⁴"'Make an altar of earth for me and sacrifice on it your burnt offerings and fellowship offerings,ᵃ your sheep and goats and your cattle. Wherever I cause my name to be honored, I will come to you and bless you. ²⁵If you make an altar of stones for me, do not build it with dressed stones, for you will defile it if you use a tool on it. ²⁶And do not go up to my altar on steps, lest your nakedness be exposed on it.'

21   "These are the laws you are to set before them:

Hebrew Servants

²"If you buy a Hebrew servant, he is to serve you for six years. But in the seventh year, he shall go free, without paying anything. ³If he comes alone, he is to go free alone; but if he has a wife when he comes, she is to go with him. ⁴If his master gives him a wife and she bears him sons or daughters, the woman and her children shall belong to her master, and only the man shall go free.

⁵"But if the servant declares, 'I love my master and my wife and children and do not want to go free,' ⁶then his master must take him before the judges.ᵇ He shall take him to

---

ᵃ4 Traditionally *peace offerings*   ᵇ6 Or *before God*

the door or the doorpost and pierce his ear with an awl. Then he will be his servant fo
life.

7"If a man sells his daughter as a servant, she is not to go free as menservants do. 8
she does not please the master who has selected her for himself,[a] he must let her b
redeemed. He has no right to sell her to foreigners, because he has broken faith with he
9If he selects her for his son, he must grant her the rights of a daughter. 10If he marrie
another woman, he must not deprive the first one of her food, clothing and marital right
11If he does not provide her with these three things, she is to go free, without an
payment of money.

Personal Injuries

12"Anyone who strikes a man and kills him shall surely be put to death. 13However,
he does not do it intentionally, but God lets it happen, he is to flee to a place I w
designate. 14But if a man schemes and kills another man deliberately, take him awa
from my altar and put him to death.

15"Anyone who attacks[b] his father or his mother must be put to death.

16"Anyone who kidnaps another and either sells him or still has him when he is caugh
must be put to death.

17"Anyone who curses his father or mother must be put to death.

18"If men quarrel and one hits the other with a stone or with his fist[c] and he does n
die but is confined to bed, 19the one who struck the blow will not be held responsible
the other gets up and walks around outside with his staff; however, he must pay th
injured man for the loss of his time and see that he is completely healed.

20"If a man beats his male or female slave with a rod and the slave dies as a dire
result, he must be punished, 21but he is not to be punished if the slave gets up after a da
or two, since the slave is his property.

22"If men who are fighting hit a pregnant woman and she gives birth prematurel
but there is no serious injury, the offender must be fined whatever the woman's husban
demands and the court allows. 23But if there is serious injury, you are to take life for lif
24eye for eye, tooth for tooth, hand for hand, foot for foot, 25burn for burn, wound f
wound, bruise for bruise.

26"If a man hits a manservant or maidservant in the eye and destroys it, he must let th
servant go free to compensate for the eye. 27And if he knocks out the tooth of a manse
vant or maidservant, he must let the servant go free to compensate for the tooth.

28"If a bull gores a man or a woman to death, the bull must be stoned, and i
meat must not be eaten. But the owner of the bull will not be held responsible. 29
however, the bull has had the habit of goring and the owner has been warned but h
not kept it penned up and it kills a man or woman, the bull must be stoned and th
owner also must be put to death. 30However, if payment is demanded of him, he ma
redeem his life by paying whatever is demanded. 31This law also applies if the bull gor
a son or a daughter. 32If the bull gores a male or female slave, the owner must pay thir
shekels[e] of silver to the master of the slave, and the bull must be stoned.

33"If a man uncovers a pit or digs one and fails to cover it and an ox or a donkey fa
into it, 34the owner of the pit must pay for the loss; he must pay its owner, and the de
animal will be his.

35"If a man's bull injures the bull of another and it dies, they are to sell the live one an
divide both the money and the dead animal equally. 36However, if it was known that th
bull had the habit of goring, yet the owner did not keep it penned up, the owner mu
pay, animal for animal, and the dead animal will be his.

Protection of Property

22 "If a man steals an ox or a sheep and slaughters it or sells it, he must pay back five head of cattle for the ox and four sheep for the sheep.

²"If a thief is caught breaking in and is struck so that he dies, the defender is not guilty of bloodshed; ³but if it happens*ᵃ* after sunrise, he is guilty of bloodshed.

"A thief must certainly make restitution, but if he has nothing, he must be sold to pay for his theft.

⁴"If the stolen animal is found alive in his possession—whether ox or donkey or sheep—he must pay back double.

⁵"If a man grazes his livestock in a field or vineyard and lets them stray and they graze in another man's field, he must make restitution from the best of his own field or vineyard.

⁶"If a fire breaks out and spreads into thornbushes so that it burns shocks of grain or standing grain or the whole field, the one who started the fire must make restitution.

⁷"If a man gives his neighbor silver or goods for safekeeping and they are stolen from the neighbor's house, the thief, if he is caught, must pay back double. ⁸But if the thief is not found, the owner of the house must appear before the judges*ᵇ* to determine whether he has laid his hands on the other man's property. ⁹In all cases of illegal possession of an ox, a donkey, a sheep, a garment, or any other lost property about which somebody says, 'This is mine,' both parties are to bring their cases before the judges. The one whom the judges declare*ᶜ* guilty must pay back double to his neighbor.

¹⁰"If a man gives a donkey, an ox, a sheep or any other animal to his neighbor for safekeeping and it dies or is injured or is taken away while no one is looking, ¹¹the issue between them will be settled by the taking of an oath before the LORD that the neighbor did not lay hands on the other person's property. The owner is to accept this, and no restitution is required. ¹²But if the animal was stolen from the neighbor, he must make restitution to the owner. ¹³If it was torn to pieces by a wild animal, he shall bring in the remains as evidence and he will not be required to pay for the torn animal.

¹⁴"If a man borrows an animal from his neighbor and it is injured or dies while the owner is not present, he must make restitution. ¹⁵But if the owner is with the animal, the borrower will not have to pay. If the animal was hired, the money paid for the hire covers the loss.

▣ ▦▦▦▦▦ REASONS TO BELIEVE ▦▦▦▦▦ ⬀

22:1–31
The Amazing Bible

The laws in this chapter show the fairness of the biblical system for handling crime. Many of these laws do not apply in our culture, but we can extract some good principles from them. For example, nonviolent criminals were required to make restitution for their crimes. Rather than being imprisoned, they had to compensate their victims.

The Bible's instruction is that punishment is meant to fit the crime. Compared to some of the law codes from the ancient Near East, the Bible's system is measurably more fair. The phrase "Eye for eye, tooth for tooth" (see chapter 21, verse 24 [page 98]) is meant to prescribe limits on punishment rather than insist on how much or what kind of punishment is appropriate.

Another timeless principle is fairness toward the "underdog" (verses 21–27; chapter 23, verses 1–9 [page 100]). Biblical law protects people who have limited means from more powerful members of society.

Furthermore, the Bible commands compassion as a way of life. God knows that a generous society is a just society.

The underlying theme of this passage demonstrates God's concern that justice, tempered with compassion, rule in human affairs.

ᵃ3 Or if he strikes him   *ᵇ8 Or before God; also in verse 9*   *ᶜ9 Or whom God declares*

Social Responsibility

¹⁶"If a man seduces a virgin who is not pledged to be married and sleeps with her, he must pay the bride-price, and she shall be his wife. ¹⁷If her father absolutely refuses to give her to him, he must still pay the bride-price for virgins.

¹⁸"Do not allow a sorceress to live.

¹⁹"Anyone who has sexual relations with an animal must be put to death.

²⁰"Whoever sacrifices to any god other than the LORD must be destroyed.ᵃ

²¹"Do not mistreat an alien or oppress him, for you were aliens in Egypt.

²²"Do not take advantage of a widow or an orphan. ²³If you do and they cry out to me, I will certainly hear their cry. ²⁴My anger will be aroused, and I will kill you with the sword; your wives will become widows and your children fatherless.

²⁵"If you lend money to one of my people among you who is needy, do not be like a moneylender; charge him no interest.ᵇ ²⁶If you take your neighbor's cloak as a pledge, return it to him by sunset, ²⁷because his cloak is the only covering he has for his body. What else will he sleep in? When he cries out to me, I will hear, for I am compassionate.

²⁸"Do not blaspheme Godᶜ or curse the ruler of your people.

²⁹"Do not hold back offerings from your granaries or your vats.ᵈ

"You must give me the firstborn of your sons. ³⁰Do the same with your cattle and your sheep. Let them stay with their mothers for seven days, but give them to me on the eighth day.

³¹"You are to be my holy people. So do not eat the meat of an animal torn by wild beasts; throw it to the dogs.

Laws of Justice and Mercy

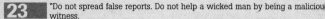 **23** "Do not spread false reports. Do not help a wicked man by being a malicious witness.

²"Do not follow the crowd in doing wrong. When you give testimony in a lawsuit, do not pervert justice by siding with the crowd, ³and do not show favoritism to a poor man in his lawsuit.

⁴"If you come across your enemy's ox or donkey wandering off, be sure to take it back to him. ⁵If you see the donkey of someone who hates you fallen down under its load, do not leave it there; be sure you help him with it.

⁶"Do not deny justice to your poor people in their lawsuits. ⁷Have nothing to do with a false charge and do not put an innocent or honest person to death, for I will not acquit the guilty.

⁸"Do not accept a bribe, for a bribe blinds those who see and twists the words of the righteous.

⁹"Do not oppress an alien; you yourselves know how it feels to be aliens, because you were aliens in Egypt.

Sabbath Laws

¹⁰"For six years you are to sow your fields and harvest the crops, ¹¹but during the seventh year let the land lie unplowed and unused. Then the poor among your people may get food from it, and the wild animals may eat what they leave. Do the same with your vineyard and your olive grove.

¹²"Six days do your work, but on the seventh day do not work, so that your ox and your donkey may rest, and the slave born in your household, and the alien as well, may be refreshed.

¹³"Be careful to do everything I have said to you. Do not invoke the names of other gods; do not let them be heard on your lips.

ᵃ20 The Hebrew term refers to the irrevocable giving over of things or persons to the LORD, often by totally destroying them.   ᵇ25 Or excessive interest   ᶜ28 Or Do not revile the judges   ᵈ29 The meaning of the Hebrew for this phrase is uncertain.

e Three Annual Festivals

¹⁴"Three times a year you are to celebrate a festival to me.

¹⁵"Celebrate the Feast of Unleavened Bread; for seven days eat bread made without ast, as I commanded you. Do this at the appointed time in the month of Abib, for in that nth you came out of Egypt.

'No one is to appear before me empty-handed.

¹⁶"Celebrate the Feast of Harvest with the firstfruits of the crops you sow in your field. 'Celebrate the Feast of Ingathering at the end of the year, when you gather in your ps from the field.

¹⁷"Three times a year all the men are to appear before the Sovereign LORD.

¹⁸"Do not offer the blood of a sacrifice to me along with anything containing yeast. 'The fat of my festival offerings must not be kept until morning.

¹⁹"Bring the best of the firstfruits of your soil to the house of the LORD your God. 'Do not cook a young goat in its mother's milk.

d's Angel to Prepare the Way

²⁰"See, I am sending an angel ahead of you to guard you along the way and to bring u to the place I have prepared. ²¹Pay attention to him and listen to what he says. Do t rebel against him; he will not forgive your rebellion, since my Name is in him. ²²If you en carefully to what he says and do all that I say, I will be an enemy to your enemies d will oppose those who oppose you. ²³My angel will go ahead of you and bring you o the land of the Amorites, Hittites, Perizzites, Canaanites, Hivites and Jebusites, and I l wipe them out. ²⁴Do not bow down before their gods or worship them or follow their ctices. You must demolish them and break their sacred stones to pieces. ²⁵Worship the ᴅ your God, and his blessing will be on your food and water. I will take away sickness m among you, ²⁶and none will miscarry or be barren in your land. I will give you a full e span.

²⁷"I will send my terror ahead of you and throw into confusion every nation you counter. I will make all your enemies turn their backs and run. ²⁸I will send the hornet ead of you to drive the Hivites, Canaanites and Hittites out of your way. ²⁹But I will not ve them out in a single year, because the land would become desolate and the wild imals too numerous for you. ³⁰Little by little I will drive them out before you, until you ve increased enough to take possession of the land.

³¹"I will establish your borders from the Red Sea*ᵃ* to the Sea of the Philistines,*ᵇ* and m the desert to the River.*ᶜ* I will hand over to you the people who live in the land and u will drive them out before you. ³²Do not make a covenant with them or with their ds. ³³Do not let them live in your land, or they will cause you to sin against me, cause the worship of their gods will certainly be a snare to you."

e Covenant Confirmed

24 Then he said to Moses, "Come up to the LORD, you and Aaron, Nadab and Abihu, and seventy of the elders of Israel. You are to worship at a distance, ut Moses alone is to approach the LORD; the others must not come near. And the people y not come up with him."

³When Moses went and told the people all the LORD's words and laws, they responded th one voice, "Everything the LORD has said we will do." ⁴Moses then wrote down erything the LORD had said.

He got up early the next morning and built an altar at the foot of the mountain and set twelve stone pillars representing the twelve tribes of Israel. ⁵Then he sent young aelite men, and they offered burnt offerings and sacrificed young bulls as fellowship erings*ᵈ* to the LORD. ⁶Moses took half of the blood and put it in bowls, and the other

Hebrew *Yam Suph*; that is, Sea of Reeds   *ᵇ31* That is, the Mediterranean   *ᶜ31* That is, the Euphrates Traditionally *peace offerings*

half he sprinkled on the altar. ⁷Then he took the Book of the Covenant and read it to people. They responded, "We will do everything the Lᴏʀᴅ has said; we will obey."

⁸Moses then took the blood, sprinkled it on the people and said, "This is the blood the covenant that the Lᴏʀᴅ has made with you in accordance with all these words."

⁹Moses and Aaron, Nadab and Abihu, and the seventy elders of Israel went up ¹⁰a saw the God of Israel. Under his feet was something like a pavement made of sapphir clear as the sky itself. ¹¹But God did not raise his hand against these leaders of Israelites; they saw God, and they ate and drank.

¹²The Lᴏʀᴅ said to Moses, "Come up to me on the mountain and stay here, and I give you the tablets of stone, with the law and commands I have written for th instruction."

¹³Then Moses set out with Joshua his aide, and Moses went up on the mountain God. ¹⁴He said to the elders, "Wait here for us until we come back to you. Aaron and are with you, and anyone involved in a dispute can go to them."

¹⁵When Moses went up on the mountain, the cloud covered it, ¹⁶and the glory of Lᴏʀᴅ settled on Mount Sinai. For six days the cloud covered the mountain, and on seventh day the Lᴏʀᴅ called to Moses from within the cloud. ¹⁷To the Israelites the glor the Lᴏʀᴅ looked like a consuming fire on top of the mountain. ¹⁸Then Moses entered cloud as he went on up the mountain. And he stayed on the mountain forty days a forty nights.

Offerings for the Tabernacle

25 The Lᴏʀᴅ said to Moses, ²"Tell the Israelites to bring me an offering. You to receive the offering for me from each man whose heart prompts him give. ³These are the offerings you are to receive from them: gold, silver and bron ⁴blue, purple and scarlet yarn and fine linen; goat hair; ⁵ram skins dyed red and hides sea cowsᵇ; acacia wood; ⁶olive oil for the light; spices for the anointing oil and for fragrant incense; ⁷and onyx stones and other gems to be mounted on the ephod breastpiece.

⁸"Then have them make a sanctuary for me, and I will dwell among them. ⁹Make tabernacle and all its furnishings exactly like the pattern I will show you.

The Ark

¹⁰"Have them make a chest of acacia wood—two and a half cubits long, a cubit an half wide, and a cubit and a half high.ᶜ ¹¹Overlay it with pure gold, both inside and and make a gold molding around it. ¹²Cast four gold rings for it and fasten them to its f feet, with two rings on one side and two rings on the other. ¹³Then make poles of aca wood and overlay them with gold. ¹⁴Insert the poles into the rings on the sides of chest to carry it. ¹⁵The poles are to remain in the rings of this ark; they are not to removed. ¹⁶Then put in the ark the Testimony, which I will give you.

¹⁷"Make an atonement coverᵈ of pure gold—two and a half cubits long and a cubit a half wide.ᵉ ¹⁸And make two cherubim out of hammered gold at the ends of the cov ¹⁹Make one cherub on one end and the second cherub on the other; make the cheru of one piece with the cover, at the two ends. ²⁰The cherubim are to have their wi spread upward, overshadowing the cover with them. The cherubim are to face e other, looking toward the cover. ²¹Place the cover on top of the ark and put in the ark Testimony, which I will give you. ²²There, above the cover between the two cheru that are over the ark of the Testimony, I will meet with you and give you all my co mands for the Israelites.

ᵃ10 Or lapis lazuli   ᵇ5 That is, dugongs   ᶜ10 That is, about 3 3/4 feet (about 1.1 meters) long and 2 1/4 feet (about 0.7 meter) wide and high   ᵈ17 Traditionally a mercy seat   ᵉ17 That is, about 3 3/4 feet (about 1.1 meters) long and 2 1/4 feet (about 0.7 meter) wide

The Table

23"Make a table of acacia wood—two cubits long, a cubit wide and a cubit and a half high.ᵃ 24Overlay it with pure gold and make a gold molding around it. 25Also make round it a rim a handbreadthᵇ wide and put a gold molding on the rim. 26Make four gold rings for the table and fasten them to the four corners, where the four legs are. 27The rings are to be close to the rim to hold the poles used in carrying the table. 28Make the poles of acacia wood, overlay them with gold and carry the table with them. 29And make its plates and dishes of pure gold, as well as its pitchers and bowls for the pouring out of offerings. 30Put the bread of the Presence on this table to be before me at all times.

The Lampstand

31"Make a lampstand of pure gold and hammer it out, base and shaft; its flower-like cups, buds and blossoms shall be of one piece with it. 32Six branches are to extend from the sides of the lampstand—three on one side and three on the other. 33Three cups shaped like almond flowers with buds and blossoms are to be on one branch, three on the next branch, and the same for all six branches extending from the lampstand. 34And on the lampstand

> ## ADDRESSING QUESTIONS
>
> ### Chapters 25—31
> ### God
>
> These chapters give instructions for the cere-monial aspects of Israel's religious obser-vances. While they may have little direct application for us today, here's one observa-tion worth pondering.
>
> These detailed instructions for worship—and for crafting articles to use in worship—show us that beauty and excellence are important to God. The God who made the wonders of creation is pleased when we do our best to serve him with the skills he's given us.
>
> There is a place for you and your abilities in God's family. According to the Bible, God made you in his image, and your creativity is a manifestation of that mark. When you're ready to trust God with your life and to com-mit yourself to him, you'll discover that he is eager to work powerfully through you as you use your talents for his glory.

there are to be four cups shaped like almond flowers with buds and blossoms. 35One bud shall be under the first pair of branches extending from the lampstand, a second bud under the second pair, and a third bud under the third pair—six branches in all. 36The buds and branches shall all be of one piece with the lampstand, hammered out of pure gold.

37Then make its seven lamps and set them up on it so that they light the space in front of it. 38Its wick trimmers and trays are to be of pure gold. 39A talentᶜ of pure gold is to be used for the lampstand and all these accessories. 40See that you make them according to the pattern shown you on the mountain.

The Tabernacle

26 "Make the tabernacle with ten curtains of finely twisted linen and blue, purple and scarlet yarn, with cherubim worked into them by a skilled crafts-man. 2All the curtains are to be the same size—twenty-eight cubits long and four cubits wide.ᵈ 3Join five of the curtains together, and do the same with the other five. 4Make loops of blue material along the edge of the end curtain in one set, and do the same with the end curtain in the other set. 5Make fifty loops on one curtain and fifty loops on the end curtain of the other set, with the loops opposite each other. 6Then make fifty gold clasps and use them to fasten the curtains together so that the tabernacle is a unit.

7"Make curtains of goat hair for the tent over the tabernacle—eleven altogether. 8All

23 That is, about 3 feet (about 0.9 meter) long and 1 1/2 feet (about 0.5 meter) wide and 2 1/4 feet (about 0.7 meter) high
ᵇ5 That is, about 3 inches (about 8 centimeters)   ᶜ39 That is, about 75 pounds (about 34 kilograms)   ᵈ2 That is, about 42 feet (about 12.5 meters) long and 6 feet (about 1.8 meters) wide

eleven curtains are to be the same size—thirty cubits long and four cubits wide.*ᵃ* ⁹Jo[in]
five of the curtains together into one set and the other six into another set. Fold the six[th]
curtain double at the front of the tent. ¹⁰Make fifty loops along the edge of the e[nd]
curtain in one set and also along the edge of the end curtain in the other set. ¹¹Th[en]
make fifty bronze clasps and put them in the loops to fasten the tent together as a un[it.]
¹²As for the additional length of the tent curtains, the half curtain that is left over is [to]
hang down at the rear of the tabernacle. ¹³The tent curtains will be a cubit*ᵇ* longer [on]
both sides; what is left will hang over the sides of tabernacle so as to cover it. ¹⁴Ma[ke]
for the tent a covering of ram skins dyed red, and over that a covering of hides of s[ea]
cows.*ᶜ*

¹⁵"Make upright frames of acacia wood for the tabernacle. ¹⁶Each frame is to be te[n]
cubits long and a cubit and a half wide,*ᵈ* ¹⁷with two projections set parallel to ea[ch]
other. Make all the frames of the tabernacle in this way. ¹⁸Make twenty frames for t[he]
south side of the tabernacle ¹⁹and make forty silver bases to go under them—two bas[es]
for each frame, one under each projection. ²⁰For the other side, the north side of th[e]
tabernacle, make twenty frames ²¹and forty silver bases—two under each frame. ²²Mak[e]
six frames for the far end, that is, the west end of the tabernacle, ²³and make two fram[es]
for the corners at the far end. ²⁴At these two corners they must be double from t[he]
bottom all the way to the top, and fitted into a single ring; both shall be like that. ²⁵[So]
there will be eight frames and sixteen silver bases—two under each frame.

²⁶"Also make crossbars of acacia wood: five for the frames on one side of the tabern[a]-
cle, ²⁷five for those on the other side, and five for the frames on the west, at the far e[nd]
of the tabernacle. ²⁸The center crossbar is to extend from end to end at the middle of t[he]
frames. ²⁹Overlay the frames with gold and make gold rings to hold the crossbars. Al[so]
overlay the crossbars with gold.

³⁰"Set up the tabernacle according to the plan shown you on the mountain.

³¹"Make a curtain of blue, purple and scarlet yarn and finely twisted linen, with cher[u]-
bim worked into it by a skilled craftsman. ³²Hang it with gold hooks on four posts [of]
acacia wood overlaid with gold and standing on four silver bases. ³³Hang the curtai[n]
from the clasps and place the ark of the Testimony behind the curtain. The curtain w[ill]
separate the Holy Place from the Most Holy Place. ³⁴Put the atonement cover on the ar[k of]
the Testimony in the Most Holy Place. ³⁵Place the table outside the curtain on the nor[th]
side of the tabernacle and put the lampstand opposite it on the south side.

³⁶"For the entrance to the tent make a curtain of blue, purple and scarlet yarn a[nd]
finely twisted linen—the work of an embroiderer. ³⁷Make gold hooks for this curtain a[nd]
five posts of acacia wood overlaid with gold. And cast five bronze bases for them.

The Altar of Burnt Offering

27   "Build an altar of acacia wood, three cubits*ᵉ* high; it is to be square, fi[ve]
cubits long and five cubits wide.*ᶠ* ²Make a horn at each of the four corner[s]
so that the horns and the altar are of one piece, and overlay the altar with bronze. ³Ma[ke]
all its utensils of bronze—its pots to remove the ashes, and its shovels, sprinkling bow[ls,]
meat forks and firepans. ⁴Make a grating for it, a bronze network, and make a bronze ri[ng]
at each of the four corners of the network. ⁵Put it under the ledge of the altar so that it [is]
halfway up the altar. ⁶Make poles of acacia wood for the altar and overlay them wi[th]
bronze. ⁷The poles are to be inserted into the rings so they will be on two sides of t[he]
altar when it is carried. ⁸Make the altar hollow, out of boards. It is to be made just as y[ou]
were shown on the mountain.

ᵃ8 That is, about 45 feet (about 13.5 meters) long and 6 feet (about 1.8 meters) wide   *ᵇ13* That is, about 1 1/2 feet (about
0.5 meter)   *ᶜ14* That is, dugongs   *ᵈ16* That is, about 15 feet (about 4.5 meters) long and 2 1/4 feet (about 0.7 meter)
wide   *ᵉ1* That is, about 4 1/2 feet (about 1.3 meters)   *ᶠ1* That is, about 7 1/2 feet (about 2.3 meters) long and wide

The Courtyard

9"Make a courtyard for the tabernacle. The south side shall be a hundred cubits[a] long and is to have curtains of finely twisted linen, 10with twenty posts and twenty bronze bases and with silver hooks and bands on the posts. 11The north side shall also be a hundred cubits long and is to have curtains, with twenty posts and twenty bronze bases and with silver hooks and bands on the posts.

12"The west end of the courtyard shall be fifty cubits[b] wide and have curtains, with ten posts and ten bases. 13On the east end, toward the sunrise, the courtyard shall also be fifty cubits wide. 14Curtains fifteen cubits[c] long are to be on one side of the entrance, with three posts and three bases, 15and curtains fifteen cubits long are to be on the other side, with three posts and three bases.

16"For the entrance to the courtyard, provide a curtain twenty cubits[d] long, of blue, purple and scarlet yarn and finely twisted linen—the work of an embroiderer—with four posts and four bases. 17All the posts around the courtyard are to have silver bands and hooks, and bronze bases. 18The courtyard shall be a hundred cubits long and fifty cubits wide,[e] with curtains of finely twisted linen five cubits[f] high, and with bronze bases. 19All the other articles used in the service of the tabernacle, whatever their function, including all the tent pegs for it and those for the courtyard, are to be of bronze.

Oil for the Lampstand

20"Command the Israelites to bring you clear oil of pressed olives for the light so that the lamps may be kept burning. 21In the Tent of Meeting, outside the curtain that is in front of the Testimony, Aaron and his sons are to keep the lamps burning before the LORD from evening till morning. This is to be a lasting ordinance among the Israelites for the generations to come.

The Priestly Garments

28 "Have Aaron your brother brought to you from among the Israelites, along with his sons Nadab and Abihu, Eleazar and Ithamar, so they may serve me as priests. 2Make sacred garments for your brother Aaron, to give him dignity and honor. 3Tell all the skilled men to whom I have given wisdom in such matters that they are to make garments for Aaron, for his consecration, so he may serve me as priest. 4These are the garments they are to make: a breastpiece, an ephod, a robe, a woven tunic, a turban and a sash. They are to make these sacred garments for your brother Aaron and his sons, so they may serve me as priests. 5Have them use gold, and blue, purple and scarlet yarn, and fine linen.

The Ephod

6"Make the ephod of gold, and of blue, purple and scarlet yarn, and of finely twisted linen—the work of a skilled craftsman. 7It is to have two shoulder pieces attached to two of its corners, so it can be fastened. 8Its skillfully woven waistband is to be like it—of one piece with the ephod and made with gold, and with blue, purple and scarlet yarn, and with finely twisted linen.

9"Take two onyx stones and engrave on them the names of the sons of Israel 10in the order of their birth—six names on one stone and the remaining six on the other. 11Engrave the names of the sons of Israel on the two stones the way a gem cutter engraves a seal. Then mount the stones in gold filigree settings 12and fasten them on the shoulder pieces of the ephod as memorial stones for the sons of Israel. Aaron is to bear the names

---

a9 That is, about 150 feet (about 46 meters); also in verse 11   b12 That is, about 75 feet (about 23 meters); also in verse 13   c14 That is, about 22 1/2 feet (about 6.9 meters); also in verse 15   d16 That is, about 30 feet (about 9 meters)   e18 That is, about 150 feet (about 46 meters) long and 75 feet (about 23 meters) wide   f18 That is, about 7 1/2 feet (about 2.3 meters)

on his shoulders as a memorial before the LORD. ¹³Make gold filigree settings ¹⁴and two braided chains of pure gold, like a rope, and attach the chains to the settings.

The Breastpiece

¹⁵"Fashion a breastpiece for making decisions—the work of a skilled craftsman. Make it like the ephod: of gold, and of blue, purple and scarlet yarn, and of finely twisted linen. ¹⁶It is to be square—a span ᵃ long and a span wide—and folded double. ¹⁷Then mount four rows of precious stones on it. In the first row there shall be a ruby, a topaz and a beryl; ¹⁸in the second row a turquoise, a sapphire ᵇ and an emerald; ¹⁹in the third row a jacinth, an agate and an amethyst; ²⁰in the fourth row a chrysolite, an onyx and a jasper. ᶜ Mount them in gold filigree settings. ²¹There are to be twelve stones, one for each of the names of the sons of Israel, each engraved like a seal with the name of one of the twelve tribes.

²²"For the breastpiece make braided chains of pure gold, like a rope. ²³Make two gold rings for it and fasten them to two corners of the breastpiece. ²⁴Fasten the two gold chains to the rings at the corners of the breastpiece, ²⁵and the other ends of the chains to the two settings, attaching them to the shoulder pieces of the ephod at the front. ²⁶Make two gold rings and attach them to the other two corners of the breastpiece on the inside edge next to the ephod. ²⁷Make two more gold rings and attach them to the bottom of the shoulder pieces on the front of the ephod, close to the seam just above the waistband of the ephod. ²⁸The rings of the breastpiece are to be tied to the rings of the ephod with blue cord, connecting it to the waistband, so that the breastpiece will not swing out from the ephod.

²⁹"Whenever Aaron enters the Holy Place, he will bear the names of the sons of Israel over his heart on the breastpiece of decision as a continuing memorial before the LORD. ³⁰Also put the Urim and the Thummim in the breastpiece, so they may be over Aaron's heart whenever he enters the presence of the LORD. Thus Aaron will always bear the means of making decisions for the Israelites over his heart before the LORD.

Other Priestly Garments

³¹"Make the robe of the ephod entirely of blue cloth, ³²with an opening for the head in its center. There shall be a woven edge like a collar ᵈ around this opening, so that it will not tear. ³³Make pomegranates of blue, purple and scarlet yarn around the hem of the robe, with gold bells between them. ³⁴The gold bells and the pomegranates are to alternate around the hem of the robe. ³⁵Aaron must wear it when he ministers. The sound of the bells will be heard when he enters the Holy Place before the LORD and when he comes out, so that he will not die.

³⁶"Make a plate of pure gold and engrave on it as on a seal: HOLY TO THE LORD. ³⁷Fasten a blue cord to it to attach it to the turban; it is to be on the front of the turban. ³⁸It will be on Aaron's forehead, and he will bear the guilt involved in the sacred gifts the Israelites consecrate, whatever their gifts may be. It will be on Aaron's forehead continually so that they will be acceptable to the LORD.

³⁹"Weave the tunic of fine linen and make the turban of fine linen. The sash is to be the work of an embroiderer. ⁴⁰Make tunics, sashes and headbands for Aaron's sons, to give them dignity and honor. ⁴¹After you put these clothes on your brother Aaron and his sons, anoint and ordain them. Consecrate them so they may serve me as priests.

⁴²"Make linen undergarments as a covering for the body, reaching from the waist to the thigh. ⁴³Aaron and his sons must wear them whenever they enter the Tent of Meeting or approach the altar to minister in the Holy Place, so that they will not incur guilt and die.

"This is to be a lasting ordinance for Aaron and his descendants.

ᵃ16 That is, about 9 inches (about 22 centimeters)   ᵇ18 Or lapis lazuli   ᶜ20 The precise identification of some of these precious stones is uncertain.   ᵈ32 The meaning of the Hebrew for this word is uncertain.

Consecration of the Priests

29 ¹"This is what you are to do to consecrate them, so they may serve me as priests: Take a young bull and two rams without defect. ²And from fine wheat flour, without yeast, make bread, and cakes mixed with oil, and wafers spread with oil. ³Put them in a basket and present them in it—along with the bull and the two rams. ⁴Then bring Aaron and his sons to the entrance to the Tent of Meeting and wash them with water. ⁵Take the garments and dress Aaron with the tunic, the robe of the ephod, the ephod itself and the breastpiece. Fasten the ephod on him by its skillfully woven waistband. ⁶Put the turban on his head and attach the sacred diadem to the turban. ⁷Take the anointing oil and anoint him by pouring it on his head. ⁸Bring his sons and dress them in tunics ⁹and put headbands on them. Then tie sashes on Aaron and his sons.ᵃ The priesthood is theirs by a lasting ordinance. In this way you shall ordain Aaron and his sons.

¹⁰"Bring the bull to the front of the Tent of Meeting, and Aaron and his sons shall lay their hands on its head. ¹¹Slaughter it in the LORD's presence at the entrance to the Tent of Meeting. ¹²Take some of the bull's blood and put it on the horns of the altar with your finger, and pour out the rest of it at the base of the altar. ¹³Then take all the fat around the inner parts, the covering of the liver, and both kidneys with the fat on them, and burn them on the altar. ¹⁴But burn the bull's flesh and its hide and its offal outside the camp. It is a sin offering.

¹⁵"Take one of the rams, and Aaron and his sons shall lay their hands on its head. ¹⁶Slaughter it and take the blood and sprinkle it against the altar on all sides. ¹⁷Cut the ram into pieces and wash the inner parts and the legs, putting them with the head and the other pieces. ¹⁸Then burn the entire ram on the altar. It is a burnt offering to the LORD, a pleasing aroma, an offeringᵇ made to the LORD by fire.

¹⁹"Take the other ram, and Aaron and his sons shall lay their hands on its head. ²⁰Slaughter it, take some of its blood and put it on the lobes of the right ears of Aaron and his sons, on the thumbs of their right hands, and on the big toes of their right feet. Then sprinkle blood against the altar on all sides. ²¹And take some of the blood on the altar and some of the anointing oil and sprinkle it on Aaron and his garments and on his sons and their garments. Then he and his sons and their garments will be consecrated.

²²"Take from this ram the fat, the fat tail, the fat around the inner parts, the covering of the liver, both kidneys with the fat on them, and the right thigh. (This is the ram for the ordination.) ²³From the basket of bread made without yeast, which is before the LORD, take a loaf, and a cake made with oil, and a wafer. ²⁴Put all these in the hands of Aaron and his sons and wave them before the LORD as a wave offering. ²⁵Then take them from their hands and burn them on the altar along with the burnt offering for a pleasing aroma to the LORD, an offering made to the LORD by fire. ²⁶After you take the breast of the ram for Aaron's ordination, wave it before the LORD as a wave offering, and it will be your share.

²⁷"Consecrate those parts of the ordination ram that belong to Aaron and his sons: the breast that was waved and the thigh that was presented. ²⁸This is always to be the regular share from the Israelites for Aaron and his sons. It is the contribution the Israelites are to make to the LORD from their fellowship offerings.ᵇ

²⁹"Aaron's sacred garments will belong to his descendants so that they can be anointed and ordained in them. ³⁰The son who succeeds him as priest and comes to the Tent of Meeting to minister in the Holy Place is to wear them seven days.

³¹"Take the ram for the ordination and cook the meat in a sacred place. ³²At the entrance to the Tent of Meeting, Aaron and his sons are to eat the meat of the ram and the bread that is in the basket. ³³They are to eat these offerings by which atonement was made for their ordination and consecration. But no one else may eat them, because they

---

ᵃ Hebrew; Septuagint on them   ᵇ 28 Traditionally peace offerings

are sacred. ³⁴And if any of the meat of the ordination ram or any bread is left over til morning, burn it up. It must not be eaten, because it is sacred.

³⁵"Do for Aaron and his sons everything I have commanded you, taking seven days to ordain them. ³⁶Sacrifice a bull each day as a sin offering to make atonement. Purify the altar by making atonement for it, and anoint it to consecrate it. ³⁷For seven days make atonement for the altar and consecrate it. Then the altar will be most holy, and whatever touches it will be holy.

³⁸"This is what you are to offer on the altar regularly each day: two lambs a year old ³⁹Offer one in the morning and the other at twilight. ⁴⁰With the first lamb offer a tenth of an ephah^a of fine flour mixed with a quarter of a hin^b of oil from pressed olives, and a quarter of a hin of wine as a drink offering. ⁴¹Sacrifice the other lamb at twilight with the same grain offering and its drink offering as in the morning—a pleasing aroma, an offering made to the LORD by fire.

⁴²"For the generations to come this burnt offering is to be made regularly at the entrance to the Tent of Meeting before the LORD. There I will meet you and speak to you ⁴³there also I will meet with the Israelites, and the place will be consecrated by my glory

⁴⁴"So I will consecrate the Tent of Meeting and the altar and will consecrate Aaron and his sons to serve me as priests. ⁴⁵Then I will dwell among the Israelites and be their God ⁴⁶They will know that I am the LORD their God, who brought them out of Egypt so that I might dwell among them. I am the LORD their God.

The Altar of Incense

30 "Make an altar of acacia wood for burning incense. ²It is to be square, a cubit long and a cubit wide, and two cubits high^c—its horns of one piece with it ³Overlay the top and all the sides and the horns with pure gold, and make a gold molding around it. ⁴Make two gold rings for the altar below the molding—two on opposite sides—to hold the poles used to carry it. ⁵Make the poles of acacia wood and overlay them with gold. ⁶Put the altar in front of the curtain that is before the ark of the Testimony—before the atonement cover that is over the Testimony—where I will meet with you.

⁷"Aaron must burn fragrant incense on the altar every morning when he tends the lamps. ⁸He must burn incense again when he lights the lamps at twilight so incense will burn regularly before the LORD for the generations to come. ⁹Do not offer on this altar any other incense or any burnt offering or grain offering, and do not pour a drink offering on it. ¹⁰Once a year Aaron shall make atonement on its horns. This annual atonement must be made with the blood of the atoning sin offering for the generations to come. It is most holy to the LORD."

Atonement Money

¹¹Then the LORD said to Moses, ¹²"When you take a census of the Israelites to count them, each one must pay the LORD a ransom for his life at the time he is counted. Then no plague will come on them when you number them. ¹³Each one who crosses over to those already counted is to give a half shekel,^d according to the sanctuary shekel, which weighs twenty gerahs. This half shekel is an offering to the LORD. ¹⁴All who cross over, those twenty years old or more, are to give an offering to the LORD. ¹⁵The rich are not to give more than a half shekel and the poor are not to give less when you make the offering to the LORD to atone for your lives. ¹⁶Receive the atonement money from the Israelites and use it for the service of the Tent of Meeting. It will be a memorial for the Israelites before the LORD, making atonement for your lives."

^a40 That is, probably about 2 quarts (about 2 liters)   ^b40 That is, probably about 1 quart (about 1 liter)   ^c2 That is, about 1 1/2 feet (about 0.5 meter) long and wide and about 3 feet (about 0.9 meter) high   ^d13 That is, about 1/5 ounce (about 6 grams); also in verse 15

Basin for Washing

¹⁷Then the LORD said to Moses, ¹⁸"Make a bronze basin, with its bronze stand, for washing. Place it between the Tent of Meeting and the altar, and put water in it. ¹⁹Aaron and his sons are to wash their hands and feet with water from it. ²⁰Whenever they enter the Tent of Meeting, they shall wash with water so that they will not die. Also, when they approach the altar to minister by presenting an offering made to the LORD by fire, ²¹they shall wash their hands and feet so that they will not die. This is to be a lasting ordinance for Aaron and his descendants for the generations to come."

Anointing Oil

²²Then the LORD said to Moses, ²³"Take the following fine spices: 500 shekels*a* of liquid myrrh, half as much (that is, 250 shekels) of fragrant cinnamon, 250 shekels of fragrant cane, ²⁴500 shekels of cassia—all according to the sanctuary shekel—and a hin*b* of olive oil. ²⁵Make these into a sacred anointing oil, a fragrant blend, the work of a perfumer. It will be the sacred anointing oil. ²⁶Then use it to anoint the Tent of Meeting, the ark of the Testimony, ²⁷the table and all its articles, the lampstand and its accessories, the altar of incense, ²⁸the altar of burnt offering and all its utensils, and the basin with its stand. ²⁹You shall consecrate them so they will be most holy, and whatever touches them will be holy.

³⁰"Anoint Aaron and his sons and consecrate them so they may serve me as priests. ³¹Say to the Israelites, 'This is to be my sacred anointing oil for the generations to come. ³²Do not pour it on men's bodies and do not make any oil with the same formula. It is sacred, and you are to consider it sacred. ³³Whoever makes perfume like it and whoever puts it on anyone other than a priest must be cut off from his people.'"

Incense

³⁴Then the LORD said to Moses, "Take fragrant spices—gum resin, onycha and galbanum—and pure frankincense, all in equal amounts, ³⁵and make a fragrant blend of incense, the work of a perfumer. It is to be salted and pure and sacred. ³⁶Grind some of it to powder and place it in front of the Testimony in the Tent of Meeting, where I will meet with you. It shall be most holy to you. ³⁷Do not make any incense with this formula for yourselves; consider it holy to the LORD. ³⁸Whoever makes any like it to enjoy its fragrance must be cut off from his people."

Bezalel and Oholiab

31 Then the LORD said to Moses, ²"See, I have chosen Bezalel son of Uri, the son of Hur, of the tribe of Judah, ³and I have filled him with the Spirit of God, with skill, ability and knowledge in all kinds of crafts— ⁴to make artistic designs for work in gold, silver and bronze, ⁵to cut and set stones, to work in wood, and to engage in all kinds of craftsmanship. ⁶Moreover, I have appointed Oholiab son of Ahisamach, of the tribe of Dan, to help him. Also I have given skill to all the craftsmen to make everything I have commanded you: ⁷the Tent of Meeting, the ark of the Testimony with the atonement cover on it, and all the other furnishings of the tent— ⁸the table and its articles, the pure gold lampstand and all its accessories, the altar of incense, ⁹the altar of burnt offering and all its utensils, the basin with its stand— ¹⁰and also the woven garments, both the sacred garments for Aaron the priest and the garments for his sons when they serve as priests, ¹¹and the anointing oil and fragrant incense for the Holy Place. They are to make them just as I commanded you."

---

a23 That is, about 12 1/2 pounds (about 6 kilograms)   *b24* That is, probably about 4 quarts (about 4 liters)

The Sabbath

¹²Then the LORD said to Moses, ¹³"Say to the Israelites, 'You must observe my Sabbaths. This will be a sign between me and you for the generations to come, so you may know that I am the LORD, who makes you holy.ᵃ

¹⁴"'Observe the Sabbath, because it is holy to you. Anyone who desecrates it must be put to death; whoever does any work on that day must be cut off from his people. ¹⁵For six days, work is to be done, but the seventh day is a Sabbath of rest, holy to the LORD. Whoever does any work on the Sabbath day must be put to death. ¹⁶The Israelites are to observe the Sabbath, celebrating it for the generations to come as a lasting covenant. ¹⁷It will be a sign between me and the Israelites forever, for in six days the LORD made the heavens and the earth, and on the seventh day he abstained from work and rested.'"

¹⁸When the LORD finished speaking to Moses on Mount Sinai, he gave him the two tablets of the Testimony, the tablets of stone inscribed by the finger of God.

The Golden Calf

32 When the people saw that Moses was so long in coming down from the mountain, they gathered around Aaron and said, "Come, make us godsᵇ who will go before us. As for this fellow Moses who brought us up out of Egypt, we don't know what has happened to him."

²Aaron answered them, "Take off the gold earrings that your wives, your sons and your daughters are wearing, and bring them to me." ³So all the people took off their earrings and brought them to Aaron. ⁴He took what they handed him and made it into an idol cast in the shape of a calf, fashioning it with a tool. Then they said, "These are your gods,ᶜ O Israel, who brought you up out of Egypt."

⁵When Aaron saw this, he built an altar in front of the calf and announced, "Tomorrow there will be a festival to the LORD." ⁶So the next day the people rose early and sacrificed burnt offerings and presented fellowship offerings.ᵈ Afterward they sat down to eat and drink and got up to indulge in revelry.

⁷Then the LORD said to Moses, "Go down, because your people, whom you brought up out of Egypt, have become corrupt. ⁸They have been quick to turn away from what I commanded them and have made themselves an idol cast in the shape of a calf. They have bowed down to it and sacrificed to it and have said, 'These are your gods, O Israel, who brought you up out of Egypt.'

⁹"I have seen these people," the LORD said to Moses, "and they are a stiff-necked people. ¹⁰Now leave me alone so that my anger may burn against them and that I may destroy them. Then I will make you into a great nation."

¹¹But Moses sought the favor of the LORD his God. "O LORD," he said, "why should your anger burn against your people, whom you brought out of Egypt with great power and a mighty hand? ¹²Why should the Egyptians say, 'It was with evil intent that he brought them out, to kill them in the mountains and to wipe them off the face of the earth'? Turn from your fierce anger; relent and do not bring disaster on your people. ¹³Remember your servants Abraham, Isaac and Israel, to whom you swore by your own self: 'I will make your descendants as numerous as the stars in the sky and I will give your descendants all this land I promised them, and it will be their inheritance forever.'" ¹⁴Then the LORD relented and did not bring on his people the disaster he had threatened.

¹⁵Moses turned and went down the mountain with the two tablets of the Testimony in his hands. They were inscribed on both sides, front and back. ¹⁶The tablets were the work of God; the writing was the writing of God, engraved on the tablets.

¹⁷When Joshua heard the noise of the people shouting, he said to Moses, "There is the sound of war in the camp."

¹⁸Moses replied:

ᵃ 13 Or *who sanctifies you; or who sets you apart as holy god; also in verse 8*   ᵇ 1 Or *a god; also in verses 23 and 31*   ᶜ 4 Or *This is your*   ᵈ 6 Traditionally *peace offerings*

"It is not the sound of victory,
   it is not the sound of defeat;
   it is the sound of singing that I hear."

¹⁹When Moses approached the camp and saw the calf and the dancing, his anger burned and he threw the tablets out of his hands, breaking them to pieces at the foot of the mountain. ²⁰And he took the calf they had made and burned in the fire; then he ground it to powder, scattered it on the water and made the Israelites drink it.

²¹He said to Aaron, "What did these people do to you, that you led them into such great sin?"

²²"Do not be angry, my lord," Aaron answered. "You know how prone these people are to evil. ²³They said to me, 'Make us gods who will go before us. As for this fellow Moses who brought us up out of Egypt, we don't know what has happened to him.' ²⁴So I told them, 'Whoever has any gold jewelry, take it off.' Then they gave me the gold, and I threw it into the fire, and out came this calf!"

²⁵Moses saw that the people were running wild and that Aaron had let them get out of control and so become a laughingstock to their enemies. ²⁶So he stood at the entrance to the camp and said, "Whoever is for the LORD, come to me." And all the Levites rallied to him.

²⁷Then he said to them, "This is what the LORD, the God of Israel, says: 'Each man strap a sword to his side. Go back and forth through the camp from one end to the other, each killing his brother and friend and neighbor.'" ²⁸The Levites did as Moses commanded, and that day about three thousand of the people died. ²⁹Then Moses said, "You have been set apart to the LORD today, for you were against your own sons and brothers, and he has blessed you this day."

³⁰The next day Moses said to the people, "You have committed a great sin. But now I will go up to the LORD; perhaps I can make atonement for your sin."

³¹So Moses went back to the LORD and said, "Oh, what a great sin these people have committed! They have made themselves gods of gold. ³²But now, please forgive their sin—but if not, then blot me out of the book you have written."

³³The LORD replied to Moses, "Whoever has sinned against me I will blot out of my book. Now go, lead the people to the place I spoke of, and my angel will go before you. However, when the time comes for me to punish, I will punish them for their sin."

³⁵And the LORD struck the people with a plague because of what they did with the calf Aaron had made.

33 Then the LORD said to Moses, "Leave this place, you and the people you brought up out of Egypt, and go up to the land I promised on oath to Abraham, Isaac and Jacob, saying, 'I will give it to your descendants.' ²I will send an angel before you and drive out the Canaanites, Amorites, Hittites, Perizzites, Hivites and Jebu-

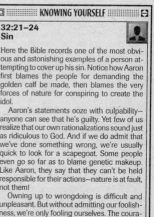

████ KNOWING YOURSELF ████

32:21–24
Sin

Here the Bible records one of the most obvious and astonishing examples of a person attempting to cover up his sin. Notice how Aaron first blames the people for demanding the golden calf be made, then blames the very forces of nature for conspiring to create the idol.

Aaron's statements ooze with culpability—anyone can see that he's guilty. Yet few of us realize that our own rationalizations sound just as ridiculous to God. And if we do admit that we've done something wrong, we're usually quick to look for a scapegoat. Some people even go so far as to blame genetic makeup. Like Aaron, they say that they can't be held responsible for their actions—nature is at fault, not them!

Owning up to wrongdoing is difficult and unpleasant. But without admitting our foolishness, we're only fooling ourselves. The courageous millions who have joined 12-step groups have discovered the value of making complete admissions. All of us need to embrace such complete honesty—with God, with others, and with ourselves.

sites. ³Go up to the land flowing with milk and honey. But I will not go with you, becau
you are a stiff-necked people and I might destroy you on the way."

⁴When the people heard these distressing words, they began to mourn and no one ▮
on any ornaments. ⁵For the LORD had said to Moses, "Tell the Israelites, 'You are a st
necked people. If I were to go with you even for a moment, I might destroy you. Now ta
off your ornaments and I will decide what to do with you.'" ⁶So the Israelites stripped
their ornaments at Mount Horeb.

The Tent of Meeting

⁷Now Moses used to take a tent and pitch it outside the camp some distance aw
calling it the "tent of meeting." Anyone inquiring of the LORD would go to the tent
meeting outside the camp. ⁸And whenever Moses went out to the tent, all the people ro
and stood at the entrances to their tents, watching Moses until he entered the tent. ⁹
Moses went into the tent, the pillar of cloud would come down and stay at the entran
while the LORD spoke with Moses. ¹⁰Whenever the people saw the pillar of cloud stand:
at the entrance to the tent, they all stood and worshiped, each at the entrance to his te
¹¹The LORD would speak to Moses face to face, as a man speaks with his friend. Th
Moses would return to the camp, but his young aide Joshua son of Nun did not leave ▮
tent.

Moses and the Glory of the LORD

¹²Moses said to the LORD, "You have been telling me, 'Lead these people,' but you ha
not let me know whom you will send with me. You have said, 'I know you by name a
you have found favor with me.' ¹³If you are pleased with me, teach me your ways s
may know you and continue to find favor with you. Remember that this nation is yo
people."

¹⁴The LORD replied, "My Presence will go with you, and I will give you rest."

¹⁵Then Moses said to him, "If your Presence does not go with us, do not send us
from here. ¹⁶How will anyone know that you are pleased with me and with your peo,
unless you go with us? What else will distinguish me and your people from all the oth
people on the face of the earth?"

¹⁷And the LORD said to Moses, "I will do the very thing you have asked, because I ▮
pleased with you and I know you by name."

¹⁸Then Moses said, "Now show me your glory."

¹⁹And the LORD said, "I will cause all my goodness to pass in front of you, and I v
proclaim my name, the LORD, in your presence. I will have mercy on whom I will ha
mercy, and I will have compassion on whom I will have compassion. ²⁰But," he said, "y
cannot see my face, for no one may see me and live."

²¹Then the LORD said, "There is a place near me where you may stand on a ro
²²When my glory passes by, I will put you in a cleft in the rock and cover you with
hand until I have passed by. ²³Then I will remove my hand and you will see my back; ▮
my face must not be seen."

The New Stone Tablets

34 The LORD said to Moses, "Chisel out two stone tablets like the first ones, a
I will write on them the words that were on the first tablets, which y
broke. ²Be ready in the morning, and then come up on Mount Sinai. Present yourself
me there on top of the mountain. ³No one is to come with you or be seen anywhere
the mountain; not even the flocks and herds may graze in front of the mountain."

⁴So Moses chiseled out two stone tablets like the first ones and went up Mount Si
early in the morning, as the LORD had commanded him; and he carried the two sto
tablets in his hands. ⁵Then the LORD came down in the cloud and stood there with h
and proclaimed his name, the LORD. ⁶And he passed in front of Moses, proclaiming, "T

LORD, the LORD, the compassionate and gracious God, slow to anger, abounding in love and faithfulness, **7**maintaining love to thousands, and forgiving wickedness, rebellion and sin. Yet he does not leave the guilty unpunished; he punishes the children and their children for the sin of the fathers to the third and fourth generation."

8Moses bowed to the ground at once and worshiped. **9**"O Lord, if I have found favor in your eyes," he said, "then let the Lord go with us. Although this is a stiff-necked people, forgive our wickedness and our sin, and take us as your inheritance."

10Then the LORD said: "I am making a covenant with you. Before all your people I will do wonders never before done in any nation in all the world. The people you live among will see how awesome is the work that I, the LORD, will do for you. **11**Obey what I command you today. I will drive out before you the Amorites, Canaanites, Hittites, Perizzites, Hivites and Jebusites. **12**Be careful not to make a treaty with those who live in the land where you are going, or they will be a snare among you. **13**Break down their altars, smash their sacred stones and cut down their Asherah poles.*ᵃ* **14**Do not worship any other god, for the LORD, whose name is Jealous, is a jealous God.

15"Be careful not to make a treaty with those who live in the land; for when they prostitute themselves to their gods and sacrifice to them, they will invite you and you will eat their sacrifices. **16**And when you choose some of their daughters as wives for your sons and those daughters prostitute themselves to their gods, they will lead your sons to do the same.

17"Do not make cast idols.

18"Celebrate the Feast of Unleavened Bread. For seven days eat bread made without yeast, as I commanded you. Do this at the appointed time in the month of Abib, for in that month you came out of Egypt.

19"The first offspring of every womb belongs to me, including all the firstborn males of your livestock, whether from herd or flock. **20**Redeem the firstborn donkey with a lamb, but if you do not redeem it, break its neck. Redeem all your firstborn sons.

"No one is to appear before me empty-handed.

21"Six days you shall labor, but on the seventh day you shall rest; even during the plowing season and harvest you must rest.

22"Celebrate the Feast of Weeks with the firstfruits of the wheat harvest, and the Feast of Ingathering at the turn of the year.*ᵇ* **23**Three times a year all your men are to appear before the Sovereign LORD, the God of Israel. **24**I will drive out nations before you and enlarge your territory, and no one will covet your land when you go up three times each year to appear before the LORD your God.

25"Do not offer the blood of a sacrifice to me along with anything containing yeast, and do not let any of the sacrifice from the Passover Feast remain until morning.

26"Bring the best of the firstfruits of your soil to the house of the LORD your God.

"Do not cook a young goat in its mother's milk."

27Then the LORD said to Moses, "Write down these words, for in accordance with these words I have made a covenant with you and with Israel." **28**Moses was there with the LORD forty days and forty nights without eating bread or drinking water. And he wrote on the tablets the words of the covenant—the Ten Commandments.

The Radiant Face of Moses

29When Moses came down from Mount Sinai with the two tablets of the Testimony in his hands, he was not aware that his face was radiant because he had spoken with the LORD. **30**When Aaron and all the Israelites saw Moses, his face was radiant, and they were afraid to come near him. **31**But Moses called to them; so Aaron and all the leaders of the community came back to him, and he spoke to them. **32**Afterward all the Israelites came near him, and he gave them all the commands the LORD had given him on Mount Sinai.

33When Moses finished speaking to them, he put a veil over his face. **34**But whenever

---

13 That is, symbols of the goddess Asherah   *ᵇ22 That is, in the fall*

he entered the LORD's presence to speak with him, he removed the veil until he came out. And when he came out and told the Israelites what he had been commanded, ³⁵they saw that his face was radiant. Then Moses would put the veil back over his face until he went in to speak with the LORD.

📖 ░░░░░ ADDRESSING QUESTIONS ░░░░░ ↩

Chapters 35–40
God

The rest of the book of Exodus deals with additional regulations concerning articles used in worship. Like chapters 25–31, these chapters give detailed descriptions of the beautiful works of art that the people were to make.

Chapter 35, verse 30, through chapter 36, verse 38 (pages 115–116) describe a particular work that God did through the artisans of Israel—the "tabernacle," or tent of worship. The whole nation banded together to work on this project, and a flood of volunteer workers and donations poured in—more than enough to complete the structure. At its completion, the nation of Israel had a vivid reminder of God's presence in their midst. They then camped around the tabernacle, further demonstrating that God was to be at the very center of their lives.

In our day, there is no tabernacle to point to as the place where God centrally manifests himself. As you keep reading in the Bible, you will discover that God's plan now is to live in the hearts and souls of his followers. He actually comes to dwell inside those who invite him in. The New Testament even says that those who put their faith in him become "the temple(s) of the living God" (2 Corinthians chapter 6, verse 16 [page 1515]).

Sabbath Regulations

35 Moses assembled the whole Israelite community and said to them, "These are the things the LORD has commanded you to do: ²For six days, work is to be done, but the seventh day shall be your holy day, a Sabbath of rest to the LORD. Whoever does any work on it must be put to death. ³Do not light a fire in any of your dwellings on the Sabbath day."

Materials for the Tabernacle

⁴Moses said to the whole Israelite community, "This is what the LORD has commanded: ⁵From what you have, take an offering for the LORD. Everyone who is willing is to bring to the LORD an offering of gold, silver and bronze; ⁶blue, purple and scarlet yarn and fine linen; goat hair; ⁷ram skins dyed red and hides of sea cows*ᵃ*; acacia wood; ⁸olive oil for the light; spices for the anointing oil and for the fragrant incense; ⁹and onyx stones and other gems to be mounted on the ephod and breastpiece.

¹⁰"All who are skilled among you are to come and make everything the LORD has commanded: ¹¹the tabernacle with its tent and its covering, clasps, frames, crossbars, posts and bases; ¹²the ark with its poles and the atonement cover and the curtain that shields it; ¹³the table with its poles and all its articles and the bread of the Presence; ¹⁴the lampstand that is for light with its accessories, lamps and oil for the light; ¹⁵the altar of incense with its poles, the anointing oil and the fragrant incense; the curtain for the doorway at the entrance to the tabernacle; ¹⁶the altar of burnt offering with its bronze grating, its poles and all its utensils; the bronze basin with its stand; ¹⁷the curtains of the courtyard with its posts and bases, and the curtain for the entrance to the courtyard; ¹⁸the tent pegs for the tabernacle and for the courtyard, and their ropes; ¹⁹the woven garments worn for ministering in the sanctuary—both the sacred garments for Aaron the priest and the garments for his sons when they serve as priests."

²⁰Then the whole Israelite community withdrew from Moses' presence, ²¹and everyone who was willing and whose heart moved him came and brought an offering to the LORD for the work on the Tent of Meeting, for all its service, and for the sacred garments. ²²All who were willing, men and women alike, came and brought gold jewelry of all kinds: brooches, earrings, rings and ornaments. They all presented their gold as a wave offering to the LORD. ²³Everyone who had blue, purple or scarlet yarn or fine linen, or goat hair, ram skins dyed red or hides of sea cows brought them. ²⁴Those presenting an offering o

ᵃ7 That is, dugongs; also in verse 23

ver or bronze brought it as an offering to the LORD, and everyone who had acacia wood
r any part of the work brought it. ²⁵Every skilled woman spun with her hands and
ought what she had spun—blue, purple or scarlet yarn or fine linen. ²⁶And all the
omen who were willing and had the skill spun the goat hair. ²⁷The leaders brought
yx stones and other gems to be mounted on the ephod and breastpiece. ²⁸They also
ought spices and olive oil for the light and for the anointing oil and for the fragrant
cense. ²⁹All the Israelite men and women who were willing brought to the LORD freewill
erings for all the work the LORD through Moses had commanded them to do.

ezalel and Oholiab

³⁰Then Moses said to the Israelites, "See, the LORD has chosen Bezalel son of Uri, the son
Hur, of the tribe of Judah, ³¹and he has filled him with the Spirit of God, with skill,
ility and knowledge in all kinds of crafts— ³²to make artistic designs for work in gold,
ver and bronze, ³³to cut and set stones, to work in wood and to engage in all kinds of
tistic craftsmanship. ³⁴And he has given both him and Oholiab son of Ahisamach, of the
be of Dan, the ability to teach others. ³⁵He has filled them with skill to do all kinds of
ork as craftsmen, designers, embroiderers in blue, purple and scarlet yarn and fine
36 linen, and weavers—all of them master craftsmen and designers. ¹So Bezalel,
Oholiab and every skilled person to whom the LORD has given skill and ability
know how to carry out all the work of constructing the sanctuary are to do the work
st as the Lord has commanded."

²Then Moses summoned Bezalel and Oholiab and every skilled person to whom the
RD had given ability and who was willing to come and do the work. ³They received
m Moses all the offerings the Israelites had brought to carry out the work of construct-
g the sanctuary. And the people continued to bring freewill offerings morning after
orning. ⁴So all the skilled craftsmen who were doing all the work on the sanctuary left
eir work ⁵and said to Moses, "The people are bringing more than enough for doing the
ork the LORD commanded to be done."

⁶Then Moses gave an order and they sent this word throughout the camp: "No man or
oman is to make anything else as an offering for the sanctuary." And so the people
ere restrained from bringing more, ⁷because what they already had was more than
ough to do all the work.

e Tabernacle

⁸All the skilled men among the workmen made the tabernacle with ten curtains of
ely twisted linen and blue, purple and scarlet yarn, with cherubim worked into them
a skilled craftsman. ⁹All the curtains were the same size—twenty-eight cubits long
d four cubits wide.ᵃ ¹⁰They joined five of the curtains together and did the same with
e other five. ¹¹Then they made loops of blue material along the edge of the end curtain
one set, and the same was done with the end curtain in the other set. ¹²They also
ade fifty loops on one curtain and fifty loops on the end curtain of the other set, with
e loops opposite each other. ¹³Then they made fifty gold clasps and used them to
sten the two sets of curtains together so that the tabernacle was a unit.

¹⁴They made curtains of goat hair for the tent over the tabernacle—eleven altogether.
ll eleven curtains were the same size—thirty cubits long and four cubits wide.ᵇ
They joined five of the curtains into one set and the other six into another set. ¹⁷Then
ey made fifty loops along the edge of the end curtain in one set and also along the
ge of the end curtain in the other set. ¹⁸They made fifty bronze clasps to fasten the tent
gether as a unit. ¹⁹Then they made for the tent a covering of ram skins dyed red, and
er that a covering of hides of sea cows.ᶜ

²⁰They made upright frames of acacia wood for the tabernacle. ²¹Each frame was ten

ᵃThat is, about 42 feet (about 12.5 meters) long and 6 feet (about 1.8 meters) wide   ᵇ15 That is, about 45 feet (about
meters) long and 6 feet (about 1.8 meters) wide   ᶜ19 That is, dugongs

cubits long and a cubit and a half wide,*a* *22*with two projections set parallel to ea
other. They made all the frames of the tabernacle in this way. *23*They made twer
frames for the south side of the tabernacle *24*and made forty silver bases to go und
them—two bases for each frame, one under each projection. *25*For the other side, t
north side of the tabernacle, they made twenty frames *26*and forty silver bases—tv
under each frame. *27*They made six frames for the far end, that is, the west end of tl
tabernacle, *28*and two frames were made for the corners of the tabernacle at the far en
*29*At these two corners the frames were double from the bottom all the way to the t
and fitted into a single ring; both were made alike. *30*So there were eight frames a
sixteen silver bases—two under each frame.

*31*They also made crossbars of acacia wood: five for the frames on one side of tl
tabernacle, *32*five for those on the other side, and five for the frames on the west, at tl
far end of the tabernacle. *33*They made the center crossbar so that it extended from e
to end at the middle of the frames. *34*They overlaid the frames with gold and made go
rings to hold the crossbars. They also overlaid the crossbars with gold.

*35*They made the curtain of blue, purple and scarlet yarn and finely twisted linen, wi
cherubim worked into it by a skilled craftsman. *36*They made four posts of acacia woo
for it and overlaid them with gold. They made gold hooks for them and cast their fo
silver bases. *37*For the entrance to the tent they made a curtain of blue, purple and scar
yarn and finely twisted linen—the work of an embroiderer; *38*and they made five po
with hooks for them. They overlaid the tops of the posts and their bands with gold a
made their five bases of bronze.

The Ark

37 Bezalel made the ark of acacia wood—two and a half cubits long, a cubit a
a half wide, and a cubit and a half high.*b* *2*He overlaid it with pure go
both inside and out, and made a gold molding around it. *3*He cast four gold rings for
and fastened them to its four feet, with two rings on one side and two rings on the oth
*4*Then he made poles of acacia wood and overlaid them with gold. *5*And he inserted t
poles into the rings on the sides of the ark to carry it.

*6*He made the atonement cover of pure gold—two and a half cubits long and a cu
and a half wide.*c* *7*Then he made two cherubim out of hammered gold at the ends of t
cover. *8*He made one cherub on one end and the second cherub on the other; at the tv
ends he made them of one piece with the cover. *9*The cherubim had their wings spre
upward, overshadowing the cover with them. The cherubim faced each other, looki
toward the cover.

The Table

*10*They*d* made the table of acacia wood—two cubits long, a cubit wide, and a cu
and a half high.*e* *11*Then they overlaid it with pure gold and made a gold moldi
around it. *12*They also made around it a rim a handbreadth*f* wide and put a go
molding on the rim. *13*They cast four gold rings for the table and fastened them to t
four corners, where the four legs were. *14*The rings were put close to the rim to hold t
poles used in carrying the table. *15*The poles for carrying the table were made of acac
wood and were overlaid with gold. *16*And they made from pure gold the articles for t
table—its plates and dishes and bowls and its pitchers for the pouring out of dri
offerings.

---

a21 That is, about 15 feet (about 4.5 meters) long and 2 1/4 feet (about 0.7 meter) wide   *b1* That is, about 3 3/4 feet (abou
1.1 meters) long and 2 1/4 feet (about 0.7 meter) wide and high   *c6* That is, about 3 3/4 feet (about 1.1 meters) long and
2 1/4 feet (about 0.7 meter) wide   *d10* Or *He*; also in verses 11-29   *e10* That is, about 3 feet (about 0.9 meter) long,
1 1/2 feet (about 0.5 meter) wide, and 2 1/4 feet (about 0.7 meter) high   *f12* That is, about 3 inches (about 8 centimeters)

e Lampstand

17They made the lampstand of pure gold and hammered it out, base and shaft; its werlike cups, buds and blossoms were of one piece with it. **18**Six branches extended om the sides of the lampstand—three on one side and three on the other. **19**Three cups aped like almond flowers with buds and blossoms were on one branch, three on the xt branch and the same for all six branches extending from the lampstand. **20**And on e lampstand were four cups shaped like almond flowers with buds and blossoms. One bud was under the first pair of branches extending from the lampstand, a second nd under the second pair, and a third bud under the third pair—six branches in all. The buds and the branches were all of one piece with the lampstand, hammered out of re gold.

23They made its seven lamps, as well as its wick trimmers and trays, of pure gold. They made the lampstand and all its accessories from one talent*a* of pure gold.

e Altar of Incense

25They made the altar of incense out of acacia wood. It was square, a cubit long and a bit wide, and two cubits high*b*—its horns of one piece with it. **26**They overlaid the top d all the sides and the horns with pure gold, and made a gold molding around it. They made two gold rings below the molding—two on opposite sides—to hold the les used to carry it. **28**They made the poles of acacia wood and overlaid them with ld.

29They also made the sacred anointing oil and the pure, fragrant incense—the work of perfumer.

e Altar of Burnt Offering

38 They*c* built the altar of burnt offering of acacia wood, three cubits*d* high; it was square, five cubits long and five cubits wide.*e* **2**They made a horn on ch of the four corners, so that the horns and the altar were of one piece, and they erlaid the altar with bronze. **3**They made all its utensils of bronze—its pots, shovels, rinkling bowls, meat forks and firepans. **4**They made a grating for the altar, a bronze etwork, to be under its ledge, halfway up the altar. **5**They cast bronze rings to hold the les for the four corners of the bronze grating. **6**They made the poles of acacia wood and erlaid them with bronze. **7**They inserted the poles into the rings so they would be on e sides of the altar for carrying it. They made it hollow, out of boards.

asin for Washing

8They made the bronze basin and its bronze stand from the mirrors of the women who rved at the entrance to the Tent of Meeting.

he Courtyard

9Next they made the courtyard. The south side was a hundred cubits*f* long and had rtains of finely twisted linen, **10**with twenty posts and twenty bronze bases, and with lver hooks and bands on the posts. **11**The north side was also a hundred cubits long and d twenty posts and twenty bronze bases, with silver hooks and bands on the posts. **12**The west end was fifty cubits*g* wide and had curtains, with ten posts and ten bases, ith silver hooks and bands on the posts. **13**The east end, toward the sunrise, was also ty cubits wide. **14**Curtains fifteen cubits*h* long were on one side of the entrance, with ree posts and three bases, **15**and curtains fifteen cubits long were on the other side of e entrance to the courtyard, with three posts and three bases. **16**All the curtains around

4 That is, about 75 pounds (about 34 kilograms)   *b25* That is, about 1 1/2 feet (about 0.5 meter) long and wide, and out 3 feet (about 0.9 meter) high   *c1* Or *He;* also in verses 2-9   *d1* That is, about 4 1/2 feet (about 1.3 meters) That is, about 7 1/2 feet (about 2.3 meters) long and wide   *f9* That is, about 150 feet (about 46 meters)   *g12* That about 75 feet (about 23 meters)   *h14* That is, about 22 1/2 feet (about 6.9 meters)

the courtyard were of finely twisted linen. ¹⁷The bases for the posts were bronze. T
hooks and bands on the posts were silver, and their tops were overlaid with silver; so
the posts of the courtyard had silver bands.

¹⁸The curtain for the entrance to the courtyard was of blue, purple and scarlet yarn a
finely twisted linen—the work of an embroiderer. It was twenty cubits*ᵃ* long and, li
the curtains of the courtyard, five cubits*ᵇ* high, ¹⁹with four posts and four bronze base
Their hooks and bands were silver, and their tops were overlaid with silver. ²⁰All the te
pegs of the tabernacle and of the surrounding courtyard were bronze.

The Materials Used

²¹These are the amounts of the materials used for the tabernacle, the tabernacle of t
Testimony, which were recorded at Moses' command by the Levites under the directi
of Ithamar son of Aaron, the priest. ²²(Bezalel son of Uri, the son of Hur, of the tribe
Judah, made everything the LORD commanded Moses; ²³with him was Oholiab son
Ahisamach, of the tribe of Dan—a craftsman and designer, and an embroiderer in blu
purple and scarlet yarn and fine linen.) ²⁴The total amount of the gold from the wa
offering used for all the work on the sanctuary was 29 talents and 730 shekel
according to the sanctuary shekel.

²⁵The silver obtained from those of the community who were counted in the cens
was 100 talents and 1,775 shekels,*ᵈ* according to the sanctuary shekel— ²⁶one beka p
person, that is, half a shekel,*ᵉ* according to the sanctuary shekel, from everyone wl
had crossed over to those counted, twenty years old or more, a total of 603,550 me
²⁷The 100 talents*ᶠ* of silver were used to cast the bases for the sanctuary and for t
curtain—100 bases from the 100 talents, one talent for each base. ²⁸They used the 1,7
shekels*ᵍ* to make the hooks for the posts, to overlay the tops of the posts, and to ma
their bands.

²⁹The bronze from the wave offering was 70 talents and 2,400 shekels.*ʰ* ³⁰They us
it to make the bases for the entrance to the Tent of Meeting, the bronze altar with
bronze grating and all its utensils, ³¹the bases for the surrounding courtyard and those
its entrance and all the tent pegs for the tabernacle and those for the surroundi
courtyard.

The Priestly Garments

39 From the blue, purple and scarlet yarn they made woven garments for mini
tering in the sanctuary. They also made sacred garments for Aaron, as t
LORD commanded Moses.

The Ephod

²They*ⁱ* made the ephod of gold, and of blue, purple and scarlet yarn, and of fine
twisted linen. ³They hammered out thin sheets of gold and cut strands to be worked in
the blue, purple and scarlet yarn and fine linen—the work of a skilled craftsman. ⁴Th
made shoulder pieces for the ephod, which were attached to two of its corners, so
could be fastened. ⁵Its skillfully woven waistband was like it—of one piece with t
ephod and made with gold, and with blue, purple and scarlet yarn, and with fine
twisted linen, as the LORD commanded Moses.

⁶They mounted the onyx stones in gold filigree settings and engraved them like a se
with the names of the sons of Israel. ⁷Then they fastened them on the shoulder pieces
the ephod as memorial stones for the sons of Israel, as the LORD commanded Moses.

*ᵃ18 That is, about 30 feet (about 9 meters)   ᵇ18 That is, about 7 1/2 feet (about 2.3 meters)   ᶜ24 The weight of the
gold was a little over one ton (about 1 metric ton).   ᵈ25 The weight of the silver was a little over 3 3/4 tons (about 3.4
metric tons).   ᵉ26 That is, about 1/5 ounce (about 5.5 grams)   ᶠ27 That is, about 3 3/4 tons (about 3.4 metric tons)
ᵍ28 That is, about 45 pounds (about 20 kilograms)   ʰ29 The weight of the bronze was about 2 1/2 tons (about 2.4 metric
tons).   ⁱ2 Or He; also in verses 7, 8 and 22*

The Breastpiece

8They fashioned the breastpiece—the work of a skilled craftsman. They made it like the ephod: of gold, and of blue, purple and scarlet yarn, and of finely twisted linen. **9**It was square—a span*a* long and a span wide—and folded double. **10**Then they mounted four rows of precious stones on it. In the first row there was a ruby, a topaz and a beryl; **11**in the second row a turquoise, a sapphire*b* and an emerald; **12**in the third row a jacinth, an agate and an amethyst; **13**in the fourth row a chrysolite, an onyx and a jasper.*c* They were mounted in gold filigree settings. **14**There were twelve stones, one for each of the names of the sons of Israel, each engraved like a seal with the name of one of the twelve tribes.

15For the breastpiece they made braided chains of pure gold, like a rope. **16**They made two gold filigree settings and two gold rings, and fastened the rings to two of the corners of the breastpiece. **17**They fastened the two gold chains to the rings at the corners of the breastpiece, **18**and the other ends of the chains to the two settings, attaching them to the shoulder pieces of the ephod at the front. **19**They made two gold rings and attached them to the other two corners of the breastpiece on the inside edge next to the ephod. **20**Then they made two more gold rings and attached them to the bottom of the shoulder pieces on the front of the ephod, close to the seam just above the waistband of the ephod. **21**They tied the rings of the breastpiece to the rings of the ephod with blue cord, connecting it to the waistband so that the breastpiece would not swing out from the ephod—as the LORD commanded Moses.

Other Priestly Garments

22They made the robe of the ephod entirely of blue cloth—the work of a weaver— **23**with an opening in the center of the robe like the opening of a collar,*d* and a band around this opening, so that it would not tear. **24**They made pomegranates of blue, purple and scarlet yarn and finely twisted linen around the hem of the robe. **25**And they made bells of pure gold and attached them around the hem between the pomegranates. **26**The bells and pomegranates alternated around the hem of the robe to be worn for ministering, as the LORD commanded Moses.

27For Aaron and his sons, they made tunics of fine linen—the work of a weaver— **28**and the turban of fine linen, the linen headbands and the undergarments of finely twisted linen. **29**The sash was of finely twisted linen and blue, purple and scarlet yarn—the work of an embroiderer—as the LORD commanded Moses.

30They made the plate, the sacred diadem, out of pure gold and engraved on it, like an inscription on a seal: HOLY TO THE LORD. **31**Then they fastened a blue cord to it to attach it to the turban, as the LORD commanded Moses.

Moses Inspects the Tabernacle

32So all the work on the tabernacle, the Tent of Meeting, was completed. The Israelites did everything just as the LORD commanded Moses. **33**Then they brought the tabernacle to Moses: the tent and all its furnishings, its clasps, frames, crossbars, posts and bases; **34**the covering of ram skins dyed red, the covering of hides of sea cows*e* and the shielding curtain; **35**the ark of the Testimony with its poles and the atonement cover; **36**the table with all its articles and the bread of the Presence; **37**the pure gold lampstand with its row of lamps and all its accessories, and the oil for the light; **38**the gold altar, the anointing oil, the fragrant incense, and the curtain for the entrance to the tent; **39**the bronze altar with its bronze grating, its poles and all its utensils; the basin with its stand; **40**the curtains of the courtyard with its posts and bases, and the curtain for the entrance to the courtyard;

a9 That is, about 9 inches (about 22 centimeters)   *b11* Or lapis lazuli   *c13* The precise identification of some of these precious stones is uncertain.   *d23* The meaning of the Hebrew for this word is uncertain.   *e34* That is, dugongs

the ropes and tent pegs for the courtyard; all the furnishings for the tabernacle, the Tent of Meeting; ⁴¹and the woven garments worn for ministering in the sanctuary, both the sacred garments for Aaron the priest and the garments for his sons when serving as priests.

⁴²The Israelites had done all the work just as the LORD had commanded Moses. ⁴³Moses inspected the work and saw that they had done it just as the LORD had commanded. So Moses blessed them.

Setting Up the Tabernacle

40 Then the LORD said to Moses: ²"Set up the tabernacle, the Tent of Meeting, on the first day of the first month. ³Place the ark of the Testimony in it and shield the ark with the curtain. ⁴Bring in the table and set out what belongs on it. Then bring in the lampstand and set up its lamps. ⁵Place the gold altar of incense in front of the ark of the Testimony and put the curtain at the entrance to the tabernacle.

⁶"Place the altar of burnt offering in front of the entrance to the tabernacle, the Tent of Meeting; ⁷place the basin between the Tent of Meeting and the altar and put water in it. ⁸Set up the courtyard around it and put the curtain at the entrance to the courtyard.

⁹"Take the anointing oil and anoint the tabernacle and everything in it; consecrate it and all its furnishings, and it will be holy. ¹⁰Then anoint the altar of burnt offering and all its utensils; consecrate the altar, and it will be most holy. ¹¹Anoint the basin and its stand and consecrate them.

¹²"Bring Aaron and his sons to the entrance to the Tent of Meeting and wash them with water. ¹³Then dress Aaron in the sacred garments, anoint him and consecrate him so he may serve me as priest. ¹⁴Bring his sons and dress them in tunics. ¹⁵Anoint them just as you anointed their father, so they may serve me as priests. Their anointing will be to a priesthood that will continue for all generations to come." ¹⁶Moses did everything just as the LORD commanded him.

¹⁷So the tabernacle was set up on the first day of the first month in the second year. ¹⁸When Moses set up the tabernacle, he put the bases in place, erected the frames, inserted the crossbars and set up the posts. ¹⁹Then he spread the tent over the tabernacle and put the covering over the tent, as the LORD commanded him.

²⁰He took the Testimony and placed it in the ark, attached the poles to the ark and put the atonement cover over it. ²¹Then he brought the ark into the tabernacle and hung the shielding curtain and shielded the ark of the Testimony, as the LORD commanded him.

²²Moses placed the table in the Tent of Meeting on the north side of the tabernacle outside the curtain ²³and set out the bread on it before the LORD, as the LORD commanded him.

²⁴He placed the lampstand in the Tent of Meeting opposite the table on the south side of the tabernacle ²⁵and set up the lamps before the LORD, as the LORD commanded him.

²⁶Moses placed the gold altar in the Tent of Meeting in front of the curtain ²⁷and burned fragrant incense on it, as the LORD commanded him. ²⁸Then he put up the curtain at the entrance to the tabernacle.

²⁹He set the altar of burnt offering near the entrance to the tabernacle, the Tent of Meeting, and offered on it burnt offerings and grain offerings, as the LORD commanded him.

³⁰He placed the basin between the Tent of Meeting and the altar and put water in it for washing, ³¹and Moses and Aaron and his sons used it to wash their hands and feet. ³²They washed whenever they entered the Tent of Meeting or approached the altar, as the LORD commanded Moses.

³³Then Moses set up the courtyard around the tabernacle and altar and put up the curtain at the entrance to the courtyard. And so Moses finished the work.

e Glory of the Lord

³⁴Then the cloud covered the Tent of Meeting, and the glory of the Lord filled the
ɔernacle. ³⁵Moses could not enter the Tent of Meeting because the cloud had settled
₀on it, and the glory of the Lord filled the tabernacle.

³⁶In all the travels of the Israelites, whenever the cloud lifted from above the taberna-
ɛ, they would set out; ³⁷but if the cloud did not lift, they did not set out—until the day
lifted. ³⁸So the cloud of the Lord was over the tabernacle by day, and fire was in the
ɔud by night, in the sight of all the house of Israel during all their travels.

LEVITICUS

Introduction

THE BOTTOM LINE

This book outlines what God wanted his ancient people, the Israelites, to do to set themselves apart from the rest of the world. Since many of the laws in this book don't apply to our culture, reading Leviticus today requires taking a mental step back and looking at the historical picture. The message that comes through loud and clear is that people who choose to live as God desires will behave differently than those who close God out of their lives. While that may be difficult, doing so not only pleases God, but it also leads to unexpected benefits.

CENTRAL IDEAS

- God desires that his people be free from the harmful effects of sin and impurity.
- The Israelites were challenged to be fully devoted to God, not to try to fit God into a self-centered way of life.
- Sin needs to be forgiven by God; there is no other remedy for its damaging effects.
- Religious rituals are meaningless unless we have a genuine, sincere relationship with God.

OUTLINE

1. Five main offerings (chs. 1–7)
2. The work of the priests (chs. 8–10)
3. Laws of cleanness (chs. 11–15)
4. Repentance and worship (chs. 16–17)
5. Moral laws (chs. 18–20)
6. Regulations for priests (21:1–24:9)
7. Judicial codes (24:10–23)
8. Times set aside for God's wor (ch. 25)
9. Results of obedience and dis obedience (ch. 26)
10. Regulations for offerings (ch. 27)

TITLE

Leviticus comes from the name "Levites," a tribe of Israelites who took care of the priestl duties for the nation. This book contains a lot of "priestly" material.

AUTHOR AND READERS

Moses was probably the author of this book, which gives instructions for Israel's social and religious life.

Eighty percent of all new restaurants fail within five years. Those that succeed do so for two primary reasons—great food and superior service.

We all know where good food comes from—a skilled chef and quality ingredients. But what about good service?

One restaurateur who has opened over 150 thriving restaurants was asked the reason for his success. His answer? "It's very simple," he replied, "I believe the customer is the boss, and I build that value into our employees. Every greeter, server, busperson, cook, and manager knows that he or she is at work to serve the customer."

Upon entering one of this man's restaurants, customers are warmly greeted within seven seconds. They are then escorted to a room where every table is clean, silverware is spotless, and service is prompt and friendly.

"Every job is crucial—even washing dishes. If customers are impressed with everything else, you don't want them to find lettuce on a fork. Each customer must be treated with

"I'll be back!"

the same honor given a boss—because each one *is* the boss!" If customers receive that kind of treatment, upon leaving the restaurant they'll utter those three magic words, "I'll be back!"*

In a very real sense, this man's values are lived out through his employees. It's no surprise that every restaurant he has opened has succeeded.

God also wants to reveal his values to the world. He desires that those who don't know him will experience what he is like from how they are treated by his "employees"—his followers.

In the book of Leviticus, we find a code of conduct that expresses God's values and character. God gave the people of Israel that code so they would be "different"—more like God. As other nations saw the character of God's people, they would be able to make some conclusions about God himself. Like customers returning to fine restaurant, others would be drawn to find out more about Israel's God.

It is an undeniable fact of history—*people become like the god they worship.* It's true in all places at all times in every culture. It's even true of you and me right now. For a look at the kind of behavior that reveals the character of the true God, turn to Leviticus chapter 19, verses 1–37 (page 145).

*Used by permission of *Bob Farrell's Pickle Production, Inc.*

TIME LINE

Moses' life (c. 1526–1406 B.C.)		The exodus from Egypt (c. 1446 B.C.)	Israel camps at Mount Sinai (c. 1444 B.C.)	Iron age begins in Asia (1400 B.C.)
1525 B.C.	**1500**	**1475**	**1450**	**1425**	**1400**
	Volcanic eruption destroys Minoan civilization of 1600 (c. 1470 B.C.)	Key events of Leviticus occur (c.1445–1444 B.C.)	Book of Leviticus written (c. 1440 B.C.)	Clocks first used in Egypt (c. 1400 B.C.)

LEVITICUS

The Burnt Offering

1 The LORD called to Moses and spoke to him from the Tent of Meeting. He said, ²"Speak to the Israelites and say to them: 'When any of you brings an offering to the LORD, bring as your offering an animal from either the herd or the flock.

³" 'If the offering is a burnt offering from the herd, he is to offer a male without defect. He must present it at the entrance to the Tent of Meeting so that it[a] will be acceptable to the LORD. ⁴He is to lay his hand on the head of the burnt offering, and it will be accepted on his behalf to make atonement for him. ⁵He is to slaughter the young bull before the LORD, and then Aaron's sons the priests shall bring the blood and sprinkle it against the altar on all sides at the entrance to the Tent of Meeting. ⁶He is to skin the burnt offering and cut it into pieces. ⁷The sons of Aaron the priest are to put fire on the altar and arrange wood on the fire. ⁸Then Aaron's sons the priests shall arrange the pieces, including the head and the fat, on the burning wood that is on the altar. ⁹He is to wash the inner parts and the legs with water, and the priest is to burn all of it on the altar. It is a burnt offering, an offering made by fire, an aroma pleasing to the LORD.

¹⁰" 'If the offering is a burnt offering from the flock, from either the sheep or the goats, he is to offer a male without defect. ¹¹He is to slaughter it at the north side of the altar before the LORD, and Aaron's sons the priests shall sprinkle its blood against the altar on all sides. ¹²He is to cut it into pieces, and the priest shall arrange them, including the head and the fat, on the burning wood that is on the altar. ¹³He is to wash the inner parts and the legs with water, and the priest is to bring all of it and burn it on the altar. It is a burnt offering, an offering made by fire, an aroma pleasing to the LORD.

¹⁴" 'If the offering to the LORD is a burnt offering of birds, he is to offer a dove or a young pigeon. ¹⁵The priest shall bring it to the altar, wring off the head and burn it on the altar; its blood shall be drained out on the side of the altar. ¹⁶He is to remove the crop with its contents[b] and throw it to the east side of the altar, where the ashes are. ¹⁷He shall tear it open by the wings, not severing it completely, and then the priest shall burn it on the wood that is on the fire on the altar. It is a burnt offering, an offering made by fire, an aroma pleasing to the LORD.

┌─────────────────────────────────────┐
│ ▣ ▓▓▓▓ **ADDRESSING QUESTIONS** ▓▓▓▓ ⊟ │
│   │
│ **1:3–5**   ┌──┐ │
│ **God**   │ Q│ │
│   └──┘ │
│ Why did God command that animals be sac- │
│ rificed as an act of worship?   │
│   These detailed regulations for slaughtering │
│ animals may seem odd—if not repugnant—to │
│ most modern readers. But God never wanted │
│ these practices to be neat and clean. God │
│ wanted to remind his people that paying for │
│ the sin that comes between humans and God │
│ is messy, gruesome and costly.   │
│   Notice that sacrificial animals had to be │
│ "without defect." This directive contains a pro- │
│ found principle: sin—imperfection—has to be │
│ paid for with perfection. Wrongs can be made │
│ right only if they are completely paid for (that's │
│ what "atonement" [verse 4] means), and only │
│ a flawless sacrifice is acceptable to present in │
│ payment.   │
│   God provided a perfect sacrifice for all peo- │
│ ple when he offered his flawless Son, Jesus │
│ Christ, on the cross. Jesus is the fulfillment of │
│ the elaborate sacrificial system, and because │
│ of him we can now be forgiven once and for │
│ all (see Hebrews chapter 7, verse 27 [page │
│ 1591]).   │
└─────────────────────────────────────┘

---

a3 Or he   b16 Or crop and the feathers; the meaning of the Hebrew for this word is uncertain.

The Grain Offering

2 ¹ "'When someone brings a grain offering to the LORD, his offering is to be of fine flour. He is to pour oil on it, put incense on it ²and take it to Aaron's sons the priests. The priest shall take a handful of the fine flour and oil, together with all the incense, and burn this as a memorial portion on the altar, an offering made by fire, an aroma pleasing to the LORD. ³The rest of the grain offering belongs to Aaron and his sons; it is a most holy part of the offerings made to the LORD by fire.

⁴ "'If you bring a grain offering baked in an oven, it is to consist of fine flour: cakes made without yeast and mixed with oil, or*ᵃ* wafers made without yeast and spread with oil. ⁵If your grain offering is prepared on a griddle, it is to be made of fine flour mixed with oil, and without yeast. ⁶Crumble it and pour oil on it; it is a grain offering. ⁷If your grain offering is cooked in a pan, it is to be made of fine flour and oil. ⁸Bring the grain offering made of these things to the LORD; present it to the priest, who shall take it to the altar. ⁹He shall take out the memorial portion from the grain offering and burn it on the altar as an offering made by fire, an aroma pleasing to the LORD. ¹⁰The rest of the grain offering belongs to Aaron and his sons; it is a most holy part of the offerings made to the LORD by fire.

¹¹ "'Every grain offering you bring to the LORD must be made without yeast, for you are not to burn any yeast or honey in an offering made to the LORD by fire. ¹²You may bring them to the LORD as an offering of the firstfruits, but they are not to be offered on the altar as a pleasing aroma. ¹³Season all your grain offerings with salt. Do not leave the salt of the covenant of your God out of your grain offerings; add salt to all your offerings.

¹⁴ "'If you bring a grain offering of firstfruits to the LORD, offer crushed heads of new grain roasted in the fire. ¹⁵Put oil and incense on it; it is a grain offering. ¹⁶The priest shall burn the memorial portion of the crushed grain and the oil, together with all the incense, as an offering made to the LORD by fire.

The Fellowship Offering

3 ¹ "'If someone's offering is a fellowship offering,*ᵇ* and he offers an animal from the herd, whether male or female, he is to present before the LORD an animal without defect. ²He is to lay his hand on the head of his offering and slaughter it at the entrance to the Tent of Meeting. Then Aaron's sons the priests shall sprinkle the blood against the altar on all sides. ³From the fellowship offering he is to bring a sacrifice made to the LORD by fire: all the fat that covers the inner parts or is connected to them, ⁴both kidneys with the fat on them near the loins, and the covering of the liver, which he will remove with the kidneys. ⁵Then Aaron's sons are to burn it on the altar on top of the burnt offering that is on the burning wood, as an offering made by fire, an aroma pleasing to the LORD.

⁶ "'If he offers an animal from the flock as a fellowship offering to the LORD, he is to offer a male or female without defect. ⁷If he offers a lamb, he is to present it before the LORD. ⁸He is to lay his hand on the head of his offering and slaughter it in front of the Tent of Meeting. Then Aaron's sons shall sprinkle its blood against the altar on all sides. ⁹From the fellowship offering he is to bring a sacrifice made to the LORD by fire: its fat, the entire fat tail cut off close to the backbone, all the fat that covers the inner parts or is connected to them, ¹⁰both kidneys with the fat on them near the loins, and the covering of the liver, which he will remove with the kidneys. ¹¹The priest shall burn them on the altar as food, an offering made to the LORD by fire.

¹² "'If his offering is a goat, he is to present it before the LORD. ¹³He is to lay his hand on its head and slaughter it in front of the Tent of Meeting. Then Aaron's sons shall sprinkle its blood against the altar on all sides. ¹⁴From what he offers he is to make this offering to the LORD by fire: all the fat that covers the inner parts or is connected to them, ¹⁵both

---

ᵃ4 Or *and*   *ᵇ1* Traditionally *peace offering*; also in verses 3, 6 and 9

kidneys with the fat on them near the loins, and the covering of the liver, which he will remove with the kidneys. ¹⁶The priest shall burn them on the altar as food, an offering made by fire, a pleasing aroma. All the fat is the LORD's.

¹⁷"'This is a lasting ordinance for the generations to come, wherever you live: You must not eat any fat or any blood.'"

The Sin Offering

4 The LORD said to Moses, ²"Say to the Israelites: 'When anyone sins unintentionally and does what is forbidden in any of the LORD's commands—

³"'If the anointed priest sins, bringing guilt on the people, he must bring to the LORD a young bull without defect as a sin offering for the sin he has committed. ⁴He is to present the bull at the entrance to the Tent of Meeting before the LORD. He is to lay his hand on its head and slaughter it before the LORD. ⁵Then the anointed priest shall take some of the bull's blood and carry it into the Tent of Meeting. ⁶He is to dip his finger into the blood and sprinkle some of it seven times before the LORD, in front of the curtain of the sanctuary. ⁷The priest shall then put some of the blood on the horns of the altar of fragrant incense that is before the LORD in the Tent of Meeting. The rest of the bull's blood he shall pour out at the base of the altar of burnt offering at the entrance to the Tent of Meeting. ⁸He shall remove all the fat from the bull of the sin offering—the fat that covers the inner parts or is connected to them, ⁹both kidneys with the fat on them near the loins, and the covering of the liver, which he will remove with the kidneys— ¹⁰just as the fat is removed from the ox ᵃ sacrificed as a fellowship offering.ᵇ Then the anointed priest shall burn them on the altar of burnt offering. ¹¹But the hide of the bull and all its flesh, as well as the head and legs, the inner parts and offal— ¹²that is, all the rest of the bull—he must take outside the camp to a place ceremonially clean, where the ashes are thrown, and burn it in a wood fire on the ash heap.

¹³"'If the whole Israelite community sins unintentionally and does what is forbidden in any of the LORD's commands, even though the community is unaware of the matter, they are guilty. ¹⁴When they become aware of the sin they committed, the assembly must bring a young bull as a sin offering and present it before the Tent of Meeting. ¹⁵The elders of the community are to lay their hands on the bull's head before the LORD, and the bull shall be slaughtered before the LORD. ¹⁶Then the anointed priest is to take some of the bull's blood into the Tent of Meeting. ¹⁷He shall dip his finger into the blood and sprinkle it before the LORD seven times in front of the curtain. ¹⁸He is to put some of the blood on the horns of the altar that is before the LORD in the Tent of Meeting. The rest of the blood he shall pour out at the base of the altar of burnt offering at the entrance to the Tent of Meeting. ¹⁹He shall remove all the fat from it and burn it on the altar, ²⁰and do with this bull just as he did with the bull for the sin offering. In this way the priest will make atonement for them, and they will be forgiven. ²¹Then he shall take the bull outside the camp and burn it as he burned the first bull. This is the sin offering for the community.

²²"'When a leader sins unintentionally and does what is forbidden in any of the commands of the LORD his God, he is guilty. ²³When he is made aware of the sin he committed, he must bring as his offering a male goat without defect. ²⁴He is to lay his hand on the goat's head and slaughter it at the place where the burnt offering is slaughtered before the LORD. It is a sin offering. ²⁵Then the priest shall take some of the blood of the sin offering with his finger and put it on the horns of the altar of burnt offering and pour out the rest of the blood at the base of the altar. ²⁶He shall burn all the fat on the altar as he burned the fat of the fellowship offering. In this way the priest will make atonement for the man's sin, and he will be forgiven.

²⁷"'If a member of the community sins unintentionally and does what is forbidden in

---

ᵃ10 The Hebrew word can include both male and female.   ᵇ10 Traditionally peace offering; also in verses 26, 31 and 35

any of the LORD's commands, he is guilty. ²⁸When he is made aware of the sin he committed, he must bring as his offering for the sin he committed a female goat without defect. ²⁹He is to lay his hand on the head of the sin offering and slaughter it at the place of the burnt offering. ³⁰Then the priest is to take some of the blood with his finger and put it on the horns of the altar of burnt offering and pour out the rest of the blood at the base of the altar. ³¹He shall remove all the fat, just as the fat is removed from the fellowship offering, and the priest shall burn it on the altar as an aroma pleasing to the LORD. In this way the priest will make atonement for him, and he will be forgiven.

³²"'If he brings a lamb as his sin offering, he is to bring a female without defect. ³³He is to lay his hand on its head and slaughter it for a sin offering at the place where the

---

▤ KNOWING YOURSELF ◪

4:1–35
Sin

During moments of quiet reflection, most of us realize we've said and done things that we don't want anyone else to know about. We're often ashamed of ourselves. We don't tell anyone about these episodes, because it doesn't seem possible that anyone else could understand our actions. Usually, we wouldn't even want anyone to try.

Shame is a powerful force in our lives. Sometimes it produces pain, which we try to deaden with alcohol, drugs, sex, overwork, overeating, gambling or a host of other numbing behaviors. Shame also hinders us from making intimate connections with other people—even those we love. It tells us, "Keep those inner struggles locked up, or people will think you're really odd!"

And what about God? Well, if other people have a hard time accepting our dark side, we surely can't expect that God will! Keeping our distance from him, then, seems to make sense.

Or does it? God created humans to live in relationship with each other and with him. Sin and shame lead to disconnection—from ourselves, from other people, and from God. The only way to restore our relationships—and to get out of that isolation—is to remove the barrier between ourselves and others. The following story illustrates sin's effect on our lives.

A man once spotted an expensive fountain pen on his coworker's desk. When the other man wasn't looking, he slipped the pen into his shirt pocket. A moment later the coworker turned around and reached for the pen. Noticing it was gone, he asked, "Have you seen my pen?"

"No, I haven't," the guilty man replied.

"Then what's that blue stain on your shirt pocket?"

Realizing he had been caught, the man sheepishly pulled the leaky pen from his pocket and handed it over. Even though the two spoke words of regret followed by words of forgiveness, the stain remained as a reminder of the man's greed. He couldn't hide it, and no washing removed it.

The Bible says that sin leaves a stain on our soul. Even if we admit our guilt, what do we do about the stain? How do we restore the broken relationship between us and God?

In this chapter we find that when the ancient Israelites sinned against God, they were commanded to offer an animal sacrifice. That seems strange to us today. Why would God prescribe the killing of an animal, when human sin was the issue?

God mandated such sacrifices to show his people the seriousness of what they'd done. By offering valuable animals up for sacrifice, the Israelites recognized that God accepted animal life as payment on their behalf. Animal sacrifices dealt with guilt only temporarily, however, which is why they had to be offered over and over again. But these sacrifices prepared Israel for the coming of Jesus Christ.

Because Jesus is the perfect Son of God (on earth he was both God and man), his sacrifice paid for our guilt once and for all. He gave his life not just for one sin, but for every sin ever committed. Through his death and shed blood, our guilt is not only covered, it's washed away. (See John chapter 1, verse 29 [page 1383] to read what one man said when he saw Jesus.)

As you try to understand this sacrificial procedure that God mandated for the ancient Israelites, keep in mind its important future significance. Animal sacrifice was a model of what a gracious God would do to solve the problem of human shame once and for all, restoring our relationship with him and with one another.

burnt offering is slaughtered. ³⁴Then the priest shall take some of the blood of the sin offering with his finger and put it on the horns of the altar of burnt offering and pour out the rest of the blood at the base of the altar. ³⁵He shall remove all the fat, just as the fat is removed from the lamb of the fellowship offering, and the priest shall burn it on the altar on top of the offerings made to the Lᴏʀᴅ by fire. In this way the priest will make atonement for him for the sin he has committed, and he will be forgiven.

5 "'If a person sins because he does not speak up when he hears a public charge to testify regarding something he has seen or learned about, he will be held responsible.

²"'Or if a person touches anything ceremonially unclean—whether the carcasses of unclean wild animals or of unclean livestock or of unclean creatures that move along the ground—even though he is unaware of it, he has become unclean and is guilty.

³"'Or if he touches human uncleanness—anything that would make him unclean—even though he is unaware of it, when he learns of it he will be guilty.

⁴"'Or if a person thoughtlessly takes an oath to do anything, whether good or evil—in any matter one might carelessly swear about—even though he is unaware of it, in any case when he learns of it he will be guilty.

⁵"'When anyone is guilty in any of these ways, he must confess in what way he has sinned ⁶and, as a penalty for the sin he has committed, he must bring to the Lᴏʀᴅ a female lamb or goat from the flock as a sin offering; and the priest shall make atonement for him for his sin.

⁷"'If he cannot afford a lamb, he is to bring two doves or two young pigeons to the Lᴏʀᴅ as a penalty for his sin—one for a sin offering and the other for a burnt offering. ⁸He is to bring them to the priest, who shall first offer the one for the sin offering. He is to wring its head from its neck, not severing it completely, ⁹and is to sprinkle some of the blood of the sin offering against the side of the altar; the rest of the blood must be drained out at the base of the altar. It is a sin offering. ¹⁰The priest shall then offer the other as a burnt offering in the prescribed way and make atonement for him for the sin he has committed, and he will be forgiven.

¹¹"'If, however, he cannot afford two doves or two young pigeons, he is to bring as an offering for his sin a tenth of an ephah*ᵃ* of fine flour for a sin offering. He must not put oil or incense on it, because it is a sin offering. ¹²He is to bring it to the priest, who shall take a handful of it as a memorial portion and burn it on the altar on top of the offerings made to the Lᴏʀᴅ by fire. It is a sin offering. ¹³In this way the priest will make atonement for him for any of these sins he has committed, and he will be forgiven. The rest of the offering will belong to the priest, as in the case of the grain offering.'"

The Guilt Offering

¹⁴The Lᴏʀᴅ said to Moses: ¹⁵"When a person commits a violation and sins unintentionally in regard to any of the Lᴏʀᴅ's holy things, he is to bring to the Lᴏʀᴅ as a penalty a ram from the flock, one without defect and of the proper value in silver, according to the sanctuary shekel.ᵇ It is a guilt offering. ¹⁶He must make restitution for what he has failed to do in regard to the holy things, add a fifth of the value to that and give it all to the priest, who will make atonement for him with the ram as a guilt offering, and he will be forgiven.

¹⁷If a person sins and does what is forbidden in any of the Lᴏʀᴅ's commands, even though he does not know it, he is guilty and will be held responsible. ¹⁸He is to bring to the priest as a guilt offering a ram from the flock, one without defect and of the proper value. In this way the priest will make atonement for him for the wrong he has commit-

---

ᵃ 11 That is, probably about 2 quarts (about 2 liters)   ᵇ 15 That is, about 2/5 ounce (about 11.5 grams)

ted unintentionally, and he will be forgiven. ¹⁹It is a guilt offering; he has been guilty of[a] wrongdoing against the LORD."

6 The LORD said to Moses: ²"If anyone sins and is unfaithful to the LORD by deceiving his neighbor about something entrusted to him or left in his care or stolen, or if he cheats him, ³or if he finds lost property and lies about it, or if he swears falsely, or if he commits any such sin that people may do— ⁴when he thus sins and becomes guilty, he must return what he has stolen or taken by extortion, or what was entrusted to him, or the lost property he found, ⁵or whatever it was he swore falsely about. He must make restitution in full, add a fifth of the value to it and give it all to the owner on the day he presents his guilt offering. ⁶And as a penalty he must bring to the priest, that is, to the LORD, his guilt offering, a ram from the flock, one without defect and of the proper value. ⁷In this way the priest will make atonement for him before the LORD, and he will be forgiven for any of these things he did that made him guilty."

The Burnt Offering

⁸The LORD said to Moses: ⁹"Give Aaron and his sons this command: 'These are the regulations for the burnt offering: The burnt offering is to remain on the altar hearth throughout the night, till morning, and the fire must be kept burning on the altar. ¹⁰The priest shall then put on his linen clothes, with linen undergarments next to his body, and shall remove the ashes of the burnt offering that the fire has consumed on the altar and place them beside the altar. ¹¹Then he is to take off these clothes and put on others, and carry the ashes outside the camp to a place that is ceremonially clean. ¹²The fire on the altar must be kept burning; it must not go out. Every morning the priest is to add firewood and arrange the burnt offering on the fire and burn the fat of the fellowship offerings[b] on it. ¹³The fire must be kept burning on the altar continuously; it must not go out.

The Grain Offering

¹⁴" 'These are the regulations for the grain offering: Aaron's sons are to bring it before the LORD, in front of the altar. ¹⁵The priest is to take a handful of fine flour and oil, together with all the incense on the grain offering, and burn the memorial portion on the altar as an aroma pleasing to the LORD. ¹⁶Aaron and his sons shall eat the rest of it, but it is to be eaten without yeast in a holy place; they are to eat it in the courtyard of the Tent of Meeting. ¹⁷It must not be baked with yeast; I have given it as their share of the offerings made to me by fire. Like the sin offering and the guilt offering, it is most holy. ¹⁸Any male descendant of Aaron may eat it. It is his regular share of the offerings made to the LORD by fire for the generations to come. Whatever touches them will become holy.[c] "

¹⁹The LORD also said to Moses, ²⁰"This is the offering Aaron and his sons are to bring to the LORD on the day he[d] is anointed: a tenth of an ephah[e] of fine flour as a regular grain offering, half of it in the morning and half in the evening. ²¹Prepare it with oil on a griddle; bring it well-mixed and present the grain offering broken[f] in pieces as an aroma pleasing to the LORD. ²²The son who is to succeed him as anointed priest shall prepare it. It is the LORD's regular share and is to be burned completely. ²³Every grain offering of a priest shall be burned completely; it must not be eaten."

The Sin Offering

²⁴The LORD said to Moses, ²⁵"Say to Aaron and his sons: 'These are the regulations for the sin offering: The sin offering is to be slaughtered before the LORD in the place the burnt offering is slaughtered; it is most holy. ²⁶The priest who offers it shall eat it; it is to

---

a 19 Or has made full expiation for his similarly in verse 27   d 20 Or each Hebrew for this word is uncertain.   b 12 Traditionally peace offerings   c 18 Or Whoever touches them must be holy; e 20 That is, probably about 2 quarts (about 2 liters)   f 21 The meaning of the

be eaten in a holy place, in the courtyard of the Tent of Meeting. ²⁷Whatever touches any of the flesh will become holy, and if any of the blood is spattered on a garment, you must wash it in a holy place. ²⁸The clay pot the meat is cooked in must be broken; but if it is cooked in a bronze pot, the pot is to be scoured and rinsed with water. ²⁹Any male in a priest's family may eat it; it is most holy. ³⁰But any sin offering whose blood is brought into the Tent of Meeting to make atonement in the Holy Place must not be eaten; it must be burned.

The Guilt Offering

7 "'These are the regulations for the guilt offering, which is most holy: ²The guilt offering is to be slaughtered in the place where the burnt offering is slaughtered, and its blood is to be sprinkled against the altar on all sides. ³All its fat shall be offered: the fat tail and the fat that covers the inner parts, ⁴both kidneys with the fat on them near the loins, and the covering of the liver, which is to be removed with the kidneys. ⁵The priest shall burn them on the altar as an offering made to the LORD by fire. It is a guilt offering. ⁶Any male in a priest's family may eat it, but it must be eaten in a holy place; it is most holy.

⁷"'The same law applies to both the sin offering and the guilt offering: They belong to the priest who makes atonement with them. ⁸The priest who offers a burnt offering for anyone may keep its hide for himself. ⁹Every grain offering baked in an oven or cooked in a pan or on a griddle belongs to the priest who offers it, ¹⁰and every grain offering, whether mixed with oil or dry, belongs equally to all the sons of Aaron.

The Fellowship Offering

¹¹"'These are the regulations for the fellowship offering*a* a person may present to the LORD:

¹²"'If he offers it as an expression of thankfulness, then along with this thank offering he is to offer cakes of bread made without yeast and mixed with oil, wafers made without yeast and spread with oil, and cakes of fine flour well-kneaded and mixed with oil. ¹³Along with his fellowship offering of thanksgiving he is to present an offering with cakes of bread made with yeast. ¹⁴He is to bring one of each kind as an offering, a contribution to the LORD; it belongs to the priest who sprinkles the blood of the fellowship offerings. ¹⁵The meat of his fellowship offering of thanksgiving must be eaten on the day it is offered; he must leave none of it till morning.

¹⁶"'If, however, his offering is the result of a vow or is a freewill offering, the sacrifice shall be eaten on the day he offers it, but anything left over may be eaten on the next day. ¹⁷Any meat of the sacrifice left over till the third day must be burned up. ¹⁸If any meat of the fellowship offering is eaten on the third day, it will not be accepted. It will not be credited to the one who offered it, for it is impure; the person who eats any of it will be held responsible.

¹⁹"'Meat that touches anything ceremonially unclean must not be eaten; it must be burned up. As for other meat, anyone ceremonially clean may eat it. ²⁰But if anyone who is unclean eats any meat of the fellowship offering belonging to the LORD, that person must be cut off from his people. ²¹If anyone touches something unclean—whether human uncleanness or an unclean animal or any unclean, detestable thing—and then eats any of the meat of the fellowship offering belonging to the LORD, that person must be cut off from his people.'"

Eating Fat and Blood Forbidden

²²The LORD said to Moses, ²³"Say to the Israelites: 'Do not eat any of the fat of cattle, sheep or goats. ²⁴The fat of an animal found dead or torn by wild animals may be used for any other purpose, but you must not eat it. ²⁵Anyone who eats the fat of an animal

a 11 Traditionally peace offering; also in verses 13-37

from which an offering by fire may be^a made to the LORD must be cut off from his people. ^{26}And wherever you live, you must not eat the blood of any bird or animal. ^{27}If anyone eats blood, that person must be cut off from his people.'"

The Priests' Share

^{28}The LORD said to Moses, ^{29}"Say to the Israelites: 'Anyone who brings a fellowship offering to the LORD is to bring part of it as his sacrifice to the LORD. ^{30}With his own hands he is to bring the offering made to the LORD by fire; he is to bring the fat, together with the breast, and wave the breast before the LORD as a wave offering. ^{31}The priest shall burn the fat on the altar, but the breast belongs to Aaron and his sons. ^{32}You are to give the right thigh of your fellowship offerings to the priest as a contribution. ^{33}The son of Aaron who offers the blood and the fat of the fellowship offering shall have the right thigh as his share. ^{34}From the fellowship offerings of the Israelites, I have taken the breast that is waved and the thigh that is presented and have given them to Aaron the priest and his sons as their regular share from the Israelites.'"

^{35}This is the portion of the offerings made to the LORD by fire that were allotted to Aaron and his sons on the day they were presented to serve the LORD as priests. ^{36}On the day they were anointed, the LORD commanded that the Israelites give this to them as their regular share for the generations to come.

^{37}These, then, are the regulations for the burnt offering, the grain offering, the sin offering, the guilt offering, the ordination offering and the fellowship offering, ^{38}which the LORD gave Moses on Mount Sinai on the day he commanded the Israelites to bring their offerings to the LORD, in the Desert of Sinai.

The Ordination of Aaron and His Sons

8 The LORD said to Moses, ^{2}"Bring Aaron and his sons, their garments, the anointing oil, the bull for the sin offering, the two rams and the basket containing bread made without yeast, ^{3}and gather the entire assembly at the entrance to the Tent of Meeting." ^{4}Moses did as the LORD commanded him, and the assembly gathered at the entrance to the Tent of Meeting.

^{5}Moses said to the assembly, "This is what the LORD has commanded to be done." ^{6}Then Moses brought Aaron and his sons forward and washed them with water. ^{7}He put the tunic on Aaron, tied the sash around him, clothed him with the robe and put the ephod on him. He also tied the ephod to him by its skillfully woven waistband; so it was fastened on him. ^{8}He placed the breastpiece on him and put the Urim and Thummim in the breastpiece. ^{9}Then he placed the turban on Aaron's head and set the gold plate, the sacred diadem, on the front of it, as the LORD commanded Moses.

^{10}Then Moses took the anointing oil and anointed the tabernacle and everything in it, and so consecrated them. ^{11}He sprinkled some of the oil on the altar seven times, anointing the altar and all its utensils and the basin with its stand, to consecrate them. ^{12}He poured some of the anointing oil on Aaron's head and anointed him to consecrate him. ^{13}Then he brought Aaron's sons forward, put tunics on them, tied sashes around them and put headbands on them, as the LORD commanded Moses.

^{14}He then presented the bull for the sin offering, and Aaron and his sons laid their hands on its head. ^{15}Moses slaughtered the bull and took some of the blood, and with his finger he put it on all the horns of the altar to purify the altar. He poured out the rest of the blood at the base of the altar. So he consecrated it to make atonement for it. ^{16}Moses also took all the fat around the inner parts, the covering of the liver, and both kidneys and their fat, and burned it on the altar. ^{17}But the bull with its hide and its flesh and its offal he burned up outside the camp, as the LORD commanded Moses.

^{18}He then presented the ram for the burnt offering, and Aaron and his sons laid their

---

$^a25$ Or *fire is*

hands on its head. [19]Then Moses slaughtered the ram and sprinkled the blood against the altar on all sides. [20]He cut the ram into pieces and burned the head, the pieces and the fat. [21]He washed the inner parts and the legs with water and burned the whole ram on the altar as a burnt offering, a pleasing aroma, an offering made to the LORD by fire, as the LORD commanded Moses.

[22]He then presented the other ram, the ram for the ordination, and Aaron and his sons laid their hands on its head. [23]Moses slaughtered the ram and took some of its blood and put it on the lobe of Aaron's right ear, on the thumb of his right hand and on the big toe of his right foot. [24]Moses also brought Aaron's sons forward and put some of the blood on the lobes of their right ears, on the thumbs of their right hands and on the big toes of their right feet. Then he sprinkled blood against the altar on all sides. [25]He took the fat, the fat tail, all the fat around the inner parts, the covering of the liver, both kidneys and their fat and the right thigh. [26]Then from the basket of bread made without yeast, which was before the LORD, he took a cake of bread, and one made with oil, and a wafer; he put these on the fat portions and on the right thigh. [27]He put all these in the hands of Aaron and his sons and waved them before the LORD as a wave offering. [28]Then Moses took them from their hands and burned them on the altar on top of the burnt offering as an ordination offering, a pleasing aroma, an offering made to the LORD by fire. [29]He also took the breast—Moses' share of the ordination ram—and waved it before the LORD as a wave offering, as the LORD commanded Moses.

[30]Then Moses took some of the anointing oil and some of the blood from the altar and sprinkled them on Aaron and his garments and on his sons and their garments. So he consecrated Aaron and his garments and his sons and their garments.

[31]Moses then said to Aaron and his sons, "Cook the meat at the entrance to the Tent of Meeting and eat it there with the bread from the basket of ordination offerings, as I commanded, saying,[a] 'Aaron and his sons are to eat it.' [32]Then burn up the rest of the meat and the bread. [33]Do not leave the entrance to the Tent of Meeting for seven days, until the days of your ordination are completed, for your ordination will last seven days. [34]What has been done today was commanded by the LORD to make atonement for you. [35]You must stay at the entrance to the Tent of Meeting day and night for seven days and do what the LORD requires, so you will not die; for that is what I have been commanded." [36]So Aaron and his sons did everything the LORD commanded through Moses.

The Priests Begin Their Ministry

9 On the eighth day Moses summoned Aaron and his sons and the elders of Israel. [2]He said to Aaron, "Take a bull calf for your sin offering and a ram for your burnt offering, both without defect, and present them before the LORD. [3]Then say to the Israelites: 'Take a male goat for a sin offering, a calf and a lamb—both a year old and without defect—for a burnt offering, [4]and an ox[b] and a ram for a fellowship offering[c] to sacrifice before the LORD, together with a grain offering mixed with oil. For today the LORD will appear to you.'"

[5]They took the things Moses commanded to the front of the Tent of Meeting, and the entire assembly came near and stood before the LORD. [6]Then Moses said, "This is what the LORD has commanded you to do, so that the glory of the LORD may appear to you."

[7]Moses said to Aaron, "Come to the altar and sacrifice your sin offering and your burnt offering and make atonement for yourself and the people; sacrifice the offering that is for the people and make atonement for them, as the LORD has commanded."

[8]So Aaron came to the altar and slaughtered the calf as a sin offering for himself. [9]His sons brought the blood to him, and he dipped his finger into the blood and put it on the horns of the altar; the rest of the blood he poured out at the base of the altar. [10]On the

---

[a]31 Or I was commanded;   [b]4 The Hebrew word can include both male and female; also in verses 18 and 19.
[c]4 Traditionally peace offering; also in verses 18 and 22

altar he burned the fat, the kidneys and the covering of the liver from the sin offering, as the LORD commanded Moses; [11]the flesh and the hide he burned up outside the camp.

[12]Then he slaughtered the burnt offering. His sons handed him the blood, and he sprinkled it against the altar on all sides. [13]They handed him the burnt offering piece by piece, including the head, and he burned them on the altar. [14]He washed the inner parts and the legs and burned them on top of the burnt offering on the altar.

[15]Aaron then brought the offering that was for the people. He took the goat for the people's sin offering and slaughtered it and offered it for a sin offering as he did with the first one.

[16]He brought the burnt offering and offered it in the prescribed way. [17]He also brought the grain offering, took a handful of it and burned it on the altar in addition to the morning's burnt offering.

[18]He slaughtered the ox and the ram as the fellowship offering for the people. His sons handed him the blood, and he sprinkled it against the altar on all sides. [19]But the fat portions of the ox and the ram—the fat tail, the layer of fat, the kidneys and the covering of the liver— [20]these they laid on the breasts, and then Aaron burned the fat on the altar. [21]Aaron waved the breasts and the right thigh before the LORD as a wave offering, as Moses commanded.

[22]Then Aaron lifted his hands toward the people and blessed them. And having sacrificed the sin offering, the burnt offering and the fellowship offering, he stepped down.

[23]Moses and Aaron then went into the Tent of Meeting. When they came out, they blessed the people; and the glory of the LORD appeared to all the people. [24]Fire came out from the presence of the LORD and consumed the burnt offering and the fat portions on the altar. And when all the people saw it, they shouted for joy and fell facedown.

The Death of Nadab and Abihu

10 Aaron's sons Nadab and Abihu took their censers, put fire in them and added incense; and they offered unauthorized fire before the LORD, contrary to his command. [2]So fire came out from the presence of the LORD and consumed them, and they died before the LORD. [3]Moses then said to Aaron, "This is what the LORD spoke of when he said:

> "'Among those who approach me
> I will show myself holy;
> in the sight of all the people
> I will be honored.'"

Aaron remained silent.

[4]Moses summoned Mishael and Elzaphan, sons of Aaron's uncle Uzziel, and said to them, "Come here; carry your cousins outside the camp, away from the front of the

---

sanctuary." ⁵So they came and carried them, still in their tunics, outside the camp, as Moses ordered.

⁶Then Moses said to Aaron and his sons Eleazar and Ithamar, "Do not let your hair become unkempt,ᵃ and do not tear your clothes, or you will die and the LORD will be angry with the whole community. But your relatives, all the house of Israel, may mourn for those the LORD has destroyed by fire. ⁷Do not leave the entrance to the Tent of Meeting or you will die, because the LORD's anointing oil is on you." So they did as Moses said.

⁸Then the LORD said to Aaron, ⁹"You and your sons are not to drink wine or other fermented drink whenever you go into the Tent of Meeting, or you will die. This is a lasting ordinance for the generations to come. ¹⁰You must distinguish between the holy and the common, between the unclean and the clean, ¹¹and you must teach the Israelites all the decrees the LORD has given them through Moses."

¹²Moses said to Aaron and his remaining sons, Eleazar and Ithamar, "Take the grain offering left over from the offerings made to the LORD by fire and eat it prepared without yeast beside the altar, for it is most holy. ¹³Eat it in a holy place, because it is your share and your sons' share of the offerings made to the LORD by fire; for so I have been commanded. ¹⁴But you and your sons and your daughters may eat the breast that was waved and the thigh that was presented. Eat them in a ceremonially clean place; they have been given to you and your children as your share of the Israelites' fellowship offerings.ᵇ ¹⁵The thigh that was presented and the breast that was waved must be brought with the fat portions of the offerings made by fire, to be waved before the LORD as a wave offering. This will be the regular share for you and your children, as the LORD has commanded."

¹⁶When Moses inquired about the goat of the sin offering and found that it had been burned up, he was angry with Eleazar and Ithamar, Aaron's remaining sons, and asked, ¹⁷"Why didn't you eat the sin offering in the sanctuary area? It is most holy; it was given to you to take away the guilt of the community by making atonement for them before the LORD. ¹⁸Since its blood was not taken into the Holy Place, you should have eaten the goat in the sanctuary area, as I commanded."

¹⁹Aaron replied to Moses, "Today they sacrificed their sin offering and their burnt offering before the LORD, but such things as this have happened to me. Would the LORD have been pleased if I had eaten the sin offering today?" ²⁰When Moses heard this, he was satisfied.

Clean and Unclean Food

11 The LORD said to Moses and Aaron, ²"Say to the Israelites: 'Of all the animals that live on land, these are the ones you may eat: ³You may eat any animal that has a split hoof completely divided and that chews the cud.

⁴"'There are some that only chew the cud or only have a split hoof, but you must not eat them. The camel, though it chews the cud, does not have a split hoof; it is ceremonially unclean for you. ⁵The coney,ᶜ though it chews the cud, does not have a split hoof; it is unclean for you. ⁶The rabbit, though it chews the cud, does not have a split hoof; it is unclean for you. ⁷And the pig, though it has a split hoof completely divided, does not chew the cud; it is unclean for you. ⁸You must not eat their meat or touch their carcasses; they are unclean for you.

⁹"'Of all the creatures living in the water of the seas and the streams, you may eat any that have fins and scales. ¹⁰But all creatures in the seas or streams that do not have fins and scales—whether among all the swarming things or among all the other living creatures in the water—you are to detest. ¹¹And since you are to detest them, you must not eat their meat and you must detest their carcasses. ¹²Anything living in the water that does not have fins and scales is to be detestable to you.

¹³"'These are the birds you are to detest and not eat because they are detestable: the

---

ᵃ 6 Or *Do not uncover your heads*   ᵇ 14 Traditionally *peace offerings*   ᶜ 5 That is, the hyrax or rock badger eagle, the vulture, the black vulture, **14**the red kite, any kind of black kite, **15**any kind of raven, **16**the horned owl, the screech owl, the gull, any kind of hawk, **17**the little owl, the cormorant, the great owl, **18**the white owl, the desert owl, the osprey, **19**the stork, any kind of heron, the hoopoe and the bat.*ᵃ*

20" 'All flying insects that walk on all fours are to be detestable to you. **21**There are, however, some winged creatures that walk on all fours that you may eat: those that have jointed legs for hopping on the ground. **22**Of these you may eat any kind of locust, katydid, cricket or grasshopper. **23**But all other winged creatures that have four legs you are to detest.

24" 'You will make yourselves unclean by these; whoever touches their carcasses will be unclean till evening. **25**Whoever picks up one of their carcasses must wash his clothes, and he will be unclean till evening.

26" 'Every animal that has a split hoof not completely divided or that does not chew the cud is unclean for you; whoever touches ⸢the carcass of⸣ any of them will be unclean. **27**Of all the animals that walk on all fours, those that walk on their paws are unclean for you; whoever touches their carcasses will be unclean till evening. **28**Anyone who picks up their carcasses must wash his clothes, and he will be unclean till evening. They are unclean for you.

29" 'Of the animals that move about on the ground, these are unclean for you: the weasel, the rat, any kind of great lizard, **30**the gecko, the monitor lizard, the wall lizard, the skink and the chameleon. **31**Of all those that move along the ground, these are unclean for you. Whoever touches them when they are dead will be unclean till evening. **32**When one of them dies and falls on something, that article, whatever its use, will be unclean, whether it is made of wood, cloth, hide or sackcloth. Put it in water; it will be unclean till evening, and then it will be clean. **33**If one of them falls into a clay pot, everything in it will be unclean, and you must break the pot. **34**Any food that could be eaten but has water on it from such a pot is unclean, and any liquid that could be drunk from it is unclean. **35**Anything that one of their carcasses falls on becomes unclean; an oven or cooking pot must be broken up. They are unclean, and you are to regard them as unclean. **36**A spring, however, or a cistern for collecting water remains clean, but anyone who touches one of these carcasses is unclean. **37**If a carcass falls on any seeds that are to be planted, they remain clean. **38**But if water has been put on the seed and a carcass falls on it, it is unclean for you.

39" 'If an animal that you are allowed to eat dies, anyone who touches the carcass will be unclean till evening. **40**Anyone who eats some of the carcass must wash his clothes, and he will be unclean till evening. Anyone who picks up the carcass must wash his clothes, and he will be unclean till evening.

41" 'Every creature that moves about on the ground is detestable; it is not to be eaten. **42**You are not to eat any creature that moves about on the ground, whether it moves on its belly or walks on all fours or on many feet; it is detestable. **43**Do not defile yourselves by any of these creatures. Do not make yourselves unclean by means of them or be made unclean by them. **44**I am the LORD your God; consecrate yourselves and be holy, because I am holy. Do not make yourselves unclean by any creature that moves about on the ground. **45**I am the LORD who brought you up out of Egypt to be your God; therefore be holy, because I am holy.

46" 'These are the regulations concerning animals, birds, every living thing that moves in the water and every creature that moves about on the ground. **47**You must distinguish between the unclean and the clean, between living creatures that may be eaten and those that may not be eaten.' "

ᵃ 19 The precise identification of some of the birds, insects and animals in this chapter is uncertain.

Purification After Childbirth

12 The LORD said to Moses, [2]"Say to the Israelites: 'A woman who becomes pregnant and gives birth to a son will be ceremonially unclean for seven days, just as she is unclean during her monthly period. [3]On the eighth day the boy is to be circumcised. [4]Then the woman must wait thirty-three days to be purified from her bleeding. She must not touch anything sacred or go to the sanctuary until the days of her purification are over. [5]If she gives birth to a daughter, for two weeks the woman will be unclean, as during her period. Then she must wait sixty-six days to be purified from her bleeding.

[6]"'When the days of her purification for a son or daughter are over, she is to bring to the priest at the entrance to the Tent of Meeting a year-old lamb for a burnt offering and a young pigeon or a dove for a sin offering. [7]He shall offer them before the LORD to make atonement for her, and then she will be ceremonially clean from her flow of blood.

[8]"'These are the regulations for the woman who gives birth to a boy or a girl. [8]If she cannot afford a lamb, she is to bring two doves or two young pigeons, one for a burnt offering and the other for a sin offering. In this way the priest will make atonement for her, and she will be clean.'"

Regulations About Infectious Skin Diseases

13 The LORD said to Moses and Aaron, [2]"When anyone has a swelling or a rash or a bright spot on his skin that may become an infectious skin disease,[a] he must be brought to Aaron the priest or to one of his sons[b] who is a priest. [3]The priest is to examine the sore on his skin, and if the hair in the sore has turned white and the sore appears to be more than skin deep,[c] it is an infectious skin disease. When the priest examines him, he shall pronounce him ceremonially unclean. [4]If the spot on his skin is white but does not appear to be more than skin deep and the hair in it has not turned white, the priest is to put the infected person in isolation for seven days. [5]On the seventh day the priest is to examine him, and if he sees that the sore is unchanged and has not spread in the skin, he is to keep him in isolation another seven days. [6]On the seventh day the priest is to examine him again, and if the sore has faded and has not spread in the skin, the priest shall pronounce him clean; it is only a rash. The man must wash his clothes, and he will be clean. [7]But if the rash does spread in his skin after he has shown himself to the priest to be pronounced clean, he must appear before the priest again. [8]The priest is to examine him, and if the rash has spread in the skin, he shall pronounce him unclean; it is an infectious disease.

[9]"When anyone has an infectious skin disease, he must be brought to the priest. [10]The priest is to examine him, and if there is a white swelling in the skin that has turned the hair white and if there is raw flesh in the swelling, [11]it is a chronic skin disease and the priest shall pronounce him unclean. He is not to put him in isolation, because he is already unclean.

[12]"If the disease breaks out all over his skin and, so far as the priest can see, it covers all the skin of the infected person from head to foot, [13]the priest is to examine him, and if the disease has covered his whole body, he shall pronounce that person clean. Since it has all turned white, he is clean. [14]But whenever raw flesh appears on him, he will be unclean. [15]When the priest sees the raw flesh, he shall pronounce him unclean. The raw flesh is unclean; he has an infectious disease. [16]Should the raw flesh change and turn white, he must go to the priest. [17]The priest is to examine him, and if the sores have turned white, the priest shall pronounce the infected person clean; then he will be clean.

[18]"When someone has a boil on his skin and it heals, [19]and in the place where the boil was, a white swelling or reddish-white spot appears, he must present himself to the priest. [20]The priest is to examine it, and if it appears to be more than skin deep and the

---

[a]2 Traditionally *leprosy*; the Hebrew word was used for various diseases affecting the skin—not necessarily leprosy; also elsewhere in this chapter.   [b]2 Or *descendants*   [c]3 Or *be lower than the rest of the skin*; also elsewhere in this chapter

hair in it has turned white, the priest shall pronounce him unclean. It is an infectious skin disease that has broken out where the boil was. [21]But if, when the priest examines it, there is no white hair in it and it is not more than skin deep and has faded, then the priest is to put him in isolation for seven days. [22]If it is spreading in the skin, the priest shall pronounce him unclean; it is infectious. [23]But if the spot is unchanged and has not spread, it is only a scar from the boil, and the priest shall pronounce him clean.

[24]"When someone has a burn on his skin and a reddish-white or white spot appears in the raw flesh of the burn, [25]the priest is to examine the spot, and if the hair in it has turned white, and it appears to be more than skin deep, it is an infectious disease that has broken out in the burn. The priest shall pronounce him unclean; it is an infectious skin disease. [26]But if the priest examines it and there is no white hair in the spot and if it is not more than skin deep and has faded, then the priest is to put him in isolation for seven days. [27]On the seventh day the priest is to examine him, and if it is spreading in the skin, the priest shall pronounce him unclean; it is an infectious skin disease. [28]If, however, the spot is unchanged and has not spread in the skin but has faded, it is a swelling from the burn, and the priest shall pronounce him clean; it is only a scar from the burn.

[29]"If a man or woman has a sore on the head or on the chin, [30]the priest is to examine the sore, and if it appears to be more than skin deep and the hair in it is yellow and thin, the priest shall pronounce that person unclean; it is an itch, an infectious disease of the head or chin. [31]But if, when the priest examines this kind of sore, it does not seem to be more than skin deep and there is no black hair in it, then the priest is to put the infected person in isolation for seven days. [32]On the seventh day the priest is to examine the sore, and if the itch has not spread and there is no yellow hair in it and it does not appear to be more than skin deep, [33]he must be shaved except for the diseased area, and the priest is to keep him in isolation another seven days. [34]On the seventh day the priest is to examine the itch, and if it has not spread in the skin and appears to be no more than skin deep, the priest shall pronounce him clean. He must wash his clothes, and he will be clean. [35]But if the itch does spread in the skin after he is pronounced clean, [36]the priest is to examine him, and if the itch has spread in the skin, the priest does not need to look for yellow hair; the person is unclean. [37]If, however, in his judgment it is unchanged and black hair has grown in it, the itch is healed. He is clean, and the priest shall pronounce him clean.

[38]"When a man or woman has white spots on the skin, [39]the priest is to examine them, and if the spots are dull white, it is a harmless rash that has broken out on the skin; that person is clean.

[40]"When a man has lost his hair and is bald, he is clean. [41]If he has lost his hair from the front of his scalp and has a bald forehead, he is clean. [42]But if he has a reddish-white sore on his bald head or forehead, it is an infectious disease breaking out on his head or forehead. [43]The priest is to examine him, and if the swollen sore on his head or forehead is reddish-white like an infectious skin disease, [44]the man is diseased and is unclean. The priest shall pronounce him unclean because of the sore on his head.

[45]"The person with such an infectious disease must wear torn clothes, let his hair be unkempt,[a] cover the lower part of his face and cry out, 'Unclean! Unclean!' [46]As long as he has the infection he remains unclean. He must live alone; he must live outside the camp.

Regulations About Mildew

[47]"If any clothing is contaminated with mildew—any woolen or linen clothing, [48]any woven or knitted material of linen or wool, any leather or anything made of leather— [49]and if the contamination in the clothing, or leather, or woven or knitted material, or any leather article, is greenish or reddish, it is a spreading mildew and must be shown to the

a45 Or clothes; uncover his head

priest. ⁵⁰The priest is to examine the mildew and isolate the affected article for seven days. ⁵¹On the seventh day he is to examine it, and if the mildew has spread in the clothing, or the woven or knitted material, or the leather, whatever its use, it is a destructive mildew; the article is unclean. ⁵²He must burn up the clothing, or the woven or knitted material of wool or linen, or any leather article that has the contamination in it, because the mildew is destructive; the article must be burned up.

⁵³"But if, when the priest examines it, the mildew has not spread in the clothing, or the woven or knitted material, or the leather article, ⁵⁴he shall order that the contaminated article be washed. Then he is to isolate it for another seven days. ⁵⁵After the affected article has been washed, the priest is to examine it, and if the mildew has not changed its appearance, even though it has not spread, it is unclean. Burn it with fire, whether the mildew has affected one side or the other. ⁵⁶If, when the priest examines it, the mildew has faded after the article has been washed, he is to tear the contaminated part out of the clothing, or the leather, or the woven or knitted material. ⁵⁷But if it reappears in the clothing, or in the woven or knitted material, or in the leather article, it is spreading, and whatever has the mildew must be burned with fire. ⁵⁸The clothing, or the woven or knitted material, or any leather article that has been washed and is rid of the mildew, must be washed again, and it will be clean."

⁵⁹These are the regulations concerning contamination by mildew in woolen or linen clothing, woven or knitted material, or any leather article, for pronouncing them clean or unclean.

Cleansing From Infectious Skin Diseases

14 The LORD said to Moses, ²"These are the regulations for the diseased person at the time of his ceremonial cleansing, when he is brought to the priest: ³The priest is to go outside the camp and examine him. If the person has been healed of his infectious skin disease,ᵃ ⁴the priest shall order that two live clean birds and some cedar wood, scarlet yarn and hyssop be brought for the one to be cleansed. ⁵Then the priest shall order that one of the birds be killed over fresh water in a clay pot. ⁶He is then to take the live bird and dip it, together with the cedar wood, the scarlet yarn and the hyssop, into the blood of the bird that was killed over the fresh water. ⁷Seven times he shall sprinkle the one to be cleansed of the infectious disease and pronounce him clean. Then he is to release the live bird in the open fields.

⁸"The person to be cleansed must wash his clothes, shave off all his hair and bathe with water; then he will be ceremonially clean. After this he may come into the camp, but he must stay outside his tent for seven days. ⁹On the seventh day he must shave off all his hair; he must shave his head, his beard, his eyebrows and the rest of his hair. He must wash his clothes and bathe himself with water, and he will be clean.

¹⁰"On the eighth day he must bring two male lambs and one ewe lamb a year old, each without defect, along with three-tenths of an ephahᵇ of fine flour mixed with oil for a grain offering, and one logᶜ of oil. ¹¹The priest who pronounces him clean shall present both the one to be cleansed and his offerings before the LORD at the entrance to the Tent of Meeting.

¹²"Then the priest is to take one of the male lambs and offer it as a guilt offering, along with the log of oil; he shall wave them before the LORD as a wave offering. ¹³He is to slaughter the lamb in the holy place where the sin offering and the burnt offering are slaughtered. Like the sin offering, the guilt offering belongs to the priest; it is most holy. ¹⁴The priest is to take some of the blood of the guilt offering and put it on the lobe of the right ear of the one to be cleansed, on the thumb of his right hand and on the big toe of his right foot. ¹⁵The priest shall then take some of the log of oil, pour it in the palm of his

---

ᵃ3 Traditionally *leprosy*; the Hebrew word was used for various diseases affecting the skin—not necessarily leprosy; also elsewhere in this chapter.   ᵇ10 That is, probably about 6 quarts (about 6.5 liters)   ᶜ10 That is, probably about 2/3 pint (about 0.3 liter); also in verses 12, 15, 21 and 24

wn left hand, ¹⁶dip his right forefinger into the oil in his palm, and with his finger
prinkle some of it before the Lᴏʀᴅ seven times. ¹⁷The priest is to put some of the oil
emaining in his palm on the lobe of the right ear of the one to be cleansed, on the
humb of his right hand and on the big toe of his right foot, on top of the blood of the
uilt offering. ¹⁸The rest of the oil in his palm the priest shall put on the head of the one
o be cleansed and make atonement for him before the Lᴏʀᴅ.

¹⁹"Then the priest is to sacrifice the sin offering and make atonement for the one to be
leansed from his uncleanness. After that, the priest shall slaughter the burnt offering
and offer it on the altar, together with the grain offering, and make atonement for him,
nd he will be clean.

²¹"If, however, he is poor and cannot afford these, he must take one male lamb as a
uilt offering to be waved to make atonement for him, together with a tenth of an
phah ᵃ of fine flour mixed with oil for a grain offering, a log of oil, ²²and two doves or
wo young pigeons, which he can afford, one for a sin offering and the other for a burnt
ffering.

²³"On the eighth day he must bring them for his cleansing to the priest at the entrance
o the Tent of Meeting, before the Lᴏʀᴅ. ²⁴The priest is to take the lamb for the guilt
ffering, together with the log of oil, and wave them before the Lᴏʀᴅ as a wave offering.
⁵He shall slaughter the lamb for the guilt offering and take some of its blood and put it
n the lobe of the right ear of the one to be cleansed, on the thumb of his right hand and
n the big toe of his right foot. ²⁶The priest is to pour some of the oil into the palm of his
wn left hand, ²⁷and with his right forefinger sprinkle some of the oil from his palm
even times before the Lᴏʀᴅ. ²⁸Some of the oil in his palm he is to put on the same places
e put the blood of the guilt offering—on the lobe of the right ear of the one to be
leansed, on the thumb of his right hand and on the big toe of his right foot. ²⁹The rest of
he oil in his palm the priest shall put on the head of the one to be cleansed, to make
tonement for him before the Lᴏʀᴅ. ³⁰Then he shall sacrifice the doves or the young
igeons, which the person can afford, ³¹one ᵇ as a sin offering and the other as a burnt
ffering, together with the grain offering. In this way the priest will make atonement
efore the Lᴏʀᴅ on behalf of the one to be cleansed."

³²These are the regulations for anyone who has an infectious skin disease and who
annot afford the regular offerings for his cleansing.

Cleansing From Mildew

³³The Lᴏʀᴅ said to Moses and Aaron, ³⁴"When you enter the land of Canaan, which I am
iving you as your possession, and I put a spreading mildew in a house in that land,
⁵the owner of the house must go and tell the priest, 'I have seen something that looks
ke mildew in my house.' ³⁶The priest is to order the house to be emptied before he goes
n to examine the mildew, so that nothing in the house will be pronounced unclean. After
his the priest is to go in and inspect the house. ³⁷He is to examine the mildew on the
valls, and if it has greenish or reddish depressions that appear to be deeper than the
urface of the wall, ³⁸the priest shall go out the doorway of the house and close it up for
even days. ³⁹On the seventh day the priest shall return to inspect the house. If the
ildew has spread on the walls, ⁴⁰he is to order that the contaminated stones be torn out
nd thrown into an unclean place outside the town. ⁴¹He must have all the inside walls
f the house scraped and the material that is scraped off dumped into an unclean place
utside the town. ⁴²Then they are to take other stones to replace these and take new
lay and plaster the house.

⁴³"If the mildew reappears in the house after the stones have been torn out and the
ouse scraped and plastered, ⁴⁴the priest is to go and examine it and, if the mildew has
pread in the house, it is a destructive mildew; the house is unclean. ⁴⁵It must be torn

ᵃ 21 That is, probably about 2 quarts (about 2 liters)   ᵇ 31 Septuagint and Syriac; Hebrew ³¹ such as the person can afford.
ne

down—its stones, timbers and all the plaster—and taken out of the town to an unclea
place.

⁴⁶"Anyone who goes into the house while it is closed up will be unclean till evenin
⁴⁷Anyone who sleeps or eats in the house must wash his clothes.

⁴⁸"But if the priest comes to examine it and the mildew has not spread after the hous
has been plastered, he shall pronounce the house clean, because the mildew is gon
⁴⁹To purify the house he is to take two birds and some cedar wood, scarlet yarn an
hyssop. ⁵⁰He shall kill one of the birds over fresh water in a clay pot. ⁵¹Then he is to tak
the cedar wood, the hyssop, the scarlet yarn and the live bird, dip them into the blood
the dead bird and the fresh water, and sprinkle the house seven times. ⁵²He shall puri
the house with the bird's blood, the fresh water, the live bird, the cedar wood, th
hyssop and the scarlet yarn. ⁵³Then he is to release the live bird in the open fiel
outside the town. In this way he will make atonement for the house, and it will b
clean."

⁵⁴These are the regulations for any infectious skin disease, for an itch, ⁵⁵for mildew i
clothing or in a house, ⁵⁶and for a swelling, a rash or a bright spot, ⁵⁷to determine whe
something is clean or unclean.

These are the regulations for infectious skin diseases and mildew.

Discharges Causing Uncleanness

15 The LORD said to Moses and Aaron, ²"Speak to the Israelites and say to ther
'When any man has a bodily discharge, the discharge is unclean. ³Whethe
it continues flowing from his body or is blocked, it will make him unclean. This is how h
discharge will bring about uncleanness:

⁴"'Any bed the man with a discharge lies on will be unclean, and anything he sits o
will be unclean. ⁵Anyone who touches his bed must wash his clothes and bathe wi
water, and he will be unclean till evening. ⁶Whoever sits on anything that the man wit
a discharge sat on must wash his clothes and bathe with water, and he will be unclea
till evening.

⁷"'Whoever touches the man who has a discharge must wash his clothes and bath
with water, and he will be unclean till evening.

⁸"'If the man with the discharge spits on someone who is clean, that person mus
wash his clothes and bathe with water, and he will be unclean till evening.

⁹"'Everything the man sits on when riding will be unclean, ¹⁰and whoever touches an
of the things that were under him will be unclean till evening; whoever picks up thos
things must wash his clothes and bathe with water, and he will be unclean till evenin

¹¹"'Anyone the man with a discharge touches without rinsing his hands with wate
must wash his clothes and bathe with water, and he will be unclean till evening.

¹²"'A clay pot that the man touches must be broken, and any wooden article is to b
rinsed with water.

¹³"'When a man is cleansed from his discharge, he is to count off seven days for hi
ceremonial cleansing; he must wash his clothes and bathe himself with fresh water, an
he will be clean. ¹⁴On the eighth day he must take two doves or two young pigeons an
come before the LORD to the entrance to the Tent of Meeting and give them to the pries
¹⁵The priest is to sacrifice them, the one for a sin offering and the other for a bur
offering. In this way he will make atonement before the LORD for the man because of hi
discharge.

¹⁶"'When a man has an emission of semen, he must bathe his whole body with wate
and he will be unclean till evening. ¹⁷Any clothing or leather that has semen on it mus
be washed with water, and it will be unclean till evening. ¹⁸When a man lies with
woman and there is an emission of semen, both must bathe with water, and they will b
unclean till evening.

⁹"'When a woman has her regular flow of blood, the impurity of her monthly period
l last seven days, and anyone who touches her will be unclean till evening.
²⁰"'Anything she lies on during her period will be unclean, and anything she sits on
ll be unclean. ²¹Whoever touches her bed must wash his clothes and bathe with
iter, and he will be unclean till evening. ²²Whoever touches anything she sits on must
ish his clothes and bathe with water, and he will be unclean till evening. ²³Whether it
he bed or anything she was sitting on, when anyone touches it, he will be unclean till
ening.

²⁴"'If a man lies with her and her monthly flow touches him, he will be unclean for
ven days; any bed he lies on will be unclean.

²⁵"'When a woman has a discharge of blood for many days at a time other than her
inthly period or has a discharge that continues beyond her period, she will be unclean
long as she has the discharge, just as in the days of her period. ²⁶Any bed she lies on
ile her discharge continues will be unclean, as is her bed during her monthly period,
d anything she sits on will be unclean, as during her period. ²⁷Whoever touches them
ll be unclean; he must wash his clothes and bathe with water, and he will be unclean
evening.

²⁸"'When she is cleansed from her discharge, she must count off seven days, and after
at she will be ceremonially clean. ²⁹On the eighth day she must take two doves or two
ung pigeons and bring them to the priest at the entrance to the Tent of Meeting. ³⁰The
est is to sacrifice one for a sin offering and the other for a burnt offering. In this way he
ll make atonement for her before the LORD for the uncleanness of her discharge.

³¹"'You must keep the Israelites separate from things that make them unclean, so
ey will not die in their uncleanness for defiling my dwelling place,ᵃ which is among
em.'"

³²These are the regulations for a man with a discharge, for anyone made unclean by
: emission of semen, ³³for a woman in her monthly period, for a man or a woman with
discharge, and for a man who lies with a woman who is ceremonially unclean.

e Day of Atonement

6 The LORD spoke to Moses after the death of the two sons of Aaron who died
when they approached the LORD. ²The LORD said to Moses: "Tell your brother
ron not to come whenever he chooses into the Most Holy Place behind the curtain in
int of the atonement cover on the ark, or else he will die, because I appear in the cloud
er the atonement cover.

³"This is how Aaron is to enter the sanctuary area: with a young bull for a sin offering
d a ram for a burnt offering. ⁴He is to put on the sacred linen tunic, with linen
dergarments next to his body; he is to tie the linen sash around him and put on the
en turban. These are sacred garments; so he must bathe himself with water before he
ts them on. ⁵From the Israelite community he is to take two male goats for a sin
'ering and a ram for a burnt offering.

⁶"Aaron is to offer the bull for his own sin offering to make atonement for himself and
s household. ⁷Then he is to take the two goats and present them before the LORD at the
trance to the Tent of Meeting. ⁸He is to cast lots for the two goats—one lot for the LORD
d the other for the scapegoat.ᵇ ⁹Aaron shall bring the goat whose lot falls to the LORD
d sacrifice it for a sin offering. ¹⁰But the goat chosen by lot as the scapegoat shall be
esented alive before the LORD to be used for making atonement by sending it into the
sert as a scapegoat.

¹¹"Aaron shall bring the bull for his own sin offering to make atonement for himself
d his household, and he is to slaughter the bull for his own sin offering. ¹²He is to take
:enser full of burning coals from the altar before the LORD and two handfuls of finely
ound fragrant incense and take them behind the curtain. ¹³He is to put the incense on

ᵃ Or my tabernacle   ᵇ 8 That is, the goat of removal; Hebrew azazel; also in verses 10 and 26

the fire before the LORD, and the smoke of the incense will conceal the atonement co
above the Testimony, so that he will not die. ¹⁴He is to take some of the bull's blood a
with his finger sprinkle it on the front of the atonement cover; then he shall sprin
some of it with his finger seven times before the atonement cover.

¹⁵"He shall then slaughter the goat for the sin offering for the people and take its blo
behind the curtain and do with it as he did with the bull's blood: He shall sprinkle it
the atonement cover and in front of it. ¹⁶In this way he will make atonement for the M
Holy Place because of the uncleanness and rebellion of the Israelites, whatever their s
have been. He is to do the same for the Tent of Meeting, which is among them in
midst of their uncleanness. ¹⁷No one is to be in the Tent of Meeting from the time Aa
goes in to make atonement in the Most Holy Place until he comes out, having ma
atonement for himself, his household and the whole community of Israel.

¹⁸"Then he shall come out to the altar that is before the LORD and make atonement
it. He shall take some of the bull's blood and some of the goat's blood and put it on all
horns of the altar. ¹⁹He shall sprinkle some of the blood on it with his finger seven tim
to cleanse it and to consecrate it from the uncleanness of the Israelites.

²⁰"When Aaron has finished making atonement for the Most Holy Place, the Tent
Meeting and the altar, he shall bring forward the live goat. ²¹He is to lay both hands
the head of the live goat and confess over it all the wickedness and rebellion of
Israelites—all their sins—and put them on the goat's head. He shall send the goat aw
into the desert in the care of a man appointed for the task. ²²The goat will carry on its
all their sins to a solitary place; and the man shall release it in the desert.

²³"Then Aaron is to go into the Tent of Meeting and take off the linen garments he
on before he entered the Most Holy Place, and he is to leave them there. ²⁴He shall bat
himself with water in a holy place and put on his regular garments. Then he shall co
out and sacrifice the burnt offering for himself and the burnt offering for the people,
make atonement for himself and for the people. ²⁵He shall also burn the fat of the
offering on the altar.

²⁶"The man who releases the goat as a scapegoat must wash his clothes and bat
himself with water; afterward he may come into the camp. ²⁷The bull and the goat
the sin offerings, whose blood was brought into the Most Holy Place to make atoneme
must be taken outside the camp; their hides, flesh and offal are to be burned up. ²⁸T

╔══════════════════ **DISCOVERING GOD** ══════════════════

16:1–10
The God Who Is There

Stroll down the aisles of a supermarket and you'll find dozens of cleansers—products to clean bodies, hair, fingernails, feet, teeth, dishes, clothing, floors, furniture, glass, cars, contact lenses, tools—
every item imaginable. But you'll search long and hard to find a product that can wash the human
soul. Yet God says that he can do just that—cleanse us from the inside out.

The book of Leviticus provided the ancient nation of Israel with a two-step process for washing away their sin. First, they were to admit what they had done—no hiding, no rationalizations.
Second, they needed to offer an animal sacrifice.

Sacrifice illustrates a very important spiritual truth: sin doesn't just evaporate into the air; it
has to be disposed of. Like nuclear waste, sin is dangerous stuff and, if not carefully handled, will
continue to do damage for a long time.

Wouldn't it be great if God could do a once-and-for-all sin disposal? Well, he could. And
some 1,400 years after Leviticus was written, he did. (Look at 1 Peter, chapter 2, verses 21–24 [page
1612], to see what happened.)

Do you want to wipe the stain from your soul? You're reading the right book. The Bible contains the only "spiritual cleanser" that's guaranteed to work. It's a promise—and provision—from
God himself.

man who burns them must wash his clothes and bathe himself with water; afterward he may come into the camp.

²⁹"This is to be a lasting ordinance for you: On the tenth day of the seventh month you must deny yourselves*ᵃ* and not do any work—whether native-born or an alien living among you— ³⁰because on this day atonement will be made for you, to cleanse you. Then, before the LORD, you will be clean from all your sins. ³¹It is a sabbath of rest, and you must deny yourselves; it is a lasting ordinance. ³²The priest who is anointed and ordained to succeed his father as high priest is to make atonement. He is to put on the sacred linen garments ³³and make atonement for the Most Holy Place, for the Tent of Meeting and the altar, and for the priests and all the people of the community.

³⁴"This is to be a lasting ordinance for you: Atonement is to be made once a year for all the sins of the Israelites."

And it was done, as the LORD commanded Moses.

Eating Blood Forbidden

17 The LORD said to Moses, ²"Speak to Aaron and his sons and to all the Israelites and say to them: 'This is what the LORD has commanded: ³Any Israelite who sacrifices an ox,*ᵇ* a lamb or a goat in the camp or outside of it ⁴instead of bringing it to the entrance to the Tent of Meeting to present it as an offering to the LORD in front of the tabernacle of the LORD—that man shall be considered guilty of bloodshed; he has shed blood and must be cut off from his people. ⁵This is so the Israelites will bring to the LORD the sacrifices they are now making in the open fields. They must bring them to the priest, that is, to the LORD, at the entrance to the Tent of Meeting and sacrifice them as fellowship offerings.*ᶜ* ⁶The priest is to sprinkle the blood against the altar of the LORD at the entrance to the Tent of Meeting and burn the fat as an aroma pleasing to the LORD. ⁷They must no longer offer any of their sacrifices to the goat idols*ᵈ* to whom they prostitute themselves. This is to be a lasting ordinance for them and for the generations to come.'

⁸"Say to them: 'Any Israelite or any alien living among them who offers a burnt offering or sacrifice ⁹and does not bring it to the entrance to the Tent of Meeting to sacrifice it to the LORD—that man must be cut off from his people.

¹⁰"'Any Israelite or any alien living among them who eats any blood—I will set my face against that person who eats blood and will cut him off from his people. ¹¹For the life of a creature is in the blood, and I have given it to you to make atonement for yourselves on the altar; it is the blood that makes atonement for one's life. ¹²Therefore I say to the Israelites, "None of you may eat blood, nor may an alien living among you eat blood."

¹³"'Any Israelite or any alien living among you who hunts any animal or bird that may be eaten must drain out the blood and cover it with earth, ¹⁴because the life of every creature is its blood. That is why I have said to the Israelites, "You must not eat the blood of any creature, because the life of every creature is its blood; anyone who eats it must be cut off."

¹⁵"'Anyone, whether native-born or alien, who eats anything found dead or torn by wild animals must wash his clothes and bathe with water, and he will be ceremonially unclean till evening; then he will be clean. ¹⁶But if he does not wash his clothes and bathe himself, he will be held responsible.'

Unlawful Sexual Relations

18 The LORD said to Moses, ²"Speak to the Israelites and say to them: 'I am the LORD your God. ³You must not do as they do in Egypt, where you used to live, and you must not do as they do in the land of Canaan, where I am bringing you. Do not follow their practices. ⁴You must obey my laws and be careful to follow my decrees. I am

ᵃ29 Or must fast; also in verse 31   ᵇ3 The Hebrew word can include both male and female.   ᶜ5 Traditionally peace offerings   ᵈ7 Or demons

the Lord your God. **5**Keep my decrees and laws, for the man who obeys them will live by them. I am the Lord.

6" 'No one is to approach any close relative to have sexual relations. I am the Lord.

7" 'Do not dishonor your father by having sexual relations with your mother. She is your mother; do not have relations with her.

8" 'Do not have sexual relations with your father's wife; that would dishonor your father.

9" 'Do not have sexual relations with your sister, either your father's daughter or your mother's daughter, whether she was born in the same home or elsewhere.

10" 'Do not have sexual relations with your son's daughter or your daughter's daughter; that would dishonor you.

11" 'Do not have sexual relations with the daughter of your father's wife, born to your father; she is your sister.

12" 'Do not have sexual relations with your father's sister; she is your father's close relative.

13" 'Do not have sexual relations with your mother's sister, because she is your mother's close relative.

14" 'Do not dishonor your father's brother by approaching his wife to have sexual relations; she is your aunt.

15" 'Do not have sexual relations with your daughter-in-law. She is your son's wife; do not have relations with her.

16" 'Do not have sexual relations with your brother's wife; that would dishonor your brother.

17" 'Do not have sexual relations with both a woman and her daughter. Do not have sexual relations with either her son's daughter or her daughter's daughter; they are her close relatives. That is wickedness.

18" 'Do not take your wife's sister as a rival wife and have sexual relations with her while your wife is living.

19" 'Do not approach a woman to have sexual relations during the uncleanness of her monthly period.

20" 'Do not have sexual relations with your neighbor's wife and defile yourself with her.

21" 'Do not give any of your children to be sacrificed*a* to Molech, for you must not profane the name of your God. I am the Lord.

22" 'Do not lie with a man as one lies with a woman; that is detestable.

23" 'Do not have sexual relations with an animal and defile yourself with it. A woman must not present herself to an animal to have sexual relations with it; that is a perversion.

24" 'Do not defile yourselves in any of these ways, because this is how the nations that I am going to drive out before you became defiled. **25**Even the land was defiled; so I punished it for its sin, and the land vomited out its inhabitants. **26**But you must keep my decrees and my laws. The native-born and the aliens living among you must not do any of these detestable things, **27**for all these things were done by the people who lived in the land before you, and the land became defiled. **28**And if you defile the land, it will vomit you out as it vomited out the nations that were before you.

29" 'Everyone who does any of these detestable things—such persons must be cut off from their people. **30**Keep my requirements and do not follow any of the detestable customs that were practiced before you came and do not defile yourselves with them. I am the Lord your God.' "

a 21 Or to be passed through the fire

Various Laws

19 The LORD said to Moses, 2"Speak to the entire assembly of Israel and say to them: 'Be holy because I, the LORD your God, am holy.

3" 'Each of you must respect his mother and father, and you must observe my Sabbaths. I am the LORD your God.

4" 'Do not turn to idols or make gods of cast metal for yourselves. I am the LORD your God.

5" 'When you sacrifice a fellowship offering*a* to the LORD, sacrifice it in such a way that it will be accepted on your behalf. 6It shall be eaten on the day you sacrifice it or on the next day; anything left over until the third day must be burned up. 7If any of it is eaten on the third day, it is impure and will not be accepted. 8Whoever eats it will be held responsible because he has desecrated what is holy to the LORD; that person must be cut off from his people.

9" 'When you reap the harvest of your land, do not reap to the very edges of your field or gather the gleanings of your harvest. 10Do not go over your vineyard a second time or pick up the grapes that have fallen. Leave them for the poor and the alien. I am the LORD your God.

11" 'Do not steal.

" 'Do not lie.

" 'Do not deceive one another.

12" 'Do not swear falsely by my name and so profane the name of your God. I am the LORD.

13" 'Do not defraud your neighbor or rob him.

" 'Do not hold back the wages of a hired man overnight.

14" 'Do not curse the deaf or put a stumbling block in front of the blind, but fear your God. I am the LORD.

15" 'Do not pervert justice; do not show partiality to the poor or favoritism to the great, but judge your neighbor fairly.

16" 'Do not go about spreading slander among your people.

" 'Do not do anything that endangers your neighbor's life. I am the LORD.

17" 'Do not hate your brother in your heart. Rebuke your neighbor frankly so you will not share in his guilt.

STRENGTHENING RELATIONSHIPS

19:11–18, 32–33
Social

Here God gives instructions concerning how men and women should treat others. As people seek to be like God, they will show God's love to others. They won't lie, steal or slander. They'll express kindness to those who experience physical disabilities. They'll see that both rich and poor people are treated justly. And they'll show respect to the elderly.

Not only will they guard their behavior, they'll also control their attitudes. Hatred and bitterness will be uprooted from their hearts. And they'll be kind to people of other races or nationalities who live among them.

Think of what would happen in the world today if everyone were to abide by these instructions!

18" 'Do not seek revenge or bear a grudge against one of your people, but love your neighbor as yourself. I am the LORD.

19" 'Keep my decrees.

" 'Do not mate different kinds of animals.

" 'Do not plant your field with two kinds of seed.

" 'Do not wear clothing woven of two kinds of material.

20" 'If a man sleeps with a woman who is a slave girl promised to another man but who has not been ransomed or given her freedom, there must be due punishment. Yet they are not to be put to death, because she had not been freed. 21The man, however, must bring a ram to the entrance to the Tent of Meeting for a guilt offering to the LORD. 22With

a 5 Traditionally peace offering

the ram of the guilt offering the priest is to make atonement for him before the LORD fo
the sin he has committed, and his sin will be forgiven.

²³ "'When you enter the land and plant any kind of fruit tree, regard its fruit as forbid
den.ᵃ For three years you are to consider it forbiddenᵃ; it must not be eaten. ²⁴In th
fourth year all its fruit will be holy, an offering of praise to the LORD. ²⁵But in the fifth ye
you may eat its fruit. In this way your harvest will be increased. I am the LORD your Go

²⁶ "'Do not eat any meat with the blood still in it.

"'Do not practice divination or sorcery.

²⁷ "'Do not cut the hair at the sides of your head or clip off the edges of your bear

²⁸ "'Do not cut your bodies for the dead or put tattoo marks on yourselves. I am the LOR

²⁹ "'Do not degrade your daughter by making her a prostitute, or the land will turn
prostitution and be filled with wickedness.

³⁰ "'Observe my Sabbaths and have reverence for my sanctuary. I am the LORD.

³¹ "'Do not turn to mediums or seek o
spiritists, for you will be defiled by them.
am the LORD your God.

³² "'Rise in the presence of the age
show respect for the elderly and rever
your God. I am the LORD.

³³ "'When an alien lives with you in you
land, do not mistreat him. ³⁴The alien livin
with you must be treated as one of you
native-born. Love him as yourself, for yo
were aliens in Egypt. I am the LORD you
God.

³⁵ "'Do not use dishonest standards whe
measuring length, weight or quantity

DISCOVERING GOD

19:31
Spiritual Fraud

Here God instructs his people to avoid occult
practitioners such as fortune-tellers, palm-
readers, channelers and astrologers. Occult
practices are not only ineffective, but they also
lead to spiritual corruption. God wants to protect people from being ripped off or—much
worse—spiritually misled and lost.

³⁶Use honest scales and honest weights, an honest ephahᵇ and an honest hin.ᶜ I ar
the LORD your God, who brought you out of Egypt.

³⁷ "'Keep all my decrees and all my laws and follow them. I am the LORD.'"

Punishments for Sin

20 The LORD said to Moses, ² "Say to the Israelites: 'Any Israelite or any alie
living in Israel who givesᵈ any of his children to Molech must be put t
death. The people of the community are to stone him. ³I will set my face against that ma
and I will cut him off from his people; for by giving his children to Molech, he has defile
my sanctuary and profaned my holy name. ⁴If the people of the community close the
eyes when that man gives one of his children to Molech and they fail to put him to death
⁵I will set my face against that man and his family and will cut off from their people bot
him and all who follow him in prostituting themselves to Molech.

⁶ "'I will set my face against the person who turns to mediums and spiritists to prosti
tute himself by following them, and I will cut him off from his people.

⁷ "'Consecrate yourselves and be holy, because I am the LORD your God. ⁸Keep m
decrees and follow them. I am the LORD, who makes you holy.ᵉ

⁹ "'If anyone curses his father or mother, he must be put to death. He has cursed hi
father or his mother, and his blood will be on his own head.

¹⁰ "'If a man commits adultery with another man's wife—with the wife of his neighbor—
both the adulterer and the adulteress must be put to death.

¹¹ "'If a man sleeps with his father's wife, he has dishonored his father. Both the ma
and the woman must be put to death; their blood will be on their own heads.

ᵃ23 Hebrew uncircumcised   ᵇ36 An ephah was a dry measure.   ᶜ36 A hin was a liquid measure.   ᵈ2 Or
sacrifices; also in verses 3 and 4   ᵉ8 Or who sanctifies you; or who sets you apart as holy

¹²"'If a man sleeps with his daughter-in-law, both of them must be put to death. What they have done is a perversion; their blood will be on their own heads.

¹³"'If a man lies with a man as one lies with a woman, both of them have done what is detestable. They must be put to death; their blood will be on their own heads.

¹⁴"'If a man marries both a woman and her mother, it is wicked. Both he and they must be burned in the fire, so that no wickedness will be among you.

¹⁵"'If a man has sexual relations with an animal, he must be put to death, and you must kill the animal.

¹⁶"'If a woman approaches an animal to have sexual relations with it, kill both the woman and the animal. They must be put to death; their blood will be on their own heads.

¹⁷"'If a man marries his sister, the daughter of either his father or his mother, and they have sexual relations, it is a disgrace. They must be cut off before the eyes of their people. He has dishonored his sister and will be held responsible.

¹⁸"'If a man lies with a woman during her monthly period and has sexual relations with her, he has exposed the source of her flow, and she has also uncovered it. Both of them must be cut off from their people.

¹⁹"'Do not have sexual relations with the sister of either your mother or your father, for that would dishonor a close relative; both of you would be held responsible.

²⁰"'If a man sleeps with his aunt, he has dishonored his uncle. They will be held responsible; they will die childless.

²¹"'If a man marries his brother's wife, it is an act of impurity; he has dishonored his brother. They will be childless.

²²"'Keep all my decrees and laws and follow them, so that the land where I am bringing you to live may not vomit you out. ²³You must not live according to the customs of the nations I am going to drive out before you. Because they did all these things, I abhorred them. ²⁴But I said to you, "You will possess their land; I will give it to you as an inheritance, a land flowing with milk and honey." I am the LORD your God, who has set you apart from the nations.

²⁵"'You must therefore make a distinction between clean and unclean animals and between unclean and clean birds. Do not defile yourselves by any animal or bird or anything that moves along the ground—those which I have set apart as unclean for you. ²⁶You are to be holy to me ᵃ because I, the LORD, am holy, and I have set you apart from the nations to be my own.

▣ ⠿⠿⠿⠿⠿ DISCOVERING GOD ⠿⠿⠿⠿⠿ ▣

20:7–8
Life with God

Because God is a spiritual being, we can't see him. But that doesn't mean we can't try to understand what he is like. The wonders of creation give us insight into God's *power*. We can gain insight into God's *character* by looking into the lives of his followers. Leviticus chapters 18–20 describe the conduct that is to characterize God's followers.

God defined the specific behavior of his people because he wanted the ancient Israelites to be different from their immoral neighbors. Many of these ancient regulations address issues that would accomplish this goal, including even such external issues as hairstyle and clothing. Not all of these cultural directives apply today, but the spirit of these instructions demonstrates the pure life that God-followers of every age are to live.

As people give God their devotion, they become more like him. And the more people act like God, the more earthly evidence there is of God's loving, caring, inviting nature. Ancient Israel's highest call was to show the world the excellence of God. That's the call of God's people today as well.

²⁷"'A man or woman who is a medium or spiritist among you must be put to death. You are to stone them; their blood will be on their own heads.'"

ᵃ⁶ Or be my holy ones

Rules for Priests

The LORD said to Moses, "Speak to the priests, the sons of Aaron, and say
them: 'A priest must not make himself ceremonially unclean for any of h
people who die, ²except for a close relative, such as his mother or father, his son
daughter, his brother, ³or an unmarried sister who is dependent on him since she has r
husband—for her he may make himself unclean. ⁴He must not make himself unclean f
people related to him by marriage,ᵃ and so defile himself.

⁵"'Priests must not shave their heads or shave off the edges of their beards or cut the
bodies. ⁶They must be holy to their God and must not profane the name of their Go
Because they present the offerings made to the LORD by fire, the food of their God, t
are to be holy.

⁷"'They must not marry women defiled by prostitution or divorced from their husband
because priests are holy to their God. ⁸Regard them as holy, because they offer up th
food of your God. Consider them holy, because I the LORD am holy—I who make yc
holy.ᵇ

⁹"'If a priest's daughter defiles herself by becoming a prostitute, she disgraces h
father; she must be burned in the fire.

¹⁰"'The high priest, the one among his brothers who has had the anointing oil poure
on his head and who has been ordained to wear the priestly garments, must not let h
hair become unkemptᶜ or tear his clothes. ¹¹He must not enter a place where there is
dead body. He must not make himself unclean, even for his father or mother, ¹²nor lea
the sanctuary of his God or desecrate it, because he has been dedicated by the anointi
oil of his God. I am the LORD.

¹³"'The woman he marries must be a virgin. ¹⁴He must not marry a widow, a divorce
woman, or a woman defiled by prostitution, but only a virgin from his own peopl
¹⁵so he will not defile his offspring among his people. I am the LORD, who makes hi
holy.ᵈ'"

¹⁶The LORD said to Moses, ¹⁷"Say to Aaron: 'For the generations to come none of yo
descendants who has a defect may come near to offer the food of his God. ¹⁸No man wl
has any defect may come near: no man who is blind or lame, disfigured or deforme
¹⁹no man with a crippled foot or hand, ²⁰or who is hunchbacked or dwarfed, or who h
any eye defect, or who has festering or running sores or damaged testicles. ²¹No desce
dant of Aaron the priest who has any defect is to come near to present the offerin
made to the LORD by fire. He has a defect; he must not come near to offer the food of h
God. ²²He may eat the most holy food of his God, as well as the holy food; ²³yet becau
of his defect, he must not go near the curtain or approach the altar, and so desecrate n
sanctuary. I am the LORD, who makes them holy.ᵉ'"

²⁴So Moses told this to Aaron and his sons and to all the Israelites.

22   The LORD said to Moses, ²"Tell Aaron and his sons to treat with respect tl
sacred offerings the Israelites consecrate to me, so they will not profane n
holy name. I am the LORD.

³"Say to them: 'For the generations to come, if any of your descendants is ceremoniall
unclean and yet comes near the sacred offerings that the Israelites consecrate to the LOF
that person must be cut off from my presence. I am the LORD.

⁴"'If a descendant of Aaron has an infectious skin diseaseᶠ or a bodily discharge, I
may not eat the sacred offerings until he is cleansed. He will also be unclean if I
touches something defiled by a corpse or by anyone who has an emission of semen, ⁵
if he touches any crawling thing that makes him unclean, or any person who makes hi

ᵃ4 Or *unclean as a leader among his people*   ᵇ8 Or *who sanctify you; or who set you apart as holy*   ᶜ10 Or *not
uncover his head*   ᵈ15 Or *who sanctifies him; or who sets him apart as holy*   ᵉ23 Or *who sanctifies them; or who sets
them apart as holy*   ᶠ4 Traditionally *leprosy*; the Hebrew word was used for various diseases affecting the skin—not
necessarily leprosy.

nclean, whatever the uncleanness may be. [6]The one who touches any such thing will
e unclean till evening. He must not eat any of the sacred offerings unless he has bathed
imself with water. [7]When the sun goes down, he will be clean, and after that he may
at the sacred offerings, for they are his food. [8]He must not eat anything found dead or
rn by wild animals, and so become unclean through it. I am the LORD.

[9]"The priests are to keep my requirements so that they do not become guilty and die
r treating them with contempt. I am the LORD, who makes them holy.[a]

[10]"No one outside a priest's family may eat the sacred offering, nor may the guest of a
riest or his hired worker eat it. [11]But if a priest buys a slave with money, or if a slave is
rn in his household, that slave may eat his food. [12]If a priest's daughter marries anyone
her than a priest, she may not eat any of the sacred contributions. [13]But if a priest's
aughter becomes a widow or is divorced, yet has no children, and she returns to live in
er father's house as in her youth, she may eat of her father's food. No unauthorized
erson, however, may eat any of it.

[14]"If anyone eats a sacred offering by mistake, he must make restitution to the priest
r the offering and add a fifth of the value to it. [15]The priests must not desecrate
e sacred offerings the Israelites present to
e LORD [16]by allowing them to eat the
acred offerings and so bring upon them
uilt requiring payment. I am the LORD, who
akes them holy.'"

nacceptable Sacrifices

[17]The LORD said to Moses, [18]"Speak to
aron and his sons and to all the Israelites
nd say to them: 'If any of you—either an
raelite or an alien living in Israel—presents
gift for a burnt offering to the LORD, either
fulfill a vow or as a freewill offering, [19]you
ust present a male without defect from the
attle, sheep or goats in order that it may be
ccepted on your behalf. [20]Do not bring
nything with a defect, because it will not
e accepted on your behalf. [21]When anyone
rings from the herd or flock a fellowship
fering[b] to the LORD to fulfill a special vow
r as a freewill offering, it must be without
efect or blemish to be acceptable. [22]Do not
fer to the LORD the blind, the injured or the
aimed, or anything with warts or festering
running sores. Do not place any of these

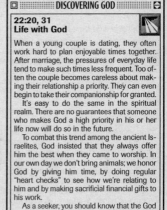

n the altar as an offering made to the LORD by fire. [23]You may, however, present as a
eewill offering an ox[c] or a sheep that is deformed or stunted, but it will not be
ccepted in fulfillment of a vow. [24]You must not offer to the LORD an animal whose
sticles are bruised, crushed, torn or cut. You must not do this in your own land, [25]and
u must not accept such animals from the hand of a foreigner and offer them as the food
your God. They will not be accepted on your behalf, because they are deformed and
ave defects.'"

Or *who sanctifies them*; or *who sets them apart as holy*; also in verse 16   [b]21 Traditionally *peace offering*
3 The Hebrew word can include both male and female.

²⁶The Lord said to Moses, ²⁷"When a calf, a lamb or a goat is born, it is to remain wi
its mother for seven days. From the eighth day on, it will be acceptable as an offerin
made to the Lord by fire. ²⁸Do not slaughter a cow or a sheep and its young on the sam
day.

²⁹"When you sacrifice a thank offering to the Lord, sacrifice it in such a way that it w
be accepted on your behalf. ³⁰It must be eaten that same day; leave none of it
morning. I am the Lord.

³¹"Keep my commands and follow them. I am the Lord. ³²Do not profane my holy nam
I must be acknowledged as holy by the Israelites. I am the Lord, who makes*a* you ho
³³and who brought you out of Egypt to be your God. I am the Lord."

23   The Lord said to Moses, ²"Speak to the Israelites and say to them: 'These a
my appointed feasts, the appointed feasts of the Lord, which you are
proclaim as sacred assemblies.

The Sabbath

³"'There are six days when you may work, but the seventh day is a Sabbath of rest,
day of sacred assembly. You are not to do any work; wherever you live, it is a Sabbath
the Lord.

The Passover and Unleavened Bread

⁴"'These are the Lord's appointed feasts, the sacred assemblies you are to proclaim
their appointed times: ⁵The Lord's Passover begins at twilight on the fourteenth day of th
first month. ⁶On the fifteenth day of that month the Lord's Feast of Unleavened Brea
begins; for seven days you must eat bread made without yeast. ⁷On the first day ho
a sacred assembly and do no regular work. ⁸For seven days present an offering ma
to the Lord by fire. And on the seventh day hold a sacred assembly and do no regul
work.'"

Firstfruits

⁹The Lord said to Moses, ¹⁰"Speak to the Israelites and say to them: 'When you enter th
land I am going to give you and you reap its harvest, bring to the priest a sheaf of the fir
grain you harvest. ¹¹He is to wave the sheaf before the Lord so it will be accepted on yo
behalf; the priest is to wave it on the day after the Sabbath. ¹²On the day you wave th
sheaf, you must sacrifice as a burnt offering to the Lord a lamb a year old without defe
¹³together with its grain offering of two-tenths of an ephah*c* of fine flour mixed with
an offering made to the Lord by fire, a pleasing aroma—and its drink offering of a quar
of a hin*d* of wine. ¹⁴You must not eat any bread, or roasted or new grain, until the ve
day you bring this offering to your God. This is to be a lasting ordinance for the generatio
to come, wherever you live.

Feast of Weeks

¹⁵"'From the day after the Sabbath, the day you brought the sheaf of the wave offerin
count off seven full weeks. ¹⁶Count off fifty days up to the day after the seventh Sabba
and then present an offering of new grain to the Lord. ¹⁷From wherever you live, bri
two loaves made of two-tenths of an ephah of fine flour, baked with yeast, as a wa
offering of firstfruits to the Lord. ¹⁸Present with this bread seven male lambs, each a ye
old and without defect, one young bull and two rams. They will be a burnt offering to th
Lord, together with their grain offerings and drink offerings—an offering made by fire,

---

a32 Or made   *b32* Or who sanctifies you; or who sets you apart as holy   *c13* That is, probably about 4 quarts (about 4
liters); also in verse 17   *d13* That is, probably about 1 quart (about 1 liter)

aroma pleasing to the LORD. ¹⁹Then sacrifice one male goat for a sin offering and two lambs, each a year old, for a fellowship offering.ᵃ ²⁰The priest is to wave the two lambs before the LORD as a wave offering, together with the bread of the firstfruits. They are a sacred offering to the LORD for the priest. ²¹On that same day you are to proclaim a sacred assembly and do no regular work. This is to be a lasting ordinance for the generations to come, wherever you live.

²²"'When you reap the harvest of your land, do not reap to the very edges of your field or gather the gleanings of your harvest. Leave them for the poor and the alien. I am the LORD your God.'"

Feast of Trumpets

²³The LORD said to Moses, ²⁴"Say to the Israelites: 'On the first day of the seventh month you are to have a day of rest, a sacred assembly commemorated with trumpet blasts. ²⁵Do no regular work, but present an offering made to the LORD by fire.'"

Day of Atonement

²⁶The LORD said to Moses, ²⁷"The tenth day of this seventh month is the Day of Atonement. Hold a sacred assembly and deny yourselves,ᵇ and present an offering made to the LORD by fire. ²⁸Do no work on that day, because it is the Day of Atonement, when atonement is made for you before the LORD your God. ²⁹Anyone who does not deny himself on that day must be cut off from his people. ³⁰I will destroy from among his people anyone who does any work on that day. ³¹You shall do no work at all. This is to be a lasting ordinance for the generations to come, wherever you live. ³²It is a sabbath of rest for you, and you must deny yourselves. From the evening of the ninth day of the month until the following evening you are to observe your sabbath."

Feast of Tabernacles

³³The LORD said to Moses, ³⁴"Say to the Israelites: 'On the fifteenth day of the seventh month the LORD's Feast of Tabernacles begins, and it lasts for seven days. ³⁵The first day is a sacred assembly; do no regular work. ³⁶For seven days present offerings made to the LORD by fire, and on the eighth day hold a sacred assembly and present an offering made to the LORD by fire. It is the closing assembly; do no regular work.

³⁷("These are the LORD's appointed feasts, which you are to proclaim as sacred assemblies for bringing offerings made to the LORD by fire—the burnt offerings and grain offerings, sacrifices and drink offerings required for each day. ³⁸These offerings are in addition to those for the LORD's Sabbaths andᶜ in addition to your gifts and whatever you have vowed and all the freewill offerings you give to the LORD.)

³⁹"'So beginning with the fifteenth day of the seventh month, after you have gathered the crops of the land, celebrate the festival to the LORD for seven days; the first day is a day of rest, and the eighth day also is a day of rest. ⁴⁰On the first day you are to take choice fruit from the trees, and palm fronds, leafy branches and poplars, and rejoice before the LORD your God for seven days. ⁴¹Celebrate this as a festival to the LORD for seven days each year. This is to be a lasting ordinance for the generations to come; celebrate it in the seventh month. ⁴²Live in booths for seven days: All native-born Israelites are to live in booths ⁴³so your descendants will know that I had the Israelites live in booths when I brought them out of Egypt. I am the LORD your God.'"

⁴⁴So Moses announced to the Israelites the appointed feasts of the LORD.

---

¹⁹ Traditionally peace offering   ᵇ27 Or and fast; also in verses 29 and 32   ᶜ38 Or These feasts are in addition to the LORD's Sabbaths, and these offerings are

Oil and Bread Set Before the LORD

24 The LORD said to Moses, 2"Command the Israelites to bring you clear oil of pressed olives for the light so that the lamps may be kept burning continually. 3Outside the curtain of the Testimony in the Tent of Meeting, Aaron is to tend the lamps before the LORD from evening till morning, continually. This is to be a lasting ordinance for the generations to come. 4The lamps on the pure gold lampstand before the LORD must be tended continually.

5"Take fine flour and bake twelve loaves of bread, using two-tenths of an ephah^a for each loaf. 6Set them in two rows, six in each row, on the table of pure gold before the LORD. 7Along each row put some pure incense as a memorial portion to represent the bread and to be an offering made to the LORD by fire. 8This bread is to be set out before the LORD regularly, Sabbath after Sabbath, on behalf of the Israelites, as a lasting covenant. 9It belongs to Aaron and his sons, who are to eat it in a holy place, because it is a most holy part of their regular share of the offerings made to the LORD by fire."

A Blasphemer Stoned

10Now the son of an Israelite mother and an Egyptian father went out among the Israelites, and a fight broke out in the camp between him and an Israelite. 11The son of the Israelite woman blasphemed the Name with a curse; so they brought him to Moses. (His mother's name was Shelomith, the daughter of Dibri the Danite.) 12They put him in custody until the will of the LORD should be made clear to them.

13Then the LORD said to Moses: 14"Take the blasphemer outside the camp. All those who heard him are to lay their hands on his head, and the entire assembly is to stone him. 15Say to the Israelites: 'If anyone curses his God, he will be held responsible; 16anyone who blasphemes the name of the LORD must be put to death. The entire assembly must stone him. Whether an alien or native-born, when he blasphemes the Name, he must be put to death.

17"'If anyone takes the life of a human being, he must be put to death. 18Anyone who takes the life of someone's animal must make restitution—life for life. 19If anyone injures his neighbor, whatever he has done must be done to him: 20fracture for fracture, eye for eye, tooth for tooth. As he has injured the other, so he is to be injured. 21Whoever kills an animal must make restitution, but whoever kills a man must be put to death. 22You are to have the same law for the alien and the native-born. I am the LORD your God.'"

23Then Moses spoke to the Israelites, and they took the blasphemer outside the camp and stoned him. The Israelites did as the LORD commanded Moses.

The Sabbath Year

25 The LORD said to Moses on Mount Sinai, 2"Speak to the Israelites and say to them: 'When you enter the land I am going to give you, the land itself must observe a sabbath to the LORD. 3For six years sow your fields, and for six years prune your vineyards and gather their crops. 4But in the seventh year the land is to have a sabbath of rest, a sabbath to the LORD. Do not sow your fields or prune your vineyards. 5Do not reap what grows of itself or harvest the grapes of your untended vines. The land is to have a year of rest. 6Whatever the land yields during the sabbath year will be food for you—for yourself, your manservant and maidservant, and the hired worker and temporary resident who live among you, 7as well as for your livestock and the wild animals in your land. Whatever the land produces may be eaten.

The Year of Jubilee

8"'Count off seven sabbaths of years—seven times seven years—so that the seven sabbaths of years amount to a period of forty-nine years. 9Then have the trumpet sound

---

^{a} 5 That is, probably about 4 quarts (about 4.5 liters)

ed everywhere on the tenth day of the seventh month; on the Day of Atonement sound the trumpet throughout your land. ¹⁰Consecrate the fiftieth year and proclaim liberty throughout the land to all its inhabitants. It shall be a jubilee for you; each one of you is to return to his family property and each to his own clan. ¹¹The fiftieth year shall be a jubilee for you; do not sow and do not reap what grows of itself or harvest the untended vines. ¹²For it is a jubilee and is to be holy for you; eat only what is taken directly from the fields.

¹³ "'In this Year of Jubilee everyone is to return to his own property.

¹⁴ "'If you sell land to one of your countrymen or buy any from him, do not take advantage of each other. ¹⁵You are to buy from your countryman on the basis of the number of years since the Jubilee. And he is to sell to you on the basis of the number of years left for harvesting crops. ¹⁶When the years are many, you are to increase the price, and when the years are few, you are to decrease the price, because what he is really selling you is the number of crops. ¹⁷Do not take advantage of each other, but fear your God. I am the LORD your God.

¹⁸ "'Follow my decrees and be careful to obey my laws, and you will live safely in the land. ¹⁹Then the land will yield its fruit, and you will eat your fill and live there in safety. ²⁰You may ask, "What will we eat in the seventh year if we do not plant or harvest our crops?" ²¹I will send you such a blessing in the sixth year that the land will yield enough for three years. ²²While you plant during the eighth year, you will eat from the old crop and will continue to eat from it until the harvest of the ninth year comes in.

²³ "'The land must not be sold permanently, because the land is mine and you are but aliens and my tenants. ²⁴Throughout the country that you hold as a possession, you must provide for the redemption of the land.

²⁵ "'If one of your countrymen becomes poor and sells some of his property, his nearest relative is to come and redeem what his countryman has sold. ²⁶If, however, a man has no one to redeem it for him but he himself prospers and acquires sufficient means to redeem it, ²⁷he is to determine the value for the years since he sold it and refund the balance to the man to whom he sold it; he can then go back to his own property. ²⁸But if he does not acquire the means to repay him, what he sold will remain in the possession of the buyer until the Year of Jubilee. It will be returned in the Jubilee, and he can then go back to his property.

²⁹ "'If a man sells a house in a walled city, he retains the right of redemption a full year after its sale. During that time he may redeem it. ³⁰If it is not redeemed before a full year has passed, the house in the walled city shall belong permanently to the buyer and his descendants. It is not to be returned in the Jubilee. ³¹But houses in villages without walls around them are to be considered as open country. They can be redeemed, and they are to be returned in the Jubilee.

³² "'The Levites always have the right to redeem their houses in the Levitical towns, which they possess. ³³So the property of the Levites is redeemable—that is, a house sold in any town they hold—and is to be returned in the Jubilee, because the houses in the towns of the Levites are their property among the Israelites. ³⁴But the pastureland belonging to their towns must not be sold; it is their permanent possession.

³⁵ "'If one of your countrymen becomes poor and is unable to support himself among you, help him as you would an alien or a temporary resident, so he can continue to live among you. ³⁶Do not take interest of any kind*a* from him, but fear your God, so that your countryman may continue to live among you. ³⁷You must not lend him money at interest or sell him food at a profit. ³⁸I am the LORD your God, who brought you out of Egypt to give you the land of Canaan and to be your God.

³⁹ "'If one of your countrymen becomes poor among you and sells himself to you, do not make him work as a slave. ⁴⁰He is to be treated as a hired worker or a temporary resident among you; he is to work for you until the Year of Jubilee. ⁴¹Then he and his children are

---

a 36 Or *take excessive interest*; similarly in verse 37

to be released, and he will go back to his own clan and to the property of his forefathers. ⁴²Because the Israelites are my servants, whom I brought out of Egypt, they must not be sold as slaves. ⁴³Do not rule over them ruthlessly, but fear your God.

⁴⁴"'Your male and female slaves are to come from the nations around you; from them you may buy slaves. ⁴⁵You may also buy some of the temporary residents living among you and members of their clans born in your country, and they will become your property. ⁴⁶You can will them to your children as inherited property and can make them slaves for life, but you must not rule over your fellow Israelites ruthlessly.

⁴⁷"'If an alien or a temporary resident among you becomes rich and one of your countrymen becomes poor and sells himself to the alien living among you or to a member of the alien's clan, ⁴⁸he retains the right of redemption after he has sold himself. One of his relatives may redeem him: ⁴⁹An uncle or a cousin or any blood relative in his clan may redeem him. Or if he prospers, he may redeem himself. ⁵⁰He and his buyer are to count the time from the year he sold himself up to the Year of Jubilee. The price for his release is to be based on the rate paid to a hired man for that number of years. ⁵¹If many years remain, he must pay for his redemption a larger share of the price paid for him. ⁵²If only a few years remain until the Year of Jubilee, he is to compute that and pay for his redemption accordingly. ⁵³He is to be treated as a man hired from year to year; you must see to it that his owner does not rule over him ruthlessly.

⁵⁴"'Even if he is not redeemed in any of these ways, he and his children are to be released in the Year of Jubilee, ⁵⁵for the Israelites belong to me as servants. They are my servants, whom I brought out of Egypt. I am the LORD your God.

Reward for Obedience

26 "'Do not make idols or set up an image or a sacred stone for yourselves, and do not place a carved stone in your land to bow down before it. I am the LORD your God.

²"'Observe my Sabbaths and have reverence for my sanctuary. I am the LORD.

³"'If you follow my decrees and are careful to obey my commands, ⁴I will send you rain in its season, and the ground will yield its crops and the trees of the field their fruit. ⁵Your threshing will continue until grape harvest and the grape harvest will continue until planting, and you will eat all the food you want and live in safety in your land.

⁶"'I will grant peace in the land, and you will lie down and no one will make you afraid. I will remove savage beasts from the land, and the sword will not pass through your country. ⁷You will pursue your enemies, and they will fall by the sword before you. ⁸Five of you will chase a hundred, and a hundred of you will chase ten thousand, and your enemies will fall by the sword before you.

⁹"'I will look on you with favor and make you fruitful and increase your numbers, and I will keep my covenant with you. ¹⁰You will still be eating last year's harvest when you will have to move it out to make room for the new. ¹¹I will put my dwelling place*ᵃ* among you, and I will not abhor you. ¹²I will walk among you and be your God, and you will be my people. ¹³I am the LORD your God, who brought you out of Egypt so that you would no longer be slaves to the Egyptians; I broke the bars of your yoke and enabled you to walk with heads held high.

Punishment for Disobedience

¹⁴"'But if you will not listen to me and carry out all these commands, ¹⁵and if you reject my decrees and abhor my laws and fail to carry out all my commands and so violate my covenant, ¹⁶then I will do this to you: I will bring upon you sudden terror, wasting diseases and fever that will destroy your sight and drain away your life. You will plant seed in vain, because your enemies will eat it. ¹⁷I will set my face against you so that you

ᵃ 11 Or my tabernacle

will be defeated by your enemies; those who hate you will rule over you, and you will flee even when no one is pursuing you.

18 " 'If after all this you will not listen to me, I will punish you for your sins seven times over. 19I will break down your stubborn pride and make the sky above you like iron and the ground beneath you like bronze. 20Your strength will be spent in vain, because your soil will not yield its crops, nor will the trees of the land yield their fruit.

21 " 'If you remain hostile toward me and refuse to listen to me, I will multiply your afflictions seven times over, as your sins deserve. 22I will send wild animals against you, and they will rob you of your children, destroy your cattle and make you so few in number that your roads will be deserted.

23 " 'If in spite of these things you do not accept my correction but continue to be hostile toward me, 24I myself will be hostile toward you and will afflict you for your sins seven times over. 25And I will bring the sword upon you to avenge the breaking of the covenant. When you withdraw into your cities, I will send a plague among you, and you will be given into enemy hands. 26When I cut off your supply of bread, ten women will be able to bake your bread in one oven, and they will dole out the bread by weight. You will eat, but you will not be satisfied.

27 " 'If in spite of this you still not listen to me but continue to be hostile toward me, 28then in my anger I will be hostile toward you, and I myself will punish you for your sins seven times over. 29You will eat the flesh of your sons and the flesh of your daughters. 30I will destroy your high places, cut down your incense altars and pile your dead bodies on the lifeless forms of your idols, and I will abhor you. 31I will turn your cities into ruins and lay waste your sanctuaries, and I will take no delight in the pleasing aroma of your offerings. 32I will lay waste the land, so that your enemies who live there will be appalled. 33I will scatter you among the nations and will draw out my sword and pursue you. Your land will be laid waste, and your cities will lie in ruins. 34Then the land will enjoy its sabbath years all the time that it lies desolate and you are in the country of your enemies; then the land will rest and enjoy its sabbaths. 35All the time that it lies desolate, the land will have the rest it did not have during the sabbaths you lived in it.

36 " 'As for those of you who are left, I will make their hearts so fearful in the lands of

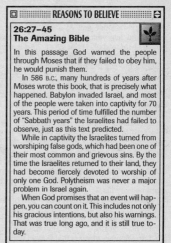

REASONS TO BELIEVE

26:27–45
The Amazing Bible

In this passage God warned the people through Moses that if they failed to obey him, he would punish them.

In 586 B.C., many hundreds of years after Moses wrote this book, that is precisely what happened. Babylon invaded Israel, and most of the people were taken into captivity for 70 years. This period of time fulfilled the number of "Sabbath years" the Israelites had failed to observe, just as this text predicted.

While in captivity the Israelites turned from worshiping false gods, which had been one of their most common and grievous sins. By the time the Israelites returned to their land, they had become fiercely devoted to worship of only one God. Polytheism was never a major problem in Israel again.

When God promises that an event will happen, you can count on it. This includes not only his gracious intentions, but also his warnings. That was true long ago, and it is still true today.

their enemies that the sound of a windblown leaf will put them to flight. They will run as though fleeing from the sword, and they will fall, even though no one is pursuing them. 37They will stumble over one another as though fleeing from the sword, even though no one is pursuing. So you will not be able to stand before your enemies. 38You will perish among the nations; the land of your enemies will devour you. 39Those of you who are left will waste away in the lands of their enemies because of their sins; also because of their fathers' sins they will waste away.

40 " 'But if they will confess their sins and the sins of their fathers—their treachery against me and their hostility toward me, 41which made me hostile toward them so that

I sent them into the land of their enemies—then when their uncircumcised hearts are humbled and they pay for their sin, ⁴²I will remember my covenant with Jacob and my covenant with Isaac and my covenant with Abraham, and I will remember the land. ⁴³For the land will be deserted by them and will enjoy its sabbaths while it lies desolate without them. They will pay for their sins because they rejected my laws and abhorred my decrees. ⁴⁴Yet in spite of this, when they are in the land of their enemies, I will not reject them or abhor them so as to destroy them completely, breaking my covenant with them. I am the LORD their God. ⁴⁵But for their sake I will remember the covenant with their ancestors whom I brought out of Egypt in the sight of the nations to be their God. I am the LORD.' "

⁴⁶These are the decrees, the laws and the regulations that the LORD established on Mount Sinai between himself and the Israelites through Moses.

Redeeming What Is the LORD's

27 The LORD said to Moses, ²"Speak to the Israelites and say to them: 'If anyone makes a special vow to dedicate persons to the LORD by giving equivalent values, ³set the value of a male between the ages of twenty and sixty at fifty shekels*ᵃ* of silver, according to the sanctuary shekel*ᵇ*; ⁴and if it is a female, set her value at thirty shekels.*ᶜ* ⁵If it is a person between the ages of five and twenty, set the value of a male at twenty shekels*ᵈ* and of a female at ten shekels.*ᵉ* ⁶If it is a person between one month and five years, set the value of a male at five shekels*ᶠ* of silver and that of a female at three shekels*ᵍ* of silver. ⁷If it is a person sixty years old or more, set the value of a male at fifteen shekels*ʰ* and of a female at ten shekels. ⁸If anyone making the vow is too poor to pay the specified amount, he is to present the person to the priest, who will set the value for him according to what the man making the vow can afford.

⁹"'If what he vowed is an animal that is acceptable as an offering to the LORD, such an animal given to the LORD becomes holy. ¹⁰He must not exchange it or substitute a good one for a bad one, or a bad one for a good one; if he should substitute one animal for another, both it and the substitute become holy. ¹¹If what he vowed is a ceremonially unclean animal—one that is not acceptable as an offering to the LORD—the animal must be presented to the priest, ¹²who will judge its quality as good or bad. Whatever value the priest then sets, that is what it will be. ¹³If the owner wishes to redeem the animal, he must add a fifth to its value.

¹⁴"'If a man dedicates his house as something holy to the LORD, the priest will judge its quality as good or bad. Whatever value the priest then sets, so it will remain. ¹⁵If the man who dedicates his house redeems it, he must add a fifth to its value, and the house will again become his.

¹⁶"'If a man dedicates to the LORD part of his family land, its value is to be set according to the amount of seed required for it—fifty shekels of silver to a homer*ⁱ* of barley seed. ¹⁷If he dedicates his field during the Year of Jubilee, the value that has been set remains. ¹⁸But if he dedicates his field after the Jubilee, the priest will determine the value according to the number of years that remain until the next Year of Jubilee, and its set value will be reduced. ¹⁹If the man who dedicates the field wishes to redeem it, he must add a fifth to its value, and the field will again become his. ²⁰If, however, he does not redeem the field, or if he has sold it to someone else, it can never be redeemed. ²¹When the field is released in the Jubilee, it will become holy, like a field devoted to the LORD; it will become the property of the priests.*ʲ*

²²"'If a man dedicates to the LORD a field he has bought, which is not part of his family land, ²³the priest will determine its value up to the Year of Jubilee, and the man must pay

ᵃ3 That is, about 1 1/4 pounds (about 0.6 kilogram); also in verse 16   ᵇ3 That is, about 12 ounces (about 0.3 kilogram)   in verse 25   ᵈ4 That is, about 110 ounces (about 0.3 kilogram)   ᵈ5 That is, about 2/5 ounce (about 11.5 grams); also   ᵉ5 That is, about 4 ounces (about 110 grams); also in verse 7   ᶠ6 That is, about 2 ounces (about 55 grams)   ᵍ6 That is, about 1 1/4 ounces (about 35 grams)   ʰ7 That is, about 6 ounces (about 170 grams)   ⁱ16 That is, probably about 6 bushels (about 220 liters)   ʲ21 Or priest

ts value on that day as something holy to the LORD. ²⁴In the Year of Jubilee the field will evert to the person from whom he bought it, the one whose land it was. ²⁵Every value is o be set according to the sanctuary shekel, twenty gerahs to the shekel.

²⁶ᵃ'No one, however, may dedicate the firstborn of an animal, since the firstborn already belongs to the LORD; whether an oxᵃ or a sheep, it is the LORD's. ²⁷If it is one of the unclean animals, he may buy it back at its set value, adding a fifth of the value to it. If he does not redeem it, it is to be sold at its set value.

²⁸ᵃ'But nothing that a man owns and devotesᵇ to the LORD—whether man or animal or amily land—may be sold or redeemed; everything so devoted is most holy to the LORD. ²⁹ᵃ'No person devoted to destructionᶜ may be ransomed; he must be put to death.

³⁰ᵃ'A tithe of everything from the land, whether grain from the soil or fruit from the rees, belongs to the LORD; it is holy to the LORD. ³¹If a man redeems any of his tithe, he nust add a fifth of the value to it. ³²The entire tithe of the herd and flock—every tenth nimal that passes under the shepherd's rod—will be holy to the LORD. ³³He must not pick out the good from the bad or make any substitution. If he does make a substitution, both he animal and its substitute become holy and cannot be redeemed.' "

³⁴These are the commands the LORD gave Moses on Mount Sinai for the Israelites.

---

26 The Hebrew word can include both male and female.   ᵇ28 The Hebrew term refers to the irrevocable giving over of ings or persons to the LORD.   ᶜ29 The Hebrew term refers to the irrevocable giving over of things or persons to the LORD, en by totally destroying them.

NUMBERS

Introduction

THE BOTTOM LINE

As a seeker, you may be frustrated by the realization of how far you fall short of God's ideals. While it's true that God has high standards, you can take comfort in the fact that you're not the first person who has disappointed him. This book details the rebellion of the Israelite people as they wandered in a hot, dusty desert for the better part of forty years. The cycle of the Israelites sinning against God, suffering the consequences of that sin, and pleading with God for forgiveness happens no less than ten times in this book alone. While God may at times appear harsh to our way of thinking, don't miss the point that God wants to protect his people. He therefore had to do some "surgery" on the nation of Israel. Any person who sins is invited to come back and be restored; however, serious consequences fall on those who refuse God's pardon.

CENTRAL IDEAS

- God's rules have been set in place to give people a measure of well-being in this world.
- Despite good intentions, no one completely obeys God.
- God is patient; he wants people to stop sinning and to return to him.
- God is not obligated to spare people from the consequences of their sin.

OUTLINE

1 Israel prepares to leave for the promised land (1:1—10:10)
2 Journey out of Sinai (10:11—12:16)
3 Israel rebels (13:1—20:13)
4 Journey to Moab (20:14—22:1)
5 Israel anticipates taking the promised land (22:2—32:42)
6 Miscellaneous instructions (chs. 33—36)

TITLE

The title relates directly to the genealogical information found in chapters 1 and 26; vast "numbers" of Israelites wander in the desert, hopefully anticipating their arrival in the new land that God has promised them.

AUTHOR AND READERS

Moses wrote this book for the people of Israel.

Let me tell you about the most horrible thing I've ever had to do as a father. Twice a day I performed an orthodontic procedure on my eleven-year-old son, David, that caused him excruciating pain.

Because his mouth wasn't large enough to house all of his teeth, it had to be made bigger. To accomplish that, a small metal bar was placed across the palate of his mouth and anchored on both sides to his upper molars. In the middle of the bar was a tiny slot into which I placed a lever. Twice a day I would crank that lever, which would spread the bar and stretch his palate. Over a period of weeks David's palate literally cracked. His mouth was enlarged, but the price was great pain.

Every morning and night David would plead with me, "Dad, do we have to do this?" Sometimes he became angry, and sometimes he questioned my love. Even though his mother and I did all we could to diminish the pain (my wife would tickle David to distract him), nothing relieved him of the hurt that accompanied the procedure.

Dad, do we have to do this?"

During these times of torment David never denied that I was his father; he was just angry about the pain, and his anger sometimes distorted his view of me. We have a similar experience with God. During difficult times in our lives we don't deny his existence, but pain and fear distort our view of him. We become angry that God allows hurtful things to happen.

The ancient people of Israel reacted in a similar manner. After God delivered them from slavery in Egypt, they wandered in the desert wilderness. Freedom from their Egyptian rulers wasn't all they had hoped it would be. "Maybe God just brought us out here to toy with us and make us suffer!" they thought. Disappointment and fear distorted their view of God.

How does God deal with such angry reactions to life's circumstances? How does God deal with *your* pain and disappointment? Turn to Numbers chapter 11, verses 1–34 (page 175), for a story that illustrates both the people's rebellion and God's firm but gracious response.

	Moses' life (c. 1526–1406 B.C.)	The exodus from Egypt (c. 1446 B.C.)	Israel's desert wanderings (c. 1446–1406 B.C.)	First period of Chinese literature (c. 1400 B.C.)		
	1500 BC	**1450**	**1400**	**1350**	**1300**
		Water buffalo domesticated in China (c. 1500 B.C.)	Exploration of Canaan (c. 1443 B.C.)	Book of Numbers written (c. 1406 B.C.)	First evidence of musical notation at Ugarit, Syria (c. 1300 B.C.)

NUMBERS

The Census

1 The LORD spoke to Moses in the Tent of Meeting in the Desert of Sinai on the first day of the second month of the second year after the Israelites came out of Egypt. He said: ²"Take a census of the whole Israelite community by their clans and families, listing every man by name, one by one. ³You and Aaron are to number by their divisions all the men in Israel twenty years old or more who are able to serve in the army. ⁴One man from each tribe, each the head of his family, is to help you. ⁵These are the names of the men who are to assist you:

from Reuben, Elizur son of Shedeur;
⁶from Simeon, Shelumiel son of Zurishaddai;
⁷from Judah, Nahshon son of Amminadab;
⁸from Issachar, Nethanel son of Zuar;
⁹from Zebulun, Eliab son of Helon;
¹⁰from the sons of Joseph:
from Ephraim, Elishama son of Ammihud;
from Manasseh, Gamaliel son of Pedahzur;
¹¹from Benjamin, Abidan son of Gideoni;
¹²from Dan, Ahiezer son of Ammishaddai;
¹³from Asher, Pagiel son of Ocran;
¹⁴from Gad, Eliasaph son of Deuel;
¹⁵from Naphtali, Ahira son of Enan."

¹⁶These were the men appointed from the community, the leaders of their ancestral tribes. They were the heads of the clans of Israel.

¹⁷Moses and Aaron took these men whose names had been given, ¹⁸and they called the whole community together on the first day of the second month. The people indicated their ancestry by their clans and families, and the men twenty years old or more were listed by name, one by one, ¹⁹as the LORD commanded Moses. And so he counted them in the Desert of Sinai:

²⁰From the descendants of Reuben the firstborn son of Israel:
All the men twenty years old or more who were able to serve in the army were listed by name, one by one, according to the records of their clans and families. ²¹The number from the tribe of Reuben was 46,500.

²²From the descendants of Simeon:
All the men twenty years old or more who were able to serve in the army were counted and listed by name, one by one, according to the records of their clans and families. ²³The number from the tribe of Simeon was 59,300.

²⁴From the descendants of Gad:
All the men twenty years old or more who were able to serve in the army were listed by name, according to the records of their clans and families. ²⁵The number from the tribe of Gad was 45,650.

²⁶From the descendants of Judah:
All the men twenty years old or more who were able to serve in the army were

listed by name, according to the records of their clans and families. ²⁷The number from the tribe of Judah was 74,600.

From the descendants of Issachar:
    All the men twenty years old or more who were able to serve in the army were listed by name, according to the records of their clans and families. ²⁹The number from the tribe of Issachar was 54,400.

From the descendants of Zebulun:
    All the men twenty years old or more who were able to serve in the army were listed by name, according to the records of their clans and families. ³¹The number from the tribe of Zebulun was 57,400.

From the sons of Joseph:
From the descendants of Ephraim:
    All the men twenty years old or more who were able to serve in the army were listed by name, according to the records of their clans and families. ³³The number from the tribe of Ephraim was 40,500.

From the descendants of Manasseh:
    All the men twenty years old or more who were able to serve in the army were listed by name, according to the records of their clans and families. ³⁵The number from the tribe of Manasseh was 32,200.

From the descendants of Benjamin:
    All the men twenty years old or more who were able to serve in the army were listed by name, according to the records of their clans and families. ³⁷The number from the tribe of Benjamin was 35,400.

From the descendants of Dan:
    All the men twenty years old or more who were able to serve in the army were listed by name, according to the records of their clans and families. ³⁹The number from the tribe of Dan was 62,700.

From the descendants of Asher:
    All the men twenty years old or more who were able to serve in the army were listed by name, according to the records of their clans and families. ⁴¹The number from the tribe of Asher was 41,500.

From the descendants of Naphtali:
    All the men twenty years old or more who were able to serve in the army were listed by name, according to the records of their clans and families. ⁴³The number from the tribe of Naphtali was 53,400.

⁴⁴These were the men counted by Moses and Aaron and the twelve leaders of Israel, each one representing his family. ⁴⁵All the Israelites twenty years old or more who were able to serve in Israel's army were counted according to their families. ⁴⁶The total number was 603,550.

⁴⁷The families of the tribe of Levi, however, were not counted along with the others. ⁴⁸The LORD had said to Moses: ⁴⁹"You must not count the tribe of Levi or include them in the census of the other Israelites. ⁵⁰Instead, appoint the Levites to be in charge of the tabernacle of the Testimony—over all its furnishings and everything belonging to it. They are to carry the tabernacle and all its furnishings; they are to take care of it and encamp around it. ⁵¹Whenever the tabernacle is to move, the Levites are to take it down, and whenever the tabernacle is to be set up, the Levites shall do it. Anyone else who goes near it shall be put to death. ⁵²The Israelites are to set up their tents by divisions, each man in his own camp under his own standard. ⁵³The Levites, however, are to set up their tents around the tabernacle of the Testimony so that wrath will not fall on the Israelite

community. The Levites are to be responsible for the care of the tabernacle of the Tes
mony."

⁵⁴The Israelites did all this just as the Lᴏʀᴅ commanded Moses.

The Arrangement of the Tribal Camps

2 The Lᴏʀᴅ said to Moses and Aaron: ²"The Israelites are to camp around t
Tent of Meeting some distance from it, each man under his standard with t
banners of his family."

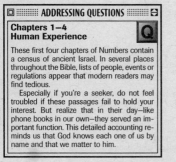

ADDRESSING QUESTIONS

**Chapters 1–4
Human Experience**

These first four chapters of Numbers contain
a census of ancient Israel. In several places
throughout the Bible, lists of people, events or
regulations appear that modern readers may
find tedious.

Especially if you're a seeker, do not feel
troubled if these passages fail to hold your
interest. But realize that in their day—like
phone books in our own—they served an important function. This detailed accounting reminds us that God knows each one of us by
name and that we matter to him.

³On the east, toward the sunrise, the
divisions of the camp of Judah are to
encamp under their standard. The
leader of the people of Judah is Nahshon son of Amminadab. ⁴His division
numbers 74,600.

⁵The tribe of Issachar will camp next
to them. The leader of the people of
Issachar is Nethanel son of Zuar. ⁶His
division numbers 54,400.

⁷The tribe of Zebulun will be next.
The leader of the people of Zebulun is
Eliab son of Helon. ⁸His division num-
bers 57,400.

⁹All the men assigned to the camp
of Judah, according to their divisions,
number 186,400. They will set out first.

¹⁰On the south will be the divisions of the camp of Reuben under their standard.
The leader of the people of Reuben is Elizur son of Shedeur. ¹¹His division numbers
46,500.

¹²The tribe of Simeon will camp next to them. The leader of the people of Simeon
is Shelumiel son of Zurishaddai. ¹³His division numbers 59,300.

¹⁴The tribe of Gad will be next. The leader of the people of Gad is Eliasaph son of
Deuel.ᵃ ¹⁵His division numbers 45,650.

¹⁶All the men assigned to the camp of Reuben, according to their divisions, number 151,450. They will set out second.

¹⁷Then the Tent of Meeting and the camp of the Levites will set out in the middle
of the camps. They will set out in the same order as they encamp, each in his own
place under his standard.

¹⁸On the west will be the divisions of the camp of Ephraim under their standard.
The leader of the people of Ephraim is Elishama son of Ammihud. ¹⁹His division
numbers 40,500.

²⁰The tribe of Manasseh will be next to them. The leader of the people of Manasseh is Gamaliel son of Pedahzur. ²¹His division numbers 32,200.

²²The tribe of Benjamin will be next. The leader of the people of Benjamin is
Abidan son of Gideoni. ²³His division numbers 35,400.

²⁴All the men assigned to the camp of Ephraim, according to their divisions, number 108,100. They will set out third.

²⁵On the north will be the divisions of the camp of Dan, under their standard. The

ᵃ14 Many manuscripts of the Masoretic Text, Samaritan Pentateuch and Vulgate (see also Num. 1:14); most manuscripts of the
Masoretic Text Reuel

leader of the people of Dan is Ahiezer son of Ammishaddai. ²⁶His division numbers 2,700.

²⁷The tribe of Asher will camp next to them. The leader of the people of Asher is agiel son of Ocran. ²⁸His division numbers 41,500.

²⁹The tribe of Naphtali will be next. The leader of the people of Naphtali is Ahira on of Enan. ³⁰His division numbers 53,400.

³¹All the men assigned to the camp of Dan number 157,600. They will set out last, nder their standards.

³²These are the Israelites, counted according to their families. All those in the amps, by their divisions, number 603,550. ³³The Levites, however, were not count-d along with the other Israelites, as the Lord commanded Moses.

⁴So the Israelites did everything the Lord commanded Moses; that is the way they amped under their standards, and that is the way they set out, each with his clan and ily.

e Levites

████ This is the account of the family of Aaron and Moses at the time the Lord talked with Moses on Mount Sinai.

The names of the sons of Aaron were Nadab the firstborn and Abihu, Eleazar and mar. ³Those were the names of Aaron's sons, the anointed priests, who were or-ned to serve as priests. ⁴Nadab and Abihu, however, fell dead before the Lord when y made an offering with unauthorized fire before him in the Desert of Sinai. They had sons; so only Eleazar and Ithamar served as priests during the lifetime of their father on.

The Lord said to Moses, ⁶"Bring the tribe of Levi and present them to Aaron the priest assist him. ⁷They are to perform duties for him and for the whole community at the t of Meeting by doing the work of the tabernacle. ⁸They are to take care of all the ishings of the Tent of Meeting, fulfilling the obligations of the Israelites by doing work of the tabernacle. ⁹Give the Levites to Aaron and his sons; they are the Israelites are to be given wholly to him.ᵃ ¹⁰Appoint Aaron and his sons to serve as priests; one else who approaches the sanctuary must be put to death."

¹The Lord also said to Moses, ¹²"I have taken the Levites from among the Israelites in ce of the first male offspring of every Israelite woman. The Levites are mine, ¹³for all firstborn are mine. When I struck down all the firstborn in Egypt, I set apart for myself ry firstborn in Israel, whether man or animal. They are to be mine. I am the Lord."

¹The Lord said to Moses in the Desert of Sinai, ¹⁵"Count the Levites by their families clans. Count every male a month old or more." ¹⁶So Moses counted them, as he was manded by the word of the Lord.

hese were the names of the sons of Levi:
Gershon, Kohath and Merari.

These were the names of the Gershonite clans:
Libni and Shimei.

he Kohathite clans:
Amram, Izhar, Hebron and Uzziel.

he Merarite clans:
Mahli and Mushi.

hese were the Levite clans, according to their families.

¹To Gershon belonged the clans of the Libnites and Shimeites; these were the Ger-nite clans. ²²The number of all the males a month old or more who were counted

ost manuscripts of the Masoretic Text; some manuscripts of the Masoretic Text, Samaritan Pentateuch and Septuagint (see fum. 8:16) to me

was 7,500. ²³The Gershonite clans were to camp on the west, behind the taberna
²⁴The leader of the families of the Gershonites was Eliasaph son of Lael. ²⁵At the Ter
Meeting the Gershonites were responsible for the care of the tabernacle and tent,
coverings, the curtain at the entrance to the Tent of Meeting, ²⁶the curtains of the co
yard, the curtain at the entrance to the courtyard surrounding the tabernacle and a
and the ropes—and everything related to their use.

²⁷To Kohath belonged the clans of the Amramites, Izharites, Hebronites and Uzziel
these were the Kohathite clans. ²⁸The number of all the males a month old or more
8,600.ᵃ The Kohathites were responsible for the care of the sanctuary. ²⁹The Kohat
clans were to camp on the south side of the tabernacle. ³⁰The leader of the families of
Kohathite clans was Elizaphan son of Uzziel. ³¹They were responsible for the care of
ark, the table, the lampstand, the altars, the articles of the sanctuary used in minister
the curtain, and everything related to their use. ³²The chief leader of the Levites
Eleazar son of Aaron, the priest. He was appointed over those who were responsible
the care of the sanctuary.

³³To Merari belonged the clans of the Mahlites and the Mushites; these were
Merarite clans. ³⁴The number of all the males a month old or more who were cou
was 6,200. ³⁵The leader of the families of the Merarite clans was Zuriel son of Abi
they were to camp on the north side of the tabernacle. ³⁶The Merarites were appointe
take care of the frames of the tabernacle, its crossbars, posts, bases, all its equipm
and everything related to their use, ³⁷as well as the posts of the surrounding court
with their bases, tent pegs and ropes.

³⁸Moses and Aaron and his sons were to camp to the east of the tabernacle, toward
sunrise, in front of the Tent of Meeting. They were responsible for the care of the sar
ary on behalf of the Israelites. Anyone else who approached the sanctuary was to be
to death.

³⁹The total number of Levites counted at the LORD's command by Moses and A
according to their clans, including every male a month old or more, was 22,000.

⁴⁰The LORD said to Moses, "Count all the firstborn Israelite males who are a month o
more and make a list of their names. ⁴¹Take the Levites for me in place of all the first
of the Israelites, and the livestock of the Levites in place of all the firstborn of
livestock of the Israelites. I am the LORD."

⁴²So Moses counted all the firstborn of the Israelites, as the LORD commanded
⁴³The total number of firstborn males a month old or more, listed by name, was 22,

⁴⁴The LORD also said to Moses, ⁴⁵"Take the Levites in place of all the firstborn of Is
and the livestock of the Levites in place of their livestock. The Levites are to be mine.
the LORD. ⁴⁶To redeem the 273 firstborn Israelites who exceed the number of the Lev
⁴⁷collect five shekelsᵇ for each one, according to the sanctuary shekel, which wei
twenty gerahs. ⁴⁸Give the money for the redemption of the additional Israelites to A
and his sons."

⁴⁹So Moses collected the redemption money from those who exceeded the nur
redeemed by the Levites. ⁵⁰From the firstborn of the Israelites he collected silver we
ing 1,365 shekels,ᶜ according to the sanctuary shekel. ⁵¹Moses gave the redemp
money to Aaron and his sons, as he was commanded by the word of the LORD.

ᵃ28 Hebrew; some Septuagint manuscripts 8,300   ᵇ47 That is, about 2 ounces (about 55 grams)   ᶜ50 That is, about
35 pounds (about 15.5 kilograms)

Kohathites

The LORD said to Moses and Aaron: [2]"Take a census of the Kohathite branch of the Levites by their clans and families. [3]Count all the men from thirty to [fifty] years of age who come to serve in the work in the Tent of Meeting.

[4]"This is the work of the Kohathites in the Tent of Meeting: the care of the most holy [thin]gs. [5]When the camp is to move, Aaron and his sons are to go in and take down the [sh]ielding curtain and cover the ark of the Testimony with it. [6]Then they are to cover this [wit]h hides of sea cows,[a] spread a cloth of solid blue over that and put the poles in place.

[7]"Over the table of the Presence they are to spread a blue cloth and put on it the plates, [dish]es and bowls, and the jars for drink offerings; the bread that is continually there is to [rem]ain on it. [8]Over these they are to spread a scarlet cloth, cover that with hides of sea [cow]s and put its poles in place.

[9]"They are to take a blue cloth and cover the lampstand that is for light, together with [its] lamps, its wick trimmers and trays, and all its jars for the oil used to supply it. [10]Then [the]y are to wrap it and all its accessories in a covering of hides of sea cows and put it on [a c]arrying frame.

[11]"Over the gold altar they are to spread a blue cloth and cover that with hides of sea [cow]s and put its poles in place.

[12]"They are to take all the articles used for ministering in the sanctuary, wrap them in [bl]ue cloth, cover that with hides of sea cows and put them on a carrying frame.

[13]"They are to remove the ashes from the bronze altar and spread a purple cloth over [it.] [14]Then they are to place on it all the utensils used for ministering at the altar, includ[ing] the firepans, meat forks, shovels and sprinkling bowls. Over it they are to spread a [cov]ering of hides of sea cows and put its poles in place.

[15]"After Aaron and his sons have finished covering the holy furnishings and all the [hol]y articles, and when the camp is ready to move, the Kohathites are to come to do the [carr]ying. But they must not touch the holy things or they will die. The Kohathites are to [carr]y those things that are in the Tent of Meeting.

[16]"Eleazar son of Aaron, the priest, is to have charge of the oil for the light, the fragrant [ince]nse, the regular grain offering and the anointing oil. He is to be in charge of the [enti]re tabernacle and everything in it, including its holy furnishings and articles."

[17]The LORD said to Moses and Aaron, [18]"See that the Kohathite tribal clans are not cut [off] from the Levites. [19]So that they may live and not die when they come near the most [hol]y things, do this for them: Aaron and his sons are to go into the sanctuary and assign [to e]ach man his work and what he is to carry. [20]But the Kohathites must not go in to look [at t]he holy things, even for a moment, or they will die."

Gershonites

[21]The LORD said to Moses, [22]"Take a census also of the Gershonites by their families and [clan]s. [23]Count all the men from thirty to fifty years of age who come to serve in the work [in t]he Tent of Meeting.

[24]"This is the service of the Gershonite clans as they work and carry burdens: [25]They [are] to carry the curtains of the tabernacle, the Tent of Meeting, its covering and the outer [cov]ering of hides of sea cows, the curtains for the entrance to the Tent of Meeting, [26]the [curt]ains of the courtyard surrounding the tabernacle and altar, the curtain for the en[tran]ce, the ropes and all the equipment used in its service. The Gershonites are to do all [that] needs to be done with these things. [27]All their service, whether carrying or doing [othe]r work, is to be done under the direction of Aaron and his sons. You shall assign to [the]m as their responsibility all they are to carry. [28]This is the service of the Gershonite [clan]s at the Tent of Meeting. Their duties are to be under the direction of Ithamar son of [Aaro]n, the priest.

[a] [that is, dugongs; also in verses 8, 10, 11, 12, 14 and 25]

The Merarites

29"Count the Merarites by their clans and families. 30Count all the men from thirty [to]
fifty years of age who come to serve in the work at the Tent of Meeting. 31This is t[he]
duty as they perform service at the Tent of Meeting: to carry the frames of the taberna[cle,]
its crossbars, posts and bases, 32as well as the posts of the surrounding courtyard v[ith]
their bases, tent pegs, ropes, all their equipment and everything related to their [use.]
Assign to each man the specific things he is to carry. 33This is the service of the Mera[rite]
clans as they work at the Tent of Meeting under the direction of Ithamar son of Aa[ron]
the priest."

The Numbering of the Levite Clans

34Moses, Aaron and the leaders of the community counted the Kohathites by their cl[ans]
and families. 35All the men from thirty to fifty years of age who came to serve in the w[ork]
in the Tent of Meeting, 36counted by clans, were 2,750. 37This was the total of all th[ose]
in the Kohathite clans who served in the Tent of Meeting. Moses and Aaron counted th[em]
according to the LORD's command through Moses.

38The Gershonites were counted by their clans and families. 39All the men from th[irty]
to fifty years of age who came to serve in the work at the Tent of Meeting, 40counted [by]
their clans and families, were 2,630. 41This was the total of those in the Gershonite cl[ans]
who served at the Tent of Meeting. Moses and Aaron counted them according to [the]
LORD's command.

42The Merarites were counted by their clans and families. 43All the men from thirty [to]
fifty years of age who came to serve in the work at the Tent of Meeting, 44counted [by]
their clans, were 3,200. 45This was the total of those in the Merarite clans. Moses [and]
Aaron counted them according to the LORD's command through Moses.

46So Moses, Aaron and the leaders of Israel counted all the Levites by their clans [and]
families. 47All the men from thirty to fifty years of age who came to do the work [of]
serving and carrying the Tent of Meeting 48numbered 8,580. 49At the LORD's comm[and]
through Moses, each was assigned his work and told what to carry.

Thus they were counted, as the LORD commanded Moses.

The Purity of the Camp

5 The LORD said to Moses, 2"Command the Israelites to send away from [the]
camp anyone who has an infectious skin disease[a] or a discharge of [any]
kind, or who is ceremonially unclean because of a dead body. 3Send away male [and]
female alike; send them outside the camp so they will not defile their camp, whe[re I]
dwell among them." 4The Israelites did this; they sent them outside the camp. They [did]
just as the LORD had instructed Moses.

Restitution for Wrongs

5The LORD said to Moses, 6"Say to the Israelites: 'When a man or woman wro[ngs]
another in any way[b] and so is unfaithful to the LORD, that person is guilty 7and [must]
confess the sin he has committed. He must make full restitution for his wrong, add [a]
fifth to it and give it all to the person he has wronged. 8But if that person has no c[lose]
relative to whom restitution can be made for the wrong, the restitution belongs to [the]
LORD and must be given to the priest, along with the ram with which atonement is m[ade]
for him. 9All the sacred contributions the Israelites bring to a priest will belong to h[im.]
10Each man's sacred gifts are his own, but what he gives to the priest will belong to [the]
priest.'"

---

a2 Traditionally leprosy; the Hebrew word was used for various diseases affecting the skin—not necessarily leprosy.   b6 Or
woman commits any wrong common to mankind

The Test for an Unfaithful Wife

[11]Then the LORD said to Moses, [12]"Speak to the Israelites and say to them: 'If a man's wife goes astray and is unfaithful to him [13]by sleeping with another man, and this is hidden from her husband and her impurity is undetected (since there is no witness against her and she has not been caught in the act), [14]and if feelings of jealousy come over her husband and he suspects his wife and she is impure—or if he is jealous and suspects her even though she is not impure— [15]then he is to take his wife to the priest. He must also take an offering of a tenth of an ephah[a] of barley flour on her behalf. He must not pour oil on it or put incense on it, because it is a grain offering for jealousy, a reminder offering to draw attention to guilt.

[16]"The priest shall bring her and have her stand before the LORD. [17]Then he shall take some holy water in a clay jar and put some dust from the tabernacle floor into the water. [18]After the priest has had the woman stand before the LORD, he shall loosen her hair and place in her hands the reminder offering, the grain offering for jealousy, while he himself holds the bitter water that brings a curse. [19]Then the priest shall put the woman under oath and say to her, "If no other man has slept with you and you have not gone astray and become impure while married to your husband, may this bitter water that brings a curse not harm you. [20]But if you have gone astray while married to your husband and you have defiled yourself by sleeping with a man other than your husband"— [21]here the priest is to put the woman under this curse

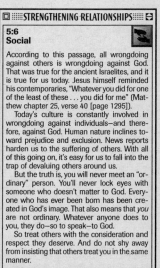

of the oath—"may the LORD cause your people to curse and denounce you when he causes your thigh to waste away and your abdomen to swell.[b] [22]May this water that brings a curse enter your body so that your abdomen swells and your thigh wastes away.[c]"

"Then the woman is to say, "Amen. So be it."

[23]"'The priest is to write these curses on a scroll and then wash them off into the bitter water. [24]He shall have the woman drink the bitter water that brings a curse, and this water will enter her and cause bitter suffering. [25]The priest is to take from her hands the grain offering for jealousy, wave it before the LORD and bring it to the altar. [26]The priest is then to take a handful of the grain offering as a memorial offering and burn it on the altar; after that, he is to have the woman drink the water. [27]If she has defiled herself and been unfaithful to her husband, then when she is made to drink the water that brings a curse, it will go into her and cause bitter suffering; her abdomen will swell and her thigh waste away,[d] and she will become accursed among her people. [28]If, however, the woman has not defiled herself and is free from impurity, she will be cleared of guilt and will be able to have children.

---

[a] 15 That is, probably about 2 quarts (about 2 liters)   [b] 21 Or causes you to have a miscarrying womb and barrenness   [c] 22 Or body and cause you to be barren and have a miscarrying womb   [d] 27 Or suffering; she will have barrenness and a miscarrying womb

²⁹"'This, then, is the law of jealousy when a woman goes astray and defiles hers
while married to her husband, ³⁰or when feelings of jealousy come over a man becau
he suspects his wife. The priest is to have her stand before the LORD and is to apply t
entire law to her. ³¹The husband will be innocent of any wrongdoing, but the wom
will bear the consequences of her sin.'"

The Nazirite

6 The LORD said to Moses, ²"Speak to the Israelites and say to them: 'If a man
woman wants to make a special vow, a vow of separation to the LORD as
Nazirite, ³he must abstain from wine and other fermented drink and must not dr
vinegar made from wine or from other fermented drink. He must not drink grape juice
eat grapes or raisins. ⁴As long as he is a Nazirite, he must not eat anything that com
from the grapevine, not even the seeds or skins.

⁵"'During the entire period of his vow of separation no razor may be used on his hea
He must be holy until the period of his separation to the LORD is over; he must let the h
of his head grow long. ⁶Throughout the period of his separation to the LORD he must
go near a dead body. ⁷Even if his own father or mother or brother or sister dies, he m
not make himself ceremonially unclean on account of them, because the symbol of
separation to God is on his head. ⁸Throughout the period of his separation he is cons
crated to the LORD.

⁹"'If someone dies suddenly in his presence, thus defiling the hair he has dedicated,
must shave his head on the day of his cleansing—the seventh day. ¹⁰Then on the eig
day he must bring two doves or two young pigeons to the priest at the entrance to
Tent of Meeting. ¹¹The priest is to offer one as a sin offering and the other as a bu
offering to make atonement for him because he sinned by being in the presence of
dead body. That same day he is to consecrate his head. ¹²He must dedicate himself to
LORD for the period of his separation and must bring a year-old male lamb as a g
offering. The previous days do not count, because he became defiled during his sepa
tion.

¹³"'Now this is the law for the Nazirite when the period of his separation is over. He
to be brought to the entrance to the Tent of Meeting. ¹⁴There he is to present
offerings to the LORD: a year-old male lamb without defect for a burnt offering, a year-
ewe lamb without defect for a sin offering, a ram without defect for a fellowship off
ing,ᵃ ¹⁵together with their grain offerings and drink offerings, and a basket of bre
made without yeast—cakes made of fine flour mixed with oil, and wafers spread with

¹⁶"The priest is to present them before the LORD and make the sin offering and
burnt offering. ¹⁷He is to present the basket of unleavened bread and is to sacrifice
ram as a fellowship offering to the LORD, together with its grain offering and drink off
ing.

¹⁸"'Then at the entrance to the Tent of Meeting, the Nazirite must shave off the h
that he dedicated. He is to take the hair and put it in the fire that is under the sacrifice
the fellowship offering.

¹⁹"'After the Nazirite has shaved off the hair of his dedication, the priest is to place
his hands a boiled shoulder of the ram, and a cake and a wafer from the basket, b
made without yeast. ²⁰The priest shall then wave them before the LORD as a wave off
ing; they are holy and belong to the priest, together with the breast that was waved a
the thigh that was presented. After that, the Nazirite may drink wine.

²¹"'This is the law of the Nazirite who vows his offering to the LORD in accordance w
his separation, in addition to whatever else he can afford. He must fulfill the vow he
made, according to the law of the Nazirite.'"

ᵃ14 Traditionally *peace offering*; also in verses 17 and 18

The Priestly Blessing

²²The LORD said to Moses, ²³"Tell Aaron and his sons, 'This is how you are to bless the Israelites. Say to them:

²⁴' "The LORD bless you
    and keep you;
²⁵the LORD make his face shine upon you
    and be gracious to you;
²⁶the LORD turn his face toward you
    and give you peace." '

²⁷"So they will put my name on the Israelites, and I will bless them."

Offerings at the Dedication of the Tabernacle

7 When Moses finished setting up the tabernacle, he anointed it and consecrated it and all its furnishings. He also anointed and consecrated the altar and all its utensils. ²Then the leaders of Israel, the heads of families who were the tribal leaders in charge of those who were counted, made offerings. ³They brought as their gifts before the LORD six covered carts and twelve oxen—an ox from each leader and a cart from every two. These they presented before the tabernacle.

⁴The LORD said to Moses, ⁵"Accept these from them, that they may be used in the work at the Tent of Meeting. Give them to the Levites as each man's work requires."

⁶So Moses took the carts and oxen and gave them to the Levites. ⁷He gave two carts and four oxen to the Gershonites, as their work required, ⁸and he gave four carts and eight oxen to the Merarites, as their work required. They were all under the direction of Ithamar son of Aaron, the priest. ⁹But Moses did not give any to the Kohathites, because they were to carry on their shoulders the holy things, for which they were responsible. ¹⁰When the altar was anointed, the leaders brought their offerings for its dedication and presented them before the altar. ¹¹For the LORD had said to Moses, "Each day one leader is to bring his offering for the dedication of the altar."

¹²The one who brought his offering on the first day was Nahshon son of Amminadab of the tribe of Judah.

¹³His offering was one silver plate weighing a hundred and thirty shekels,[a] and one silver sprinkling bowl weighing seventy shekels,[b] both according to the sanctuary shekel, each filled with fine flour mixed with oil as a grain offering; ¹⁴one gold dish weighing ten shekels,[c] filled with incense; ¹⁵one young bull, one ram and one male lamb a year old, for a burnt offering; ¹⁶one male goat for a sin offering; ¹⁷and two oxen, five rams, five male goats and five male lambs a year old, to be sacrificed as a fellowship offering.[d] This was the offering of Nahshon son of Amminadab.

¹⁸On the second day Nethanel son of Zuar, the leader of Issachar, brought his offering. ¹⁹The offering he brought was one silver plate weighing a hundred and thirty shekels, and one silver sprinkling bowl weighing seventy shekels, both according to the sanctuary shekel, each filled with fine flour mixed with oil as a grain offering; ²⁰one gold dish weighing ten shekels, filled with incense; ²¹one young bull, one ram and one male lamb a year old, for a burnt offering; ²²one male goat for a sin offering; ²³and two oxen, five rams, five male goats and five male lambs a year old, to be sacrificed as a fellowship offering. This was the offering of Nethanel son of Zuar.

²⁴On the third day, Eliab son of Helon, the leader of the people of Zebulun, brought his offering.

a 13 That is, about 3 1/4 pounds (about 1.5 kilograms); also elsewhere in this chapter   b 13 That is, about 1 3/4 pounds (about 0.8 kilogram); also elsewhere in this chapter   c 14 That is, about 4 ounces (about 110 grams); also elsewhere in this chapter   d 17 Traditionally *peace offering*; also elsewhere in this chapter

[25]His offering was one silver plate weighing a hundred and thirty shekels, and one silver sprinkling bowl weighing seventy shekels, both according to the sanctuary shekel, each filled with fine flour mixed with oil as a grain offering; [26]one gold dish weighing ten shekels, filled with incense; [27]one young bull, one ram and one male lamb a year old, for a burnt offering; [28]one male goat for a sin offering; [29]and two oxen, five rams, five male goats and five male lambs a year old, to be sacrificed as a fellowship offering. This was the offering of Eliab son of Helon.

[30]On the fourth day Elizur son of Shedeur, the leader of the people of Reuben, brought his offering.

[31]His offering was one silver plate weighing a hundred and thirty shekels, and one silver sprinkling bowl weighing seventy shekels, both according to the sanctuary shekel, each filled with fine flour mixed with oil as a grain offering; [32]one gold dish weighing ten shekels, filled with incense; [33]one young bull, one ram and one male lamb a year old, for a burnt offering; [34]one male goat for a sin offering; [35]and two oxen, five rams, five male goats and five male lambs a year old, to be sacrificed as a fellowship offering. This was the offering of Elizur son of Shedeur.

[36]On the fifth day Shelumiel son of Zurishaddai, the leader of the people of Simeon, brought his offering.

[37]His offering was one silver plate weighing a hundred and thirty shekels, and one silver sprinkling bowl weighing seventy shekels, both according to the sanctuary shekel, each filled with fine flour mixed with oil as a grain offering; [38]one gold dish weighing ten shekels, filled with incense; [39]one young bull, one ram and one male lamb a year old, for a burnt offering; [40]one male goat for a sin offering; [41]and two oxen, five rams, five male goats and five male lambs a year old, to be sacrificed as a fellowship offering. This was the offering of Shelumiel son of Zurishaddai.

[42]On the sixth day Eliasaph son of Deuel, the leader of the people of Gad, brought his offering.

[43]His offering was one silver plate weighing a hundred and thirty shekels, and one silver sprinkling bowl weighing seventy shekels, both according to the sanctuary shekel, each filled with fine flour mixed with oil as a grain offering; [44]one gold dish weighing ten shekels, filled with incense; [45]one young bull, one ram and one male lamb a year old, for a burnt offering; [46]one male goat for a sin offering; [47]and two oxen, five rams, five male goats and five male lambs a year old, to be sacrificed as a fellowship offering. This was the offering of Eliasaph son of Deuel.

[48]On the seventh day Elishama son of Ammihud, the leader of the people of Ephraim, brought his offering.

[49]His offering was one silver plate weighing a hundred and thirty shekels, and one silver sprinkling bowl weighing seventy shekels, both according to the sanctuary shekel, each filled with fine flour mixed with oil as a grain offering; [50]one gold dish weighing ten shekels, filled with incense; [51]one young bull, one ram and one male lamb a year old, for a burnt offering; [52]one male goat for a sin offering; [53]and two oxen, five rams, five male goats and five male lambs a year old, to be sacrificed as a fellowship offering. This was the offering of Elishama son of Ammihud.

[54]On the eighth day Gamaliel son of Pedahzur, the leader of the people of Manasseh, brought his offering.

[55]His offering was one silver plate weighing a hundred and thirty shekels, and one silver sprinkling bowl weighing seventy shekels, both according to the sanctuary shekel, each filled with fine flour mixed with oil as a grain offering; [56]one gold dish weighing ten shekels, filled with incense; [57]one young bull, one ram and one male lamb a year old, for a burnt offering; [58]one male goat for a sin offering; [59]and two

oxen, five rams, five male goats and five male lambs a year old, to be sacrificed as a fellowship offering. This was the offering of Gamaliel son of Pedahzur.

⁶⁰On the ninth day Abidan son of Gideoni, the leader of the people of Benjamin, brought his offering.

⁶¹His offering was one silver plate weighing a hundred and thirty shekels, and one silver sprinkling bowl weighing seventy shekels, both according to the sanctuary shekel, each filled with fine flour mixed with oil as a grain offering; ⁶²one gold dish weighing ten shekels, filled with incense; ⁶³one young bull, one ram and one male lamb a year old, for a burnt offering; ⁶⁴one male goat for a sin offering; ⁶⁵and two oxen, five rams, five male goats and five male lambs a year old, to be sacrificed as a fellowship offering. This was the offering of Abidan son of Gideoni.

⁶⁶On the tenth day Ahiezer son of Ammishaddai, the leader of the people of Dan, brought his offering.

⁶⁷His offering was one silver plate weighing a hundred and thirty shekels, and one silver sprinkling bowl weighing seventy shekels, both according to the sanctuary shekel, each filled with fine flour mixed with oil as a grain offering; ⁶⁸one gold dish weighing ten shekels, filled with incense; ⁶⁹one young bull, one ram and one male lamb a year old, for a burnt offering; ⁷⁰one male goat for a sin offering; ⁷¹and two oxen, five rams, five male goats and five male lambs a year old, to be sacrificed as a fellowship offering. This was the offering of Ahiezer son of Ammishaddai.

⁷²On the eleventh day Pagiel son of Ocran, the leader of the people of Asher, brought his offering.

⁷³His offering was one silver plate weighing a hundred and thirty shekels, and one silver sprinkling bowl weighing seventy shekels, both according to the sanctuary shekel, each filled with fine flour mixed with oil as a grain offering; ⁷⁴one gold dish weighing ten shekels, filled with incense; ⁷⁵one young bull, one ram and one male lamb a year old, for a burnt offering; ⁷⁶one male goat for a sin offering; ⁷⁷and two oxen, five rams, five male goats and five male lambs a year old, to be sacrificed as a fellowship offering. This was the offering of Pagiel son of Ocran.

⁷⁸On the twelfth day Ahira son of Enan, the leader of the people of Naphtali, brought his offering.

⁷⁹His offering was one silver plate weighing a hundred and thirty shekels, and one silver sprinkling bowl weighing seventy shekels, both according to the sanctuary shekel, each filled with fine flour mixed with oil as a grain offering; ⁸⁰one gold dish weighing ten shekels, filled with incense; ⁸¹one young bull, one ram and one male lamb a year old, for a burnt offering; ⁸²one male goat for a sin offering; ⁸³and two oxen, five rams, five male goats and five male lambs a year old, to be sacrificed as a fellowship offering. This was the offering of Ahira son of Enan.

⁸⁴These were the offerings of the Israelite leaders for the dedication of the altar when it was anointed: twelve silver plates, twelve silver sprinkling bowls and twelve gold dishes. ⁸⁵Each silver plate weighed a hundred and thirty shekels, and each sprinkling bowl seventy shekels. Altogether, the silver dishes weighed two thousand four hundred shekels,ᵃ according to the sanctuary shekel. ⁸⁶The twelve gold dishes filled with incense weighed ten shekels each, according to the sanctuary shekel. Altogether, the gold dishes weighed a hundred and twenty shekels.ᵇ ⁸⁷The total number of animals for the burnt offering came to twelve young bulls, twelve rams and twelve male lambs a year old,

ᵃ85 That is, about 60 pounds (about 28 kilograms)   ᵇ86 That is, about 3 pounds (about 1.4 kilograms) together with their grain offering. Twelve male goats were used for the sin offering. **88**The total number of animals for the sacrifice of the fellowship offering came to twenty-four oxen, sixty rams, sixty male goats and sixty male lambs a year old. These were the offerings for the dedication of the altar after it was anointed.

89When Moses entered the Tent of Meeting to speak with the LORD, he heard the voice speaking to him from between the two cherubim above the atonement cover on the ark of the Testimony. And he spoke with him.

Setting Up the Lamps

8 The LORD said to Moses, **2**"Speak to Aaron and say to him, 'When you set up the seven lamps, they are to light the area in front of the lampstand.'"

3Aaron did so; he set up the lamps so that they faced forward on the lampstand, just as the LORD commanded Moses. **4**This is how the lampstand was made: It was made of hammered gold—from its base to its blossoms. The lampstand was made exactly like the pattern the LORD had shown Moses.

The Setting Apart of the Levites

5The LORD said to Moses: **6**"Take the Levites from among the other Israelites and make them ceremonially clean. **7**To purify them, do this: Sprinkle the water of cleansing on them; then have them shave their whole bodies and wash their clothes, and so purify themselves. **8**Have them take a young bull with its grain offering of fine flour mixed with oil; then you are to take a second young bull for a sin offering. **9**Bring the Levites to the front of the Tent of Meeting and assemble the whole Israelite community. **10**You are to bring the Levites before the LORD, and the Israelites are to lay their hands on them. **11**Aaron is to present the Levites before the LORD as a wave offering from the Israelites, so that they may be ready to do the work of the LORD.

12"After the Levites lay their hands on the heads of the bulls, use the one for a sin offering to the LORD and the other for a burnt offering, to make atonement for the Levites. **13**Have the Levites stand in front of Aaron and his sons and then present them as a wave offering to the LORD. **14**In this way you are to set the Levites apart from the other Israelites, and the Levites will be mine.

15"After you have purified the Levites and presented them as a wave offering, they are to come to do their work at the Tent of Meeting. **16**They are the Israelites who are to be given wholly to me. I have taken them as my own in place of the firstborn, the first male offspring from every Israelite woman. **17**Every firstborn male in Israel, whether man or animal, is mine. When I struck down all the firstborn in Egypt, I set them apart for myself. **18**And I have taken the Levites in place of all the firstborn sons in Israel. **19**Of all the Israelites, I have given the Levites as gifts to Aaron and his sons to do the work at the Tent of Meeting on behalf of the Israelites and to make atonement for them so that no plague will strike the Israelites when they go near the sanctuary."

20Moses, Aaron and the whole Israelite community did with the Levites just as the LORD commanded Moses. **21**The Levites purified themselves and washed their clothes. Then Aaron presented them as a wave offering before the LORD and made atonement for them to purify them. **22**After that, the Levites came to do their work at the Tent of Meeting under the supervision of Aaron and his sons. They did with the Levites just as the LORD commanded Moses.

23The LORD said to Moses, **24**"This applies to the Levites: Men twenty-five years old or more shall come to take part in the work at the Tent of Meeting, **25**but at the age of fifty, they must retire from their regular service and work no longer. **26**They may assist their brothers in performing their duties at the Tent of Meeting, but they themselves must not do the work. This, then, is how you are to assign the responsibilities of the Levites."

The Passover

9 The LORD spoke to Moses in the Desert of Sinai in the first month of the second year after they came out of Egypt. He said, [2]"Have the Israelites celebrate the Passover at the appointed time. [3]Celebrate it at the appointed time, at twilight on the fourteenth day of this month, in accordance with all its rules and regulations."

[4]So Moses told the Israelites to celebrate the Passover, [5]and they did so in the Desert of Sinai at twilight on the fourteenth day of the first month. The Israelites did everything just as the LORD commanded Moses.

[6]But some of them could not celebrate the Passover on that day because they were ceremonially unclean on account of a dead body. So they came to Moses and Aaron that same day [7]and said to Moses, "We have become unclean because of a dead body, but why should we be kept from presenting the LORD's offering with the other Israelites at the appointed time?"

[8]Moses answered them, "Wait until I find out what the LORD commands concerning you."

[9]Then the LORD said to Moses, [10]"Tell the Israelites: 'When any of you or your descendants are unclean because of a dead body or are away on a journey, they may still celebrate the LORD's Passover. [11]They are to celebrate it on the fourteenth day of the second month at twilight. They are to eat the lamb, together with unleavened bread and bitter herbs. [12]They must not leave any of it till morning or break any of its bones. When they celebrate the Passover, they must follow all the regulations. [13]But if a man who is ceremonially clean and not on a journey fails to celebrate the Passover, that person must be cut off from his people because he did not present the LORD's offering at the appointed time. That man will bear the consequences of his sin.

[14]" 'An alien living among you who wants to celebrate the LORD's Passover must do so in accordance with its rules and regulations. You must have the same regulations for the alien and the native-born.' "

DISCOVERING GOD

9:15–23
The God Who Is There

During this period of Israel's history, God guided the nation with a constant and miraculous display of his power. The cloud of God's presence showed the people exactly where to go and when.

This divine manifestation served as a training tool, preparing the Israelites for their coming responsibilities. God only led the people with the cloud while they were in the desert. But what the Israelites learned through this experience served them well when God's leadership methods later changed.

As they watched the cloud, the nation could not help but see that God was part of their daily routine. No matter where people were in the camp, whether it was day or night, they could see the cloud and remember that God was near. The cloud also made the Israelites responsive to God. They were keenly aware that yesterday's guidance was for that day, and that they had to follow God afresh with each new day.

In every age, those of us who want to live in a relationship with God must be willing to do the same. This prospect may be a bit intimidating at first, but following the lead of the God who desires to work in the life of every individual on the planet can lead to some of the most surprising and exhilarating experiences a person can have!

The Cloud Above the Tabernacle

[15]On the day the tabernacle, the Tent of the Testimony, was set up, the cloud covered it. From evening till morning the cloud above the tabernacle looked like fire. [16]That is how it continued to be; the cloud covered it, and at night it looked like fire. [17]Whenever the cloud lifted from above the Tent, the Israelites set out; wherever the cloud settled, the Israelites encamped. [18]At the LORD's command the Israelites set out, and at his command they encamped. As long as the cloud stayed over the tabernacle, they remained in camp. [19]When the cloud remained over the tabernacle a long time, the Israelites obeyed the LORD's order and did not set out. [20]Sometimes the cloud was over the tabernacle only a

few days; at the LORD's command they would encamp, and then at his command the
would set out. ²¹Sometimes the cloud stayed only from evening till morning, and when
lifted in the morning, they set out. Whether by day or by night, whenever the cloud lifted
they set out. ²²Whether the cloud stayed over the tabernacle for two days or a month
a year, the Israelites would remain in camp and not set out; but when it lifted, the
would set out. ²³At the LORD's command they encamped, and at the LORD's command the
set out. They obeyed the LORD's order, in accordance with his command through Mose

The Silver Trumpets

10 The LORD said to Moses: ²"Make two trumpets of hammered silver, and us
them for calling the community together and for having the camps set ou
³When both are sounded, the whole community is to assemble before you at the entranc
to the Tent of Meeting. ⁴If only one is sounded, the leaders—the heads of the clans
Israel—are to assemble before you. ⁵When a trumpet blast is sounded, the tribes campin
on the east are to set out. ⁶At the sounding of a second blast, the camps on the south ar
to set out. The blast will be the signal for setting out. ⁷To gather the assembly, blow th
trumpets, but not with the same signal.

⁸"The sons of Aaron, the priests, are to blow the trumpets. This is to be a lastin
ordinance for you and the generations to come. ⁹When you go into battle in your ow
land against an enemy who is oppressing you, sound a blast on the trumpets. Then yo
will be remembered by the LORD your God and rescued from your enemies. ¹⁰Also at you
times of rejoicing—your appointed feasts and New Moon festivals—you are to sound th
trumpets over your burnt offerings and fellowship offerings,ᵃ and they will be a memori
al for you before your God. I am the LORD your God."

The Israelites Leave Sinai

¹¹On the twentieth day of the second month of the second year, the cloud lifted fror
above the tabernacle of the Testimony. ¹²Then the Israelites set out from the Desert c
Sinai and traveled from place to place until the cloud came to rest in the Desert of Parar
¹³They set out, this first time, at the LORD's command through Moses.

¹⁴The divisions of the camp of Judah went first, under their standard. Nahshon son c
Amminadab was in command. ¹⁵Nethanel son of Zuar was over the division of the tribe c
Issachar, ¹⁶and Eliab son of Helon was over the division of the tribe of Zebulun. ¹⁷The
the tabernacle was taken down, and the Gershonites and Merarites, who carried it, se
out.

¹⁸The divisions of the camp of Reuben went next, under their standard. Elizur son c
Shedeur was in command. ¹⁹Shelumiel son of Zurishaddai was over the division of th
tribe of Simeon, ²⁰and Eliasaph son of Deuel was over the division of the tribe of Gad
²¹Then the Kohathites set out, carrying the holy things. The tabernacle was to be set u
before they arrived.

²²The divisions of the camp of Ephraim went next, under their standard. Elishama so
of Ammihud was in command. ²³Gamaliel son of Pedahzur was over the division of th
tribe of Manasseh, ²⁴and Abidan son of Gideoni was over the division of the tribe o
Benjamin.

²⁵Finally, as the rear guard for all the units, the divisions of the camp of Dan set out
under their standard. Ahiezer son of Ammishaddai was in command. ²⁶Pagiel son c
Ocran was over the division of the tribe of Asher, ²⁷and Ahira son of Enan was over the
division of the tribe of Naphtali. ²⁸This was the order of march for the Israelite division
as they set out.

²⁹Now Moses said to Hobab son of Reuel the Midianite, Moses' father-in-law, "We are

ᵃ10 Traditionally peace offerings

etting out for the place about which the LORD said, 'I will give it to you.' Come with us and we will treat you well, for the LORD has promised good things to Israel."

³⁰He answered, "No, I will not go; I am going back to my own land and my own people."

³¹But Moses said, "Please do not leave us. You know where we should camp in the desert, and you can be our eyes. ³²If you come with us, we will share with you whatever good things the LORD gives us."

³³So they set out from the mountain of the LORD and traveled for three days. The ark of the covenant of the LORD went before them during those three days to find them a place to rest. ³⁴The cloud of the LORD was over them by day when they set out from the camp. ³⁵Whenever the ark set out, Moses said,

> "Rise up, O LORD!
>   May your enemies be scattered;
>   may your foes flee before you."

³⁶Whenever it came to rest, he said,

> "Return, O LORD,
>   to the countless thousands of Israel."

Fire From the LORD

11 Now the people complained about their hardships in the hearing of the LORD, and when he heard them his anger was aroused. Then fire from the LORD burned among them and consumed some of the outskirts of the camp. ²When the people cried out to Moses, he prayed to the LORD and the fire died down. ³So that place was called Taberah,ᵃ because fire from the LORD had burned among them.

Quail From the LORD

⁴The rabble with them began to crave other food, and again the Israelites started wailing and said, "If only we had meat to eat! ⁵We remember the fish we ate in Egypt at no cost—also the cucumbers, melons, leeks, onions and garlic. ⁶But now we have lost our appetite; we never see anything but this manna!"

⁷The manna was like coriander seed and looked like resin. ⁸The people went around gathering it, and then ground it in a handmill or crushed it in a mortar. They cooked it in a pot or made it into cakes. And it tasted like something made with olive oil. ⁹When the dew settled on the camp at night, the manna also came down.

¹⁰Moses heard the people of every family wailing, each at the entrance to his tent. The LORD became exceedingly angry, and Moses was troubled. ¹¹He asked the LORD, "Why did you bring this trouble on your servant? What have I done to displease you that you put the burden of all these people on me? ¹²Did I conceive all these people? Did I give them birth? Why do you tell me to carry them in my arms, as a nurse carries an infant, to the land you promised on oath to their forefathers? ¹³Where can I get meat for all these people? They keep wailing to me, 'Give us meat to eat!' ¹⁴I cannot carry all these people by myself; the burden is too heavy for me. ¹⁵If this is how you are going to treat me, put me to death right now—if I have found favor in your eyes—and do not let me face my own ruin."

¹⁶The LORD said to Moses: "Bring me seventy of Israel's elders who are known to you as leaders and officials among the people. Have them come to the Tent of Meeting, that they may stand there with you. ¹⁷I will come down and speak with you there, and I will take of the Spirit that is on you and put the Spirit on them. They will help you carry the burden of the people so that you will not have to carry it alone.

¹⁸"Tell the people: 'Consecrate yourselves in preparation for tomorrow, when you will

---

ᵃ3 *Taberah* means burning.

eat meat. The LORD heard you when you wailed, "If only we had meat to eat! We were better off in Egypt!" Now the LORD will give you meat, and you will eat it. [19]You will not eat it for just one day, or two days, or five, ten or twenty days, [20]but for a whole month—until it comes out of your nostrils and you loathe it—because you have rejected the LORD, who is among you, and have wailed before him, saying, "Why did we ever leave Egypt?" '"

[21]But Moses said, "Here I am among six hundred thousand men on foot, and you say, 'I will give them meat to eat for a whole month!' [22]Would they have enough if flocks and herds were slaughtered for them? Would they have enough if all the fish in the sea were caught for them?"

[23]The LORD answered Moses, "Is the LORD's arm too short? You will now see whether or not what I say will come true for you."

[24]So Moses went out and told the people what the LORD had said. He brought together seventy of their elders and had them stand around the Tent. [25]Then the LORD came down in the cloud and spoke with him, and he took of the Spirit that was on him and put the Spirit on the seventy elders. When the Spirit rested on them, they prophesied, but they did not do so again.[a]

[26]However, two men, whose names were Eldad and Medad, had remained in the camp. They were listed among the elders, but did not go out to the Tent. Yet the Spirit also rested on them, and they prophesied in the camp. [27]A young man ran and told Moses, "Eldad and Medad are prophesying in the camp."

[28]Joshua son of Nun, who had been Moses' aide since youth, spoke up and said, "Moses, my lord, stop them!"

a25 Or prophesied and continued to do so

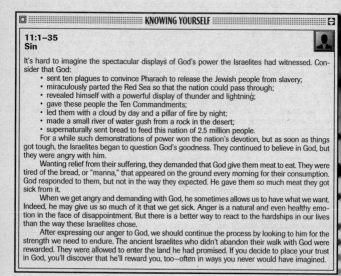

KNOWING YOURSELF

11:1–35
Sin

It's hard to imagine the spectacular displays of God's power the Israelites had witnessed. Consider that God:

- sent ten plagues to convince Pharaoh to release the Jewish people from slavery;
- miraculously parted the Red Sea so that the nation could pass through;
- revealed himself with a powerful display of thunder and lightning;
- gave these people the Ten Commandments;
- led them with a cloud by day and a pillar of fire by night;
- made a small river of water gush from a rock in the desert;
- supernaturally sent bread to feed this nation of 2.5 million people.

For a while such demonstrations of power won the nation's devotion, but as soon as things got tough, the Israelites began to question God's goodness. They continued to believe in God, but they were angry with him.

Wanting relief from their suffering, they demanded that God give them meat to eat. They were tired of the bread, or "manna," that appeared on the ground every morning for their consumption. God responded to them, but not in the way they expected. He gave them so much meat they got sick from it.

When we get angry and demanding with God, he sometimes allows us to have what we want. Indeed, he may give us so much of it that we get sick. Anger is a natural and even healthy emotion in the face of disappointment. But there is a better way to react to the hardships in our lives than the way these Israelites chose.

After expressing our anger to God, we should continue the process by looking to him for the strength we need to endure. The ancient Israelites who didn't abandon their walk with God were rewarded. They were allowed to enter the land he had promised. If you decide to place your trust in God, you'll discover that he'll reward you, too—often in ways you never would have imagined.

²⁹But Moses replied, "Are you jealous for my sake? I wish that all the LORD's people were prophets and that the LORD would put his Spirit on them!" ³⁰Then Moses and the elders of Israel returned to the camp.

³¹Now a wind went out from the LORD and drove quail in from the sea. It brought them*ᵃ* down all around the camp to about three feet*ᵇ* above the ground, as far as a day's walk in any direction. ³²All that day and night and all the next day the people went out and gathered quail. No one gathered less than ten homers.*ᶜ* Then they spread them out all around the camp. ³³But while the meat was still between their teeth and before it could be consumed, the anger of the LORD burned against the people, and he struck them with a severe plague. ³⁴Therefore the place was named Kibroth Hattaavah,*ᵈ* because there they buried the people who had craved other food.

³⁵From Kibroth Hattaavah the people traveled to Hazeroth and stayed there.

Miriam and Aaron Oppose Moses

12 Miriam and Aaron began to talk against Moses because of his Cushite wife, for he had married a Cushite. ²"Has the LORD spoken only through Moses?" they asked. "Hasn't he also spoken through us?" And the LORD heard this.

³(Now Moses was a very humble man, more humble than anyone else on the face of the earth.)

⁴At once the LORD said to Moses, Aaron and Miriam, "Come out to the Tent of Meeting, all three of you." So the three of them came out. ⁵Then the LORD came down in a pillar of cloud; he stood at the entrance to the Tent and summoned Aaron and Miriam. When both of them stepped forward, ⁶he said, "Listen to my words:

> "When a prophet of the LORD is among you,
>   I reveal myself to him in visions,
>   I speak to him in dreams.
> ⁷But this is not true of my servant Moses;
>   he is faithful in all my house.
> ⁸With him I speak face to face,
>   clearly and not in riddles;
>   he sees the form of the LORD.
> Why then were you not afraid
>   to speak against my servant Moses?"

⁹The anger of the LORD burned against them, and he left them.

¹⁰When the cloud lifted from above the Tent, there stood Miriam—leprous,*ᵉ* like snow. Aaron turned toward her and saw that she had leprosy; ¹¹and he said to Moses, "Please, my lord, do not hold against us the sin we have so foolishly committed. ¹²Do not let her be like a stillborn infant coming from its mother's womb with its flesh half eaten away."

¹³So Moses cried out to the LORD, "O God, please heal her!"

¹⁴The LORD replied to Moses, "If her father had spit in her face, would she not have been in disgrace for seven days? Confine her outside the camp for seven days; after that she can be brought back." ¹⁵So Miriam was confined outside the camp for seven days, and the people did not move on till she was brought back.

¹⁶After that, the people left Hazeroth and encamped in the Desert of Paran.

---

a31 Or *They flew*   *b31* Hebrew *two cubits* (about 1 meter)   *c32* That is, probably about 60 bushels (about 2.2 kiloliters)   *d34* *Kibroth Hattaavah* means *graves of craving.*   *e10* The Hebrew word was used for various diseases affecting the skin—not necessarily leprosy.

Exploring Canaan

13 The LORD said to Moses, ²"Send some men to explore the land of Canaan, which I am giving to the Israelites. From each ancestral tribe send one of its leaders."

³So at the LORD's command Moses sent them out from the Desert of Paran. All of them were leaders of the Israelites. ⁴These are their names:

from the tribe of Reuben, Shammua son of Zaccur;
⁵from the tribe of Simeon, Shaphat son of Hori;
⁶from the tribe of Judah, Caleb son of Jephunneh;
⁷from the tribe of Issachar, Igal son of Joseph;
⁸from the tribe of Ephraim, Hoshea son of Nun;
⁹from the tribe of Benjamin, Palti son of Raphu;
¹⁰from the tribe of Zebulun, Gaddiel son of Sodi;
¹¹from the tribe of Manasseh (a tribe of Joseph), Gaddi son of Susi;
¹²from the tribe of Dan, Ammiel son of Gemalli;
¹³from the tribe of Asher, Sethur son of Michael;
¹⁴from the tribe of Naphtali, Nahbi son of Vophsi;
¹⁵from the tribe of Gad, Geuel son of Maki.

¹⁶These are the names of the men Moses sent to explore the land. (Moses gave Hoshea son of Nun the name Joshua.)

¹⁷When Moses sent them to explore Canaan, he said, "Go up through the Negev and on into the hill country. ¹⁸See what the land is like and whether the people who live there are strong or weak, few or many. ¹⁹What kind of land do they live in? Is it good or bad? What kind of towns do they live in? Are they unwalled or fortified? ²⁰How is the soil? Is it fertile or poor? Are there trees on it or not? Do your best to bring back some of the fruit of the land." (It was the season for the first ripe grapes.)

²¹So they went up and explored the land from the Desert of Zin as far as Rehob, toward Lebo*ᵃ* Hamath. ²²They went up through the Negev and came to Hebron, where Ahiman, Sheshai and Talmai, the descendants of Anak, lived. (Hebron had been built seven years before Zoan in Egypt.) ²³When they reached the Valley of Eshcol,*ᵇ* they cut off a branch bearing a single cluster of grapes. Two of them carried it on a pole between them, along with some pomegranates and figs. ²⁴That place was called the Valley of Eshcol because of the cluster of grapes the Israelites cut off there. ²⁵At the end of forty days they returned from exploring the land.

Report on the Exploration

²⁶They came back to Moses and Aaron and the whole Israelite community at Kadesh in the Desert of Paran. There they reported to them and to the whole assembly and showed them the fruit of the land. ²⁷They gave Moses this account: "We went into the land to which you sent us, and it does flow with milk and honey! Here is its fruit. ²⁸But the people who live there are powerful, and the cities are fortified and very large. We even saw descendants of Anak there. ²⁹The Amalekites live in the Negev; the Hittites, Jebusites and Amorites live in the hill country; and the Canaanites live near the sea and along the Jordan."

³⁰Then Caleb silenced the people before Moses and said, "We should go up and take possession of the land, for we can certainly do it."

³¹But the men who had gone up with him said, "We can't attack those people; they are stronger than we are." ³²And they spread among the Israelites a bad report about the land they had explored. They said, "The land we explored devours those living in it. All the people we saw there are of great size. ³³We saw the Nephilim there (the descendants

ᵃ21 Or toward the entrance to   ᵇ23 Eshcol means cluster; also in verse 24.

of Anak come from the Nephilim). We seemed like grasshoppers in our own eyes, and we looked the same to them."

The People Rebel

14 That night all the people of the community raised their voices and wept aloud. ²All the Israelites grumbled against Moses and Aaron, and the whole assembly said to them, "If only we had died in Egypt! Or in this desert! ³Why is the LORD bringing us to this land only to let us fall by the sword? Our wives and children will be taken as plunder. Wouldn't it be better for us to go back to Egypt?" ⁴And they said to each other, "We should choose a leader and go back to Egypt."

⁵Then Moses and Aaron fell facedown in front of the whole Israelite assembly gathered there. ⁶Joshua son of Nun and Caleb son of Jephunneh, who were among those who had explored the land, tore their clothes ⁷and said to the entire Israelite assembly, "The land we passed through and explored is exceedingly good. ⁸If the LORD is pleased with us, he will lead us into that land, a land flowing with milk and honey, and will give it to us. ⁹Only do not rebel against the LORD. And do not be afraid of the people of the land, because we will swallow them up. Their protection is gone, but the LORD is with us. Do not be afraid of them."

¹⁰But the whole assembly talked about stoning them. Then the glory of the LORD appeared at the Tent of Meeting to all the Israelites. ¹¹The LORD said to Moses, "How long will these people treat me with contempt? How long will they refuse to believe in me, in spite of all the miraculous signs I have performed among them? ¹²I will strike them down with a plague and destroy them, but I will make you into a nation greater and stronger than they."

¹³Moses said to the LORD, "Then the Egyptians will hear about it! By your power you brought these people up from among them. ¹⁴And they will tell the inhabitants of this land about it. They have already heard that you, O LORD, are with these people and that you, O LORD, have been seen face to face, that your cloud stays over them, and that you go

---

▣ :::::::::::::::::::::::::: **STRENGTHENING RELATIONSHIPS** :::::::::::::::::::::::::: ⬌

14:1–23
Leadership

This should have been Moses' greatest leadership moment. He had led the fledgling nation of slaves out of captivity in Egypt and now stood on the border of the land God had promised to give them.

After sending a band of spies to explore Canaan, their new homeland, God himself assured the Israelites that, with his help, they could conquer it. But then something went wrong—10 of the 12 spies crumbled in despair, telling their friends and families that the enemy was too strong to defeat. Crippled by fear, the whole nation suddenly turned against both God and Moses (verses 3–4).

What does a good leader do in such a situation? Perhaps as a test, God suggested starting over from scratch to make a new nation. But Moses considered the needs of his followers before his own, asking God for mercy and forgiveness for the people. And, being completely sensitive to God's perspective, he framed the whole problem in the context of God's reputation. God's response to Moses included both forgiveness and discipline (verses 20–23).

Moses could have used his position either to advance himself or to benefit the nation. As a godly leader, he made the correct choice. Such a choice isn't always easy—especially when a small compromise holds the promise of money, power or fame. If you're a leader, you'll do well to follow Moses' example. Ask yourself, "Which decision will benefit the people I lead, rather than allowing me to position myself more favorably?" Then choose to do what's right, no matter how great the sacrifice. In the long run, you'll never regret such a choice.

Actually, this *was* Moses' greatest leadership moment!

before them in a pillar of cloud by day and a pillar of fire by night. ¹⁵If you put these people to death all at one time, the nations who have heard this report about you will say, ¹⁶'The LORD was not able to bring these people into the land he promised them on oath; so he slaughtered them in the desert.'

¹⁷"Now may the Lord's strength be displayed, just as you have declared: ¹⁸'The LORD is slow to anger, abounding in love and forgiving sin and rebellion. Yet he does not leave the guilty unpunished; he punishes the children for the sin of the fathers to the third and fourth generation.' ¹⁹In accordance with your great love, forgive the sin of these people, just as you have pardoned them from the time they left Egypt until now."

²⁰The LORD replied, "I have forgiven them, as you asked. ²¹Nevertheless, as surely as I live and as surely as the glory of the LORD fills the whole earth, ²²not one of the men who saw my glory and the miraculous signs I performed in Egypt and in the desert but who disobeyed me and tested me ten times— ²³not one of them will ever see the land I promised on oath to their forefathers. No one who has treated me with contempt will ever see it. ²⁴But because my servant Caleb has a different spirit and follows me wholeheartedly, I will bring him into the land he went to, and his descendants will inherit it ²⁵Since the Amalekites and Canaanites are living in the valleys, turn back tomorrow and set out toward the desert along the route to the Red Sea.ᵃ"

²⁶The LORD said to Moses and Aaron: ²⁷"How long will this wicked community grumble against me? I have heard the complaints of these grumbling Israelites. ²⁸So tell them, 'As surely as I live, declares the LORD, I will do to you the very things I heard you say: ²⁹In this desert your bodies will fall—every one of you twenty years old or more who was counted in the census and who has grumbled against me. ³⁰Not one of you will enter the land I swore with uplifted hand to make your home, except Caleb son of Jephunneh and Joshua son of Nun. ³¹As for your children that you said would be taken as plunder, I will bring them in to enjoy the land you have rejected. ³²But you—your bodies will fall in this desert. ³³Your children will be shepherds here for forty years, suffering for your unfaithfulness, until the last of your bodies lies in the desert. ³⁴For forty years—one year for each of the forty days you explored the land—you will suffer for your sins and know what it is like to have me against you.' ³⁵I, the LORD, have spoken, and I will surely do these things to this whole wicked community, which has banded together against me. They will meet their end in this desert; here they will die."

³⁶So the men Moses had sent to explore the land, who returned and made the whole community grumble against him by spreading a bad report about it— ³⁷these men responsible for spreading the bad report about the land were struck down and died of a plague before the LORD. ³⁸Of the men who went to explore the land, only Joshua son of Nun and Caleb son of Jephunneh survived.

³⁹When Moses reported this to all the Israelites, they mourned bitterly. ⁴⁰Early the next morning they went up toward the high hill country. "We have sinned," they said. "We will go up to the place the LORD promised."

⁴¹But Moses said, "Why are you disobeying the LORD's command? This will not succeed! ⁴²Do not go up, because the LORD is not with you. You will be defeated by your enemies, ⁴³for the Amalekites and Canaanites will face you there. Because you have turned away from the LORD, he will not be with you and you will fall by the sword."

⁴⁴Nevertheless, in their presumption they went up toward the high hill country, though neither Moses nor the ark of the LORD's covenant moved from the camp. ⁴⁵Then the Amalekites and Canaanites who lived in that hill country came down and attacked them and beat them down all the way to Hormah.

ᵃ25 Hebrew *Yam Suph*; that is, Sea of Reeds

Supplementary Offerings

15 The LORD said to Moses, **2**"Speak to the Israelites and say to them: 'After you enter the land I am giving you as a home **3**and you present to the LORD offerings made by fire, from the herd or the flock, as an aroma pleasing to the LORD— whether burnt offerings or sacrifices, for special vows or freewill offerings or festival offerings— **4**then the one who brings his offering shall present to the LORD a grain offering of a tenth of an ephah*a* of fine flour mixed with a quarter of a hin*b* of oil, **5**With each lamb for the burnt offering or the sacrifice, prepare a quarter of a hin of wine as a drink offering.

6"'With a ram prepare a grain offering of two-tenths of an ephah*c* of fine flour mixed with a third of a hin*d* of oil, **7**and a third of a hin of wine as a drink offering. Offer it as an aroma pleasing to the LORD.

8"'When you prepare a young bull as a burnt offering or sacrifice, for a special vow or a fellowship offering*e* to the LORD, **9**bring with the bull a grain offering of three-tenths of an ephah*f* of fine flour mixed with half a hin*g* of oil. **10**Also bring half a hin of wine as a drink offering. It will be an offering made by fire, an aroma pleasing to the LORD. **11**Each bull or ram, each lamb or young goat, is to be prepared in this manner. **12**Do this for each one, for as many as you prepare.

13"'Everyone who is native-born must do these things in this way when he brings an offering made by fire as an aroma pleasing to the LORD. **14**For the generations to come, whenever an alien or anyone else living among you presents an offering made by fire as an aroma pleasing to the LORD, he must do exactly as you do. **15**The community is to have the same rules for you and for the alien living among you; this is a lasting ordinance for the generations to come. You and the alien shall be the same before the LORD: **16**The same laws and regulations will apply both to you and to the alien living among you.'"

17The LORD said to Moses, **18**"Speak to the Israelites and say to them: 'When you enter the land to which I am taking you **19**and you eat the food of the land, present a portion as an offering to the LORD. **20**Present a cake from the first of your ground meal and present it as an offering from the threshing floor. **21**Throughout the generations to come you are to give this offering to the LORD from the first of your ground meal.

Offerings for Unintentional Sins

22"'Now if you unintentionally fail to keep any of these commands the LORD gave Moses— **23**any of the LORD's commands to you through him, from the day the LORD gave them and continuing through the generations to come— **24**and if this is done unintentionally without the community being aware of it, then the whole community is to offer a young bull for a burnt offering as an aroma pleasing to the LORD, along with its prescribed grain offering and drink offering, and a male goat for a sin offering. **25**The priest is to make atonement for the whole Israelite community, and they will be forgiven, for it was not intentional and they have brought to the LORD for their wrong an offering made by fire and a sin offering. **26**The whole Israelite community and the aliens living among them will be forgiven, because all the people were involved in the unintentional wrong.

27"'But if just one person sins unintentionally, he must bring a year-old female goat for a sin offering. **28**The priest is to make atonement before the LORD for the one who erred by sinning unintentionally, and when atonement has been made for him, he will be forgiven. **29**One and the same law applies to everyone who sins unintentionally, whether he is a native-born Israelite or an alien.

30"'But anyone who sins defiantly, whether native-born or alien, blasphemes the LORD, and that person must be cut off from his people. **31**Because he has despised the LORD's

a4 That is, probably about 2 quarts (about 2 liters)   *b4* That is, probably about 1 quart (about 1 liter); also in verse 5
c6 That is, probably about 4 quarts (about 4.5 liters)   *d6* That is, probably about 1 1/4 quarts (about 1.2 liters); also in
verse 7   *e8* Traditionally *peace offering*   *f9* That is, probably about 6 quarts (about 6.5 liters)   *g9* That is,
probably about 2 quarts (about 2 liters); also in verse 10

word and broken his commands, that person must surely be cut off; his guilt remains on him.'"

The Sabbath-Breaker Put to Death

³²While the Israelites were in the desert, a man was found gathering wood on the Sabbath day. ³³Those who found him gathering wood brought him to Moses and Aaron and the whole assembly, ³⁴and they kept him in custody, because it was not clear what should be done to him. ³⁵Then the LORD said to Moses, "The man must die. The whole assembly must stone him outside the camp." ³⁶So the assembly took him outside the camp and stoned him to death, as the LORD commanded Moses.

⊡ ▦▦▦ STRENGTHENING RELATIONSHIPS ▦▦▦ ⊟

15:37–40
Parenting

Here God commanded that the people of Israel wear a physical reminder of their need to obey him. The tassels on their garments served as a check on their behavior, specifically in regard to lust. Committing adultery, for example, would have been pretty difficult without the individuals seeing the tassels and knowing that God forbade what they were about to do.

Reminders of moral behavior can be a great idea—not only for ourselves, but for our children. Some parents help their kids stay sexually pure until marriage by giving them a ring, or some other jewelry, that the teenager wears until he or she gets married. When on a date, such a tangible sign can point to a higher and better commitment, overruling the decision that may seem unavoidable in the passion of the moment.

Tassels on Garments

³⁷The LORD said to Moses, ³⁸"Speak to the Israelites and say to them: 'Throughout the generations to come you are to make tassels on the corners of your garments, with a blue cord on each tassel. ³⁹You will have these tassels to look at and so you will remember all the commands of the LORD, that you may obey them and not prostitute yourselves by going after the lusts of your own hearts and eyes. ⁴⁰Then you will remember to obey all my commands and will be consecrated to your God. ⁴¹I am the LORD your God, who brought you out of Egypt to be your God. I am the LORD your God.'"

Korah, Dathan and Abiram

16 Korah son of Izhar, the son of Kohath, the son of Levi, and certain Reubenites—Dathan and Abiram, sons of Eliab, and On son of Peleth—became insolent[a] ²and rose up against Moses. With them were 250 Israelite men, well-known community leaders who had been appointed members of the council. ³They came as a group to oppose Moses and Aaron and said to them, "You have gone too far! The whole community is holy, every one of them, and the LORD is with them. Why then do you set yourselves above the LORD's assembly?"

⁴When Moses heard this, he fell facedown. ⁵Then he said to Korah and all his followers: "In the morning the LORD will show who belongs to him and who is holy, and he will have that person come near him. The man he chooses he will cause to come near him. ⁶You, Korah, and all your followers are to do this: Take censers ⁷and tomorrow put fire and incense in them before the LORD. The man the LORD chooses will be the one who is holy. You Levites have gone too far!"

⁸Moses also said to Korah, "Now listen, you Levites! ⁹Isn't it enough for you that the God of Israel has separated you from the rest of the Israelite community and brought you near himself to do the work at the LORD's tabernacle and to stand before the community and minister to them? ¹⁰He has brought you and all your fellow Levites near himself, but now you are trying to get the priesthood too. ¹¹It is against the LORD that you and all your followers have banded together. Who is Aaron that you should grumble against him?"

¹²Then Moses summoned Dathan and Abiram, the sons of Eliab. But they said, "We will

---

a 1 Or Peleth—took ,men,

not come! ¹³Isn't it enough that you have brought us up out of a land flowing with milk and honey to kill us in the desert? And now you also want to lord it over us? ¹⁴Moreover, you haven't brought us into a land flowing with milk and honey or given us an inheritance of fields and vineyards. Will you gouge out the eyes of*ᵃ* these men? No, we will not come!"

¹⁵Then Moses became very angry and said to the LORD, "Do not accept their offering. I have not taken so much as a donkey from them, nor have I wronged any of them."

¹⁶Moses said to Korah, "You and all your followers are to appear before the LORD tomorrow—you and they and Aaron. ¹⁷Each man is to take his censer and put incense in it—250 censers in all—and present it before the LORD. You and Aaron are to present your censers also." ¹⁸So each man took his censer, put fire and incense in it, and stood with Moses and Aaron at the entrance to the Tent of Meeting. ¹⁹When Korah had gathered all his followers in opposition to them at the entrance to the Tent of Meeting, the glory of the LORD appeared to the entire assembly. ²⁰The LORD said to Moses and Aaron, ²¹"Separate yourselves from this assembly so I can put an end to them at once."

²²But Moses and Aaron fell facedown and cried out, "O God, God of the spirits of all mankind, will you be angry with the entire assembly when only one man sins?"

²³Then the LORD said to Moses, ²⁴"Say to the assembly, 'Move away from the tents of Korah, Dathan and Abiram.'"

²⁵Moses got up and went to Dathan and Abiram, and the elders of Israel followed him. ²⁶He warned the assembly, "Move back from the tents of these wicked men! Do not touch anything belonging to them, or you will be swept away because of all their sins." ²⁷So they moved away from the tents of Korah, Dathan and Abiram. Dathan and Abiram had come out and were standing with their wives, children and little ones at the entrances to their tents.

²⁸Then Moses said, "This is how you will know that the LORD has sent me to do all these things and that it was not my idea: ²⁹If these men die a natural death and experience only what usually happens to men, then the LORD has not sent me. ³⁰But if the LORD brings about something totally new, and the earth opens its mouth and swallows them, with everything that belongs to them, and they go down alive into the grave,*ᵇ* then you will know that these men have treated the LORD with contempt."

³¹As soon as he finished saying all this, the ground under them split apart ³²and the earth opened its mouth and swallowed them, with their households and all Korah's men and all their possessions. ³³They went down alive into the grave, with everything they owned; the earth closed over them, and they perished and were gone from the community. ³⁴At their cries, all the Israelites around them fled, shouting, "The earth is going to swallow us too!"

³⁵And fire came out from the LORD and consumed the 250 men who were offering incense.

³⁶The LORD said to Moses, ³⁷"Tell Eleazar son of Aaron, the priest, to take the censers out of the smoldering remains and scatter the coals some distance away, for the censers are holy— ³⁸the censers of the men who sinned at the cost of their lives. Hammer the censers into sheets to overlay the altar, for they were presented before the LORD and have become holy. Let them be a sign to the Israelites."

³⁹So Eleazar the priest collected the bronze censers brought by those who had been burned up, and he had them hammered out to overlay the altar, ⁴⁰as the LORD directed him through Moses. This was to remind the Israelites that no one except a descendant of Aaron should come to burn incense before the LORD, or he would become like Korah and his followers.

⁴¹The next day the whole Israelite community grumbled against Moses and Aaron. "You have killed the LORD's people," they said.

⁴²But when the assembly gathered in opposition to Moses and Aaron and turned

ᵃ 14 Or you make slaves of; or you deceive   ᵇ 30 Hebrew Sheol; also in verse 33

toward the Tent of Meeting, suddenly the cloud covered it and the glory of the Lord appeared. ⁴³Then Moses and Aaron went to the front of the Tent of Meeting, ⁴⁴and the Lord said to Moses, ⁴⁵"Get away from this assembly so I can put an end to them at once." And they fell facedown.

⁴⁶Then Moses said to Aaron, "Take your censer and put incense in it, along with fire from the altar, and hurry to the assembly to make atonement for them. Wrath has come out from the Lord; the plague has started." ⁴⁷So Aaron did as Moses said, and ran into the midst of the assembly. The plague had already started among the people, but Aaron offered the incense and made atonement for them. ⁴⁸He stood between the living and the dead, and the plague stopped. ⁴⁹But 14,700 people died from the plague, in addition to those who had died because of Korah. ⁵⁰Then Aaron returned to Moses at the entrance to the Tent of Meeting, for the plague had stopped.

The Budding of Aaron's Staff

17 The Lord said to Moses, ²"Speak to the Israelites and get twelve staffs from them, one from the leader of each of their ancestral tribes. Write the name of each man on his staff. ³On the staff of Levi write Aaron's name, for there must be one staff for the head of each ancestral tribe. ⁴Place them in the Tent of Meeting in front of the Testimony, where I meet with you. ⁵The staff belonging to the man I choose will sprout, and I will rid myself of this constant grumbling against you by the Israelites."

⁶So Moses spoke to the Israelites, and their leaders gave him twelve staffs, one for the leader of each of their ancestral tribes, and Aaron's staff was among them. ⁷Moses placed the staffs before the Lord in the Tent of the Testimony.

⁸The next day Moses entered the Tent of the Testimony and saw that Aaron's staff, which represented the house of Levi, had not only sprouted but had budded, blossomed and produced almonds. ⁹Then Moses brought out all the staffs from the Lord's presence to all the Israelites. They looked at them, and each man took his own staff.

¹⁰The Lord said to Moses, "Put back Aaron's staff in front of the Testimony, to be kept as a sign to the rebellious. This will put an end to their grumbling against me, so that they will not die." ¹¹Moses did just as the Lord commanded him.

¹²The Israelites said to Moses, "We will die! We are lost, we are all lost! ¹³Anyone who even comes near the tabernacle of the Lord will die. Are we all going to die?"

Duties of Priests and Levites

18 The Lord said to Aaron, "You, your sons and your father's family are to bear the responsibility for offenses against the sanctuary, and you and your sons alone are to bear the responsibility for offenses against the priesthood. ²Bring your fellow Levites from your ancestral tribe to join you and assist you when you and your sons minister before the Tent of the Testimony. ³They are to be responsible to you and are to perform all the duties of the Tent, but they must not go near the furnishings of the sanctuary or the altar, or both they and you will die. ⁴They are to join you and be responsible for the care of the Tent of Meeting—all the work at the Tent—and no one else may come near where you are.

⁵"You are to be responsible for the care of the sanctuary and the altar, so that wrath will not fall on the Israelites again. ⁶I myself have selected your fellow Levites from among the Israelites as a gift to you, dedicated to the Lord to do the work at the Tent of Meeting. ⁷But only you and your sons may serve as priests in connection with everything at the altar and inside the curtain. I am giving you the service of the priesthood as a gift. Anyone else who comes near the sanctuary must be put to death."

Offerings for Priests and Levites

⁸Then the Lord said to Aaron, "I myself have put you in charge of the offerings presented to me; all the holy offerings the Israelites give me I give to you and your sons as your

portion and regular share. ⁹You are to have the part of the most holy offerings that is kept from the fire. From all the gifts they bring me as most holy offerings, whether grain or sin or guilt offerings, that part belongs to you and your sons. ¹⁰Eat it as something most holy; every male shall eat it. You must regard it as holy.

¹¹"This also is yours: whatever is set aside from the gifts of all the wave offerings of the Israelites. I give this to you and your sons and daughters as your regular share. Everyone in your household who is ceremonially clean may eat it.

¹²"I give you all the finest olive oil and all the finest new wine and grain they give the LORD as the firstfruits of their harvest. ¹³All the land's firstfruits that they bring to the LORD will be yours. Everyone in your household who is ceremonially clean may eat it.

¹⁴"Everything in Israel that is devoted*ᵃ* to the LORD is yours. ¹⁵The first offspring of every womb, both man and animal, that is offered to the LORD is yours. But you must redeem every firstborn son and every firstborn male of unclean animals. ¹⁶When they are a month old, you must redeem them at the redemption price set at five shekels*ᵇ* of silver, according to the sanctuary shekel, which weighs twenty gerahs.

¹⁷"But you must not redeem the firstborn of an ox, a sheep or a goat; they are holy. Sprinkle their blood on the altar and burn their fat as an offering made by fire, an aroma pleasing to the LORD. ¹⁸Their meat is to be yours, just as the breast of the wave offering and the right thigh are yours. ¹⁹Whatever is set aside from the holy offerings the Israelites present to the LORD I give to you and your sons and daughters as your regular share. It is an everlasting covenant of salt before the LORD for both you and your offspring."

²⁰The LORD said to Aaron, "You will have no inheritance in their land, nor will you have any share among them; I am your share and your inheritance among the Israelites.

²¹"I give to the Levites all the tithes in Israel as their inheritance in return for the work they do while serving at the Tent of Meeting. ²²From now on the Israelites must not go near the Tent of Meeting, or they will bear the consequences of their sin and will die. ²³It is the Levites who are to do the work at the Tent of Meeting and bear the responsibility for offenses against it. This is a lasting ordinance for the generations to come. They will receive no inheritance among the Israelites. ²⁴Instead, I give to the Levites as their inheritance the tithes that the Israelites present as an offering to the LORD. That is why I said concerning them: 'They will have no inheritance among the Israelites.'"

²⁵The LORD said to Moses, ²⁶"Speak to the Levites and say to them: 'When you receive from the Israelites the tithe I give you as your inheritance, you must present a tenth of that tithe as the LORD's offering. ²⁷Your offering will be reckoned to you as grain from the threshing floor or juice from the winepress. ²⁸In this way you also will present an offering to the LORD from all the tithes you receive from the Israelites. From these tithes you must give the LORD's portion to Aaron the priest. ²⁹You must present as the LORD's portion the best and holiest part of everything given to you.'

³⁰"Say to the Levites: 'When you present the best part, it will be reckoned to you as the product of the threshing floor or the winepress. ³¹You and your households may eat the rest of it anywhere, for it is your wages for your work at the Tent of Meeting. ³²By presenting the best part of it you will not be guilty in this matter; then you will not defile the holy offerings of the Israelites, and you will not die.'"

The Water of Cleansing

19 The LORD said to Moses and Aaron: ²"This is a requirement of the law that the LORD has commanded: Tell the Israelites to bring you a red heifer without defect or blemish and that has never been under a yoke. ³Give it to Eleazar the priest; it is to be taken outside the camp and slaughtered in his presence. ⁴Then Eleazar the priest is to take some of its blood on his finger and sprinkle it seven times toward the front of the Tent of Meeting. ⁵While he watches, the heifer is to be burned—its hide, flesh, blood

---

ᵃ14 The Hebrew term refers to the irrevocable giving over of things or persons to the LORD.   *ᵇ16* That is, about 2 ounces (about 55 grams)

and offal. ⁶The priest is to take some cedar wood, hyssop and scarlet wool and throw them onto the burning heifer. ⁷After that, the priest must wash his clothes and bathe himself with water. He may then come into the camp, but he will be ceremonially unclean till evening. ⁸The man who burns it must also wash his clothes and bathe with water, and he too will be unclean till evening.

⁹"A man who is clean shall gather up the ashes of the heifer and put them in a ceremonially clean place outside the camp. They shall be kept by the Israelite community for use in the water of cleansing; it is for purification from sin. ¹⁰The man who gathers up the ashes of the heifer must also wash his clothes, and he too will be unclean till evening. This will be a lasting ordinance both for the Israelites and for the aliens living among them.

¹¹"Whoever touches the dead body of anyone will be unclean for seven days. ¹²He must purify himself with the water on the third day and on the seventh day; then he will be clean. But if he does not purify himself on the third and seventh days, he will not be clean. ¹³Whoever touches the dead body of anyone and fails to purify himself defiles the LORD's tabernacle. That person must be cut off from Israel. Because the water of cleansing has not been sprinkled on him, he is unclean; his uncleanness remains on him.

¹⁴"This is the law that applies when a person dies in a tent: Anyone who enters the tent and anyone who is in it will be unclean for seven days, ¹⁵and every open container without a lid fastened on it will be unclean.

¹⁶"Anyone out in the open who touches someone who has been killed with a sword or someone who has died a natural death, or anyone who touches a human bone or a grave, will be unclean for seven days.

¹⁷"For the unclean person, put some ashes from the burned purification offering into a jar and pour fresh water over them. ¹⁸Then a man who is ceremonially clean is to take some hyssop, dip it in the water and sprinkle the tent and all the furnishings and the people who were there. He must also sprinkle anyone who has touched a human bone or a grave or someone who has been killed or someone who has died a natural death. ¹⁹The man who is clean is to sprinkle the unclean person on the third and seventh days, and on the seventh day he is to purify him. The person being cleansed must wash his clothes and bathe with water, and that evening he will be clean. ²⁰But if a person who is unclean does not purify himself, he must be cut off from the community, because he has defiled the sanctuary of the LORD. The water of cleansing has not been sprinkled on him, and he is unclean. ²¹This is a lasting ordinance for them.

"The man who sprinkles the water of cleansing must also wash his clothes, and anyone who touches the water of cleansing will be unclean till evening. ²²Anything that an unclean person touches becomes unclean, and anyone who touches it becomes unclean till evening."

Water From the Rock

20 In the first month the whole Israelite community arrived at the Desert of Zin, and they stayed at Kadesh. There Miriam died and was buried.

²Now there was no water for the community, and the people gathered in opposition to Moses and Aaron. ³They quarreled with Moses and said, "If only we had died when our brothers fell dead before the LORD! ⁴Why did you bring the LORD's community into this desert, that we and our livestock should die here? ⁵Why did you bring us up out of Egypt to this terrible place? It has no grain or figs, grapevines or pomegranates. And there is no water to drink!"

⁶Moses and Aaron went from the assembly to the entrance to the Tent of Meeting and fell facedown, and the glory of the LORD appeared to them. ⁷The LORD said to Moses, ⁸"Take the staff, and you and your brother Aaron gather the assembly together. Speak to that rock before their eyes and it will pour out its water. You will bring water out of the rock for the community so they and their livestock can drink."

⁹So Moses took the staff from the LORD's presence, just as he commanded him. ¹⁰He and Aaron gathered the assembly together in front of the rock and Moses said to them, "Listen, you rebels, must we bring you water out of this rock?" ¹¹Then Moses raised his arm and struck the rock twice with his staff. Water gushed out, and the community and their livestock drank.

¹²But the LORD said to Moses and Aaron, "Because you did not trust in me enough to honor me as holy in the sight of the Israelites, you will not bring this community into the land I give them."

¹³These were the waters of Meribah,ᵃ where the Israelites quarreled with the LORD and where he showed himself holy among them.

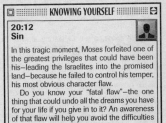

▣ ▦▦▦▦▦▦ **KNOWING YOURSELF** ▦▦▦▦▦▦ ⊟

20:12
Sin

In this tragic moment, Moses forfeited one of the greatest privileges that could have been his—leading the Israelites into the promised land—because he failed to control his temper, his most obvious character flaw.

Do you know your "fatal flaw"—the one thing that could undo all the dreams you have for your life if you give in to it? An awareness of that flaw will help you avoid the difficulties associated with it.

You must not only face squarely what you could fall into, but also take precautionary steps to protect yourself from that weakness. Otherwise, in spite of all your accomplishments, you could leave a legacy of "unfinished business" along the lines of Moses' experience.

Edom Denies Israel Passage

¹⁴Moses sent messengers from Kadesh to the king of Edom, saying:

"This is what your brother Israel says: You know about all the hardships that have come upon us. ¹⁵Our forefathers went down into Egypt, and we lived there many years. The Egyptians mistreated us and our fathers, ¹⁶but when we cried out to the LORD, he heard our cry and sent an angel and brought us out of Egypt.

"Now we are here at Kadesh, a town on the edge of your territory. ¹⁷Please let us pass through your country. We will not go through any field or vineyard, or drink water from any well. We will travel along the king's highway and not turn to the right or to the left until we have passed through your territory."

¹⁸But Edom answered:

"You may not pass through here; if you try, we will march out and attack you with the sword."

¹⁹The Israelites replied:

"We will go along the main road, and if we or our livestock drink any of your water, we will pay for it. We only want to pass through on foot—nothing else."

²⁰Again they answered:

"You may not pass through."

Then Edom came out against them with a large and powerful army. ²¹Since Edom refused to let them go through their territory, Israel turned away from them.

The Death of Aaron

²²The whole Israelite community set out from Kadesh and came to Mount Hor. ²³At Mount Hor, near the border of Edom, the LORD said to Moses and Aaron, ²⁴"Aaron will be gathered to his people. He will not enter the land I give the Israelites, because both of you rebelled against my command at the waters of Meribah. ²⁵Get Aaron and his son

ᵃ13 Meribah means quarreling.

Eleazar and take them up Mount Hor. ²⁶Remove Aaron's garments and put them on his son Eleazar, for Aaron will be gathered to his people; he will die there."

²⁷Moses did as the LORD commanded: They went up Mount Hor in the sight of the whole community. ²⁸Moses removed Aaron's garments and put them on his son Eleazar. And Aaron died there on top of the mountain. Then Moses and Eleazar came down from the mountain, ²⁹and when the whole community learned that Aaron had died, the entire house of Israel mourned for him thirty days.

Arad Destroyed

21 When the Canaanite king of Arad, who lived in the Negev, heard that Israel was coming along the road to Atharim, he attacked the Israelites and captured some of them. ²Then Israel made this vow to the LORD: "If you will deliver these people into our hands, we will totally destroy*ᵃ* their cities." ³The LORD listened to Israel's plea and gave the Canaanites over to them. They completely destroyed them and their towns; so the place was named Hormah.*ᵇ*

The Bronze Snake

⁴They traveled from Mount Hor along the route to the Red Sea,*ᶜ* to go around Edom. But the people grew impatient on the way; ⁵they spoke against God and against Moses, and said, "Why have you brought us up out of Egypt to die in the desert? There is no bread! There is no water! And we detest this miserable food!"

⁶Then the LORD sent venomous snakes among them; they bit the people and many Israelites died. ⁷The people came to Moses and said, "We sinned when we spoke against the LORD and against you. Pray that the LORD will take the snakes away from us." So Moses prayed for the people.

⁸The LORD said to Moses, "Make a snake and put it up on a pole; anyone who is bitten

---

ᵃ2 The Hebrew term refers to the irrevocable giving over of things or persons to the LORD, often by totally destroying them; also in verse 3.   *ᵇ3* *Hormah* means *destruction*.   *ᶜ4* Hebrew *Yam Suph*; that is, Sea of Reeds

---

▦▦▦ DISCOVERING GOD ▦▦▦

21:8–9
Life with God

This unusual incident contains very important lessons of faith that still apply to us today.

According to this passage, ancient Israel experienced a plague of snakes because of their sin. They literally were dying because they had rejected God. But God did for them what they couldn't do for themselves—supplied a miraculous cure. This provision was very simple; it did not involve elaborate rituals or regulations. They only needed to look at the snake on the pole and *believe.* Simple trust in God's power was their only hope.

We are all like the Israelites in the wilderness. Sin has invaded our lives and bitten us. Its venom has fatally poisoned us. What do we do—heal ourselves? Try harder? Get religious?

Like the ancient Israelites, our only recourse is God's provision. We must put faith in his solution—believe it, claim it, and completely trust in it.

What is that solution? Later in history, God lifted up another substitute on a pole for the whole world to look at and trust in (see John chapter 3, verses 14–16 [page 1385]). Jesus himself became the sin-disfigured offering for us. The life-giving response to that gift is to simply *believe*—trust in, rely on, cling to—that provision.

Someone once asked Jesus, "What must we do to do the works God requires?" Jesus' response startled people who assumed that God's antidote for sin contained a list of do's and don'ts. His reply—strikingly similar to God's command to Israel in this story—stands as the divine provision for all who want to be forgiven and find a new beginning. "The work of God is this: to believe in the one he has sent" (John chapter 6, verses 28–29 [page 1392]).

...n look at it and live." 9So Moses made a bronze snake and put it up on a pole. Then ...hen anyone was bitten by a snake and looked at the bronze snake, he lived.

...he Journey to Moab

10The Israelites moved on and camped at Oboth. 11Then they set out from Oboth and ...amped in Iye Abarim, in the desert that faces Moab toward the sunrise. 12From there ...ey moved on and camped in the Zered Valley. 13They set out from there and camped ...ongside the Arnon, which is in the desert extending into Amorite territory. The Arnon is ...e border of Moab, between Moab and the Amorites. 14That is why the Book of the Wars ... the LORD says:

> ". . . Waheb in Suphah*a* and the ravines,
>   the Arnon 15and*b* the slopes of the ravines
> that lead to the site of Ar
>   and lie along the border of Moab."

...From there they continued on to Beer, the well where the LORD said to Moses, "Gather ...e people together and I will give them water."

17Then Israel sang this song:

> "Spring up, O well!
>   Sing about it,
> 18about the well that the princes dug,
>   that the nobles of the people sank—
> the nobles with scepters and staffs."

...hen they went from the desert to Mattanah, 19from Mattanah to Nahaliel, from Nahaliel ...o Bamoth, 20and from Bamoth to the valley in Moab where the top of Pisgah overlooks ...e wasteland.

...efeat of Sihon and Og

21Israel sent messengers to say to Sihon king of the Amorites:

22"Let us pass through your country. We will not turn aside into any field or vineyard, or drink water from any well. We will travel along the king's highway until we have passed through your territory."

23But Sihon would not let Israel pass through his territory. He mustered his entire army ...nd marched out into the desert against Israel. When he reached Jahaz, he fought with ...srael. 24Israel, however, put him to the sword and took over his land from the Arnon to ...ne Jabbok, but only as far as the Ammonites, because their border was fortified. 25Israel ...aptured all the cities of the Amorites and occupied them, including Heshbon and all its ...urrounding settlements. 26Heshbon was the city of Sihon king of the Amorites, who had ...ought against the former king of Moab and had taken from him all his land as far as the ...rnon.

27That is why the poets say:

> "Come to Heshbon and let it be rebuilt;
>   let Sihon's city be restored.
>
> 28"Fire went out from Heshbon,
>   a blaze from the city of Sihon.
> It consumed Ar of Moab,
>   the citizens of Arnon's heights.
> 29Woe to you, O Moab!

---

a 14 The meaning of the Hebrew for this phrase is uncertain.   *b 14,15* Or *"I have been given from Suphah and the ravines /* *of the Arnon 15to*

You are destroyed, O people of Chemosh!
He has given up his sons as fugitives
    and his daughters as captives
    to Sihon king of the Amorites.

³⁰"But we have overthrown them;
    Heshbon is destroyed all the way to Dibon.
We have demolished them as far as Nophah,
    which extends to Medeba."

³¹So Israel settled in the land of the Amorites.

³²After Moses had sent spies to Jazer, the Israelites captured its surrounding settlements and drove out the Amorites who were there. ³³Then they turned and went up along the road toward Bashan, and Og king of Bashan and his whole army marched out to meet them in battle at Edrei.

³⁴The LORD said to Moses, "Do not be afraid of him, for I have handed him over to you, with his whole army and his land. Do to him what you did to Sihon king of the Amorites, who reigned in Heshbon."

³⁵So they struck him down, together with his sons and his whole army, leaving them no survivors. And they took possession of his land.

Balak Summons Balaam

22 Then the Israelites traveled to the plains of Moab and camped along the Jordan across from Jericho.ᵃ

²Now Balak son of Zippor saw all that Israel had done to the Amorites, ³and Moab was terrified because there were so many people. Indeed, Moab was filled with dread because of the Israelites.

⁴The Moabites said to the elders of Midian, "This horde is going to lick up everything around us, as an ox licks up the grass of the field."

So Balak son of Zippor, who was king of Moab at that time, ⁵sent messengers to summon Balaam son of Beor, who was at Pethor, near the River,ᵇ in his native land. Balak said:

"A people has come out of Egypt; they cover the face of the land and have settled next to me. ⁶Now come and put a curse on these people, because they are too powerful for me. Perhaps then I will be able to defeat them and drive them out of the country. For I know that those you bless are blessed, and those you curse are cursed."

⁷The elders of Moab and Midian left, taking with them the fee for divination. When they came to Balaam, they told him what Balak had said.

⁸"Spend the night here," Balaam said to them, "and I will bring you back the answer the LORD gives me." So the Moabite princes stayed with him.

⁹God came to Balaam and asked, "Who are these men with you?"

¹⁰Balaam said to God, "Balak son of Zippor, king of Moab, sent me this message: ¹¹'A people that has come out of Egypt covers the face of the land. Now come and put a curse on them for me. Perhaps then I will be able to fight them and drive them away.'"

¹²But God said to Balaam, "Do not go with them. You must not put a curse on those people, because they are blessed."

¹³The next morning Balaam got up and said to Balak's princes, "Go back to your own country, for the LORD has refused to let me go with you."

¹⁴So the Moabite princes returned to Balak and said, "Balaam refused to come with us."

¹⁵Then Balak sent other princes, more numerous and more distinguished than the first ¹⁶They came to Balaam and said:

ᵃ 1 Hebrew *Jordan of Jericho*; possibly an ancient name for the Jordan River   ᵇ 5 That is, the Euphrates

"This is what Balak son of Zippor says: Do not let anything keep you from coming to me, ¹⁷because I will reward you handsomely and do whatever you say. Come and put a curse on these people for me."

¹⁸But Balaam answered them, "Even if Balak gave me his palace filled with silver and gold, I could not do anything great or small to go beyond the command of the LORD my God. ¹⁹Now stay here tonight as the others did, and I will find out what else the LORD will tell me."

²⁰That night God came to Balaam and said, "Since these men have come to summon you, go with them, but do only what I tell you."

Balaam's Donkey

²¹Balaam got up in the morning, saddled his donkey and went with the princes of Moab. ²²But God was very angry when he went, and the angel of the LORD stood in the road to oppose him. Balaam was riding on his donkey, and his two servants were with him. ²³When the donkey saw the angel of the LORD standing in the road with a drawn sword in his hand, she turned off the road into a field. Balaam beat her to get her back on the road.

²⁴Then the angel of the LORD stood in a narrow path between two vineyards, with walls on both sides. ²⁵When the donkey saw the angel of the LORD, she pressed close to the wall, crushing Balaam's foot against it. So he beat her again.

²⁶Then the angel of the LORD moved on ahead and stood in a narrow place where there was no room to turn, either to the right or to the left. ²⁷When the donkey saw the angel of the LORD, she lay down under Balaam, and he was angry and beat her with his staff. ²⁸Then the LORD opened the donkey's mouth, and she said to Balaam, "What have I done to you to make you beat me these three times?"

²⁹Balaam answered the donkey, "You have made a fool of me! If I had a sword in my hand, I would kill you right now."

³⁰The donkey said to Balaam, "Am I not your own donkey, which you have always ridden, to this day? Have I been in the habit of doing this to you?"

"No," he said.

³¹Then the LORD opened Balaam's eyes, and he saw the angel of the LORD standing in the road with his sword drawn. So he bowed low and fell facedown.

³²The angel of the LORD asked him, "Why have you beaten your donkey these three times? I have come here to oppose you because your path is a reckless one before me.ᵃ ³³The donkey saw me and turned away from me these three times. If she had not turned away, I would certainly have killed you by now, but I would have spared her."

³⁴Balaam said to the angel of the LORD, "I have sinned. I did not realize you were standing in the road to oppose me. Now if you are displeased, I will go back."

³⁵The angel of the LORD said to Balaam, "Go with the men, but speak only what I tell you." So Balaam went with the princes of Balak.

³⁶When Balak heard that Balaam was coming, he went out to meet him at the Moabite town on the Arnon border, at the edge of his territory. ³⁷Balak said to Balaam, "Did I not send you an urgent summons? Why didn't you come to me? Am I really not able to reward you?"

³⁸"Well, I have come to you now," Balaam replied. "But can I say just anything? I must speak only what God puts in my mouth."

³⁹Then Balaam went with Balak to Kiriath Huzoth. ⁴⁰Balak sacrificed cattle and sheep, and gave some to Balaam and the princes who were with him. ⁴¹The next morning Balak took Balaam up to Bamoth Baal, and from there he saw part of the people.

ᵃ32 The meaning of the Hebrew for this clause is uncertain.

Balaam's First Oracle

23 Balaam said, "Build me seven altars here, and prepare seven bulls and seven rams for me." [2]Balak did as Balaam said, and the two of them offered a bull and a ram on each altar.

[3]Then Balaam said to Balak, "Stay here beside your offering while I go aside. Perhaps the LORD will come to meet with me. Whatever he reveals to me I will tell you." Then he went off to a barren height.

[4]God met with him, and Balaam said, "I have prepared seven altars, and on each altar I have offered a bull and a ram."

[5]The LORD put a message in Balaam's mouth and said, "Go back to Balak and give him this message."

[6]So he went back to him and found him standing beside his offering, with all the princes of Moab. [7]Then Balaam uttered his oracle:

> "Balak brought me from Aram,
>   the king of Moab from the eastern mountains.
> 'Come,' he said, 'curse Jacob for me;
>   come, denounce Israel.'
> [8]How can I curse
>   those whom God has not cursed?
> How can I denounce
>   those whom the LORD has not denounced?
> [9]From the rocky peaks I see them,
>   from the heights I view them.
> I see a people who live apart
>   and do not consider themselves one of the nations.
> [10]Who can count the dust of Jacob
>   or number the fourth part of Israel?
> Let me die the death of the righteous,
>   and may my end be like theirs!"

[11]Balak said to Balaam, "What have you done to me? I brought you to curse my enemies, but you have done nothing but bless them!"

[12]He answered, "Must I not speak what the LORD puts in my mouth?"

Balaam's Second Oracle

[13]Then Balak said to him, "Come with me to another place where you can see them; you will see only a part but not all of them. And from there, curse them for me." [14]So he took him to the field of Zophim on the top of Pisgah, and there he built seven altars and offered a bull and a ram on each altar.

[15]Balaam said to Balak, "Stay here beside your offering while I meet with him over there."

[16]The LORD met with Balaam and put a message in his mouth and said, "Go back to Balak and give him this message."

[17]So he went to him and found him standing beside his offering, with the princes of Moab. Balak asked him, "What did the LORD say?"

[18]Then he uttered his oracle:

> "Arise, Balak, and listen;
>   hear me, son of Zippor.
> [19]God is not a man, that he should lie,
>   nor a son of man, that he should change his mind.
> Does he speak and then not act?
>   Does he promise and not fulfill?

²⁰I have received a command to bless;
    he has blessed, and I cannot change it.

²¹"No misfortune is seen in Jacob,
    no misery observed in Israel.ᵃ
The Lᴏʀᴅ their God is with them;
    the shout of the King is among them.
²²God brought them out of Egypt;
    they have the strength of a wild ox.
²³There is no sorcery against Jacob,
    no divination against Israel.
It will now be said of Jacob
    and of Israel, 'See what God has done!'
²⁴The people rise like a lioness;
    they rouse themselves like a lion
that does not rest till he devours his prey
    and drinks the blood of his victims."

²⁵Then Balak said to Balaam, "Neither curse them at all nor bless them at all!"

²⁶Balaam answered, "Did I not tell you I must do whatever the Lᴏʀᴅ says?"

Balaam's Third Oracle

²⁷Then Balak said to Balaam, "Come, let me take you to another place. Perhaps it will please God to let you curse them for me from there." ²⁸And Balak took Balaam to the top of Peor, overlooking the wasteland.

²⁹Balaam said, "Build me seven altars here, and prepare seven bulls and seven rams for me." ³⁰Balak did as Balaam had said, and offered a bull and a ram on each altar.

24 Now when Balaam saw that it pleased the Lᴏʀᴅ to bless Israel, he did not resort to sorcery as at other times, but turned his face toward the desert. ²When Balaam looked out and saw Israel encamped tribe by tribe, the Spirit of God came upon him ³and he uttered his oracle:

"The oracle of Balaam son of Beor,
    the oracle of one whose eye sees clearly,
⁴the oracle of one who hears the words of God,
    who sees a vision from the Almighty,ᵇ
    who falls prostrate, and whose eyes are opened:

⁵"How beautiful are your tents, O Jacob,
    your dwelling places, O Israel!

⁶"Like valleys they spread out,
    like gardens beside a river,
like aloes planted by the Lᴏʀᴅ,
    like cedars beside the waters.
⁷Water will flow from their buckets;
    their seed will have abundant water.

"Their king will be greater than Agag;
    their kingdom will be exalted.

⁸"God brought them out of Egypt;
    they have the strength of a wild ox.
They devour hostile nations
    and break their bones in pieces;

ᵃ21 Or He has not looked on Jacob's offenses / or on the wrongs found in Israel.   ᵇ4 Hebrew Shaddai; also in verse 16

with their arrows they pierce them.
⁹Like a lion they crouch and lie down,
like a lioness—who dares to rouse them?

"May those who bless you be blessed
and those who curse you be cursed!"

¹⁰Then Balak's anger burned against Balaam. He struck his hands together and said to him, "I summoned you to curse my enemies, but you have blessed them these three times. ¹¹Now leave at once and go home! I said I would reward you handsomely, but the LORD has kept you from being rewarded."

¹²Balaam answered Balak, "Did I not tell the messengers you sent me, ¹³'Even if Balak gave me his palace filled with silver and gold, I could not do anything of my own accord, good or bad, to go beyond the command of the LORD—and I must say only what the LORD says'? ¹⁴Now I am going back to my people, but come, let me warn you of what this people will do to your people in days to come."

Balaam's Fourth Oracle

¹⁵Then he uttered his oracle:

"The oracle of Balaam son of Beor,
the oracle of one whose eye sees clearly,
¹⁶the oracle of one who hears the words of God,
who has knowledge from the Most High,
who sees a vision from the Almighty,
who falls prostrate, and whose eyes are opened:

¹⁷"I see him, but not now;
I behold him, but not near.
A star will come out of Jacob;
a scepter will rise out of Israel.
He will crush the foreheads of Moab,
the skulls*a* of*b* all the sons of Sheth.*c*
¹⁸Edom will be conquered;
Seir, his enemy, will be conquered,
but Israel will grow strong.
¹⁹A ruler will come out of Jacob
and destroy the survivors of the city."

Balaam's Final Oracles

²⁰Then Balaam saw Amalek and uttered his oracle:

"Amalek was first among the nations,
but he will come to ruin at last."

²¹Then he saw the Kenites and uttered his oracle:

"Your dwelling place is secure,
your nest is set in a rock;
²²yet you Kenites will be destroyed
when Asshur takes you captive."

²³Then he uttered his oracle:

---

a 17 Samaritan Pentateuch (see also Jer. 48:45); the meaning of the word in the Masoretic Text is uncertain.   *b 17* Or
possibly *Moab, / batter*   *c 17* Or *all the noisy boasters*

"Ah, who can live when God does this?[a]
24 Ships will come from the shores of Kittim;
    they will subdue Asshur and Eber,
      but they too will come to ruin."

25Then Balaam got up and returned home and Balak went his own way.

Moab Seduces Israel

25 While Israel was staying in Shittim, the men began to indulge in sexual immorality with Moabite women, 2who invited them to the sacrifices to their gods. The people ate and bowed down before these gods. 3So Israel joined in worshiping the Baal of Peor. And the LORD's anger burned against them.

4The LORD said to Moses, "Take all the leaders of these people, kill them and expose them in broad daylight before the LORD, so that the LORD's fierce anger may turn away from Israel."

5So Moses said to Israel's judges, "Each of you must put to death those of your men who have joined in worshiping the Baal of Peor."

6Then an Israelite man brought to his family a Midianite woman right before the eyes of Moses and the whole assembly of Israel while they were weeping at the entrance to the Tent of Meeting. 7When Phinehas son of Eleazar, the son of Aaron, the priest, saw this, he left the assembly, took a spear in his hand 8and followed the Israelite into the tent. He drove the spear through both of them—through the Israelite and into the woman's body. Then the plague against the Israelites was stopped; 9but those who died in the plague numbered 24,000.

10The LORD said to Moses, 11"Phinehas son of Eleazar, the son of Aaron, the priest, has turned my anger away from the Israelites; for he was as zealous as I am for my honor among them, so that in my zeal I did not put an end to them. 12Therefore tell him I am making my covenant of peace with him. 13He and his descendants will have a covenant of a lasting priesthood, because he was zealous for the honor of his God and made atonement for the Israelites."

14The name of the Israelite who was killed with the Midianite woman was Zimri son of Salu, the leader of a Simeonite family. 15And the name of the Midianite woman who was put to death was Cozbi daughter of Zur, a tribal chief of a Midianite family.

16The LORD said to Moses, 17"Treat the Midianites as enemies and kill them, 18because they treated you as enemies when they deceived you in the affair of Peor and their sister Cozbi, the daughter of a Midianite leader, the woman who was killed when the plague came as a result of Peor."

23 Masoretic Text; with a different word division of the Hebrew *A people will gather from the north.*

The Second Census

26 After the plague the LORD said to Moses and Eleazar son of Aaron, the priest, ²"Take a census of the whole Israelite community by families—all those twenty years old or more who are able to serve in the army of Israel." ³So on the plains of Moab by the Jordan across from Jericho,ᵃ Moses and Eleazar the priest spoke with them and said, ⁴"Take a census of the men twenty years old or more, as the LORD commanded Moses."

These were the Israelites who came out of Egypt:

⁵The descendants of Reuben, the firstborn son of Israel, were:
   through Hanoch, the Hanochite clan;
   through Pallu, the Palluite clan;
   ⁶through Hezron, the Hezronite clan;
   through Carmi, the Carmite clan.
⁷These were the clans of Reuben; those numbered were 43,730.

⁸The son of Pallu was Eliab, ⁹and the sons of Eliab were Nemuel, Dathan and Abiram. The same Dathan and Abiram were the community officials who rebelled against Moses and Aaron and were among Korah's followers when they rebelled against the LORD. ¹⁰The earth opened its mouth and swallowed them along with Korah, whose followers died when the fire devoured the 250 men. And they served as a warning sign. ¹¹The line of Korah, however, did not die out.

¹²The descendants of Simeon by their clans were:
   through Nemuel, the Nemuelite clan;
   through Jamin, the Jaminite clan;
   through Jakin, the Jakinite clan;
   ¹³through Zerah, the Zerahite clan;
   through Shaul, the Shaulite clan.
¹⁴These were the clans of Simeon; there were 22,200 men.

¹⁵The descendants of Gad by their clans were:
   through Zephon, the Zephonite clan;
   through Haggi, the Haggite clan;
   through Shuni, the Shunite clan;
   ¹⁶through Ozni, the Oznite clan;
   through Eri, the Erite clan;
   ¹⁷through Arodi,ᵇ the Arodite clan;
   through Areli, the Arelite clan.
¹⁸These were the clans of Gad; those numbered were 40,500.

¹⁹Er and Onan were sons of Judah, but they died in Canaan.
²⁰The descendants of Judah by their clans were:
   through Shelah, the Shelanite clan;
   through Perez, the Perezite clan;
   through Zerah, the Zerahite clan;
   ²¹The descendants of Perez were:
      through Hezron, the Hezronite clan;
      through Hamul, the Hamulite clan.
²²These were the clans of Judah; those numbered were 76,500.

²³The descendants of Issachar by their clans were:
   through Tola, the Tolaite clan;

ᵃ3 Hebrew *Jordan of Jericho*; possibly an ancient name for the Jordan River; also in verse 63 and Syriac (see also Gen. 46:16); Masoretic Text *Arod*   ᵇ17 Samaritan Pentateuch

through Puah, the Puite[a] clan;
[24]through Jashub, the Jashubite clan;
through Shimron, the Shimronite clan.
These were the clans of Issachar; those numbered were 64,300.

The descendants of Zebulun by their clans were:
through Sered, the Seredite clan;
through Elon, the Elonite clan;
through Jahleel, the Jahleelite clan.
These were the clans of Zebulun; those numbered were 60,500.

The descendants of Joseph by their clans through Manasseh and Ephraim were:

The descendants of Manasseh:
through Makir, the Makirite clan (Makir was the father of Gilead);
through Gilead, the Gileadite clan.
[30]These were the descendants of Gilead:
through Iezer, the Iezerite clan;
through Helek, the Helekite clan;
[31]through Asriel, the Asrielite clan;
through Shechem, the Shechemite clan;
[32]through Shemida, the Shemidaite clan;
through Hepher, the Hepherite clan.
[33](Zelophehad son of Hepher had no sons; he had only daughters, whose names were Mahlah, Noah, Hoglah, Milcah and Tirzah.)
These were the clans of Manasseh; those numbered were 52,700.

These were the descendants of Ephraim by their clans:
through Shuthelah, the Shuthelahite clan;
through Beker, the Bekerite clan;
through Tahan, the Tahanite clan.
[36]These were the descendants of Shuthelah:
through Eran, the Eranite clan.
These were the clans of Ephraim; those numbered were 32,500.

These were the descendants of Joseph by their clans.

The descendants of Benjamin by their clans were:
through Bela, the Belaite clan;
through Ashbel, the Ashbelite clan;
through Ahiram, the Ahiramite clan;
[39]through Shupham,[b] the Shuphamite clan;
through Hupham, the Huphamite clan.
[40]The descendants of Bela through Ard and Naaman were:
through Ard,[c] the Ardite clan;
through Naaman, the Naamite clan.
These were the clans of Benjamin; those numbered were 45,600.

These were the descendants of Dan by their clans:
through Shuham, the Shuhamite clan.
These were the clans of Dan: [43]All of them were Shuhamite clans; and those numbered were 64,400.

The descendants of Asher by their clans were:

[23] Samaritan Pentateuch, Septuagint, Vulgate and Syriac (see also 1 Chron. 7:1); Masoretic Text *through Puvah, the Punite*
[39] A few manuscripts of the Masoretic Text, Samaritan Pentateuch, Vulgate and Syriac (see also Septuagint); most manuscripts of the Masoretic Text *Shephupham*   [c]40 Samaritan Pentateuch and Vulgate (see also Septuagint); Masoretic Text does not have *through Ard*.

through Imnah, the Imnite clan;
through Ishvi, the Ishvite clan;
through Beriah, the Beriite clan;
[45]and through the descendants of Beriah:
   through Heber, the Heberite clan;
   through Malkiel, the Malkielite clan.
[46](Asher had a daughter named Serah.)
[47]These were the clans of Asher; those numbered were 53,400.

[48]The descendants of Naphtali by their clans were:
   through Jahzeel, the Jahzeelite clan;
   through Guni, the Gunite clan;
   [49]through Jezer, the Jezerite clan;
   through Shillem, the Shillemite clan.
[50]These were the clans of Naphtali; those numbered were 45,400.

[51]The total number of the men of Israel was 601,730.

[52]The LORD said to Moses, [53]"The land is to be allotted to them as an inheritance base on the number of names. [54]To a larger group give a larger inheritance, and to a small group a smaller one; each is to receive its inheritance according to the number of tho. listed. [55]Be sure that the land is distributed by lot. What each group inherits will b according to the names for its ancestral tribe. [56]Each inheritance is to be distributed b lot among the larger and smaller groups."

[57]These were the Levites who were counted by their clans:
   through Gershon, the Gershonite clan;
   through Kohath, the Kohathite clan;
   through Merari, the Merarite clan.
[58]These also were Levite clans:
  the Libnite clan,
  the Hebronite clan,
  the Mahlite clan,
  the Mushite clan,
  the Korahite clan.
(Kohath was the forefather of Amram; [59]the name of Amram's wife was Jochebed, a descendant of Levi, who was born to the Levites[a] in Egypt. To Amram she bore Aaron, Moses and their sister Miriam. [60]Aaron was the father of Nadab and Abihu, Eleazar and Ithamar. [61]But Nadab and Abihu died when they made an offering before the LORD with unauthorized fire.)

[62]All the male Levites a month old or more numbered 23,000. They were not counte along with the other Israelites because they received no inheritance among them.

[63]These are the ones counted by Moses and Eleazar the priest when they counted th Israelites on the plains of Moab by the Jordan across from Jericho. [64]Not one of them wa among those counted by Moses and Aaron the priest when they counted the Israelites the Desert of Sinai. [65]For the LORD had told those Israelites they would surely die in t desert, and not one of them was left except Caleb son of Jephunneh and Joshua son Nun.

---

[a] 59 Or Jochebed, a daughter of Levi, who was born to Levi

Zelophehad's Daughters

27 The daughters of Zelophehad son of Hepher, the son of Gilead, the son of Makir, the son of Manasseh, belonged to the clans of Manasseh son of Joseph. The names of the daughters were Mahlah, Noah, Hoglah, Milcah and Tirzah. They approached ²the entrance to the Tent of Meeting and stood before Moses, Eleazar the priest, the leaders and the whole assembly, and said, ³"Our father died in the desert. He was not among Korah's followers, who banded together against the LORD, but he died for his own sin and left no sons. ⁴Why should our father's name disappear from his clan because he had no son? Give us property among our father's relatives."

⁵So Moses brought their case before the LORD ⁶and the LORD said to him, ⁷"What Zelophehad's daughters are saying is right. You must certainly give them property as an inheritance among their father's relatives and turn their father's inheritance over to them.

⁸"Say to the Israelites, 'If a man dies and leaves no son, turn his inheritance over to his daughter. ⁹If he has no daughter, give his inheritance to his brothers. ¹⁰If he has no brothers, give his inheritance to his father's brothers. ¹¹If his father had no brothers, give his inheritance to the nearest relative in his clan, that he may possess it. This is to be a legal requirement for the Israelites, as the LORD commanded Moses.'"

Joshua to Succeed Moses

¹²Then the LORD said to Moses, "Go up this mountain in the Abarim range and see the land I have given the Israelites. ¹³After you have seen it, you too will be gathered to your people, as your brother Aaron was, ¹⁴for when the community rebelled at the waters in the Desert of Zin, both of you disobeyed my command to honor me as holy before their eyes." (These were the waters of Meribah Kadesh, in the Desert of Zin.)

¹⁵Moses said to the LORD, ¹⁶"May the LORD, the God of the spirits of all mankind, appoint a man over this community ¹⁷to go out and come in before them, one who will lead them out and bring them in, so the LORD's people will not be like sheep without a shepherd." ¹⁸So the LORD said to Moses, "Take Joshua son of Nun, a man in whom is the spirit,[a] and lay your hand on him. ¹⁹Have him stand before Eleazar the priest and the entire assembly and commission him in their presence. ²⁰Give him some of your authority so the whole Israelite community will obey him. ²¹He is to stand before Eleazar the priest, who will obtain decisions for him by inquiring of the Urim before the LORD. At his command he and the entire community of the Israelites will go out, and at his command they will come in."

²²Moses did as the LORD commanded him. He took Joshua and had him stand before Eleazar the priest and the whole assembly. ²³Then he laid his hands on him and commissioned him, as the LORD instructed through Moses.

Daily Offerings

28 The LORD said to Moses, ²"Give this command to the Israelites and say to them: 'See that you present to me at the appointed time the food for my offerings made by fire, as an aroma pleasing to me.' ³Say to them: 'This is the offering made by fire that you are to present to the LORD: two lambs a year old without defect, as a regular burnt offering each day. ⁴Prepare one lamb in the morning and the other at twilight, ⁵together with a grain offering of a tenth of an ephah[b] of fine flour mixed with a quarter of a hin[c] of oil from pressed olives. ⁶This is the regular burnt offering instituted at Mount Sinai as a pleasing aroma, an offering made to the LORD by fire. ⁷The accompanying drink offering is to be a quarter of a hin of fermented drink with each lamb. Pour out the drink offering to the LORD at the sanctuary. ⁸Prepare the second lamb at twilight, along with the same kind of grain offering and drink offering that you prepare in the morning. This is an offering made by fire, an aroma pleasing to the LORD.

---

18 Or *Spirit*   *b 5* That is, probably about 2 quarts (about 2 liters); also in verses 13, 21 and 29   *c 5* That is, probably about 1 quart (about 1 liter); also in verses 7 and 14

Sabbath Offerings

⁹"'On the Sabbath day, make an offering of two lambs a year old without defec together with its drink offering and a grain offering of two-tenths of an ephah[a] of fin flour mixed with oil. ¹⁰This is the burnt offering for every Sabbath, in addition to th regular burnt offering and its drink offering.

Monthly Offerings

¹¹"'On the first of every month, present to the LORD a burnt offering of two young bull one ram and seven male lambs a year old, all without defect. ¹²With each bull there is t be a grain offering of three-tenths of an ephah[b] of fine flour mixed with oil; with th ram, a grain offering of two-tenths of an ephah of fine flour mixed with oil; ¹³and wit each lamb, a grain offering of a tenth of an ephah of fine flour mixed with oil. This is fo a burnt offering, a pleasing aroma, an offering made to the LORD by fire. ¹⁴With each bu there is to be a drink offering of half a hin[c] of wine; with the ram, a third of a hin[d]; an with each lamb, a quarter of a hin. This is the monthly burnt offering to be made at eac new moon during the year. ¹⁵Besides the regular burnt offering with its drink offerin one male goat is to be presented to the LORD as a sin offering.

The Passover

¹⁶"'On the fourteenth day of the first month the LORD's Passover is to be held. ¹⁷On th fifteenth day of this month there is to be a festival; for seven days eat bread mad without yeast. ¹⁸On the first day hold a sacred assembly and do no regular work ¹⁹Present to the LORD an offering made by fire, a burnt offering of two young bulls, on ram and seven male lambs a year old, all without defect. ²⁰With each bull prepare a grai offering of three-tenths of an ephah of fine flour mixed with oil; with the ram, two tenths; ²¹and with each of the seven lambs, one-tenth. ²²Include one male goat as a si offering to make atonement for you. ²³Prepare these in addition to the regular mornin burnt offering. ²⁴In this way prepare the food for the offering made by fire every day fo seven days as an aroma pleasing to the LORD; it is to be prepared in addition to the regula burnt offering and its drink offering. ²⁵On the seventh day hold a sacred assembly and d no regular work.

Feast of Weeks

²⁶"'On the day of firstfruits, when you present to the LORD an offering of new grai during the Feast of Weeks, hold a sacred assembly and do no regular work. ²⁷Present burnt offering of two young bulls, one ram and seven male lambs a year old as an arom pleasing to the LORD. ²⁸With each bull there is to be a grain offering of three-tenths of a ephah of fine flour mixed with oil; with the ram, two-tenths; ²⁹and with each of th seven lambs, one-tenth. ³⁰Include one male goat to make atonement for you. ³¹Prepar these together with their drink offerings, in addition to the regular burnt offering and it grain offering. Be sure the animals are without defect.

Feast of Trumpets

29 "'On the first day of the seventh month hold a sacred assembly and do n regular work. It is a day for you to sound the trumpets. ²As an aroma pleas ing to the LORD, prepare a burnt offering of one young bull, one ram and seven male lamb a year old, all without defect. ³With the bull prepare a grain offering of three-tenths of a ephah[e] of fine flour mixed with oil; with the ram, two-tenths[f]; ⁴and with each of th seven lambs, one-tenth.[g] ⁵Include one male goat as a sin offering to make atonemer

---

[a]9 That is, probably about 4 quarts (about 4.5 liters); also in verses 12, 20 and 28   [b]12 That is, probably about 6 quarts (about 6.5 liters); also in verses 20 and 28   [c]14 That is, probably about 2 quarts (about 2 liters)   [d]14 That is, probably about 1 1/4 quarts (about 1.2 liters)   [e]3 That is, probably about 6 quarts (about 6.5 liters); also in verses 9 and 14   [f]3 That is, probably about 4 quarts (about 4.5 liters); also in verses 9 and 14   [g]4 That is, probably about 2 quarts (about 2 liters); also in verses 10 and 15

for you. ⁶These are in addition to the monthly and daily burnt offerings with their grain offerings and drink offerings as specified. They are offerings made to the Lᴏʀᴅ by fire—a pleasing aroma.

Day of Atonement

⁷"'On the tenth day of this seventh month hold a sacred assembly. You must deny yourselvesᵃ and do no work. ⁸Present as an aroma pleasing to the Lᴏʀᴅ a burnt offering of one young bull, one ram and seven male lambs a year old, all without defect. ⁹With the bull prepare a grain offering of three-tenths of an ephah of fine flour mixed with oil; with the ram, two-tenths; ¹⁰and with each of the seven lambs, one-tenth. ¹¹Include one male goat as a sin offering, in addition to the sin offering for atonement and the regular burnt offering with its grain offering, and their drink offerings.

Feast of Tabernacles

¹²"'On the fifteenth day of the seventh month, hold a sacred assembly and do no regular work. Celebrate a festival to the Lᴏʀᴅ for seven days. ¹³Present an offering made by fire as an aroma pleasing to the Lᴏʀᴅ, a burnt offering of thirteen young bulls, two rams and fourteen male lambs a year old, all without defect. ¹⁴With each of the thirteen bulls prepare a grain offering of three-tenths of an ephah of fine flour mixed with oil; with each of the two rams, two-tenths; ¹⁵and with each of the fourteen lambs, one-tenth. ¹⁶Include one male

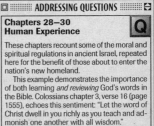

▣ ▦▦▦▦ **ADDRESSING QUESTIONS** ▦▦▦▦ ⊟

Chapters 28–30
Human Experience   **Q**

These chapters recount some of the moral and spiritual regulations in ancient Israel, repeated here for the benefit of those about to enter the nation's new homeland.

   This example demonstrates the importance of both learning *and reviewing* God's words in the Bible. Colossians chapter 3, verse 16 (page 1555), echoes this sentiment: "Let the word of Christ dwell in you richly as you teach and admonish one another with all wisdom."

   God's words in the Bible provide us with the ultimate textbook on life. Millions of people—from the oldest scholars to the littlest children—benefit from the Bible's wisdom for living every day. As you continue to read through this book, realize that centuries of examination and explanation have not yet exhausted the wealth of insight contained in these pages.

goat as a sin offering, in addition to the regular burnt offering with its grain offering and drink offering.

¹⁷"'On the second day prepare twelve young bulls, two rams and fourteen male lambs a year old, all without defect. ¹⁸With the bulls, rams and lambs, prepare their grain offerings and drink offerings according to the number specified. ¹⁹Include one male goat as a sin offering, in addition to the regular burnt offering with its grain offering, and their drink offerings.

²⁰"'On the third day prepare eleven bulls, two rams and fourteen male lambs a year old, all without defect. ²¹With the bulls, rams and lambs, prepare their grain offerings and drink offerings according to the number specified. ²²Include one male goat as a sin offering, in addition to the regular burnt offering with its grain offering and drink offering.

²³"'On the fourth day prepare ten bulls, two rams and fourteen male lambs a year old, all without defect. ²⁴With the bulls, rams and lambs, prepare their grain offerings and drink offerings according to the number specified. ²⁵Include one male goat as a sin offering, in addition to the regular burnt offering with its grain offering and drink offering.

²⁶"'On the fifth day prepare nine bulls, two rams and fourteen male lambs a year old, all without defect. ²⁷With the bulls, rams and lambs, prepare their grain offerings and drink offerings according to the number specified. ²⁸Include one male goat as a sin offering, in addition to the regular burnt offering with its grain offering and drink offering.

²⁹"'On the sixth day prepare eight bulls, two rams and fourteen male lambs a year old,

all without defect. ³⁰With the bulls, rams and lambs, prepare their grain offerings and drink offerings according to the number specified. ³¹Include one male goat as a sin offering, in addition to the regular burnt offering with its grain offering and drink offering.

³²" 'On the seventh day prepare seven bulls, two rams and fourteen male lambs a year old, all without defect. ³³With the bulls, rams and lambs, prepare their grain offerings and drink offerings according to the number specified. ³⁴Include one male goat as a sin offering, in addition to the regular burnt offering with its grain offering and drink offering.

³⁵" 'On the eighth day hold an assembly and do no regular work. ³⁶Present an offering made by fire as an aroma pleasing to the LORD, a burnt offering of one bull, one ram and seven male lambs a year old, all without defect. ³⁷With the bull, the ram and the lambs, prepare their grain offerings and drink offerings according to the number specified. ³⁸Include one male goat as a sin offering, in addition to the regular burnt offering with its grain offering and drink offering.

³⁹" 'In addition to what you vow and your freewill offerings, prepare these for the LORD at your appointed feasts: your burnt offerings, grain offerings, drink offerings and fellowship offerings.*^a*' "

⁴⁰Moses told the Israelites all that the LORD commanded him.

Vows

30 Moses said to the heads of the tribes of Israel: "This is what the LORD commands: ²When a man makes a vow to the LORD or takes an oath to obligate himself by a pledge, he must not break his word but must do everything he said.

³"When a young woman still living in her father's house makes a vow to the LORD or obligates herself by a pledge ⁴and her father hears about her vow or pledge but says nothing to her, then all her vows and every pledge by which she obligated herself will stand. ⁵But if her father forbids her when he hears about it, none of her vows or the pledges by which she obligated herself will stand; the LORD will release her because her father has forbidden her.

⁶"If she marries after she makes a vow or after her lips utter a rash promise by which she obligates herself ⁷and her husband hears about it but says nothing to her, then her vows or the pledges by which she obligated herself will stand. ⁸But if her husband forbids her when he hears about it, he nullifies the vow that obligates her or the rash promise by which she obligates herself, and the LORD will release her.

⁹"Any vow or obligation taken by a widow or divorced woman will be binding on her.

¹⁰"If a woman living with her husband makes a vow or obligates herself by a pledge under oath ¹¹and her husband hears about it but says nothing to her and does not forbid her, then all her vows or the pledges by which she obligated herself will stand. ¹²But if her husband nullifies them when he hears about them, then none of the vows or pledges that came from her lips will stand. Her husband has nullified them, and the LORD will release her. ¹³Her husband may confirm or nullify any vow she makes or any sworn pledge to deny herself. ¹⁴But if her husband says nothing to her about it from day to day, then he confirms all her vows or the pledges binding on her. He confirms them by saying nothing to her when he hears about them. ¹⁵If, however, he nullifies them some time after he hears about them, then he is responsible for her guilt."

¹⁶These are the regulations the LORD gave Moses concerning relationships between a man and his wife, and between a father and his young daughter still living in his house.

Vengeance on the Midianites

31 The LORD said to Moses, ²"Take vengeance on the Midianites for the Israelites. After that, you will be gathered to your people."

³So Moses said to the people, "Arm some of your men to go to war against the Midianites and to carry out the LORD's vengeance on them. ⁴Send into battle a thousand men

a 39 Traditionally *peace offerings*

rom each of the tribes of Israel." ⁵So twelve thousand men armed for battle, a thousand 'rom each tribe, were supplied from the clans of Israel. ⁶Moses sent them into battle, a housand from each tribe, along with Phinehas son of Eleazar, the priest, who took with him articles from the sanctuary and the trumpets for signaling.

⁷They fought against Midian, as the LORD commanded Moses, and killed every man. ⁸Among their victims were Evi, Rekem, Zur, Hur and Reba—the five kings of Midian. They also killed Balaam son of Beor with the sword. ⁹The Israelites captured the Midianite women and children and took all the Midianite herds, flocks and goods as plunder. ¹⁰They burned all the towns where the Midianites had settled, as well as all their camps. ¹¹They took all the plunder and spoils, including the people and animals, ¹²and brought the captives, spoils and plunder to Moses and Eleazar the priest and the Israelite assembly at their camp on the plains of Moab, by the Jordan across from Jericho.ᵃ

¹³Moses, Eleazar the priest and all the leaders of the community went to meet them outside the camp. ¹⁴Moses was angry with the officers of the army—the commanders of thousands and commanders of hundreds—who returned from the battle.

¹⁵"Have you allowed all the women to live?" he asked them. ¹⁶"They were the ones who followed Balaam's advice and were the means of turning the Israelites away from the LORD in what happened at Peor, so that a plague struck the LORD's people. ¹⁷Now kill all the boys. And kill every woman who has slept with a man, ¹⁸but save for yourselves every girl who has never slept with a man.

¹⁹"All of you who have killed anyone or touched anyone who was killed must stay outside the camp seven days. On the third and seventh days you must purify yourselves and your captives. ²⁰Purify every garment as well as everything made of leather, goat hair or wood."

²¹Then Eleazar the priest said to the soldiers who had gone into battle, "This is the requirement of the law that the LORD gave Moses: ²²Gold, silver, bronze, iron, tin, lead ²³and anything else that can withstand fire must be put through the fire, and then it will be clean. But it must also be purified with the water of cleansing. And whatever cannot withstand fire must be put through that water. ²⁴On the seventh day wash your clothes and you will be clean. Then you may come into the camp."

Dividing the Spoils

²⁵The LORD said to Moses, ²⁶"You and Eleazar the priest and the family heads of the community are to count all the people and animals that were captured. ²⁷Divide the spoils between the soldiers who took part in the battle and the rest of the community. ²⁸From the soldiers who fought in the battle, set apart as tribute for the LORD one out of every five hundred, whether persons, cattle, donkeys, sheep or goats. ²⁹Take this tribute from their half share and give it to Eleazar the priest as the LORD's part. ³⁰From the Israelites' half, select one out of every fifty, whether persons, cattle, donkeys, sheep, goats or other animals. Give them to the Levites, who are responsible for the care of the LORD's tabernacle." ³¹So Moses and Eleazar the priest did as the LORD commanded Moses.

³²The plunder remaining from the spoils that the soldiers took was 675,000 sheep, ³³372,000 cattle, ³⁴61,000 donkeys ³⁵and 32,000 women who had never slept with a man.

³⁶The half share of those who fought in the battle was:

　337,500 sheep, ³⁷of which the tribute for the LORD was 675;

³⁸36,000 cattle, of which the tribute for the LORD was 72;

³⁹30,500 donkeys, of which the tribute for the LORD was 61;

⁴⁰16,000 people, of which the tribute for the LORD was 32.

⁴¹Moses gave the tribute to Eleazar the priest as the LORD's part, as the LORD commanded Moses.

12 Hebrew *Jordan of Jericho*; possibly an ancient name for the Jordan River

⁴²The half belonging to the Israelites, which Moses set apart from that of the fighting men— ⁴³the community's half—was 337,500 sheep, ⁴⁴36,000 cattle, ⁴⁵30,500 donkeys ⁴⁶and 16,000 people. ⁴⁷From the Israelites' half, Moses selected one out of every fifty persons and animals, as the LORD commanded him, and gave them to the Levites, who were responsible for the care of the LORD's tabernacle.

⁴⁸Then the officers who were over the units of the army—the commanders of thousands and commanders of hundreds—went to Moses ⁴⁹and said to him, "Your servants have counted the soldiers under our command, and not one is missing. ⁵⁰So we have brought as an offering to the LORD the gold articles each of us acquired—armlets, bracelets, signet rings, earrings and necklaces—to make atonement for ourselves before the LORD."

⁵¹Moses and Eleazar the priest accepted from them the gold—all the crafted articles. ⁵²All the gold from the commanders of thousands and commanders of hundreds that Moses and Eleazar presented as a gift to the LORD weighed 16,750 shekels.ᵃ ⁵³Each soldier had taken plunder for himself. ⁵⁴Moses and Eleazar the priest accepted the gold from the commanders of thousands and commanders of hundreds and brought it into the Tent of Meeting as a memorial for the Israelites before the LORD.

The Transjordan Tribes

32 The Reubenites and Gadites, who had very large herds and flocks, saw that the lands of Jazer and Gilead were suitable for livestock. ²So they came to Moses and Eleazar the priest and to the leaders of the community, and said, ³"Ataroth, Dibon, Jazer, Nimrah, Heshbon, Elealeh, Sebam, Nebo and Beon— ⁴the land the LORD subdued before the people of Israel—are suitable for livestock, and your servants have livestock. ⁵If we have found favor in your eyes," they said, "let this land be given to your servants as our possession. Do not make us cross the Jordan."

⁶Moses said to the Gadites and Reubenites, "Shall your countrymen go to war while you sit here? ⁷Why do you discourage the Israelites from going over into the land the LORD has given them? ⁸This is what your fathers did when I sent them from Kadesh Barnea to look over the land. ⁹After they went up to the Valley of Eshcol and viewed the land, they discouraged the Israelites from entering the land the LORD had given them. ¹⁰The LORD's anger was aroused that day and he swore this oath: ¹¹'Because they have not followed me wholeheartedly, not one of the men twenty years old or more who came up out of Egypt will see the land I promised on oath to Abraham, Isaac and Jacob— ¹²not one except Caleb son of Jephunneh the Kenizzite and Joshua son of Nun, for they followed the LORD wholeheartedly.' ¹³The LORD's anger burned against Israel and he made them wander in the desert forty years, until the whole generation of those who had done evil in his sight was gone.

¹⁴"And here you are, a brood of sinners, standing in the place of your fathers and making the LORD even more angry with Israel. ¹⁵If you turn away from following him, he will again leave all this people in the desert, and you will be the cause of their destruction."

¹⁶Then they came up to him and said, "We would like to build pens here for our livestock and cities for our women and children. ¹⁷But we are ready to arm ourselves and go ahead of the Israelites until we have brought them to their place. Meanwhile our women and children will live in fortified cities, for protection from the inhabitants of the land. ¹⁸We will not return to our homes until every Israelite has received his inheritance. ¹⁹We will not receive any inheritance with them on the other side of the Jordan, because our inheritance has come to us on the east side of the Jordan."

²⁰Then Moses said to them, "If you will do this—if you will arm yourselves before the LORD for battle, ²¹and if all of you will go armed over the Jordan before the LORD until he has driven his enemies out before him— ²²then when the land is subdued before the

ᵃ52 That is, about 420 pounds (about 190 kilograms)

LORD, you may return and be free from your obligation to the LORD and to Israel. And this land will be your possession before the LORD.

²³"But if you fail to do this, you will be sinning against the LORD; and you may be sure that your sin will find you out. ²⁴Build cities for your women and children, and pens for your flocks, but do what you have promised."

²⁵The Gadites and Reubenites said to Moses, "We your servants will do as our lord commands. ²⁶Our children and wives, our flocks and herds will remain here in the cities of Gilead. ²⁷But your servants, every man armed for battle, will cross over to fight before the LORD, just as our lord says."

²⁸Then Moses gave orders about them to Eleazar the priest and Joshua son of Nun and to the family heads of the Israelite tribes. ²⁹He said to them, "If the Gadites and Reubenites, every man armed for battle, cross over the Jordan with you before the LORD, then when the land is subdued before you, give them the land of Gilead as their possession. ³⁰But if they do not cross over with you armed, they must accept their possession with you in Canaan."

³¹The Gadites and Reubenites answered, "Your servants will do what the LORD has said. ³²We will cross over before the LORD into Canaan armed, but the property we inherit will be on this side of the Jordan."

³³Then Moses gave to the Gadites, the Reubenites and the half-tribe of Manasseh son of Joseph the kingdom of Sihon king of the Amorites and the kingdom of Og king of Bashan—the whole land with its cities and the territory around them.

³⁴The Gadites built up Dibon, Ataroth, Aroer, ³⁵Atroth Shophan, Jazer, Jogbehah, ³⁶Beth Nimrah and Beth Haran as fortified cities, and built pens for their flocks. ³⁷And the Reubenites rebuilt Heshbon, Elealeh and Kiriathaim, ³⁸as well as Nebo and Baal Meon (these names were changed) and Sibmah. They gave names to the cities they rebuilt.

³⁹The descendants of Makir son of Manasseh went to Gilead, captured it and drove out the Amorites who were there. ⁴⁰So Moses gave Gilead to the Makirites, the descendants of Manasseh, and they settled there. ⁴¹Jair, a descendant of Manasseh, captured their settlements and called them Havvoth Jair.ᵃ ⁴²And Nobah captured Kenath and its surrounding settlements and called it Nobah after himself.

Stages in Israel's Journey

33 Here are the stages in the journey of the Israelites when they came out of Egypt by divisions under the leadership of Moses and Aaron. ²At the LORD's command Moses recorded the stages in their journey. This is their journey by stages:

³The Israelites set out from Rameses on the fifteenth day of the first month, the day after the Passover. They marched out boldly in full view of all the Egyptians, ⁴who were burying all their firstborn, whom the LORD had struck down among them; for the LORD had brought judgment on their gods.

⁵The Israelites left Rameses and camped at Succoth.

⁶They left Succoth and camped at Etham, on the edge of the desert.

⁷They left Etham, turned back to Pi Hahiroth, to the east of Baal Zephon, and camped near Migdol.

⁸They left Pi Hahirothᵇ and passed through the sea into the desert, and when they had traveled for three days in the Desert of Etham, they camped at Marah.

⁹They left Marah and went to Elim, where there were twelve springs and seventy palm trees, and they camped there.

¹⁰They left Elim and camped by the Red Sea.ᶜ

¹¹They left the Red Sea and camped in the Desert of Sin.

¹²They left the Desert of Sin and camped at Dophkah.

ᵃ41 Or them the settlements of Jair   ᵇ8 Many manuscripts of the Masoretic Text, Samaritan Pentateuch and Vulgate; most manuscripts of the Masoretic Text left from before Hahiroth   ᶜ10 Hebrew Yam Suph; that is, Sea of Reeds; also in verse 11

¹³They left Dophkah and camped at Alush.

¹⁴They left Alush and camped at Rephidim, where there was no water for the people to drink.

¹⁵They left Rephidim and camped in the Desert of Sinai.

¹⁶They left the Desert of Sinai and camped at Kibroth Hattaavah.

¹⁷They left Kibroth Hattaavah and camped at Hazeroth.

¹⁸They left Hazeroth and camped at Rithmah.

¹⁹They left Rithmah and camped at Rimmon Perez.

²⁰They left Rimmon Perez and camped at Libnah.

²¹They left Libnah and camped at Rissah.

²²They left Rissah and camped at Kehelathah.

²³They left Kehelathah and camped at Mount Shepher.

²⁴They left Mount Shepher and camped at Haradah.

²⁵They left Haradah and camped at Makheloth.

²⁶They left Makheloth and camped at Tahath.

²⁷They left Tahath and camped at Terah.

²⁸They left Terah and camped at Mithcah.

²⁹They left Mithcah and camped at Hashmonah.

³⁰They left Hashmonah and camped at Moseroth.

³¹They left Moseroth and camped at Bene Jaakan.

³²They left Bene Jaakan and camped at Hor Haggidgad.

³³They left Hor Haggidgad and camped at Jotbathah.

³⁴They left Jotbathah and camped at Abronah.

³⁵They left Abronah and camped at Ezion Geber.

³⁶They left Ezion Geber and camped at Kadesh, in the Desert of Zin.

³⁷They left Kadesh and camped at Mount Hor, on the border of Edom. ³⁸At the LORD's command Aaron the priest went up Mount·Hor, where he died on the first day of the fifth month of the fortieth year after the Israelites came out of Egypt. ³⁹Aaron was a hundred and twenty-three years old when he died on Mount Hor.

⁴⁰The Canaanite king of Arad, who lived in the Negev of Canaan, heard that the Israelites were coming.

⁴¹They left Mount Hor and camped at Zalmonah.

⁴²They left Zalmonah and camped at Punon.

⁴³They left Punon and camped at Oboth.

⁴⁴They left Oboth and camped at Iye Abarim, on the border of Moab.

⁴⁵They left Iyim ᵃ and camped at Dibon Gad.

⁴⁶They left Dibon Gad and camped at Almon Diblathaim.

⁴⁷They left Almon Diblathaim and camped in the mountains of Abarim, near Nebo.

⁴⁸They left the mountains of Abarim and camped on the plains of Moab by the Jordan across from Jericho.ᵇ ⁴⁹There on the plains of Moab they camped along the Jordan from Beth Jeshimoth to Abel Shittim.

⁵⁰On the plains of Moab by the Jordan across from Jericho the LORD said to Moses, ⁵¹"Speak to the Israelites and say to them: 'When you cross the Jordan into Canaan, ⁵²drive out all the inhabitants of the land before you. Destroy all their carved images and their cast idols, and demolish all their high places. ⁵³Take possession of the land and settle in it, for I have given you the land to possess. ⁵⁴Distribute the land by lot, according to your clans. To a larger group give a larger inheritance, and to a smaller group a smaller one. Whatever falls to them by lot will be theirs. Distribute it according to your ancestral tribes.

⁵⁵"'But if you do not drive out the inhabitants of the land, those you allow to remain

ᵃ45 That is, Iye Abarim   ᵇ48 Hebrew *Jordan of Jericho*; possibly an ancient name for the Jordan River; also in verse 50

will become barbs in your eyes and thorns in your sides. They will give you trouble in the
land where you will live. **56**And then I will do to you what I plan to do to them.' "

Boundaries of Canaan

34 The LORD said to Moses, **2**"Command the Israelites and say to them: 'When
you enter Canaan, the land that will be allotted to you as an inheritance will
have these boundaries:

3" 'Your southern side will include some of the Desert of Zin along the border of Edom.
On the east, your southern boundary will start from the end of the Salt Sea,*a* **4**cross south
of Scorpion*b* Pass, continue on to Zin and go south of Kadesh Barnea. Then it will go to
Hazar Addar and over to Azmon, **5**where it will turn, join the Wadi of Egypt and end at
the Sea.*c*

6" 'Your western boundary will be the coast of the Great Sea. This will be your boundary on the west.

7" 'For your northern boundary, run a line from the Great Sea to Mount Hor **8**and from
Mount Hor to Lebo*d* Hamath. Then the boundary will go to Zedad, **9**continue to Ziphron
and end at Hazar Enan. This will be your boundary on the north.

10" 'For your eastern boundary, run a line from Hazar Enan to Shepham. **11**The boundary will go down from Shepham to Riblah on the east side of Ain and continue along the
slopes east of the Sea of Kinnereth.*e* **12**Then the boundary will go down along the
Jordan and end at the Salt Sea.

" 'This will be your land, with its boundaries on every side.' "

13Moses commanded the Israelites: "Assign this land by lot as an inheritance. The LORD
has ordered that it be given to the nine and a half tribes, **14**because the families of the
tribe of Reuben, the tribe of Gad and the half-tribe of Manasseh have received their
inheritance. **15**These two and a half tribes have received their inheritance on the east
side of the Jordan of Jericho,*f* toward the sunrise."

16The LORD said to Moses, **17**"These are the names of the men who are to assign the
land for you as an inheritance: Eleazar the priest and Joshua son of Nun. **18**And appoint
one leader from each tribe to help assign the land. **19**These are their names:

Caleb son of Jephunneh,
　　from the tribe of Judah;
20Shemuel son of Ammihud,
　　from the tribe of Simeon;
21Elidad son of Kislon,
　　from the tribe of Benjamin;
22Bukki son of Jogli,
　　the leader from the tribe of Dan;
23Hanniel son of Ephod,
　　the leader from the tribe of Manasseh son of Joseph;
24Kemuel son of Shiphtan,
　　the leader from the tribe of Ephraim son of Joseph;
25Elizaphan son of Parnach,
　　the leader from the tribe of Zebulun;
26Paltiel son of Azzan,
　　the leader from the tribe of Issachar;
27Ahihud son of Shelomi,
　　the leader from the tribe of Asher;

a3 That is, the Dead Sea; also in verse 12　　*b4 Hebrew Akrabbim*　　*c5 That is, the Mediterranean; also in verses 6 and 7*
d8 Or to the entrance to　　*e11 That is, Galilee*　　*f15 Jordan of Jericho was possibly an ancient name for the*
Jordan River.

²⁸Pedahel son of Ammihud,
the leader from the tribe of Naphtali."

²⁹These are the men the LORD commanded to assign the inheritance to the Israelites in the land of Canaan.

Towns for the Levites

35 On the plains of Moab by the Jordan across from Jericho,ᵃ the LORD said to Moses, ²"Command the Israelites to give the Levites towns to live in from the inheritance the Israelites will possess. And give them pasturelands around the towns. ³Then they will have towns to live in and pasturelands for their cattle, flocks and all their other livestock.

⁴"The pasturelands around the towns that you give the Levites will extend out fifteen hundred feetᵇ from the town wall. ⁵Outside the town, measure three thousand feetᶜ on the east side, three thousand on the south side, three thousand on the west and three thousand on the north, with the town in the center. They will have this area as pasture-land for the towns.

Cities of Refuge

⁶"Six of the towns you give the Levites will be cities of refuge, to which a person who has killed someone may flee. In addition, give them forty-two other towns. ⁷In all you must give the Levites forty-eight towns, together with their pasturelands. ⁸The towns you give the Levites from the land the Israelites possess are to be given in proportion to the inheritance of each tribe: Take many towns from a tribe that has many, but few from one that has few."

⁹Then the LORD said to Moses: ¹⁰"Speak to the Israelites and say to them: 'When you cross the Jordan into Canaan, ¹¹select some towns to be your cities of refuge, to which a person who has killed someone accidentally may flee. ¹²They will be places of refuge from the avenger, so that a person accused of murder may not die before he stands trial before the assembly. ¹³These six towns you give will be your cities of refuge. ¹⁴Give three on this side of the Jordan and three in Canaan as cities of refuge. ¹⁵These six towns will be a place of refuge for Israelites, aliens and any other people living among them, so that anyone who has killed another accidentally can flee there.

¹⁶"'If a man strikes someone with an iron object so that he dies, he is a murderer; the murderer shall be put to death. ¹⁷Or if anyone has a stone in his hand that could kill, and he strikes someone so that he dies, he is a murderer; the murderer shall be put to death. ¹⁸Or if anyone has a wooden object in his hand that could kill, and he hits someone so that he dies, he is a murderer; the murderer shall be put to death. ¹⁹The avenger of blood shall put the murderer to death; when he meets him, he shall put him to death. ²⁰If anyone with malice aforethought shoves another or throws something at him intentionally so that he dies ²¹or if in hostility he hits him with his fist so that he dies, that person shall be put to death; he is a murderer. The avenger of blood shall put the murderer to death when he meets him.

²²"'But if without hostility someone suddenly shoves another or throws something at him unintentionally, ²³or, without seeing him, drops a stone on him that could kill him, and he dies, then since he was not his enemy and he did not intend to harm him, ²⁴the assembly must judge between him and the avenger of blood according to these regulations. ²⁵The assembly must protect the one accused of murder from the avenger of blood and send him back to the city of refuge to which he fled. He must stay there until the death of the high priest, who was anointed with the holy oil.

²⁶"'But if the accused ever goes outside the limits of the city of refuge to which he ha

---

ᵃ1 Hebrew *Jordan of Jericho*; possibly an ancient name for the Jordan River   ᵇ4 Hebrew *a thousand cubits* (about 450 meters)   ᶜ5 Hebrew *two thousand cubits* (about 900 meters)

fled ²⁷and the avenger of blood finds him outside the city, the avenger of blood may kill the accused without being guilty of murder. ²⁸The accused must stay in his city of refuge until the death of the high priest; only after the death of the high priest may he return to his own property.

²⁹"These are to be legal requirements for you throughout the generations to come, wherever you live.

³⁰"Anyone who kills a person is to be put to death as a murderer only on the testimony of witnesses. But no one is to be put to death on the testimony of only one witness.

³¹"Do not accept a ransom for the life of a murderer, who deserves to die. He must surely be put to death.

³²"Do not accept a ransom for anyone who has fled to a city of refuge and so allow him to go back and live on his own land before the death of the high priest.

³³"Do not pollute the land where you are. Bloodshed pollutes the land, and atonement cannot be made for the land on which blood has been shed, except by the blood of the one who shed it. ³⁴Do not defile the land where you live and where I dwell, for I, the LORD, dwell among the Israelites.'"

Inheritance of Zelophehad's Daughters

36 The family heads of the clan of Gilead son of Makir, the son of Manasseh, who were from the clans of the descendants of Joseph, came and spoke before Moses and the leaders, the heads of the Israelite families. ²They said, "When the LORD commanded my lord to give the land as an inheritance to the Israelites by lot, he ordered you to give the inheritance of our brother Zelophehad to his daughters. ³Now suppose they marry men from other Israelite tribes; then their inheritance will be taken from our ancestral inheritance and added to that of the tribe they marry into. And so part of the inheritance allotted to us will be taken away. ⁴When the Year of Jubilee for the Israelites comes, their inheritance will be added to that of the tribe into which they marry, and their property will be taken from the tribal inheritance of our forefathers."

⁵Then at the LORD's command Moses gave this order to the Israelites: "What the tribe of the descendants of Joseph is saying is right. ⁶This is what the LORD commands for Zelophehad's daughters: They may marry anyone they please as long as they marry within the tribal clan of their father. ⁷No inheritance in Israel is to pass from tribe to tribe, for every Israelite shall keep the tribal land inherited from his forefathers. ⁸Every daughter who inherits land in any Israelite tribe must marry someone in her father's tribal clan, so that every Israelite will possess the inheritance of his fathers. ⁹No inheritance may pass from tribe to tribe, for each Israelite tribe is to keep the land it inherits."

¹⁰So Zelophehad's daughters did as the LORD commanded Moses. ¹¹Zelophehad's

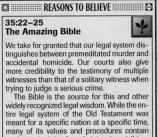

daughters—Mahlah, Tirzah, Hoglah, Milcah and Noah—married their cousins on their father's side. [12]They married within the clans of the descendants of Manasseh son of Joseph, and their inheritance remained in their father's clan and tribe.

[13]These are the commands and regulations the LORD gave through Moses to the Israelites on the plains of Moab by the Jordan across from Jericho. [a]

---

[a] 13 Hebrew *Jordan of Jericho*; possibly an ancient name for the Jordan River

I was raised in your basic reformed Jewish home. We celebrated all the major holidays and I had my Bas Mitzvah at age 13, but none of these activities impacted me spiritually. My family rarely discussed God or what he meant to our lives.

I believe that many of the negative events of my early life were directly related to my lack of a spiritual connection. I was a hyperactive kid, and I turned into a selectively hyperactive teenager. I was a good student when I chose to be—a choice I didn't make very often. I found myself searching for acceptance and love in all the wrong places and became entrenched in a wild, hedonistic lifestyle. I honestly didn't believe I would live past the age of 21. Eventually I married a man who I believed was my "knight in shining armor," but the marriage lasted only a few years.

Still searching for the perfect man to complete my life and fill the void in my heart, I became involved in another intense relationship. Since our religious beliefs were different, my boyfriend and I decided to compromise and search for a new church altogether. We joined a large non-denominational church, and our relationship grew. He moved in with me, and we even discussed marriage. The church, however, had different ideas about us living together. We thought about joining a small group for couples, but decided against it because we didn't want to be confronted with our living situation.

I continued to go to church without my boyfriend and joined a seeker small group. That's where I found what I needed—loving leaders and group members who were gentle yet firm with me about my relationship with my boyfriend and my relationship with God. I began to see that my relationship with my boyfriend was going nowhere and was really beginning to drag me down. In the meantime God continued to knock at my door by placing wonderful Christian women in every area of my life. My relationship with God grew, and I asked my boyfriend to move out. We began premarital counseling with the church, but after two sessions we decided it simply wasn't going to work.

The day I broke up with my boyfriend is the day I accepted Jesus Christ as my Messiah. I knew I couldn't continue in this painful pattern of destructive relationships, and that only the love of Jesus and the guidance of his Holy Spirit would allow me to break that pattern. Throughout this process the members of my small group encouraged me in my own spiritual and emotional growth. The message I heard from them was that there was only one perfect man who could completely fill the void in my life—Jesus Christ himself. What a gift that realization has been!

I am so incredibly grateful to have received the gift of salvation, the love of Jesus and the blessing of the Holy Spirit. I wish I could say that my seeker small group had all the answers for my life. They couldn't answer all my questions, and I'm still searching for some of those answers. What they did give me, however, was infinitely more valuable than just answers to my questions. They showed me the love of Jesus through their actions, a love that has penetrated my heart and soul. I now know that the Bible is God's Word, and that Jesus is the way and the truth and the life (John 14:6)!

DEUTERONOMY

Introduction

THE BOTTOM LINE

All trade agreements, whether as large as a nation's international policy or as small as a contract from the local used car lot, include a series of regulations and stipulations—"We promise this if you do that." In this book, Moses spells out God's agreement (or "covenant") with the people of Israel. The main terms are simple: Israel is to love and obey God, being careful to show his character to the world. In turn, God will establish them in the land he had promised to their ancestor Abraham. God extends a similar offer to us today. He wants us to love him above all else, and to rely on Jesus for forgiveness. To those who do so, God grants total pardon from sin (Hebrews chapter 10, verses 10, 16–18 [p. 1594]).

CENTRAL IDEAS

- God's agreement with Israel: "I will preserve your nation if you obey me."
- We must reject anything that takes away from devotion to God.
- God reaches out to people—not because they're deserving, but because he's gracious.
- Moses restates the Ten Commandments (chapter 5).

OUTLINE

1 Preamble (1:1–5)
2 Historical prologue (1:6–4:43)
3 God's agreement with his people (4:44—26:19)
4 Results of obedience and disobedience (chs. 27–30)
5 Leadership transferred (chs. 31–34)

TITLE

Deuteronomy means "the second law" – Moses gives his final sermon and tells the Israelites God's commandments for the second (and his last) time.

AUTHOR AND READERS

Moses wrote this book as his final words to the people of Israel.

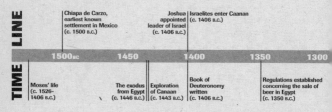

TIME LINE					
	Chiapa de Carzo, earliest known settlement in Mexico (c. 1500 B.C.)		Joshua appointed leader of Israel (c. 1406 B.C.)	Israelites enter Caanan (c. 1406 B.C.)	
1500 BC	**1450**		**1400**	**1350**	**1300**
Moses' life (c. 1526–1406 B.C.)		The exodus from Egypt (c. 1446 B.C.)	Exploration of Canaan (c. 1443 B.C.)	Book of Deuteronomy written (c. 1406 B.C.)	Regulations established concerning the sale of beer in Egypt (c. 1350 B.C.)

A certain college professor had his sociology class collect case histories from 200 young boys in a Baltimore slum. The class was asked to write an evaluation of each boy's future. In every case the students wrote, "He hasn't got a chance."

Twenty-five years later another sociology professor came across the earlier study. He had his students follow up on the project to see what had happened to these boys. With the exception of 20 boys who had moved away or died, the students learned that 176 of the remaining 180 had achieved more than ordinary success as lawyers, doctors, and businessmen.

The professor was astonished and decided to pursue the matter further. Since all of the men were in the area, he was able to ask each one, "How do you account for your success?" In each case the reply began with the same words: "There was this teacher...."

Fortunately, the teacher was still alive, so the professor sought her out. He asked the elderly woman what magic formula she had used to pull these boys out of the slums and into success and achievement.

*"I loved **those boys.**"*

The teacher's eyes sparkled and her lips broke into a gentle smile. "It's really very simple," she said, "I *loved* those boys."

Human love is a powerful force. It can somehow take kids who seem destined to fail and transform them into success stories. Divine love is an even greater power. It takes spiritually dead people and gives them life. God's love causes people to hunger to know him. Once they know him, his love creates within them a desire for his leadership in every facet of life.

As the Israelite people prepared to enter the land God had promised them, God used his spokesman Moses to give them guidance for their new life. In this book, which is actually Moses' farewell speech, Moses reiterates the primary principle upon which the nation will be built—the law of loving God above all else because he loves them. After repeating the famous "Ten Commandments," he teaches them how to apply that law of love and how to pass it on to the next generation. Turn to Deuteronomy chapter 6, verses 4–9 (page 223), to find that guidance.

Eric Butterworth, "Love: The One Creative Force," quoted in *Chicken Soup for the Soul,* ed. Jack Cranfield and Mark Victor Hansen (Deerfield Beach, Fla.: Health Communications, [1993]), pp. 3–4.

DEUTERONOMY

The Command to Leave Horeb

1 These are the words Moses spoke to all Israel in the desert east of th
Jordan—that is, in the Arabah—opposite Suph, between Paran and Tophe
Laban, Hazeroth and Dizahab. ²(It takes eleven days to go from Horeb to Kadesh Barne
by the Mount Seir road.)

³In the fortieth year, on the first day of the eleventh month, Moses proclaimed to th
Israelites all that the LORD had commanded him concerning them. ⁴This was after he ha
defeated Sihon king of the Amorites, who reigned in Heshbon, and at Edrei had defeate
Og king of Bashan, who reigned in Ashtaroth.

⁵East of the Jordan in the territory of Moab, Moses began to expound this law, saying

⁶The LORD our God said to us at Horeb, "You have stayed long enough at this mountain
⁷Break camp and advance into the hill country of the Amorites; go to all the neighborin
peoples in the Arabah, in the mountains, in the western foothills, in the Negev and alon
the coast, to the land of the Canaanites and to Lebanon, as far as the great river, th
Euphrates. ⁸See, I have given you this land. Go in and take possession of the land tha
the LORD swore he would give to your fathers—to Abraham, Isaac and Jacob—and to the
descendants after them."

The Appointment of Leaders

⁹At that time I said to you, "You are too heavy a burden for me to carry alone. ¹⁰Th
LORD your God has increased your numbers so that today you are as many as the stars i
the sky. ¹¹May the LORD, the God of your fathers, increase you a thousand times and bles
you as he has promised! ¹²But how can I bear your problems and your burdens and you
disputes all by myself? ¹³Choose some wise, understanding and respected men fron
each of your tribes, and I will set them over you."

¹⁴You answered me, "What you propose to do is good."

¹⁵So I took the leading men of your tribes, wise and respected men, and appointe
them to have authority over you—as commanders of thousands, of hundreds, of fifties and
of tens and as tribal officials. ¹⁶And I charged your judges at that time: Hear the dispute
between your brothers and judge fairly, whether the case is between brother Israelites o
between one of them and an alien. ¹⁷Do not show partiality in judging; hear both smal
and great alike. Do not be afraid of any man, for judgment belongs to God. Bring me an
case too hard for you, and I will hear it. ¹⁸And at that time I told you everything you wer
to do.

Spies Sent Out

¹⁹Then, as the LORD our God commanded us, we set out from Horeb and went towar
the hill country of the Amorites through all that vast and dreadful desert that you have
seen, and so we reached Kadesh Barnea. ²⁰Then I said to you, "You have reached the hil
country of the Amorites, which the LORD our God is giving us. ²¹See, the LORD your God ha
given you the land. Go up and take possession of it as the LORD, the God of your fathers
told you. Do not be afraid; do not be discouraged."

²²Then all of you came to me and said, "Let us send men ahead to spy out the land fo
us and bring back a report about the route we are to take and the towns we wil
come to."

23The idea seemed good to me; so I selected twelve of you, one man from each tribe. 24They left and went up into the hill country, and came to the Valley of Eshcol and explored it. 25Taking with them some of the fruit of the land, they brought it down to us and reported, "It is a good land that the LORD our God is giving us."

Rebellion Against the LORD

26But you were unwilling to go up; you rebelled against the command of the LORD your God. 27You grumbled in your tents and said, "The LORD hates us; so he brought us out of Egypt to deliver us into the hands of the Amorites to destroy us. 28Where can we go? Our brothers have made us lose heart. They say, 'The people are stronger and taller than we are; the cities are large, with walls up to the sky. We even saw the Anakites there.'"

29Then I said to you, "Do not be terrified; do not be afraid of them. 30The LORD your God, who is going before you, will fight for you, as he did for you in Egypt, before your very eyes, 31and in the desert. There you saw how the LORD your God carried you, as a father carries his son, all the way you went until you reached this place."

32In spite of this, you did not trust in the LORD your God, 33who went ahead of you on your journey, in fire by night and in a cloud by day, to search out places for you to camp and to show you the way you should go.

34When the LORD heard what you said, he was angry and solemnly swore: 35"Not a man of this evil generation shall see the good land I swore to give your forefathers, 36except Caleb son of Jephunneh. He will see it, and I will give him and his descendants the land he set his feet on, because he followed the LORD wholeheartedly."

37Because of you the LORD became angry with me also and said, "You shall not enter it, either. 38But your assistant, Joshua son of Nun, will enter it. Encourage him, because he will lead Israel to inherit it. 39And the little ones that you said would be taken captive, your children who do not yet know good from bad—they will enter the land. I will give it to them and they will take possession of it. 40But as for you, turn around and set out toward the desert along the route to the Red Sea.[a]"

41Then you replied, "We have sinned against the LORD. We will go up and fight, as the LORD our God commanded us." So every one of you put on his weapons, thinking it easy to go up into the hill country.

42But the LORD said to me, "Tell them, 'Do not go up and fight, because I will not be with you. You will be defeated by your enemies.'"

43So I told you, but you would not listen. You rebelled against the LORD's command and in your arrogance you marched up into the hill country. 44The Amorites who lived in those hills came out against you; they chased you like a swarm of bees and beat you down from Seir all the way to Hormah. 45You came back and wept before the LORD, but he

> ### ▣ ⦙⦙⦙⦙⦙STRENGTHENING RELATIONSHIPS⦙⦙⦙⦙⦙ ⬅
>
> #### 1:15–17
> #### Leadership
>
> One function of leaders in Old Testament times was to help settle disagreements. These leaders needed to be wise and discerning as they heard both sides of a story, sorted through details, and determined a fair and impartial solution. Their God-given objective was to give the "little people" in their society the same kind of hearing they gave to the rich and powerful.
>
> What about leaders today? Good leaders in business, government and education must be able to cut to the core of an issue, be open to all points of view until all the evidence is in, and be utterly fair and unbiased.
>
> But notice that the spiritual dimension is lacking in many who wield power in our day. Ultimately, leaders answer to God, not just to those whom they lead. Think of how much better the government and marketplace would function if men and women were to recognize that they were accountable to an all-seeing, impartial God who will someday judge *them!*

a40 Hebrew *Yam Suph;* that is, Sea of Reeds

paid no attention to your weeping and turned a deaf ear to you. ⁴⁶And so you stayed in Kadesh many days—all the time you spent there.

Wanderings in the Desert

2 Then we turned back and set out toward the desert along the route to the Red Sea,ª as the LORD had directed me. For a long time we made our way around the hill country of Seir.

²Then the LORD said to me, ³"You have made your way around this hill country long enough; now turn north. ⁴Give the people these orders: 'You are about to pass through the territory of your brothers the descendants of Esau, who live in Seir. They will be afraid of you, but be very careful. ⁵Do not provoke them to war, for I will not give you any of their land, not even enough to put your foot on. I have given Esau the hill country of Seir as his own. ⁶You are to pay them in silver for the food you eat and the water you drink.'"

⁷The LORD your God has blessed you in all the work of your hands. He has watched over your journey through this vast desert. These forty years the LORD your God has been with you, and you have not lacked anything.

⁸So we went on past our brothers the descendants of Esau, who live in Seir. We turned from the Arabah road, which comes up from Elath and Ezion Geber, and traveled along the desert road of Moab.

⁹Then the LORD said to me, "Do not harass the Moabites or provoke them to war, for I will not give you any part of their land. I have given Ar to the descendants of Lot as a possession."

¹⁰(The Emites used to live there—a people strong and numerous, and as tall as the Anakites. ¹¹Like the Anakites, they too were considered Rephaites, but the Moabites called them Emites. ¹²Horites used to live in Seir, but the descendants of Esau drove them out. They destroyed the Horites from before them and settled in their place, just as Israel did in the land the LORD gave them as their possession.)

¹³And the LORD said, "Now get up and cross the Zered Valley." So we crossed the valley.

¹⁴Thirty-eight years passed from the time we left Kadesh Barnea until we crossed the Zered Valley. By then, that entire generation of fighting men had perished from the camp, as the LORD had sworn to them. ¹⁵The LORD's hand was against them until he had completely eliminated them from the camp.

¹⁶Now when the last of these fighting men among the people had died, ¹⁷the LORD said to me, ¹⁸"Today you are to pass by the region of Moab at Ar. ¹⁹When you come to the Ammonites, do not harass them or provoke them to war, for I will not give you possession of any land belonging to the Ammonites. I have given it as a possession to the descendants of Lot."

²⁰(That too was considered a land of the Rephaites, who used to live there; but the Ammonites called them Zamzummites. ²¹They were a people strong and numerous, and as tall as the Anakites. The LORD destroyed them from before the Ammonites, who drove them out and settled in their place. ²²The LORD had done the same for the descendants of Esau, who lived in Seir, when he destroyed the Horites from before them. They drove them out and have lived in their place to this day. ²³And as for the Avvites who lived in villages as far as Gaza, the Caphtorites coming out from Caphtorᵇ destroyed them and settled in their place.)

Defeat of Sihon King of Heshbon

²⁴"Set out now and cross the Arnon Gorge. See, I have given into your hand Sihon the Amorite, king of Heshbon, and his country. Begin to take possession of it and engage him in battle. ²⁵This very day I will begin to put the terror and fear of you on all the nations

---

ª 1 Hebrew *Yam Suph*; that is, Sea of Reeds   ᵇ 23 That is, Crete

under heaven. They will hear reports of you and will tremble and be in anguish because of you."

26From the desert of Kedemoth I sent messengers to Sihon king of Heshbon offering peace and saying, 27"Let us pass through your country. We will stay on the main road; we will not turn aside to the right or to the left. 28Sell us food to eat and water to drink or their price in silver. Only let us pass through on foot— 29as the descendants of Esau, who live in Seir, and the Moabites, who live in Ar, did for us—until we cross the Jordan into the land the LORD our God is giving us." 30But Sihon king of Heshbon refused to let us pass through. For the LORD your God had made his spirit stubborn and his heart obstinate in order to give him into your hands, as he has now done.

31The LORD said to me, "See, I have begun to deliver Sihon and his country over to you. Now begin to conquer and possess his land."

32When Sihon and all his army came out to meet us in battle at Jahaz, 33the LORD our God delivered him over to us and we struck him down, together with his sons and his whole army. 34At that time we took all his towns and completely destroyed*a* them—men, women and children. We left no survivors.

35But the livestock and the plunder from the towns we had captured we carried off for ourselves. 36From Aroer on the rim of the Arnon Gorge, and from the town in the gorge, even as far as Gilead, not one town was too strong for us. The LORD our God gave us all of them. 37But in accordance with the command of the LORD our God, you did not encroach on any of the land of the Ammonites, neither the land along the course of the Jabbok nor that around the towns in the hills.

Defeat of Og King of Bashan

3 Next we turned and went up along the road toward Bashan, and Og king of Bashan with his whole army marched out to meet us in battle at Edrei. 2The LORD said to me, "Do not be afraid of him, for I have handed him over to you with his whole army and his land. Do to him what you did to Sihon king of the Amorites, who reigned in Heshbon."

3So the LORD our God also gave into our hands Og king of Bashan and all his army. We struck them down, leaving no survivors. 4At that time we took all his cities. There was not one of the sixty cities that we did not take from them—the whole region of Argob, Og's kingdom in Bashan. 5All these cities were fortified with high walls and with gates and bars, and there were also a great many unwalled villages. 6We completely destroyed*a* them, as we had done with Sihon king of Heshbon, destroying*a* every city—men, women and children. 7But all the livestock and the plunder from their cities we carried off for ourselves.

8So at that time we took from these two kings of the Amorites the territory east of the

---

a 34,6 The Hebrew term refers to the irrevocable giving over of things or persons to the LORD, often by totally destroying them.

Jordan, from the Arnon Gorge as far as Mount Hermon. ⁹(Hermon is called Sirion by the Sidonians; the Amorites call it Senir.) ¹⁰We took all the towns on the plateau, and all Gilead, and all Bashan as far as Salecah and Edrei, towns of Og's kingdom in Bashan ¹¹(Only Og king of Bashan was left of the remnant of the Rephaites. His bed*a* was made of iron and was more than thirteen feet long and six feet wide.*b* It is still in Rabbah of the Ammonites.)

Division of the Land

¹²Of the land that we took over at that time, I gave the Reubenites and the Gadites the territory north of Aroer by the Arnon Gorge, including half the hill country of Gilead together with its towns. ¹³The rest of Gilead and also all of Bashan, the kingdom of Og, I gave to the half tribe of Manasseh. (The whole region of Argob in Bashan used to be known as a land of the Rephaites. ¹⁴Jair, a descendant of Manasseh, took the whole region of Argob as far as the border of the Geshurites and the Maacathites; it was named after him, so that to this day Bashan is called Havvoth Jair.*c*) ¹⁵And I gave Gilead to Makir. ¹⁶But to the Reubenites and the Gadites I gave the territory extending from Gilead down to the Arnon Gorge (the middle of the gorge being the border) and out to the Jabbok River, which is the border of the Ammonites. ¹⁷Its western border was the Jordan in the Arabah, from Kinnereth to the Sea of the Arabah (the Salt Sea*d*), below the slopes of Pisgah.

¹⁸I commanded you at that time: "The LORD your God has given you this land to take possession of it. But all your able-bodied men, armed for battle, must cross over ahead of your brother Israelites. ¹⁹However, your wives, your children and your livestock (I know you have much livestock) may stay in the towns I have given you, ²⁰until the LORD gives rest to your brothers as he has to you, and they too have taken over the land that the LORD your God is giving them, across the Jordan. After that, each of you may go back to the possession I have given you."

Moses Forbidden to Cross the Jordan

²¹At that time I commanded Joshua: "You have seen with your own eyes all that the LORD your God has done to these two kings. The LORD will do the same to all the kingdoms over there where you are going. ²²Do not be afraid of them; the LORD your God himself will fight for you."

²³At that time I pleaded with the LORD: ²⁴"O Sovereign LORD, you have begun to show to your servant your greatness and your strong hand. For what god is there in heaven or on earth who can do the deeds and mighty works you do? ²⁵Let me go over and see the good land beyond the Jordan—that fine hill country and Lebanon."

²⁶But because of you the LORD was angry with me and would not listen to me. "That is enough," the LORD said. "Do not speak to me anymore about this matter. ²⁷Go up to the top of Pisgah and look west and north and south and east. Look at the land with your own eyes, since you are not going to cross this Jordan. ²⁸But commission Joshua, and encourage and strengthen him, for he will lead this people across and will cause them to inherit the land that you will see." ²⁹So we stayed in the valley near Beth Peor.

Obedience Commanded

4 Hear now, O Israel, the decrees and laws I am about to teach you. Follow them so that you may live and may go in and take possession of the land that the LORD, the God of your fathers, is giving you. ²Do not add to what I command you and do not subtract from it, but keep the commands of the LORD your God that I give you ³You saw with your own eyes what the LORD did at Baal Peor. The LORD your God

---

a 11 Or *sarcophagus*   *b 11* Hebrew *nine cubits long and four cubits wide* (about 4 meters long and 1.8 meters wide)
c 14 Or *called the settlements of Jair*   *d 17* That is, the Dead Sea

estroyed from among you everyone who followed the Baal of Peor, **4**but all of you who
eld fast to the L ORD your God are still alive today.

5See, I have taught you decrees and laws as the L ORD my God commanded me, so that
ou may follow them in the land you are entering to take possession of it. **6**Observe them
arefully, for this will show your wisdom and understanding to the nations, who will
ear about all these decrees and say, "Surely this great nation is a wise and understand-
g people." **7**What other nation is so great as to have their gods near them the way the
ORD our God is near us whenever we pray to him? **8**And what other nation is so great as
 have such righteous decrees and laws as this body of laws I am setting before you
day?

9Only be careful, and watch yourselves closely so that you do not forget the things your
yes have seen or let them slip from your heart as long as you live. Teach them to your
hildren and to their children after them. **10**Remember the day you stood before the L ORD
our God at Horeb, when he said to me,
Assemble the people before me to hear my
ords so that they may learn to revere me
s long as they live in the land and may
ach them to their children." **11**You came
ear and stood at the foot of the mountain
hile it blazed with fire to the very heav-
ns, with black clouds and deep darkness.
Then the L ORD spoke to you out of the fire.
ou heard the sound of words but saw no
rm; there was only a voice. **13**He declared
 you his covenant, the Ten Command-
ents, which he commanded you to follow
nd then wrote them on two stone tablets.
And the L ORD directed me at that time to
ach you the decrees and laws you are to
llow in the land that you are crossing the
ordan to possess.

> □ ::::::::::::::: **DISCOVERING GOD** ::::::::::::::: ↔
>
> **4:2**
> **Spiritual Fraud**
>
> Adding to what God has said in the Bible is
> just as wrong as taking away from it or ignor-
> ing his commandments. Some "religious"
> people are good at taking God's words and
> making more out of them than was originally
> intended. They create rules and regulations for
> conduct that God never intended for his peo-
> ple. Others tend to minimize God's commands,
> sometimes even labeling them as irrelevant to
> today's world.
>
> If you're a seeker, don't assume that every-
> thing your "spiritual" friends say is what God
> commands. Check the source for yourself and
> see what the Bible *really* says.

Idolatry Forbidden

15You saw no form of any kind the day the L ORD spoke to you at Horeb out of the fire.
herefore watch yourselves very carefully, **16**so that you do not become corrupt and make
r yourselves an idol, an image of any shape, whether formed like a man or a woman,
or like any animal on earth or any bird that flies in the air, **18**or like any creature that
oves along the ground or any fish in the waters below. **19**And when you look up to the
ky and see the sun, the moon and the stars—all the heavenly array—do not be enticed
to bowing down to them and worshiping things the L ORD your God has apportioned to
l the nations under heaven. **20**But as for you, the L ORD took you and brought you out of
e iron-smelting furnace, out of Egypt, to be the people of his inheritance, as you now
re.

21The L ORD was angry with me because of you, and he solemnly swore that I would not
oss the Jordan and enter the good land the L ORD your God is giving you as your inheri-
nce. **22**I will die in this land; I will not cross the Jordan; but you are about to cross over
nd take possession of that good land. **23**Be careful not to forget the covenant of the L ORD
our God that he made with you; do not make for yourselves an idol in the form of
nything the L ORD your God has forbidden. **24**For the L ORD your God is a consuming fire, a
alous God.

25After you have had children and grandchildren and have lived in the land a long
ne—if you then become corrupt and make any kind of idol, doing evil in the eyes of the
ORD your God and provoking him to anger, **26**I call heaven and earth as witnesses against

you this day that you will quickly perish from the land that you are crossing the Jordan ▮ possess. You will not live there long but will certainly be destroyed. ²⁷The LORD wi▮ scatter you among the peoples, and only a few of you will survive among the nations t▮ which the LORD will drive you. ²⁸There you will worship man-made gods of wood an▮ stone, which cannot see or hear or eat ▮ smell. ²⁹But if from there you seek the LOR▮ your God, you will find him if you look fo▮ him with all your heart and with all you▮ soul. ³⁰When you are in distress and a▮ these things have happened to you, then i▮ later days you will return to the LORD you▮ God and obey him. ³¹For the LORD your Go▮ is a merciful God; he will not abandon ▮ destroy you or forget the covenant wit▮ your forefathers, which he confirmed ▮ them by oath.

═══ DISCOVERING GOD ═══

4:28–31
Life with God

Here's a verse every seeker should learn by heart! God promises that people can find him even when they've gone far astray spiritually (in this case, by worshipping other gods).

Although we may not bow down to stone idols today, all of us have allowed things or people in our lives to become more important than God. That's the essence of idolatry. So this verse applies more directly than we might think at first.

But if the bad news applies, so does the good news. Mercy is at the very heart of God's character. He would much rather welcome back a wandering soul than allow that person to live apart from him forever. So on the authority of this verse, consider yourself personally and formally invited to seek God with all your heart and soul. And be comforted by the promise that he is merciful and eager to be in a relationship with you forever.

The LORD Is God

³²Ask now about the former days, lon▮ before your time, from the day God create▮ man on the earth; ask from one end of th▮ heavens to the other. Has anything so grea▮ as this ever happened, or has anything lik▮ it ever been heard of? ³³Has any othe▮ people heard the voice of God*a* speakin▮ out of fire, as you have, and lived? ³⁴Ha▮ any god ever tried to take for himself on▮ nation out of another nation, by testing▮ by miraculous signs and wonders, by wa▮ by a mighty hand and an outstretched arm▮ or by great and awesome deeds, like all the things the LORD your God did for you in Egy▮ before your very eyes?

³⁵You were shown these things so that you might know that the LORD is God; beside▮ him there is no other. ³⁶From heaven he made you hear his voice to discipline you. C▮ earth he showed you his great fire, and you heard his words from out of the fire. ³⁷Be▮ cause he loved your forefathers and chose their descendants after them, he brought yo▮ out of Egypt by his Presence and his great strength, ³⁸to drive out before you natio▮ greater and stronger than you and to bring you into their land to give it to you for yo▮ inheritance, as it is today.

³⁹Acknowledge and take to heart this day that the LORD is God in heaven above and ▮ the earth below. There is no other. ⁴⁰Keep his decrees and commands, which I am givin▮ you today, so that it may go well with you and your children after you and that you ma▮ live long in the land the LORD your God gives you for all time.

Cities of Refuge

⁴¹Then Moses set aside three cities east of the Jordan, ⁴²to which anyone who ha▮ killed a person could flee if he had unintentionally killed his neighbor without mali▮ aforethought. He could flee into one of these cities and save his life. ⁴³The cities we▮ these: Bezer in the desert plateau, for the Reubenites; Ramoth in Gilead, for the Gadite▮ and Golan in Bashan, for the Manassites.

a 33 Or of a god

Introduction to the Law

44This is the law Moses set before the Israelites. **45**These are the stipulations, decrees and laws Moses gave them when they came out of Egypt **46**and were in the valley near Beth Peor east of the Jordan, in the land of Sihon king of the Amorites, who reigned in Heshbon and was defeated by Moses and the Israelites as they came out of Egypt. **47**They took possession of his land and the land of Og king of Bashan, the two Amorite kings east of the Jordan. **48**This land extended from Aroer on the rim of the Arnon Gorge to Mount Siyon*a* (that is, Hermon), **49**and included all the Arabah east of the Jordan, as far as the Sea of the Arabah,*b* below the slopes of Pisgah.

The Ten Commandments

5 Moses summoned all Israel and said:

Hear, O Israel, the decrees and laws I declare in your hearing today. Learn them and be sure to follow them. **2**The LORD our God made a covenant with us at Horeb. **3**It was not with our fathers that the LORD made this covenant, but with us, with all of us who are alive here today. **4**The LORD spoke to you face to face out of the fire on the mountain. **5**(At that time I stood between the LORD and you to declare to you the word of the LORD, because you were afraid of the fire and did not go up the mountain.) And he said:

6"I am the LORD your God, who brought you out of Egypt, out of the land of slavery.

7"You shall have no other gods before*c* me.

8"You shall not make for yourself an idol in the form of anything in heaven above or on the earth beneath or in the waters below. **9**You shall not bow down to them or worship them; for I, the LORD your God, am a jealous God, punishing the children for the sin of the fathers to the third and fourth generation of those who hate me, **10**but showing love to a thousand ⌊generations⌋ of those who love me and keep my commandments.

11"You shall not misuse the name of the LORD your God, for the LORD will not hold anyone guiltless who misuses his name.

12"Observe the Sabbath day by keeping it holy, as the LORD your God has commanded you. **13**Six days you shall labor and do all your work, **14**but the seventh day is a Sabbath to the LORD your God. On it you shall not do any work, neither you, nor your son or daughter, nor your manservant or maidservant, nor your ox, your donkey or any of your animals, nor the alien within your gates, so that your manservant and maidservant may rest, as you do. **15**Remember that you were slaves in Egypt and that the LORD your God brought you out of there with a mighty hand and an outstretched arm. Therefore the LORD your God has commanded you to observe the Sabbath day.

16"Honor your father and your mother, as the LORD your God has commanded you, so that you may live long and that it may go well with you in the land the LORD your God is giving you.

17"You shall not murder.

18"You shall not commit adultery.

19"You shall not steal.

20"You shall not give false testimony against your neighbor.

21"You shall not covet your neighbor's wife. You shall not set your desire on your neighbor's house or land, his manservant or maidservant, his ox or donkey, or anything that belongs to your neighbor."

22These are the commandments the LORD proclaimed in a loud voice to your whole

a 8 Hebrew; Syriac (see also Deut. 3:9) Sirion   b 49 That is, the Dead Sea   c 7 Or besides

5:6–21
Sin

Of all the "Top 10" lists ever written, these "Ten Commandments" are the most famous. They briefly sum up the essence of everything God wants people to do to live in harmony with him and with every other person on the planet.

So to succeed in life, just follow these precepts, right? Sounds simple enough—that is, until you actually *try.*

Maybe you think you can do better than most. And perhaps you can. But before you get too self-assured, take a closer look at this moral yardstick. How well are you *really* doing? (Warning: This self-examination is not for the faint of heart!)

- Number One—No Other Gods

Have you ever spent an inappropriate amount of time, energy or money on something less important than God?

- Number Two—No Idols

Have you ever attributed good luck to some object (such as a crystal, an article of clothing or a rabbit's foot) or considered a religious statue or picture to be of some spiritual benefit to you?

- Number Three—Don't Misuse God's Name

Have you ever cursed anyone in God's name or said "God" like it was an expletive?

- Number Four—Take a Day Out of Every Seven for God

Have you ever exhibited workaholic tendencies—unable to "unplug" for days on end—or been so preoccupied with your own activities that you rarely gave a thought to what your soul and God need from you?

- Number Five—Honor Your Parents

Have you ever lied to, deceived or treated your parents with disrespect?

- Number Six—Don't Murder

Maybe you haven't actually killed anyone, but have you ever wished that someone were dead? The Bible compares hate to the sin of murder.

- Number Seven—Don't Commit Adultery

Jesus made it clear that God prohibits not only the physical act of adultery but also the mental act—playing it out in our minds (see Matthew chapter 5, verses 27–28 [page 1264]).

- Number Eight—Don't Steal

Have you ever taken something that wasn't yours, cheated on taxes or on an expense account or been inconsiderate of someone else's time?

- Number Nine—Don't Lie

Have you ever bent the truth in your favor, exaggerated a story "to make it more interesting," or covered up wrongdoing with a lie—even a "little white lie"?

- Number Ten—Don't Covet

Have you ever wanted something that someone else had so you wouldn't feel inferior, bought something for the sheer sake of what others would think of you or jealously compared your clothing or car to someone else's?

No need to get morbid here, but you have to admit that the picture this paints of your commandment-keeping tendencies is pretty bleak. Interestingly, the Bible is clear that God is not surprised by how you stack up.

Here's the amazing thing. This character yardstick—which shows where you stand and takes away any false hope of innate goodness—actually leads you right where you need to be. By recognizing that consistent goodness isn't just hard, it's impossible, you can now approach God in the right frame of mind. Now you can humbly seek him and his mercy instead of trying to chalk up enough spiritual "brownie points." That attitude of weakness and brokenness is the starting place for every seeker who wants to meet God personally.

ssembly there on the mountain from out of the fire, the cloud and the deep darkness;
nd he added nothing more. Then he wrote them on two stone tablets and gave them
o me.

²³When you heard the voice out of the darkness, while the mountain was ablaze with
re, all the leading men of your tribes and your elders came to me. ²⁴And you said, "The
ᴏʀᴅ our God has shown us his glory and his majesty, and we have heard his voice from
he fire. Today we have seen that a man can live even if God speaks with him. ²⁵But
ow, why should we die? This great fire will consume us, and we will die if we hear the
oice of the Lᴏʀᴅ our God any longer. ²⁶For what mortal man has ever heard the voice of
he living God speaking out of fire, as we have, and survived? ²⁷Go near and listen to all
hat the Lᴏʀᴅ our God says. Then tell us whatever the Lᴏʀᴅ our God tells you. We will listen
nd obey."

²⁸The Lᴏʀᴅ heard you when you spoke to me and the Lᴏʀᴅ said to me, "I have heard
vhat this people said to you. Everything they said was good. ²⁹Oh, that their hearts
vould be inclined to fear me and keep all my commands always, so that it might go well
vith them and their children forever!

³⁰"Go, tell them to return to their tents. ³¹But you stay here with me so that I may give
ou all the commands, decrees and laws you are to teach them to follow in the land I am
iving them to possess."

³²So be careful to do what the Lᴏʀᴅ your God has commanded you; do not turn aside to
he right or to the left. ³³Walk in all the way that the Lᴏʀᴅ your God has commanded you,
o that you may live and prosper and prolong your days in the land that you will possess.

ove the Lᴏʀᴅ Your God

6 These are the commands, decrees and laws the Lᴏʀᴅ your God directed me to
teach you to observe in the land that you are crossing the Jordan to possess,
so that you, your children and their children after them may fear the Lᴏʀᴅ your God as
ong as you live by keeping all his decrees and commands that I give you, and so that you
nay enjoy long life. ³Hear, O Israel, and be careful to obey so that it may go well with
ou and that you may increase greatly in a land flowing with milk and honey, just as the
ᴏʀᴅ, the God of your fathers, promised you.

⁴Hear, O Israel: The Lᴏʀᴅ our God, the Lᴏʀᴅ is one.ᵃ ⁵Love the Lᴏʀᴅ your God with all
our heart and with all your soul and with all your strength. ⁶These commandments that
give you today are to be upon your hearts. ⁷Impress them on your children. Talk about
nem when you sit at home and when you walk along the road, when you lie down and
vhen you get up. ⁸Tie them as symbols on your hands and bind them on your foreheads.
Write them on the doorframes of your houses and on your gates.

¹⁰When the Lᴏʀᴅ your God brings you into the land he swore to your fathers, to Abra-
am, Isaac and Jacob, to give you—a land with large, flourishing cities you did not build,
¹houses filled with all kinds of good things you did not provide, wells you did not dig,
nd vineyards and olive groves you did not plant—then when you eat and are satisfied,
²be careful that you do not forget the Lᴏʀᴅ, who brought you out of Egypt, out of the land
f slavery.

¹³Fear the Lᴏʀᴅ your God, serve him only and take your oaths in his name. ¹⁴Do not
ollow other gods, the gods of the peoples around you; ¹⁵for the Lᴏʀᴅ your God, who is
mong you, is a jealous God and his anger will burn against you, and he will destroy you
rom the face of the land. ¹⁶Do not test the Lᴏʀᴅ your God as you did at Massah. ¹⁷Be sure
o keep the commands of the Lᴏʀᴅ your God and the stipulations and decrees he has
iven you. ¹⁸Do what is right and good in the Lᴏʀᴅ's sight, so that it may go well with you
nd you may go in and take over the good land that the Lᴏʀᴅ promised on oath to your
orefathers, ¹⁹thrusting out all your enemies before you, as the Lᴏʀᴅ said.

²⁰In the future, when your son asks you, "What is the meaning of the stipulations,

---

4 Or *The Lᴏʀᴅ our God is one Lᴏʀᴅ*; or *The Lᴏʀᴅ is our God, the Lᴏʀᴅ is one*; or *The Lᴏʀᴅ is our God, the Lᴏʀᴅ alone*

decrees and laws the Lord our God has commanded you?" ²¹tell him: "We were slaves ‹
Pharaoh in Egypt, but the Lord brought us out of Egypt with a mighty hand. ²²Before o‹
eyes the Lord sent miraculous signs and wonders—great and terrible—upon Egypt ar
Pharaoh and his whole household. ²³But he brought us out from there to bring us in an
give us the land that he promised on oath to our forefathers. ²⁴The Lord commanded us ‹
obey all these decrees and to fear the Lord our God, so that we might always prosper an
be kept alive, as is the case today. ²⁵And if we are careful to obey all this law before th
Lord our God, as he has commanded us, that will be our righteousness."

Driving Out the Nations

7 When the Lord your God brings you into the land you are entering to posse‹
and drives out before you many nations—the Hittites, Girgashites, Amorite
Canaanites, Perizzites, Hivites and Jebusites, seven nations larger and stronger tha
you— ²and when the Lord your God has delivered them over to you and you hav
defeated them, then you must destroy them totally.ᵃ Make no treaty with them, ar
show them no mercy. ³Do not intermarry with them. Do not give your daughters to the
sons or take their daughters for your sons, ⁴for they will turn your sons away fro‹
following me to serve other gods, and the Lord's anger will burn against you and w
quickly destroy you. ⁵This is what you are to do to them: Break down their altars, smas
their sacred stones, cut down their Asherah polesᵇ and burn their idols in the fire. ⁶F‹
you are a people holy to the Lord your God. The Lord your God has chosen you out of a
the peoples on the face of the earth to be his people, his treasured possession.

⁷The Lord did not set his affection on you and choose you because you were mo‹
numerous than other peoples, for you were the fewest of all peoples. ⁸But it was becaus
the Lord loved you and kept the oath he swore to your forefathers that he brought you o
with a mighty hand and redeemed you from the land of slavery, from the power
Pharaoh king of Egypt. ⁹Know therefore that the Lord your God is God; he is the faithf‹

ᵃ2 The Hebrew term refers to the irrevocable giving over of things or persons to the Lord, often by totally destroying them; also in
verse 26.   ᵇ5 That is, symbols of the goddess Asherah; here and elsewhere in Deuteronomy

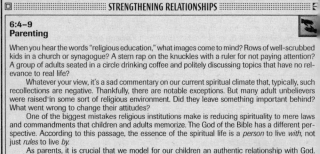

▦ ⋮⋮⋮⋮⋮⋮⋮⋮⋮⋮ STRENGTHENING RELATIONSHIPS ⋮⋮⋮⋮⋮⋮⋮⋮⋮ E

6:4–9
Parenting

When you hear the words "religious education," what images come to mind? Rows of well-scrubbed kids in a church or synagogue? A stern rap on the knuckles with a ruler for not paying attention? A group of adults seated in a circle drinking coffee and politely discussing topics that have no relevance to real life?

Whatever your view, it's a sad commentary on our current spiritual climate that, typically, such recollections are negative. Thankfully, there are notable exceptions. But many adult unbelievers were raised in some sort of religious environment. Did they leave something important behind? What went wrong to change their attitudes?

One of the biggest mistakes religious institutions make is reducing spirituality to mere laws and commandments that children and adults memorize. The God of the Bible has a different perspective. According to this passage, the essence of the spiritual life is a *person* to live *with*, not just *rules* to live *by*.

As parents, it is crucial that we model for our children an authentic relationship with God. The attempt to indoctrinate our children, hoping that they'll somehow embrace beliefs that we obviously don't live out, is an exercise in futility.

That's why this passage emphasizes *lifestyle* teaching rather than academics. There is a need for both. But the place to ground a child's spiritual life is in everyday events. That's where kids sort through what's mere theory and what Mom and Dad really live out.

God, keeping his covenant of love to a thousand generations of those who love him and keep his commands. ¹⁰But

> those who hate him he will repay to their face by destruction;
> he will not be slow to repay to their face those who hate him.

¹¹Therefore, take care to follow the commands, decrees and laws I give you today.

¹²If you pay attention to these laws and are careful to follow them, then the LORD your God will keep his covenant of love with you, as he swore to your forefathers. ¹³He will love you and bless you and increase your numbers. He will bless the fruit of your womb, the crops of your land—your grain, new wine and oil—the calves of your herds and the lambs of your flocks in the land that he swore to your forefathers to give you. ¹⁴You will be blessed more than any other people; none of your men or women will be childless, nor any of your livestock without young. ¹⁵The LORD will keep you free from every disease. He will not inflict on you the horrible diseases you knew in Egypt, but he will inflict them on all who hate you. ¹⁶You must destroy all the peoples the LORD your God gives over to you. Do not look on them with pity and do not serve their gods, for that will be a snare to you.

¹⁷You may say to yourselves, "These nations are stronger than we are. How can we drive them out?" ¹⁸But do not be afraid of them; remember well what the LORD your God did to Pharaoh and to all Egypt. ¹⁹You saw with your own eyes the great trials, the miraculous signs and wonders, the mighty hand and outstretched arm, with which the LORD your God brought you out. The LORD your God will do the same to all the peoples you now fear. ²⁰Moreover, the LORD your God will send the hornet among them until even the survivors who hide from you have perished. ²¹Do not be terrified by them, for the LORD your God, who is among you, is a great and awesome God. ²²The LORD your God will drive out those nations before you, little by little. You will not be allowed to eliminate them all at once, or the wild animals will multiply around you. ²³But the LORD your God will deliver them over to you, throwing them into great confusion until they are destroyed. ²⁴He will give their kings into your hand, and you will wipe out their names from under heaven. No one will be able to stand up against you; you will destroy them. ²⁵The images of their gods you are to burn in the fire. Do not covet the silver and gold on them, and do not take it for yourselves, or you will be ensnared by it, for it is detestable to the LORD your God. ²⁶Do not bring a detestable thing into your house or you, like it, will be set apart for destruction. Utterly abhor and detest it, for it is set apart for destruction.

Do Not Forget the LORD

8 Be careful to follow every command I am giving you today, so that you may live and increase and may enter and possess the land that the LORD promised on oath to your forefathers. ²Remember how the LORD your God led you all the way in the desert these forty years, to humble you and to test you in order to know what was in your heart, whether or not you would keep his commands. ³He humbled you, causing you to hunger and then feeding you with manna, which neither you nor your fathers had known, to teach you that man does not live on bread alone but on every word that comes from the mouth of the LORD. ⁴Your clothes did not wear out and your feet did not swell during these forty years. ⁵Know then in your heart that as a man disciplines his son, so the LORD your God disciplines you.

⁶Observe the commands of the LORD your God, walking in his ways and revering him. ⁷For the LORD your God is bringing you into a good land—a land with streams and pools of water, with springs flowing in the valleys and hills; ⁸a land with wheat and barley, vines and fig trees, pomegranates, olive oil and honey; ⁹a land where bread will not be scarce and you will lack nothing; a land where the rocks are iron and you can dig copper out of the hills.

¹⁰When you have eaten and are satisfied, praise the LORD your God for the good land he

has given you. ¹¹Be careful that you do not forget the LORD your God, failing to observe hi
commands, his laws and his decrees that I am giving you this day. ¹²Otherwise, whe
you eat and are satisfied, when you build fine houses and settle down, ¹³and when you
herds and flocks grow large and your silver and gold increase and all you have i
multiplied, ¹⁴then your heart will become proud and you will forget the LORD your Goc
who brought you out of Egypt, out of the land of slavery. ¹⁵He led you through the vas
and dreadful desert, that thirsty and waterless land, with its venomous snakes an
scorpions. He brought you water out of hard rock. ¹⁶He gave you manna to eat in th
desert, something your fathers had never known, to humble and to test you so that in th
end it might go well with you. ¹⁷You may say to yourself, "My power and the strength o
my hands have produced this wealth fo
me." ¹⁸But remember the LORD your God, fo
it is he who gives you the ability to pro
duce wealth, and so confirms his covenan
which he swore to your forefathers, as it i
today.

¹⁹If you ever forget the LORD your God an
follow other gods and worship and bow
down to them, I testify against you toda
that you will surely be destroyed. ²⁰Lik
the nations the LORD destroyed before yo
so you will be destroyed for not obeyin
the LORD your God.

Not Because of Israel's Righteousness

9 Hear, O Israel. You are now
about to cross the Jordan to g
in and dispossess nations greater an
stronger than you, with large cities tha
have walls up to the sky. ²The people ar
strong and tall—Anakites! You know abo
them and have heard it said: "Who ca
stand up against the Anakites?" ³But be as
sured today that the LORD your God is th
one who goes across ahead of you like
devouring fire. He will destroy them; h
will subdue them before you. And you wi
drive them out and annihilate them quick
ly, as the LORD has promised you.

⁴After the LORD your God has driven the
out before you, do not say to yourself, "Th
LORD has brought me here to take posses

sion of this land because of my righteousness." No, it is on account of the wickedness
these nations that the LORD is going to drive them out before you. ⁵It is not because of you
righteousness or your integrity that you are going in to take possession of their land; b
on account of the wickedness of these nations, the LORD your God will drive them o
before you, to accomplish what he swore to your fathers, to Abraham, Isaac and Jacol
⁶Understand, then, that it is not because of your righteousness that the LORD your God
giving you this good land to possess, for you are a stiff-necked people.

The Golden Calf

⁷Remember this and never forget how you provoked the LORD your God to anger in th
desert. From the day you left Egypt until you arrived here, you have been rebelliou

gainst the LORD. **8**At Horeb you aroused the LORD's wrath so that he was angry enough to estroy you. **9**When I went up on the mountain to receive the tablets of stone, the tablets f the covenant that the LORD had made with you, I stayed on the mountain forty days and rty nights; I ate no bread and drank no water. **10**The LORD gave me two stone tablets scribed by the finger of God. On them were all the commandments the LORD proclaimed you on the mountain out of the fire, on the day of the assembly.

11At the end of the forty days and forty nights, the LORD gave me the two stone tablets, e tablets of the covenant. **12**Then the LORD told me, "Go down from here at once, ecause your people whom you brought out of Egypt have become corrupt. They have rned away quickly from what I commanded them and have made a cast idol for them- elves."

13And the LORD said to me, "I have seen this people, and they are a stiff-necked people deed! **14**Let me alone, so that I may destroy them and blot out their name from under eaven. And I will make you into a nation stronger and more numerous than they."

15So I turned and went down from the mountain while it was ablaze with fire. And the vo tablets of the covenant were in my hands.*a* **16**When I looked, I saw that you had nned against the LORD your God; you had made for yourselves an idol cast in the shape a calf. You had turned aside quickly from the way that the LORD had commanded you. So I took the two tablets and threw them out of my hands, breaking them to pieces efore your eyes.

18Then once again I fell prostrate before the LORD for forty days and forty nights; I ate bread and drank no water, because of all the sin you had committed, doing what was vil in the LORD's sight and so provoking him to anger. **19**I feared the anger and wrath of e LORD, for he was angry enough with you to destroy you. But again the LORD listened to e. **20**And the LORD was angry enough with Aaron to destroy him, but at that time I rayed for Aaron too. **21**Also I took that sinful thing of yours, the calf you had made, and rned it in the fire. Then I crushed it and ground it to powder as fine as dust and threw e dust into a stream that flowed down the mountain.

22You also made the LORD angry at Taberah, at Massah and at Kibroth Hattaavah.

23And when the LORD sent you out from Kadesh Barnea, he said, "Go up and take ssession of the land I have given you." But you rebelled against the command of the RD your God. You did not trust him or obey him. **24**You have been rebellious against the RD ever since I have known you.

25I lay prostrate before the LORD those forty days and forty nights because the LORD had id he would destroy you. **26**I prayed to the LORD and said, "O Sovereign LORD, do not stroy your people, your own inheritance that you redeemed by your great power and ought out of Egypt with a mighty hand. **27**Remember your servants Abraham, Isaac and cob. Overlook the stubbornness of this people, their wickedness and their sin. **28**Other- se, the country from which you brought us will say, 'Because the LORD was not able to ke them into the land he had promised them, and because he hated them, he brought em out to put them to death in the desert.' **29**But they are your people, your inheritance at you brought out by your great power and your outstretched arm."

ablets Like the First Ones

10 At that time the LORD said to me, "Chisel out two stone tablets like the first ones and come up to me on the mountain. Also make a wooden chest.*b* **2**I ll write on the tablets the words that were on the first tablets, which you broke. Then u are to put them in the chest."

3So I made the ark out of acacia wood and chiseled out two stone tablets like the first es, and I went up on the mountain with the two tablets in my hands. **4**The LORD wrote these tablets what he had written before, the Ten Commandments he had proclaimed you on the mountain, out of the fire, on the day of the assembly. And the LORD gave

5 Or And I had the two tablets of the covenant with me, one in each hand   *b 1 That is, an ark*

them to me. ⁵Then I came back down the mountain and put the tablets in the ark I ha[
made, as the LORD commanded me, and they are there now.

⁶(The Israelites traveled from the wells of the Jaakanites to Moserah. There Aaron die[
and was buried, and Eleazar his son succeeded him as priest. ⁷From there they travele[
to Gudgodah and on to Jotbathah, a land with streams of water. ⁸At that time the LORD s[
apart the tribe of Levi to carry the ark of the covenant of the LORD, to stand before the Lo[
to minister and to pronounce blessings in his name, as they still do today. ⁹That is wh[
the Levites have no share or inheritance among their brothers; the LORD is their inher[
tance, as the LORD your God told them.)

¹⁰Now I had stayed on the mountain forty days and nights, as I did the first time, an[
the LORD listened to me at this time also. It was not his will to destroy you. ¹¹"Go," the Lo[
said to me, "and lead the people on the
way, so that they may enter and possess th[
land that I swore to their fathers to give them[

Fear the LORD

¹²And now, O Israel, what does the Lo[
your God ask of you but to fear the Lo[
your God, to walk in all his ways, to lo[
him, to serve the LORD your God with a[
your heart and with all your soul, ¹³and [
observe the LORD's commands and decre[
that I am giving you today for your ow[
good?

¹⁴To the LORD your God belong the heav[
ens, even the highest heavens, the ear[
and everything in it. ¹⁵Yet the LORD set h[
affection on your forefathers and love[
them, and he chose you, their descendant[
above all the nations, as it is today. ¹⁶Ci[
cumcise your hearts, therefore, and do n[
be stiff-necked any longer. ¹⁷For the Lo[
your God is God of gods and Lord of lord[
the great God, mighty and awesome, wh[
shows no partiality and accepts no bribe[
¹⁸He defends the cause of the fatherle[
and the widow, and loves the alien, givin[
him food and clothing. ¹⁹And you are [
love those who are aliens, for you your[
selves were aliens in Egypt. ²⁰Fear the Lo[
your God and serve him. Hold fast to hi[
and take your oaths in his name. ²¹He [
your praise; he is your God, who performe[

for you those great and awesome wonders you saw with your own eyes. ²²Your forefathe[
who went down into Egypt were seventy in all, and now the LORD your God has made y[
as numerous as the stars in the sky.

Love and Obey the LORD

11 Love the LORD your God and keep his requirements, his decrees, his laws a[
his commands always. ²Remember today that your children were not t[
ones who saw and experienced the discipline of the LORD your God: his majesty, h[
mighty hand, his outstretched arm; ³the signs he performed and the things he did in th[

heart of Egypt, both to Pharaoh king of Egypt and to his whole country; ⁴what he did to the Egyptian army, to its horses and chariots, how he overwhelmed them with the waters of the Red Sea *a* as they were pursuing you, and how the LORD brought lasting ruin on them. ⁵It was not your children who saw what he did for you in the desert until you arrived at this place, ⁶and what he did to Dathan and Abiram, sons of Eliab the Reubenite, when the earth opened its mouth right in the middle of all Israel and swallowed them up with their households, their tents and every living thing that belonged to them. ⁷But it was your own eyes that saw all these great things the LORD has done.

⁸Observe therefore all the commands I am giving you today, so that you may have the strength to go in and take over the land that you are crossing the Jordan to possess, ⁹and so that you may live long in the land that the LORD swore to your forefathers to give to them and their descendants, a land flowing with milk and honey. ¹⁰The land you are entering to take over is not like the land of Egypt, from which you have come, where you planted your seed and irrigated it by foot as in a vegetable garden. ¹¹But the land you are crossing the Jordan to take possession of is a land of mountains and valleys that drinks rain from heaven. ¹²It is a land the LORD your God cares for; the eyes of the LORD your God are continually on it from the beginning of the year to its end.

¹³So if you faithfully obey the commands I am giving you today—to love the LORD your God and to serve him with all your heart and with all your soul— ¹⁴then I will send rain on your land in its season, both autumn and spring rains, so that you may gather in your grain, new wine and oil. ¹⁵I will provide grass in the fields for your cattle, and you will eat and be satisfied.

¹⁶Be careful, or you will be enticed to turn away and worship other gods and bow down to them. ¹⁷Then the LORD's anger will burn against you, and he will shut the heavens so that it will not rain and the ground will yield no produce, and you will soon perish from the good land the LORD is giving you. ¹⁸Fix these words of mine in your hearts and minds; tie them as symbols on your hands and bind them on your foreheads. ¹⁹Teach them to your children, talking about them when you sit at home and when you walk along the road, when you lie down and when you get up. ²⁰Write them on the doorframes of your houses and on your gates, ²¹so that your days and the days of your children may be many in the land that the LORD swore to give your forefathers, as many as the days that the heavens are above the earth.

²²If you carefully observe all these commands I am giving you to follow—to love the LORD your God, to walk in all his ways and to hold fast to him— ²³then the LORD will drive out all these nations before you, and you will dispossess nations larger and stronger than you. ²⁴Every place where you set your foot will be yours: Your territory will extend from the desert to Lebanon, and from the Euphrates River to the western sea.*b* ²⁵No man will be able to stand against you. The LORD your God, as he promised you, will put the terror and fear of you on the whole land, wherever you go.

²⁶See, I am setting before you today a blessing and a curse— ²⁷the blessing if you obey the commands of the LORD your God that I am giving you today; ²⁸the curse if you disobey the commands of the LORD your God and turn from the way that I command you today by following other gods, which you have not known. ²⁹When the LORD your God has brought you into the land you are entering to possess, you are to proclaim on Mount Gerizim the blessings, and on Mount Ebal the curses. ³⁰As you know, these mountains are across the Jordan, west of the road,*c* toward the setting sun, near the great trees of Moreh, in the territory of those Canaanites living in the Arabah in the vicinity of Gilgal. ³¹You are about to cross the Jordan to enter and take possession of the land the LORD your God is giving you. When you have taken it over and are living there, ³²be sure that you obey all the decrees and laws I am setting before you today.

a 4 Hebrew *Yam Suph;* that is, Sea of Reeds   *b* 24 That is, the Mediterranean   *c* 30 Or *Jordan, westward*

The One Place of Worship

12 These are the decrees and laws you must be careful to follow in the land that the LORD, the God of your fathers, has given you to possess—as long as you live in the land. ²Destroy completely all the places on the high mountains and on the hills and under every spreading tree where the nations you are dispossessing worship their gods. ³Break down their altars, smash their sacred stones and burn their Asherah poles in the fire; cut down the idols of their gods and wipe out their names from those places.

⁴You must not worship the LORD your God in their way. ⁵But you are to seek the place the LORD your God will choose from among all your tribes to put his Name there for his dwelling. To that place you must go; ⁶there bring your burnt offerings and sacrifices, your tithes and special gifts, what you have vowed to give and your freewill offerings, and the firstborn of your herds and flocks. ⁷There, in the presence of the LORD your God, you and your families shall eat and shall rejoice in everything you have put your hand to, because the LORD your God has blessed you.

⁸You are not to do as we do here today, everyone as he sees fit, ⁹since you have not yet reached the resting place and the inheritance the LORD your God is giving you. ¹⁰But you will cross the Jordan and settle in the land the LORD your God is giving you as an inheritance, and he will give you rest from all your enemies around you so that you will live in safety. ¹¹Then to the place the LORD your God will choose as a dwelling for his Name—there you are to bring everything I command you: your burnt offerings and sacrifices, your tithes and special gifts, and all the choice possessions you have vowed to the LORD. ¹²And there rejoice before the LORD your God, you, your sons and daughters, your menservants and maidservants, and the Levites from your towns, who have no allotment or inheritance of their own. ¹³Be careful not to sacrifice your burnt offerings anywhere you please. ¹⁴Offer them only at the place the LORD will choose in one of your tribes, and there observe everything I command you.

¹⁵Nevertheless, you may slaughter your animals in any of your towns and eat as much of the meat as you want, as if it were gazelle or deer, according to the blessing the LORD your God gives you. Both the ceremonially unclean and the clean may eat it. ¹⁶But you must not eat the blood; pour it out on the ground like water. ¹⁷You must not eat in you own towns the tithe of your grain and new wine and oil, or the firstborn of your herds and flocks, or whatever you have vowed to give, or your freewill offerings or special gifts ¹⁸Instead, you are to eat them in the presence of the LORD your God at the place the LORD your God will choose—you, your sons and daughters, your menservants and maidservants, and the Levites from your towns—and you are to rejoice before the LORD your God in everything you put your hand to. ¹⁹Be careful not to neglect the Levites as long as you live in your land.

²⁰When the LORD your God has enlarged your territory as he promised you, and you crave meat and say, "I would like some meat," then you may eat as much of it as you want. ²¹If the place where the LORD your God chooses to put his Name is too far away from you, you may slaughter animals from the herds and flocks the LORD has given you, as I have commanded you, and in your own towns you may eat as much of them as you want ²²Eat them as you would gazelle or deer. Both the ceremonially unclean and the clean may eat. ²³But be sure you do not eat the blood, because the blood is the life, and you must not eat the life with the meat. ²⁴You must not eat the blood; pour it out on the ground like water. ²⁵Do not eat it, so that it may go well with you and your children after you, because you will be doing what is right in the eyes of the LORD.

²⁶But take your consecrated things and whatever you have vowed to give, and go to the place the LORD will choose. ²⁷Present your burnt offerings on the altar of the LORD your God, both the meat and the blood. The blood of your sacrifices must be poured beside the altar of the LORD your God, but you may eat the meat. ²⁸Be careful to obey all these regulations I am giving you, so that it may always go well with you and your children

after you, because you will be doing what is good and right in the eyes of the Lord your God.

²⁹The Lord your God will cut off before you the nations you are about to invade and dispossess. But when you have driven them out and settled in their land, ³⁰and after they have been destroyed before you, be careful not to be ensnared by inquiring about their gods, saying, "How do these nations serve their gods? We will do the same." ³¹You must not worship the Lord your God in their way, because in worshiping their gods, they do all kinds of detestable things the Lord hates. They even burn their sons and daughters in the fire as sacrifices to their gods.

³²See that you do all I command you; do not add to it or take away from it.

Worshiping Other Gods

13 If a prophet, or one who foretells by dreams, appears among you and announces to you a miraculous sign or wonder, ²and if the sign or wonder of which he has spoken takes place, and he says, "Let us follow other gods" (gods you have not known) "and let us worship them," ³you must not listen to the words of that prophet or dreamer. The Lord your God is testing you to find out whether you love him with all your heart and with all your soul. ⁴It is the Lord your God you must follow, and him you must revere. Keep his commands and obey him; serve him and hold fast to him. ⁵That prophet or dreamer must be put to death, because he preached rebellion against the Lord your God, who brought you out of Egypt and redeemed you from the land of slavery; he has tried to turn you from the way the Lord your God commanded you to follow. You must purge the evil from among you.

⁶If your very own brother, or your son or daughter, or the wife you love, or your closest friend secretly entices you, saying,

▣ ::::::::::: DISCOVERING GOD ::::::::::: ▣

13:1–5
Spiritual Fraud

Everything supernatural is not from God.

Some people naively assume that if a person has predictive abilities or other supernatural powers, he or she must have some sort of divine enablement. But the Bible emphasizes that, just as there are frauds in other spheres, spiritual deception ensnares unsuspecting people.

If such unusual activity is not a guarantee of God's work, how can a person know what is from God? This passage gives one of the main tests: If the "miracle worker" calls you to follow a god different from the God of the Bible, then reject the message and the messenger.

While that may seem like a strong reaction—perhaps even smacking of closed-mindedness—it makes sense when you realize what's at stake. If someone takes you in with a phony business scam, you lose your money. If someone lures you with false promises, you may suffer a broken heart. But if someone leads you to a false god, you will lose your soul.

"Let us go and worship other gods" (gods that neither you nor your fathers have known, ⁷gods of the peoples around you, whether near or far, from one end of the land to the other), ⁸do not yield to him or listen to him. Show him no pity. Do not spare him or shield him. ⁹You must certainly put him to death. Your hand must be the first in putting him to death, and then the hands of all the people. ¹⁰Stone him to death, because he tried to turn you away from the Lord your God, who brought you out of Egypt, out of the land of slavery. ¹¹Then all Israel will hear and be afraid, and no one among you will do such an evil thing again.

¹²If you hear it said about one of the towns the Lord your God is giving you to live in ¹³that wicked men have arisen among you and have led the people of their town astray, saying, "Let us go and worship other gods" (gods you have not known), ¹⁴then you must inquire, probe and investigate it thoroughly. And if it is true and it has been proved that this detestable thing has been done among you, ¹⁵you must certainly put to the sword all who live in that town. Destroy it completely,ᵃ both its people and its livestock. ¹⁶Gather

---

ᵃ15 The Hebrew term refers to the irrevocable giving over of things or persons to the Lord, often by totally destroying them.

all the plunder of the town into the middle of the public square and completely burn the town and all its plunder as a whole burnt offering to the LORD your God. It is to remain a ruin forever, never to be rebuilt. [17]None of those condemned things[a] shall be found in your hands, so that the LORD will turn from his fierce anger; he will show you mercy, have compassion on you, and increase your numbers, as he promised on oath to your forefathers, [18]because you obey the LORD your God, keeping all his commands that I am giving you today and doing what is right in his eyes.

Clean and Unclean Food

14 You are the children of the LORD your God. Do not cut yourselves or shave the front of your heads for the dead, [2]for you are a people holy to the LORD your God. Out of all the peoples on the face of the earth, the LORD has chosen you to be his treasured possession.

[3]Do not eat any detestable thing. [4]These are the animals you may eat: the ox, the sheep, the goat, [5]the deer, the gazelle, the roe deer, the wild goat, the ibex, the antelope and the mountain sheep.[b] [6]You may eat any animal that has a split hoof divided in two and that chews the cud. [7]However, of those that chew the cud or that have a split hoof completely divided you may not eat the camel, the rabbit or the coney.[c] Although they chew the cud, they do not have a split hoof; they are ceremonially unclean for you. [8]The pig is also unclean; although it has a split hoof, it does not chew the cud. You are not to eat their meat or touch their carcasses.

[9]Of all the creatures living in the water, you may eat any that has fins and scales. [10]But anything that does not have fins and scales you may not eat; for you it is unclean.

[11]You may eat any clean bird. [12]But these you may not eat: the eagle, the vulture, the black vulture, [13]the red kite, the black kite, any kind of falcon, [14]any kind of raven, [15]the horned owl, the screech owl, the gull, any kind of hawk, [16]the little owl, the great owl, the white owl, [17]the desert owl, the osprey, the cormorant, [18]the stork, any kind of heron, the hoopoe and the bat.

[19]All flying insects that swarm are unclean to you; do not eat them. [20]But any winged creature that is clean you may eat.

[21]Do not eat anything you find already dead. You may give it to an alien living in any of your towns, and he may eat it, or you may sell it to a foreigner. But you are a people holy to the LORD your God.

Do not cook a young goat in its mother's milk.

Tithes

[22]Be sure to set aside a tenth of all that your fields produce each year. [23]Eat the tithe of your grain, new wine and oil, and the firstborn of your herds and flocks in the presence of the LORD your God at the place he will choose as a dwelling for his Name, so that you may learn to revere the LORD your God always. [24]But if that place is too distant and you have been blessed by the LORD your God and cannot carry your tithe (because the place where the LORD will choose to put his Name is so far away), [25]then exchange your tithe for silver, and take the silver with you and go to the place the LORD your God will choose. [26]Use the silver to buy whatever you like: cattle, sheep, wine or other fermented drink, or anything you wish. Then you and your household shall eat there in the presence of the LORD your God and rejoice. [27]And do not neglect the Levites living in your towns, for they have no allotment or inheritance of their own.

[28]At the end of every three years, bring all the tithes of that year's produce and store it in your towns, [29]so that the Levites (who have no allotment or inheritance of their own) and the aliens, the fatherless and the widows who live in your towns may come and eat

[a] 17 The Hebrew term refers to the irrevocable giving over of things or persons to the LORD, often by totally destroying them.   [b] 5 The precise identification of some of the birds and animals in this chapter is uncertain.   [c] 7 That is, the hyrax or rock badger

and be satisfied, and so that the Lord your God may bless you in all the work of your hands.

The Year for Canceling Debts

15 At the end of every seven years you must cancel debts. ²This is how it is to be done: Every creditor shall cancel the loan he has made to his fellow Israelite. He shall not require payment from his fellow Israelite or brother, because the Lord's time for canceling debts has been proclaimed. ³You may require payment from a foreigner, but you must cancel any debt your brother owes you. ⁴However, there should be no poor among you, for in the land the Lord your God is giving you to possess as your inheritance, he will richly bless you, ⁵if only you fully obey the Lord your God and are careful to follow all these commands I am giving you today. ⁶For the Lord your God will bless you as he has promised, and you will lend to many nations but will borrow from none. You will rule over many nations but none will rule over you.

⁷If there is a poor man among your brothers in any of the towns of the land that the Lord your God is giving you, do not be hardhearted or tightfisted toward your poor brother. ⁸Rather be openhanded and freely lend him whatever he needs. ⁹Be careful not to harbor this wicked thought: "The seventh year, the year for canceling debts, is near," so that you do not show ill will toward your needy brother and give him nothing. He may then appeal to the Lord against you, and you will be found guilty of sin. ¹⁰Give generously to him and do so without a grudging heart; then because of this the Lord your God will bless you in all your work and in everything you put your hand to. ¹¹There will always be poor people in the land. Therefore I command you to be openhanded toward your brothers and toward the poor and needy in your land.

Freeing Servants

¹²If a fellow Hebrew, a man or a woman, sells himself to you and serves you six years, in the seventh year you must let him go free. ¹³And when you release him, do not send him away empty-handed. ¹⁴Supply him liberally from your flock, your threshing floor and your winepress. Give to him as the Lord your God has blessed you. ¹⁵Remember that you were slaves in Egypt and the Lord your God redeemed you. That is why I give you this command today.

¹⁶But if your servant says to you, "I do not want to leave you," because he loves you and your family and is well off with you, ¹⁷then take an awl and push it through his ear lobe into the door, and he will become your servant for life. Do the same for your maidservant.

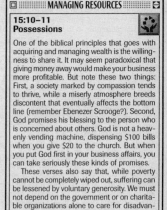

MANAGING RESOURCES

**15:10–11
Possessions**

One of the biblical principles that goes with acquiring and managing wealth is the willingness to share it. It may seem paradoxical that giving money away would make your business more profitable. But note these two things: First, a society marked by compassion tends to thrive, while a miserly atmosphere breeds discontent that eventually affects the bottom line (remember Ebenezer Scrooge?). Second, God promises his blessing to the person who is concerned about others. God is not a heavenly vending machine, dispensing $100 bills when you give $20 to the church. But when you put God first in your business affairs, you can take seriously these kinds of promises.

These verses also say that, while poverty cannot be completely wiped out, suffering can be lessened by voluntary generosity. We must not depend on the government or on charitable organizations alone to care for disadvantaged individuals.

In short, if you want your business and your society to succeed, don't be tightfisted toward people who need assistance.

¹⁸Do not consider it a hardship to set your servant free, because his service to you these six years has been worth twice as much as that of a hired hand. And the Lord your God will bless you in everything you do.

The Firstborn Animals

¹⁹Set apart for the LORD your God every firstborn male of your herds and flocks. Do not put the firstborn of your oxen to work, and do not shear the firstborn of your sheep. ²⁰Each year you and your family are to eat them in the presence of the LORD your God at the place he will choose. ²¹If an animal has a defect, is lame or blind, or has any serious flaw, you must not sacrifice it to the LORD your God. ²²You are to eat it in your own towns. Both the ceremonially unclean and the clean may eat it, as if it were gazelle or deer. ²³But you must not eat the blood; pour it out on the ground like water.

Passover

16 Observe the month of Abib and celebrate the Passover of the LORD your God, because in the month of Abib he brought you out of Egypt by night. ²Sacrifice as the Passover to the LORD your God an animal from your flock or herd at the place the LORD will choose as a dwelling for his Name. ³Do not eat it with bread made with yeast, but for seven days eat unleavened bread, the bread of affliction, because you left Egypt in haste—so that all the days of your life you may remember the time of your departure from Egypt. ⁴Let no yeast be found in your possession in all your land for seven days. Do not let any of the meat you sacrifice on the evening of the first day remain until morning.

⁵You must not sacrifice the Passover in any town the LORD your God gives you ⁶except in the place he will choose as a dwelling for his Name. There you must sacrifice the Passover in the evening, when the sun goes down, on the anniversary*a* of your departure from Egypt. ⁷Roast it and eat it at the place the LORD your God will choose. Then in the morning return to your tents. ⁸For six days eat unleavened bread and on the seventh day hold an assembly to the LORD your God and do no work.

Feast of Weeks

⁹Count off seven weeks from the time you begin to put the sickle to the standing grain. ¹⁰Then celebrate the Feast of Weeks to the LORD your God by giving a freewill offering in proportion to the blessings the LORD your God has given you. ¹¹And rejoice before the LORD your God at the place he will choose as a dwelling for his Name—you, your sons and daughters, your menservants and maidservants, the Levites in your towns, and the aliens, the fatherless and the widows living among you. ¹²Remember that you were slaves in Egypt, and follow carefully these decrees.

Feast of Tabernacles

¹³Celebrate the Feast of Tabernacles for seven days after you have gathered the produce of your threshing floor and your winepress. ¹⁴Be joyful at your Feast—you, your sons and daughters, your menservants and maidservants, and the Levites, the aliens, the fatherless and the widows who live in your towns. ¹⁵For seven days celebrate the Feast to the LORD your God at the place the LORD will choose. For the LORD your God will bless you in all your harvest and in all the work of your hands, and your joy will be complete.

¹⁶Three times a year all your men must appear before the LORD your God at the place he will choose: at the Feast of Unleavened Bread, the Feast of Weeks and the Feast of Tabernacles. No man should appear before the LORD empty-handed: ¹⁷Each of you must bring a gift in proportion to the way the LORD your God has blessed you.

Judges

¹⁸Appoint judges and officials for each of your tribes in every town the LORD your God is giving you, and they shall judge the people fairly. ¹⁹Do not pervert justice or show partiality. Do not accept a bribe, for a bribe blinds the eyes of the wise and twists the

a 6 Or down, at the time of day

words of the righteous. [20]Follow justice and justice alone, so that you may live and possess the land the LORD your God is giving you.

Worshiping Other Gods

[21]Do not set up any wooden Asherah pole[a] beside the altar you build to the LORD your God, [22]and do not erect a sacred stone, for these the LORD your God hates.

17 Do not sacrifice to the LORD your God an ox or a sheep that has any defect or flaw in it, for that would be detestable to him.

[2]If a man or woman living among you in one of the towns the LORD gives you is found doing evil in the eyes of the LORD your God in violation of his covenant, [3]and contrary to my command has worshiped other gods, bowing down to them or to the sun or the moon or the stars of the sky, [4]and this has been brought to your attention, then you must investigate it thoroughly. If it is true and it has been proved that this detestable thing has been done in Israel, [5]take the man or woman who has done this evil deed to your city gate and stone that person to death. [6]On the testimony of two or three witnesses a man shall be put to death, but no one shall be put to death on the testimony of only one witness. [7]The hands of the witnesses must be the first in putting him to death, and then the hands of all the people. You must purge the evil from among you.

Law Courts

[8]If cases come before your courts that are too difficult for you to judge—whether bloodshed, lawsuits or assaults—take them to the place the LORD your God will choose. [9]Go to the priests, who are Levites, and to the judge who is in office at that time. Inquire of them and they will give you the verdict. [10]You must act according to the decisions they give you at the place the LORD will choose. Be careful to do everything they direct you to do. [11]Act according to the law they teach you and the decisions they give you. Do not turn aside from what they tell you, to the right or to the left. [12]The man who shows contempt for the judge or for the priest who stands ministering there to the LORD your God must be put to death. You must purge the evil from Israel. [13]All the people will hear and be afraid, and will not be contemptuous again.

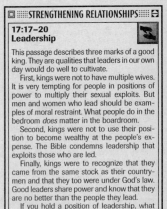

STRENGTHENING RELATIONSHIPS

17:17-20
Leadership

This passage describes three marks of a good king. They are qualities that leaders in our own day would do well to cultivate.

First, kings were not to have multiple wives. It is very tempting for people in positions of power to multiply their sexual exploits. But men and women who lead should be examples of moral restraint. What people do in the bedroom *does* matter in the boardroom.

Second, kings were not to use their position to become wealthy at the people's expense. The Bible condemns leadership that exploits those who are led.

Finally, kings were to recognize that they came from the same stock as their countrymen and that they too were under God's law. Good leaders share power and know that they are no better than the people they lead.

If you hold a position of leadership, what kind of leader are you?

The King

[14]When you enter the land the LORD your God is giving you and have taken possession of it and settled in it, and you say, "Let us set a king over us like all the nations around us," [15]be sure to appoint over you the king the LORD your God chooses. He must be from among your own brothers. Do not place a foreigner over you, one who is not a brother Israelite. [16]The king, moreover, must not acquire great numbers of horses for himself or make the people return to Egypt to get more of them, for the LORD has told you, "You are not to go back that way again." [17]He must not take many wives, or his heart will be led astray. He must not accumulate large amounts of silver and gold.

a 21 Or Do not plant any tree dedicated to Asherah

[18]When he takes the throne of his kingdom, he is to write for himself on a scroll a copy of this law, taken from that of the priests, who are Levites. [19]It is to be with him, and he is to read it all the days of his life so that he may learn to revere the LORD his God and follow carefully all the words of this law and these decrees [20]and not consider himself better than his brothers and turn from the law to the right or to the left. Then he and his descendants will reign a long time over his kingdom in Israel.

Offerings for Priests and Levites

18 The priests, who are Levites—indeed the whole tribe of Levi—are to have no allotment or inheritance with Israel. They shall live on the offerings made to the LORD by fire, for that is their inheritance. [2]They shall have no inheritance among their brothers; the LORD is their inheritance, as he promised them.

[3]This is the share due the priests from the people who sacrifice a bull or a sheep: the shoulder, the jowls and the inner parts. [4]You are to give them the firstfruits of your grain, new wine and oil, and the first wool from the shearing of your sheep, [5]for the LORD your God has chosen them and their descendants out of all your tribes to stand and minister in the LORD's name always.

[6]If a Levite moves from one of your towns anywhere in Israel where he is living, and comes in all earnestness to the place the LORD will choose, [7]he may minister in the name of the LORD his God like all his fellow Levites who serve there in the presence of the LORD. [8]He is to share equally in their benefits, even though he has received money from the sale of family possessions.

Detestable Practices

[9]When you enter the land the LORD your God is giving you, do not learn to imitate the detestable ways of the nations there. [10]Let no one be found among you who sacrifices his son or daughter in[a] the fire, who practices divination or sorcery, interprets omens, engages in witchcraft, [11]or casts spells, or who is a medium or spiritist or who consults the dead. [12]Anyone who does these things is detestable to the LORD, and because of these detestable practices the LORD your God will drive out those nations before you. [13]You must be blameless before the LORD your God.

The Prophet

[14]The nations you will dispossess listen to those who practice sorcery or divination. But as for you, the LORD your God has not permitted you to do so. [15]The LORD your God will raise up for you a prophet like me from among your own brothers. You must listen to him. [16]For this is what you asked of the LORD your God at Horeb on the day of the assembly when you said, "Let us not hear the voice of the LORD our God nor see this great fire anymore, or we will die."

[17]The LORD said to me: "What they say is good. [18]I will raise up for them a prophet like you from among their brothers; I will put my words in his mouth, and he will tell them

DISCOVERING GOD

18:10–13
Spiritual Fraud

God is very concerned that his people not participate in those forms of spiritual experience commonly known as occult practices. While some occult practices are fake, others actually work because of the evil forces behind them. Such practices are dangerous and are to be avoided.

The Bible gives us plenty of evidence for the existence of unseen evil forces. Jesus encountered a real devil (see Matthew chapter 4, verses 1–11 [page 1261]), and the apostle Paul made it clear that there is an invisible spiritual battle going on all around us (Ephesians chapter 6, verses 11–13 [page 1539]).

Just as a person doesn't need to experiment with illegal drugs to know that they are harmful, spiritual seekers don't need to dabble in the occult to understand that it is evil. God is not to be found there.

a 10 Or who makes his son or daughter pass through

everything I command him. ¹⁹If anyone does not listen to my words that the prophet speaks in my name, I myself will call him to account. ²⁰But a prophet who presumes to speak in my name anything I have not commanded him to say, or a prophet who speaks in the name of other gods, must be put to death."

²¹You may say to yourselves, "How can we know when a message has not been spoken by the LORD?" ²²If what a prophet proclaims in the name of the LORD does not take place or come true, that is a message the LORD has not spoken. That prophet has spoken presumptuously. Do not be afraid of him.

Cities of Refuge

19 When the LORD your God has destroyed the nations whose land he is giving you, and when you have driven them out and settled in their towns and houses, ²then set aside for yourselves three cities centrally located in the land the LORD your God is giving you to possess. ³Build roads to them and divide into three parts the land the LORD your God is giving you as an inheritance, so that anyone who kills a man may flee there.

⁴This is the rule concerning the man who kills another and flees there to save his life—one who kills his neighbor unintentionally, without malice aforethought. ⁵For instance, a man may go into the forest with his neighbor to cut wood, and as he swings his ax to fell a tree, the head may fly off and hit his neighbor and kill him. That man may flee to one of these cities and save his life. ⁶Otherwise, the avenger of blood might

DISCOVERING GOD

18:21–22
Spiritual Fraud

Here is another way to discover spiritual counterfeits. The Biblical test for a prophet is 100 percent accuracy. Just one deviation from that standard and the prophet is to be disregarded.

Many so-called prophets predict events in our own day. They seem to think they have a "gift" when they do better than 50 percent. But not one of them has anywhere near 100 percent accuracy. On the other hand, true Biblical prophets *never* made an erroneous prediction. Their information source was the most reliable one in the universe—God himself.

The next time you thumb through the tabloids at the checkout counter, remember this test: without complete accuracy, any so-called prophet is not from God. Don't waste your time or money on someone who does not have God's endorsement. Rather, invest your energy in studying this Bible—it's the proven source of God's revelation.

pursue him in a rage, overtake him if the distance is too great, and kill him even though he is not deserving of death, since he did it to his neighbor without malice aforethought. ⁷This is why I command you to set aside for yourselves three cities.

⁸If the LORD your God enlarges your territory, as he promised on oath to your forefathers, and gives you the whole land he promised them, ⁹because you carefully follow all these laws I command you today—to love the LORD your God and to walk always in his ways—then you are to set aside three more cities. ¹⁰Do this so that innocent blood will not be shed in your land, which the LORD your God is giving you as your inheritance, and so that you will not be guilty of bloodshed.

¹¹But if a man hates his neighbor and lies in wait for him, assaults and kills him, and then flees to one of these cities, ¹²the elders of his town shall send for him, bring him back from the city, and hand him over to the avenger of blood to die. ¹³Show him no pity. You must purge from Israel the guilt of shedding innocent blood, so that it may go well with you.

¹⁴Do not move your neighbor's boundary stone set up by your predecessors in the inheritance you receive in the land the LORD your God is giving you to possess.

Witnesses

¹⁵One witness is not enough to convict a man accused of any crime or offense he ma[...] have committed. A matter must be established by the testimony of two or three wi[...] nesses.

¹⁶If a malicious witness takes the stand to accuse a man of a crime, ¹⁷the two me[...] involved in the dispute must stand in the presence of the LORD before the priests and th[...] judges who are in office at the time. ¹⁸The judges must make a thorough investigatio[...] and if the witness proves to be a liar, giving false testimony against his brother, ¹⁹the[...] do to him as he intended to do to his brother. You must purge the evil from among yo[...] ²⁰The rest of the people will hear of this and be afraid, and never again will such an ev[...] thing be done among you. ²¹Show no pity: life for life, eye for eye, tooth for tooth, har[...] for hand, foot for foot.

Going to War

20 When you go to war against your enemies and see horses and chariots an[...] an army greater than yours, do not be afraid of them, because the LORD yo[...] God, who brought you up out of Egypt, will be with you. ²When you are about to go in[...] battle, the priest shall come forward and address the army. ³He shall say: "Hear, O Israe[...] today you are going into battle against your enemies. Do not be fainthearted or afraid; c[...] not be terrified or give way to panic before them. ⁴For the LORD your God is the one wh[...] goes with you to fight for you against your enemies to give you victory."

⁵The officers shall say to the army: "Has anyone built a new house and not dedicate[...] it? Let him go home, or he may die in battle and someone else may dedicate it. ⁶H[...] anyone planted a vineyard and not begun to enjoy it? Let him go home, or he may die i[...] battle and someone else enjoy it. ⁷Has anyone become pledged to a woman and n[...] married her? Let him go home, or he may die in battle and someone else marry he[...] ⁸Then the officers shall add, "Is any man afraid or fainthearted? Let him go home so th[...] his brothers will not become disheartened too." ⁹When the officers have finished speak[...] ing to the army, they shall appoint commanders over it.

⊡ ▒▒▒▒ ADDRESSING QUESTIONS ▒▒▒▒ ⤴

20:10–18
God   **Q**

Remember, the God of the Bible hates war-fare. But at this crucial point in history, these unique, never-to-be-repeated actions served God's justice and gave his nation a foothold in a corner of the world that was filled with abuse and evil (see the note on Deuteronomy chapter 2, verse 34 [page 217]).

¹⁰When you march up to attack a cit[...] make its people an offer of peace. ¹¹If the[...] accept and open their gates, all the peop[...] in it shall be subject to forced labor an[...] shall work for you. ¹²If they refuse to mak[...] peace and they engage you in battle, la[...] siege to that city. ¹³When the LORD your Go[...] delivers it into your hand, put to the swor[...] all the men in it. ¹⁴As for the women, th[...] children, the livestock and everything els[...] in the city, you may take these as plund[...] for yourselves. And you may use the plu[...] der the LORD your God gives you from you[...] enemies. ¹⁵This is how you are to treat a[...] the cities that are at a distance from you and do not belong to the nations nearby.

¹⁶However, in the cities of the nations the LORD your God is giving you as an inher[...] tance, do not leave alive anything that breathes. ¹⁷Completely destroy*ᵃ* them—the Hi[...] tites, Amorites, Canaanites, Perizzites, Hivites and Jebusites—as the LORD your God ha[...] commanded you. ¹⁸Otherwise, they will teach you to follow all the detestable things the[...] do in worshiping their gods, and you will sin against the LORD your God.

¹⁹When you lay siege to a city for a long time, fighting against it to capture it, do n[...] destroy its trees by putting an ax to them, because you can eat their fruit. Do not cut the[...]

ᵃ 17 The Hebrew term refers to the irrevocable giving over of things or persons to the LORD, often by totally destroying them.

down. Are the trees of the field people, that you should besiege them?[a] ²⁰However, you may cut down trees that you know are not fruit trees and use them to build siege works until the city at war with you falls.

Atonement for an Unsolved Murder

21 If a man is found slain, lying in a field in the land the LORD your God is giving you to possess, and it is not known who killed him, ²your elders and judges shall go out and measure the distance from the body to the neighboring towns. ³Then the elders of the town nearest the body shall take a heifer that has never been worked and has never worn a yoke ⁴and lead her down to a valley that has not been plowed or planted and where there is a flowing stream. There in the valley they are to break the heifer's neck. ⁵The priests, the sons of Levi, shall step forward, for the LORD your God has chosen them to minister and to pronounce blessings in the name of the LORD and to decide all cases of dispute and assault. ⁶Then all the elders of the town nearest the body shall wash their hands over the heifer whose neck was broken in the valley, ⁷and they shall declare: "Our hands did not shed this blood, nor did our eyes see it done. ⁸Accept this atonement for your people Israel, whom you have redeemed, O LORD, and do not hold your people guilty of the blood of an innocent man." And the bloodshed will be atoned for. ⁹So you will purge from yourselves the guilt of shedding innocent blood, since you have done what is right in the eyes of the LORD.

Marrying a Captive Woman

¹⁰When you go to war against your enemies and the LORD your God delivers them into your hands and you take captives, ¹¹if you notice among the captives a beautiful woman and are attracted to her, you may take her as your wife. ¹²Bring her into your home and have her shave her head, trim her nails ¹³and put aside the clothes she was wearing when captured. After she has lived in your house and mourned her father and mother for a full month, then you may go to her and be her husband and she shall be your wife. ¹⁴If you are not pleased with her, let her go wherever she wishes. You must not sell her or treat her as a slave, since you have dishonored her.

The Right of the Firstborn

¹⁵If a man has two wives, and he loves one but not the other, and both bear him sons but the firstborn is the son of the wife he does not love, ¹⁶when he wills his property to his sons, he must not give the rights of the firstborn to the son of the wife he loves in preference to his actual firstborn, the son of the wife he does not love. ¹⁷He must acknowledge the son of his unloved wife as the firstborn by giving him a double share of all he has. That son is the first sign of his father's strength. The right of the firstborn belongs to him.

A Rebellious Son

¹⁸If a man has a stubborn and rebellious son who does not obey his father and mother and will not listen to them when they discipline him, ¹⁹his father and mother shall take hold of him and bring him to the elders at the gate of his town. ²⁰They shall say to the elders, "This son of ours is stubborn and rebellious. He will not obey us. He is a profligate and a drunkard." ²¹Then all the men of his town shall stone him to death. You must purge the evil from among you. All Israel will hear of it and be afraid.

Various Laws

²²If a man guilty of a capital offense is put to death and his body is hung on a tree, ²³you must not leave his body on the tree overnight. Be sure to bury him that same day,

---

[a]19 Or down to use in the siege, for the fruit trees are for the benefit of man.

because anyone who is hung on a tree is under God's curse. You must not desecrate the land the Lord your God is giving you as an inheritance.

22 If you see your brother's ox or sheep straying, do not ignore it but be sure to take it back to him. [2]If the brother does not live near you or if you do not know who he is, take it home with you and keep it until he comes looking for it. Then give it back to him. [3]Do the same if you find your brother's donkey or his cloak or anything he loses. Do not ignore it.

[4]If you see your brother's donkey or his ox fallen on the road, do not ignore it. Help him get it to its feet.

[5]A woman must not wear men's clothing, nor a man wear women's clothing, for the Lord your God detests anyone who does this.

[6]If you come across a bird's nest beside the road, either in a tree or on the ground, and the mother is sitting on the young or on the eggs, do not take the mother with the young. [7]You may take the young, but be sure to let the mother go, so that it may go well with you and you may have a long life.

[8]When you build a new house, make a parapet around your roof so that you may not bring the guilt of bloodshed on your house if someone falls from the roof.

[9]Do not plant two kinds of seed in your vineyard; if you do, not only the crops you plant but also the fruit of the vineyard will be defiled.[a]

[10]Do not plow with an ox and a donkey yoked together.

[11]Do not wear clothes of wool and linen woven together.

[12]Make tassels on the four corners of the cloak you wear.

Marriage Violations

[13]If a man takes a wife and, after lying with her, dislikes her [14]and slanders her and gives her a bad name, saying, "I married this woman, but when I approached her, I did not find proof of her virginity," [15]then the girl's father and mother shall bring proof that she was a virgin to the town elders at the gate. [16]The girl's father will say to the elders, "I gave my daughter in marriage to this man, but he dislikes her. [17]Now he has slandered her and said, 'I did not find your daughter to be a virgin.' But here is the proof of my daughter's virginity." Then her parents shall display the cloth before the elders of the town, [18]and the elders shall take the man and punish him. [19]They shall fine him a hundred shekels of silver[b] and give them to the girl's father, because this man has given an Israelite virgin a bad name. She shall continue to

STRENGTHENING RELATIONSHIPS

22:13–30
Marriage

These strict laws about sexual purity sound harsh in our permissive age. But behind their rigidity lies a timeless principle: God intends that marriage be permanent and that both husband and wife remain faithful to one another.

When people commit adultery, pain spreads out like ripples in a pond. Understand that God doesn't hate sin because he wants to limit our fun or freedom; he hates sin because of the human suffering that results.

Jesus, in the Gospel of John, gives us further instructions for dealing with sin—specifically, the sin of adultery (please turn to John chapter 8, verses 1–11 [page 1395]). In that story, Jesus clarifies the point of the harsh law that we read in this passage—completely eliminating all traces of this sin from your marriage.

This woman, however, had already committed adultery. Instead of condemning her, Jesus commanded her to "Go now and leave your life of sin." That's a picture of God's willingness to forgive us when we do wrong—a benefit that we can all enjoy when we commit our lives and marriages to him.

Is your marriage a permanent bond? Or are you connected with your spouse only until someone better comes along? Most people see marriage as a positive arrangement as long as two people are in love. But according to God's design, it's a committed marriage that keeps love alive, not the other way around.

---

[a]9 Or be forfeited to the sanctuary   [b]19 That is, about 2 1/2 pounds (about 1 kilogram)

e his wife; he must not divorce her as long as he lives.

20If, however, the charge is true and no proof of the girl's virginity can be found, 21she shall be brought to the door of her father's house and there the men of her town shall stone her to death. She has done a disgraceful thing in Israel by being promiscuous while till in her father's house. You must purge the evil from among you.

22If a man is found sleeping with another man's wife, both the man who slept with her and the woman must die. You must purge the evil from Israel.

23If a man happens to meet in a town a virgin pledged to be married and he sleeps with her, 24you shall take both of them to the gate of that town and stone them to death—the girl because she was in a town and did not scream for help, and the man because he violated another man's wife. You must purge the evil from among you.

25But if out in the country a man happens to meet a girl pledged to be married and rapes her, only the man who has done this shall die. 26Do nothing to the girl; she has committed no sin deserving death. This case is like that of someone who attacks and murders his neighbor, 27for the man found the girl out in the country, and though the betrothed girl screamed, there was no one to rescue her.

28If a man happens to meet a virgin who is not pledged to be married and rapes her and they are discovered, 29he shall pay the girl's father fifty shekels of silver.*a* He must marry the girl, for he has violated her. He can never divorce her as long as he lives.

30A man is not to marry his father's wife; he must not dishonor his father's bed.

Exclusion From the Assembly

23 No one who has been emasculated by crushing or cutting may enter the assembly of the LORD.

2No one born of a forbidden marriage*b* nor any of his descendants may enter the assembly of the LORD, even down to the tenth generation.

3No Ammonite or Moabite or any of his descendants may enter the assembly of the LORD, even down to the tenth generation. 4For they did not come to meet you with bread and water on your way when you came out of Egypt, and they hired Balaam son of Beor from Pethor in Aram Naharaim*c* to pronounce a curse on you. 5However, the LORD your God would not listen to Balaam but turned the curse into a blessing for you, because the LORD your God loves you. 6Do not seek a treaty of friendship with them as long as you live.

7Do not abhor an Edomite, for he is your brother. Do not abhor an Egyptian, because you lived as an alien in his country. 8The third generation of children born to them may enter the assembly of the LORD.

Uncleanness in the Camp

9When you are encamped against your enemies, keep away from everything impure. 10If one of your men is unclean because of a nocturnal emission, he is to go outside the camp and stay there. 11But as evening approaches he is to wash himself, and at sunset he may return to the camp.

12Designate a place outside the camp where you can go to relieve yourself. 13As part of your equipment have something to dig with, and when you relieve yourself, dig a hole and cover up your excrement. 14For the LORD your God moves about in your camp to protect you and to deliver your enemies to you. Your camp must be holy, so that he will not see among you anything indecent and turn away from you.

Miscellaneous Laws

15If a slave has taken refuge with you, do not hand him over to his master. 16Let him live among you wherever he likes and in whatever town he chooses. Do not oppress him.

---

29 That is, about 1 1/4 pounds (about 0.6 kilogram)　　*b2 Or one of illegitimate birth*　　*c4 That is, Northwest Mesopotamia*

¹⁷No Israelite man or woman is to become a shrine prostitute. ¹⁸You must not bring the earnings of a female prostitute or of a male prostitute*ᵃ* into the house of the Lᴏʀᴅ your God to pay any vow, because the Lᴏʀᴅ your God detests them both.

¹⁹Do not charge your brother interest, whether on money or food or anything else that may earn interest. ²⁰You may charge a foreigner interest, but not a brother Israelite, so that the Lᴏʀᴅ your God may bless you in everything you put your hand to in the land you are entering to possess.

²¹If you make a vow to the Lᴏʀᴅ your God, do not be slow to pay it, for the Lᴏʀᴅ your God will certainly demand it of you and you will be guilty of sin. ²²But if you refrain from making a vow, you will not be guilty. ²³Whatever your lips utter you must be sure to do because you made your vow freely to the Lᴏʀᴅ your God with your own mouth.

²⁴If you enter your neighbor's vineyard, you may eat all the grapes you want, but do not put any in your basket. ²⁵If you enter your neighbor's grainfield, you may pick kernels with your hands, but you must not put a sickle to his standing grain.

24 If a man marries a woman who becomes displeasing to him because he finds something indecent about her, and he writes her a certificate of divorce, gives it to her and sends her from his house, ²and if after she leaves his house she becomes the wife of another man, ³and her second husband dislikes her and writes her a certificate of divorce, gives it to her and sends her from his house, or if he dies, ⁴then her first husband, who divorced her, is not allowed to marry her again after she has been defiled. That would be detestable in the eyes of the Lᴏʀᴅ. Do not bring sin upon the land the Lᴏʀᴅ your God is giving you as an inheritance.

⁵If a man has recently married, he must not be sent to war or have any other duty laid on him. For one year he is to be free to stay at home and bring happiness to the wife he has married.

⁶Do not take a pair of millstones—not even the upper one—as security for a debt, because that would be taking a man's livelihood as security.

⁷If a man is caught kidnapping one of his brother Israelites and treats him as a slave or sells him, the kidnapper must die. You must purge the evil from among you.

⁸In cases of leprous*ᵇ* diseases be very careful to do exactly as the priests, who are Levites, instruct you. You must follow carefully what I have commanded them. ⁹Remember what the Lᴏʀᴅ your God did to Miriam along the way after you came out of Egypt.

¹⁰When you make a loan of any kind to your neighbor, do not go into his house to get what he is offering as a pledge. ¹¹Stay outside and let the man to whom you are making the loan bring the pledge out to you. ¹²If the man is poor, do not go to sleep with his pledge in your possession. ¹³Return his cloak to him by sunset so that he may sleep in it. Then he will thank you, and it will be regarded as a righteous act in the sight of the Lᴏʀᴅ your God.

¹⁴Do not take advantage of a hired man who is poor and needy, whether he is a brother Israelite or an alien living in one of your towns. ¹⁵Pay him his wages each day before sunset, because he is poor and is counting on it. Otherwise he may cry to the Lᴏʀᴅ against you, and you will be guilty of sin.

▣ ⫴⫴⫴⫴ MANAGING RESOURCES ⫴⫴⫴⫴ ⬓

**24:14–15
Business**

If you are an employer, God is concerned that you are not only fair, but also compassionate. The practice of paying wages each day ensured that poor individuals who lived literally hand-to-mouth would not be stuck waiting for their pay. Such a delay might have been permissible, but cold-hearted.

What a wonderful reputation you would make for yourself if your business treated all employees with dignity and—don't fall down here—paid all its bills on time!

¹⁶Fathers shall not be put to death for their children, nor children put to death for their fathers; each is to die for his own sin.

ᵃ 18 Hebrew *of a dog*   *ᵇ 8* The Hebrew word was used for various diseases affecting the skin—not necessarily leprosy.

¹⁷Do not deprive the alien or the fatherless of justice, or take the cloak of the widow as a pledge. ¹⁸Remember that you were slaves in Egypt and the LORD your God redeemed you from there. That is why I command you to do this.

¹⁹When you are harvesting in your field and you overlook a sheaf, do not go back to get it. Leave it for the alien, the fatherless and the widow, so that the LORD your God may bless you in all the work of your hands. ²⁰When you beat the olives from your trees, do not go over the branches a second time. Leave what remains for the alien, the fatherless and the widow. ²¹When you harvest the grapes in your vineyard, do not go over the vines again. Leave what remains for the alien, the fatherless and the widow. ²²Remember that you were slaves in Egypt. That is why I command you to do this.

25 When men have a dispute, they are to take it to court and the judges will decide the case, acquitting the innocent and condemning the guilty. ²If the guilty man deserves to be beaten, the judge shall make him lie down and have him flogged in his presence with the number of lashes his crime deserves, ³but he must not give him more than forty lashes. If he is flogged more than that, your brother will be degraded in your eyes.

⁴Do not muzzle an ox while it is treading out the grain.

⁵If brothers are living together and one of them dies without a son, his widow must not marry outside the family. Her husband's brother shall take her and marry her and fulfill the duty of a brother-in-law to her. ⁶The first son she bears shall carry on the name of the dead brother so that his name will not be blotted out from Israel.

⁷However, if a man does not want to marry his brother's wife, she shall go to the elders at the town gate and say, "My husband's brother refuses to carry on his brother's name in Israel. He will not fulfill the duty of a brother-in-law to me." ⁸Then the elders of his town shall summon him and talk to him. If he persists in saying, "I do not want to marry her," ⁹his brother's widow shall go up to him in the presence of the elders, take off one of his sandals, spit in his face and say, "This is what is done to the man who will not build up his brother's family line." ¹⁰That man's line shall be known in Israel as The Family of the Unsandaled.

¹¹If two men are fighting and the wife of one of them comes to rescue her husband from his assailant, and she reaches out and seizes him by his private parts, ¹²you shall cut off her hand. Show her no pity.

¹³Do not have two differing weights in your bag—one heavy, one light. ¹⁴Do not have two differing measures in your house—one large, one small. ¹⁵You must have accurate and honest weights and measures, so that you may live long in the land the LORD your God is giving you. ¹⁶For the LORD your God detests anyone who does these things, anyone who deals dishonestly.

¹⁷Remember what the Amalekites did to you along the way when you came out of Egypt. ¹⁸When you were weary and worn out, they met you on your journey and cut off all who were lagging behind; they had no fear of God. ¹⁹When the LORD your God gives you rest from all the enemies around you in the land he is giving you to possess as an inheritance, you shall blot out the memory of Amalek from under heaven. Do not forget!

Firstfruits and Tithes

26 When you have entered the land the LORD your God is giving you as an inheritance and have taken possession of it and settled in it, ²take some of the firstfruits of all that you produce from the soil of the land the LORD your God is giving you and put them in a basket. Then go to the place the LORD your God will choose as a dwelling for his Name ³and say to the priest in office at the time, "I declare today to the LORD your God that I have come to the land the LORD swore to our forefathers to give us." ⁴The priest shall take the basket from your hands and set it down in front of the altar of the LORD your God. ⁵Then you shall declare before the LORD your God: "My father was a wandering Aramean, and he went down into Egypt with a few people and lived there and became a great nation, powerful and numerous. ⁶But the Egyptians mistreated u' and made us suffer, putting us to hard labor. ⁷Then we cried out to the LORD, the God o' our fathers, and the LORD heard our voice and saw our misery, toil and oppression. ⁸So th' LORD brought us out of Egypt with a mighty hand and an outstretched arm, with grea' terror and with miraculous signs and wonders. ⁹He brought us to this place and gave u' this land, a land flowing with milk and honey; ¹⁰and now I bring the firstfruits of the so' that you, O LORD, have given me." Place the basket before the LORD your God and bov' down before him. ¹¹And you and the Levites and the aliens among you shall rejoice in a' the good things the LORD your God has given to you and your household.

¹²When you have finished setting aside a tenth of all your produce in the third yea' the year of the tithe, you shall give it to the Levite, the alien, the fatherless and th' widow, so that they may eat in your towns and be satisfied. ¹³Then say to the LORD you' God: "I have removed from my house the sacred portion and have given it to the Levite the alien, the fatherless and the widow, according to all you commanded. I have no' turned aside from your commands nor have I forgotten any of them. ¹⁴I have not eate' any of the sacred portion while I was in mourning, nor have I removed any of it while was unclean, nor have I offered any of it to the dead. I have obeyed the LORD my God; have done everything you commanded me. ¹⁵Look down from heaven, your holy dwell ing place, and bless your people Israel and the land you have given us as you promise' on oath to our forefathers, a land flowing with milk and honey."

Follow the LORD's Commands

¹⁶The LORD your God commands you this day to follow these decrees and laws; carefull' observe them with all your heart and with all your soul. ¹⁷You have declared this day tha' the LORD is your God and that you will walk in his ways, that you will keep his decrees commands and laws, and that you will obey him. ¹⁸And the LORD has declared this da' that you are his people, his treasured possession as he promised, and that you are to keep all his commands. ¹⁹He has declared that he will set you in praise, fame and hono' high above all the nations he has made and that you will be a people holy to the LOR' your God, as he promised.

The Altar on Mount Ebal

27 Moses and the elders of Israel commanded the people: "Keep all these com mands that I give you today. ²When you have crossed the Jordan into th' land the LORD your God is giving you, set up some large stones and coat them with plaster ³Write on them all the words of this law when you have crossed over to enter the lan' the LORD your God is giving you, a land flowing with milk and honey, just as the LORD, th' God of your fathers, promised. ⁴And when you have crossed the Jordan, set up thes' stones on Mount Ebal, as I command you today, and coat them with plaster. ⁵Build ther' an altar to the LORD your God, an altar of stones. Do not use any iron tool upon them ⁶Build the altar of the LORD your God with fieldstones and offer burnt offerings on it to th' LORD your God. ⁷Sacrifice fellowship offerings*ᵃ* there, eating them and rejoicing in th' presence of the LORD your God. ⁸And you shall write very clearly all the words of this law on these stones you have set up."

Curses From Mount Ebal

⁹Then Moses and the priests, who are Levites, said to all Israel, "Be silent, O Israel, an' listen! You have now become the people of the LORD your God. ¹⁰Obey the LORD your Go' and follow his commands and decrees that I give you today."

¹¹On the same day Moses commanded the people:

¹²When you have crossed the Jordan, these tribes shall stand on Mount Gerizim t' bless the people: Simeon, Levi, Judah, Issachar, Joseph and Benjamin. ¹³And these tribe'

ᵃ 7 Traditionally *peace offerings*

shall stand on Mount Ebal to pronounce curses: Reuben, Gad, Asher, Zebulun, Dan and Naphtali.

¹⁴The Levites shall recite to all the people of Israel in a loud voice:

¹⁵"Cursed is the man who carves an image or casts an idol—a thing detestable to the LORD, the work of the craftsman's hands—and sets it up in secret."

Then all the people shall say, "Amen!"

¹⁶"Cursed is the man who dishonors his father or his mother."

Then all the people shall say, "Amen!"

¹⁷"Cursed is the man who moves his neighbor's boundary stone."

Then all the people shall say, "Amen!"

¹⁸"Cursed is the man who leads the blind astray on the road."

Then all the people shall say, "Amen!"

¹⁹"Cursed is the man who withholds justice from the alien, the fatherless or the widow."

Then all the people shall say, "Amen!"

²⁰"Cursed is the man who sleeps with his father's wife, for he dishonors his father's bed."

Then all the people shall say, "Amen!"

²¹"Cursed is the man who has sexual relations with any animal."

Then all the people shall say, "Amen!"

²²"Cursed is the man who sleeps with his sister, the daughter of his father or the daughter of his mother."

Then all the people shall say, "Amen!"

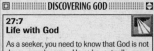

DISCOVERING GOD

27:7
Life with God

As a seeker, you need to know that God is not down on pleasure. Here he actually commands Israel to enjoy a steak dinner during worship!

If you perceive church as being dull and boring, realize that it's not supposed to be that way. God wants people to see time with him as something enjoyable and desirable. This passage shows us that a whole range of human emotions can be expressed during worship, including excitement, awe, joy, and wonder.

The challenge of accepting God is one of the most exciting and dangerous propositions humans can ever face. It calls for a radical, revolutionary life-change, and forces people to consider living for a cause outside of themselves. It involves tapping into the power of the very God who created the universe and all that is in it. People who devote their lives to the cause of Christ find thrills and chills that last—not just for a moment, but for eternity. What better reason could there be for celebration?

Are you ready for the thrill of a lifetime?

²³"Cursed is the man who sleeps with his mother-in-law."

Then all the people shall say, "Amen!"

²⁴"Cursed is the man who kills his neighbor secretly."

Then all the people shall say, "Amen!"

²⁵"Cursed is the man who accepts a bribe to kill an innocent person."

Then all the people shall say, "Amen!"

²⁶"Cursed is the man who does not uphold the words of this law by carrying them out."

Then all the people shall say, "Amen!"

Blessings for Obedience

28 If you fully obey the LORD your God and carefully follow all his commands I give you today, the LORD your God will set you high above all the nations on earth. ²All these blessings will come upon you and accompany you if you obey the LORD your God:

³You will be blessed in the city and blessed in the country.

⁴The fruit of your womb will be blessed, and the crops of your land and the young of your livestock—the calves of your herds and the lambs of your flocks.

⁵Your basket and your kneading trough will be blessed.

⁶You will be blessed when you come in and blessed when you go out.

⁷The Lord will grant that the enemies who rise up against you will be defeated befor you. They will come at you from one direction but flee from you in seven.

⁸The Lord will send a blessing on your barns and on everything you put your hand t The Lord your God will bless you in the land he is giving you.

⁹The Lord will establish you as his holy people, as he promised you on oath, if you kee the commands of the Lord your God and walk in his ways. ¹⁰Then all the peoples on ear will see that you are called by the name of the Lord, and they will fear you. ¹¹The Lor will grant you abundant prosperity—in the fruit of your womb, the young of your livestoc and the crops of your ground—in the land he swore to your forefathers to give you.

¹²The Lord will open the heavens, the storehouse of his bounty, to send rain on yo land in season and to bless all the work of your hands. You will lend to many nations b will borrow from none. ¹³The Lord will make you the head, not the tail. If you pa attention to the commands of the Lord your God that I give you this day and carefull follow them, you will always be at the top, never at the bottom. ¹⁴Do not turn aside fro any of the commands I give you today, to the right or to the left, following other gods ar serving them.

Curses for Disobedience

¹⁵However, if you do not obey the Lord your God and do not carefully follow all h commands and decrees I am giving you today, all these curses will come upon you ar overtake you:

¹⁶You will be cursed in the city and cursed in the country.

¹⁷Your basket and your kneading trough will be cursed.

¹⁸The fruit of your womb will be cursed, and the crops of your land, and the calves of your herds and the lambs of your flocks.

¹⁹You will be cursed when you come in and cursed when you go out.

²⁰The Lord will send on you curses, confusion and rebuke in everything you put yo hand to, until you are destroyed and come to sudden ruin because of the evil you hav done in forsaking him.ᵃ ²¹The Lord will plague you with diseases until he has destroye you from the land you are entering to possess. ²²The Lord will strike you with wastir disease, with fever and inflammation, with scorching heat and drought, with blight ar mildew, which will plague you until you perish. ²³The sky over your head will be bronz the ground beneath you iron. ²⁴The Lord will turn the rain of your country into dust ar powder; it will come down from the skies until you are destroyed.

²⁵The Lord will cause you to be defeated before your enemies. You will come at the from one direction but flee from them in seven, and you will become a thing of horror all the kingdoms on earth. ²⁶Your carcasses will be food for all the birds of the air and t beasts of the earth, and there will be no one to frighten them away. ²⁷The Lord will affli you with the boils of Egypt and with tumors, festering sores and the itch, from which yo cannot be cured. ²⁸The Lord will afflict you with madness, blindness and confusion mind. ²⁹At midday you will grope about like a blind man in the dark. You will ▌ unsuccessful in everything you do; day after day you will be oppressed and robbed, wi no one to rescue you.

³⁰You will be pledged to be married to a woman, but another will take her and ravis her. You will build a house, but you will not live in it. You will plant a vineyard, but yo

ᵃ20 Hebrew *me*

will not even begin to enjoy its fruit. ³¹Your ox will be slaughtered before your eyes, but you will eat none of it. Your donkey will be forcibly taken from you and will not be returned. Your sheep will be given to your enemies, and no one will rescue them. ³²Your sons and daughters will be given to another nation, and you will wear out your eyes watching for them day after day, powerless to lift a hand. ³³A people that you do not know will eat what your land and labor produce, and you will have nothing but cruel oppression all your days. ³⁴The sights you see will drive you mad. ³⁵The LORD will afflict your knees and legs with painful boils that cannot be cured, spreading from the soles of your feet to the top of your head.

³⁶The LORD will drive you and the king you set over you to a nation unknown to you or your fathers. There you will worship other gods, gods of wood and stone. ³⁷You will become a thing of horror and an object of scorn and ridicule to all the nations where the LORD will drive you.

³⁸You will sow much seed in the field but you will harvest little, because locusts will devour it. ³⁹You will plant vineyards and cultivate them but you will not drink the wine or gather the grapes, because worms will eat them. ⁴⁰You will have olive trees throughout your country but you will not use the oil, because the olives will drop off. ⁴¹You will have sons and daughters but you will not keep them, because they will go into captivity. ⁴²Swarms of locusts will take over all your trees and the crops of your land.

⁴³The alien who lives among you will rise above you higher and higher, but you will sink lower and lower. ⁴⁴He will lend to you, but you will not lend to him. He will be the head, but you will be the tail.

⁴⁵All these curses will come upon you. They will pursue you and overtake you until you are destroyed, because you did not obey the LORD your God and observe the commands and decrees he gave you. ⁴⁶They will be a sign and a wonder to you and your descendants forever. ⁴⁷Because you did not serve the LORD your God joyfully and gladly in the time of prosperity, ⁴⁸therefore in hunger and thirst, in nakedness and dire poverty, you will serve the enemies the LORD sends against you. He will put an iron yoke on your neck until he has destroyed you.

⁴⁹The LORD will bring a nation against you from far away, from the ends of the earth, like an eagle swooping down, a nation whose language you will not understand, ⁵⁰a fierce-looking nation without respect for the old or pity for the young. ⁵¹They will devour the young of your livestock and the crops of your land until you are destroyed. They will leave you no grain, new wine or oil, nor any calves of your herds or lambs of your flocks until you are ruined. ⁵²They will lay siege to all the cities throughout your land until the high fortified walls in which you trust fall down. They will besiege all the cities throughout the land the LORD your God is giving you.

⁵³Because of the suffering that your enemy will inflict on you during the siege, you will eat the fruit of the womb, the flesh of the sons and daughters the LORD your God has given you. ⁵⁴Even the most gentle and sensitive man among you will have no compassion on his own brother or the wife he loves or his surviving children, ⁵⁵and he will not give to one of them any of the flesh of his children that he is eating. It will be all he has left because of the suffering your enemy will inflict on you during the siege of all your cities. ⁵⁶The most gentle and sensitive woman among you—so sensitive and gentle that she would not venture to touch the ground with the sole of her foot—will begrudge the husband she loves and her own son or daughter ⁵⁷the afterbirth from her womb and the children she bears. For she intends to eat them secretly during the siege and in the distress that your enemy will inflict on you in your cities.

⁵⁸If you do not carefully follow all the words of this law, which are written in this book, and do not revere this glorious and awesome name—the LORD your God— ⁵⁹the LORD will send fearful plagues on you and your descendants, harsh and prolonged disasters, and severe and lingering illnesses. ⁶⁰He will bring upon you all the diseases of Egypt that you dreaded, and they will cling to you. ⁶¹The LORD will also bring on you every kind of

sickness and disaster not recorded in this Book of the Law, until you are destroyed. ⁶²Yo
who were as numerous as the stars in the sky will be left but few in number, becaus
you did not obey the LORD your God. ⁶³Just as it pleased the LORD to make you prosper an
increase in number, so it will please him to ruin and destroy you. You will be uproote
from the land you are entering to possess.

⁶⁴Then the LORD will scatter you among all nations, from one end of the earth to th
other. There you will worship other gods—gods of wood and stone, which neither yo
nor your fathers have known. ⁶⁵Among those nations you will find no repose, no restir
place for the sole of your foot. There the LORD will give you an anxious mind, eyes wea
with longing, and a despairing heart. ⁶⁶You will live in constant suspense, filled wit
dread both night and day, never sure of your life. ⁶⁷In the morning you will say, "If on
it were evening!" and in the evening, "If only it were morning!"—because of the terr
that will fill your hearts and the sights that your eyes will see. ⁶⁸The LORD will send yo
back in ships to Egypt on a journey I said you should never make again. There you wi
offer yourselves for sale to your enemies as male and female slaves, but no one will bu
you.

Renewal of the Covenant

29 These are the terms of the covenant the LORD commanded Moses to mak
with the Israelites in Moab, in addition to the covenant he had made wit
them at Horeb.

²Moses summoned all the Israelites and said to them:

Your eyes have seen all that the LORD did in Egypt to Pharaoh, to all his officials and
all his land. ³With your own eyes you saw those great trials, those miraculous signs an
great wonders. ⁴But to this day the LORD has not given you a mind that understands
eyes that see or ears that hear. ⁵During the forty years that I led you through the dese
your clothes did not wear out, nor did the sandals on your feet. ⁶You ate no bread an
drank no wine or other fermented drink. I did this so that you might know that I am th
LORD your God.

⁷When you reached this place, Sihon king of Heshbon and Og king of Bashan came ou
to fight against us, but we defeated them. ⁸We took their land and gave it as an inher
tance to the Reubenites, the Gadites and the half-tribe of Manasseh.

⁹Carefully follow the terms of this covenant, so that you may prosper in everything yo
do. ¹⁰All of you are standing today in the presence of the LORD your God—your leaders an
chief men, your elders and officials, and all the other men of Israel, ¹¹together with yo
children and your wives, and the aliens living in your camps who chop your wood an
carry your water. ¹²You are standing here in order to enter into a covenant with the LOR
your God, a covenant the LORD is making with you this day and sealing with an oath, ¹³¹
confirm you this day as his people, that he may be your God as he promised you and a
he swore to your fathers, Abraham, Isaac and Jacob. ¹⁴I am making this covenant, with i
oath, not only with you ¹⁵who are standing here with us today in the presence of the LOR
our God but also with those who are not here today.

¹⁶You yourselves know how we lived in Egypt and how we passed through the coun
tries on the way here. ¹⁷You saw among them their detestable images and idols of woo
and stone, of silver and gold. ¹⁸Make sure there is no man or woman, clan or tribe amon
you today whose heart turns away from the LORD our God to go and worship the gods
those nations; make sure there is no root among you that produces such bitter poiso

¹⁹When such a person hears the words of this oath, he invokes a blessing on himse
and therefore thinks, "I will be safe, even though I persist in going my own way." Thi
will bring disaster on the watered land as well as the dry.ᵃ ²⁰The LORD will never b
willing to forgive him; his wrath and zeal will burn against that man. All the curse

ᵃ19 Or way, in order to add drunkenness to thirst."

written in this book will fall upon him, and the LORD will blot out his name from under heaven. ²¹The LORD will single him out from all the tribes of Israel for disaster, according to all the curses of the covenant written in this Book of the Law.

²²Your children who follow you in later generations and foreigners who come from distant lands will see the calamities that have fallen on the land and the diseases with which the LORD has afflicted it. ²³The whole land will be a burning waste of salt and sulfur—nothing planted, nothing sprouting, no vegetation growing on it. It will be like the destruction of Sodom and Gomorrah, Admah and Zeboiim, which the LORD overthrew in fierce anger. ²⁴All the nations will ask: "Why has the LORD done this to this land? Why this fierce, burning anger?"

²⁵And the answer will be: "It is because this people abandoned the covenant of the LORD, the God of their fathers, the covenant he made with them when he brought them out of Egypt. ²⁶They went off and worshiped other gods and bowed down to them, gods they did not know, gods he had not given them. ²⁷Therefore the LORD's anger burned against this land, so that he brought on it all the curses written in this book. ²⁸In furious anger and in great wrath the LORD uprooted them from their land and thrust them into another land, as it is now."

²⁹The secret things belong to the LORD our God, but the things revealed belong to us and to our children forever, that we may follow all the words of this law.

Prosperity After Turning to the LORD

30 When all these blessings and curses I have set before you come upon you and you take them to heart wherever the LORD your God disperses you among the nations, ²and when you and your children return to the LORD your God and obey him with all your heart and with all your soul according to everything I command you today, ³then the LORD your God will restore your fortunes*ᵃ* and have compassion on you and gather you again from all the nations where he scattered you. ⁴Even if you have been banished to the most distant land under the heavens, from there the LORD your God will gather you and bring you back. ⁵He will bring you to the land that belonged to your fathers, and you will take possession of it. He will make you

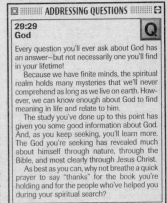

⊞ ADDRESSING QUESTIONS ⊞

**29:29
God**   **Q**

Every question you'll ever ask about God has an answer—but not necessarily one you'll find in your lifetime!

Because we have finite minds, the spiritual realm holds many mysteries that we'll never comprehend as long as we live on earth. However, we can know enough about God to find meaning in life and relate to him.

The study you've done up to this point has given you some good information about God. And, as you keep seeking, you'll learn more. The God you're seeking has revealed much about himself through nature, through the Bible, and most clearly through Jesus Christ.

As best as you can, why not breathe a quick prayer to say "thanks" for the book you're holding and for the people who've helped you during your spiritual search?

more prosperous and numerous than your fathers. ⁶The LORD your God will circumcise your hearts and the hearts of your descendants, so that you may love him with all your heart and with all your soul, and live. ⁷The LORD your God will put all these curses on your enemies who hate and persecute you. ⁸You will again obey the LORD and follow all his commands I am giving you today. ⁹Then the LORD your God will make you most prosperous in all the work of your hands and in the fruit of your womb, the young of your livestock and the crops of your land. The LORD will again delight in you and make you prosperous, just as he delighted in your fathers, ¹⁰if you obey the LORD your God and keep his commands and decrees that are written in this Book of the Law and turn to the LORD your God with all your heart and with all your soul.

ᵃ 3 Or will bring you back from captivity

The Offer of Life or Death

¹¹Now what I am commanding you today is not too difficult for you or beyond your reach. ¹²It is not up in heaven, so that you have to ask, "Who will ascend into heaven to get it and proclaim it to us so we may obey it?" ¹³Nor is it beyond the sea, so that you have to ask, "Who will cross the sea to get it and proclaim it to us so we may obey it?" ¹⁴No, the word is very near you; it is in your mouth and in your heart so you may obey it.

¹⁵See, I set before you today life and prosperity, death and destruction. ¹⁶For I command you today to love the LORD your God, to walk in his ways, and to keep his commands, decrees and laws; then you will live and increase, and the LORD your God will bless you in the land you are entering to possess.

¹⁷But if your heart turns away and you are not obedient, and if you are drawn away to bow down to other gods and worship them, ¹⁸I declare to you this day that you will certainly be destroyed. You will not live long in the land you are crossing the Jordan to enter and possess.

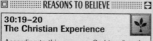

░░░░░ REASONS TO BELIEVE ░░░░░

30:19–20
The Christian Experience

According to this passage, God is a "gentleman"—he does not force anyone to follow him. He offers people the choice of accepting his love—and with it, eternal life.

God gave that choice to the people of ancient Israel. In the verses preceding this passage, God spoke forthrightly to these people, warning them that hard times would come if they disobeyed. He also promised wonderful blessings if they would remain faithful to him.

This challenge was uttered more than three millennia ago to a rag-tag band of ex-slaves. But a timeless principle remains: God has set before you today—even as you read this—life or death, a blessing or a curse.

Choose life, so that you may really live!

---

¹⁹This day I call heaven and earth as witnesses against you that I have set before you life and death, blessings and curses. Now choose life, so that you and your children may live ²⁰and that you may love the LORD your God, listen to his voice, and hold fast to him. For the LORD is your life, and he will give you many years in the land he swore to give to your fathers, Abraham, Isaac and Jacob.

Joshua to Succeed Moses

31 Then Moses went out and spoke these words to all Israel: ²"I am now a hundred and twenty years old and I am no longer able to lead you. The LORD has said to me, 'You shall not cross the Jordan.' ³The LORD your God himself will cross over ahead of you. He will destroy these nations before you, and you will take possession of their land. Joshua also will cross over ahead of you, as the LORD said. ⁴And the LORD will do to them what he did to Sihon and Og, the kings of the Amorites, whom he destroyed along with their land. ⁵The LORD will deliver them to you, and you must do to them all that I have commanded you. ⁶Be strong and courageous. Do not be afraid or terrified because of them, for the LORD your God goes with you; he will never leave you nor forsake you."

⁷Then Moses summoned Joshua and said to him in the presence of all Israel, "Be strong and courageous, for you must go with this people into the land that the LORD swore to their forefathers to give them, and you must divide it among them as their inheritance. ⁸The LORD himself goes before you and will be with you; he will never leave you nor forsake you. Do not be afraid; do not be discouraged."

The Reading of the Law

⁹So Moses wrote down this law and gave it to the priests, the sons of Levi, who carried the ark of the covenant of the LORD, and to all the elders of Israel. ¹⁰Then Moses commanded them: "At the end of every seven years, in the year for canceling debts, during the Feast of Tabernacles, ¹¹when all Israel comes to appear before the LORD your God at the place he will choose, you shall read this law before them in their hearing. ¹²Assemble

he people—men, women and children, and the aliens living in your towns—so they can listen and learn to fear the LORD your God and follow carefully all the words of this law. ³Their children, who do not know this law, must hear it and learn to fear the LORD your God as long as you live in the land you are crossing the Jordan to possess."

Israel's Rebellion Predicted

¹⁴The LORD said to Moses, "Now the day of your death is near. Call Joshua and present yourselves at the Tent of Meeting, where I will commission him." So Moses and Joshua came and presented themselves at the Tent of Meeting.

¹⁵Then the LORD appeared at the Tent in a pillar of cloud, and the cloud stood over the entrance to the Tent. ¹⁶And the LORD said to Moses: "You are going to rest with your fathers, and these people will soon prostitute themselves to the foreign gods of the land they are entering. They will forsake me and break the covenant I made with them. ¹⁷On that day I will become angry with them and forsake them; I will hide my face from them, and they will be destroyed. Many disasters and difficulties will come upon them, and on that day they will ask, 'Have not these disasters come upon us because our God is not with us?' ¹⁸And I will certainly hide my face on that day because of all their wickedness in turning to other gods.

¹⁹"Now write down for yourselves this song and teach it to the Israelites and have them sing it, so that it may be a witness for me against them. ²⁰When I have brought them into the land flowing with milk and honey, the land I promised on oath to their forefathers, and when they eat their fill and thrive, they will turn to other gods and worship them, rejecting me and breaking my covenant. ²¹And when many disasters and difficulties come upon them, this song will testify against them, because it will not be forgotten by their descendants. I know what they are disposed to do, even before I bring them into the land I promised them on oath." ²²So Moses wrote down this song that day and taught it to the Israelites.

²³The LORD gave this command to Joshua son of Nun: "Be strong and courageous, for you will bring the Israelites into the land I promised them on oath, and I myself will be with you."

²⁴After Moses finished writing in a book the words of this law from beginning to end, ²⁵he gave this command to the Levites who carried the ark of the covenant of the LORD: ²⁶"Take this Book of the Law and place it beside the ark of the covenant of the LORD your God. There it will remain as a witness against you. ²⁷For I know how rebellious and stiff-necked you are. If you have been rebellious against the LORD while I am still alive and with you, how much more will you rebel after I die! ²⁸Assemble before me all the elders of your tribes and all your officials, so that I can speak these words in their hearing and call heaven and earth to testify against them. ²⁹For I know that after my death you are sure to become utterly corrupt and to turn from the way I have commanded you. In days to come, disaster will fall upon you because you will do evil in the sight of the LORD and provoke him to anger by what your hands have made."

The Song of Moses

³⁰And Moses recited the words of this song from beginning to end in the hearing of the whole assembly of Israel:

32   Listen, O heavens, and I will speak;
       hear, O earth, the words of my mouth.
 ²Let my teaching fall like rain
     and my words descend like dew,
   like showers on new grass,
     like abundant rain on tender plants.

 ³I will proclaim the name of the LORD.

Oh, praise the greatness of our God!
⁴He is the Rock, his works are perfect,
    and all his ways are just.
A faithful God who does no wrong,
    upright and just is he.

⁵They have acted corruptly toward him;
    to their shame they are no longer his children,
    but a warped and crooked generation. ᵃ
⁶Is this the way you repay the LORD,
    O foolish and unwise people?
Is he not your Father, your Creator, ᵇ
    who made you and formed you?

⁷Remember the days of old;
    consider the generations long past.
Ask your father and he will tell you,
    your elders, and they will explain to you.
⁸When the Most High gave the nations their inheritance,
    when he divided all mankind,
he set up boundaries for the peoples
    according to the number of the sons of Israel. ᶜ
⁹For the LORD's portion is his people,
    Jacob his allotted inheritance.

¹⁰In a desert land he found him,
    in a barren and howling waste.
He shielded him and cared for him;
    he guarded him as the apple of his eye,
¹¹like an eagle that stirs up its nest
    and hovers over its young,
that spreads its wings to catch them
    and carries them on its pinions.
¹²The LORD alone led him;
    no foreign god was with him.

¹³He made him ride on the heights of the land
    and fed him with the fruit of the fields.
He nourished him with honey from the rock,
    and with oil from the flinty crag,
¹⁴with curds and milk from herd and flock
    and with fattened lambs and goats,
with choice rams of Bashan
    and the finest kernels of wheat.
You drank the foaming blood of the grape.

¹⁵Jeshurunᵈ grew fat and kicked;
    filled with food, he became heavy and sleek.
He abandoned the God who made him
    and rejected the Rock his Savior.
¹⁶They made him jealous with their foreign gods
    and angered him with their detestable idols.
¹⁷They sacrificed to demons, which are not God—

ᵃ5 Or Corrupt are they and not his children, / a generation warped and twisted to their shame   ᵇ6 Or Father, who bought you   ᶜ8 Masoretic Text; Dead Sea Scrolls (see also Septuagint) sons of God   ᵈ15 Jeshurun means the upright one, that is, Israel.

gods they had not known,
gods that recently appeared,
gods your fathers did not fear.
¹⁸You deserted the Rock, who fathered you;
you forgot the God who gave you birth.

¹⁹The LORD saw this and rejected them
because he was angered by his sons and daughters.
²⁰"I will hide my face from them," he said,
"and see what their end will be;
for they are a perverse generation,
children who are unfaithful.
²¹They made me jealous by what is no god
and angered me with their worthless idols.
I will make them envious by those who are not a people;
I will make them angry by a nation that has no understanding.
²²For a fire has been kindled by my wrath,
one that burns to the realm of death ᵃ below.
It will devour the earth and its harvests
and set afire the foundations of the mountains.

²³"I will heap calamities upon them
and spend my arrows against them.
²⁴I will send wasting famine against them,
consuming pestilence and deadly plague;
I will send against them the fangs of wild beasts,
the venom of vipers that glide in the dust.
²⁵In the street the sword will make them childless;
in their homes terror will reign.
Young men and young women will perish,
infants and gray-haired men.
²⁶I said I would scatter them
and blot out their memory from mankind,
²⁷but I dreaded the taunt of the enemy,
lest the adversary misunderstand
and say, 'Our hand has triumphed;
the LORD has not done all this.'"

²⁸They are a nation without sense,
there is no discernment in them.
²⁹If only they were wise and would understand this
and discern what their end will be!
³⁰How could one man chase a thousand,
or two put ten thousand to flight,
unless their Rock had sold them,
unless the LORD had given them up?
³¹For their rock is not like our Rock,
as even our enemies concede.
³²Their vine comes from the vine of Sodom
and from the fields of Gomorrah.
Their grapes are filled with poison,
and their clusters with bitterness.

ᵃ22 Hebrew *to Sheol*

[33]Their wine is the venom of serpents,
  the deadly poison of cobras.

[34]"Have I not kept this in reserve
  and sealed it in my vaults?
[35]It is mine to avenge; I will repay.
  In due time their foot will slip;
their day of disaster is near
  and their doom rushes upon them."

[36]The LORD will judge his people
  and have compassion on his servants
when he sees their strength is gone
  and no one is left, slave or free.
[37]He will say: "Now where are their gods,
  the rock they took refuge in,
[38]the gods who ate the fat of their sacrifices
  and drank the wine of their drink offerings?
Let them rise up to help you!
  Let them give you shelter!

[39]"See now that I myself am He!
  There is no god besides me.
I put to death and I bring to life,
  I have wounded and I will heal,
  and no one can deliver out of my hand.
[40]I lift my hand to heaven and declare:
  As surely as I live forever,
[41]when I sharpen my flashing sword
  and my hand grasps it in judgment,
I will take vengeance on my adversaries
  and repay those who hate me.
[42]I will make my arrows drunk with blood,
  while my sword devours flesh:
the blood of the slain and the captives,
  the heads of the enemy leaders."

[43]Rejoice, O nations, with his people,[a,b]
  for he will avenge the blood of his servants;
he will take vengeance on his enemies
  and make atonement for his land and people.

[44]Moses came with Joshua[c] son of Nun and spoke all the words of this song in the hearing of the people. [45]When Moses finished reciting all these words to all Israel, [46]he said to them, "Take to heart all the words I have solemnly declared to you this day, so that you may command your children to obey carefully all the words of this law. [47]They are not just idle words for you—they are your life. By them you will live long in the land you are crossing the Jordan to possess."

Moses to Die on Mount Nebo

[48]On that same day the LORD told Moses, [49]"Go up into the Abarim Range to Mount Nebo in Moab, across from Jericho, and view Canaan, the land I am giving the Israelites as their own possession. [50]There on the mountain that you have climbed you will die and

---

[a]43 Or *Make his people rejoice, O nations*   [b]43 Masoretic Text; Dead Sea Scrolls (see also Septuagint) *people, / and let all the angels worship him /*   [c]44 Hebrew *Hoshea,* a variant of *Joshua*

be gathered to your people, just as your brother Aaron died on Mount Hor and was gathered to his people. ⁵¹This is because both of you broke faith with me in the presence of the Israelites at the waters of Meribah Kadesh in the Desert of Zin and because you did not uphold my holiness among the Israelites. ⁵²Therefore, you will see the land only from a distance; you will not enter the land I am giving to the people of Israel."

Moses Blesses the Tribes

33 This is the blessing that Moses the man of God pronounced on the Israelites before his death. ²He said:

"The LORD came from Sinai
    and dawned over them from Seir;
he shone forth from Mount Paran.
He came with ᵃ myriads of holy ones
    from the south, from his mountain slopes.ᵇ
³Surely it is you who love the people;
    all the holy ones are in your hand.
At your feet they all bow down,
    and from you receive instruction,
⁴the law that Moses gave us,
    the possession of the assembly of Jacob.
⁵He was king over Jeshurunᶜ
    when the leaders of the people assembled,
    along with the tribes of Israel.

⁶"Let Reuben live and not die,
    norᵈ his men be few."

⁷And this he said about Judah:

"Hear, O LORD, the cry of Judah;

ᵃ2 Or from   ᵇ2 The meaning of the Hebrew for this phrase is uncertain.   ᶜ5 Jeshurun means the upright one, that is, Israel; also in verse 26.   ᵈ6 Or but let

---

⬛ ▦▦▦▦▦▦▦▦▦▦▦▦▦ **KNOWING YOURSELF** ▦▦▦▦▦▦▦▦▦▦▦▦▦ ⬔

32:52
Emotions

Great leaders often have one or more serious character flaws. In Moses' case, it was his temper.

When Moses was a young man, he commited murder in an outburst of anger, killing an Egyptian who was beating a Hebrew slave. When he came down from the mountain with the original Ten Commandments, he was so angry at Israel's disobedience that he smashed the stone tablets that had God's very words on them. And in one of his most costly outbursts, he struck a rock with the symbol of his leadership authority—the staff he carried—in direct disobedience to God's command.

The result of that last action was especially painful for Moses. At the end of Moses' life, after decades of faithful service, he was not allowed to see the land he had led his people to possess. God made it clear why this was so (verse 51): Moses' temper had cost him the privilege.

Is there an underlying rage in your soul that leaks out at inopportune times? Anger is not necessarily sin, but if your anger has led you to actions you regret, maybe it's time to take a closer look at what's going on deep inside of you.

Learn from this sad picture of Moses, seeing his dream at a distance but never living to experience it. Don't let the anger boiling inside you scald those you care about. Find help so you can get to the root of your rage—and root it out.

bring him to his people.
With his own hands he defends his cause.
Oh, be his help against his foes!"

8About Levi he said:

"Your Thummim and Urim belong
 to the man you favored.
You tested him at Massah;
 you contended with him at the waters of Meribah.
9He said of his father and mother,
 'I have no regard for them.'
He did not recognize his brothers
 or acknowledge his own children,
but he watched over your word
 and guarded your covenant.
10He teaches your precepts to Jacob
 and your law to Israel.
He offers incense before you
 and whole burnt offerings on your altar.
11Bless all his skills, O LORD,
 and be pleased with the work of his hands.
Smite the loins of those who rise up against him;
 strike his foes till they rise no more."

12About Benjamin he said:

"Let the beloved of the LORD rest secure in him,
 for he shields him all day long,
 and the one the LORD loves rests between his shoulders."

13About Joseph he said:

"May the LORD bless his land
 with the precious dew from heaven above
 and with the deep waters that lie below;
14with the best the sun brings forth
 and the finest the moon can yield;
15with the choicest gifts of the ancient mountains
 and the fruitfulness of the everlasting hills;
16with the best gifts of the earth and its fullness
 and the favor of him who dwelt in the burning bush.
Let all these rest on the head of Joseph,
 on the brow of the prince among*a* his brothers.
17In majesty he is like a firstborn bull;
 his horns are the horns of a wild ox.
With them he will gore the nations,
 even those at the ends of the earth.
Such are the ten thousands of Ephraim;
 such are the thousands of Manasseh."

18About Zebulun he said:

"Rejoice, Zebulun, in your going out,
 and you, Issachar, in your tents.
19They will summon peoples to the mountain

a16 Or *of the one separated from*

and there offer sacrifices of righteousness;
they will feast on the abundance of the seas,
on the treasures hidden in the sand."

²⁰About Gad he said:

"Blessed is he who enlarges Gad's domain!
Gad lives there like a lion,
tearing at arm or head.
²¹He chose the best land for himself;
the leader's portion was kept for him.
When the heads of the people assembled,
he carried out the LORD's righteous will,
and his judgments concerning Israel."

²²About Dan he said:

"Dan is a lion's cub,
springing out of Bashan."

²³About Naphtali he said:

"Naphtali is abounding with the favor of the LORD
and is full of his blessing;
he will inherit southward to the lake."

²⁴About Asher he said:

"Most blessed of sons is Asher;
let him be favored by his brothers,
and let him bathe his feet in oil.
²⁵The bolts of your gates will be iron and bronze,
and your strength will equal your days.

²⁶"There is no one like the God of Jeshurun,
who rides on the heavens to help you
and on the clouds in his majesty.
²⁷The eternal God is your refuge,
and underneath are the everlasting arms.
He will drive out your enemy before you,
saying, 'Destroy him!'
²⁸So Israel will live in safety alone;
Jacob's spring is secure
in a land of grain and new wine,
where the heavens drop dew.
²⁹Blessed are you, O Israel!
Who is like you,
a people saved by the LORD?
He is your shield and helper
and your glorious sword.
Your enemies will cower before you,
and you will trample down their high places. ^a"

---

^a29 Or will tread upon their bodies

The Death of Moses

34 Then Moses climbed Mount Nebo from the plains of Moab to the top of Pisgah, across from Jericho. There the LORD showed him the whole land—from Gilead to Dan, ²all of Naphtali, the territory of Ephraim and Manasseh, all the land of Judah as far as the western sea,ᵃ ³the Negev and the whole region from the Valley of Jericho, the City of Palms, as far as Zoar. ⁴Then the LORD said to him, "This is the land I promised on oath to Abraham, Isaac and Jacob when I said, 'I will give it to your descendants.' I have let you see it with your eyes, but you will not cross over into it."

⁵And Moses the servant of the LORD died there in Moab, as the LORD had said. ⁶He buried himᵇ in Moab, in the valley opposite Beth Peor, but to this day no one knows where his grave is. ⁷Moses was a hundred and twenty years old when he died, yet his eyes were not weak nor his strength gone. ⁸The Israelites grieved for Moses in the plains of Moab thirty days, until the time of weeping and mourning was over.

⁹Now Joshua son of Nun was filled with the spiritᶜ of wisdom because Moses had laid his hands on him. So the Israelites listened to him and did what the LORD had commanded Moses.

🖥 ▓▓▓▓▓▓ DISCOVERING GOD ▓▓▓▓▓▓ 🔀

34:10–12
Life with God

This last chapter of Deuteronomy was probably written by Joshua, Moses' successor. He used several key phrases to sum up Moses' life's work: "miraculous signs," "mighty power" and "awesome deeds."

All those phrases make for an impressive tombstone inscription. But notice the most important phrase of all, the one that tops the list of accomplishments. Joshua said of Moses, "the LORD knew [him] face to face."

When all is said and done, the most significant human experience is to live in a relationship with the God who created us. To know God and enjoy him forever is the reason we were created. To a large extent, we can have what Moses had if we will seek it with all our hearts.

---

¹⁰Since then, no prophet has risen in Israel like Moses, whom the LORD knew face to face, ¹¹who did all those miraculous signs and wonders the LORD sent him to do in Egypt—to Pharaoh and to all his officials and to his whole land. ¹²For no one has ever shown the mighty power or performed the awesome deeds that Moses did in the sight of all Israel.

ᵃ2 That is, the Mediterranean   ᵇ6 Or *He was buried*   ᶜ9 Or *Spirit*

=== EPILOGUE ===

As a seeker, no more important goal exists for you than to be able to say, "I have found what I was looking for."

You were made to know God. Your sin, like everybody else's, is the main barrier between you and God. But God has graciously offered to take it away and to give you a new start.

Through this book—the second in the "Five Alive" series that summarizes the whole Bible's message—pictures of a great God, a great leader (Moses), and a great nation (Israel) come into focus. God didn't set this nation aside simply because he wanted to encourage a small earthly population to be totally devoted to him. God chose this nation as his instrument—the people who would eventually reach out to the world and invite them to know God.

In time one particular Israelite would embody everything God wanted to say to the world. You can read about this ultimate manifestation of God in the second part of the Bible, called the New Testament. Some 1,400 years after Moses, Jesus of Nazareth showed the world what God was like. He followed every one of God's commandments perfectly. He did miraculous deeds, as Moses had. And then he did what no one else had done: After his execution he rose from the dead, never to die again.

To read an account of Jesus' life and teachings, turn to the book called "The Gospel of John" (page 1382). There you'll meet the most famous person in all of history. Jesus' influence has changed the lives of millions of individuals over the centuries. He is still alive today, and he invites you to know him and to experience the new life he offers.

JOSHUA

Introduction

THE BOTTOM LINE

The book of Joshua shows God's power on earth at a pivotal point in history. Here we find a nomadic people with a new, untested leader moving into hostile territory. Yet, despite all of their disadvantages, the Israelites have a secret weapon: the God of the universe is on their side. As you read these stories, note how God's power—not human effort—allows the people to inhabit the land. God can help you "conquer" the hostile territory you experience every day.

CENTRAL IDEAS

- God's purposes are worked out by the cooperation of human and supernatural means.
- The Israelites developed great trust in God as they faced overwhelming odds.
- God gave Israel a second chance to conquer the promised land; this time, they succeeded.
- At certain times, God intervenes to limit society's evil (in this case, the wicked Canaanites' practices).

OUTLINE

1. Israel enters the promised land (1:1–5:12)
2. The conquest of the land (5:13–12:24)
3. Distribution of the land (chs. 13–21)
4. Epilogue—tribal unity; loyalty to the Lord (chs. 22–24)

TITLE

This book is named after Joshua, who was Israel's military and spiritual leader as the people moved in and conquered their new homeland.

AUTHOR AND READERS

The author is not mentioned; Joshua himself may or may not have been the writer here.

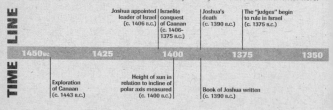

TIME LINE

	Joshua appointed leader of Israel (c. 1406 B.C.)	Israelite conquest of Canaan (c. 1406–1375 B.C.)	Joshua's death (c. 1390 B.C.)	The "judges" begin to rule in Israel (c. 1375 B.C.)
1450 B.C.	**1425**	**1400**	**1375**	**1350**
	Exploration of Canaan (c. 1443 B.C.)	Height of sun in relation to incline of polar axis measured (c. 1400 B.C.)	Book of Joshua written (c. 1390 B.C.)	

On May 9, 1841, the first wagon train to California departed from Missouri. Sixty-eight people left behind the life they knew to begin the life they longed for. They elected John Bartleson as their captain for the simple reason that he was the only one with a map. His "map" was a crude drawing with some scribbled instructions from a Dr. Marsh who lived in California. This simple document was their only guide for crossing half a continent.

Shortly after they had begun their journey, they joined up with a party of missionaries. These intrepid folks were led by a mountain man, Thomas "Broken Hand" Fitzpatrick, who knew the route west as far as what would later be known as Soda Springs, Idaho.

This simple document was their only guide for crossing half a continent.

After encountering massive herds of buffalo, a near-catastrophic twister-like waterspout, and numerous other dangers, they reached Soda Springs. At that point less than half of the people were willing to continue the journey.

The remaining group members set out again for California; the only advice they had been given was not to venture south into the desert or north into steep canyons. As the wagon train pushed westward, the trail became increasingly difficult. Unable to carry sufficient food, they traded with the natives for berries and a sweet, honey-like confection—until they realized that its main ingredient was mashed insects. In the toughest part of the journey, the pioneers virtually clawed their way across the Sierras. Before they reached the other side, their remaining horses had been stolen. They were forced to travel by foot and live off the land eating crows, wildcats, and whatever else they could find.

On November 4, 1841, the surviving pioneers unexpectedly stumbled into a valley abundantly filled with wild grapes, deer, and antelope. Even more astonishing than their sudden good fortune was the fact that at the end of the valley lay the farm of Dr. Marsh—the very man whose letter they had carried from Missouri. Thirty-one men and one woman had finished the trek in the strength of their admirable determination.*

Long before the American West was settled, the people of Israel dreamed of a homeland—the one God had promised their forefather Abraham. After waiting some 400 years as slaves in Egypt (almost twice the length of time the United States has been a nation!) these fledgling pioneers were led out of Egypt, through the wilderness, and to the boundary of their new home. Their newly appointed leader, Joshua, prepared to lead the charge.

Conquering that land would require moral strength and courage as well as military victories. The book of Joshua tells the story of how the Israelites came into their land, divided it among the twelve tribes, and established a foothold for a new nation. It wasn't paradise any more than the American frontier was paradise. But with God as their ultimate leader, this nation began to fulfill its divine role as a spiritual light to the surrounding nations.

Even though you're not trying to start a new country, you probably face challenges that test the limits of your endurance and leadership abilities. Joshua's legacy and the struggles of the nation he led contain many practical lessons you can use today. And behind all of Joshua's successes there lay a central focus, a foundation upon which everything else was built. Turn to Joshua chapter 1, verses 6–9 (page 262), to learn where you too can find that foundation for a lifetime of meaningful accomplishments.

* *Strange Stories, Amazing Facts of America's Past*, Jim Dwyer, ed. (Pleasantville, N.Y.: The Reader's Digest Association, 1989), p. 284.

JOSHUA

The LORD Commands Joshua

1 After the death of Moses the servant of the LORD, the LORD said to Joshua son of Nun, Moses' aide: ²"Moses my servant is dead. Now then, you and all these people, get ready to cross the Jordan River into the land I am about to give to them—to the Israelites. ³I will give you every place where you set your foot, as I promised Moses. ⁴Your territory will extend from the desert to Lebanon, and from the great river, the Euphrates—all the Hittite country—to the Great Sea*a* on the west. ⁵No one will be able to stand up against you all the days of your life. As I was with Moses, so I will be with you; I will never leave you nor forsake you.

⁶"Be strong and courageous, because you will lead these people to inherit the land I swore to their forefathers to give them. ⁷Be strong and very courageous. Be careful to obey all the law my servant Moses gave you; do not turn from it to the right or to the left, that you may be successful wherever you go. ⁸Do not let this Book of the Law depart from your mouth; meditate on it day and night, so that you may be careful to do everything written in it. Then you will be prosperous and successful. ⁹Have I not commanded you?

a 4 That is, the Mediterranean

▓▓▓▓ KNOWING YOURSELF ▓▓▓▓

1:1–9
Character

If you've ever faced a seemingly impossible task, then you'll be able to identify with Joshua. God appointed him to lead the wandering tribes of ancient Israel into a new homeland. Not only would Joshua have to contend with tough military powers secured within walled cities, but also with his own people comparing him to his great predecessor, Moses.

Three times God told Joshua to "be strong and courageous." But God did more than give him a pep talk. He gave Joshua specific guidance that was designed to ensure Joshua's success.

First, God promised to support Joshua in his new responsibilities (verses 5, 9). Second, he encouraged him to remember that he was a promise-keeping God. Joshua's forefathers had received God's promise of a new homeland centuries before, and God wasn't about to go back on his word (verses 3–6). These words assured Joshua that military victory didn't depend on human courage or strength, but on God's faithfulness. Third, God told Joshua to constantly mull over the words Moses had written in the first five books of the Bible (verses 7–8). For Joshua, these books held the key to God's wisdom, comfort, and encouragement, just as they had for Moses.

Sneak a peak at the end of this book, and you'll see what happened as a result of Joshua rigorously living out these principles. In chapter 23, verse 14 (page 288), Joshua pointed out how God had been faithful to him and to Israel. Then he recommitted himself to the Lord—even if no one else around him chose to follow (chapter 24, verse 15 [page 289]). By the time Joshua died (chapter 24, verses 29–31 [page 290]), his courageous leadership had shaped a rag-tag band of former slaves into a nation that was to become a major political and spiritual power in that part of the world for centuries. Not a bad legacy!

Joshua's source of courage is also available to you. Keep reading this book, and you'll be able to get a better picture of how Joshua's God made him into a dynamic leader. And remember, God has not changed over the centuries—the promises that he made to Joshua still apply today.

Be strong and courageous. Do not be terrified; do not be discouraged, for the LORD your God will be with you wherever you go."

10So Joshua ordered the officers of the people: 11"Go through the camp and tell the people, 'Get your supplies ready. Three days from now you will cross the Jordan here to go in and take possession of the land the LORD your God is giving you for your own.'"

12But to the Reubenites, the Gadites and the half-tribe of Manasseh, Joshua said, 13"Remember the command that Moses the servant of the LORD gave you: 'The LORD your God is giving you rest and has granted you this land.' 14Your wives, your children and your livestock may stay in the land that Moses gave you east of the Jordan, but all your fighting men, fully armed, must cross over ahead of your brothers. You are to help your brothers 15until the LORD gives them rest, as he has done for you, and until they too have taken possession of the land that the LORD your God is giving them. After that, you may go back and occupy your own land, which Moses the servant of the LORD gave you east of the Jordan toward the sunrise."

16Then they answered Joshua, "Whatever you have commanded us we will do, and wherever you send us we will go. 17Just as we fully obeyed Moses, so we will obey you. Only may the LORD your God be with you as he was with Moses. 18Whoever rebels against your word and does not obey your words, whatever you may command them, will be put to death. Only be strong and courageous!"

Rahab and the Spies

2 Then Joshua son of Nun secretly sent two spies from Shittim. "Go, look over the land," he said, "especially Jericho." So they went and entered the house of a prostitute*a* named Rahab and stayed there.

2The king of Jericho was told, "Look! Some of the Israelites have come here tonight to spy out the land." 3So the king of Jericho sent this message to Rahab: "Bring out the men who came to you and entered your house, because they have come to spy out the whole land."

4But the woman had taken the two men and hidden them. She said, "Yes, the men came to me, but I did not know where they had come from. 5At dusk, when it was time to close the city gate, the men left. I don't know which way they went. Go after them quickly. You may catch up with them." 6(But she had taken them up to the roof and hidden them under the stalks of flax she had laid out on the roof.) 7So the men set out in pursuit of the spies on the road that leads to the fords of the Jordan, and as soon as the pursuers had gone out, the gate was shut.

8Before the spies lay down for the night, she went up on the roof 9and said to them, "I know that the LORD has given this land to you and that a great fear of you has fallen on us, so that all who live in this country are melting in fear because of you. 10We have heard how the LORD dried up the water of the Red Sea*b* for you when you came out of Egypt, and what you did to Sihon and Og, the two kings of the Amorites east of the Jordan, whom you completely destroyed.*c* 11When we heard of it, our hearts melted and everyone's courage failed because of you, for the LORD your God is God in heaven above and on the earth below. 12Now then, please swear to me by the LORD that you will show kindness to my family, because I have shown kindness to you. Give me a sure sign 13that you will spare the lives of my father and mother, my brothers and sisters, and all who belong to them, and that you will save us from death."

14"Our lives for your lives!" the men assured her. "If you don't tell what we are doing, we will treat you kindly and faithfully when the LORD gives us the land."

15So she let them down by a rope through the window, for the house she lived in was part of the city wall. 16Now she had said to them, "Go to the hills so the pursuers will not find you. Hide yourselves there three days until they return, and then go on your way."

---

a 1 Or possibly *an innkeeper*   *b 10* Hebrew *Yam Suph;* that is, Sea of Reeds   *c 10* The Hebrew term refers to the irrevocable giving over of things or persons to the LORD, often by totally destroying them.

¹⁷The men said to her, "This oath you made us swear will not be binding on us ¹⁸unless, when we enter the land, you have tied this scarlet cord in the window through which you let us down, and unless you have brought your father and mother, your brothers and all your family into your house. ¹⁹If anyone goes outside your house into the street, his blood will be on his own head; we will not be responsible. As for anyone who is in the house with you, his blood will be on our head if a hand is laid on him. ²⁰But if you tell what we are doing, we will be released from the oath you made us swear."

²¹"Agreed," she replied. "Let it be as you say." So she sent them away and they departed. And she tied the scarlet cord in the window.

²²When they left, they went into the hills and stayed there three days, until the pursuers had searched all along the road and returned without finding them. ²³Then the two men started back. They went down out of the hills, forded the river and came to Joshua son of Nun and told him everything that had happened to them. ²⁴They said to Joshua, "The LORD has surely given the whole land into our hands; all the people are melting in fear because of us."

Crossing the Jordan

3 Early in the morning Joshua and all the Israelites set out from Shittim and went to the Jordan, where they camped before crossing over. ²After three days the officers went throughout the camp, ³giving orders to the people: "When you see the ark of the covenant of the LORD your God, and the priests, who are Levites, carrying it, you are to move out from your positions and follow it. ⁴Then you will know which way to go, since you have never been this way before. But keep a distance of about a thousand yards*ᵃ* between you and the ark; do not go near it."

ᵃ 4 Hebrew *about two thousand cubits* (about 900 meters)

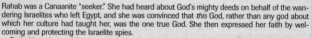

▣	**DISCOVERING GOD** ⬌

2:8–13
Life with God

Rahab was a Canaanite "seeker." She had heard about God's mighty deeds on behalf of the wandering Israelites who left Egypt, and she was convinced that *this* God, rather than any god about which her culture had taught her, was the one true God. She then expressed her faith by welcoming and protecting the Israelite spies.

Both this action and the request she made of these men showed the depth of her commitment. She literally put her life—and the lives of her family members—on the line by throwing in her lot with the Israelites. And the soldiers honored that commitment. When they raided the city, they were careful to save Rahab's life.

You may not have to risk your life to show your faith in God. You will, however, have to do as Rahab did and turn your ultimate loyalty to the God of the Bible. As the first of God's Ten Commandments says, "You shall have no other gods before me" (Exodus chapter 20, verse 3 [page 96]). If, for example, you've devoted your life solely to your career at the cost of all other considerations, then your career is the "god" that needs to take a lower priority in your life.

Crossing the line of faith will also mean trusting God with your spiritual life. Like every sincere seeker, you will probably at some point recognize that if God doesn't come through on his promises, you will be lost. But if he does come through, you will have a relationship with him that cannot be broken even by death. That risk is definitely worth taking, because God always keeps his promises (see chapter 23, verse 14 [page 288]).

Rahab took that step of trust and was not only spared, but also had a significant place in redemptive history—she eventually married an Israelite and became a direct ancestor of Jesus Christ (see Matthew chapter 1, verse 5 [page 1258]). If you decide to take this step, you too will have a place in God's unfolding drama. And while your name will not necessarily be recorded in world history books, it'll be written forever in heaven (see Revelation chapter 3, verse 5 [page 1637]).

⁵Joshua told the people, "Consecrate yourselves, for tomorrow the LORD will do amazing things among you."

⁶Joshua said to the priests, "Take up the ark of the covenant and pass on ahead of the people." So they took it up and went ahead of them.

⁷And the LORD said to Joshua, "Today I will begin to exalt you in the eyes of all Israel, so they may know that I am with you as I was with Moses. ⁸Tell the priests who carry the ark of the covenant: 'When you reach the edge of the Jordan's waters, go and stand in the river.'"

⁹Joshua said to the Israelites, "Come here and listen to the words of the LORD your God. ¹⁰This is how you will know that the living God is among you and that he will certainly drive out before you the Canaanites, Hittites, Hivites, Perizzites, Girgashites, Amorites and Jebusites. ¹¹See, the ark of the covenant of the Lord of all the earth will go into the Jordan ahead of you. ¹²Now then, choose twelve men from the tribes of Israel, one from each tribe. ¹³And as soon as the priests who carry the ark of the LORD—the Lord of all the earth—set foot in the Jordan, its waters flowing downstream will be cut off and stand up in a heap."

¹⁴So when the people broke camp to cross the Jordan, the priests carrying the ark of the covenant went ahead of them. ¹⁵Now the Jordan is at flood stage all during harvest. Yet as soon as the priests who carried the ark reached the Jordan and their feet touched the water's edge, ¹⁶the water from upstream stopped flowing. It piled up in a heap a great distance away, at a town called Adam in the vicinity of Zarethan, while the water flowing down to the Sea of the Arabah (the Salt Sea ᵍ) was completely cut off. So the people crossed over opposite Jericho. ¹⁷The priests who carried the ark of the covenant of the LORD stood firm on dry ground in the middle of the Jordan, while all Israel passed by until the whole nation had completed the crossing on dry ground.

4 When the whole nation had finished crossing the Jordan, the LORD said to Joshua, ²"Choose twelve men from among the people, one from each tribe, ³and tell them to take up twelve stones from the middle of the Jordan from right where the priests stood and to carry them over with you and put them down at the place where you stay tonight."

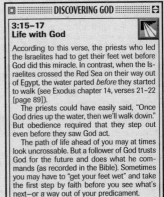

DISCOVERING GOD

3:15–17
Life with God

According to this verse, the priests who led the Israelites had to get their feet wet before God did this miracle. In contrast, when the Israelites crossed the Red Sea on their way out of Egypt, the water parted *before* they started to walk (see Exodus chapter 14, verses 21–22 [page 89]).

The priests could have easily said, "Once God dries up the water, then we'll walk down." But obedience required that they step out even before they saw God act.

The path of life ahead of you may at times look uncrossable. But a follower of God trusts God for the future and does what he commands (as recorded in the Bible). Sometimes you may have to "get your feet wet" and take the first step by faith before you see what's next—or a way out of your predicament.

⁴So Joshua called together the twelve men he had appointed from the Israelites, one from each tribe, ⁵and said to them, "Go over before the ark of the LORD your God into the middle of the Jordan. Each of you is to take up a stone on his shoulder, according to the number of the tribes of the Israelites, ⁶to serve as a sign among you. In the future, when your children ask you, 'What do these stones mean?' ⁷tell them that the flow of the Jordan was cut off before the ark of the covenant of the LORD. When it crossed the Jordan, the waters of the Jordan were cut off. These stones are to be a memorial to the people of Israel forever."

⁸So the Israelites did as Joshua commanded them. They took twelve stones from the middle of the Jordan, according to the number of the tribes of the Israelites, as the LORD

ᵃ16 That is, the Dead Sea

had told Joshua; and they carried them over with them to their camp, where they put them down. ⁹Joshua set up the twelve stones that had been[a] in the middle of the Jordan at the spot where the priests who carried the ark of the covenant had stood. And they are there to this day.

¹⁰Now the priests who carried the ark remained standing in the middle of the Jordan until everything the Lord had commanded Joshua was done by the people, just as Moses had directed Joshua. The people hurried over, ¹¹and as soon as all of them had crossed, the ark of the Lord and the priests came to the other side while the people watched. ¹²The men of Reuben, Gad and the half-tribe of Manasseh crossed over, armed, in front of the Israelites, as Moses had directed them. ¹³About forty thousand armed for battle crossed over before the Lord to the plains of Jericho for war.

¹⁴That day the Lord exalted Joshua in the sight of all Israel; and they revered him all the days of his life, just as they had revered Moses.

¹⁵Then the Lord said to Joshua, ¹⁶"Command the priests carrying the ark of the Testimony to come up out of the Jordan."

¹⁷So Joshua commanded the priests, "Come up out of the Jordan."

¹⁸And the priests came up out of the river carrying the ark of the covenant of the Lord. No sooner had they set their feet on the dry ground than the waters of the Jordan returned to their place and ran at flood stage as before.

¹⁹On the tenth day of the first month the people went up from the Jordan and camped at Gilgal on the eastern border of Jericho. ²⁰And Joshua set up at Gilgal the twelve stones they had taken out of the Jordan. ²¹He said to the Israelites, "In the future when your descendants ask their fathers, 'What do these stones mean?' ²²tell them, 'Israel crossed the Jordan on dry ground.' ²³For the Lord your God dried up the Jordan before you until you had crossed over. The Lord your God did to the Jordan just what he had done to the Red Sea[b] when he dried it up before us until we had crossed over. ²⁴He did this so that all the peoples of the earth might know that the hand of the Lord is powerful and so that you might always fear the Lord your God."

Circumcision at Gilgal

5 Now when all the Amorite kings west of the Jordan and all the Canaanite kings along the coast heard how the Lord had dried up the Jordan before the Israelites until we had crossed over, their hearts melted and they no longer had the courage to face the Israelites.

²At that time the Lord said to Joshua, "Make flint knives and circumcise the Israelites again." ³So Joshua made flint knives and circumcised the Israelites at Gibeath Haaraloth.[c]

⁴Now this is why he did so: All those who came out of Egypt—all the men of military age—died in the desert on the way after leaving Egypt. ⁵All the people that came out had been circumcised, but all the people born in the desert during the journey from Egypt had not. ⁶The Israelites had moved about in the desert forty years until all the men who were of military age when they left Egypt had died, since they had not obeyed the Lord. For the Lord had sworn to them that they would not see the land that he had solemnly promised their fathers to give us, a land flowing with milk and honey. ⁷So he raised up their sons in their place, and these were the ones Joshua circumcised. They were still uncircumcised because they had not been circumcised on the way. ⁸And after the whole nation had been circumcised, they remained where they were in camp until they were healed.

⁹Then the Lord said to Joshua, "Today I have rolled away the reproach of Egypt from you." So the place has been called Gilgal[d] to this day.

¹⁰On the evening of the fourteenth day of the month, while camped at Gilgal on the plains of Jericho, the Israelites celebrated the Passover. ¹¹The day after the Passover, that

---

a 9 Or *Joshua also set up twelve stones*   b 23 Hebrew *Yam Suph*; that is, Sea of Reeds   c 3 *Gibeath Haaraloth* means *hill of foreskins.*   d 9 *Gilgal* sounds like the Hebrew for *roll.*

very day, they ate some of the produce of the land: unleavened bread and roasted grain. ¹²The manna stopped the day after*a* they ate this food from the land; there was no longer any manna for the Israelites, but that year they ate of the produce of Canaan.

The Fall of Jericho

¹³Now when Joshua was near Jericho, he looked up and saw a man standing in front of him with a drawn sword in his hand. Joshua went up to him and asked, "Are you for us or for our enemies?"

¹⁴"Neither," he replied, "but as commander of the army of the LORD I have now come." Then Joshua fell facedown to the ground in reverence, and asked him, "What message does my Lord*b* have for his servant?"

¹⁵The commander of the LORD's army replied, "Take off your sandals, for the place where you are standing is holy." And Joshua did so.

6 Now Jericho was tightly shut up because of the Israelites. No one went out and no one came in.

²Then the LORD said to Joshua, "See, I have delivered Jericho into your hands, along with its king and its fighting men. ³March around the city once with all the armed men. Do this for six days. ⁴Have seven priests carry trumpets of rams' horns in front of the ark. On the seventh day, march around the city seven times, with the priests blowing the trumpets. ⁵When you hear them sound a long blast on the trumpets, have all the people give a loud shout; then the wall of the city will collapse and the people will go up, every man straight in."

⁶So Joshua son of Nun called the priests and said to them, "Take up the ark of the covenant of the LORD and have seven priests carry trumpets in front of it." ⁷And he ordered the people, "Advance! March around the city, with the armed guard going ahead of the ark of the LORD."

⁸When Joshua had spoken to the people, the seven priests carrying the seven trumpets before the LORD went forward, blowing their trumpets, and the ark of the LORD's covenant followed them. ⁹The armed guard marched ahead of the priests who blew the trumpets, and the rear guard followed the ark. All this time the trumpets were sounding. ¹⁰But Joshua had commanded the people, "Do not give a war cry, do not raise your voices, do not say a word until the day I tell you to shout. Then shout!" ¹¹So he had the ark of the LORD carried around the city, circling it once. Then the people returned to camp and spent the night there.

¹²Joshua got up early the next morning and the priests took up the ark of the LORD. ¹³The seven priests carrying the seven trumpets went forward, marching before the ark of the LORD and blowing the trumpets. The armed men went ahead of them and the rear guard followed the ark of the LORD, while the trumpets kept sounding. ¹⁴So on the second day they marched around the city once and returned to the camp. They did this for six days.

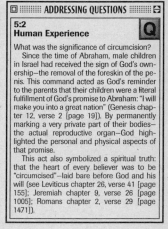

ADDRESSING QUESTIONS

5:2
Human Experience

Q

What was the significance of circumcision?

Since the time of Abraham, male children in Israel had received the sign of God's ownership—the removal of the foreskin of the penis. This command acted as God's reminder to the parents that their children were a literal fulfillment of God's promise to Abraham: "I will make you into a great nation" (Genesis chapter 12, verse 2 [page 19]). By permanently marking a very private part of their bodies—the actual reproductive organ—God highlighted the personal and physical aspects of that promise.

This act also symbolized a spiritual truth: that the heart of every believer was to be "circumcised"—laid bare before God and his will (see Leviticus chapter 26, verse 41 [page 155]; Jeremiah chapter 9, verse 26 [page 1005]; Romans chapter 2, verse 29 [page 1471]).

a12 Or the day   b14 Or lord

¹⁵On the seventh day, they got up at daybreak and marched around the city seven times in the same manner, except that on that day they circled the city seven times. ¹⁶The seventh time around, when the priests sounded the trumpet blast, Joshua commanded the people, "Shout! For the LORD has given you the city! ¹⁷The city and all that is in it are to be devoted^a to the LORD. Only Rahab the prostitute^b and all who are with her in her house shall be spared, because she hid the spies we sent. ¹⁸But keep away from the devoted things, so that you will not bring about your own destruction by taking any of them. Otherwise you will make the camp of Israel liable to destruction and bring trouble on it. ¹⁹All the silver and gold and the articles of bronze and iron are sacred to the LORD and must go into his treasury."

²⁰When the trumpets sounded, the people shouted, and at the sound of the trumpet, when the people gave a loud shout, the wall collapsed; so every man charged straight in, and they took the city. ²¹They devoted the city to the LORD and destroyed with the sword every living thing in it—men and women, young and old, cattle, sheep and donkeys.

²²Joshua said to the two men who had spied out the land, "Go into the prostitute's house and bring her out and all who belong to her, in accordance with your oath to her." ²³So the young men who had done the spying went in and brought out Rahab, her father and mother and brothers and all who belonged to her. They brought out her entire family and put them in a place outside the camp of Israel.

²⁴Then they burned the whole city and everything in it, but they put the silver and gold and the articles of bronze and iron into the treasury of the LORD's house. ²⁵But Joshua spared Rahab the prostitute, with her family and all who belonged to her, because she hid the men Joshua had sent as spies to Jericho—and she lives among the Israelites to this day.

²⁶At that time Joshua pronounced this solemn oath: "Cursed before the LORD is the man who undertakes to rebuild this city, Jericho:

"At the cost of his firstborn son
    will he lay its foundations;
at the cost of his youngest
    will he set up its gates."

²⁷So the LORD was with Joshua, and his fame spread throughout the land.

Achan's Sin

7 But the Israelites acted unfaithfully in regard to the devoted things^c; Achan son of Carmi, the son of Zimri,^d the son of Zerah, of the tribe of Judah, took some of them. So the LORD's anger burned against Israel.

²Now Joshua sent men from Jericho to Ai, which is near Beth Aven to the east of Bethel, and told them, "Go up and spy out the region." So the men went up and spied out Ai.

³When they returned to Joshua, they said, "Not all the people will have to go up against Ai. Send two or three thousand men to take it and do not weary all the people, for only a few men are there." ⁴So about three thousand men went up; but they were routed by the men of Ai, ⁵who killed about thirty-six of them. They chased the Israelites

^a17 The Hebrew term refers to the irrevocable giving over of things or persons to the LORD, often by totally destroying them; also in verses 18 and 21.   ^b17 Or possibly *innkeeper*; also in verses 22 and 25   ^c1 The Hebrew term refers to the irrevocable giving over of things or persons to the LORD, often by totally destroying them; also in verses 11, 12, 13 and 15.
^d1 See Septuagint and 1 Chron. 2:6; Hebrew *Zabdi*; also in verses 17 and 18.

from the city gate as far as the stone quarries*a* and struck them down on the slopes. At this the hearts of the people melted and became like water.

⁶Then Joshua tore his clothes and fell facedown to the ground before the ark of the LORD, remaining there till evening. The elders of Israel did the same, and sprinkled dust on their heads. ⁷And Joshua said, "Ah, Sovereign LORD, why did you ever bring this people across the Jordan to deliver us into the hands of the Amorites to destroy us? If only we had been content to stay on the other side of the Jordan! ⁸O Lord, what can I say, now that Israel has been routed by its enemies? ⁹The Canaanites and the other people of the country will hear about this and they will surround us and wipe out our name from the earth. What then will you do for your own great name?"

¹⁰The LORD said to Joshua, "Stand up! What are you doing down on your face? ¹¹Israel has sinned; they have violated my covenant, which I commanded them to keep. They have taken some of the devoted things; they have stolen, they have lied, they have put them with their own possessions. ¹²That is why the Israelites cannot stand against their enemies; they turn their backs and run because they have been made liable to destruction. I will not be with you anymore unless you destroy whatever among you is devoted to destruction.

¹³"Go, consecrate the people. Tell them, 'Consecrate yourselves in preparation for tomorrow; for this is what the LORD, the God of Israel, says: That which is devoted is among you, O Israel. You cannot stand against your enemies until you remove it.

¹⁴" 'In the morning, present yourselves tribe by tribe. The tribe that the LORD takes shall come forward clan by clan; the clan that the LORD takes shall come forward family by family; and the family that the LORD takes shall come forward man by man. ¹⁵He who is caught with the devoted things shall be destroyed by fire, along with all that belongs to him. He has violated the covenant of the LORD and has done a disgraceful thing in Israel!' "

¹⁶Early the next morning Joshua had Israel come forward by tribes, and Judah was taken. ¹⁷The clans of Judah came forward, and he took the Zerahites. He had the clan of the Zerahites come forward by families, and Zimri was taken. ¹⁸Joshua had his family come forward man by man, and Achan son of Carmi, the son of Zimri, the son of Zerah, of the tribe of Judah, was taken.

¹⁹Then Joshua said to Achan, "My son, give glory to the LORD,*b* the God of Israel, and give him the praise.*c* Tell me what you have done; do not hide it from me."

²⁰Achan replied, "It is true! I have sinned against the LORD, the God of Israel. This is what I have done: ²¹When I saw in the plunder a beautiful robe from Babylonia,*d* two hundred shekels*e* of silver and a wedge of gold weighing fifty shekels,*f* I coveted them and took them. They are hidden in the ground inside my tent, with the silver underneath."

²²So Joshua sent messengers, and they ran to the tent, and there it was, hidden in his tent, with the silver underneath. ²³They took the things from the tent, brought them to Joshua and all the Israelites and spread them out before the LORD.

²⁴Then Joshua, together with all Israel, took Achan son of Zerah, the silver, the robe, the gold wedge, his sons and daughters, his cattle, donkeys and sheep, his tent and all that he had, to the Valley of Achor. ²⁵Joshua said, "Why have you brought this trouble on us? The LORD will bring trouble on you today."

Then all Israel stoned him, and after they had stoned the rest, they burned them. ²⁶Over Achan they heaped up a large pile of rocks, which remains to this day. Then the LORD turned from his fierce anger. Therefore that place has been called the Valley of Achor*g* ever since.

---

a5 Or as far as Shebarim   *b19* A solemn charge to tell the truth   *c19* Or and confess to him   *d21* Hebrew Shinar
e21 That is, about 5 pounds (about 2.3 kilograms)   *f21* That is, about 1 1/4 pounds (about 0.6 kilogram)
g26 Achor means trouble.

Ai Destroyed

8 Then the LORD said to Joshua, "Do not be afraid; do not be discouraged. Take the whole army with you, and go up and attack Ai. For I have delivered into your hands the king of Ai, his people, his city and his land. ²You shall do to Ai and its king as you did to Jericho and its king, except that you may carry off their plunder and livestock for yourselves. Set an ambush behind the city."

³So Joshua and the whole army moved out to attack Ai. He chose thirty thousand of his best fighting men and sent them out at night ⁴with these orders: "Listen carefully. You are to set an ambush behind the city. Don't go very far from it. All of you be on the alert. ⁵I and all those with me will advance on the city, and when the men come out against us, as they did before, we will flee from them. ⁶They will pursue us until we have lured them away from the city, for they will say, 'They are running away from us as they did before.' So when we flee from them, ⁷you are to rise up from ambush and take the city. The LORD your God will give it into your hand. ⁸When you have taken the city, set it on fire. Do what the LORD has commanded. See to it; you have my orders."

⁹Then Joshua sent them off, and they went to the place of ambush and lay in wait between Bethel and Ai, to the west of Ai—but Joshua spent that night with the people.

¹⁰Early the next morning Joshua mustered his men, and he and the leaders of Israel marched before them to Ai. ¹¹The entire force that was with him marched up and approached the city and arrived in front of it. They set up camp north of Ai, with the valley between them and the city. ¹²Joshua had taken about five thousand men and set them in ambush between Bethel and Ai, to the west of the city. ¹³They had the soldiers take up their positions—all those in the camp to the north of the city and the ambush to the west of it. That night Joshua went into the valley.

¹⁴When the king of Ai saw this, he and all the men of the city hurried out early in the morning to meet Israel in battle at a certain place overlooking the Arabah. But he did not know that an ambush had been set against him behind the city. ¹⁵Joshua and all Israel let themselves be driven back before them, and they fled toward the desert. ¹⁶All the men of Ai were called to pursue them, and they pursued Joshua and were lured away from the city. ¹⁷Not a man remained in Ai or Bethel who did not go after Israel. They left the city open and went in pursuit of Israel.

¹⁸Then the LORD said to Joshua, "Hold out toward Ai the javelin that is in your hand, for into your hand I will deliver the city." So Joshua held out his javelin toward Ai. ¹⁹As soon as he did this, the men in the ambush rose quickly from their position and rushed forward. They entered the city and captured it and quickly set it on fire.

²⁰The men of Ai looked back and saw the smoke of the city rising against the sky, but they had no chance to escape in any direction, for the Israelites who had been fleeing toward the desert had turned back against their pursuers. ²¹For when Joshua and all Israel saw that the ambush had taken the city and that smoke was going up from the city, they turned around and attacked the men of Ai. ²²The men of the ambush also came out of the city against them, so that they were caught in the middle, with Israelites on both sides. Israel cut them down, leaving them neither survivors nor fugitives. ²³But they took the king of Ai alive and brought him to Joshua.

²⁴When Israel had finished killing all the men of Ai in the fields and in the desert where they had chased them, and when every one of them had been put to the sword, all the Israelites returned to Ai and killed those who were in it. ²⁵Twelve thousand men and women fell that day—all the people of Ai. ²⁶For Joshua did not draw back the hand that held out his javelin until he had destroyed[a] all who lived in Ai. ²⁷But Israel did carry off for themselves the livestock and plunder of this city, as the LORD had instructed Joshua.

²⁸So Joshua burned Ai and made it a permanent heap of ruins, a desolate place to this day. ²⁹He hung the king of Ai on a tree and left him there until evening. At sunset, Joshua

---

a26 The Hebrew term refers to the irrevocable giving over of things or persons to the LORD, often by totally destroying them.

ordered them to take his body from the tree and throw it down at the entrance of the city gate. And they raised a large pile of rocks over it, which remains to this day.

The Covenant Renewed at Mount Ebal

30Then Joshua built on Mount Ebal an altar to the LORD, the God of Israel, 31as Moses the servant of the LORD had commanded the Israelites. He built it according to what is written in the Book of the Law of Moses—an altar of uncut stones, on which no iron tool had been used. On it they offered to the LORD burnt offerings and sacrificed fellowship offerings.[a] 32There, in the presence of the Israelites, Joshua copied on stones the law of Moses, which he had written. 33All Israel, aliens and citizens alike, with their elders, officials and judges, were standing on both sides of the ark of the covenant of the LORD, facing those who carried it—the priests, who were Levites. Half of the people stood in front of Mount Gerizim and half of them in front of Mount Ebal, as Moses the servant of the LORD had formerly commanded when he gave instructions to bless the people of Israel.

34Afterward, Joshua read all the words of the law—the blessings and the curses—just as it is written in the Book of the Law. 35There was not a word of all that Moses had commanded that Joshua did not read to the whole assembly of Israel, including the women and children, and the aliens who lived among them.

The Gibeonite Deception

9 Now when all the kings west of the Jordan heard about these things—those in the hill country, in the western foothills, and along the entire coast of the Great Sea[b] as far as Lebanon (the kings of the Hittites, Amorites, Canaanites, Perizzites, Hivites and Jebusites)— 2they came together to make war against Joshua and Israel.

3However, when the people of Gibeon heard what Joshua had done to Jericho and Ai, 4they resorted to a ruse: They went as a delegation whose donkeys were loaded[c] with worn-out sacks and old wineskins, cracked and mended. 5The men put worn and patched sandals on their feet and wore old clothes. All the bread of their food supply was dry and moldy. 6Then they went to Joshua in the camp at Gilgal and said to him and the men of Israel, "We have come from a distant country; make a treaty with us."

7The men of Israel said to the Hivites, "But perhaps you live near us. How then can we make a treaty with you?"

8"We are your servants," they said to Joshua.

But Joshua asked, "Who are you and where do you come from?"

9They answered: "Your servants have come from a very distant country because of the fame of the LORD your God. For we have heard reports of him: all that he did in Egypt, 10and all that he did to the two kings of the Amorites east of the Jordan—Sihon king of Heshbon, and Og king of Bashan, who reigned in Ashtaroth. 11And our elders and all those living in our country said to us, 'Take provisions for your journey; go and meet them and say to them, "We are your servants; make a treaty with us." ' 12This bread of ours was warm when we packed it at home on the day we left to come to you. But now see how dry and moldy it is. 13And these wineskins that we filled were new, but see how cracked they are. And our clothes and sandals are worn out by the very long journey."

14The men of Israel sampled their provisions but did not inquire of the LORD. 15Then Joshua made a treaty of peace with them to let them live, and the leaders of the assembly ratified it by oath.

16Three days after they made the treaty with the Gibeonites, the Israelites heard that they were neighbors, living near them. 17So the Israelites set out and on the third day came to their cities: Gibeon, Kephirah, Beeroth and Kiriath Jearim. 18But the Israelites did

---

a 31 Traditionally *peace offerings*   *b 1* That is, the Mediterranean   *c 4* Most Hebrew manuscripts; some Hebrew manuscripts, Vulgate and Syriac (see also Septuagint) *They prepared provisions and loaded their donkeys*

not attack them, because the leaders of the assembly had sworn an oath to them by the LORD, the God of Israel.

The whole assembly grumbled against the leaders, ¹⁹but all the leaders answered, "We have given them our oath by the LORD, the God of Israel, and we cannot touch them now. ²⁰This is what we will do to them: We will let them live, so that wrath will not fall on us for breaking the oath we swore to them." ²¹They continued, "Let them live, but let them be woodcutters and water carriers for the entire community." So the leaders' promise to them was kept.

²²Then Joshua summoned the Gibeonites and said, "Why did you deceive us by saying, 'We live a long way from you,' while actually you live near us? ²³You are now under a curse: You will never cease to serve as woodcutters and water carriers for the house of my God."

²⁴They answered Joshua, "Your servants were clearly told how the LORD your God had commanded his servant Moses to give you the whole land and to wipe out all its inhabitants from before you. So we feared for our lives because of you, and that is why we did this. ²⁵We are now in your hands. Do to us whatever seems good and right to you."

²⁶So Joshua saved them from the Israelites, and they did not kill them. ²⁷That day he made the Gibeonites woodcutters and water carriers for the community and for the altar of the LORD at the place the LORD would choose. And that is what they are to this day.

The Sun Stands Still

10 Now Adoni-Zedek king of Jerusalem heard that Joshua had taken Ai and totally destroyed*ᵃ* it, doing to Ai and its king as he had done to Jericho and its king, and that the people of Gibeon had made a treaty of peace with Israel and were living near them. ²He and his people were very much alarmed at this, because Gibeon was an important city, like one of the royal cities; it was larger than Ai, and all its men were good fighters. ³So Adoni-Zedek king of Jerusalem appealed to Hoham king of Hebron, Piram king of Jarmuth, Japhia king of Lachish and Debir king of Eglon. ⁴"Come up and help me attack Gibeon," he said, "because it has made peace with Joshua and the Israelites."

⁵Then the five kings of the Amorites—the kings of Jerusalem, Hebron, Jarmuth, Lachish and Eglon—joined forces. They moved up with all their troops and took up positions against Gibeon and attacked it.

⁶The Gibeonites then sent word to Joshua in the camp at Gilgal: "Do not abandon your servants. Come up to us quickly and save us! Help us, because all the Amorite kings from the hill country have joined forces against us."

⁷So Joshua marched up from Gilgal with his entire army, including all the best fighting men. ⁸The LORD said to Joshua, "Do not be afraid of them; I have given them into your hand. Not one of them will be able to withstand you."

⁹After an all-night march from Gilgal, Joshua took them by surprise. ¹⁰The LORD threw them into confusion before Israel, who defeated them in a great victory at Gibeon. Israel pursued them along the road going up to Beth Horon and cut them down all the way to Azekah and Makkedah. ¹¹As they fled before Israel on the road down from Beth Horon to Azekah, the LORD hurled large hailstones down on them from the sky, and more of them died from the hailstones than were killed by the swords of the Israelites.

¹²On the day the LORD gave the Amorites over to Israel, Joshua said to the LORD in the presence of Israel:

> "O sun, stand still over Gibeon,
>   O moon, over the Valley of Aijalon."
> ¹³So the sun stood still,

ᵃ 1 The Hebrew term refers to the irrevocable giving over of things or persons to the LORD, often by totally destroying them; also in verses 28, 35, 37, 39 and 40.

> and the moon stopped,
> till the nation avenged itself on*a* its enemies,

as it is written in the Book of Jashar.

The sun stopped in the middle of the sky and delayed going down about a full day. **14**There has never been a day like it before or since, a day when the LORD listened to a man. Surely the LORD was fighting for Israel!

15Then Joshua returned with all Israel to the camp at Gilgal.

Five Amorite Kings Killed

16Now the five kings had fled and hidden in the cave at Makkedah. **17**When Joshua was told that the five kings had been found hiding in the cave at Makkedah, **18**he said, "Roll large rocks up to the mouth of the cave, and post some men there to guard it. **19**But don't stop! Pursue your enemies, attack them from the rear and don't let them reach their cities, for the LORD your God has given them into your hand."

20So Joshua and the Israelites destroyed them completely—almost to a man—but the few who were left reached their fortified cities. **21**The whole army then returned safely to Joshua in the camp at Makkedah, and no one uttered a word against the Israelites.

22Joshua said, "Open the mouth of the cave and bring those five kings out to me." **23**So they brought the five kings out of the cave—the kings of Jerusalem, Hebron, Jarmuth, Lachish and Eglon. **24**When they had brought these kings to Joshua, he summoned all the men of Israel and said to the army commanders who had come with him, "Come here and put your feet on the necks of these kings." So they came forward and placed their feet on their necks.

25Joshua said to them, "Do not be afraid; do not be discouraged. Be strong and courageous. This is what the LORD will do to all the enemies you are going to fight." **26**Then Joshua struck and killed the kings and hung them on five trees, and they were left hanging on the trees until evening.

27At sunset Joshua gave the order and they took them down from the trees and threw them into the cave where they had been hiding. At the mouth of the cave they placed large rocks, which are there to this day.

⊡ ▦▦▦▦ ADDRESSING QUESTIONS ▦▦▦▦ ⬒

10:12–14
God

Does this text really mean that the sun stood still in the sky?

In evaluating difficult passages like this one, we must ask ourselves two questions: First, "What does the text actually say?"; second, "If the passage indicates that something unusual happened, is it possible, with what we know of God, for such an occurrence to take place?"

In some ways, the second question is easier to answer. If what we know of God so far is true—that he created the universe and everything in it out of nothing—then it is certainly possible for him to freeze the rotation of the earth, keep everything from spinning off, and then start it up again. Surely the God who created quasars and galaxies has such power.

But is that the best understanding of this passage? Scholars studying these verses have suggested at least a dozen alternative interpretations. However, there is nothing wrong with concluding that we *can't* firmly conclude anything yet about the particular details of this passage. Because so many other parts of the Bible are clear, we can focus on those sections until more research sheds light on the vocabulary and background of less clear passages such as this one.

We *can* conclude, however, that in this situation God did a mighty miracle to intervene on behalf of his people. It's an amazing story about an amazing, caring God—the same God who still works miracles in the lives of individuals today.

28That day Joshua took Makkedah. He put the city and its king to the sword and totally destroyed everyone in it. He left no survivors. And he did to the king of Makkedah as he had done to the king of Jericho.

Southern Cities Conquered

29Then Joshua and all Israel with him moved on from Makkedah to Libnah and attacked it. **30**The LORD also gave that city and its king into Israel's hand. The city and everyone in it Joshua put to the sword. He left no survivors there. And he did to its king as he had done to the king of Jericho.

31Then Joshua and all Israel with him moved on from Libnah to Lachish; he took up positions against it and attacked it. **32**The LORD handed Lachish over to Israel, and Joshua took it on the second day. The city and everyone in it he put to the sword, just as he had done to Libnah. **33**Meanwhile, Horam king of Gezer had come up to help Lachish, but Joshua defeated him and his army—until no survivors were left.

34Then Joshua and all Israel with him moved on from Lachish to Eglon; they took up positions against it and attacked it. **35**They captured it that same day and put it to the sword and totally destroyed everyone in it, just as they had done to Lachish.

36Then Joshua and all Israel with him went up from Eglon to Hebron and attacked it. **37**They took the city and put it to the sword, together with its king, its villages and everyone in it. They left no survivors. Just as at Eglon, they totally destroyed it and everyone in it.

38Then Joshua and all Israel with him turned around and attacked Debir. **39**They took the city, its king and its villages, and put them to the sword. Everyone in it they totally destroyed. They left no survivors. They did to Debir and its king as they had done to Libnah and its king and to Hebron.

40So Joshua subdued the whole region, including the hill country, the Negev, the western foothills and the mountain slopes, together with all their kings. He left no survivors. He totally destroyed all who breathed, just as the LORD, the God of Israel, had commanded. **41**Joshua subdued them from Kadesh Barnea to Gaza and from the whole region of Goshen to Gibeon. **42**All these kings and their lands Joshua conquered in one campaign, because the LORD, the God of Israel, fought for Israel.

43Then Joshua returned with all Israel to the camp at Gilgal.

Northern Kings Defeated

11 When Jabin king of Hazor heard of this, he sent word to Jobab king of Madon, to the kings of Shimron and Acshaph, **2**and to the northern kings who were in the mountains, in the Arabah south of Kinnereth, in the western foothills and in Naphoth Dor*a* on the west; **3**to the Canaanites in the east and west; to the Amorites, Hittites, Perizzites and Jebusites in the hill country; and to the Hivites below Hermon in the region of Mizpah. **4**They came out with all their troops and a large number of horses and chariots—a huge army, as numerous as the sand on the seashore. **5**All these kings joined forces and made camp together at the Waters of Merom, to fight against Israel.

6The LORD said to Joshua, "Do not be afraid of them, because by this time tomorrow I will hand all of them over to Israel, slain. You are to hamstring their horses and burn their chariots."

7So Joshua and his whole army came against them suddenly at the Waters of Merom and attacked them, **8**and the LORD gave them into the hand of Israel. They defeated them and pursued them all the way to Greater Sidon, to Misrephoth Maim, and to the Valley of Mizpah on the east, until no survivors were left. **9**Joshua did to them as the LORD had directed: He hamstrung their horses and burned their chariots.

10At that time Joshua turned back and captured Hazor and put its king to the sword. (Hazor had been the head of all these kingdoms.) **11**Everyone in it they put to the sword. They totally destroyed*b* them, not sparing anything that breathed, and he burned up Hazor itself.

---

a 2 Or *in the heights of Dor*   *b 11* The Hebrew term refers to the irrevocable giving over of things or persons to the LORD, often by totally destroying them; also in verses 12, 20 and 21.

¹²Joshua took all these royal cities and their kings and put them to the sword. He totally destroyed them, as Moses the servant of the LORD had commanded. ¹³Yet Israel did not burn any of the cities built on their mounds—except Hazor, which Joshua burned. ¹⁴The Israelites carried off for themselves all the plunder and livestock of these cities, but all the people they put to the sword until they completely destroyed them, not sparing anyone that breathed. ¹⁵As the LORD commanded his servant Moses, so Moses commanded Joshua, and Joshua did it; he left nothing undone of all that the LORD commanded Moses.

¹⁶So Joshua took this entire land: the hill country, all the Negev, the whole region of Goshen, the western foothills, the Arabah and the mountains of Israel with their foothills, ¹⁷from Mount Halak, which rises toward Seir, to Baal Gad in the Valley of Lebanon below Mount Hermon. He captured all their kings and struck them down, putting them to death. ¹⁸Joshua waged war against all these kings for a long time. ¹⁹Except for the Hivites living in Gibeon, not one city made a treaty of peace with the Israelites, who took them all in battle. ²⁰For it was the LORD himself who hardened their hearts to wage war against Israel, so that he might destroy them totally, exterminating them without mercy, as the LORD had commanded Moses.

²¹At that time Joshua went and destroyed the Anakites from the hill country: from Hebron, Debir and Anab, from all the hill country of Judah, and from all the hill country of Israel. Joshua totally destroyed them and their towns. ²²No Anakites were left in Israelite territory; only in Gaza, Gath and Ashdod did any survive. ²³So Joshua took the entire land, just as the LORD had directed Moses, and he gave it as an inheritance to Israel according to their tribal divisions.

Then the land had rest from war.

List of Defeated Kings

12 These are the kings of the land whom the Israelites had defeated and whose territory they took over east of the Jordan, from the Arnon Gorge to Mount Hermon, including all the eastern side of the Arabah:

²Sihon king of the Amorites,
　who reigned in Heshbon. He ruled from Aroer on the rim of the Arnon Gorge—from the middle of the gorge—to the Jabbok River, which is the border of the Ammonites. This included half of Gilead. ³He also ruled over the eastern Arabah from the Sea of Kinnereth*ᵃ* to the Sea of the Arabah (the Salt Sea*ᵇ*), to Beth Jeshimoth, and then southward below the slopes of Pisgah.

⁴And the territory of Og king of Bashan,
　one of the last of the Rephaites, who reigned in Ashtaroth and Edrei. ⁵He ruled over Mount Hermon, Salecah, all of Bashan to the border of the people of Geshur and Maacah, and half of Gilead to the border of Sihon king of Heshbon.

⁶Moses, the servant of the LORD, and the Israelites conquered them. And Moses the servant of the LORD gave their land to the Reubenites, the Gadites and the half-tribe of Manasseh to be their possession.

⁷These are the kings of the land that Joshua and the Israelites conquered on the west side of the Jordan, from Baal Gad in the Valley of Lebanon to Mount Halak, which rises toward Seir (their lands Joshua gave as an inheritance to the tribes of Israel according to their tribal divisions— ⁸the hill country, the western foothills, the Arabah, the mountain slopes, the desert and the Negev—the lands of the Hittites, Amorites, Canaanites, Perizzites, Hivites and Jebusites):

⁹the king of Jericho	one
the king of Ai (near Bethel)	one

ᵃ3 That is, Galilee　　*ᵇ3* That is, the Dead Sea

¹⁰the king of Jerusalem	one
the king of Hebron	one
¹¹the king of Jarmuth	one
the king of Lachish	one
¹²the king of Eglon	one
the king of Gezer	one
¹³the king of Debir	one
the king of Geder	one
¹⁴the king of Hormah	one
the king of Arad	one
¹⁵the king of Libnah	one
the king of Adullam	one
¹⁶the king of Makkedah	one
the king of Bethel	one
¹⁷the king of Tappuah	one
the king of Hepher	one
¹⁸the king of Aphek	one
the king of Lasharon	one
¹⁹the king of Madon	one
the king of Hazor	one
²⁰the king of Shimron Meron	one
the king of Acshaph	one
²¹the king of Taanach	one
the king of Megiddo	one
²²the king of Kedesh	one
the king of Jokneam in Carmel	one
²³the king of Dor (in Naphoth Dorᵃ)	one
the king of Goyim in Gilgal	one
²⁴the king of Tirzah	one

thirty-one kings in all.

ADDRESSING QUESTIONS

Chapters 13—21
Human Experience

These chapters were intended as a land-title record for the emerging nation of Israel. They contain detailed information about who was to receive what property. This "database"—though probably not of much interest to readers in our day—was of vital concern to those who settled the new land.

Land Still to Be Taken

13 When Joshua was old and well advanced in years, the LORD said to him, "You are very old, and there are still very large areas of land to be taken over.

²"This is the land that remains: all the regions of the Philistines and Geshurites: ³from the Shihor River on the east of Egypt to the territory of Ekron on the north, all of it counted as Canaanite (the territory of the five Philistine rulers in Gaza, Ashdod, Ashkelon, Gath and Ekron—that of the Avvites); ⁴from the south, all the land of the Canaanites, from Arah of the Sidonians as far as Aphek, the region of the Amorites, ⁵the area of the Gebalitesᵇ; and all Lebanon to the east, from Baal Gad below Mount Hermon to Leboᶜ Hamath.

⁶"As for all the inhabitants of the mountain regions from Lebanon to Misrephoth Maim, that is, all the Sidonians, I myself will drive them out before the Israelites. Be sure to

---

ᵃ23 Or in the heights of Dor   ᵇ5 That is, the area of Byblos   ᶜ5 Or to the entrance to

allocate this land to Israel for an inheritance, as I have instructed you, [7]and divide it as an inheritance among the nine tribes and half of the tribe of Manasseh."

Division of the Land East of the Jordan

[8]The other half of Manasseh, [a] the Reubenites and the Gadites had received the inheritance that Moses had given them east of the Jordan, as he, the servant of the LORD, had assigned it to them.

[9]It extended from Aroer on the rim of the Arnon Gorge, and from the town in the middle of the gorge, and included the whole plateau of Medeba as far as Dibon, [10]and all the towns of Sihon king of the Amorites, who ruled in Heshbon, out to the border of the Ammonites. [11]It also included Gilead, the territory of the people of Geshur and Maacah, all of Mount Hermon and all Bashan as far as Salecah— [12]that is, the whole kingdom of Og in Bashan, who had reigned in Ashtaroth and Edrei and had survived as one of the last of the Rephaites. Moses had defeated them and taken over their land. [13]But the Israelites did not drive out the people of Geshur and Maacah, so they continue to live among the Israelites to this day.

[14]But to the tribe of Levi he gave no inheritance, since the offerings made by fire to the LORD, the God of Israel, are their inheritance, as he promised them.

[15]This is what Moses had given to the tribe of Reuben, clan by clan:

[16]The territory from Aroer on the rim of the Arnon Gorge, and from the town in the middle of the gorge, and the whole plateau past Medeba [17]to Heshbon and all its towns on the plateau, including Dibon, Bamoth Baal, Beth Baal Meon, [18]Jahaz, Kedemoth, Mephaath, [19]Kiriathaim, Sibmah, Zereth Shahar on the hill in the valley, [20]Beth Peor, the slopes of Pisgah, and Beth Jeshimoth [21]—all the towns on the plateau and the entire realm of Sihon king of the Amorites, who ruled at Heshbon. Moses had defeated him and the Midianite chiefs, Evi, Rekem, Zur, Hur and Reba—princes allied with Sihon—who lived in that country. [22]In addition to those slain in battle, the Israelites had put to the sword Balaam son of Beor, who practiced divination. [23]The boundary of the Reubenites was the bank of the Jordan. These towns and their villages were the inheritance of the Reubenites, clan by clan.

[24]This is what Moses had given to the tribe of Gad, clan by clan:

[25]The territory of Jazer, all the towns of Gilead and half the Ammonite country as far as Aroer, near Rabbah; [26]and from Heshbon to Ramath Mizpah and Betonim, and from Mahanaim to the territory of Debir; [27]and in the valley, Beth Haram, Beth Nimrah, Succoth and Zaphon with the rest of the realm of Sihon king of Heshbon (the east side of the Jordan, the territory up to the end of the Sea of Kinnereth [b]). [28]These towns and their villages were the inheritance of the Gadites, clan by clan.

[29]This is what Moses had given to the half-tribe of Manasseh, that is, to half the family of the descendants of Manasseh, clan by clan:

[30]The territory extending from Mahanaim and including all of Bashan, the entire realm of Og king of Bashan—all the settlements of Jair in Bashan, sixty towns, [31]half of Gilead, and Ashtaroth and Edrei (the royal cities of Og in Bashan). This was for the descendants of Makir son of Manasseh—for half of the sons of Makir, clan by clan.

[32]This is the inheritance Moses had given when he was in the plains of Moab across the Jordan east of Jericho. [33]But to the tribe of Levi, Moses had given no inheritance; the LORD, the God of Israel, is their inheritance, as he promised them.

[a]8 Hebrew *With it* (that is, with the other half of Manasseh)   [b]27 That is, Galilee

Division of the Land West of the Jordan

14 Now these are the areas the Israelites received as an inheritance in the land of Canaan, which Eleazar the priest, Joshua son of Nun and the heads of the tribal clans of Israel allotted to them. ²Their inheritances were assigned by lot to the nine-and-a-half tribes, as the LORD had commanded through Moses. ³Moses had granted the two-and-a-half tribes their inheritance east of the Jordan but had not granted the Levites an inheritance among the rest, ⁴for the sons of Joseph had become two tribes—Manasseh and Ephraim. The Levites received no share of the land but only towns to live in, with pasturelands for their flocks and herds. ⁵So the Israelites divided the land, just as the LORD had commanded Moses.

Hebron Given to Caleb

⁶Now the men of Judah approached Joshua at Gilgal, and Caleb son of Jephunneh the Kenizzite said to him, "You know what the LORD said to Moses the man of God at Kadesh Barnea about you and me. ⁷I was forty years old when Moses the servant of the LORD sent me from Kadesh Barnea to explore the land. And I brought him back a report according to my convictions, ⁸but my brothers who went up with me made the hearts of the people melt with fear. I, however, followed the LORD my God wholeheartedly. ⁹So on that day Moses swore to me, 'The land on which your feet have walked will be your inheritance and that of your children forever, because you have followed the LORD my God wholeheartedly.'*ᵃ*

¹⁰"Now then, just as the LORD promised, he has kept me alive for forty-five years since the time he said this to Moses, while Israel moved about in the desert. So here I am today, eighty-five years old! ¹¹I am still as strong today as the day Moses sent me out; I'm just as vigorous to go out to battle now as I was then. ¹²Now give me this hill country that the LORD promised me that day. You yourself heard then that the Anakites were there and their cities were large and fortified, but, the LORD helping me, I will drive them out just as he said."

¹³Then Joshua blessed Caleb son of Jephunneh and gave him Hebron as his inheritance. ¹⁴So Hebron has belonged to Caleb son of Jephunneh the Kenizzite ever since, because he followed the LORD, the God of Israel, wholeheartedly. ¹⁵(Hebron used to be called Kiriath Arba after Arba, who was the greatest man among the Anakites.)

Then the land had rest from war.

Allotment for Judah

15 The allotment for the tribe of Judah, clan by clan, extended down to the territory of Edom, to the Desert of Zin in the extreme south.

²Their southern boundary started from the bay at the southern end of the Salt Sea,ᵇ ³crossed south of Scorpionᶜ Pass, continued on to Zin and went over to the south of Kadesh Barnea. Then it ran past Hezron up to Addar and curved around to Karka. ⁴It then passed along to Azmon and joined the Wadi of Egypt, ending at the sea. This is theirᵈ southern boundary.

⁵The eastern boundary is the Salt Sea as far as the mouth of the Jordan.

The northern boundary started from the bay of the sea at the mouth of the Jordan, ⁶went up to Beth Hoglah and continued north of Beth Arabah to the Stone of Bohan son of Reuben. ⁷The boundary then went up to Debir from the Valley of Achor and turned north to Gilgal, which faces the Pass of Adummim south of the gorge. It continued along to the waters of En Shemesh and came out at En Rogel. ⁸Then it ran up the Valley of Ben Hinnom along the southern slope of the Jebusite city (that is, Jerusalem). From there it climbed to the top of the hill west of the Hinnom Valley at the northern end of the Valley of Rephaim. ⁹From the hilltop the boundary headed

ᵃ9 Deut. 1:36   ᵇ2 That is, the Dead Sea; also in verse 5   ᶜ3 Hebrew Akrabbim   ᵈ4 Hebrew your

toward the spring of the waters of Nephtoah, came out at the towns of Mount Ephron and went down toward Baalah (that is, Kiriath Jearim). [10]Then it curved westward from Baalah to Mount Seir, ran along the northern slope of Mount Jearim (that is, Kesalon), continued down to Beth Shemesh and crossed to Timnah. [11]It went to the northern slope of Ekron, turned toward Shikkeron, passed along to Mount Baalah and reached Jabneel. The boundary ended at the sea.

[12]The western boundary is the coastline of the Great Sea.[a]
These are the boundaries around the people of Judah by their clans.

[13]In accordance with the LORD's command to him, Joshua gave to Caleb son of Jephunneh a portion in Judah—Kiriath Arba, that is, Hebron. (Arba was the forefather of Anak.) [14]From Hebron Caleb drove out the three Anakites—Sheshai, Ahiman and Talmai—descendants of Anak. [15]From there he marched against the people living in Debir (formerly called Kiriath Sepher). [16]And Caleb said, "I will give my daughter Acsah in marriage to the man who attacks and captures Kiriath Sepher." [17]Othniel son of Kenaz, Caleb's brother, took it; so Caleb gave his daughter Acsah to him in marriage.

[18]One day when she came to Othniel, she urged him[b] to ask her father for a field. When she got off her donkey, Caleb asked her, "What can I do for you?"

[19]She replied, "Do me a special favor. Since you have given me land in the Negev, give me also springs of water." So Caleb gave her the upper and lower springs.

[20]This is the inheritance of the tribe of Judah, clan by clan:

[21]The southernmost towns of the tribe of Judah in the Negev toward the boundary of Edom were:

Kabzeel, Eder, Jagur, [22]Kinah, Dimonah, Adadah, [23]Kedesh, Hazor, Ithnan, [24]Ziph, Telem, Bealoth, [25]Hazor Hadattah, Kerioth Hezron (that is, Hazor), [26]Amam, Shema, Moladah, [27]Hazar Gaddah, Heshmon, Beth Pelet, [28]Hazar Shual, Beersheba, Biziothiah, [29]Baalah, Iim, Ezem, [30]Eltolad, Kesil, Hormah, [31]Ziklag, Madmannah, Sansannah, [32]Lebaoth, Shilhim, Ain and Rimmon—a total of twenty-nine towns and their villages.

[33]In the western foothills:

Eshtaol, Zorah, Ashnah, [34]Zanoah, En Gannim, Tappuah, Enam, [35]Jarmuth, Adullam, Socoh, Azekah, [36]Shaaraim, Adithaim and Gederah (or Gederothaim)[c]—fourteen towns and their villages.

[37]Zenan, Hadashah, Migdal Gad, [38]Dilean, Mizpah, Joktheel, [39]Lachish, Bozkath, Eglon, [40]Cabbon, Lahmas, Kitlish, [41]Gederoth, Beth Dagon, Naamah and Makkedah—sixteen towns and their villages.

[42]Libnah, Ether, Ashan, [43]Iphtah, Ashnah, Nezib, [44]Keilah, Aczib and Mareshah—nine towns and their villages.

[45]Ekron, with its surrounding settlements and villages; [46]west of Ekron, all that were in the vicinity of Ashdod, together with their villages; [47]Ashdod, its surrounding settlements and villages; and Gaza, its settlements and villages, as far as the Wadi of Egypt and the coastline of the Great Sea.

[48]In the hill country:

Shamir, Jattir, Socoh, [49]Dannah, Kiriath Sannah (that is, Debir), [50]Anab, Eshtemoh, Anim, [51]Goshen, Holon and Giloh—eleven towns and their villages.

[52]Arab, Dumah, Eshan, [53]Janim, Beth Tappuah, Aphekah, [54]Humtah, Kiriath Arba (that is, Hebron) and Zior—nine towns and their villages.

[55]Maon, Carmel, Ziph, Juttah, [56]Jezreel, Jokdeam, Zanoah, [57]Kain, Gibeah and Timnah—ten towns and their villages.

---

[a]12 That is, the Mediterranean; also in verse 47   [b]18 Hebrew and some Septuagint manuscripts; other Septuagint manuscripts (see also note at Judges 1:14) Othniel, he urged her   [c]36 Or Gederah and Gederothaim

⁵⁸Halhul, Beth Zur, Gedor, ⁵⁹Maarath, Beth Anoth and Eltekon—six towns and their villages.

⁶⁰Kiriath Baal (that is, Kiriath Jearim) and Rabbah—two towns and their villages.

⁶¹In the desert:

Beth Arabah, Middin, Secacah, ⁶²Nibshan, the City of Salt and En Gedi—six towns and their villages.

⁶³Judah could not dislodge the Jebusites, who were living in Jerusalem; to this day the Jebusites live there with the people of Judah.

Allotment for Ephraim and Manasseh

16 The allotment for Joseph began at the Jordan of Jericho,ᵃ east of the waters of Jericho, and went up from there through the desert into the hill country of Bethel. ²It went on from Bethel (that is, Luz),ᵇ crossed over to the territory of the Arkites in Ataroth, ³descended westward to the territory of the Japhletites as far as the region of Lower Beth Horon and on to Gezer, ending at the sea.

⁴So Manasseh and Ephraim, the descendants of Joseph, received their inheritance.

⁵This was the territory of Ephraim, clan by clan:

The boundary of their inheritance went from Ataroth Addar in the east to Upper Beth Horon ⁶and continued to the sea. From Micmethath on the north it curved eastward to Taanath Shiloh, passing by it to Janoah on the east. ⁷Then it went down from Janoah to Ataroth and Naarah, touched Jericho and came out at the Jordan. ⁸From Tappuah the border went west to the Kanah Ravine and ended at the sea. This was the inheritance of the tribe of the Ephraimites, clan by clan. ⁹It also included all the towns and their villages that were set aside for the Ephraimites within the inheritance of the Manassites.

¹⁰They did not dislodge the Canaanites living in Gezer; to this day the Canaanites live among the people of Ephraim but are required to do forced labor.

17 This was the allotment for the tribe of Manasseh as Joseph's firstborn, that is, for Makir, Manasseh's firstborn. Makir was the ancestor of the Gileadites, who had received Gilead and Bashan because the Makirites were great soldiers. ²So this allotment was for the rest of the people of Manasseh—the clans of Abiezer, Helek, Asriel, Shechem, Hepher and Shemida. These are the other male descendants of Manasseh son of Joseph by their clans.

³Now Zelophehad son of Hepher, the son of Gilead, the son of Makir, the son of Manasseh, had no sons but only daughters, whose names were Mahlah, Noah, Hoglah, Milcah and Tirzah. ⁴They went to Eleazar the priest, Joshua son of Nun, and the leaders and said, "The LORD commanded Moses to give us an inheritance among our brothers." So Joshua gave them an inheritance along with the brothers of their father, according to the LORD's command. ⁵Manasseh's share consisted of ten tracts of land besides Gilead and Bashan east of the Jordan, ⁶because the daughters of the tribe of Manasseh received an inheritance among the sons. The land of Gilead belonged to the rest of the descendants of Manasseh.

⁷The territory of Manasseh extended from Asher to Micmethath east of Shechem. The boundary ran southward from there to include the people living at En Tappuah. ⁸(Manasseh had the land of Tappuah, but Tappuah itself, on the boundary of Manasseh, belonged to the Ephraimites.) ⁹Then the boundary continued south to the Kanah Ravine. There were towns belonging to Ephraim lying among the towns of Manasseh, but the boundary of Manasseh was the northern side of the ravine and ended at the sea. ¹⁰On the south the land belonged to Ephraim, on the north to Manasseh. The

---

ᵃ1 *Jordan of Jericho* was possibly an ancient name for the Jordan River.   ᵇ2 Septuagint; Hebrew *Bethel to Luz*

territory of Manasseh reached the sea and bordered Asher on the north and Issachar on the east.

¹¹Within Issachar and Asher, Manasseh also had Beth Shan, Ibleam and the people of Dor, Endor, Taanach and Megiddo, together with their surrounding settlements (the third in the list is Naphoth*a*).

¹²Yet the Manassites were not able to occupy these towns, for the Canaanites were determined to live in that region. ¹³However, when the Israelites grew stronger, they subjected the Canaanites to forced labor but did not drive them out completely.

¹⁴The people of Joseph said to Joshua, "Why have you given us only one allotment and one portion for an inheritance? We are a numerous people and the LORD has blessed us abundantly."

¹⁵"If you are so numerous," Joshua answered, "and if the hill country of Ephraim is too small for you, go up into the forest and clear land for yourselves there in the land of the Perizzites and Rephaites."

¹⁶The people of Joseph replied, "The hill country is not enough for us, and all the Canaanites who live in the plain have iron chariots, both those in Beth Shan and its settlements and those in the Valley of Jezreel."

¹⁷But Joshua said to the house of Joseph—to Ephraim and Manasseh—"You are numerous and very powerful. You will have not only one allotment ¹⁸but the forested hill country as well. Clear it, and its farthest limits will be yours; though the Canaanites have iron chariots and though they are strong, you can drive them out."

Division of the Rest of the Land

18 The whole assembly of the Israelites gathered at Shiloh and set up the Tent of Meeting there. The country was brought under their control, ²but there were still seven Israelite tribes who had not yet received their inheritance.

³So Joshua said to the Israelites: "How long will you wait before you begin to take possession of the land that the LORD, the God of your fathers, has given you? ⁴Appoint three men from each tribe. I will send them out to make a survey of the land and to write a description of it, according to the inheritance of each. Then they will return to me. ⁵You are to divide the land into seven parts. Judah is to remain in its territory on the south and the house of Joseph in its territory on the north. ⁶After you have written descriptions of the seven parts of the land, bring them here to me and I will cast lots for you in the presence of the LORD our God. ⁷The Levites, however, do not get a portion among you, because the priestly service of the LORD is their inheritance. And Gad, Reuben and the half-tribe of Manasseh have already received their inheritance on the east side of the Jordan. Moses the servant of the LORD gave it to them."

⁸As the men started on their way to map out the land, Joshua instructed them, "Go and make a survey of the land and write a description of it. Then return to me, and I will cast lots for you here at Shiloh in the presence of the LORD." ⁹So the men left and went through the land. They wrote its description on a scroll, town by town, in seven parts, and returned to Joshua in the camp at Shiloh. ¹⁰Joshua then cast lots for them in Shiloh in the presence of the LORD, and there he distributed the land to the Israelites according to their tribal divisions.

Allotment for Benjamin

¹¹The lot came up for the tribe of Benjamin, clan by clan. Their allotted territory lay between the tribes of Judah and Joseph:

¹²On the north side their boundary began at the Jordan, passed the northern slope of Jericho and headed west into the hill country, coming out at the desert of Beth Aven. ¹³From there it crossed to the south slope of Luz (that is, Bethel) and went down to Ataroth Addar on the hill south of Lower Beth Horon.

a 11 That is, Naphoth Dor

¹⁴From the hill facing Beth Horon on the south the boundary turned south along the western side and came out at Kiriath Baal (that is, Kiriath Jearim), a town of the people of Judah. This was the western side.

¹⁵The southern side began at the outskirts of Kiriath Jearim on the west, and the boundary came out at the spring of the waters of Nephtoah. ¹⁶The boundary went down to the foot of the hill facing the Valley of Ben Hinnom, north of the Valley of Rephaim. It continued down the Hinnom Valley along the southern slope of the Jebusite city and so to En Rogel. ¹⁷It then curved north, went to En Shemesh, continued to Geliloth, which faces the Pass of Adummim, and ran down to the Stone of Bohan son of Reuben. ¹⁸It continued to the northern slope of Beth Arabah ᵃ and on down into the Arabah. ¹⁹It then went to the northern slope of Beth Hoglah and came out at the northern bay of the Salt Sea, ᵇ at the mouth of the Jordan in the south. This was the southern boundary.

²⁰The Jordan formed the boundary on the eastern side.

These were the boundaries that marked out the inheritance of the clans of Benjamin on all sides.

²¹The tribe of Benjamin, clan by clan, had the following cities:

Jericho, Beth Hoglah, Emek Keziz, ²²Beth Arabah, Zemaraim, Bethel, ²³Avvim, Parah, Ophrah, ²⁴Kephar Ammoni, Ophni and Geba—twelve towns and their villages.

²⁵Gibeon, Ramah, Beeroth, ²⁶Mizpah, Kephirah, Mozah, ²⁷Rekem, Irpeel, Taralah, ²⁸Zelah, Haeleph, the Jebusite city (that is, Jerusalem), Gibeah and Kiriath—fourteen towns and their villages.

This was the inheritance of Benjamin for its clans.

Allotment for Simeon

19 The second lot came out for the tribe of Simeon, clan by clan. Their inheritance lay within the territory of Judah. ²It included:

Beersheba (or Sheba), ᶜ Moladah, ³Hazar Shual, Balah, Ezem, ⁴Eltolad, Bethul, Hormah, ⁵Ziklag, Beth Marcaboth, Hazar Susah, ⁶Beth Lebaoth and Sharuhen—thirteen towns and their villages;

⁷Ain, Rimmon, Ether and Ashan—four towns and their villages— ⁸and all the villages around these towns as far as Baalath Beer (Ramah in the Negev).

This was the inheritance of the tribe of the Simeonites, clan by clan. ⁹The inheritance of the Simeonites was taken from the share of Judah, because Judah's portion was more than they needed. So the Simeonites received their inheritance within the territory of Judah.

Allotment for Zebulun

¹⁰The third lot came up for Zebulun, clan by clan:

The boundary of their inheritance went as far as Sarid. ¹¹Going west it ran to Maralah, touched Dabbesheth, and extended to the ravine near Jokneam. ¹²It turned east from Sarid toward the sunrise to the territory of Kisloth Tabor and went on to Daberath and up to Japhia. ¹³Then it continued eastward to Gath Hepher and Eth Kazin; it came out at Rimmon and turned toward Neah. ¹⁴There the boundary went around on the north to Hannathon and ended at the Valley of Iphtah El. ¹⁵Included were Kattath, Nahalal, Shimron, Idalah and Bethlehem. There were twelve towns and their villages.

¹⁶These towns and their villages were the inheritance of Zebulun, clan by clan.

ᵃ18 Septuagint; Hebrew *slope facing the Arabah*   ᵇ19 That is, the Dead Sea   ᶜ2 Or *Beersheba, Sheba*; 1 Chron. 4:28 does not have *Sheba*.

Allotment for Issachar

¹⁷The fourth lot came out for Issachar, clan by clan. ¹⁸Their territory included:

Jezreel, Kesulloth, Shunem, ¹⁹Hapharaim, Shion, Anaharath, ²⁰Rabbith, Kishion, Ebez, ²¹Remeth, En Gannim, En Haddah and Beth Pazzez. ²²The boundary touched Tabor, Shahazumah and Beth Shemesh, and ended at the Jordan. There were sixteen towns and their villages.

²³These towns and their villages were the inheritance of the tribe of Issachar, clan by clan.

Allotment for Asher

²⁴The fifth lot came out for the tribe of Asher, clan by clan. ²⁵Their territory included:

Helkath, Hali, Beten, Acshaph, ²⁶Allammelech, Amad and Mishal. On the west the boundary touched Carmel and Shihor Libnath. ²⁷It then turned east toward Beth Dagon, touched Zebulun and the Valley of Iphtah El, and went north to Beth Emek and Neiel, passing Cabul on the left. ²⁸It went to Abdon,ᵃ Rehob, Hammon and Kanah, as far as Greater Sidon. ²⁹The boundary then turned back toward Ramah and went to the fortified city of Tyre, turned toward Hosah and came out at the sea in the region of Aczib, ³⁰Ummah, Aphek and Rehob. There were twenty-two towns and their villages.

³¹These towns and their villages were the inheritance of the tribe of Asher, clan by clan.

Allotment for Naphtali

³²The sixth lot came out for Naphtali, clan by clan:

³³Their boundary went from Heleph and the large tree in Zaanannim, passing Adami Nekeb and Jabneel to Lakkum and ending at the Jordan. ³⁴The boundary ran west through Aznoth Tabor and came out at Hukkok. It touched Zebulun on the south, Asher on the west and the Jordanᵇ on the east. ³⁵The fortified cities were Ziddim, Zer, Hammath, Rakkath, Kinnereth, ³⁶Adamah, Ramah, Hazor, ³⁷Kedesh, Edrei, En Hazor, ³⁸Iron, Migdal El, Horem, Beth Anath and Beth Shemesh. There were nineteen towns and their villages.

³⁹These towns and their villages were the inheritance of the tribe of Naphtali, clan by clan.

Allotment for Dan

⁴⁰The seventh lot came out for the tribe of Dan, clan by clan. ⁴¹The territory of their inheritance included:

Zorah, Eshtaol, Ir Shemesh, ⁴²Shaalabbin, Aijalon, Ithlah, ⁴³Elon, Timnah, Ekron, ⁴⁴Eltekeh, Gibbethon, Baalath, ⁴⁵Jehud, Bene Berak, Gath Rimmon, ⁴⁶Me Jarkon and Rakkon, with the area facing Joppa.

⁴⁷(But the Danites had difficulty taking possession of their territory, so they went up and attacked Leshem, took it, put it to the sword and occupied it. They settled in Leshem and named it Dan after their forefather.)

⁴⁸These towns and their villages were the inheritance of the tribe of Dan, clan by clan.

Allotment for Joshua

⁴⁹When they had finished dividing the land into its allotted portions, the Israelites gave Joshua son of Nun an inheritance among them, ⁵⁰as the Lᴏʀᴅ had commanded. They gave him the town he asked for—Timnath Serahᶜ in the hill country of Ephraim. And he built up the town and settled there.

⁵¹These are the territories that Eleazar the priest, Joshua son of Nun and the heads of

---

ᵃ28 Some Hebrew manuscripts (see also Joshua 21:30); most Hebrew manuscripts *Ebron*   ᵇ34 Septuagint; Hebrew *west, and Judah, the Jordan.*   ᶜ50 Also known as *Timnath Heres* (see Judges 2:9)

the tribal clans of Israel assigned by lot at Shiloh in the presence of the LORD at the entrance to the Tent of Meeting. And so they finished dividing the land.

Cities of Refuge

20 Then the LORD said to Joshua: ²"Tell the Israelites to designate the cities of refuge, as I instructed you through Moses, ³so that anyone who kills a person accidentally and unintentionally may flee there and find protection from the avenger of blood.

⁴"When he flees to one of these cities, he is to stand in the entrance of the city gate and state his case before the elders of that city. Then they are to admit him into their city and give him a place to live with them. ⁵If the avenger of blood pursues him, they must not surrender the one accused, because he killed his neighbor unintentionally and without malice aforethought. ⁶He is to stay in that city until he has stood trial before the assembly and until the death of the high priest who is serving at that time. Then he may go back to his own home in the town from which he fled."

⁷So they set apart Kedesh in Galilee in the hill country of Naphtali, Shechem in the hill country of Ephraim, and Kiriath Arba (that is, Hebron) in the hill country of Judah. ⁸On the east side of the Jordan of Jericho^a they designated Bezer in the desert on the plateau in the tribe of Reuben, Ramoth in Gilead in the tribe of Gad, and Golan in Bashan in the tribe of Manasseh. ⁹Any of the Israelites or any alien living among them who killed someone accidentally could flee to these designated cities and not be killed by the avenger of blood prior to standing trial before the assembly.

REASONS TO BELIEVE

20:1–9
The Amazing Bible

We take for granted due process when it comes to legal matters. In ancient Israel a similar system offered shelter from unjust prosecution or revenge.

The "cities of refuge," as they were called (verse 2), afforded sanctuary for people guilty of involuntary manslaughter but not murder. These designated areas gave such people a safe place to flee when pursued by hotheaded relatives of the deceased. Without a standing police force, this provision ensured justice for all. This is another testimony to the remarkable wisdom contained in the Bible.

Towns for the Levites

21 Now the family heads of the Levites approached Eleazar the priest, Joshua son of Nun, and the heads of the other tribal families of Israel ²at Shiloh in Canaan and said to them, "The LORD commanded through Moses that you give us towns to live in, with pasturelands for our livestock." ³So, as the LORD had commanded, the Israelites gave the Levites the following towns and pasturelands out of their own inheritance:

⁴The first lot came out for the Kohathites, clan by clan. The Levites who were descendants of Aaron the priest were allotted thirteen towns from the tribes of Judah, Simeon and Benjamin. ⁵The rest of Kohath's descendants were allotted ten towns from the clans of the tribes of Ephraim, Dan and half of Manasseh.

⁶The descendants of Gershon were allotted thirteen towns from the clans of the tribes of Issachar, Asher, Naphtali and the half-tribe of Manasseh in Bashan.

⁷The descendants of Merari, clan by clan, received twelve towns from the tribes of Reuben, Gad and Zebulun.

⁸So the Israelites allotted to the Levites these towns and their pasturelands, as the LORD had commanded through Moses.

⁹From the tribes of Judah and Simeon they allotted the following towns by name ¹⁰(these towns were assigned to the descendants of Aaron who were from the Kohathite clans of the Levites, because the first lot fell to them):

---

^a 8 *Jordan of Jericho* was possibly an ancient name for the Jordan River.

¹¹They gave them Kiriath Arba (that is, Hebron), with its surrounding pastureland, in the hill country of Judah. (Arba was the forefather of Anak.) ¹²But the fields and villages around the city they had given to Caleb son of Jephunneh as his possession.

¹³So to the descendants of Aaron the priest they gave Hebron (a city of refuge for one accused of murder), Libnah, ¹⁴Jattir, Eshtemoa, ¹⁵Holon, Debir, ¹⁶Ain, Juttah and Beth Shemesh, together with their pasturelands—nine towns from these two tribes.

¹⁷And from the tribe of Benjamin they gave them Gibeon, Geba, ¹⁸Anathoth and Almon, together with their pasturelands—four towns.

¹⁹All the towns for the priests, the descendants of Aaron, were thirteen, together with their pasturelands.

²⁰The rest of the Kohathite clans of the Levites were allotted towns from the tribe of Ephraim:

²¹In the hill country of Ephraim they were given Shechem (a city of refuge for one accused of murder) and Gezer, ²²Kibzaim and Beth Horon, together with their pasturelands—four towns.

²³Also from the tribe of Dan they received Eltekeh, Gibbethon, ²⁴Aijalon and Gath Rimmon, together with their pasturelands—four towns.

²⁵From half the tribe of Manasseh they received Taanach and Gath Rimmon, together with their pasturelands—two towns.

²⁶All these ten towns and their pasturelands were given to the rest of the Kohathite clans.

²⁷The Levite clans of the Gershonites were given:
from the half-tribe of Manasseh,
Golan in Bashan (a city of refuge for one accused of murder) and Be Eshtarah, together with their pasturelands—two towns;
²⁸from the tribe of Issachar,
Kishion, Daberath, ²⁹Jarmuth and En Gannim, together with their pasturelands—four towns;
³⁰from the tribe of Asher,
Mishal, Abdon, ³¹Helkath and Rehob, together with their pasturelands—four towns;
³²from the tribe of Naphtali,
Kedesh in Galilee (a city of refuge for one accused of murder), Hammoth Dor and Kartan, together with their pasturelands—three towns.

³³All the towns of the Gershonite clans were thirteen, together with their pasturelands.

³⁴The Merarite clans (the rest of the Levites) were given:
from the tribe of Zebulun,
Jokneam, Kartah, ³⁵Dimnah and Nahalal, together with their pasturelands—four towns;
³⁶from the tribe of Reuben,
Bezer, Jahaz, ³⁷Kedemoth and Mephaath, together with their pasturelands—four towns;
³⁸from the tribe of Gad,
Ramoth in Gilead (a city of refuge for one accused of murder), Mahanaim, ³⁹Heshbon and Jazer, together with their pasturelands—four towns in all.

⁴⁰All the towns allotted to the Merarite clans, who were the rest of the Levites, were twelve.

⁴¹The towns of the Levites in the territory held by the Israelites were forty-eight in all, together with their pasturelands. ⁴²Each of these towns had pasturelands surrounding it; this was true for all these towns.

⁴³So the Lord gave Israel all the land he had sworn to give their forefathers, and they took possession of it and settled there. ⁴⁴The Lord gave them rest on every side, just as he

had sworn to their forefathers. Not one of their enemies withstood them; the Lord handed all their enemies over to them. ⁴⁵Not one of all the Lord's good promises to the house of Israel failed; every one was fulfilled.

Eastern Tribes Return Home

22 Then Joshua summoned the Reubenites, the Gadites and the half-tribe of Manasseh ²and said to them, "You have done all that Moses the servant of the Lord commanded, and you have obeyed me in everything I commanded. ³For a long time now—to this very day—you have not deserted your brothers but have carried out the mission the Lord your God gave you. ⁴Now that the Lord your God has given your brothers rest as he promised, return to your homes in the land that Moses the servant of the Lord gave you on the other side of the Jordan. ⁵But be very careful to keep the commandment and the law that Moses the servant of the Lord gave you: to love the Lord your God, to walk in all his ways, to obey his commands, to hold fast to him and to serve him with all your heart and all your soul."

⁶Then Joshua blessed them and sent them away, and they went to their homes. ⁷(To the half-tribe of Manasseh Moses had given land in Bashan, and to the other half of the tribe Joshua gave land on the west side of the Jordan with their brothers.) When Joshua sent them home, he blessed them, ⁸saying, "Return to your homes with your great wealth—with large herds of livestock, with silver, gold, bronze and iron, and a great quantity of clothing—and divide with your brothers the plunder from your enemies."

⁹So the Reubenites, the Gadites and the half-tribe of Manasseh left the Israelites at Shiloh in Canaan to return to Gilead, their own land, which they had acquired in accordance with the command of the Lord through Moses.

¹⁰When they came to Geliloth near the Jordan in the land of Canaan, the Reubenites, the Gadites and the half-tribe of Manasseh built an imposing altar there by the Jordan. ¹¹And when the Israelites heard that they had built the altar on the border of Canaan at Geliloth near the Jordan on the Israelite side, ¹²the whole assembly of Israel gathered at Shiloh to go to war against them.

¹³So the Israelites sent Phinehas son of Eleazar, the priest, to the land of Gilead—to Reuben, Gad and the half-tribe of Manasseh. ¹⁴With him they sent ten of the chief men, one for each of the tribes of Israel, each the head of a family division among the Israelite clans.

¹⁵When they went to Gilead—to Reuben, Gad and the half-tribe of Manasseh—they said to them: ¹⁶"The whole assembly of the Lord says: 'How could you break faith with the God of Israel like this? How could you turn away from the Lord and build yourselves an altar in rebellion against him now? ¹⁷Was not the sin of Peor enough for us? Up to this very day we have not cleansed ourselves from that sin, even though a plague fell on the community of the Lord! ¹⁸And are you now turning away from the Lord?

"'If you rebel against the Lord today, tomorrow he will be angry with the whole community of Israel. ¹⁹If the land you possess is defiled, come over to the Lord's land, where the Lord's tabernacle stands, and share the land with us. But do not rebel against the Lord or against us by building an altar for yourselves, other than the altar of the Lord our God. ²⁰When Achan son of Zerah acted unfaithfully regarding the devoted things,ᵃ did not wrath come upon the whole community of Israel? He was not the only one who died for his sin.'"

²¹Then Reuben, Gad and the half-tribe of Manasseh replied to the heads of the clans of Israel: ²²"The Mighty One, God, the Lord! The Mighty One, God, the Lord! He knows! And let Israel know! If this has been in rebellion or disobedience to the Lord, do not spare us this day. ²³If we have built our own altar to turn away from the Lord and to offer burnt

---

ᵃ20 The Hebrew term refers to the irrevocable giving over of things or persons to the Lord, often by totally destroying them.

offerings and grain offerings, or to sacrifice fellowship offerings[a] on it, may the LORD himself call us to account.

²⁴"No! We did it for fear that some day your descendants might say to ours, 'What do you have to do with the LORD, the God of Israel? ²⁵The LORD has made the Jordan a boundary between us and you—you Reubenites and Gadites! You have no share in the LORD.' So your descendants might cause ours to stop fearing the LORD.

²⁶"That is why we said, 'Let us get ready and build an altar—but not for burnt offerings or sacrifices.' ²⁷On the contrary, it is to be a witness between us and you and the generations that follow, that we will worship the LORD at his sanctuary with our burnt offerings, sacrifices and fellowship offerings. Then in the future your descendants will not be able to say to ours, 'You have no share in the LORD.'

²⁸"And we said, 'If they ever say this to us, or to our descendants, we will answer: Look at the replica of the LORD's altar, which our fathers built, not for burnt offerings and sacrifices, but as a witness between us and you.'

²⁹"Far be it from us to rebel against the LORD and turn away from him today by building an altar for burnt offerings, grain offerings and sacrifices, other than the altar of the LORD our God that stands before his tabernacle."

³⁰When Phinehas the priest and the leaders of the community—the heads of the clans of the Israelites—heard what Reuben, Gad and Manasseh had to say, they were pleased. ³¹And Phinehas son of Eleazar, the priest, said to Reuben, Gad and Manasseh, "Today we know that the LORD is with us, because you have not acted unfaithfully toward the LORD in this matter. Now you have rescued the Israelites from the LORD's hand."

³²Then Phinehas son of Eleazar, the priest, and the leaders returned to Canaan from their meeting with the Reubenites and Gadites in Gilead and reported to the Israelites. ³³They were glad to hear the report and praised God. And they talked no more about going to war against them to devastate the country where the Reubenites and the Gadites lived.

³⁴And the Reubenites and the Gadites gave the altar this name: A Witness Between Us that the LORD is God.

Joshua's Farewell to the Leaders

23 After a long time had passed and the LORD had given Israel rest from all their enemies around them, Joshua, by then old and well advanced in years, ²summoned all Israel—their elders, leaders, judges and officials—and said to them: "I am old and well advanced in years. ³You yourselves have seen everything the LORD your God has done to all these nations for your sake; it was the LORD your God who fought for you. ⁴Remember how I have allotted as an inheritance for your tribes all the land of the nations that remain—the nations I conquered—between the Jordan and the Great Sea[b] in the west. ⁵The LORD your God himself will drive them out of your way. He will push them out before you, and you will take possession of their land, as the LORD your God promised you.

⁶"Be very strong; be careful to obey all that is written in the Book of the Law of Moses, without turning aside to the right or to the left. ⁷Do not associate with these nations that remain among you; do not invoke the names of their gods or swear by them. You must not serve them or bow down to them. ⁸But you are to hold fast to the LORD your God, as you have until now.

⁹"The LORD has driven out before you great and powerful nations; to this day no one has been able to withstand you. ¹⁰One of you routs a thousand, because the LORD your God fights for you, just as he promised. ¹¹So be very careful to love the LORD your God.

¹²"But if you turn away and ally yourselves with the survivors of these nations that remain among you and if you intermarry with them and associate with them, ¹³then you may be sure that the LORD your God will no longer drive out these nations before you.

---

a 23 Traditionally *peace offerings*; also in verse 27   *b 4* That is, the Mediterranean

Instead, they will become snares and traps for you, whips on your backs and thorns in your eyes, until you perish from this good land, which the LORD your God has given you.

¹⁴"Now I am about to go the way of all the earth. You know with all your heart and soul that not one of all the good promises the LORD your God gave you has failed. Every promise has been fulfilled; not one has failed. ¹⁵But just as every good promise of the LORD your God has come true, so the LORD will bring on you all the evil he has threatened, until he has destroyed you from this good land he has given you. ¹⁶If you violate the covenant of the LORD your God, which he commanded you, and go and serve other gods and bow down to them, the LORD's anger will burn against you, and you will quickly perish from the good land he has given you."

The Covenant Renewed at Shechem

24 Then Joshua assembled all the tribes of Israel at Shechem. He summoned the elders, leaders, judges and officials of Israel, and they presented themselves before God.

²Joshua said to all the people, "This is what the LORD, the God of Israel, says: 'Long ago your forefathers, including Terah the father of Abraham and Nahor, lived beyond the River*a* and worshiped other gods. ³But I took your father Abraham from the land beyond the River and led him throughout Canaan and gave him many descendants. I gave him Isaac, ⁴and to Isaac I gave Jacob and Esau. I assigned the hill country of Seir to Esau, but Jacob and his sons went down to Egypt.

⁵"'Then I sent Moses and Aaron, and I afflicted the Egyptians by what I did there, and I brought you out. ⁶When I brought your fathers out of Egypt, you came to the sea, and the Egyptians pursued them with chariots and horsemen*b* as far as the Red Sea.*c* ⁷But they cried to the LORD for help, and he put darkness between you and the Egyptians; he brought the sea over them and covered them. You saw with your own eyes what I did to the Egyptians. Then you lived in the desert for a long time.

⁸"'I brought you to the land of the Amorites who lived east of the Jordan. They fought against you, but I gave them into your hands. I destroyed them from before you, and you took possession of their land. ⁹When Balak son of Zippor, the king of Moab, prepared to fight against Israel, he sent for Balaam son of Beor to put a curse on you. ¹⁰But I would

---

a2 That is, the Euphrates; also in verses 3, 14 and 15   *b6* Or *charioteers*   *c6* Hebrew *Yam Suph*; that is, Sea of Reeds

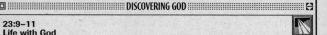

not listen to Balaam, so he blessed you again and again, and I delivered you out of his hand.

¹¹"Then you crossed the Jordan and came to Jericho. The citizens of Jericho fought against you, as did also the Amorites, Perizzites, Canaanites, Hittites, Girgashites, Hivites and Jebusites, but I gave them into your hands. ¹²I sent the hornet ahead of you, which drove them out before you—also the two Amorite kings. You did not do it with your own sword and bow. ¹³So I gave you a land on which you did not toil and cities you did not build; and you live in them and eat from vineyards and olive groves that you did not plant.'

¹⁴"Now fear the Lord and serve him with all faithfulness. Throw away the gods your forefathers worshiped beyond the River and in Egypt, and serve the Lord. ¹⁵But if serving the Lord seems undesirable to you, then choose for yourselves this day whom you will serve, whether the gods your forefathers served beyond the River, or the gods of the Amorites, in whose land you are living. But as for me and my household, we will serve the Lord."

¹⁶Then the people answered, "Far be it from us to forsake the Lord to serve other gods! ¹⁷It was the Lord our God himself who brought us and our fathers up out of Egypt, from that land of slavery, and performed those great signs before our eyes. He protected us on our entire journey and among all the nations through which we traveled. ¹⁸And the Lord drove out before us all the nations, including the Amorites, who lived in the land. We too will serve the Lord, because he is our God."

¹⁹Joshua said to the people, "You are not able to serve the Lord. He is a holy God; he is a jealous God. He will not forgive your rebellion and your sins. ²⁰If you forsake the Lord and serve foreign gods, he will turn and bring disaster on you and make an end of you, after he has been good to you."

²¹But the people said to Joshua, "No! We will serve the Lord."

²²Then Joshua said, "You are witnesses against yourselves that you have chosen to serve the Lord."

"Yes, we are witnesses," they replied.

▣ ⠿⠿⠿ DISCOVERING GOD ⠿⠿⠿ ▣

24:15
Life with God

In this passage Joshua offers the people of Israel a choice; in a sense, giving them freedom of religion. But in doing so, Joshua—and more importantly, God—doesn't imply that Israel could select any one of several ways to God. Joshua's challenge is much more cut and dried than that—either accept God or reject him. "Choice" is God's gift to humanity, intended as a means of giving us the opportunity to respond to him in love.

God wants you to choose him. He won't force you—you have the right to make the wrong choice. But his desire is that you would turn to him and reject all the false things you've been trusting in. He wants your exclusive devotion, knowing that anything else to which you give yourself will ultimately disappoint you.

Hear what Joshua says to his countrymen, and realize that these are God's words to you today. Who are you serving right now? Are you satisfied? If not, why keep paying the price of going that direction? Follow the true God—millions who have done so throughout the centuries have found him faithful. You will too!

---

²³"Now then," said Joshua, "throw away the foreign gods that are among you and yield your hearts to the Lord, the God of Israel."

²⁴And the people said to Joshua, "We will serve the Lord our God and obey him."

²⁵On that day Joshua made a covenant for the people, and there at Shechem he drew up for them decrees and laws. ²⁶And Joshua recorded these things in the Book of the Law of God. Then he took a large stone and set it up there under the oak near the holy place of the Lord.

²⁷"See!" he said to all the people. "This stone will be a witness against us. It has heard all the words the Lord has said to us. It will be a witness against you if you are untrue to your God."

Buried in the Promised Land

²⁸Then Joshua sent the people away, each to his own inheritance.

²⁹After these things, Joshua son of Nun, the servant of the LORD, died at the age of a hundred and ten. ³⁰And they buried him in the land of his inheritance, at Timnath Serah*ᵃ* in the hill country of Ephraim, north of Mount Gaash.

³¹Israel served the LORD throughout the lifetime of Joshua and of the elders who outlived him and who had experienced everything the LORD had done for Israel.

³²And Joseph's bones, which the Israelites had brought up from Egypt, were buried at Shechem in the tract of land that Jacob bought for a hundred pieces of silver*ᵇ* from the sons of Hamor, the father of Shechem. This became the inheritance of Joseph's descendants.

³³And Eleazar son of Aaron died and was buried at Gibeah, which had been allotted to his son Phinehas in the hill country of Ephraim.

ᵃ30 Also known as *Timnath Heres* (see Judges 2:9)   *ᵇ32* Hebrew *hundred kesitahs*; a kesitah was a unit of money of unknown weight and value.

For most of my adult life I have been a workaholic. I am now 41 years old. My early career blossomed at the expense of my family while I spent ten years traveling on business. By the time I realized what was happening, my first marriage was ending in divorce. This left a void in the lives of each family member including our only daughter, who was seven years old at the time.

At about that time a friend asked me to come to a Sunday "Seeker service" at his church. I can't remember much about that first service, other than the fact that I really enjoyed it. That year I attended a church-sponsored marriage and divorce workshop where I learned about God's views on marriage, divorce and relationships. What I learned there made me think especially of the relationship I had with my daughter.

In September of 1993 I knelt before God and asked him to be my personal Savior. I asked him to forgive me of my sins, to help me with my selfishness and to guide me to mend my broken relationships. Since that time I have worked hard to gain a Biblical perspective on my life and my relationships. Sometimes I feel that God is trying to break me of my old habits and help me learn new ones, much as a parent would a child who is learning these things for the first time. I am growing each day in Christ and, with the help of Sunday and midweek services, I stay better focused.

Even though my business is doing poorly, my relationship with my daughter is still broken, and several other traumatic conditions continue to plague my life, my faith in Christ has never been stronger. In the midst of all this turmoil I have a lot to be thankful for, including the baby my new wife and I are going to have this fall.

Introduction

THE BOTTOM LINE

The books of Judges and Ruth describe a crucial era in Israel's early history. During this time, the nation had no king. Each person was free to do "as he saw fit" (Judges chapter 21, verse 25 [p. 323]). This freedom led to evil practices—especially wicked religious acts. In the midst of rampant perversity, God raised up a series of leaders, called "judges." These men and women called Israel back to the one true God and helped the people overcome their oppressors. Yet as soon as each judge died, the people returned to their ruinous ways. If you want to discover how to live as a God-follower in an age when "anything goes," settle into these two books. They provide worthy examples of strong character that not only helped to deliver Israel, but also helped the people return to God.

CENTRAL IDEAS

- God uses imperfect people to champion his cause on earth.
- Judges graphically depicts the human capacity for sin and shows how evil periodically encounters God's judgment.
- In spite of sin, God shows love both to his people and to those who want to become God-followers.

TITLES

Judges is named after the leaders who governed Israel before they had kings; Ruth was a woman of faith who lived during this time.

AUTHORS AND READERS

Samuel is traditionally credited with writing the historical book of the Judges of Israel, but the author was probably one of his close associates. The author who recorded the story of Ruth is unknown; the book was probably written after 1000 B.C.

TIME LINE

The "judges" begin to rule Israel (c. 1375 B.C.)	Egyptian tombs display perils of the afterlife (c. 1300 B.C.)			Book of Judges written (c. 1000 B.C.)	David establishes Jerusalem as his capital city (c. 1000 B.C.)
1400 BC	**1300**	**1200**	**1100**	**1000**	**900**
Egyptian slaves connect the Nile and the Red Sea with a canal (c. 1380 B.C.)		Troy is destroyed in the Trojan War (c. 1183 B.C.)		Book of Ruth written (c. 1000 B.C.)	First verified date of poppies grown in Egypt (c. 950 B.C.)

I'll only be gone a few minutes," Miss Harris, our sixth-grade teacher, said. "Behave while I'm gone."

Fat chance, I said to myself. Her request was reasonable enough. The problem was that we were a bunch of twelve-year-old kids. And while the cat was away, the mice were going to play. No sooner was Miss Harris out of the room than Ernie Bellone ran over to the door. "I'll stand guard," he said. Tony Stewart wadded up a piece of paper and hit Dave Carr in the back of the head. Bob Noack interpreted that as a declaration of war and quickly began wadding up pieces of paper and throwing them as fast and hard as he could. Within seconds, a hail of paper projectiles turned that classroom into a cellulose snowstorm. A few kids refused to join in. "You're gonna get us all in trouble," they complained.

"Here she comes!" gasped Ernie in a high-decibel whisper. In a flash we all raced to our desks, picked up our pencils, and started scribbling.

> **"Here she comes!" gasped Ernie in a high-decibel whisper.**

Miss Harris was impressed at our apparent order—for about a second. Then she saw the floor covered with wadded paper balls. Needless to say, everyone had to stay after school—even those who had been noncombatants.

Most of us aren't surprised when kids prefer anarchy over order. They'll do what *they* think is fun in almost every situation. Adults often do the same thing, but there's a difference. Kids usually know when they're doing wrong and try to hide it from authority figures. We adults, however, typically redefine right and wrong according to our preferences. It's much easier to say, "It's okay as long as nobody gets hurt" than, "I know I'm doing wrong even if I temporarily escape the consequences." We are masters of rationalization.

Actually, we're a lot like the ancient Israelites right after they settled in their new homeland. Without a king to direct them, they did whatever they felt like doing. Many turned to the false gods and goddesses of the land, such as Baal, a rain and fertility god, or Ashtoreth, Baal's female counterpart. The "worship" of these false gods and goddesses included sexual immorality and even human sacrifice. In spite of this, the people convinced themselves that their behavior was necessary to insure a productive harvest. "We'd better cover our bases with the local deities in case our God doesn't come through for us!" they reasoned.

The book of Judges tells of the repeated cycles in which the nation of Israel rebelled against God, suffered defeat at the hands of an enemy, cried out to God for help, and then was delivered by a judge (a spiritual and military leader). The book of Ruth, however, tells about one woman during this period who remained faithful to God in spite of hardship.

Have you perfected the art of rationalizing your wrongdoing? God can see through the act. But don't lose hope. He is ready to help you face the truth of your cover-ups and to set a new course for the future. Turn to Judges chapter 6, verses 31–32 (page 302), to see how one family boldly confronted the self-deceptive futility of idol worship and challenged the people to turn back to the real God.

JUDGES

Israel Fights the Remaining Canaanites

1 After the death of Joshua, the Israelites asked the LORD, "Who will be the fir to go up and fight for us against the Canaanites?"

²The LORD answered, "Judah is to go; I have given the land into their hands."

³Then the men of Judah said to the Simeonites their brothers, "Come up with us in the territory allotted to us, to fight against the Canaanites. We in turn will go with yo into yours." So the Simeonites went with them.

⁴When Judah attacked, the LORD gave the Canaanites and Perizzites into their han and they struck down ten thousand men at Bezek. ⁵It was there that they found Adon Bezek and fought against him, putting to rout the Canaanites and Perizzites. ⁶Adoni-Be zek fled, but they chased him and caught him, and cut off his thumbs and big toes.

⁷Then Adoni-Bezek said, "Seventy kings with their thumbs and big toes cut off hav picked up scraps under my table. Now God has paid me back for what I did to them They brought him to Jerusalem, and he died there.

⁸The men of Judah attacked Jerusalem also and took it. They put the city to the swor and set it on fire.

⁹After that, the men of Judah went down to fight against the Canaanites living in th hill country, the Negev and the western foothills. ¹⁰They advanced against the Canaa ites living in Hebron (formerly called Kiriath Arba) and defeated Sheshai, Ahiman an Talmai.

¹¹From there they advanced against the people living in Debir (formerly called Kiria Sepher). ¹²And Caleb said, "I will give my daughter Acsah in marriage to the man wh attacks and captures Kiriath Sepher." ¹³Othniel son of Kenaz, Caleb's younger brothe took it; so Caleb gave him his daughter Acsah to him in marriage.

¹⁴One day when she came to Othniel, she urged him*ᵃ* to ask her father for a fiel When she got off her donkey, Caleb asked her, "What can I do for you?"

¹⁵She replied, "Do me a special favor. Since you have given me land in the Negev, gi me also springs of water." Then Caleb gave her the upper and lower springs.

¹⁶The descendants of Moses' father-in-law, the Kenite, went up from the City Palms*ᵇ* with the men of Judah to live among the people of the Desert of Judah in th Negev near Arad.

¹⁷Then the men of Judah went with the Simeonites their brothers and attacked th Canaanites living in Zephath, and they totally destroyed*ᶜ* the city. Therefore it wa called Hormah.*ᵈ* ¹⁸The men of Judah also took*ᵉ* Gaza, Ashkelon and Ekron—each ci with its territory.

¹⁹The LORD was with the men of Judah. They took possession of the hill country, b they were unable to drive the people from the plains, because they had iron chario ²⁰As Moses had promised, Hebron was given to Caleb, who drove from it the three so of Anak. ²¹The Benjamites, however, failed to dislodge the Jebusites, who were living Jerusalem; to this day the Jebusites live there with the Benjamites.

²²Now the house of Joseph attacked Bethel, and the LORD was with them. ²³When the sent men to spy out Bethel (formerly called Luz), ²⁴the spies saw a man coming out of th city and they said to him, "Show us how to get into the city and we will see that you a

---

ᵃ 14 Hebrew; Septuagint and Vulgate *Othniel, he urged her*   *ᵇ 16* That is, Jericho   *ᶜ 17* The Hebrew term refers to the irrevocable giving over of things or persons to the LORD, often by totally destroying them.   *ᵈ 17* *Hormah* means *destruction.*
ᵉ 18 Hebrew; Septuagint *Judah did not take*

eated well." ²⁵So he showed them, and they put the city to the sword but spared the man and his whole family. ²⁶He then went to the land of the Hittites, where he built a city and called it Luz, which is its name to this day.

²⁷But Manasseh did not drive out the people of Beth Shan or Taanach or Dor or Ibleam r Megiddo and their surrounding settlements, for the Canaanites were determined to ve in that land. ²⁸When Israel became strong, they pressed the Canaanites into forced abor but never drove them out completely. ²⁹Nor did Ephraim drive out the Canaanites ving in Gezer, but the Canaanites continued to live there among them. ³⁰Neither did ebulun drive out the Canaanites living in Kitron or Nahalol, who remained among them; ut they did subject them to forced labor. ³¹Nor did Asher drive out those living in Acco or idon or Ahlab or Aczib or Helbah or Aphek or Rehob, ³²and because of this the people of Asher lived among the Canaanite inhabitants of the land. ³³Neither did Naphtali drive out hose living in Beth Shemesh or Beth Anath; but the Naphtalites too lived among the Canaanite inhabitants of the land, and those living in Beth Shemesh and Beth Anath ecame forced laborers for them. ³⁴The Amorites confined the Danites to the hill country, ot allowing them to come down into the plain. ³⁵And the Amorites were determined also to hold out in Mount Heres, Aijalon and Shaalbim, but when the power of the house f Joseph increased, they too were pressed into forced labor. ³⁶The boundary of the Amorites was from Scorpion*a* Pass to Sela and beyond.

The Angel of the LORD at Bokim

2 The angel of the LORD went up from Gilgal to Bokim and said, I brought you up out of Egypt and led you nto the land that I swore to give to your prefathers. I said, 'I will never break my ovenant with you, ²and you shall not nake a covenant with the people of this and, but you shall break down their altars.' et you have disobeyed me. Why have you lone this? ³Now therefore I tell you that I vill not drive them out before you; they vill be ⸤thorns⸥ in your sides and their gods vill be a snare to you."

⁴When the angel of the LORD had spoken hese things to all the Israelites, the people wept aloud, ⁵and they called that place Bo-im.*b* There they offered sacrifices to the LORD.

Disobedience and Defeat

⁶After Joshua had dismissed the Israel-tes, they went to take possession of the and, each to his own inheritance. ⁷The people served the LORD throughout the life-ime of Joshua and of the elders who outlived him and who had seen all the great things he LORD had done for Israel.

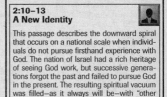

⁸Joshua son of Nun, the servant of the LORD, died at the age of a hundred and ten. ⁹And hey buried him in the land of his inheritance, at Timnath Heres*c* in the hill country of phraim, north of Mount Gaash.

¹⁰After that whole generation had been gathered to their fathers, another generation grew up, who knew neither the LORD nor what he had done for Israel. ¹¹Then the Israel-

36 Hebrew Akrabbim   *b5 Bokim means weepers.*   *c9 Also known as Timnath Serah (see Joshua 19:50 and 24:30)*

ites did evil in the eyes of the LORD and served the Baals. ¹²They forsook the LORD, the Go
of their fathers, who had brought them out of Egypt. They followed and worshipe
various gods of the peoples around them. They provoked the LORD to anger ¹³because the
forsook him and served Baal and the Ashtoreths. ¹⁴In his anger against Israel the LOR
handed them over to raiders who plundered them. He sold them to their enemies a
around, whom they were no longer able to resist. ¹⁵Whenever Israel went out to figh
the hand of the LORD was against them to defeat them, just as he had sworn to them
They were in great distress.

¹⁶Then the LORD raised up judges,ᵃ who saved them out of the hands of these raiders
¹⁷Yet they would not listen to their judges but prostituted themselves to other gods an
worshiped them. Unlike their fathers, they quickly turned from the way in which thei
fathers had walked, the way of obedience to the LORD's commands. ¹⁸Whenever the LOR
raised up a judge for them, he was with the judge and saved them out of the hands c
their enemies as long as the judge lived; for the LORD had compassion on them as the
groaned under those who oppressed and afflicted them. ¹⁹But when the judge died, th
people returned to ways even more corrupt than those of their fathers, following othe
gods and serving and worshiping them. They refused to give up their evil practices an
stubborn ways.

²⁰Therefore the LORD was very angry with Israel and said, "Because this nation ha
violated the covenant that I laid down for their forefathers and has not listened to me, ²
will no longer drive out before them any of the nations Joshua left when he died. ²²I wil
use them to test Israel and see whether they will keep the way of the LORD and walk in
as their forefathers did." ²³The LORD had allowed those nations to remain; he did not driv
them out at once by giving them into the hands of Joshua.

3 These are the nations the LORD left to test all those Israelites who had nc
experienced any of the wars in Canaan ²(he did this only to teach warfare t
the descendants of the Israelites who had not had previous battle experience): ³the fiv
rulers of the Philistines, all the Canaanites, the Sidonians, and the Hivites living in th
Lebanon mountains from Mount Baal Hermon to Leboᵇ Hamath. ⁴They were left to tes
the Israelites to see whether they would obey the LORD's commands, which he had give
their forefathers through Moses.

⁵The Israelites lived among the Canaanites, Hittites, Amorites, Perizzites, Hivites an
Jebusites. ⁶They took their daughters in marriage and gave their own daughters to thei
sons, and served their gods.

Othniel

⁷The Israelites did evil in the eyes of the LORD; they forgot the LORD their God and serve
the Baals and the Asherahs. ⁸The anger of the LORD burned against Israel so that he sol
them into the hands of Cushan-Rishathaim king of Aram Naharaim,ᶜ to whom th
Israelites were subject for eight years. ⁹But when they cried out to the LORD, he raised u
for them a deliverer, Othniel son of Kenaz, Caleb's younger brother, who saved them
¹⁰The Spirit of the LORD came upon him, so that he became Israel's judgeᵈ and went t
war. The LORD gave Cushan-Rishathaim king of Aram into the hands of Othniel, wh
overpowered him. ¹¹So the land had peace for forty years, until Othniel son of Kena
died.

Ehud

¹²Once again the Israelites did evil in the eyes of the LORD, and because they did thi
evil the LORD gave Eglon king of Moab power over Israel. ¹³Getting the Ammonites an
Amalekites to join him, Eglon came and attacked Israel, and they took possession of th
City of Palms.ᵉ ¹⁴The Israelites were subject to Eglon king of Moab for eighteen years

---

ᵃ16 Or leaders; similarly in verses 17–19   ᵇ3 Or to the entrance to   ᶜ8 That is, Northwest Mesopotamia   ᵈ10 Or
leader   ᵉ13 That is, Jericho

¹⁵Again the Israelites cried out to the LORD, and he gave them a deliverer—Ehud, a left-handed man, the son of Gera the Benjamite. The Israelites sent him with tribute to Eglon king of Moab. ¹⁶Now Ehud had made a double-edged sword about a foot and a half[a] long, which he strapped to his right thigh under his clothing. ¹⁷He presented the tribute to Eglon king of Moab, who was a very fat man. ¹⁸After Ehud had presented the tribute, he sent on their way the men who had carried it. ¹⁹At the idols[b] near Gilgal he himself turned back and said, "I have a secret message for you, O king."

The king said, "Quiet!" And all his attendants left him.

²⁰Ehud then approached him while he was sitting alone in the upper room of his summer palace[c] and said, "I have a message from God for you." As the king rose from his seat, ²¹Ehud reached with his left hand, drew the sword from his right thigh and plunged it into the king's belly. ²²Even the handle sank in after the blade, which came out his back. Ehud did not pull the sword out, and the fat closed in over it. ²³Then Ehud went out to the porch[d]; he shut the doors of the upper room behind him and locked them.

²⁴After he had gone, the servants came and found the doors of the upper room locked. They said, "He must be relieving himself in the inner room of the house." ²⁵They waited to the point of embarrassment, but when he did not open the doors of the room, they took a key and unlocked them. There they saw their lord fallen to the floor, dead.

²⁶While they waited, Ehud got away. He passed by the idols and escaped to Seirah. ²⁷When he arrived there, he blew a trumpet in the hill country of Ephraim, and the Israelites went down with him from the hills, with him leading them.

²⁸"Follow me," he ordered, "for the LORD has given Moab, your enemy, into your hands." So they followed him down and, taking possession of the fords of the Jordan that led to Moab, they allowed no one to cross over. ²⁹At that time they struck down about ten thousand Moabites, all vigorous and strong; not a man escaped. ³⁰That day Moab was made subject to Israel, and the land had peace for eighty years.

Shamgar

³¹After Ehud came Shamgar son of Anath, who struck down six hundred Philistines with an oxgoad. He too saved Israel.

Deborah

4 After Ehud died, the Israelites once again did evil in the eyes of the LORD. ²So the LORD sold them into the hands of Jabin, a king of Canaan, who reigned in Hazor. The commander of his army was Sisera, who lived in Harosheth Haggoyim. ³Because he had nine hundred iron chariots and had cruelly oppressed the Israelites for twenty years, they cried to the LORD for help.

⁴Deborah, a prophetess, the wife of Lappidoth, was leading[e] Israel at that time. ⁵She held court under the Palm of Deborah between Ramah and Bethel in the hill country of Ephraim, and the Israelites came to her to have their disputes decided. ⁶She sent for Barak son of Abinoam from Kedesh in Naphtali and said to him, "The LORD, the God of Israel, commands you: 'Go, take with you ten thousand men of Naphtali and Zebulun and lead the way to Mount Tabor. ⁷I will lure Sisera, the commander of Jabin's army, with his chariots and his troops to the Kishon River and give him into your hands.'"

⁸Barak said to her, "If you go with me, I will go; but if you don't go with me, I won't go."

⁹"Very well," Deborah said, "I will go with you. But because of the way you are going about this,[f] the honor will not be yours, for the LORD will hand Sisera over to a woman." So Deborah went with Barak to Kedesh, ¹⁰where he summoned Zebulun and Naphtali. Ten thousand men followed him, and Deborah also went with him.

---

[a]16 Hebrew *a cubit* (about 0.5 meter)   [b]19 Or *the stone quarries*; also in verse 26   [c]20 The meaning of the Hebrew for this phrase is uncertain.   [d]23 The meaning of the Hebrew for this word is uncertain.   [e]4 Traditionally *judging*
[f]9 Or *But on the expedition you are undertaking*

¹¹Now Heber the Kenite had left the other Kenites, the descendants of Hobab, Moses' brother-in-law,ᵃ and pitched his tent by the great tree in Zaanannim near Kedesh.

¹²When they told Sisera that Barak son of Abinoam had gone up to Mount Tabor, ¹³Sisera gathered together his nine hundred iron chariots and all the men with him, from Harosheth Haggoyim to the Kishon River.

¹⁴Then Deborah said to Barak, "Go! This is the day the Lᴏʀᴅ has given Sisera into your hands. Has not the Lᴏʀᴅ gone ahead of you?" So Barak went down Mount Tabor, followed by ten thousand men. ¹⁵At Barak's advance, the Lᴏʀᴅ routed Sisera and all his chariots and army by the sword, and Sisera abandoned his chariot and fled on foot. ¹⁶But Barak pursued the chariots and army as far as Harosheth Haggoyim. All the troops of Sisera fell by the sword; not a man was left.

¹⁷Sisera, however, fled on foot to the tent of Jael, the wife of Heber the Kenite, because there were friendly relations between Jabin king of Hazor and the clan of Heber the Kenite.

¹⁸Jael went out to meet Sisera and said to him, "Come, my lord, come right in. Don't be afraid." So he entered her tent, and she put a covering over him.

¹⁹"I'm thirsty," he said. "Please give me some water." She opened a skin of milk, gave him a drink, and covered him up.

²⁰"Stand in the doorway of the tent," he told her. "If someone comes by and asks you, 'Is anyone here?' say 'No.'"

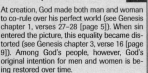

ADDRESSING QUESTIONS

4:4–5
Human Experience

Q

At creation, God made both man and woman to co-rule over his perfect world (see Genesis chapter 1, verses 27–28 [page 5]). When sin entered the picture, this equality became distorted (see Genesis chapter 3, verse 16 [page 9]). Among God's people, however, God's original intention for men and women is being restored over time.

This passage shows us one early example of this restoration. Here we find a gifted woman named Deborah using her abilities as a judge to lead Israel. Though women rarely held such leadership positions, God affirmed this arrangement by making Deborah a prophetess (verses 6–7) and by using her unique, God-given capabilities to direct the affairs of his people.

²¹But Jael, Heber's wife, picked up a tent peg and a hammer and went quietly to him while he lay fast asleep, exhausted. She drove the peg through his temple into the ground, and he died.

²²Barak came by in pursuit of Sisera, and Jael went out to meet him. "Come," she said, "I will show you the man you're looking for." So he went in with her, and there lay Sisera with the tent peg through his temple—dead.

²³On that day God subdued Jabin, the Canaanite king, before the Israelites. ²⁴And the hand of the Israelites grew stronger and stronger against Jabin, the Canaanite king, until they destroyed him.

The Song of Deborah

5 On that day Deborah and Barak son of Abinoam sang this song:

²"When the princes in Israel take the lead,
  when the people willingly offer themselves—
  praise the Lᴏʀᴅ!

³"Hear this, you kings! Listen, you rulers!
  I will sing toᵇ the Lᴏʀᴅ, I will sing;
  I will make music toᶜ the Lᴏʀᴅ, the God of Israel.

⁴"O Lᴏʀᴅ, when you went out from Seir,
  when you marched from the land of Edom,

ᵃ11 Or father-in-law   ᵇ3 Or of   ᶜ3 Or / with song I will praise

the earth shook, the heavens poured,
    the clouds poured down water.
⁵The mountains quaked before the LORD, the One of Sinai,
    before the LORD, the God of Israel.

⁶"In the days of Shamgar son of Anath,
    in the days of Jael, the roads were abandoned;
    travelers took to winding paths.
⁷Village life*ᵃ* in Israel ceased,
    ceased until I,*ᵇ* Deborah, arose,
    arose a mother in Israel.
⁸When they chose new gods,
    war came to the city gates,
  and not a shield or spear was seen
    among forty thousand in Israel.
⁹My heart is with Israel's princes,
    with the willing volunteers among the people.
    Praise the LORD!

¹⁰"You who ride on white donkeys,
    sitting on your saddle blankets,
    and you who walk along the road,
  consider ¹¹the voice of the singers*ᶜ* at the watering places.
    They recite the righteous acts of the LORD,
    the righteous acts of his warriors*ᵈ* in Israel.

"Then the people of the LORD
    went down to the city gates.
¹²'Wake up, wake up, Deborah!
    Wake up, wake up, break out in song!
  Arise, O Barak!
    Take captive your captives, O son of Abinoam.'

¹³"Then the men who were left
    came down to the nobles;
  the people of the LORD
    came to me with the mighty.
¹⁴Some came from Ephraim, whose roots were in Amalek;
    Benjamin was with the people who followed you.
  From Makir captains came down,
    from Zebulun those who bear a commander's staff.
¹⁵The princes of Issachar were with Deborah;
    yes, Issachar was with Barak,
    rushing after him into the valley.
  In the districts of Reuben
    there was much searching of heart.
¹⁶Why did you stay among the campfires*ᵉ*
    to hear the whistling for the flocks?
  In the districts of Reuben
    there was much searching of heart.
¹⁷Gilead stayed beyond the Jordan.
    And Dan, why did he linger by the ships?
  Asher remained on the coast

ᵃ7 Or Warriors   *ᵇ7 Or you*   *ᶜ11 Or archers; the meaning of the Hebrew for this word is uncertain.*   *ᵈ11 Or*
illagers   *ᵉ16 Or saddlebags*

and stayed in his coves.
¹⁸The people of Zebulun risked their very lives;
    so did Naphtali on the heights of the field.

¹⁹"Kings came, they fought;
    the kings of Canaan fought
  at Taanach by the waters of Megiddo,
    but they carried off no silver, no plunder.
²⁰From the heavens the stars fought,
    from their courses they fought against Sisera.
²¹The river Kishon swept them away,
    the age-old river, the river Kishon.
    March on, my soul; be strong!
²²Then thundered the horses' hoofs—
    galloping, galloping go his mighty steeds.
²³'Curse Meroz,' said the angel of the LORD.
    'Curse its people bitterly,
  because they did not come to help the LORD,
    to help the LORD against the mighty.'

²⁴"Most blessed of women be Jael,
    the wife of Heber the Kenite,
    most blessed of tent-dwelling women.
²⁵He asked for water, and she gave him milk;
    in a bowl fit for nobles she brought him curdled milk.
²⁶Her hand reached for the tent peg,
    her right hand for the workman's hammer.
  She struck Sisera, she crushed his head,
    she shattered and pierced his temple.
²⁷At her feet he sank,
    he fell; there he lay.
  At her feet he sank, he fell;
    where he sank, there he fell—dead.

²⁸"Through the window peered Sisera's mother;
    behind the lattice she cried out,
  'Why is his chariot so long in coming?
    Why is the clatter of his chariots delayed?'
²⁹The wisest of her ladies answer her;
    indeed, she keeps saying to herself,
³⁰'Are they not finding and dividing the spoils:
    a girl or two for each man,
    colorful garments as plunder for Sisera,
    colorful garments embroidered,
    highly embroidered garments for my neck—
  all this as plunder?'

³¹"So may all your enemies perish, O LORD!
    But may they who love you be like the sun
    when it rises in its strength."

Then the land had peace forty years.

Gideon

6 Again the Israelites did evil in the eyes of the LORD, and for seven years he gave them into the hands of the Midianites. ²Because the power of Midian was so oppressive, the Israelites prepared shelters for themselves in mountain clefts, caves and strongholds. ³Whenever the Israelites planted their crops, the Midianites, Amalekites and other eastern peoples invaded the country. ⁴They camped on the land and ruined the crops all the way to Gaza and did not spare a living thing for Israel, neither sheep nor cattle nor donkeys. ⁵They came up with their livestock and their tents like swarms of locusts. It was impossible to count the men and their camels; they invaded the land to ravage it. ⁶Midian so impoverished the Israelites that they cried out to the LORD for help.

⁷When the Israelites cried to the LORD because of Midian, ⁸he sent them a prophet, who said, "This is what the LORD, the God of Israel, says: I brought you up out of Egypt, out of the land of slavery. ⁹I snatched you from the power of Egypt and from the hand of all your oppressors. I drove them from before you and gave you their land. ¹⁰I said to you, 'I am the LORD your God; do not worship the gods of the Amorites, in whose land you live.' But you have not listened to me."

::::::::::::::::::::: **KNOWING YOURSELF** :::::::::::::::::::::

6:1–40
A New Identity

Heroes sometimes come wrapped in unlikely packages, and Gideon is a good example of that.

After 40 years of peace, the ancient nation of Israel turned from God and suffered the painful consequences of that choice. For seven years Israel's enemies, the Midianites and their allies, trampled the people and ravaged their land (verses 1–6). Terrified, the people of Israel hid from the invaders by living on cliffs and in caves.

Nobody would have picked Gideon as Israel's hero. When we first see Gideon, he's working in a secluded location, fearful of losing his grain to the invading Midianites. So when God's angel initially greets him as "mighty warrior" (verse 12), we might imagine Gideon looking around to see who the angel meant! By his own admission, Gideon came from the least significant family in the nation. He certainly didn't see himself as "mighty warrior" material.

Two things happened that enabled Gideon to rise to the occasion. One involved his relationship with God; the other involved his relationship with his family.

First, God proved, then allowed Gideon to test, his call to service. Modern readers might puzzle over Gideon's need for repeated reassurance, but God was patient in answering those requests. After the initial display of divine fire (verses 20–21), Gideon was convinced of God's call. Later, however, Gideon double-checked, then *triple-checked* God's directives (verses 37 and 39). After this time of testing, Gideon knew that he could proceed with the full assurance of God's powerful, guiding presence.

Second, under God's direction, Gideon tore down his father's pagan altars, thereby destroying the means by which his family worshiped false gods. This action established Gideon's revolutionary cause and served as a wake-up call to the people of Israel, assuring them of the divine origin of Gideon's leadership.

The same God who reassured Gideon of his presence does the same thing today for those who seek him. While he may not send fire from heaven at our request, God is willing and able to identify himself. He reveals himself through various means: through creation, through the words of the Bible, through Jesus Christ, and through his followers.

God also strengthens his followers and enables them to remove from their lives any barriers that stand in the way of giving their full devotion to him. Gideon found out that tearing down the idols in his life involved a great deal of personal risk. Doing so with your own personal "idols" may involve the same for you. But, as Gideon also discovered, putting aside his fear and entering into a relationship with God was well worth the effort.

Are you willing to risk it?

¹¹The angel of the Lord came and sat down under the oak in Ophrah that belonged to Joash the Abiezrite, where his son Gideon was threshing wheat in a winepress to keep it from the Midianites. ¹²When the angel of the Lord appeared to Gideon, he said, "The Lord is with you, mighty warrior."

¹³"But sir," Gideon replied, "if the Lord is with us, why has all this happened to us? Where are all his wonders that our fathers told us about when they said, 'Did not the Lord bring us up out of Egypt?' But now the Lord has abandoned us and put us into the hand of Midian."

¹⁴The Lord turned to him and said, "Go in the strength you have and save Israel out of Midian's hand. Am I not sending you?"

¹⁵"But Lord,ᵃ" Gideon asked, "how can I save Israel? My clan is the weakest in Manasseh, and I am the least in my family."

¹⁶The Lord answered, "I will be with you, and you will strike down all the Midianites together."

¹⁷Gideon replied, "If now I have found favor in your eyes, give me a sign that it is really you talking to me. ¹⁸Please do not go away until I come back and bring my offering and set it before you."

And the Lord said, "I will wait until you return."

¹⁹Gideon went in, prepared a young goat, and from an ephahᵇ of flour he made bread without yeast. Putting the meat in a basket and its broth in a pot, he brought them out and offered them to him under the oak.

²⁰The angel of God said to him, "Take the meat and the unleavened bread, place them on this rock, and pour out the broth." And Gideon did so. ²¹With the tip of the staff that was in his hand, the angel of the Lord touched the meat and the unleavened bread. Fire flared from the rock, consuming the meat and the bread. And the angel of the Lord disappeared. ²²When Gideon realized that it was the angel of the Lord, he exclaimed, "Ah, Sovereign Lord! I have seen the angel of the Lord face to face!"

²³But the Lord said to him, "Peace! Do not be afraid. You are not going to die."

²⁴So Gideon built an altar to the Lord there and called it The Lord is Peace. To this day it stands in Ophrah of the Abiezrites.

²⁵That same night the Lord said to him, "Take the second bull from your father's herd, the one seven years old.ᶜ Tear down your father's altar to Baal and cut down the Asherah poleᵈ beside it. ²⁶Then build a proper kind ofᵉ altar to the Lord your God on the top of this height. Using the wood of the Asherah pole that you cut down, offer the secondᶠ bull as a burnt offering."

²⁷So Gideon took ten of his servants and did as the Lord told him. But because he was afraid of his family and the men of the town, he did it at night rather than in the daytime.

²⁸In the morning when the men of the town got up, there was Baal's altar, demolished, with the Asherah pole beside it cut down and the second bull sacrificed on the newly built altar!

²⁹They asked each other, "Who did this?"

When they carefully investigated, they were told, "Gideon son of Joash did it."

³⁰The men of the town demanded of Joash, "Bring out your son. He must die, because he has broken down Baal's altar and cut down the Asherah pole beside it."

³¹But Joash replied to the hostile crowd around him, "Are you going to plead Baal's cause? Are you trying to save him? Whoever fights for him shall be put to death by morning! If Baal really is a god, he can defend himself when someone breaks down his altar." ³²So that day they called Gideon "Jerub-Baal,ᵍ" saying, "Let Baal contend with him," because he broke down Baal's altar.

³³Now all the Midianites, Amalekites and other eastern peoples joined forces and

---

ᵃ15 Or sir   ᵇ19 That is, probably about 3/5 bushel (about 22 liters)   ᶜ25 Or Take a full-grown, mature bull from your father's herd   ᵈ25 That is, a symbol of the goddess Asherah; here and elsewhere in Judges   ᵉ26 Or build with layers of stone an   ᶠ26 Or full-grown; also in verse 28   ᵍ32 Jerub-Baal means let Baal contend.

crossed over the Jordan and camped in the Valley of Jezreel. ³⁴Then the Spirit of the LORD came upon Gideon, and he blew a trumpet, summoning the Abiezrites to follow him. ³⁵He sent messengers throughout Manasseh, calling them to arms, and also into Asher, Zebulun and Naphtali, so that they too went up to meet them.

³⁶Gideon said to God, "If you will save Israel by my hand as you have promised— ³⁷look, I will place a wool fleece on the threshing floor. If there is dew only on the fleece and all the ground is dry, then I will know that you will save Israel by my hand, as you said." ³⁸And that is what happened. Gideon rose early the next day; he squeezed the fleece and wrung out the dew—a bowlful of water.

³⁹Then Gideon said to God, "Do not be angry with me. Let me make just one more request. Allow me one more test with the fleece. This time make the fleece dry and the ground covered with dew." ⁴⁰That night God did so. Only the fleece was dry; all the ground was covered with dew.

Gideon Defeats the Midianites

7 Early in the morning, Jerub-Baal (that is, Gideon) and all his men camped at the spring of Harod. The camp of Midian was north of them in the valley near the hill of Moreh. ²The LORD said to Gideon, "You have too many men for me to deliver Midian into their hands. In order that Israel may not boast against me that her own strength has saved her, ³announce now to the people, 'Anyone who trembles with fear may turn back and leave Mount Gilead.'" So twenty-two thousand men left, while ten thousand remained.

⁴But the LORD said to Gideon, "There are still too many men. Take them down to the water, and I will sift them for you there. If I say, 'This one shall go with you,' he shall go; but if I say, 'This one shall not go with you,' he shall not go."

⁵So Gideon took the men down to the water. There the LORD told him, "Separate those who lap the water with their tongues like a dog from those who kneel down to drink." ⁶Three hundred men lapped with their hands to their mouths. All the rest got down on their knees to drink.

⁷The LORD said to Gideon, "With the three hundred men that lapped I will save you and give the Midianites into your hands. Let all the other men go, each to his own place." ⁸So Gideon sent the rest of the Israelites to their tents but kept the three hundred, who took over the provisions and trumpets of the others.

Now the camp of Midian lay below him

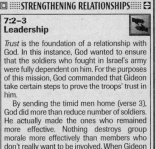

STRENGTHENING RELATIONSHIPS

7:2-3
Leadership

Trust is the foundation of a relationship with God. In this instance, God wanted to ensure that the soldiers who fought in Israel's army were fully dependent on him. For the purposes of this mission, God commanded that Gideon take certain steps to prove the troops' trust in him.

By sending the timid men home (verse 3), God did more than reduce number of soldiers. He actually made the ones who remained more effective. Nothing destroys group morale more effectively than members who don't really want to be involved. When Gideon announced that the frightened men could leave, over two-thirds of the army went home! Think of the impact that such an overwhelming majority of frightened soldiers would have had on the campaign against the Midianites.

There's a leadership principle here: When you're called to work in a team setting, work with those who are willing. A small number of committed people working on a task will always be more effective than a larger, but halfhearted, team.

in the valley. ⁹During that night the LORD said to Gideon, "Get up, go down against the camp, because I am going to give it into your hands. ¹⁰If you are afraid to attack, go down to the camp with your servant Purah ¹¹and listen to what they are saying. Afterward, you will be encouraged to attack the camp." So he and Purah his servant went down to the outposts of the camp. ¹²The Midianites, the Amalekites and all the other eastern peoples had settled in the valley, thick as locusts. Their camels could no more be counted than the sand on the seashore.

¹³Gideon arrived just as a man was telling a friend his dream. "I had a dream," he was saying. "A round loaf of barley bread came tumbling into the Midianite camp. It struck the tent with such force that the tent overturned and collapsed."

¹⁴His friend responded, "This can be nothing other than the sword of Gideon son of Joash, the Israelite. God has given the Midianites and the whole camp into his hands."

¹⁵When Gideon heard the dream and its interpretation, he worshiped God. He returned to the camp of Israel and called out, "Get up! The Lord has given the Midianite camp into your hands." ¹⁶Dividing the three hundred men into three companies, he placed trumpets and empty jars in the hands of all of them, with torches inside.

¹⁷"Watch me," he told them. "Follow my lead. When I get to the edge of the camp, do exactly as I do. ¹⁸When I and all who are with me blow our trumpets, then from all around the camp blow yours and shout, 'For the Lord and for Gideon.'"

¹⁹Gideon and the hundred men with him reached the edge of the camp at the beginning of the middle watch, just after they had changed the guard. They blew their trumpets and broke the jars that were in their hands. ²⁰The three companies blew the trumpets and smashed the jars. Grasping the torches in their left hands and holding in their right hands the trumpets they were to blow, they shouted, "A sword for the Lord and for Gideon!" ²¹While each man held his position around the camp, all the Midianites ran, crying out as they fled.

²²When the three hundred trumpets sounded, the Lord caused the men throughout the camp to turn on each other with their swords. The army fled to Beth Shittah toward Zererah as far as the border of Abel Meholah near Tabbath. ²³Israelites from Naphtali, Asher and all Manasseh were called out, and they pursued the Midianites. ²⁴Gideon sent messengers throughout the hill country of Ephraim, saying, "Come down against the Midianites and seize the waters of the Jordan ahead of them as far as Beth Barah."

So all the men of Ephraim were called out and they took the waters of the Jordan as far as Beth Barah. ²⁵They also captured two of the Midianite leaders, Oreb and Zeeb. They killed Oreb at the rock of Oreb, and Zeeb at the winepress of Zeeb. They pursued the Midianites and brought the heads of Oreb and Zeeb to Gideon, who was by the Jordan.

Zebah and Zalmunna

8 Now the Ephraimites asked Gideon, "Why have you treated us like this? Why didn't you call us when you went to fight Midian?" And they criticized him sharply.

²But he answered them, "What have I accomplished compared to you? Aren't the gleanings of Ephraim's grapes better than the full grape harvest of Abiezer? ³God gave Oreb and Zeeb, the Midianite leaders, into your hands. What was I able to do compared to you?" At this, their resentment against him subsided.

⁴Gideon and his three hundred men, exhausted yet keeping up the pursuit, came to the Jordan and crossed it. ⁵He said to the men of Succoth, "Give my troops some bread; they are worn out, and I am still pursuing Zebah and Zalmunna, the kings of Midian."

⁶But the officials of Succoth said, "Do you already have the hands of Zebah and Zalmunna in your possession? Why should we give bread to your troops?"

⁷Then Gideon replied, "Just for that, when the Lord has given Zebah and Zalmunna into my hand, I will tear your flesh with desert thorns and briers."

⁸From there he went up to Peniel*a* and made the same request of them, but they answered as the men of Succoth had. ⁹So he said to the men of Peniel, "When I return in triumph, I will tear down this tower."

¹⁰Now Zebah and Zalmunna were in Karkor with a force of about fifteen thousand men, all that were left of the armies of the eastern peoples; a hundred and twenty

---

a 8 Hebrew *Penuel*, a variant of *Peniel*; also in verses 9 and 17

thousand swordsmen had fallen. ¹¹Gideon went up by the route of the nomads east of Nobah and Jogbehah and fell upon the unsuspecting army. ¹²Zebah and Zalmunna, the two kings of Midian, fled, but he pursued them and captured them, routing their entire army.

¹³Gideon son of Joash then returned from the battle by the Pass of Heres. ¹⁴He caught a young man of Succoth and questioned him, and the young man wrote down for him the names of the seventy-seven officials of Succoth, the elders of the town. ¹⁵Then Gideon came and said to the men of Succoth, "Here are Zebah and Zalmunna, about whom you taunted me by saying, 'Do you already have the hands of Zebah and Zalmunna in your possession? Why should we give bread to your exhausted men?'" ¹⁶He took the elders of the town and taught the men of Succoth a lesson by punishing them with desert thorns and briers. ¹⁷He also pulled down the tower of Peniel and killed the men of the town.

¹⁸Then he asked Zebah and Zalmunna, "What kind of men did you kill at Tabor?"

"Men like you," they answered, "each one with the bearing of a prince."

¹⁹Gideon replied, "Those were my brothers, the sons of my own mother. As surely as the LORD lives, if you had spared their lives, I would not kill you." ²⁰Turning to Jether, his oldest son, he said, "Kill them!" But Jether did not draw his sword, because he was only a boy and was afraid.

²¹Zebah and Zalmunna said, "Come, do it yourself. 'As is the man, so is his strength.'" So Gideon stepped forward and killed them, and took the ornaments off their camels' necks.

Gideon's Ephod

²²The Israelites said to Gideon, "Rule over us—you, your son and your grandson—because you have saved us out of the hand of Midian."

²³But Gideon told them, "I will not rule over you, nor will my son rule over you. The LORD will rule over you." ²⁴And he said, "I do have one request, that each of you give me an earring from your share of the plunder." (It was the custom of the Ishmaelites to wear gold earrings.)

²⁵They answered, "We'll be glad to give them." So they spread out a garment, and each man threw a ring from his plunder onto it. ²⁶The weight of the gold rings he asked for came to seventeen hundred shekels,ᵃ not counting the ornaments, the pendants and the purple garments worn by the kings of Midian or the chains that were on their camels' necks. ²⁷Gideon made the gold into an ephod, which he placed in Ophrah, his town. All Israel prostituted themselves by worshiping it there, and it became a snare to Gideon and his family.

Gideon's Death

²⁸Thus Midian was subdued before the Israelites and did not raise its head again. During Gideon's lifetime, the land enjoyed peace forty years.

²⁹Jerub-Baal son of Joash went back home to live. ³⁰He had seventy sons of his own, for he had many wives. ³¹His concubine, who lived in Shechem, also bore him a son, whom he named Abimelech. ³²Gideon son of Joash died at a good old age and was buried in the tomb of his father Joash in Ophrah of the Abiezrites.

³³No sooner had Gideon died than the Israelites again prostituted themselves to the Baals. They set up Baal-Berith as their god and ³⁴did not remember the LORD their God, who had rescued them from the hands of all their enemies on every side. ³⁵They also failed to show kindness to the family of Jerub-Baal (that is, Gideon) for all the good things he had done for them.

ᵃ26 That is, about 43 pounds (about 19.5 kilograms)

Abimelech

9 Abimelech son of Jerub-Baal went to his mother's brothers in Shechem and said to them and to all his mother's clan, ²"Ask all the citizens of Shechem, 'Which is better for you: to have all seventy of Jerub-Baal's sons rule over you, or just one man?' Remember, I am your flesh and blood."

³When the brothers repeated all this to the citizens of Shechem, they were inclined to follow Abimelech, for they said, "He is our brother." ⁴They gave him seventy shekels*ᵃ* of silver from the temple of Baal-Berith, and Abimelech used it to hire reckless adventurers, who became his followers. ⁵He went to his father's home in Ophrah and on one stone murdered his seventy brothers, the sons of Jerub-Baal. But Jotham, the youngest son of Jerub-Baal, escaped by hiding. ⁶Then all the citizens of Shechem and Beth Millo gathered beside the great tree at the pillar in Shechem to crown Abimelech king.

⁷When Jotham was told about this, he climbed up on the top of Mount Gerizim and shouted to them, "Listen to me, citizens of Shechem, so that God may listen to you. ⁸One day the trees went out to anoint a king for themselves. They said to the olive tree, 'Be our king.'

⁹"But the olive tree answered, 'Should I give up my oil, by which both gods and men are honored, to hold sway over the trees?'

¹⁰"Next, the trees said to the fig tree, 'Come and be our king.'

¹¹"But the fig tree replied, 'Should I give up my fruit, so good and sweet, to hold sway over the trees?'

¹²"Then the trees said to the vine, 'Come and be our king.'

¹³"But the vine answered, 'Should I give up my wine, which cheers both gods and men, to hold sway over the trees?'

¹⁴"Finally all the trees said to the thornbush, 'Come and be our king.'

¹⁵"The thornbush said to the trees, 'If you really want to anoint me king over you, come and take refuge in my shade; but if not, then let fire come out of the thornbush and consume the cedars of Lebanon!'

¹⁶"Now if you have acted honorably and in good faith when you made Abimelech king, and if you have been fair to Jerub-Baal and his family, and if you have treated him as he deserves— ¹⁷and to think that my father fought for you, risked his life to rescue you from the hand of Midian ¹⁸(but today you have revolted against my father's family, murdered his seventy sons on a single stone, and made Abimelech, the son of his slave girl, king over the citizens of Shechem because he is your brother)— ¹⁹if then you have acted honorably and in good faith toward Jerub-Baal and his family today, may Abimelech be your joy, and may you be his, too! ²⁰But if you have not, let fire come out from Abimelech and consume you, citizens of Shechem and Beth Millo, and let fire come out from you, citizens of Shechem and Beth Millo, and consume Abimelech!"

²¹Then Jotham fled, escaping to Beer, and he lived there because he was afraid of his brother Abimelech.

²²After Abimelech had governed Israel three years, ²³God sent an evil spirit between Abimelech and the citizens of Shechem, who acted treacherously against Abimelech. ²⁴God did this in order that the crime against Jerub-Baal's seventy sons, the shedding of their blood, might be avenged on their brother Abimelech and on the citizens of Shechem, who had helped him murder his brothers. ²⁵In opposition to him these citizens of Shechem set men on the hilltops to ambush and rob everyone who passed by, and this was reported to Abimelech.

²⁶Now Gaal son of Ebed moved with his brothers into Shechem, and its citizens put their confidence in him. ²⁷After they had gone out into the fields and gathered the grapes and trodden them, they held a festival in the temple of their god. While they were eating and drinking, they cursed Abimelech. ²⁸Then Gaal son of Ebed said, "Who is Abimelech,

ᵃ 4 That is, about 1 3/4 pounds (about 0.8 kilogram)

and who is Shechem, that we should be subject to him? Isn't he Jerub-Baal's son, and isn't Zebul his deputy? Serve the men of Hamor, Shechem's father! Why should we serve Abimelech? ²⁹If only this people were under my command! Then I would get rid of him. I would say to Abimelech, 'Call out your whole army!'"ᵃ

³⁰When Zebul the governor of the city heard what Gaal son of Ebed said, he was very angry. ³¹Under cover he sent messengers to Abimelech, saying, "Gaal son of Ebed and his brothers have come to Shechem and are stirring up the city against you. ³²Now then, during the night you and your men should come and lie in wait in the fields. ³³In the morning at sunrise, advance against the city. When Gaal and his men come out against you, do whatever your hand finds to do."

³⁴So Abimelech and all his troops set out by night and took up concealed positions near Shechem in four companies. ³⁵Now Gaal son of Ebed had gone out and was standing at the entrance to the city gate just as Abimelech and his soldiers came out from their hiding place.

³⁶When Gaal saw them, he said to Zebul, "Look, people are coming down from the tops of the mountains!"

Zebul replied, "You mistake the shadows of the mountains for men."

³⁷But Gaal spoke up again: "Look, people are coming down from the center of the land, and a company is coming from the direction of the soothsayers' tree."

³⁸Then Zebul said to him, "Where is your big talk now, you who said, 'Who is Abimelech that we should be subject to him?' Aren't these the men you ridiculed? Go out and fight them!"

³⁹So Gaal led outᵇ the citizens of Shechem and fought Abimelech. ⁴⁰Abimelech chased him, and many fell wounded in the flight—all the way to the entrance to the gate. ⁴¹Abimelech stayed in Arumah, and Zebul drove Gaal and his brothers out of Shechem.

⁴²The next day the people of Shechem went out to the fields, and this was reported to Abimelech. ⁴³So he took his men, divided them into three companies and set an ambush in the fields. When he saw the people coming out of the city, he rose to attack them. ⁴⁴Abimelech and the companies with him rushed forward to a position at the entrance to the city gate. Then two companies rushed upon those in the fields and struck them down. ⁴⁵All that day Abimelech pressed his attack against the city until he had captured it and killed its people. Then he destroyed the city and scattered salt over it.

⁴⁶On hearing this, the citizens in the tower of Shechem went into the stronghold of the temple of El-Berith. ⁴⁷When Abimelech heard that they had assembled there, ⁴⁸he and all his men went up Mount Zalmon. He took an ax and cut off some branches, which he lifted to his shoulders. He ordered the men with him, "Quick! Do what you have seen me do!" ⁴⁹So all the men cut branches and followed Abimelech. They piled them against the stronghold and set it on fire over the people inside. So all the people in the tower of Shechem, about a thousand men and women, also died.

⁵⁰Next Abimelech went to Thebez and besieged it and captured it. ⁵¹Inside the city, however, was a strong tower, to which all the men and women—all the people of the city—fled. They locked themselves in and climbed up on the tower roof. ⁵²Abimelech went to the tower and stormed it. But as he approached the entrance to the tower to set it on fire, ⁵³a woman dropped an upper millstone on his head and cracked his skull.

⁵⁴Hurriedly he called to his armor-bearer, "Draw your sword and kill me, so that they can't say, 'A woman killed him.'" So his servant ran him through, and he died. ⁵⁵When the Israelites saw that Abimelech was dead, they went home.

⁵⁶Thus God repaid the wickedness that Abimelech had done to his father by murdering his seventy brothers. ⁵⁷God also made the men of Shechem pay for all their wickedness. The curse of Jotham son of Jerub-Baal came on them.

29 Septuagint; Hebrew him." Then he said to Abimelech, "Call out your whole army!"   ᵇ39 Or Gaal went out in the sight of

Tola

10 After the time of Abimelech a man of Issachar, Tola son of Puah, the son c Dodo, rose to save Israel. He lived in Shamir, in the hill country of Ephraim. ²He led*ᵃ* Israel twenty-three years; then he died, and was buried in Shamir.

Jair

³He was followed by Jair of Gilead, who led Israel twenty-two years. ⁴He had thirt sons, who rode thirty donkeys. They controlled thirty towns in Gilead, which to this da are called Havvoth Jair.*ᵇ* ⁵When Jair died, he was buried in Kamon.

Jephthah

⁶Again the Israelites did evil in the eyes of the LORD. They served the Baals and th Ashtoreths, and the gods of Aram, the gods of Sidon, the gods of Moab, the gods of th Ammonites and the gods of the Philistines. And because the Israelites forsook the LORD and no longer served him, ⁷he became angry with them. He sold them into the hands c the Philistines and the Ammonites, ⁸who that year shattered and crushed them. Fo eighteen years they oppressed all the Isra elites on the east side of the Jordan in Gile ad, the land of the Amorites. ⁹The Ammon ites also crossed the Jordan to fight agains Judah, Benjamin and the house of Ephraim and Israel was in great distress. ¹⁰Then the Israelites cried out to the LORD, "We hav sinned against you, forsaking our God and serving the Baals."

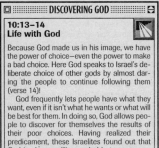

□ ▓▓▓▓ DISCOVERING GOD ▓▓▓▓ ⛶

10:13–14
Life with God

Because God made us in his image, we have the power of choice—even the power to make a bad choice. Here God speaks to Israel's de liberate choice of other gods by almost dar ing the people to continue following them (verse 14)!

God frequently lets people have what they want, even if it isn't what he wants or what will be best for them. In doing so, God allows peo ple to discover for themselves the results of their poor choices. Having realized their predicament, these Israelites found out that God is always willing and able to save peo ple—no matter how dire their circumstances— when they decide to place their trust in him (read chapter 11, verses 21 and 22).

As one embarking on a search for truth, re alize that the worst thing that can happen in the spiritual realm is for God to allow you to persist in your rebellion and to have your own way. Have the results of your life-choices left you empty or injured? Even if you've never ac knowledged God in your life up to this point, he stands ready to listen to you and to help you make a new start.

¹¹The LORD replied, "When the Egyptians the Amorites, the Ammonites, the Philis tines, ¹²the Sidonians, the Amalekites an the Maonites*ᶜ* oppressed you and you cried to me for help, did I not save you from their hands? ¹³But you have forsaken m and served other gods, so I will no longe save you. ¹⁴Go and cry out to the gods yo have chosen. Let them save you when yo are in trouble!"

¹⁵But the Israelites said to the LORD, "W have sinned. Do with us whatever yo think best, but please rescue us now. ¹⁶Then they got rid of the foreign god among them and served the LORD. And h could bear Israel's misery no longer.

¹⁷When the Ammonites were called t arms and camped in Gilead, the Israelite assembled and camped at Mizpah. ¹⁸Th leaders of the people of Gilead said to eac other, "Whoever will launch the attac against the Ammonites will be the head of all those living in Gilead."

11 Jephthah the Gileadite was a mighty warrior. His father was Gilead; hi mother was a prostitute. ²Gilead's wife also bore him sons, and when the were grown up, they drove Jephthah away. "You are not going to get any inheritance i our family," they said, "because you are the son of another woman." ³So Jephthah fle

ᵃ2 Traditionally *judged*; also in verse 3   *ᵇ4* Or *called the settlements of Jair*   *ᶜ12* Hebrew; some Septuagint manuscripts *Midianites*

rom his brothers and settled in the land of Tob, where a group of adventurers gathered round him and followed him.

⁴Some time later, when the Ammonites made war on Israel, ⁵the elders of Gilead went o get Jephthah from the land of Tob. ⁶"Come," they said, "be our commander, so we can ight the Ammonites."

⁷Jephthah said to them, "Didn't you hate me and drive me from my father's house? Vhy do you come to me now, when you're in trouble?"

⁸The elders of Gilead said to him, "Nevertheless, we are turning to you now; come with us to fight the Ammonites, and you will be our head over all who live in Gilead."

⁹Jephthah answered, "Suppose you take me back to fight the Ammonites and the LORD gives them to me—will I really be your head?"

¹⁰The elders of Gilead replied, "The LORD is our witness; we will certainly do as you ay." ¹¹So Jephthah went with the elders of Gilead, and the people made him head and ommander over them. And he repeated all his words before the LORD in Mizpah.

¹²Then Jephthah sent messengers to the Ammonite king with the question: "What do vou have against us that you have attacked our country?"

¹³The king of the Ammonites answered Jephthah's messengers, "When Israel came up ut of Egypt, they took away my land from the Arnon to the Jabbok, all the way to the ordan. Now give it back peaceably."

¹⁴Jephthah sent back messengers to the Ammonite king, ¹⁵saying:

"This is what Jephthah says: Israel did not take the land of Moab or the land of the Ammonites. ¹⁶But when they came up out of Egypt, Israel went through the desert to the Red Sea ᵃ and on to Kadesh. ¹⁷Then Israel sent messengers to the king of Edom, saying, 'Give us permission to go through your country,' but the king of Edom would not listen. They sent also to the king of Moab, and he refused. So Israel stayed at Kadesh.

¹⁸"Next they traveled through the desert, skirted the lands of Edom and Moab, passed along the eastern side of the country of Moab, and camped on the other side of the Arnon. They did not enter the territory of Moab, for the Arnon was its border.

¹⁹"Then Israel sent messengers to Sihon king of the Amorites, who ruled in Heshbon, and said to him, 'Let us pass through your country to our own place.' ²⁰Sihon, however, did not trust Israel ᵇ to pass through his territory. He mustered all his men and encamped at Jahaz and fought with Israel.

²¹"Then the LORD, the God of Israel, gave Sihon and all his men into Israel's hands, and they defeated them. Israel took over all the land of the Amorites who lived in that country, ²²capturing all of it from the Arnon to the Jabbok and from the desert to the Jordan.

²³"Now since the LORD, the God of Israel, has driven the Amorites out before his people Israel, what right have you to take it over? ²⁴Will you not take what your god Chemosh gives you? Likewise, whatever the LORD our God has given us, we will possess. ²⁵Are you better than Balak son of Zippor, king of Moab? Did he ever quarrel with Israel or fight with them? ²⁶For three hundred years Israel occupied Heshbon, Aroer, the surrounding settlements and all the towns along the Arnon. Why didn't you retake them during that time? ²⁷I have not wronged you, but you are doing me wrong by waging war against me. Let the LORD, the Judge,ᶜ decide the dispute this day between the Israelites and the Ammonites."

⁸The king of Ammon, however, paid no attention to the message Jephthah sent him.

²⁹Then the Spirit of the LORD came upon Jephthah. He crossed Gilead and Manasseh, assed through Mizpah of Gilead, and from there he advanced against the Ammonites. ⁰And Jephthah made a vow to the LORD: "If you give the Ammonites into my hands,

16 Hebrew Yam Suph; that is, Sea of Reeds   ᵇ20 Or however, would not make an agreement for Israel   ᶜ27 Or Ruler

³¹whatever comes out of the door of my house to meet me when I return in triumph from the Ammonites will be the LORD's, and I will sacrifice it as a burnt offering."

³²Then Jephthah went over to fight the Ammonites, and the LORD gave them into his hands. ³³He devastated twenty towns from Aroer to the vicinity of Minnith, as far as Abel Keramim. Thus Israel subdued Ammon.

³⁴When Jephthah returned to his home in Mizpah, who should come out to meet him but his daughter, dancing to the sound of tambourines! She was an only child. Except for her he had neither son nor daughter. ³⁵When he saw her, he tore his clothes and cried, "Oh! My daughter! You have made me miserable and wretched, because I have made a vow to the LORD that I cannot break."

³⁶"My father," she replied, "you have given your word to the LORD. Do to me just as you promised, now that the LORD has avenged you of your enemies, the Ammonites. ³⁷But grant me this one request," she said. "Give me two months to roam the hills and weep with my friends, because I will never marry."

³⁸"You may go," he said. And he let her go for two months. She and the girls went into the hills and wept because she would never marry. ³⁹After the two months, she returned to her father and he did to her as he had vowed. And she was a virgin.

From this comes the Israelite custom ⁴⁰that each year the young women of Israel go out for four days to commemorate the daughter of Jephthah the Gileadite.

Jephthah and Ephraim

12 The men of Ephraim called out their forces, crossed over to Zaphon and said to Jephthah, "Why did you go to fight the Ammonites without calling us to go with you? We're going to burn down your house over your head."

²Jephthah answered, "I and my people were engaged in a great struggle with the Ammonites, and although I called, you didn't save me out of their hands. ³When I saw that you wouldn't help, I took my life in my hands and crossed over to fight the Ammonites, and the LORD gave me the victory over them. Now why have you come up today to fight me?"

⁴Jephthah then called together the men of Gilead and fought against Ephraim. The Gileadites struck them down because the Ephraimites had said, "You Gileadites are renegades from Ephraim and Manasseh." ⁵The Gileadites captured the fords of the Jordan leading to Ephraim, and whenever a survivor of Ephraim said, "Let me cross over," the men of Gilead asked him, "Are you an Ephraimite?" If he replied, "No," ⁶they said, "All right, say 'Shibboleth.'" If he said, "Sibboleth," because he could not pronounce the word correctly, they seized him and killed him at the fords of the Jordan. Forty-two thousand Ephraimites were killed at that time.

⁷Jephthah led ᵃ Israel six years. Then Jephthah the Gileadite died, and was buried in a town in Gilead.

Ibzan, Elon and Abdon

⁸After him, Ibzan of Bethlehem led Israel. ⁹He had thirty sons and thirty daughters. He gave his daughters away in marriage to those outside his clan, and for his sons he brought in thirty young women as wives from outside his clan. Ibzan led Israel seven years. ¹⁰Then Ibzan died, and was buried in Bethlehem.

¹¹After him, Elon the Zebulunite led Israel ten years. ¹²Then Elon died, and was buried in Aijalon in the land of Zebulun.

¹³After him, Abdon son of Hillel, from Pirathon, led Israel. ¹⁴He had forty sons and thirty grandsons, who rode on seventy donkeys. He led Israel eight years. ¹⁵Then Abdon son of Hillel died, and was buried at Pirathon in Ephraim, in the hill country of the Amalekites.

ᵃ7 Traditionally *judged*; also in verses 8-14

The Birth of Samson

13 Again the Israelites did evil in the eyes of the LORD, so the LORD delivered them into the hands of the Philistines for forty years.

²A certain man of Zorah, named Manoah, from the clan of the Danites, had a wife who was sterile and remained childless. ³The angel of the LORD appeared to her and said, "You are sterile and childless, but you are going to conceive and have a son. ⁴Now see to it that you drink no wine or other fermented drink and that you do not eat anything unclean, ⁵because you will conceive and give birth to a son. No razor may be used on his head, because the boy is to be a Nazirite, set apart to God from birth, and he will begin the deliverance of Israel from the hands of the Philistines."

⁶Then the woman went to her husband and told him, "A man of God came to me. He looked like an angel of God, very awesome. I didn't ask him where he came from, and he didn't tell me his name. ⁷But he said to me, 'You will conceive and give birth to a son. Now then, drink no wine or other fermented drink and do not eat anything unclean, because the boy will be a Nazirite of God from birth until the day of his death.'"

⁸Then Manoah prayed to the LORD: "O Lord, I beg you, let the man of God you sent to us come again to teach us how to bring up the boy who is to be born."

⁹God heard Manoah, and the angel of God came again to the woman while she was out in the field; but her husband Manoah was not with her. ¹⁰The woman hurried to tell her husband, "He's here! The man who appeared to me the other day!"

¹¹Manoah got up and followed his wife. When he came to the man, he said, "Are you the one who talked to my wife?"

"I am," he said.

¹²So Manoah asked him, "When your words are fulfilled, what is to be the rule for the boy's life and work?"

¹³The angel of the LORD answered, "Your wife must do all that I have told her. ¹⁴She must not eat anything that comes from the grapevine, nor drink any wine or other fermented drink nor eat anything unclean. She must do everything I have commanded her."

¹⁵Manoah said to the angel of the LORD, "We would like you to stay until we prepare a young goat for you."

¹⁶The angel of the LORD replied, "Even though you detain me, I will not eat any of your food. But if you prepare a burnt offering, offer it to the LORD." (Manoah did not realize that it was the angel of the LORD.)

¹⁷Then Manoah inquired of the angel of the LORD, "What is your name, so that we may honor you when your word comes true?"

¹⁸He replied, "Why do you ask my name? It is beyond understanding.ᵃ" ¹⁹Then Manoah took a young goat, together with the grain offering, and sacrificed it on a rock to the

---

> ▣ ░░░░░░░ **REASONS TO BELIEVE** ░░░░░░░ ⬧
>
> ### Chapters 13—16
> ### The Amazing Bible
>
> These chapters contain the fascinating but tragic story of Samson. His life is the stuff of Hollywood movies, full of lust, greed, treachery, violence and murder. The Bible doesn't seek to gloss over the negative aspects of the story, and paints this hero of the faith with the most realistic colors. While the Spirit of God works through Samson to deliver Israel from some of its enemies, his God-given physical strength seems to be the only thing Samson ever uses for good. The other essential qualities of a leader—character, self-discipline, wisdom and willingness to serve others—are tragically lacking.
>
> While you'll be able to draw many lessons from reading these chapters, most of them will be in the category of pitfalls to avoid. Get ready to meet "the world's weakest strong man."

ᵃ 18 Or *is wonderful*

LORD. And the LORD did an amazing thing while Manoah and his wife watched: ²⁰As the flame blazed up from the altar toward heaven, the angel of the LORD ascended in the flame. Seeing this, Manoah and his wife fell with their faces to the ground. ²¹When the angel of the LORD did not show himself again to Manoah and his wife, Manoah realized that it was the angel of the LORD.

²²"We are doomed to die!" he said to his wife. "We have seen God!"

²³But his wife answered, "If the LORD had meant to kill us, he would not have accepted a burnt offering and grain offering from our hands, nor shown us all these things or now told us this."

²⁴The woman gave birth to a boy and named him Samson. He grew and the LORD blessed him, ²⁵and the Spirit of the LORD began to stir him while he was in Mahaneh Dan, between Zorah and Eshtaol.

Samson's Marriage

14 Samson went down to Timnah and saw there a young Philistine woman. ²When he returned, he said to his father and mother, "I have seen a Philistine woman in Timnah; now get her for me as my wife."

³His father and mother replied, "Isn't there an acceptable woman among your relatives or among all our people? Must you go to the uncircumcised Philistines to get a wife?"

But Samson said to his father, "Get her for me. She's the right one for me." ⁴(His parents did not know that this was from the LORD, who was seeking an occasion to confront the Philistines; for at that time they were ruling over Israel.) ⁵Samson went down to Timnah together with his father and mother. As they approached the vineyards of Timnah, suddenly a young lion came roaring toward him. ⁶The Spirit of the LORD came upon him in power so that he tore the lion apart with his bare hands as he might have torn a young goat. But he told neither his father nor his mother what he had done. ⁷Then he went down and talked with the woman, and he liked her.

⁸Some time later, when he went back to marry her, he turned aside to look at the lion's carcass. In it was a swarm of bees and some honey, ⁹which he scooped out with his hands and ate as he went along. When he rejoined his parents, he gave them some, and they too ate it. But he did not tell them that he had taken the honey from the lion's carcass.

¹⁰Now his father went down to see the woman. And Samson made a feast there, as was customary for bridegrooms. ¹¹When he appeared, he was given thirty companions.

¹²"Let me tell you a riddle," Samson said to them. "If you can give me the answer within the seven days of the feast, I will give you thirty linen garments and thirty sets of clothes. ¹³If you can't tell me the answer, you must give me thirty linen garments and thirty sets of clothes."

"Tell us your riddle," they said. "Let's hear it."

¹⁴He replied,

> "Out of the eater, something to eat;
>   out of the strong, something sweet."

For three days they could not give the answer.

¹⁵On the fourth ᵃ day, they said to Samson's wife, "Coax your husband into explaining the riddle for us, or we will burn you and your father's household to death. Did you invite us here to rob us?"

¹⁶Then Samson's wife threw herself on him, sobbing, "You hate me! You don't really love me. You've given my people a riddle, but you haven't told me the answer."

"I haven't even explained it to my father or mother," he replied, "so why should I explain it to you?" ¹⁷She cried the whole seven days of the feast. So on the seventh day

ᵃ15 Some Septuagint manuscripts and Syriac; Hebrew *seventh*

he finally told her, because she continued to press him. She in turn explained the riddle to her people.

¹⁸Before sunset on the seventh day the men of the town said to him,

> "What is sweeter than honey?
>   What is stronger than a lion?"

Samson said to them,

> "If you had not plowed with my heifer,
>   you would not have solved my riddle."

¹⁹Then the Spirit of the LORD came upon him in power. He went down to Ashkelon, struck down thirty of their men, stripped them of their belongings and gave their clothes to those who had explained the riddle. Burning with anger, he went up to his father's house. ²⁰And Samson's wife was given to the friend who had attended him at his wedding.

Samson's Vengeance on the Philistines

15 Later on, at the time of wheat harvest, Samson took a young goat and went to visit his wife. He said, "I'm going to my wife's room." But her father would not let him go in.

²"I was so sure you thoroughly hated her," he said, "that I gave her to your friend. Isn't her younger sister more attractive? Take her instead."

³Samson said to them, "This time I have a right to get even with the Philistines; I will really harm them." ⁴So he went out and caught three hundred foxes and tied them tail to tail in pairs. He then fastened a torch to every pair of tails, ⁵lit the torches and let the foxes loose in the standing grain of the Philistines. He burned up the shocks and standing grain, together with the vineyards and olive groves.

⁶When the Philistines asked, "Who did this?" they were told, "Samson, the Timnite's son-in-law, because his wife was given to his friend."

So the Philistines went up and burned her and her father to death. ⁷Samson said to them, "Since you've acted like this, I won't stop until I get my revenge on you." ⁸He attacked them viciously and slaughtered many of them. Then he went down and stayed in a cave in the rock of Etam.

⁹The Philistines went up and camped in Judah, spreading out near Lehi. ¹⁰The men of Judah asked, "Why have you come to fight us?"

"We have come to take Samson prisoner," they answered, "to do to him as he did to us."

¹¹Then three thousand men from Judah went down to the cave in the rock of Etam and said to Samson, "Don't you realize that the Philistines are rulers over us? What have you done to us?"

He answered, "I merely did to them what they did to me."

¹²They said to him, "We've come to tie you up and hand you over to the Philistines."

Samson said, "Swear to me that you won't kill me yourselves."

¹³"Agreed," they answered. "We will only tie you up and hand you over to them. We will not kill you." So they bound him with two new ropes and led him up from the rock. ¹⁴As he approached Lehi, the Philistines came toward him shouting. The Spirit of the LORD came upon him in power. The ropes on his arms became like charred flax, and the bindings dropped from his hands. ¹⁵Finding a fresh jawbone of a donkey, he grabbed it and struck down a thousand men.

¹⁶Then Samson said,

"With a donkey's jawbone
I have made donkeys of them. *a*
With a donkey's jawbone
I have killed a thousand men."

¹⁷When he finished speaking, he threw away the jawbone; and the place was called Ramath Lehi. *b*

¹⁸Because he was very thirsty, he cried out to the LORD, "You have given your servant this great victory. Must I now die of thirst and fall into the hands of the uncircumcised?" ¹⁹Then God opened up the hollow place in Lehi, and water came out of it. When Samson drank, his strength returned and he revived. So the spring was called En Hakkore, *c* and it is still there in Lehi.

²⁰Samson led *d* Israel for twenty years in the days of the Philistines.

Samson and Delilah

16 One day Samson went to Gaza, where he saw a prostitute. He went in to spend the night with her. ²The people of Gaza were told, "Samson is here!" So they surrounded the place and lay in wait for him all night at the city gate. They made no move during the night, saying, "At dawn we'll kill him."

³But Samson lay there only until the middle of the night. Then he got up and took hold of the doors of the city gate, together with the two posts, and tore them loose, bar and all. He lifted them to his shoulders and carried them to the top of the hill that faces Hebron.

⁴Some time later, he fell in love with a woman in the Valley of Sorek whose name was Delilah. ⁵The rulers of the Philistines went to her and said, "See if you can lure him into showing you the secret of his great strength and how we can overpower him so we may tie him up and subdue him. Each one of us will give you eleven hundred shekels *e* of silver."

⁶So Delilah said to Samson, "Tell me the secret of your great strength and how you can be tied up and subdued."

⁷Samson answered her, "If anyone ties me with seven fresh thongs *f* that have not been dried, I'll become as weak as any other man."

⁸Then the rulers of the Philistines brought her seven fresh thongs that had not been dried, and she tied him with them. ⁹With men hidden in the room, she called to him, "Samson, the Philistines are upon you!" But he snapped the thongs as easily as a piece of string snaps when it comes close to a flame. So the secret of his strength was not discovered.

¹⁰Then Delilah said to Samson, "You have made a fool of me; you lied to me. Come now, tell me how you can be tied."

¹¹He said, "If anyone ties me securely with new ropes that have never been used, I'll become as weak as any other man."

¹²So Delilah took new ropes and tied him with them. Then, with men hidden in the room, she called to him, "Samson, the Philistines are upon you!" But he snapped the ropes off his arms as if they were threads.

¹³Delilah then said to Samson, "Until now, you have been making a fool of me and lying to me. Tell me how you can be tied."

He replied, "If you weave the seven braids of my head into the fabric ⌊on the loom⌋ and tighten it with the pin, I'll become as weak as any other man." So while he was sleeping, Delilah took the seven braids of his head, wove them into the fabric ¹⁴and *g* tightened it with the pin.

---

a 16 Or *made a heap or two; the Hebrew for donkey sounds like the Hebrew for heap.*   *b 17 Ramath Lehi* means *jawbone hill.*   *c 19 En Hakkore* means *caller's spring.*   *d 20* Traditionally *judged*   *e 5* That is, about 28 pounds (about 13 kilograms)   *f 7* Or *bowstrings;* also in verses 8 and 9   *g 13,14* Some Septuagint manuscripts; Hebrew "*I can, if you weave the seven braids of my head into the fabric ⌊on the loom.⌋*" *¹⁴So she*

Again she called to him, "Samson, the Philistines are upon you!" He awoke from his sleep and pulled up the pin and the loom, with the fabric.

¹⁵Then she said to him, "How can you say, 'I love you,' when you won't confide in me? This is the third time you have made a fool of me and haven't told me the secret of your great strength." ¹⁶With such nagging she prodded him day after day until he was tired to death.

¹⁷So he told her everything. "No razor has ever been used on my head," he said, "because I have been a Nazirite set apart to God since birth. If my head were shaved, my strength would leave me, and I would become as weak as any other man."

¹⁸When Delilah saw that he had told her everything, she sent word to the rulers of the Philistines, "Come back once more; he has told me everything." So the rulers of the Philistines returned with the silver in their hands. ¹⁹Having put him to sleep on her lap, she called a man to shave off the seven braids of his hair, and so began to subdue him.ᵃ And his strength left him.

²⁰Then she called, "Samson, the Philistines are upon you!"

He awoke from his sleep and thought, "I'll go out as before and shake myself free." But he did not know that the LORD had left him.

ᵃ19 Hebrew; some Septuagint manuscripts and he began to weaken

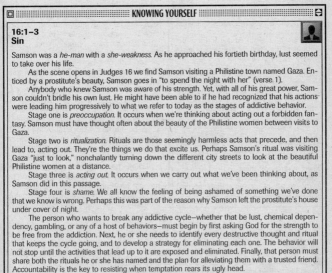

KNOWING YOURSELF

16:1–3
Sin

Samson was a *he-man* with a *she-weakness.* As he approached his fortieth birthday, lust seemed to take over his life.

As the scene opens in Judges 16 we find Samson visiting a Philistine town named Gaza. Enticed by a prostitute's beauty, Samson goes in "to spend the night with her" (verse 1).

Anybody who knew Samson was aware of his strength. Yet, with all of his great power, Samson couldn't bridle his own lust. He might have been able to if he had recognized that his actions were leading him progressively to what we refer to today as the stages of addictive behavior.

Stage one is *preoccupation.* It occurs when we're thinking about acting out a forbidden fantasy. Samson must have thought often about the beauty of the Philistine women between visits to Gaza.

Stage two is *ritualization.* Rituals are those seemingly harmless acts that precede, and then lead to, acting out. They're the things we do that excite us. Perhaps Samson's ritual was visiting Gaza "just to look," nonchalantly turning down the different city streets to look at the beautiful Philistine women at a distance.

Stage three is *acting out.* It occurs when we carry out what we've been thinking about, as Samson did in this passage.

Stage four is *shame.* We all know the feeling of being ashamed of something we've done that we know is wrong. Perhaps this was part of the reason why Samson left the prostitute's house under cover of night.

The person who wants to break any addictive cycle—whether that be lust, chemical dependency, gambling, or any of a host of behaviors—must begin by first asking God for the strength to be free from the addiction. Next, he or she needs to identify every destructive thought and ritual that keeps the cycle going, and to develop a strategy for eliminating each one. The behavior will not stop until the activities that lead up to it are exposed and eliminated. Finally, that person must share both the rituals he or she has named and the plan for alleviating them with a trusted friend. Accountability is the key to resisting when temptation rears its ugly head.

Think about how different Samson's life might have been if he had taken the steps to break the cycle of his addiction! Instead of turning to God for help and insight, he chose to let his destructive appetite get the best of him. If you're heading down that same path, learn from Samson's example.

²¹Then the Philistines seized him, gouged out his eyes and took him down to Gaza. Binding him with bronze shackles, they set him to grinding in the prison. ²²But the hair on his head began to grow again after it had been shaved.

The Death of Samson

²³Now the rulers of the Philistines assembled to offer a great sacrifice to Dagon their god and to celebrate, saying, "Our god has delivered Samson, our enemy, into our hands."

²⁴When the people saw him, they praised their god, saying,

> "Our god has delivered our enemy
>   into our hands,
> the one who laid waste our land
>   and multiplied our slain."

²⁵While they were in high spirits, they shouted, "Bring out Samson to entertain us." So they called Samson out of the prison, and he performed for them.

When they stood him among the pillars, ²⁶Samson said to the servant who held his hand, "Put me where I can feel the pillars that support the temple, so that I may lean against them." ²⁷Now the temple was crowded with men and women; all the rulers of the Philistines were there, and on the roof were about three thousand men and women watching Samson perform. ²⁸Then Samson prayed to the LORD, "O Sovereign LORD, remember me. O God, please strengthen me just once more, and let me with one blow get revenge on the Philistines for my two eyes." ²⁹Then Samson reached toward the two central pillars on which the temple stood. Bracing himself against them, his right hand on the one and his left hand on the other, ³⁰Samson said, "Let me die with the Philistines!" Then he pushed with all his might, and down came the temple on the rulers and all the people in it. Thus he killed many more when he died than while he lived.

³¹Then his brothers and his father's whole family went down to get him. They brought him back and buried him between Zorah and Eshtaol in the tomb of Manoah his father. He had led ᵃ Israel twenty years.

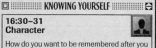

KNOWING YOURSELF

16:30-31
Character

How do you want to be remembered after you die?

Samson is remembered as a destroyer, not a builder. He killed people and animals, burned crops and tore down buildings.

He is remembered for strength, but not self-control. He lived by his biceps instead of his precepts. Samson could *get* women, for example, but he couldn't *keep* them. He refused to be loyal and was easily manipulated. He didn't let God-honoring core values dictate his actions.

What are you building that will really last? Is your life ordered by higher principles? Are you faithful to your spouse (or friends or other family members) and devoted to his or her well-being? Do you conduct yourself ethically in the workplace? Letting God lead you into a life that appropriately answers these and other questions can assure you a life of meaning and purpose—and no regrets.

Micah's Idols

17 Now a man named Micah from the hill country of Ephraim ²said to his mother, "The eleven hundred shekels ᵇ of silver that were taken from you and about which I heard you utter a curse—I have that silver with me; I took it."

Then his mother said, "The LORD bless you, my son!"

³When he returned the eleven hundred shekels of silver to his mother, she said, "I solemnly consecrate my silver to the LORD for my son to make a carved image and a cast idol. I will give it back to you."

ᵃ31 Traditionally *judged*   ᵇ2 That is, about 28 pounds (about 13 kilograms)

⁴So he returned the silver to his mother, and she took two hundred shekels^a of silver and gave them to a silversmith, who made them into the image and the idol. And they were put in Micah's house.

⁵Now this man Micah had a shrine, and he made an ephod and some idols and installed one of his sons as his priest. ⁶In those days Israel had no king; everyone did as he saw fit.

⁷A young Levite from Bethlehem in Judah, who had been living within the clan of Judah, ⁸left that town in search of some other place to stay. On his way^b he came to Micah's house in the hill country of Ephraim.

⁹Micah asked him, "Where are you from?"

"I'm a Levite from Bethlehem in Judah," he said, "and I'm looking for a place to stay."

¹⁰Then Micah said to him, "Live with me and be my father and priest, and I'll give you ten shekels^c of silver a year, your clothes and your food." ¹¹So the Levite agreed to live with him, and the young man was to him like one of his sons. ¹²Then Micah installed the Levite, and the young man became his priest and lived in his house. ¹³And Micah said, "Now I know that the LORD will be good to me, since this Levite has become my priest."

Danites Settle in Laish

18 In those days Israel had no king.

And in those days the tribe of the Danites was seeking a place of their own where they might settle, because they had not yet come into an inheritance among the tribes of Israel. ²So the Danites sent five warriors from Zorah and Eshtaol to spy out the land and explore it. These men represented all their clans. They told them, "Go, explore the land."

The men entered the hill country of Ephraim and came to the house of Micah, where they spent the night. ³When they were near Micah's house, they recognized the voice of the young Levite; so they turned in there and asked him, "Who brought you here? What are you doing in this place? Why are you here?"

⁴He told them what Micah had done for him, and said, "He has hired me and I am his priest."

⁵Then they said to him, "Please inquire of God to learn whether our journey will be successful."

⁶The priest answered them, "Go in peace. Your journey has the LORD's approval."

⁷So the five men left and came to Laish, where they saw that the people were living in safety, like the Sidonians, unsuspecting and secure. And since their land lacked nothing, they were prosperous.^d Also, they lived a long way from the Sidonians and had no relationship with anyone else.^e

⁸When they returned to Zorah and Eshtaol, their brothers asked them, "How did you find things?"

⁹They answered, "Come on, let's attack them! We have seen that the land is very good. Aren't you going to do something? Don't hesitate to go there and take it over. ¹⁰When you get there, you will find an unsuspecting people and a spacious land that God has put into your hands, a land that lacks nothing whatever."

¹¹Then six hundred men from the clan of the Danites, armed for battle, set out from Zorah and Eshtaol. ¹²On their way they set up camp near Kiriath Jearim in Judah. This is why the place west of Kiriath Jearim is called Mahaneh Dan^f to this day. ¹³From there they went on to the hill country of Ephraim and came to Micah's house.

¹⁴Then the five men who had spied out the land of Laish said to their brothers, "Do you know that one of these houses has an ephod, other household gods, a carved image and a cast idol? Now you know what to do." ¹⁵So they turned in there and went to the house

---

^a4 That is, about 5 pounds (about 2.3 kilograms)   ^b8 Or To carry on his profession   ^c10 That is, about 4 ounces (about 110 grams)   ^d7 The meaning of the Hebrew for this clause is uncertain.   ^e7 Hebrew; some Septuagint manuscripts with the Arameans   ^f12 Mahaneh Dan means Dan's camp.

of the young Levite at Micah's place and greeted him. [16]The six hundred Danites, armed for battle, stood at the entrance to the gate. [17]The five men who had spied out the land went inside and took the carved image, the ephod, the other household gods and the cast idol while the priest and the six hundred armed men stood at the entrance to the gate.

[18]When these men went into Micah's house and took the carved image, the ephod, the other household gods and the cast idol, the priest said to them, "What are you doing?"

[19]They answered him, "Be quiet! Don't say a word. Come with us, and be our father and priest. Isn't it better that you serve a tribe and clan in Israel as priest rather than just one man's household?" [20]Then the priest was glad. He took the ephod, the other household gods and the carved image and went along with the people. [21]Putting their little children, their livestock and their possessions in front of them, they turned away and left.

[22]When they had gone some distance from Micah's house, the men who lived near Micah were called together and overtook the Danites. [23]As they shouted after them, the Danites turned and said to Micah, "What's the matter with you that you called out your men to fight?"

[24]He replied, "You took the gods I made, and my priest, and went away. What else do I have? How can you ask, 'What's the matter with you?'"

[25]The Danites answered, "Don't argue with us, or some hot-tempered men will attack you, and you and your family will lose your lives." [26]So the Danites went their way, and Micah, seeing that they were too strong for him, turned around and went back home.

[27]Then they took what Micah had made, and his priest, and went on to Laish, against a peaceful and unsuspecting people. They attacked them with the sword and burned down their city. [28]There was no one to rescue them because they lived a long way from Sidon and had no relationship with anyone else. The city was in a valley near Beth Rehob.

The Danites rebuilt the city and settled there. [29]They named it Dan after their forefather Dan, who was born to Israel—though the city used to be called Laish. [30]There the Danites set up for themselves the idols, and Jonathan son of Gershom, the son of Moses,[a] and his sons were priests for the tribe of Dan until the time of the captivity of the land. [31]They continued to use the idols Micah had made, all the time the house of God was in Shiloh.

A Levite and His Concubine

19 In those days Israel had no king.

Now a Levite who lived in a remote area in the hill country of Ephraim took a concubine from Bethlehem in Judah. [2]But she was unfaithful to him. She left him and went back to her father's house in Bethlehem, Judah. After she had been there four months, [3]her husband went to her to persuade her to return. He had with him his servant and two donkeys. She took him into her father's house, and when her father saw him, he gladly welcomed him. [4]His father-in-law, the girl's father, prevailed upon him to stay; so he remained with him three days, eating and drinking, and sleeping there.

[5]On the fourth day they got up early and he prepared to leave, but the girl's father said to his son-in-law, "Refresh yourself with something to eat; then you can go." [6]So the two of them sat down to eat and drink together. Afterward the girl's father said, "Please stay tonight and enjoy yourself." [7]And when the man got up to go, his father-in-law persuaded him, so he stayed there that night. [8]On the morning of the fifth day, when he rose to go, the girl's father said, "Refresh yourself. Wait till afternoon!" So the two of them ate together.

[9]Then when the man, with his concubine and his servant, got up to leave, his father-in-law, the girl's father, said, "Now look, it's almost evening. Spend the night here; the day is nearly over. Stay and enjoy yourself. Early tomorrow morning you can get up and

---

[a] *30* An ancient Hebrew scribal tradition, some Septuagint manuscripts and Vulgate; Masoretic Text *Manasseh*

be on your way home." ¹⁰But, unwilling to stay another night, the man left and went toward Jebus (that is, Jerusalem), with his two saddled donkeys and his concubine. ¹¹When they were near Jebus and the day was almost gone, the servant said to his master, "Come, let's stop at this city of the Jebusites and spend the night." ¹²His master replied, "No. We won't go into an alien city, whose people are not Israelites. We will go on to Gibeah." ¹³He added, "Come, let's try to reach Gibeah or Ramah and spend the night in one of those places." ¹⁴So they went on, and the sun set as they neared Gibeah in Benjamin. ¹⁵There they stopped to spend the night. They went and sat in the city square, but no one took them into his home for the night.

¹⁶That evening an old man from the hill country of Ephraim, who was living in Gibeah (the men of the place were Benjamites), came in from his work in the fields. ¹⁷When he looked and saw the traveler in the city square, the old man asked, "Where are you going? Where did you come from?"

¹⁸He answered, "We are on our way from Bethlehem in Judah to a remote area in the hill country of Ephraim where I live. I have been to Bethlehem in Judah and now I am going to the house of the LORD. No one has taken me into his house. ¹⁹We have both straw and fodder for our donkeys and bread and wine for ourselves your servants—me, your maidservant, and the young man with us. We don't need anything."

²⁰"You are welcome at my house," the old man said. "Let me supply whatever you need. Only don't spend the night in the square." ²¹So he took him into his house and fed his donkeys. After they had washed their feet, they had something to eat and drink.

²²While they were enjoying themselves, some of the wicked men of the city surrounded the house. Pounding on the door, they shouted to the old man who owned the house, "Bring out the man who came to your house so we can have sex with him."

²³The owner of the house went outside and said to them, "No, my friends, don't be so vile. Since this man is my guest, don't do this disgraceful thing. ²⁴Look, here is my virgin daughter, and his concubine. I will bring them out to you now, and you can use them and do to them whatever you wish. But to this man, don't do such a disgraceful thing."

²⁵But the men would not listen to him. So the man took his concubine and sent her outside to them, and they raped her and abused her throughout the night, and at dawn they let her go. ²⁶At daybreak the woman went back to the house where her master was staying, fell down at the door and lay there until daylight.

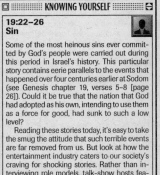

KNOWING YOURSELF

19:22–26
Sin

Some of the most heinous sins ever committed by God's people were carried out during this period in Israel's history. This particular story contains eerie parallels to the events that happened over four centuries earlier at Sodom (see Genesis chapter 19, verses 5–8 [page 26]). Could it be true that the nation that God had adopted as his own, intending to use them as a force for good, had sunk to such a low level?

Reading these stories today, it's easy to take the smug the attitude that such terrible events are far removed from us. But look at how the entertainment industry caters to our society's craving for shocking stories. Rather than interviewing role models, talk-show hosts feature people whose lifestyles are far from healthy and decent. We tend to gawk at them, either tolerating their excesses under the banner of pluralism or dismissing them as so bizarre that we feel relief that we're not that "messed up." In any event, we walk away feeling better about ourselves than we ought, and fail to recognize our own shortcomings.

The only good thing to note about this passage is the reaction of the people who heard of these events (verse 30). They were appalled and took steps to punish the evildoers. But this nation didn't recognize that it was drinking the poison it sought to eliminate—a problem we have in our day as well.

²⁷When her master got up in the morning and opened the door of the house and stepped out to continue on his way, there lay his concubine, fallen in the doorway of the house, with her hands on the threshold. ²⁸He said to her, "Get up; let's go." But there was no answer. Then the man put her on his donkey and set out for home.

²⁹When he reached home, he took a knife and cut up his concubine, limb by limb, into twelve parts and sent them into all the areas of Israel. ³⁰Everyone who saw it said, "Such a thing has never been seen or done, not since the day the Israelites came up out of Egypt. Think about it! Consider it! Tell us what to do!"

Israelites Fight the Benjamites

20 Then all the Israelites from Dan to Beersheba and from the land of Gilead came out as one man and assembled before the LORD in Mizpah. ²The leaders of all the people of the tribes of Israel took their places in the assembly of the people of God, four hundred thousand soldiers armed with swords. ³(The Benjamites heard that the Israelites had gone up to Mizpah.) Then the Israelites said, "Tell us how this awful thing happened."

⁴So the Levite, the husband of the murdered woman, said, "I and my concubine came to Gibeah in Benjamin to spend the night. ⁵During the night the men of Gibeah came after me and surrounded the house, intending to kill me. They raped my concubine, and she died. ⁶I took my concubine, cut her into pieces and sent one piece to each region of Israel's inheritance, because they committed this lewd and disgraceful act in Israel. ⁷Now, all you Israelites, speak up and give your verdict."

⁸All the people rose as one man, saying, "None of us will go home. No, not one of us will return to his house. ⁹But now this is what we'll do to Gibeah: We'll go up against it as the lot directs. ¹⁰We'll take ten men out of every hundred from all the tribes of Israel, and a hundred from a thousand, and a thousand from ten thousand, to get provisions for the army. Then, when the army arrives at Gibeah*ᵃ* in Benjamin, it can give them what they deserve for all this vileness done in Israel." ¹¹So all the men of Israel got together and united as one man against the city.

¹²The tribes of Israel sent men throughout the tribe of Benjamin, saying, "What about this awful crime that was committed among you? ¹³Now surrender those wicked men of Gibeah so that we may put them to death and purge the evil from Israel."

But the Benjamites would not listen to their fellow Israelites. ¹⁴From their towns they came together at Gibeah to fight against the Israelites. ¹⁵At once the Benjamites mobilized twenty-six thousand swordsmen from their towns, in addition to seven hundred chosen men from those living in Gibeah. ¹⁶Among all these soldiers there were seven hundred chosen men who were left-handed, each of whom could sling a stone at a hair and not miss.

¹⁷Israel, apart from Benjamin, mustered four hundred thousand swordsmen, all of them fighting men.

¹⁸The Israelites went up to Bethel*ᵇ* and inquired of God. They said, "Who of us shall go first to fight against the Benjamites?"

The LORD replied, "Judah shall go first."

¹⁹The next morning the Israelites got up and pitched camp near Gibeah. ²⁰The men of Israel went out to fight the Benjamites and took up battle positions against them at Gibeah. ²¹The Benjamites came out of Gibeah and cut down twenty-two thousand Israelites on the battlefield that day. ²²But the men of Israel encouraged one another and again took up their positions where they had stationed themselves the first day. ²³The Israelites

---

ᵃ10 One Hebrew manuscript; most Hebrew manuscripts *Geba*, a variant of *Gibeah*   *ᵇ18* Or *to the house of God*; also in verse 26

went up and wept before the LORD until evening, and they inquired of the LORD. They said, "Shall we go up again to battle against the Benjamites, our brothers?"

The LORD answered, "Go up against them."

²⁴Then the Israelites drew near to Benjamin the second day. ²⁵This time, when the Benjamites came out from Gibeah to oppose them, they cut down another eighteen thousand Israelites, all of them armed with swords.

²⁶Then the Israelites, all the people, went up to Bethel, and there they sat weeping before the LORD. They fasted that day until evening and presented burnt offerings and fellowship offeringsᵃ to the LORD. ²⁷And the Israelites inquired of the LORD. (In those days the ark of the covenant of God was there, ²⁸with Phinehas son of Eleazar, the son of Aaron, ministering before it.) They asked, "Shall we go up again to battle with Benjamin our brother, or not?"

The LORD responded, "Go, for tomorrow I will give them into your hands."

²⁹Then Israel set an ambush around Gibeah. ³⁰They went up against the Benjamites on the third day and took up positions against Gibeah as they had done before. ³¹The Benjamites came out to meet them and were drawn away from the city. They began to inflict casualties on the Israelites as before, so that about thirty men fell in the open field and on the roads—the one leading to Bethel and the other to Gibeah.

³²While the Benjamites were saying, "We are defeating them as before," the Israelites were saying, "Let's retreat and draw them away from the city to the roads."

³³All the men of Israel moved from their places and took up positions at Baal Tamar, and the Israelite ambush charged out of its place on the westᵇ of Gibeah.ᶜ ³⁴Then ten thousand of Israel's finest men made a frontal attack on Gibeah. The fighting was so heavy that the Benjamites did not realize how near disaster was. ³⁵The LORD defeated Benjamin before Israel, and on that day the Israelites struck down 25,100 Benjamites, all armed with swords. ³⁶Then the Benjamites saw that they were beaten.

Now the men of Israel had given way before Benjamin, because they relied on the ambush they had set near Gibeah. ³⁷The men who had been in ambush made a sudden dash into Gibeah, spread out and put the whole city to the sword. ³⁸The men of Israel had arranged with the ambush that they should send up a great cloud of smoke from the city, ³⁹and then the men of Israel would turn in the battle.

The Benjamites had begun to inflict casualties on the men of Israel (about thirty), and they said, "We are defeating them as in the first battle." ⁴⁰But when the column of smoke began to rise from the city, the Benjamites turned and saw the smoke of the whole city going up into the sky. ⁴¹Then the men of Israel turned on them, and the men of Benjamin were terrified, because they realized that disaster had come upon them. ⁴²So they fled before the Israelites in the direction of the desert, but they could not escape the battle. And the men of Israel who came out of the towns cut them down there. ⁴³They surrounded the Benjamites, chased them and easilyᵈ overran them in the vicinity of Gibeah on the east. ⁴⁴Eighteen thousand Benjamites fell, all of them valiant fighters. ⁴⁵As they turned and fled toward the desert to the rock of Rimmon, the Israelites cut down five thousand men along the roads. They kept pressing after the Benjamites as far as Gidom and struck down two thousand more.

⁴⁶On that day twenty-five thousand Benjamite swordsmen fell, all of them valiant fighters. ⁴⁷But six hundred men turned and fled into the desert to the rock of Rimmon, where they stayed four months. ⁴⁸The men of Israel went back to Benjamin and put all the towns to the sword, including the animals and everything else they found. All the towns they came across they set on fire.

ᵃ26 Traditionally *peace offerings*   ᵇ33 Some Septuagint manuscripts and Vulgate; the meaning of the Hebrew for this word is uncertain.   ᶜ33 Hebrew *Geba*, a variant of *Gibeah*   ᵈ43 The meaning of the Hebrew for this word is uncertain.

Wives for the Benjamites

21 The men of Israel had taken an oath at Mizpah: "Not one of us will give his daughter in marriage to a Benjamite."

²The people went to Bethel,*ᵃ* where they sat before God until evening, raising their voices and weeping bitterly. ³"O LORD, the God of Israel," they cried, "why has this happened to Israel? Why should one tribe be missing from Israel today?"

⁴Early the next day the people built an altar and presented burnt offerings and fellowship offerings.*ᵇ*

⁵Then the Israelites asked, "Who from all the tribes of Israel has failed to assemble before the LORD?" For they had taken a solemn oath that anyone who failed to assemble before the LORD at Mizpah should certainly be put to death.

⁶Now the Israelites grieved for their brothers, the Benjamites. "Today one tribe is cut off from Israel," they said. ⁷"How can we provide wives for those who are left, since we have taken an oath by the LORD not to give them any of our daughters in marriage?" ⁸Then they asked, "Which one of the tribes of Israel failed to assemble before the LORD at Mizpah?" They discovered that no one from Jabesh Gilead had come to the camp for the assembly. ⁹For when they counted the people, they found that none of the people of Jabesh Gilead were there.

❑ ▦▦▦▦ ADDRESSING QUESTIONS ▦▦▦▦ ⮂
21:25 **Human Experience** **Q** Wouldn't it be great to have the freedom to do whatever you wanted? Wouldn't the ideal society be one that had no restraints? According to the book of Judges, Israel had that kind of a society—and it was a disaster. They experienced what we all need to discover: *True freedom is not the right to do anything; it's the power to do the right thing.* Is that kind of power at work in your life? Do you exercise your freedom to do what's right, or do you find yourself regretting actions that seemed acceptable or even necessary at the time? God offers the freedom that will enable you to act out of principle rather than appetite. You need only to invite him into your life and ask him to set you free from sin's stranglehold. After you've asked him to be your leader and to give you his power, he'll give you the strength to obey his commands found in the Bible. When you align yourself with God's principles and use them to direct your life, "doing as you see fit" will lead to a life less hampered by regret.

¹⁰So the assembly sent twelve thousand fighting men with instructions to go to Jabesh Gilead and put to the sword those living there, including the women and children. ¹¹"This is what you are to do," they said. "Kill every male and every woman who is not a virgin." ¹²They found among the people living in Jabesh Gilead four hundred young women who had never slept with a man, and they took them to the camp at Shiloh in Canaan.

¹³Then the whole assembly sent an offer of peace to the Benjamites at the rock of Rimmon. ¹⁴So the Benjamites returned at that time and were given the women of Jabesh Gilead who had been spared. But there were not enough for all of them.

¹⁵The people grieved for Benjamin, because the LORD had made a gap in the tribes of Israel. ¹⁶And the elders of the assembly said, "With the women of Benjamin destroyed, how shall we provide wives for the men who are left?" ¹⁷The Benjamite survivors must have heirs," they said, "so that a tribe of Israel will not be wiped out. ¹⁸We can't give them our daughters as wives, since we Israelites have taken this oath: 'Cursed be anyone who gives a wife to a Benjamite.' ¹⁹But look, there is the annual festival of the LORD in Shiloh, to the north of Bethel, and east of the road that goes from Bethel to Shechem, and to the south of Lebonah."

ᵃ2 Or to the house of God   ᵇ4 Traditionally peace offerings

²⁰So they instructed the Benjamites, saying, "Go and hide in the vineyards ²¹and watch. When the girls of Shiloh come out to join in the dancing, then rush from the vineyards and each of you seize a wife from the girls of Shiloh and go to the land of Benjamin. ²²When their fathers or brothers complain to us, we will say to them, 'Do us a kindness by helping them, because we did not get wives for them during the war, and you are innocent, since you did not give your daughters to them.'"

²³So that is what the Benjamites did. While the girls were dancing, each man caught one and carried her off to be his wife. Then they returned to their inheritance and rebuilt the towns and settled in them.

²⁴At that time the Israelites left that place and went home to their tribes and clans, each to his own inheritance.

²⁵In those days Israel had no king; everyone did as he saw fit.

RUTH

Naomi and Ruth

1 In the days when the judges ruled,[a] there was a famine in the land, and a man from Bethlehem in Judah, together with his wife and two sons, went to live for a while in the country of Moab. ²The man's name was Elimelech, his wife's name Naomi, and the names of his two sons were Mahlon and Kilion. They were Ephrathites from Bethlehem, Judah. And they went to Moab and lived there.

³Now Elimelech, Naomi's husband, died, and she was left with her two sons. ⁴They married Moabite women, one named Orpah and the other Ruth. After they had lived there about ten years, ⁵both Mahlon and Kilion also died, and Naomi was left without her two sons and her husband.

⁶When she heard in Moab that the LORD had come to the aid of his people by providing food for them, Naomi and her daughters-in-law prepared to return home from there.

⁷With her two daughters-in-law she left the place where she had been living and set out on the road that would take them back to the land of Judah.

⁸Then Naomi said to her two daughters-in-law, "Go back, each of you, to your mother's home. May the LORD show kindness to you, as you have shown to your dead and to me. ⁹May the LORD grant that each of you will find rest in the home of another husband."

Then she kissed them and they wept aloud ¹⁰and said to her, "We will go back with you to your people."

¹¹But Naomi said, "Return home, my daughters. Why would you come with me? Am I going to have any more sons, who could become your husbands? ¹²Return home, my daughters; I am too old to have another husband. Even if I thought there was still hope for me—even if I had a husband tonight and then gave birth to sons—¹³would you wait until they grew up? Would you remain unmarried for them? No, my daughters. It is more bitter for me than for you, because the LORD's hand has gone out against me!"

>
>
> ## ▣ ▦STRENGTHENING RELATIONSHIPS▦ ⮂
>
> ### 1:16–17
> ### Marriage/Family
>
> Many people want the benefits of strong relationships, but they can't seem to find a working formula. They fail to realize that satisfying relationships don't magically become stronger—rather, *strong relationships become more satisfying.* If you first set out to make a relationship strong, then it will be fulfilling. And the key to relational strength is commitment.
>
> Ruth committed herself to Naomi. And at the core of that pledge was a shared spirituality—she was firmly tied to God as well as to her mother-in-law. It was out of the deep-rooted strength of that commitment that the joy of their partnership grew.
>
> Rather than thinking you have to "trade in" your spouse, friends, or family members to find happiness, work from the foundation of strong commitment to those individuals. As Ruth discovered, happiness will then take care of itself.

¹⁴At this they wept again. Then Orpah kissed her mother-in-law good-by, but Ruth clung to her.

¹⁵"Look," said Naomi, "your sister-in-law is going back to her people and her gods. Go back with her."

¹⁶But Ruth replied, "Don't urge me to leave you or to turn back from you. Where you go

---

I will go, and where you stay I will stay. Your people will be my people and your God my God. [17]Where you die I will die, and there I will be buried. May the LORD deal with me, be it ever so severely, if anything but death separates you and me." [18]When Naomi realized that Ruth was determined to go with her, she stopped urging her.

[19]So the two women went on until they came to Bethlehem. When they arrived in Bethlehem, the whole town was stirred because of them, and the women exclaimed, "Can this be Naomi?"

[20]"Don't call me Naomi,[a]" she told them. "Call me Mara,[b] because the Almighty[c] has made my life very bitter. [21]I went away full, but the LORD has brought me back empty. Why call me Naomi? The LORD has afflicted[d] me; the Almighty has brought misfortune upon me."

[22]So Naomi returned from Moab accompanied by Ruth the Moabitess, her daughter-in-law, arriving in Bethlehem as the barley harvest was beginning.

Ruth Meets Boaz

2 Now Naomi had a relative on her husband's side, from the clan of Elimelech, a man of standing, whose name was Boaz.

[2]And Ruth the Moabitess said to Naomi, "Let me go to the fields and pick up the leftover grain behind anyone in whose eyes I find favor."

Naomi said to her, "Go ahead, my daughter." [3]So she went out and began to glean in the fields behind the harvesters. As it turned out, she found herself working in a field belonging to Boaz, who was from the clan of Elimelech.

[4]Just then Boaz arrived from Bethlehem and greeted the harvesters, "The LORD be with you!"

"The LORD bless you!" they called back.

[5]Boaz asked the foreman of his harvesters, "Whose young woman is that?"

[6]The foreman replied, "She is the Moabitess who came back from Moab with Naomi. [7]She said, 'Please let me glean and gather among the sheaves behind the harvesters.' She went into the field and has worked steadily from morning till now, except for a short rest in the shelter."

[8]So Boaz said to Ruth, "My daughter, listen to me. Don't go and glean in another field and don't go away from here. Stay here with my servant girls. [9]Watch the field where the men are harvesting, and follow along after the girls. I have told the men not to touch you. And whenever you are thirsty, go and get a drink from the water jars the men have filled."

[10]At this, she bowed down with her face to the ground. She exclaimed, "Why have I found such favor in your eyes that you notice me—a foreigner?"

[11]Boaz replied, "I've been told all about what you have done for your mother-in-law since the death of your husband—how you left your father and mother and your homeland and came to live with a people you did not know before. [12]May the LORD repay you

---

▦▦▦▦ **MANAGING RESOURCES** ▦▦▦▦

2:3
Possessions

Out of his great compassion for poor people, God commanded the ancient Israelites to purposefully leave behind some produce and to leave the edges of their fields unharvested (see Leviticus chapter 23, verse 22 [page 151]). This allowed those who were less fortunate to gather what they needed from those who had more than enough.

This system reinforced two key values. First, it provided a dignified way for poor people to meet their own needs—they had to work for what they ate. Second, this system taught those who had an abundance not to hoard. By walking away from an incompletely harvested field, these landowners cultivated a spirit of compassion even as they maintained their business concerns.

---

a20 Naomi means pleasant; also in verse 21.   *b20 Mara means bitter.*   *c20 Hebrew Shaddai; also in verse 21*
d21 Or has testified against

for what you have done. May you be richly rewarded by the LORD, the God of Israel, under whose wings you have come to take refuge."

¹³"May I continue to find favor in your eyes, my lord," she said. "You have given me comfort and have spoken kindly to your servant—though I do not have the standing of one of your servant girls."

¹⁴At mealtime Boaz said to her, "Come over here. Have some bread and dip it in the wine vinegar."

When she sat down with the harvesters, he offered her some roasted grain. She ate all she wanted and had some left over. ¹⁵As she got up to glean, Boaz gave orders to his men, "Even if she gathers among the sheaves, don't embarrass her. ¹⁶Rather, pull out some stalks for her from the bundles and leave them for her to pick up, and don't rebuke her."

¹⁷So Ruth gleaned in the field until evening. Then she threshed the barley she had gathered, and it amounted to about an ephah.ᵃ ¹⁸She carried it back to town, and her mother-in-law saw how much she had gathered. Ruth also brought out and gave her what she had left over after she had eaten enough.

¹⁹Her mother-in-law asked her, "Where did you glean today? Where did you work? Blessed be the man who took notice of you!"

Then Ruth told her mother-in-law about the one at whose place she had been working. "The name of the man I worked with today is Boaz," she said.

²⁰"The LORD bless him!" Naomi said to her daughter-in-law. "He has not stopped showing his kindness to the living and the dead." She added, "That man is our close relative; he is one of our kinsman-redeemers."

²¹Then Ruth the Moabitess said, "He even said to me, 'Stay with my workers until they finish harvesting all my grain.'"

²²Naomi said to Ruth her daughter-in-law, "It will be good for you, my daughter, to go with his girls, because in someone else's field you might be harmed."

²³So Ruth stayed close to the servant girls of Boaz to glean until the barley and wheat harvests were finished. And she lived with her mother-in-law.

Ruth and Boaz at the Threshing Floor

3 One day Naomi her mother-in-law said to her, "My daughter, should I not try to find a homeᵇ for you, where you will be well provided for? ²Is not Boaz, with whose servant girls you have been, a kinsman of ours? Tonight he will be winnowing barley on the threshing floor. ³Wash and perfume yourself, and put on your best clothes. Then go down to the threshing floor, but don't let him know you are there until he has finished eating and drinking. ⁴When he lies down, note the place where he is lying. Then go and uncover his feet and lie down. He will tell you what to do."

⁵"I will do whatever you say," Ruth answered. ⁶So she went down to the threshing floor and did everything her mother-in-law told her to do.

⁷When Boaz had finished eating and drinking and was in good spirits, he went over to lie down at the far end of the grain pile. Ruth approached quietly, uncovered his feet and lay down. ⁸In the middle of the night something startled the man, and he turned and discovered a woman lying at his feet.

⁹"Who are you?" he asked.

"I am your servant Ruth," she said. "Spread the corner of your garment over me, since you are a kinsman-redeemer."

¹⁰"The LORD bless you, my daughter," he replied. "This kindness is greater than that which you showed earlier: You have not run after the younger men, whether rich or poor. ¹¹And now, my daughter, don't be afraid. I will do for you all you ask. All my fellow townsmen know that you are a woman of noble character. ¹²Although it is true that I am near of kin, there is a kinsman-redeemer nearer than I. ¹³Stay here for the night, and in

---

ᵃ17 That is, probably about 3/5 bushel (about 22 liters)   ᵇ1 Hebrew find rest (see Ruth 1:9)

the morning if he wants to redeem, good; let him redeem. But if he is not willing, as surely as the Lord lives I will do it. Lie here until morning."

¹⁴So she lay at his feet until morning, but got up before anyone could be recognized; and he said, "Don't let it be known that a woman came to the threshing floor."

¹⁵He also said, "Bring me the shawl you are wearing and hold it out." When she did so, he poured into it six measures of barley and put it on her. Then he ᵃ went back to town.

¹⁶When Ruth came to her mother-in-law, Naomi asked, "How did it go, my daughter?"

Then she told her everything Boaz had done for her ¹⁷and added, "He gave me these six measures of barley, saying, 'Don't go back to your mother-in-law empty-handed.'"

¹⁸Then Naomi said, "Wait, my daughter, until you find out what happens. For the man will not rest until the matter is settled today."

Boaz Marries Ruth

4 Meanwhile Boaz went up to the town gate and sat there. When the kinsman-redeemer he had mentioned came along, Boaz said, "Come over here, my friend, and sit down." So he went over and sat down.

²Boaz took ten of the elders of the town and said, "Sit here," and they did so. ³Then he said to the kinsman-redeemer, "Naomi, who has come back from Moab, is selling the piece of land that belonged to our brother Elimelech. ⁴I thought I should bring the matter to your attention and suggest that you buy it in the presence of these seated here and in the presence of the elders of my people. If you will redeem it, do so. But if you ᵇ will not, tell me, so I will know. For no one has the right to do it except you, and I am next in line."

"I will redeem it," he said.

⁵Then Boaz said, "On the day you buy the land from Naomi and from Ruth the Moabitess, you acquire ᶜ the dead man's widow, in order to maintain the name of the dead with his property."

⁶At this, the kinsman-redeemer said, "Then I cannot redeem it because I might endanger my own estate. You redeem it yourself. I cannot do it."

⁷(Now in earlier times in Israel, for the redemption and transfer of property to become final, one party took off his sandal and gave it to the other. This was the method of legalizing transactions in Israel.)

ADDRESSING QUESTIONS

4:17
Human Experience

Q

The "David" mentioned in this passage (the great-grandson of Ruth) is the well-known King David—of "David and Goliath" fame. And King David was one of the direct ancestors of the Messiah, Jesus Christ.

When Ruth originally made her commitment to Naomi and Naomi's God, she had no way of knowing where that commitment would lead. But God rewarded her faithfulness well beyond her lifetime. The same holds true for all people who put their trust in God and live according to his truth.

⁸So the kinsman-redeemer said to Boaz, "Buy it yourself." And he removed his sandal.

⁹Then Boaz announced to the elders and all the people, "Today you are witnesses that I have bought from Naomi all the property of Elimelech, Kilion and Mahlon. ¹⁰I have also acquired Ruth the Moabitess, Mahlon's widow, as my wife, in order to maintain the name of the dead with his property, so that his name will not disappear from among his family or from the town records. Today you are witnesses!"

¹¹Then the elders and all those at the gate said, "We are witnesses. May the Lord make the woman who is coming into your home like Rachel and Leah, who together built up the house of Israel. May you have standing in Ephrathah and be famous in Bethlehem.

ᵃ15 Most Hebrew manuscripts; many Hebrew manuscripts, Vulgate and Syriac she   ᵇ4 Many Hebrew manuscripts, Septuagint, Vulgate and Syriac; most Hebrew manuscripts he   ᶜ5 Hebrew; Vulgate and Syriac Naomi, you acquire Ruth the Moabitess,

¹²Through the offspring the LORD gives you by this young woman, may your family be like that of Perez, whom Tamar bore to Judah."

The Genealogy of David

¹³So Boaz took Ruth and she became his wife. Then he went to her, and the LORD enabled her to conceive, and she gave birth to a son. ¹⁴The women said to Naomi: "Praise be to the LORD, who this day has not left you without a kinsman-redeemer. May he become famous throughout Israel! ¹⁵He will renew your life and sustain you in your old age. For your daughter-in-law, who loves you and who is better to you than seven sons, has given him birth."

¹⁶Then Naomi took the child, laid him in her lap and cared for him. ¹⁷The women living there said, "Naomi has a son." And they named him Obed. He was the father of Jesse, the father of David.

¹⁸This, then, is the family line of Perez:

Perez was the father of Hezron,
¹⁹Hezron the father of Ram,
Ram the father of Amminadab,
²⁰Amminadab the father of Nahshon,
Nahshon the father of Salmon,[a]
²¹Salmon the father of Boaz,
Boaz the father of Obed,
²²Obed the father of Jesse,
and Jesse the father of David.

---

a20 A few Hebrew manuscripts, some Septuagint manuscripts and Vulgate (see also verse 21 and Septuagint of 1 Chron. 2:11); most Hebrew manuscripts *Salma*

Anyone who saw me in years past would never have suspected anything.

By all outward appearances I was living a normal life. But my life was a lie, both inside my home and outside. I didn't feel I had a choice, however; I was stuck in an abusive situation, and couldn't see a way out of it. At times I even contemplated suicide as I searched in vain for inward peace. I thought an affair would satisfy the lack of love I was experiencing and fill that void in my heart. But when it was over, I had only lost respect for myself.

In May of 1991 I was sitting at a worship service, listening to the pastor's message. He explained how much I mattered to God and that by my own efforts, nothing I did or could do would earn me eternal life. For the first time I clearly understood that salvation was a gift, and that I only had to confess my sins and ask Jesus to come live in me to accept that gift for myself.

What joy I felt! I knew Jesus could do better with my life than I was doing if I would just surrender it to him. And he has! Since that time, several individuals and small groups in the church have helped me rebuild my life. The love that they've selflessly given has made me feel whole again. And now the Spirit has led me to grow in the Lord by helping others who experience the same kind of despair that I felt.

In August 1994 I lost my sister, my only sibling, in a tragic auto accident. It came only thirteen short months after losing my mother to cancer. Nine years prior I had lost my father. Suddenly, at the age of 32, I found myself an orphan with no siblings. Although I have two beautiful sons and a wonderful husband, I still had this terribly frightening loneliness in the back of my mind—I was the sole survivor of my birth family.

My husband and children couldn't fill this pit of loneliness. I decided to trust in Jesus, the only one who could heal my broken heart. I was raised in a Christian family, but had never decided to have a personal relationship with Christ until last fall. Now I marvel more at the beauty in life and appreciate life's joys in a way I never have before. The tragedy and loss in my life has compelled me to seek God, and he is helping me. I still have a long journey ahead of me, but I know I'm not alone in spite of the fact that my dad, mom and sister have gone through heaven's gates before me.

Introduction

THE BOTTOM LINE

Someone once said, "Power corrupts; absolute power corrupts absolutely." That statement holds particular weight for these two books. The people of Israel weren't content to have God as their king. They begged him, through the judges, to let them have a human king; they wanted to be like all the nations around them. God allowed this, and these books tell the story of this transitional era in Israel's history. Samuel was the last of the judges; Saul and David were the first and second Israelite kings, respectively. The nation paid a price for its refusal to live by faith in the unseen God. Though a godly king was a powerful force for good, every king had his weaknesses. Whether you wield authority or must yield to it, these stories from God's Word will open your eyes to sobering lessons about the uses and abuses of power.

CENTRAL IDEAS

- God's hand is evident in this people's history—from a childless woman's plea to David's crowning as king.
- Leaders must answer to those they lead, and ultimately to God, who judges all.
- God honors total dependence on him.
- Character is built in secret, and no amount of talent or charisma can make up for its deficiency.

TITLES

Samuel was the last of the judges in Israel; these two books cover the transitional period between the rule of the judges and the rule of the kings.

AUTHOR AND READERS

Most scholars believe that the unnamed historian(s) who wrote these books combined the records of the prophets Samuel, Nathan, and Gad in recording this portion of Israel's history.

TIME LINE

	1300 BC	1200	1100	1000	900
Above line	The "judges" begin to rule Israel (c. 1375 B.C.)		David establishes Jerusalem as his capital city (c. 1000 B.C.)	Solomon's fleet trades on the African continent (c. 965 B.C.)	Carthage founded as trading center with Tyre (c. 813 B.C.)
Below line			Saul named Israel's first king (c. 1050 B.C.)	David kills Goliath (c. 1025 B.C.)	Absalom rebels against David (978 B.C.)	1 and 2 Samuel written (c. 930 B.C.)

It was a classic mismatch. At 45 years of age, George Foreman seemed too old to compete against the reigning world heavyweight champion, Michael Moorer. The champion was 26 years old and unbeaten in 35 fights.

After nine rounds Moorer had the fight wrapped up. He jabbed and danced and made Foreman look like a 45-year-old has-been. Foreman's face was lopsided from Moorer's right jabs and hooks. His left eye was swelling shut, and he was huffing and puffing.

Then, in the tenth round, with shocking suddenness, Foreman blew Moorer's house down.

"He never should have stood in front of me," the 250-pound Foreman said later.

For one brief moment Moorer stood in the wrong place, and Foreman clipped the champion with the "ol' one-two" jab followed by a short but straight-down-the-pipe right hand that nailed Moorer in the mouth.

"The only pain I felt was my son crying."

"The only pain I felt," the defeated Moorer said afterward, "was my son crying." The punch was *that* fast and *that* hard. Broadcaster Gil Clancy acclaimed it as the most significant punch in the history of boxing.

Funny how we are drawn to root for the underdog, isn't it? Maybe it's because no matter how "together" we are on the outside there are times we've felt outweighed and outgunned by our competition. In school there was always someone a little smarter. Athletically, someone eventually broke our records. In the marketplace, somebody sold more or earned more than we did. When George Foreman knocked out Michael Moorer, every underdog in the world gained a glimpse of hope and thought, *Hey, if a long shot like that can win, maybe I can too.*

Many people overlooked a brief but significant moment in the mayhem that followed that incredible knockout punch. While Moorer was spread out on the canvas, George Foreman walked over to a neutral corner. There he knelt and prayed. George Foreman the puncher is also a preacher. He wanted to thank the "God of the underdog" for letting him win.

Of course, underdogs don't always win, and God doesn't take the side of every winning athlete. If that were true, there would be no such thing as an underdog! But God is ready to stand with us in *any* circumstance. He gives us his power to win a victory with humility or to endure defeat with dignity. I suspect that if Foreman had lost, he would have thanked God for enabling him to fight in the first place. And he would have looked for ways to find God's hand at work in that difficult moment.

Perhaps no story in the Bible demonstrates God's support for the underdog like the battle between David and Goliath. This was a military mismatch on every level. Yet the courageous young David was certain that the God who had been with him in the field as he tended sheep would be with him now as his companion—and champion. For inspiration and insight about how God is able to help *you* face the challenges in your life, turn to 1 Samuel chapter 17, verses 1–54 (page 350), and read this famous story of courage and faith.

1 SAMUEL

The Birth of Samuel

1 There was a certain man from Ramathaim, a Zuphite*a* from the hill country of Ephraim, whose name was Elkanah son of Jeroham, the son of Elihu, the son of Tohu, the son of Zuph, an Ephraimite. ²He had two wives; one was called Hannah and the other Peninnah. Peninnah had children, but Hannah had none.

³Year after year this man went up from his town to worship and sacrifice to the Lord Almighty at Shiloh, where Hophni and Phinehas, the two sons of Eli, were priests of the Lord. ⁴Whenever the day came for Elkanah to sacrifice, he would give portions of the meat to his wife Peninnah and to all her sons and daughters. ⁵But to Hannah he gave a double portion because he loved her, and the Lord had closed her womb. ⁶And because the Lord had closed her womb, her rival kept provoking her in order to irritate her. ⁷This went on year after year. Whenever Hannah went up to the house of the Lord, her rival provoked her till she wept and would not eat. ⁸Elkanah her husband would say to her, "Hannah, why are you weeping? Why don't you eat? Why are you downhearted? Don't I mean more to you than ten sons?"

⁹Once when they had finished eating and drinking in Shiloh, Hannah stood up. Now Eli the priest was sitting on a chair by the doorpost of the Lord's temple.*b* ¹⁰In bitterness of soul Hannah wept much and prayed to the Lord. ¹¹And she made a vow, saying, "O Lord Almighty, if you will only look upon your servant's misery and remember me, and not forget your servant but give her a son, then I will give him to the Lord for all the days of his life, and no razor will ever be used on his head."

¹²As she kept on praying to the Lord, Eli observed her mouth. ¹³Hannah was praying in her heart, and her lips were moving but her voice was not heard. Eli thought she was drunk ¹⁴and said to her, "How long will you keep on getting drunk? Get rid of your wine."

¹⁵"Not so, my lord," Hannah replied, "I am a woman who is deeply troubled. I have not been drinking wine or beer; I was pouring out my soul to the Lord. ¹⁶Do not take your servant for a wicked woman; I have been praying here out of my great anguish and grief."

¹⁷Eli answered, "Go in peace, and may the God of Israel grant you what you have asked of him."

¹⁸She said, "May your servant find favor in your eyes." Then she went her way and ate something, and her face was no longer downcast.

¹⁹Early the next morning they arose and worshiped before the Lord and then went back to their home at Ramah. Elkanah lay with Hannah his wife, and the Lord remembered her. ²⁰So in the course of time Hannah conceived and gave birth to a son. She named him Samuel,*c* saying, "Because I asked the Lord for him."

Hannah Dedicates Samuel

²¹When the man Elkanah went up with all his family to offer the annual sacrifice to the Lord and to fulfill his vow, ²²Hannah did not go. She said to her husband, "After the boy is weaned, I will take him and present him before the Lord, and he will live there always."

²³"Do what seems best to you," Elkanah her husband told her. "Stay here until you

---

a 1 Or from Ramathaim Zuphim   *b 9 That is, tabernacle*   *c 20 Samuel sounds like the Hebrew for heard of God.*

have weaned him; only may the Lord make good his*a* word." So the woman stayed at home and nursed her son until she had weaned him.

²⁴After he was weaned, she took the boy with her, young as he was, along with a three-year-old bull,*b* an ephah*c* of flour and a skin of wine, and brought him to the house of the Lord at Shiloh. ²⁵When they had slaughtered the bull, they brought the boy to Eli, ²⁶and she said to him, "As surely as you live, my lord, I am the woman who stood here beside you praying to the Lord. ²⁷I prayed for this child, and the Lord has granted me what I asked of him. ²⁸So now I give him to the Lord. For his whole life he will be given over to the Lord." And he worshiped the Lord there.

Hannah's Prayer

2 Then Hannah prayed and said:

"My heart rejoices in the Lord;
  in the Lord my horn*d* is lifted high.
My mouth boasts over my enemies,
  for I delight in your deliverance.

²"There is no one holy*e* like the Lord;
  there is no one besides you;
  there is no Rock like our God.

³"Do not keep talking so proudly
  or let your mouth speak such arrogance,
for the Lord is a God who knows,
  and by him deeds are weighed.

⁴"The bows of the warriors are broken,
  but those who stumbled are armed with strength.
⁵Those who were full hire themselves out for food,
  but those who were hungry hunger no more.
She who was barren has borne seven children,
  but she who has had many sons pines away.

⁶"The Lord brings death and makes alive;
  he brings down to the grave*f* and raises up.
⁷The Lord sends poverty and wealth;
  he humbles and he exalts.
⁸He raises the poor from the dust
  and lifts the needy from the ash heap;
he seats them with princes
  and has them inherit a throne of honor.

"For the foundations of the earth are the Lord's;
  upon them he has set the world.
⁹He will guard the feet of his saints,
  but the wicked will be silenced in darkness.

"It is not by strength that one prevails;
¹⁰ those who oppose the Lord will be shattered.
He will thunder against them from heaven;
  the Lord will judge the ends of the earth.

---

a23 Masoretic Text; Dead Sea Scrolls, Septuagint and Syriac *your*   *b24* Dead Sea Scrolls, Septuagint and Syriac; Masoretic Text *with three bulls*   *c24* That is, probably about 3/5 bushel (about 22 liters)   *d1* *Horn* here symbolizes strength; also in verse 10.   *e2* Or *no Holy One*   *f6* Hebrew *Sheol*

> "He will give strength to his king
>   and exalt the horn of his anointed."

¹¹Then Elkanah went home to Ramah, but the boy ministered before the LORD under Eli the priest.

Eli's Wicked Sons

¹²Eli's sons were wicked men; they had no regard for the LORD. ¹³Now it was the practice of the priests with the people that whenever anyone offered a sacrifice and while the meat was being boiled, the servant of the priest would come with a three-pronged fork in his hand. ¹⁴He would plunge it into the pan or kettle or caldron or pot, and the priest would take for himself whatever the fork brought up. This is how they treated all the Israelites who came to Shiloh. ¹⁵But even before the fat was burned, the servant of the priest would come and say to the man who was sacrificing, "Give the priest some meat to roast; he won't accept boiled meat from you, but only raw."

¹⁶If the man said to him, "Let the fat be burned up first, and then take whatever you want," the servant would then answer, "No, hand it over now; if you don't, I'll take it by force."

¹⁷This sin of the young men was very great in the LORD's sight, for they*ᵃ* were treating the LORD's offering with contempt.

¹⁸But Samuel was ministering before the LORD—a boy wearing a linen ephod. ¹⁹Each year his mother made him a little robe and took it to him when she went up with her husband to offer the annual sacrifice. ²⁰Eli would bless Elkanah and his wife, saying, "May the LORD give you children by this woman to take the place of the one she prayed for and gave to the LORD." Then they would go home. ²¹And the LORD was gracious to Hannah; she conceived and gave birth to three sons and two daughters. Meanwhile, the boy Samuel grew up in the presence of the LORD.

²²Now Eli, who was very old, heard about everything his sons were doing to all Israel and how they slept with the women who served at the entrance to the Tent of Meeting. ²³So he said to them, "Why do you do such things? I hear from all the people about these wicked deeds of yours. ²⁴No, my sons; it is not a good report that I hear spreading among the LORD's people. ²⁵If a man sins against another man, God*ᵇ* may mediate for him; but if a man sins against the LORD, who will intercede for him?" His sons, however, did not listen to their father's rebuke, for it was the LORD's will to put them to death.

²⁶And the boy Samuel continued to grow in stature and in favor with the LORD and with men.

Prophecy Against the House of Eli

²⁷Now a man of God came to Eli and said to him, "This is what the LORD says: 'Did I not clearly reveal myself to your father's house when they were in Egypt under Pharaoh? ²⁸I chose your father out of all the tribes of Israel to be my priest, to go up to my altar, to burn incense, and to wear an ephod in my presence. I also gave your father's house all the offerings made with fire by the Israelites. ²⁹Why do you*ᶜ* scorn my sacrifice and offering that I prescribed for my dwelling? Why do you honor your sons more than me by fattening yourselves on the choice parts of every offering made by my people Israel?'

³⁰"Therefore the LORD, the God of Israel, declares: 'I promised that your house and your father's house would minister before me forever.' But now the LORD declares: 'Far be it from me! Those who honor me I will honor, but those who despise me will be disdained. ³¹The time is coming when I will cut short your strength and the strength of your father's

house, so that there will not be an old man in your family line ³²and you will see distress in my dwelling. Although good will be done to Israel, in your family line there will never be an old man. ³³Every one of you that I do not cut off from my altar will be spared only to blind your eyes with tears and to grieve your heart, and all your descendants will die in the prime of life.

³⁴"'And what happens to your two sons, Hophni and Phinehas, will be a sign to you—they will both die on the same day. ³⁵I will raise up for myself a faithful priest, who will do according to what is in my heart and mind. I will firmly establish his house, and he will minister before my anointed one always. ³⁶Then everyone left in your family line will come and bow down before him for a piece of silver and a crust of bread and plead, "Appoint me to some priestly office so I can have food to eat." '"

The LORD Calls Samuel

3 The boy Samuel ministered before the LORD under Eli. In those days the word of the LORD was rare; there were not many visions.

²One night Eli, whose eyes were becoming so weak that he could barely see, was lying down in his usual place. ³The lamp of God had not yet gone out, and Samuel was lying down in the temple*a* of the LORD, where the ark of God was. ⁴Then the LORD called Samuel.

Samuel answered, "Here I am." ⁵And he ran to Eli and said, "Here I am; you called me."

But Eli said, "I did not call; go back and lie down." So he went and lay down.

⁶Again the LORD called, "Samuel!" And Samuel got up and went to Eli and said, "Here I am; you called me."

"My son," Eli said, "I did not call; go back and lie down."

⁷Now Samuel did not yet know the LORD: The word of the LORD had not yet been revealed to him.

⁸The LORD called Samuel a third time, and Samuel got up and went to Eli and said, "Here I am; you called me."

Then Eli realized that the LORD was calling the boy. ⁹So Eli told Samuel, "Go and lie down, and if he calls you, say, 'Speak, LORD, for your servant is listening.'" So Samuel went and lay down in his place.

¹⁰The LORD came and stood there, calling as at the other times, "Samuel! Samuel!"

Then Samuel said, "Speak, for your servant is listening."

¹¹And the LORD said to Samuel: "See, I am about to do something in Israel that will make the ears of everyone who hears of it tingle. ¹²At that time I will carry out against Eli everything I spoke against his family—from beginning to end. ¹³For I told him that I would judge his family forever because of the sin he knew about; his sons made them-

STRENGTHENING RELATIONSHIPS

3:13
Parenting

Eli held a privileged position in Israel. He had access to God's laws, and knew well the history and power of God's workings with his people. Yet he couldn't manage his own sons in accordance with what he knew was right.

Eli's tragic inability to restrain his sons was an affront to God. (Chapter 2 discusses the role these two men had in conducting and corrupting Israel's worship.) Notice that the passage doesn't say that Eli was supposed to *control* his sons, as if he should have had some sort of power over their wills. But Eli could have taken steps to assure that their actions wouldn't continue to spoil Israelite worship.

If you are a parent, one of the roles God has for you is to teach your children how to *do* what is right, not just *know* what is right. When their behavior harms others, you are called to step in with firm love and limit the effects of their disobedience. If you want to be a leader in the world, you first need to be a leader at home.

a3 That is, tabernacle

selves contemptible,^{a} and he failed to restrain them. [14]Therefore, I swore to the house of Eli, 'The guilt of Eli's house will never be atoned for by sacrifice or offering.'"

[15]Samuel lay down until morning and then opened the doors of the house of the LORD. He was afraid to tell Eli the vision, [16]but Eli called him and said, "Samuel, my son."

Samuel answered, "Here I am."

[17]"What was it he said to you?" Eli asked. "Do not hide it from me. May God deal with you, be it ever so severely, if you hide from me anything he told you." [18]So Samuel told him everything, hiding nothing from him. Then Eli said, "He is the LORD; let him do what is good in his eyes."

[19]The LORD was with Samuel as he grew up, and he let none of his words fall to the ground. [20]And all Israel from Dan to Beersheba recognized that Samuel was attested as a prophet of the LORD. [21]The LORD continued to appear at Shiloh, and there he revealed himself to Samuel through his word.

 4   And Samuel's word came to all Israel.

The Philistines Capture the Ark

Now the Israelites went out to fight against the Philistines. The Israelites camped at Ebenezer, and the Philistines at Aphek. [2]The Philistines deployed their forces to meet Israel, and as the battle spread, Israel was defeated by the Philistines, who killed about four thousand of them on the battlefield. [3]When the soldiers returned to camp, the elders of Israel asked, "Why did the LORD bring defeat upon us today before the Philistines? Let us bring the ark of the LORD's covenant from Shiloh, so that it^b may go with us and save us from the hand of our enemies."

[4]So the people sent men to Shiloh, and they brought back the ark of the covenant of the LORD Almighty, who is enthroned between the cherubim. And Eli's two sons, Hophni and Phinehas, were there with the ark of the covenant of God.

[5]When the ark of the LORD's covenant came into the camp, all Israel raised such a great shout that the ground shook. [6]Hearing the uproar, the Philistines asked, "What's all this shouting in the Hebrew camp?"

When they learned that the ark of the LORD had come into the camp, [7]the Philistines were afraid. "A god has come into the camp," they said. "We're in trouble! Nothing like this has happened before. [8]Woe to us! Who will deliver us from the hand of these mighty gods? They are the gods who struck the Egyptians with all kinds of plagues in the desert. [9]Be strong, Philistines! Be men, or you will be subject to the Hebrews, as they have been to you. Be men, and fight!"

[10]So the Philistines fought, and the Israelites were defeated and every man fled to his tent. The slaughter was very great; Israel lost thirty thousand foot soldiers. [11]The ark of God was captured, and Eli's two sons, Hophni and Phinehas, died.

Death of Eli

[12]That same day a Benjamite ran from the battle line and went to Shiloh, his clothes torn and dust on his head. [13]When he arrived, there was Eli sitting on his chair by the side of the road, watching, because his heart feared for the ark of God. When the man entered the town and told what had happened, the whole town sent up a cry.

[14]Eli heard the outcry and asked, "What is the meaning of this uproar?"

The man hurried over to Eli, [15]who was ninety-eight years old and whose eyes were set so that he could not see. [16]He told Eli, "I have just come from the battle line; I fled from it this very day."

Eli asked, "What happened, my son?"

[17]The man who brought the news replied, "Israel fled before the Philistines, and the

---

^{a}13 Masoretic Text; an ancient Hebrew scribal tradition and Septuagint *sons blasphemed God* ^{b}3 Or *he*

army has suffered heavy losses. Also your two sons, Hophni and Phinehas, are dead, and the ark of God has been captured."

18When he mentioned the ark of God, Eli fell backward off his chair by the side of the gate. His neck was broken and he died, for he was an old man and heavy. He had led[a] Israel forty years.

19His daughter-in-law, the wife of Phinehas, was pregnant and near the time of delivery. When she heard the news that the ark of God had been captured and that her father-in-law and her husband were dead, she went into labor and gave birth, but was overcome by her labor pains. 20As she was dying, the women attending her said, "Don't despair; you have given birth to a son." But she did not respond or pay any attention.

21She named the boy Ichabod,[b] saying, "The glory has departed from Israel"—because of the capture of the ark of God and the deaths of her father-in-law and her husband. 22She said, "The glory has departed from Israel, for the ark of God has been captured."

The Ark in Ashdod and Ekron

5 After the Philistines had captured the ark of God, they took it from Ebenezer to Ashdod. 2Then they carried the ark into Dagon's temple and set it beside Dagon. 3When the people of Ashdod rose early the next day, there was Dagon, fallen on his face on the ground before the ark of the LORD! They took Dagon and put him back in his place. 4But the following morning when they rose, there was Dagon, fallen on his face on the ground before the ark of the LORD! His head and hands had been broken off and were lying on the threshold; only his body remained. 5That is why to this day neither the priests of Dagon nor any others who enter Dagon's temple at Ashdod step on the threshold.

6The LORD's hand was heavy upon the people of Ashdod and its vicinity; he brought devastation upon them and afflicted them with tumors.[c] 7When the men of Ashdod saw what was happening, they said, "The ark of the god of Israel must not stay here with us, because his hand is heavy upon us and upon Dagon our god." 8So they called together all the rulers of the Philistines and asked them, "What shall we do with the ark of the god of Israel?"

They answered, "Have the ark of the god of Israel moved to Gath." So they moved the ark of the God of Israel.

9But after they had moved it, the LORD's hand was against that city, throwing it into a great panic. He afflicted the people of the city, both young and old, with an outbreak of tumors.[d] 10So they sent the ark of God to Ekron.

As the ark of God was entering Ekron, the people of Ekron cried out, "They have brought the ark of the god of Israel around to us to kill us and our people." 11So they called together all the rulers of the Philistines and said, "Send the ark of the god of Israel away; let it go back to its own place, or it[e] will kill us and our people." For death had filled the city with panic; God's hand was very heavy upon it. 12Those who did not die were afflicted with tumors, and the outcry of the city went up to heaven.

The Ark Returned to Israel

6 When the ark of the LORD had been in Philistine territory seven months, 2the Philistines called for the priests and the diviners and said, "What shall we do with the ark of the LORD? Tell us how we should send it back to its place."

3They answered, "If you return the ark of the god of Israel, do not send it away empty, but by all means send a guilt offering to him. Then you will be healed, and you will know why his hand has not been lifted from you."

4The Philistines asked, "What guilt offering should we send to him?"

---

a 18 Traditionally judged   *b 21 Ichabod means no glory.*   *c 6 Hebrew; Septuagint and Vulgate tumors. And rats appeared in their land, and death and destruction were throughout the city*   *d 9 Or with tumors in the groin (see Septuagint)*   *e 11 Or he*

They replied, "Five gold tumors and five gold rats, according to the number of the Philistine rulers, because the same plague has struck both you and your rulers. ⁵Make models of the tumors and of the rats that are destroying the country, and pay honor to Israel's god. Perhaps he will lift his hand from you and your gods and your land. ⁶Why do you harden your hearts as the Egyptians and Pharaoh did? When heᵃ treated them harshly, did they not send the Israelites out so they could go on their way?

⁷"Now then, get a new cart ready, with two cows that have calved and have never been yoked. Hitch the cows to the cart, but take their calves away and pen them up. ⁸Take the ark of the Lᴏʀᴅ and put it on the cart, and in a chest beside it put the gold objects you are sending back to him as a guilt offering. Send it on its way, ⁹but keep watching it. If it goes up to its own territory, toward Beth Shemesh, then the Lᴏʀᴅ has brought this great disaster on us. But if it does not, then we will know that it was not his hand that struck us and that it happened to us by chance."

¹⁰So they did this. They took two such cows and hitched them to the cart and penned up their calves. ¹¹They placed the ark of the Lᴏʀᴅ on the cart and along with it the chest containing the gold rats and the models of the tumors. ¹²Then the cows went straight up toward Beth Shemesh, keeping on the road and lowing all the way; they did not turn to the right or to the left. The rulers of the Philistines followed them as far as the border of Beth Shemesh.

¹³Now the people of Beth Shemesh were harvesting their wheat in the valley, and when they looked up and saw the ark, they rejoiced at the sight. ¹⁴The cart came to the field of Joshua of Beth Shemesh, and there it stopped beside a large rock. The people chopped up the wood of the cart and sacrificed the cows as a burnt offering to the Lᴏʀᴅ. ¹⁵The Levites took down the ark of the Lᴏʀᴅ, together with the chest containing the gold objects, and placed them on the large rock. On that day the people of Beth Shemesh offered burnt offerings and made sacrifices to the Lᴏʀᴅ. ¹⁶The five rulers of the Philistines saw all this and then returned that same day to Ekron.

¹⁷These are the gold tumors the Philistines sent as a guilt offering to the Lᴏʀᴅ—one each for Ashdod, Gaza, Ashkelon, Gath and Ekron. ¹⁸And the number of the gold rats was according to the number of Philistine towns belonging to the five rulers—the fortified towns with their country villages. The large rock, on whichᵇ they set the ark of the Lᴏʀᴅ, is a witness to this day in the field of Joshua of Beth Shemesh.

¹⁹But God struck down some of the men of Beth Shemesh, putting seventyᶜ of them to death because they had looked into the ark of the Lᴏʀᴅ. The people mourned because of the heavy blow the Lᴏʀᴅ had dealt them, ²⁰and the men of Beth Shemesh asked, "Who can stand in the presence of the Lᴏʀᴅ, this holy God? To whom will the ark go up from here?"

²¹Then they sent messengers to the people of Kiriath Jearim, saying, "The Philistines have returned the ark of the Lᴏʀᴅ. Come down and take it up to your place." ¹So the men of Kiriath Jearim came and took up the ark of the Lᴏʀᴅ. They took it to Abinadab's house on the hill and consecrated Eleazar his son to guard the ark of the Lᴏʀᴅ.

Samuel Subdues the Philistines at Mizpah

²It was a long time, twenty years in all, that the ark remained at Kiriath Jearim, and all the people of Israel mourned and sought after the Lᴏʀᴅ. ³And Samuel said to the whole house of Israel, "If you are returning to the Lᴏʀᴅ with all your hearts, then rid yourselves of the foreign gods and the Ashtoreths and commit yourselves to the Lᴏʀᴅ and serve him only, and he will deliver you out of the hand of the Philistines." ⁴So the Israelites put away their Baals and Ashtoreths, and served the Lᴏʀᴅ only.

⁵Then Samuel said, "Assemble all Israel at Mizpah and I will intercede with the Lᴏʀᴅ for you." ⁶When they had assembled at Mizpah, they drew water and poured it out before

---

ᵃ6 That is, God Abel, where   ᵇ18 A few Hebrew manuscripts (see also Septuagint); most Hebrew manuscripts *villages as far as Greater*   ᶜ19 A few Hebrew manuscripts; most Hebrew manuscripts and Septuagint 50,070

the LORD. On that day they fasted and there they confessed, "We have sinned against the LORD." And Samuel was leader*a* of Israel at Mizpah.

⁷When the Philistines heard that Israel had assembled at Mizpah, the rulers of the Philistines came up to attack them. And when the Israelites heard of it, they were afraid because of the Philistines. ⁸They said to Samuel, "Do not stop crying out to the LORD our God for us, that he may rescue us from the hand of the Philistines." ⁹Then Samuel took a suckling lamb and offered it up as a whole burnt offering to the LORD. He cried out to the LORD on Israel's behalf, and the LORD answered him.

¹⁰While Samuel was sacrificing the burnt offering, the Philistines drew near to engage Israel in battle. But that day the LORD thundered with loud thunder against the Philistines and threw them into such a panic that they were routed before the Israelites. ¹¹The men of Israel rushed out of Mizpah and pursued the Philistines, slaughtering them along the way to a point below Beth Car.

¹²Then Samuel took a stone and set it up between Mizpah and Shen. He named it Ebenezer,*b* saying, "Thus far has the LORD helped us." ¹³So the Philistines were subdued and did not invade Israelite territory again.

Throughout Samuel's lifetime, the hand of the LORD was against the Philistines. ¹⁴The towns from Ekron to Gath that the Philistines had captured from Israel were restored to her, and Israel delivered the neighboring territory from the power of the Philistines. And there was peace between Israel and the Amorites.

¹⁵Samuel continued as judge over Israel all the days of his life. ¹⁶From year to year he went on a circuit from Bethel to Gilgal to Mizpah, judging Israel in all those places. ¹⁷But he always went back to Ramah, where his home was, and there he also judged Israel. And he built an altar there to the LORD.

Israel Asks for a King

8 When Samuel grew old, he appointed his sons as judges for Israel. ²The name of his firstborn was Joel and the name of his second was Abijah, and they served at Beersheba. ³But his sons did not walk in his ways. They turned aside after dishonest gain and accepted bribes and perverted justice.

⁴So all the elders of Israel gathered together and came to Samuel at Ramah. They said to him, "You are old, and your sons do not walk in your ways; now appoint a king to lead*c* us, such as all the other nations have."

⁶But when they said, "Give us a king to lead us," this displeased Samuel; so he prayed to the LORD. ⁷And the LORD told him: "Listen to all that the people are saying to you; it is not you they have rejected, but they have rejected me as their king. ⁸As they have done from the day I brought them up out of Egypt until this day, forsaking me and serving

---

▣ ░░░░░ KNOWING YOURSELF ░░░░░ ⬅

8:4–20
Sin

Peer pressure is a powerful force among teenagers. They'll almost anything to be included in whatever group they want to be a part of. Isn't it great to know that we as adults grow out of that stage and gain the ability to shrug off peer pressure?

Or do we?

Listen to the adolescent whine coming from the people of Israel in this passage as they plead for a king. Even their rationale—to "be like all the other nations"—is pure childishness. Where is their common sense? Can't they see their attitude for what it is?

No, they can't. And neither can most of us when we get caught up in the desire to have something that we think will make us feel secure. The Israelites listen to Samuel's warning about what a king will do to change their society and spending habits (verses 10–18), but they don't really *hear* the warning. They stubbornly reiterate their demand (verses 19–20).

Be careful what you pray for—you just may get it. Better to first ask God what he wants for you, and trust that his answer will be in your best interests. And whatever you do, don't whine!

---

a 6 Traditionally judge   *b 12 Ebenezer means stone of help.*   *c 5 Traditionally judge; also in verses 6 and 20*

other gods, so they are doing to you. ⁹Now listen to them; but warn them solemnly and let them know what the king who will reign over them will do."

¹⁰Samuel told all the words of the LORD to the people who were asking him for a king. ¹¹He said, "This is what the king who will reign over you will do: He will take your sons and make them serve with his chariots and horses, and they will run in front of his chariots. ¹²Some he will assign to be commanders of thousands and commanders of fifties, and others to plow his ground and reap his harvest, and still others to make weapons of war and equipment for his chariots. ¹³He will take your daughters to be perfumers and cooks and bakers. ¹⁴He will take the best of your fields and vineyards and olive groves and give them to his attendants. ¹⁵He will take a tenth of your grain and of your vintage and give it to his officials and attendants. ¹⁶Your menservants and maidservants and the best of your cattle*ᵃ* and donkeys he will take for his own use. ¹⁷He will take a tenth of your flocks, and you yourselves will become his slaves. ¹⁸When that day comes, you will cry out for relief from the king you have chosen, and the LORD will not answer you in that day."

¹⁹But the people refused to listen to Samuel. "No!" they said. "We want a king over us. ²⁰Then we will be like all the other nations, with a king to lead us and to go out before us and fight our battles."

²¹When Samuel heard all that the people said, he repeated it before the LORD. ²²The LORD answered, "Listen to them and give them a king."

Then Samuel said to the men of Israel, "Everyone go back to his town."

Samuel Anoints Saul

9 There was a Benjamite, a man of standing, whose name was Kish son of Abiel, the son of Zeror, the son of Becorath, the son of Aphiah of Benjamin. ²He had a son named Saul, an impressive young man without equal among the Israelites—a head taller than any of the others.

³Now the donkeys belonging to Saul's father Kish were lost, and Kish said to his son Saul, "Take one of the servants with you and go and look for the donkeys." ⁴So he passed through the hill country of Ephraim and through the area around Shalisha, but they did not find them. They went on into the district of Shaalim, but the donkeys were not there. Then he passed through the territory of Benjamin, but they did not find them.

⁵When they reached the district of Zuph, Saul said to the servant who was with him, "Come, let's go back, or my father will stop thinking about the donkeys and start worrying about us."

⁶But the servant replied, "Look, in this town there is a man of God; he is highly respected, and everything he says comes true. Let's go there now. Perhaps he will tell us what way to take."

⁷Saul said to his servant, "If we go, what can we give the man? The food in our sacks is gone. We have no gift to take to the man of God. What do we have?"

⁸The servant answered him again. "Look," he said, "I have a quarter of a shekel*ᵇ* of silver. I will give it to the man of God so that he will tell us what way to take." ⁹(Formerly in Israel, if a man went to inquire of God, he would say, "Come, let us go to the seer," because the prophet of today used to be called a seer.)

¹⁰"Good," Saul said to his servant. "Come, let's go." So they set out for the town where the man of God was.

¹¹As they were going up the hill to the town, they met some girls coming out to draw water, and they asked them, "Is the seer here?"

¹²"He is," they answered. "He's ahead of you. Hurry now; he has just come to our town today, for the people have a sacrifice at the high place. ¹³As soon as you enter the town, you will find him before he goes up to the high place to eat. The people will not begin

---

ᵃ 16 Septuagint; Hebrew *young men*   *ᵇ 8* That is, about 1/10 ounce (about 3 grams)

ating until he comes, because he must bless the sacrifice; afterward, those who are invited will eat. Go up now; you should find him about this time."

¹⁴They went up to the town, and as they were entering it, there was Samuel, coming toward them on his way up to the high place.

¹⁵Now the day before Saul came, the LORD had revealed this to Samuel: ¹⁶"About this time tomorrow I will send you a man from the land of Benjamin. Anoint him leader over my people Israel; he will deliver my people from the hand of the Philistines. I have looked upon my people, for their cry has reached me."

¹⁷When Samuel caught sight of Saul, the LORD said to him, "This is the man I spoke to you about; he will govern my people."

¹⁸Saul approached Samuel in the gateway and asked, "Would you please tell me where the seer's house is?"

¹⁹"I am the seer," Samuel replied. "Go up ahead of me to the high place, for today you are to eat with me, and in the morning I will let you go and will tell you all that is in your heart. ²⁰As for the donkeys you lost three days ago, do not worry about them; they have been found. And to whom is all the desire of Israel turned, if not to you and all your father's family?"

²¹Saul answered, "But am I not a Benjamite, from the smallest tribe of Israel, and is not my clan the least of all the clans of the tribe of Benjamin? Why do you say such a thing to me?"

²²Then Samuel brought Saul and his servant into the hall and seated them at the head of those who were invited—about thirty in number. ²³Samuel said to the cook, "Bring the piece of meat I gave you, the one I told you to lay aside."

²⁴So the cook took up the leg with what was on it and set it in front of Saul. Samuel said, "Here is what has been kept for you. Eat, because it was set aside for you for this occasion, from the time I said, 'I have invited guests.'" And Saul dined with Samuel that day.

²⁵After they came down from the high place to the town, Samuel talked with Saul on the roof of his house. ²⁶They rose about daybreak and Samuel called to Saul on the roof, "Get ready, and I will send you on your way." When Saul got ready, he and Samuel went outside together. ²⁷As they were going down to the edge of the town, Samuel said to Saul, "Tell the servant to go on ahead of us"—and the servant did so—"but you stay here awhile, so that I may give you a message from God."

10 Then Samuel took a flask of oil and poured it on Saul's head and kissed him, saying, "Has not the LORD anointed you leader over his inheritance?ᵃ ²When you leave me today, you will meet two men near Rachel's tomb, at Zelzah on the border of Benjamin. They will say to you, 'The donkeys you set out to look for have been found. And now your father has stopped thinking about them and is worried about you. He is asking, "What shall I do about my son?"'

³"Then you will go on from there until you reach the great tree of Tabor. Three men going up to God at Bethel will meet you there. One will be carrying three young goats, another three loaves of bread, and another a skin of wine. ⁴They will greet you and offer you two loaves of bread, which you will accept from them.

⁵"After that you will go to Gibeah of God, where there is a Philistine outpost. As you approach the town, you will meet a procession of prophets coming down from the high place with lyres, tambourines, flutes and harps being played before them, and they will be prophesying. ⁶The Spirit of the LORD will come upon you in power, and you will prophesy with them; and you will be changed into a different person. ⁷Once these signs are fulfilled, do whatever your hand finds to do, for God is with you.

⁸"Go down ahead of me to Gilgal. I will surely come down to you to sacrifice burnt

---

I Hebrew; Septuagint and Vulgate over his people Israel? You will reign over the LORD's people and save them from the power of their enemies round about. And this will be a sign to you that the LORD has anointed you leader over his inheritance:

offerings and fellowship offerings,ᵃ but you must wait seven days until I come to yo and tell you what you are to do."

Saul Made King

⁹As Saul turned to leave Samuel, God changed Saul's heart, and all these signs wer fulfilled that day. ¹⁰When they arrived at Gibeah, a procession of prophets met him; th Spirit of God came upon him in power, and he joined in their prophesying. ¹¹When a those who had formerly known him saw him prophesying with the prophets, they aske each other, "What is this that has happened to the son of Kish? Is Saul also among th prophets?"

¹²A man who lived there answered, "And who is their father?" So it became a sayin "Is Saul also among the prophets?" ¹³After Saul stopped prophesying, he went to the hig place.

¹⁴Now Saul's uncle asked him and his servant, "Where have you been?"

"Looking for the donkeys," he said. "But when we saw they were not to be found, w went to Samuel."

¹⁵Saul's uncle said, "Tell me what Samuel said to you."

¹⁶Saul replied, "He assured us that the donkeys had been found." But he did not tell h uncle what Samuel had said about the kingship.

¹⁷Samuel summoned the people of Israel to the LORD at Mizpah ¹⁸and said to them, "Th is what the LORD, the God of Israel, says: 'I brought Israel up out of Egypt, and I delivere you from the power of Egypt and all the kingdoms that oppressed you.' ¹⁹But you hav now rejected your God, who saves you out of all your calamities and distresses. And y have said, 'No, set a king over us.' So now present yourselves before the LORD by you tribes and clans."

²⁰When Samuel brought all the tribes of Israel near, the tribe of Benjamin was chose ²¹Then he brought forward the tribe of Benjamin, clan by clan, and Matri's clan wa chosen. Finally Saul son of Kish was chosen. But when they looked for him, he was n to be found. ²²So they inquired further of the LORD, "Has the man come here yet?"

And the LORD said, "Yes, he has hidden himself among the baggage."

²³They ran and brought him out, and as he stood among the people he was a hea taller than any of the others. ²⁴Samuel said to all the people, "Do you see the man th LORD has chosen? There is no one like him among all the people."

Then the people shouted, "Long live the king!"

²⁵Samuel explained to the people the regulations of the kingship. He wrote them dow on a scroll and deposited it before the LORD. Then Samuel dismissed the people, each t his own home.

²⁶Saul also went to his home in Gibeah, accompanied by valiant men whose hear God had touched. ²⁷But some troublemakers said, "How can this fellow save us?" The despised him and brought him no gifts. But Saul kept silent.

Saul Rescues the City of Jabesh

11 Nahash the Ammonite went up and besieged Jabesh Gilead. And all the me of Jabesh said to him, "Make a treaty with us, and we will be subject to you

²But Nahash the Ammonite replied, "I will make a treaty with you only on the conditic that I gouge out the right eye of every one of you and so bring disgrace on all Israel

³The elders of Jabesh said to him, "Give us seven days so we can send messenger throughout Israel; if no one comes to rescue us, we will surrender to you."

⁴When the messengers came to Gibeah of Saul and reported these terms to the peopl they all wept aloud. ⁵Just then Saul was returning from the fields, behind his oxen, an he asked, "What is wrong with the people? Why are they weeping?" Then they repeate to him what the men of Jabesh had said.

ᵃ 8 Traditionally *peace offerings*

⁶When Saul heard their words, the Spirit of God came upon him in power, and he burned with anger. ⁷He took a pair of oxen, cut them into pieces, and sent the pieces by messengers throughout Israel, proclaiming, "This is what will be done to the oxen of anyone who does not follow Saul and Samuel." Then the terror of the LORD fell on the people, and they turned out as one man. ⁸When Saul mustered them at Bezek, the men of Israel numbered three hundred thousand and the men of Judah thirty thousand.

⁹They told the messengers who had come, "Say to the men of Jabesh Gilead, 'By the time the sun is hot tomorrow, you will be delivered.'" When the messengers went and reported this to the men of Jabesh, they were elated. ¹⁰They said to the Ammonites, "Tomorrow we will surrender to you, and you can do to us whatever seems good to you."

¹¹The next day Saul separated his men into three divisions; during the last watch of the night they broke into the camp of the Ammonites and slaughtered them until the heat of the day. Those who survived were scattered, so that no two of them were left together.

Saul Confirmed as King

¹²The people then said to Samuel, "Who was it that asked, 'Shall Saul reign over us?' Bring these men to us and we will put them to death."

¹³But Saul said, "No one shall be put to death today, for this day the LORD has rescued Israel."

¹⁴Then Samuel said to the people, "Come, let us go to Gilgal and there reaffirm the kingship." ¹⁵So all the people went to Gilgal and confirmed Saul as king in the presence of the LORD. There they sacrificed fellowship offeringsª before the LORD, and Saul and all the Israelites held a great celebration.

Samuel's Farewell Speech

12 Samuel said to all Israel, "I have listened to everything you said to me and have set a king over you. ²Now you have a king as your leader. As for me, I am old and gray, and my sons are here with you. I have been your leader from my youth until this day. ³Here I stand. Testify against me in the presence of the LORD and his anointed. Whose ox have I taken? Whose donkey have I taken? Whom have I cheated? Whom have I oppressed? From whose hand have I accepted a bribe to make me shut my eyes? If I have done any of these, I will make it right."

⁴"You have not cheated or oppressed us," they replied. "You have not taken anything from anyone's hand."

⁵Samuel said to them, "The LORD is witness against you, and also his anointed is witness this day, that you have not found anything in my hand."

"He is witness," they said.

⁶Then Samuel said to the people, "It is the LORD who appointed Moses and Aaron and brought your forefathers up out of Egypt. ⁷Now then, stand here, because I am going to

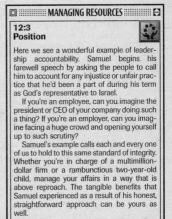

▣ ░░░░░░░ **MANAGING RESOURCES** ░░░░░░░ ◩

**12:3
Position**

Here we see a wonderful example of leadership accountability. Samuel begins his farewell speech by asking the people to call him to account for any injustice or unfair practice that he'd been a part of during his term as God's representative to Israel.

If you're an employee, can you imagine the president or CEO of your company doing such a thing? If you're an employer, can you imagine facing a huge crowd and opening yourself up to such scrutiny?

Samuel's example calls each and every one of us to hold to this same standard of integrity. Whether you're in charge of a multimillion-dollar firm or a rambunctious two-year-old child, manage your affairs in a way that is above reproach. The tangible benefits that Samuel experienced as a result of his honest, straightforward approach can be yours as well.

confront you with evidence before the LORD as to all the righteous acts performed by the LORD for you and your fathers.

[8]"After Jacob entered Egypt, they cried to the LORD for help, and the LORD sent Moses and Aaron, who brought your forefathers out of Egypt and settled them in this place.

[9]"But they forgot the LORD their God; so he sold them into the hand of Sisera, the commander of the army of Hazor, and into the hands of the Philistines and the king of Moab, who fought against them. [10]They cried out to the LORD and said, 'We have sinned; we have forsaken the LORD and served the Baals and the Ashtoreths. But now deliver us from the hands of our enemies, and we will serve you.' [11]Then the LORD sent Jerub-Baal,[a] Barak,[b] Jephthah and Samuel,[c] and he delivered you from the hands of your enemies on every side, so that you lived securely.

[12]"But when you saw that Nahash king of the Ammonites was moving against you, you said to me, 'No, we want a king to rule over us'—even though the LORD your God was your king. [13]Now here is the king you have chosen, the one you asked for; see, the LORD has set a king over you. [14]If you fear the LORD and serve and obey him and do not rebel against his commands, and if both you and the king who reigns over you follow the LORD your God—good! [15]But if you do not obey the LORD, and if you rebel against his commands, his hand will be against you, as it was against your fathers.

[16]"Now then, stand still and see this great thing the LORD is about to do before your eyes! [17]Is it not wheat harvest now? I will call upon the LORD to send thunder and rain. And you will realize what an evil thing you did in the eyes of the LORD when you asked for a king."

[18]Then Samuel called upon the LORD, and that same day the LORD sent thunder and rain. So all the people stood in awe of the LORD and of Samuel.

[19]The people all said to Samuel, "Pray to the LORD your God for your servants so that we will not die, for we have added to all our other sins the evil of asking for a king."

[20]"Do not be afraid," Samuel replied. "You have done all this evil; yet do not turn away from the LORD, but serve the LORD with all your heart. [21]Do not turn away after useless idols. They can do you no good, nor can they rescue you, because they are useless. [22]For the sake of his great name the LORD will not reject his people, because the LORD was pleased to make you his own. [23]As for me, far be it from me that I should sin against the LORD by failing to pray for you. And I will teach you the way that is good and right. [24]But be sure to fear the LORD and serve him faithfully with all your heart; consider what great things he has done for you. [25]Yet if you persist in doing evil, both you and your king will be swept away."

Samuel Rebukes Saul

13 Saul was ⌊thirty⌋[d] years old when he became king, and he reigned over Israel ⌊forty-⌋[e] two years.

[2]Saul[f] chose three thousand men from Israel; two thousand were with him at Micmash and in the hill country of Bethel, and a thousand were with Jonathan at Gibeah in Benjamin. The rest of the men he sent back to their homes.

[3]Jonathan attacked the Philistine outpost at Geba, and the Philistines heard about it. Then Saul had the trumpet blown throughout the land and said, "Let the Hebrews hear!" [4]So all Israel heard the news: "Saul has attacked the Philistine outpost, and now Israel has become a stench to the Philistines." And the people were summoned to join Saul at Gilgal.

[5]The Philistines assembled to fight Israel, with three thousand[g] chariots, six thousand charioteers, and soldiers as numerous as the sand on the seashore. They went up and camped at Micmash, east of Beth Aven. [6]When the men of Israel saw that their situation

---

a 11 Also called *Gideon*   *b 11* Some Septuagint manuscripts and Syriac; Hebrew *Bedan*   *c 11* Hebrew; some Septuagint manuscripts and Syriac *Samson*   *d 1* A few late manuscripts of the Septuagint; Hebrew does not have *thirty*.   *e 1* See the round number in Acts 13:21; Hebrew does not have *forty-*.   *f 1,2* Or *and when he had reigned over Israel two years,* *²he*   *g 5* Some Septuagint manuscripts and Syriac; Hebrew *thirty thousand*

was critical and that their army was hard pressed, they hid in caves and thickets, among the rocks, and in pits and cisterns. [7]Some Hebrews even crossed the Jordan to the land of Gad and Gilead.

Saul remained at Gilgal, and all the troops with him were quaking with fear. [8]He waited seven days, the time set by Samuel; but Samuel did not come to Gilgal, and Saul's men began to scatter. [9]So he said, "Bring me the burnt offering and the fellowship offerings.ᵃ" And Saul offered up the burnt offering. [10]Just as he finished making the offering, Samuel arrived, and Saul went out to greet him.

[11]"What have you done?" asked Samuel.

Saul replied, "When I saw that the men were scattering, and that you did not come at the set time, and that the Philistines were assembling at Micmash, [12]I thought, 'Now the Philistines will come down against me at Gilgal, and I have not sought the LORD's favor.' So I felt compelled to offer the burnt offering."

[13]"You acted foolishly," Samuel said. "You have not kept the command the LORD your God gave you; if you had, he would have established your kingdom over Israel for all time. [14]But now your kingdom will not endure; the LORD has sought out a man after his own heart and appointed him leader of his people, because you have not kept the LORD's command."

[15]Then Samuel left Gilgalᵇ and went up to Gibeah in Benjamin, and Saul counted the men who were with him. They numbered about six hundred.

Israel Without Weapons

[16]Saul and his son Jonathan and the men with them were staying in Gibeahᶜ in Benjamin, while the Philistines camped at Micmash. [17]Raiding parties went out from the Philistine camp in three detachments. One turned toward Ophrah in the vicinity of Shual, [18]another toward Beth Horon, and the third toward the borderland overlooking the Valley of Zeboim facing the desert.

[19]Not a blacksmith could be found in the whole land of Israel, because the Philistines had said, "Otherwise the Hebrews will make swords or spears!" [20]So all Israel went down to the Philistines to have their plowshares, mattocks, axes and sicklesᵈ sharpened. [21]The price was two thirds of a shekelᵉ for sharpening plowshares and mattocks, and a third of a shekelᶠ for sharpening forks and axes and for repointing goads.

[22]So on the day of the battle not a soldier with Saul and Jonathan had a sword or spear in his hand; only Saul and his son Jonathan had them.

Jonathan Attacks the Philistines

14 [23]Now a detachment of Philistines had gone out to the pass at Micmash. [1]One day Jonathan son of Saul said to the young man bearing his armor, "Come, let's go over to the Philistine outpost on the other side." But he did not tell his father.

[2]Saul was staying on the outskirts of Gibeah under a pomegranate tree in Migron. With him were about six hundred men, [3]among whom was Ahijah, who was wearing an ephod. He was a son of Ichabod's brother Ahitub son of Phinehas, the son of Eli, the LORD's priest in Shiloh. No one was aware that Jonathan had left.

[4]On each side of the pass that Jonathan intended to cross to reach the Philistine outpost was a cliff; one was called Bozez, and the other Seneh. [5]One cliff stood to the north toward Micmash, the other to the south toward Geba.

[6]Jonathan said to his young armor-bearer, "Come, let's go over to the outpost of those uncircumcised fellows. Perhaps the LORD will act in our behalf. Nothing can hinder the LORD from saving, whether by many or by few."

ᵃ9 Traditionally peace offerings   ᵇ15 Hebrew; Septuagint *Gilgal and went his way; the rest of the people went after Saul to meet the army, and they went out of Gilgal*   ᶜ16 Two Hebrew manuscripts; most Hebrew manuscripts *Geba*, a variant of *Gibeah*   ᵈ20 Septuagint; Hebrew *plowshares*   ᵉ21 Hebrew *pim*; that is, about 1/4 ounce (about 8 grams)   ᶠ21 That is, about 1/8 ounce (about 4 grams)

7"Do all that you have in mind," his armor-bearer said. "Go ahead; I am with you heart and soul."

8Jonathan said, "Come, then; we will cross over toward the men and let them see us. 9If they say to us, 'Wait there until we come to you,' we will stay where we are and not go up to them. 10But if they say, 'Come up to us,' we will climb up, because that will be our sign that the LORD has given them into our hands."

11So both of them showed themselves to the Philistine outpost. "Look!" said the Philistines. "The Hebrews are crawling out of the holes they were hiding in." 12The men of the outpost shouted to Jonathan and his armor-bearer, "Come up to us and we'll teach you a lesson."

So Jonathan said to his armor-bearer, "Climb up after me; the LORD has given them into the hand of Israel."

13Jonathan climbed up, using his hands and feet, with his armor-bearer right behind him. The Philistines fell before Jonathan, and his armor-bearer followed and killed behind him. 14In that first attack Jonathan and his armor-bearer killed some twenty men in an area of about half an acre.[a]

Israel Routs the Philistines

15Then panic struck the whole army—those in the camp and field, and those in the outposts and raiding parties—and the ground shook. It was a panic sent by God.[b]

16Saul's lookouts at Gibeah in Benjamin saw the army melting away in all directions. 17Then Saul said to the men who were with him, "Muster the forces and see who has left us." When they did, it was Jonathan and his armor-bearer who were not there.

18Saul said to Ahijah, "Bring the ark of God." (At that time it was with the Israelites.)[c] 19While Saul was talking to the priest, the tumult in the Philistine camp increased more and more. So Saul said to the priest, "Withdraw your hand."

20Then Saul and all his men assembled and went to the battle. They found the Philistines in total confusion, striking each other with their swords. 21Those Hebrews who had previously been with the Philistines and had gone up with them to their camp went over to the Israelites who were with Saul and Jonathan. 22When all the Israelites who had hidden in the hill country of Ephraim heard that the Philistines were on the run, they joined the battle in hot pursuit. 23So the LORD rescued Israel that day, and the battle moved on beyond Beth Aven.

Jonathan Eats Honey

24Now the men of Israel were in distress that day, because Saul had bound the people under an oath, saying, "Cursed be any man who eats food before evening comes, before I have avenged myself on my enemies!" So none of the troops tasted food.

25The entire army[d] entered the woods, and there was honey on the ground. 26When they went into the woods, they saw the honey oozing out, yet no one put his hand to his mouth, because they feared the oath. 27But Jonathan had not heard that his father had bound the people with the oath, so he reached out the end of the staff that was in his hand and dipped it into the honeycomb. He raised his hand to his mouth, and his eyes brightened.[e] 28Then one of the soldiers told him, "Your father bound the army under a strict oath, saying, 'Cursed be any man who eats food today!' That is why the men are faint."

29Jonathan said, "My father has made trouble for the country. See how my eyes brightened[f] when I tasted a little of this honey. 30How much better it would have been if the men had eaten today some of the plunder they took from their enemies. Would not the slaughter of the Philistines have been even greater?"

---

[a]14 Hebrew half a yoke; a "yoke" was the land plowed by a yoke of oxen in one day.   [b]15 Or a terrible panic   [c]18 Hebrew; Septuagint "Bring the ephod." (At that time he wore the ephod before the Israelites.)   [d]25 Or Now all the people of the land   [e]27 Or his strength was renewed   [f]29 Or my strength was renewed

³¹That day, after the Israelites had struck down the Philistines from Micmash to Aijalon, they were exhausted. ³²They pounced on the plunder and, taking sheep, cattle and calves, they butchered them on the ground and ate them, together with the blood. ³³Then someone said to Saul, "Look, the men are sinning against the LORD by eating meat that has blood in it."

"You have broken faith," he said. "Roll a large stone over here at once." ³⁴Then he said, "Go out among the men and tell them, 'Each of you bring me your cattle and sheep, and slaughter them here and eat them. Do not sin against the LORD by eating meat with blood still in it.' "

So everyone brought his ox that night and slaughtered it there. ³⁵Then Saul built an altar to the LORD; it was the first time he had done this.

³⁶Saul said, "Let us go down after the Philistines by night and plunder them till dawn, and let us not leave one of them alive."

"Do whatever seems best to you," they replied.

But the priest said, "Let us inquire of God here."

³⁷So Saul asked God, "Shall I go down after the Philistines? Will you give them into Israel's hand?" But God did not answer him that day.

³⁸Saul therefore said, "Come here, all you who are leaders of the army, and let us find out what sin has been committed today. ³⁹As surely as the LORD who rescues Israel lives, even if it lies with my son Jonathan, he must die." But not one of the men said a word.

⁴⁰Saul then said to all the Israelites, "You stand over there; I and Jonathan my son will stand over here."

"Do what seems best to you," the men replied.

⁴¹Then Saul prayed to the LORD, the God of Israel, "Give me the right answer."ᵃ And Jonathan and Saul were taken by lot, and the men were cleared. ⁴²Saul said, "Cast the lot between me and Jonathan my son." And Jonathan was taken.

⁴³Then Saul said to Jonathan, "Tell me what you have done."

So Jonathan told him, "I merely tasted a little honey with the end of my staff. And now must I die?"

⁴⁴Saul said, "May God deal with me, be it ever so severely, if you do not die, Jonathan."

⁴⁵But the men said to Saul, "Should Jonathan die—he who has brought about this great deliverance in Israel? Never! As surely as the LORD lives, not a hair of his head will fall to the ground, for he did this today with God's help." So the men rescued Jonathan, and he was not put to death.

⁴⁶Then Saul stopped pursuing the Philistines, and they withdrew to their own land.

⁴⁷After Saul had assumed rule over Israel, he fought against their enemies on every side: Moab, the Ammonites, Edom, the kingsᵇ of Zobah, and the Philistines. Wherever he turned, he inflicted punishment on them.ᶜ ⁴⁸He fought valiantly and defeated the Amalekites, delivering Israel from the hands of those who had plundered them.

Saul's Family

⁴⁹Saul's sons were Jonathan, Ishvi and Malki-Shua. The name of his older daughter was Merab, and that of the younger was Michal. ⁵⁰His wife's name was Ahinoam daughter of Ahimaaz. The name of the commander of Saul's army was Abner son of Ner, and Ner was Saul's uncle. ⁵¹Saul's father Kish and Abner's father Ner were sons of Abiel.

⁵²All the days of Saul there was bitter war with the Philistines, and whenever Saul saw a mighty or brave man, he took him into his service.

ᵃ41 Hebrew; Septuagint *"Why have you not answered your servant today? If the fault is in me or my son Jonathan, respond with Urim, but if the men of Israel are at fault, respond with Thummim."*   ᵇ47 Masoretic Text; Dead Sea Scrolls and Septuagint *king*   ᶜ47 Hebrew; Septuagint *he was victorious*

The LORD Rejects Saul as King

15 Samuel said to Saul, "I am the one the LORD sent to anoint you king over his people Israel; so listen now to the message from the LORD. ²This is what the LORD Almighty says: 'I will punish the Amalekites for what they did to Israel when they waylaid them as they came up from Egypt. ³Now go, attack the Amalekites and totally destroy^a everything that belongs to them. Do not spare them; put to death men and women, children and infants, cattle and sheep, camels and donkeys.'"

⁴So Saul summoned the men and mustered them at Telaim—two hundred thousand foot soldiers and ten thousand men from Judah. ⁵Saul went to the city of Amalek and set an ambush in the ravine. ⁶Then he said to the Kenites, "Go away, leave the Amalekites so that I do not destroy you along with them; for you showed kindness to all the Israelites when they came up out of Egypt." So the Kenites moved away from the Amalekites.

⁷Then Saul attacked the Amalekites all the way from Havilah to Shur, to the east of Egypt. ⁸He took Agag king of the Amalekites alive, and all his people he totally destroyed with the sword. ⁹But Saul and the army spared Agag and the best of the sheep and cattle, the fat calves^b and lambs—everything that was good. These they were unwilling to destroy completely, but everything that was despised and weak they totally destroyed.

¹⁰Then the word of the LORD came to Samuel: ¹¹"I am grieved that I have made Saul king, because he has turned away from me and has not carried out my instructions." Samuel was troubled, and he cried out to the LORD all that night.

¹²Early in the morning Samuel got up and went to meet Saul, but he was told, "Saul has gone to Carmel. There he has set up a monument in his own honor and has turned and gone on down to Gilgal."

¹³When Samuel reached him, Saul said, "The LORD bless you! I have carried out the LORD's instructions."

¹⁴But Samuel said, "What then is this bleating of sheep in my ears? What is this lowing of cattle that I hear?"

¹⁵Saul answered, "The soldiers brought them from the Amalekites; they spared the best of the sheep and cattle to sacrifice to the LORD your God, but we totally destroyed the rest."

¹⁶"Stop!" Samuel said to Saul. "Let me tell you what the LORD said to me last night."

"Tell me," Saul replied.

¹⁷Samuel said, "Although you were once small in your own eyes, did you not become the head of the tribes of Israel? The LORD anointed you king over Israel. ¹⁸And he sent you on a mission, saying, 'Go and completely destroy those wicked people, the Amalekites; make war on them until you have wiped them out.' ¹⁹Why did you not obey the LORD? Why did you pounce on the plunder and do evil in the eyes of the LORD?"

²⁰"But I did obey the LORD," Saul said. "I went on the mission the LORD assigned me. I completely destroyed the Amalekites and brought back Agag their king. ²¹The soldiers took sheep and cattle from the plunder, the best of what was devoted to God, in order to sacrifice them to the LORD your God at Gilgal."

²²But Samuel replied:

> "Does the LORD delight in burnt offerings and sacrifices
>   as much as in obeying the voice of the LORD?
> To obey is better than sacrifice,
>   and to heed is better than the fat of rams.
> ²³For rebellion is like the sin of divination,
>   and arrogance like the evil of idolatry.
> Because you have rejected the word of the LORD,
>   he has rejected you as king."

a3 The Hebrew term refers to the irrevocable giving over of things or persons to the LORD, often by totally destroying them; also in verses 8, 9, 15, 18, 20 and 21.   b9 Or the grown bulls; the meaning of the Hebrew for this phrase is uncertain.

²⁴Then Saul said to Samuel, "I have sinned. I violated the Lᴏʀᴅ's command and your instructions. I was afraid of the people and so I gave in to them. ²⁵Now I beg you, forgive my sin and come back with me, so that I may worship the Lᴏʀᴅ."

²⁶But Samuel said to him, "I will not go back with you. You have rejected the word of the Lᴏʀᴅ, and the Lᴏʀᴅ has rejected you as king over Israel!"

²⁷As Samuel turned to leave, Saul caught hold of the hem of his robe, and it tore. ²⁸Samuel said to him, "The Lᴏʀᴅ has torn the kingdom of Israel from you today and has given it to one of your neighbors—to one better than you. ²⁹He who is the Glory of Israel does not lie or change his mind; for he is not a man, that he should change his mind."

³⁰Saul replied, "I have sinned. But please honor me before the elders of my people and before Israel; come back with me, so that I may worship the Lᴏʀᴅ your God." ³¹So Samuel went back with Saul, and Saul worshiped the Lᴏʀᴅ.

³²Then Samuel said, "Bring me Agag king of the Amalekites."

Agag came to him confidently,ᵃ thinking, "Surely the bitterness of death is past."

³³But Samuel said,

> "As your sword has made women childless,
> so will your mother be childless among women."

And Samuel put Agag to death before the Lᴏʀᴅ at Gilgal.

³⁴Then Samuel left for Ramah, but Saul went up to his home in Gibeah of Saul. ³⁵Until the day Samuel died, he did not go to see Saul again, though Samuel mourned for him. And the Lᴏʀᴅ was grieved that he had made Saul king over Israel.

Samuel Anoints David

16 The Lᴏʀᴅ said to Samuel, "How long will you mourn for Saul, since I have rejected him as king over Israel? Fill your horn with oil and be on your way; I am sending you to Jesse of Bethlehem. I have chosen one of his sons to be king."

²But Samuel said, "How can I go? Saul will hear about it and kill me."

The Lᴏʀᴅ said, "Take a heifer with you and say, 'I have come to sacrifice to the Lᴏʀᴅ.' ³Invite Jesse to the sacrifice, and I will show you what to do. You are to anoint for me the one I indicate."

⁴Samuel did what the Lᴏʀᴅ said. When he arrived at Bethlehem, the elders of the town trembled when they met him. They asked, "Do you come in peace?"

⁵Samuel replied, "Yes, in peace; I have come to sacrifice to the Lᴏʀᴅ. Consecrate yourselves and come to the sacrifice with me." Then he consecrated Jesse and his sons and invited them to the sacrifice.

⁶When they arrived, Samuel saw Eliab and thought, "Surely the Lᴏʀᴅ's anointed stands here before the Lᴏʀᴅ."

⁷But the Lᴏʀᴅ said to Samuel, "Do not consider his appearance or his height, for I have

---

▣ ═══════ DISCOVERING GOD ═══════ ◪

15:22
Life with God

There's a saying, "It's easier to ask for forgiveness than permission." That's a popular line with people who, for example, want to "borrow" something from the office for personal use.

Some people even talk like that about their moral and spiritual life. They figure they can always ask God for forgiveness, so why not go ahead and sin? "To err is human, to forgive, divine." Forgiveness is God's *job*, right?

The mistake that lies at the heart of that approach is this: If we truly care about another, we will take that person's feelings into account when choosing a course of action. The bottom line is that our disobedience shows that we value ourselves more than we value God.

The stories and teachings of this book make it abundantly clear that following and obeying God is the best—and most rewarding—way to live. That goes for this life and the next.

ᵃ *32 Or him trembling, yet*

rejected him. The LORD does not look at the things man looks at. Man looks at the outward appearance, but the LORD looks at the heart."

⁸Then Jesse called Abinadab and had him pass in front of Samuel. But Samuel said, "The LORD has not chosen this one either." ⁹Jesse then had Shammah pass by, but Samuel said, "Nor has the LORD chosen this one." ¹⁰Jesse had seven of his sons pass before Samuel, but Samuel said to him, "The LORD has not chosen these." ¹¹So he asked Jesse, "Are these all the sons you have?"

"There is still the youngest," Jesse answered, "but he is tending the sheep."

Samuel said, "Send for him; we will not sit down*a* until he arrives."

¹²So he sent and had him brought in. He was ruddy, with a fine appearance and handsome features.

Then the LORD said, "Rise and anoint him; he is the one."

¹³So Samuel took the horn of oil and anointed him in the presence of his brothers, and from that day on the Spirit of the LORD came upon David in power. Samuel then went to Ramah.

David in Saul's Service

¹⁴Now the Spirit of the LORD had departed from Saul, and an evil*b* spirit from the LORD tormented him.

¹⁵Saul's attendants said to him, "See, an evil spirit from God is tormenting you. ¹⁶Let our lord command his servants here to search for someone who can play the harp. He will play when the evil spirit from God comes upon you, and you will feel better."

¹⁷So Saul said to his attendants, "Find someone who plays well and bring him to me."

¹⁸One of the servants answered, "I have seen a son of Jesse of Bethlehem who knows how to play the harp. He is a brave man and a warrior. He speaks well and is a fine-looking man. And the LORD is with him."

¹⁹Then Saul sent messengers to Jesse and said, "Send me your son David, who is with the sheep." ²⁰So Jesse took a donkey loaded with bread, a skin of wine and a young goat and sent them with his son David to Saul.

²¹David came to Saul and entered his service. Saul liked him very much, and David became one of his armor-bearers. ²²Then Saul sent word to Jesse, saying, "Allow David to remain in my service, for I am pleased with him."

²³Whenever the spirit from God came upon Saul, David would take his harp and play. Then relief would come to Saul; he would feel better, and the evil spirit would leave him.

David and Goliath

17 Now the Philistines gathered their forces for war and assembled at Socoh in Judah. They pitched camp at Ephes Dammim, between Socoh and Azekah. ²Saul and the Israelites assembled and camped in the Valley of Elah and drew up their battle line to meet the Philistines. ³The Philistines occupied one hill and the Israelites another, with the valley between them.

⁴A champion named Goliath, who was from Gath, came out of the Philistine camp. He was over nine feet*c* tall. ⁵He had a bronze helmet on his head and wore a coat of scale armor of bronze weighing five thousand shekels*d*; ⁶on his legs he wore bronze greaves and a bronze javelin was slung on his back. ⁷His spear shaft was like a weaver's rod, and its iron point weighed six hundred shekels.*e* His shield bearer went ahead of him.

⁸Goliath stood and shouted to the ranks of Israel, "Why do you come out and line up for battle? Am I not a Philistine, and are you not the servants of Saul? Choose a man and have him come down to me. ⁹If he is able to fight and kill me, we will become your subjects; but if I overcome him and kill him, you will become our subjects and serve us.

*a 11 Some Septuagint manuscripts; Hebrew not gather around   b 14 Or injurious; also in verses 15, 16 and 23
c 4 Hebrew was six cubits and a span (about 3 meters)   d 5 That is, about 125 pounds (about 57 kilograms)   e 7 That is, about 15 pounds (about 7 kilograms)*

¹⁰Then the Philistine said, "This day I defy the ranks of Israel! Give me a man and let us fight each other." ¹¹On hearing the Philistine's words, Saul and all the Israelites were dismayed and terrified.

¹²Now David was the son of an Ephrathite named Jesse, who was from Bethlehem in Judah. Jesse had eight sons, and in Saul's time he was old and well advanced in years. ¹³Jesse's three oldest sons had followed Saul to the war: The firstborn was Eliab; the second, Abinadab; and the third, Shammah. ¹⁴David was the youngest. The three oldest followed Saul, ¹⁵but David went back and forth from Saul to tend his father's sheep at Bethlehem.

¹⁶For forty days the Philistine came forward every morning and evening and took his stand.

¹⁷Now Jesse said to his son David, "Take this ephah*a* of roasted grain and these ten loaves of bread for your brothers and hurry to their camp. ¹⁸Take along these ten cheeses to the commander of their unit.*b* See how your brothers are and bring back some assurance*c* from them. ¹⁹They are with Saul and all the men of Israel in the Valley of Elah, fighting against the Philistines."

²⁰Early in the morning David left the flock with a shepherd, loaded up and set out, as Jesse had directed. He reached the camp as the army was going out to its battle positions, shouting the war cry. ²¹Israel and the Philistines were drawing up their lines facing each other. ²²David left his

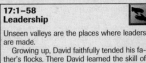

things with the keeper of supplies, ran to the battle lines and greeted his brothers. ²³As he was talking with them, Goliath, the Philistine champion from Gath, stepped out from his lines and shouted his usual defiance, and David heard it. ²⁴When the Israelites saw the man, they all ran from him in great fear.

²⁵Now the Israelites had been saying, "Do you see how this man keeps coming out? He comes out to defy Israel. The king will give great wealth to the man who kills him. He will also give him his daughter in marriage and will exempt his father's family from taxes in Israel."

²⁶David asked the men standing near him, "What will be done for the man who kills this Philistine and removes this disgrace from Israel? Who is this uncircumcised Philistine that he should defy the armies of the living God?"

²⁷They repeated to him what they had been saying and told him, "This is what will be done for the man who kills him."

²⁸When Eliab, David's oldest brother, heard him speaking with the men, he burned with anger at him and asked, "Why have you come down here? And with whom did you leave those few sheep in the desert? I know how conceited you are and how wicked your heart is; you came down only to watch the battle."

²⁹"Now what have I done?" said David. "Can't I even speak?" ³⁰He then turned away to

a 17 That is, probably about 3/5 bushel (about 22 liters) of spoils   *b 18 Hebrew thousand*   *c 18 Or some token; or some pledge* someone else and brought up the same matter, and the men answered him as before. ³¹What David said was overheard and reported to Saul, and Saul sent for him.

³²David said to Saul, "Let no one lose heart on account of this Philistine; your servant will go and fight him."

³³Saul replied, "You are not able to go out against this Philistine and fight him; you are only a boy, and he has been a fighting man from his youth."

³⁴But David said to Saul, "Your servant has been keeping his father's sheep. When a lion or a bear came and carried off a sheep from the flock, ³⁵I went after it, struck it and rescued the sheep from its mouth. When it turned on me, I seized it by its hair, struck it and killed it. ³⁶Your servant has killed both the lion and the bear; this uncircumcised Philistine will be like one of them, because he has defied the armies of the living God. ³⁷The LORD who delivered me from the paw of the lion and the paw of the bear will deliver me from the hand of this Philistine."

Saul said to David, "Go, and the LORD be with you."

³⁸Then Saul dressed David in his own tunic. He put a coat of armor on him and a bronze helmet on his head. ³⁹David fastened on his sword over the tunic and tried walking around, because he was not used to them.

"I cannot go in these," he said to Saul, "because I am not used to them." So he took them off. ⁴⁰Then he took his staff in his hand, chose five smooth stones from the stream, put them in the pouch of his shepherd's bag and, with his sling in his hand, approached the Philistine.

⁴¹Meanwhile, the Philistine, with his shield bearer in front of him, kept coming closer to David. ⁴²He looked David over and saw that he was only a boy, ruddy and handsome, and he despised him. ⁴³He said to David, "Am I a dog, that you come at me with sticks?" And the Philistine cursed David by his gods. ⁴⁴"Come here," he said, "and I'll give your flesh to the birds of the air and the beasts of the field!"

⁴⁵David said to the Philistine, "You come against me with sword and spear and javelin, but I come against you in the name of the LORD Almighty, the God of the armies of Israel, whom you have defied. ⁴⁶This day the LORD will hand you over to me, and I'll strike you down and cut off your head. Today I will give the carcasses of the Philistine army to the birds of the air and the beasts of the earth, and the whole world will know that there is a God in Israel. ⁴⁷All those gathered here will know that it is not by sword or spear that the LORD saves; for the battle is the LORD's, and he will give all of you into our hands."

⁴⁸As the Philistine moved closer to attack him, David ran quickly toward the battle line to meet him. ⁴⁹Reaching into his bag and taking out a stone, he slung it and struck the Philistine on the forehead. The stone sank into his forehead, and he fell facedown on the ground.

⁵⁰So David triumphed over the Philistine with a sling and a stone; without a sword in his hand he struck down the Philistine and killed him.

⁵¹David ran and stood over him. He took hold of the Philistine's sword and drew it from the scabbard. After he killed him, he cut off his head with the sword.

When the Philistines saw that their hero was dead, they turned and ran. ⁵²Then the men of Israel and Judah surged forward with a shout and pursued the Philistines to the entrance of Gathᵃ and to the gates of Ekron. Their dead were strewn along the Shaaraim road to Gath and Ekron. ⁵³When the Israelites returned from chasing the Philistines, they plundered their camp. ⁵⁴David took the Philistine's head and brought it to Jerusalem, and he put the Philistine's weapons in his own tent.

⁵⁵As Saul watched David going out to meet the Philistine, he said to Abner, commander of the army, "Abner, whose son is that young man?"

Abner replied, "As surely as you live, O king, I don't know."

⁵⁶The king said, "Find out whose son this young man is."

ᵃ52 Some Septuagint manuscripts; Hebrew *a valley*

⁵⁷As soon as David returned from killing the Philistine, Abner took him and brought him before Saul, with David still holding the Philistine's head.

⁵⁸"Whose son are you, young man?" Saul asked him.

David said, "I am the son of your servant Jesse of Bethlehem."

Saul's Jealousy of David

18 After David had finished talking with Saul, Jonathan became one in spirit with David, and he loved him as himself. ²From that day Saul kept David with him and did not let him return to his father's house. ³And Jonathan made a covenant with David because he loved him as himself. ⁴Jonathan took off the robe he was wearing and gave it to David, along with his tunic, and even his sword, his bow and his belt.

⁵Whatever Saul sent him to do, David did it so successfully*ᵃ* that Saul gave him a high rank in the army. This pleased all the people, and Saul's officers as well.

⁶When the men were returning home after David had killed the Philistine, the women came out from all the towns of Israel to meet King Saul with singing and dancing, with joyful songs and with tambourines and lutes. ⁷As they danced, they sang:

> "Saul has slain his thousands,
>   and David his tens of thousands."

⁸Saul was very angry; this refrain galled him. "They have credited David with tens of thousands," he thought, "but me with only thousands. What more can he get but the kingdom?" ⁹And from that time on Saul kept a jealous eye on David.

¹⁰The next day an evil*ᵇ* spirit from God came forcefully upon Saul. He was prophesying in his house, while David was playing the harp, as he usually did. Saul had a spear in his hand ¹¹and he hurled it, saying to himself, "I'll pin David to the wall." But David eluded him twice.

¹²Saul was afraid of David, because the LORD was with David but had left Saul. ¹³So he sent David away from him and gave him command over a thousand men, and David led the troops in their campaigns. ¹⁴In everything he did he had great success,*ᶜ* because the LORD was with him. ¹⁵When Saul saw how successful*ᵈ* he was, he was afraid of him. ¹⁶But all Israel and Judah loved David, because he led them in their campaigns.

¹⁷Saul said to David, "Here is my older daughter Merab. I will give her to you in marriage; only serve me bravely and fight the battles of the LORD." For Saul said to himself, "I will not raise a hand against him. Let the Philistines do that!"

¹⁸But David said to Saul, "Who am I, and what is my family or my father's clan in Israel, that I should become the king's son-in-law?" ¹⁹So*ᵉ* when the time came for Merab, Saul's daughter, to be given to David, she was given in marriage to Adriel of Meholah.

²⁰Now Saul's daughter Michal was in love with David, and when they told Saul about it, he was pleased. ²¹"I will give her to him," he thought, "so that she may be a snare to him and so that the hand of the Philistines may be against him." So Saul said to David, "Now you have a second opportunity to become my son-in-law."

²²Then Saul ordered his attendants: "Speak to David privately and say, 'Look, the king is pleased with you, and his attendants all like you; now become his son-in-law.'"

²³They repeated these words to David. But David said, "Do you think it is a small matter to become the king's son-in-law? I'm only a poor man and little known."

²⁴When Saul's servants told him what David had said, ²⁵Saul replied, "Say to David, 'The king wants no other price for the bride than a hundred Philistine foreskins, to take revenge on his enemies.'" Saul's plan was to have David fall by the hands of the Philistines.

²⁶When the attendants told David these things, he was pleased to become the king's son-in-law. So before the allotted time elapsed, ²⁷David and his men went out and killed

---

ᵃ5 Or wisely   *ᵇ10 Or injurious*   *ᶜ14 Or he was very wise*   *ᵈ15 Or wise*   *ᵉ19 Or However,*

two hundred Philistines. He brought their foreskins and presented the full number to the king so that he might become the king's son-in-law. Then Saul gave him his daughter Michal in marriage.

²⁸When Saul realized that the LORD was with David and that his daughter Michal loved David, ²⁹Saul became still more afraid of him, and he remained his enemy the rest of his days.

³⁰The Philistine commanders continued to go out to battle, and as often as they did, David met with more success*a* than the rest of Saul's officers, and his name became well known.

Saul Tries to Kill David

19 Saul told his son Jonathan and all the attendants to kill David. But Jonathan was very fond of David ²and warned him, "My father Saul is looking for a chance to kill you. Be on your guard tomorrow morning; go into hiding and stay there. ³I will go out and stand with my father in the field where you are. I'll speak to him about you and will tell you what I find out."

⁴Jonathan spoke well of David to Saul his father and said to him, "Let not the king do wrong to his servant David; he has not wronged you, and what he has done has benefited you greatly. ⁵He took his life in his hands when he killed the Philistine. The LORD won a great victory for all Israel, and you saw it and were glad. Why then would you do wrong to an innocent man like David by killing him for no reason?"

⁶Saul listened to Jonathan and took this oath: "As surely as the LORD lives, David will not be put to death."

⁷So Jonathan called David and told him the whole conversation. He brought him to Saul, and David was with Saul as before.

⁸Once more war broke out, and David went out and fought the Philistines. He struck them with such force that they fled before him.

⁹But an evil*b* spirit from the LORD came upon Saul as he was sitting in his house with his spear in his hand. While David was playing the harp, ¹⁰Saul tried to pin him to the wall with his spear, but David eluded him as Saul drove the spear into the wall. That night David made good his escape.

¹¹Saul sent men to David's house to watch it and to kill him in the morning. But Michal, David's wife, warned him, "If you don't run for your life tonight, tomorrow you'll be killed." ¹²So Michal let David down through a window, and he fled and escaped. ¹³Then Michal took an idol*c* and laid it on the bed, covering it with a garment and putting some goats' hair at the head.

¹⁴When Saul sent the men to capture David, Michal said, "He is ill."

¹⁵Then Saul sent the men back to see David and told them, "Bring him up to me in his bed so that I may kill him." ¹⁶But when the men entered, there was the idol in the bed, and at the head was some goats' hair.

¹⁷Saul said to Michal, "Why did you deceive me like this and send my enemy away so that he escaped?"

Michal told him, "He said to me, 'Let me get away. Why should I kill you?'"

¹⁸When David had fled and made his escape, he went to Samuel at Ramah and told him all that Saul had done to him. Then he and Samuel went to Naioth and stayed there. ¹⁹Word came to Saul: "David is in Naioth at Ramah"; ²⁰so he sent men to capture him. But when they saw a group of prophets prophesying, with Samuel standing there as their leader, the Spirit of God came upon Saul's men and they also prophesied. ²¹Saul was told about it, and he sent more men, and they prophesied too. Saul sent men a third time, and they also prophesied. ²²Finally, he himself left for Ramah and went to the great cistern at Secu. And he asked, "Where are Samuel and David?"

"Over in Naioth at Ramah," they said.

---

a 30 Or *David acted more wisely*   *b 9* Or *injurious*   *c 13* Hebrew *teraphim;* also in verse 16

²³So Saul went to Naioth at Ramah. But the Spirit of God came even upon him, and he walked along prophesying until he came to Naioth. ²⁴He stripped off his robes and also prophesied in Samuel's presence. He lay that way all that day and night. This is why people say, "Is Saul also among the prophets?"

David and Jonathan

20 Then David fled from Naioth at Ramah and went to Jonathan and asked, "What have I done? What is my crime? How have I wronged your father, that he is trying to take my life?"

²"Never!" Jonathan replied. "You are not going to die! Look, my father doesn't do anything, great or small, without confiding in me. Why would he hide this from me? It's not so!"

³But David took an oath and said, "Your father knows very well that I have found favor in your eyes, and he has said to himself, 'Jonathan must not know this or he will be grieved.' Yet as surely as the LORD lives and as you live, there is only a step between me and death."

⁴Jonathan said to David, "Whatever you want me to do, I'll do for you."

⁵So David said, "Look, tomorrow is the New Moon festival, and I am supposed to dine with the king; but let me go and hide in the field until the evening of the day after tomorrow. ⁶If your father misses me at all, tell him, 'David earnestly asked my permission to hurry to Bethlehem, his hometown, because an annual sacrifice is being made there for his whole clan.' ⁷If he says, 'Very well,' then your servant is safe. But if he loses his temper, you can be sure that he is determined to harm me. ⁸As for you, show kindness to your servant, for you have brought him into a covenant with you before the LORD. If I am guilty, then kill me yourself! Why hand me over to your father?"

⁹"Never!" Jonathan said. "If I had the least inkling that my father was determined to harm you, wouldn't I tell you?"

¹⁰David asked, "Who will tell me if your father answers you harshly?"

¹¹"Come," Jonathan said, "let's go out into the field." So they went there together.

¹²Then Jonathan said to David: "By the LORD, the God of Israel, I will surely sound out my father by this time the day after tomorrow! If he is favorably disposed toward you, will I not send you word and let you know? ¹³But if my father is inclined to harm you, may the LORD deal with me, be it ever so severely, if I do not let you know and send you away safely. May the LORD be with you as he has been with my father. ¹⁴But show me unfailing kindness like that of the LORD as long as I live, so that I may not be killed, ¹⁵and do not ever cut off your kindness from my family—not even when the LORD has cut off every one of David's enemies from the face of the earth."

¹⁶So Jonathan made a covenant with the house of David, saying, "May the LORD call David's enemies to account." ¹⁷And Jonathan had David reaffirm his oath out of love for him, because he loved him as he loved himself.

¹⁸Then Jonathan said to David: "Tomorrow is the New Moon festival. You will be missed, because your seat will be empty. ¹⁹The day after tomorrow, toward evening, go to the place where you hid when this trouble began, and wait by the stone Ezel. ²⁰I will shoot three arrows to the side of it, as though I were shooting at a target. ²¹Then I will send a boy and say, 'Go, find the arrows.' If I say to him, 'Look, the arrows are on this side of you; bring them here,' then come, because, as surely as the LORD lives, you are safe; there is no danger. ²²But if I say to the boy, 'Look, the arrows are beyond you,' then you must go, because the LORD has sent you away. ²³And about the matter you and I discussed—remember, the LORD is witness between you and me forever."

²⁴So David hid in the field, and when the New Moon festival came, the king sat down to eat. ²⁵He sat in his customary place by the wall, opposite Jonathan,ᵃ and Abner sat next to Saul, but David's place was empty. ²⁶Saul said nothing that day, for he thought,

---

ᵃ25 Septuagint; Hebrew *wall. Jonathan arose*

"Something must have happened to David to make him ceremonially unclean—surely he is unclean." 27But the next day, the second day of the month, David's place was empty again. Then Saul said to his son Jonathan, "Why hasn't the son of Jesse come to the meal, either yesterday or today?"

28Jonathan answered, "David earnestly asked me for permission to go to Bethlehem. 29He said, 'Let me go, because our family is observing a sacrifice in the town and my brother has ordered me to be there. If I have found favor in your eyes, let me get away to see my brothers.' That is why he has not come to the king's table."

30Saul's anger flared up at Jonathan and he said to him, "You son of a perverse and rebellious woman! Don't I know that you have sided with the son of Jesse to your own shame and to the shame of the mother who bore you? 31As long as the son of Jesse lives on this earth, neither you nor your kingdom will be established. Now send and bring him to me, for he must die!"

32"Why should he be put to death? What has he done?" Jonathan asked his father. 33But Saul hurled his spear at him to kill him. Then Jonathan knew that his father intended to kill David.

34Jonathan got up from the table in fierce anger; on that second day of the month he did not eat, because he was grieved at his father's shameful treatment of David.

35In the morning Jonathan went out to the field for his meeting with David. He had a small boy with him, 36and he said to the boy, "Run and find the arrows I shoot." As the boy ran, he shot an arrow beyond him. 37When the boy came to the place where Jonathan's arrow had fallen, Jonathan called out after him, "Isn't the arrow beyond you?" 38Then he shouted, "Hurry! Go quickly! Don't stop!" The boy picked up the arrow and returned to his master. 39(The boy knew nothing of all this; only Jonathan and David knew.) 40Then Jonathan gave his weapons to the boy and said, "Go, carry them back to town."

41After the boy had gone, David got up from the south side ˏof the stone˒ and bowed down before Jonathan three times, with his face to the ground. Then they kissed each other and wept together—but David wept the most.

42Jonathan said to David, "Go in peace, for we have sworn friendship with each other in the name of the LORD, saying, 'The LORD is witness between you and me, and between your descendants and my descendants forever.'" Then David left, and Jonathan went back to the town.

David at Nob

21 David went to Nob, to Ahimelech the priest. Ahimelech trembled when he met him, and asked, "Why are you alone? Why is no one with you?"

2David answered Ahimelech the priest, "The king charged me with a certain matter and said to me, 'No one is to know anything about your mission and your instructions.' As for my men, I have told them to meet me at a certain place. 3Now then, what do you have on hand? Give me five loaves of bread, or whatever you can find."

4But the priest answered David, "I don't have any ordinary bread on hand; however, there is some consecrated bread here—provided the men have kept themselves from women."

5David replied, "Indeed women have been kept from us, as usual whenever ª I set out. The men's thingsᵇ are holy even on missions that are not holy. How much more so today!" 6So the priest gave him the consecrated bread, since there was no bread there except the bread of the Presence that had been removed from before the LORD and replaced by hot bread on the day it was taken away.

7Now one of Saul's servants was there that day, detained before the LORD; he was Doeg the Edomite, Saul's head shepherd.

⁸David asked Ahimelech, "Don't you have a spear or a sword here? I haven't brought my sword or any other weapon, because the king's business was urgent."

⁹The priest replied, "The sword of Goliath the Philistine, whom you killed in the Valley of Elah, is here; it is wrapped in a cloth behind the ephod. If you want it, take it; there is no sword here but that one."

David said, "There is none like it; give it to me."

David at Gath

¹⁰That day David fled from Saul and went to Achish king of Gath. ¹¹But the servants of Achish said to him, "Isn't this David, the king of the land? Isn't he the one they sing about in their dances:

> "'Saul has slain his thousands,
>   and David his tens of thousands'?"

¹²David took these words to heart and was very much afraid of Achish king of Gath. ¹³So he pretended to be insane in their presence; and while he was in their hands he acted like a madman, making marks on the doors of the gate and letting saliva run down his beard.

¹⁴Achish said to his servants, "Look at the man! He is insane! Why bring him to me? ¹⁵Am I so short of madmen that you have to bring this fellow here to carry on like this in front of me? Must this man come into my house?"

David at Adullam and Mizpah

22 David left Gath and escaped to the cave of Adullam. When his brothers and his father's household heard about it, they went down to him there. ²All those who were in distress or in debt or discontented gathered around him, and he became their leader. About four hundred men were with him.

³From there David went to Mizpah in Moab and said to the king of Moab, "Would you let my father and mother come and stay with you until I learn what God will do for me?" ⁴So he left them with the king of Moab, and they stayed with him as long as David was in the stronghold.

⁵But the prophet Gad said to David, "Do not stay in the stronghold. Go into the land of Judah." So David left and went to the forest of Hereth.

Saul Kills the Priests of Nob

⁶Now Saul heard that David and his men had been discovered. And Saul, spear in hand, was seated under the tamarisk tree on the hill at Gibeah, with all his officials standing around him. ⁷Saul said to them, "Listen, men of Benjamin! Will the son of Jesse give all of you fields and vineyards? Will he make all of you commanders of thousands and commanders of hundreds? ⁸Is that why you have all conspired against me? No one tells me when my son makes a covenant with the son of Jesse. None of you is concerned about me or tells me that my son has incited my servant to lie in wait for me, as he does today."

⁹But Doeg the Edomite, who was standing with Saul's officials, said, "I saw the son of Jesse come to Ahimelech son of Ahitub at Nob. ¹⁰Ahimelech inquired of the LORD for him; he also gave him provisions and the sword of Goliath the Philistine."

¹¹Then the king sent for the priest Ahimelech son of Ahitub and his father's whole family, who were the priests at Nob, and they all came to the king. ¹²Saul said, "Listen now, son of Ahitub."

"Yes, my lord," he answered.

¹³Saul said to him, "Why have you conspired against me, you and the son of Jesse, giving him bread and a sword and inquiring of God for him, so that he has rebelled against me and lies in wait for me, as he does today?"

¹⁴Ahimelech answered the king, "Who of all your servants is as loyal as David, the king's son-in-law, captain of your bodyguard and highly respected in your household? ¹⁵Was that day the first time I inquired of God for him? Of course not! Let not the king accuse your servant or any of his father's family, for your servant knows nothing at all about this whole affair."

¹⁶But the king said, "You will surely die, Ahimelech, you and your father's whole family."

¹⁷Then the king ordered the guards at his side: "Turn and kill the priests of the LORD, because they too have sided with David. They knew he was fleeing, yet they did not tell me."

But the king's officials were not willing to raise a hand to strike the priests of the LORD.

¹⁸The king then ordered Doeg, "You turn and strike down the priests." So Doeg the Edomite turned and struck them down. That day he killed eighty-five men who wore the linen ephod. ¹⁹He also put to the sword Nob, the town of the priests, with its men and women, its children and infants, and its cattle, donkeys and sheep.

²⁰But Abiathar, a son of Ahimelech son of Ahitub, escaped and fled to join David. ²¹He told David that Saul had killed the priests of the LORD. ²²Then David said to Abiathar: "That day, when Doeg the Edomite was there, I knew he would be sure to tell Saul. I am responsible for the death of your father's whole family. ²³Stay with me; don't be afraid; the man who is seeking your life is seeking mine also. You will be safe with me."

David Saves Keilah

23 When David was told, "Look, the Philistines are fighting against Keilah and are looting the threshing floors," ²he inquired of the LORD, saying, "Shall I go and attack these Philistines?"

The LORD answered him, "Go, attack the Philistines and save Keilah."

³But David's men said to him, "Here in Judah we are afraid. How much more, then, if we go to Keilah against the Philistine forces!"

⁴Once again David inquired of the LORD, and the LORD answered him, "Go down to Keilah, for I am going to give the Philistines into your hand." ⁵So David and his men went to Keilah, fought the Philistines and carried off their livestock. He inflicted heavy losses on the Philistines and saved the people of Keilah. ⁶(Now Abiathar son of Ahimelech had brought the ephod down with him when he fled to David at Keilah.)

Saul Pursues David

⁷Saul was told that David had gone to Keilah, and he said, "God has handed him over to me, for David has imprisoned himself by entering a town with gates and bars." ⁸And Saul called up all his forces for battle, to go down to Keilah to besiege David and his men.

⁹When David learned that Saul was plotting against him, he said to Abiathar the priest, "Bring the ephod." ¹⁰David said, "O LORD, God of Israel, your servant has heard definitely that Saul plans to come to Keilah and destroy the town on account of me. ¹¹Will the citizens of Keilah surrender me to him? Will Saul come down, as your servant has heard? O LORD, God of Israel, tell your servant."

And the LORD said, "He will."

¹²Again David asked, "Will the citizens of Keilah surrender me and my men to Saul?"

And the LORD said, "They will."

¹³So David and his men, about six hundred in number, left Keilah and kept moving from place to place. When Saul was told that David had escaped from Keilah, he did not go there.

¹⁴David stayed in the desert strongholds and in the hills of the Desert of Ziph. Day after day Saul searched for him, but God did not give David into his hands.

¹⁵While David was at Horesh in the Desert of Ziph, he learned that Saul had come out to take his life. ¹⁶And Saul's son Jonathan went to David at Horesh and helped him find

strength in God. ¹⁷"Don't be afraid," he said. "My father Saul will not lay a hand on you. You will be king over Israel, and I will be second to you. Even my father Saul knows this." ¹⁸The two of them made a covenant before the LORD. Then Jonathan went home, but David remained at Horesh.

¹⁹The Ziphites went up to Saul at Gibeah and said, "Is not David hiding among us in the strongholds at Horesh, on the hill of Hakilah, south of Jeshimon? ²⁰Now, O king, come down whenever it pleases you to do so, and we will be responsible for handing him over to the king."

²¹Saul replied, "The LORD bless you for your concern for me. ²²Go and make further preparation. Find out where David usually goes and who has seen him there. They tell me he is very crafty. ²³Find out about all the hiding places he uses and come back to me with definite information.ᵃ Then I will go with you; if he is in the area, I will track him down among all the clans of Judah."

²⁴So they set out and went to Ziph ahead of Saul. Now David and his men were in the Desert of Maon, in the Arabah south of Jeshimon. ²⁵Saul and his men began the search, and when David was told about it, he went down to the rock and stayed in the Desert of Maon. When Saul heard this, he went into the Desert of Maon in pursuit of David.

²⁶Saul was going along one side of the mountain, and David and his men were on the other side, hurrying to get away from Saul. As Saul and his forces were closing in on David and his men to capture them, ²⁷a messenger came to Saul, saying, "Come quickly! The Philistines are raiding the land." ²⁸Then Saul broke off his pursuit of David and went to meet the Philistines. That is why they call this place Sela Hammahlekoth.ᵇ ²⁹And David went up from there and lived in the strongholds of En Gedi.

David Spares Saul's Life

24 After Saul returned from pursuing the Philistines, he was told, "David is in the Desert of En Gedi." ²So Saul took three thousand chosen men from all Israel and set out to look for David and his men near the Crags of the Wild Goats.

³He came to the sheep pens along the way; a cave was there, and Saul went in to relieve himself. David and his men were far back in the cave. ⁴The men said, "This is the day the LORD spoke of when he saidᶜ to you, 'I will give your enemy into your hands for you to deal with as you wish.'" Then David crept up unnoticed and cut off a corner of Saul's robe.

⁵Afterward, David was conscience-stricken for having cut off a corner of his robe. ⁶He said to his men, "The LORD forbid that I should do such a thing to my master, the LORD's anointed, or lift my hand against him; for he is the anointed of the LORD." ⁷With these words David rebuked his men and did not allow them to attack Saul. And Saul left the cave and went his way.

⁸Then David went out of the cave and called out to Saul, "My lord the king!" When Saul looked behind him, David bowed down and prostrated himself with his face to the ground. ⁹He said to Saul, "Why do you listen when men say, 'David is bent on harming you'? ¹⁰This day you have seen with your own eyes how the LORD delivered you into my hands in the cave. Some urged me to kill you, but I spared you; I said, 'I will not lift my hand against my master, because he is the LORD's anointed.' ¹¹See, my father, look at this piece of your robe in my hand! I cut off the corner of your robe but did not kill you. Now understand and recognize that I am not guilty of wrongdoing or rebellion. I have not wronged you, but you are hunting me down to take my life. ¹²May the LORD judge between you and me. And may the LORD avenge the wrongs you have done to me, but my hand will not touch you. ¹³As the old saying goes, 'From evildoers come evil deeds,' so my hand will not touch you.

¹⁴"Against whom has the king of Israel come out? Whom are you pursuing? A dead

ᵃ23 Or me at Nacon   ᵇ28 Sela Hammahlekoth means rock of parting.   ᶜ4 Or "Today the LORD is saying

dog? A flea? ¹⁵May the Lᴏʀᴅ be our judge and decide between us. May he consider my cause and uphold it; may he vindicate me by delivering me from your hand."

¹⁶When David finished saying this, Saul asked, "Is that your voice, David my son?" And he wept aloud. ¹⁷"You are more righteous than I," he said. "You have treated me well, but I have treated you badly. ¹⁸You have just now told me of the good you did to me; the Lᴏʀᴅ delivered me into your hands, but you did not kill me. ¹⁹When a man finds his enemy, does he let him get away unharmed? May the Lᴏʀᴅ reward you well for the way you treated me today. ²⁰I know that you will surely be king and that the kingdom of Israel will be established in your hands. ²¹Now swear to me by the Lᴏʀᴅ that you will not cut off my descendants or wipe out my name from my father's family."

²²So David gave his oath to Saul. Then Saul returned home, but David and his men went up to the stronghold.

David, Nabal and Abigail

25 Now Samuel died, and all Israel assembled and mourned for him; and they buried him at his home in Ramah.

Then David moved down into the Desert of Maon.ᵃ ²A certain man in Maon, who had property there at Carmel, was very wealthy. He had a thousand goats and three thousand sheep, which he was shearing in Carmel. ³His name was Nabal and his wife's name was Abigail. She was an intelligent and beautiful woman, but her husband, a Calebite, was surly and mean in his dealings.

⁴While David was in the desert, he heard that Nabal was shearing sheep. ⁵So he sent ten young men and said to them, "Go up to Nabal at Carmel and greet him in my name. ⁶Say to him: 'Long life to you! Good health to you and your household! And good health to all that is yours!

⁷"'Now I hear that it is sheep-shearing time. When your shepherds were with us, we

---

ᵃ *1* Some Septuagint manuscripts; Hebrew *Paran*

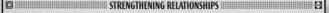

▣ ░░░ STRENGTHENING RELATIONSHIPS ░░░ ⮌

24:1–4
Social

If ever anyone had a good reason to seek revenge, it was David.

David had served as King Saul's armor bearer (chapter 16, verse 21 [page 350]). He played his harp to comfort the king when he was troubled (chapter 16, verse 23 [page 350]). And David rallied the king's army by killing their enemy Goliath (chapter 17 [page 350]). David even married the king's daughter (chapter 18, verse 27 [page 353]).

In spite of all of this, Saul drove David from his palace and hunted him as if he was an animal. Time and again David barely escaped Saul's murderous pursuit. But finally a moment came when the hunted became the hunter. As David and his rag-tag army hid in a cave, the king walked right into their hiding place without even knowing it. David's men urged their leader to finally be rid of his tormentor. They even assured David that God would bless him for killing Saul.

But instead of killing Saul, David sneaked up behind him and sliced off a corner of his robe. Moments later, his conscience pricked, David followed Saul out of the cave and reassured the king of his loyalty.

In doing so, David took a great risk. Saul could have ordered him to be killed on the spot. But forgiveness requires taking chances and being honest about how you feel (as David was in verses 8–15). It demands going out on a limb with only the hope—not the certainty—of reconciliation.

Is there someone in your life you should write a note to or call on the phone and express your willingness to forgive? While that first step may be hard to take, doing so will put you on the path to a restored relationship.

did not mistreat them, and the whole time they were at Carmel nothing of theirs was missing. ⁸Ask your own servants and they will tell you. Therefore be favorable toward my young men, since we come at a festive time. Please give your servants and your son David whatever you can find for them.'"

⁹When David's men arrived, they gave Nabal this message in David's name. Then they waited.

¹⁰Nabal answered David's servants, "Who is this David? Who is this son of Jesse? Many servants are breaking away from their masters these days. ¹¹Why should I take my bread and water, and the meat I have slaughtered for my shearers, and give it to men coming from who knows where?"

¹²David's men turned around and went back. When they arrived, they reported every word. ¹³David said to his men, "Put on your swords!" So they put on their swords, and David put on his. About four hundred men went up with David, while two hundred stayed with the supplies.

¹⁴One of the servants told Nabal's wife Abigail: "David sent messengers from the desert to give our master his greetings, but he hurled insults at them. ¹⁵Yet these men were very good to us. They did not mistreat us, and the whole time we were out in the fields near them nothing was missing. ¹⁶Night and day they were a wall around us all the time we were herding our sheep near them. ¹⁷Now think it over and see what you can do, because disaster is hanging over our master and his whole household. He is such a wicked man that no one can talk to him."

¹⁸Abigail lost no time. She took two hundred loaves of bread, two skins of wine, five dressed sheep, five seahs*ᵃ* of roasted grain, a hundred cakes of raisins and two hundred cakes of pressed figs, and loaded them on donkeys. ¹⁹Then she told her servants, "Go on ahead; I'll follow you." But she did not tell her husband Nabal.

²⁰As she came riding her donkey into a mountain ravine, there were David and his men descending toward her, and she met them. ²¹David had just said, "It's been useless—all my watching over this fellow's property in the desert so that nothing of his was missing. He has paid me back evil for good. ²²May God deal with David,*ᵇ* be it ever so severely, if by morning I leave alive one male of all who belong to him!"

²³When Abigail saw David, she quickly got off her donkey and bowed down before David with her face to the ground. ²⁴She fell at his feet and said: "My lord, let the blame be on me alone. Please let your servant speak to you; hear what your servant has to say. ²⁵May my lord pay no attention to that wicked man Nabal. He is just like his name—his name is Fool, and folly goes with him. But as for me, your servant, I did not see the men my master sent.

²⁶"Now since the LORD has kept you, my master, from bloodshed and from avenging yourself with your own hands, as surely as the LORD lives and as you live, may your enemies and all who intend to harm my master be like Nabal. ²⁷And let this gift, which your servant has brought to my master, be given to the men who follow you. ²⁸Please forgive your servant's offense, for the LORD will certainly make a lasting dynasty for my master, because he fights the LORD's battles. Let no wrongdoing be found in you as long as you live. ²⁹Even though someone is pursuing you to take your life, the life of my master will be bound securely in the bundle of the living by the LORD your God. But the lives of your enemies he will hurl away as from the pocket of a sling. ³⁰When the LORD has done for my master every good thing he promised concerning him and has appointed him leader over Israel, ³¹my master will not have on his conscience the staggering burden of needless bloodshed or of having avenged himself. And when the LORD has brought my master success, remember your servant."

³²David said to Abigail, "Praise be to the LORD, the God of Israel, who has sent you today to meet me. ³³May you be blessed for your good judgment and for keeping me from bloodshed this day and from avenging myself with my own hands. ³⁴Otherwise, as surely

---

ᵃ 18 That is, probably about a bushel (about 37 liters)   *ᵇ 22* Some Septuagint manuscripts; Hebrew *with David's enemies*

as the LORD, the God of Israel, lives, who has kept me from harming you, if you had not come quickly to meet me, not one male belonging to Nabal would have been left alive by daybreak."

³⁵Then David accepted from her hand what she had brought him and said, "Go home in peace. I have heard your words and granted your request."

³⁶When Abigail went to Nabal, he was in the house holding a banquet like that of a king. He was in high spirits and very drunk. So she told him nothing until daybreak. ³⁷Then in the morning, when Nabal was sober, his wife told him all these things, and his heart failed him and he became like a stone. ³⁸About ten days later, the LORD struck Nabal and he died.

³⁹When David heard that Nabal was dead, he said, "Praise be to the LORD, who has upheld my cause against Nabal for treating me with contempt. He has kept his servant from doing wrong and has brought Nabal's wrongdoing down on his own head."

Then David sent word to Abigail, asking her to become his wife. ⁴⁰His servants went to Carmel and said to Abigail, "David has sent us to you to take you to become his wife."

⁴¹She bowed down with her face to the ground and said, "Here is your maidservant, ready to serve you and wash the feet of my master's servants." ⁴²Abigail quickly got on a donkey and, attended by her five maids, went with David's messengers and became his wife. ⁴³David had also married Ahinoam of Jezreel, and they both were his wives. ⁴⁴But Saul had given his daughter Michal, David's wife, to Paltiel^a son of Laish, who was from Gallim.

David Again Spares Saul's Life

26 The Ziphites went to Saul at Gibeah and said, "Is not David hiding on the hill of Hakilah, which faces Jeshimon?"

²So Saul went down to the Desert of Ziph, with his three thousand chosen men of Israel, to search there for David. ³Saul made his camp beside the road on the hill of Hakilah facing Jeshimon, but David stayed in the desert. When he saw that Saul had followed him there, ⁴he sent out scouts and learned that Saul had definitely arrived.^b

⁵Then David set out and went to the place where Saul had camped. He saw where Saul and Abner son of Ner, the commander of the army, had lain down. Saul was lying inside the camp, with the army encamped around him.

⁶David then asked Ahimelech the Hittite and Abishai son of Zeruiah, Joab's brother, "Who will go down into the camp with me to Saul?"

"I'll go with you," said Abishai.

⁷So David and Abishai went to the army by night, and there was Saul, lying asleep inside the camp with his spear stuck in the ground near his head. Abner and the soldiers were lying around him.

⁸Abishai said to David, "Today God has delivered your enemy into your hands. Now let me pin him to the ground with one thrust of my spear; I won't strike him twice."

⁹But David said to Abishai, "Don't destroy him! Who can lay a hand on the LORD's anointed and be guiltless? ¹⁰As surely as the LORD lives," he said, "the LORD himself will strike him; either his time will come and he will die, or he will go into battle and perish. ¹¹But the LORD forbid that I should lay a hand on the LORD's anointed. Now get the spear and water jug that are near his head, and let's go."

¹²So David took the spear and water jug near Saul's head, and they left. No one saw or knew about it, nor did anyone wake up. They were all sleeping, because the LORD had put them into a deep sleep.

¹³Then David crossed over to the other side and stood on top of the hill some distance away; there was a wide space between them. ¹⁴He called out to the army and to Abner son of Ner, "Aren't you going to answer me, Abner?"

Abner replied, "Who are you who calls to the king?"

^a44 Hebrew *Palti,* a variant of *Paltiel*   ^b4 Or *had come to Nacon*

¹⁵David said, "You're a man, aren't you? And who is like you in Israel? Why didn't you guard your lord the king? Someone came to destroy your lord the king. ¹⁶What you have done is not good. As surely as the LORD lives, you and your men deserve to die, because you did not guard your master, the LORD's anointed. Look around you. Where are the king's spear and water jug that were near his head?"

¹⁷Saul recognized David's voice and said, "Is that your voice, David my son?"

David replied, "Yes it is, my lord the king." ¹⁸And he added, "Why is my lord pursuing his servant? What have I done, and what wrong am I guilty of? ¹⁹Now let my lord the king listen to his servant's words. If the LORD has incited you against me, then may he accept an offering. If, however, men have done it, may they be cursed before the LORD! They have now driven me from my share in the LORD's inheritance and have said, 'Go, serve other gods.' ²⁰Now do not let my blood fall to the ground far from the presence of the LORD. The king of Israel has come out to look for a flea—as one hunts a partridge in the mountains."

²¹Then Saul said, "I have sinned. Come back, David my son. Because you considered my life precious today, I will not try to harm you again. Surely I have acted like a fool and have erred greatly."

²²"Here is the king's spear," David answered. "Let one of your young men come over and get it. ²³The LORD rewards every man for his righteousness and faithfulness. The LORD delivered you into my hands today, but I would not lay a hand on the LORD's anointed. ²⁴As surely as I valued your life today, so may the LORD value my life and deliver me from all trouble."

²⁵Then Saul said to David, "May you be blessed, my son David; you will do great things and surely triumph."

So David went on his way, and Saul returned home.

David Among the Philistines

27 But David thought to himself, "One of these days I will be destroyed by the hand of Saul. The best thing I can do is to escape to the land of the Philistines. Then Saul will give up searching for me anywhere in Israel, and I will slip out of his hand."

²So David and the six hundred men with him left and went over to Achish son of Maoch king of Gath. ³David and his men settled in Gath with Achish. Each man had his family with him, and David had his two wives: Ahinoam of Jezreel and Abigail of Carmel, the widow of Nabal. ⁴When Saul was told that David had fled to Gath, he no longer searched for him.

⁵Then David said to Achish, "If I have found favor in your eyes, let a place be assigned to me in one of the country towns, that I may live there. Why should your servant live in the royal city with you?"

⁶So on that day Achish gave him Ziklag, and it has belonged to the kings of Judah ever since. ⁷David lived in Philistine territory a year and four months.

⁸Now David and his men went up and raided the Geshurites, the Girzites and the Amalekites. (From ancient times these peoples had lived in the land extending to Shur and Egypt.) ⁹Whenever David attacked an area, he did not leave a man or woman alive, but took sheep and cattle, donkeys and camels, and clothes. Then he returned to Achish.

¹⁰When Achish asked, "Where did you go raiding today?" David would say, "Against the Negev of Judah" or "Against the Negev of Jerahmeel" or "Against the Negev of the Kenites." ¹¹He did not leave a man or woman alive to be brought to Gath, for he thought, "They might inform on us and say, 'This is what David did.'" And such was his practice as long as he lived in Philistine territory. ¹²Achish trusted David and said to himself, "He has become so odious to his people, the Israelites, that he will be my servant forever."

Saul and the Witch of Endor

28 In those days the Philistines gathered their forces to fight against Israel. Achish said to David, "You must understand that you and your men will accompany me in the army."

²David said, "Then you will see for yourself what your servant can do."

Achish replied, "Very well, I will make you my bodyguard for life."

³Now Samuel was dead, and all Israel had mourned for him and buried him in his own town of Ramah. Saul had expelled the mediums and spiritists from the land.

⁴The Philistines assembled and came and set up camp at Shunem, while Saul gathered all the Israelites and set up camp at Gilboa. ⁵When Saul saw the Philistine army, he was afraid; terror filled his heart. ⁶He inquired of the LORD, but the LORD did not answer him by dreams or Urim or prophets. ⁷Saul then said to his attendants, "Find me a woman who is a medium, so I may go and inquire of her."

"There is one in Endor," they said.

⁸So Saul disguised himself, putting on other clothes, and at night he and two men went to the woman. "Consult a spirit for me," he said, "and bring up for me the one I name."

⁹But the woman said to him, "Surely you know what Saul has done. He has cut off the mediums and spiritists from the land. Why have you set a trap for my life to bring about my death?"

¹⁰Saul swore to her by the LORD, "As surely as the LORD lives, you will not be punished for this."

¹¹Then the woman asked, "Whom shall I bring up for you?"

"Bring up Samuel," he said.

¹²When the woman saw Samuel, she cried out at the top of her voice and said to Saul, "Why have you deceived me? You are Saul!"

DISCOVERING GOD

28:1–7
Spiritual Fraud

Fear has a powerful effect on humans. When we need consolation and reassurance, we can sometimes go to incredible lengths to find it. And if we happen to be running from God at the time, our fragile—and foolish—human hearts are even more apparent.

Consider Saul. The king of God's chosen people blatantly disobeyed God to try to get the inside scoop on the next day's battle. He wanted to talk to Samuel, who had on many occasions given him divinely inspired information. But Samuel was dead, so he employed the services of a medium who he hoped would be able to inform him.

Was the appearance of Samuel (verse 12) really Samuel? The Bible strictly forbids this kind of activity (see Deuteronomy chapter 18, verses 10–12 [page 236]). This is the only place in the Bible where we read details of a medium in action. As in our own day, people can pull off amazing feats of deception knowing full well they are tricking their victims. It is also possible, because we're dealing here with forbidden spiritual powers, that a demon appeared in Samuel's form and deceived everyone, including the medium.

What was the end result of this experience? Saul was shaken, and was far worse off than he had been before. This act of disobedience put one more wedge between Saul and the God he should have been serving.

---

¹³The king said to her, "Don't be afraid. What do you see?"

The woman said, "I see a spirit*ᵃ* coming up out of the ground."

¹⁴"What does he look like?" he asked.

"An old man wearing a robe is coming up," she said.

Then Saul knew it was Samuel, and he bowed down and prostrated himself with his face to the ground.

¹⁵Samuel said to Saul, "Why have you disturbed me by bringing me up?"

"I am in great distress," Saul said. "The Philistines are fighting against me, and God has

---

ᵃ 13 Or see spirits; or see gods

turned away from me. He no longer answers me, either by prophets or by dreams. So I have called on you to tell me what to do."

¹⁶Samuel said, "Why do you consult me, now that the LORD has turned away from you and become your enemy? ¹⁷The LORD has done what he predicted through me. The LORD has torn the kingdom out of your hands and given it to one of your neighbors—to David. ¹⁸Because you did not obey the LORD or carry out his fierce wrath against the Amalekites, the LORD has done this to you today. ¹⁹The LORD will hand over both Israel and you to the Philistines, and tomorrow you and your sons will be with me. The LORD will also hand over the army of Israel to the Philistines."

²⁰Immediately Saul fell full length on the ground, filled with fear because of Samuel's words. His strength was gone, for he had eaten nothing all that day and night.

²¹When the woman came to Saul and saw that he was greatly shaken, she said, "Look, your maidservant has obeyed you. I took my life in my hands and did what you told me to do. ²²Now please listen to your servant and let me give you some food so you may eat and have the strength to go on your way."

²³He refused and said, "I will not eat."

But his men joined the woman in urging him, and he listened to them. He got up from the ground and sat on the couch.

²⁴The woman had a fattened calf at the house, which she butchered at once. She took some flour, kneaded it and baked bread without yeast. ²⁵Then she set it before Saul and his men, and they ate. That same night they got up and left.

Achish Sends David Back to Ziklag

29 The Philistines gathered all their forces at Aphek, and Israel camped by the spring in Jezreel. ²As the Philistine rulers marched with their units of hundreds and thousands, David and his men were marching at the rear with Achish. ³The commanders of the Philistines asked, "What about these Hebrews?"

Achish replied, "Is this not David, who was an officer of Saul king of Israel? He has already been with me for over a year, and from the day he left Saul until now, I have found no fault in him."

⁴But the Philistine commanders were angry with him and said, "Send the man back, that he may return to the place you assigned him. He must not go with us into battle, or he will turn against us during the fighting. How better could he regain his master's favor than by taking the heads of our own men? ⁵Isn't this the David they sang about in their dances:

> " 'Saul has slain his thousands,
>   and David his tens of thousands'?"

⁶So Achish called David and said to him, "As surely as the LORD lives, you have been reliable, and I would be pleased to have you serve with me in the army. From the day you came to me until now, I have found no fault in you, but the rulers don't approve of you. ⁷Turn back and go in peace; do nothing to displease the Philistine rulers."

⁸"But what have I done?" asked David. "What have you found against your servant from the day I came to you until now? Why can't I go and fight against the enemies of my lord the king?"

⁹Achish answered, "I know that you have been as pleasing in my eyes as an angel of God; nevertheless, the Philistine commanders have said, 'He must not go up with us into battle.' ¹⁰Now get up early, along with your master's servants who have come with you, and leave in the morning as soon as it is light."

¹¹So David and his men got up early in the morning to go back to the land of the Philistines, and the Philistines went up to Jezreel.

David Destroys the Amalekites

30 David and his men reached Ziklag on the third day. Now the Amalekites had raided the Negev and Ziklag. They had attacked Ziklag and burned it, ²and had taken captive the women and all who were in it, both young and old. They killed none of them, but carried them off as they went on their way.

³When David and his men came to Ziklag, they found it destroyed by fire and their wives and sons and daughters taken captive. ⁴So David and his men wept aloud until they had no strength left to weep. ⁵David's two wives had been captured—Ahinoam of Jezreel and Abigail, the widow of Nabal of Carmel. ⁶David was greatly distressed because the men were talking of stoning him; each one was bitter in spirit because of his sons and daughters. But David found strength in the LORD his God.

⁷Then David said to Abiathar the priest, the son of Ahimelech, "Bring me the ephod." Abiathar brought it to him, ⁸and David inquired of the LORD, "Shall I pursue this raiding party? Will I overtake them?"

"Pursue them," he answered. "You will certainly overtake them and succeed in the rescue."

⁹David and the six hundred men with him came to the Besor Ravine, where some stayed behind, ¹⁰for two hundred men were too exhausted to cross the ravine. But David and four hundred men continued the pursuit.

¹¹They found an Egyptian in a field and brought him to David. They gave him water to drink and food to eat— ¹²part of a cake of pressed figs and two cakes of raisins. He ate and was revived, for he had not eaten any food or drunk any water for three days and three nights.

¹³David asked him, "To whom do you belong, and where do you come from?"

He said, "I am an Egyptian, the slave of an Amalekite. My master abandoned me when I became ill three days ago. ¹⁴We raided the Negev of the Kerethites and the territory belonging to Judah and the Negev of Caleb. And we burned Ziklag."

¹⁵David asked him, "Can you lead me down to this raiding party?"

He answered, "Swear to me before God that you will not kill me or hand me over to my master, and I will take you down to them."

¹⁶He led David down, and there they were, scattered over the countryside, eating, drinking and reveling because of the great amount of plunder they had taken from the land of the Philistines and from Judah. ¹⁷David fought them from dusk until the evening of the next day, and none of them got away, except four hundred young men who rode off on camels and fled. ¹⁸David recovered everything the Amalekites had taken, including his two wives. ¹⁹Nothing was missing: young or old, boy or girl, plunder or anything else they had taken. David brought everything back. ²⁰He took all the flocks and herds, and his men drove them ahead of the other livestock, saying, "This is David's plunder."

²¹Then David came to the two hundred men who had been too exhausted to follow him and who were left behind at the Besor Ravine. They came out to meet David and the people with him. As David and his men approached, he greeted them. ²²But all the evil men and troublemakers among David's followers said, "Because they did not go out with us, we will not share with them the plunder we recovered. However, each man may take his wife and children and go."

²³David replied, "No, my brothers, you must not do that with what the LORD has given us. He has protected us and handed over to us the forces that came against us. ²⁴Who will listen to what you say? The share of the man who stayed with the supplies is to be the same as that of him who went down to the battle. All will share alike." ²⁵David made this a statute and ordinance for Israel from that day to this.

²⁶When David arrived in Ziklag, he sent some of the plunder to the elders of Judah, who were his friends, saying, "Here is a present for you from the plunder of the LORD's enemies."

²⁷He sent it to those who were in Bethel, Ramoth Negev and Jattir; ²⁸to those in Aroer,

Siphmoth, Eshtemoa ²⁹and Racal; to those in the towns of the Jerahmeelites and the Kenites; ³⁰to those in Hormah, Bor Ashan, Athach ³¹and Hebron; and to those in all the other places where David and his men had roamed.

Saul Takes His Life

31 Now the Philistines fought against Israel; the Israelites fled before them, and many fell slain on Mount Gilboa. ²The Philistines pressed hard after Saul and his sons, and they killed his sons Jonathan, Abinadab and Malki-Shua. ³The fighting grew fierce around Saul, and when the archers overtook him, they wounded him critically.

⁴Saul said to his armor-bearer, "Draw your sword and run me through, or these uncircumcised fellows will come and run me through and abuse me."

But his armor-bearer was terrified and would not do it; so Saul took his own sword and fell on it. ⁵When the armor-bearer saw that Saul was dead, he too fell on his sword and died with him. ⁶So Saul and his three sons and his armor-bearer and all his men died together that same day.

⁷When the Israelites along the valley and those across the Jordan saw that the Israelite army had fled and that Saul and his sons had died, they abandoned their towns and fled. And the Philistines came and occupied them.

⁸The next day, when the Philistines came to strip the dead, they found Saul and his three sons fallen on Mount Gilboa. ⁹They cut off his head and stripped off his armor, and they sent messengers throughout the land of the Philistines to proclaim the news in the temple of their idols and among their people. ¹⁰They put his armor in the temple of the Ashtoreths and fastened his body to the wall of Beth Shan.

¹¹When the people of Jabesh Gilead heard of what the Philistines had done to Saul, ¹²all their valiant men journeyed through the night to Beth Shan. They took down the bodies of Saul and his sons from the wall of Beth Shan and went to Jabesh, where they burned them. ¹³Then they took their bones and buried them under a tamarisk tree at Jabesh, and they fasted seven days.

2 SAMUEL

David Hears of Saul's Death

1 After the death of Saul, David returned from defeating the Amalekites and stayed in Ziklag two days. ²On the third day a man arrived from Saul's camp, with his clothes torn and with dust on his head. When he came to David, he fell to the ground to pay him honor.

³"Where have you come from?" David asked him.

He answered, "I have escaped from the Israelite camp."

⁴"What happened?" David asked. "Tell me."

He said, "The men fled from the battle. Many of them fell and died. And Saul and his son Jonathan are dead."

⁵Then David said to the young man who brought him the report, "How do you know that Saul and his son Jonathan are dead?"

⁶"I happened to be on Mount Gilboa," the young man said, "and there was Saul, leaning on his spear, with the chariots and riders almost upon him. ⁷When he turned around and saw me, he called out to me, and I said, 'What can I do?'

⁸"He asked me, 'Who are you?'

"'An Amalekite,' I answered.

⁹"Then he said to me, 'Stand over me and kill me! I am in the throes of death, but I'm still alive.'

¹⁰"So I stood over him and killed him, because I knew that after he had fallen he could not survive. And I took the crown that was on his head and the band on his arm and have brought them here to my lord."

¹¹Then David and all the men with him took hold of their clothes and tore them. ¹²They mourned and wept and fasted till evening for Saul and his son Jonathan, and for the army of the LORD and the house of Israel, because they had fallen by the sword.

¹³David said to the young man who brought him the report, "Where are you from?"

"I am the son of an alien, an Amalekite," he answered.

¹⁴David asked him, "Why were you not afraid to lift your hand to destroy the LORD's anointed?"

¹⁵Then David called one of his men and said, "Go, strike him down!" So he struck him down, and he died. ¹⁶For David had said to him, "Your blood be on your own head. Your own mouth testified against you when you said, 'I killed the LORD's anointed.'"

David's Lament for Saul and Jonathan

¹⁷David took up this lament concerning Saul and his son Jonathan, ¹⁸and ordered that the men of Judah be taught this lament of the bow (it is written in the Book of Jashar):

¹⁹"Your glory, O Israel, lies slain on your heights.
How the mighty have fallen!

²⁰"Tell it not in Gath,
proclaim it not in the streets of Ashkelon,
lest the daughters of the Philistines be glad,
lest the daughters of the uncircumcised rejoice.

²¹"O mountains of Gilboa,
may you have neither dew nor rain,

nor fields that yield offerings ⌊of grain⌋.
For there the shield of the mighty was defiled,
⠀⠀the shield of Saul—no longer rubbed with oil.
22From the blood of the slain,
⠀⠀from the flesh of the mighty,
the bow of Jonathan did not turn back,
⠀⠀the sword of Saul did not return unsatisfied.

23"Saul and Jonathan—
⠀⠀in life they were loved and gracious,
⠀⠀and in death they were not parted.
They were swifter than eagles,
⠀⠀they were stronger than lions.

24"O daughters of Israel,
⠀⠀weep for Saul,
who clothed you in scarlet and finery,
⠀⠀who adorned your garments with ornaments of gold.

25"How the mighty have fallen in battle!
⠀⠀Jonathan lies slain on your heights.
26I grieve for you, Jonathan my brother;
⠀⠀you were very dear to me.
Your love for me was wonderful,
⠀⠀more wonderful than that of women.

27"How the mighty have fallen!
⠀⠀The weapons of war have perished!"

David Anointed King Over Judah

2 In the course of time, David inquired of the LORD. "Shall I go up to one of the towns of Judah?" he asked.

The LORD said, "Go up."

David asked, "Where shall I go?"

"To Hebron," the LORD answered.

2So David went up there with his two wives, Ahinoam of Jezreel and Abigail, the widow of Nabal of Carmel. 3David also took the men who were with him, each with his family, and they settled in Hebron and its towns. 4Then the men of Judah came to Hebron and there they anointed David king over the house of Judah.

When David was told that it was the men of Jabesh Gilead who had buried Saul, 5he sent messengers to the men of Jabesh Gilead to say to them, "The LORD bless you for showing this kindness to Saul your master by burying him. 6May the LORD now show you kindness and faithfulness, and I too will show you the same favor because you have done this. 7Now then, be strong and brave, for Saul your master is dead, and the house of Judah has anointed me king over them."

War Between the Houses of David and Saul

8Meanwhile, Abner son of Ner, the commander of Saul's army, had taken Ish-Bosheth son of Saul and brought him over to Mahanaim. 9He made him king over Gilead, Ashuri[a] and Jezreel, and also over Ephraim, Benjamin and all Israel.

10Ish-Bosheth son of Saul was forty years old when he became king over Israel, and he reigned two years. The house of Judah, however, followed David. 11The length of time David was king in Hebron over the house of Judah was seven years and six months.

12Abner son of Ner, together with the men of Ish-Bosheth son of Saul, left Mahanaim

a9 Or *Asher*

and went to Gibeon. ¹³Joab son of Zeruiah and David's men went out and met them at the pool of Gibeon. One group sat down on one side of the pool and one group on the other side.

¹⁴Then Abner said to Joab, "Let's have some of the young men get up and fight hand to hand in front of us."

"All right, let them do it," Joab said.

¹⁵So they stood up and were counted off—twelve men for Benjamin and Ish-Bosheth son of Saul, and twelve for David. ¹⁶Then each man grabbed his opponent by the head and thrust his dagger into his opponent's side, and they fell down together. So that place in Gibeon was called Helkath Hazzurim. ᵃ

¹⁷The battle that day was very fierce, and Abner and the men of Israel were defeated by David's men.

¹⁸The three sons of Zeruiah were there: Joab, Abishai and Asahel. Now Asahel was as fleet-footed as a wild gazelle. ¹⁹He chased Abner, turning neither to the right nor to the left as he pursued him. ²⁰Abner looked behind him and asked, "Is that you, Asahel?"

"It is," he answered.

²¹Then Abner said to him, "Turn aside to the right or to the left; take on one of the young men and strip him of his weapons." But Asahel would not stop chasing him.

²²Again Abner warned Asahel, "Stop chasing me! Why should I strike you down? How could I look your brother Joab in the face?"

²³But Asahel refused to give up the pursuit; so Abner thrust the butt of his spear into Asahel's stomach, and the spear came out through his back. He fell there and died on the spot. And every man stopped when he came to the place where Asahel had fallen and died.

²⁴But Joab and Abishai pursued Abner, and as the sun was setting, they came to the hill of Ammah, near Giah on the way to the wasteland of Gibeon. ²⁵Then the men of Benjamin rallied behind Abner. They formed themselves into a group and took their stand on top of a hill.

²⁶Abner called out to Joab, "Must the sword devour forever? Don't you realize that this will end in bitterness? How long before you order your men to stop pursuing their brothers?"

²⁷Joab answered, "As surely as God lives, if you had not spoken, the men would have continued the pursuit of their brothers until morning.ᵇ"

²⁸So Joab blew the trumpet, and all the men came to a halt; they no longer pursued Israel, nor did they fight anymore.

²⁹All that night Abner and his men marched through the Arabah. They crossed the Jordan, continued through the whole Bithronᶜ and came to Mahanaim.

³⁰Then Joab returned from pursuing Abner and assembled all his men. Besides Asahel, nineteen of David's men were found missing. ³¹But David's men had killed three hundred and sixty Benjamites who were with Abner. ³²They took Asahel and buried him in his father's tomb at Bethlehem. Then Joab and his men marched all night and arrived at Hebron by daybreak.

3 The war between the house of Saul and the house of David lasted a long time. David grew stronger and stronger, while the house of Saul grew weaker and weaker.

²Sons were born to David in Hebron:

His firstborn was Amnon the son of Ahinoam of Jezreel;

³his second, Kileab the son of Abigail the widow of Nabal of Carmel;

the third, Absalom the son of Maacah daughter of Talmai king of Geshur;

⁴the fourth, Adonijah the son of Haggith;

ᵃ16 Helkath Hazzurim means field of daggers or field of hostilities.   ᵇ27 Or spoken this morning, the men would not have taken up the pursuit of their brothers; or spoken, the men would have given up the pursuit of their brothers by morning   ᶜ29 Or morning; or ravine; the meaning of the Hebrew for this word is uncertain.

the fifth, Shephatiah the son of Abital;
⁵and the sixth, Ithream the son of David's wife Eglah.
These were born to David in Hebron.

Abner Goes Over to David

⁶During the war between the house of Saul and the house of David, Abner had been strengthening his own position in the house of Saul. ⁷Now Saul had had a concubine named Rizpah daughter of Aiah. And Ish-Bosheth said to Abner, "Why did you sleep with my father's concubine?"

⁸Abner was very angry because of what Ish-Bosheth said and he answered, "Am I a dog's head—on Judah's side? This very day I am loyal to the house of your father Saul and to his family and friends. I haven't handed you over to David. Yet now you accuse me of an offense involving this woman! ⁹May God deal with Abner, be it ever so severely, if I do not do for David what the LORD promised him on oath ¹⁰and transfer the kingdom from the house of Saul and establish David's throne over Israel and Judah from Dan to Beersheba." ¹¹Ish-Bosheth did not dare to say another word to Abner, because he was afraid of him.

¹²Then Abner sent messengers on his behalf to say to David, "Whose land is it? Make an agreement with me, and I will help you bring all Israel over to you."

¹³"Good," said David. "I will make an agreement with you. But I demand one thing of you: Do not come into my presence unless you bring Michal daughter of Saul when you come to see me." ¹⁴Then David sent messengers to Ish-Bosheth son of Saul, demanding, "Give me my wife Michal, whom I betrothed to myself for the price of a hundred Philistine foreskins."

¹⁵So Ish-Bosheth gave orders and had her taken away from her husband Paltiel son of Laish. ¹⁶Her husband, however, went with her, weeping behind her all the way to Bahurim. Then Abner said to him, "Go back home!" So he went back.

¹⁷Abner conferred with the elders of Israel and said, "For some time you have wanted to make David your king. ¹⁸Now do it! For the LORD promised David, 'By my servant David I will rescue my people Israel from the hand of the Philistines and from the hand of all their enemies.'"

¹⁹Abner also spoke to the Benjamites in person. Then he went to Hebron to tell David everything that Israel and the whole house of Benjamin wanted to do. ²⁰When Abner, who had twenty men with him, came to David at Hebron, David prepared a feast for him and his men. ²¹Then Abner said to David, "Let me go at once and assemble all Israel for my lord the king, so that they may make a compact with you, and that you may rule over all that your heart desires." So David sent Abner away, and he went in peace.

Joab Murders Abner

²²Just then David's men and Joab returned from a raid and brought with them a great deal of plunder. But Abner was no longer with David in Hebron, because David had sent him away, and he had gone in peace. ²³When Joab and all the soldiers with him arrived, he was told that Abner son of Ner had come to the king and that the king had sent him away and that he had gone in peace.

²⁴So Joab went to the king and said, "What have you done? Look, Abner came to you. Why did you let him go? Now he is gone! ²⁵You know Abner son of Ner; he came to deceive you and observe your movements and find out everything you are doing."

²⁶Joab then left David and sent messengers after Abner, and they brought him back from the well of Sirah. But David did not know it. ²⁷Now when Abner returned to Hebron, Joab took him aside into the gateway, as though to speak with him privately. And there, to avenge the blood of his brother Asahel, Joab stabbed him in the stomach, and he died.

²⁸Later, when David heard about this, he said, "I and my kingdom are forever innocent before the LORD concerning the blood of Abner son of Ner. ²⁹May his blood fall upon the

head of Joab and upon all his father's house! May Joab's house never be without some-one who has a running sore or leprosy*a* or who leans on a crutch or who falls by the sword or who lacks food."

³⁰(Joab and his brother Abishai murdered Abner because he had killed their brother Asahel in the battle at Gibeon.)

³¹Then David said to Joab and all the people with him, "Tear your clothes and put on sackcloth and walk in mourning in front of Abner." King David himself walked behind the bier. ³²They buried Abner in Hebron, and the king wept aloud at Abner's tomb. All the people wept also.

³³The king sang this lament for Abner:

"Should Abner have died as the lawless die?
³⁴   Your hands were not bound,
        your feet were not fettered.
    You fell as one falls before wicked men."

And all the people wept over him again.

³⁵Then they all came and urged David to eat something while it was still day; but David took an oath, saying, "May God deal with me, be it ever so severely, if I taste bread or anything else before the sun sets!"

³⁶All the people took note and were pleased; indeed, everything the king did pleased them. ³⁷So on that day all the people and all Israel knew that the king had no part in the murder of Abner son of Ner.

³⁸Then the king said to his men, "Do you not realize that a prince and a great man has fallen in Israel this day? ³⁹And today, though I am the anointed king, I am weak, and these sons of Zeruiah are too strong for me. May the LORD repay the evildoer according to his evil deeds!"

Ish-Bosheth Murdered

4 When Ish-Bosheth son of Saul heard that Abner had died in Hebron, he lost courage, and all Israel became alarmed. ²Now Saul's son had two men who were leaders of raiding bands. One was named Baanah and the other Recab; they were sons of Rimmon the Beerothite from the tribe of Benjamin—Beeroth is considered part of Benjamin, ³because the people of Beeroth fled to Gittaim and have lived there as aliens to this day.

⁴(Jonathan son of Saul had a son who was lame in both feet. He was five years old when the news about Saul and Jonathan came from Jezreel. His nurse picked him up and fled, but as she hurried to leave, he fell and became crippled. His name was Mephibo-sheth.)

⁵Now Recab and Baanah, the sons of Rimmon the Beerothite, set out for the house of Ish-Bosheth, and they arrived there in the heat of the day while he was taking his noonday rest. ⁶They went into the inner part of the house as if to get some wheat, and they stabbed him in the stomach. Then Recab and his brother Baanah slipped away.

⁷They had gone into the house while he was lying on the bed in his bedroom. After they stabbed and killed him, they cut off his head. Taking it with them, they traveled all night by way of the Arabah. ⁸They brought the head of Ish-Bosheth to David at Hebron and said to the king, "Here is the head of Ish-Bosheth son of Saul, your enemy, who tried to take your life. This day the LORD has avenged my lord the king against Saul and his offspring."

⁹David answered Recab and his brother Baanah, the sons of Rimmon the Beerothite, "As surely as the LORD lives, who has delivered me out of all trouble, ¹⁰when a man told me, 'Saul is dead,' and thought he was bringing good news, I seized him and put him to death in Ziklag. That was the reward I gave him for his news! ¹¹How much more—when

a 29 The Hebrew word was used for various diseases affecting the skin—not necessarily leprosy.

wicked men have killed an innocent man in his own house and on his own bed—should I not now demand his blood from your hand and rid the earth of you!"

¹²So David gave an order to his men, and they killed them. They cut off their hands and feet and hung the bodies by the pool in Hebron. But they took the head of Ish-Bo-sheth and buried it in Abner's tomb at Hebron.

David Becomes King Over Israel

5 All the tribes of Israel came to David at Hebron and said, "We are your own flesh and blood. ²In the past, while Saul was king over us, you were the one who led Israel on their military campaigns. And the LORD said to you, 'You will shepherd my people Israel, and you will become their ruler.'"

³When all the elders of Israel had come to King David at Hebron, the king made a compact with them at Hebron before the LORD, and they anointed David king over Israel. ⁴David was thirty years old when he became king, and he reigned forty years. ⁵In Hebron he reigned over Judah seven years and six months, and in Jerusalem he reigned over all Israel and Judah thirty-three years.

David Conquers Jerusalem

⁶The king and his men marched to Jerusalem to attack the Jebusites, who lived there. The Jebusites said to David, "You will not get in here; even the blind and the lame can ward you off." They thought, "David cannot get in here." ⁷Nevertheless, David captured the fortress of Zion, the City of David.

⁸On that day, David said, "Anyone who conquers the Jebusites will have to use the water shaft*ᵃ* to reach those 'lame and blind' who are David's enemies.*ᵇ*" That is why they say, "The 'blind and lame' will not enter the palace."

⁹David then took up residence in the fortress and called it the City of David. He built up the area around it, from the supporting terraces*ᶜ* inward. ¹⁰And he became more and more powerful, because the LORD God Almighty was with him.

¹¹Now Hiram king of Tyre sent messengers to David, along with cedar logs and carpenters and stonemasons, and they built a palace for David. ¹²And David knew that the LORD had established him as king over Israel and had exalted his kingdom for the sake of his people Israel.

¹³After he left Hebron, David took more concubines and wives in Jerusalem, and more sons and daughters were born to him. ¹⁴These are the names of the children born to him there: Shammua, Shobab, Nathan, Solomon, ¹⁵Ibhar, Elishua, Nepheg, Japhia, ¹⁶Elishama, Eliada and Eliphelet.

David Defeats the Philistines

¹⁷When the Philistines heard that David had been anointed king over Israel, they went up in full force to search for him, but David heard about it and went down to the stronghold. ¹⁸Now the Philistines had come and spread out in the Valley of Rephaim; ¹⁹so David inquired of the LORD, "Shall I go and attack the Philistines? Will you hand them over to me?"

The LORD answered him, "Go, for I will surely hand the Philistines over to you."

²⁰So David went to Baal Perazim, and there he defeated them. He said, "As waters break out, the LORD has broken out against my enemies before me." So that place was called Baal Perazim.*ᵈ* ²¹The Philistines abandoned their idols there, and David and his men carried them off.

²²Once more the Philistines came up and spread out in the Valley of Rephaim; ²³so David inquired of the LORD, and he answered, "Do not go straight up, but circle around behind them and attack them in front of the balsam trees. ²⁴As soon as you hear the

---

ᵃ8 Or use scaling hooks   *ᵇ8 Or are hated by David*   *ᶜ9 Or the Millo*   *ᵈ20 Baal Perazim means the lord who breaks out.*

sound of marching in the tops of the balsam trees, move quickly, because that will mean the LORD has gone out in front of you to strike the Philistine army." ²⁵So David did as the LORD commanded him, and he struck down the Philistines all the way from Gibeon*a* to Gezer.

The Ark Brought to Jerusalem

6 David again brought together out of Israel chosen men, thirty thousand in all. ²He and all his men set out from Baalah of Judah*b* to bring up from there the ark of God, which is called by the Name,*c* the name of the LORD Almighty, who is enthroned between the cherubim that are on the ark. ³They set the ark of God on a new cart and brought it from the house of Abinadab, which was on the hill. Uzzah and Ahio, sons of Abinadab, were guiding the new cart ⁴with the ark of God on it,*d* and Ahio was walking in front of it. ⁵David and the whole house of Israel were celebrating with all their might before the LORD, with songs*e* and with harps, lyres, tambourines, sistrums and cymbals.

⁶When they came to the threshing floor of Nacon, Uzzah reached out and took hold of the ark of God, because the oxen stumbled. ⁷The LORD's anger burned against Uzzah because of his irreverent act; therefore God struck him down and he died there beside the ark of God.

⁸Then David was angry because the LORD's wrath had broken out against Uzzah, and to this day that place is called Perez Uzzah.*f*

⁹David was afraid of the LORD that day and said, "How can the ark of the LORD ever come to me?" ¹⁰He was not willing to take the ark of the LORD to be with him in the City of David. Instead, he took it aside to the house of Obed-Edom the Gittite. ¹¹The ark of the LORD remained in the house of Obed-Edom the Gittite for three months, and the LORD blessed him and his entire household.

¹²Now King David was told, "The LORD has blessed the household of Obed-Edom and everything he has, because of the ark of God." So David went down and brought up the ark of God from the house of Obed-Edom to the City of David with rejoicing. ¹³When those who were carrying the ark of the LORD had taken six steps, he sacrificed a bull and a fattened calf. ¹⁴David, wearing a linen ephod, danced before the LORD with all his might, ¹⁵while he and the entire house of Israel brought up the ark of the LORD with shouts and the sound of trumpets.

¹⁶As the ark of the LORD was entering the City of David, Michal daughter of Saul watched from a window. And when she saw King David leaping and dancing before the LORD, she despised him in her heart.

¹⁷They brought the ark of the LORD and set it in its place inside the tent that David had pitched for it, and David sacrificed burnt offerings and fellowship offerings*g* before the LORD. ¹⁸After he had finished sacrificing the burnt offerings and fellowship offerings, he blessed the people in the name of the LORD Almighty. ¹⁹Then he gave a loaf of bread, a cake of dates and a cake of raisins to each person in the whole crowd of Israelites, both men and women. And all the people went to their homes.

²⁰When David returned home to bless his household, Michal daughter of Saul came out to meet him and said, "How the king of Israel has distinguished himself today, disrobing in the sight of the slave girls of his servants as any vulgar fellow would!"

²¹David said to Michal, "It was before the LORD, who chose me rather than your father or anyone from his house when he appointed me ruler over the LORD's people Israel—I will celebrate before the LORD. ²²I will become even more undignified than this, and I will be

---

a 25 Septuagint (see also 1 Chron. 14:16); Hebrew *Geba*   *b 2* That is, Kiriath Jearim; Hebrew *Baale Judah*, a variant of *Baalah of Judah*   *c 2* Hebrew; Septuagint and Vulgate do not have *the Name*.   *d 3,4* Dead Sea Scrolls and some Septuagint manuscripts; Masoretic Text *cart* *4and they brought it with the ark of God from the house of Abinadab, which was on the hill*   *e 5* See Dead Sea Scrolls, Septuagint and 1 Chronicles 13:8; Masoretic Text *celebrating before the LORD with all kinds of instruments made of pine.*   *f 8* Perez Uzzah means *outbreak against Uzzah.*   *g 17* Traditionally *peace offerings*; also in verse 18

humiliated in my own eyes. But by these slave girls you spoke of, I will be held in honor."
²³And Michal daughter of Saul had no children to the day of her death.

God's Promise to David

7 After the king was settled in his palace and the LORD had given him rest from all his enemies around him, ²he said to Nathan the prophet, "Here I am, living in a palace of cedar, while the ark of God remains in a tent."

³Nathan replied to the king, "Whatever you have in mind, go ahead and do it, for the LORD is with you."

⁴That night the word of the LORD came to Nathan, saying:

⁵"Go and tell my servant David, 'This is what the LORD says: Are you the one to build me a house to dwell in? ⁶I have not dwelt in a house from the day I brought the Israelites up out of Egypt to this day. I have been moving from place to place with a tent as my dwelling. ⁷Wherever I have moved with all the Israelites, did I ever say to any of their rulers whom I commanded to shepherd my people Israel, "Why have you not built me a house of cedar?" '

⁸"Now then, tell my servant David, 'This is what the LORD Almighty says: I took you from the pasture and from following the flock to be ruler over my people Israel. ⁹I have been with you wherever you have gone, and I have cut off all your enemies from before you. Now I will make your name great, like the names of the greatest men of the earth. ¹⁰And I will provide a place for my people Israel and will plant them so that they can have a home of their own and no longer be disturbed. Wicked people will not oppress them anymore, as they did at the beginning ¹¹and have done ever since the time I appointed leadersᵃ over my people Israel. I will also give you rest from all your enemies.

" 'The LORD declares to you that the LORD himself will establish a house for you: ¹²When your days are over and you rest with your fathers, I will raise up your offspring to succeed you, who will come from your own body, and I will establish his kingdom. ¹³He is the one who will build a house for my Name, and I will establish the throne of his kingdom forever. ¹⁴I will be his father, and he will be my son. When he does wrong, I will punish him with the rod of men, with floggings inflicted by men. ¹⁵But my love will never be taken away from him, as I took it away from Saul, whom I removed from before you. ¹⁶Your house and your kingdom will endure forever before meᵇ; your throne will be established forever.' "

¹⁷Nathan reported to David all the words of this entire revelation.

David's Prayer

¹⁸Then King David went in and sat before the LORD, and he said:

"Who am I, O Sovereign LORD, and what is my family, that you have brought me this far? ¹⁹And as if this were not enough in your sight, O Sovereign LORD, you have also spoken about the future of the house of your servant. Is this your usual way of dealing with man, O Sovereign LORD?

²⁰"What more can David say to you? For you know your servant, O Sovereign LORD. ²¹For the sake of your word and according to your will, you have done this great thing and made it known to your servant.

²²"How great you are, O Sovereign LORD! There is no one like you, and there is no God but you, as we have heard with our own ears. ²³And who is like your people Israel—the one nation on earth that God went out to redeem as a people for himself, and to make a name for himself, and to perform great and awesome wonders by

---

ᵃ11 Traditionally *judges*   ᵇ16 Some Hebrew manuscripts and Septuagint; most Hebrew manuscripts *you*

driving out nations and their gods from before your people, whom you redeemed from Egypt?[a] 24You have established your people Israel as your very own forever, and you, O LORD, have become their God.

25"And now, LORD God, keep forever the promise you have made concerning your servant and his house. Do as you promised, 26so that your name will be great forever. Then men will say, 'The LORD Almighty is God over Israel!' And the house of your servant David will be established before you.

27"O LORD Almighty, God of Israel, you have revealed this to your servant, saying, 'I will build a house for you.' So your servant has found courage to offer you this prayer. 28O Sovereign LORD, you are God! Your words are trustworthy, and you have promised these good things to your servant. 29Now be pleased to bless the house of your servant, that it may continue forever in your sight; for you, O Sovereign LORD, have spoken, and with your blessing the house of your servant will be blessed forever."

---

a 23 See Septuagint and 1 Chron. 17:21; Hebrew *wonders for your land and before your people, whom you redeemed from Egypt, from the nations and their gods.*

ADDRESSING QUESTIONS

7:11–17
Human Experience

October 27, 1993 was a terrible day for the people of Laguna Beach, California. Smoke-filled skies loomed in the east, warning them that a raging fire was coming closer to their community. Of course, everyone hoped this fire would pass by their beautiful city. Other fires had. But this one, pushed by desert winds, raced through the canyon directly toward the city.

The residents knew they had to get out of town, but what would they take with them? And what would be left when they returned? The cedar-shake roofs that decorated their exclusive homes looked beautiful, but they proved to be nothing more than dry kindling. One spark, and they erupted into flames.

A picture that appeared in newspapers across the country revealed the extent of the damage. The shot, taken from a helicopter, showed block after block of burned-out homes. Nothing remained of the palatial homes but foundations, chimneys, and ashes.

Except one particular white house. It stood in the middle of a burned-out neighborhood, unharmed amid homes that had burned to the ground. Its owner, contractor To Bui, had planned ahead. He had built the house himself, and he had built it to last, constructing the roof out of concrete and tile. The flames had threatened his house, but they never hurt it.

It's no wonder so many people approached Bui after the fire and asked him to rebuild their homes. The fact that his house stood while others fell testified to the reliability of his work.

In a sense, the same thing could be said about God. While nations rise and fall, God is building a kingdom that will endure forever. This passage shows how God was preparing for that kingdom 3000 years ago.

These verses promise that a son of David will reign on David's throne *forever*. We might consider this an overstatement, except that in Christ it literally—in every aspect—came to pass. Jesus received the blood right to David's *earthly* throne through his mother, Mary, and the legal right through his stepfather, Joseph, who were both of David's line.

In 70 A.D. the Roman army destroyed the temple in Jerusalem. At that time, all of Israel's ancient birth records were lost. If someone today would claim to be the Messiah, the son of David, he would have no way to prove it. Whoever the Messiah was, he had to live before 70 A.D. so his Davidic lineage could be authenticated. So in an earthly sense, Jesus meets the qualifications of the Messiah.

What about Jesus' *eternal* throne? Only an eternal being can reign forever. And Jesus, as we learn from the New Testament, is the eternal Son of God (see 1 John 5:20 [page 1626]).

The kingdom is already here, though it is still "under construction." Wouldn't you like to be a part of it? You can, if you'll simply accept the leadership of its king, Jesus Christ.

David's Victories

8 In the course of time, David defeated the Philistines and subdued them, and he took Metheg Ammah from the control of the Philistines.

²David also defeated the Moabites. He made them lie down on the ground and measured them off with a length of cord. Every two lengths of them were put to death, and the third length was allowed to live. So the Moabites became subject to David and brought tribute.

³Moreover, David fought Hadadezer son of Rehob, king of Zobah, when he went to restore his control along the Euphrates River. ⁴David captured a thousand of his chariots, seven thousand charioteers*a* and twenty thousand foot soldiers. He hamstrung all but a hundred of the chariot horses.

⁵When the Arameans of Damascus came to help Hadadezer king of Zobah, David struck down twenty-two thousand of them. ⁶He put garrisons in the Aramean kingdom of Damascus, and the Arameans became subject to him and brought tribute. The LORD gave David victory wherever he went.

⁷David took the gold shields that belonged to the officers of Hadadezer and brought them to Jerusalem. ⁸From Tebah*b* and Berothai, towns that belonged to Hadadezer, King David took a great quantity of bronze.

⁹When Tou*c* king of Hamath heard that David had defeated the entire army of Hadadezer, ¹⁰he sent his son Joram*d* to King David to greet him and congratulate him on his victory in battle over Hadadezer, who had been at war with Tou. Joram brought with him articles of silver and gold and bronze.

¹¹King David dedicated these articles to the LORD, as he had done with the silver and gold from all the nations he had subdued: ¹²Edom*e* and Moab, the Ammonites and the Philistines, and Amalek. He also dedicated the plunder taken from Hadadezer son of Rehob, king of Zobah.

¹³And David became famous after he returned from striking down eighteen thousand Edomites*f* in the Valley of Salt.

¹⁴He put garrisons throughout Edom, and all the Edomites became subject to David. The LORD gave David victory wherever he went.

David's Officials

¹⁵David reigned over all Israel, doing what was just and right for all his people. ¹⁶Joab son of Zeruiah was over the army; Jehoshaphat son of Ahilud was recorder; ¹⁷Zadok son of Ahitub and Ahimelech son of Abiathar were priests; Seraiah was secretary; ¹⁸Benaiah son of Jehoiada was over the Kerethites and Pelethites; and David's sons were royal advisers.*g*

David and Mephibosheth

9 David asked, "Is there anyone still left of the house of Saul to whom I can show kindness for Jonathan's sake?"

²Now there was a servant of Saul's household named Ziba. They called him to appear before David, and the king said to him, "Are you Ziba?"

"Your servant," he replied.

³The king asked, "Is there no one still left of the house of Saul to whom I can show God's kindness?"

Ziba answered the king, "There is still a son of Jonathan; he is crippled in both feet."

⁴"Where is he?" the king asked.

Ziba answered, "He is at the house of Makir son of Ammiel in Lo Debar."

---

a 4 Septuagint (see also Dead Sea Scrolls and 1 Chron. 18:4); Masoretic Text *captured seventeen hundred of his charioteers*
b 8 See some Septuagint manuscripts (see also 1 Chron. 18:8); Hebrew *Betah.*   *c 9* Hebrew *Toi,* a variant of *Tou;* also in verse 10   *d 10* A variant of *Hadoram*   *e 12* Some Hebrew manuscripts, Septuagint and Syriac (see also 1 Chron. 18:11); most Hebrew manuscripts *Aram*   *f 13* A few Hebrew manuscripts, Septuagint and Syriac (see also 1 Chron. 18:12); most Hebrew manuscripts *Aram* (that is, Arameans)   *g 18* Or *were priests*

⁵So King David had him brought from Lo Debar, from the house of Makir son of Ammiel. ⁶When Mephibosheth son of Jonathan, the son of Saul, came to David, he bowed down to pay him honor.

David said, "Mephibosheth!"

"Your servant," he replied.

⁷"Don't be afraid," David said to him, "for I will surely show you kindness for the sake of your father Jonathan. I will restore to you all the land that belonged to your grandfather Saul, and you will always eat at my table."

⁸Mephibosheth bowed down and said, "What is your servant, that you should notice a dead dog like me?"

⁹Then the king summoned Ziba, Saul's servant, and said to him, "I have given your master's grandson everything that belonged to Saul and his family. ¹⁰You and your sons and your servants are to farm the land for him and bring in the crops, so that your master's grandson may be provided for. And Mephibosheth, grandson of your master, will always eat at my table." (Now Ziba had fifteen sons and twenty servants.)

¹¹Then Ziba said to the king, "Your servant will do whatever my lord the king commands his servant to do." So Mephibosheth ate at David's*ᵃ* table like one of the king's sons.

¹²Mephibosheth had a young son named Mica, and all the members of Ziba's household were servants of Mephibosheth. ¹³And Mephibosheth lived in Jerusalem, because he always ate at the king's table, and he was crippled in both feet.

David Defeats the Ammonites

10 In the course of time, the king of the Ammonites died, and his son Hanun succeeded him as king. ²David thought, "I will show kindness to Hanun son of Nahash, just as his father showed kindness to me." So David sent a delegation to express his sympathy to Hanun concerning his father.

When David's men came to the land of the Ammonites, ³the Ammonite nobles said to Hanun their lord, "Do you think David is honoring your father by sending men to you to express sympathy? Hasn't David sent them to you to explore the city and spy it out and overthrow it?" ⁴So Hanun seized David's men, shaved off half of each man's beard, cut off their garments in the middle at the buttocks, and sent them away.

⁵When David was told about this, he sent messengers to meet the men, for they were greatly humiliated. The king said, "Stay at Jericho till your beards have grown, and then come back."

⁶When the Ammonites realized that they had become a stench in David's nostrils, they hired twenty thousand Aramean foot soldiers from Beth Rehob and Zobah, as well as the king of Maacah with a thousand men, and also twelve thousand men from Tob.

⁷On hearing this, David sent Joab out with the entire army of fighting men. ⁸The Ammonites came out and drew up in battle formation at the entrance to their city gate, while the Arameans of Zobah and Rehob and the men of Tob and Maacah were by themselves in the open country.

⁹Joab saw that there were battle lines in front of him and behind him; so he selected some of the best troops in Israel and deployed them against the Arameans. ¹⁰He put the rest of the men under the command of Abishai his brother and deployed them against the Ammonites. ¹¹Joab said, "If the Arameans are too strong for me, then you are to come to my rescue; but if the Ammonites are too strong for you, then I will come to rescue you. ¹²Be strong and let us fight bravely for our people and the cities of our God. The LORD will do what is good in his sight."

¹³Then Joab and the troops with him advanced to fight the Arameans, and they fled

ᵃ 11 Septuagint; Hebrew *my*

before him. ¹⁴When the Ammonites saw that the Arameans were fleeing, they fled before Abishai and went inside the city. So Joab returned from fighting the Ammonites and came to Jerusalem.

¹⁵After the Arameans saw that they had been routed by Israel, they regrouped. ¹⁶Hadadezer had Arameans brought from beyond the River*ᵃ*; they went to Helam, with Shobach the commander of Hadadezer's army leading them.

¹⁷When David was told of this, he gathered all Israel, crossed the Jordan and went to Helam. The Arameans formed their battle lines to meet David and fought against him. ¹⁸But they fled before Israel, and David killed seven hundred of their charioteers and forty thousand of their foot soldiers.*ᵇ* He also struck down Shobach the commander of their army, and he died there. ¹⁹When all the kings who were vassals of Hadadezer saw that they had been defeated by Israel, they made peace with the Israelites and became subject to them.

So the Arameans were afraid to help the Ammonites anymore.

David and Bathsheba

11 In the spring, at the time when kings go off to war, David sent Joab out with the king's men and the whole Israelite army. They destroyed the Ammonites and besieged Rabbah. But David remained in Jerusalem.

²One evening David got up from his bed and walked around on the roof of the palace. From the roof he saw a woman bathing. The woman was very beautiful, ³and David sent someone to find out about her. The man said, "Isn't this Bathsheba, the daughter of Eliam and the wife of Uriah the Hittite?" ⁴Then David sent messengers to get her. She came to

---

ᵃ16 That is, the Euphrates   *ᵇ18* Some Septuagint manuscripts (see also 1 Chron. 19:18); Hebrew *horsemen*

▒▒▒ KNOWING YOURSELF ▒▒▒

11:1–27
Sin

If anybody ever seemed safe from the lure of sexual temptation, it was King David. Time and again he demonstrated his disciplined devotion to God. Yet in many ways David was no different than any other man or woman. He was vulnerable to the appeal of illicit sensual pleasure. His tragic mistake stands as a stark reminder that such dangers must be avoided.

As the story opens in chapter 11, we find that David stayed home while his army went to battle. After overcoming some of his greatest opponents, David may have felt like he deserved a break. He may have been tired, a circumstance that provided the perfect setup for a fall.

One evening while strolling on the roof of the palace, the king saw something that forever changed his life. Actually, he saw some*one*—a beautiful woman bathing.

Did he know she would be there? Did he plan his walk to allow himself a peek? We'll never know. But we do know that he was in the wrong place at the wrong time.

When most God-followers find themselves in morally compromising situations, they look for ways to get out as fast as they can. David didn't do that. Instead, he pursued the situation further. He found out who the woman was. Then he invited her to his room, and he slept with her.

When she discovered she was pregnant, David brought her husband home in an attempt to create a cover-up. But the soldier refused to sleep with his wife while his comrades were risking their lives in battle. So David had to take his scheme one step further. During the next battle, the king gave orders to have the woman's husband killed on the front lines.

David's severe actions demonstrate how unbridled sexual appetites can destroy people, causing them to do things that were previously unthinkable. But people who struggle with sin in this area can still come to God for forgiveness. David ran from God for almost an entire year before finally admitting what he had done. He writes about the joy of God's forgiveness in the book of Psalms, chapters 32 (page 681) and 51 (page 701). The mercy David found is available to us today if we'll just reach out for it.

him, and he slept with her. (She had purified herself from her uncleanness.) Then[a] she went back home. [5]The woman conceived and sent word to David, saying, "I am pregnant."

[6]So David sent this word to Joab: "Send me Uriah the Hittite." And Joab sent him to David. [7]When Uriah came to him, David asked him how Joab was, how the soldiers were and how the war was going. [8]Then David said to Uriah, "Go down to your house and wash your feet." So Uriah left the palace, and a gift from the king was sent after him. [9]But Uriah slept at the entrance to the palace with all his master's servants and did not go down to his house.

[10]When David was told, "Uriah did not go home," he asked him, "Haven't you just come from a distance? Why didn't you go home?"

[11]Uriah said to David, "The ark and Israel and Judah are staying in tents, and my master Joab and my lord's men are camped in the open fields. How could I go to my house to eat and drink and lie with my wife? As surely as you live, I will not do such a thing!"

[12]Then David said to him, "Stay here one more day, and tomorrow I will send you back." So Uriah remained in Jerusalem that day and the next. [13]At David's invitation, he ate and drank with him, and David made him drunk. But in the evening Uriah went out to sleep on his mat among his master's servants; he did not go home.

[14]In the morning David wrote a letter to Joab and sent it with Uriah. [15]In it he wrote, "Put Uriah in the front line where the fighting is fiercest. Then withdraw from him so he will be struck down and die."

[16]So while Joab had the city under siege, he put Uriah at a place where he knew the strongest defenders were. [17]When the men of the city came out and fought against Joab, some of the men in David's army fell; moreover, Uriah the Hittite died.

[18]Joab sent David a full account of the battle. [19]He instructed the messenger: "When you have finished giving the king this account of the battle, [20]the king's anger may flare up, and he may ask you, 'Why did you get so close to the city to fight? Didn't you know they would shoot arrows from the wall? [21]Who killed Abimelech son of Jerub-Besheth[b]? Didn't a woman throw an upper millstone on him from the wall, so that he died in Thebez? Why did you get so close to the wall?' If he asks you this, then say to him, 'Also, your servant Uriah the Hittite is dead.'"

[22]The messenger set out, and when he arrived he told David everything Joab had sent him to say. [23]The messenger said to David, "The men overpowered us and came out against us in the open, but we drove them back to the entrance to the city gate. [24]Then the archers shot arrows at your servants from the wall, and some of the king's men died. Moreover, your servant Uriah the Hittite is dead."

[25]David told the messenger, "Say this to Joab: 'Don't let this upset you; the sword devours one as well as another. Press the attack against the city and destroy it.' Say this to encourage Joab."

[26]When Uriah's wife heard that her husband was dead, she mourned for him. [27]After the time of mourning was over, David had her brought to his house, and she became his wife and bore him a son. But the thing David had done displeased the LORD.

Nathan Rebukes David

12 The LORD sent Nathan to David. When he came to him, he said, "There were two men in a certain town, one rich and the other poor. [2]The rich man had a very large number of sheep and cattle, [3]but the poor man had nothing except one little ewe lamb he had bought. He raised it, and it grew up with him and his children. It shared his food, drank from his cup and even slept in his arms. It was like a daughter to him.

[4]"Now a traveler came to the rich man, but the rich man refrained from taking one of

---

[a]4 Or with her. When she purified herself from her uncleanness.   [b]21 Also known as Jerub-Baal (that is, Gideon)

his own sheep or cattle to prepare a meal for the traveler who had come to him. Instead, he took the ewe lamb that belonged to the poor man and prepared it for the one who had come to him."

⁵David burned with anger against the man and said to Nathan, "As surely as the LORD lives, the man who did this deserves to die! ⁶He must pay for that lamb four times over, because he did such a thing and had no pity."

⁷Then Nathan said to David, "You are the man! This is what the LORD, the God of Israel, says: 'I anointed you king over Israel, and I delivered you from the hand of Saul. ⁸I gave your master's house to you, and your master's wives into your arms. I gave you the house of Israel and Judah. And if all this had been too little, I would have given you even more. ⁹Why did you despise the word of the LORD by doing what is evil in his eyes? You struck down Uriah the Hittite with the sword and took his wife to be your own. You killed him with the sword of the Ammonites. ¹⁰Now, therefore, the sword will never depart from your house, because you despised me and took the wife of Uriah the Hittite to be your own.'

¹¹"This is what the LORD says: 'Out of your own household I am going to bring calamity upon you. Before your very eyes I will take your wives and give them to one who is close to you, and he will lie with your wives in broad daylight. ¹²You did it in secret, but I will do this thing in broad daylight before all Israel.'"

¹³Then David said to Nathan, "I have sinned against the LORD."

Nathan replied, "The LORD has taken away your sin. You are not going to die. ¹⁴But because by doing this you have made the enemies of the LORD show utter contempt,ᵃ the son born to you will die."

¹⁵After Nathan had gone home, the LORD struck the child that Uriah's wife had borne to David, and he became ill. ¹⁶David pleaded with God for the child. He fasted and went into his house and spent the nights lying on the ground. ¹⁷The elders of his household stood beside him to get him up from the ground, but he refused, and he would not eat any food with them.

¹⁸On the seventh day the child died. David's servants were afraid to tell him that the child was dead, for they thought, "While the child was still living, we spoke to David but he would not listen to us. How can we tell him the child is dead? He may do something desperate."

¹⁹David noticed that his servants were whispering among themselves and he realized the child was dead. "Is the child dead?" he asked.

"Yes," they replied, "he is dead."

²⁰Then David got up from the ground. After he had washed, put on lotions and changed his clothes, he went into the house of the LORD and worshiped. Then he went to his own house, and at his request they served him food, and he ate.

²¹His servants asked him, "Why are you acting this way? While the child was alive, you fasted and wept, but now that the child is dead, you get up and eat!"

²²He answered, "While the child was still alive, I fasted and wept. I thought, 'Who knows? The LORD may be gracious to me and let the child live.' ²³But now that he is dead, why should I fast? Can I bring him back again? I will go to him, but he will not return to me."

²⁴Then David comforted his wife Bathsheba, and he went to her and lay with her. She gave birth to a son, and they named him Solomon. The LORD loved him; ²⁵and because the LORD loved him, he sent word through Nathan the prophet to name him Jedidiah.ᵇ

²⁶Meanwhile Joab fought against Rabbah of the Ammonites and captured the royal citadel. ²⁷Joab then sent messengers to David, saying, "I have fought against Rabbah and taken its water supply. ²⁸Now muster the rest of the troops and besiege the city and capture it. Otherwise I will take the city, and it will be named after me."

ᵃ*14* Masoretic Text; an ancient Hebrew scribal tradition *this you have shown utter contempt for the LORD*   ᵇ*25* *Jedidiah* means *loved by the LORD.*

²⁹So David mustered the entire army and went to Rabbah, and attacked and captured it. ³⁰He took the crown from the head of their king*ᵃ*—its weight was a talent*ᵇ* of gold, and it was set with precious stones—and it was placed on David's head. He took a great quantity of plunder from the city ³¹and brought out the people who were there, consigning them to labor with saws and with iron picks and axes, and he made them work at brickmaking.*ᶜ* He did this to all the Ammonite towns. Then David and his entire army returned to Jerusalem.

Amnon and Tamar

13 In the course of time, Amnon son of David fell in love with Tamar, the beautiful sister of Absalom son of David.

²Amnon became frustrated to the point of illness on account of his sister Tamar, for she was a virgin, and it seemed impossible for him to do anything to her.

³Now Amnon had a friend named Jonadab son of Shimeah, David's brother. Jonadab was a very shrewd man. ⁴He asked Amnon, "Why do you, the king's son, look so haggard morning after morning? Won't you tell me?"

Amnon said to him, "I'm in love with Tamar, my brother Absalom's sister."

⁵"Go to bed and pretend to be ill," Jonadab said. "When your father comes to see you, say to him, 'I would like my sister Tamar to come and give me something to eat. Let her prepare the food in my sight so I may watch her and then eat it from her hand.'"

⁶So Amnon lay down and pretended to be ill. When the king came to see him, Amnon said to him, "I would like my sister Tamar to come and make some special bread in my sight, so I may eat from her hand."

⁷David sent word to Tamar at the palace: "Go to the house of your brother Amnon and prepare some food for him." ⁸So Tamar went to the house of her brother Amnon, who was lying down. She took some dough, kneaded it, made the bread in his sight and baked it. ⁹Then she took the pan and served him the bread, but he refused to eat.

"Send everyone out of here," Amnon said. So everyone left him. ¹⁰Then Amnon said to Tamar, "Bring the food here into my bedroom so I may eat from your hand." And Tamar took the bread she had prepared and brought it to her brother Amnon in his bedroom. ¹¹But when she took it to him to eat, he grabbed her and said, "Come to bed with me, my sister."

¹²"Don't, my brother!" she said to him. "Don't force me. Such a thing should not be done in Israel! Don't do this wicked thing. ¹³What about me? Where could I get rid of my disgrace? And what about you? You would be like one of the wicked fools in Israel. Please speak to the king; he will not keep me from being married to you." ¹⁴But he refused to listen to her, and since he was stronger than she, he raped her.

¹⁵Then Amnon hated her with intense hatred. In fact, he hated her more than he had loved her. Amnon said to her, "Get up and get out!"

¹⁶"No!" she said to him. "Sending me away would be a greater wrong than what you have already done to me."

But he refused to listen to her. ¹⁷He called his personal servant and said, "Get this woman out of here and bolt the door after her." ¹⁸So his servant put her out and bolted the door after her. She was wearing a richly ornamented*ᵈ* robe, for this was the kind of garment the virgin daughters of the king wore. ¹⁹Tamar put ashes on her head and tore the ornamented*ᵉ* robe she was wearing. She put her hand on her head and went away, weeping aloud as she went.

²⁰Her brother Absalom said to her, "Has that Amnon, your brother, been with you? Be quiet now, my sister; he is your brother. Don't take this thing to heart." And Tamar lived in her brother Absalom's house, a desolate woman.

ᵃ30 Or *of Milcom* (that is, Molech) Hebrew for this clause is uncertain.   *ᵇ30* That is, about 75 pounds (about 34 kilograms)   *ᶜ31* The meaning of the Hebrew for this word is uncertain.   *ᵈ18* The meaning of the Hebrew for this phrase is uncertain.   *ᵉ19* The meaning of

²¹When King David heard all this, he was furious. ²²Absalom never said a word to Amnon, either good or bad; he hated Amnon because he had disgraced his sister Tamar.

Absalom Kills Amnon

²³Two years later, when Absalom's sheepshearers were at Baal Hazor near the border of Ephraim, he invited all the king's sons to come there. ²⁴Absalom went to the king and said, "Your servant has had shearers come. Will the king and his officials please join me?"

²⁵"No, my son," the king replied. "All of us should not go; we would only be a burden to you." Although Absalom urged him, he still refused to go, but gave him his blessing.

²⁶Then Absalom said, "If not, please let my brother Amnon come with us."

The king asked him, "Why should he go with you?" ²⁷But Absalom urged him, so he sent with him Amnon and the rest of the king's sons.

²⁸Absalom ordered his men, "Listen! When Amnon is in high spirits from drinking wine and I say to you, 'Strike Amnon down,' then kill him. Don't be afraid. Have not I given you this order? Be strong and brave." ²⁹So Absalom's men did to Amnon what Absalom had ordered. Then all the king's sons got up, mounted their mules and fled.

³⁰While they were on their way, the report came to David: "Absalom has struck down all the king's sons; not one of them is left." ³¹The king stood up, tore his clothes and lay down on the ground; and all his servants stood by with their clothes torn.

³²But Jonadab son of Shimeah, David's brother, said, "My lord should not think that they killed all the princes; only Amnon is dead. This has been Absalom's expressed intention ever since the day Amnon raped his sister Tamar. ³³My lord the king should not be concerned about the report that all the king's sons are dead. Only Amnon is dead."

³⁴Meanwhile, Absalom had fled.

Now the man standing watch looked up and saw many people on the road west of him, coming down the side of the hill. The watchman went and told the king, "I see men in the direction of Horonaim, on the side of the hill."ᵃ

³⁵Jonadab said to the king, "See, the king's sons are here; it has happened just as your servant said."

³⁶As he finished speaking, the king's sons came in, wailing loudly. The king, too, and all his servants wept very bitterly.

³⁷Absalom fled and went to Talmai son of Ammihud, the king of Geshur. But King David mourned for his son every day.

³⁸After Absalom fled and went to Geshur, he stayed there three years. ³⁹And the spirit of the kingᵇ longed to go to Absalom, for he was consoled concerning Amnon's death.

Absalom Returns to Jerusalem

14 Joab son of Zeruiah knew that the king's heart longed for Absalom. ²So Joab sent someone to Tekoa and had a wise woman brought from there. He said to her, "Pretend you are in mourning. Dress in mourning clothes, and don't use any cosmetic lotions. Act like a woman who has spent many days grieving for the dead. ³Then go to the king and speak these words to him." And Joab put the words in her mouth.

⁴When the woman from Tekoa wentᶜ to the king, she fell with her face to the ground to pay him honor, and she said, "Help me, O king!"

⁵The king asked her, "What is troubling you?"

She said, "I am indeed a widow; my husband is dead. ⁶I your servant had two sons. They got into a fight with each other in the field, and no one was there to separate them. One struck the other and killed him. ⁷Now the whole clan has risen up against your servant; they say, 'Hand over the one who struck his brother down, so that we may put

---

ᵃ34 Septuagint; Hebrew does not have this sentence.   ᵇ39 Dead Sea Scrolls and some Septuagint manuscripts; Masoretic Text *But the spirit of,* David the king   ᶜ4 Many Hebrew manuscripts, Septuagint, Vulgate and Syriac; most Hebrew manuscripts *spoke*

him to death for the life of his brother whom he killed; then we will get rid of the heir as well.' They would put out the only burning coal I have left, leaving my husband neither name nor descendant on the face of the earth."

⁸The king said to the woman, "Go home, and I will issue an order in your behalf."

⁹But the woman from Tekoa said to him, "My lord the king, let the blame rest on me and on my father's family, and let the king and his throne be without guilt."

¹⁰The king replied, "If anyone says anything to you, bring him to me, and he will not bother you again."

¹¹She said, "Then let the king invoke the Lᴏʀᴅ his God to prevent the avenger of blood from adding to the destruction, so that my son will not be destroyed."

"As surely as the Lᴏʀᴅ lives," he said, "not one hair of your son's head will fall to the ground."

¹²Then the woman said, "Let your servant speak a word to my lord the king."

"Speak," he replied.

¹³The woman said, "Why then have you devised a thing like this against the people of God? When the king says this, does he not convict himself, for the king has not brought back his banished son? ¹⁴Like water spilled on the ground, which cannot be recovered, so we must die. But God does not take away life; instead, he devises ways so that a banished person may not remain estranged from him.

¹⁵"And now I have come to say this to my lord the king because the people have made me afraid. Your servant thought, 'I will speak to the king; perhaps he will do what his servant asks. ¹⁶Perhaps the king will agree to deliver his servant from the hand of the man who is trying to cut off both me and my son from the inheritance God gave us.'

¹⁷"And now your servant says, 'May the word of my lord the king bring me rest, for my lord the king is like an angel of God in discerning good and evil. May the Lᴏʀᴅ your God be with you.'"

¹⁸Then the king said to the woman, "Do not keep from me the answer to what I am going to ask you."

"Let my lord the king speak," the woman said.

¹⁹The king asked, "Isn't the hand of Joab with you in all this?"

The woman answered, "As surely as you live, my lord the king, no one can turn to the right or to the left from anything my lord the king says. Yes, it was your servant Joab who instructed me to do this and who put all these words into the mouth of your servant. ²⁰Your servant Joab did this to change the present situation. My lord has wisdom like that of an angel of God—he knows everything that happens in the land."

²¹The king said to Joab, "Very well, I will do it. Go, bring back the young man Absalom."

²²Joab fell with his face to the ground to pay him honor, and he blessed the king. Joab said, "Today your servant knows that he has found favor in your eyes, my lord the king, because the king has granted his servant's request."

²³Then Joab went to Geshur and brought Absalom back to Jerusalem. ²⁴But the king said, "He must go to his own house; he must not see my face." So Absalom went to his own house and did not see the face of the king.

²⁵In all Israel there was not a man so highly praised for his handsome appearance as Absalom. From the top of his head to the sole of his foot there was no blemish in him. ²⁶Whenever he cut the hair of his head—he used to cut his hair from time to time when it became too heavy for him—he would weigh it, and its weight was two hundred shekels[a] by the royal standard.

²⁷Three sons and a daughter were born to Absalom. The daughter's name was Tamar, and she became a beautiful woman.

²⁸Absalom lived two years in Jerusalem without seeing the king's face. ²⁹Then Absalom sent for Joab in order to send him to the king, but Joab refused to come to him. So he

a26 That is, about 5 pounds (about 2.3 kilograms)

sent a second time, but he refused to come. ³⁰Then he said to his servants, "Look, Joab's field is next to mine, and he has barley there. Go and set it on fire." So Absalom's servants set the field on fire.

³¹Then Joab did go to Absalom's house and he said to him, "Why have your servants set my field on fire?"

³²Absalom said to Joab, "Look, I sent word to you and said, 'Come here so I can send you to the king to ask, "Why have I come from Geshur? It would be better for me if I were still there!" ' Now then, I want to see the king's face, and if I am guilty of anything, let him put me to death."

³³So Joab went to the king and told him this. Then the king summoned Absalom, and he came in and bowed down with his face to the ground before the king. And the king kissed Absalom.

Absalom's Conspiracy

15 In the course of time, Absalom provided himself with a chariot and horses and with fifty men to run ahead of him. ²He would get up early and stand by the side of the road leading to the city gate. Whenever anyone came with a complaint to be placed before the king for a decision, Absalom would call out to him, "What town are you from?" He would answer, "Your servant is from one of the tribes of Israel." ³Then Absalom would say to him, "Look, your claims are valid and proper, but there is no representative of the king to hear you." ⁴And Absalom would add, "If only I were appointed judge in the land! Then everyone who has a complaint or case could come to me and I would see that he gets justice."

⁵Also, whenever anyone approached him to bow down before him, Absalom would reach out his hand, take hold of him and kiss him. ⁶Absalom behaved in this way toward all the Israelites who came to the king asking for justice, and so he stole the hearts of the men of Israel.

⁷At the end of four*ᵃ* years, Absalom said to the king, "Let me go to Hebron and fulfill a vow I made to the LORD. ⁸While your servant was living at Geshur in Aram, I made this vow: 'If the LORD takes me back to Jerusalem, I will worship the LORD in Hebron.*ᵇ* ' "

⁹The king said to him, "Go in peace." So he went to Hebron.

¹⁰Then Absalom sent secret messengers throughout the tribes of Israel to say, "As soon as you hear the sound of the trumpets, then say, 'Absalom is king in Hebron.' " ¹¹Two hundred men from Jerusalem had accompanied Absalom. They had been invited as guests and went quite innocently, knowing nothing about the matter. ¹²While Absalom was offering sacrifices, he also sent for Ahithophel the Gilonite, David's counselor, to come from Giloh, his hometown. And so the conspiracy gained strength, and Absalom's following kept on increasing.

David Flees

¹³A messenger came and told David, "The hearts of the men of Israel are with Absalom."

¹⁴Then David said to all his officials who were with him in Jerusalem, "Come! We must flee, or none of us will escape from Absalom. We must leave immediately, or he will move quickly to overtake us and bring ruin upon us and put the city to the sword."

¹⁵The king's officials answered him, "Your servants are ready to do whatever our lord the king chooses."

¹⁶The king set out, with his entire household following him; but he left ten concubines to take care of the palace. ¹⁷So the king set out, with all the people following him, and they halted at a place some distance away. ¹⁸All his men marched past him, along with

---

ᵃ 7 Some Septuagint manuscripts, Syriac and Josephus; Hebrew *forty* have *in Hebron.*   *ᵇ 8* Some Septuagint manuscripts; Hebrew does not

all the Kerethites and Pelethites; and all the six hundred Gittites who had accompanied him from Gath marched before the king.

¹⁹The king said to Ittai the Gittite, "Why should you come along with us? Go back and stay with King Absalom. You are a foreigner, an exile from your homeland. ²⁰You came only yesterday. And today shall I make you wander about with us, when I do not know where I am going? Go back, and take your countrymen. May kindness and faithfulness be with you."

²¹But Ittai replied to the king, "As surely as the LORD lives, and as my lord the king lives, wherever my lord the king may be, whether it means life or death, there will your servant be."

²²David said to Ittai, "Go ahead, march on." So Ittai the Gittite marched on with all his men and the families that were with him.

²³The whole countryside wept aloud as all the people passed by. The king also crossed the Kidron Valley, and all the people moved on toward the desert.

²⁴Zadok was there, too, and all the Levites who were with him were carrying the ark of the covenant of God. They set down the ark of God, and Abiathar offered sacrifices*a* until all the people had finished leaving the city.

²⁵Then the king said to Zadok, "Take the ark of God back into the city. If I find favor in the LORD's eyes, he will bring me back and let me see it and his dwelling place again. ²⁶But if he says, 'I am not pleased with you,' then I am ready; let him do to me whatever seems good to him."

²⁷The king also said to Zadok the priest, "Aren't you a seer? Go back to the city in peace, with your son Ahimaaz and Jonathan son of Abiathar. You and Abiathar take your two sons with you. ²⁸I will wait at the fords in the desert until word comes from you to inform me." ²⁹So Zadok and Abiathar took the ark of God back to Jerusalem and stayed there.

³⁰But David continued up the Mount of Olives, weeping as he went; his head was covered and he was barefoot. All the people with him covered their heads too and were weeping as they went up. ³¹Now David had been told, "Ahithophel is among the conspirators with Absalom." So David prayed, "O LORD, turn Ahithophel's counsel into foolishness."

³²When David arrived at the summit, where people used to worship God, Hushai the Arkite was there to meet him, his robe torn and dust on his head. ³³David said to him, "If you go with me, you will be a burden to me. ³⁴But if you return to the city and say to Absalom, 'I will be your servant, O king; I was your father's servant in the past, but now I will be your servant,' then you can help me by frustrating Ahithophel's advice. ³⁵Won't the priests Zadok and Abiathar be there with you? Tell them anything you hear in the king's palace. ³⁶Their two sons, Ahimaaz son of Zadok and Jonathan son of Abiathar, are there with them. Send them to me with anything you hear."

³⁷So David's friend Hushai arrived at Jerusalem as Absalom was entering the city.

David and Ziba

16 When David had gone a short distance beyond the summit, there was Ziba, the steward of Mephibosheth, waiting to meet him. He had a string of donkeys saddled and loaded with two hundred loaves of bread, a hundred cakes of raisins, a hundred cakes of figs and a skin of wine.

²The king asked Ziba, "Why have you brought these?"

Ziba answered, "The donkeys are for the king's household to ride on, the bread and fruit are for the men to eat, and the wine is to refresh those who become exhausted in the desert."

³The king then asked, "Where is your master's grandson?"

a24 Or Abiathar went up

Ziba said to him, "He is staying in Jerusalem, because he thinks, 'Today the house of Israel will give me back my grandfather's kingdom.'"

⁴Then the king said to Ziba, "All that belonged to Mephibosheth is now yours."

"I humbly bow," Ziba said. "May I find favor in your eyes, my lord the king."

Shimei Curses David

⁵As King David approached Bahurim, a man from the same clan as Saul's family came out from there. His name was Shimei son of Gera, and he cursed as he came out. ⁶He pelted David and all the king's officials with stones, though all the troops and the special guard were on David's right and left. ⁷As he cursed, Shimei said, "Get out, get out, you man of blood, you scoundrel! ⁸The LORD has repaid you for all the blood you shed in the household of Saul, in whose place you have reigned. The LORD has handed the kingdom over to your son Absalom. You have come to ruin because you are a man of blood!"

⁹Then Abishai son of Zeruiah said to the king, "Why should this dead dog curse my lord the king? Let me go over and cut off his head."

¹⁰But the king said, "What do you and I have in common, you sons of Zeruiah? If he is cursing because the LORD said to him, 'Curse David,' who can ask, 'Why do you do this?'"

¹¹David then said to Abishai and all his officials, "My son, who is of my own flesh, is trying to take my life. How much more, then, this Benjamite! Leave him alone; let him curse, for the LORD has told him to. ¹²It may be that the LORD will see my distress and repay me with good for the cursing I am receiving today."

¹³So David and his men continued along the road while Shimei was going along the hillside opposite him, cursing as he went and throwing stones at him and showering him with dirt. ¹⁴The king and all the people with him arrived at their destination exhausted. And there he refreshed himself.

The Advice of Hushai and Ahithophel

¹⁵Meanwhile, Absalom and all the men of Israel came to Jerusalem, and Ahithophel was with him. ¹⁶Then Hushai the Arkite, David's friend, went to Absalom and said to him, "Long live the king! Long live the king!"

¹⁷Absalom asked Hushai, "Is this the love you show your friend? Why didn't you go with your friend?"

¹⁸Hushai said to Absalom, "No, the one chosen by the LORD, by these people, and by all the men of Israel—his I will be, and I will remain with him. ¹⁹Furthermore, whom should I serve? Should I not serve the son? Just as I served your father, so I will serve you."

²⁰Absalom said to Ahithophel, "Give us your advice. What should we do?"

²¹Ahithophel answered, "Lie with your father's concubines whom he left to take care of the palace. Then all Israel will hear that you have made yourself a stench in your father's nostrils, and the hands of everyone with you will be strengthened." ²²So they pitched a tent for Absalom on the roof, and he lay with his father's concubines in the sight of all Israel.

²³Now in those days the advice Ahithophel gave was like that of one who inquires of God. That was how both David and Absalom regarded all of Ahithophel's advice.

17 Ahithophel said to Absalom, "I would[a] choose twelve thousand men and set out tonight in pursuit of David. ²I would[b] attack him while he is weary and weak. I would[b] strike him with terror, and then all the people with him will flee. I would[b] strike down only the king ³and bring all the people back to you. The death of the man you seek will mean the return of all; all the people will be unharmed." ⁴This plan seemed good to Absalom and to all the elders of Israel.

⁵But Absalom said, "Summon also Hushai the Arkite, so we can hear what he has to say." ⁶When Hushai came to him, Absalom said, "Ahithophel has given this advice. Should we do what he says? If not, give us your opinion."

a 1 Or Let me   b 2 Or will

⁷Hushai replied to Absalom, "The advice Ahithophel has given is not good this time. ⁸You know your father and his men; they are fighters, and as fierce as a wild bear robbed of her cubs. Besides, your father is an experienced fighter; he will not spend the night with the troops. ⁹Even now, he is hidden in a cave or some other place. If he should attack your troops first,ᵃ whoever hears about it will say, 'There has been a slaughter among the troops who follow Absalom.' ¹⁰Then even the bravest soldier, whose heart is like the heart of a lion, will melt with fear, for all Israel knows that your father is a fighter and that those with him are brave.

¹¹"So I advise you: Let all Israel, from Dan to Beersheba—as numerous as the sand on the seashore—be gathered to you, with you yourself leading them into battle. ¹²Then we will attack him wherever he may be found, and we will fall on him as dew settles on the ground. Neither he nor any of his men will be left alive. ¹³If he withdraws into a city, then all Israel will bring ropes to that city, and we will drag it down to the valley until not even a piece of it can be found."

¹⁴Absalom and all the men of Israel said, "The advice of Hushai the Arkite is better than that of Ahithophel." For the Lord had determined to frustrate the good advice of Ahithophel in order to bring disaster on Absalom.

¹⁵Hushai told Zadok and Abiathar, the priests, "Ahithophel has advised Absalom and the elders of Israel to do such and such, but I have advised them to do so and so. ¹⁶Now send a message immediately and tell David, 'Do not spend the night at the fords in the desert; cross over without fail, or the king and all the people with him will be swallowed up.'"

¹⁷Jonathan and Ahimaaz were staying at En Rogel. A servant girl was to go and inform them, and they were to go and tell King David, for they could not risk being seen entering the city. ¹⁸But a young man saw them and told Absalom. So the two of them left quickly and went to the house of a man in Bahurim. He had a well in his courtyard, and they climbed down into it. ¹⁹His wife took a covering and spread it out over the opening of the well and scattered grain over it. No one knew anything about it.

²⁰When Absalom's men came to the woman at the house, they asked, "Where are Ahimaaz and Jonathan?"

The woman answered them, "They crossed over the brook."ᵇ The men searched but found no one, so they returned to Jerusalem.

²¹After the men had gone, the two climbed out of the well and went to inform King David. They said to him, "Set out and cross the river at once; Ahithophel has advised such and such against you." ²²So David and all the people with him set out and crossed the Jordan. By daybreak, no one was left who had not crossed the Jordan.

²³When Ahithophel saw that his advice had not been followed, he saddled his donkey and set out for his house in his hometown. He put his house in order and then hanged himself. So he died and was buried in his father's tomb.

²⁴David went to Mahanaim, and Absalom crossed the Jordan with all the men of Israel. ²⁵Absalom had appointed Amasa over the army in place of Joab. Amasa was the son of a man named Jether,ᶜ an Israeliteᵈ who had married Abigail,ᵉ the daughter of Nahash and sister of Zeruiah the mother of Joab. ²⁶The Israelites and Absalom camped in the land of Gilead.

²⁷When David came to Mahanaim, Shobi son of Nahash from Rabbah of the Ammonites, and Makir son of Ammiel from Lo Debar, and Barzillai the Gileadite from Rogelim ²⁸brought bedding and bowls and articles of pottery. They also brought wheat and barley, flour and roasted grain, beans and lentils,ᶠ ²⁹honey and curds, sheep, and cheese from cows' milk for David and his people to eat. For they said, "The people have become hungry and tired and thirsty in the desert."

ᵃ9 Or *When some of the men fall at the first attack*   ᵇ20 Or *"They passed by the sheep pen toward the water."*
ᶜ25 Hebrew *Ithra,* a variant of *Jether*   ᵈ25 Hebrew and some Septuagint manuscripts; other Septuagint manuscripts (see also 1 Chron. 2:17) *Ishmaelite* or *Jezreelite*   ᵉ25 Hebrew *Abigal,* a variant of *Abigail*   ᶠ28 Most Septuagint manuscripts and Syriac; Hebrew *lentils, and roasted grain*

Absalom's Death

18 David mustered the men who were with him and appointed over them commanders of thousands and commanders of hundreds. ²David sent the troops out—a third under the command of Joab, a third under Joab's brother Abishai son of Zeruiah, and a third under Ittai the Gittite. The king told the troops, "I myself will surely march out with you."

³But the men said, "You must not go out; if we are forced to flee, they won't care about us. Even if half of us die, they won't care; but you are worth ten thousand of us.ᵃ It would be better now for you to give us support from the city."

⁴The king answered, "I will do whatever seems best to you."

So the king stood beside the gate while all the men marched out in units of hundreds and of thousands. ⁵The king commanded Joab, Abishai and Ittai, "Be gentle with the young man Absalom for my sake." And all the troops heard the king giving orders concerning Absalom to each of the commanders.

⁶The army marched into the field to fight Israel, and the battle took place in the forest of Ephraim. ⁷There the army of Israel was defeated by David's men, and the casualties that day were great—twenty thousand men. ⁸The battle spread out over the whole countryside, and the forest claimed more lives that day than the sword.

⁹Now Absalom happened to meet David's men. He was riding his mule, and as the mule went under the thick branches of a large oak, Absalom's head got caught in the tree. He was left hanging in midair, while the mule he was riding kept on going.

¹⁰When one of the men saw this, he told Joab, "I just saw Absalom hanging in an oak tree."

¹¹Joab said to the man who had told him this, "What! You saw him? Why didn't you strike him to the ground right there? Then I would have had to give you ten shekelsᵇ of silver and a warrior's belt."

¹²But the man replied, "Even if a thousand shekelsᶜ were weighed out into my hands, I would not lift my hand against the king's son. In our hearing the king commanded you and Abishai and Ittai, 'Protect the young man Absalom for my sake.'ᵈ ¹³And if I had put my life in jeopardyᵉ—and nothing is hidden from the king—you would have kept your distance from me."

¹⁴Joab said, "I'm not going to wait like this for you." So he took three javelins in his hand and plunged them into Absalom's heart while Absalom was still alive in the oak tree. ¹⁵And ten of Joab's armor-bearers surrounded Absalom, struck him and killed him.

¹⁶Then Joab sounded the trumpet, and the troops stopped pursuing Israel, for Joab halted them. ¹⁷They took Absalom, threw him into a big pit in the forest and piled up a large heap of rocks over him. Meanwhile, all the Israelites fled to their homes.

¹⁸During his lifetime Absalom had taken a pillar and erected it in the King's Valley as a monument to himself, for he thought, "I have no son to carry on the memory of my name." He named the pillar after himself, and it is called Absalom's Monument to this day.

David Mourns

¹⁹Now Ahimaaz son of Zadok said, "Let me run and take the news to the king that the Lᴏʀᴅ has delivered him from the hand of his enemies."

²⁰"You are not the one to take the news today," Joab told him. "You may take the news another time, but you must not do so today, because the king's son is dead."

²¹Then Joab said to a Cushite, "Go, tell the king what you have seen." The Cushite bowed down before Joab and ran off.

ᵃ3 Two Hebrew manuscripts, some Septuagint manuscripts and Vulgate; most Hebrew manuscripts *care; for now there are ten thousand like us*   ᵇ11 That is, about 4 ounces (about 115 grams)   ᶜ12 That is, about 25 pounds (about 11 kilograms)   ᵈ12 A few Hebrew manuscripts, Septuagint, Vulgate and Syriac; most Hebrew manuscripts may be translated *Absalom, whoever you may be.*   ᵉ13 Or *Otherwise, if I had acted treacherously toward him*

²²Ahimaaz son of Zadok again said to Joab, "Come what may, please let me run behind the Cushite."

But Joab replied, "My son, why do you want to go? You don't have any news that will bring you a reward."

²³He said, "Come what may, I want to run."

So Joab said, "Run!" Then Ahimaaz ran by way of the plain*a* and outran the Cushite.

²⁴While David was sitting between the inner and outer gates, the watchman went up to the roof of the gateway by the wall. As he looked out, he saw a man running alone.
²⁵The watchman called out to the king and reported it.

The king said, "If he is alone, he must have good news." And the man came closer and closer.

²⁶Then the watchman saw another man running, and he called down to the gatekeeper, "Look, another man running alone!"

The king said, "He must be bringing good news, too."

²⁷The watchman said, "It seems to me that the first one runs like Ahimaaz son of Zadok."

"He's a good man," the king said. "He comes with good news."

²⁸Then Ahimaaz called out to the king, "All is well!" He bowed down before the king with his face to the ground and said, "Praise be to the LORD your God! He has delivered up the men who lifted their hands against my lord the king."

²⁹The king asked, "Is the young man Absalom safe?"

Ahimaaz answered, "I saw great confusion just as Joab was about to send the king's servant and me, your servant, but I don't know what it was."

³⁰The king said, "Stand aside and wait here." So he stepped aside and stood there.

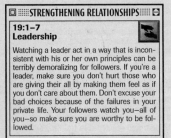

▣ ⫸STRENGTHENING RELATIONSHIPS⫷ ⮂

19:1–7
Leadership

Watching a leader act in a way that is inconsistent with his or her own principles can be terribly demoralizing for followers. If you're a leader, make sure you don't hurt those who are giving their all by making them feel as if you don't care about them. Don't excuse your bad choices because of the failures in your private life. Your followers watch you—all of you—so make sure you are worthy to be followed.

³¹Then the Cushite arrived and said, "My lord the king, hear the good news! The LORD has delivered you today from all who rose up against you."

³²The king asked the Cushite, "Is the young man Absalom safe?"

The Cushite replied, "May the enemies of my lord the king and all who rise up to harm you be like that young man."

³³The king was shaken. He went up to the room over the gateway and wept. As he went, he said: "O my son Absalom! My son, my son Absalom! If only I had died instead of you—O Absalom, my son, my son!"

19 Joab was told, "The king is weeping and mourning for Absalom." ²And for the whole army the victory that day was turned into mourning, because on that day the troops heard it said, "The king is grieving for his son." ³The men stole into the city that day as men steal in who are ashamed when they flee from battle. ⁴The king covered his face and cried aloud, "O my son Absalom! O Absalom, my son, my son!"

⁵Then Joab went into the house to the king and said, "Today you have humiliated all your men, who have just saved your life and the lives of your sons and daughters and the lives of your wives and concubines. ⁶You love those who hate you and hate those who love you. You have made it clear today that the commanders and their men mean nothing to you. I see that you would be pleased if Absalom were alive today and all of us were dead. ⁷Now go out and encourage your men. I swear by the LORD that if you don't go out

a 23 That is, the plain of the Jordan

not a man will be left with you by nightfall. This will be worse for you than all the calamities that have come upon you from your youth till now."

⁸So the king got up and took his seat in the gateway. When the men were told, "The king is sitting in the gateway," they all came before him.

David Returns to Jerusalem

Meanwhile, the Israelites had fled to their homes. ⁹Throughout the tribes of Israel, the people were all arguing with each other, saying, "The king delivered us from the hand of our enemies; he is the one who rescued us from the hand of the Philistines. But now he has fled the country because of Absalom; ¹⁰and Absalom, whom we anointed to rule over us, has died in battle. So why do you say nothing about bringing the king back?"

¹¹King David sent this message to Zadok and Abiathar, the priests: "Ask the elders of Judah, 'Why should you be the last to bring the king back to his palace, since what is being said throughout Israel has reached the king at his quarters? ¹²You are my brothers, my own flesh and blood. So why should you be the last to bring back the king?' ¹³And say to Amasa, 'Are you not my own flesh and blood? May God deal with me, be it ever so severely, if from now on you are not the commander of my army in place of Joab.'"

¹⁴He won over the hearts of all the men of Judah as though they were one man. They sent word to the king, "Return, you and all your men." ¹⁵Then the king returned and went as far as the Jordan.

Now the men of Judah had come to Gilgal to go out and meet the king and bring him across the Jordan. ¹⁶Shimei son of Gera, the Benjamite from Bahurim, hurried down with the men of Judah to meet King David. ¹⁷With him were a thousand Benjamites, along with Ziba, the steward of Saul's household, and his fifteen sons and twenty servants. They rushed to the Jordan, where the king was. ¹⁸They crossed at the ford to take the king's household over and to do whatever he wished.

When Shimei son of Gera crossed the Jordan, he fell prostrate before the king ¹⁹and said to him, "May my lord not hold me guilty. Do not remember how your servant did wrong on the day my lord the king left Jerusalem. May the king put it out of his mind. ²⁰For I your servant know that I have sinned, but today I have come here as the first of the whole house of Joseph to come down and meet my lord the king."

²¹Then Abishai son of Zeruiah said, "Shouldn't Shimei be put to death for this? He cursed the LORD's anointed."

²²David replied, "What do you and I have in common, you sons of Zeruiah? This day you have become my adversaries! Should anyone be put to death in Israel today? Do I not know that today I am king over Israel?" ²³So the king said to Shimei, "You shall not die." And the king promised him on oath.

²⁴Mephibosheth, Saul's grandson, also went down to meet the king. He had not taken care of his feet or trimmed his mustache or washed his clothes from the day the king left until the day he returned safely. ²⁵When he came from Jerusalem to meet the king, the king asked him, "Why didn't you go with me, Mephibosheth?"

²⁶He said, "My lord the king, since I your servant am lame, I said, 'I will have my donkey saddled and will ride on it, so I can go with the king.' But Ziba my servant betrayed me. ²⁷And he has slandered your servant to my lord the king. My lord the king is like an angel of God; so do whatever pleases you. ²⁸All my grandfather's descendants deserved nothing but death from my lord the king, but you gave your servant a place among those who eat at your table. So what right do I have to make any more appeals to the king?"

²⁹The king said to him, "Why say more? I order you and Ziba to divide the fields."

³⁰Mephibosheth said to the king, "Let him take everything, now that my lord the king has arrived home safely."

³¹Barzillai the Gileadite also came down from Rogelim to cross the Jordan with the king and to send him on his way from there. ³²Now Barzillai was a very old man, eighty years

of age. He had provided for the king during his stay in Mahanaim, for he was a very wealthy man. ³³The king said to Barzillai, "Cross over with me and stay with me in Jerusalem, and I will provide for you."

³⁴But Barzillai answered the king, "How many more years will I live, that I should go up to Jerusalem with the king? ³⁵I am now eighty years old. Can I tell the difference between what is good and what is not? Can your servant taste what he eats and drinks? Can I still hear the voices of men and women singers? Why should your servant be an added burden to my lord the king? ³⁶Your servant will cross over the Jordan with the king for a short distance, but why should the king reward me in this way? ³⁷Let your servant return, that I may die in my own town near the tomb of my father and mother. But here is your servant Kimham. Let him cross over with my lord the king. Do for him whatever pleases you."

³⁸The king said, "Kimham shall cross over with me, and I will do for him whatever pleases you. And anything you desire from me I will do for you."

³⁹So all the people crossed the Jordan, and then the king crossed over. The king kissed Barzillai and gave him his blessing, and Barzillai returned to his home.

⁴⁰When the king crossed over to Gilgal, Kimham crossed with him. All the troops of Judah and half the troops of Israel had taken the king over.

⁴¹Soon all the men of Israel were coming to the king and saying to him, "Why did our brothers, the men of Judah, steal the king away and bring him and his household across the Jordan, together with all his men?"

⁴²All the men of Judah answered the men of Israel, "We did this because the king is closely related to us. Why are you angry about it? Have we eaten any of the king's provisions? Have we taken anything for ourselves?"

⁴³Then the men of Israel answered the men of Judah, "We have ten shares in the king; and besides, we have a greater claim on David than you have. So why do you treat us with contempt? Were we not the first to speak of bringing back our king?"

But the men of Judah responded even more harshly than the men of Israel.

Sheba Rebels Against David

20 Now a troublemaker named Sheba son of Bicri, a Benjamite, happened to be there. He sounded the trumpet and shouted,

> "We have no share in David,
>   no part in Jesse's son!
> Every man to his tent, O Israel!"

²So all the men of Israel deserted David to follow Sheba son of Bicri. But the men of Judah stayed by their king all the way from the Jordan to Jerusalem.

³When David returned to his palace in Jerusalem, he took the ten concubines he had left to take care of the palace and put them in a house under guard. He provided for them, but did not lie with them. They were kept in confinement till the day of their death, living as widows.

⁴Then the king said to Amasa, "Summon the men of Judah to come to me within three days, and be here yourself." ⁵But when Amasa went to summon Judah, he took longer than the time the king had set for him.

⁶David said to Abishai, "Now Sheba son of Bicri will do us more harm than Absalom did. Take your master's men and pursue him, or he will find fortified cities and escape from us." ⁷So Joab's men and the Kerethites and Pelethites and all the mighty warriors went out under the command of Abishai. They marched out from Jerusalem to pursue Sheba son of Bicri.

⁸While they were at the great rock in Gibeon, Amasa came to meet them. Joab was wearing his military tunic, and strapped over it at his waist was a belt with a dagger in its sheath. As he stepped forward, it dropped out of its sheath.

⁹Joab said to Amasa, "How are you, my brother?" Then Joab took Amasa by the beard with his right hand to kiss him. ¹⁰Amasa was not on his guard against the dagger in Joab's hand, and Joab plunged it into his belly, and his intestines spilled out on the ground. Without being stabbed again, Amasa died. Then Joab and his brother Abishai pursued Sheba son of Bicri.

¹¹One of Joab's men stood beside Amasa and said, "Whoever favors Joab, and whoever is for David, let him follow Joab!" ¹²Amasa lay wallowing in his blood in the middle of the road, and the man saw that all the troops came to a halt there. When he realized that everyone who came up to Amasa stopped, he dragged him from the road into a field and threw a garment over him. ¹³After Amasa had been removed from the road, all the men went on with Joab to pursue Sheba son of Bicri.

¹⁴Sheba passed through all the tribes of Israel to Abel Beth Maacah[a] and through the entire region of the Berites, who gathered together and followed him. ¹⁵All the troops with Joab came and besieged Sheba in Abel Beth Maacah. They built a siege ramp up to the city, and it stood against the outer fortifications. While they were battering the wall to bring it down, ¹⁶a wise woman called from the city, "Listen! Listen! Tell Joab to come here so I can speak to him." ¹⁷He went toward her, and she asked, "Are you Joab?"

"I am," he answered.

She said, "Listen to what your servant has to say."

"I'm listening," he said.

¹⁸She continued, "Long ago they used to say, 'Get your answer at Abel,' and that settled it. ¹⁹We are the peaceful and faithful in Israel. You are trying to destroy a city that is a mother in Israel. Why do you want to swallow up the LORD's inheritance?"

²⁰"Far be it from me!" Joab replied, "Far be it from me to swallow up or destroy! ²¹That is not the case. A man named Sheba son of Bicri, from the hill country of Ephraim, has lifted up his hand against the king, against David. Hand over this one man, and I'll withdraw from the city."

The woman said to Joab, "His head will be thrown to you from the wall."

²²Then the woman went to all the people with her wise advice, and they cut off the head of Sheba son of Bicri and threw it to Joab. So he sounded the trumpet, and his men dispersed from the city, each returning to his home. And Joab went back to the king in Jerusalem.

²³Joab was over Israel's entire army; Benaiah son of Jehoiada was over the Kerethites and Pelethites; ²⁴Adoniram[b] was in charge of forced labor; Jehoshaphat son of Ahilud was recorder; ²⁵Sheva was secretary; Zadok and Abiathar were priests; ²⁶and Ira the Jairite was David's priest.

The Gibeonites Avenged

21 During the reign of David, there was a famine for three successive years; so David sought the face of the LORD. The LORD said, "It is on account of Saul and his blood-stained house; it is because he put the Gibeonites to death."

²The king summoned the Gibeonites and spoke to them. (Now the Gibeonites were not a part of Israel but were survivors of the Amorites; the Israelites had sworn to ˌspareˌ them, but Saul in his zeal for Israel and Judah had tried to annihilate them.) ³David asked the Gibeonites, "What shall I do for you? How shall I make amends so that you will bless the LORD's inheritance?"

⁴The Gibeonites answered him, "We have no right to demand silver or gold from Saul or his family, nor do we have the right to put anyone in Israel to death."

"What do you want me to do for you?" David asked.

⁵They answered the king, "As for the man who destroyed us and plotted against us so that we have been decimated and have no place anywhere in Israel, ⁶let seven of his

---

a 14 Or Abel, even Beth Maacah; also in verse 15   *b 24 Some Septuagint manuscripts (see also 1 Kings 4:6 and 5:14);*
Hebrew Adoram

male descendants be given to us to be killed and exposed before the LORD at Gibeah of Saul—the LORD's chosen one."

So the king said, "I will give them to you."

⁷The king spared Mephibosheth son of Jonathan, the son of Saul, because of the oath before the LORD between David and Jonathan son of Saul. ⁸But the king took Armoni and Mephibosheth, the two sons of Aiah's daughter Rizpah, whom she had borne to Saul, together with the five sons of Saul's daughter Merab,ᵃ whom she had borne to Adriel son of Barzillai the Meholathite. ⁹He handed them over to the Gibeonites, who killed and exposed them on a hill before the LORD. All seven of them fell together; they were put to death during the first days of the harvest, just as the barley harvest was beginning.

¹⁰Rizpah daughter of Aiah took sackcloth and spread it out for herself on a rock. From the beginning of the harvest till the rain poured down from the heavens on the bodies, she did not let the birds of the air touch them by day or the wild animals by night. ¹¹When David was told what Aiah's daughter Rizpah, Saul's concubine, had done, ¹²he went and took the bones of Saul and his son Jonathan from the citizens of Jabesh Gilead. (They had taken them secretly from the public square at Beth Shan, where the Philistines had hung them after they struck Saul down on Gilboa.) ¹³David brought the bones of Saul and his son Jonathan from there, and the bones of those who had been killed and exposed were gathered up.

¹⁴They buried the bones of Saul and his son Jonathan in the tomb of Saul's father Kish, at Zela in Benjamin, and did everything the king commanded. After that, God answered prayer in behalf of the land.

Wars Against the Philistines

¹⁵Once again there was a battle between the Philistines and Israel. David went down with his men to fight against the Philistines, and he became exhausted. ¹⁶And Ishbi-Benob, one of the descendants of Rapha, whose bronze spearhead weighed three hundred shekelsᵇ and who was armed with a new ˌswordˌ, said he would kill David. ¹⁷But Abishai son of Zeruiah came to David's rescue; he struck the Philistine down and killed him. Then David's men swore to him, saying, "Never again will you go out with us to battle, so that the lamp of Israel will not be extinguished."

¹⁸In the course of time, there was another battle with the Philistines, at Gob. At that time Sibbecai the Hushathite killed Saph, one of the descendants of Rapha.

¹⁹In another battle with the Philistines at Gob, Elhanan son of Jaare-Oregimᶜ the Bethlehemite killed Goliathᵈ the Gittite, who had a spear with a shaft like a weaver's rod.

²⁰In still another battle, which took place at Gath, there was a huge man with six fingers on each hand and six toes on each foot—twenty-four in all. He also was descended from Rapha. ²¹When he taunted Israel, Jonathan son of Shimeah, David's brother, killed him.

²²These four were descendants of Rapha in Gath, and they fell at the hands of David and his men.

David's Song of Praise

 David sang to the LORD the words of this song when the LORD delivered him from the hand of all his enemies and from the hand of Saul. ²He said:

> "The LORD is my rock, my fortress and my deliverer;
> 3   my God is my rock, in whom I take refuge,
>   my shield and the hornᵉ of my salvation.

ᵃ8 Two Hebrew manuscripts, some Septuagint manuscripts and Syriac (see also 1 Samuel 18:19); most Hebrew and Septuagint manuscripts *Michal*   ᵇ16 That is, about 7 1/2 pounds (about 3.5 kilograms)   ᶜ19 Or *son of Jair the weaver*   ᵈ19 Hebrew and Septuagint; cf. 1 Chron. 20:5 *son of Jair killed Lahmi the brother of Goliath*   ᵉ3 Horn here symbolizes strength.

He is my stronghold, my refuge and my savior—
    from violent men you save me.
⁴I call to the LORD, who is worthy of praise,
    and I am saved from my enemies.

⁵"The waves of death swirled about me;
    the torrents of destruction overwhelmed me.
⁶The cords of the grave*a* coiled around me;
    the snares of death confronted me.
⁷In my distress I called to the LORD;
    I called out to my God.
From his temple he heard my voice;
    my cry came to his ears.

⁸"The earth trembled and quaked,
    the foundations of the heavens*b* shook;
    they trembled because he was angry.
⁹Smoke rose from his nostrils;
    consuming fire came from his mouth,
    burning coals blazed out of it.
¹⁰He parted the heavens and came down;
    dark clouds were under his feet.
¹¹He mounted the cherubim and flew;
    he soared*c* on the wings of the wind.
¹²He made darkness his canopy around him—
    the dark*d* rain clouds of the sky.
¹³Out of the brightness of his presence
    bolts of lightning blazed forth.
¹⁴The LORD thundered from heaven;
    the voice of the Most High resounded.
¹⁵He shot arrows and scattered the enemies,
    bolts of lightning and routed them.
¹⁶The valleys of the sea were exposed
    and the foundations of the earth laid bare
at the rebuke of the LORD,
    at the blast of breath from his nostrils.

¹⁷"He reached down from on high and took hold of me;
    he drew me out of deep waters.
¹⁸He rescued me from my powerful enemy,
    from my foes, who were too strong for me.
¹⁹They confronted me in the day of my disaster,
    but the LORD was my support.
²⁰He brought me out into a spacious place;
    he rescued me because he delighted in me.

²¹"The LORD has dealt with me according to my righteousness;
    according to the cleanness of my hands he has rewarded me.
²²For I have kept the ways of the LORD;
    I have not done evil by turning from my God.
²³All his laws are before me;
    I have not turned away from his decrees.

---

a 6 Hebrew *Sheol*   *b 8* Hebrew; Vulgate and Syriac (see also Psalm 18:7) *mountains*   *c 11* Many Hebrew manuscripts (see also Psalm 18:10); most Hebrew manuscripts *appeared*   *d 12* Septuagint and Vulgate (see also Psalm 18:11); Hebrew *massed*

²⁴I have been blameless before him
   and have kept myself from sin.
²⁵The Lord has rewarded me according to my righteousness,
   according to my cleanness*ᵃ* in his sight.

²⁶"To the faithful you show yourself faithful,
   to the blameless you show yourself blameless,
²⁷to the pure you show yourself pure,
   but to the crooked you show yourself shrewd.
²⁸You save the humble,
   but your eyes are on the haughty to bring them low.
²⁹You are my lamp, O Lord;
   the Lord turns my darkness into light.
³⁰With your help I can advance against a troop*ᵇ*;
   with my God I can scale a wall.

³¹"As for God, his way is perfect;
   the word of the Lord is flawless.
   He is a shield
   for all who take refuge in him.
³²For who is God besides the Lord?
   And who is the Rock except our God?
³³It is God who arms me with strength*ᶜ*
   and makes my way perfect.
³⁴He makes my feet like the feet of a deer;
   he enables me to stand on the heights.
³⁵He trains my hands for battle;
   my arms can bend a bow of bronze.
³⁶You give me your shield of victory;
   you stoop down to make me great.
³⁷You broaden the path beneath me,
   so that my ankles do not turn.

³⁸"I pursued my enemies and crushed them;
   I did not turn back till they were destroyed.
³⁹I crushed them completely, and they could not rise;
   they fell beneath my feet.
⁴⁰You armed me with strength for battle;
   you made my adversaries bow at my feet.
⁴¹You made my enemies turn their backs in flight,
   and I destroyed my foes.
⁴²They cried for help, but there was no one to save them—
   to the Lord, but he did not answer.
⁴³I beat them as fine as the dust of the earth;
   I pounded and trampled them like mud in the streets.

⁴⁴"You have delivered me from the attacks of my people;
   you have preserved me as the head of nations.
   People I did not know are subject to me,
⁴⁵   and foreigners come cringing to me;
   as soon as they hear me, they obey me.

ᵃ25 Hebrew; Septuagint and Vulgate (see also Psalm 18:24) *to the cleanness of my hands*   *ᵇ30* Or *can run through a barricade*   *ᶜ33* Dead Sea Scrolls, some Septuagint manuscripts, Vulgate and Syriac (see also Psalm 18:32); Masoretic Text *who is my strong refuge*

⁴⁶They all lose heart;
   they come trembling*ᵃ* from their strongholds.

⁴⁷"The Lᴏʀᴅ lives! Praise be to my Rock!
   Exalted be God, the Rock, my Savior!
⁴⁸He is the God who avenges me,
   who puts the nations under me,
⁴⁹ who sets me free from my enemies.
You exalted me above my foes;
   from violent men you rescued me.
⁵⁰Therefore I will praise you, O Lᴏʀᴅ, among the nations;
   I will sing praises to your name.
⁵¹He gives his king great victories;
   he shows unfailing kindness to his anointed,
   to David and his descendants forever."

The Last Words of David

23   These are the last words of David:

   "The oracle of David son of Jesse,
     the oracle of the man exalted by the Most High,
   the man anointed by the God of Jacob,
     Israel's singer of songs*ᵇ*:

²"The Spirit of the Lᴏʀᴅ spoke through me;
   his word was on my tongue.
³The God of Israel spoke,
   the Rock of Israel said to me:
'When one rules over men in righteousness,
   when he rules in the fear of God,
⁴he is like the light of morning at sunrise
   on a cloudless morning,
like the brightness after rain
   that brings the grass from the earth.'

⁵"Is not my house right with God?
   Has he not made with me an everlasting covenant,
   arranged and secured in every part?
Will he not bring to fruition my salvation
   and grant me my every desire?
⁶But evil men are all to be cast aside like thorns,
   which are not gathered with the hand.
⁷Whoever touches thorns
   uses a tool of iron or the shaft of a spear;
   they are burned up where they lie."

David's Mighty Men

⁸These are the names of David's mighty men:

Josheb-Basshebeth,*ᶜ* a Tahkemonite,*ᵈ* was chief of the Three; he raised his spear against eight hundred men, whom he killed*ᵉ* in one encounter.
⁹Next to him was Eleazar son of Dodai the Ahohite. As one of the three mighty men, he

---

ᵃ46 Some Septuagint manuscripts and Vulgate (see also Psalm 18:45); Masoretic Text *they arm themselves.*   *ᵇ1* Or *Israel's beloved singer*   *ᶜ8* Hebrew; some Septuagint manuscripts suggest *Ish-Bosheth,* that is, *Esh-Baal* (see also 1 Chron. 11:11 *Jashobeam*).   *ᵈ8* Probably a variant of *Hacmonite* (see 1 Chron. 11:11)   *ᵉ8* Some Septuagint manuscripts (see also 1 Chron. 11:11); Hebrew and other Septuagint manuscripts *Three; it was Adino the Eznite who killed eight hundred men*

was with David when they taunted the Philistines gathered ₍at Pas Dammim,ᵃ for battle. Then the men of Israel retreated, ¹⁰but he stood his ground and struck down the Philistines till his hand grew tired and froze to the sword. The LORD brought about a great victory that day. The troops returned to Eleazar, but only to strip the dead.

¹¹Next to him was Shammah son of Agee the Hararite. When the Philistines banded together at a place where there was a field full of lentils, Israel's troops fled from them. ¹²But Shammah took his stand in the middle of the field. He defended it and struck the Philistines down, and the LORD brought about a great victory.

¹³During harvest time, three of the thirty chief men came down to David at the cave of Adullam, while a band of Philistines was encamped in the Valley of Rephaim. ¹⁴At that time David was in the stronghold, and the Philistine garrison was at Bethlehem. ¹⁵David longed for water and said, "Oh, that someone would get me a drink of water from the well near the gate of Bethlehem!" ¹⁶So the three mighty men broke through the Philistine lines, drew water from the well near the gate of Bethlehem and carried it back to David. But he refused to drink it; instead, he poured it out before the LORD. ¹⁷"Far be it from me, O LORD, to do this!" he said. "Is it not the blood of men who went at the risk of their lives?" And David would not drink it.

Such were the exploits of the three mighty men.

¹⁸Abishai the brother of Joab son of Zeruiah was chief of the Three.ᵇ He raised his spear against three hundred men, whom he killed, and so he became as famous as the Three. ¹⁹Was he not held in greater honor than the Three? He became their commander, even though he was not included among them.

²⁰Benaiah son of Jehoiada was a valiant fighter from Kabzeel, who performed great exploits. He struck down two of Moab's best men. He also went down into a pit on a snowy day and killed a lion. ²¹And he struck down a huge Egyptian. Although the Egyptian had a spear in his hand, Benaiah went against him with a club. He snatched the spear from the Egyptian's hand and killed him with his own spear. ²²Such were the exploits of Benaiah son of Jehoiada; he too was as famous as the three mighty men. ²³He was held in greater honor than any of the Thirty, but he was not included among the Three. And David put him in charge of his bodyguard.

²⁴Among the Thirty were:
Asahel the brother of Joab,
Elhanan son of Dodo from Bethlehem,
²⁵Shammah the Harodite,
Elika the Harodite,
²⁶Helez the Paltite,
Ira son of Ikkesh from Tekoa,
²⁷Abiezer from Anathoth,
Mebunnaiᶜ the Hushathite,
²⁸Zalmon the Ahohite,
Maharai the Netophathite,
²⁹Heledᵈ son of Baanah the Netophathite,
Ithai son of Ribai from Gibeah in Benjamin,
³⁰Benaiah the Pirathonite,
Hiddaiᵉ from the ravines of Gaash,
³¹Abi-Albon the Arbathite,
Azmaveth the Barhumite,
³²Eliahba the Shaalbonite,
the sons of Jashen,

ᵃ9 See 1 Chron. 11:13; Hebrew gathered there.   ᵇ18 Most Hebrew manuscripts (see also 1 Chron. 11:20); two Hebrew manuscripts and Syriac Thirty   ᶜ27 Hebrew; some Septuagint manuscripts (see also 1 Chron. 11:29) Sibbecai   ᵈ29 Some Hebrew manuscripts and Vulgate (see also 1 Chron. 11:30); most Hebrew manuscripts Heleb   ᵉ30 Hebrew; some Septuagint manuscripts (see also 1 Chron. 11:32) Hurai

Jonathan ³³son of^{*a*} Shammah the Hararite,
Ahiam son of Sharar^{*b*} the Hararite,
³⁴Eliphelet son of Ahasbai the Maacathite,
Eliam son of Ahithophel the Gilonite,
³⁵Hezro the Carmelite,
Paarai the Arbite,
³⁶Igal son of Nathan from Zobah,
the son of Hagri,^{*c*}
³⁷Zelek the Ammonite,
Naharai the Beerothite, the armor-bearer of Joab son of Zeruiah,
³⁸Ira the Ithrite,
Gareb the Ithrite
³⁹and Uriah the Hittite.
There were thirty-seven in all.

David Counts the Fighting Men

24 Again the anger of the LORD burned against Israel, and he incited David against them, saying, "Go and take a census of Israel and Judah."

²So the king said to Joab and the army commanders^{*d*} with him, "Go throughout the tribes of Israel from Dan to Beersheba and enroll the fighting men, so that I may know how many there are."

³But Joab replied to the king, "May the LORD your God multiply the troops a hundred times over, and may the eyes of my lord the king see it. But why does my lord the king want to do such a thing?"

⁴The king's word, however, overruled Joab and the army commanders; so they left the presence of the king to enroll the fighting men of Israel.

⁵After crossing the Jordan, they camped near Aroer, south of the town in the gorge, and then went through Gad and on to Jazer. ⁶They went to Gilead and the region of Tahtim Hodshi, and on to Dan Jaan and around toward Sidon. ⁷Then they went toward the fortress of Tyre and all the towns of the Hivites and Canaanites. Finally, they went on to Beersheba in the Negev of Judah.

⁸After they had gone through the entire land, they came back to Jerusalem at the end of nine months and twenty days.

⁹Joab reported the number of the fighting men to the king: In Israel there were eight hundred thousand able-bodied men who could handle a sword, and in Judah five hundred thousand.

¹⁰David was conscience-stricken after he had counted the fighting men, and he said to the LORD, "I have sinned greatly in what I have done. Now, O LORD, I beg you, take away the guilt of your servant. I have done a very foolish thing."

¹¹Before David got up the next morning, the word of the LORD had come to Gad the

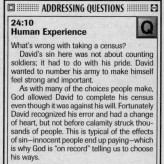

ADDRESSING QUESTIONS

24:10
Human Experience

Q

What's wrong with taking a census?
David's sin here was not about counting soldiers; it had to do with his pride. David wanted to number his army to make himself feel strong and important.

As with many of the choices people make, God allowed David to complete his census even though it was against his will. Fortunately David recognized his error and had a change of heart, but not before calamity struck thousands of people. This is typical of the effects of sin—innocent people end up paying—which is why God is "on record" telling us to choose his ways.

prophet, David's seer: ¹²"Go and tell David, 'This is what the LORD says: I am giving you three options. Choose one of them for me to carry out against you.'"

¹³So Gad went to David and said to him, "Shall there come upon you three^a years of famine in your land? Or three months of fleeing from your enemies while they pursue you? Or three days of plague in your land? Now then, think it over and decide how I should answer the one who sent me."

¹⁴David said to Gad, "I am in deep distress. Let us fall into the hands of the LORD, for his mercy is great; but do not let me fall into the hands of men."

¹⁵So the LORD sent a plague on Israel from that morning until the end of the time designated, and seventy thousand of the people from Dan to Beersheba died. ¹⁶When the angel stretched out his hand to destroy Jerusalem, the LORD was grieved because of the calamity and said to the angel who was afflicting the people, "Enough! Withdraw your hand." The angel of the LORD was then at the threshing floor of Araunah the Jebusite.

¹⁷When David saw the angel who was striking down the people, he said to the LORD, "I am the one who has sinned and done wrong. These are but sheep. What have they done? Let your hand fall upon me and my family."

David Builds an Altar

¹⁸On that day Gad went to David and said to him, "Go up and build an altar to the LORD on the threshing floor of Araunah the Jebusite." ¹⁹So David went up, as the LORD had commanded through Gad. ²⁰When Araunah looked and saw the king and his men coming toward him, he went out and bowed down before the king with his face to the ground.

²¹Araunah said, "Why has my lord the king come to his servant?"

"To buy your threshing floor," David answered, "so I can build an altar to the LORD, that the plague on the people may be stopped."

²²Araunah said to David, "Let my lord the king take whatever pleases him and offer it up. Here are oxen for the burnt offering, and here are threshing sledges and ox yokes for the wood. ²³O king, Araunah gives all this to the king." Araunah also said to him, "May the LORD your God accept you."

²⁴But the king replied to Araunah, "No, I insist on paying you for it. I will not sacrifice to the LORD my God burnt offerings that cost me nothing."

So David bought the threshing floor and the oxen and paid fifty shekels^b of silver for them. ²⁵David built an altar to the LORD there and sacrificed burnt offerings and fellowship offerings.^c Then the LORD answered prayer in behalf of the land, and the plague on Israel was stopped.

---

^a 13 Septuagint (see also 1 Chron. 21:12); Hebrew *seven*   ^b 24 That is, about 1 1/4 pounds (about 0.6 kilogram)   ^c 25 Traditionally *peace offerings*

SEEKER STORIES

Although I had considerable religious exposure when I was growing up, I drifted away from commitment to God in my 20's and 30's. I was divorced after being unfaithful to my wife and subsequently became involved in a substantial amount of immoral behavior. Through the encouragement of some friends I "tested the waters" at a local church, and eventually came to see how unhappy and unsatisfying my life truly was.

I made the decision to follow Christ while sitting in a worship service, listening to a pastor speak about Romans 6:23—that God's gift of salvation and everlasting life through Jesus Christ is available only if I reach out and accept it. My life has been a tremendous journey since I made the decision to accept Christ and give God control. Each day I have grown stronger and have come closer to the Lord.

This year I had some major health problems, and God's presence allowed me to deal with them confidently and with little fear. Perhaps the biggest change in my life is the inner peace that I now feel. God's love for me is so constant, so reliable and so strong that I feel safe from anything that might threaten to harm me. Because I have other, more important goals, my earthly successes or failures are much less important to me. The more I have come to know about God, his love for me, and the path he wants me to follow, the simpler and happier my life has become.

I accepted Christ as a young boy at the age of 15. Since then my life has had many highs and lows, but God has always been with me to celebrate the good times and to help me through the bad times.

My Christianity has made a real difference in my life. Relying on Jesus, I have lived through three very difficult experiences: The loss of my child in an accident, the loss of my family due to divorce, and the loss of my health due to cancer.

I have survived these events only because of the grace and love of my Lord. Today I can truly say that my life is an ongoing celebration. It is a testimony not only of God's ability to save souls, but of his ability to salvage and rebuild the lives of individuals.

1 KINGS/2 KINGS

Introduction

THE BOTTOM LINE

hese two books provide us with valuable insight into how prone human nature is to sin—especially when a person holds a position of power. Many of the kings of Israel were led away from the path of following God by their surrounding culture. They turned to worshiping idols, participating in pagan religious rituals, and doing other kinds of "evil in the eyes of the Lord." In so doing, they led the people of Israel astray as well. The world around us wants to squeeze us into its mold, just as it did to some of these ancient leaders. Only a close relationship with God can protect us from the corruption that presses in around us.

CENTRAL IDEAS

- The Jewish kings who followed God's directives experienced blessings; those who chose to rebel against God faced serious consequences.
- One king, Solomon, asked God for wisdom; his discretion is now legendary.
- God never stopped sending messengers to try to convince his people to turn from their wicked ways.
- The consequences of Israel's repeated sin against God were civil war and eventual captivity by foreign powers.

TITLES

These books record the acts of King Solomon – the last ruler before civil war divided ancient Israel – and the subsequent kings of the divided kingdom.

AUTHOR AND READERS

Jewish tradition cites the prophet Jeremiah as the author of these historical books. The writer wanted the people to learn their history and to remember the results of disobedience against God.

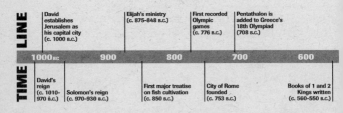

TIME LINE

	David establishes Jerusalem as his capital city (c. 1000 B.C.)	Elijah's ministry (c. 875-848 B.C.)	First recorded Olympic games (c. 776 B.C.)	Pentathalon is added to Greece's 18th Olympiad (708 B.C.)	
1000 B.C.	**900**	**800**	**700**	**600**	
David's reign (c. 1010-970 B.C.)	Solomon's reign (c. 970-930 B.C.)	First major treatise on fish cultivation (c. 850 B.C.)	City of Rome founded (c. 753 B.C.)	Books of 1 and 2 Kings written (c. 560-550 B.C.)	

As kids it was fun to imagine what three wishes we would ask for if we found a magic lamp with a genie inside. Sometimes we even play that game as adults. Of course it's just a game, but wouldn't it be great to wish for anything and get it?

One night Solomon, the wise and famous king of ancient Israel, had a chance to do just that. God spoke to him in a dream just after Solomon began his rule and said, "Ask for whatever you want, and I'll give it to you."

If God made that promise to you, what would you ask for? An estate in the country? Vacation homes in Vail, Palm Springs, and the French Riviera? How about a jet to speed you from one destination to another? Maybe you'd want fame—so that everyone in the world would recognize your face. Or power—so that no world leader could make a decision without your approval.

Solomon was allowed to ask for only one thing. Which would it be—money, fame, or power? Surprisingly, he didn't ask for any of those. Instead, he thanked God for his goodness and then said, "Give your servant a discerning heart" (1 Kings chapter 3, verse 9 [page 408]). In other words, Solomon asked for wisdom! Why? Because as a king he felt inadequate for the task at hand. He took his position seriously and knew he needed God's help to lead effectively. Solomon's choice was selfless and honorable. He surrendered his personal wants to benefit those he led.

> ## "Ask for whatever you want, and I'll give it to you."

God was pleased with Solomon's response. He expanded his original offer by pledging to grant Solomon's request and to add to it. God not only made Solomon incredibly wise, but also overwhelmingly rich and powerful.

While God doesn't make such open-ended offers to us, he does promise to help us make good decisions. He is very willing to enable us to carry out our responsibilities with wisdom. The primary way he does this is through what he has told us in the Bible. And while the Bible doesn't address all of our specific issues, it does provide us with a moral framework and practical insights to guide us as we chart our life's course.

The books of 1 and 2 Kings tell us about the exploits of the kings of Israel. Some of them had wise hearts and followed God. Others were foolish and ignored God. Each of us can benefit from observing these kings' choices—and the consequences that followed. Turn to 1 Kings chapter 3, verses 16–28 (page 408), for an example of a tough problem solved by Solomon's God-given wisdom. Realize that the same God who made Solomon so competent is willing to work through you.

1 KINGS

Adonijah Sets Himself Up as King

1 When King David was old and well advanced in years, he could not keep warm even when they put covers over him. ²So his servants said to him, "Let us look for a young virgin to attend the king and take care of him. She can lie beside him so that our lord the king may keep warm."

³Then they searched throughout Israel for a beautiful girl and found Abishag, a Shunammite, and brought her to the king. ⁴The girl was very beautiful; she took care of the king and waited on him, but the king had no intimate relations with her.

⁵Now Adonijah, whose mother was Haggith, put himself forward and said, "I will be king." So he got chariots and horses*ª* ready, with fifty men to run ahead of him. ⁶(His father had never interfered with him by asking, "Why do you behave as you do?" He was also very handsome and was born next after Absalom.)

⁷Adonijah conferred with Joab son of Zeruiah and with Abiathar the priest, and they gave him their support. ⁸But Zadok the priest, Benaiah son of Jehoiada, Nathan the prophet, Shimei and Rei*ᵇ* and David's special guard did not join Adonijah.

⁹Adonijah then sacrificed sheep, cattle and fattened calves at the Stone of Zoheleth near En Rogel. He invited all his brothers, the king's sons, and all the men of Judah who were royal officials, ¹⁰but he did not invite Nathan the prophet or Benaiah or the special guard or his brother Solomon.

¹¹Then Nathan asked Bathsheba, Solomon's mother, "Have you not heard that Adonijah, the son of Haggith, has become king without our lord David's knowing it? ¹²Now then, let me advise you how you can save your own life and the life of your son Solomon. ¹³Go in to King David and say to him, 'My lord the king, did you not swear to me your servant: "Surely Solomon your son shall be king after me, and he will sit on my throne"? Why then has Adonijah become king?' ¹⁴While you are still there talking to the king, I will come in and confirm what you have said."

¹⁵So Bathsheba went to see the aged king in his room, where Abishag the Shunammite was attending him. ¹⁶Bathsheba bowed low and knelt before the king.

"What is it you want?" the king asked.

¹⁷She said to him, "My lord, you yourself swore to me your servant by the LORD your God: 'Solomon your son shall be king after me, and he will sit on my throne.' ¹⁸But now Adonijah has become king, and you, my lord the king, do not know about it. ¹⁹He has sacrificed great numbers of cattle, fattened calves, and sheep, and has invited all the king's sons, Abiathar the priest and Joab the commander of the army, but he has not invited Solomon your servant. ²⁰My lord the king, the eyes of all Israel are on you, to learn from you who will sit on the throne of my lord the king after him. ²¹Otherwise, as soon as my lord the king is laid to rest with his fathers, I and my son Solomon will be treated as criminals."

²²While she was still speaking with the king, Nathan the prophet arrived. ²³And they told the king, "Nathan the prophet is here." So he went before the king and bowed with his face to the ground.

²⁴Nathan said, "Have you, my lord the king, declared that Adonijah shall be king after you, and that he will sit on your throne? ²⁵Today he has gone down and sacrificed great numbers of cattle, fattened calves, and sheep. He has invited all the king's sons, the

---

ª5 Or charioteers   *ᵇ8 Or and his friends*

commanders of the army and Abiathar the priest. Right now they are eating and drinking with him and saying, 'Long live King Adonijah!' ²⁶But me your servant, and Zadok the priest, and Benaiah son of Jehoiada, and your servant Solomon he did not invite. ²⁷Is this something my lord the king has done without letting his servants know who should sit on the throne of my lord the king after him?"

David Makes Solomon King

²⁸Then King David said, "Call in Bathsheba." So she came into the king's presence and stood before him.

²⁹The king then took an oath: "As surely as the LORD lives, who has delivered me out of every trouble, ³⁰I will surely carry out today what I swore to you by the LORD, the God of Israel: Solomon your son shall be king after me, and he will sit on my throne in my place."

³¹Then Bathsheba bowed low with her face to the ground and, kneeling before the king, said, "May my lord King David live forever!"

³²King David said, "Call in Zadok the priest, Nathan the prophet and Benaiah son of Jehoiada." When they came before the king, ³³he said to them: "Take your lord's servants with you and set Solomon my son on my own mule and take him down to Gihon. ³⁴There have Zadok the priest and Nathan the prophet anoint him king over Israel. Blow the trumpet and shout, 'Long live King Solomon!' ³⁵Then you are to go up with him, and he is to come and sit on my throne and reign in my place. I have appointed him ruler over Israel and Judah."

³⁶Benaiah son of Jehoiada answered the king, "Amen! May the LORD, the God of my lord the king, so declare it. ³⁷As the LORD was with my lord the king, so may he be with Solomon to make his throne even greater than the throne of my lord King David!"

³⁸So Zadok the priest, Nathan the prophet, Benaiah son of Jehoiada, the Kerethites and the Pelethites went down and put Solomon on King David's mule and escorted him to Gihon. ³⁹Zadok the priest took the horn of oil from the sacred tent and anointed Solomon. Then they sounded the trumpet and all the people shouted, "Long live King Solomon!" ⁴⁰And all the people went up after him, playing flutes and rejoicing greatly, so that the ground shook with the sound.

⁴¹Adonijah and all the guests who were with him heard it as they were finishing their feast. On hearing the sound of the trumpet, Joab asked, "What's the meaning of all the noise in the city?"

⁴²Even as he was speaking, Jonathan son of Abiathar the priest arrived. Adonijah said, "Come in. A worthy man like you must be bringing good news."

⁴³"Not at all!" Jonathan answered. "Our lord King David has made Solomon king. ⁴⁴The king has sent with him Zadok the priest, Nathan the prophet, Benaiah son of Jehoiada, the Kerethites and the Pelethites, and they have put him on the king's mule, ⁴⁵and Zadok the priest and Nathan the prophet have anointed him king at Gihon. From there they have gone up cheering, and the city resounds with it. That's the noise you hear. ⁴⁶Moreover, Solomon has taken his seat on the royal throne. ⁴⁷Also, the royal officials have come to congratulate our lord King David, saying, 'May your God make Solomon's name more famous than yours and his throne greater than yours!' And the king bowed in worship on his bed ⁴⁸and said, 'Praise be to the LORD, the God of Israel, who has allowed my eyes to see a successor on my throne today.'"

⁴⁹At this, all Adonijah's guests rose in alarm and dispersed. ⁵⁰But Adonijah, in fear of Solomon, went and took hold of the horns of the altar. ⁵¹Then Solomon was told, "Adonijah is afraid of King Solomon and is clinging to the horns of the altar. He says, 'Let King Solomon swear to me today that he will not put his servant to death with the sword.'"

⁵²Solomon replied, "If he shows himself to be a worthy man, not a hair of his head will fall to the ground; but if evil is found in him, he will die." ⁵³Then King Solomon sent men,

and they brought him down from the altar. And Adonijah came and bowed down to King Solomon, and Solomon said, "Go to your home."

David's Charge to Solomon

2 When the time drew near for David to die, he gave a charge to Solomon his son.

²"I am about to go the way of all the earth," he said. "So be strong, show yourself a man, ³and observe what the LORD your God requires: Walk in his ways, and keep his decrees and commands, his laws and requirements, as written in the Law of Moses, so that you may prosper in all you do and wherever you go, ⁴and that the LORD may keep his promise to me: 'If your descendants watch how they live, and if they walk faithfully before me with all their heart and soul, you will never fail to have a man on the throne of Israel.'

⁵"Now you yourself know what Joab son of Zeruiah did to me—what he did to the two commanders of Israel's armies, Abner son of Ner and Amasa son of Jether. He killed them, shedding their blood in peacetime as if in battle, and with that blood stained the belt around his waist and the sandals on his feet. ⁶Deal with him according to your wisdom, but do not let his gray head go down to the grave ᵃ in peace.

⁷"But show kindness to the sons of Barzillai of Gilead and let them be among those who eat at your table. They stood by me when I fled from your brother Absalom.

⁸"And remember, you have with you Shimei son of Gera, the Benjamite from Bahurim, who called down bitter curses on me the day I went to Mahanaim. When he came down to meet me at the Jordan, I swore to him by the LORD: 'I will not put you to death by the sword.' ⁹But now, do not consider him innocent. You are a man of wisdom; you will know what to do to him. Bring his gray head down to the grave in blood."

¹⁰Then David rested with his fathers and was buried in the City of David. ¹¹He had reigned forty years over Israel—seven years in Hebron and thirty-three in Jerusalem. ¹²So Solomon sat on the throne of his father David, and his rule was firmly established.

Solomon's Throne Established

¹³Now Adonijah, the son of Haggith, went to Bathsheba, Solomon's mother. Bathsheba asked him, "Do you come peacefully?"

He answered, "Yes, peacefully." ¹⁴Then he added, "I have something to say to you."

"You may say it," she replied.

¹⁵"As you know," he said, "the kingdom was mine. All Israel looked to me as their king. But things changed, and the kingdom has gone to my brother; for it has come to him from the LORD. ¹⁶Now I have one request to make of you. Do not refuse me."

"You may make it," she said.

¹⁷So he continued, "Please ask King Solomon—he will not refuse you—to give me Abishag the Shunammite as my wife."

¹⁸"Very well," Bathsheba replied, "I will speak to the king for you."

¹⁹When Bathsheba went to King Solomon to speak to him for Adonijah, the king stood up to meet her, bowed down to her and sat down on his throne. He had a throne brought for the king's mother, and she sat down at his right hand.

²⁰"I have one small request to make of you," she said. "Do not refuse me."

The king replied, "Make it, my mother; I will not refuse you."

²¹So she said, "Let Abishag the Shunammite be given in marriage to your brother Adonijah."

²²King Solomon answered his mother, "Why do you request Abishag the Shunammite for Adonijah? You might as well request the kingdom for him—after all, he is my older brother—yes, for him and for Abiathar the priest and Joab son of Zeruiah!"

ᵃ6 Hebrew *Sheol*; also in verse 9

²³Then King Solomon swore by the LORD: "May God deal with me, be it ever so severely, if Adonijah does not pay with his life for this request! ²⁴And now, as surely as the LORD lives—he who has established me securely on the throne of my father David and has founded a dynasty for me as he promised—Adonijah shall be put to death today!" ²⁵So King Solomon gave orders to Benaiah son of Jehoiada, and he struck down Adonijah and he died.

²⁶To Abiathar the priest the king said, "Go back to your fields in Anathoth. You deserve to die, but I will not put you to death now, because you carried the ark of the Sovereign LORD before my father David and shared all my father's hardships." ²⁷So Solomon removed Abiathar from the priesthood of the LORD, fulfilling the word the LORD had spoken at Shiloh about the house of Eli.

²⁸When the news reached Joab, who had conspired with Adonijah though not with Absalom, he fled to the tent of the LORD and took hold of the horns of the altar. ²⁹King Solomon was told that Joab had fled to the tent of the LORD and was beside the altar. Then Solomon ordered Benaiah son of Jehoiada, "Go, strike him down!"

³⁰So Benaiah entered the tent of the LORD and said to Joab, "The king says, 'Come out!' "

But he answered, "No, I will die here."

Benaiah reported to the king, "This is how Joab answered me."

³¹Then the king commanded Benaiah, "Do as he says. Strike him down and bury him, and so clear me and my father's house of the guilt of the innocent blood that Joab shed. ³²The LORD will repay him for the blood he shed, because without the knowledge of my father David he attacked two men and killed them with the sword. Both of them—Abner son of Ner, commander of Israel's army, and Amasa son of Jether, commander of Judah's army—were better men and more upright than he. ³³May the guilt of their blood rest on the head of Joab and his descendants forever. But on David and his descendants, his house and his throne, may there be the LORD's peace forever."

³⁴So Benaiah son of Jehoiada went up and struck down Joab and killed him, and he was buried on his own land ᵃ in the desert. ³⁵The king put Benaiah son of Jehoiada over the army in Joab's position and replaced Abiathar with Zadok the priest.

³⁶Then the king sent for Shimei and said to him, "Build yourself a house in Jerusalem and live there, but do not go anywhere else. ³⁷The day you leave and cross the Kidron Valley, you can be sure you will die; your blood will be on your own head."

³⁸Shimei answered the king, "What you say is good. Your servant will do as my lord the king has said." And Shimei stayed in Jerusalem for a long time.

³⁹But three years later, two of Shimei's slaves ran off to Achish son of Maacah, king of Gath, and Shimei was told, "Your slaves are in Gath." ⁴⁰At this, he saddled his donkey and went to Achish at Gath in search of his slaves. So Shimei went away and brought the slaves back from Gath.

⁴¹When Solomon was told that Shimei had gone from Jerusalem to Gath and had returned, ⁴²the king summoned Shimei and said to him, "Did I not make you swear by the LORD and warn you, 'On the day you leave to go anywhere else, you can be sure you will die'? At that time you said to me, 'What you say is good. I will obey.' ⁴³Why then did you not keep your oath to the LORD and obey the command I gave you?"

⁴⁴The king also said to Shimei, "You know in your heart all the wrong you did to my father David. Now the LORD will repay you for your wrongdoing. ⁴⁵But King Solomon will be blessed, and David's throne will remain secure before the LORD forever."

⁴⁶Then the king gave the order to Benaiah son of Jehoiada, and he went out and struck Shimei down and killed him.

The kingdom was now firmly established in Solomon's hands.

ᵃ34 Or buried in his tomb

Solomon Asks for Wisdom

3 Solomon made an alliance with Pharaoh king of Egypt and married his daughter. He brought her to the City of David until he finished building his palace and the temple of the LORD, and the wall around Jerusalem. ²The people, however, were still sacrificing at the high places, because a temple had not yet been built for the Name of the LORD. ³Solomon showed his love for the LORD by walking according to the statutes of his father David, except that he offered sacrifices and burned incense on the high places.

⁴The king went to Gibeon to offer sacrifices, for that was the most important high place, and Solomon offered a thousand burnt offerings on that altar. ⁵At Gibeon the LORD appeared to Solomon during the night in a dream, and God said, "Ask for whatever you want me to give you."

⁶Solomon answered, "You have shown great kindness to your servant, my father David, because he was faithful to you and righteous and upright in heart. You have continued this great kindness to him and have given him a son to sit on his throne this very day.

⁷"Now, O LORD my God, you have made your servant king in place of my father David. But I am only a little child and do not know how to carry out my duties. ⁸Your servant is here among the people you have chosen, a great people, too numerous to count or number. ⁹So give your servant a discerning heart to govern your people and to distinguish between right and wrong. For who is able to govern this great people of yours?"

¹⁰The Lord was pleased that Solomon had asked for this. ¹¹So God said to him, "Since you have asked for this and not for long life or wealth for yourself, nor have asked for the death of your enemies but for discernment in administering justice, ¹²I will do what you have asked. I will give you a wise and discerning heart, so that there will never have been anyone like you, nor will there ever be. ¹³Moreover, I will give you what you have not asked for—both riches and honor—so that in your lifetime you will have no equal among kings. ¹⁴And if you walk in my ways and obey my statutes and commands as David your father did, I will give you a long life." ¹⁵Then Solomon awoke—and he realized it had been a dream.

He returned to Jerusalem, stood before the ark of the Lord's covenant and sacrificed burnt offerings and fellowship offerings.ᵃ Then he gave a feast for all his court.

A Wise Ruling

¹⁶Now two prostitutes came to the king and stood before him. ¹⁷One of them said, "My lord, this woman and I live in the same house. I had a baby while she was there with me. ¹⁸The third day after my child was born, this woman also had a baby. We were alone; there was no one in the house but the two of us.

¹⁹"During the night this woman's son died because she lay on him. ²⁰So she got up in the middle of the night and took my son from my side while I your servant was asleep. She put him by her breast and put her dead son by my breast. ²¹The next morning, I got up to nurse my son—and he was dead! But when I looked at him closely in the morning light, I saw that it wasn't the son I had borne."

²²The other woman said, "No! The living one is my son; the dead one is yours."

But the first one insisted, "No! The dead one is yours; the living one is mine." And so they argued before the king.

²³The king said, "This one says, 'My son is alive and your son is dead,' while that one says, 'No! Your son is dead and mine is alive.'"

²⁴Then the king said, "Bring me a sword." So they brought a sword for the king. ²⁵He then gave an order: "Cut the living child in two and give half to one and half to the other."

ᵃ15 Traditionally *peace offerings*

²⁶The woman whose son was alive was filled with compassion for her son and said to the king, "Please, my lord, give her the living baby! Don't kill him!"

But the other said, "Neither I nor you shall have him. Cut him in two!"

²⁷Then the king gave his ruling: "Give the living baby to the first woman. Do not kill him; she is his mother."

²⁸When all Israel heard the verdict the king had given, they held the king in awe, because they saw that he had wisdom from God to administer justice.

Solomon's Officials and Governors

4 So King Solomon ruled over all Israel. ²And these were his chief officials:

Azariah son of Zadok—the priest;

³Elihoreph and Ahijah, sons of Shisha—secretaries;

Jehoshaphat son of Ahilud—recorder;

⁴Benaiah son of Jehoiada—commander in chief;

Zadok and Abiathar—priests;

⁵Azariah son of Nathan—in charge of the district officers;

Zabud son of Nathan—a priest and personal adviser to the king;

⁶Ahishar—in charge of the palace;

Adoniram son of Abda—in charge of forced labor.

⁷Solomon also had twelve district governors over all Israel, who supplied provisions for the king and the royal household. Each one had to provide supplies for one month in the year. ⁸These are their names:

Ben-Hur—in the hill country of Ephraim;

⁹Ben-Deker—in Makaz, Shaalbim, Beth Shemesh and Elon Bethhanan;

¹⁰Ben-Hesed—in Arubboth (Socoh and all the land of Hepher were his);

¹¹Ben-Abinadab—in Naphoth Dorᵃ (he was married to Taphath daughter of Solomon);

ᵃ11 Or in the heights of Dor

MANAGING RESOURCES

3:16–28
Position

If you could have anything you wished for, what would it be? Money? Power? Fame? Sometimes such a proposition is fun to dream about. For Solomon, King David's son, this dream became a reality.

One day, in a dream, God told Solomon, "Ask for whatever you want me to give you" (chapter 3, verse 5). But instead of asking for the things many of us would request, Solomon asked for wisdom so he could govern wisely and know the difference between right and wrong. Pleased with his request, God gave him this wisdom (chapter 3, verses 10–12).

This passage tells the story of how Solomon's wisdom was put to the test. The two prostitutes who approached Solomon with their dispute needed a definitive answer to their problem, but there was virtually no evidence available to support either woman's case. Acting as an impartial judge, Solomon gave a seemingly cold and harsh answer to their problem—but his underlying intentions were wise and compassionate. By drawing out the real mother's concern for the life of her child, he was able to make the correct decision. Those who heard about it were amazed, because they realized that the wisdom Solomon exhibited came from God (verse 28).

The next time a tough decision stares you in the face, don't tackle it alone. Why not ask God for the wisdom to know what to do?

¹²Baana son of Ahilud—in Taanach and Megiddo, and in all of Beth Shan next to Zarethan below Jezreel, from Beth Shan to Abel Meholah across to Jokmeam;

¹³Ben-Geber—in Ramoth Gilead (the settlements of Jair son of Manasseh in Gilead were his, as well as the district of Argob in Bashan and its sixty large walled cities with bronze gate bars);

¹⁴Ahinadab son of Iddo—in Mahanaim;

¹⁵Ahimaaz—in Naphtali (he had married Basemath daughter of Solomon);

¹⁶Baana son of Hushai—in Asher and in Aloth;

¹⁷Jehoshaphat son of Paruah—in Issachar;

¹⁸Shimei son of Ela—in Benjamin;

¹⁹Geber son of Uri—in Gilead (the country of Sihon king of the Amorites and the country of Og king of Bashan). He was the only governor over the district.

Solomon's Daily Provisions

²⁰The people of Judah and Israel were as numerous as the sand on the seashore; they ate, they drank and they were happy. ²¹And Solomon ruled over all the kingdoms from the River[a] to the land of the Philistines, as far as the border of Egypt. These countries brought tribute and were Solomon's subjects all his life.

²²Solomon's daily provisions were thirty cors[b] of fine flour and sixty cors[c] of meal, ²³ten head of stall-fed cattle, twenty of pasture-fed cattle and a hundred sheep and goats, as well as deer, gazelles, roebucks and choice fowl. ²⁴For he ruled over all the kingdoms west of the River, from Tiphsah to Gaza, and had peace on all sides. ²⁵During Solomon's lifetime Judah and Israel, from Dan to Beersheba, lived in safety, each man under his own vine and fig tree.

²⁶Solomon had four[d] thousand stalls for chariot horses, and twelve thousand horses.[e]

²⁷The district officers, each in his month, supplied provisions for King Solomon and all who came to the king's table. They saw to it that nothing was lacking. ²⁸They also brought to the proper place their quotas of barley and straw for the chariot horses and the other horses.

Solomon's Wisdom

²⁹God gave Solomon wisdom and very great insight, and a breadth of understanding as measureless as the sand on the seashore. ³⁰Solomon's wisdom was greater than the wisdom of all the men of the East, and greater than all the wisdom of Egypt. ³¹He was wiser than any other man, including Ethan the Ezrahite—wiser than Heman, Calcol and Darda, the sons of Mahol. And his fame spread to all the surrounding nations. ³²He spoke three thousand proverbs and his songs numbered a thousand and five. ³³He described plant life, from the cedar of Lebanon to the hyssop that grows out of walls. He also taught about animals and birds, reptiles and fish. ³⁴Men of all nations came to listen to Solomon's wisdom, sent by all the kings of the world, who had heard of his wisdom.

Preparations for Building the Temple

5 When Hiram king of Tyre heard that Solomon had been anointed king to succeed his father David, he sent his envoys to Solomon, because he had always been on friendly terms with David. ²Solomon sent back this message to Hiram:

³"You know that because of the wars waged against my father David from all sides, he could not build a temple for the Name of the Lord his God until the Lord put his enemies under his feet. ⁴But now the Lord my God has given me rest on every side, and there is no adversary or disaster. ⁵I intend, therefore, to build a temple for the Name of the Lord my God, as the Lord told my father David, when he said, 'Your

---

a21 That is, the Euphrates; also in verse 24   b22 That is, probably about 185 bushels (about 6.6 kiloliters)   c22 That is, probably about 375 bushels (about 13.2 kiloliters)   d26 Some Septuagint manuscripts (see also 2 Chron. 9:25); Hebrew forty   e26 Or charioteers

son whom I will put on the throne in your place will build the temple for my Name.'

⁶"So give orders that cedars of Lebanon be cut for me. My men will work with yours, and I will pay you for your men whatever wages you set. You know that we have no one so skilled in felling timber as the Sidonians."

⁷When Hiram heard Solomon's message, he was greatly pleased and said, "Praise be to the Lord today, for he has given David a wise son to rule over this great nation."

⁸So Hiram sent word to Solomon:

"I have received the message you sent me and will do all you want in providing the cedar and pine logs. ⁹My men will haul them down from Lebanon to the sea, and I will float them in rafts by sea to the place you specify. There I will separate them and you can take them away. And you are to grant my wish by providing food for my royal household."

¹⁰In this way Hiram kept Solomon supplied with all the cedar and pine logs he wanted, ¹¹and Solomon gave Hiram twenty thousand cors*a* of wheat as food for his household, in addition to twenty thousand baths*b,c* of pressed olive oil. Solomon continued to do this for Hiram year after year. ¹²The Lord gave Solomon wisdom, just as he had promised him. There were peaceful relations between Hiram and Solomon, and the two of them made a treaty.

¹³King Solomon conscripted laborers from all Israel—thirty thousand men. ¹⁴He sent them off to Lebanon in shifts of ten thousand a month, so that they spent one month in Lebanon and two months at home. Adoniram was in charge of the forced labor. ¹⁵Solomon had seventy thousand carriers and eighty thousand stonecutters in the hills, ¹⁶as well as thirty-three hundred*d* foremen who supervised the project and directed the workmen. ¹⁷At the king's command they removed from the quarry large blocks of quality stone to provide a foundation of dressed stone for the temple. ¹⁸The craftsmen of Solomon and Hiram and the men of Gebal*e* cut and prepared the timber and stone for the building of the temple.

Solomon Builds the Temple

6 In the four hundred and eightieth*f* year after the Israelites had come out of Egypt, in the fourth year of Solomon's reign over Israel, in the month of Ziv, the second month, he began to build the temple of the Lord.

²The temple that King Solomon built for the Lord was sixty cubits long, twenty wide and thirty high.*g* ³The portico at the front of the main hall of the temple extended the width of the temple, that is twenty cubits,*h* and projected ten cubits*i* from the front of the temple. ⁴He made narrow clerestory windows in the temple. ⁵Against the walls of the main hall and inner sanctuary he built a structure around the building, in which there were side rooms. ⁶The lowest floor was five cubits*j* wide, the middle floor six cubits*k* and the third floor seven.*l* He made offset ledges around the outside of the temple so that nothing would be inserted into the temple walls.

⁷In building the temple, only blocks dressed at the quarry were used, and no hammer, chisel or any other iron tool was heard at the temple site while it was being built.

⁸The entrance to the lowest*m* floor was on the south side of the temple; a stairway led up to the middle level and from there to the third. ⁹So he built the temple and completed it, roofing it with beams and cedar planks. ¹⁰And he built the side rooms all along the

---

a11 That is, probably about 125,000 bushels (about 4,400 kiloliters)   *b11* Septuagint (see also 2 Chron. 2:10); Hebrew twenty cors   *c11* That is, about 115,000 gallons (about 440 kiloliters)   *d16* Hebrew; some Septuagint manuscripts (see also 2 Chron. 2:2, 18) thirty-six hundred   *e18* That is, Byblos   *f1* Hebrew; Septuagint four hundred and fortieth   *g2* That is, about 90 feet (about 27 meters) long and 30 feet (about 9 meters) wide and 45 feet (about 13.5 meters) high   *h3* That is, about 30 feet (about 9 meters)   *i3* That is, about 15 feet (about 4.5 meters)   *j6* That is, about 7 1/2 feet (about 2.3 meters); also in verses 10 and 24   *k6* That is, about 9 feet (about 2.7 meters)   *l6* That is, about 10 1/2 feet (about 3.1 meters)   *m8* Septuagint; Hebrew middle

temple. The height of each was five cubits, and they were attached to the temple by beams of cedar.

¹¹The word of the LORD came to Solomon: ¹²"As for this temple you are building, if you follow my decrees, carry out my regulations and keep all my commands and obey them, I will fulfill through you the promise I gave to David your father. ¹³And I will live among the Israelites and will not abandon my people Israel."

¹⁴So Solomon built the temple and completed it. ¹⁵He lined its interior walls with cedar boards, paneling them from the floor of the temple to the ceiling, and covered the floor of the temple with planks of pine. ¹⁶He partitioned off twenty cubits*a* at the rear of the temple with cedar boards from floor to ceiling to form within the temple an inner sanctuary, the Most Holy Place. ¹⁷The main hall in front of this room was forty cubits*b* long. ¹⁸The inside of the temple was cedar, carved with gourds and open flowers. Everything was cedar; no stone was to be seen.

¹⁹He prepared the inner sanctuary within the temple to set the ark of the covenant of the LORD there. ²⁰The inner sanctuary was twenty cubits long, twenty wide and twenty high.*c* He overlaid the inside with pure gold, and he also overlaid the altar of cedar. ²¹Solomon covered the inside of the temple with pure gold, and he extended gold chains across the front of the inner sanctuary, which was overlaid with gold. ²²So he overlaid the whole interior with gold. He also overlaid with gold the altar that belonged to the inner sanctuary.

²³In the inner sanctuary he made a pair of cherubim of olive wood, each ten cubits*d* high. ²⁴One wing of the first cherub was five cubits long, and the other wing five cubits— ten cubits from wing tip to wing tip. ²⁵The second cherub also measured ten cubits, for the two cherubim were identical in size and shape. ²⁶The height of each cherub was ten cubits. ²⁷He placed the cherubim inside the innermost room of the temple, with their wings spread out. The wing of one cherub touched one wall, while the wing of the other touched the other wall, and their wings touched each other in the middle of the room. ²⁸He overlaid the cherubim with gold.

²⁹On the walls all around the temple, in both the inner and outer rooms, he carved cherubim, palm trees and open flowers. ³⁰He also covered the floors of both the inner and outer rooms of the temple with gold.

³¹For the entrance of the inner sanctuary he made doors of olive wood with five-sided jambs. ³²And on the two olive wood doors he carved cherubim, palm trees and open flowers, and overlaid the cherubim and palm trees with beaten gold. ³³In the same way he made four-sided jambs of olive wood for the entrance to the main hall. ³⁴He also made two pine doors, each having two leaves that turned in sockets. ³⁵He carved cherubim, palm trees and open flowers on them and overlaid them with gold hammered evenly over the carvings.

³⁶And he built the inner courtyard of three courses of dressed stone and one course of trimmed cedar beams.

³⁷The foundation of the temple of the LORD was laid in the fourth year, in the month of Ziv. ³⁸In the eleventh year in the month of Bul, the eighth month, the temple was finished in all its details according to its specifications. He had spent seven years building it.

Solomon Builds His Palace

7 It took Solomon thirteen years, however, to complete the construction of his palace. ²He built the Palace of the Forest of Lebanon a hundred cubits long, fifty wide and thirty high,*e* with four rows of cedar columns supporting trimmed cedar beams. ³It was roofed with cedar above the beams that rested on the columns—forty-five

---

a 16 That is, about 30 feet (about 9 meters)   *b 17* That is, about 60 feet (about 18 meters)   *c 20* That is, about 30 feet (about 9 meters) long, wide and high   *d 23* That is, about 15 feet (about 4.5 meters)   *e 2* That is, about 150 feet (about 46 meters) long, 75 feet (about 23 meters) wide and 45 feet (about 13.5 meters) high

beams, fifteen to a row. **4**Its windows were placed high in sets of three, facing each other. **5**All the doorways had rectangular frames; they were in the front part in sets of three, facing each other.ᵃ

6He made a colonnade fifty cubits long and thirty wide.ᵇ In front of it was a portico, and in front of that were pillars and an overhanging roof.

7He built the throne hall, the Hall of Justice, where he was to judge, and he covered it with cedar from 'floor to ceiling.ᶜ **8**And the palace in which he was to live, set farther back, was similar in design. Solomon also made a palace like this hall for Pharaoh's daughter, whom he had married.

9All these structures, from the outside to the great courtyard and from foundation to eaves, were made of blocks of high-grade stone cut to size and trimmed with a saw on their inner and outer faces. **10**The foundations were laid with large stones of good quality, some measuring ten cubitsᵈ and some eight.ᵉ **11**Above were high-grade stones, cut to size, and cedar beams. **12**The great courtyard was surrounded by a wall of three courses of dressed stone and one course of trimmed cedar beams, as was the inner courtyard of the temple of the Lᴏʀᴅ with its portico.

The Temple's Furnishings

13King Solomon sent to Tyre and brought Huram,ᶠ **14**whose mother was a widow from the tribe of Naphtali and whose father was a man of Tyre and a craftsman in bronze. Huram was highly skilled and experienced in all kinds of bronze work. He came to King Solomon and did all the work assigned to him.

15He cast two bronze pillars, each eighteen cubits high and twelve cubits around,ᵍ by line. **16**He also made two capitals of cast bronze to set on the tops of the pillars; each capital was five cubitsʰ high. **17**A network of interwoven chains festooned the capitals on top of the pillars, seven for each capital. **18**He made pomegranates in two rowsⁱ encircling each network to decorate the capitals on top of the pillars.ʲ He did the same for each capital. **19**The capitals on top of the pillars in the portico were in the shape of lilies, four cubitsᵏ high. **20**On the capitals of both pillars, above the bowl-shaped part next to the network, were the two hundred pomegranates in rows all around. **21**He erected the pillars at the portico of the temple. The pillar to the south he named Jakinˡ and the one to the north Boaz.ᵐ **22**The capitals on top were in the shape of lilies. And so the work on the pillars was completed.

23He made the Sea of cast metal, circular in shape, measuring ten cubitsᵈ from rim to rim and five cubits high. It took a line of thirty cubitsⁿ to measure around it. **24**Below the rim, gourds encircled it—ten to a cubit. The gourds were cast in two rows in one piece with the Sea.

25The Sea stood on twelve bulls, three facing north, three facing west, three facing south and three facing east. The Sea rested on top of them, and their hindquarters were toward the center. **26**It was a handbreadthᵒ in thickness, and its rim was like the rim of a cup, like a lily blossom. It held two thousand baths.ᵖ

27He also made ten movable stands of bronze; each was four cubits long, four wide and three high. q **28**This is how the stands were made: They had side panels attached to uprights. **29**On the panels between the uprights were lions, bulls and cherubim—and on the uprights as well. Above and below the lions and bulls were wreaths of hammered work. **30**Each stand had four bronze wheels with bronze axles, and each had a basin

ᵃ5 The meaning of the Hebrew for this verse is uncertain.   ᵇ6 That is, about 75 feet (about 23 meters) long and 45 feet (about 13.5 meters) wide   ᶜ7 Vulgate and Syriac; Hebrew *floor*   ᵈ10,23 That is, about 15 feet (about 4.5 meters)   ᵉ10 That is, about 12 feet (about 3.6 meters)   ᶠ13 Hebrew *Hiram,* a variant of *Huram;* also in verses 40 and 45   ᵍ15 That is, about 27 feet (about 8.1 meters) high and 18 feet (about 5.4 meters) around   ʰ16 That is, about 7 1/2 feet (about 2.3 meters); also in verse 23   ⁱ18 Two Hebrew manuscripts and Septuagint; most Hebrew manuscripts *made the pillars, and there were two rows*   ʲ18 Many Hebrew manuscripts and Syriac; most Hebrew manuscripts *pomegranates*   ᵏ19 That is, about 6 feet (about 1.8 meters); also in verse 38   ˡ21 *Jakin* probably means *he establishes.*   ᵐ21 *Boaz* probably means *in him is strength.*   ⁿ23 That is, about 45 feet (about 13.5 meters)   ᵒ26 That is, about 3 inches (about 8 centimeters)   ᵖ26 That is, probably about 11,500 gallons (about 44 kiloliters); the Septuagint does not have this sentence.   q27 That is, about 6 feet (about 1.8 meters) long and wide and about 4 1/2 feet (about 1.3 meters) high resting on four supports, cast with wreaths on each side. ³¹On the inside of the stand there was an opening that had a circular frame one cubit*a* deep. This opening was round, and with its basework it measured a cubit and a half.*b* Around its opening there was engraving. The panels of the stands were square, not round. ³²The four wheels were under the panels, and the axles of the wheels were attached to the stand. The diameter of each wheel was a cubit and a half. ³³The wheels were made like chariot wheels; the axles, rims, spokes and hubs were all of cast metal.

³⁴Each stand had four handles, one on each corner, projecting from the stand. ³⁵At the top of the stand there was a circular band half a cubit*c* deep. The supports and panels were attached to the top of the stand. ³⁶He engraved cherubim, lions and palm trees on the surfaces of the supports and on the panels, in every available space, with wreaths all around. ³⁷This is the way he made the ten stands. They were all cast in the same molds and were identical in size and shape.

³⁸He then made ten bronze basins, each holding forty baths*d* and measuring four cubits across, one basin to go on each of the ten stands. ³⁹He placed five of the stands on the south side of the temple and five on the north. He placed the Sea on the south side, at the southeast corner of the temple. ⁴⁰He also made the basins and shovels and sprinkling bowls.

So Huram finished all the work he had undertaken for King Solomon in the temple of the LORD:

⁴¹the two pillars;

  the two bowl-shaped capitals on top of the pillars;

  the two sets of network decorating the two bowl-shaped capitals on top of the pillars;

⁴²the four hundred pomegranates for the two sets of network (two rows of pomegranates for each network, decorating the bowl-shaped capitals on top of the pillars);

⁴³the ten stands with their ten basins;

⁴⁴the Sea and the twelve bulls under it;

⁴⁵the pots, shovels and sprinkling bowls.

All these objects that Huram made for King Solomon for the temple of the LORD were of burnished bronze. ⁴⁶The king had them cast in clay molds in the plain of the Jordan between Succoth and Zarethan. ⁴⁷Solomon left all these things unweighed, because there were so many; the weight of the bronze was not determined.

⁴⁸Solomon also made all the furnishings that were in the LORD's temple:

  the golden altar;

  the golden table on which was the bread of the Presence;

⁴⁹the lampstands of pure gold (five on the right and five on the left, in front of the inner sanctuary);

  the gold floral work and lamps and tongs;

⁵⁰the pure gold basins, wick trimmers, sprinkling bowls, dishes and censers;

  and the gold sockets for the doors of the innermost room, the Most Holy Place, and also for the doors of the main hall of the temple.

⁵¹When all the work King Solomon had done for the temple of the LORD was finished, he brought in the things his father David had dedicated—the silver and gold and the furnishings—and he placed them in the treasuries of the LORD's temple.

---

a31 That is, about 1 1/2 feet (about 0.5 meter)   *b31* That is, about 2 1/4 feet (about 0.7 meter); also in verse 32
c35 That is, about 3/4 foot (about 0.2 meter)   *d38* That is, about 230 gallons (about 880 liters)

The Ark Brought to the Temple

8 Then King Solomon summoned into his presence at Jerusalem the elders of Israel, all the heads of the tribes and the chiefs of the Israelite families, to bring up the ark of the LORD's covenant from Zion, the City of David. ²All the men of Israel came together to King Solomon at the time of the festival in the month of Ethanim, the seventh month.

³When all the elders of Israel had arrived, the priests took up the ark, ⁴and they brought up the ark of the LORD and the Tent of Meeting and all the sacred furnishings in it. The priests and Levites carried them up, ⁵and King Solomon and the entire assembly of Israel that had gathered about him were before the ark, sacrificing so many sheep and cattle that they could not be recorded or counted.

⁶The priests then brought the ark of the LORD's covenant to its place in the inner sanctuary of the temple, the Most Holy Place, and put it beneath the wings of the cherubim. ⁷The cherubim spread their wings over the place of the ark and overshadowed the ark and its carrying poles. ⁸These poles were so long that their ends could be seen from the Holy Place in front of the inner sanctuary, but not from outside the Holy Place; and they are still there today. ⁹There was nothing in the ark except the two stone tablets that Moses had placed in it at Horeb, where the LORD made a covenant with the Israelites after they came out of Egypt.

¹⁰When the priests withdrew from the Holy Place, the cloud filled the temple of the LORD. ¹¹And the priests could not perform their service because of the cloud, for the glory of the LORD filled his temple.

¹²Then Solomon said, "The LORD has said that he would dwell in a dark cloud; ¹³I have indeed built a magnificent temple for you, a place for you to dwell forever."

¹⁴While the whole assembly of Israel was standing there, the king turned around and blessed them. ¹⁵Then he said:

"Praise be to the LORD, the God of Israel, who with his own hand has fulfilled what he promised with his own mouth to my father David. For he said, ¹⁶'Since the day I brought my people Israel out of Egypt, I have not chosen a city in any tribe of Israel to have a temple built for my Name to be there, but I have chosen David to rule my people Israel.'

¹⁷"My father David had it in his heart to build a temple for the Name of the LORD, the God of Israel. ¹⁸But the LORD said to my father David, 'Because it was in your heart to build a temple for my Name, you did well to have this in your heart. ¹⁹Nevertheless, you are not the one to build the temple, but your son, who is your own flesh and blood—he is the one who will build the temple for my Name.'

²⁰"The LORD has kept the promise he made: I have succeeded David my father and now I sit on the throne of Israel, just as the LORD promised, and I have built the temple for the Name of the LORD, the God of Israel. ²¹I have provided a place there for the ark, in which is the covenant of the LORD that he made with our fathers when he brought them out of Egypt."

Solomon's Prayer of Dedication

²²Then Solomon stood before the altar of the LORD in front of the whole assembly of Israel, spread out his hands toward heaven ²³and said:

"O LORD, God of Israel, there is no God like you in heaven above or on earth below—you who keep your covenant of love with your servants who continue wholeheartedly in your way. ²⁴You have kept your promise to your servant David my father; with your mouth you have promised and with your hand you have fulfilled it—as it is today.

²⁵"Now LORD, God of Israel, keep for your servant David my father the promises you made to him when you said, 'You shall never fail to have a man to sit before me on

the throne of Israel, if only your sons are careful in all they do to walk before me as you have done.' ²⁶And now, O God of Israel, let your word that you promised your servant David my father come true.

²⁷"But will God really dwell on earth? The heavens, even the highest heaven, cannot contain you. How much less this temple I have built! ²⁸Yet give attention to your servant's prayer and his plea for mercy, O LORD my God. Hear the cry and the prayer that your servant is praying in your presence this day. ²⁹May your eyes be open toward this temple night and day, this place of which you said, 'My Name shall be there,' so that you will hear the prayer your servant prays toward this place. ³⁰Hear the supplication of your servant and of your people Israel when they pray toward this place. Hear from heaven, your dwelling place, and when you hear, forgive.

³¹"When a man wrongs his neighbor and is required to take an oath and he comes and swears the oath before your altar in this temple, ³²then hear from heaven and act. Judge between your servants, condemning the guilty and bringing down on his own head what he has done. Declare the innocent not guilty, and so establish his innocence.

³³"When your people Israel have been defeated by an enemy because they have sinned against you, and when they turn back to you and confess your name, praying and making supplication to you in this temple, ³⁴then hear from heaven and forgive the sin of your people Israel and bring them back to the land you gave to their fathers.

³⁵"When the heavens are shut up and there is no rain because your people have sinned against you, and when they pray toward this place and confess your name and turn from their sin because you have afflicted them, ³⁶then hear from heaven and forgive the sin of your servants, your people Israel. Teach them the right way to live, and send rain on the land you gave your people for an inheritance.

³⁷"When famine or plague comes to the land, or blight or mildew, locusts or grasshoppers, or when an enemy besieges them in any of their cities, whatever disaster or disease may come, ³⁸and when a prayer or plea is made by any of your people Israel—each one aware of the afflictions of his own heart, and spreading out his hands toward this temple— ³⁹then hear from heaven, your dwelling place. Forgive and act; deal with each man according to all he does, since you know his heart (for you alone know the hearts of all men), ⁴⁰so that they will fear you all the time they live in the land you gave our fathers.

⁴¹"As for the foreigner who does not belong to your people Israel but has come from a distant land because of your name— ⁴²for men will hear of your great name and your mighty hand and your outstretched arm—when he comes and prays toward this temple, ⁴³then hear from heaven, your dwelling place, and do whatever the foreigner asks of you, so that all the peoples of the earth may know your name and fear you, as do your own people Israel, and may know that this house I have built bears your Name.

⁴⁴"When your people go to war against their enemies, wherever you send them, and when they pray to the LORD toward the city you have chosen and the temple I have built for your Name, ⁴⁵then hear from heaven their prayer and their plea, and uphold their cause.

⁴⁶"When they sin against you—for there is no one who does not sin—and you become angry with them and give them over to the enemy, who takes them captive to his own land, far away or near; ⁴⁷and if they have a change of heart in the land where they are held captive, and repent and plead with you in the land of their conquerors and say, 'We have sinned, we have done wrong, we have acted wickedly'; ⁴⁸and if they turn back to you with all their heart and soul in the land of their enemies who took them captive, and pray to you toward the land you gave their

fathers, toward the city you have chosen and the temple I have built for your Name; ⁴⁹then from heaven, your dwelling place, hear their prayer and their plea, and uphold their cause. ⁵⁰And forgive your people, who have sinned against you; forgive all the offenses they have committed against you, and cause their conquerors to show them mercy; ⁵¹for they are your people and your inheritance, whom you brought out of Egypt, out of that iron-smelting furnace.

⁵²"May your eyes be open to your servant's plea and to the plea of your people Israel, and may you listen to them whenever they cry out to you. ⁵³For you singled them out from all the nations of the world to be your own inheritance, just as you declared through your servant Moses when you, O Sovereign Lord, brought our fathers out of Egypt."

⁵⁴When Solomon had finished all these prayers and supplications to the Lord, he rose from before the altar of the Lord, where he had been kneeling with his hands spread out toward heaven. ⁵⁵He stood and blessed the whole assembly of Israel in a loud voice, saying:

⁵⁶"Praise be to the Lord, who has given rest to his people Israel just as he promised. Not one word has failed of all the good promises he gave through his servant Moses. ⁵⁷May the Lord our God be with us as he was with our fathers; may he never leave us nor forsake us. ⁵⁸May he turn our hearts to him, to walk in all his ways and to keep the commands, decrees and regulations he gave our fathers. ⁵⁹And may these words of mine, which I have prayed before the Lord, be near to the Lord our God day and night, that he may uphold the cause of his servant and the cause of his people Israel according to each day's need, ⁶⁰so that all the peoples of the earth may know that the Lord is God and that there is no other. ⁶¹But your hearts must be fully committed to the Lord our God, to live by his decrees and obey his commands, as at this time."

The Dedication of the Temple

⁶²Then the king and all Israel with him offered sacrifices before the Lord. ⁶³Solomon offered a sacrifice of fellowship offerings*a* to the Lord: twenty-two thousand cattle and a hundred and twenty thousand sheep and goats. So the king and all the Israelites dedicated the temple of the Lord.

⁶⁴On that same day the king consecrated the middle part of the courtyard in front of the temple of the Lord, and there he offered burnt offerings, grain offerings and the fat of the fellowship offerings, because the bronze altar before the Lord was too small to hold the burnt offerings, the grain offerings and the fat of the fellowship offerings.

⁶⁵So Solomon observed the festival at that time, and all Israel with him—a vast assembly, people from Lebo*b* Hamath to the Wadi of Egypt. They celebrated it before the Lord our God for seven days and seven days more, fourteen days in all. ⁶⁶On the following day he sent the people away. They blessed the king and then went home, joyful and glad in heart for all the good things the Lord had done for his servant David and his people Israel.

The Lord Appears to Solomon

9 When Solomon had finished building the temple of the Lord and the royal palace, and had achieved all he had desired to do, ²the Lord appeared to him a second time, as he had appeared to him at Gibeon. ³The Lord said to him:

"I have heard the prayer and plea you have made before me; I have consecrated this temple, which you have built, by putting my Name there forever. My eyes and my heart will always be there.

⁴"As for you, if you walk before me in integrity of heart and uprightness, as David

a 63 Traditionally *peace offerings*; also in verse 64   *b 65* Or *from the entrance to*

your father did, and do all I command and observe my decrees and laws, ⁵I will establish your royal throne over Israel forever, as I promised David your father when I said, 'You shall never fail to have a man on the throne of Israel.'

⁶"But if you*ᵃ* or your sons turn away from me and do not observe the commands and decrees I have given you*ᵃ* and go off to serve other gods and worship them, ⁷then I will cut off Israel from the land I have given them and will reject this temple I have consecrated for my Name. Israel will then become a byword and an object of ridicule among all peoples. ⁸And though this temple is now imposing, all who pass by will be appalled and will scoff and say, 'Why has the Lᴏʀᴅ done such a thing to this land and to this temple?' ⁹People will answer, 'Because they have forsaken the Lᴏʀᴅ their God, who brought their fathers out of Egypt, and have embraced other gods, worshiping and serving them—that is why the Lᴏʀᴅ brought all this disaster on them.' "

Solomon's Other Activities

¹⁰At the end of twenty years, during which Solomon built these two buildings—the temple of the Lᴏʀᴅ and the royal palace— ¹¹King Solomon gave twenty towns in Galilee to Hiram king of Tyre, because Hiram had supplied him with all the cedar and pine and gold he wanted. ¹²But when Hiram went from Tyre to see the towns that Solomon had given him, he was not pleased with them. ¹³"What kind of towns are these you have given me, my brother?" he asked. And he called them the Land of Cabul,*ᵇ* a name they have to this day. ¹⁴Now Hiram had sent to the king 120 talents*ᶜ* of gold.

¹⁵Here is the account of the forced labor King Solomon conscripted to build the Lᴏʀᴅ's temple, his own palace, the supporting terraces,*ᵈ* the wall of Jerusalem, and Hazor, Megiddo and Gezer. ¹⁶(Pharaoh king of Egypt had attacked and captured Gezer. He had set it on fire. He killed its Canaanite inhabitants and then gave it as a wedding gift to his daughter, Solomon's wife. ¹⁷And Solomon rebuilt Gezer.) He built up Lower Beth Horon, ¹⁸Baalath, and Tadmor*ᵉ* in the desert, within his land, ¹⁹as well as all his store cities and the towns for his chariots and for his horses*ᶠ*—whatever he desired to build in Jerusalem, in Lebanon and throughout all the territory he ruled.

²⁰All the people left from the Amorites, Hittites, Perizzites, Hivites and Jebusites (these peoples were not Israelites), ²¹that is, their descendants remaining in the land, whom the Israelites could not exterminate*ᵍ*—these Solomon conscripted for his slave labor force, as it is to this day. ²²But Solomon did not make slaves of any of the Israelites; they were his fighting men, his government officials, his officers, his captains, and the commanders of his chariots and charioteers. ²³They were also the chief officials in charge of Solomon's projects—550 officials supervising the men who did the work.

²⁴After Pharaoh's daughter had come up from the City of David to the palace Solomon had built for her, he constructed the supporting terraces.

²⁵Three times a year Solomon sacrificed burnt offerings and fellowship offerings*ʰ* on the altar he had built for the Lᴏʀᴅ, burning incense before the Lᴏʀᴅ along with them, and so fulfilled the temple obligations.

²⁶King Solomon also built ships at Ezion Geber, which is near Elath in Edom, on the shore of the Red Sea.*ᶦ* ²⁷And Hiram sent his men—sailors who knew the sea—to serve in the fleet with Solomon's men. ²⁸They sailed to Ophir and brought back 420 talents*ʲ* of gold, which they delivered to King Solomon.

ᵃ6 The Hebrew is plural.   *ᵇ13* Cabul sounds like the Hebrew for good-for-nothing.   *ᶜ14* That is, about 4 1/2 tons (about 4 metric tons)   *ᵈ15* Or the Millo; also in verse 24   *ᵉ18* The Hebrew may also be read Tamar.   *ᶠ19* Or charioteers   *ᵍ21* The Hebrew term refers to the irrevocable giving over of things or persons to the Lᴏʀᴅ, often by totally destroying them.   *ʰ25* Traditionally peace offerings   *ᶦ26* Hebrew Yam Suph; that is, Sea of Reeds   *ʲ28* That is, about 16 tons (about 14.5 metric tons)

The Queen of Sheba Visits Solomon

10 When the queen of Sheba heard about the fame of Solomon and his relation to the name of the LORD, she came to test him with hard questions. ²Arriving at Jerusalem with a very great caravan—with camels carrying spices, large quantities of gold, and precious stones—she came to Solomon and talked with him about all that she had on her mind. ³Solomon answered all her questions; nothing was too hard for the king to explain to her. ⁴When the queen of Sheba saw all the wisdom of Solomon and the palace he had built, ⁵the food on his table, the seating of his officials, the attending servants in their robes, his cupbearers, and the burnt offerings he made at*ᵃ* the temple of the LORD, she was overwhelmed.

⁶She said to the king, "The report I heard in my own country about your achievements and your wisdom is true. ⁷But I did not believe these things until I came and saw with my own eyes. Indeed, not even half was told me; in wisdom and wealth you have far exceeded the report I heard. ⁸How happy your men must be! How happy your officials, who continually stand before you and hear your wisdom! ⁹Praise be to the LORD your God, who has delighted in you and placed you on the throne of Israel. Because of the LORD's eternal love for Israel, he has made you king, to maintain justice and righteousness."

¹⁰And she gave the king 120 talents*ᵇ* of gold, large quantities of spices, and precious stones. Never again were so many spices brought in as those the queen of Sheba gave to King Solomon.

¹¹(Hiram's ships brought gold from Ophir; and from there they brought great cargoes of almugwood*ᶜ* and precious stones. ¹²The king used the almugwood to make supports for the temple of the LORD and for the royal palace, and to make harps and lyres for the musicians. So much almugwood has never been imported or seen since that day.)

¹³King Solomon gave the queen of Sheba all she desired and asked for, besides what he had given her out of his royal bounty. Then she left and returned with her retinue to her own country.

Solomon's Splendor

¹⁴The weight of the gold that Solomon received yearly was 666 talents,*ᵈ* ¹⁵not including the revenues from merchants and traders and from all the Arabian kings and the governors of the land.

¹⁶King Solomon made two hundred large shields of hammered gold; six hundred bekas*ᵉ* of gold went into each shield. ¹⁷He also made three hundred small shields of hammered gold, with three minas*ᶠ* of gold in each shield. The king put them in the Palace of the Forest of Lebanon.

¹⁸Then the king made a great throne inlaid with ivory and overlaid with fine gold. ¹⁹The throne had six steps, and its back had a rounded top. On both sides of the seat were armrests, with a lion standing beside each of them. ²⁰Twelve lions stood on the six steps, one at either end of each step. Nothing like it had ever been made for any other kingdom. ²¹All King Solomon's goblets were gold, and all the household articles in the Palace of the Forest of Lebanon were pure gold. Nothing was made of silver, because silver was considered of little value in Solomon's days. ²²The king had a fleet of trading ships*ᵍ* at sea along with the ships of Hiram. Once every three years it returned, carrying gold, silver and ivory, and apes and baboons.

²³King Solomon was greater in riches and wisdom than all the other kings of the earth. ²⁴The whole world sought audience with Solomon to hear the wisdom God had put in his heart. ²⁵Year after year, everyone who came brought a gift—articles of silver and gold, robes, weapons and spices, and horses and mules.

²⁶Solomon accumulated chariots and horses; he had fourteen hundred chariots and

---

ᵃ5 Or *the ascent by which he went up to*   *ᵇ10* That is, about 4 1/2 tons (about 4 metric tons)   *ᶜ11* Probably a variant of *algumwood;* also in verse 12   *ᵈ14* That is, about 25 tons (about 23 metric tons)   *ᵉ16* That is, about 7 1/2 pounds (about 3.5 kilograms)   *ᶠ17* That is, about 3 3/4 pounds (about 1.7 kilograms)   *ᵍ22* Hebrew *of ships of Tarshish*

twelve thousand horses,ᵃ which he kept in the chariot cities and also with him in Jerusalem. ²⁷The king made silver as common in Jerusalem as stones, and cedar as plentiful as sycamore-fig trees in the foothills. ²⁸Solomon's horses were imported from Egyptᵇ and from Kueᶜ—the royal merchants purchased them from Kue. ²⁹They imported a chariot from Egypt for six hundred shekelsᵈ of silver, and a horse for a hundred and fifty.ᵉ They also exported them to all the kings of the Hittites and of the Arameans.

:::::: STRENGTHENING RELATIONSHIPS :::::: ⬅

11:1–6
Marriage

The sheer number of Solomon's wives and concubines probably amazes all who read this account. But more serious is how these wives and concubines drew him away from the true God to serve the gods of their particular family backgrounds (verse 4).

Solomon made two mistakes when it came to marriage. First, he ignored the fact that God designed marriage as an institution that allows two people to commit to build an exclusive relationship together. Second, he ignored the basis for a solid marriage—love for God and love for one's spouse. In God's eyes, following the various other gods of his many wives was his greatest offense—one that he paid for dearly (verse 11).

This story may sound foreign to our modern ears, but we can learn from Solomon's negative example what God truly intends for marriage and what can happen when those intentions are ignored.

Solomon's Wives

11 King Solomon, however, loved many foreign women besides Pharaoh's daughter—Moabites, Ammonites, Edomites, Sidonians and Hittites. ²They were from nations about which the LORD had told the Israelites, "You must not intermarry with them, because they will surely turn your hearts after their gods." Nevertheless, Solomon held fast to them in love. ³He had seven hundred wives of royal birth and three hundred concubines, and his wives led him astray. ⁴As Solomon grew old, his wives turned his heart after other gods, and his heart was not fully devoted to the LORD his God, as the heart of David his father had been. ⁵He followed Ashtoreth the goddess of the Sidonians, and Molechᶠ the detestable god of the Ammonites. ⁶So Solomon did evil in the eyes of the LORD; he did not follow the LORD completely, as David his father had done.

⁷On a hill east of Jerusalem, Solomon built a high place for Chemosh the detestable god of Moab, and for Molech the detestable god of the Ammonites. ⁸He did the same for all his foreign wives, who burned incense and offered sacrifices to their gods.

⁹The LORD became angry with Solomon because his heart had turned away from the LORD, the God of Israel, who had appeared to him twice. ¹⁰Although he had forbidden Solomon to follow other gods, Solomon did not keep the LORD's command. ¹¹So the LORD said to Solomon, "Since this is your attitude and you have not kept my covenant and my decrees, which I commanded you, I will most certainly tear the kingdom away from you and give it to one of your subordinates. ¹²Nevertheless, for the sake of David your father, I will not do it during your lifetime. I will tear it out of the hand of your son. ¹³Yet I will not tear the whole kingdom from him, but will give him one tribe for the sake of David my servant and for the sake of Jerusalem, which I have chosen."

Solomon's Adversaries

¹⁴Then the LORD raised up against Solomon an adversary, Hadad the Edomite, from the royal line of Edom. ¹⁵Earlier when David was fighting with Edom, Joab the commander of the army, who had gone up to bury the dead, had struck down all the men in Edom. ¹⁶Joab and all the Israelites stayed there for six months, until they had destroyed all the men in Edom. ¹⁷But Hadad, still only a boy, fled to Egypt with some Edomite officials who

---

ᵃ26 Or charioteers ᵇ28 Or possibly Muzur, a region in Cilicia; also in verse 29 ᶜ28 Probably Cilicia ᵈ29 That is, about 15 pounds (about 7 kilograms) ᵉ29 That is, about 3 3/4 pounds (about 1.7 kilograms) ᶠ5 Hebrew Milcom; also in verse 33

had served his father. ¹⁸They set out from Midian and went to Paran. Then taking men from Paran with them, they went to Egypt, to Pharaoh king of Egypt, who gave Hadad a house and land and provided him with food.

¹⁹Pharaoh was so pleased with Hadad that he gave him a sister of his own wife, Queen Tahpenes, in marriage. ²⁰The sister of Tahpenes bore him a son named Genubath, whom Tahpenes brought up in the royal palace. There Genubath lived with Pharaoh's own children.

²¹While he was in Egypt, Hadad heard that David rested with his fathers and that Joab the commander of the army was also dead. Then Hadad said to Pharaoh, "Let me go, that I may return to my own country."

²²"What have you lacked here that you want to go back to your own country?" Pharaoh asked.

"Nothing," Hadad replied, "but do let me go!"

²³And God raised up against Solomon another adversary, Rezon son of Eliada, who had fled from his master, Hadadezer king of Zobah. ²⁴He gathered men around him and became the leader of a band of rebels when David destroyed the forces*ᵃ* ˌof Zobahˌ; the rebels went to Damascus, where they settled and took control. ²⁵Rezon was Israel's adversary as long as Solomon lived, adding to the trouble caused by Hadad. So Rezon ruled in Aram and was hostile toward Israel.

Jeroboam Rebels Against Solomon

²⁶Also, Jeroboam son of Nebat rebelled against the king. He was one of Solomon's officials, an Ephraimite from Zeredah, and his mother was a widow named Zeruah.

²⁷Here is the account of how he rebelled against the king: Solomon had built the supporting terraces*ᵇ* and had filled in the gap in the wall of the city of David his father. ²⁸Now Jeroboam was a man of standing, and when Solomon saw how well the young man did his work, he put him in charge of the whole labor force of the house of Joseph.

²⁹About that time Jeroboam was going out of Jerusalem, and Ahijah the prophet of Shiloh met him on the way, wearing a new cloak. The two of them were alone out in the country, ³⁰and Ahijah took hold of the new cloak he was wearing and tore it into twelve pieces. ³¹Then he said to Jeroboam, "Take ten pieces for yourself, for this is what the LORD, the God of Israel, says: 'See, I am going to tear the kingdom out of Solomon's hand and give you ten tribes. ³²But for the sake of my servant David and the city of Jerusalem, which I have chosen out of all the tribes of Israel, he will have one tribe. ³³I will do this because they have*ᶜ* forsaken me and worshiped Ashtoreth the goddess of the Sidonians, Chemosh the god of the Moabites, and Molech the god of the Ammonites, and have not walked in my ways, nor done what is right in my eyes, nor kept my statutes and laws as David, Solomon's father, did.

³⁴" 'But I will not take the whole kingdom out of Solomon's hand; I have made him ruler all the days of his life for the sake of David my servant, whom I chose and who observed my commands and statutes. ³⁵I will take the kingdom from his son's hands and give you ten tribes. ³⁶I will give one tribe to his son so that David my servant may always have a lamp before me in Jerusalem, the city where I chose to put my Name. ³⁷However, as for you, I will take you, and you will rule over all that your heart desires; you will be king over Israel. ³⁸If you do whatever I command you and walk in my ways and do what is right in my eyes by keeping my statutes and commands, as David my servant did, I will be with you. I will build you a dynasty as enduring as the one I built for David and will give Israel to you. ³⁹I will humble David's descendants because of this, but not forever.' "

⁴⁰Solomon tried to kill Jeroboam, but Jeroboam fled to Egypt, to Shishak the king, and stayed there until Solomon's death.

ᵃ24 Hebrew *destroyed them*   *ᵇ27* Or *the Millo*   *ᶜ33* Hebrew; Septuagint, Vulgate and Syriac *because he has*

Solomon's Death

⁴¹As for the other events of Solomon's reign—all he did and the wisdom he displayed— are they not written in the book of the annals of Solomon? ⁴²Solomon reigned in Jerusalem over all Israel forty years. ⁴³Then he rested with his fathers and was buried in the city of David his father. And Rehoboam his son succeeded him as king.

Israel Rebels Against Rehoboam

12 Rehoboam went to Shechem, for all the Israelites had gone there to make him king. ²When Jeroboam son of Nebat heard this (he was still in Egypt, where he had fled from King Solomon), he returned from*ᵃ* Egypt. ³So they sent for Jeroboam, and he and the whole assembly of Israel went to Rehoboam and said to him: ⁴"Your father put a heavy yoke on us, but now lighten the harsh labor and the heavy yoke he put on us, and we will serve you."

⁵Rehoboam answered, "Go away for three days and then come back to me." So the people went away.

⁶Then King Rehoboam consulted the elders who had served his father Solomon during his lifetime. "How would you advise me to answer these people?" he asked.

⁷They replied, "If today you will be a servant to these people and serve them and give them a favorable answer, they will always be your servants."

⁸But Rehoboam rejected the advice the elders gave him and consulted the young men who had grown up with him and were serving him. ⁹He asked them, "What is your advice? How should we answer these people who say to me, 'Lighten the yoke your father put on us'?"

¹⁰The young men who had grown up with him replied, "Tell these people who have said to you, 'Your father put a heavy yoke on us, but make our yoke lighter'—tell them, 'My little finger is thicker than my father's waist. ¹¹My father laid on you a heavy yoke; I will make it even heavier. My father scourged you with whips; I will scourge you with scorpions.'"

¹²Three days later Jeroboam and all the people returned to Rehoboam, as the king had said, "Come back to me in three days." ¹³The king answered the people harshly. Rejecting the advice given him by the elders, ¹⁴he followed the advice of the young men and said, "My father made your yoke heavy; I will make it even heavier. My father scourged you with whips; I will scourge you with scorpions." ¹⁵So the king did not listen to the people, for this turn of events was from the LORD, to fulfill the word the LORD had spoken to Jeroboam son of Nebat through Ahijah the Shilonite.

¹⁶When all Israel saw that the king refused to listen to them, they answered the king:

> "What share do we have in David,
>   what part in Jesse's son?
> To your tents, O Israel!
>   Look after your own house, O David!"

So the Israelites went home. ¹⁷But as for the Israelites who were living in the towns of Judah, Rehoboam still ruled over them.

¹⁸King Rehoboam sent out Adoniram,*ᵇ* who was in charge of forced labor, but all Israel stoned him to death. King Rehoboam, however, managed to get into his chariot and escape to Jerusalem. ¹⁹So Israel has been in rebellion against the house of David to this day.

²⁰When all the Israelites heard that Jeroboam had returned, they sent and called him to the assembly and made him king over all Israel. Only the tribe of Judah remained loyal to the house of David.

²¹When Rehoboam arrived in Jerusalem, he mustered the whole house of Judah and

---

ᵃ2 Or *he remained in*   *ᵇ18* Some Septuagint manuscripts and Syriac (see also 1 Kings 4:6 and 5:14); Hebrew *Adoram* the tribe of Benjamin—a hundred and eighty thousand fighting men—to make war against the house of Israel and to regain the kingdom for Rehoboam son of Solomon.

²²But this word of God came to Shemaiah the man of God: ²³"Say to Rehoboam son of Solomon king of Judah, to the whole house of Judah and Benjamin, and to the rest of the people, ²⁴'This is what the LORD says: Do not go up to fight against your brothers, the Israelites. Go home, every one of you, for this is my doing.'" So they obeyed the word of the LORD and went home again, as the LORD had ordered.

Golden Calves at Bethel and Dan

²⁵Then Jeroboam fortified Shechem in the hill country of Ephraim and lived there. From there he went out and built up Peniel.*ᵃ*

²⁶Jeroboam thought to himself, "The kingdom will now likely revert to the house of David. ²⁷If these people go up to offer sacrifices at the temple of the LORD in Jerusalem, they will again give their allegiance to their lord, Rehoboam king of Judah. They will kill me and return to King Rehoboam."

²⁸After seeking advice, the king made two golden calves. He said to the people, "It is too much for you to go up to Jerusalem. Here are your gods, O Israel, who brought you up out of Egypt." ²⁹One he set up in Bethel, and the other in Dan. ³⁰And this thing became a sin; the people went even as far as Dan to worship the one there.

³¹Jeroboam built shrines on high places and appointed priests from all sorts of people, even though they were not Levites. ³²He instituted a festival on the fifteenth day of the eighth month, like the festival held in Judah, and offered sacrifices on the altar. This he did in Bethel, sacrificing to the calves he had made. And at Bethel he also installed priests at the high places he had made. ³³On the fifteenth day of the eighth month, a month of his own choosing, he offered sacrifices on the altar he had built at Bethel. So he instituted the festival for the Israelites and went up to the altar to make offerings.

The Man of God From Judah

13 By the word of the LORD a man of God came from Judah to Bethel, as Jeroboam was standing by the altar to make an offering. ²He cried out against the altar by the word of the LORD: "O altar, altar! This is what the LORD says: 'A son named Josiah will be born to the house of David. On you he will sacrifice the priests of the high places who now make offerings here, and human bones will be burned on you.'" ³That same day the man of God gave a sign: "This is the sign the LORD has declared: The altar will be split apart and the ashes on it will be poured out."

⁴When King Jeroboam heard what the man of God cried out against the altar at Bethel, he stretched out his hand from the altar and said, "Seize him!" But the hand he stretched out toward the man shriveled up, so that he could not pull it back. ⁵Also, the altar was split apart and its ashes poured out according to the sign given by the man of God by the word of the LORD.

⁶Then the king said to the man of God, "Intercede with the LORD your God and pray for me that my hand may be restored." So the man of God interceded with the LORD, and the king's hand was restored and became as it was before.

⁷The king said to the man of God, "Come home with me and have something to eat, and I will give you a gift."

⁸But the man of God answered the king, "Even if you were to give me half your possessions, I would not go with you, nor would I eat bread or drink water here. ⁹For I was commanded by the word of the LORD: 'You must not eat bread or drink water or return by the way you came.'" ¹⁰So he took another road and did not return by the way he had come to Bethel.

¹¹Now there was a certain old prophet living in Bethel, whose sons came and told him all that the man of God had done there that day. They also told their father what he had

ᵃ25 Hebrew Penuel, a variant of Peniel

said to the king. ¹²Their father asked them, "Which way did he go?" And his sons showed him which road the man of God from Judah had taken. ¹³So he said to his sons, "Saddle the donkey for me." And when they had saddled the donkey for him, he mounted it ¹⁴and rode after the man of God. He found him sitting under an oak tree and asked, "Are you the man of God who came from Judah?"

"I am," he replied.

¹⁵So the prophet said to him, "Come home with me and eat."

¹⁶The man of God said, "I cannot turn back and go with you, nor can I eat bread or drink water with you in this place. ¹⁷I have been told by the word of the LORD: 'You must not eat bread or drink water there or return by the way you came.'"

¹⁸The old prophet answered, "I too am a prophet, as you are. And an angel said to me by the word of the LORD: 'Bring him back with you to your house so that he may eat bread and drink water.'" (But he was lying to him.) ¹⁹So the man of God returned with him and ate and drank in his house.

²⁰While they were sitting at the table, the word of the LORD came to the old prophet who had brought him back. ²¹He cried out to the man of God who had come from Judah, "This is what the LORD says: 'You have defied the word of the LORD and have not kept the command the LORD your God gave you. ²²You came back and ate bread and drank water in the place where he told you not to eat or drink. Therefore your body will not be buried in the tomb of your fathers.'"

²³When the man of God had finished eating and drinking, the prophet who had brought him back saddled his donkey for him. ²⁴As he went on his way, a lion met him on the road and killed him, and his body was thrown down on the road, with both the donkey and the lion standing beside it. ²⁵Some people who passed by saw the body thrown down there, with the lion standing beside the body, and they went and reported it in the city where the old prophet lived.

²⁶When the prophet who had brought him back from his journey heard of it, he said, "It is the man of God who defied the word of the LORD. The LORD has given him over to the lion, which has mauled him and killed him, as the word of the LORD had warned him."

²⁷The prophet said to his sons, "Saddle the donkey for me," and they did so. ²⁸Then he went out and found the body thrown down on the road, with the donkey and the lion standing beside it. The lion had neither eaten the body nor mauled the donkey. ²⁹So the prophet picked up the body of the man of God, laid it on the donkey, and brought it back to his own city to mourn for him and bury him. ³⁰Then he laid the body in his own tomb, and they mourned over him and said, "Oh, my brother!"

³¹After burying him, he said to his sons, "When I die, bury me in the grave where the man of God is buried; lay my bones beside his bones. ³²For the message he declared by the word of the LORD against the altar in Bethel and against all the shrines on the high places in the towns of Samaria will certainly come true."

³³Even after this, Jeroboam did not change his evil ways, but once more appointed priests for the high places from all sorts of people. Anyone who wanted to become a priest he consecrated for the high places. ³⁴This was the sin of the house of Jeroboam that led to its downfall and to its destruction from the face of the earth.

Ahijah's Prophecy Against Jeroboam

14 At that time Abijah son of Jeroboam became ill, ²and Jeroboam said to his wife, "Go, disguise yourself, so you won't be recognized as the wife of Jeroboam. Then go to Shiloh. Ahijah the prophet is there—the one who told me I would be king over this people. ³Take ten loaves of bread with you, some cakes and a jar of honey, and go to him. He will tell you what will happen to the boy." ⁴So Jeroboam's wife did what he said and went to Ahijah's house in Shiloh.

Now Ahijah could not see; his sight was gone because of his age. ⁵But the LORD had told Ahijah, "Jeroboam's wife is coming to ask you about her son, for he is ill, and you are to give her such and such an answer. When she arrives, she will pretend to be someone else."

⁶So when Ahijah heard the sound of her footsteps at the door, he said, "Come in, wife of Jeroboam. Why this pretense? I have been sent to you with bad news. ⁷Go, tell Jeroboam that this is what the Lᴏʀᴅ, the God of Israel, says: 'I raised you up from among the people and made you a leader over my people Israel. ⁸I tore the kingdom away from the house of David and gave it to you, but you have not been like my servant David, who kept my commands and followed me with all his heart, doing only what was right in my eyes. ⁹You have done more evil than all who lived before you. You have made for yourself other gods, idols made of metal; you have provoked me to anger and thrust me behind your back.

¹⁰"'Because of this, I am going to bring disaster on the house of Jeroboam. I will cut off from Jeroboam every last male in Israel—slave or free. I will burn up the house of Jeroboam as one burns dung, until it is all gone. ¹¹Dogs will eat those belonging to Jeroboam who die in the city, and the birds of the air will feed on those who die in the country. The Lᴏʀᴅ has spoken!'

¹²"As for you, go back home. When you set foot in your city, the boy will die. ¹³All Israel will mourn for him and bury him. He is the only one belonging to Jeroboam who will be buried, because he is the only one in the house of Jeroboam in whom the Lᴏʀᴅ, the God of Israel, has found anything good.

¹⁴"The Lᴏʀᴅ will raise up for himself a king over Israel who will cut off the family of Jeroboam. This is the day! What? Yes, even now.ᵃ ¹⁵And the Lᴏʀᴅ will strike Israel, so that it will be like a reed swaying in the water. He will uproot Israel from this good land that he gave to their forefathers and scatter them beyond the River,ᵇ because they provoked the Lᴏʀᴅ to anger by making Asherah poles.ᶜ ¹⁶And he will give Israel up because of the sins Jeroboam has committed and has caused Israel to commit."

¹⁷Then Jeroboam's wife got up and left and went to Tirzah. As soon as she stepped over the threshold of the house, the boy died. ¹⁸They buried him, and all Israel mourned for him, as the Lᴏʀᴅ had said through his servant the prophet Ahijah.

¹⁹The other events of Jeroboam's reign, his wars and how he ruled, are written in the book of the annals of the kings of Israel. ²⁰He reigned for twenty-two years and then rested with his fathers. And Nadab his son succeeded him as king.

Rehoboam King of Judah

²¹Rehoboam son of Solomon was king in Judah. He was forty-one years old when he became king, and he reigned seventeen years in Jerusalem, the city the Lᴏʀᴅ had chosen out of all the tribes of Israel in which to put his Name. His mother's name was Naamah; she was an Ammonite.

²²Judah did evil in the eyes of the Lᴏʀᴅ. By the sins they committed they stirred up his jealous anger more than their fathers had done. ²³They also set up for themselves high places, sacred stones and Asherah poles on every high hill and under every spreading tree. ²⁴There were even male shrine prostitutes in the land; the people engaged in all the detestable practices of the nations the Lᴏʀᴅ had driven out before the Israelites.

²⁵In the fifth year of King Rehoboam, Shishak king of Egypt attacked Jerusalem. ²⁶He carried off the treasures of the temple of the Lᴏʀᴅ and the treasures of the royal palace. He took everything, including all the gold shields Solomon had made. ²⁷So King Rehoboam made bronze shields to replace them and assigned these to the commanders of the guard on duty at the entrance to the royal palace. ²⁸Whenever the king went to the Lᴏʀᴅ's temple, the guards bore the shields, and afterward they returned them to the guardroom.

²⁹As for the other events of Rehoboam's reign, and all he did, are they not written in the book of the annals of the kings of Judah? ³⁰There was continual warfare between

---

ᵃ14 The meaning of the Hebrew for this sentence is uncertain.   ᵇ15 That is, the Euphrates   ᶜ15 That is, symbols of the goddess Asherah; here and elsewhere in 1 Kings

Rehoboam and Jeroboam. ³¹And Rehoboam rested with his fathers and was buried with them in the City of David. His mother's name was Naamah; she was an Ammonite. And Abijah*ᵃ* his son succeeded him as king.

Abijah King of Judah

15 In the eighteenth year of the reign of Jeroboam son of Nebat, Abijah*ᵇ* became king of Judah, ²and he reigned in Jerusalem three years. His mother's name was Maacah daughter of Abishalom.*ᶜ*

³He committed all the sins his father had done before him; his heart was not fully devoted to the LORD his God, as the heart of David his forefather had been. ⁴Nevertheless, for David's sake the LORD his God gave him a lamp in Jerusalem by raising up a son to succeed him and by making Jerusalem strong. ⁵For David had done what was right in the eyes of the LORD and had not failed to keep any of the LORD's commands all the days of his life—except in the case of Uriah the Hittite.

⁶There was war between Rehoboam*ᵈ* and Jeroboam throughout ⌊Abijah's⌋ lifetime. ⁷As for the other events of Abijah's reign, and all he did, are they not written in the book of the annals of the kings of Judah? There was war between Abijah and Jeroboam. ⁸And Abijah rested with his fathers and was buried in the City of David. And Asa his son succeeded him as king.

Asa King of Judah

⁹In the twentieth year of Jeroboam king of Israel, Asa became king of Judah, ¹⁰and he reigned in Jerusalem forty-one years. His grandmother's name was Maacah daughter of Abishalom.

¹¹Asa did what was right in the eyes of the LORD, as his father David had done. ¹²He expelled the male shrine prostitutes from the land and got rid of all the idols his fathers had made. ¹³He even deposed his grandmother Maacah from her position as queen mother, because she had made a repulsive Asherah pole. Asa cut the pole down and burned it in the Kidron Valley. ¹⁴Although he did not remove the high places, Asa's heart was fully committed to the LORD all his life. ¹⁵He brought into the temple of the LORD the silver and gold and the articles that he and his father had dedicated.

¹⁶There was war between Asa and Baasha king of Israel throughout their reigns. ¹⁷Baasha king of Israel went up against Judah and fortified Ramah to prevent anyone from leaving or entering the territory of Asa king of Judah.

¹⁸Asa then took all the silver and gold that was left in the treasuries of the LORD's temple and of his own palace. He entrusted it to his officials and sent them to Ben-Hadad son of Tabrimmon, the son of Hezion, the king of Aram, who was ruling in Damascus. ¹⁹"Let there be a treaty between me and you," he said, "as there was between my father and your father. See, I am sending you a gift of silver and gold. Now break your treaty with Baasha king of Israel so he will withdraw from me."

²⁰Ben-Hadad agreed with King Asa and sent the commanders of his forces against the towns of Israel. He conquered Ijon, Dan, Abel Beth Maacah and all Kinnereth in addition to Naphtali. ²¹When Baasha heard this, he stopped building Ramah and withdrew to Tirzah. ²²Then King Asa issued an order to all Judah—no one was exempt—and they carried away from Ramah the stones and timber Baasha had been using there. With them King Asa built up Geba in Benjamin, and also Mizpah.

²³As for all the other events of Asa's reign, all his achievements, all he did and the cities he built, are they not written in the book of the annals of the kings of Judah? In his old age, however, his feet became diseased. ²⁴Then Asa rested with his fathers and was

---

ᵃ31 Some Hebrew manuscripts and Septuagint (see also 2 Chron. 12:16); most Hebrew manuscripts *Abijam*   *ᵇ1* Some Hebrew manuscripts and Septuagint (see also 2 Chron. 12:16); most Hebrew manuscripts *Abijam*; also in verses 7 and 8   *ᶜ2* A variant of *Absalom*; also in verse 10   *ᵈ6* Most Hebrew manuscripts; some Hebrew manuscripts and Syriac *Abijam* (that is, Abijah)

buried with them in the city of his father David. And Jehoshaphat his son succeeded him as king.

Nadab King of Israel

²⁵Nadab son of Jeroboam became king of Israel in the second year of Asa king of Judah, and he reigned over Israel two years. ²⁶He did evil in the eyes of the LORD, walking in the ways of his father and in his sin, which he had caused Israel to commit.

²⁷Baasha son of Ahijah of the house of Issachar plotted against him, and he struck him down at Gibbethon, a Philistine town, while Nadab and all Israel were besieging it. ²⁸Baasha killed Nadab in the third year of Asa king of Judah and succeeded him as king.

²⁹As soon as he began to reign, he killed Jeroboam's whole family. He did not leave Jeroboam anyone that breathed, but destroyed them all, according to the word of the LORD given through his servant Ahijah the Shilonite— ³⁰because of the sins Jeroboam had committed and had caused Israel to commit, and because he provoked the LORD, the God of Israel, to anger.

³¹As for the other events of Nadab's reign, and all he did, are they not written in the book of the annals of the kings of Israel? ³²There was war between Asa and Baasha king of Israel throughout their reigns.

Baasha King of Israel

³³In the third year of Asa king of Judah, Baasha son of Ahijah became king of all Israel in Tirzah, and he reigned twenty-four years. ³⁴He did evil in the eyes of the LORD, walking in the ways of Jeroboam and in his sin, which he had caused Israel to commit.

16 Then the word of the LORD came to Jehu son of Hanani against Baasha: ²"I lifted you up from the dust and made you leader of my people Israel, but you walked in the ways of Jeroboam and caused my people Israel to sin and to provoke me to anger by their sins. ³So I am about to consume Baasha and his house, and I will make your house like that of Jeroboam son of Nebat. ⁴Dogs will eat those belonging to Baasha who die in the city, and the birds of the air will feed on those who die in the country."

⁵As for the other events of Baasha's reign, what he did and his achievements, are they not written in the book of the annals of the kings of Israel? ⁶Baasha rested with his fathers and was buried in Tirzah. And Elah his son succeeded him as king.

⁷Moreover, the word of the LORD came through the prophet Jehu son of Hanani to Baasha and his house, because of all the evil he had done in the eyes of the LORD, provoking him to anger by the things he did, and becoming like the house of Jeroboam— and also because he destroyed it.

Elah King of Israel

⁸In the twenty-sixth year of Asa king of Judah, Elah son of Baasha became king of Israel, and he reigned in Tirzah two years.

⁹Zimri, one of his officials, who had command of half his chariots, plotted against him. Elah was in Tirzah at the time, getting drunk in the home of Arza, the man in charge of the palace at Tirzah. ¹⁰Zimri came in, struck him down and killed him in the twenty-seventh year of Asa king of Judah. Then he succeeded him as king.

¹¹As soon as he began to reign and was seated on the throne, he killed off Baasha's whole family. He did not spare a single male, whether relative or friend. ¹²So Zimri destroyed the whole family of Baasha, in accordance with the word of the LORD spoken against Baasha through the prophet Jehu— ¹³because of all the sins Baasha and his son Elah had committed and had caused Israel to commit, so that they provoked the LORD, the God of Israel, to anger by their worthless idols.

¹⁴As for the other events of Elah's reign, and all he did, are they not written in the book of the annals of the kings of Israel?

Zimri King of Israel

¹⁵In the twenty-seventh year of Asa king of Judah, Zimri reigned in Tirzah seven days. The army was encamped near Gibbethon, a Philistine town. ¹⁶When the Israelites in the camp heard that Zimri had plotted against the king and murdered him, they proclaimed Omri, the commander of the army, king over Israel that very day there in the camp. ¹⁷Then Omri and all the Israelites with him withdrew from Gibbethon and laid siege to Tirzah. ¹⁸When Zimri saw that the city was taken, he went into the citadel of the royal palace and set the palace on fire around him. So he died, ¹⁹because of the sins he had committed, doing evil in the eyes of the LORD and walking in the ways of Jeroboam and in the sin he had committed and had caused Israel to commit.

²⁰As for the other events of Zimri's reign, and the rebellion he carried out, are they not written in the book of the annals of the kings of Israel?

Omri King of Israel

²¹Then the people of Israel were split into two factions; half supported Tibni son of Ginath for king, and the other half supported Omri. ²²But Omri's followers proved stronger than those of Tibni son of Ginath. So Tibni died and Omri became king.

²³In the thirty-first year of Asa king of Judah, Omri became king of Israel, and he reigned twelve years, six of them in Tirzah. ²⁴He bought the hill of Samaria from Shemer for two talents*ᵃ* of silver and built a city on the hill, calling it Samaria, after Shemer, the name of the former owner of the hill.

²⁵But Omri did evil in the eyes of the LORD and sinned more than all those before him. ²⁶He walked in all the ways of Jeroboam son of Nebat and in his sin, which he had caused Israel to commit, so that they provoked the LORD, the God of Israel, to anger by their worthless idols.

²⁷As for the other events of Omri's reign, what he did and the things he achieved, are they not written in the book of the annals of the kings of Israel? ²⁸Omri rested with his fathers and was buried in Samaria. And Ahab his son succeeded him as king.

Ahab Becomes King of Israel

²⁹In the thirty-eighth year of Asa king of Judah, Ahab son of Omri became king of Israel, and he reigned in Samaria over Israel twenty-two years. ³⁰Ahab son of Omri did more evil in the eyes of the LORD than any of those before him. ³¹He not only considered it trivial to commit the sins of Jeroboam son of Nebat, but he also married Jezebel daughter of Ethbaal king of the Sidonians, and began to serve Baal and worship him. ³²He set up an altar for Baal in the temple of Baal that he built in Samaria. ³³Ahab also made an Asherah pole and did more to provoke the LORD, the God of Israel, to anger than did all the kings of Israel before him.

³⁴In Ahab's time, Hiel of Bethel rebuilt Jericho. He laid its foundations at the cost of his firstborn son Abiram, and he set up its gates at the cost of his youngest son Segub, in accordance with the word of the LORD spoken by Joshua son of Nun.

Elijah Fed by Ravens

17 Now Elijah the Tishbite, from Tishbe*ᵇ* in Gilead, said to Ahab, "As the LORD, the God of Israel, lives, whom I serve, there will be neither dew nor rain in the next few years except at my word."

²Then the word of the LORD came to Elijah: ³"Leave here, turn eastward and hide in the Kerith Ravine, east of the Jordan. ⁴You will drink from the brook, and I have ordered the ravens to feed you there."

⁵So he did what the LORD had told him. He went to the Kerith Ravine, east of the

---

ᵃ24 That is, about 150 pounds (about 70 kilograms)   *ᵇ1 Or Tishbite, of the settlers*

Jordan, and stayed there. ⁶The ravens brought him bread and meat in the morning and bread and meat in the evening, and he drank from the brook.

The Widow at Zarephath

⁷Some time later the brook dried up because there had been no rain in the land. ⁸Then the word of the LORD came to him: ⁹"Go at once to Zarephath of Sidon and stay there. I have commanded a widow in that place to supply you with food." ¹⁰So he went to Zarephath. When he came to the town gate, a widow was there gathering sticks. He called to her and asked, "Would you bring me a little water in a jar so I may have a drink?" ¹¹As she was going to get it, he called, "And bring me, please, a piece of bread."

¹²"As surely as the LORD your God lives," she replied, "I don't have any bread—only a handful of flour in a jar and a little oil in a jug. I am gathering a few sticks to take home and make a meal for myself and my son, that we may eat it—and die."

¹³Elijah said to her, "Don't be afraid. Go home and do as you have said. But first make a small cake of bread for me from what you have and bring it to me, and then make something for yourself and your son. ¹⁴For this is what the LORD, the God of Israel, says: 'The jar of flour will not be used up and the jug of oil will not run dry until the day the LORD gives rain on the land.'"

¹⁵She went away and did as Elijah had told her. So there was food every day for Elijah and for the woman and her family. ¹⁶For the jar of flour was not used up and the jug of oil did not run dry, in keeping with the word of the LORD spoken by Elijah.

¹⁷Some time later the son of the woman who owned the house became ill. He grew worse and worse, and finally stopped breathing. ¹⁸She said to Elijah, "What do you have against me, man of God? Did you come to remind me of my sin and kill my son?"

¹⁹"Give me your son," Elijah replied. He took him from her arms, carried him to the upper room where he was staying, and laid him on his bed. ²⁰Then he cried out to the LORD, "O LORD my God, have you brought tragedy also upon this widow I am staying with, by causing her son to die?" ²¹Then he stretched himself out on the boy three times and cried to the LORD, "O LORD my God, let this boy's life return to him!"

²²The LORD heard Elijah's cry, and the boy's life returned to him, and he lived. ²³Elijah picked up the child and carried him down from the room into the house. He gave him to his mother and said, "Look, your son is alive!"

²⁴Then the woman said to Elijah, "Now I know that you are a man of God and that the word of the LORD from your mouth is the truth."

Elijah and Obadiah

18 After a long time, in the third year, the word of the LORD came to Elijah: "Go and present yourself to Ahab, and I will send rain on the land." ²So Elijah went to present himself to Ahab.

Now the famine was severe in Samaria, ³and Ahab had summoned Obadiah, who was in charge of his palace. (Obadiah was a devout believer in the LORD. ⁴While Jezebel was killing off the LORD's prophets, Obadiah had taken a hundred prophets and hidden them in two caves, fifty in each, and had supplied them with food and water.) ⁵Ahab had said to Obadiah, "Go through the land to all the springs and valleys. Maybe we can find some grass to keep the horses and mules alive so we will not have to kill any of our animals." ⁶So they divided the land they were to cover, Ahab going in one direction and Obadiah in another.

⁷As Obadiah was walking along, Elijah met him. Obadiah recognized him, bowed down to the ground, and said, "Is it really you, my lord Elijah?"

⁸"Yes," he replied. "Go tell your master, 'Elijah is here.'"

⁹"What have I done wrong," asked Obadiah, "that you are handing your servant over to Ahab to be put to death? ¹⁰As surely as the LORD your God lives, there is not a nation or kingdom where my master has not sent someone to look for you. And whenever a nation

or kingdom claimed you were not there, he made them swear they could not find you. ¹¹But now you tell me to go to my master and say, 'Elijah is here.' ¹²I don't know where the Spirit of the Lord may carry you when I leave you. If I go and tell Ahab and he doesn't find you, he will kill me. Yet I your servant have worshiped the Lord since my youth. ¹³Haven't you heard, my lord, what I did while Jezebel was killing the prophets of the Lord? I hid a hundred of the Lord's prophets in two caves, fifty in each, and supplied them with food and water. ¹⁴And now you tell me to go to my master and say, 'Elijah is here.' He will kill me!"

¹⁵Elijah said, "As the Lord Almighty lives, whom I serve, I will surely present myself to Ahab today."

Elijah on Mount Carmel

¹⁶So Obadiah went to meet Ahab and told him, and Ahab went to meet Elijah. ¹⁷When he saw Elijah, he said to him, "Is that you, you troubler of Israel?"

¹⁸"I have not made trouble for Israel," Elijah replied. "But you and your father's family have. You have abandoned the Lord's commands and have followed the Baals. ¹⁹Now summon the people from all over Israel to meet me on Mount Carmel. And bring the four hundred and fifty prophets of Baal and the four hundred prophets of Asherah, who eat at Jezebel's table."

²⁰So Ahab sent word throughout all Israel and assembled the prophets on Mount Carmel. ²¹Elijah went before the people and said, "How long will you waver between two opinions? If the Lord is God, follow him; but if Baal is God, follow him."

But the people said nothing.

²²Then Elijah said to them, "I am the only one of the Lord's prophets left, but Baal has four hundred and fifty prophets. ²³Get two bulls for us. Let them choose one for themselves, and let them cut it into pieces and put it on the wood but not set fire to it. I will prepare the other bull and put it on the wood but not set fire to it. ²⁴Then you call on the name of your god, and I will call on the name of the Lord. The god who answers by fire—he is God."

Then all the people said, "What you say is good."

²⁵Elijah said to the prophets of Baal, "Choose one of the bulls and prepare it first, since there are so many of you. Call on the name of your god, but do not light the fire." ²⁶So they took the bull given them and prepared it.

Then they called on the name of Baal from morning till noon. "O Baal, answer us!" they shouted. But there was no response; no one answered. And they danced around the altar they had made.

²⁷At noon Elijah began to taunt them. "Shout louder!" he said. "Surely he is a god! Perhaps he is deep in thought, or busy, or traveling. Maybe he is sleeping and must be awakened." ²⁸So they shouted louder and slashed themselves with swords and spears, as was their custom, until their blood flowed. ²⁹Midday passed, and they continued their frantic prophesying until the time for the evening sacrifice. But there was no response, no one answered, no one paid attention.

³⁰Then Elijah said to all the people, "Come here to me." They came to him, and he repaired the altar of the Lord, which was in ruins. ³¹Elijah took twelve stones, one for each of the tribes descended from Jacob, to whom the word of the Lord had come, saying, "Your name shall be Israel." ³²With the stones he built an altar in the name of the Lord, and he dug a trench around it large enough to hold two seahs*ᵃ* of seed. ³³He arranged the wood, cut the bull into pieces and laid it on the wood. Then he said to them, "Fill four large jars with water and pour it on the offering and on the wood."

³⁴"Do it again," he said, and they did it again.

"Do it a third time," he ordered, and they did it the third time. ³⁵The water ran down around the altar and even filled the trench.

ᵃ32 That is, probably about 13 quarts (about 15 liters)

³⁶At the time of sacrifice, the prophet Elijah stepped forward and prayed: "O LORD, God of Abraham, Isaac and Israel, let it be known today that you are God in Israel and that I am your servant and have done all these things at your command. ³⁷Answer me, O LORD, answer me, so these people will know that you, O LORD, are God, and that you are turning their hearts back again."

³⁸Then the fire of the LORD fell and burned up the sacrifice, the wood, the stones and the soil, and also licked up the water in the trench.

³⁹When all the people saw this, they fell prostrate and cried, "The LORD—he is God! The LORD—he is God!"

⁴⁰Then Elijah commanded them, "Seize the prophets of Baal. Don't let anyone get away!" They seized them, and Elijah had them brought down to the Kishon Valley and slaughtered there.

⁴¹And Elijah said to Ahab, "Go, eat and drink, for there is the sound of a heavy rain." ⁴²So Ahab went off to eat and drink, but Elijah climbed to the top of Carmel, bent down to the ground and put his face between his knees.

⁴³"Go and look toward the sea," he told his servant. And he went up and looked.

"There is nothing there," he said.

Seven times Elijah said, "Go back."

⁴⁴The seventh time the servant reported, "A cloud as small as a man's hand is rising from the sea."

So Elijah said, "Go and tell Ahab, 'Hitch up your chariot and go down before the rain stops you.'"

⁴⁵Meanwhile, the sky grew black with clouds, the wind rose, a heavy rain came on and Ahab rode off to Jezreel. ⁴⁶The power of the LORD came upon Elijah and, tucking his cloak into his belt, he ran ahead of Ahab all the way to Jezreel.

ADDRESSING QUESTIONS

18:28–29
God

All we need to be accepted by God is to be sincere, right?

If anybody demonstrated true sincerity in their religious practices, it was the priests of Baal. They went so far as to literally cut themselves and shed their own blood as a sign of dedication to their god.

But sincere people can be sincerely *wrong.* In calling out to their god, these men were calling out to nobody. This story dramatically exposes the false idea that all religions are the same and that all paths lead to the same God. God wouldn't answer the priests' misdirected request, because "Baal" is not another name for "God." Read on in this chapter to discover whose prayer God actually honored.

As you search for the truth about God, make sure your efforts are keyed into the God whom this book describes. Don't allow yourself to be swayed by any group that places an individual or a collection of writings on a parallel with God and the Bible. As Elijah discovered, if you search sincerely for the true God of the Bible, you'll find the answers that you're looking for.

Elijah Flees to Horeb

19 Now Ahab told Jezebel everything Elijah had done and how he had killed all the prophets with the sword. ²So Jezebel sent a messenger to Elijah to say, "May the gods deal with me, be it ever so severely, if by this time tomorrow I do not make your life like that of one of them."

³Elijah was afraid^a and ran for his life. When he came to Beersheba in Judah, he left his servant there, ⁴while he himself went a day's journey into the desert. He came to a broom tree, sat down under it and prayed that he might die. "I have had enough, LORD," he said. "Take my life; I am no better than my ancestors." ⁵Then he lay down under the tree and fell asleep.

All at once an angel touched him and said, "Get up and eat." ⁶He looked around, and there by his head was a cake of bread baked over hot coals, and a jar of water. He ate and drank and then lay down again.

⁷The angel of the LORD came back a second time and touched him and said, "Get up and eat, for the journey is too much for you." ⁸So he got up and ate and drank. Strengthened

^a3 Or Elijah saw

by that food, he traveled forty days and forty nights until he reached Horeb, the mountain of God. ⁹There he went into a cave and spent the night.

The LORD Appears to Elijah

And the word of the LORD came to him: "What are you doing here, Elijah?"

¹⁰He replied, "I have been very zealous for the LORD God Almighty. The Israelites have rejected your covenant, broken down your altars, and put your prophets to death with the sword. I am the only one left, and now they are trying to kill me too."

¹¹The LORD said, "Go out and stand on the mountain in the presence of the LORD, for the LORD is about to pass by."

Then a great and powerful wind tore the mountains apart and shattered the rocks before the LORD, but the LORD was not in the wind. After the wind there was an earthquake, but the LORD was not in the earthquake. ¹²After the earthquake came a fire, but the LORD was not in the fire. And after the fire came a gentle whisper. ¹³When Elijah heard it, he pulled his cloak over his face and went out and stood at the mouth of the cave.

Then a voice said to him, "What are you doing here, Elijah?"

¹⁴He replied, "I have been very zealous for the LORD God Almighty. The Israelites have rejected your covenant, broken down your altars, and put your prophets to death with the sword. I am the only one left, and now they are trying to kill me too."

¹⁵The LORD said to him, "Go back the way you came, and go to the Desert of Damascus. When you get there, anoint Hazael king over Aram. ¹⁶Also, anoint Jehu son of Nimshi king over Israel, and anoint Elisha son of Shaphat from Abel Meholah to succeed you as prophet. ¹⁷Jehu will put to death any who escape the sword of Hazael, and Elisha will put to death any who escape the sword of Jehu. ¹⁸Yet I reserve seven thousand in Israel—all whose knees have not bowed down to Baal and all whose mouths have not kissed him."

The Call of Elisha

¹⁹So Elijah went from there and found Elisha son of Shaphat. He was plowing with twelve yoke of oxen, and he himself was driving the twelfth pair. Elijah went up to him and threw his cloak around him. ²⁰Elisha then left his oxen and ran after Elijah. "Let me kiss my father and mother good-by," he said, "and then I will come with you."

"Go back," Elijah replied. "What have I done to you?"

²¹So Elisha left him and went back. He took his yoke of oxen and slaughtered them. He burned the plowing equipment to cook the meat and gave it to the people, and they ate. Then he set out to follow Elijah and became his attendant.

Ben-Hadad Attacks Samaria

20 Now Ben-Hadad king of Aram mustered his entire army. Accompanied by thirty-two kings with their horses and chariots, he went up and besieged Samaria and attacked it. ²He sent messengers into the city to Ahab king of Israel, saying, "This is what Ben-Hadad says: ³'Your silver and gold are mine, and the best of your wives and children are mine.'"

⁴The king of Israel answered, "Just as you say, my lord the king. I and all I have are yours."

⁵The messengers came again and said, "This is what Ben-Hadad says: 'I sent to demand your silver and gold, your wives and your children. ⁶But about this time tomorrow I am going to send my officials to search your palace and the houses of your officials. They will seize everything you value and carry it away.'"

⁷The king of Israel summoned all the elders of the land and said to them, "See how this man is looking for trouble! When he sent for my wives and my children, my silver and my gold, I did not refuse him."

⁸The elders and the people all answered, "Don't listen to him or agree to his demands."

⁹So he replied to Ben-Hadad's messengers, "Tell my lord the king, 'Your servant will do all you demanded the first time, but this demand I cannot meet.'" They left and took the answer back to Ben-Hadad.

¹⁰Then Ben-Hadad sent another message to Ahab: "May the gods deal with me, be it ever so severely, if enough dust remains in Samaria to give each of my men a handful."

¹¹The king of Israel answered, "Tell him: 'One who puts on his armor should not boast like one who takes it off.'"

¹²Ben-Hadad heard this message while he and the kings were drinking in their tents,ᵃ and he ordered his men: "Prepare to attack." So they prepared to attack the city.

Ahab Defeats Ben-Hadad

¹³Meanwhile a prophet came to Ahab king of Israel and announced, "This is what the LORD says: 'Do you see this vast army? I will give it into your hand today, and then you will know that I am the LORD.'"

¹⁴"But who will do this?" asked Ahab.

The prophet replied, "This is what the LORD says: 'The young officers of the provincial commanders will do it.'"

"And who will start the battle?" he asked.

The prophet answered, "You will."

¹⁵So Ahab summoned the young officers of the provincial commanders, 232 men. Then he assembled the rest of the Israelites, 7,000 in all. ¹⁶They set out at noon while Ben-Hadad and the 32 kings allied with him were in their tents getting drunk. ¹⁷The young officers of the provincial commanders went out first.

Now Ben-Hadad had dispatched scouts, who reported, "Men are advancing from Samaria."

¹⁸He said, "If they have come out for peace, take them alive; if they have come out for war, take them alive."

¹⁹The young officers of the provincial commanders marched out of the city with the army behind them ²⁰and each one struck down his opponent. At that, the Arameans fled, with the Israelites in pursuit. But Ben-Hadad king of Aram escaped on horseback with some of his horsemen. ²¹The king of Israel advanced and overpowered the horses and chariots and inflicted heavy losses on the Arameans.

²²Afterward, the prophet came to the king of Israel and said, "Strengthen your position and see what must be done, because next spring the king of Aram will attack you again."

²³Meanwhile, the officials of the king of Aram advised him, "Their gods are gods of the hills. That is why they were too strong for us. But if we fight them on the plains, surely we will be stronger than they. ²⁴Do this: Remove all the kings from their commands and replace them with other officers. ²⁵You must also raise an army like the one you lost— horse for horse and chariot for chariot—so we can fight Israel on the plains. Then surely we will be stronger than they." He agreed with them and acted accordingly.

²⁶The next spring Ben-Hadad mustered the Arameans and went up to Aphek to fight against Israel. ²⁷When the Israelites were also mustered and given provisions, they marched out to meet them. The Israelites camped opposite them like two small flocks of goats, while the Arameans covered the countryside.

²⁸The man of God came up and told the king of Israel, "This is what the LORD says: 'Because the Arameans think the LORD is a god of the hills and not a god of the valleys, I will deliver this vast army into your hands, and you will know that I am the LORD.'"

²⁹For seven days they camped opposite each other, and on the seventh day the battle was joined. The Israelites inflicted a hundred thousand casualties on the Aramean foot soldiers in one day. ³⁰The rest of them escaped to the city of Aphek, where the wall collapsed on twenty-seven thousand of them. And Ben-Hadad fled to the city and hid in an inner room.

ᵃ 12 Or in Succoth; also in verse 16

³¹His officials said to him, "Look, we have heard that the kings of the house of Israel are merciful. Let us go to the king of Israel with sackcloth around our waists and ropes around our heads. Perhaps he will spare your life."

³²Wearing sackcloth around their waists and ropes around their heads, they went to the king of Israel and said, "Your servant Ben-Hadad says: 'Please let me live.'"

The king answered, "Is he still alive? He is my brother."

³³The men took this as a good sign and were quick to pick up his word. "Yes, your brother Ben-Hadad!" they said.

"Go and get him," the king said. When Ben-Hadad came out, Ahab had him come up into his chariot.

³⁴"I will return the cities my father took from your father," Ben-Hadad offered. "You may set up your own market areas in Damascus, as my father did in Samaria."

⌊Ahab said,⌋ "On the basis of a treaty I will set you free." So he made a treaty with him, and let him go.

A Prophet Condemns Ahab

³⁵By the word of the LORD one of the sons of the prophets said to his companion, "Strike me with your weapon," but the man refused.

³⁶So the prophet said, "Because you have not obeyed the LORD, as soon as you leave me a lion will kill you." And after the man went away, a lion found him and killed him.

³⁷The prophet found another man and said, "Strike me, please." So the man struck him and wounded him. ³⁸Then the prophet went and stood by the road waiting for the king. He disguised himself with his headband down over his eyes. ³⁹As the king passed by, the prophet called out to him, "Your servant went into the thick of the battle, and someone came to me with a captive and said, 'Guard this man. If he is missing, it will be your life for his life, or you must pay a talent*a* of silver.' ⁴⁰While your servant was busy here and there, the man disappeared."

"That is your sentence," the king of Israel said. "You have pronounced it yourself."

⁴¹Then the prophet quickly removed the headband from his eyes, and the king of Israel recognized him as one of the prophets. ⁴²He said to the king, "This is what the LORD says: 'You have set free a man I had determined should die.*b* Therefore it is your life for his life, your people for his people.'" ⁴³Sullen and angry, the king of Israel went to his palace in Samaria.

Naboth's Vineyard

21 Some time later there was an incident involving a vineyard belonging to Naboth the Jezreelite. The vineyard was in Jezreel, close to the palace of Ahab king of Samaria. ²Ahab said to Naboth, "Let me have your vineyard to use for a vegetable garden, since it is close to my palace. In exchange I will give you a better vineyard or, if you prefer, I will pay you whatever it is worth."

³But Naboth replied, "The LORD forbid that I should give you the inheritance of my fathers."

⁴So Ahab went home, sullen and angry because Naboth the Jezreelite had said, "I will not give you the inheritance of my fathers." He lay on his bed sulking and refused to eat.

⁵His wife Jezebel came in and asked him, "Why are you so sullen? Why won't you eat?"

⁶He answered her, "Because I said to Naboth the Jezreelite, 'Sell me your vineyard; or if you prefer, I will give you another vineyard in its place.' But he said, 'I will not give you my vineyard.'"

⁷Jezebel his wife said, "Is this how you act as king over Israel? Get up and eat! Cheer up. I'll get you the vineyard of Naboth the Jezreelite."

---

a 39 That is, about 75 pounds (about 34 kilograms)   *b 42* The Hebrew term refers to the irrevocable giving over of things or persons to the LORD, often by totally destroying them.

⁸So she wrote letters in Ahab's name, placed his seal on them, and sent them to the elders and nobles who lived in Naboth's city with him. ⁹In those letters she wrote:

"Proclaim a day of fasting and seat Naboth in a prominent place among the people. ¹⁰But seat two scoundrels opposite him and have them testify that he has cursed both God and the king. Then take him out and stone him to death."

¹¹So the elders and nobles who lived in Naboth's city did as Jezebel directed in the letters she had written to them. ¹²They proclaimed a fast and seated Naboth in a prominent place among the people. ¹³Then two scoundrels came and sat opposite him and brought charges against Naboth before the people, saying, "Naboth has cursed both God and the king." So they took him outside the city and stoned him to death. ¹⁴Then they sent word to Jezebel: "Naboth has been stoned and is dead."

¹⁵As soon as Jezebel heard that Naboth had been stoned to death, she said to Ahab, "Get up and take possession of the vineyard of Naboth the Jezreelite that he refused to sell you. He is no longer alive, but dead." ¹⁶When Ahab heard that Naboth was dead, he got up and went down to take possession of Naboth's vineyard.

¹⁷Then the word of the LORD came to Elijah the Tishbite: ¹⁸"Go down to meet Ahab king of Israel, who rules in Samaria. He is now in Naboth's vineyard, where he has gone to take possession of it. ¹⁹Say to him, 'This is what the LORD says: Have you not murdered a man and seized his property?' Then say to him, 'This is what the LORD says: In the place where dogs licked up Naboth's blood, dogs will lick up your blood—yes, yours!'"

²⁰Ahab said to Elijah, "So you have found me, my enemy!"

"I have found you," he answered, "because you have sold yourself to do evil in the eyes of the LORD. ²¹I am going to bring disaster on you. I will consume your descendants and cut off from Ahab every last male in Israel—slave or free. ²²I will make your house like that of Jeroboam son of Nebat and that of Baasha son of Ahijah, because you have provoked me to anger and have caused Israel to sin.'

²³"And also concerning Jezebel the LORD says: 'Dogs will devour Jezebel by the wall of*a* Jezreel.'

²⁴"Dogs will eat those belonging to Ahab who die in the city, and the birds of the air will feed on those who die in the country."

²⁵(There was never a man like Ahab, who sold himself to do evil in the eyes of the LORD, urged on by Jezebel his wife. ²⁶He behaved in the vilest manner by going after idols, like the Amorites the LORD drove out before Israel.)

□ ▓▓▓▓▓ MANAGING RESOURCES ▓▓▓▓▓ ⧉

21:1–19
Business

In this story, King Ahab demonstrates the reasoning behind his label as Israel's "vilest" king (see verses 25 and 26). Not only did he sulk like a child when Naboth wouldn't sell him an attractive piece of real estate, he also sat quietly by while his wife arranged Naboth's murder. When it was all over, Ahab immediately jumped up and claimed Naboth's field as his own (verse 16).

This story, placed in the Bible to show us just how far King Ahab had strayed from God's way, is the perfect example of unscrupulous business practices. Corporate leaders who allow others to do their immoral (and many times illegal) "dirty work" behind the scenes do not absolve themselves of responsibility for those actions. Just as Ahab could be seen as a silent accomplice to Naboth's murder, so the corporate president who hires "hatchet" employees to clear out competition must ultimately answer for their actions.

Elijah's harsh message for Ahab (verse 19) gives us a clear picture of what God thinks of cutthroat, immoral business practices. In your business and in your personal life, conduct your affairs in a way that is pleasing to God. In the end, you'll be much better off.

---

a 23 Most Hebrew manuscripts; a few Hebrew manuscripts, Vulgate and Syriac (see also 2 Kings 9:26) *the plot of ground at*

²⁷When Ahab heard these words, he tore his clothes, put on sackcloth and fasted. He lay in sackcloth and went around meekly.

²⁸Then the word of the LORD came to Elijah the Tishbite: ²⁹"Have you noticed how Ahab has humbled himself before me? Because he has humbled himself, I will not bring this disaster in his day, but I will bring it on his house in the days of his son."

Micaiah Prophesies Against Ahab

22 For three years there was no war between Aram and Israel. ²But in the third year Jehoshaphat king of Judah went down to see the king of Israel. ³The king of Israel had said to his officials, "Don't you know that Ramoth Gilead belongs to us and yet we are doing nothing to retake it from the king of Aram?"

⁴So he asked Jehoshaphat, "Will you go with me to fight against Ramoth Gilead?"

Jehoshaphat replied to the king of Israel, "I am as you are, my people as your people, my horses as your horses." ⁵But Jehoshaphat also said to the king of Israel, "First seek the counsel of the LORD."

⁶So the king of Israel brought together the prophets—about four hundred men—and asked them, "Shall I go to war against Ramoth Gilead, or shall I refrain?"

"Go," they answered, "for the Lord will give it into the king's hand."

⁷But Jehoshaphat asked, "Is there not a prophet of the LORD here whom we can inquire of?"

⁸The king of Israel answered Jehoshaphat, "There is still one man through whom we can inquire of the LORD, but I hate him because he never prophesies anything good about me, but always bad. He is Micaiah son of Imlah."

"The king should not say that," Jehoshaphat replied.

⁹So the king of Israel called one of his officials and said, "Bring Micaiah son of Imlah at once."

¹⁰Dressed in their royal robes, the king of Israel and Jehoshaphat king of Judah were sitting on their thrones at the threshing floor by the entrance of the gate of Samaria, with all the prophets prophesying before them. ¹¹Now Zedekiah son of Kenaanah had made iron horns and he declared, "This is what the LORD says: 'With these you will gore the Arameans until they are destroyed.'"

¹²All the other prophets were prophesying the same thing. "Attack Ramoth Gilead and be victorious," they said, "for the LORD will give it into the king's hand."

¹³The messenger who had gone to summon Micaiah said to him, "Look, as one man the other prophets are predicting success for the king. Let your word agree with theirs, and speak favorably."

¹⁴But Micaiah said, "As surely as the LORD lives, I can tell him only what the LORD tells me."

¹⁵When he arrived, the king asked him, "Micaiah, shall we go to war against Ramoth Gilead, or shall I refrain?"

"Attack and be victorious," he answered, "for the LORD will give it into the king's hand."

¹⁶The king said to him, "How many times must I make you swear to tell me nothing but the truth in the name of the LORD?"

¹⁷Then Micaiah answered, "I saw all Israel scattered on the hills like sheep without a shepherd, and the LORD said, 'These people have no master. Let each one go home in peace.'"

¹⁸The king of Israel said to Jehoshaphat, "Didn't I tell you that he never prophesies anything good about me, but only bad?"

¹⁹Micaiah continued, "Therefore hear the word of the LORD: I saw the LORD sitting on his throne with all the host of heaven standing around him on his right and on his left. ²⁰And the LORD said, 'Who will entice Ahab into attacking Ramoth Gilead and going to his death there?'

"One suggested this, and another that. ²¹Finally, a spirit came forward, stood before the LORD and said, 'I will entice him.'

²²"'By what means?' the LORD asked.

"'I will go out and be a lying spirit in the mouths of all his prophets,' he said.

"'You will succeed in enticing him,' said the LORD. 'Go and do it.'

²³"So now the LORD has put a lying spirit in the mouths of all these prophets of yours. The LORD has decreed disaster for you."

²⁴Then Zedekiah son of Kenaanah went up and slapped Micaiah in the face. "Which way did the spirit from*a* the LORD go when he went from me to speak to you?" he asked.

²⁵Micaiah replied, "You will find out on the day you go to hide in an inner room."

²⁶The king of Israel then ordered, "Take Micaiah and send him back to Amon the ruler of the city and to Joash the king's son ²⁷and say, 'This is what the king says: Put this fellow in prison and give him nothing but bread and water until I return safely.'"

²⁸Micaiah declared, "If you ever return safely, the LORD has not spoken through me." Then he added, "Mark my words, all you people!"

Ahab Killed at Ramoth Gilead

²⁹So the king of Israel and Jehoshaphat king of Judah went up to Ramoth Gilead. ³⁰The king of Israel said to Jehoshaphat, "I will enter the battle in disguise, but you wear your royal robes." So the king of Israel disguised himself and went into battle.

³¹Now the king of Aram had ordered his thirty-two chariot commanders, "Do not fight with anyone, small or great, except the king of Israel." ³²When the chariot commanders saw Jehoshaphat, they thought, "Surely this is the king of Israel." So they turned to attack him, but when Jehoshaphat cried out, ³³the chariot commanders saw that he was not the king of Israel and stopped pursuing him.

³⁴But someone drew his bow at random and hit the king of Israel between the sections of his armor. The king told his chariot driver, "Wheel around and get me out of the fighting. I've been wounded." ³⁵All day long the battle raged, and the king was propped up in his chariot facing the Arameans. The blood from his wound ran onto the floor of the chariot, and that evening he died. ³⁶As the sun was setting, a cry spread through the army: "Every man to his town; everyone to his land!"

³⁷So the king died and was brought to Samaria, and they buried him there. ³⁸They washed the chariot at a pool in Samaria (where the prostitutes bathed),*b* and the dogs licked up his blood, as the word of the LORD had declared.

³⁹As for the other events of Ahab's reign, including all he did, the palace he built and inlaid with ivory, and the cities he fortified, are they not written in the book of the annals of the kings of Israel? ⁴⁰Ahab rested with his fathers. And Ahaziah his son succeeded him as king.

Jehoshaphat King of Judah

⁴¹Jehoshaphat son of Asa became king of Judah in the fourth year of Ahab king of Israel. ⁴²Jehoshaphat was thirty-five years old when he became king, and he reigned in Jerusalem twenty-five years. His mother's name was Azubah daughter of Shilhi. ⁴³In everything he walked in the ways of his father Asa and did not stray from them; he did what was right in the eyes of the LORD. The high places, however, were not removed, and the people continued to offer sacrifices and burn incense there. ⁴⁴Jehoshaphat was also at peace with the king of Israel.

⁴⁵As for the other events of Jehoshaphat's reign, the things he achieved and his military exploits, are they not written in the book of the annals of the kings of Judah? ⁴⁶He rid the land of the rest of the male shrine prostitutes who remained there even after the reign of his father Asa. ⁴⁷There was then no king in Edom; a deputy ruled.

⁴⁸Now Jehoshaphat built a fleet of trading ships*c* to go to Ophir for gold, but they

---

*a*24 Or *Spirit of*   *b*38 Or *Samaria and cleaned the weapons*   *c*48 Hebrew *of ships of Tarshish* never set sail—they were wrecked at Ezion Geber. 49At that time Ahaziah son of Ahab said to Jehoshaphat, "Let my men sail with your men," but Jehoshaphat refused.

50Then Jehoshaphat rested with his fathers and was buried with them in the city of David his father. And Jehoram his son succeeded him.

Ahaziah King of Israel

51Ahaziah son of Ahab became king of Israel in Samaria in the seventeenth year of Jehoshaphat king of Judah, and he reigned over Israel two years. 52He did evil in the eyes of the LORD, because he walked in the ways of his father and mother and in the ways of Jeroboam son of Nebat, who caused Israel to sin. 53He served and worshiped Baal and provoked the LORD, the God of Israel, to anger, just as his father had done.

The LORD's Judgment on Ahaziah

1 After Ahab's death, Moab rebelled against Israel. ²Now Ahaziah had fallen through the lattice of his upper room in Samaria and injured himself. So he sent messengers, saying to them, "Go and consult Baal-Zebub, the god of Ekron, to see if I will recover from this injury."

³But the angel of the LORD said to Elijah the Tishbite, "Go up and meet the messengers of the king of Samaria and ask them, 'Is it because there is no God in Israel that you are going off to consult Baal-Zebub, the god of Ekron?' ⁴Therefore this is what the LORD says: 'You will not leave the bed you are lying on. You will certainly die!'" So Elijah went.

⁵When the messengers returned to the king, he asked them, "Why have you come back?"

⁶"A man came to meet us," they replied. "And he said to us, 'Go back to the king who sent you and tell him, "This is what the LORD says: Is it because there is no God in Israel that you are sending men to consult Baal-Zebub, the god of Ekron? Therefore you will not leave the bed you are lying on. You will certainly die!"'"

⁷The king asked them, "What kind of man was it who came to meet you and told you this?"

⁸They replied, "He was a man with a garment of hair and with a leather belt around his waist."

The king said, "That was Elijah the Tishbite."

⁹Then he sent to Elijah a captain with his company of fifty men. The captain went up to Elijah, who was sitting on the top of a hill, and said to him, "Man of God, the king says, 'Come down!'"

¹⁰Elijah answered the captain, "If I am a man of God, may fire come down from heaven and consume you and your fifty men!" Then fire fell from heaven and consumed the captain and his men.

¹¹At this the king sent to Elijah another captain with his fifty men. The captain said to him, "Man of God, this is what the king says, 'Come down at once!'"

¹²"If I am a man of God," Elijah replied, "may fire come down from heaven and consume you and your fifty men!" Then the fire of God fell from heaven and consumed him and his fifty men.

¹³So the king sent a third captain with his fifty men. This third captain went up and fell on his knees before Elijah. "Man of God," he begged, "please have respect for my life and the lives of these fifty men, your servants! ¹⁴See, fire has fallen from heaven and consumed the first two captains and all their men. But now have respect for my life!"

¹⁵The angel of the LORD said to Elijah, "Go down with him; do not be afraid of him." So Elijah got up and went down with him to the king.

¹⁶He told the king, "This is what the LORD says: Is it because there is no God in Israel for you to consult that you have sent messengers to consult Baal-Zebub, the god of Ekron? Because you have done this, you will never leave the bed you are lying on. You will certainly die!" ¹⁷So he died, according to the word of the LORD that Elijah had spoken.

Because Ahaziah had no son, Joram*ᵃ* succeeded him as king in the second year of Jehoram son of Jehoshaphat king of Judah. ¹⁸As for all the other events of Ahaziah's

ᵃ 17 Hebrew Jehoram, a variant of Joram

reign, and what he did, are they not written in the book of the annals of the kings of Israel?

Elijah Taken Up to Heaven

2 When the LORD was about to take Elijah up to heaven in a whirlwind, Elijah and Elisha were on their way from Gilgal. ²Elijah said to Elisha, "Stay here; the LORD has sent me to Bethel."

But Elisha said, "As surely as the LORD lives and as you live, I will not leave you." So they went down to Bethel.

³The company of the prophets at Bethel came out to Elisha and asked, "Do you know that the LORD is going to take your master from you today?"

"Yes, I know," Elisha replied, "but do not speak of it."

⁴Then Elijah said to him, "Stay here, Elisha; the LORD has sent me to Jericho."

And he replied, "As surely as the LORD lives and as you live, I will not leave you." So they went to Jericho.

⁵The company of the prophets at Jericho went up to Elisha and asked him, "Do you know that the LORD is going to take your master from you today?"

"Yes, I know," he replied, "but do not speak of it."

⁶Then Elijah said to him, "Stay here; the LORD has sent me to the Jordan."

And he replied, "As surely as the LORD lives and as you live, I will not leave you." So the two of them walked on.

⁷Fifty men of the company of the prophets went and stood at a distance, facing the place where Elijah and Elisha had stopped at the Jordan. ⁸Elijah took his cloak, rolled it up and struck the water with it. The water divided to the right and to the left, and the two of them crossed over on dry ground.

⁹When they had crossed, Elijah said to Elisha, "Tell me, what can I do for you before I am taken from you?"

"Let me inherit a double portion of your spirit," Elisha replied.

¹⁰"You have asked a difficult thing," Elijah said, "yet if you see me when I am taken from you, it will be yours—otherwise not."

¹¹As they were walking along and talking together, suddenly a chariot of fire and horses of fire appeared and separated the two of them, and Elijah went up to heaven in a whirlwind. ¹²Elisha saw this and cried out, "My father! My father! The chariots and horsemen of Israel!" And Elisha saw him no more. Then he took hold of his own clothes and tore them apart.

¹³He picked up the cloak that had fallen from Elijah and went back and stood on the bank of the Jordan. ¹⁴Then he took the cloak that had fallen from him and struck the water with it. "Where now is the LORD, the God of Elijah?" he asked. When he struck the water, it divided to the right and to the left, and he crossed over.

¹⁵The company of the prophets from Jericho, who were watching, said, "The spirit of Elijah is resting on Elisha." And they went to meet him and bowed to the ground before him. ¹⁶"Look," they said, "we your servants have fifty able men. Let them go and look for your master. Perhaps the Spirit of the LORD has picked him up and set him down on some mountain or in some valley."

"No," Elisha replied, "do not send them."

¹⁷But they persisted until he was too ashamed to refuse. So he said, "Send them." And they sent fifty men, who searched for three days but did not find him. ¹⁸When they returned to Elisha, who was staying in Jericho, he said to them, "Didn't I tell you not to go?"

Healing of the Water

¹⁹The men of the city said to Elisha, "Look, our lord, this town is well situated, as you can see, but the water is bad and the land is unproductive."

²⁰"Bring me a new bowl," he said, "and put salt in it." So they brought it to him.

²¹Then he went out to the spring and threw the salt into it, saying, "This is what the LORD says: 'I have healed this water. Never again will it cause death or make the land unproductive.'" ²²And the water has remained wholesome to this day, according to the word Elisha had spoken.

Elisha Is Jeered

²³From there Elisha went up to Bethel. As he was walking along the road, some youths came out of the town and jeered at him. "Go on up, you baldhead!" they said. "Go on up, you baldhead!" ²⁴He turned around, looked at them and called down a curse on them in the name of the LORD. Then two bears came out of the woods and mauled forty-two of the youths. ²⁵And he went on to Mount Carmel and from there returned to Samaria.

Moab Revolts

3 Joram*ᵃ* son of Ahab became king of Israel in Samaria in the eighteenth year of Jehoshaphat king of Judah, and he reigned twelve years. ²He did evil in the eyes of the LORD, but not as his father and mother had done. He got rid of the sacred stone of Baal that his father had made. ³Nevertheless he clung to the sins of Jeroboam son of Nebat, which he had caused Israel to commit; he did not turn away from them.

⁴Now Mesha king of Moab raised sheep, and he had to supply the king of Israel with a hundred thousand lambs and with the wool of a hundred thousand rams. ⁵But after Ahab died, the king of Moab rebelled against the king of Israel. ⁶So at that time King Joram set out from Samaria and mobilized all Israel. ⁷He also sent this message to Jehoshaphat king of Judah: "The king of Moab has rebelled against me. Will you go with me to fight against Moab?"

"I will go with you," he replied. "I am as you are, my people as your people, my horses as your horses."

⁸"By what route shall we attack?" he asked.

"Through the Desert of Edom," he answered.

⁹So the king of Israel set out with the king of Judah and the king of Edom. After a roundabout march of seven days, the army had no more water for themselves or for the animals with them.

¹⁰"What!" exclaimed the king of Israel. "Has the LORD called us three kings together only to hand us over to Moab?"

¹¹But Jehoshaphat asked, "Is there no prophet of the LORD here, that we may inquire of the LORD through him?"

An officer of the king of Israel answered, "Elisha son of Shaphat is here. He used to pour water on the hands of Elijah.*ᵇ*"

¹²Jehoshaphat said, "The word of the LORD is with him." So the king of Israel and Jehoshaphat and the king of Edom went down to him.

¹³Elisha said to the king of Israel, "What do we have to do with each other? Go to the prophets of your father and the prophets of your mother."

"No," the king of Israel answered, "because it was the LORD who called us three kings together to hand us over to Moab."

¹⁴Elisha said, "As surely as the LORD Almighty lives, whom I serve, if I did not have respect for the presence of Jehoshaphat king of Judah, I would not look at you or even notice you. ¹⁵But now bring me a harpist."

While the harpist was playing, the hand of the LORD came upon Elisha ¹⁶and he said, "This is what the LORD says: Make this valley full of ditches. ¹⁷For this is what the LORD says: You will see neither wind nor rain, yet this valley will be filled with water, and you, your cattle and your other animals will drink. ¹⁸This is an easy thing in the eyes of the LORD; he will also hand Moab over to you. ¹⁹You will overthrow every fortified city and

---

ᵃ 1 Hebrew *Jehoram,* a variant of *Joram;* also in verse 6   *ᵇ 11* That is, he was Elijah's personal servant.

every major town. You will cut down every good tree, stop up all the springs, and ruin every good field with stones."

²⁰The next morning, about the time for offering the sacrifice, there it was—water flowing from the direction of Edom! And the land was filled with water.

²¹Now all the Moabites had heard that the kings had come to fight against them; so every man, young and old, who could bear arms was called up and stationed on the border. ²²When they got up early in the morning, the sun was shining on the water. To the Moabites across the way, the water looked red—like blood. ²³"That's blood!" they said. "Those kings must have fought and slaughtered each other. Now to the plunder, Moab!"

²⁴But when the Moabites came to the camp of Israel, the Israelites rose up and fought them until they fled. And the Israelites invaded the land and slaughtered the Moabites. ²⁵They destroyed the towns, and each man threw a stone on every good field until it was covered. They stopped up all the springs and cut down every good tree. Only Kir Hareseth was left with its stones in place, but men armed with slings surrounded it and attacked it as well.

²⁶When the king of Moab saw that the battle had gone against him, he took with him seven hundred swordsmen to break through to the king of Edom, but they failed. ²⁷Then he took his firstborn son, who was to succeed him as king, and offered him as a sacrifice on the city wall. The fury against Israel was great; they withdrew and returned to their own land.

The Widow's Oil

 The wife of a man from the company of the prophets cried out to Elisha, "Your servant my husband is dead, and you know that he revered the LORD. But now his creditor is coming to take my two boys as his slaves."

²Elisha replied to her, "How can I help you? Tell me, what do you have in your house?"

"Your servant has nothing there at all," she said, "except a little oil."

³Elisha said, "Go around and ask all your neighbors for empty jars. Don't ask for just a few. ⁴Then go inside and shut the door behind you and your sons. Pour oil into all the jars, and as each is filled, put it to one side."

⁵She left him and afterward shut the door behind her and her sons. They brought the jars to her and she kept pouring. ⁶When all the jars were full, she said to her son, "Bring me another one."

But he replied, "There is not a jar left." Then the oil stopped flowing.

⁷She went and told the man of God, and he said, "Go, sell the oil and pay your debts. You and your sons can live on what is left."

The Shunammite's Son Restored to Life

⁸One day Elisha went to Shunem. And a well-to-do woman was there, who urged him to stay for a meal. So whenever he came by, he stopped there to eat. ⁹She said to her

husband, "I know that this man who often comes our way is a holy man of God. ¹⁰Let's make a small room on the roof and put in it a bed and a table, a chair and a lamp for him. Then he can stay there whenever he comes to us."

¹¹One day when Elisha came, he went up to his room and lay down there. ¹²He said to his servant Gehazi, "Call the Shunammite." So he called her, and she stood before him. ¹³Elisha said to him, "Tell her, 'You have gone to all this trouble for us. Now what can be done for you? Can we speak on your behalf to the king or the commander of the army?'"

She replied, "I have a home among my own people."

¹⁴"What can be done for her?" Elisha asked.

Gehazi said, "Well, she has no son and her husband is old."

¹⁵Then Elisha said, "Call her." So he called her, and she stood in the doorway. ¹⁶"About this time next year," Elisha said, "you will hold a son in your arms."

"No, my lord," she objected. "Don't mislead your servant, O man of God!"

¹⁷But the woman became pregnant, and the next year about that same time she gave birth to a son, just as Elisha had told her.

¹⁸The child grew, and one day he went out to his father, who was with the reapers. ¹⁹"My head! My head!" he said to his father.

His father told a servant, "Carry him to his mother." ²⁰After the servant had lifted him up and carried him to his mother, the boy sat on her lap until noon, and then he died. ²¹She went up and laid him on the bed of the man of God, then shut the door and went out.

²²She called her husband and said, "Please send me one of the servants and a donkey so I can go to the man of God quickly and return."

²³"Why go to him today?" he asked. "It's not the New Moon or the Sabbath."

"It's all right," she said.

²⁴She saddled the donkey and said to her servant, "Lead on; don't slow down for me unless I tell you." ²⁵So she set out and came to the man of God at Mount Carmel.

When he saw her in the distance, the man of God said to his servant Gehazi, "Look! There's the Shunammite! ²⁶Run to meet her and ask her, 'Are you all right? Is your husband all right? Is your child all right?'"

"Everything is all right," she said.

²⁷When she reached the man of God at the mountain, she took hold of his feet. Gehazi came over to push her away, but the man of God said, "Leave her alone! She is in bitter distress, but the LORD has hidden it from me and has not told me why."

²⁸"Did I ask you for a son, my lord?" she said. "Didn't I tell you, 'Don't raise my hopes'?"

²⁹Elisha said to Gehazi, "Tuck your cloak into your belt, take my staff in your hand and run. If you meet anyone, do not greet him, and if anyone greets you, do not answer. Lay my staff on the boy's face."

³⁰But the child's mother said, "As surely as the LORD lives and as you live, I will not leave you." So he got up and followed her.

³¹Gehazi went on ahead and laid the staff on the boy's face, but there was no sound or response. So Gehazi went back to meet Elisha and told him, "The boy has not awakened."

³²When Elisha reached the house, there was the boy lying dead on his couch. ³³He went in, shut the door on the two of them and prayed to the LORD. ³⁴Then he got on the bed and lay upon the boy, mouth to mouth, eyes to eyes, hands to hands. As he stretched himself out upon him, the boy's body grew warm. ³⁵Elisha turned away and walked back and forth in the room and then got on the bed and stretched out upon him once more. The boy sneezed seven times and opened his eyes.

³⁶Elisha summoned Gehazi and said, "Call the Shunammite." And he did. When she came, he said, "Take your son." ³⁷She came in, fell at his feet and bowed to the ground. Then she took her son and went out.

Death in the Pot

38Elisha returned to Gilgal and there was a famine in that region. While the company of the prophets was meeting with him, he said to his servant, "Put on the large pot and cook some stew for these men."

39One of them went out into the fields to gather herbs and found a wild vine. He gathered some of its gourds and filled the fold of his cloak. When he returned, he cut them up into the pot of stew, though no one knew what they were. **40**The stew was poured out for the men, but as they began to eat it, they cried out, "O man of God, there is death in the pot!" And they could not eat it.

41Elisha said, "Get some flour." He put it into the pot and said, "Serve it to the people to eat." And there was nothing harmful in the pot.

Feeding of a Hundred

42A man came from Baal Shalishah, bringing the man of God twenty loaves of barley bread baked from the first ripe grain, along with some heads of new grain. "Give it to the people to eat," Elisha said.

43"How can I set this before a hundred men?" his servant asked.

But Elisha answered, "Give it to the people to eat. For this is what the LORD says: 'They will eat and have some left over.'" **44**Then he set it before them, and they ate and had some left over, according to the word of the LORD.

Naaman Healed of Leprosy

5 Now Naaman was commander of the army of the king of Aram. He was a great man in the sight of his master and highly regarded, because through him the LORD had given victory to Aram. He was a valiant soldier, but he had leprosy.*ᵃ*

2Now bands from Aram had gone out and had taken captive a young girl from Israel, and she served Naaman's wife. **3**She said to her mistress, "If only my master would see the prophet who is in Samaria! He would cure him of his leprosy."

4Naaman went to his master and told him what the girl from Israel had said. **5**"By all means, go," the king of Aram replied. "I will send a letter to the king of Israel." So Naaman left, taking with him ten talents*ᵇ* of silver, six thousand shekels*ᶜ* of gold and ten sets of clothing. **6**The letter that he took to the king of Israel read: "With this letter I am sending my servant Naaman to you so that you may cure him of his leprosy."

7As soon as the king of Israel read the letter, he tore his robes and said, "Am I God? Can I kill and bring back to life? Why does this fellow send someone to me to be cured of his leprosy? See how he is trying to pick a quarrel with me!"

8When Elisha the man of God heard that the king of Israel had torn his robes, he sent him this message: "Why have you torn your robes? Have the man come to me and he will know that there is a prophet in Israel." **9**So Naaman went with his horses and chariots and stopped at the door of Elisha's house. **10**Elisha sent a messenger to say to him, "Go, wash yourself seven times in the Jordan, and your flesh will be restored and you will be cleansed."

11But Naaman went away angry and said, "I thought that he would surely come out to me and stand and call on the name of the LORD his God, wave his hand over the spot and cure me of my leprosy. **12**Are not Abana and Pharpar, the rivers of Damascus, better than any of the waters of Israel? Couldn't I wash in them and be cleansed?" So he turned and went off in a rage.

13Naaman's servants went to him and said, "My father, if the prophet had told you to do some great thing, would you not have done it? How much more, then, when he tells you, 'Wash and be cleansed'!" **14**So he went down and dipped himself in the Jordan

---

ᵃ 1 The Hebrew word was used for various diseases affecting the skin—not necessarily leprosy; also in verses 3, 6, 7, 11 and 27.
ᵇ 5 That is, about 750 pounds (about 340 kilograms)   *ᶜ 5* That is, about 150 pounds (about 70 kilograms)

seven times, as the man of God had told him, and his flesh was restored and became clean like that of a young boy.

¹⁵Then Naaman and all his attendants went back to the man of God. He stood before him and said, "Now I know that there is no God in all the world except in Israel. Please accept now a gift from your servant."

¹⁶The prophet answered, "As surely as the LORD lives, whom I serve, I will not accept a thing." And even though Naaman urged him, he refused.

¹⁷"If you will not," said Naaman, "please let me, your servant, be given as much earth as a pair of mules can carry, for your servant will never again make burnt offerings and sacrifices to any other god but the LORD. ¹⁸But may the LORD forgive your servant for this one thing: When my master enters the temple of Rimmon to bow down and he is leaning on my arm and I bow there also—when I bow down in the temple of Rimmon, may the LORD forgive your servant for this."

¹⁹"Go in peace," Elisha said.

After Naaman had traveled some distance, ²⁰Gehazi, the servant of Elisha the man of God, said to himself, "My master was too easy on Naaman, this Aramean, by not accepting from him what he brought. As surely as the LORD lives, I will run after him and get something from him."

²¹So Gehazi hurried after Naaman. When Naaman saw him running toward him, he got down from the chariot to meet him. "Is everything all right?" he asked.

²²"Everything is all right," Gehazi answered. "My master sent me to say, 'Two young men from the company of the prophets have just come to me from the hill country of Ephraim. Please give them a talent*a* of silver and two sets of clothing.' "

²³"By all means, take two talents," said Naaman. He urged Gehazi to accept them, and then tied up the two talents of silver in two bags, with two sets of clothing. He gave them to two of his servants, and they carried them ahead of Gehazi. ²⁴When Gehazi came to the hill, he took the things from the servants and put them away in the house. He sent the men away and they left. ²⁵Then he went in and stood before his master Elisha.

"Where have you been, Gehazi?" Elisha asked.

"Your servant didn't go anywhere," Gehazi answered.

²⁶But Elisha said to him, "Was not my spirit with you when the man got down from his chariot to meet you? Is this the time to take money, or to accept clothes, olive groves, vineyards, flocks, herds, or menservants and maidservants? ²⁷Naaman's leprosy will cling to you and to your descendants forever." Then Gehazi went from Elisha's presence and he was leprous, as white as snow.

An Axhead Floats

6 The company of the prophets said to Elisha, "Look, the place where we meet with you is too small for us. ²Let us go to the Jordan, where each of us can get a pole; and let us build a place there for us to live."

And he said, "Go."

³Then one of them said, "Won't you please come with your servants?"

"I will," Elisha replied. ⁴And he went with them.

They went to the Jordan and began to cut down trees. ⁵As one of them was cutting down a tree, the iron axhead fell into the water. "Oh, my lord," he cried out, "it was borrowed!"

⁶The man of God asked, "Where did it fall?" When he showed him the place, Elisha cut a stick and threw it there, and made the iron float. ⁷"Lift it out," he said. Then the man reached out his hand and took it.

a 22 That is, about 75 pounds (about 34 kilograms)

Elisha Traps Blinded Arameans

⁸Now the king of Aram was at war with Israel. After conferring with his officers, he said, "I will set up my camp in such and such a place."

⁹The man of God sent word to the king of Israel: "Beware of passing that place, because the Arameans are going down there." ¹⁰So the king of Israel checked on the place indicated by the man of God. Time and again Elisha warned the king, so that he was on his guard in such places.

¹¹This enraged the king of Aram. He summoned his officers and demanded of them, "Will you not tell me which of us is on the side of the king of Israel?"

¹²"None of us, my lord the king," said one of his officers, "but Elisha, the prophet who is in Israel, tells the king of Israel the very words you speak in your bedroom."

¹³"Go, find out where he is," the king ordered, "so I can send men and capture him." The report came back: "He is in Dothan." ¹⁴Then he sent horses and chariots and a strong force there. They went by night and surrounded the city.

□ ▦▦▦▦ ADDRESSING QUESTIONS ▦▦▦▦ ▷◁

**6:8–23
Unseen Realities**

Q

This story powerfully illustrates the existence of spiritual beings and shows that they operate "behind the scenes" in response to God's directives.

Elisha knew that God was at work in the crisis the Israelites faced, but his servant couldn't see any hope. When Elisha prayed, his servant's spiritual "eyes" were "opened," and he grasped the reality of the spiritual realm.

The Bible teaches that beyond our material world there is also a spiritual world. Each reality parallels the other. In short, *there's more to the universe than meets the eye.*

---

¹⁵When the servant of the man of God got up and went out early the next morning, an army with horses and chariots had surrounded the city. "Oh, my lord, what shall we do?" the servant asked.

¹⁶"Don't be afraid," the prophet answered. "Those who are with us are more than those who are with them."

¹⁷And Elisha prayed, "O LORD, open his eyes so he may see." Then the LORD opened the servant's eyes, and he looked and saw the hills full of horses and chariots of fire all around Elisha.

¹⁸As the enemy came down toward him, Elisha prayed to the LORD, "Strike these people with blindness." So he struck them with blindness, as Elisha had asked.

¹⁹Elisha told them, "This is not the road and this is not the city. Follow me, and I will lead you to the man you are looking for." And he led them to Samaria.

²⁰After they entered the city, Elisha said, "LORD, open the eyes of these men so they can see." Then the LORD opened their eyes and they looked, and there they were, inside Samaria.

²¹When the king of Israel saw them, he asked Elisha, "Shall I kill them, my father? Shall I kill them?"

²²"Do not kill them," he answered. "Would you kill men you have captured with your own sword or bow? Set food and water before them so that they may eat and drink and then go back to their master." ²³So he prepared a great feast for them, and after they had finished eating and drinking, he sent them away, and they returned to their master. So the bands from Aram stopped raiding Israel's territory.

Famine in Besieged Samaria

²⁴Some time later, Ben-Hadad king of Aram mobilized his entire army and marched up and laid siege to Samaria. ²⁵There was a great famine in the city; the siege lasted so long that a donkey's head sold for eighty shekels*ᵃ* of silver, and a quarter of a cab*ᵇ* of seed pods*ᶜ* for five shekels.*ᵈ*

ᵃ25 That is, about 2 pounds (about 1 kilogram)   *ᵇ25* That is, probably about 1/2 pint (about 0.3 liter)   *ᶜ25* Or of dove's dung   *ᵈ25* That is, about 2 ounces (about 55 grams)

²⁶As the king of Israel was passing by on the wall, a woman cried to him, "Help me, my lord the king!"

²⁷The king replied, "If the LORD does not help you, where can I get help for you? From the threshing floor? From the winepress?" ²⁸Then he asked her, "What's the matter?"

She answered, "This woman said to me, 'Give up your son so we may eat him today, and tomorrow we'll eat my son.' ²⁹So we cooked my son and ate him. The next day I said to her, 'Give up your son so we may eat him,' but she had hidden him."

³⁰When the king heard the woman's words, he tore his robes. As he went along the wall, the people looked, and there, underneath, he had sackcloth on his body. ³¹He said, "May God deal with me, be it ever so severely, if the head of Elisha son of Shaphat remains on his shoulders today!"

³²Now Elisha was sitting in his house, and the elders were sitting with him. The king sent a messenger ahead, but before he arrived, Elisha said to the elders, "Don't you see how this murderer is sending someone to cut off my head? Look, when the messenger comes, shut the door and hold it shut against him. Is not the sound of his master's footsteps behind him?"

³³While he was still talking to them, the messenger came down to him. And ⌞the king⌟ said, "This disaster is from the LORD. Why should I wait for the LORD any longer?"

7 Elisha said, "Hear the word of the LORD. This is what the LORD says: About this time tomorrow, a seah*ᵃ* of flour will sell for a shekel*ᵇ* and two seahs*ᶜ* of barley for a shekel at the gate of Samaria."

²The officer on whose arm the king was leaning said to the man of God, "Look, even if the LORD should open the floodgates of the heavens, could this happen?"

"You will see it with your own eyes," answered Elisha, "but you will not eat any of it!"

The Siege Lifted

³Now there were four men with leprosy*ᵈ* at the entrance of the city gate. They said to each other, "Why stay here until we die? ⁴If we say, 'We'll go into the city'—the famine is there, and we will die. And if we stay here, we will die. So let's go over to the camp of the Arameans and surrender. If they spare us, we live; if they kill us, then we die."

⁵At dusk they got up and went to the camp of the Arameans. When they reached the edge of the camp, not a man was there, ⁶for the Lord had caused the Arameans to hear the sound of chariots and horses and a great army, so that they said to one another, "Look, the king of Israel has hired the Hittite and Egyptian kings to attack us!" ⁷So they got up and fled in the dusk and abandoned their tents and their horses and donkeys. They left the camp as it was and ran for their lives.

⁸The men who had leprosy reached the edge of the camp and entered one of the tents. They ate and drank, and carried away silver, gold and clothes, and went off and hid them. They returned and entered another tent and took some things from it and hid them also.

⁹Then they said to each other, "We're not doing right. This is a day of good news and we are keeping it to ourselves. If we wait until daylight, punishment will overtake us. Let's go at once and report this to the royal palace."

¹⁰So they went and called out to the city gatekeepers and told them, "We went into the Aramean camp and not a man was there—not a sound of anyone—only tethered horses and donkeys, and the tents left just as they were." ¹¹The gatekeepers shouted the news, and it was reported within the palace.

¹²The king got up in the night and said to his officers, "I will tell you what the Arameans have done to us. They know we are starving; so they have left the camp to

---

ᵃ1 That is, probably about 7 quarts (about 7.3 liters); also in verses 16 and 18   *ᵇ1* That is, about 2/5 ounce (about 11 grams); also in verses 16 and 18   *ᶜ1* That is, probably about 13 quarts (about 15 liters); also in verses 16 and 18
ᵈ3 The Hebrew word is used for various diseases affecting the skin—not necessarily leprosy; also in verse 8.

hide in the countryside, thinking, 'They will surely come out, and then we will take them alive and get into the city.'"

¹³One of his officers answered, "Have some men take five of the horses that are left in the city. Their plight will be like that of all the Israelites left here—yes, they will only be like all these Israelites who are doomed. So let us send them to find out what happened."

¹⁴So they selected two chariots with their horses, and the king sent them after the Aramean army. He commanded the drivers, "Go and find out what has happened." ¹⁵They followed them as far as the Jordan, and they found the whole road strewn with the clothing and equipment the Arameans had thrown away in their headlong flight. So the messengers returned and reported to the king. ¹⁶Then the people went out and plundered the camp of the Arameans. So a seah of flour sold for a shekel, and two seahs of barley sold for a shekel, as the LORD had said.

¹⁷Now the king had put the officer on whose arm he leaned in charge of the gate, and the people trampled him in the gateway, and he died, just as the man of God had foretold when the king came down to his house. ¹⁸It happened as the man of God had said to the king: "About this time tomorrow, a seah of flour will sell for a shekel and two seahs of barley for a shekel at the gate of Samaria."

¹⁹The officer had said to the man of God, "Look, even if the LORD should open the floodgates of the heavens, could this happen?" The man of God had replied, "You will see it with your own eyes, but you will not eat any of it!" ²⁰And that is exactly what happened to him, for the people trampled him in the gateway, and he died.

The Shunammite's Land Restored

8 Now Elisha had said to the woman whose son he had restored to life, "Go away with your family and stay for a while wherever you can, because the LORD has decreed a famine in the land that will last seven years." ²The woman proceeded to do as the man of God said. She and her family went away and stayed in the land of the Philistines seven years.

³At the end of the seven years she came back from the land of the Philistines and went to the king to beg for her house and land. ⁴The king was talking to Gehazi, the servant of the man of God, and had said, "Tell me about all the great things Elisha has done." ⁵Just as Gehazi was telling the king how Elisha had restored the dead to life, the woman whose son Elisha had brought back to life came to beg the king for her house and land.

Gehazi said, "This is the woman, my lord the king, and this is her son whom Elisha restored to life." ⁶The king asked the woman about it, and she told him.

Then he assigned an official to her case and said to him, "Give back everything that belonged to her, including all the income from her land from the day she left the country until now."

Hazael Murders Ben-Hadad

⁷Elisha went to Damascus, and Ben-Hadad king of Aram was ill. When the king was told, "The man of God has come all the way up here," ⁸he said to Hazael, "Take a gift with you and go to meet the man of God. Consult the LORD through him; ask him, 'Will I recover from this illness?'"

⁹Hazael went to meet Elisha, taking with him as a gift forty camel-loads of all the finest wares of Damascus. He went in and stood before him, and said, "Your son Ben-Hadad king of Aram has sent me to ask, 'Will I recover from this illness?'"

¹⁰Elisha answered, "Go and say to him, 'You will certainly recover'; but ᵃ the LORD has revealed to me that he will in fact die." ¹¹He stared at him with a fixed gaze until Hazael felt ashamed. Then the man of God began to weep.

¹²"Why is my lord weeping?" asked Hazael.

"Because I know the harm you will do to the Israelites," he answered. "You will set fire

---

ᵃ10 The Hebrew may also be read *Go and say, 'You will certainly not recover,'* for.

to their fortified places, kill their young men with the sword, dash their little children to the ground, and rip open their pregnant women."

¹³Hazael said, "How could your servant, a mere dog, accomplish such a feat?"

"The LORD has shown me that you will become king of Aram," answered Elisha.

¹⁴Then Hazael left Elisha and returned to his master. When Ben-Hadad asked, "What did Elisha say to you?" Hazael replied, "He told me that you would certainly recover." ¹⁵But the next day he took a thick cloth, soaked it in water and spread it over the king's face, so that he died. Then Hazael succeeded him as king.

Jehoram King of Judah

¹⁶In the fifth year of Joram son of Ahab king of Israel, when Jehoshaphat was king of Judah, Jehoram son of Jehoshaphat began his reign as king of Judah. ¹⁷He was thirty-two years old when he became king, and he reigned in Jerusalem eight years. ¹⁸He walked in the ways of the kings of Israel, as the house of Ahab had done, for he married a daughter of Ahab. He did evil in the eyes of the LORD. ¹⁹Nevertheless, for the sake of his servant David, the LORD was not willing to destroy Judah. He had promised to maintain a lamp for David and his descendants forever.

²⁰In the time of Jehoram, Edom rebelled against Judah and set up its own king. ²¹So Jehoram*ᵃ* went to Zair with all his chariots. The Edomites surrounded him and his chariot commanders, but he rose up and broke through by night; his army, however, fled back home. ²²To this day Edom has been in rebellion against Judah. Libnah revolted at the same time.

²³As for the other events of Jehoram's reign, and all he did, are they not written in the book of the annals of the kings of Judah? ²⁴Jehoram rested with his fathers and was buried with them in the City of David. And Ahaziah his son succeeded him as king.

Ahaziah King of Judah

²⁵In the twelfth year of Joram son of Ahab king of Israel, Ahaziah son of Jehoram king of Judah began to reign. ²⁶Ahaziah was twenty-two years old when he became king, and he reigned in Jerusalem one year. His mother's name was Athaliah, a granddaughter of Omri king of Israel. ²⁷He walked in the ways of the house of Ahab and did evil in the eyes of the LORD, as the house of Ahab had done, for he was related by marriage to Ahab's family.

²⁸Ahaziah went with Joram son of Ahab to war against Hazael king of Aram at Ramoth Gilead. The Arameans wounded Joram; ²⁹so King Joram returned to Jezreel to recover from the wounds the Arameans had inflicted on him at Ramoth*ᵇ* in his battle with Hazael king of Aram.

Then Ahaziah son of Jehoram king of Judah went down to Jezreel to see Joram son of Ahab, because he had been wounded.

Jehu Anointed King of Israel

9   The prophet Elisha summoned a man from the company of the prophets and said to him, "Tuck your cloak into your belt, take this flask of oil with you and go to Ramoth Gilead. ²When you get there, look for Jehu son of Jehoshaphat, the son of Nimshi. Go to him, get him away from his companions and take him into an inner room. ³Then take the flask and pour the oil on his head and declare, 'This is what the LORD says: I anoint you king over Israel.' Then open the door and run; don't delay!"

⁴So the young man, the prophet, went to Ramoth Gilead. ⁵When he arrived, he found the army officers sitting together. "I have a message for you, commander," he said.

"For which of us?" asked Jehu.

"For you, commander," he replied.

⁶Jehu got up and went into the house. Then the prophet poured the oil on Jehu's head

---

ᵃ21 Hebrew *Joram*, a variant of *Jehoram*; also in verses 23 and 24   *ᵇ29* Hebrew *Ramah*, a variant of *Ramoth*

and declared, "This is what the LORD, the God of Israel, says: 'I anoint you king over the LORD's people Israel. [7]You are to destroy the house of Ahab your master, and I will avenge the blood of my servants the prophets and the blood of all the LORD's servants shed by Jezebel. [8]The whole house of Ahab will perish. I will cut off from Ahab every last male in Israel—slave or free. [9]I will make the house of Ahab like the house of Jeroboam son of Nebat and like the house of Baasha son of Ahijah. [10]As for Jezebel, dogs will devour her on the plot of ground at Jezreel, and no one will bury her.'" Then he opened the door and ran.

[11]When Jehu went out to his fellow officers, one of them asked him, "Is everything all right? Why did this madman come to you?"

"You know the man and the sort of things he says," Jehu replied.

[12]"That's not true!" they said. "Tell us."

Jehu said, "Here is what he told me: 'This is what the LORD says: I anoint you king over Israel.'"

[13]They hurried and took their cloaks and spread them under him on the bare steps. Then they blew the trumpet and shouted, "Jehu is king!"

Jehu Kills Joram and Ahaziah

[14]So Jehu son of Jehoshaphat, the son of Nimshi, conspired against Joram. (Now Joram and all Israel had been defending Ramoth Gilead against Hazael king of Aram, [15]but King Joram[a] had returned to Jezreel to recover from the wounds the Arameans had inflicted on him in the battle with Hazael king of Aram.) Jehu said, "If this is the way you feel, don't let anyone slip out of the city to go and tell the news in Jezreel." [16]Then he got into his chariot and rode to Jezreel, because Joram was resting there and Ahaziah king of Judah had gone down to see him.

[17]When the lookout standing on the tower in Jezreel saw Jehu's troops approaching, he called out, "I see some troops coming."

"Get a horseman," Joram ordered. "Send him to meet them and ask, 'Do you come in peace?'"

[18]The horseman rode off to meet Jehu and said, "This is what the king says: 'Do you come in peace?'"

"What do you have to do with peace?" Jehu replied. "Fall in behind me."

The lookout reported, "The messenger has reached them, but he isn't coming back."

[19]So the king sent out a second horseman. When he came to them he said, "This is what the king says: 'Do you come in peace?'"

Jehu replied, "What do you have to do with peace? Fall in behind me."

[20]The lookout reported, "He has reached them, but he isn't coming back either. The driving is like that of Jehu son of Nimshi—he drives like a madman."

[21]"Hitch up my chariot," Joram ordered. And when it was hitched up, Joram king of Israel and Ahaziah king of Judah rode out, each in his own chariot, to meet Jehu. They met him at the plot of ground that had belonged to Naboth the Jezreelite. [22]When Joram saw Jehu he asked, "Have you come in peace, Jehu?"

"How can there be peace," Jehu replied, "as long as all the idolatry and witchcraft of your mother Jezebel abound?"

[23]Joram turned about and fled, calling out to Ahaziah, "Treachery, Ahaziah!"

[24]Then Jehu drew his bow and shot Joram between the shoulders. The arrow pierced his heart and he slumped down in his chariot. [25]Jehu said to Bidkar, his chariot officer, "Pick him up and throw him on the field that belonged to Naboth the Jezreelite. Remember how you and I were riding together in chariots behind Ahab his father when the LORD made this prophecy about him: [26]'Yesterday I saw the blood of Naboth and the blood of his sons, declares the LORD, and I will surely make you pay for it on this plot of ground,

---

[a] 15 Hebrew *Jehoram*, a variant of *Joram*; also in verses 17 and 21-24

declares the Lord.'*a* Now then, pick him up and throw him on that plot, in accordance with the word of the Lord."

²⁷When Ahaziah king of Judah saw what had happened, he fled up the road to Beth Haggan.*b* Jehu chased him, shouting, "Kill him too!" They wounded him in his chariot on the way up to Gur near Ibleam, but he escaped to Megiddo and died there. ²⁸His servants took him by chariot to Jerusalem and buried him with his fathers in his tomb in the City of David. ²⁹(In the eleventh year of Joram son of Ahab, Ahaziah had become king of Judah.)

Jezebel Killed

³⁰Then Jehu went to Jezreel. When Jezebel heard about it, she painted her eyes, arranged her hair and looked out of a window. ³¹As Jehu entered the gate, she asked, "Have you come in peace, Zimri, you murderer of your master?"*c*

³²He looked up at the window and called out, "Who is on my side? Who?" Two or three eunuchs looked down at him. ³³"Throw her down!" Jehu said. So they threw her down, and some of her blood spattered the wall and the horses as they trampled her underfoot.

³⁴Jehu went in and ate and drank. "Take care of that cursed woman," he said, "and bury her, for she was a king's daughter." ³⁵But when they went out to bury her, they found nothing except her skull, her feet and her hands. ³⁶They went back and told Jehu, who said, "This is the word of the Lord that he spoke through his servant Elijah the Tishbite: On the plot of ground at Jezreel dogs will devour Jezebel's flesh.*d* ³⁷Jezebel's body will be like refuse on the ground in the plot at Jezreel, so that no one will be able to say, 'This is Jezebel.'"

Ahab's Family Killed

10 Now there were in Samaria seventy sons of the house of Ahab. So Jehu wrote letters and sent them to Samaria: to the officials of Jezreel,*e* to the elders and to the guardians of Ahab's children. He said, ²"As soon as this letter reaches you, since your master's sons are with you and you have chariots and horses, a fortified city and weapons, ³choose the best and most worthy of your master's sons and set him on his father's throne. Then fight for your master's house."

⁴But they were terrified and said, "If two kings could not resist him, how can we?"

⁵So the palace administrator, the city governor, the elders and the guardians sent this message to Jehu: "We are your servants and we will do anything you say. We will not appoint anyone as king; you do whatever you think best."

⁶Then Jehu wrote them a second letter, saying, "If you are on my side and will obey me, take the heads of your master's sons and come to me in Jezreel by this time tomorrow."

Now the royal princes, seventy of them, were with the leading men of the city, who were rearing them. ⁷When the letter arrived, these men took the princes and slaughtered all seventy of them. They put their heads in baskets and sent them to Jehu in Jezreel. ⁸When the messenger arrived, he told Jehu, "They have brought the heads of the princes."

Then Jehu ordered, "Put them in two piles at the entrance of the city gate until morning."

⁹The next morning Jehu went out. He stood before all the people and said, "You are innocent. It was I who conspired against my master and killed him, but who killed all these? ¹⁰Know then, that not a word the Lord has spoken against the house of Ahab will fail. The Lord has done what he promised through his servant Elijah." ¹¹So Jehu killed everyone in Jezreel who remained of the house of Ahab, as well as all his chief men, his close friends and his priests, leaving him no survivor.

a 26 See 1 Kings 21:19.   *b 27* Or *fled by way of the garden house*   *c 31* Or *"Did Zimri have peace, who murdered his master?"*   *d 36* See 1 Kings 21:23.   *e 1* Hebrew; some Septuagint manuscripts and Vulgate *of the city*

¹²Jehu then set out and went toward Samaria. At Beth Eked of the Shepherds, ¹³he met some relatives of Ahaziah king of Judah and asked, "Who are you?"

They said, "We are relatives of Ahaziah, and we have come down to greet the families of the king and of the queen mother."

¹⁴"Take them alive!" he ordered. So they took them alive and slaughtered them by the well of Beth Eked—forty-two men. He left no survivor.

¹⁵After he left there, he came upon Jehonadab son of Recab, who was on his way to meet him. Jehu greeted him and said, "Are you in accord with me, as I am with you?"

"I am," Jehonadab answered.

"If so," said Jehu, "give me your hand." So he did, and Jehu helped him up into the chariot. ¹⁶Jehu said, "Come with me and see my zeal for the LORD." Then he had him ride along in his chariot.

¹⁷When Jehu came to Samaria, he killed all who were left there of Ahab's family; he destroyed them, according to the word of the LORD spoken to Elijah.

Ministers of Baal Killed

¹⁸Then Jehu brought all the people together and said to them, "Ahab served Baal a little; Jehu will serve him much. ¹⁹Now summon all the prophets of Baal, all his ministers and all his priests. See that no one is missing, because I am going to hold a great sacrifice for Baal. Anyone who fails to come will no longer live." But Jehu was acting deceptively in order to destroy the ministers of Baal.

²⁰Jehu said, "Call an assembly in honor of Baal." So they proclaimed it. ²¹Then he sent word throughout Israel, and all the ministers of Baal came; not one stayed away. They crowded into the temple of Baal until it was full from one end to the other. ²²And Jehu said to the keeper of the wardrobe, "Bring robes for all the ministers of Baal." So he brought out robes for them.

²³Then Jehu and Jehonadab son of Recab went into the temple of Baal. Jehu said to the ministers of Baal, "Look around and see that no servants of the LORD are here with you—only ministers of Baal." ²⁴So they went in to make sacrifices and burnt offerings. Now Jehu had posted eighty men outside with this warning: "If one of you lets any of the men I am placing in your hands escape, it will be your life for his life."

²⁵As soon as Jehu had finished making the burnt offering, he ordered the guards and officers: "Go in and kill them; let no one escape." So they cut them down with the sword. The guards and officers threw the bodies out and then entered the inner shrine of the temple of Baal. ²⁶They brought the sacred stone out of the temple of Baal and burned it. ²⁷They demolished the sacred stone of Baal and tore down the temple of Baal, and people have used it for a latrine to this day.

²⁸So Jehu destroyed Baal worship in Israel. ²⁹However, he did not turn away from the sins of Jeroboam son of Nebat, which he had caused Israel to commit—the worship of the golden calves at Bethel and Dan.

³⁰The LORD said to Jehu, "Because you have done well in accomplishing what is right in my eyes and have done to the house of Ahab all I had in mind to do, your descendants will sit on the throne of Israel to the fourth generation." ³¹Yet Jehu was not careful to keep the law of the LORD, the God of Israel, with all his heart. He did not turn away from the sins of Jeroboam, which he had caused Israel to commit.

³²In those days the LORD began to reduce the size of Israel. Hazael overpowered the Israelites throughout their territory ³³east of the Jordan in all the land of Gilead (the region of Gad, Reuben and Manasseh), from Aroer by the Arnon Gorge through Gilead to Bashan.

³⁴As for the other events of Jehu's reign, all he did, and all his achievements, are they not written in the book of the annals of the kings of Israel?

³⁵Jehu rested with his fathers and was buried in Samaria. And Jehoahaz his son

succeeded him as king. ³⁶The time that Jehu reigned over Israel in Samaria was twenty-eight years.

Athaliah and Joash

11 When Athaliah the mother of Ahaziah saw that her son was dead, she proceeded to destroy the whole royal family. ²But Jehosheba, the daughter of King Jehoram*a* and sister of Ahaziah, took Joash son of Ahaziah and stole him away from among the royal princes, who were about to be murdered. She put him and his nurse in a bedroom to hide him from Athaliah; so he was not killed. ³He remained hidden with his nurse at the temple of the LORD for six years while Athaliah ruled the land.

⁴In the seventh year Jehoiada sent for the commanders of units of a hundred, the Carites and the guards and had them brought to him at the temple of the LORD. He made a covenant with them and put them under oath at the temple of the LORD. Then he showed them the king's son. ⁵He commanded them, saying, "This is what you are to do: You who are in the three companies that are going on duty on the Sabbath—a third of you guarding the royal palace, ⁶a third at the Sur Gate, and a third at the gate behind the guard, who take turns guarding the temple— ⁷and you who are in the other two companies that normally go off Sabbath duty are all to guard the temple for the king. ⁸Station yourselves around the king, each man with his weapon in his hand. Anyone who approaches your ranks*b* must be put to death. Stay close to the king wherever he goes."

⁹The commanders of units of a hundred did just as Jehoiada the priest ordered. Each one took his men—those who were going on duty on the Sabbath and those who were going off duty—and came to Jehoiada the priest. ¹⁰Then he gave the commanders the spears and shields that had belonged to King David and that were in the temple of the LORD. ¹¹The guards, each with his weapon in his hand, stationed themselves around the king—near the altar and the temple, from the south side to the north side of the temple.

¹²Jehoiada brought out the king's son and put the crown on him; he presented him with a copy of the covenant and proclaimed him king. They anointed him, and the people clapped their hands and shouted, "Long live the king!"

¹³When Athaliah heard the noise made by the guards and the people, she went to the people at the temple of the LORD. ¹⁴She looked and there was the king, standing by the pillar, as the custom was. The officers and the trumpeters were beside the king, and all the people of the land were rejoicing and blowing trumpets. Then Athaliah tore her robes and called out, "Treason! Treason!"

¹⁵Jehoiada the priest ordered the commanders of units of a hundred, who were in

a 2 Hebrew *Joram,* a variant of *Jehoram*　　*b* 8 Or *approaches the precincts* charge of the troops: "Bring her out between the ranks[a] and put to the sword anyone who follows her." For the priest had said, "She must not be put to death in the temple of the LORD." [16]So they seized her as she reached the place where the horses enter the palace grounds, and there she was put to death.

[17]Jehoiada then made a covenant between the LORD and the king and people that they would be the LORD's people. He also made a covenant between the king and the people. [18]All the people of the land went to the temple of Baal and tore it down. They smashed the altars and idols to pieces and killed Mattan the priest of Baal in front of the altars.

Then Jehoiada the priest posted guards at the temple of the LORD. [19]He took with him the commanders of hundreds, the Carites, the guards and all the people of the land, and together they brought the king down from the temple of the LORD and went into the palace, entering by way of the gate of the guards. The king then took his place on the royal throne, [20]and all the people of the land rejoiced. And the city was quiet, because Athaliah had been slain with the sword at the palace.

[21]Joash[b] was seven years old when he began to reign.

Joash Repairs the Temple

12 In the seventh year of Jehu, Joash[c] became king, and he reigned in Jerusalem forty years. His mother's name was Zibiah; she was from Beersheba. [2]Joash did what was right in the eyes of the LORD all the years Jehoiada the priest instructed him. [3]The high places, however, were not removed; the people continued to offer sacrifices and burn incense there.

[4]Joash said to the priests, "Collect all the money that is brought as sacred offerings to the temple of the LORD—the money collected in the census, the money received from personal vows and the money brought voluntarily to the temple. [5]Let every priest receive the money from one of the treasurers, and let it be used to repair whatever damage is found in the temple."

[6]But by the twenty-third year of King Joash the priests still had not repaired the temple. [7]Therefore King Joash summoned Jehoiada the priest and the other priests and asked them, "Why aren't you repairing the damage done to the temple? Take no more money from your treasurers, but hand it over for repairing the temple." [8]The priests agreed that they would not collect any more money from the people and that they would not repair the temple themselves.

[9]Jehoiada the priest took a chest and bored a hole in its lid. He placed it beside the altar, on the right side as one enters the temple of the LORD. The priests who guarded the entrance put into the chest all the money that was brought to the temple of the LORD. [10]Whenever they saw that there was a large amount of money in the chest, the royal secretary and the high priest came, counted the money that had been brought into the temple of the LORD and put it into bags. [11]When the amount had been determined, they gave the money to the men appointed to supervise the work on the temple. With it they paid those who worked on the temple of the LORD—the carpenters and builders, [12]the masons and stonecutters. They purchased timber and dressed stone for the repair of the temple of the LORD, and met all the other expenses of restoring the temple.

[13]The money brought into the temple was not spent for making silver basins, wick trimmers, sprinkling bowls, trumpets or any other articles of gold or silver for the temple of the LORD; [14]it was paid to the workmen, who used it to repair the temple. [15]They did not require an accounting from those to whom they gave the money to pay the workers, because they acted with complete honesty. [16]The money from the guilt offerings and sin offerings was not brought into the temple of the LORD; it belonged to the priests.

[17]About this time Hazael king of Aram went up and attacked Gath and captured it. Then he turned to attack Jerusalem. [18]But Joash king of Judah took all the sacred objects

---

[a]15 Or *out from the precincts*   [b]21 Hebrew *Jehoash,* a variant of *Joash*   [c]1 Hebrew *Jehoash,* a variant of *Joash;* also in verses 2, 4, 6, 7 and 18

dedicated by his fathers—Jehoshaphat, Jehoram and Ahaziah, the kings of Judah—and the gifts he himself had dedicated and all the gold found in the treasuries of the temple of the LORD and of the royal palace, and he sent them to Hazael king of Aram, who then withdrew from Jerusalem.

¹⁹As for the other events of the reign of Joash, and all he did, are they not written in the book of the annals of the kings of Judah? ²⁰His officials conspired against him and assassinated him at Beth Millo, on the road down to Silla. ²¹The officials who murdered him were Jozabad son of Shimeath and Jehozabad son of Shomer. He died and was buried with his fathers in the City of David. And Amaziah his son succeeded him as king.

Jehoahaz King of Israel

13 In the twenty-third year of Joash son of Ahaziah king of Judah, Jehoahaz son of Jehu became king of Israel in Samaria, and he reigned seventeen years. ²He did evil in the eyes of the LORD by following the sins of Jeroboam son of Nebat, which he had caused Israel to commit, and he did not turn away from them. ³So the LORD's anger burned against Israel, and for a long time he kept them under the power of Hazael king of Aram and Ben-Hadad his son.

⁴Then Jehoahaz sought the LORD's favor, and the LORD listened to him, for he saw how severely the king of Aram was oppressing Israel. ⁵The LORD provided a deliverer for Israel, and they escaped from the power of Aram. So the Israelites lived in their own homes as they had before. ⁶But they did not turn away from the sins of the house of Jeroboam, which he had caused Israel to commit; they continued in them. Also, the Asherah pole[a] remained standing in Samaria.

⁷Nothing had been left of the army of Jehoahaz except fifty horsemen, ten chariots and ten thousand foot soldiers, for the king of Aram had destroyed the rest and made them like the dust at threshing time.

⁸As for the other events of the reign of Jehoahaz, all he did and his achievements, are they not written in the book of the annals of the kings of Israel? ⁹Jehoahaz rested with his fathers and was buried in Samaria. And Jehoash[b] his son succeeded him as king.

Jehoash King of Israel

¹⁰In the thirty-seventh year of Joash king of Judah, Jehoash son of Jehoahaz became king of Israel in Samaria, and he reigned sixteen years. ¹¹He did evil in the eyes of the LORD and did not turn away from any of the sins of Jeroboam son of Nebat, which he had caused Israel to commit; he continued in them.

¹²As for the other events of the reign of Jehoash, all he did and his achievements, including his war against Amaziah king of Judah, are they not written in the book of the annals of the kings of Israel? ¹³Jehoash rested with his fathers, and Jeroboam succeeded him on the throne. Jehoash was buried in Samaria with the kings of Israel.

¹⁴Now Elisha was suffering from the illness from which he died. Jehoash king of Israel went down to see him and wept over him. "My father! My father!" he cried. "The chariots and horsemen of Israel!"

¹⁵Elisha said, "Get a bow and some arrows," and he did so. ¹⁶"Take the bow in your hands," he said to the king of Israel. When he had taken it, Elisha put his hands on the king's hands.

¹⁷"Open the east window," he said, and he opened it. "Shoot!" Elisha said, and he shot. "The LORD's arrow of victory, the arrow of victory over Aram!" Elisha declared. "You will completely destroy the Arameans at Aphek."

¹⁸Then he said, "Take the arrows," and the king took them. Elisha told him, "Strike the ground." He struck it three times and stopped. ¹⁹The man of God was angry with him and

---

a6 That is, a symbol of the goddess Asherah; here and elsewhere in 2 Kings   *b9* Hebrew *Joash*, a variant of *Jehoash*; also in verses 12-14 and 25

said, "You should have struck the ground five or six times; then you would have defeated Aram and completely destroyed it. But now you will defeat it only three times."

²⁰Elisha died and was buried.

Now Moabite raiders used to enter the country every spring. ²¹Once while some Israelites were burying a man, suddenly they saw a band of raiders; so they threw the man's body into Elisha's tomb. When the body touched Elisha's bones, the man came to life and stood up on his feet.

²²Hazael king of Aram oppressed Israel throughout the reign of Jehoahaz. ²³But the LORD was gracious to them and had compassion and showed concern for them because of his covenant with Abraham, Isaac and Jacob. To this day he has been unwilling to destroy them or banish them from his presence.

²⁴Hazael king of Aram died, and Ben-Hadad his son succeeded him as king. ²⁵Then Jehoash son of Jehoahaz recaptured from Ben-Hadad son of Hazael the towns he had taken in battle from his father Jehoahaz. Three times Jehoash defeated him, and so he recovered the Israelite towns.

Amaziah King of Judah

14 In the second year of Jehoash[a] son of Jehoahaz king of Israel, Amaziah son of Joash king of Judah began to reign. ²He was twenty-five years old when he became king, and he reigned in Jerusalem twenty-nine years. His mother's name was Jehoaddin; she was from Jerusalem. ³He did what was right in the eyes of the LORD, but not as his father David had done. In everything he followed the example of his father Joash. ⁴The high places, however, were not removed; the people continued to offer sacrifices and burn incense there.

⁵After the kingdom was firmly in his grasp, he executed the officials who had murdered his father the king. ⁶Yet he did not put the sons of the assassins to death, in accordance with what is written in the Book of the Law of Moses where the LORD commanded: "Fathers shall not be put to death for their children, nor children put to death for their fathers; each is to die for his own sins."[b]

⁷He was the one who defeated ten thousand Edomites in the Valley of Salt and captured Sela in battle, calling it Joktheel, the name it has to this day.

⁸Then Amaziah sent messengers to Jehoash son of Jehoahaz, the son of Jehu, king of Israel, with the challenge: "Come, meet me face to face."

⁹But Jehoash king of Israel replied to Amaziah king of Judah: "A thistle in Lebanon sent a message to a cedar in Lebanon, 'Give your daughter to my son in marriage.' Then a wild beast in Lebanon came along and trampled the thistle underfoot. ¹⁰You have indeed defeated Edom and now you are arrogant. Glory in your victory, but stay at home! Why ask for trouble and cause your own downfall and that of Judah also?"

¹¹Amaziah, however, would not listen, so Jehoash king of Israel attacked. He and Amaziah king of Judah faced each other at Beth Shemesh in Judah. ¹²Judah was routed by Israel, and every man fled to his home. ¹³Jehoash king of Israel captured Amaziah king of Judah, the son of Joash, the son of Ahaziah, at Beth Shemesh. Then Jehoash went to Jerusalem and broke down the wall of Jerusalem from the Ephraim Gate to the Corner Gate—a section about six hundred feet long.[c] ¹⁴He took all the gold and silver and all the articles found in the temple of the LORD and in the treasuries of the royal palace. He also took hostages and returned to Samaria.

¹⁵As for the other events of the reign of Jehoash, what he did and his achievements, including his war against Amaziah king of Judah, are they not written in the book of the annals of the kings of Israel? ¹⁶Jehoash rested with his fathers and was buried in Samaria with the kings of Israel. And Jeroboam his son succeeded him as king.

¹⁷Amaziah son of Joash king of Judah lived for fifteen years after the death of Jehoash

---

[a]1 Hebrew *Joash*, a variant of *Jehoash*; also in verses 13, 23 and 27   [b]6 Deut. 24:16   [c]13 Hebrew *four hundred cubits* (about 180 meters)

son of Jehoahaz king of Israel. ¹⁸As for the other events of Amaziah's reign, are they not written in the book of the annals of the kings of Judah?

¹⁹They conspired against him in Jerusalem, and he fled to Lachish, but they sent men after him to Lachish and killed him there. ²⁰He was brought back by horse and was buried in Jerusalem with his fathers, in the City of David.

²¹Then all the people of Judah took Azariah,ᵃ who was sixteen years old, and made him king in place of his father Amaziah. ²²He was the one who rebuilt Elath and restored it to Judah after Amaziah rested with his fathers.

Jeroboam II King of Israel

²³In the fifteenth year of Amaziah son of Joash king of Judah, Jeroboam son of Jehoash king of Israel became king in Samaria, and he reigned forty-one years. ²⁴He did evil in the eyes of the LORD and did not turn away from any of the sins of Jeroboam son of Nebat, which he had caused Israel to commit. ²⁵He was the one who restored the boundaries of Israel from Leboᵇ Hamath to the Sea of the Arabah,ᶜ in accordance with the word of the LORD, the God of Israel, spoken through his servant Jonah son of Amittai, the prophet from Gath Hepher.

²⁶The LORD had seen how bitterly everyone in Israel, whether slave or free, was suffering; there was no one to help them. ²⁷And since the LORD had not said he would blot out the name of Israel from under heaven, he saved them by the hand of Jeroboam son of Jehoash.

²⁸As for the other events of Jeroboam's reign, all he did, and his military achievements, including how he recovered for Israel both Damascus and Hamath, which had belonged to Yaudi,ᵈ are they not written in the book of the annals of the kings of Israel? ²⁹Jeroboam rested with his fathers, the kings of Israel. And Zechariah his son succeeded him as king.

Azariah King of Judah

15 In the twenty-seventh year of Jeroboam king of Israel, Azariah son of Amaziah king of Judah began to reign. ²He was sixteen years old when he became king, and he reigned in Jerusalem fifty-two years. His mother's name was Jecoliah; she was from Jerusalem. ³He did what was right in the eyes of the LORD, just as his father Amaziah had done. ⁴The high places, however, were not removed; the people continued to offer sacrifices and burn incense there.

⁵The LORD afflicted the king with leprosyᵉ until the day he died, and he lived in a separate house.ᶠ Jotham the king's son had charge of the palace and governed the people of the land.

⁶As for the other events of Azariah's reign, and all he did, are they not written in the book of the annals of the kings of Judah? ⁷Azariah rested with his fathers and was buried near them in the City of David. And Jotham his son succeeded him as king.

Zechariah King of Israel

⁸In the thirty-eighth year of Azariah king of Judah, Zechariah son of Jeroboam became king of Israel in Samaria, and he reigned six months. ⁹He did evil in the eyes of the LORD, as his fathers had done. He did not turn away from the sins of Jeroboam son of Nebat, which he had caused Israel to commit.

¹⁰Shallum son of Jabesh conspired against Zechariah. He attacked him in front of the people,ᵍ assassinated him and succeeded him as king. ¹¹The other events of Zechariah's reign are written in the book of the annals of the kings of Israel. ¹²So the word of the LORD

---

a21 Also called *Uzziah*   *b25* Or *from the entrance to*   *c25* That is, the Dead Sea   *d28* Or *Judah*   *e5* The Hebrew word was used for various diseases affecting the skin—not necessarily leprosy.   *f5* Or *in a house where he was relieved of responsibility*   *g10* Hebrew; some Septuagint manuscripts *in Ibleam*

spoken to Jehu was fulfilled: "Your descendants will sit on the throne of Israel to the fourth generation." [a]

Shallum King of Israel

[13]Shallum son of Jabesh became king in the thirty-ninth year of Uzziah king of Judah, and he reigned in Samaria one month. [14]Then Menahem son of Gadi went from Tirzah up to Samaria. He attacked Shallum son of Jabesh in Samaria, assassinated him and succeeded him as king.

[15]The other events of Shallum's reign, and the conspiracy he led, are written in the book of the annals of the kings of Israel.

[16]At that time Menahem, starting out from Tirzah, attacked Tiphsah and everyone in the city and its vicinity, because they refused to open their gates. He sacked Tiphsah and ripped open all the pregnant women.

Menahem King of Israel

[17]In the thirty-ninth year of Azariah king of Judah, Menahem son of Gadi became king of Israel, and he reigned in Samaria ten years. [18]He did evil in the eyes of the LORD. During his entire reign he did not turn away from the sins of Jeroboam son of Nebat, which he had caused Israel to commit.

[19]Then Pul [b] king of Assyria invaded the land, and Menahem gave him a thousand talents [c] of silver to gain his support and strengthen his own hold on the kingdom. [20]Menahem exacted this money from Israel. Every wealthy man had to contribute fifty shekels [d] of silver to be given to the king of Assyria. So the king of Assyria withdrew and stayed in the land no longer.

[21]As for the other events of Menahem's reign, and all he did, are they not written in the book of the annals of the kings of Israel? [22]Menahem rested with his fathers. And Pekahiah his son succeeded him as king.

Pekahiah King of Israel

[23]In the fiftieth year of Azariah king of Judah, Pekahiah son of Menahem became king of Israel in Samaria, and he reigned two years. [24]Pekahiah did evil in the eyes of the LORD. He did not turn away from the sins of Jeroboam son of Nebat, which he had caused Israel to commit. [25]One of his chief officers, Pekah son of Remaliah, conspired against him. Taking fifty men of Gilead with him, he assassinated Pekahiah, along with Argob and Arieh, in the citadel of the royal palace at Samaria. So Pekah killed Pekahiah and succeeded him as king.

[26]The other events of Pekahiah's reign, and all he did, are written in the book of the annals of the kings of Israel.

Pekah King of Israel

[27]In the fifty-second year of Azariah king of Judah, Pekah son of Remaliah became king of Israel in Samaria, and he reigned twenty years. [28]He did evil in the eyes of the LORD. He did not turn away from the sins of Jeroboam son of Nebat, which he had caused Israel to commit.

[29]In the time of Pekah king of Israel, Tiglath-Pileser king of Assyria came and took Ijon, Abel Beth Maacah, Janoah, Kedesh and Hazor. He took Gilead and Galilee, including all the land of Naphtali, and deported the people to Assyria. [30]Then Hoshea son of Elah conspired against Pekah son of Remaliah. He attacked and assassinated him, and then succeeded him as king in the twentieth year of Jotham son of Uzziah.

[31]As for the other events of Pekah's reign, and all he did, are they not written in the book of the annals of the kings of Israel?

a 12 2 Kings 10:30   *b 19* Also called *Tiglath-Pileser*   *c 19* That is, about 37 tons (about 34 metric tons)   *d 20* That is, about 1 1/4 pounds (about 0.6 kilogram)

Jotham King of Judah

³²In the second year of Pekah son of Remaliah king of Israel, Jotham son of Uzziah king of Judah began to reign. ³³He was twenty-five years old when he became king, and he reigned in Jerusalem sixteen years. His mother's name was Jerusha daughter of Zadok. ³⁴He did what was right in the eyes of the LORD, just as his father Uzziah had done. ³⁵The high places, however, were not removed; the people continued to offer sacrifices and burn incense there. Jotham rebuilt the Upper Gate of the temple of the LORD.

³⁶As for the other events of Jotham's reign, and what he did, are they not written in the book of the annals of the kings of Judah? ³⁷(In those days the LORD began to send Rezin king of Aram and Pekah son of Remaliah against Judah.) ³⁸Jotham rested with his fathers and was buried with them in the City of David, the city of his father. And Ahaz his son succeeded him as king.

Ahaz King of Judah

16 In the seventeenth year of Pekah son of Remaliah, Ahaz son of Jotham king of Judah began to reign. ²Ahaz was twenty years old when he became king, and he reigned in Jerusalem sixteen years. Unlike David his father, he did not do what was right in the eyes of the LORD his God. ³He walked in the ways of the kings of Israel and even sacrificed his son in*a* the fire, following the detestable ways of the nations the LORD had driven out before the Israelites. ⁴He offered sacrifices and burned incense at the high places, on the hilltops and under every spreading tree.

⁵Then Rezin king of Aram and Pekah son of Remaliah king of Israel marched up to fight against Jerusalem and besieged Ahaz, but they could not overpower him. ⁶At that time, Rezin king of Aram recovered Elath for Aram by driving out the men of Judah. Edomites then moved into Elath and have lived there to this day.

⁷Ahaz sent messengers to say to Tiglath-Pileser king of Assyria, "I am your servant and vassal. Come up and save me out of the hand of the king of Aram and of the king of Israel, who are attacking me." ⁸And Ahaz took the silver and gold found in the temple of the LORD and in the treasuries of the royal palace and sent it as a gift to the king of Assyria. ⁹The king of Assyria complied by attacking Damascus and capturing it. He deported its inhabitants to Kir and put Rezin to death.

¹⁰Then King Ahaz went to Damascus to meet Tiglath-Pileser king of Assyria. He saw an altar in Damascus and sent to Uriah the priest a sketch of the altar, with detailed plans for its construction. ¹¹So Uriah the priest built an altar in accordance with all the plans that King Ahaz had sent from Damascus and finished it before King Ahaz returned. ¹²When the king came back from Damascus and saw the altar, he approached it and presented offerings*b* on it. ¹³He offered up his burnt offering and grain offering, poured out his drink offering, and sprinkled the blood of his fellowship offerings*c* on the altar. ¹⁴The bronze altar that stood before the LORD he brought from the front of the temple—from between the new altar and the temple of the LORD—and put it on the north side of the new altar.

¹⁵King Ahaz then gave these orders to Uriah the priest: "On the large new altar, offer the morning burnt offering and the evening grain offering, the king's burnt offering and his grain offering, and the burnt offering of all the people of the land, and their grain offering and their drink offering. Sprinkle on the altar all the blood of the burnt offerings and sacrifices. But I will use the bronze altar for seeking guidance." ¹⁶And Uriah the priest did just as King Ahaz had ordered.

¹⁷King Ahaz took away the side panels and removed the basins from the movable stands. He removed the Sea from the bronze bulls that supported it and set it on a stone base. ¹⁸He took away the Sabbath canopy*d* that had been built at the temple and

a3 Or even made his son pass through   *b12* Or and went up   *c13* Traditionally peace offerings   *d18* Or the dais
of his throne (see Septuagint)

removed the royal entryway outside the temple of the LORD, in deference to the king of Assyria.

¹⁹As for the other events of the reign of Ahaz, and what he did, are they not written in the book of the annals of the kings of Judah? ²⁰Ahaz rested with his fathers and was buried with them in the City of David. And Hezekiah his son succeeded him as king.

Hoshea Last King of Israel

17 In the twelfth year of Ahaz king of Judah, Hoshea son of Elah became king of Israel in Samaria, and he reigned nine years. ²He did evil in the eyes of the LORD, but not like the kings of Israel who preceded him.

³Shalmaneser king of Assyria came up to attack Hoshea, who had been Shalmaneser's vassal and had paid him tribute. ⁴But the king of Assyria discovered that Hoshea was a traitor, for he had sent envoys to So*ᵃ* king of Egypt, and he no longer paid tribute to the king of Assyria, as he had done year by year. Therefore Shalmaneser seized him and put him in prison. ⁵The king of Assyria invaded the entire land, marched against Samaria and laid siege to it for three years. ⁶In the ninth year of Hoshea, the king of Assyria captured Samaria and deported the Israelites to Assyria. He settled them in Halah, in Gozan on the Habor River and in the towns of the Medes.

Israel Exiled Because of Sin

⁷All this took place because the Israelites had sinned against the LORD their God, who had brought them up out of Egypt from under the power of Pharaoh king of Egypt. They worshiped other gods ⁸and followed the practices of the nations the LORD had driven out before them, as well as the practices that the kings of Israel had introduced. ⁹The Israelites secretly did things against the LORD their God that were not right. From watchtower to fortified city they built themselves high places in all their towns. ¹⁰They set up sacred stones and Asherah poles on every high hill and under every spreading tree. ¹¹At every high place they burned incense, as the nations whom the LORD had driven out before them had done. They did wicked things that provoked the LORD to anger. ¹²They worshiped idols, though the LORD had said, "You shall not do this."*ᵇ* ¹³The LORD warned Israel and Judah through all his prophets and seers: "Turn from your evil ways. Observe my commands and decrees, in accordance with the entire Law that I commanded your fathers to obey and that I delivered to you through my servants the prophets."

¹⁴But they would not listen and were as stiff-necked as their fathers, who did not trust in the LORD their God. ¹⁵They rejected his decrees and the covenant he had made with their fathers and the warnings he had given them. They followed worthless idols and themselves became worthless. They imitated the nations around them although the LORD had ordered them, "Do not do as they do," and they did the things the LORD had forbidden them to do.

¹⁶They forsook all the commands of the LORD their God and made for themselves two idols cast in the shape of calves, and an Asherah pole. They bowed down to all the starry hosts, and they worshiped Baal. ¹⁷They sacrificed their sons and daughters in*ᶜ* the fire. They practiced divination and sorcery and sold themselves to do evil in the eyes of the LORD, provoking him to anger.

¹⁸So the LORD was very angry with Israel and removed them from his presence. Only the tribe of Judah was left, ¹⁹and even Judah did not keep the commands of the LORD their God. They followed the practices Israel had introduced. ²⁰Therefore the LORD rejected all the people of Israel; he afflicted them and gave them into the hands of plunderers, until he thrust them from his presence.

ᵃ4 Or *to Sais, to the; So* is possibly an abbreviation for *Osorkon.*   *ᵇ12* Exodus 20:4, 5   *ᶜ17* Or *They made their sons and daughters pass through*

²¹When he tore Israel away from the house of David, they made Jeroboam son of Nebat their king. Jeroboam enticed Israel away from following the Lᴏʀᴅ and caused them to commit a great sin. ²²The Israelites persisted in all the sins of Jeroboam and did not turn away from them ²³until the Lᴏʀᴅ removed them from his presence, as he had warned through all his servants the prophets. So the people of Israel were taken from their homeland into exile in Assyria, and they are still there.

Samaria Resettled

²⁴The king of Assyria brought people from Babylon, Cuthah, Avva, Hamath and Sepharvaim and settled them in the towns of Samaria to replace the Israelites. They took over Samaria and lived in its towns. ²⁵When they first lived there, they did not worship the Lᴏʀᴅ; so he sent lions among them and they killed some of the people. ²⁶It was reported to the king of Assyria: "The people you deported and resettled in the towns of Samaria do not know what the god of that country requires. He has sent lions among them, which are killing them off, because the people do not know what he requires."

²⁷Then the king of Assyria gave this order: "Have one of the priests you took captive from Samaria go back to live there and teach the people what the god of the land requires." ²⁸So one of the priests who had been exiled from Samaria came to live in Bethel and taught them how to worship the Lᴏʀᴅ.

²⁹Nevertheless, each national group made its own gods in the several towns where they settled, and set them up in the shrines the people of Samaria had made at the high places. ³⁰The men from Babylon made Succoth Benoth, the men from Cuthah made Nergal, and the men from Hamath made Ashima; ³¹the Avvites made Nibhaz and Tartak, and the Sepharvites burned their children in the fire as sacrifices to Adrammelech and Anammelech, the gods of Sepharvaim. ³²They worshiped the Lᴏʀᴅ, but they also appointed all sorts of their own people to officiate for them as priests in the shrines at the high places. ³³They worshiped the Lᴏʀᴅ, but they also served their own gods in accordance with the customs of the nations from which they had been brought.

◻ ⬛DISCOVERING GOD⬛ ⊟

17:40–41
Spiritual Fraud

What an indictment! These people were serving idols while they were worshiping God. This is the origin of the sect and nationality known as the Samaritans, who still lived in Israel in Jesus' day.

If you're a seeker, note how disdainfully the Scriptures speak of this type of spiritual compromise. If you come to the point where you choose to follow God, do it wholeheartedly. Don't be double-minded as these people were.

³⁴To this day they persist in their former practices. They neither worship the Lᴏʀᴅ nor adhere to the decrees and ordinances, the laws and commands that the Lᴏʀᴅ gave the descendants of Jacob, whom he named Israel. ³⁵When the Lᴏʀᴅ made a covenant with the Israelites, he commanded them: "Do not worship any other gods or bow down to them, serve them or sacrifice to them. ³⁶But the Lᴏʀᴅ, who brought you up out of Egypt with mighty power and outstretched arm, is the one you must worship. To him you shall bow down and to him offer sacrifices. ³⁷You must always be careful to keep the decrees and ordinances, the laws and commands he wrote for you. Do not worship other gods. ³⁸Do not forget the covenant I have made with you, and do not worship other gods. ³⁹Rather, worship the Lᴏʀᴅ your God; it is he who will deliver you from the hand of all your enemies."

⁴⁰They would not listen, however, but persisted in their former practices. ⁴¹Even while these people were worshiping the Lᴏʀᴅ, they were serving their idols. To this day their children and grandchildren continue to do as their fathers did.

Hezekiah King of Judah

18 In the third year of Hoshea son of Elah king of Israel, Hezekiah son of Ahaz king of Judah began to reign. ²He was twenty-five years old when he became king, and he reigned in Jerusalem twenty-nine years. His mother's name was Abijah*a* daughter of Zechariah. ³He did what was right in the eyes of the LORD, just as his father David had done. ⁴He removed the high places, smashed the sacred stones and cut down the Asherah poles. He broke into pieces the bronze snake Moses had made, for up to that time the Israelites had been burning incense to it. (It was called*b* Nehushtan.*c*

⁵Hezekiah trusted in the LORD, the God of Israel. There was no one like him among all the kings of Judah, either before him or after him. ⁶He held fast to the LORD and did not cease to follow him; he kept the commands the LORD had given Moses. ⁷And the LORD was with him; he was successful in whatever he undertook. He rebelled against the king of Assyria and did not serve him. ⁸From watchtower to fortified city, he defeated the Philistines, as far as Gaza and its territory.

⁹In King Hezekiah's fourth year, which was the seventh year of Hoshea son of Elah king of Israel, Shalmaneser king of Assyria marched against Samaria and laid siege to it. ¹⁰At the end of three years the Assyrians took it. So Samaria was captured in Hezekiah's sixth year, which was the ninth year of Hoshea king of Israel. ¹¹The king of Assyria deported Israel to Assyria and settled them in Halah, in Gozan on the Habor River and in towns of the Medes. ¹²This happened because they had not obeyed the LORD their God, but had violated his covenant—all that Moses the servant of the LORD commanded. They neither listened to the commands nor carried them out.

¹³In the fourteenth year of King Hezekiah's reign, Sennacherib king of Assyria attacked all the fortified cities of Judah and captured them. ¹⁴So Hezekiah king of Judah sent this message to the king of Assyria at Lachish: "I have done wrong. Withdraw from me, and I will pay whatever you demand of me." The king of Assyria exacted from Hezekiah king of Judah three hundred talents*d* of silver and thirty talents*e* of gold. ¹⁵So Hezekiah gave him all the silver that was found in the temple of the LORD and in the treasuries of the royal palace.

¹⁶At this time Hezekiah king of Judah stripped off the gold with which he had covered the doors and doorposts of the temple of the LORD, and gave it to the king of Assyria.

Sennacherib Threatens Jerusalem

¹⁷The king of Assyria sent his supreme commander, his chief officer and his field commander with a large army, from Lachish to King Hezekiah at Jerusalem. They came up to Jerusalem and stopped at the aqueduct of the Upper Pool, on the road to the Washerman's Field. ¹⁸They called for the king; and Eliakim son of Hilkiah the palace administrator, Shebna the secretary, and Joah son of Asaph the recorder went out to them.

¹⁹The field commander said to them, "Tell Hezekiah:

" 'This is what the great king, the king of Assyria, says: On what are you basing this confidence of yours? ²⁰You say you have strategy and military strength—but you speak only empty words. On whom are you depending, that you rebel against me? ²¹Look now, you are depending on Egypt, that splintered reed of a staff, which pierces a man's hand and wounds him if he leans on it! Such is Pharaoh king of Egypt to all who depend on him. ²²And if you say to me, "We are depending on the LORD our God"—isn't he the one whose high places and altars Hezekiah removed, saying to Judah and Jerusalem, "You must worship before this altar in Jerusalem"?

²³" 'Come now, make a bargain with my master, the king of Assyria: I will give you two thousand horses—if you can put riders on them! ²⁴How can you repulse one

---

*a*2 Hebrew *Abi,* a variant of *Abijah*   *b*4 Or *He called it*   *c*4 *Nehushtan* sounds like the Hebrew for *bronze* and *snake* and *unclean thing.*   *d*14 That is, about 11 tons (about 10 metric tons)   *e*14 That is, about 1 ton (about 1 metric ton)

officer of the least of my master's officials, even though you are depending on Egypt for chariots and horsemen[a]? 25Furthermore, have I come to attack and destroy this place without word from the LORD? The LORD himself told me to march against this country and destroy it.'"

26Then Eliakim son of Hilkiah, and Shebna and Joah said to the field commander, "Please speak to your servants in Aramaic, since we understand it. Don't speak to us in Hebrew in the hearing of the people on the wall."

27But the commander replied, "Was it only to your master and you that my master sent me to say these things, and not to the men sitting on the wall—who, like you, will have to eat their own filth and drink their own urine?"

28Then the commander stood and called out in Hebrew: "Hear the word of the great king, the king of Assyria! 29This is what the king says: Do not let Hezekiah deceive you. He cannot deliver you from my hand. 30Do not let Hezekiah persuade you to trust in the LORD when he says, 'The LORD will surely deliver us; this city will not be given into the hand of the king of Assyria.'

31"Do not listen to Hezekiah. This is what the king of Assyria says: Make peace with me and come out to me. Then every one of you will eat from his own vine and fig tree and drink water from his own cistern, 32until I come and take you to a land like your own, a land of grain and new wine, a land of bread and vineyards, a land of olive trees and honey. Choose life and not death!

"Do not listen to Hezekiah, for he is misleading you when he says, 'The LORD will deliver us.' 33Has the god of any nation ever delivered his land from the hand of the king of Assyria? 34Where are the gods of Hamath and Arpad? Where are the gods of Sepharvaim, Hena and Ivvah? Have they rescued Samaria from my hand? 35Who of all the gods of these countries has been able to save his land from me? How then can the LORD deliver Jerusalem from my hand?"

36But the people remained silent and said nothing in reply, because the king had commanded, "Do not answer him."

37Then Eliakim son of Hilkiah the palace administrator, Shebna the secretary and Joah son of Asaph the recorder went to Hezekiah, with their clothes torn, and told him what the field commander had said.

Jerusalem's Deliverance Foretold

19 When King Hezekiah heard this, he tore his clothes and put on sackcloth and went into the temple of the LORD. 2He sent Eliakim the palace administrator, Shebna the secretary and the leading priests, all wearing sackcloth, to the prophet Isaiah son of Amoz. 3They told him, "This is what Hezekiah says: This day is a day of distress and rebuke and disgrace, as when children come to the point of birth and there is no strength to deliver them. 4It may be that the LORD your God will hear all the words of the field commander, whom his master, the king of Assyria, has sent to ridicule the living God, and that he will rebuke him for the words the LORD your God has heard. Therefore pray for the remnant that still survives."

5When King Hezekiah's officials came to Isaiah, 6Isaiah said to them, "Tell your master, 'This is what the LORD says: Do not be afraid of what you have heard—those words with which the underlings of the king of Assyria have blasphemed me. 7Listen! I am going to put such a spirit in him that when he hears a certain report, he will return to his own country, and there I will have him cut down with the sword.'"

8When the field commander heard that the king of Assyria had left Lachish, he withdrew and found the king fighting against Libnah.

9Now Sennacherib received a report that Tirhakah, the Cushite[b] king ⌊of Egypt⌋ was marching out to fight against him. So he again sent messengers to Hezekiah with this

a24 Or charioteers   b9 That is, from the upper Nile region

word: ¹⁰"Say to Hezekiah king of Judah: Do not let the god you depend on deceive you when he says, 'Jerusalem will not be handed over to the king of Assyria.' ¹¹Surely you have heard what the kings of Assyria have done to all the countries, destroying them completely. And will you be delivered? ¹²Did the gods of the nations that were destroyed by my forefathers deliver them: the gods of Gozan, Haran, Rezeph and the people of Eden who were in Tel Assar? ¹³Where is the king of Hamath, the king of Arpad, the king of the city of Sepharvaim, or of Hena or Ivvah?"

Hezekiah's Prayer

¹⁴Hezekiah received the letter from the messengers and read it. Then he went up to the temple of the LORD and spread it out before the LORD. ¹⁵And Hezekiah prayed to the LORD: "O LORD, God of Israel, enthroned between the cherubim, you alone are God over all the kingdoms of the earth. You have made heaven and earth. ¹⁶Give ear, O LORD, and hear; open your eyes, O LORD, and see; listen to the words Sennacherib has sent to insult the living God.

¹⁷"It is true, O LORD, that the Assyrian kings have laid waste these nations and their lands. ¹⁸They have thrown their gods into the fire and destroyed them, for they were not gods but only wood and stone, fashioned by men's hands. ¹⁹Now, O LORD our God, deliver us from his hand, so that all kingdoms on earth may know that you alone, O LORD, are God."

Isaiah Prophesies Sennacherib's Fall

²⁰Then Isaiah son of Amoz sent a message to Hezekiah: "This is what the LORD, the God of Israel, says: I have heard your prayer concerning Sennacherib king of Assyria. ²¹This is the word that the LORD has spoken against him:

> " 'The Virgin Daughter of Zion
>   despises you and mocks you.
> The Daughter of Jerusalem
>   tosses her head as you flee.
> ²²Who is it you have insulted and blasphemed?
>   Against whom have you raised your voice
> and lifted your eyes in pride?
>   Against the Holy One of Israel!
> ²³By your messengers
>   you have heaped insults on the Lord.
> And you have said,
>   "With my many chariots
> I have ascended the heights of the mountains,
>   the utmost heights of Lebanon.
> I have cut down its tallest cedars,
>   the choicest of its pines.
> I have reached its remotest parts,
>   the finest of its forests.
> ²⁴I have dug wells in foreign lands
>   and drunk the water there.
> With the soles of my feet
>   I have dried up all the streams of Egypt."
>
> ²⁵" 'Have you not heard?
>   Long ago I ordained it.
> In days of old I planned it;
>   now I have brought it to pass,
> that you have turned fortified cities

into piles of stone.
^{26}Their people, drained of power,
  are dismayed and put to shame.
They are like plants in the field,
  like tender green shoots,
like grass sprouting on the roof,
  scorched before it grows up.

^{27}" 'But I know where you stay
  and when you come and go
  and how you rage against me.
^{28}Because you rage against me
  and your insolence has reached my ears,
I will put my hook in your nose
  and my bit in your mouth,
and I will make you return
  by the way you came.'

^{29}"This will be the sign for you, O Hezekiah:

"This year you will eat what grows by itself,
  and the second year what springs from that.
But in the third year sow and reap,
  plant vineyards and eat their fruit.
^{30}Once more a remnant of the house of Judah
  will take root below and bear fruit above.
^{31}For out of Jerusalem will come a remnant,
  and out of Mount Zion a band of survivors.

The zeal of the LORD Almighty will accomplish this.

^{32}"Therefore this is what the LORD says concerning the king of Assyria:

"He will not enter this city
  or shoot an arrow here.
He will not come before it with shield
  or build a siege ramp against it.
^{33}By the way that he came he will return;
  he will not enter this city,

                                    declares the LORD.
^{34}I will defend this city and save it,
  for my sake and for the sake of David my servant."

^{35}That night the angel of the LORD went out and put to death a hundred and eighty-five thousand men in the Assyrian camp. When the people got up the next morning—there were all the dead bodies! ^{36}So Sennacherib king of Assyria broke camp and withdrew. He returned to Nineveh and stayed there.

^{37}One day, while he was worshiping in the temple of his god Nisroch, his sons Adrammelech and Sharezer cut him down with the sword, and they escaped to the land of Ararat. And Esarhaddon his son succeeded him as king.

Hezekiah's Illness

20 In those days Hezekiah became ill and was at the point of death. The prophet Isaiah son of Amoz went to him and said, "This is what the LORD says: Put your house in order, because you are going to die; you will not recover."

^{2}Hezekiah turned his face to the wall and prayed to the LORD, ^{3}"Remember, O LORD, how

I have walked before you faithfully and with wholehearted devotion and have done what is good in your eyes." And Hezekiah wept bitterly.

⁴Before Isaiah had left the middle court, the word of the LORD came to him: ⁵"Go back and tell Hezekiah, the leader of my people, 'This is what the LORD, the God of your father David, says: I have heard your prayer and seen your tears; I will heal you. On the third day from now you will go up to the temple of the LORD. ⁶I will add fifteen years to your life. And I will deliver you and this city from the hand of the king of Assyria. I will defend this city for my sake and for the sake of my servant David.'"

⁷Then Isaiah said, "Prepare a poultice of figs." They did so and applied it to the boil, and he recovered.

⁸Hezekiah had asked Isaiah, "What will be the sign that the LORD will heal me and that I will go up to the temple of the LORD on the third day from now?"

⁹Isaiah answered, "This is the LORD's sign to you that the LORD will do what he has promised: Shall the shadow go forward ten steps, or shall it go back ten steps?"

¹⁰"It is a simple matter for the shadow to go forward ten steps," said Hezekiah. "Rather, have it go back ten steps."

¹¹Then the prophet Isaiah called upon the LORD, and the LORD made the shadow go back the ten steps it had gone down on the stairway of Ahaz.

Envoys From Babylon

¹²At that time Merodach-Baladan son of Baladan king of Babylon sent Hezekiah letters and a gift, because he had heard of Hezekiah's illness. ¹³Hezekiah received the messengers and showed them all that was in his storehouses—the silver, the gold, the spices and the fine oil—his armory and everything found among his treasures. There was nothing in his palace or in all his kingdom that Hezekiah did not show them.

¹⁴Then Isaiah the prophet went to King Hezekiah and asked, "What did those men say, and where did they come from?"

"From a distant land," Hezekiah replied. "They came from Babylon."

¹⁵The prophet asked, "What did they see in your palace?"

"They saw everything in my palace," Hezekiah said. "There is nothing among my treasures that I did not show them."

¹⁶Then Isaiah said to Hezekiah, "Hear the word of the LORD: ¹⁷The time will surely come when everything in your palace, and all that your fathers have stored up until this day, will be carried off to Babylon. Nothing will be left, says the LORD. ¹⁸And some of your descendants, your own flesh and blood, that will be born to you, will be taken away, and they will become eunuchs in the palace of the king of Babylon."

¹⁹"The word of the LORD you have spoken is good," Hezekiah replied. For he thought, "Will there not be peace and security in my lifetime?"

²⁰As for the other events of Hezekiah's reign, all his achievements and how he made the pool and the tunnel by which he brought water into the city, are they not written in the book of the annals of the kings of Judah? ²¹Hezekiah rested with his fathers. And Manasseh his son succeeded him as king.

Manasseh King of Judah

21 Manasseh was twelve years old when he became king, and he reigned in Jerusalem fifty-five years. His mother's name was Hephzibah. ²He did evil in the eyes of the LORD, following the detestable practices of the nations the LORD had driven out before the Israelites. ³He rebuilt the high places his father Hezekiah had destroyed; he also erected altars to Baal and made an Asherah pole, as Ahab king of Israel had done. He bowed down to all the starry hosts and worshiped them. ⁴He built altars in the temple of the LORD, of which the LORD had said, "In Jerusalem I will put my Name." ⁵In both courts of the temple of the LORD, he built altars to all the starry hosts. ⁶He sacrificed his own son in[a] the fire, practiced sorcery and divination, and consulted mediums and spiritists. He did much evil in the eyes of the LORD, provoking him to anger.

[7]He took the carved Asherah pole he had made and put it in the temple, of which the LORD had said to David and to his son Solomon, "In this temple and in Jerusalem, which I have chosen out of all the tribes of Israel, I will put my Name forever. [8]I will not again make the feet of the Israelites wander from the land I gave their forefathers, if only they will be careful to do everything I commanded them and will keep the whole Law that my servant Moses gave them." [9]But the people did not listen. Manasseh led them astray, so that they did more evil than the nations the LORD had destroyed before the Israelites.

[10]The LORD said through his servants the prophets: [11]"Manasseh king of Judah has committed these detestable sins. He has done more evil than the Amorites who preceded him and has led Judah into sin with his idols. [12]Therefore this is what the LORD, the God of Israel, says: I am going to bring such disaster on Jerusalem and Judah that the ears of everyone who hears of it will tingle. [13]I will stretch out over Jerusalem the measuring line used against Samaria and the plumb line used against the house of Ahab. I will wipe out Jerusalem as one wipes a dish, wiping it and turning it upside down. [14]I will forsake the remnant of my inheritance and hand them over to their enemies. They will be looted and plundered by all their foes, [15]because they have done evil in my eyes and have provoked me to anger from the day their forefathers came out of Egypt until this day."

[16]Moreover, Manasseh also shed so much innocent blood that he filled Jerusalem from end to end—besides the sin that he had caused Judah to commit, so that they did evil in the eyes of the LORD.

[17]As for the other events of Manasseh's reign, and all he did, including the sin he committed, are they not written in the book of the annals of the kings of Judah? [18]Manasseh rested with his fathers and was buried in his palace garden, the garden of Uzza. And Amon his son succeeded him as king.

▩ ▦▦▦▦▦▦▦ DISCOVERING GOD ▦▦▦▦▦▦▦ ▣

21:5–6
Spiritual Fraud

King Manasseh indulged in just about every evil practice you can imagine. This was no pagan king—he was part of God's chosen nation. He knew better. And he led others into his wickedness.

Spiritual fraud can come from anywhere—even the very people who call themselves God's followers. It can show up in a church; it can come from the leadership of a religious group; it can come from the smiling individual at your doorstep.

Don't be naive about the reality of people's inclination to pervert authentic spirituality. Whether you're a seeker or a believer, determine you won't let this kind of religious compromise pull you into its unholy mire.

Amon King of Judah

[19]Amon was twenty-two years old when he became king, and he reigned in Jerusalem two years. His mother's name was Meshullemeth daughter of Haruz; she was from Jotbah. [20]He did evil in the eyes of the LORD, as his father Manasseh had done. [21]He walked in all the ways of his father; he worshiped the idols his father had worshiped, and bowed down to them. [22]He forsook the LORD, the God of his fathers, and did not walk in the way of the LORD.

[23]Amon's officials conspired against him and assassinated the king in his palace. [24]Then the people of the land killed all who had plotted against King Amon, and they made Josiah his son king in his place.

[25]As for the other events of Amon's reign, and what he did, are they not written in the book of the annals of the kings of Judah? [26]He was buried in his grave in the garden of Uzza. And Josiah his son succeeded him as king.

[a] 6 Or He made his own son pass through

The Book of the Law Found

22 Josiah was eight years old when he became king, and he reigned in Jerusalem thirty-one years. His mother's name was Jedidah daughter of Adaiah; she was from Bozkath. ²He did what was right in the eyes of the LORD and walked in all the ways of his father David, not turning aside to the right or to the left.

³In the eighteenth year of his reign, King Josiah sent the secretary, Shaphan son of Azaliah, the son of Meshullam, to the temple of the LORD. He said: ⁴"Go up to Hilkiah the high priest and have him get ready the money that has been brought into the temple of the LORD, which the doorkeepers have collected from the people. ⁵Have them entrust it to the men appointed to supervise the work on the temple. And have these men pay the workers who repair the temple of the LORD— ⁶the carpenters, the builders and the masons. Also have them purchase timber and dressed stone to repair the temple. ⁷But they need not account for the money entrusted to them, because they are acting faithfully."

⁸Hilkiah the high priest said to Shaphan the secretary, "I have found the Book of the Law in the temple of the LORD." He gave it to Shaphan, who read it. ⁹Then Shaphan the secretary went to the king and reported to him: "Your officials have paid out the money that was in the temple of the LORD and have entrusted it to the workers and supervisors at the temple." ¹⁰Then Shaphan the secretary informed the king, "Hilkiah the priest has given me a book." And Shaphan read from it in the presence of the king.

¹¹When the king heard the words of the Book of the Law, he tore his robes. ¹²He gave these orders to Hilkiah the priest, Ahikam son of Shaphan, Acbor son of Micaiah, Shaphan the secretary and Asaiah the king's attendant: ¹³"Go and inquire of the LORD for me and for the people and for all Judah about what is written in this book that has been found. Great is the LORD's anger that burns against us because our fathers have not obeyed the words of this book; they have not acted in accordance with all that is written there concerning us."

¹⁴Hilkiah the priest, Ahikam, Acbor, Shaphan and Asaiah went to speak to the prophetess Huldah, who was the wife of Shallum son of Tikvah, the son of Harhas, keeper of the wardrobe. She lived in Jerusalem, in the Second District.

¹⁵She said to them, "This is what the LORD, the God of Israel, says: Tell the man who sent you to me, ¹⁶'This is what the LORD says: I am going to bring disaster on this place and its people, according to everything written in the book the king of Judah has read. ¹⁷Because they have forsaken me and burned incense to other gods and provoked me to anger by all the idols their hands have made,ᵃ my anger will burn against this place and will not be quenched.' ¹⁸Tell the king of Judah, who sent you to inquire of the LORD, 'This is what the LORD, the God of Israel, says concerning the words you heard: ¹⁹Because your heart was responsive and you humbled yourself before the LORD when you heard what I have spoken against this place and its people, that they would become accursed and laid waste, and because you tore your robes and wept in my presence, I have heard you, declares the LORD. ²⁰Therefore I will gather you to your fathers, and you will be buried in peace. Your eyes will not see all the disaster I am going to bring on this place.'"

So they took her answer back to the king.

Josiah Renews the Covenant

23 Then the king called together all the elders of Judah and Jerusalem. ²He went up to the temple of the LORD with the men of Judah, the people of Jerusalem, the priests and the prophets—all the people from the least to the greatest. He read in their hearing all the words of the Book of the Covenant, which had been found in the temple of the LORD. ³The king stood by the pillar and renewed the covenant in the presence of the LORD—to follow the LORD and keep his commands, regulations and decrees

ᵃ *17 Or by everything they have done*

with all his heart and all his soul, thus confirming the words of the covenant written in this book. Then all the people pledged themselves to the covenant.

⁴The king ordered Hilkiah the high priest, the priests next in rank and the doorkeepers to remove from the temple of the LORD all the articles made for Baal and Asherah and all the starry hosts. He burned them outside Jerusalem in the fields of the Kidron Valley and took the ashes to Bethel. ⁵He did away with the pagan priests appointed by the kings of Judah to burn incense on the high places of the towns of Judah and on those around Jerusalem—those who burned incense to Baal, to the sun and moon, to the constellations and to all the starry hosts. ⁶He took the Asherah pole from the temple of the LORD to the Kidron Valley outside Jerusalem and burned it there. He ground it to powder and scattered the dust over the graves of the common people. ⁷He also tore down the quarters of the male shrine prostitutes, which were in the temple of the LORD and where women did weaving for Asherah.

⁸Josiah brought all the priests from the towns of Judah and desecrated the high places, from Geba to Beersheba, where the priests had burned incense. He broke down the shrines*a* at the gates—at the entrance to the Gate of Joshua, the city governor, which is on the left of the city gate. ⁹Although the priests of the high places did not serve at the altar of the LORD in Jerusalem, they ate unleavened bread with their fellow priests.

¹⁰He desecrated Topheth, which was in the Valley of Ben Hinnom, so no one could use it to sacrifice his son or daughter in*b* the fire to Molech. ¹¹He removed from the entrance to the temple of the LORD the horses that the kings of Judah had dedicated to the sun. They were in the court near the room of an official named Nathan-Melech. Josiah then burned the chariots dedicated to the sun.

¹²He pulled down the altars the kings of Judah had erected on the roof near the upper room of Ahaz, and the altars Manasseh had built in the two courts of the temple of the LORD. He removed them from there, smashed them to pieces and threw the rubble into the Kidron Valley. ¹³The king also desecrated the high places that were east of Jerusalem on the south of the Hill of Corruption—the ones Solomon king of Israel had built for Ashtoreth the vile goddess of the Sidonians, for Chemosh the vile god of Moab, and for Molech*c* the detestable god of the people of Ammon. ¹⁴Josiah smashed the sacred stones and cut down the Asherah poles and covered the sites with human bones.

¹⁵Even the altar at Bethel, the high place made by Jeroboam son of Nebat, who had caused Israel to sin—even that altar and high place he demolished. He burned the high place and ground it to powder, and burned the Asherah pole also. ¹⁶Then Josiah looked around, and when he saw the tombs that were there on the hillside, he had the bones removed from them and burned on the altar to defile it, in accordance with the word of the LORD proclaimed by the man of God who foretold these things.

¹⁷The king asked, "What is that tombstone I see?"

The men of the city said, "It marks the tomb of the man of God who came from Judah and pronounced against the altar of Bethel the very things you have done to it."

¹⁸"Leave it alone," he said. "Don't let anyone disturb his bones." So they spared his bones and those of the prophet who had come from Samaria.

¹⁹Just as he had done at Bethel, Josiah removed and defiled all the shrines at the high places that the kings of Israel had built in the towns of Samaria that had provoked the LORD to anger. ²⁰Josiah slaughtered all the priests of those high places on the altars and burned human bones on them. Then he went back to Jerusalem.

²¹The king gave this order to all the people: "Celebrate the Passover to the LORD your God, as it is written in this Book of the Covenant." ²²Not since the days of the judges who led Israel, nor throughout the days of the kings of Israel and the kings of Judah, had any such Passover been observed. ²³But in the eighteenth year of King Josiah, this Passover was celebrated to the LORD in Jerusalem.

²⁴Furthermore, Josiah got rid of the mediums and spiritists, the household gods, the

---

a 8 Or *high places*   *b 10* Or *to make his son or daughter pass through*   *c 13* Hebrew *Milcom*

idols and all the other detestable things seen in Judah and Jerusalem. This he did to fulfill the requirements of the law written in the book that Hilkiah the priest had discovered in the temple of the LORD. 25Neither before nor after Josiah was there a king like him who turned to the LORD as he did—with all his heart and with all his soul and with all his strength, in accordance with all the Law of Moses.

26Nevertheless, the LORD did not turn away from the heat of his fierce anger, which burned against Judah because of all that Manasseh had done to provoke him to anger. 27So the LORD said, "I will remove Judah also from my presence as I removed Israel, and I will reject Jerusalem, the city I chose, and this temple, about which I said, 'There shall my Name be.'ᵃ"

28As for the other events of Josiah's reign, and all he did, are they not written in the book of the annals of the kings of Judah?

29While Josiah was king, Pharaoh Neco king of Egypt went up to the Euphrates River to help the king of Assyria. King Josiah marched out to meet him in battle, but Neco faced him and killed him at Megiddo. 30Josiah's servants brought his body in a chariot from Megiddo to Jerusalem and buried him in his own tomb. And the people of the land took Jehoahaz son of Josiah and anointed him and made him king in place of his father.

Jehoahaz King of Judah

31Jehoahaz was twenty-three years old when he became king, and he reigned in Jerusalem three months. His mother's name was Hamutal daughter of Jeremiah; she was from Libnah. 32He did evil in the eyes of the LORD, just as his fathers had done. 33Pharaoh Neco put him in chains at Riblah in the land of Hamathᵇ so that he might not reign in Jerusalem, and he imposed on Judah a levy of a hundred talentsᶜ of silver and a talentᵈ of gold. 34Pharaoh Neco made Eliakim son of Josiah king in place of his father Josiah and changed Eliakim's name to Jehoiakim. But he took Jehoahaz and carried him off to Egypt, and there he died. 35Jehoiakim paid Pharaoh Neco the silver and gold he demanded. In order to do so, he taxed the land and exacted the silver and gold from the people of the land according to their assessments.

Jehoiakim King of Judah

36Jehoiakim was twenty-five years old when he became king, and he reigned in Jerusalem eleven years. His mother's name was Zebidah daughter of Pedaiah; she was from Rumah. 37And he did evil in the eyes of the LORD, just as his fathers had done.

24 During Jehoiakim's reign, Nebuchadnezzar king of Babylon invaded the land, and Jehoiakim became his vassal for three years. But then he changed his mind and rebelled against Nebuchadnezzar. 2The LORD sent Babylonian,ᵉ Aramean, Moabite and Ammonite raiders against him. He sent them to destroy Judah, in accordance with the word of the LORD proclaimed by his servants the prophets. 3Surely these things happened to Judah according to the LORD's command, in order to remove them from his presence because of the sins of Manasseh and all he had done, 4including the shedding of innocent blood. For he had filled Jerusalem with innocent blood, and the LORD was not willing to forgive.

5As for the other events of Jehoiakim's reign, and all he did, are they not written in the book of the annals of the kings of Judah? 6Jehoiakim rested with his fathers. And Jehoiachin his son succeeded him as king.

7The king of Egypt did not march out from his own country again, because the king of Babylon had taken all his territory, from the Wadi of Egypt to the Euphrates River.

ᵃ27 1 Kings 8:29   ᵇ33 Hebrew; Septuagint (see also 2 Chron. 36:3) *Neco at Riblah in Hamath removed him*   ᶜ33 That is, about 3 3/4 tons (about 3.4 metric tons)   ᵈ33 That is, about 75 pounds (about 34 kilograms)   ᵉ2 Or *Chaldean*

Jehoiachin King of Judah

8Jehoiachin was eighteen years old when he became king, and he reigned in Jerusalem three months. His mother's name was Nehushta daughter of Elnathan; she was from Jerusalem. **9**He did evil in the eyes of the LORD, just as his father had done.

10At that time the officers of Nebuchadnezzar king of Babylon advanced on Jerusalem and laid siege to it, **11**and Nebuchadnezzar himself came up to the city while his officers were besieging it. **12**Jehoiachin king of Judah, his mother, his attendants, his nobles and his officials all surrendered to him.

In the eighth year of the reign of the king of Babylon, he took Jehoiachin prisoner. **13**As the LORD had declared, Nebuchadnezzar removed all the treasures from the temple of the LORD and from the royal palace, and took away all the gold articles that Solomon king of Israel had made for the temple of the LORD. **14**He carried into exile all Jerusalem: all the officers and fighting men, and all the craftsmen and artisans—a total of ten thousand. Only the poorest people of the land were left.

15Nebuchadnezzar took Jehoiachin captive to Babylon. He also took from Jerusalem to Babylon the king's mother, his wives, his officials and the leading men of the land. **16**The king of Babylon also deported to Babylon the entire force of seven thousand fighting men, strong and fit for war, and a thousand craftsmen and artisans. **17**He made Mattaniah, Jehoiachin's uncle, king in his place and changed his name to Zedekiah.

Zedekiah King of Judah

18Zedekiah was twenty-one years old when he became king, and he reigned in Jerusalem eleven years. His mother's name was Hamutal daughter of Jeremiah; she was from Libnah. **19**He did evil in the eyes of the LORD, just as Jehoiakim had done. **20**It was because of the LORD's anger that all this happened to Jerusalem and Judah, and in the end he thrust them from his presence.

The Fall of Jerusalem

Now Zedekiah rebelled against the king of Babylon.

25 So in the ninth year of Zedekiah's reign, on the tenth day of the tenth month, Nebuchadnezzar king of Babylon marched against Jerusalem with his whole army. He encamped outside the city and built siege works all around it. **2**The city was kept under siege until the eleventh year of King Zedekiah. **3**By the ninth day of the fourth,ᵃ month the famine in the city had become so severe that there was no food for the people to eat. **4**Then the city wall was broken through, and the whole army fled at night through the gate between the two walls near the king's garden, though the Babyloniansᵇ were surrounding the city. They fled toward the Arabah,ᶜ **5**but the Babylonianᵈ army pursued the king and overtook him in the plains of Jericho. All his soldiers were separated from him and scattered, **6**and he was captured. He was taken to the king of Babylon at Riblah, where sentence was pronounced on him. **7**They killed the sons of Zedekiah before his eyes. Then they put out his eyes, bound him with bronze shackles and took him to Babylon.

8On the seventh day of the fifth month, in the nineteenth year of Nebuchadnezzar king of Babylon, Nebuzaradan commander of the imperial guard, an official of the king of Babylon, came to Jerusalem. **9**He set fire to the temple of the LORD, the royal palace and all the houses of Jerusalem. Every important building he burned down. **10**The whole Babylonian army, under the commander of the imperial guard, broke down the walls around Jerusalem. **11**Nebuzaradan the commander of the guard carried into exile the people who remained in the city, along with the rest of the populace and those who had gone over to the king of Babylon. **12**But the commander left behind some of the poorest people of the land to work the vineyards and fields.

ᵃ3 See Jer. 52:6.   ᵇ4 Or *Chaldeans*; also in verses 13, 25 and 26   ᶜ4 Or *the Jordan Valley*   ᵈ5 Or *Chaldean*; also in verses 10 and 24

¹³The Babylonians broke up the bronze pillars, the movable stands and the bronze Sea that were at the temple of the LORD and they carried the bronze to Babylon. ¹⁴They also took away the pots, shovels, wick trimmers, dishes and all the bronze articles used in temple service. ¹⁵The commander of the imperial guard took away the censers and sprinkling bowls—all that were made of pure gold or silver.

¹⁶The bronze from the two pillars, the Sea and the movable stands, which Solomon had made for the temple of the LORD, was more than could be weighed. ¹⁷Each pillar was twenty-seven feet*a* high. The bronze capital on top of one pillar was four and a half feet*b* high and was decorated with a network and pomegranates of bronze all around. The other pillar, with its network, was similar.

¹⁸The commander of the guard took as prisoners Seraiah the chief priest, Zephaniah the priest next in rank and the three doorkeepers. ¹⁹Of those still in the city, he took the officer in charge of the fighting men and five royal advisers. He also took the secretary who was chief officer in charge of conscripting the people of the land and sixty of his men who were found in the city. ²⁰Nebuzaradan the commander took them all and brought them to the king of Babylon at Riblah. ²¹There at Riblah, in the land of Hamath, the king had them executed.

So Judah went into captivity, away from her land.

²²Nebuchadnezzar king of Babylon appointed Gedaliah son of Ahikam, the son of Shaphan, to be over the people he had left behind in Judah. ²³When all the army officers and their men heard that the king of Babylon had appointed Gedaliah as governor, they came to Gedaliah at Mizpah—Ishmael son of Nethaniah, Johanan son of Kareah, Seraiah son of Tanhumeth the Netophathite, Jaazaniah the son of the Maacathite, and their men. ²⁴Gedaliah took an oath to reassure them and their men. "Do not be afraid of the Babylonian officials," he said. "Settle down in the land and serve the king of Babylon, and it will go well with you."

²⁵In the seventh month, however, Ishmael son of Nethaniah, the son of Elishama, who was of royal blood, came with ten men and assassinated Gedaliah and also the men of Judah and the Babylonians who were with him at Mizpah. ²⁶At this, all the people from the least to the greatest, together with the army officers, fled to Egypt for fear of the Babylonians.

Jehoiachin Released

²⁷In the thirty-seventh year of the exile of Jehoiachin king of Judah, in the year Evil-Merodach*c* became king of Babylon, he released Jehoiachin from prison on the twenty-seventh day of the twelfth month. ²⁸He spoke kindly to him and gave him a seat of honor higher than those of the other kings who were with him in Babylon. ²⁹So Jehoiachin put aside his prison clothes and for the rest of his life ate regularly at the king's table. ³⁰Day by day the king gave Jehoiachin a regular allowance as long as he lived.

---

a 17 Hebrew *eighteen cubits* (about 8.1 meters)   *b 17* Hebrew *three cubits* (about 1.3 meters)   *c 27* Also called
Amel-Marduk

Before accepting Christ as my Savior, I believed that God was very distant from me. My interpretation of having a relationship with God was very legalistic. I believed that a person entered heaven by doing good works and by observing rules. Although I believed in God and followed the rules, I always had doubts and felt I should be doing more. Sometimes the rules would change, which made me begin to question what it really meant to be a Christian. I became increasingly skeptical about religion and participated solely out of moral obligation.

I still wanted to believe in God, but trying so hard to be faithful left me feeling frustrated. Then a friend from college invited me to a continuing Bible study, which I attended on a regular basis. During one meeting one of the group members talked about being "saved." My initial reaction was that this person must be very arrogant to be so sure of his salvation, but his assurance made me begin to doubt what I had believed since childhood. Later, a Christian friend from work invited me to a small group Bible study that met in his home. It was as a member of that group that I made the decision to accept Christ and trust in God's guidance for my life.

That decision has made a huge difference in my life. I know now that being a Christian is not just about obeying rules and attending church; it's about having a real relationship with God. Knowing I have received the gift of salvation has given me an overwhelming sense of thankfulness, freedom, and relief. I am now more content with my life and more caring toward other people. I appreciate the power of prayer, and look forward to attending church. In addition, I have put God in charge of my finances, something I never would have done before accepting Christ.

I am 62 years old and have spent most of my adult life wandering in God's neighborhood wondering if he really exists and, if so, where might I find him. I have attended various churches (primarily on religious holidays) hoping that somewhere, somehow, someone could help me find what my wife and so many others have already found.

Four years ago my son invited my wife and I to his church. I have attended on a regular basis ever since. I am through wandering. I have found my salvation in Christ. I feel and see his love reflected in my wife, children, grandchildren, and others around me. Now I have a happiness inside me that I did not realize could ever exist.

1 CHRONICLES/2 CHRONICLES

Introduction

THE BOTTOM LINE

Modern technology provides us with on-line services, fax machines, and telecommunications systems that connect us with individuals all over the globe. Yet it's easy to feel lost in the crowd. Who hasn't asked at one time or another, "With all this electronic noise in the world, where does *my* voice fit in?" Although the ancient Israelites didn't have modern technology, they knew what it was like to feel insignificant. After decades spent in foreign captivity, their small voice had been drowned out by the major superpowers of that time. The books of 1 and 2 Chronicles served to reconnect these people with their past. The detailed genealogies, rules and regulations may seem like so many fussy details to our eyes; yet they centered the people's thoughts on God's personal involvement in making them a nation. In today's fast-paced world, God wants to give you that same personal assurance and "grounding."

CENTRAL IDEAS

- This summary of Jewish history was intended to unify a disjointed and disorganized people.
- The genealogical record connected the Israelites to their past "glory days" and instilled hope for the future.
- The author intended to set a good example by focusing on the kings who did what was right in God's eyes.
- These books show a strong correlation between doing God's will and receiving God's blessing.

TITLE

The title of these books refers to the purpose of the books — to chronicle the history of God's work in the lives of the Israelites.

AUTHOR AND READERS

Jewish tradition credits Ezra as the author of these books. They were written for the Jews who had returned to their homeland from exile.

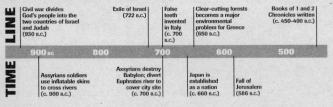

TIME LINE

Civil war divides God's people into the two countries of Israel and Judah (930 B.C.)	Exile of Israel (722 B.C.)	False teeth invented in Italy (c. 700 B.C.)	Clear-cutting forests becomes a major environmental problem for Greece (650 B.C.)	Books of 1 and 2 Chronicles written (c. 450-400 B.C.)
900 BC	**800**	**700**	**600**	**500**
Assyrians soldiers use inflatable skins to cross rivers (c. 900 B.C.)	Assyrians destroy Babylon; divert Euphrates river to cover city site (c. 700 B.C.)	Japan is established as a nation (c. 660 B.C.)	Fall of Jerusalem (586 B.C.)	

A story is told about a man who sat at a diner one night lamenting the horrible condition of his life. "My wife left me yesterday, and today I lost my job," he moaned.

Sitting beside him at the counter was a handsome, dark-haired man wearing glasses. "I'll tell you what I do when I'm depressed," he said. "On the roof of the building next door is a spot were a person can dive into open space, fall toward the street below, and float back to the roof again."

"That's ridiculous," the depressed man said.

"It sounds impossible, but it works," said the stranger. "When I'm depressed I jump off that roof, and it lifts my spirit. If you don't believe me, let's go up there, and I'll show you."

In a short time the two men were standing on the roof of a 50-story building. The handsome young man walked over to the edge and dove off. Just before he hit the street he spread his legs and arms and floated back to the roof.

Realizing his companion was skeptical, he repeated the jump. As before, he stopped just before hitting the pavement and floated effortlessly back to the roof.

In a short time the two men were standing on the roof of a 50-story building.

Convinced he could do the same thing, the despondent man leaped from the roof and spread his arms and legs. But unlike the other man, he didn't float back to the roof.

The good-looking man returned to the diner and sat down—alone. The waitress, who knew him well, shook her head in disgust. "You know, Superman, you can be a real jerk when you put your mind to it!"

This entertaining story illustrates the ease with which power can be abused. Because most of us have power over someone, we need to be careful how we exercise that power. The books of 1 and 2 Chronicles tell about the kings of Israel and Judah from God's perspective (1 and 2 Samuel and 1 and 2 Kings tell the same stories from a human perspective). Sometimes these powerful kings exercised their authority in honorable ways. On other occasions they acted contemptibly.

Few biblical characters provide us with a better example of how to correct a personal misuse of power than David. Turn to 1 Chronicles chapter 11, verses 10–19 (page 494), to see how David stumbled and then regained his footing. Then think about how you can apply the lessons of his experience to relationships in your own life.

1 CHRONICLES

Historical Records From Adam to Abraham

To Noah's Sons

1 Adam, Seth, Enosh, ²Kenan, Mahalalel, Jared, ³Enoch, Methuselah, Lamech, Noah.

⁴The sons of Noah:ᵃ
Shem, Ham and Japheth.

The Japhethites

⁵The sonsᵇ of Japheth:
Gomer, Magog, Madai, Javan, Tubal, Meshech and Tiras.

⁶The sons of Gomer:
Ashkenaz, Riphathᶜ and Togarmah.

⁷The sons of Javan:
Elishah, Tarshish, the Kittim and the Rodanim.

The Hamites

⁸The sons of Ham:
Cush, Mizraim,ᵈ Put and Canaan.

⁹The sons of Cush:
Seba, Havilah, Sabta, Raamah and Sabteca.

The sons of Raamah:
Sheba and Dedan.

¹⁰Cush was the fatherᵉ of
Nimrod, who grew to be a mighty warrior on earth.

ADDRESSING QUESTIONS

**Chapters 1—9
Human Experience** **Q**

These first nine chapters contain genealogies and reference material that was very important to the people of ancient Israel. By making such a detailed list, the Israelites traced their history all the way back to the first man, Adam. This helped them to remember that God had created them and that he had his hand on their past, present, and future.

Don't feel guilty if you're inclined to skip over this material. Go on ahead to chapter 10 where the stories begin!

---

¹¹Mizraim was the father of
the Ludites, Anamites, Lehabites, Naphtuhites, ¹²Pathrusites, Casluhites (from whom the Philistines came) and Caphtorites.

¹³Canaan was the father of
Sidon his firstborn,ᶠ and of the Hittites, ¹⁴Jebusites, Amorites, Girgashites, ¹⁵Hivites, Arkites, Sinites, ¹⁶Arvadites, Zemarites and Hamathites.

The Semites

¹⁷The sons of Shem:
Elam, Asshur, Arphaxad, Lud and Aram.
The sons of Aramᵍ:
Uz, Hul, Gether and Meshech.

ᵃ4 Septuagint; Hebrew does not have *The sons of Noah:*   ᵇ5 *Sons* may mean *descendants* or *successors* or *nations*; also in verses 6-10, 17 and 20.   ᶜ6 Many Hebrew manuscripts and Vulgate (see also Septuagint and Gen. 10:3); most Hebrew manuscripts *Diphath*   ᵈ8 That is, Egypt; also in verse 11   ᵉ10 *Father* may mean *ancestor* or *predecessor* or *founder*; also in verses 11, 13, 18 and 20.   ᶠ13 Or *of the Sidonians, the foremost*   ᵍ17 One Hebrew manuscript and some Septuagint manuscripts (see also Gen. 10:23); most Hebrew manuscripts do not have this line.

¹⁸Arphaxad was the father of Shelah,
   and Shelah the father of Eber.
¹⁹Two sons were born to Eber:
   One was named Peleg,^a because in his time the earth was divided; his brother
   was named Joktan.
²⁰Joktan was the father of
   Almodad, Sheleph, Hazarmaveth, Jerah, ²¹Hadoram, Uzal, Diklah, ²²Obal,^b Abimael, Sheba, ²³Ophir, Havilah and Jobab. All these were sons of Joktan.

   ²⁴Shem, Arphaxad,^c Shelah,
   ²⁵Eber, Peleg, Reu,
   ²⁶Serug, Nahor, Terah
   ²⁷and Abram (that is, Abraham).

The Family of Abraham

²⁸The sons of Abraham:
   Isaac and Ishmael.

Descendants of Hagar

²⁹These were their descendants:
   Nebaioth the firstborn of Ishmael, Kedar, Adbeel, Mibsam, ³⁰Mishma, Dumah,
   Massa, Hadad, Tema, ³¹Jetur, Naphish and Kedemah. These were the sons of
   Ishmael.

Descendants of Keturah

³²The sons born to Keturah, Abraham's concubine:
   Zimran, Jokshan, Medan, Midian, Ishbak and Shuah.
   The sons of Jokshan:
   Sheba and Dedan.
³³The sons of Midian:
   Ephah, Epher, Hanoch, Abida and Eldaah.
   All these were descendants of Keturah.

Descendants of Sarah

³⁴Abraham was the father of Isaac.
   The sons of Isaac:
   Esau and Israel.

Esau's Sons

³⁵The sons of Esau:
   Eliphaz, Reuel, Jeush, Jalam and Korah.
³⁶The sons of Eliphaz:
   Teman, Omar, Zepho,^d Gatam and Kenaz;
   by Timna: Amalek.^e
³⁷The sons of Reuel:
   Nahath, Zerah, Shammah and Mizzah.

The People of Seir in Edom

³⁸The sons of Seir:
   Lotan, Shobal, Zibeon, Anah, Dishon, Ezer and Dishan.

---

^a19 *Peleg* means division.   ^b22 Some Hebrew manuscripts and Syriac (see also Gen. 10:28); most Hebrew manuscripts *Ebal*
^c24 Hebrew; some Septuagint manuscripts *Arphaxad, Cainan* (see also note at Gen. 11:10)   ^d36 Many Hebrew manuscripts,
some Septuagint manuscripts and Syriac (see also Gen. 36:11); most Hebrew manuscripts *Zephi*   ^e36 Some Septuagint
manuscripts (see also Gen. 36:12); Hebrew *Gatam, Kenaz, Timna and Amalek*

³⁹The sons of Lotan:
Hori and Homam. Timna was Lotan's sister.
⁴⁰The sons of Shobal:
Alvan,ᵃ Manahath, Ebal, Shepho and Onam.
The sons of Zibeon:
Aiah and Anah.
⁴¹The son of Anah:
Dishon.
The sons of Dishon:
Hemdan,ᵇ Eshban, Ithran and Keran.
⁴²The sons of Ezer:
Bilhan, Zaavan and Akan.ᶜ
The sons of Dishanᵈ:
Uz and Aran.

The Rulers of Edom

⁴³These were the kings who reigned in Edom before any Israelite king reignedᵉ:
Bela son of Beor, whose city was named Dinhabah.
⁴⁴When Bela died, Jobab son of Zerah from Bozrah succeeded him as king.
⁴⁵When Jobab died, Husham from the land of the Temanites succeeded him as king.
⁴⁶When Husham died, Hadad son of Bedad, who defeated Midian in the country of
Moab, succeeded him as king. His city was named Avith.
⁴⁷When Hadad died, Samlah from Masrekah succeeded him as king.
⁴⁸When Samlah died, Shaul from Rehoboth on the riverᶠ succeeded him as king.
⁴⁹When Shaul died, Baal-Hanan son of Acbor succeeded him as king.
⁵⁰When Baal-Hanan died, Hadad succeeded him as king. His city was named Pau,ᵍ
and his wife's name was Mehetabel daughter of Matred, the daughter of Me-Zahab. **⁵¹**Hadad also died.

The chiefs of Edom were:
Timna, Alvah, Jetheth, **⁵²**Oholibamah, Elah, Pinon, **⁵³**Kenaz, Teman, Mibzar,
⁵⁴Magdiel and Iram. These were the chiefs of Edom.

Israel's Sons

2 These were the sons of Israel:
Reuben, Simeon, Levi, Judah, Issachar, Zebulun, **²**Dan, Joseph, Benjamin,
Naphtali, Gad and Asher.

Judah

To Hezron's Sons

³The sons of Judah:
Er, Onan and Shelah. These three were born to him by a Canaanite woman, the
daughter of Shua. Er, Judah's firstborn, was wicked in the LORD's sight; so the LORD
put him to death. **⁴**Tamar, Judah's daughter-in-law, bore him Perez and Zerah.
Judah had five sons in all.

⁵The sons of Perez:
Hezron and Hamul.
⁶The sons of Zerah:

ᵃ40 Many Hebrew manuscripts and some Septuagint manuscripts (see also Gen. 36:23); most Hebrew manuscripts *Alian*
ᵇ41 Many Hebrew manuscripts and some Septuagint manuscripts (see also Gen. 36:26); most Hebrew manuscripts *Hamran*
ᶜ42 Many Hebrew and Septuagint manuscripts (see also Gen. 36:27); most Hebrew manuscripts *Zaavan, Jaakan*
ᵈ42 Hebrew *Dishon*, a variant of *Dishan*   ᵉ43 Or *before an Israelite king reigned over them*   ᶠ48 Possibly the
Euphrates   ᵍ50 Many Hebrew manuscripts, some Septuagint manuscripts, Vulgate and Syriac (see also Gen. 36:39); most
Hebrew manuscripts *Pai*

Zimri, Ethan, Heman, Calcol and Darda[a]—five in all.

⁷The son of Carmi:

Achar,[b] who brought trouble on Israel by violating the ban on taking devoted things.[c]

⁸The son of Ethan:

Azariah.

⁹The sons born to Hezron were:

Jerahmeel, Ram and Caleb.[d]

From Ram Son of Hezron

¹⁰Ram was the father of

Amminadab, and Amminadab the father of Nahshon, the leader of the people of Judah. ¹¹Nahshon was the father of Salmon,[e] Salmon the father of Boaz, ¹²Boaz the father of Obed and Obed the father of Jesse.

¹³Jesse was the father of

Eliab his firstborn; the second son was Abinadab, the third Shimea, ¹⁴the fourth Nethanel, the fifth Raddai, ¹⁵the sixth Ozem and the seventh David. ¹⁶Their sisters were Zeruiah and Abigail. Zeruiah's three sons were Abishai, Joab and Asahel. ¹⁷Abigail was the mother of Amasa, whose father was Jether the Ishmaelite.

Caleb Son of Hezron

¹⁸Caleb son of Hezron had children by his wife Azubah (and by Jerioth). These were her sons: Jesher, Shobab and Ardon. ¹⁹When Azubah died, Caleb married Ephrath, who bore him Hur. ²⁰Hur was the father of Uri, and Uri the father of Bezalel.

²¹Later, Hezron lay with the daughter of Makir the father of Gilead (he had married her when he was sixty years old), and she bore him Segub. ²²Segub was the father of Jair, who controlled twenty-three towns in Gilead. ²³(But Geshur and Aram captured Havvoth Jair,[f] as well as Kenath with its surrounding settlements—sixty towns.) All these were descendants of Makir the father of Gilead.

²⁴After Hezron died in Caleb Ephrathah, Abijah the wife of Hezron bore him Ashhur the father[g] of Tekoa.

Jerahmeel Son of Hezron

²⁵The sons of Jerahmeel the firstborn of Hezron:

Ram his firstborn, Bunah, Oren, Ozem and[h] Ahijah. ²⁶Jerahmeel had another wife, whose name was Atarah; she was the mother of Onam.

²⁷The sons of Ram the firstborn of Jerahmeel:

Maaz, Jamin and Eker.

²⁸The sons of Onam:

Shammai and Jada.

The sons of Shammai:

Nadab and Abishur.

²⁹Abishur's wife was named Abihail, who bore him Ahban and Molid.

³⁰The sons of Nadab:

Seled and Appaim. Seled died without children.

³¹The son of Appaim:

Ishi, who was the father of Sheshan.

Sheshan was the father of Ahlai.

---

a6 Many Hebrew manuscripts, some Septuagint manuscripts and Syriac (see also 1 Kings 4:31); most Hebrew manuscripts *Dara*   *b7* *Achar* means *trouble; Achar* is called *Achan* in Joshua.   *c7* The Hebrew term refers to the irrevocable giving over of things or persons to the Lᴏʀᴅ, often by totally destroying them.   *d9* Hebrew *Kelubai,* a variant of *Caleb*   *e11* Septuagint (see also Ruth 4:21); Hebrew *Salma*   *f23* Or *captured the settlements of Jair*   *g24* *Father* may mean *civic leader* or *military leader;* also in verses 42, 45, 49-52 and possibly elsewhere.   *h25* Or *Oren and Ozem, by*

³²The sons of Jada, Shammai's brother:

Jether and Jonathan. Jether died without children.

³³The sons of Jonathan:

Peleth and Zaza.

These were the descendants of Jerahmeel.

³⁴Sheshan had no sons—only daughters.

He had an Egyptian servant named Jarha. ³⁵Sheshan gave his daughter in marriage to his servant Jarha, and she bore him Attai.

³⁶Attai was the father of Nathan,

Nathan the father of Zabad,

³⁷Zabad the father of Ephlal,

Ephlal the father of Obed,

³⁸Obed the father of Jehu,

Jehu the father of Azariah,

³⁹Azariah the father of Helez,

Helez the father of Eleasah,

⁴⁰Eleasah the father of Sismai,

Sismai the father of Shallum,

⁴¹Shallum the father of Jekamiah,

and Jekamiah the father of Elishama.

The Clans of Caleb

⁴²The sons of Caleb the brother of Jerahmeel:

Mesha his firstborn, who was the father of Ziph, and his son Mareshah,ᵃ who was the father of Hebron.

⁴³The sons of Hebron:

Korah, Tappuah, Rekem and Shema. ⁴⁴Shema was the father of Raham, and Raham the father of Jorkeam. Rekem was the father of Shammai. ⁴⁵The son of Shammai was Maon, and Maon was the father of Beth Zur.

⁴⁶Caleb's concubine Ephah was the mother of Haran, Moza and Gazez. Haran was the father of Gazez.

⁴⁷The sons of Jahdai:

Regem, Jotham, Geshan, Pelet, Ephah and Shaaph.

⁴⁸Caleb's concubine Maacah was the mother of Sheber and Tirhanah. ⁴⁹She also gave birth to Shaaph the father of Madmannah and to Sheva the father of Macbenah and Gibea. Caleb's daughter was Acsah. ⁵⁰These were the descendants of Caleb.

The sons of Hur the firstborn of Ephrathah:

Shobal the father of Kiriath Jearim, ⁵¹Salma the father of Bethlehem, and Hareph the father of Beth Gader.

⁵²The descendants of Shobal the father of Kiriath Jearim were:

Haroeh, half the Manahathites, ⁵³and the clans of Kiriath Jearim: the Ithrites, Puthites, Shumathites and Mishraites. From these descended the Zorathites and Eshtaolites.

⁵⁴The descendants of Salma:

Bethlehem, the Netophathites, Atroth Beth Joab, half the Manahathites, the Zorites, ⁵⁵and the clans of scribesᵇ who lived at Jabez: the Tirathites, Shimeathites and Sucathites. These are the Kenites who came from Hammath, the father of the house of Recab.ᶜ

ᵃ *42 The meaning of the Hebrew for this phrase is uncertain.*   ᵇ *55 Or of the Sopherites*   ᶜ *55 Or father of Beth Recab*

The Sons of David

3 These were the sons of David born to him in Hebron:
The firstborn was Amnon the son of Ahinoam of Jezreel;
the second, Daniel the son of Abigail of Carmel;
²the third, Absalom the son of Maacah daughter of Talmai king of Geshur;
the fourth, Adonijah the son of Haggith;
³the fifth, Shephatiah the son of Abital;
and the sixth, Ithream, by his wife Eglah.
⁴These six were born to David in Hebron, where he reigned seven years and six months.

David reigned in Jerusalem thirty-three years, ⁵and these were the children born to him there:

Shammua,ᵃ Shobab, Nathan and Solomon. These four were by Bathshebaᵇ daughter of Ammiel. ⁶There were also Ibhar, Elishua,ᶜ Eliphelet, ⁷Nogah, Nepheg, Japhia, ⁸Elishama, Eliada and Eliphelet—nine in all. ⁹All these were the sons of David, besides his sons by his concubines. And Tamar was their sister.

The Kings of Judah

¹⁰Solomon's son was Rehoboam,
Abijah his son,
Asa his son,
Jehoshaphat his son,
¹¹Jehoramᵈ his son,
Ahaziah his son,
Joash his son,
¹²Amaziah his son,
Azariah his son,
Jotham his son,
¹³Ahaz his son,
Hezekiah his son,
Manasseh his son,
¹⁴Amon his son,
Josiah his son.
¹⁵The sons of Josiah:
Johanan the firstborn,
Jehoiakim the second son,
Zedekiah the third,
Shallum the fourth.
¹⁶The successors of Jehoiakim:
Jehoiachinᵉ his son,
and Zedekiah.

The Royal Line After the Exile

¹⁷The descendants of Jehoiachin the captive:
Shealtiel his son, ¹⁸Malkiram, Pedaiah, Shenazzar, Jekamiah, Hoshama and Nedabiah.
¹⁹The sons of Pedaiah:
Zerubbabel and Shimei.
The sons of Zerubbabel:

ᵃ5 Hebrew *Shimea,* a variant of *Shammua* 11:3); most Hebrew manuscripts *Bathshua*　　ᵇ5 One Hebrew manuscript and Vulgate (see also Septuagint and 2 Samuel 11:3); most Hebrew manuscripts *Bathshua*　　ᶜ6 Two Hebrew manuscripts (see also 2 Samuel 5:15 and 1 Chron. 14:5); most Hebrew manuscripts *Elishama*　　ᵈ11 Hebrew *Joram,* a variant of *Jehoram*　　ᵉ16 Hebrew *Jeconiah,* a variant of *Jehoiachin;* also in verse 17

Meshullam and Hananiah.
Shelomith was their sister.
²⁰There were also five others:
Hashubah, Ohel, Berekiah, Hasadiah and Jushab-Hesed.
²¹The descendants of Hananiah:
Pelatiah and Jeshaiah, and the sons of Rephaiah, of Arnan, of Obadiah and of Shecaniah.
²²The descendants of Shecaniah:
Shemaiah and his sons:
Hattush, Igal, Bariah, Neariah and Shaphat—six in all.
²³The sons of Neariah:
Elioenai, Hizkiah and Azrikam—three in all.
²⁴The sons of Elioenai:
Hodaviah, Eliashib, Pelaiah, Akkub, Johanan, Delaiah and Anani—seven in all.

Other Clans of Judah

4 The descendants of Judah:
Perez, Hezron, Carmi, Hur and Shobal.

²Reaiah son of Shobal was the father of Jahath, and Jahath the father of Ahumai and Lahad. These were the clans of the Zorathites.

³These were the sons*ᵃ* of Etam:
Jezreel, Ishma and Idbash. Their sister was named Hazzelelponi. ⁴Penuel was the father of Gedor, and Ezer the father of Hushah.

These were the descendants of Hur, the firstborn of Ephrathah and father*ᵇ* of Bethlehem.

⁵Ashhur the father of Tekoa had two wives, Helah and Naarah.

⁶Naarah bore him Ahuzzam, Hepher, Temeni and Haahashtari. These were the descendants of Naarah.

⁷The sons of Helah:
Zereth, Zohar, Ethnan, ⁸and Koz, who was the father of Anub and Hazzobebah and of the clans of Aharhel son of Harum.

⁹Jabez was more honorable than his brothers. His mother had named him Jabez,*ᶜ* saying, "I gave birth to him in pain." ¹⁰Jabez cried out to the God of Israel, "Oh, that you would bless me and enlarge my territory! Let your hand be with me, and keep me from harm so that I will be free from pain." And God granted his request.

¹¹Kelub, Shuhah's brother, was the father of Mehir, who was the father of Eshton. ¹²Eshton was the father of Beth Rapha, Paseah and Tehinnah the father of Ir Nahash.*ᵈ* These were the men of Recah.

¹³The sons of Kenaz:
Othniel and Seraiah.
The sons of Othniel:
Hathath and Meonothai.*ᵉ* ¹⁴Meonothai was the father of Ophrah.
Seraiah was the father of Joab,
the father of Ge Harashim.*ᶠ* It was called this because its people were craftsmen.

¹⁵The sons of Caleb son of Jephunneh:
Iru, Elah and Naam.
The son of Elah:
Kenaz.

ᵃ3 Some Septuagint manuscripts (see also Vulgate); Hebrew *father*   *ᵇ4* *Father* may mean *civic leader* or *military leader*; also in verses 12, 14, 17, 18 and possibly elsewhere.   *ᶜ9* *Jabez* sounds like the Hebrew for *pain*.   *ᵈ12* Or *of the city of Nahash*   *ᵉ13* Some Septuagint manuscripts and Vulgate; Hebrew does not have *and Meonothai*.   *ᶠ14* *Ge Harashim* means *valley of craftsmen*.

¹⁶The sons of Jehallelel:

Ziph, Ziphah, Tiria and Asarel.

¹⁷The sons of Ezrah:

Jether, Mered, Epher and Jalon. One of Mered's wives gave birth to Miriam, Shammai and Ishbah the father of Eshtemoa. ¹⁸(His Judean wife gave birth to Jered the father of Gedor, Heber the father of Soco, and Jekuthiel the father of Zanoah.) These were the children of Pharaoh's daughter Bithiah, whom Mered had married.

¹⁹The sons of Hodiah's wife, the sister of Naham:

the father of Keilah the Garmite, and Eshtemoa the Maacathite.

²⁰The sons of Shimon:

Amnon, Rinnah, Ben-Hanan and Tilon.

The descendants of Ishi:

Zoheth and Ben-Zoheth.

²¹The sons of Shelah son of Judah:

Er the father of Lecah, Laadah the father of Mareshah and the clans of the linen workers at Beth Ashbea, ²²Jokim, the men of Cozeba, and Joash and Saraph, who ruled in Moab and Jashubi Lehem. (These records are from ancient times.) ²³They were the potters who lived at Netaim and Gederah; they stayed there and worked for the king.

Simeon

²⁴The descendants of Simeon:

Nemuel, Jamin, Jarib, Zerah and Shaul;

²⁵Shallum was Shaul's son, Mibsam his son and Mishma his son.

²⁶The descendants of Mishma:

Hammuel his son, Zaccur his son and Shimei his son.

²⁷Shimei had sixteen sons and six daughters, but his brothers did not have many children; so their entire clan did not become as numerous as the people of Judah. ²⁸They lived in Beersheba, Moladah, Hazar Shual, ²⁹Bilhah, Ezem, Tolad, ³⁰Bethuel, Hormah, Ziklag, ³¹Beth Marcaboth, Hazar Susim, Beth Biri and Shaaraim. These were their towns until the reign of David. ³²Their surrounding villages were Etam, Ain, Rimmon, Token and Ashan—five towns— ³³and all the villages around these towns as far as Baalath.ᵃ These were their settlements. And they kept a genealogical record.

³⁴Meshobab, Jamlech, Joshah son of Amaziah, ³⁵Joel, Jehu son of Joshibiah, the son of Seraiah, the son of Asiel, ³⁶also Elioenai, Jaakobah, Jeshohaiah, Asaiah, Adiel, Jesimiel, Benaiah, ³⁷and Ziza son of Shiphi, the son of Allon, the son of Jedaiah, the son of Shimri, the son of Shemaiah.

³⁸The men listed above by name were leaders of their clans. Their families increased greatly, ³⁹and they went to the outskirts of Gedor to the east of the valley in search of pasture for their flocks. ⁴⁰They found rich, good pasture, and the land was spacious, peaceful and quiet. Some Hamites had lived there formerly.

⁴¹The men whose names were listed came in the days of Hezekiah king of Judah. They attacked the Hamites in their dwellings and also the Meunites who were there and completely destroyedᵇ them, as is evident to this day. Then they settled in their place, because there was pasture for their flocks. ⁴²And five hundred of these Simeonites, led by Pelatiah, Neariah, Rephaiah and Uzziel, the sons of Ishi, invaded the hill country of Seir. ⁴³They killed the remaining Amalekites who had escaped, and they have lived there to this day.

ᵃ33 Some Septuagint manuscripts (see also Joshua 19:8); Hebrew *Baal*   ᵇ41 The Hebrew term refers to the irrevocable giving over of things or persons to the Lord, often by totally destroying them.

Reuben

5 The sons of Reuben the firstborn of Israel (he was the firstborn, but when he defiled his father's marriage bed, his rights as firstborn were given to the sons of Joseph son of Israel; so he could not be listed in the genealogical record in accordance with his birthright, ²and though Judah was the strongest of his brothers and a ruler came from him, the rights of the firstborn belonged to Joseph)— ³the sons of Reuben the firstborn of Israel:

Hanoch, Pallu, Hezron and Carmi.

⁴The descendants of Joel:

Shemaiah his son, Gog his son,
Shimei his son, ⁵Micah his son,
Reaiah his son, Baal his son,

⁶and Beerah his son, whom Tiglath-Pileser*a* king of Assyria took into exile. Bee-rah was a leader of the Reubenites.

⁷Their relatives by clans, listed according to their genealogical records:

Jeiel the chief, Zechariah, ⁸and Bela son of Azaz, the son of Shema, the son of Joel. They settled in the area from Aroer to Nebo and Baal Meon. ⁹To the east they occupied the land up to the edge of the desert that extends to the Euphrates River, because their livestock had increased in Gilead.

¹⁰During Saul's reign they waged war against the Hagrites, who were defeated at their hands; they occupied the dwellings of the Hagrites throughout the entire region east of Gilead.

Gad

¹¹The Gadites lived next to them in Bashan, as far as Salecah:

¹²Joel was the chief, Shapham the second, then Janai and Shaphat, in Bashan.

¹³Their relatives, by families, were:

Michael, Meshullam, Sheba, Jorai, Jacan, Zia and Eber—seven in all.

¹⁴These were the sons of Abihail son of Huri, the son of Jaroah, the son of Gilead, the son of Michael, the son of Jeshishai, the son of Jahdo, the son of Buz.

¹⁵Ahi son of Abdiel, the son of Guni, was head of their family.

¹⁶The Gadites lived in Gilead, in Bashan and its outlying villages, and on all the pasturelands of Sharon as far as they extended.

¹⁷All these were entered in the genealogical records during the reigns of Jotham king of Judah and Jeroboam king of Israel.

¹⁸The Reubenites, the Gadites and the half-tribe of Manasseh had 44,760 men ready for military service—able-bodied men who could handle shield and sword, who could use a bow, and who were trained for battle. ¹⁹They waged war against the Hagrites, Jetur, Naphish and Nodab. ²⁰They were helped in fighting them, and God handed the Hagrites and all their allies over to them, because they cried out to him during the battle. He answered their prayers, because they trusted in him. ²¹They seized the livestock of the Hagrites—fifty thousand camels, two hundred fifty thousand sheep and two thousand donkeys. They also took one hundred thousand people captive, ²²and many others fell slain, because the battle was God's. And they occupied the land until the exile.

The Half-Tribe of Manasseh

²³The people of the half-tribe of Manasseh were numerous; they settled in the land from Bashan to Baal Hermon, that is, to Senir (Mount Hermon).

²⁴These were the heads of their families: Epher, Ishi, Eliel, Azriel, Jeremiah, Hodaviah and Jahdiel. They were brave warriors, famous men, and heads of their families. ²⁵But they were unfaithful to the God of their fathers and prostituted themselves to the gods of

a 6 Hebrew Tilgath-Pilneser, a variant of Tiglath-Pileser; also in verse 26

the peoples of the land, whom God had destroyed before them. ²⁶So the God of Israel stirred up the spirit of Pul king of Assyria (that is, Tiglath-Pileser king of Assyria), who took the Reubenites, the Gadites and the half-tribe of Manasseh into exile. He took them to Halah, Habor, Hara and the river of Gozan, where they are to this day.

Levi

6 The sons of Levi:
Gershon, Kohath and Merari.

²The sons of Kohath:
Amram, Izhar, Hebron and Uzziel.

³The children of Amram:
Aaron, Moses and Miriam.

The sons of Aaron:
Nadab, Abihu, Eleazar and Ithamar.

⁴Eleazar was the father of Phinehas,
Phinehas the father of Abishua,

⁵Abishua the father of Bukki,
Bukki the father of Uzzi,

⁶Uzzi the father of Zerahiah,
Zerahiah the father of Meraioth,

⁷Meraioth the father of Amariah,
Amariah the father of Ahitub,

⁸Ahitub the father of Zadok,
Zadok the father of Ahimaaz,

⁹Ahimaaz the father of Azariah,
Azariah the father of Johanan,

¹⁰Johanan the father of Azariah (it was he who served as priest in the temple Solomon built in Jerusalem),

¹¹Azariah the father of Amariah,
Amariah the father of Ahitub,

¹²Ahitub the father of Zadok,
Zadok the father of Shallum,

¹³Shallum the father of Hilkiah,
Hilkiah the father of Azariah,

¹⁴Azariah the father of Seraiah,
and Seraiah the father of Jehozadak.

¹⁵Jehozadak was deported when the LORD sent Judah and Jerusalem into exile by the hand of Nebuchadnezzar.

¹⁶The sons of Levi:
Gershon,ᵃ Kohath and Merari.

¹⁷These are the names of the sons of Gershon:
Libni and Shimei.

¹⁸The sons of Kohath:
Amram, Izhar, Hebron and Uzziel.

¹⁹The sons of Merari:
Mahli and Mushi.

These are the clans of the Levites listed according to their fathers:

²⁰Of Gershon:
Libni his son, Jehath his son,
Zimmah his son, ²¹Joah his son,
Iddo his son, Zerah his son

ᵃ16 Hebrew *Gershom*, a variant of *Gershon*; also in verses 17, 20, 43, 62 and 71

and Jeatherai his son.
²²The descendants of Kohath:
Amminadab his son, Korah his son,
Assir his son, ²³Elkanah his son,
Ebiasaph his son, Assir his son,
²⁴Tahath his son, Uriel his son,
Uzziah his son and Shaul his son.
²⁵The descendants of Elkanah:
Amasai, Ahimoth,
²⁶Elkanah his son,ᵃ Zophai his son,
Nahath his son, ²⁷Eliab his son,
Jeroham his son, Elkanah his son
and Samuel his son.ᵇ
²⁸The sons of Samuel:
Joelᶜ the firstborn
and Abijah the second son.
²⁹The descendants of Merari:
Mahli, Libni his son,
Shimei his son, Uzzah his son,
³⁰Shimea his son, Haggiah his son
and Asaiah his son.

The Temple Musicians

³¹These are the men David put in charge of the music in the house of the LORD after the ark came to rest there. ³²They ministered with music before the tabernacle, the Tent of Meeting, until Solomon built the temple of the LORD in Jerusalem. They performed their duties according to the regulations laid down for them.

³³Here are the men who served, together with their sons:
From the Kohathites:
Heman, the musician,
the son of Joel, the son of Samuel,
³⁴the son of Elkanah, the son of Jeroham,
the son of Eliel, the son of Toah,
³⁵the son of Zuph, the son of Elkanah,
the son of Mahath, the son of Amasai,
³⁶the son of Elkanah, the son of Joel,
the son of Azariah, the son of Zephaniah,
³⁷the son of Tahath, the son of Assir,
the son of Ebiasaph, the son of Korah,
³⁸the son of Izhar, the son of Kohath,
the son of Levi, the son of Israel;
³⁹and Heman's associate Asaph, who served at his right hand:
Asaph son of Berekiah, the son of Shimea,
⁴⁰the son of Michael, the son of Baaseiah,ᵈ
the son of Malkijah, ⁴¹the son of Ethni,
the son of Zerah, the son of Adaiah,
⁴²the son of Ethan, the son of Zimmah,
the son of Shimei, ⁴³the son of Jahath,
the son of Gershon, the son of Levi;
⁴⁴and from their associates, the Merarites, at his left hand:

ᵃ26 Some Hebrew manuscripts, Septuagint and Syriac; most Hebrew manuscripts *Ahimoth* ²⁶*and Elkanah. The sons of Elkanah:*
ᵇ27 Some Septuagint manuscripts (see also 1 Samuel 1:19,20 and 1 Chron. 6:33,34); Hebrew does not have *and Samuel his son.*
ᶜ28 Some Septuagint manuscripts and Syriac (see also 1 Samuel 8:2 and 1 Chron. 6:33); Hebrew does not have *Joel.*
ᵈ40 Most Hebrew manuscripts; some Hebrew manuscripts, one Septuagint manuscript and Syriac *Maaseiah*

Ethan son of Kishi, the son of Abdi,
  the son of Malluch, **45**the son of Hashabiah,
  the son of Amaziah, the son of Hilkiah,
46the son of Amzi, the son of Bani,
  the son of Shemer, **47**the son of Mahli,
  the son of Mushi, the son of Merari,
  the son of Levi.

48Their fellow Levites were assigned to all the other duties of the tabernacle, the house of God. **49**But Aaron and his descendants were the ones who presented offerings on the altar of burnt offering and on the altar of incense in connection with all that was done in the Most Holy Place, making atonement for Israel, in accordance with all that Moses the servant of God had commanded.

50These were the descendants of Aaron:
  Eleazar his son, Phinehas his son,
  Abishua his son, **51**Bukki his son,
  Uzzi his son, Zerahiah his son,
52Meraioth his son, Amariah his son,
  Ahitub his son, **53**Zadok his son
  and Ahimaaz his son.

54These were the locations of their settlements allotted as their territory (they were assigned to the descendants of Aaron who were from the Kohathite clan, because the first lot was for them):
  55They were given Hebron in Judah with its surrounding pasturelands. **56**But the fields and villages around the city were given to Caleb son of Jephunneh.
  57So the descendants of Aaron were given Hebron (a city of refuge), and Libnah,*a* Jattir, Eshtemoa, **58**Hilen, Debir, **59**Ashan, Juttah*b* and Beth Shemesh, together with their pasturelands. **60**And from the tribe of Benjamin they were given Gibeon,*c* Geba, Alemeth and Anathoth, together with their pasturelands.
  These towns, which were distributed among the Kohathite clans, were thirteen in all.
  61The rest of Kohath's descendants were allotted ten towns from the clans of half the tribe of Manasseh.
  62The descendants of Gershon, clan by clan, were allotted thirteen towns from the tribes of Issachar, Asher and Naphtali, and from the part of the tribe of Manasseh that is in Bashan.
  63The descendants of Merari, clan by clan, were allotted twelve towns from the tribes of Reuben, Gad and Zebulun.
  64So the Israelites gave the Levites these towns and their pasturelands. **65**From the tribes of Judah, Simeon and Benjamin they allotted the previously named towns.
  66Some of the Kohathite clans were given as their territory towns from the tribe of Ephraim.
  67In the hill country of Ephraim they were given Shechem (a city of refuge), and Gezer,*d* **68**Jokmeam, Beth Horon, **69**Aijalon and Gath Rimmon, together with their pasturelands.
  70And from half the tribe of Manasseh the Israelites gave Aner and Bileam, together with their pasturelands, to the rest of the Kohathite clans.

71The Gershonites received the following:
  From the clan of the half-tribe of Manasseh

---

a 57 See Joshua 21:13; Hebrew *given the cities of refuge: Hebron, Libnah.*   *b 59* Syriac (see also Septuagint and Joshua 21:16); Hebrew does not have *Juttah.*   *c 60* See Joshua 21:17; Hebrew does not have *Gibeon.*   *d 67* See Joshua 21:21; Hebrew *given the cities of refuge: Shechem, Gezer.*

they received Golan in Bashan and also Ashtaroth, together with their pasturelands;
⁷²from the tribe of Issachar
they received Kedesh, Daberath, ⁷³Ramoth and Anem, together with their pasturelands;
⁷⁴from the tribe of Asher
they received Mashal, Abdon, ⁷⁵Hukok and Rehob, together with their pasturelands;
⁷⁶and from the tribe of Naphtali
they received Kedesh in Galilee, Hammon and Kiriathaim, together with their pasturelands.

⁷⁷The Merarites (the rest of the Levites) received the following:
From the tribe of Zebulun
they received Jokneam, Kartah,ᵃ Rimmono and Tabor, together with their pasturelands;
⁷⁸from the tribe of Reuben across the Jordan east of Jericho
they received Bezer in the desert, Jahzah, ⁷⁹Kedemoth and Mephaath, together with their pasturelands;
⁸⁰and from the tribe of Gad
they received Ramoth in Gilead, Mahanaim, ⁸¹Heshbon and Jazer, together with their pasturelands.

Issachar

7 The sons of Issachar:
Tola, Puah, Jashub and Shimron—four in all.
²The sons of Tola:
Uzzi, Rephaiah, Jeriel, Jahmai, Ibsam and Samuel—heads of their families. During the reign of David, the descendants of Tola listed as fighting men in their genealogy numbered 22,600.
³The son of Uzzi:
Izrahiah.
The sons of Izrahiah:
Michael, Obadiah, Joel and Isshiah. All five of them were chiefs. ⁴According to their family genealogy, they had 36,000 men ready for battle, for they had many wives and children.
⁵The relatives who were fighting men belonging to all the clans of Issachar, as listed in their genealogy, were 87,000 in all.

Benjamin

⁶Three sons of Benjamin:
Bela, Beker and Jediael.
⁷The sons of Bela:
Ezbon, Uzzi, Uzziel, Jerimoth and Iri, heads of families—five in all. Their genealogical record listed 22,034 fighting men.
⁸The sons of Beker:
Zemirah, Joash, Eliezer, Elioenai, Omri, Jeremoth, Abijah, Anathoth and Alemeth. All these were the sons of Beker. ⁹Their genealogical record listed the heads of families and 20,200 fighting men.
¹⁰The son of Jediael:
Bilhan.
The sons of Bilhan:

ᵃ 77 See Septuagint and Joshua 21:34; Hebrew does not have *Jokneam, Kartah*.

Jeush, Benjamin, Ehud, Kenaanah, Zethan, Tarshish and Ahishahar. ¹¹All these sons of Jediael were heads of families. There were 17,200 fighting men ready to go out to war.

¹²The Shuppites and Huppites were the descendants of Ir, and the Hushites the descendants of Aher.

Naphtali

¹³The sons of Naphtali:
Jahziel, Guni, Jezer and Shillem*ᵃ*—the descendants of Bilhah.

Manasseh

¹⁴The descendants of Manasseh:
Asriel was his descendant through his Aramean concubine. She gave birth to Makir the father of Gilead. ¹⁵Makir took a wife from among the Huppites and Shuppites. His sister's name was Maacah.
Another descendant was named Zelophehad, who had only daughters.
¹⁶Makir's wife Maacah gave birth to a son and named him Peresh. His brother was named Sheresh, and his sons were Ulam and Rakem.
¹⁷The son of Ulam:
Bedan.
These were the sons of Gilead son of Makir, the son of Manasseh. ¹⁸His sister Hammoleketh gave birth to Ishhod, Abiezer and Mahlah.
¹⁹The sons of Shemida were:
Ahian, Shechem, Likhi and Aniam.

Ephraim

²⁰The descendants of Ephraim:
Shuthelah, Bered his son,
Tahath his son, Eleadah his son,
Tahath his son, ²¹Zabad his son
and Shuthelah his son.
Ezer and Elead were killed by the native-born men of Gath, when they went down to seize their livestock. ²²Their father Ephraim mourned for them many days, and his relatives came to comfort him. ²³Then he lay with his wife again, and she became pregnant and gave birth to a son. He named him Beriah,*ᵇ* because there had been misfortune in his family. ²⁴His daughter was Sheerah, who built Lower and Upper Beth Horon as well as Uzzen Sheerah.
²⁵Rephah was his son, Resheph his son,*ᶜ*
Telah his son, Tahan his son,
²⁶Ladan his son, Ammihud his son,
Elishama his son, ²⁷Nun his son
and Joshua his son.
²⁸Their lands and settlements included Bethel and its surrounding villages, Naaran to the east, Gezer and its villages to the west, and Shechem and its villages all the way to Ayyah and its villages. ²⁹Along the borders of Manasseh were Beth Shan, Taanach, Megiddo and Dor, together with their villages. The descendants of Joseph son of Israel lived in these towns.

Asher

³⁰The sons of Asher:
Imnah, Ishvah, Ishvi and Beriah. Their sister was Serah.

ᵃ 13 Some Hebrew and Septuagint manuscripts (see also Gen. 46:24 and Num. 26:49); most Hebrew manuscripts *Shallum*　　*ᵇ 23* *Beriah* sounds like the Hebrew for *misfortune.*　　*ᶜ 25* Some Septuagint manuscripts; Hebrew does not have *his son.*

³¹The sons of Beriah:

   Heber and Malkiel, who was the father of Birzaith.

³²Heber was the father of Japhlet, Shomer and Hotham and of their sister Shua.

³³The sons of Japhlet:

   Pasach, Bimhal and Ashvath.

   These were Japhlet's sons.

³⁴The sons of Shomer:

   Ahi, Rohgah,ᵃ Hubbah and Aram.

³⁵The sons of his brother Helem:

   Zophah, Imna, Shelesh and Amal.

³⁶The sons of Zophah:

   Suah, Harnepher, Shual, Beri, Imrah, ³⁷Bezer, Hod, Shamma, Shilshah, Ithranᵇ and Beera.

³⁸The sons of Jether:

   Jephunneh, Pispah and Ara.

³⁹The sons of Ulla:

   Arah, Hanniel and Rizia.

⁴⁰All these were descendants of Asher—heads of families, choice men, brave warriors and outstanding leaders. The number of men ready for battle, as listed in their genealogy, was 26,000.

The Genealogy of Saul the Benjamite

8 Benjamin was the father of Bela his firstborn,

   Ashbel the second son, Aharah the third,

²Nohah the fourth and Rapha the fifth.

³The sons of Bela were:

   Addar, Gera, Abihud,ᶜ ⁴Abishua, Naaman, Ahoah, ⁵Gera, Shephuphan and Huram.

⁶These were the descendants of Ehud, who were heads of families of those living in Geba and were deported to Manahath:

⁷Naaman, Ahijah, and Gera, who deported them and who was the father of Uzza and Ahihud.

⁸Sons were born to Shaharaim in Moab after he had divorced his wives Hushim and Baara. ⁹By his wife Hodesh he had Jobab, Zibia, Mesha, Malcam, ¹⁰Jeuz, Sakia and Mirmah. These were his sons, heads of families. ¹¹By Hushim he had Abitub and Elpaal.

¹²The sons of Elpaal:

   Eber, Misham, Shemed (who built Ono and Lod with its surrounding villages), ¹³and Beriah and Shema, who were heads of families of those living in Aijalon and who drove out the inhabitants of Gath.

¹⁴Ahio, Shashak, Jeremoth, ¹⁵Zebadiah, Arad, Eder, ¹⁶Michael, Ishpah and Joha were the sons of Beriah.

¹⁷Zebadiah, Meshullam, Hizki, Heber, ¹⁸Ishmerai, Izliah and Jobab were the sons of Elpaal.

¹⁹Jakim, Zicri, Zabdi, ²⁰Elienai, Zillethai, Eliel, ²¹Adaiah, Beraiah and Shimrath were the sons of Shimei.

²²Ishpan, Eber, Eliel, ²³Abdon, Zicri, Hanan, ²⁴Hananiah, Elam, Anthothijah, ²⁵Iphdeiah and Penuel were the sons of Shashak.

²⁶Shamsherai, Shehariah, Athaliah, ²⁷Jaareshiah, Elijah and Zicri were the sons of Jeroham.

²⁸All these were heads of families, chiefs as listed in their genealogy, and they lived in Jerusalem.

ᵃ34 Or of his brother Shomer: Rohgah   ᵇ37 Possibly a variant of Jether   ᶜ3 Or Gera the father of Ehud

²⁹Jeiel^{*a*} the father^{*b*} of Gibeon lived in Gibeon.

His wife's name was Maacah, ³⁰and his firstborn son was Abdon, followed by Zur, Kish, Baal, Ner,^{*c*} Nadab, ³¹Gedor, Ahio, Zeker ³²and Mikloth, who was the father of Shimeah. They too lived near their relatives in Jerusalem.

³³Ner was the father of Kish, Kish the father of Saul, and Saul the father of Jonathan, Malki-Shua, Abinadab and Esh-Baal.^{*d*}

³⁴The son of Jonathan:

Merib-Baal,^{*e*} who was the father of Micah.

³⁵The sons of Micah:

Pithon, Melech, Tarea and Ahaz.

³⁶Ahaz was the father of Jehoaddah, Jehoaddah was the father of Alemeth, Azmaveth and Zimri, and Zimri was the father of Moza. ³⁷Moza was the father of Binea; Raphah was his son, Eleasah his son and Azel his son.

³⁸Azel had six sons, and these were their names:

Azrikam, Bokeru, Ishmael, Sheariah, Obadiah and Hanan. All these were the sons of Azel.

³⁹The sons of his brother Eshek:

Ulam his firstborn, Jeush the second son and Eliphelet the third. ⁴⁰The sons of Ulam were brave warriors who could handle the bow. They had many sons and grandsons—150 in all.

All these were the descendants of Benjamin.

 All Israel was listed in the genealogies recorded in the book of the kings of Israel.

The People in Jerusalem

The people of Judah were taken captive to Babylon because of their unfaithfulness. ²Now the first to resettle on their own property in their own towns were some Israelites, priests, Levites and temple servants.

³Those from Judah, from Benjamin, and from Ephraim and Manasseh who lived in Jerusalem were:

⁴Uthai son of Ammihud, the son of Omri, the son of Imri, the son of Bani, a descendant of Perez son of Judah.

⁵Of the Shilonites:

Asaiah the firstborn and his sons.

⁶Of the Zerahites:

Jeuel.

The people from Judah numbered 690.

⁷Of the Benjamites:

Sallu son of Meshullam, the son of Hodaviah, the son of Hassenuah;

⁸Ibneiah son of Jeroham; Elah son of Uzzi, the son of Micri; and Meshullam son of Shephatiah, the son of Reuel, the son of Ibnijah;

⁹The people from Benjamin, as listed in their genealogy, numbered 956. All these men were heads of their families.

¹⁰Of the priests:

Jedaiah; Jehoiarib; Jakin;

¹¹Azariah son of Hilkiah, the son of Meshullam, the son of Zadok, the son of Meraioth, the son of Ahitub, the official in charge of the house of God;

¹²Adaiah son of Jeroham, the son of Pashhur, the son of Malkijah; and Maasai son

a 29 Some Septuagint manuscripts (see also 1 Chron. 9:35); Hebrew does not have *Jeiel.*   *b 29 Father* may mean *civic leader* or *military leader.*   *c 30* Some Septuagint manuscripts (see also 1 Chron. 9:36); Hebrew does not have *Ner.*   *d 33* Also known as *Ish-Bosheth*   *e 34* Also known as *Mephibosheth*

of Adiel, the son of Jahzerah, the son of Meshullam, the son of Meshillemith, the son of Immer.

¹³The priests, who were heads of families, numbered 1,760. They were able men, responsible for ministering in the house of God.

¹⁴Of the Levites:

Shemaiah son of Hasshub, the son of Azrikam, the son of Hashabiah, a Merarite; ¹⁵Bakbakkar, Heresh, Galal and Mattaniah son of Mica, the son of Zicri, the son of Asaph; ¹⁶Obadiah son of Shemaiah, the son of Galal, the son of Jeduthun; and Berekiah son of Asa, the son of Elkanah, who lived in the villages of the Netophathites.

¹⁷The gatekeepers:

Shallum, Akkub, Talmon, Ahiman and their brothers, Shallum their chief ¹⁸being stationed at the King's Gate on the east, up to the present time. These were the gatekeepers belonging to the camp of the Levites. ¹⁹Shallum son of Kore, the son of Ebiasaph, the son of Korah, and his fellow gatekeepers from his family (the Korahites) were responsible for guarding the thresholds of the Tent*ᵃ* just as their fathers had been responsible for guarding the entrance to the dwelling of the Lᴏʀᴅ. ²⁰In earlier times Phinehas son of Eleazar was in charge of the gatekeepers, and the Lᴏʀᴅ was with him. ²¹Zechariah son of Meshelemiah was the gatekeeper at the entrance to the Tent of Meeting.

²²Altogether, those chosen to be gatekeepers at the thresholds numbered 212. They were registered by genealogy in their villages. The gatekeepers had been assigned to their positions of trust by David and Samuel the seer. ²³They and their descendants were in charge of guarding the gates of the house of the Lᴏʀᴅ—the house called the Tent. ²⁴The gatekeepers were on the four sides: east, west, north and south. ²⁵Their brothers in their villages had to come from time to time and share their duties for seven-day periods. ²⁶But the four principal gatekeepers, who were Levites, were entrusted with the responsibility for the rooms and treasuries in the house of God. ²⁷They would spend the night stationed around the house of God, because they had to guard it; and they had charge of the key for opening it each morning.

²⁸Some of them were in charge of the articles used in the temple service; they counted them when they were brought in and when they were taken out. ²⁹Others were assigned to take care of the furnishings and all the other articles of the sanctuary, as well as the flour and wine, and the oil, incense and spices. ³⁰But some of the priests took care of mixing the spices. ³¹A Levite named Mattithiah, the firstborn son of Shallum the Korahite, was entrusted with the responsibility for baking the offering bread. ³²Some of their Kohathite brothers were in charge of preparing for every Sabbath the bread set out on the table.

³³Those who were musicians, heads of Levite families, stayed in the rooms of the temple and were exempt from other duties because they were responsible for the work day and night.

³⁴All these were heads of Levite families, chiefs as listed in their genealogy, and they lived in Jerusalem.

The Genealogy of Saul

³⁵Jeiel the father*ᵇ* of Gibeon lived in Gibeon.

His wife's name was Maacah, ³⁶and his firstborn son was Abdon, followed by Zur, Kish, Baal, Ner, Nadab, ³⁷Gedor, Ahio, Zechariah and Mikloth. ³⁸Mikloth was the father of Shimeam. They too lived near their relatives in Jerusalem.

³⁹Ner was the father of Kish, Kish the father of Saul, and Saul the father of Jonathan, Malki-Shua, Abinadab and Esh-Baal.*ᶜ*

ᵃ 19 That is, the temple; also in verses 21 and 23   *ᵇ 35 Father* may mean *civic leader* or *military leader.*   *ᶜ 39* Also known as *Ish-Bosheth*

40The son of Jonathan:

Merib-Baal,^{a} who was the father of Micah.

41The sons of Micah:

Pithon, Melech, Tahrea and Ahaz.^{b}

42Ahaz was the father of Jadah, Jadah^c was the father of Alemeth, Azmaveth and Zimri, and Zimri was the father of Moza. **43**Moza was the father of Binea; Rephaiah was his son, Eleasah his son and Azel his son.

44Azel had six sons, and these were their names:

Azrikam, Bokeru, Ishmael, Sheariah, Obadiah and Hanan. These were the sons of Azel.

Saul Takes His Life

10 Now the Philistines fought against Israel; the Israelites fled before them, and many fell slain on Mount Gilboa. **2**The Philistines pressed hard after Saul and his sons, and they killed his sons Jonathan, Abinadab and Malki-Shua. **3**The fighting grew fierce around Saul, and when the archers overtook him, they wounded him.

4Saul said to his armor-bearer, "Draw your sword and run me through, or these uncircumcised fellows will come and abuse me."

But his armor-bearer was terrified and would not do it; so Saul took his own sword and fell on it. **5**When the armor-bearer saw that Saul was dead, he too fell on his sword and died. **6**So Saul and his three sons died, and all his house died together.

7When all the Israelites in the valley saw that the army had fled and that Saul and his sons had died, they abandoned their towns and fled. And the Philistines came and occupied them.

8The next day, when the Philistines came to strip the dead, they found Saul and his sons fallen on Mount Gilboa. **9**They stripped him and took his head and his armor, and sent messengers throughout the land of the Philistines to proclaim the news among their idols and their people. **10**They put his armor in the temple of their gods and hung up his head in the temple of Dagon.

11When all the inhabitants of Jabesh Gilead heard of everything the Philistines had done to Saul, **12**all their valiant men went and took the bodies of Saul and his sons and brought them to Jabesh. Then they buried their bones under the great tree in Jabesh, and they fasted seven days.

13Saul died because he was unfaithful to the LORD; he did not keep the word of the LORD and even consulted a medium for guidance, **14**and did not inquire of the LORD. So the LORD put him to death and turned the kingdom over to David son of Jesse.

David Becomes King Over Israel

11 All Israel came together to David at Hebron and said, "We are your own flesh and blood. **2**In the past, even while Saul was king, you were the one who led Israel on their military campaigns. And the LORD your God said to you, 'You will shepherd my people Israel, and you will become their ruler.'"

3When all the elders of Israel had come to King David at Hebron, he made a compact with them at Hebron before the LORD, and they anointed David king over Israel, as the LORD had promised through Samuel.

David Conquers Jerusalem

4David and all the Israelites marched to Jerusalem (that is, Jebus). The Jebusites who lived there **5**said to David, "You will not get in here." Nevertheless, David captured the fortress of Zion, the City of David.

$^a40$ Also known as *Mephibosheth* $^b41$ Vulgate and Syriac (see also Septuagint and 1 Chron. 8:35); Hebrew does not have *and Ahaz*. $^c42$ Some Hebrew manuscripts and Septuagint (see also 1 Chron. 8:36); most Hebrew manuscripts *Jarah, Jarah*

⁶David had said, "Whoever leads the attack on the Jebusites will become commander-in-chief." Joab son of Zeruiah went up first, and so he received the command.

⁷David then took up residence in the fortress, and so it was called the City of David. ⁸He built up the city around it, from the supporting terraces*ᵃ* to the surrounding wall, while Joab restored the rest of the city. ⁹And David became more and more powerful, because the LORD Almighty was with him.

David's Mighty Men

¹⁰These were the chiefs of David's mighty men—they, together with all Israel, gave his kingship strong support to extend it over the whole land, as the LORD had promised— ¹¹this is the list of David's mighty men:

Jashobeam,*ᵇ* a Hacmonite, was chief of the officers*ᶜ*; he raised his spear against three hundred men, whom he killed in one encounter.

¹²Next to him was Eleazar son of Dodai the Ahohite, one of the three mighty men. ¹³He was with David at Pas Dammim when the Philistines gathered there for battle. At a place where there was a field full of barley, the troops fled from the Philistines. ¹⁴But they took their stand in the middle of the field. They defended it and struck the Philistines down, and the LORD brought about a great victory.

¹⁵Three of the thirty chiefs came down to David to the rock at the cave of Adullam, while a band of Philistines was encamped in the Valley of Rephaim. ¹⁶At that time David was in the stronghold, and the Philistine garrison was at Bethlehem. ¹⁷David longed for water and said, "Oh, that someone would get me a drink of water from the well near the gate of Bethlehem!" ¹⁸So the Three broke through the Philistine lines, drew water from the well near the gate of Bethlehem and carried it back to David. But he refused to drink it; instead, he poured it out before the LORD. ¹⁹"God forbid that I should do this!" he said. "Should I drink the blood of these men who went at the risk of their lives?" Because they risked their lives to bring it back, David would not drink it.

Such were the exploits of the three mighty men.

²⁰Abishai the brother of Joab was chief of the Three. He raised his spear against three hundred men, whom he killed, and so he became as famous as the Three. ²¹He was

ᵃ8 Or the Millo   *ᵇ11 Possibly a variant of Jashob-Baal*   *ᶜ11 Or Thirty; some Septuagint manuscripts Three (see also 2 Samuel 23:8)*

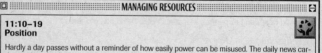

▣ ⬚⬚⬚⬚⬚ MANAGING RESOURCES ⬚⬚⬚⬚⬚ ↔

11:10–19
Position

Hardly a day passes without a reminder of how easily power can be misused. The daily news carries stories of politicians, policemen, teachers, clergy and coaches who inappropriately use their positions. In this story, however, King David gives us a lesson in the appropriate use of leadership authority.

When three of David's loyal followers interpreted his longing for a drink of water as a command, they risked their lives to fulfill his wish. They broke through enemy lines to draw some water from the well in David's occupied hometown of Bethlehem.

David's response to this action may seem strange to us—he poured the water out on the ground, sacrificing it as an offering to God instead of refreshing himself with it. In doing so, David did these men a great honor, acknowledging their extraordinary courage and loyalty. As a result, their story was often retold among their fellow soldiers.

Here David displayed a key ingredient to successful leadership: valuing the contributions of those he led and rewarding their sacrifices publicly. If you have the benefit, as David did, of a few dedicated people following you—whether that be in a business or a family setting—follow David's example. Honor those people, even at your own expense, for the work they do. They've earned it.

doubly honored above the Three and became their commander, even though he was not included among them.

²²Benaiah son of Jehoiada was a valiant fighter from Kabzeel, who performed great exploits. He struck down two of Moab's best men. He also went down into a pit on a snowy day and killed a lion. ²³And he struck down an Egyptian who was seven and a half feet*ᵃ* tall. Although the Egyptian had a spear like a weaver's rod in his hand, Benaiah went against him with a club. He snatched the spear from the Egyptian's hand and killed him with his own spear. ²⁴Such were the exploits of Benaiah son of Jehoiada; he too was as famous as the three mighty men. ²⁵He was held in greater honor than any of the Thirty, but he was not included among the Three. And David put him in charge of his bodyguard.

²⁶The mighty men were:
    Asahel the brother of Joab,
    Elhanan son of Dodo from Bethlehem,
²⁷Shammoth the Harorite,
    Helez the Pelonite,
²⁸Ira son of Ikkesh from Tekoa,
    Abiezer from Anathoth,
²⁹Sibbecai the Hushathite,
    Ilai the Ahohite,
³⁰Maharai the Netophathite,
    Heled son of Baanah the Netophathite,
³¹Ithai son of Ribai from Gibeah in Benjamin,
    Benaiah the Pirathonite,
³²Hurai from the ravines of Gaash,
    Abiel the Arbathite,
³³Azmaveth the Baharumite,
    Eliahba the Shaalbonite,
³⁴the sons of Hashem the Gizonite,
    Jonathan son of Shagee the Hararite,
³⁵Ahiam son of Sacar the Hararite,
    Eliphal son of Ur,
³⁶Hepher the Mekerathite,
    Ahijah the Pelonite,
³⁷Hezro the Carmelite,
    Naarai son of Ezbai,
³⁸Joel the brother of Nathan,
    Mibhar son of Hagri,
³⁹Zelek the Ammonite,
    Naharai the Berothite, the armor-bearer of Joab son of Zeruiah,
⁴⁰Ira the Ithrite,
    Gareb the Ithrite,
⁴¹Uriah the Hittite,
    Zabad son of Ahlai,
⁴²Adina son of Shiza the Reubenite, who was chief of the Reubenites, and the thirty with him,
⁴³Hanan son of Maacah,
    Joshaphat the Mithnite,
⁴⁴Uzzia the Ashterathite,
    Shama and Jeiel the sons of Hotham the Aroerite,
⁴⁵Jediael son of Shimri,

ᵃ23 Hebrew five cubits *(about 2.3 meters)*

his brother Joha the Tizite,
⁴⁶Eliel the Mahavite,
Jeribai and Joshaviah the sons of Elnaam,
Ithmah the Moabite,
⁴⁷Eliel, Obed and Jaasiel the Mezobaite.

Warriors Join David

12 These were the men who came to David at Ziklag, while he was banished from the presence of Saul son of Kish (they were among the warriors who helped him in battle; ²they were armed with bows and were able to shoot arrows or to sling stones right-handed or left-handed; they were kinsmen of Saul from the tribe of Benjamin):

³Ahiezer their chief and Joash the sons of Shemaah the Gibeathite; Jeziel and Pelet the sons of Azmaveth; Beracah, Jehu the Anathothite, ⁴and Ishmaiah the Gibeonite, a mighty man among the Thirty, who was a leader of the Thirty; Jeremiah, Jahaziel, Johanan, Jozabad the Gederathite, ⁵Eluzai, Jerimoth, Bealiah, Shemariah and Sheph-atiah the Haruphite; ⁶Elkanah, Isshiah, Azarel, Joezer and Jashobeam the Korahites; ⁷and Joelah and Zebadiah the sons of Jeroham from Gedor.

⁸Some Gadites defected to David at his stronghold in the desert. They were brave warriors, ready for battle and able to handle the shield and spear. Their faces were the faces of lions, and they were as swift as gazelles in the mountains.

⁹Ezer was the chief,
   Obadiah the second in command, Eliab the third,
¹⁰Mishmannah the fourth, Jeremiah the fifth,
¹¹Attai the sixth, Eliel the seventh,
¹²Johanan the eighth, Elzabad the ninth,
¹³Jeremiah the tenth and Macbannai the eleventh.

¹⁴These Gadites were army commanders; the least was a match for a hundred, and the greatest for a thousand. ¹⁵It was they who crossed the Jordan in the first month when it was overflowing all its banks, and they put to flight everyone living in the valleys, to the east and to the west.

¹⁶Other Benjamites and some men from Judah also came to David in his stronghold. ¹⁷David went out to meet them and said to them, "If you have come to me in peace, to help me, I am ready to have you unite with me. But if you have come to betray me to my enemies when my hands are free from violence, may the God of our fathers see it and judge you."

¹⁸Then the Spirit came upon Amasai, chief of the Thirty, and he said:

"We are yours, O David!
   We are with you, O son of Jesse!
Success, success to you,
   and success to those who help you,
      for your God will help you."

So David received them and made them leaders of his raiding bands.

¹⁹Some of the men of Manasseh defected to David when he went with the Philistines to fight against Saul. (He and his men did not help the Philistines because, after consulta-tion, their rulers sent him away. They said, "It will cost us our heads if he deserts to his master Saul.") ²⁰When David went to Ziklag, these were the men of Manasseh who defected to him: Adnah, Jozabad, Jediael, Michael, Jozabad, Elihu and Zillethai, leaders of units of a thousand in Manasseh. ²¹They helped David against raiding bands, for all of

them were brave warriors, and they were commanders in his army. ²²Day after day men came to help David, until he had a great army, like the army of God.ᵃ

Others Join David at Hebron

²³These are the numbers of the men armed for battle who came to David at Hebron to turn Saul's kingdom over to him, as the LORD had said:

²⁴men of Judah, carrying shield and spear—6,800 armed for battle;

²⁵men of Simeon, warriors ready for battle—7,100;

²⁶men of Levi—4,600, ²⁷including Jehoiada, leader of the family of Aaron, with 3,700 men, ²⁸and Zadok, a brave young warrior, with 22 officers from his family;

²⁹men of Benjamin, Saul's kinsmen—3,000, most of whom had remained loyal to Saul's house until then;

³⁰men of Ephraim, brave warriors, famous in their own clans—20,800;

³¹men of half the tribe of Manasseh, designated by name to come and make David king—18,000;

³²men of Issachar, who understood the times and knew what Israel should do—200 chiefs, with all their relatives under their command;

³³men of Zebulun, experienced soldiers prepared for battle with every type of weapon, to help David with undivided loyalty—50,000;

³⁴men of Naphtali—1,000 officers, together with 37,000 men carrying shields and spears;

³⁵men of Dan, ready for battle—28,600;

³⁶men of Asher, experienced soldiers prepared for battle—40,000;

³⁷and from east of the Jordan, men of Reuben, Gad and the half-tribe of Manasseh, armed with every type of weapon—120,000.

³⁸All these were fighting men who volunteered to serve in the ranks. They came to Hebron fully determined to make David king over all Israel. All the rest of the Israelites were also of one mind to make David king. ³⁹The men spent three days there with David, eating and drinking, for their families had supplied provisions for them. ⁴⁰Also, their neighbors from as far away as Issachar, Zebulun and Naphtali came bringing food on donkeys, camels, mules and oxen. There were plentiful supplies of flour, fig cakes, raisin cakes, wine, oil, cattle and sheep, for there was joy in Israel.

Bringing Back the Ark

13 David conferred with each of his officers, the commanders of thousands and commanders of hundreds. ²He then said to the whole assembly of Israel, "If it seems good to you and if it is the will of the LORD our God, let us send word far and wide to the rest of our brothers throughout the territories of Israel, and also to the priests and Levites who are with them in their towns and pasturelands, to come and join us. ³Let us bring the ark of our God back to us, for we did not inquire ofᵇ itᶜ during the reign of Saul." ⁴The whole assembly agreed to do this, because it seemed right to all the people.

⁵So David assembled all the Israelites, from the Shihor River in Egypt to Leboᵈ Hamath, to bring the ark of God from Kiriath Jearim. ⁶David and all the Israelites with him went to Baalah of Judah (Kiriath Jearim) to bring up from there the ark of God the LORD, who is enthroned between the cherubim—the ark that is called by the Name.

⁷They moved the ark of God from Abinadab's house on a new cart, with Uzzah and Ahio guiding it. ⁸David and all the Israelites were celebrating with all their might before God, with songs and with harps, lyres, tambourines, cymbals and trumpets.

⁹When they came to the threshing floor of Kidon, Uzzah reached out his hand to steady the ark, because the oxen stumbled. ¹⁰The LORD's anger burned against Uzzah, and he struck him down because he had put his hand on the ark. So he died there before God.

¹¹Then David was angry because the LORD's wrath had broken out against Uzzah, and to this day that place is called Perez Uzzah.ᵃ

¹²David was afraid of God that day and asked, "How can I ever bring the ark of God to me?" ¹³He did not take the ark to be with him in the City of David. Instead, he took it aside to the house of Obed-Edom the Gittite. ¹⁴The ark of God remained with the family of Obed-Edom in his house for three months, and the LORD blessed his household and everything he had.

David's House and Family

14 Now Hiram king of Tyre sent messengers to David, along with cedar logs, stonemasons and carpenters to build a palace for him. ²And David knew that the LORD had established him as king over Israel and that his kingdom had been highly exalted for the sake of his people Israel.

³In Jerusalem David took more wives and became the father of more sons and daughters. ⁴These are the names of the children born to him there: Shammua, Shobab, Nathan, Solomon, ⁵Ibhar, Elishua, Elpelet, ⁶Nogah, Nepheg, Japhia, ⁷Elishama, Beeliadaᵇ and Eliphelet.

David Defeats the Philistines

⁸When the Philistines heard that David had been anointed king over all Israel, they went up in full force to search for him, but David heard about it and went out to meet them. ⁹Now the Philistines had come and raided the Valley of Rephaim; ¹⁰so David inquired of God: "Shall I go and attack the Philistines? Will you hand them over to me?"

The LORD answered him, "Go, I will hand them over to you."

¹¹So David and his men went up to Baal Perazim, and there he defeated them. He said, "As waters break out, God has broken out against my enemies by my hand." So that place was called Baal Perazim.ᶜ ¹²The Philistines had abandoned their gods there, and David gave orders to burn them in the fire.

¹³Once more the Philistines raided the valley; ¹⁴so David inquired of God again, and God answered him, "Do not go straight up, but circle around them and attack them in front of the balsam trees. ¹⁵As soon as you hear the sound of marching in the tops of the balsam trees, move out to battle, because that will mean God has gone out in front of you to strike the Philistine army." ¹⁶So David did as God commanded him, and they struck down the Philistine army, all the way from Gibeon to Gezer.

¹⁷So David's fame spread throughout every land, and the LORD made all the nations fear him.

The Ark Brought to Jerusalem

15 After David had constructed buildings for himself in the City of David, he prepared a place for the ark of God and pitched a tent for it. ²Then David said, "No one but the Levites may carry the ark of God, because the LORD chose them to carry the ark of the LORD and to minister before him forever."

³David assembled all Israel in Jerusalem to bring up the ark of the LORD to the place he had prepared for it. ⁴He called together the descendants of Aaron and the Levites:

⁵From the descendants of Kohath,

Uriel the leader and 120 relatives;

⁶from the descendants of Merari,

Asaiah the leader and 220 relatives;

⁷from the descendants of Gershon,ᵈ

Joel the leader and 130 relatives;

⁸from the descendants of Elizaphan,

ᵃ 11 *Perez Uzzah* means *outbreak against Uzzah.*   ᵇ 7 A variant of *Eliada*   ᶜ 11 *Baal Perazim* means *the lord who breaks out.*   ᵈ 7 Hebrew *Gershom,* a variant of *Gershon*

Shemaiah the leader and 200 relatives;
⁹from the descendants of Hebron,
Eliel the leader and 80 relatives;
¹⁰from the descendants of Uzziel,
Amminadab the leader and 112 relatives.

¹¹Then David summoned Zadok and Abiathar the priests, and Uriel, Asaiah, Joel, She-maiah, Eliel and Amminadab the Levites. ¹²He said to them, "You are the heads of the Levitical families; you and your fellow Levites are to consecrate yourselves and bring up the ark of the LORD, the God of Israel, to the place I have prepared for it. ¹³It was because you, the Levites, did not bring it up the first time that the LORD our God broke out in anger against us. We did not inquire of him about how to do it in the prescribed way." ¹⁴So the priests and Levites consecrated themselves in order to bring up the ark of the LORD, the God of Israel. ¹⁵And the Levites carried the ark of God with the poles on their shoulders, as Moses had commanded in accordance with the word of the LORD.

¹⁶David told the leaders of the Levites to appoint their brothers as singers to sing joyful songs, accompanied by musical instruments: lyres, harps and cymbals.

¹⁷So the Levites appointed Heman son of Joel; from his brothers, Asaph son of Bereki-ah; and from their brothers the Merarites, Ethan son of Kushaiah; ¹⁸and with them their brothers next in rank: Zechariah,ᵃ Jaaziel, Shemiramoth, Jehiel, Unni, Eliab, Benaiah, Maaseiah, Mattithiah, Eliphelehu, Mikneiah, Obed-Edom and Jeiel,ᵇ the gatekeepers.

¹⁹The musicians Heman, Asaph and Ethan were to sound the bronze cymbals; ²⁰Zecha-riah, Aziel, Shemiramoth, Jehiel, Unni, Eliab, Maaseiah and Benaiah were to play the lyres according to alamoth,ᶜ ²¹and Mattithiah, Eliphelehu, Mikneiah, Obed-Edom, Jeiel and Azaziah were to play the harps, directing according to sheminith.ᶜ ²²Kenaniah the head Levite was in charge of the singing; that was his responsibility because he was skillful at it.

²³Berekiah and Elkanah were to be doorkeepers for the ark. ²⁴Shebaniah, Joshaphat, Nethanel, Amasai, Zechariah, Benaiah and Eliezer the priests were to blow trumpets before the ark of God. Obed-Edom and Jehiah were also to be doorkeepers for the ark.

²⁵So David and the elders of Israel and the commanders of units of a thousand went to bring up the ark of the covenant of the LORD from the house of Obed-Edom, with rejoicing. ²⁶Because God had helped the Levites who were carrying the ark of the covenant of the LORD, seven bulls and seven rams were sacrificed. ²⁷Now David was clothed in a robe of fine linen, as were all the Levites who were carrying the ark, and as were the singers, and Kenaniah, who was in charge of the singing of the choirs. David also wore a linen ephod. ²⁸So all Israel brought up the ark of the covenant of the LORD with shouts, with the sounding of rams' horns and trumpets, and of cymbals, and the playing of lyres and harps.

²⁹As the ark of the covenant of the LORD was entering the City of David, Michal daughter of Saul watched from a window. And when she saw King David dancing and celebrating, she despised him in her heart.

16 They brought the ark of God and set it inside the tent that David had pitched for it, and they presented burnt offerings and fellowship offeringsᵈ before God. ²After David had finished sacrificing the burnt offerings and fellowship offerings, he blessed the people in the name of the LORD. ³Then he gave a loaf of bread, a cake of dates and a cake of raisins to each Israelite man and woman.

⁴He appointed some of the Levites to minister before the ark of the LORD, to make petition, to give thanks, and to praise the LORD, the God of Israel: ⁵Asaph was the chief, Zechariah second, then Jeiel, Shemiramoth, Jehiel, Mattithiah, Eliab, Benaiah, Obed-Edom and Jeiel. They were to play the lyres and harps, Asaph was to sound the cymbals,

---

ᵃ18 Three Hebrew manuscripts and most Septuagint manuscripts (see also verse 20 and 1 Chron. 16:5); most Hebrew manuscripts Zechariah son and or Zechariah, Ben and   ᵇ18 Hebrew; Septuagint (see also verse 21) Jeiel and Azaziah   ᶜ20,21 Probably a musical term   ᵈ1 Traditionally peace offerings; also in verse 2

⁶and Benaiah and Jahaziel the priests were to blow the trumpets regularly before the ark of the covenant of God.

David's Psalm of Thanks

⁷That day David first committed to Asaph and his associates this psalm of thanks to the LORD:

⁸Give thanks to the LORD, call on his name;
  make known among the nations what he has done.
⁹Sing to him, sing praise to him;
  tell of all his wonderful acts.
¹⁰Glory in his holy name;
  let the hearts of those who seek the LORD rejoice.
¹¹Look to the LORD and his strength;
  seek his face always.
¹²Remember the wonders he has done,
  his miracles, and the judgments he pronounced,
¹³O descendants of Israel his servant,
  O sons of Jacob, his chosen ones.

¹⁴He is the LORD our God;
  his judgments are in all the earth.
¹⁵He remembers ᵃ his covenant forever,
  the word he commanded, for a thousand generations,
¹⁶the covenant he made with Abraham,
  the oath he swore to Isaac.
¹⁷He confirmed it to Jacob as a decree,
  to Israel as an everlasting covenant:
¹⁸"To you I will give the land of Canaan
  as the portion you will inherit."

¹⁹When they were but few in number,
  few indeed, and strangers in it,
²⁰they ᵇ wandered from nation to nation,
  from one kingdom to another.
²¹He allowed no man to oppress them;
  for their sake he rebuked kings:
²²"Do not touch my anointed ones;
  do my prophets no harm."

²³Sing to the LORD, all the earth;
  proclaim his salvation day after day.
²⁴Declare his glory among the nations,
  his marvelous deeds among all peoples.
²⁵For great is the LORD and most worthy of praise;
  he is to be feared above all gods.
²⁶For all the gods of the nations are idols,
  but the LORD made the heavens.
²⁷Splendor and majesty are before him;
  strength and joy in his dwelling place.
²⁸Ascribe to the LORD, O families of nations,
  ascribe to the LORD glory and strength,

ᵃ15 Some Septuagint manuscripts (see also Psalm 105:8); Hebrew *Remember*   ᵇ18-20 One Hebrew manuscript, Septuagint and Vulgate (see also Psalm 105:12); most Hebrew manuscripts *inherit, / ¹⁹though you are but few in number, / few indeed, and strangers in it." / ²⁰They*

29   ascribe to the LORD the glory due his name.
   Bring an offering and come before him;
      worship the LORD in the splendor of his*a* holiness.
30Tremble before him, all the earth!
     The world is firmly established; it cannot be moved.
31Let the heavens rejoice, let the earth be glad;
     let them say among the nations, "The LORD reigns!"
32Let the sea resound, and all that is in it;
     let the fields be jubilant, and everything in them!
33Then the trees of the forest will sing,
     they will sing for joy before the LORD,
     for he comes to judge the earth.

34Give thanks to the LORD, for he is good;
     his love endures forever.
35Cry out, "Save us, O God our Savior;
     gather us and deliver us from the nations,
   that we may give thanks to your holy name,
   that we may glory in your praise."
36Praise be to the LORD, the God of Israel,
     from everlasting to everlasting.

Then all the people said "Amen" and "Praise the LORD."

37David left Asaph and his associates before the ark of the covenant of the LORD to minister there regularly, according to each day's requirements. 38He also left Obed-Edom and his sixty-eight associates to minister with them. Obed-Edom son of Jeduthun, and also Hosah, were gatekeepers.

39David left Zadok the priest and his fellow priests before the tabernacle of the LORD at the high place in Gibeon 40to present burnt offerings to the LORD on the altar of burnt offering regularly, morning and evening, in accordance with everything written in the Law of the LORD, which he had given Israel. 41With them were Heman and Jeduthun and the rest of those chosen and designated by name to give thanks to the LORD, "for his love endures forever." 42Heman and Jeduthun were responsible for the sounding of the trumpets and cymbals and for the playing of the other instruments for sacred song. The sons of Jeduthun were stationed at the gate.

43Then all the people left, each for his own home, and David returned home to bless his family.

God's Promise to David

17 After David was settled in his palace, he said to Nathan the prophet, "Here I am, living in a palace of cedar, while the ark of the covenant of the LORD is under a tent."

2Nathan replied to David, "Whatever you have in mind, do it, for God is with you."

3That night the word of God came to Nathan, saying:

4"Go and tell my servant David, 'This is what the LORD says: You are not the one to build me a house to dwell in. 5I have not dwelt in a house from the day I brought Israel up out of Egypt to this day. I have moved from one tent site to another, from one dwelling place to another. 6Wherever I have moved with all the Israelites, did I ever say to any of their leaders*b* whom I commanded to shepherd my people, "Why have you not built me a house of cedar?" '

7"Now then, tell my servant David, 'This is what the LORD Almighty says: I took you from the pasture and from following the flock, to be ruler over my people Israel. 8I

a 29 Or LORD *with the splendor of*   *b 6* Traditionally *judges*; also in verse 10

have been with you wherever you have gone, and I have cut off all your enemies from before you. Now I will make your name like the names of the greatest men of the earth. ⁹And I will provide a place for my people Israel and will plant them so that they can have a home of their own and no longer be disturbed. Wicked people will not oppress them anymore, as they did at the beginning ¹⁰and have done ever since the time I appointed leaders over my people Israel. I will also subdue all your enemies.

"'I declare to you that the LORD will build a house for you: ¹¹When your days are over and you go to be with your fathers, I will raise up your offspring to succeed you, one of your own sons, and I will establish his kingdom. ¹²He is the one who will build a house for me, and I will establish his throne forever. ¹³I will be his father, and he will be my son. I will never take my love away from him, as I took it away from your predecessor. ¹⁴I will set him over my house and my kingdom forever; his throne will be established forever.'"

¹⁵Nathan reported to David all the words of this entire revelation.

David's Prayer

¹⁶Then King David went in and sat before the LORD, and he said:

"Who am I, O LORD God, and what is my family, that you have brought me this far? ¹⁷And as if this were not enough in your sight, O God, you have spoken about the future of the house of your servant. You have looked on me as though I were the most exalted of men, O LORD God.

¹⁸"What more can David say to you for honoring your servant? For you know your servant, ¹⁹O LORD. For the sake of your servant and according to your will, you have done this great thing and made known all these great promises.

²⁰"There is no one like you, O LORD, and there is no God but you, as we have heard with our own ears. ²¹And who is like your people Israel—the one nation on earth whose God went out to redeem a people for himself, and to make a name for yourself, and to perform great and awesome wonders by driving out nations from before your people, whom you redeemed from Egypt? ²²You made your people Israel your very own forever, and you, O LORD, have become their God.

²³"And now, LORD, let the promise you have made concerning your servant and his house be established forever. Do as you promised, ²⁴so that it will be established and that your name will be great forever. Then men will say, 'The LORD Almighty, the God over Israel, is Israel's God!' And the house of your servant David will be established before you.

²⁵"You, my God, have revealed to your servant that you will build a house for him. So your servant has found courage to pray to you. ²⁶O LORD, you are God! You have

promised these good things to your servant. ²⁷Now you have been pleased to bless the house of your servant, that it may continue forever in your sight; for you, O LORD, have blessed it, and it will be blessed forever."

David's Victories

18 In the course of time, David defeated the Philistines and subdued them, and he took Gath and its surrounding villages from the control of the Philistines. ²David also defeated the Moabites, and they became subject to him and brought tribute.

³Moreover, David fought Hadadezer king of Zobah, as far as Hamath, when he went to establish his control along the Euphrates River. ⁴David captured a thousand of his chariots, seven thousand charioteers and twenty thousand foot soldiers. He hamstrung all but a hundred of the chariot horses.

⁵When the Arameans of Damascus came to help Hadadezer king of Zobah, David struck down twenty-two thousand of them. ⁶He put garrisons in the Aramean kingdom of Damascus, and the Arameans became subject to him and brought tribute. The LORD gave David victory everywhere he went.

⁷David took the gold shields carried by the officers of Hadadezer and brought them to Jerusalem. ⁸From Tebah*ᵃ* and Cun, towns that belonged to Hadadezer, David took a great quantity of bronze, which Solomon used to make the bronze Sea, the pillars and various bronze articles.

⁹When Tou king of Hamath heard that David had defeated the entire army of Hadadezer king of Zobah, ¹⁰he sent his son Hadoram to King David to greet him and congratulate him on his victory in battle over Hadadezer, who had been at war with Tou. Hadoram brought all kinds of articles of gold and silver and bronze.

¹¹King David dedicated these articles to the LORD, as he had done with the silver and gold he had taken from all these nations: Edom and Moab, the Ammonites and the Philistines, and Amalek.

¹²Abishai son of Zeruiah struck down eighteen thousand Edomites in the Valley of Salt. ¹³He put garrisons in Edom, and all the Edomites became subject to David. The LORD gave David victory everywhere he went.

David's Officials

¹⁴David reigned over all Israel, doing what was just and right for all his people. ¹⁵Joab son of Zeruiah was over the army; Jehoshaphat son of Ahilud was recorder; ¹⁶Zadok son of Ahitub and Ahimelech*ᵇ* son of Abiathar were priests; Shavsha was secretary; ¹⁷Benaiah son of Jehoiada was over the Kerethites and Pelethites; and David's sons were chief officials at the king's side.

The Battle Against the Ammonites

19 In the course of time, Nahash king of the Ammonites died, and his son succeeded him as king. ²David thought, "I will show kindness to Hanun son of Nahash, because his father showed kindness to me." So David sent a delegation to express his sympathy to Hanun concerning his father.

When David's men came to Hanun in the land of the Ammonites to express sympathy to him, ³the Ammonite nobles said to Hanun, "Do you think David is honoring your father by sending men to you to express sympathy? Haven't his men come to you to explore and spy out the country and overthrow it?" ⁴So Hanun seized David's men, shaved them, cut off their garments in the middle at the buttocks, and sent them away.

⁵When someone came and told David about the men, he sent messengers to meet

ᵃ8 Hebrew Tibhath, a variant of Tebah   ᵇ16 Some Hebrew manuscripts, Vulgate and Syriac (see also 2 Samuel 8:17); most Hebrew manuscripts Abimelech

them, for they were greatly humiliated. The king said, "Stay at Jericho till your beards have grown, and then come back."

⁶When the Ammonites realized that they had become a stench in David's nostrils, Hanun and the Ammonites sent a thousand talents*a* of silver to hire chariots and charioteers from Aram Naharaim,*b* Aram Maacah and Zobah. ⁷They hired thirty-two thousand chariots and charioteers, as well as the king of Maacah with his troops, who came and camped near Medeba, while the Ammonites were mustered from their towns and moved out for battle.

⁸On hearing this, David sent Joab out with the entire army of fighting men. ⁹The Ammonites came out and drew up in battle formation at the entrance to their city, while the kings who had come were by themselves in the open country.

¹⁰Joab saw that there were battle lines in front of him and behind him; so he selected some of the best troops in Israel and deployed them against the Arameans. ¹¹He put the rest of the men under the command of Abishai his brother, and they were deployed against the Ammonites. ¹²Joab said, "If the Arameans are too strong for me, then you are to rescue me; but if the Ammonites are too strong for you, then I will rescue you. ¹³Be strong and let us fight bravely for our people and the cities of our God. The Lord will do what is good in his sight."

¹⁴Then Joab and the troops with him advanced to fight the Arameans, and they fled before him. ¹⁵When the Ammonites saw that the Arameans were fleeing, they too fled before his brother Abishai and went inside the city. So Joab went back to Jerusalem.

¹⁶After the Arameans saw that they had been routed by Israel, they sent messengers and had Arameans brought from beyond the River,*c* with Shophach the commander of Hadadezer's army leading them.

¹⁷When David was told of this, he gathered all Israel and crossed the Jordan; he advanced against them and formed his battle lines opposite them. David formed his lines to meet the Arameans in battle, and they fought against him. ¹⁸But they fled before Israel, and David killed seven thousand of their charioteers and forty thousand of their foot soldiers. He also killed Shophach the commander of their army.

¹⁹When the vassals of Hadadezer saw that they had been defeated by Israel, they made peace with David and became subject to him.

So the Arameans were not willing to help the Ammonites anymore.

The Capture of Rabbah

20 In the spring, at the time when kings go off to war, Joab led out the armed forces. He laid waste the land of the Ammonites and went to Rabbah and besieged it, but David remained in Jerusalem. Joab attacked Rabbah and left it in ruins. ²David took the crown from the head of their king*d*—its weight was found to be a talent*e* of gold, and it was set with precious stones—and it was placed on David's head. He took a great quantity of plunder from the city ³and brought out the people who were there, consigning them to labor with saws and with iron picks and axes. David did this to all the Ammonite towns. Then David and his entire army returned to Jerusalem.

War With the Philistines

⁴In the course of time, war broke out with the Philistines, at Gezer. At that time Sibbecai the Hushathite killed Sippai, one of the descendants of the Rephaites, and the Philistines were subjugated.

⁵In another battle with the Philistines, Elhanan son of Jair killed Lahmi the brother of Goliath the Gittite, who had a spear with a shaft like a weaver's rod.

⁶In still another battle, which took place at Gath, there was a huge man with six fingers on each hand and six toes on each foot—twenty-four in all. He also was descend-

a6 That is, about 37 tons (about 34 metric tons)   *b6* That is, Northwest Mesopotamia   *c16* That is, the Euphrates
d2 Or of Milcom, that is, Molech   *e2* That is, about 75 pounds (about 34 kilograms)

ed from Rapha. ⁷When he taunted Israel, Jonathan son of Shimea, David's brother, killed him.

⁸These were descendants of Rapha in Gath, and they fell at the hands of David and his men.

David Numbers the Fighting Men

21 Satan rose up against Israel and incited David to take a census of Israel. ²So David said to Joab and the commanders of the troops, "Go and count the Israelites from Beersheba to Dan. Then report back to me so that I may know how many there are."

³But Joab replied, "May the LORD multiply his troops a hundred times over. My lord the king, are they not all my lord's subjects? Why does my lord want to do this? Why should he bring guilt on Israel?"

⁴The king's word, however, overruled Joab; so Joab left and went throughout Israel and then came back to Jerusalem. ⁵Joab reported the number of the fighting men to David: In all Israel there were one million one hundred thousand men who could handle a sword, including four hundred and seventy thousand in Judah.

⁶But Joab did not include Levi and Benjamin in the numbering, because the king's command was repulsive to him. ⁷This command was also evil in the sight of God; so he punished Israel.

⁸Then David said to God, "I have sinned greatly by doing this. Now, I beg you, take away the guilt of your servant. I have done a very foolish thing."

⁹The LORD said to Gad, David's seer, ¹⁰"Go and tell David, 'This is what the LORD says: I am giving you three options. Choose one of them for me to carry out against you.'"

¹¹So Gad went to David and said to him, "This is what the LORD says: 'Take your choice: ¹²three years of famine, three months of being swept away[a] before your enemies, with their swords overtaking you, or three days of the sword of the LORD—days of plague in the land, with the angel of the LORD ravaging every part of Israel.' Now then, decide how I should answer the one who sent me."

¹³David said to Gad, "I am in deep distress. Let me fall into the hands of the LORD, for his mercy is very great; but do not let me fall into the hands of men."

¹⁴So the LORD sent a plague on Israel, and seventy thousand men of Israel fell dead. ¹⁵And God sent an angel to destroy Jerusalem. But as the angel was doing so, the LORD saw it and was grieved because of the calamity and said to the angel who was destroying the people, "Enough! Withdraw your hand." The angel of the LORD was then standing at the threshing floor of Araunah[b] the Jebusite.

¹⁶David looked up and saw the angel of the LORD standing between heaven and earth, with a drawn sword in his hand extended over Jerusalem. Then David and the elders, clothed in sackcloth, fell facedown.

¹⁷David said to God, "Was it not I who ordered the fighting men to be counted? I am the one who has sinned and done wrong. These are but sheep. What have they done? O LORD my God, let your hand fall upon me and my family, but do not let this plague remain on your people."

¹⁸Then the angel of the LORD ordered Gad to tell David to go up and build an altar to the LORD on the threshing floor of Araunah the Jebusite. ¹⁹So David went up in obedience to the word that Gad had spoken in the name of the LORD.

²⁰While Araunah was threshing wheat, he turned and saw the angel; his four sons who were with him hid themselves. ²¹Then David approached, and when Araunah looked and saw him, he left the threshing floor and bowed down before David with his face to the ground.

²²David said to him, "Let me have the site of your threshing floor so I can build an altar

---

a 12 Hebrew; Septuagint and Vulgate (see also 2 Samuel 24:13) *of fleeing*   b 15 Hebrew *Ornan*, a variant of *Araunah*; also in verses 18–28

to the LORD, that the plague on the people may be stopped. Sell it to me at the full price."

²³Araunah said to David, "Take it! Let my lord the king do whatever pleases him. Look, I will give the oxen for the burnt offerings, the threshing sledges for the wood, and the wheat for the grain offering. I will give all this."

²⁴But King David replied to Araunah, "No, I insist on paying the full price. I will not take for the LORD what is yours, or sacrifice a burnt offering that costs me nothing."

²⁵So David paid Araunah six hundred shekels*a* of gold for the site. ²⁶David built an altar to the LORD there and sacrificed burnt offerings and fellowship offerings.*b* He called on the LORD, and the LORD answered him with fire from heaven on the altar of burnt offering.

²⁷Then the LORD spoke to the angel, and he put his sword back into its sheath. ²⁸At that time, when David saw that the LORD had answered him on the threshing floor of Araunah the Jebusite, he offered sacrifices there. ²⁹The tabernacle of the LORD, which Moses had made in the desert, and the altar of burnt offering were at that time on the high place at Gibeon. ³⁰But David could not go before it to inquire of God, because he was afraid of the sword of the angel of the LORD.

22 Then David said, "The house of the LORD God is to be here, and also the altar of burnt offering for Israel."

Preparations for the Temple

²So David gave orders to assemble the aliens living in Israel, and from among them he appointed stonecutters to prepare dressed stone for building the house of God. ³He provided a large amount of iron to make nails for the doors of the gateways and for the fittings, and more bronze than could be weighed. ⁴He also provided more cedar logs than could be counted, for the Sidonians and Tyrians had brought large numbers of them to David.

⁵David said, "My son Solomon is young and inexperienced, and the house to be built for the LORD should be of great magnificence and fame and splendor in the sight of all the nations. Therefore I will make preparations for it." So David made extensive preparations before his death.

⁶Then he called for his son Solomon and charged him to build a house for the LORD, the God of Israel. ⁷David said to Solomon: "My son, I had it in my heart to build a house for the Name of the LORD my God. ⁸But this word of the LORD came to me: 'You have shed much blood and have fought many wars. You are not to build a house for my Name, because you have shed much blood on the earth in my sight. ⁹But you will have a son who will be a man of peace and rest, and I will give him rest from all his enemies on every side. His name will be Solomon,*c* and I will grant Israel peace and quiet during his reign. ¹⁰He is the one who will build a house for my Name. He will be my son, and I will be his father. And I will establish the throne of his kingdom over Israel forever.'

¹¹"Now, my son, the LORD be with you, and may you have success and build the house of the LORD your God, as he said you would. ¹²May the LORD give you discretion and understanding when he puts you in command over Israel, so that you may keep the law of the LORD your God. ¹³Then you will have success if you are careful to observe the decrees and laws that the LORD gave Moses for Israel. Be strong and courageous. Do not be afraid or discouraged.

¹⁴"I have taken great pains to provide for the temple of the LORD a hundred thousand talents*d* of gold, a million talents*e* of silver, quantities of bronze and iron too great to be weighed, and wood and stone. And you may add to them. ¹⁵You have many workmen: stonecutters, masons and carpenters, as well as men skilled in every kind of work ¹⁶in

a25 That is, about 15 pounds (about 7 kilograms)   *b26* Traditionally peace offerings   *c9* Solomon sounds like and may be derived from the Hebrew for peace.   *d14* That is, about 3,750 tons (about 3,450 metric tons)   *e14* That is, about 37,500 tons (about 34,500 metric tons)

gold and silver, bronze and iron—craftsmen beyond number. Now begin the work, and the LORD be with you."

[17]Then David ordered all the leaders of Israel to help his son Solomon. [18]He said to them, "Is not the LORD your God with you? And has he not granted you rest on every side? For he has handed the inhabitants of the land over to me, and the land is subject to the LORD and to his people. [19]Now devote your heart and soul to seeking the LORD your God. Begin to build the sanctuary of the LORD God, so that you may bring the ark of the covenant of the LORD and the sacred articles belonging to God into the temple that will be built for the Name of the LORD."

The Levites

23 When David was old and full of years, he made his son Solomon king over Israel.

[2]He also gathered together all the leaders of Israel, as well as the priests and Levites. [3]The Levites thirty years old or more were counted, and the total number of men was thirty-eight thousand. [4]David said, "Of these, twenty-four thousand are to supervise the work of the temple of the LORD and six thousand are to be officials and judges. [5]Four thousand are to be gatekeepers and four thousand are to praise the LORD with the musical instruments I have provided for that purpose."

[6]David divided the Levites into groups corresponding to the sons of Levi: Gershon, Kohath and Merari.

Gershonites

[7]Belonging to the Gershonites:
Ladan and Shimei.
[8]The sons of Ladan:
Jehiel the first, Zetham and Joel—three in all.
[9]The sons of Shimei:
Shelomoth, Haziel and Haran—three in all.
These were the heads of the families of Ladan.
[10]And the sons of Shimei:
Jahath, Ziza,[a] Jeush and Beriah.
These were the sons of Shimei—four in all.
[11]Jahath was the first and Ziza the second, but Jeush and Beriah did not have many sons; so they were counted as one family with one assignment.

Kohathites

[12]The sons of Kohath:
Amram, Izhar, Hebron and Uzziel—four in all.
[13]The sons of Amram:
Aaron and Moses.
Aaron was set apart, he and his descendants forever, to consecrate the most holy things, to offer sacrifices before the LORD, to minister before him and to pronounce blessings in his name forever. [14]The sons of Moses the man of God were counted as part of the tribe of Levi.
[15]The sons of Moses:
Gershom and Eliezer.
[16]The descendants of Gershom:
Shubael was the first.
[17]The descendants of Eliezer:
Rehabiah was the first.
Eliezer had no other sons, but the sons of Rehabiah were very numerous.

a 10 One Hebrew manuscript, Septuagint and Vulgate (see also verse 11); most Hebrew manuscripts Zina

¹⁸The sons of Izhar:

Shelomith was the first.

¹⁹The sons of Hebron:

Jeriah the first, Amariah the second, Jahaziel the third and Jekameam the fourth.

²⁰The sons of Uzziel:

Micah the first and Isshiah the second.

Merarites

²¹The sons of Merari:

Mahli and Mushi.

The sons of Mahli:

Eleazar and Kish.

²²Eleazar died without having sons: he had only daughters. Their cousins, the sons of Kish, married them.

²³The sons of Mushi:

Mahli, Eder and Jerimoth—three in all.

²⁴These were the descendants of Levi by their families—the heads of families as they were registered under their names and counted individually, that is, the workers twenty years old or more who served in the temple of the LORD. ²⁵For David had said, "Since the LORD, the God of Israel, has granted rest to his people and has come to dwell in Jerusalem forever, ²⁶the Levites no longer need to carry the tabernacle or any of the articles used in its service." ²⁷According to the last instructions of David, the Levites were counted from those twenty years old or more.

²⁸The duty of the Levites was to help Aaron's descendants in the service of the temple of the LORD: to be in charge of the courtyards, the side rooms, the purification of all sacred things and the performance of other duties at the house of God. ²⁹They were in charge of the bread set out on the table, the flour for the grain offerings, the unleavened wafers, the baking and the mixing, and all measurements of quantity and size. ³⁰They were also to stand every morning to thank and praise the LORD. They were to do the same in the evening ³¹and whenever burnt offerings were presented to the LORD on Sabbaths and at New Moon festivals and at appointed feasts. They were to serve before the LORD regularly in the proper number and in the way prescribed for them.

▣ ▦▦▦▦ **KNOWING YOURSELF** ▦▦▦ ⊟

23:28–29
A New Identity

Who were these people, and how is it that they got recognized in the Bible?

These individuals were the "little people" who attended to the daily worship operations of Israel. The fact that this and the next few chapters detail the responsibilities of such people is important for us today. This listing clearly indicates that God uses all kinds of people for his service—not just the visionaries. To be sure, God honors the "big names" of this world; but he also honors the millions who work quietly behind the scenes to build his kingdom.

As you continue to seek God, try to discover which of your abilities can be used in his service. Are you a skilled carpenter? Perhaps you could work on a low-income housing project. Are you a shrewd businessperson? Maybe you could use that ability to help a colleague get out of debt. Do you have a knack for taking care of children? Why not take some pressure off of that struggling single parent down the street? Whatever your talent, God wants to use it for his service.

---

³²And so the Levites carried out their responsibilities for the Tent of Meeting, for the Holy Place and, under their brothers the descendants of Aaron, for the service of the temple of the LORD.

The Divisions of Priests

24 These were the divisions of the sons of Aaron:

The sons of Aaron were Nadab, Abihu, Eleazar and Ithamar. ²But Nadab and Abihu died before their father did, and they had no sons; so Eleazar and Ithamar served as the priests. ³With the help of Zadok a descendant of Eleazar and Ahimelech a descendant of Ithamar, David separated them into divisions for their appointed order of ministering. ⁴A larger number of leaders were found among Eleazar's descendants than among Ithamar's, and they were divided accordingly: sixteen heads of families from Eleazar's descendants and eight heads of families from Ithamar's descendants. ⁵They divided them impartially by drawing lots, for there were officials of the sanctuary and officials of God among the descendants of both Eleazar and Ithamar.

⁶The scribe Shemaiah son of Nethanel, a Levite, recorded their names in the presence of the king and of the officials: Zadok the priest, Ahimelech son of Abiathar and the heads of families of the priests and of the Levites—one family being taken from Eleazar and then one from Ithamar.

⁷The first lot fell to Jehoiarib,
  the second to Jedaiah,
⁸the third to Harim,
  the fourth to Seorim,
⁹the fifth to Malkijah,
  the sixth to Mijamin,
¹⁰the seventh to Hakkoz,
  the eighth to Abijah,
¹¹the ninth to Jeshua,
  the tenth to Shecaniah,
¹²the eleventh to Eliashib,
  the twelfth to Jakim,
¹³the thirteenth to Huppah,
  the fourteenth to Jeshebeab,
¹⁴the fifteenth to Bilgah,
  the sixteenth to Immer,
¹⁵the seventeenth to Hezir,
  the eighteenth to Happizzez,
¹⁶the nineteenth to Pethahiah,
  the twentieth to Jehezkel,
¹⁷the twenty-first to Jakin,
  the twenty-second to Gamul,
¹⁸the twenty-third to Delaiah
  and the twenty-fourth to Maaziah.

¹⁹This was their appointed order of ministering when they entered the temple of the Lord, according to the regulations prescribed for them by their forefather Aaron, as the Lord, the God of Israel, had commanded him.

The Rest of the Levites

²⁰As for the rest of the descendants of Levi:
  from the sons of Amram: Shubael;
    from the sons of Shubael: Jehdeiah.
  ²¹As for Rehabiah, from his sons:
    Isshiah was the first.
²²From the Izharites: Shelomoth;
    from the sons of Shelomoth: Jahath.

²³The sons of Hebron: Jeriah the first,ᵃ Amariah the second, Jahaziel the third and Jekameam the fourth.
²⁴The son of Uzziel: Micah;
from the sons of Micah: Shamir.
²⁵The brother of Micah: Isshiah;
from the sons of Isshiah: Zechariah.
²⁶The sons of Merari: Mahli and Mushi.
The son of Jaaziah: Beno.
²⁷The sons of Merari:
from Jaaziah: Beno, Shoham, Zaccur and Ibri.
²⁸From Mahli: Eleazar, who had no sons.
²⁹From Kish: the son of Kish:
Jerahmeel.
³⁰And the sons of Mushi: Mahli, Eder and Jerimoth.

These were the Levites, according to their families. ³¹They also cast lots, just as their brothers the descendants of Aaron did, in the presence of King David and of Zadok, Ahimelech, and the heads of families of the priests and of the Levites. The families of the oldest brother were treated the same as those of the youngest.

The Singers

25 David, together with the commanders of the army, set apart some of the sons of Asaph, Heman and Jeduthun for the ministry of prophesying, accompanied by harps, lyres and cymbals. Here is the list of the men who performed this service:

²From the sons of Asaph:
Zaccur, Joseph, Nethaniah and Asarelah. The sons of Asaph were under the supervision of Asaph, who prophesied under the king's supervision.
³As for Jeduthun, from his sons:
Gedaliah, Zeri, Jeshaiah, Shimei,ᵇ Hashabiah and Mattithiah, six in all, under the supervision of their father Jeduthun, who prophesied, using the harp in thanking and praising the LORD.
⁴As for Heman, from his sons:
Bukkiah, Mattaniah, Uzziel, Shubael and Jerimoth; Hananiah, Hanani, Eliathah, Giddalti and Romamti-Ezer; Joshbekashah, Mallothi, Hothir and Mahazioth. ⁵All these were sons of Heman the king's seer. They were given him through the promises of God to exalt him.ᶜ God gave Heman fourteen sons and three daughters.

⁶All these men were under the supervision of their fathers for the music of the temple of the LORD, with cymbals, lyres and harps, for the ministry at the house of God. Asaph, Jeduthun and Heman were under the supervision of the king. ⁷Along with their relatives—all of them trained and skilled in music for the LORD—they numbered 288. ⁸Young and old alike, teacher as well as student, cast lots for their duties.

⁹The first lot, which was for Asaph, fell to Joseph, his sons and relatives,ᵈ	12ᵉ
the second to Gedaliah, he and his relatives and sons,	12
¹⁰the third to Zaccur, his sons and relatives,	12
¹¹the fourth to Izri,ᶠ his sons and relatives,	12

ᵃ23 Two Hebrew manuscripts and some Septuagint manuscripts (see also 1 Chron. 23:19); most Hebrew manuscripts *The sons of Jeriah:*   ᵇ3 One Hebrew manuscript and some Septuagint manuscripts (see also verse 17); most Hebrew manuscripts do not have *Shimei.*   ᶜ5 Hebrew *exalt the horn*   ᵈ9 See Septuagint; Hebrew does not have *his sons and relatives.*   ᵉ9 See the total in verse 7; Hebrew does not have *twelve.*   ᶠ11 A variant of *Zeri*

¹²the fifth to Nethaniah,
    his sons and relatives,   12
¹³the sixth to Bukkiah,
    his sons and relatives,   12
¹⁴the seventh to Jesarelah,ᵃ
    his sons and relatives,   12
¹⁵the eighth to Jeshaiah,
    his sons and relatives,   12
¹⁶the ninth to Mattaniah,
    his sons and relatives,   12
¹⁷the tenth to Shimei,
    his sons and relatives,   12
¹⁸the eleventh to Azarel,ᵇ
    his sons and relatives,   12
¹⁹the twelfth to Hashabiah,
    his sons and relatives,   12
²⁰the thirteenth to Shubael,
    his sons and relatives,   12
²¹the fourteenth to Mattithiah,
    his sons and relatives,   12
²²the fifteenth to Jerimoth,
    his sons and relatives,   12
²³the sixteenth to Hananiah,
    his sons and relatives,   12
²⁴the seventeenth to Joshbekashah,
    his sons and relatives,   12
²⁵the eighteenth to Hanani,
    his sons and relatives,   12
²⁶the nineteenth to Mallothi,
    his sons and relatives,   12
²⁷the twentieth to Eliathah,
    his sons and relatives,   12
²⁸the twenty-first to Hothir,
    his sons and relatives,   12
²⁹the twenty-second to Giddalti,
    his sons and relatives,   12
³⁰the twenty-third to Mahazioth,
    his sons and relatives,   12
³¹the twenty-fourth to Romamti-Ezer,
    his sons and relatives,   12

The Gatekeepers

26 The divisions of the gatekeepers:

From the Korahites: Meshelemiah son of Kore, one of the sons of Asaph.
²Meshelemiah had sons:
    Zechariah the firstborn,
    Jediael the second,
    Zebadiah the third,
    Jathniel the fourth,
    ³Elam the fifth,
    Jehohanan the sixth

ᵃ 14 A variant of *Asarelah*   ᵇ 18 A variant of *Uzziel*

and Eliehoenai the seventh.
⁴Obed-Edom also had sons:
Shemaiah the firstborn,
Jehozabad the second,
Joah the third,
Sacar the fourth,
Nethanel the fifth,
⁵Ammiel the sixth,
Issachar the seventh
and Peullethai the eighth.
(For God had blessed Obed-Edom.)

⁶His son Shemaiah also had sons, who were leaders in their father's family because they were very capable men. ⁷The sons of Shemaiah: Othni, Rephael, Obed and Elzabad; his relatives Elihu and Semakiah were also able men. ⁸All these were descendants of Obed-Edom; they and their sons and their relatives were capable men with the strength to do the work—descendants of Obed-Edom, 62 in all. ⁹Meshelemiah had sons and relatives, who were able men—18 in all.

¹⁰Hosah the Merarite had sons: Shimri the first (although he was not the firstborn, his father had appointed him the first), ¹¹Hilkiah the second, Tabaliah the third and Zechariah the fourth. The sons and relatives of Hosah were 13 in all.

¹²These divisions of the gatekeepers, through their chief men, had duties for ministering in the temple of the LORD, just as their relatives had. ¹³Lots were cast for each gate, according to their families, young and old alike.

¹⁴The lot for the East Gate fell to Shelemiah.ᵃ Then lots were cast for his son Zechariah, a wise counselor, and the lot for the North Gate fell to him. ¹⁵The lot for the South Gate fell to Obed-Edom, and the lot for the storehouse fell to his sons. ¹⁶The lots for the West Gate and the Shalleketh Gate on the upper road fell to Shuppim and Hosah.

Guard was alongside of guard: ¹⁷There were six Levites a day on the east, four a day on the north, four a day on the south and two at a time at the storehouse. ¹⁸As for the court to the west, there were four at the road and two at the court itself.

¹⁹These were the divisions of the gatekeepers who were descendants of Korah and Merari.

The Treasurers and Other Officials

²⁰Their fellow Levites wereᵇ in charge of the treasuries of the house of God and the treasuries for the dedicated things.

²¹The descendants of Ladan, who were Gershonites through Ladan and who were heads of families belonging to Ladan the Gershonite, were Jehieli, ²²the sons of Jehieli, Zetham and his brother Joel. They were in charge of the treasuries of the temple of the LORD.

²³From the Amramites, the Izharites, the Hebronites and the Uzzielites:

²⁴Shubael, a descendant of Gershom the son of Moses, was the officer in charge of the treasuries. ²⁵His relatives through Eliezer: Rehabiah his son, Jeshaiah his son, Joram his son, Zicri his son and Shelomith his son. ²⁶Shelomith and his relatives were in charge of all the treasuries for the things dedicated by King David, by the heads of families who were the commanders of thousands and commanders of hundreds, and by the other army commanders. ²⁷Some of the plunder taken in battle they dedicated for the repair of the temple of the LORD. ²⁸And everything dedicated by Samuel the seer and by Saul son of Kish, Abner son of Ner and Joab

---

ᵃ 14 A variant of *Meshelemiah*   ᵇ 20 Septuagint; Hebrew *As for the Levites, Ahijah was*

son of Zeruiah, and all the other dedicated things were in the care of Shelomith and his relatives.

²⁹From the Izharites: Kenaniah and his sons were assigned duties away from the temple, as officials and judges over Israel.

³⁰From the Hebronites: Hashabiah and his relatives—seventeen hundred able men—were responsible in Israel west of the Jordan for all the work of the LORD and for the king's service. ³¹As for the Hebronites, Jeriah was their chief according to the genealogical records of their families. In the fortieth year of David's reign a search was made in the records, and capable men among the Hebronites were found at Jazer in Gilead. ³²Jeriah had twenty-seven hundred relatives, who were able men and heads of families, and King David put them in charge of the Reubenites, the Gadites and the half-tribe of Manasseh for every matter pertaining to God and for the affairs of the king.

Army Divisions

27 This is the list of the Israelites—heads of families, commanders of thousands and commanders of hundreds, and their officers, who served the king in all that concerned the army divisions that were on duty month by month throughout the year. Each division consisted of 24,000 men.

²In charge of the first division, for the first month, was Jashobeam son of Zabdiel. There were 24,000 men in his division. ³He was a descendant of Perez and chief of all the army officers for the first month.

⁴In charge of the division for the second month was Dodai the Ahohite; Mikloth was the leader of his division. There were 24,000 men in his division.

⁵The third army commander, for the third month, was Benaiah son of Jehoiada the priest. He was chief and there were 24,000 men in his division. ⁶This was the Benaiah who was a mighty man among the Thirty and was over the Thirty. His son Ammizabad was in charge of his division.

⁷The fourth, for the fourth month, was Asahel the brother of Joab; his son Zebadiah was his successor. There were 24,000 men in his division.

⁸The fifth, for the fifth month, was the commander Shamhuth the Izrahite. There were 24,000 men in his division.

⁹The sixth, for the sixth month, was Ira the son of Ikkesh the Tekoite. There were 24,000 men in his division.

¹⁰The seventh, for the seventh month, was Helez the Pelonite, an Ephraimite. There were 24,000 men in his division.

¹¹The eighth, for the eighth month, was Sibbecai the Hushathite, a Zerahite. There were 24,000 men in his division.

¹²The ninth, for the ninth month, was Abiezer the Anathothite, a Benjamite. There were 24,000 men in his division.

¹³The tenth, for the tenth month, was Maharai the Netophathite, a Zerahite. There were 24,000 men in his division.

¹⁴The eleventh, for the eleventh month, was Benaiah the Pirathonite, an Ephraimite. There were 24,000 men in his division.

¹⁵The twelfth, for the twelfth month, was Heldai the Netophathite, from the family of Othniel. There were 24,000 men in his division.

Officers of the Tribes

¹⁶The officers over the tribes of Israel:

over the Reubenites: Eliezer son of Zicri;
over the Simeonites: Shephatiah son of Maacah;
¹⁷over Levi: Hashabiah son of Kemuel;

over Aaron: Zadok;
¹⁸over Judah: Elihu, a brother of David;
over Issachar: Omri son of Michael;
¹⁹over Zebulun: Ishmaiah son of Obadiah;
over Naphtali: Jerimoth son of Azriel;
²⁰over the Ephraimites: Hoshea son of Azaziah;
over half the tribe of Manasseh: Joel son of Pedaiah;
²¹over the half-tribe of Manasseh in Gilead: Iddo son of Zechariah;
over Benjamin: Jaasiel son of Abner;
²²over Dan: Azarel son of Jeroham.
These were the officers over the tribes of Israel.

²³David did not take the number of the men twenty years old or less, because the LORD had promised to make Israel as numerous as the stars in the sky. ²⁴Joab son of Zeruiah began to count the men but did not finish. Wrath came on Israel on account of this numbering, and the number was not entered in the book^a of the annals of King David.

The King's Overseers

²⁵Azmaveth son of Adiel was in charge of the royal storehouses.
Jonathan son of Uzziah was in charge of the storehouses in the outlying districts, in the towns, the villages and the watchtowers.
²⁶Ezri son of Kelub was in charge of the field workers who farmed the land.
²⁷Shimei the Ramathite was in charge of the vineyards.
Zabdi the Shiphmite was in charge of the produce of the vineyards for the wine vats.
²⁸Baal-Hanan the Gederite was in charge of the olive and sycamore-fig trees in the western foothills.
Joash was in charge of the supplies of olive oil.
²⁹Shitrai the Sharonite was in charge of the herds grazing in Sharon.
Shaphat son of Adlai was in charge of the herds in the valleys.
³⁰Obil the Ishmaelite was in charge of the camels.
Jehdeiah the Meronothite was in charge of the donkeys.
³¹Jaziz the Hagrite was in charge of the flocks.
All these were the officials in charge of King David's property.

³²Jonathan, David's uncle, was a counselor, a man of insight and a scribe. Jehiel son of Hacmoni took care of the king's sons.
³³Ahithophel was the king's counselor.
Hushai the Arkite was the king's friend. ³⁴Ahithophel was succeeded by Jehoiada son of Benaiah and by Abiathar.
Joab was the commander of the royal army.

David's Plans for the Temple

28 David summoned all the officials of Israel to assemble at Jerusalem: the officers over the tribes, the commanders of the divisions in the service of the king, the commanders of thousands and commanders of hundreds, and the officials in charge of all the property and livestock belonging to the king and his sons, together with the palace officials, the mighty men and all the brave warriors.

²King David rose to his feet and said: "Listen to me, my brothers and my people. I had it in my heart to build a house as a place of rest for the ark of the covenant of the LORD, for the footstool of our God, and I made plans to build it. ³But God said to me, 'You are not to build a house for my Name, because you are a warrior and have shed blood.'

⁴"Yet the LORD, the God of Israel, chose me from my whole family to be king over Israel forever. He chose Judah as leader, and from the house of Judah he chose my family, and

^a24 Septuagint; Hebrew number

from my father's sons he was pleased to make me king over all Israel. ⁵Of all my sons—and the LORD has given me many—he has chosen my son Solomon to sit on the throne of the kingdom of the LORD over Israel. ⁶He said to me: 'Solomon your son is the one who will build my house and my courts, for I have chosen him to be my son, and I will be his father. ⁷I will establish his kingdom forever if he is unswerving in carrying out my commands and laws, as is being done at this time.'

⁸"So now I charge you in the sight of all Israel and of the assembly of the LORD, and in the hearing of our God: Be careful to follow all the commands of the LORD your God, that you may possess this good land and pass it on as an inheritance to your descendants forever.

⁹"And you, my son Solomon, acknowledge the God of your father, and serve him with wholehearted devotion and with a willing mind, for the LORD searches every heart and understands every motive behind the thoughts. If you seek him, he will be found by you; but if you forsake him, he will reject you forever. ¹⁰Consider now, for the LORD has chosen you to build a temple as a sanctuary. Be strong and do the work."

¹¹Then David gave his son Solomon the plans for the portico of the temple, its buildings, its storerooms, its upper parts, its inner rooms and the place of atonement. ¹²He gave him the plans of all that the Spirit had put in his mind for the courts of the temple of the LORD and all the surrounding rooms, for the treasuries of the temple of God and for the treasuries for the dedicated things. ¹³He gave him instructions for the divisions of the priests and Levites, and for all the work of serving in the temple of the LORD, as well as for all the articles to be used in its service. ¹⁴He designated the

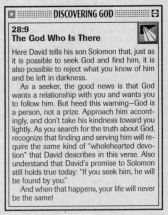

┌─ DISCOVERING GOD ─┐

28:9
The God Who Is There

Here David tells his son Solomon that, just as it is possible to seek God and find him, it is also possible to reject what you know of him and be left in darkness.

As a seeker, the good news is that God wants a relationship with you and wants you to follow him. But heed this warning—God is a person, not a prize. Approach him accordingly, and don't take his kindness toward you lightly. As you search for the truth about God, recognize that finding and serving him will require the same kind of "wholehearted devotion" that David describes in this verse. Also understand that David's promise to Solomon still holds true today: "If you seek him, he will be found by you."

And when that happens, your life will never be the same!

weight of gold for all the gold articles to be used in various kinds of service, and the weight of silver for all the silver articles to be used in various kinds of service: ¹⁵the weight of gold for the gold lampstands and their lamps, with the weight for each lampstand and its lamps; and the weight of silver for each silver lampstand and its lamps, according to the use of each lampstand; ¹⁶the weight of gold for each table for consecrated bread; the weight of silver for the silver tables; ¹⁷the weight of pure gold for the forks, sprinkling bowls and pitchers; the weight of gold for each gold dish; the weight of silver for each silver dish; ¹⁸and the weight of the refined gold for the altar of incense. He also gave him the plan for the chariot, that is, the cherubim of gold that spread their wings and shelter the ark of the covenant of the LORD.

¹⁹"All this," David said, "I have in writing from the hand of the LORD upon me, and he gave me understanding in all the details of the plan."

²⁰David also said to Solomon his son, "Be strong and courageous, and do the work. Do not be afraid or discouraged, for the LORD God, my God, is with you. He will not fail you or forsake you until all the work for the service of the temple of the LORD is finished. ²¹The divisions of the priests and Levites are ready for all the work on the temple of God, and every willing man skilled in any craft will help you in all the work. The officials and all the people will obey your every command."

Gifts for Building the Temple

29 Then King David said to the whole assembly: "My son Solomon, the one whom God has chosen, is young and inexperienced. The task is great, because this palatial structure is not for man but for the LORD God. ²With all my resources I have provided for the temple of my God—gold for the gold work, silver for the silver, bronze for the bronze, iron for the iron and wood for the wood, as well as onyx for the settings, turquoise,ᵃ stones of various colors, and all kinds of fine stone and marble—all of these in large quantities. ³Besides, in my devotion to the temple of my God I now give my personal treasures of gold and silver for the temple of my God, over and above everything I have provided for this holy temple: ⁴three thousand talentsᵇ of gold (gold of Ophir) and seven thousand talentsᶜ of refined silver, for the overlaying of the walls of the buildings, ⁵for the gold work and the silver work, and for all the work to be done by the craftsmen. Now, who is willing to consecrate himself today to the LORD?"

⁶Then the leaders of families, the officers of the tribes of Israel, the commanders of thousands and commanders of hundreds, and the officials in charge of the king's work gave willingly. ⁷They gave toward the work on the temple of God five thousand talentsᵈ and ten thousand daricsᵉ of gold, ten thousand talentsᶠ of silver, eighteen thousand talentsᵍ of bronze and a hundred thousand talentsʰ of iron. ⁸Any who had precious stones gave them to the treasury of the temple of the LORD in the custody of Jehiel the Gershonite. ⁹The people rejoiced at the willing response of their leaders, for they had given freely and wholeheartedly to the LORD. David the king also rejoiced greatly.

David's Prayer

¹⁰David praised the LORD in the presence of the whole assembly, saying,

> "Praise be to you, O LORD,
>   God of our father Israel,
>   from everlasting to everlasting.
> ¹¹Yours, O LORD, is the greatness and the power
>   and the glory and the majesty and the splendor,
>   for everything in heaven and earth is yours.
> Yours, O LORD, is the kingdom;
>   you are exalted as head over all.
> ¹²Wealth and honor come from you;
>   you are the ruler of all things.
> In your hands are strength and power
>   to exalt and give strength to all.
> ¹³Now, our God, we give you thanks,
>   and praise your glorious name.

¹⁴"But who am I, and who are my people, that we should be able to give as generously as this? Everything comes from you, and we have given you only what comes from your hand. ¹⁵We are aliens and strangers in your sight, as were all our forefathers. Our days on earth are like a shadow, without hope. ¹⁶O LORD our God, as for all this abundance that we have provided for building you a temple for your Holy Name, it comes from your hand, and all of it belongs to you. ¹⁷I know, my God, that you test the heart and are pleased with integrity. All these things have I given willingly and with honest intent. And now I have seen with joy how willingly your people who are here have given to you. ¹⁸O LORD, God of our fathers Abraham, Isaac and Israel, keep this desire in the hearts of your people forever, and keep their hearts loyal to you. ¹⁹And give my son Solomon the wholehearted

---

ᵃ2 The meaning of the Hebrew for this word is uncertain.   ᵇ4 That is, about 110 tons (about 100 metric tons)   ᶜ4 That is, about 260 tons (about 240 metric tons)   ᵈ7 That is, about 190 tons (about 170 metric tons)   ᵉ7 That is, about 185 pounds (about 84 kilograms)   ᶠ7 That is, about 375 tons (about 345 metric tons)   ᵍ7 That is, about 675 tons (about 610 metric tons)   ʰ7 That is, about 3,750 tons (about 3,450 metric tons)

devotion to keep your commands, requirements and decrees and to do everything to build the palatial structure for which I have provided."

²⁰Then David said to the whole assembly, "Praise the LORD your God." So they all praised the LORD, the God of their fathers; they bowed low and fell prostrate before the LORD and the king.

Solomon Acknowledged as King

²¹The next day they made sacrifices to the LORD and presented burnt offerings to him: a thousand bulls, a thousand rams and a thousand male lambs, together with their drink offerings, and other sacrifices in abundance for all Israel. ²²They ate and drank with great joy in the presence of the LORD that day.

Then they acknowledged Solomon son of David as king a second time, anointing him before the LORD to be ruler and Zadok to be priest. ²³So Solomon sat on the throne of the LORD as king in place of his father David. He prospered and all Israel obeyed him. ²⁴All the officers and mighty men, as well as all of King David's sons, pledged their submission to King Solomon.

²⁵The LORD highly exalted Solomon in the sight of all Israel and bestowed on him royal splendor such as no king over Israel ever had before.

The Death of David

²⁶David son of Jesse was king over all Israel. ²⁷He ruled over Israel forty years—seven in Hebron and thirty-three in Jerusalem. ²⁸He died at a good old age, having enjoyed long life, wealth and honor. His son Solomon succeeded him as king.

²⁹As for the events of King David's reign, from beginning to end, they are written in the records of Samuel the seer, the records of Nathan the prophet and the records of Gad the seer, ³⁰together with the details of his reign and power, and the circumstances that surrounded him and Israel and the kingdoms of all the other lands.

2 CHRONICLES

Solomon Asks for Wisdom

1 Solomon son of David established himself firmly over his kingdom, for the LORD his God was with him and made him exceedingly great.

²Then Solomon spoke to all Israel—to the commanders of thousands and commanders of hundreds, to the judges and to all the leaders in Israel, the heads of families— ³and Solomon and the whole assembly went to the high place at Gibeon, for God's Tent of Meeting was there, which Moses the LORD's servant had made in the desert. ⁴Now David had brought up the ark of God from Kiriath Jearim to the place he had prepared for it, because he had pitched a tent for it in Jerusalem. ⁵But the bronze altar that Bezalel son of Uri, the son of Hur, had made was in Gibeon in front of the tabernacle of the LORD; so Solomon and the assembly inquired of him there. ⁶Solomon went up to the bronze altar before the LORD in the Tent of Meeting and offered a thousand burnt offerings on it.

⁷That night God appeared to Solomon and said to him, "Ask for whatever you want me to give you."

⁸Solomon answered God, "You have shown great kindness to David my father and have made me king in his place. ⁹Now, LORD God, let your promise to my father David be confirmed, for you have made me king over a people who are as numerous as the dust of the earth. ¹⁰Give me wisdom and knowledge, that I may lead this people, for who is able to govern this great people of yours?"

¹¹God said to Solomon, "Since this is your heart's desire and you have not asked for wealth, riches or honor, nor for the death of your enemies, and since you have not asked for a long life but for wisdom and knowledge to govern my people over whom I have made you king, ¹²therefore wisdom and knowledge will be given you. And I will also give you wealth, riches and honor, such as no king who was before you ever had and none after you will have."

¹³Then Solomon went to Jerusalem from the high place at Gibeon, from before the Tent of Meeting. And he reigned over Israel.

¹⁴Solomon accumulated chariots and horses; he had fourteen hundred chariots and twelve thousand horses,ᵃ which he kept in the chariot cities and also with him in Jerusalem. ¹⁵The king made silver and gold as common in Jerusalem as stones, and cedar as plentiful as sycamore-fig trees in the foothills. ¹⁶Solomon's horses were imported from Egyptᵇ and from Kueᶜ—the royal merchants purchased them from Kue. ¹⁷They imported a chariot from Egypt for six hundred shekelsᵈ of silver, and a horse for a hundred and fifty.ᵉ They also exported them to all the kings of the Hittites and of the Arameans.

Preparations for Building the Temple

2 Solomon gave orders to build a temple for the Name of the LORD and a royal palace for himself. ²He conscripted seventy thousand men as carriers and eighty thousand as stonecutters in the hills and thirty-six hundred as foremen over them. ³Solomon sent this message to Hiramᶠ king of Tyre:

"Send me cedar logs as you did for my father David when you sent him cedar to build a palace to live in. ⁴Now I am about to build a temple for the Name of the LORD

ᵃ14 Or *charioteers*   ᵇ16 Or possibly *Muzur*, a region in Cilicia; also in verse 17   ᶜ16 Probably Cilicia   ᵈ17 That is, about 15 pounds (about 7 kilograms)   ᵉ17 That is, about 3 3/4 pounds (about 1.7 kilograms)   ᶠ3 Hebrew *Huram*, a variant of *Hiram*; also in verses 11 and 12

my God and to dedicate it to him for burning fragrant incense before him, for setting out the consecrated bread regularly, and for making burnt offerings every morning and evening and on Sabbaths and New Moons and at the appointed feasts of the LORD our God. This is a lasting ordinance for Israel.

5"The temple I am going to build will be great, because our God is greater than all other gods. 6But who is able to build a temple for him, since the heavens, even the highest heavens, cannot contain him? Who then am I to build a temple for him, except as a place to burn sacrifices before him?

7"Send me, therefore, a man skilled to work in gold and silver, bronze and iron, and in purple, crimson and blue yarn, and experienced in the art of engraving, to work in Judah and Jerusalem with my skilled craftsmen, whom my father David provided.

8"Send me also cedar, pine and algum*a* logs from Lebanon, for I know that your men are skilled in cutting timber there. My men will work with yours 9to provide me with plenty of lumber, because the temple I build must be large and magnificent. 10I will give your servants, the woodsmen who cut the timber, twenty thousand cors*b* of ground wheat, twenty thousand cors of barley, twenty thousand baths*c* of wine and twenty thousand baths of olive oil."

11Hiram king of Tyre replied by letter to Solomon:

"Because the LORD loves his people, he has made you their king."

12And Hiram added:

"Praise be to the LORD, the God of Israel, who made heaven and earth! He has given King David a wise son, endowed with intelligence and discernment, who will build a temple for the LORD and a palace for himself.

13"I am sending you Huram-Abi, a man of great skill, 14whose mother was from Dan and whose father was from Tyre. He is trained to work in gold and silver, bronze and iron, stone and wood, and with purple and blue and crimson yarn and fine linen. He is experienced in all kinds of engraving and can execute any design given to him. He will work with your craftsmen and with those of my lord, David your father.

15"Now let my lord send his servants the wheat and barley and the olive oil and wine he promised, 16and we will cut all the logs from Lebanon that you need and will float them in rafts by sea down to Joppa. You can then take them up to Jerusalem."

17Solomon took a census of all the aliens who were in Israel, after the census his father David had taken; and they were found to be 153,600. 18He assigned 70,000 of them to be carriers and 80,000 to be stonecutters in the hills, with 3,600 foremen over them to keep the people working.

Solomon Builds the Temple

3 Then Solomon began to build the temple of the LORD in Jerusalem on Mount Moriah, where the LORD had appeared to his father David. It was on the threshing floor of Araunah*d* the Jebusite, the place provided by David. 2He began building on the second day of the second month in the fourth year of his reign.

3The foundation Solomon laid for building the temple of God was sixty cubits long and twenty cubits wide*e* (using the cubit of the old standard). 4The portico at the front of the

---

a8 Probably a variant of *almug;* possibly juniper   *b10* That is, probably about 125,000 bushels (about 4,400 kiloliters)   *c10* That is, probably about 115,000 gallons (about 440 kiloliters)   *d1* Hebrew *Ornan,* a variant of *Araunah*   *e3* That is, about 90 feet (about 27 meters) long and 30 feet (about 9 meters) wide

temple was twenty cubits[a] long across the width of the building and twenty cubits[b] high.

He overlaid the inside with pure gold. [5]He paneled the main hall with pine and covered it with fine gold and decorated it with palm tree and chain designs. [6]He adorned the temple with precious stones. And the gold he used was gold of Parvaim. [7]He overlaid the ceiling beams, doorframes, walls and doors of the temple with gold, and he carved cherubim on the walls.

[8]He built the Most Holy Place, its length corresponding to the width of the temple—twenty cubits long and twenty cubits wide. He overlaid the inside with six hundred talents[c] of fine gold. [9]The gold nails weighed fifty shekels.[d] He also overlaid the upper parts with gold.

[10]In the Most Holy Place he made a pair of sculptured cherubim and overlaid them with gold. [11]The total wingspan of the cherubim was twenty cubits. One wing of the first cherub was five cubits[e] long and touched the temple wall, while its other wing, also five cubits long, touched the wing of the other cherub. [12]Similarly one wing of the second cherub was five cubits long and touched the other temple wall, and its other wing, also five cubits long, touched the wing of the first cherub. [13]The wings of these cherubim extended twenty cubits. They stood on their feet, facing the main hall.[f]

[14]He made the curtain of blue, purple and crimson yarn and fine linen, with cherubim worked into it.

[15]In the front of the temple he made two pillars, which together, were thirty-five cubits[g] long, each with a capital on top measuring five cubits. [16]He made interwoven chains[h] and put them on top of the pillars. He also made a hundred pomegranates and attached them to the chains. [17]He erected the pillars in the front of the temple, one to the south and one to the north. The one to the south he named Jakin[i] and the one to the north Boaz.[j]

The Temple's Furnishings

4 He made a bronze altar twenty cubits long, twenty cubits wide and ten cubits high.[k] [2]He made the Sea of cast metal, circular in shape, measuring ten cubits from rim to rim and five cubits[l] high. It took a line of thirty cubits[m] to measure around it. [3]Below the rim, figures of bulls encircled it—ten to a cubit.[n] The bulls were cast in two rows in one piece with the Sea.

[4]The Sea stood on twelve bulls, three facing north, three facing west, three facing south and three facing east. The Sea rested on top of them, and their hindquarters were

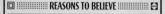
[a]4 That is, about 30 feet (about 9 meters); also in verses 8, 11 and 13   [b]4 Some Septuagint and Syriac manuscripts; Hebrew *and a hundred and twenty*   [c]8 That is, about 23 tons (about 21 metric tons)   [d]9 That is, about 1 1/4 pounds (about 0.6 kilogram)   [e]11 That is, about 7 1/2 feet (about 2.3 meters); also in verse 15   [f]13 Or *facing inward*   [g]15 That is, about 52 feet (about 16 meters)   [h]16 Or possibly *made chains in the inner sanctuary*; the meaning of the Hebrew for this phrase is uncertain.   [i]17 *Jakin* probably means *he establishes.*   [j]17 *Boaz* probably means *in him is strength.*   [k]1 That is, about 30 feet (about 9 meters) long and wide, and about 15 feet (about 4.5 meters) high   [l]2 That is, about 7 1/2 feet (about 2.3 meters)   [m]2 That is, about 45 feet (about 13.5 meters)   [n]3 That is, about 1 1/2 feet (about 0.5 meter)

toward the center. ⁵It was a handbreadth*ᵃ* in thickness, and its rim was like the rim of a cup, like a lily blossom. It held three thousand baths.*ᵇ*

⁶He then made ten basins for washing and placed five on the south side and five on the north. In them the things to be used for the burnt offerings were rinsed, but the Sea was to be used by the priests for washing.

⁷He made ten gold lampstands according to the specifications for them and placed them in the temple, five on the south side and five on the north.

⁸He made ten tables and placed them in the temple, five on the south side and five on the north. He also made a hundred gold sprinkling bowls.

⁹He made the courtyard of the priests, and the large court and the doors for the court, and overlaid the doors with bronze. ¹⁰He placed the Sea on the south side, at the southeast corner.

¹¹He also made the pots and shovels and sprinkling bowls.

So Huram finished the work he had undertaken for King Solomon in the temple of God:

¹²the two pillars;
  the two bowl-shaped capitals on top of the pillars;
  the two sets of network decorating the two bowl-shaped capitals on top of the pillars;
¹³the four hundred pomegranates for the two sets of network (two rows of pomegranates for each network, decorating the bowl-shaped capitals on top of the pillars);
¹⁴the stands with their basins;
¹⁵the Sea and the twelve bulls under it;
¹⁶the pots, shovels, meat forks and all related articles.

All the objects that Huram-Abi made for King Solomon for the temple of the LORD were of polished bronze. ¹⁷The king had them cast in clay molds in the plain of the Jordan between Succoth and Zarethan.*ᶜ* ¹⁸All these things that Solomon made amounted to so much that the weight of the bronze was not determined.

¹⁹Solomon also made all the furnishings that were in God's temple:

  the golden altar;
  the tables on which was the bread of the Presence;
²⁰the lampstands of pure gold with their lamps, to burn in front of the inner sanctuary as prescribed;
²¹the gold floral work and lamps and tongs (they were solid gold);
²²the pure gold wick trimmers, sprinkling bowls, dishes and censers; and the gold doors of the temple: the inner doors to the Most Holy Place and the doors of the main hall.

5 When all the work Solomon had done for the temple of the LORD was finished, he brought in the things his father David had dedicated—the silver and gold and all the furnishings—and he placed them in the treasuries of God's temple.

The Ark Brought to the Temple

²Then Solomon summoned to Jerusalem the elders of Israel, all the heads of the tribes and the chiefs of the Israelite families, to bring up the ark of the LORD's covenant from Zion, the City of David. ³And all the men of Israel came together to the king at the time of the festival in the seventh month.

⁴When all the elders of Israel had arrived, the Levites took up the ark, ⁵and they brought up the ark and the Tent of Meeting and all the sacred furnishings in it. The priests, who were Levites, carried them up; ⁶and King Solomon and the entire assembly

---

ᵃ5 That is, about 3 inches (about 8 centimeters)   *ᵇ5* That is, about 17,500 gallons (about 66 kiloliters)   *ᶜ17* Hebrew *Zeredatha,* a variant of *Zarethan*

of Israel that had gathered about him were before the ark, sacrificing so many sheep and cattle that they could not be recorded or counted.

⁷The priests then brought the ark of the LORD's covenant to its place in the inner sanctuary of the temple, the Most Holy Place, and put it beneath the wings of the cherubim. ⁸The cherubim spread their wings over the place of the ark and covered the ark and its carrying poles. ⁹These poles were so long that their ends, extending from the ark, could be seen from in front of the inner sanctuary, but not from outside the Holy Place; and they are still there today. ¹⁰There was nothing in the ark except the two tablets that Moses had placed in it at Horeb, where the LORD made a covenant with the Israelites after they came out of Egypt.

¹¹The priests then withdrew from the Holy Place. All the priests who were there had consecrated themselves, regardless of their divisions. ¹²All the Levites who were musicians—Asaph, Heman, Jeduthun and their sons and relatives—stood on the east side of the altar, dressed in fine linen and playing cymbals, harps and lyres. They were accompanied by 120 priests sounding trumpets. ¹³The trumpeters and singers joined in unison, as with one voice, to give praise and thanks to the LORD. Accompanied by trumpets, cymbals and other instruments, they raised their voices in praise to the LORD and sang:

> "He is good;
>   his love endures forever."

Then the temple of the LORD was filled with a cloud, ¹⁴and the priests could not perform their service because of the cloud, for the glory of the LORD filled the temple of God.

6 Then Solomon said, "The LORD has said that he would dwell in a dark cloud; ²I have built a magnificent temple for you, a place for you to dwell forever."

³While the whole assembly of Israel was standing there, the king turned around and blessed them. ⁴Then he said:

"Praise be to the LORD, the God of Israel, who with his hands has fulfilled what he promised with his mouth to my father David. For he said, ⁵'Since the day I brought my people out of Egypt, I have not chosen a city in any tribe of Israel to have a temple built for my Name to be there, nor have I chosen anyone to be the leader over my people Israel. ⁶But now I have chosen Jerusalem for my Name to be there, and I have chosen David to rule my people Israel.'

⁷"My father David had it in his heart to build a temple for the Name of the LORD, the God of Israel. ⁸But the LORD said to my father David, 'Because it was in your heart to build a temple for my Name, you did well to have this in your heart. ⁹Nevertheless, you are not the one to build the temple, but your son, who is your own flesh and blood—he is the one who will build the temple for my Name.'

¹⁰"The LORD has kept the promise he made. I have succeeded David my father and now I sit on the throne of Israel, just as the LORD promised, and I have built the temple for the Name of the LORD, the God of Israel. ¹¹There I have placed the ark, in which is the covenant of the LORD that he made with the people of Israel."

Solomon's Prayer of Dedication

¹²Then Solomon stood before the altar of the LORD in front of the whole assembly of Israel and spread out his hands. ¹³Now he had made a bronze platform, five cubits^a long, five cubits wide and three cubits^b high, and had placed it in the center of the outer court. He stood on the platform and then knelt down before the whole assembly of Israel and spread out his hands toward heaven. ¹⁴He said:

"O LORD, God of Israel, there is no God like you in heaven or on earth—you who keep your covenant of love with your servants who continue wholeheartedly in your

---

^a 13 That is, about 7 1/2 feet (about 2.3 meters)   ^b 13 That is, about 4 1/2 feet (about 1.3 meters)

way. ¹⁵You have kept your promise to your servant David my father; with your mouth you have promised and with your hand you have fulfilled it—as it is today.

¹⁶"Now Lord, God of Israel, keep for your servant David my father the promises you made to him when you said, 'You shall never fail to have a man to sit before me on the throne of Israel, if only your sons are careful in all they do to walk before me according to my law, as you have done.' ¹⁷And now, O Lord, God of Israel, let your word that you promised your servant David come true.

¹⁸"But will God really dwell on earth with men? The heavens, even the highest heavens, cannot contain you. How much less this temple I have built! ¹⁹Yet give attention to your servant's prayer and his plea for mercy, O Lord my God. Hear the cry and the prayer that your servant is praying in your presence. ²⁰May your eyes be open toward this temple day and night, this place of which you said you would put your Name there. May you hear the prayer your servant prays toward this place. ²¹Hear the supplications of your servant and of your people Israel when they pray toward this place. Hear from heaven, your dwelling place; and when you hear, forgive.

²²"When a man wrongs his neighbor and is required to take an oath and he comes and swears the oath before your altar in this temple, ²³then hear from heaven and act. Judge between your servants, repaying the guilty by bringing down on his own head what he has done. Declare the innocent not guilty and so establish his innocence.

²⁴"When your people Israel have been defeated by an enemy because they have sinned against you and when they turn back and confess your name, praying and making supplication before you in this temple, ²⁵then hear from heaven and forgive the sin of your people Israel and bring them back to the land you gave to them and their fathers.

²⁶"When the heavens are shut up and there is no rain because your people have sinned against you, and when they pray toward this place and confess your name and turn from their sin because you have afflicted them, ²⁷then hear from heaven and forgive the sin of your servants, your people Israel. Teach them the right way to live, and send rain on the land you gave your people for an inheritance.

²⁸"When famine or plague comes to the land, or blight or mildew, locusts or grasshoppers, or when enemies besiege them in any of their cities, whatever disaster or disease may come, ²⁹and when a prayer or plea is made by any of your people Israel—each one aware of his afflictions and pains, and spreading out his hands toward this temple— ³⁰then hear from heaven, your dwelling place. Forgive, and deal with each man according to all he does, since you know his heart (for you alone know the hearts of men), ³¹so that they will fear you and walk in your ways all the time they live in the land you gave our fathers.

³²"As for the foreigner who does not belong to your people Israel but has come from a distant land because of your great name and your mighty hand and your outstretched arm—when he comes and prays toward this temple, ³³then hear from heaven, your dwelling place, and do whatever the foreigner asks of you, so that all the peoples of the earth may know your name and fear you, as do your own people Israel, and may know that this house I have built bears your Name.

³⁴"When your people go to war against their enemies, wherever you send them, and when they pray to you toward this city you have chosen and the temple I have built for your Name, ³⁵then hear from heaven their prayer and their plea, and uphold their cause.

³⁶"When they sin against you—for there is no one who does not sin—and you become angry with them and give them over to the enemy, who takes them captive to a land far away or near; ³⁷and if they have a change of heart in the land where they are held captive, and repent and plead with you in the land of their captivity

and say, 'We have sinned, we have done wrong and acted wickedly'; [38]and if they turn back to you with all their heart and soul in the land of their captivity where they were taken, and pray toward the land you gave their fathers, toward the city you have chosen and toward the temple I have built for your Name; [39]then from heaven, your dwelling place, hear their prayer and their pleas, and uphold their cause. And forgive your people, who have sinned against you.

[40]"Now, my God, may your eyes be open and your ears attentive to the prayers offered in this place.

[41]"Now arise, O LORD God, and come to your resting place,
    you and the ark of your might.
May your priests, O LORD God, be clothed with salvation,
    may your saints rejoice in your goodness.
[42]O LORD God, do not reject your anointed one.
    Remember the great love promised to David your servant."

The Dedication of the Temple

7 When Solomon finished praying, fire came down from heaven and consumed the burnt offering and the sacrifices, and the glory of the LORD filled the temple. [2]The priests could not enter the temple of the LORD because the glory of the LORD filled it. [3]When all the Israelites saw the fire coming down and the glory of the LORD above the temple, they knelt on the pavement with their faces to the ground, and they worshiped and gave thanks to the LORD, saying,

"He is good;
    his love endures forever."

[4]Then the king and all the people offered sacrifices before the LORD. [5]And King Solomon offered a sacrifice of twenty-two thousand head of cattle and a hundred and twenty thousand sheep and goats. So the king and all the people dedicated the temple of God. [6]The priests took their positions, as did the Levites with the LORD's musical instruments, which King David had made for praising the LORD and which were used when he gave thanks, saying, "His love endures forever." Opposite the Levites, the priests blew their trumpets, and all the Israelites were standing.

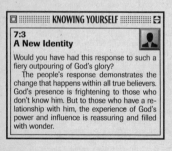

KNOWING YOURSELF

7:3
A New Identity

Would you have had this response to such a fiery outpouring of God's glory?

The people's response demonstrates the change that happens within all true believers. God's presence is frightening to those who don't know him. But to those who have a relationship with him, the experience of God's power and influence is reassuring and filled with wonder.

[7]Solomon consecrated the middle part of the courtyard in front of the temple of the LORD, and there he offered burnt offerings and the fat of the fellowship offerings,[a] because the bronze altar he had made could not hold the burnt offerings, the grain offerings and the fat portions.

[8]So Solomon observed the festival at that time for seven days, and all Israel with him—a vast assembly, people from Lebo[b] Hamath to the Wadi of Egypt. [9]On the eighth day they held an assembly, for they had celebrated the dedication of the altar for seven days and the festival for seven days more. [10]On the twenty-third day of the seventh month he sent the people to their homes, joyful and glad in heart for the good things the LORD had done for David and Solomon and for his people Israel.

[a]7 Traditionally *peace offerings*   [b]8 Or *from the entrance to*

The LORD Appears to Solomon

11When Solomon had finished the temple of the LORD and the royal palace, and had succeeded in carrying out all he had in mind to do in the temple of the LORD and in his own palace, 12the LORD appeared to him at night and said:

"I have heard your prayer and have chosen this place for myself as a temple for sacrifices.

13"When I shut up the heavens so that there is no rain, or command locusts to devour the land or send a plague among my people, 14if my people, who are called by my name, will humble themselves and pray and seek my face and turn from their wicked ways, then will I hear from heaven and will forgive their sin and will heal their land. 15Now my eyes will be open and my ears attentive to the prayers offered in this place. 16I have chosen and consecrated this temple so that my Name may be there forever. My eyes and my heart will always be there.

17"As for you, if you walk before me as David your father did, and do all I command, and observe my decrees and laws, 18I will establish your royal throne, as I covenanted with David your father when I said, 'You shall never fail to have a man to rule over Israel.'

19"But if you*a* turn away and forsake the decrees and commands I have given you*a* and go off to serve other gods and worship them, 20then I will uproot Israel from my land, which I have given them, and will reject this temple I have consecrated for my Name. I will make it a byword and an object of ridicule among all peoples. 21And though this temple is now so imposing, all who pass by will be appalled and say, 'Why has the LORD done such a thing to this land and to this temple?' 22People will answer, 'Because they have forsaken the LORD, the God of their fathers, who brought them out of Egypt, and have embraced other gods, worshiping and serving them—that is why he brought all this disaster on them.'"

Solomon's Other Activities

8 At the end of twenty years, during which Solomon built the temple of the LORD and his own palace, 2Solomon rebuilt the villages that Hiram*b* had given him, and settled Israelites in them. 3Solomon then went to Hamath Zobah and captured it. 4He also built up Tadmor in the desert and all the store cities he had built in Hamath. 5He rebuilt Upper Beth Horon and Lower Beth Horon as fortified cities, with walls and with gates and bars, 6as well as Baalath and all his store cities, and all the cities for his chariots and for his horses*c*—whatever he desired to build in Jerusalem, in Lebanon and throughout all the territory he ruled.

7All the people left from the Hittites, Amorites, Perizzites, Hivites and Jebusites (these peoples were not Israelites), 8that is, their descendants remaining in the land, whom the Israelites had not destroyed—these Solomon conscripted for his slave labor force, as it is to this day. 9But Solomon did not make slaves of the Israelites for his work; they were his fighting men, commanders of his captains, and commanders of his chariots and charioteers. 10They were also King Solomon's chief officials—two hundred and fifty officials supervising the men.

11Solomon brought Pharaoh's daughter up from the City of David to the palace he had built for her, for he said, "My wife must not live in the palace of David king of Israel, because the places the ark of the LORD has entered are holy."

12On the altar of the LORD that he had built in front of the portico, Solomon sacrificed burnt offerings to the LORD, 13according to the daily requirement for offerings commanded by Moses for Sabbaths, New Moons and the three annual feasts—the Feast of Unleavened Bread, the Feast of Weeks and the Feast of Tabernacles. 14In keeping with the ordinance of his father David, he appointed the divisions of the priests for their duties, and the

---

a19 The Hebrew is plural.   *b2 Hebrew Huram, a variant of Hiram; also in verse 18*   *c6 Or charioteers*

Levites to lead the praise and to assist the priests according to each day's requirement. He also appointed the gatekeepers by divisions for the various gates, because this was what David the man of God had ordered. ¹⁵They did not deviate from the king's commands to the priests or to the Levites in any matter, including that of the treasuries.

¹⁶All Solomon's work was carried out, from the day the foundation of the temple of the LORD was laid until its completion. So the temple of the LORD was finished.

¹⁷Then Solomon went to Ezion Geber and Elath on the coast of Edom. ¹⁸And Hiram sent him ships commanded by his own officers, men who knew the sea. These, with Solomon's men, sailed to Ophir and brought back four hundred and fifty talents ᵃ of gold, which they delivered to King Solomon.

The Queen of Sheba Visits Solomon

9 When the queen of Sheba heard of Solomon's fame, she came to Jerusalem to test him with hard questions. Arriving with a very great caravan—with camels carrying spices, large quantities of gold, and precious stones—she came to Solomon and talked with him about all she had on her mind. ²Solomon answered all her questions; nothing was too hard for him to explain to her. ³When the queen of Sheba saw the wisdom of Solomon, as well as the palace he had built, ⁴the food on his table, the seating of his officials, the attending servants in their robes, the cupbearers in their robes and the burnt offerings he made at ᵇ the temple of the LORD, she was overwhelmed.

⁵She said to the king, "The report I heard in my own country about your achievements and your wisdom is true. ⁶But I did not believe what they said until I came and saw with my own eyes. Indeed, not even half the greatness of your wisdom was told me; you have far exceeded the report I heard. ⁷How happy your men must be! How happy your officials, who continually stand before you and hear your wisdom! ⁸Praise be to the LORD your God, who has delighted in you and placed you on his throne as king to rule for the LORD your God. Because of the love of your God for Israel and his desire to uphold them forever, he has made you king over them, to maintain justice and righteousness."

⁹Then she gave the king 120 talents ᶜ of gold, large quantities of spices, and precious stones. There had never been such spices as those the queen of Sheba gave to King Solomon.

¹⁰(The men of Hiram and the men of Solomon brought gold from Ophir; they also brought algumwood ᵈ and precious stones. ¹¹The king used the algumwood to make steps for the temple of the LORD and for the royal palace, and to make harps and lyres for the musicians. Nothing like them had ever been seen in Judah.)

¹²King Solomon gave the queen of Sheba all she desired and asked for; he gave her more than she had brought to him. Then she left and returned with her retinue to her own country.

Solomon's Splendor

¹³The weight of the gold that Solomon received yearly was 666 talents, ᵉ ¹⁴not including the revenues brought in by merchants and traders. Also all the kings of Arabia and the governors of the land brought gold and silver to Solomon.

¹⁵King Solomon made two hundred large shields of hammered gold; six hundred bekas ᶠ of hammered gold went into each shield. ¹⁶He also made three hundred small shields of hammered gold, with three hundred bekas ᵍ of gold in each shield. The king put them in the Palace of the Forest of Lebanon.

¹⁷Then the king made a great throne inlaid with ivory and overlaid with pure gold. ¹⁸The throne had six steps, and a footstool of gold was attached to it. On both sides of the seat were armrests, with a lion standing beside each of them. ¹⁹Twelve lions stood on

---

ᵃ 18 That is, about 17 tons (about 16 metric tons)   ᵇ 4 Or the ascent by which he went up to   ᶜ 9 That is, about 4 1/2 tons (about 4 metric tons)   ᵈ 10 Probably a variant of almugwood   ᵉ 13 That is, about 25 tons (about 23 metric tons)   ᶠ 15 That is, about 7 1/2 pounds (about 3.5 kilograms)   ᵍ 16 That is, about 3 3/4 pounds (about 1.7 kilograms)

the six steps, one at either end of each step. Nothing like it had ever been made for any other kingdom. 20All King Solomon's goblets were gold, and all the household articles in the Palace of the Forest of Lebanon were pure gold. Nothing was made of silver, because silver was considered of little value in Solomon's day. 21The king had a fleet of trading ships*a* manned by Hiram's*b* men. Once every three years it returned, carrying gold, silver and ivory, and apes and baboons.

22King Solomon was greater in riches and wisdom than all the other kings of the earth. 23All the kings of the earth sought audience with Solomon to hear the wisdom God had put in his heart. 24Year after year, everyone who came brought a gift—articles of silver and gold, and robes, weapons and spices, and horses and mules.

25Solomon had four thousand stalls for horses and chariots, and twelve thousand horses,*c* which he kept in the chariot cities and also with him in Jerusalem. 26He ruled over all the kings from the River*d* to the land of the Philistines, as far as the border of Egypt. 27The king made silver as common in Jerusalem as stones, and cedar as plentiful as sycamore-fig trees in the foothills. 28Solomon's horses were imported from Egypt*e* and from all other countries.

Solomon's Death

29As for the other events of Solomon's reign, from beginning to end, are they not written in the records of Nathan the prophet, in the prophecy of Ahijah the Shilonite and in the visions of Iddo the seer concerning Jeroboam son of Nebat? 30Solomon reigned in Jerusalem over all Israel forty years. 31Then he rested with his fathers and was buried in the city of David his father. And Rehoboam his son succeeded him as king.

Israel Rebels Against Rehoboam

10 Rehoboam went to Shechem, for all the Israelites had gone there to make him king. 2When Jeroboam son of Nebat heard this (he was in Egypt, where he had fled from King Solomon), he returned from Egypt. 3So they sent for Jeroboam, and he and all Israel went to Rehoboam and said to him: 4"Your father put a heavy yoke on us, but now lighten the harsh labor and the heavy yoke he put on us, and we will serve you."

5Rehoboam answered, "Come back to me in three days." So the people went away.

6Then King Rehoboam consulted the elders who had served his father Solomon during his lifetime. "How would you advise me to answer these people?" he asked.

7They replied, "If you will be kind to these people and please them and give them a favorable answer, they will always be your servants."

8But Rehoboam rejected the advice the elders gave him and consulted the young men who had grown up with him and were serving him. 9He asked them, "What is your advice? How should we answer these people who say to me, 'Lighten the yoke your father put on us'?"

10The young men who had grown up with him replied, "Tell the people who have said to you, 'Your father put a heavy yoke on us, but make our yoke lighter'—tell them, 'My little finger is thicker than my father's waist. 11My father laid on you a heavy yoke; I will make it even heavier. My father scourged you with whips; I will scourge you with scorpions.'"

12Three days later Jeroboam and all the people returned to Rehoboam, as the king had said, "Come back to me in three days." 13The king answered them harshly. Rejecting the advice of the elders, 14he followed the advice of the young men and said, "My father made your yoke heavy; I will make it even heavier. My father scourged you with whips; I will scourge you with scorpions." 15So the king did not listen to the people, for this turn

a21 Hebrew of *ships that could go to Tarshish*   *b21* Hebrew *Huram,* a variant of *Hiram*   *c25* Or *charioteers*
d26 That is, the Euphrates   *e28* Or possibly *Muzur,* a region in Cilicia

of events was from God, to fulfill the word the LORD had spoken to Jeroboam son of Nebat through Ahijah the Shilonite.

¹⁶When all Israel saw that the king refused to listen to them, they answered the king:

> "What share do we have in David,
>   what part in Jesse's son?
> To your tents, O Israel!
>   Look after your own house, O David!"

So all the Israelites went home. ¹⁷But as for the Israelites who were living in the towns of Judah, Rehoboam still ruled over them.

¹⁸King Rehoboam sent out Adoniram,ᵃ who was in charge of forced labor, but the Israelites stoned him to death. King Rehoboam, however, managed to get into his chariot and escape to Jerusalem. ¹⁹So Israel has been in rebellion against the house of David to this day.

11 When Rehoboam arrived in Jerusalem, he mustered the house of Judah and Benjamin—a hundred and eighty thousand fighting men—to make war against Israel and to regain the kingdom for Rehoboam.

²But this word of the LORD came to Shemaiah the man of God: ³"Say to Rehoboam son of Solomon king of Judah and to all the Israelites in Judah and Benjamin, ⁴'This is what the LORD says: Do not go up to fight against your brothers. Go home, every one of you, for this is my doing.'" So they obeyed the words of the LORD and turned back from marching against Jeroboam.

Rehoboam Fortifies Judah

⁵Rehoboam lived in Jerusalem and built up towns for defense in Judah: ⁶Bethlehem, Etam, Tekoa, ⁷Beth Zur, Soco, Adullam, ⁸Gath, Mareshah, Ziph, ⁹Adoraim, Lachish, Azekah, ¹⁰Zorah, Aijalon and Hebron. These were fortified cities in Judah and Benjamin. ¹¹He strengthened their defenses and put commanders in them, with supplies of food, olive oil and wine. ¹²He put shields and spears in all the cities, and made them very strong. So Judah and Benjamin were his.

¹³The priests and Levites from all their districts throughout Israel sided with him. ¹⁴The Levites even abandoned their pasturelands and property, and came to Judah and Jerusalem because Jeroboam and his sons had rejected them as priests of the LORD. ¹⁵And he appointed his own priests for the high places and for the goat and calf idols he had made. ¹⁶Those from every tribe of Israel who set their hearts on seeking the LORD, the God of Israel, followed the Levites to Jerusalem to offer sacrifices to the LORD, the God of their fathers. ¹⁷They strengthened the kingdom of Judah and supported Rehoboam son of Solomon three years, walking in the ways of David and Solomon during this time.

Rehoboam's Family

¹⁸Rehoboam married Mahalath, who was the daughter of David's son Jerimoth and of Abihail, the daughter of Jesse's son Eliab. ¹⁹She bore him sons: Jeush, Shemariah and Zaham. ²⁰Then he married Maacah daughter of Absalom, who bore him Abijah, Attai, Ziza and Shelomith. ²¹Rehoboam loved Maacah daughter of Absalom more than any of his other wives and concubines. In all, he had eighteen wives and sixty concubines, twenty-eight sons and sixty daughters.

²²Rehoboam appointed Abijah son of Maacah to be the chief prince among his brothers, in order to make him king. ²³He acted wisely, dispersing some of his sons throughout the districts of Judah and Benjamin, and to all the fortified cities. He gave them abundant provisions and took many wives for them.

ᵃ 18 Hebrew *Hadoram*, a variant of *Adoniram*

Shishak Attacks Jerusalem

12 After Rehoboam's position as king was established and he had become strong, he and all Israel[a] with him abandoned the law of the LORD. ²Because they had been unfaithful to the LORD, Shishak king of Egypt attacked Jerusalem in the fifth year of King Rehoboam. ³With twelve hundred chariots and sixty thousand horsemen and the innumerable troops of Libyans, Sukkites and Cushites[b] that came with him from Egypt, ⁴he captured the fortified cities of Judah and came as far as Jerusalem.

⁵Then the prophet Shemaiah came to Rehoboam and to the leaders of Judah who had assembled in Jerusalem for fear of Shishak, and he said to them, "This is what the LORD says, 'You have abandoned me; therefore, I now abandon you to Shishak.'"

⁶The leaders of Israel and the king humbled themselves and said, "The LORD is just."

⁷When the LORD saw that they humbled themselves, this word of the LORD came to Shemaiah: "Since they have humbled themselves, I will not destroy them but will soon give them deliverance. My wrath will not be poured out on Jerusalem through Shishak. ⁸They will, however, become subject to him, so that they may learn the difference between serving me and serving the kings of other lands."

⁹When Shishak king of Egypt attacked Jerusalem, he carried off the treasures of the temple of the LORD and the treasures of the royal palace. He took everything, including the gold shields Solomon had made. ¹⁰So King Rehoboam made bronze shields to replace them and assigned these to the commanders of the guard on duty at the entrance to the royal palace. ¹¹Whenever the king went to the LORD's temple, the guards went with him, bearing the shields, and afterward they returned them to the guardroom.

¹²Because Rehoboam humbled himself, the LORD's anger turned from him, and he was not totally destroyed. Indeed, there was some good in Judah.

¹³King Rehoboam established himself firmly in Jerusalem and continued as king. He was forty-one years old when he became king, and he reigned seventeen years in Jerusalem, the city the LORD had chosen out of all the tribes of Israel in which to put his Name. His mother's name was Naamah; she was an Ammonite. ¹⁴He did evil because he had not set his heart on seeking the LORD.

¹⁵As for the events of Rehoboam's reign, from beginning to end, are they not written in the records of Shemaiah the prophet and of Iddo the seer that deal with genealogies? There was continual warfare between Rehoboam and Jeroboam. ¹⁶Rehoboam rested with his fathers and was buried in the City of David. And Abijah his son succeeded him as king.

Abijah King of Judah

13 In the eighteenth year of the reign of Jeroboam, Abijah became king of Judah, ²and he reigned in Jerusalem three years. His mother's name was Maacah,[c] a daughter[d] of Uriel of Gibeah.

There was war between Abijah and Jeroboam. ³Abijah went into battle with a force of four hundred thousand able fighting men, and Jeroboam drew up a battle line against him with eight hundred thousand able troops.

⁴Abijah stood on Mount Zemaraim, in the hill country of Ephraim, and said, "Jeroboam and all Israel, listen to me! ⁵Don't you know that the LORD, the God of Israel, has given the kingship of Israel to David and his descendants forever by a covenant of salt? ⁶Yet Jeroboam son of Nebat, an official of Solomon son of David, rebelled against his master. ⁷Some worthless scoundrels gathered around him and opposed Rehoboam son of Solomon when he was young and indecisive and not strong enough to resist them.

⁸"And now you plan to resist the kingdom of the LORD, which is in the hands of David's descendants. You are indeed a vast army and have with you the golden calves that Jeroboam made to be your gods. ⁹But didn't you drive out the priests of the LORD, the sons

---

[a] 1 That is, Judah, as frequently in 2 Chronicles   [b] 3 That is, people from the upper Nile region   [c] 2 Most Septuagint manuscripts and Syriac (see also 2 Chron. 11:20 and 1 Kings 15:2); Hebrew *Micaiah*   [d] 2 Or *granddaughter*

of Aaron, and the Levites, and make priests of your own as the peoples of other lands do? Whoever wants to consecrate himself with a young bull and seven rams may become a priest of what are not gods.

¹⁰"As for us, the LORD is our God, and we have not forsaken him. The priests who serve the LORD are sons of Aaron, and the Levites assist them. ¹¹Every morning and evening they present burnt offerings and fragrant incense to the LORD. They set out the bread on the ceremonially clean table and light the lamps on the gold lampstand every evening. We are observing the requirements of the LORD our God. But you have forsaken him. ¹²God is with us; he is our leader. His priests with their trumpets will sound the battle cry against you. Men of Israel, do not fight against the LORD, the God of your fathers, for you will not succeed."

¹³Now Jeroboam had sent troops around to the rear, so that while he was in front of Judah the ambush was behind them. ¹⁴Judah turned and saw that they were being attacked at both front and rear. Then they cried out to the LORD. The priests blew their trumpets ¹⁵and the men of Judah raised the battle cry. At the sound of their battle cry, God routed Jeroboam and all Israel before Abijah and Judah. ¹⁶The Israelites fled before Judah, and God delivered them into their hands. ¹⁷Abijah and his men inflicted heavy losses on them, so that there were five hundred thousand casualties among Israel's able men. ¹⁸The men of Israel were subdued on that occasion, and the men of Judah were victorious because they relied on the LORD, the God of their fathers.

¹⁹Abijah pursued Jeroboam and took from him the towns of Bethel, Jeshanah and Ephron, with their surrounding villages. ²⁰Jeroboam did not regain power during the time of Abijah. And the LORD struck him down and he died.

²¹But Abijah grew in strength. He married fourteen wives and had twenty-two sons and sixteen daughters.

²²The other events of Abijah's reign, what he did and what he said, are written in the annotations of the prophet Iddo.

14 And Abijah rested with his fathers and was buried in the City of David. Asa his son succeeded him as king, and in his days the country was at peace for ten years.

Asa King of Judah

²Asa did what was good and right in the eyes of the LORD his God. ³He removed the foreign altars and the high places, smashed the sacred stones and cut down the Asherah poles.ᵃ ⁴He commanded Judah to seek the LORD, the God of their fathers, and to obey his laws and commands. ⁵He removed the high places and incense altars in every town in Judah, and the kingdom was at peace under him. ⁶He built up the fortified cities of Judah, since the land was at peace. No one was at war with him during those years, for the LORD gave him rest.

⁷"Let us build up these towns," he said to Judah, "and put walls around them, with towers, gates and bars. The land is still ours, because we have sought the LORD our God; we sought him and he has given us rest on every side." So they built and prospered.

⁸Asa had an army of three hundred thousand men from Judah, equipped with large shields and with spears, and two hundred and eighty thousand from Benjamin, armed with small shields and with bows. All these were brave fighting men.

⁹Zerah the Cushite marched out against them with a vast armyᵇ and three hundred chariots, and came as far as Mareshah. ¹⁰Asa went out to meet him, and they took up battle positions in the Valley of Zephathah near Mareshah.

¹¹Then Asa called to the LORD his God and said, "LORD, there is no one like you to help the powerless against the mighty. Help us, O LORD our God, for we rely on you, and in

ᵃ 3 That is, symbols of the goddess Asherah; here and elsewhere in 2 Chronicles   ᵇ 9 Hebrew with an army of a thousand thousands or with an army of thousands upon thousands

your name we have come against this vast army. O LORD, you are our God; do not let man prevail against you."

[12]The LORD struck down the Cushites before Asa and Judah. The Cushites fled, [13]and Asa and his army pursued them as far as Gerar. Such a great number of Cushites fell that they could not recover; they were crushed before the LORD and his forces. The men of Judah carried off a large amount of plunder. [14]They destroyed all the villages around Gerar, for the terror of the LORD had fallen upon them. They plundered all these villages, since there was much booty there. [15]They also attacked the camps of the herdsmen and carried off droves of sheep and goats and camels. Then they returned to Jerusalem.

Asa's Reform

15 The Spirit of God came upon Azariah son of Oded. [2]He went out to meet Asa and said to him, "Listen to me, Asa and all Judah and Benjamin. The LORD is with you when you are with him. If you seek him, he will be found by you, but if you forsake him, he will forsake you. [3]For a long time Israel was without the true God, without a priest to teach and without the law. [4]But in their distress they turned to the LORD, the God of Israel, and sought him, and he was found by them. [5]In those days it was not safe to travel about, for all the inhabitants of the lands were in great turmoil. [6]One nation was being crushed by another and one city by another, because God was troubling them with every kind of distress. [7]But as for you, be strong and do not give up, for your work will be rewarded."

[8]When Asa heard these words and the prophecy of Azariah son of[a] Oded the prophet, he took courage. He removed the detestable idols from the whole land of Judah and Benjamin and from the towns he had captured in the hills of Ephraim. He repaired the altar of the LORD that was in front of the portico of the LORD's temple.

[9]Then he assembled all Judah and Benjamin and the people from Ephraim, Manasseh and Simeon who had settled among them, for large numbers had come over to him from Israel when they saw that the LORD his God was with him.

[10]They assembled at Jerusalem in the third month of the fifteenth year of Asa's reign. [11]At that time they sacrificed to the LORD seven hundred head of cattle and seven thousand sheep and goats from the plunder they had brought back. [12]They entered into a covenant to seek the LORD, the God of their fathers, with all their heart and soul. [13]All who would not seek the LORD, the God of Israel, were to be put to death, whether small or great, man or woman. [14]They took an oath to the LORD with loud acclamation, with shouting and with trumpets and horns. [15]All Judah rejoiced about the oath because they had sworn it wholeheartedly. They sought God eagerly, and he was found by them. So the LORD gave them rest on every side.

[16]King Asa also deposed his grandmother Maacah from her position as queen mother, because she had made a repulsive Asherah pole. Asa cut the pole down, broke it up and burned it in the Kidron Valley. [17]Although he did not remove the high places from Israel, Asa's heart was fully committed ⸤to the LORD⸥ all his life. [18]He brought into the temple of God the silver and gold and the articles that he and his father had dedicated.

[19]There was no more war until the thirty-fifth year of Asa's reign.

Asa's Last Years

16 In the thirty-sixth year of Asa's reign Baasha king of Israel went up against Judah and fortified Ramah to prevent anyone from leaving or entering the territory of Asa king of Judah.

[2]Asa then took the silver and gold out of the treasuries of the LORD's temple and of his own palace and sent it to Ben-Hadad king of Aram, who was ruling in Damascus. [3]"Let there be a treaty between me and you," he said, "as there was between my father and

a 8 Vulgate and Syriac (see also Septuagint and verse 1); Hebrew does not have Azariah son of.

your father. See, I am sending you silver and gold. Now break your treaty with Baasha king of Israel so he will withdraw from me."

⁴Ben-Hadad agreed with King Asa and sent the commanders of his forces against the towns of Israel. They conquered Ijon, Dan, Abel Maim*ᵃ* and all the store cities of Naphtali. ⁵When Baasha heard this, he stopped building Ramah and abandoned his work. ⁶Then King Asa brought all the men of Judah, and they carried away from Ramah the stones and timber Baasha had been using. With them he built up Geba and Mizpah.

⁷At that time Hanani the seer came to Asa king of Judah and said to him: "Because you relied on the king of Aram and not on the LORD your God, the army of the king of Aram has escaped from your hand. ⁸Were not the Cushites*ᵇ* and Libyans a mighty army with great numbers of chariots and horsemen*ᶜ*? Yet when you relied on the LORD, he delivered them into your hand. ⁹For the eyes of the LORD range throughout the earth to strengthen those whose hearts are fully committed to him. You have done a foolish thing, and from now on you will be at war."

¹⁰Asa was angry with the seer because of this; he was so enraged that he put him in prison. At the same time Asa brutally oppressed some of the people.

¹¹The events of Asa's reign, from beginning to end, are written in the book of the kings of Judah and Israel. ¹²In the thirty-ninth year of his reign Asa was afflicted with a disease in his feet. Though his disease was severe, even in his illness he did not seek help from the LORD, but only from the physicians. ¹³Then in the forty-first year of his reign Asa died and rested with his fathers. ¹⁴They buried him in the tomb that he had cut out for himself in the City of David. They laid him on a bier covered with spices and various blended perfumes, and they made a huge fire in his honor.

◻ ▦ ADDRESSING QUESTIONS ▦ ⬒

16:12
Human Experience
Q

Was Asa wrong to go to a doctor?

The issue here is not what Asa did, but what he *didn't* do. For some reason, he did not pray about the matter. He decided to trust his own doctors rather than trusting in God's healing.

Nowhere in Scripture are medicines forbidden (see 1 Timothy chapter 5, verse 23 [page 1573]). In fact, Luke, the Gospel writer, was himself a doctor (Colossians chapter 4, verse 14 [page 1556]). So God doesn't frown on the medical profession in general. As he does with other earthly institutions, God has used advances in medicine over the years in his service.

Asa was wise to have used the medical experts in his day to look after his disease. But he shouldn't have closed God out of this area of his life. And neither should we, when we experience similar circumstances.

Jehoshaphat King of Judah

17 Jehoshaphat his son succeeded him as king and strengthened himself against Israel. ²He stationed troops in all the fortified cities of Judah and put garrisons in Judah and in the towns of Ephraim that his father Asa had captured.

³The LORD was with Jehoshaphat because in his early years he walked in the ways his father David had followed. He did not consult the Baals ⁴but sought the God of his father and followed his commands rather than the practices of Israel. ⁵The LORD established the kingdom under his control; and all Judah brought gifts to Jehoshaphat, so that he had great wealth and honor. ⁶His heart was devoted to the ways of the LORD; furthermore, he removed the high places and the Asherah poles from Judah.

⁷In the third year of his reign he sent his officials Ben-Hail, Obadiah, Zechariah, Nethanel and Micaiah to teach in the towns of Judah. ⁸With them were certain Levites—Shemaiah, Nethaniah, Zebadiah, Asahel, Shemiramoth, Jehonathan, Adonijah, Tobijah and Tob-Adonijah—and the priests Elishama and Jehoram. ⁹They taught throughout Judah, taking with them the Book of the Law of the LORD; they went around to all the towns of Judah and taught the people.

ᵃ4 Also known as *Abel Beth Maacah*   *ᵇ8* That is, people from the upper Nile region   *ᶜ8* Or *charioteers*

¹⁰The fear of the LORD fell on all the kingdoms of the lands surrounding Judah, so that they did not make war with Jehoshaphat. ¹¹Some Philistines brought Jehoshaphat gifts and silver as tribute, and the Arabs brought him flocks: seven thousand seven hundred rams and seven thousand seven hundred goats.

¹²Jehoshaphat became more and more powerful; he built forts and store cities in Judah ¹³and had large supplies in the towns of Judah. He also kept experienced fighting men in Jerusalem. ¹⁴Their enrollment by families was as follows:

> From Judah, commanders of units of 1,000:
>> Adnah the commander, with 300,000 fighting men;
> ¹⁵next, Jehohanan the commander, with 280,000;
> ¹⁶next, Amasiah son of Zicri, who volunteered himself for the service of the LORD, with 200,000.
> ¹⁷From Benjamin:
>> Eliada, a valiant soldier, with 200,000 men armed with bows and shields;
> ¹⁸next, Jehozabad, with 180,000 men armed for battle.

¹⁹These were the men who served the king, besides those he stationed in the fortified cities throughout Judah.

Micaiah Prophesies Against Ahab

18 Now Jehoshaphat had great wealth and honor, and he allied himself with Ahab by marriage. ²Some years later he went down to visit Ahab in Samaria. Ahab slaughtered many sheep and cattle for him and the people with him and urged him to attack Ramoth Gilead. ³Ahab king of Israel asked Jehoshaphat king of Judah, "Will you go with me against Ramoth Gilead?"

Jehoshaphat replied, "I am as you are, and my people as your people; we will join you in the war." ⁴But Jehoshaphat also said to the king of Israel, "First seek the counsel of the LORD."

⁵So the king of Israel brought together the prophets—four hundred men—and asked them, "Shall we go to war against Ramoth Gilead, or shall I refrain?"

"Go," they answered, "for God will give it into the king's hand."

⁶But Jehoshaphat asked, "Is there not a prophet of the LORD here whom we can inquire of?"

⁷The king of Israel answered Jehoshaphat, "There is still one man through whom we can inquire of the LORD, but I hate him because he never prophesies anything good about me, but always bad. He is Micaiah son of Imlah."

"The king should not say that," Jehoshaphat replied.

⁸So the king of Israel called one of his officials and said, "Bring Micaiah son of Imlah at once."

⁹Dressed in their royal robes, the king of Israel and Jehoshaphat king of Judah were sitting on their thrones at the threshing floor by the entrance to the gate of Samaria, with all the prophets prophesying before them. ¹⁰Now Zedekiah son of Kenaanah had made iron horns, and he declared, "This is what the LORD says: 'With these you will gore the Arameans until they are destroyed.'"

¹¹All the other prophets were prophesying the same thing. "Attack Ramoth Gilead and be victorious," they said, "for the LORD will give it into the king's hand."

¹²The messenger who had gone to summon Micaiah said to him, "Look, as one man the other prophets are predicting success for the king. Let your word agree with theirs, and speak favorably."

¹³But Micaiah said, "As surely as the LORD lives, I can tell him only what my God says."

¹⁴When he arrived, the king asked him, "Micaiah, shall we go to war against Ramoth Gilead, or shall I refrain?"

"Attack and be victorious," he answered, "for they will be given into your hand."

¹⁵The king said to him, "How many times must I make you swear to tell me nothing but the truth in the name of the LORD?"

¹⁶Then Micaiah answered, "I saw all Israel scattered on the hills like sheep without a shepherd, and the LORD said, 'These people have no master. Let each one go home in peace.'"

¹⁷The king of Israel said to Jehoshaphat, "Didn't I tell you that he never prophesies anything good about me, but only bad?"

¹⁸Micaiah continued, "Therefore hear the word of the LORD: I saw the LORD sitting on his throne with all the host of heaven standing on his right and on his left. ¹⁹And the LORD said, 'Who will entice Ahab king of Israel into attacking Ramoth Gilead and going to his death there?'

"One suggested this, and another that. ²⁰Finally, a spirit came forward, stood before the LORD and said, 'I will entice him.'

"'By what means?' the LORD asked.

²¹"'I will go and be a lying spirit in the mouths of all his prophets,' he said.

"'You will succeed in enticing him,' said the LORD. 'Go and do it.'

²²"So now the LORD has put a lying spirit in the mouths of these prophets of yours. The LORD has decreed disaster for you."

²³Then Zedekiah son of Kenaanah went up and slapped Micaiah in the face. "Which way did the spirit from[a] the LORD go when he went from me to speak to you?" he asked.

²⁴Micaiah replied, "You will find out on the day you go to hide in an inner room."

²⁵The king of Israel then ordered, "Take Micaiah and send him back to Amon the ruler of the city and to Joash the king's son, ²⁶and say, 'This is what the king says: Put this fellow in prison and give him nothing but bread and water until I return safely.'"

²⁷Micaiah declared, "If you ever return safely, the LORD has not spoken through me." Then he added, "Mark my words, all you people!"

Ahab Killed at Ramoth Gilead

²⁸So the king of Israel and Jehoshaphat king of Judah went up to Ramoth Gilead. ²⁹The king of Israel said to Jehoshaphat, "I will enter the battle in disguise, but you wear your royal robes." So the king of Israel disguised himself and went into battle.

³⁰Now the king of Aram had ordered his chariot commanders, "Do not fight with anyone, small or great, except the king of Israel." ³¹When the chariot commanders saw Jehoshaphat, they thought, "This is the king of Israel." So they turned to attack him, but Jehoshaphat cried out, and the LORD helped him. God drew them away from him, ³²for when the chariot commanders saw that he was not the king of Israel, they stopped pursuing him.

³³But someone drew his bow at random and hit the king of Israel between the sections of his armor. The king told the chariot driver, "Wheel around and get me out of the fighting. I've been wounded." ³⁴All day long the battle raged, and the king of Israel propped himself up in his chariot facing the Arameans until evening. Then at sunset he died.

19 When Jehoshaphat king of Judah returned safely to his palace in Jerusalem, ²Jehu the seer, the son of Hanani, went out to meet him and said to the king, "Should you help the wicked and love[b] those who hate the LORD? Because of this, the wrath of the LORD is upon you. ³There is, however, some good in you, for you have rid the land of the Asherah poles and have set your heart on seeking God."

Jehoshaphat Appoints Judges

⁴Jehoshaphat lived in Jerusalem, and he went out again among the people from Beersheba to the hill country of Ephraim and turned them back to the LORD, the God of their fathers. ⁵He appointed judges in the land, in each of the fortified cities of Judah. ⁶He told

---

a 23 Or Spirit of   b 2 Or and make alliances with

them, "Consider carefully what you do, because you are not judging for man but for the LORD, who is with you whenever you give a verdict. ⁷Now let the fear of the LORD be upon you. Judge carefully, for with the LORD our God there is no injustice or partiality or bribery."

⁸In Jerusalem also, Jehoshaphat appointed some of the Levites, priests and heads of Israelite families to administer the law of the LORD and to settle disputes. And they lived in Jerusalem. ⁹He gave them these orders: "You must serve faithfully and wholeheartedly in the fear of the LORD. ¹⁰In every case that comes before you from your fellow countrymen who live in the cities—whether bloodshed or other concerns of the law, commands, decrees or ordinances—you are to warn them not to sin against the LORD; otherwise his wrath will come on you and your brothers. Do this, and you will not sin.

¹¹Amariah the chief priest will be over you in any matter concerning the LORD, and Zebadiah son of Ishmael, the leader of the tribe of Judah, will be over you in any matter concerning the king, and the Levites will serve as officials before you. Act with courage, and may the LORD be with those who do well."

Jehoshaphat Defeats Moab and Ammon

20 After this, the Moabites and Ammonites with some of the Meunites*ᵃ* came to make war on Jehoshaphat.

²Some men came and told Jehoshaphat, "A vast army is coming against you from Edom,*ᵇ* from the other side of the Sea.*ᶜ* It is already in Hazazon Tamar" (that is, En Gedi). ³Alarmed, Jehoshaphat resolved to inquire of the LORD, and he proclaimed a fast for all Judah. ⁴The people of Judah came together to seek help from the LORD; indeed, they came from every town in Judah to seek him.

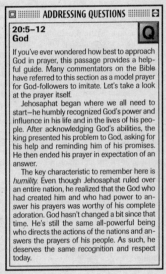

ADDRESSING QUESTIONS

20:5–12
God **Q**

If you've ever wondered how best to approach God in prayer, this passage provides a helpful guide. Many commentators on the Bible have referred to this section as a model prayer for God-followers to imitate. Let's take a look at the prayer itself.

Jehosaphat began where we all need to start—he humbly recognized God's power and influence in his life and in the lives of his people. After acknowledging God's abilities, the king presented his problem to God, asking for his help and reminding him of his promises. He then ended his prayer in expectation of an answer.

The key characteristic to remember here is *humility*. Even though Jehosaphat ruled over an entire nation, he realized that the God who had created him and who had power to answer his prayers was worthy of his complete adoration. God hasn't changed a bit since that time. He's still the same all-powerful being who directs the actions of the nations and answers the prayers of his people. As such, he deserves the same recognition and respect today.

⁵Then Jehoshaphat stood up in the assembly of Judah and Jerusalem at the temple of the LORD in the front of the new courtyard ⁶and said:

"O LORD, God of our fathers, are you not the God who is in heaven? You rule over all the kingdoms of the nations. Power and might are in your hand, and no one can withstand you. ⁷O our God, did you not drive out the inhabitants of this land before your people Israel and give it forever to the descendants of Abraham your friend? ⁸They have lived in it and have built in it a sanctuary for your Name, saying, ⁹'If calamity comes upon us, whether the sword of judgment, or plague or famine, we will stand in your presence before this temple that bears your Name and will cry out to you in our distress, and you will hear us and save us.'

¹⁰"But now here are men from Ammon, Moab and Mount Seir, whose territory you

ᵃ1 Some Septuagint manuscripts; Hebrew *Ammonites*   *ᵇ2* One Hebrew manuscript; most Hebrew manuscripts, Septuagint and Vulgate *Aram*   *ᶜ2* That is, the Dead Sea

would not allow Israel to invade when they came from Egypt; so they turned away from them and did not destroy them. ¹¹See how they are repaying us by coming to drive us out of the possession you gave us as an inheritance. ¹²O our God, will you not judge them? For we have no power to face this vast army that is attacking us. We do not know what to do, but our eyes are upon you."

¹³All the men of Judah, with their wives and children and little ones, stood there before the LORD.

¹⁴Then the Spirit of the LORD came upon Jahaziel son of Zechariah, the son of Benaiah, the son of Jeiel, the son of Mattaniah, a Levite and descendant of Asaph, as he stood in the assembly.

¹⁵He said: "Listen, King Jehoshaphat and all who live in Judah and Jerusalem! This is what the LORD says to you: 'Do not be afraid or discouraged because of this vast army. For the battle is not yours, but God's. ¹⁶Tomorrow march down against them. They will be climbing up by the Pass of Ziz, and you will find them at the end of the gorge in the Desert of Jeruel. ¹⁷You will not have to fight this battle. Take up your positions; stand firm and see the deliverance the LORD will give you, O Judah and Jerusalem. Do not be afraid; do not be discouraged. Go out to face them tomorrow, and the LORD will be with you.'"

¹⁸Jehoshaphat bowed with his face to the ground, and all the people of Judah and Jerusalem fell down in worship before the LORD. ¹⁹Then some Levites from the Kohathites and Korahites stood up and praised the LORD, the God of Israel, with very loud voice.

²⁰Early in the morning they left for the Desert of Tekoa. As they set out, Jehoshaphat stood and said, "Listen to me, Judah and people of Jerusalem! Have faith in the LORD your God and you will be upheld; have faith in his prophets and you will be successful." ²¹After consulting the people, Jehoshaphat appointed men to sing to the LORD and to praise him for the splendor of his^a holiness as they went out at the head of the army, saying:

> "Give thanks to the LORD,
>   for his love endures forever."

²²As they began to sing and praise, the LORD set ambushes against the men of Ammon and Moab and Mount Seir who were invading Judah, and they were defeated. ²³The men of Ammon and Moab rose up against the men from Mount Seir to destroy and annihilate them. After they finished slaughtering the men from Seir, they helped to destroy one another.

²⁴When the men of Judah came to the place that overlooks the desert and looked toward the vast army, they saw only dead bodies lying on the ground; no one had escaped. ²⁵So Jehoshaphat and his men went to carry off their plunder, and they found among them a great amount of equipment and clothing^b and also articles of value—more than they could take away. There was so much plunder that it took three days to collect it. ²⁶On the fourth day they assembled in the Valley of Beracah, where they praised the LORD. This is why it is called the Valley of Beracah^c to this day.

²⁷Then, led by Jehoshaphat, all the men of Judah and Jerusalem returned joyfully to Jerusalem, for the LORD had given them cause to rejoice over their enemies. ²⁸They entered Jerusalem and went to the temple of the LORD with harps and lutes and trumpets.

²⁹The fear of God came upon all the kingdoms of the countries when they heard how the LORD had fought against the enemies of Israel. ³⁰And the kingdom of Jehoshaphat was at peace, for his God had given him rest on every side.

---

^a21 Or him with the splendor of   ^b25 Some Hebrew manuscripts and Vulgate; most Hebrew manuscripts corpses
^c26 Beracah means praise.

The End of Jehoshaphat's Reign

³¹So Jehoshaphat reigned over Judah. He was thirty-five years old when he became king of Judah, and he reigned in Jerusalem twenty-five years. His mother's name was Azubah daughter of Shilhi. ³²He walked in the ways of his father Asa and did not stray from them; he did what was right in the eyes of the LORD. ³³The high places, however, were not removed, and the people still had not set their hearts on the God of their fathers.

³⁴The other events of Jehoshaphat's reign, from beginning to end, are written in the annals of Jehu son of Hanani, which are recorded in the book of the kings of Israel.

³⁵Later, Jehoshaphat king of Judah made an alliance with Ahaziah king of Israel, who was guilty of wickedness. ³⁶He agreed with him to construct a fleet of trading ships.ᵃ After these were built at Ezion Geber, ³⁷Eliezer son of Dodavahu of Mareshah prophesied against Jehoshaphat, saying, "Because you have made an alliance with Ahaziah, the LORD will destroy what you have made." The ships were wrecked and were not able to set sail to trade.ᵇ

21 Then Jehoshaphat rested with his fathers and was buried with them in the City of David. And Jehoram his son succeeded him as king. ²Jehoram's brothers, the sons of Jehoshaphat, were Azariah, Jehiel, Zechariah, Azariahu, Michael and Shephatiah. All these were sons of Jehoshaphat king of Israel.ᶜ ³Their father had given them many gifts of silver and gold and articles of value, as well as fortified cities in Judah, but he had given the kingdom to Jehoram because he was his firstborn son.

Jehoram King of Judah

⁴When Jehoram established himself firmly over his father's kingdom, he put all his brothers to the sword along with some of the princes of Israel. ⁵Jehoram was thirty-two years old when he became king, and he reigned in Jerusalem eight years. ⁶He walked in the ways of the kings of Israel, as the house of Ahab had done, for he married a daughter of Ahab. He did evil in the eyes of the LORD. ⁷Nevertheless, because of the covenant the LORD had made with David, the LORD was not willing to destroy the house of David. He had promised to maintain a lamp for him and his descendants forever.

⁸In the time of Jehoram, Edom rebelled against Judah and set up its own king. ⁹So Jehoram went there with his officers and all his chariots. The Edomites surrounded him and his chariot commanders, but he rose up and broke through by night. ¹⁰To this day Edom has been in rebellion against Judah.

Libnah revolted at the same time, because Jehoram had forsaken the LORD, the God of his fathers. ¹¹He had also built high places on the hills of Judah and had caused the people of Jerusalem to prostitute themselves and had led Judah astray.

¹²Jehoram received a letter from Elijah the prophet, which said:

"This is what the LORD, the God of your father David, says: 'You have not walked in the ways of your father Jehoshaphat or of Asa king of Judah. ¹³But you have walked in the ways of the kings of Israel, and you have led Judah and the people of Jerusalem to prostitute themselves, just as the house of Ahab did. You have also murdered your own brothers, members of your father's house, men who were better than you. ¹⁴So now the LORD is about to strike your people, your sons, your wives and everything that is yours, with a heavy blow. ¹⁵You yourself will be very ill with a lingering disease of the bowels, until the disease causes your bowels to come out.'"

¹⁶The LORD aroused against Jehoram the hostility of the Philistines and of the Arabs who lived near the Cushites. ¹⁷They attacked Judah, invaded it and carried off all the goods found in the king's palace, together with his sons and wives. Not a son was left to him except Ahaziah,ᵈ the youngest.

ᵃ36 Hebrew *of ships that could go to Tarshish*   ᵇ37 Hebrew *sail for Tarshish*   ᶜ2 That is, Judah, as frequently in 2 Chronicles   ᵈ17 Hebrew *Jehoahaz*, a variant of *Ahaziah*

¹⁸After all this, the LORD afflicted Jehoram with an incurable disease of the bowels. ¹⁹In the course of time, at the end of the second year, his bowels came out because of the disease, and he died in great pain. His people made no fire in his honor, as they had for his fathers.

²⁰Jehoram was thirty-two years old when he became king, and he reigned in Jerusalem eight years. He passed away, to no one's regret, and was buried in the City of David, but not in the tombs of the kings.

Ahaziah King of Judah

22 The people of Jerusalem made Ahaziah, Jehoram's youngest son, king in his place, since the raiders, who came with the Arabs into the camp, had killed all the older sons. So Ahaziah son of Jehoram king of Judah began to reign.

²Ahaziah was twenty-two years old[a] when he became king, and he reigned in Jerusalem one year. His mother's name was Athaliah, a granddaughter of Omri.

³He too walked in the ways of the house of Ahab, for his mother encouraged him in doing wrong. ⁴He did evil in the eyes of the LORD, as the house of Ahab had done, for after his father's death they became his advisers, to his undoing. ⁵He also followed their counsel when he went with Joram[b] son of Ahab king of Israel to war against Hazael king of Aram at Ramoth Gilead. The Arameans wounded Joram; ⁶so he returned to Jezreel to recover from the wounds they had inflicted on him at Ramoth[c] in his battle with Hazael king of Aram.

Then Ahaziah[d] son of Jehoram king of Judah went down to Jezreel to see Joram son of Ahab because he had been wounded.

⁷Through Ahaziah's visit to Joram, God brought about Ahaziah's downfall. When Ahaziah arrived, he went out with Joram to meet Jehu son of Nimshi, whom the LORD had anointed to destroy the house of Ahab. ⁸While Jehu was executing judgment on the house of Ahab, he found the princes of Judah and the sons of Ahaziah's relatives, who had been attending Ahaziah, and he killed them. ⁹He then went in search of Ahaziah, and his men captured him while he was hiding in Samaria. He was brought to Jehu and put to death. They buried him, for they said, "He was a son of Jehoshaphat, who sought the LORD with all his heart." So there was no one in the house of Ahaziah powerful enough to retain the kingdom.

Athaliah and Joash

¹⁰When Athaliah the mother of Ahaziah saw that her son was dead, she proceeded to destroy the whole royal family of the house of Judah. ¹¹But Jehosheba,[e] the daughter of King Jehoram, took Joash son of Ahaziah and stole him away from among the royal princes who were about to be murdered and put him and his nurse in a bedroom. Because Jehosheba,[e] the daughter of King Jehoram and wife of the priest Jehoiada, was Ahaziah's sister, she hid the child from Athaliah so she could not kill him. ¹²He remained hidden with them at the temple of God for six years while Athaliah ruled the land.

23 In the seventh year Jehoiada showed his strength. He made a covenant with the commanders of units of a hundred: Azariah son of Jeroham, Ishmael son of Jehohanan, Azariah son of Obed, Maaseiah son of Adaiah, and Elishaphat son of Zicri. ²They went throughout Judah and gathered the Levites and the heads of Israelite families from all the towns. When they came to Jerusalem, ³the whole assembly made a covenant with the king at the temple of God.

Jehoiada said to them, "The king's son shall reign, as the LORD promised concerning the descendants of David. ⁴Now this is what you are to do: A third of you priests and Levites who are going on duty on the Sabbath are to keep watch at the doors, ⁵a third of you at

---

[a]2 Some Septuagint manuscripts and Syriac (see also 2 Kings 8:26); Hebrew *forty-two*   [b]5 Hebrew *Jehoram*, a variant of *Joram*; also in verses 6 and 7   [c]6 Hebrew *Ramah*, a variant of *Ramoth*   [d]6 Some Hebrew manuscripts, Septuagint, Vulgate and Syriac (see also 2 Kings 8:29); most Hebrew manuscripts *Azariah*   [e]11 Hebrew *Jehoshabeath*, a variant of *Jehosheba*

the royal palace and a third at the Foundation Gate, and all the other men are to be in the courtyards of the temple of the LORD. ⁶No one is to enter the temple of the LORD except the priests and Levites on duty; they may enter because they are consecrated, but all the other men are to guard what the LORD has assigned to them.ᵃ ⁷The Levites are to station themselves around the king, each man with his weapons in his hand. Anyone who enters the temple must be put to death. Stay close to the king wherever he goes."

⁸The Levites and all the men of Judah did just as Jehoiada the priest ordered. Each one took his men—those who were going on duty on the Sabbath and those who were going off duty—for Jehoiada the priest had not released any of the divisions. ⁹Then he gave the commanders of units of a hundred the spears and the large and small shields that had belonged to King David and that were in the temple of God. ¹⁰He stationed all the men, each with his weapon in his hand, around the king—near the altar and the temple, from the south side to the north side of the temple.

¹¹Jehoiada and his sons brought out the king's son and put the crown on him; they presented him with a copy of the covenant and proclaimed him king. They anointed him and shouted, "Long live the king!"

¹²When Athaliah heard the noise of the people running and cheering the king, she went to them at the temple of the LORD. ¹³She looked, and there was the king, standing by his pillar at the entrance. The officers and the trumpeters were beside the king, and all the people of the land were rejoicing and blowing trumpets, and singers with musical instruments were leading the praises. Then Athaliah tore her robes and shouted, "Treason! Treason!"

¹⁴Jehoiada the priest sent out the commanders of units of a hundred, who were in charge of the troops, and said to them: "Bring her out between the ranksᵇ and put to the sword anyone who follows her." For the priest had said, "Do not put her to death at the temple of the LORD." ¹⁵So they seized her as she reached the entrance of the Horse Gate on the palace grounds, and there they put her to death.

¹⁶Jehoiada then made a covenant that he and the people and the kingᶜ would be the LORD's people. ¹⁷All the people went to the temple of Baal and tore it down. They smashed the altars and idols and killed Mattan the priest of Baal in front of the altars.

¹⁸Then Jehoiada placed the oversight of the temple of the LORD in the hands of the priests, who were Levites, to whom David had made assignments in the temple, to present the burnt offerings of the LORD as written in the Law of Moses, with rejoicing and singing, as David had ordered. ¹⁹He also stationed doorkeepers at the gates of the LORD's temple so that no one who was in any way unclean might enter.

²⁰He took with him the commanders of hundreds, the nobles, the rulers of the people and all the people of the land and brought the king down from the temple of the LORD. They went into the palace through the Upper Gate and seated the king on the royal throne, ²¹and all the people of the land rejoiced. And the city was quiet, because Athaliah had been slain with the sword.

Joash Repairs the Temple

24 Joash was seven years old when he became king, and he reigned in Jerusalem forty years. His mother's name was Zibiah; she was from Beersheba. ²Joash did what was right in the eyes of the LORD all the years of Jehoiada the priest. ³Jehoiada chose two wives for him, and he had sons and daughters.

⁴Some time later Joash decided to restore the temple of the LORD. ⁵He called together the priests and Levites and said to them, "Go to the towns of Judah and collect the money due annually from all Israel, to repair the temple of your God. Do it now." But the Levites did not act at once.

⁶Therefore the king summoned Jehoiada the chief priest and said to him, "Why haven't

ᵃ6 Or to observe the LORD's command ˌnot to enterˌ   ᵇ14 Or out from the precincts   ᶜ16 Or covenant between ˌthe LORDˌ and the people and the king that they (see 2 Kings 11:17)

you required the Levites to bring in from Judah and Jerusalem the tax imposed by Moses the servant of the LORD and by the assembly of Israel for the Tent of the Testimony?"

⁷Now the sons of that wicked woman Athaliah had broken into the temple of God and had used even its sacred objects for the Baals.

⁸At the king's command, a chest was made and placed outside, at the gate of the temple of the LORD. ⁹A proclamation was then issued in Judah and Jerusalem that they should bring to the LORD the tax that Moses the servant of God had required of Israel in the desert. ¹⁰All the officials and all the people brought their contributions gladly, dropping them into the chest until it was full. ¹¹Whenever the chest was brought in by the Levites to the king's officials and they saw that there was a large amount of money, the royal secretary and the officer of the chief priest would come and empty the chest and carry it back to its place. They did this regularly and collected a great amount of money. ¹²The king and Jehoiada gave it to the men who carried out the work required for the temple of the LORD. They hired masons and carpenters to restore the LORD's temple, and also workers in iron and bronze to repair the temple.

¹³The men in charge of the work were diligent, and the repairs progressed under them. They rebuilt the temple of God according to its original design and reinforced it. ¹⁴When they had finished, they brought the rest of the money to the king and Jehoiada, and with it were made articles for the LORD's temple: articles for the service and for the burnt offerings, and also dishes and other objects of gold and silver. As long as Jehoiada lived, burnt offerings were presented continually in the temple of the LORD.

¹⁵Now Jehoiada was old and full of years, and he died at the age of a hundred and thirty. ¹⁶He was buried with the kings in the City of David, because of the good he had done in Israel for God and his temple.

The Wickedness of Joash

¹⁷After the death of Jehoiada, the officials of Judah came and paid homage to the king, and he listened to them. ¹⁸They abandoned the temple of the LORD, the God of their fathers, and worshiped Asherah poles and idols. Because of their guilt, God's anger came upon Judah and Jerusalem. ¹⁹Although the LORD sent prophets to the people to bring them back to him, and though they testified against them, they would not listen.

²⁰Then the Spirit of God came upon Zechariah son of Jehoiada the priest. He stood before the people and said, "This is what God says: 'Why do you disobey the LORD's commands? You will not prosper. Because you have forsaken the LORD, he has forsaken you.'"

²¹But they plotted against him, and by order of the king they stoned him to death in the courtyard of the LORD's temple. ²²King Joash did not remember the kindness Zechariah's father Jehoiada had shown him but killed his son, who said as he lay dying, "May the LORD see this and call you to account."

²³At the turn of the year,ᵃ the army of Aram marched against Joash; it invaded Judah and Jerusalem and killed all the leaders of the people. They sent all the plunder to their king in Damascus. ²⁴Although the Aramean army had come with only a few men, the LORD delivered into their hands a much larger army. Because Judah had forsaken the LORD, the God of their fathers, judgment was executed on Joash. ²⁵When the Arameans withdrew, they left Joash severely wounded. His officials conspired against him for murdering the son of Jehoiada the priest, and they killed him in his bed. So he died and was buried in the City of David, but not in the tombs of the kings.

²⁶Those who conspired against him were Zabad,ᵇ son of Shimeath an Ammonite woman, and Jehozabad, son of Shimrithᶜ a Moabite woman. ²⁷The account of his sons, the many prophecies about him, and the record of the restoration of the temple of God are written in the annotations on the book of the kings. And Amaziah his son succeeded him as king.

ᵃ23 Probably in the spring   ᵇ26 A variant of Jozabad   ᶜ26 A variant of Shomer

Amaziah King of Judah

25 Amaziah was twenty-five years old when he became king, and he reigned in Jerusalem twenty-nine years. His mother's name was Jehoaddin[a]; she was from Jerusalem. [2]He did what was right in the eyes of the LORD, but not wholeheartedly. [3]After the kingdom was firmly in his control, he executed the officials who had murdered his father the king. [4]Yet he did not put their sons to death, but acted in accordance with what is written in the Law, in the Book of Moses, where the LORD commanded: "Fathers shall not be put to death for their children, nor children put to death for their fathers; each is to die for his own sins."[b]

[5]Amaziah called the people of Judah together and assigned them according to their families to commanders of thousands and commanders of hundreds for all Judah and Benjamin. He then mustered those twenty years old or more and found that there were three hundred thousand men ready for military service, able to handle the spear and shield. [6]He also hired a hundred thousand fighting men from Israel for a hundred talents[c] of silver.

[7]But a man of God came to him and said, "O king, these troops from Israel must not march with you, for the LORD is not with Israel—not with any of the people of Ephraim. [8]Even if you go and fight courageously in battle, God will overthrow you before the enemy, for God has the power to help or to overthrow."

[9]Amaziah asked the man of God, "But what about the hundred talents I paid for these Israelite troops?"

The man of God replied, "The LORD can give you much more than that."

[10]So Amaziah dismissed the troops who had come to him from Ephraim and sent them home. They were furious with Judah and left for home in a great rage.

[11]Amaziah then marshaled his strength and led his army to the Valley of Salt, where he killed ten thousand men of Seir. [12]The army of Judah also captured ten thousand men alive, took them to the top of a cliff and threw them down so that all were dashed to pieces.

[13]Meanwhile the troops that Amaziah had sent back and had not allowed to take part in the war raided Judean towns from Samaria to Beth Horon. They killed three thousand people and carried off great quantities of plunder.

[14]When Amaziah returned from slaughtering the Edomites, he brought back the gods of the people of Seir. He set them up as his own gods, bowed down to them and burned sacrifices to them. [15]The anger of the LORD burned against Amaziah, and he sent a prophet to him, who said, "Why do you consult this people's gods, which could not save their own people from your hand?"

[16]While he was still speaking, the king said to him, "Have we appointed you an adviser to the king? Stop! Why be struck down?"

So the prophet stopped but said, "I know that God has determined to destroy you, because you have done this and have not listened to my counsel."

[17]After Amaziah king of Judah consulted his advisers, he sent this challenge to Jehoash[d] son of Jehoahaz, the son of Jehu, king of Israel: "Come, meet me face to face."

[18]But Jehoash king of Israel replied to Amaziah king of Judah: "A thistle in Lebanon sent a message to a cedar in Lebanon, 'Give your daughter to my son in marriage.' Then a wild beast in Lebanon came along and trampled the thistle underfoot. [19]You say to yourself that you have defeated Edom, and now you are arrogant and proud. But stay at home! Why ask for trouble and cause your own downfall and that of Judah also?"

[20]Amaziah, however, would not listen, for God so worked that he might hand them over to ⌊Jehoash⌋, because they sought the gods of Edom. [21]So Jehoash king of Israel attacked. He and Amaziah king of Judah faced each other at Beth Shemesh in Judah. [22]Judah was routed by Israel, and every man fled to his home. [23]Jehoash king of Israel

---

[a]1 Hebrew *Jehoaddan*, a variant of *Jehoaddin*   [b]4 Deut. 24:16   [c]6 That is, about 3 3/4 tons (about 3.4 metric tons); also in verse 9   [d]17 Hebrew *Joash*, a variant of *Jehoash*; also in verses 18, 21, 23 and 25

captured Amaziah king of Judah, the son of Joash, the son of Ahaziah,[a] at Beth She-mesh. Then Jehoash brought him to Jerusalem and broke down the wall of Jerusalem from the Ephraim Gate to the Corner Gate—a section about six hundred feet[b] long. 24He took all the gold and silver and all the articles found in the temple of God that had been in the care of Obed-Edom, together with the palace treasures and the hostages, and returned to Samaria.

25Amaziah son of Joash king of Judah lived for fifteen years after the death of Jehoash son of Jehoahaz king of Israel. 26As for the other events of Amaziah's reign, from begin-ning to end, are they not written in the book of the kings of Judah and Israel? 27From the time that Amaziah turned away from following the LORD, they conspired against him in Jerusalem and he fled to Lachish, but they sent men after him to Lachish and killed him there. 28He was brought back by horse and was buried with his fathers in the City of Judah.

Uzziah King of Judah

26 Then all the people of Judah took Uzziah,[c] who was sixteen years old, and made him king in place of his father Amaziah. 2He was the one who rebuilt Elath and restored it to Judah after Amaziah rested with his fathers.

3Uzziah was sixteen years old when he became king, and he reigned in Jerusalem fifty-two years. His mother's name was Jecoliah; she was from Jerusalem. 4He did what was right in the eyes of the LORD, just as his father Amaziah had done. 5He sought God during the days of Zechariah, who in-structed him in the fear[d] of God. As long as he sought the LORD, God gave him suc-cess.

6He went to war against the Philistines and broke down the walls of Gath, Jabneh and Ashdod. He then rebuilt towns near Ashdod and elsewhere among the Philis-tines. 7God helped him against the Philis-tines and against the Arabs who lived in Gur Baal and against the Meunites. 8The Ammonites brought tribute to Uzziah, and his fame spread as far as the border of Egypt, because he had become very pow-erful.

9Uzziah built towers in Jerusalem at the Corner Gate, at the Valley Gate and at the angle of the wall, and he fortified them. 10He also built towers in the desert and dug many cisterns, because he had much livestock in the foothills and in the plain. He had people working his fields and vineyards in the hills and in the fertile lands, for he loved the soil.

11Uzziah had a well-trained army, ready to go out by divisions according to their numbers as mustered by Jeiel the secretary and Maaseiah the officer under the direction of Hananiah, one of the royal officials. 12The total number of family leaders over the fighting men was 2,600. 13Under their command was an army of 307,500 men trained for war, a powerful force to support the king against his enemies. 14Uzziah provided

> ### ▣ ▒▒▒ REASONS TO BELIEVE ▒▒▒ ⮀
>
> **26:3–5**
> **The Christian Experience**
>
> Does seeking God guarantee success, as this passage seems to imply? You may get that im-pression from some religious organizations that promise material blessings from heaven in return for the financial support of their min-istry. Such a "health and wealth" gospel, as it is sometimes called, hardly expresses the whole truth of God's intentions for his followers.
>
> While God may choose to bless those who seek him with the things that society sees as signs of success—money, status, prestige—he never guarantees that such material things will flow from a relationship with him. What he does guarantee, however, is that people who seek him will find his love, his peace and his goodness, whatever their financial status.
>
> Becoming a follower of God involves find-ing a much richer treasure than any bank ac-count or stock portfolio could ever hold.

---

a23 Hebrew *Jehoahaz,* a variant of *Ahaziah*   b23 Hebrew *four hundred cubits* (about 180 meters)   c1 Also called *Azariah*   d5 Many Hebrew manuscripts, Septuagint and Syriac; other Hebrew manuscripts *vision*

shields, spears, helmets, coats of armor, bows and slingstones for the entire army. ¹⁵In Jerusalem he made machines designed by skillful men for use on the towers and on the corner defenses to shoot arrows and hurl large stones. His fame spread far and wide, for he was greatly helped until he became powerful.

¹⁶But after Uzziah became powerful, his pride led to his downfall. He was unfaithful to the Lord his God, and entered the temple of the Lord to burn incense on the altar of incense. ¹⁷Azariah the priest with eighty other courageous priests of the Lord followed him in. ¹⁸They confronted him and said, "It is not right for you, Uzziah, to burn incense to the Lord. That is for the priests, the descendants of Aaron, who have been consecrated to burn incense. Leave the sanctuary, for you have been unfaithful; and you will not be honored by the Lord God."

¹⁹Uzziah, who had a censer in his hand ready to burn incense, became angry. While he was raging at the priests in their presence before the incense altar in the Lord's temple, leprosyᵃ broke out on his forehead. ²⁰When Azariah the chief priest and all the other priests looked at him, they saw that he had leprosy on his forehead, so they hurried him out. Indeed, he himself was eager to leave, because the Lord had afflicted him.

²¹King Uzziah had leprosy until the day he died. He lived in a separate houseᵇ—leprous, and excluded from the temple of the Lord. Jotham his son had charge of the palace and governed the people of the land.

²²The other events of Uzziah's reign, from beginning to end, are recorded by the prophet Isaiah son of Amoz. ²³Uzziah rested with his fathers and was buried near them in a field for burial that belonged to the kings, for people said, "He had leprosy." And Jotham his son succeeded him as king.

Jotham King of Judah

27 Jotham was twenty-five years old when he became king, and he reigned in Jerusalem sixteen years. His mother's name was Jerusha daughter of Zadok. ²He did what was right in the eyes of the Lord, just as his father Uzziah had done, but unlike him he did not enter the temple of the Lord. The people, however, continued their corrupt practices. ³Jotham rebuilt the Upper Gate of the temple of the Lord and did extensive work on the wall at the hill of Ophel. ⁴He built towns in the Judean hills and forts and towers in the wooded areas.

⁵Jotham made war on the king of the Ammonites and conquered them. That year the Ammonites paid him a hundred talentsᶜ of silver, ten thousand corsᵈ of wheat and ten thousand cors of barley. The Ammonites brought him the same amount also in the second and third years.

⁶Jotham grew powerful because he walked steadfastly before the Lord his God.

⁷The other events in Jotham's reign, including all his wars and the other things he did, are written in the book of the kings of Israel and Judah. ⁸He was twenty-five years old when he became king, and he reigned in Jerusalem sixteen years. ⁹Jotham rested with his fathers and was buried in the City of David. And Ahaz his son succeeded him as king.

Ahaz King of Judah

28 Ahaz was twenty years old when he became king, and he reigned in Jerusalem sixteen years. Unlike David his father, he did not do what was right in the eyes of the Lord. ²He walked in the ways of the kings of Israel and also made cast idols for worshiping the Baals. ³He burned sacrifices in the Valley of Ben Hinnom and sacrificed his sons in the fire, following the detestable ways of the nations the Lord had driven out before the Israelites. ⁴He offered sacrifices and burned incense at the high places, on the hilltops and under every spreading tree.

ᵃ19 The Hebrew word was used for various diseases affecting the skin—not necessarily leprosy; also in verses 20, 21 and 23.
ᵇ21 Or in a house where he was relieved of responsibilities   ᶜ5 That is, about 3 3/4 tons (about 3.4 metric tons)
ᵈ5 That is, probably about 62,000 bushels (about 2,200 kiloliters)

[5]Therefore the LORD his God handed him over to the king of Aram. The Arameans defeated him and took many of his people as prisoners and brought them to Damascus.

He was also given into the hands of the king of Israel, who inflicted heavy casualties on him. [6]In one day Pekah son of Remaliah killed a hundred and twenty thousand soldiers in Judah—because Judah had forsaken the LORD, the God of their fathers. [7]Zicri, an Ephraimite warrior, killed Maaseiah the king's son, Azrikam the officer in charge of the palace, and Elkanah, second to the king. [8]The Israelites took captive from their kinsmen two hundred thousand wives, sons and daughters. They also took a great deal of plunder, which they carried back to Samaria.

[9]But a prophet of the LORD named Oded was there, and he went out to meet the army when it returned to Samaria. He said to them, "Because the LORD, the God of your fathers, was angry with Judah, he gave them into your hand. But you have slaughtered them in a rage that reaches to heaven. [10]And now you intend to make the men and women of Judah and Jerusalem your slaves. But aren't you also guilty of sins against the LORD your God? [11]Now listen to me! Send back your fellow countrymen you have taken as prisoners, for the LORD's fierce anger rests on you."

[12]Then some of the leaders in Ephraim—Azariah son of Jehohanan, Berekiah son of Meshillemoth, Jehizkiah son of Shallum, and Amasa son of Hadlai—confronted those who were arriving from the war. [13]"You must not bring those prisoners here," they said, "or we will be guilty before the LORD. Do you intend to add to our sin and guilt? For our guilt is already great, and his fierce anger rests on Israel."

[14]So the soldiers gave up the prisoners and plunder in the presence of the officials and all the assembly. [15]The men designated by name took the prisoners, and from the plunder they clothed all who were naked. They provided them with clothes and sandals, food and drink, and healing balm. All those who were weak they put on donkeys. So they took them back to their fellow countrymen at Jericho, the City of Palms, and returned to Samaria.

[16]At that time King Ahaz sent to the king[a] of Assyria for help. [17]The Edomites had again come and attacked Judah and carried away prisoners, [18]while the Philistines had raided towns in the foothills and in the Negev of Judah. They captured and occupied Beth Shemesh, Aijalon and Gederoth, as well as Soco, Timnah and Gimzo, with their surrounding villages. [19]The LORD had humbled Judah because of Ahaz king of Israel,[b] for he had promoted wickedness in Judah and had been most unfaithful to the LORD. [20]Tiglath-Pileser[c] king of Assyria came to him, but he gave him trouble instead of help. [21]Ahaz took some of the things from the temple of the LORD and from the royal palace and from the princes and presented them to the king of Assyria, but that did not help him.

[22]In his time of trouble King Ahaz became even more unfaithful to the LORD. [23]He offered sacrifices to the gods of Damascus, who had defeated him; for he thought, "Since the gods of the kings of Aram have helped them, I will sacrifice to them so they will help me." But they were his downfall, and the downfall of all Israel.

[24]Ahaz gathered together the furnishings from the temple of God and took them away.[d] He shut the doors of the LORD's temple and set up altars at every street corner in Jerusalem. [25]In every town in Judah he built high places to burn sacrifices to other gods and provoked the LORD, the God of his fathers, to anger.

[26]The other events of his reign and all his ways, from beginning to end, are written in the book of the kings of Judah and Israel. [27]Ahaz rested with his fathers and was buried in the city of Jerusalem, but he was not placed in the tombs of the kings of Israel. And Hezekiah his son succeeded him as king.

---

[a]16 One Hebrew manuscript, Septuagint and Vulgate (see also 2 Kings 16:7); most Hebrew manuscripts *kings*   [b]19 That is, Judah, as frequently in 2 Chronicles   [c]20 Hebrew *Tilgath-Pilneser*, a variant of *Tiglath-Pileser*   [d]24 Or *and cut them up*

Hezekiah Purifies the Temple

29 Hezekiah was twenty-five years old when he became king, and he reigned in Jerusalem twenty-nine years. His mother's name was Abijah daughter of Zechariah. ²He did what was right in the eyes of the LORD, just as his father David had done.

³In the first month of the first year of his reign, he opened the doors of the temple of the LORD and repaired them. ⁴He brought in the priests and the Levites, assembled them in the square on the east side ⁵and said: "Listen to me, Levites! Consecrate yourselves now and consecrate the temple of the LORD, the God of your fathers. Remove all defilement from the sanctuary. ⁶Our fathers were unfaithful; they did evil in the eyes of the LORD our God and forsook him. They turned their faces away from the LORD's dwelling place and turned their backs on him. ⁷They also shut the doors of the portico and put out the lamps. They did not burn incense or present any burnt offerings at the sanctuary to the God of Israel. ⁸Therefore, the anger of the LORD has fallen on Judah and Jerusalem; he has made them an object of dread and horror and scorn, as you can see with your own eyes. ⁹This is why our fathers have fallen by the sword and why our sons and daughters and our wives are in captivity. ¹⁰Now I intend to make a covenant with the LORD, the God of Israel, so that his fierce anger will turn away from us. ¹¹My sons, do not be negligent now, for the LORD has chosen you to stand before him and serve him, to minister before him and to burn incense."

¹²Then these Levites set to work:

from the Kohathites,
    Mahath son of Amasai and Joel son of Azariah;
from the Merarites,
    Kish son of Abdi and Azariah son of Jehallelel;
from the Gershonites,
    Joah son of Zimmah and Eden son of Joah;
¹³from the descendants of Elizaphan,
    Shimri and Jeiel;
from the descendants of Asaph,
    Zechariah and Mattaniah;
¹⁴from the descendants of Heman,
    Jehiel and Shimei;
from the descendants of Jeduthun,
    Shemaiah and Uzziel.

¹⁵When they had assembled their brothers and consecrated themselves, they went in to purify the temple of the LORD, as the king had ordered, following the word of the LORD. ¹⁶The priests went into the sanctuary of the LORD to purify it. They brought out to the courtyard of the LORD's temple everything unclean that they found in the temple of the LORD. The Levites took it and carried it out to the Kidron Valley. ¹⁷They began the consecration on the first day of the first month, and by the eighth day of the month they reached the portico of the LORD. For eight more days they consecrated the temple of the LORD itself, finishing on the sixteenth day of the first month.

¹⁸Then they went in to King Hezekiah and reported: "We have purified the entire temple of the LORD, the altar of burnt offering with all its utensils, and the table for setting out the consecrated bread, with all its articles. ¹⁹We have prepared and consecrated all the articles that King Ahaz removed in his unfaithfulness while he was king. They are now in front of the LORD's altar."

²⁰Early the next morning King Hezekiah gathered the city officials together and went up to the temple of the LORD. ²¹They brought seven bulls, seven rams, seven male lambs and seven male goats as a sin offering for the kingdom, for the sanctuary and for Judah. The king commanded the priests, the descendants of Aaron, to offer these on the altar of

the Lord. ²²So they slaughtered the bulls, and the priests took the blood and sprinkled it on the altar; next they slaughtered the rams and sprinkled their blood on the altar; then they slaughtered the lambs and sprinkled their blood on the altar. ²³The goats for the sin offering were brought before the king and the assembly, and they laid their hands on them. ²⁴The priests then slaughtered the goats and presented their blood on the altar for a sin offering to atone for all Israel, because the king had ordered the burnt offering and the sin offering for all Israel.

²⁵He stationed the Levites in the temple of the Lord with cymbals, harps and lyres in the way prescribed by David and Gad the king's seer and Nathan the prophet; this was commanded by the Lord through his prophets. ²⁶So the Levites stood ready with David's instruments, and the priests with their trumpets.

²⁷Hezekiah gave the order to sacrifice the burnt offering on the altar. As the offering began, singing to the Lord began also, accompanied by trumpets and the instruments of David king of Israel. ²⁸The whole assembly bowed in worship, while the singers sang and the trumpeters played. All this continued until the sacrifice of the burnt offering was completed.

²⁹When the offerings were finished, the king and everyone present with him knelt down and worshiped. ³⁰King Hezekiah and his officials ordered the Levites to praise the Lord with the words of David and of Asaph the seer. So they sang praises with gladness and bowed their heads and worshiped.

³¹Then Hezekiah said, "You have now dedicated yourselves to the Lord. Come and bring sacrifices and thank offerings to the temple of the Lord." So the assembly brought sacrifices and thank offerings, and all whose hearts were willing brought burnt offerings.

³²The number of burnt offerings the assembly brought was seventy bulls, a hundred rams and two hundred male lambs—all of them for burnt offerings to the Lord. ³³The animals consecrated as sacrifices amounted to six hundred bulls and three thousand sheep and goats. ³⁴The priests, however, were too few to skin all the burnt offerings; so their kinsmen the Levites helped them until the task was finished and until other priests had been consecrated, for the Levites had been more conscientious in consecrating themselves than the priests had been. ³⁵There were burnt offerings in abundance, together with the fat of the fellowship offerings^a and the drink offerings that accompanied the burnt offerings.

So the service of the temple of the Lord was reestablished. ³⁶Hezekiah and all the people rejoiced at what God had brought about for his people, because it was done so quickly.

Hezekiah Celebrates the Passover

30 Hezekiah sent word to all Israel and Judah and also wrote letters to Ephraim and Manasseh, inviting them to come to the temple of the Lord in Jerusalem and celebrate the Passover to the Lord, the God of Israel. ²The king and his officials and the whole assembly in Jerusalem decided to celebrate the Passover in the second month. ³They had not been able to celebrate it at the regular time because not enough priests had consecrated themselves and the people had not assembled in Jerusalem. ⁴The plan seemed right both to the king and to the whole assembly. ⁵They decided to send a proclamation throughout Israel, from Beersheba to Dan, calling the people to come to Jerusalem and celebrate the Passover to the Lord, the God of Israel. It had not been celebrated in large numbers according to what was written.

⁶At the king's command, couriers went throughout Israel and Judah with letters from the king and from his officials, which read:

"People of Israel, return to the Lord, the God of Abraham, Isaac and Israel, that he

^a35 Traditionally *peace offerings*

may return to you who are left, who have escaped from the hand of the kings of Assyria. ⁷Do not be like your fathers and brothers, who were unfaithful to the LORD, the God of their fathers, so that he made them an object of horror, as you see. ⁸Do not be stiff-necked, as your fathers were; submit to the LORD. Come to the sanctuary, which he has consecrated forever. Serve the LORD your God, so that his fierce anger will turn away from you. ⁹If you return to the LORD, then your brothers and your children will be shown compassion by their captors and will come back to this land, for the LORD your God is gracious and compassionate. He will not turn his face from you if you return to him."

¹⁰The couriers went from town to town in Ephraim and Manasseh, as far as Zebulun, but the people scorned and ridiculed them. ¹¹Nevertheless, some men of Asher, Manasseh and Zebulun humbled themselves and went to Jerusalem. ¹²Also in Judah the hand of God was on the people to give them unity of mind to carry out what the king and his officials had ordered, following the word of the LORD.

¹³A very large crowd of people assembled in Jerusalem to celebrate the Feast of Unleavened Bread in the second month. ¹⁴They removed the altars in Jerusalem and cleared away the incense altars and threw them into the Kidron Valley.

¹⁵They slaughtered the Passover lamb on the fourteenth day of the second month. The priests and the Levites were ashamed and consecrated themselves and brought burnt offerings to the temple of the LORD. ¹⁶Then they took up their regular positions as prescribed in the Law of Moses the man of God. The priests sprinkled the blood handed to them by the Levites. ¹⁷Since many in the crowd had not consecrated themselves, the Levites had to kill the Passover lambs for all those who were not ceremonially clean and could not consecrate ⌊their lambs⌋ to the LORD. ¹⁸Although most of the many people who came from Ephraim, Manasseh, Issachar and Zebulun had not purified themselves, yet they ate the Passover, contrary to what was written. But Hezekiah prayed for them, saying, "May the LORD, who is good, pardon everyone ¹⁹who sets his heart on seeking God—the LORD, the God of his fathers—even if he is not clean according to the rules of the sanctuary." ²⁰And the LORD heard Hezekiah and healed the people.

²¹The Israelites who were present in Jerusalem celebrated the Feast of Unleavened Bread for seven days with great rejoicing, while the Levites and priests sang to the LORD every day, accompanied by the LORD's instruments of praise.ᵃ

²²Hezekiah spoke encouragingly to all the Levites, who showed good understanding of the service of the LORD. For the seven days they ate their assigned portion and offered fellowship offeringsᵇ and praised the LORD, the God of their fathers.

²³The whole assembly then agreed to celebrate the festival seven more days; so for another seven days they celebrated joyfully. ²⁴Hezekiah king of Judah provided a thousand bulls and seven thousand sheep and goats for the assembly, and the officials provided them with a thousand bulls and ten thousand sheep and goats. A great number of priests consecrated themselves. ²⁵The entire assembly of Judah rejoiced, along with the priests and Levites and all who had assembled from Israel, including the aliens who had come from Israel and those who lived in Judah. ²⁶There was great joy in Jerusalem, for since the days of Solomon son of David king of Israel there had been nothing like this in Jerusalem. ²⁷The priests and the Levites stood to bless the people, and God heard them, for their prayer reached heaven, his holy dwelling place.

31 When all this had ended, the Israelites who were there went out to the towns of Judah, smashed the sacred stones and cut down the Asherah poles. They destroyed the high places and the altars throughout Judah and Benjamin and in

ᵃ21 Or *priests praised the LORD every day with resounding instruments belonging to the LORD*   ᵇ22 Traditionally *peace offerings*

Ephraim and Manasseh. After they had destroyed all of them, the Israelites returned to their own towns and to their own property.

Contributions for Worship

²Hezekiah assigned the priests and Levites to divisions—each of them according to their duties as priests or Levites—to offer burnt offerings and fellowship offerings,ᵃ to minister, to give thanks and to sing praises at the gates of the LORD's dwelling. ³The king contributed from his own possessions for the morning and evening burnt offerings and for the burnt offerings on the Sabbaths, New Moons and appointed feasts as written in the Law of the LORD. ⁴He ordered the people living in Jerusalem to give the portion due the priests and Levites so they could devote themselves to the Law of the LORD. ⁵As soon as the order went out, the Israelites generously gave the firstfruits of their grain, new wine, oil and honey and all that the fields produced. They brought a great amount, a tithe of everything. ⁶The men of Israel and Judah who lived in the towns of Judah also brought a tithe of their herds and flocks and a tithe of the holy things dedicated to the LORD their God, and they piled them in heaps. ⁷They began doing this in the third month and finished in the seventh month. ⁸When Hezekiah and his officials came and saw the heaps, they praised the LORD and blessed his people Israel.

⁹Hezekiah asked the priests and Levites about the heaps; ¹⁰and Azariah the chief priest, from the family of Zadok, answered, "Since the people began to bring their contributions to the temple of the LORD, we have had enough to eat and plenty to spare, because the LORD has blessed his people, and this great amount is left over."

¹¹Hezekiah gave orders to prepare storerooms in the temple of the LORD, and this was done. ¹²Then they faithfully brought in the contributions, tithes and dedicated gifts. Conaniah, a Levite, was in charge of these things, and his brother Shimei was next in rank. ¹³Jehiel, Azaziah, Nahath, Asahel, Jerimoth, Jozabad, Eliel, Ismakiah, Mahath and Benaiah were supervisors under Conaniah and Shimei his brother, by appointment of King Hezekiah and Azariah the official in charge of the temple of God.

¹⁴Kore son of Imnah the Levite, keeper of the East Gate, was in charge of the freewill offerings given to God, distributing the contributions made to the LORD and also the consecrated gifts. ¹⁵Eden, Miniamin, Jeshua, Shemaiah, Amariah and Shecaniah assisted him faithfully in the towns of the priests, distributing to their fellow priests according to their divisions, old and young alike.

¹⁶In addition, they distributed to the males three years old or more whose names were in the genealogical records—all who would enter the temple of the LORD to perform the daily duties of their various tasks, according to their responsibilities and their divisions. ¹⁷And they distributed to the priests enrolled by their families in the genealogical records and likewise to the Levites twenty years old or more, according to their responsibilities and their divisions. ¹⁸They included all the little ones, the wives, and the sons and daughters of the whole community listed in these genealogical records. For they were faithful in consecrating themselves.

¹⁹As for the priests, the descendants of Aaron, who lived on the farm lands around their towns or in any other towns, men were designated by name to distribute portions to every male among them and to all who were recorded in the genealogies of the Levites.

²⁰This is what Hezekiah did throughout Judah, doing what was good and right and faithful before the LORD his God. ²¹In everything that he undertook in the service of God's temple and in obedience to the law and the commands, he sought his God and worked wholeheartedly. And so he prospered.

ᵃ2 Traditionally *peace offerings*

Sennacherib Threatens Jerusalem

32 After all that Hezekiah had so faithfully done, Sennacherib king of Assyria came and invaded Judah. He laid siege to the fortified cities, thinking to conquer them for himself. ²When Hezekiah saw that Sennacherib had come and that he intended to make war on Jerusalem, ³he consulted with his officials and military staff about blocking off the water from the springs outside the city, and they helped him. ⁴A large force of men assembled, and they blocked all the springs and the stream that flowed through the land. "Why should the kings*ᵃ* of Assyria come and find plenty of water?" they said. ⁵Then he worked hard repairing all the broken sections of the wall and building towers on it. He built another wall outside that one and reinforced the supporting terraces*ᵇ* of the City of David. He also made large numbers of weapons and shields.

⁶He appointed military officers over the people and assembled them before him in the square at the city gate and encouraged them with these words: ⁷"Be strong and courageous. Do not be afraid or discouraged because of the king of Assyria and the vast army with him, for there is a greater power with us than with him. ⁸With him is only the arm of flesh, but with us is the Lᴏʀᴅ our God to help us and to fight our battles." And the people gained confidence from what Hezekiah the king of Judah said.

⁹Later, when Sennacherib king of Assyria and all his forces were laying siege to Lachish, he sent his officers to Jerusalem with this message for Hezekiah king of Judah and for all the people of Judah who were there:

¹⁰"This is what Sennacherib king of Assyria says: On what are you basing your confidence, that you remain in Jerusalem under siege? ¹¹When Hezekiah says, 'The Lᴏʀᴅ our God will save us from the hand of the king of Assyria,' he is misleading you, to let you die of hunger and thirst. ¹²Did not Hezekiah himself remove this god's high places and altars, saying to Judah and Jerusalem, 'You must worship before one altar and burn sacrifices on it'?

¹³"Do you not know what I and my fathers have done to all the peoples of the other lands? Were the gods of those nations ever able to deliver their land from my hand? ¹⁴Who of all the gods of these nations that my fathers destroyed has been able to save his people from me? How then can your god deliver you from my hand? ¹⁵Now do not let Hezekiah deceive you and mislead you like this. Do not believe him, for no god of any nation or kingdom has been able to deliver his people from my hand or the hand of my fathers. How much less will your god deliver you from my hand!"

¹⁶Sennacherib's officers spoke further against the Lᴏʀᴅ God and against his servant Hezekiah. ¹⁷The king also wrote letters insulting the Lᴏʀᴅ, the God of Israel, and saying this against him: "Just as the gods of the peoples of the other lands did not rescue their people from my hand, so the god of Hezekiah will not rescue his people from my hand." ¹⁸Then they called out in Hebrew to the people of Jerusalem who were on the wall, to terrify them and make them afraid in order to capture the city. ¹⁹They spoke about the God of Jerusalem as they did about the gods of the other peoples of the world—the work of men's hands.

²⁰King Hezekiah and the prophet Isaiah son of Amoz cried out in prayer to heaven about this. ²¹And the Lᴏʀᴅ sent an angel, who annihilated all the fighting men and the leaders and officers in the camp of the Assyrian king. So he withdrew to his own land in disgrace. And when he went into the temple of his god, some of his sons cut him down with the sword.

²²So the Lᴏʀᴅ saved Hezekiah and the people of Jerusalem from the hand of Sennacherib king of Assyria and from the hand of all others. He took care of them*ᶜ* on every side.

ᵃ4 Hebrew; Septuagint and Syriac *king*   *ᵇ5* Or *the Millo*   *ᶜ22* Hebrew; Septuagint and Vulgate *He gave them rest*

²³Many brought offerings to Jerusalem for the Lord and valuable gifts for Hezekiah king of Judah. From then on he was highly regarded by all the nations.

Hezekiah's Pride, Success and Death

²⁴In those days Hezekiah became ill and was at the point of death. He prayed to the Lord, who answered him and gave him a miraculous sign. ²⁵But Hezekiah's heart was proud and he did not respond to the kindness shown him; therefore the Lord's wrath was on him and on Judah and Jerusalem. ²⁶Then Hezekiah repented of the pride of his heart, as did the people of Jerusalem; therefore the Lord's wrath did not come upon them during the days of Hezekiah.

²⁷Hezekiah had very great riches and honor, and he made treasuries for his silver and gold and for his precious stones, spices, shields and all kinds of valuables. ²⁸He also made buildings to store the harvest of grain, new wine and oil; and he made stalls for various kinds of cattle, and pens for the flocks. ²⁹He built villages and acquired great numbers of flocks and herds, for God had given him very great riches.

³⁰It was Hezekiah who blocked the upper outlet of the Gihon spring and channeled the water down to the west side of the City of David. He succeeded in everything he undertook. ³¹But when envoys were sent by the rulers of Babylon to ask him about the miraculous sign that had occurred in the land, God left him to test him and to know everything that was in his heart.

³²The other events of Hezekiah's reign and his acts of devotion are written in the vision of the prophet Isaiah son of Amoz in the book of the kings of Judah and Israel. ³³Hezekiah rested with his fathers and was buried on the hill where the tombs of David's descendants are. All Judah and the people of Jerusalem honored him when he died. And Manasseh his son succeeded him as king.

Manasseh King of Judah

33 Manasseh was twelve years old when he became king, and he reigned in Jerusalem fifty-five years. ²He did evil in the eyes of the Lord, following the detestable practices of the nations the Lord had driven out before the Israelites. ³He rebuilt the high places his father Hezekiah had demolished; he also erected altars to the Baals and made Asherah poles. He bowed down to all the starry hosts and worshiped them. ⁴He built altars in the temple of the Lord, of which the Lord had said, "My Name will remain in Jerusalem forever." ⁵In both courts of the temple of the Lord, he built altars to all the starry hosts. ⁶He sacrificed his sons in[a] the fire in the Valley of Ben Hinnom, practiced sorcery, divination and witchcraft, and consulted mediums and spiritists. He did much evil in the eyes of the Lord, provoking him to anger.

⁷He took the carved image he had made and put it in God's temple, of which God had said to David and to his son Solomon, "In this temple and in Jerusalem, which I have chosen out of all the tribes of Israel, I will put my Name forever. ⁸I will not again make the feet of the Israelites leave the land I assigned to your forefathers, if only they will be careful to do everything I commanded them concerning all the laws, decrees and ordinances given through Moses." ⁹But Manasseh led Judah and the people of Jerusalem astray, so that they did more evil than the nations the Lord had destroyed before the Israelites.

¹⁰The Lord spoke to Manasseh and his people, but they paid no attention. ¹¹So the Lord brought against them the army commanders of the king of Assyria, who took Manasseh prisoner, put a hook in his nose, bound him with bronze shackles and took him to Babylon. ¹²In his distress he sought the favor of the Lord his God and humbled himself greatly before the God of his fathers. ¹³And when he prayed to him, the Lord was moved by his entreaty and listened to his plea; so he brought him back to Jerusalem and to his kingdom. Then Manasseh knew that the Lord is God.

a 6 Or He made his sons pass through

¹⁴Afterward he rebuilt the outer wall of the City of David, west of the Gihon spring in the valley, as far as the entrance of the Fish Gate and encircling the hill of Ophel; he also made it much higher. He stationed military commanders in all the fortified cities in Judah.

¹⁵He got rid of the foreign gods and removed the image from the temple of the LORD, as well as all the altars he had built on the temple hill and in Jerusalem; and he threw them out of the city. ¹⁶Then he restored the altar of the LORD and sacrificed fellowship offerings*a* and thank offerings on it, and told Judah to serve the LORD, the God of Israel. ¹⁷The people, however, continued to sacrifice at the high places, but only to the LORD their God.

¹⁸The other events of Manasseh's reign, including his prayer to his God and the words the seers spoke to him in the name of the LORD, the God of Israel, are written in the annals of the kings of Israel.*b* ¹⁹His prayer and how God was moved by his entreaty, as well as all his sins and unfaithfulness, and the sites where he built high places and set up Asherah poles and idols before he humbled himself—all are written in the records of the seers.*c* ²⁰Manasseh rested with his fathers and was buried in his palace. And Amon his son succeeded him as king.

Amon King of Judah

²¹Amon was twenty-two years old when he became king, and he reigned in Jerusalem two years. ²²He did evil in the eyes of the LORD, as his father Manasseh had done. Amon worshiped and offered sacrifices to all the idols Manasseh had made. ²³But unlike his father Manasseh, he did not humble himself before the LORD; Amon increased his guilt.

²⁴Amon's officials conspired against him and assassinated him in his palace. ²⁵Then the people of the land killed all who had plotted against King Amon, and they made Josiah his son king in his place.

Josiah's Reforms

34 Josiah was eight years old when he became king, and he reigned in Jerusalem thirty-one years. ²He did what was right in the eyes of the LORD and walked in the ways of his father David, not turning aside to the right or to the left.

³In the eighth year of his reign, while he was still young, he began to seek the God of his father David. In his twelfth year he began to purge Judah and Jerusalem of high places, Asherah poles, carved idols and cast images. ⁴Under his direction the altars of the Baals were torn down; he cut to pieces the incense altars that were above them, and smashed the Asherah poles, the idols and the images. These he broke to pieces and scattered over the graves of those who had sacrificed to them. ⁵He burned the bones of the priests on their altars, and so he purged Judah and Jerusalem. ⁶In the towns of Manasseh, Ephraim and Simeon, as far as Naphtali, and in the ruins around them, ⁷he tore down the altars and the Asherah poles and crushed the idols to powder and cut to pieces all the incense altars throughout Israel. Then he went back to Jerusalem.

⁸In the eighteenth year of Josiah's reign, to purify the land and the temple, he sent

---

a 16 Traditionally *peace offerings*   *b 18* That is, Judah, as frequently in 2 Chronicles   *c 19* One Hebrew manuscript and Septuagint; most Hebrew manuscripts of Hozai

Shaphan son of Azaliah and Maaseiah the ruler of the city, with Joah son of Joahaz, the recorder, to repair the temple of the LORD his God.

⁹They went to Hilkiah the high priest and gave him the money that had been brought into the temple of God, which the Levites who were the doorkeepers had collected from the people of Manasseh, Ephraim and the entire remnant of Israel and from all the people of Judah and Benjamin and the inhabitants of Jerusalem. ¹⁰Then they entrusted it to the men appointed to supervise the work on the LORD's temple. These men paid the workers who repaired and restored the temple. ¹¹They also gave money to the carpenters and builders to purchase dressed stone, and timber for joists and beams for the buildings that the kings of Judah had allowed to fall into ruin.

¹²The men did the work faithfully. Over them to direct them were Jahath and Obadiah, Levites descended from Merari, and Zechariah and Meshullam, descended from Kohath. The Levites—all who were skilled in playing musical instruments— ¹³had charge of the laborers and supervised all the workers from job to job. Some of the Levites were secretaries, scribes and doorkeepers.

The Book of the Law Found

¹⁴While they were bringing out the money that had been taken into the temple of the LORD, Hilkiah the priest found the Book of the Law of the LORD that had been given through Moses. ¹⁵Hilkiah said to Shaphan the secretary, "I have found the Book of the Law in the temple of the LORD." He gave it to Shaphan.

¹⁶Then Shaphan took the book to the king and reported to him: "Your officials are doing everything that has been committed to them. ¹⁷They have paid out the money that was in the temple of the LORD and have entrusted it to the supervisors and workers." ¹⁸Then Shaphan the secretary informed the king, "Hilkiah the priest has given me a book." And Shaphan read from it in the presence of the king.

¹⁹When the king heard the words of the Law, he tore his robes. ²⁰He gave these orders to Hilkiah, Ahikam son of Shaphan, Abdon son of Micah,ᵃ Shaphan the secretary and Asaiah the king's attendant: ²¹"Go and inquire of the LORD for me and for the remnant in Israel and Judah about what is written in this book that has been found. Great is the LORD's anger that is poured out on us because our fathers have not kept the word of the LORD; they have not acted in accordance with all that is written in this book."

²²Hilkiah and those the king sent with himᵇ went to speak to the prophetess Huldah, who was the wife of Shallum son of Tokhath,ᶜ the son of Hasrah,ᵈ keeper of the wardrobe. She lived in Jerusalem, in the Second District.

²³She said to them, "This is what the LORD, the God of Israel, says: Tell the man who sent you to me, ²⁴'This is what the LORD says: I am going to bring disaster on this place and its people—all the curses written in the book that has been read in the presence of the king of Judah. ²⁵Because they have forsaken me and burned incense to other gods and provoked me to anger by all that their hands have made,ᵉ my anger will be poured out on this place and will not be quenched.' ²⁶Tell the king of Judah, who sent you to inquire of the LORD, 'This is what the LORD, the God of Israel, says concerning the words you heard: ²⁷Because your heart was responsive and you humbled yourself before God when you heard what he spoke against this place and its people, and because you humbled yourself before me and tore your robes and wept in my presence, I have heard you, declares the LORD. ²⁸Now I will gather you to your fathers, and you will be buried in peace. Your eyes will not see all the disaster I am going to bring on this place and on those who live here.'"

So they took her answer back to the king.

²⁹Then the king called together all the elders of Judah and Jerusalem. ³⁰He went up to the temple of the LORD with the men of Judah, the people of Jerusalem, the priests and the

ᵃ20 Also called Acbor son of Micaiah   ᵇ22 One Hebrew manuscript, Vulgate and Syriac; most Hebrew manuscripts do not have had sent with him.   ᶜ22 Also called Tikvah   ᵈ22 Also called Harhas   ᵉ25 Or by everything they have done

Levites—all the people from the least to the greatest. He read in their hearing all the words of the Book of the Covenant, which had been found in the temple of the LORD. ³¹The king stood by his pillar and renewed the covenant in the presence of the LORD—to follow the LORD and keep his commands, regulations and decrees with all his heart and all his soul, and to obey the words of the covenant written in this book.

³²Then he had everyone in Jerusalem and Benjamin pledge themselves to it; the people of Jerusalem did this in accordance with the covenant of God, the God of their fathers.

³³Josiah removed all the detestable idols from all the territory belonging to the Israelites, and he had all who were present in Israel serve the LORD their God. As long as he lived, they did not fail to follow the LORD, the God of their fathers.

Josiah Celebrates the Passover

35 Josiah celebrated the Passover to the LORD in Jerusalem, and the Passover lamb was slaughtered on the fourteenth day of the first month. ²He appointed the priests to their duties and encouraged them in the service of the LORD's temple. ³He said to the Levites, who instructed all Israel and who had been consecrated to the LORD: "Put the sacred ark in the temple that Solomon son of David king of Israel built. It is not to be carried about on your shoulders. Now serve the LORD your God and his people Israel. ⁴Prepare yourselves by families in your divisions, according to the directions written by David king of Israel and by his son Solomon.

⁵"Stand in the holy place with a group of Levites for each subdivision of the families of your fellow countrymen, the lay people. ⁶Slaughter the Passover lambs, consecrate yourselves and prepare ˌthe lambsˌ for your fellow countrymen, doing what the LORD commanded through Moses."

⁷Josiah provided for all the lay people who were there a total of thirty thousand sheep and goats for the Passover offerings, and also three thousand cattle—all from the king's own possessions.

⁸His officials also contributed voluntarily to the people and the priests and Levites. Hilkiah, Zechariah and Jehiel, the administrators of God's temple, gave the priests twenty-six hundred Passover offerings and three hundred cattle. ⁹Also Conaniah along with Shemaiah and Nethanel, his brothers, and Hashabiah, Jeiel and Jozabad, the leaders of the Levites, provided five thousand Passover offerings and five hundred head of cattle for the Levites.

¹⁰The service was arranged and the priests stood in their places with the Levites in their divisions as the king had ordered. ¹¹The Passover lambs were slaughtered, and the priests sprinkled the blood handed to them, while the Levites skinned the animals. ¹²They set aside the burnt offerings to give them to the subdivisions of the families of the people to offer to the LORD, as is written in the Book of Moses. They did the same with the cattle. ¹³They roasted the Passover animals over the fire as prescribed, and boiled the holy offerings in pots, caldrons and pans and served them quickly to all the people. ¹⁴After this, they made preparations for themselves and for the priests, because the priests, the descendants of Aaron, were sacrificing the burnt offerings and the fat portions until nightfall. So the Levites made preparations for themselves and for the Aaronic priests.

¹⁵The musicians, the descendants of Asaph, were in the places prescribed by David, Asaph, Heman and Jeduthun the king's seer. The gatekeepers at each gate did not need to leave their posts, because their fellow Levites made the preparations for them.

¹⁶So at that time the entire service of the LORD was carried out for the celebration of the Passover and the offering of burnt offerings on the altar of the LORD, as King Josiah had ordered. ¹⁷The Israelites who were present celebrated the Passover at that time and observed the Feast of Unleavened Bread for seven days. ¹⁸The Passover had not been observed like this in Israel since the days of the prophet Samuel; and none of the kings

of Israel had ever celebrated such a Passover as did Josiah, with the priests, the Levites and all Judah and Israel who were there with the people of Jerusalem. ¹⁹This Passover was celebrated in the eighteenth year of Josiah's reign.

The Death of Josiah

²⁰After all this, when Josiah had set the temple in order, Neco king of Egypt went up to fight at Carchemish on the Euphrates, and Josiah marched out to meet him in battle. ²¹But Neco sent messengers to him, saying, "What quarrel is there between you and me, O king of Judah? It is not you I am attacking at this time, but the house with which I am at war. God has told me to hurry; so stop opposing God, who is with me, or he will destroy you."

²²Josiah, however, would not turn away from him, but disguised himself to engage him in battle. He would not listen to what Neco had said at God's command but went to fight him on the plain of Megiddo.

²³Archers shot King Josiah, and he told his officers, "Take me away; I am badly wounded." ²⁴So they took him out of his chariot, put him in the other chariot he had and brought him to Jerusalem, where he died. He was buried in the tombs of his fathers, and all Judah and Jerusalem mourned for him.

²⁵Jeremiah composed laments for Josiah, and to this day all the men and women singers commemorate Josiah in the laments. These became a tradition in Israel and are written in the Laments.

²⁶The other events of Josiah's reign and his acts of devotion, according to what is written in the Law of the LORD— ²⁷all the events, from beginning to end, are written in the book of the kings of Israel and Judah. **36** ¹And the people of the land took Jehoahaz son of Josiah and made him king in Jerusalem in place of his father.

Jehoahaz King of Judah

²Jehoahaz*ᵃ* was twenty-three years old when he became king, and he reigned in Jerusalem three months. ³The king of Egypt dethroned him in Jerusalem and imposed on Judah a levy of a hundred talents*ᵇ* of silver and a talent*ᶜ* of gold. ⁴The king of Egypt made Eliakim, a brother of Jehoahaz, king over Judah and Jerusalem and changed Eliakim's name to Jehoiakim. But Neco took Eliakim's brother Jehoahaz and carried him off to Egypt.

Jehoiakim King of Judah

⁵Jehoiakim was twenty-five years old when he became king, and he reigned in Jerusalem eleven years. He did evil in the eyes of the LORD his God. ⁶Nebuchadnezzar king of Babylon attacked him and bound him with bronze shackles to take him to Babylon. ⁷Nebuchadnezzar also took to Babylon articles from the temple of the LORD and put them in his temple*ᵈ* there.

⁸The other events of Jehoiakim's reign, the detestable things he did and all that was found against him, are written in the book of the kings of Israel and Judah. And Jehoiachin his son succeeded him as king.

Jehoiachin King of Judah

⁹Jehoiachin was eighteen*ᵉ* years old when he became king, and he reigned in Jerusalem three months and ten days. He did evil in the eyes of the LORD. ¹⁰In the spring, King Nebuchadnezzar sent for him and brought him to Babylon, together with articles of value

---

ᵃ2 Hebrew *Joahaz,* a variant of *Jehoahaz;* also in verse 4   *ᵇ3* That is, about 3 3/4 tons (about 3.4 metric tons)
ᶜ3 That is, about 75 pounds (about 34 kilograms)   *ᵈ7 Or palace*   *ᵉ9* One Hebrew manuscript, some Septuagint manuscripts and Syriac (see also 2 Kings 24:8); most Hebrew manuscripts *eight*

from the temple of the LORD, and he made Jehoiachin's uncle,[a] Zedekiah, king over Judah and Jerusalem.

Zedekiah King of Judah

[11]Zedekiah was twenty-one years old when he became king, and he reigned in Jerusalem eleven years. [12]He did evil in the eyes of the LORD his God and did not humble himself before Jeremiah the prophet, who spoke the word of the LORD. [13]He also rebelled against King Nebuchadnezzar, who had made him take an oath in God's name. He became stiff-necked and hardened his heart and would not turn to the LORD, the God of Israel. [14]Furthermore, all the leaders of the priests and the people became more and more unfaithful, following all the detestable practices of the nations and defiling the temple of the LORD, which he had consecrated in Jerusalem.

The Fall of Jerusalem

[15]The LORD, the God of their fathers, sent word to them through his messengers again and again, because he had pity on his people and on his dwelling place. [16]But they mocked God's messengers, despised his words and scoffed at his prophets until the wrath of the LORD was aroused against his people and there was no remedy. [17]He brought up against them the king of the Babylonians,[b] who killed their young men with the sword in the sanctuary, and spared neither young man nor young woman, old man or aged. God handed all of them over to Nebuchadnezzar. [18]He carried to Babylon all the articles from the temple of God, both large and small, and the treasures of the LORD's temple and the treasures of the king and his officials. [19]They set fire to God's temple and broke down the wall of Jerusalem; they burned all the palaces and destroyed everything of value there.

[20]He carried into exile to Babylon the remnant, who escaped from the sword, and they became servants to him and his sons until the kingdom of Persia came to power. [21]The land enjoyed its sabbath rests; all the time of its desolation it rested, until the seventy years were completed in fulfillment of the word of the LORD spoken by Jeremiah.

[22]In the first year of Cyrus king of Persia, in order to fulfill the word of the LORD spoken by Jeremiah, the LORD moved the heart of Cyrus king of Persia to make a proclamation throughout his realm and to put it in writing:

[23]"This is what Cyrus king of Persia says:

"'The LORD, the God of heaven, has given me all the kingdoms of the earth and he has appointed me to build a temple for him at Jerusalem in Judah. Anyone of his people among you—may the LORD his God be with him, and let him go up.'"

---

a 10 Hebrew *brother,* that is, relative (see 2 Kings 24:17)   *b 17* Or *Chaldeans*

Introduction

THE BOTTOM LINE

These books provide us with fascinating character studies of three Jewish leaders. Even though their personalities were vastly different, God used their unique abilities and orchestrated his work through them. Ezra was a quiet leader, and one of the first Jews to return to Jerusalem from captivity in Babylon. His behind-the-scenes encouragement kept a disjointed band of Israelites working together. Nehemiah was a fiery leader who demanded that the Jews live up to their calling as the people of God. Esther was a beautiful queen who risked her own life to stop the treacherous plans of a genocidal maniac. Although these books detail the lives of Jewish heroes, God was clearly the author of their successes. He is just as ready today to write a chapter through you if you'll let him.

CENTRAL IDEAS

■ God's care for his people extends beyond circumstantial, political or military boundaries.
■ God can use even non-believers to further his purposes.
■ Even the worst human treachery cannot thwart God's involvement in the affairs of his people.
■ Leaders who rely on God achieve what is impossible to accomplish on their own.

TITLES

The titles of these books name the three individuals whose fascinating stories they recount.

AUTHOR AND READERS

These fascinating historical records were probably compiled from personal memoirs. The author of Ezra and Nehemiah is considered to be Ezra himself, and some scholars speculate that he wrote Esther as well. However, no one knows for certain.

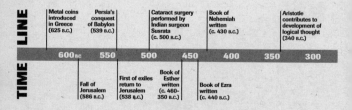

TIME LINE

Metal coins introduced in Greece (625 B.C.)	Persia's conquest of Babylon (539 B.C.)	Cataract surgery performed by Indian surgeon Susrata (c. 500 B.C.)	Book of Nehemiah written (c. 430 B.C.)	Aristotle contributes to development of logical thought (340 B.C.)

600 B.C.	550	500	450	400	350	300

	Fall of Jerusalem (586 B.C.)	First of exiles return to Jerusalem (538 B.C.)	Book of Esther written (c. 460-350 B.C.)	Book of Ezra written (c. 440 B.C.)

It was the most important document he would ever sign—The Emancipation Proclamation. At precisely 12:00 noon on January 1, 1863, it was placed before him.

President Lincoln looked at the document and picked up the pen. Then, sensing that something wasn't right, he laid down the pen.

A few moments later he again took up the pen to sign the document. Once more he laid it back down. Turning to the secretary of state, Lincoln said, "I've been shaking hands since nine o'clock this morning, and my right arm is almost paralyzed. If my name ever goes into history, it will be for this act, and my whole soul is in it. If my hand trembles when I sign the Proclamation, all who examine the document hereafter will say, 'He hesitated.'"

Lincoln picked up the pen a third time, leaned forward, and slowly but firmly wrote his signature.*

Leadership without trembling. That's what Lincoln gave the United States during some of its most difficult years. Of course, that doesn't mean there weren't days when Lincoln feared for himself and the nation. Rather, it means he stood with unflinching courage for what he believed was right. That's what every leader needs to provide those under his or her charge. And that's certainly what Ezra, Nehemiah, and Esther gave the Jewish people during some of the most difficult days in Israel's history.

> **Lincoln stood with unflinching courage for what he believed was right.**

Ezra and Nehemiah returned to Jerusalem from exile: Ezra in 458 B.C., Nehemiah in 445 B.C. Ezra returned to spiritually rebuild the people and to reconstruct the temple. Nehemiah was commissioned to rebuild the walls of the city. Esther was a Jewish woman who lived in Persia before Ezra or Nehemiah returned to Jerusalem. She married the king and took bold steps to preserve the Jewish people living in Persia.

Each of these three provide us with an excellent example of leadership. If you would like some insight into how you can be an effective leader during crisis, turn to Nehemiah chapter 5 (page 563).

*The Little Brown Book of Anecdotes, Clifton Fadiman, ed. (Boston: Little, Brown & Co., 1985), p 359.

EZRA

Cyrus Helps the Exiles to Return

1 In the first year of Cyrus king of Persia, in order to fulfill the word of the LORD spoken by Jeremiah, the LORD moved the heart of Cyrus king of Persia to make a proclamation throughout his realm and to put it in writing:

²"This is what Cyrus king of Persia says:

"'The LORD, the God of heaven, has given me all the kingdoms of the earth and he has appointed me to build a temple for him at Jerusalem in Judah. ³Anyone of his people among you—may his God be with him, and let him go up to Jerusalem in Judah and build the temple of the LORD, the God of Israel, the God who is in Jerusalem. ⁴And the people of any place where survivors may now be living are to provide him with silver and gold, with goods and livestock, and with freewill offerings for the temple of God in Jerusalem.'"

⁵Then the family heads of Judah and Benjamin, and the priests and Levites—everyone whose heart God had moved—prepared to go up and build the house of the LORD in Jerusalem. ⁶All their neighbors assisted them with articles of silver and gold, with goods and livestock, and with valuable gifts, in addition to all the freewill offerings. ⁷Moreover, King Cyrus brought out the articles belonging to the temple of the LORD, which Nebuchadnezzar had carried away from Jerusalem and had placed in the temple of his god.*ᵃ*

ᵃ 7 Or gods

REASONS TO BELIEVE

1:1–2
The Amazing Bible

Nothing demonstrates the reliability of the Bible more than the fulfillment of prophecies made hundreds (and sometimes thousands) of years before the event occurred.

Biblical prophets made such predictions after receiving special messages from God concerning future or contemporary events. It's important to understand that God's prophets weren't trying to guess what might happen or what they should say. On the contrary, God revealed to them what would *definitely* happen, and gave them the words to speak for him when the time came.

The book of Ezra opens with fulfilled prophecy—a copy of a proclamation by Cyrus, the king of Persia, stating that the Jewish people in his kingdom could return to Jerusalem and rebuild the temple of the Lord. This king's edict fulfilled the predictions that the prophets Jeremiah and Isaiah had made hundreds of years earlier.

Jeremiah had predicted that the Jewish people would be allowed to return from captivity to rebuild their temple, which was destroyed during his ministry. More specifically, he had said that the people would be allowed to return to Jerusalem after 70 years of captivity. Calculate the years from the destruction of the temple in 586 B.C. to its completion in 516 B.C. and you'll discover that exactly 70 years had passed (see Jeremiah chapter 29, verse 10 [page 1032]).

That's an amazing prediction. But even more amazing is the fact that Isaiah, who lived over a hundred years before Cyrus, had predicted that a king named Cyrus would allow Jerusalem to be rebuilt (see Isaiah chapter 44, verse 28 [page 948]).

Prophecies such as these demonstrate the Bible's divine inspiration. When it comes to revelation from God, the Bible is the real thing!

⁸Cyrus king of Persia had them brought by Mithredath the treasurer, who counted them out to Sheshbazzar the prince of Judah.

⁹This was the inventory:

gold dishes	30
silver dishes	1,000
silver pans^a	29
¹⁰gold bowls	30
matching silver bowls	410
other articles	1,000

¹¹In all, there were 5,400 articles of gold and of silver. Sheshbazzar brought all these along when the exiles came up from Babylon to Jerusalem.

The List of the Exiles Who Returned

2 Now these are the people of the province who came up from the captivity of the exiles, whom Nebuchadnezzar king of Babylon had taken captive to Babylon (they returned to Jerusalem and Judah, each to his own town, ²in company with Zerubbabel, Jeshua, Nehemiah, Seraiah, Reelaiah, Mordecai, Bilshan, Mispar, Bigvai, Rehum and Baanah):

The list of the men of the people of Israel:

³the descendants of Parosh	2,172
⁴of Shephatiah	372
⁵of Arah	775
⁶of Pahath-Moab (through the line of Jeshua and Joab)	2,812
⁷of Elam	1,254
⁸of Zattu	945
⁹of Zaccai	760
¹⁰of Bani	642
¹¹of Bebai	623
¹²of Azgad	1,222
¹³of Adonikam	666
¹⁴of Bigvai	2,056
¹⁵of Adin	454
¹⁶of Ater (through Hezekiah)	98
¹⁷of Bezai	323
¹⁸of Jorah	112
¹⁹of Hashum	223
²⁰of Gibbar	95
²¹the men of Bethlehem	123
²²of Netophah	56
²³of Anathoth	128
²⁴of Azmaveth	42
²⁵of Kiriath Jearim,^b Kephirah and Beeroth	743
²⁶of Ramah and Geba	621
²⁷of Micmash	122
²⁸of Bethel and Ai	223
²⁹of Nebo	52
³⁰of Magbish	156
³¹of the other Elam	1,254
³²of Harim	320

^a9 The meaning of the Hebrew for this word is uncertain.   ^b25 See Septuagint (see also Neh. 7:29); Hebrew *Kiriath Arim*.

³³of Lod, Hadid and Ono	725
³⁴of Jericho	345
³⁵of Senaah	3,630

³⁶The priests:

the descendants of Jedaiah (through the family of Jeshua)	973
³⁷of Immer	1,052
³⁸of Pashhur	1,247
³⁹of Harim	1,017

⁴⁰The Levites:

the descendants of Jeshua and Kadmiel (through the line of Hodaviah)	74

⁴¹The singers:

the descendants of Asaph	128

⁴²The gatekeepers of the temple:

the descendants of Shallum, Ater, Talmon, Akkub, Hatita and Shobai	139

⁴³The temple servants:

the descendants of
Ziha, Hasupha, Tabbaoth,
⁴⁴Keros, Siaha, Padon,
⁴⁵Lebanah, Hagabah, Akkub,
⁴⁶Hagab, Shalmai, Hanan,
⁴⁷Giddel, Gahar, Reaiah,
⁴⁸Rezin, Nekoda, Gazzam,
⁴⁹Uzza, Paseah, Besai,
⁵⁰Asnah, Meunim, Nephussim,
⁵¹Bakbuk, Hakupha, Harhur,
⁵²Bazluth, Mehida, Harsha,
⁵³Barkos, Sisera, Temah,
⁵⁴Neziah and Hatipha

⁵⁵The descendants of the servants of Solomon:

the descendants of
Sotai, Hassophereth, Peruda,
⁵⁶Jaala, Darkon, Giddel,
⁵⁷Shephatiah, Hattil,
Pokereth-Hazzebaim and Ami

⁵⁸The temple servants and the descendants of the servants of Solomon	392

⁵⁹The following came up from the towns of Tel Melah, Tel Harsha, Kerub, Addon and Immer, but they could not show that their families were descended from Israel:

⁶⁰The descendants of Delaiah, Tobiah and Nekoda	652

⁶¹And from among the priests:

The descendants of

Hobaiah, Hakkoz and Barzillai (a man who had married a daughter of Barzillai the Gileadite and was called by that name).

⁶²These searched for their family records, but they could not find them and so were excluded from the priesthood as unclean. ⁶³The governor ordered them not to eat any of the most sacred food until there was a priest ministering with the Urim and Thummim.

⁶⁴The whole company numbered 42,360, ⁶⁵besides their 7,337 menservants and maidservants; and they also had 200 men and women singers. ⁶⁶They had 736 horses, 245 mules, ⁶⁷435 camels and 6,720 donkeys.

⁶⁸When they arrived at the house of the LORD in Jerusalem, some of the heads of the families gave freewill offerings toward the rebuilding of the house of God on its site. ⁶⁹According to their ability they gave to the treasury for this work 61,000 drachmas*a* of gold, 5,000 minas*b* of silver and 100 priestly garments.

⁷⁰The priests, the Levites, the singers, the gatekeepers and the temple servants settled in their own towns, along with some of the other people, and the rest of the Israelites settled in their towns.

Rebuilding the Altar

3 When the seventh month came and the Israelites had settled in their towns, the people assembled as one man in Jerusalem. ²Then Jeshua son of Jozadak and his fellow priests and Zerubbabel son of Shealtiel and his associates began to build the altar of the God of Israel to sacrifice burnt offerings on it, in accordance with what is written in the Law of Moses the man of God. ³Despite their fear of the peoples around them, they built the altar on its foundation and sacrificed burnt offerings on it to the LORD, both the morning and evening sacrifices. ⁴Then in accordance with what is written, they celebrated the Feast of Tabernacles with the required number of burnt offerings prescribed for each day. ⁵After that, they presented the regular burnt offerings, the New Moon sacrifices and the sacrifices for all the appointed sacred feasts of the LORD, as well as those brought as freewill offerings to the LORD. ⁶On the first day of the seventh month they began to offer burnt offerings to the LORD, though the foundation of the LORD's temple had not yet been laid.

Rebuilding the Temple

⁷Then they gave money to the masons and carpenters, and gave food and drink and oil to the people of Sidon and Tyre, so that they would bring cedar logs by sea from Lebanon to Joppa, as authorized by Cyrus king of Persia.

⁸In the second month of the second year after their arrival at the house of God in Jerusalem, Zerubbabel son of Shealtiel, Jeshua son of Jozadak and the rest of their brothers (the priests and the Levites and all who had returned from the captivity to Jerusalem) began the work, appointing Levites twenty years of age and older to supervise the building of the house of the LORD. ⁹Jeshua and his sons and brothers and Kadmiel and his sons (descendants of Hodaviah*c*) and the sons of Henadad and their sons and brothers—all Levites—joined together in supervising those working on the house of God.

¹⁰When the builders laid the foundation of the temple of the LORD, the priests in their vestments and with trumpets, and the Levites (the sons of Asaph) with cymbals, took their places to praise the LORD, as prescribed by David king of Israel. ¹¹With praise and thanksgiving they sang to the LORD:

> "He is good;
> his love to Israel endures forever."

---

*a*69 That is, about 1,100 pounds (about 500 kilograms)   *b*69 That is, about 3 tons (about 2.9 metric tons)   *c*9 Hebrew *Yehudah*, probably a variant of *Hodaviah*

And all the people gave a great shout of praise to the LORD, because the foundation of the house of the LORD was laid. ¹²But many of the older priests and Levites and family heads, who had seen the former temple, wept aloud when they saw the foundation of this temple being laid, while many others shouted for joy. ¹³No one could distinguish the sound of the shouts of joy from the sound of weeping, because the people made so much noise. And the sound was heard far away.

Opposition to the Rebuilding

4 When the enemies of Judah and Benjamin heard that the exiles were building a temple for the LORD, the God of Israel, ²they came to Zerubbabel and to the heads of the families and said, "Let us help you build because, like you, we seek your God and have been sacrificing to him since the time of Esarhaddon king of Assyria, who brought us here."

³But Zerubbabel, Jeshua and the rest of the heads of the families of Israel answered, "You have no part with us in building a temple to our God. We alone will build it for the LORD, the God of Israel, as King Cyrus, the king of Persia, commanded us."

⁴Then the peoples around them set out to discourage the people of Judah and make them afraid to go on building.ᵃ ⁵They hired counselors to work against them and frustrate their plans during the entire reign of Cyrus king of Persia and down to the reign of Darius king of Persia.

Later Opposition Under Xerxes and Artaxerxes

⁶At the beginning of the reign of Xerxes,ᵇ they lodged an accusation against the people of Judah and Jerusalem.

⁷And in the days of Artaxerxes king of Persia, Bishlam, Mithredath, Tabeel and the rest of his associates wrote a letter to Artaxerxes. The letter was written in Aramaic script and in the Aramaic language.ᶜ,ᵈ

⁸Rehum the commanding officer and Shimshai the secretary wrote a letter against Jerusalem to Artaxerxes the king as follows:

⁹Rehum the commanding officer and Shimshai the secretary, together with the rest of their associates—the judges and officials over the men from Tripolis, Persia,ᵉ Erech and Babylon, the Elamites of Susa, ¹⁰and the other people whom the great and honorable Ashurbanipalᶠ deported and settled in the city of Samaria and elsewhere in Trans-Euphrates.

¹¹(This is a copy of the letter they sent him.)

To King Artaxerxes,

From your servants, the men of Trans-Euphrates:

¹²The king should know that the Jews who came up to us from you have gone to Jerusalem and are rebuilding that rebellious and wicked city. They are restoring the walls and repairing the foundations.

¹³Furthermore, the king should know that if this city is built and its walls are restored, no more taxes, tribute or duty will be paid, and the royal revenues will suffer. ¹⁴Now since we are under obligation to the palace and it is not proper for us to see the king dishonored, we are sending this message to inform the king, ¹⁵so that a search may be made in the archives of your predecessors. In these records you will find that this city is a rebellious city, troublesome to kings and provinces, a place of rebellion from ancient times. That is why this city was destroyed. ¹⁶We inform the

ᵃ4 Or and troubled them as they built   ᵇ6 Hebrew Ahasuerus, a variant of Xerxes' Persian name   ᶜ7 Or written in Aramaic and translated   ᵈ7 The text of Ezra 4:8–6:18 is in Aramaic.   ᵉ9 Or officials, magistrates and governors over the men from   ᶠ10 Aramaic Osnappar, a variant of Ashurbanipal

king that if this city is built and its walls are restored, you will be left with nothing in Trans-Euphrates.

[17]The king sent this reply:

To Rehum the commanding officer, Shimshai the secretary and the rest of their associates living in Samaria and elsewhere in Trans-Euphrates:

Greetings.

[18]The letter you sent us has been read and translated in my presence. [19]I issued an order and a search was made, and it was found that this city has a long history of revolt against kings and has been a place of rebellion and sedition. [20]Jerusalem has had powerful kings ruling over the whole of Trans-Euphrates, and taxes, tribute and duty were paid to them. [21]Now issue an order to these men to stop work, so that this city will not be rebuilt until I so order. [22]Be careful not to neglect this matter. Why let this threat grow, to the detriment of the royal interests?

[23]As soon as the copy of the letter of King Artaxerxes was read to Rehum and Shimshai the secretary and their associates, they went immediately to the Jews in Jerusalem and compelled them by force to stop.

[24]Thus the work on the house of God in Jerusalem came to a standstill until the second year of the reign of Darius king of Persia.

Tattenai's Letter to Darius

5 Now Haggai the prophet and Zechariah the prophet, a descendant of Iddo, prophesied to the Jews in Judah and Jerusalem in the name of the God of Israel, who was over them. [2]Then Zerubbabel son of Shealtiel and Jeshua son of Jozadak set to work to rebuild the house of God in Jerusalem. And the prophets of God were with them, helping them.

[3]At that time Tattenai, governor of Trans-Euphrates, and Shethar-Bozenai and their associates went to them and asked, "Who authorized you to rebuild this temple and restore this structure?" [4]They also asked, "What are the names of the men constructing this building?"[a] [5]But the eye of their God was watching over the elders of the Jews, and they were not stopped until a report could go to Darius and his written reply be received.

[6]This is a copy of the letter that Tattenai, governor of Trans-Euphrates, and Shethar-Bozenai and their associates, the officials of Trans-Euphrates, sent to King Darius. [7]The report they sent him read as follows:

To King Darius:

Cordial greetings.

[8]The king should know that we went to the district of Judah, to the temple of the great God. The people are building it with large stones and placing the timbers in the walls. The work is being carried on with diligence and is making rapid progress under their direction.

[9]We questioned the elders and asked them, "Who authorized you to rebuild this temple and restore this structure?" [10]We also asked them their names, so that we could write down the names of their leaders for your information.

[11]This is the answer they gave us:

"We are the servants of the God of heaven and earth, and we are rebuilding the temple that was built many years ago, one that a great king of Israel built and finished. [12]But because our fathers angered the God of heaven, he handed them over

---

a 4 See Septuagint; Aramaic *4We told them the names of the men constructing this building.*

to Nebuchadnezzar the Chaldean, king of Babylon, who destroyed this temple and deported the people to Babylon.

¹³"However, in the first year of Cyrus king of Babylon, King Cyrus issued a decree to rebuild this house of God. ¹⁴He even removed from the temple^a of Babylon the gold and silver articles of the house of God, which Nebuchadnezzar had taken from the temple in Jerusalem and brought to the temple^a in Babylon.

"Then King Cyrus gave them to a man named Sheshbazzar, whom he had appointed governor, ¹⁵and he told him, 'Take these articles and go and deposit them in the temple in Jerusalem. And rebuild the house of God on its site.' ¹⁶So this Sheshbazzar came and laid the foundations of the house of God in Jerusalem. From that day to the present it has been under construction but is not yet finished."

¹⁷Now if it pleases the king, let a search be made in the royal archives of Babylon to see if King Cyrus did in fact issue a decree to rebuild this house of God in Jerusalem. Then let the king send us his decision in this matter.

The Decree of Darius

6 King Darius then issued an order, and they searched in the archives stored in the treasury at Babylon. ²A scroll was found in the citadel of Ecbatana in the province of Media, and this was written on it:

Memorandum:

³In the first year of King Cyrus, the king issued a decree concerning the temple of God in Jerusalem:

Let the temple be rebuilt as a place to present sacrifices, and let its foundations be laid. It is to be ninety feet^b high and ninety feet wide, ⁴with three courses of large stones and one of timbers. The costs are to be paid by the royal treasury. ⁵Also, the gold and silver articles of the house of God, which Nebuchadnezzar took from the temple in Jerusalem and brought to Babylon, are to be returned to their places in the temple in Jerusalem; they are to be deposited in the house of God.

⁶Now then, Tattenai, governor of Trans-Euphrates, and Shethar-Bozenai and you, their fellow officials of that province, stay away from there. ⁷Do not interfere with the work on this temple of God. Let the governor of the Jews and the Jewish elders rebuild this house of God on its site.

⁸Moreover, I hereby decree what you are to do for these elders of the Jews in the construction of this house of God:

The expenses of these men are to be fully paid out of the royal treasury, from the revenues of Trans-Euphrates, so that the work will not stop. ⁹Whatever is needed—young bulls, rams, male lambs for burnt offerings to the God of heaven, and wheat, salt, wine and oil, as requested by the priests in Jerusalem—must be given them daily without fail, ¹⁰so that they may offer sacrifices pleasing to the God of heaven and pray for the well-being of the king and his sons.

¹¹Furthermore, I decree that if anyone changes this edict, a beam is to be pulled from his house and he is to be lifted up and impaled on it. And for this crime his house is to be made a pile of rubble. ¹²May God, who has caused his Name to dwell there, overthrow any king or people who lifts a hand to change this decree or to destroy this temple in Jerusalem.

I Darius have decreed it. Let it be carried out with diligence.

^a14 Or palace   ^b3 Aramaic sixty cubits (about 27 meters)

Completion and Dedication of the Temple

¹³Then, because of the decree King Darius had sent, Tattenai, governor of Trans-Euphrates, and Shethar-Bozenai and their associates carried it out with diligence. ¹⁴So the elders of the Jews continued to build and prosper under the preaching of Haggai the prophet and Zechariah, a descendant of Iddo. They finished building the temple according to the command of the God of Israel and the decrees of Cyrus, Darius and Artaxerxes, kings of Persia. ¹⁵The temple was completed on the third day of the month Adar, in the sixth year of the reign of King Darius.

¹⁶Then the people of Israel—the priests, the Levites and the rest of the exiles—celebrated the dedication of the house of God with joy. ¹⁷For the dedication of this house of God they offered a hundred bulls, two hundred rams, four hundred male lambs and, as a sin offering for all Israel, twelve male goats, one for each of the tribes of Israel. ¹⁸And they installed the priests in their divisions and the Levites in their groups for the service of God at Jerusalem, according to what is written in the Book of Moses.

The Passover

¹⁹On the fourteenth day of the first month, the exiles celebrated the Passover. ²⁰The priests and Levites had purified themselves and were all ceremonially clean. The Levites slaughtered the Passover lamb for all the exiles, for their brothers the priests and for themselves. ²¹So the Israelites who had returned from the exile ate it, together with all who had separated themselves from the unclean practices of their Gentile neighbors in order to seek the LORD, the God of Israel. ²²For seven days they celebrated with joy the Feast of Unleavened Bread, because the LORD had filled them with joy by changing the attitude of the king of Assyria, so that he assisted them in the work on the house of God, the God of Israel.

Ezra Comes to Jerusalem

7 After these things, during the reign of Artaxerxes king of Persia, Ezra son of Seraiah, the son of Azariah, the son of Hilkiah, ²the son of Shallum, the son of Zadok, the son of Ahitub, ³the son of Amariah, the son of Azariah, the son of Meraioth, ⁴the son of Zerahiah, the son of Uzzi, the son of Bukki, ⁵the son of Abishua, the son of Phinehas, the son of Eleazar, the son of Aaron the chief priest— ⁶this Ezra came up from Babylon. He was a teacher well versed in the Law of Moses, which the LORD, the God of Israel, had given. The king had granted him everything he asked, for the hand of the LORD his God was on him. ⁷Some of the Israelites, including priests, Levites, singers, gatekeepers and temple servants, also came up to Jerusalem in the seventh year of King Artaxerxes.

⁸Ezra arrived in Jerusalem in the fifth month of the seventh year of the king. ⁹He had begun his journey from Babylon on the first day of the first month, and he arrived in Jerusalem on the first day of the fifth month, for the gracious hand of his God was on him. ¹⁰For Ezra had devoted himself to the study and observance of the Law of the LORD, and to teaching its decrees and laws in Israel.

King Artaxerxes' Letter to Ezra

¹¹This is a copy of the letter King Artaxerxes had given to Ezra the priest and teacher, a man learned in matters concerning the commands and decrees of the LORD for Israel:

¹²ᵃArtaxerxes, king of kings,

To Ezra the priest, a teacher of the Law of the God of heaven:

Greetings.

ᵃ12 The text of Ezra 7:12-26 is in Aramaic.

¹³Now I decree that any of the Israelites in my kingdom, including priests and Levites, who wish to go to Jerusalem with you, may go. ¹⁴You are sent by the king and his seven advisers to inquire about Judah and Jerusalem with regard to the Law of your God, which is in your hand. ¹⁵Moreover, you are to take with you the silver and gold that the king and his advisers have freely given to the God of Israel, whose dwelling is in Jerusalem, ¹⁶together with all the silver and gold you may obtain from the province of Babylon, as well as the freewill offerings of the people and priests for the temple of their God in Jerusalem. ¹⁷With this money be sure to buy bulls, rams and male lambs, together with their grain offerings and drink offerings, and sacrifice them on the altar of the temple of your God in Jerusalem.

¹⁸You and your brother Jews may then do whatever seems best with the rest of the silver and gold, in accordance with the will of your God. ¹⁹Deliver to the God of Jerusalem all the articles entrusted to you for worship in the temple of your God. ²⁰And anything else needed for the temple of your God that you may have occasion to supply, you may provide from the royal treasury.

²¹Now I, King Artaxerxes, order all the treasurers of Trans-Euphrates to provide with diligence whatever Ezra the priest, a teacher of the Law of the God of heaven, may ask of you— ²²up to a hundred talents*a* of silver, a hundred cors*b* of wheat, a hundred baths*c* of wine, a hundred baths*c* of olive oil, and salt without limit. ²³Whatever the God of heaven has prescribed, let it be done with diligence for the temple of the God of heaven. Why should there be wrath against the realm of the king and of his sons? ²⁴You are also to know that you have no authority to impose taxes, tribute or duty on any of the priests, Levites, singers, gatekeepers, temple servants or other workers at this house of God.

²⁵And you, Ezra, in accordance with the wisdom of your God, which you possess, appoint magistrates and judges to administer justice to all the people of Trans-Euphrates—all who know the laws of your God. And you are to teach any who do not know them. ²⁶Whoever does not obey the law of your God and the law of the king must surely be punished by death, banishment, confiscation of property, or imprisonment.

²⁷Praise be to the LORD, the God of our fathers, who has put it into the king's heart to bring honor to the house of the LORD in Jerusalem in this way ²⁸and who has extended his good favor to me before the king and his advisers and all the king's powerful officials. Because the hand of the LORD my God was on me, I took courage and gathered leading men from Israel to go up with me.

List of the Family Heads Returning With Ezra

8 These are the family heads and those registered with them who came up with me from Babylon during the reign of King Artaxerxes:

²of the descendants of Phinehas, Gershom;

of the descendants of Ithamar, Daniel;

of the descendants of David, Hattush ³of the descendants of Shecaniah;

of the descendants of Parosh, Zechariah, and with him were registered 150 men;
⁴of the descendants of Pahath-Moab, Eliehoenai son of Zerahiah, and with him 200 men;
⁵of the descendants of Zattu,*d* Shecaniah son of Jahaziel, and with him 300 men;
⁶of the descendants of Adin, Ebed son of Jonathan, and with him 50 men;
⁷of the descendants of Elam, Jeshaiah son of Athaliah, and with him 70 men;
⁸of the descendants of Shephatiah, Zebadiah son of Michael, and with him 80 men;

---

a 22 That is, about 3 3/4 tons (about 3.4 metric tons)   *b 22* That is, probably about 600 bushels (about 22 kiloliters)   *c 22* That is, probably about 600 gallons (about 2.2 kiloliters)   *d 5* Some Septuagint manuscripts (also 1 Esdras 8:32); Hebrew does not have *Zattu.*

⁹of the descendants of Joab, Obadiah son of Jehiel, and with him 218 men;

¹⁰of the descendants of Bani,ᵃ Shelomith son of Josiphiah, and with him 160 men;

¹¹of the descendants of Bebai, Zechariah son of Bebai, and with him 28 men;

¹²of the descendants of Azgad, Johanan son of Hakkatan, and with him 110 men;

¹³of the descendants of Adonikam, the last ones, whose names were Eliphelet, Jeuel and Shemaiah, and with them 60 men;

¹⁴of the descendants of Bigvai, Uthai and Zaccur, and with them 70 men.

The Return to Jerusalem

¹⁵I assembled them at the canal that flows toward Ahava, and we camped there three days. When I checked among the people and the priests, I found no Levites there. ¹⁶So I summoned Eliezer, Ariel, Shemaiah, Elnathan, Jarib, Elnathan, Nathan, Zechariah and Meshullam, who were leaders, and Joiarib and Elnathan, who were men of learning, ¹⁷and I sent them to Iddo, the leader in Casiphia. I told them what to say to Iddo and his kinsmen, the temple servants in Casiphia, so that they might bring attendants to us for the house of our God. ¹⁸Because the gracious hand of our God was on us, they brought us Sherebiah, a capable man, from the descendants of Mahli son of Levi, the son of Israel, and Sherebiah's sons and brothers, 18 men; ¹⁹and Hashabiah, together with Jeshaiah from the descendants of Merari, and his brothers and nephews, 20 men. ²⁰They also brought 220 of the temple servants—a body that David and the officials had established to assist the Levites. All were registered by name.

²¹There, by the Ahava Canal, I proclaimed a fast, so that we might humble ourselves before our God and ask him for a safe journey for us and our children, with all our possessions. ²²I was ashamed to ask the king for soldiers and horsemen to protect us from enemies on the road, because we had told the king, "The gracious hand of our God is on everyone who looks to him, but his great anger is against all who forsake him." ²³So we fasted and petitioned our God about this, and he answered our prayer.

²⁴Then I set apart twelve of the leading priests, together with Sherebiah, Hashabiah and ten of their brothers, ²⁵and I weighed out to them the offering of silver and gold and the articles that the king, his advisers, his officials and all Israel present there had donated for the house of our God. ²⁶I weighed out to them 650 talentsᵇ of silver, silver articles weighing 100 talents,ᶜ 100 talentsᶜ of gold, ²⁷20 bowls of gold valued at 1,000 darics,ᵈ and two fine articles of polished bronze, as precious as gold.

²⁸I said to them, "You as well as these articles are consecrated to the LORD. The silver and gold are a freewill offering to the LORD, the God of your fathers. ²⁹Guard them carefully until you weigh them out in the chambers of the house of the LORD in Jerusalem before the leading priests and the Levites and the family heads of Israel." ³⁰Then the priests and Levites received the silver and gold and sacred articles that had been weighed out to be taken to the house of our God in Jerusalem.

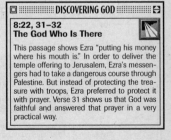

📖 ⬚⬚⬚ **DISCOVERING GOD** ⬚⬚⬚ ⬛

8:22, 31–32
The God Who Is There

This passage shows Ezra "putting his money where his mouth is." In order to deliver the temple offering to Jerusalem, Ezra's messengers had to take a dangerous course through Palestine. But instead of protecting the treasure with troops, Ezra preferred to protect it with prayer. Verse 31 shows us that God was faithful and answered that prayer in a very practical way.

³¹On the twelfth day of the first month we set out from the Ahava Canal to go to Jerusalem. The hand of our God was on us, and he protected us from enemies and bandits along the way. ³²So we arrived in Jerusalem, where we rested three days.

ᵃ10 Some Septuagint manuscripts (also 1 Esdras 8:36); Hebrew does not have Bani.   ᵇ26 That is, about 25 tons (about 22 metric tons)   ᶜ26 That is, about 3 3/4 tons (about 3.4 metric tons)   ᵈ27 That is, about 19 pounds (about 8.5 kilograms)

³³On the fourth day, in the house of our God, we weighed out the silver and gold and the sacred articles into the hands of Meremoth son of Uriah, the priest. Eleazar son of Phinehas was with him, and so were the Levites Jozabad son of Jeshua and Noadiah son of Binnui. ³⁴Everything was accounted for by number and weight, and the entire weight was recorded at that time.

³⁵Then the exiles who had returned from captivity sacrificed burnt offerings to the God of Israel: twelve bulls for all Israel, ninety-six rams, seventy-seven male lambs and, as a sin offering, twelve male goats. All this was a burnt offering to the LORD. ³⁶They also delivered the king's orders to the royal satraps and to the governors of Trans-Euphrates, who then gave assistance to the people and to the house of God.

Ezra's Prayer About Intermarriage

9 After these things had been done, the leaders came to me and said, "The people of Israel, including the priests and the Levites, have not kept themselves separate from the neighboring peoples with their detestable practices, like those of the Canaanites, Hittites, Perizzites, Jebusites, Ammonites, Moabites, Egyptians and Amorites. ²They have taken some of their daughters as wives for themselves and their sons, and have mingled the holy race with the peoples around them. And the leaders and officials have led the way in this unfaithfulness."

³When I heard this, I tore my tunic and cloak, pulled hair from my head and beard and sat down appalled. ⁴Then everyone who trembled at the words of the God of Israel gathered around me because of this unfaithfulness of the exiles. And I sat there appalled until the evening sacrifice.

⁵Then, at the evening sacrifice, I rose from my self-abasement, with my tunic and cloak torn, and fell on my knees with my hands spread out to the LORD my God ⁶and prayed:

"O my God, I am too ashamed and disgraced to lift up my face to you, my God, because our sins are higher than our heads and our guilt has reached to the heavens. ⁷From the days of our forefathers until now, our guilt has been great. Because of our sins, we and our kings and our priests have been subjected to the sword and captivity, to pillage and humiliation at the hand of foreign kings, as it is today.

⁸"But now, for a brief moment, the LORD our God has been gracious in leaving us a

---

KNOWING YOURSELF

9:5-15
Sin

This passage gives us a great example of frank, open confession to God. If you're looking for a good model of owning up to your own wrongdoing, there's none better than this prayer of Ezra.

Notice that Ezra maintains no sugar-coated delusions about humanity's inherent goodness. He knows his nation has a history of sin, in spite of God's favor on them. Ezra highlights how good God has been to his people despite how badly the people have behaved. What's more, he gets very specific about the wrongs done—no meaningless generalizations here. And he refuses to blame God or quarrel with his righteousness. This is about his people's disobedience, plain and simple.

Ezra's confession had an immediate and profound effect on the people. Those who saw their leader in true repentance joined him and recommitted themselves to God's service (see chapter 10, verses 1-3).

Wouldn't it be great if we would all be so forthright in admitting our errors and faults? Take a cue from this passage, and be honest and up-front with people whom you have wronged. Be honest and direct with God, as well. He knows your heart, and he's ready to forgive you when you turn to him and ask for forgiveness.

remnant and giving us a firm place in his sanctuary, and so our God gives light to our eyes and a little relief in our bondage. 9Though we are slaves, our God has not deserted us in our bondage. He has shown us kindness in the sight of the kings of Persia: He has granted us new life to rebuild the house of our God and repair its ruins, and he has given us a wall of protection in Judah and Jerusalem.

10"But now, O our God, what can we say after this? For we have disregarded the commands 11you gave through your servants the prophets when you said: 'The land you are entering to possess is a land polluted by the corruption of its peoples. By their detestable practices they have filled it with their impurity from one end to the other. 12Therefore, do not give your daughters in marriage to their sons or take their daughters for your sons. Do not seek a treaty of friendship with them at any time, that you may be strong and eat the good things of the land and leave it to your children as an everlasting inheritance.'

13"What has happened to us is a result of our evil deeds and our great guilt, and yet, our God, you have punished us less than our sins have deserved and have given us a remnant like this. 14Shall we again break your commands and intermarry with the peoples who commit such detestable practices? Would you not be angry enough with us to destroy us, leaving us no remnant or survivor? 15O LORD, God of Israel, you are righteous! We are left this day as a remnant. Here we are before you in our guilt, though because of it not one of us can stand in your presence."

The People's Confession of Sin

10 While Ezra was praying and confessing, weeping and throwing himself down before the house of God, a large crowd of Israelites—men, women and children—gathered around him. They too wept bitterly. 2Then Shecaniah son of Jehiel, one of the descendants of Elam, said to Ezra, "We have been unfaithful to our God by marrying foreign women from the peoples around us. But in spite of this, there is still hope for Israel. 3Now let us make a covenant before our God to send away all these women and their children, in accordance with the counsel of my lord and of those who fear the commands of our God. Let it be done according to the Law. 4Rise up; this matter is in your hands. We will support you, so take courage and do it."

5So Ezra rose up and put the leading priests and Levites and all Israel under oath to do what had been suggested. And they took the oath. 6Then Ezra withdrew from before the house of God and went to the room of Jehohanan son of Eliashib. While he was there, he ate no food and drank no water, because he continued to mourn over the unfaithfulness of the exiles.

7A proclamation was then issued throughout Judah and Jerusalem for all the exiles to assemble in Jerusalem. 8Anyone who failed to appear within three days would forfeit all his property, in accordance with the decision of the officials and elders, and would himself be expelled from the assembly of the exiles.

9Within the three days, all the men of Judah and Benjamin had gathered in Jerusalem. And on the twentieth day of the ninth month, all the people were sitting in the square before the house of God, greatly distressed by the occasion and because of the rain. 10Then Ezra the priest stood up and said to them, "You have been unfaithful; you have married foreign women, adding to Israel's guilt. 11Now make confession to the LORD, the God of your fathers, and do his will. Separate yourselves from the peoples around you and from your foreign wives."

12The whole assembly responded with a loud voice: "You are right! We must do as you say. 13But there are many people here and it is the rainy season; so we cannot stand outside. Besides, this matter cannot be taken care of in a day or two, because we have sinned greatly in this thing. 14Let our officials act for the whole assembly. Then let everyone in our towns who has married a foreign woman come at a set time, along with the elders and judges of each town, until the fierce anger of our God in this matter is turned away from us." ¹⁵Only Jonathan son of Asahel and Jahzeiah son of Tikvah, supported by Meshullam and Shabbethai the Levite, opposed this.

¹⁶So the exiles did as was proposed. Ezra the priest selected men who were family heads, one from each family division, and all of them designated by name. On the first day of the tenth month they sat down to investigate the cases, ¹⁷and by the first day of the first month they finished dealing with all the men who had married foreign women.

Those Guilty of Intermarriage

¹⁸Among the descendants of the priests, the following had married foreign women:

From the descendants of Jeshua son of Jozadak, and his brothers: Maaseiah, Eliezer, Jarib and Gedaliah. ¹⁹(They all gave their hands in pledge to put away their wives, and for their guilt they each presented a ram from the flock as a guilt offering.)

²⁰From the descendants of Immer:
Hanani and Zebadiah.
²¹From the descendants of Harim:
Maaseiah, Elijah, Shemaiah, Jehiel and Uzziah.
²²From the descendants of Pashhur:
Elioenai, Maaseiah, Ishmael, Nethanel, Jozabad and Elasah.

²³Among the Levites:

Jozabad, Shimei, Kelaiah (that is, Kelita), Pethahiah, Judah and Eliezer.
²⁴From the singers:
Eliashib.
From the gatekeepers:
Shallum, Telem and Uri.

²⁵And among the other Israelites:

From the descendants of Parosh:
Ramiah, Izziah, Malkijah, Mijamin, Eleazar, Malkijah and Benaiah.
²⁶From the descendants of Elam:
Mattaniah, Zechariah, Jehiel, Abdi, Jeremoth and Elijah.
²⁷From the descendants of Zattu:
Elioenai, Eliashib, Mattaniah, Jeremoth, Zabad and Aziza.
²⁸From the descendants of Bebai:
Jehohanan, Hananiah, Zabbai and Athlai.
²⁹From the descendants of Bani:
Meshullam, Malluch, Adaiah, Jashub, Sheal and Jeremoth.
³⁰From the descendants of Pahath-Moab:
Adna, Kelal, Benaiah, Maaseiah, Mattaniah, Bezalel, Binnui and Manasseh.
³¹From the descendants of Harim:
Eliezer, Ishijah, Malkijah, Shemaiah, Shimeon, ³²Benjamin, Malluch and Shemariah.
³³From the descendants of Hashum:
Mattenai, Mattattah, Zabad, Eliphelet, Jeremai, Manasseh and Shimei.
³⁴From the descendants of Bani:
Maadai, Amram, Uel, ³⁵Benaiah, Bedeiah, Keluhi, ³⁶Vaniah, Meremoth, Eliashib, ³⁷Mattaniah, Mattenai and Jaasu.

[38]From the descendants of Binnui:[a]

Shimei, [39]Shelemiah, Nathan, Adaiah, [40]Macnadebai, Shashai, Sharai, [41]Azarel, Shelemiah, Shemariah, [42]Shallum, Amariah and Joseph.

[43]From the descendants of Nebo:

Jeiel, Mattithiah, Zabad, Zebina, Jaddai, Joel and Benaiah.

[44]All these had married foreign women, and some of them had children by these wives.[b]

NEHEMIAH

Nehemiah's Prayer

1 The words of Nehemiah son of Hacaliah:

In the month of Kislev in the twentieth year, while I was in the citadel of Susa, ²Hanani, one of my brothers, came from Judah with some other men, and I questioned them about the Jewish remnant that survived the exile, and also about Jerusalem.

³They said to me, "Those who survived the exile and are back in the province are in great trouble and disgrace. The wall of Jerusalem is broken down, and its gates have been burned with fire."

⁴When I heard these things, I sat down and wept. For some days I mourned and fasted and prayed before the God of heaven. ⁵Then I said:

"O LORD, God of heaven, the great and awesome God, who keeps his covenant of love with those who love him and obey his commands, ⁶let your ear be attentive and your eyes open to hear the prayer your servant is praying before you day and night for your servants, the people of Israel. I confess the sins we Israelites, including myself and my father's house, have committed against you. ⁷We have acted very wickedly toward you. We have not obeyed the commands, decrees and laws you gave your servant Moses.

⁸"Remember the instruction you gave your servant Moses, saying, 'If you are unfaithful, I will scatter you among the nations, ⁹but if you return to me and obey my commands, then even if your exiled people are at the farthest horizon, I will gather them from there and bring them to the place I have chosen as a dwelling for my Name.'

¹⁰"They are your servants and your people, whom you redeemed by your great strength and your mighty hand. ¹¹O Lord, let your ear be attentive to the prayer of this your servant and to the prayer of your servants who delight in revering your name. Give your servant success today by granting him favor in the presence of this man."

I was cupbearer to the king.

Artaxerxes Sends Nehemiah to Jerusalem

2 In the month of Nisan in the twentieth year of King Artaxerxes, when wine was brought for him, I took the wine and gave it to the king. I had not been sad in his presence before; ²so the king asked me, "Why does your face look so sad when you are not ill? This can be nothing but sadness of heart."

I was very much afraid, ³but I said to the king, "May the king live forever! Why should my face not look sad when the city where my fathers are buried lies in ruins, and its gates have been destroyed by fire?"

⁴The king said to me, "What is it you want?"

Then I prayed to the God of heaven, ⁵and I answered the king, "If it pleases the king and if your servant has found favor in his sight, let him send me to the city in Judah where my fathers are buried so that I can rebuild it."

⁶Then the king, with the queen sitting beside him, asked me, "How long will your journey take, and when will you get back?" It pleased the king to send me; so I set a time.

⁷I also said to him, "If it pleases the king, may I have letters to the governors of Trans-Euphrates, so that they will provide me safe-conduct until I arrive in Judah? ⁸And may I have a letter to Asaph, keeper of the king's forest, so he will give me timber to make beams for the gates of the citadel by the temple and for the city wall and for the residence I will occupy?" And because the gracious hand of my God was upon me, the king granted my requests. ⁹So I went to the governors of Trans-Euphrates and gave them the king's letters. The king had also sent army officers and cavalry with me.

¹⁰When Sanballat the Horonite and Tobiah the Ammonite official heard about this, they were very much disturbed that someone had come to promote the welfare of the Israelites.

Nehemiah Inspects Jerusalem's Walls

¹¹I went to Jerusalem, and after staying there three days ¹²I set out during the night with a few men. I had not told anyone what my God had put in my heart to do for Jerusalem. There were no mounts with me except the one I was riding on.

¹³By night I went out through the Valley Gate toward the Jackal[a] Well and the Dung Gate, examining the walls of Jerusalem, which had been broken down, and its gates, which had been destroyed by fire. ¹⁴Then I moved on toward the Fountain Gate and the King's Pool, but there was not enough room for my mount to get through; ¹⁵so I went up the valley by night, examining the wall. Finally, I turned back and re-entered through the Valley Gate. ¹⁶The officials did not know where I had gone or what I was doing, because as yet I had said nothing to the Jews or the priests or nobles or officials or any others who would be doing the work.

◻ ▥▥▥ **STRENGTHENING RELATIONSHIPS** ▥▥▥ ◨

2:11–16
Leadership

Good leadership is often proven in the most unusual places. For example, Nehemiah began his important mission in Jerusalem by quietly, without fanfare, sizing up the scope of the problem he needed to address. Late at night, he walked among the ruins he had to repair to give himself some perspective. No doubt he used this time to create mental images—not just of the obstacles he faced, but of what the wall would look like when his task was done.

If you're a leader, have you taken a "solitary ride" through the challenges you face to get a clear picture of what you're up against? Have you constructed in your mind a vision of what you're creating so you can instill that vision in others? Good leaders take the time they need to develop a strong purpose and clear goal.

---

¹⁷Then I said to them, "You see the trouble we are in: Jerusalem lies in ruins, and its gates have been burned with fire. Come, let us rebuild the wall of Jerusalem, and we will no longer be in disgrace." ¹⁸I also told them about the gracious hand of my God upon me and what the king had said to me.

They replied, "Let us start rebuilding." So they began this good work.

¹⁹But when Sanballat the Horonite, Tobiah the Ammonite official and Geshem the Arab heard about it, they mocked and ridiculed us. "What is this you are doing?" they asked. "Are you rebelling against the king?"

²⁰I answered them by saying, "The God of heaven will give us success. We his servants will start rebuilding, but as for you, you have no share in Jerusalem or any claim or historic right to it."

Builders of the Wall

3 Eliashib the high priest and his fellow priests went to work and rebuilt the Sheep Gate. They dedicated it and set its doors in place, building as far as the Tower of the Hundred, which they dedicated, and as far as the Tower of Hananel. ²The men of Jericho built the adjoining section, and Zaccur son of Imri built next to them.

a 13 Or Serpent or Fig

³The Fish Gate was rebuilt by the sons of Hassenaah. They laid its beams and put its doors and bolts and bars in place. ⁴Meremoth son of Uriah, the son of Hakkoz, repaired the next section. Next to him Meshullam son of Berekiah, the son of Meshezabel, made repairs, and next to him Zadok son of Baana also made repairs. ⁵The next section was repaired by the men of Tekoa, but their nobles would not put their shoulders to the work under their supervisors.ᵃ

⁶The Jeshanahᵇ Gate was repaired by Joiada son of Paseah and Meshullam son of Besodeiah. They laid its beams and put its doors and bolts and bars in place. ⁷Next to them, repairs were made by men from Gibeon and Mizpah—Melatiah of Gibeon and Jadon of Meronoth—places under the authority of the governor of Trans-Euphrates. ⁸Uzziel son of Harhaiah, one of the goldsmiths, repaired the next section; and Hananiah, one of the perfume-makers, made repairs next to that. They restoredᶜ Jerusalem as far as the Broad Wall. ⁹Rephaiah son of Hur, ruler of a half-district of Jerusalem, repaired the next section. ¹⁰Adjoining this, Jedaiah son of Harumaph made repairs opposite his house, and Hattush son of Hashabneiah made repairs next to him. ¹¹Malkijah son of Harim and Hasshub son of Pahath-Moab repaired another section and the Tower of the Ovens. ¹²Shallum son of Hallohesh, ruler of a half-district of Jerusalem, repaired the next section with the help of his daughters.

¹³The Valley Gate was repaired by Hanun and the residents of Zanoah. They rebuilt it and put its doors and bolts and bars in place. They also repaired five hundred yardsᵈ of the wall as far as the Dung Gate.

¹⁴The Dung Gate was repaired by Malkijah son of Recab, ruler of the district of Beth Hakkerem. He rebuilt it and put its doors and bolts and bars in place.

¹⁵The Fountain Gate was repaired by Shallun son of Col-Hozeh, ruler of the district of Mizpah. He rebuilt it, roofing it over and putting its doors and bolts and bars in place. He also repaired the wall of the Pool of Siloam,ᵉ by the King's Garden, as far as the steps going down from the City of David. ¹⁶Beyond him, Nehemiah son of Azbuk, ruler of a half-district of Beth Zur, made repairs up to a point opposite the tombsᶠ of David, as far as the artificial pool and the House of the Heroes.

¹⁷Next to him, the repairs were made by the Levites under Rehum son of Bani. Beside him, Hashabiah, ruler of half the district of Keilah, carried out repairs for his district. ¹⁸Next to him, the repairs were made by their countrymen under Binnuiᵍ son of Henadad, ruler of the other half-district of Keilah. ¹⁹Next to him, Ezer son of Jeshua, ruler of Mizpah, repaired another section, from a point facing the ascent to the armory as far as the angle. ²⁰Next to him, Baruch son of Zabbai zealously repaired another section, from the angle to the entrance of the house of Eliashib the high priest. ²¹Next to him, Meremoth son of Uriah, the son of Hakkoz, repaired another section, from the entrance of Eliashib's house to the end of it.

²²The repairs next to him were made by the priests from the surrounding region. ²³Beyond them, Benjamin and Hasshub made repairs in front of their house; and next to them, Azariah son of Maaseiah, the son of Ananiah, made repairs beside his house. ²⁴Next to him, Binnui son of Henadad repaired another section, from Azariah's house to the angle and the corner, ²⁵and Palal son of Uzai worked opposite the angle and the tower projecting from the upper palace near the court of the guard. Next to him, Pedaiah son of Parosh ²⁶and the temple servants living on the hill of Ophel made repairs up to a point opposite the Water Gate toward the east and the projecting tower. ²⁷Next to them, the men of Tekoa repaired another section, from the great projecting tower to the wall of Ophel.

ᵃ5 Or their Lord or, the governor   ᵇ6 Or Old   ᶜ8 Or They left out part of   ᵈ13 Hebrew a thousand cubits (about 450 meters)   ᵉ15 Hebrew Shelah, a variant of Shiloah, that is, Siloam   ᶠ16 Hebrew; Septuagint, some Vulgate manuscripts and Syriac tomb   ᵍ18 Two Hebrew manuscripts and Syriac (see also Septuagint and verse 24); most Hebrew manuscripts Bavvai

28Above the Horse Gate, the priests made repairs, each in front of his own house. 29Next to them, Zadok son of Immer made repairs opposite his house. Next to him, Shemaiah son of Shecaniah, the guard at the East Gate, made repairs. 30Next to him, Hananiah son of Shelemiah, and Hanun, the sixth son of Zalaph, repaired another section. Next to them, Meshullam son of Berekiah made repairs opposite his living quarters. 31Next to him, Malkijah, one of the goldsmiths, made repairs as far as the house of the temple servants and the merchants, opposite the Inspection Gate, and as far as the room above the corner; 32and between the room above the corner and the Sheep Gate the goldsmiths and merchants made repairs.

Opposition to the Rebuilding

4 When Sanballat heard that we were rebuilding the wall, he became angry and was greatly incensed. He ridiculed the Jews, 2and in the presence of his associates and the army of Samaria, he said, "What are those feeble Jews doing? Will they restore their wall? Will they offer sacrifices? Will they finish in a day? Can they bring the stones back to life from those heaps of rubble—burned as they are?"

3Tobiah the Ammonite, who was at his side, said, "What they are building—if even a fox climbed up on it, he would break down their wall of stones!"

4Hear us, O our God, for we are despised. Turn their insults back on their own heads. Give them over as plunder in a land of captivity. 5Do not cover up their guilt or blot out their sins from your sight, for they have thrown insults in the face of*a* the builders.

6So we rebuilt the wall till all of it reached half its height, for the people worked with all their heart.

7But when Sanballat, Tobiah, the Arabs, the Ammonites and the men of Ashdod heard that the repairs to Jerusalem's walls had gone ahead and that the gaps were being closed, they were very angry. 8They all plotted together to come and fight against Jerusalem and stir up trouble against it. 9But we prayed to our God and posted a guard day and night to meet this threat.

10Meanwhile, the people in Judah said, "The strength of the laborers is giving out, and there is so much rubble that we cannot rebuild the wall."

11Also our enemies said, "Before they know it or see us, we will be right there among them and will kill them and put an end to the work."

12Then the Jews who lived near them came and told us ten times over, "Wherever you turn, they will attack us."

13Therefore I stationed some of the people behind the lowest points of the wall at the exposed places, posting them by families, with their swords, spears and bows. 14After I looked things over, I stood up and said to the nobles, the officials and the rest of the people, "Don't be afraid of them. Remember the Lord, who is great and awesome, and fight for your brothers, your sons and your daughters, your wives and your homes."

15When our enemies heard that we were aware of their plot and that God had frustrated it, we all returned to the wall, each to his own work.

16From that day on, half of my men did the work, while the other half were equipped with spears, shields, bows and armor. The officers posted themselves behind all the people of Judah 17who were building the wall. Those who carried materials did their work with one hand and held a weapon in the other, 18and each of the builders wore his sword at his side as he worked. But the man who sounded the trumpet stayed with me.

19Then I said to the nobles, the officials and the rest of the people, "The work is extensive and spread out, and we are widely separated from each other along the wall. 20Wherever you hear the sound of the trumpet, join us there. Our God will fight for us!"

21So we continued the work with half the men holding spears, from the first light of dawn till the stars came out. 22At that time I also said to the people, "Have every man and

a 5 Or have provoked you to anger before

his helper stay inside Jerusalem at night, so they can serve us as guards by night and workmen by day." ²³Neither I nor my brothers nor my men nor the guards with me took off our clothes; each had his weapon, even when he went for water.ᵃ

Nehemiah Helps the Poor

5 Now the men and their wives raised a great outcry against their Jewish brothers. ²Some were saying, "We and our sons and daughters are numerous; in order for us to eat and stay alive, we must get grain."

³Others were saying, "We are mortgaging our fields, our vineyards and our homes to get grain during the famine."

⁴Still others were saying, "We have had to borrow money to pay the king's tax on our fields and vineyards. ⁵Although we are of the same flesh and blood as our countrymen and though our sons are as good as theirs, yet we have to subject our sons and daughters to slavery. Some of our daughters have already been enslaved, but we are powerless, because our fields and our vineyards belong to others."

⁶When I heard their outcry and these charges, I was very angry. ⁷I pondered them in my mind and then accused the nobles and officials. I told them, "You are exacting usury from your own countrymen!" So I called together a large meeting to deal with them ⁸and said: "As far as possible, we have bought back our Jewish brothers who were sold to the Gentiles. Now you are selling your brothers, only for them to be sold back to us!" They kept quiet, because they could find nothing to say.

⁹So I continued, "What you are doing is not right. Shouldn't you walk in the fear of our God to avoid the reproach of our Gentile enemies? ¹⁰I and my brothers and my men are also lending the people money and grain. But let the exacting of usury stop! ¹¹Give back to them immediately their fields, vineyards, olive groves and houses, and also the usury you are charging them—the hundredth part of the money, grain, new wine and oil."

¹²"We will give it back," they said. "And we will not demand anything more from them. We will do as you say."

Then I summoned the priests and made the nobles and officials take an oath to do

ᵃ23 The meaning of the Hebrew for this clause is uncertain.

▤ ⬛⬛⬛ STRENGTHENING RELATIONSHIPS ⬛⬛⬛ ⬛

5:1–19
Leadership

Problems that can't be seen, like cracks in the foundation of a building, are often the most dangerous. The issues Nehemiah faced in this chapter had to be rooted out and brought into the open. In facing these problems, Nehemiah provided us with a timeless example that can help us lead successfully as well.

Nehemiah began with *contemplation* (verses 6–7). After hearing the complaints about how the Jewish leaders were charging poor people criminally high interest rates, Nehemiah "pondered" what he had heard. He thought before he acted.

Next, he *confronted* the wrongdoers (verses 7–9). Nehemiah was angry because of the injustice he saw. He realized that God's reputation was being damaged as powerful Jews oppressed their poorer Jewish brothers and sisters. As the chosen people, the Jews' behavior was supposed to reflect God's own character. Nehemiah dealt firmly with the people who were at fault.

Finally, Nehemiah *corrected* the problem (verses 10–19). He demanded that these oppressive practices stop and that the guilty parties give back what they had taken. And to bring his point home, Nehemiah noted that during his 12 years as the governor of Judah he had taken no salary (verses 14–16). His unselfish example set a standard for others to follow.

Take a moment and review these three steps. How could they help you successfully resolve a leadership challenge?

what they had promised. ¹³I also shook out the folds of my robe and said, "In this way may God shake out of his house and possessions every man who does not keep this promise. So may such a man be shaken out and emptied!"

At this the whole assembly said, "Amen," and praised the LORD. And the people did as they had promised.

¹⁴Moreover, from the twentieth year of King Artaxerxes, when I was appointed to be their governor in the land of Judah, until his thirty-second year—twelve years—neither I nor my brothers ate the food allotted to the governor. ¹⁵But the earlier governors—those preceding me—placed a heavy burden on the people and took forty shekels*a* of silver from them in addition to food and wine. Their assistants also lorded it over the people. But out of reverence for God I did not act like that. ¹⁶Instead, I devoted myself to the work on this wall. All my men were assembled there for the work; we*b* did not acquire any land.

¹⁷Furthermore, a hundred and fifty Jews and officials ate at my table, as well as those who came to us from the surrounding nations. ¹⁸Each day one ox, six choice sheep and some poultry were prepared for me, and every ten days an abundant supply of wine of all kinds. In spite of all this, I never demanded the food allotted to the governor, because the demands were heavy on these people.

¹⁹Remember me with favor, O my God, for all I have done for these people.

Further Opposition to the Rebuilding

6 When word came to Sanballat, Tobiah, Geshem the Arab and the rest of our enemies that I had rebuilt the wall and not a gap was left in it—though up to that time I had not set the doors in the gates— ²Sanballat and Geshem sent me this message: "Come, let us meet together in one of the villages*c* on the plain of Ono."

But they were scheming to harm me; ³so I sent messengers to them with this reply: "I am carrying on a great project and cannot go down. Why should the work stop while I leave it and go down to you?" ⁴Four times they sent me the same message, and each time I gave them the same answer.

⁵Then, the fifth time, Sanballat sent his aide to me with the same message, and in his hand was an unsealed letter ⁶in which was written:

"It is reported among the nations—and Geshem*d* says it is true—that you and the Jews are plotting to revolt, and therefore you are building the wall. Moreover, according to these reports you are about to become their king ⁷and have even appointed prophets to make this proclamation about you in Jerusalem: 'There is a king in Judah!' Now this report will get back to the king; so come, let us confer together."

⁸I sent him this reply: "Nothing like what you are saying is happening; you are just making it up out of your head."

⁹They were all trying to frighten us, thinking, "Their hands will get too weak for the work, and it will not be completed."

ₗBut I prayed,ₗ "Now strengthen my hands."

¹⁰One day I went to the house of Shemaiah son of Delaiah, the son of Mehetabel, who was shut in at his home. He said, "Let us meet in the house of God, inside the temple, and let us close the temple doors, because men are coming to kill you—by night they are coming to kill you."

¹¹But I said, "Should a man like me run away? Or should one like me go into the temple to save his life? I will not go!" ¹²I realized that God had not sent him, but that he had prophesied against me because Tobiah and Sanballat had hired him. ¹³He had been hired to intimidate me so that I would commit a sin by doing this, and then they would give me a bad name to discredit me.

---

a15 That is, about 1 pound (about 0.5 kilogram)   *b16* Most Hebrew manuscripts; some Hebrew manuscripts, Septuagint, Vulgate and Syriac *I*   *c2* Or *in Kephirim*   *d6* Hebrew *Gashmu*, a variant of *Geshem*

¹⁴Remember Tobiah and Sanballat, O my God, because of what they have done; remember also the prophetess Noadiah and the rest of the prophets who have been trying to intimidate me.

The Completion of the Wall

¹⁵So the wall was completed on the twenty-fifth of Elul, in fifty-two days. ¹⁶When all our enemies heard about this, all the surrounding nations were afraid and lost their self-confidence, because they realized that this work had been done with the help of our God.

¹⁷Also, in those days the nobles of Judah were sending many letters to Tobiah, and replies from Tobiah kept coming to them. ¹⁸For many in Judah were under oath to him, since he was son-in-law to Shecaniah son of Arah, and his son Jehohanan had married the daughter of Meshullam son of Berekiah. ¹⁹Moreover, they kept reporting to me his good deeds and then telling him what I said. And Tobiah sent letters to intimidate me.

7 After the wall had been rebuilt and I had set the doors in place, the gatekeepers and the singers and the Levites were appointed. ²I put in charge of Jerusalem my brother Hanani, along with*ᵃ* Hananiah the commander of the citadel, because he was a man of integrity and feared God more than most men do. ³I said to them, "The gates of Jerusalem are not to be opened until the sun is hot. While the gatekeepers are still on duty, have them shut the doors and bar them. Also appoint residents of Jerusalem as guards, some at their posts and some near their own houses."

The List of the Exiles Who Returned

⁴Now the city was large and spacious, but there were few people in it, and the houses had not yet been rebuilt. ⁵So my God put it into my heart to assemble the nobles, the officials and the common people for registration by families. I found the genealogical record of those who had been the first to return. This is what I found written there:

⁶These are the people of the province who came up from the captivity of the exiles whom Nebuchadnezzar king of Babylon had taken captive (they returned to Jerusalem and Judah, each to his own town, ⁷in company with Zerubbabel, Jeshua, Nehemiah, Azariah, Raamiah, Nahamani, Mordecai, Bilshan, Mispereth, Bigvai, Nehum and Baanah):

The list of the men of Israel:

⁸the descendants of Parosh	2,172
⁹of Shephatiah	372
¹⁰of Arah	652
¹¹of Pahath-Moab (through the line of Jeshua and Joab)	2,818
¹²of Elam	1,254
¹³of Zattu	845
¹⁴of Zaccai	760
¹⁵of Binnui	648
¹⁶of Bebai	628
¹⁷of Azgad	2,322
¹⁸of Adonikam	667
¹⁹of Bigvai	2,067
²⁰of Adin	655
²¹of Ater (through Hezekiah)	98
²²of Hashum	328
²³of Bezai	324

ᵃ2 Or Hanani, that is,

[24]of Hariph	112
[25]of Gibeon	95
[26]the men of Bethlehem and Netophah	188
[27]of Anathoth	128
[28]of Beth Azmaveth	42
[29]of Kiriath Jearim, Kephirah and Beeroth	743
[30]of Ramah and Geba	621
[31]of Micmash	122
[32]of Bethel and Ai	123
[33]of the other Nebo	52
[34]of the other Elam	1,254
[35]of Harim	320
[36]of Jericho	345
[37]of Lod, Hadid and Ono	721
[38]of Senaah	3,930

[39]The priests:

the descendants of Jedaiah (through the family of Jeshua)	973
[40]of Immer	1,052
[41]of Pashhur	1,247
[42]of Harim	1,017

[43]The Levites:

the descendants of Jeshua (through Kadmiel through the line of Hodaviah)	74

[44]The singers:

the descendants of Asaph	148

[45]The gatekeepers:

the descendants of Shallum, Ater, Talmon, Akkub, Hatita and Shobai	138

[46]The temple servants:

the descendants of
Ziha, Hasupha, Tabbaoth,
[47]Keros, Sia, Padon,
[48]Lebana, Hagaba, Shalmai,
[49]Hanan, Giddel, Gahar,
[50]Reaiah, Rezin, Nekoda,
[51]Gazzam, Uzza, Paseah,
[52]Besai, Meunim, Nephussim,
[53]Bakbuk, Hakupha, Harhur,
[54]Bazluth, Mehida, Harsha,
[55]Barkos, Sisera, Temah,
[56]Neziah and Hatipha

[57]The descendants of the servants of Solomon:

the descendants of
Sotai, Sophereth, Perida,
[58]Jaala, Darkon, Giddel,
[59]Shephatiah, Hattil,
Pokereth-Hazzebaim and Amon

⁶⁰The temple servants and the descendants of the servants of
    Solomon   392

⁶¹The following came up from the towns of Tel Melah, Tel Harsha, Kerub, Addon
and Immer, but they could not show that their families were descended from Israel:

⁶²the descendants of
    Delaiah, Tobiah and Nekoda   642

⁶³And from among the priests:

the descendants of
    Hobaiah, Hakkoz and Barzillai (a man who had married a daughter
    of Barzillai the Gileadite and was called by that name).

⁶⁴These searched for their family records, but they could not find them and so
were excluded from the priesthood as unclean. ⁶⁵The governor, therefore, ordered
them not to eat any of the most sacred food until there should be a priest ministering
with the Urim and Thummim.

⁶⁶The whole company numbered 42,360, ⁶⁷besides their 7,337 menservants and
maidservants; and they also had 245 men and women singers. ⁶⁸There were 736
horses, 245 mules,ᵃ ⁶⁹435 camels and 6,720 donkeys.

⁷⁰Some of the heads of the families contributed to the work. The governor gave to
the treasury 1,000 drachmasᵇ of gold, 50 bowls and 530 garments for priests.
⁷¹Some of the heads of the families gave to the treasury for the work 20,000 drach-
masᶜ of gold and 2,200 minasᵈ of silver. ⁷²The total given by the rest of the people
was 20,000 drachmas of gold, 2,000 minasᵉ of silver and 67 garments for priests.

⁷³The priests, the Levites, the gatekeepers, the singers and the temple servants,
along with certain of the people and the rest of the Israelites, settled in their own
towns.

Ezra Reads the Law

8 When the seventh month came and the Israelites had settled in their towns, ¹all
the people assembled as one man in the square before the Water Gate. They
told Ezra the scribe to bring out the Book of the Law of Moses, which the Lᴏʀᴅ had
commanded for Israel.

²So on the first day of the seventh month Ezra the priest brought the Law before the
assembly, which was made up of men and women and all who were able to understand.
³He read it aloud from daybreak till noon as he faced the square before the Water Gate in
the presence of the men, women and others who could understand. And all the people
listened attentively to the Book of the Law.

⁴Ezra the scribe stood on a high wooden platform built for the occasion. Beside him on
his right stood Mattithiah, Shema, Anaiah, Uriah, Hilkiah and Maaseiah; and on his left
were Pedaiah, Mishael, Malkijah, Hashum, Hashbaddanah, Zechariah and Meshullam.

⁵Ezra opened the book. All the people could see him because he was standing above
them; and as he opened it, the people all stood up. ⁶Ezra praised the Lᴏʀᴅ, the great God;
and all the people lifted their hands and responded, "Amen! Amen!" Then they bowed
down and worshiped the Lᴏʀᴅ with their faces to the ground.

⁷The Levites—Jeshua, Bani, Sherebiah, Jamin, Akkub, Shabbethai, Hodiah, Maaseiah,
Kelita, Azariah, Jozabad, Hanan and Pelaiah—instructed the people in the Law while the
people were standing there. ⁸They read from the Book of the Law of God, making it

---

ᵃ68 Some Hebrew manuscripts (see also Ezra 2:66); most Hebrew manuscripts do not have this verse.   ᵇ70 That is, about
19 pounds (about 8.5 kilograms)   ᶜ71 That is, about 375 pounds (about 170 kilograms); also in verse 72   ᵈ71 That is,
about 1 1/3 tons (about 1.2 metric tons)   ᵉ72 That is, about 1 1/4 tons (about 1.1 metric tons)

clear[a] and giving the meaning so that the people could understand what was being read.

[9]Then Nehemiah the governor, Ezra the priest and scribe, and the Levites who were instructing the people said to them all, "This day is sacred to the LORD your God. Do not mourn or weep." For all the people had been weeping as they listened to the words of the Law.

[10]Nehemiah said, "Go and enjoy choice food and sweet drinks, and send some to those who have nothing prepared. This day is sacred to our Lord. Do not grieve, for the joy of the LORD is your strength."

[11]The Levites calmed all the people, saying, "Be still, for this is a sacred day. Do not grieve."

[12]Then all the people went away to eat and drink, to send portions of food and to celebrate with great joy, because they now understood the words that had been made known to them.

[13]On the second day of the month, the heads of all the families, along with the priests and the Levites, gathered around Ezra the scribe to give attention to the words of the Law. [14]They found written in the Law, which the LORD had commanded through Moses, that the Israelites were to live in booths during the feast of the seventh month [15]and that they should proclaim this word and spread it throughout their towns and in Jerusalem: "Go out into the hill country and bring back branches from olive and wild olive trees, and from myrtles, palms and shade trees, to make booths"—as it is written.[b]

[16]So the people went out and brought back branches and built themselves booths on their own roofs, in their courtyards, in the courts of the house of God and in the square by the Water Gate and the one by the Gate of Ephraim. [17]The whole company that had returned from exile built booths and lived in them. From the days of Joshua son of Nun until that day, the Israelites had not celebrated it like this. And their joy was very great.

[18]Day after day, from the first day to the last, Ezra read from the Book of the Law of God. They celebrated the feast for seven days, and on the eighth day, in accordance with the regulation, there was an assembly.

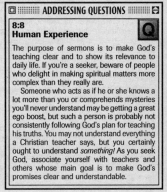

▓▓▓▓ ADDRESSING QUESTIONS ▓▓▓▓ 🔄

8:8
Human Experience

The purpose of sermons is to make God's teaching clear and to show its relevance to daily life. If you're a seeker, beware of people who delight in making spiritual matters more complex than they really are.

Someone who acts as if he or she knows a lot more than you or comprehends mysteries you'll never understand may be getting a great ego boost, but such a person is probably not consistently following God's plan for teaching his truths. You may not understand everything a Christian teacher says, but you certainly ought to understand *something!* As you seek God, associate yourself with teachers and others whose main goal is to make God's promises clear and understandable.

The Israelites Confess Their Sins

9 On the twenty-fourth day of the same month, the Israelites gathered together, fasting and wearing sackcloth and having dust on their heads. [2]Those of Israelite descent had separated themselves from all foreigners. They stood in their places and confessed their sins and the wickedness of their fathers. [3]They stood where they were and read from the Book of the Law of the LORD their God for a quarter of the day, and spent another quarter in confession and in worshiping the LORD their God. [4]Standing on the stairs were the Levites—Jeshua, Bani, Kadmiel, Shebaniah, Bunni, Sherebiah, Bani and Kenani—who called with loud voices to the LORD their God. [5]And the Levites—Jeshua,

[a]8 Or God, translating it   [b]15 See Lev. 23:37-40.

Kadmiel, Bani, Hashabneiah, Sherebiah, Hodiah, Shebaniah and Pethahiah—said: "Stand up and praise the Lord your God, who is from everlasting to everlasting.*"

"Blessed be your glorious name, and may it be exalted above all blessing and praise. 6You alone are the Lord. You made the heavens, even the highest heavens, and all their starry host, the earth and all that is on it, the seas and all that is in them. You give life to everything, and the multitudes of heaven worship you.

7"You are the Lord God, who chose Abram and brought him out of Ur of the Chaldeans and named him Abraham. 8You found his heart faithful to you, and you made a covenant with him to give to his descendants the land of the Canaanites, Hittites, Amorites, Perizzites, Jebusites and Girgashites. You have kept your promise because you are righteous.

9"You saw the suffering of our forefathers in Egypt; you heard their cry at the Red Sea.b 10You sent miraculous signs and wonders against Pharaoh, against all his officials and all the people of his land, for you knew how arrogantly the Egyptians treated them. You made a name for yourself, which remains to this day. 11You divided the sea before them, so that they passed through it on dry ground, but you hurled their pursuers into the depths, like a stone into mighty waters. 12By day you led them with a pillar of cloud, and by night with a pillar of fire to give them light on the way they were to take.

13"You came down on Mount Sinai; you spoke to them from heaven. You gave them regulations and laws that are just and right, and decrees and commands that are good. 14You made known to them your holy Sabbath and gave them commands, decrees and laws through your servant Moses. 15In their hunger you gave them bread from heaven and in their thirst you brought them water from the rock; you told them to go in and take possession of the land you had sworn with uplifted hand to give them.

16"But they, our forefathers, became arrogant and stiff-necked, and did not obey your commands. 17They refused to listen and failed to remember the miracles you performed among them. They became stiff-necked and in their rebellion appointed a leader in order to return to their slavery. But you are a forgiving God, gracious and compassionate, slow to anger and abounding in love. Therefore you did not desert them, 18even when they cast for themselves an image of a calf and said, 'This is your god, who brought you up out of Egypt,' or when they committed awful blasphemies.

19"Because of your great compassion you did not abandon them in the desert. By day the pillar of cloud did not cease to guide them on their path, nor the pillar of fire by night to shine on the way they were to take. 20You gave your good Spirit to instruct them. You did not withhold your manna from their mouths, and you gave them water for their thirst. 21For forty years you sustained them in the desert; they lacked nothing, their clothes did not wear out nor did their feet become swollen.

22"You gave them kingdoms and nations, allotting to them even the remotest frontiers. They took over the country of Sihonc king of Heshbon and the country of Og king of Bashan. 23You made their sons as numerous as the stars in the sky, and you brought them into the land that you told their fathers to enter and possess. 24Their sons went in and took possession of the land. You subdued before them the Canaanites, who lived in the land; you handed the Canaanites over to them, along with their kings and the peoples of the land, to deal with them as they pleased. 25They captured fortified cities and fertile land; they took possession of houses filled with all kinds of good things, wells already dug, vineyards, olive groves and fruit trees in abundance. They ate to the full and were well-nourished; they reveled in your great goodness.

---

*5 Or God for ever and ever   b9 Hebrew Yam Suph; that is, Sea of Reeds   c22 One Hebrew manuscript and Septuagint; most Hebrew manuscripts Sihon, that is, the country of the

²⁶"But they were disobedient and rebelled against you; they put your law behind their backs. They killed your prophets, who had admonished them in order to turn them back to you; they committed awful blasphemies. ²⁷So you handed them over to their enemies, who oppressed them. But when they were oppressed they cried out to you. From heaven you heard them, and in your great compassion you gave them deliverers, who rescued them from the hand of their enemies.

²⁸"But as soon as they were at rest, they again did what was evil in your sight. Then you abandoned them to the hand of their enemies so that they ruled over them. And when they cried out to you again, you heard from heaven, and in your compassion you delivered them time after time.

²⁹"You warned them to return to your law, but they became arrogant and disobeyed your commands. They sinned against your ordinances, by which a man will live if he obeys them. Stubbornly they turned their backs on you, became stiff-necked and refused to listen. ³⁰For many years you were patient with them. By your Spirit you admonished them through your prophets. Yet they paid no attention, so you handed them over to the neighboring peoples. ³¹But in your great mercy you did not put an end to them or abandon them, for you are a gracious and merciful God.

³²"Now therefore, O our God, the great, mighty and awesome God, who keeps his covenant of love, do not let all this hardship seem trifling in your eyes—the hardship that has come upon us, upon our kings and leaders, upon our priests and prophets, upon our fathers and all your people, from the days of the kings of Assyria until today. ³³In all that has happened to us, you have been just; you have acted faithfully, while we did wrong. ³⁴Our kings, our leaders, our priests and our fathers did not follow your law; they did not pay attention to your commands or the warnings you gave them. ³⁵Even while they were in their kingdom, enjoying your great goodness to them in the spacious and fertile land you gave them, they did not serve you or turn from their evil ways.

³⁶"But see, we are slaves today, slaves in the land you gave our forefathers so they could eat its fruit and the other good things it produces. ³⁷Because of our sins, its abundant harvest goes to the kings you have placed over us. They rule over our bodies and our cattle as they please. We are in great distress.

The Agreement of the People

³⁸"In view of all this, we are making a binding agreement, putting it in writing, and our leaders, our Levites and our priests are affixing their seals to it."

10 Those who sealed it were:

Nehemiah the governor, the son of Hacaliah.

Zedekiah, ²Seraiah, Azariah, Jeremiah,
³Pashhur, Amariah, Malkijah,
⁴Hattush, Shebaniah, Malluch,
⁵Harim, Meremoth, Obadiah,
⁶Daniel, Ginnethon, Baruch,
⁷Meshullam, Abijah, Mijamin,
⁸Maaziah, Bilgai and Shemaiah.
These were the priests.

⁹The Levites:

Jeshua son of Azaniah, Binnui of the sons of Henadad, Kadmiel,
¹⁰and their associates: Shebaniah,
Hodiah, Kelita, Pelaiah, Hanan,
¹¹Mica, Rehob, Hashabiah,

¹²Zaccur, Sherebiah, Shebaniah,
¹³Hodiah, Bani and Beninu.

¹⁴The leaders of the people:

Parosh, Pahath-Moab, Elam, Zattu, Bani,
¹⁵Bunni, Azgad, Bebai,
¹⁶Adonijah, Bigvai, Adin,
¹⁷Ater, Hezekiah, Azzur,
¹⁸Hodiah, Hashum, Bezai,
¹⁹Hariph, Anathoth, Nebai,
²⁰Magpiash, Meshullam, Hezir,
²¹Meshezabel, Zadok, Jaddua,
²²Pelatiah, Hanan, Anaiah,
²³Hoshea, Hananiah, Hasshub,
²⁴Hallohesh, Pilha, Shobek,
²⁵Rehum, Hashabnah, Maaseiah,
²⁶Ahiah, Hanan, Anan,
²⁷Malluch, Harim and Baanah.

²⁸"The rest of the people—priests, Levites, gatekeepers, singers, temple servants and all who separated themselves from the neighboring peoples for the sake of the Law of God, together with their wives and all their sons and daughters who are able to understand— ²⁹all these now join their brothers the nobles, and bind themselves with a curse and an oath to follow the Law of God given through Moses the servant of God and to obey carefully all the commands, regulations and decrees of the Lord our Lord.

³⁰"We promise not to give our daughters in marriage to the peoples around us or take their daughters for our sons.

³¹"When the neighboring peoples bring merchandise or grain to sell on the Sabbath, we will not buy from them on the Sabbath or on any holy day. Every seventh year we will forgo working the land and will cancel all debts.

³²"We assume the responsibility for carrying out the commands to give a third of a shekel[a] each year for the service of the house of our God: ³³for the bread set out on the table; for the regular grain offerings and burnt offerings; for the offerings on the Sabbaths, New Moon festivals and appointed feasts; for the holy offerings; for sin offerings to make atonement for Israel; and for all the duties of the house of our God.

³⁴"We—the priests, the Levites and the people—have cast lots to determine when each of our families is to bring to the house of our God at set times each year a contribution of wood to burn on the altar of the Lord our God, as it is written in the Law.

³⁵"We also assume responsibility for bringing to the house of the Lord each year the firstfruits of our crops and of every fruit tree.

³⁶"As it is also written in the Law, we will bring the firstborn of our sons and of our cattle, of our herds and of our flocks to the house of our God, to the priests ministering there.

³⁷"Moreover, we will bring to the storerooms of the house of our God, to the priests, the first of our ground meal, of our ₗgrainₗ offerings, of the fruit of all our trees and of our new wine and oil. And we will bring a tithe of our crops to the Levites, for it is the Levites who collect the tithes in all the towns where we work. ³⁸A priest descended from Aaron is to accompany the Levites when they receive the tithes, and the Levites are to bring a tenth of the tithes up to the house of our God, to the storerooms of the treasury. ³⁹The people of Israel, including the Levites, are to

ᵃ32 That is, about 1/8 ounce (about 4 grams)

bring their contributions of grain, new wine and oil to the storerooms where the articles for the sanctuary are kept and where the ministering priests, the gatekeepers and the singers stay.

"We will not neglect the house of our God."

The New Residents of Jerusalem

11 Now the leaders of the people settled in Jerusalem, and the rest of the people cast lots to bring one out of every ten to live in Jerusalem, the holy city, while the remaining nine were to stay in their own towns. ²The people commended all the men who volunteered to live in Jerusalem.

³These are the provincial leaders who settled in Jerusalem (now some Israelites, priests, Levites, temple servants and descendants of Solomon's servants lived in the towns of Judah, each on his own property in the various towns, ⁴while other people from both Judah and Benjamin lived in Jerusalem):

From the descendants of Judah:

Athaiah son of Uzziah, the son of Zechariah, the son of Amariah, the son of Shephatiah, the son of Mahalalel, a descendant of Perez; ⁵and Maaseiah son of Baruch, the son of Col-Hozeh, the son of Hazaiah, the son of Adaiah, the son of Joiarib, the son of Zechariah, a descendant of Shelah. ⁶The descendants of Perez who lived in Jerusalem totaled 468 able men.

⁷From the descendants of Benjamin:

Sallu son of Meshullam, the son of Joed, the son of Pedaiah, the son of Kolaiah, the son of Maaseiah, the son of Ithiel, the son of Jeshaiah, ⁸and his followers, Gabbai and Sallai—928 men. ⁹Joel son of Zicri was their chief officer, and Judah son of Hassenuah was over the Second District of the city.

¹⁰From the priests:

Jedaiah; the son of Joiarib; Jakin; ¹¹Seraiah son of Hilkiah, the son of Meshullam, the son of Zadok, the son of Meraioth, the son of Ahitub, supervisor in the house of God, ¹²and their associates, who carried on work for the temple—822 men; Adaiah son of Jeroham, the son of Pelaliah, the son of Amzi, the son of Zechariah, the son of Pashhur, the son of Malkijah, ¹³and his associates, who were heads of families—242 men; Amashsai son of Azarel, the son of Ahzai, the son of Meshillemoth, the son of Immer, ¹⁴and his^a associates, who were able men—128. Their chief officer was Zabdiel son of Haggedolim.

¹⁵From the Levites:

Shemaiah son of Hasshub, the son of Azrikam, the son of Hashabiah, the son of Bunni; ¹⁶Shabbethai and Jozabad, two of the heads of the Levites, who had charge of the outside work of the house of God; ¹⁷Mattaniah son of Mica, the son of Zabdi, the son of Asaph, the director who led in thanksgiving and prayer; Bakbukiah, second among his associates; and Abda son of Shammua, the son of Galal, the son of Jeduthun. ¹⁸The Levites in the holy city totaled 284.

¹⁹The gatekeepers:

Akkub, Talmon and their associates, who kept watch at the gates—172 men.

²⁰The rest of the Israelites, with the priests and Levites, were in all the towns of Judah, each on his ancestral property.

---

^a 14 Most Septuagint manuscripts; Hebrew *their*

²¹The temple servants lived on the hill of Ophel, and Ziha and Gishpa were in charge of them.

²²The chief officer of the Levites in Jerusalem was Uzzi son of Bani, the son of Hashabiah, the son of Mattaniah, the son of Mica. Uzzi was one of Asaph's descendants, who were the singers responsible for the service of the house of God. ²³The singers were under the king's orders, which regulated their daily activity.

²⁴Pethahiah son of Meshezabel, one of the descendants of Zerah son of Judah, was the king's agent in all affairs relating to the people.

²⁵As for the villages with their fields, some of the people of Judah lived in Kiriath Arba and its surrounding settlements, in Dibon and its settlements, in Jekabzeel and its villages, ²⁶in Jeshua, in Moladah, in Beth Pelet, ²⁷in Hazar Shual, in Beersheba and its settlements, ²⁸in Ziklag, in Meconah and its settlements, ²⁹in En Rimmon, in Zorah, in Jarmuth, ³⁰Zanoah, Adullam and their villages, in Lachish and its fields, and in Azekah and its settlements. So they were living all the way from Beersheba to the Valley of Hinnom.

³¹The descendants of the Benjamites from Geba lived in Micmash, Aija, Bethel and its settlements, ³²in Anathoth, Nob and Ananiah, ³³in Hazor, Ramah and Gittaim, ³⁴in Hadid, Zeboim and Neballat, ³⁵in Lod and Ono, and in the Valley of the Craftsmen.

³⁶Some of the divisions of the Levites of Judah settled in Benjamin.

Priests and Levites

12 These were the priests and Levites who returned with Zerubbabel son of Shealtiel and with Jeshua:

Seraiah, Jeremiah, Ezra,
²Amariah, Malluch, Hattush,
³Shecaniah, Rehum, Meremoth,
⁴Iddo, Ginnethon,ᵃ Abijah,
⁵Mijamin,ᵇ Moadiah, Bilgah,
⁶Shemaiah, Joiarib, Jedaiah,
⁷Sallu, Amok, Hilkiah and Jedaiah.

These were the leaders of the priests and their associates in the days of Jeshua.

⁸The Levites were Jeshua, Binnui, Kadmiel, Sherebiah, Judah, and also Mattaniah, who, together with his associates, was in charge of the songs of thanksgiving. ⁹Bakbukiah and Unni, their associates, stood opposite them in the services.

¹⁰Jeshua was the father of Joiakim, Joiakim the father of Eliashib, Eliashib the father of Joiada, ¹¹Joiada the father of Jonathan, and Jonathan the father of Jaddua.

¹²In the days of Joiakim, these were the heads of the priestly families:

of Seraiah's family, Meraiah;
of Jeremiah's, Hananiah;
¹³of Ezra's, Meshullam;
of Amariah's, Jehohanan;
¹⁴of Malluch's, Jonathan;
of Shecaniah's,ᶜ Joseph;
¹⁵of Harim's, Adna;
of Meremoth's,ᵈ Helkai;
¹⁶of Iddo's, Zechariah;
of Ginnethon's, Meshullam;
¹⁷of Abijah's, Zicri;
of Miniamin's and of Moadiah's, Piltai;
¹⁸of Bilgah's, Shammua;

ᵃ4 Many Hebrew manuscripts and Vulgate (see also Neh. 12:16); most Hebrew manuscripts *Ginnethoi*   ᵇ5 A variant of *Miniamin*   ᶜ14 Very many Hebrew manuscripts, some Septuagint manuscripts and Syriac (see also Neh. 12:3); most Hebrew manuscripts *Shebaniah's*   ᵈ15 Some Septuagint manuscripts (see also Neh. 12:3); Hebrew *Meraioth's*

of Shemaiah's, Jehonathan;
¹⁹of Joiarib's, Mattenai;
of Jedaiah's, Uzzi;
²⁰of Sallu's, Kallai;
of Amok's, Eber;
²¹of Hilkiah's, Hashabiah;
of Jedaiah's, Nethanel.

²²The family heads of the Levites in the days of Eliashib, Joiada, Johanan and Jaddua, as well as those of the priests, were recorded in the reign of Darius the Persian. ²³The family heads among the descendants of Levi up to the time of Johanan son of Eliashib were recorded in the book of the annals. ²⁴And the leaders of the Levites were Hashabiah, Sherebiah, Jeshua son of Kadmiel, and their associates, who stood opposite them to give praise and thanksgiving, one section responding to the other, as prescribed by David the man of God.

²⁵Mattaniah, Bakbukiah, Obadiah, Meshullam, Talmon and Akkub were gatekeepers who guarded the storerooms at the gates. ²⁶They served in the days of Joiakim son of Jeshua, the son of Jozadak, and in the days of Nehemiah the governor and of Ezra the priest and scribe.

Dedication of the Wall of Jerusalem

²⁷At the dedication of the wall of Jerusalem, the Levites were sought out from where they lived and were brought to Jerusalem to celebrate joyfully the dedication with songs of thanksgiving and with the music of cymbals, harps and lyres. ²⁸The singers also were brought together from the region around Jerusalem—from the villages of the Netophathites, ²⁹from Beth Gilgal, and from the area of Geba and Azmaveth, for the singers had built villages for themselves around Jerusalem. ³⁰When the priests and Levites had purified themselves ceremonially, they purified the people, the gates and the wall.

³¹I had the leaders of Judah go up on top*a* of the wall. I also assigned two large choirs to give thanks. One was to proceed on top*b* of the wall to the right, toward the Dung Gate. ³²Hoshaiah and half the leaders of Judah followed them, ³³along with Azariah, Ezra, Meshullam, ³⁴Judah, Benjamin, Shemaiah, Jeremiah, ³⁵as well as some

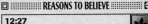

┌─────────────────────────────────────┐
│ ▦▦▦▦▦ **REASONS TO BELIEVE** ▦▦▦▦▦ │
│   │
│ **12:27**   │
│ **The Christian Experience**   │
│   │
│ Celebration is one of the key principles of life with God. │
│   Does that sound strange to you? Perhaps in the past you've experienced worship that didn't seem much like celebration to you. But believers in God have reason to celebrate every single day! │
│   This chapter shows how Nehemiah staged a huge victory party after the wall around Jerusalem had been rebuilt. After accomplishing their task, the Israelites took time to worship God, who had blessed their work. When today's Christians get together, they celebrate the fact that, through Jesus, the wall between us and God has been broken down. And that reality adds a pervasive aspect of celebration to the Christian's life. As you continue to seek God, you'll want to look into places of fellowship that openly celebrate that reality. │
└─────────────────────────────────────┘

priests with trumpets, and also Zechariah son of Jonathan, the son of Shemaiah, the son of Mattaniah, the son of Micaiah, the son of Zaccur, the son of Asaph, ³⁶and his associates—Shemaiah, Azarel, Milalai, Gilalai, Maai, Nethanel, Judah and Hanani—with musical instruments ⌐prescribed by⌐ David the man of God. Ezra the scribe led the procession. ³⁷At the Fountain Gate they continued directly up the steps of the City of David on the ascent to the wall and passed above the house of David to the Water Gate on the east.

³⁸The second choir proceeded in the opposite direction. I followed them on top*c* of the wall, together with half the people—past the Tower of the Ovens to the Broad Wall, ³⁹over the Gate of Ephraim, the Jeshanah*d* Gate, the Fish Gate, the Tower of Hananel

a31 Or go alongside   b31 Or proceed alongside   c38 Or them alongside   d39 Or Old

and the Tower of the Hundred, as far as the Sheep Gate. At the Gate of the Guard they stopped.

40The two choirs that gave thanks then took their places in the house of God; so did I, together with half the officials, **41**as well as the priests—Eliakim, Maaseiah, Miniamin, Micaiah, Elioenai, Zechariah and Hananiah with their trumpets— **42**and also Maaseiah, Shemaiah, Eleazar, Uzzi, Jehohanan, Malkijah, Elam and Ezer. The choirs sang under the direction of Jezrahiah. **43**And on that day they offered great sacrifices, rejoicing because God had given them great joy. The women and children also rejoiced. The sound of rejoicing in Jerusalem could be heard far away.

44At that time men were appointed to be in charge of the storerooms for the contributions, firstfruits and tithes. From the fields around the towns they were to bring into the storerooms the portions required by the Law for the priests and the Levites, for Judah was pleased with the ministering priests and Levites. **45**They performed the service of their God and the service of purification, as did also the singers and gatekeepers, according to the commands of David and his son Solomon. **46**For long ago, in the days of David and Asaph, there had been directors for the singers and for the songs of praise and thanksgiving to God. **47**So in the days of Zerubbabel and of Nehemiah, all Israel contributed the daily portions for the singers and gatekeepers. They also set aside the portion for the other Levites, and the Levites set aside the portion for the descendants of Aaron.

Nehemiah's Final Reforms

13 On that day the Book of Moses was read aloud in the hearing of the people and there it was found written that no Ammonite or Moabite should ever be admitted into the assembly of God, **2**because they had not met the Israelites with food and water but had hired Balaam to call a curse down on them. (Our God, however, turned the curse into a blessing.) **3**When the people heard this law, they excluded from Israel all who were of foreign descent.

4Before this, Eliashib the priest had been put in charge of the storerooms of the house of our God. He was closely associated with Tobiah, **5**and he had provided him with a large room formerly used to store the grain offerings and incense and temple articles, and also the tithes of grain, new wine and oil prescribed for the Levites, singers and gatekeepers, as well as the contributions for the priests.

6But while all this was going on, I was not in Jerusalem, for in the thirty-second year of Artaxerxes king of Babylon I had returned to the king. Some time later I asked his permission **7**and came back to Jerusalem. Here I learned about the evil thing Eliashib had done in providing Tobiah a room in the courts of the house of God. **8**I was greatly displeased and threw all Tobiah's household goods out of the room. **9**I gave orders to purify the rooms, and then I put back into them the equipment of the house of God, with the grain offerings and the incense.

10I also learned that the portions assigned to the Levites had not been given to them, and that all the Levites and singers responsible for the service had gone back to their own fields. **11**So I rebuked the officials and asked them, "Why is the house of God neglected?" Then I called them together and stationed them at their posts.

12All Judah brought the tithes of grain, new wine and oil into the storerooms. **13**I put Shelemiah the priest, Zadok the scribe, and a Levite named Pedaiah in charge of the storerooms and made Hanan son of Zaccur, the son of Mattaniah, their assistant, because these men were considered trustworthy. They were made responsible for distributing the supplies to their brothers.

14Remember me for this, O my God, and do not blot out what I have so faithfully done for the house of my God and its services.

15In those days I saw men in Judah treading winepresses on the Sabbath and bringing in grain and loading it on donkeys, together with wine, grapes, figs and all other kinds of loads. And they were bringing all this into Jerusalem on the Sabbath. Therefore I warned them against selling food on that day. [16]Men from Tyre who lived in Jerusalem were bringing in fish and all kinds of merchandise and selling them in Jerusalem on the Sabbath to the people of Judah. [17]I rebuked the nobles of Judah and said to them, "What is this wicked thing you are doing—desecrating the Sabbath day? [18]Didn't your forefathers do the same things, so that our God brought all this calamity upon us and upon this city? Now you are stirring up more wrath against Israel by desecrating the Sabbath."

[19]When evening shadows fell on the gates of Jerusalem before the Sabbath, I ordered the doors to be shut and not opened until the Sabbath was over. I stationed some of my own men at the gates so that no load could be brought in on the Sabbath day. [20]Once or twice the merchants and sellers of all kinds of goods spent the night outside Jerusalem. [21]But I warned them and said, "Why do you spend the night by the wall? If you do this again, I will lay hands on you." From that time on they no longer came on the Sabbath. [22]Then I commanded the Levites to purify themselves and go and guard the gates in order to keep the Sabbath day holy.

Remember me for this also, O my God, and show mercy to me according to your great love.

[23]Moreover, in those days I saw men of Judah who had married women from Ashdod, Ammon and Moab. [24]Half of their children spoke the language of Ashdod or the language of one of the other peoples, and did not know how to speak the language of Judah. [25]I rebuked them and called curses down on them. I beat some of the men and pulled out their hair. I made them take an oath in God's name and said: "You are not to give your daughters in marriage to their sons, nor are you to take their daughters in marriage for your sons or for yourselves. [26]Was it not because of marriages like these that Solomon king of Israel sinned? Among the many nations there was no king like him. He was loved by his God, and God made him king over all Israel, but even he was led into sin by foreign women. [27]Must we hear now that you too are doing all this terrible wickedness and are being unfaithful to our God by marrying foreign women?"

[28]One of the sons of Joiada son of Eliashib the high priest was son-in-law to Sanballat the Horonite. And I drove him away from me.

[29]Remember them, O my God, because they defiled the priestly office and the covenant of the priesthood and of the Levites.

[30]So I purified the priests and the Levites of everything foreign, and assigned them duties, each to his own task. [31]I also made provision for contributions of wood at designated times, and for the firstfruits.

Remember me with favor, O my God.

ESTHER

Queen Vashti Deposed

1 This is what happened during the time of Xerxes,[a] the Xerxes who ruled over 127 provinces stretching from India to Cush[b]: ²At that time King Xerxes reigned from his royal throne in the citadel of Susa, ³and in the third year of his reign he gave a banquet for all his nobles and officials. The military leaders of Persia and Media, the princes, and the nobles of the provinces were present.

⁴For a full 180 days he displayed the vast wealth of his kingdom and the splendor and glory of his majesty. ⁵When these days were over, the king gave a banquet, lasting seven days, in the enclosed garden of the king's palace, for all the people from the least to the greatest, who were in the citadel of Susa. ⁶The garden had hangings of white and blue linen, fastened with cords of white linen and purple material to silver rings on marble pillars. There were couches of gold and silver on a mosaic pavement of porphyry, marble, mother-of-pearl and other costly stones. ⁷Wine was served in goblets of gold, each one different from the other, and the royal wine was abundant, in keeping with the king's liberality. ⁸By the king's command each guest was allowed to drink in his own way, for the king instructed all the wine stewards to serve each man what he wished.

⁹Queen Vashti also gave a banquet for the women in the royal palace of King Xerxes.

¹⁰On the seventh day, when King Xerxes was in high spirits from wine, he commanded the seven eunuchs who served him—Mehuman, Biztha, Harbona, Bigtha, Abagtha, Zethar and Carcas— ¹¹to bring before him Queen Vashti, wearing her royal crown, in order to display her beauty to the people and nobles, for she was lovely to look at. ¹²But when the attendants delivered the king's command, Queen Vashti refused to come. Then the king became furious and burned with anger.

¹³Since it was customary for the king to consult experts in matters of law and justice, he spoke with the wise men who understood the times ¹⁴and were closest to the king—Carshena, Shethar, Admatha, Tarshish, Meres, Marsena and Memucan, the seven nobles of Persia and Media who had special access to the king and were highest in the kingdom.

¹⁵"According to law, what must be done to Queen Vashti?" he asked. "She has not obeyed the command of King Xerxes that the eunuchs have taken to her."

¹⁶Then Memucan replied in the presence of the king and the nobles, "Queen Vashti has done wrong, not only against the king but also against all the nobles and the peoples of all the provinces of King Xerxes. ¹⁷For the queen's conduct will become known to all the women, and so they will despise their husbands and say, 'King Xerxes commanded Queen Vashti to be brought before him, but she would not come.' ¹⁸This very day the Persian and Median women of the nobility who have heard about the queen's conduct will respond to all the king's nobles in the same way. There will be no end of disrespect and discord.

¹⁹"Therefore, if it pleases the king, let him issue a royal decree and let it be written in the laws of Persia and Media, which cannot be repealed, that Vashti is never again to enter the presence of King Xerxes. Also let the king give her royal position to someone else who is better than she. ²⁰Then when the king's edict is proclaimed throughout all his vast realm, all the women will respect their husbands, from the least to the greatest."

²¹The king and his nobles were pleased with this advice, so the king did as Memucan

---

[a] 1 Hebrew *Ahasuerus*, a variant of Xerxes' Persian name; here and throughout Esther   [b] 1 That is, the upper Nile region

proposed. ²²He sent dispatches to all parts of the kingdom, to each province in its own script and to each people in its own language, proclaiming in each people's tongue that every man should be ruler over his own household.

Esther Made Queen

2 Later when the anger of King Xerxes had subsided, he remembered Vashti and what she had done and what he had decreed about her. ²Then the king's personal attendants proposed, "Let a search be made for beautiful young virgins for the king. ³Let the king appoint commissioners in every province of his realm to bring all these beautiful girls into the harem at the citadel of Susa. Let them be placed under the care of Hegai, the king's eunuch, who is in charge of the women; and let beauty treatments be given to them. ⁴Then let the girl who pleases the king be queen instead of Vashti." This advice appealed to the king, and he followed it.

⁵Now there was in the citadel of Susa a Jew of the tribe of Benjamin, named Mordecai son of Jair, the son of Shimei, the son of Kish, ⁶who had been carried into exile from Jerusalem by Nebuchadnezzar king of Babylon, among those taken captive with Jehoia-chin*a* king of Judah. ⁷Mordecai had a cousin named Hadassah, whom he had brought up because she had neither father nor mother. This girl, who was also known as Esther, was lovely in form and features, and Mordecai had taken her as his own daughter when her father and mother died.

⁸When the king's order and edict had been proclaimed, many girls were brought to the citadel of Susa and put under the care of Hegai. Esther also was taken to the king's palace and entrusted to Hegai, who had charge of the harem. ⁹The girl pleased him and won his favor. Immediately he provided her with her beauty treatments and special food. He assigned to her seven maids selected from the king's palace and moved her and her maids into the best place in the harem.

¹⁰Esther had not revealed her nationality and family background, because Mordecai had forbidden her to do so. ¹¹Every day he walked back and forth near the courtyard of the harem to find out how Esther was and what was happening to her.

¹²Before a girl's turn came to go in to King Xerxes, she had to complete twelve months of beauty treatments prescribed for the women, six months with oil of myrrh and six with perfumes and cosmetics. ¹³And this is how she would go to the king: Anything she wanted was given her to take with her from the harem to the king's palace. ¹⁴In the evening she would go there and in the morning return to another part of the harem to the care of Shaashgaz, the king's eunuch who was in charge of the concubines. She would not return to the king unless he was pleased with her and summoned her by name.

¹⁵When the turn came for Esther (the girl Mordecai had adopted, the daughter of his uncle Abihail) to go to the king, she asked for nothing other than what Hegai, the king's eunuch who was in charge of the harem, suggested. And Esther won the favor of every-one who saw her. ¹⁶She was taken to King Xerxes in the royal residence in the tenth month, the month of Tebeth, in the seventh year of his reign.

¹⁷Now the king was attracted to Esther more than to any of the other women, and she won his favor and approval more than any of the other virgins. So he set a royal crown on her head and made her queen instead of Vashti. ¹⁸And the king gave a great banquet, Esther's banquet, for all his nobles and officials. He proclaimed a holiday throughout the provinces and distributed gifts with royal liberality.

Mordecai Uncovers a Conspiracy

¹⁹When the virgins were assembled a second time, Mordecai was sitting at the king's gate. ²⁰But Esther had kept secret her family background and nationality just as Mordecai

a6 Hebrew *Jeconiah,* a variant of *Jehoiachin*

had told her to do, for she continued to follow Mordecai's instructions as she had done when he was bringing her up.

²¹During the time Mordecai was sitting at the king's gate, Bigthana[a] and Teresh, two of the king's officers who guarded the doorway, became angry and conspired to assassinate King Xerxes. ²²But Mordecai found out about the plot and told Queen Esther, who in turn reported it to the king, giving credit to Mordecai. ²³And when the report was investigated and found to be true, the two officials were hanged on a gallows.[b] All this was recorded in the book of the annals in the presence of the king.

Haman's Plot to Destroy the Jews

3 After these events, King Xerxes honored Haman son of Hammedatha, the Agagite, elevating him and giving him a seat of honor higher than that of all the other nobles. ²All the royal officials at the king's gate knelt down and paid honor to Haman, for the king had commanded this concerning him. But Mordecai would not kneel down or pay him honor.

³Then the royal officials at the king's gate asked Mordecai, "Why do you disobey the king's command?" ⁴Day after day they spoke to him but he refused to comply. Therefore they told Haman about it to see whether Mordecai's behavior would be tolerated, for he had told them he was a Jew.

⁵When Haman saw that Mordecai would not kneel down or pay him honor, he was enraged. ⁶Yet having learned who Mordecai's people were, he scorned the idea of killing only Mordecai. Instead Haman looked for a way to destroy all Mordecai's people, the Jews, throughout the whole kingdom of Xerxes.

⁷In the twelfth year of King Xerxes, in the first month, the month of Nisan, they cast the *pur* (that is, the lot) in the presence of Haman to select a day and month. And the lot fell on[c] the twelfth month, the month of Adar.

⁸Then Haman said to King Xerxes, "There is a certain people dispersed and scattered among the peoples in all the provinces of your kingdom whose customs are different from those of all other people and who do not obey the king's laws; it is not in the king's best interest to tolerate them. ⁹If it pleases the king, let a decree be issued to destroy them, and I will put ten thousand talents[d] of silver into the royal treasury for the men who carry out this business."

¹⁰So the king took his signet ring from his finger and gave it to Haman son of Hammedatha, the Agagite, the enemy of the Jews. ¹¹"Keep the money," the king said to Haman, "and do with the people as you please."

¹²Then on the thirteenth day of the first month the royal secretaries were summoned. They wrote out in the script of each province and in the language of each people all Haman's orders to the king's satraps, the governors of the various provinces and the nobles of the various peoples. These were written in the name of King Xerxes himself and sealed with his own ring. ¹³Dispatches were sent by couriers to all the king's provinces with the order to destroy, kill and annihilate all the Jews—young and old, women and little children—on a single day, the thirteenth day of the twelfth month, the month of Adar, and to plunder their goods. ¹⁴A copy of the text of the edict was to be issued as law in every province and made known to the people of every nationality so they would be ready for that day.

¹⁵Spurred on by the king's command, the couriers went out, and the edict was issued in the citadel of Susa. The king and Haman sat down to drink, but the city of Susa was bewildered.

---

a21 Hebrew *Bigthan*, a variant of *Bigthana*   *b23* Or *were hung* (or *impaled*) *on poles;* similarly elsewhere in Esther
c7 Septuagint; Hebrew does not have *And the lot fell on.*   *d9* That is, about 375 tons (about 345 metric tons)

Mordecai Persuades Esther to Help

4 When Mordecai learned of all that had been done, he tore his clothes, put on sackcloth and ashes, and went out into the city, wailing loudly and bitterly. ²But he went only as far as the king's gate, because no one clothed in sackcloth was allowed to enter it. ³In every province to which the edict and order of the king came, there was great mourning among the Jews, with fasting, weeping and wailing. Many lay in sackcloth and ashes.

⁴When Esther's maids and eunuchs came and told her about Mordecai, she was in great distress. She sent clothes for him to put on instead of his sackcloth, but he would not accept them. ⁵Then Esther summoned Hathach, one of the king's eunuchs assigned to attend her, and ordered him to find out what was troubling Mordecai and why.

⁶So Hathach went out to Mordecai in the open square of the city in front of the king's gate. ⁷Mordecai told him everything that had happened to him, including the exact amount of money Haman had promised to pay into the royal treasury for the destruction of the Jews. ⁸He also gave him a copy of the text of the edict for their annihilation, which had been published in Susa, to show to Esther and explain it to her, and he told him to urge her to go into the king's presence to beg for mercy and plead with him for her people.

⁹Hathach went back and reported to Esther what Mordecai had said. ¹⁰Then she instructed him to say to Mordecai, ¹¹"All the king's officials and the people of the royal provinces know that for any man or woman who approaches the king in the inner court without being summoned the king has but one law: that he be put to death. The only exception to this is for the king to extend the gold scepter to him and spare his life. But thirty days have passed since I was called to go to the king."

¹²When Esther's words were reported to Mordecai, ¹³he sent back this answer: "Do not think that because you are in the king's house you alone of all the Jews will escape. ¹⁴For if you remain silent at this time, relief and deliverance for the Jews will arise from another place, but you and your father's family will perish. And who knows but that you have come to royal position for such a time as this?"

¹⁵Then Esther sent this reply to Mordecai: ¹⁶"Go, gather together all the Jews who are in Susa, and fast for me. Do not eat or drink for three days, night or day. I and my maids will fast as you do. When this is done, I will go to the king, even though it is against the law. And if I perish, I perish."

¹⁷So Mordecai went away and carried out all of Esther's instructions.

▣ ▦▦▦▦ ADDRESSING QUESTIONS ▦▦▦▦ ⬔

4:14
God **Q**

Esther is the only book in the Bible that doesn't contain the word "God." That's an ironic omission, because the book is full of circumstances and events that point to God's sovereign work behind the scenes at this pivotal time in Israel's history.

God is always busy in the lives of his followers, but his actions aren't always readily apparent. Sometimes people need the perspective of time before they can begin to see evidence of his hand in the tapestry of their lives.

In this story, Esther was able to see God at work in her life even as events unfolded. She probably understood that she did not receive her influential position by accident. The God who watches over his people was using her as his agent in the midst of the current crisis.

If you're a seeker, you need to know that God has been at work in your life, silently moving behind the scenes to make it clear that he wants a relationship with you. And when you allow him access, he will do amazing things through you. As with Esther, your life will sometimes lead you to important crossroads. When that happens, God will be waiting, ready to give you the courage to do what is needed at that time.

Esther's Request to the King

5 On the third day Esther put on her royal robes and stood in the inner court of the palace, in front of the king's hall. The king was sitting on his royal throne in the hall, facing the entrance. ²When he saw Queen Esther standing in the court, he was pleased with her and held out to her the gold scepter that was in his hand. So Esther approached and touched the tip of the scepter.

³Then the king asked, "What is it, Queen Esther? What is your request? Even up to half the kingdom, it will be given you."

⁴"If it pleases the king," replied Esther, "let the king, together with Haman, come today to a banquet I have prepared for him."

⁵"Bring Haman at once," the king said, "so that we may do what Esther asks."

So the king and Haman went to the banquet Esther had prepared. ⁶As they were drinking wine, the king again asked Esther, "Now what is your petition? It will be given you. And what is your request? Even up to half the kingdom, it will be granted."

⁷Esther replied, "My petition and my request is this: ⁸If the king regards me with favor and if it pleases the king to grant my petition and fulfill my request, let the king and Haman come tomorrow to the banquet I will prepare for them. Then I will answer the king's question."

Haman's Rage Against Mordecai

⁹Haman went out that day happy and in high spirits. But when he saw Mordecai at the king's gate and observed that he neither rose nor showed fear in his presence, he was filled with rage against Mordecai. ¹⁰Nevertheless, Haman restrained himself and went home.

Calling together his friends and Zeresh, his wife, ¹¹Haman boasted to them about his vast wealth, his many sons, and all the ways the king had honored him and how he had elevated him above the other nobles and officials. ¹²"And that's not all," Haman added. "I'm the only person Queen Esther invited to accompany the king to the banquet she gave. And she has invited me along with the king tomorrow. ¹³But all this gives me no satisfaction as long as I see that Jew Mordecai sitting at the king's gate."

¹⁴His wife Zeresh and all his friends said to him, "Have a gallows built, seventy-five feet*a* high, and ask the king in the morning to have Mordecai hanged on it. Then go with the king to the dinner and be happy." This suggestion delighted Haman, and he had the gallows built.

Mordecai Honored

6 That night the king could not sleep; so he ordered the book of the chronicles, the record of his reign, to be brought in and read to him. ²It was found recorded there that Mordecai had exposed Bigthana and Teresh, two of the king's officers who guarded the doorway, who had conspired to assassinate King Xerxes.

³"What honor and recognition has Mordecai received for this?" the king asked.

"Nothing has been done for him," his attendants answered.

⁴The king said, "Who is in the court?" Now Haman had just entered the outer court of the palace to speak to the king about hanging Mordecai on the gallows he had erected for him.

⁵His attendants answered, "Haman is standing in the court."

"Bring him in," the king ordered.

⁶When Haman entered, the king asked him, "What should be done for the man the king delights to honor?"

Now Haman thought to himself, "Who is there that the king would rather honor than me?" ⁷So he answered the king, "For the man the king delights to honor, ⁸have them

a 14 Hebrew fifty cubits (about 23 meters)

bring a royal robe the king has worn and a horse the king has ridden, one with a royal crest placed on its head. ⁹Then let the robe and horse be entrusted to one of the king's most noble princes. Let them robe the man the king delights to honor, and lead him on the horse through the city streets, proclaiming before him, 'This is what is done for the man the king delights to honor!' "

¹⁰"Go at once," the king commanded Haman. "Get the robe and the horse and do just as you have suggested for Mordecai the Jew, who sits at the king's gate. Do not neglect anything you have recommended."

¹¹So Haman got the robe and the horse. He robed Mordecai, and led him on horseback through the city streets, proclaiming before him, "This is what is done for the man the king delights to honor!"

¹²Afterward Mordecai returned to the king's gate. But Haman rushed home, with his head covered in grief, ¹³and told Zeresh his wife and all his friends everything that had happened to him.

His advisers and his wife Zeresh said to him, "Since Mordecai, before whom your downfall has started, is of Jewish origin, you cannot stand against him—you will surely come to ruin!" ¹⁴While they were still talking with him, the king's eunuchs arrived and hurried Haman away to the banquet Esther had prepared.

Haman Hanged

7 So the king and Haman went to dine with Queen Esther, ²and as they were drinking wine on that second day, the king again asked, "Queen Esther, what is your petition? It will be given you. What is your request? Even up to half the kingdom, it will be granted."

³Then Queen Esther answered, "If I have found favor with you, O king, and if it pleases your majesty, grant me my life—this is my petition. And spare my people—this is my request. ⁴For I and my people have been sold for destruction and slaughter and annihilation. If we had merely been sold as male and female slaves, I would have kept quiet, because no such distress would justify disturbing the king.ᵃ"

⁵King Xerxes asked Queen Esther, "Who is he? Where is the man who has dared to do such a thing?"

⁶Esther said, "The adversary and enemy is this vile Haman."

Then Haman was terrified before the king and queen. ⁷The king got up in a rage, left his wine and went out into the palace garden. But Haman, realizing that the king had already decided his fate, stayed behind to beg Queen Esther for his life.

⁸Just as the king returned from the palace garden to the banquet hall, Haman was falling on the couch where Esther was reclining.

▣ ::::::::: KNOWING YOURSELF ::::::::: ▣

7:3–10
Character

This story gives us two illustrations of character—one positive and one negative.

Under God's inspiration, Queen Esther dug deep to find the courage to accuse Haman, the king's right-hand man, of the evil plot to wipe out the Jews. Until this time, Haman's plan to exterminate the Persian Jews had proceeded without resistance. Esther had risked her life to request the king's audience initially (see chapter 4, verse 16 [page 593]), and here again risked rejection and death if the king decided to favor Haman over her.

Haman's impulsive reaction to the Queen's words showed his true character. Realizing his fate, he begged Queen Esther to save his life, falling on her just as the king returned from the garden. In Haman's case, one bad event led to another until he was finally hung on the gallows he had hatefully prepared for his enemy, Mordecai.

It's easy to see why this story holds a special place in the hearts of Jews around the world. Esther's courage, combined with God's divine plan, saved the Jewish population at a crucial juncture in their history. The events in this story make this one of the Bible's most dramatic and exciting accounts of God's work in our world.

ᵃ4 Or quiet, but the compensation our adversary offers cannot be compared with the loss the king would suffer

The king exclaimed, "Will he even molest the queen while she is with me in the house?"

As soon as the word left the king's mouth, they covered Haman's face. [9]Then Harbona, one of the eunuchs attending the king, said, "A gallows seventy-five feet[a] high stands by Haman's house. He had it made for Mordecai, who spoke up to help the king."

The king said, "Hang him on it!" [10]So they hanged Haman on the gallows he had prepared for Mordecai. Then the king's fury subsided.

The King's Edict in Behalf of the Jews

8 That same day King Xerxes gave Queen Esther the estate of Haman, the enemy of the Jews. And Mordecai came into the presence of the king, for Esther had told how he was related to her. [2]The king took off his signet ring, which he had reclaimed from Haman, and presented it to Mordecai. And Esther appointed him over Haman's estate.

[3]Esther again pleaded with the king, falling at his feet and weeping. She begged him to put an end to the evil plan of Haman the Agagite, which he had devised against the Jews. [4]Then the king extended the gold scepter to Esther and she arose and stood before him.

[5]"If it pleases the king," she said, "and if he regards me with favor and thinks it the right thing to do, and if he is pleased with me, let an order be written overruling the dispatches that Haman son of Hammedatha, the Agagite, devised and wrote to destroy the Jews in all the king's provinces. [6]For how can I bear to see disaster fall on my people? How can I bear to see the destruction of my family?"

[7]King Xerxes replied to Queen Esther and to Mordecai the Jew, "Because Haman attacked the Jews, I have given his estate to Esther, and they have hanged him on the gallows. [8]Now write another decree in the king's name in behalf of the Jews as seems best to you, and seal it with the king's signet ring—for no document written in the king's name and sealed with his ring can be revoked."

[9]At once the royal secretaries were summoned—on the twenty-third day of the third month, the month of Sivan. They wrote out all Mordecai's orders to the Jews, and to the satraps, governors and nobles of the 127 provinces stretching from India to Cush.[b] These orders were written in the script of each province and the language of each people and also to the Jews in their own script and language. [10]Mordecai wrote in the name of King Xerxes, sealed the dispatches with the king's signet ring, and sent them by mounted couriers, who rode fast horses especially bred for the king.

[11]The king's edict granted the Jews in every city the right to assemble and protect themselves; to destroy, kill and annihilate any armed force of any nationality or province that might attack them and their women and children; and to plunder the property of their enemies. [12]The day appointed for the Jews to do this in all the provinces of King Xerxes was the thirteenth day of the twelfth month, the month of Adar. [13]A copy of the text of the edict was to be issued as law in every province and made known to the people of every nationality so that the Jews would be ready on that day to avenge themselves on their enemies.

[14]The couriers, riding the royal horses, raced out, spurred on by the king's command. And the edict was also issued in the citadel of Susa.

[15]Mordecai left the king's presence wearing royal garments of blue and white, a large crown of gold and a purple robe of fine linen. And the city of Susa held a joyous celebration. [16]For the Jews it was a time of happiness and joy, gladness and honor. [17]In every province and in every city, wherever the edict of the king went, there was joy and gladness among the Jews, with feasting and celebrating. And many people of other nationalities became Jews because fear of the Jews had seized them.

---

[a]9 Hebrew *fifty cubits* (about 23 meters)   [b]9 That is, the upper Nile region

Triumph of the Jews

9 On the thirteenth day of the twelfth month, the month of Adar, the edict commanded by the king was to be carried out. On this day the enemies of the Jews had hoped to overpower them, but now the tables were turned and the Jews got the upper hand over those who hated them. ²The Jews assembled in their cities in all the provinces of King Xerxes to attack those seeking their destruction. No one could stand against them, because the people of all the other nationalities were afraid of them. ³And all the nobles of the provinces, the satraps, the governors and the king's administrators helped the Jews, because fear of Mordecai had seized them. ⁴Mordecai was prominent in the palace; his reputation spread throughout the provinces, and he became more and more powerful.

⁵The Jews struck down all their enemies with the sword, killing and destroying them, and they did what they pleased to those who hated them. ⁶In the citadel of Susa, the Jews killed and destroyed five hundred men. ⁷They also killed Parshandatha, Dalphon, Aspatha, ⁸Poratha, Adalia, Aridatha, ⁹Parmashta, Arisai, Aridai and Vaizatha, ¹⁰the ten sons of Haman son of Hammedatha, the enemy of the Jews. But they did not lay their hands on the plunder.

¹¹The number of those slain in the citadel of Susa was reported to the king that same day. ¹²The king said to Queen Esther, "The Jews have killed and destroyed five hundred men and the ten sons of Haman in the citadel of Susa. What have they done in the rest of the king's provinces? Now what is your petition? It will be given you. What is your request? It will also be granted."

¹³"If it pleases the king," Esther answered, "give the Jews in Susa permission to carry out this day's edict tomorrow also, and let Haman's ten sons be hanged on gallows."

¹⁴So the king commanded that this be done. An edict was issued in Susa, and they hanged the ten sons of Haman. ¹⁵The Jews in Susa came together on the fourteenth day of the month of Adar, and they put to death in Susa three hundred men, but they did not lay their hands on the plunder.

¹⁶Meanwhile, the remainder of the Jews who were in the king's provinces also assembled to protect themselves and get relief from their enemies. They killed seventy-five thousand of them but did not lay their hands on the plunder. ¹⁷This happened on the thirteenth day of the month of Adar, and on the fourteenth they rested and made it a day of feasting and joy.

Purim Celebrated

¹⁸The Jews in Susa, however, had assembled on the thirteenth and fourteenth, and then on the fifteenth they rested and made it a day of feasting and joy.

¹⁹That is why rural Jews—those living in villages—observe the fourteenth of the month of Adar as a day of joy and feasting, a day for giving presents to each other.

²⁰Mordecai recorded these events, and he sent letters to all the Jews throughout the provinces of King Xerxes, near and far, ²¹to have them celebrate annually the fourteenth and fifteenth days of the month of Adar ²²as the time when the Jews got relief from their enemies, and as the month when their sorrow was turned into joy and their mourning into a day of celebration. He wrote them to observe the days as days of feasting and joy and giving presents of food to one another and gifts to the poor.

²³So the Jews agreed to continue the celebration they had begun, doing what Mordecai had written to them. ²⁴For Haman son of Hammedatha, the Agagite, the enemy of all the Jews, had plotted against the Jews to destroy them and had cast the *pur* (that is, the lot) for their ruin and destruction. ²⁵But when the plot came to the king's attention,ᵃ he issued written orders that the evil scheme Haman had devised against the Jews should come back onto his own head, and that he and his sons should be hanged on the

ᵃ25 Or *when Esther came before the king*

gallows. 26(Therefore these days were called Purim, from the word *pur*.) Because of everything written in this letter and because of what they had seen and what had happened to them, 27the Jews took it upon themselves to establish the custom that they and their descendants and all who join them should without fail observe these two days every year, in the way prescribed and at the time appointed. 28These days should be remembered and observed in every generation by every family, and in every province and in every city. And these days of Purim should never cease to be celebrated by the Jews, nor should the memory of them die out among their descendants.

29So Queen Esther, daughter of Abihail, along with Mordecai the Jew, wrote with full authority to confirm this second letter concerning Purim. 30And Mordecai sent letters to all the Jews in the 127 provinces of the kingdom of Xerxes—words of goodwill and assurance— 31to establish these days of Purim at their designated times, as Mordecai the Jew and Queen Esther had decreed for them, and as they had established for themselves and their descendants in regard to their times of fasting and lamentation. 32Esther's decree confirmed these regulations about Purim, and it was written down in the records.

The Greatness of Mordecai

10 King Xerxes imposed tribute throughout the empire, to its distant shores. 2And all his acts of power and might, together with a full account of the greatness of Mordecai to which the king had raised him, are they not written in the book of the annals of the kings of Media and Persia? 3Mordecai the Jew was second in rank to King Xerxes, preeminent among the Jews, and held in high esteem by his many fellow Jews, because he worked for the good of his people and spoke up for the welfare of all the Jews.

I spent my early years living on the road with my mother and stepfather, who were carnival workers. At one state fair where my parents were working some women rented a booth in the convention building, decorated it to resemble a miniature living room, and told Bible stories. That's where I first heard about Jesus. As I remember, the booth was very cozy and inviting. I became such a permanent fixture there that I finally began telling Bible stories about Jesus and heaven to other children.

When I reached first grade I was forced to live with my stepfather and his girlfriend. Since he was a long-haul truck driver, our family spent the next 12 years or so roaming from town to town and job to job. I attended 14 schools prior to college. But in each town I always made arrangements for the family to go to church. And there was always a neighbor, a friend's parent, or someone from school who was happy to point us in the right direction.

The churches that I found most exciting were those where the preacher asked the people to come to the front and be saved. Sunday after Sunday I went down to the front of the church, got on my knees, and prayed for Jesus to be my personal Savior. "Save me Jesus! Save me Jesus!" I pleaded with all my heart, praying that the torment of my daily life would end, praying that I would wake up one day to a sane world.

My prayers were never answered the way I thought they would be, however, and as teenager I became deeply confused. The emotional, physical and sexual abuse in my life became a burden that was too heavy for me to carry. In each town my parents seemed to hate me more and more as I grew older, and I fell into deep despair. One day when I was about 17, after a senseless beating from my stepmother, I shredded my Bible and ran to my closet. I remember sitting there in the dark for hours.

I stopped going to church, and I stopped pleading with God and Jesus. Clearly they weren't going to help me. I began to follow in my stepparents' footsteps, using drugs and alcohol and engaging in meaningless sexual relationships. I found I wasn't very good at it, but I soon learned to pretend that I was a bad girl. Yet even though I talked tough, on the inside I was a jumbled mess of insecurities and fears.

My greatest fear was loss of self-control, so I eventually managed to "get on top of it"—to stay sober and straight and not pregnant. To me, drugs and children signified the ultimate loss of control. By taking control of myself and my life, I was able to go on to college and get a good job. I met a man who loved me, and we were married.

I had always thought that I'd be able to walk away from my past, that I could easily separate myself from my parents' influence. But I soon found out that it wasn't so easy. I spent years with the support of my husband and his family changing my life and reversing these behaviors. During that time I worked hard to develop my spirituality, which centered around New-Age philosophies. I refused to consider God and Jesus because I was deeply angry and disappointed with them. In my mind, they had abandoned me when I needed them most. Part of me hated myself for trusting God; the other part hated God for leaving me. Still, I always had a sense that I was unfulfilled. No program or book or person or thing could fill me up. Nothing made me feel whole.

About two years ago, God sent me an incredible gift. He put me in a college class with an unusually spiritually sensitive Christian. Her mind and heart and vision of God were big enough to discuss my ideas of spirituality, and her Biblical knowledge was great enough to help me see that I needed to personally walk through the narrow gates to Jesus. At the end of 1993 I kneeled with her and asked Jesus again to be my personal Savior. I confessed my sins. And I acknowledged the existence and the power of God.

That decision touched off what has been for me an intense journey of spiritual renewal, awakening and acceptance. God has been direct with me, allowing me the freedom to express my anger and fury and rage. He has allowed me my pain and resentment, and has given me a new understanding of my life. I see the value of my past; I also see God's continual presence with me through all those years. Words cannot express the wonderful things that have happened in my heart and mind and life as God has helped me see that, rather than magically taking away life's troubles, he helps those who seek him to live through those troubles in the strength of his Spirit.

JOB

Introduction

THE BOTTOM LINE

This book attempts to answer one of life's hardest questions: "How could a loving God allow people to suffer?" Seekers as well as believers have asked this question for literally thousands of years. For some people, the presence of suffering proves there cannot be an all-loving, yet all-powerful God. The hero of this story is a good man who suffers extreme personal loss and physical agony. His friends develop various explanations for his pain. In the final chapters, God himself makes an appearance, and Job and his friends hear firsthand the answers to their speculations. If you've ever suffered or heard others try to explain suffering, this is a book you can't afford to miss.

CENTRAL IDEAS

- Sometimes good people suffer.
- Not all suffering can be explained as the result of some wrong we've done.
- Life in this messed-up world is not fair; but "life" is not God.
- God speaks to us in the middle of our pain.

OUTLINE

1. Job is tested (chs. 1–2)
2. Job's friends try to explain his sufferings (chs. 3–27)
3. Interlude on wisdom (ch. 28)
4. Monologues: Job, Elihu, and God (29:1–42:6)
5. God's verdict; Job's restoration (42:7-17)

TITLE

Although this book might first appear to be on the topic of employment, it is actually the name of the main character of this book.

AUTHOR AND READERS

Many scholars believe that this story was passed down through oral tradition until it was written down by an Israelite and added to the Hebrew canon. It is probably the oldest literature in the Bible, and one of the most universally appealing stories.

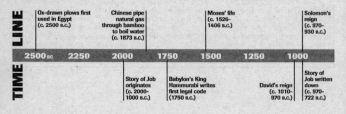

TIME LINE							
Ox-drawn plows first used in Egypt (c. 2500 B.C.)		Chinese pipe natural gas through bamboo to boil water (c. 1873 B.C.)		Moses' life (c. 1526–1406 B.C.)			Solomon's reign (c. 970–930 B.C.)
2500 BC	**2250**	**2000**	**1750**	**1500**	**1250**	**1000**	
		Story of Job originates (c. 2000–1000 B.C.)	Babylon's King Hammurabi writes first legal code (1750 B.C.)		David's reign (c. 1010–970 B.C.)		Story of Job written down (c. 970–722 B.C.)

Mr. Perkins?" The woman's voice on the phone sounded formal and stiff. "I'm Jill Smith. I work for security at Washington Square Shopping Mall."

The moment after she identified herself, I wondered if someone I knew had been mugged—or caught shoplifting.

"Your wife's okay," the caller said, interrupting my thoughts, "but she has been in an automobile accident. She needs you to pick her up." She described how our car had been smashed like an accordion. But Cindy, my wife, was unharmed.

After I hung up the phone, I took a moment to catch my breath. Suddenly I realized how empty my life would be without Cindy. Our home would be empty without her smile. Our sons would be devastated without her hugs. The absence of her laughter would be deafening.

As I pulled into the parking lot of the shopping center, Cindy was standing by our once-beautiful car. Tears streamed down her face. I hugged her, and we wept. In that moment I had a new appreciation for my wife and a compelling desire to say, "I love you."

Suddenly I realized how empty my life would be without Cindy.

Sometimes we have to lose—or almost lose—someone before we realize how much we care for her or him. During a serious illness, or after a life-threatening accident, or following the death of a loved one, we find out how connected we are to those around us. And we learn how fragile life is and how every good thing on this earth is temporary.

"Why this?" "Why now?" "Why me?" Those questions scream for answers when tragedy strikes. There are no easy answers to such plaintive cries. But the Bible does give us help—and hope. A man named Job suffered mind-numbing losses and personal hardships. From his despair we can learn valuable lessons about suffering and about how to view God when our world falls apart. Turn to Job chapter 1, verses 6–22 (page 603), for details about Job's hardships and for a glimpse at one of the forces behind human pain.

JOB

Prologue

1 In the land of Uz there lived a man whose name was Job. This man was blameless and upright; he feared God and shunned evil. ²He had seven sons and three daughters, ³and he owned seven thousand sheep, three thousand camels, five hundred yoke of oxen and five hundred donkeys, and had a large number of servants. He was the greatest man among all the people of the East.

⁴His sons used to take turns holding feasts in their homes, and they would invite their three sisters to eat and drink with them. ⁵When a period of feasting had run its course, Job would send and have them purified. Early in the morning he would sacrifice a burnt offering for each of them, thinking, "Perhaps my children have sinned and cursed God in their hearts." This was Job's regular custom.

⬚ ▦▦▦▦▦▦▦▦▦▦▦ **ADDRESSING QUESTIONS** ▦▦▦▦▦▦▦▦▦▦▦ ⬚

1:1–22
Human Experience

Q

This is the story of Job (pronounced "jobe," not "jahb"). It is probably the oldest literature in the Bible. How fitting, then, that it deals with humankind's oldest and most troubling question: *Why does God allow people to suffer?*

Job had everything a person would want—wealth, power, a good reputation, servants, land, livestock, a loving family and good health (verses 1–5). On top of that, he was devout—worshiping and revering God was very important to him. His name was synonymous with integrity and spirituality.

Suddenly, without warning, Job lost everything. Gone were his livestock, crops, land, servants and, to his great sorrow, his ten children. A short time later a horrible disease covered him with boils. As he sat among the ashes of his home and his life, his wife urged him to "curse God and die!" (chapter 2, verse 9). Later, his friends tried to explain his suffering by accusing him of sinning against God. What else could explain such hardship?

This is the story of how a God-follower struggles with tragedy, and how those watching a broken person try to make sense of what's happening. If there were no God, this story would have no meaning, nor would it matter. If the universe was nothing more than the random movement of atoms and molecules, there would be no logical reason to be troubled by suffering. But precisely because all the players in this story believe in a fair and compassionate God, they attempt to make the pieces fit.

The opening chapters of the story provide two important spiritual principles that help us understand Job's situation—and by extension, ours as well. First, *God allows evil but is not the author of it.* Satan, the devil, inflicts pain—not God. That's an important distinction, because it upholds what the Bible consistently says about God: He is utterly good and righteous. Second, *Satan is limited and restrained by God.* Were there to be a cosmic "face off," God would be the absolute and immediate victor. He hasn't done so yet—there's the quandary —but these introductory chapters (as well as the rest of the Bible) leave no doubt as to who's in charge.

As the story of Job unfolds, keep these points before you. And as you face your own difficulties in life, hang on to these principles. There are more lessons ahead in this book, but these truths have to be the starting point for bringing into focus the answer to the problem of suffering.

Job's First Test

⁶One day the angels[a] came to present themselves before the Lord, and Satan[b] also came with them. ⁷The Lord said to Satan, "Where have you come from?"

Satan answered the Lord, "From roaming through the earth and going back and forth in it."

⁸Then the Lord said to Satan, "Have you considered my servant Job? There is no one on earth like him; he is blameless and upright, a man who fears God and shuns evil."

⁹"Does Job fear God for nothing?" Satan replied. ¹⁰"Have you not put a hedge around him and his household and everything he has? You have blessed the work of his hands, so that his flocks and herds are spread throughout the land. ¹¹But stretch out your hand and strike everything he has, and he will surely curse you to your face."

¹²The Lord said to Satan, "Very well, then, everything he has is in your hands, but on the man himself do not lay a finger."

Then Satan went out from the presence of the Lord.

¹³One day when Job's sons and daughters were feasting and drinking wine at the oldest brother's house, ¹⁴a messenger came to Job and said, "The oxen were plowing and the donkeys were grazing nearby, ¹⁵and the Sabeans attacked and carried them off. They put the servants to the sword, and I am the only one who has escaped to tell you!"

¹⁶While he was still speaking, another messenger came and said, "The fire of God fell from the sky and burned up the sheep and the servants, and I am the only one who has escaped to tell you!"

¹⁷While he was still speaking, another messenger came and said, "The Chaldeans formed three raiding parties and swept down on your camels and carried them off. They put the servants to the sword, and I am the only one who has escaped to tell you!"

¹⁸While he was still speaking, yet another messenger came and said, "Your sons and daughters were feasting and drinking wine at the oldest brother's house, ¹⁹when suddenly a mighty wind swept in from the desert and struck the four corners of the house. It collapsed on them and they are dead, and I am the only one who has escaped to tell you!"

²⁰At this, Job got up and tore his robe and shaved his head. Then he fell to the ground in worship ²¹and said:

> "Naked I came from my mother's womb,
>   and naked I will depart.[c]
> The Lord gave and the Lord has taken away;
>   may the name of the Lord be praised."

²²In all this, Job did not sin by charging God with wrongdoing.

Job's Second Test

2 On another day the angels[a] came to present themselves before the Lord, and Satan also came with them to present himself before him. ²And the Lord said to Satan, "Where have you come from?"

Satan answered the Lord, "From roaming through the earth and going back and forth in it."

³Then the Lord said to Satan, "Have you considered my servant Job? There is no one on earth like him; he is blameless and upright, a man who fears God and shuns evil. And he

---

a 6,1 Hebrew the sons of God   *b 6 Satan means accuser.*   *c 21 Or will return there*

still maintains his integrity, though you incited me against him to ruin him without any reason."

⁴"Skin for skin!" Satan replied. "A man will give all he has for his own life. ⁵But stretch out your hand and strike his flesh and bones, and he will surely curse you to your face."

⁶The LORD said to Satan, "Very well, then, he is in your hands; but you must spare his life."

⁷So Satan went out from the presence of the LORD and afflicted Job with painful sores from the soles of his feet to the top of his head. ⁸Then Job took a piece of broken pottery and scraped himself with it as he sat among the ashes.

⁹His wife said to him, "Are you still holding on to your integrity? Curse God and die!"

¹⁰He replied, "You are talking like a foolish*a* woman. Shall we accept good from God, and not trouble?"

In all this, Job did not sin in what he said.

Job's Three Friends

¹¹When Job's three friends, Eliphaz the Temanite, Bildad the Shuhite and Zophar the Naamathite, heard about all the troubles that had come upon him, they set out from their homes and met together by agreement to go and sympathize with him and comfort him. ¹²When they saw him from a distance, they could hardly recognize him; they began to weep aloud, and they tore their robes and sprinkled dust on their heads. ¹³Then they sat on the ground with him for seven days and seven nights. No one said a word to him, because they saw how great his suffering was.

▣ ⠿⠿STRENGTHENING RELATIONSHIPS⠿⠿ ⇱

2:13
Social

What's the proper response to grief?

When Job's friends first visited him after hearing the news of his troubles, they were so overwhelmed that they just sat with him in silence. By the end of the book you'll realize that this was their finest hour! For when they started to talk, they changed from caring friends to amateur theologians—and became next to useless.

Have you ever approached a suffering friend and thought, *What can I say?* Don't feel that you have to say anything! Just be with that person. Come alongside, and if need be, sit in silence with that person for a long time. That's one of the best responses to suffering that you can give in the early stages of grief.

Job Speaks

3 After this, Job opened his mouth and cursed the day of his birth. ²He said:

³"May the day of my birth perish,
    and the night it was said, 'A boy
        is born!'
⁴That day—may it turn to darkness;
    may God above not care about
        it;
    may no light shine upon it.
⁵May darkness and deep shadow*b* claim
        it once more;
    may a cloud settle over it;
    may blackness overwhelm its light.
⁶That night—may thick darkness seize it;
    may it not be included among the days of the year
    nor be entered in any of the months.
⁷May that night be barren;
    may no shout of joy be heard in it.
⁸May those who curse days*c* curse that day,
    those who are ready to rouse Leviathan.

---

a 10 The Hebrew word rendered *foolish* denotes moral deficiency.   *b 5* Or *and the shadow of death*   *c 8* Or *the sea*

9May its morning stars become dark;
  may it wait for daylight in vain
  and not see the first rays of dawn,
10for it did not shut the doors of the womb on me
  to hide trouble from my eyes.
11"Why did I not perish at birth,
  and die as I came from the womb?
12Why were there knees to receive me
  and breasts that I might be nursed?
13For now I would be lying down
    in peace;
  I would be asleep and at
    rest
14with kings and counselors
    of the earth,
  who built for themselves places
    now lying in ruins,
15with rulers who had gold,
  who filled their houses with
    silver.
16Or why was I not hidden in
    the ground like
  a stillborn child,
  like an infant who never saw
    the light of day?
17There the wicked cease from
    turmoil,
  and there the weary are at
    rest.
18Captives also enjoy their ease;
  they no longer hear the slave
    driver's shout.
19The small and the great are
    there,
  and the slave is freed from
    his master.

20"Why is light given to those in
    misery,
  and life to the bitter of soul,
21to those who long for death that
    does not come,
  who search for it more than
    for hidden treasure,
22who are filled with gladness
  and rejoice when they reach the grave?
23Why is life given to a man
    whose way is hidden,
  whom God has hedged in?
24For sighing comes to me instead of food;
  my groans pour out like water.
25What I feared has come upon me;

🔲 ▓▓▓▓▓▓▓ DISCOVERING GOD ▓▓▓▓▓▓▓ ⬛

Chapters 3–37
The God Who Is There

The majority of the book of Job contains several rounds of speeches. Job talks, the friends respond; Job rebuts, the friends accuse. The thrust of the arguments center on what Job must have done to deserve God's punishment, and Job keeps trying to point out that he has done nothing. Job's friends are scandalized by such a thought—surely God wouldn't have allowed this if it weren't for some sin in Job's life.

After many rounds the arguments are finally exhausted, and the speakers are all back where they started, each entrenched in his original position. At this point, God brings a dramatic resolution to the story (beginning with chapter 38 [page 643]).

As you read through this series of monologues, remember that God was listening too. While these individuals tried to force God's actions into a human rationale of fairness, God prepared his own statement that turned the discussion around.

As the author of what is truly "fair" in the universe, sometimes God's actions in our life don't seem to make sense. We can't always see beyond our immediate circumstances to get a vision for God's plan in our lives. But, as Elihu said, "In his justice and great righteousness, he does not oppress. Therefore, men revere him . . ." (chapter 37, verses 23–24 [page 643]).

what I dreaded has happened to me.
²⁶I have no peace, no quietness;
    I have no rest, but only turmoil."

Eliphaz

4   Then Eliphaz the Temanite replied:

²"If someone ventures a word with you, will you be impatient?
    But who can keep from speaking?
³Think how you have instructed many,
    how you have strengthened feeble hands.
⁴Your words have supported those who stumbled;
    you have strengthened faltering knees.
⁵But now trouble comes to you, and you are discouraged;
    it strikes you, and you are dismayed.
⁶Should not your piety be your confidence
    and your blameless ways your hope?

⁷"Consider now: Who, being innocent, has ever perished?
    Where were the upright ever destroyed?
⁸As I have observed, those who plow evil
    and those who sow trouble reap it.
⁹At the breath of God they are destroyed;
    at the blast of his anger they perish.
¹⁰The lions may roar and growl,
    yet the teeth of the great lions are broken.
¹¹The lion perishes for lack of prey,
    and the cubs of the lioness are scattered.

¹²"A word was secretly brought to me,
    my ears caught a whisper of it.
¹³Amid disquieting dreams in the night,
    when deep sleep falls on men,
¹⁴fear and trembling seized me
    and made all my bones shake.
¹⁵A spirit glided past my face,
    and the hair on my body stood on end.
¹⁶It stopped,
    but I could not tell what it was.
  A form stood before my eyes,
    and I heard a hushed voice:
¹⁷'Can a mortal be more righteous than God?
    Can a man be more pure than his Maker?
¹⁸If God places no trust in his servants,
    if he charges his angels with error,
¹⁹how much more those who live in houses of clay,
    whose foundations are in the dust,
    who are crushed more readily than a moth!
²⁰Between dawn and dusk they are broken to pieces;
    unnoticed, they perish forever.
²¹Are not the cords of their tent pulled up,
    so that they die without wisdom?' ^a

---

^a21 Some interpreters end the quotation after verse 17.

5 "Call if you will, but who will answer you?
To which of the holy ones will you turn?
²Resentment kills a fool,
and envy slays the simple.
³I myself have seen a fool taking root,
but suddenly his house was cursed.
⁴His children are far from safety,
crushed in court without a defender.
⁵The hungry consume his harvest,
taking it even from among thorns,
and the thirsty pant after his wealth.
⁶For hardship does not spring from the soil,
nor does trouble sprout from the ground.
⁷Yet man is born to trouble
as surely as sparks fly upward.

⁸"But if it were I, I would appeal to God;
I would lay my cause before him.
⁹He performs wonders that cannot be fathomed,
miracles that cannot be counted.
¹⁰He bestows rain on the earth;
he sends water upon the countryside.
¹¹The lowly he sets on high,
and those who mourn are lifted to safety.
¹²He thwarts the plans of the crafty,
so that their hands achieve no success.
¹³He catches the wise in their craftiness,
and the schemes of the wily are swept away.
¹⁴Darkness comes upon them in the daytime;
at noon they grope as in the night.
¹⁵He saves the needy from the sword in their mouth;
he saves them from the clutches of the powerful.
¹⁶So the poor have hope,
and injustice shuts its mouth.

¹⁷"Blessed is the man whom God corrects;
so do not despise the discipline of the Almighty.ᵃ
¹⁸For he wounds, but he also binds up;
he injures, but his hands also heal.
¹⁹From six calamities he will rescue you;
in seven no harm will befall you.
²⁰In famine he will ransom you from death,
and in battle from the stroke of the sword.
²¹You will be protected from the lash of the tongue,
and need not fear when destruction comes.
²²You will laugh at destruction and famine,
and need not fear the beasts of the earth.
²³For you will have a covenant with the stones of the field,
and the wild animals will be at peace with you.
²⁴You will know that your tent is secure;
you will take stock of your property and find nothing missing.
²⁵You will know that your children will be many,
and your descendants like the grass of the earth.

ᵃ 17 Hebrew *Shaddai*; here and throughout Job

²⁶You will come to the grave in full vigor,
    like sheaves gathered in season.

²⁷"We have examined this, and it is true.
    So hear it and apply it to yourself."

Job

6   Then Job replied:

²"If only my anguish could be weighed
    and all my misery be placed on the scales!
³It would surely outweigh the sand of the seas—
    no wonder my words have been impetuous.
⁴The arrows of the Almighty are in me,
    my spirit drinks in their poison;
    God's terrors are marshaled against me.
⁵Does a wild donkey bray when it has grass,
    or an ox bellow when it has fodder?
⁶Is tasteless food eaten without salt,
    or is there flavor in the white of an egg*ᵃ*?
⁷I refuse to touch it;
    such food makes me ill.

⁸"Oh, that I might have my request,
    that God would grant what I hope for,
⁹that God would be willing to crush me,
    to let loose his hand and cut me off!
¹⁰Then I would still have this consolation—
    my joy in unrelenting pain—
    that I had not denied the words of the Holy One.

¹¹"What strength do I have, that I should still hope?
    What prospects, that I should be patient?
¹²Do I have the strength of stone?
    Is my flesh bronze?
¹³Do I have any power to help myself,
    now that success has been driven from me?

¹⁴"A despairing man should have the devotion of his friends,
    even though he forsakes the fear of the Almighty.
¹⁵But my brothers are as undependable as intermittent streams,
    as the streams that overflow
¹⁶when darkened by thawing ice
    and swollen with melting snow,
¹⁷but that cease to flow in the dry season,
    and in the heat vanish from their channels.
¹⁸Caravans turn aside from their routes;
    they go up into the wasteland and perish.
¹⁹The caravans of Tema look for water,
    the traveling merchants of Sheba look in hope.
²⁰They are distressed, because they had been confident;
    they arrive there, only to be disappointed.
²¹Now you too have proved to be of no help;
    you see something dreadful and are afraid.

ᵃ 6 The meaning of the Hebrew for this phrase is uncertain.

²²Have I ever said, 'Give something on my behalf,
  pay a ransom for me from your wealth,
²³deliver me from the hand of the enemy,
  ransom me from the clutches of the ruthless'?

²⁴"Teach me, and I will be quiet;
  show me where I have been wrong.
²⁵How painful are honest words!
  But what do your arguments prove?
²⁶Do you mean to correct what I say,
  and treat the words of a despairing man as wind?
²⁷You would even cast lots for the fatherless
  and barter away your friend.

²⁸"But now be so kind as to look at me.
  Would I lie to your face?
²⁹Relent, do not be unjust;
  reconsider, for my integrity is at stake. ᵃ
³⁰Is there any wickedness on my lips?
  Can my mouth not discern malice?

7 "Does not man have hard service on earth?
  Are not his days like those of a hired man?
²Like a slave longing for the evening shadows,
  or a hired man waiting eagerly for his wages,
³so I have been allotted months of futility,
  and nights of misery have been assigned to me.
⁴When I lie down I think, 'How long before I get up?'
  The night drags on, and I toss till dawn.
⁵My body is clothed with worms and scabs,
  my skin is broken and festering.

⁶"My days are swifter than a weaver's shuttle,
  and they come to an end without hope.
⁷Remember, O God, that my life is but a breath;
  my eyes will never see happiness again.
⁸The eye that now sees me will see me no longer;
  you will look for me, but I will be no more.
⁹As a cloud vanishes and is gone,
  so he who goes down to the grave ᵇ does not return.
¹⁰He will never come to his house again;
  his place will know him no more.

¹¹"Therefore I will not keep silent;
  I will speak out in the anguish of my spirit,
  I will complain in the bitterness of my soul.
¹²Am I the sea, or the monster of the deep,
  that you put me under guard?
¹³When I think my bed will comfort me
  and my couch will ease my complaint,
¹⁴even then you frighten me with dreams
  and terrify me with visions,
¹⁵so that I prefer strangling and death,
  rather than this body of mine.

ᵃ29 Or my righteousness still stands   ᵇ9 Hebrew Sheol

¹⁶I despise my life; I would not live forever.
    Let me alone; my days have no meaning.

¹⁷"What is man that you make so much of him,
    that you give him so much attention,
¹⁸that you examine him every morning
    and test him every moment?
¹⁹Will you never look away from me,
    or let me alone even for an instant?
²⁰If I have sinned, what have I done to you,
    O watcher of men?
Why have you made me your target?
    Have I become a burden to you?^a
²¹Why do you not pardon my offenses
    and forgive my sins?
For I will soon lie down in the dust;
    you will search for me, but I will be no more."

Bildad

8 Then Bildad the Shuhite replied:

²"How long will you say such things?
    Your words are a blustering wind.
³Does God pervert justice?
    Does the Almighty pervert what is right?
⁴When your children sinned against him,
    he gave them over to the penalty of their sin.
⁵But if you will look to God
    and plead with the Almighty,
⁶if you are pure and upright,
    even now he will rouse himself on your behalf
    and restore you to your rightful place.
⁷Your beginnings will seem humble,
    so prosperous will your future be.

⁸"Ask the former generations
    and find out what their fathers learned,
⁹for we were born only yesterday and know nothing,
    and our days on earth are but a shadow.
¹⁰Will they not instruct you and tell you?
    Will they not bring forth words from their understanding?
¹¹Can papyrus grow tall where there is no marsh?
    Can reeds thrive without water?
¹²While still growing and uncut,
    they wither more quickly than grass.
¹³Such is the destiny of all who forget God;
    so perishes the hope of the godless.
¹⁴What he trusts in is fragile^b;
    what he relies on is a spider's web.
¹⁵He leans on his web, but it gives way;
    he clings to it, but it does not hold.
¹⁶He is like a well-watered plant in the sunshine,

---

^a20 A few manuscripts of the Masoretic Text, an ancient Hebrew scribal tradition and Septuagint; most manuscripts of the Masoretic Text *I have become a burden to myself.*   ^b14 The meaning of the Hebrew for this word is uncertain.

spreading its shoots over the garden;
¹⁷it entwines its roots around a pile of rocks
   and looks for a place among the stones.
¹⁸But when it is torn from its spot,
   that place disowns it and says, 'I never saw you.'
¹⁹Surely its life withers away,
   andᵃ from the soil other plants grow.

²⁰"Surely God does not reject a blameless man
   or strengthen the hands of evildoers.
²¹He will yet fill your mouth with laughter
   and your lips with shouts of joy.
²²Your enemies will be clothed in shame,
   and the tents of the wicked will be no more."

Job

9   Then Job replied:

²"Indeed, I know that this is true.
   But how can a mortal be righteous before God?
³Though one wished to dispute with him,
   he could not answer him one time out of a thousand.
⁴His wisdom is profound, his power is vast.
   Who has resisted him and come out unscathed?
⁵He moves mountains without their knowing it
   and overturns them in his anger.
⁶He shakes the earth from its place
   and makes its pillars tremble.
⁷He speaks to the sun and it does not shine;
   he seals off the light of the stars.
⁸He alone stretches out the heavens
   and treads on the waves of the sea.
⁹He is the Maker of the Bear and Orion,
   the Pleiades and the constellations of the south.
¹⁰He performs wonders that cannot be fathomed,
   miracles that cannot be counted.
¹¹When he passes me, I cannot see him;
   when he goes by, I cannot perceive him.
¹²If he snatches away, who can stop him?
   Who can say to him, 'What are you doing?'
¹³God does not restrain his anger;
   even the cohorts of Rahab cowered at his feet.

¹⁴"How then can I dispute with him?
   How can I find words to argue with him?
¹⁵Though I were innocent, I could not answer him;
   I could only plead with my Judge for mercy.
¹⁶Even if I summoned him and he responded,
   I do not believe he would give me a hearing.
¹⁷He would crush me with a storm
   and multiply my wounds for no reason.
¹⁸He would not let me regain my breath
   but would overwhelm me with misery.

ᵃ19 Or Surely all the joy it has / is that

¹⁹If it is a matter of strength, he is mighty!
  And if it is a matter of justice, who will summon him*ᵃ*?
²⁰Even if I were innocent, my mouth would condemn me;
  if I were blameless, it would pronounce me guilty.

²¹"Although I am blameless,
  I have no concern for myself;
  I despise my own life.
²²It is all the same; that is why I say,
  'He destroys both the blameless and the wicked.'
²³When a scourge brings sudden death,
  he mocks the despair of the innocent.
²⁴When a land falls into the hands of the wicked,
  he blindfolds its judges.
  If it is not he, then who is it?

²⁵"My days are swifter than a runner;
  they fly away without a glimpse of joy.
²⁶They skim past like boats of papyrus,
  like eagles swooping down on their prey.
²⁷If I say, 'I will forget my complaint,
  I will change my expression, and smile,'
²⁸I still dread all my sufferings,
  for I know you will not hold me innocent.
²⁹Since I am already found guilty,
  why should I struggle in vain?
³⁰Even if I washed myself with soapᵇ
  and my hands with washing soda,
³¹you would plunge me into a slime pit
  so that even my clothes would detest me.

³²"He is not a man like me that I might answer him,
  that we might confront each other in court.
³³If only there were someone to arbitrate between us,
  to lay his hand upon us both,
³⁴someone to remove God's rod from me,
  so that his terror would frighten me no more.
³⁵Then I would speak up without fear of him,
  but as it now stands with me, I cannot.

10 "I loathe my very life;
  therefore I will give free rein to my complaint
  and speak out in the bitterness of my soul.
²I will say to God: Do not condemn me,
  but tell me what charges you have against me.
³Does it please you to oppress me,
  to spurn the work of your hands,
  while you smile on the schemes of the wicked?
⁴Do you have eyes of flesh?
  Do you see as a mortal sees?
⁵Are your days like those of a mortal
  or your years like those of a man,
⁶that you must search out my faults
  and probe after my sin—

ᵃ 19 See Septuagint; Hebrew *me.*   *ᵇ 30* Or *snow*

7though you know that I am not guilty
　　and that no one can rescue me from your hand?

8"Your hands shaped me and made me.
　　Will you now turn and destroy me?
9Remember that you molded me like clay.
　　Will you now turn me to dust again?
10Did you not pour me out like milk
　　and curdle me like cheese,
11clothe me with skin and flesh
　　and knit me together with bones and sinews?
12You gave me life and showed me kindness,
　　and in your providence watched over my spirit.

13"But this is what you concealed in your heart,
　　and I know that this was in your mind:
14If I sinned, you would be watching me
　　and would not let my offense go unpunished.
15If I am guilty—woe to me!
　　Even if I am innocent, I cannot lift my head,
　for I am full of shame
　　and drowned in*a* my affliction.
16If I hold my head high, you stalk me like a lion
　　and again display your awesome power against me.
17You bring new witnesses against me
　　and increase your anger toward me;
　　your forces come against me wave upon wave.

18"Why then did you bring me out of the womb?
　　I wish I had died before any eye saw me.
19If only I had never come into being,
　　or had been carried straight from the womb to the grave!
20Are not my few days almost over?
　　Turn away from me so I can have a moment's joy
21before I go to the place of no return,
　　to the land of gloom and deep shadow,*b*
22to the land of deepest night,
　　of deep shadow and disorder,
　　where even the light is like darkness."

Zophar

11 Then Zophar the Naamathite replied:

2"Are all these words to go unanswered?
　　Is this talker to be vindicated?
3Will your idle talk reduce men to silence?
　　Will no one rebuke you when you mock?
4You say to God, 'My beliefs are flawless
　　and I am pure in your sight.'
5Oh, how I wish that God would speak,
　　that he would open his lips against you
6and disclose to you the secrets of wisdom,

a15 Or and aware of   b21 Or and the shadow of death; also in verse 22

for true wisdom has two sides.
Know this: God has even forgotten some of your sin.

⁷"Can you fathom the mysteries of God?
    Can you probe the limits of the Almighty?
⁸They are higher than the heavens—what can you do?
    They are deeper than the depths of the grave*ᵃ*—what can you
        know?
⁹Their measure is longer than the earth
    and wider than the sea.

¹⁰"If he comes along and confines you in prison
    and convenes a court, who can oppose him?
¹¹Surely he recognizes deceitful men;
    and when he sees evil, does he not take note?
¹²But a witless man can no more become wise
    than a wild donkey's colt can be born a man.*ᵇ*

¹³"Yet if you devote your heart to him
    and stretch out your hands to him,
¹⁴if you put away the sin that is in your hand
    and allow no evil to dwell in your tent,
¹⁵then you will lift up your face without shame;
    you will stand firm and without fear.
¹⁶You will surely forget your trouble,
    recalling it only as waters gone by.
¹⁷Life will be brighter than noonday,
    and darkness will become like morning.
¹⁸You will be secure, because there is hope;
    you will look about you and take your rest in safety.
¹⁹You will lie down, with no one to make you afraid,
    and many will court your favor.
²⁰But the eyes of the wicked will fail,
    and escape will elude them;
    their hope will become a dying gasp."

Job

12   Then Job replied:

²"Doubtless you are the people,
    and wisdom will die with you!
³But I have a mind as well as you;
    I am not inferior to you.
    Who does not know all these things?

⁴"I have become a laughingstock to my friends,
    though I called upon God and he answered—
    a mere laughingstock, though righteous and blameless!
⁵Men at ease have contempt for misfortune
    as the fate of those whose feet are slipping.
⁶The tents of marauders are undisturbed,
    and those who provoke God are secure—
    those who carry their god in their hands.*ᶜ*

ᵃ8 Hebrew *than Sheol*   *ᵇ12* Or *wild donkey can be born tame*   *ᶜ6* Or *secure / in what God's hand brings them*

⁷"But ask the animals, and they will teach you,
   or the birds of the air, and they will tell you;
⁸or speak to the earth, and it will teach you,
   or let the fish of the sea inform you.
⁹Which of all these does not know
   that the hand of the Lord has done this?
¹⁰In his hand is the life of every creature
   and the breath of all mankind.
¹¹Does not the ear test words
   as the tongue tastes food?
¹²Is not wisdom found among the aged?
   Does not long life bring understanding?

¹³"To God belong wisdom and power;
   counsel and understanding are his.
¹⁴What he tears down cannot be rebuilt;
   the man he imprisons cannot be released.
¹⁵If he holds back the waters, there is drought;
   if he lets them loose, they devastate the land.
¹⁶To him belong strength and victory;
   both deceived and deceiver are his.
¹⁷He leads counselors away stripped
   and makes fools of judges.
¹⁸He takes off the shackles put on by kings
   and ties a loincloth ᵃ around their waist.
¹⁹He leads priests away stripped
   and overthrows men long established.
²⁰He silences the lips of trusted advisers
   and takes away the discernment of elders.
²¹He pours contempt on nobles
   and disarms the mighty.
²²He reveals the deep things of darkness
   and brings deep shadows into the light.
²³He makes nations great, and destroys them;
   he enlarges nations, and disperses them.
²⁴He deprives the leaders of the earth of their reason;
   he sends them wandering through a trackless waste.
²⁵They grope in darkness with no light;
   he makes them stagger like drunkards.

13 "My eyes have seen all this,
   my ears have heard and understood it.
²What you know, I also know;
   I am not inferior to you.
³But I desire to speak to the Almighty
   and to argue my case with God.
⁴You, however, smear me with lies;
   you are worthless physicians, all of you!
⁵If only you would be altogether silent!
   For you, that would be wisdom.
⁶Hear now my argument;
   listen to the plea of my lips.
⁷Will you speak wickedly on God's behalf?

ᵃ 18 Or *shackles of kings / and ties a belt*

Will you speak deceitfully for him?
⁸Will you show him partiality?
Will you argue the case for God?
⁹Would it turn out well if he examined you?
Could you deceive him as you might deceive men?
¹⁰He would surely rebuke you
if you secretly showed partiality.
¹¹Would not his splendor terrify you?
Would not the dread of him fall on you?
¹²Your maxims are proverbs of ashes;
your defenses are defenses of clay.

¹³"Keep silent and let me speak;
then let come to me what may.
¹⁴Why do I put myself in jeopardy
and take my life in my hands?
¹⁵Though he slay me, yet will I hope in him;
I will surely *ᵃ* defend my ways to his face.
¹⁶Indeed, this will turn out for my deliverance,
for no godless man would dare come before him!
¹⁷Listen carefully to my words;
let your ears take in what I say.
¹⁸Now that I have prepared my case,
I know I will be vindicated.
¹⁹Can anyone bring charges against me?
If so, I will be silent and die.

²⁰"Only grant me these two things, O God,
and then I will not hide from you:
²¹Withdraw your hand far from me,
and stop frightening me with your terrors.
²²Then summon me and I will answer,
or let me speak, and you reply.
²³How many wrongs and sins have I committed?
Show me my offense and my sin.
²⁴Why do you hide your face
and consider me your enemy?
²⁵Will you torment a windblown leaf?
Will you chase after dry chaff?
²⁶For you write down bitter things against me
and make me inherit the sins of my youth.
²⁷You fasten my feet in shackles;
you keep close watch on all my paths
by putting marks on the soles of my feet.

²⁸"So man wastes away like something rotten,
like a garment eaten by moths.

14

"Man born of woman
is of few days and full of trouble.
²He springs up like a flower and withers away;
like a fleeting shadow, he does not endure.

ᵃ15 Or *He will surely slay me; I have no hope — / yet I will*

³Do you fix your eye on such a one?
    Will you bring him*a* before you for judgment?
⁴Who can bring what is pure from the impure?
    No one!
⁵Man's days are determined;
    you have decreed the number of his months
    and have set limits he cannot exceed.
⁶So look away from him and let him alone,
    till he has put in his time like a hired man.

⁷"At least there is hope for a tree:
    If it is cut down, it will sprout again,
    and its new shoots will not fail.
⁸Its roots may grow old in the ground
    and its stump die in the soil,
⁹yet at the scent of water it will bud
    and put forth shoots like a plant.
¹⁰But man dies and is laid low;
    he breathes his last and is no more.
¹¹As water disappears from the sea
    or a riverbed becomes parched and dry,
¹²so man lies down and does not rise;
    till the heavens are no more, men will not awake
    or be roused from their sleep.

¹³"If only you would hide me in the grave*b*
    and conceal me till your anger has passed!
    If only you would set me a time
    and then remember me!
¹⁴If a man dies, will he live again?
    All the days of my hard service
    I will wait for my renewal*c* to come.
¹⁵You will call and I will answer you;
    you will long for the creature your hands have made.
¹⁶Surely then you will count my steps
    but not keep track of my sin.
¹⁷My offenses will be sealed up in a bag;
    you will cover over my sin.

¹⁸"But as a mountain erodes and crumbles
    and as a rock is moved from its place,
¹⁹as water wears away stones
    and torrents wash away the soil,
    so you destroy man's hope.
²⁰You overpower him once for all, and he is gone;
    you change his countenance and send him away.
²¹If his sons are honored, he does not know it;
    if they are brought low, he does not see it.
²²He feels but the pain of his own body
    and mourns only for himself."

---

a3 Septuagint, Vulgate and Syriac; Hebrew *me*   *b13* Hebrew *Sheol*   *c14* Or *release*

Eliphaz

15

Then Eliphaz the Temanite replied:

2"Would a wise man answer with empty notions
  or fill his belly with the hot east wind?
3Would he argue with useless words,
  with speeches that have no value?
4But you even undermine piety
  and hinder devotion to God.
5Your sin prompts your mouth;
  you adopt the tongue of the crafty.
6Your own mouth condemns you, not mine;
  your own lips testify against you.

7"Are you the first man ever born?
  Were you brought forth before the hills?
8Do you listen in on God's council?
  Do you limit wisdom to yourself?
9What do you know that we do not know?
  What insights do you have that we do not have?
10The gray-haired and the aged are on our side,
  men even older than your father.
11Are God's consolations not enough for you,
  words spoken gently to you?
12Why has your heart carried you away,
  and why do your eyes flash,
13so that you vent your rage against God
  and pour out such words from your mouth?

14"What is man, that he could be pure,
  or one born of woman, that he could be righteous?
15If God places no trust in his holy ones,
  if even the heavens are not pure in his eyes,
16how much less man, who is vile and corrupt,
  who drinks up evil like water!

17"Listen to me and I will explain to you;
  let me tell you what I have seen,
18what wise men have declared,
  hiding nothing received from their fathers
19(to whom alone the land was given
  when no alien passed among them):
20All his days the wicked man suffers torment,
  the ruthless through all the years stored up for him.
21Terrifying sounds fill his ears;
  when all seems well, marauders attack him.
22He despairs of escaping the darkness;
  he is marked for the sword.
23He wanders about—food for vultures[a];
  he knows the day of darkness is at hand.
24Distress and anguish fill him with terror;
  they overwhelm him, like a king poised to attack,
25because he shakes his fist at God

a23 Or about, looking for food

and vaunts himself against the Almighty,
26defiantly charging against him
 with a thick, strong shield.

27"Though his face is covered with fat
 and his waist bulges with flesh,
28he will inhabit ruined towns
 and houses where no one lives,
 houses crumbling to rubble.
29He will no longer be rich and his wealth will not endure,
 nor will his possessions spread over the land.
30He will not escape the darkness;
 a flame will wither his shoots,
 and the breath of God's mouth will carry him away.
31Let him not deceive himself by trusting what is worthless,
 for he will get nothing in return.
32Before his time he will be paid in full,
 and his branches will not flourish.
33He will be like a vine stripped of its unripe grapes,
 like an olive tree shedding its blossoms.
34For the company of the godless will be barren,
 and fire will consume the tents of those who love bribes.
35They conceive trouble and give birth to evil;
 their womb fashions deceit."

Job

16 Then Job replied:

2"I have heard many things like these;
 miserable comforters are you all!
3Will your long-winded speeches never end?
 What ails you that you keep on arguing?
4I also could speak like you,
 if you were in my place;
 I could make fine speeches against you
 and shake my head at you.
5But my mouth would encourage you;
 comfort from my lips would bring you relief.

6"Yet if I speak, my pain is not relieved;
 and if I refrain, it does not go away.
7Surely, O God, you have worn me out;
 you have devastated my entire household.
8You have bound me—and it has become a witness;
 my gauntness rises up and testifies against me.
9God assails me and tears me in his anger
 and gnashes his teeth at me;
 my opponent fastens on me his piercing eyes.
10Men open their mouths to jeer at me;
 they strike my cheek in scorn
 and unite together against me.
11God has turned me over to evil men
 and thrown me into the clutches of the wicked.
12All was well with me, but he shattered me;

he seized me by the neck and crushed me.
He has made me his target;
13   his archers surround me.
Without pity, he pierces my kidneys
    and spills my gall on the ground.
¹⁴Again and again he bursts upon me;
    he rushes at me like a warrior.

¹⁵"I have sewed sackcloth over my skin
    and buried my brow in the dust.
¹⁶My face is red with weeping,
    deep shadows ring my eyes;
¹⁷yet my hands have been free of violence
    and my prayer is pure.

¹⁸"O earth, do not cover my blood;
    may my cry never be laid to rest!
¹⁹Even now my witness is in heaven;
    my advocate is on high.
²⁰My intercessor is my friend *ᵃ*
    as my eyes pour out tears to God;
²¹on behalf of a man he pleads with God
    as a man pleads for his friend.

²²"Only a few years will pass
    before I go on the journey of no return.

17 ¹My spirit is broken,
    my days are cut short,
    the grave awaits me.
²Surely mockers surround me;
    my eyes must dwell on their hostility.

³"Give me, O God, the pledge you demand.
    Who else will put up security for me?
⁴You have closed their minds to understanding;
    therefore you will not let them triumph.
⁵If a man denounces his friends for reward,
    the eyes of his children will fail.

⁶"God has made me a byword to everyone,
    a man in whose face people spit.
⁷My eyes have grown dim with grief;
    my whole frame is but a shadow.
⁸Upright men are appalled at this;
    the innocent are aroused against the ungodly.
⁹Nevertheless, the righteous will hold to their ways,
    and those with clean hands will grow stronger.

¹⁰"But come on, all of you, try again!
    I will not find a wise man among you.
¹¹My days have passed, my plans are shattered,
    and so are the desires of my heart.
¹²These men turn night into day;
    in the face of darkness they say, 'Light is near.'
¹³If the only home I hope for is the grave, *ᵇ*

ᵃ20 Or *My friends treat me with scorn*   *ᵇ13* Hebrew *Sheol*

if I spread out my bed in darkness,
¹⁴if I say to corruption, 'You are my father,'
and to the worm, 'My mother' or 'My sister,'
¹⁵where then is my hope?
Who can see any hope for me?
¹⁶Will it go down to the gates of death^a?
Will we descend together into the dust?"

Bildad

18 Then Bildad the Shuhite replied:

²"When will you end these speeches?
Be sensible, and then we can talk.
³Why are we regarded as cattle
and considered stupid in your sight?
⁴You who tear yourself to pieces in your anger,
is the earth to be abandoned for your sake?
Or must the rocks be moved from their place?

⁵"The lamp of the wicked is snuffed out;
the flame of his fire stops burning.
⁶The light in his tent becomes dark;
the lamp beside him goes out.
⁷The vigor of his step is weakened;
his own schemes throw him down.
⁸His feet thrust him into a net
and he wanders into its mesh.
⁹A trap seizes him by the heel;
a snare holds him fast.
¹⁰A noose is hidden for him on the ground;
a trap lies in his path.
¹¹Terrors startle him on every side
and dog his every step.
¹²Calamity is hungry for him;
disaster is ready for him when he falls.
¹³It eats away parts of his skin;
death's firstborn devours his limbs.
¹⁴He is torn from the security of his tent
and marched off to the king of terrors.
¹⁵Fire resides^b in his tent;
burning sulfur is scattered over his dwelling.
¹⁶His roots dry up below
and his branches wither above.
¹⁷The memory of him perishes from the earth;
he has no name in the land.
¹⁸He is driven from light into darkness
and is banished from the world.
¹⁹He has no offspring or descendants among his people,
no survivor where once he lived.
²⁰Men of the west are appalled at his fate;
men of the east are seized with horror.

^a16 Hebrew Sheol   ^b15 Or Nothing he had remains

²¹Surely such is the dwelling of an evil man;
  such is the place of one who knows not God."

Job

19

Then Job replied:

²"How long will you torment me
  and crush me with words?
³Ten times now you have reproached me;
  shamelessly you attack me.
⁴If it is true that I have gone astray,
  my error remains my concern alone.
⁵If indeed you would exalt yourselves above me
  and use my humiliation against me,
⁶then know that God has wronged me
  and drawn his net around me.

⁷"Though I cry, 'I've been wronged!' I get no response;
  though I call for help, there is no justice.
⁸He has blocked my way so I cannot pass;
  he has shrouded my paths in darkness.
⁹He has stripped me of my honor
  and removed the crown from my head.
¹⁰He tears me down on every side till I am gone;
  he uproots my hope like a tree.
¹¹His anger burns against me;
  he counts me among his enemies.
¹²His troops advance in force;
  they build a siege ramp against me
  and encamp around my tent.

¹³"He has alienated my brothers from me;
  my acquaintances are completely estranged from me.
¹⁴My kinsmen have gone away;
  my friends have forgotten me.
¹⁵My guests and my maidservants count me a stranger;
  they look upon me as an alien.
¹⁶I summon my servant, but he does not answer,
  though I beg him with my own mouth.
¹⁷My breath is offensive to my wife;
  I am loathsome to my own brothers.
¹⁸Even the little boys scorn me;
  when I appear, they ridicule me.
¹⁹All my intimate friends detest me;
  those I love have turned against me.
²⁰I am nothing but skin and bones;
  I have escaped with only the skin of my teeth. [a]

²¹"Have pity on me, my friends, have pity,
  for the hand of God has struck me.
²²Why do you pursue me as God does?
  Will you never get enough of my flesh?

²³"Oh, that my words were recorded,

[a] 20 Or *only my gums*

that they were written on a scroll,
²⁴that they were inscribed with an iron tool on*ᵃ* lead,
        or engraved in rock forever!
²⁵I know that my Redeemer*ᵇ* lives,
        and that in the end he will stand upon the earth.*ᶜ*
²⁶And after my skin has been destroyed,
        yet*ᵈ* in*ᵉ* my flesh I will see God;
²⁷I myself will see him
        with my own eyes—I, and not another.
        How my heart yearns within me!

²⁸"If you say, 'How we will hound him,
        since the root of the trouble lies in him,*ᶠ*'
²⁹you should fear the sword yourselves;
        for wrath will bring punishment by the sword,
        and then you will know that there is judgment.*ᵍ*"

Zophar

20 Then Zophar the Naamathite replied:

²"My troubled thoughts prompt me to answer
        because I am greatly disturbed.
³I hear a rebuke that dishonors me,
        and my understanding inspires me to reply.

⁴"Surely you know how it has been from of old,
        ever since man*ʰ* was placed on the earth,
⁵that the mirth of the wicked is brief,
        the joy of the godless lasts but a moment.
⁶Though his pride reaches to the heavens
        and his head touches the clouds,
⁷he will perish forever, like his own dung;
        those who have seen him will say, 'Where is he?'
⁸Like a dream he flies away, no more to be found,
        banished like a vision of the night.
⁹The eye that saw him will not see him again;
        his place will look on him no more.
¹⁰His children must make amends to the poor;
        his own hands must give back his wealth.
¹¹The youthful vigor that fills his bones
        will lie with him in the dust.

¹²"Though evil is sweet in his mouth
        and he hides it under his tongue,
¹³though he cannot bear to let it go
        and keeps it in his mouth,
¹⁴yet his food will turn sour in his stomach;
        it will become the venom of serpents within him.
¹⁵He will spit out the riches he swallowed;
        God will make his stomach vomit them up.
¹⁶He will suck the poison of serpents;
        the fangs of an adder will kill him.

ᵃ24 Or *and destroyed, / then*   *ᵇ25* Or *defender*   *ᶜ25* Or *upon my grave*   *ᵈ26* Or *And after I awake, / though this body, has been destroyed, / then*   *ᵉ26* Or / *apart from*   *ᶠ28* Many Hebrew manuscripts, Septuagint and Vulgate; most Hebrew manuscripts *me*   *ᵍ29* Or / *that you may come to know the Almighty*   *ʰ4* Or *Adam*

¹⁷He will not enjoy the streams,
the rivers flowing with honey and cream.
¹⁸What he toiled for he must give back uneaten;
he will not enjoy the profit from his trading.
¹⁹For he has oppressed the poor and left them destitute;
he has seized houses he did not build.

²⁰"Surely he will have no respite from his craving;
he cannot save himself by his treasure.
²¹Nothing is left for him to devour;
his prosperity will not endure.
²²In the midst of his plenty, distress will overtake him;
the full force of misery will come upon him.
²³When he has filled his belly,
God will vent his burning anger against him
and rain down his blows upon him.
²⁴Though he flees from an iron weapon,
a bronze-tipped arrow pierces him.
²⁵He pulls it out of his back,
the gleaming point out of his liver.
Terrors will come over him;
²⁶ total darkness lies in wait for his treasures.
A fire unfanned will consume him
and devour what is left in his tent.
²⁷The heavens will expose his guilt;
the earth will rise up against him.
²⁸A flood will carry off his house,
rushing waters^a on the day of God's wrath.
²⁹Such is the fate God allots the wicked,
the heritage appointed for them by God."

Job

21

Then Job replied:

²"Listen carefully to my words;
let this be the consolation you give me.
³Bear with me while I speak,
and after I have spoken, mock on.

⁴"Is my complaint directed to man?
Why should I not be impatient?
⁵Look at me and be astonished;
clap your hand over your mouth.
⁶When I think about this, I am terrified;
trembling seizes my body.
⁷Why do the wicked live on,
growing old and increasing in power?
⁸They see their children established around them,
their offspring before their eyes.
⁹Their homes are safe and free from fear;
the rod of God is not upon them.
¹⁰Their bulls never fail to breed;
their cows calve and do not miscarry.

a 28 Or *The possessions in his house will be carried off, / washed away*

¹¹They send forth their children as a flock;
  their little ones dance about.
¹²They sing to the music of tambourine and harp;
  they make merry to the sound of the flute.
¹³They spend their years in prosperity
  and go down to the grave ᵃ in peace. ᵇ
¹⁴Yet they say to God, 'Leave us alone!
  We have no desire to know your ways.
¹⁵Who is the Almighty, that we should serve him?
  What would we gain by praying to him?'
¹⁶But their prosperity is not in their own hands,
  so I stand aloof from the counsel of the wicked.

¹⁷"Yet how often is the lamp of the wicked snuffed out?
  How often does calamity come upon them,
  the fate God allots in his anger?
¹⁸How often are they like straw before the wind,
  like chaff swept away by a gale?
¹⁹It is said, 'God stores up a man's punishment for his sons.'
  Let him repay the man himself, so that he will know it!
²⁰Let his own eyes see his destruction;
  let him drink of the wrath of the Almighty. ᶜ
²¹For what does he care about the family he leaves behind
  when his allotted months come to an end?

²²"Can anyone teach knowledge to God,
  since he judges even the highest?
²³One man dies in full vigor,
  completely secure and at ease,
²⁴his body ᵈ well nourished,
  his bones rich with marrow.
²⁵Another man dies in bitterness of soul,
  never having enjoyed anything good.
²⁶Side by side they lie in the dust,
  and worms cover them both.

²⁷"I know full well what you are thinking,
  the schemes by which you would wrong me.
²⁸You say, 'Where now is the great man's house,
  the tents where wicked men lived?'
²⁹Have you never questioned those who travel?
  Have you paid no regard to their accounts—
³⁰that the evil man is spared from the day of calamity,
  that he is delivered from ᵉ the day of wrath?
³¹Who denounces his conduct to his face?
  Who repays him for what he has done?
³²He is carried to the grave,
  and watch is kept over his tomb.
³³The soil in the valley is sweet to him;
  all men follow after him,
  and a countless throng goes ᶠ before him.

ᵃ 13 Hebrew Sheol   ᵇ 13 Or in an instant   ᶜ 17–20 Verses 17 and 18 may be taken as exclamations and 19 and 20 as declarations.   ᵈ 24 The meaning of the Hebrew for this word is uncertain.   ᵉ 30 Or man is reserved for the day of calamity, / that he is brought forth to   ᶠ 33 Or / as a countless throng went

³⁴"So how can you console me with your nonsense?
　　Nothing is left of your answers but falsehood!"

Eliphaz

22 Then Eliphaz the Temanite replied:

²"Can a man be of benefit to God?
　　Can even a wise man benefit him?
³What pleasure would it give the Almighty if you were righteous?
　　What would he gain if your ways were blameless?

⁴"Is it for your piety that he rebukes you
　　and brings charges against you?
⁵Is not your wickedness great?
　　Are not your sins endless?
⁶You demanded security from your brothers for no reason;
　　you stripped men of their clothing, leaving them naked.
⁷You gave no water to the weary
　　and you withheld food from the hungry,
⁸though you were a powerful man, owning land—
　　an honored man, living on it.
⁹And you sent widows away empty-handed
　　and broke the strength of the fatherless.
¹⁰That is why snares are all around you,
　　why sudden peril terrifies you,
¹¹why it is so dark you cannot see,
　　and why a flood of water covers you.

¹²"Is not God in the heights of heaven?
　　And see how lofty are the highest stars!
¹³Yet you say, 'What does God know?
　　Does he judge through such darkness?
¹⁴Thick clouds veil him, so he does not see us
　　as he goes about in the vaulted heavens.'
¹⁵Will you keep to the old path
　　that evil men have trod?
¹⁶They were carried off before their time,
　　their foundations washed away by a flood.
¹⁷They said to God, 'Leave us alone!
　　What can the Almighty do to us?'
¹⁸Yet it was he who filled their houses with good things,
　　so I stand aloof from the counsel of the wicked.

¹⁹"The righteous see their ruin and rejoice;
　　the innocent mock them, saying,
²⁰'Surely our foes are destroyed,
　　and fire devours their wealth.'

²¹"Submit to God and be at peace with him;
　　in this way prosperity will come to you.
²²Accept instruction from his mouth
　　and lay up his words in your heart.
²³If you return to the Almighty, you will be restored:
　　If you remove wickedness far from your tent
²⁴and assign your nuggets to the dust,

your gold of Ophir to the rocks in the ravines,
²⁵then the Almighty will be your gold,
   the choicest silver for you.
²⁶Surely then you will find delight in the Almighty
   and will lift up your face to God.
²⁷You will pray to him, and he will hear you,
   and you will fulfill your vows.
²⁸What you decide on will be done,
   and light will shine on your ways.
²⁹When men are brought low and you say, 'Lift them up!'
   then he will save the downcast.
³⁰He will deliver even one who is not innocent,
   who will be delivered through the cleanness of your hands."

Job

23

Then Job replied:

²"Even today my complaint is bitter;
   his hand*ᵃ* is heavy in spite of*ᵇ* my groaning.
³If only I knew where to find him;
   if only I could go to his dwelling!
⁴I would state my case before him
   and fill my mouth with arguments.
⁵I would find out what he would answer me,
   and consider what he would say.
⁶Would he oppose me with great power?
   No, he would not press charges against me.
⁷There an upright man could present his case before him,
   and I would be delivered forever from my judge.

⁸"But if I go to the east, he is not there;
   if I go to the west, I do not find him.
⁹When he is at work in the north, I do not see him;
   when he turns to the south, I catch no glimpse of him.
¹⁰But he knows the way that I take;
   when he has tested me, I will come forth as gold.
¹¹My feet have closely followed his steps;
   I have kept to his way without turning aside.
¹²I have not departed from the commands of his lips;
   I have treasured the words of his mouth more than my daily
      bread.

¹³"But he stands alone, and who can oppose him?
   He does whatever he pleases.
¹⁴He carries out his decree against me,
   and many such plans he still has in store.
¹⁵That is why I am terrified before him;
   when I think of all this, I fear him.
¹⁶God has made my heart faint;
   the Almighty has terrified me.
¹⁷Yet I am not silenced by the darkness,
   by the thick darkness that covers my face.

ᵃ2 Septuagint and Syriac; Hebrew / *the hand on me*   *ᵇ2* Or *heavy on me in*

24 "Why does the Almighty not set times for judgment?
Why must those who know him look in vain for such days?
²Men move boundary stones;
they pasture flocks they have stolen.
³They drive away the orphan's donkey
and take the widow's ox in pledge.
⁴They thrust the needy from the path
and force all the poor of the land into hiding.
⁵Like wild donkeys in the desert,
the poor go about their labor of foraging food;
the wasteland provides food for their children.
⁶They gather fodder in the fields
and glean in the vineyards of the wicked.
⁷Lacking clothes, they spend the night naked;
they have nothing to cover themselves in the cold.
⁸They are drenched by mountain rains
and hug the rocks for lack of shelter.
⁹The fatherless child is snatched from the breast;
the infant of the poor is seized for a debt.
¹⁰Lacking clothes, they go about naked;
they carry the sheaves, but still go hungry.
¹¹They crush olives among the terraces*a*;
they tread the winepresses, yet suffer thirst.
¹²The groans of the dying rise from the city,
and the souls of the wounded cry out for help.
But God charges no one with wrongdoing.

¹³"There are those who rebel against the light,
who do not know its ways
or stay in its paths.
¹⁴When daylight is gone, the murderer rises up
and kills the poor and needy;
in the night he steals forth like a thief.
¹⁵The eye of the adulterer watches for dusk;
he thinks, 'No eye will see me,'
and he keeps his face concealed.
¹⁶In the dark, men break into houses,
but by day they shut themselves in;
they want nothing to do with the light.
¹⁷For all of them, deep darkness is their morning*b*;
they make friends with the terrors of darkness.*c*

¹⁸"Yet they are foam on the surface of the water;
their portion of the land is cursed,
so that no one goes to the vineyards.
¹⁹As heat and drought snatch away the melted snow,
so the grave*d* snatches away those who have sinned.
²⁰The womb forgets them,
the worm feasts on them;
evil men are no longer remembered
but are broken like a tree.
²¹They prey on the barren and childless woman,

---

a 11 Or olives between the millstones; the meaning of the Hebrew for this word is uncertain.   *b 17 Or them, their morning is like the shadow of death*   *c 17 Or of the shadow of death*   *d 19 Hebrew Sheol*

and to the widow show no kindness.
²²But God drags away the mighty by his power;
  though they become established, they have no assurance of life.
²³He may let them rest in a feeling of security,
  but his eyes are on their ways.
²⁴For a little while they are exalted, and then they are gone;
  they are brought low and gathered up like all others;
  they are cut off like heads of grain.

²⁵"If this is not so, who can prove me false
  and reduce my words to nothing?"

Bildad

25 Then Bildad the Shuhite replied:

²"Dominion and awe belong to God;
  he establishes order in the heights of heaven.
³Can his forces be numbered?
  Upon whom does his light not rise?
⁴How then can a man be righteous before God?
  How can one born of woman be pure?
⁵If even the moon is not bright
  and the stars are not pure in his eyes,
⁶how much less man, who is but a maggot—
  a son of man, who is only a worm!"

Job

26 Then Job replied:

²"How you have helped the powerless!
  How you have saved the arm that is feeble!
³What advice you have offered to one without wisdom!
  And what great insight you have displayed!
⁴Who has helped you utter these words?
  And whose spirit spoke from your mouth?

⁵"The dead are in deep anguish,
  those beneath the waters and all that live in them.
⁶Death ᵃ is naked before God;
  Destruction ᵇ lies uncovered.
⁷He spreads out the northern ˻skies˼ over empty space;
  he suspends the earth over nothing.
⁸He wraps up the waters in his clouds,
  yet the clouds do not burst under their weight.
⁹He covers the face of the full moon,
  spreading his clouds over it.
¹⁰He marks out the horizon on the face of the waters
  for a boundary between light and darkness.
¹¹The pillars of the heavens quake,
  aghast at his rebuke.
¹²By his power he churned up the sea;
  by his wisdom he cut Rahab to pieces.
¹³By his breath the skies became fair;

ᵃ6 Hebrew *Sheol*   ᵇ6 Hebrew *Abaddon*

his hand pierced the gliding serpent.
¹⁴And these are but the outer fringe of his works;
    how faint the whisper we hear of him!
    Who then can understand the thunder of his power?"

27 And Job continued his discourse:

²"As surely as God lives, who has denied me justice,
    the Almighty, who has made me taste bitterness of soul,
³as long as I have life within me,
    the breath of God in my nostrils,
⁴my lips will not speak wickedness,
    and my tongue will utter no deceit.
⁵I will never admit you are in the right;
    till I die, I will not deny my integrity.
⁶I will maintain my righteousness and never let go of it;
    my conscience will not reproach me as long as I live.

⁷"May my enemies be like the wicked,
    my adversaries like the unjust!
⁸For what hope has the godless when he is cut off,
    when God takes away his life?
⁹Does God listen to his cry
    when distress comes upon him?
¹⁰Will he find delight in the Almighty?
    Will he call upon God at all times?

¹¹"I will teach you about the power of God;
    the ways of the Almighty I will not conceal.
¹²You have all seen this yourselves.
    Why then this meaningless talk?

¹³"Here is the fate God allots to the wicked,
    the heritage a ruthless man receives from the Almighty:
¹⁴However many his children, their fate is the sword;
    his offspring will never have enough to eat.
¹⁵The plague will bury those who survive him,
    and their widows will not weep for them.
¹⁶Though he heaps up silver like dust
    and clothes like piles of clay,
¹⁷what he lays up the righteous will wear,
    and the innocent will divide his silver.
¹⁸The house he builds is like a moth's cocoon,
    like a hut made by a watchman.
¹⁹He lies down wealthy, but will do so no more;
    when he opens his eyes, all is gone.
²⁰Terrors overtake him like a flood;
    a tempest snatches him away in the night.
²¹The east wind carries him off, and he is gone;
    it sweeps him out of his place.
²²It hurls itself against him without mercy
    as he flees headlong from its power.
²³It claps its hands in derision
    and hisses him out of his place.

28

"There is a mine for silver
and a place where gold is refined.
²Iron is taken from the earth,
and copper is smelted from ore.
³Man puts an end to the darkness;
he searches the farthest recesses
for ore in the blackest darkness.
⁴Far from where people dwell he cuts a shaft,
in places forgotten by the foot of man;
far from men he dangles and sways.
⁵The earth, from which food comes,
is transformed below as by fire;
⁶sapphiresᵃ come from its rocks,
and its dust contains nuggets of gold.
⁷No bird of prey knows that hidden path,
no falcon's eye has seen it.
⁸Proud beasts do not set foot on it,
and no lion prowls there.
⁹Man's hand assaults the flinty rock
and lays bare the roots of the mountains.
¹⁰He tunnels through the rock;
his eyes see all its treasures.
¹¹He searchesᵇ the sources of the rivers
and brings hidden things to light.

¹²"But where can wisdom be found?
Where does understanding dwell?
¹³Man does not comprehend its worth;
it cannot be found in the land of the living.
¹⁴The deep says, 'It is not in me';
the sea says, 'It is not with me.'
¹⁵It cannot be bought with the finest gold,
nor can its price be weighed in silver.
¹⁶It cannot be bought with the gold of Ophir,
with precious onyx or sapphires.
¹⁷Neither gold nor crystal can compare with it,
nor can it be had for jewels of gold.
¹⁸Coral and jasper are not worthy of mention;
the price of wisdom is beyond rubies.
¹⁹The topaz of Cush cannot compare with it;
it cannot be bought with pure gold.

²⁰"Where then does wisdom come from?
Where does understanding dwell?
²¹It is hidden from the eyes of every living thing,
concealed even from the birds of the air.
²²Destructionᶜ and Death say,
'Only a rumor of it has reached our ears.'
²³God understands the way to it
and he alone knows where it dwells,
²⁴for he views the ends of the earth
and sees everything under the heavens.
²⁵When he established the force of the wind

ᵃ6 Or lapis lazuli; also in verse 16   ᵇ11 Septuagint, Aquila and Vulgate; Hebrew He dams up   ᶜ22 Hebrew Abaddon

and measured out the waters,
²⁶when he made a decree for the rain
    and a path for the thunderstorm,
²⁷then he looked at wisdom and appraised it;
    he confirmed it and tested it.
²⁸And he said to man,
    'The fear of the Lord—that is wisdom,
    and to shun evil is understanding.' "

29   Job continued his discourse:

²"How I long for the months gone by,
    for the days when God watched over me,
³when his lamp shone upon my head
    and by his light I walked through darkness!
⁴Oh, for the days when I was in my prime,
    when God's intimate friendship blessed my house,
⁵when the Almighty was still with me
    and my children were around me,
⁶when my path was drenched with cream
    and the rock poured out for me streams of olive oil.

⁷"When I went to the gate of the city
    and took my seat in the public square,
⁸the young men saw me and stepped aside
    and the old men rose to their feet;
⁹the chief men refrained from speaking
    and covered their mouths with their hands;
¹⁰the voices of the nobles were hushed,
    and their tongues stuck to the roof of their mouths.
¹¹Whoever heard me spoke well of me,
    and those who saw me commended me,
¹²because I rescued the poor who cried for help,
    and the fatherless who had none to assist him.
¹³The man who was dying blessed me;
    I made the widow's heart sing.
¹⁴I put on righteousness as my clothing;
    justice was my robe and my turban.
¹⁵I was eyes to the blind
    and feet to the lame.
¹⁶I was a father to the needy;
    I took up the case of the stranger.
¹⁷I broke the fangs of the wicked
    and snatched the victims from their teeth.

¹⁸"I thought, 'I will die in my own house,
    my days as numerous as the grains of sand.
¹⁹My roots will reach to the water,
    and the dew will lie all night on my branches.
²⁰My glory will remain fresh in me,
    the bow ever new in my hand.'

²¹"Men listened to me expectantly,
    waiting in silence for my counsel.
²²After I had spoken, they spoke no more;

my words fell gently on their ears.
²³They waited for me as for showers
    and drank in my words as the spring rain.
²⁴When I smiled at them, they scarcely believed it;
    the light of my face was precious to them. *a*
²⁵I chose the way for them and sat as their chief;
    I dwelt as a king among his troops;
    I was like one who comforts mourners.

30 "But now they mock me,
        men younger than I,
    whose fathers I would have disdained
        to put with my sheep dogs.
²Of what use was the strength of their hands to me,
    since their vigor had gone from them?
³Haggard from want and hunger,
    they roamed *b* the parched land
    in desolate wastelands at night.
⁴In the brush they gathered salt herbs,
    and their food *c* was the root of the broom tree.
⁵They were banished from their fellow men,
    shouted at as if they were thieves.
⁶They were forced to live in the dry stream beds,
    among the rocks and in holes in the ground.
⁷They brayed among the bushes
    and huddled in the undergrowth.
⁸A base and nameless brood,
    they were driven out of the land.

⁹"And now their sons mock me in song;
    I have become a byword among them.
¹⁰They detest me and keep their distance;
    they do not hesitate to spit in my face.
¹¹Now that God has unstrung my bow and afflicted me,
    they throw off restraint in my presence.
¹²On my right the tribe *d* attacks;
    they lay snares for my feet,
    they build their siege ramps against me.
¹³They break up my road;
    they succeed in destroying me—
    without anyone's helping them. *e*
¹⁴They advance as through a gaping breach;
    amid the ruins they come rolling in.
¹⁵Terrors overwhelm me;
    my dignity is driven away as by the wind,
    my safety vanishes like a cloud.

¹⁶"And now my life ebbs away;
    days of suffering grip me.
¹⁷Night pierces my bones;
    my gnawing pains never rest.
¹⁸In his great power ⌊God⌋ becomes like clothing to me *f*;

---

a 24 The meaning of the Hebrew for this clause is uncertain.   *b 3* Or *gnawed*   *c 4* Or *fuel*   *d 12* The meaning of the Hebrew for this word is uncertain.   *e 13* Or *me. / 'No one can help him,' they say,*   *f 18* Hebrew; Septuagint ⌊*God*⌋ *grasps my clothing*

he binds me like the neck of my garment.
¹⁹He throws me into the mud,
and I am reduced to dust and ashes.

²⁰"I cry out to you, O God, but you do not answer;
I stand up, but you merely look at me.
²¹You turn on me ruthlessly;
with the might of your hand you attack me.
²²You snatch me up and drive me before the wind;
you toss me about in the storm.
²³I know you will bring me down to death,
to the place appointed for all the living.

²⁴"Surely no one lays a hand on a broken man
when he cries for help in his distress.
²⁵Have I not wept for those in trouble?
Has not my soul grieved for the poor?
²⁶Yet when I hoped for good, evil came;
when I looked for light, then came darkness.
²⁷The churning inside me never stops;
days of suffering confront me.
²⁸I go about blackened, but not by the sun;
I stand up in the assembly and cry for help.
²⁹I have become a brother of jackals,
a companion of owls.
³⁰My skin grows black and peels;
my body burns with fever.
³¹My harp is tuned to mourning,
and my flute to the sound of wailing.

31 "I made a covenant with my eyes
not to look lustfully at a girl.
²For what is man's lot from God above,
his heritage from the Almighty on high?
³Is it not ruin for the wicked,
disaster for those who do wrong?
⁴Does he not see my ways
and count my every step?

⁵"If I have walked in falsehood
or my foot has hurried after deceit—
⁶let God weigh me in honest scales
and he will know that I am blameless—
⁷if my steps have turned from the path,
if my heart has been led by my eyes,
or if my hands have been defiled,
⁸then may others eat what I have sown,
and may my crops be uprooted.

⁹"If my heart has been enticed by a woman,
or if I have lurked at my neighbor's door,
¹⁰then may my wife grind another man's grain,
and may other men sleep with her.
¹¹For that would have been shameful,
a sin to be judged.

¹²It is a fire that burns to Destruction[a];
   it would have uprooted my harvest.

¹³"If I have denied justice to my menservants and maidservants
   when they had a grievance against me,
¹⁴what will I do when God confronts me?
   What will I answer when called to account?
¹⁵Did not he who made me in the womb make them?
   Did not the same one form us both within our mothers?

¹⁶"If I have denied the desires of the poor
   or let the eyes of the widow grow weary,
¹⁷if I have kept my bread to myself,
   not sharing it with the fatherless—
¹⁸but from my youth I reared him as would a father,
   and from my birth I guided the widow—
¹⁹if I have seen anyone perishing for lack of clothing,
   or a needy man without a garment,
²⁰and his heart did not bless me
   for warming him with the fleece from my sheep,
²¹if I have raised my hand against the fatherless,
   knowing that I had influence in court,
²²then let my arm fall from the shoulder,
   let it be broken off at the joint.
²³For I dreaded destruction from God,
   and for fear of his splendor I could not do such things.

²⁴"If I have put my trust in gold
   or said to pure gold, 'You are my security,'
²⁵if I have rejoiced over my great wealth,
   the fortune my hands had gained,
²⁶if I have regarded the sun in its radiance
   or the moon moving in splendor,
²⁷so that my heart was secretly enticed
   and my hand offered them a kiss of homage,
²⁸then these also would be sins to be judged,
   for I would have been unfaithful to God on high.

²⁹"If I have rejoiced at my enemy's misfortune
   or gloated over the trouble that came to him—
³⁰I have not allowed my mouth to sin
   by invoking a curse against his life—
³¹if the men of my household have never said,
   'Who has not had his fill of Job's meat?'—
³²but no stranger had to spend the night in the street,
   for my door was always open to the traveler—
³³if I have concealed my sin as men do,[b]
   by hiding my guilt in my heart
³⁴because I so feared the crowd
   and so dreaded the contempt of the clans
   that I kept silent and would not go outside

³⁵("Oh, that I had someone to hear me!
   I sign now my defense—let the Almighty answer me;

---

[a]12 Hebrew *Abaddon*   [b]33 Or *as Adam did*

let my accuser put his indictment in writing.
³⁶Surely I would wear it on my shoulder,
    I would put it on like a crown.
³⁷I would give him an account of my every step;
    like a prince I would approach him.)—

³⁸"if my land cries out against me
    and all its furrows are wet with tears,
³⁹if I have devoured its yield without payment
    or broken the spirit of its tenants,
⁴⁰then let briers come up instead of wheat
    and weeds instead of barley."

The words of Job are ended.

Elihu

32 So these three men stopped answering Job, because he was righteous in his
own eyes. ²But Elihu son of Barakel the Buzite, of the family of Ram, became
very angry with Job for justifying himself rather than God. ³He was also angry with the
three friends, because they had found no way to refute Job, and yet had condemned
him.ᵃ ⁴Now Elihu had waited before speaking to Job because they were older than he.
⁵But when he saw that the three men had nothing more to say, his anger was aroused.

⁶So Elihu son of Barakel the Buzite said:

"I am young in years,
    and you are old;
that is why I was fearful,
    not daring to tell you what I know.
⁷I thought, 'Age should speak;
    advanced years should teach wisdom.'
⁸But it is the spiritᵇ in a man,
    the breath of the Almighty, that gives him understanding.
⁹It is not only the oldᶜ who are wise,
    not only the aged who understand what is right.

¹⁰"Therefore I say: Listen to me;
    I too will tell you what I know.
¹¹I waited while you spoke,
    I listened to your reasoning;
    while you were searching for words,
¹² I gave you my full attention.
    But not one of you has proved Job wrong;
    none of you has answered his arguments.
¹³Do not say, 'We have found wisdom;
    let God refute him, not man.'
¹⁴But Job has not marshaled his words against me,
    and I will not answer him with your arguments.

¹⁵"They are dismayed and have no more to say;
    words have failed them.
¹⁶Must I wait, now that they are silent,
    now that they stand there with no reply?
¹⁷I too will have my say;

ᵃ3 Masoretic Text; an ancient Hebrew scribal tradition *Job, and so had condemned God*   ᵇ8 Or *Spirit*; also in verse 18
ᶜ9 Or *many*; or *great*

I too will tell what I know.
¹⁸For I am full of words,
    and the spirit within me compels me;
¹⁹inside I am like bottled-up wine,
    like new wineskins ready to burst.
²⁰I must speak and find relief;
    I must open my lips and reply.
²¹I will show partiality to no one,
    nor will I flatter any man;
²²for if I were skilled in flattery,
    my Maker would soon take me away.

33 "But now, Job, listen to my words;
    pay attention to everything I say.
²I am about to open my mouth;
    my words are on the tip of my tongue.
³My words come from an upright heart;
    my lips sincerely speak what I know.
⁴The Spirit of God has made me;
    the breath of the Almighty gives me life.
⁵Answer me then, if you can;
    prepare yourself and confront me.
⁶I am just like you before God;
    I too have been taken from clay.
⁷No fear of me should alarm you,
    nor should my hand be heavy upon you.

⁸"But you have said in my hearing—
    I heard the very words—
⁹'I am pure and without sin;
    I am clean and free from guilt.
¹⁰Yet God has found fault with me;
    he considers me his enemy.
¹¹He fastens my feet in shackles;
    he keeps close watch on all my paths.'

¹²"But I tell you, in this you are not right,
    for God is greater than man.
¹³Why do you complain to him
    that he answers none of man's words*a*?
¹⁴For God does speak—now one way, now another—
    though man may not perceive it.
¹⁵In a dream, in a vision of the night,
    when deep sleep falls on men
    as they slumber in their beds,
¹⁶he may speak in their ears
    and terrify them with warnings,
¹⁷to turn man from wrongdoing
    and keep him from pride,
¹⁸to preserve his soul from the pit,*b*
    his life from perishing by the sword.*c*
¹⁹Or a man may be chastened on a bed of pain

a13 Or that he does not answer for any of his actions   *b18* Or preserve him from the grave   *c18* Or from crossing the River

with constant distress in his bones,
²⁰so that his very being finds food repulsive
and his soul loathes the choicest meal.
²¹His flesh wastes away to nothing,
and his bones, once hidden, now stick out.
²²His soul draws near to the pit,[a]
and his life to the messengers of death.[b]

²³"Yet if there is an angel on his side
as a mediator, one out of a thousand,
to tell a man what is right for him,
²⁴to be gracious to him and say,
'Spare him from going down to the pit[c];
I have found a ransom for him'—
²⁵then his flesh is renewed like a child's;
it is restored as in the days of his youth.
²⁶He prays to God and finds favor with him,
he sees God's face and shouts for joy;
he is restored by God to his righteous state.
²⁷Then he comes to men and says,
'I sinned, and perverted what was right,
but I did not get what I deserved.
²⁸He redeemed my soul from going down to the pit,[d]
and I will live to enjoy the light.'

²⁹"God does all these things to a man—
twice, even three times—
³⁰to turn back his soul from the pit,[e]
that the light of life may shine on him.

³¹"Pay attention, Job, and listen to me;
be silent, and I will speak.
³²If you have anything to say, answer me;
speak up, for I want you to be cleared.
³³But if not, then listen to me;
be silent, and I will teach you wisdom."

34   Then Elihu said:

²"Hear my words, you wise men;
listen to me, you men of learning.
³For the ear tests words
as the tongue tastes food.
⁴Let us discern for ourselves what is right;
let us learn together what is good.

⁵"Job says, 'I am innocent,
but God denies me justice.
⁶Although I am right,
I am considered a liar;
although I am guiltless,
his arrow inflicts an incurable wound.'
⁷What man is like Job,

---

[a]22 Or *He draws near to the grave*   [b]22 Or *to the dead*   [c]24 Or *grave*   [d]28 Or *redeemed me from going down to the grave*   [e]30 Or *turn him back from the grave*

who drinks scorn like water?
⁸He keeps company with evildoers;
  he associates with wicked men.
⁹For he says, 'It profits a man nothing
  when he tries to please God.'

¹⁰"So listen to me, you men of understanding.
  Far be it from God to do evil,
  from the Almighty to do wrong.
¹¹He repays a man for what he has done;
  he brings upon him what his conduct deserves.
¹²It is unthinkable that God would do wrong,
  that the Almighty would pervert justice.
¹³Who appointed him over the earth?
  Who put him in charge of the whole world?
¹⁴If it were his intention
  and he withdrew his spirit ᵃ and breath,
¹⁵all mankind would perish together
  and man would return to the dust.

¹⁶"If you have understanding, hear this;
  listen to what I say.
¹⁷Can he who hates justice govern?
  Will you condemn the just and mighty One?
¹⁸Is he not the One who says to kings, 'You are worthless,'
  and to nobles, 'You are wicked,'
¹⁹who shows no partiality to princes
  and does not favor the rich over the poor,
  for they are all the work of his hands?
²⁰They die in an instant, in the middle of the night;
  the people are shaken and they pass away;
  the mighty are removed without human hand.

²¹"His eyes are on the ways of men;
  he sees their every step.
²²There is no dark place, no deep shadow,
  where evildoers can hide.
²³God has no need to examine men further,
  that they should come before him for judgment.
²⁴Without inquiry he shatters the mighty
  and sets up others in their place.
²⁵Because he takes note of their deeds,
  he overthrows them in the night and they are crushed.
²⁶He punishes them for their wickedness
  where everyone can see them,
²⁷because they turned from following him
  and had no regard for any of his ways.
²⁸They caused the cry of the poor to come before him,
  so that he heard the cry of the needy.
²⁹But if he remains silent, who can condemn him?
  If he hides his face, who can see him?
  Yet he is over man and nation alike,

ᵃ 14 Or Spirit

30   to keep a godless man from ruling,
        from laying snares for the people.

31"Suppose a man says to God,
      'I am guilty but will offend no more.
32Teach me what I cannot see;
      if I have done wrong, I will not do so again.'
33Should God then reward you on your terms,
      when you refuse to repent?
    You must decide, not I;
      so tell me what you know.

34"Men of understanding declare,
      wise men who hear me say to me,
35'Job speaks without knowledge;
      his words lack insight.'
36Oh, that Job might be tested to the utmost
      for answering like a wicked man!
37To his sin he adds rebellion;
      scornfully he claps his hands among us
      and multiplies his words against God."

35   Then Elihu said:

2"Do you think this is just?
      You say, 'I will be cleared by God.ᵃ'
3Yet you ask him, 'What profit is it to me,ᵇ
      and what do I gain by not sinning?'

4"I would like to reply to you
      and to your friends with you.
5Look up at the heavens and see;
      gaze at the clouds so high above you.
6If you sin, how does that affect him?
      If your sins are many, what does that do to him?
7If you are righteous, what do you give to him,
      or what does he receive from your hand?
8Your wickedness affects only a man like yourself,
      and your righteousness only the sons of men.

9"Men cry out under a load of oppression;
      they plead for relief from the arm of the powerful.
10But no one says, 'Where is God my Maker,
      who gives songs in the night,
11who teaches more to us than toᶜ the beasts of the earth
      and makes us wiser thanᵈ the birds of the air?'
12He does not answer when men cry out
      because of the arrogance of the wicked.
13Indeed, God does not listen to their empty plea;
      the Almighty pays no attention to it.
14How much less, then, will he listen
      when you say that you do not see him,
    that your case is before him
      and you must wait for him,

ᵃ2 Or My righteousness is more than God's   ᵇ3 Or you   ᶜ11 Or teaches us by   ᵈ11 Or us wise by

¹⁵and further, that his anger never punishes
and he does not take the least notice of wickedness.ᵃ
¹⁶So Job opens his mouth with empty talk;
without knowledge he multiplies words."

36

Elihu continued:

²"Bear with me a little longer and I will show you
that there is more to be said in God's behalf.
³I get my knowledge from afar;
I will ascribe justice to my Maker.
⁴Be assured that my words are not false;
one perfect in knowledge is with you.

⁵"God is mighty, but does not despise men;
he is mighty, and firm in his purpose.
⁶He does not keep the wicked alive
but gives the afflicted their rights.
⁷He does not take his eyes off the righteous;
he enthrones them with kings
and exalts them forever.
⁸But if men are bound in chains,
held fast by cords of affliction,
⁹he tells them what they have done—
that they have sinned arrogantly.
¹⁰He makes them listen to correction
and commands them to repent of their evil.
¹¹If they obey and serve him,
they will spend the rest of their days in prosperity
and their years in contentment.
¹²But if they do not listen,
they will perish by the swordᵇ
and die without knowledge.

¹³"The godless in heart harbor resentment;
even when he fetters them, they do not cry for help.
¹⁴They die in their youth,
among male prostitutes of the shrines.
¹⁵But those who suffer he delivers in their suffering;
he speaks to them in their affliction.

¹⁶"He is wooing you from the jaws of distress
to a spacious place free from restriction,
to the comfort of your table laden with choice food.
¹⁷But now you are laden with the judgment due the wicked;
judgment and justice have taken hold of you.
¹⁸Be careful that no one entices you by riches;
do not let a large bribe turn you aside.
¹⁹Would your wealth
or even all your mighty efforts
sustain you so you would not be in distress?
²⁰Do not long for the night,

ᵃ15 Symmachus, Theodotion and Vulgate; the meaning of the Hebrew for this word is uncertain.   ᵇ12 Or *will cross the River*

to drag people away from their homes.[a]
²¹Beware of turning to evil,
    which you seem to prefer to affliction.

²²"God is exalted in his power.
    Who is a teacher like him?
²³Who has prescribed his ways for him,
    or said to him, 'You have done wrong'?
²⁴Remember to extol his work,
    which men have praised in song.
²⁵All mankind has seen it;
    men gaze on it from afar.
²⁶How great is God—beyond our understanding!
    The number of his years is past finding out.

²⁷"He draws up the drops of water,
    which distill as rain to the streams[b];
²⁸the clouds pour down their moisture
    and abundant showers fall on mankind.
²⁹Who can understand how he spreads out the clouds,
    how he thunders from his pavilion?
³⁰See how he scatters his lightning about him,
    bathing the depths of the sea.
³¹This is the way he governs[c] the nations
    and provides food in abundance.
³²He fills his hands with lightning
    and commands it to strike its mark.
³³His thunder announces the coming storm;
    even the cattle make known its approach.[d]

37 "At this my heart pounds
    and leaps from its place.
²Listen! Listen to the roar of his voice,
    to the rumbling that comes from his mouth.
³He unleashes his lightning beneath the whole heaven
    and sends it to the ends of the earth.
⁴After that comes the sound of his roar;
    he thunders with his majestic voice.
When his voice resounds,
    he holds nothing back.
⁵God's voice thunders in marvelous ways;
    he does great things beyond our understanding.
⁶He says to the snow, 'Fall on the earth,'
    and to the rain shower, 'Be a mighty downpour.'
⁷So that all men he has made may know his work,
    he stops every man from his labor.[e]
⁸The animals take cover;
    they remain in their dens.
⁹The tempest comes out from its chamber,
    the cold from the driving winds.
¹⁰The breath of God produces ice,
    and the broad waters become frozen.

---

a20 The meaning of the Hebrew for verses 18-20 is uncertain.   *b27* Or *distill from the mist as rain*   *c31* Or *nourishes*
d33 Or *announces his coming—/ the One zealous against evil*   *e7* Or / *he fills all men with fear by his power*

¹¹He loads the clouds with moisture;
    he scatters his lightning through them.
¹²At his direction they swirl around
    over the face of the whole earth
    to do whatever he commands them.
¹³He brings the clouds to punish men,
    or to water his earth*ᵃ* and show his love.

¹⁴"Listen to this, Job;
    stop and consider God's wonders.
¹⁵Do you know how God controls the clouds
    and makes his lightning flash?
¹⁶Do you know how the clouds hang poised,
    those wonders of him who is perfect in knowledge?
¹⁷You who swelter in your clothes
    when the land lies hushed under the south wind,
¹⁸can you join him in spreading out the skies,
    hard as a mirror of cast bronze?

¹⁹"Tell us what we should say to him;
    we cannot draw up our case because of our darkness.
²⁰Should he be told that I want to speak?
    Would any man ask to be swallowed up?
²¹Now no one can look at the sun,
    bright as it is in the skies
    after the wind has swept them clean.
²²Out of the north he comes in golden splendor;
    God comes in awesome majesty.
²³The Almighty is beyond our reach and exalted in power;
    in his justice and great righteousness, he does not oppress.
²⁴Therefore, men revere him,
    for does he not have regard for all the wise in heart?*ᵇ*"

The LORD Speaks

38 Then the LORD answered Job out of the storm. He said:

²"Who is this that darkens my counsel
    with words without knowledge?
³Brace yourself like a man;
    I will question you,
    and you shall answer me.

⁴"Where were you when I laid the earth's foundation?
    Tell me, if you understand.
⁵Who marked off its dimensions? Surely you know!
    Who stretched a measuring line across it?
⁶On what were its footings set,
    or who laid its cornerstone—
⁷while the morning stars sang together
    and all the angels*ᶜ* shouted for joy?

ᵃ 13 Or to favor them   *ᵇ 24 Or for he does not have regard for any who think they are wise.*   *ᶜ 7 Hebrew the sons of God*

⁸"Who shut up the sea behind doors
    when it burst forth from the womb,
⁹when I made the clouds its garment
    and wrapped it in thick darkness,
¹⁰when I fixed limits for it
    and set its doors and bars in place,
¹¹when I said, 'This far you may come and no farther;
    here is where your proud waves halt'?

¹²"Have you ever given orders to the morning,
    or shown the dawn its place,
¹³that it might take the earth by the edges
    and shake the wicked out of it?
¹⁴The earth takes shape like clay under a seal;
    its features stand out like those of a garment.
¹⁵The wicked are denied their light,
    and their upraised arm is broken.

¹⁶"Have you journeyed to the springs of the sea
    or walked in the recesses of the deep?
¹⁷Have the gates of death been shown to you?
    Have you seen the gates of the shadow of death^a?
¹⁸Have you comprehended the vast expanses of the earth?
    Tell me, if you know all this.

¹⁹"What is the way to the abode of light?
    And where does darkness reside?
²⁰Can you take them to their places?
    Do you know the paths to their dwellings?
²¹Surely you know, for you were already born!
    You have lived so many years!

┌──────────────────────────────────────┐
│ **DISCOVERING GOD**

38:4–7
Life with God

God does not mind our questions. He listens when we express our pain and confusion honestly. But we cross the line of appropriateness when we accuse God and believe things about him that are untrue.

That's what God is responding to as he begins his reply to Job. The ideas and theories expressed in the previous discussion have painted a distorted picture of who God is and how he works in the lives of his people. Here God helps Job understand that he works on a cosmic scale that we sometimes don't understand. In the process he provides the most beautiful and picturesque images of his own creative power to be found in the Bible (chapter 38, verse 4 through chapter 40, verse 2).

Throughout this book, Job maintains his innocence and righteousness and questions the suffering that he experiences. But, as Job discovers, a little humility goes a long way in the presence of the creator of the universe (see chapter 40, verses 4–5 [page 647] and chapter 42, verses 5–6 [page 649]).

The same holds true for us. When we wrestle with God, we need to remember who we're talking to.
└──────────────────────────────────────┘

---

²²"Have you entered the storehouses of the snow
    or seen the storehouses of the hail,
²³which I reserve for times of trouble,
    for days of war and battle?
²⁴What is the way to the place where the lightning is dispersed,
    or the place where the east winds are scattered over the earth?
²⁵Who cuts a channel for the torrents of rain,
    and a path for the thunderstorm,
²⁶to water a land where no man lives,

^a17 Or *gates of deep shadows*

a desert with no one in it,
27to satisfy a desolate wasteland
    and make it sprout with grass?
28Does the rain have a father?
    Who fathers the drops of dew?
29From whose womb comes the ice?
    Who gives birth to the frost from the heavens
30when the waters become hard as stone,
    when the surface of the deep is frozen?

31"Can you bind the beautiful*a* Pleiades?
    Can you loose the cords of Orion?
32Can you bring forth the constellations in their seasons*b*
    or lead out the Bear*c* with its cubs?
33Do you know the laws of the heavens?
    Can you set up ⌊God's*d*⌋ dominion over the earth?

34"Can you raise your voice to the clouds
    and cover yourself with a flood of water?
35Do you send the lightning bolts on their way?
    Do they report to you, 'Here we are'?
36Who endowed the heart*e* with wisdom
    or gave understanding to the mind*e*?
37Who has the wisdom to count the clouds?
    Who can tip over the water jars of the heavens
38when the dust becomes hard
    and the clods of earth stick together?

39"Do you hunt the prey for the lioness
    and satisfy the hunger of the lions
40when they crouch in their dens
    or lie in wait in a thicket?
41Who provides food for the raven
    when its young cry out to God
    and wander about for lack of food?

39 "Do you know when the mountain goats give birth?
    Do you watch when the doe bears her fawn?
2Do you count the months till they bear?
    Do you know the time they give birth?
3They crouch down and bring forth their young;
    their labor pains are ended.
4Their young thrive and grow strong in the wilds;
    they leave and do not return.

5"Who let the wild donkey go free?
    Who untied his ropes?
6I gave him the wasteland as his home,
    the salt flats as his habitat.
7He laughs at the commotion in the town;
    he does not hear a driver's shout.

a31 Or *the twinkling;* or *the chains of the their*   *b32* Or *the morning star in its season*   *c32* Or *out Leo*   *d33* Or *his;* or
e36 The meaning of the Hebrew for this word is uncertain.

⁸He ranges the hills for his pasture
and searches for any green thing.

⁹"Will the wild ox consent to serve you?
Will he stay by your manger at night?
¹⁰Can you hold him to the furrow with a harness?
Will he till the valleys behind you?
¹¹Will you rely on him for his great strength?
Will you leave your heavy work to him?
¹²Can you trust him to bring in your grain
and gather it to your threshing floor?

¹³"The wings of the ostrich flap joyfully,
but they cannot compare with the pinions and feathers of the
stork.   .
¹⁴She lays her eggs on the ground
and lets them warm in the sand,
¹⁵unmindful that a foot may crush them,
that some wild animal may trample them.
¹⁶She treats her young harshly, as if they were not hers;
she cares not that her labor was in vain,
¹⁷for God did not endow her with wisdom
or give her a share of good sense.
¹⁸Yet when she spreads her feathers to run,
she laughs at horse and rider.

¹⁹"Do you give the horse his strength
or clothe his neck with a flowing mane?
²⁰Do you make him leap like a locust,
striking terror with his proud snorting?
²¹He paws fiercely, rejoicing in his strength,
and charges into the fray.
²²He laughs at fear, afraid of nothing;
he does not shy away from the sword.
²³The quiver rattles against his side,
along with the flashing spear and lance.
²⁴In frenzied excitement he eats up the ground;
he cannot stand still when the trumpet sounds.
²⁵At the blast of the trumpet he snorts, 'Aha!'
He catches the scent of battle from afar,
the shout of commanders and the battle cry.

²⁶"Does the hawk take flight by your wisdom
and spread his wings toward the south?
²⁷Does the eagle soar at your command
and build his nest on high?
²⁸He dwells on a cliff and stays there at night;
a rocky crag is his stronghold.
²⁹From there he seeks out his food;
his eyes detect it from afar.
³⁰His young ones feast on blood,
and where the slain are, there is he."

40

The LORD said to Job:

2"Will the one who contends with the Almighty correct him?
  Let him who accuses God answer him!"

3Then Job answered the LORD:

4"I am unworthy—how can I reply to you?
  I put my hand over my mouth.
5I spoke once, but I have no answer—
  twice, but I will say no more."

6Then the LORD spoke to Job out of the storm:

7"Brace yourself like a man;
  I will question you,
  and you shall answer me.

8"Would you discredit my justice?
  Would you condemn me to justify yourself?
9Do you have an arm like God's,
  and can your voice thunder like his?
10Then adorn yourself with glory and splendor,
  and clothe yourself in honor and majesty.
11Unleash the fury of your wrath,
  look at every proud man and bring him low,
12look at every proud man and humble him,
  crush the wicked where they stand.
13Bury them all in the dust together;
  shroud their faces in the grave.
14Then I myself will admit to you
  that your own right hand can save you.

15"Look at the behemoth,ᵃ
  which I made along with you
  and which feeds on grass like an ox.
16What strength he has in his loins,
  what power in the muscles of his belly!
17His tailᵇ sways like a cedar;
  the sinews of his thighs are close-knit.
18His bones are tubes of bronze,
  his limbs like rods of iron.
19He ranks first among the works of God,
  yet his Maker can approach him with his sword.
20The hills bring him their produce,
  and all the wild animals play nearby.
21Under the lotus plants he lies,
  hidden among the reeds in the marsh.
22The lotuses conceal him in their shadow;
  the poplars by the stream surround him.
23When the river rages, he is not alarmed;
  he is secure, though the Jordan should surge against his mouth.
24Can anyone capture him by the eyes,ᶜ
  or trap him and pierce his nose?

ᵃ15 Possibly the hippopotamus or the elephant   ᵇ17 Possibly trunk   ᶜ24 Or by a water hole

41 "Can you pull in the leviathan[a] with a fishhook
or tie down his tongue with a rope?
²Can you put a cord through his nose
or pierce his jaw with a hook?
³Will he keep begging you for mercy?
Will he speak to you with gentle words?
⁴Will he make an agreement with you
for you to take him as your slave for life?
⁵Can you make a pet of him like a bird
or put him on a leash for your girls?
⁶Will traders barter for him?
Will they divide him up among the merchants?
⁷Can you fill his hide with harpoons
or his head with fishing spears?
⁸If you lay a hand on him,
you will remember the struggle and never do it again!
⁹Any hope of subduing him is false;
the mere sight of him is overpowering.
¹⁰No one is fierce enough to rouse him.
Who then is able to stand against me?
¹¹Who has a claim against me that I must pay?
Everything under heaven belongs to me.

¹²"I will not fail to speak of his limbs,
his strength and his graceful form.
¹³Who can strip off his outer coat?
Who would approach him with a bridle?
¹⁴Who dares open the doors of his mouth,
ringed about with his fearsome teeth?
¹⁵His back has[b] rows of shields
tightly sealed together;
¹⁶each is so close to the next
that no air can pass between.
¹⁷They are joined fast to one another;
they cling together and cannot be parted.
¹⁸His snorting throws out flashes of light;
his eyes are like the rays of dawn.
¹⁹Firebrands stream from his mouth;
sparks of fire shoot out.
²⁰Smoke pours from his nostrils
as from a boiling pot over a fire of reeds.
²¹His breath sets coals ablaze,
and flames dart from his mouth.
²²Strength resides in his neck;
dismay goes before him.
²³The folds of his flesh are tightly joined;
they are firm and immovable.
²⁴His chest is hard as rock,
hard as a lower millstone.
²⁵When he rises up, the mighty are terrified;
they retreat before his thrashing.
²⁶The sword that reaches him has no effect,

---

a 1 Possibly the crocodile   b 15 Or *His pride is his*

nor does the spear or the dart or the javelin.
27Iron he treats like straw
  and bronze like rotten wood.
28Arrows do not make him flee;
  slingstones are like chaff to him.
29A club seems to him but a piece of straw;
  he laughs at the rattling of the lance.
30His undersides are jagged potsherds,
  leaving a trail in the mud like a threshing sledge.
31He makes the depths churn like a boiling caldron
  and stirs up the sea like a pot of ointment.
32Behind him he leaves a glistening wake;
  one would think the deep had white hair.
33Nothing on earth is his equal—
  a creature without fear.
34He looks down on all that are haughty;
  he is king over all that are proud."

Job

42   Then Job replied to the LORD:

2"I know that you can do all things;
  no plan of yours can be thwarted.
3 You asked, 'Who is this that obscures my counsel without
        knowledge?'
  Surely I spoke of things I did not understand,
  things too wonderful for me to know.

4 "You said, 'Listen now, and I will speak;
  I will question you,
  and you shall answer me.'
5My ears had heard of you
  but now my eyes have seen you.
6Therefore I despise myself
  and repent in dust and ashes."

Epilogue

7After the LORD had said these things to Job, he said to Eliphaz the Temanite, "I am angry with you and your two friends, because you have not spoken of me what is right, as my servant Job has. 8So now take seven bulls and seven rams and go to my servant Job and sacrifice a burnt offering for yourselves. My servant Job will pray for you, and I will accept his prayer and not deal with you according to your folly. You have not spoken of me what is right, as my servant Job has." 9So Eliphaz the Temanite, Bildad the Shuhite and Zophar the Naamathite did what the LORD told them; and the LORD accepted Job's prayer.

10After Job had prayed for his friends, the LORD made him prosperous again and gave him twice as much as he had before. 11All his brothers and sisters and everyone who had known him before came and ate with him in his house. They comforted and consoled him over all the trouble the LORD had brought upon him, and each one gave him a piece of silver*a* and a gold ring.

12The LORD blessed the latter part of Job's life more than the first. He had fourteen thousand sheep, six thousand camels, a thousand yoke of oxen and a thousand donkeys.

---

a 11 Hebrew *him a kesitah*; a kesitah was a unit of money of unknown weight and value.

¹³And he also had seven sons and three daughters. ¹⁴The first daughter he named Jemimah, the second Keziah and the third Keren-Happuch. ¹⁵Nowhere in all the land were there found women as beautiful as Job's daughters, and their father granted them an inheritance along with their brothers.

¹⁶After this, Job lived a hundred and forty years; he saw his children and their children to the fourth generation. ¹⁷And so he died, old and full of years.

DISCOVERING GOD

42:7–17
Life with God

When God rebuked Job, his friends may have felt a bit smug. Ironically, however, they were more in error than Job was. Job may not have understood his suffering, but the friends made the more serious error of misunderstanding God. Only when Job prayed for them did God forgive them of their folly (verse 8).

Job found restoration from his suffering in three ways. First, while he was still in his pain with no relief in sight, Job made his peace with God (verse 6). He chose to place his absolute trust in God based on facts rather than on the emotions generated by his painful situation.

Second, Job prayed for his friends. He obeyed God and extended himself to help others even though he was hurting. In effect, he prayed for those who persecuted him—something Jesus taught us to do as well (see Matthew chapter 5, verse 44 [page 1264]). Through that outward focus, Job ended up helping himself.

Third, God chose to restore Job's family and fortunes (verses 12–17). This ending brings the story of Job full circle, giving us as modern-day readers some positive resolution to the questions that are raised throughout this book.

As you grapple further with the question of suffering in this world, remember the two principles laid out at the beginning of this book: First, *God allows evil but is not the author of it.* Second, *Satan is limited and restrained by God.* While we in this world still struggle with pain, we need to realize that the one who created us is good and that he is ready to help us when we turn to him. Like Job, we can experience God's peace and restoration in our lives.

I did not have the benefit of a strong Christian upbringing and had become an "agnostic"—as I used to coyly refer to myself—by age 14. I spent the next 15 years focusing on the hypocrisy of some of the more notorious so-called Christian leaders. Each new revelation of their impropriety helped me build my case against Christianity. I felt that I didn't want or need to be associated with a group of people who acted as they did. Through this time, I never stopped to see what Christianity was really all about. Then several friends of mine encouraged me to look a little deeper and investigate a personal relationship with Christ. I had a great deal of respect for these people, and felt the inclination to at least check it out.

One weekend while out of town on business, I attended a nondenominational service at the hotel in which I was staying. The service was actually geared toward seekers, and I felt as if the pastor was talking to me alone. He challenged those of us gathered there to ignore the actions of others and investigate Christianity for ourselves. When this pastor called to the front those who wanted to accept Christ as their personal Savior, I was too embarrassed to join the others. I chose instead to repeat the prayer from where I was seated.

Being a fairly analytical person, I felt it was important to learn about Christianity as soon as possible. I immediately purchased a Bible and started to study it. My wife and I also started to look for a church. It was important to me that the church we attended was Bible-based in order to avoid the interpretations of any self-serving religious figures. (At this point in my search I was very cynical.) Eventually we found the church where we're now attending, and through our pastor's teaching I've learned a lot about what God says in the Bible.

Since I have accepted Christ, things just seem to make a lot more sense. I once heard someone say that without Christ a person may experience periods of happiness, but that person will never know true joy. I believe that statement is true. I've also found it very comforting to turn my challenges over to the Lord, and can honestly say that he has given me clarity to deal with many of the problems I've faced. In addition, my relationship with my wife has improved tremendously during this period; that's a gift for which I will be forever grateful.

PSALMS

Introduction

THE BOTTOM LINE

Have you ever wondered what's the "right way" to talk with God? This book, the longest one in the Bible, contains 150 prayers to God in the form of songs. Interestingly, there is no one "formula" for these prayers—some are long, some are short; some sound formal, some conversational. And what a range of emotions! The writers rage against their enemies, lay their hearts out in sorrow for their sin, and shout their praises to God at the top of their lungs. What's the "right way" to pray? Apparently, it's the "real" way. Whatever our emotions—anger, doubt, fear, joy, frustration—God wants us to be honest, trusting that he'll be "big enough" to handle whatever we have to say.

CENTRAL IDEAS

- No matter what our concerns or joys, we can bring them all to God.
- God desires that we be completely honest when we pray to him.
- God enjoys our praise and worship
- The language of the Psalms is poetry—the expressive language of the heart.

OUTLINE

1. Book 1 (chs. 1–41)
2. Book 2 (chs. 42–72)
3. Book 3 (chs. 73–89)
4. Book 4 (chs. 90–106)
5. Book 5 (chs. 107–150)

TITLE

The title of this book comes from a Greek word that referred to songs that were accompanied by stringed instruments.

AUTHORS AND READERS

The Book of Psalms has several authors, most of which are named in the introductions to their works. About a third of the psalms are anonymous. These collected psalms were compiled to direct the worship of the Jewish people.

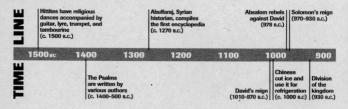

TIME LINE

Hittites have religious dances accompanied by guitar, lyre, trumpet, and tambourine (c. 1500 B.C.)

Abulfaraj, Syrian historian, compiles the first encyclopedia (c. 1270 B.C.)

Absalom rebels against David (978 B.C.)

Solomon's reign (970–930 B.C.)

| 1500 BC | 1400 | 1300 | 1200 | 1100 | 1000 | 900 |

The Psalms are written by various authors (c. 1400–500 B.C.)

David's reign (1010–970 B.C.)

Chinese cut ice and use it for refrigeration (c. 1000 B.C.)

Division of the kingdom (930 B.C.)

The songwriter Harold Arlen was riding in a New York taxicab several years ago when the cabby, who didn't know him, began whistling one of Arlen's most enduring tunes, "Stormy Weather." As the composer listened to the song, he couldn't resist speaking up.

"Do you know who wrote that song?" he asked the driver.

"Sure," the cabby answered, "Irving Berlin."

"Wrong," Arlen informed him, "but I'll give you two more guesses."

"Well, uh…," stammered the driver.

"How about Cole Porter?" Arlen prompted.

"Yeah! I was just going to say him."

"Wrong again," Arlen replied. After a pause he finally broke the silence. "*I* wrote 'Stormy Weather.' I'm Harold Arlen," he said proudly.

The cabby turned around for a closer look at his distinguished passenger. "Who?" he asked.

In these writings you will find joy, anger, fear, hate, sadness, and ecstasy.

We've all experienced moments when others have made us feel insignificant. At such times our credentials don't help. On other occasions we may feel insignificant because we don't think we've done anything important.

Problems occur when we let our significance be determined by what we've accomplished or by what others think of us. No matter what we've done, there will always be people who don't value us. But the God who made us also knows us and loves us deeply. We fare much better when we derive our significance from him, because that is how we were originally designed to function. And he is also quite ready to accept us, regardless of our emotional state.

One of the wonders of the book of Psalms is the wide range of feelings that inspired these 150 songs. In these writings you will find joy, anger, fear, hate, sadness, and ecstasy. God isn't upset by our need to openly express what we feel. The one thing these songs all have in common is that whatever the author felt, *he brought it to God.*

If you find it hard to think of God as someone who cares about you just as you are, this is the book for you. Especially if you feel undervalued, you will find great comfort in the writings of those who poured their hearts out to God and found him willing to listen. Turn to Psalm 139 (page 788), where you'll discover one picture of God's love for you.

PSALMS

BOOK I
Psalms 1–41

Psalm

¹Blessed is the man
who does not walk in the counsel of the wicked
or stand in the way of sinners
or sit in the seat of mockers.
²But his delight is in the law of the LORD,
and on his law he meditates day and night.
³He is like a tree planted by streams of water,
which yields its fruit in season
and whose leaf does not wither.
Whatever he does prospers.

⁴Not so the wicked!
They are like chaff
that the wind blows away.
⁵Therefore the wicked will not stand in the judgment,
nor sinners in the assembly of the righteous.

⁶For the LORD watches over the way of the righteous,
but the way of the wicked will perish.

Psalm

¹Why do the nations conspire*ᵃ*
and the peoples plot in vain?
²The kings of the earth take their stand
and the rulers gather together
against the LORD
and against his Anointed One.*ᵇ*
³"Let us break their chains," they say,
"and throw off their fetters."

⁴The One enthroned in heaven laughs;
the Lord scoffs at them.
⁵Then he rebukes them in his anger
and terrifies them in his wrath, saying,
⁶"I have installed my King*ᶜ*
on Zion, my holy hill."

ᵃ1 Hebrew; Septuagint *rage*   *ᵇ2* Or *anointed one*   *ᶜ6* Or *king*

⁷I will proclaim the decree of the Lord:

He said to me, "You are my Son*ᵃ*;
  today I have become your Father.*ᵇ*
⁸Ask of me,
  and I will make the nations your inheritance,
  the ends of the earth your possession.
⁹You will rule them with an iron scepter*ᶜ*;
  you will dash them to pieces like pottery."

¹⁰Therefore, you kings, be wise;
  be warned, you rulers of the earth.
¹¹Serve the Lord with fear
  and rejoice with trembling.
¹²Kiss the Son, lest he be angry
  and you be destroyed in
    your way,
for his wrath can flare up in a
    moment.
  Blessed are all who take
    refuge in him.

Psalm

A psalm of David. When he fled
from his son Absalom.

¹O Lord, how many are my foes!
  How many rise up against
    me!
²Many are saying of me,
  "God will not deliver him."
                    Selahᵈ

³But you are a shield around
    me, O Lord;
  you bestow glory on me and
    lift*ᵉ* up my head.
⁴To the Lord I cry aloud,
  and he answers me from his
    holy hill.

⁵I lie down and sleep;
  I wake again, because the Lord sustains me.
⁶I will not fear the tens of thousands
  drawn up against me on every side.

⁷Arise, O Lord!
  Deliver me, O my God!
Strike all my enemies on the jaw;
  break the teeth of the wicked.

                              Selah

ᵃ7 Or *son;* also in verse 12   ᵇ7 Or *have begotten you*   ᶜ9 Or *will break them with a rod of iron*   ᵈ2 A word of
uncertain meaning, occurring frequently in the Psalms; possibly a musical term   ᵉ3 Or *Lord, / my Glorious One, who lifts*

⁸From the LORD comes deliverance.
  May your blessing be on your people.   *Selah*

Psalm

For the director of music. With stringed instruments. A psalm of David.

¹Answer me when I call to you,
  O my righteous God.
 Give me relief from my distress;
  be merciful to me and hear my prayer.

²How long, O men, will you turn my glory into shame*ª*?
  How long will you love delusions and seek false gods*ᵇ*?   *Selah*
³Know that the LORD has set apart the godly for himself;
  the LORD will hear when I call to him.

⁴In your anger do not sin;
  when you are on your beds,
  search your hearts and be silent.   *Selah*
⁵Offer right sacrifices
  and trust in the LORD.

⁶Many are asking, "Who can show us any good?"
  Let the light of your face shine upon us, O LORD.
⁷You have filled my heart with greater joy
  than when their grain and new wine abound.
⁸I will lie down and sleep in peace,
  for you alone, O LORD,
  make me dwell in safety.

Psalm

For the director of music. For flutes. A psalm of David.

¹Give ear to my words, O LORD,
  consider my sighing.
²Listen to my cry for help,
  my King and my God,
  for to you I pray.
³In the morning, O LORD, you hear my voice;
  in the morning I lay my requests before you
  and wait in expectation.

⁴You are not a God who takes pleasure in evil;
  with you the wicked cannot dwell.
⁵The arrogant cannot stand in your presence;
  you hate all who do wrong.
⁶You destroy those who tell lies;
  bloodthirsty and deceitful men
  the LORD abhors.

ª2 Or you dishonor my Glorious One   *ᵇ2 Or seek lies*

7But I, by your great mercy,
   will come into your house;
in reverence will I bow down
   toward your holy temple.
8Lead me, O Lord, in your righteousness
   because of my enemies—
   make straight your way before me.

9Not a word from their mouth can be trusted;
   their heart is filled with destruction.
Their throat is an open grave;
   with their tongue they speak deceit.
10Declare them guilty, O God!
   Let their intrigues be their downfall.
Banish them for their many sins,
   for they have rebelled against you.

11But let all who take refuge in you be glad;
   let them ever sing for joy.
Spread your protection over them,
   that those who love your name may rejoice in you.
12For surely, O Lord, you bless the righteous;
   you surround them with your favor as with a shield.

Psalm

6

For the director of music. With stringed instruments. According to *sheminith.*ᵃ
A psalm of David.

1O Lord, do not rebuke me in your anger
   or discipline me in your wrath.
2Be merciful to me, Lord, for I am faint;
   O Lord, heal me, for my bones are in agony.
3My soul is in anguish.
   How long, O Lord, how long?

4Turn, O Lord, and deliver me;
   save me because of your unfailing love.
5No one remembers you when he is dead.
   Who praises you from the graveᵇ?

6I am worn out from groaning;
   all night long I flood my bed with weeping
   and drench my couch with tears.
7My eyes grow weak with sorrow;
   they fail because of all my foes.

8Away from me, all you who do evil,
   for the Lord has heard my weeping.
9The Lord has heard my cry for mercy;
   the Lord accepts my prayer.
10All my enemies will be ashamed and dismayed;
   they will turn back in sudden disgrace.

ᵃTitle: Probably a musical term   ᵇ5 Hebrew *Sheol*

Psalm

A *shiggaion*[a] of David, which he sang to the L ORD concerning Cush,
a Benjamite.

¹O L ORD my God, I take refuge in you;
  save and deliver me from all who pursue me,
²or they will tear me like a lion
  and rip me to pieces with no one to rescue me.

³O L ORD my God, if I have done this
  and there is guilt on my hands—
⁴if I have done evil to him who is at peace with me
  or without cause have robbed my foe—
⁵then let my enemy pursue and overtake me;
  let him trample my life to the ground
  and make me sleep in the dust.   *Selah*

⁶Arise, O L ORD, in your anger;
  rise up against the rage of my enemies.
  Awake, my God; decree justice.
⁷Let the assembled peoples gather around you.
  Rule over them from on high;
⁸ let the L ORD judge the peoples.
  Judge me, O L ORD, according to my righteousness,
  according to my integrity, O Most High.
⁹O righteous God,
  who searches minds and hearts,
  bring to an end the violence of the wicked
  and make the righteous secure.

¹⁰My shield[b] is God Most High,
  who saves the upright in heart.
¹¹God is a righteous judge,
  a God who expresses his wrath every day.
¹²If he does not relent,
  he[c] will sharpen his sword;
  he will bend and string his bow.
¹³He has prepared his deadly weapons;
  he makes ready his flaming arrows.

¹⁴He who is pregnant with evil
  and conceives trouble gives birth to disillusionment.
¹⁵He who digs a hole and scoops it out
  falls into the pit he has made.
¹⁶The trouble he causes recoils on himself;
  his violence comes down on his own head.

¹⁷I will give thanks to the L ORD because of his righteousness
  and will sing praise to the name of the L ORD Most High.

---

*a*Title: Probably a literary or musical term   *b 10* Or *sovereign*   *c 12* Or *If a man does not repent, / God*

Psalm

8

For the director of music. According to *gittith.ᵃ* A psalm of David.

¹O Lᴏʀᴅ, our Lord,
  how majestic is your name in all the earth!

You have set your glory
  above the heavens.
²From the lips of children and infants
  you have ordained praiseᵇ
because of your enemies,
  to silence the foe and the avenger.

³When I consider your heavens,
  the work of your fingers,
the moon and the stars,
  which you have set in place,
⁴what is man that you are
    mindful of him,
  the son of man that you care
    for him?
⁵You made him a little lower
    than the heavenly
    beingsᶜ
  and crowned him with glory
    and honor.

⁶You made him ruler over the
    works of your hands;
  you put everything under his
    feet:
⁷all flocks and herds,
  and the beasts of the field,
⁸the birds of the air,
  and the fish of the sea,
  all that swim the paths of the seas.

⁹O Lᴏʀᴅ, our Lord,
  how majestic is your name in all the earth!

> ▦▦▦▦▦ **DISCOVERING GOD** ▦▦▦▦▦
>
> **8:3–4**
> **Life with God**
>
> The dazzle of a starry night has set many a person to wondering about his or her place in the grand scheme of things. While God's great power and creativity can be seen in what he has made, even more remarkable is that small, seemingly insignificant beings like us matter so much to him.
>
> The consistent message of the Bible points to an awe-inspiring, majestic, creative God who is at the same time a caring Father. This wonder-filled God wants to have a close relationship with every one of his human creatures who will ask him to do so.

Psalmᵈ

9

For the director of music. To ˌthe tune ofˌ "The Death of the Son."
A psalm of David.

¹I will praise you, O Lᴏʀᴅ, with all my heart;
  I will tell of all your wonders.
²I will be glad and rejoice in you;
  I will sing praise to your name, O Most High.

ᵃTitle: Probably a musical term   ᵇ2 Or *strength*   ᶜ5 Or *than God*   ᵈPsalms 9 and 10 may have been originally a single acrostic poem, the stanzas of which begin with the successive letters of the Hebrew alphabet. In the Septuagint they constitute one psalm.

³My enemies turn back;
　　they stumble and perish before you.
⁴For you have upheld my right and my cause;
　　you have sat on your throne, judging righteously.
⁵You have rebuked the nations and destroyed the wicked;
　　you have blotted out their name for ever and ever.
⁶Endless ruin has overtaken the enemy,
　　you have uprooted their cities;
　　even the memory of them has perished.

⁷The LORD reigns forever;
　　he has established his throne for judgment.
⁸He will judge the world in righteousness;
　　he will govern the peoples with justice.
⁹The LORD is a refuge for the oppressed,
　　a stronghold in times of trouble.
¹⁰Those who know your name will trust in you,
　　for you, LORD, have never forsaken those who seek you.

¹¹Sing praises to the LORD, enthroned in Zion;
　　proclaim among the nations what he has done.
¹²For he who avenges blood remembers;
　　he does not ignore the cry of the afflicted.

¹³O LORD, see how my enemies persecute me!
　　Have mercy and lift me up from the gates of death,
¹⁴that I may declare your praises
　　in the gates of the Daughter of Zion
　　and there rejoice in your salvation.
¹⁵The nations have fallen into the pit they have dug;
　　their feet are caught in the net they have hidden.
¹⁶The LORD is known by his justice;
　　the wicked are ensnared by the work of their hands.　　　　*Higgaion.ᵃ Selah*
¹⁷The wicked return to the grave,ᵇ
　　all the nations that forget God.
¹⁸But the needy will not always be forgotten,
　　nor the hope of the afflicted ever perish.

¹⁹Arise, O LORD, let not man triumph;
　　let the nations be judged in your presence.
²⁰Strike them with terror, O LORD;
　　let the nations know they are but men.　　　　　　　　　　　　*Selah*

Psalmᶜ
10

¹Why, O LORD, do you stand far off?
　　Why do you hide yourself in times of trouble?

²In his arrogance the wicked man hunts down the weak,
　　who are caught in the schemes he devises.
³He boasts of the cravings of his heart;

ᵃ*16* Or *Meditation*; possibly a musical notation　　　ᵇ*17* Hebrew *Sheol*　　　ᶜPsalms 9 and 10 may have been originally a single acrostic poem, the stanzas of which begin with the successive letters of the Hebrew alphabet. In the Septuagint they constitute one psalm.

    he blesses the greedy and reviles the LORD.
4In his pride the wicked does not seek him;
    in all his thoughts there is no room for God.
5His ways are always prosperous;
    he is haughty and your laws are far from him;
    he sneers at all his enemies.
6He says to himself, "Nothing will shake me;
    I'll always be happy and never have trouble."
7His mouth is full of curses and lies and threats;
    trouble and evil are under his tongue.
8He lies in wait near the villages;
    from ambush he murders the innocent,
    watching in secret for his victims.
9He lies in wait like a lion in cover;
    he lies in wait to catch the helpless;
    he catches the helpless and drags them off in his net.
10His victims are crushed, they collapse;
    they fall under his strength.
11He says to himself, "God has forgotten;
    he covers his face and never sees."

12Arise, LORD! Lift up your hand, O God.
    Do not forget the helpless.
13Why does the wicked man revile God?
    Why does he say to himself,
    "He won't call me to account"?
14But you, O God, do see trouble and grief;
    you consider it to take it in hand.
  The victim commits himself to you;
    you are the helper of the fatherless.
15Break the arm of the wicked and evil man;
    call him to account for his wickedness
    that would not be found out.

16The LORD is King for ever and ever;
    the nations will perish from his land.
17You hear, O LORD, the desire of the afflicted;
    you encourage them, and you listen to their cry,
18defending the fatherless and the oppressed,
    in order that man, who is of the earth, may terrify no more.

Psalm

For the director of music. Of David.

1In the LORD I take refuge.
    How then can you say to me:
    "Flee like a bird to your mountain.
2For look, the wicked bend their bows;
    they set their arrows against the strings
  to shoot from the shadows
    at the upright in heart.

³When the foundations are being destroyed,
  what can the righteous do^a?"

⁴The LORD is in his holy temple;
  the LORD is on his heavenly throne.
 He observes the sons of men;
  his eyes examine them.
⁵The LORD examines the righteous,
  but the wicked^b and those who love violence
  his soul hates.
⁶On the wicked he will rain
  fiery coals and burning sulfur;
  a scorching wind will be their lot.

⁷For the LORD is righteous,
  he loves justice;
  upright men will see his face.

Psalm

For the director of music. According to *sheminith.*^c A psalm of David.

¹Help, LORD, for the godly are no more;
  the faithful have vanished from among men.
²Everyone lies to his neighbor;
  their flattering lips speak with deception.

³May the LORD cut off all flattering lips
  and every boastful tongue
⁴that says, "We will triumph with our tongues;
  we own our lips^d—who is our master?"

⁵"Because of the oppression of the weak
  and the groaning of the needy,
 I will now arise," says the LORD.
  "I will protect them from those who malign them."
⁶And the words of the LORD are flawless,
  like silver refined in a furnace of clay,
  purified seven times.

⁷O LORD, you will keep us safe
  and protect us from such people forever.
⁸The wicked freely strut about
  when what is vile is honored among men.

Psalm

For the director of music. A psalm of David.

¹How long, O LORD? Will you forget me forever?
  How long will you hide your face from me?

^a3 Or *what is the Righteous One doing*   ^b5 Or *The LORD, the Righteous One, examines the wicked. /*   ^cTitle: Probably a
musical term   ^d4 Or / *our lips are our plowshares*

2How long must I wrestle with my thoughts
  and every day have sorrow in my heart?
How long will my enemy triumph over me?

3Look on me and answer, O LORD my God.
  Give light to my eyes, or I will sleep in death;
4my enemy will say, "I have overcome him,"
  and my foes will rejoice when I fall.

5But I trust in your unfailing love;
  my heart rejoices in your salvation.
6I will sing to the LORD,
  for he has been good to me.

Psalm

14

For the director of music. Of David.

1The fool*a* says in his heart,
  "There is no God."
They are corrupt, their deeds are vile;
  there is no one who does good.

2The LORD looks down from
    heaven
  on the sons of men
to see if there are any who
    understand,
  any who seek God.
3All have turned aside,
  they have together become
    corrupt;
there is no one who does good,
  not even one.

4Will evildoers never learn—
  those who devour my people
    as men eat bread
  and who do not call on the
    LORD?
5There they are, overwhelmed
    with dread,
  for God is present in the
    company of the
    righteous.
6You evildoers frustrate the plans of the poor,
  but the LORD is their refuge.

7Oh, that salvation for Israel would come out of Zion!
  When the LORD restores the fortunes of his people,
  let Jacob rejoice and Israel be glad!

> ▣ ::::::::::::::: **KNOWING YOURSELF** ::::::::::::::: ⬆
>
> **14:1**
> **Sin**
>
> Believing or not believing in God is always an intellectual matter, right? Not according to this psalm.
>
> Sometimes not believing in God has more to do with matters of the will than with lack of evidence. In this passage, the "fool" is said to dismiss God—not because he or she doesn't have reasons for belief, but because acknowledging God would mean that he or she would have to change corrupt living patterns (example: verses 4 and 6).
>
> If you're a seeker, don't get trapped into thinking all your issues with God are limited to "head" matters. You may have a "heart" obstacle that's clouding your judgment and standing in the way of a rich, vital relationship with the God who loves you.

---

a 1 The Hebrew words rendered *fool* in Psalms denote one who is morally deficient.

Psalm

A psalm of David.

¹LORD, who may dwell in your sanctuary?
  Who may live on your holy hill?

²He whose walk is blameless
  and who does what is righteous,
who speaks the truth from his heart
³   and has no slander on his tongue,
who does his neighbor no wrong
  and casts no slur on his fellowman,
⁴who despises a vile man
  but honors those who fear the LORD,
who keeps his oath
  even when it hurts,
⁵who lends his money without usury
  and does not accept a bribe against the innocent.

He who does these things
  will never be shaken.

Psalm

A *miktam*ᵃ of David.

¹Keep me safe, O God,
  for in you I take refuge.

²I said to the LORD, "You are my Lord;
  apart from you I have no good thing."
³As for the saints who are in the land,
  they are the glorious ones in whom is all my delight.ᵇ
⁴The sorrows of those will increase
  who run after other gods.
 I will not pour out their libations of blood
  or take up their names on my lips.

⁵LORD, you have assigned me my portion and my cup;
  you have made my lot secure.
⁶The boundary lines have fallen for me in pleasant places;
  surely I have a delightful inheritance.

⁷I will praise the LORD, who counsels me;
  even at night my heart instructs me.
⁸I have set the LORD always before me.
  Because he is at my right hand,
  I will not be shaken.

⁹Therefore my heart is glad and my tongue rejoices;
  my body also will rest secure,

ᵃTitle: Probably a literary or musical term   ᵇ3 Or *As for the pagan priests who are in the land / and the nobles in whom all delight, I said:*

¹⁰because you will not abandon me to the grave,[a]
    nor will you let your Holy One[b] see decay.
¹¹You have made[c] known to me the path of life;
    you will fill me with joy in your presence,
    with eternal pleasures at your right hand.

Psalm

17

A prayer of David.

¹Hear, O LORD, my righteous plea;
    listen to my cry.
Give ear to my prayer—
    it does not rise from deceitful lips.
²May my vindication come from you;
    may your eyes see what is right.

³Though you probe my heart and examine me at night,
    though you test me, you will find nothing;
    I have resolved that my mouth will not sin.
⁴As for the deeds of men—
    by the word of your lips
I have kept myself
    from the ways of the violent.
⁵My steps have held to your paths;
    my feet have not slipped.

⁶I call on you, O God, for you will answer me;
    give ear to me and hear my prayer.
⁷Show the wonder of your great love,
    you who save by your right hand
    those who take refuge in you from their foes.
⁸Keep me as the apple of your eye;
    hide me in the shadow of your wings
⁹from the wicked who assail me,
    from my mortal enemies who surround me.

¹⁰They close up their callous hearts,
    and their mouths speak with arrogance.
¹¹They have tracked me down, they now surround me,
    with eyes alert, to throw me to the ground.
¹²They are like a lion hungry for prey,
    like a great lion crouching in cover.

¹³Rise up, O LORD, confront them, bring them down;
    rescue me from the wicked by your sword.
¹⁴O LORD, by your hand save me from such men,
    from men of this world whose reward is in this life.

You still the hunger of those you cherish;
    their sons have plenty,
    and they store up wealth for their children.

---

a 10 Hebrew *Sheol*   *b 10* Or *your faithful one*   *c 11* Or *You will make*

¹⁵And I—in righteousness I will see your face;
  when I awake, I will be satisfied with seeing your likeness.

Psalm

For the director of music. Of David the servant of the LORD. He sang to the LORD
the words of this song when the LORD delivered him from the hand of all his
enemies and from the hand of Saul. He said:

¹I love you, O LORD, my strength.

²The LORD is my rock, my fortress and my deliverer;
  my God is my rock, in whom I take refuge.
He is my shield and the horn*ᵃ* of my salvation, my stronghold.
³I call to the LORD, who is worthy of praise,
  and I am saved from my enemies.

⁴The cords of death entangled me;
  the torrents of destruction overwhelmed me.
⁵The cords of the grave*ᵇ* coiled around me;
  the snares of death confronted me.
⁶In my distress I called to the LORD;
  I cried to my God for help.
From his temple he heard my voice;
  my cry came before him, into his ears.

⁷The earth trembled and quaked,
  and the foundations of the mountains shook;
  they trembled because he was angry.
⁸Smoke rose from his nostrils;
  consuming fire came from his mouth,
  burning coals blazed out of it.
⁹He parted the heavens and came down;
  dark clouds were under his feet.
¹⁰He mounted the cherubim and flew;
  he soared on the wings of the wind.
¹¹He made darkness his covering, his canopy around him—
  the dark rain clouds of the sky.
¹²Out of the brightness of his presence clouds advanced,
  with hailstones and bolts of lightning.
¹³The LORD thundered from heaven;
  the voice of the Most High resounded.*ᶜ*
¹⁴He shot his arrows and scattered ⌊the enemies⌋,
  great bolts of lightning and routed them.
¹⁵The valleys of the sea were exposed
  and the foundations of the earth laid bare
at your rebuke, O LORD,
  at the blast of breath from your nostrils.

¹⁶He reached down from on high and took hold of me;
  he drew me out of deep waters.
¹⁷He rescued me from my powerful enemy,

ᵃ2 Horn here symbolizes strength.   *ᵇ5* Hebrew *Sheol*   *ᶜ13* Some Hebrew manuscripts and Septuagint (see also
2 Samuel 22:14); most Hebrew manuscripts *resounded, / amid hailstones and bolts of lightning*

from my foes, who were too strong for me.
¹⁸They confronted me in the day of my disaster,
  but the LORD was my support.
¹⁹He brought me out into a spacious place;
  he rescued me because he delighted in me.

²⁰The LORD has dealt with me according to my righteousness;
  according to the cleanness of my hands he has rewarded me.
²¹For I have kept the ways of the LORD;
  I have not done evil by turning from my God.
²²All his laws are before me;
  I have not turned away from his decrees.
²³I have been blameless before him
  and have kept myself from sin.
²⁴The LORD has rewarded me according to my righteousness,
  according to the cleanness of my hands in his sight.

²⁵To the faithful you show yourself faithful,
  to the blameless you show yourself blameless,
²⁶to the pure you show yourself pure,
  but to the crooked you show yourself shrewd.
²⁷You save the humble
  but bring low those whose eyes are haughty.
²⁸You, O LORD, keep my lamp burning;
  my God turns my darkness into light.
²⁹With your help I can advance against a troop ᵃ;
  with my God I can scale a wall.

³⁰As for God, his way is perfect;
  the word of the LORD is flawless.
 He is a shield
  for all who take refuge in him.
³¹For who is God besides the LORD?
  And who is the Rock except our God?
³²It is God who arms me with strength
  and makes my way perfect.
³³He makes my feet like the feet of a deer;
  he enables me to stand on the heights.
³⁴He trains my hands for battle;
  my arms can bend a bow of bronze.
³⁵You give me your shield of victory,
  and your right hand sustains me;
  you stoop down to make me great.
³⁶You broaden the path beneath me,
  so that my ankles do not turn.

³⁷I pursued my enemies and overtook them;
  I did not turn back till they were destroyed.
³⁸I crushed them so that they could not rise;
  they fell beneath my feet.
³⁹You armed me with strength for battle;
  you made my adversaries bow at my feet.
⁴⁰You made my enemies turn their backs in flight,

ᵃ 29 Or *can run through a barricade*

and I destroyed my foes.
⁴¹They cried for help, but there was no one to save them—
to the LORD, but he did not answer.
⁴²I beat them as fine as dust borne on the wind;
I poured them out like mud in the streets.

⁴³You have delivered me from the attacks of the people;
you have made me the head of nations;
people I did not know are subject to me.
⁴⁴As soon as they hear me, they obey me;
foreigners cringe before me.

DISCOVERING GOD

19:1–14
The God Who Is There

If you're a seeker, try this experiment. The next time you look up at a clear night sky, say to God, "If you're there, and if you created all of this, make yourself known to me." Don't expect a flash of lightning or a booming voice. But as you read through sections of this Bible, expect God to start getting through to you.

That's the twofold theme of this psalm: God sends his message through *creation* (verses 1–6) and through written *revelation* (verses 7–11); that is, the Bible you're holding in your hand.

---

⁴⁵They all lose heart;
they come trembling from their
strongholds.
⁴⁶The LORD lives! Praise be to my Rock!
Exalted be God my Savior!
⁴⁷He is the God who avenges me,
who subdues nations under me,
⁴⁸   who saves me from my enemies.
You exalted me above my foes;
from violent men you rescued me.
⁴⁹Therefore I will praise you among the
nations, O LORD;
I will sing praises to your name.
⁵⁰He gives his king great victories;
he shows unfailing kindness to his
anointed,
to David and his descendants
forever.

Psalm

19

For the director of music. A psalm of David.

¹The heavens declare the glory of God;
the skies proclaim the work of his hands.
²Day after day they pour forth speech;
night after night they display knowledge.
³There is no speech or language
where their voice is not heard.ᵃ
⁴Their voiceᵇ goes out into all the earth,
their words to the ends of the world.

In the heavens he has pitched a tent for the sun,
⁵   which is like a bridegroom coming forth from his pavilion,
like a champion rejoicing to run his course.
⁶It rises at one end of the heavens
and makes its circuit to the other;
nothing is hidden from its heat.

⁷The law of the LORD is perfect,

ᵃ3 Or They have no speech, there are no words; / no sound is heard from them   ᵇ4 Septuagint, Jerome and Syriac; Hebrew
line

reviving the soul.
The statutes of the Lord are trustworthy,
  making wise the simple.
8The precepts of the Lord are right,
  giving joy to the heart.
The commands of the Lord are radiant,
  giving light to the eyes.
9The fear of the Lord is pure,
  enduring forever.
The ordinances of the Lord are sure
  and altogether righteous.
10They are more precious than gold,
  than much pure gold;
they are sweeter than honey,
  than honey from the comb.
11By them is your servant warned;
  in keeping them there is great reward.

12Who can discern his errors?
  Forgive my hidden faults.
13Keep your servant also from willful sins;
  may they not rule over me.
Then will I be blameless,
  innocent of great transgression.

14May the words of my mouth and the meditation of my heart
  be pleasing in your sight,
  O Lord, my Rock and my Redeemer.

Psalm

20

For the director of music. A psalm of David.

1May the Lord answer you when you are in distress;
  may the name of the God of Jacob protect you.
2May he send you help from the sanctuary
  and grant you support from Zion.
3May he remember all your sacrifices
  and accept your burnt offerings.   *Selah*
4May he give you the desire of your heart
  and make all your plans succeed.
5We will shout for joy when you are victorious
  and will lift up our banners in the name of our God.
May the Lord grant all your requests.

6Now I know that the Lord saves his anointed;
  he answers him from his holy heaven
  with the saving power of his right hand.
7Some trust in chariots and some in horses,
  but we trust in the name of the Lord our God.
8They are brought to their knees and fall,
  but we rise up and stand firm.

⁹O Lᴏʀᴅ, save the king!
   Answer*a* us when we call!

Psalm

For the director of music. A psalm of David.

¹O Lᴏʀᴅ, the king rejoices in your strength.
   How great is his joy in the victories you give!
²You have granted him the desire of his heart
   and have not withheld the request of his lips.   *Selah*
³You welcomed him with rich blessings
   and placed a crown of pure gold on his head.
⁴He asked you for life, and you gave it to him—
   length of days, for ever and ever.
⁵Through the victories you gave, his glory is great;
   you have bestowed on him splendor and majesty.
⁶Surely you have granted him eternal blessings
   and made him glad with the joy of your presence.
⁷For the king trusts in the Lᴏʀᴅ;
   through the unfailing love of the Most High
   he will not be shaken.

⁸Your hand will lay hold on all your enemies;
   your right hand will seize your foes.
⁹At the time of your appearing
   you will make them like a fiery furnace.
 In his wrath the Lᴏʀᴅ will swallow them up,
   and his fire will consume them.
¹⁰You will destroy their descendants from the earth,
   their posterity from mankind.
¹¹Though they plot evil against you
   and devise wicked schemes, they cannot succeed;
¹²for you will make them turn their backs
   when you aim at them with drawn bow.

¹³Be exalted, O Lᴏʀᴅ, in your strength;
   we will sing and praise your might.

Psalm

For the director of music. To ⌊the tune of⌋ "The Doe of the Morning." A psalm
of David.

¹My God, my God, why have you forsaken me?
   Why are you so far from saving me,
   so far from the words of my groaning?
²O my God, I cry out by day, but you do not answer,
   by night, and am not silent.

³Yet you are enthroned as the Holy One;

---
a9 Or save! / O King, answer

you are the praise of Israel. [a]

⁴In you our fathers put their trust;
　　they trusted and you delivered them.
⁵They cried to you and were saved;
　　in you they trusted and were not disappointed.

⁶But I am a worm and not a man,
　　scorned by men and despised by the people.
⁷All who see me mock me;
　　they hurl insults, shaking their heads:
⁸"He trusts in the LORD;
　　let the LORD rescue him.
　Let him deliver him,
　　since he delights in him."

⁹Yet you brought me out of the womb;
　　you made me trust in you
　　even at my mother's breast.
¹⁰From birth I was cast upon you;
　　from my mother's womb you have been my God.
¹¹Do not be far from me,
　　for trouble is near
　　and there is no one to help.

¹²Many bulls surround me;
　　strong bulls of Bashan encircle me.

a 3 Or Yet you are holy, / enthroned on the praises of Israel

---

▣ ⦂⦂⦂⦂⦂⦂⦂⦂⦂⦂⦂⦂⦂⦂⦂⦂⦂⦂⦂⦂⦂⦂⦂ REASONS TO BELIEVE ⦂⦂⦂⦂⦂⦂⦂⦂⦂⦂⦂⦂⦂⦂⦂⦂⦂⦂⦂⦂⦂⦂⦂ ⊠

22:1–31
The Amazing Bible

Fulfilled prophecy is one of the most stunning features of the Bible, one that sets it apart from all
the other "holy books" in the world.

　　Consider the prophecies found just in this psalm. Hundreds of years before the Romans came
to power, David prophesied that the Jewish Messiah would be crucified (crucifixion as a state punishment hadn't even been invented yet!). The details he included were nothing short of amazing.
Check the following out for yourself:

Prophecy	Fulfillment
• Messiah would be forsaken (verse 1)	Matthew 27:46 (page 1300)
• The Messiah would cry out in darkness (verse 2)	Matthew 27:45–46 (page 1300)
• The Messiah would be mocked (verses 6–8)	Matthew 27:39–40, 43–44 (page 1300)
• The Messiah would be "poured out like water" (verse 14)	John 19:34 (page 1415)
• The Messiah would be thirsty (verse 15)	John 19:28 (page 1415)
• The Messiah would be crucified by non-Jews ("dogs") (verse 16)	Matthew 27:27–31,35–36 (page 1299)
• The Messiah's hands and feet would be pierced (verse 16)	John 19:18; 20:25–29 (page 1415)
• The Messiah's executioners would gamble for his robe (verse 18)	Matthew 27:35 (page 1300)

　　God made sure that future seekers could look at Jesus and know for sure that he is the One
they're looking for.

¹³Roaring lions tearing their prey
    open their mouths wide against me.
¹⁴I am poured out like water,
    and all my bones are out of joint.
My heart has turned to wax;
    it has melted away within me.
¹⁵My strength is dried up like a potsherd,
    and my tongue sticks to the roof of my mouth;
    you lay me*ᵃ* in the dust of death.
¹⁶Dogs have surrounded me;
    a band of evil men has encircled me,
    they have pierced*ᵇ* my hands and my feet.
¹⁷I can count all my bones;
    people stare and gloat over me.
¹⁸They divide my garments among them
    and cast lots for my clothing.

¹⁹But you, O LORD, be not far off;
    O my Strength, come quickly to help me.
²⁰Deliver my life from the sword,
    my precious life from the power of the dogs.
²¹Rescue me from the mouth of the lions;
    save*ᶜ* me from the horns of the wild oxen.

²²I will declare your name to my brothers;
    in the congregation I will praise you.
²³You who fear the LORD, praise him!
    All you descendants of Jacob, honor him!
    Revere him, all you descendants of Israel!
²⁴For he has not despised or disdained
    the suffering of the afflicted one;
he has not hidden his face from him
    but has listened to his cry for help.

²⁵From you comes the theme of my praise in the great assembly;
    before those who fear you*ᵈ* will I fulfill my vows.
²⁶The poor will eat and be satisfied;
    they who seek the LORD will praise him—
    may your hearts live forever!
²⁷All the ends of the earth
    will remember and turn to the LORD,
and all the families of the nations
    will bow down before him,
²⁸for dominion belongs to the LORD
    and he rules over the nations.

²⁹All the rich of the earth will feast and worship;
    all who go down to the dust will kneel before him—
    those who cannot keep themselves alive.
³⁰Posterity will serve him;
    future generations will be told about the Lord.
³¹They will proclaim his righteousness

ᵃ15 Or */ I am laid*   *ᵇ16* Some Hebrew manuscripts, Septuagint and Syriac; most Hebrew manuscripts */ like the lion,*
ᶜ21 Or */ you have heard*   *ᵈ25* Hebrew *him*

to a people yet unborn—
for he has done it.

Psalm

A psalm of David.

¹The LORD is my shepherd, I shall not be in want.
² He makes me lie down in green pastures,
he leads me beside quiet waters,
³ he restores my soul.
He guides me in paths of righteousness
for his name's sake.
⁴Even though I walk
through the valley of the shadow of death,ᵃ
I will fear no evil,
for you are with me;
your rod and your staff,
they comfort me.

⁵You prepare a table before me
in the presence of my
enemies.
You anoint my head with oil;
my cup overflows.
⁶Surely goodness and love will
follow me
all the days of my life,
and I will dwell in the house
of the LORD
forever.

┌─────────────────────────────────────┐
│ ▦ ▦▦▦▦▦ **DISCOVERING GOD** ▦▦▦▦▦ ⮐ │
│   │
│ **23:1–6**   │
│ **Life with God**   │
│   │
│ This is the most famous psalm in all │
│ the Bible. As you read it, can you   │
│ spot the reason for its popularity?   │
│   Actually, it isn't hard to see.   │
│ This refreshing picture of a caring   │
│ shepherd is an unforgettable image   │
│ of God. Compared to the angry,   │
│ unforgiving figure many of us have   │
│ imagined him to be, wouldn't you   │
│ rather live in *this* God's house   │
│ forever (verse 6)?   │
└─────────────────────────────────────┘

Psalm

Of David. A psalm.

¹The earth is the LORD's, and everything in it,
the world, and all who live in it;
²for he founded it upon the seas
and established it upon the waters.

³Who may ascend the hill of the LORD?
Who may stand in his holy place?
⁴He who has clean hands and a pure heart,
who does not lift up his soul to an idol
or swear by what is false.ᵇ
⁵He will receive blessing from the LORD
and vindication from God his Savior.
⁶Such is the generation of those who seek him,
who seek your face, O God of Jacob.ᶜ

Selah

ᵃ4 Or *through the darkest valley*   ᵇ4 Or *swear falsely*   ᶜ6 Two Hebrew manuscripts and Syriac (see also Septuagint);
most Hebrew manuscripts *face, Jacob*

⁷Lift up your heads, O you gates;
    be lifted up, you ancient doors,
    that the King of glory may come in.
⁸Who is this King of glory?
    The Lord strong and mighty,
    the Lord mighty in battle.
⁹Lift up your heads, O you gates;
    lift them up, you ancient doors,
    that the King of glory may come in.
¹⁰Who is he, this King of glory?
    The Lord Almighty—
    he is the King of glory.

Selah

Psalm[a]

25

Of David.

¹To you, O Lord, I lift up my soul;
²   in you I trust, O my God.
 Do not let me be put to shame,
    nor let my enemies triumph over me.
³No one whose hope is in you
    will ever be put to shame,
 but they will be put to shame
    who are treacherous without excuse.

⁴Show me your ways, O Lord,
    teach me your paths;
⁵guide me in your truth and teach me,
    for you are God my Savior,
    and my hope is in you all day long.
⁶Remember, O Lord, your great mercy and love,
    for they are from of old.
⁷Remember not the sins of my youth
    and my rebellious ways;
 according to your love remember me,
    for you are good, O Lord.

⁸Good and upright is the Lord;
    therefore he instructs sinners in his ways.
⁹He guides the humble in what is right
    and teaches them his way.
¹⁰All the ways of the Lord are loving and faithful
    for those who keep the demands of his covenant.
¹¹For the sake of your name, O Lord,
    forgive my iniquity, though it is great.
¹²Who, then, is the man that fears the Lord?
    He will instruct him in the way chosen for him.
¹³He will spend his days in prosperity,
    and his descendants will inherit the land.
¹⁴The Lord confides in those who fear him;
    he makes his covenant known to them.

---

[a]This psalm is an acrostic poem, the verses of which begin with the successive letters of the Hebrew alphabet.

¹⁵My eyes are ever on the LORD,
　　for only he will release my feet from the snare.

¹⁶Turn to me and be gracious to me,
　　for I am lonely and afflicted.
¹⁷The troubles of my heart have multiplied;
　　free me from my anguish.
¹⁸Look upon my affliction and my distress
　　and take away all my sins.
¹⁹See how my enemies have increased
　　and how fiercely they hate me!
²⁰Guard my life and rescue me;
　　let me not be put to shame,
　　for I take refuge in you.
²¹May integrity and uprightness protect me,
　　because my hope is in you.

²²Redeem Israel, O God,
　　from all their troubles!

Psalm

26

Of David.

¹Vindicate me, O LORD,
　　for I have led a blameless life;
　I have trusted in the LORD
　　without wavering.
²Test me, O LORD, and try me,
　　examine my heart and my mind;
³for your love is ever before me,
　　and I walk continually in your truth.
⁴I do not sit with deceitful men,
　　nor do I consort with hypocrites;
⁵I abhor the assembly of evildoers
　　and refuse to sit with the wicked.
⁶I wash my hands in innocence,
　　and go about your altar, O LORD,
⁷proclaiming aloud your praise
　　and telling of all your wonderful deeds.
⁸I love the house where you live, O LORD,
　　the place where your glory dwells.

⁹Do not take away my soul along with sinners,
　　my life with bloodthirsty men,
¹⁰in whose hands are wicked schemes,
　　whose right hands are full of bribes.
¹¹But I lead a blameless life;
　　redeem me and be merciful to me.

¹²My feet stand on level ground;
　　in the great assembly I will praise the LORD.

Psalm

Of David.

¹The Lord is my light and my salvation—
  whom shall I fear?
The Lord is the stronghold of my life—
  of whom shall I be afraid?
²When evil men advance against me
  to devour my flesh,ᵃ
when my enemies and my foes attack me,
  they will stumble and fall.
³Though an army besiege me,
  my heart will not fear;
though war break out against me,
  even then will I be confident.

⁴One thing I ask of the Lord,
  this is what I seek:
that I may dwell in the house of the Lord
  all the days of my life,
to gaze upon the beauty of the Lord
  and to seek him in his temple.
⁵For in the day of trouble
  he will keep me safe in his dwelling;
he will hide me in the shelter of his tabernacle
  and set me high upon a rock.
⁶Then my head will be exalted
  above the enemies who surround me;
at his tabernacle will I sacrifice with shouts of joy;
  I will sing and make music to the Lord.

⁷Hear my voice when I call, O Lord;
  be merciful to me and answer me.
⁸My heart says of you, "Seek hisᵇ face!"
  Your face, Lord, I will seek.
⁹Do not hide your face from me,
  do not turn your servant away in anger;
  you have been my helper.
Do not reject me or forsake me,
  O God my Savior.
¹⁰Though my father and mother forsake me,
  the Lord will receive me.
¹¹Teach me your way, O Lord;
  lead me in a straight path
  because of my oppressors.
¹²Do not turn me over to the desire of my foes,
  for false witnesses rise up against me,
  breathing out violence.

¹³I am still confident of this:
  I will see the goodness of the Lord

ᵃ2 Or to slander me   ᵇ8 Or To you, O my heart, he has said, "Seek my

in the land of the living.
¹⁴Wait for the LORD;
  be strong and take heart
  and wait for the LORD.

Psalm

Of David.

¹To you I call, O LORD my Rock;
  do not turn a deaf ear to me.
 For if you remain silent,
  I will be like those who have gone down to the pit.
²Hear my cry for mercy
  as I call to you for help,
 as I lift up my hands
  toward your Most Holy Place.

³Do not drag me away with the wicked,
  with those who do evil,
 who speak cordially with their neighbors
  but harbor malice in their hearts.
⁴Repay them for their deeds
  and for their evil work;
 repay them for what their hands have done
  and bring back upon them what they deserve.
⁵Since they show no regard for the works of the LORD
  and what his hands have done,
 he will tear them down
  and never build them up again.

⁶Praise be to the LORD,
  for he has heard my cry for mercy.
⁷The LORD is my strength and my shield;
  my heart trusts in him, and I am helped.
 My heart leaps for joy
  and I will give thanks to him in song.

⁸The LORD is the strength of his people,
  a fortress of salvation for his anointed one.
⁹Save your people and bless your inheritance;
  be their shepherd and carry them forever.

Psalm

A psalm of David.

¹Ascribe to the LORD, O mighty ones,
  ascribe to the LORD glory and strength.
²Ascribe to the LORD the glory due his name;
  worship the LORD in the splendor of his*a* holiness.

a2 Or LORD with the splendor of

³The voice of the Lord is over the waters;
　　the God of glory thunders,
　　the Lord thunders over the mighty waters.
⁴The voice of the Lord is powerful;
　　the voice of the Lord is majestic.
⁵The voice of the Lord breaks the cedars;
　　the Lord breaks in pieces the cedars of Lebanon.
⁶He makes Lebanon skip like a calf,
　　Sirion *ᵃ* like a young wild ox.
⁷The voice of the Lord strikes
　　with flashes of lightning.
⁸The voice of the Lord shakes the desert;
　　the Lord shakes the Desert of Kadesh.
⁹The voice of the Lord twists the oaks *ᵇ*
　　and strips the forests bare.
And in his temple all cry, "Glory!"

¹⁰The Lord sits *ᶜ* enthroned over the flood;
　　the Lord is enthroned as King forever.
¹¹The Lord gives strength to his people;
　　the Lord blesses his people with peace.

Psalm

30

A psalm. A song. For the dedication of the temple. *ᵈ* Of David.

¹I will exalt you, O Lord,
　　for you lifted me out of the depths
　　and did not let my enemies gloat over me.
²O Lord my God, I called to you for help
　　and you healed me.
³O Lord, you brought me up from the grave *ᵉ*;
　　you spared me from going down into the pit.

⁴Sing to the Lord, you saints of his;
　　praise his holy name.
⁵For his anger lasts only a moment,
　　but his favor lasts a lifetime;
weeping may remain for a night,
　　but rejoicing comes in the morning.

⁶When I felt secure, I said,
　　"I will never be shaken."
⁷O Lord, when you favored me,
　　you made my mountain *ᶠ* stand firm;
but when you hid your face,
　　I was dismayed.

⁸To you, O Lord, I called;
　　to the Lord I cried for mercy:
⁹"What gain is there in my destruction, *ᵍ*
　　in my going down into the pit?

ᵃ6 That is, Mount Hermon　　*ᵇ9* Or *Lord makes the deer give birth*　　*ᶜ10* Or *sat*　　*ᵈTitle:* Or *palace*　　*ᵉ3* Hebrew
Sheol　　*ᶠ7* Or *hill country*　　*ᵍ9* Or *there if I am silenced*

Will the dust praise you?
   Will it proclaim your faithfulness?
¹⁰Hear, O L<small>ORD</small>, and be merciful to me;
   O L<small>ORD</small>, be my help."

¹¹You turned my wailing into dancing;
   you removed my sackcloth and clothed me with joy,
¹²that my heart may sing to you and not be silent.
   O L<small>ORD</small> my God, I will give you thanks forever.

Psalm 31

For the director of music. A psalm of David.

¹In you, O L<small>ORD</small>, I have taken refuge;
   let me never be put to shame;
   deliver me in your righteousness.
²Turn your ear to me,
   come quickly to my rescue;
   be my rock of refuge,
   a strong fortress to save me.
³Since you are my rock and my
      fortress,
   for the sake of your name
      lead and guide me.
⁴Free me from the trap that is
      set for me,
   for you are my refuge.
⁵Into your hands I commit my
      spirit;
   redeem me, O L<small>ORD</small>, the God
      of truth.

⁶I hate those who cling to
      worthless idols;
   I trust in the L<small>ORD</small>.
⁷I will be glad and rejoice in
      your love,
   for you saw my affliction
   and knew the anguish of my
      soul.
⁸You have not handed me over
      to the enemy
   but have set my feet in a
      spacious place.

⁹Be merciful to me, O L<small>ORD</small>, for I am in distress;
   my eyes grow weak with sorrow,
   my soul and my body with grief.
¹⁰My life is consumed by anguish
   and my years by groaning;

▣ ▦▦▦▦▦ KNOWING YOURSELF ▦▦▦▦▦ ⬦

30:5
Emotions

God has designed human beings to experience a wide range of emotions. This psalm's author, Israel's King David, describes several emotional states, all centering around his relationship with God.

David's honesty in this psalm is a good example for all of us to follow. He describes times in his life where he felt that God had "hid [his] face" (verse 7), times when David felt abandoned. During such times David cried out in desperation and frustration, asking God for mercy, comfort and restoration.

That kind of honesty is the key to processing our feelings toward God. We shouldn't deny our emotions (either positive or negative!) or let them rule over us and cloud our perception of God. God wants us to express our emotions honestly before him. He is perfectly capable of handling anything we need to say.

my strength fails because of my affliction,[a]
and my bones grow weak.
¹¹Because of all my enemies,
I am the utter contempt of my neighbors;
I am a dread to my friends—
those who see me on the street flee from me.
¹²I am forgotten by them as though I were dead;
I have become like broken pottery.
¹³For I hear the slander of many;
there is terror on every side;
they conspire against me
and plot to take my life.

¹⁴But I trust in you, O LORD;
I say, "You are my God."
¹⁵My times are in your hands;
deliver me from my enemies
and from those who pursue me.
¹⁶Let your face shine on your servant;
save me in your unfailing love.
¹⁷Let me not be put to shame, O LORD,
for I have cried out to you;
but let the wicked be put to shame
and lie silent in the grave.[b]
¹⁸Let their lying lips be silenced,
for with pride and contempt
they speak arrogantly against the righteous.

¹⁹How great is your goodness,
which you have stored up for those who fear you,
which you bestow in the sight of men
on those who take refuge in you.
²⁰In the shelter of your presence you hide them
from the intrigues of men;
in your dwelling you keep them safe
from accusing tongues.

²¹Praise be to the LORD,
for he showed his wonderful love to me
when I was in a besieged city.
²²In my alarm I said,
"I am cut off from your sight!"
Yet you heard my cry for mercy
when I called to you for help.

²³Love the LORD, all his saints!
The LORD preserves the faithful,
but the proud he pays back in full.
²⁴Be strong and take heart,
all you who hope in the LORD.

---

a 10 Or *guilt*   *b* 17 Hebrew *Sheol*

Psalm

Of David. A *maskil.*[a]

¹Blessed is he
　whose transgressions are forgiven,
　whose sins are covered.
²Blessed is the man
　whose sin the LORD does not count against him
　and in whose spirit is no deceit.

³When I kept silent,
　my bones wasted away
　through my groaning all day
　　long.
⁴For day and night
　your hand was heavy upon
　　me;
　my strength was sapped
　as in the heat of summer.
　　　　　　　　　　　　Selah
⁵Then I acknowledged my sin
　　to you
　and did not cover up my
　　iniquity.
　I said, "I will confess
　my transgressions to the
　　LORD"—
　and you forgave
　the guilt of my sin.　*Selah*

⁶Therefore let everyone who is
　　godly pray to you
　while you may be found;
　surely when the mighty
　　waters rise,
　they will not reach him.
⁷You are my hiding place;
　you will protect me from
　　trouble
　and surround me with songs of deliverance.　*Selah*

⁸I will instruct you and teach you in the way you should go;
　I will counsel you and watch over you.
⁹Do not be like the horse or the mule,
　which have no understanding
　but must be controlled by bit and bridle
　or they will not come to you.
¹⁰Many are the woes of the wicked,
　but the LORD's unfailing love
　surrounds the man who trusts in him.

KNOWING YOURSELF

32:3–5
Sin

Perhaps you've heard the old adage "Confession is good for the soul." But unrecognized guilt can have real physical consequences as well. David, the writer of this psalm, gives evidence to that fact. That's one reason why God doesn't want us walking around with a load of guilt.

God has provided a way out from under the weight of guilt. That way begins with basic acknowledgment, continues with confession and remorse, and ends with accepting his forgiveness. He wants us to recognize that we've done wrong and tell him about it. Because he already knows our thoughts and actions, we shouldn't expect that he'll be shocked.

Do you know what forgiveness feels like? Have you ever experienced it? Why not agree with God about your sin? Go ahead and let him know what you've been trying to hide. He has promised to provide a safe place for you to get it all out in the open—and to get rid of it. That's when you'll experience the same kind of relief that David felt.

ᵃTitle: Probably a literary or musical term

¹¹Rejoice in the LORD and be glad, you righteous;
  sing, all you who are upright in heart!

Psalm

33

¹Sing joyfully to the LORD, you righteous;
  it is fitting for the upright to praise him.
²Praise the LORD with the harp;
  make music to him on the ten-stringed lyre.
³Sing to him a new song;
  play skillfully, and shout for joy.

⁴For the word of the LORD is right and true;
  he is faithful in all he does.
⁵The LORD loves righteousness and justice;
  the earth is full of his unfailing love.

⁶By the word of the LORD were the heavens made,
  their starry host by the breath of his mouth.
⁷He gathers the waters of the sea into jars*a*;
  he puts the deep into storehouses.
⁸Let all the earth fear the LORD;
  let all the people of the world revere him.
⁹For he spoke, and it came to be;
  he commanded, and it stood firm.
¹⁰The LORD foils the plans of the nations;
  he thwarts the purposes of the peoples.
¹¹But the plans of the LORD stand firm forever,
  the purposes of his heart through all generations.

¹²Blessed is the nation whose God is the LORD,
  the people he chose for his inheritance.
¹³From heaven the LORD looks down
  and sees all mankind;
¹⁴from his dwelling place he watches
  all who live on earth—
¹⁵he who forms the hearts of all,
  who considers everything they do.
¹⁶No king is saved by the size of his army;
  no warrior escapes by his great strength.
¹⁷A horse is a vain hope for deliverance;
  despite all its great strength it cannot save.
¹⁸But the eyes of the LORD are on those who fear him,
  on those whose hope is in his unfailing love,
¹⁹to deliver them from death
  and keep them alive in famine.

²⁰We wait in hope for the LORD;
  he is our help and our shield.
²¹In him our hearts rejoice,
  for we trust in his holy name.

a 7 Or *sea as into a heap*

²²May your unfailing love rest upon us, O LORD,
  even as we put our hope in you.

Psalm *a*

Of David. When he pretended to be insane before Abimelech, who drove him
away, and he left.

¹I will extol the LORD at all times;
  his praise will always be on my lips.
²My soul will boast in the LORD;
  let the afflicted hear and rejoice.
³Glorify the LORD with me;
  let us exalt his name together.

⁴I sought the LORD, and he answered me;
  he delivered me from all my fears.
⁵Those who look to him are radiant;
  their faces are never covered with shame.
⁶This poor man called, and the LORD heard him;
  he saved him out of all his troubles.
⁷The angel of the LORD encamps around those who fear him,
  and he delivers them.

⁸Taste and see that the LORD is good;
  blessed is the man who takes refuge in him.
⁹Fear the LORD, you his saints,
  for those who fear him lack nothing.
¹⁰The lions may grow weak and hungry,
  but those who seek the LORD lack no good thing.

¹¹Come, my children, listen to me;
  I will teach you the fear of the LORD.
¹²Whoever of you loves life
  and desires to see many good days,
¹³keep your tongue from evil
  and your lips from speaking lies.
¹⁴Turn from evil and do good;
  seek peace and pursue it.

¹⁵The eyes of the LORD are on the righteous
  and his ears are attentive to their cry;
¹⁶the face of the LORD is against those who do evil,
  to cut off the memory of them from the earth.

¹⁷The righteous cry out, and the LORD hears them;
  he delivers them from all their troubles.
¹⁸The LORD is close to the brokenhearted
  and saves those who are crushed in spirit.

¹⁹A righteous man may have many troubles,
  but the LORD delivers him from them all;
²⁰he protects all his bones,
  not one of them will be broken.

*a*This psalm is an acrostic poem, the verses of which begin with the successive letters of the Hebrew alphabet.

²¹Evil will slay the wicked;
    the foes of the righteous will be condemned.
²²The Lᴏʀᴅ redeems his servants;
    no one will be condemned who takes refuge in him.

Psalm

35

Of David.

¹Contend, O Lᴏʀᴅ, with those who contend with me;
    fight against those who fight against me.
²Take up shield and buckler;
    arise and come to my aid.
³Brandish spear and javelin*ᵃ*
    against those who pursue me.
  Say to my soul,
    "I am your salvation."

⁴May those who seek my life
    be disgraced and put to shame;
  may those who plot my ruin
    be turned back in dismay.
⁵May they be like chaff before the wind,
    with the angel of the Lᴏʀᴅ driving them away;
⁶may their path be dark and slippery,
    with the angel of the Lᴏʀᴅ pursuing them.
⁷Since they hid their net for me without cause
    and without cause dug a pit for me,
⁸may ruin overtake them by surprise—
    may the net they hid entangle them,
    may they fall into the pit, to their ruin.
⁹Then my soul will rejoice in the Lᴏʀᴅ
    and delight in his salvation.
¹⁰My whole being will exclaim,
    "Who is like you, O Lᴏʀᴅ?
  You rescue the poor from those too strong for them,
    the poor and needy from those who rob them."

¹¹Ruthless witnesses come forward;
    they question me on things I know nothing about.
¹²They repay me evil for good
    and leave my soul forlorn.
¹³Yet when they were ill, I put on sackcloth
    and humbled myself with fasting.
  When my prayers returned to me unanswered,
¹⁴ I went about mourning
    as though for my friend or brother.
  I bowed my head in grief
    as though weeping for my mother.
¹⁵But when I stumbled, they gathered in glee;
    attackers gathered against me when I was unaware.
    They slandered me without ceasing.

ᵃ3 Or and block the way

16Like the ungodly they maliciously mocked*a*;
  they gnashed their teeth at me.
17O Lord, how long will you look on?
  Rescue my life from their ravages,
    my precious life from these lions.
18I will give you thanks in the great assembly;
  among throngs of people I will praise you.

19Let not those gloat over me
  who are my enemies without cause;
let not those who hate me without reason
  maliciously wink the eye.
20They do not speak peaceably,
  but devise false accusations
    against those who live quietly in the land.
21They gape at me and say, "Aha! Aha!
  With our own eyes we have seen it."

22O LORD, you have seen this; be not silent.
  Do not be far from me, O Lord.
23Awake, and rise to my defense!
  Contend for me, my God and Lord.
24Vindicate me in your righteousness, O LORD my God;
  do not let them gloat over me.
25Do not let them think, "Aha, just what we wanted!"
  or say, "We have swallowed him up."

26May all who gloat over my distress
  be put to shame and confusion;
may all who exalt themselves over me
  be clothed with shame and disgrace.
27May those who delight in my vindication
  shout for joy and gladness;
may they always say, "The LORD be exalted,
  who delights in the well-being of his servant."
28My tongue will speak of your righteousness
  and of your praises all day long.

Psalm

36

For the director of music. Of David the servant of the LORD.

1An oracle is within my heart
  concerning the sinfulness of the wicked:*b*
There is no fear of God
  before his eyes.
2For in his own eyes he flatters himself
  too much to detect or hate his sin.
3The words of his mouth are wicked and deceitful;
  he has ceased to be wise and to do good.
4Even on his bed he plots evil;

---

a16 Septuagint; Hebrew may mean *ungodly circle of mockers.*   *b1* Or *heart:* / *Sin proceeds from the wicked.*

he commits himself to a sinful course
and does not reject what is wrong.

5Your love, O LORD, reaches to the heavens,
your faithfulness to the skies.
6Your righteousness is like the mighty mountains,
your justice like the great deep.
O LORD, you preserve both man and beast.
7   How priceless is your unfailing love!
Both high and low among men
find*a* refuge in the shadow of your wings.
8They feast on the abundance of your house;
you give them drink from your river of delights.
9For with you is the fountain of life;
in your light we see light.

10Continue your love to those who know you,
your righteousness to the upright in heart.
11May the foot of the proud not come against me,
nor the hand of the wicked drive me away.
12See how the evildoers lie fallen—
thrown down, not able to rise!

Psalm *b*

37

Of David.

1Do not fret because of evil men
or be envious of those who do wrong;
2for like the grass they will soon wither,
like green plants they will soon die away.

3Trust in the LORD and do good;
dwell in the land and enjoy safe pasture.
4Delight yourself in the LORD
and he will give you the desires of your heart.

5Commit your way to the LORD;
trust in him and he will do this:
6He will make your righteousness shine like the dawn,
the justice of your cause like the noonday sun.

7Be still before the LORD and wait patiently for him;
do not fret when men succeed in their ways,
when they carry out their wicked schemes.

8Refrain from anger and turn from wrath;
do not fret—it leads only to evil.
9For evil men will be cut off,
but those who hope in the LORD will inherit the land.

10A little while, and the wicked will be no more;
though you look for them, they will not be found.

a 7 Or *love, O God!* / *Men find*; or *love!* / *Both heavenly beings and men* / *find*   *b* This psalm is an acrostic poem, the stanzas
of which begin with the successive letters of the Hebrew alphabet.

¹¹But the meek will inherit the land
   and enjoy great peace.

¹²The wicked plot against the righteous
   and gnash their teeth at them;
¹³but the Lord laughs at the wicked,
   for he knows their day is coming.

¹⁴The wicked draw the sword
   and bend the bow
 to bring down the poor and needy,
   to slay those whose ways are upright.
¹⁵But their swords will pierce
      their own hearts,
   and their bows will be
      broken.

¹⁶Better the little that the
      righteous have
   than the wealth of many
      wicked;
¹⁷for the power of the wicked
      will be broken,
   but the LORD upholds the
      righteous.

¹⁸The days of the blameless are
      known to the LORD,
   and their inheritance will
      endure forever.
¹⁹In times of disaster they will
      not wither;
   in days of famine they will
      enjoy plenty.

²⁰But the wicked will perish:
   The LORD's enemies will be
      like the beauty of the
      fields,
   they will vanish—vanish like
      smoke.

²¹The wicked borrow and do not repay,
   but the righteous give generously;
²²those the LORD blesses will inherit the land,
   but those he curses will be cut off.

²³If the LORD delights in a man's way,
   he makes his steps firm;
²⁴though he stumble, he will not fall,
   for the LORD upholds him with his hand.

²⁵I was young and now I am old,
   yet I have never seen the righteous forsaken
   or their children begging bread.
²⁶They are always generous and lend freely;
   their children will be blessed.

ADDRESSING QUESTIONS

**37:1–9
God**

A group of simple but devout farmers stood by a dusty truck and expressed their frustration. One of their peers—a very irreligious man—had avoided church, gotten drunk on weekends, and generally rejected God. Yet here it was October, and he had the best crop in the county. Why had God rewarded this man's work when he flaunted his disregard for God's way? The conversation was intense, and the men seriously questioned their faith.

Finally one farmer who hadn't said much spoke up. "Fellas, I don't know everything 'bout the Bible, but I'm sure it ain't written in there that God settles all his accounts in October!"

People who follow God don't always see the immediate benefits of that trust. Worse, they sometimes have to watch others get away with doing evil. This psalm promises that, in time, living God's way will give you "the desires of your heart" (verse 4).

But not necessarily in October!

²⁷Turn from evil and do good;
  then you will dwell in the land forever.
²⁸For the Lᴏʀᴅ loves the just
  and will not forsake his faithful ones.

  They will be protected forever,
  but the offspring of the wicked will be cut off;
²⁹the righteous will inherit the land
  and dwell in it forever.

³⁰The mouth of the righteous man utters wisdom,
  and his tongue speaks what is just.
³¹The law of his God is in his heart;
  his feet do not slip.

³²The wicked lie in wait for the righteous,
  seeking their very lives;
³³but the Lᴏʀᴅ will not leave them in their power
  or let them be condemned when brought to trial.

³⁴Wait for the Lᴏʀᴅ
  and keep his way.
He will exalt you to inherit the land;
  when the wicked are cut off, you will see it.

³⁵I have seen a wicked and ruthless man
  flourishing like a green tree in its native soil,
³⁶but he soon passed away and was no more;
  though I looked for him, he could not be found.

³⁷Consider the blameless, observe the upright;
  there is a future ᵃ for the man of peace.
³⁸But all sinners will be destroyed;
  the future ᵇ of the wicked will be cut off.

³⁹The salvation of the righteous comes from the Lᴏʀᴅ;
  he is their stronghold in time of trouble.
⁴⁰The Lᴏʀᴅ helps them and delivers them;
  he delivers them from the wicked and saves them,
  because they take refuge in him.

Psalm

38

A psalm of David. A petition.

¹O Lᴏʀᴅ, do not rebuke me in your anger
  or discipline me in your wrath.
²For your arrows have pierced me,
  and your hand has come down upon me.
³Because of your wrath there is no health in my body;
  my bones have no soundness because of my sin.
⁴My guilt has overwhelmed me
  like a burden too heavy to bear.

⁵My wounds fester and are loathsome

ᵃ37 Or there will be posterity   ᵇ38 Or posterity

because of my sinful folly.
⁶I am bowed down and brought very low;
  all day long I go about mourning.
⁷My back is filled with searing pain;
  there is no health in my body.
⁸I am feeble and utterly crushed;
  I groan in anguish of heart.

⁹All my longings lie open before you, O Lord;
  my sighing is not hidden from you.
¹⁰My heart pounds, my strength fails me;
  even the light has gone from my eyes.
¹¹My friends and companions avoid me because of my wounds;
  my neighbors stay far away.
¹²Those who seek my life set their traps,
  those who would harm me talk of my ruin;
  all day long they plot deception.

¹³I am like a deaf man, who cannot hear,
  like a mute, who cannot open his mouth;
¹⁴I have become like a man who does not hear,
  whose mouth can offer no reply.
¹⁵I wait for you, O LORD;
  you will answer, O Lord my God.
¹⁶For I said, "Do not let them gloat
  or exalt themselves over me when my foot slips."

¹⁷For I am about to fall,
  and my pain is ever with me.
¹⁸I confess my iniquity;
  I am troubled by my sin.
¹⁹Many are those who are my vigorous enemies;
  those who hate me without reason are numerous.
²⁰Those who repay my good with evil
  slander me when I pursue what is good.

²¹O LORD, do not forsake me;
  be not far from me, O my God.
²²Come quickly to help me,
  O Lord my Savior.

Psalm

39

For the director of music. For Jeduthun. A psalm of David.

¹I said, "I will watch my ways
  and keep my tongue from sin;
I will put a muzzle on my mouth
  as long as the wicked are in my presence."
²But when I was silent and still,
  not even saying anything good,
  my anguish increased.
³My heart grew hot within me,

and as I meditated, the fire burned;
    then I spoke with my tongue:

⁴"Show me, O LORD, my life's end
    and the number of my days;
    let me know how fleeting is my life.
⁵You have made my days a mere handbreadth;
    the span of my years is as nothing before you.
    Each man's life is but a breath.   *Selah*

⁶Man is a mere phantom as he goes to
        and fro:
    He bustles about, but only in vain;
    he heaps up wealth, not knowing
        who will get it.

⁷"But now, Lord, what do I look for?
    My hope is in you.
⁸Save me from all my transgressions;
    do not make me the scorn of fools.
⁹I was silent; I would not open my mouth,
    for you are the one who has done this.
¹⁰Remove your scourge from me;
    I am overcome by the blow of your
        hand.
¹¹You rebuke and discipline men for
        their sin;
    you consume their wealth like a
        moth—
    each man is but a breath.   *Selah*

¹²"Hear my prayer, O LORD,
    listen to my cry for help;
    be not deaf to my weeping.
For I dwell with you as an alien,
    a stranger, as all my fathers were.
¹³Look away from me, that I may rejoice
        again
    before I depart and am no more."

MANAGING RESOURCES

39:4–7
Time

In the busyness of modern life we can easily forget how short our time on earth really is. Those of us who have children have constant reminders of the passing of time—one day the kids are tiny; the next day it seems they're all grown-up. We exclaim with surprise, "Look how much you've grown!" But why are we so shocked to see something as common and natural as a child growing older?

Middle age also has a way of showing us how quickly life passes. Suddenly our government leaders and other trusted authorities look like teenagers. And older people don't seem quite as aged as they used to. Before we know it, we're eligible for the senior citizen's discount at the local fast-food restaurant.

God doesn't intend for this psalm to create despair. He just wants us to be aware of the brevity of life so that we don't waste it. The simple yet profound conviction that gives meaning to our lives is this: Hope in God (verse 7).

Psalm

40

For the director of music. Of David. A psalm.

¹I waited patiently for the LORD;
    he turned to me and heard my cry.
²He lifted me out of the slimy pit,
    out of the mud and mire;
    he set my feet on a rock
    and gave me a firm place to stand.
³He put a new song in my mouth,
    a hymn of praise to our God.
Many will see and fear
    and put their trust in the LORD.

⁴Blessed is the man
  who makes the LORD his trust,
who does not look to the proud,
  to those who turn aside to false gods. *a*
⁵Many, O LORD my God,
  are the wonders you have done.
The things you planned for us
  no one can recount to you;
were I to speak and tell of them,
  they would be too many to declare.

⁶Sacrifice and offering you did not desire,
  but my ears you have pierced *b, c*;
burnt offerings and sin offerings
  you did not require.
⁷Then I said, "Here I am, I have come—
  it is written about me in the scroll. *d*
⁸I desire to do your will, O my God;
  your law is within my heart."

⁹I proclaim righteousness in the great assembly;
  I do not seal my lips,
  as you know, O LORD.
¹⁰I do not hide your righteousness in my heart;
  I speak of your faithfulness and salvation.
I do not conceal your love and your truth
  from the great assembly.

¹¹Do not withhold your mercy from me, O LORD;
  may your love and your truth always protect me.
¹²For troubles without number surround me;
  my sins have overtaken me, and I cannot see.
They are more than the hairs of my head,
  and my heart fails within me.

¹³Be pleased, O LORD, to save me;
  O LORD, come quickly to help me.
¹⁴May all who seek to take my life
  be put to shame and confusion;
may all who desire my ruin
  be turned back in disgrace.
¹⁵May those who say to me, "Aha! Aha!"
  be appalled at their own shame.
¹⁶But may all who seek you
  rejoice and be glad in you;
may those who love your salvation always say,
  "The LORD be exalted!"

¹⁷Yet I am poor and needy;
  may the Lord think of me.
You are my help and my deliverer;
  O my God, do not delay.

---

a 4 Or *to falsehood*   *b 6* Hebrew; Septuagint *but a body you have prepared for me* (see also Symmachus and Theodotion)
c 6 Or *opened*   *d 7* Or *come / with the scroll written for me*

Psalm

For the director of music. A psalm of David.

¹Blessed is he who has regard for the weak;
  the LORD delivers him in times of trouble.
²The LORD will protect him and preserve his life;
  he will bless him in the land
  and not surrender him to the desire of his foes.
³The LORD will sustain him on his sickbed
  and restore him from his bed of illness.

⁴I said, "O LORD, have mercy on me;
  heal me, for I have sinned against you."
⁵My enemies say of me in malice,
  "When will he die and his name perish?"
⁶Whenever one comes to see me,
  he speaks falsely, while his heart gathers slander;
  then he goes out and spreads it abroad.

⁷All my enemies whisper together against me;
  they imagine the worst for me, saying,
⁸"A vile disease has beset him;
  he will never get up from the place where he lies."
⁹Even my close friend, whom I trusted,
  he who shared my bread,
  has lifted up his heel against me.

¹⁰But you, O LORD, have mercy on me;
  raise me up, that I may repay them.
¹¹I know that you are pleased with me,
  for my enemy does not triumph over me.
¹²In my integrity you uphold me
  and set me in your presence forever.

¹³Praise be to the LORD, the God of Israel,
  from everlasting to everlasting.
                    Amen and Amen.

BOOK II

Psalms 42–72

Psalm*ᵃ*

For the director of music. A *maskil*ᵇ of the Sons of Korah.

¹As the deer pants for streams of water,
  so my soul pants for you, O God.
²My soul thirsts for God, for the living God.
  When can I go and meet with God?

ᵃIn many Hebrew manuscripts Psalms 42 and 43 constitute one psalm.   ᵇTitle: Probably a literary or musical term

³My tears have been my food
    day and night,
while men say to me all day long,
    "Where is your God?"
⁴These things I remember
    as I pour out my soul:
how I used to go with the multitude,
    leading the procession to the house of God,
with shouts of joy and thanksgiving
    among the festive throng.

⁵Why are you downcast, O my soul?
    Why so disturbed within me?
Put your hope in God,
    for I will yet praise him,
    my Savior and ⁶my God.

My ᵃ soul is downcast within me;
    therefore I will remember you
from the land of the Jordan,
    the heights of Hermon—from Mount Mizar.
⁷Deep calls to deep
    in the roar of your
        waterfalls;
all your waves and breakers
    have swept over me.

⁸By day the LORD directs his
        love,
    at night his song is with
        me—
a prayer to the God of my
        life.

⁹I say to God my Rock,
    "Why have you forgotten
        me?
Why must I go about
        mourning,
    oppressed by the enemy?"
¹⁰My bones suffer mortal agony
    as my foes taunt me,
saying to me all day long,
    "Where is your God?"

¹¹Why are you downcast, O my soul?
    Why so disturbed within me?
Put your hope in God,
    for I will yet praise him,
    my Savior and my God.

▦ ▨▨▨▨▨ REASONS TO BELIEVE ▨▨▨▨▨ ⬍

42:1–3
The Christian Experience

Even when things go wrong—*especially* when
things go wrong—those who have a relationship with God long for a sense of his near-
ness. They know that the only sure thing in life
is the reality of God.

That's one of the benefits of becoming a
God-follower and placing your trust in him.
God's love and concern for you is like an anchor that keeps you grounded, no matter how
the storms of life throw you. Once you've experienced the security and comfort of his
presence in the midst of crisis, you'll never
want to be without him again.

ᵃ⁵,⁶ A few Hebrew manuscripts, Septuagint and Syriac; most Hebrew manuscripts *praise him for his saving help. /*
⁶*O my God, my*

Psalm[a]

43

¹Vindicate me, O God,
    and plead my cause against an ungodly nation;
    rescue me from deceitful and wicked men.
²You are God my stronghold.
    Why have you rejected me?
 Why must I go about mourning,
    oppressed by the enemy?
³Send forth your light and your truth,
    let them guide me;
 let them bring me to your holy mountain,
    to the place where you dwell.
⁴Then will I go to the altar of God,
    to God, my joy and my delight.
 I will praise you with the harp,
    O God, my God.

⁵Why are you downcast, O my soul?
    Why so disturbed within me?
 Put your hope in God,
    for I will yet praise him,
    my Savior and my God.

Psalm

44

For the director of music. Of the Sons of Korah. A *maskil.*[b]

¹We have heard with our ears, O God;
    our fathers have told us
 what you did in their days,
    in days long ago.
²With your hand you drove out the nations
    and planted our fathers;
 you crushed the peoples
    and made our fathers flourish.
³It was not by their sword that they won the land,
    nor did their arm bring them victory;
 it was your right hand, your arm,
    and the light of your face, for you loved them.

⁴You are my King and my God,
    who decrees[c] victories for Jacob.
⁵Through you we push back our enemies;
    through your name we trample our foes.
⁶I do not trust in my bow,
    my sword does not bring me victory;
⁷but you give us victory over our enemies,
    you put our adversaries to shame.

---

⁸In God we make our boast all day long,
    and we will praise your name forever.   *Selah*

⁹But now you have rejected and humbled us;
    you no longer go out with our armies.
¹⁰You made us retreat before the enemy,
    and our adversaries have plundered us.
¹¹You gave us up to be devoured like sheep
    and have scattered us among the nations.
¹²You sold your people for a pittance,
    gaining nothing from their sale.

¹³You have made us a reproach to our neighbors,
    the scorn and derision of those around us.
¹⁴You have made us a byword among the nations;
    the peoples shake their heads at us.
¹⁵My disgrace is before me all day long,
    and my face is covered with shame
¹⁶at the taunts of those who reproach and revile me,
    because of the enemy, who is bent on revenge.

¹⁷All this happened to us,
    though we had not forgotten you
    or been false to your covenant.
¹⁸Our hearts had not turned back;
    our feet had not strayed from your path.
¹⁹But you crushed us and made us a haunt for jackals
    and covered us over with deep darkness.

²⁰If we had forgotten the name of our God
    or spread out our hands to a foreign god,
²¹would not God have discovered it,
    since he knows the secrets of the heart?
²²Yet for your sake we face death all day long;
    we are considered as sheep to be slaughtered.

²³Awake, O Lord! Why do you sleep?
    Rouse yourself! Do not reject us forever.
²⁴Why do you hide your face
    and forget our misery and oppression?

²⁵We are brought down to the dust;
    our bodies cling to the ground.
²⁶Rise up and help us;
    redeem us because of your unfailing love.

Psalm

For the director of music. To ˌthe tune of ˌ"Lilies." Of the Sons of Korah.
A *maskil.*^a A wedding song.

¹My heart is stirred by a noble theme
    as I recite my verses for the king;
    my tongue is the pen of a skillful writer.

^aTitle: Probably a literary or musical term

²You are the most excellent of men
  and your lips have been anointed with grace,
  since God has blessed you forever.
³Gird your sword upon your side, O mighty one;
  clothe yourself with splendor and majesty.
⁴In your majesty ride forth victoriously
  in behalf of truth, humility and righteousness;
  let your right hand display awesome deeds.
⁵Let your sharp arrows pierce the hearts of the king's enemies;
  let the nations fall beneath your feet.
⁶Your throne, O God, will last for ever and ever;
  a scepter of justice will be the scepter of your kingdom.
⁷You love righteousness and hate wickedness;
  therefore God, your God, has set you above your companions
  by anointing you with the oil of joy.
⁸All your robes are fragrant with myrrh and aloes and cassia;
  from palaces adorned with ivory
  the music of the strings makes you glad.
⁹Daughters of kings are among your honored women;
  at your right hand is the royal bride in gold of Ophir.

¹⁰Listen, O daughter, consider and give ear:
  Forget your people and your father's house.
¹¹The king is enthralled by your beauty;
  honor him, for he is your lord.
¹²The Daughter of Tyre will come with a gift,ᵃ
  men of wealth will seek your favor.

¹³All glorious is the princess within ̗her chamber ̗;
  her gown is interwoven with gold.
¹⁴In embroidered garments she is led to the king;
  her virgin companions follow her
  and are brought to you.
¹⁵They are led in with joy and gladness;
  they enter the palace of the king.

¹⁶Your sons will take the place of your fathers;
  you will make them princes throughout the land.
¹⁷I will perpetuate your memory through all generations;
  therefore the nations will praise you for ever and ever.

Psalm

46

For the director of music. Of the Sons of Korah. According to *alamoth*.ᵇ A song.

¹God is our refuge and strength,
  an ever-present help in trouble.
²Therefore we will not fear, though the earth give way
  and the mountains fall into the heart of the sea,
³though its waters roar and foam
  and the mountains quake with their surging.   *Selah*

⁴There is a river whose streams make glad the city of God,

ᵃ12 Or *A Tyrian robe is among the gifts*   ᵇTitle: Probably a musical term

the holy place where the Most High dwells.
⁵God is within her, she will not fall;
  God will help her at break of day.
⁶Nations are in uproar,
    kingdoms fall;
  he lifts his voice, the earth
    melts.

⁷The Lord Almighty is with us;
  the God of Jacob is our
    fortress.   *Selah*

⁸Come and see the works of
    the Lord,
  the desolations he has
    brought on the earth.
⁹He makes wars cease to the
    ends of the earth;
  he breaks the bow and
    shatters the spear,
  he burns the shields*ᵃ* with
    fire.
¹⁰"Be still, and know that I am
    God;
  I will be exalted among the
    nations,
  I will be exalted in the
    earth."

¹¹The Lord Almighty is with us;
  the God of Jacob is our
    fortress.   *Selah*

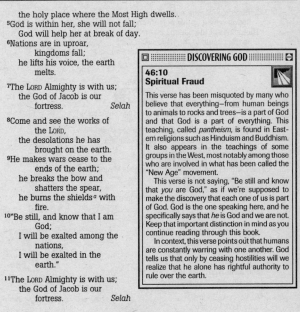

▣ ▦▦▦▦▦ DISCOVERING GOD ▦▦▦▦▦ ⮧

46:10
Spiritual Fraud

This verse has been misquoted by many who believe that everything—from human beings to animals to rocks and trees—is a part of God and that God is a part of everything. This teaching, called *pantheism*, is found in Eastern religions such as Hinduism and Buddhism. It also appears in the teachings of some groups in the West, most notably among those who are involved in what has been called the "New Age" movement.

This verse is not saying, "Be still and know that *you* are God," as if we're supposed to make the discovery that each one of us is part of God. God is the one speaking here, and he specifically says that *he* is God and we are not. Keep that important distinction in mind as you continue reading through this book.

In context, this verse points out that humans are constantly warring with one another. God tells us that only by ceasing hostilities will we realize that he alone has rightful authority to rule over the earth.

Psalm

47

For the director of music. Of the Sons of Korah. A psalm.

¹Clap your hands, all you nations;
  shout to God with cries of joy.
²How awesome is the Lord Most High,
  the great King over all the earth!
³He subdued nations under us,
  peoples under our feet.
⁴He chose our inheritance for us,
  the pride of Jacob, whom he loved.   *Selah*

⁵God has ascended amid shouts of joy,
  the Lord amid the sounding of trumpets.
⁶Sing praises to God, sing praises;
  sing praises to our King, sing praises.

⁷For God is the King of all the earth;
  sing to him a psalm*ᵇ* of praise.

ᵃ9 Or *chariots*   *ᵇ7* Or *a maskil* (probably a literary or musical term)

[8]God reigns over the nations;
    God is seated on his holy throne.
[9]The nobles of the nations assemble
    as the people of the God of Abraham,
for the kings[a] of the earth belong to God;
    he is greatly exalted.

Psalm

A song. A psalm of the Sons of Korah.

[1]Great is the LORD, and most worthy of praise,
    in the city of our God, his holy mountain.
[2]It is beautiful in its loftiness,
    the joy of the whole earth.
Like the utmost heights of Zaphon[b] is Mount Zion,
    the[c] city of the Great King.
[3]God is in her citadels;
    he has shown himself to be her fortress.

[4]When the kings joined forces,
    when they advanced together,
[5]they saw ⌊her⌋ and were astounded;
    they fled in terror.
[6]Trembling seized them there,
    pain like that of a woman in labor.
[7]You destroyed them like ships of Tarshish
    shattered by an east wind.

[8]As we have heard,
    so have we seen
in the city of the LORD Almighty,
    in the city of our God:
God makes her secure forever.   *Selah*

[9]Within your temple, O God,
    we meditate on your unfailing love.
[10]Like your name, O God,
    your praise reaches to the ends of the earth;
    your right hand is filled with righteousness.
[11]Mount Zion rejoices,
    the villages of Judah are glad
    because of your judgments.

[12]Walk about Zion, go around her,
    count her towers,
[13]consider well her ramparts,
    view her citadels,
    that you may tell of them to the next generation.
[14]For this God is our God for ever and ever;
    he will be our guide even to the end.

---

[a]9 Or *shields*   [b]2 *Zaphon* can refer to a sacred mountain or the direction north.   [c]2 Or *earth, / Mount Zion, on the northern side / of the*

Psalm

49

For the director of music. Of the Sons of Korah. A psalm.

¹Hear this, all you peoples;
   listen, all who live in this world,
²both low and high,
   rich and poor alike:
³My mouth will speak words of wisdom;
   the utterance from my heart will give understanding.
⁴I will turn my ear to a proverb;
   with the harp I will expound my riddle:

⁵Why should I fear when evil days come,
   when wicked deceivers surround me—
⁶those who trust in their wealth
   and boast of their great riches?
⁷No man can redeem the life of another
   or give to God a ransom for him—
⁸the ransom for a life is costly,
   no payment is ever enough—
⁹that he should live on forever
   and not see decay.

¹⁰For all can see that wise men
     die;
   the foolish and the senseless
     alike perish
   and leave their wealth to
     others.
¹¹Their tombs will remain their
     houses*a* forever,
   their dwellings for endless
     generations,
   though they had*b* named
     lands after themselves.

¹²But man, despite his riches,
   does not endure;
   he is*c* like the beasts that
     perish.

¹³This is the fate of those who
     trust in themselves,
   and of their followers, who
     approve their sayings.
           Selah
¹⁴Like sheep they are destined for the grave,*d*
   and death will feed on them.
The upright will rule over them in the morning;
   their forms will decay in the grave,*d*
   far from their princely mansions.

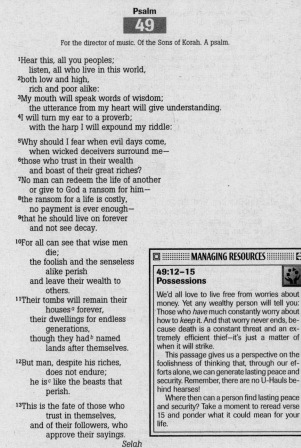

▣ ▓▓▓▓▓▓ MANAGING RESOURCES ▓▓▓▓▓▓ ⇄

49:12–15
Possessions

We'd all love to live free from worries about money. Yet any wealthy person will tell you: Those who *have* much constantly worry about how to *keep* it. And that worry never ends, because death is a constant threat and an extremely efficient thief—it's just a matter of when it will strike.

This passage gives us a perspective on the foolishness of thinking that, through our efforts alone, we can generate lasting peace and security. Remember, there are no U-Hauls behind hearses!

Where then can a person find lasting peace and security? Take a moment to reread verse 15 and ponder what it could mean for your life.

---

a 11 Septuagint and Syriac; Hebrew *In their thoughts their houses will remain*   *b 11* Or */ for they have*
Septuagint and Syriac read verse 12 the same as verse 20.   *d 14* Hebrew *Sheol*; also in verse 15   *c 12* Hebrew;

¹⁵But God will redeem my life[a] from the grave;
he will surely take me to himself.

Selah

¹⁶Do not be overawed when a man grows rich,
when the splendor of his house increases;
¹⁷for he will take nothing with him when he dies,
his splendor will not descend with him.
¹⁸Though while he lived he counted himself blessed—
and men praise you when you prosper—
¹⁹he will join the generation of his fathers,
who will never see the light ˌof lifeˌ.

²⁰A man who has riches without understanding
is like the beasts that perish.

Psalm

A psalm of Asaph.

¹The Mighty One, God, the LORD,
speaks and summons the earth
from the rising of the sun to the place where it sets.
²From Zion, perfect in beauty,
God shines forth.
³Our God comes and will not be silent;
a fire devours before him,
and around him a tempest rages.
⁴He summons the heavens above,
and the earth, that he may judge his people:
⁵"Gather to me my consecrated ones,
who made a covenant with me by sacrifice."
⁶And the heavens proclaim his righteousness,
for God himself is judge.

Selah

⁷"Hear, O my people, and I will speak,
O Israel, and I will testify against you:
I am God, your God.
⁸I do not rebuke you for your sacrifices
or your burnt offerings, which are ever before me.
⁹I have no need of a bull from your stall
or of goats from your pens,
¹⁰for every animal of the forest is mine,
and the cattle on a thousand hills.
¹¹I know every bird in the mountains,
and the creatures of the field are mine.
¹²If I were hungry I would not tell you,
for the world is mine, and all that is in it.
¹³Do I eat the flesh of bulls
or drink the blood of goats?
¹⁴Sacrifice thank offerings to God,
fulfill your vows to the Most High,

¹⁵and call upon me in the day of trouble;
   I will deliver you, and you will honor me."

¹⁶But to the wicked, God says:

   "What right have you to recite my laws
     or take my covenant on your lips?
¹⁷You hate my instruction
   and cast my words behind you.
¹⁸When you see a thief, you join with him;
   you throw in your lot with adulterers.
¹⁹You use your mouth for evil
   and harness your tongue to deceit.
²⁰You speak continually against your brother
   and slander your own mother's son.
²¹These things you have done and I kept silent;
   you thought I was altogether^a like you.
But I will rebuke you
   and accuse you to your face.

²²"Consider this, you who forget God,
   or I will tear you to pieces, with none to rescue:
²³He who sacrifices thank offerings honors me,
   and he prepares the way
   so that I may show him^b the salvation of God."

Psalm

51

For the director of music. A psalm of David. When the prophet Nathan came to
him after David had committed adultery with Bathsheba.

¹Have mercy on me, O God,
   according to your unfailing love;
according to your great compassion
   blot out my transgressions.
²Wash away all my iniquity
   and cleanse me from my sin.

³For I know my transgressions,
   and my sin is always before me.
⁴Against you, you only, have I sinned
   and done what is evil in your sight,
so that you are proved right when you speak
   and justified when you judge.
⁵Surely I was sinful at birth,
   sinful from the time my mother conceived me.
⁶Surely you desire truth in the inner parts^c;
   you teach^d me wisdom in the inmost place.

⁷Cleanse me with hyssop, and I will be clean;
   wash me, and I will be whiter than snow.
⁸Let me hear joy and gladness;
   let the bones you have crushed rejoice.

---

^{a}21 Or thought the 'I AM' was ^{b}23 Or and to him who considers his way / I will show ^{c}6 The meaning of the
Hebrew for this phrase is uncertain. ^{d}6 Or you desired . . . ; / you taught

⁹Hide your face from my sins
　and blot out all my iniquity.

¹⁰Create in me a pure heart, O God,
　and renew a steadfast spirit within me.

¹¹Do not cast me from your presence
　or take your Holy Spirit from me.

¹²Restore to me the joy of your salvation
　and grant me a willing spirit, to sustain me.

¹³Then I will teach transgressors your ways,
　and sinners will turn back to you.

¹⁴Save me from bloodguilt, O God,
　the God who saves me,
　and my tongue will sing of your righteousness.

¹⁵O Lord, open my lips,
　and my mouth will declare your praise.

¹⁶You do not delight in sacrifice, or I would bring it;
　you do not take pleasure in burnt offerings.

¹⁷The sacrifices of God are*ᵃ* a broken spirit;
　a broken and contrite heart,
　O God, you will not despise.

¹⁸In your good pleasure make Zion prosper;

ᵃ 17 Or My sacrifice, O God, is

▦ KNOWING YOURSELF

51:1–19
Sin

Guilt has both positive and negative aspects. It's painful, but it serves a purpose because it tells us that something is wrong. In that sense, it's like a warning light on a car dashboard. The problem is that most of us don't like heeding that warning and dealing with the actions behind our guilt. Many of us don't even know how to begin. That's probably why we would rather ignore, deny, or run away from our guilt than face up to it.

That's what Israel's king David did. After committing adultery and murder, David ignored his sin for almost a year. When God sent the prophet Nathan to confront David, he finally confessed his sin (see 2 Samuel chapters 11–12). After admitting his wrongdoing, David wrote this psalm and poured out his heart to God. And in his prayer we find insights that will help us deal with our guilt.

The order of David's prayer is significant. He began by recounting God's merciful, unfailing love (verses 1–2) as he reflected on the severity of his sin. He asked for forgiveness from a forgiving God.

Then he candidly and frankly admitted his sin (verses 3–6). David refused to excuse his behavior or downplay his evil actions. He also asked God for help in addressing the core issues that produced his sinful actions: his inner thoughts and feelings.

Next he movingly asked God to cleanse him of that sin (verses 7–12). David wanted his heart purified. He knew that only God could do that kind of "heart surgery."

Finally, he pledged himself to a life of service (verses 13–19). He truly wanted to help others see the benefits of living in union with God instead of fighting him all the time.

Perhaps you too feel the pain of guilt as you read these words. If so, God is trying to tell you that something is wrong—your "warning light" is flashing. Don't ignore it, as David chose to do for a time. Instead, learn from David's example: Tell God what you've done and thank him for his willingness to forgive you.

build up the walls of Jerusalem.
¹⁹Then there will be righteous sacrifices,
    whole burnt offerings to delight you;
    then bulls will be offered on your altar.

Psalm

52

For the director of music. A *maskil*ᵃ of David. When Doeg the Edomite had
gone to Saul and told him: "David has gone to the house of Ahimelech."

¹Why do you boast of evil, you mighty man?
    Why do you boast all day long,
    you who are a disgrace in the eyes of God?
²Your tongue plots destruction;
    it is like a sharpened razor,
    you who practice deceit.
³You love evil rather than good,
    falsehood rather than speaking the truth.   *Selah*
⁴You love every harmful word,
    O you deceitful tongue!

⁵Surely God will bring you down to everlasting ruin:
    He will snatch you up and tear you from your tent;
    he will uproot you from the land of the living.   *Selah*
⁶The righteous will see and fear;
    they will laugh at him, saying,
⁷"Here now is the man
    who did not make God his stronghold
 but trusted in his great wealth
    and grew strong by destroying others!"

⁸But I am like an olive tree
    flourishing in the house of God;
 I trust in God's unfailing love
    for ever and ever.
⁹I will praise you forever for what you have done;
    in your name I will hope, for your name is good.
    I will praise you in the presence of your saints.

Psalm

53

For the director of music. According to *mahalath*.ᵇ A *maskil*ᵃ of David.

¹The fool says in his heart,
    "There is no God."
They are corrupt, and their ways are vile;
    there is no one who does good.

²God looks down from heaven
    on the sons of men
to see if there are any who understand,

ᵃTitle: Probably a literary or musical term   ᵇTitle: Probably a musical term

any who seek God.
3Everyone has turned away,
   they have together become corrupt;
there is no one who does good,
   not even one.

4Will the evildoers never learn—
   those who devour my people as men eat bread
   and who do not call on God?
5There they were, overwhelmed with dread,
   where there was nothing to dread.
God scattered the bones of those who attacked you;
   you put them to shame, for God despised them.

6Oh, that salvation for Israel would come out of Zion!
   When God restores the fortunes of his people,
   let Jacob rejoice and Israel be glad!

Psalm

54

For the director of music. With stringed instruments. A *maskil*[a] of David. When
the Ziphites had gone to Saul and said, "Is not David hiding among us?"

1Save me, O God, by your name;
   vindicate me by your might.
2Hear my prayer, O God;
   listen to the words of my mouth.

3Strangers are attacking me;
   ruthless men seek my life—
   men without regard for God.   *Selah*

4Surely God is my help;
   the Lord is the one who sustains me.

5Let evil recoil on those who slander me;
   in your faithfulness destroy them.

6I will sacrifice a freewill offering to you;
   I will praise your name, O LORD,
   for it is good.
7For he has delivered me from all my troubles,
   and my eyes have looked in triumph on my foes.

Psalm

55

For the director of music. With stringed instruments. A *maskil*[a] of David.

1Listen to my prayer, O God,
   do not ignore my plea;
2   hear me and answer me.
My thoughts trouble me and I am distraught
3   at the voice of the enemy,

---

[a] Title: Probably a literary or musical term

at the stares of the wicked;
for they bring down suffering upon me
and revile me in their anger.

4My heart is in anguish within me;
the terrors of death assail me.
5Fear and trembling have beset me;
horror has overwhelmed me.
6I said, "Oh, that I had the wings of a dove!
I would fly away and be at rest—
7I would flee far away
and stay in the desert;   *Selah*
8I would hurry to my place of shelter,
far from the tempest and storm."

9Confuse the wicked, O Lord, confound their speech,
for I see violence and strife in the city.
10Day and night they prowl about on its walls;
malice and abuse are within it.
11Destructive forces are at work in the city;
threats and lies never leave its streets.

12If an enemy were insulting me,
I could endure it;
if a foe were raising himself against me,
I could hide from him.
13But it is you, a man like myself,
my companion, my close friend,
14with whom I once enjoyed sweet fellowship
as we walked with the throng at the house of God.

15Let death take my enemies by surprise;
let them go down alive to the grave, *a*
for evil finds lodging among them.

16But I call to God,
and the Lord saves me.
17Evening, morning and noon
I cry out in distress,
and he hears my voice.
18He ransoms me unharmed
from the battle waged against me,
even though many oppose me.
19God, who is enthroned forever,
will hear them and afflict them—   *Selah*
men who never change their ways
and have no fear of God.

20My companion attacks his friends;
he violates his covenant.
21His speech is smooth as butter,
yet war is in his heart;
his words are more soothing than oil,
yet they are drawn swords.

a 15 Hebrew *Sheol*

²²Cast your cares on the LORD
    and he will sustain you;
    he will never let the righteous fall.
²³But you, O God, will bring down the wicked
    into the pit of corruption;
bloodthirsty and deceitful men
    will not live out half their days.

But as for me, I trust in you.

Psalm

For the director of music. To ⌊the tune of⌋ "A Dove on Distant Oaks." Of David.
A *miktam.*ᵃ When the Philistines had seized him in Gath.

¹Be merciful to me, O God, for men hotly pursue me;
    all day long they press their attack.
²My slanderers pursue me all day long;
    many are attacking me in their pride.

³When I am afraid,
    I will trust in you.
⁴In God, whose word I praise,
    in God I trust; I will not be afraid.
    What can mortal man do to me?

⁵All day long they twist my words;
    they are always plotting to harm me.
⁶They conspire, they lurk,
    they watch my steps,
    eager to take my life.

⁷On no account let them escape;
    in your anger, O God, bring down the nations.
⁸Record my lament;
    list my tears on your scrollᵇ—
    are they not in your record?

⁹Then my enemies will turn back
    when I call for help.
    By this I will know that God is for me.
¹⁰In God, whose word I praise,
    in the LORD, whose word I praise—
¹¹in God I trust; I will not be afraid.
    What can man do to me?

¹²I am under vows to you, O God;
    I will present my thank offerings to you.
¹³For you have delivered meᶜ from death
    and my feet from stumbling,
that I may walk before God
    in the light of life.ᵈ

ᵃTitle: Probably a literary or musical term   ᵇ8 Or / put my tears in your wineskin   ᶜ13 Or my soul   ᵈ13 Or the
land of the living

Psalm

57

For the director of music. ⌞To the tune of⌟ "Do Not Destroy." Of David.
A *miktam.* ᵃ When he had fled from Saul into the cave.

¹Have mercy on me, O God, have mercy on me,
   for in you my soul takes refuge.
 I will take refuge in the shadow of your wings
   until the disaster has passed.

²I cry out to God Most High,
   to God, who fulfills ⌞his purpose⌟ for me.
³He sends from heaven and
      saves me,
   rebuking those who hotly
      pursue me;   *Selah*
 God sends his love and his
      faithfulness.

⁴I am in the midst of lions;
   I lie among ravenous
      beasts—
 men whose teeth are spears
      and arrows,
   whose tongues are sharp
      swords.

⁵Be exalted, O God, above the
      heavens;
   let your glory be over all the
      earth.

⁶They spread a net for my
      feet—
   I was bowed down in
      distress.
 They dug a pit in my path—
   but they have fallen into it
      themselves.   *Selah*

⁷My heart is steadfast, O God,
   my heart is steadfast;
 I will sing and make music.
⁸Awake, my soul!
 Awake, harp and lyre!
   I will awaken the dawn.

⁹I will praise you, O Lord,
      among the nations;
   I will sing of you among the peoples.
¹⁰For great is your love, reaching to the heavens;
   your faithfulness reaches to the skies.

ᵃTitle: Probably a literary or musical term

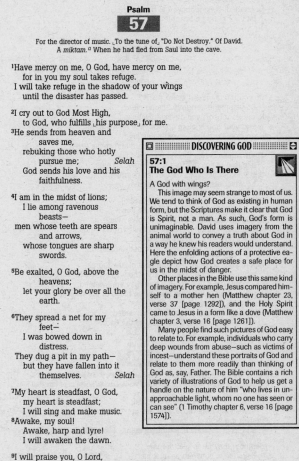

▣ ▦▦▦▦▦▦▦ **DISCOVERING GOD** ▦▦▦▦▦▦▦ ⬒

57:1
The God Who Is There

A God with wings?
   This image may seem strange to most of us.
We tend to think of God as existing in human
form, but the Scriptures make it clear that God
is Spirit, not a man. As such, God's form is
unimaginable. David uses imagery from the
animal world to convey a truth about God in
a way he knew his readers would understand.
Here the enfolding actions of a protective eagle depict how God creates a safe place for
us in the midst of danger.
   Other places in the Bible use this same kind
of imagery. For example, Jesus compared himself to a mother hen (Matthew chapter 23,
verse 37 [page 1292]), and the Holy Spirit
came to Jesus in a form like a dove (Matthew
chapter 3, verse 16 [page 1261]).
   Many people find such pictures of God easy
to relate to. For example, individuals who carry
deep wounds from abuse—such as victims of
incest—understand these portraits of God and
relate to them more readily than thinking of
God as, say, Father. The Bible contains a rich
variety of illustrations of God to help us get a
handle on the nature of him "who lives in unapproachable light, whom no one has seen or
can see" (1 Timothy chapter 6, verse 16 [page
1574]).

¹¹Be exalted, O God, above the heavens;
    let your glory be over all the earth.

Psalm

58

For the director of music. ⌞To the tune of⌟ "Do Not Destroy." Of David.
    A *miktam.* ᵃ

¹Do you rulers indeed speak justly?
    Do you judge uprightly among men?
²No, in your heart you devise injustice,
    and your hands mete out violence on the earth.
³Even from birth the wicked go astray;
    from the womb they are wayward and speak lies.
⁴Their venom is like the venom of a snake,
    like that of a cobra that has stopped its ears,
⁵that will not heed the tune of the charmer,
    however skillful the enchanter may be.

⁶Break the teeth in their mouths, O God;
    tear out, O LORD, the fangs of the lions!
⁷Let them vanish like water that flows away;
    when they draw the bow, let their arrows be blunted.
⁸Like a slug melting away as it moves along,
    like a stillborn child, may they not see the sun.

⁹Before your pots can feel ⌞the heat of⌟ the thorns—
    whether they be green or dry—the wicked will be swept away. ᵇ
¹⁰The righteous will be glad when they are avenged,
    when they bathe their feet in the blood of the wicked.
¹¹Then men will say,
    "Surely the righteous still are rewarded;
    surely there is a God who judges the earth."

Psalm

59

For the director of music. ⌞To the tune of⌟ "Do Not Destroy." Of David.
A *miktam.* ᵃ When Saul had sent men to watch David's house in order to kill him.

¹Deliver me from my enemies, O God;
    protect me from those who rise up against me.
²Deliver me from evildoers
    and save me from bloodthirsty men.

³See how they lie in wait for me!
    Fierce men conspire against me
    for no offense or sin of mine, O LORD.
⁴I have done no wrong, yet they are ready to attack me.
    Arise to help me; look on my plight!
⁵O LORD God Almighty, the God of Israel,

ᵃTitle: Probably a literary or musical term   ᵇ9 The meaning of the Hebrew for this verse is uncertain.

rouse yourself to punish all the nations;
show no mercy to wicked traitors.   *Selah*

⁶They return at evening,
snarling like dogs,
and prowl about the city.
⁷See what they spew from their mouths—
they spew out swords from their lips,
and they say, "Who can hear us?"
⁸But you, O LORD, laugh at them;
you scoff at all those nations.

⁹O my Strength, I watch for you;
you, O God, are my fortress, ¹⁰my loving God.

God will go before me
and will let me gloat over those who slander me.
¹¹But do not kill them, O Lord our shield,ᵃ
or my people will forget.
In your might make them wander about,
and bring them down.
¹²For the sins of their mouths,
for the words of their lips,
let them be caught in their pride.
For the curses and lies they utter,
¹³   consume them in wrath,
consume them till they are no more.
Then it will be known to the ends of the earth
that God rules over Jacob.   *Selah*

¹⁴They return at evening,
snarling like dogs,
and prowl about the city.
¹⁵They wander about for food
and howl if not satisfied.
¹⁶But I will sing of your strength,
in the morning I will sing of your love;
for you are my fortress,
my refuge in times of trouble.

¹⁷O my Strength, I sing praise to you;
you, O God, are my fortress, my loving God.

Psalm

For the director of music. To ˌthe tune of˒ "The Lily of the Covenant." A
*miktam*ᵇ of David. For teaching. When he fought Aram Naharaimᶜ and Aram
Zobah,ᵈ and when Joab returned and struck down twelve thousand Edomites
in the Valley of Salt.

¹You have rejected us, O God, and burst forth upon us;
you have been angry—now restore us!
²You have shaken the land and torn it open;

ᵃ11 Or *sovereign*   ᵇTitle: Probably a literary or musical term   ᶜTitle: That is, Arameans of Northwest Mesopotamia
ᵈTitle: That is, Arameans of central Syria

mend its fractures, for it is quaking.
[3]You have shown your people desperate times;
　　you have given us wine that makes us stagger.

[4]But for those who fear you, you have raised a banner
　　to be unfurled against the bow.　　　　　　　　　　*Selah*

[5]Save us and help us with your right hand,
　　that those you love may be delivered.
[6]God has spoken from his sanctuary:
　　"In triumph I will parcel out Shechem
　　and measure off the Valley of Succoth.
[7]Gilead is mine, and Manasseh is mine;
　　Ephraim is my helmet,
　　Judah my scepter.
[8]Moab is my washbasin,
　　upon Edom I toss my sandal;
　　over Philistia I shout in triumph."

[9]Who will bring me to the fortified city?
　　Who will lead me to Edom?
[10]Is it not you, O God, you who have rejected us
　　and no longer go out with our armies?
[11]Give us aid against the enemy,
　　for the help of man is worthless.
[12]With God we will gain the victory,
　　and he will trample down our enemies.

Psalm

61

For the director of music. With stringed instruments. Of David.

[1]Hear my cry, O God;
　　listen to my prayer.

[2]From the ends of the earth I call to you,
　　I call as my heart grows faint;
　　lead me to the rock that is higher than I.
[3]For you have been my refuge,
　　a strong tower against the foe.

[4]I long to dwell in your tent forever
　　and take refuge in the shelter of your wings.　　　　*Selah*
[5]For you have heard my vows, O God;
　　you have given me the heritage of those who fear your name.

[6]Increase the days of the king's life,
　　his years for many generations.
[7]May he be enthroned in God's presence forever;
　　appoint your love and faithfulness to protect him.

[8]Then will I ever sing praise to your name
　　and fulfill my vows day after day.

Psalm

For the director of music. For Jeduthun. A psalm of David.

¹My soul finds rest in God alone;
  my salvation comes from him.
²He alone is my rock and my salvation;
  he is my fortress, I will never be shaken.

³How long will you assault a man?
  Would all of you throw him down—
  this leaning wall, this tottering fence?
⁴They fully intend to topple him
  from his lofty place;
  they take delight in lies.
With their mouths they bless,
  but in their hearts they
    curse.   *Selah*

⁵Find rest, O my soul, in God
    alone;
  my hope comes from him.
⁶He alone is my rock and my
    salvation;
  he is my fortress, I will not
    be shaken.
⁷My salvation and my honor
    depend on God*ᵃ*;
  he is my mighty rock, my
    refuge.
⁸Trust in him at all times,
    O people;
  pour out your hearts to him,
  for God is our refuge.   *Selah*

⁹Lowborn men are but a breath,
  the highborn are but a lie;
  if weighed on a balance, they
    are nothing;
  together they are only a
    breath.
¹⁰Do not trust in extortion
  or take pride in stolen goods;
  though your riches increase,
  do not set your heart on them.

¹¹One thing God has spoken,
  two things have I heard:
  that you, O God, are strong,
¹² and that you, O Lord, are loving.
  Surely you will reward each person
  according to what he has done.

▓ ░░░░░░ MANAGING RESOURCES ░░░░░░ ⬆

62:9–10
Position and Possessions

Position and possessions. Consciously or unconsciously we think they will provide us with a security we don't now possess. But even if we have lots of both, we always end up wanting just a bit more. That's the nature of these two commodities. Since they can literally be taken from us in an instant, there is no lasting sense of security in either one of them. We can never be absolutely sure that we've obtained a secure position in life or an adequate amount of wealth.

God is certainly not opposed to position or possessions. What he opposes is *trusting* in them. Why? Because he loves us, and he knows that if we trust in what is untrustworthy, we'll be disappointed. He wants to spare us the heartbreak of throwing away the only life we have on the wrong pursuits.

The richest, most secure person in the world is the one who places his or her trust in God regardless of his or her financial circumstances or social status. God is the only entity that we can truly rely on for lasting security (verse 1).

---

*ᵃ*7 Or / God Most High is my salvation and my honor

Psalm

A psalm of David. When he was in the Desert of Judah.

[1]O God, you are my God,
      earnestly I seek you;
my soul thirsts for you,
      my body longs for you,
in a dry and weary land
      where there is no water.

[2]I have seen you in the sanctuary
      and beheld your power and your glory.
[3]Because your love is better than life,
      my lips will glorify you.
[4]I will praise you as long as I live,
      and in your name I will lift up my hands.
[5]My soul will be satisfied as with the richest of foods;
      with singing lips my mouth will praise you.

[6]On my bed I remember you;
      I think of you through the watches of the night.
[7]Because you are my help,
      I sing in the shadow of your wings.
[8]My soul clings to you;
      your right hand upholds me.

[9]They who seek my life will be destroyed;
      they will go down to the depths of the earth.
[10]They will be given over to the sword
      and become food for jackals.

[11]But the king will rejoice in God;
      all who swear by God's name will praise him,
      while the mouths of liars will be silenced.

Psalm

For the director of music. A psalm of David.

[1]Hear me, O God, as I voice my complaint;
      protect my life from the threat of the enemy.
[2]Hide me from the conspiracy of the wicked,
      from that noisy crowd of evildoers.

[3]They sharpen their tongues like swords
      and aim their words like deadly arrows.
[4]They shoot from ambush at the innocent man;
      they shoot at him suddenly, without fear.

[5]They encourage each other in evil plans,
      they talk about hiding their snares;
      they say, "Who will see them*a*?"

a5 Or us

⁶They plot injustice and say,
　"We have devised a perfect plan!"
　Surely the mind and heart of man are cunning.

⁷But God will shoot them with arrows;
　suddenly they will be struck down.
⁸He will turn their own tongues against them
　and bring them to ruin;
　all who see them will shake their heads in scorn.

⁹All mankind will fear;
　they will proclaim the works of God
　and ponder what he has done.
¹⁰Let the righteous rejoice in the Lord
　and take refuge in him;
　let all the upright in heart praise him!

Psalm

65

For the director of music. A psalm of David. A song.

¹Praise awaits*ᵃ* you, O God, in Zion;
　to you our vows will be fulfilled.
²O you who hear prayer,
　to you all men will come.
³When we were overwhelmed by sins,
　you forgave*ᵇ* our transgressions.
⁴Blessed are those you choose
　and bring near to live in your courts!
We are filled with the good things of your house,
　of your holy temple.

⁵You answer us with awesome deeds of righteousness,
　O God our Savior,
‑the hope of all the ends of the earth
　and of the farthest seas,
⁶who formed the mountains by your power,
　having armed yourself with strength,
⁷who stilled the roaring of the seas,
　the roaring of their waves,
　and the turmoil of the nations.
⁸Those living far away fear your wonders;
　where morning dawns and evening fades
　you call forth songs of joy.

⁹You care for the land and water it;
　you enrich it abundantly.
The streams of God are filled with water
　to provide the people with grain,
　for so you have ordained it.*ᶜ*
¹⁰You drench its furrows
　and level its ridges;

ᵃ 1 Or befits; the meaning of the Hebrew for this word is uncertain.
you prepare the land　　　*ᵇ 3 Or made atonement for*　　*ᶜ 9 Or for that is how*

you soften it with showers
  and bless its crops.
¹¹You crown the year with your bounty,
  and your carts overflow with abundance.
¹²The grasslands of the desert overflow;
  the hills are clothed with gladness.
¹³The meadows are covered with flocks
  and the valleys are mantled with grain;
  they shout for joy and sing.

Psalm

66

For the director of music. A song. A psalm.

¹Shout with joy to God, all the earth!
² Sing the glory of his name;
  make his praise glorious!
³Say to God, "How awesome are your deeds!
  So great is your power
  that your enemies cringe before you.
⁴All the earth bows down to you;
  they sing praise to you,
  they sing praise to your name."   *Selah*

⁵Come and see what God has done,
  how awesome his works in man's behalf!
⁶He turned the sea into dry land,
  they passed through the waters on foot—
  come, let us rejoice in him.
⁷He rules forever by his power,
  his eyes watch the nations—
  let not the rebellious rise up against him.   *Selah*

⁸Praise our God, O peoples,
  let the sound of his praise be heard;
⁹he has preserved our lives
  and kept our feet from slipping.
¹⁰For you, O God, tested us;
  you refined us like silver.
¹¹You brought us into prison
  and laid burdens on our backs.
¹²You let men ride over our heads;
  we went through fire and water,
  but you brought us to a place of abundance.

¹³I will come to your temple with burnt offerings
  and fulfill my vows to you—
¹⁴vows my lips promised and my mouth spoke
  when I was in trouble.
¹⁵I will sacrifice fat animals to you
  and an offering of rams;
  I will offer bulls and goats.   *Selah*

¹⁶Come and listen, all you who fear God;

let me tell you what he has done for me.
¹⁷I cried out to him with my mouth;
　　his praise was on my tongue.
¹⁸If I had cherished sin in my heart,
　　the Lord would not have listened;
¹⁹but God has surely listened
　　and heard my voice in prayer.
²⁰Praise be to God,
　　who has not rejected my prayer
　　or withheld his love from me!

Psalm

67

For the director of music. With stringed instruments. A psalm. A song.

¹May God be gracious to us and bless us
　　and make his face shine upon us,　　　　　　　　　*Selah*
²that your ways may be known
　　　　on earth,
　　your salvation among all
　　　　nations.

³May the peoples praise you,
　　O God;
　　may all the peoples praise
　　　　you.
⁴May the nations be glad and
　　　　sing for joy,
　　for you rule the peoples
　　　　justly
　　and guide the nations of the
　　　　earth.　　　　　　*Selah*
⁵May the peoples praise you,
　　O God;
　　may all the peoples praise
　　　　you.
⁶Then the land will yield its
　　　　harvest,
　　and God, our God, will bless
　　　　us.
⁷God will bless us,
　　and all the ends of the earth
　　　　will fear him.

▣ ::::::::::: **KNOWING YOURSELF** ::::::::::: ⬌

66:18
Sin

Why are some prayers not answered?

Generally, God answers every prayer—although sometimes he says no. This verse mentions the only exception to that rule: When we harbor sin in our hearts, God withholds his answer until we first give up that "cherished" sin (compare similar teaching in Isaiah chapter 59, verses 1–2 [page 970], and 1 Peter chapter 3, verse 7 [page 1613]).

If you're a seeker, understand that it's best to deal with the subject of sin before you deal with the subject of prayer. When you ask God to forgive you for the things you've done, your sin will no longer be a barrier in your relationship with him. If you are already a believer, don't cherish the things God despises. A relationship with God is too valuable to short-circuit on something that will hurt you in the long run anyway.

Psalm

68

For the director of music. Of David. A psalm. A song.

¹May God arise, may his enemies be scattered;
　　may his foes flee before him.
²As smoke is blown away by the wind,
　　may you blow them away;

as wax melts before the fire,
may the wicked perish before God.
³But may the righteous be glad
and rejoice before God;
may they be happy and joyful.

⁴Sing to God, sing praise to his name,
extol him who rides on the clouds^a—
his name is the LORD—
and rejoice before him.
⁵A father to the fatherless, a defender of widows,
is God in his holy dwelling.
⁶God sets the lonely in families,^b
he leads forth the prisoners with singing;
but the rebellious live in a sun-scorched land.

⁷When you went out before your people, O God,
when you marched through the wasteland,   *Selah*
⁸the earth shook,
the heavens poured down rain,
before God, the One of Sinai,
before God, the God of Israel.
⁹You gave abundant showers, O God;
you refreshed your weary inheritance.
¹⁰Your people settled in it,
and from your bounty, O God, you provided for the poor.

¹¹The Lord announced the word,
and great was the company of those who proclaimed it:
¹²"Kings and armies flee in haste;
in the camps men divide the plunder.
¹³Even while you sleep among the campfires,^c
the wings of ˻my˼ dove are sheathed with silver,
its feathers with shining gold."
¹⁴When the Almighty^d scattered the kings in the land,
it was like snow fallen on Zalmon.

¹⁵The mountains of Bashan are majestic mountains;
rugged are the mountains of Bashan.
¹⁶Why gaze in envy, O rugged mountains,
at the mountain where God chooses to reign,
where the LORD himself will dwell forever?
¹⁷The chariots of God are tens of thousands
and thousands of thousands;
the Lord ˻has come˼ from Sinai into his sanctuary.
¹⁸When you ascended on high,
you led captives in your train;
you received gifts from men,
even from^e the rebellious—
that you,^f O LORD God, might dwell there.

¹⁹Praise be to the Lord, to God our Savior,
who daily bears our burdens.   *Selah*

---

^a4 Or / prepare the way for him who rides through the deserts   ^b6 Or the desolate in a homeland   ^c13 Or saddlebags
^d14 Hebrew Shaddai   ^e18 Or gifts for men, / even   ^f18 Or they

²⁰Our God is a God who saves;
  from the Sovereign LORD comes escape from death.

²¹Surely God will crush the heads of his enemies,
  the hairy crowns of those who go on in their sins.
²²The Lord says, "I will bring them from Bashan;
  I will bring them from the depths of the sea,
²³that you may plunge your feet in the blood of your foes,
  while the tongues of your dogs have their share."

²⁴Your procession has come into view, O God,
  the procession of my God and King into the sanctuary.
²⁵In front are the singers, after them the musicians;
  with them are the maidens playing tambourines.
²⁶Praise God in the great congregation;
  praise the LORD in the assembly of Israel.
²⁷There is the little tribe of Benjamin, leading them,
  there the great throng of Judah's princes,
  and there the princes of Zebulun and of Naphtali.

²⁸Summon your power, O God*a*;
  show us your strength, O God, as you have done before.
²⁹Because of your temple at Jerusalem
  kings will bring you gifts.
³⁰Rebuke the beast among the reeds,
  the herd of bulls among the calves of the nations.
 Humbled, may it bring bars of silver.
  Scatter the nations who delight in war.
³¹Envoys will come from Egypt;
  Cush*b* will submit herself to God.

³²Sing to God, O kingdoms of the earth,
  sing praise to the Lord,   *Selah*
³³to him who rides the ancient skies above,
  who thunders with mighty voice.
³⁴Proclaim the power of God,
  whose majesty is over Israel,
  whose power is in the skies.
³⁵You are awesome, O God, in your sanctuary;
  the God of Israel gives power and strength to his people.

 Praise be to God!

Psalm

69

For the director of music. To ₌the tune of₌ "Lilies." Of David.

¹Save me, O God,
  for the waters have come up to my neck.
²I sink in the miry depths,
  where there is no foothold.
 I have come into the deep waters;

---

a 28 Many Hebrew manuscripts, Septuagint and Syriac; most Hebrew manuscripts *Your God has summoned power for you*
b 31 That is, the upper Nile region

    the floods engulf me.
³I am worn out calling for help;
    my throat is parched.
My eyes fail,
    looking for my God.
⁴Those who hate me without reason
    outnumber the hairs of my head;
many are my enemies without cause,
    those who seek to destroy me.
I am forced to restore
    what I did not steal.

⁵You know my folly, O God;
    my guilt is not hidden from you.

⁶May those who hope in you
    not be disgraced because of me,
    O Lord, the LORD Almighty;
may those who seek you
    not be put to shame because of me,
    O God of Israel.
⁷For I endure scorn for your sake,
    and shame covers my face.
⁸I am a stranger to my brothers,
    an alien to my own mother's sons;
⁹for zeal for your house consumes me,
    and the insults of those who insult you fall on me.
¹⁰When I weep and fast,
    I must endure scorn;
¹¹when I put on sackcloth,
    people make sport of me.
¹²Those who sit at the gate mock me,
    and I am the song of the drunkards.

¹³But I pray to you, O LORD,
    in the time of your favor;
in your great love, O God,
    answer me with your sure salvation.
¹⁴Rescue me from the mire,
    do not let me sink;
deliver me from those who hate me,
    from the deep waters.
¹⁵Do not let the floodwaters engulf me
    or the depths swallow me up
    or the pit close its mouth over me.
¹⁶Answer me, O LORD, out of the goodness of your love;
    in your great mercy turn to me.
¹⁷Do not hide your face from your servant;
    answer me quickly, for I am in trouble.
¹⁸Come near and rescue me;
    redeem me because of my foes.

¹⁹You know how I am scorned, disgraced and shamed;
    all my enemies are before you.
²⁰Scorn has broken my heart

and has left me helpless;
I looked for sympathy, but there was none,
    for comforters, but I found none.
²¹They put gall in my food
    and gave me vinegar for my thirst.

²²May the table set before them become a snare;
    may it become retribution and*ᵃ* a trap.
²³May their eyes be darkened so they cannot see,
    and their backs be bent forever.
²⁴Pour out your wrath on them;
    let your fierce anger overtake them.
²⁵May their place be deserted;
    let there be no one to dwell in their tents.
²⁶For they persecute those you wound
    and talk about the pain of those you hurt.
²⁷Charge them with crime upon crime;
    do not let them share in your salvation.
²⁸May they be blotted out of the book of life
    and not be listed with the righteous.

²⁹I am in pain and distress;
    may your salvation, O God, protect me.

³⁰I will praise God's name in song
    and glorify him with thanksgiving.
³¹This will please the LORD more than an ox,
    more than a bull with its horns and hoofs.
³²The poor will see and be glad—
    you who seek God, may your hearts live!
³³The LORD hears the needy
    and does not despise his captive people.

³⁴Let heaven and earth praise him,
    the seas and all that move in them,
³⁵for God will save Zion
    and rebuild the cities of Judah.
  Then people will settle there and possess it;
³⁶   the children of his servants will inherit it,
    and those who love his name will dwell there.

Psalm

For the director of music. Of David. A petition.

¹Hasten, O God, to save me;
    O LORD, come quickly to help me.
²May those who seek my life
    be put to shame and confusion;
  may all who desire my ruin
    be turned back in disgrace.
³May those who say to me, "Aha! Aha!"
    turn back because of their shame.

ᵃ22 Or snare / and their fellowship become

⁴But may all who seek you
 rejoice and be glad in you;
may those who love your salvation always say,
 "Let God be exalted!"

⁵Yet I am poor and needy;
 come quickly to me, O God.
You are my help and my deliverer;
 O Lᴏʀᴅ, do not delay.

Psalm

71

¹In you, O Lᴏʀᴅ, I have taken refuge;
 let me never be put to shame.
²Rescue me and deliver me in your righteousness;
 turn your ear to me and save me.
³Be my rock of refuge,
 to which I can always go;
 give the command to save me,
 for you are my rock and my fortress.
⁴Deliver me, O my God, from the hand of the wicked,
 from the grasp of evil and cruel men.

⁵For you have been my hope, O Sovereign Lᴏʀᴅ,
 my confidence since my youth.
⁶From birth I have relied on you;
 you brought me forth from my mother's womb.
 I will ever praise you.
⁷I have become like a portent to many,
 but you are my strong refuge.
⁸My mouth is filled with your praise,
 declaring your splendor all day long.

⁹Do not cast me away when I am old;
 do not forsake me when my strength is gone.
¹⁰For my enemies speak against me;
 those who wait to kill me conspire together.
¹¹They say, "God has forsaken him;
 pursue him and seize him,
 for no one will rescue him."
¹²Be not far from me, O God;
 come quickly, O my God, to help me.
¹³May my accusers perish in shame;
 may those who want to harm me
 be covered with scorn and disgrace.

¹⁴But as for me, I will always have hope;
 I will praise you more and more.
¹⁵My mouth will tell of your righteousness,
 of your salvation all day long,
 though I know not its measure.
¹⁶I will come and proclaim your mighty acts, O Sovereign Lᴏʀᴅ;
 I will proclaim your righteousness, yours alone.
¹⁷Since my youth, O God, you have taught me,

and to this day I declare your marvelous deeds.
¹⁸Even when I am old and gray,
   do not forsake me, O God,
till I declare your power to the next generation,
   your might to all who are to come.

¹⁹Your righteousness reaches to the skies, O God,
   you who have done great things.
   Who, O God, is like you?
²⁰Though you have made me see troubles, many and bitter,
   you will restore my life again;
from the depths of the earth
   you will again bring me up.
²¹You will increase my honor
   and comfort me once again.

²²I will praise you with the harp
   for your faithfulness, O my God;
I will sing praise to you with the lyre,
   O Holy One of Israel.
²³My lips will shout for joy
   when I sing praise to you—
   I, whom you have redeemed.
²⁴My tongue will tell of your righteous acts
   all day long,
for those who wanted to harm me
   have been put to shame and confusion.

Psalm

72

Of Solomon.

¹Endow the king with your justice, O God,
   the royal son with your righteousness.
²He will*ᵃ* judge your people in righteousness,
   your afflicted ones with justice.
³The mountains will bring prosperity to the people,
   the hills the fruit of righteousness.
⁴He will defend the afflicted among the people
   and save the children of the needy;
   he will crush the oppressor.

⁵He will endure*ᵇ* as long as the sun,
   as long as the moon, through all generations.
⁶He will be like rain falling on a mown field,
   like showers watering the earth.
⁷In his days the righteous will flourish;
   prosperity will abound till the moon is no more.

⁸He will rule from sea to sea
   and from the River*ᶜ* to the ends of the earth.*ᵈ*
⁹The desert tribes will bow before him

ᵃ2 Or *May he; similarly in verses 3–11 and 17*   *ᵇ5* Septuagint; Hebrew *You will be feared*   *ᶜ8* That is, the Euphrates
ᵈ8 Or *the end of the land*

and his enemies will lick the dust.
¹⁰The kings of Tarshish and of distant shores
    will bring tribute to him;
  the kings of Sheba and Seba
    will present him gifts.
¹¹All kings will bow down to him
    and all nations will serve him.

¹²For he will deliver the needy who cry out,
    the afflicted who have no one to help.

¹³He will take pity on the weak and the
      needy
    and save the needy from death.
¹⁴He will rescue them from oppression
      and violence,
    for precious is their blood in his
      sight.

¹⁵Long may he live!
    May gold from Sheba be given him.
  May people ever pray for him
    and bless him all day long.
¹⁶Let grain abound throughout the land;
    on the tops of the hills may it sway.
  Let its fruit flourish like Lebanon;
    let it thrive like the grass of the
      field.
¹⁷May his name endure forever;
    may it continue as long as the sun.

  All nations will be blessed through
      him,
    and they will call him blessed.

□ ░░░STRENGTHENING RELATIONSHIPS░░░ ⮂

72:4
Leadership

One key leadership responsibility is to see that all individuals receive fair treatment. Individuals in leadership positions need to speak up for those who don't have a voice and frustrate those who try to use their power to exploit others.

Whether you're a corporate CEO, a kindergarten teacher, or a parent, there are some areas in your life in which you need to exhibit leadership. How would people working under you characterize your leadership? Do those with little influence feel that you are their champion? Do those who take advantage of others know that if you find out about it, they're in trouble? According to the Bible, God's kind of leader is able to answer yes to both of those questions.

---

¹⁸Praise be to the Lᴏʀᴅ God, the God of Israel,
    who alone does marvelous deeds.
¹⁹Praise be to his glorious name forever;
    may the whole earth be filled with his glory.
                        Amen and Amen.

²⁰This concludes the prayers of David son of Jesse.

BOOK III

Psalms 73–89

Psalm

73

A psalm of Asaph.

¹Surely God is good to Israel,
    to those who are pure in heart.

²But as for me, my feet had almost slipped;

I had nearly lost my foothold.
³For I envied the arrogant
    when I saw the prosperity of the wicked.

⁴They have no struggles;
    their bodies are healthy and strong.ᵃ
⁵They are free from the burdens common to man;
    they are not plagued by human ills.
⁶Therefore pride is their necklace;
    they clothe themselves with violence.
⁷From their callous hearts comes iniquityᵇ;
    the evil conceits of their minds know no limits.
⁸They scoff, and speak with malice;
    in their arrogance they threaten oppression.
⁹Their mouths lay claim to heaven,
    and their tongues take possession of the earth.
¹⁰Therefore their people turn to them
    and drink up waters in abundance.ᶜ
¹¹They say, "How can God know?
    Does the Most High have knowledge?"

¹²This is what the wicked are like—
    always carefree, they increase in wealth.

¹³Surely in vain have I kept my heart pure;
    in vain have I washed my hands in innocence.
¹⁴All day long I have been plagued;
    I have been punished every morning.

¹⁵If I had said, "I will speak thus,"
    I would have betrayed your children.
¹⁶When I tried to understand all this,
    it was oppressive to me
¹⁷till I entered the sanctuary of God;
    then I understood their final destiny.

¹⁸Surely you place them on slippery ground;
    you cast them down to ruin.
¹⁹How suddenly are they destroyed,
    completely swept away by terrors!
²⁰As a dream when one awakes,
    so when you arise, O Lord,
    you will despise them as fantasies.

²¹When my heart was grieved
    and my spirit embittered,
²²I was senseless and ignorant;
    I was a brute beast before you.

²³Yet I am always with you;
    you hold me by my right hand.
²⁴You guide me with your counsel,
    and afterward you will take me into glory.

ᵃ4 With a different word division of the Hebrew; Masoretic Text *struggles at their death; / their bodies are healthy*
ᵇ7 Syriac (see also Septuagint); Hebrew *Their eyes bulge with fat*   ᶜ10 The meaning of the Hebrew for this verse is uncertain.

²⁵Whom have I in heaven but you?
    And earth has nothing I desire besides you.
²⁶My flesh and my heart may fail,
    but God is the strength of my heart
    and my portion forever.

²⁷Those who are far from you will perish;
    you destroy all who are unfaithful to you.
²⁸But as for me, it is good to be near God.
    I have made the Sovereign LORD my refuge;
    I will tell of all your deeds.

Psalm

74

A maskil^a of Asaph.

¹Why have you rejected us forever, O God?
    Why does your anger smolder against the sheep of your pasture?
²Remember the people you purchased of old,
    the tribe of your inheritance, whom you redeemed—
    Mount Zion, where you dwelt.
³Turn your steps toward these everlasting ruins,
    all this destruction the enemy has brought on the sanctuary.

⁴Your foes roared in the place where you met with us;
    they set up their standards as signs.
⁵They behaved like men wielding axes
    to cut through a thicket of trees.
⁶They smashed all the carved paneling
    with their axes and hatchets.
⁷They burned your sanctuary to the ground;
    they defiled the dwelling place of your Name.
⁸They said in their hearts, "We will crush them completely!"
    They burned every place where God was worshiped in the land.
⁹We are given no miraculous signs;
    no prophets are left,
    and none of us knows how long this will be.

¹⁰How long will the enemy mock you, O God?
    Will the foe revile your name forever?
¹¹Why do you hold back your hand, your right hand?
    Take it from the folds of your garment and destroy them!

¹²But you, O God, are my king from of old;
    you bring salvation upon the earth.
¹³It was you who split open the sea by your power;
    you broke the heads of the monster in the waters.
¹⁴It was you who crushed the heads of Leviathan
    and gave him as food to the creatures of the desert.
¹⁵It was you who opened up springs and streams;
    you dried up the ever flowing rivers.

---

^aTitle: Probably a literary or musical term

¹⁶The day is yours, and yours also the night;
    you established the sun and moon.
¹⁷It was you who set all the boundaries of the earth;
    you made both summer and winter.

¹⁸Remember how the enemy has mocked you, O LORD,
    how foolish people have reviled your name.
¹⁹Do not hand over the life of your dove to wild beasts;
    do not forget the lives of your afflicted people forever.
²⁰Have regard for your covenant,
    because haunts of violence fill the dark places of the land.
²¹Do not let the oppressed retreat in disgrace;
    may the poor and needy praise your name.

²²Rise up, O God, and defend your cause;
    remember how fools mock you all day long.
²³Do not ignore the clamor of your adversaries,
    the uproar of your enemies, which rises continually.

Psalm

For the director of music. To the tune of, "Do Not Destroy." A psalm of Asaph.
A song.

¹We give thanks to you, O God,
    we give thanks, for your Name is near;
    men tell of your wonderful deeds.

²You say, "I choose the appointed time;
    it is I who judge uprightly.
³When the earth and all its people quake,
    it is I who hold its pillars firm.   *Selah*
⁴To the arrogant I say, 'Boast no more,'
    and to the wicked, 'Do not lift up your horns.
⁵Do not lift your horns against heaven;
    do not speak with outstretched neck.'"

⁶No one from the east or the west
    or from the desert can exalt a man.
⁷But it is God who judges:
    He brings one down, he exalts another.
⁸In the hand of the LORD is a cup
    full of foaming wine mixed with spices;
   he pours it out, and all the wicked of the earth
    drink it down to its very dregs.

⁹As for me, I will declare this forever;
    I will sing praise to the God of Jacob.
¹⁰I will cut off the horns of all the wicked,
    but the horns of the righteous will be lifted up.

Psalm

For the director of music. With stringed instruments.
A psalm of Asaph. A song.

[1]In Judah God is known;
  his name is great in Israel.
[2]His tent is in Salem,
  his dwelling place in Zion.
[3]There he broke the flashing arrows,
  the shields and the swords, the weapons of war.   *Selah*

[4]You are resplendent with light,
  more majestic than mountains rich with game.
[5]Valiant men lie plundered,
  they sleep their last sleep;
not one of the warriors
  can lift his hands.
[6]At your rebuke, O God of Jacob,
  both horse and chariot lie still.
[7]You alone are to be feared.
  Who can stand before you when you are angry?
[8]From heaven you pronounced judgment,
  and the land feared and was quiet—
[9]when you, O God, rose up to judge,
  to save all the afflicted of the land.   *Selah*
[10]Surely your wrath against men brings you praise,
  and the survivors of your wrath are restrained.[a]

[11]Make vows to the LORD your God and fulfill them;
  let all the neighboring lands
  bring gifts to the One to be feared.
[12]He breaks the spirit of rulers;
  he is feared by the kings of the earth.

Psalm

For the director of music. For Jeduthun. Of Asaph. A psalm.

[1]I cried out to God for help;
  I cried out to God to hear me.
[2]When I was in distress, I sought the Lord;
  at night I stretched out untiring hands
  and my soul refused to be comforted.

[3]I remembered you, O God, and I groaned;
  I mused, and my spirit grew faint.   *Selah*

a 10 Or *Surely the wrath of men brings you praise, / and with the remainder of wrath you arm yourself*

4You kept my eyes from closing;
    I was too troubled to speak.
5I thought about the former days,
    the years of long ago;
6I remembered my songs in the night.
    My heart mused and my spirit inquired:

7"Will the Lord reject forever?
    Will he never show his favor again?
8Has his unfailing love vanished forever?
    Has his promise failed for all time?
9Has God forgotten to be merciful?
    Has he in anger withheld his compassion?"   *Selah*

10Then I thought, "To this I will appeal:
    the years of the right hand of the Most High."
11I will remember the deeds of the LORD;
    yes, I will remember your miracles of long ago.
12I will meditate on all your works
    and consider all your mighty deeds.

13Your ways, O God, are holy.
    What god is so great as our
        God?
14You are the God who performs
        miracles;
    you display your power
        among the peoples.
15With your mighty arm you
        redeemed your people,
    the descendants of Jacob
        and Joseph.   *Selah*

16The waters saw you, O God,
    the waters saw you and
        writhed;
    the very depths were
        convulsed.
17The clouds poured down
        water,
    the skies resounded with thunder;
    your arrows flashed back and forth.
18Your thunder was heard in the whirlwind,
    your lightning lit up the world;
    the earth trembled and quaked.
19Your path led through the sea,
    your way through the mighty waters,
    though your footprints were not seen.

20You led your people like a flock
    by the hand of Moses and Aaron.

▣ ▦▦▦▦▦ DISCOVERING GOD ▦▦▦▦▦ ⬌

77:7–14
The God Who Is There

When hard times come and it seems that God is nowhere near, what do you think about most?

This psalm urges us to think back and remember the way God has worked in the past. By recalling his power, we can be reminded of his faithfulness even if current circumstances don't give evidence of his activity. These memories prompt us to recall the comforting truth that God promises to act on his followers' behalf—even if it takes time.

Psalm

A maskil[a] of Asaph.

¹O my people, hear my teaching;
  listen to the words of my mouth.
²I will open my mouth in parables,
  I will utter hidden things, things from of old—
³what we have heard and known,
  what our fathers have told us.
⁴We will not hide them from their children;
  we will tell the next generation
the praiseworthy deeds of the LORD,
  his power, and the wonders he has done.
⁵He decreed statutes for Jacob
  and established the law in Israel,
which he commanded our forefathers
  to teach their children,
⁶so the next generation would know them,
  even the children yet to be born,
  and they in turn would tell their children.
⁷Then they would put their trust in God
  and would not forget his deeds
  but would keep his commands.
⁸They would not be like their forefathers—
  a stubborn and rebellious generation,
whose hearts were not loyal to God,
  whose spirits were not faithful to him.

⁹The men of Ephraim, though armed with bows,
  turned back on the day of battle;
¹⁰they did not keep God's covenant
  and refused to live by his law.
¹¹They forgot what he had done,
  the wonders he had shown them.
¹²He did miracles in the sight of their fathers
  in the land of Egypt, in the region of Zoan.
¹³He divided the sea and led them through;
  he made the water stand firm like a wall.
¹⁴He guided them with the cloud by day
  and with light from the fire all night.
¹⁵He split the rocks in the desert
  and gave them water as abundant as the seas;
¹⁶he brought streams out of a rocky crag
  and made water flow down like rivers.

¹⁷But they continued to sin against him,
  rebelling in the desert against the Most High.
¹⁸They willfully put God to the test
  by demanding the food they craved.
¹⁹They spoke against God, saying,

ᵃTitle: Probably a literary or musical term

"Can God spread a table in the desert?
²⁰When he struck the rock, water gushed out,
    and streams flowed abundantly.
  But can he also give us food?
    Can he supply meat for his people?"
²¹When the LORD heard them, he was very angry;
    his fire broke out against Jacob,
    and his wrath rose against Israel,
²²for they did not believe in God
    or trust in his deliverance.
²³Yet he gave a command to the skies above
    and opened the doors of the heavens;
²⁴he rained down manna for the people to eat,
    he gave them the grain of heaven.
²⁵Men ate the bread of angels;
    he sent them all the food they could eat.
²⁶He let loose the east wind from the heavens
    and led forth the south wind by his power.
²⁷He rained meat down on them like dust,
    flying birds like sand on the seashore.
²⁸He made them come down inside their camp,
    all around their tents.
²⁹They ate till they had more than enough,
    for he had given them what they craved.
³⁰But before they turned from the food they craved,
    even while it was still in their mouths,
³¹God's anger rose against them;
    he put to death the sturdiest among them,
    cutting down the young men of Israel.

³²In spite of all this, they kept on sinning;
    in spite of his wonders, they did not believe.
³³So he ended their days in futility
    and their years in terror.
³⁴Whenever God slew them, they would seek him;
    they eagerly turned to him again.
³⁵They remembered that God was their Rock,
    that God Most High was their Redeemer.
³⁶But then they would flatter him with their mouths,
    lying to him with their tongues;
³⁷their hearts were not loyal to him,
    they were not faithful to his covenant.
³⁸Yet he was merciful;
    he forgave their iniquities
    and did not destroy them.
  Time after time he restrained his anger
    and did not stir up his full wrath.
³⁹He remembered that they were but flesh,
    a passing breeze that does not return.

⁴⁰How often they rebelled against him in the desert
    and grieved him in the wasteland!
⁴¹Again and again they put God to the test;
    they vexed the Holy One of Israel.

⁴²They did not remember his power—
  the day he redeemed them from the oppressor,
⁴³the day he displayed his miraculous signs in Egypt,
  his wonders in the region of Zoan.
⁴⁴He turned their rivers to blood;
  they could not drink from their streams.
⁴⁵He sent swarms of flies that devoured them,
  and frogs that devastated them.
⁴⁶He gave their crops to the grasshopper,
  their produce to the locust.
⁴⁷He destroyed their vines with hail
  and their sycamore-figs with sleet.
⁴⁸He gave over their cattle to the hail,
  their livestock to bolts of lightning.
⁴⁹He unleashed against them his hot anger,
  his wrath, indignation and hostility—
  a band of destroying angels.
⁵⁰He prepared a path for his anger;
  he did not spare them from death
  but gave them over to the plague.
⁵¹He struck down all the firstborn of Egypt,
  the firstfruits of manhood in the tents of Ham.
⁵²But he brought his people out like a flock;
  he led them like sheep through the desert.
⁵³He guided them safely, so they were unafraid;
  but the sea engulfed their enemies.
⁵⁴Thus he brought them to the border of his holy land,
  to the hill country his right hand had taken.
⁵⁵He drove out nations before them
  and allotted their lands to them as an inheritance;
  he settled the tribes of Israel in their homes.

⁵⁶But they put God to the test
  and rebelled against the Most High;
  they did not keep his statutes.
⁵⁷Like their fathers they were disloyal and faithless,
  as unreliable as a faulty bow.
⁵⁸They angered him with their high places;
  they aroused his jealousy with their idols.
⁵⁹When God heard them, he was very angry;
  he rejected Israel completely.
⁶⁰He abandoned the tabernacle of Shiloh,
  the tent he had set up among men.
⁶¹He sent ⌊the ark of⌋ his might into captivity,
  his splendor into the hands of the enemy.
⁶²He gave his people over to the sword;
  he was very angry with his inheritance.
⁶³Fire consumed their young men,
  and their maidens had no wedding songs;
⁶⁴their priests were put to the sword,
  and their widows could not weep.

⁶⁵Then the Lord awoke as from sleep,
  as a man wakes from the stupor of wine.

⁶⁶He beat back his enemies;
  he put them to everlasting shame.
⁶⁷Then he rejected the tents of Joseph,
  he did not choose the tribe of Ephraim;
⁶⁸but he chose the tribe of Judah,
  Mount Zion, which he loved.
⁶⁹He built his sanctuary like the heights,
  like the earth that he established forever.
⁷⁰He chose David his servant
  and took him from the sheep pens;
⁷¹from tending the sheep he brought him
  to be the shepherd of his people Jacob,
  of Israel his inheritance.
⁷²And David shepherded them with integrity of heart;
  with skillful hands he led them.

Psalm

79

A psalm of Asaph.

¹O God, the nations have invaded your inheritance;
  they have defiled your holy temple,
  they have reduced Jerusalem to rubble.
²They have given the dead bodies of your servants
  as food to the birds of the air,
  the flesh of your saints to the beasts of the earth.
³They have poured out blood like water
  all around Jerusalem,
  and there is no one to bury the dead.
⁴We are objects of reproach to our neighbors,
  of scorn and derision to those around us.

⁵How long, O LORD? Will you be angry forever?
  How long will your jealousy burn like fire?
⁶Pour out your wrath on the nations
  that do not acknowledge you,
 on the kingdoms
  that do not call on your name;
⁷for they have devoured Jacob
  and destroyed his homeland.
⁸Do not hold against us the sins of the fathers;
  may your mercy come quickly to meet us,
  for we are in desperate need.

⁹Help us, O God our Savior,
  for the glory of your name;
 deliver us and forgive our sins
  for your name's sake.
¹⁰Why should the nations say,
  "Where is their God?"
 Before our eyes, make known among the nations
  that you avenge the outpoured blood of your servants.
¹¹May the groans of the prisoners come before you;

by the strength of your arm
preserve those condemned to die.

¹²Pay back into the laps of our neighbors seven times
the reproach they have hurled at you, O Lord.
¹³Then we your people, the sheep of your pasture,
will praise you forever;
from generation to generation
we will recount your praise.

Psalm

For the director of music. To ˌthe tune of¸ "The Lilies of the Covenant."
Of Asaph. A psalm.

¹Hear us, O Shepherd of Israel,
you who lead Joseph like a flock;
you who sit enthroned between the cherubim, shine forth
² before Ephraim, Benjamin and Manasseh.
Awaken your might;
come and save us.

³Restore us, O God;
make your face shine upon us,
that we may be saved.

⁴O Lᴏʀᴅ God Almighty,
how long will your anger smolder
against the prayers of your people?
⁵You have fed them with the bread of tears;
you have made them drink tears by the bowlful.
⁶You have made us a source of contention to our neighbors,
and our enemies mock us.

⁷Restore us, O God Almighty;
make your face shine upon us,
that we may be saved.

⁸You brought a vine out of Egypt;
you drove out the nations and planted it.
⁹You cleared the ground for it,
and it took root and filled the land.
¹⁰The mountains were covered with its shade,
the mighty cedars with its branches.
¹¹It sent out its boughs to the Sea,ᵃ
its shoots as far as the River.ᵇ

¹²Why have you broken down its walls
so that all who pass by pick its grapes?
¹³Boars from the forest ravage it
and the creatures of the field feed on it.
¹⁴Return to us, O God Almighty!
Look down from heaven and see!
Watch over this vine,

ᵃ*11* Probably the Mediterranean   ᵇ*11* That is, the Euphrates

15   the root your right hand has planted,
       the son[a] you have raised up for yourself.

16Your vine is cut down, it is burned with fire;
       at your rebuke your people perish.
17Let your hand rest on the man at your right hand,
       the son of man you have raised up for yourself.
18Then we will not turn away from you;
       revive us, and we will call on your name.

19Restore us, O Lord God Almighty;
       make your face shine upon us,
       that we may be saved.

Psalm

81

For the director of music. According to *gittith*.[b] Of Asaph.

1Sing for joy to God our strength;
       shout aloud to the God of Jacob!
2Begin the music, strike the tambourine,
       play the melodious harp and lyre.

3Sound the ram's horn at the New Moon,
       and when the moon is full, on the day of our Feast;
4this is a decree for Israel,
       an ordinance of the God of Jacob.
5He established it as a statute for Joseph
       when he went out against Egypt,
       where we heard a language we did not understand.[c]

6He says, "I removed the burden from their shoulders;
       their hands were set free from the basket.
7In your distress you called and I rescued you,
       I answered you out of a thundercloud;
       I tested you at the waters of Meribah.   *Selah*

8"Hear, O my people, and I will warn you—
       if you would but listen to me, O Israel!
9You shall have no foreign god among you;
       you shall not bow down to an alien god.
10I am the Lord your God,
       who brought you up out of Egypt.
       Open wide your mouth and I will fill it.

11"But my people would not listen to me;
       Israel would not submit to me.
12So I gave them over to their stubborn hearts
       to follow their own devices.

13"If my people would but listen to me,
       if Israel would follow my ways,
14how quickly would I subdue their enemies
       and turn my hand against their foes!

---

a 15 Or *branch*   *b Title:* Probably a musical term   *c 5* Or / *and we heard a voice we had not known*

¹⁵Those who hate the Lᴏʀᴅ would cringe before him,
and their punishment would last forever.
¹⁶But you would be fed with the finest of wheat;
with honey from the rock I would satisfy you."

Psalm

A psalm of Asaph.

¹God presides in the great assembly;
he gives judgment among the "gods":

²"How long will you*ᵃ* defend the unjust
and show partiality to the wicked?   *Selah*
³Defend the cause of the weak and fatherless;
maintain the rights of the poor and oppressed.
⁴Rescue the weak and needy;
deliver them from the hand of the wicked.

⁵"They know nothing, they understand nothing.
They walk about in darkness;
all the foundations of the earth are shaken.

⬚ ▒▒▒ DISCOVERING GOD ▒▒▒ ↻

82:6–7
Spiritual Fraud

Is this psalm saying that all people are "gods"—on their way to full godhood?

Not even close. In fact, this verse actually mocks that idea. Yes, we are created in God's image, but that's the point: We've been *created* by the *Creator*, and he alone is God—*un*-created. Verse 7 is clear: We will die. We are corrupt (verse 2) and willfully ignorant about what matters most (verse 5). Hardly a description of a god!

Take no comfort if some religious person flatters you with promises about being able to attain godhood. The Bible offers no such hope. Instead, be glad there is one Creator who is holy and just, and who wants to be in relationship with people. In his hands we can confidently rest. Through his power we can become fully human.

---

⁶"I said, 'You are "gods";
you are all sons of the Most High.'
⁷But you will die like mere men;
you will fall like every other ruler."

⁸Rise up, O God, judge the earth,
for all the nations are your
inheritance.

Psalm

A song. A psalm of Asaph.

¹O God, do not keep silent;
be not quiet, O God, be not still.
²See how your enemies are astir,
how your foes rear their heads.
³With cunning they conspire against
your people;
they plot against those you cherish.
⁴"Come," they say, "let us destroy them
as a nation,
that the name of Israel be
remembered no more."

⁵With one mind they plot together;
they form an alliance against you—
⁶the tents of Edom and the Ishmaelites,
of Moab and the Hagrites,

ᵃ2 The Hebrew is plural.

⁷Gebal,ᵃ Ammon and Amalek,
  Philistia, with the people of Tyre.
⁸Even Assyria has joined them
  to lend strength to the descendants of Lot.   *Selah*

⁹Do to them as you did to Midian,
  as you did to Sisera and Jabin at the river Kishon,
¹⁰who perished at Endor
  and became like refuse on the ground.
¹¹Make their nobles like Oreb and Zeeb,
  all their princes like Zebah and Zalmunna,
¹²who said, "Let us take possession
  of the pasturelands of God."

¹³Make them like tumbleweed, O my God,
  like chaff before the wind.
¹⁴As fire consumes the forest
  or a flame sets the mountains ablaze,
¹⁵so pursue them with your tempest
  and terrify them with your storm.
¹⁶Cover their faces with shame
  so that men will seek your name, O LORD.

¹⁷May they ever be ashamed and dismayed;
  may they perish in disgrace.
¹⁸Let them know that you, whose name is the LORD—
  that you alone are the Most High over all the earth.

Psalm

84

For the director of music. According to *gittith.ᵇ* Of the Sons of Korah. A psalm.

¹How lovely is your dwelling place,
  O LORD Almighty!
²My soul yearns, even faints,
  for the courts of the LORD;
my heart and my flesh cry out
  for the living God.

³Even the sparrow has found a home,
  and the swallow a nest for herself,
  where she may have her young—
a place near your altar,
  O LORD Almighty, my King and my God.
⁴Blessed are those who dwell in your house;
  they are ever praising you.   *Selah*

⁵Blessed are those whose strength is in you,
  who have set their hearts on pilgrimage.
⁶As they pass through the Valley of Baca,
  they make it a place of springs;
  the autumn rains also cover it with pools.ᶜ

ᵃ7 That is, Byblos   ᵇTitle: Probably a musical term   ᶜ6 Or *blessings*

⁷They go from strength to strength,
    till each appears before God in Zion.

⁸Hear my prayer, O Lᴏʀᴅ God Almighty;
    listen to me, O God of Jacob.   *Selah*
⁹Look upon our shield,ᵃ O God;
    look with favor on your anointed one.

¹⁰Better is one day in your courts
    than a thousand elsewhere;
I would rather be a doorkeeper in the house of my God
    than dwell in the tents of the wicked.
¹¹For the Lᴏʀᴅ God is a sun and shield;
    the Lᴏʀᴅ bestows favor and honor;
no good thing does he withhold
    from those whose walk is blameless.

¹²O Lᴏʀᴅ Almighty,
    blessed is the man who trusts in you.

Psalm

85

For the director of music. Of the Sons of Korah. A psalm.

¹You showed favor to your land, O Lᴏʀᴅ;
    you restored the fortunes of Jacob.
²You forgave the iniquity of your people
    and covered all their sins.   *Selah*
³You set aside all your wrath
    and turned from your fierce anger.

⁴Restore us again, O God our Savior,
    and put away your displeasure toward us.
⁵Will you be angry with us forever?
    Will you prolong your anger through all generations?
⁶Will you not revive us again,
    that your people may rejoice in you?
⁷Show us your unfailing love, O Lᴏʀᴅ,
    and grant us your salvation.

⁸I will listen to what God the Lᴏʀᴅ will say;
    he promises peace to his people, his saints—
    but let them not return to folly.
⁹Surely his salvation is near those who fear him,
    that his glory may dwell in our land.

¹⁰Love and faithfulness meet together;
    righteousness and peace kiss each other.
¹¹Faithfulness springs forth from the earth,
    and righteousness looks down from heaven.
¹²The Lᴏʀᴅ will indeed give what is good,
    and our land will yield its harvest.
¹³Righteousness goes before him
    and prepares the way for his steps.

ᵃ9 Or *sovereign*

Psalm

A prayer of David.

¹Hear, O Lᴏʀᴅ, and answer me,
for I am poor and needy.
²Guard my life, for I am devoted to you.
You are my God; save your servant
who trusts in you.
³Have mercy on me, O Lord,
for I call to you all day long.
⁴Bring joy to your servant,
for to you, O Lord,
I lift up my soul.

⁵You are forgiving and good, O Lord,
abounding in love to all who call to you.
⁶Hear my prayer, O Lᴏʀᴅ;
listen to my cry for mercy.
⁷In the day of my trouble I will call to you,
for you will answer me.

⁸Among the gods there is none like you, O Lord;
no deeds can compare with yours.
⁹All the nations you have made
will come and worship before you, O Lord;
they will bring glory to your name.
¹⁰For you are great and do marvelous deeds;
you alone are God.

¹¹Teach me your way, O Lᴏʀᴅ,
and I will walk in your truth;
give me an undivided heart,
that I may fear your name.
¹²I will praise you, O Lord my God, with all my heart;
I will glorify your name forever.
¹³For great is your love toward me;
you have delivered me from the depths of the grave.ᵃ

¹⁴The arrogant are attacking me, O God;
a band of ruthless men seeks my life—
men without regard for you.
¹⁵But you, O Lord, are a compassionate and gracious God,
slow to anger, abounding in love and faithfulness.
¹⁶Turn to me and have mercy on me;
grant your strength to your servant
and save the son of your maidservant.ᵇ
¹⁷Give me a sign of your goodness,
that my enemies may see it and be put to shame,
for you, O Lᴏʀᴅ, have helped me and comforted me.

ᵃ13 Hebrew Sheol   ᵇ16 Or save your faithful son

Psalm

Of the Sons of Korah. A psalm. A song.

¹He has set his foundation on the holy mountain;
² the LORD loves the gates of Zion
    more than all the dwellings of Jacob.
³Glorious things are said of you,
    O city of God: *Selah*
⁴"I will record Rahab*ᵃ* and Babylon
    among those who acknowledge me—
Philistia too, and Tyre, along with Cush*ᵇ*—
    and will say, 'This*ᶜ* one was born in Zion.'"

⁵Indeed, of Zion it will be said,
    "This one and that one were born in her,
    and the Most High himself will establish her."
⁶The LORD will write in the register of the peoples:
    "This one was born in Zion."   *Selah*
⁷As they make music they will sing,
    "All my fountains are in you."

Psalm

A song. A psalm of the Sons of Korah. For the director of music. According to
*mahalath leannoth.*ᵈ A *maskil*ᵉ of Heman the Ezrahite.

¹O LORD, the God who saves me,
    day and night I cry out before you.
²May my prayer come before you;
    turn your ear to my cry.

³For my soul is full of trouble
    and my life draws near the grave.*ᶠ*
⁴I am counted among those who go down to the pit;
    I am like a man without strength.
⁵I am set apart with the dead,
    like the slain who lie in the grave,
whom you remember no more,
    who are cut off from your care.

⁶You have put me in the lowest pit,
    in the darkest depths.
⁷Your wrath lies heavily upon me;
    you have overwhelmed me with all your waves.   *Selah*
⁸You have taken from me my closest friends
    and have made me repulsive to them.
I am confined and cannot escape;
⁹ my eyes are dim with grief.

ᵃ4 A poetic name for Egypt   ᵇ4 That is, the upper Nile region   ᶜ4 Or "O Rahab and Babylon, / Philistia, Tyre and
Cush, / I will record concerning those who acknowledge me: / This   ᵈTitle: Possibly a tune, "The Suffering of Affliction"
ᵉTitle: Probably a literary or musical term   ᶠ3 Hebrew Sheol

I call to you, O LORD, every day;
    I spread out my hands to you.
¹⁰Do you show your wonders to the dead?
    Do those who are dead rise up and praise you?   *Selah*
¹¹Is your love declared in the grave,
    your faithfulness in Destruction*ᵃ*?
¹²Are your wonders known in the place of darkness,
    or your righteous deeds in the land of oblivion?

¹³But I cry to you for help, O LORD;
    in the morning my prayer comes before you.
¹⁴Why, O LORD, do you reject me
    and hide your face from me?

¹⁵From my youth I have been afflicted and close to death;
    I have suffered your terrors and am in despair.
¹⁶Your wrath has swept over me;
    your terrors have destroyed me.
¹⁷All day long they surround me like a flood;
    they have completely engulfed me.
¹⁸You have taken my companions and loved ones from me;
    the darkness is my closest friend.

Psalm

89

A *maskil*ᵇ of Ethan the Ezrahite.

¹I will sing of the LORD's great love forever;
    with my mouth I will make your faithfulness known through all
        generations.
²I will declare that your love stands firm forever,
    that you established your faithfulness in heaven itself.

³You said, "I have made a covenant with my chosen one,
    I have sworn to David my servant,
⁴'I will establish your line forever
    and make your throne firm through all generations.'"   *Selah*

⁵The heavens praise your wonders, O LORD,
    your faithfulness too, in the assembly of the holy ones.
⁶For who in the skies above can compare with the LORD?
    Who is like the LORD among the heavenly beings?
⁷In the council of the holy ones God is greatly feared;
    he is more awesome than all who surround him.
⁸O LORD God Almighty, who is like you?
    You are mighty, O LORD, and your faithfulness surrounds you.

⁹You rule over the surging sea;
    when its waves mount up, you still them.
¹⁰You crushed Rahab like one of the slain;
    with your strong arm you scattered your enemies.
¹¹The heavens are yours, and yours also the earth;
    you founded the world and all that is in it.

ᵃ11 Hebrew *Abaddon*   *ᵇ*Title: Probably a literary or musical term

¹²You created the north and the south;
  Tabor and Hermon sing for joy at your name.
¹³Your arm is endued with power;
  your hand is strong, your right hand exalted.

¹⁴Righteousness and justice are the foundation of your throne;
  love and faithfulness go before you.
¹⁵Blessed are those who have learned to acclaim you,
  who walk in the light of your presence, O LORD.
¹⁶They rejoice in your name all day long;
  they exult in your righteousness.
¹⁷For you are their glory and strength,
  and by your favor you exalt our horn.ᵃ
¹⁸Indeed, our shieldᵇ belongs to the LORD,
  our king to the Holy One of Israel.

¹⁹Once you spoke in a vision,
  to your faithful people you said:
 "I have bestowed strength on a warrior;
  I have exalted a young man from among the people.
²⁰I have found David my servant;
  with my sacred oil I have anointed him.
²¹My hand will sustain him;
  surely my arm will strengthen him.
²²No enemy will subject him to tribute;
  no wicked man will oppress him.
²³I will crush his foes before him
  and strike down his adversaries.
²⁴My faithful love will be with him,
  and through my name his hornᶜ will be exalted.
²⁵I will set his hand over the sea,
  his right hand over the rivers.
²⁶He will call out to me, 'You are my Father,
  my God, the Rock my Savior.'
²⁷I will also appoint him my firstborn,
  the most exalted of the kings of the earth.
²⁸I will maintain my love to him forever,
  and my covenant with him will never fail.
²⁹I will establish his line forever,
  his throne as long as the heavens endure.

³⁰"If his sons forsake my law
  and do not follow my statutes,
³¹if they violate my decrees
  and fail to keep my commands,
³²I will punish their sin with the rod,
  their iniquity with flogging;
³³but I will not take my love from him,
  nor will I ever betray my faithfulness.
³⁴I will not violate my covenant
  or alter what my lips have uttered.
³⁵Once for all, I have sworn by my holiness—
  and I will not lie to David—

ᵃ17 *Horn* here symbolizes strong one.   ᵇ18 Or *sovereign*   ᶜ24 *Horn* here symbolizes strength.

³⁶that his line will continue forever
   and his throne endure before me like the sun;
³⁷it will be established forever like the moon,
   the faithful witness in the sky."   *Selah*

³⁸But you have rejected, you have spurned,
   you have been very angry with your anointed one.
³⁹You have renounced the covenant with your servant
   and have defiled his crown in the dust.
⁴⁰You have broken through all his walls
   and reduced his strongholds to ruins.
⁴¹All who pass by have plundered him;
   he has become the scorn of his neighbors.
⁴²You have exalted the right hand of his foes;
   you have made all his enemies rejoice.
⁴³You have turned back the edge of his sword
   and have not supported him in battle.
⁴⁴You have put an end to his splendor
   and cast his throne to the ground.
⁴⁵You have cut short the days of his youth;
   you have covered him with a mantle of shame.   *Selah*

⁴⁶How long, O LORD? Will you hide yourself forever?
   How long will your wrath burn like fire?
⁴⁷Remember how fleeting is my life.
   For what futility you have created all men!
⁴⁸What man can live and not see death,
   or save himself from the power of the grave *ᵃ*?   *Selah*
⁴⁹O Lord, where is your former great love,
   which in your faithfulness you swore to David?
⁵⁰Remember, Lord, how your servant has *ᵇ* been mocked,
   how I bear in my heart the taunts of all the nations,
⁵¹the taunts with which your enemies have mocked, O LORD,
   with which they have mocked every step of your anointed one.

⁵²Praise be to the LORD forever!
               Amen and Amen.

BOOK IV

Psalms 90–106

Psalm

90

A prayer of Moses the man of God.

¹Lord, you have been our dwelling place
   throughout all generations.
²Before the mountains were born
   or you brought forth the earth and the world,
   from everlasting to everlasting you are God.

ᵃ48 Hebrew *Sheol*   *ᵇ50* Or *your servants have*

³You turn men back to dust,
    saying, "Return to dust, O sons of men."
⁴For a thousand years in your sight
    are like a day that has just gone by,
    or like a watch in the night.
⁵You sweep men away in the sleep of death;
    they are like the new grass of the morning—
⁶though in the morning it springs up new,
    by evening it is dry and withered.

⁷We are consumed by your anger
    and terrified by your indignation.
⁸You have set our iniquities before you,
    our secret sins in the light of your presence.
⁹All our days pass away under your wrath;
    we finish our years with a moan.
¹⁰The length of our days is seventy years—
    or eighty, if we have the strength;
    yet their span*a* is but trouble and sorrow,
    for they quickly pass, and we fly away.

¹¹Who knows the power of your anger?
    For your wrath is as great as the fear that is due you.
¹²Teach us to number our days aright,
    that we may gain a heart of wisdom.

¹³Relent, O Lᴏʀᴅ! How long will it be?
    Have compassion on your servants.
¹⁴Satisfy us in the morning with your unfailing love,
    that we may sing for joy and be glad all our days.
¹⁵Make us glad for as many days as you have afflicted us,
    for as many years as we have seen trouble.
¹⁶May your deeds be shown to your servants,
    your splendor to their children.

¹⁷May the favor*b* of the Lord our God rest upon us;
    establish the work of our hands for us—
    yes, establish the work of our hands.

Psalm 91

¹He who dwells in the shelter of the Most High
    will rest in the shadow of the Almighty.*c*
²I will say*d* of the Lᴏʀᴅ, "He is my refuge and my fortress,
    my God, in whom I trust."

³Surely he will save you from the fowler's snare
    and from the deadly pestilence.
⁴He will cover you with his feathers,
    and under his wings you will find refuge;
    his faithfulness will be your shield and rampart.
⁵You will not fear the terror of night,
    nor the arrow that flies by day,

---

a 10 Or *yet the best of them*   *b 17* Or *beauty*   *c 1* Hebrew *Shaddai*   *d 2* Or *He says*

⁶nor the pestilence that stalks in the darkness,
    nor the plague that destroys at midday.
⁷A thousand may fall at your side,
    ten thousand at your right hand,
    but it will not come near you.
⁸You will only observe with your eyes
    and see the punishment of the wicked.

⁹If you make the Most High your dwelling—
    even the LORD, who is my refuge—
¹⁰then no harm will befall you,
    no disaster will come near
        your tent.
¹¹For he will command his
        angels concerning you
    to guard you in all your
        ways;
¹²they will lift you up in their
        hands,
    so that you will not strike
        your foot against a
        stone.
¹³You will tread upon the lion
        and the cobra;
    you will trample the great
        lion and the serpent.

¹⁴"Because he loves me," says
        the LORD, "I will rescue
        him;
    I will protect him, for he acknowledges my name.
¹⁵He will call upon me, and I will answer him;
    I will be with him in trouble,
    I will deliver him and honor him.
¹⁶With long life will I satisfy him
    and show him my salvation."

> ### ▣ ▥▥▥ ADDRESSING QUESTIONS ▥▥▥ ◨
>
> **91:1–16**
> ## Human Experience   **Q**
>
> The psalmist didn't mean here that those who know God won't ever have to die or face terrifying circumstances. Instead, he was saying that no matter what happens, those who trust in God can have confidence in his care. Because God is strong enough to defeat death, no difficulty is so great that it can overpower God's love and support for his people. As God says in verse 15, he will be with his people "*in* trouble"; they won't necessarily be preserved *from* it.
>
> If you're a seeker, wouldn't you like to have that kind of assurance?

Psalm

92

A psalm. A song. For the Sabbath day.

¹It is good to praise the LORD
    and make music to your name, O Most High,
²to proclaim your love in the morning
    and your faithfulness at night,
³to the music of the ten-stringed lyre
    and the melody of the harp.

⁴For you make me glad by your deeds, O LORD;
    I sing for joy at the works of your hands.
⁵How great are your works, O LORD,
    how profound your thoughts!
⁶The senseless man does not know,
    fools do not understand,

⁷that though the wicked spring up like grass
    and all evildoers flourish,
they will be forever destroyed.

⁸But you, O Lord, are exalted forever.

⁹For surely your enemies, O Lord,
    surely your enemies will perish;
    all evildoers will be scattered.
¹⁰You have exalted my horn*a* like that of a wild ox;
    fine oils have been poured upon me.
¹¹My eyes have seen the defeat of my adversaries;
    my ears have heard the rout of my wicked foes.

¹²The righteous will flourish like a palm tree,
    they will grow like a cedar of Lebanon;
¹³planted in the house of the Lord,
    they will flourish in the courts of our God.
¹⁴They will still bear fruit in old age,
    they will stay fresh and green,
¹⁵proclaiming, "The Lord is upright;
    he is my Rock, and there is no wickedness in him."

Psalm

93

¹The Lord reigns, he is robed in majesty;
    the Lord is robed in majesty
    and is armed with strength.
The world is firmly established;
    it cannot be moved.
²Your throne was established long ago;
    you are from all eternity.

³The seas have lifted up, O Lord,
    the seas have lifted up their voice;
    the seas have lifted up their pounding waves.
⁴Mightier than the thunder of the great waters,
    mightier than the breakers of the sea—
    the Lord on high is mighty.

⁵Your statutes stand firm;
    holiness adorns your house
    for endless days, O Lord.

Psalm

94

¹O Lord, the God who avenges,
    O God who avenges, shine forth.
²Rise up, O Judge of the earth;
    pay back to the proud what they deserve.
³How long will the wicked, O Lord,
    how long will the wicked be jubilant?

---

a 10 Horn here symbolizes strength.

⁴They pour out arrogant words;
   all the evildoers are full of boasting.
⁵They crush your people, O Lᴏʀᴅ;
   they oppress your inheritance.
⁶They slay the widow and the alien;
   they murder the fatherless.
⁷They say, "The Lᴏʀᴅ does not see;
   the God of Jacob pays no heed."

⁸Take heed, you senseless ones among the people;
   you fools, when will you become wise?
⁹Does he who implanted the ear not hear?
   Does he who formed the eye not see?
¹⁰Does he who disciplines nations not punish?
   Does he who teaches man lack knowledge?
¹¹The Lᴏʀᴅ knows the thoughts of man;
   he knows that they are futile.

¹²Blessed is the man you discipline, O Lᴏʀᴅ,
   the man you teach from your law;
¹³you grant him relief from days of trouble,
   till a pit is dug for the wicked.
¹⁴For the Lᴏʀᴅ will not reject his people;
   he will never forsake his inheritance.
¹⁵Judgment will again be founded on righteousness,
   and all the upright in heart will follow it.

¹⁶Who will rise up for me against the wicked?
   Who will take a stand for me against evildoers?
¹⁷Unless the Lᴏʀᴅ had given me help,
   I would soon have dwelt in the silence of death.
¹⁸When I said, "My foot is slipping,"
   your love, O Lᴏʀᴅ, supported me.
¹⁹When anxiety was great within me,
   your consolation brought joy to my soul.

²⁰Can a corrupt throne be allied with you—
   one that brings on misery by its decrees?
²¹They band together against the righteous
   and condemn the innocent to death.
²²But the Lᴏʀᴅ has become my fortress,
   and my God the rock in whom I take refuge.
²³He will repay them for their sins
   and destroy them for their wickedness;
   the Lᴏʀᴅ our God will destroy them.

Psalm

95

¹Come, let us sing for joy to the Lᴏʀᴅ;
   let us shout aloud to the Rock of our salvation.
²Let us come before him with thanksgiving
   and extol him with music and song.

³For the Lᴏʀᴅ is the great God,
   the great King above all gods.

⁴In his hand are the depths of the earth,
  and the mountain peaks belong to him.
⁵The sea is his, for he made it,
  and his hands formed the dry land.

⁶Come, let us bow down in worship,
  let us kneel before the LORD our Maker;
⁷for he is our God
  and we are the people of his pasture,
  the flock under his care.

  Today, if you hear his voice,
⁸ do not harden your hearts as you did at Meribah,ᵃ
  as you did that day at Massahᵇ in the desert,
⁹where your fathers tested and tried me,
  though they had seen what I did.
¹⁰For forty years I was angry with that generation;
  I said, "They are a people whose hearts go astray,
  and they have not known my ways."
¹¹So I declared on oath in my anger,
  "They shall never enter my rest."

Psalm 96

¹Sing to the LORD a new song;
  sing to the LORD, all the earth.
²Sing to the LORD, praise his name;
  proclaim his salvation day after day.
³Declare his glory among the nations,
  his marvelous deeds among all peoples.

⁴For great is the LORD and most worthy of praise;
  he is to be feared above all gods.
⁵For all the gods of the nations are idols,
  but the LORD made the heavens.
⁶Splendor and majesty are before him;
  strength and glory are in his sanctuary.

⁷Ascribe to the LORD, O families of nations,
  ascribe to the LORD glory and strength.
⁸Ascribe to the LORD the glory due his name;
  bring an offering and come into his courts.
⁹Worship the LORD in the splendor of hisᶜ holiness;
  tremble before him, all the earth.

¹⁰Say among the nations, "The LORD reigns."
  The world is firmly established, it cannot be moved;
  he will judge the peoples with equity.
¹¹Let the heavens rejoice, let the earth be glad;
  let the sea resound, and all that is in it;
¹² let the fields be jubilant, and everything in them.
  Then all the trees of the forest will sing for joy;
¹³ they will sing before the LORD, for he comes,

ᵃ8 *Meribah* means *quarreling.*   ᵇ8 *Massah* means *testing.*   ᶜ9 Or LORD *with the splendor of*

he comes to judge the earth.
He will judge the world in righteousness
and the peoples in his truth.

Psalm

¹The Lord reigns, let the earth be glad;
let the distant shores rejoice.

²Clouds and thick darkness surround him;
righteousness and justice are the foundation of his throne.
³Fire goes before him
and consumes his foes on every side.
⁴His lightning lights up the world;
the earth sees and trembles.
⁵The mountains melt like wax before the Lord,
before the Lord of all the earth.
⁶The heavens proclaim his
righteousness,
and all the peoples see his
glory.

⁷All who worship images are
put to shame,
those who boast in idols—
worship him, all you gods!

⁸Zion hears and rejoices
and the villages of Judah are
glad
because of your judgments,
O Lord.
⁹For you, O Lord, are the Most
High over all the earth;
you are exalted far above all gods.

¹⁰Let those who love the Lord hate evil,
for he guards the lives of his faithful ones
and delivers them from the hand of the wicked.
¹¹Light is shed upon the righteous
and joy on the upright in heart.
¹²Rejoice in the Lord, you who are righteous,
and praise his holy name.

Psalm

98

A psalm.

¹Sing to the Lord a new song,
for he has done marvelous things;
his right hand and his holy arm
have worked salvation for him.
²The Lord has made his salvation known

■ DISCOVERING GOD ■

96:10–13
Life with God

The Bible says over and over that God is fair and that he can be trusted to do what is right when it comes to judgment. This blanket statement can help us cope with the tough questions that we have that the Bible does not address directly. Since God, by his very nature, *cannot* do what is unjust, we have the assurance of his purely moral and just action in our lives.

and revealed his righteousness to the nations.
³He has remembered his love
   and his faithfulness to the house of Israel;
all the ends of the earth have seen
   the salvation of our God.

⁴Shout for joy to the Lᴏʀᴅ, all the earth,
   burst into jubilant song with music;
⁵make music to the Lᴏʀᴅ with the harp,
   with the harp and the sound of singing,
⁶with trumpets and the blast of the ram's horn—
   shout for joy before the Lᴏʀᴅ, the King.

⁷Let the sea resound, and everything in it,
   the world, and all who live in it.
⁸Let the rivers clap their hands,
   let the mountains sing together for joy;
⁹let them sing before the Lᴏʀᴅ,
   for he comes to judge the earth.
He will judge the world in righteousness
   and the peoples with equity.

Psalm

99

¹The Lᴏʀᴅ reigns,
   let the nations tremble;
he sits enthroned between the cherubim,
   let the earth shake.
²Great is the Lᴏʀᴅ in Zion;
   he is exalted over all the nations.
³Let them praise your great and awesome name—
   he is holy.

⁴The King is mighty, he loves justice—
   you have established equity;
in Jacob you have done
   what is just and right.
⁵Exalt the Lᴏʀᴅ our God
   and worship at his footstool;
   he is holy.

⁶Moses and Aaron were among his priests,
   Samuel was among those who called on his name;
they called on the Lᴏʀᴅ
   and he answered them.
⁷He spoke to them from the pillar of cloud;
   they kept his statutes and the decrees he gave them.

⁸O Lᴏʀᴅ our God,
   you answered them;
you were to Israel ᵃ a forgiving God,
   though you punished their misdeeds. ᵇ
⁹Exalt the Lᴏʀᴅ our God

ᵃ8 Hebrew them   ᵇ8 Or / an avenger of the wrongs done to them

and worship at his holy mountain,
for the LORD our God is holy.

Psalm

A psalm. For giving thanks.

¹Shout for joy to the LORD, all the earth.
² Worship the LORD with gladness;
come before him with joyful songs.
³Know that the LORD is God.
It is he who made us, and we are his[a]
we are his people, the sheep of his pasture.

⁴Enter his gates with
thanksgiving
and his courts with praise;
give thanks to him and
praise his name.
⁵For the LORD is good and his
love endures forever;
his faithfulness continues
through all generations.

Psalm

Of David. A psalm.

¹I will sing of your love and
justice;
to you, O LORD, I will sing
praise.
²I will be careful to lead a
blameless life—
when will you come to me?

I will walk in my house
with blameless heart.
³I will set before my eyes
no vile thing.

The deeds of faithless men I
hate;
they will not cling to me.
⁴Men of perverse heart shall be far from me;
I will have nothing to do with evil.

⁵Whoever slanders his neighbor in secret,
him will I put to silence;
whoever has haughty eyes and a proud heart,
him will I not endure.

> ▣ ▦▦▦▦▦ **KNOWING YOURSELF** ▦▦▦▦▦ ⮂
>
> **101:1–6**
> **Sin**
>
> Almost everyone struggles with some form of
> compulsive behavior. David's words offer in-
> sight into how we can successfully overcome
> habits that enslave us.
>
> First, we need to strike at our duplicity—our
> tendency to live and behave differently when
> no one is looking. David makes it clear that
> we must strive to make both our private and
> public lives blameless (verse 2).
>
> Second, we need to avoid flirting with the
> object of our compulsion. David says he won't
> even look at any "vile thing" (verse 3).
>
> Third, we need to stay away from people
> who pull us into destructive patterns. Whether
> in business or in our social lives, we must
> not let the objectionable behaviors of those
> around us determine our actions—even if we
> have to break off relationships that drag us
> down (verses 3–5).
>
> Finally, we need to look for good role mod-
> els. Instead of idolizing TV characters who
> demonstrate lifestyles we would never want
> to imitate, we must look for inspiration from
> the "faithful of the land" (verse 6).

ᵃ3 Or and not we ourselves

⁶My eyes will be on the faithful in the land,
   that they may dwell with me;
he whose walk is blameless
   will minister to me.

⁷No one who practices deceit
   will dwell in my house;
no one who speaks falsely
   will stand in my presence.

⁸Every morning I will put to silence
   all the wicked in the land;
I will cut off every evildoer
   from the city of the LORD.

Psalm

102

*A prayer of an afflicted man. When he is faint and pours out
his lament before the LORD.*

¹Hear my prayer, O LORD;
   let my cry for help come to you.
²Do not hide your face from me
   when I am in distress.
Turn your ear to me;
   when I call, answer me quickly.

³For my days vanish like smoke;
   my bones burn like glowing embers.
⁴My heart is blighted and withered like grass;
   I forget to eat my food.
⁵Because of my loud groaning
   I am reduced to skin and bones.
⁶I am like a desert owl,
   like an owl among the ruins.
⁷I lie awake; I have become
   like a bird alone on a roof.
⁸All day long my enemies taunt me;
   those who rail against me use my name as a curse.
⁹For I eat ashes as my food
   and mingle my drink with tears
¹⁰because of your great wrath,
   for you have taken me up and thrown me aside.
¹¹My days are like the evening shadow;
   I wither away like grass.

¹²But you, O LORD, sit enthroned forever;
   your renown endures through all generations.
¹³You will arise and have compassion on Zion,
   for it is time to show favor to her;
   the appointed time has come.
¹⁴For her stones are dear to your servants;
   her very dust moves them to pity.
¹⁵The nations will fear the name of the LORD,
   all the kings of the earth will revere your glory.

¹⁶For the LORD will rebuild Zion
and appear in his glory.
¹⁷He will respond to the prayer of the destitute;
he will not despise their plea.

¹⁸Let this be written for a future generation,
that a people not yet created may praise the LORD:
¹⁹"The LORD looked down from his sanctuary on high,
from heaven he viewed the earth,
²⁰to hear the groans of the prisoners
and release those condemned to death."
²¹So the name of the LORD will be declared in Zion
and his praise in Jerusalem
²²when the peoples and the
kingdoms
assemble to worship the
LORD.

²³In the course of my life*a* he
broke my strength;
he cut short my days.
²⁴So I said:
"Do not take me away, O my
God, in the midst of my
days;
your years go on through all
generations.
²⁵In the beginning you laid the
foundations of the earth,
and the heavens are the
work of your hands.
²⁶They will perish, but you
remain;
they will all wear out like a
garment.
Like clothing you will change
them
and they will be discarded.
²⁷But you remain the same,
and your years will never
end.

> ### ▣ ▦▦▦▦ DISCOVERING GOD ▦▦▦▦ ⬧
>
> **102:25–27**
> **Jesus, the God-Man**
>
> Verses like these that describe God's role as creator and his unchanging nature are common in the Old Testament. What is unusual is that the New Testament writers apply verses like these to Jesus. They use these passages to support the claim that Jesus was God for all eternity before being born on earth and taking on a human nature and name.
>
> The writer of the New Testament book of Hebrews quotes these verses in describing Jesus' office as creator (Hebrews chapter 1, verses 10–12 [page 1586]). John picks up the same theme of Jesus as co-Creator of the universe (John 1:1–3, 14 [page 1382]), as does Paul (Colossians chapter 1, verses 16–17 [page 1552]).
>
> If you're a seeker, you may not yet be convinced that Jesus was God in human form. But make no mistake about it, that's exactly what the Bible claims. There is simply no way to seek the God of the Bible without dealing with the question, "Who is Jesus?"

²⁸The children of your servants will live in your presence;
their descendants will be established before you."

Psalm

103

Of David.

¹Praise the LORD, O my soul;
all my inmost being, praise his holy name.
²Praise the LORD, O my soul,
and forget not all his benefits—

a23 Or By his power

³who forgives all your sins
and heals all your diseases,
⁴who redeems your life from the pit
and crowns you with love and compassion,
⁵who satisfies your desires with good things
so that your youth is renewed like the eagle's.

⁶The LORD works righteousness
and justice for all the oppressed.

⁷He made known his ways to Moses,
his deeds to the people of Israel:
⁸The LORD is compassionate and gracious,
slow to anger, abounding in love.
⁹He will not always accuse,
nor will he harbor his anger forever;

¹⁰he does not treat us as our sins
deserve
or repay us according to our
iniquities.
¹¹For as high as the heavens are above
the earth,
so great is his love for those who
fear him;
¹²as far as the east is from the west,
so far has he removed our
transgressions from us.
¹³As a father has compassion on his
children,
so the LORD has compassion on those
who fear him;
¹⁴for he knows how we are formed,
he remembers that we are dust.
¹⁵As for man, his days are like grass,
he flourishes like a flower of the
field;
¹⁶the wind blows over it and it is gone,
and its place remembers it no more.
¹⁷But from everlasting to everlasting
the LORD's love is with those who
fear him,
and his righteousness with their
children's children—

◻ :::::::::::::::: **DISCOVERING GOD** :::::::::::::::: ⊟

103:10–14
Life with God

One thing that keeps many seekers away from God is the fear that he could never forgive them of the things they've done. Has that thought ever concerned you? If so, this passage contains some great news.

While many people anesthetize guilt feelings with alcohol, drugs, sex, food, work, or a host of other things, God has offered to show compassion and remove your guilt completely—"as far as the east is from the west."

So what's the catch? You are! God wants you to become his child, to be adopted into his family. He wants you to personally experience all of these benefits.

Jesus Christ paid for your sin in full when he died on the cross. His power to do so was evidenced in his resurrection from the dead. Why not ask him to come into your life and remove your sin forever? Then memorize these verses so that they can comfort and encourage you.

---

¹⁸with those who keep his covenant
and remember to obey his precepts.

¹⁹The LORD has established his throne in heaven,
and his kingdom rules over all.

²⁰Praise the LORD, you his angels,
you mighty ones who do his bidding,
who obey his word.
²¹Praise the LORD, all his heavenly hosts,
you his servants who do his will.

²²Praise the LORD, all his works
  everywhere in his dominion.

Praise the LORD, O my soul.

Psalm

¹Praise the LORD, O my soul.

O LORD my God, you are very great;
  you are clothed with splendor and majesty.
²He wraps himself in light as with a garment;
  he stretches out the heavens like a tent
³ and lays the beams of his upper chambers on their waters.
He makes the clouds his chariot
  and rides on the wings of the wind.
⁴He makes winds his messengers,ᵃ
  flames of fire his servants.

ᵃ4 Or angels

▦ ═══════ REASONS TO BELIEVE ═══════ ◪

104:2
The Christian Experience

It is just as impossible to comprehend the vastness of God as it is to comprehend the vastness of the universe.

For instance, the nearest star to the earth (besides our sun) is Alpha Centauri, which is 4.5 light years away. That means that light, traveling at the speed of 186,000 miles per second, takes 4.5 years to travel from that star to the earth. And flung out into space are stars whose light is just now coming into our vision after thousands of years.

Or to look at it another way, our earth is part of the Milky Way galaxy, which consists of 1,200 billion stars. Our sun is just one of those stars, and is 93 million miles away from our earth. The surface of the sun is almost 12,000 times greater than that of the earth, and the sun's volume is 1,300,000 times the volume of the earth. That means that if you had a pile of earths and dropped one into the sun every second, filling the sun would take 15 days.

But there's more. The largest star we know about is called Alpha Hercules. It is so large that 512 million suns or 670 million million earths could fit into it. If we could take that same pile of earths and drop one into Alpha Hercules every second, filling that star would take 21 million years. Yet, when seen through a telescope, this gigantic heavenly body appears as a tiny dot of light.

Is your mind short-circuiting yet?

As vast as the universe may be, God is greater. He had to be in order to create it. This psalm speaks of God in elemental terms, as the complete master over everything in the heavens and on the earth. The picture of God using light as a garment and the heavens as a tent is one of the more memorable images in the Bible. And the advanced space-watching technology from which we modern readers benefit makes our picture of God just that much more awesome and mind-boggling.

Though he is wonderful beyond comprehension, this amazing God has decided to make himself available to us, his creatures. He is vitally interested in the lives of each of us as we move about on this planet, tucked away as we are in a small corner of the universe. This psalm tells us that God actually takes delight in what every individual feels when worshiping him (verse 34)! That intimate, two-way relationship is the hope of every God-follower.

Isn't this God worth getting to know?

⁵He set the earth on its foundations;
   it can never be moved.
⁶You covered it with the deep as with a garment;
   the waters stood above the mountains.
⁷But at your rebuke the waters fled,
   at the sound of your thunder they took to flight;
⁸they flowed over the mountains,
   they went down into the valleys,
   to the place you assigned for them.
⁹You set a boundary they cannot cross;
   never again will they cover the earth.

¹⁰He makes springs pour water into the ravines;
   it flows between the mountains.
¹¹They give water to all the beasts of the field;
   the wild donkeys quench their thirst.
¹²The birds of the air nest by the waters;
   they sing among the branches.
¹³He waters the mountains from his upper chambers;
   the earth is satisfied by the fruit of his work.
¹⁴He makes grass grow for the cattle,
   and plants for man to cultivate—
   bringing forth food from the earth:
¹⁵wine that gladdens the heart of man,
   oil to make his face shine,
   and bread that sustains his heart.
¹⁶The trees of the Lᴏʀᴅ are well watered,
   the cedars of Lebanon that he planted.
¹⁷There the birds make their nests;
   the stork has its home in the pine trees.
¹⁸The high mountains belong to the wild goats;
   the crags are a refuge for the coneys.ᵃ

¹⁹The moon marks off the seasons,
   and the sun knows when to go down.
²⁰You bring darkness, it becomes night,
   and all the beasts of the forest prowl.
²¹The lions roar for their prey
   and seek their food from God.
²²The sun rises, and they steal away;
   they return and lie down in their dens.
²³Then man goes out to his work,
   to his labor until evening.

²⁴How many are your works, O Lᴏʀᴅ!
   In wisdom you made them all;
   the earth is full of your creatures.
²⁵There is the sea, vast and spacious,
   teeming with creatures beyond number—
   living things both large and small.
²⁶There the ships go to and fro,
   and the leviathan, which you formed to frolic there.

ᵃ *18* That is, the hyrax or rock badger

²⁷These all look to you
     to give them their food at the proper time.
²⁸When you give it to them,
     they gather it up;
 when you open your hand,
     they are satisfied with good things.
²⁹When you hide your face,
     they are terrified;
 when you take away their breath,
     they die and return to the dust.
³⁰When you send your Spirit,
     they are created,
     and you renew the face of the earth.

³¹May the glory of the LORD endure forever;
     may the LORD rejoice in his works—
³²he who looks at the earth, and it trembles,
     who touches the mountains, and they smoke.

³³I will sing to the LORD all my life;
     I will sing praise to my God as long as I live.
³⁴May my meditation be pleasing to him,
     as I rejoice in the LORD.
³⁵But may sinners vanish from the earth
     and the wicked be no more.

 Praise the LORD, O my soul.

 Praise the LORD.ᵃ

Psalm

105

¹Give thanks to the LORD, call on his name;
     make known among the nations what he has done.
²Sing to him, sing praise to him;
     tell of all his wonderful acts.
³Glory in his holy name;
     let the hearts of those who seek the LORD rejoice.
⁴Look to the LORD and his strength;
     seek his face always.

⁵Remember the wonders he has done,
     his miracles, and the judgments he pronounced,
⁶O descendants of Abraham his servant,
     O sons of Jacob, his chosen ones.
⁷He is the LORD our God;
     his judgments are in all the earth.

⁸He remembers his covenant forever,
     the word he commanded, for a thousand generations,
⁹the covenant he made with Abraham,
     the oath he swore to Isaac.
¹⁰He confirmed it to Jacob as a decree,

ᵃ35 Hebrew *Hallelu Yah*; in the Septuagint this line stands at the beginning of Psalm 105.

to Israel as an everlasting covenant:
¹¹"To you I will give the land of Canaan
  as the portion you will inherit."

¹²When they were but few in number,
  few indeed, and strangers in it,
¹³they wandered from nation to nation,
  from one kingdom to another.
¹⁴He allowed no one to oppress them;
  for their sake he rebuked kings:
¹⁵"Do not touch my anointed ones;
  do my prophets no harm."

¹⁶He called down famine on the land
  and destroyed all their supplies of food;
¹⁷and he sent a man before them—
  Joseph, sold as a slave.
¹⁸They bruised his feet with shackles,
  his neck was put in irons,
¹⁹till what he foretold came to pass,
  till the word of the LORD proved him true.
²⁰The king sent and released him,
  the ruler of peoples set him free.
²¹He made him master of his household,
  ruler over all he possessed,
²²to instruct his princes as he pleased
  and teach his elders wisdom.

²³Then Israel entered Egypt;
  Jacob lived as an alien in the land of Ham.
²⁴The LORD made his people very fruitful;
  he made them too numerous for their foes,
²⁵whose hearts he turned to hate his people,
  to conspire against his servants.
²⁶He sent Moses his servant,
  and Aaron, whom he had chosen.
²⁷They performed his miraculous signs among them,
  his wonders in the land of Ham.
²⁸He sent darkness and made the land dark—
  for had they not rebelled against his words?
²⁹He turned their waters into blood,
  causing their fish to die.
³⁰Their land teemed with frogs,
  which went up into the bedrooms of their rulers.
³¹He spoke, and there came swarms of flies,
  and gnats throughout their country.
³²He turned their rain into hail,
  with lightning throughout their land;
³³he struck down their vines and fig trees
  and shattered the trees of their country.
³⁴He spoke, and the locusts came,
  grasshoppers without number;
³⁵they ate up every green thing in their land,
  ate up the produce of their soil.

³⁶Then he struck down all the firstborn in their land,
   the firstfruits of all their manhood.

³⁷He brought out Israel, laden with silver and gold,
   and from among their tribes no one faltered.
³⁸Egypt was glad when they left,
   because dread of Israel had fallen on them.
³⁹He spread out a cloud as a covering,
   and a fire to give light at night.
⁴⁰They asked, and he brought them quail
   and satisfied them with the bread of heaven.
⁴¹He opened the rock, and water gushed out;
   like a river it flowed in the desert.

⁴²For he remembered his holy promise
   given to his servant Abraham.
⁴³He brought out his people with rejoicing,
   his chosen ones with shouts of joy;
⁴⁴he gave them the lands of the nations,
   and they fell heir to what others had toiled for—
⁴⁵that they might keep his precepts
   and observe his laws.

Praise the LORD. ^{*a*}

Psalm

106

¹Praise the LORD. ^{*b*}

  Give thanks to the LORD, for he is good;
   his love endures forever.
²Who can proclaim the mighty acts of the LORD
   or fully declare his praise?
³Blessed are they who maintain justice,
   who constantly do what is right.

⁴Remember me, O LORD, when you show favor to your people,
   come to my aid when you save them,
⁵that I may enjoy the prosperity of your chosen ones,
   that I may share in the joy of your nation
   and join your inheritance in giving praise.

⁶We have sinned, even as our fathers did;
   we have done wrong and acted wickedly.
⁷When our fathers were in Egypt,
   they gave no thought to your miracles;
  they did not remember your many kindnesses,
   and they rebelled by the sea, the Red Sea. ^{*c*}
⁸Yet he saved them for his name's sake,
   to make his mighty power known.
⁹He rebuked the Red Sea, and it dried up;
   he led them through the depths as through a desert.
¹⁰He saved them from the hand of the foe;

a 45 Hebrew *Hallelu Yah*   *b 1* Hebrew *Hallelu Yah*; also in verse 48   *c 7* Hebrew *Yam Suph*; that is, Sea of Reeds; also
in verses 9 and 22

from the hand of the enemy he redeemed them.
¹¹The waters covered their adversaries;
    not one of them survived.
¹²Then they believed his promises
    and sang his praise.

¹³But they soon forgot what he had done
    and did not wait for his counsel.
¹⁴In the desert they gave in to their craving;
    in the wasteland they put God to the test.
¹⁵So he gave them what they asked for,
    but sent a wasting disease upon them.

¹⁶In the camp they grew envious of Moses
    and of Aaron, who was consecrated to the Lord.
¹⁷The earth opened up and swallowed Dathan;
    it buried the company of Abiram.
¹⁸Fire blazed among their followers;
    a flame consumed the wicked.

¹⁹At Horeb they made a calf
    and worshiped an idol cast from metal.
²⁰They exchanged their Glory
    for an image of a bull, which eats grass.
²¹They forgot the God who saved them,
    who had done great things in Egypt,
²²miracles in the land of Ham
    and awesome deeds by the Red Sea.
²³So he said he would destroy them—
    had not Moses, his chosen one,
stood in the breach before him
    to keep his wrath from destroying them.

²⁴Then they despised the pleasant land;
    they did not believe his promise.
²⁵They grumbled in their tents
    and did not obey the Lord.
²⁶So he swore to them with uplifted hand
    that he would make them fall in the desert,
²⁷make their descendants fall among the nations
    and scatter them throughout the lands.

²⁸They yoked themselves to the Baal of Peor
    and ate sacrifices offered to lifeless gods;
²⁹they provoked the Lord to anger by their wicked deeds,
    and a plague broke out among them.
³⁰But Phinehas stood up and intervened,
    and the plague was checked.
³¹This was credited to him as righteousness
    for endless generations to come.

³²By the waters of Meribah they angered the Lord,
    and trouble came to Moses because of them;

³³for they rebelled against the Spirit of God,
and rash words came from Moses' lips. ^a

³⁴They did not destroy the peoples
as the L<small>ORD</small> had commanded them,
³⁵but they mingled with the nations
and adopted their customs.
³⁶They worshiped their idols,
which became a snare to them.
³⁷They sacrificed their sons
and their daughters to demons.
³⁸They shed innocent blood,
the blood of their sons and daughters,
whom they sacrificed to the idols of Canaan,
and the land was desecrated by their blood.
³⁹They defiled themselves by what they did;
by their deeds they prostituted themselves.

⁴⁰Therefore the L<small>ORD</small> was angry with his people
and abhorred his inheritance.
⁴¹He handed them over to the nations,
and their foes ruled over them.
⁴²Their enemies oppressed them
and subjected them to their power.
⁴³Many times he delivered them,
but they were bent on rebellion
and they wasted away in their sin.

⁴⁴But he took note of their distress
when he heard their cry;
⁴⁵for their sake he remembered his covenant
and out of his great love he relented.
⁴⁶He caused them to be pitied
by all who held them captive.

⁴⁷Save us, O L<small>ORD</small> our God,
and gather us from the nations,
that we may give thanks to your holy name
and glory in your praise.

⁴⁸Praise be to the L<small>ORD</small>, the God of Israel,
from everlasting to everlasting.
Let all the people say, "Amen!"

Praise the L<small>ORD</small>.

BOOK V

Psalms 107–150

Psalm

¹Give thanks to the L<small>ORD</small>, for he is good;
his love endures forever.

---

^a 33 Or *against his spirit, / and rash words came from his lips*

²Let the redeemed of the LORD say this—
    those he redeemed from the hand of the foe,
³those he gathered from the lands,
    from east and west, from north and south.ᵃ

⁴Some wandered in desert wastelands,
    finding no way to a city where they could settle.
⁵They were hungry and thirsty,
    and their lives ebbed away.
⁶Then they cried out to the LORD in their trouble,
    and he delivered them from their distress.
⁷He led them by a straight way
    to a city where they could settle.
⁸Let them give thanks to the LORD for his unfailing love
    and his wonderful deeds for men,
⁹for he satisfies the thirsty
    and fills the hungry with good things.

¹⁰Some sat in darkness and the deepest gloom,
    prisoners suffering in iron chains,
¹¹for they had rebelled against the words of God
    and despised the counsel of the Most High.
¹²So he subjected them to bitter labor;
    they stumbled, and there was no one to help.
¹³Then they cried to the LORD in their trouble,
    and he saved them from their distress.
¹⁴He brought them out of darkness and the deepest gloom
    and broke away their chains.
¹⁵Let them give thanks to the LORD for his unfailing love
    and his wonderful deeds for men,
¹⁶for he breaks down gates of bronze
    and cuts through bars of iron.

¹⁷Some became fools through their rebellious ways
    and suffered affliction because of their iniquities.
¹⁸They loathed all food
    and drew near the gates of death.
¹⁹Then they cried to the LORD in their trouble,
    and he saved them from their distress.
²⁰He sent forth his word and healed them;
    he rescued them from the grave.
²¹Let them give thanks to the LORD for his unfailing love
    and his wonderful deeds for men.
²²Let them sacrifice thank offerings
    and tell of his works with songs of joy.

²³Others went out on the sea in ships;
    they were merchants on the mighty waters.
²⁴They saw the works of the LORD,
    his wonderful deeds in the deep.
²⁵For he spoke and stirred up a tempest
    that lifted high the waves.
²⁶They mounted up to the heavens and went down to the depths;

ᵃ3 Hebrew *north and the sea*

in their peril their courage melted away.
²⁷They reeled and staggered like drunken men;
they were at their wits' end.
²⁸Then they cried out to the LORD in their trouble,
and he brought them out of their distress.
²⁹He stilled the storm to a whisper;
the waves of the sea were hushed.
³⁰They were glad when it grew
calm,
and he guided them to their
desired haven.
³¹Let them give thanks to the
LORD for his unfailing
love
and his wonderful deeds for
men.
³²Let them exalt him in the
assembly of the people
and praise him in the
council of the elders.

▣ ⬚⬚⬚⬚⬚⬚ DISCOVERING GOD ⬚⬚⬚⬚⬚⬚ ⬡

107:29
Jesus, the God-Man

God is the only one powerful enough to still a
storm.
    No wonder Jesus' friends just about fell out
of the boat when he did that very thing! They
rightfully questioned, "What kind of man is
this? Even the winds and the waves obey him!"
(Matthew chapter 8, verse 27 [page 1269]).
    What kind of man? Well, the God-Man!

---

³³He turned rivers into a desert,
flowing springs into thirsty
ground,
³⁴and fruitful land into a salt waste,
because of the wickedness of those who lived there.
³⁵He turned the desert into pools of water
and the parched ground into flowing springs;
³⁶there he brought the hungry to live,
and they founded a city where they could settle.
³⁷They sowed fields and planted vineyards
that yielded a fruitful harvest;
³⁸he blessed them, and their numbers greatly increased,
and he did not let their herds diminish.

³⁹Then their numbers decreased, and they were humbled
by oppression, calamity and sorrow;
⁴⁰he who pours contempt on nobles
made them wander in a trackless waste.
⁴¹But he lifted the needy out of their affliction
and increased their families like flocks.
⁴²The upright see and rejoice,
but all the wicked shut their mouths.

⁴³Whoever is wise, let him heed these things
and consider the great love of the LORD.

Psalm

108

A song. A psalm of David.

¹My heart is steadfast, O God;
I will sing and make music with all my soul.
²Awake, harp and lyre!

I will awaken the dawn.
3I will praise you, O LORD, among the nations;
    I will sing of you among the peoples.
4For great is your love, higher than the heavens;
    your faithfulness reaches to the skies.
5Be exalted, O God, above the heavens,
    and let your glory be over all the earth.

6Save us and help us with your right hand,
    that those you love may be delivered.
7God has spoken from his sanctuary:
    "In triumph I will parcel out Shechem
    and measure off the Valley of Succoth.
8Gilead is mine, Manasseh is mine;
    Ephraim is my helmet,
    Judah my scepter.
9Moab is my washbasin,
    upon Edom I toss my sandal;
    over Philistia I shout in triumph."

10Who will bring me to the fortified city?
    Who will lead me to Edom?
11Is it not you, O God, you who have rejected us
    and no longer go out with our armies?
12Give us aid against the enemy,
    for the help of man is worthless.
13With God we will gain the victory,
    and he will trample down our enemies.

Psalm

109

For the director of music. Of David. A psalm.

1O God, whom I praise,
    do not remain silent,
2for wicked and deceitful men
    have opened their mouths against me;
    they have spoken against me with lying tongues.
3With words of hatred they surround me;
    they attack me without cause.
4In return for my friendship they accuse me,
    but I am a man of prayer.
5They repay me evil for good,
    and hatred for my friendship.

6Appoint*a* an evil man*b* to oppose him;
    let an accuser*c* stand at his right hand.
7When he is tried, let him be found guilty,
    and may his prayers condemn him.
8May his days be few;
    may another take his place of leadership.
9May his children be fatherless

---

a6 Or _They say:_ "Appoint (with quotation marks at the end of verse 19)   *b6* Or _the Evil One_   *c6* Or _let Satan_

and his wife a widow.
¹⁰May his children be wandering beggars;
    may they be driven*a* from their ruined homes.
¹¹May a creditor seize all he has;
    may strangers plunder the fruits of his labor.
¹²May no one extend kindness to him
    or take pity on his fatherless children.
¹³May his descendants be cut off,
    their names blotted out from the next generation.
¹⁴May the iniquity of his fathers be remembered before the LORD;
    may the sin of his mother never be blotted out.
¹⁵May their sins always remain before the LORD,
    that he may cut off the memory of them from the earth.

¹⁶For he never thought of doing a kindness,
    but hounded to death the poor
    and the needy and the brokenhearted.
¹⁷He loved to pronounce a curse—
    may it*b* come on him;
  he found no pleasure in blessing—
    may it be*c* far from him.
¹⁸He wore cursing as his garment;
    it entered into his body like water,
    into his bones like oil.
¹⁹May it be like a cloak wrapped about him,
    like a belt tied forever around him.
²⁰May this be the LORD's payment to my accusers,
    to those who speak evil of me.

²¹But you, O Sovereign LORD,
    deal well with me for your name's sake;
    out of the goodness of your love, deliver me.
²²For I am poor and needy,
    and my heart is wounded within me.
²³I fade away like an evening shadow;
    I am shaken off like a locust.
²⁴My knees give way from fasting;
    my body is thin and gaunt.
²⁵I am an object of scorn to my accusers;
    when they see me, they shake their heads.

²⁶Help me, O LORD my God;
    save me in accordance with your love.
²⁷Let them know that it is your hand,
    that you, O LORD, have done it.
²⁸They may curse, but you will bless;
    when they attack they will be put to shame,
    but your servant will rejoice.
²⁹My accusers will be clothed with disgrace
    and wrapped in shame as in a cloak.

³⁰With my mouth I will greatly extol the LORD;
    in the great throng I will praise him.

a 10 Septuagint; Hebrew *sought*   *b 17* Or *curse, / and it has*   *c 17* Or *blessing, / and it is*

31For he stands at the right hand of the needy one,
   to save his life from those who condemn him.

Psalm

Of David. A psalm.

1The Lord says to my Lord:
   "Sit at my right hand
until I make your enemies
   a footstool for your feet."

2The Lord will extend your mighty scepter from Zion;
   you will rule in the midst of your enemies.
3Your troops will be willing
   on your day of battle.
Arrayed in holy majesty,
   from the womb of the dawn
   you will receive the dew of your youth.a

4The Lord has sworn
   and will not change his mind:
"You are a priest forever,
   in the order of Melchizedek."

5The Lord is at your right hand;
   he will crush kings on the day of his wrath.
6He will judge the nations, heaping up the dead
   and crushing the rulers of the whole earth.
7He will drink from a brook beside the wayb;
   therefore he will lift up his head.

Psalmc

1Praise the Lord.d

I will extol the Lord with all my heart
   in the council of the upright and in the assembly.

2Great are the works of the Lord;
   they are pondered by all who delight in them.
3Glorious and majestic are his deeds,
   and his righteousness endures forever.
4He has caused his wonders to be remembered;
   the Lord is gracious and compassionate.
5He provides food for those who fear him;
   he remembers his covenant forever.
6He has shown his people the power of his works,
   giving them the lands of other nations.
7The works of his hands are faithful and just;

a3 Or / your young men will come to you like the dew   b7 Or / The One who grants succession will set him in authority
cThis psalm is an acrostic poem, the lines of which begin with the successive letters of the Hebrew alphabet.   d1 Hebrew
Hallelu Yah

all his precepts are trustworthy.
8They are steadfast for ever and ever,
   done in faithfulness and uprightness.
9He provided redemption for his people;
   he ordained his covenant forever—
   holy and awesome is his name.

10The fear of the LORD is the beginning of wisdom;
   all who follow his precepts have good understanding.
   To him belongs eternal praise.

Psalm^a

1Praise the LORD.^b

Blessed is the man who fears the LORD,
   who finds great delight in his commands.

2His children will be mighty in the land;
   the generation of the upright will be blessed.
3Wealth and riches are in his house,
   and his righteousness endures forever.
4Even in darkness light dawns for the upright,
   for the gracious and compassionate and righteous man.^c
5Good will come to him who is generous and lends freely,
   who conducts his affairs with justice.
6Surely he will never be shaken;
   a righteous man will be remembered forever.
7He will have no fear of bad news;
   his heart is steadfast, trusting in the LORD.
8His heart is secure, he will have no fear;
   in the end he will look in triumph on his foes.
9He has scattered abroad his gifts to the poor,
   his righteousness endures forever;
   his horn^d will be lifted high in honor.

10The wicked man will see and be vexed,
   he will gnash his teeth and waste away;
   the longings of the wicked will come to nothing.

Psalm

1Praise the LORD.^e

Praise, O servants of the LORD,
   praise the name of the LORD.
2Let the name of the LORD be praised,
   both now and forevermore.
3From the rising of the sun to the place where it sets,
   the name of the LORD is to be praised.

---

^aThis psalm is an acrostic poem, the lines of which begin with the successive letters of the Hebrew alphabet.   ^b1 Hebrew *Hallelu Yah*   ^c4 Or *for the* LORD, *is gracious and compassionate and righteous*   ^d9 *Horn* here symbolizes dignity. ^e1 Hebrew *Hallelu Yah*; also in verse 9

⁴The LORD is exalted over all the nations,
    his glory above the heavens.
⁵Who is like the LORD our God,
    the One who sits enthroned on high,
⁶who stoops down to look
    on the heavens and the earth?

⁷He raises the poor from the dust
    and lifts the needy from the ash heap;
⁸he seats them with princes,
    with the princes of their people.
⁹He settles the barren woman in her home
    as a happy mother of children.

 Praise the LORD.

Psalm

¹When Israel came out of Egypt,
    the house of Jacob from a people of foreign tongue,
²Judah became God's sanctuary,
    Israel his dominion.

³The sea looked and fled,
    the Jordan turned back;
⁴the mountains skipped like rams,
    the hills like lambs.

⁵Why was it, O sea, that you fled,
    O Jordan, that you turned back,
⁶you mountains, that you skipped like rams,
    you hills, like lambs?

⁷Tremble, O earth, at the presence of the Lord,
    at the presence of the God of Jacob,
⁸who turned the rock into a pool,
    the hard rock into springs of water.

Psalm

¹Not to us, O LORD, not to us
    but to your name be the glory,
    because of your love and faithfulness.

²Why do the nations say,
    "Where is their God?"
³Our God is in heaven;
    he does whatever pleases him.
⁴But their idols are silver and gold,
    made by the hands of men.
⁵They have mouths, but cannot speak,
    eyes, but they cannot see;
⁶they have ears, but cannot hear,
    noses, but they cannot smell;

⁷they have hands, but cannot feel,
    feet, but they cannot walk;
    nor can they utter a sound with their throats.
⁸Those who make them will be like them,
    and so will all who trust in them.

⁹O house of Israel, trust in the LORD—
    he is their help and shield.
¹⁰O house of Aaron, trust in the LORD—
    he is their help and shield.
¹¹You who fear him, trust in the LORD—
    he is their help and shield.

¹²The LORD remembers us and will bless us:
    He will bless the house of Israel,
    he will bless the house of Aaron,
¹³he will bless those who fear the LORD—
    small and great alike.

¹⁴May the LORD make you increase,
    both you and your children.
¹⁵May you be blessed by the LORD,
    the Maker of heaven and earth.

¹⁶The highest heavens belong to the LORD,
    but the earth he has given to man.
¹⁷It is not the dead who praise
        the LORD,
    those who go down to
        silence;
¹⁸it is we who extol the LORD,
    both now and forevermore.

Praise the LORD. ᵃ

Psalm
116

¹I love the LORD, for he heard
    my voice;
    he heard my cry for mercy.
²Because he turned his ear to
        me,
    I will call on him as long as
        I live.

³The cords of death entangled
        me,
    the anguish of the grave ᵇ came upon me;
    I was overcome by trouble and sorrow.
⁴Then I called on the name of the LORD:
    "O LORD, save me!"

⁵The LORD is gracious and righteous;
    our God is full of compassion.

:::: DISCOVERING GOD ::::

116:1–6
The God Who Is There

Sometimes we have to reach a point of despair before we call out to God.

If you're a seeker, you may be reluctant to do that. You may figure that if you don't serve God when things are going well, it would be presumptuous to ask him for help during bad times. But God knows that we sometimes need to hit bottom before he can get our attention. He'd rather have you turn to him then than never.

If you're at your wits' end, don't hesitate to reach out to God as best you know how. He's waiting for you.

ᵃ 18 Hebrew *Hallelu Yah*   ᵇ 3 Hebrew *Sheol*

⁶The LORD protects the simplehearted;
  when I was in great need, he saved me.

⁷Be at rest once more, O my soul,
  for the LORD has been good to you.

⁸For you, O LORD, have delivered my soul from death,
  my eyes from tears,
  my feet from stumbling,
⁹that I may walk before the LORD
  in the land of the living.
¹⁰I believed; therefore*a* I said,
  "I am greatly afflicted."
¹¹And in my dismay I said,
  "All men are liars."

¹²How can I repay the LORD
  for all his goodness to me?
¹³I will lift up the cup of salvation
  and call on the name of the LORD.
¹⁴I will fulfill my vows to the LORD
  in the presence of all his people.

¹⁵Precious in the sight of the LORD
  is the death of his saints.
¹⁶O LORD, truly I am your servant;
  I am your servant, the son of your maidservant*b*;
  you have freed me from my chains.

¹⁷I will sacrifice a thank offering to you
  and call on the name of the LORD.
¹⁸I will fulfill my vows to the LORD
  in the presence of all his people,
¹⁹in the courts of the house of the LORD—
  in your midst, O Jerusalem.

  Praise the LORD.*c*

Psalm

¹Praise the LORD, all you nations;
  extol him, all you peoples.
²For great is his love toward us,
  and the faithfulness of the LORD endures forever.

  Praise the LORD.*c*

Psalm

¹Give thanks to the LORD, for he is good;
  his love endures forever.

²Let Israel say:

---

a 10 Or *believed even when*   *b 16* Or *servant, your faithful son*   *c 19,2* Hebrew *Hallelu Yah*

"His love endures forever."
³Let the house of Aaron say:
  "His love endures forever."
⁴Let those who fear the LORD say:
  "His love endures forever."

⁵In my anguish I cried to the LORD,
  and he answered by setting me free.
⁶The LORD is with me; I will not be afraid.
  What can man do to me?
⁷The LORD is with me; he is my helper.
  I will look in triumph on my enemies.

⁸It is better to take refuge in the LORD
  than to trust in man.
⁹It is better to take refuge in the LORD
  than to trust in princes.

¹⁰All the nations surrounded me,
  but in the name of the LORD I cut them off.
¹¹They surrounded me on every side,
  but in the name of the LORD I cut them off.
¹²They swarmed around me like bees,
  but they died out as quickly as burning thorns;
  in the name of the LORD I cut them off.

¹³I was pushed back and about to
  fall,
  but the LORD helped me.
¹⁴The LORD is my strength and my
  song;
  he has become my salvation.

¹⁵Shouts of joy and victory
  resound in the tents of the
  righteous:
  "The LORD's right hand has done
    mighty things!
¹⁶ The LORD's right hand is lifted
    high;
  the LORD's right hand has done
    mighty things!"

¹⁷I will not die but live,
  and will proclaim what the
    LORD has done.
¹⁸The LORD has chastened me
  severely,
  but he has not given me over
    to death.

¹⁹Open for me the gates of righteousness;
  I will enter and give thanks to the LORD.
²⁰This is the gate of the LORD
  through which the righteous may enter.
²¹I will give you thanks, for you answered me;
  you have become my salvation.

▣ ⠿⠿⠿⠿⠿ DISCOVERING GOD ⠿⠿⠿⠿⠿ ⬙

118:22–23
Jesus, the God-Man

"The first will be last"—that's a very well-known phrase. But this biblical theme was taught long before Jesus said it in that memorable way (see Matthew 20:16 [page 1286]).

That theme is played out here metaphorically as a cast-off stone becomes the one God selects for the capstone of his building. Jesus applied this text to himself, noting how so many in his day were ready to dismiss his claim to be the Messiah (Matthew chapter 21, verse 42 [page 1289]). Yet the time was coming when everyone would see just how important Jesus was to the building of the kingdom of God. As he was the "last" one many thought could be the Messiah, through his resurrection from the dead he has now taken his position as the "first"—the one and only Messiah, the foundation of God's kingdom.

²²The stone the builders rejected
    has become the capstone;
²³the LORD has done this,
    and it is marvelous in our eyes.
²⁴This is the day the LORD has made;
    let us rejoice and be glad in it.
²⁵O LORD, save us;
    O LORD, grant us success.
²⁶Blessed is he who comes in the name of the LORD.
    From the house of the LORD we bless you. ᵃ
²⁷The LORD is God,
    and he has made his light shine upon us.
    With boughs in hand, join in the festal procession
    up ᵇ to the horns of the altar.

²⁸You are my God, and I will give you thanks;
    you are my God, and I will exalt you.

²⁹Give thanks to the LORD, for he is good;
    his love endures forever.

Psalm ᶜ
119

א   Aleph

¹Blessed are they whose ways are blameless,
    who walk according to the law of the LORD.
²Blessed are they who keep his statutes
    and seek him with all their heart.
³They do nothing wrong;
    they walk in his ways.
⁴You have laid down precepts
    that are to be fully obeyed.
⁵Oh, that my ways were steadfast
    in obeying your decrees!
⁶Then I would not be put to shame
    when I consider all your commands.
⁷I will praise you with an upright heart
    as I learn your righteous laws.
⁸I will obey your decrees;
    do not utterly forsake me.

ב   Beth

⁹How can a young man keep his way pure?
    By living according to your word.
¹⁰I seek you with all my heart;
    do not let me stray from your commands.
¹¹I have hidden your word in my heart
    that I might not sin against you.
¹²Praise be to you, O LORD;
    teach me your decrees.
¹³With my lips I recount
    all the laws that come from your mouth.

ᵃ26 The Hebrew is plural.   ᵇ27 Or *Bind the festal sacrifice with ropes / and take it*   ᶜThis psalm is an acrostic poem;
the verses of each stanza begin with the same letter of the Hebrew alphabet.

¹⁴I rejoice in following your statutes
  as one rejoices in great riches.
¹⁵I meditate on your precepts
  and consider your ways.
¹⁶I delight in your decrees;
  I will not neglect your word.

ג   Gimel

¹⁷Do good to your servant, and I will live;
  I will obey your word.
¹⁸Open my eyes that I may see
  wonderful things in your law.
¹⁹I am a stranger on earth;
  do not hide your commands from me.
²⁰My soul is consumed with longing
  for your laws at all times.
²¹You rebuke the arrogant, who are cursed
  and who stray from your commands.
²²Remove from me scorn and contempt,
  for I keep your statutes.
²³Though rulers sit together and slander me,
  your servant will meditate on your decrees.
²⁴Your statutes are my delight;
  they are my counselors.

ד   Daleth

²⁵I am laid low in the dust;
  preserve my life according to
    your word.
²⁶I recounted my ways and you
    answered me;
  teach me your decrees.
²⁷Let me understand the teaching
    of your precepts;
  then I will meditate on your
    wonders.
²⁸My soul is weary with sorrow;
  strengthen me according to
    your word.
²⁹Keep me from deceitful ways;
  be gracious to me through
    your law.
³⁰I have chosen the way of truth;
  I have set my heart on your laws.
³¹I hold fast to your statutes, O Lᴏʀᴅ;
  do not let me be put to shame.
³²I run in the path of your commands,
  for you have set my heart free.

ה   He

³³Teach me, O Lᴏʀᴅ, to follow your decrees;
  then I will keep them to the end.
³⁴Give me understanding, and I will keep your law

▣ ┊┊┊┊┊┊ **REASONS TO BELIEVE** ┊┊┊┊┊┊ ↕

119:1–176
The Amazing Bible

Psalm 119 is the longest psalm—and the
longest chapter—in the whole Bible. And to
what does the writer devote all this space?
God's Word! This chapter is all about the Bible.
  As you flip through these 176 verses, you'll
be hard-pressed to find one that doesn't talk
about God's written revelation in some form.
This psalm celebrates the wonderful reality
that God has communicated to us in this way.
  If you're a seeker, you probably have this
Bible because you're wondering if God will use
it to help you find him. Rest assured—and keep
seeking—because that's exactly what he's going to do!

and obey it with all my heart.
³⁵Direct me in the path of your commands,
for there I find delight.
³⁶Turn my heart toward your statutes
and not toward selfish gain.
³⁷Turn my eyes away from worthless things;
preserve my life according to your word.[a]
³⁸Fulfill your promise to your servant,
so that you may be feared.
³⁹Take away the disgrace I dread,
for your laws are good.
⁴⁰How I long for your precepts!
Preserve my life in your righteousness.

ו Waw

⁴¹May your unfailing love come to me, O LORD,
your salvation according to your promise;
⁴²then I will answer the one who taunts me,
for I trust in your word.
⁴³Do not snatch the word of truth from my mouth,
for I have put my hope in your laws.
⁴⁴I will always obey your law,
for ever and ever.
⁴⁵I will walk about in freedom,
for I have sought out your precepts.
⁴⁶I will speak of your statutes before kings
and will not be put to shame,
⁴⁷for I delight in your commands
because I love them.
⁴⁸I lift up my hands to[b] your commands, which I love,
and I meditate on your decrees.

ז Zayin

⁴⁹Remember your word to your servant,
for you have given me hope.
⁵⁰My comfort in my suffering is this:
Your promise preserves my life.
⁵¹The arrogant mock me without restraint,
but I do not turn from your law.
⁵²I remember your ancient laws, O LORD,
and I find comfort in them.
⁵³Indignation grips me because of the wicked,
who have forsaken your law.
⁵⁴Your decrees are the theme of my song
wherever I lodge.
⁵⁵In the night I remember your name, O LORD,
and I will keep your law.
⁵⁶This has been my practice:
I obey your precepts.

[a] 37 Two manuscripts of the Masoretic Text and Dead Sea Scrolls; most manuscripts of the Masoretic Text *life in your way*
[b] 48 Or *for*

ח   Heth

⁵⁷You are my portion, O Lᴏʀᴅ;
    I have promised to obey your words.
⁵⁸I have sought your face with all my heart;
    be gracious to me according to your promise.
⁵⁹I have considered my ways
    and have turned my steps to your statutes.
⁶⁰I will hasten and not delay
    to obey your commands.
⁶¹Though the wicked bind me with ropes,
    I will not forget your law.
⁶²At midnight I rise to give you thanks
    for your righteous laws.
⁶³I am a friend to all who fear you,
    to all who follow your precepts.
⁶⁴The earth is filled with your love, O Lᴏʀᴅ;
    teach me your decrees.

ט   Teth

⁶⁵Do good to your servant
    according to your word, O Lᴏʀᴅ.
⁶⁶Teach me knowledge and good judgment,
    for I believe in your commands.
⁶⁷Before I was afflicted I went astray,
    but now I obey your word.
⁶⁸You are good, and what you do is good;
    teach me your decrees.
⁶⁹Though the arrogant have smeared me with lies,
    I keep your precepts with all my heart.
⁷⁰Their hearts are callous and unfeeling,
    but I delight in your law.
⁷¹It was good for me to be afflicted
    so that I might learn your decrees.
⁷²The law from your mouth is more precious to me
    than thousands of pieces of silver and gold.

י   Yodh

⁷³Your hands made me and formed me;
    give me understanding to learn your commands.
⁷⁴May those who fear you rejoice when they see me,
    for I have put my hope in your word.
⁷⁵I know, O Lᴏʀᴅ, that your laws are righteous,
    and in faithfulness you have afflicted me.
⁷⁶May your unfailing love be my comfort,
    according to your promise to your servant.
⁷⁷Let your compassion come to me that I may live,
    for your law is my delight.
⁷⁸May the arrogant be put to shame for wronging me without cause;
    but I will meditate on your precepts.
⁷⁹May those who fear you turn to me,
    those who understand your statutes.
⁸⁰May my heart be blameless toward your decrees,
    that I may not be put to shame.

כ   Kaph

⁸¹My soul faints with longing for your salvation,
     but I have put my hope in your word.
⁸²My eyes fail, looking for your promise;
     I say, "When will you comfort me?"
⁸³Though I am like a wineskin in the smoke,
     I do not forget your decrees.
⁸⁴How long must your servant wait?
     When will you punish my persecutors?
⁸⁵The arrogant dig pitfalls for me,
     contrary to your law.
⁸⁶All your commands are trustworthy;
     help me, for men persecute me without cause.
⁸⁷They almost wiped me from the earth,
     but I have not forsaken your precepts.
⁸⁸Preserve my life according to your love,
     and I will obey the statutes of your mouth.

ל   Lamedh

⁸⁹Your word, O Lᴏʀᴅ, is eternal;
     it stands firm in the heavens.
⁹⁰Your faithfulness continues through all generations;
     you established the earth, and it endures.
⁹¹Your laws endure to this day,
     for all things serve you.
⁹²If your law had not been my delight,
     I would have perished in my affliction.
⁹³I will never forget your precepts,
     for by them you have preserved my life.
⁹⁴Save me, for I am yours;
     I have sought out your precepts.
⁹⁵The wicked are waiting to destroy me,
     but I will ponder your statutes.
⁹⁶To all perfection I see a limit;
     but your commands are boundless.

מ   Mem

⁹⁷Oh, how I love your law!
     I meditate on it all day long.
⁹⁸Your commands make me wiser than my enemies,
     for they are ever with me.
⁹⁹I have more insight than all my teachers,
     for I meditate on your statutes.
¹⁰⁰I have more understanding than the elders,
     for I obey your precepts.
¹⁰¹I have kept my feet from every evil path
     so that I might obey your word.
¹⁰²I have not departed from your laws,
     for you yourself have taught me.
¹⁰³How sweet are your words to my taste,
     sweeter than honey to my mouth!
¹⁰⁴I gain understanding from your precepts;
     therefore I hate every wrong path.

ב   Nun

105Your word is a lamp to my feet
    and a light for my path.
106I have taken an oath and confirmed it,
    that I will follow your righteous laws.
107I have suffered much;
    preserve my life, O LORD, according to your word.
108Accept, O LORD, the willing praise of my mouth,
    and teach me your laws.
109Though I constantly take my life in my hands,
    I will not forget your law.
110The wicked have set a snare for me,
    but I have not strayed from your precepts.
111Your statutes are my heritage forever;
    they are the joy of my heart.
112My heart is set on keeping your decrees
    to the very end.

ס   Samekh

113I hate double-minded men,
    but I love your law.
114You are my refuge and my shield;
    I have put my hope in your word.
115Away from me, you evildoers,
    that I may keep the commands of my God!
116Sustain me according to your promise, and I will live;
    do not let my hopes be dashed.
117Uphold me, and I will be delivered;
    I will always have regard for your decrees.
118You reject all who stray from your decrees,
    for their deceitfulness is in vain.
119All the wicked of the earth you discard like dross;
    therefore I love your statutes.
120My flesh trembles in fear of you;
    I stand in awe of your laws.

ע   Ayin

121I have done what is righteous and just;
    do not leave me to my oppressors.
122Ensure your servant's well-being;
    let not the arrogant oppress me.
123My eyes fail, looking for your salvation,
    looking for your righteous promise.
124Deal with your servant according to your love
    and teach me your decrees.
125I am your servant; give me discernment
    that I may understand your statutes.
126It is time for you to act, O LORD;
    your law is being broken.
127Because I love your commands
    more than gold, more than pure gold,
128and because I consider all your precepts right,
    I hate every wrong path.

 פ   Pe

¹²⁹Your statutes are wonderful;
    therefore I obey them.
¹³⁰The unfolding of your words gives light;
    it gives understanding to the simple.
¹³¹I open my mouth and pant,
    longing for your commands.
¹³²Turn to me and have mercy on me,
    as you always do to those who love your name.
¹³³Direct my footsteps according to your word;
    let no sin rule over me.
¹³⁴Redeem me from the oppression of men,
    that I may obey your precepts.
¹³⁵Make your face shine upon your servant
    and teach me your decrees.
¹³⁶Streams of tears flow from my eyes,
    for your law is not obeyed.

צ   Tsadhe

¹³⁷Righteous are you, O Lord,
    and your laws are right.
¹³⁸The statutes you have laid down are righteous;
    they are fully trustworthy.
¹³⁹My zeal wears me out,
    for my enemies ignore your words.
¹⁴⁰Your promises have been thoroughly tested,
    and your servant loves them.
¹⁴¹Though I am lowly and despised,
    I do not forget your precepts.
¹⁴²Your righteousness is everlasting
    and your law is true.
¹⁴³Trouble and distress have come upon me,
    but your commands are my delight.
¹⁴⁴Your statutes are forever right;
    give me understanding that I may live.

ק   Qoph

¹⁴⁵I call with all my heart; answer me, O Lord,
    and I will obey your decrees.
¹⁴⁶I call out to you; save me
    and I will keep your statutes.
¹⁴⁷I rise before dawn and cry for help;
    I have put my hope in your word.
¹⁴⁸My eyes stay open through the watches of the night,
    that I may meditate on your promises.
¹⁴⁹Hear my voice in accordance with your love;
    preserve my life, O Lord, according to your laws.
¹⁵⁰Those who devise wicked schemes are near,
    but they are far from your law.
¹⁵¹Yet you are near, O Lord,
    and all your commands are true.
¹⁵²Long ago I learned from your statutes
    that you established them to last forever.

ר   Resh

¹⁵³Look upon my suffering and deliver me,
  for I have not forgotten your law.
¹⁵⁴Defend my cause and redeem me;
  preserve my life according to your promise.
¹⁵⁵Salvation is far from the wicked,
  for they do not seek out your decrees.
¹⁵⁶Your compassion is great, O Lord;
  preserve my life according to your laws.
¹⁵⁷Many are the foes who persecute me,
  but I have not turned from your statutes.
¹⁵⁸I look on the faithless with loathing,
  for they do not obey your word.
¹⁵⁹See how I love your precepts;
  preserve my life, O Lord, according to your love.
¹⁶⁰All your words are true;
  all your righteous laws are eternal.

שׂ   Sin and Shin

¹⁶¹Rulers persecute me without cause,
  but my heart trembles at your word.
¹⁶²I rejoice in your promise
  like one who finds great spoil.
¹⁶³I hate and abhor falsehood
  but I love your law.
¹⁶⁴Seven times a day I praise you
  for your righteous laws.
¹⁶⁵Great peace have they who love your law,
  and nothing can make them stumble.
¹⁶⁶I wait for your salvation, O Lord,
  and I follow your commands.
¹⁶⁷I obey your statutes,
  for I love them greatly.
¹⁶⁸I obey your precepts and your statutes,
  for all my ways are known to you.

ת   Taw

¹⁶⁹May my cry come before you, O Lord;
  give me understanding according to your word.
¹⁷⁰May my supplication come before you;
  deliver me according to your promise.
¹⁷¹May my lips overflow with praise,
  for you teach me your decrees.
¹⁷²May my tongue sing of your word,
  for all your commands are righteous.
¹⁷³May your hand be ready to help me,
  for I have chosen your precepts.
¹⁷⁴I long for your salvation, O Lord,
  and your law is my delight.
¹⁷⁵Let me live that I may praise you,
  and may your laws sustain me.

¹⁷⁶I have strayed like a lost sheep.
    Seek your servant,
    for I have not forgotten your commands.

Psalm

A song of ascents.

¹I call on the LORD in my distress,
    and he answers me.
²Save me, O LORD, from lying lips
    and from deceitful tongues.

³What will he do to you,
    and what more besides, O deceitful tongue?
⁴He will punish you with a warrior's sharp arrows,
    with burning coals of the broom tree.

⁵Woe to me that I dwell in Meshech,
    that I live among the tents of Kedar!
⁶Too long have I lived
    among those who hate peace.
⁷I am a man of peace;
    but when I speak, they are for war.

Psalm

A song of ascents.

¹I lift up my eyes to the hills—
    where does my help come from?
²My help comes from the LORD,
    the Maker of heaven and earth.

³He will not let your foot slip—
    he who watches over you will not slumber;
⁴indeed, he who watches over Israel
    will neither slumber nor sleep.

⁵The LORD watches over you—
    the LORD is your shade at your right hand;
⁶the sun will not harm you by day,
    nor the moon by night.

⁷The LORD will keep you from all harm—
    he will watch over your life;
⁸the LORD will watch over your coming and going
    both now and forevermore.

Psalm

A song of ascents. Of David.

¹I rejoiced with those who said to me,
  "Let us go to the house of the LORD."
²Our feet are standing
  in your gates, O Jerusalem.

³Jerusalem is built like a city
  that is closely compacted together.
⁴That is where the tribes go up,
  the tribes of the LORD,
 to praise the name of the LORD
  according to the statute given to Israel.
⁵There the thrones for judgment stand,
  the thrones of the house of David.

⁶Pray for the peace of Jerusalem:
  "May those who love you be secure.
⁷May there be peace within your walls
  and security within your citadels."
⁸For the sake of my brothers and friends,
  I will say, "Peace be within you."
⁹For the sake of the house of the LORD our God,
  I will seek your prosperity.

Psalm

A song of ascents.

¹I lift up my eyes to you,
  to you whose throne is in heaven.
²As the eyes of slaves look to the hand of their master,
  as the eyes of a maid look to the hand of her mistress,
 so our eyes look to the LORD our God,
  till he shows us his mercy.

³Have mercy on us, O LORD, have mercy on us,
  for we have endured much contempt.
⁴We have endured much ridicule from the proud,
  much contempt from the arrogant.

Psalm

A song of ascents. Of David.

¹If the LORD had not been on our side—
  let Israel say—
²if the LORD had not been on our side
  when men attacked us,
³when their anger flared against us,

they would have swallowed us alive;
⁴the flood would have engulfed us,
    the torrent would have swept over us,
⁵the raging waters
    would have swept us away.

⁶Praise be to the Lᴏʀᴅ,
    who has not let us be torn by their teeth.
⁷We have escaped like a bird
    out of the fowler's snare;
the snare has been broken,
    and we have escaped.
⁸Our help is in the name of the Lᴏʀᴅ,
    the Maker of heaven and earth.

Psalm

A song of ascents.

¹Those who trust in the Lᴏʀᴅ are like Mount Zion,
    which cannot be shaken but endures forever.
²As the mountains surround Jerusalem,
    so the Lᴏʀᴅ surrounds his people
    both now and forevermore.

³The scepter of the wicked will not remain
    over the land allotted to the righteous,
for then the righteous might use
    their hands to do evil.

⁴Do good, O Lᴏʀᴅ, to those who are good,
    to those who are upright in heart.
⁵But those who turn to crooked ways
    the Lᴏʀᴅ will banish with the evildoers.

Peace be upon Israel.

Psalm

A song of ascents.

¹When the Lᴏʀᴅ brought back the captives toᵃ Zion,
    we were like men who dreamed.ᵇ
²Our mouths were filled with laughter,
    our tongues with songs of joy.
Then it was said among the nations,
    "The Lᴏʀᴅ has done great things for them."
³The Lᴏʀᴅ has done great things for us,
    and we are filled with joy.

⁴Restore our fortunes,ᶜ O Lᴏʀᴅ,
    like streams in the Negev.

ᵃ1 Or Lᴏʀᴅ restored the fortunes of   ᵇ1 Or men restored to health   ᶜ4 Or Bring back our captives

⁵Those who sow in tears
  will reap with songs of joy.
⁶He who goes out weeping,
  carrying seed to sow,
will return with songs of joy,
  carrying sheaves with him.

Psalm

A song of ascents. Of Solomon.

¹Unless the LORD builds the house,
  its builders labor in vain.
Unless the LORD watches over the city,
  the watchmen stand guard in vain.
²In vain you rise early
  and stay up late,
toiling for food to eat—
  for he grants sleep to[a]
    those he loves.

³Sons are a heritage from the
    LORD,
  children a reward from him.
⁴Like arrows in the hands of a
    warrior
  are sons born in one's
    youth.
⁵Blessed is the man
  whose quiver is full of them.
They will not be put to shame
  when they contend with
    their enemies in the
    gate.

Psalm

A song of ascents.

¹Blessed are all who fear the
    LORD,
  who walk in his ways.
²You will eat the fruit of your labor;
  blessings and prosperity will be yours.
³Your wife will be like a fruitful vine
  within your house;
your sons will be like olive shoots
  around your table.
⁴Thus is the man blessed
  who fears the LORD.

▣ ▥▥▥▥▥▥ **KNOWING YOURSELF** ▥▥▥▥▥▥ ▤

**127:1–2
Character**

How often have we wanted to do something significant—start a business, raise a family, write a book or whatever—that would have value and importance beyond our present sphere? That desire is inborn. God created us to yearn for things that last, which is part of what it means to be made in his image.

The problem that so many of us run into is that we don't include God in our plans. If anything, God is an afterthought. Worse, we may actually cut God out of our plans because we know that he wouldn't approve of our actions.

This psalm contains a somber warning to believers and seekers alike: Anything done apart from God will not endure. In the grand scheme of things, all of our hard work, planning, and dreaming will come to nothing if we don't allow God to be an integral part of the process from start to finish.

---

a2 Or eat— / for while they sleep he provides for

⁵May the LORD bless you from Zion
    all the days of your life;
may you see the prosperity of Jerusalem,
  ⁶ and may you live to see your children's children.

  Peace be upon Israel.

Psalm

A song of ascents.

¹They have greatly oppressed me from my youth—
    let Israel say—
²they have greatly oppressed me from my youth,
    but they have not gained the victory over me.
³Plowmen have plowed my back
    and made their furrows long.
⁴But the LORD is righteous;
    he has cut me free from the cords of the wicked.

⁵May all who hate Zion
    be turned back in shame.
⁶May they be like grass on the roof,
    which withers before it can grow;
⁷with it the reaper cannot fill his hands,
    nor the one who gathers fill his arms.
⁸May those who pass by not say,
    "The blessing of the LORD be upon you;
    we bless you in the name of the LORD."

Psalm

A song of ascents.

¹Out of the depths I cry to you, O LORD;
  ² O Lord, hear my voice.
Let your ears be attentive
    to my cry for mercy.

³If you, O LORD, kept a record of sins,
    O Lord, who could stand?
⁴But with you there is forgiveness;
    therefore you are feared.

⁵I wait for the LORD, my soul waits,
    and in his word I put my hope.
⁶My soul waits for the Lord
    more than watchmen wait for the morning,
    more than watchmen wait for the morning.

⁷O Israel, put your hope in the LORD,
    for with the LORD is unfailing love
    and with him is full redemption.

⁸He himself will redeem Israel
　　from all their sins.

Psalm

A song of ascents. Of David.

¹My heart is not proud, O Lᴏʀᴅ,
　　my eyes are not haughty;
I do not concern myself with great matters
　　or things too wonderful for me.
²But I have stilled and quieted
　　my soul;
　　like a weaned child with its
　　　mother,
　　like a weaned child is my
　　　soul within me.

³O Israel, put your hope in the
　　Lᴏʀᴅ
　　both now and forevermore.

Psalm

A song of ascents.

¹O Lᴏʀᴅ, remember David
　　and all the hardships he
　　　endured.

²He swore an oath to the Lᴏʀᴅ
　　and made a vow to the
　　　Mighty One of Jacob:
³"I will not enter my house
　　or go to my bed—
⁴I will allow no sleep to my
　　eyes,
　　no slumber to my eyelids,
⁵till I find a place for the Lᴏʀᴅ,
　　a dwelling for the Mighty One of Jacob."

⁶We heard it in Ephrathah,
　　we came upon it in the fields of Jaarᵃ;ᵇ
⁷"Let us go to his dwelling place;
　　let us worship at his footstool—
⁸arise, O Lᴏʀᴅ, and come to your resting place,
　　you and the ark of your might.
⁹May your priests be clothed with righteousness;
　　may your saints sing for joy."

▣ ▦▦▦▦▦▦ DISCOVERING GOD ▦▦▦▦▦▦ ⟳

130:3–4
The God Who Is There

Some of us take great comfort in knowing that God sees everything done in secret, thinking that God will pay back those who've wronged us during our lifetime and seemingly got away with it. While that is certainly true, it also means that God sees *our* wrongdoing. What about the account we will have to give for our *own* actions?

In that light, this psalm gives us especially welcome news. Each of us has the opportunity to ask God to forgive us for every wrong thing we've ever done. Written down, thinking those offenses would add up to a monumental list. Who could stand if God shoved a copy of that list in our face? But these verses assure us that if we hope in his forgiveness, instead of in our "goodness," we can find full redemption (verse 7).

ᵃ6 That is, Kiriath Jearim　　ᵇ6 Or *heard of it in Ephrathah, / we found it in the fields of Jaar.* (And no quotes around verses 7–9)

¹⁰For the sake of David your servant,
do not reject your anointed one.

¹¹The LORD swore an oath to David,
a sure oath that he will not revoke:
"One of your own descendants
I will place on your throne—
¹²if your sons keep my covenant
and the statutes I teach them,
then their sons will sit
on your throne for ever and ever."

¹³For the LORD has chosen Zion,
he has desired it for his dwelling:
¹⁴"This is my resting place for ever and ever;
here I will sit enthroned, for I have desired it—
¹⁵I will bless her with abundant provisions;
her poor will I satisfy with food.
¹⁶I will clothe her priests with salvation,
and her saints will ever sing for joy.

¹⁷"Here I will make a horn^{*a*} grow for David
and set up a lamp for my anointed one.
¹⁸I will clothe his enemies with shame,
but the crown on his head will be resplendent."

Psalm

133

A song of ascents. Of David.

¹How good and pleasant it is
when brothers live together in unity!
²It is like precious oil poured on the head,
running down on the beard,
running down on Aaron's beard,
down upon the collar of his robes.
³It is as if the dew of Hermon
were falling on Mount Zion.
For there the LORD bestows his blessing,
even life forevermore.

Psalm

134

A song of ascents.

¹Praise the LORD, all you servants of the LORD
who minister by night in the house of the LORD.
²Lift up your hands in the sanctuary
and praise the LORD.

³May the LORD, the Maker of heaven and earth,
bless you from Zion.

---

a 17 Horn here symbolizes *strong one,* that is, king.

Psalm
135

¹Praise the LORD.[a]

Praise the name of the LORD;
   praise him, you servants of the LORD,
²you who minister in the house of the LORD,
   in the courts of the house of our God.

³Praise the LORD, for the LORD is good;
   sing praise to his name, for that is pleasant.
⁴For the LORD has chosen Jacob to be his own,
   Israel to be his treasured possession.

⁵I know that the LORD is great,
   that our Lord is greater than all gods.
⁶The LORD does whatever pleases him,
   in the heavens and on the earth,
   in the seas and all their depths.
⁷He makes clouds rise from the ends of the earth;
   he sends lightning with the rain
   and brings out the wind from his storehouses.

⁸He struck down the firstborn of Egypt,
   the firstborn of men and animals.
⁹He sent his signs and wonders into your midst, O Egypt,
   against Pharaoh and all his servants.
¹⁰He struck down many nations
   and killed mighty kings—
¹¹Sihon king of the Amorites,
   Og king of Bashan
   and all the kings of Canaan—
¹²and he gave their land as an inheritance,
   an inheritance to his people Israel.

¹³Your name, O LORD, endures forever,
   your renown, O LORD, through all generations.
¹⁴For the LORD will vindicate his people
   and have compassion on his servants.

¹⁵The idols of the nations are silver and gold,
   made by the hands of men.
¹⁶They have mouths, but cannot speak,
   eyes, but they cannot see;
¹⁷they have ears, but cannot hear,
   nor is there breath in their mouths.
¹⁸Those who make them will be like them,
   and so will all who trust in them.

¹⁹O house of Israel, praise the LORD;
   O house of Aaron, praise the LORD;
²⁰O house of Levi, praise the LORD;
   you who fear him, praise the LORD.

a 1 Hebrew *Hallelu Yah*; also in verses 3 and 21

²¹Praise be to the LORD from Zion,
to him who dwells in Jerusalem.

Praise the LORD.

Psalm
136

¹Give thanks to the LORD, for he is good.

His love endures forever.

²Give thanks to the God of gods.

His love endures forever.

³Give thanks to the Lord of lords:

His love endures forever.

⁴to him who alone does great wonders,

His love endures forever.

⁵who by his understanding made the heavens,

His love endures forever.

⁶who spread out the earth upon the waters,

His love endures forever.

⁷who made the great lights—

His love endures forever.

⁸the sun to govern the day,

His love endures forever.

⁹the moon and stars to govern the night;

His love endures forever.

¹⁰to him who struck down the firstborn of Egypt

His love endures forever.

¹¹and brought Israel out from among them

His love endures forever.

¹²with a mighty hand and outstretched arm;

His love endures forever.

¹³to him who divided the Red Sea ᵃ asunder

His love endures forever.

¹⁴and brought Israel through the midst of it,

His love endures forever.

¹⁵but swept Pharaoh and his army into the Red Sea;

His love endures forever.

¹⁶to him who led his people through the desert,

His love endures forever.

¹⁷who struck down great kings,

His love endures forever.

¹⁸and killed mighty kings—

His love endures forever.

¹⁹Sihon king of the Amorites

His love endures forever.

²⁰and Og king of Bashan—

His love endures forever.

²¹and gave their land as an inheritance,

His love endures forever.

ᵃ 13 Hebrew *Yam Suph*; that is, Sea of Reeds; also in verse 15

²²an inheritance to his servant Israel;

His love endures forever.

²³to the One who remembered us in our low estate

His love endures forever.

²⁴and freed us from our enemies,

His love endures forever.

²⁵and who gives food to every creature.

His love endures forever.

²⁶Give thanks to the God of heaven.

His love endures forever.

Psalm

137

¹By the rivers of Babylon we sat and wept
   when we remembered Zion.
²There on the poplars
   we hung our harps,
³for there our captors asked us for songs,
   our tormentors demanded songs of joy;
   they said, "Sing us one of the songs of Zion!"

⁴How can we sing the songs of the LORD
   while in a foreign land?
⁵If I forget you, O Jerusalem,
   may my right hand forget ⸢its skill⸣.
⁶May my tongue cling to the roof of my mouth
   if I do not remember you,
   if I do not consider Jerusalem
   my highest joy.

⁷Remember, O LORD, what the Edomites did
   on the day Jerusalem fell.
"Tear it down," they cried,
   "tear it down to its foundations!"

⁸O Daughter of Babylon, doomed to destruction,
   happy is he who repays you
   for what you have done to us—
⁹he who seizes your infants
   and dashes them against the rocks.

Psalm

138

Of David.

¹I will praise you, O LORD, with all my heart;
   before the "gods" I will sing your praise.
²I will bow down toward your holy temple
   and will praise your name
   for your love and your faithfulness,
for you have exalted above all things
   your name and your word.

³When I called, you answered me;
  you made me bold and stouthearted.

⁴May all the kings of the earth praise you, O Lᴏʀᴅ,
  when they hear the words of your mouth.
⁵May they sing of the ways of the Lᴏʀᴅ,
  for the glory of the Lᴏʀᴅ is great.

⁶Though the Lᴏʀᴅ is on high, he looks upon the lowly,
  but the proud he knows from afar.

▣ ⦙⦙⦙⦙⦙⦙⦙⦙ KNOWING YOURSELF ⦙⦙⦙⦙⦙⦙⦙⦙ ◧

139:1–24
A New Identity

All of us can think of something we would like to change about ourselves—our height, weight, strength, intelligence, personality, or something else. But when we berate ourselves, we fail to take into account that we were designed and created by God himself. Verse 13 of this psalm brings that fact into sharp focus.

At conception, each of us was smaller than the period at the end of this sentence. Yet the genetic code for everything we are and will be was contained in that small dot. Nine months later we were born as tiny human beings. What a miracle!

It's easy to understand why many people start seeking God after the birth of a child. They've participated in the most incredible creative experience humans can have. But the wonder and love we feel at holding a new little life is barely a dim reflection of what God feels for each one of us!

The next time you become overly critical of yourself, read Psalm 139 again. After you've done that, consider thanking God for his involvement in your life and for caring about you with an unending love.

---

⁷Though I walk in the midst of trouble,
  you preserve my life;
you stretch out your hand against the
    anger of my foes,
  with your right hand you save me.
⁸The Lᴏʀᴅ will fulfill ⌊his purpose⌋ for
    me;
  your love, O Lᴏʀᴅ, endures forever—
  do not abandon the works of your
    hands.

Psalm

139

For the director of music.
Of David. A psalm.

¹O Lᴏʀᴅ, you have searched me
  and you know me.
²You know when I sit and when I rise;
  you perceive my thoughts from afar.
³You discern my going out and my lying
    down;
  you are familiar with all my ways.
⁴Before a word is on my tongue
  you know it completely, O Lᴏʀᴅ.

⁵You hem me in—behind and before;
  you have laid your hand upon me.
⁶Such knowledge is too wonderful for
    me,
  too lofty for me to attain.

⁷Where can I go from your Spirit?
  Where can I flee from your presence?
⁸If I go up to the heavens, you are there;
  if I make my bed in the depths,ᵃ you are there.
⁹If I rise on the wings of the dawn,
  if I settle on the far side of the sea,
¹⁰even there your hand will guide me,
  your right hand will hold me fast.

¹¹If I say, "Surely the darkness will hide me

ᵃ8 Hebrew *Sheol*

and the light become night around me,"
[12]even the darkness will not be dark to you;
    the night will shine like the day,
    for darkness is as light to you.

[13]For you created my inmost being;
    you knit me together in my mother's womb.
[14]I praise you because I am fearfully and wonderfully made;
    your works are wonderful,
    I know that full well.
[15]My frame was not hidden from you
    when I was made in the secret place.
When I was woven together in the depths of the earth,
[16]   your eyes saw my unformed body.
All the days ordained for me
    were written in your book
    before one of them came to be.

[17]How precious to[a] me are your thoughts, O God!
    How vast is the sum of them!
[18]Were I to count them,
    they would outnumber the grains of sand.
When I awake,
    I am still with you.

[19]If only you would slay the wicked, O God!
    Away from me, you bloodthirsty men!
[20]They speak of you with evil intent;
    your adversaries misuse your name.
[21]Do I not hate those who hate you, O LORD,
    and abhor those who rise up against you?
[22]I have nothing but hatred for them;
    I count them my enemies.

[23]Search me, O God, and know my heart;
    test me and know my anxious thoughts.
[24]See if there is any offensive way in me,
    and lead me in the way everlasting.

Psalm

140

For the director of music. A psalm of David.

[1]Rescue me, O LORD, from evil men;
    protect me from men of violence,
[2]who devise evil plans in their hearts
    and stir up war every day.
[3]They make their tongues as sharp as a serpent's;
    the poison of vipers is on their lips.   *Selah*

[4]Keep me, O LORD, from the hands of the wicked;
    protect me from men of violence
    who plan to trip my feet.

---

[a] 17 Or *concerning*

⁵Proud men have hidden a snare for me;
   they have spread out the cords of their net
   and have set traps for me along my path.   *Selah*

⁶O Lord, I say to you, "You are my God."
   Hear, O Lord, my cry for mercy.
⁷O Sovereign Lord, my strong deliverer,
   who shields my head in the day of battle—
⁸do not grant the wicked their desires, O Lord;
   do not let their plans succeed,
   or they will become proud.   *Selah*

⁹Let the heads of those who surround me
   be covered with the trouble their lips have caused.
¹⁰Let burning coals fall upon them;
   may they be thrown into the fire,
   into miry pits, never to rise.
¹¹Let slanderers not be established in the land;
   may disaster hunt down men of violence.

¹²I know that the Lord secures justice for the poor
   and upholds the cause of the needy.
¹³Surely the righteous will praise your name
   and the upright will live before you.

Psalm

A psalm of David.

¹O Lord, I call to you; come quickly to me.
   Hear my voice when I call to you.
²May my prayer be set before you like incense;
   may the lifting up of my hands be like the evening sacrifice.

³Set a guard over my mouth, O Lord;
   keep watch over the door of my lips.
⁴Let not my heart be drawn to what is evil,
   to take part in wicked deeds
with men who are evildoers;
   let me not eat of their delicacies.

⁵Let a righteous man*ᵃ* strike me—it is a kindness;
   let him rebuke me—it is oil on my head.
   My head will not refuse it.

Yet my prayer is ever against the deeds of evildoers;
⁶   their rulers will be thrown down from the cliffs,
   and the wicked will learn that my words were well spoken.
⁷They will say, "As one plows and breaks up the earth,
   so our bones have been scattered at the mouth of the grave.*ᵇ*"

⁸But my eyes are fixed on you, O Sovereign Lord;
   in you I take refuge—do not give me over to death.
⁹Keep me from the snares they have laid for me,

ᵃ5 Or Let the Righteous One   *ᵇ7 Hebrew Sheol*

from the traps set by evildoers.
¹⁰Let the wicked fall into their own nets,
   while I pass by in safety.

Psalm

A maskil[a] *of David. When he was in the cave. A prayer.*

¹I cry aloud to the LORD;
   I lift up my voice to the LORD for mercy.
²I pour out my complaint before him;
   before him I tell my trouble.

³When my spirit grows faint within me,
   it is you who know my way.
In the path where I walk
   men have hidden a snare for me.
⁴Look to my right and see;
   no one is concerned for me.
I have no refuge;
   no one cares for my life.

⁵I cry to you, O LORD;
   I say, "You are my refuge,
   my portion in the land of the living."
⁶Listen to my cry,
   for I am in desperate need;
rescue me from those who pursue me,
   for they are too strong for me.
⁷Set me free from my prison,
   that I may praise your name.

Then the righteous will gather about me
   because of your goodness to me.

Psalm

A psalm of David.

¹O LORD, hear my prayer,
   listen to my cry for mercy;
in your faithfulness and righteousness
   come to my relief.
²Do not bring your servant into judgment,
   for no one living is righteous before you.

³The enemy pursues me,
   he crushes me to the ground;
he makes me dwell in darkness
   like those long dead.
⁴So my spirit grows faint within me;
   my heart within me is dismayed.

a Title: Probably a literary or musical term

⁵I remember the days of long ago;
  I meditate on all your works
  and consider what your hands have done.
⁶I spread out my hands to you;
  my soul thirsts for you like a parched land.   *Selah*

⁷Answer me quickly, O LORD;
  my spirit fails.
 Do not hide your face from me
  or I will be like those who go down to the pit.
⁸Let the morning bring me word of your unfailing love,
  for I have put my trust in you.
 Show me the way I should go,
  for to you I lift up my soul.
⁹Rescue me from my enemies, O LORD,
  for I hide myself in you.
¹⁰Teach me to do your will,
  for you are my God;
 may your good Spirit
  lead me on level ground.

¹¹For your name's sake, O LORD, preserve my life;
  in your righteousness, bring me out of trouble.
¹²In your unfailing love, silence my enemies;
  destroy all my foes,
  for I am your servant.

Psalm

144

Of David.

¹Praise be to the LORD my Rock,
  who trains my hands for war,
  my fingers for battle.
²He is my loving God and my fortress,
  my stronghold and my deliverer,
 my shield, in whom I take refuge,
  who subdues peoples*ᵃ* under me.

³O LORD, what is man that you care for him,
  the son of man that you think of him?
⁴Man is like a breath;
  his days are like a fleeting shadow.

⁵Part your heavens, O LORD, and come down;
  touch the mountains, so that they smoke.
⁶Send forth lightning and scatter ⌊the enemies⌋;
  shoot your arrows and rout them.
⁷Reach down your hand from on high;
  deliver me and rescue me
 from the mighty waters,
  from the hands of foreigners

ᵃ2 Many manuscripts of the Masoretic Text, Dead Sea Scrolls, Aquila, Jerome and Syriac; most manuscripts of the Masoretic Text *subdues my people*

⁸whose mouths are full of lies,
　　whose right hands are deceitful.

⁹I will sing a new song to you, O God;
　　on the ten-stringed lyre I will make music to you,
¹⁰to the One who gives victory to kings,
　　who delivers his servant David from the deadly sword.

¹¹Deliver me and rescue me
　　from the hands of foreigners
　whose mouths are full of lies,
　　whose right hands are deceitful.

¹²Then our sons in their youth
　　will be like well-nurtured plants,
　and our daughters will be like pillars
　　carved to adorn a palace.
¹³Our barns will be filled
　　with every kind of provision.
　Our sheep will increase by thousands,
　　by tens of thousands in our fields;
¹⁴　our oxen will draw heavy loads.ᵃ
　There will be no breaching of walls,
　　no going into captivity,
　　no cry of distress in our streets.

¹⁵Blessed are the people of whom this is true;
　　blessed are the people whose God is the LORD.

Psalmᵇ

A psalm of praise. Of David.

¹I will exalt you, my God the King;
　　I will praise your name for ever and ever.
²Every day I will praise you
　　and extol your name for ever and ever.

³Great is the LORD and most worthy of praise;
　　his greatness no one can fathom.
⁴One generation will commend your works to another;
　　they will tell of your mighty acts.
⁵They will speak of the glorious splendor of your majesty,
　　and I will meditate on your wonderful works.ᶜ
⁶They will tell of the power of your awesome works,
　　and I will proclaim your great deeds.
⁷They will celebrate your abundant goodness
　　and joyfully sing of your righteousness.

⁸The LORD is gracious and compassionate,
　　slow to anger and rich in love.
⁹The LORD is good to all;

ᵃ14 Or our chieftains will be firmly established　　ᵇThis psalm is an acrostic poem, the verses of which (including verse 13b) begin with the successive letters of the Hebrew alphabet.　　ᶜ5 Dead Sea Scrolls and Syriac (see also Septuagint); Masoretic Text *On the glorious splendor of your majesty / and on your wonderful works I will meditate*

he has compassion on all he has made.
¹⁰All you have made will praise you, O LORD;
your saints will extol you.
¹¹They will tell of the glory of your kingdom
and speak of your might,
¹²so that all men may know of your mighty acts
and the glorious splendor of your kingdom.
¹³Your kingdom is an everlasting kingdom,
and your dominion endures through all generations.

The LORD is faithful to all his promises
and loving toward all he has made.ᵃ
¹⁴The LORD upholds all those who fall
and lifts up all who are bowed down.
¹⁵The eyes of all look to you,
and you give them their food at the proper time.

⌦ ▦▦▦▦▦▦ **DISCOVERING GOD** ▦▦▦▦▦▦ ⎀

145:17–20
Life with God

God loves everyone (verse 17), but he will not let people who persist in rejecting him spoil his creation forever. He openly welcomes all who turn to him, no matter what their condition; verse 20 makes that clear. But God wants people to cooperate with his design instead of fighting it. Make no mistake—God will eventually destroy those who continually oppose him.

Which are you? Which do you want to be? You don't have to persist in fighting God anymore. It's as easy as saying, "Lord, I surrender!" Come to him and accept his invitation to be your forgiver and leader.

---

¹⁶You open your hand
and satisfy the desires of every living thing.

¹⁷The LORD is righteous in all his ways
and loving toward all he has made.
¹⁸The LORD is near to all who call on him,
to all who call on him in truth.
¹⁹He fulfills the desires of those who fear him;
he hears their cry and saves them.
²⁰The LORD watches over all who love him,
but all the wicked he will destroy.

²¹My mouth will speak in praise of the LORD.
Let every creature praise his holy name
for ever and ever.

Psalm

146

¹Praise the LORD.ᵇ

Praise the LORD, O my soul.
² I will praise the LORD all my life;
I will sing praise to my God as long as I live.

³Do not put your trust in princes,
in mortal men, who cannot save.
⁴When their spirit departs, they return to the ground;
on that very day their plans come to nothing.

⁵Blessed is he whose help is the God of Jacob,
whose hope is in the LORD his God,
⁶the Maker of heaven and earth,
the sea, and everything in them—

ᵃ13 One manuscript of the Masoretic Text, Dead Sea Scrolls and Syriac (see also Septuagint); most manuscripts of the Masoretic Text do not have the last two lines of verse 13.   ᵇ1 Hebrew Hallelu Yah; also in verse 10

the LORD, who remains faithful forever.
⁷He upholds the cause of the oppressed
    and gives food to the hungry.
The LORD sets prisoners free,
⁸   the LORD gives sight to the blind,
the LORD lifts up those who are bowed down,
    the LORD loves the righteous.
⁹The LORD watches over the alien
    and sustains the fatherless and the widow,
    but he frustrates the ways of the wicked.

¹⁰The LORD reigns forever,
    your God, O Zion, for all generations.

Praise the LORD.

Psalm

147

¹Praise the LORD. *ᵃ*

How good it is to sing praises to our God,
    how pleasant and fitting to praise him!

²The LORD builds up Jerusalem;
    he gathers the exiles of Israel.
³He heals the brokenhearted
    and binds up their wounds.
⁴He determines the number of the stars
    and calls them each by name.
⁵Great is our Lord and mighty in power;
    his understanding has no limit.
⁶The LORD sustains the humble
    but casts the wicked to the ground.

⁷Sing to the LORD with thanksgiving;
    make music to our God on the harp.
⁸He covers the sky with clouds;
    he supplies the earth with rain
    and makes grass grow on the hills.
⁹He provides food for the cattle
    and for the young ravens when they call.

¹⁰His pleasure is not in the strength of the horse,
    nor his delight in the legs of a man;
¹¹the LORD delights in those who fear him,
    who put their hope in his unfailing love.

¹²Extol the LORD, O Jerusalem;
    praise your God, O Zion,
¹³for he strengthens the bars of your gates
    and blesses your people within you.
¹⁴He grants peace to your borders
    and satisfies you with the finest of wheat.

ᵃ 1   Hebrew *Hallelu Yah;* also in verse 20

¹⁵He sends his command to the earth;
  his word runs swiftly.
¹⁶He spreads the snow like wool
  and scatters the frost like ashes.
¹⁷He hurls down his hail like pebbles.
  Who can withstand his icy blast?
¹⁸He sends his word and melts them;
  he stirs up his breezes, and the waters flow.

¹⁹He has revealed his word to Jacob,
  his laws and decrees to Israel.
²⁰He has done this for no other nation;
  they do not know his laws.

  Praise the Lord.

Psalm

148

¹Praise the Lord.ᵃ

  Praise the Lord from the heavens,
    praise him in the heights above.
²Praise him, all his angels,
    praise him, all his heavenly hosts.
³Praise him, sun and moon,
    praise him, all you shining stars.
⁴Praise him, you highest heavens
    and you waters above the skies.
⁵Let them praise the name of the Lord,
    for he commanded and they were created.
⁶He set them in place for ever and ever;
    he gave a decree that will never pass away.

⁷Praise the Lord from the earth,
    you great sea creatures and all ocean depths,
⁸lightning and hail, snow and clouds,
    stormy winds that do his bidding,
⁹you mountains and all hills,
    fruit trees and all cedars,
¹⁰wild animals and all cattle,
    small creatures and flying birds,
¹¹kings of the earth and all nations,
    you princes and all rulers on earth,
¹²young men and maidens,
    old men and children.

¹³Let them praise the name of the Lord,
    for his name alone is exalted;
    his splendor is above the earth and the heavens.
¹⁴He has raised up for his people a horn,ᵇ

ᵃ1 Hebrew *Hallelu Yah*; also in verse 14   ᵇ14 *Horn* here symbolizes strong one, that is, king.

the praise of all his saints,
of Israel, the people close to his heart.

Praise the LORD.

Psalm

¹Praise the LORD.ᵃ

Sing to the LORD a new song,
his praise in the assembly of the saints.

²Let Israel rejoice in their
Maker;
let the people of Zion be
glad in their King.
³Let them praise his name with
dancing
and make music to him with
tambourine and harp.
⁴For the LORD takes delight in
his people;
he crowns the humble with
salvation.
⁵Let the saints rejoice in this
honor
and sing for joy on their
beds.

⁶May the praise of God be in
their mouths
and a double-edged sword
in their hands,
⁷to inflict vengeance on the
nations
and punishment on the
peoples,
⁸to bind their kings with fetters,
their nobles with shackles of
iron,
⁹to carry out the sentence
written against them.
This is the glory of all his
saints.

Praise the LORD.

▣ ▨▨▨▨▨ **ADDRESSING QUESTIONS** ▨▨▨▨▨ ⧉

150:1–6
Human Experience

They paint their faces. They don ridiculous-
looking hats and other bizarre costumes.
Sometimes they go without shirts in freezing
weather. They carry signs and shout until
they're hoarse. They're called *fans.* And they
show up at football games.

Why do these people do all this? What great
benefit will they receive, or what humanitar-
ian cause will they further for all their sacrifice?

Well, uh . . . none.

So why is it that when someone gets a little excited about what God has done, most of
us consider such a person a *fanatic?* Maybe
we've got it turned around.

This closing psalm is an exuberant, pull-
out-all-the-stops celebration of God's power
and greatness. If we were to obey all the commands of this passage of Scripture, we'd make
some serious noise!

People will probably never stop acting crazy
at football games. But is it too much to hope
that people will give God a little credit for all
he's done—and maybe even raise a cheer for
his sake? That was this psalmist's intention. If
the truth in this book has broadened your
knowledge of God and helped you place your
trust in him, why not make it yours as well?

Psalm

¹Praise the LORD.ᵇ

Praise God in his sanctuary;

ᵃ1 Hebrew *Hallelu Yah;* also in verse 9   ᵇ1 Hebrew *Hallelu Yah;* also in verse 6

    praise him in his mighty heavens.
²Praise him for his acts of power;
    praise him for his surpassing greatness.
³Praise him with the sounding of the trumpet,
    praise him with the harp and lyre,
⁴praise him with tambourine and dancing,
    praise him with the strings and flute,
⁵praise him with the clash of cymbals,
    praise him with resounding cymbals.

⁶Let everything that has breath praise the LORD.

  Praise the LORD.

If this story sounds like a confession, that's because it is one.

I spent the past 15 years heavily involved in just about every criminal activity one can imagine. During that time right and wrong, good and evil, truth and lies became blurred and distorted. I spent most of the time in a drug-induced haze, unable to deal with reality when sober.

The lie came crashing down around me one night when a S.W.A.T. team, armed with machine guns and tear gas, broke my door down. They seized drugs, cash, my car, and about 30 guns. I now face two very serious felony charges.

The Sunday after the raid my fiancée (thank God she didn't leave me!) brought me to a worship service at her church. The opening music touched my heart and opened me up to hear God's truth as the soloist sang about God's ways being higher than mine. As the pastor preached his message, I began to realize how God, in his wisdom, had been working in my life. At that very moment—a moment I will never forget, a moment I could never begin to describe—God reached out to me with open arms and drew me close to himself.

The feeling of being touched by God is indescribable. I sobbed tears of pure joy, as well as tears of sadness. I had been away from my Father for too long. I had denied Christ in my heart for too long. But all of that changed in a single moment. I was the prodigal son, returning home after years of wandering away from God. God, my Father, saw me coming. He ran to me with open arms and embraced me. I embraced him as well, and at that moment felt a love so pure that I will never let go.

The change in my life could only be described as a complete turnaround. I am a new person, or perhaps I've become the *real* person God has always intended me to be. I no longer live the lie of evil. I've invited God to fill the void in my heart in a way that only he can. My life has become a walk *with* Christ instead of one away from Him. I surround myself with other believers. I need them to help me grow and flourish. I pray every day that God will make himself known to me more and more so that I'll be able to take his will for my life and make it my own.

PROVERBS/ECCLESIASTES

Introduction

THE BOTTOM LINE

Pick up these books and you'll find it hard to believe that the words you're reading were written almost 3000 years ago. Proverbs includes "street-wise," no-nonsense advice on relationships, money, sex, business—just about every topic that affects daily life. Ecclesiastes takes a look at the futility of pursuing material things, and points to God as the only source of real meaning. Are these books so applicable to our lives because the world's problems haven't changed much over the centuries? Perhaps. But an even better explanation is that God's character and truth have remained unchanged since the beginning of time.

CENTRAL IDEAS

- God's Biblical directives make good sense for our lives today.
- Running after pleasure, fame, knowledge, or riches is futile.
- In this life, meaning only comes from living a life that's devoted to God.
- Practical wisdom from God is the only sure guide for life, and it's worth every investment to acquire.

TITLES

Proverbs describes the short bits of insight into human behavior contained in the book. The word Ecclesiastes, in the Greek, refers to an assembly of people — people who would be listening to the words of "the Teacher."

AUTHORS AND READERS

The primary author of Proverbs is Solomon, but others also made contributions to the text. The wisdom of this book was intended for young Israelites, but its down-to-earth and sometimes witty advice applies to people of all times and places. Ecclesiastes has been traditionally ascribed to Solomon too, although it may have been written by a close observer of his life.

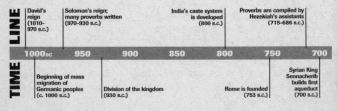

TIME LINE

David's reign (1010-970 B.C.)	Solomon's reign; many proverbs written (970-930 B.C.)		India's caste system is developed (800 B.C.)	Proverbs are compiled by Hezekiah's assistants (715-686 B.C.)	
1000 BC	**950**	**900**	**850**	**800**	**750**	**700**
	Beginning of mass migration of Germanic peoples (c. 1000 B.C.)	Division of the kingdom (930 B.C.)		Rome is founded (753 B.C.)	Syrian King Sennacherib builds first aqueduct (700 B.C.)

An episode of the television program "The Twilight Zone" told of an east-coast gangster who died. Following his death, the hoodlum found himself in a beautiful penthouse in a high-rise gambling casino. As an attendant led him around the glittering room, the gangster thought to himself, *I'm in heaven!*

Eager to try his luck, he wagered some money. Every time he placed a bet, he won. The man had never had such a run of good luck. He couldn't imagine that things could get any better than this—but they did.

Not only was he having a run of luck at the tables, he was doing all right with the women. In fact, one beautiful woman showered him with affection and laughed at all of his jokes. The gangster had everything he ever thought would make him happy.

Then, slowly, something began to change. No, it wasn't his luck that ran out; he continued to win at every table. What changed was his ability to enjoy winning. Without the risk of losing, winning was no fun. His female companion also began to bore him. He wished she wouldn't laugh at his every joke and agree with his every comment.

The gangster thought to himself, **I'm in heaven!**

What the man needed was a challenge—something to end his boredom. Eventually, he asked his gray-haired attendant if God hadn't made a mistake by sending him to heaven.

"Heaven?" the attendant asked in surprise. "You haven't been sent to heaven. You're in hell!"

While this isn't a biblical story, it does make an important point. True satisfaction doesn't come from heaping up wealth or pleasure. A meaningful life involves much more.

A thousand years before Christ was born, the wisest man in Israel's history, King Solomon, made his mark by leaving behind a body of wisdom unparalleled in the ancient world. Through his writings, Solomon intended to teach his readers how to live a truly meaningful life. Three thousand years later, Proverbs and Ecclesiastes are among the most widely read books in the Old Testament. In them you will find practical wisdom to help you in virtually every area of life—money, sex, power, business, relationships, marriage, recreation, parenting, and more.

Want a taste of ancient learning that is as contemporary as the latest television show? See what happened to a man who didn't have to die before he experienced events similar to those in the "Twilight Zone" episode. Ecclesiastes chapter 2, verses 1–11 (page 851), describe Solomon's perspective on "the good life." He found that if a person has abundance without God's gift of contentment, life is less like heaven than it is like hell.

But keep reading. This story has a happy ending (see Ecclesiastes chapter 12; page 863).

PROVERBS

Prologue: Purpose and Theme

1 The proverbs of Solomon son of David, king of Israel:

²for attaining wisdom and discipline;
  for understanding words of insight;
³for acquiring a disciplined and prudent life,
  doing what is right and just and fair;
⁴for giving prudence to the simple,
  knowledge and discretion to the young—
⁵let the wise listen and add to their learning,
  and let the discerning get guidance—
⁶for understanding proverbs and parables,
  the sayings and riddles of the wise.

⁷The fear of the LORD is the beginning of
  knowledge,
  but fools*ᵃ* despise wisdom and
    discipline.

Exhortations to Embrace Wisdom

Warning Against Enticement

⁸Listen, my son, to your father's
  instruction
  and do not forsake your mother's
    teaching.
⁹They will be a garland to grace your
  head
  and a chain to adorn your neck.

¹⁰My son, if sinners entice you,
  do not give in to them.
¹¹If they say, "Come along with us;
  let's lie in wait for someone's blood,
  let's waylay some harmless soul;
¹²let's swallow them alive, like the
  grave,*ᵇ*
  and whole, like those who go down
    to the pit;
¹³we will get all sorts of valuable things
  and fill our houses with plunder;
¹⁴throw in your lot with us,
  and we will share a common purse"—
¹⁵my son, do not go along with them,

MANAGING RESOURCES

1:7
Education

What does this author mean when he writes about "the fear of the LORD," and what does it have to do with gaining wisdom?

Fear, in this context, doesn't mean cowering before God. He is not some celestial schoolmaster who stands over us demanding that we learn his ways—or else. When we *fear* God, we acknowledge his power and love for us and our ultimate dependence on him. That knowledge frames and permeates all that we do. When we try to live our lives without that most basic of all truths, our search for wisdom starts out using the wrong "database."

As the creator of the universe, God is the source of all wisdom and all knowledge. As you seek to expand your knowledge of him and of his world, recognize that truth, and honor him in whatever field of education you pursue.

ᵃ7 The Hebrew words rendered *fool* in Proverbs, and often elsewhere in the Old Testament, denote one who is morally deficient.
ᵇ12 Hebrew *Sheol*

do not set foot on their paths;
¹⁶for their feet rush into sin,
    they are swift to shed blood.
¹⁷How useless to spread a net
    in full view of all the birds!
¹⁸These men lie in wait for their own blood;
    they waylay only themselves!
¹⁹Such is the end of all who go after ill-gotten gain;
    it takes away the lives of those who get it.

Warning Against Rejecting Wisdom

²⁰Wisdom calls aloud in the street,
    she raises her voice in the public squares;
²¹at the head of the noisy streetsᵃ she cries out,
    in the gateways of the city she makes her speech:

²²"How long will you simple onesᵇ love your simple ways?
    How long will mockers delight in mockery
    and fools hate knowledge?
²³If you had responded to my rebuke,
    I would have poured out my heart to you
    and made my thoughts known to you.
²⁴But since you rejected me when I called
    and no one gave heed when I stretched out my hand,
²⁵since you ignored all my advice
    and would not accept my rebuke,
²⁶I in turn will laugh at your disaster;
    I will mock when calamity overtakes you—
²⁷when calamity overtakes you like a storm,
    when disaster sweeps over you like a whirlwind,
    when distress and trouble overwhelm you.

²⁸"Then they will call to me but I will not answer;
    they will look for me but will not find me.
²⁹Since they hated knowledge
    and did not choose to fear the LORD,
³⁰since they would not accept my advice
    and spurned my rebuke,
³¹they will eat the fruit of their ways
    and be filled with the fruit of their schemes.
³²For the waywardness of the simple will kill them,
    and the complacency of fools will destroy them;
³³but whoever listens to me will live in safety
    and be at ease, without fear of harm."

Moral Benefits of Wisdom

2 My son, if you accept my words
    and store up my commands within you,
²turning your ear to wisdom
    and applying your heart to understanding,
³and if you call out for insight
    and cry aloud for understanding,

ᵃ21 Hebrew; Septuagint / *on the tops of the walls*   ᵇ22 The Hebrew word rendered *simple* in Proverbs generally denotes
one without moral direction and inclined to evil.

⁴and if you look for it as for silver
    and search for it as for hidden treasure,
⁵then you will understand the fear of the LORD
    and find the knowledge of God.
⁶For the LORD gives wisdom,
    and from his mouth come knowledge and understanding.

⁷He holds victory in store for the
    upright,
    he is a shield to those whose walk
        is blameless,
⁸for he guards the course of the just
    and protects the way of his faithful
        ones.

⁹Then you will understand what is right
    and just
    and fair—every good path.
¹⁰For wisdom will enter your heart,
    and knowledge will be pleasant to
        your soul.
¹¹Discretion will protect you,
    and understanding will guard you.

¹²Wisdom will save you from the ways
    of wicked men,
    from men whose words are perverse,
¹³who leave the straight paths
    to walk in dark ways,
¹⁴who delight in doing wrong
    and rejoice in the perverseness of
        evil,
¹⁵whose paths are crooked
    and who are devious in their ways.

¹⁶It will save you also from the
    adulteress,
    from the wayward wife with her
        seductive words,

MANAGING RESOURCES

2:1–9
Education

Mal Fisher was a sunken-treasure hunter—a *patient* one.

One sunken cargo in particular captured his interest. When he read about a hurricane that had destroyed a fleet of Spanish ships loaded with gold and silver just off the Florida coast in 1622, Mal spent more than 16 years with a team of divers scouring the sea floor in search of the treasure. After expending all that time and energy, Fisher's underwater camera spotted an estimated 300 tons of gold, silver, artifacts, and ship remnants. While the 16 years had been long and difficult, for Mal Fisher this discovery was worth every second.

Solomon felt the same way about the riches of God's wisdom. He even compared wisdom's benefits to "hidden treasure" (verse 4). He wrote that God's wisdom gives its possessors the ability to discern between good and evil (verse 9), to avoid the snares of others who plot to drag them down (verses 12 and 16) and, most important, to know God (verse 5). But unlike Mal Fisher's divers, we have a map showing the exact location of this treasure! We find wisdom by searching for it in God's revelation, the Bible (see verse 6).

---

¹⁷who has left the partner of her youth
    and ignored the covenant she made before God.ᵃ
¹⁸For her house leads down to death
    and her paths to the spirits of the dead.
¹⁹None who go to her return
    or attain the paths of life.

²⁰Thus you will walk in the ways of good men
    and keep to the paths of the righteous.
²¹For the upright will live in the land,
    and the blameless will remain in it;
²²but the wicked will be cut off from the land,
    and the unfaithful will be torn from it.

ᵃ17 Or covenant of her God

Further Benefits of Wisdom

3
My son, do not forget my teaching,
but keep my commands in your heart,
[2]for they will prolong your life many years
and bring you prosperity.

[3]Let love and faithfulness never
leave you;
bind them around your neck,
write them on the tablet of
your heart.
[4]Then you will win favor and a
good name
in the sight of God and man.

[5]Trust in the LORD with all your
heart
and lean not on your own
understanding;
[6]in all your ways acknowledge
him,
and he will make your paths
straight.[a]

[7]Do not be wise in your own
eyes;
fear the LORD and shun evil.
[8]This will bring health to your
body
and nourishment to your
bones.

[9]Honor the LORD with your
wealth,
with the firstfruits of all your
crops;
[10]then your barns will be filled
to overflowing,
and your vats will brim over with new wine.

[11]My son, do not despise the LORD's discipline
and do not resent his rebuke,
[12]because the LORD disciplines those he loves,
as a father[b] the son he delights in.

[13]Blessed is the man who finds wisdom,
the man who gains understanding,
[14]for she is more profitable than silver
and yields better returns than gold.
[15]She is more precious than rubies;
nothing you desire can compare with her.
[16]Long life is in her right hand;
in her left hand are riches and honor.
[17]Her ways are pleasant ways,

▦ MANAGING RESOURCES ▦ ▤

**3:9–10, 27–28
Possessions**

A principle found throughout Scripture is that those who hold most tightly to their money can't seem to keep it, while those who use their wealth compassionately prosper in the long run. In other words, the generous among us receive generosity (compare chapter 11, verse 24 [page 818]).

These verses teach two important Biblical principles: First, when we acknowledge God's part in our success, we owe a certain amount back to his service (the historical biblical standard is 10 percent of our income). Second, we need to pay our bills on time without forcing people to wait unnecessarily. These are good policies for companies as well as individuals, because they foster an attitude of compassion and generosity toward others.

As you'll see, the book of Proverbs contains many guidelines for money management. But just implementing these two will radically change the way we live and the impact we have on others.

Are your money management principles working? If not, why not consider the principles found in this book for your own situation?

---

a 6 Or will direct your paths   *b 12 Hebrew; Septuagint / and he punishes*

and all her paths are peace.
¹⁸She is a tree of life to those who embrace her;
   those who lay hold of her will be blessed.

¹⁹By wisdom the LORD laid the earth's foundations,
   by understanding he set the heavens in place;
²⁰by his knowledge the deeps were divided,
   and the clouds let drop the dew.

²¹My son, preserve sound judgment and discernment,
   do not let them out of your sight;

²²they will be life for you,
   an ornament to grace your neck.
²³Then you will go on your way in safety,
   and your foot will not stumble;
²⁴when you lie down, you will not be afraid;
   when you lie down, your sleep will be sweet.
²⁵Have no fear of sudden disaster
   or of the ruin that overtakes the wicked,
²⁶for the LORD will be your confidence
   and will keep your foot from being snared.

²⁷Do not withhold good from those who deserve it,
   when it is in your power to act.
²⁸Do not say to your neighbor,
   "Come back later; I'll give it tomorrow"—
   when you now have it with you.

²⁹Do not plot harm against your neighbor,
   who lives trustfully near you.

▣ ▒▒▒▒▒▒ DISCOVERING GOD ▒▒▒▒▒▒ ⬌

3:11–12
Life with God

It's hard for a parent to discipline a child. Why? Because he or she knows it's painful. Yet the parent intends only to help the child realize that bad decisions bring unfavorable consequences, so that the child will avoid bad decisions in the future.

Similarly, God sometimes disciplines us. We make a foolish or sinful choice and find that it costs us a business account, a friendship, or even our health. Such natural consequences may be God's way of disciplining us.

But God goes one step further with his followers. He may actually carry out *supernatural* consequences to get our attention. He doesn't punish his followers—all punishment for their sin has already been laid on Jesus Christ. But God will at times orchestrate events so that his followers realize their error and get back on the right track. As a caring Father, he lovingly does that which is best for his people (see also Hebrews chapter 12, verses 4–13 [page 1598]).

---

³⁰Do not accuse a man for no reason—
   when he has done you no harm.

³¹Do not envy a violent man
   or choose any of his ways,
³²for the LORD detests a perverse man
   but takes the upright into his confidence.

³³The LORD's curse is on the house of the wicked,
   but he blesses the home of the righteous.
³⁴He mocks proud mockers
   but gives grace to the humble.
³⁵The wise inherit honor,
   but fools he holds up to shame.

Wisdom Is Supreme

4 Listen, my sons, to a father's instruction;
pay attention and gain understanding.
²I give you sound learning,
so do not forsake my teaching.
³When I was a boy in my father's house,
still tender, and an only child of my mother,
⁴he taught me and said,
"Lay hold of my words with all your heart;
keep my commands and you will live.
⁵Get wisdom, get understanding;
do not forget my words or swerve from them.
⁶Do not forsake wisdom, and she will protect you;
love her, and she will watch over you.
⁷Wisdom is supreme; therefore get wisdom.
Though it cost all you have,ᵃ get understanding.
⁸Esteem her, and she will exalt you;
embrace her, and she will honor you.
⁹She will set a garland of grace on your head
and present you with a crown of splendor."

¹⁰Listen, my son, accept what I say,
and the years of your life will be many.
¹¹I guide you in the way of wisdom
and lead you along straight paths.
¹²When you walk, your steps will not be hampered;
when you run, you will not stumble.
¹³Hold on to instruction, do not let it go;
guard it well, for it is your life.
¹⁴Do not set foot on the path of the wicked
or walk in the way of evil men.
¹⁵Avoid it, do not travel on it;
turn from it and go on your way.
¹⁶For they cannot sleep till they do evil;
they are robbed of slumber till they make someone fall.
¹⁷They eat the bread of wickedness
and drink the wine of violence.

¹⁸The path of the righteous is like the first gleam of dawn,
shining ever brighter till the full light of day.
¹⁹But the way of the wicked is like deep darkness;
they do not know what makes them stumble.

²⁰My son, pay attention to what I say;
listen closely to my words.
²¹Do not let them out of your sight,
keep them within your heart;
²²for they are life to those who find them
and health to a man's whole body.
²³Above all else, guard your heart,
for it is the wellspring of life.
²⁴Put away perversity from your mouth;
keep corrupt talk far from your lips.

ᵃ7 Or Whatever else you get

²⁵Let your eyes look straight ahead,
  fix your gaze directly before you.
²⁶Make level^a paths for your feet
  and take only ways that are firm.
²⁷Do not swerve to the right or the left;
  keep your foot from evil.

Warning Against Adultery

5 My son, pay attention to my wisdom,
  listen well to my words of insight,
²that you may maintain discretion
  and your lips may preserve knowledge.
³For the lips of an adulteress drip honey,
  and her speech is smoother than oil;
⁴but in the end she is bitter as gall,
  sharp as a double-edged sword.
⁵Her feet go down to death;
  her steps lead straight to the grave.^b

⁶She gives no thought to the way of life;
  her paths are crooked, but she knows it not.

⁷Now then, my sons, listen to me;
  do not turn aside from what I say.
⁸Keep to a path far from her,
  do not go near the door of her house,
⁹lest you give your best strength to others
  and your years to one who is cruel,
¹⁰lest strangers feast on your wealth
  and your toil enrich another man's house.
¹¹At the end of your life you will groan,
  when your flesh and body are spent.
¹²You will say, "How I hated discipline!
  How my heart spurned correction!
¹³I would not obey my teachers
  or listen to my instructors.
¹⁴I have come to the brink of utter ruin
  in the midst of the whole assembly."

¹⁵Drink water from your own cistern,
  running water from your own well.
¹⁶Should your springs overflow in the streets,
  your streams of water in the public squares?

STRENGTHENING RELATIONSHIPS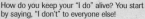

5:18–20
Marriage

How do you keep your "I do" alive? You start by saying, "I don't" to everyone else!

Solomon urges couples to rejoice in their marriage partners—even as they begin to age. He warns against the danger of diluting romantic affection by giving it to someone other than a spouse. A husband should be romantically intoxicated with the "wife of [his] youth." Rather than comparing her to others, he should choose to focus on her beauty alone and allow his heart to be captured by her love. This advice goes for wives as well as husbands.

This advice may seem outdated in our age. The divorce rate stands at just above 50 percent in North America, and it sometimes seems like people swap partners as if marriage were nothing more than a square dance. Yet God's plan has always been that marriage be an exclusive, lifelong relationship between a man and a woman.

Do you want to strengthen your marriage? The best way to begin is by strengthening your own personal commitment to your spouse.

---

¹⁷Let them be yours alone,
  never to be shared with strangers.
¹⁸May your fountain be blessed,

---

^a 26 Or *Consider the*   ^b 5 Hebrew *Sheol*

and may you rejoice in the wife of your youth.
¹⁹A loving doe, a graceful deer—
    may her breasts satisfy you always,
    may you ever be captivated by her love.
²⁰Why be captivated, my son, by an adulteress?
    Why embrace the bosom of another man's wife?

²¹For a man's ways are in full view of the LORD,
    and he examines all his paths.
²²The evil deeds of a wicked man ensnare him;
    the cords of his sin hold him fast.
²³He will die for lack of discipline,
    led astray by his own great folly.

Warnings Against Folly

6 My son, if you have put up security for your neighbor,
    if you have struck hands in pledge for another,
²if you have been trapped by
        what you said,
    ensnared by the words of
        your mouth,
³then do this, my son, to free
        yourself,
    since you have fallen into
        your neighbor's hands:
Go and humble yourself;
    press your plea with your
        neighbor!
⁴Allow no sleep to your eyes,
    no slumber to your eyelids.
⁵Free yourself, like a gazelle
        from the hand of the
        hunter,
    like a bird from the snare of
        the fowler.

⁶Go to the ant, you sluggard;
    consider its ways and be wise!
⁷It has no commander,
    no overseer or ruler,
⁸yet it stores its provisions in summer
    and gathers its food at harvest.

⁹How long will you lie there, you sluggard?
    When will you get up from your sleep?
¹⁰A little sleep, a little slumber,
    a little folding of the hands to rest—
¹¹and poverty will come on you like a bandit
    and scarcity like an armed man.ᵃ

¹²A scoundrel and villain,
    who goes about with a corrupt mouth,
¹³ who winks with his eye,

> ◻ ▦▦▦▦ **MANAGING RESOURCES** ▦▦▦▦ ⬆
>
> **6:1–5**
> **Possessions**
>
> This passage provides us with a wonderful example of the Bible's practical wisdom.
>
> Here Solomon warns us against the danger of signing for someone else's financial obligation. If that person doesn't pay the debt, we'll be in jeopardy. That exposes us to unnecessary risk and can keep someone who needs to become more financially responsible from being forced to do so.
>
> If you have already put your resources on the line in this way, Solomon's advice is to get out of the obligation as quickly as you can.

ᵃ 11 Or like a vagrant / and scarcity like a beggar

signals with his feet
and motions with his fingers,
¹⁴ who plots evil with deceit in his heart—
he always stirs up dissension.
¹⁵Therefore disaster will overtake him in an instant;
he will suddenly be destroyed—without remedy.

¹⁶There are six things the LORD hates,
seven that are detestable to him:
¹⁷ haughty eyes,
a lying tongue,
hands that shed innocent blood,
¹⁸ a heart that devises wicked schemes,
feet that are quick to rush into evil,
¹⁹ a false witness who pours out lies
and a man who stirs up dissension among brothers.

Warning Against Adultery

²⁰My son, keep your father's commands
and do not forsake your mother's teaching.
²¹Bind them upon your heart forever;
fasten them around your neck.

▣ ▦▦▦▦▦▦ KNOWING YOURSELF ▦▦▦▦▦▦ ⮀

6:6–11
Character

One of Solomon's favorite themes in the book of Proverbs is laziness. Some of his most colorful descriptions of human character flaws can be found in the passages that talk about the "sluggard."

Here Solomon says that the essential problem of laziness is the inability to be a self-starter. The ant doesn't have a boss but does all the work necessary to provide for itself. That's the model for productivity that he encourages us to follow. In addition, the ant practices delayed gratification. It plans for hard times by storing up resources for the future.

What do your work habits and savings show about your character? Does a common ant have one up on you?

---

²²When you walk, they will guide you;
when you sleep, they will watch
over you;
when you awake, they will speak to
you.
²³For these commands are a lamp,
this teaching is a light,
and the corrections of discipline
are the way to life,
²⁴keeping you from the immoral woman,
from the smooth tongue of the
wayward wife.
²⁵Do not lust in your heart after her
beauty
or let her captivate you with her
eyes,
²⁶for the prostitute reduces you to a loaf
of bread,
and the adulteress preys upon your
very life.
²⁷Can a man scoop fire into his lap
without his clothes being burned?
²⁸Can a man walk on hot coals
without his feet being scorched?
²⁹So is he who sleeps with another man's wife;
no one who touches her will go unpunished.

³⁰Men do not despise a thief if he steals
to satisfy his hunger when he is starving.
³¹Yet if he is caught, he must pay sevenfold;
though it costs him all the wealth of his house.
³²But a man who commits adultery lacks judgment;

whoever does so destroys himself.
33Blows and disgrace are his lot,
and his shame will never be wiped away;
34for jealousy arouses a husband's fury,
and he will show no mercy when he takes revenge.
35He will not accept any compensation;
he will refuse the bribe, however great it is.

Warning Against the Adulteress

7 My son, keep my words
and store up my commands within you.
2Keep my commands and you will live;
guard my teachings as the apple of your eye.
3Bind them on your fingers;
write them on the tablet of your heart.
4Say to wisdom, "You are my sister,"
and call understanding your kinsman;
5they will keep you from the adulteress,
from the wayward wife with her seductive words.

6At the window of my house
I looked out through the lattice.
7I saw among the simple,
I noticed among the young men,
a youth who lacked judgment.
8He was going down the street near her corner,
walking along in the direction of her house
9at twilight, as the day was fading,
as the dark of night set in.

10Then out came a woman to meet him,

▦ KNOWING YOURSELF ▦

7:6–27
Sin

We could title this section of Proverbs "The Anatomy of a Seduction." The purpose is not so much to condemn the sensuous woman as it is to point out the foolishness of the young man she entices.

The seduction begins with a willing "victim." Why is the young man going near her house? He knows what he's flirting with but covers up his intentions under the cloak of night (verse 9). The woman's dress and actions say, "Take me—I'm available." To avoid her advances, all the young man has to do is keep walking. But he loves her attention, her brazenness. He feels desirable, and that's all he cares about. She fills his ears with explicit talk and visions of pleasure. Then, like an animal being led to the slaughter, he follows her home. Only later does he realize the high price he must pay (verse 23). He has sacrificed everything for one night of indulgence. (These verses take on an eerie literalism when we consider the reality of sexually transmitted diseases!)

Where did the young man go wrong? Back when it was easy to turn away—when he first played with the harmless idea of "just strolling by her place. I won't stop; surely there's no harm in just looking!"

There's no virtue in getting close to adultery without falling. The time to reckon with consequences is not when you're already in a lover's arms. Who can think clearly in the heat of passion? Solomon wisely warns us: Don't get that close in the first place. If you play with fire, you'll get burned.

dressed like a prostitute and with crafty intent.
[11](She is loud and defiant,
  her feet never stay at home;
[12]now in the street, now in the squares,
  at every corner she lurks.)
[13]She took hold of him and kissed him
  and with a brazen face she said:

[14]"I have fellowship offerings[a] at home;
  today I fulfilled my vows.
[15]So I came out to meet you;
  I looked for you and have found you!
[16]I have covered my bed
  with colored linens from Egypt.
[17]I have perfumed my bed
  with myrrh, aloes and cinnamon.
[18]Come, let's drink deep of love till morning;
  let's enjoy ourselves with love!
[19]My husband is not at home;
  he has gone on a long journey.
[20]He took his purse filled with money
  and will not be home till full moon."

[21]With persuasive words she led him astray;
  she seduced him with her smooth talk.
[22]All at once he followed her
  like an ox going to the slaughter,
  like a deer[b] stepping into a noose[c]
[23] till an arrow pierces his liver,
  like a bird darting into a snare,
  little knowing it will cost him his life.

[24]Now then, my sons, listen to me;
  pay attention to what I say.
[25]Do not let your heart turn to her ways
  or stray into her paths.
[26]Many are the victims she has brought down;
  her slain are a mighty throng.
[27]Her house is a highway to the grave,[d]
  leading down to the chambers of death.

Wisdom's Call

8 Does not wisdom call out?
  Does not understanding raise her voice?
[2]On the heights along the way,
  where the paths meet, she takes her stand;
[3]beside the gates leading into the city,
  at the entrances, she cries aloud:
[4]"To you, O men, I call out;
  I raise my voice to all mankind.
[5]You who are simple, gain prudence;
  you who are foolish, gain understanding.

---

[a]14 Traditionally *peace offerings*   [b]22 Syriac (see also Septuagint); Hebrew *fool*   [c]22 The meaning of the Hebrew for this line is uncertain.   [d]27 Hebrew *Sheol*

⁶Listen, for I have worthy things to say;
    I open my lips to speak what is right.
⁷My mouth speaks what is true,
    for my lips detest wickedness.
⁸All the words of my mouth are just;
    none of them is crooked or perverse.
⁹To the discerning all of them are right;
    they are faultless to those who have knowledge.
¹⁰Choose my instruction instead of silver,
    knowledge rather than choice gold,
¹¹for wisdom is more precious than rubies,
    and nothing you desire can compare with her.

¹²"I, wisdom, dwell together with prudence;
    I possess knowledge and discretion.
¹³To fear the LORD is to hate evil;
    I hate pride and arrogance,
    evil behavior and perverse speech.
¹⁴Counsel and sound judgment are mine;
    I have understanding and power.
¹⁵By me kings reign
    and rulers make laws that are just;
¹⁶by me princes govern,
    and all nobles who rule on earth. ᵃ
¹⁷I love those who love me,
    and those who seek me find me.
¹⁸With me are riches and honor,
    enduring wealth and prosperity.
¹⁹My fruit is better than fine gold;
    what I yield surpasses choice silver.
²⁰I walk in the way of righteousness,
    along the paths of justice,
²¹bestowing wealth on those who love me
    and making their treasuries full.

²²"The LORD brought me forth as the first of his works,ᵇ, ᶜ
    before his deeds of old;
²³I was appointedᵈ from eternity,
    from the beginning, before the world began.
²⁴When there were no oceans, I was given birth,
    when there were no springs abounding with water;
²⁵before the mountains were settled in place,
    before the hills, I was given birth,
²⁶before he made the earth or its fields
    or any of the dust of the world.
²⁷I was there when he set the heavens in place,
    when he marked out the horizon on the face of the deep,
²⁸when he established the clouds above
    and fixed securely the fountains of the deep,
²⁹when he gave the sea its boundary
    so the waters would not overstep his command,

ᵃ16 Many Hebrew manuscripts and Septuagint; most Hebrew manuscripts *and nobles—all righteous rulers*   ᵇ22 Or *way;* or *dominion*   ᶜ22 Or *The LORD possessed me at the beginning of his work;* or *The LORD brought me forth at the beginning of his work*   ᵈ23 Or *fashioned*

and when he marked out the foundations of the earth.
30   Then I was the craftsman at his side.
I was filled with delight day after day,
    rejoicing always in his presence,
31rejoicing in his whole world
    and delighting in mankind.

32"Now then, my sons, listen to me;
    blessed are those who keep my ways.
33Listen to my instruction and be wise;
    do not ignore it.
34Blessed is the man who listens to me,
    watching daily at my doors,
    waiting at my doorway.
35For whoever finds me finds life
    and receives favor from the Lord.
36But whoever fails to find me harms himself;
    all who hate me love death."

Invitations of Wisdom and of Folly

9   Wisdom has built her house;
    she has hewn out its seven pillars.
2She has prepared her meat and mixed her wine;
    she has also set her table.
3She has sent out her maids, and she calls
    from the highest point of the city.
4"Let all who are simple come in here!"
    she says to those who lack judgment.
5"Come, eat my food
    and drink the wine I have mixed.
6Leave your simple ways and you will live;
    walk in the way of understanding.

7"Whoever corrects a mocker invites insult;
    whoever rebukes a wicked man incurs abuse.
8Do not rebuke a mocker or he will hate you;
    rebuke a wise man and he will love you.
9Instruct a wise man and he will be wiser still;
    teach a righteous man and he will add to his learning.

10"The fear of the Lord is the beginning of wisdom,
    and knowledge of the Holy One is understanding.
11For through me your days will be many,
    and years will be added to your life.
12If you are wise, your wisdom will reward you;
    if you are a mocker, you alone will suffer."

13The woman Folly is loud;
    she is undisciplined and without knowledge.
14She sits at the door of her house,
    on a seat at the highest point of the city,
15calling out to those who pass by,
    who go straight on their way.
16"Let all who are simple come in here!"
    she says to those who lack judgment.

¹⁷"Stolen water is sweet;
  food eaten in secret is delicious!"
¹⁸But little do they know that the dead are there,
  that her guests are in the depths of the grave.ᵃ

Proverbs of Solomon

10 The proverbs of Solomon:

A wise son brings joy to his father,
  but a foolish son grief to his mother.

²Ill-gotten treasures are of no value,
  but righteousness delivers from death.

³The Lᴏʀᴅ does not let the righteous go hungry
  but he thwarts the craving of the wicked.

⁴Lazy hands make a man poor,
  but diligent hands bring
    wealth.

⁵He who gathers crops in
    summer is a wise son,
  but he who sleeps during
    harvest is a disgraceful
    son.

⁶Blessings crown the head of
    the righteous,
  but violence overwhelms the
    mouth of the wicked.ᵇ

⁷The memory of the righteous
    will be a blessing,
  but the name of the wicked
    will rot.

⁸The wise in heart accept
    commands,
  but a chattering fool comes
    to ruin.

⁹The man of integrity walks
    securely,
  but he who takes crooked paths will be found out.

¹⁰He who winks maliciously causes grief,
  and a chattering fool comes to ruin.

¹¹The mouth of the righteous is a fountain of life,
  but violence overwhelms the mouth of the wicked.

¹²Hatred stirs up dissension,
  but love covers over all wrongs.

¹³Wisdom is found on the lips of the discerning,
  but a rod is for the back of him who lacks judgment.

▣ STRENGTHENING RELATIONSHIPS ⮂

9:8–9
Social

Two defining characteristics of wise people
are an openness to criticism and a continual
desire for self-improvement. It's worth noting
that no mention is made of the quality of the
criticism or the critic. Wise people hear whatever comes, even if it's presented poorly. They
realize that the only way to grow is to listen to
others, and they appreciate those who care
enough to correct them.

"Fools," on the other hand, hate both criticism and those who criticize. The pain of having their flaws pointed out is so great that they
retaliate. Verse 12 talks about the kind of "solitary confinement" in which such people place
themselves. Again, the Bible's practical wisdom shines through: If you want to strengthen
your relationships, follow God's guidance on
this issue.

ᵃ18 Hebrew *Sheol*   ᵇ6 Or *but the mouth of the wicked conceals violence; also in verse 11*

¹⁴Wise men store up knowledge,
  but the mouth of a fool invites ruin.

¹⁵The wealth of the rich is their fortified city,
  but poverty is the ruin of the poor.

¹⁶The wages of the righteous bring them life,
  but the income of the wicked brings them punishment.

¹⁷He who heeds discipline shows the way to life,
  but whoever ignores correction leads others astray.

¹⁸He who conceals his hatred has lying lips,
  and whoever spreads slander is a fool.

¹⁹When words are many, sin is not absent,
  but he who holds his tongue is wise.

²⁰The tongue of the righteous is choice silver,
  but the heart of the wicked is of little value.

²¹The lips of the righteous nourish many,
  but fools die for lack of judgment.

²²The blessing of the LORD brings wealth,
  and he adds no trouble to it.

²³A fool finds pleasure in evil conduct,
  but a man of understanding delights in wisdom.

²⁴What the wicked dreads will overtake him;
  what the righteous desire will be granted.

²⁵When the storm has swept by, the wicked are gone,
  but the righteous stand firm forever.

²⁶As vinegar to the teeth and smoke to the eyes,
  so is a sluggard to those who send him.

²⁷The fear of the LORD adds length to life,
  but the years of the wicked are cut short.

²⁸The prospect of the righteous is joy,
  but the hopes of the wicked come to nothing.

²⁹The way of the LORD is a refuge for the righteous,
  but it is the ruin of those who do evil.

³⁰The righteous will never be uprooted,
  but the wicked will not remain in the land.

³¹The mouth of the righteous brings forth wisdom,
  but a perverse tongue will be cut out.

³²The lips of the righteous know what is fitting,
  but the mouth of the wicked only what is perverse.

11 The LORD abhors dishonest scales,
  but accurate weights are his delight.

²When pride comes, then comes disgrace,
  but with humility comes wisdom.

³The integrity of the upright guides them,
but the unfaithful are destroyed by their duplicity.

⁴Wealth is worthless in the day of wrath,
but righteousness delivers from death.

⁵The righteousness of the blameless makes a straight way for them,
but the wicked are brought down by their own wickedness.

⁶The righteousness of the upright delivers them,
but the unfaithful are trapped by evil desires.

⁷When a wicked man dies, his hope perishes;
all he expected from his power comes to nothing.

⁸The righteous man is rescued from trouble,
and it comes on the wicked instead.

⁹With his mouth the godless destroys his neighbor,
but through knowledge the righteous escape.

¹⁰When the righteous prosper, the city rejoices;
when the wicked perish, there are shouts of joy.

¹¹Through the blessing of the upright a city is exalted,
but by the mouth of the wicked it is destroyed.

¹²A man who lacks judgment derides his neighbor,
but a man of understanding holds his tongue.

¹³A gossip betrays a confidence,
but a trustworthy man keeps a secret.

¹⁴For lack of guidance a nation falls,
but many advisers make victory sure.

¹⁵He who puts up security for another will surely suffer,
but whoever refuses to strike hands in pledge is safe.

¹⁶A kindhearted woman gains respect,
but ruthless men gain only wealth.

¹⁷A kind man benefits himself,
but a cruel man brings trouble on himself.

¹⁸The wicked man earns deceptive wages,
but he who sows righteousness reaps a sure reward.

¹⁹The truly righteous man attains life,
but he who pursues evil goes to his death.

²⁰The LORD detests men of perverse heart
but he delights in those whose ways are blameless.

²¹Be sure of this: The wicked will not go unpunished,
but those who are righteous will go free.

²²Like a gold ring in a pig's snout
is a beautiful woman who shows no discretion.

²³The desire of the righteous ends only in good,
but the hope of the wicked only in wrath.

²⁴One man gives freely, yet gains even more;
    another withholds unduly, but comes to poverty.

²⁵A generous man will prosper;
    he who refreshes others will himself be refreshed.

²⁶People curse the man who hoards grain,
    but blessing crowns him who is willing to sell.

²⁷He who seeks good finds goodwill,
    but evil comes to him who searches for it.

²⁸Whoever trusts in his riches will fall,
    but the righteous will thrive like a green leaf.

²⁹He who brings trouble on his family will inherit only wind,
    and the fool will be servant to the wise.

³⁰The fruit of the righteous is a tree of life,
    and he who wins souls is wise.

³¹If the righteous receive their due on earth,
    how much more the ungodly and the sinner!

12 Whoever loves discipline loves knowledge,
    but he who hates correction is stupid.

²A good man obtains favor from the LORD,
    but the LORD condemns a crafty man.

³A man cannot be established through wickedness,
    but the righteous cannot be uprooted.

⁴A wife of noble character is her husband's crown,
    but a disgraceful wife is like decay in his bones.

⁵The plans of the righteous are just,
    but the advice of the wicked is deceitful.

⁶The words of the wicked lie in wait for blood,
    but the speech of the upright rescues them.

⁷Wicked men are overthrown and are no more,
    but the house of the righteous stands firm.

⁸A man is praised according to his wisdom,
    but men with warped minds are despised.

⁹Better to be a nobody and yet have a servant
    than pretend to be somebody and have no food.

¹⁰A righteous man cares for the needs of his animal,
    but the kindest acts of the wicked are cruel.

¹¹He who works his land will have abundant food,
    but he who chases fantasies lacks judgment.

¹²The wicked desire the plunder of evil men,
    but the root of the righteous flourishes.

¹³An evil man is trapped by his sinful talk,
    but a righteous man escapes trouble.

¹⁴From the fruit of his lips a man is filled with good things
  as surely as the work of his hands rewards him.

¹⁵The way of a fool seems right to him,
  but a wise man listens to advice.

¹⁶A fool shows his annoyance at once,
  but a prudent man overlooks an insult.

¹⁷A truthful witness gives honest testimony,
  but a false witness tells lies.

¹⁸Reckless words pierce like a sword,
  but the tongue of the wise brings healing.

¹⁹Truthful lips endure forever,
  but a lying tongue lasts only a moment.

²⁰There is deceit in the hearts of
      those who plot evil,
  but joy for those who
      promote peace.

²¹No harm befalls the righteous,
  but the wicked have their
      fill of trouble.

²²The LORD detests lying lips,
  but he delights in men who
      are truthful.

²³A prudent man keeps his
      knowledge to himself,
  but the heart of fools blurts
      out folly.

²⁴Diligent hands will rule,
  but laziness ends in slave labor.

²⁵An anxious heart weighs a man down,
  but a kind word cheers him up.

²⁶A righteous man is cautious in friendship,ᵃ
  but the way of the wicked leads them astray.

²⁷The lazy man does not roastᵇ his game,
  but the diligent man prizes his possessions.

²⁸In the way of righteousness there is life;
  along that path is immortality.

13 A wise son heeds his father's instruction,
  but a mocker does not listen to rebuke.

²From the fruit of his lips a man enjoys good things,
  but the unfaithful have a craving for violence.

³He who guards his lips guards his life,
  but he who speaks rashly will come to ruin.

☐ ▦▦▦▦▦ **MANAGING RESOURCES** ▦▦▦▦▦ ⬘

12:15
Business

This recommendation applies both to the business and personal setting. The best way to manage the decisions you have to make is to get advice from wise people. The better the counsel, the better the decision. Even if you decide to go with your own hunch, at least you'll have the assurance of knowing your decision was an informed one.

ᵃ26 Or *man is a guide to his neighbor*   ᵇ27 The meaning of the Hebrew for this word is uncertain.

⁴The sluggard craves and gets nothing,
  but the desires of the diligent are fully satisfied.

⁵The righteous hate what is false,
  but the wicked bring shame and disgrace.

⁶Righteousness guards the man of integrity,
  but wickedness overthrows the sinner.

⁷One man pretends to be rich, yet has nothing;
  another pretends to be poor, yet has great wealth.

⁸A man's riches may ransom his life,
  but a poor man hears no threat.

⁹The light of the righteous shines brightly,
  but the lamp of the wicked is snuffed out.

¹⁰Pride only breeds quarrels,
  but wisdom is found in those who take advice.

¹¹Dishonest money dwindles away,
  but he who gathers money little by little makes it grow.

¹²Hope deferred makes the heart sick,
  but a longing fulfilled is a tree of life.

¹³He who scorns instruction will pay for it,
  but he who respects a command is rewarded.

¹⁴The teaching of the wise is a fountain of life,
  turning a man from the snares of death.

¹⁵Good understanding wins favor,
  but the way of the unfaithful is hard. ᵃ

¹⁶Every prudent man acts out of knowledge,
  but a fool exposes his folly.

¹⁷A wicked messenger falls into trouble,
  but a trustworthy envoy brings healing.

¹⁸He who ignores discipline comes to poverty and shame,
  but whoever heeds correction is honored.

¹⁹A longing fulfilled is sweet to the soul,
  but fools detest turning from evil.

²⁰He who walks with the wise grows wise,
  but a companion of fools suffers harm.

²¹Misfortune pursues the sinner,
  but prosperity is the reward of the righteous.

²²A good man leaves an inheritance for his children's children,
  but a sinner's wealth is stored up for the righteous.

²³A poor man's field may produce abundant food,
  but injustice sweeps it away.

ᵃ 15 Or *unfaithful does not endure*

²⁴He who spares the rod hates his son,
    but he who loves him is careful to discipline him.

²⁵The righteous eat to their hearts' content,
    but the stomach of the wicked goes hungry.

14 The wise woman builds her house,
    but with her own hands the foolish one tears hers down.

²He whose walk is upright fears the LORD,
    but he whose ways are devious despises him.

³A fool's talk brings a rod to his back,
    but the lips of the wise protect them.

⁴Where there are no oxen, the manger is empty,
    but from the strength of an ox comes an abundant harvest.

⁵A truthful witness does not deceive,
    but a false witness pours out lies.

⁶The mocker seeks wisdom and finds none,
    but knowledge comes easily to the discerning.

⁷Stay away from a foolish man,
    for you will not find knowledge on his lips.

⁸The wisdom of the prudent is to give thought to their ways,
    but the folly of fools is deception.

⁹Fools mock at making amends for sin,
    but goodwill is found among the upright.

¹⁰Each heart knows its own bitterness,
    and no one else can share its joy.

¹¹The house of the wicked will be destroyed,
    but the tent of the upright will flourish.

¹²There is a way that seems right to a man,
    but in the end it leads to death.

¹³Even in laughter the heart may ache,
    and joy may end in grief.

¹⁴The faithless will be fully repaid for their ways,
    and the good man rewarded for his.

¹⁵A simple man believes anything,
    but a prudent man gives thought to his steps.

¹⁶A wise man fears the LORD and shuns evil,
    but a fool is hotheaded and reckless.

¹⁷A quick-tempered man does foolish things,
    and a crafty man is hated.

¹⁸The simple inherit folly,
    but the prudent are crowned with knowledge.

¹⁹Evil men will bow down in the presence of the good,
    and the wicked at the gates of the righteous.

²⁰The poor are shunned even by their neighbors,
  but the rich have many friends.

²¹He who despises his neighbor sins,
  but blessed is he who is kind to the needy.

²²Do not those who plot evil go astray?
  But those who plan what is good find*a* love and faithfulness.

²³All hard work brings a profit,
  but mere talk leads only to poverty.

²⁴The wealth of the wise is their crown,
  but the folly of fools yields folly.

²⁵A truthful witness saves lives,
  but a false witness is deceitful.

²⁶He who fears the LORD has a secure fortress,
  and for his children it will be a refuge.

²⁷The fear of the LORD is a fountain of life,
  turning a man from the snares of death.

²⁸A large population is a king's glory,
  but without subjects a prince is ruined.

²⁹A patient man has great understanding,
  but a quick-tempered man displays folly.

³⁰A heart at peace gives life to the body,
  but envy rots the bones.

³¹He who oppresses the poor shows contempt for their Maker,
  but whoever is kind to the needy honors God.

³²When calamity comes, the wicked are brought down,
  but even in death the righteous have a refuge.

³³Wisdom reposes in the heart of the discerning
  and even among fools she lets herself be known.*b*

³⁴Righteousness exalts a nation,
  but sin is a disgrace to any people.

³⁵A king delights in a wise servant,
  but a shameful servant incurs his wrath.

15 A gentle answer turns away wrath,
  but a harsh word stirs up anger.

²The tongue of the wise commends knowledge,
  but the mouth of the fool gushes folly.

³The eyes of the LORD are everywhere,
  keeping watch on the wicked and the good.

⁴The tongue that brings healing is a tree of life,
  but a deceitful tongue crushes the spirit.

a 22 Or *show*   *b 33* Hebrew; Septuagint and Syriac / *but in the heart of fools she is not known*

⁵A fool spurns his father's discipline,
    but whoever heeds correction shows prudence.

⁶The house of the righteous contains great treasure,
    but the income of the wicked brings them trouble.

⁷The lips of the wise spread knowledge;
    not so the hearts of fools.

⁸The LORD detests the sacrifice of the wicked,
    but the prayer of the upright pleases him.

⁹The LORD detests the way of the wicked
    but he loves those who pursue righteousness.

¹⁰Stern discipline awaits him
        who leaves the path;
    he who hates correction will
        die.

¹¹Death and Destruction*a* lie
        open before the LORD—
    how much more the hearts
        of men!

¹²A mocker resents correction;
    he will not consult the wise.

¹³A happy heart makes the face
        cheerful,
    but heartache crushes the
        spirit.

¹⁴The discerning heart seeks
        knowledge,
    but the mouth of a fool feeds
        on folly.

▣ ⫸STRENGTHENING RELATIONSHIPS⫷ ⮂

15:1
Social

This memorable proverb gives us a good lesson in conflict management: *The easiest way to prevent an argument is to diffuse it before it explodes.* That's not so easy when people vent their anger directly at us. But it is possible if we allow people to express their feelings without feeling judged. Such a gentle reaction—caring for people without getting caught up in their anger—is a helpful first step toward managing the conflict at hand.

Think of it this way: A "harsh word," however small it may seem, is like a match. When we keep it in the box, it remains harmless. When we strike it, we risk turning a volatile situation into an inferno.

---

¹⁵All the days of the oppressed
        are wretched,
    but the cheerful heart has a continual feast.

¹⁶Better a little with the fear of the LORD
    than great wealth with turmoil.

¹⁷Better a meal of vegetables where there is love
    than a fattened calf with hatred.

¹⁸A hot-tempered man stirs up dissension,
    but a patient man calms a quarrel.

¹⁹The way of the sluggard is blocked with thorns,
    but the path of the upright is a highway.

²⁰A wise son brings joy to his father,
    but a foolish man despises his mother.

²¹Folly delights a man who lacks judgment,
    but a man of understanding keeps a straight course.

a 11 Hebrew *Sheol and Abaddon*

²²Plans fail for lack of counsel,
  but with many advisers they succeed.

²³A man finds joy in giving an apt reply—
  and how good is a timely word!

²⁴The path of life leads upward for the wise
  to keep him from going down to the grave.ᵃ

²⁵The LORD tears down the proud man's house
  but he keeps the widow's boundaries intact.

²⁶The LORD detests the thoughts of the wicked,
  but those of the pure are pleasing to him.

²⁷A greedy man brings trouble to his family,
  but he who hates bribes will live.

²⁸The heart of the righteous weighs its answers,
  but the mouth of the wicked gushes evil.

²⁹The LORD is far from the wicked
  but he hears the prayer of the righteous.

³⁰A cheerful look brings joy to the heart,
  and good news gives health to the bones.

³¹He who listens to a life-giving rebuke
  will be at home among the wise.

³²He who ignores discipline despises himself,
  but whoever heeds correction gains understanding.

³³The fear of the LORD teaches a man wisdom,ᵇ
  and humility comes before honor.

16 To man belong the plans of the heart,
  but from the LORD comes the reply of the tongue.

²All a man's ways seem innocent to him,
  but motives are weighed by the LORD.

³Commit to the LORD whatever you do,
  and your plans will succeed.

⁴The LORD works out everything for his own ends—
  even the wicked for a day of disaster.

⁵The LORD detests all the proud of heart.
  Be sure of this: They will not go unpunished.

⁶Through love and faithfulness sin is atoned for;
  through the fear of the LORD a man avoids evil.

⁷When a man's ways are pleasing to the LORD,
  he makes even his enemies live at peace with him.

⁸Better a little with righteousness
  than much gain with injustice.

ᵃ24 Hebrew *Sheol*   ᵇ33 Or *Wisdom teaches the fear of the LORD*

⁹In his heart a man plans his course,
but the Lᴏʀᴅ determines his steps.

¹⁰The lips of a king speak as an oracle,
and his mouth should not betray justice.

¹¹Honest scales and balances are from the Lᴏʀᴅ;
all the weights in the bag are of his making.

¹²Kings detest wrongdoing,
for a throne is established through righteousness.

¹³Kings take pleasure in honest lips;
they value a man who speaks the truth.

¹⁴A king's wrath is a messenger of death,
but a wise man will appease it.

¹⁵When a king's face brightens, it means life;
his favor is like a rain cloud in spring.

¹⁶How much better to get wisdom than gold,
to choose understanding rather than silver!

¹⁷The highway of the upright avoids evil;
he who guards his way guards his life.

¹⁸Pride goes before destruction,
a haughty spirit before a fall.

¹⁹Better to be lowly in spirit and among the oppressed
than to share plunder with the proud.

²⁰Whoever gives heed to instruction prospers,
and blessed is he who trusts in the Lᴏʀᴅ.

²¹The wise in heart are called discerning,
and pleasant words promote instruction. ᵃ

²²Understanding is a fountain of life to those who have it,
but folly brings punishment to fools.

²³A wise man's heart guides his mouth,
and his lips promote instruction. ᵇ

²⁴Pleasant words are a honeycomb,
sweet to the soul and healing to the bones.

²⁵There is a way that seems right to a man,
but in the end it leads to death.

²⁶The laborer's appetite works for him;
his hunger drives him on.

²⁷A scoundrel plots evil,
and his speech is like a scorching fire.

²⁸A perverse man stirs up dissension,
and a gossip separates close friends.

ᵃ 21 Or words make a man persuasive   ᵇ 23 Or mouth / and makes his lips persuasive

²⁹A violent man entices his neighbor
  and leads him down a path that is not good.

³⁰He who winks with his eye is plotting perversity;
  he who purses his lips is bent on evil.

³¹Gray hair is a crown of splendor;
  it is attained by a righteous life.

³²Better a patient man than a warrior,
  a man who controls his temper than one who takes a city.

³³The lot is cast into the lap,
  but its every decision is from the LORD.

17 Better a dry crust with peace and quiet
  than a house full of feasting,^a with strife.

²A wise servant will rule over a disgraceful son,
  and will share the inheritance as one of the brothers.

³The crucible for silver and the furnace for gold,
  but the LORD tests the heart.

⁴A wicked man listens to evil lips;
  a liar pays attention to a malicious tongue.

⁵He who mocks the poor shows contempt for their Maker;
  whoever gloats over disaster will not go unpunished.

⁶Children's children are a crown to the aged,
  and parents are the pride of their children.

⁷Arrogant^b lips are unsuited to a fool—
  how much worse lying lips to a ruler!

⁸A bribe is a charm to the one who gives it;
  wherever he turns, he succeeds.

⁹He who covers over an offense promotes love,
  but whoever repeats the matter separates close friends.

¹⁰A rebuke impresses a man of discernment
  more than a hundred lashes a fool.

¹¹An evil man is bent only on rebellion;
  a merciless official will be sent against him.

¹²Better to meet a bear robbed of her cubs
  than a fool in his folly.

¹³If a man pays back evil for good,
  evil will never leave his house.

¹⁴Starting a quarrel is like breaching a dam;
  so drop the matter before a dispute breaks out.

¹⁵Acquitting the guilty and condemning the innocent—
  the LORD detests them both.

---

^a 1 Hebrew *sacrifices*   ^b 7 Or *Eloquent*

¹⁶Of what use is money in the hand of a fool,
    since he has no desire to get wisdom?

¹⁷A friend loves at all times,
    and a brother is born for adversity.

¹⁸A man lacking in judgment strikes hands in pledge
    and puts up security for his neighbor.

¹⁹He who loves a quarrel loves sin;
    he who builds a high gate invites destruction.

²⁰A man of perverse heart does not prosper;
    he whose tongue is deceitful falls into trouble.

²¹To have a fool for a son brings grief;
    there is no joy for the father of a fool.

²²A cheerful heart is good medicine,
    but a crushed spirit dries up the bones.

²³A wicked man accepts a bribe in secret
    to pervert the course of justice.

²⁴A discerning man keeps wisdom in view,
    but a fool's eyes wander to the ends of the earth.

²⁵A foolish son brings grief to his father
    and bitterness to the one who bore him.

²⁶It is not good to punish an innocent man,
    or to flog officials for their integrity.

²⁷A man of knowledge uses
      words with restraint,
    and a man of understanding
      is even-tempered.

²⁸Even a fool is thought wise if
      he keeps silent,
    and discerning if he holds
      his tongue.

18   An unfriendly man pursues
    selfish ends;
    he defies all sound judgment.

²A fool finds no pleasure in
      understanding
    but delights in airing his own opinions.

³When wickedness comes, so does contempt,
    and with shame comes disgrace.

⁴The words of a man's mouth are deep waters,
    but the fountain of wisdom is a bubbling brook.

⁵It is not good to be partial to the wicked
    or to deprive the innocent of justice.

⁶A fool's lips bring him strife,
    and his mouth invites a beating.

▣ ▥▥▥ STRENGTHENING RELATIONSHIPS ▥▥▥ ▣

17:27–28
Social

The lesson of this problem extends into all areas of life. How often have you regretted saying too much about a certain subject? Better to keep quiet and leave the other person unsure of whether you're foolish than to open your mouth and remove all doubt!

⁷A fool's mouth is his undoing,
    and his lips are a snare to his soul.

⁸The words of a gossip are like choice morsels;
    they go down to a man's inmost parts.

⁹One who is slack in his work
    is brother to one who destroys.

¹⁰The name of the LORD is a strong tower;
    the righteous run to it and are safe.

¹¹The wealth of the rich is their fortified city;
    they imagine it an unscalable wall.

¹²Before his downfall a man's heart is proud,
    but humility comes before honor.

¹³He who answers before listening—
    that is his folly and his shame.

☐ ▦STRENGTHENING RELATIONSHIPS▦ ⇄

**18:13
Social**

Solomon here helps us brush up on our interpersonal skills. We all need somebody to listen to us—someone to whom we can pour out our hearts. But the door swings both ways—we also need to listen to others who need us.

Learning to listen involves restraining our thoughts and reactions. In fact, Solomon says it's pure foolishness to give an answer before we've completely heard what the other person has to say. After all, God gave us two ears and one mouth. Following that cue, we'll do well to listen twice as much as we speak!

---

¹⁴A man's spirit sustains him in sickness,
    but a crushed spirit who can bear?

¹⁵The heart of the discerning acquires knowledge;
    the ears of the wise seek it out.

¹⁶A gift opens the way for the giver
    and ushers him into the presence of the great.

¹⁷The first to present his case seems right,
    till another comes forward and questions him.

¹⁸Casting the lot settles disputes
    and keeps strong opponents apart.

¹⁹An offended brother is more unyielding than a fortified city,
    and disputes are like the barred gates of a citadel.

²⁰From the fruit of his mouth a man's stomach is filled;
    with the harvest from his lips he is satisfied.

²¹The tongue has the power of life and death,
    and those who love it will eat its fruit.

²²He who finds a wife finds what is good
    and receives favor from the LORD.

²³A poor man pleads for mercy,
    but a rich man answers harshly.

²⁴A man of many companions may come to ruin,
    but there is a friend who sticks closer than a brother.

19 Better a poor man whose walk is blameless
than a fool whose lips are perverse.

²It is not good to have zeal without knowledge,
nor to be hasty and miss the way.

³A man's own folly ruins his life,
yet his heart rages against the LORD.

⁴Wealth brings many friends,
but a poor man's friend deserts him.

⁵A false witness will not go unpunished,
and he who pours out lies will not go free.

⁶Many curry favor with a ruler,
and everyone is the friend of a man who gives gifts.

⁷A poor man is shunned by all his relatives—
how much more do his friends avoid him!
Though he pursues them with pleading,
they are nowhere to be found. ᵃ

⁸He who gets wisdom loves his own soul;
he who cherishes understanding prospers.

⁹A false witness will not go unpunished,
and he who pours out lies will perish.

¹⁰It is not fitting for a fool to live in luxury—
how much worse for a slave to rule over princes!

¹¹A man's wisdom gives him patience;
it is to his glory to overlook an offense.

¹²A king's rage is like the roar of a lion,
but his favor is like dew on the grass.

¹³A foolish son is his father's ruin,
and a quarrelsome wife is like a constant dripping.

¹⁴Houses and wealth are inherited from parents,
but a prudent wife is from the LORD.

¹⁵Laziness brings on deep sleep,
and the shiftless man goes hungry.

¹⁶He who obeys instructions guards his life,
but he who is contemptuous of his ways will die.

¹⁷He who is kind to the poor lends to the LORD,
and he will reward him for what he has done.

¹⁸Discipline your son, for in that there is hope;
do not be a willing party to his death.

¹⁹A hot-tempered man must pay the penalty;
if you rescue him, you will have to do it again.

²⁰Listen to advice and accept instruction,
and in the end you will be wise.

ᵃ7 The meaning of the Hebrew for this sentence is uncertain.

²¹Many are the plans in a man's heart,
  but it is the Lord's purpose that prevails.

²²What a man desires is unfailing love*ᵃ*;
  better to be poor than a liar.

²³The fear of the Lord leads to life:
  Then one rests content, untouched by trouble.

²⁴The sluggard buries his hand in the dish;
  he will not even bring it back to his mouth!

²⁵Flog a mocker, and the simple will learn prudence;
  rebuke a discerning man, and he will gain knowledge.

²⁶He who robs his father and drives out his mother
  is a son who brings shame and disgrace.

²⁷Stop listening to instruction, my son,
  and you will stray from the words of knowledge.

²⁸A corrupt witness mocks at justice,
  and the mouth of the wicked gulps down evil.

²⁹Penalties are prepared for mockers,
  and beatings for the backs of fools.

20 Wine is a mocker and beer a brawler;
  whoever is led astray by them is not wise.

²A king's wrath is like the roar of a lion;
  he who angers him forfeits his life.

³It is to a man's honor to avoid strife,
  but every fool is quick to quarrel.

⁴A sluggard does not plow in season;
  so at harvest time he looks but finds nothing.

⁵The purposes of a man's heart are deep waters,
  but a man of understanding draws them out.

⁶Many a man claims to have unfailing love,
  but a faithful man who can find?

⁷The righteous man leads a blameless life;
  blessed are his children after him.

⁸When a king sits on his throne to judge,
  he winnows out all evil with his eyes.

⁹Who can say, "I have kept my heart pure;
  I am clean and without sin"?

¹⁰Differing weights and differing measures—
  the Lord detests them both.

¹¹Even a child is known by his actions,
  by whether his conduct is pure and right.

ᵃ 22 Or A man's greed is his shame

¹²Ears that hear and eyes that see—
  the Lord has made them both.

¹³Do not love sleep or you will grow poor;
  stay awake and you will have food to spare.

¹⁴"It's no good, it's no good!" says the buyer;
  then off he goes and boasts about his purchase.

¹⁵Gold there is, and rubies in abundance,
  but lips that speak knowledge are a rare jewel.

¹⁶Take the garment of one who
    puts up security for a
    stranger;
  hold it in pledge if he does
    it for a wayward
    woman.

¹⁷Food gained by fraud tastes
    sweet to a man,
  but he ends up with a
    mouth full of gravel.

¹⁸Make plans by seeking advice;
  if you wage war, obtain
    guidance.

¹⁹A gossip betrays a confidence;
  so avoid a man who talks
    too much.

²⁰If a man curses his father or
    mother,
  his lamp will be snuffed out
    in pitch darkness.

> ### ▦ MANAGING RESOURCES ▦
>
> **20:10**
> **Business**
>
> In the ancient world retailers used scales when making or receiving payments. On one side they placed their weights, and on the other side they placed an equal weight of silver or gold. Dishonest retailers used a weight that was heavier or lighter than labeled—whichever was to their advantage—when buying something or making a payment. This verse says that God hates such dishonesty.
>
> What you do in the marketplace really does matter to God. Are there any "dishonest weights" in your business? If so, why not correct the situation right now? Having people recognize that you run your business with integrity is much more valuable than any money you might gain by being dishonest.

²¹An inheritance quickly gained at the beginning
  will not be blessed at the end.

²²Do not say, "I'll pay you back for this wrong!"
  Wait for the Lord, and he will deliver you.

²³The Lord detests differing weights,
  and dishonest scales do not please him.

²⁴A man's steps are directed by the Lord.
  How then can anyone understand his own way?

²⁵It is a trap for a man to dedicate something rashly
  and only later to consider his vows.

²⁶A wise king winnows out the wicked;
  he drives the threshing wheel over them.

²⁷The lamp of the Lord searches the spirit of a man*a*;
  it searches out his inmost being.

---

a27 Or The spirit of man is the Lord's lamp

²⁸Love and faithfulness keep a king safe;
   through love his throne is made secure.

²⁹The glory of young men is their strength,
   gray hair the splendor of the old.

³⁰Blows and wounds cleanse away evil,
   and beatings purge the inmost being.

21 The king's heart is in the hand of the LORD;
   he directs it like a watercourse wherever he pleases.

²All a man's ways seem right to him,
   but the LORD weighs the heart.

³To do what is right and just
   is more acceptable to the LORD than sacrifice.

⁴Haughty eyes and a proud heart,
   the lamp of the wicked, are sin!

⁵The plans of the diligent lead to profit
   as surely as haste leads to poverty.

⁶A fortune made by a lying tongue
   is a fleeting vapor and a deadly snare.ᵃ

⁷The violence of the wicked will drag them away,
   for they refuse to do what is right.

⁸The way of the guilty is devious,
   but the conduct of the innocent is upright.

⁹Better to live on a corner of the roof
   than share a house with a quarrelsome wife.

¹⁰The wicked man craves evil;
   his neighbor gets no mercy from him.

¹¹When a mocker is punished, the simple gain wisdom;
   when a wise man is instructed, he gets knowledge.

¹²The Righteous Oneᵇ takes note of the house of the wicked
   and brings the wicked to ruin.

¹³If a man shuts his ears to the cry of the poor,
   he too will cry out and not be answered.

¹⁴A gift given in secret soothes anger,
   and a bribe concealed in the cloak pacifies great wrath.

¹⁵When justice is done, it brings joy to the righteous
   but terror to evildoers.

¹⁶A man who strays from the path of understanding
   comes to rest in the company of the dead.

¹⁷He who loves pleasure will become poor;
   whoever loves wine and oil will never be rich.

ᵃ6 Some Hebrew manuscripts, Septuagint and Vulgate; most Hebrew manuscripts *vapor for those who seek death*   ᵇ12 Or *The righteous man*

¹⁸The wicked become a ransom for the righteous,
and the unfaithful for the upright.

¹⁹Better to live in a desert
than with a quarrelsome and ill-tempered wife.

²⁰In the house of the wise are stores of choice food and oil,
but a foolish man devours all he has.

²¹He who pursues righteousness and love
finds life, prosperity*ᵃ* and honor.

²²A wise man attacks the city of the mighty
and pulls down the stronghold in which they trust.

²³He who guards his mouth and his tongue
keeps himself from calamity.

²⁴The proud and arrogant man—"Mocker" is his name;
he behaves with overweening pride.

²⁵The sluggard's craving will be the death of him,
because his hands refuse to work.

²⁶All day long he craves for more,
but the righteous give without sparing.

²⁷The sacrifice of the wicked is detestable—
how much more so when brought with evil intent!

²⁸A false witness will perish,
and whoever listens to him will be destroyed forever.*ᵇ*

²⁹A wicked man puts up a bold front,
but an upright man gives thought to his ways.

³⁰There is no wisdom, no insight, no plan
that can succeed against the LORD.

³¹The horse is made ready for the day of battle,
but victory rests with the LORD.

22 A good name is more desirable than great riches;
to be esteemed is better than silver or gold.

²Rich and poor have this in common:
The LORD is the Maker of them all.

³A prudent man sees danger and takes refuge,
but the simple keep going and suffer for it.

⁴Humility and the fear of the LORD
bring wealth and honor and life.

⁵In the paths of the wicked lie thorns and snares,
but he who guards his soul stays far from them.

⁶Train*ᶜ* a child in the way he should go,
and when he is old he will not turn from it.

⁷The rich rule over the poor,
and the borrower is servant to the lender.

ᵃ21 Or righteousness   ᵇ28 Or / but the words of an obedient man will live on   ᶜ6 Or Start

⁸He who sows wickedness reaps trouble,
    and the rod of his fury will be destroyed.

⁹A generous man will himself be blessed,
    for he shares his food with the poor.

¹⁰Drive out the mocker, and out goes strife;
    quarrels and insults are ended.

STRENGTHENING RELATIONSHIPS

22:6
Parenting

This verse does not promise that a child will consistently follow where a parent leads. For example, if a parent takes a child to church all the years he or she is growing up, that child may still choose to change that habit later in life. Many of the people reading these very words provide living proof to support that fact.

One way to look at this verse is in terms of finding out how children are "wired." A parent who works to discover his or her child's unique talents and abilities can then guide that in-born energy toward the right direction—a way that honors God and follows a course that is consistent with how God designed that child. A child who sees that God's way makes sense for his or her life has a better chance of following in that way.

If you're a parent, do you know your child well? Are you aware of his or her distinctive abilities and temperaments? Are you pointing your child in the direction that fits him or her—or are you squeezing your child into your mold? When you honor and validate the special way God created your child, you can help lead him or her into a fulfilling adult life.

---

¹¹He who loves a pure heart and whose
        speech is gracious
    will have the king for his friend.

¹²The eyes of the LORD keep watch over
        knowledge,
    but he frustrates the words of the
        unfaithful.

¹³The sluggard says, "There is a lion
        outside!"
    or, "I will be murdered in the
        streets!"

¹⁴The mouth of an adulteress is a deep
        pit;
    he who is under the LORD's wrath
        will fall into it.

¹⁵Folly is bound up in the heart of a
        child,
    but the rod of discipline will drive it
        far from him.

¹⁶He who oppresses the poor to increase
        his wealth
    and he who gives gifts to the rich—
        both come to poverty.

Sayings of the Wise

¹⁷Pay attention and listen to the sayings
        of the wise;
    apply your heart to what I teach,

¹⁸for it is pleasing when you
        keep them in your heart
    and have all of them ready on your lips.
¹⁹So that your trust may be in the LORD,
    I teach you today, even you.
²⁰Have I not written thirty[a] sayings for you,
    sayings of counsel and knowledge,
²¹teaching you true and reliable words,
    so that you can give sound answers
    to him who sent you?

²²Do not exploit the poor because they are poor
    and do not crush the needy in court,

[a] 20 Or not formerly written; or not written excellent

²³for the LORD will take up their case
  and will plunder those who plunder them.

²⁴Do not make friends with a hot-tempered man,
  do not associate with one easily angered,
²⁵or you may learn his ways
  and get yourself ensnared.

²⁶Do not be a man who strikes hands in pledge
  or puts up security for debts;
²⁷if you lack the means to pay,
  your very bed will be snatched from under you.

²⁸Do not move an ancient boundary stone
  set up by your forefathers.

²⁹Do you see a man skilled in his work?
  He will serve before kings;
  he will not serve before obscure men.

23 When you sit to dine with a ruler,
  note well what *ᵃ* is before you,
²and put a knife to your throat
  if you are given to gluttony.
³Do not crave his delicacies,
  for that food is deceptive.

⁴Do not wear yourself out to get rich;
  have the wisdom to show restraint.
⁵Cast but a glance at riches, and they are gone,
  for they will surely sprout wings
  and fly off to the sky like an eagle.

⁶Do not eat the food of a stingy man,
  do not crave his delicacies;
⁷for he is the kind of man
  who is always thinking about the cost. *ᵇ*
 "Eat and drink," he says to you,
  but his heart is not with you.
⁸You will vomit up the little you have eaten
  and will have wasted your compliments.

⁹Do not speak to a fool,
  for he will scorn the wisdom of your words.

¹⁰Do not move an ancient boundary stone
  or encroach on the fields of the fatherless,
¹¹for their Defender is strong;
  he will take up their case against you.

¹²Apply your heart to instruction
  and your ears to words of knowledge.

¹³Do not withhold discipline from a child;
  if you punish him with the rod, he will not die.
¹⁴Punish him with the rod
  and save his soul from death. *ᶜ*

ᵃ1 Or *who*   *ᵇ7* Or *for as he thinks within himself, / so he is;* or *for as he puts on a feast, / so he is*   *ᶜ14* Hebrew *Sheol*

¹⁵My son, if your heart is wise,
    then my heart will be glad;
¹⁶my inmost being will rejoice
    when your lips speak what is right.

¹⁷Do not let your heart envy sinners,
    but always be zealous for the fear of the LORD.
¹⁸There is surely a future hope for you,
    and your hope will not be cut off.

¹⁹Listen, my son, and be wise,
    and keep your heart on the right path.
²⁰Do not join those who drink too much wine
    or gorge themselves on meat,
²¹for drunkards and gluttons become poor,
    and drowsiness clothes them in rags.

²²Listen to your father, who gave you life,
    and do not despise your mother when she is old.
²³Buy the truth and do not sell it;
    get wisdom, discipline and understanding.
²⁴The father of a righteous man has great joy;
    he who has a wise son delights in him.
²⁵May your father and mother be glad;
    may she who gave you birth rejoice!

²⁶My son, give me your heart
    and let your eyes keep to my ways,
²⁷for a prostitute is a deep pit
    and a wayward wife is a narrow well.
²⁸Like a bandit she lies in wait,
    and multiplies the unfaithful among men.

²⁹Who has woe? Who has sorrow?
    Who has strife? Who has complaints?
    Who has needless bruises? Who has bloodshot eyes?
³⁰Those who linger over wine,
    who go to sample bowls of mixed wine.
³¹Do not gaze at wine when it is red,
    when it sparkles in the cup,
    when it goes down smoothly!
³²In the end it bites like a snake
    and poisons like a viper.
³³Your eyes will see strange sights
    and your mind imagine confusing things.
³⁴You will be like one sleeping on the high seas,
    lying on top of the rigging.
³⁵"They hit me," you will say, "but I'm not hurt!
    They beat me, but I don't feel it!
When will I wake up
    so I can find another drink?"

 Do not envy wicked men,
    do not desire their company;
²for their hearts plot violence,
    and their lips talk about making trouble.

³By wisdom a house is built,
   and through understanding it is established;
⁴through knowledge its rooms are filled
   with rare and beautiful treasures.

⁵A wise man has great power,
   and a man of knowledge increases strength;
⁶for waging war you need guidance,
   and for victory many advisers.

⁷Wisdom is too high for a fool;
   in the assembly at the gate he has nothing to say.

⁸He who plots evil
   will be known as a schemer.
⁹The schemes of folly are sin,
   and men detest a mocker.

¹⁰If you falter in times of trouble,
   how small is your strength!

¹¹Rescue those being led away to death;
   hold back those staggering toward slaughter.
¹²If you say, "But we knew nothing about this,"
   does not he who weighs the heart perceive it?
Does not he who guards your life know it?
   Will he not repay each person according to what he has done?

¹³Eat honey, my son, for it is good;
   honey from the comb is sweet to your taste.
¹⁴Know also that wisdom is sweet to your soul;
   if you find it, there is a future hope for you,
   and your hope will not be cut off.

¹⁵Do not lie in wait like an outlaw against a righteous man's house,
   do not raid his dwelling place;
¹⁶for though a righteous man falls seven times, he rises again,
   but the wicked are brought down by calamity.

¹⁷Do not gloat when your enemy falls;
   when he stumbles, do not let your heart rejoice,
¹⁸or the LORD will see and disapprove
   and turn his wrath away from him.

¹⁹Do not fret because of evil men
   or be envious of the wicked,
²⁰for the evil man has no future hope,
   and the lamp of the wicked will be snuffed out.

²¹Fear the LORD and the king, my son,
   and do not join with the rebellious,
²²for those two will send sudden destruction upon them,
   and who knows what calamities they can bring?

Further Sayings of the Wise

²³These also are sayings of the wise:

   To show partiality in judging is not good:

²⁴Whoever says to the guilty, "You are innocent"—
    peoples will curse him and nations denounce him.
²⁵But it will go well with those who convict the guilty,
    and rich blessing will come upon them.

²⁶An honest answer
    is like a kiss on the lips.

²⁷Finish your outdoor work
    and get your fields ready;
    after that, build your house.

²⁸Do not testify against your neighbor without cause,
    or use your lips to deceive.
²⁹Do not say, "I'll do to him as he has done to me;
    I'll pay that man back for what he did."

³⁰I went past the field of the sluggard,
    past the vineyard of the man who lacks judgment;
³¹thorns had come up everywhere,
    the ground was covered with weeds,
    and the stone wall was in ruins.
³²I applied my heart to what I observed
    and learned a lesson from what I saw:
³³A little sleep, a little slumber,
    a little folding of the hands to rest—
³⁴and poverty will come on you like a bandit
    and scarcity like an armed man. ^a

More Proverbs of Solomon

25 These are more proverbs of Solomon, copied by the men of Hezekiah king of Judah:

²It is the glory of God to conceal a matter;
    to search out a matter is the glory of kings.

³As the heavens are high and the earth is deep,
    so the hearts of kings are unsearchable.

⁴Remove the dross from the silver,
    and out comes material for^b the silversmith;
⁵remove the wicked from the king's presence,
    and his throne will be established through righteousness.

⁶Do not exalt yourself in the king's presence,
    and do not claim a place among great men;
⁷it is better for him to say to you, "Come up here,"
    than for him to humiliate you before a nobleman.

What you have seen with your eyes
⁸   do not bring^c hastily to court,
    for what will you do in the end
    if your neighbor puts you to shame?

⁹If you argue your case with a neighbor,

---

^a34 Or like a vagrant / and scarcity like a beggar   ^b4 Or comes a vessel from   ^c7,8 Or nobleman / on whom you had
set your eyes. / ⁸Do not go

do not betray another man's confidence,
[10]or he who hears it may shame you
  and you will never lose your bad reputation.

[11]A word aptly spoken
  is like apples of gold in settings of silver.

[12]Like an earring of gold or an ornament of fine gold
  is a wise man's rebuke to a listening ear.

[13]Like the coolness of snow at harvest time
  is a trustworthy messenger to those who send him;
  he refreshes the spirit of his masters.

[14]Like clouds and wind without rain
  is a man who boasts of gifts he does not give.

[15]Through patience a ruler can be persuaded,
  and a gentle tongue can break a bone.

[16]If you find honey, eat just enough—
  too much of it, and you will vomit.
[17]Seldom set foot in your neighbor's house—
  too much of you, and he will hate you.

[18]Like a club or a sword or a sharp arrow
  is the man who gives false testimony against his neighbor.

[19]Like a bad tooth or a lame foot
  is reliance on the unfaithful in times of trouble.

[20]Like one who takes away a
    garment on a cold day,
  or like vinegar poured on
    soda,
  is one who sings songs to a
    heavy heart.

[21]If your enemy is hungry, give
    him food to eat;
  if he is thirsty, give him
    water to drink.
[22]In doing this, you will heap
    burning coals on his
    head,
  and the LORD will reward
    you.

[23]As a north wind brings rain,
  so a sly tongue brings angry looks.

[24]Better to live on a corner of the roof
  than share a house with a quarrelsome wife.

[25]Like cold water to a weary soul
  is good news from a distant land.

[26]Like a muddied spring or a polluted well
  is a righteous man who gives way to the wicked.

▣ ∷∷∷∷∷∷ KNOWING YOURSELF ∷∷∷∷∷∷ ⬌

**25:13
Character**

Sometimes it seems that reliable people—
those who give their word and can be counted
on to follow through—are in short supply today. If you're an employee, this verse makes it
clear that keeping your word and being reliable is the way to succeed in your job.

  If you own a business and want to have
people lining up to work with you, simply fulfill your promises to your employees and to
your customers. Chances are you'll stand
head and shoulders above the competition!

²⁷It is not good to eat too much honey,
  nor is it honorable to seek one's own honor.

²⁸Like a city whose walls are broken down
  is a man who lacks self-control.

26 Like snow in summer or rain in harvest,
  honor is not fitting for a fool.

²Like a fluttering sparrow or a darting swallow,
  an undeserved curse does not come to rest.

³A whip for the horse, a halter for the donkey,
  and a rod for the backs of fools!

⁴Do not answer a fool according to his folly,
  or you will be like him yourself.

⁵Answer a fool according to his folly,
  or he will be wise in his own eyes.

⁶Like cutting off one's feet or drinking violence
  is the sending of a message by the hand of a fool.

⁷Like a lame man's legs that hang limp
  is a proverb in the mouth of a fool.

⁸Like tying a stone in a sling
  is the giving of honor to a fool.

⁹Like a thornbush in a drunkard's hand
  is a proverb in the mouth of a fool.

¹⁰Like an archer who wounds at random
  is he who hires a fool or any passer-by.

¹¹As a dog returns to its vomit,
  so a fool repeats his folly.

¹²Do you see a man wise in his own eyes?
  There is more hope for a fool than for him.

¹³The sluggard says, "There is a lion in the road,
  a fierce lion roaming the streets!"

¹⁴As a door turns on its hinges,
  so a sluggard turns on his bed.

¹⁵The sluggard buries his hand in the dish;
  he is too lazy to bring it back to his mouth.

¹⁶The sluggard is wiser in his own eyes
  than seven men who answer discreetly.

¹⁷Like one who seizes a dog by the ears
  is a passer-by who meddles in a quarrel not his own.

¹⁸Like a madman shooting
  firebrands or deadly arrows
¹⁹is a man who deceives his neighbor
  and says, "I was only joking!"

²⁰Without wood a fire goes out;
  without gossip a quarrel dies down.

²¹As charcoal to embers and as wood to fire,
  so is a quarrelsome man for kindling strife.

²²The words of a gossip are like choice morsels;
  they go down to a man's inmost parts.

²³Like a coating of glaze ᵃ over earthenware
  are fervent lips with an evil heart.

²⁴A malicious man disguises himself with his lips,
  but in his heart he harbors deceit.
²⁵Though his speech is charming, do not believe him,
  for seven abominations fill his heart.
²⁶His malice may be concealed by deception,
  but his wickedness will be exposed in the assembly.

²⁷If a man digs a pit, he will fall into it;
  if a man rolls a stone, it will roll back on him.

²⁸A lying tongue hates those it hurts,
  and a flattering mouth works ruin.

27 Do not boast about tomorrow,
  for you do not know what a day may bring forth.

²Let another praise you, and not your own mouth;
  someone else, and not your own lips.

³Stone is heavy and sand a burden,
  but provocation by a fool is heavier than both.

⁴Anger is cruel and fury overwhelming,
  but who can stand before jealousy?

⁵Better is open rebuke
  than hidden love.

⁶Wounds from a friend can be trusted,
  but an enemy multiplies kisses.

⁷He who is full loathes honey,
  but to the hungry even what is bitter tastes sweet.

⁸Like a bird that strays from its nest
  is a man who strays from his home.

⁹Perfume and incense bring joy to the heart,
  and the pleasantness of one's friend springs from his earnest counsel.

¹⁰Do not forsake your friend and the friend of your father,
  and do not go to your brother's house when disaster strikes you—
  better a neighbor nearby than a brother far away.

¹¹Be wise, my son, and bring joy to my heart;
  then I can answer anyone who treats me with contempt.

ᵃ23 With a different word division of the Hebrew; Masoretic Text *of silver dross*

¹²The prudent see danger and take refuge,
　　but the simple keep going and suffer for it.

¹³Take the garment of one who puts up security for a stranger;
　　hold it in pledge if he does it for a wayward woman.

¹⁴If a man loudly blesses his neighbor early in the morning,
　　it will be taken as a curse.

¹⁵A quarrelsome wife is like
　　a constant dripping on a rainy day;
¹⁶restraining her is like restraining the wind
　　or grasping oil with the hand.

¹⁷As iron sharpens iron,
　　so one man sharpens another.

¹⁸He who tends a fig tree will eat its fruit,
　　and he who looks after his master will be honored.

¹⁹As water reflects a face,
　　so a man's heart reflects the man.

²⁰Death and Destruction[a] are never satisfied,
　　and neither are the eyes of man.

²¹The crucible for silver and the furnace for gold,
　　but man is tested by the praise he receives.

²²Though you grind a fool in a mortar,
　　grinding him like grain with a pestle,
　　you will not remove his folly from him.

²³Be sure you know the condition of your flocks,
　　give careful attention to your herds;
²⁴for riches do not endure forever,
　　and a crown is not secure for all generations.
²⁵When the hay is removed and new growth appears
　　and the grass from the hills is gathered in,
²⁶the lambs will provide you with clothing,
　　and the goats with the price of a field.
²⁷You will have plenty of goats' milk
　　to feed you and your family
　　and to nourish your servant girls.

28 The wicked man flees though no one pursues,
　　but the righteous are as bold as a lion.

²When a country is rebellious, it has many rulers,
　　but a man of understanding and knowledge maintains order.

³A ruler[b] who oppresses the poor
　　is like a driving rain that leaves no crops.

⁴Those who forsake the law praise the wicked,
　　but those who keep the law resist them.

⁵Evil men do not understand justice,
　　but those who seek the LORD understand it fully.

---

[a]20 Hebrew *Sheol* and *Abaddon*　　[b]3 Or *A poor man*

⁶Better a poor man whose walk is blameless
than a rich man whose ways are perverse.

⁷He who keeps the law is a discerning son,
but a companion of gluttons disgraces his father.

⁸He who increases his wealth by exorbitant interest
amasses it for another, who will be kind to the poor.

⁹If anyone turns a deaf ear to the law,
even his prayers are detestable.

¹⁰He who leads the upright along an evil path
will fall into his own trap,
but the blameless will receive a good inheritance.

¹¹A rich man may be wise in his own eyes,
but a poor man who has discernment sees through him.

¹²When the righteous triumph, there is great elation;
but when the wicked rise to power, men go into hiding.

¹³He who conceals his sins does not prosper,
but whoever confesses and renounces them finds mercy.

¹⁴Blessed is the man who always fears the Lord,
but he who hardens his heart falls into trouble.

¹⁵Like a roaring lion or a charging bear
is a wicked man ruling over a helpless people.

¹⁶A tyrannical ruler lacks judgment,
but he who hates ill-gotten gain will enjoy a long life.

¹⁷A man tormented by the guilt of murder
will be a fugitive till death;
let no one support him.

¹⁸He whose walk is blameless is kept safe,
but he whose ways are perverse will suddenly fall.

¹⁹He who works his land will have abundant food,
but the one who chases fantasies will have his fill of poverty.

²⁰A faithful man will be richly blessed,
but one eager to get rich will not go unpunished.

²¹To show partiality is not good—
yet a man will do wrong for a piece of bread.

²²A stingy man is eager to get rich
and is unaware that poverty awaits him.

²³He who rebukes a man will in the end gain more favor
than he who has a flattering tongue.

²⁴He who robs his father or mother
and says, "It's not wrong"—
he is partner to him who destroys.

²⁵A greedy man stirs up dissension,
but he who trusts in the Lord will prosper.

²⁶He who trusts in himself is a fool,
　　but he who walks in wisdom is kept safe.

²⁷He who gives to the poor will lack nothing,
　　but he who closes his eyes to them receives many curses.

²⁸When the wicked rise to power, people go into hiding;
　　but when the wicked perish, the righteous thrive.

29　A man who remains stiff-necked after many rebukes
　　will suddenly be destroyed—without remedy.

²When the righteous thrive, the people rejoice;
　　when the wicked rule, the people groan.

³A man who loves wisdom brings joy to his father,
　　but a companion of prostitutes squanders his wealth.

⁴By justice a king gives a country stability,
　　but one who is greedy for bribes tears it down.

⁵Whoever flatters his neighbor
　　is spreading a net for his feet.

⁶An evil man is snared by his own sin,
　　but a righteous one can sing and be glad.

⁷The righteous care about justice for the poor,
　　but the wicked have no such concern.

⁸Mockers stir up a city,
　　but wise men turn away anger.

⁹If a wise man goes to court with a fool,
　　the fool rages and scoffs, and there is no peace.

¹⁰Bloodthirsty men hate a man of integrity
　　and seek to kill the upright.

¹¹A fool gives full vent to his anger,
　　but a wise man keeps himself under control.

¹²If a ruler listens to lies,
　　all his officials become wicked.

¹³The poor man and the oppressor have this in common:
　　The LORD gives sight to the eyes of both.

¹⁴If a king judges the poor with fairness,
　　his throne will always be secure.

¹⁵The rod of correction imparts wisdom,
　　but a child left to himself disgraces his mother.

¹⁶When the wicked thrive, so does sin,
　　but the righteous will see their downfall.

¹⁷Discipline your son, and he will give you peace;
　　he will bring delight to your soul.

¹⁸Where there is no revelation, the people cast off restraint;
　　but blessed is he who keeps the law.

¹⁹A servant cannot be corrected by mere words;
  though he understands, he will not respond.

²⁰Do you see a man who speaks in haste?
  There is more hope for a fool than for him.

²¹If a man pampers his servant from youth,
  he will bring grief*ᵃ* in the end.

²²An angry man stirs up dissension,
  and a hot-tempered one commits many sins.

²³A man's pride brings him low,
  but a man of lowly spirit gains honor.

²⁴The accomplice of a thief is his own enemy;
  he is put under oath and dare not testify.

²⁵Fear of man will prove to be a snare,
  but whoever trusts in the LORD is kept safe.

²⁶Many seek an audience with a ruler,
  but it is from the LORD that man gets justice.

²⁷The righteous detest the dishonest;
  the wicked detest the upright.

Sayings of Agur

30 The sayings of Agur son of Jakeh—an oracle*ᵇ*:

This man declared to Ithiel,
  to Ithiel and to Ucal:*ᶜ*

²"I am the most ignorant of men;
  I do not have a man's understanding.
³I have not learned wisdom,
  nor have I knowledge of the Holy One.
⁴Who has gone up to heaven and come down?
  Who has gathered up the wind in the hollow of his hands?
 Who has wrapped up the waters in his cloak?
  Who has established all the ends of the earth?
 What is his name, and the name of his son?
  Tell me if you know!

⁵"Every word of God is flawless;
  he is a shield to those who take refuge in him.
⁶Do not add to his words,
  or he will rebuke you and prove you a liar.

⁷"Two things I ask of you, O LORD;
  do not refuse me before I die:
⁸Keep falsehood and lies far from me;
  give me neither poverty nor riches,
  but give me only my daily bread.

ᵃ21 The meaning of the Hebrew for this word is uncertain.   *ᵇ1* Or *Jakeh of Massa*   *ᶜ1* Masoretic Text; with a different word division of the Hebrew *declared, "I am weary, O God; / I am weary, O God, and faint.*

⁹Otherwise, I may have too much and disown you
    and say, 'Who is the LORD?'
Or I may become poor and steal,
    and so dishonor the name of my God.

▣ ▒▒▒ MANAGING RESOURCES ▒▒▒ ⬌

30:7–9
Possessions

What a wonderful world it would be if we
would content ourselves with what we have
instead of wasting our lives always striving after "more."

This verse describes a wonderful goal: To
have simply "enough." Not so much abundance that we become arrogant; not so little
that we become a burden or act foolishly out
of desperation.

How does this prospect sound to you?
Would this be a worthy and rewarding goal for
you to adopt? If you want to pray this same
prayer, God is ready to listen.

---

¹⁰"Do not slander a servant to his master,
    or he will curse you, and you will
        pay for it.

¹¹"There are those who curse their
        fathers
    and do not bless their mothers;
¹²those who are pure in their own eyes
    and yet are not cleansed of their
        filth;
¹³those whose eyes are ever so haughty,
    whose glances are so disdainful;
¹⁴those whose teeth are swords
    and whose jaws are set with
        knives
to devour the poor from the earth,
    the needy from among mankind.

¹⁵"The leech has two daughters.
    'Give! Give!' they cry.

"There are three things that are never
        satisfied,
    four that never say, 'Enough!':
¹⁶the grave,ᵃ the barren womb,
    land, which is never satisfied with water,
    and fire, which never says, 'Enough!'

¹⁷"The eye that mocks a father,
    that scorns obedience to a mother,
will be pecked out by the ravens of the valley,
    will be eaten by the vultures.

¹⁸"There are three things that are too amazing
        for me,
    four that I do not understand:
¹⁹the way of an eagle in the sky,
    the way of a snake on a rock,
the way of a ship on the high seas,
    and the way of a man with a maiden.

²⁰"This is the way of an adulteress:
    She eats and wipes her mouth
    and says, 'I've done nothing wrong.'

²¹"Under three things the earth trembles,
    under four it cannot bear up:
²²a servant who becomes king,
    a fool who is full of food,

ᵃ16 Hebrew Sheol

²³an unloved woman who is married,
    and a maidservant who displaces her mistress.

²⁴"Four things on earth are small,
    yet they are extremely wise:
²⁵Ants are creatures of little strength,
    yet they store up their food in the summer;
²⁶coneys^a are creatures of little power,
    yet they make their home in the crags;
²⁷locusts have no king,
    yet they advance together in ranks;
²⁸a lizard can be caught with the hand,
    yet it is found in kings' palaces.

²⁹"There are three things that are stately in their stride,
    four that move with stately bearing:
³⁰a lion, mighty among beasts,
    who retreats before nothing;
³¹a strutting rooster, a he-goat,
    and a king with his army around him.^b

³²"If you have played the fool and exalted yourself,
    or if you have planned evil,
    clap your hand over your mouth!
³³For as churning the milk produces butter,
    and as twisting the nose produces blood,
    so stirring up anger produces strife."

Sayings of King Lemuel

31 The sayings of King Lemuel—an oracle^c his mother taught him:

²"O my son, O son of my womb,
    O son of my vows,^d
³do not spend your strength on women,
    your vigor on those who ruin kings.

⁴"It is not for kings, O Lemuel—
    not for kings to drink wine,
    not for rulers to crave beer,
⁵lest they drink and forget what the law decrees,
    and deprive all the oppressed of their rights.
⁶Give beer to those who are perishing,
    wine to those who are in anguish;
⁷let them drink and forget their poverty
    and remember their misery no more.

⁸"Speak up for those who cannot speak for themselves,
    for the rights of all who are destitute.

---

^a26 That is, the hyrax or rock badger   ^b31 Or king secure against revolt   ^c1 Or of Lemuel king of Massa, which
^d2 Or / the answer to my prayers

⁹Speak up and judge fairly;
  defend the rights of the poor and needy."

Epilogue: The Wife of Noble Character

¹⁰ᵃA wife of noble character who can find?
  She is worth far more than rubies.
¹¹Her husband has full confidence in her
  and lacks nothing of value.
¹²She brings him good, not harm,
  all the days of her life.

▣ KNOWING YOURSELF ↔

31:10–31
Character

Although our cultural situation is quite different from the one implied in this passage, this description of "the wife of noble character" still speaks to us today.

For example, this woman has developed competence in many areas of life (verses 16 and 19). She is compassionate (verse 20) and cares for people both inside and outside of her own household (verse 21). She prepares for the future (verse 25). Also note that she refuses to get caught up in society's fixation with youth and beauty (verse 30). She cultivates inner character and spiritual strength, which give her a lasting elegance that others recognize (verses 28 and 29).

Does this seem like an impossible standard to live up to? Notice where such a woman begins—by fearing the LORD (verse 30). As Solomon mentioned at the beginning of this book of proverbs, that's where all true wisdom begins (see chapter 1, verse 7 and note [page 802]).

---

¹³She selects wool and flax
  and works with eager hands.
¹⁴She is like the merchant ships,
  bringing her food from afar.
¹⁵She gets up while it is still dark;
  she provides food for her family
  and portions for her servant girls.
¹⁶She considers a field and buys it;
  out of her earnings she plants a
  vineyard.
¹⁷She sets about her work vigorously;
  her arms are strong for her tasks.
¹⁸She sees that her trading is profitable,
  and her lamp does not go out at
  night.
¹⁹In her hand she holds the distaff
  and grasps the spindle with her
  fingers.
²⁰She opens her arms to the poor
  and extends her hands to the needy.
²¹When it snows, she has no fear for her
  household;
  for all of them are clothed in scarlet.
²²She makes coverings for her bed;
  she is clothed in fine linen and
  purple.
²³Her husband is respected at the city
  gate,
  where he takes his seat among the
  elders of the land.
²⁴She makes linen garments and sells them,
  and supplies the merchants with sashes.
²⁵She is clothed with strength and dignity;
  she can laugh at the days to come.
²⁶She speaks with wisdom,
  and faithful instruction is on her tongue.
²⁷She watches over the affairs of her household
  and does not eat the bread of idleness.
²⁸Her children arise and call her blessed;
  her husband also, and he praises her:

ᵃ10 Verses 10–31 are an acrostic, each verse beginning with a successive letter of the Hebrew alphabet.

²⁹"Many women do noble things,
   but you surpass them all."
³⁰Charm is deceptive, and beauty is fleeting;
   but a woman who fears the Lord is to be praised.
³¹Give her the reward she has earned,
   and let her works bring her praise at the city gate.

ECCLESIASTES

Everything Is Meaningless

1 The words of the Teacher,[a] son of David, king in Jerusalem:

² "Meaningless! Meaningless!"
     says the Teacher.
  "Utterly meaningless!
     Everything is meaningless."

³ What does man gain from all
     his labor
  at which he toils under the
     sun?
⁴ Generations come and
     generations go,
  but the earth remains forever.
⁵ The sun rises and the sun sets,
  and hurries back to where it
     rises.
⁶ The wind blows to the south
  and turns to the north;
  round and round it goes,
  ever returning on its course.
⁷ All streams flow into the sea,
  yet the sea is never full.
  To the place the streams come
     from,
  there they return again.
⁸ All things are wearisome,
  more than one can say.
  The eye never has enough of
     seeing,
  nor the ear its fill of hearing.
⁹ What has been will be again,
  what has been done will be
     done again;
  there is nothing new under
     the sun.

¹⁰ Is there anything of which one can say,
     "Look! This is something new"?
  It was here already, long ago;
     it was here before our time.
¹¹ There is no remembrance of men of old,
     and even those who are yet to come
  will not be remembered
     by those who follow.

Wisdom Is Meaningless

¹²I, the Teacher, was king over Israel in Jerusalem. ¹³I devoted myself to study and to explore by wisdom all that is done under heaven. What a heavy burden God has laid on men! ¹⁴I have seen all the things that are done under the sun; all of them are meaningless, a chasing after the wind.

> ¹⁵What is twisted cannot be straightened;
> what is lacking cannot be counted.

¹⁶I thought to myself, "Look, I have grown and increased in wisdom more than anyone who has ruled over Jerusalem before me; I have experienced much of wisdom and knowledge." ¹⁷Then I applied myself to the understanding of wisdom, and also of madness and folly, but I learned that this, too, is a chasing after the wind.

> ¹⁸For with much wisdom comes much sorrow;
> the more knowledge, the more grief.

Pleasures Are Meaningless

2 I thought in my heart, "Come now, I will test you with pleasure to find out what is good." But that also proved to be meaningless. ²"Laughter," I said, "is foolish. And what does pleasure accomplish?" ³I tried cheering myself with wine, and embracing folly—my mind still guiding me with wisdom. I wanted to see what was worthwhile for men to do under heaven during the few days of their lives.

⁴I undertook great projects: I built houses for myself and planted vineyards. ⁵I made gardens and parks and planted all kinds of fruit trees in them. ⁶I made reservoirs to water groves of flourishing trees. ⁷I bought male and female slaves and had other slaves who were born in my house. I also owned more herds and flocks than anyone in Jerusalem before me. ⁸I amassed silver and gold for myself, and the treasure of kings and provinces. I acquired men and women singers, and a harem*ᵃ* as well— the delights of the heart of man. ⁹I became greater by far than anyone in Jerusalem before me. In all this my wisdom stayed with me.

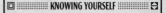

KNOWING YOURSELF

**2:1–11
Character**

Solomon discovered what many others have learned through the ages: No matter how much we have, it's never enough to satisfy. In spite of indulging himself in every pleasure of mind and body, he found no ultimate satisfaction.

We might naturally conclude that Solomon's experimentation left him a skeptic. But unlike many hedonists of our own day, he actually sought and found his answer. He concluded that only God gives satisfaction. That's why he finally wrote that we should simply "fear God and keep his commandments" (chapter 12, verse 13 [page 864]).

Solomon's insight helps us understand the source of lasting purpose and joy. That source isn't found in acquiring more and better "things." It is only found in a relationship with the living God.

> ¹⁰I denied myself nothing my eyes desired;
> I refused my heart no pleasure.
> My heart took delight in all my work,
> and this was the reward for all my labor.
> ¹¹Yet when I surveyed all that my hands had done
> and what I had toiled to achieve,
> everything was meaningless, a chasing after the wind;
> nothing was gained under the sun.

ᵃ8 The meaning of the Hebrew for this phrase is uncertain.

Wisdom and Folly Are Meaningless

¹²Then I turned my thoughts to consider wisdom,
    and also madness and folly.
  What more can the king's successor do
    than what has already been done?
¹³I saw that wisdom is better than folly,
    just as light is better than darkness.
¹⁴The wise man has eyes in his head,
    while the fool walks in the darkness;
  but I came to realize
    that the same fate overtakes them both.

¹⁵Then I thought in my heart,

  "The fate of the fool will overtake me also.
    What then do I gain by being wise?"
  I said in my heart,
    "This too is meaningless."
¹⁶For the wise man, like the fool, will not be long remembered;
    in days to come both will be forgotten.
  Like the fool, the wise man too must die!

Toil Is Meaningless

¹⁷So I hated life, because the work that is done under the sun was grievous to me. All of it is meaningless, a chasing after the wind. ¹⁸I hated all the things I had toiled for under the sun, because I must leave them to the one who comes after me. ¹⁹And who knows whether he will be a wise man or a fool? Yet he will have control over all the work into which I have poured my effort and skill under the sun. This too is meaningless. ²⁰So my heart began to despair over all my toilsome labor under the sun. ²¹For a man may do his work with wisdom, knowledge and skill, and then he must leave all he owns to someone who has not worked for it. This too is meaningless and a great misfortune. ²²What does a man get for all the toil and anxious striving with which he labors under the sun? ²³All his days his work is pain and grief; even at night his mind does not rest. This too is meaningless.

²⁴A man can do nothing better than to eat and drink and find satisfaction in his work. This too, I see, is from the hand of God, ²⁵for without him, who can eat or find enjoyment? ²⁶To the man who pleases him, God gives wisdom, knowledge and happiness, but to the sinner he gives the task of gathering and storing up wealth to hand it over to the one who pleases God. This too is meaningless, a chasing after the wind.

 DISCOVERING GOD

2:24–25
The God Who Is There

This passage emphasizes the fact that everything we do and have and enjoy comes from God's hand. Without God's enabling, none of us would have the ability to enjoy the work we do or the things we've acquired—something like having a beautiful, expensive home theater package with a big-screen TV and surround-sound speakers, but no electricity. Solomon implies that the very capacity to say "Ah!" and enjoy life is a gracious gift from God (see also chapter 3, verse 13).

A Time for Everything

3 There is a time for everything,
    and a season for every activity under heaven:

² a time to be born and a time to die,
    a time to plant and a time to uproot,
³ a time to kill and a time to heal,

a time to tear down and a time to build,
4   a time to weep and a time to laugh,
a time to mourn and a time to dance,
5   a time to scatter stones and a time to gather them,
a time to embrace and a time to refrain,
6   a time to search and a time to give up,
a time to keep and a time to throw away,
7   a time to tear and a time to mend,
a time to be silent and a time to speak,
8   a time to love and a time to hate,
a time for war and a time for peace.

⁹What does the worker gain from his toil? ¹⁰I have seen the burden God has laid on men. ¹¹He has made everything beautiful in its time. He has also set eternity in the hearts of men; yet they cannot fathom what God has done from beginning to end. ¹²I know that there is nothing better for men than to be happy and do good while they live. ¹³That everyone may eat and drink, and find satisfaction in all his toil—this is the gift of God. ¹⁴I know that everything God does will endure forever; nothing can be added to it and nothing taken from it. God does it so that men will revere him.

¹⁵Whatever is has already been,
and what will be has been before;
and God will call the past to account.ᵃ

¹⁶And I saw something else under the sun:

In the place of judgment—wickedness was there,
in the place of justice—wickedness was there.

ᵃ15 Or God calls back the past

::::::::::::::::::::::: **ADDRESSING QUESTIONS** :::::::::::::::::::::::

3:1–11
Human Experience   **Q**

Dave Dravecky seemed to have the world at his feet. The left-handed pitcher for the San Francisco Giants was destined for greatness.

Then doctors removed a large mass of cancerous tissue from the muscle of Dravecky's left arm in October of 1988. Few thought he would ever return to baseball. But on August 10, 1989, he again stood on the mound and did his stuff. Sadly, his comeback ended several games later when his weakened arm snapped under the strain of a pitch. In one moment, Dave Dravecky saw the seasons of his life change.

While we live on this earth, we'll never fully know the reasons why God allows windfalls or tragedies to change our lives so drastically. But we can have hope in spite of changing circumstances. Solomon tells us that God "has made *everything* beautiful in its time" (verse 11). So the current circumstances we're experiencing fit perfectly into a larger plan for our lives.

Our problem is that we possess only a few pieces of the puzzle and can't see how they fit together. The good news is that a bigger picture does exist, and that God has given us all an inner urge to pursue that reality. We all are born with an awareness that we are made for something greater than just this life with its unanswered questions. In other words, God has "set eternity in [our] hearts . . ." (verse 11).

When you think back on some of the experiences of your life, can you detect God's hand leading you in a certain direction? Perhaps the circumstances that have lead you to read this book have all been a part of his plan for your life. If you think that's true, then it's no great leap to realize that he has plans for the rest of your life. If you choose to follow him, he'll help you fit the pieces of your life together until one day, when the "big picture" is finally revealed.

[17]I thought in my heart,

> "God will bring to judgment
>   both the righteous and the wicked,
> for there will be a time for every activity,
>   a time for every deed."

[18]I also thought, "As for men, God tests them so that they may see that they are like the animals. [19]Man's fate is like that of the animals; the same fate awaits them both: As one dies, so dies the other. All have the same breath[a]; man has no advantage over the animal. Everything is meaningless. [20]All go to the same place; all come from dust, and to dust all return. [21]Who knows if the spirit of man rises upward and if the spirit of the animal[b] goes down into the earth?"

[22]So I saw that there is nothing better for a man than to enjoy his work, because that is his lot. For who can bring him to see what will happen after him?

Oppression, Toil, Friendlessness

 Again I looked and saw all the oppression that was taking place under the sun:

> I saw the tears of the oppressed—
>   and they have no comforter;
> power was on the side of their oppressors—
>   and they have no comforter.
> [2]And I declared that the dead,
>   who had already died,
> are happier than the living,
>   who are still alive.
> [3]But better than both
>   is he who has not yet been,
> who has not seen the evil
>   that is done under the sun.

[4]And I saw that all labor and all achievement spring from man's envy of his neighbor. This too is meaningless, a chasing after the wind.

> [5]The fool folds his hands
>   and ruins himself.
> [6]Better one handful with tranquillity
>   than two handfuls with toil
>   and chasing after the wind.

[7]Again I saw something meaningless under the sun:

> [8]There was a man all alone;
>   he had neither son nor brother.
> There was no end to his toil,
>   yet his eyes were not content with his wealth.
> "For whom am I toiling," he asked,
>   "and why am I depriving myself of enjoyment?"
> This too is meaningless—
>   a miserable business!

> [9]Two are better than one,
>   because they have a good return for their work:

---

[a] 19 Or *spirit*   [b] 21 Or *Who knows the spirit of man, which rises upward, or the spirit of the animal, which*

¹⁰If one falls down,
>   his friend can help him up.
> But pity the man who falls
>   and has no one to help him up!

¹¹Also, if two lie down together, they will keep warm.
>   But how can one keep warm alone?

¹²Though one may be overpowered,
>   two can defend themselves.
> A cord of three strands is not quickly broken.

Advancement Is Meaningless

¹³Better a poor but wise youth than an old but foolish king who no longer knows how to take warning. ¹⁴The youth may have come from prison to the kingship, or he may have been born in poverty within his kingdom. ¹⁵I saw that all who lived and walked under the sun followed the youth, the king's successor. ¹⁶There was no end to all the people who were before them. But those who came later were not pleased with the successor. This too is meaningless, a chasing after the wind.

Stand in Awe of God

5 Guard your steps when you go to the house of God. Go near to listen rather than to offer the sacrifice of fools, who do not know that they do wrong.

²Do not be quick with your mouth,
>   do not be hasty in your heart
>   to utter anything before God.
> God is in heaven
>   and you are on earth,
>   so let your words be few.

³As a dream comes when there are many cares,
>   so the speech of a fool when there are many words.

⁴When you make a vow to God, do not delay in fulfilling it. He has no pleasure in fools; fulfill your vow. ⁵It is better not to vow than to make a vow and not fulfill it. ⁶Do not let your mouth lead you into sin. And do not protest to the ⌊temple⌋ messenger, "My vow was a mistake." Why should God be angry at what you say and destroy the work of your hands? ⁷Much dreaming and many words are meaningless. Therefore stand in awe of God.

Riches Are Meaningless

⁸If you see the poor oppressed in a district, and justice and rights denied, do not be surprised at such things; for one official is eyed by a higher one, and over them both are others higher still. ⁹The increase from the land is taken by all; the king himself profits from the fields.

¹⁰Whoever loves money never has
>   money enough;
>   whoever loves wealth is never
>   satisfied with his income.
> This too is meaningless.

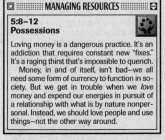

▣ ░░░░░░░ **MANAGING RESOURCES** ░░░░░░░ ⬧

5:8–12
Possessions

Loving money is a dangerous practice. It's an addiction that requires constant new "fixes." It's a raging thirst that's impossible to quench.

Money, in and of itself, isn't bad—we all need some form of currency to function in society. But we get in trouble when we *love* money and expend our energies in pursuit of a relationship with what is by nature nonpersonal. Instead, we should love people and use things—not the other way around.

¹¹As goods increase,
so do those who consume them.
And what benefit are they to the owner
except to feast his eyes on them?

¹²The sleep of a laborer is sweet,
whether he eats little or much,
but the abundance of a rich man
permits him no sleep.

¹³I have seen a grievous evil under the sun:

wealth hoarded to the harm of its owner,
¹⁴   or wealth lost through some misfortune,
so that when he has a son
there is nothing left for him.
¹⁵Naked a man comes from his mother's womb,
and as he comes, so he departs.
He takes nothing from his labor
that he can carry in his hand.

¹⁶This too is a grievous evil:

As a man comes, so he departs,
and what does he gain,
since he toils for the wind?
¹⁷All his days he eats in darkness,
with great frustration, affliction and anger.

¹⁸Then I realized that it is good and proper for a man to eat and drink, and to find satisfaction in his toilsome labor under the sun during the few days of life God has given him—for this is his lot. ¹⁹Moreover, when God gives any man wealth and possessions, and enables him to enjoy them, to accept his lot and be happy in his work—this is a gift of God. ²⁰He seldom reflects on the days of his life, because God keeps him occupied with gladness of heart.

6 I have seen another evil under the sun, and it weighs heavily on men: ²God gives a man wealth, possessions and honor, so that he lacks nothing his heart desires, but God does not enable him to enjoy them, and a stranger enjoys them instead. This is meaningless, a grievous evil.

³A man may have a hundred children and live many years; yet no matter how long he lives, if he cannot enjoy his prosperity and does not receive proper burial, I say that a stillborn child is better off than he. ⁴It comes without meaning, it departs in darkness, and in darkness its name is shrouded. ⁵Though it never saw the sun or knew anything, it has more rest than does that man— ⁶even if he lives a thousand years twice over but fails to enjoy his prosperity. Do not all go to the same place?

⁷All man's efforts are for his mouth,
yet his appetite is never satisfied.
⁸What advantage has a wise man
over a fool?
What does a poor man gain
by knowing how to conduct himself before others?
⁹Better what the eye sees
than the roving of the appetite.

This too is meaningless,
a chasing after the wind.

[10]Whatever exists has already been named,
and what man is has been known;
no man can contend
with one who is stronger than he.
[11]The more the words,
the less the meaning,
and how does that profit anyone?

[12]For who knows what is good for a man in life, during the few and meaningless days he passes through like a shadow? Who can tell him what will happen under the sun after he is gone?

Wisdom

7
A good name is better than
fine perfume,
and the day of death better
than the day of birth.
[2]It is better to go to a house of
mourning
than to go to a house of
feasting,
for death is the destiny of every
man;
the living should take this to
heart.
[3]Sorrow is better than laughter,
because a sad face is good for
the heart.
[4]The heart of the wise is in the house of mourning,
but the heart of fools is in the house of pleasure.
[5]It is better to heed a wise man's rebuke
than to listen to the song of fools.
[6]Like the crackling of thorns under the pot,
so is the laughter of fools.
This too is meaningless.

[7]Extortion turns a wise man into a fool,
and a bribe corrupts the heart.

[8]The end of a matter is better than its beginning,
and patience is better than pride.
[9]Do not be quickly provoked in your spirit,
for anger resides in the lap of fools.

[10]Do not say, "Why were the old days better than these?"
For it is not wise to ask such questions.

[11]Wisdom, like an inheritance, is a good thing
and benefits those who see the sun.
[12]Wisdom is a shelter
as money is a shelter,

▣ ▒▒▒▒▒ ADDRESSING QUESTIONS ▒▒▒▒▒ ◈

7:1
Human Experience   **Q**

How can the "day of death" be better than the "day of birth"?

Solomon's point here is that sad times teach us more about our condition in life than happy times. At a funeral we're forced to reflect on the serious matters of life. The death of a loved one is a reality that interrupts our dreams and brings us back to earth. It reminds us of life's limits. And it causes us to consider God more seriously.

Solomon uses these images to make his readers think about life and its troubles, pointing them to the real hope that believers have in the reality that lies beyond this world.

but the advantage of knowledge is this:
that wisdom preserves the life of its possessor.

¹³Consider what God has done:

Who can straighten
what he has made crooked?
¹⁴When times are good, be happy;
but when times are bad, consider:
God has made the one
as well as the other.
Therefore, a man cannot discover
anything about his future.

¹⁵In this meaningless life of mine I have seen both of these:

a righteous man perishing in his righteousness,
and a wicked man living long in his wickedness.
¹⁶Do not be overrighteous,
neither be overwise—
why destroy yourself?
¹⁷Do not be overwicked,
and do not be a fool—
why die before your time?
¹⁸It is good to grasp the one
and not let go of the other.
The man who fears God will avoid all ⌞extremes⌟.ᵃ

¹⁹Wisdom makes one wise man more powerful
than ten rulers in a city.

²⁰There is not a righteous man on earth
who does what is right and never sins.

²¹Do not pay attention to every word people say,
or you may hear your servant cursing you—
²²for you know in your heart
that many times you yourself have cursed others.

²³All this I tested by wisdom and I said,

"I am determined to be wise"—
but this was beyond me.
²⁴Whatever wisdom may be,
it is far off and most profound—
who can discover it?
²⁵So I turned my mind to understand,
to investigate and to search out wisdom and the scheme of things
and to understand the stupidity of wickedness
and the madness of folly.

²⁶I find more bitter than death
the woman who is a snare,
whose heart is a trap
and whose hands are chains.
The man who pleases God will escape her,
but the sinner she will ensnare.

ᵃ 18 Or will follow them both

²⁷"Look," says the Teacher,ᵃ "this is what I have discovered:

> "Adding one thing to another to discover the scheme of things—
> ²⁸ while I was still searching
> but not finding—
> I found one ⌊upright⌋ man among a thousand,
> but not one ⌊upright⌋ woman among them all.

²⁹This only have I found:

> God made mankind upright,
> but men have gone in search
> of many schemes."

8
> Who is like the wise man?
> Who knows the explanation
> of things?
> Wisdom brightens a man's face
> and changes its hard
> appearance.

▭ ▥▥▥▥▥▥ **KNOWING YOURSELF** ▥▥▥▥▥▥ ↩

**7:29
Sin**

Have truer words than these ever been written? How many times have we been amazed at the extent to which human evil will go? If there's any area in which we humans show amazing creativity, it's in the capacity for producing new ways to avoid God or to promote ourselves to the harm of others.

   God is not responsible for our sin—the Bible makes it clear that *we* are the ones who "have gone in search of many schemes" and have chosen what is wrong. But God is eager to help us reverse that pattern in our lives.

Obey the King

²Obey the king's command, I say, because you took an oath before God. ³Do not be in a hurry to leave the king's presence. Do not stand up for a bad cause, for he will do whatever he pleases. ⁴Since a king's word is supreme, who can say to him, "What are you doing?"

> ⁵Whoever obeys his command will come to no harm,
> and the wise heart will know the proper time and procedure.
> ⁶For there is a proper time and procedure for every matter,
> though a man's misery weighs heavily upon him.

> ⁷Since no man knows the future,
> who can tell him what is to come?
> ⁸No man has power over the wind to contain itᵇ;
> so no one has power over the day of his death.
> As no one is discharged in time of war,
> so wickedness will not release those who practice it.

⁹All this I saw, as I applied my mind to everything done under the sun. There is a time when a man lords it over others to his ownᶜ hurt. ¹⁰Then too, I saw the wicked buried— those who used to come and go from the holy place and receive praiseᵈ in the city where they did this. This too is meaningless.

¹¹When the sentence for a crime is not quickly carried out, the hearts of the people are filled with schemes to do wrong. ¹²Although a wicked man commits a hundred crimes and still lives a long time, I know that it will go better with God-fearing men, who are reverent before God. ¹³Yet because the wicked do not fear God, it will not go well with them, and their days will not lengthen like a shadow.

¹⁴There is something else meaningless that occurs on earth: righteous men who get what the wicked deserve, and wicked men who get what the righteous deserve. This too, I say, is meaningless. ¹⁵So I commend the enjoyment of life, because nothing is better for a man under the sun than to eat and drink and be glad. Then joy will accompany him in his work all the days of the life God has given him under the sun.

ᵃ27 Or *leader of the assembly*   ᵇ8 Or *over his spirit to retain it*   ᶜ9 Or *to their*   ᵈ10 Some Hebrew manuscripts and Septuagint (Aquila); most Hebrew manuscripts *and are forgotten*

¹⁶When I applied my mind to know wisdom and to observe man's labor on earth—his eyes not seeing sleep day or night— ¹⁷then I saw all that God has done. No one can comprehend what goes on under the sun. Despite all his efforts to search it out, man cannot discover its meaning. Even if a wise man claims he knows, he cannot really comprehend it.

A Common Destiny for All

9 So I reflected on all this and concluded that the righteous and the wise and what they do are in God's hands, but no man knows whether love or hate awaits him. ²All share a common destiny—the righteous and the wicked, the good and the bad,ᵃ the clean and the unclean, those who offer sacrifices and those who do not.

> As it is with the good man,
>   so with the sinner;
> as it is with those who take oaths,
>   so with those who are afraid to take them.

³This is the evil in everything that happens under the sun: The same destiny overtakes all. The hearts of men, moreover, are full of evil and there is madness in their hearts while they live, and afterward they join the dead. ⁴Anyone who is among the living has hopeᵇ—even a live dog is better off than a dead lion!

> ⁵For the living know that they will die,
>   but the dead know nothing;
> they have no further reward,
>   and even the memory of them is forgotten.
> ⁶Their love, their hate
>   and their jealousy have long since vanished;
> never again will they have a part
>   in anything that happens under the sun.

⁷Go, eat your food with gladness, and drink your wine with a joyful heart, for it is now that God favors what you do. ⁸Always be clothed in white, and always anoint your head with oil. ⁹Enjoy life with your wife, whom you love, all the days of this meaningless life that God has given you under the sun— all your meaningless days. For this is your lot in life and in your toilsome labor under the sun. ¹⁰Whatever your hand finds to do, do it with all your might, for in the grave,ᶜ where you are going, there is neither working nor planning nor knowledge nor wisdom.

¹¹I have seen something else under the sun:

> The race is not to the swift
>   or the battle to the strong,
> nor does food come to the wise
>   or wealth to the brilliant
>   or favor to the learned;
> but time and chance happen to them all.

¹²Moreover, no man knows when his hour will come:

> As fish are caught in a cruel net,
>   or birds are taken in a snare,

ᵃ2 Septuagint (Aquila), Vulgate and Syriac; Hebrew does not have *and the bad,* who live, there is hope   ᶜ10 Hebrew *Sheol*   ᵇ4 Or *What then is to be chosen? With all*

so men are trapped by evil times
   that fall unexpectedly upon them.

Wisdom Better Than Folly

¹³I also saw under the sun this example of wisdom that greatly impressed me: ¹⁴There was once a small city with only a few people in it. And a powerful king came against it, surrounded it and built huge siegeworks against it. ¹⁵Now there lived in that city a man poor but wise, and he saved the city by his wisdom. But nobody remembered that poor man. ¹⁶So I said, "Wisdom is better than strength." But the poor man's wisdom is despised, and his words are no longer heeded.

¹⁷The quiet words of the wise are more to be heeded
   than the shouts of a ruler of fools.
¹⁸Wisdom is better than weapons of war,
   but one sinner destroys much good.

10 As dead flies give perfume a bad smell,
   so a little folly outweighs wisdom and honor.
²The heart of the wise inclines to the right,
   but the heart of the fool to the left.
³Even as he walks along the road,
   the fool lacks sense
   and shows everyone how stupid he is.
⁴If a ruler's anger rises against you,
   do not leave your post;
   calmness can lay great errors to rest.

⁵There is an evil I have seen under the sun,
   the sort of error that arises from a ruler:
⁶Fools are put in many high positions,
   while the rich occupy the low ones.
⁷I have seen slaves on horseback,
   while princes go on foot like slaves.

⁸Whoever digs a pit may fall into it;
   whoever breaks through a wall may be bitten by a snake.
⁹Whoever quarries stones may be injured by them;
   whoever splits logs may be endangered by them.

¹⁰If the ax is dull
   and its edge unsharpened,
more strength is needed
   but skill will bring success.

¹¹If a snake bites before it is charmed,
   there is no profit for the charmer.

¹²Words from a wise man's mouth are gracious,
   but a fool is consumed by his own lips.
¹³At the beginning his words are folly;
   at the end they are wicked madness—
¹⁴   and the fool multiplies words.

No one knows what is coming—
   who can tell him what will happen after him?

¹⁵A fool's work wearies him;
   he does not know the way to town.

¹⁶Woe to you, O land whose king was a servant[a]
    and whose princes feast in the morning.
¹⁷Blessed are you, O land whose king is of noble birth
    and whose princes eat at a proper time—
        for strength and not for drunkenness.

¹⁸If a man is lazy, the rafters sag;
    if his hands are idle, the house leaks.

¹⁹A feast is made for laughter,
    and wine makes life merry,
        but money is the answer for everything.

²⁰Do not revile the king even in your thoughts,
    or curse the rich in your bedroom,
because a bird of the air may carry your words,
    and a bird on the wing may report what you say.

Bread Upon the Waters

11 Cast your bread upon the waters,
    for after many days you will find it again.
²Give portions to seven, yes to eight,
    for you do not know what disaster may come upon the land.

³If clouds are full of water,
    they pour rain upon the earth.
Whether a tree falls to the south or to the north,
    in the place where it falls, there will it lie.
⁴Whoever watches the wind will not plant;
    whoever looks at the clouds will not reap.

⁵As you do not know the path of the wind,
    or how the body is formed[b] in a mother's womb,
so you cannot understand the work of God,
    the Maker of all things.

⁶Sow your seed in the morning,
    and at evening let not your hands be idle,
for you do not know which will succeed,
    whether this or that,
        or whether both will do equally well.

Remember Your Creator While Young

⁷Light is sweet,
    and it pleases the eyes to see the sun.
⁸However many years a man may live,
    let him enjoy them all.
But let him remember the days of darkness,
    for they will be many.
        Everything to come is meaningless.

⁹Be happy, young man, while you are young,
    and let your heart give you joy in the days of your youth.

---

a 16 Or king is a child   b 5 Or know how life (or the spirit) / enters the body being formed

Follow the ways of your heart
and whatever your eyes see,
but know that for all these things
God will bring you to judgment.
[10]So then, banish anxiety from your heart
and cast off the troubles of your body,
for youth and vigor are meaningless.

12 Remember your Creator
in the days of your youth,
before the days of trouble come
and the years approach when you will say,
"I find no pleasure in them"—
[2]before the sun and the light
and the moon and the stars
grow dark,
and the clouds return after the
rain;
[3]when the keepers of the house
tremble,
and the strong men stoop,
when the grinders cease
because they are few,
and those looking through the
windows grow dim;
[4]when the doors to the street are
closed
and the sound of grinding
fades;
when men rise up at the sound
of birds,
but all their songs grow faint;
[5]when men are afraid of heights
and of dangers in the streets;
when the almond tree blossoms
and the grasshopper drags
himself along
and desire no longer is stirred.
Then man goes to his eternal home
and mourners go about the streets.

[6]Remember him—before the silver cord is severed,
or the golden bowl is broken;
before the pitcher is shattered at the spring,
or the wheel broken at the well,
[7]and the dust returns to the ground it came from,
and the spirit returns to God who gave it.
[8]"Meaningless! Meaningless!" says the Teacher.[a]
"Everything is meaningless!"

▣ ▦▦▦▦ DISCOVERING GOD ▦▦▦▦ ⬍

**12:13–14
Life with God**

Throughout the book of Ecclesiastes, Solomon points out the futility of life. He walks down several paths as he looks for meaning in life—pleasure, wealth, wisdom and work. Not many of us will ever possess the time or the resources to do the kind of searching that Solomon did, so this book gives us the benefit of his experience by allowing us to peek at the end of the story. His conclusion? No matter how hard we try to manufacture meaning in life, time passes and we all die.

But don't despair! Solomon also gives us the ultimate answer and directs us to the ultimate source for finding meaning in life: knowing and living with God.

Think of unanswered questions as doors that slam in our faces. With gut-wrenching accuracy, Solomon forces us to look at our lives and recognize that these obstacles exist. But instead of trying to supply us with keys to open those doors ourselves, Solomon points us to God, the Architect who built the house. Ultimately, true meaning in life can be found only in a relationship with God—a relationship that is the "whole duty of man" (verse 13).

---

[a] Or the leader of the assembly; also in verses 9 and 10

The Conclusion of the Matter

⁹Not only was the Teacher wise, but also he imparted knowledge to the people. He pondered and searched out and set in order many proverbs. ¹⁰The Teacher searched to find just the right words, and what he wrote was upright and true.

¹¹The words of the wise are like goads, their collected sayings like firmly embedded nails—given by one Shepherd. ¹²Be warned, my son, of anything in addition to them.

Of making many books there is no end, and much study wearies the body.

> ¹³Now all has been heard;
>   here is the conclusion of the matter:
>   Fear God and keep his commandments,
>   for this is the whole ˻duty˼ of man.
> ¹⁴For God will bring every deed into judgment,
>   including every hidden thing,
>   whether it is good or evil.

My husband and I have been married for over three years now, and this letter is long overdue. I'm writing to thank the church for insisting that Chris and I move apart after we became Christians. Even though we had been living together for six and a half years and were engaged, the church exhorted us to establish a pattern of purity before getting married. I am so grateful—though I never would have predicted I would be! Allow me to explain.

The idea of living apart after such a long time together seemed impossible at first. After all, Chris and I had recently invested in a new house together! Still, the leaders of the church asked us to honor their wishes, even offering to help with the costs of finding a new place to live, if need be. We reluctantly trusted them, thinking that they probably had our best interests in mind. I moved out of the house for the five months that remained before our wedding.

During those five months we discovered a lot of things to be thankful for. First, we had the joy of knowing that we were obeying our church leaders, whom we had really come to admire since we became involved in the church community. Second, our decision to live apart was an immediate public testimony to the transformation that Christ had made in our lives. As it happened, our relationship became a strong, silent witness to three of my siblings about God's views on living together before marriage. Third, we now look at our relationship as if it had two phases—before Christ and after Christ. Doing so has allowed us to see many of the negative patterns that we had established before we were married, and has given us a new perspective on our lives together. Sure, during those five months I missed my fiancé, my dog, and my house, but the long-term benefits of our decision far outweigh any short-term inconveniences we experienced.

Being married is a lot different than simply living together, and I'm glad the distinction between the two phases of our relationship has been so clear-cut for me. When we lived together, Chris and I were committed to each other as long as we were in love; now we're in love because we're committed!

While our married life is not perfect, many of the problems we're experiencing are a result of our past life together. I believe that, had we waited to live together until marriage, we would have had greater respect for one another. We would have also learned to negotiate and to resolve our differences more constructively. When we lived together, we approached each conflict as one that might end our relationship. Doing so seriously hampered trust and intimacy in our relationship, and encouraged fantasies about living alone. Now that splitting up is no longer an option for us we face our problems head-on, knowing that our old ways of dealing with them are inappropriate. We want our marriage to be God-glorifying, so we're getting help with our problems and are learning new communication skills.

We believe that marriage is a wonderful part of God's plan for the life of a man and a woman who want to live in a committed relationship. Our experience has shown us that living together before marriage makes the process of making that commitment more difficult, and we're convinced that others who experience the same kinds of problems that we faced will come to the same conclusion that we have. Thank you, once again, for your guidance. With God's help, we'll be able to continue to do our best to honor him in our marriage.

Introduction

THE BOTTOM LINE

Who would expect to find a sexually explicit love poem in the Bible? Well, for starters, the one who invented sex—God. After all, God was the one who created humans as sexual beings. Ever since the beginning of time, however, various influences have distorted this awesome gift. This book offers its readers a refreshing break from the perversion of our surrounding culture. It allows us to look again on sexuality as it was originally intended—desperately exciting, endlessly fascinating, intensely joyful, and exclusively experienced between a husband and wife.

CENTRAL IDEAS

- Sexuality is one of God's most wonderful gifts to us.
- Sinful culture has distorted sexuality.
- Sexuality is designed for the exclusive, committed marriage relationship.

OUTLINE

1 The first meeting (1:2–2:7)
2 The second meeting (2:8–3:5)
3 The third meeting (3:6–5:1)
4 The fourth meeting (5:2–6:3)
5 The fifth meeting (6:4–8:4)
6 The literary turning point (8:5–7)
7 Conclusion (8:8–14)

TITLE

The phrase Song of Songs means "the greatest of songs" – a fitting title for the most beautiful love song ever written.

AUTHOR AND READERS

This book, by virtue of its first verse, has been ascribed to Solomon. However, it may have been written for him as a wedding present by an undisclosed author. Or it may have been in a part of a body of love poetry ascribed to Solomon's era.

TIME LINE					
Pinto Indians build wood and reed huts in California (c. 1000 B.C.)	Song of Songs written (c. 950 B.C.)	Celts invade Britain (900 B.C.)		In Ephesus, construction begins on the temple of Artemis, one of the seven wonders of the ancient world (772 B.C.)	
1000 BC	**950**	**900**	**850**	**800**	**750**
Solomon's reign (970–930 B.C.)	Solomon's fleet trades on the African continent (c. 965 B.C.)	Division of the kingdom (930 B.C.)	Elijah's ministry in Israel (c. 875–848 B.C.)		

In his book *The Mystery of Marriage* author Mike Mason tells of an experience he and his wife had during their honeymoon. They spotted, at the end of a country lane, above a ripe field of wheat, two dots in the sky. A pair of hawks were gliding high above the tree-tops. As the birds descended in lazy swoops, they looked as if they were putting on a show. One turned clockwise and the other counterclockwise, spiraling lower and lower in the afternoon stillness.

The longer the Masons watched, the clearer it became that the graceful, open-winged dance of the hawks had absolutely no practical value. The birds weren't hunting, looking for anything, or going anywhere. They were playing—simply enjoying the pleasure of flying together.

God gives his creatures the capacity to experience uncensored pleasure.

Whether birds in the sky or newlyweds on their honeymoon, living beings are endowed with more than just the ability to survive. We learn something about God's nature when we realize that he gives his creatures the capacity to experience uncensored pleasure. By his decree, pairs of hawks—and humans—love "flying" together!

Scattered throughout the pages of the Bible are words intended to help men and women derive the greatest possible pleasure from their physical relationship. But no one book in the Bible discusses the sexual dimension between a husband and wife more frankly than the Song of Songs. And no portion of the Bible shows God's approval of appropriate sexual activity more than this book. Turn to Song of Songs chapter 5, verse 1 (page 873). There you'll read how one lover describes his bride in wonderfully sensual terms, and hear God's response to the honeymooning couple as told through the voices of the newlyweds' friends.

SONG OF SONGS

 Solomon's Song of Songs.

Beloved[a]

    2Let him kiss me with the kisses of his mouth—
      for your love is more delightful than wine.
    3Pleasing is the fragrance of your perfumes;
      your name is like perfume poured out.
    No wonder the maidens love you!
    4Take me away with you—let us hurry!
      Let the king bring me into his chambers.

Friends

    We rejoice and delight in you[b];
      we will praise your love more than wine.

Beloved

    How right they are to adore you!

    5Dark am I, yet lovely,
      O daughters of Jerusalem,
    dark like the tents of Kedar,
      like the tent curtains of Solomon.[c]
    6Do not stare at me because I am dark,
      because I am darkened by the sun.
    My mother's sons were angry with me
      and made me take care of the vineyards;
      my own vineyard I have neglected.
    7Tell me, you whom I love, where you graze your flock
      and where you rest your sheep at midday.
    Why should I be like a veiled woman
      beside the flocks of your friends?

Friends

    8If you do not know, most beautiful of women,
      follow the tracks of the sheep
    and graze your young goats
      by the tents of the shepherds.

Lover

    9I liken you, my darling, to a mare
      harnessed to one of the chariots of Pharaoh.
    10Your cheeks are beautiful with earrings,
      your neck with strings of jewels.

---

[a]Primarily on the basis of the gender of the Hebrew pronouns used, male and female speakers are indicated in the margins by the captions *Lover* and *Beloved* respectively. The words of others are marked *Friends*. In some instances the divisions and their captions are debatable.   [b]4 The Hebrew is masculine singular.   [c]5 Or *Salma*

¹¹We will make you earrings of gold,
   studded with silver.

Beloved

¹²While the king was at his table,
   my perfume spread its fragrance.
¹³My lover is to me a sachet of myrrh
   resting between my breasts.
¹⁴My lover is to me a cluster of henna blossoms
   from the vineyards of En Gedi.

Lover

¹⁵How beautiful you are, my darling!
   Oh, how beautiful!
   Your eyes are doves.

Beloved

¹⁶How handsome you are, my lover!
   Oh, how charming!
   And our bed is verdant.

Lover

¹⁷The beams of our house are cedars;
   our rafters are firs.

*Beloved*ᵃ

 I am a roseᵇ of Sharon,
   a lily of the valleys.

Lover

²Like a lily among thorns
   is my darling among the maidens.

Beloved

³Like an apple tree among the trees of the forest
   is my lover among the young men.
 I delight to sit in his shade,
   and his fruit is sweet to my taste.
⁴He has taken me to the banquet hall,
   and his banner over me is love.
⁵Strengthen me with raisins,
   refresh me with apples,
   for I am faint with love.
⁶His left arm is under my head,
   and his right arm embraces me.
⁷Daughters of Jerusalem, I charge you
   by the gazelles and by the does of the field:
 Do not arouse or awaken love
   until it so desires.

ᵃ 1 Or *Lover*   ᵇ 1 Possibly a member of the crocus family

⁸Listen! My lover!
    Look! Here he comes,
  leaping across the mountains,
    bounding over the hills.
⁹My lover is like a gazelle or a young stag.
    Look! There he stands behind our wall,
  gazing through the windows,
    peering through the lattice.

◻ ▒▒▒▒ STRENGTHENING RELATIONSHIPS ▒▒▒▒ ⤧

2:4
Marriage

Love is meant to accompany sex. Within the protective confines of a marriage—in the arms of a devoted spouse and under the safe "banner of love"—sex is a wonderful and pleasurable gift from God.

Our culture has separated the notion of love from sex. In its most common distortion, sex is a form of recreation to be enjoyed between consenting partners—with or without the benefit of marriage. In its more perverted form, sex is about exploitation and power. Both of these corrupt sexual practices lead to guilt and pain, not pleasure.

Have you tried to quench your sexual thirst in your own way instead of following God's design? Then you may have already learned about the pain and regret that accompany that choice. If you are not married, wait to have sex until you are. If you are married, build a strong relationship with your spouse to protect this precious gift from God.

---

¹⁰My lover spoke and said to me,
    "Arise, my darling,
      my beautiful one, and come with
        me.
¹¹See! The winter is past;
    the rains are over and gone.
¹²Flowers appear on the earth;
    the season of singing has come,
  the cooing of doves
    is heard in our land.
¹³The fig tree forms its early fruit;
    the blossoming vines spread their
      fragrance.
  Arise, come, my darling;
    my beautiful one, come with me."

Lover

¹⁴My dove in the clefts of the rock,
    in the hiding places on the
      mountainside,
  show me your face,
    let me hear your voice;
  for your voice is sweet,
    and your face is lovely.

¹⁵Catch for us the foxes,
    the little foxes
  that ruin the vineyards,
    our vineyards that are in bloom.

Beloved

¹⁶My lover is mine and I am his;
    he browses among the lilies.
¹⁷Until the day breaks
    and the shadows flee,
  turn, my lover,
    and be like a gazelle
  or like a young stag
    on the rugged hills.ᵃ

3 All night long on my bed
    I looked for the one my heart loves;

ᵃ 17 Or *the hills of Bether*

I looked for him but did not find him.
²I will get up now and go about the city,
　through its streets and squares;
I will search for the one my heart loves.
　So I looked for him but did not find him.
³The watchmen found me
　as they made their rounds in the city.
　"Have you seen the one my heart loves?"
⁴Scarcely had I passed them
　when I found the one my heart loves.
I held him and would not let him go
　till I had brought him to my
　　mother's house,
　to the room of the one who
　　conceived me.
⁵Daughters of Jerusalem, I
　　charge you
　by the gazelles and by the
　　does of the field:
Do not arouse or awaken love
　until it so desires.

⁶Who is this coming up from the
　　desert
　like a column of smoke,
perfumed with myrrh and
　　incense
　made from all the spices of
　　the merchant?
⁷Look! It is Solomon's carriage,
　escorted by sixty warriors,
　the noblest of Israel,
⁸all of them wearing the sword,
　all experienced in battle,
each with his sword at his side,
　prepared for the terrors of the night.
⁹King Solomon made for himself the carriage;
　he made it of wood from Lebanon.
¹⁰Its posts he made of silver,
　its base of gold.
Its seat was upholstered with purple,
　its interior lovingly inlaid
　byᵃ the daughters of Jerusalem.
¹¹Come out, you daughters of Zion,
　and look at King Solomon wearing the crown,
　the crown with which his mother crowned him
on the day of his wedding,
　the day his heart rejoiced.

▣ ▦▦▦ STRENGTHENING RELATIONSHIPS ▦▦▦ ↘

3:5
Marriage

How often do two people fall in love and want to hurry their relationship along? Whether they move too quickly toward marriage or add sex to the relationship before marriage, a couple's relationship potential is damaged by "awakening love before it desires."

Don't try to force the person you're with into a level of commitment that he or she is not ready to accept. And don't buy into the lie that premarital sex will accelerate that level of commitment. If you and your partner have all the basic ingredients for a great relationship, it will be more satisfying if you wait for your love to "bake" for as long as it needs!

ᵃ 10 Or *its inlaid interior a gift of love / from*

Lover

4 How beautiful you are, my darling!
Oh, how beautiful!
Your eyes behind your veil are doves.
Your hair is like a flock of goats
descending from Mount Gilead.
[2]Your teeth are like a flock of sheep just shorn,
coming up from the washing.
Each has its twin;
not one of them is alone.
[3]Your lips are like a scarlet ribbon;
your mouth is lovely.
Your temples behind your veil
are like the halves of a pomegranate.
[4]Your neck is like the tower of David,
built with elegance[a];
on it hang a thousand shields,
all of them shields of warriors.
[5]Your two breasts are like two fawns,
like twin fawns of a gazelle
that browse among the lilies.
[6]Until the day breaks
and the shadows flee,
I will go to the mountain of myrrh
and to the hill of incense.
[7]All beautiful you are, my darling;
there is no flaw in you.

[8]Come with me from Lebanon, my bride,
come with me from Lebanon.
Descend from the crest of Amana,
from the top of Senir, the summit of Hermon,
from the lions' dens
and the mountain haunts of the leopards.
[9]You have stolen my heart, my sister, my bride;
you have stolen my heart
with one glance of your eyes,
with one jewel of your necklace.
[10]How delightful is your love, my sister, my bride!
How much more pleasing is your love than wine,
and the fragrance of your perfume than any spice!
[11]Your lips drop sweetness as the honeycomb, my bride;
milk and honey are under your tongue.
The fragrance of your garments is like that of Lebanon.
[12]You are a garden locked up, my sister, my bride;
you are a spring enclosed, a sealed fountain.
[13]Your plants are an orchard of pomegranates
with choice fruits,
with henna and nard,
[14]   nard and saffron,
calamus and cinnamon,
with every kind of incense tree,

---

a 4 The meaning of the Hebrew for this word is uncertain.

with myrrh and aloes
and all the finest spices.
¹⁵You are ᵃ a garden fountain,
a well of flowing water
streaming down from Lebanon.

Beloved

¹⁶Awake, north wind,
and come, south wind!
Blow on my garden,
that its fragrance may spread abroad.
Let my lover come into his garden
and taste its choice fruits.

Lover

5 I have come into my garden, my sister, my bride;
I have gathered my myrrh with my spice.
I have eaten my honeycomb and my honey;
I have drunk my wine and my milk.

Friends

Eat, O friends, and drink;
drink your fill, O lovers.

Beloved

²I slept but my heart was awake.
Listen! My lover is knocking:

ᵃ15 Or *I am* (spoken by the *Beloved*)

▣ ▦▦▦▦▦▦▦▦ **STRENGTHENING RELATIONSHIPS** ▦▦▦▦▦▦▦▦ ⬍

5:1
Marriage

No sculptor could have fashioned two people better suited for one another than these. He is the king of a great nation, and she is his chosen bride. Their love has been the talk of the court, truly a romance for all seasons. And God approves of their love as they consummate it on their wedding day.

Recognizing God's approval lifts sex to a sacred level. No wonder Solomon uses such poetic delicacy and modesty to extol the beauty of their first night together. He compares his bride to a lovely garden and fountain (chapter 4, verses 12–15) that has been sealed and locked because Solomon's bride has kept herself for him. The king praises her for waiting while at the same time gently requesting that she give herself to him as his wife.

Her response is equally poetic and clear (chapter 4, verse 16). When the newlyweds have consummated their marriage, Solomon declares his joy by using similar imagery. His bride is overwhelmingly beautiful, as refreshing as enchanting spices and as intoxicating as wine, and the king delights in her.

Their experience is a mystery created by the God who says, through the voice of the friends, "Drink your fill, O lovers" (chapter 5, verse 1). With those words, God shows his approval of the sexual pleasure Solomon and his bride give and receive.

The sensual imagery included in these chapters is intended to give us a picture of the wonderful nature of human sexuality. When carried out in the appropriate framework of marriage, sex is truly a celebration!

"Open to me, my sister, my darling,
  my dove, my flawless one.
My head is drenched with dew,
  my hair with the dampness of the night."
³I have taken off my robe—
  must I put it on again?
I have washed my feet—
  must I soil them again?
⁴My lover thrust his hand through the latch-opening;
  my heart began to pound for him.
⁵I arose to open for my lover,
  and my hands dripped with myrrh,
my fingers with flowing myrrh,
  on the handles of the lock.
⁶I opened for my lover,
  but my lover had left; he was gone.
  My heart sank at his departure.ᵃ
I looked for him but did not find him.
I called him but he did not answer.
⁷The watchmen found me
  as they made their rounds in the city.
They beat me, they bruised me;
  they took away my cloak,
  those watchmen of the walls!
⁸O daughters of Jerusalem, I charge you—
  if you find my lover,
what will you tell him?
  Tell him I am faint with love.

Friends

⁹How is your beloved better than others,
  most beautiful of women?
How is your beloved better than others,
  that you charge us so?

Beloved

¹⁰My lover is radiant and ruddy,
  outstanding among ten thousand.
¹¹His head is purest gold;
  his hair is wavy
  and black as a raven.
¹²His eyes are like doves
  by the water streams,
washed in milk,
  mounted like jewels.
¹³His cheeks are like beds of spice
  yielding perfume.
His lips are like lilies
  dripping with myrrh.
¹⁴His arms are rods of gold
  set with chrysolite.

ᵃ6 Or heart had gone out to him when he spoke

His body is like polished ivory
  decorated with sapphires. [a]
[15]His legs are pillars of marble
  set on bases of pure gold.
His appearance is like Lebanon,
  choice as its cedars.
[16]His mouth is sweetness itself;
  he is altogether lovely.
This is my lover, this my friend,
  O daughters of Jerusalem.

Friends

6 Where has your lover gone,
  most beautiful of women?
Which way did your lover
    turn,
  that we may look for him
    with you?

Beloved

[2]My lover has gone down to
    his garden,
  to the beds of spices,
to browse in the gardens
  and to gather lilies.
[3]I am my lover's and my lover
    is mine;
  he browses among the lilies.

Lover

[4]You are beautiful, my darling, as Tirzah,
  lovely as Jerusalem,
  majestic as troops with banners.
[5]Turn your eyes from me;
  they overwhelm me.
Your hair is like a flock of goats
  descending from Gilead.
[6]Your teeth are like a flock of sheep
  coming up from the washing.
Each has its twin,
  not one of them is alone.
[7]Your temples behind your veil
  are like the halves of a pomegranate.
[8]Sixty queens there may be,
  and eighty concubines,
  and virgins beyond number;
[9]but my dove, my perfect one, is unique,
  the only daughter of her mother,
  the favorite of the one who bore her.
The maidens saw her and called her blessed;
  the queens and concubines praised her.

▣ ▦▦▦▦ STRENGTHENING RELATIONSHIPS ▦▦▦▦ ⬍

5:16
Marriage

What kind of person makes the best lover—
one who has had a lot of "experience"? One
who's read the books and knows the techniques?

According to this passage, the best lover is
a member of the opposite sex whom you consider your *friend*. A marriage partner should
be someone you trust, someone you like to be
with. Romance flourishes in an atmosphere of
trust, not performance.

In other words, strong love creates great
sex—not the other way around!

---

a 14 Or lapis lazuli

Friends

10Who is this that appears like the dawn,
    fair as the moon, bright as the sun,
    majestic as the stars in procession?

Lover

11I went down to the grove of nut trees
    to look at the new growth in the valley,
  to see if the vines had budded
    or the pomegranates were in bloom.
12Before I realized it,
    my desire set me among the royal chariots of my people.*a*

Friends

13Come back, come back, O Shulammite;
    come back, come back, that we may gaze on you!

Lover

Why would you gaze on the Shulammite
    as on the dance of Mahanaim?

7 How beautiful your sandaled feet,
    O prince's daughter!
Your graceful legs are like jewels,
    the work of a craftsman's hands.
2Your navel is a rounded goblet
    that never lacks blended wine.
Your waist is a mound of wheat
    encircled by lilies.
3Your breasts are like two fawns,
    twins of a gazelle.
4Your neck is like an ivory tower.
Your eyes are the pools of Heshbon
    by the gate of Bath Rabbim.
Your nose is like the tower of Lebanon
    looking toward Damascus.
5Your head crowns you like Mount Carmel.
    Your hair is like royal tapestry;
    the king is held captive by its tresses.
6How beautiful you are and how pleasing,
    O love, with your delights!
7Your stature is like that of the palm,
    and your breasts like clusters of fruit.
8I said, "I will climb the palm tree;
    I will take hold of its fruit."
May your breasts be like the clusters of the vine,
    the fragrance of your breath like apples,
9   and your mouth like the best wine.

a 12 Or *among the chariots of Amminadab*; or *among the chariots of the people of the prince*

Beloved

May the wine go straight to my lover,
   flowing gently over lips and teeth. *a*
¹⁰I belong to my lover,
   and his desire is for me.
¹¹Come, my lover, let us go to the countryside,
   let us spend the night in the villages. *b*
¹²Let us go early to the vineyards
   to see if the vines have budded,
if their blossoms have opened,
   and if the pomegranates are in bloom—
there I will give you my love.
¹³The mandrakes send out their fragrance,
   and at our door is every delicacy,
both new and old,
   that I have stored up for you, my lover.

8 If only you were to me like a brother,
   who was nursed at my mother's breasts!
Then, if I found you outside,
   I would kiss you,
   and no one would despise me.
²I would lead you
   and bring you to my mother's
     house—
   she who has taught me.
I would give you spiced wine to
     drink,
   the nectar of my pomegranates.
³His left arm is under my head
   and his right arm embraces
     me.
⁴Daughters of Jerusalem, I charge
     you:
   Do not arouse or awaken love
   until it so desires.

🖵 ▦▦▦▦ **ADDRESSING QUESTIONS** ▦▦▦▦ ↩

8:6–7
Human Experience **Q**

This passage describes true love in all of its glory—its power rivals death; it burns like a consuming fire; it stands strong against the storms of life; it can't be bought. In other words, love isn't something we can toy with. We must treat it with utmost care and respect, since it so deeply affects the core of our human experience.

Friends

⁵Who is this coming up from the desert
   leaning on her lover?

Beloved

Under the apple tree I roused you;
   there your mother conceived you,
   there she who was in labor gave you birth.
⁶Place me like a seal over your heart,
   like a seal on your arm;
for love is as strong as death,

     its jealousy*a* unyielding as the grave.*b*
  It burns like blazing fire,
     like a mighty flame.*c*
 7Many waters cannot quench love;
     rivers cannot wash it away.
  If one were to give
     all the wealth of his house for love,
     it*d* would be utterly scorned.

Friends

 8We have a young sister,
     and her breasts are not yet grown.
  What shall we do for our sister
     for the day she is spoken for?
 9If she is a wall,
     we will build towers of silver on her.
  If she is a door,
     we will enclose her with panels of cedar.

Beloved

 10I am a wall,
     and my breasts are like towers.
  Thus I have become in his eyes
     like one bringing contentment.
 11Solomon had a vineyard in Baal Hamon;
     he let out his vineyard to tenants.
  Each was to bring for its fruit
     a thousand shekels*e* of silver.
 12But my own vineyard is mine to give;
     the thousand shekels are for you, O Solomon,
     and two hundred*f* are for those who tend its fruit.

Lover

 13You who dwell in the gardens
     with friends in attendance,
     let me hear your voice!

Beloved

 14Come away, my lover,
     and be like a gazelle
  or like a young stag
     on the spice-laden mountains.

---

a6 Or *ardor*   *b6* Hebrew *Sheol*   *c6* Or / *like the very flame of the* LORD   *d7* Or *he*   *e11* That is, about 25 pounds (about 11.5 kilograms); also in verse 12   *f12* That is, about 5 pounds (about 2.3 kilograms)

Let me start by saying I was born and raised in a religious family. As a youth I attended parochial schools, and participated in all the rituals of my religion. I was even married in a church. I always believed in God, but I never realized that I didn't really know him. I never truly learned what the Bible taught as a result, and was never fully satisfied with my beliefs. I quit going to church, except for on religious holidays, when I was a teen.

In later years I married and my wife began studying the Bible with a woman who was a Jehovah's Witness. When she became confused about their teachings, she asked if I would join the study. She felt I would be more knowledgeable about the Bible and better able to evaluate what the woman was teaching. I discovered that I didn't know as much about the Bible as I thought I did! We continued to study with this woman and her husband for four years.

During the third year of our study we began to have doubts about what we were being taught. Still we stuck with our mentors, fearful that they held the only truth and that people who weren't Jehovah's Witnesses would be destroyed at Armageddon.

I was fortunate enough to work with a Christian man at my job, and we discussed religious matters whenever we worked together. I would hit him with questions and he would return with Biblical perspectives on my questions the next day. We had no idea that while we were doing this we were searching the Word of God and becoming much stronger because of it. My newfound hunger for the Bible made me realize that nothing in my early education or in my four years of Bible study had shown me how to be saved. I reached a point where I wanted to find out.

We knew a Christian pastor who lived in our neighborhood, so we called him up and told him we were studying with the Witnesses and that we were confused about the things we were learning. We asked if he would meet with us, and he came over that evening. That night, as the hours went on, he explained to us how we could gain salvation. We learned that a person is saved only by grace, through faith and not by works (Ephesians 2:8–9). I wasn't completely sure what all this conversation meant, but I definitely knew the Witnesses were wrong.

We began attending a nondenominational church, and shortly thereafter joined a small group within the church. As I was sitting in a service one day, the pastor's message struck me. He talked about how Christ's death covers all of our sins and shortcomings no matter what they are, and how each and every person who comes to the cross is on equal footing before him. I finally realized how much Christ loved me and what a fool I had been all of my life. I finally realized that I needed Jesus to save me and that I couldn't save myself. That night, all the puzzle pieces snapped into place.

My wife and I are now involved in an outreach to Jehovah's Witnesses. We hope to help some of those people break free from the Watchtower Society. We also want to help families whose loved ones are Witnesses to understand their teachings and show them how to Biblically counter those teachings.

I thank the Lord every day for the change he has made in my life, and for all he has done for me and my family. I surrender my life to him every day, and he never fails to amaze me.

ISAIAH

Introduction

THE BOTTOM LINE

In this book you'll come face-to-face with a "no compromise" approach to spirituality: Either follow God or fully renounce him. Isaiah spoke to a divided Israel during a time when success, luxury and complacency had dulled the minds of those who said they knew God. Their worship was a mere formality—a simple matter of going through the motions. Into such a setting, the God who often comforts the disturbed had to disturb the comfortable. Through Isaiah, God's Spirit lit a fire that burns to this day. Step into its light, and let it burn away any exterior of pride and complacency that may cover your life. Like purified gold, you'll find a rich deposit of precious ore at the end of the encounter.

CENTRAL IDEAS

■ People who are outwardly "religious" yet refuse to let God affect their lifestyle are subject to God's discipline.

■ God is just, yet shows mercy; he is justifiably angry toward his sinful people, yet he loves them tenderly.

■ Although many people turn away, God always sustains a "remnant" who remain loyal to him.

■ Isaiah foresaw a time when the Messiah would come to set things right.

OUTLINE

1 Part 1: Judgment (chs. 1–39)

A Messages of rebuke and promise (chs. 1–6)

B Prophecies regarding Judah (chs. 7–12)

C Judgment and promise of God's kingdom (chs. 13–27)

D Consequences of unfaithfulness (chs. 28–35)

E Historical transition (chs. 36–39)

2 Part 2: Comfort (chs. 40–66)

A Deliverance and restoration (chs. 40–48)

B The suffering servant's ministry (the Messiah); Israel's restoration (chs. 49–57)

C Everlasting deliverance/Everlasting judgment (chs. 58–66)

TITLE

Isaiah is often referred to as the greatest of Israel's prophets. This is his story.

AUTHOR AND READERS

Isaiah wrote this book to the people of Judah (southern Israel). The revelations and visions contained in this book speak to their historical setting, yet the warnings and promises are timeless in their application to God's people in all ages.

When Dan Piske strolled out of the post office in Bend, Oregon, he had no idea what he carried in his hands. He thought it was just a sheet of 29-cent stamps. It was that—but much more.

On that sheet, which commemorated 20 heroes of the Old West, was one stamp that bore the image of Bill Pickett—or what was *supposed* to be the image of Bill Pickett. Earlier, when surviving Pickett family members had seen the stamp, they noticed that the picture was of Bill's brother, Ben. They immediately brought the error to the attention of postal authorities, who scratched their heads and scrambled to fix the problem. The misprint marked the first time in 147 years that the Postal Service had issued a stamp with an incorrect image. Not wanting to break their winning streak, the Postal Service recalled the 250 million sheets in the series.

But a few sheets had slipped out anyway. And Dan Piske happened to pick up one for a few dollars. Dan's father, a retired postal worker, spotted the rare stamp and told Dan not to use it. It was good advice—*the stamp was worth close to one million dollars!*

That day a million-dollar stamp carried a utility bill to its destination!

At about the same time Dan was celebrating his good fortune, another man bought one of the few sheets containing the Ben-not-Bill Pickett stamp. Not knowing what he had, he tore it off the sheet, licked it, and placed it on an envelope. That day a million-dollar stamp carried a utility bill to its destination!

Imagine yourself being that man. You stare at the place where the torn-off stamp had been and feel sick when you think that you once owned such a rare item—and treated it as something common. It had so much more to offer you, yet you used it in such an ordinary way, not even beginning to experience its rich potential.

That's similar to what the prophet Isaiah felt. He knew what spiritual treasure he had in his relationship with God. What caused him anguish was knowing that his countrymen had no such appreciation for God. They viewed their role within God's plan as no big deal. "God will always be there for us," they presumed. But they had turned away from him. And the time was coming—either because of death or national calamity—that their opportunity to know God in this life would pass.

Have you understood God's wish to have a relationship with you? Have you sensed his desire to come into your life and make an eternal difference? What have you done with that offer—set it aside for later? Considered it an inconvenience, or even a disruption? This is your opportunity, says Isaiah. Don't miss it. So much is at stake. And if you send God away, even a million dollars will seem a tolerable loss in comparison.

Turn to Isaiah chapter 55, verses 6–7 (page 965) for more on God's invitation through the prophet Isaiah.

TIME LINE					
	The poet Homer's *Iliad* and *Odyssey* written down (760 B.C.)	Book of Isaiah written (c. 700–680 B.C.)		Greek lawmaker Draco establishes harsh ("Draconian") law code—death for nearly every crime (621 B.C.)	The mathematician Pythagoras studies musical harmonics (540 B.C.)
800 BC	750	700	650	600	550	500
	Rome is founded (753 B.C.)	Isaiah's ministry to Judah (c. 740–681 B.C.)	Soldering of iron invented (c. 650)	Jeremiah's ministry in Judah (c. 626–585 B.C.)	Fall of Jerusalem (586 B.C.)

ISAIAH

1 The vision concerning Judah and Jerusalem that Isaiah son of Amoz saw during the reigns of Uzziah, Jotham, Ahaz and Hezekiah, kings of Judah.

A Rebellious Nation

²Hear, O heavens! Listen, O earth!
  For the LORD has spoken:
"I reared children and brought them up,
  but they have rebelled against me.
³The ox knows his master,
  the donkey his owner's manger,
but Israel does not know,
  my people do not understand."

⁴Ah, sinful nation,
  a people loaded with guilt,
a brood of evildoers,
  children given to corruption!
They have forsaken the LORD;
  they have spurned the Holy One of Israel
  and turned their backs on him.

⁵Why should you be beaten anymore?
  Why do you persist in rebellion?
Your whole head is injured,
  your whole heart afflicted.
⁶From the sole of your foot to the top of your head
  there is no soundness—
only wounds and welts
  and open sores,
not cleansed or bandaged
  or soothed with oil.

⁷Your country is desolate,
  your cities burned with fire;
your fields are being stripped by foreigners
  right before you,
  laid waste as when overthrown by strangers.
⁸The Daughter of Zion is left
  like a shelter in a vineyard,
like a hut in a field of melons,
  like a city under siege.
⁹Unless the LORD Almighty
  had left us some survivors,
we would have become like Sodom,
  we would have been like Gomorrah.

¹⁰Hear the word of the LORD,
  you rulers of Sodom;

listen to the law of our God,
  you people of Gomorrah!
11"The multitude of your sacrifices—
  what are they to me?" says the LORD.
"I have more than enough of burnt offerings,
  of rams and the fat of fattened animals;
I have no pleasure
  in the blood of bulls and lambs and goats.
12When you come to appear before me,
  who has asked this of you,
  this trampling of my courts?
13Stop bringing meaningless offerings!
  Your incense is detestable to me.
New Moons, Sabbaths and convocations—
  I cannot bear your evil assemblies.
14Your New Moon festivals and your appointed feasts
  my soul hates.
They have become a burden to me;
  I am weary of bearing them.
15When you spread out your hands in prayer,
  I will hide my eyes from you;
even if you offer many prayers,
  I will not listen.
Your hands are full of blood;
16   wash and make yourselves clean.
Take your evil deeds
  out of my sight!
Stop doing wrong,
17   learn to do right!
Seek justice,
  encourage the oppressed. a
Defend the cause of the fatherless,
  plead the case of the widow.

18"Come now, let us reason together,"
  says the LORD.
"Though your sins are like scarlet,
  they shall be as white as snow;
though they are red as crimson,
  they shall be like wool.
19If you are willing and obedient,
  you will eat the best from the land;
20but if you resist and rebel,
  you will be devoured by the sword."
                    For the mouth of the LORD has spoken.

21See how the faithful city
  has become a harlot!
She once was full of justice;
  righteousness used to dwell in her—
  but now murderers!
22Your silver has become dross,
  your choice wine is diluted with water.

a 17 Or / rebuke the oppressor

23Your rulers are rebels,
    companions of thieves;
they all love bribes
    and chase after gifts.
They do not defend the cause of the fatherless;
    the widow's case does not come before them.
24Therefore the Lord, the LORD Almighty,
    the Mighty One of Israel, declares:
"Ah, I will get relief from my foes
    and avenge myself on my enemies.
25I will turn my hand against you;
    I will thoroughly purge away your dross
    and remove all your impurities.

26I will restore your judges as in days of
        old,
    your counselors as at the beginning.
Afterward you will be called
    the City of Righteousness,
    the Faithful City."

27Zion will be redeemed with justice,
    her penitent ones with righteousness.
28But rebels and sinners will both be
        broken,
    and those who forsake the LORD
        will perish.

29"You will be ashamed because of the
        sacred oaks
    in which you have delighted;
you will be disgraced because of the
        gardens
    that you have chosen.
30You will be like an oak with fading
        leaves,
    like a garden without water.

 REASONS TO BELIEVE

1:18
The Christian Experience

This passage shows us that believing and trusting in God makes good sense.

Through the prophet Isaiah, God puts this challenge before us. Loosely paraphrased, God says to us, "Let's sit down and talk about this. The truth is that I can offer you freedom from your sin, no matter how much it has stained your life. You can either accept that forgiveness and enjoy its benefits (verse 19) or reject it and face the consequences" (verse 20).

It is "reasonable" to admit our sinfulness. God invites us to do so—to stop running from him. Through his power, our sin can be changed from scarlet to white. That's not a transformation we can accomplish on our own. But the Bible's message is that God can and will do it for us—if we turn to him and ask.

31The mighty man will become tinder
    and his work a spark;
both will burn together,
    with no one to quench the fire."

The Mountain of the LORD

2 This is what Isaiah son of Amoz saw concerning Judah and Jerusalem:

2In the last days

the mountain of the LORD's temple will be established
    as chief among the mountains;
it will be raised above the hills,
    and all nations will stream to it.

3Many peoples will come and say,

"Come, let us go up to the mountain of the LORD,
　to the house of the God of Jacob.
He will teach us his ways,
　so that we may walk in his paths."
The law will go out from Zion,
　the word of the LORD from Jerusalem.
⁴He will judge between the nations
　and will settle disputes for many peoples.
They will beat their swords into plowshares
　and their spears into pruning hooks.
Nation will not take up sword against nation,
　nor will they train for war anymore.

⁵Come, O house of Jacob,
　let us walk in the light of the LORD.

The Day of the LORD

⁶You have abandoned your people,
　the house of Jacob.
They are full of superstitions from the East;
　they practice divination like the Philistines
　and clasp hands with pagans.
⁷Their land is full of silver and gold;
　there is no end to their treasures.
Their land is full of horses;
　there is no end to their chariots.
⁸Their land is full of idols;
　they bow down to the work of their hands,
　to what their fingers have made.
⁹So man will be brought low
　and mankind humbled—
　do not forgive them.ᵃ

¹⁰Go into the rocks,
　hide in the ground
from dread of the LORD
　and the splendor of his majesty!
¹¹The eyes of the arrogant man will be humbled
　and the pride of men brought low;
　the LORD alone will be exalted in that day.

¹²The LORD Almighty has a day in store
　for all the proud and lofty,
　for all that is exalted
　(and they will be humbled),
¹³for all the cedars of Lebanon, tall and lofty,
　and all the oaks of Bashan,
¹⁴for all the towering mountains
　and all the high hills,
¹⁵for every lofty tower
　and every fortified wall,
¹⁶for every trading shipᵇ
　and every stately vessel.

ᵃ9 Or not raise them up   ᵇ16 Hebrew every ship of Tarshish

¹⁷The arrogance of man will be brought low
 and the pride of men humbled;
 the Lord alone will be exalted in that day,
¹⁸ and the idols will totally disappear.

¹⁹Men will flee to caves in the rocks
 and to holes in the ground
from dread of the Lord
 and the splendor of his majesty,
 when he rises to shake the earth.
²⁰In that day men will throw away
 to the rodents and bats
their idols of silver and idols of gold,
 which they made to worship.
²¹They will flee to caverns in the rocks
 and to the overhanging crags
from dread of the Lord
 and the splendor of his majesty,
 when he rises to shake the earth.

²²Stop trusting in man,
 who has but a breath in his nostrils.
Of what account is he?

Judgment on Jerusalem and Judah

3 See now, the Lord,
 the Lord Almighty,
is about to take from Jerusalem and Judah
 both supply and support:
all supplies of food and all supplies of water,
² the hero and warrior,
the judge and prophet,
 the soothsayer and elder,
³the captain of fifty and man of rank,
 the counselor, skilled craftsman and clever enchanter.

⁴I will make boys their officials;
 mere children will govern them.
⁵People will oppress each other—
 man against man, neighbor against neighbor.
The young will rise up against the old,
 the base against the honorable.

⁶A man will seize one of his brothers
 at his father's home, and say,
"You have a cloak, you be our leader;
 take charge of this heap of ruins!"
⁷But in that day he will cry out,
 "I have no remedy.
I have no food or clothing in my house;
 do not make me the leader of the people."

⁸Jerusalem staggers,
 Judah is falling;
their words and deeds are against the Lord,
 defying his glorious presence.

⁹The look on their faces testifies against them;
    they parade their sin like Sodom;
    they do not hide it.
Woe to them!
    They have brought disaster upon themselves.

¹⁰Tell the righteous it will be well with them,
    for they will enjoy the fruit of their deeds.
¹¹Woe to the wicked! Disaster is upon them!
    They will be paid back for what their hands have done.

¹²Youths oppress my people,
    women rule over them.
O my people, your guides lead you astray;
    they turn you from the path.

¹³The LORD takes his place in court;
    he rises to judge the people.
¹⁴The LORD enters into judgment
    against the elders and leaders of his people:
"It is you who have ruined my vineyard;
    the plunder from the poor is in your houses.
¹⁵What do you mean by crushing my people
    and grinding the faces of the poor?"
                    declares the Lord, the LORD Almighty.

¹⁶The LORD says,
    "The women of Zion are haughty,
walking along with outstretched necks,
    flirting with their eyes,
tripping along with mincing steps,
    with ornaments jingling on their ankles.
¹⁷Therefore the Lord will bring sores on the heads of the women of
        Zion;
    the LORD will make their scalps bald."

¹⁸In that day the Lord will snatch away their finery: the bangles and headbands and crescent necklaces, ¹⁹the earrings and bracelets and veils, ²⁰the headdresses and ankle chains and sashes, the perfume bottles and charms, ²¹the signet rings and nose rings, ²²the fine robes and the capes and cloaks, the purses ²³and mirrors, and the linen garments and tiaras and shawls.

²⁴Instead of fragrance there will be a stench;
    instead of a sash, a rope;
instead of well-dressed hair, baldness;
    instead of fine clothing, sackcloth;
    instead of beauty, branding.
²⁵Your men will fall by the sword,
    your warriors in battle.
²⁶The gates of Zion will lament and mourn;
    destitute, she will sit on the ground.

4 In that day seven women
    will take hold of one man
and say, "We will eat our own food
    and provide our own clothes;

> only let us be called by your name.
> Take away our disgrace!"

The Branch of the LORD

²In that day the Branch of the LORD will be beautiful and glorious, and the fruit of the land will be the pride and glory of the survivors in Israel. ³Those who are left in Zion, who remain in Jerusalem, will be called holy, all who are recorded among the living in Jerusalem. ⁴The Lord will wash away the filth of the women of Zion; he will cleanse the bloodstains from Jerusalem by a spirit[a] of judgment and a spirit[a] of fire. ⁵Then the LORD will create over all of Mount Zion and over those who assemble there a cloud of smoke by day and a glow of flaming fire by night; over all the glory will be a canopy. ⁶It will be a shelter and shade from the heat of the day, and a refuge and hiding place from the storm and rain.

The Song of the Vineyard

> ## 5
>
> I will sing for the one I love
>   a song about his vineyard:
> My loved one had a vineyard
>   on a fertile hillside.
> ²He dug it up and cleared it of stones
>   and planted it with the choicest vines.
> He built a watchtower in it
>   and cut out a winepress as well.
> Then he looked for a crop of good grapes,
>   but it yielded only bad fruit.
>
> ³"Now you dwellers in Jerusalem and men of Judah,
>   judge between me and my vineyard.
> ⁴What more could have been done for my vineyard
>   than I have done for it?
> When I looked for good grapes,
>   why did it yield only bad?
> ⁵Now I will tell you
>   what I am going to do to my vineyard:
> I will take away its hedge,
>   and it will be destroyed;
> I will break down its wall,
>   and it will be trampled.
> ⁶I will make it a wasteland,
>   neither pruned nor cultivated,
>   and briers and thorns will grow there.
> I will command the clouds
>   not to rain on it."
>
> ⁷The vineyard of the LORD Almighty
>   is the house of Israel,
> and the men of Judah
>   are the garden of his delight.
> And he looked for justice, but saw bloodshed;
>   for righteousness, but heard cries of distress.

ᵃ 4 Or the Spirit

Woes and Judgments

8Woe to you who add house to house
    and join field to field
till no space is left
    and you live alone in the land.

9The LORD Almighty has declared in my hearing:

"Surely the great houses will become desolate,
    the fine mansions left without occupants.
10A ten-acre*a* vineyard will produce only a bath*b* of wine,
    a homer*c* of seed only an ephah*d* of grain."

11Woe to those who rise early in the morning
    to run after their drinks,
who stay up late at night
    till they are inflamed with wine.
12They have harps and lyres at their banquets,
    tambourines and flutes and wine,
but they have no regard for the deeds of the LORD,
    no respect for the work of his hands.
13Therefore my people will go into exile
    for lack of understanding;
their men of rank will die of hunger
    and their masses will be parched with thirst.
14Therefore the grave*e* enlarges its appetite
    and opens its mouth without limit;
into it will descend their nobles and masses
    with all their brawlers and revelers.
15So man will be brought low
    and mankind humbled,
    the eyes of the arrogant humbled.
16But the LORD Almighty will be exalted by his justice,
    and the holy God will show himself holy by his righteousness.
17Then sheep will graze as in their own pasture;
    lambs will feed*f* among the ruins of the rich.

18Woe to those who draw sin along with cords of deceit,
    and wickedness as with cart ropes,
19to those who say, "Let God hurry,
    let him hasten his work
    so we may see it.
Let it approach,
    let the plan of the Holy One of Israel come,
    so we may know it."

20Woe to those who call evil good
    and good evil,
who put darkness for light
    and light for darkness,

a10 Hebrew *ten-yoke,* that is, the land plowed by 10 yoke of oxen in one day   *b10* That is, probably about 6 gallons (about 22 liters)   *c10* That is, probably about 6 bushels (about 220 liters)   *d10* That is, probably about 3/5 bushel (about 22 liters)   *e14* Hebrew *Sheol*   *f17* Septuagint; Hebrew / *strangers will eat*

who put bitter for sweet
　and sweet for bitter.
21Woe to those who are wise in their own eyes
　and clever in their own sight.

22Woe to those who are heroes at drinking wine
　and champions at mixing drinks,
23who acquit the guilty for a bribe,
　but deny justice to the innocent.
24Therefore, as tongues of fire lick up straw
　and as dry grass sinks down in the flames,
so their roots will decay
　and their flowers blow away like dust;
for they have rejected the law of the LORD Almighty
　and spurned the word of the Holy One of Israel.
25Therefore the LORD's anger burns against his people;
　his hand is raised and he strikes them down.
The mountains shake,
　and the dead bodies are like refuse in the streets.

Yet for all this, his anger is not turned away,
　his hand is still upraised.

26He lifts up a banner for the distant nations,
　he whistles for those at the ends of the earth.
Here they come,
　swiftly and speedily!
27Not one of them grows tired or stumbles,
　not one slumbers or sleeps;
not a belt is loosened at the waist,
　not a sandal thong is broken.
28Their arrows are sharp,
　all their bows are strung;
their horses' hoofs seem like flint,
　their chariot wheels like a whirlwind.
29Their roar is like that of the lion,
　they roar like young lions;
they growl as they seize their prey
　and carry it off with no one to rescue.
30In that day they will roar over it
　like the roaring of the sea.
And if one looks at the land,
　he will see darkness and distress;
　even the light will be darkened by the clouds.

Isaiah's Commission

6 In the year that King Uzziah died, I saw the Lord seated on a throne, high and exalted, and the train of his robe filled the temple. 2Above him were seraphs, each with six wings: With two wings they covered their faces, with two they covered their feet, and with two they were flying. 3And they were calling to one another:

"Holy, holy, holy is the LORD Almighty;
　the whole earth is full of his glory."

⁴At the sound of their voices the doorposts and thresholds shook and the temple was filled with smoke.

⁵"Woe to me!" I cried. "I am ruined! For I am a man of unclean lips, and I live among a people of unclean lips, and my eyes have seen the King, the LORD Almighty."

⁶Then one of the seraphs flew to me with a live coal in his hand, which he had taken with tongs from the altar. ⁷With it he touched my mouth and said, "See, this has touched your lips; your guilt is taken away and your sin atoned for."

⁸Then I heard the voice of the Lord saying, "Whom shall I send? And who will go for us?"
And I said, "Here am I. Send me!"

⁹He said, "Go and tell this people:

> " 'Be ever hearing, but never
>   understanding;
> be ever seeing, but never
>   perceiving.'
> ¹⁰Make the heart of this people
>   calloused;
> make their ears dull
>   and close their eyes.ᵃ
> Otherwise they might see with
>   their eyes,
> hear with their ears,
> understand with their hearts,
> and turn and be healed."

¹¹Then I said, "For how long, O Lord?"
And he answered:

> "Until the cities lie ruined
>   and without inhabitant,
> until the houses are left
>   deserted
>   and the fields ruined and
>   ravaged,
> ¹²until the LORD has sent everyone
>   far away
>   and the land is utterly
>   forsaken.
> ¹³And though a tenth remains in the land,
>   it will again be laid waste.
> But as the terebinth and oak
>   leave stumps when they are cut down,
>   so the holy seed will be the stump in the land."

The Sign of Immanuel

7 When Ahaz son of Jotham, the son of Uzziah, was king of Judah, King Rezin of Aram and Pekah son of Remaliah king of Israel marched up to fight against Jerusalem, but they could not overpower it.

²Now the house of David was told, "Aram has allied itself withᵇ Ephraim"; so the hearts of Ahaz and his people were shaken, as the trees of the forest are shaken by the wind.

ᵃ9,10 Hebrew; Septuagint 'You will be ever hearing, but never understanding; / you will be ever seeing, but never perceiving.' / ¹⁰This people's heart has become calloused; / they hardly hear with their ears, / and they have closed their eyes   ᵇ2 Or has set up camp in

³Then the LORD said to Isaiah, "Go out, you and your son Shear-Jashub,ᵃ to meet Ahaz at the end of the aqueduct of the Upper Pool, on the road to the Washerman's Field. ⁴Say to him, 'Be careful, keep calm and don't be afraid. Do not lose heart because of these two smoldering stubs of firewood—because of the fierce anger of Rezin and Aram and of the son of Remaliah. ⁵Aram, Ephraim and Remaliah's son have plotted your ruin, saying, ⁶"Let us invade Judah; let us tear it apart and divide it among ourselves, and make the son of Tabeel king over it." ⁷Yet this is what the Sovereign LORD says:

> " 'It will not take place,
>   it will not happen,
> ⁸for the head of Aram is Damascus,
>   and the head of Damascus is only Rezin.
> Within sixty-five years
>   Ephraim will be too shattered to be a people.
> ⁹The head of Ephraim is Samaria,
>   and the head of Samaria is only Remaliah's son.
> If you do not stand firm in your faith,
>   you will not stand at all.' "

¹⁰Again the LORD spoke to Ahaz, ¹¹"Ask the LORD your God for a sign, whether in the deepest depths or in the highest heights."

¹²But Ahaz said, "I will not ask; I will not put the LORD to the test."

¹³Then Isaiah said, "Hear now, you house of David! Is it not enough to try the patience of men? Will you try the patience of my God also? ¹⁴Therefore the Lord himself will give youᵇ a sign: The virgin will be with child and will give birth to a son, andᶜ will call him Immanuel.ᵈ ¹⁵He will eat curds and honey when he knows enough to reject the wrong and choose the right. ¹⁶But before the boy knows enough to reject the wrong and choose the right, the land of the two kings you dread will be laid waste. ¹⁷The LORD will bring on you and on your people and on the house of your father a time unlike any since Ephraim broke away from Judah—he will bring the king of Assyria."

¹⁸In that day the LORD will whistle for flies from the distant streams of Egypt and for bees from the land of Assyria. ¹⁹They will all come and settle in the steep ravines and in the crevices in the rocks, on all the thornbushes and at all the water holes. ²⁰In that day the Lord will use a razor hired from beyond the Riverᵉ—the king of Assyria—to shave your head and the hair of your legs, and to take off your beards also. ²¹In that day, a man will keep alive a young cow and two goats. ²²And because of the abundance of the milk they give, he will have curds to eat. All who remain in the land will eat curds and honey. ²³In that day, in every place where there were a thousand vines worth a thousand silver shekels,ᶠ there will be only briers and thorns. ²⁴Men will go there with bow and arrow, for the land will be covered with briers and thorns. ²⁵As for all the hills once cultivated by the hoe, you will no longer go there for fear of the briers and thorns; they will become places where cattle are turned loose and where sheep run.

Assyria, the LORD's Instrument

8 The LORD said to me, "Take a large scroll and write on it with an ordinary pen: Maher-Shalal-Hash-Baz.ᵍ ²And I will call in Uriah the priest and Zechariah son of Jeberekiah as reliable witnesses for me."

³Then I went to the prophetess, and she conceived and gave birth to a son. And the LORD said to me, "Name him Maher-Shalal-Hash-Baz. ⁴Before the boy knows how to say 'My father' or 'My mother,' the wealth of Damascus and the plunder of Samaria will be carried off by the king of Assyria."

ᵃ3 Shear-Jashub means a remnant will return.   ᵇ14 The Hebrew is plural.   ᶜ14 Masoretic Text; Dead Sea Scrolls and he or and they   ᵈ14 Immanuel means God with us.   ᵉ20 That is, the Euphrates   ᶠ23 That is, about 25 pounds (about 11.5 kilograms)   ᵍ1 Maher-Shalal-Hash-Baz means quick to the plunder, swift to the spoil; also in verse 3.

⁵The Lord spoke to me again:

> ⁶"Because this people has rejected
>   the gently flowing waters of Shiloah
> and rejoices over Rezin
>   and the son of Remaliah,
> ⁷therefore the Lord is about to bring against them
>   the mighty floodwaters of the River [a]—
>   the king of Assyria with all his pomp.
> It will overflow all its channels,
>   run over all its banks
> ⁸and sweep on into Judah, swirling over it,
>   passing through it and reaching up to the neck.
> Its outspread wings will cover the breadth of your land,
>   O Immanuel [b]!"

> ⁹Raise the war cry, [c] you nations, and be shattered!
>   Listen, all you distant lands.
> Prepare for battle, and be shattered!
>   Prepare for battle, and be shattered!
> ¹⁰Devise your strategy, but it will be thwarted;
>   propose your plan, but it will not stand,
>   for God is with us. [d]

Fear God

¹¹The Lord spoke to me with his strong hand upon me, warning me not to follow the way of this people. He said:

> ¹²"Do not call conspiracy
>   everything that these people call conspiracy [e];
> do not fear what they fear,
>   and do not dread it.
> ¹³The Lord Almighty is the one you are to regard as holy,
>   he is the one you are to fear,
>   he is the one you are to dread,
> ¹⁴and he will be a sanctuary;
>   but for both houses of Israel he will be
> a stone that causes men to stumble
>   and a rock that makes them fall.
> And for the people of Jerusalem he will be
>   a trap and a snare.
> ¹⁵Many of them will stumble;
>   they will fall and be broken,
>   they will be snared and captured."

> ¹⁶Bind up the testimony
>   and seal up the law among my disciples.
> ¹⁷I will wait for the Lord,
>   who is hiding his face from the house of Jacob.
> I will put my trust in him.

¹⁸Here am I, and the children the Lord has given me. We are signs and symbols in Israel from the Lord Almighty, who dwells on Mount Zion.

ᵃ7 That is, the Euphrates   ᵇ8 *Immanuel* means *God with us.*   ᶜ9 Or *Do your worst*   ᵈ10 Hebrew *Immanuel*
ᵉ12 Or *Do not call for a treaty / every time these people call for a treaty*

¹⁹When men tell you to consult mediums and spiritists, who whisper and mutter, should not a people inquire of their God? Why consult the dead on behalf of the living? ²⁰To the law and to the testimony! If they do not speak according to this word, they have no light of dawn. ²¹Distressed and hungry, they will roam through the land; when they are famished, they will become enraged and, looking upward, will curse their king and their God. ²²Then they will look toward the earth and see only distress and darkness and fearful gloom, and they will be thrust into utter darkness.

To Us a Child Is Born

9 Nevertheless, there will be no more gloom for those who were in distress. In the past he humbled the land of Zebulun and the land of Naphtali, but in the future he will honor Galilee of the Gentiles, by the way of the sea, along the Jordan—

²The people walking in darkness
  have seen a great light;
on those living in the land of the shadow of death[a]
  a light has dawned.
³You have enlarged the nation
  and increased their joy;
they rejoice before you
  as people rejoice at the harvest,
as men rejoice
  when dividing the plunder.
⁴For as in the day of Midian's defeat,
  you have shattered
the yoke that burdens them,
  the bar across their shoulders,
  the rod of their oppressor.
⁵Every warrior's boot used in battle
  and every garment rolled in blood
will be destined for burning,
  will be fuel for the fire.
⁶For to us a child is born,
  to us a son is given,
  and the government will be on his shoulders.
And he will be called
  Wonderful Counselor,[b] Mighty God,
  Everlasting Father, Prince of Peace.
⁷Of the increase of his government and peace
  there will be no end.
He will reign on David's throne
  and over his kingdom,
establishing and upholding it
  with justice and righteousness
  from that time on and forever.
The zeal of the LORD Almighty
  will accomplish this.

The LORD's Anger Against Israel

⁸The Lord has sent a message against Jacob;
  it will fall on Israel.

a 2 Or *land of darkness*   *b 6* Or *Wonderful, Counselor*

⁹All the people will know it—
    Ephraim and the inhabitants of Samaria—
who say with pride
    and arrogance of heart,
¹⁰"The bricks have fallen down,
    but we will rebuild with
        dressed stone;
the fig trees have been felled,
    but we will replace them with
        cedars."
¹¹But the LORD has strengthened
    Rezin's foes against
        them
    and has spurred their enemies
        on.
¹²Arameans from the east and
    Philistines from the
        west
have devoured Israel with
    open mouth.

Yet for all this, his anger is
    not turned away,
    his hand is still upraised.

¹³But the people have not returned
    to him who struck them,
nor have they sought the
    LORD Almighty.
¹⁴So the LORD will cut off from Israel
    head and tail,
both palm branch and reed in a single day;
¹⁵the elders and prominent men are the head,
    the prophets who teach lies are the tail.
¹⁶Those who guide this people mislead them,
    and those who are guided are led astray.
¹⁷Therefore the Lord will take no pleasure in the young men,
    nor will he pity the fatherless and widows,
for everyone is ungodly and wicked,
    every mouth speaks vileness.

Yet for all this, his anger is not turned away,
    his hand is still upraised.

¹⁸Surely wickedness burns like a fire;
    it consumes briers and thorns,
it sets the forest thickets ablaze,
    so that it rolls upward in a column of smoke.
¹⁹By the wrath of the LORD Almighty
    the land will be scorched
and the people will be fuel for the fire;
    no one will spare his brother.

▣ ▦▦▦▦▦ REASONS TO BELIEVE ▦▦▦▦▦ ⮂

9:6–7
The Amazing Bible

Handel's *Messiah* is sung around the world each Christmas, and every year we hear again the wonderful news that the child born in Bethlehem's stable is the "Wonderful Counselor, Mighty God, Everlasting Father, Prince of Peace" that Isaiah names here.

This prediction of Jesus' coming is particularly remarkable because it pinpoints where the Messiah would live. Verse 1 tells us "Galilee of the Gentiles" would be the place from which this great light would begin to shine—precisely where Jesus grew up and began his ministry! (See Matthew chapter 4, verses 13–16 [page 1262].)

You hold in your hands a most remarkable book. It not only tells about the "Mighty God" who came as a child, but it also contains accurate predictions—made hundreds of years before Jesus was born on earth—that set it apart from all other "holy" books in the world.

²⁰On the right they will devour,
    but still be hungry;
on the left they will eat,
    but not be satisfied.
Each will feed on the flesh of his own offspring^a:
²¹ Manasseh will feed on Ephraim, and Ephraim on Manasseh;
    together they will turn against Judah.

Yet for all this, his anger is not turned away,
    his hand is still upraised.

10   Woe to those who make unjust laws,
    to those who issue oppressive decrees,
²to deprive the poor of their rights
    and withhold justice from the oppressed of my people,
making widows their prey
    and robbing the fatherless.
³What will you do on the day of reckoning,
    when disaster comes from afar?
To whom will you run for help?
    Where will you leave your riches?
⁴Nothing will remain but to cringe among the captives
    or fall among the slain.

Yet for all this, his anger is not turned away,
    his hand is still upraised.

God's Judgment on Assyria

⁵"Woe to the Assyrian, the rod of my anger,
    in whose hand is the club of my wrath!
⁶I send him against a godless nation,
    I dispatch him against a people who anger me,
to seize loot and snatch plunder,
    and to trample them down like mud in the streets.
⁷But this is not what he intends,
    this is not what he has in mind;
his purpose is to destroy,
    to put an end to many nations.
⁸'Are not my commanders all kings?' he says.
⁹ 'Has not Calno fared like Carchemish?
Is not Hamath like Arpad,
    and Samaria like Damascus?
¹⁰As my hand seized the kingdoms of the idols,
    kingdoms whose images excelled those of Jerusalem and
        Samaria—
¹¹shall I not deal with Jerusalem and her images
    as I dealt with Samaria and her idols?'"

¹²When the Lord has finished all his work against Mount Zion and Jerusalem, he will say, "I will punish the king of Assyria for the willful pride of his heart and the haughty look in his eyes. ¹³For he says:

"'By the strength of my hand I have done this,
    and by my wisdom, because I have understanding.

---

^a20 Or *arm*

I removed the boundaries of nations,
  I plundered their treasures;
  like a mighty one I subdued^a their kings.
¹⁴As one reaches into a nest,
  so my hand reached for the wealth of the nations;
as men gather abandoned eggs,
  so I gathered all the countries;
not one flapped a wing,
  or opened its mouth to chirp.' "

¹⁵Does the ax raise itself above him who swings it,
  or the saw boast against him who uses it?
As if a rod were to wield him who lifts it up,
  or a club brandish him who is not wood!
¹⁶Therefore, the Lord, the LORD Almighty,
  will send a wasting disease upon his sturdy warriors;
under his pomp a fire will be kindled
  like a blazing flame.
¹⁷The Light of Israel will become a fire,
  their Holy One a flame;
in a single day it will burn and consume
  his thorns and his briers.
¹⁸The splendor of his forests and fertile fields
  it will completely destroy,
  as when a sick man wastes away.
¹⁹And the remaining trees of his forests will be so few
  that a child could write them down.

The Remnant of Israel

²⁰In that day the remnant of Israel,
  the survivors of the house of Jacob,
will no longer rely on him
  who struck them down
but will truly rely on the LORD,
  the Holy One of Israel.
²¹A remnant will return,^b a remnant of Jacob
  will return to the Mighty God.
²²Though your people, O Israel, be like the sand by the sea,
  only a remnant will return.
Destruction has been decreed,
  overwhelming and righteous.
²³The Lord, the LORD Almighty, will carry out
  the destruction decreed upon the whole land.

²⁴Therefore, this is what the Lord, the LORD Almighty, says:

  "O my people who live in Zion,
    do not be afraid of the Assyrians,
  who beat you with a rod
    and lift up a club against you, as Egypt did.
²⁵Very soon my anger against you will end
    and my wrath will be directed to their destruction."

^a13 Or / I subdued the mighty.   ^b21 Hebrew shear-jashub; also in verse 22

²⁶The Lᴏʀᴅ Almighty will lash them with a whip,
    as when he struck down Midian at the rock of Oreb;
and he will raise his staff over the waters,
    as he did in Egypt.
²⁷In that day their burden will be lifted from your shoulders,
    their yoke from your neck;
the yoke will be broken
    because you have grown so fat.ᵃ

²⁸They enter Aiath;
    they pass through Migron;
    they store supplies at Micmash.
²⁹They go over the pass, and say,
    "We will camp overnight at Geba."
Ramah trembles;
    Gibeah of Saul flees.
³⁰Cry out, O Daughter of Gallim!
    Listen, O Laishah!
    Poor Anathoth!
³¹Madmenah is in flight;
    the people of Gebim take cover.
³²This day they will halt at Nob;
    they will shake their fist
at the mount of the Daughter of Zion,
    at the hill of Jerusalem.

³³See, the Lord, the Lᴏʀᴅ Almighty,
    will lop off the boughs with great power.
The lofty trees will be felled,
    the tall ones will be brought low.
³⁴He will cut down the forest thickets with an ax;
    Lebanon will fall before the Mighty One.

The Branch From Jesse

11 A shoot will come up from the stump of Jesse;
    from his roots a Branch will bear fruit.
²The Spirit of the Lᴏʀᴅ will rest on him—
    the Spirit of wisdom and of understanding,
    the Spirit of counsel and of power,
    the Spirit of knowledge and of the fear of the Lᴏʀᴅ—
³and he will delight in the fear of the Lᴏʀᴅ.

He will not judge by what he sees with his eyes,
    or decide by what he hears with his ears;
⁴but with righteousness he will judge the needy,
    with justice he will give decisions for the poor of the earth.
He will strike the earth with the rod of his mouth;
    with the breath of his lips he will slay the wicked.
⁵Righteousness will be his belt
    and faithfulness the sash around his waist.

⁶The wolf will live with the lamb,
    the leopard will lie down with the goat,
the calf and the lion and the yearlingᵇ together;

ᵃ27 Hebrew; Septuagint *broken / from your shoulders*   ᵇ6 Hebrew; Septuagint *lion will feed*

and a little child will lead them.
⁷The cow will feed with the bear,
their young will lie down together,
and the lion will eat straw like the ox.
⁸The infant will play near the hole of the cobra,
and the young child put his hand into the viper's nest.
⁹They will neither harm nor destroy
on all my holy mountain,
for the earth will be full of the knowledge of the Lᴏʀᴅ
as the waters cover the sea.

¹⁰In that day the Root of Jesse will stand as a banner for the peoples; the nations will rally to him, and his place of rest will be glorious. ¹¹In that day the Lord will reach out his hand a second time to reclaim the remnant that is left of his people from Assyria, from Lower Egypt, from Upper Egypt,ᵃ from Cush,ᵇ from Elam, from Babylonia,ᶜ from Hamath and from the islands of the sea.

¹²He will raise a banner for the nations
and gather the exiles of Israel;
he will assemble the scattered people of Judah
from the four quarters of the earth.
¹³Ephraim's jealousy will vanish,
and Judah's enemiesᵈ will be cut off;
Ephraim will not be jealous of Judah,
nor Judah hostile toward Ephraim.
¹⁴They will swoop down on the slopes of Philistia to the west;
together they will plunder the people to the east.
They will lay hands on Edom and Moab,
and the Ammonites will be subject to them.
¹⁵The Lᴏʀᴅ will dry up
the gulf of the Egyptian sea;
with a scorching wind he will sweep his hand
over the Euphrates River.ᵉ
He will break it up into seven streams
so that men can cross over in sandals.
¹⁶There will be a highway for the remnant of his people
that is left from Assyria,
as there was for Israel
when they came up from Egypt.

Songs of Praise

12 In that day you will say:

"I will praise you, O Lᴏʀᴅ.
Although you were angry with me,
your anger has turned away
and you have comforted me.
²Surely God is my salvation;
I will trust and not be afraid.
The Lᴏʀᴅ, the Lᴏʀᴅ, is my strength and my song;
he has become my salvation."

ᵃ11 Hebrew from Pathros   ᵇ11 That is, the upper Nile region   ᶜ11 Hebrew Shinar   ᵈ13 Or hostility
ᵉ15 Hebrew the River

³With joy you will draw water
    from the wells of salvation.

⁴In that day you will say:

"Give thanks to the LORD, call on his name;
    make known among the nations what he has done,
    and proclaim that his name is exalted.
⁵Sing to the LORD, for he has done glorious things;
    let this be known to all the world.
⁶Shout aloud and sing for joy, people of Zion,
    for great is the Holy One of Israel among you."

A Prophecy Against Babylon

13 An oracle concerning Babylon that Isaiah son of Amoz saw:

²Raise a banner on a bare hilltop,
    shout to them;
beckon to them
    to enter the gates of the nobles.
³I have commanded my holy ones;
    I have summoned my warriors to carry out my wrath—
    those who rejoice in my triumph.

⁴Listen, a noise on the mountains,
    like that of a great multitude!
Listen, an uproar among the kingdoms,
    like nations massing together!
The LORD Almighty is mustering
    an army for war.
⁵They come from faraway lands,
    from the ends of the heavens—
the LORD and the weapons of his wrath—
    to destroy the whole country.

⁶Wail, for the day of the LORD is near;
    it will come like destruction from the Almighty.^a
⁷Because of this, all hands will go limp,
    every man's heart will melt.
⁸Terror will seize them,
    pain and anguish will grip them;
    they will writhe like a woman in labor.
They will look aghast at each other,
    their faces aflame.

⁹See, the day of the LORD is coming
    —a cruel day, with wrath and fierce anger—
to make the land desolate
    and destroy the sinners within it.
¹⁰The stars of heaven and their constellations
    will not show their light.
The rising sun will be darkened
    and the moon will not give its light.

^a6 Hebrew *Shaddai*

¹¹I will punish the world for its evil,
  the wicked for their sins.
 I will put an end to the arrogance of the haughty
  and will humble the pride of the ruthless.
¹²I will make man scarcer than pure gold,
  more rare than the gold of Ophir.
¹³Therefore I will make the heavens tremble;
  and the earth will shake from its place
 at the wrath of the LORD Almighty,
  in the day of his burning anger.

¹⁴Like a hunted gazelle,
  like sheep without a shepherd,
 each will return to his own people,
  each will flee to his native land.
¹⁵Whoever is captured will be thrust through;
  all who are caught will fall by the sword.
¹⁶Their infants will be dashed to pieces before their eyes;
  their houses will be looted and their wives ravished.

¹⁷See, I will stir up against them the Medes,
  who do not care for silver
  and have no delight in gold.
¹⁸Their bows will strike down the young men;
  they will have no mercy on infants
  nor will they look with compassion on children.
¹⁹Babylon, the jewel of kingdoms,
  the glory of the Babylonians'ᵃ pride,
 will be overthrown by God
  like Sodom and Gomorrah.
²⁰She will never be inhabited
  or lived in through all generations;
 no Arab will pitch his tent there,
  no shepherd will rest his flocks there.
²¹But desert creatures will lie there,
  jackals will fill her houses;
 there the owls will dwell,
  and there the wild goats will leap about.
²²Hyenas will howl in her strongholds,
  jackals in her luxurious palaces.
 Her time is at hand,
  and her days will not be prolonged.

14 The LORD will have compassion on Jacob;
  once again he will choose Israel
 and will settle them in their own land.
 Aliens will join them
  and unite with the house of Jacob.
²Nations will take them
  and bring them to their own place.
 And the house of Israel will possess the nations
  as menservants and maidservants in the LORD's land.

ᵃ*19* Or *Chaldeans'*

They will make captives of their captors
    and rule over their oppressors.

³On the day the Lᴏʀᴅ gives you relief from suffering and turmoil and cruel bondage,
⁴you will take up this taunt against the king of Babylon:

How the oppressor has come to an end!
    How his fury*a* has ended!
⁵The Lᴏʀᴅ has broken the rod of the wicked,
    the scepter of the rulers,
⁶which in anger struck down peoples
    with unceasing blows,
and in fury subdued nations
    with relentless aggression.
⁷All the lands are at rest and at peace;
    they break into singing.
⁸Even the pine trees and the cedars of Lebanon
    exult over you and say,
"Now that you have been laid low,
    no woodsman comes to cut us down."

⁹The grave*b* below is all astir
    to meet you at your coming;
it rouses the spirits of the departed to greet you—
    all those who were leaders in the world;
it makes them rise from their thrones—
    all those who were kings over the nations.
¹⁰They will all respond,
    they will say to you,
"You also have become weak, as we are;
    you have become like us."
¹¹All your pomp has been brought down to the grave,
    along with the noise of your harps;
maggots are spread out beneath you
    and worms cover you.

¹²How you have fallen from heaven,
    O morning star, son of the dawn!
You have been cast down to the earth,
    you who once laid low the nations!
¹³You said in your heart,
    "I will ascend to heaven;
I will raise my throne
    above the stars of God;
I will sit enthroned on the mount of assembly,
    on the utmost heights of the sacred mountain.*c*
¹⁴I will ascend above the tops of the clouds;
    I will make myself like the Most High."
¹⁵But you are brought down to the grave,
    to the depths of the pit.

¹⁶Those who see you stare at you,
    they ponder your fate:

a4 Dead Sea Scrolls, Septuagint and Syriac; the meaning of the word in the Masoretic Text is uncertain.   *b9* Hebrew *Sheol*;
also in verses 11 and 15   *c13* Or *the north*; Hebrew *Zaphon*

"Is this the man who shook the earth
    and made kingdoms tremble,
¹⁷the man who made the world a desert,
    who overthrew its cities
    and would not let his captives go home?"

¹⁸All the kings of the nations lie in state,
    each in his own tomb.
¹⁹But you are cast out of your tomb
    like a rejected branch;
you are covered with the slain,
    with those pierced by the
        sword,
    those who descend to the
        stones of the pit.
Like a corpse trampled underfoot,
²⁰   you will not join them in
        burial,
for you have destroyed your land
    and killed your people.

The offspring of the wicked
    will never be mentioned again.
²¹Prepare a place to slaughter his
        sons
    for the sins of their forefathers;
they are not to rise to inherit the
        land
    and cover the earth with their cities.

²²"I will rise up against them,"
    declares the LORD Almighty.
"I will cut off from Babylon her name and survivors,
    her offspring and descendants,"

                              declares the LORD.

²³"I will turn her into a place for owls
    and into swampland;
I will sweep her with the broom of destruction,"
    declares the LORD Almighty.

◰ ▒▒▒▒▒▒ ADDRESSING QUESTIONS ▒▒▒▒▒▒ ⬍

14:12–15
Unseen Realities   **Q**

This passage refers to the wicked king of
Babylon as the "morning star," or "Lucifer." As
verse 3 indicates, this king arrogantly wanted
to rise to the level of a god but was condemned
for his pride-filled intentions.

Many commentators have compared this
king to Satan, the devil, originally a good angel who wanted to be like God (you may recall that the serpent promised Eve that she
had the potential to "be like God" in Genesis
chapter 3, verse 5 [page 7]).

Whether a man or an angel, no created
thing can ever assume the position that belongs to God alone by virtue of his uncreated,
infinite nature.

A Prophecy Against Assyria

²⁴The LORD Almighty has sworn,

"Surely, as I have planned, so it will be,
    and as I have purposed, so it will stand.
²⁵I will crush the Assyrian in my land;
    on my mountains I will trample him down.
His yoke will be taken from my people,
    and his burden removed from their shoulders."

²⁶This is the plan determined for the whole world;
    this is the hand stretched out over all nations.
²⁷For the LORD Almighty has purposed, and who can thwart him?
    His hand is stretched out, and who can turn it back?

A Prophecy Against the Philistines

²⁸This oracle came in the year King Ahaz died:

²⁹Do not rejoice, all you Philistines,
    that the rod that struck you is broken;
from the root of that snake will spring up a viper,
    its fruit will be a darting, venomous serpent.
³⁰The poorest of the poor will find pasture,
    and the needy will lie down in safety.
But your root I will destroy by famine;
    it will slay your survivors.

³¹Wail, O gate! Howl, O city!
    Melt away, all you Philistines!
A cloud of smoke comes from the north,
    and there is not a straggler in its ranks.
³²What answer shall be given
    to the envoys of that nation?
"The Lord has established Zion,
    and in her his afflicted people will find refuge."

A Prophecy Against Moab

15 An oracle concerning Moab:

Ar in Moab is ruined,
    destroyed in a night!
Kir in Moab is ruined,
    destroyed in a night!
²Dibon goes up to its temple,
    to its high places to weep;
Moab wails over Nebo and Medeba.
Every head is shaved
    and every beard cut off.
³In the streets they wear sackcloth;
    on the roofs and in the public squares
they all wail,
    prostrate with weeping.
⁴Heshbon and Elealeh cry out,
    their voices are heard all the way to Jahaz.
Therefore the armed men of Moab cry out,
    and their hearts are faint.

⁵My heart cries out over Moab;
    her fugitives flee as far as Zoar,
    as far as Eglath Shelishiyah.
They go up the way to Luhith,
    weeping as they go;
on the road to Horonaim
    they lament their destruction.
⁶The waters of Nimrim are dried up
    and the grass is withered;
the vegetation is gone
    and nothing green is left.
⁷So the wealth they have acquired and stored up

they carry away over the Ravine of the Poplars.
⁸Their outcry echoes along the border of Moab;
  their wailing reaches as far as Eglaim,
  their lamentation as far as Beer Elim.
⁹Dimon's *a* waters are full of blood,
  but I will bring still more upon Dimon *a*—
a lion upon the fugitives of Moab
  and upon those who remain in the land.

16 Send lambs as tribute
  to the ruler of the land,
from Sela, across the desert,
  to the mount of the Daughter of Zion.
²Like fluttering birds
  pushed from the nest,
so are the women of Moab
  at the fords of the Arnon.

³"Give us counsel,
  render a decision.
Make your shadow like night—
  at high noon.
Hide the fugitives,
  do not betray the refugees.
⁴Let the Moabite fugitives stay with you;
  be their shelter from the destroyer."

The oppressor will come to an end,
  and destruction will cease;
  the aggressor will vanish from the land.
⁵In love a throne will be established;
  in faithfulness a man will sit on it—
  one from the house *b* of David—
one who in judging seeks justice
  and speeds the cause of righteousness.

⁶We have heard of Moab's pride—
  her overweening pride and conceit,
her pride and her insolence—
  but her boasts are empty.
⁷Therefore the Moabites wail,
  they wail together for Moab.
Lament and grieve
  for the men *c* of Kir Hareseth.
⁸The fields of Heshbon wither,
  the vines of Sibmah also.
The rulers of the nations
  have trampled down the choicest vines,
which once reached Jazer
  and spread toward the desert.

---

a 9 Masoretic Text; Dead Sea Scrolls, some Septuagint manuscripts and Vulgate *Dibon*   *b 5* Hebrew *tent*   *c 7* Or "*raisin cakes*," a wordplay

Their shoots spread out
and went as far as the sea.
⁹So I weep, as Jazer weeps,
for the vines of Sibmah.
O Heshbon, O Elealeh,
I drench you with tears!
The shouts of joy over your ripened fruit
and over your harvests have been stilled.
¹⁰Joy and gladness are taken away from the orchards;
no one sings or shouts in the vineyards;
no one treads out wine at the presses,
for I have put an end to the shouting.
¹¹My heart laments for Moab like a harp,
my inmost being for Kir Hareseth.
¹²When Moab appears at her high place,
she only wears herself out;
when she goes to her shrine to pray,
it is to no avail.

¹³This is the word the Lord has already spoken concerning Moab. ¹⁴But now the Lord says: "Within three years, as a servant bound by contract would count them, Moab's splendor and all her many people will be despised, and her survivors will be very few and feeble."

An Oracle Against Damascus

17 An oracle concerning Damascus:

"See, Damascus will no longer be a city
but will become a heap of ruins.
²The cities of Aroer will be deserted
and left to flocks, which will lie down,
with no one to make them afraid.
³The fortified city will disappear from Ephraim,
and royal power from Damascus;
the remnant of Aram will be
like the glory of the Israelites,"

declares the Lord Almighty.

⁴"In that day the glory of Jacob will fade;
the fat of his body will waste away.
⁵It will be as when a reaper gathers the standing grain
and harvests the grain with his arm—
as when a man gleans heads of grain
in the Valley of Rephaim.
⁶Yet some gleanings will remain,
as when an olive tree is beaten,
leaving two or three olives on the topmost branches,
four or five on the fruitful boughs,"

declares the Lord, the God of Israel.

⁷In that day men will look to their Maker
and turn their eyes to the Holy One of Israel.
⁸They will not look to the altars,
the work of their hands,

and they will have no regard for the Asherah poles[a]
and the incense altars their fingers have made.

⁹In that day their strong cities, which they left because of the Israelites, will be like places abandoned to thickets and undergrowth. And all will be desolation.

¹⁰You have forgotten God your Savior;
   you have not remembered the Rock, your fortress.
Therefore, though you set out the finest plants
   and plant imported vines,
¹¹though on the day you set them out, you make them grow,
   and on the morning when you plant them, you bring them to bud,
yet the harvest will be as nothing
   in the day of disease and incurable pain.

¹²Oh, the raging of many nations—
   they rage like the raging sea!
Oh, the uproar of the peoples—
   they roar like the roaring of great waters!
¹³Although the peoples roar like the roar of surging waters,
   when he rebukes them they flee far away,
driven before the wind like chaff on the hills,
   like tumbleweed before a gale.
¹⁴In the evening, sudden terror!
   Before the morning, they are gone!
This is the portion of those who loot us,
   the lot of those who plunder us.

A Prophecy Against Cush

18 Woe to the land of whirring wings[b]
      along the rivers of Cush,[c]
²which sends envoys by sea
   in papyrus boats over the water.

Go, swift messengers,
to a people tall and smooth-skinned,
   to a people feared far and wide,
an aggressive nation of strange speech,
   whose land is divided by rivers.

³All you people of the world,
   you who live on the earth,
when a banner is raised on the mountains,
   you will see it,
and when a trumpet sounds,
   you will hear it.
⁴This is what the LORD says to me:
   "I will remain quiet and will look on from my dwelling place,
like shimmering heat in the sunshine,
   like a cloud of dew in the heat of harvest."
⁵For, before the harvest, when the blossom is gone
   and the flower becomes a ripening grape,
he will cut off the shoots with pruning knives,
   and cut down and take away the spreading branches.

---

a 8 That is, symbols of the goddess Asherah   *b 1* Or *of locusts*   *c 1* That is, the upper Nile region

⁶They will all be left to the mountain birds of prey
　　and to the wild animals;
the birds will feed on them all summer,
　　the wild animals all winter.

⁷At that time gifts will be brought to the Lᴏʀᴅ Almighty

　　from a people tall and smooth-skinned,
　　　　from a people feared far and wide,
　　an aggressive nation of strange speech,
　　　　whose land is divided by rivers—

the gifts will be brought to Mount Zion, the place of the Name of the Lᴏʀᴅ Almighty.

A Prophecy About Egypt

19 An oracle concerning Egypt:

See, the Lᴏʀᴅ rides on a swift cloud
　　and is coming to Egypt.
The idols of Egypt tremble before him,
　　and the hearts of the Egyptians melt within them.

²"I will stir up Egyptian against Egyptian—
　　brother will fight against brother,
　　neighbor against neighbor,
　　city against city,
　　kingdom against kingdom.
³The Egyptians will lose heart,
　　and I will bring their plans to nothing;
they will consult the idols and the spirits of the dead,
　　the mediums and the spiritists.
⁴I will hand the Egyptians over
　　to the power of a cruel master,
and a fierce king will rule over them,"
　　declares the Lord, the Lᴏʀᴅ Almighty.

⁵The waters of the river will dry up,
　　and the riverbed will be parched and dry.
⁶The canals will stink;
　　the streams of Egypt will dwindle and dry up.
The reeds and rushes will wither,
⁷　　also the plants along the Nile,
　　at the mouth of the river.
Every sown field along the Nile
　　will become parched, will blow away and be no more.
⁸The fishermen will groan and lament,
　　all who cast hooks into the Nile;
those who throw nets on the water
　　will pine away.
⁹Those who work with combed flax will despair,
　　the weavers of fine linen will lose hope.
¹⁰The workers in cloth will be dejected,
　　and all the wage earners will be sick at heart.

¹¹The officials of Zoan are nothing but fools;
　　the wise counselors of Pharaoh give senseless advice.

How can you say to Pharaoh,
"I am one of the wise men,
a disciple of the ancient kings"?

¹²Where are your wise men now?
Let them show you and make known
what the Lord Almighty
has planned against Egypt.
¹³The officials of Zoan have become fools,
the leaders of Memphis*a* are deceived;
the cornerstones of her peoples
have led Egypt astray.
¹⁴The Lord has poured into them
a spirit of dizziness;
they make Egypt stagger in all that she does,
as a drunkard staggers around in his vomit.
¹⁵There is nothing Egypt can do—
head or tail, palm branch or reed.

¹⁶In that day the Egyptians will be like women. They will shudder with fear at the uplifted hand that the Lord Almighty raises against them. ¹⁷And the land of Judah will bring terror to the Egyptians; everyone to whom Judah is mentioned will be terrified, because of what the Lord Almighty is planning against them.

¹⁸In that day five cities in Egypt will speak the language of Canaan and swear allegiance to the Lord Almighty. One of them will be called the City of Destruction.*b*

¹⁹In that day there will be an altar to the Lord in the heart of Egypt, and a monument to the Lord at its border. ²⁰It will be a sign and witness to the Lord Almighty in the land of Egypt. When they cry out to the Lord because of their oppressors, he will send them a savior and defender, and he will rescue them. ²¹So the Lord will make himself known to the Egyptians, and in that day they will acknowledge the Lord. They will worship with sacrifices and grain offerings; they will make vows to the Lord and keep them. ²²The Lord will strike Egypt with a plague; he will strike them and heal them. They will turn to the Lord, and he will respond to their pleas and heal them.

²³In that day there will be a highway from Egypt to Assyria. The Assyrians will go to Egypt and the Egyptians to Assyria. The Egyptians and Assyrians will worship together. ²⁴In that day Israel will be the third, along with Egypt and Assyria, a blessing on the earth. ²⁵The Lord Almighty will bless them, saying, "Blessed be Egypt my people, Assyria my handiwork, and Israel my inheritance."

A Prophecy Against Egypt and Cush

20 In the year that the supreme commander, sent by Sargon king of Assyria, came to Ashdod and attacked and captured it— ²at that time the Lord spoke through Isaiah son of Amoz. He said to him, "Take off the sackcloth from your body and the sandals from your feet." And he did so, going around stripped and barefoot.

³Then the Lord said, "Just as my servant Isaiah has gone stripped and barefoot for three years, as a sign and portent against Egypt and Cush,*c* ⁴so the king of Assyria will lead away stripped and barefoot the Egyptian captives and Cushite exiles, young and old, with buttocks bared—to Egypt's shame. ⁵Those who trusted in Cush and boasted in Egypt will be afraid and put to shame. ⁶In that day the people who live on this coast will say, 'See what has happened to those we relied on, those we fled to for help and deliverance from the king of Assyria! How then can we escape?'"

---

13 Hebrew *Noph*   *b 18* Most manuscripts of the Masoretic Text; some manuscripts of the Masoretic Text, Dead Sea Scrolls and Vulgate *City of the Sun* (that is, Heliopolis)   *c 3* That is, the upper Nile region; also in verse 5

A Prophecy Against Babylon

21 An oracle concerning the Desert by the Sea:

Like whirlwinds sweeping through the southland,
    an invader comes from the desert,
    from a land of terror.

²A dire vision has been shown to me:
    The traitor betrays, the looter takes loot.
Elam, attack! Media, lay siege!
    I will bring to an end all the groaning she caused.

³At this my body is racked with pain,
    pangs seize me, like those of a woman in labor;
I am staggered by what I hear,
    I am bewildered by what I see.
⁴My heart falters,
    fear makes me tremble;
the twilight I longed for
    has become a horror to me.

⁵They set the tables,
    they spread the rugs,
    they eat, they drink!
Get up, you officers,
    oil the shields!

⁶This is what the Lord says to me:

"Go, post a lookout
    and have him report what he sees.
⁷When he sees chariots
    with teams of horses,
riders on donkeys
    or riders on camels,
let him be alert,
    fully alert."

⁸And the lookout*ᵃ* shouted,

"Day after day, my lord, I stand on the watchtower;
    every night I stay at my post.
⁹Look, here comes a man in a chariot
    with a team of horses.
And he gives back the answer:
    'Babylon has fallen, has fallen!
All the images of its gods
    lie shattered on the ground!'"

¹⁰O my people, crushed on the threshing floor,
    I tell you what I have heard
from the LORD Almighty,
    from the God of Israel.

ᵃ8 Dead Sea Scrolls and Syriac; Masoretic Text *A lion*

A Prophecy Against Edom

¹¹An oracle concerning Dumah^a:

> Someone calls to me from Seir,
>> "Watchman, what is left of the night?
>> Watchman, what is left of the night?"
> ¹²The watchman replies,
>> "Morning is coming, but also the night.
>> If you would ask, then ask;
>>> and come back yet again."

A Prophecy Against Arabia

¹³An oracle concerning Arabia:

> You caravans of Dedanites,
>> who camp in the thickets of Arabia,
> ¹⁴   bring water for the thirsty;
> you who live in Tema,
>> bring food for the fugitives.
> ¹⁵They flee from the sword,
>> from the drawn sword,
> from the bent bow
>> and from the heat of battle.

¹⁶This is what the Lord says to me: "Within one year, as a servant bound by contract would count it, all the pomp of Kedar will come to an end. ¹⁷The survivors of the bowmen, the warriors of Kedar, will be few." The LORD, the God of Israel, has spoken.

A Prophecy About Jerusalem

22 An oracle concerning the Valley of Vision:

> What troubles you now,
>> that you have all gone up on the roofs,
> ²O town full of commotion,
>> O city of tumult and revelry?
> Your slain were not killed by the sword,
>> nor did they die in battle.
> ³All your leaders have fled together;
>> they have been captured without using the bow.
> All you who were caught were taken prisoner together,
>> having fled while the enemy was still far away.
> ⁴Therefore I said, "Turn away from me;
>> let me weep bitterly.
> Do not try to console me
>> over the destruction of my people."
>
> ⁵The Lord, the LORD Almighty, has a day
>> of tumult and trampling and terror
>> in the Valley of Vision,
> a day of battering down walls
>> and of crying out to the mountains.
> ⁶Elam takes up the quiver,
>> with her charioteers and horses;
> Kir uncovers the shield.

^a 11 *Dumah* means *silence* or *stillness,* a wordplay on *Edom.*

7Your choicest valleys are full of chariots,
  and horsemen are posted at the city gates;
8   the defenses of Judah are stripped away.

And you looked in that day
  to the weapons in the Palace of the Forest;
9you saw that the City of David
  had many breaches in its defenses;
you stored up water
  in the Lower Pool.
10You counted the buildings in Jerusalem
  and tore down houses to strengthen the wall.
11You built a reservoir between the two walls
  for the water of the Old Pool,
but you did not look to the One who made it,
  or have regard for the One who planned it long ago.

12The Lord, the LORD Almighty,
  called you on that day
to weep and to wail,
  to tear out your hair and put on sackcloth.
13But see, there is joy and revelry,
  slaughtering of cattle and killing of sheep,
  eating of meat and drinking of wine!
"Let us eat and drink," you say,
  "for tomorrow we die!"

14The LORD Almighty has revealed this in my hearing: "Till your dying day this sin will not be atoned for," says the Lord, the LORD Almighty.

15This is what the Lord, the LORD Almighty, says:

"Go, say to this steward,
  to Shebna, who is in charge of the palace:
16What are you doing here and who gave you permission
  to cut out a grave for yourself here,
hewing your grave on the height
  and chiseling your resting place in the rock?

17"Beware, the LORD is about to take firm hold of you
  and hurl you away, O you mighty man.
18He will roll you up tightly like a ball
  and throw you into a large country.
There you will die
  and there your splendid chariots will remain—
  you disgrace to your master's house!
19I will depose you from your office,
  and you will be ousted from your position.

20"In that day I will summon my servant, Eliakim son of Hilkiah. 21I will clothe him with your robe and fasten your sash around him and hand your authority over to him. He will be a father to those who live in Jerusalem and to the house of Judah. 22I will place on his shoulder the key to the house of David; what he opens no one can shut, and what he shuts no one can open. 23I will drive him like a peg into a firm place; he will be a seat^a

of honor for the house of his father. **24**All the glory of his family will hang on him: its offspring and offshoots—all its lesser vessels, from the bowls to all the jars.

25"In that day," declares the LORD Almighty, "the peg driven into the firm place will give way; it will be sheared off and will fall, and the load hanging on it will be cut down." The LORD has spoken.

A Prophecy About Tyre

23 An oracle concerning Tyre:

Wail, O ships of Tarshish!
For Tyre is destroyed
and left without house or harbor.
From the land of Cyprus*a*
word has come to them.

2Be silent, you people of the island
and you merchants of Sidon,
whom the seafarers have enriched.
3On the great waters
came the grain of the Shihor;
the harvest of the Nile*b* was the revenue of Tyre,
and she became the marketplace of the nations.

4Be ashamed, O Sidon, and you, O fortress of the sea,
for the sea has spoken:
"I have neither been in labor nor given birth;
I have neither reared sons nor brought up daughters."
5When word comes to Egypt,
they will be in anguish at the report from Tyre.

6Cross over to Tarshish;
wail, you people of the island.
7Is this your city of revelry,
the old, old city,
whose feet have taken her
to settle in far-off lands?
8Who planned this against Tyre,
the bestower of crowns,
whose merchants are princes,
whose traders are renowned in the earth?
9The LORD Almighty planned it,
to bring low the pride of all glory
and to humble all who are renowned on the earth.

10Till*c* your land as along the Nile,
O Daughter of Tarshish,
for you no longer have a harbor.
11The LORD has stretched out his hand over the sea
and made its kingdoms tremble.
He has given an order concerning Phoenicia*d*
that her fortresses be destroyed.
12He said, "No more of your reveling,

---

a 1 Hebrew *Kittim*   *b 2,3* Masoretic Text; one Dead Sea Scroll *Sidon, / who cross over the sea; / your envoys* **3***are on the great waters. / The grain of the Shihor, / the harvest of the Nile,*   *c 10* Dead Sea Scrolls and some Septuagint manuscripts; Masoretic Text *Go through*   *d 11* Hebrew *Canaan*

O Virgin Daughter of Sidon, now crushed!

"Up, cross over to Cyprus^a;
    even there you will find no rest."
¹³Look at the land of the Babylonians,^b
    this people that is now of no account!
The Assyrians have made it
    a place for desert creatures;
they raised up their siege towers,
    they stripped its fortresses bare
    and turned it into a ruin.

¹⁴Wail, you ships of Tarshish;
    your fortress is destroyed!

¹⁵At that time Tyre will be forgotten for seventy years, the span of a king's life. But at the end of these seventy years, it will happen to Tyre as in the song of the prostitute:

¹⁶"Take up a harp, walk through the city,
    O prostitute forgotten;
play the harp well, sing many a song,
    so that you will be remembered."

¹⁷At the end of seventy years, the LORD will deal with Tyre. She will return to her hire as a prostitute and will ply her trade with all the kingdoms on the face of the earth. ¹⁸Yet her profit and her earnings will be set apart for the LORD; they will not be stored up or hoarded. Her profits will go to those who live before the LORD, for abundant food and fine clothes.

The LORD's Devastation of the Earth

24 See, the LORD is going to lay waste the earth
    and devastate it;
he will ruin its face
    and scatter its inhabitants—
²it will be the same
    for priest as for people,
    for master as for servant,
    for mistress as for maid,
    for seller as for buyer,
    for borrower as for lender,
    for debtor as for creditor.
³The earth will be completely laid waste
    and totally plundered.

The LORD has spoken this word.

⁴The earth dries up and withers,
    the world languishes and withers,
    the exalted of the earth languish.
⁵The earth is defiled by its people;
    they have disobeyed the laws,
    violated the statutes
    and broken the everlasting covenant.
⁶Therefore a curse consumes the earth;
    its people must bear their guilt.
Therefore earth's inhabitants are burned up,

^a12 Hebrew Kittim   ^b13 Or Chaldeans

and very few are left.
⁷The new wine dries up and the vine withers;
all the merrymakers groan.
⁸The gaiety of the tambourines is stilled,
the noise of the revelers has stopped,
the joyful harp is silent.
⁹No longer do they drink wine with a song;
the beer is bitter to its drinkers.
¹⁰The ruined city lies desolate;
the entrance to every house is barred.
¹¹In the streets they cry out for wine;
all joy turns to gloom,
all gaiety is banished from the earth.
¹²The city is left in ruins,
its gate is battered to pieces.
¹³So will it be on the earth
and among the nations,
as when an olive tree is beaten,
or as when gleanings are left after the grape harvest.

¹⁴They raise their voices, they shout for joy;
from the west they acclaim the LORD's majesty.
¹⁵Therefore in the east give glory to the LORD;
exalt the name of the LORD, the God of Israel,
in the islands of the sea.
¹⁶From the ends of the earth we hear singing:
"Glory to the Righteous One."

But I said, "I waste away, I waste away!
Woe to me!
The treacherous betray!
With treachery the treacherous betray!"
¹⁷Terror and pit and snare await you,
O people of the earth.
¹⁸Whoever flees at the sound of terror
will fall into a pit;
whoever climbs out of the pit
will be caught in a snare.

The floodgates of the heavens are opened,
the foundations of the earth shake.
¹⁹The earth is broken up,
the earth is split asunder,
the earth is thoroughly shaken.
²⁰The earth reels like a drunkard,
it sways like a hut in the wind;
so heavy upon it is the guilt of its rebellion
that it falls—never to rise again.

²¹In that day the LORD will punish
the powers in the heavens above
and the kings on the earth below.
²²They will be herded together
like prisoners bound in a dungeon;
they will be shut up in prison

and be punished^a after many days.
²³The moon will be abashed, the sun ashamed;
    for the LORD Almighty will reign
on Mount Zion and in Jerusalem,
    and before its elders, gloriously.

Praise to the LORD

25 O LORD, you are my God;
    I will exalt you and praise your name,
for in perfect faithfulness
    you have done marvelous things,
    things planned long ago.
²You have made the city a heap of rubble,
    the fortified town a ruin,
the foreigners' stronghold a city no more;
    it will never be rebuilt.
³Therefore strong peoples will honor you;
    cities of ruthless nations will revere you.
⁴You have been a refuge for the poor,
    a refuge for the needy in his distress,
a shelter from the storm
    and a shade from the heat.
For the breath of the ruthless
    is like a storm driving against a wall
⁵   and like the heat of the desert.
You silence the uproar of foreigners;
    as heat is reduced by the shadow of a cloud,
    so the song of the ruthless is stilled.

⁶On this mountain the LORD Almighty will prepare
    a feast of rich food for all peoples,
a banquet of aged wine—
    the best of meats and the finest of wines.
⁷On this mountain he will destroy
    the shroud that enfolds all peoples,
the sheet that covers all nations;
⁸   he will swallow up death forever.
The Sovereign LORD will wipe away the tears
    from all faces;
he will remove the disgrace of his people
    from all the earth.

The LORD has spoken.

⁹In that day they will say,

"Surely this is our God;
    we trusted in him, and he saved us.
This is the LORD, we trusted in him;
    let us rejoice and be glad in his salvation."

¹⁰The hand of the LORD will rest on this mountain;
    but Moab will be trampled under him
    as straw is trampled down in the manure.
¹¹They will spread out their hands in it,

^a22 Or released

as a swimmer spreads out his hands to swim.
God will bring down their pride
   despite the cleverness[a] of their hands.
¹²He will bring down your high fortified walls
   and lay them low;
he will bring them down to the ground,
   to the very dust.

A Song of Praise

26 In that day this song will be sung in the land of Judah:

We have a strong city;
   God makes salvation
   its walls and ramparts.
²Open the gates
   that the righteous nation may enter,
   the nation that keeps faith.
³You will keep in perfect peace
   him whose mind is steadfast,
   because he trusts in you.
⁴Trust in the LORD forever,
   for the LORD, the LORD, is the Rock eternal.
⁵He humbles those who dwell on high,
   he lays the lofty city low;
he levels it to the ground
   and casts it down to the dust.
⁶Feet trample it down—
   the feet of the oppressed,
   the footsteps of the poor.

⁷The path of the righteous is level;
   O upright One, you make the way of the righteous smooth.
⁸Yes, LORD, walking in the way of your laws,[b]
   we wait for you;
your name and renown
   are the desire of our hearts.
⁹My soul yearns for you in the night;
   in the morning my spirit longs for you.
When your judgments come upon the earth,
   the people of the world learn righteousness.
¹⁰Though grace is shown to the wicked,
   they do not learn righteousness;
even in a land of uprightness they go on doing evil
   and regard not the majesty of the LORD.
¹¹O LORD, your hand is lifted high,
   but they do not see it.
Let them see your zeal for your people and be put to shame;
   let the fire reserved for your enemies consume them.

¹²LORD, you establish peace for us;
   all that we have accomplished you have done for us.

---

a 11 The meaning of the Hebrew for this word is uncertain.   *b 8* Or *judgments*

¹³O Lᴏʀᴅ, our God, other lords besides you have ruled over us,
but your name alone do we honor.
¹⁴They are now dead, they live no more;
those departed spirits do not rise.
You punished them and brought them to ruin;
you wiped out all memory of them.
¹⁵You have enlarged the nation, O Lᴏʀᴅ;
you have enlarged the nation.
You have gained glory for yourself;
you have extended all the borders of the land.

¹⁶Lᴏʀᴅ, they came to you in their distress;
when you disciplined them,
they could barely whisper a prayer.ᵃ
¹⁷As a woman with child and about to give birth
writhes and cries out in her pain,
so were we in your presence, O Lᴏʀᴅ.
¹⁸We were with child, we writhed in pain,
but we gave birth to wind.
We have not brought salvation to the earth;
we have not given birth to people of the world.

¹⁹But your dead will live;
their bodies will rise.
You who dwell in the dust,
wake up and shout for joy.
Your dew is like the dew of the morning;
the earth will give birth to her dead.

²⁰Go, my people, enter your rooms
and shut the doors behind you;
hide yourselves for a little while
until his wrath has passed by.

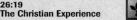

REASONS TO BELIEVE

26:19
The Christian Experience

This passage is one of a few in the Old Testament that announces the hope of everyone who places their trust in God. While in its immediate context this verse predicts the restoration of Israel, it also points to the day when all believers will have the ultimate victory over humankind's worst enemy—death itself.

²¹See, the Lᴏʀᴅ is coming out of his dwelling
to punish the people of the earth for their sins.
The earth will disclose the blood shed upon her;
she will conceal her slain no longer.

Deliverance of Israel

27 In that day,

the Lᴏʀᴅ will punish with his sword,
his fierce, great and powerful sword,
Leviathan the gliding serpent,
Leviathan the coiling serpent;
he will slay the monster of the sea.

²In that day—

"Sing about a fruitful vineyard:
³ I, the Lᴏʀᴅ, watch over it;

ᵃ16 The meaning of the Hebrew for this clause is uncertain.

I water it continually.
I guard it day and night
   so that no one may harm it.
4 I am not angry.
If only there were briers and thorns confronting me!
   I would march against them in battle;
   I would set them all on fire.
⁵Or else let them come to me for refuge;
   let them make peace with me,
   yes, let them make peace with me."

⁶In days to come Jacob will take root,
   Israel will bud and blossom
   and fill all the world with fruit.

⁷Has ⌊the Lord⌋ struck her
   as he struck down those who struck her?
Has she been killed
   as those were killed who killed her?
⁸By warfare*a* and exile you contend with her—
   with his fierce blast he drives her out,
   as on a day the east wind blows.
⁹By this, then, will Jacob's guilt be atoned for,
   and this will be the full fruitage of the removal of his sin:
When he makes all the altar stones
   to be like chalk stones crushed to pieces,
no Asherah poles*b* or incense altars
   will be left standing.
¹⁰The fortified city stands desolate,
   an abandoned settlement, forsaken like the desert;
there the calves graze,
   there they lie down;
   they strip its branches bare.
¹¹When its twigs are dry, they are broken off
   and women come and make fires with them.
For this is a people without understanding;
   so their Maker has no compassion on them,
   and their Creator shows them no favor.

¹²In that day the Lord will thresh from the flowing Euphrates*c* to the Wadi of Egypt, and you, O Israelites, will be gathered up one by one. ¹³And in that day a great trumpet will sound. Those who were perishing in Assyria and those who were exiled in Egypt will come and worship the Lord on the holy mountain in Jerusalem.

Woe to Ephraim

28 Woe to that wreath, the pride of Ephraim's drunkards,
   to the fading flower, his glorious beauty,
set on the head of a fertile valley—
   to that city, the pride of those laid low by wine!
²See, the Lord has one who is powerful and strong.
   Like a hailstorm and a destructive wind,
   like a driving rain and a flooding downpour,

a8 See Septuagint; the meaning of the Hebrew for this word is uncertain.   *b9* That is, symbols of the goddess Asherah
c12 Hebrew *River*

he will throw it forcefully to the ground.
³That wreath, the pride of Ephraim's drunkards,
     will be trampled underfoot.
⁴That fading flower, his glorious beauty,
     set on the head of a fertile valley,
will be like a fig ripe before harvest—
     as soon as someone sees it and takes it in his hand,
     he swallows it.

⁵In that day the Lᴏʀᴅ Almighty
     will be a glorious crown,
a beautiful wreath
     for the remnant of his people.
⁶He will be a spirit of justice
     to him who sits in judgment,
a source of strength
     to those who turn back the battle at the gate.

⁷And these also stagger from wine
     and reel from beer:
Priests and prophets stagger from beer
     and are befuddled with wine;
they reel from beer,
     they stagger when seeing visions,
     they stumble when rendering decisions.
⁸All the tables are covered with vomit
     and there is not a spot without filth.

⁹"Who is it he is trying to teach?
     To whom is he explaining his message?
To children weaned from their milk,
     to those just taken from the breast?
¹⁰For it is:
     Do and do, do and do,
     rule on rule, rule on rule ᵃ;
     a little here, a little there."

¹¹Very well then, with foreign lips and strange tongues
     God will speak to this people,
¹²to whom he said,
     "This is the resting place, let the weary rest";
and, "This is the place of repose"—
     but they would not listen.
¹³So then, the word of the Lᴏʀᴅ to them will become:
     Do and do, do and do,
     rule on rule, rule on rule;
     a little here, a little there—
so that they will go and fall backward,
     be injured and snared and captured.

¹⁴Therefore hear the word of the Lᴏʀᴅ, you scoffers
     who rule this people in Jerusalem.
¹⁵You boast, "We have entered into a covenant with death,

ᵃ10 Hebrew / sav lasav sav lasav / kav lakav kav lakav (possibly meaningless sounds; perhaps a mimicking of the prophet's words); also in verse 13

with the grave[a] we have made an agreement.
When an overwhelming scourge sweeps by,
    it cannot touch us,
for we have made a lie our refuge
    and falsehood[b] our hiding place."

16So this is what the Sovereign Lord says:

"See, I lay a stone in Zion,
    a tested stone,
a precious cornerstone for a sure foundation;
    the one who trusts will never be dismayed.
17I will make justice the measuring line
    and righteousness the plumb line;
hail will sweep away your refuge, the lie,
    and water will overflow your hiding place.
18Your covenant with death will be annulled;
    your agreement with the grave will not stand.
When the overwhelming scourge sweeps by,
    you will be beaten down by it.
19As often as it comes it will carry you away;
    morning after morning, by day and by night,
    it will sweep through."

The understanding of this message
    will bring sheer terror.
20The bed is too short to stretch out on,
    the blanket too narrow to wrap around you.
21The Lord will rise up as he did at Mount Perazim,
    he will rouse himself as in the Valley of Gibeon—
to do his work, his strange work,
    and perform his task, his alien task.
22Now stop your mocking,
    or your chains will become heavier;
the Lord, the Lord Almighty, has told me
    of the destruction decreed against the whole land.

23Listen and hear my voice;
    pay attention and hear what I say.
24When a farmer plows for planting, does he plow continually?
    Does he keep on breaking up and harrowing the soil?
25When he has leveled the surface,
    does he not sow caraway and scatter cummin?
Does he not plant wheat in its place,[c]
    barley in its plot,[c]
    and spelt in its field?
26His God instructs him
    and teaches him the right way.

27Caraway is not threshed with a sledge,
    nor is a cartwheel rolled over cummin;
caraway is beaten out with a rod,
    and cummin with a stick.
28Grain must be ground to make bread;

---

a15 Hebrew *Sheol;* also in verse 18   *b15* Or *false gods*   *c25* The meaning of the Hebrew for this word is uncertain.

so one does not go on threshing it forever.
Though he drives the wheels of his threshing cart over it,
　　his horses do not grind it.
²⁹All this also comes from the Lᴏʀᴅ Almighty,
　　wonderful in counsel and magnificent in wisdom.

Woe to David's City

29 Woe to you, Ariel, Ariel,
　　the city where David settled!
Add year to year
　　and let your cycle of festivals go on.
²Yet I will besiege Ariel;
　　she will mourn and lament,
　　she will be to me like an altar hearth.ᵃ
³I will encamp against you all around;
　　I will encircle you with towers
　　and set up my siege works against you.
⁴Brought low, you will speak from the ground;
　　your speech will mumble out of the dust.
Your voice will come ghostlike from the earth;
　　out of the dust your speech will whisper.

⁵But your many enemies will become like fine dust,
　　the ruthless hordes like blown chaff.
Suddenly, in an instant,
⁶　the Lᴏʀᴅ Almighty will come
　with thunder and earthquake and great noise,
　　with windstorm and tempest and flames of a devouring fire.
⁷Then the hordes of all the nations that fight against Ariel,
　　that attack her and her fortress and besiege her,
will be as it is with a dream,
　　with a vision in the night—
⁸as when a hungry man dreams that he is eating,
　　but he awakens, and his hunger remains;
as when a thirsty man dreams that he is drinking,
　　but he awakens faint, with his thirst unquenched.
So will it be with the hordes of all the nations
　　that fight against Mount Zion.

⁹Be stunned and amazed,
　　blind yourselves and be sightless;
be drunk, but not from wine,
　　stagger, but not from beer.
¹⁰The Lᴏʀᴅ has brought over you a deep sleep:
　　He has sealed your eyes (the prophets);
　　he has covered your heads (the seers).

¹¹For you this whole vision is nothing but words sealed in a scroll. And if you give the scroll to someone who can read, and say to him, "Read this, please," he will answer, "I can't; it is sealed." ¹²Or if you give the scroll to someone who cannot read, and say, "Read this, please," he will answer, "I don't know how to read."

¹³The Lord says:

ᵃ2 The Hebrew for *altar hearth* sounds like the Hebrew for *Ariel.*

"These people come near to me with their mouth
 and honor me with their lips,
 but their hearts are far from me.
Their worship of me
 is made up only of rules taught by men.*ᵃ*
¹⁴Therefore once more I will astound these people
 with wonder upon wonder;
the wisdom of the wise will perish,
 the intelligence of the intelligent will vanish."
¹⁵Woe to those who go to great depths
 to hide their plans from the LORD,
who do their work in darkness and think,
 "Who sees us? Who will know?"
¹⁶You turn things upside down,
 as if the potter were thought to be like the clay!
Shall what is formed say to him who formed it,
 "He did not make me"?
Can the pot say of the potter,
 "He knows nothing"?

¹⁷In a very short time, will not Lebanon be turned into a fertile field
 and the fertile field seem like a forest?
¹⁸In that day the deaf will hear the words of the scroll,
 and out of gloom and darkness
 the eyes of the blind will see.
¹⁹Once more the humble will rejoice in the LORD;
 the needy will rejoice in the Holy One of Israel.
²⁰The ruthless will vanish,
 the mockers will disappear,
 and all who have an eye for evil will be cut down—
²¹those who with a word make a man out to be guilty,
 who ensnare the defender in court
 and with false testimony deprive the innocent of justice.

²²Therefore this is what the LORD, who redeemed Abraham, says to the house of Jacob:

"No longer will Jacob be ashamed;
 no longer will their faces grow pale.
²³When they see among them their children,
 the work of my hands,
they will keep my name holy;
 they will acknowledge the holiness of the Holy One of Jacob,
 and will stand in awe of the God of Israel.
²⁴Those who are wayward in spirit will gain understanding;
 those who complain will accept instruction."

Woe to the Obstinate Nation

30 "Woe to the obstinate children,"
 declares the LORD,
"to those who carry out plans that are not mine, \
 forming an alliance, but not by my Spirit,
 heaping sin upon sin;
²who go down to Egypt

ᵃ 13 Hebrew; Septuagint *They worship me in vain, / their teachings are but rules taught by men*

without consulting me;
who look for help to Pharaoh's protection,
    to Egypt's shade for refuge.
³But Pharaoh's protection will be to your shame,
    Egypt's shade will bring you disgrace.
⁴Though they have officials in Zoan
    and their envoys have arrived in Hanes,
⁵everyone will be put to shame
    because of a people useless to them,
who bring neither help nor advantage,
    but only shame and disgrace."

⁶An oracle concerning the animals of the Negev:

Through a land of hardship and distress,
    of lions and lionesses,
    of adders and darting snakes,
the envoys carry their riches on donkeys' backs,
    their treasures on the humps of camels,
to that unprofitable nation,
⁷   to Egypt, whose help is utterly useless.
Therefore I call her
    Rahab the Do-Nothing.

⁸Go now, write it on a tablet for them,
    inscribe it on a scroll,
that for the days to come
    it may be an everlasting witness.
⁹These are rebellious people, deceitful children,
    children unwilling to listen to the LORD's instruction.
¹⁰They say to the seers,
    "See no more visions!"
and to the prophets,
    "Give us no more visions of what is right!
Tell us pleasant things,
    prophesy illusions.
¹¹Leave this way,
    get off this path,
and stop confronting us
    with the Holy One of Israel!"

¹²Therefore, this is what the Holy One of Israel says:

"Because you have rejected this message,
    relied on oppression
    and depended on deceit,
¹³this sin will become for you
    like a high wall, cracked and bulging,
    that collapses suddenly, in an instant.
¹⁴It will break in pieces like pottery,
    shattered so mercilessly
that among its pieces not a fragment will be found
    for taking coals from a hearth
    or scooping water out of a cistern."

¹⁵This is what the Sovereign LORD, the Holy One of Israel, says:

"In repentance and rest is your salvation,
  in quietness and trust is your strength,
  but you would have none of it.
¹⁶You said, 'No, we will flee on horses.'
  Therefore you will flee!
You said, 'We will ride off on swift horses.'
  Therefore your pursuers will be swift!
¹⁷A thousand will flee
  at the threat of one;
at the threat of five
  you will all flee away,
till you are left
  like a flagstaff on a mountaintop,
  like a banner on a hill."

¹⁸Yet the LORD longs to be gracious to you;
  he rises to show you compassion.
For the LORD is a God of justice.
  Blessed are all who wait for him!

¹⁹O people of Zion, who live in Jerusalem, you will weep no more. How gracious he
will be when you cry for help! As soon as he hears, he will answer you. ²⁰Although the
Lord gives you the bread of adversity and the water of affliction, your teachers will be
hidden no more; with your own eyes you will see them. ²¹Whether you turn to the right
or to the left, your ears will hear a voice behind you, saying, "This is the way; walk in it."
²²Then you will defile your idols overlaid with silver and your images covered with gold;
you will throw them away like a menstrual cloth and say to them, "Away with you!"

²³He will also send you rain for the seed you sow in the ground, and the food that
comes from the land will be rich and plentiful. In that day your cattle will graze in broad
meadows. ²⁴The oxen and donkeys that work the soil will eat fodder and mash, spread
out with fork and shovel. ²⁵In the day of great slaughter, when the towers fall, streams of
water will flow on every high mountain and every lofty hill. ²⁶The moon will shine like
the sun, and the sunlight will be seven times brighter, like the light of seven full days,
when the LORD binds up the bruises of his people and heals the wounds he inflicted.

²⁷See, the Name of the LORD comes from afar,
  with burning anger and dense clouds of smoke;
his lips are full of wrath,
  and his tongue is a consuming fire.
²⁸His breath is like a rushing torrent,
  rising up to the neck.
He shakes the nations in the sieve of destruction;
  he places in the jaws of the peoples
  a bit that leads them astray.
²⁹And you will sing
  as on the night you celebrate a holy festival;
your hearts will rejoice
  as when people go up with flutes
to the mountain of the LORD,
  to the Rock of Israel.
³⁰The LORD will cause men to hear his majestic voice
  and will make them see his arm coming down
with raging anger and consuming fire,
  with cloudburst, thunderstorm and hail.

³¹The voice of the LORD will shatter Assyria;
    with his scepter he will strike them down.
³²Every stroke the LORD lays on them
    with his punishing rod
will be to the music of tambourines and harps,
    as he fights them in battle with the blows of his arm.
³³Topheth has long been prepared;
    it has been made ready for the king.
Its fire pit has been made deep and wide,
    with an abundance of fire and wood;
the breath of the LORD,
    like a stream of burning sulfur,
    sets it ablaze.

Woe to Those Who Rely on Egypt

31 Woe to those who go down to Egypt for help,
    who rely on horses,
who trust in the multitude of their chariots
    and in the great strength of their horsemen,
but do not look to the Holy One of Israel,
    or seek help from the LORD.
²Yet he too is wise and can bring disaster;
    he does not take back his words.
He will rise up against the house of the wicked,
    against those who help evildoers.
³But the Egyptians are men and not God;
    their horses are flesh and not spirit.
When the LORD stretches out his hand,
    he who helps will stumble,
    he who is helped will fall;
    both will perish together.

⁴This is what the LORD says to me:

"As a lion growls,
    a great lion over his prey—
and though a whole band of shepherds
    is called together against him,
he is not frightened by their shouts
    or disturbed by their clamor—
so the LORD Almighty will come down
    to do battle on Mount Zion and on its heights.
⁵Like birds hovering overhead,
    the LORD Almighty will shield Jerusalem;
he will shield it and deliver it,
    he will 'pass over' it and will rescue it."

⁶Return to him you have so greatly revolted against, O Israelites. ⁷For in that day every one of you will reject the idols of silver and gold your sinful hands have made.

⁸"Assyria will fall by a sword that is not of man;
    a sword, not of mortals, will devour them.
They will flee before the sword
    and their young men will be put to forced labor.
⁹Their stronghold will fall because of terror;

at sight of the battle standard their commanders will panic,"
declares the LORD,
  whose fire is in Zion,
  whose furnace is in Jerusalem.

The Kingdom of Righteousness

32 See, a king will reign in righteousness
  and rulers will rule with justice.
²Each man will be like a shelter from the wind
  and a refuge from the storm,
  like streams of water in the desert
  and the shadow of a great rock in a thirsty land.

³Then the eyes of those who see will no longer be closed,
  and the ears of those who hear will listen.
⁴The mind of the rash will know and understand,
  and the stammering tongue will be fluent and clear.
⁵No longer will the fool be called noble
  nor the scoundrel be highly respected.
⁶For the fool speaks folly,
  his mind is busy with evil:
He practices ungodliness
  and spreads error concerning the LORD;
the hungry he leaves empty
  and from the thirsty he withholds water.
⁷The scoundrel's methods are wicked,
  he makes up evil schemes
to destroy the poor with lies,
  even when the plea of the needy is just.
⁸But the noble man makes noble plans,
  and by noble deeds he stands.

The Women of Jerusalem

⁹You women who are so complacent,
  rise up and listen to me;
you daughters who feel secure,
  hear what I have to say!
¹⁰In little more than a year
  you who feel secure will tremble;
the grape harvest will fail,
  and the harvest of fruit will not come.
¹¹Tremble, you complacent women;
  shudder, you daughters who feel secure!
Strip off your clothes,
  put sackcloth around your waists.
¹²Beat your breasts for the pleasant fields,
  for the fruitful vines
¹³and for the land of my people,
  a land overgrown with thorns and briers—
yes, mourn for all houses of merriment
  and for this city of revelry.
¹⁴The fortress will be abandoned,
  the noisy city deserted;
citadel and watchtower will become a wasteland forever,

the delight of donkeys, a pasture for flocks,
¹⁵till the Spirit is poured upon us from on high,
    and the desert becomes a fertile field,
    and the fertile field seems like a forest.
¹⁶Justice will dwell in the desert
    and righteousness live in the fertile field.
¹⁷The fruit of righteousness will be peace;
    the effect of righteousness will be quietness and confidence
        forever.
¹⁸My people will live in peaceful dwelling places,
    in secure homes,
    in undisturbed places of rest.
¹⁹Though hail flattens the forest
    and the city is leveled completely,
²⁰how blessed you will be,
    sowing your seed by every stream,
    and letting your cattle and donkeys range free.

Distress and Help

33 Woe to you, O destroyer,
        you who have not been destroyed!
Woe to you, O traitor,
    you who have not been betrayed!
When you stop destroying,
    you will be destroyed;
when you stop betraying,
    you will be betrayed.

²O LORD, be gracious to us;
    we long for you.
Be our strength every morning,
    our salvation in time of distress.
³At the thunder of your voice, the peoples flee;
    when you rise up, the nations scatter.
⁴Your plunder, O nations, is harvested as by young locusts;
    like a swarm of locusts men pounce on it.

⁵The LORD is exalted, for he dwells on high;
    he will fill Zion with justice and righteousness.
⁶He will be the sure foundation for your times,
    a rich store of salvation and wisdom and knowledge;
    the fear of the LORD is the key to this treasure.ᵃ

⁷Look, their brave men cry aloud in the streets;
    the envoys of peace weep bitterly.
⁸The highways are deserted,
    no travelers are on the roads.
The treaty is broken,
    its witnessesᵇ are despised,
    no one is respected.
⁹The land mournsᶜ and wastes away,
    Lebanon is ashamed and withers;

ᵃ6 Or is a treasure from him   ᵇ8 Dead Sea Scrolls; Masoretic Text / the cities   ᶜ9 Or dries up

Sharon is like the Arabah,
and Bashan and Carmel drop their leaves.

¹⁰"Now will I arise," says the LORD.
"Now will I be exalted;
now will I be lifted up.
¹¹You conceive chaff,
you give birth to straw;
your breath is a fire that consumes you.
¹²The peoples will be burned as if to lime;
like cut thornbushes they will be set ablaze."

¹³You who are far away, hear what I have done;
you who are near, acknowledge my power!
¹⁴The sinners in Zion are terrified;
trembling grips the godless:
"Who of us can dwell with the consuming fire?
Who of us can dwell with everlasting burning?"
¹⁵He who walks righteously
and speaks what is right,
who rejects gain from extortion
and keeps his hand from accepting bribes,
who stops his ears against plots of murder
and shuts his eyes against contemplating evil—
¹⁶this is the man who will dwell on the heights,
whose refuge will be the mountain fortress.
His bread will be supplied,
and water will not fail him.

¹⁷Your eyes will see the king in his beauty
and view a land that stretches afar.
¹⁸In your thoughts you will ponder the former terror:
"Where is that chief officer?
Where is the one who took the revenue?
Where is the officer in charge of the towers?"
¹⁹You will see those arrogant people no more,
those people of an obscure speech,
with their strange, incomprehensible tongue.

²⁰Look upon Zion, the city of our festivals;
your eyes will see Jerusalem,
a peaceful abode, a tent that will not be moved;
its stakes will never be pulled up,
nor any of its ropes broken.
²¹There the LORD will be our Mighty One.
It will be like a place of broad rivers and streams.
No galley with oars will ride them,
no mighty ship will sail them.
²²For the LORD is our judge,
the LORD is our lawgiver,
the LORD is our king;
it is he who will save us.

²³Your rigging hangs loose:
The mast is not held secure,
the sail is not spread.

Then an abundance of spoils will be divided
and even the lame will carry off plunder.
²⁴No one living in Zion will say, "I am ill";
and the sins of those who dwell there will be forgiven.

Judgment Against the Nations

34 Come near, you nations, and listen;
pay attention, you peoples!
Let the earth hear, and all that is in it,
the world, and all that comes out of it!
²The Lord is angry with all nations;
his wrath is upon all their armies.
He will totally destroy*ᵃ* them,
he will give them over to slaughter.
³Their slain will be thrown out,
their dead bodies will send up a stench;
the mountains will be soaked with their blood.
⁴All the stars of the heavens will be dissolved
and the sky rolled up like a scroll;
all the starry host will fall
like withered leaves from the vine,
like shriveled figs from the fig tree.

⁵My sword has drunk its fill in the heavens;
see, it descends in judgment on Edom,
the people I have totally destroyed.
⁶The sword of the Lord is bathed in blood,
it is covered with fat—
the blood of lambs and goats,
fat from the kidneys of rams.
For the Lord has a sacrifice in Bozrah
and a great slaughter in Edom.
⁷And the wild oxen will fall with them,
the bull calves and the great bulls.
Their land will be drenched with blood,
and the dust will be soaked with fat.

⁸For the Lord has a day of vengeance,
a year of retribution, to uphold Zion's cause.
⁹Edom's streams will be turned into pitch,
her dust into burning sulfur;
her land will become blazing pitch!
¹⁰It will not be quenched night and day;
its smoke will rise forever.
From generation to generation it will lie desolate;
no one will ever pass through it again.
¹¹The desert owlᵇ and screech owlᵇ will possess it;
the great owlᵇ and the raven will nest there.
God will stretch out over Edom
the measuring line of chaos

ᵃ 2 The Hebrew term refers to the irrevocable giving over of things or persons to the Lord, often by totally destroying them; also in verse 5.   *ᵇ 11* The precise identification of these birds is uncertain.

and the plumb line of desolation.
¹²Her nobles will have nothing there to be called a kingdom,
    all her princes will vanish away.
¹³Thorns will overrun her citadels,
    nettles and brambles her strongholds.
She will become a haunt for jackals,
    a home for owls.
¹⁴Desert creatures will meet with hyenas,
    and wild goats will bleat to each other;
there the night creatures will also repose
    and find for themselves places of rest.
¹⁵The owl will nest there and lay eggs,
    she will hatch them, and care for her young under the
        shadow of her wings;
there also the falcons will gather,
    each with its mate.

¹⁶Look in the scroll of the Lord and read:

None of these will be missing,
    not one will lack her mate.
For it is his mouth that has given the order,
    and his Spirit will gather them together.
¹⁷He allots their portions;
    his hand distributes them by measure.
They will possess it forever
    and dwell there from generation to generation.

Joy of the Redeemed

35 The desert and the parched land will be glad;
    the wilderness will rejoice and blossom.
Like the crocus, ²it will burst into bloom;
    it will rejoice greatly and shout for joy.
The glory of Lebanon will be given to it,
    the splendor of Carmel and Sharon;
they will see the glory of the Lord,
    the splendor of our God.

³Strengthen the feeble hands,
    steady the knees that give way;
⁴say to those with fearful hearts,
    "Be strong, do not fear;
your God will come,
    he will come with vengeance;
with divine retribution
    he will come to save you."

⁵Then will the eyes of the blind be opened
    and the ears of the deaf unstopped.
⁶Then will the lame leap like a deer,
    and the mute tongue shout for joy.
Water will gush forth in the wilderness
    and streams in the desert.
⁷The burning sand will become a pool,

the thirsty ground bubbling springs.
In the haunts where jackals once lay,
    grass and reeds and papyrus will grow.
[8]And a highway will be there;
    it will be called the Way of Holiness.
The unclean will not journey on it;

it will be for those who walk in that
        Way;
    wicked fools will not go about
        on it.[a]
[9]No lion will be there,
    nor will any ferocious beast get up
        on it;
    they will not be found there.
But only the redeemed will walk there,
[10]   and the ransomed of the LORD will
        return.
They will enter Zion with singing;
    everlasting joy will crown their heads.
Gladness and joy will overtake them,
    and sorrow and sighing will flee away.

▣ ▒▒▒▒▒▒▒▒▒ REASONS TO BELIEVE ▒▒▒▒▒▒▒▒▒ ⮂

35:4–6
The Amazing Bible

Here Isaiah predicts the signs of the Messianic Age—the time when God would send the Messiah to save his people. Jesus performed these miracles during his ministry on earth (see "Miracles of Jesus," page 1700). These demonstrations revealed Jesus' identity as the one who came to save all people who would believe in him and lead them into a place of "everlasting joy" (verse 10).

Sennacherib Threatens Jerusalem

36 In the fourteenth year of King Hezekiah's reign, Sennacherib king of Assyria attacked all the fortified cities of Judah and captured them. [2]Then the king of Assyria sent his field commander with a large army from Lachish to King Hezekiah at Jerusalem. When the commander stopped at the aqueduct of the Upper Pool, on the road to the Washerman's Field, [3]Eliakim son of Hilkiah the palace administrator, Shebna the secretary, and Joah son of Asaph the recorder went out to him.

[4]The field commander said to them, "Tell Hezekiah,

" 'This is what the great king, the king of Assyria, says: On what are you basing this confidence of yours? [5]You say you have strategy and military strength—but you speak only empty words. On whom are you depending, that you rebel against me? [6]Look now, you are depending on Egypt, that splintered reed of a staff, which pierces a man's hand and wounds him if he leans on it! Such is Pharaoh king of Egypt to all who depend on him. [7]And if you say to me, "We are depending on the LORD our God"—isn't he the one whose high places and altars Hezekiah removed, saying to Judah and Jerusalem, "You must worship before this altar"?

[8]" 'Come now, make a bargain with my master, the king of Assyria: I will give you two thousand horses—if you can put riders on them! [9]How then can you repulse one officer of the least of my master's officials, even though you are depending on Egypt for chariots and horsemen? [10]Furthermore, have I come to attack and destroy this land without the LORD? The LORD himself told me to march against this country and destroy it.' "

[11]Then Eliakim, Shebna and Joah said to the field commander, "Please speak to your servants in Aramaic, since we understand it. Don't speak to us in Hebrew in the hearing of the people on the wall."

[12]But the commander replied, "Was it only to your master and you that my master sent me to say these things, and not to the men sitting on the wall—who, like you, will have to eat their own filth and drink their own urine?"

[13]Then the commander stood and called out in Hebrew, "Hear the words of the great

---

[a]8 Or / the simple will not stray from it

king, the king of Assyria! ¹⁴This is what the king says: Do not let Hezekiah deceive you. He cannot deliver you! ¹⁵Do not let Hezekiah persuade you to trust in the LORD when he says, 'The LORD will surely deliver us; this city will not be given into the hand of the king of Assyria.'

¹⁶"Do not listen to Hezekiah. This is what the king of Assyria says: Make peace with me and come out to me. Then every one of you will eat from his own vine and fig tree and drink water from his own cistern, ¹⁷until I come and take you to a land like your own—a land of grain and new wine, a land of bread and vineyards.

¹⁸"Do not let Hezekiah mislead you when he says, 'The LORD will deliver us.' Has the god of any nation ever delivered his land from the hand of the king of Assyria? ¹⁹Where are the gods of Hamath and Arpad? Where are the gods of Sepharvaim? Have they rescued Samaria from my hand? ²⁰Who of all the gods of these countries has been able to save his land from me? How then can the LORD deliver Jerusalem from my hand?"

²¹But the people remained silent and said nothing in reply, because the king had commanded, "Do not answer him."

²²Then Eliakim son of Hilkiah the palace administrator, Shebna the secretary, and Joah son of Asaph the recorder went to Hezekiah, with their clothes torn, and told him what the field commander had said.

Jerusalem's Deliverance Foretold

37 When King Hezekiah heard this, he tore his clothes and put on sackcloth and went into the temple of the LORD. ²He sent Eliakim the palace administrator, Shebna the secretary, and the leading priests, all wearing sackcloth, to the prophet Isaiah son of Amoz. ³They told him, "This is what Hezekiah says: This day is a day of distress and rebuke and disgrace, as when children come to the point of birth and there is no strength to deliver them. ⁴It may be that the LORD your God will hear the words of the field commander, whom his master, the king of Assyria, has sent to ridicule the living God, and that he will rebuke him for the words the LORD your God has heard. Therefore pray for the remnant that still survives."

⁵When King Hezekiah's officials came to Isaiah, ⁶Isaiah said to them, "Tell your master, 'This is what the LORD says: Do not be afraid of what you have heard—those words with which the underlings of the king of Assyria have blasphemed me. ⁷Listen! I am going to put a spirit in him so that when he hears a certain report, he will return to his own country, and there I will have him cut down with the sword.'"

⁸When the field commander heard that the king of Assyria had left Lachish, he withdrew and found the king fighting against Libnah.

⁹Now Sennacherib received a report that Tirhakah, the Cushite*ᵃ* king ⌊of Egypt⌋, was marching out to fight against him. When he heard it, he sent messengers to Hezekiah with this word: ¹⁰"Say to Hezekiah king of Judah: Do not let the god you depend on deceive you when he says, 'Jerusalem will not be handed over to the king of Assyria.' ¹¹Surely you have heard what the kings of Assyria have done to all the countries, destroying them completely. And will you be delivered? ¹²Did the gods of the nations that were destroyed by my forefathers deliver them—the gods of Gozan, Haran, Rezeph and the people of Eden who were in Tel Assar? ¹³Where is the king of Hamath, the king of Arpad, the king of the city of Sepharvaim, or of Hena or Ivvah?"

Hezekiah's Prayer

¹⁴Hezekiah received the letter from the messengers and read it. Then he went up to the temple of the LORD and spread it out before the LORD. ¹⁵And Hezekiah prayed to the LORD: ¹⁶"O LORD Almighty, God of Israel, enthroned between the cherubim, you alone are God over all the kingdoms of the earth. You have made heaven and earth. ¹⁷Give ear,

ᵃ9 That is, from the upper Nile region

O Lord, and hear; open your eyes, O Lord, and see; listen to all the words Sennacherib has sent to insult the living God.

¹⁸"It is true, O Lord, that the Assyrian kings have laid waste all these peoples and their lands. ¹⁹They have thrown their gods into the fire and destroyed them, for they were not gods but only wood and stone, fashioned by human hands. ²⁰Now, O Lord our God, deliver us from his hand, so that all kingdoms on earth may know that you alone, O Lord, are God.ᵃ"

Sennacherib's Fall

²¹Then Isaiah son of Amoz sent a message to Hezekiah: "This is what the Lord, the God of Israel, says: Because you have prayed to me concerning Sennacherib king of Assyria, ²²this is the word the Lord has spoken against him:

> "The Virgin Daughter of Zion
>   despises and mocks you.
> The Daughter of Jerusalem
>   tosses her head as you flee.
> ²³Who is it you have insulted and blasphemed?
>   Against whom have you raised your voice
> and lifted your eyes in pride?
>   Against the Holy One of Israel!
> ²⁴By your messengers
>   you have heaped insults on the Lord.
> And you have said,
>   'With my many chariots
> I have ascended the heights of the mountains,
>   the utmost heights of Lebanon.
> I have cut down its tallest cedars,
>   the choicest of its pines.
> I have reached its remotest heights,
>   the finest of its forests.
> ²⁵I have dug wells in foreign landsᵇ
>   and drunk the water there.
> With the soles of my feet
>   I have dried up all the streams of Egypt.'
>
> ²⁶"Have you not heard?
>   Long ago I ordained it.
> In days of old I planned it;
>   now I have brought it to pass,
> that you have turned fortified cities
>   into piles of stone.
> ²⁷Their people, drained of power,
>   are dismayed and put to shame.
> They are like plants in the field,
>   like tender green shoots,
> like grass sprouting on the roof,
>   scorchedᶜ before it grows up.
>
> ²⁸"But I know where you stay
>   and when you come and go
>   and how you rage against me.

ᵃ20 Dead Sea Scrolls (see also 2 Kings 19:19); Masoretic Text *alone are the Lord*   ᵇ25 Dead Sea Scrolls (see also 2 Kings 19:24); Masoretic Text does not have *in foreign lands.*   ᶜ27 Some manuscripts of the Masoretic Text, Dead Sea Scrolls and some Septuagint manuscripts (see also 2 Kings 19:26); most manuscripts of the Masoretic Text *roof / and terraced fields*

²⁹Because you rage against me
    and because your insolence has reached my ears,
I will put my hook in your nose
    and my bit in your mouth,
and I will make you return
    by the way you came.

³⁰"This will be the sign for you, O Hezekiah:

"This year you will eat what grows by itself,
    and the second year what springs from that.
But in the third year sow and reap,
    plant vineyards and eat their fruit.
³¹Once more a remnant of the house of Judah
    will take root below and bear fruit above.
³²For out of Jerusalem will come a remnant,
    and out of Mount Zion a band of survivors.
The zeal of the Lord Almighty
    will accomplish this.

³³"Therefore this is what the Lord says concerning the king of Assyria:

"He will not enter this city
    or shoot an arrow here.
He will not come before it with shield
    or build a siege ramp against it.
³⁴By the way that he came he will return;
    he will not enter this city,"

                        declares the Lord.

³⁵"I will defend this city and save it,
    for my sake and for the sake of David my servant!"

³⁶Then the angel of the Lord went out and put to death a hundred and eighty-five thousand men in the Assyrian camp. When the people got up the next morning—there were all the dead bodies! ³⁷So Sennacherib king of Assyria broke camp and withdrew. He returned to Nineveh and stayed there.

³⁸One day, while he was worshiping in the temple of his god Nisroch, his sons Adrammelech and Sharezer cut him down with the sword, and they escaped to the land of Ararat. And Esarhaddon his son succeeded him as king.

Hezekiah's Illness

38 In those days Hezekiah became ill and was at the point of death. The prophet Isaiah son of Amoz went to him and said, "This is what the Lord says: Put your house in order, because you are going to die; you will not recover."

²Hezekiah turned his face to the wall and prayed to the Lord, ³"Remember, O Lord, how I have walked before you faithfully and with wholehearted devotion and have done what is good in your eyes." And Hezekiah wept bitterly.

⁴Then the word of the Lord came to Isaiah: ⁵"Go and tell Hezekiah, 'This is what the Lord, the God of your father David, says: I have heard your prayer and seen your tears; I will add fifteen years to your life. ⁶And I will deliver you and this city from the hand of the king of Assyria. I will defend this city.

⁷"'This is the Lord's sign to you that the Lord will do what he has promised: ⁸I will make the shadow cast by the sun go back the ten steps it has gone down on the stairway of Ahaz.'" So the sunlight went back the ten steps it had gone down.

⁹A writing of Hezekiah king of Judah after his illness and recovery:

¹⁰I said, "In the prime of my life
    must I go through the gates of death*ᵃ*
    and be robbed of the rest of my years?"
¹¹I said, "I will not again see the LORD,
    the LORD, in the land of the living;
no longer will I look on mankind,
    or be with those who now dwell in this world.*ᵇ*
¹²Like a shepherd's tent my house
    has been pulled down and taken from me.
Like a weaver I have rolled up my life,
    and he has cut me off from the loom;
    day and night you made an end of me.
¹³I waited patiently till dawn,
    but like a lion he broke all my bones;
    day and night you made an end of me.
¹⁴I cried like a swift or thrush,
    I moaned like a mourning dove.
My eyes grew weak as I looked to the heavens.
    I am troubled; O Lord, come to my aid!"

¹⁵But what can I say?
    He has spoken to me, and he himself has done this.
I will walk humbly all my years
    because of this anguish of my soul.
¹⁶Lord, by such things men live;
    and my spirit finds life in them too.
You restored me to health
    and let me live.
¹⁷Surely it was for my benefit
    that I suffered such anguish.
In your love you kept me
    from the pit of destruction;
    you have put all my sins
    behind your back.
¹⁸For the grave*ᵃ* cannot praise you,
    death cannot sing your praise;
those who go down to the pit
    cannot hope for your faithfulness.
¹⁹The living, the living—they praise you,
    as I am doing today;
fathers tell their children
    about your faithfulness.

²⁰The LORD will save me,
    and we will sing with stringed instruments
all the days of our lives
    in the temple of the LORD.

²¹Isaiah had said, "Prepare a poultice of figs and apply it to the boil, and he will recover."
²²Hezekiah had asked, "What will be the sign that I will go up to the temple of the LORD?"

ᵃ10,18 Hebrew *Sheol*   *ᵇ11* A few Hebrew manuscripts; most Hebrew manuscripts *in the place of cessation*

Envoys From Babylon

39 At that time Merodach-Baladan son of Baladan king of Babylon sent Hezekiah letters and a gift, because he had heard of his illness and recovery. [2]Hezekiah received the envoys gladly and showed them what was in his storehouses—the silver, the gold, the spices, the fine oil, his entire armory and everything found among his treasures. There was nothing in his palace or in all his kingdom that Hezekiah did not show them.

[3]Then Isaiah the prophet went to King Hezekiah and asked, "What did those men say, and where did they come from?"

"From a distant land," Hezekiah replied. "They came to me from Babylon."

[4]The prophet asked, "What did they see in your palace?"

"They saw everything in my palace," Hezekiah said. "There is nothing among my treasures that I did not show them."

[5]Then Isaiah said to Hezekiah, "Hear the word of the LORD Almighty: [6]The time will surely come when everything in your palace, and all that your fathers have stored up until this day, will be carried off to Babylon. Nothing will be left, says the LORD. [7]And some of your descendants, your own flesh and blood who will be born to you, will be taken away, and they will become eunuchs in the palace of the king of Babylon."

[8]"The word of the LORD you have spoken is good," Hezekiah replied. For he thought, "There will be peace and security in my lifetime."

Comfort for God's People

40 Comfort, comfort my people,
    says your God.
[2]Speak tenderly to Jerusalem,
    and proclaim to her
that her hard service has been completed,
    that her sin has been paid for,
that she has received from the LORD's hand
    double for all her sins.

[3]A voice of one calling:
"In the desert prepare
    the way for the LORD[a];
make straight in the wilderness
    a highway for our God.[b]
[4]Every valley shall be raised up,
    every mountain and hill made low;
the rough ground shall become level,
    the rugged places a plain.
[5]And the glory of the LORD will be revealed,
    and all mankind together will see it.
                For the mouth of the LORD has spoken."

[6]A voice says, "Cry out."
    And I said, "What shall I cry?"

"All men are like grass,
    and all their glory is like the flowers of the field.
[7]The grass withers and the flowers fall,
    because the breath of the LORD blows on them.
    Surely the people are grass.

---

a 3 Or *A voice of one calling in the desert: / "Prepare the way for the* LORD   *b 3* Hebrew; Septuagint *make straight the paths of our God*

[8]The grass withers and the flowers fall,
　　but the word of our God stands forever."

[9]You who bring good tidings to Zion,
　　go up on a high mountain.
You who bring good tidings to Jerusalem,[a]
　　lift up your voice with a shout,
lift it up, do not be afraid;
　　say to the towns of Judah,
　　"Here is your God!"

[10]See, the Sovereign LORD comes
　　　with power,
　　and his arm rules for him.
See, his reward is with him,
　　and his recompense accompanies
　　　him.
[11]He tends his flock like a shepherd:
　　He gathers the lambs in his arms
and carries them close to his heart;
　　he gently leads those that have
　　　young.

[12]Who has measured the waters in the
　　　hollow of his hand,
　　or with the breadth of his hand
　　　marked off the heavens?
Who has held the dust of the earth in a
　　　basket,
　　or weighed the mountains on the scales
　　　and the hills in a balance?

▣ ▦▦▦▦▦ REASONS TO BELIEVE ▦▦▦▦▦ ⇄

40:1–3
The Amazing Bible

This chapter signifies a turning point in Isaiah's prophecy—a dramatic change in tone that lasts through the end of the book. Isaiah's stinging message is now tempered by words of comfort and hope. Perhaps after all the "bad news" that came before in this book, God wanted Isaiah to point out the good things in store for the faithful remnant of his people.

Note that verse 3 talks about a voice preparing a way in the desert. This is exactly what John the Baptist did in preparation for Jesus—another fulfilled biblical prediction (see Mark chapter 1, verses 1–8 [page 1306]).

---

[13]Who has understood the mind[b] of the LORD,
　　or instructed him as his counselor?
[14]Whom did the LORD consult to enlighten him,
　　and who taught him the right way?
Who was it that taught him knowledge
　　or showed him the path of understanding?

[15]Surely the nations are like a drop in a bucket;
　　they are regarded as dust on the scales;
　　he weighs the islands as though they were fine dust.
[16]Lebanon is not sufficient for altar fires,
　　nor its animals enough for burnt offerings.
[17]Before him all the nations are as nothing;
　　they are regarded by him as worthless
　　and less than nothing.

[18]To whom, then, will you compare God?
　　What image will you compare him to?

---

[a]9 Or O Zion, bringer of good tidings, / go up on a high mountain. / O Jerusalem, bringer of good tidings　　[b]13 Or Spirit; or spirit

¹⁹As for an idol, a craftsman casts it,
  and a goldsmith overlays it with gold
  and fashions silver chains for it.
²⁰A man too poor to present such an offering
  selects wood that will not rot.
He looks for a skilled craftsman
  to set up an idol that will not topple.

²¹Do you not know?
  Have you not heard?
Has it not been told you from the beginning?
  Have you not understood since the earth was founded?
²²He sits enthroned above the circle of the earth,
  and its people are like grasshoppers.
He stretches out the heavens like a canopy,
  and spreads them out like a tent to live in.
²³He brings princes to naught
  and reduces the rulers of this world to nothing.
²⁴No sooner are they planted,
  no sooner are they sown,
  no sooner do they take root in the ground,
than he blows on them and they wither,
  and a whirlwind sweeps them away like chaff.

²⁵"To whom will you compare me?
  Or who is my equal?" says the Holy One.
²⁶Lift your eyes and look to the heavens:
  Who created all these?
He who brings out the starry host one by one,
  and calls them each by name.
Because of his great power and mighty strength,
  not one of them is missing.

²⁷Why do you say, O Jacob,
  and complain, O Israel,
"My way is hidden from the LORD;
  my cause is disregarded by my God"?
²⁸Do you not know?
  Have you not heard?
The LORD is the everlasting God,
  the Creator of the ends of the earth.
He will not grow tired or weary,
  and his understanding no one can fathom.
²⁹He gives strength to the weary
  and increases the power of the weak.
³⁰Even youths grow tired and weary,
  and young men stumble and fall;
³¹but those who hope in the LORD
  will renew their strength.
They will soar on wings like eagles;
  they will run and not grow weary,
  they will walk and not be faint.

The Helper of Israel

41 "Be silent before me, you islands!
Let the nations renew their strength!
Let them come forward and speak;
   let us meet together at the place of judgment.

²"Who has stirred up one from the east,
   calling him in righteousness to his service*ᵃ*?
He hands nations over to him
   and subdues kings before him.
He turns them to dust with his sword,
   to windblown chaff with his bow.
³He pursues them and moves on unscathed,
   by a path his feet have not traveled before.
⁴Who has done this and carried it through,
   calling forth the generations from the beginning?
I, the LORD—with the first of them
   and with the last—I am he."

⁵The islands have seen it and fear;
   the ends of the earth tremble.
They approach and come forward;
⁶   each helps the other
   and says to his brother, "Be strong!"
⁷The craftsman encourages the goldsmith,
   and he who smooths with the hammer
   spurs on him who strikes the anvil.
He says of the welding, "It is good."
   He nails down the idol so it will not topple.

⁸"But you, O Israel, my servant,
   Jacob, whom I have chosen,
   you descendants of Abraham my friend,
⁹I took you from the ends of the earth,
   from its farthest corners I called you.
I said, 'You are my servant';
   I have chosen you and have not rejected you.
¹⁰So do not fear, for I am with you;
   do not be dismayed, for I am your God.
I will strengthen you and help you;
   I will uphold you with my righteous right hand.

¹¹"All who rage against you
   will surely be ashamed and disgraced;
those who oppose you
   will be as nothing and perish.
¹²Though you search for your enemies,
   you will not find them.
Those who wage war against you
   will be as nothing at all.
¹³For I am the LORD, your God,
   who takes hold of your right hand
and says to you, Do not fear;

ᵃ2 Or / whom victory meets at every step

I will help you.
¹⁴Do not be afraid, O worm Jacob,
    O little Israel,
  for I myself will help you," declares the LORD,
    your Redeemer, the Holy One of Israel.
¹⁵"See, I will make you into a threshing sledge,
    new and sharp, with many teeth.
  You will thresh the mountains and crush them,
    and reduce the hills to chaff.
¹⁶You will winnow them, the wind will pick them up,
    and a gale will blow them away.
  But you will rejoice in the LORD
    and glory in the Holy One of Israel.

¹⁷"The poor and needy search for water,
    but there is none;
    their tongues are parched with thirst.
  But I the LORD will answer them;
    I, the God of Israel, will not forsake them.
¹⁸I will make rivers flow on barren heights,
    and springs within the valleys.
  I will turn the desert into pools of water,
    and the parched ground into springs.
¹⁹I will put in the desert
    the cedar and the acacia, the myrtle and the olive.
  I will set pines in the wasteland,
    the fir and the cypress together,
²⁰so that people may see and know,
    may consider and understand,
  that the hand of the LORD has done this,
    that the Holy One of Israel has created it.

²¹"Present your case," says the LORD.
    "Set forth your arguments," says Jacob's King.
²²"Bring in ⌞your idols⌟ to tell us
    what is going to happen.
  Tell us what the former things were,
    so that we may consider them
    and know their final outcome.
  Or declare to us the things to come,
²³   tell us what the future holds,
    so we may know that you are gods.
  Do something, whether good or bad,
    so that we will be dismayed and filled with fear.
²⁴But you are less than nothing
    and your works are utterly worthless;
    he who chooses you is detestable.

²⁵"I have stirred up one from the north, and he comes—
    one from the rising sun who calls on my name.
  He treads on rulers as if they were mortar,
    as if he were a potter treading the clay.
²⁶Who told of this from the beginning, so we could know,
    or beforehand, so we could say, 'He was right'?
  No one told of this,

no one foretold it,
no one heard any words from you.
²⁷I was the first to tell Zion, 'Look, here they are!'
I gave to Jerusalem a messenger of good tidings.
²⁸I look but there is no one—
no one among them to give counsel,
no one to give answer when I ask them.
²⁹See, they are all false!
Their deeds amount to nothing;
their images are but wind and confusion.

The Servant of the LORD

42 "Here is my servant, whom I uphold,
my chosen one in whom I delight;
I will put my Spirit on him
and he will bring justice to the nations.
²He will not shout or cry out,
or raise his voice in the streets.
³A bruised reed he will not break,
and a smoldering wick he will not snuff out.
In faithfulness he will bring forth justice;
⁴   he will not falter or be discouraged
till he establishes justice on earth.
In his law the islands will put their hope."

⁵This is what God the LORD says—
he who created the heavens and stretched them out,
who spread out the earth and all that comes out of it,
who gives breath to its people,
and life to those who walk on it:
⁶"I, the LORD, have called you in righteousness;
I will take hold of your hand.
I will keep you and will make you
to be a covenant for the people
and a light for the Gentiles,
⁷to open eyes that are blind,
to free captives from prison
and to release from the dungeon those who sit in darkness.

⁸"I am the LORD; that is my name!
I will not give my glory to another
or my praise to idols.
⁹See, the former things have taken place,
and new things I declare;
before they spring into being
I announce them to you."

Song of Praise to the LORD

¹⁰Sing to the LORD a new song,
his praise from the ends of the earth,
you who go down to the sea, and all that is in it,
you islands, and all who live in them.
¹¹Let the desert and its towns raise their voices;
let the settlements where Kedar lives rejoice.

Let the people of Sela sing for joy;
 let them shout from the mountaintops.
¹²Let them give glory to the LORD
 and proclaim his praise in the islands.
¹³The LORD will march out like a mighty man,
 like a warrior he will stir up his zeal;
with a shout he will raise the battle cry
 and will triumph over his enemies.

¹⁴"For a long time I have kept silent,
 I have been quiet and held myself back.
But now, like a woman in childbirth,
 I cry out, I gasp and pant.
¹⁵I will lay waste the mountains and hills
 and dry up all their vegetation;
I will turn rivers into islands
 and dry up the pools.
¹⁶I will lead the blind by ways they have not known,
 along unfamiliar paths I will guide them;
I will turn the darkness into light before them
 and make the rough places smooth.
These are the things I will do;
 I will not forsake them.
¹⁷But those who trust in idols,
 who say to images, 'You are our gods,'
 will be turned back in utter shame.

Israel Blind and Deaf

¹⁸"Hear, you deaf;
 look, you blind, and see!
¹⁹Who is blind but my servant,
 and deaf like the messenger I send?
Who is blind like the one committed to me,
 blind like the servant of the LORD?
²⁰You have seen many things, but have paid no attention;
 your ears are open, but you hear nothing."
²¹It pleased the LORD
 for the sake of his righteousness
 to make his law great and glorious.
²²But this is a people plundered and looted,
 all of them trapped in pits
 or hidden away in prisons.
They have become plunder,
 with no one to rescue them;
they have been made loot,
 with no one to say, "Send them back."

²³Which of you will listen to this
 or pay close attention in time to come?
²⁴Who handed Jacob over to become loot,
 and Israel to the plunderers?
Was it not the LORD,
 against whom we have sinned?
For they would not follow his ways;

they did not obey his law.
²⁵So he poured out on them his burning anger,
  the violence of war.
It enveloped them in flames, yet they did not understand;
  it consumed them, but they did not take it to heart.

Israel's Only Savior

43 But now, this is what the Lord says—
  he who created you, O Jacob,
  he who formed you, O Israel:
"Fear not, for I have redeemed you;
  I have summoned you by name; you are mine.
²When you pass through the waters,
  I will be with you;
and when you pass through the rivers,
  they will not sweep over you.
When you walk through the fire,
  you will not be burned;
  the flames will not set you ablaze.
³For I am the Lord, your God,
  the Holy One of Israel, your Savior;
I give Egypt for your ransom,
  Cushᵃ and Seba in your stead.
⁴Since you are precious and honored in my sight,
  and because I love you,
I will give men in exchange for you,
  and people in exchange for your life.
⁵Do not be afraid, for I am with you;
  I will bring your children from the east
and gather you from the west.
⁶I will say to the north, 'Give them up!'
  and to the south, 'Do not hold them back.'
Bring my sons from afar
  and my daughters from the ends of the earth—
⁷everyone who is called by my name,
  whom I created for my glory,
  whom I formed and made."

⁸Lead out those who have eyes but are blind,
  who have ears but are deaf.
⁹All the nations gather together
  and the peoples assemble.
Which of them foretold this
  and proclaimed to us the former things?
Let them bring in their witnesses to prove they were right,
  so that others may hear and say, "It is true."
¹⁰"You are my witnesses," declares the Lord,
  "and my servant whom I have chosen,
so that you may know and believe me
  and understand that I am he.
Before me no god was formed,
  nor will there be one after me.

ᵃ3 That is, the upper Nile region

11I, even I, am the Lord,
and apart from me there is no savior.
12I have revealed and saved and proclaimed—
I, and not some foreign god among you.
You are my witnesses," declares the Lord, "that I am God.
13 Yes, and from ancient days I am he.
No one can deliver out of my hand.
When I act, who can reverse it?"

God's Mercy and Israel's Unfaithfulness

14This is what the Lord says—
your Redeemer, the Holy One of Israel:
"For your sake I will send to Babylon
and bring down as fugitives all the Babylonians,[a]
in the ships in which they took pride.
15I am the Lord, your Holy One,
Israel's Creator, your King."

16This is what the Lord says—
he who made a way through the sea,
a path through the mighty waters,
17who drew out the chariots and horses,
the army and reinforcements together,
and they lay there, never to rise again,
extinguished, snuffed out like a wick:
18"Forget the former things;
do not dwell on the past.
19See, I am doing a new thing!
Now it springs up; do you not perceive it?
I am making a way in the desert
and streams in the wasteland.
20The wild animals honor me,
the jackals and the owls,
because I provide water in the desert
and streams in the wasteland,
to give drink to my people, my chosen,
21 the people I formed for myself
that they may proclaim my praise.

22"Yet you have not called upon me, O Jacob,
you have not wearied yourselves for me, O Israel.
23You have not brought me sheep for burnt offerings,
nor honored me with your sacrifices.
I have not burdened you with grain offerings
nor wearied you with demands for incense.
24You have not bought any fragrant calamus for me,
or lavished on me the fat of your sacrifices.
But you have burdened me with your sins
and wearied me with your offenses.

25"I, even I, am he who blots out
your transgressions, for my own sake,
and remembers your sins no more.

a 14 Or Chaldeans

²⁶Review the past for me,
  let us argue the matter together;
  state the case for your innocence.
²⁷Your first father sinned;
  your spokesmen rebelled against me.
²⁸So I will disgrace the dignitaries of your temple,
  and I will consign Jacob to destruction*ᵃ*
  and Israel to scorn.

Israel the Chosen

44 "But now listen, O Jacob, my servant,
  Israel, whom I have chosen.
²This is what the LORD says—
  he who made you, who formed you in the womb,
  and who will help you:
 Do not be afraid, O Jacob, my servant,
  Jeshurun, whom I have chosen.
³For I will pour water on the thirsty land,
  and streams on the dry ground;
 I will pour out my Spirit on your offspring,
  and my blessing on your descendants.
⁴They will spring up like grass in a meadow,
  like poplar trees by flowing streams.
⁵One will say, 'I belong to the LORD';
  another will call himself by the name of Jacob;
 still another will write on his hand, 'The LORD's,'
  and will take the name Israel.

The LORD, Not Idols

⁶"This is what the LORD says—
  Israel's King and Redeemer, the LORD Almighty:
 I am the first and I am the last;
  apart from me there is no God.
⁷Who then is like me? Let him proclaim it.
  Let him declare and lay out before me
 what has happened since I established my ancient people,
  and what is yet to come—
  yes, let him foretell what will come.
⁸Do not tremble, do not be afraid.
  Did I not proclaim this and foretell it long ago?
 You are my witnesses. Is there any God besides me?
  No, there is no other Rock; I know not one."

⁹All who make idols are nothing,
  and the things they treasure are worthless.
 Those who would speak up for them are blind;
  they are ignorant, to their own shame.
¹⁰Who shapes a god and casts an idol,
  which can profit him nothing?
¹¹He and his kind will be put to shame;
  craftsmen are nothing but men.

ᵃ28 The Hebrew term refers to the irrevocable giving over of things or persons to the LORD, often by totally destroying them.

Let them all come together and take their stand;
  they will be brought down to terror and infamy.

12The blacksmith takes a tool
  and works with it in the coals;
he shapes an idol with hammers,
  he forges it with the might of his arm.
He gets hungry and loses his strength;
  he drinks no water and grows faint.
13The carpenter measures with a line
  and makes an outline with a marker;
he roughs it out with chisels
  and marks it with compasses.
He shapes it in the form of man,
  of man in all his glory,
  that it may dwell in a shrine.
14He cut down cedars,
  or perhaps took a cypress or oak.
He let it grow among the trees of the forest,
  or planted a pine, and the rain made it grow.
15It is man's fuel for burning;
  some of it he takes and warms himself,
  he kindles a fire and bakes bread.
But he also fashions a god and worships it;
  he makes an idol and bows down to it.
16Half of the wood he burns in the fire;
  over it he prepares his meal,
  he roasts his meat and eats his fill.
He also warms himself and says,
  "Ah! I am warm; I see the fire."
17From the rest he makes a god, his idol;
  he bows down to it and worships.
He prays to it and says,
  "Save me; you are my god."
18They know nothing, they understand nothing;
  their eyes are plastered over so they cannot see,
  and their minds closed so they cannot understand.
19No one stops to think,
  no one has the knowledge or understanding to say,
"Half of it I used for fuel;
  I even baked bread over its coals,
  I roasted meat and I ate.
Shall I make a detestable thing from what is left?
  Shall I bow down to a block of wood?"
20He feeds on ashes, a deluded heart misleads him;
  he cannot save himself, or say,
  "Is not this thing in my right hand a lie?"

21"Remember these things, O Jacob,
  for you are my servant, O Israel.
I have made you, you are my servant;
  O Israel, I will not forget you.
22I have swept away your offenses like a cloud,
  your sins like the morning mist.

Return to me,
for I have redeemed you."

²³Sing for joy, O heavens, for the LORD has done this;
shout aloud, O earth beneath.
Burst into song, you mountains,
you forests and all your trees,
for the LORD has redeemed Jacob,
he displays his glory in Israel.

Jerusalem to Be Inhabited

²⁴"This is what the LORD says—
your Redeemer, who formed you in the womb:

I am the LORD,
who has made all things,
who alone stretched out the heavens,
who spread out the earth by myself,

²⁵who foils the signs of false prophets
and makes fools of diviners,
who overthrows the learning of the wise
and turns it into nonsense,
²⁶who carries out the words of his servants
and fulfills the predictions of his messengers,

who says of Jerusalem, 'It shall be inhabited,'
of the towns of Judah, 'They shall be built,'
and of their ruins, 'I will restore them,'
²⁷who says to the watery deep, 'Be dry,
and I will dry up your streams,'
²⁸who says of Cyrus, 'He is my shepherd
and will accomplish all that I please;
he will say of Jerusalem, "Let it be rebuilt,"
and of the temple, "Let its foundations be laid." '

45 "This is what the LORD says to his anointed,
to Cyrus, whose right hand I take hold of
to subdue nations before him
and to strip kings of their armor,
to open doors before him
so that gates will not be shut:
²I will go before you
and will level the mountains*a*;
I will break down gates of bronze
and cut through bars of iron.
³I will give you the treasures of darkness,
riches stored in secret places,
so that you may know that I am the LORD,
the God of Israel, who summons you by name.
⁴For the sake of Jacob my servant,
of Israel my chosen,
I summon you by name
and bestow on you a title of honor,

a 2 Dead Sea Scrolls and Septuagint; the meaning of the word in the Masoretic Text is uncertain.

though you do not acknowledge me.
⁵I am the Lord, and there is no other;
    apart from me there is no God.
I will strengthen you,
    though you have not acknowledged me,
⁶so that from the rising of the sun
    to the place of its setting
men may know there is none besides me.
    I am the Lord, and there is no other.
⁷I form the light and create darkness,
    I bring prosperity and create disaster;
    I, the Lord, do all these things.

⁸"You heavens above, rain down righteousness;
    let the clouds shower it down.
Let the earth open wide,
    let salvation spring up,
let righteousness grow with it;
    I, the Lord, have created it.

⁹"Woe to him who quarrels with his Maker,
    to him who is but a potsherd among the potsherds on the ground.
Does the clay say to the potter,
    'What are you making?'
Does your work say,
    'He has no hands'?
¹⁰Woe to him who says to his father,
    'What have you begotten?'
or to his mother,
    'What have you brought to birth?'

¹¹"This is what the Lord says—
    the Holy One of Israel, and its Maker:
Concerning things to come,
    do you question me about my children,
    or give me orders about the work of my hands?
¹²It is I who made the earth
    and created mankind upon it.
My own hands stretched out the heavens;
    I marshaled their starry hosts.
¹³I will raise up Cyrus[a] in my righteousness:
    I will make all his ways straight.
He will rebuild my city
    and set my exiles free,
but not for a price or reward,
    says the Lord Almighty."

¹⁴This is what the Lord says:

"The products of Egypt and the merchandise of Cush,[b]
    and those tall Sabeans—
they will come over to you
    and will be yours;
they will trudge behind you,

coming over to you in chains.
They will bow down before you
   and plead with you, saying,
'Surely God is with you, and there is no other;
   there is no other god.'"

15Truly you are a God who hides himself,
   O God and Savior of Israel.
16All the makers of idols will be put to shame and disgraced;
   they will go off into disgrace together.
17But Israel will be saved by the LORD
   with an everlasting salvation;
you will never be put to shame or disgraced,
   to ages everlasting.

18For this is what the LORD says—
he who created the heavens,
   he is God;
he who fashioned and made the earth,
   he founded it;
he did not create it to be empty,
   but formed it to be inhabited—
he says:
"I am the LORD,
   and there is no other.
19I have not spoken in secret,
   from somewhere in a land of darkness;
I have not said to Jacob's descendants,
   'Seek me in vain.'
I, the LORD, speak the truth;
   I declare what is right.

20"Gather together and come;
   assemble, you fugitives from the nations.
Ignorant are those who carry about idols of wood,
   who pray to gods that cannot save.
21Declare what is to be, present it—
   let them take counsel together.
Who foretold this long ago,
   who declared it from the distant past?
Was it not I, the LORD?
   And there is no God apart from me,
a righteous God and a Savior;
   there is none but me.

22"Turn to me and be saved,
   all you ends of the earth;
for I am God, and there is no other.
23By myself I have sworn,
   my mouth has uttered in all integrity
   a word that will not be revoked:
Before me every knee will bow;
   by me every tongue will swear.
24They will say of me, 'In the LORD alone
   are righteousness and strength.'"

All who have raged against him
will come to him and be put to shame.
²⁵But in the Lᴏʀᴅ all the descendants of Israel
will be found righteous and will exult.

Gods of Babylon

46 Bel bows down, Nebo stoops low;
their idols are borne by beasts of burden. ᵃ
The images that are carried about are burdensome,
a burden for the weary.
²They stoop and bow down together;
unable to rescue the burden,
they themselves go off into captivity.

³"Listen to me, O house of Jacob,
all you who remain of the house of Israel,
you whom I have upheld since you were conceived,
and have carried since your birth.
⁴Even to your old age and gray hairs
I am he, I am he who will sustain you.
I have made you and I will carry you;
I will sustain you and I will rescue you.

⁵"To whom will you compare me or count me equal?
To whom will you liken me that we may be compared?
⁶Some pour out gold from their bags
and weigh out silver on the scales;
they hire a goldsmith to make it into a god,
and they bow down and worship it.
⁷They lift it to their shoulders and carry it;
they set it up in its place, and there it stands.
From that spot it cannot move.
Though one cries out to it, it does not answer;
it cannot save him from his troubles.

⁸"Remember this, fix it in mind,
take it to heart, you rebels.
⁹Remember the former things, those of long ago;
I am God, and there is no other;
I am God, and there is none like me.
¹⁰I make known the end from the beginning,
from ancient times, what is still to come.
I say: My purpose will stand,
and I will do all that I please.
¹¹From the east I summon a bird of prey;
from a far-off land, a man to fulfill my purpose.
What I have said, that will I bring about;
what I have planned, that will I do.
¹²Listen to me, you stubborn-hearted,
you who are far from righteousness.
¹³I am bringing my righteousness near,
it is not far away;
and my salvation will not be delayed.

ᵃ *1 Or are but beasts and cattle*

I will grant salvation to Zion,
   my splendor to Israel.

The Fall of Babylon

47 "Go down, sit in the dust,
   Virgin Daughter of Babylon;
sit on the ground without a throne,
   Daughter of the Babylonians. [a]
No more will you be called
   tender or delicate.
2Take millstones and grind flour;
   take off your veil.
Lift up your skirts, bare your legs,
   and wade through the streams.
3Your nakedness will be exposed
   and your shame uncovered.
I will take vengeance;
   I will spare no one."

4Our Redeemer—the Lord Almighty is his name—
   is the Holy One of Israel.

5"Sit in silence, go into darkness,
   Daughter of the Babylonians;
no more will you be called
   queen of kingdoms.
6I was angry with my people
   and desecrated my inheritance;
I gave them into your hand,
   and you showed them no mercy.
Even on the aged
   you laid a very heavy yoke.
7You said, 'I will continue forever—
   the eternal queen!'
But you did not consider these things
   or reflect on what might happen.

8"Now then, listen, you wanton creature,
   lounging in your security
and saying to yourself,
   'I am, and there is none besides me.
I will never be a widow
   or suffer the loss of children.'
9Both of these will overtake you
   in a moment, on a single day:
   loss of children and widowhood.
They will come upon you in full measure,
   in spite of your many sorceries
   and all your potent spells.
10You have trusted in your wickedness
   and have said, 'No one sees me.'
Your wisdom and knowledge mislead you
   when you say to yourself,

---

a 1 Or *Chaldeans*; also in verse 5

'I am, and there is none besides me.'
¹¹Disaster will come upon you,
      and you will not know how to conjure it away.
  A calamity will fall upon you
      that you cannot ward off with a ransom;
  a catastrophe you cannot foresee
      will suddenly come upon you.

¹²"Keep on, then, with your magic spells
      and with your many sorceries,
      which you have labored at since childhood.
  Perhaps you will succeed,
      perhaps you will cause terror.
¹³All the counsel you have received has only worn you out!
      Let your astrologers come forward,
  those stargazers who make predictions month by month,
      let them save you from what is coming upon you.
¹⁴Surely they are like stubble;
      the fire will burn them up.
  They cannot even save themselves
      from the power of the flame.
  Here are no coals to warm anyone;
      here is no fire to sit by.
¹⁵That is all they can do for you—
      these you have labored with
      and trafficked with since childhood.
  Each of them goes on in his error;
      there is not one that can save you.

Stubborn Israel

48 "Listen to this, O house of Jacob,
      you who are called by the name of Israel
      and come from the line of Judah,
  you who take oaths in the name of the LORD
      and invoke the God of Israel—
      but not in truth or righteousness—
²you who call yourselves citizens of the holy city
      and rely on the God of Israel—
      the LORD Almighty is his name:
³I foretold the former things long ago,
      my mouth announced them and I made them known;
      then suddenly I acted, and they came to pass.
⁴For I knew how stubborn you were;
      the sinews of your neck were iron,
      your forehead was bronze.
⁵Therefore I told you these things long ago;
      before they happened I announced them to you
  so that you could not say,
      'My idols did them;
      my wooden image and metal god ordained them.'
⁶You have heard these things; look at them all.
      Will you not admit them?

  "From now on I will tell you of new things,

of hidden things unknown to you.
[7]They are created now, and not long ago;
  you have not heard of them before today.
So you cannot say,
  'Yes, I knew of them.'
[8]You have neither heard nor understood;
  from of old your ear has not been open.
Well do I know how treacherous you are;
  you were called a rebel from birth.
[9]For my own name's sake I delay my wrath;
  for the sake of my praise I hold it back from you,
  so as not to cut you off.
[10]See, I have refined you, though not as silver;
  I have tested you in the furnace of affliction.
[11]For my own sake, for my own sake, I do this.
  How can I let myself be defamed?
  I will not yield my glory to another.

Israel Freed

[12]"Listen to me, O Jacob,
  Israel, whom I have called:
I am he;
  I am the first and I am the last.
[13]My own hand laid the foundations of the earth,
  and my right hand spread out the heavens;
when I summon them,
  they all stand up together.

[14]"Come together, all of you, and listen:
  Which of ˎthe idolsˎ has foretold these things?
The Lord's chosen ally
  will carry out his purpose against Babylon;
  his arm will be against the Babylonians.[a]
[15]I, even I, have spoken;
  yes, I have called him.
I will bring him,
  and he will succeed in his mission.

[16]"Come near me and listen to this:

  "From the first announcement I have not spoken in secret;
    at the time it happens, I am there."

And now the Sovereign Lord has sent me,
  with his Spirit.

[17]This is what the Lord says—
  your Redeemer, the Holy One of Israel:
"I am the Lord your God,
  who teaches you what is best for you,
  who directs you in the way you should go.
[18]If only you had paid attention to my commands,
  your peace would have been like a river,
  your righteousness like the waves of the sea.

---

[a]14 Or Chaldeans; also in verse 20

19Your descendants would have been like the sand,
  your children like its numberless grains;
their name would never be cut off
  nor destroyed from before me."

20Leave Babylon,
  flee from the Babylonians!
Announce this with shouts of joy
  and proclaim it.
Send it out to the ends of the earth;
  say, "The LORD has redeemed his servant Jacob."
21They did not thirst when he led them through the deserts;
  he made water flow for them from the rock;
he split the rock
  and water gushed out.

22"There is no peace," says the LORD, "for the wicked."

The Servant of the LORD

49 Listen to me, you islands;
  hear this, you distant nations:
Before I was born the LORD called me;
  from my birth he has made mention of my name.
2He made my mouth like a sharpened sword,
  in the shadow of his hand he hid me;
he made me into a polished arrow
  and concealed me in his quiver.
3He said to me, "You are my servant,
  Israel, in whom I will display my splendor."
4But I said, "I have labored to no purpose;
  I have spent my strength in vain and for nothing.
Yet what is due me is in the LORD's hand,
  and my reward is with my God."

5And now the LORD says—
  he who formed me in the womb to be his servant
to bring Jacob back to him
  and gather Israel to himself,
for I am honored in the eyes of the LORD
  and my God has been my strength—
6he says:
  "It is too small a thing for you to be my servant
  to restore the tribes of Jacob
  and bring back those of Israel I have kept.
I will also make you a light for the Gentiles,
  that you may bring my salvation to the ends of the earth."

7This is what the LORD says—
  the Redeemer and Holy One of Israel—
to him who was despised and abhorred by the nation,
  to the servant of rulers:
"Kings will see you and rise up,
  princes will see and bow down,
because of the LORD, who is faithful,
  the Holy One of Israel, who has chosen you."

Restoration of Israel

⁸This is what the LORD says:

> "In the time of my favor I will answer you,
>   and in the day of salvation I will help you;
> I will keep you and will make you
>   to be a covenant for the people,
> to restore the land
>   and to reassign its desolate inheritances,
> ⁹to say to the captives, 'Come out,'
>   and to those in darkness, 'Be free!'
>
> "They will feed beside the roads
>   and find pasture on every barren hill.
> ¹⁰They will neither hunger nor thirst,
>   nor will the desert heat or the sun beat upon them.
> He who has compassion on them will guide them
>   and lead them beside springs of water.
> ¹¹I will turn all my mountains into roads,
>   and my highways will be raised up.
> ¹²See, they will come from afar—
>   some from the north, some from the west,
>   some from the region of Aswan. ᵃ"
>
> ¹³Shout for joy, O heavens;
>   rejoice, O earth;
>   burst into song, O mountains!
> For the LORD comforts his people
>   and will have compassion on his afflicted ones.
>
> ¹⁴But Zion said, "The LORD has forsaken me,
>   the Lord has forgotten me."
>
> ¹⁵"Can a mother forget the baby at her breast
>   and have no compassion on the child she has borne?
> Though she may forget,
>   I will not forget you!
> ¹⁶See, I have engraved you on the palms of my hands;
>   your walls are ever before me.
> ¹⁷Your sons hasten back,
>   and those who laid you waste depart from you.
> ¹⁸Lift up your eyes and look around;
>   all your sons gather and come to you.
> As surely as I live," declares the LORD,
>   "you will wear them all as ornaments;
>   you will put them on, like a bride.
>
> ¹⁹"Though you were ruined and made desolate
>   and your land laid waste,
> now you will be too small for your people,
>   and those who devoured you will be far away.
> ²⁰The children born during your bereavement
>   will yet say in your hearing,

ᵃ *12* Dead Sea Scrolls; Masoretic Text *Sinim*

'This place is too small for us;
    give us more space to live in.'
²¹Then you will say in your heart,
    'Who bore me these?
I was bereaved and barren;
    I was exiled and rejected.
Who brought these up?
I was left all alone,
    but these—where have they come from?'"

²²This is what the Sovereign LORD says:

"See, I will beckon to the Gentiles,
    I will lift up my banner to the peoples;
they will bring your sons in their arms
    and carry your daughters on their shoulders.
²³Kings will be your foster fathers,
    and their queens your nursing mothers.
They will bow down before you with their faces to the ground;
    they will lick the dust at your feet.
Then you will know that I am the LORD;
    those who hope in me will not be disappointed."

²⁴Can plunder be taken from warriors,
    or captives rescued from the fierce*ᵃ*?

²⁵But this is what the LORD says:

"Yes, captives will be taken from warriors,
    and plunder retrieved from the fierce;
I will contend with those who contend with you,
    and your children I will save.
²⁶I will make your oppressors eat their own flesh;
    they will be drunk on their own blood, as with wine.
Then all mankind will know
    that I, the LORD, am your Savior,
    your Redeemer, the Mighty One of Jacob."

Israel's Sin and the Servant's Obedience

50 This is what the LORD says:

"Where is your mother's certificate of divorce
    with which I sent her away?
Or to which of my creditors
    did I sell you?
Because of your sins you were sold;
    because of your transgressions your mother was sent away.
²When I came, why was there no one?
    When I called, why was there no one to answer?
Was my arm too short to ransom you?
    Do I lack the strength to rescue you?
By a mere rebuke I dry up the sea,

ᵃ *24* Dead Sea Scrolls, Vulgate and Syriac (see also Septuagint and verse 25); Masoretic Text *righteous*

I turn rivers into a desert;
their fish rot for lack of water
and die of thirst.
[3]I clothe the sky with darkness
and make sackcloth its covering."

[4]The Sovereign LORD has given me an instructed tongue,
to know the word that sustains the weary.

He wakens me morning by morning,
wakens my ear to listen like
one being taught.
[5]The Sovereign LORD has opened my ears,
and I have not been rebellious;
I have not drawn back.
[6]I offered my back to those who beat me,
my cheeks to those who pulled out my
beard;
I did not hide my face
from mocking and spitting.
[7]Because the Sovereign LORD helps me,
I will not be disgraced.
Therefore have I set my face like flint,
and I know I will not be put to shame.
[8]He who vindicates me is near.
Who then will bring charges against me?
Let us face each other!
Who is my accuser?
Let him confront me!
[9]It is the Sovereign LORD who helps me.
Who is he that will condemn me?
They will all wear out like a garment;
the moths will eat them up.

[10]Who among you fears the LORD
and obeys the word of his servant?
Let him who walks in the dark,
who has no light,
trust in the name of the LORD
and rely on his God.
[11]But now, all you who light fires
and provide yourselves with flaming torches,
go, walk in the light of your fires
and of the torches you have set ablaze.
This is what you shall receive from my hand:
You will lie down in torment.

Everlasting Salvation for Zion

51 "Listen to me, you who pursue righteousness
and who seek the LORD:
Look to the rock from which you were cut
and to the quarry from which you were hewn;
[2]look to Abraham, your father,
and to Sarah, who gave you birth.

□ ▦▦▦▦▦ **REASONS TO BELIEVE** ▦▦▦▦▦ ⊟

50:6
The Amazing Bible

Isaiah predicted that the Messiah would be
beaten on the back and in the face, that his
beard would be plucked out, and that he
would be mocked and spat upon. This is exactly the kind of treatment Jesus received at
the hands of the Roman soldiers just before
he was crucified (see Matthew chapter 27,
verses 26–31 [page 1299]).

When I called him he was but one,
  and I blessed him and made him many.
³The LORD will surely comfort Zion
  and will look with compassion on all her ruins;
he will make her deserts like Eden,
  her wastelands like the garden of the LORD.
Joy and gladness will be found in her,
  thanksgiving and the sound of singing.

⁴"Listen to me, my people;
  hear me, my nation:
The law will go out from me;
  my justice will become a light to the nations.
⁵My righteousness draws near speedily,
  my salvation is on the way,
  and my arm will bring justice to the nations.
The islands will look to me
  and wait in hope for my arm.
⁶Lift up your eyes to the heavens,
  look at the earth beneath;
the heavens will vanish like smoke,
  the earth will wear out like a garment
  and its inhabitants die like flies.
But my salvation will last forever,
  my righteousness will never fail.

⁷"Hear me, you who know what is right,
  you people who have my law in your hearts:
Do not fear the reproach of men
  or be terrified by their insults.
⁸For the moth will eat them up like a garment;
  the worm will devour them like wool.
But my righteousness will last forever,
  my salvation through all generations."

⁹Awake, awake! Clothe yourself with strength,
  O arm of the LORD;
awake, as in days gone by,
  as in generations of old.
Was it not you who cut Rahab to pieces,
  who pierced that monster through?
¹⁰Was it not you who dried up the sea,
  the waters of the great deep,
who made a road in the depths of the sea
  so that the redeemed might cross over?
¹¹The ransomed of the LORD will return.
  They will enter Zion with singing;
everlasting joy will crown their heads.
  Gladness and joy will overtake them,
  and sorrow and sighing will flee away.

¹²"I, even I, am he who comforts you.
  Who are you that you fear mortal men,
  the sons of men, who are but grass,
¹³that you forget the LORD your Maker,

who stretched out the heavens
and laid the foundations of the earth,
that you live in constant terror every day
because of the wrath of the oppressor,
who is bent on destruction? ·
For where is the wrath of the oppressor?
14 The cowering prisoners will soon be set free;
they will not die in their dungeon,
nor will they lack bread.
15For I am the LORD your God,
who churns up the sea so that its waves roar—
the LORD Almighty is his name.
16I have put my words in your mouth
and covered you with the shadow of my hand—
I who set the heavens in place,
who laid the foundations of the earth,
and who say to Zion, 'You are my people.'"

The Cup of the LORD's Wrath

17Awake, awake!
Rise up, O Jerusalem,
you who have drunk from the hand of the LORD
the cup of his wrath,
you who have drained to its dregs
the goblet that makes men stagger.
18Of all the sons she bore
there was none to guide her;
of all the sons she reared
there was none to take her by the hand.
19These double calamities have come upon you—
who can comfort you?—
ruin and destruction, famine and sword—
who can*a* console you?
20Your sons have fainted;
they lie at the head of every street,
like antelope caught in a net.
They are filled with the wrath of the LORD
and the rebuke of your God.

21Therefore hear this, you afflicted one,
made drunk, but not with wine.
22This is what your Sovereign LORD says,
your God, who defends his people:
"See, I have taken out of your hand
the cup that made you stagger;
from that cup, the goblet of my wrath,
you will never drink again.
23I will put it into the hands of your tormentors,
who said to you,
'Fall prostrate that we may walk over you.'
And you made your back like the ground,
like a street to be walked over."

a 19 Dead Sea Scrolls, Septuagint, Vulgate and Syriac; Masoretic Text / *how can I*

52

Awake, awake, O Zion,
   clothe yourself with strength.
Put on your garments of splendor,
   O Jerusalem, the holy city.
The uncircumcised and defiled
   will not enter you again.
²Shake off your dust;
   rise up, sit enthroned, O Jerusalem.
Free yourself from the chains on your neck,
   O captive Daughter of Zion.

³For this is what the LORD says:

   "You were sold for nothing,
      and without money you will be redeemed."

⁴For this is what the Sovereign LORD says:

   "At first my people went down to Egypt to live;
      lately, Assyria has oppressed them.

⁵"And now what do I have here?" declares the LORD.

   "For my people have been taken away for nothing,
      and those who rule them mock,ᵃ"

declares the LORD.

   "And all day long
      my name is constantly blasphemed.
⁶Therefore my people will know my name;
   therefore in that day they will know
that it is I who foretold it.
   Yes, it is I."

⁷How beautiful on the mountains
   are the feet of those who bring good news,
who proclaim peace,
   who bring good tidings,
   who proclaim salvation,
who say to Zion,
   "Your God reigns!"
⁸Listen! Your watchmen lift up their voices;
   together they shout for joy.
When the LORD returns to Zion,
   they will see it with their own eyes.
⁹Burst into songs of joy together,
   you ruins of Jerusalem,
for the LORD has comforted his people,
   he has redeemed Jerusalem.
¹⁰The LORD will lay bare his holy arm
   in the sight of all the nations,
and all the ends of the earth will see
   the salvation of our God.

¹¹Depart, depart, go out from there!
   Touch no unclean thing!
Come out from it and be pure,

ᵃ 5 Dead Sea Scrolls and Vulgate; Masoretic Text *wail*

you who carry the vessels of the LORD.
¹²But you will not leave in haste
or go in flight;
for the LORD will go before you,
the God of Israel will be your rear guard.

The Suffering and Glory of the Servant

¹³See, my servant will act wisely*a*;
he will be raised and lifted up and highly exalted.
¹⁴Just as there were many who were appalled at him*b*—
his appearance was so disfigured beyond that of any man
and his form marred beyond human likeness—
¹⁵so will he sprinkle many nations,*c*
and kings will shut their mouths because of him.
For what they were not told, they will see,
and what they have not heard, they will understand.

53 Who has believed our message
and to whom has the arm of the LORD been revealed?
²He grew up before him like a tender shoot,
and like a root out of dry ground.
He had no beauty or majesty to attract us to him,
nothing in his appearance that we should desire him.
³He was despised and rejected by men,
a man of sorrows, and familiar with suffering.
Like one from whom men hide their faces
he was despised, and we esteemed him not.

⁴Surely he took up our infirmities
and carried our sorrows,
yet we considered him stricken by God,
smitten by him, and afflicted.
⁵But he was pierced for our transgressions,
he was crushed for our iniquities;
the punishment that brought us peace was upon him,

a13 Or *will prosper*   *b14* Hebrew *you*   *c15* Hebrew; Septuagint *so will many nations marvel at him*

▦ REASONS TO BELIEVE ▦

53:1–12
The Amazing Bible

This is one of the most important chapters in the Old Testament. Written over 700 years before Jesus' birth, it details several events that were part of the crucifixion, death, and burial of the Messiah. *Each of these predictions was fulfilled in Jesus of Nazareth!*

• Rejected by his own people (verse 3)	Fulfilled: John 7:5, 48 (page 1393)
• Pierced (verse 5)	Fulfilled: John 19:34–37; 20:25–29 (page 1415)
• Wounded (verse 5)	Fulfilled: Matthew 27:26 (page 1299)
• Took our sin on himself (verses 5, 10, 11)	Fulfilled: 1 Peter 2:24 (page 1612)
• Silent before accusers (verse 7)	Fulfilled: Matthew 27:12–14 (page 1299)
• Buried by a rich man (verse 9)	Fulfilled: Matthew 27:57–60 (page 1300)
• Prayed for his persecutors (verse 12)	Fulfilled: Luke 23:34 (page 1377)
• Crucified with thieves (verse 12)	Fulfilled: Matthew 27:38 (page 1300)
• Killed, though still sees life (verses 10–12)	Fulfilled: Matthew 28:5–7 (page 1301)

and by his wounds we are healed.
⁶We all, like sheep, have gone astray,
    each of us has turned to his own way;
and the LORD has laid on him
    the iniquity of us all.

⁷He was oppressed and afflicted,
    yet he did not open his mouth;
he was led like a lamb to the slaughter,
    and as a sheep before her shearers is silent,
    so he did not open his mouth.
⁸By oppression*a* and judgment he was taken away.
    And who can speak of his descendants?
For he was cut off from the land of the living;
    for the transgression of my people he was stricken.*b*
⁹He was assigned a grave with the wicked,
    and with the rich in his death,
though he had done no violence,
    nor was any deceit in his mouth.

¹⁰Yet it was the LORD's will to crush him and cause him to suffer,
    and though the LORD makes*c* his life a guilt offering,
he will see his offspring and prolong his days,
    and the will of the LORD will prosper in his hand.
¹¹After the suffering of his soul,
    he will see the light ⌊of life⌋*d* and be satisfied*e*;
by his knowledge*f* my righteous servant will justify many,
    and he will bear their iniquities.
¹²Therefore I will give him a portion among the great,*g*
    and he will divide the spoils with the strong,*h*
because he poured out his life unto death,
    and was numbered with the transgressors.
For he bore the sin of many,
    and made intercession for the transgressors.

The Future Glory of Zion

54 "Sing, O barren woman,
    you who never bore a child;
burst into song, shout for joy,
    you who were never in labor;
because more are the children of the desolate woman
    than of her who has a husband,"

                    says the LORD.

²"Enlarge the place of your tent,
    stretch your tent curtains wide,
    do not hold back;
lengthen your cords,
    strengthen your stakes.
³For you will spread out to the right and to the left;
    your descendants will dispossess nations
    and settle in their desolate cities.

---

a 8 Or *From arrest*   *b 8* Or *away. / Yet who of his generation considered / that he was cut off from the land of the living / for the transgression of my people. / to whom the blow was due?*   *c 10* Hebrew *though you make*   *d 11* Dead Sea Scrolls (see also Septuagint); Masoretic Text does not have *the light ⌊of life⌋*   *e 11* Or (with Masoretic Text) *11He will see the result of the suffering of his soul / and be satisfied*   *f 11* Or *by knowledge of him*   *g 12* Or *many*   *h 12* Or *numerous*

⁴"Do not be afraid; you will not suffer shame.
  Do not fear disgrace; you will not be humiliated.
You will forget the shame of your youth
  and remember no more the reproach of your widowhood.
⁵For your Maker is your husband—
  the LORD Almighty is his name—
the Holy One of Israel is your Redeemer;
  he is called the God of all the earth.
⁶The LORD will call you back
  as if you were a wife deserted and distressed in spirit—
a wife who married young,
  only to be rejected," says your God.
⁷"For a brief moment I abandoned you,
  but with deep compassion I will bring you back.
⁸In a surge of anger
  I hid my face from you for a moment,
but with everlasting kindness
  I will have compassion on you,"
    says the LORD your Redeemer.

⁹"To me this is like the days of Noah,
  when I swore that the waters of Noah would never again cover
      the earth.
So now I have sworn not to be angry with you,
  never to rebuke you again.
¹⁰Though the mountains be shaken
  · and the hills be removed,
yet my unfailing love for you will not be shaken
  nor my covenant of peace be removed,"
    says the LORD, who has compassion on you.

¹¹"O afflicted city, lashed by storms and not comforted,
  I will build you with stones of turquoise,ᵃ
  your foundations with sapphires.ᵇ
¹²I will make your battlements of rubies,
  your gates of sparkling jewels,
  and all your walls of precious stones.
¹³All your sons will be taught by the LORD,
  and great will be your children's peace.
¹⁴In righteousness you will be established:
  Tyranny will be far from you;
    you will have nothing to fear.
  Terror will be far removed;
    it will not come near you.
¹⁵If anyone does attack you, it will not be my doing;
  whoever attacks you will surrender to you.

¹⁶"See, it is I who created the blacksmith
  who fans the coals into flame
  and forges a weapon fit for its work.
And it is I who have created the destroyer to work havoc;
¹⁷ no weapon forged against you will prevail,
  and you will refute every tongue that accuses you.

ᵃ 11 The meaning of the Hebrew for this word is uncertain.   ᵇ 11 Or *lapis lazuli*

This is the heritage of the servants of the Lᴏʀᴅ,
  and this is their vindication from me,"

declares the Lᴏʀᴅ.

Invitation to the Thirsty

55 "Come, all you who are thirsty,
  come to the waters;
and you who have no money,
  come, buy and eat!
Come, buy wine and milk
  without money and without cost.
²Why spend money on what is not bread,
  and your labor on what does not satisfy?
Listen, listen to me, and eat what is good,
  and your soul will delight in the richest of fare.
³Give ear and come to me;
  hear me, that your soul may live.
I will make an everlasting covenant with you,
  my faithful love promised to David.
⁴See, I have made him a witness to the peoples,
  a leader and commander of the peoples.
⁵Surely you will summon nations you know not,
  and nations that do not know you will hasten to you,
because of the Lᴏʀᴅ your God,
  the Holy One of Israel,
  for he has endowed you with splendor."

⁶Seek the Lᴏʀᴅ while he may be found;
  call on him while he is near.
⁷Let the wicked forsake his way
  and the evil man his thoughts.
Let him turn to the Lᴏʀᴅ, and he will have mercy on him,
  and to our God, for he will freely pardon.

⁸"For my thoughts are not your thoughts,
  neither are your ways my ways,"

declares the Lᴏʀᴅ.

⁹"As the heavens are higher than the earth,
  so are my ways higher than your ways
  and my thoughts than your thoughts.
¹⁰As the rain and the snow
  come down from heaven,
and do not return to it
  without watering the earth
and making it bud and flourish,
  so that it yields seed for the sower and bread for the eater,
¹¹so is my word that goes out from my mouth:
  It will not return to me empty,
but will accomplish what I desire
  and achieve the purpose for which I sent it.
¹²You will go out in joy
  and be led forth in peace;
the mountains and hills
  will burst into song before you,

and all the trees of the field
    will clap their hands.
¹³Instead of the thornbush will grow the pine tree,
    and instead of briers the myrtle will grow.
This will be for the LORD's renown,
    for an everlasting sign,
    which will not be destroyed."

Salvation for Others

56 This is what the LORD says:

"Maintain justice
    and do what is right,
for my salvation is close at hand
    and my righteousness will soon be revealed.
²Blessed is the man who does this,
    the man who holds it fast,
who keeps the Sabbath without desecrating it,
    and keeps his hand from doing any evil."

³Let no foreigner who has bound himself to the LORD say,
    "The LORD will surely exclude me from his people."
And let not any eunuch complain,
    "I am only a dry tree."

⁴For this is what the LORD says:

"To the eunuchs who keep my Sabbaths,
    who choose what pleases me
    and hold fast to my covenant—
⁵to them I will give within my temple and its walls
    a memorial and a name
    better than sons and daughters;
I will give them an everlasting name
    that will not be cut off.
⁶And foreigners who bind themselves to the LORD
    to serve him,
to love the name of the LORD,
    and to worship him,
all who keep the Sabbath without desecrating it
    and who hold fast to my covenant—
⁷these I will bring to my holy mountain
    and give them joy in my house of prayer.
Their burnt offerings and sacrifices
    will be accepted on my altar;
for my house will be called
    a house of prayer for all nations."
⁸The Sovereign LORD declares—
    he who gathers the exiles of Israel:
"I will gather still others to them
    besides those already gathered."

God's Accusation Against the Wicked

⁹Come, all you beasts of the field,
    come and devour, all you beasts of the forest!

¹⁰Israel's watchmen are blind,
⠀⠀they all lack knowledge;
they are all mute dogs,
⠀⠀they cannot bark;
they lie around and dream,
⠀⠀they love to sleep.
¹¹They are dogs with mighty appetites;
⠀⠀they never have enough.
They are shepherds who lack understanding;
⠀⠀they all turn to their own way,
⠀⠀each seeks his own gain.
¹²"Come," each one cries, "let me get wine!
⠀⠀Let us drink our fill of beer!
And tomorrow will be like today,
⠀⠀or even far better."

57⠀⠀The righteous perish,
⠀⠀and no one ponders it in his heart;
devout men are taken away,
⠀⠀and no one understands
that the righteous are taken away
⠀⠀to be spared from evil.
²Those who walk uprightly
⠀⠀enter into peace;
⠀⠀they find rest as they lie in death.

³"But you—come here, you sons of a sorceress,
⠀⠀you offspring of adulterers and prostitutes!
⁴Whom are you mocking?
⠀⠀At whom do you sneer
⠀⠀and stick out your tongue?
Are you not a brood of rebels,
⠀⠀the offspring of liars?
⁵You burn with lust among the oaks
⠀⠀and under every spreading tree;
you sacrifice your children in the ravines
⠀⠀and under the overhanging crags.
⁶The idols₋ among the smooth stones of the ravines are your portion;
⠀⠀they, they are your lot.
Yes, to them you have poured out drink offerings
⠀⠀and offered grain offerings.
⠀⠀In the light of these things, should I relent?
⁷You have made your bed on a high and lofty hill;
⠀⠀there you went up to offer your sacrifices.
⁸Behind your doors and your doorposts
⠀⠀you have put your pagan symbols.
Forsaking me, you uncovered your bed,
⠀⠀you climbed into it and opened it wide;
you made a pact with those whose beds you love,
⠀⠀and you looked on their nakedness.
⁹You went to Molech*ᵃ* with olive oil
⠀⠀and increased your perfumes.

ᵃ9 Or to the king

You sent your ambassadors[a] far away;
    you descended to the grave[b] itself!
¹⁰You were wearied by all your ways,
    but you would not say, 'It is hopeless.'
You found renewal of your strength,
    and so you did not faint.

¹¹"Whom have you so dreaded and feared
    that you have been false to me,
and have neither remembered me
    nor pondered this in your hearts?
Is it not because I have long been silent
    that you do not fear me?
¹²I will expose your righteousness and your works,
    and they will not benefit you.
¹³When you cry out for help,
    let your collection ⌊of idols⌋ save you!
The wind will carry all of them off,
    a mere breath will blow them away.
But the man who makes me his refuge
    will inherit the land
    and possess my holy mountain."

Comfort for the Contrite

¹⁴And it will be said:

"Build up, build up, prepare the road!
    Remove the obstacles out of the way of my people."
¹⁵For this is what the high and lofty One says—
    he who lives forever, whose name is holy:
"I live in a high and holy place,
    but also with him who is contrite and lowly in spirit,
to revive the spirit of the lowly
    and to revive the heart of the contrite.
¹⁶I will not accuse forever,
    nor will I always be angry,
for then the spirit of man would grow faint before me—
    the breath of man that I have created.
¹⁷I was enraged by his sinful greed;
    I punished him, and hid my face in anger,
    yet he kept on in his willful ways.
¹⁸I have seen his ways, but I will heal him;
    I will guide him and restore comfort to him,
¹⁹   creating praise on the lips of the mourners in Israel.
Peace, peace, to those far and near,"
    says the LORD. "And I will heal them."
²⁰But the wicked are like the tossing sea,
    which cannot rest,
    whose waves cast up mire and mud.
²¹"There is no peace," says my God, "for the wicked."

---

a 9 Or *idols*   *b 9* Hebrew *Sheol*

True Fasting

58 "Shout it aloud, do not hold back.
  Raise your voice like a trumpet.
Declare to my people their rebellion
  and to the house of Jacob their sins.
²For day after day they seek me out;
  they seem eager to know my ways,
as if they were a nation that does what is right
  and has not forsaken the commands of its God.
They ask me for just decisions
  and seem eager for God to come near them.
³'Why have we fasted,' they say,
  'and you have not seen it?
Why have we humbled ourselves,
  and you have not noticed?'

"Yet on the day of your fasting, you do as you please
  and exploit all your workers.
⁴Your fasting ends in quarreling and strife,
  and in striking each other with wicked fists.
You cannot fast as you do today
  and expect your voice to be heard on high.
⁵Is this the kind of fast I have chosen,
  only a day for a man to humble himself?
Is it only for bowing one's head like a reed
  and for lying on sackcloth and ashes?
Is that what you call a fast,
  a day acceptable to the LORD?

⁶"Is not this the kind of fasting I have chosen:
to loose the chains of injustice
  and untie the cords of the yoke,
to set the oppressed free
  and break every yoke?
⁷Is it not to share your food with the hungry
  and to provide the poor wanderer with shelter—
when you see the naked, to clothe him,
  and not to turn away from your own flesh and blood?
⁸Then your light will break forth like the dawn,
  and your healing will quickly appear;
then your righteousness*a* will go before you,
  and the glory of the LORD will be your rear guard.
⁹Then you will call, and the LORD will answer;
  you will cry for help, and he will say: Here am I.

"If you do away with the yoke of oppression,
  with the pointing finger and malicious talk,
¹⁰and if you spend yourselves in behalf of the hungry
  and satisfy the needs of the oppressed,
then your light will rise in the darkness,
  and your night will become like the noonday.
¹¹The LORD will guide you always;
  he will satisfy your needs in a sun-scorched land

---

a8 Or your righteous One

and will strengthen your frame.
You will be like a well-watered garden,
    like a spring whose waters never fail.
¹²Your people will rebuild the ancient ruins
    and will raise up the age-old foundations;
you will be called Repairer of Broken Walls,
    Restorer of Streets with Dwellings.

¹³"If you keep your feet from breaking the Sabbath
    and from doing as you please on my holy day,
if you call the Sabbath a delight
    and the LORD's holy day honorable,
and if you honor it by not going your own way
    and not doing as you please or speaking idle words,
¹⁴then you will find your joy in the LORD,
    and I will cause you to ride on the heights of the land
    and to feast on the inheritance of your father Jacob."
                    The mouth of the LORD has spoken.

Sin, Confession and Redemption

59 Surely the arm of the LORD is not too short to save,
    nor his ear too dull to hear.
²But your iniquities have separated
    you from your God;
your sins have hidden his face from you,
    so that he will not hear.
³For your hands are stained with blood,
    your fingers with guilt.
Your lips have spoken lies,
    and your tongue mutters wicked things.
⁴No one calls for justice;
    no one pleads his case with integrity.
They rely on empty arguments and speak lies;
    they conceive trouble and give birth to evil.
⁵They hatch the eggs of vipers
    and spin a spider's web.
Whoever eats their eggs will die,
    and when one is broken, an adder is hatched.
⁶Their cobwebs are useless for clothing;
    they cannot cover themselves with what they make.
Their deeds are evil deeds,
    and acts of violence are in their hands.
⁷Their feet rush into sin;
    they are swift to shed innocent blood.
Their thoughts are evil thoughts;
    ruin and destruction mark their ways.
⁸The way of peace they do not know;
    there is no justice in their paths.
They have turned them into crooked roads;
    no one who walks in them will know peace.

⁹So justice is far from us,
    and righteousness does not reach us.
We look for light, but all is darkness;

for brightness, but we walk in deep shadows.
¹⁰Like the blind we grope along the wall,
    feeling our way like men without eyes.
At midday we stumble as if it were twilight;
    among the strong, we are like the dead.
¹¹We all growl like bears;
    we moan mournfully like doves.
We look for justice, but find none;
    for deliverance, but it is far away.

¹²For our offenses are many in your sight,
    and our sins testify against us.
Our offenses are ever with us,
    and we acknowledge our iniquities:
¹³rebellion and treachery against the Lord,
    turning our backs on our God,
fomenting oppression and revolt,
    uttering lies our hearts have conceived.
¹⁴So justice is driven back,
    and righteousness stands at a distance;
truth has stumbled in the streets,
    honesty cannot enter.
¹⁵Truth is nowhere to be found,
    and whoever shuns evil becomes a prey.

The Lord looked and was displeased
    that there was no justice.
¹⁶He saw that there was no one,
    he was appalled that there was no one to intervene;
so his own arm worked salvation for him,
    and his own righteousness sustained him.
¹⁷He put on righteousness as his breastplate,
    and the helmet of salvation on his head;
he put on the garments of vengeance
    and wrapped himself in zeal as in a cloak.
¹⁸According to what they have done,
    so will he repay
wrath to his enemies
    and retribution to his foes;
he will repay the islands their due.
¹⁹From the west, men will fear the name of the Lord,
    and from the rising of the sun, they will revere his glory.
For he will come like a pent-up flood
    that the breath of the Lord drives along. ᵃ

²⁰"The Redeemer will come to Zion,
    to those in Jacob who repent of their sins,"

                    declares the Lord.

²¹"As for me, this is my covenant with them," says the Lord. "My Spirit, who is on you, and my words that I have put in your mouth will not depart from your mouth, or from the mouths of your children, or from the mouths of their descendants from this time on and forever," says the Lord.

ᵃ 19 Or When the enemy comes in like a flood, / the Spirit of the Lord will put him to flight

The Glory of Zion

60 ¹"Arise, shine, for your light has come,
and the glory of the LORD rises upon you.
²See, darkness covers the earth
and thick darkness is over the peoples,
but the LORD rises upon you
and his glory appears over you.
³Nations will come to your light,
and kings to the brightness of your dawn.

⁴"Lift up your eyes and look about you:
All assemble and come to you;
your sons come from afar,
and your daughters are carried on the arm.
⁵Then you will look and be radiant,
your heart will throb and swell with joy;
the wealth on the seas will be brought to you,
to you the riches of the nations will come.
⁶Herds of camels will cover your land,
young camels of Midian and Ephah.
And all from Sheba will come,
bearing gold and incense
and proclaiming the praise of the LORD.
⁷All Kedar's flocks will be gathered to you,
the rams of Nebaioth will serve you;
they will be accepted as offerings on my altar,
and I will adorn my glorious temple.

⁸"Who are these that fly along like clouds,
like doves to their nests?
⁹Surely the islands look to me;
in the lead are the ships of Tarshish, ᵃ
bringing your sons from afar,
with their silver and gold,
to the honor of the LORD your God,
the Holy One of Israel,
for he has endowed you with splendor.

¹⁰"Foreigners will rebuild your walls,
and their kings will serve you.
Though in anger I struck you,
in favor I will show you compassion.
¹¹Your gates will always stand open,
they will never be shut, day or night,
so that men may bring you the wealth of the nations—
their kings led in triumphal procession.
¹²For the nation or kingdom that will not serve you will perish;
it will be utterly ruined.

¹³"The glory of Lebanon will come to you,
the pine, the fir and the cypress together,

ᵃ9 Or the trading ships

to adorn the place of my sanctuary;
and I will glorify the place of my feet.
[14]The sons of your oppressors will come bowing before you;
all who despise you will bow down at your feet
and will call you the City of the LORD,
Zion of the Holy One of Israel.

[15]"Although you have been forsaken and hated,
with no one traveling through,
I will make you the everlasting pride
and the joy of all generations.
[16]You will drink the milk of nations
and be nursed at royal breasts.
Then you will know that I, the LORD, am your Savior,
your Redeemer, the Mighty One of Jacob.
[17]Instead of bronze I will bring you gold,
and silver in place of iron.
Instead of wood I will bring you bronze,
and iron in place of stones.
I will make peace your governor
and righteousness your ruler.
[18]No longer will violence be heard in your land,
nor ruin or destruction within your borders,
but you will call your walls Salvation
and your gates Praise.
[19]The sun will no more be your light by day,
nor will the brightness of the moon shine on you,
for the LORD will be your everlasting light,
and your God will be your glory.
[20]Your sun will never set again,
and your moon will wane no more;
the LORD will be your everlasting light,
and your days of sorrow will end.
[21]Then will all your people be righteous
and they will possess the land forever.
They are the shoot I have planted,
the work of my hands,
for the display of my splendor.
[22]The least of you will become a thousand,
the smallest a mighty nation.
I am the LORD;
in its time I will do this swiftly."

The Year of the LORD's Favor

61 The Spirit of the Sovereign LORD is on me,
because the LORD has anointed me
to preach good news to the poor.
He has sent me to bind up the brokenhearted,
to proclaim freedom for the captives
and release from darkness for the prisoners,[a]
[2]to proclaim the year of the LORD's favor

---

[a] 1 Hebrew; Septuagint the blind

and the day of vengeance of our God,
to comfort all who mourn,
³ and provide for those who grieve in Zion—
to bestow on them a crown of beauty
    instead of ashes,
the oil of gladness
    instead of mourning,
and a garment of praise
    instead of a spirit of despair.
They will be called oaks of righteousness,
    a planting of the LORD
for the display of his splendor.

⁴They will rebuild the ancient ruins
    and restore the places long devastated;
they will renew the ruined cities
    that have been devastated for
      generations.
⁵Aliens will shepherd your flocks;
    foreigners will work your fields
    and vineyards.
⁶And you will be called priests of the
    LORD,
    you will be named ministers of our
      God.
You will feed on the wealth of nations,
    and in their riches you will boast.

⁷Instead of their shame
    my people will receive a double
      portion,
and instead of disgrace
    they will rejoice in their inheritance;
and so they will inherit a double
      portion in their land,
    and everlasting joy will be theirs.

⁸"For I, the LORD, love justice;
    I hate robbery and iniquity.
In my faithfulness I will reward them
    and make an everlasting covenant
      with them.

DISCOVERING GOD

61:1–2
Jesus, the God-Man

Jesus began his public ministry by quoting these verses (see Luke 4:18–19 [page 1343]). He stopped short of the last phrases in verse 2 because his mission was to bring hope and salvation, not judgment. At least not *yet*.

There is coming a time, however, when he will return to fulfill his mission, as prophesied in this verse. In his first appearance, Jesus came as the life-giving suffering Servant, but when he comes again he will bring history to its consummation as the "KING OF KINGS AND LORD OF LORDS" (Revelation chapter 19, verses 11–21 [page 1652]).

The Messiah came to earth once, and he will come a second time to judge the people of all nations. The Bible tells us that if we have a loving relationship with Jesus, we need not fear that day (see 1 John chapter 4, verses 16–18 [page 1625]). What could be more important than being ready for his arrival?

---

⁹Their descendants will be known among the nations
    and their offspring among the peoples.
All who see them will acknowledge
    that they are a people the LORD has blessed."

¹⁰I delight greatly in the LORD;
    my soul rejoices in my God.
For he has clothed me with garments of salvation
    and arrayed me in a robe of righteousness,
as a bridegroom adorns his head like a priest,
    and as a bride adorns herself with her jewels.
¹¹For as the soil makes the sprout come up
    and a garden causes seeds to grow,

so the Sovereign LORD will make righteousness and praise
    spring up before all nations.

Zion's New Name

62 For Zion's sake I will not keep silent,
    for Jerusalem's sake I will not remain quiet,
till her righteousness shines out like the dawn,
    her salvation like a blazing torch.
²The nations will see your righteousness,
    and all kings your glory;
you will be called by a new name
    that the mouth of the LORD will bestow.
³You will be a crown of splendor in the LORD's hand,
    a royal diadem in the hand of your God.
⁴No longer will they call you Deserted,
    or name your land Desolate.
But you will be called Hephzibah,[a]
    and your land Beulah[b];
for the LORD will take delight in you,
    and your land will be married.
⁵As a young man marries a maiden,
    so will your sons[c] marry you;
as a bridegroom rejoices over his bride,
    so will your God rejoice over you.

⁶I have posted watchmen on your walls, O Jerusalem;
    they will never be silent day or night.
You who call on the LORD,
    give yourselves no rest,
⁷and give him no rest till he establishes Jerusalem
    and makes her the praise of the earth.

⁸The LORD has sworn by his right hand
    and by his mighty arm:
"Never again will I give your grain
    as food for your enemies,
and never again will foreigners drink the new wine
    for which you have toiled;
⁹but those who harvest it will eat it
    and praise the LORD,
and those who gather the grapes will drink it
    in the courts of my sanctuary."

¹⁰Pass through, pass through the gates!
    Prepare the way for the people.
Build up, build up the highway!
    Remove the stones.
Raise a banner for the nations.

¹¹The LORD has made proclamation
    to the ends of the earth:
"Say to the Daughter of Zion,
    'See, your Savior comes!

---

a 4 Hephzibah means my delight is in her.   *b 4 Beulah means married.*   *c 5 Or Builder*

See, his reward is with him,
  and his recompense accompanies him.'"
¹²They will be called the Holy People,
  the Redeemed of the LORD;
and you will be called Sought After,
  the City No Longer Deserted.

God's Day of Vengeance and Redemption

63 Who is this coming from Edom,
  from Bozrah, with his garments stained crimson?
Who is this, robed in splendor,
  striding forward in the greatness of his strength?

"It is I, speaking in righteousness,
  mighty to save."

²Why are your garments red,
  like those of one treading the winepress?

³"I have trodden the winepress alone;
  from the nations no one was with me.
I trampled them in my anger
  and trod them down in my wrath;
their blood spattered my garments,
  and I stained all my clothing.
⁴For the day of vengeance was in my heart,
  and the year of my redemption has come.
⁵I looked, but there was no one to help,
  I was appalled that no one gave support;
so my own arm worked salvation for me,
  and my own wrath sustained me.
⁶I trampled the nations in my anger;
  in my wrath I made them drunk
  and poured their blood on the ground."

Praise and Prayer

⁷I will tell of the kindnesses of the LORD,
  the deeds for which he is to be praised,
  according to all the LORD has done for us—
yes, the many good things he has done
  for the house of Israel,
  according to his compassion and many kindnesses.
⁸He said, "Surely they are my people,
  sons who will not be false to me";
  and so he became their Savior.
⁹In all their distress he too was distressed,
  and the angel of his presence saved them.
In his love and mercy he redeemed them;
  he lifted them up and carried them
  all the days of old.
¹⁰Yet they rebelled
  and grieved his Holy Spirit.
So he turned and became their enemy
  and he himself fought against them.

¹¹Then his people recalled[a] the days of old,
    the days of Moses and his people—
where is he who brought them through the sea,
    with the shepherd of his flock?
Where is he who set
    his Holy Spirit among them,
¹²who sent his glorious arm of power
    to be at Moses' right hand,
who divided the waters before them,
    to gain for himself everlasting renown,
¹³who led them through the depths?
Like a horse in open country,
    they did not stumble;
¹⁴like cattle that go down to the plain,
    they were given rest by the Spirit of the LORD.
This is how you guided your people
    to make for yourself a glorious name.

¹⁵Look down from heaven and see
    from your lofty throne, holy and glorious.
Where are your zeal and your might?
    Your tenderness and compassion are withheld from us.
¹⁶But you are our Father,
    though Abraham does not know us
    or Israel acknowledge us;
you, O LORD, are our Father,
    our Redeemer from of old is your name.
¹⁷Why, O LORD, do you make us wander from your ways
    and harden our hearts so we do not revere you?
Return for the sake of your servants,
    the tribes that are your inheritance.
¹⁸For a little while your people possessed your holy place,
    but now our enemies have trampled down your sanctuary.
¹⁹We are yours from of old;
    but you have not ruled over them,
    they have not been called by your name.[b]

64 Oh, that you would rend the heavens and come down,
    that the mountains would tremble before you!
²As when fire sets twigs ablaze
    and causes water to boil,
come down to make your name known to your enemies
    and cause the nations to quake before you!
³For when you did awesome things that we did not expect,
    you came down, and the mountains trembled before you.
⁴Since ancient times no one has heard,
    no ear has perceived,
no eye has seen any God besides you,
    who acts on behalf of those who wait for him.
⁵You come to the help of those who gladly do right,
    who remember your ways.
But when we continued to sin against them,

---

a 11 Or *But may he recall*   *b 19* Or *We are like those you have never ruled, / like those never called by your name*

you were angry.
How then can we be saved?
⁶All of us have become like one who is unclean,
    and all our righteous acts are like filthy rags;
we all shrivel up like a leaf,
    and like the wind our sins sweep us away.
⁷No one calls on your name
    or strives to lay hold of you;
for you have hidden your face from us
    and made us waste away because of our sins.

⁸Yet, O LORD, you are our Father.
    We are the clay, you are the potter;
    we are all the work of your hand.
⁹Do not be angry beyond measure, O LORD;
    do not remember our sins forever.
Oh, look upon us, we pray,
    for we are all your people.
¹⁰Your sacred cities have become a desert;
    even Zion is a desert, Jerusalem a desolation.
¹¹Our holy and glorious temple, where our fathers praised you,
    has been burned with fire,
    and all that we treasured lies in ruins.
¹²After all this, O LORD, will you hold yourself back?
    Will you keep silent and punish us beyond measure?

Judgment and Salvation

65 "I revealed myself to those who did not ask for me;
    I was found by those who did not seek me.
To a nation that did not call on my name,
    I said, 'Here am I, here am I.'
²All day long I have held out my hands
    to an obstinate people,
who walk in ways not good,
    pursuing their own imaginations—
³a people who continually provoke me
    to my very face,
offering sacrifices in gardens
    and burning incense on altars of brick;
⁴who sit among the graves
    and spend their nights keeping secret vigil;
who eat the flesh of pigs,
    and whose pots hold broth of unclean meat;
⁵who say, 'Keep away; don't come near me,
    for I am too sacred for you!'
Such people are smoke in my nostrils,
    a fire that keeps burning all day.

⁶"See, it stands written before me:
    I will not keep silent but will pay back in full;
    I will pay it back into their laps—
⁷both your sins and the sins of your fathers,"
    says the LORD.

"Because they burned sacrifices on the mountains
   and defied me on the hills,
I will measure into their laps
   the full payment for their former deeds."

⁸This is what the LORD says:

"As when juice is still found in a cluster of grapes
   and men say, 'Don't destroy it,
   there is yet some good in it,'
so will I do in behalf of my servants;
   I will not destroy them all.
⁹I will bring forth descendants from Jacob,
   and from Judah those who will possess my mountains;
my chosen people will inherit them,
   and there will my servants live.
¹⁰Sharon will become a pasture for flocks,
   and the Valley of Achor a resting place for herds,
   for my people who seek me.

¹¹"But as for you who forsake the LORD
   and forget my holy mountain,
who spread a table for Fortune
   and fill bowls of mixed wine for Destiny,
¹²I will destine you for the sword,
   and you will all bend down for the slaughter;
for I called but you did not answer,
   I spoke but you did not listen.
You did evil in my sight
   and chose what displeases me."

¹³Therefore this is what the Sovereign LORD says:

"My servants will eat,
   but you will go hungry;
my servants will drink,
   but you will go thirsty;
my servants will rejoice,
   but you will be put to shame.
¹⁴My servants will sing
   out of the joy of their hearts,
but you will cry out
   from anguish of heart
   and wail in brokenness of spirit.
¹⁵You will leave your name
   to my chosen ones as a curse;
the Sovereign LORD will put you to death,
   but to his servants he will give another name.
¹⁶Whoever invokes a blessing in the land
   will do so by the God of truth;
he who takes an oath in the land
   will swear by the God of truth.

For the past troubles will be forgotten
and hidden from my eyes.

New Heavens and a New Earth

17"Behold, I will create
new heavens and a new earth.
The former things will not be remembered,
nor will they come to mind.
18But be glad and rejoice forever
in what I will create,
for I will create Jerusalem to be a delight
and its people a joy.
19I will rejoice over Jerusalem
and take delight in my people;
the sound of weeping and of crying
will be heard in it no more.

20"Never again will there be in it
an infant who lives but a few days,
or an old man who does not live out his years;
he who dies at a hundred
will be thought a mere youth;
he who fails to reach*a* a hundred
will be considered accursed.
21They will build houses and dwell in them;
they will plant vineyards and eat their fruit.
22No longer will they build houses and others live in them,
or plant and others eat.
For as the days of a tree,
so will be the days of my people;
my chosen ones will long enjoy
the works of their hands.
23They will not toil in vain
or bear children doomed to misfortune;
for they will be a people blessed by the LORD,
they and their descendants with them.
24Before they call I will answer;
while they are still speaking I will hear.
25The wolf and the lamb will feed together,
and the lion will eat straw like the ox,
but dust will be the serpent's food.
They will neither harm nor destroy
on all my holy mountain,"

says the LORD.

Judgment and Hope

66 This is what the LORD says:

"Heaven is my throne,
and the earth is my footstool.
Where is the house you will build for me?

a20 Or / the sinner who reaches

Where will my resting place be?
²Has not my hand made all these things,
and so they came into being?"

declares the LORD.

"This is the one I esteem:
he who is humble and contrite in spirit,
and trembles at my word.
³But whoever sacrifices a bull
is like one who kills a man,
and whoever offers a lamb,
like one who breaks a dog's
neck;
whoever makes a grain offering
is like one who presents pig's
blood,
and whoever burns memorial
incense,
like one who worships an
idol.
They have chosen their own
ways,
and their souls delight in
their abominations;
⁴so I also will choose harsh
treatment for them
and will bring upon them what
they dread.
For when I called, no one
answered,
when I spoke, no one
listened.
They did evil in my sight
and chose what displeases
me."

⁵Hear the word of the LORD,
you who tremble at his word:
"Your brothers who hate you,
and exclude you because of my name, have said,
'Let the LORD be glorified,
that we may see your joy!'
Yet they will be put to shame.
⁶Hear that uproar from the city,
hear that noise from the temple!
It is the sound of the LORD
repaying his enemies all they deserve.

⁷"Before she goes into labor,
she gives birth;
before the pains come upon her,
she delivers a son.
⁸Who has ever heard of such a thing?
Who has ever seen such things?

DISCOVERING GOD

66:1–2
Life with God

God is bigger than the universe itself.

Sometimes we forget that, foolishly believing that we can "localize" God to places such as church buildings. But God is not interested in merely meeting his people once a week in *any* building, no matter how beautiful or ornate it is. He's more interested in walking with them every day. As this passage says, he wants to be with people who take his words seriously and recognize his role as the Creator.

Jesus faced this same kind of limited thinking when he spoke with a seeker in his day. A woman who lived in Samaria asked Jesus to tell her the proper place to worship God. Jesus replied that the ground we stand on is far less important than the condition of our souls when we worship: "True worshipers . . . worship the Father in spirit and truth, for they are the kind of worshipers the Father seeks. God is spirit, and his worshipers must worship in spirit and in truth" (see John chapter 4, verses 19–24 [page 1388]).

Rather than limiting God to a place, Jesus says that we must remind ourselves of his spiritual nature and live openly and honestly before him every day, wherever we are.

> Can a country be born in a day
>> or a nation be brought forth in a moment?
> Yet no sooner is Zion in labor
>> than she gives birth to her children.
> ⁹Do I bring to the moment of birth
>> and not give delivery?" says the LORD.
> "Do I close up the womb
>> when I bring to delivery?" says your God.
> ¹⁰"Rejoice with Jerusalem and be glad for her,
>> all you who love her;
> rejoice greatly with her,
>> all you who mourn over her.
> ¹¹For you will nurse and be satisfied
>> at her comforting breasts;
> you will drink deeply
>> and delight in her overflowing abundance."

¹²For this is what the LORD says:

> "I will extend peace to her like a river,
>> and the wealth of nations like a flooding stream;
> you will nurse and be carried on her arm
>> and dandled on her knees.
> ¹³As a mother comforts her child,
>> so will I comfort you;
> and you will be comforted over Jerusalem."

> ¹⁴When you see this, your heart will rejoice
>> and you will flourish like grass;
> the hand of the LORD will be made known to his servants,
>> but his fury will be shown to his foes.
> ¹⁵See, the LORD is coming with fire,
>> and his chariots are like a whirlwind;
> he will bring down his anger with fury,
>> and his rebuke with flames of fire.
> ¹⁶For with fire and with his sword
>> the LORD will execute judgment upon all men,
> and many will be those slain by the LORD.

¹⁷"Those who consecrate and purify themselves to go into the gardens, following the one in the midst of*ᵃ* those who eat the flesh of pigs and rats and other abominable things—they will meet their end together," declares the LORD.

¹⁸"And I, because of their actions and their imaginations, am about to come*ᵇ* and gather all nations and tongues, and they will come and see my glory.

¹⁹"I will set a sign among them, and I will send some of those who survive to the nations—to Tarshish, to the Libyans*ᶜ* and Lydians (famous as archers), to Tubal and Greece, and to the distant islands that have not heard of my fame or seen my glory. They will proclaim my glory among the nations. ²⁰And they will bring all your brothers, from all the nations, to my holy mountain in Jerusalem as an offering to the LORD—on horses, in chariots and wagons, and on mules and camels," says the LORD. "They will bring them, as the Israelites bring their grain offerings, to the temple of the LORD in ceremonially

---

ᵃ17 Or *gardens behind one of your temples, and*   ᵇ18 The meaning of the Hebrew for this clause is uncertain.
ᶜ19 Some Septuagint manuscripts *Put* (Libyans); Hebrew *Pul*

clean vessels. [21]And I will select some of them also to be priests and Levites," says the LORD.

[22]"As the new heavens and the new earth that I make will endure before me," declares the LORD, "so will your name and descendants endure. [23]From one New Moon to another and from one Sabbath to another, all mankind will come and bow down before me," says the LORD. [24]"And they will go out and look upon the dead bodies of those who rebelled against me; their worm will not die, nor will their fire be quenched, and they will be loathsome to all mankind."

JEREMIAH/LAMENTATIONS

Introduction

THE BOTTOM LINE

Have you ever had to tell someone something that you knew they wouldn't want to hear? That experience is painful enough; but that pain is much sharper when that person refuses to accept what you've got to say. God called Jeremiah to the unenviable task of telling God's people that, if they refused to turn from their evil practices, their comfortable way of life was soon to end at the hand of a foreign power. Jeremiah received only hatred and scorn in return from his family, friends and countrymen. Through it all, however, this prophet remained obedient to God—an example of true servanthood if there ever was one. Has God placed a "Jeremiah" in your life—someone who's been encouraging you to follow God? That person could very well be listening to a higher call. If so, he or she deserves a closer hearing.

CENTRAL IDEAS

- God calls human messengers to turn people back to him.
- Individuals who refuse to turn from their wicked practices will face severe consequences.
- Sincere devotion to God and his directives leads to divine favor.
- God's heart is grieved when his people turn away (see Lamentations chapter 2 verse 11 [p. 1078]).

TITLES

Jeremiah recounts the prophet's story; Lamentations refers to the author's "lament" over the destruction of Jerusalem.

AUTHOR AND READERS

These two books recount the life of Jeremiah, and were written by the prophet's faithful secretary, Baruch. Jeremiah challenged the people of ancient Judah (southern Israel) during a time of rampant religious complacency and social injustice.

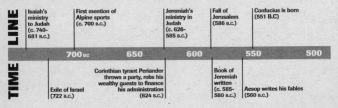

	Isaiah's ministry to Judah (c. 740-681 B.C.)	First mention of Alpine sports (c. 700 B.C.)		Jeremiah's ministry in Judah (c. 626-585 B.C.)	Fall of Jerusalem (586 B.C.)	Confucius is born (551 B.C)	
TIME LINE			700 BC	650	600	550	500
		Exile of Israel (722 B.C.)	Corinthian tyrant Periander throws a party, robs his wealthy guests to finance his administration (624 B.C.)		Book of Jeremiah written (c. 585-580 B.C.)	Aesop writes his fables (560 B.C.)	

Many boxing enthusiasts believe Muhammad Ali was the greatest fighter ever to step into a ring. Three times, from 1964 until 1980, he reigned as the heavyweight champion of the world. As impressive as Ali was in the ring with his fancy footwork and lightning-quick jab, he was equally adroit with his tongue outside the ring.

In the film *Rocky II* a character much like the real-life Muhammad Ali taunts the hero with the words, "I'll destroy you. I am the master of disaster." After seeing the film, Ali wistfully said, "I wish I'd thought of that!"

Actually, when it came to bragging, there were few things that Ali didn't think of. Irritated by his perpetual boasts of "I am the greatest," a colleague once asked the boxer how he was at golf. "I'm the best," replied Ali. "I just haven't played yet."

On one occasion, however, the boxer was actually silenced by a flight attendant. Just before takeoff, the attractive young woman reminded Ali to fasten his seat belt. "Superman don't need no seat belt," replied Ali. "Superman don't need no airplane, either," retorted the flight attendant. Ali fastened his belt without a word.*

"Superman don't need no airplane, either."

Boasting can be amusing or it can be annoying, but it always reveals a great deal about the person doing it. Surprisingly, God doesn't condemn all kinds of boasting. In fact, one type that God actually encourages is boasting in who he is and what he has done for us. Why? Because that kind of boasting is actually a verbal expression of faith. Obviously, we shouldn't boast about something that will one day let us down—such as our strength, talent, or wisdom. But confidence in God is a virtue.

Jeremiah understood that. The prophet lived in dire circumstances, and his writings are filled with despair. That's why he is called "The Weeping Prophet." Instead of turning to God, the people formed political alliances and devised false assurances designed to keep themselves from facing the moral and spiritual bankruptcy of their day. Surrounded by devastation, rejected by the very ones to whom he tried to minister, and sometimes insecure about his own mission, Jeremiah didn't seem to have much reason to boast. But turn to Jeremiah chapter 9, verses 23–24 (page 1004), and you'll discover what God encouraged him—and us—to brag about even when all seemed lost.

---

* *The Little Brown Book of Anecdotes*, Clifton Fadiman, ed. (Boston: Little, Brown & Co., 1985), p. 14.

JEREMIAH

1 The words of Jeremiah son of Hilkiah, one of the priests at Anathoth in the territory of Benjamin. ²The word of the LORD came to him in the thirteenth year of the reign of Josiah son of Amon king of Judah, ³and through the reign of Jehoiakim son of Josiah king of Judah, down to the fifth month of the eleventh year of Zedekiah son of Josiah king of Judah, when the people of Jerusalem went into exile.

The Call of Jeremiah

⁴The word of the LORD came to me, saying,

> ⁵"Before I formed you in the womb I knew*ᵃ* you,
>   before you were born I set you apart;
>   I appointed you as a prophet to the nations."

⁶"Ah, Sovereign LORD," I said, "I do not know how to speak; I am only a child."

⁷But the LORD said to me, "Do not say, 'I am only a child.' You must go to everyone I send you to and say whatever I command you. ⁸Do not be afraid of them, for I am with you and will rescue you," declares the LORD.

⁹Then the LORD reached out his hand and touched my mouth and said to me, "Now, I have put my words in your mouth. ¹⁰See, today I appoint you over nations and kingdoms to uproot and tear down, to destroy and overthrow, to build and to plant."

¹¹The word of the LORD came to me: "What do you see, Jeremiah?"

"I see the branch of an almond tree," I replied.

¹²The LORD said to me, "You have seen correctly, for I am watching*ᵇ* to see that my word is fulfilled."

¹³The word of the LORD came to me again: "What do you see?"

"I see a boiling pot, tilting away from the north," I answered.

¹⁴The LORD said to me, "From the north disaster will be poured out on all who live in the land. ¹⁵I am about to summon all the peoples of the northern kingdoms," declares the LORD.

> "Their kings will come and set up their thrones
>   in the entrance of the gates of Jerusalem;
> they will come against all her surrounding walls
>   and against all the towns of Judah.
> ¹⁶I will pronounce my judgments on my people
>   because of their wickedness in forsaking me,
> in burning incense to other gods
>   and in worshiping what their hands have made.

¹⁷"Get yourself ready! Stand up and say to them whatever I command you. Do not be terrified by them, or I will terrify you before them. ¹⁸Today I have made you a fortified city, an iron pillar and a bronze wall to stand against the whole land—against the kings of Judah, its officials, its priests and the people of the land. ¹⁹They will fight against you but will not overcome you, for I am with you and will rescue you," declares the LORD.

ᵃ5 Or *chose*   *ᵇ12* The Hebrew for *watching* sounds like the Hebrew for *almond tree.*

Israel Forsakes God

2 The word of the LORD came to me: ²"Go and proclaim in the hearing of Jerusalem:

" 'I remember the devotion of your youth,
    how as a bride you loved me
and followed me through the desert,
    through a land not sown.
³Israel was holy to the LORD,
    the firstfruits of his harvest;
all who devoured her were held guilty,
    and disaster overtook them,' "

declares the LORD.

⁴Hear the word of the LORD, O house of Jacob,
    all you clans of the house of Israel.

⁵This is what the LORD says:

"What fault did your fathers find in me,
    that they strayed so far from me?
They followed worthless idols
    and became worthless themselves.
⁶They did not ask, 'Where is the LORD,
    who brought us up out of Egypt
and led us through the barren wilderness,
    through a land of deserts and rifts,
a land of drought and darkness,ᵃ
    a land where no one travels and no one lives?'
⁷I brought you into a fertile land
    to eat its fruit and rich produce.
But you came and defiled my land
    and made my inheritance detestable.
⁸The priests did not ask,
    'Where is the LORD?'
Those who deal with the law did not know me;
    the leaders rebelled against me.
The prophets prophesied by Baal,
    following worthless idols.

⁹"Therefore I bring charges against you again,"

declares the LORD.

"And I will bring charges against your children's children.
¹⁰Cross over to the coasts of Kittimᵇ and look,
    send to Kedarᶜ and observe closely;
    see if there has ever been anything like this:
¹¹Has a nation ever changed its gods?
    (Yet they are not gods at all.)
But my people have exchanged theirᵈ Glory
    for worthless idols.
¹²Be appalled at this, O heavens,
    and shudder with great horror,"

declares the LORD.

ᵃ6 Or *and the shadow of death*   ᵇ10 That is, Cyprus and western coastlands   ᶜ10 The home of Bedouin tribes in the Syro-Arabian desert   ᵈ11 Masoretic Text; an ancient Hebrew scribal tradition *my*

¹³"My people have committed two sins:
  They have forsaken me,
    the spring of living water,
  and have dug their own cisterns,
    broken cisterns that cannot hold water.
¹⁴Is Israel a servant, a slave by birth?
  Why then has he become plunder?
¹⁵Lions have roared;
    they have growled at him.
  They have laid waste his land;
    his towns are burned and deserted.
¹⁶Also, the men of Memphis*a* and Tahpanhes
    have shaved the crown of your head.*b*
¹⁷Have you not brought this on yourselves
  by forsaking the LORD your God
    when he led you in the way?
¹⁸Now why go to Egypt
    to drink water from the Shihor*c*?
  And why go to Assyria
    to drink water from the River*d*?
¹⁹Your wickedness will punish you;
    your backsliding will rebuke you.
  Consider then and realize
    how evil and bitter it is for you
  when you forsake the LORD your God
    and have no awe of me,"

                        declares the Lord, the LORD Almighty.

²⁰"Long ago you broke off your yoke
    and tore off your bonds;
  you said, 'I will not serve you!'
  Indeed, on every high hill
    and under every spreading tree
  you lay down as a prostitute.
²¹I had planted you like a choice vine
    of sound and reliable stock.
  How then did you turn against me
    into a corrupt, wild vine?
²²Although you wash yourself with soda
    and use an abundance of soap,
    the stain of your guilt is still before me,"

                        declares the Sovereign LORD.

²³"How can you say, 'I am not defiled;
    I have not run after the Baals'?
  See how you behaved in the valley;
    consider what you have done.
  You are a swift she-camel
    running here and there,
²⁴a wild donkey accustomed to the desert,
    sniffing the wind in her craving—

---

a16 Hebrew *Noph*   *b16* Or *have cracked your skull*   *c18* That is, a branch of the Nile   *d18* That is, the Euphrates

in her heat who can restrain her?
Any males that pursue her need not tire themselves;
   at mating time they will find her.
²⁵Do not run until your feet are bare
   and your throat is dry.
But you said, 'It's no use!
I love foreign gods,
   and I must go after them.'

²⁶"As a thief is disgraced when he
     is caught,
  so the house of Israel is
     disgraced—
they, their kings and their
     officials,
  their priests and their prophets.
²⁷They say to wood, 'You are my
     father,'
  and to stone, 'You gave me
     birth.'
They have turned their backs to
     me
  and not their faces;
yet when they are in trouble,
     they say,
  'Come and save us!'
²⁸Where then are the gods you
     made for yourselves?
Let them come if they can
     save you
  when you are in trouble!
For you have as many gods
     as you have towns, O Judah.

²⁹"Why do you bring charges
     against me?
You have all rebelled against
     me,"

                 declares the LORD.
³⁰"In vain I punished your people;
  they did not respond to correction.
Your sword has devoured your prophets
   like a ravening lion.

³¹"You of this generation, consider the word of the LORD:

  "Have I been a desert to Israel
   or a land of great darkness?
Why do my people say, 'We are free to roam;
   we will come to you no more'?
³²Does a maiden forget her jewelry,
   a bride her wedding ornaments?
Yet my people have forgotten me,

▣ ▦▦▦▦▦▦ KNOWING YOURSELF ▦▦▦▦▦▦ ↹

2:20–22
Sin

God used the prophet Jeremiah to speak to
the people of Israel. Jeremiah was called the
"weeping prophet" because so much of what
he had to say conveyed God's judgment on
Israel's sin, and because he himself was so utterly despised and rejected by his peers.

In this chapter Jeremiah used various images to tell the people how they had rejected
God. Specifically, Jeremiah addressed their
worship of pagan deities, which included ritual sex—so verse 20 is both figuratively and
literally true. God intended his people be
like a cultivated vine, but they chose to follow
their "wild" nature instead (verse 21) as they
gave themselves over to idol worship.

This sin was like a stain on Israel in God's
eyes (verse 22). And no amount of outward
ritual cleansing or acts of worship could remove that stain. Only God would be able to
make the people clean and change them from
the inside out.

That is also true today. No detergent can
bleach our sin stain. No amount of good
deeds—no matter how wonderful they may
be—can take away the sin in our lives. Only a
new heart given by God will provide a new
start and the new behavior that flows from a
changed life.

days without number.
³³How skilled you are at pursuing love!
    Even the worst of women can learn from your ways.
³⁴On your clothes men find
    the lifeblood of the innocent poor,
    though you did not catch them breaking in.
    Yet in spite of all this
³⁵ you say, 'I am innocent;
    he is not angry with me.'
    But I will pass judgment on you
    because you say, 'I have not sinned.'
³⁶Why do you go about so much,
    changing your ways?
    You will be disappointed by Egypt
    as you were by Assyria.
³⁷You will also leave that place
    with your hands on your head,
    for the Lᴏʀᴅ has rejected those you trust;
    you will not be helped by them.

3   "If a man divorces his wife
    and she leaves him and marries another man,
    should he return to her again?
    Would not the land be completely defiled?
    But you have lived as a prostitute with many lovers—
    would you now return to me?"

                                            declares the Lᴏʀᴅ.

²"Look up to the barren heights and see.
    Is there any place where you have not been ravished?
    By the roadside you sat waiting for lovers,
    sat like a nomad*ᵃ* in the desert.
    You have defiled the land
    with your prostitution and wickedness.
³Therefore the showers have been withheld,
    and no spring rains have fallen.
    Yet you have the brazen look of a prostitute;
    you refuse to blush with shame.
⁴Have you not just called to me:
    'My Father, my friend from my youth,
⁵will you always be angry?
    Will your wrath continue forever?'
    This is how you talk,
    but you do all the evil you can."

Unfaithful Israel

⁶During the reign of King Josiah, the Lᴏʀᴅ said to me, "Have you seen what faithless Israel has done? She has gone up on every high hill and under every spreading tree and has committed adultery there. ⁷I thought that after she had done all this she would return to me but she did not, and her unfaithful sister Judah saw it. ⁸I gave faithless Israel her certificate of divorce and sent her away because of all her adulteries. Yet I saw that her unfaithful sister Judah had no fear; she also went out and committed adultery. ⁹Because

ᵃ2 Or an Arab

Israel's immorality mattered so little to her, she defiled the land and committed adultery with stone and wood. [10]In spite of all this, her unfaithful sister Judah did not return to me with all her heart, but only in pretense," declares the LORD.

[11]The LORD said to me, "Faithless Israel is more righteous than unfaithful Judah. [12]Go, proclaim this message toward the north:

> " 'Return, faithless Israel,' declares the LORD,
> 'I will frown on you no longer,
> for I am merciful,' declares the LORD,
> 'I will not be angry forever.
> [13]Only acknowledge your guilt—
> you have rebelled against the LORD your God,
> you have scattered your favors to foreign gods
> under every spreading tree,
> and have not obeyed me,' "

declares the LORD.

[14]"Return, faithless people," declares the LORD, "for I am your husband. I will choose you—one from a town and two from a clan—and bring you to Zion. [15]Then I will give you shepherds after my own heart, who will lead you with knowledge and understanding. [16]In those days, when your numbers have increased greatly in the land," declares the LORD, "men will no longer say, 'The ark of the covenant of the LORD.' It will never enter their minds or be remembered; it will not be missed, nor will another one be made. [17]At that time they will call Jerusalem The Throne of the LORD, and all nations will gather in Jerusalem to honor the name of the LORD. No longer will they follow the stubbornness of their evil hearts. [18]In those days the house of Judah will join the house of Israel, and together they will come from a northern land to the land I gave your forefathers as an inheritance.

[19]"I myself said,

> " 'How gladly would I treat you like sons
> and give you a desirable land,
> the most beautiful inheritance of any nation.'
> I thought you would call me 'Father'
> and not turn away from following me.
> [20]But like a woman unfaithful to her husband,
> so you have been unfaithful to me, O house of Israel,"

declares the LORD.

> [21]A cry is heard on the barren heights,
> the weeping and pleading of the people of Israel,
> because they have perverted their ways
> and have forgotten the LORD their God.

> [22]"Return, faithless people;
> I will cure you of backsliding."

> "Yes, we will come to you,
> for you are the LORD our God.
> [23]Surely the ⌊idolatrous⌋ commotion on the hills
> and mountains is a deception;
> surely in the LORD our God
> is the salvation of Israel.
> [24]From our youth shameful gods have consumed
> the fruits of our fathers' labor—

their flocks and herds,
    their sons and daughters.
²⁵Let us lie down in our shame,
    and let our disgrace cover us.
We have sinned against the LORD our God,
    both we and our fathers;
from our youth till this day
    we have not obeyed the LORD our God."

4   "If you will return, O Israel,
    return to me,"

declares the LORD.

"If you put your detestable idols out of my sight
    and no longer go astray,
²and if in a truthful, just and righteous way
    you swear, 'As surely as the LORD lives,'
then the nations will be blessed by him
    and in him they will glory."

³This is what the LORD says to the men of Judah and to Jerusalem:

"Break up your unplowed ground
    and do not sow among thorns.
⁴Circumcise yourselves to the LORD,
    circumcise your hearts,
    you men of Judah and people of Jerusalem,
or my wrath will break out and burn like fire
    because of the evil you have done—
    burn with no one to quench it.

Disaster From the North

⁵"Announce in Judah and proclaim in Jerusalem and say:
    'Sound the trumpet throughout the land!'
Cry aloud and say:
    'Gather together!
    Let us flee to the fortified cities!'
⁶Raise the signal to go to Zion!
    Flee for safety without delay!
For I am bringing disaster from the north,
    even terrible destruction."

⁷A lion has come out of his lair;
    a destroyer of nations has set out.
He has left his place
    to lay waste your land.
Your towns will lie in ruins
    without inhabitant.
⁸So put on sackcloth,
    lament and wail,
for the fierce anger of the LORD
    has not turned away from us.

⁹"In that day," declares the LORD,
    "the king and the officials will lose heart,

the priests will be horrified,
and the prophets will be appalled."

¹⁰Then I said, "Ah, Sovereign LORD, how completely you have deceived this people and Jerusalem by saying, 'You will have peace,' when the sword is at our throats."

¹¹At that time this people and Jerusalem will be told, "A scorching wind from the barren heights in the desert blows toward my people, but not to winnow or cleanse; ¹²a wind too strong for that comes from me.ᵃ Now I pronounce my judgments against them."

¹³Look! He advances like the clouds,
his chariots come like a whirlwind,
his horses are swifter than eagles.
Woe to us! We are ruined!
¹⁴O Jerusalem, wash the evil from your heart and be saved.
How long will you harbor wicked thoughts?
¹⁵A voice is announcing from Dan,
proclaiming disaster from the hills of Ephraim.
¹⁶"Tell this to the nations,
proclaim it to Jerusalem:
'A besieging army is coming from a distant land,
raising a war cry against the cities of Judah.
¹⁷They surround her like men guarding a field,
because she has rebelled against me,'"

declares the LORD.

¹⁸"Your own conduct and actions
have brought this upon you.
This is your punishment.
How bitter it is!
How it pierces to the heart!"

¹⁹Oh, my anguish, my anguish!
I writhe in pain.
Oh, the agony of my heart!
My heart pounds within me,
I cannot keep silent.
For I have heard the sound of the trumpet;
I have heard the battle cry.
²⁰Disaster follows disaster;
the whole land lies in ruins.
In an instant my tents are destroyed,
my shelter in a moment.
²¹How long must I see the battle standard
and hear the sound of the trumpet?

²²"My people are fools;
they do not know me.
They are senseless children;
they have no understanding.
They are skilled in doing evil;
they know not how to do good."

²³I looked at the earth,
and it was formless and empty;
and at the heavens,

ᵃ12 Or comes at my command

and their light was gone.
24I looked at the mountains,
  and they were quaking;
  all the hills were swaying.
25I looked, and there were no people;
  every bird in the sky had flown away.
26I looked, and the fruitful land was a desert;
  all its towns lay in ruins
  before the LORD, before his fierce anger.

27This is what the LORD says:

"The whole land will be ruined,
  though I will not destroy it completely.
28Therefore the earth will mourn
  and the heavens above grow dark,
because I have spoken and will not relent,
  I have decided and will not turn back."

29At the sound of horsemen and archers
  every town takes to flight.
Some go into the thickets;
  some climb up among the rocks.
All the towns are deserted;
  no one lives in them.

30What are you doing, O devastated one?
  Why dress yourself in scarlet
  and put on jewels of gold?
Why shade your eyes with paint?
  You adorn yourself in vain.
Your lovers despise you;
  they seek your life.

31I hear a cry as of a woman in labor,
  a groan as of one bearing her first child—
the cry of the Daughter of Zion gasping for breath,
  stretching out her hands and saying,
"Alas! I am fainting;
  my life is given over to murderers."

Not One Is Upright

5 "Go up and down the streets of Jerusalem,
  look around and consider,
  search through her squares.
If you can find but one person
  who deals honestly and seeks the truth,
  I will forgive this city.
2Although they say, 'As surely as the LORD lives,'
  still they are swearing falsely."

3O LORD, do not your eyes look for truth?
  You struck them, but they felt no pain;
  you crushed them, but they refused correction.
They made their faces harder than stone
  and refused to repent.

⁴I thought, "These are only the poor;
  they are foolish,
for they do not know the way of the LORD,
  the requirements of their God.
⁵So I will go to the leaders
  and speak to them;
surely they know the way of the LORD,
  the requirements of their God."
But with one accord they too had broken off the yoke
  and torn off the bonds.
⁶Therefore a lion from the forest will attack them,
  a wolf from the desert will ravage them,
a leopard will lie in wait near their towns
  to tear to pieces any who venture out,
for their rebellion is great
  and their backslidings many.

⁷"Why should I forgive you?
  Your children have forsaken me
  and sworn by gods that are not gods.
I supplied all their needs,
  yet they committed adultery
  and thronged to the houses of prostitutes.
⁸They are well-fed, lusty stallions,
  each neighing for another man's wife.
⁹Should I not punish them for this?"
  declares the LORD.
"Should I not avenge myself
  on such a nation as this?

¹⁰"Go through her vineyards and ravage them,
  but do not destroy them completely.
Strip off her branches,
  for these people do not belong to the LORD.
¹¹The house of Israel and the house of Judah
  have been utterly unfaithful to me,"

declares the LORD.

¹²They have lied about the LORD;
  they said, "He will do nothing!
No harm will come to us;
  we will never see sword or famine.
¹³The prophets are but wind
  and the word is not in them;
  so let what they say be done to them."

¹⁴Therefore this is what the LORD God Almighty says:

"Because the people have spoken these words,
  I will make my words in your mouth a fire
  and these people the wood it consumes.
¹⁵O house of Israel," declares the LORD,
  "I am bringing a distant nation against you—
an ancient and enduring nation,
  a people whose language you do not know,
  whose speech you do not understand.

¹⁶Their quivers are like an open grave;
  all of them are mighty warriors.
¹⁷They will devour your harvests and food,
  devour your sons and daughters;
 they will devour your flocks and herds,
  devour your vines and fig trees.
 With the sword they will destroy
  the fortified cities in which you trust.

¹⁸"Yet even in those days," declares the LORD, "I will not destroy you completely. ¹⁹And when the people ask, 'Why has the LORD our God done all this to us?' you will tell them, 'As you have forsaken me and served foreign gods in your own land, so now you will serve foreigners in a land not your own.'

²⁰"Announce this to the house of Jacob
  and proclaim it in Judah:
²¹Hear this, you foolish and senseless people,
  who have eyes but do not see,
  who have ears but do not hear:
²²Should you not fear me?" declares the LORD.
  "Should you not tremble in my presence?
 I made the sand a boundary for the sea,
  an everlasting barrier it cannot cross.
 The waves may roll, but they cannot prevail;
  they may roar, but they cannot cross it.
²³But these people have stubborn and rebellious hearts;
  they have turned aside and gone away.
²⁴They do not say to themselves,
  'Let us fear the LORD our God,
 who gives autumn and spring rains in season,
  who assures us of the regular weeks of harvest.'
²⁵Your wrongdoings have kept these away;
  your sins have deprived you of good.

²⁶"Among my people are wicked men
  who lie in wait like men who snare birds
  and like those who set traps to catch men.
²⁷Like cages full of birds,
  their houses are full of deceit;
 they have become rich and powerful
²⁸ and have grown fat and sleek.
 Their evil deeds have no limit;
  they do not plead the case of the fatherless to win it,
  they do not defend the rights of the poor.
²⁹Should I not punish them for this?"
  declares the LORD.
 "Should I not avenge myself
  on such a nation as this?

³⁰"A horrible and shocking thing
  has happened in the land:
³¹The prophets prophesy lies,
  the priests rule by their own authority,
 and my people love it this way.
  But what will you do in the end?

Jerusalem Under Siege

6
"Flee for safety, people of Benjamin!
    Flee from Jerusalem!
Sound the trumpet in Tekoa!
    Raise the signal over Beth Hakkerem!
For disaster looms out of the north,
    even terrible destruction.
²I will destroy the Daughter of Zion,
    so beautiful and delicate.
³Shepherds with their flocks will come against her;
    they will pitch their tents around her,
    each tending his own portion."

⁴"Prepare for battle against her!
    Arise, let us attack at noon!
But, alas, the daylight is fading,
    and the shadows of evening grow long.
⁵So arise, let us attack at night
    and destroy her fortresses!"

⁶This is what the LORD Almighty says:

"Cut down the trees
    and build siege ramps against Jerusalem.
This city must be punished;
    it is filled with oppression.
⁷As a well pours out its water,
    so she pours out her wickedness.
Violence and destruction resound in her;
    her sickness and wounds are ever before me.
⁸Take warning, O Jerusalem,
    or I will turn away from you
and make your land desolate
    so no one can live in it."

⁹This is what the LORD Almighty says:

"Let them glean the remnant of Israel
    as thoroughly as a vine;
pass your hand over the branches again,
    like one gathering grapes."

¹⁰To whom can I speak and give warning?
    Who will listen to me?
Their ears are closed*ᵃ*
    so they cannot hear.
The word of the LORD is offensive to them;
    they find no pleasure in it.
¹¹But I am full of the wrath of the LORD,
    and I cannot hold it in.

"Pour it out on the children in the street
    and on the young men gathered together;
both husband and wife will be caught in it,
    and the old, those weighed down with years.

ᵃ 10 Hebrew *uncircumcised*

¹²Their houses will be turned over to others,
    together with their fields and their wives,
when I stretch out my hand
    against those who live in the land,"

declares the LORD.

¹³"From the least to the greatest,
    all are greedy for gain;
prophets and priests alike,
    all practice deceit.
¹⁴They dress the wound of my people
    as though it were not serious.
'Peace, peace,' they say,
    when there is no peace.
¹⁵Are they ashamed of their loathsome conduct?
    No, they have no shame at all;
    they do not even know how to blush.
So they will fall among the fallen;
    they will be brought down when I punish them,"

says the LORD.

¹⁶This is what the LORD says:

    "Stand at the crossroads and look;
        ask for the ancient paths,
ask where the good way is, and walk in it,
    and you will find rest for your souls.
    But you said, 'We will not walk in it.'
¹⁷I appointed watchmen over you and said,
    'Listen to the sound of the trumpet!'
    But you said, 'We will not listen.'
¹⁸Therefore hear, O nations;
    observe, O witnesses,
    what will happen to them.
¹⁹Hear, O earth:
I am bringing disaster on this people,
    the fruit of their schemes,
because they have not listened to my words
    and have rejected my law.
²⁰What do I care about incense from Sheba
    or sweet calamus from a distant land?
Your burnt offerings are not acceptable;
    your sacrifices do not please me."

²¹Therefore this is what the LORD says:

    "I will put obstacles before this people.
    Fathers and sons alike will stumble over them;
    neighbors and friends will perish."

²²This is what the LORD says:

    "Look, an army is coming
        from the land of the north;
a great nation is being stirred up
    from the ends of the earth.
²³They are armed with bow and spear;

they are cruel and show no mercy.
They sound like the roaring sea
    as they ride on their horses;
they come like men in battle formation
    to attack you, O Daughter of Zion."

24We have heard reports about them,
    and our hands hang limp.
Anguish has gripped us,
    pain like that of a woman in labor.
25Do not go out to the fields
    or walk on the roads,
for the enemy has a sword,
    and there is terror on every side.
26O my people, put on sackcloth
    and roll in ashes;
mourn with bitter wailing
    as for an only son,
for suddenly the destroyer
    will come upon us.

27"I have made you a tester of metals
    and my people the ore,
that you may observe
    and test their ways.
28They are all hardened rebels,
    going about to slander.
They are bronze and iron;
    they all act corruptly.
29The bellows blow fiercely
    to burn away the lead with fire,
but the refining goes on in vain;
    the wicked are not purged out.
30They are called rejected silver,
    because the LORD has rejected them."

False Religion Worthless

7 This is the word that came to Jeremiah from the LORD: 2"Stand at the gate of the LORD's house and there proclaim this message:

" 'Hear the word of the LORD, all you people of Judah who come through these gates to worship the LORD. 3This is what the LORD Almighty, the God of Israel, says: Reform your ways and your actions, and I will let you live in this place. 4Do not trust in deceptive words and say, "This is the temple of the LORD, the temple of the LORD, the temple of the LORD!" 5If you really change your ways and your actions and deal with each other justly, 6if you do not oppress the alien, the fatherless or the widow and do not shed innocent blood in this place, and if you do not follow other gods to your own harm, 7then I will let you live in this place, in the land I gave your forefathers for ever and ever. 8But look, you are trusting in deceptive words that are worthless.

9" 'Will you steal and murder, commit adultery and perjury,ᵃ burn incense to Baal and follow other gods you have not known, 10and then come and stand before me in this house, which bears my Name, and say, "We are safe"—safe to do all these detestable things? 11Has this house, which bears my Name, become a den of robbers to you? But I have been watching! declares the LORD.

ᵃ9 Or and swear by false gods

¹²"'Go now to the place in Shiloh where I first made a dwelling for my Name, and see what I did to it because of the wickedness of my people Israel. ¹³While you were doing all these things, declares the LORD, I spoke to you again and again, but you did not listen; I called you, but you did not answer. ¹⁴Therefore, what I did to Shiloh I will now do to the house that bears my Name, the temple you trust in, the place I gave to you and your fathers. ¹⁵I will thrust you from my presence, just as I did all your brothers, the people of Ephraim.'

¹⁶"So do not pray for this people nor offer any plea or petition for them; do not plead with me, for I will not listen to you. ¹⁷Do you not see what they are doing in the towns of Judah and in the streets of Jerusalem? ¹⁸The children gather wood, the fathers light the fire, and the women knead the dough and make cakes of bread for the Queen of Heaven. They pour out drink offerings to other gods to provoke me to anger. ¹⁹But am I the one they are provoking? declares the LORD. Are they not rather harming themselves, to their own shame?

²⁰"Therefore this is what the Sovereign LORD says: My anger and my wrath will be poured out on this place, on man and beast, on the trees of the field and on the fruit of the ground, and it will burn and not be quenched.

²¹"This is what the LORD Almighty, the God of Israel, says: Go ahead, add your burnt offerings to your other sacrifices and eat the meat yourselves! ²²For when I brought your forefathers out of Egypt and spoke to them, I did not just give them commands about burnt offerings and sacrifices, ²³but I gave them this command: Obey me, and I will be your God and you will be my people. Walk in all the ways I command you, that it may go well with you. ²⁴But they did not listen or pay attention; instead, they followed the stubborn inclinations of their evil hearts. They went backward and not forward. ²⁵From the time your forefathers left Egypt until now, day after day, again and again I sent you my servants the prophets. ²⁶But they did not listen to me or pay attention. They were stiff-necked and did more evil than their forefathers.'

²⁷"When you tell them all this, they will not listen to you; when you call to them, they will not answer. ²⁸Therefore say to them, 'This is the nation that has not obeyed the LORD its God or responded to correction. Truth has perished; it has vanished from their lips. ²⁹Cut off your hair and throw it away; take up a lament on the barren heights, for the LORD has rejected and abandoned this generation that is under his wrath.

The Valley of Slaughter

³⁰"The people of Judah have done evil in my eyes, declares the LORD. They have set up their detestable idols in the house that bears my Name and have defiled it. ³¹They have built the high places of Topheth in the Valley of Ben Hinnom to burn their sons and daughters in the fire—something I did not command, nor did it enter my mind. ³²So beware, the days are coming, declares the LORD, when people will no longer call it Topheth or the Valley of Ben Hinnom, but the Valley of Slaughter, for they will bury the

---

⧉ ⦙⦙⦙⦙⦙⦙⦙ KNOWING YOURSELF ⦙⦙⦙⦙⦙⦙⦙ ⊟

7:9–11
Sin

Some people take God for a fool! They think they can totally ignore his commands and dabble in pagan practices, figuring that they can always revert back to God if their "new religion" doesn't work.

Not that God won't receive repentant seekers—of course he will. But the people Jeremiah condemned here weren't repentant—they wanted to have it both ways.

Are you looking for the freedom to experiment in behaviors, practices, or lifestyles that you know are wrong—and then to cozy up to God when things get tough? That's a dangerous practice! It's an indication of a heart that needs to be touched by God's grace and trained by his truth. Don't wait any longer—let God know that you want him to forgive you and help you live in ways that are not only right, but are also the best for you.

dead in Topheth until there is no more room. ³³Then the carcasses of this people will become food for the birds of the air and the beasts of the earth, and there will be no one voices of bride and bridegroom in the towns of Judah and the streets of Jerusalem, for the land will become desolate.

8 " 'At that time, declares the LORD, the bones of the kings and officials of Judah, the bones of the priests and prophets, and the bones of the people of Jerusalem will be removed from their graves. ²They will be exposed to the sun and the moon and all the stars of the heavens, which they have loved and served and which they have followed and consulted and worshiped. They will not be gathered up or buried, but will be like refuse lying on the ground. ³Wherever I banish them, all the survivors of this evil nation will prefer death to life, declares the LORD Almighty.'

Sin and Punishment

⁴"Say to them, 'This is what the LORD says:

" 'When men fall down, do they not get up?
   When a man turns away, does he not return?
⁵Why then have these people turned away?
   Why does Jerusalem always turn away?
They cling to deceit;
   they refuse to return.
⁶I have listened attentively,
   but they do not say what is right.
No one repents of his wickedness,
   saying, "What have I done?"
Each pursues his own course
   like a horse charging into battle.
⁷Even the stork in the sky
   knows her appointed seasons,
and the dove, the swift and the thrush
   observe the time of their migration.
But my people do not know
   the requirements of the LORD.

⁸" 'How can you say, "We are wise,
   for we have the law of the LORD,"
when actually the lying pen of the scribes
   has handled it falsely?
⁹The wise will be put to shame;
   they will be dismayed and trapped.
Since they have rejected the word of the LORD,
   what kind of wisdom do they have?
¹⁰Therefore I will give their wives to other men
   and their fields to new owners.
From the least to the greatest,
   all are greedy for gain;
prophets and priests alike,
   all practice deceit.
¹¹They dress the wound of my people
   as though it were not serious.
"Peace, peace," they say,
   when there is no peace.

¹²Are they ashamed of their loathsome conduct?
  No, they have no shame at all;
  they do not even know how to blush.
So they will fall among the fallen;
  they will be brought down when they are punished,

                                        says the LORD.

¹³" 'I will take away their harvest,

                                        declares the LORD.

  There will be no grapes on the vine.
  There will be no figs on the tree,
    and their leaves will wither.
  What I have given them
    will be taken from them.ᵃ' "

¹⁴"Why are we sitting here?
    Gather together!
  Let us flee to the fortified cities
    and perish there!
  For the LORD our God has doomed us to perish
    and given us poisoned water to drink,
    because we have sinned against him.
¹⁵We hoped for peace
    but no good has come,
  for a time of healing
    but there was only terror.
¹⁶The snorting of the enemy's horses
    is heard from Dan;
  at the neighing of their stallions
    the whole land trembles.
  They have come to devour
    the land and everything in it,
    the city and all who live there."

¹⁷"See, I will send venomous snakes among you,
    vipers that cannot be charmed,
    and they will bite you,"

                                        declares the LORD.

¹⁸O my Comforterᵇ in sorrow,
    my heart is faint within me.
¹⁹Listen to the cry of my people
    from a land far away:
  "Is the LORD not in Zion?
    Is her King no longer there?"

  "Why have they provoked me to anger with their images,
    with their worthless foreign idols?"

²⁰"The harvest is past,
    the summer has ended,
    and we are not saved."

ᵃ13 The meaning of the Hebrew for this sentence is uncertain.   ᵇ18 The meaning of the Hebrew for this word is uncertain.

²¹Since my people are crushed, I am crushed;
  I mourn, and horror grips me.
²²Is there no balm in Gilead?
  Is there no physician there?
Why then is there no healing
  for the wound of my people?

9
¹Oh, that my head were a spring of water
  and my eyes a fountain of tears!
I would weep day and night
  for the slain of my people.
²Oh, that I had in the desert
  a lodging place for travelers,
so that I might leave my people
  and go away from them;
for they are all adulterers,
  a crowd of unfaithful people.

³"They make ready their tongue
  like a bow, to shoot lies;
it is not by truth
  that they triumph*ª* in the land.
They go from one sin to another;
  they do not acknowledge me,"

                              declares the Lord.

⁴"Beware of your friends;
  do not trust your brothers.
For every brother is a deceiver,*ᵇ*
  and every friend a slanderer.
⁵Friend deceives friend,
  and no one speaks the truth.
They have taught their tongues to lie;
  they weary themselves with sinning.
⁶You*ᶜ* live in the midst of deception;
  in their deceit they refuse to acknowledge me,"

                              declares the Lord.

⁷Therefore this is what the Lord Almighty says:

  "See, I will refine and test them,
    for what else can I do
    because of the sin of my people?
⁸Their tongue is a deadly arrow;
    it speaks with deceit.
With his mouth each speaks cordially to his neighbor,
    but in his heart he sets a trap for him.
⁹Should I not punish them for this?"
    declares the Lord.
  "Should I not avenge myself
    on such a nation as this?"

¹⁰I will weep and wail for the mountains
  and take up a lament concerning the desert pastures.
They are desolate and untraveled,

ª3 Or lies; / they are not valiant for truth   *ᵇ4 Or a deceiving Jacob*   *ᶜ6 That is, Jeremiah (the Hebrew is singular)*

and the lowing of cattle is not heard.
The birds of the air have fled
    and the animals are gone.

11"I will make Jerusalem a heap of ruins,
    a haunt of jackals;
and I will lay waste the towns of Judah
    so no one can live there."

12What man is wise enough to understand this? Who has been instructed by the Lord and can explain it? Why has the land been ruined and laid waste like a desert that no one can cross?

13The Lord said, "It is because they have forsaken my law, which I set before them; they have not obeyed me or followed my law. 14Instead, they have followed the stubbornness of their hearts; they have followed the Baals, as their fathers taught them." 15Therefore, this is what the Lord Almighty, the God of Israel, says: "See, I will make this people eat bitter food and drink poisoned water. 16I will scatter them among nations that neither they nor their fathers have known, and I will pursue them with the sword until I have destroyed them."

17This is what the Lord Almighty says:

"Consider now! Call for the wailing women to come;
    send for the most skillful of them.
18Let them come quickly
    and wail over us
till our eyes overflow with tears
    and water streams from our eyelids.
19The sound of wailing is heard from Zion:
    'How ruined we are!
    How great is our shame!
We must leave our land
    because our houses are in ruins.'"

20Now, O women, hear the word of the Lord;
    open your ears to the words of his mouth.
Teach your daughters how to wail;
    teach one another a lament.
21Death has climbed in through our windows
    and has entered our fortresses;
it has cut off the children from the streets
    and the young men from the public squares.

22Say, "This is what the Lord declares:

"'The dead bodies of men will lie
    like refuse on the open field,
like cut grain behind the reaper,
    with no one to gather them.'"

23This is what the Lord says:

"Let not the wise man boast of his wisdom
    or the strong man boast of his strength
    or the rich man boast of his riches,
24but let him who boasts boast about this:
    that he understands and knows me,

> that I am the LORD, who exercises kindness,
>   justice and righteousness on earth,
>   for in these I delight," ⎯/

>   declares the LORD.

²⁵"The days are coming," declares the LORD, "when I will punish all who are circumcised only in the flesh— ²⁶Egypt, Judah, Edom, Ammon, Moab and all who live in the desert in distant places.ᵃ For all these nations are really uncircumcised, and even the whole house of Israel is uncircumcised in heart."

God and Idols

10 Hear what the LORD says to you, O house of Israel. ²This is what the LORD says:

> "Do not learn the ways of the nations
>   or be terrified by signs in the sky,
>   though the nations are terrified by them.
> ³For the customs of the peoples are worthless;
>   they cut a tree out of the forest,
>   and a craftsman shapes it
>   with his chisel.
> ⁴They adorn it with silver and gold
>   they fasten it with hammer
>   and nails
>   so it will not totter.
> ⁵Like a scarecrow in a melon patch,
>   their idols cannot speak;
> they must be carried
>   because they cannot walk.
> Do not fear them;
>   they can do no harm
>   nor can they do any good."

> ⁶No one is like you, O LORD;
>   you are great,
>   and your name is mighty in power.
> ⁷Who should not revere you,
>   O King of the nations?
>   This is your due.
> Among all the wise men of the nations
>   and in all their kingdoms,
>   there is no one like you.
> ⁸They are all senseless and foolish;
>   they are taught by worthless wooden idols.
> ⁹Hammered silver is brought from Tarshish
>   and gold from Uphaz.
> What the craftsman and goldsmith have made
>   is then dressed in blue and purple—
>   all made by skilled workers.
> ¹⁰But the LORD is the true God;

🔲 ▒▒▒▒ KNOWING YOURSELF ▒▒▒▒ ⮐

9:23–24
A New Identity

What do you think makes you attractive? What are you drawn to in others? When asked this question, most of us name qualities that can fit under the three categories mentioned in this passage: wisdom (intelligence, education, savvy), strength (nice physique, good looks, youthfulness, power, control) or riches (wealth, position, status, respect).

   But God says that the most important quality a human being can have is an understanding and knowledge of God. We need more than knowledge *about* God; we need to have an experiential connection *with* God. As we experience God's influence in our lives, we'll want to mirror his character qualities: kindness, justice, and righteousness.

   Those are the characteristics that are worth bragging about—the ones that reflect God's own character in our lives.

ᵃ26 Or desert and who clip the hair by their foreheads

he is the living God, the eternal King.
When he is angry, the earth trembles;
the nations cannot endure his wrath.

¹¹"Tell them this: 'These gods, who did not make the heavens and the earth, will perish from the earth and from under the heavens.'"ᵃ

¹²But God made the earth by his power;
he founded the world by his wisdom
and stretched out the heavens by his understanding.
¹³When he thunders, the waters in the heavens roar;
he makes clouds rise from the ends of the earth.
He sends lightning with the rain
and brings out the wind from his storehouses.

¹⁴Everyone is senseless and without knowledge;
every goldsmith is shamed by his idols.
His images are a fraud;
they have no breath in them.
¹⁵They are worthless, the objects of mockery;
when their judgment comes, they will perish.
¹⁶He who is the Portion of Jacob is not like these,
for he is the Maker of all things,
including Israel, the tribe of his inheritance—
the LORD Almighty is his name.

Coming Destruction

¹⁷Gather up your belongings to leave the land,
you who live under siege.
¹⁸For this is what the LORD says:
"At this time I will hurl out
those who live in this land;
I will bring distress on them
so that they may be captured."

¹⁹Woe to me because of my injury!
My wound is incurable!
Yet I said to myself,
"This is my sickness, and I must endure it."
²⁰My tent is destroyed;
all its ropes are snapped.
My sons are gone from me and are no more;
no one is left now to pitch my tent
or to set up my shelter.
²¹The shepherds are senseless
and do not inquire of the LORD;
so they do not prosper
and all their flock is scattered.
²²Listen! The report is coming—
a great commotion from the land of the north!
It will make the towns of Judah desolate,
a haunt of jackals.

ᵃ 11 The text of this verse is in Aramaic.

Jeremiah's Prayer

²³I know, O LORD, that a man's life is not his own;
    it is not for man to direct his steps.
²⁴Correct me, LORD, but only with justice—
    not in your anger,
    lest you reduce me to nothing.
²⁵Pour out your wrath on the nations
    that do not acknowledge you,
    on the peoples who do not call on your name.
For they have devoured Jacob;
    they have devoured him completely
    and destroyed his homeland.

The Covenant Is Broken

11 This is the word that came to Jeremiah from the LORD: ²"Listen to the terms of this covenant and tell them to the people of Judah and to those who live in Jerusalem. ³Tell them that this is what the LORD, the God of Israel, says: 'Cursed is the man who does not obey the terms of this covenant— ⁴the terms I commanded your forefathers when I brought them out of Egypt, out of the iron-smelting furnace.' I said, 'Obey me and do everything I command you, and you will be my people, and I will be your God. ⁵Then I will fulfill the oath I swore to your forefathers, to give them a land flowing with milk and honey'—the land you possess today."

I answered, "Amen, LORD."

⁶The LORD said to me, "Proclaim all these words in the towns of Judah and in the streets of Jerusalem: 'Listen to the terms of this covenant and follow them. ⁷From the time I brought your forefathers up from Egypt until today, I warned them again and again, saying, "Obey me." ⁸But they did not listen or pay attention; instead, they followed the stubbornness of their evil hearts. So I brought on them all the curses of the covenant I had commanded them to follow but that they did not keep.'"

⁹Then the LORD said to me, "There is a conspiracy among the people of Judah and those who live in Jerusalem. ¹⁰They have returned to the sins of their forefathers, who refused to listen to my words. They have followed other gods to serve them. Both the house of Israel and the house of Judah have broken the covenant I made with their forefathers. ¹¹Therefore this is what the LORD says: 'I will bring on them a disaster they cannot escape. Although they cry out to me, I will not listen to them. ¹²The towns of Judah and the people of Jerusalem will go and cry out to the gods to whom they burn incense, but they will not help them at all when disaster strikes. ¹³You have as many gods as you have towns, O Judah; and the altars you have set up to burn incense to that shameful god Baal are as many as the streets of Jerusalem.'

¹⁴"Do not pray for this people nor offer any plea or petition for them, because I will not listen when they call to me in the time of their distress.

¹⁵"What is my beloved doing in my temple
    as she works out her evil schemes with many?
Can consecrated meat avert ˻your punishment˼?
When you engage in your wickedness,
    then you rejoice.ᵃ"

¹⁶The LORD called you a thriving olive tree
    with fruit beautiful in form.
But with the roar of a mighty storm

ᵃ15 Or *Could consecrated meat avert your punishment? / Then you would rejoice*

> he will set it on fire,
> and its branches will be broken.

¹⁷The LORD Almighty, who planted you, has decreed disaster for you, because the house of Israel and the house of Judah have done evil and provoked me to anger by burning incense to Baal.

Plot Against Jeremiah

¹⁸Because the LORD revealed their plot to me, I knew it, for at that time he showed me what they were doing. ¹⁹I had been like a gentle lamb led to the slaughter; I did not realize that they had plotted against me, saying,

> "Let us destroy the tree and its fruit;
> let us cut him off from the land of the living,
> that his name be remembered no more."
> ²⁰But, O LORD Almighty, you who judge righteously
> and test the heart and mind,
> let me see your vengeance upon them,
> for to you I have committed my cause.

²¹"Therefore this is what the LORD says about the men of Anathoth who are seeking your life and saying, 'Do not prophesy in the name of the LORD or you will die by our hands'— ²²therefore this is what the LORD Almighty says: 'I will punish them. Their young men will die by the sword, their sons and daughters by famine. ²³Not even a remnant will be left to them, because I will bring disaster on the men of Anathoth in the year of their punishment.'"

Jeremiah's Complaint

12 You are always righteous, O LORD,
> when I bring a case before you.
> Yet I would speak with you about your justice:
> Why does the way of the wicked prosper?
> Why do all the faithless live at ease?
> ²You have planted them, and they have taken root;
> they grow and bear fruit.
> You are always on their lips
> but far from their hearts.
> ³Yet you know me, O LORD;
> you see me and test my thoughts about you.
> Drag them off like sheep to be butchered!
> Set them apart for the day of slaughter!
> ⁴How long will the land lie parched ᵃ
> and the grass in every field be withered?
> Because those who live in it are wicked,
> the animals and birds have perished.
> Moreover, the people are saying,
> "He will not see what happens to us."

God's Answer

> ⁵"If you have raced with men on foot
> and they have worn you out,
> how can you compete with horses?
> If you stumble in safe country, ᵇ

ᵃ4 Or *land mourn*   ᵇ5 Or *If you put your trust in a land of safety*

how will you manage in the thickets by*a* the Jordan?
⁶Your brothers, your own family—
  even they have betrayed you;
  they have raised a loud cry against you.
 Do not trust them,
  though they speak well of you.

⁷"I will forsake my house,
  abandon my inheritance;
 I will give the one I love
  into the hands of her enemies.
⁸My inheritance has become to me
  like a lion in the forest.
 She roars at me;
  therefore I hate her.
⁹Has not my inheritance become to me
  like a speckled bird of prey
  that other birds of prey surround and attack?
 Go and gather all the wild beasts;
  bring them to devour.
¹⁰Many shepherds will ruin my vineyard
  and trample down my field;
 they will turn my pleasant field
  into a desolate wasteland.
¹¹It will be made a wasteland,
  parched and desolate before me;
 the whole land will be laid waste
  because there is no one who cares.
¹²Over all the barren heights in the desert
  destroyers will swarm,
 for the sword of the LORD will devour
  from one end of the land to the other;
  no one will be safe.
¹³They will sow wheat but reap thorns;
  they will wear themselves out but gain nothing.
 So bear the shame of your harvest
  because of the LORD's fierce anger."

¹⁴This is what the LORD says: "As for all my wicked neighbors who seize the inheritance I gave my people Israel, I will uproot them from their lands and I will uproot the house of Judah from among them. ¹⁵But after I uproot them, I will again have compassion and will bring each of them back to his own inheritance and his own country. ¹⁶And if they learn well the ways of my people and swear by my name, saying, 'As surely as the LORD lives'—even as they once taught my people to swear by Baal—then they will be established among my people. ¹⁷But if any nation does not listen, I will completely uproot and destroy it," declares the LORD.

A Linen Belt

13 This is what the LORD said to me: "Go and buy a linen belt and put it around your waist, but do not let it touch water." ²So I bought a belt, as the LORD directed, and put it around my waist.

³Then the word of the LORD came to me a second time: ⁴"Take the belt you bought and

a5 Or the flooding of ___

are wearing around your waist, and go now to Perath^a and hide it there in a crevice in the rocks." ⁵So I went and hid it at Perath, as the LORD told me.

⁶Many days later the LORD said to me, "Go now to Perath and get the belt I told you to hide there." ⁷So I went to Perath and dug up the belt and took it from the place where I had hidden it, but now it was ruined and completely useless.

⁸Then the word of the LORD came to me: ⁹"This is what the LORD says: 'In the same way I will ruin the pride of Judah and the great pride of Jerusalem. ¹⁰These wicked people, who refuse to listen to my words, who follow the stubbornness of their hearts and go after other gods to serve and worship them, will be like this belt—completely useless! ¹¹For as a belt is bound around a man's waist, so I bound the whole house of Israel and the whole house of Judah to me,' declares the LORD, 'to be my people for my renown and praise and honor. But they have not listened.'

Wineskins

¹²"Say to them: 'This is what the LORD, the God of Israel, says: Every wineskin should be filled with wine.' And if they say to you, 'Don't we know that every wineskin should be filled with wine?' ¹³then tell them, 'This is what the LORD says: I am going to fill with drunkenness all who live in this land, including the kings who sit on David's throne, the priests, the prophets and all those living in Jerusalem. ¹⁴I will smash them one against the other, fathers and sons alike, declares the LORD. I will allow no pity or mercy or compassion to keep me from destroying them.'"

Threat of Captivity

¹⁵Hear and pay attention,
    do not be arrogant,
    for the LORD has spoken.
¹⁶Give glory to the LORD your God
    before he brings the darkness,
before your feet stumble
    on the darkening hills.
You hope for light,
    but he will turn it to thick darkness
    and change it to deep gloom.
¹⁷But if you do not listen,
    I will weep in secret
    because of your pride;
my eyes will weep bitterly,
    overflowing with tears,
    because the LORD's flock will be taken captive.

¹⁸Say to the king and to the queen mother,
    "Come down from your thrones,
for your glorious crowns
    will fall from your heads."
¹⁹The cities in the Negev will be shut up,
    and there will be no one to open them.
All Judah will be carried into exile,
    carried completely away.

²⁰Lift up your eyes and see
    those who are coming from the north.
Where is the flock that was entrusted to you,
    the sheep of which you boasted?

^a 4 Or possibly *the Euphrates*; also in verses 5-7

²¹What will you say when ˌthe Lord₎ sets over you
    those you cultivated as your special allies?
Will not pain grip you
    like that of a woman in labor?
²²And if you ask yourself,
    "Why has this happened to me?"—
it is because of your many sins
    that your skirts have been torn off
    and your body mistreated.
²³Can the Ethiopian*ᵃ* change his skin
    or the leopard its spots?
Neither can you do good
    who are accustomed to doing evil.

²⁴"I will scatter you like chaff
    driven by the desert wind.
²⁵This is your lot,
    the portion I have decreed for you,"

                             declares the Lord,

"because you have forgotten me
    and trusted in false gods.
²⁶I will pull up your skirts over your face
    that your shame may be seen—
²⁷your adulteries and lustful neighings,
    your shameless prostitution!
I have seen your detestable acts
    on the hills and in the fields.
Woe to you, O Jerusalem!
    How long will you be unclean?"

Drought, Famine, Sword

14 This is the word of the Lord to Jeremiah concerning the drought:

²"Judah mourns,
    her cities languish;
they wail for the land,
    and a cry goes up from Jerusalem.
³The nobles send their servants for water;
    they go to the cisterns
    but find no water.
They return with their jars unfilled;
    dismayed and despairing,
    they cover their heads.
⁴The ground is cracked
    because there is no rain in the land;
the farmers are dismayed
    and cover their heads.
⁵Even the doe in the field
    deserts her newborn fawn
    because there is no grass.

ᵃ23 Hebrew Cushite *(probably a person from the upper Nile region)*

⁶Wild donkeys stand on the barren heights
    and pant like jackals;
their eyesight fails
    for lack of pasture."

⁷Although our sins testify against us,
    O Lᴏʀᴅ, do something for the sake of your name.
For our backsliding is great;
    we have sinned against you.
⁸O Hope of Israel,
    its Savior in times of distress,
why are you like a stranger in the land,
    like a traveler who stays only a night?
⁹Why are you like a man taken by surprise,
    like a warrior powerless to save?
You are among us, O Lᴏʀᴅ,
    and we bear your name;
    do not forsake us!

¹⁰This is what the Lᴏʀᴅ says about this people:

    "They greatly love to wander;
        they do not restrain their feet.
    So the Lᴏʀᴅ does not accept them;
        he will now remember their wickedness
        and punish them for their sins."

¹¹Then the Lᴏʀᴅ said to me, "Do not pray for the well-being of this people. ¹²Although they fast, I will not listen to their cry; though they offer burnt offerings and grain offerings, I will not accept them. Instead, I will destroy them with the sword, famine and plague."

¹³But I said, "Ah, Sovereign Lᴏʀᴅ, the prophets keep telling them, 'You will not see the sword or suffer famine. Indeed, I will give you lasting peace in this place.'"

¹⁴Then the Lᴏʀᴅ said to me, "The prophets are prophesying lies in my name. I have not sent them or appointed them or spoken to them. They are prophesying to you false visions, divinations, idolatries ᵃ and the delusions of their own minds. ¹⁵Therefore, this is what the Lᴏʀᴅ says about the prophets who are prophesying in my name: I did not send them, yet they are saying, 'No sword or famine will touch this land.' Those same prophets will perish by sword and famine. ¹⁶And the people they are prophesying to will be thrown out into the streets of Jerusalem because of the famine and sword. There will be no one to bury them or their wives, their sons or their daughters. I will pour out on them the calamity they deserve.

¹⁷"Speak this word to them:

    "'Let my eyes overflow with tears
        night and day without ceasing;
    for my virgin daughter—my people—
        has suffered a grievous wound,
        a crushing blow.
    ¹⁸If I go into the country,
        I see those slain by the sword;

ᵃ 14 Or *visions, worthless divinations*

if I go into the city,
  I see the ravages of famine.
Both prophet and priest
  have gone to a land they know not.' "

19Have you rejected Judah completely?
  Do you despise Zion?
Why have you afflicted us
  so that we cannot be healed?
We hoped for peace
  but no good has come,
for a time of healing
  but there is only terror.
20O LORD, we acknowledge our wickedness
  and the guilt of our fathers;
  we have indeed sinned against you.
21For the sake of your name do not despise us;
  do not dishonor your glorious throne.
Remember your covenant with us
  and do not break it.
22Do any of the worthless idols of the nations bring rain?
  Do the skies themselves send down showers?
No, it is you, O LORD our God.
  Therefore our hope is in you,
  for you are the one who does all this.

15 Then the LORD said to me: "Even if Moses and Samuel were to stand before me, my heart would not go out to this people. Send them away from my presence! Let them go! 2And if they ask you, 'Where shall we go?' tell them, 'This is what the LORD says:

" 'Those destined for death, to death;
  those for the sword, to the sword;
  those for starvation, to starvation;
  those for captivity, to captivity.'

3"I will send four kinds of destroyers against them," declares the LORD, "the sword to kill and the dogs to drag away and the birds of the air and the beasts of the earth to devour and destroy. 4I will make them abhorrent to all the kingdoms of the earth because of what Manasseh son of Hezekiah king of Judah did in Jerusalem.

5"Who will have pity on you, O Jerusalem?
  Who will mourn for you?
  Who will stop to ask how you are?
6You have rejected me," declares the LORD.
  "You keep on backsliding.
So I will lay hands on you and destroy you;
  I can no longer show compassion.
7I will winnow them with a winnowing fork
  at the city gates of the land.
I will bring bereavement and destruction on my people,
  for they have not changed their ways.
8I will make their widows more numerous
  than the sand of the sea.

At midday I will bring a destroyer
    against the mothers of their young men;
suddenly I will bring down on them
    anguish and terror.
[9]The mother of seven will grow faint
    and breathe her last.
Her sun will set while it is still day;
    she will be disgraced and humiliated.
I will put the survivors to the sword
    before their enemies,"

                                        declares the LORD.

[10]Alas, my mother, that you gave me birth,
    a man with whom the whole land strives and contends!
I have neither lent nor borrowed,
    yet everyone curses me.

[11]The LORD said,

"Surely I will deliver you for a good purpose;
    surely I will make your enemies plead with you
    in times of disaster and times of distress.

[12]"Can a man break iron—
    iron from the north—or bronze?
[13]Your wealth and your treasures
    I will give as plunder, without charge,
because of all your sins
    throughout your country.
[14]I will enslave you to your enemies
    in[a] a land you do not know,
for my anger will kindle a fire
    that will burn against you."

[15]You understand, O LORD;
    remember me and care for me.
    Avenge me on my persecutors.
You are long-suffering—do not take me away;
    think of how I suffer reproach for your sake.
[16]When your words came, I ate them;
    they were my joy and my heart's delight,
for I bear your name,
    O LORD God Almighty.
[17]I never sat in the company of revelers,
    never made merry with them;
I sat alone because your hand was on me
    and you had filled me with indignation.
[18]Why is my pain unending
    and my wound grievous and incurable?
Will you be to me like a deceptive brook,
    like a spring that fails?

_a 14_ Some Hebrew manuscripts, Septuagint and Syriac (see also Jer. 17:4); most Hebrew manuscripts _I will cause your enemies to bring you / into_

¹⁹Therefore this is what the Lord says:

> "If you repent, I will restore you
>   that you may serve me;
> if you utter worthy, not worthless, words,
>   you will be my spokesman.
> Let this people turn to you,
>   but you must not turn to them.
> ²⁰I will make you a wall to this people,
>   a fortified wall of bronze;
> they will fight against you
>   but will not overcome you,
> for I am with you
>   to rescue and save you,"

declares the Lord.

> ²¹"I will save you from the hands of the wicked
>   and redeem you from the grasp of the cruel."

Day of Disaster

16 Then the word of the Lord came to me: ²"You must not marry and have sons or daughters in this place." ³For this is what the Lord says about the sons and daughters born in this land and about the women who are their mothers and the men who are their fathers: ⁴"They will die of deadly diseases. They will not be mourned or buried but will be like refuse lying on the ground. They will perish by sword and famine, and their dead bodies will become food for the birds of the air and the beasts of the earth."

⁵For this is what the Lord says: "Do not enter a house where there is a funeral meal; do not go to mourn or show sympathy, because I have withdrawn my blessing, my love and my pity from this people," declares the Lord. ⁶"Both high and low will die in this land. They will not be buried or mourned, and no one will cut himself or shave his head for them. ⁷No one will offer food to comfort those who mourn for the dead—not even for a father or a mother—nor will anyone give them a drink to console them.

⁸"And do not enter a house where there is feasting and sit down to eat and drink. ⁹For this is what the Lord Almighty, the God of Israel, says: Before your eyes and in your days I will bring an end to the sounds of joy and gladness and to the voices of bride and bridegroom in this place.

¹⁰"When you tell these people all this and they ask you, 'Why has the Lord decreed such a great disaster against us? What wrong have we done? What sin have we committed against the Lord our God?' ¹¹then say to them, 'It is because your fathers forsook me,' declares the Lord, 'and followed other gods and served and worshiped them. They forsook me and did not keep my law. ¹²But you have behaved more wickedly than your fathers. See how each of you is following the stubbornness of his evil heart instead of obeying me. ¹³So I will throw you out of this land into a land neither you nor your fathers have known, and there you will serve other gods day and night, for I will show you no favor.'

¹⁴"However, the days are coming," declares the Lord, "when men will no longer say, 'As surely as the Lord lives, who brought the Israelites up out of Egypt,' ¹⁵but they will say, 'As surely as the Lord lives, who brought the Israelites up out of the land of the north and out of all the countries where he had banished them.' For I will restore them to the land I gave their forefathers.

¹⁶"But now I will send for many fishermen," declares the Lord, "and they will catch them. After that I will send for many hunters, and they will hunt them down on every mountain and hill and from the crevices of the rocks. ¹⁷My eyes are on all their ways; they are not hidden from me, nor is their sin concealed from my eyes. ¹⁸I will repay them

double for their wickedness and their sin, because they have defiled my land with the lifeless forms of their vile images and have filled my inheritance with their detestable idols."

¹⁹O LORD, my strength and my fortress,
    my refuge in time of distress,
to you the nations will come
    from the ends of the earth and say,
"Our fathers possessed nothing but false gods,
    worthless idols that did them no good.
²⁰Do men make their own gods?
    Yes, but they are not gods!"

²¹"Therefore I will teach them—
    this time I will teach them
    my power and might.
Then they will know
    that my name is the LORD.

17   "Judah's sin is engraved with an iron tool,
    inscribed with a flint point,
on the tablets of their hearts
    and on the horns of their altars.
²Even their children remember
    their altars and Asherah poles^a
beside the spreading trees
    and on the high hills.
³My mountain in the land
    and your^b wealth and all your treasures
I will give away as plunder,
    together with your high places,
    because of sin throughout your country.
⁴Through your own fault you will lose
    the inheritance I gave you.
I will enslave you to your enemies
    in a land you do not know,
for you have kindled my anger,
    and it will burn forever."

⁵This is what the LORD says:

"Cursed is the one who trusts in man,
    who depends on flesh for his strength
    and whose heart turns away from the LORD.
⁶He will be like a bush in the wastelands;
    he will not see prosperity when it comes.
He will dwell in the parched places of the desert,
    in a salt land where no one lives.

⁷"But blessed is the man who trusts in the LORD,
    whose confidence is in him.
⁸He will be like a tree planted by the water
    that sends out its roots by the stream.
It does not fear when heat comes;
    its leaves are always green.

a 2 That is, symbols of the goddess Asherah   *b 2,3* Or *hills /* ³*and the mountains of the land. / Your*

It has no worries in a year of drought
  and never fails to bear fruit."

⁹The heart is deceitful above all things
  and beyond cure.
  Who can understand it?

¹⁰"I the LORD search the heart
  and examine the mind,
to reward a man according to his conduct,
  according to what his deeds deserve."

¹¹Like a partridge that hatches eggs it did not lay
  is the man who gains riches by unjust means.
When his life is half gone, they will desert him,
  and in the end he will prove to be a fool.

¹²A glorious throne, exalted from the beginning,
  is the place of our sanctuary.
¹³O LORD, the hope of Israel,
  all who forsake you will be
    put to shame.
Those who turn away from you
    will be written in the dust
  because they have forsaken
    the LORD,
  the spring of living water.

¹⁴Heal me, O LORD, and I will be
    healed;
  save me and I will be saved,
  for you are the one I praise.
¹⁵They keep saying to me,
  "Where is the word of the
    LORD?
  Let it now be fulfilled!"
¹⁶I have not run away from being
    your shepherd;
  you know I have not desired
    the day of despair.
  What passes my lips is open
    before you.
¹⁷Do not be a terror to me;
  you are my refuge in the day of disaster.
¹⁸Let my persecutors be put to shame,
  but keep me from shame;
let them be terrified,
  but keep me from terror.
Bring on them the day of disaster;
  destroy them with double destruction.

▣ ⬚⬚⬚⬚⬚ KNOWING YOURSELF ⬚⬚⬚⬚⬚ ⬚

17:9
Sin

This verse describes the human heart apart from God. Try as we might, we can never completely sift through our motives and determine why we do things. Our hearts are just too deceitful.

Perhaps you, like many other people, believe that you're basically honest. But ask yourself this question, *Do I have to work harder at speaking the truth or distorting the truth?* Isn't it more difficult to be consistently truthful? Of course. Our natural tendency is to make ourselves look good, even if we have to stretch a few facts or lie to protect ourselves from unfavorable consequences.

This verse doesn't give us the cure for our "heart disease," but it's a great diagnostic tool. No more self-deceit—we have a problem, and we need help.

Keep reading—there's a solution!

Keeping the Sabbath Holy

¹⁹This is what the LORD said to me: "Go and stand at the gate of the people, through which the kings of Judah go in and out; stand also at all the other gates of Jerusalem. ²⁰Say to them, 'Hear the word of the LORD, O kings of Judah and all people of Judah and everyone living in Jerusalem who come through these gates. ²¹This is what the LORD says:

Be careful not to carry a load on the Sabbath day or bring it through the gates of Jerusalem. ²²Do not bring a load out of your houses or do any work on the Sabbath, but keep the Sabbath day holy, as I commanded your forefathers. ²³Yet they did not listen or pay attention; they were stiff-necked and would not listen or respond to discipline. ²⁴But if you are careful to obey me, declares the LORD, and bring no load through the gates of this city on the Sabbath, but keep the Sabbath day holy by not doing any work on it, ²⁵then kings who sit on David's throne will come through the gates of this city with their officials. They and their officials will come riding in chariots and on horses, accompanied by the men of Judah and those living in Jerusalem, and this city will be inhabited forever. ²⁶People will come from the towns of Judah and the villages around Jerusalem, from the territory of Benjamin and the western foothills, from the hill country and the Negev, bringing burnt offerings and sacrifices, grain offerings, incense and thank offerings to the house of the LORD. ²⁷But if you do not obey me to keep the Sabbath day holy by not carrying any load as you come through the gates of Jerusalem on the Sabbath day, then I will kindle an unquenchable fire in the gates of Jerusalem that will consume her fortresses.' "

At the Potter's House

18 This is the word that came to Jeremiah from the LORD: ²"Go down to the potter's house, and there I will give you my message." ³So I went down to the potter's house, and I saw him working at the wheel. ⁴But the pot he was shaping from the clay was marred in his hands; so the potter formed it into another pot, shaping it as seemed best to him.

⁵Then the word of the LORD came to me: ⁶"O house of Israel, can I not do with you as this potter does?" declares the LORD. "Like clay in the hand of the potter, so are you in my hand, O house of Israel. ⁷If at any time I announce that a nation or kingdom is to be uprooted, torn down and destroyed, ⁸and if that nation I warned repents of its evil, then I will relent and not inflict on it the disaster I had planned. ⁹And if at another time I announce that a nation or kingdom is to be built up and planted, ¹⁰and if it does evil in my sight and does not obey me, then I will reconsider the good I had intended to do for it.

¹¹"Now therefore say to the people of Judah and those living in Jerusalem, 'This is what the LORD says: Look! I am preparing a disaster for you and devising a plan against you. So turn from your evil ways, each one of you, and reform your ways and your actions.' ¹²But they will reply, 'It's no use. We will continue with our own plans; each of us will follow the stubbornness of his evil heart.' "

¹³Therefore this is what the LORD says:

> "Inquire among the nations:
>   Who has ever heard anything like this?
> A most horrible thing has been done
>   by Virgin Israel.
> ¹⁴Does the snow of Lebanon
>   ever vanish from its rocky slopes?
> Do its cool waters from distant sources
>   ever cease to flow?ᵃ
> ¹⁵Yet my people have forgotten me;
>   they burn incense to worthless idols,
> which made them stumble in their ways
>   and in the ancient paths.
> They made them walk in bypaths
>   and on roads not built up.

ᵃ14 The meaning of the Hebrew for this sentence is uncertain.

¹⁶Their land will be laid waste,
   an object of lasting scorn;
all who pass by will be appalled
   and will shake their heads.
¹⁷Like a wind from the east,
   I will scatter them before their enemies;
I will show them my back and not my face
   in the day of their disaster."

¹⁸They said, "Come, let's make plans against Jeremiah; for the teaching of the law by the priest will not be lost, nor will counsel from the wise, nor the word from the prophets. So come, let's attack him with our tongues and pay no attention to anything he says."

¹⁹Listen to me, O LORD;
   hear what my accusers are saying!
²⁰Should good be repaid with evil?
   Yet they have dug a pit for me.
Remember that I stood before you
   and spoke in their behalf
   to turn your wrath away from them.
²¹So give their children over to famine;
   hand them over to the power of the sword.
Let their wives be made childless and widows;
   let their men be put to death,
   their young men slain by the sword in battle.
²²Let a cry be heard from their houses
   when you suddenly bring invaders against them,
for they have dug a pit to capture me
   and have hidden snares for my feet.
²³But you know, O LORD,
   all their plots to kill me.
Do not forgive their crimes
   or blot out their sins from your sight.
Let them be overthrown before you;
   deal with them in the time of your anger.

19 This is what the LORD says: "Go and buy a clay jar from a potter. Take along some of the elders of the people and of the priests ²and go out to the Valley of Ben Hinnom, near the entrance of the Potsherd Gate. There proclaim the words I tell you, ³and say, 'Hear the word of the LORD, O kings of Judah and people of Jerusalem. This is what the LORD Almighty, the God of Israel, says: Listen! I am going to bring a disaster on this place that will make the ears of everyone who hears of it tingle. ⁴For they have forsaken me and made this a place of foreign gods; they have burned sacrifices in it to gods that neither they nor their fathers nor the kings of Judah ever knew, and they have filled this place with the blood of the innocent. ⁵They have built the high places of Baal to burn their sons in the fire as offerings to Baal—something I did not command or mention, nor did it enter my mind. ⁶So beware, the days are coming, declares the LORD, when people will no longer call this place Topheth or the Valley of Ben Hinnom, but the Valley of Slaughter.

⁷"'In this place I will ruin^a the plans of Judah and Jerusalem. I will make them fall by the sword before their enemies, at the hands of those who seek their lives, and I will give their carcasses as food to the birds of the air and the beasts of the earth. ⁸I will devastate this city and make it an object of scorn; all who pass by will be appalled and will scoff

_____

^a7 The Hebrew for _ruin_ sounds like the Hebrew for _jar_ (see verses 1 and 10).

because of all its wounds. ⁹I will make them eat the flesh of their sons and daughters, and they will eat one another's flesh during the stress of the siege imposed on them by the enemies who seek their lives.'

¹⁰"Then break the jar while those who go with you are watching, ¹¹and say to them, 'This is what the LORD Almighty says: I will smash this nation and this city just as this potter's jar is smashed and cannot be repaired. They will bury the dead in Topheth until there is no more room. ¹²This is what I will do to this place and to those who live here, declares the LORD. I will make this city like Topheth. ¹³The houses in Jerusalem and those of the kings of Judah will be defiled like this place, Topheth—all the houses where they burned incense on the roofs to all the starry hosts and poured out drink offerings to other gods.'"

¹⁴Jeremiah then returned from Topheth, where the LORD had sent him to prophesy, and stood in the court of the LORD's temple and said to all the people, ¹⁵"This is what the LORD Almighty, the God of Israel, says: 'Listen! I am going to bring on this city and the villages around it every disaster I pronounced against them, because they were stiff-necked and would not listen to my words.'"

Jeremiah and Pashhur

20 When the priest Pashhur son of Immer, the chief officer in the temple of the LORD, heard Jeremiah prophesying these things, ²he had Jeremiah the prophet beaten and put in the stocks at the Upper Gate of Benjamin at the LORD's temple. ³The next day, when Pashhur released him from the stocks, Jeremiah said to him, "The LORD's name for you is not Pashhur, but Magor-Missabib.ᵃ ⁴For this is what the LORD says: 'I will make you a terror to yourself and to all your friends; with your own eyes you will see them fall by the sword of their enemies. I will hand all Judah over to the king of Babylon, who will carry them away to Babylon or put them to the sword. ⁵I will hand over to their enemies all the wealth of this city—all its products, all its valuables and all the treasures of the kings of Judah. They will take it away as plunder and carry it off to Babylon. ⁶And you, Pashhur, and all who live in your house will go into exile to Babylon. There you will die and be buried, you and all your friends to whom you have prophesied lies.'"

Jeremiah's Complaint

⁷O LORD, you deceivedᵇ me, and I was deceivedᵇ;
  you overpowered me and prevailed.
I am ridiculed all day long;
  everyone mocks me.
⁸Whenever I speak, I cry out
  proclaiming violence and destruction.
So the word of the LORD has brought me
  insult and reproach all day long.
⁹But if I say, "I will not mention him
  or speak any more in his name,"
his word is in my heart like a fire,
  a fire shut up in my bones.
I am weary of holding it in;
  indeed, I cannot.
¹⁰I hear many whispering,
  "Terror on every side!
  Report him! Let's report him!"
All my friends
  are waiting for me to slip, saying,

ᵃ3 *Magor-Missabib* means *terror on every side.*   ᵇ7 Or *persuaded*

"Perhaps he will be deceived;
    then we will prevail over him
    and take our revenge on him."

¹¹But the LORD is with me like a mighty warrior;
    so my persecutors will stumble and not prevail.
They will fail and be thoroughly disgraced;
    their dishonor will never be forgotten.
¹²O LORD Almighty, you who examine the righteous
    and probe the heart and mind,
let me see your vengeance upon them,
    for to you I have committed my cause.

¹³Sing to the LORD!
    Give praise to the LORD!
He rescues the life of the needy
    from the hands of the wicked.

¹⁴Cursed be the day I was born!
    May the day my mother bore me not be blessed!
¹⁵Cursed be the man who brought my father the news,
    who made him very glad, saying,
    "A child is born to you—a son!"
¹⁶May that man be like the towns
    the LORD overthrew without pity.
May he hear wailing in the morning,
    a battle cry at noon.
¹⁷For he did not kill me in the womb,
    with my mother as my grave,
    her womb enlarged forever.
¹⁸Why did I ever come out of the womb
    to see trouble and sorrow
    and to end my days in shame?

God Rejects Zedekiah's Request

21 The word came to Jeremiah from the LORD when King Zedekiah sent to him Pashhur son of Malkijah and the priest Zephaniah son of Maaseiah. They said: ²"Inquire now of the LORD for us because Nebuchadnezzar^a king of Babylon is attacking us. Perhaps the LORD will perform wonders for us as in times past so that he will withdraw from us."

³But Jeremiah answered them, "Tell Zedekiah, ⁴'This is what the LORD, the God of Israel, says: I am about to turn against you the weapons of war that are in your hands, which you are using to fight the king of Babylon and the Babylonians^b who are outside the wall besieging you. And I will gather them inside this city. ⁵I myself will fight against you with an outstretched hand and a mighty arm in anger and fury and great wrath. ⁶I will strike down those who live in this city—both men and animals—and they will die of a terrible plague. ⁷After that, declares the LORD, I will hand over Zedekiah king of Judah, his officials and the people in this city who survive the plague, sword and famine, to Nebuchadnezzar king of Babylon and to their enemies who seek their lives. He will put them to the sword; he will show them no mercy or pity or compassion.'

^a2 Hebrew *Nebuchadrezzar*, of which *Nebuchadnezzar* is a variant; here and often in Jeremiah and Ezekiel   ^b4 Or
Chaldeans; also in verse 9

⁸"Furthermore, tell the people, 'This is what the LORD says: See, I am setting before you the way of life and the way of death. ⁹Whoever stays in this city will die by the sword, famine or plague. But whoever goes out and surrenders to the Babylonians who are besieging you will live; he will escape with his life. ¹⁰I have determined to do this city harm and not good, declares the LORD. It will be given into the hands of the king of Babylon, and he will destroy it with fire.'

¹¹"Moreover, say to the royal house of Judah, 'Hear the word of the LORD; ¹²O house of David, this is what the LORD says:

> "'Administer justice every morning;
>   rescue from the hand of his oppressor
>   the one who has been robbed,
> or my wrath will break out and burn like fire
>   because of the evil you have done—
>   burn with no one to quench it.
> ¹³I am against you, ⌊Jerusalem,⌋
>   you who live above this valley
>   on the rocky plateau,
>
>   declares the LORD—
>
> you who say, "Who can come against us?
>   Who can enter our refuge?"
> ¹⁴I will punish you as your deeds deserve,
>
>   declares the LORD.
>
>   I will kindle a fire in your forests
>   that will consume everything around you.'"

Judgment Against Evil Kings

22 This is what the LORD says: "Go down to the palace of the king of Judah and proclaim this message there: ²'Hear the word of the·LORD, O king of Judah, you who sit on David's throne—you, your officials and your people who come through these gates. ³This is what the LORD says: Do what is just and right. Rescue from the hand of his oppressor the one who has been robbed. Do no wrong or violence to the alien, the fatherless or the widow, and do not shed innocent blood in this place. ⁴For if you are careful to carry out these commands, then kings who sit on David's throne will come through the gates of this palace, riding in chariots and on horses, accompanied by their officials and their people. ⁵But if you do not obey these commands, declares the LORD, I swear by myself that this palace will become a ruin.'"

⁶For this is what the LORD says about the palace of the king of Judah:

> "Though you are like Gilead to me,
>   like the summit of Lebanon,
> I will surely make you like a desert,
>   like towns not inhabited.
> ⁷I will send destroyers against you,
>   each man with his weapons,
> and they will cut up your fine cedar beams
>   and throw them into the fire.

⁸"People from many nations will pass by this city and will ask one another, 'Why has the LORD done such a thing to this great city?' ⁹And the answer will be: 'Because they have forsaken the covenant of the LORD their God and have worshiped and served other gods.'"

¹⁰Do not weep for the dead ˻king˼ or mourn his loss;
  rather, weep bitterly for him who is exiled,
because he will never return
  nor see his native land again.

¹¹For this is what the Lord says about Shallum^a son of Josiah, who succeeded his father as king of Judah but has gone from this place: "He will never return. ¹²He will die in the place where they have led him captive; he will not see this land again."

¹³"Woe to him who builds his palace by unrighteousness,
  his upper rooms by injustice,
making his countrymen work for nothing,
  not paying them for their labor.
¹⁴He says, 'I will build myself a great palace
  with spacious upper rooms.'
So he makes large windows in it,
  panels it with cedar
  and decorates it in red.

¹⁵"Does it make you a king
  to have more and more cedar?
Did not your father have food and drink?
  He did what was right and just,
  so all went well with him.
¹⁶He defended the cause of the poor and needy,
  and so all went well.
Is that not what it means to know me?"
  declares the Lord.
¹⁷"But your eyes and your heart
  are set only on dishonest gain,
on shedding innocent blood
  and on oppression and extortion."

¹⁸Therefore this is what the Lord says about Jehoiakim son of Josiah king of Judah:

"They will not mourn for him:
  'Alas, my brother! Alas, my sister!'
They will not mourn for him:
  'Alas, my master! Alas, his splendor!'
¹⁹He will have the burial of a donkey—
  dragged away and thrown
  outside the gates of Jerusalem."

²⁰"Go up to Lebanon and cry out,
  let your voice be heard in Bashan,
cry out from Abarim,
  for all your allies are crushed.
²¹I warned you when you felt secure,
  but you said, 'I will not listen!'
This has been your way from your youth;
  you have not obeyed me.
²²The wind will drive all your shepherds away,
  and your allies will go into exile.
Then you will be ashamed and disgraced

^a *11* Also called *Jehoahaz*

because of all your wickedness.
²³You who live in 'Lebanon,ᵃ'
    who are nestled in cedar buildings,
how you will groan when pangs come upon you,
    pain like that of a woman in labor!

²⁴"As surely as I live," declares the LORD, "even if you, Jehoiachinᵇ son of Jehoiakim king of Judah, were a signet ring on my right hand, I would still pull you off. ²⁵I will hand you over to those who seek your life, those you fear—to Nebuchadnezzar king of Babylon and to the Babylonians.ᶜ ²⁶I will hurl you and the mother who gave you birth into another country, where neither of you was born, and there you both will die. ²⁷You will never come back to the land you long to return to."

²⁸Is this man Jehoiachin a despised, broken pot,
    an object no one wants?
Why will he and his children be hurled out,
    cast into a land they do not know?
²⁹O land, land, land,
    hear the word of the LORD!
³⁰This is what the LORD says:
"Record this man as if childless,
    a man who will not prosper in his lifetime,
for none of his offspring will prosper,
    none will sit on the throne of David
    or rule anymore in Judah."

The Righteous Branch

23 "Woe to the shepherds who are destroying and scattering the sheep of my pasture!" declares the LORD. ²Therefore this is what the LORD, the God of Israel, says to the shepherds who tend my people: "Because you have scattered my flock and driven them away and have not bestowed care on them, I will bestow punishment on you for the evil you have done," declares the LORD. ³"I myself will gather the remnant of my flock out of all the countries where I have driven them and will bring them back to their pasture, where they will be fruitful and increase in number. ⁴I will place shepherds over them who will tend them, and they will no longer be afraid or terrified, nor will any be missing," declares the LORD.

⁵"The days are coming," declares the LORD,
    "when I will raise up to Davidᵈ a
        righteous Branch,
a King who will reign wisely
    and do what is just and right in the
        land.
⁶In his days Judah will be saved
    and Israel will live in safety.
This is the name by which he will be called:
    The LORD Our Righteousness.

DISCOVERING GOD

23:5–6
Jesus, the God-Man

One aspect of messianic hope, based firmly on this and similar passages, was the promise of a righteous king. When the Jews of Jesus' day expected the Messiah to be a political leader, they weren't entirely off base. At Jesus' second coming, he *will* rule over the earth as this verse promises. What they failed to understand was the need to solve their spiritual problems before any political change would benefit them.

Jesus' mission was not just to save his people from oppressive earthly powers; it was primarily to save his people from the oppression of sin. He can fulfill that role for anyone who asks him—as he does right now for Christians all over the world.

ᵃ23 That is, the palace in Jerusalem (see 1 Kings 7:2)   ᵇ24 Hebrew *Coniah,* a variant of *Jehoiachin;* also in verse 28   ᶜ25 Or *Chaldeans*   ᵈ5 Or *up from David's line*

7"So then, the days are coming," declares the LORD, "when people will no longer say, 'As surely as the LORD lives, who brought the Israelites up out of Egypt,' **8**but they will say, 'As surely as the LORD lives, who brought the descendants of Israel up out of the land of the north and out of all the countries where he had banished them.' Then they will live in their own land."

Lying Prophets

9Concerning the prophets:

> My heart is broken within me;
>   all my bones tremble.
> I am like a drunken man,
>   like a man overcome by wine,
> because of the LORD
>   and his holy words.
> **10**The land is full of adulterers;
>   because of the curse*a* the land lies parched*b*
>   and the pastures in the desert are withered.
> The ⌞prophets⌟ follow an evil course
>   and use their power unjustly.

> **11**"Both prophet and priest are godless;
>   even in my temple I find their wickedness,"

>   declares the LORD.

> **12**"Therefore their path will become slippery;
>   they will be banished to darkness
>   and there they will fall.
> I will bring disaster on them
>   in the year they are punished,"

>   declares the LORD.

> **13**"Among the prophets of Samaria
>   I saw this repulsive thing:
> They prophesied by Baal
>   and led my people Israel astray.
> **14**And among the prophets of Jerusalem
>   I have seen something horrible:
> They commit adultery and live a lie.
>   They strengthen the hands of evildoers,
>   so that no one turns from his wickedness.
> They are all like Sodom to me;
>   the people of Jerusalem are like Gomorrah."

15Therefore, this is what the LORD Almighty says concerning the prophets:

> "I will make them eat bitter food
>   and drink poisoned water,
> because from the prophets of Jerusalem
>   ungodliness has spread throughout the land."

16This is what the LORD Almighty says:

---

a 10 Or *because of these things*   *b 10* Or *land mourns*

"Do not listen to what the prophets are prophesying to you;
    they fill you with false hopes.
They speak visions from their own minds,
    not from the mouth of the LORD.
17They keep saying to those who despise me,
    'The LORD says: You will have peace.'
And to all who follow the stubbornness of their hearts
    they say, 'No harm will come to you.'
18But which of them has stood in the council of the LORD
    to see or to hear his word?
    Who has listened and heard his word?
19See, the storm of the LORD
    will burst out in wrath,
a whirlwind swirling down
    on the heads of the wicked.
20The anger of the LORD will not turn back
    until he fully accomplishes
    the purposes of his heart.
In days to come
    you will understand it clearly.
21I did not send these prophets,
    yet they have run with their message;
I did not speak to them,
    yet they have prophesied.
22But if they had stood in my council,
    they would have proclaimed my words to my people
and would have turned them from their evil ways
    and from their evil deeds.

23"Am I only a God nearby,"

                      declares the LORD,

    "and not a God far away?
24Can anyone hide in secret places
    so that I cannot see him?"

                      declares the LORD.

    "Do not I fill heaven and earth?"

                      declares the LORD.

25"I have heard what the prophets say who prophesy lies in my name. They say, 'I had a dream! I had a dream!' 26How long will this continue in the hearts of these lying prophets, who prophesy the delusions of their own minds? 27They think the dreams they tell one another will make my people forget my name, just as their fathers forgot my name through Baal worship. 28Let the prophet who has a dream tell his dream, but let the one who has my word speak it faithfully. For what has straw to do with grain?" declares the LORD. 29"Is not my word like fire," declares the LORD, "and like a hammer that breaks a rock in pieces?

30"Therefore," declares the LORD, "I am against the prophets who steal from one another words supposedly from me. 31Yes," declares the LORD, "I am against the prophets who wag their own tongues and yet declare, 'The LORD declares.' 32Indeed, I am against those who prophesy false dreams," declares the LORD. "They tell them and lead my people astray with their reckless lies, yet I did not send or appoint them. They do not benefit these people in the least," declares the LORD.

False Oracles and False Prophets

33"When these people, or a prophet or a priest, ask you, 'What is the oracle[a] of the LORD?' say to them, 'What oracle?[b] I will forsake you, declares the LORD.' **34**If a prophet or a priest or anyone else claims, 'This is the oracle of the LORD,' I will punish that man and his household. **35**This is what each of you keeps on saying to his friend or relative: 'What is the LORD's answer?' or 'What has the LORD spoken?' **36**But you must not mention 'the oracle of the LORD' again, because every man's own word becomes his oracle and so you distort the words of the living God, the LORD Almighty, our God. **37**This is what you keep saying to a prophet: 'What is the LORD's answer to you?' or 'What has the LORD spoken?' **38**Although you claim, 'This is the oracle of the LORD,' this is what the LORD says: You used the words, 'This is the oracle of the LORD,' even though I told you that you must not claim, 'This is the oracle of the LORD.' **39**Therefore, I will surely forget you and cast you out of my presence along with the city I gave to you and your fathers. **40**I will bring upon you everlasting disgrace—everlasting shame that will not be forgotten."

Two Baskets of Figs

24 After Jehoiachin[c] son of Jehoiakim king of Judah and the officials, the craftsmen and the artisans of Judah were carried into exile from Jerusalem to Babylon by Nebuchadnezzar king of Babylon, the LORD showed me two baskets of figs placed in front of the temple of the LORD. **2**One basket had very good figs, like those that ripen early; the other basket had very poor figs, so bad they could not be eaten.

3Then the LORD asked me, "What do you see, Jeremiah?"

"Figs," I answered. "The good ones are very good, but the poor ones are so bad they cannot be eaten."

4Then the word of the LORD came to me: **5**"This is what the LORD, the God of Israel, says: 'Like these good figs, I regard as good the exiles from Judah, whom I sent away from this place to the land of the Babylonians.[d] **6**My eyes will watch over them for their good, and I will bring them back to this land. I will build them up and not tear them down; I will plant them and not uproot them. **7**I will give them a heart to know me, that I am the LORD. They will be my people, and I will be their God, for they will return to me with all their heart.

8"But like the poor figs, which are so bad they cannot be eaten,' says the LORD, 'so will I deal with Zedekiah king of Judah, his officials and the survivors from Jerusalem, whether they remain in this land or live in Egypt. **9**I will make them abhorrent and an offense to all the kingdoms of the earth, a reproach and a byword, an object of ridicule and cursing, wherever I banish them. **10**I will send the sword, famine and plague against them until they are destroyed from the land I gave to them and their fathers.'"

Seventy Years of Captivity

25 The word came to Jeremiah concerning all the people of Judah in the fourth year of Jehoiakim son of Josiah king of Judah, which was the first year of Nebuchadnezzar king of Babylon. **2**So Jeremiah the prophet said to all the people of Judah and to all those living in Jerusalem: **3**For twenty-three years—from the thirteenth year of Josiah son of Amon king of Judah until this very day—the word of the LORD has come to me and I have spoken to you again and again, but you have not listened.

4And though the LORD has sent all his servants the prophets to you again and again, you have not listened or paid any attention. **5**They said, "Turn now, each of you, from your evil ways and your evil practices, and you can stay in the land the LORD gave to you and your fathers for ever and ever. **6**Do not follow other gods to serve and worship them; do not provoke me to anger with what your hands have made. Then I will not harm you."

---

a 33 Or *burden* (see Septuagint and Vulgate)   *b 33* Hebrew; Septuagint and Vulgate *You are the burden.* (The Hebrew for oracle and burden is the same.)   *c 1* Hebrew *Jeconiah,* a variant of *Jehoiachin*   *d 5* Or *Chaldeans*

⁷"But you did not listen to me," declares the LORD, "and you have provoked me with what your hands have made, and you have brought harm to yourselves."

⁸Therefore the LORD Almighty says this: "Because you have not listened to my words, ⁹I will summon all the peoples of the north and my servant Nebuchadnezzar king of Babylon," declares the LORD, "and I will bring them against this land and its inhabitants and against all the surrounding nations. I will completely destroyᵃ them and make them an object of horror and scorn, and an everlasting ruin. ¹⁰I will banish from them the sounds of joy and gladness, the voices of bride and bridegroom, the sound of millstones and the light of the lamp. ¹¹This whole country will become a desolate wasteland, and these nations will serve the king of Babylon seventy years.

¹²"But when the seventy years are fulfilled, I will punish the king of Babylon and his nation, the land of the Babylonians,ᵇ for their guilt," declares the LORD, "and will make it desolate forever. ¹³I will bring upon that land all the things I have spoken against it, all that are written in this book and prophesied by Jeremiah against all the nations. ¹⁴They themselves will be enslaved by many nations and great kings; I will repay them according to their deeds and the work of their hands."

The Cup of God's Wrath

¹⁵This is what the LORD, the God of Israel, said to me: "Take from my hand this cup filled with the wine of my wrath and make all the nations to whom I send you drink it. ¹⁶When they drink it, they will stagger and go mad because of the sword I will send among them."

¹⁷So I took the cup from the LORD's hand and made all the nations to whom he sent me drink it: ¹⁸Jerusalem and the towns of Judah, its kings and officials, to make them a ruin and an object of horror and scorn and cursing, as they are today; ¹⁹Pharaoh king of Egypt, his attendants, his officials and all his people, ²⁰and all the foreign people there; all the kings of Uz; all the kings of the Philistines (those of Ashkelon, Gaza, Ekron, and the people left at Ashdod); ²¹Edom, Moab and Ammon; ²²all the kings of Tyre and Sidon; the kings of the coastlands across the sea; ²³Dedan, Tema, Buz and all who are in distant placesᶜ; ²⁴all the kings of Arabia and all the kings of the foreign people who live in the desert; ²⁵all the kings of Zimri, Elam and Media; ²⁶and all the kings of the north, near and far, one after the other—all the kingdoms on the face of the earth. And after all of them, the king of Sheshachᵈ will drink it too.

²⁷"Then tell them, 'This is what the LORD Almighty, the God of Israel, says: Drink, get drunk and vomit, and fall to rise no more because of the sword I will send among you.' ²⁸But if they refuse to take the cup from your hand and drink, tell them, 'This is what the LORD Almighty says: You must drink it! ²⁹See, I am beginning to bring disaster on the city that bears my Name, and will you indeed go unpunished? You will not go unpunished, for I am calling down a sword upon all who live on the earth, declares the LORD Almighty.'

³⁰"Now prophesy all these words against them and say to them:

"'The LORD will roar from on high;
    he will thunder from his holy dwelling
    and roar mightily against his land.
He will shout like those who tread the grapes,
    shout against all who live on the earth.
³¹The tumult will resound to the ends of the earth,
    for the LORD will bring charges against the nations;
he will bring judgment on all mankind
    and put the wicked to the sword,'"

declares the LORD.

ᵃ9 The Hebrew term refers to the irrevocable giving over of things or persons to the LORD, often by totally destroying them.   ᵇ12 Or Chaldeans   ᶜ23 Or who clip the hair by their foreheads   ᵈ26 Sheshach is a cryptogram for Babylon.

³²This is what the LORD Almighty says:

> "Look! Disaster is spreading
> from nation to nation;
> a mighty storm is rising
> from the ends of the earth."

³³At that time those slain by the LORD will be everywhere—from one end of the earth to the other. They will not be mourned or gathered up or buried, but will be like refuse lying on the ground.

> ³⁴Weep and wail, you shepherds;
> roll in the dust, you leaders of the flock.
> For your time to be slaughtered has come;
> you will fall and be shattered like fine pottery.
> ³⁵The shepherds will have nowhere to flee,
> the leaders of the flock no place to escape.
> ³⁶Hear the cry of the shepherds,
> the wailing of the leaders of the flock,
> for the LORD is destroying their pasture.
> ³⁷The peaceful meadows will be laid waste
> because of the fierce anger of the LORD.
> ³⁸Like a lion he will leave his lair,
> and their land will become desolate
> because of the sword ᵃ of the oppressor
> and because of the LORD's fierce anger.

Jeremiah Threatened With Death

26 Early in the reign of Jehoiakim son of Josiah king of Judah, this word came from the LORD: ²"This is what the LORD says: Stand in the courtyard of the LORD's house and speak to all the people of the towns of Judah who come to worship in the house of the LORD. Tell them everything I command you; do not omit a word. ³Perhaps they will listen and each will turn from his evil way. Then I will relent and not bring on them the disaster I was planning because of the evil they have done. ⁴Say to them, 'This is what the LORD says: If you do not listen to me and follow my law, which I have set before you, ⁵and if you do not listen to the words of my servants the prophets, whom I have sent to you again and again (though you have not listened), ⁶then I will make this house like Shiloh and this city an object of cursing among all the nations of the earth.'"

⁷The priests, the prophets and all the people heard Jeremiah speak these words in the house of the LORD. ⁸But as soon as Jeremiah finished telling all the people everything the LORD had commanded him to say, the priests, the prophets and all the people seized him and said, "You must die! ⁹Why do you prophesy in the LORD's name that this house will be like Shiloh and this city will be desolate and deserted?" And all the people crowded around Jeremiah in the house of the LORD.

¹⁰When the officials of Judah heard about these things, they went up from the royal palace to the house of the LORD and took their places at the entrance of the New Gate of the LORD's house. ¹¹Then the priests and the prophets said to the officials and all the people, "This man should be sentenced to death because he has prophesied against this city. You have heard it with your own ears!"

¹²Then Jeremiah said to all the officials and all the people: "The LORD sent me to prophesy against this house and this city all the things you have heard. ¹³Now reform your ways and your actions and obey the LORD your God. Then the LORD will relent and not bring the disaster he has pronounced against you. ¹⁴As for me, I am in your hands; do

ᵃ38 Some Hebrew manuscripts and Septuagint (see also Jer. 46:16 and 50:16); most Hebrew manuscripts *anger*

with me whatever you think is good and right. [15]Be assured, however, that if you put me to death, you will bring the guilt of innocent blood on yourselves and on this city and on those who live in it, for in truth the LORD has sent me to you to speak all these words in your hearing."

[16]Then the officials and all the people said to the priests and the prophets, "This man should not be sentenced to death! He has spoken to us in the name of the LORD our God."

[17]Some of the elders of the land stepped forward and said to the entire assembly of people, [18]"Micah of Moresheth prophesied in the days of Hezekiah king of Judah. He told all the people of Judah, 'This is what the LORD Almighty says:

> "'Zion will be plowed like a field,
>   Jerusalem will become a heap of rubble,
>   the temple hill a mound overgrown with thickets.'[a]

[19]"Did Hezekiah king of Judah or anyone else in Judah put him to death? Did not Hezekiah fear the LORD and seek his favor? And did not the LORD relent, so that he did not bring the disaster he pronounced against them? We are about to bring a terrible disaster on ourselves!"

[20](Now Uriah son of Shemaiah from Kiriath Jearim was another man who prophesied in the name of the LORD; he prophesied the same things against this city and this land as Jeremiah did. [21]When King Jehoiakim and all his officers and officials heard his words, the king sought to put him to death. But Uriah heard of it and fled in fear to Egypt. [22]King Jehoiakim, however, sent Elnathan son of Acbor to Egypt, along with some other men. [23]They brought Uriah out of Egypt and took him to King Jehoiakim, who had him struck down with a sword and his body thrown into the burial place of the common people.)

[24]Furthermore, Ahikam son of Shaphan supported Jeremiah, and so he was not handed over to the people to be put to death.

Judah to Serve Nebuchadnezzar

27 Early in the reign of Zedekiah[b] son of Josiah king of Judah, this word came to Jeremiah from the LORD: [2]This is what the LORD said to me: "Make a yoke out of straps and crossbars and put it on your neck. [3]Then send word to the kings of Edom, Moab, Ammon, Tyre and Sidon through the envoys who have come to Jerusalem to Zedekiah king of Judah. [4]Give them a message for their masters and say, 'This is what the LORD Almighty, the God of Israel, says: "Tell this to your masters: [5]With my great power and outstretched arm I made the earth and its people and the animals that are on it, and I give it to anyone I please. [6]Now I will hand all your countries over to my servant Nebuchadnezzar king of Babylon; I will make even the wild animals subject to him. [7]All nations will serve him and his son and his grandson until the time for his land comes; then many nations and great kings will subjugate him.

[8]" 'If, however, any nation or kingdom will not serve Nebuchadnezzar king of Babylon or bow its neck under his yoke, I will punish that nation with the sword, famine and plague, declares the LORD, until I destroy it by his hand. [9]So do not listen to your prophets, your diviners, your interpreters of dreams, your mediums or your sorcerers who tell you, 'You will not serve the king of Babylon.' [10]They prophesy lies to you that will only serve to remove you far from your lands; I will banish you and you will perish. [11]But if any nation will bow its neck under the yoke of the king of Babylon and serve him, I will let that nation remain in its own land to till it and to live there, declares the LORD.' ' "

[12]I gave the same message to Zedekiah king of Judah. I said, "Bow your neck under the yoke of the king of Babylon; serve him and his people, and you will live. [13]Why will you and your people die by the sword, famine and plague with which the LORD has threatened any nation that will not serve the king of Babylon? [14]Do not listen to the words of

---

a 18 Micah 3:12   *b 1* A few Hebrew manuscripts and Syriac (see also Jer. 27:3, 12 and 28:1); most Hebrew manuscripts *Jehoiakim* (Most Septuagint manuscripts do not have this verse.)

the prophets who say to you, 'You will not serve the king of Babylon,' for they are prophesying lies to you. ¹⁵'I have not sent them,' declares the Lord. 'They are prophesying lies in my name. Therefore, I will banish you and you will perish, both you and the prophets who prophesy to you.'"

¹⁶Then I said to the priests and all these people, "This is what the Lord says: Do not listen to the prophets who say, 'Very soon now the articles from the Lord's house will be brought back from Babylon.' They are prophesying lies to you. ¹⁷Do not listen to them. Serve the king of Babylon, and you will live. Why should this city become a ruin? ¹⁸If they are prophets and have the word of the Lord, let them plead with the Lord Almighty that the furnishings remaining in the house of the Lord and in the palace of the king of Judah and in Jerusalem not be taken to Babylon. ¹⁹For this is what the Lord Almighty says about the pillars, the Sea, the movable stands and the other furnishings that are left in this city, ²⁰which Nebuchadnezzar king of Babylon did not take away when he carried Jehoiachin*ᵃ* son of Jehoiakim king of Judah into exile from Jerusalem to Babylon, along with all the nobles of Judah and Jerusalem— ²¹yes, this is what the Lord Almighty, the God of Israel, says about the things that are left in the house of the Lord and in the palace of the king of Judah and in Jerusalem: ²²'They will be taken to Babylon and there they will remain until the day I come for them,' declares the Lord. 'Then I will bring them back and restore them to this place.'"

The False Prophet Hananiah

28 In the fifth month of that same year, the fourth year, early in the reign of Zedekiah king of Judah, the prophet Hananiah son of Azzur, who was from Gibeon, said to me in the house of the Lord in the presence of the priests and all the people: ²"This is what the Lord Almighty, the God of Israel, says: 'I will break the yoke of the king of Babylon. ³Within two years I will bring back to this place all the articles of the Lord's house that Nebuchadnezzar king of Babylon removed from here and took to Babylon. ⁴I will also bring back to this place Jehoiachin*ᵃ* son of Jehoiakim king of Judah and all the other exiles from Judah who went to Babylon,' declares the Lord, 'for I will break the yoke of the king of Babylon.'"

⁵Then the prophet Jeremiah replied to the prophet Hananiah before the priests and all the people who were standing in the house of the Lord. ⁶He said, "Amen! May the Lord do so! May the Lord fulfill the words you have prophesied by bringing the articles of the Lord's house and all the exiles back to this place from Babylon. ⁷Nevertheless, listen to what I have to say in your hearing and in the hearing of all the people: ⁸From early times the prophets who preceded you and me have prophesied war, disaster and plague against many countries and great kingdoms. ⁹But the prophet who prophesies peace will be recognized as one truly sent by the Lord only if his prediction comes true."

¹⁰Then the prophet Hananiah took the yoke off the neck of the prophet Jeremiah and broke it, ¹¹and he said before all the people, "This is what the Lord says: 'In the same way will I break the yoke of Nebuchadnezzar king of Babylon off the neck of all the nations within two years.'" At this, the prophet Jeremiah went on his way.

¹²Shortly after the prophet Hananiah had broken the yoke off the neck of the prophet Jeremiah, the word of the Lord came to Jeremiah: ¹³"Go and tell Hananiah, 'This is what the Lord says: You have broken a wooden yoke, but in its place you will get a yoke of iron. ¹⁴This is what the Lord Almighty, the God of Israel, says: I will put an iron yoke on the necks of all these nations to make them serve Nebuchadnezzar king of Babylon, and they will serve him. I will even give him control over the wild animals.'"

¹⁵Then the prophet Jeremiah said to Hananiah the prophet, "Listen, Hananiah! The Lord has not sent you, yet you have persuaded this nation to trust in lies. ¹⁶Therefore, this is

ᵃ20,4 Hebrew Jeconiah, a variant of Jehoiachin

what the LORD says: 'I am about to remove you from the face of the earth. This very year you are going to die, because you have preached rebellion against the LORD.' "

¹⁷In the seventh month of that same year, Hananiah the prophet died.

A Letter to the Exiles

29 This is the text of the letter that the prophet Jeremiah sent from Jerusalem to the surviving elders among the exiles and to the priests, the prophets and all the other people Nebuchadnezzar had carried into exile from Jerusalem to Babylon. ²(This was after King Jehoiachin*ᵃ* and the queen mother, the court officials and the leaders of Judah and Jerusalem, the craftsmen and the artisans had gone into exile from Jerusalem.) ³He entrusted the letter to Elasah son of Shaphan and to Gemariah son of Hilkiah, whom Zedekiah king of Judah sent to King Nebuchadnezzar in Babylon. It said:

⁴This is what the LORD Almighty, the God of Israel, says to all those I carried into exile from Jerusalem to Babylon: ⁵"Build houses and settle down; plant gardens and eat what they produce. ⁶Marry and have sons and daughters; find wives for your sons and give your daughters in marriage, so that they too may have sons and daughters. Increase in number there; do not decrease. ⁷Also, seek the peace and prosperity of the city to which I have carried you into exile. Pray to the LORD for it, because if it prospers, you too will prosper." ⁸Yes, this is what the LORD Almighty, the God of Israel, says: "Do not let the prophets and diviners among you deceive you. Do not listen to the dreams you encourage them to have. ⁹They are prophesying lies to you in my name. I have not sent them," declares the LORD.

¹⁰This is what the LORD says: "When seventy years are completed for Babylon, I will come to you and fulfill my gracious promise to bring you back to this place. ¹¹For

I know the plans I have for you," declares the LORD, "plans to prosper you and not to harm you, plans to give you hope and a future. ¹²Then you will call upon me and come and pray to me, and I will listen to you. ¹³You will seek me and find me when you seek me with all your heart. ¹⁴I will be found by you," declares the LORD, "and will bring you back from captivity.*ᵇ* I will gather you from all the nations and places where I have banished you," declares the LORD, "and will bring you back to the place from which I carried you into exile."

¹⁵You may say, "The LORD has raised up prophets for us in Babylon," ¹⁶but this is what the LORD says about the king who sits on David's throne and all the people who remain in this city, your countrymen who did not go with you into exile— ¹⁷yes, this is what the

---

□ ▒▒▒▒▒▒▒ DISCOVERING GOD ▒▒▒▒▒▒▒ ▣

29:11–14
Life with God

Finally! A message of hope for the people of Israel! For those who had strayed far from their religious roots and knew they had done wrong, this word from God must have been a great relief.

This message holds a promise for every seeker today as well. God doesn't say that seekers *might* find him if they look hard enough. His promise is rock-solid: "I *will* be found by you" (verse 14). This promise contains a spiritual principle that's true at all times with all people: God stands ready to welcome back any person who seeks and trusts in him wholeheartedly. God wants us to turn to him, recognizing him as the only source for "hope and a future" (verse 11).

LORD Almighty says: "I will send the sword, famine and plague against them and I will make them like poor figs that are so bad they cannot be eaten. ¹⁸I will pursue them with the sword, famine and plague and will make them abhorrent to all the kingdoms of the earth and an object of cursing and horror, of scorn and reproach, among all the nations where I drive them. ¹⁹For they have not listened to my words,"

ᵃ 2 Hebrew Jeconiah, a variant of Jehoiachin   ᵇ 14 Or will restore your fortunes

declares the LORD, "words that I sent to them again and again by my servants the prophets. And you exiles have not listened either," declares the LORD.

²⁰Therefore, hear the word of the LORD, all you exiles whom I have sent away from Jerusalem to Babylon. ²¹This is what the LORD Almighty, the God of Israel, says about Ahab son of Kolaiah and Zedekiah son of Maaseiah, who are prophesying lies to you in my name: "I will hand them over to Nebuchadnezzar king of Babylon, and he will put them to death before your very eyes. ²²Because of them, all the exiles from Judah who are in Babylon will use this curse: 'The LORD treat you like Zedekiah and Ahab, whom the king of Babylon burned in the fire.' ²³For they have done outrageous things in Israel; they have committed adultery with their neighbors' wives and in my name have spoken lies, which I did not tell them to do. I know it and am a witness to it," declares the LORD.

Message to Shemaiah

²⁴Tell Shemaiah the Nehelamite, ²⁵"This is what the LORD Almighty, the God of Israel, says: You sent letters in your own name to all the people in Jerusalem, to Zephaniah son of Maaseiah the priest, and to all the other priests. You said to Zephaniah, ²⁶"The LORD has appointed you priest in place of Jehoiada to be in charge of the house of the LORD; you should put any madman who acts like a prophet into the stocks and neck-irons. ²⁷So why have you not reprimanded Jeremiah from Anathoth, who poses as a prophet among you? ²⁸He has sent this message to us in Babylon: It will be a long time. Therefore build houses and settle down; plant gardens and eat what they produce.'"

²⁹Zephaniah the priest, however, read the letter to Jeremiah the prophet. ³⁰Then the word of the LORD came to Jeremiah: ³¹"Send this message to all the exiles: 'This is what the LORD says about Shemaiah the Nehelamite: Because Shemaiah has prophesied to you, even though I did not send him, and has led you to believe a lie, ³²this is what the LORD says: I will surely punish Shemaiah the Nehelamite and his descendants. He will have no one left among this people, nor will he see the good things I will do for my people, declares the LORD, because he has preached rebellion against me.'"

Restoration of Israel

30 This is the word that came to Jeremiah from the LORD: ²"This is what the LORD, the God of Israel, says: 'Write in a book all the words I have spoken to you. ³The days are coming,' declares the LORD, 'when I will bring my people Israel and Judah back from captivity[a] and restore them to the land I gave their forefathers to possess,' says the LORD."

⁴These are the words the LORD spoke concerning Israel and Judah: ⁵"This is what the LORD says:

" 'Cries of fear are heard—
    terror, not peace.
⁶Ask and see:
    Can a man bear children?
Then why do I see every strong man
    with his hands on his stomach like a woman in labor,
    every face turned deathly pale?
⁷How awful that day will be!
    None will be like it.
It will be a time of trouble for Jacob,
    but he will be saved out of it.

⁸" 'In that day,' declares the LORD Almighty,
    'I will break the yoke off their necks

a 3 Or will restore the fortunes of my people Israel and Judah

and will tear off their bonds;
　　no longer will foreigners enslave them.
[9]Instead, they will serve the LORD their God
　　and David their king,
　　whom I will raise up for them.

[10]'So do not fear, O Jacob my servant;
　　do not be dismayed, O Israel,'

　　　　　　　　　　　　　　　　declares the LORD.

'I will surely save you out of a distant place,
　　your descendants from the land of their exile.
Jacob will again have peace and security,
　　and no one will make him afraid.
[11]I am with you and will save you,'
　　declares the LORD.
'Though I completely destroy all the nations
　　among which I scatter you,
　　I will not completely destroy you.
I will discipline you but only with justice;
　　I will not let you go entirely unpunished.'

[12]"This is what the LORD says:

"'Your wound is incurable,
　　your injury beyond healing.
[13]There is no one to plead your cause,
　　no remedy for your sore,
　　no healing for you.
[14]All your allies have forgotten you;
　　they care nothing for you.
I have struck you as an enemy would
　　and punished you as would the cruel,
because your guilt is so great
　　and your sins so many.
[15]Why do you cry out over your wound,
　　your pain that has no cure?
Because of your great guilt and many sins
　　I have done these things to you.

[16]"But all who devour you will be devoured;
　　all your enemies will go into exile.
Those who plunder you will be plundered;
　　all who make spoil of you I will despoil.
[17]But I will restore you to health
　　and heal your wounds,'

　　　　　　　　　　　　　　　　declares the LORD,

'because you are called an outcast,
　　Zion for whom no one cares.'

[18]"This is what the LORD says:

"'I will restore the fortunes of Jacob's tents
　　and have compassion on his dwellings;
the city will be rebuilt on her ruins,
　　and the palace will stand in its proper place.
[19]From them will come songs of thanksgiving

and the sound of rejoicing.
I will add to their numbers,
 and they will not be decreased;
I will bring them honor,
 and they will not be disdained.
²⁰Their children will be as in days of old,
 and their community will be established before me;
 I will punish all who oppress them.
²¹Their leader will be one of their own;
 their ruler will arise from among them.
I will bring him near and he will come close to me,
 for who is he who will devote himself
 to be close to me?'

            declares the LORD.

²²"'So you will be my people,
 and I will be your God.'"

²³See, the storm of the LORD
 will burst out in wrath,
a driving wind swirling down
 on the heads of the wicked.
²⁴The fierce anger of the LORD will not turn back
 until he fully accomplishes
 the purposes of his heart.
In days to come
 you will understand this.

31 "At that time," declares the LORD, "I will be the God of all the clans of Israel,
and they will be my people."

²This is what the LORD says:

 "The people who survive the sword
  will find favor in the desert;
 I will come to give rest to Israel."

³The LORD appeared to us in the past,ᵃ saying:

 "I have loved you with an everlasting love;
  I have drawn you with loving-kindness.
 ⁴I will build you up again
  and you will be rebuilt, O Virgin Israel.
 Again you will take up your tambourines
  and go out to dance with the joyful.
 ⁵Again you will plant vineyards
  on the hills of Samaria;
 the farmers will plant them
  and enjoy their fruit.
 ⁶There will be a day when watchmen cry out
  on the hills of Ephraim,
 'Come, let us go up to Zion,
  to the LORD our God.'"

⁷This is what the LORD says:

 "Sing with joy for Jacob;

ᵃ3 Or LORD has appeared to us from afar

shout for the foremost of the nations.
Make your praises heard, and say,
  'O LORD, save your people,
  the remnant of Israel.'
[8]See, I will bring them from the land of the north
  and gather them from the ends of the earth.
Among them will be the blind and the lame,
  expectant mothers and women in labor;
  a great throng will return.
[9]They will come with weeping;
  they will pray as I bring them back.
I will lead them beside streams of water
  on a level path where they will not stumble,
because I am Israel's father,
  and Ephraim is my firstborn son.

[10]"Hear the word of the LORD, O nations;
  proclaim it in distant coastlands:
'He who scattered Israel will gather them
  and will watch over his flock like a shepherd.'
[11]For the LORD will ransom Jacob
  and redeem them from the hand of those stronger than they.
[12]They will come and shout for joy on the heights of Zion;
  they will rejoice in the bounty of the LORD—
the grain, the new wine and the oil,
  the young of the flocks and herds.
They will be like a well-watered garden,
  and they will sorrow no more.
[13]Then maidens will dance and be glad,
  young men and old as well.
I will turn their mourning into gladness;
  I will give them comfort and joy instead of sorrow.
[14]I will satisfy the priests with abundance,
  and my people will be filled with my bounty,"

declares the LORD.

[15]This is what the LORD says:

"A voice is heard in Ramah,
  mourning and great weeping,
Rachel weeping for her children
  and refusing to be comforted,
  because her children are no more."

[16]This is what the LORD says:

"Restrain your voice from weeping
  and your eyes from tears,
for your work will be rewarded,"

declares the LORD.

"They will return from the land of the enemy.
[17]So there is hope for your future,"

declares the LORD.

"Your children will return to their own land.

[18]"I have surely heard Ephraim's moaning:

'You disciplined me like an unruly calf,
    and I have been disciplined.
Restore me, and I will return,
    because you are the LORD my God.
¹⁹After I strayed,
    I repented;
after I came to understand,
    I beat my breast.
I was ashamed and humiliated
    because I bore the disgrace of my youth.'
²⁰Is not Ephraim my dear son,
    the child in whom I delight?
Though I often speak against him,
    I still remember him.
Therefore my heart yearns for him;
    I have great compassion for him,"

                                        declares the LORD.

²¹"Set up road signs;
    put up guideposts.
Take note of the highway,
    the road that you take.
Return, O Virgin Israel,
    return to your towns.
²²How long will you wander,
    O unfaithful daughter?
The LORD will create a new thing on earth—
    a woman will surround^a a man."

²³This is what the LORD Almighty, the God of Israel, says: "When I bring them back from captivity,^b the people in the land of Judah and in its towns will once again use these words: 'The LORD bless you, O righteous dwelling, O sacred mountain.' ²⁴People will live together in Judah and all its towns—farmers and those who move about with their flocks. ²⁵I will refresh the weary and satisfy the faint."

²⁶At this I awoke and looked around. My sleep had been pleasant to me.

²⁷"The days are coming," declares the LORD, "when I will plant the house of Israel and the house of Judah with the offspring of men and of animals. ²⁸Just as I watched over them to uproot and tear down, and to overthrow, destroy and bring disaster, so I will watch over them to build and to plant," declares the LORD. ²⁹"In those days people will no longer say,

'The fathers have eaten sour grapes,
    and the children's teeth are set on edge.'

³⁰Instead, everyone will die for his own sin; whoever eats sour grapes—his own teeth will be set on edge.

³¹"The time is coming," declares the LORD,
    "when I will make a new covenant
with the house of Israel
    and with the house of Judah.
³²It will not be like the covenant
    I made with their forefathers

---

^a22 Or will go about ,seeking,; or will protect   ^b23 Or I restore their fortunes

when I took them by the hand
    to lead them out of Egypt,
because they broke my covenant,
    though I was a husband to*ᵃ* them,*ᵇ*"

                  declares the LORD.

³³"This is the covenant I will make with the house of Israel
    after that time," declares the LORD.
"I will put my law in their minds
    and write it on their hearts.
I will be their God,
    and they will be my people.

³⁴No longer will a man teach his
      neighbor,
    or a man his brother, saying,
      'Know the LORD,'
because they will all know me,
    from the least of them to the
      greatest,"
                declares the LORD.
"For I will forgive their
      wickedness
    and will remember their sins
      no more."

³⁵This is what the LORD says,

he who appoints the sun
    to shine by day,
who decrees the moon and stars
    to shine by night,
who stirs up the sea
    so that its waves roar—
    the LORD Almighty is his name:
³⁶"Only if these decrees vanish
      from my sight,"
    declares the LORD,

ADDRESSING QUESTIONS

31:31–34

The basis for calling the second part of the
Bible the New Testament is found in these
verses. Jesus' coming inaugurated the new
covenant, or New Testament.

    Notice all that is included in this covenant:
- God's law will be in our hearts and minds.
- We will be God's people, and he will be
  our God.
- God will be widely known.
- Our sins will be forgiven and forgotten.

The whole of the new covenant can be
boiled down to this: *God will have a personal
relationship with us.* That's exactly what Jesus
has made possible by forgiving our sin and
sending the Holy Spirit to live inside us.

    You can be part of this new covenant. Just
ask God to forgive your sins on the basis of
what Jesus, the mediator of the new agreement, did for you on the cross. Then you will
become a member of the biggest family ever—
the family of God.

    "will the descendants of Israel
      ever cease
    to be a nation before me."

³⁷This is what the LORD says:

    "Only if the heavens above can be measured
      and the foundations of the earth below be searched out
    will I reject all the descendants of Israel
      because of all they have done,"

                  declares the LORD.

³⁸"The days are coming," declares the LORD, "when this city will be rebuilt for me from
the Tower of Hananel to the Corner Gate. ³⁹The measuring line will stretch from there
straight to the hill of Gareb and then turn to Goah. ⁴⁰The whole valley where dead bodies
and ashes are thrown, and all the terraces out to the Kidron Valley on the east as far as

---

ᵃ32 Hebrew; Septuagint and Syriac / *and I turned away from*   *ᵇ32* Or *was their master*

the corner of the Horse Gate, will be holy to the Lord. The city will never again be uprooted or demolished."

Jeremiah Buys a Field

32 This is the word that came to Jeremiah from the Lord in the tenth year of Zedekiah king of Judah, which was the eighteenth year of Nebuchadnezzar. ²The army of the king of Babylon was then besieging Jerusalem, and Jeremiah the prophet was confined in the courtyard of the guard in the royal palace of Judah.

³Now Zedekiah king of Judah had imprisoned him there, saying, "Why do you prophesy as you do? You say, 'This is what the Lord says: I am about to hand this city over to the king of Babylon, and he will capture it. ⁴Zedekiah king of Judah will not escape out of the hands of the Babylonians*ᵃ* but will certainly be handed over to the king of Babylon, and will speak with him face to face and see him with his own eyes. ⁵He will take Zedekiah to Babylon, where he will remain until I deal with him, declares the Lord. If you fight against the Babylonians, you will not succeed.' "

⁶Jeremiah said, "The word of the Lord came to me: ⁷Hanamel son of Shallum your uncle is going to come to you and say, 'Buy my field at Anathoth, because as nearest relative it is your right and duty to buy it.'

⁸"Then, just as the Lord had said, my cousin Hanamel came to me in the courtyard of the guard and said, 'Buy my field at Anathoth in the territory of Benjamin. Since it is your right to redeem it and possess it, buy it for yourself.'

"I knew that this was the word of the Lord; ⁹so I bought the field at Anathoth from my cousin Hanamel and weighed out for him seventeen shekels*ᵇ* of silver. ¹⁰I signed and sealed the deed, had it witnessed, and weighed out the silver on the scales. ¹¹I took the deed of purchase—the sealed copy containing the terms and conditions, as well as the unsealed copy— ¹²and I gave this deed to Baruch son of Neriah, the son of Mahseiah, in the presence of my cousin Hanamel and of the witnesses who had signed the deed and of all the Jews sitting in the courtyard of the guard.

¹³"In their presence I gave Baruch these instructions: ¹⁴'This is what the Lord Almighty, the God of Israel, says: Take these documents, both the sealed and unsealed copies of the deed of purchase, and put them in a clay jar so they will last a long time. ¹⁵For this is what the Lord Almighty, the God of Israel, says: Houses, fields and vineyards will again be bought in this land.'

¹⁶"After I had given the deed of purchase to Baruch son of Neriah, I prayed to the Lord:

¹⁷"Ah, Sovereign Lord, you have made the heavens and the earth by your great power and outstretched arm. Nothing is too hard for you. ¹⁸You show love to thousands but bring the punishment for the fathers' sins into the laps of their children after them. O great and powerful God, whose name is the Lord Almighty, ¹⁹great are your purposes and mighty are your deeds. Your eyes are open to all the ways of men; you reward everyone according to his conduct and as his deeds deserve. ²⁰You performed miraculous signs and wonders in Egypt and have continued them to this day, both in Israel and among all mankind, and have gained the renown that is still yours. ²¹You brought your people Israel out of Egypt with signs and wonders, by a mighty hand and an outstretched arm and with great terror. ²²You gave them this land you had sworn to give their forefathers, a land flowing with milk and honey. ²³They came in and took possession of it, but they did not obey you or follow your law; they did not do what you commanded them to do. So you brought all this disaster upon them.

²⁴"See how the siege ramps are built up to take the city. Because of the sword, famine and plague, the city will be handed over to the Babylonians who are attacking it. What you said has happened, as you now see. ²⁵And though the city will be

---

ᵃ4 Or *Chaldeans;* also in verses 5, 24, 25, 28, 29 and 43   *ᵇ9* That is, about 7 ounces (about 200 grams)

handed over to the Babylonians, you, O Sovereign LORD, say to me, 'Buy the field with silver and have the transaction witnessed.' "

²⁶Then the word of the LORD came to Jeremiah: ²⁷"I am the LORD, the God of all mankind. Is anything too hard for me? ²⁸Therefore, this is what the LORD says: I am about to hand this city over to the Babylonians and to Nebuchadnezzar king of Babylon, who will capture it. ²⁹The Babylonians who are attacking this city will come in and set it on fire; they will burn it down, along with the houses where the people provoked me to anger by burning incense on the roofs to Baal and by pouring out drink offerings to other gods.

³⁰"The people of Israel and Judah have done nothing but evil in my sight from their youth; indeed, the people of Israel have done nothing but provoke me with what their hands have made, declares the LORD. ³¹From the day it was built until now, this city has so aroused my anger and wrath that I must remove it from my sight. ³²The people of Israel and Judah have provoked me by all the evil they have done—they, their kings and officials, their priests and prophets, the men of Judah and the people of Jerusalem. ³³They turned their backs to me and not their faces; though I taught them again and again, they would not listen or respond to discipline. ³⁴They set up their abominable idols in the house that bears my Name and defiled it. ³⁵They built high places for Baal in the Valley of Ben Hinnom to sacrifice their sons and daughters[a] to Molech, though I never commanded, nor did it enter my mind, that they should do such a detestable thing and so make Judah sin.

³⁶"You are saying about this city, 'By the sword, famine and plague it will be handed over to the king of Babylon'; but this is what the LORD, the God of Israel, says: ³⁷I will surely gather them from all the lands where I banish them in my furious anger and great wrath; I will bring them back to this place and let them live in safety. ³⁸They will be my people, and I will be their God. ³⁹I will give them singleness of heart and action, so that they will always fear me for their own good and the good of their children after them. ⁴⁰I will make an everlasting covenant with them: I will never stop doing good to them, and I will inspire them to fear me, so that they will never turn away from me. ⁴¹I will rejoice in doing them good and will assuredly plant them in this land with all my heart and soul.

⁴²"This is what the LORD says: As I have brought all this great calamity on this people, so I will give them all the prosperity I have promised them. ⁴³Once more fields will be bought in this land of which you say, 'It is a desolate waste, without men or animals; for it has been handed over to the Babylonians.' ⁴⁴Fields will be bought for silver, and deeds will be signed, sealed and witnessed in the territory of Benjamin, in the villages around Jerusalem, in the towns of Judah and in the towns of the hill country, of the western foothills and of the Negev, because I will restore their fortunes,[b] declares the LORD."

Promise of Restoration

33 While Jeremiah was still confined in the courtyard of the guard, the word of the LORD came to him a second time: ²"This is what the LORD says, he who made the earth, the LORD who formed it and established it—the LORD is his name: ³'Call to me and I will answer you and tell you great and unsearchable things you do not know.' ⁴For this is what the LORD, the God of Israel, says about the houses in this city and the royal palaces of Judah that have been torn down to be used against the siege ramps and the sword ⁵in the fight with the Babylonians[c]: 'They will be filled with the dead bodies of the men I will slay in my anger and wrath. I will hide my face from this city because of all its wickedness.

⁶"'Nevertheless, I will bring health and healing to it; I will heal my people and will let them enjoy abundant peace and security. ⁷I will bring Judah and Israel back from

---

a 35 Or to make their sons and daughters pass through ⌊the fire⌋,   *b 44 Or will bring them back from captivity*   *c 5 Or* *Chaldeans*

captivity^a and will rebuild them as they were before. ⁸I will cleanse them from all the sin they have committed against me and will forgive all their sins of rebellion against me. ⁹Then this city will bring me renown, joy, praise and honor before all nations on earth that hear of all the good things I do for it; and they will be in awe and will tremble at the abundant prosperity and peace I provide for it.'

¹⁰"This is what the LORD says: 'You say about this place, "It is a desolate waste, without men or animals." Yet in the towns of Judah and the streets of Jerusalem that are deserted, inhabited by neither men nor animals, there will be heard once more ¹¹the sounds of joy and gladness, the voices of bride and bridegroom, and the voices of those who bring thank offerings to the house of the LORD, saying,

> "Give thanks to the LORD Almighty,
>   for the LORD is good;
>   his love endures forever."

For I will restore the fortunes of the land as they were before,' says the LORD.

¹²"This is what the LORD Almighty says: 'In this place, desolate and without men or animals—in all its towns there will again be pastures for shepherds to rest their flocks. ¹³In the towns of the hill country, of the western foothills and of the Negev, in the territory of Benjamin, in the villages around Jerusalem and in the towns of Judah, flocks will again pass under the hand of the one who counts them,' says the LORD.

¹⁴"'The days are coming,' declares the LORD, 'when I will fulfill the gracious promise I made to the house of Israel and to the house of Judah.

> ¹⁵"'In those days and at that time
>   I will make a righteous Branch sprout from David's line;
>   he will do what is just and right in the land.
> ¹⁶In those days Judah will be saved
>   and Jerusalem will live in safety.
> This is the name by which it^b will be called:
>   The LORD Our Righteousness.'

¹⁷For this is what the LORD says: 'David will never fail to have a man to sit on the throne of the house of Israel, ¹⁸nor will the priests, who are Levites, ever fail to have a man to stand before me continually to offer burnt offerings, to burn grain offerings and to present sacrifices.'"

¹⁹The word of the LORD came to Jeremiah: ²⁰"This is what the LORD says: 'If you can break my covenant with the day and my covenant with the night, so that day and night no longer come at their appointed time, ²¹then my covenant with David my servant—and my covenant with the Levites who are priests ministering before me—can be broken and David will no longer have a descendant to reign on his throne. ²²I will make the descendants of David my servant and the Levites who minister before me as countless as the stars of the sky and as measureless as the sand on the seashore.'"

²³The word of the LORD came to Jeremiah: ²⁴"Have you not noticed that these people are saying, 'The LORD has rejected the two kingdoms^c he chose'? So they despise my people and no longer regard them as a nation. ²⁵This is what the LORD says: 'If I have not established my covenant with day and night and the fixed laws of heaven and earth, ²⁶then I will reject the descendants of Jacob and David my servant and will not choose one of his sons to rule over the descendants of Abraham, Isaac and Jacob. For I will restore their fortunes^d and have compassion on them.'"

---

^a7 Or will restore the fortunes of Judah and Israel   ^b16 Or he   ^c24 Or families   ^d26 Or will bring them back from captivity

Warning to Zedekiah

34 While Nebuchadnezzar king of Babylon and all his army and all the kingdoms and peoples in the empire he ruled were fighting against Jerusalem and all its surrounding towns, this word came to Jeremiah from the LORD: ²"This is what the LORD, the God of Israel, says: Go to Zedekiah king of Judah and tell him, 'This is what the LORD says: I am about to hand this city over to the king of Babylon, and he will burn it down. ³You will not escape from his grasp but will surely be captured and handed over to him. You will see the king of Babylon with your own eyes, and he will speak with you face to face. And you will go to Babylon.

⁴"'Yet hear the promise of the LORD, O Zedekiah king of Judah. This is what the LORD says concerning you: You will not die by the sword; ⁵you will die peacefully. As people made a funeral fire in honor of your fathers, the former kings who preceded you, so they will make a fire in your honor and lament, "Alas, O master!" I myself make this promise, declares the LORD.'"

⁶Then Jeremiah the prophet told all this to Zedekiah king of Judah, in Jerusalem, ⁷while the army of the king of Babylon was fighting against Jerusalem and the other cities of Judah that were still holding out—Lachish and Azekah. These were the only fortified cities left in Judah.

Freedom for Slaves

⁸The word came to Jeremiah from the LORD after King Zedekiah had made a covenant with all the people in Jerusalem to proclaim freedom for the slaves. ⁹Everyone was to free his Hebrew slaves, both male and female; no one was to hold a fellow Jew in bondage. ¹⁰So all the officials and people who entered into this covenant agreed that they would free their male and female slaves and no longer hold them in bondage. They agreed, and set them free. ¹¹But afterward they changed their minds and took back the slaves they had freed and enslaved them again.

¹²Then the word of the LORD came to Jeremiah: ¹³"This is what the LORD, the God of Israel, says: I made a covenant with your forefathers when I brought them out of Egypt, out of the land of slavery. I said, ¹⁴'Every seventh year each of you must free any fellow Hebrew who has sold himself to you. After he has served you six years, you must let him go free.'[a] Your fathers, however, did not listen to me or pay attention to me. ¹⁵Recently you repented and did what is right in my sight: Each of you proclaimed freedom to his countrymen. You even made a covenant before me in the house that bears my Name. ¹⁶But now you have turned around and profaned my name; each of you has taken back the male and female slaves you had set free to go where they wished. You have forced them to become your slaves again.

¹⁷"Therefore, this is what the LORD says: You have not obeyed me; you have not proclaimed freedom for your fellow countrymen. So I now proclaim 'freedom' for you, declares the LORD—'freedom' to fall by the sword, plague and famine. I will make you abhorrent to all the kingdoms of the earth. ¹⁸The men who have violated my covenant and have not fulfilled the terms of the covenant they made before me, I will treat like the calf they cut in two and then walked between its pieces. ¹⁹The leaders of Judah and Jerusalem, the court officials, the priests and all the people of the land who walked between the pieces of the calf, ²⁰I will hand over to their enemies who seek their lives. Their dead bodies will become food for the birds of the air and the beasts of the earth.

²¹"I will hand Zedekiah king of Judah and his officials over to their enemies who seek their lives, to the army of the king of Babylon, which has withdrawn from you. ²²I am going to give the order, declares the LORD, and I will bring them back to this city. They will fight against it, take it and burn it down. And I will lay waste the towns of Judah so no one can live there."

---

a 14 Deut. 15:12

The Recabites

35 This is the word that came to Jeremiah from the LORD during the reign of Jehoiakim son of Josiah king of Judah: ²"Go to the Recabite family and invite them to come to one of the side rooms of the house of the LORD and give them wine to drink."

³So I went to get Jaazaniah son of Jeremiah, the son of Habazziniah, and his brothers and all his sons—the whole family of the Recabites. ⁴I brought them into the house of the LORD, into the room of the sons of Hanan son of Igdaliah the man of God. It was next to the room of the officials, which was over that of Maaseiah son of Shallum the doorkeeper. ⁵Then I set bowls full of wine and some cups before the men of the Recabite family and said to them, "Drink some wine."

⁶But they replied, "We do not drink wine, because our forefather Jonadab son of Recab gave us this command: 'Neither you nor your descendants must ever drink wine. ⁷Also you must never build houses, sow seed or plant vineyards; you must never have any of these things, but must always live in tents. Then you will live a long time in the land where you are nomads.' ⁸We have obeyed everything our forefather Jonadab son of Recab commanded us. Neither we nor our wives nor our sons and daughters have ever drunk wine ⁹or built houses to live in or had vineyards, fields or crops. ¹⁰We have lived in tents and have fully obeyed everything our forefather Jonadab commanded us. ¹¹But when Nebuchadnezzar king of Babylon invaded this land, we said, 'Come, we must go to Jerusalem to escape the Babylonian*ᵃ* and Aramean armies.' So we have remained in Jerusalem."

¹²Then the word of the LORD came to Jeremiah, saying: ¹³"This is what the LORD Almighty, the God of Israel, says: Go and tell the men of Judah and the people of Jerusalem, 'Will you not learn a lesson and obey my words?' declares the LORD. ¹⁴'Jonadab son of Recab ordered his sons not to drink wine and this command has been kept. To this day they do not drink wine, because they obey their forefather's command. But I have spoken to you again and again, yet you have not obeyed me. ¹⁵Again and again I sent all my servants the prophets to you. They said, "Each of you must turn from your wicked ways and reform your actions; do not follow other gods to serve them. Then you will live in the land I have given to you and your fathers." But you have not paid attention or listened to me. ¹⁶The descendants of Jonadab son of Recab have carried out the command their forefather gave them, but these people have not obeyed me.'

¹⁷"Therefore, this is what the LORD God Almighty, the God of Israel, says: 'Listen! I am going to bring on Judah and on everyone living in Jerusalem every disaster I pronounced against them. I spoke to them, but they did not listen; I called to them, but they did not answer.' "

¹⁸Then Jeremiah said to the family of the Recabites, "This is what the LORD Almighty, the God of Israel, says: 'You have obeyed the command of your forefather Jonadab and have followed all his instructions and have done everything he ordered.' ¹⁹Therefore, this is what the LORD Almighty, the God of Israel, says: 'Jonadab son of Recab will never fail to have a man to serve me.' "

Jehoiakim Burns Jeremiah's Scroll

36 In the fourth year of Jehoiakim son of Josiah king of Judah, this word came to Jeremiah from the LORD: ²"Take a scroll and write on it all the words I have spoken to you concerning Israel, Judah and all the other nations from the time I began speaking to you in the reign of Josiah till now. ³Perhaps when the people of Judah hear about every disaster I plan to inflict on them, each of them will turn from his wicked way; then I will forgive their wickedness and their sin."

⁴So Jeremiah called Baruch son of Neriah, and while Jeremiah dictated all the words

ᵃ 11 Or *Chaldean*

the LORD had spoken to him, Baruch wrote them on the scroll. ⁵Then Jeremiah told Baruch, "I am restricted; I cannot go to the LORD's temple. ⁶So you go to the house of the LORD on a day of fasting and read to the people from the scroll the words of the LORD that you wrote as I dictated. Read them to all the people of Judah who come in from their towns. ⁷Perhaps they will bring their petition before the LORD, and each will turn from his wicked ways, for the anger and wrath pronounced against this people by the LORD are great."

⁸Baruch son of Neriah did everything Jeremiah the prophet told him to do; at the LORD's temple he read the words of the LORD from the scroll. ⁹In the ninth month of the fifth year of Jehoiakim son of Josiah king of Judah, a time of fasting before the LORD was proclaimed for all the people in Jerusalem and those who had come from the towns of Judah. ¹⁰From the room of Gemariah son of Shaphan the secretary, which was in the upper courtyard at the entrance of the New Gate of the temple, Baruch read to all the people at the LORD's temple the words of Jeremiah from the scroll.

¹¹When Micaiah son of Gemariah, the son of Shaphan, heard all the words of the LORD from the scroll, ¹²he went down to the secretary's room in the royal palace, where all the officials were sitting: Elishama the secretary, Delaiah son of Shemaiah, Elnathan son of Acbor, Gemariah son of Shaphan, Zedekiah son of Hananiah, and all the other officials. ¹³After Micaiah told them everything he had heard Baruch read to the people from the scroll, ¹⁴all the officials sent Jehudi son of Nethaniah, the son of Shelemiah, the son of Cushi, to say to Baruch, "Bring the scroll from which you have read to the people and come." So Baruch son of Neriah went to them with the scroll in his hand. ¹⁵They said to him, "Sit down, please, and read it to us."

So Baruch read it to them. ¹⁶When they heard all these words, they looked at each other in fear and said to Baruch, "We must report all these words to the king." ¹⁷Then they asked Baruch, "Tell us, how did you come to write all this? Did Jeremiah dictate it?"

¹⁸"Yes," Baruch replied, "he dictated all these words to me, and I wrote them in ink on the scroll."

¹⁹Then the officials said to Baruch, "You and Jeremiah, go and hide. Don't let anyone know where you are."

²⁰After they put the scroll in the room of Elishama the secretary, they went to the king in the courtyard and reported everything to him. ²¹The king sent Jehudi to get the scroll, and Jehudi brought it from the room of Elishama the secretary and read it to the king and all the officials standing beside him. ²²It was the ninth month and the king was sitting in the winter apartment, with a fire burning in the firepot in front of him. ²³Whenever Jehudi had read three or four columns of the scroll, the king cut them off with a scribe's knife and threw them into the firepot, until the entire scroll was burned in the fire. ²⁴The king and all his attendants who heard all these words showed no fear, nor did they tear their clothes. ²⁵Even though Elnathan, Delaiah and Gemariah urged the king not to burn the scroll, he would not listen to them. ²⁶Instead, the king commanded Jerahmeel, a son of the king, Seraiah son of Azriel and Shelemiah son of Abdeel to arrest Baruch the scribe and Jeremiah the prophet. But the LORD had hidden them.

²⁷After the king burned the scroll containing the words that Baruch had written at Jeremiah's dictation, the word of the LORD came to Jeremiah: ²⁸"Take another scroll and write on it all the words that were on the first scroll, which Jehoiakim king of Judah burned up. ²⁹Also tell Jehoiakim king of Judah, 'This is what the LORD says: You burned that scroll and said, "Why did you write on it that the king of Babylon would certainly come and destroy this land and cut off both men and animals from it?" ³⁰Therefore, this is what the LORD says about Jehoiakim king of Judah: He will have no one to sit on the throne of David; his body will be thrown out and exposed to the heat by day and the frost by night. ³¹I will punish him and his children and his attendants for their wickedness; I will bring on them and those living in Jerusalem and the people of Judah every disaster I pronounced against them, because they have not listened.'"

³²So Jeremiah took another scroll and gave it to the scribe Baruch son of Neriah, and as

Jeremiah dictated, Baruch wrote on it all the words of the scroll that Jehoiakim king of Judah had burned in the fire. And many similar words were added to them.

Jeremiah in Prison

37 Zedekiah son of Josiah was made king of Judah by Nebuchadnezzar king of Babylon; he reigned in place of Jehoiachin[a] son of Jehoiakim. ²Neither he nor his attendants nor the people of the land paid any attention to the words the LORD had spoken through Jeremiah the prophet.

³King Zedekiah, however, sent Jehucal son of Shelemiah with the priest Zephaniah son of Maaseiah to Jeremiah the prophet with this message: "Please pray to the LORD our God for us."

⁴Now Jeremiah was free to come and go among the people, for he had not yet been put in prison. ⁵Pharaoh's army had marched out of Egypt, and when the Babylonians[b] who were besieging Jerusalem heard the report about them, they withdrew from Jerusalem.

⁶Then the word of the LORD came to Jeremiah the prophet: ⁷"This is what the LORD, the God of Israel, says: Tell the king of Judah, who sent you to inquire of me, 'Pharaoh's army, which has marched out to support you, will go back to its own land, to Egypt. ⁸Then the Babylonians will return and attack this city; they will capture it and burn it down.'

⁹"This is what the LORD says: Do not deceive yourselves, thinking, 'The Babylonians will surely leave us.' They will not! ¹⁰Even if you were to defeat the entire Babylonian[c] army that is attacking you and only wounded men were left in their tents, they would come out and burn this city down."

¹¹After the Babylonian army had withdrawn from Jerusalem because of Pharaoh's army, ¹²Jeremiah started to leave the city to go to the territory of Benjamin to get his share of the property among the people there. ¹³But when he reached the Benjamin Gate, the captain of the guard, whose name was Irijah son of Shelemiah, the son of Hananiah, arrested him and said, "You are deserting to the Babylonians!"

¹⁴"That's not true!" Jeremiah said. "I am not deserting to the Babylonians." But Irijah would not listen to him; instead, he arrested Jeremiah and brought him to the officials. ¹⁵They were angry with Jeremiah and had him beaten and imprisoned in the house of Jonathan the secretary, which they had made into a prison.

¹⁶Jeremiah was put into a vaulted cell in a dungeon, where he remained a long time. ¹⁷Then King Zedekiah sent for him and had him brought to the palace, where he asked him privately, "Is there any word from the LORD?"

"Yes," Jeremiah replied, "you will be handed over to the king of Babylon."

¹⁸Then Jeremiah said to King Zedekiah, "What crime have I committed against you or your officials or this people, that you have put me in prison? ¹⁹Where are your prophets who prophesied to you, 'The king of Babylon will not attack you or this land'? ²⁰But now, my lord the king, please listen. Let me bring my petition before you: Do not send me back to the house of Jonathan the secretary, or I will die there."

²¹King Zedekiah then gave orders for Jeremiah to be placed in the courtyard of the guard and given bread from the street of the bakers each day until all the bread in the city was gone. So Jeremiah remained in the courtyard of the guard.

Jeremiah Thrown Into a Cistern

38 Shephatiah son of Mattan, Gedaliah son of Pashhur, Jehucal[d] son of Shelemiah, and Pashhur son of Malkijah heard what Jeremiah was telling all the people when he said, ²"This is what the LORD says: 'Whoever stays in this city will die by the sword, famine or plague, but whoever goes over to the Babylonians[e] will live. He

---

a 1 Hebrew *Coniah,* a variant of *Jehoiachin*   *b 5* Or *Chaldeans;* also in verses 8, 9, 13 and 14   *c 10* Or *Chaldean;* also in verse 11   *d 1* Hebrew *Jucal,* a variant of *Jehucal*   *e 2* Or *Chaldeans;* also in verses 18, 19 and 23

will escape with his life; he will live.' ³And this is what the LORD says: 'This city will certainly be handed over to the army of the king of Babylon, who will capture it.'"

⁴Then the officials said to the king, "This man should be put to death. He is discouraging the soldiers who are left in this city, as well as all the people, by the things he is saying to them. This man is not seeking the good of these people but their ruin."

⁵"He is in your hands," King Zedekiah answered. "The king can do nothing to oppose you."

⁶So they took Jeremiah and put him into the cistern of Malkijah, the king's son, which was in the courtyard of the guard. They lowered Jeremiah by ropes into the cistern; it had no water in it, only mud, and Jeremiah sank down into the mud.

⁷But Ebed-Melech, a Cushite,ᵃ an officialᵇ in the royal palace, heard that they had put Jeremiah into the cistern. While the king was sitting in the Benjamin Gate, ⁸Ebed-Melech went out of the palace and said to him, ⁹"My lord the king, these men have acted wickedly in all they have done to Jeremiah the prophet. They have thrown him into a cistern, where he will starve to death when there is no longer any bread in the city."

¹⁰Then the king commanded Ebed-Melech the Cushite, "Take thirty men from here with you and lift Jeremiah the prophet out of the cistern before he dies."

¹¹So Ebed-Melech took the men with him and went to a room under the treasury in the palace. He took some old rags and worn-out clothes from there and let them down with ropes to Jeremiah in the cistern. ¹²Ebed-Melech the Cushite said to Jeremiah, "Put these old rags and worn-out clothes under your arms to pad the ropes." Jeremiah did so, ¹³and they pulled him up with the ropes and lifted him out of the cistern. And Jeremiah remained in the courtyard of the guard.

Zedekiah Questions Jeremiah Again

¹⁴Then King Zedekiah sent for Jeremiah the prophet and had him brought to the third entrance to the temple of the LORD. "I am going to ask you something," the king said to Jeremiah. "Do not hide anything from me."

¹⁵Jeremiah said to Zedekiah, "If I give you an answer, will you not kill me? Even if I did give you counsel, you would not listen to me."

¹⁶But King Zedekiah swore this oath secretly to Jeremiah: "As surely as the LORD lives, who has given us breath, I will neither kill you nor hand you over to those who are seeking your life."

¹⁷Then Jeremiah said to Zedekiah, "This is what the LORD God Almighty, the God of Israel, says: 'If you surrender to the officers of the king of Babylon, your life will be spared and this city will not be burned down; you and your family will live. ¹⁸But if you will not surrender to the officers of the king of Babylon, this city will be handed over to the Babylonians and they will burn it down; you yourself will not escape from their hands.'"

¹⁹King Zedekiah said to Jeremiah, "I am afraid of the Jews who have gone over to the Babylonians, for the Babylonians may hand me over to them and they will mistreat me."

²⁰"They will not hand you over," Jeremiah replied. "Obey the LORD by doing what I tell you. Then it will go well with you, and your life will be spared. ²¹But if you refuse to surrender, this is what the LORD has revealed to me: ²²All the women left in the palace of the king of Judah will be brought out to the officials of the king of Babylon. Those women will say to you:

> "'They misled you and overcame you—
> those trusted friends of yours.
> Your feet are sunk in the mud;
> your friends have deserted you.'

²³"All your wives and children will be brought out to the Babylonians. You yourself will

---

ᵃ 7 Probably from the upper Nile region   ᵇ 7 Or *a eunuch* not escape from their hands but will be captured by the king of Babylon; and this city will*a* be burned down."

²⁴Then Zedekiah said to Jeremiah, "Do not let anyone know about this conversation, or you may die. ²⁵If the officials hear that I talked with you, and they come to you and say, 'Tell us what you said to the king and what the king said to you; do not hide it from us or we will kill you,' ²⁶then tell them, 'I was pleading with the king not to send me back to Jonathan's house to die there.'"

²⁷All the officials did come to Jeremiah and question him, and he told them everything the king had ordered him to say. So they said no more to him, for no one had heard his conversation with the king.

²⁸And Jeremiah remained in the courtyard of the guard until the day Jerusalem was captured.

The Fall of Jerusalem

39 This is how Jerusalem was taken: ¹In the ninth year of Zedekiah king of Judah, in the tenth month, Nebuchadnezzar king of Babylon marched against Jerusalem with his whole army and laid siege to it. ²And on the ninth day of the fourth month of Zedekiah's eleventh year, the city wall was broken through. ³Then all the officials of the king of Babylon came and took seats in the Middle Gate: Nergal-Sharezer of Samgar, Nebo-Sarsekim*b* a chief officer, Nergal-Sharezer a high official and all the other officials of the king of Babylon. ⁴When Zedekiah king of Judah and all the soldiers saw them, they fled; they left the city at night by way of the king's garden, through the gate between the two walls, and headed toward the Arabah.*c*

⁵But the Babylonian*d* army pursued them and overtook Zedekiah in the plains of Jericho. They captured him and took him to Nebuchadnezzar king of Babylon at Riblah in the land of Hamath, where he pronounced sentence on him. ⁶There at Riblah the king of Babylon slaughtered the sons of Zedekiah before his eyes and also killed all the nobles of Judah. ⁷Then he put out Zedekiah's eyes and bound him with bronze shackles to take him to Babylon.

⁸The Babylonians*e* set fire to the royal palace and the houses of the people and broke down the walls of Jerusalem. ⁹Nebuzaradan commander of the imperial guard carried into exile to Babylon the people who remained in the city, along with those who had gone over to him, and the rest of the people. ¹⁰But Nebuzaradan the commander of the guard left behind in the land of Judah some of the poor people, who owned nothing; and at that time he gave them vineyards and fields.

¹¹Now Nebuchadnezzar king of Babylon had given these orders about Jeremiah through Nebuzaradan commander of the imperial guard: ¹²"Take him and look after him; don't harm him but do for him whatever he asks." ¹³So Nebuzaradan the commander of the guard, Nebushazban a chief officer, Nergal-Sharezer a high official and all the other officers of the king of Babylon ¹⁴sent and had Jeremiah taken out of the courtyard of the guard. They turned him over to Gedaliah son of Ahikam, the son of Shaphan, to take him back to his home. So he remained among his own people.

¹⁵While Jeremiah had been confined in the courtyard of the guard, the word of the Lord came to him: ¹⁶"Go and tell Ebed-Melech the Cushite, 'This is what the Lord Almighty, the God of Israel, says: I am about to fulfill my words against this city through disaster, not prosperity. At that time they will be fulfilled before your eyes. ¹⁷But I will rescue you on that day, declares the Lord; you will not be handed over to those you fear. ¹⁸I will save you; you will not fall by the sword but will escape with your life, because you trust in me, declares the Lord.'"

*a 23 Or and you will cause this city to   b 3 Or Nergal-Sharezer, Samgar-Nebo, Sarsekim   c 4 Or the Jordan Valley
d 5 Or Chaldean   e 8 Or Chaldeans*

Jeremiah Freed

40 The word came to Jeremiah from the LORD after Nebuzaradan commander of the imperial guard had released him at Ramah. He had found Jeremiah bound in chains among all the captives from Jerusalem and Judah who were being carried into exile to Babylon. [2]When the commander of the guard found Jeremiah, he said to him, "The LORD your God decreed this disaster for this place. [3]And now the LORD has brought it about; he has done just as he said he would. All this happened because you people sinned against the LORD and did not obey him. [4]But today I am freeing you from the chains on your wrists. Come with me to Babylon, if you like, and I will look after you; but if you do not want to, then don't come. Look, the whole country lies before you; go wherever you please." [5]However, before Jeremiah turned to go,[a] Nebuzaradan added, "Go back to Gedaliah son of Ahikam, the son of Shaphan, whom the king of Babylon has appointed over the towns of Judah, and live with him among the people, or go anywhere else you please."

Then the commander gave him provisions and a present and let him go. [6]So Jeremiah went to Gedaliah son of Ahikam at Mizpah and stayed with him among the people who were left behind in the land.

Gedaliah Assassinated

[7]When all the army officers and their men who were still in the open country heard that the king of Babylon had appointed Gedaliah son of Ahikam as governor over the land and had put him in charge of the men, women and children who were the poorest in the land and who had not been carried into exile to Babylon, [8]they came to Gedaliah at Mizpah—Ishmael son of Nethaniah, Johanan and Jonathan the sons of Kareah, Seraiah son of Tanhumeth, the sons of Ephai the Netophathite, and Jaazaniah[b] the son of the Maacathite, and their men. [9]Gedaliah son of Ahikam, the son of Shaphan, took an oath to reassure them and their men. "Do not be afraid to serve the Babylonians,[c]" he said. "Settle down in the land and serve the king of Babylon, and it will go well with you. [10]I myself will stay at Mizpah to represent you before the Babylonians who come to us, but you are to harvest the wine, summer fruit and oil, and put them in your storage jars, and live in the towns you have taken over."

[11]When all the Jews in Moab, Ammon, Edom and all the other countries heard that the king of Babylon had left a remnant in Judah and had appointed Gedaliah son of Ahikam, the son of Shaphan, as governor over them, [12]they all came back to the land of Judah, to Gedaliah at Mizpah, from all the countries where they had been scattered. And they harvested an abundance of wine and summer fruit.

[13]Johanan son of Kareah and all the army officers still in the open country came to Gedaliah at Mizpah [14]and said to him, "Don't you know that Baalis king of the Ammonites has sent Ishmael son of Nethaniah to take your life?" But Gedaliah son of Ahikam did not believe them.

[15]Then Johanan son of Kareah said privately to Gedaliah in Mizpah, "Let me go and kill Ishmael son of Nethaniah, and no one will know it. Why should he take your life and cause all the Jews who are gathered around you to be scattered and the remnant of Judah to perish?"

[16]But Gedaliah son of Ahikam said to Johanan son of Kareah, "Don't do such a thing! What you are saying about Ishmael is not true."

41 In the seventh month Ishmael son of Nethaniah, the son of Elishama, who was of royal blood and had been one of the king's officers, came with ten men to Gedaliah son of Ahikam at Mizpah. While they were eating together there, [2]Ishmael son of Nethaniah and the ten men who were with him got up and struck down

---

a 5 Or Jeremiah answered   b 8 Hebrew Jezaniah, a variant of Jaazaniah   c 9 Or Chaldeans; also in verse 10

Gedaliah son of Ahikam, the son of Shaphan, with the sword, killing the one whom the king of Babylon had appointed as governor over the land. ³Ishmael also killed all the Jews who were with Gedaliah at Mizpah, as well as the Babylonian*a* soldiers who were there.

⁴The day after Gedaliah's assassination, before anyone knew about it, ⁵eighty men who had shaved off their beards, torn their clothes and cut themselves came from Shechem, Shiloh and Samaria, bringing grain offerings and incense with them to the house of the LORD. ⁶Ishmael son of Nethaniah went out from Mizpah to meet them, weeping as he went. When he met them, he said, "Come to Gedaliah son of Ahikam." ⁷When they went into the city, Ishmael son of Nethaniah and the men who were with him slaughtered them and threw them into a cistern. ⁸But ten of them said to Ishmael, "Don't kill us! We have wheat and barley, oil and honey, hidden in a field." So he let them alone and did not kill them with the others. ⁹Now the cistern where he threw all the bodies of the men he had killed along with Gedaliah was the one King Asa had made as part of his defense against Baasha king of Israel. Ishmael son of Nethaniah filled it with the dead.

¹⁰Ishmael made captives of all the rest of the people who were in Mizpah—the king's daughters along with all the others who were left there, over whom Nebuzaradan commander of the imperial guard had appointed Gedaliah son of Ahikam. Ishmael son of Nethaniah took them captive and set out to cross over to the Ammonites.

¹¹When Johanan son of Kareah and all the army officers who were with him heard about all the crimes Ishmael son of Nethaniah had committed, ¹²they took all their men and went to fight Ishmael son of Nethaniah. They caught up with him near the great pool in Gibeon. ¹³When all the people Ishmael had with him saw Johanan son of Kareah and the army officers who were with him, they were glad. ¹⁴All the people Ishmael had taken captive at Mizpah turned and went over to Johanan son of Kareah. ¹⁵But Ishmael son of Nethaniah and eight of his men escaped from Johanan and fled to the Ammonites.

Flight to Egypt

¹⁶Then Johanan son of Kareah and all the army officers who were with him led away all the survivors from Mizpah whom he had recovered from Ishmael son of Nethaniah after he had assassinated Gedaliah son of Ahikam: the soldiers, women, children and court officials he had brought from Gibeon. ¹⁷And they went on, stopping at Geruth Kimham near Bethlehem on their way to Egypt ¹⁸to escape the Babylonians.*b* They were afraid of them because Ishmael son of Nethaniah had killed Gedaliah son of Ahikam, whom the king of Babylon had appointed as governor over the land.

42 Then all the army officers, including Johanan son of Kareah and Jezaniah*c* son of Hoshaiah, and all the people from the least to the greatest approached ²Jeremiah the prophet and said to him, "Please hear our petition and pray to the LORD your God for this entire remnant. For as you now see, though we were once many, now only a few are left. ³Pray that the LORD your God will tell us where we should go and what we should do."

⁴"I have heard you," replied Jeremiah the prophet. "I will certainly pray to the LORD your God as you have requested; I will tell you everything the LORD says and will keep nothing back from you."

⁵Then they said to Jeremiah, "May the LORD be a true and faithful witness against us if we do not act in accordance with everything the LORD your God sends you to tell us. ⁶Whether it is favorable or unfavorable, we will obey the LORD our God, to whom we are sending you, so that it will go well with us, for we will obey the LORD our God."

⁷Ten days later the word of the LORD came to Jeremiah. ⁸So he called together Johanan son of Kareah and all the army officers who were with him and all the people from the least to the greatest. ⁹He said to them, "This is what the LORD, the God of Israel, to whom

a 3 Or Chaldean   b 18 Or Chaldeans   c 1 Hebrew; Septuagint (see also 43:2) Azariah

you sent me to present your petition, says: **10**'If you stay in this land, I will build you up and not tear you down; I will plant you and not uproot you, for I am grieved over the disaster I have inflicted on you. **11**Do not be afraid of the king of Babylon, whom you now fear. Do not be afraid of him, declares the LORD, for I am with you and will save you and deliver you from his hands. **12**I will show you compassion so that he will have compassion on you and restore you to your land.'

13"However, if you say, 'We will not stay in this land,' and so disobey the LORD your God, **14**and if you say, 'No, we will go and live in Egypt, where we will not see war or hear the trumpet or be hungry for bread,' **15**then hear the word of the LORD, O remnant of Judah. This is what the LORD Almighty, the God of Israel, says: 'If you are determined to go to Egypt and you do go to settle there, **16**then the sword you fear will overtake you there, and the famine you dread will follow you into Egypt, and there you will die. **17**Indeed, all who are determined to go to Egypt to settle there will die by the sword, famine and plague; not one of them will survive or escape the disaster I will bring on them.' **18**This is what the LORD Almighty, the God of Israel, says: 'As my anger and wrath have been poured out on those who lived in Jerusalem, so will my wrath be poured out on you when you go to Egypt. You will be an object of cursing and horror, of condemnation and reproach; you will never see this place again.'

19"O remnant of Judah, the LORD has told you, 'Do not go to Egypt.' Be sure of this: I warn you today **20**that you made a fatal mistake*a* when you sent me to the LORD your God and said, 'Pray to the LORD our God for us; tell us everything he says and we will do it.' **21**I have told you today, but you still have not obeyed the LORD your God in all he sent me to tell you. **22**So now, be sure of this: You will die by the sword, famine and plague in the place where you want to go to settle."

43   When Jeremiah finished telling the people all the words of the LORD their God—everything the LORD had sent him to tell them— **2**Azariah son of Hoshaiah and Johanan son of Kareah and all the arrogant men said to Jeremiah, "You are lying! The LORD our God has not sent you to say, 'You must not go to Egypt to settle there.' **3**But Baruch son of Neriah is inciting you against us to hand us over to the Babylonians,*b* so they may kill us or carry us into exile to Babylon."

4So Johanan son of Kareah and all the army officers and all the people disobeyed the LORD's command to stay in the land of Judah. **5**Instead, Johanan son of Kareah and all the army officers led away all the remnant of Judah who had come back to live in the land of Judah from all the nations where they had been scattered. **6**They also led away all the men, women and children and the king's daughters whom Nebuzaradan commander of the imperial guard had left with Gedaliah son of Ahikam, the son of Shaphan, and Jeremiah the prophet and Baruch son of Neriah. **7**So they entered Egypt in disobedience to the LORD and went as far as Tahpanhes.

8In Tahpanhes the word of the LORD came to Jeremiah: **9**"While the Jews are watching, take some large stones with you and bury them in clay in the brick pavement at the entrance to Pharaoh's palace in Tahpanhes. **10**Then say to them, 'This is what the LORD Almighty, the God of Israel, says: I will send for my servant Nebuchadnezzar king of Babylon, and I will set his throne over these stones I have buried here; he will spread his royal canopy above them. **11**He will come and attack Egypt, bringing death to those destined for death, captivity to those destined for captivity, and the sword to those destined for the sword. **12**He*c* will set fire to the temples of the gods of Egypt; he will burn their temples and take their gods captive. As a shepherd wraps his garment around him, so will he wrap Egypt around himself and depart from there unscathed. **13**There in the temple of the sun*d* in Egypt he will demolish the sacred pillars and will burn down the temples of the gods of Egypt.'"

---

a 20 Or *you erred in your hearts*   *b 3* Or *Chaldeans*   *c 12* Or *I*   *d 13* Or *in Heliopolis*

Disaster Because of Idolatry

44 This word came to Jeremiah concerning all the Jews living in Lower Egypt—in Migdol, Tahpanhes and Memphis[a]—and in Upper Egypt[b]: ²"This is what the LORD Almighty, the God of Israel, says: You saw the great disaster I brought on Jerusalem and on all the towns of Judah. Today they lie deserted and in ruins ³because of the evil they have done. They provoked me to anger by burning incense and by worshiping other gods that neither they nor you nor your fathers ever knew. ⁴Again and again I sent my servants the prophets, who said, 'Do not do this detestable thing that I hate!' ⁵But they did not listen or pay attention; they did not turn from their wickedness or stop burning incense to other gods. ⁶Therefore, my fierce anger was poured out; it raged against the towns of Judah and the streets of Jerusalem and made them the desolate ruins they are today.

⁷"Now this is what the LORD God Almighty, the God of Israel, says: Why bring such great disaster on yourselves by cutting off from Judah the men and women, the children and infants, and so leave yourselves without a remnant? ⁸Why provoke me to anger with what your hands have made, burning incense to other gods in Egypt, where you have come to live? You will destroy yourselves and make yourselves an object of cursing and reproach among all the nations on earth. ⁹Have you forgotten the wickedness committed by your fathers and by the kings and queens of Judah and the wickedness committed by you and your wives in the land of Judah and the streets of Jerusalem? ¹⁰To this day they have not humbled themselves or shown reverence, nor have they followed my law and the decrees I set before you and your fathers.

¹¹"Therefore, this is what the LORD Almighty, the God of Israel, says: I am determined to bring disaster on you and to destroy all Judah. ¹²I will take away the remnant of Judah who were determined to go to Egypt to settle there. They will all perish in Egypt; they will fall by the sword or die from famine. From the least to the greatest, they will die by sword or famine. They will become an object of cursing and horror, of condemnation and reproach. ¹³I will punish those who live in Egypt with the sword, famine and plague, as I punished Jerusalem. ¹⁴None of the remnant of Judah who have gone to live in Egypt will escape or survive to return to the land of Judah, to which they long to return and live; none will return except a few fugitives."

¹⁵Then all the men who knew that their wives were burning incense to other gods, along with all the women who were present—a large assembly—and all the people living in Lower and Upper Egypt,[c] said to Jeremiah, ¹⁶"We will not listen to the message you have spoken to us in the

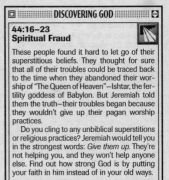

╠ ▒ DISCOVERING GOD ▒ ╣

44:16–23
Spiritual Fraud

These people found it hard to let go of their superstitious beliefs. They thought for sure that all of their troubles could be traced back to the time when they abandoned their worship of "The Queen of Heaven"—Ishtar, the fertility goddess of Babylon. But Jeremiah told them the truth—their troubles began because they wouldn't give up their pagan worship practices.

Do you cling to any unbiblical superstitions or religious practices? Jeremiah would tell you in the strongest words: *Give them up.* They're not helping you, and they won't help anyone else. Find out how strong God is by putting your faith in him instead of in your old ways.

name of the LORD! ¹⁷We will certainly do everything we said we would: We will burn incense to the Queen of Heaven and will pour out drink offerings to her just as we and our fathers, our kings and our officials did in the towns of Judah and in the streets of Jerusalem. At that time we had plenty of food and were well off and suffered no harm. ¹⁸But ever since we stopped burning incense to the Queen of Heaven and pouring out

---

a 1 Hebrew *Noph*   *b 1* Hebrew *in Pathros*   *c 15* Hebrew *in Egypt and Pathros*

drink offerings to her, we have had nothing and have been perishing by sword and famine."

¹⁹The women added, "When we burned incense to the Queen of Heaven and poured out drink offerings to her, did not our husbands know that we were making cakes like her image and pouring out drink offerings to her?"

²⁰Then Jeremiah said to all the people, both men and women, who were answering him, ²¹"Did not the LORD remember and think about the incense burned in the towns of Judah and the streets of Jerusalem by you and your fathers, your kings and your officials and the people of the land? ²²When the LORD could no longer endure your wicked actions and the detestable things you did, your land became an object of cursing and a desolate waste without inhabitants, as it is today. ²³Because you have burned incense and have sinned against the LORD and have not obeyed him or followed his law or his decrees or his stipulations, this disaster has come upon you, as you now see."

²⁴Then Jeremiah said to all the people, including the women, "Hear the word of the LORD, all you people of Judah in Egypt. ²⁵This is what the LORD Almighty, the God of Israel, says: You and your wives have shown by your actions what you promised when you said, 'We will certainly carry out the vows we made to burn incense and pour out drink offerings to the Queen of Heaven.'

"Go ahead then, do what you promised! Keep your vows! ²⁶But hear the word of the LORD, all Jews living in Egypt: 'I swear by my great name,' says the LORD, 'that no one from Judah living anywhere in Egypt will ever again invoke my name or swear, "As surely as the Sovereign LORD lives." ²⁷For I am watching over them for harm, not for good; the Jews in Egypt will perish by sword and famine until they are all destroyed. ²⁸Those who escape the sword and return to the land of Judah from Egypt will be very few. Then the whole remnant of Judah who came to live in Egypt will know whose word will stand—mine or theirs.

²⁹"'This will be the sign to you that I will punish you in this place,' declares the LORD, 'so that you will know that my threats of harm against you will surely stand.' ³⁰This is what the LORD says: 'I am going to hand Pharaoh Hophra king of Egypt over to his enemies who seek his life, just as I handed Zedekiah king of Judah over to Nebuchadnezzar king of Babylon, the enemy who was seeking his life.'"

A Message to Baruch

45 This is what Jeremiah the prophet told Baruch son of Neriah in the fourth year of Jehoiakim son of Josiah king of Judah, after Baruch had written on a scroll the words Jeremiah was then dictating: ²"This is what the LORD, the God of Israel, says to you, Baruch: ³You said, 'Woe to me! The LORD has added sorrow to my pain; I am worn out with groaning and find no rest.'"

⁴The LORD said, "Say this to him: 'This is what the LORD says: I will overthrow what I have built and uproot what I have planted, throughout the land. ⁵Should you then seek great things for yourself? Seek them not. For I will bring disaster on all people, declares the LORD, but wherever you go I will let you escape with your life.'"

A Message About Egypt

46 This is the word of the LORD that came to Jeremiah the prophet concerning the nations:

²Concerning Egypt:

This is the message against the army of Pharaoh Neco king of Egypt, which was defeated at Carchemish on the Euphrates River by Nebuchadnezzar king of Babylon in the fourth year of Jehoiakim son of Josiah king of Judah:

³"Prepare your shields, both large and small,

and march out for battle!
⁴Harness the horses,
    mount the steeds!
Take your positions
    with helmets on!
Polish your spears,
    put on your armor!
⁵What do I see?
    They are terrified,
they are retreating,
    their warriors are defeated.
They flee in haste
    without looking back,
    and there is terror on every side,"

declares the LORD.

⁶"The swift cannot flee
    nor the strong escape.
In the north by the River Euphrates
    they stumble and fall.

⁷"Who is this that rises like the Nile,
    like rivers of surging waters?
⁸Egypt rises like the Nile,
    like rivers of surging waters.
She says, 'I will rise and cover the earth;
    I will destroy cities and their people.'
⁹Charge, O horses!
    Drive furiously, O charioteers!
March on, O warriors—
    men of Cush*a* and Put who carry shields,
    men of Lydia who draw the bow.
¹⁰But that day belongs to the Lord, the LORD Almighty—
    a day of vengeance, for vengeance on his foes.
The sword will devour till it is satisfied,
    till it has quenched its thirst with blood.
For the Lord, the LORD Almighty, will offer sacrifice
    in the land of the north by the River Euphrates.

¹¹"Go up to Gilead and get balm,
    O Virgin Daughter of Egypt.
But you multiply remedies in vain;
    there is no healing for you.
¹²The nations will hear of your shame;
    your cries will fill the earth.
One warrior will stumble over another;
    both will fall down together."

¹³This is the message the LORD spoke to Jeremiah the prophet about the coming of Nebuchadnezzar king of Babylon to attack Egypt:

¹⁴"Announce this in Egypt, and proclaim it in Migdol;
    proclaim it also in Memphis*b* and Tahpanhes:
'Take your positions and get ready,
    for the sword devours those around you.'

a 9 That is, the upper Nile region   *b 14 Hebrew Noph; also in verse 19*

¹⁵Why will your warriors be laid low?
    They cannot stand, for the LORD will push them down.
¹⁶They will stumble repeatedly;
    they will fall over each other.
    They will say, 'Get up, let us go back
    to our own people and our native lands,
    away from the sword of the oppressor.'
¹⁷There they will exclaim,
    'Pharaoh king of Egypt is only a loud noise;
    he has missed his opportunity.'

¹⁸"As surely as I live," declares the King,
    whose name is the LORD Almighty,
    "one will come who is like Tabor among the mountains,
    like Carmel by the sea.
¹⁹Pack your belongings for exile,
    you who live in Egypt,
    for Memphis will be laid waste
    and lie in ruins without inhabitant.

²⁰"Egypt is a beautiful heifer,
    but a gadfly is coming
    against her from the north.
²¹The mercenaries in her ranks
    are like fattened calves.
    They too will turn and flee together,
    they will not stand their ground,
    for the day of disaster is coming upon them,
    the time for them to be punished.
²²Egypt will hiss like a fleeing serpent
    as the enemy advances in force;
    they will come against her with axes,
    like men who cut down trees.
²³They will chop down her forest,"

                                        declares the LORD,

    "dense though it be.
    They are more numerous than locusts,
    they cannot be counted.
²⁴The Daughter of Egypt will be put to shame,
    handed over to the people of the north."

²⁵The LORD Almighty, the God of Israel, says: "I am about to bring punishment on Amon*
god of Thebes,ᵃ on Pharaoh, on Egypt and her gods and her kings, and on those who
rely on Pharaoh. ²⁶I will hand them over to those who seek their lives, to Nebuchadnezzar king of Babylon and his officers. Later, however, Egypt will be inhabited as in times
past," declares the LORD.

²⁷"Do not fear, O Jacob my servant;
    do not be dismayed, O Israel.
    I will surely save you out of a distant place,
    your descendants from the land of their exile.
    Jacob will again have peace and security,
    and no one will make him afraid.
²⁸Do not fear, O Jacob my servant,

ᵃ25 Hebrew *No*

for I am with you," declares the LORD.
"Though I completely destroy all the nations
    among which I scatter you,
I will not completely destroy you.
I will discipline you but only with justice;
    I will not let you go entirely unpunished."

Message About the Philistines

47 This is the word of the LORD that came to Jeremiah the prophet concerning the Philistines before Pharaoh attacked Gaza:

²This is what the LORD says:

"See how the waters are rising in the north;
    they will become an overflowing torrent.
They will overflow the land and everything in it,
    the towns and those who live in them.
The people will cry out;
    all who dwell in the land will wail
³at the sound of the hoofs of galloping steeds,
    at the noise of enemy chariots
    and the rumble of their wheels.
Fathers will not turn to help their children;
    their hands will hang limp.
⁴For the day has come
    to destroy all the Philistines
and to cut off all survivors
    who could help Tyre and Sidon.
The LORD is about to destroy the Philistines,
    the remnant from the coasts of Caphtor.ᵃ
⁵Gaza will shave her head in mourning;
    Ashkelon will be silenced.
O remnant on the plain,
    how long will you cut yourselves?
⁶" 'Ah, sword of the LORD,' ⌊you cry,⌋
    'how long till you rest?
Return to your scabbard;
    cease and be still.'
⁷But how can it rest
    when the LORD has commanded it,
when he has ordered it
    to attack Ashkelon and the coast?"

Message About Moab

48 Concerning Moab:

This is what the LORD Almighty, the God of Israel, says:

"Woe to Nebo, for it will be ruined.
    Kiriathaim will be disgraced and captured;
the strongholdᵇ will be disgraced and shattered.
²Moab will be praised no more;
    in Heshbonᶜ men will plot her downfall:

---

⁴ That is, Crete   ᵇ 1 Or / Misgab   ᶜ 2 The Hebrew for Heshbon sounds like the Hebrew for plot.

'Come, let us put an end to that nation.'
You too, O Madmen, *a* will be silenced;
     the sword will pursue you.
³Listen to the cries from Horonaim,
     cries of great havoc and destruction.
⁴Moab will be broken;
     her little ones will cry out. *b*
⁵They go up the way to Luhith,
     weeping bitterly as they go;
on the road down to Horonaim
     anguished cries over the destruction are heard.
⁶Flee! Run for your lives;
     become like a bush*c* in the desert.
⁷Since you trust in your deeds and riches,
     you too will be taken captive,
and Chemosh will go into exile,
     together with his priests and officials.
⁸The destroyer will come against every town,
     and not a town will escape.
The valley will be ruined
     and the plateau destroyed,
because the Lord has spoken.
⁹Put salt on Moab,
     for she will be laid waste*d*;
her towns will become desolate,
     with no one to live in them.

¹⁰"A curse on him who is lax in doing the Lord's work!
     A curse on him who keeps his sword from bloodshed!

¹¹"Moab has been at rest from youth,
     like wine left on its dregs,
not poured from one jar to another—
     she has not gone into exile.
So she tastes as she did,
     and her aroma is unchanged.
¹²But days are coming,"
     declares the Lord,
"when I will send men who pour from jars,
     and they will pour her out;
they will empty her jars
     and smash her jugs.
¹³Then Moab will be ashamed of Chemosh,
     as the house of Israel was ashamed
     when they trusted in Bethel.

¹⁴"How can you say, 'We are warriors,
     men valiant in battle'?
¹⁵Moab will be destroyed and her towns invaded;
     her finest young men will go down in the slaughter,"
     declares the King, whose name is the Lord Almighty.
¹⁶"The fall of Moab is at hand;

---

*a*2 The name of the Moabite town Madmen sounds like the Hebrew for *be silenced.*   *b*4 Hebrew; Septuagint / *proclaim it to* Zoar   *c*6 Or *like Aroer*   *d*9 Or *Give wings to Moab, / for she will fly away*

her calamity will come quickly.
¹⁷Mourn for her, all who live around her,
    all who know her fame;
  say, 'How broken is the mighty scepter,
    how broken the glorious staff!'

¹⁸"Come down from your glory
    and sit on the parched ground,
    O inhabitants of the Daughter of Dibon,
  for he who destroys Moab
    will come up against you
    and ruin your fortified cities.
¹⁹Stand by the road and watch,
    you who live in Aroer.
  Ask the man fleeing and the woman escaping,
    ask them, 'What has happened?'
²⁰Moab is disgraced, for she is shattered.
    Wail and cry out!
  Announce by the Arnon
    that Moab is destroyed.
²¹Judgment has come to the plateau—
    to Holon, Jahzah and Mephaath,
²²   to Dibon, Nebo and Beth Diblathaim,
²³   to Kiriathaim, Beth Gamul and Beth Meon,
²⁴   to Kerioth and Bozrah—
    to all the towns of Moab, far and near.
²⁵Moab's horn^a is cut off;
    her arm is broken,"

declares the Lord.

²⁶"Make her drunk,
    for she has defied the Lord.
  Let Moab wallow in her vomit;
    let her be an object of ridicule.
²⁷Was not Israel the object of your ridicule?
    Was she caught among thieves,
  that you shake your head in scorn
    whenever you speak of her?
²⁸Abandon your towns and dwell among the rocks,
    you who live in Moab.
  Be like a dove that makes its nest
    at the mouth of a cave.

²⁹"We have heard of Moab's pride—
    her overweening pride and conceit,
  her pride and arrogance
    and the haughtiness of her heart.
³⁰I know her insolence but it is futile,"

declares the Lord,

  "and her boasts accomplish nothing.
³¹Therefore I wail over Moab,
    for all Moab I cry out,
    I moan for the men of Kir Hareseth.

²⁵ *Horn* here symbolizes strength.

³²I weep for you, as Jazer weeps,
O vines of Sibmah.
Your branches spread as far as the sea;
they reached as far as the sea of Jazer.
The destroyer has fallen
on your ripened fruit and grapes.
³³Joy and gladness are gone
from the orchards and fields of Moab.
I have stopped the flow of wine from the presses;
no one treads them with shouts of joy.
Although there are shouts,
they are not shouts of joy.

³⁴"The sound of their cry rises
from Heshbon to Elealeh and Jahaz,
from Zoar as far as Horonaim and Eglath Shelishiyah,
for even the waters of Nimrim are dried up.
³⁵In Moab I will put an end
to those who make offerings on the high places
and burn incense to their gods,"

declares the LORD.

³⁶"So my heart laments for Moab like a flute;
it laments like a flute for the men of Kir Hareseth.
The wealth they acquired is gone.
³⁷Every head is shaved
and every beard cut off;
every hand is slashed
and every waist is covered with sackcloth.
³⁸On all the roofs in Moab
and in the public squares
there is nothing but mourning,
for I have broken Moab
like a jar that no one wants,"

declares the LORD.

³⁹"How shattered she is! How they wail!
How Moab turns her back in shame!
Moab has become an object of ridicule,
an object of horror to all those around her."

⁴⁰This is what the LORD says:

"Look! An eagle is swooping down,
spreading its wings over Moab.
⁴¹Kerioth^a will be captured
and the strongholds taken.
In that day the hearts of Moab's warriors
will be like the heart of a woman in labor.
⁴²Moab will be destroyed as a nation
because she defied the LORD.
⁴³Terror and pit and snare await you,
O people of Moab,"

declares the LORD.

⁴⁴"Whoever flees from the terror

^a41 Or *The cities*

   will fall into a pit,
whoever climbs out of the pit
   will be caught in a snare;
for I will bring upon Moab
   the year of her punishment,"

declares the Lord.

⁴⁵"In the shadow of Heshbon
   the fugitives stand helpless,
for a fire has gone out from Heshbon,
   a blaze from the midst of Sihon;
it burns the foreheads of Moab,
   the skulls of the noisy boasters.
⁴⁶Woe to you, O Moab!
   The people of Chemosh are destroyed;
your sons are taken into exile
   and your daughters into captivity.

⁴⁷"Yet I will restore the fortunes of Moab
   in days to come,"

declares the Lord.

Here ends the judgment on Moab.

A Message About Ammon

49 Concerning the Ammonites:

This is what the Lord says:

   "Has Israel no sons?
      Has she no heirs?
   Why then has Molech*ᵃ* taken possession of Gad?
      Why do his people live in its towns?
   ²But the days are coming,"
      declares the Lord,
   "when I will sound the battle cry
      against Rabbah of the Ammonites;
   it will become a mound of ruins,
      and its surrounding villages will be set on fire.
   Then Israel will drive out
      those who drove her out,"

says the Lord.

   ³"Wail, O Heshbon, for Ai is destroyed!
      Cry out, O inhabitants of Rabbah!
   Put on sackcloth and mourn;
      rush here and there inside the walls,
   for Molech will go into exile,
      together with his priests and officials.
   ⁴Why do you boast of your valleys,
      boast of your valleys so fruitful?
   O unfaithful daughter,
      you trust in your riches and say,
      'Who will attack me?'
   ⁵I will bring terror on you

ᵃ 1 Or their king; Hebrew malcam; also in verse 3

from all those around you,"

> declares the Lord, the Lord Almighty.

"Every one of you will be driven away,
  and no one will gather the fugitives.

⁶"Yet afterward, I will restore the fortunes of the Ammonites,"

> declares the Lord.

A Message About Edom

⁷Concerning Edom:

This is what the Lord Almighty says:

> "Is there no longer wisdom in Teman?
>   Has counsel perished from the prudent?
>   Has their wisdom decayed?
> ⁸Turn and flee, hide in deep caves,
>   you who live in Dedan,
> for I will bring disaster on Esau
>   at the time I punish him.
> ⁹If grape pickers came to you,
>   would they not leave a few grapes?
> If thieves came during the night,
>   would they not steal only as much as they wanted?
> ¹⁰But I will strip Esau bare;
>   I will uncover his hiding places,
>   so that he cannot conceal himself.
> His children, relatives and neighbors will perish,
>   and he will be no more.
> ¹¹Leave your orphans; I will protect their lives.
>   Your widows too can trust in me."

¹²This is what the Lord says: "If those who do not deserve to drink the cup must drink it, why should you go unpunished? You will not go unpunished, but must drink it. ¹³I swear by myself," declares the Lord, "that Bozrah will become a ruin and an object of horror, of reproach and of cursing; and all its towns will be in ruins forever."

¹⁴I have heard a message from the Lord:
  An envoy was sent to the nations to say,
  "Assemble yourselves to attack it!
    Rise up for battle!"

¹⁵"Now I will make you small among the nations,
  despised among men.
¹⁶The terror you inspire
  and the pride of your heart have deceived you,
you who live in the clefts of the rocks,
  who occupy the heights of the hill.
Though you build your nest as high as the eagle's,
  from there I will bring you down,"

> declares the Lord.

¹⁷"Edom will become an object of horror;
  all who pass by will be appalled and will scoff
  because of all its wounds.
¹⁸As Sodom and Gomorrah were overthrown,

along with their neighboring towns,"

says the LORD,

"so no one will live there;
no man will dwell in it.

¹⁹"Like a lion coming up from Jordan's thickets
to a rich pastureland,
I will chase Edom from its land in an instant.
Who is the chosen one I will appoint for this?
Who is like me and who can challenge me?
And what shepherd can stand against me?"

²⁰Therefore, hear what the LORD has planned against Edom,
what he has purposed against those who live in Teman:
The young of the flock will be dragged away;
he will completely destroy their pasture because of them.

²¹At the sound of their fall the earth will tremble;
their cry will resound to the Red Sea.ᵃ

²²Look! An eagle will soar and swoop down,
spreading its wings over Bozrah.
In that day the hearts of Edom's warriors
will be like the heart of a woman in labor.

A Message About Damascus

²³Concerning Damascus:

"Hamath and Arpad are dismayed,
for they have heard bad news.
They are disheartened,
troubled likeᵇ the restless sea.

²⁴Damascus has become feeble,
she has turned to flee
and panic has gripped her;
anguish and pain have seized her,
pain like that of a woman in labor.

²⁵Why has the city of renown not been abandoned,
the town in which I delight?

²⁶Surely, her young men will fall in the streets;
all her soldiers will be silenced in that day,"

declares the LORD Almighty.

²⁷"I will set fire to the walls of Damascus;
it will consume the fortresses of Ben-Hadad."

A Message About Kedar and Hazor

²⁸Concerning Kedar and the kingdoms of Hazor, which Nebuchadnezzar king of Babylon attacked:

This is what the LORD says:

"Arise, and attack Kedar
and destroy the people of the East.

²⁹Their tents and their flocks will be taken;
their shelters will be carried off
with all their goods and camels.

ᵃ21 Hebrew *Yam Suph*; that is, Sea of Reeds   ᵇ23 Hebrew *on* or *by*

> Men will shout to them,
>   'Terror on every side!'

> 30"Flee quickly away!
>   Stay in deep caves, you who live in Hazor,"

declares the LORD.

> "Nebuchadnezzar king of Babylon has plotted against you;
>   he has devised a plan against you.

> 31"Arise and attack a nation at ease,
>   which lives in confidence,"

declares the LORD,

> "a nation that has neither gates nor bars;
>   its people live alone.
> 32Their camels will become plunder,
>   and their large herds will be booty.
> I will scatter to the winds those who are in distant places*a*
>   and will bring disaster on them from every side,"

declares the LORD.

> 33"Hazor will become a haunt of jackals,
>   a desolate place forever.
> No one will live there;
>   no man will dwell in it."

A Message About Elam

34This is the word of the LORD that came to Jeremiah the prophet concerning Elam, early in the reign of Zedekiah king of Judah:

35This is what the LORD Almighty says:

> "See, I will break the bow of Elam,
>   the mainstay of their might.
> 36I will bring against Elam the four winds
>   from the four quarters of the heavens;
> I will scatter them to the four winds,
>   and there will not be a nation
>   where Elam's exiles do not go.
> 37I will shatter Elam before their foes,
>   before those who seek their lives;
> I will bring disaster upon them,
>   even my fierce anger,"

declares the LORD.

> "I will pursue them with the sword
>   until I have made an end of them.
> 38I will set my throne in Elam
>   and destroy her king and officials,"

declares the LORD.

> 39"Yet I will restore the fortunes of Elam
>   in days to come,"

declares the LORD.

a32 Or who clip the hair by their foreheads

A Message About Babylon

50 This is the word the LORD spoke through Jeremiah the prophet concerning Babylon and the land of the Babylonians[a]:

2"Announce and proclaim among the nations,
   lift up a banner and proclaim it;
   keep nothing back, but say,
'Babylon will be captured;
   Bel will be put to shame,
   Marduk filled with terror.
Her images will be put to shame
   and her idols filled with terror.'
3A nation from the north will attack her
   and lay waste her land.
No one will live in it;
   both men and animals will flee away.

4"In those days, at that time,"
   declares the LORD,
"the people of Israel and the people of Judah together
   will go in tears to seek the LORD their God.
5They will ask the way to Zion
   and turn their faces toward it.
They will come and bind themselves to the LORD
   in an everlasting covenant
   that will not be forgotten.

6"My people have been lost sheep;
   their shepherds have led them astray
   and caused them to roam on the mountains.
They wandered over mountain and hill
   and forgot their own resting place.
7Whoever found them devoured them;
   their enemies said, 'We are not guilty,
for they sinned against the LORD, their true pasture,
   the LORD, the hope of their fathers.'

8"Flee out of Babylon;
   leave the land of the Babylonians,
   and be like the goats that lead the flock.
9For I will stir up and bring against Babylon
   an alliance of great nations from the land of the north.
They will take up their positions against her,
   and from the north she will be captured.
Their arrows will be like skilled warriors
   who do not return empty-handed.
10So Babylonia[b] will be plundered;
   all who plunder her will have their fill,"

                                        declares the LORD.

11"Because you rejoice and are glad,
   you who pillage my inheritance,
because you frolic like a heifer threshing grain
   and neigh like stallions,

---

a1 Or *Chaldeans*; also in verses 8, 25, 35 and 45   b10 Or *Chaldea*

¹²your mother will be greatly ashamed;
    she who gave you birth will be disgraced.
She will be the least of the nations—
    a wilderness, a dry land, a desert.
¹³Because of the Lord's anger she will not be inhabited
    but will be completely desolate.
All who pass Babylon will be horrified and scoff
    because of all her wounds.

¹⁴"Take up your positions around Babylon,
    all you who draw the bow.
Shoot at her! Spare no arrows,
    for she has sinned against the Lord.
¹⁵Shout against her on every side!
    She surrenders, her towers fall,
    her walls are torn down.
Since this is the vengeance of the Lord,
    take vengeance on her;
    do to her as she has done to others.
¹⁶Cut off from Babylon the sower,
    and the reaper with his sickle at harvest.
Because of the sword of the oppressor
    let everyone return to his own people,
    let everyone flee to his own land.

¹⁷"Israel is a scattered flock
    that lions have chased away.
The first to devour him
    was the king of Assyria;
the last to crush his bones
    was Nebuchadnezzar king of Babylon."

¹⁸Therefore this is what the Lord Almighty, the God of Israel, says:

"I will punish the king of Babylon and his land
    as I punished the king of Assyria.
¹⁹But I will bring Israel back to his own pasture
    and he will graze on Carmel and Bashan;
his appetite will be satisfied
    on the hills of Ephraim and Gilead.
²⁰In those days, at that time,"
    declares the Lord,
"search will be made for Israel's guilt,
    but there will be none,
and for the sins of Judah,
    but none will be found,
    for I will forgive the remnant I spare.

²¹"Attack the land of Merathaim
    and those who live in Pekod.
Pursue, kill and completely destroy*ᵃ* them,"
                                                    declares the Lord.

    "Do everything I have commanded you.

---

a21 The Hebrew term refers to the irrevocable giving over of things or persons to the Lord, often by totally destroying them; also in verse 26.

²²The noise of battle is in the land,
  the noise of great destruction!
²³How broken and shattered
  is the hammer of the whole earth!
How desolate is Babylon
  among the nations!
²⁴I set a trap for you, O Babylon,
  and you were caught before you knew it;
you were found and captured
  because you opposed the LORD.
²⁵The LORD has opened his arsenal
  and brought out the weapons of his wrath,
for the Sovereign LORD Almighty has work to do
  in the land of the Babylonians.
²⁶Come against her from afar.
  Break open her granaries;
pile her up like heaps of grain.
  Completely destroy her
  and leave her no remnant.
²⁷Kill all her young bulls;
  let them go down to the slaughter!
Woe to them! For their day has come,
  the time for them to be punished.
²⁸Listen to the fugitives and refugees from Babylon
  declaring in Zion
how the LORD our God has taken vengeance,
  vengeance for his temple.

²⁹"Summon archers against Babylon,
  all those who draw the bow.
Encamp all around her;
  let no one escape.
Repay her for her deeds;
  do to her as she has done.
For she has defied the LORD,
  the Holy One of Israel.
³⁰Therefore, her young men will fall in the streets;
  all her soldiers will be silenced in that day,"

declares the LORD.

³¹"See, I am against you, O arrogant one,"
  declares the Lord, the LORD Almighty,
"for your day has come,
  the time for you to be punished.
³²The arrogant one will stumble and fall
  and no one will help her up;
I will kindle a fire in her towns
  that will consume all who are around her."

³³This is what the LORD Almighty says:

"The people of Israel are oppressed,
  and the people of Judah as well.
All their captors hold them fast,
  refusing to let them go.
³⁴Yet their Redeemer is strong;

the LORD Almighty is his name.
He will vigorously defend their cause
    so that he may bring rest to their land,
    but unrest to those who live in Babylon.

³⁵"A sword against the Babylonians!"
    declares the LORD—
"against those who live in Babylon
    and against her officials and wise men!
³⁶A sword against her false prophets!
    They will become fools.
A sword against her warriors!
    They will be filled with terror.
³⁷A sword against her horses and chariots
    and all the foreigners in her ranks!
    They will become women.
A sword against her treasures!
    They will be plundered.
³⁸A drought on*ᵃ* her waters!
    They will dry up.
For it is a land of idols,
    idols that will go mad with terror.

³⁹"So desert creatures and hyenas will live there,
    and there the owl will dwell.
It will never again be inhabited
    or lived in from generation to generation.
⁴⁰As God overthrew Sodom and Gomorrah
    along with their neighboring towns,"

                            declares the LORD,

"so no one will live there;
    no man will dwell in it.

⁴¹"Look! An army is coming from the north;
    a great nation and many kings
    are being stirred up from the ends of the earth.
⁴²They are armed with bows and spears;
    they are cruel and without mercy.
They sound like the roaring sea
    as they ride on their horses;
they come like men in battle formation
    to attack you, O Daughter of Babylon.
⁴³The king of Babylon has heard reports about them,
    and his hands hang limp.
Anguish has gripped him,
    pain like that of a woman in labor.
⁴⁴Like a lion coming up from Jordan's thickets
    to a rich pastureland,
I will chase Babylon from its land in an instant.
    Who is the chosen one I will appoint for this?
Who is like me and who can challenge me?
    And what shepherd can stand against me?"
⁴⁵Therefore, hear what the LORD has planned against Babylon,

ᵃ 38 Or A sword against

what he has purposed against the land of the Babylonians:
The young of the flock will be dragged away;
    he will completely destroy their pasture because of them.
⁴⁶At the sound of Babylon's capture the earth will tremble;
    its cry will resound among the nations.

51 This is what the LORD says:

"See, I will stir up the spirit of a destroyer
    against Babylon and the people of Leb Kamai.ᵃ
²I will send foreigners to Babylon
    to winnow her and to devastate her land;
they will oppose her on every side
    in the day of her disaster.
³Let not the archer string his bow,
    nor let him put on his armor.
Do not spare her young men;
    completely destroyᵇ her army.
⁴They will fall down slain in Babylon,ᶜ
    fatally wounded in her streets.
⁵For Israel and Judah have not been forsaken
    by their God, the LORD Almighty,
though their landᵈ is full of guilt
    before the Holy One of Israel.

⁶"Flee from Babylon!
    Run for your lives!
    Do not be destroyed because of her sins.
It is time for the LORD's vengeance;
    he will pay her what she deserves.
⁷Babylon was a gold cup in the LORD's hand;
    she made the whole earth drunk.
The nations drank her wine;
    therefore they have now gone mad.
⁸Babylon will suddenly fall and be broken.
    Wail over her!
Get balm for her pain;
    perhaps she can be healed.

⁹"'We would have healed Babylon,
    but she cannot be healed;
let us leave her and each go to his own land,
    for her judgment reaches to the skies,
    it rises as high as the clouds.'

¹⁰"'The LORD has vindicated us;
    come, let us tell in Zion
    what the LORD our God has done.'

¹¹"Sharpen the arrows,
    take up the shields!
The LORD has stirred up the kings of the Medes,

ᵃ1 *Leb Kamai* is a cryptogram for Chaldea, that is, Babylonia.
things or persons to the LORD, often by totally destroying them.
Babylonians,

ᵇ3 The Hebrew term refers to the irrevocable giving over of
ᶜ4 Or *Chaldea*   ᵈ5 Or / *and the land . of the*

because his purpose is to destroy Babylon.
The LORD will take vengeance,
vengeance for his temple.
¹²Lift up a banner against the walls of Babylon!
Reinforce the guard,
station the watchmen,
prepare an ambush!
The LORD will carry out his purpose,
his decree against the people of Babylon.
¹³You who live by many waters
and are rich in treasures,
your end has come,
the time for you to be cut off.
¹⁴The LORD Almighty has sworn by himself:
I will surely fill you with men, as with a swarm of locusts,
and they will shout in triumph over you.

¹⁵"He made the earth by his power;
he founded the world by his wisdom
and stretched out the heavens by his understanding.
¹⁶When he thunders, the waters in the heavens roar;
he makes clouds rise from the ends of the earth.
He sends lightning with the rain
and brings out the wind from his storehouses.

¹⁷"Every man is senseless and without knowledge;
every goldsmith is shamed by his idols.
His images are a fraud;
they have no breath in them.
¹⁸They are worthless, the objects of mockery;
when their judgment comes, they will perish.
¹⁹He who is the Portion of Jacob is not like these,
for he is the Maker of all things,
including the tribe of his inheritance—
the LORD Almighty is his name.

²⁰"You are my war club,
my weapon for battle—
with you I shatter nations,
with you I destroy kingdoms,
²¹with you I shatter horse and rider,
with you I shatter chariot and driver,
²²with you I shatter man and woman,
with you I shatter old man and youth,
with you I shatter young man and maiden,
²³with you I shatter shepherd and flock,
with you I shatter farmer and oxen,
with you I shatter governors and officials.

²⁴"Before your eyes I will repay Babylon and all who live in Babylonia*ᵃ* for all the wrong they have done in Zion," declares the LORD.

²⁵"I am against you, O destroying mountain,

ᵃ24 Or *Chaldea;* also in verse 35

you who destroy the whole earth,"

declares the LORD.

"I will stretch out my hand against you,
    roll you off the cliffs,
    and make you a burned-out mountain.
26No rock will be taken from you for a cornerstone,
    nor any stone for a foundation,
    for you will be desolate forever,"

declares the LORD.

27"Lift up a banner in the land!
    Blow the trumpet among the nations!
Prepare the nations for battle against her;
    summon against her these kingdoms:
    Ararat, Minni and Ashkenaz.
Appoint a commander against her;
    send up horses like a swarm of locusts.
28Prepare the nations for battle against her—
    the kings of the Medes,
their governors and all their officials,
    and all the countries they rule.
29The land trembles and writhes,
    for the LORD's purposes against Babylon stand—
to lay waste the land of Babylon
    so that no one will live there.
30Babylon's warriors have stopped fighting;
    they remain in their strongholds.
Their strength is exhausted;
    they have become like women.
Her dwellings are set on fire;
    the bars of her gates are broken.
31One courier follows another
    and messenger follows messenger
to announce to the king of Babylon
    that his entire city is captured,
32the river crossings seized,
    the marshes set on fire,
    and the soldiers terrified."

33This is what the LORD Almighty, the God of Israel, says:

"The Daughter of Babylon is like a threshing floor
    at the time it is trampled;
    the time to harvest her will soon come."

34"Nebuchadnezzar king of Babylon has devoured us,
    he has thrown us into confusion,
    he has made us an empty jar.
Like a serpent he has swallowed us
    and filled his stomach with our delicacies,
    and then has spewed us out.
35May the violence done to our flesha be upon Babylon,"
    say the inhabitants of Zion.

a35 Or done to us and to our children

"May our blood be on those who live in Babylonia,"
  says Jerusalem.

36Therefore, this is what the LORD says:

"See, I will defend your cause
  and avenge you;
I will dry up her sea
  and make her springs dry.
37Babylon will be a heap of ruins,
  a haunt of jackals,
an object of horror and scorn,
  a place where no one lives.
38Her people all roar like young lions,
  they growl like lion cubs.
39But while they are aroused,
  I will set out a feast for them
  and make them drunk,
so that they shout with laughter—
  then sleep forever and not awake,"

                              declares the LORD.

40"I will bring them down
  like lambs to the slaughter,
  like rams and goats.

41"How Sheshach[a] will be captured,
  the boast of the whole earth seized!
What a horror Babylon will be
  among the nations!
42The sea will rise over Babylon;
  its roaring waves will cover her.
43Her towns will be desolate,
  a dry and desert land,
a land where no one lives,
  through which no man travels.
44I will punish Bel in Babylon
  and make him spew out what he has swallowed.
The nations will no longer stream to him.
  And the wall of Babylon will fall.

45"Come out of her, my people!
  Run for your lives!
  Run from the fierce anger of the LORD.
46Do not lose heart or be afraid
  when rumors are heard in the land;
one rumor comes this year, another the next,
  rumors of violence in the land
  and of ruler against ruler.
47For the time will surely come
  when I will punish the idols of Babylon;
her whole land will be disgraced
  and her slain will all lie fallen within her.
48Then heaven and earth and all that is in them
  will shout for joy over Babylon,

for out of the north
  destroyers will attack her,"

declares the Lord.

⁴⁹"Babylon must fall because of Israel's slain,
  just as the slain in all the earth
  have fallen because of Babylon.
⁵⁰You who have escaped the sword,
  leave and do not linger!
Remember the Lord in a distant land,
  and think on Jerusalem."

⁵¹"We are disgraced,
  for we have been insulted
  and shame covers our faces,
because foreigners have entered
  the holy places of the Lord's house."

⁵²"But days are coming," declares the Lord,
  "when I will punish her idols,
and throughout her land
  the wounded will groan.
⁵³Even if Babylon reaches the sky
  and fortifies her lofty stronghold,
  I will send destroyers against her,"

declares the Lord.

⁵⁴"The sound of a cry comes from Babylon,
  the sound of great destruction
  from the land of the Babylonians.ᵃ
⁵⁵The Lord will destroy Babylon;
  he will silence her noisy din.
Waves ⌊of enemies⌋ will rage like great waters;
  the roar of their voices will resound.
⁵⁶A destroyer will come against Babylon;
  her warriors will be captured,
  and their bows will be broken.
For the Lord is a God of retribution;
  he will repay in full.
⁵⁷I will make her officials and wise men drunk,
  her governors, officers and warriors as well;
they will sleep forever and not awake,"
  declares the King, whose name is the Lord Almighty.

⁵⁸This is what the Lord Almighty says:

  "Babylon's thick wall will be leveled
    and her high gates set on fire;
  the peoples exhaust themselves for nothing,
    the nations' labor is only fuel for the flames."

⁵⁹This is the message Jeremiah gave to the staff officer Seraiah son of Neriah, the son of Mahseiah, when he went to Babylon with Zedekiah king of Judah in the fourth year of his reign. ⁶⁰Jeremiah had written on a scroll about all the disasters that would come upon Babylon—all that had been recorded concerning Babylon. ⁶¹He said to Seraiah, "When

ᵃ54 Or *Chaldeans*

you get to Babylon, see that you read all these words aloud. ⁶²Then say, 'O LORD, you have said you will destroy this place, so that neither man nor animal will live in it; it will be desolate forever.' ⁶³When you finish reading this scroll, tie a stone to it and throw it into the Euphrates. ⁶⁴Then say, 'So will Babylon sink to rise no more because of the disaster I will bring upon her. And her people will fall.'"

The words of Jeremiah end here.

The Fall of Jerusalem

52 Zedekiah was twenty-one years old when he became king, and he reigned in Jerusalem eleven years. His mother's name was Hamutal daughter of Jeremiah; she was from Libnah. ²He did evil in the eyes of the LORD, just as Jehoiakim had done. ³It was because of the LORD's anger that all this happened to Jerusalem and Judah, and in the end he thrust them from his presence.

Now Zedekiah rebelled against the king of Babylon.

⁴So in the ninth year of Zedekiah's reign, on the tenth day of the tenth month, Nebuchadnezzar king of Babylon marched against Jerusalem with his whole army. They camped outside the city and built siege works all around it. ⁵The city was kept under siege until the eleventh year of King Zedekiah.

⁶By the ninth day of the fourth month the famine in the city had become so severe that there was no food for the people to eat. ⁷Then the city wall was broken through, and the whole army fled. They left the city at night through the gate between the two walls near the king's garden, though the Babylonians*ᵃ* were surrounding the city. They fled toward the Arabah,*ᵇ* ⁸but the Babylonian*ᶜ* army pursued King Zedekiah and overtook him in the plains of Jericho. All his soldiers were separated from him and scattered, ⁹and he was captured.

He was taken to the king of Babylon at Riblah in the land of Hamath, where he pronounced sentence on him. ¹⁰There at Riblah the king of Babylon slaughtered the sons of Zedekiah before his eyes; he also killed all the officials of Judah. ¹¹Then he put out Zedekiah's eyes, bound him with bronze shackles and took him to Babylon, where he put him in prison till the day of his death.

¹²On the tenth day of the fifth month, in the nineteenth year of Nebuchadnezzar king of Babylon, Nebuzaradan commander of the imperial guard, who served the king of Babylon, came to Jerusalem. ¹³He set fire to the temple of the LORD, the royal palace and all the houses of Jerusalem. Every important building he burned down. ¹⁴The whole Babylonian army under the commander of the imperial guard broke down all the walls around Jerusalem. ¹⁵Nebuzaradan the commander of the guard carried into exile some of the poorest people and those who remained in the city, along with the rest of the craftsmen*ᵈ* and those who had gone over to the king of Babylon. ¹⁶But Nebuzaradan left behind the rest of the poorest people of the land to work the vineyards and fields.

¹⁷The Babylonians broke up the bronze pillars, the movable stands and the bronze Sea that were at the temple of the LORD and they carried all the bronze to Babylon. ¹⁸They also took away the pots, shovels, wick trimmers, sprinkling bowls, dishes and all the bronze articles used in the temple service. ¹⁹The commander of the imperial guard took away the basins, censers, sprinkling bowls, pots, lampstands, dishes and bowls used for drink offerings—all that were made of pure gold or silver.

²⁰The bronze from the two pillars, the Sea and the twelve bronze bulls under it, and the movable stands, which King Solomon had made for the temple of the LORD, was more than could be weighed. ²¹Each of the pillars was eighteen cubits high and twelve cubits in circumference*ᵉ*; each was four fingers thick, and hollow. ²²The bronze capital on top of the one pillar was five cubits*ᶠ* high and was decorated with a network and pome-

ᵃ7 Or Chaldeans; also in verse 17   ᵇ7 Or the Jordan Valley   ᶜ8 Or Chaldean; also in verse 14   ᵈ15 Or populace
ᵉ21 That is, about 27 feet (about 8.1 meters) high and 18 feet (about 5.4 meters) in circumference   ᶠ22 That is, about 7 1/2 feet (about 2.3 meters)

granates of bronze all around. The other pillar, with its pomegranates, was similar. [23]There were ninety-six pomegranates on the sides; the total number of pomegranates above the surrounding network was a hundred.

[24]The commander of the guard took as prisoners Seraiah the chief priest, Zephaniah the priest next in rank and the three doorkeepers. [25]Of those still in the city, he took the officer in charge of the fighting men, and seven royal advisers. He also took the secretary who was chief officer in charge of conscripting the people of the land and sixty of his men who were found in the city. [26]Nebuzaradan the commander took them all and brought them to the king of Babylon at Riblah. [27]There at Riblah, in the land of Hamath, the king had them executed.

So Judah went into captivity, away from her land. [28]This is the number of the people Nebuchadnezzar carried into exile:

> in the seventh year, 3,023 Jews;
> [29]in Nebuchadnezzar's eighteenth year,
>   832 people from Jerusalem;
> [30]in his twenty-third year,
>   745 Jews taken into exile by Nebuzaradan the commander of the imperial guard.
> There were 4,600 people in all.

Jehoiachin Released

[31]In the thirty-seventh year of the exile of Jehoiachin king of Judah, in the year Evil-Merodach[a] became king of Babylon, he released Jehoiachin king of Judah and freed him from prison on the twenty-fifth day of the twelfth month. [32]He spoke kindly to him and gave him a seat of honor higher than those of the other kings who were with him in Babylon. [33]So Jehoiachin put aside his prison clothes and for the rest of his life ate regularly at the king's table. [34]Day by day the king of Babylon gave Jehoiachin a regular allowance as long as he lived, till the day of his death.

---

[a]31 Also called *Amel-Marduk*

LAMENTATIONS

1[a] How deserted lies the city,
    once so full of people!
How like a widow is she,
    who once was great among the nations!
She who was queen among the provinces
    has now become a slave.

2 Bitterly she weeps at night,
    tears are upon her cheeks.
Among all her lovers
    there is none to comfort her.
All her friends have betrayed her;
    they have become her enemies.

3 After affliction and harsh labor,
    Judah has gone into exile.
She dwells among the nations;
    she finds no resting place.
All who pursue her have overtaken her
    in the midst of her distress.

4 The roads to Zion mourn,
    for no one comes to her appointed feasts.
All her gateways are desolate,
    her priests groan,
her maidens grieve,
    and she is in bitter anguish.

5 Her foes have become her masters;
    her enemies are at ease.
The LORD has brought her grief
    because of her many sins.
Her children have gone into exile,
    captive before the foe.

6 All the splendor has departed
    from the Daughter of Zion.
Her princes are like deer
    that find no pasture;
in weakness they have fled
    before the pursuer.

7 In the days of her affliction and wandering
    Jerusalem remembers all the treasures
    that were hers in days of old.
When her people fell into enemy hands,
    there was no one to help her.

[a] This chapter is an acrostic poem, the verses of which begin with the successive letters of the Hebrew alphabet.

Her enemies looked at her
    and laughed at her destruction.

⁸Jerusalem has sinned greatly
    and so has become unclean.
All who honored her despise her,
    for they have seen her nakedness;
she herself groans
    and turns away.

⁹Her filthiness clung to her skirts;
    she did not consider her future.
Her fall was astounding;
    there was none to comfort her.
"Look, O Lord, on my affliction,
    for the enemy has triumphed."

¹⁰The enemy laid hands
    on all her treasures;
she saw pagan nations
    enter her sanctuary—
those you had forbidden
    to enter your assembly.

¹¹All her people groan
    as they search for bread;
they barter their treasures for food
    to keep themselves alive.
"Look, O Lord, and consider,
    for I am despised."

¹²"Is it nothing to you, all you who pass by?
    Look around and see.
Is any suffering like my suffering
    that was inflicted on me,
that the Lord brought on me
    in the day of his fierce anger?

¹³"From on high he sent fire,
    sent it down into my bones.
He spread a net for my feet
    and turned me back.
He made me desolate,
    faint all the day long.

¹⁴"My sins have been bound into a yoke ᵃ;
    by his hands they were woven together.
They have come upon my neck
    and the Lord has sapped my strength.
He has handed me over
    to those I cannot withstand.

¹⁵"The Lord has rejected
    all the warriors in my midst;
he has summoned an army against me
    to ᵇ crush my young men.

ᵃ 14 Most Hebrew manuscripts; Septuagint *He kept watch over my sins*   ᵇ 15 Or *has set a time for me / when he will*

In his winepress the Lord has trampled
the Virgin Daughter of Judah.

16"This is why I weep
and my eyes overflow with tears.
No one is near to comfort me,
no one to restore my spirit.
My children are destitute
because the enemy has prevailed."

17Zion stretches out her hands,
but there is no one to comfort her.
The LORD has decreed for Jacob
that his neighbors become his foes;
Jerusalem has become
an unclean thing among them.

18"The LORD is righteous,
yet I rebelled against his command.
Listen, all you peoples;
look upon my suffering.
My young men and maidens
have gone into exile.

19"I called to my allies
but they betrayed me.
My priests and my elders
perished in the city
while they searched for food
to keep themselves alive.

20"See, O LORD, how distressed I am!
I am in torment within,
and in my heart I am disturbed,
for I have been most rebellious.
Outside, the sword bereaves;
inside, there is only death.

21"People have heard my groaning,
but there is no one to comfort me.
All my enemies have heard of my distress;
they rejoice at what you have done.
May you bring the day you have announced
so they may become like me.

22"Let all their wickedness come before you;
deal with them
as you have dealt with me
because of all my sins.
My groans are many
and my heart is faint."

2^a   How the Lord has covered the Daughter of Zion
          with the cloud of his anger^b!
   He has hurled down the splendor of Israel
       from heaven to earth;
   he has not remembered his footstool
       in the day of his anger.

²Without pity the Lord has swallowed up
       all the dwellings of Jacob;
   in his wrath he has torn down
       the strongholds of the Daughter of Judah.
   He has brought her kingdom and its princes
       down to the ground in dishonor.

³In fierce anger he has cut off
       every horn^c of Israel.
   He has withdrawn his right hand
       at the approach of the enemy.
   He has burned in Jacob like a flaming fire
       that consumes everything around it.

⁴Like an enemy he has strung his bow;
       his right hand is ready.
   Like a foe he has slain
       all who were pleasing to the eye;
   he has poured out his wrath like fire
       on the tent of the Daughter of Zion.

⁵The Lord is like an enemy;
       he has swallowed up Israel.
   He has swallowed up all her palaces
       and destroyed her strongholds.
   He has multiplied mourning and lamentation
       for the Daughter of Judah.

⁶He has laid waste his dwelling like a garden;
       he has destroyed his place of meeting.
   The Lᴏʀᴅ has made Zion forget
       her appointed feasts and her Sabbaths;
   in his fierce anger he has spurned
       both king and priest.

⁷The Lord has rejected his altar
       and abandoned his sanctuary.
   He has handed over to the enemy
       the walls of her palaces;
   they have raised a shout in the house of the Lᴏʀᴅ
       as on the day of an appointed feast.

⁸The Lᴏʀᴅ determined to tear down
       the wall around the Daughter of Zion.
   He stretched out a measuring line
       and did not withhold his hand from destroying.

^aThis chapter is an acrostic poem, the verses of which begin with the successive letters of the Hebrew alphabet.   ^b1 Or *How the Lord in his anger / has treated the Daughter of Zion with contempt*   ^c3 Or */ all the strength*; or *every king*; *horn* here symbolizes strength.

He made ramparts and walls lament;
    together they wasted away.

9Her gates have sunk into the ground;
    their bars he has broken and destroyed.
Her king and her princes are exiled among the nations,
    the law is no more,
and her prophets no longer find
    visions from the LORD.

10The elders of the Daughter of Zion
    sit on the ground in silence;
they have sprinkled dust on their heads
    and put on sackcloth.
The young women of Jerusalem
    have bowed their heads to the ground.

11My eyes fail from weeping,
    I am in torment within,
my heart is poured out on the ground
    because my people are destroyed,
because children and infants faint
    in the streets of the city.

12They say to their mothers,
    "Where is bread and wine?"
as they faint like wounded men
    in the streets of the city,
as their lives ebb away
    in their mothers' arms.

13What can I say for you?
    With what can I compare you,
    O Daughter of Jerusalem?
To what can I liken you,
    that I may comfort you,
    O Virgin Daughter of Zion?
Your wound is as deep as the sea.
    Who can heal you?

14The visions of your prophets
    were false and worthless;
they did not expose your sin
    to ward off your captivity.
The oracles they gave you
    were false and misleading.

15All who pass your way
    clap their hands at you;
they scoff and shake their heads
    at the Daughter of Jerusalem:
"Is this the city that was called
    the perfection of beauty,
    the joy of the whole earth?"

16All your enemies open their mouths
    wide against you;

they scoff and gnash their teeth
  and say, "We have swallowed her up.
This is the day we have waited for;
  we have lived to see it."

¹⁷The LORD has done what he planned;
  he has fulfilled his word,
  which he decreed long ago.
He has overthrown you without pity,
  he has let the enemy gloat over you,
  he has exalted the horn^a of your foes.

¹⁸The hearts of the people
  cry out to the Lord.
O wall of the Daughter of Zion,
  let your tears flow like a river
    day and night;
give yourself no relief,
  your eyes no rest.

¹⁹Arise, cry out in the night,
  as the watches of the night begin;
pour out your heart like water
  in the presence of the Lord.
Lift up your hands to him
  for the lives of your children,
who faint from hunger
  at the head of every street.

²⁰"Look, O LORD, and consider:
  Whom have you ever treated like this?
Should women eat their offspring,
  the children they have cared for?
Should priest and prophet be killed
  in the sanctuary of the Lord?

²¹"Young and old lie together
  in the dust of the streets;
my young men and maidens
  have fallen by the sword.
You have slain them in the day of your anger;
  you have slaughtered them without pity.

²²"As you summon to a feast day,
  so you summoned against me terrors on every side.
In the day of the LORD's anger
  no one escaped or survived;
those I cared for and reared,
  my enemy has destroyed."

3^b I am the man who has seen affliction
  by the rod of his wrath.
²He has driven me away and made me walk
  in darkness rather than light;

---

^a 17 *Horn* here symbolizes strength.   ^bThis chapter is an acrostic poem; the verses of each stanza begin with the successive letters of the Hebrew alphabet, and the verses within each stanza begin with the same letter.

³indeed, he has turned his hand against me
again and again, all day long.

⁴He has made my skin and my flesh grow old
and has broken my bones.
⁵He has besieged me and surrounded me
with bitterness and hardship.
⁶He has made me dwell in darkness
like those long dead.

⁷He has walled me in so I cannot escape;
he has weighed me down with chains.
⁸Even when I call out or cry for help,
he shuts out my prayer.
⁹He has barred my way with blocks of stone;
he has made my paths crooked.

¹⁰Like a bear lying in wait,
like a lion in hiding,
¹¹he dragged me from the path and mangled me
and left me without help.
¹²He drew his bow
and made me the target for his arrows.

¹³He pierced my heart
with arrows from his quiver.
¹⁴I became the laughingstock of all my people;
they mock me in song all day long.
¹⁵He has filled me with bitter herbs
and sated me with gall.

¹⁶He has broken my teeth with gravel;
he has trampled me in the dust.
¹⁷I have been deprived of peace;
I have forgotten what prosperity is.
¹⁸So I say, "My splendor is gone
and all that I had hoped from the LORD."

¹⁹I remember my affliction and my wandering,
the bitterness and the gall.
²⁰I well remember them,
and my soul is downcast within me.
²¹Yet this I call to mind
and therefore I have hope:

²²Because of the LORD's great love we are not consumed,
for his compassions never fail.
²³They are new every morning;
great is your faithfulness.
²⁴I say to myself, "The LORD is my portion;
therefore I will wait for him."

²⁵The LORD is good to those whose hope is in him,
to the one who seeks him;
²⁶it is good to wait quietly
for the salvation of the LORD.

27It is good for a man to bear the yoke
    while he is young.

28Let him sit alone in silence,
    for the LORD has laid it on him.
29Let him bury his face in the dust—
    there may yet be hope.
30Let him offer his cheek to one who would strike him,
    and let him be filled with disgrace.

31For men are not cast off
    by the Lord forever.
32Though he brings grief, he will
        show compassion,
    so great is his unfailing love.
33For he does not willingly bring
        affliction
    or grief to the children of men.

34To crush underfoot
    all prisoners in the land,
35to deny a man his rights
    before the Most High,
36to deprive a man of justice—
    would not the Lord see such
        things?

37Who can speak and have it
        happen
    if the Lord has not decreed it?
38Is it not from the mouth of the
        Most High
    that both calamities and good
        things come?
39Why should any living man
        complain
    when punished for his sins?

40Let us examine our ways and test
        them,
    and let us return to the LORD.
41Let us lift up our hearts and our
        hands
    to God in heaven, and say:
42"We have sinned and rebelled
    and you have not forgiven.

43"You have covered yourself with anger and pursued us;
    you have slain without pity.
44You have covered yourself with a cloud
    so that no prayer can get through.
45You have made us scum and refuse
    among the nations.

46"All our enemies have opened their mouths
    wide against us.

🖩 ▓▓▓▓▓▓ **DISCOVERING GOD** ▓▓▓▓▓▓ ⬅

3:19–23
Life with God

The prophet Jeremiah wrote Lamentations to record his overwhelming grief as he scanned the desolation of Jerusalem (see Jeremiah chapter 52 [page 1072]). His people had not listened to God's warnings, and now the once-proud city sat in ruins, its temple destroyed and its inhabitants in exile. In spite of the seemingly hopeless situation, however, two things gave the prophet hope—God's compassion and love.

Jeremiah knew that God would keep his promise to restore his people to Jerusalem. He knew that God would preserve a remnant of the Jewish people who would return and rebuild the ruined walls. (The books of Ezra and Nehemiah tell the story of God's fulfilled promises to Israel.) Jeremiah relied on the strength of God's promises, which he found consistently faithful and uplifting.

In the same way, God's promises to us are "new every morning." God is faithful, and promises to care for us even when our world caves in upon us. We need only to rely on him for the strength to get through each day—especially on our most difficult days.

Jeremiah's optimism can be ours today. After all, these aren't the theoretical words of an academic theologian; they're the testimony of a real-life sufferer who found God's goodness in spite of his pain.

47We have suffered terror and pitfalls,
   ruin and destruction."
48Streams of tears flow from my eyes
   because my people are destroyed.

49My eyes will flow unceasingly,
   without relief,
50until the LORD looks down
   from heaven and sees.
51What I see brings grief to my soul
   because of all the women of my city.

52Those who were my enemies without cause
   hunted me like a bird.
53They tried to end my life in a pit
   and threw stones at me;
54the waters closed over my head,
   and I thought I was about to be cut off.

55I called on your name, O LORD,
   from the depths of the pit.
56You heard my plea: "Do not close your ears
   to my cry for relief."
57You came near when I called you,
   and you said, "Do not fear."

58O Lord, you took up my case;
   you redeemed my life.
59You have seen, O LORD, the wrong done to me.
   Uphold my cause!
60You have seen the depth of their vengeance,
   all their plots against me.

61O LORD, you have heard their insults,
   all their plots against me—
62what my enemies whisper and mutter
   against me all day long.
63Look at them! Sitting or standing,
   they mock me in their songs.

64Pay them back what they deserve, O LORD,
   for what their hands have done.
65Put a veil over their hearts,
   and may your curse be on them!
66Pursue them in anger and destroy them
   from under the heavens of the LORD.

4ᵃ   How the gold has lost its luster,
   the fine gold become dull!
The sacred gems are scattered
   at the head of every street.

2How the precious sons of Zion,

ᵃThis chapter is an acrostic poem, the verses of which begin with the successive letters of the Hebrew alphabet.

once worth their weight in gold,
are now considered as pots of clay,
the work of a potter's hands!

³Even jackals offer their breasts
to nurse their young,
but my people have become heartless
like ostriches in the desert.

⁴Because of thirst the infant's tongue
sticks to the roof of its mouth;
the children beg for bread,
but no one gives it to them.

⁵Those who once ate delicacies
are destitute in the streets.
Those nurtured in purple
now lie on ash heaps.

⁶The punishment of my people
is greater than that of Sodom,
which was overthrown in a moment
without a hand turned to help her.

⁷Their princes were brighter than snow
and whiter than milk,
their bodies more ruddy than rubies,
their appearance like sapphires.ᵃ

⁸But now they are blacker than soot;
they are not recognized in the streets.
Their skin has shriveled on their bones;
it has become as dry as a stick.

⁹Those killed by the sword are better off
than those who die of famine;
racked with hunger, they waste away
for lack of food from the field.

¹⁰With their own hands compassionate women
have cooked their own children,
who became their food
when my people were destroyed.

¹¹The Lᴏʀᴅ has given full vent to his wrath;
he has poured out his fierce anger.
He kindled a fire in Zion
that consumed her foundations.

¹²The kings of the earth did not believe,
nor did any of the world's people,
that enemies and foes could enter
the gates of Jerusalem.

¹³But it happened because of the sins of her prophets

ᵃ 7 Or *lapis lazuli*

and the iniquities of her priests,
who shed within her
the blood of the righteous.

[14]Now they grope through the streets
like men who are blind.
They are so defiled with blood
that no one dares to touch their garments.

[15]"Go away! You are unclean!" men cry to them.
"Away! Away! Don't touch us!"
When they flee and wander about,
people among the nations say,
"They can stay here no longer."

[16]The Lord himself has scattered them;
he no longer watches over them.
The priests are shown no honor,
the elders no favor.

[17]Moreover, our eyes failed,
looking in vain for help;
from our towers we watched
for a nation that could not save us.

[18]Men stalked us at every step,
so we could not walk in our streets.
Our end was near, our days were numbered,
for our end had come.

[19]Our pursuers were swifter
than eagles in the sky;
they chased us over the mountains
and lay in wait for us in the desert.

[20]The Lord's anointed, our very life breath,
was caught in their traps.
We thought that under his shadow
we would live among the nations.

[21]Rejoice and be glad, O Daughter of Edom,
you who live in the land of Uz.
But to you also the cup will be passed;
you will be drunk and stripped naked.

[22]O Daughter of Zion, your punishment will end;
he will not prolong your exile.
But, O Daughter of Edom, he will punish your sin
and expose your wickedness.

5 Remember, O Lord, what has happened to us;
look, and see our disgrace.
[2]Our inheritance has been turned over to aliens,
our homes to foreigners.

³We have become orphans and fatherless,
   our mothers like widows.
⁴We must buy the water we drink;
   our wood can be had only at a price.
⁵Those who pursue us are at our heels;
   we are weary and find no rest.
⁶We submitted to Egypt and Assyria
   to get enough bread.
⁷Our fathers sinned and are no more,
   and we bear their punishment.
⁸Slaves rule over us,
   and there is none to free us from their hands.
⁹We get our bread at the risk of our lives
   because of the sword in the desert.
¹⁰Our skin is hot as an oven,
   feverish from hunger.
¹¹Women have been ravished in Zion,
   and virgins in the towns of Judah.
¹²Princes have been hung up by their hands;
   elders are shown no respect.
¹³Young men toil at the millstones;
   boys stagger under loads of wood.
¹⁴The elders are gone from the city gate;
   the young men have stopped their music.
¹⁵Joy is gone from our hearts;
   our dancing has turned to mourning.
¹⁶The crown has fallen from our head.
   Woe to us, for we have sinned!
¹⁷Because of this our hearts are faint,
   because of these things our eyes grow dim
¹⁸for Mount Zion, which lies desolate,
   with jackals prowling over it.

¹⁹You, O Lord, reign forever;
   your throne endures from generation to generation.
²⁰Why do you always forget us?
   Why do you forsake us so long?
²¹Restore us to yourself, O Lord, that we may return;
   renew our days as of old
²²unless you have utterly rejected us
   and are angry with us beyond measure.

Introduction

THE BOTTOM LINE

The people of Israel lived in exile in the land of Babylon. Wrenched from their homeland, defeated and oppressed, life had lost most of its purpose and joy. Ezekiel and Daniel spoke to the people during this time through their writings, instilling hope and telling amazing stories of God's awesome power and protection for his people. Maybe you feel oppressed at times, too. Perhaps your daily stresses sometimes make you feel that you'd be better off just staying in bed all day with the shades pulled down. The amazing accounts in these books give us a glimpse of several people who didn't let their situation get them down. They moved ahead, trusting that God would bless them. And he did. Read on to find a timeless message of God's love for those who follow him, and of God's power over the events of our lives.

CENTRAL IDEAS

- God would rather forgive us than judge us.
- God remains faithful to us during times when we aren't faithful to him.
- God has control over all the events in this world; he can and does use evil circumstances to accomplish greater good.
- God helps those who are loyal to him to get through any difficult time.

TITLES

These two books recount the amazing stories of the lives of these two individuals.

AUTHORS AND READERS

Ezekiel was a priest who was taken to Babylon when Jerusalem was captured. He wrote the accounts of his visions to the exiled people of Israel. Daniel also wrote his book to the exiles in Babylon to encourage them with a reminder that God controls all the events of this world.

TIME LINE

625 BC	600	575	550	525	500
Greece's currency changes from grain to metal, which is easier to carry and doesn't mold (625 B.C.)	Ezekiel's ministry to Judah (c. 593–571 B.C.)	Book of Ezekiel written (c. 571 B.C.)	Milo of Crotona is crowned six times at the Olympic Games (536 B.C.)	Book of Daniel written (c. 536–530 B.C.)	
	Daniel taken captive to Babylon (c. 605 B.C.)	Nebuchadnezzar II builds Babylon's "hanging gardens," one of the seven wonders of the ancient world (580 B.C.)	Thales of Miletus writes that magnets attract iron (c. 545 B.C.)		

It didn't seem like any big deal really. I just needed directions from my house to a cabinetmaker's shop on the other side of town.

The lady on the phone had a friendly voice. Her confidence reassured me as she directed me west on a major freeway "until you're way out of town." She told me to "exit at the Forest Grove sign and then go left over the freeway."

"So far, so good," I thought.

And then she did something totally unsettling.

"Hey, Bob!" I heard her yell at someone in the office. "Does he go left or right on that street? You know, the one out in the middle of nowhere!"

"Oh great!" I said to myself. "She doesn't know what she's talking about."

From that moment until the time I pulled into the parking lot of the cabinet shop, I didn't know whether I should trust that lady. What if she was unwittingly directing me to Canada?

What if she was unwittingly directing me to Canada?

We've all faced situations in which we had to trust in people when we weren't sure about their reliability. At such times we wonder, "Should I trust them and keep on driving or give up?"

Sometimes we even feel that way about God. When everything is going wrong, it's natural to wonder if God can be trusted. Will he really get me through this mess? Should I trust in him or take off on my own?

The prophets Ezekiel and Daniel spoke to a nation wrestling with these issues. In fact, three of Daniel's friends faced exactly that question. Along with Daniel they had been taken captive to Babylon. While there, they had to make a tough choice: trust God and possibly lose their lives or denounce God so they could live. Their response provides an inspiring example of faith being put into action—and being rewarded as a result. Turn to Daniel chapter 3 (page 1149) for their story.

EZEKIEL

The Living Creatures and the Glory of the LORD

1 In the[a] thirtieth year, in the fourth month on the fifth day, while I was among the exiles by the Kebar River, the heavens were opened and I saw visions of God.

²On the fifth of the month—it was the fifth year of the exile of King Jehoiachin— ³the word of the LORD came to Ezekiel the priest, the son of Buzi,[b] by the Kebar River in the land of the Babylonians.[c] There the hand of the LORD was upon him.

⁴I looked, and I saw a windstorm coming out of the north—an immense cloud with flashing lightning and surrounded by brilliant light. The center of the fire looked like glowing metal, ⁵and in the fire was what looked like four living creatures. In appearance their form was that of a man, ⁶but each of them had four faces and four wings. ⁷Their legs were straight; their feet were like those of a calf and gleamed like burnished bronze. ⁸Under their wings on their four sides they had the hands of a man. All four of them had faces and wings, ⁹and their wings touched one another. Each one went straight ahead; they did not turn as they moved.

¹⁰Their faces looked like this: Each of the four had the face of a man, and on the right side each had the face of a lion, and on the left the face of an ox; each also had the face of an eagle. ¹¹Such were their faces. Their wings were spread out upward; each had two wings, one touching the wing of another creature on either side, and two wings covering its body. ¹²Each one went straight ahead. Wherever the spirit would go, they would go, without turning as they went. ¹³The appearance of the living creatures was like burning coals of fire or like torches. Fire moved back and forth among the creatures; it was bright, and lightning flashed out of it. ¹⁴The creatures sped back and forth like flashes of lightning.

¹⁵As I looked at the living creatures, I saw a wheel on the ground beside each creature with its four faces. ¹⁶This was the appearance and structure of the wheels: They sparkled like chrysolite, and all four looked alike. Each appeared to be made like a wheel intersecting a wheel. ¹⁷As they moved, they would go in any one of the four directions the creatures faced; the wheels did not turn about[d] as the creatures went. ¹⁸Their rims were high and awesome, and all four rims were full of eyes all around.

¹⁹When the living creatures moved, the wheels beside them moved; and when the living creatures rose from the ground, the wheels also rose. ²⁰Wherever the spirit would go, they would go, and the wheels would rise along with them, because the spirit of the living creatures was in the wheels. ²¹When the creatures moved, they also moved; when the creatures stood still, they also stood still; and when the creatures rose from the ground, the wheels rose along with them, because the spirit of the living creatures was in the wheels.

²²Spread out above the heads of the living creatures was what looked like an expanse, sparkling like ice, and awesome. ²³Under the expanse their wings were stretched out one toward the other, and each had two wings covering its body. ²⁴When the creatures moved, I heard the sound of their wings, like the roar of rushing waters, like the voice of the Almighty,[e] like the tumult of an army. When they stood still, they lowered their wings.

²⁵Then there came a voice from above the expanse over their heads as they stood with

lowered wings. [26]Above the expanse over their heads was what looked like a throne of sapphire,[a] and high above on the throne was a figure like that of a man. [27]I saw that from what appeared to be his waist up he looked like glowing metal, as if full of fire, and that from there down he looked like fire; and brilliant light surrounded him. [28]Like the appearance of a rainbow in the clouds on a rainy day, so was the radiance around him.

This was the appearance of the likeness of the glory of the LORD. When I saw it, I fell facedown, and I heard the voice of one speaking.

Ezekiel's Call

2 He said to me, "Son of man, stand up on your feet and I will speak to you." [2]As he spoke, the Spirit came into me and raised me to my feet, and I heard him speaking to me.

[3]He said: "Son of man, I am sending you to the Israelites, to a rebellious nation that has rebelled against me; they and their fathers have been in revolt against me to this very day. [4]The people to whom I am sending you are obstinate and stubborn. Say to them, 'This is what the Sovereign LORD says.' [5]And whether they listen or fail to listen—for they are a rebellious house—they will know that a prophet has been among them. [6]And you, son of man, do not be afraid of them or their words. Do not be afraid, though briers and thorns are all around you and you live among scorpions. Do not be afraid of what they say or terrified by them, though they are a rebellious house. [7]You must speak my words to them, whether they listen or fail to listen, for they are rebellious. [8]But you, son of man, listen to what I say to you. Do not rebel like that rebellious house; open your mouth and eat what I give you."

[9]Then I looked, and I saw a hand stretched out to me. In it was a scroll, [10]which he unrolled before me. On both sides of it were written words of lament and mourning and woe.

3 And he said to me, "Son of man, eat what is before you, eat this scroll; then go and speak to the house of Israel." [2]So I opened my mouth, and he gave me the scroll to eat.

[3]Then he said to me, "Son of man, eat this scroll I am giving you and fill your stomach with it." So I ate it, and it tasted as sweet as honey in my mouth.

[4]He then said to me: "Son of man, go now to the house of Israel and speak my words to them. [5]You are not being sent to a people of obscure speech and difficult language, but to the house of Israel— [6]not to many peoples of obscure speech and difficult language, whose words you cannot understand. Surely if I had sent you to them, they would have listened to you. [7]But the house of Israel is not willing to listen to you because they are not willing to listen to me, for the whole house of Israel is hardened and obstinate. [8]But I will make you as unyielding and hardened as they are. [9]I will make your forehead like the hardest stone, harder than flint. Do not be afraid of them or terrified by them, though they are a rebellious house."

[10]And he said to me, "Son of man, listen carefully and take to heart all the words I speak to you. [11]Go now to your countrymen in exile and speak to them. Say to them, 'This is what the Sovereign LORD says,' whether they listen or fail to listen."

[12]Then the Spirit lifted me up, and I heard behind me a loud rumbling sound—May the glory of the LORD be praised in his dwelling place!— [13]the sound of the wings of the living creatures brushing against each other and the sound of the wheels beside them, a loud rumbling sound. [14]The Spirit then lifted me up and took me away, and I went in bitterness and in the anger of my spirit, with the strong hand of the LORD upon me. [15]I came to the exiles who lived at Tel Abib near the Kebar River. And there, where they were living, I sat among them for seven days—overwhelmed.

[a]26 Or lapis lazuli

Warning to Israel

¹⁶At the end of seven days the word of the LORD came to me: ¹⁷"Son of man, I have made you a watchman for the house of Israel; so hear the word I speak and give them warning from me. ¹⁸When I say to a wicked man, 'You will surely die,' and you do not warn him or speak out to dissuade him from his evil ways in order to save his life, that wicked man will die for*ᵃ* his sin, and I will hold you accountable for his blood. ¹⁹But if you do warn the wicked man and he does not turn from his wickedness or from his evil ways, he will die for his sin; but you will have saved yourself.

²⁰"Again, when a righteous man turns from his righteousness and does evil, and I put a stumbling block before him, he will die. Since you did not warn him, he will die for his sin. The righteous things he did will not be remembered, and I will hold you accountable for his blood. ²¹But if you do warn the righteous man not to sin and he does not sin, he will surely live because he took warning, and you will have saved yourself."

²²The hand of the LORD was upon me there, and he said to me, "Get up and go out to the plain, and there I will speak to you." ²³So I got up and went out to the plain. And the glory of the LORD was standing there, like the glory I had seen by the Kebar River, and I fell facedown.

²⁴Then the Spirit came into me and raised me to my feet. He spoke to me and said: "Go, shut yourself inside your house. ²⁵And you, son of man, they will tie with ropes; you will be bound so that you cannot go out among the people. ²⁶I will make your tongue stick to the roof of your mouth so that you will be silent and unable to rebuke them, though they are a rebellious house. ²⁷But when I speak to you, I will open your mouth and you shall say to them, 'This is what the Sovereign LORD says.' Whoever will listen let him listen, and whoever will refuse let him refuse; for they are a rebellious house.

Siege of Jerusalem Symbolized

4 "Now, son of man, take a clay tablet, put it in front of you and draw the city of Jerusalem on it. ²Then lay siege to it: Erect siege works against it, build a ramp up to it, set up camps against it and put battering rams around it. ³Then take an iron pan, place it as an iron wall between you and the city and turn your face toward it. It will be under siege, and you shall besiege it. This will be a sign to the house of Israel.

⁴"Then lie on your left side and put the sin of the house of Israel upon yourself.*ᵇ* You are to bear their sin for the number of days you lie on your side. ⁵I have assigned you the same number of days as the years of their sin. So for 390 days you will bear the sin of the house of Israel.

⁶"After you have finished this, lie down again, this time on your right side, and bear the sin of the house of Judah. I have assigned you 40 days, a day for each year. ⁷Turn your face toward the siege of Jerusalem and with bared arm prophesy against her. ⁸I will tie you up with ropes so that you cannot turn from one side to the other until you have finished the days of your siege.

⁹"Take wheat and barley, beans and lentils, millet and spelt; put them in a storage jar and use them to make bread for yourself. You are to eat it during the 390 days you lie on your side. ¹⁰Weigh out twenty shekels*ᶜ* of food to eat each day and eat it at set times. ¹¹Also measure out a sixth of a hin*ᵈ* of water and drink it at set times. ¹²Eat the food as you would a barley cake; bake it in the sight of the people, using human excrement for fuel." ¹³The LORD said, "In this way the people of Israel will eat defiled food among the nations where I will drive them."

¹⁴Then I said, "Not so, Sovereign LORD! I have never defiled myself. From my youth until now I have never eaten anything found dead or torn by wild animals. No unclean meat has ever entered my mouth."

ᵃ18 Or in; also in verses 19 and 20   *ᵇ4* Or your side   *ᶜ10* That is, about 8 ounces (about 0.2 kilogram)
ᵈ11 That is, about 2/3 quart (about 0.6 liter)

¹⁵"Very well," he said, "I will let you bake your bread over cow manure instead of human excrement."

¹⁶He then said to me: "Son of man, I will cut off the supply of food in Jerusalem. The people will eat rationed food in anxiety and drink rationed water in despair, ¹⁷for food and water will be scarce. They will be appalled at the sight of each other and will waste away because of*ª* their sin.

5 "Now, son of man, take a sharp sword and use it as a barber's razor to shave your head and your beard. Then take a set of scales and divide up the hair. ²When the days of your siege come to an end, burn a third of the hair with fire inside the city. Take a third and strike it with the sword all around the city. And scatter a third to the wind. For I will pursue them with drawn sword. ³But take a few strands of hair and tuck them away in the folds of your garment. ⁴Again, take a few of these and throw them into the fire and burn them up. A fire will spread from there to the whole house of Israel.

⁵"This is what the Sovereign LORD says: This is Jerusalem, which I have set in the center of the nations, with countries all around her. ⁶Yet in her wickedness she has rebelled against my laws and decrees more than the nations and countries around her. She has rejected my laws and has not followed my decrees.

⁷"Therefore this is what the Sovereign LORD says: You have been more unruly than the nations around you and have not followed my decrees or kept my laws. You have not even*ᵇ* conformed to the standards of the nations around you.

⁸"Therefore this is what the Sovereign LORD says: I myself am against you, Jerusalem, and I will inflict punishment on you in the sight of the nations. ⁹Because of all your detestable idols, I will do to you what I have never done before and will never do again. ¹⁰Therefore in your midst fathers will eat their children, and children will eat their fathers. I will inflict punishment on you and will scatter all your survivors to the winds. ¹¹Therefore as surely as I live, declares the Sovereign LORD, because you have defiled my sanctuary with all your vile images and detestable practices, I myself will withdraw my favor; I will not look on you with pity or spare you. ¹²A third of your people will die of the plague or perish by famine inside you; a third will fall by the sword outside your walls; and a third I will scatter to the winds and pursue with drawn sword.

¹³"Then my anger will cease and my wrath against them will subside, and I will be avenged. And when I have spent my wrath upon them, they will know that I the LORD have spoken in my zeal.

¹⁴"I will make you a ruin and a reproach among the nations around you, in the sight of all who pass by. ¹⁵You will be a reproach and a taunt, a warning and an object of horror to the nations around you when I inflict punishment on you in anger and in wrath and with stinging rebuke. I the LORD have spoken. ¹⁶When I shoot at you with my deadly and destructive arrows of famine, I will shoot to destroy you. I will bring more and more

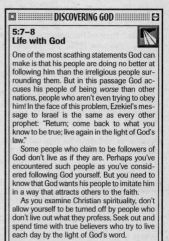

▣ ▦▦▦▦ DISCOVERING GOD ▦▦▦ ⬔

5:7–8
Life with God

One of the most scathing statements God can make is that his people are doing no better at following him than the irreligious people surrounding them. But in this passage God accuses his people of being *worse* than other nations, people who aren't even trying to obey him! In the face of this problem, Ezekiel's message to Israel is the same as every other prophet: "Return; come back to what you know to be true; live again in the light of God's law."

Some people who claim to be followers of God don't live as if they are. Perhaps you've encountered such people as you've considered following God yourself. But you need to know that God wants his people to imitate him in a way that attracts others to the faith.

As you examine Christian spirituality, don't allow yourself to be turned off by people who don't live out what they profess. Seek out and spend time with true believers who try to live each day by the light of God's word.

ª17 Or away in   *ᵇ7 Most Hebrew manuscripts; some Hebrew manuscripts and Syriac You have*

famine upon you and cut off your supply of food. ¹⁷I will send famine and wild beasts against you, and they will leave you childless. Plague and bloodshed will sweep through you, and I will bring the sword against you. I the LORD have spoken."

A Prophecy Against the Mountains of Israel

6 The word of the LORD came to me: ²"Son of man, set your face against the mountains of Israel; prophesy against them ³and say: 'O mountains of Israel, hear the word of the Sovereign LORD. This is what the Sovereign LORD says to the mountains and hills, to the ravines and valleys: I am about to bring a sword against you, and I will destroy your high places. ⁴Your altars will be demolished and your incense altars will be smashed; and I will slay your people in front of your idols. ⁵I will lay the dead bodies of the Israelites in front of their idols, and I will scatter your bones around your altars. ⁶Wherever you live, the towns will be laid waste and the high places demolished, so that your altars will be laid waste and devastated, your idols smashed and ruined, your incense altars broken down, and what you have made wiped out. ⁷Your people will fall slain among you, and you will know that I am the LORD.

⁸"'But I will spare some, for some of you will escape the sword when you are scattered among the lands and nations. ⁹Then in the nations where they have been carried captive, those who escape will remember me—how I have been grieved by their adulterous hearts, which have turned away from me, and by their eyes, which have lusted after their idols. They will loathe themselves for the evil they have done and for all their detestable practices. ¹⁰And they will know that I am the LORD; I did not threaten in vain to bring this calamity on them.

¹¹"This is what the Sovereign LORD says: Strike your hands together and stamp your feet and cry out "Alas!" because of all the wicked and detestable practices of the house of Israel, for they will fall by the sword, famine and plague. ¹²He that is far away will die of the plague, and he that is near will fall by the sword, and he that survives and is spared will die of famine. So will I spend my wrath upon them. ¹³And they will know that I am the LORD, when their people lie slain among their idols around their altars, on every high hill and on all the mountaintops, under every spreading tree and every leafy oak—places where they offered fragrant incense to all their idols. ¹⁴And I will stretch out my hand against them and make the land a desolate waste from the desert to Diblah[a]—wherever they live. Then they will know that I am the LORD.'"

The End Has Come

7 The word of the LORD came to me: ²"Son of man, this is what the Sovereign LORD says to the land of Israel: The end! The end has come upon the four corners of the land. ³The end is now upon you and I will unleash my anger against you. I will judge you according to your conduct and repay you for all your detestable practices. ⁴I will not look on you with pity or spare you; I will surely repay you for your conduct and the detestable practices among you. Then you will know that I am the LORD.

⁵"This is what the Sovereign LORD says: Disaster! An unheard-of[b] disaster is coming. ⁶The end has come! The end has come! It has roused itself against you. It has come! ⁷Doom has come upon you—you who dwell in the land. The time has come, the day is near; there is panic, not joy, upon the mountains. ⁸I am about to pour out my wrath on you and spend my anger against you; I will judge you according to your conduct and repay you for all your detestable practices. ⁹I will not look on you with pity or spare you; I will repay you in accordance with your conduct and the detestable practices among you. Then you will know that it is I the LORD who strikes the blow.

¹⁰"The day is here! It has come! Doom has burst forth, the rod has budded, arrogance has blossomed! ¹¹Violence has grown into[c] a rod to punish wickedness; none of the

a 14 Most Hebrew manuscripts; a few Hebrew manuscripts *Riblah* and Syriac   *Disaster after*   *c 11* Or *The violent one has become*   *b 5* Most Hebrew manuscripts; some Hebrew manuscripts

people will be left, none of that crowd—no wealth, nothing of value. ¹²The time has come, the day has arrived. Let not the buyer rejoice nor the seller grieve, for wrath is upon the whole crowd. ¹³The seller will not recover the land he has sold as long as both of them live, for the vision concerning the whole crowd will not be reversed. Because of their sins, not one of them will preserve his life. ¹⁴Though they blow the trumpet and get everything ready, no one will go into battle, for my wrath is upon the whole crowd.

¹⁵"Outside is the sword, inside are plague and famine; those in the country will die by the sword, and those in the city will be devoured by famine and plague. ¹⁶All who survive and escape will be in the mountains, moaning like doves of the valleys, each because of his sins. ¹⁷Every hand will go limp, and every knee will become as weak as water. ¹⁸They will put on sackcloth and be clothed with terror. Their faces will be covered with shame and their heads will be shaved. ¹⁹They will throw their silver into the streets, and their gold will be an unclean thing. Their silver and gold will not be able to save them in the day of the LORD's wrath. They will not satisfy their hunger or fill their stomachs with it, for it has made them stumble into sin. ²⁰They were proud of their beautiful jewelry and used it to make their detestable idols and vile images. Therefore I will turn these into an unclean thing for them. ²¹I will hand it all over as plunder to foreigners and as loot to the wicked of the earth, and they will defile it. ²²I will turn my face away from them, and they will desecrate my treasured place; robbers will enter it and desecrate it.

²³"Prepare chains, because the land is full of bloodshed and the city is full of violence. ²⁴I will bring the most wicked of the nations to take possession of their houses; I will put an end to the pride of the mighty, and their sanctuaries will be desecrated. ²⁵When terror comes, they will seek peace, but there will be none. ²⁶Calamity upon calamity will come, and rumor upon rumor. They will try to get a vision from the prophet; the teaching of the law by the priest will be lost, as will the counsel of the elders. ²⁷The king will mourn, the prince will be clothed with despair, and the hands of the people of the land will tremble. I will deal with them according to their conduct, and by their own standards I will judge them. Then they will know that I am the LORD."

Idolatry in the Temple

8 In the sixth year, in the sixth month on the fifth day, while I was sitting in my house and the elders of Judah were sitting before me, the hand of the Sovereign LORD came upon me there. ²I looked, and I saw a figure like that of a man.ᵃ From what appeared to be his waist down he was like fire, and from there up his appearance was as bright as glowing metal. ³He stretched out what looked like a hand and took me by the hair of my head. The Spirit lifted me up between earth and heaven and in visions of God he took me to Jerusalem, to the entrance to the north gate of the inner court, where the idol that provokes to jealousy stood. ⁴And there before me was the glory of the God of Israel, as in the vision I had seen in the plain.

⁵Then he said to me, "Son of man, look toward the north." So I looked, and in the entrance north of the gate of the altar I saw this idol of jealousy.

⁶And he said to me, "Son of man, do you see what they are doing—the utterly detestable things the house of Israel is doing here, things that will drive me far from my sanctuary? But you will see things that are even more detestable."

⁷Then he brought me to the entrance to the court. I looked, and I saw a hole in the wall. ⁸He said to me, "Son of man, now dig into the wall." So I dug into the wall and saw a doorway there.

⁹And he said to me, "Go in and see the wicked and detestable things they are doing here." ¹⁰So I went in and looked, and I saw portrayed all over the walls all kinds of crawling things and detestable animals and all the idols of the house of Israel. ¹¹In front of them stood seventy elders of the house of Israel, and Jaazaniah son of Shaphan was

ᵃ2 Or *saw a fiery figure*

standing among them. Each had a censer in his hand, and a fragrant cloud of incense was rising.

¹²He said to me, "Son of man, have you seen what the elders of the house of Israel are doing in the darkness, each at the shrine of his own idol? They say, 'The LORD does not see us; the LORD has forsaken the land.'" ¹³Again, he said, "You will see them doing things that are even more detestable."

¹⁴Then he brought me to the entrance to the north gate of the house of the LORD, and I saw women sitting there, mourning for Tammuz. ¹⁵He said to me, "Do you see this, son of man? You will see things that are even more detestable than this."

¹⁶He then brought me into the inner court of the house of the LORD, and there at the entrance to the temple, between the portico and the altar, were about twenty-five men. With their backs toward the temple of the LORD and their faces toward the east, they were bowing down to the sun in the east.

¹⁷He said to me, "Have you seen this, son of man? Is it a trivial matter for the house of Judah to do the detestable things they are doing here? Must they also fill the land with violence and continually provoke me to anger? Look at them putting the branch to their nose! ¹⁸Therefore I will deal with them in anger; I will not look on them with pity or spare them. Although they shout in my ears, I will not listen to them."

Idolaters Killed

9 Then I heard him call out in a loud voice, "Bring the guards of the city here, each with a weapon in his hand." ²And I saw six men coming from the direction of the upper gate, which faces north, each with a deadly weapon in his hand. With them was a man clothed in linen who had a writing kit at his side. They came in and stood beside the bronze altar.

³Now the glory of the God of Israel went up from above the cherubim, where it had been, and moved to the threshold of the temple. Then the LORD called to the man clothed in linen who had the writing kit at his side ⁴and said to him, "Go throughout the city of Jerusalem and put a mark on the foreheads of those who grieve and lament over all the detestable things that are done in it."

⁵As I listened, he said to the others, "Follow him through the city and kill, without showing pity or compassion. ⁶Slaughter old men, young men and maidens, women and children, but do not touch anyone who has the mark. Begin at my sanctuary." So they began with the elders who were in front of the temple.

⁷Then he said to them, "Defile the temple and fill the courts with the slain. Go!" So they went out and began killing throughout the city. ⁸While they were killing and I was left alone, I fell facedown, crying out, "Ah, Sovereign LORD! Are you going to destroy the entire remnant of Israel in this outpouring of your wrath on Jerusalem?"

⁹He answered me, "The sin of the house of Israel and Judah is exceedingly great; the land is full of bloodshed and the city is full of injustice. They say, 'The LORD has forsaken the land; the LORD does not see.' ¹⁰So I will not look on them with pity or spare them, but I will bring down on their own heads what they have done."

¹¹Then the man in linen with the writing kit at his side brought back word, saying, "I have done as you commanded."

The Glory Departs From the Temple

10 I looked, and I saw the likeness of a throne of sapphire *a* above the expanse that was over the heads of the cherubim. ²The LORD said to the man clothed in linen, "Go in among the wheels beneath the cherubim. Fill your hands with burning coals from among the cherubim and scatter them over the city." And as I watched, he went in.

³Now the cherubim were standing on the south side of the temple when the man went

a 1 Or lapis lazuli

in, and a cloud filled the inner court. ⁴Then the glory of the LORD rose from above the cherubim and moved to the threshold of the temple. The cloud filled the temple, and the court was full of the radiance of the glory of the LORD. ⁵The sound of the wings of the cherubim could be heard as far away as the outer court, like the voice of God Almighty*a* when he speaks.

⁶When the LORD commanded the man in linen, "Take fire from among the wheels, from among the cherubim," the man went in and stood beside a wheel. ⁷Then one of the cherubim reached out his hand to the fire that was among them. He took up some of it and put it into the hands of the man in linen, who took it and went out. ⁸(Under the wings of the cherubim could be seen what looked like the hands of a man.)

⁹I looked, and I saw beside the cherubim four wheels, one beside each of the cherubim; the wheels sparkled like chrysolite. ¹⁰As for their appearance, the four of them looked alike; each was like a wheel intersecting a wheel. ¹¹As they moved, they would go in any one of the four directions the cherubim faced; the wheels did not turn about*b* as the cherubim went. The cherubim went in whatever direction the head faced, without turning as they went. ¹²Their entire bodies, including their backs, their hands and their wings, were completely full of eyes, as were their four wheels. ¹³I heard the wheels being called "the whirling wheels." ¹⁴Each of the cherubim had four faces: One face was that of a cherub, the second the face of a man, the third the face of a lion, and the fourth the face of an eagle.

¹⁵Then the cherubim rose upward. These were the living creatures I had seen by the Kebar River. ¹⁶When the cherubim moved, the wheels beside them moved; and when the cherubim spread their wings to rise from the ground, the wheels did not leave their side. ¹⁷When the cherubim stood still, they also stood still; and when the cherubim rose, they rose with them, because the spirit of the living creatures was in them.

¹⁸Then the glory of the LORD departed from over the threshold of the temple and stopped above the cherubim. ¹⁹While I watched, the cherubim spread their wings and rose from the ground, and as they went, the wheels went with them. They stopped at the entrance to the east gate of the LORD's house, and the glory of the God of Israel was above them.

²⁰These were the living creatures I had seen beneath the God of Israel by the Kebar River, and I realized that they were cherubim. ²¹Each had four faces and four wings, and under their wings was what looked like the hands of a man. ²²Their faces had the same appearance as those I had seen by the Kebar River. Each one went straight ahead.

Judgment on Israel's Leaders

11 Then the Spirit lifted me up and brought me to the gate of the house of the LORD that faces east. There at the entrance to the gate were twenty-five men, and I saw among them Jaazaniah son of Azzur and Pelatiah son of Benaiah, leaders of the people. ²The LORD said to me, "Son of man, these are the men who are plotting evil and giving wicked advice in this city. ³They say, 'Will it not soon be time to build houses?*c* This city is a cooking pot, and we are the meat.' ⁴Therefore prophesy against them; prophesy, son of man."

⁵Then the Spirit of the LORD came upon me, and he told me to say: "This is what the LORD says: That is what you are saying, O house of Israel, but I know what is going through your mind. ⁶You have killed many people in this city and filled its streets with the dead.

⁷"Therefore this is what the Sovereign LORD says: The bodies you have thrown there are the meat and this city is the pot, but I will drive you out of it. ⁸You fear the sword, and the sword is what I will bring against you, declares the Sovereign LORD. ⁹I will drive you out of the city and hand you over to foreigners and inflict punishment on you. ¹⁰You will fall by the sword, and I will execute judgment on you at the borders of Israel. Then you will

a 5 Hebrew *El-Shaddai*   *b 11* Or *aside*   *c 3* Or *This is not the time to build houses.*

know that I am the LORD. ¹¹This city will not be a pot for you, nor will you be the meat in it; I will execute judgment on you at the borders of Israel. ¹²And you will know that I am the LORD, for you have not followed my decrees or kept my laws but have conformed to the standards of the nations around you."

¹³Now as I was prophesying, Pelatiah son of Benaiah died. Then I fell facedown and cried out in a loud voice, "Ah, Sovereign LORD! Will you completely destroy the remnant of Israel?"

¹⁴The word of the LORD came to me: ¹⁵"Son of man, your brothers—your brothers who are your blood relatives[a] and the whole house of Israel—are those of whom the people of Jerusalem have said, 'They are[b] far away from the LORD; this land was given to us as our possession.'

Promised Return of Israel

¹⁶"Therefore say: 'This is what the Sovereign LORD says: Although I sent them far away among the nations and scattered them among the countries, yet for a little while I have been a sanctuary for them in the countries where they have gone.'

¹⁷"Therefore say: 'This is what the Sovereign LORD says: I will gather you from the nations and bring you back from the countries where you have been scattered, and I will give you back the land of Israel again.'

¹⁸"They will return to it and remove all its vile images and detestable idols. ¹⁹I will give them an undivided heart and put a new spirit in them; I will remove from them their heart of stone and give them a heart of flesh. ²⁰Then they will follow my decrees and be careful to keep my laws. They will be my people, and I will be their God. ²¹But as for those whose hearts are devoted to their vile images and detestable idols, I will bring down on their own heads what they have done, declares the Sovereign LORD."

²²Then the cherubim, with the wheels beside them, spread their wings, and the glory of the God of Israel was above them. ²³The glory of the LORD went up from within the city and stopped above the mountain east of it. ²⁴The Spirit lifted me up and brought me to the exiles in Babylonia[c] in the vision given by the Spirit of God.

Then the vision I had seen went up from me, ²⁵and I told the exiles everything the LORD had shown me.

The Exile Symbolized

12 The word of the LORD came to me: ²"Son of man, you are living among a rebellious people. They have eyes to see but do not see and ears to hear but do not hear, for they are a rebellious people.

³"Therefore, son of man, pack your belongings for exile and in the daytime, as they watch, set out and go from where you are to another place. Perhaps they will understand, though they are a rebellious house. ⁴During the daytime, while they watch, bring out your belongings packed for exile. Then in the evening, while they are watching, go out like those who go into exile. ⁵While they watch, dig through the wall and take your belongings out through it. ⁶Put them on your shoulder as they are watching and carry them out at dusk. Cover your face so that you cannot see the land, for I have made you a sign to the house of Israel."

⁷So I did as I was commanded. During the day I brought out my things packed for exile. Then in the evening I dug through the wall with my hands. I took my belongings out at dusk, carrying them on my shoulders while they watched.

⁸In the morning the word of the LORD came to me: ⁹"Son of man, did not that rebellious house of Israel ask you, 'What are you doing?'

¹⁰"Say to them, 'This is what the Sovereign LORD says: This oracle concerns the prince

---

[a] 15 Or *are in exile with you* (see Septuagint and Syriac)   [b] 15 Or *those to whom the people of Jerusalem have said, 'Stay*
[c] 24 Or *Chaldea*

in Jerusalem and the whole house of Israel who are there.' ¹¹Say to them, 'I am a sign to you.'

"As I have done, so it will be done to them. They will go into exile as captives.

¹²"The prince among them will put his things on his shoulder at dusk and leave, and a hole will be dug in the wall for him to go through. He will cover his face so that he cannot see the land. ¹³I will spread my net for him, and he will be caught in my snare; I will bring him to Babylonia, the land of the Chaldeans, but he will not see it, and there he will die. ¹⁴I will scatter to the winds all those around him—his staff and all his troops—and I will pursue them with drawn sword.

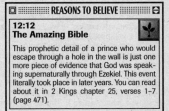

⫙⫙⫙⫙⫙ REASONS TO BELIEVE ⫙⫙⫙⫙⫙

12:12
The Amazing Bible

This prophetic detail of a prince who would escape through a hole in the wall is just one more piece of evidence that God was speaking supernaturally through Ezekiel. This event literally took place in later years. You can read about it in 2 Kings chapter 25, verses 1-7 (page 471).

¹⁵"They will know that I am the LORD, when I disperse them among the nations and scatter them through the countries. ¹⁶But I will spare a few of them from the sword, famine and plague, so that in the nations where they go they may acknowledge all their detestable practices. Then they will know that I am the LORD."

¹⁷The word of the LORD came to me: ¹⁸"Son of man, tremble as you eat your food, and shudder in fear as you drink your water. ¹⁹Say to the people of the land: 'This is what the Sovereign LORD says about those living in Jerusalem and in the land of Israel: They will eat their food in anxiety and drink their water in despair, for their land will be stripped of everything in it because of the violence of all who live there. ²⁰The inhabited towns will be laid waste and the land will be desolate. Then you will know that I am the LORD.'"

²¹The word of the LORD came to me: ²²"Son of man, what is this proverb you have in the land of Israel: 'The days go by and every vision comes to nothing'? ²³Say to them, 'This is what the Sovereign LORD says: I am going to put an end to this proverb, and they will no longer quote it in Israel.' Say to them, 'The days are near when every vision will be fulfilled. ²⁴For there will be no more false visions or flattering divinations among the people of Israel. ²⁵But I the LORD will speak what I will, and it shall be fulfilled without delay. For in your days, you rebellious house, I will fulfill whatever I say, declares the Sovereign LORD.'"

²⁶The word of the LORD came to me: ²⁷"Son of man, the house of Israel is saying, 'The vision he sees is for many years from now, and he prophesies about the distant future.'

²⁸"Therefore say to them, 'This is what the Sovereign LORD says: None of my words will be delayed any longer; whatever I say will be fulfilled, declares the Sovereign LORD.'"

False Prophets Condemned

13 The word of the LORD came to me: ²"Son of man, prophesy against the prophets of Israel who are now prophesying. Say to those who prophesy out of their own imagination: 'Hear the word of the LORD! ³This is what the Sovereign LORD says: Woe to the foolish*ᵃ* prophets who follow their own spirit and have seen nothing! ⁴Your prophets, O Israel, are like jackals among ruins. ⁵You have not gone up to the breaks in the wall to repair it for the house of Israel so that it will stand firm in the battle on the day of the LORD. ⁶Their visions are false and their divinations a lie. They say, "The LORD declares," when the LORD has not sent them; yet they expect their words to be fulfilled. ⁷Have you not seen false visions and uttered lying divinations when you say, "The LORD declares," though I have not spoken?

⁸"Therefore this is what the Sovereign LORD says: Because of your false words and lying visions, I am against you, declares the Sovereign LORD. ⁹My hand will be against the

ᵃ3 Or wicked

prophets who see false visions and utter lying divinations. They will not belong to the council of my people or be listed in the records of the house of Israel, nor will they enter the land of Israel. Then you will know that I am the Sovereign LORD.

¹⁰"'Because they lead my people astray, saying, "Peace," when there is no peace, and because, when a flimsy wall is built, they cover it with whitewash, ¹¹therefore tell those who cover it with whitewash that it is going to fall. Rain will come in torrents, and I will send hailstones hurtling down, and violent winds will burst forth. ¹²When the wall collapses, will people not ask you, "Where is the whitewash you covered it with?"

¹³"'Therefore this is what the Sovereign LORD says: In my wrath I will unleash a violent wind, and in my anger hailstones and torrents of rain will fall with destructive fury. ¹⁴I will tear down the wall you have covered with whitewash and will level it to the ground so that its foundation will be laid bare. When it*a* falls, you will be destroyed in it; and you will know that I am the LORD. ¹⁵So I will spend my wrath against the wall and against those who covered it with whitewash. I will say to you, "The wall is gone and so are those who whitewashed it, ¹⁶those prophets of Israel who prophesied to Jerusalem and saw visions of peace for her when there was no peace, declares the Sovereign LORD." '

¹⁷"Now, son of man, set your face against the daughters of your people who prophesy out of their own imagination. Prophesy against them ¹⁸and say, 'This is what the Sovereign LORD says: Woe to the women who sew magic charms on all their wrists and make veils of various lengths for their heads in order to ensnare people. Will you ensnare the lives of my people but preserve your own? ¹⁹You have profaned me among my people for a few handfuls of barley and scraps of bread. By lying to my people, who listen to lies, you have killed those who should not have died and have spared those who should not live.

²⁰"'Therefore this is what the Sovereign LORD says: I am against your magic charms with which you ensnare people like birds and I will tear them from your arms; I will set free the people that you ensnare like birds. ²¹I will tear off your veils and save my people from your hands, and they will no longer fall prey to your power. Then you will know that I am the LORD. ²²Because you disheartened the righteous with your lies, when I had brought them no grief, and because you encouraged the wicked not to turn from their evil ways and so save their lives, ²³therefore you will no longer see false visions or practice divination. I will save my people from your hands. And then you will know that I am the LORD.' "

Idolaters Condemned

14 Some of the elders of Israel came to me and sat down in front of me. ²Then the word of the LORD came to me: ³"Son of man, these men have set up idols in their hearts and put wicked stumbling blocks before their faces. Should I let them inquire of me at all? ⁴Therefore speak to them and tell them, 'This is what the Sovereign LORD says: When any Israelite sets up idols in his heart and puts a wicked stumbling block before his face and then goes to a prophet, I the LORD will answer him myself in keeping with his great idolatry. ⁵I will do this to recapture the hearts of the people of Israel, who have all deserted me for their idols.'

⁶"Therefore say to the house of Israel, 'This is what the Sovereign LORD says: Repent! Turn from your idols and renounce all your detestable practices!

⁷"'When any Israelite or any alien living in Israel separates himself from me and sets up idols in his heart and puts a wicked stumbling block before his face and then goes to a prophet to inquire of me, I the LORD will answer him myself. ⁸I will set my face against that man and make him an example and a byword. I will cut him off from my people. Then you will know that I am the LORD.

⁹"'And if the prophet is enticed to utter a prophecy, I the LORD have enticed that prophet, and I will stretch out my hand against him and destroy him from among my

a 14 Or the city

people Israel. ¹⁰They will bear their guilt—the prophet will be as guilty as the one who consults him. ¹¹Then the people of Israel will no longer stray from me, nor will they defile themselves anymore with all their sins. They will be my people, and I will be their God, declares the Sovereign LORD.'"

Judgment Inescapable

¹²The word of the LORD came to me: ¹³"Son of man, if a country sins against me by being unfaithful and I stretch out my hand against it to cut off its food supply and send famine upon it and kill its men and their animals, ¹⁴even if these three men—Noah, Daniel*a* and Job—were in it, they could save only themselves by their righteousness, declares the Sovereign LORD.

¹⁵"Or if I send wild beasts through that country and they leave it childless and it becomes desolate so that no one can pass through it because of the beasts, ¹⁶as surely as I live, declares the Sovereign LORD, even if these three men were in it, they could not save their own sons or daughters. They alone would be saved, but the land would be desolate.

¹⁷"Or if I bring a sword against that country and say, 'Let the sword pass throughout the land,' and I kill its men and their animals, ¹⁸as surely as I live, declares the Sovereign LORD, even if these three men were in it, they could not save their own sons or daughters. They alone would be saved.

¹⁹"Or if I send a plague into that land and pour out my wrath upon it through bloodshed, killing its men and their animals, ²⁰as surely as I live, declares the Sovereign LORD, even if Noah, Daniel and Job were in it, they could save neither son nor daughter. They would save only themselves by their righteousness.

²¹"For this is what the Sovereign LORD says: How much worse will it be when I send against Jerusalem my four dreadful judgments—sword and famine and wild beasts and plague—to kill its men and their animals! ²²Yet there will be some survivors—sons and daughters who will be brought out of it. They will come to you, and when you see their conduct and their actions, you will be consoled regarding the disaster I have brought upon Jerusalem—every disaster I have brought upon it. ²³You will be consoled when you see their conduct and their actions, for you will know that I have done nothing in it without cause, declares the Sovereign LORD."

Jerusalem, A Useless Vine

15 The word of the LORD came to me: ²"Son of man, how is the wood of a vine better than that of a branch on any of the trees in the forest? ³Is wood ever taken from it to make anything useful? Do they make pegs from it to hang things on? ⁴And after it is thrown on the fire as fuel and the fire burns both ends and chars the middle, is it then useful for anything? ⁵If it was not useful for anything when it was whole, how much less can it be made into something useful when the fire has burned it and it is charred?

⁶"Therefore this is what the Sovereign LORD says: As I have given the wood of the vine among the trees of the forest as fuel for the fire, so will I treat the people living in Jerusalem. ⁷I will set my face against them. Although they have come out of the fire, the fire will yet consume them. And when I set my face against them, you will know that I am the LORD. ⁸I will make the land desolate because they have been unfaithful, declares the Sovereign LORD."

An Allegory of Unfaithful Jerusalem

16 The word of the LORD came to me: ²"Son of man, confront Jerusalem with her detestable practices ³and say, 'This is what the Sovereign LORD says to Jerusalem: Your ancestry and birth were in the land of the Canaanites; your father was an Amorite and your mother a Hittite. ⁴On the day you were born your cord was not cut, nor

---

a 14 Or *Daniel*; the Hebrew spelling may suggest a person other than the prophet Daniel; also in verse 20.

were you washed with water to make you clean, nor were you rubbed with salt or wrapped in cloths. ⁵No one looked on you with pity or had compassion enough to do any of these things for you. Rather, you were thrown out into the open field, for on the day you were born you were despised.

⁶"'Then I passed by and saw you kicking about in your blood, and as you lay there in your blood I said to you, "Live!"ᵃ ⁷I made you grow like a plant of the field. You grew up and developed and became the most beautiful of jewels.ᵇ Your breasts were formed and your hair grew, you who were naked and bare.

⁸"'Later I passed by, and when I looked at you and saw that you were old enough for love, I spread the corner of my garment over you and covered your nakedness. I gave you my solemn oath and entered into a covenant with you, declares the Sovereign LORD, and you became mine.

⁹"'I bathedᶜ you with water and washed the blood from you and put ointments on you. ¹⁰I clothed you with an embroidered dress and put leather sandals on you. I dressed you in fine linen and covered you with costly garments. ¹¹I adorned you with jewelry: I put bracelets on your arms and a necklace around your neck, ¹²and I put a ring on your nose, earrings on your ears and a beautiful crown on your head. ¹³So you were adorned with gold and silver; your clothes were of fine linen and costly fabric and embroidered cloth. Your food was fine flour, honey and olive oil. You became very beautiful and rose to be a queen. ¹⁴And your fame spread among the nations on account of your beauty, because the splendor I had given you made your beauty perfect, declares the Sovereign LORD.

¹⁵"'But you trusted in your beauty and used your fame to become a prostitute. You lavished your favors on anyone who passed by and your beauty became his.ᵈ ¹⁶You took some of your garments to make gaudy high places, where you carried on your prostitution. Such things should not happen, nor should they ever occur. ¹⁷You also took the fine jewelry I gave you, the jewelry made of my gold and silver, and you made for yourself male idols and engaged in prostitution with them. ¹⁸And you took your embroidered clothes to put on them, and you offered my oil and incense before them. ¹⁹Also the food I provided for you—the fine flour, olive oil and honey I gave you to eat—you offered as fragrant incense before them. That is what happened, declares the Sovereign LORD.

²⁰"'And you took your sons and daughters whom you bore to me and sacrificed them as food to the idols. Was your prostitution not enough? ²¹You slaughtered my children and sacrificed themᵉ to the idols. ²²In all your detestable practices and your prostitution you did not remember the days of your youth, when you were naked and bare, kicking about in your blood.

²³"'Woe! Woe to you, declares the Sovereign LORD. In addition to all your other wickedness, ²⁴you built a mound for yourself and made a lofty shrine in every public square. ²⁵At the head of every street you built your lofty shrines and degraded your beauty, offering your body with increasing promiscuity to anyone who passed by. ²⁶You engaged in prostitution with the Egyptians, your lustful neighbors, and provoked me to anger with your increasing promiscuity. ²⁷So I stretched out my hand against you and reduced your territory; I gave you over to the greed of your enemies, the daughters of the Philistines, who were shocked by your lewd conduct. ²⁸You engaged in prostitution with the Assyrians too, because you were insatiable; and even after that, you still were not satisfied. ²⁹Then you increased your promiscuity to include Babylonia,ᶠ a land of merchants, but even with this you were not satisfied.

³⁰"'How weak-willed you are, declares the Sovereign LORD, when you do all these things, acting like a brazen prostitute! ³¹When you built your mounds at the head of

---

ᵃ6 A few Hebrew manuscripts, Septuagint and Syriac; most Hebrew manuscripts *"Live!" And as you lay there in your blood I said to you, "Live!"*   ᵇ7 Or *became mature*   ᶜ9 Or *I had bathed*   ᵈ15 Most Hebrew manuscripts; one Hebrew manuscript (see some Septuagint manuscripts) *by. Such a thing should not happen*   ᵉ21 Or *and made them pass through the fire*   ᶠ29 Or *Chaldea*

very street and made your lofty shrines in every public square, you were unlike a rostitute, because you scorned payment.

32 "You adulterous wife! You prefer strangers to your own husband! **33**Every prostitute eceives a fee, but you give gifts to all your lovers, bribing them to come to you from verywhere for your illicit favors. **34**So in your prostitution you are the opposite of others; o one runs after you for your favors. You are the very opposite, for you give payment and one is given to you.

35 "Therefore, you prostitute, hear the word of the LORD! **36**This is what the Sovereign ORD says: Because you poured out your wealth*a* and exposed your nakedness in your romiscuity with your lovers, and because of all your detestable idols, and because you ave them your children's blood, **37**therefore I am going to gather all your lovers, with whom you found pleasure, those you loved as well as those you hated. I will gather them gainst you from all around and will strip you in front of them, and they will see all your akedness. **38**I will sentence you to the punishment of women who commit adultery and ho shed blood; I will bring upon you the blood vengeance of my wrath and jealous nger. **39**Then I will hand you over to your lovers, and they will tear down your mounds nd destroy your lofty shrines. They will strip you of your clothes and take your fine ewelry and leave you naked and bare. **40**They will bring a mob against you, who will tone you and hack you to pieces with their swords. **41**They will burn down your houses nd inflict punishment on you in the sight of many women. I will put a stop to your rostitution, and you will no longer pay your lovers. **42**Then my wrath against you will ubside and my jealous anger will turn away from you; I will be calm and no longer ngry.

43 "Because you did not remember the days of your youth but enraged me with all ese things, I will surely bring down on your head what you have done, declares the overeign LORD. Did you not add lewdness to all your other detestable practices?

44 "Everyone who quotes proverbs will quote this proverb about you: 'Like mother, like aughter.' **45**You are a true daughter of your mother, who despised her husband and her hildren; and you are a true sister of your sisters, who despised their husbands and their hildren. Your mother was a Hittite and your father an Amorite. **46**Your older sister was amaria, who lived to the north of you with her daughters; and your younger sister, who ved to the south of you with her daughters, was Sodom. **47**You not only walked in their ays and copied their detestable practices, but in all your ways you soon became more epraved than they. **48**As surely as I live, declares the Sovereign LORD, your sister Sodom nd her daughters never did what you and your daughters have done.

49 "Now this was the sin of your sister Sodom: She and her daughters were arrogant, verfed and unconcerned; they did not help the poor and needy. **50**They were haughty nd did detestable things before me. Therefore I did away with them as you have seen. Samaria did not commit half the sins you did. You have done more detestable things an they, and have made your sisters seem righteous by all these things you have done. Bear your disgrace, for you have furnished some justification for your sisters. Because our sins were more vile than theirs, they appear more righteous than you. So then, be shamed and bear your disgrace, for you have made your sisters appear righteous.

53 "However, I will restore the fortunes of Sodom and her daughters and of Samaria nd her daughters, and your fortunes along with them, **54**so that you may bear your isgrace and be ashamed of all you have done in giving them comfort. **55**And your sisters, odom with her daughters and Samaria with her daughters, will return to what they ere before; and you and your daughters will return to what you were before. **56**You ould not even mention your sister Sodom in the day of your pride, **57**before your wick- dness was uncovered. Even so, you are now scorned by the daughters of Edom*b* and all er neighbors and the daughters of the Philistines—all those around you who despise

6 Or lust   *b 57 Many Hebrew manuscripts and Syriac; most Hebrew manuscripts, Septuagint and Vulgate Aram*

you. 58You will bear the consequences of your lewdness and your detestable practices, declares the LORD.

59"'This is what the Sovereign LORD says: I will deal with you as you deserve, because you have despised my oath by breaking the covenant. 60Yet I will remember the covenant I made with you in the days of your youth, and I will establish an everlasting covenant with you. 61Then you will remember your ways and be ashamed when you receive your sisters, both those who are older than you and those who are younger. I will give them to you as daughters, but not on the basis of my covenant with you. 62So I will establish my covenant with you, and you will know that I am the LORD. 63Then, when I make atonement for you for all you have done, you will remember and be ashamed and never again open your mouth because of your humiliation, declares the Sovereign LORD.'"

Two Eagles and a Vine

17 The word of the LORD came to me: 2"Son of man, set forth an allegory and tell the house of Israel a parable. 3Say to them, 'This is what the Sovereign LORD says: A great eagle with powerful wings, long feathers and full plumage of varied colors came to Lebanon. Taking hold of the top of a cedar, 4he broke off its topmost shoot and carried it away to a land of merchants, where he planted it in a city of traders.

5"'He took some of the seed of your land and put it in fertile soil. He planted it like a willow by abundant water, 6and it sprouted and became a low, spreading vine. Its branches turned toward him, but its roots remained under it. So it became a vine and produced branches and put out leafy boughs.

7"'But there was another great eagle with powerful wings and full plumage. The vine now sent out its roots toward him from the plot where it was planted and stretched out its branches to him for water. 8It had been planted in good soil by abundant water so that it would produce branches, bear fruit and become a splendid vine.'

9"Say to them, 'This is what the Sovereign LORD says: Will it thrive? Will it not be uprooted and stripped of its fruit so that it withers? All its new growth will wither. It will not take a strong arm or many people to pull it up by the roots. 10Even if it is transplanted, will it thrive? Will it not wither completely when the east wind strikes it—wither away in the plot where it grew?'"

11Then the word of the LORD came to me: 12"Say to this rebellious house, 'Do you not know what these things mean?' Say to them: 'The king of Babylon went to Jerusalem and carried off her king and her nobles, bringing them back with him to Babylon. 13Then he took a member of the royal family and made a treaty with him, putting him under oath. He also carried away the leading men of the land, 14so that the kingdom would be brought low, unable to rise again, surviving only by keeping his treaty. 15But the king rebelled against him by sending his envoys to Egypt to get horses and a large army. Will he succeed? Will he who does such things escape? Will he break the treaty and yet escape?

16"'As surely as I live, declares the Sovereign LORD, he shall die in Babylon, in the land of the king who put him on the throne, whose oath he despised and whose treaty he broke. 17Pharaoh with his mighty army and great horde will be of no help to him in war, when ramps are built and siege works erected to destroy many lives. 18He despised the oath by breaking the covenant. Because he had given his hand in pledge and yet did all these things, he shall not escape.

19"'Therefore this is what the Sovereign LORD says: As surely as I live, I will bring down on his head my oath that he despised and my covenant that he broke. 20I will spread my net for him, and he will be caught in my snare. I will bring him to Babylon and execute judgment upon him there because he was unfaithful to me. 21All his fleeing troops will fall by the sword, and the survivors will be scattered to the winds. Then you will know that I the LORD have spoken.

²²"'This is what the Sovereign LORD says: I myself will take a shoot from the very top of cedar and plant it; I will break off a tender sprig from its topmost shoots and plant it on high and lofty mountain. ²³On the mountain heights of Israel I will plant it; it will roduce branches and bear fruit and become a splendid cedar. Birds of every kind will est in it; they will find shelter in the shade of its branches. ²⁴All the trees of the field vill know that I the LORD bring down the tall tree and make the low tree grow tall. I dry p the green tree and make the dry tree flourish.

"'I the LORD have spoken, and I will do it.'"

he Soul Who Sins Will Die

18 The word of the LORD came to me: ²"What do you people mean by quoting this proverb about the land of Israel:

" 'The fathers eat sour grapes,
  and the children's teeth are set on edge'?

³"As surely as I live, declares the Sovereign LORD, you will no longer quote this proverb n Israel. ⁴For every living soul belongs to me, the father as well as the son—both alike elong to me. The soul who sins is the one who will die.

⁵"Suppose there is a righteous man
  who does what is just and right.
⁶He does not eat at the mountain shrines
  or look to the idols of the house of Israel.
He does not defile his neighbor's wife
  or lie with a woman during her period.
⁷He does not oppress anyone,
  but returns what he took in pledge for a loan.
He does not commit robbery
  but gives his food to the hungry
  and provides clothing for the naked.
⁸He does not lend at usury
  or take excessive interest.ᵃ
He withholds his hand from doing wrong
  and judges fairly between man and man.
⁹He follows my decrees
  and faithfully keeps my laws.
That man is righteous;
  he will surely live,

                                        declares the Sovereign LORD.

¹⁰"Suppose he has a violent son, who sheds blood or does any of these other thingsᵇ
ᵃ(though the father has done none of them):

"He eats at the mountain shrines.
He defiles his neighbor's wife.
¹²He oppresses the poor and needy.
He commits robbery.
He does not return what he took in pledge.
He looks to the idols.
He does detestable things.
¹³He lends at usury and takes excessive interest.

_____
ᵃ 8 Or *take interest; similarly in verses 13 and 17*   ᵇ 10 Or *things to a brother*

Will such a man live? He will not! Because he has done all these detestable things, he will surely be put to death and his blood will be on his own head.

¹⁴"But suppose this son has a son who sees all the sins his father commits, and though he sees them, he does not do such things:

> ¹⁵"He does not eat at the mountain shrines
>   or look to the idols of the house of Israel.
> He does not defile his neighbor's wife.
> ¹⁶He does not oppress anyone
>   or require a pledge for a loan.
> He does not commit robbery
>   but gives his food to the hungry
>   and provides clothing for the naked.
> ¹⁷He withholds his hand from sin*ᵃ*
>   and takes no usury or excessive interest.
> He keeps my laws and follows my decrees.

He will not die for his father's sin; he will surely live. ¹⁸But his father will die for his own sin, because he practiced extortion, robbed his brother and did what was wrong among his people.

¹⁹"Yet you ask, 'Why does the son not share the guilt of his father?' Since the son has done what is just and right and has been careful to keep all my decrees, he will surely live. ²⁰The soul who sins is the one who will die. The son will not share the guilt of the father, nor will the father share the guilt of the son. The righteousness of the righteous man will be credited to him, and the wickedness of the wicked will be charged against him.

²¹"But if a wicked man turns away from all the sins he has committed and keeps all my decrees and does what is just and right, he will surely live; he will not die. ²²None of the offenses he has committed will be remembered against him. Because of the righteous things he has done, he will live. ²³Do I take any pleasure in the death of the wicked? declares the Sovereign Lᴏʀᴅ. Rather, am I not pleased when they turn from their ways and live?

²⁴"But if a righteous man turns from his righteousness and commits sin and does the same detestable things the wicked man does, will he live? None of the righteous things he has done will be remembered. Because of the unfaithfulness he is guilty of and because of the sins he has committed, he will die.

²⁵"Yet you say, 'The way of the Lord is not just.' Hear, O house of Israel: Is my way unjust? Is it not your ways that are unjust? ²⁶If a righteous man turns from his righteousness and commits sin, he will die for it; because of the sin he has committed he will die. ²⁷But if a wicked man turns away from the wickedness he has committed and does what is just and right, he will save his life. ²⁸Because he considers all the offenses he has committed and turns away from them, he will surely live; he will not die. ²⁹Yet the house of Israel says, 'The way of the Lord is not just.' Are my ways unjust, O house of Israel? Is it not your ways that are unjust?

³⁰"Therefore, O house of Israel, I will judge you, each one according to his ways, declares the Sovereign Lᴏʀᴅ. Repent! Turn away from all your offenses; then sin will not be your downfall. ³¹Rid yourselves of all the offenses you have committed, and get a new heart and a new spirit. Why will you die, O house of Israel? ³²For I take no pleasure in the death of anyone, declares the Sovereign Lᴏʀᴅ. Repent and live!

ᵃ 17 Septuagint (see also verse 8); Hebrew *from the poor*

A Lament for Israel's Princes

19   ¹"Take up a lament concerning the princes of Israel ²and say:

> "'What a lioness was your mother
>   among the lions!
> She lay down among the young lions
>   and reared her cubs.
> ³She brought up one of her cubs,
>   and he became a strong lion.
> He learned to tear the prey
>   and he devoured men.
> ⁴The nations heard about him,
>   and he was trapped in their
>   pit.
> They led him with hooks
>   to the land of Egypt.
>
> ⁵"'When she saw her hope
>   unfulfilled,
>   her expectation gone,
> she took another of her cubs
>   and made him a strong lion.
> ⁶He prowled among the lions,
>   for he was now a strong
>   lion.
> He learned to tear the prey
>   and he devoured men.
> ⁷He broke down*ᵃ* their
>   strongholds
>   and devastated their towns.
> The land and all who were in it
>   were terrified by his roaring.
> ⁸Then the nations came against him,
>   those from regions round about.
> They spread their net for him,
>   and he was trapped in their pit.
> ⁹With hooks they pulled him into a cage
>   and brought him to the king of Babylon.
> They put him in prison,
>   so his roar was heard no longer
>   on the mountains of Israel.
>
> ¹⁰"'Your mother was like a vine in your vineyard*ᵇ*
>   planted by the water;
> it was fruitful and full of branches
>   because of abundant water.
> ¹¹Its branches were strong,
>   fit for a ruler's scepter.
> It towered high
>   above the thick foliage,

▣ ░░░░░░░░░░ **DISCOVERING GOD** ░░░░░░░░░░ ⬌

18:32
The God Who Is There

Some people assume that if God judges sin, he must in some way enjoy doing so. That assumption is simply not true. In this passage God clearly states that he would much rather have people leave their sin than stay separated from him in their disobedience.

If you're a seeker, you may gather that this prophetic book calls people who already believe in God back to the truth they've left behind. You, on the other hand, may be looking into Christianity for the first time in your life. Still, God's call to people in both situations is the same. He wants all people to turn to him, seeking his fellowship and reaping the benefits of a two-way relationship. That's the invitation extended to you today.

ᵃ7 Targum (see Septuagint); Hebrew He knew   *ᵇ10 Two Hebrew manuscripts; most Hebrew manuscripts* your blood

conspicuous for its height
and for its many branches.
¹²But it was uprooted in fury
and thrown to the ground.
The east wind made it shrivel,
it was stripped of its fruit;
its strong branches withered
and fire consumed them.
¹³Now it is planted in the desert,
in a dry and thirsty land.
¹⁴Fire spread from one of its main*a* branches
and consumed its fruit.
No strong branch is left on it
fit for a ruler's scepter.'

This is a lament and is to be used as a lament."

Rebellious Israel

20 In the seventh year, in the fifth month on the tenth day, some of the elders of Israel came to inquire of the LORD, and they sat down in front of me.

²Then the word of the LORD came to me: ³"Son of man, speak to the elders of Israel and say to them, 'This is what the Sovereign LORD says: Have you come to inquire of me? As surely as I live, I will not let you inquire of me, declares the Sovereign LORD.'

⁴"Will you judge them? Will you judge them, son of man? Then confront them with the detestable practices of their fathers ⁵and say to them: 'This is what the Sovereign LORD says: On the day I chose Israel, I swore with uplifted hand to the descendants of the house of Jacob and revealed myself to them in Egypt. With uplifted hand I said to them, "I am the LORD your God." ⁶On that day I swore to them that I would bring them out of Egypt into a land I had searched out for them, a land flowing with milk and honey, the most beautiful of all lands. ⁷And I said to them, "Each of you, get rid of the vile images you have set your eyes on, and do not defile yourselves with the idols of Egypt. I am the LORD your God."

⁸"'But they rebelled against me and would not listen to me; they did not get rid of the vile images they had set their eyes on, nor did they forsake the idols of Egypt. So I said I would pour out my wrath on them and spend my anger against them in Egypt. ⁹But for the sake of my name I did what would keep it from being profaned in the eyes of the nations they lived among and in whose sight I had revealed myself to the Israelites by bringing them out of Egypt. ¹⁰Therefore I led them out of Egypt and brought them into the desert. ¹¹I gave them my decrees and made known to them my laws, for the man who obeys them will live by them. ¹²Also I gave them my Sabbaths as a sign between us, so they would know that I the LORD made them holy.

¹³"'Yet the people of Israel rebelled against me in the desert. They did not follow my decrees but rejected my laws—although the man who obeys them will live by them—and they utterly desecrated my Sabbaths. So I said I would pour out my wrath on them and destroy them in the desert. ¹⁴But for the sake of my name I did what would keep it from being profaned in the eyes of the nations in whose sight I had brought them out. ¹⁵Also with uplifted hand I swore to them in the desert that I would not bring them into the land I had given them—a land flowing with milk and honey, most beautiful of all lands—¹⁶because they rejected my laws and did not follow my decrees and desecrated my Sabbaths. For their hearts were devoted to their idols. ¹⁷Yet I looked on them with pity and did not destroy them or put an end to them in the desert. ¹⁸I said to their children in

a 14 Or from under its

the desert, "Do not follow the statutes of your fathers or keep their laws or defile your-selves with their idols. ¹⁹I am the LORD your God; follow my decrees and be careful to keep my laws. ²⁰Keep my Sabbaths holy, that they may be a sign between us. Then you will know that I am the LORD your God."

²¹"But the children rebelled against me: They did not follow my decrees, they were not careful to keep my laws—although the man who obeys them will live by them—and they desecrated my Sabbaths. So I said I would pour out my wrath on them and spend my anger against them in the desert. ²²But I withheld my hand, and for the sake of my name I did what would keep it from being profaned in the eyes of the nations in whose sight I had brought them out. ²³Also with uplifted hand I swore to them in the desert that I would disperse them among the nations and scatter them through the countries, ²⁴be-cause they had not obeyed my laws but had rejected my decrees and desecrated my Sabbaths, and their eyes ₗusted₌ after their fathers' idols. ²⁵I also gave them over to statutes that were not good and laws they could not live by; ²⁶I let them become defiled through their gifts—the sacrifice of every firstborn ᵃ—that I might fill them with horror so they would know that I am the LORD.'

²⁷"Therefore, son of man, speak to the people of Israel and say to them, 'This is what the Sovereign LORD says: In this also your fathers blasphemed me by forsaking me: ²⁸When I brought them into the land I had sworn to give them and they saw any high hill or any leafy tree, there they offered their sacrifices, made offerings that provoked me to anger, presented their fragrant incense and poured out their drink offerings. ²⁹Then I said to them: What is this high place you go to?'" (It is called Bamah ᵇ to this day.)

Judgment and Restoration

³⁰"Therefore say to the house of Israel: 'This is what the Sovereign LORD says: Will you defile yourselves the way your fathers did and lust after their vile images? ³¹When you offer your gifts—the sacrifice of your sons in ᶜ the fire—you continue to defile yourselves with all your idols to this day. Am I to let you inquire of me, O house of Israel? As surely as I live, declares the Sovereign LORD, I will not let you inquire of me.

³²"'You say, "We want to be like the nations, like the peoples of the world, who serve wood and stone." But what you have in mind will never happen. ³³As surely as I live, declares the Sovereign LORD, I will rule over you with a mighty hand and an outstretched arm and with outpoured wrath. ³⁴I will bring you from the nations and gather you from the countries where you have been scattered—with a mighty hand and an outstretched arm and with outpoured wrath. ³⁵I will bring you into the desert of the nations and there, face to face, I will execute judgment upon you. ³⁶As I judged your fathers in the desert of the land of Egypt, so I will judge you, declares the Sovereign LORD. ³⁷I will take note of you as you pass under my rod, and I will bring you into the bond of the covenant. ³⁸I will purge you of those who revolt and rebel against me. Although I will bring them out of the land where they are living, yet they will not enter the land of Israel. Then you will know that I am the LORD.

³⁹"'As for you, O house of Israel, this is what the Sovereign LORD says: Go and serve your idols, every one of you! But afterward you will surely listen to me and no longer profane my holy name with your gifts and idols. ⁴⁰For on my holy mountain, the high mountain of Israel, declares the Sovereign LORD, there in the land the entire house of Israel will serve me, and there I will accept them. There I will require your offerings and your choice gifts,ᵈ along with all your holy sacrifices. ⁴¹I will accept you as fragrant incense when I bring you out from the nations and gather you from the countries where you have been scattered, and I will show myself holy among you in the sight of the nations. ⁴²Then you will know that I am the LORD, when I bring you into the land of Israel, the land I had sworn with uplifted hand to give to your fathers. ⁴³There you will remem-

---

ᵃ26 Or —making every firstborn pass through ₗthe fire,   ᵇ29 Bamah means high place.   ᶜ31 Or —making your sons
pass through   ᵈ40 Or and the gifts of your firstfruits

ber your conduct and all the actions by which you have defiled yourselves, and you will loathe yourselves for all the evil you have done. ⁴⁴You will know that I am the LORD, when I deal with you for my name's sake and not according to your evil ways and your corrupt practices, O house of Israel, declares the Sovereign LORD.'"

Prophecy Against the South

⁴⁵The word of the LORD came to me: ⁴⁶"Son of man, set your face toward the south; preach against the south and prophesy against the forest of the southland. ⁴⁷Say to the southern forest: 'Hear the word of the LORD. This is what the Sovereign LORD says: I am about to set fire to you, and it will consume all your trees, both green and dry. The blazing flame will not be quenched, and every face from south to north will be scorched by it. ⁴⁸Everyone will see that I the LORD have kindled it; it will not be quenched.'"

⁴⁹Then I said, "Ah, Sovereign LORD! They are saying of me, 'Isn't he just telling parables?'"

Babylon, God's Sword of Judgment

21 The word of the LORD came to me: ²"Son of man, set your face against Jerusalem and preach against the land of Israel ³and say to her: 'This is what the LORD says: I am against you. I will draw my sword from its scabbard and cut off from you both the righteous and the wicked. ⁴Because I am going to cut off the righteous and the wicked, my sword will be unsheathed against everyone from south to north. ⁵Then all people will know that I the LORD have drawn my sword from its scabbard; it will not return again.'

⁶"Therefore groan, son of man! Groan before them with broken heart and bitter grief. ⁷And when they ask you, 'Why are you groaning?' you shall say, 'Because of the news that is coming. Every heart will melt and every hand go limp; every spirit will become faint and every knee become as weak as water.' It is coming! It will surely take place, declares the Sovereign LORD."

⁸The word of the LORD came to me: ⁹"Son of man, prophesy and say, 'This is what the Lord says:

> "'A sword, a sword,
>   sharpened and polished—
> ¹⁰sharpened for the slaughter,
>   polished to flash like lightning!

"'Shall we rejoice in the scepter of my son ⌊Judah⌋? The sword despises every such stick.

> ¹¹"'The sword is appointed to be polished,
>   to be grasped with the hand;
> it is sharpened and polished,
>   made ready for the hand of the slayer.
> ¹²Cry out and wail, son of man,
>   for it is against my people;
> it is against all the princes of Israel.
> They are thrown to the sword
>   along with my people.
> Therefore beat your breast.

¹³"'Testing will surely come. And what if the scepter ⌊of Judah⌋, which the sword despises, does not continue? declares the Sovereign LORD.'

¹⁴"So then, son of man, prophesy

and strike your hands together.
Let the sword strike twice,
     even three times.
It is a sword for slaughter—
     a sword for great slaughter,
     closing in on them from every side.
¹⁵So that hearts may melt
     and the fallen be many,
I have stationed the sword for slaughter*a*
     at all their gates.
Oh! It is made to flash like lightning,
     it is grasped for slaughter.
¹⁶O sword, slash to the right,
     then to the left,
     wherever your blade is turned.
¹⁷I too will strike my hands together,
     and my wrath will subside.
I the LORD have spoken."

¹⁸The word of the LORD came to me: ¹⁹"Son of man, mark out two roads for the sword of the king of Babylon to take, both starting from the same country. Make a signpost where the road branches off to the city. ²⁰Mark out one road for the sword to come against Rabbah of the Ammonites and another against Judah and fortified Jerusalem. ²¹For the king of Babylon will stop at the fork in the road, at the junction of the two roads, to seek an omen: He will cast lots with arrows, he will consult his idols, he will examine the liver. ²²Into his right hand will come the lot for Jerusalem, where he is to set up battering rams, to give the command to slaughter, to sound the battle cry, to set battering rams against the gates, to build a ramp and to erect siege works. ²³It will seem like a false omen to those who have sworn allegiance to him, but he will remind them of their guilt and take them captive.

²⁴"Therefore this is what the Sovereign LORD says: 'Because you people have brought to mind your guilt by your open rebellion, revealing your sins in all that you do—because you have done this, you will be taken captive.

²⁵"'O profane and wicked prince of Israel, whose day has come, whose time of punishment has reached its climax, ²⁶this is what the Sovereign LORD says: Take off the turban, remove the crown. It will not be as it was: The lowly will be exalted and the exalted will be brought low. ²⁷A ruin! A ruin! I will make it a ruin! It will not be restored until he comes to whom it rightfully belongs; to him I will give it.'

²⁸"And you, son of man, prophesy and say, 'This is what the Sovereign LORD says about the Ammonites and their insults:

" 'A sword, a sword,
     drawn for the slaughter,
polished to consume
     and to flash like lightning!
²⁹Despite false visions concerning you
     and lying divinations about you,
it will be laid on the necks
     of the wicked who are to be slain,
whose day has come,
     whose time of punishment has reached its climax.
³⁰Return the sword to its scabbard.
     In the place where you were created,

a 15 Septuagint; the meaning of the Hebrew for this word is uncertain.

in the land of your ancestry,
   I will judge you.
³¹I will pour out my wrath upon you
   and breathe out my fiery anger against you;
   I will hand you over to brutal men,
   men skilled in destruction.
³²You will be fuel for the fire,
   your blood will be shed in your land,
   you will be remembered no more;
   for I the LORD have spoken.'"

Jerusalem's Sins

22 The word of the LORD came to me: ²"Son of man, will you judge her? Will you judge this city of bloodshed? Then confront her with all her detestable practices ³and say: 'This is what the Sovereign LORD says: O city that brings on herself doom by shedding blood in her midst and defiles herself by making idols, ⁴you have become guilty because of the blood you have shed and have become defiled by the idols you have made. You have brought your days to a close, and the end of your years has come. Therefore I will make you an object of scorn to the nations and a laughingstock to all the countries. ⁵Those who are near and those who are far away will mock you, O infamous city, full of turmoil.

⁶"'See how each of the princes of Israel who are in you uses his power to shed blood. ⁷In you they have treated father and mother with contempt; in you they have oppressed the alien and mistreated the fatherless and the widow. ⁸You have despised my holy things and desecrated my Sabbaths. ⁹In you are slanderous men bent on shedding blood; in you are those who eat at the mountain shrines and commit lewd acts. ¹⁰In you are those who dishonor their fathers' bed; in you are those who violate women during their period, when they are ceremonially unclean. ¹¹In you one man commits a detestable offense with his neighbor's wife, another shamefully defiles his daughter-in-law, and another violates his sister, his own father's daughter. ¹²In you men accept bribes to shed blood; you take usury and excessive interest^a and make unjust gain from your neighbors by extortion. And you have forgotten me, declares the Sovereign LORD.

¹³"'I will surely strike my hands together at the unjust gain you have made and at the blood you have shed in your midst. ¹⁴Will your courage endure or your hands be strong in the day I deal with you? I the LORD have spoken, and I will do it. ¹⁵I will disperse you among the nations and scatter you through the countries; and I will put an end to your uncleanness. ¹⁶When you have been defiled^b in the eyes of the nations, you will know that I am the LORD.'"

¹⁷Then the word of the LORD came to me: ¹⁸"Son of man, the house of Israel has become dross to me; all of them are the copper, tin, iron and lead left inside a furnace. They are but the dross of silver. ¹⁹Therefore this is what the Sovereign LORD says: 'Because you have all become dross, I will gather you into Jerusalem. ²⁰As men gather silver, copper, iron, lead and tin into a furnace to melt it with a fiery blast, so will I gather you in my anger and my wrath and put you inside the city and melt you. ²¹I will gather you and I will blow on you with my fiery wrath, and you will be melted inside her. ²²As silver is melted in a furnace, so you will be melted inside her, and you will know that I the LORD have poured out my wrath upon you.'"

²³Again the word of the LORD came to me: ²⁴"Son of man, say to the land, 'You are a land that has had no rain or showers^c in the day of wrath.' ²⁵There is a conspiracy of her princes^d within her like a roaring lion tearing its prey; they devour people, take treasures and precious things and make many widows within her. ²⁶Her priests do vio-

---

^a12 Or *usury and interest*   ^b16 Or *When I have allotted you your inheritance*   ^c24 Septuagint; Hebrew *has not been cleansed or rained on*   ^d25 Septuagint; Hebrew *prophets*

lence to my law and profane my holy things; they do not distinguish between the holy and the common; they teach that there is no difference between the unclean and the clean; and they shut their eyes to the keeping of my Sabbaths, so that I am profaned among them. ²⁷Her officials within her are like wolves tearing their prey; they shed blood and kill people to make unjust gain. ²⁸Her prophets whitewash these deeds for them by false visions and lying divinations. They say, 'This is what the Sovereign LORD says'—when the LORD has not spoken. ²⁹The people of the land practice extortion and commit robbery; they oppress the poor and needy and mistreat the alien, denying them justice.

³⁰"I looked for a man among them who would build up the wall and stand before me in the gap on behalf of the land so I would not have to destroy it, but I found none. ³¹So I will pour out my wrath on them and consume them with my fiery anger, bringing down on their own heads all they have done, declares the Sovereign LORD."

Two Adulterous Sisters

23 The word of the LORD came to me: ²"Son of man, there were two women, daughters of the same mother. ³They became prostitutes in Egypt, engaging in prostitution from their youth. In that land their breasts were fondled and their virgin bosoms caressed. ⁴The older was named Oholah, and her sister was Oholibah. They were mine and gave birth to sons and daughters. Oholah is Samaria, and Oholibah is Jerusalem.

⁵"Oholah engaged in prostitution while she was still mine; and she lusted after her lovers, the Assyrians—warriors ⁶clothed in blue, governors and commanders, all of them handsome young men, and mounted horsemen. ⁷She gave herself as a prostitute to all the elite of the Assyrians and defiled herself with all the idols of everyone she lusted after. ⁸She did not give up the prostitution she began in Egypt, when during her youth men slept with her, caressed her virgin bosom and poured out their lust upon her.

⁹"Therefore I handed her over to her lovers, the Assyrians, for whom she lusted. ¹⁰They stripped her naked, took away her sons and daughters and killed her with the sword. She became a byword among women, and punishment was inflicted on her.

¹¹"Her sister Oholibah saw this, yet in her lust and prostitution she was more depraved than her sister. ¹²She too lusted after the Assyrians—governors and commanders, warriors in full dress, mounted horsemen, all handsome young men. ¹³I saw that she too defiled herself; both of them went the same way.

¹⁴"But she carried her prostitution still further. She saw men portrayed on a wall, figures of Chaldeans*a* portrayed in red, ¹⁵with belts around their waists and flowing turbans on their heads; all of them looked like Babylonian chariot officers, natives of Chaldea.*b* ¹⁶As soon as she saw them, she lusted after them and sent messengers to them in Chaldea. ¹⁷Then the Babylonians came to her, to the bed of love, and in their lust they defiled her. After she had been defiled by them, she turned away from them in disgust. ¹⁸When she carried on her prostitution openly and exposed her nakedness, I turned away from her in disgust, just as I had turned away from her sister. ¹⁹Yet she became more and more promiscuous as she recalled the days of her youth, when she was a prostitute in Egypt. ²⁰There she lusted after her lovers, whose genitals were like those of donkeys and whose emission was like that of horses. ²¹So you longed for the lewdness of your youth, when in Egypt your bosom was caressed and your young breasts fondled.*c*

²²"Therefore, Oholibah, this is what the Sovereign LORD says: I will stir up your lovers against you, those you turned away from in disgust, and I will bring them against you from every side— ²³the Babylonians and all the Chaldeans, the men of Pekod and Shoa and Koa, and all the Assyrians with them, handsome young men, all of them governors and commanders, chariot officers and men of high rank, all mounted on horses. ²⁴They

---

a14 Or *Babylonians; your young breasts*   *b15* Or *Babylonia; also in verse 16*   *c21* Syriac (see also verse 3); Hebrew *caressed because of*

will come against you with weapons,ᵃ chariots and wagons and with a throng of people; they will take up positions against you on every side with large and small shields and with helmets. I will turn you over to them for punishment, and they will punish you according to their standards. ²⁵I will direct my jealous anger against you, and they will deal with you in fury. They will cut off your noses and your ears, and those of you who are left will fall by the sword. They will take away your sons and daughters, and those of you who are left will be consumed by fire. ²⁶They will also strip you of your clothes and take your fine jewelry. ²⁷So I will put a stop to the lewdness and prostitution you began in Egypt. You will not look on these things with longing or remember Egypt anymore.

²⁸For this is what the Sovereign LORD says: I am about to hand you over to those you hate, to those you turned away from in disgust. ²⁹They will deal with you in hatred and take away everything you have worked for. They will leave you naked and bare, and the shame of your prostitution will be exposed. Your lewdness and promiscuity ³⁰have brought this upon you, because you lusted after the nations and defiled yourself with their idols. ³¹You have gone the way of your sister; so I will put her cup into your hand.

³²This is what the Sovereign LORD says:

> "You will drink your sister's cup,
>   a cup large and deep;
> it will bring scorn and derision,
>   for it holds so much.
> ³³You will be filled with drunkenness and sorrow,
>   the cup of ruin and desolation,
>   the cup of your sister Samaria.
> ³⁴You will drink it and drain it dry;
>   you will dash it to pieces
>   and tear your breasts.

I have spoken, declares the Sovereign LORD.

³⁵Therefore this is what the Sovereign LORD says: Since you have forgotten me and thrust me behind your back, you must bear the consequences of your lewdness and prostitution."

³⁶The LORD said to me: "Son of man, will you judge Oholah and Oholibah? Then confront them with their detestable practices, ³⁷for they have committed adultery and blood is on their hands. They committed adultery with their idols; they even sacrificed their children, whom they bore to me,ᵇ as food for them. ³⁸They have also done this to me: At that same time they defiled my sanctuary and desecrated my Sabbaths. ³⁹On the very day they sacrificed their children to their idols, they entered my sanctuary and desecrated it. That is what they did in my house.

⁴⁰They even sent messengers for men who came from far away, and when they arrived you bathed yourself for them, painted your eyes and put on your jewelry. ⁴¹You sat on an elegant couch, with a table spread before it on which you had placed the incense and oil that belonged to me.

⁴²The noise of a carefree crowd was around her; Sabeansᶜ were brought from the desert along with men from the rabble, and they put bracelets on the arms of the woman and her sister and beautiful crowns on their heads. ⁴³Then I said about the one worn out by adultery, 'Now let them use her as a prostitute, for that is all she is.' ⁴⁴And they slept with her. As men sleep with a prostitute, so they slept with those lewd women, Oholah and Oholibah. ⁴⁵But righteous men will sentence them to the punishment of women who commit adultery and shed blood, because they are adulterous and blood is on their hands.

ᵃ24 The meaning of the Hebrew for this word is uncertain.   ᵇ37 Or even made the children they bore to me pass through
the fire,   ᶜ42 Or drunkards

⁴⁶"This is what the Sovereign Lᴏʀᴅ says: Bring a mob against them and give them over to terror and plunder. ⁴⁷The mob will stone them and cut them down with their swords; they will kill their sons and daughters and burn down their houses.

⁴⁸"So I will put an end to lewdness in the land, that all women may take warning and not imitate you. ⁴⁹You will suffer the penalty for your lewdness and bear the consequences of your sins of idolatry. Then you will know that I am the Sovereign Lᴏʀᴅ."

The Cooking Pot

24 In the ninth year, in the tenth month on the tenth day, the word of the Lᴏʀᴅ came to me: ²"Son of man, record this date, this very date, because the king of Babylon has laid siege to Jerusalem this very day. ³Tell this rebellious house a parable and say to them: 'This is what the Sovereign Lᴏʀᴅ says:

" 'Put on the cooking pot; put
        it on
    and pour water into it.
⁴Put into it the pieces of meat,
    all the choice pieces—the
        leg and the shoulder.
Fill it with the best of these bones;
⁵   take the pick of the flock.
Pile wood beneath it for the bones;
    bring it to a boil
    and cook the bones in it.

⁶"'For this is what the Sovereign Lᴏʀᴅ says:

" 'Woe to the city of bloodshed,
    to the pot now encrusted,
    whose deposit will not go away!
Empty it piece by piece
    without casting lots for them.

⁷"'For the blood she shed is in her midst:
    She poured it on the bare rock;
she did not pour it on the ground,
    where the dust would cover it.
⁸To stir up wrath and take revenge
    I put her blood on the bare rock,
    so that it would not be covered.

⁹"'Therefore this is what the Sovereign Lᴏʀᴅ says:

" 'Woe to the city of bloodshed!
    I, too, will pile the wood high.
¹⁰So heap on the wood
    and kindle the fire.
Cook the meat well,
    mixing in the spices;
    and let the bones be charred.

▣ ▓▓▓▓▓▓▓▓ **REASONS TO BELIEVE** ▓▓▓▓▓▓▓▓ ◨

24:1–2
The Amazing Bible

These verses show us that God wants to give even his disobedient children evidence that he is trying to get through to them.

By having Ezekiel record this specific date, the prophet would be able to prove that God was speaking supernaturally through him. In that era, when news took months to travel long distances, Ezekiel's written record of the exact date of the siege of Jerusalem—even though Ezekiel was far away in Babylon at the time—would confirm his prophetic office.

> ¹¹Then set the empty pot on the coals
> till it becomes hot and its copper glows
> so its impurities may be melted
> and its deposit burned away.
> ¹²It has frustrated all efforts;
> its heavy deposit has not been removed,
> not even by fire.

¹³"'Now your impurity is lewdness. Because I tried to cleanse you but you would not be cleansed from your impurity, you will not be clean again until my wrath against you has subsided.

¹⁴"'I the LORD have spoken. The time has come for me to act. I will not hold back; I will not have pity, nor will I relent. You will be judged according to your conduct and your actions, declares the Sovereign LORD.'"

Ezekiel's Wife Dies

¹⁵The word of the LORD came to me: ¹⁶"Son of man, with one blow I am about to take away from you the delight of your eyes. Yet do not lament or weep or shed any tears. ¹⁷Groan quietly; do not mourn for the dead. Keep your turban fastened and your sandals on your feet; do not cover the lower part of your face or eat the customary food ˌof mourners˺."

¹⁸So I spoke to the people in the morning, and in the evening my wife died. The next morning I did as I had been commanded.

¹⁹Then the people asked me, "Won't you tell us what these things have to do with us?"

²⁰So I said to them, "The word of the LORD came to me: ²¹Say to the house of Israel, 'This is what the Sovereign LORD says: I am about to desecrate my sanctuary—the stronghold in which you take pride, the delight of your eyes, the object of your affection. The sons and daughters you left behind will fall by the sword. ²²And you will do as I have done. You will not cover the lower part of your face or eat the customary food ˌof mourners˺. ²³You will keep your turbans on your heads and your sandals on your feet. You will not mourn or weep but will waste away because of^a your sins and groan among yourselves. ²⁴Ezekiel will be a sign to you; you will do just as he has done. When this happens, you will know that I am the Sovereign LORD.'

²⁵"And you, son of man, on the day I take away their stronghold, their joy and glory, the delight of their eyes, their heart's desire, and their sons and daughters as well— ²⁶on that day a fugitive will come to tell you the news. ²⁷At that time your mouth will be opened; you will speak with him and will no longer be silent. So you will be a sign to them, and they will know that I am the LORD."

A Prophecy Against Ammon

25 The word of the LORD came to me: ²"Son of man, set your face against the Ammonites and prophesy against them. ³Say to them, 'Hear the word of the Sovereign LORD. This is what the Sovereign LORD says: Because you said "Aha!" over my sanctuary when it was desecrated and over the land of Israel when it was laid waste and over the people of Judah when they went into exile, ⁴therefore I am going to give you to the people of the East as a possession. They will set up their camps and pitch their tents among you; they will eat your fruit and drink your milk. ⁵I will turn Rabbah into a pasture for camels and Ammon into a resting place for sheep. Then you will know that I am the LORD. ⁶For this is what the Sovereign LORD says: Because you have clapped your hands and stamped your feet, rejoicing with all the malice of your heart against the land of Israel, ⁷therefore I will stretch out my hand against you and give you as plunder to the nations.

---

^a23 Or away in

I will cut you off from the nations and exterminate you from the countries. I will destroy you, and you will know that I am the LORD.' "

A Prophecy Against Moab

8"This is what the Sovereign LORD says: 'Because Moab and Seir said, "Look, the house of Judah has become like all the other nations," 9therefore I will expose the flank of Moab, beginning at its frontier towns—Beth Jeshimoth, Baal Meon and Kiriathaim—the glory of that land. 10I will give Moab along with the Ammonites to the people of the East as a possession, so that the Ammonites will not be remembered among the nations; 11and I will inflict punishment on Moab. Then they will know that I am the LORD.' "

A Prophecy Against Edom

12"This is what the Sovereign LORD says: 'Because Edom took revenge on the house of Judah and became very guilty by doing so, 13therefore this is what the Sovereign LORD says: I will stretch out my hand against Edom and kill its men and their animals. I will lay it waste, and from Teman to Dedan they will fall by the sword. 14I will take vengeance on Edom by the hand of my people Israel, and they will deal with Edom in accordance with my anger and my wrath; they will know my vengeance, declares the Sovereign LORD.' "

A Prophecy Against Philistia

15"This is what the Sovereign LORD says: 'Because the Philistines acted in vengeance and took revenge with malice in their hearts, and with ancient hostility sought to destroy Judah, 16therefore this is what the Sovereign LORD says: I am about to stretch out my hand against the Philistines, and I will cut off the Kerethites and destroy those remaining along the coast. 17I will carry out great vengeance on them and punish them in my wrath. Then they will know that I am the LORD, when I take vengeance on them.' "

A Prophecy Against Tyre

26 In the eleventh year, on the first day of the month, the word of the LORD came to me: 2"Son of man, because Tyre has said of Jerusalem, 'Aha! The gate to the nations is broken, and its doors have swung open to me; now that she lies in ruins I will prosper,' 3therefore this is what the Sovereign LORD says: I am against you, O Tyre, and I will bring many nations against you, like the sea casting up its waves. 4They will destroy the walls of Tyre and pull down her towers; I will scrape away her rubble and make her a bare rock. 5Out in the sea she will become a place to spread fishnets, for I have spoken, declares the Sovereign LORD. She will become plunder for the nations, 6and her settlements on the mainland will be ravaged by the sword. Then they will know that I am the LORD.

7"For this is what the Sovereign LORD says: From the north I am going to bring against Tyre Nebuchadnezzar*a* king of

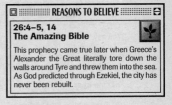

░░░ REASONS TO BELIEVE ░░░

26:4–5, 14
The Amazing Bible

This prophecy came true later when Greece's Alexander the Great literally tore down the walls around Tyre and threw them into the sea. As God predicted through Ezekiel, the city has never been rebuilt.

Babylon, king of kings, with horses and chariots, with horsemen and a great army. 8He will ravage your settlements on the mainland with the sword; he will set up siege works against you, build a ramp up to your walls and raise his shields against you. 9He will direct the blows of his battering rams against your walls and demolish your towers with his weapons. 10His horses will be so many that they will cover you with dust. Your walls will tremble at the noise of the war horses, wagons and chariots when he enters your gates as men enter a city whose walls have been broken through. 11The hoofs of his

a7 Hebrew Nebuchadrezzar, of which Nebuchadnezzar is a variant; here and often in Ezekiel and Jeremiah

horses will trample all your streets; he will kill your people with the sword, and your strong pillars will fall to the ground. ¹²They will plunder your wealth and loot your merchandise; they will break down your walls and demolish your fine houses and throw your stones, timber and rubble into the sea. ¹³I will put an end to your noisy songs, and the music of your harps will be heard no more. ¹⁴I will make you a bare rock, and you will become a place to spread fishnets. You will never be rebuilt, for I the LORD have spoken, declares the Sovereign LORD.

¹⁵"This is what the Sovereign LORD says to Tyre: Will not the coastlands tremble at the sound of your fall, when the wounded groan and the slaughter takes place in you? ¹⁶Then all the princes of the coast will step down from their thrones and lay aside their robes and take off their embroidered garments. Clothed with terror, they will sit on the ground, trembling every moment, appalled at you. ¹⁷Then they will take up a lament concerning you and say to you:

> " 'How you are destroyed, O city of renown,
>   peopled by men of the sea!
> You were a power on the seas,
>   you and your citizens;
> you put your terror
>   on all who lived there.
> ¹⁸Now the coastlands tremble
>   on the day of your fall;
>   the islands in the sea
>   are terrified at your collapse.'

¹⁹"This is what the Sovereign LORD says: When I make you a desolate city, like cities no longer inhabited, and when I bring the ocean depths over you and its vast waters cover you, ²⁰then I will bring you down with those who go down to the pit, to the people of long ago. I will make you dwell in the earth below, as in ancient ruins, with those who go down to the pit, and you will not return or take your place*a* in the land of the living. ²¹I will bring you to a horrible end and you will be no more. You will be sought, but you will never again be found, declares the Sovereign LORD."

A Lament for Tyre

27 The word of the LORD came to me: ²"Son of man, take up a lament concerning Tyre. ³Say to Tyre, situated at the gateway to the sea, merchant of peoples on many coasts, 'This is what the Sovereign LORD says:

> " 'You say, O Tyre,
>   "I am perfect in beauty."
> ⁴Your domain was on the high seas;
>   your builders brought your beauty to perfection.
> ⁵They made all your timbers
>   of pine trees from Senir*b*;
> they took a cedar from Lebanon
>   to make a mast for you.
> ⁶Of oaks from Bashan
>   they made your oars;
> of cypress wood*c* from the coasts of Cyprus*d*
>   they made your deck, inlaid with ivory.
> ⁷Fine embroidered linen from Egypt was your sail
>   and served as your banner;

a20 Septuagint; Hebrew *return, and I will give glory*   *b5* That is, Hermon   *c6* Targum; the Masoretic Text has a different division of the consonants.   *d6* Hebrew *Kittim*

your awnings were of blue and purple
    from the coasts of Elishah.
[8]Men of Sidon and Arvad were your oarsmen;
    your skilled men, O Tyre, were aboard as your seamen.
[9]Veteran craftsmen of Gebal[a] were on board
    as shipwrights to caulk your seams.
All the ships of the sea and their sailors
    came alongside to trade for your wares.

[10]"Men of Persia, Lydia and Put
    served as soldiers in your army.
They hung their shields and helmets on your walls,
    bringing you splendor.
[11]Men of Arvad and Helech
    manned your walls on every side;
men of Gammad
    were in your towers.
They hung their shields around your walls;
    they brought your beauty to perfection.

[12]"Tarshish did business with you because of your great wealth of goods; they exchanged silver, iron, tin and lead for your merchandise.
[13]"Greece, Tubal and Meshech traded with you; they exchanged slaves and articles of bronze for your wares.
[14]"Men of Beth Togarmah exchanged work horses, war horses and mules for your merchandise.
[15]"The men of Rhodes[b] traded with you, and many coastlands were your customers; they paid you with ivory tusks and ebony.
[16]"Aram[c] did business with you because of your many products; they exchanged turquoise, purple fabric, embroidered work, fine linen, coral and rubies for your merchandise.
[17]"Judah and Israel traded with you; they exchanged wheat from Minnith and confections,[d] honey, oil and balm for your wares.
[18]"Damascus, because of your many products and great wealth of goods, did business with you in wine from Helbon and wool from Zahar.
[19]"Danites and Greeks from Uzal bought your merchandise; they exchanged wrought iron, cassia and calamus for your wares.
[20]"Dedan traded in saddle blankets with you.
[21]"Arabia and all the princes of Kedar were your customers; they did business with you in lambs, rams and goats.
[22]"The merchants of Sheba and Raamah traded with you; for your merchandise they exchanged the finest of all kinds of spices and precious stones, and gold.
[23]"Haran, Canneh and Eden and merchants of Sheba, Asshur and Kilmad traded with you. [24]In your marketplace they traded with you beautiful garments, blue fabric, embroidered work and multicolored rugs with cords twisted and tightly knotted.

[25]"The ships of Tarshish serve
    as carriers for your wares.
You are filled with heavy cargo
    in the heart of the sea.
[26]Your oarsmen take you
    out to the high seas.

---

[a]9 That is, Byblos   [b]15 Septuagint; Hebrew *Dedan*   [c]16 Most Hebrew manuscripts; some Hebrew manuscripts and Syriac *Edom*   [d]17 The meaning of the Hebrew for this word is uncertain.

But the east wind will break you to pieces
   in the heart of the sea.
²⁷Your wealth, merchandise and wares,
   your mariners, seamen and shipwrights,
your merchants and all your soldiers,
   and everyone else on board
will sink into the heart of the sea
   on the day of your shipwreck.
²⁸The shorelands will quake
   when your seamen cry out.
²⁹All who handle the oars
   will abandon their ships;
the mariners and all the seamen
   will stand on the shore.
³⁰They will raise their voice
   and cry bitterly over you;
they will sprinkle dust on their heads
   and roll in ashes.
³¹They will shave their heads because of you
   and will put on sackcloth.
They will weep over you with anguish of soul
   and with bitter mourning.
³²As they wail and mourn over you,
   they will take up a lament concerning you:
"Who was ever silenced like Tyre,
   surrounded by the sea?"
³³When your merchandise went out on the seas,
   you satisfied many nations;
with your great wealth and your wares
   you enriched the kings of the earth.
³⁴Now you are shattered by the sea
   in the depths of the waters;
your wares and all your company
   have gone down with you.
³⁵All who live in the coastlands
   are appalled at you;
their kings shudder with horror
   and their faces are distorted with fear.
³⁶The merchants among the nations hiss at you;
   you have come to a horrible end
   and will be no more.' "

A Prophecy Against the King of Tyre

 The word of the LORD came to me: ²"Son of man, say to the ruler of Tyre, 'This is what the Sovereign LORD says:

" 'In the pride of your heart
   you say, "I am a god;
I sit on the throne of a god
   in the heart of the seas."
But you are a man and not a god,
   though you think you are as wise as a god.

³Are you wiser than Daniel*ᵃ*?
   Is no secret hidden from you?
⁴By your wisdom and understanding
   you have gained wealth for yourself
and amassed gold and silver
   in your treasuries.
⁵By your great skill in trading
   you have increased your wealth,
and because of your wealth
   your heart has grown proud.

⁶"'Therefore this is what the Sovereign Lᴏʀᴅ says:

  "'Because you think you are wise,
     as wise as a god,
⁷I am going to bring foreigners against you,
   the most ruthless of nations;
they will draw their swords against your beauty and wisdom
   and pierce your shining splendor.
⁸They will bring you down to the pit,
   and you will die a violent death
   in the heart of the seas.
⁹Will you then say, "I am a god,"
   in the presence of those who kill you?
You will be but a man, not a god,
   in the hands of those who slay you.
¹⁰You will die the death of the uncircumcised
   at the hands of foreigners.

I have spoken, declares the Sovereign Lᴏʀᴅ.'"

¹¹The word of the Lᴏʀᴅ came to me:
¹²"Son of man, take up a lament concerning the king of Tyre and say to him: 'This is what the Sovereign Lᴏʀᴅ says:

  "'You were the model of
     perfection,
   full of wisdom and perfect in
     beauty.
¹³You were in Eden,
   the garden of God;
every precious stone adorned
     you:
ruby, topaz and emerald,
chrysolite, onyx and jasper,
sapphire,ᵇ turquoise and beryl.ᶜ
Your settings and mountingsᵈ
     were made of gold;
on the day you were created they were prepared.
¹⁴You were anointed as a guardian cherub,
   for so I ordained you.

▣ ▦ ADDRESSING QUESTIONS ▦ ⮐

28:12–19
Unseen Realities **Q**

This passage, like the 14th chapter of Isaiah (page 901), speaks of a human tyrant, but seems to have a deeper application. By pointing back to the garden of Eden (verse 13), the prophet seems to refer to the image of Satan, the serpent. He too was created good, but rebelled and experienced God's rejection.

  Though the Bible says little about the origins and history of Satan, one thing is clear. He is a real power, and we need to avoid him and his ways at all costs.

ᵃ3 Or *Daniel*; the Hebrew spelling may suggest a person other than the prophet Daniel.   *ᵇ13* Or *lapis lazuli*   *ᶜ13* The precise identification of some of these precious stones is uncertain.   *ᵈ13* The meaning of the Hebrew for this phrase is uncertain.

You were on the holy mount of God;
  you walked among the fiery stones.
¹⁵You were blameless in your ways
    from the day you were created
    till wickedness was found in you.
¹⁶Through your widespread trade
    you were filled with violence,
    and you sinned.
  So I drove you in disgrace from the mount of God,
    and I expelled you, O guardian cherub,
    from among the fiery stones.
¹⁷Your heart became proud
    on account of your beauty,
  and you corrupted your wisdom ·
    because of your splendor.
  So I threw you to the earth;
    I made a spectacle of you before kings.
¹⁸By your many sins and dishonest trade
    you have desecrated your sanctuaries.
  So I made a fire come out from you,
    and it consumed you,
  and I reduced you to ashes on the ground
    in the sight of all who were watching.
¹⁹All the nations who knew you
    are appalled at you;
  you have come to a horrible end
    and will be no more.' "

A Prophecy Against Sidon

²⁰The word of the LORD came to me: ²¹"Son of man, set your face against Sidon; prophesy against her ²²and say: 'This is what the Sovereign LORD says:

  " 'I am against you, O Sidon,
    and I will gain glory within you.
  They will know that I am the LORD,
    when I inflict punishment on her
    and show myself holy within her.
  ²³I will send a plague upon her
    and make blood flow in her streets.
  The slain will fall within her,
    with the sword against her on every side.
  Then they will know that I am the LORD.

²⁴" 'No longer will the people of Israel have malicious neighbors who are painful briers
and sharp thorns. Then they will know that I am the Sovereign LORD.
²⁵" 'This is what the Sovereign LORD says: When I gather the people of Israel from the
nations where they have been scattered, I will show myself holy among them in the
sight of the nations. Then they will live in their own land, which I gave to my servant
Jacob. ²⁶They will live there in safety and will build houses and plant vineyards; they
will live in safety when I inflict punishment on all their neighbors who maligned them.
Then they will know that I am the LORD their God.' "

A Prophecy Against Egypt

29 In the tenth year, in the tenth month on the twelfth day, the word of the LORD came to me: **2**"Son of man, set your face against Pharaoh king of Egypt and prophesy against him and against all Egypt. **3**Speak to him and say: 'This is what the Sovereign LORD says:

> " 'I am against you, Pharaoh king of Egypt,
>   you great monster lying among your streams.
> You say, "The Nile is mine;
>   I made it for myself."
> **4**But I will put hooks in your jaws
>   and make the fish of your streams stick to your scales.
> I will pull you out from among your streams,
>   with all the fish sticking to your scales.
> **5**I will leave you in the desert,
>   you and all the fish of your streams.
> You will fall on the open field
>   and not be gathered or picked up.
> I will give you as food
>   to the beasts of the earth and the birds of the air.

6Then all who live in Egypt will know that I am the LORD.

" 'You have been a staff of reed for the house of Israel. **7**When they grasped you with their hands, you splintered and you tore open their shoulders; when they leaned on you, you broke and their backs were wrenched.[a]

8"Therefore this is what the Sovereign LORD says: I will bring a sword against you and kill your men and their animals. **9**Egypt will become a desolate wasteland. Then they will know that I am the LORD.

" 'Because you said, "The Nile is mine; I made it," **10**therefore I am against you and against your streams, and I will make the land of Egypt a ruin and a desolate waste from Migdol to Aswan, as far as the border of Cush.[b] **11**No foot of man or animal will pass through it; no one will live there for forty years. **12**I will make the land of Egypt desolate among devastated lands, and her cities will lie desolate forty years among ruined cities. And I will disperse the Egyptians among the nations and scatter them through the countries.

13"Yet this is what the Sovereign LORD says: At the end of forty years I will gather the Egyptians from the nations where they were scattered. **14**I will bring them back from captivity and return them to Upper Egypt,[c] the land of their ancestry. There they will be a lowly kingdom. **15**It will be the lowliest of kingdoms and will never again exalt itself above the other nations. I will make it so weak that it will never again rule over the nations. **16**Egypt will no longer be a source of confidence for the people of Israel but will be a reminder of their sin in turning to her for help. Then they will know that I am the Sovereign LORD.' "

17In the twenty-seventh year, in the first month on the first day, the word of the LORD came to me: **18**"Son of man, Nebuchadnezzar king of Babylon drove his army in a hard campaign against Tyre; every head was rubbed bare and every shoulder made raw. Yet he and his army got no reward from the campaign he led against Tyre. **19**Therefore this is what the Sovereign LORD says: I am going to give Egypt to Nebuchadnezzar king of Babylon, and he will carry off its wealth. He will loot and plunder the land as pay for his army. **20**I have given him Egypt as a reward for his efforts because he and his army did it for me, declares the Sovereign LORD.

a 7 Syriac (see also Septuagint and Vulgate); Hebrew *and you caused their backs to stand*   *b 10* That is, the upper Nile region   *c 14* Hebrew *to Pathros*

²¹"On that day I will make a horn[a] grow for the house of Israel, and I will open your mouth among them. Then they will know that I am the LORD."

A Lament for Egypt

 The word of the LORD came to me: ²"Son of man, prophesy and say: 'This is what the Sovereign LORD says:

" 'Wail and say,
   "Alas for that day!"
³For the day is near,
   the day of the LORD is near—
a day of clouds,
   a time of doom for the nations.
⁴A sword will come against Egypt,
   and anguish will come upon Cush.[b]
When the slain fall in Egypt,
   her wealth will be carried away
   and her foundations torn down.

⁵Cush and Put, Lydia and all Arabia, Libya[c] and the people of the covenant land will fall by the sword along with Egypt.

⁶"'This is what the LORD says:

" 'The allies of Egypt will fall
   and her proud strength will fail.
From Migdol to Aswan
   they will fall by the sword within her,

                                    declares the Sovereign LORD.

⁷"'They will be desolate
   among desolate lands,
and their cities will lie
   among ruined cities.
⁸Then they will know that I am the LORD,
   when I set fire to Egypt
   and all her helpers are crushed.

⁹"'On that day messengers will go out from me in ships to frighten Cush out of her complacency. Anguish will take hold of them on the day of Egypt's doom, for it is sure to come.

¹⁰"'This is what the Sovereign LORD says:

" 'I will put an end to the hordes of Egypt
   by the hand of Nebuchadnezzar king of Babylon.
¹¹He and his army—the most ruthless of nations—
   will be brought in to destroy the land.
They will draw their swords against Egypt
   and fill the land with the slain.
¹²I will dry up the streams of the Nile
   and sell the land to evil men;
by the hand of foreigners
   I will lay waste the land and everything in it.

I the LORD have spoken.

¹³"'This is what the Sovereign LORD says:

---

a 21 Horn here symbolizes strength.   *b 4* That is, the upper Nile region; also in verses 5 and 9   *c 5* Hebrew Cub

" 'I will destroy the idols
    and put an end to the images in Memphis. *a*
No longer will there be a prince in Egypt,
    and I will spread fear throughout the land.
¹⁴I will lay waste Upper Egypt, *b*
    set fire to Zoan
    and inflict punishment on Thebes. *c*
¹⁵I will pour out my wrath on Pelusium, *d*
    the stronghold of Egypt,
    and cut off the hordes of Thebes.
¹⁶I will set fire to Egypt;
    Pelusium will writhe in agony.
Thebes will be taken by storm;
    Memphis will be in constant distress.
¹⁷The young men of Heliopolis *e* and Bubastis *f*
    will fall by the sword,
    and the cities themselves will go into captivity.
¹⁸Dark will be the day at Tahpanhes
    when I break the yoke of Egypt;
    there her proud strength will come to an end.
She will be covered with clouds,
    and her villages will go into captivity.
¹⁹So I will inflict punishment on Egypt,
    and they will know that I am the LORD.' "

²⁰In the eleventh year, in the first month on the seventh day, the word of the LORD came to me: ²¹"Son of man, I have broken the arm of Pharaoh king of Egypt. It has not been bound up for healing or put in a splint so as to become strong enough to hold a sword. ²²Therefore this is what the Sovereign LORD says: I am against Pharaoh king of Egypt. I will break both his arms, the good arm as well as the broken one, and make the sword fall from his hand. ²³I will disperse the Egyptians among the nations and scatter them through the countries. ²⁴I will strengthen the arms of the king of Babylon and put my sword in his hand, but I will break the arms of Pharaoh, and he will groan before him like a mortally wounded man. ²⁵I will strengthen the arms of the king of Babylon, but the arms of Pharaoh will fall limp. Then they will know that I am the LORD, when I put my sword into the hand of the king of Babylon and he brandishes it against Egypt. ²⁶I will disperse the Egyptians among the nations and scatter them through the countries. Then they will know that I am the LORD."

A Cedar in Lebanon

31 In the eleventh year, in the third month on the first day, the word of the LORD came to me: ²"Son of man, say to Pharaoh king of Egypt and to his hordes:

" 'Who can be compared with you in majesty?
³Consider Assyria, once a cedar in Lebanon,
    with beautiful branches overshadowing the forest;
it towered on high,
    its top above the thick foliage.
⁴The waters nourished it,
    deep springs made it grow tall;
    their streams flowed
    all around its base

---

a 13 Hebrew *Noph;* also in verse 16   *b* 14 Hebrew *waste Pathros*   *c* 14 Hebrew *No;* also in verses 15 and 16
d 15 Hebrew *Sin;* also in verse 16   *e* 17 Hebrew *Awen* (or *On*)   *f* 17 Hebrew *Pi Beseth*

and sent their channels
  to all the trees of the field.
⁵So it towered higher
  than all the trees of the field;
its boughs increased
  and its branches grew long,
  spreading because of abundant waters.
⁶All the birds of the air
  nested in its boughs,
all the beasts of the field
  gave birth under its branches;
all the great nations
  lived in its shade.
⁷It was majestic in beauty,
  with its spreading boughs,
for its roots went down
  to abundant waters.
⁸The cedars in the garden of God
  could not rival it,
nor could the pine trees
  equal its boughs,
nor could the plane trees
  compare with its branches—
no tree in the garden of God
  could match its beauty.
⁹I made it beautiful
  with abundant branches,
the envy of all the trees of Eden
  in the garden of God.

¹⁰"'Therefore this is what the Sovereign LORD says: Because it towered on high, lifting its top above the thick foliage, and because it was proud of its height, ¹¹I handed it over to the ruler of the nations, for him to deal with according to its wickedness. I cast it aside, ¹²and the most ruthless of foreign nations cut it down and left it. Its boughs fell on the mountains and in all the valleys; its branches lay broken in all the ravines of the land. All the nations of the earth came out from under its shade and left it. ¹³All the birds of the air settled on the fallen tree, and all the beasts of the field were among its branches. ¹⁴Therefore no other trees by the waters are ever to tower proudly on high, lifting their tops above the thick foliage. No other trees so well-watered are ever to reach such a height; they are all destined for death, for the earth below, among mortal men, with those who go down to the pit.

¹⁵"'This is what the Sovereign LORD says: On the day it was brought down to the grave*ᵃ* I covered the deep springs with mourning for it; I held back its streams, and its abundant waters were restrained. Because of it I clothed Lebanon with gloom, and all the trees of the field withered away. ¹⁶I made the nations tremble at the sound of its fall when I brought it down to the grave with those who go down to the pit. Then all the trees of Eden, the choicest and best of Lebanon, all the trees that were well-watered, were consoled in the earth below. ¹⁷Those who lived in its shade, its allies among the nations, had also gone down to the grave with it, joining those killed by the sword.

¹⁸"'Which of the trees of Eden can be compared with you in splendor and majesty? Yet

---

ᵃ 15 Hebrew *Sheol;* also in verses 16 and 17

you, too, will be brought down with the trees of Eden to the earth below; you will lie among the uncircumcised, with those killed by the sword.

" 'This is Pharaoh and all his hordes, declares the Sovereign LORD.' "

A Lament for Pharaoh

32 In the twelfth year, in the twelfth month on the first day, the word of the LORD came to me: [2]"Son of man, take up a lament concerning Pharaoh king of Egypt and say to him:

" 'You are like a lion among the nations;
      you are like a monster in the seas
   thrashing about in your streams,
      churning the water with your feet
      and muddying the streams.

[3]" 'This is what the Sovereign LORD says:

" 'With a great throng of people
      I will cast my net over you,
      and they will haul you up in my net.
[4]I will throw you on the land
      and hurl you on the open field.
   I will let all the birds of the air settle on you
      and all the beasts of the earth gorge themselves on you.
[5]I will spread your flesh on the mountains
      and fill the valleys with your remains.
[6]I will drench the land with your flowing blood
      all the way to the mountains,
      and the ravines will be filled with your flesh.
[7]When I snuff you out, I will cover the heavens
      and darken their stars;
   I will cover the sun with a cloud,
      and the moon will not give its light.
[8]All the shining lights in the heavens
      I will darken over you;
   I will bring darkness over your land,

                    declares the Sovereign LORD.
[9]I will trouble the hearts of many peoples
      when I bring about your destruction among the nations,
      among[a] lands you have not known.
[10]I will cause many peoples to be appalled at you,
      and their kings will shudder with horror because of you
      when I brandish my sword before them.
   On the day of your downfall
      each of them will tremble
      every moment for his life.

[11]" 'For this is what the Sovereign LORD says:

" 'The sword of the king of Babylon
      will come against you.
[12]I will cause your hordes to fall
      by the swords of mighty men—
      the most ruthless of all nations.

---

[a]9 Hebrew; Septuagint *bring you into captivity among the nations, / to*

They will shatter the pride of Egypt,
  and all her hordes will be overthrown.
¹³I will destroy all her cattle
  from beside abundant waters
no longer to be stirred by the foot of man
  or muddied by the hoofs of cattle.
¹⁴Then I will let her waters settle
  and make her streams flow like oil,

declares the Sovereign Lord.

¹⁵When I make Egypt desolate
  and strip the land of everything in it,
when I strike down all who live there,
  then they will know that I am the Lord.'

¹⁶"This is the lament they will chant for her. The daughters of the nations will chant it; for Egypt and all her hordes they will chant it, declares the Sovereign Lord."

¹⁷In the twelfth year, on the fifteenth day of the month, the word of the Lord came to me: ¹⁸"Son of man, wail for the hordes of Egypt and consign to the earth below both her and the daughters of mighty nations, with those who go down to the pit. ¹⁹Say to them, 'Are you more favored than others? Go down and be laid among the uncircumcised.' ²⁰They will fall among those killed by the sword. The sword is drawn; let her be dragged off with all her hordes. ²¹From within the grave*ᵃ* the mighty leaders will say of Egypt and her allies, 'They have come down and they lie with the uncircumcised, with those killed by the sword.'

²²"Assyria is there with her whole army; she is surrounded by the graves of all her slain, all who have fallen by the sword. ²³Their graves are in the depths of the pit and her army lies around her grave. All who had spread terror in the land of the living are slain, fallen by the sword.

²⁴"Elam is there, with all her hordes around her grave. All of them are slain, fallen by the sword. All who had spread terror in the land of the living went down uncircumcised to the earth below. They bear their shame with those who go down to the pit. ²⁵A bed is made for her among the slain, with all her hordes around her grave. All of them are uncircumcised, killed by the sword. Because their terror had spread in the land of the living, they bear their shame with those who go down to the pit; they are laid among the slain.

²⁶"Meshech and Tubal are there, with all their hordes around their graves. All of them are uncircumcised, killed by the sword because they spread their terror in the land of the living. ²⁷Do they not lie with the other uncircumcised warriors who have fallen, who went down to the grave with their weapons of war, whose swords were placed under their heads? The punishment for their sins rested on their bones, though the terror of these warriors had stalked through the land of the living.

²⁸"You too, O Pharaoh, will be broken and will lie among the uncircumcised, with those killed by the sword.

²⁹"Edom is there, her kings and all her princes; despite their power, they are laid with those killed by the sword. They lie with the uncircumcised, with those who go down to the pit.

³⁰"All the princes of the north and all the Sidonians are there; they went down with the slain in disgrace despite the terror caused by their power. They lie uncircumcised with those killed by the sword and bear their shame with those who go down to the pit.

³¹"Pharaoh—he and all his army—will see them and he will be consoled for all his hordes that were killed by the sword, declares the Sovereign Lord. ³²Although I had him

---

ᵃ21 Hebrew Sheol; also in verse 27

spread terror in the land of the living, Pharaoh and all his hordes will be laid among the uncircumcised, with those killed by the sword, declares the Sovereign LORD."

Ezekiel a Watchman

33 The word of the LORD came to me: ²"Son of man, speak to your countrymen and say to them: 'When I bring the sword against a land, and the people of the land choose one of their men and make him their watchman, ³and he sees the sword coming against the land and blows the trumpet to warn the people, ⁴then if anyone hears the trumpet but does not take warning and the sword comes and takes his life, his blood will be on his own head. ⁵Since he heard the sound of the trumpet but did not take warning, his blood will be on his own head. If he had taken warning, he would have saved himself. ⁶But if the watchman sees the sword coming and does not blow the trumpet to warn the people and the sword comes and takes the life of one of them, that man will be taken away because of his sin, but I will hold the watchman accountable for his blood.'

⁷"Son of man, I have made you a watchman for the house of Israel; so hear the word I speak and give them warning from me. ⁸When I say to the wicked, 'O wicked man, you will surely die,' and you do not speak out to dissuade him from his ways, that wicked man will die for[a] his sin, and I will hold you accountable for his blood. ⁹But if you do warn the wicked man to turn from his ways and he does not do so, he will die for his sin, but you will have saved yourself.

¹⁰"Son of man, say to the house of Israel, 'This is what you are saying: "Our offenses and sins weigh us down, and we are wasting away because of[b] them. How then can we live?"' ¹¹Say to them, 'As surely as I live, declares the Sovereign LORD, I take no pleasure in the death of the wicked, but rather that they turn from their ways and live. Turn! Turn from your evil ways! Why will you die, O house of Israel?'

¹²"Therefore, son of man, say to your countrymen, 'The righteousness of the righteous man will not save him when he disobeys, and the wickedness of the wicked man will not cause him to fall when he turns from it. The righteous man, if he sins, will not be allowed to live because of his former righteousness.' ¹³If I tell the righteous man that he will surely live, but then he trusts in his righteousness and does evil, none of the righteous things he has done will be remembered; he will die for the evil he has done. ¹⁴And if I say to the wicked man, 'You will surely die,' but he then turns away from his sin and does what is just and right— ¹⁵if he gives back what he took in pledge for a loan, returns what he has stolen, follows the decrees that give life, and does no evil, he will surely live; he will not die. ¹⁶None of the sins he has committed will be remembered against him. He has done what is just and right; he will surely live.

¹⁷"Yet your countrymen say, 'The way of the Lord is not just.' But it is their way that is not just. ¹⁸If a righteous man turns from his righteousness and does evil, he will die for it. ¹⁹And if a wicked man turns away from his wickedness and does what is just and right, he will live by doing so. ²⁰Yet, O house of Israel, you say, 'The way of the Lord is not just.' But I will judge each of you according to his own ways."

Jerusalem's Fall Explained

²¹In the twelfth year of our exile, in the tenth month on the fifth day, a man who had escaped from Jerusalem came to me and said, "The city has fallen!" ²²Now the evening before the man arrived, the hand of the LORD was upon me, and he opened my mouth before the man came to me in the morning. So my mouth was opened and I was no longer silent.

²³Then the word of the LORD came to me: ²⁴"Son of man, the people living in those ruins in the land of Israel are saying, 'Abraham was only one man, yet he possessed the land. But we are many; surely the land has been given to us as our possession.' ²⁵Therefore

a 8 Or *in*; also in verse 9   *b 10* Or *away in*

say to them, 'This is what the Sovereign LORD says: Since you eat meat with the blood still in it and look to your idols and shed blood, should you then possess the land? ²⁶You rely on your sword, you do detestable things, and each of you defiles his neighbor's wife. Should you then possess the land?'

²⁷Say this to them: 'This is what the Sovereign LORD says: As surely as I live, those who are left in the ruins will fall by the sword, those out in the country I will give to the wild animals to be devoured, and those in strongholds and caves will die of a plague. ²⁸I will make the land a desolate waste, and her proud strength will come to an end, and the mountains of Israel will become desolate so that no one will cross them. ²⁹Then they will know that I am the LORD, when I have made the land a desolate waste because of all the detestable things they have done.'

³⁰"As for you, son of man, your countrymen are talking together about you by the walls and at the doors of the houses, saying to each other, 'Come and hear the message that has come from the LORD.' ³¹My people come to you, as they usually do, and sit before you to listen to your words, but they do not put them into practice. With their mouths they express devotion, but their hearts are greedy for unjust gain. ³²Indeed, to them you are nothing more than one who sings love songs with a beautiful voice and plays an instrument well, for they hear your words but do not put them into practice.

³³"When all this comes true—and it surely will—then they will know that a prophet has been among them."

Shepherds and Sheep

34 The word of the LORD came to me: ²"Son of man, prophesy against the shepherds of Israel; prophesy and say to them: 'This is what the Sovereign LORD says: Woe to the shepherds of Israel who only take care of themselves! Should not shepherds take care of the flock? ³You eat the curds, clothe yourselves with the wool and slaughter the choice animals, but you do not take care of the flock. ⁴You have not strengthened the weak or healed the sick or bound up the injured. You have not brought back the strays or searched for the lost. You have ruled them harshly and brutally. ⁵So they were scattered because there was no shepherd, and when they were scattered they became food for all the wild animals. ⁶My sheep wandered over all the mountains and on every high hill. They were scattered over the whole earth, and no one searched or looked for them.

⁷"'Therefore, you shepherds, hear the word of the LORD: ⁸As surely as I live, declares the Sovereign LORD, because my flock lacks a shepherd and so has been plundered and has become food for all the wild animals, and because my shepherds did not search for my flock but cared for themselves rather than for my flock, ⁹therefore, O shepherds, hear the word of the LORD: ¹⁰This is what the Sovereign LORD says: I am against the shepherds and will hold them accountable for my flock. I will remove them from tending the flock so that the shepherds can no longer feed themselves. I will rescue my flock from their mouths, and it will no longer be food for them.

¹¹"'For this is what the Sovereign LORD says: I myself will search for my sheep and look after them. ¹²As a shepherd looks after his scattered flock when he is with them, so will I look after my sheep. I will rescue them from all the places where they were scattered on a day of clouds and darkness. ¹³I will bring them out from the nations and gather them from the countries, and I will bring them into their own land. I will pasture them on the mountains of Israel, in the ravines and in all the settlements in the land. ¹⁴I will tend them in a good pasture, and the mountain heights of Israel will be their grazing land. There they will lie down in good grazing land, and there they will feed in a rich pasture on the mountains of Israel. ¹⁵I myself will tend my sheep and have them lie down, declares the Sovereign LORD. ¹⁶I will search for the lost and bring back the strays. I will bind up the injured and strengthen the weak, but the sleek and the strong I will destroy. I will shepherd the flock with justice.

¹⁷"'As for you, my flock, this is what the Sovereign Lord says: I will judge between one sheep and another, and between rams and goats. ¹⁸Is it not enough for you to feed on the good pasture? Must you also trample the rest of your pasture with your feet? Is it not enough for you to drink clear water? Must you also muddy the rest with your feet? ¹⁹Must my flock feed on what you have trampled and drink what you have muddied with your feet?

²⁰"'Therefore this is what the Sovereign Lord says to them: See, I myself will judge between the fat sheep and the lean sheep. ²¹Because you shove with flank and shoulder, butting all the weak sheep with your horns until you have driven them away, ²²I will save my flock, and they will no longer be plundered. I will judge between one sheep and another. ²³I will place over them one shepherd, my servant David, and he will tend them; he will tend them and be their shepherd. ²⁴I the Lord will be their God, and my servant David will be prince among them. I the Lord have spoken.

²⁵"'I will make a covenant of peace with them and rid the land of wild beasts so that they may live in the desert and sleep in the forests in safety. ²⁶I will bless them and the places surrounding my hill.^a I will send down showers in season; there will be showers of blessing. ²⁷The trees of the field will yield their fruit and the ground will yield its crops; the people will be secure in their land. They will know that I am the Lord, when I break the bars of their yoke and rescue them from the hands of those who enslaved them. ²⁸They will no longer be plundered by the nations, nor will wild animals devour them. They will live in safety, and no one will make them afraid. ²⁹I will provide for them a land renowned for its crops, and they will no longer be victims of famine in the land or bear the scorn of the nations. ³⁰Then they will know that I, the Lord their God, am with them and that they, the house of Israel, are my people, declares the Sovereign Lord. ³¹You my sheep, the sheep of my pasture, are people, and I am your God,' declares the Sovereign Lord.'"

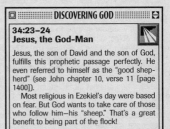

:::::: DISCOVERING GOD ::::::

34:23–24
Jesus, the God-Man

Jesus, the son of David and the son of God, fulfills this prophetic passage perfectly. He even referred to himself as the "good shepherd" (see John chapter 10, verse 11 [page 1400]).

Most religious in Ezekiel's day were based on fear. But God wants to take care of those who follow him—his "sheep." That's a great benefit to being part of the flock!

A Prophecy Against Edom

35 The word of the Lord came to me: ²"Son of man, set your face against Mount Seir; prophesy against it ³and say: 'This is what the Sovereign Lord says: I am against you, Mount Seir, and I will stretch out my hand against you and make you a desolate waste. ⁴I will turn your towns into ruins and you will be desolate. Then you will know that I am the Lord.

⁵"'Because you harbored an ancient hostility and delivered the Israelites over to the sword at the time of their calamity, the time their punishment reached its climax, ⁶therefore as surely as I live, declares the Sovereign Lord, I will give you over to bloodshed and it will pursue you. Since you did not hate bloodshed, bloodshed will pursue you. ⁷I will make Mount Seir a desolate waste and cut off from it all who come and go. ⁸I will fill your mountains with the slain; those killed by the sword will fall on your hills and in your valleys and in all your ravines. ⁹I will make you desolate forever; your towns will not be inhabited. Then you will know that I am the Lord.

¹⁰"'Because you have said, "These two nations and countries will be ours and we will take possession of them," even though I the Lord was there, ¹¹therefore as surely as I live, declares the Sovereign Lord, I will treat you in accordance with the anger and jealousy

^a26 Or I will make them and the places surrounding my hill a blessing

you showed in your hatred of them and I will make myself known among them when I judge you. ¹²Then you will know that I the LORD have heard all the contemptible things you have said against the mountains of Israel. You said, "They have been laid waste and have been given over to us to devour." ¹³You boasted against me and spoke against me without restraint, and I heard it. ¹⁴This is what the Sovereign LORD says: While the whole earth rejoices, I will make you desolate. ¹⁵Because you rejoiced when the inheritance of the house of Israel became desolate, that is how I will treat you. You will be desolate, O Mount Seir, you and all of Edom. Then they will know that I am the LORD.'"

A Prophecy to the Mountains of Israel

36 "Son of man, prophesy to the mountains of Israel and say, 'O mountains of Israel, hear the word of the LORD. ²This is what the Sovereign LORD says: The enemy said of you, "Aha! The ancient heights have become our possession." ' ³Therefore prophesy and say, 'This is what the Sovereign LORD says: Because they ravaged and hounded you from every side so that you became the possession of the rest of the nations and the object of people's malicious talk and slander, ⁴therefore, O mountains of Israel, hear the word of the Sovereign LORD: This is what the Sovereign LORD says to the mountains and hills, to the ravines and valleys, to the desolate ruins and the deserted towns that have been plundered and ridiculed by the rest of the nations around you— ⁵this is what the Sovereign LORD says: In my burning zeal I have spoken against the rest of the nations, and against all Edom, for with glee and with malice in their hearts they made my land their own possession so that they might plunder its pastureland.' ⁶Therefore prophesy concerning the land of Israel and say to the mountains and hills, to the ravines and valleys: 'This is what the Sovereign LORD says: I speak in my jealous wrath because you have suffered the scorn of the nations. ⁷Therefore this is what the Sovereign LORD says: I swear with uplifted hand that the nations around you will also suffer scorn.

⁸" 'But you, O mountains of Israel, will produce branches and fruit for my people Israel, for they will soon come home. ⁹I am concerned for you and will look on you with favor; you will be plowed and sown, ¹⁰and I will multiply the number of people upon you, even the whole house of Israel. The towns will be inhabited and the ruins rebuilt. ¹¹I will increase the number of men and animals upon you, and they will be fruitful and become numerous. I will settle people on you as in the past and will make you prosper more than before. Then you will know that I am the LORD. ¹²I will cause people, my people Israel, to walk upon you. They will possess you, and you will be their inheritance; you will never again deprive them of their children.

¹³"This is what the Sovereign LORD says: Because people say to you, "You devour men and deprive your nation of its children," ¹⁴therefore you will no longer devour men or make your nation childless, declares the Sovereign LORD. ¹⁵No longer will I make you hear the taunts of the nations, and no longer will you suffer the scorn of the peoples or cause your nation to fall, declares the Sovereign LORD.'"

¹⁶Again the word of the LORD came to me: ¹⁷"Son of man, when the people of Israel were living in their own land, they defiled it by their conduct and their actions. Their conduct was like a woman's monthly uncleanness in my sight. ¹⁸So I poured out my wrath on them because they had shed blood in the land and because they had defiled it with their idols. ¹⁹I dispersed them among the nations, and they were scattered through the countries; I judged them according to their conduct and their actions. ²⁰And wherever they went among the nations they profaned my holy name, for it was said of them, 'These are the LORD's people, and yet they had to leave his land.' ²¹I had concern for my holy name, which the house of Israel profaned among the nations where they had gone.

²²"Therefore say to the house of Israel, 'This is what the Sovereign LORD says: It is not for your sake, O house of Israel, that I am going to do these things, but for the sake of my holy name, which you have profaned among the nations where you have gone. ²³I will show the holiness of my great name, which has been profaned among the nations, the

name you have profaned among them. Then the nations will know that I am the Lord, declares the Sovereign Lord, when I show myself holy through you before their eyes.

²⁴"'For I will take you out of the nations; I will gather you from all the countries and bring you back into your own land. ²⁵I will sprinkle clean water on you, and you will be clean; I will cleanse you from all your impurities and from all your idols. ²⁶I will give you a new heart and put a new spirit in you; I will remove from you your heart of stone and give you a heart of flesh. ²⁷And I will put my Spirit in you and move you to follow my decrees and be careful to keep my laws. ²⁸You will live in the land I gave your forefathers; you will be my people, and I will be your God. ²⁹I will save you from all your uncleanness. I will call for the grain and make it plentiful and will not bring famine upon you. ³⁰I will increase the fruit of the trees and the crops of the field, so that you will no longer suffer disgrace among the nations because of famine. ³¹Then you will remember your evil ways and wicked deeds, and you will loathe yourselves for your sins and detestable practices. ³²I want you to know that I am not doing this for your sake, declares the Sovereign Lord. Be ashamed and disgraced for your conduct, O house of Israel!

³³"'This is what the Sovereign Lord says: On the day I cleanse you from all your sins, I will resettle your towns, and the ruins will be rebuilt. ³⁴The desolate land will be cultivated instead of lying desolate in the sight of all who pass through it. ³⁵They will say, "This land that was laid waste has become like the garden of Eden; the cities that were lying in ruins, desolate and destroyed, are now fortified and inhabited." ³⁶Then the nations around you that remain will know that I the Lord have rebuilt what was destroyed and have replanted what was desolate. I the Lord have spoken, and I will do it.'

³⁷"This is what the Sovereign Lord says: Once again I will yield to the plea of the house of Israel and do this for them: I will make their people as numerous as sheep, ³⁸as numerous as the flocks for offerings at Jerusalem during her appointed feasts. So will the ruined cities be filled with flocks of people. Then they will know that I am the Lord."

The Valley of Dry Bones

37 The hand of the Lord was upon me, and he brought me out by the Spirit of the Lord and set me in the middle of a valley; it was full of bones. ²He led me back and forth among them, and I saw a great many bones on the floor of the valley, bones that were very dry. ³He asked me, "Son of man, can these bones live?"

I said, "O Sovereign Lord, you alone know."

⁴Then he said to me, "Prophesy to these bones and say to them, 'Dry bones, hear the word of the Lord! ⁵This is what the Sovereign Lord says to these bones: I will make breath*ᵃ* enter you, and you will come to life. ⁶I will attach tendons to you and make flesh come upon you and cover you with skin; I will put breath in you, and you will come to life. Then you will know that I am the Lord.'"

⁷So I prophesied as I was commanded. And as I was prophesying, there was a noise, a rattling sound, and the bones came together, bone to bone. ⁸I looked, and tendons and flesh appeared on them and skin covered them, but there was no breath in them.

⁹Then he said to me, "Prophesy to the breath; prophesy, son of man, and say to it, 'This is what the Sovereign Lord says: Come from the four winds, O breath, and breathe into these slain, that they may live.'" ¹⁰So I prophesied as he commanded me, and breath entered them; they came to life and stood up on their feet—a vast army.

¹¹Then he said to me: "Son of man, these bones are the whole house of Israel. They say, 'Our bones are dried up and our hope is gone; we are cut off.' ¹²Therefore prophesy and say to them: 'This is what the Sovereign Lord says: O my people, I am going to open your graves and bring you up from them; I will bring you back to the land of Israel. ¹³Then you, my people, will know that I am the Lord, when I open your graves and bring you up from them. ¹⁴I will put my Spirit in you and you will live, and I will settle you in

_____

ᵃ 5 The Hebrew for this word can also mean *wind* or *spirit* (see verses 6-14).

your own land. Then you will know that I the LORD have spoken, and I have done it, declares the LORD.'"

One Nation Under One King

¹⁵The word of the LORD came to me: ¹⁶"Son of man, take a stick of wood and write on it, 'Belonging to Judah and the Israelites associated with him.' Then take another stick of wood, and write on it, 'Ephraim's stick, belonging to Joseph and all the house of Israel associated with him.' ¹⁷Join them together into one stick so that they will become one in your hand.

¹⁸"When your countrymen ask you, 'Won't you tell us what you mean by this?' ¹⁹say to them, 'This is what the Sovereign LORD says: I am going to take the stick of Joseph—which is in Ephraim's hand—and of the Israelite tribes associated with him, and join it to Judah's stick, making them a single stick of wood, and they will become one in my hand.' ²⁰Hold before their eyes the sticks you have written on ²¹and say to them, 'This is what the Sovereign LORD says: I will take the Israelites out of the nations where they have gone. I will gather them from all around and bring them back into their own land. ²²I will make them one nation in the land, on the mountains of Israel. There will be one king over all of them and they will never again be two nations or be divided into two kingdoms. ²³They will no longer defile themselves with their idols and vile images or with any of their offenses, for I will save them from all their sinful backsliding,ᵃ and I will cleanse them. They will be my people, and I will be their God.

²⁴"'My servant David will be king over them, and they will all have one shepherd. They will follow my laws and be careful to keep my decrees. ²⁵They will live in the land I gave to my servant Jacob, the land where your fathers lived. They and their children and their children's children will live there forever, and David my servant will be their prince forever. ²⁶I will make a covenant of peace with them; it will be an everlasting covenant. I will establish them and increase their numbers, and I will put my sanctuary among them forever. ²⁷My dwelling place will be with them; I will be their God, and they will be my people. ²⁸Then the nations will know that I the LORD make Israel holy, when my sanctuary is among them forever.'"

A Prophecy Against Gog

38 The word of the LORD came to me: ²"Son of man, set your face against Gog, of the land of Magog, the chief prince ofᵇ Meshech and Tubal; prophesy against him ³and say: 'This is what the Sovereign LORD says: I am against you, O Gog, chief prince ofᶜ Meshech and Tubal. ⁴I will turn you around, put hooks in your jaws and bring you out with your whole army—your horses, your horsemen fully armed, and a great horde with large and small shields, all of them brandishing their swords. ⁵Persia, Cushᵈ and Put will be with them, all with shields and helmets, ⁶also Gomer with all its troops, and Beth Togarmah from the far north with all its troops—the many nations with you.

⁷"'Get ready; be prepared, you and all the hordes gathered about you, and take command of them. ⁸After many days you will be called to arms. In future years you will invade a land that has recovered from war, whose people were gathered from many nations to the mountains of Israel, which had long been desolate. They had been brought out from the nations, and now all of them live in safety. ⁹You and all your troops and the many nations with you will go up, advancing like a storm; you will be like a cloud covering the land.

¹⁰"'This is what the Sovereign LORD says: On that day thoughts will come into your mind and you will devise an evil scheme. ¹¹You will say, "I will invade a land of unwalled villages; I will attack a peaceful and unsuspecting people—all of them living without

---

ᵃ23 Many Hebrew manuscripts (see also Septuagint); most Hebrew manuscripts *all their dwelling places where they sinned*
ᵇ2 Or *the prince of Rosh,*   ᶜ3 Or *Gog, prince of Rosh,*   ᵈ5 That is, the upper Nile region

walls and without gates and bars. ¹²I will plunder and loot and turn my hand against the resettled ruins and the people gathered from the nations, rich in livestock and goods, living at the center of the land." ¹³Sheba and Dedan and the merchants of Tarshish and all her villages*ᵃ* will say to you, "Have you come to plunder? Have you gathered your hordes to loot, to carry off silver and gold, to take away livestock and goods and to seize much plunder?" '

¹⁴"Therefore, son of man, prophesy and say to Gog: 'This is what the Sovereign Lord says: In that day, when my people Israel are living in safety, will you not take notice of it? ¹⁵You will come from your place in the far north, you and many nations with you, all of them riding on horses, a great horde, a mighty army. ¹⁶You will advance against my people Israel like a cloud that covers the land. In days to come, O Gog, I will bring you against my land, so that the nations may know me when I show myself holy through you before their eyes.

¹⁷" 'This is what the Sovereign Lord says: Are you not the one I spoke of in former days by my servants the prophets of Israel? At that time they prophesied for years that I would bring you against them. ¹⁸This is what will happen in that day: When Gog attacks the land of Israel, my hot anger will be aroused, declares the Sovereign Lord. ¹⁹In my zeal and fiery wrath I declare that at that time there will be a great earthquake in the land of Israel. ²⁰The fish of the sea, the birds of the air, the beasts of the field, every creature that moves along the ground, and all the people on the face of the earth will tremble at my presence. The mountains will be overturned, the cliffs will crumble and every wall will fall to the ground. ²¹I will summon a sword against Gog on all my mountains, declares the Sovereign Lord. Every man's sword will be against his brother. ²²I will execute judgment upon him with plague and bloodshed; I will pour down torrents of rain, hailstones and burning sulfur on him and on his troops and on the many nations with him. ²³And so I will show my greatness and my holiness, and I will make myself known in the sight of many nations. Then they will know that I am the Lord.'

39 "Son of man, prophesy against Gog and say: 'This is what the Sovereign Lord says: I am against you, O Gog, chief prince of*ᵇ* Meshech and Tubal. ²I will turn you around and drag you along. I will bring you from the far north and send you against the mountains of Israel. ³Then I will strike your bow from your left hand and make your arrows drop from your right hand. ⁴On the mountains of Israel you will fall, you and all your troops and the nations with you. I will give you as food to all kinds of carrion birds and to the wild animals. ⁵You will fall in the open field, for I have spoken, declares the Sovereign Lord. ⁶I will send fire on Magog and on those who live in safety in the coastlands, and they will know that I am the Lord.

⁷" 'I will make known my holy name among my people Israel. I will no longer let my holy name be profaned, and the nations will know that I the Lord am the Holy One in Israel. ⁸It is coming! It will surely take place, declares the Sovereign Lord. This is the day I have spoken of.

⁹" 'Then those who live in the towns of Israel will go out and use the weapons for fuel and burn them up—the small and large shields, the bows and arrows, the war clubs and spears. For seven years they will use them for fuel. ¹⁰They will not need to gather wood from the fields or cut it from the forests, because they will use the weapons for fuel. And they will plunder those who plundered them and loot those who looted them, declares the Sovereign Lord.

¹¹" 'On that day I will give Gog a burial place in Israel, in the valley of those who travel east toward*ᶜ* the Sea.*ᵈ* It will block the way of travelers, because Gog and all his hordes will be buried there. So it will be called the Valley of Hamon Gog.*ᵉ*

¹²" 'For seven months the house of Israel will be burying them in order to cleanse the

---

ᵃ13 Or *her strong lions*   *ᵇ1* Or *Gog, prince of Rosh.*   *ᶜ11* Or *of*   *ᵈ11* That is, the Dead Sea   *ᵉ11* Hamon Gog
means hordes of Gog.

land. [13]All the people of the land will bury them, and the day I am glorified will be a memorable day for them, declares the Sovereign LORD.

[14]"Men will be regularly employed to cleanse the land. Some will go throughout the land and, in addition to them, others will bury those that remain on the ground. At the end of the seven months they will begin their search. [15]As they go through the land and one of them sees a human bone, he will set up a marker beside it until the gravediggers have buried it in the Valley of Hamon Gog. [16](Also a town called Hamonah[a] will be there.) And so they will cleanse the land.'

[17]"Son of man, this is what the Sovereign LORD says: Call out to every kind of bird and all the wild animals: 'Assemble and come together from all around to the sacrifice I am preparing for you, the great sacrifice on the mountains of Israel. There you will eat flesh and drink blood. [18]You will eat the flesh of mighty men and drink the blood of the princes of the earth as if they were rams and lambs, goats and bulls—all of them fattened animals from Bashan. [19]At the sacrifice I am preparing for you, you will eat fat till you are glutted and drink blood till you are drunk. [20]At my table you will eat your fill of horses and riders, mighty men and soldiers of every kind,' declares the Sovereign LORD.

[21]"I will display my glory among the nations, and all the nations will see the punishment I inflict and the hand I lay upon them. [22]From that day forward the house of Israel will know that I am the LORD their God. [23]And the nations will know that the people of Israel went into exile for their sin, because they were unfaithful to me. So I hid my face from them and handed them over to their enemies, and they all fell by the sword. [24]I dealt with them according to their uncleanness and their offenses, and I hid my face from them.

[25]"Therefore this is what the Sovereign LORD says: I will now bring Jacob back from captivity[b] and will have compassion on all the people of Israel, and I will be zealous for my holy name. [26]They will forget their shame and all the unfaithfulness they showed toward me when they lived in safety in their land with no one to make them afraid. [27]When I have brought them back from the nations and have gathered them from the countries of their enemies, I will show myself holy through them in the sight of many nations. [28]Then they will know that I am the LORD their God, for though I sent them into exile among the nations, I will gather them to their own land, not leaving any behind. [29]I will no longer hide my face from them, for I will pour out my Spirit on the house of Israel, declares the Sovereign LORD."

The New Temple Area

40 In the twenty-fifth year of our exile, at the beginning of the year, on the tenth of the month, in the fourteenth year after the fall of the city—on that very day the hand of the LORD was upon me and he took me there. [2]In visions of God he took me to the land of Israel and set me on a very high mountain, on whose south side were some buildings that looked like a city. [3]He took me there, and I saw a man whose appearance was like bronze; he was standing in the gateway with a linen cord and a measuring rod in his hand. [4]The man said to me, "Son of man, look with your eyes and hear with your ears and pay attention to everything I am going to show you, for that is why you have been brought here. Tell the house of Israel everything you see."

The East Gate to the Outer Court

[5]I saw a wall completely surrounding the temple area. The length of the measuring rod in the man's hand was six long cubits, each of which was a cubit[c] and a handbreadth.[d] He measured the wall; it was one measuring rod thick and one rod high.

[6]Then he went to the gate facing east. He climbed its steps and measured the thresh-

---

[a]16 Hamonah means horde.   [b]25 Or now restore the fortunes of Jacob   [c]5 The common cubit was about 1 1/2 feet (about 0.5 meter).   [d]5 That is, about 3 inches (about 8 centimeters)

old of the gate; it was one rod deep.*ᵃ* ⁷The alcoves for the guards were one rod long and one rod wide, and the projecting walls between the alcoves were five cubits thick. And the threshold of the gate next to the portico facing the temple was one rod deep.

⁸Then he measured the portico of the gateway; ⁹it*ᵇ* was eight cubits deep and its jambs were two cubits thick. The portico of the gateway faced the temple.

¹⁰Inside the east gate were three alcoves on each side; the three had the same measurements, and the faces of the projecting walls on each side had the same measurements. ¹¹Then he measured the width of the entrance to the gateway; it was ten cubits and its length was thirteen cubits. ¹²In front of each alcove was a wall one cubit high, and the alcoves were six cubits square. ¹³Then he measured the gateway from the top of the rear wall of one alcove to the top of the opposite one; the distance was twenty-five cubits from one parapet opening to the opposite one. ¹⁴He measured along the faces of the projecting walls all around the inside of the gateway—sixty cubits. The measurement was up to the portico*ᶜ* facing the courtyard.*ᵈ* ¹⁵The distance from the entrance of the gateway to the far end of its portico was fifty cubits. ¹⁶The alcoves and the projecting walls inside the gateway were surmounted by narrow parapet openings all around, as was the portico; the openings all around faced inward. The faces of the projecting walls were decorated with palm trees.

The Outer Court

¹⁷Then he brought me into the outer court. There I saw some rooms and a pavement that had been constructed all around the court; there were thirty rooms along the pavement. ¹⁸It abutted the sides of the gateways and was as wide as they were long; this was the lower pavement. ¹⁹Then he measured the distance from the inside of the lower gateway to the outside of the inner court; it was a hundred cubits on the east side as well as on the north.

The North Gate

²⁰Then he measured the length and width of the gate facing north, leading into the outer court. ²¹Its alcoves—three on each side—its projecting walls and its portico had the same measurements as those of the first gateway. It was fifty cubits long and twenty-five cubits wide. ²²Its openings, its portico and its palm tree decorations had the same measurements as those of the gate facing east. Seven steps led up to it, with its portico opposite them. ²³There was a gate to the inner court facing the north gate, just as there was on the east. He measured from one gate to the opposite one; it was a hundred cubits.

The South Gate

²⁴Then he led me to the south side and I saw a gate facing south. He measured its jambs and its portico, and they had the same measurements as the others. ²⁵The gateway and its portico had narrow openings all around, like the openings of the others. It was fifty cubits long and twenty-five cubits wide. ²⁶Seven steps led up to it, with its portico opposite them; it had palm tree decorations on the faces of the projecting walls on each side. ²⁷The inner court also had a gate facing south, and he measured from this gate to the outer gate on the south side; it was a hundred cubits.

Gates to the Inner Court

²⁸Then he brought me into the inner court through the south gate, and he measured the south gate; it had the same measurements as the others. ²⁹Its alcoves, its projecting walls and its portico had the same measurements as the others. The gateway and its portico had openings all around. It was fifty cubits long and twenty-five cubits wide.

ᵃ6 Septuagint; Hebrew *deep, the first threshold, one rod deep*   *ᵇ8,9* Many Hebrew manuscripts, Septuagint, Vulgate and Syriac; most Hebrew manuscripts *gateway facing the temple; it was one rod deep.* ⁹*Then he measured the portico of the gateway; it*   *ᶜ14* Septuagint; Hebrew *projecting wall*   *ᵈ14* The meaning of the Hebrew for this verse is uncertain.

³⁰(The porticoes of the gateways around the inner court were twenty-five cubits wide and five cubits deep.) ³¹Its portico faced the outer court; palm trees decorated its jambs, and eight steps led up to it.

³²Then he brought me to the inner court on the east side, and he measured the gateway; it had the same measurements as the others. ³³Its alcoves, its projecting walls and its portico had the same measurements as the others. The gateway and its portico had openings all around. It was fifty cubits long and twenty-five cubits wide. ³⁴Its portico faced the outer court; palm trees decorated the jambs on either side, and eight steps led up to it.

³⁵Then he brought me to the north gate and measured it. It had the same measurements as the others, ³⁶as did its alcoves, its projecting walls and its portico, and it had openings all around. It was fifty cubits long and twenty-five cubits wide. ³⁷Its portico[a] faced the outer court; palm trees decorated the jambs on either side, and eight steps led up to it.

The Rooms for Preparing Sacrifices

³⁸A room with a doorway was by the portico in each of the inner gateways, where the burnt offerings were washed. ³⁹In the portico of the gateway were two tables on each side, on which the burnt offerings, sin offerings and guilt offerings were slaughtered. ⁴⁰By the outside wall of the portico of the gateway, near the steps at the entrance to the north gateway were two tables, and on the other side of the steps were two tables. ⁴¹So there were four tables on one side of the gateway and four on the other—eight tables in all—on which the sacrifices were slaughtered. ⁴²There were also four tables of dressed stone for the burnt offerings, each a cubit and a half long, a cubit and a half wide and a cubit high. On them were placed the utensils for slaughtering the burnt offerings and the other sacrifices. ⁴³And double-pronged hooks, each a handbreadth long, were attached to the wall all around. The tables were for the flesh of the offerings.

Rooms for the Priests

⁴⁴Outside the inner gate, within the inner court, were two rooms, one[b] at the side of the north gate and facing south, and another at the side of the south[c] gate and facing north. ⁴⁵He said to me, "The room facing south is for the priests who have charge of the temple, ⁴⁶and the room facing north is for the priests who have charge of the altar. These are the sons of Zadok, who are the only Levites who may draw near to the LORD to minister before him."

⁴⁷Then he measured the court: It was square—a hundred cubits long and a hundred cubits wide. And the altar was in front of the temple.

The Temple

⁴⁸He brought me to the portico of the temple and measured the jambs of the portico; they were five cubits wide on either side. The width of the entrance was fourteen cubits and its projecting walls were[d] three cubits wide on either side. ⁴⁹The portico was twenty cubits wide, and twelve[e] cubits from front to back. It was reached by a flight of stairs,[f] and there were pillars on each side of the jambs.

41 Then the man brought me to the outer sanctuary and measured the jambs; the width of the jambs was six cubits[g] on each side.[h] ²The entrance was ten cubits wide, and the projecting walls on each side of it were five cubits wide. He also measured the outer sanctuary; it was forty cubits long and twenty cubits wide.

³Then he went into the inner sanctuary and measured the jambs of the entrance; each was two cubits wide. The entrance was six cubits wide, and the projecting walls on each

a 37 Septuagint (see also verses 31 and 34); Hebrew *jambs*   b 44 Septuagint; Hebrew *were rooms for singers, which were*   c 44 Septuagint; Hebrew *east*   d 48 Septuagint; Hebrew *entrance was*   e 49 Septuagint; Hebrew *eleven*   f 49 Hebrew; Septuagint *Ten steps led up to it*   g 1 The common cubit was about 1 1/2 feet (about 0.5 meter).   h 1 One Hebrew manuscript and Septuagint; most Hebrew manuscripts *side, the width of the tent* side of it were seven cubits wide. ⁴And he measured the length of the inner sanctuary; it was twenty cubits, and its width was twenty cubits across the end of the outer sanctuary. He said to me, "This is the Most Holy Place."

⁵Then he measured the wall of the temple; it was six cubits thick, and each side room around the temple was four cubits wide. ⁶The side rooms were on three levels, one above another, thirty on each level. There were ledges all around the wall of the temple to serve as supports for the side rooms, so that the supports were not inserted into the wall of the temple. ⁷The side rooms all around the temple were wider at each successive level. The structure surrounding the temple was built in ascending stages, so that the rooms widened as one went upward. A stairway went up from the lowest floor to the top floor through the middle floor.

⁸I saw that the temple had a raised base all around it, forming the foundation of the side rooms. It was the length of the rod, six long cubits. ⁹The outer wall of the side rooms was five cubits thick. The open area between the side rooms of the temple ¹⁰and the ⌞priests'⌟ rooms was twenty cubits wide all around the temple. ¹¹There were entrances to the side rooms from the open area, one on the north and another on the south; and the base adjoining the open area was five cubits wide all around.

¹²The building facing the temple courtyard on the west side was seventy cubits wide. The wall of the building was five cubits thick all around, and its length was ninety cubits.

¹³Then he measured the temple; it was a hundred cubits long, and the temple courtyard and the building with its walls were also a hundred cubits long. ¹⁴The width of the temple courtyard on the east, including the front of the temple, was a hundred cubits.

¹⁵Then he measured the length of the building facing the courtyard at the rear of the temple, including its galleries on each side; it was a hundred cubits.

The outer sanctuary, the inner sanctuary and the portico facing the court, ¹⁶as well as the thresholds and the narrow windows and galleries around the three of them—everything beyond and including the threshold was covered with wood. The floor, the wall up to the windows, and the windows were covered. ¹⁷In the space above the outside of the entrance to the inner sanctuary and on the walls at regular intervals all around the inner and outer sanctuary ¹⁸were carved cherubim and palm trees. Palm trees alternated with cherubim. Each cherub had two faces: ¹⁹the face of a man toward the palm tree on one side and the face of a lion toward the palm tree on the other. They were carved all around the whole temple. ²⁰From the floor to the area above the entrance, cherubim and palm trees were carved on the wall of the outer sanctuary.

²¹The outer sanctuary had a rectangular doorframe, and the one at the front of the Most Holy Place was similar. ²²There was a wooden altar three cubits high and two cubits square^a; its corners, its base^b and its sides were of wood. The man said to me, "This is the table that is before the Lᴏʀᴅ." ²³Both the outer sanctuary and the Most Holy Place had double doors. ²⁴Each door had two leaves—two hinged leaves for each door. ²⁵And on the doors of the outer sanctuary were carved cherubim and palm trees like those carved on the walls, and there was a wooden overhang on the front of the portico. ²⁶On the sidewalls of the portico were narrow windows with palm trees carved on each side. The side rooms of the temple also had overhangs.

Rooms for the Priests

42 Then the man led me northward into the outer court and brought me to the rooms opposite the temple courtyard and opposite the outer wall on the north side. ²The building whose door faced north was a hundred cubits^c long and fifty cubits wide. ³Both in the section twenty cubits from the inner court and in the section opposite the pavement of the outer court, gallery faced gallery at the three levels. ⁴In front of the rooms was an inner passageway ten cubits wide and a hundred cubits^d

^a22 Septuagint; Hebrew *long*   ^b22 Septuagint; Hebrew *length*   ^c2 The common cubit was about 1 1/2 feet (about 0.5 meter).   ^d4 Septuagint and Syriac; Hebrew *and one cubit*

long. Their doors were on the north. ⁵Now the upper rooms were narrower, for the galleries took more space from them than from the rooms on the lower and middle floors of the building. ⁶The rooms on the third floor had no pillars, as the courts had; so they were smaller in floor space than those on the lower and middle floors. ⁷There was an outer wall parallel to the rooms and the outer court; it extended in front of the rooms for fifty cubits. ⁸While the row of rooms on the side next to the outer court was fifty cubits long, the row on the side nearest the sanctuary was a hundred cubits long. ⁹The lower rooms had an entrance on the east side as one enters them from the outer court.

¹⁰On the south side[a] along the length of the wall of the outer court, adjoining the temple courtyard and opposite the outer wall, were rooms ¹¹with a passageway in front of them. These were like the rooms on the north; they had the same length and width, with similar exits and dimensions. Similar to the doorways on the north ¹²were the doorways of the rooms on the south. There was a doorway at the beginning of the passageway that was parallel to the corresponding wall extending eastward, by which one enters the rooms.

¹³Then he said to me, "The north and south rooms facing the temple courtyard are the priests' rooms, where the priests who approach the Lord will eat the most holy offerings. There they will put the most holy offerings—the grain offerings, the sin offerings and the guilt offerings—for the place is holy. ¹⁴Once the priests enter the holy precincts, they are not to go into the outer court until they leave behind the garments in which they minister, for these are holy. They are to put on other clothes before they go near the places that are for the people."

¹⁵When he had finished measuring what was inside the temple area, he led me out by the east gate and measured the area all around: ¹⁶He measured the east side with the measuring rod; it was five hundred cubits. ¹⁷He measured the north side; it was five hundred cubits[c] by the measuring rod. ¹⁸He measured the south side; it was five hundred cubits by the measuring rod. ¹⁹Then he turned to the west side and measured; it was five hundred cubits by the measuring rod. ²⁰So he measured the area on all four sides. It had a wall around it, five hundred cubits long and five hundred cubits wide, to separate the holy from the common.

The Glory Returns to the Temple

43 Then the man brought me to the gate facing east, ²and I saw the glory of the God of Israel coming from the east. His voice was like the roar of rushing waters, and the land was radiant with his glory. ³The vision I saw was like the vision I had seen when he[d] came to destroy the city and like the visions I had seen by the Kebar River, and I fell facedown. ⁴The glory of the Lord entered the temple through the gate facing east. ⁵Then the Spirit lifted me up and brought me into the inner court, and the glory of the Lord filled the temple.

⁶While the man was standing beside me, I heard someone speaking to me from inside the temple. ⁷He said: "Son of man, this is the place of my throne and the place for the soles of my feet. This is where I will live among the Israelites forever. The house of Israel will never again defile my holy name—neither they nor their kings—by their prostitution[e] and the lifeless idols[f] of their kings at their high places. ⁸When they placed their threshold next to my threshold and their doorposts beside my doorposts, with only a wall between me and them, they defiled my holy name by their detestable practices. So I destroyed them in my anger. ⁹Now let them put away from me their prostitution and the lifeless idols of their kings, and I will live among them forever.

¹⁰"Son of man, describe the temple to the people of Israel, that they may be ashamed

---

a 10 Septuagint; Hebrew *Eastward*   *b 16* See Septuagint of verse 17; Hebrew *rods*; also in verses 18 and 19.
c 17 Septuagint; Hebrew *rods*   *d 3* Some Hebrew manuscripts and Vulgate; most Hebrew manuscripts *I*   *e 7* Or *their*
spiritual adultery; also in verse 9   *f 7* Or *the corpses*; also in verse 9

of their sins. Let them consider the plan, ¹¹and if they are ashamed of all they have done, make known to them the design of the temple—its arrangement, its exits and entrances—its whole design and all its regulations*a* and laws. Write these down before them so that they may be faithful to its design and follow all its regulations.

¹²"This is the law of the temple: All the surrounding area on top of the mountain will be most holy. Such is the law of the temple.

The Altar

¹³"These are the measurements of the altar in long cubits, that cubit being a cubit*b* and a handbreadth*c*: Its gutter is a cubit deep and a cubit wide, with a rim of one span*d* around the edge. And this is the height of the altar: ¹⁴From the gutter on the ground up to the lower ledge it is two cubits high and a cubit wide, and from the smaller ledge up to the larger ledge it is four cubits high and a cubit wide. ¹⁵The altar hearth is four cubits high, and four horns project upward from the hearth. ¹⁶The altar hearth is square, twelve cubits long and twelve cubits wide. ¹⁷The upper ledge also is square, fourteen cubits long and fourteen cubits wide, with a rim of half a cubit and a gutter of a cubit all around. The steps of the altar face east."

¹⁸Then he said to me, "Son of man, this is what the Sovereign Lord says: These will be the regulations for sacrificing burnt offerings and sprinkling blood upon the altar when it is built: ¹⁹You are to give a young bull as a sin offering to the priests, who are Levites, of the family of Zadok, who come near to minister before me, declares the Sovereign Lord. ²⁰You are to take some of its blood and put it on the four horns of the altar and on the four corners of the upper ledge and all around the rim, and so purify the altar and make atonement for it. ²¹You are to take the bull for the sin offering and burn it in the designated part of the temple area outside the sanctuary.

²²"On the second day you are to offer a male goat without defect for a sin offering, and the altar is to be purified as it was purified with the bull. ²³When you have finished purifying it, you are to offer a young bull and a ram from the flock, both without defect. ²⁴You are to offer them before the Lord, and the priests are to sprinkle salt on them and sacrifice them as a burnt offering to the Lord.

²⁵"For seven days you are to provide a male goat daily for a sin offering; you are also to provide a young bull and a ram from the flock, both without defect. ²⁶For seven days they are to make atonement for the altar and cleanse it; thus they will dedicate it. ²⁷At the end of these days, from the eighth day on, the priests are to present your burnt offerings and fellowship offerings*e* on the altar. Then I will accept you, declares the Sovereign Lord."

The Prince, the Levites, the Priests

44 Then the man brought me back to the outer gate of the sanctuary, the one facing east, and it was shut. ²The Lord said to me, "This gate is to remain shut. It must not be opened; no one may enter through it. It is to remain shut because the Lord, the God of Israel, has entered through it. ³The prince himself is the only one who may sit inside the gateway to eat in the presence of the Lord. He is to enter by way of the portico of the gateway and go out the same way."

⁴Then the man brought me by way of the north gate to the front of the temple. I looked and saw the glory of the Lord filling the temple of the Lord, and I fell facedown.

⁵The Lord said to me, "Son of man, look carefully, listen closely and give attention to everything I tell you concerning all the regulations regarding the temple of the Lord. Give attention to the entrance of the temple and all the exits of the sanctuary. ⁶Say to the rebellious house of Israel, 'This is what the Sovereign Lord says: Enough of your detest-

---

a11 Some Hebrew manuscripts and Septuagint; most Hebrew manuscripts *regulations and its whole design*   *b13* The common cubit was about 1 1/2 feet (about 0.5 meter).   *c13* That is, about 3 inches (about 8 centimeters)   *d13* That is, about 9 inches (about 22 centimeters)   *e27* Traditionally *peace offerings*

able practices, O house of Israel! ⁷In addition to all your other detestable practices, you brought foreigners uncircumcised in heart and flesh into my sanctuary, desecrating my temple while you offered me food, fat and blood, and you broke my covenant. ⁸Instead of carrying out your duty in regard to my holy things, you put others in charge of my sanctuary. ⁹This is what the Sovereign LORD says: No foreigner uncircumcised in heart and flesh is to enter my sanctuary, not even the foreigners who live among the Israelites.

¹⁰"The Levites who went far from me when Israel went astray and who wandered from me after their idols must bear the consequences of their sin. ¹¹They may serve in my sanctuary, having charge of the gates of the temple and serving in it; they may slaughter the burnt offerings and sacrifices for the people and stand before the people and serve them. ¹²But because they served them in the presence of their idols and made the house of Israel fall into sin, therefore I have sworn with uplifted hand that they must bear the consequences of their sin, declares the Sovereign LORD. ¹³They are not to come near to serve me as priests or come near any of my holy things or my most holy offerings; they must bear the shame of their detestable practices. ¹⁴Yet I will put them in charge of the duties of the temple and all the work that is to be done in it.

¹⁵"But the priests, who are Levites and descendants of Zadok and who faithfully carried out the duties of my sanctuary when the Israelites went astray from me, are to come near to minister before me; they are to stand before me to offer sacrifices of fat and blood, declares the Sovereign LORD. ¹⁶They alone are to enter my sanctuary; they alone are to come near my table to minister before me and perform my service.

¹⁷"When they enter the gates of the inner court, they are to wear linen clothes; they must not wear any woolen garment while ministering at the gates of the inner court or inside the temple. ¹⁸They are to wear linen turbans on their heads and linen undergarments around their waists. They must not wear anything that makes them perspire. ¹⁹When they go out into the outer court where the people are, they are to take off the clothes they have been ministering in and are to leave them in the sacred rooms, and put on other clothes, so that they do not consecrate the people by means of their garments.

²⁰"They must not shave their heads or let their hair grow long, but they are to keep the hair of their heads trimmed. ²¹No priest is to drink wine when he enters the inner court. ²²They must not marry widows or divorced women; they may marry only virgins of Israelite descent or widows of priests. ²³They are to teach my people the difference between the holy and the common and show them how to distinguish between the unclean and the clean.

²⁴"In any dispute, the priests are to serve as judges and decide it according to my ordinances. They are to keep my laws and my decrees for all my appointed feasts, and they are to keep my Sabbaths holy.

²⁵"'A priest must not defile himself by going near a dead person; however, if the dead person was his father or mother, son or daughter, brother or unmarried sister, then he may defile himself. ²⁶After he is cleansed, he must wait seven days. ²⁷On the day he goes into the inner court of the sanctuary to minister in the sanctuary, he is to offer a sin offering for himself, declares the Sovereign LORD.

²⁸"I am to be the only inheritance the priests have. You are to give them no possession in Israel; I will be their possession. ²⁹They will eat the grain offerings, the sin offerings and the guilt offerings; and everything in Israel devoted* to the LORD will belong to them. ³⁰The best of all the firstfruits and of all your special gifts will belong to the priests. You are to give them the first portion of your ground meal so that a blessing may rest on your household. ³¹The priests must not eat anything, bird or animal, found dead or torn by wild animals.

---

a 29 The Hebrew term refers to the irrevocable giving over of things or persons to the LORD.

Division of the Land

45 "'When you allot the land as an inheritance, you are to present to the Lord a portion of the land as a sacred district, 25,000 cubits long and 20,000[a] cubits wide; the entire area will be holy. [2]Of this, a section 500 cubits square is to be for the sanctuary, with 50 cubits around it for open land. [3]In the sacred district, measure off a section 25,000 cubits[b] long and 10,000 cubits[c] wide. In it will be the sanctuary, the Most Holy Place. [4]It will be the sacred portion of the land for the priests, who minister in the sanctuary and who draw near to minister before the Lord. It will be a place for their houses as well as a holy place for the sanctuary. [5]An area 25,000 cubits long and 10,000 cubits wide will belong to the Levites, who serve in the temple, as their possession for towns to live in.[d]

[6]"'You are to give the city as its property an area 5,000 cubits wide and 25,000 cubits long, adjoining the sacred portion; it will belong to the whole house of Israel.

[7]"'The prince will have the land bordering each side of the area formed by the sacred district and the property of the city. It will extend westward from the west side and eastward from the east side, running lengthwise from the western to the eastern border parallel to one of the tribal portions. [8]This land will be his possession in Israel. And my princes will no longer oppress my people but will allow the house of Israel to possess the land according to their tribes.

[9]"'This is what the Sovereign Lord says: You have gone far enough, O princes of Israel! Give up your violence and oppression and do what is just and right. Stop dispossessing my people, declares the Sovereign Lord. [10]You are to use accurate scales, an accurate ephah[e] and an accurate bath.[f] [11]The ephah and the bath are to be the same size, the bath containing a tenth of a homer[g] and the ephah a tenth of a homer; the homer is to be the standard measure for both. [12]The shekel[h] is to consist of twenty gerahs. Twenty shekels plus twenty-five shekels plus fifteen shekels equal one mina.[i]

Offerings and Holy Days

[13]"'This is the special gift you are to offer: a sixth of an ephah from each homer of wheat and a sixth of an ephah from each homer of barley. [14]The prescribed portion of oil, measured by the bath, is a tenth of a bath from each cor (which consists of ten baths or one homer, for ten baths are equivalent to a homer). [15]Also one sheep is to be taken from every flock of two hundred from the well-watered pastures of Israel. These will be used for the grain offerings, burnt offerings and fellowship offerings[j] to make atonement for the people, declares the Sovereign Lord. [16]All the people of the land will participate in this special gift for the use of the prince in Israel. [17]It will be the duty of the prince to provide the burnt offerings, grain offerings and drink offerings at the festivals, the New Moons and the Sabbaths—at all the appointed feasts of the house of Israel. He will provide the sin offerings, grain offerings, burnt offerings and fellowship offerings to make atonement for the house of Israel.

[18]"'This is what the Sovereign Lord says: In the first month on the first day you are to take a young bull without defect and purify the sanctuary. [19]The priest is to take some of the blood of the sin offering and put it on the doorposts of the temple, on the four corners of the upper ledge of the altar and on the gateposts of the inner court. [20]You are to do the same on the seventh day of the month for anyone who sins unintentionally or through ignorance; so you are to make atonement for the temple.

[21]"'In the first month on the fourteenth day you are to observe the Passover, a feast lasting seven days, during which you shall eat bread made without yeast. [22]On that day the prince is to provide a bull as a sin offering for himself and for all the people of the

---

[a]1 Septuagint (see also verses 3 and 5 and 48:9); Hebrew *10,000*   [b]3 That is, about 7 miles (about 12 kilometers)   [c]3 That is, about 3 miles (about 5 kilometers)   [d]5 Septuagint; Hebrew *temple; they will have as their possession 20 rooms*   [e]10 An ephah was a dry measure.   [f]10 A bath was a liquid measure.   [g]11 A homer was a dry measure.   [h]12 A shekel weighed about 2/5 ounce (about 11.5 grams).   [i]12 That is, 60 shekels; the common mina was 50 shekels.   [j]15 Traditionally *peace offerings*; also in verse 17

land. ²³Every day during the seven days of the Feast he is to provide seven bulls and seven rams without defect as a burnt offering to the LORD, and a male goat for a sin offering. ²⁴He is to provide as a grain offering an ephah for each bull and an ephah for each ram, along with a hin*a* of oil for each ephah.

²⁵"During the seven days of the Feast, which begins in the seventh month on the fifteenth day, he is to make the same provision for sin offerings, burnt offerings, grain offerings and oil.

46 "This is what the Sovereign LORD says: The gate of the inner court facing east is to be shut on the six working days, but on the Sabbath day and on the day of the New Moon it is to be opened. ²The prince is to enter from the outside through the portico of the gateway and stand by the gatepost. The priests are to sacrifice his burnt offering and his fellowship offerings.*b* He is to worship at the threshold of the gateway and then go out, but the gate will not be shut until evening. ³On the Sabbaths and New Moons the people of the land are to worship in the presence of the LORD at the entrance to that gateway. ⁴The burnt offering the prince brings to the LORD on the Sabbath day is to be six male lambs and a ram, all without defect. ⁵The grain offering given with the ram is to be an ephah,*c* and the grain offering with the lambs is to be as much as he pleases, along with a hin*a* of oil for each ephah. ⁶On the day of the New Moon he is to offer a young bull, six lambs and a ram, all without defect. ⁷He is to provide as a grain offering one ephah with the bull, one ephah with the ram, and with the lambs as much as he wants to give, along with a hin of oil with each ephah. ⁸When the prince enters, he is to go in through the portico of the gateway, and he is to come out the same way.

⁹"When the people of the land come before the LORD at the appointed feasts, whoever enters by the north gate to worship is to go out the south gate; and whoever enters by the south gate is to go out the north gate. No one is to return through the gate by which he entered, but each is to go out the opposite gate. ¹⁰The prince is to be among them, going in when they go in and going out when they go out.

¹¹"At the festivals and the appointed feasts, the grain offering is to be an ephah with a bull, an ephah with a ram, and with the lambs as much as one pleases, along with a hin of oil for each ephah. ¹²When the prince provides a freewill offering to the LORD—whether a burnt offering or fellowship offerings—the gate facing east is to be opened for him. He shall offer his burnt offering or his fellowship offerings as he does on the Sabbath day. Then he shall go out, and after he has gone out, the gate will be shut.

¹³"Every day you are to provide a year-old lamb without defect for a burnt offering to the LORD; morning by morning you shall provide it. ¹⁴You are also to provide with it morning by morning a grain offering, consisting of a sixth of an ephah with a third of a hin of oil to moisten the flour. The presenting of this grain offering to the LORD is a lasting ordinance. ¹⁵So the lamb and the grain offering and the oil shall be provided morning by morning for a regular burnt offering.

¹⁶"This is what the Sovereign LORD says: If the prince makes a gift from his inheritance to one of his sons, it will also belong to his descendants; it is to be their property by inheritance. ¹⁷If, however, he makes a gift from his inheritance to one of his servants, the servant may keep it until the year of freedom; then it will revert to the prince. His inheritance belongs to his sons only; it is theirs. ¹⁸The prince must not take any of the inheritance of the people, driving them off their property. He is to give his sons their inheritance out of his own property, so that none of my people will be separated from his property.'"

¹⁹Then the man brought me through the entrance at the side of the gate to the sacred rooms facing north, which belonged to the priests, and showed me a place at the western end. ²⁰He said to me, "This is the place where the priests will cook the guilt offering

---

a 24,5 That is, probably about 4 quarts (about 4 liters)   *b 2* Traditionally *peace offerings;* also in verse 12   *c 5* That is, probably about 3/5 bushel (about 22 liters)

and the sin offering and bake the grain offering, to avoid bringing them into the outer court and consecrating the people."

²¹He then brought me to the outer court and led me around to its four corners, and I saw in each corner another court. ²²In the four corners of the outer court were enclosed^a courts, forty cubits long and thirty cubits wide; each of the courts in the four corners was the same size. ²³Around the inside of each of the four courts was a ledge of stone, with places for fire built all around under the ledge. ²⁴He said to me, "These are the kitchens where those who minister at the temple will cook the sacrifices of the people."

The River From the Temple

47 The man brought me back to the entrance of the temple, and I saw water coming out from under the threshold of the temple toward the east (for the temple faced east). The water was coming down from under the south side of the temple, south of the altar. ²He then brought me out through the north gate and led me around the outside to the outer gate facing east, and the water was flowing from the south side.

³As the man went eastward with a measuring line in his hand, he measured off a thousand cubits^b and then led me through water that was ankle-deep. ⁴He measured off another thousand cubits and led me through water that was knee-deep. He measured off another thousand and led me through water that was up to the waist. ⁵He measured off another thousand, but now it was a river that I could not cross, because the water had risen and was deep enough to swim in—a river that no one could cross. ⁶He asked me, "Son of man, do you see this?"

Then he led me back to the bank of the river. ⁷When I arrived there, I saw a great number of trees on each side of the river. ⁸He said to me, "This water flows toward the eastern region and goes down into the Arabah,^c where it enters the Sea.^d When it empties into the Sea,^d the water there becomes fresh. ⁹Swarms of living creatures will live wherever the river flows. There will be large numbers of fish, because this water flows there and makes the salt water fresh; so where the river flows everything will live. ¹⁰Fishermen will stand along the shore; from En Gedi to En Eglaim there will be places for spreading nets. The fish will be of many kinds—like the fish of the Great Sea.^e ¹¹But the swamps and marshes will not become fresh; they will be left for salt. ¹²Fruit trees of all kinds will grow on both banks of the river. Their leaves will not wither, nor will their fruit fail. Every month they will bear, because the water from the sanctuary flows to them. Their fruit will serve for food and their leaves for healing."

The Boundaries of the Land

¹³This is what the Sovereign Lord says: "These are the boundaries by which you are to divide the land for an inheritance among the twelve tribes of Israel, with two portions for Joseph. ¹⁴You are to divide it equally among them. Because I swore with uplifted hand to give it to your forefathers, this land will become your inheritance.

¹⁵"This is to be the boundary of the land:

"On the north side it will run from the Great Sea by the Hethlon road past Lebo^f Hamath to Zedad, ¹⁶Berothah^g and Sibraim (which lies on the border between Damascus and Hamath), as far as Hazer Hatticon, which is on the border of Hauran. ¹⁷The boundary will extend from the sea to Hazar Enan,^h along the northern border of Damascus, with the border of Hamath to the north. This will be the north boundary.

¹⁸"On the east side the boundary will run between Hauran and Damascus, along the

---

^a22 The meaning of the Hebrew for this word is uncertain.　　^b3 That is, about 1,500 feet (about 450 meters)　　^c8 Or the Jordan Valley　　^d8 That is, the Dead Sea　　^e10 That is, the Mediterranean; also in verses 15, 19 and 20　　^f15 Or past the entrance to　　^g15,16 See Septuagint and Ezekiel 48:1; Hebrew road to go into Zedad, ¹⁶Hamath, Berothah　　^h17 Hebrew Enon, a variant of Enan

Jordan between Gilead and the land of Israel, to the eastern sea and as far as Tamar.[a] This will be the east boundary.

¹⁹"On the south side it will run from Tamar as far as the waters of Meribah Kadesh, then along the Wadi ⌊of Egypt⌋ to the Great Sea. This will be the south boundary.

²⁰"On the west side, the Great Sea will be the boundary to a point opposite Lebo[b] Hamath. This will be the west boundary.

²¹"You are to distribute this land among yourselves according to the tribes of Israel. ²²You are to allot it as an inheritance for yourselves and for the aliens who have settled among you and who have children. You are to consider them as native-born Israelites; along with you they are to be allotted an inheritance among the tribes of Israel. ²³In whatever tribe the alien settles, there you are to give him his inheritance," declares the Sovereign LORD.

The Division of the Land

48 "These are the tribes, listed by name: At the northern frontier, Dan will have one portion; it will follow the Hethlon road to Lebo[c] Hamath; Hazar Enan and the northern border of Damascus next to Hamath will be part of its border from the east side to the west side.

²"Asher will have one portion; it will border the territory of Dan from east to west.

³"Naphtali will have one portion; it will border the territory of Asher from east to west.

⁴"Manasseh will have one portion; it will border the territory of Naphtali from east to west.

⁵"Ephraim will have one portion; it will border the territory of Manasseh from east to west.

⁶"Reuben will have one portion; it will border the territory of Ephraim from east to west.

⁷"Judah will have one portion; it will border the territory of Reuben from east to west.

⁸"Bordering the territory of Judah from east to west will be the portion you are to present as a special gift. It will be 25,000 cubits[d] wide, and its length from east to west will equal one of the tribal portions; the sanctuary will be in the center of it.

⁹"The special portion you are to offer to the LORD will be 25,000 cubits long and 10,000 cubits[e] wide. ¹⁰This will be the sacred portion for the priests. It will be 25,000 cubits long on the north side, 10,000 cubits wide on the west side, 10,000 cubits wide on the east side and 25,000 cubits long on the south side. In the center of it will be the sanctuary of the LORD. ¹¹This will be for the consecrated priests, the Zadokites, who were faithful in serving me and did not go astray as the Levites did when the Israelites went astray. ¹²It will be a special gift to them from the sacred portion of the land, a most holy portion, bordering the territory of the Levites.

¹³"Alongside the territory of the priests, the Levites will have an allotment 25,000 cubits long and 10,000 cubits wide. Its total length will be 25,000 cubits and its width 10,000 cubits. ¹⁴They must not sell or exchange any of it. This is the best of the land and must not pass into other hands, because it is holy to the LORD.

¹⁵"The remaining area, 5,000 cubits wide and 25,000 cubits long, will be for the common use of the city, for houses and for pastureland. The city will be in the center of it ¹⁶and will have these measurements: the north side 4,500 cubits, the south side 4,500 cubits, the east side 4,500 cubits, and the west side 4,500 cubits. ¹⁷The pastureland for the city will be 250 cubits on the north, 250 cubits on the south, 250 cubits on the east, and 250 cubits on the west. ¹⁸What remains of the area, bordering on the sacred portion and running the length of it, will be 10,000 cubits on the east side and 10,000 cubits on the west side. Its produce will supply food for the workers of the city. ¹⁹The workers from

ᵃ18 Septuagint and Syriac; Hebrew *Israel. You will measure to the eastern sea*   ᵇ20 Or *opposite the entrance to*
ᶜ1 Or *to the entrance to*   ᵈ8 That is, about 7 miles (about 12 kilometers)   ᵉ9 That is, about 3 miles (about 5 kilometers)

the city who farm it will come from all the tribes of Israel. **20**The entire portion will be a square, 25,000 cubits on each side. As a special gift you will set aside the sacred portion, along with the property of the city.

21"What remains on both sides of the area formed by the sacred portion and the city property will belong to the prince. It will extend eastward from the 25,000 cubits of the sacred portion to the eastern border, and westward from the 25,000 cubits to the western border. Both these areas running the length of the tribal portions will belong to the prince, and the sacred portion with the temple sanctuary will be in the center of them. **22**So the property of the Levites and the property of the city will lie in the center of the area that belongs to the prince. The area belonging to the prince will lie between the border of Judah and the border of Benjamin.

23"As for the rest of the tribes: Benjamin will have one portion; it will extend from the east side to the west side.

24"Simeon will have one portion; it will border the territory of Benjamin from east to west.

25"Issachar will have one portion; it will border the territory of Simeon from east to west.

26"Zebulun will have one portion; it will border the territory of Issachar from east to west.

27"Gad will have one portion; it will border the territory of Zebulun from east to west.

28"The southern boundary of Gad will run south from Tamar to the waters of Meribah Kadesh, then along the Wadi ₒof Egypt₎ to the Great Sea.*a*

29"This is the land you are to allot as an inheritance to the tribes of Israel, and these will be their portions," declares the Sovereign LORD.

The Gates of the City

30"These will be the exits of the city: Beginning on the north side, which is 4,500 cubits long, **31**the gates of the city will be named after the tribes of Israel. The three gates on the north side will be the gate of Reuben, the gate of Judah and the gate of Levi.

32"On the east side, which is 4,500 cubits long, will be three gates: the gate of Joseph, the gate of Benjamin and the gate of Dan.

33"On the south side, which measures 4,500 cubits, will be three gates: the gate of Simeon, the gate of Issachar and the gate of Zebulun.

34"On the west side, which is 4,500 cubits long, will be three gates: the gate of Gad, the gate of Asher and the gate of Naphtali.

35"The distance all around will be 18,000 cubits.

"And the name of the city from that time on will be:

THE LORD IS THERE."

---

a28 That is, the Mediterranean

DANIEL

Daniel's Training in Babylon

1 In the third year of the reign of Jehoiakim king of Judah, Nebuchadnezzar king of Babylon came to Jerusalem and besieged it. ²And the Lord delivered Jehoiakim king of Judah into his hand, along with some of the articles from the temple of God. These he carried off to the temple of his god in Babylonia*ᵃ* and put in the treasure house of his god.

³Then the king ordered Ashpenaz, chief of his court officials, to bring in some of the Israelites from the royal family and the nobility— ⁴young men without any physical defect, handsome, showing aptitude for every kind of learning, well informed, quick to understand, and qualified to serve in the king's palace. He was to teach them the language and literature of the Babylonians.*ᵇ* ⁵The king assigned them a daily amount of food and wine from the king's table. They were to be trained for three years, and after that they were to enter the king's service.

⁶Among these were some from Judah: Daniel, Hananiah, Mishael and Azariah. ⁷The chief official gave them new names: to Daniel, the name Belteshazzar; to Hananiah, Shadrach; to Mishael, Meshach; and to Azariah, Abednego.

⁸But Daniel resolved not to defile himself with the royal food and wine, and he asked the chief official for permission not to defile himself this way. ⁹Now God had caused the official to show favor and sympathy to Daniel, ¹⁰but the official told Daniel, "I am afraid of my lord the king, who has assigned your*ᶜ* food and drink. Why should he see you looking worse than the other young men your age? The king would then have my head because of you."

¹¹Daniel then said to the guard whom the chief official had appointed over Daniel, Hananiah, Mishael and Azariah, ¹²"Please test your servants for ten days: Give us nothing but vegetables to eat and water to drink. ¹³Then compare our appearance with that of the young men who eat the royal food, and treat your servants in accordance with what you see." ¹⁴So he agreed to this and tested them for ten days.

¹⁵At the end of the ten days they looked healthier and better nourished than any of the young men who ate the royal food. ¹⁶So the guard took away their choice food and the wine they were to drink and gave them vegetables instead.

¹⁷To these four young men God gave knowledge and understanding of all kinds of literature and learning. And Daniel could understand visions and dreams of all kinds.

¹⁸At the end of the time set by the king to bring them in, the chief official presented them to Nebuchadnezzar. ¹⁹The king talked with them, and he found none equal to Daniel, Hananiah, Mishael and Azariah; so they entered the king's service. ²⁰In every matter of wisdom and understanding about which the king questioned them, he found them ten times better than all the magicians and enchanters in his whole kingdom.

²¹And Daniel remained there until the first year of King Cyrus.

ᵃ2 Hebrew *Shinar*   *ᵇ4* Or *Chaldeans*   *ᶜ10* The Hebrew for *your* and *you* in this verse is plural.

Nebuchadnezzar's Dream

2 In the second year of his reign, Nebuchadnezzar had dreams; his mind was troubled and he could not sleep. ²So the king summoned the magicians, enchanters, sorcerers and astrologers*ᵃ* to tell him what he had dreamed. When they came in and stood before the king, ³he said to them, "I have had a dream that troubles me and I want to know what it means.*ᵇ*"

⁴Then the astrologers answered the king in Aramaic,*ᶜ* "O king, live forever! Tell your servants the dream, and we will interpret it."

⁵The king replied to the astrologers, "This is what I have firmly decided: If you do not tell me what my dream was and interpret it, I will have you cut into pieces and your houses turned into piles of rubble. ⁶But if you tell me the dream and explain it, you will receive from me gifts and rewards and great honor. So tell me the dream and interpret it for me."

⁷Once more they replied, "Let the king tell his servants the dream, and we will interpret it."

⁸Then the king answered, "I am certain that you are trying to gain time, because you realize that this is what I have firmly decided: ⁹If you do not tell me the dream, there is just one penalty for you. You have conspired to tell me misleading and wicked things, hoping the situation will change. So then, tell me the dream, and I will know that you can interpret it for me."

¹⁰The astrologers answered the king, "There is not a man on earth who can do what the king asks! No king, however great and mighty, has ever asked such a thing of any magician or enchanter or astrologer. ¹¹What the king asks is too difficult. No one can reveal it to the king except the gods, and they do not live among men."

¹²This made the king so angry and furious that he ordered the execution of all the wise men of Babylon. ¹³So the decree was issued to put the wise men to death, and men were sent to look for Daniel and his friends to put them to death.

¹⁴When Arioch, the commander of the king's guard, had gone out to put to death the wise men of Babylon, Daniel spoke to him with wisdom and tact. ¹⁵He asked the king's officer, "Why did the king issue such a harsh decree?" Arioch then explained the matter to Daniel. ¹⁶At this, Daniel went in to the king and asked for time, so that he might interpret the dream for him.

¹⁷Then Daniel returned to his house and explained the matter to his friends Hananiah, Mishael and Azariah. ¹⁸He urged them to plead for mercy from the God of heaven concerning this mystery, so that he and his friends might not be executed with the rest of the wise men of Babylon. ¹⁹During the night the mystery was revealed to Daniel in a vision. Then Daniel praised the God of heaven ²⁰and said:

> "Praise be to the name of God for ever and ever;
>   wisdom and power are his.
> ²¹He changes times and seasons;
>   he sets up kings and deposes them.
> He gives wisdom to the wise
>   and knowledge to the discerning.
> ²²He reveals deep and hidden things;
>   he knows what lies in darkness,
>   and light dwells with him.
> ²³I thank and praise you, O God of my fathers:
>   You have given me wisdom and power,
> you have made known to me what we asked of you,
>   you have made known to us the dream of the king."

ᵃ2 Or *Chaldeans;* also in verses 4, 5 and 10   *ᵇ3* Or *was*   *ᶜ4* The text from here through chapter 7 is in Aramaic.

Daniel Interprets the Dream

²⁴Then Daniel went to Arioch, whom the king had appointed to execute the wise men of Babylon, and said to him, "Do not execute the wise men of Babylon. Take me to the king, and I will interpret his dream for him."

²⁵Arioch took Daniel to the king at once and said, "I have found a man among the exiles from Judah who can tell the king what his dream means."

²⁶The king asked Daniel (also called Belteshazzar), "Are you able to tell me what I saw in my dream and interpret it?"

²⁷Daniel replied, "No wise man, enchanter, magician or diviner can explain to the king the mystery he has asked about, ²⁸but there is a God in heaven who reveals mysteries. He has shown King Nebuchadnezzar what will happen in days to come. Your dream and the visions that passed through your mind as you lay on your bed are these:

²⁹"As you were lying there, O king, your mind turned to things to come, and the revealer of mysteries showed you what is going to happen. ³⁰As for me, this mystery has been revealed to me, not because I have greater wisdom than other living men, but so that you, O king, may know the interpretation and that you may understand what went through your mind.

³¹"You looked, O king, and there before you stood a large statue—an enormous, dazzling statue, awesome in appearance. ³²The head of the statue was made of pure gold, its chest and arms of silver, its belly and thighs of bronze, ³³its legs of iron, its feet partly of iron and partly of baked clay. ³⁴While you were watching, a rock was cut out, but not by human hands. It struck the statue on its feet of iron and clay and smashed them. ³⁵Then the iron, the clay, the bronze, the silver and the gold were broken to pieces at the same time and became like chaff on a threshing floor in the summer. The wind swept them away without leaving a trace. But the rock that struck the statue became a huge mountain and filled the whole earth.

³⁶"This was the dream, and now we will interpret it to the king. ³⁷You, O king, are the king of kings. The God of heaven has given you dominion and power and might and glory; ³⁸in your hands he has placed mankind and the beasts of the field and the birds of the air. Wherever they live, he has made you ruler over them all. You are that head of gold.

³⁹"After you, another kingdom will rise, inferior to yours. Next, a third kingdom, one of bronze, will rule over the whole earth. ⁴⁰Finally, there will be a fourth kingdom, strong as iron—for iron breaks and smashes everything—and as iron breaks things to pieces, so it will crush and break all the others. ⁴¹Just as you saw that the feet and toes were partly of baked clay and partly of iron, so this will be a divided kingdom; yet it will have some of the strength of iron in it, even as you saw iron mixed with clay. ⁴²As the toes were partly iron and partly clay, so this kingdom will be partly strong and partly brittle. ⁴³And just as you saw the iron mixed with baked clay, so the people will be a mixture and will not remain united, any more than iron mixes with clay.

⁴⁴"In the time of those kings, the God of heaven will set up a kingdom that will never be destroyed, nor will it be left to another people. It will crush all those kingdoms and bring them to an end, but it will itself endure forever. ⁴⁵This is the meaning of the vision of the rock cut out of a mountain, but not by human hands—a rock that broke the iron, the bronze, the clay, the silver and the gold to pieces.

"The great God has shown the king what will take place in the future. The dream is true and the interpretation is trustworthy."

⁴⁶Then King Nebuchadnezzar fell prostrate before Daniel and paid him honor and ordered that an offering and incense be presented to him. ⁴⁷The king said to Daniel, "Surely your God is the God of gods and the Lord of kings and a revealer of mysteries, for you were able to reveal this mystery."

⁴⁸Then the king placed Daniel in a high position and lavished many gifts on him. He made him ruler over the entire province of Babylon and placed him in charge of all its

wise men. ⁴⁹Moreover, at Daniel's request the king appointed Shadrach, Meshach and Abednego administrators over the province of Babylon, while Daniel himself remained at the royal court.

The Image of Gold and the Fiery Furnace

3 King Nebuchadnezzar made an image of gold, ninety feet high and nine feet*ᵃ* wide, and set it up on the plain of Dura in the province of Babylon. ²He then summoned the satraps, prefects, governors, advisers, treasurers, judges, magistrates and all the other provincial officials to come to the dedication of the image he had set up. ³So the satraps, prefects, governors, advisers, treasurers, judges, magistrates and all the other provincial officials assembled for the dedication of the image that King Nebuchadnezzar had set up, and they stood before it.

⁴Then the herald loudly proclaimed, "This is what you are commanded to do, O peoples, nations and men of every language: ⁵As soon as you hear the sound of the horn, flute, zither, lyre, harp, pipes and all kinds of music, you must fall down and worship the image of gold that King Nebuchadnezzar has set up. ⁶Whoever does not fall down and worship will immediately be thrown into a blazing furnace."

⁷Therefore, as soon as they heard the sound of the horn, flute, zither, lyre, harp and all kinds of music, all the peoples, nations and men of every language fell down and worshiped the image of gold that King Nebuchadnezzar had set up.

⁸At this time some astrologers*ᵇ* came forward and denounced the Jews. ⁹They said to King Nebuchadnezzar, "O king, live forever! ¹⁰You have issued a decree, O king, that everyone who hears the sound of the horn, flute, zither, lyre, harp, pipes and all kinds of music must fall down and worship the image of gold, ¹¹and that whoever does not fall down and worship will be thrown into a blazing furnace. ¹²But there are some Jews whom you have set over the affairs of the province of Babylon—Shadrach, Meshach and Abednego—who pay no attention to you, O king. They neither serve your gods nor worship the image of gold you have set up."

¹³Furious with rage, Nebuchadnezzar summoned Shadrach, Meshach and Abednego. So these men were brought before the king, ¹⁴and Nebuchadnezzar said to them, "Is it true, Shadrach, Meshach and Abednego, that you do not serve my gods or worship the image of gold I have set up? ¹⁵Now when you hear the sound of the horn, flute, zither,

---

1 Aramaic *sixty cubits high and six cubits wide* (about 27 meters high and 2.7 meters wide)   *ᵇ 8* Or *Chaldeans*

╔══════════════════ **DISCOVERING GOD** ══════════════════╗

3:1–30
Life with God

Daniel's three friends faced an unimaginable choice. They could bow down to an idol and live, or refuse to bow and die. The king who forced their decision left no other options. He even went so far as to tell them the method of their execution: They would be thrown into a blazing furnace. Taunting them, the king asked, "Then what god will be able to rescue you from my hand?"

It would have been easy for Daniel's friends to look for a way around the problem. They might have said to themselves, *Forget God; following him got us into this mess!* They might have, at the very least, been tempted to bend down to adjust their sandals at the appointed time!

Instead, they respectfully stood up to the king and expressed their faith that God could save their lives. Then they added an astounding statement: "Even if he does not [rescue us]. . . we will not serve your gods" (verse 18). They would trust in God's good plan for their lives, even if circumstances turned against them.

Knowing God doesn't automatically deliver a person from hardship. But it does deliver him or her from despair. Even in life's greatest difficulties, when everything imaginable goes wrong, God is still good—and he can be trusted.

╚═══╝

lyre, harp, pipes and all kinds of music, if you are ready to fall down and worship the image I made, very good. But if you do not worship it, you will be thrown immediately into a blazing furnace. Then what god will be able to rescue you from my hand?"

¹⁶Shadrach, Meshach and Abednego replied to the king, "O Nebuchadnezzar, we do not need to defend ourselves before you in this matter. ¹⁷If we are thrown into the blazing furnace, the God we serve is able to save us from it, and he will rescue us from your hand, O king. ¹⁸But even if he does not, we want you to know, O king, that we will not serve your gods or worship the image of gold you have set up."

¹⁹Then Nebuchadnezzar was furious with Shadrach, Meshach and Abednego, and his attitude toward them changed. He ordered the furnace heated seven times hotter than usual ²⁰and commanded some of the strongest soldiers in his army to tie up Shadrach, Meshach and Abednego and throw them into the blazing furnace. ²¹So these men, wearing their robes, trousers, turbans and other clothes, were bound and thrown into the blazing furnace. ²²The king's command was so urgent and the furnace so hot that the flames of the fire killed the soldiers who took up Shadrach, Meshach and Abednego, ²³and these three men, firmly tied, fell into the blazing furnace.

²⁴Then King Nebuchadnezzar leaped to his feet in amazement and asked his advisers, "Weren't there three men that we tied up and threw into the fire?"

They replied, "Certainly, O king."

²⁵He said, "Look! I see four men walking around in the fire, unbound and unharmed, and the fourth looks like a son of the gods."

²⁶Nebuchadnezzar then approached the opening of the blazing furnace and shouted, "Shadrach, Meshach and Abednego, servants of the Most High God, come out! Come here!"

So Shadrach, Meshach and Abednego came out of the fire, ²⁷and the satraps, prefects, governors and royal advisers crowded around them. They saw that the fire had not harmed their bodies, nor was a hair of their heads singed; their robes were not scorched, and there was no smell of fire on them.

²⁸Then Nebuchadnezzar said, "Praise be to the God of Shadrach, Meshach and Abednego, who has sent his angel and rescued his servants! They trusted in him and defied the king's command and were willing to give up their lives rather than serve or worship any god except their own God. ²⁹Therefore I decree that the people of any nation or language who say anything against the God of Shadrach, Meshach and Abednego be cut into pieces and their houses be turned into piles of rubble, for no other god can save in this way."

³⁰Then the king promoted Shadrach, Meshach and Abednego in the province of Babylon.

Nebuchadnezzar's Dream of a Tree

4 King Nebuchadnezzar,

To the peoples, nations and men of every language, who live in all the world:

May you prosper greatly!

²It is my pleasure to tell you about the miraculous signs and wonders that the Most High God has performed for me.

³How great are his signs,
 how mighty his wonders!
His kingdom is an eternal kingdom;
 his dominion endures from generation to generation.

⁴I, Nebuchadnezzar, was at home in my palace, contented and prosperous. ⁵I had a dream that made me afraid. As I was lying in my bed, the images and visions that

passed through my mind terrified me. ⁶So I commanded that all the wise men of Babylon be brought before me to interpret the dream for me. ⁷When the magicians, enchanters, astrologers*ᵃ* and diviners came, I told them the dream, but they could not interpret it for me. ⁸Finally, Daniel came into my presence and I told him the dream. (He is called Belteshazzar, after the name of my god, and the spirit of the holy gods is in him.)

⁹I said, "Belteshazzar, chief of the magicians, I know that the spirit of the holy gods is in you, and no mystery is too difficult for you. Here is my dream; interpret it for me. ¹⁰These are the visions I saw while lying in my bed: I looked, and there before me stood a tree in the middle of the land. Its height was enormous. ¹¹The tree grew large and strong and its top touched the sky; it was visible to the ends of the earth. ¹²Its leaves were beautiful, its fruit abundant, and on it was food for all. Under it the beasts of the field found shelter, and the birds of the air lived in its branches; from it every creature was fed.

¹³"In the visions I saw while lying in my bed, I looked, and there before me was a messenger,*ᵇ* a holy one, coming down from heaven. ¹⁴He called in a loud voice: 'Cut down the tree and trim off its branches; strip off its leaves and scatter its fruit. Let the animals flee from under it and the birds from its branches. ¹⁵But let the stump and its roots, bound with iron and bronze, remain in the ground, in the grass of the field.

" 'Let him be drenched with the dew of heaven, and let him live with the animals among the plants of the earth. ¹⁶Let his mind be changed from that of a man and let him be given the mind of an animal, till seven times*ᶜ* pass by for him.

¹⁷"'The decision is announced by messengers, the holy ones declare the verdict, so that the living may know that the Most High is sovereign over the kingdoms of men and gives them to anyone he wishes and sets over them the lowliest of men.'

¹⁸"This is the dream that I, King Nebuchadnezzar, had. Now, Belteshazzar, tell me what it means, for none of the wise men in my kingdom can interpret it for me. But you can, because the spirit of the holy gods is in you."

Daniel Interprets the Dream

¹⁹Then Daniel (also called Belteshazzar) was greatly perplexed for a time, and his thoughts terrified him. So the king said, "Belteshazzar, do not let the dream or its meaning alarm you."

Belteshazzar answered, "My lord, if only the dream applied to your enemies and its meaning to your adversaries! ²⁰The tree you saw, which grew large and strong, with its top touching the sky, visible to the whole earth, ²¹with beautiful leaves and abundant fruit, providing food for all, giving shelter to the beasts of the field, and having nesting places in its branches for the birds of the air— ²²you, O king, are that tree! You have become great and strong; your greatness has grown until it reaches the sky, and your dominion extends to distant parts of the earth.

²³"You, O king, saw a messenger, a holy one, coming down from heaven and saying, 'Cut down the tree and destroy it, but leave the stump, bound with iron and bronze, in the grass of the field, while its roots remain in the ground. Let him be drenched with the dew of heaven; let him live like the wild animals, until seven times pass by for him.'

²⁴"This is the interpretation, O king, and this is the decree the Most High has issued against my lord the king: ²⁵You will be driven away from people and will live with the wild animals; you will eat grass like cattle and be drenched with the dew of heaven. Seven times will pass by for you until you acknowledge that the Most High is sovereign over the kingdoms of men and gives them to anyone he wishes. ²⁶The command to leave the stump of the tree with its roots means that your king-

ᵃ7 Or *Chaldeans*   *ᵇ13* Or *watchman*; also in verses 17 and 23   *ᶜ16* Or *years*; also in verses 23, 25 and 32

dom will be restored to you when you acknowledge that Heaven rules. 27Therefore, O king, be pleased to accept my advice: Renounce your sins by doing what is right, and your wickedness by being kind to the oppressed. It may be that then your prosperity will continue."

The Dream Is Fulfilled

28All this happened to King Nebuchadnezzar. 29Twelve months later, as the king was walking on the roof of the royal palace of Babylon, 30he said, "Is not this the great Babylon I have built as the royal residence, by my mighty power and for the glory of my majesty?"

31The words were still on his lips when a voice came from heaven, "This is what is decreed for you, King Nebuchadnezzar: Your royal authority has been taken from you. 32You will be driven away from people and will live with the wild animals; you will eat grass like cattle. Seven times will pass by for you until you acknowledge that the Most High is sovereign over the kingdoms of men and gives them to anyone he wishes."

33Immediately what had been said about Nebuchadnezzar was fulfilled. He was driven away from people and ate grass like cattle. His body was drenched with the dew of heaven until his hair grew like the feathers of an eagle and his nails like the claws of a bird.

34At the end of that time, I, Nebuchadnezzar, raised my eyes toward heaven, and my sanity was restored. Then I praised the Most High; I honored and glorified him who lives forever.

> His dominion is an eternal dominion;
> his kingdom endures from generation to generation.
> 35All the peoples of the earth
> are regarded as nothing.
> He does as he pleases
> with the powers of heaven
> and the peoples of the earth.
> No one can hold back his hand
> or say to him: "What have you done?"

36At the same time that my sanity was restored, my honor and splendor were returned to me for the glory of my kingdom. My advisers and nobles sought me out, and I was restored to my throne and became even greater than before. 37Now I, Nebuchadnezzar, praise and exalt and glorify the King of heaven, because everything he does is right and all his ways are just. And those who walk in pride he is able to humble.

The Writing on the Wall

5 King Belshazzar gave a great banquet for a thousand of his nobles and drank wine with them. 2While Belshazzar was drinking his wine, he gave orders to bring in the gold and silver goblets that.Nebuchadnezzar his father*a* had taken from the temple in Jerusalem, so that the king and his nobles, his wives and his concubines might drink from them. 3So they brought in the gold goblets that had been taken from the temple of God in Jerusalem, and the king and his nobles, his wives and his concubines drank from them. 4As they drank the wine, they praised the gods of gold and silver, of bronze, iron, wood and stone.

5Suddenly the fingers of a human hand appeared and wrote on the plaster of the wall, near the lampstand in the royal palace. The king watched the hand as it wrote. 6His face

a2 Or ancestor; *or* predecessor; *also in verses 11, 13 and 18* turned pale and he was so frightened that his knees knocked together and his legs gave way.

[7]The king called out for the enchanters, astrologers[a] and diviners to be brought and said to these wise men of Babylon, "Whoever reads this writing and tells me what it means will be clothed in purple and have a gold chain placed around his neck, and he will be made the third highest ruler in the kingdom."

[8]Then all the king's wise men came in, but they could not read the writing or tell the king what it meant. [9]So King Belshazzar became even more terrified and his face grew more pale. His nobles were baffled.

[10]The queen,[b] hearing the voices of the king and his nobles, came into the banquet hall. "O king, live forever!" she said. "Don't be alarmed! Don't look so pale! [11]There is a man in your kingdom who has the spirit of the holy gods in him. In the time of your father he was found to have insight and intelligence and wisdom like that of the gods. King Nebuchadnezzar your father—your father the king, I say—appointed him chief of the magicians, enchanters, astrologers and diviners. [12]This man Daniel, whom the king called Belteshazzar, was found to have a keen mind and knowledge and understanding, and also the ability to interpret dreams, explain riddles and solve difficult problems. Call for Daniel, and he will tell you what the writing means."

[13]So Daniel was brought before the king, and the king said to him, "Are you Daniel, one of the exiles my father the king brought from Judah? [14]I have heard that the spirit of the gods is in you and that you have insight, intelligence and outstanding wisdom. [15]The wise men and enchanters were brought before me to read this writing and tell me what it means, but they could not explain it. [16]Now I have heard that you are able to give interpretations and to solve difficult problems. If you can read this writing and tell me what it means, you will be clothed in purple and have a gold chain placed around your neck, and you will be made the third highest ruler in the kingdom."

[17]Then Daniel answered the king, "You may keep your gifts for yourself and give your rewards to someone else. Nevertheless, I will read the writing for the king and tell him what it means.

[18]"O king, the Most High God gave your father Nebuchadnezzar sovereignty and greatness and glory and splendor. [19]Because of the high position he gave him, all the peoples and nations and men of every language dreaded and feared him. Those the king wanted to put to death, he put to death; those he wanted to spare, he spared; those he wanted to promote, he promoted; and those he wanted to humble, he humbled. [20]But when his heart became arrogant and hardened with pride, he was deposed from his royal throne and stripped of his glory. [21]He was driven away from people and given the mind of an animal; he lived with the wild donkeys and ate grass like cattle; and his body was drenched with the dew of heaven, until he acknowledged that the Most High God is sovereign over the kingdoms of men and sets over them anyone he wishes.

[22]"But you his son,[c] O Belshazzar, have not humbled yourself, though you knew all this. [23]Instead, you have set yourself up against the Lord of heaven. You had the goblets from his temple brought to you, and you and your nobles, your wives and your concubines drank wine from them. You praised the gods of silver and gold, of bronze, iron, wood and stone, which cannot see or hear or understand. But you did not honor the God who holds in his hand your life and all your ways. [24]Therefore he sent the hand that wrote the inscription.

[25]"This is the inscription that was written:

MENE, MENE, TEKEL, PARSIN[d]

[26]"This is what these words mean:

---

[a]7 Or Chaldeans; also in verse 11   [b]10 Or queen mother   [c]22 Or descendant; or successor   [d]25 Aramaic UPARSIN (that is, AND PARSIN)

Mene[a]: God has numbered the days of your reign and brought it to an end.
²⁷*Tekel*[b]: You have been weighed on the scales and found wanting.
²⁸*Peres*[c]: Your kingdom is divided and given to the Medes and Persians."

²⁹Then at Belshazzar's command, Daniel was clothed in purple, a gold chain was placed around his neck, and he was proclaimed the third highest ruler in the kingdom. ³⁰That very night Belshazzar, king of the Babylonians,[d] was slain, ³¹and Darius the Mede took over the kingdom, at the age of sixty-two.

DISCOVERING GOD

6:1–28
The God Who Is There

This story, one of the most popular and well-known stories from the Bible, provides us with another example of God's provision and protection in the lives of his followers. It shows us that God is able to rescue those who turn to him in prayer (verse 11), no matter how hopeless the circumstances look.

Did you turn to the pages of this book because of some painful or desperate personal situation? If so, realize that the same God who rescued Daniel is ready to work in you as well. He can enter your experience despite the adverse circumstances in your life—you are not beyond his reach. All you need to do is turn to God, trusting that he will never abandon you once you've placed your life in his hands.

Daniel in the Den of Lions

6 It pleased Darius to appoint 120 satraps to rule throughout the kingdom, ²with three administrators over them, one of whom was Daniel. The satraps were made accountable to them so that the king might not suffer loss. ³Now Daniel so distinguished himself among the administrators and the satraps by his exceptional qualities that the king planned to set him over the whole kingdom. ⁴At this, the administrators and the satraps tried to find grounds for charges against Daniel in his conduct of government affairs, but they were unable to do so. They could find no corruption in him, because he was trustworthy and neither corrupt nor negligent. ⁵Finally these men said, "We will never find any basis for charges against this man Daniel unless it has something to do with the law of his God."

⁶So the administrators and the satraps went as a group to the king and said: "O King Darius, live forever! ⁷The royal administrators, prefects, satraps, advisers and governors have all agreed that the king should issue an edict and enforce the decree that anyone who prays to any god or man during the next thirty days, except to you, O king, shall be thrown into the lions' den. ⁸Now, O king, issue the decree and put it in writing so that it cannot be altered—in accordance with the laws of the Medes and Persians, which cannot be repealed." ⁹So King Darius put the decree in writing.

¹⁰Now when Daniel learned that the decree had been published, he went home to his upstairs room where the windows opened toward Jerusalem. Three times a day he got down on his knees and prayed, giving thanks to his God, just as he had done before. ¹¹Then these men went as a group and found Daniel praying and asking God for help. ¹²So they went to the king and spoke to him about his royal decree: "Did you not publish a decree that during the next thirty days anyone who prays to any god or man except to you, O king, would be thrown into the lions' den?"

The king answered, "The decree stands—in accordance with the laws of the Medes and Persians, which cannot be repealed."

¹³Then they said to the king, "Daniel, who is one of the exiles from Judah, pays no attention to you, O king, or to the decree you put in writing. He still prays three times a day." ¹⁴When the king heard this, he was greatly distressed; he was determined to rescue Daniel and made every effort until sundown to save him.

¹⁵Then the men went as a group to the king and said to him, "Remember, O king, that

---

[a] 26 *Mene* can mean *numbered* or *mina* (a unit of money).   [b] 27 *Tekel* can mean *weighed* or *shekel*.   [c] 28 *Peres* (the singular of *Parsin*) can mean *divided* or *Persia* or *a half mina* or *a half shekel*.   [d] 30 Or *Chaldeans*

according to the law of the Medes and Persians no decree or edict that the king issues can be changed."

¹⁶So the king gave the order, and they brought Daniel and threw him into the lions' den. The king said to Daniel, "May your God, whom you serve continually, rescue you!"

¹⁷A stone was brought and placed over the mouth of the den, and the king sealed it with his own signet ring and with the rings of his nobles, so that Daniel's situation might not be changed. ¹⁸Then the king returned to his palace and spent the night without eating and without any entertainment being brought to him. And he could not sleep.

¹⁹At the first light of dawn, the king got up and hurried to the lions' den. ²⁰When he came near the den, he called to Daniel in an anguished voice, "Daniel, servant of the living God, has your God, whom you serve continually, been able to rescue you from the lions?"

²¹Daniel answered, "O king, live forever! ²²My God sent his angel, and he shut the mouths of the lions. They have not hurt me, because I was found innocent in his sight. Nor have I ever done any wrong before you, O king."

²³The king was overjoyed and gave orders to lift Daniel out of the den. And when Daniel was lifted from the den, no wound was found on him, because he had trusted in his God.

²⁴At the king's command, the men who had falsely accused Daniel were brought in and thrown into the lions' den, along with their wives and children. And before they reached the floor of the den, the lions overpowered them and crushed all their bones.

²⁵Then King Darius wrote to all the peoples, nations and men of every language throughout the land:

"May you prosper greatly!

²⁶"I issue a decree that in every part of my kingdom people must fear and reverence the God of Daniel.

"For he is the living God
    and he endures forever;
his kingdom will not be destroyed,
    his dominion will never end.
²⁷He rescues and he saves;
    he performs signs and wonders
    in the heavens and on the earth.
He has rescued Daniel
    from the power of the lions."

²⁸So Daniel prospered during the reign of Darius and the reign of Cyrus[a] the Persian.

Daniel's Dream of Four Beasts

7 In the first year of Belshazzar king of Babylon, Daniel had a dream, and visions passed through his mind as he was lying on his bed. He wrote down the substance of his dream.

²Daniel said: "In my vision at night I looked, and there before me were the four winds of heaven churning up the great sea. ³Four great beasts, each different from the others, came up out of the sea.

⁴"The first was like a lion, and it had the wings of an eagle. I watched until its wings were torn off and it was lifted from the ground so that it stood on two feet like a man, and the heart of a man was given to it.

⁵"And there before me was a second beast, which looked like a bear. It was raised up on one of its sides, and it had three ribs in its mouth between its teeth. It was told, 'Get up and eat your fill of flesh!'

a 28 Or Darius, that is, the reign of Cyrus

⁶"After that, I looked, and there before me was another beast, one that looked like a leopard. And on its back it had four wings like those of a bird. This beast had four heads, and it was given authority to rule.

⁷"After that, in my vision at night I looked, and there before me was a fourth beast—terrifying and frightening and very powerful. It had large iron teeth; it crushed and devoured its victims and trampled underfoot whatever was left. It was different from all the former beasts, and it had ten horns.

⁸"While I was thinking about the horns, there before me was another horn, a little one, which came up among them; and three of the first horns were uprooted before it. This horn had eyes like the eyes of a man and a mouth that spoke boastfully.

⁹"As I looked,

> "thrones were set in place,
>   and the Ancient of Days took his seat.
> His clothing was as white as snow;
>   the hair of his head was white like wool.
> His throne was flaming with fire,
>   and its wheels were all ablaze.
> ¹⁰A river of fire was flowing,
>   coming out from before him.
> Thousands upon thousands attended him;
>   ten thousand times ten thousand stood before him.
> The court was seated,
>   and the books were opened.

¹¹"Then I continued to watch because of the boastful words the horn was speaking. I kept looking until the beast was slain and its body destroyed and thrown into the blazing fire. ¹²(The other beasts had been stripped of their authority, but were allowed to live for a period of time.)

¹³"In my vision at night I looked, and there before me was one like a son of man, coming with the clouds of heaven. He approached the Ancient of Days and was led into his presence. ¹⁴He was given authority, glory and sovereign power; all peoples, nations and men of every language worshiped him. His dominion is an everlasting dominion that will not pass away, and his kingdom is one that will never be destroyed.

The Interpretation of the Dream

¹⁵"I, Daniel, was troubled in spirit, and the visions that passed through my mind disturbed me. ¹⁶I approached one of those standing there and asked him the true meaning of all this.

"So he told me and gave me the interpretation of these things: ¹⁷'The four great beasts are four kingdoms that will rise from the earth. ¹⁸But the saints of the Most High will receive the kingdom and will possess it forever—yes, for ever and ever.'

¹⁹"Then I wanted to know the true meaning of the fourth beast, which was different from all the others and most terrifying, with its iron teeth and bronze claws—the beast that crushed and devoured its victims and trampled underfoot whatever was left. ²⁰I also wanted to know about the ten horns on its head and about the other horn that came up, before which three of them fell—the horn that looked more imposing than the others and that had eyes and a mouth that spoke boastfully. ²¹As I watched, this horn was waging war against the saints and defeating them, ²²until the Ancient of Days came and pronounced judgment in favor of the saints of the Most High, and the time came when they possessed the kingdom.

²³"He gave me this explanation: 'The fourth beast is a fourth kingdom that will appear on earth. It will be different from all the other kingdoms and will devour the whole earth, trampling it down and crushing it. ²⁴The ten horns are ten kings who will come from this

kingdom. After them another king will arise, different from the earlier ones; he will subdue three kings. ²⁵He will speak against the Most High and oppress his saints and try to change the set times and the laws. The saints will be handed over to him for a time, times and half a time. *ᵃ*

²⁶"'But the court will sit, and his power will be taken away and completely destroyed forever. ²⁷Then the sovereignty, power and greatness of the kingdoms under the whole heaven will be handed over to the saints, the people of the Most High. His kingdom will be an everlasting kingdom, and all rulers will worship and obey him.'

²⁸"This is the end of the matter. I, Daniel, was deeply troubled by my thoughts, and my face turned pale, but I kept the matter to myself."

Daniel's Vision of a Ram and a Goat

8 In the third year of King Belshazzar's reign, I, Daniel, had a vision, after the one that had already appeared to me. ²In my vision I saw myself in the citadel of Susa in the province of Elam; in the vision I was beside the Ulai Canal. ³I looked up, and there before me was a ram with two horns, standing beside the canal, and the horns were long. One of the horns was longer than the other but grew up later. ⁴I watched the ram as he charged toward the west and the north and the south. No animal could stand against him, and none could rescue from his power. He did as he pleased and became great.

⁵As I was thinking about this, suddenly a goat with a prominent horn between his eyes came from the west, crossing the whole earth without touching the ground. ⁶He came toward the two-horned ram I had seen standing beside the canal and charged at him in great rage. ⁷I saw him attack the ram furiously, striking the ram and shattering his two horns. The ram was powerless to stand against him; the goat knocked him to the ground and trampled on him, and none could rescue the ram from his power. ⁸The goat became very great, but at the height of his power his large horn was broken off, and in its place four prominent horns grew up toward the four winds of heaven.

⁹Out of one of them came another horn, which started small but grew in power to the south and to the east and toward the Beautiful Land. ¹⁰It grew until it reached the host of the heavens, and it threw some of the starry host down to the earth and trampled on them. ¹¹It set itself up to be as great as the Prince of the host; it took away the daily sacrifice from him, and the place of his sanctuary was brought low. ¹²Because of rebellion, the host ∟of the saints⌉*ᵇ* and the daily sacrifice were given over to it. It prospered in everything it did, and truth was thrown to the ground.

¹³Then I heard a holy one speaking, and another holy one said to him, "How long will it take for the vision to be fulfilled—the vision concerning the daily sacrifice, the rebellion that causes desolation, and the surrender of the sanctuary and of the host that will be trampled underfoot?"

¹⁴He said to me, "It will take 2,300 evenings and mornings; then the sanctuary will be reconsecrated."

The Interpretation of the Vision

¹⁵While I, Daniel, was watching the vision and trying to understand it, there before me stood one who looked like a man. ¹⁶And I heard a man's voice from the Ulai calling, "Gabriel, tell this man the meaning of the vision."

¹⁷As he came near the place where I was standing, I was terrified and fell prostrate. "Son of man," he said to me, "understand that the vision concerns the time of the end."

¹⁸While he was speaking to me, I was in a deep sleep, with my face to the ground. Then he touched me and raised me to my feet.

¹⁹He said: "I am going to tell you what will happen later in the time of wrath, because

ᵃ25 Or for a year, two years and half a year   ᵇ12 Or rebellion, the armies

the vision concerns the appointed time of the end.^a ²⁰The two-horned ram that you saw represents the kings of Media and Persia. ²¹The shaggy goat is the king of Greece, and the large horn between his eyes is the first king. ²²The four horns that replaced the one that was broken off represent four kingdoms that will emerge from his nation but will not have the same power.

²³"In the latter part of their reign, when rebels have become completely wicked, a stern-faced king, a master of intrigue, will arise. ²⁴He will become very strong, but not by his own power. He will cause astounding devastation and will succeed in whatever he does. He will destroy the mighty men and the holy people. ²⁵He will cause deceit to prosper, and he will consider himself superior. When they feel secure, he will destroy many and take his stand against the Prince of princes. Yet he will be destroyed, but not by human power.

²⁶"The vision of the evenings and mornings that has been given you is true, but seal up the vision, for it concerns the distant future."

²⁷I, Daniel, was exhausted and lay ill for several days. Then I got up and went about the king's business. I was appalled by the vision; it was beyond understanding.

Daniel's Prayer

9 In the first year of Darius son of Xerxes^b (a Mede by descent), who was made ruler over the Babylonian^c kingdom— ²in the first year of his reign, I, Daniel, understood from the Scriptures, according to the word of the LORD given to Jeremiah the prophet, that the desolation of Jerusalem would last seventy years. ³So I turned to the Lord God and pleaded with him in prayer and petition, in fasting, and in sackcloth and ashes.

⁴I prayed to the LORD my God and confessed:

"O Lord, the great and awesome God, who keeps his covenant of love with all who love him and obey his commands, ⁵we have sinned and done wrong. We have been wicked and have rebelled; we have turned away from your commands and laws. ⁶We have not listened to your servants the prophets, who spoke in your name to our kings, our princes and our fathers, and to all the people of the land.

⁷"Lord, you are righteous, but this day we are covered with shame—the men of Judah and people of Jerusalem and all Israel, both near and far, in all the countries where you have scattered us because of our unfaithfulness to you. ⁸O LORD, we and our kings, our princes and our fathers are covered with shame because we have sinned against you. ⁹The Lord our God is merciful and forgiving, even though we have rebelled against him; ¹⁰we have not obeyed the LORD our God or kept the laws he gave us through his servants the prophets. ¹¹All Israel has transgressed your law and turned away, refusing to obey you.

"Therefore the curses and sworn judgments written in the Law of Moses, the servant of God, have been poured out on us, because we have sinned against you. ¹²You have fulfilled the words spoken against us and against our rulers by bringing upon us great disaster. Under the whole heaven nothing has ever been done like what has been done to Jerusalem. ¹³Just as it is written in the Law of Moses, all this disaster has come upon us, yet we have not sought the favor of the LORD our God by turning from our sins and giving attention to your truth. ¹⁴The LORD did not hesitate to bring the disaster upon us, for the LORD our God is righteous in everything he does; yet we have not obeyed him.

¹⁵"Now, O Lord our God, who brought your people out of Egypt with a mighty hand and who made for yourself a name that endures to this day, we have sinned, we have done wrong. ¹⁶O Lord, in keeping with all your righteous acts, turn away your anger and your wrath from Jerusalem, your city, your holy hill. Our sins and the

---

^a 19 Or because the end will be at the appointed time   ^b 1 Hebrew Ahasuerus   ^c 1 Or Chaldean

iniquities of our fathers have made Jerusalem and your people an object of scorn to all those around us.

17"Now, our God, hear the prayers and petitions of your servant. For your sake, O Lord, look with favor on your desolate sanctuary. 18Give ear, O God, and hear; open your eyes and see the desolation of the city that bears your Name. We do not make requests of you because we are righteous, but because of your great mercy. 19O Lord, listen! O Lord, forgive! O Lord, hear and act! For your sake, O my God, do not delay, because your city and your people bear your Name."

The Seventy "Sevens"

20While I was speaking and praying, confessing my sin and the sin of my people Israel and making my request to the LORD my God for his holy hill— 21while I was still in prayer, Gabriel, the man I had seen in the earlier vision, came to me in swift flight about the time of the evening sacrifice. 22He instructed me and said to me, "Daniel, I have now come to give you insight and understanding. 23As soon as you began to pray, an answer was given, which I have come to tell you, for you are highly esteemed. Therefore, consider the message and understand the vision:

24"Seventy 'sevens'ª are decreed for your people and your holy city to finishᵇ transgression, to put an end to sin, to atone for wickedness, to bring in everlasting righteousness, to seal up vision and prophecy and to anoint the most holy.ᶜ

25"Know and understand this: From the issuing of the decreeᵈ to restore and rebuild Jerusalem until the Anointed One,ᵉ the ruler, comes, there will be seven 'sevens,' and sixty-two 'sevens.' It will be rebuilt with streets and a trench, but in times of trouble. 26After the sixty-two 'sevens,' the Anointed One will be cut off and will have nothing.ᶠ The people of the ruler who will come will destroy the city and the sanctuary. The end will come like a flood: War will continue until the end, and desolations have been decreed. 27He will confirm a covenant with many for one 'seven.'ᵍ In the middle of the 'seven'ᵍ he will put an end to sacrifice and offering. And on a wing ⌊of the temple⌋ he will set up an abomination that causes desolation, until the end that is decreed is poured out on him.ʰ"ⁱ

Daniel's Vision of a Man

10 In the third year of Cyrus king of Persia, a revelation was given to Daniel (who was called Belteshazzar). Its message was true and it concerned a great war.ʲ The understanding of the message came to him in a vision.

2At that time I, Daniel, mourned for three weeks. 3I ate no choice food; no meat or wine touched my lips; and I used no lotions at all until the three weeks were over.

4On the twenty-fourth day of the first month, as I was standing on the bank of the great river, the Tigris, 5I looked up and there before me was a man dressed in linen, with a belt of the finest gold around his waist. 6His body was like chrysolite, his face like lightning, his eyes like flaming torches, his arms and legs like the gleam of burnished bronze, and his voice like the sound of a multitude.

7I, Daniel, was the only one who saw the vision; the men with me did not see it, but such terror overwhelmed them that they fled and hid themselves. 8So I was left alone, gazing at this great vision; I had no strength left, my face turned deathly pale and I was helpless. 9Then I heard him speaking, and as I listened to him, I fell into a deep sleep, my face to the ground.

10A hand touched me and set me trembling on my hands and knees. 11He said, "Daniel, you who are highly esteemed, consider carefully the words I am about to speak to you,

ª24 Or 'weeks'; also in verses 25 and 26   ᵇ24 Or restrain   ᶜ24 Or Most Holy Place; or most holy One   ᵈ25 Or word   ᵉ25 Or an anointed one; also in verse 26   ᶠ26 Or off and will have no one; or off, but not for himself   ᵍ27 Or 'week'   ʰ27 Or it   ⁱ27 Or And one who causes desolation will come upon the pinnacle of the abominable ⌊temple⌋ until the end that is decreed is poured out on the desolated ⌊city⌋   ʲ1 Or true and burdensome

and stand up, for I have now been sent to you." And when he said this to me, I stood up trembling.

[12]Then he continued, "Do not be afraid, Daniel. Since the first day that you set your mind to gain understanding and to humble yourself before your God, your words were heard, and I have come in response to them. [13]But the prince of the Persian kingdom resisted me twenty-one days. Then Michael, one of the chief princes, came to help me, because I was detained there with the king of Persia. [14]Now I have come to explain to you what will happen to your people in the future, for the vision concerns a time yet to come."

[15]While he was saying this to me, I bowed with my face toward the ground and was speechless. [16]Then one who looked like a man[a] touched my lips, and I opened my mouth and began to speak. I said to the one standing before me, "I am overcome with anguish because of the vision, my lord, and I am helpless. [17]How can I, your servant, talk with you, my lord? My strength is gone and I can hardly breathe."

[18]Again the one who looked like a man touched me and gave me strength. [19]"Do not be afraid, O man highly esteemed," he said. "Peace! Be strong now; be strong."

When he spoke to me, I was strengthened and said, "Speak, my lord, since you have given me strength."

[20]So he said, "Do you know why I have come to you? Soon I will return to fight against the prince of Persia, and when I go, the prince of Greece will come; [21]but first I will tell you what is written in the Book of Truth. (No one supports me against them except Michael, your prince. [1]And in the first year of Darius the Mede, I took my stand to support and protect him.)

The Kings of the South and the North

[2]"Now then, I tell you the truth: Three more kings will appear in Persia, and then a fourth, who will be far richer than all the others. When he has gained power by his wealth, he will stir up everyone against the kingdom of Greece. [3]Then a mighty king will appear, who will rule with great power and do as he pleases. [4]After he has appeared, his empire will be broken up and parceled out toward the four winds of heaven. It will not go to his descendants, nor will it have the power he exercised, because his empire will be uprooted and given to others.

[5]"The king of the South will become strong, but one of his commanders will become even stronger than he and will rule his own kingdom with great power. [6]After some years, they will become allies. The daughter of the king of the South will go to the king of the North to make an alliance, but she will not retain her power, and he and his power[b] will not last. In those days she will be handed over, together with her royal escort and her father[c] and the one who supported her.

[7]"One from her family line will arise to take her place. He will attack the forces of the king of the North and enter his fortress; he will fight against them and be victorious. [8]He will also seize their gods, their metal images and their valuable articles of silver and gold and carry them off to Egypt. For some years he will leave the king of the North alone. [9]Then the king of the North will invade the realm of the king of the South but will retreat to his own country. [10]His sons will prepare for war and assemble a great army, which will sweep on like an irresistible flood and carry the battle as far as his fortress.

[11]"Then the king of the South will march out in a rage and fight against the king of the North, who will raise a large army, but it will be defeated. [12]When the army is carried off, the king of the South will be filled with pride and will slaughter many thousands, yet he will not remain triumphant. [13]For the king of the North will muster another army, larger than the first; and after several years, he will advance with a huge army fully equipped.

[14]"In those times many will rise against the king of the South. The violent men among

[a]16 Most manuscripts of the Masoretic Text; one manuscript of the Masoretic Text, Dead Sea Scrolls and Septuagint *Then something that looked like a man's hand*   [b]6 Or *offspring*   [c]6 Or *child* (see Vulgate and Syriac)

your own people will rebel in fulfillment of the vision, but without success. ¹⁵Then the king of the North will come and build up siege ramps and will capture a fortified city. The forces of the South will be powerless to resist; even their best troops will not have the strength to stand. ¹⁶The invader will do as he pleases; no one will be able to stand against him. He will establish himself in the Beautiful Land and will have the power to destroy it. ¹⁷He will determine to come with the might of his entire kingdom and will make an alliance with the king of the South. And he will give him a daughter in marriage in order to overthrow the kingdom, but his plans*ᵃ* will not succeed or help him. ¹⁸Then he will turn his attention to the coastlands and will take many of them, but a commander will put an end to his insolence and will turn his insolence back upon him. ¹⁹After this, he will turn back toward the fortresses of his own country but will stumble and fall, to be seen no more.

²⁰"His successor will send out a tax collector to maintain the royal splendor. In a few years, however, he will be destroyed, yet not in anger or in battle.

²¹"He will be succeeded by a contemptible person who has not been given the honor of royalty. He will invade the kingdom when its people feel secure, and he will seize it through intrigue. ²²Then an overwhelming army will be swept away before him; both it and a prince of the covenant will be destroyed. ²³After coming to an agreement with him, he will act deceitfully, and with only a few people he will rise to power. ²⁴When the richest provinces feel secure, he will invade them and will achieve what neither his fathers nor his forefathers did. He will distribute plunder, loot and wealth among his followers. He will plot the overthrow of fortresses—but only for a time.

²⁵"With a large army he will stir up his strength and courage against the king of the South. The king of the South will wage war with a large and very powerful army, but he will not be able to stand because of the plots devised against him. ²⁶Those who eat from the king's provisions will try to destroy him; his army will be swept away, and many will fall in battle. ²⁷The two kings, with their hearts bent on evil, will sit at the same table and lie to each other, but to no avail, because an end will still come at the appointed time. ²⁸The king of the North will return to his own country with great wealth, but his heart will be set against the holy covenant. He will take action against it and then return to his own country.

²⁹"At the appointed time he will invade the South again, but this time the outcome will be different from what it was before. ³⁰Ships of the western coastlands*ᵇ* will oppose him, and he will lose heart. Then he will turn back and vent his fury against the holy covenant. He will return and show favor to those who forsake the holy covenant. ³¹His armed forces will rise up to desecrate the temple fortress and will abolish the daily sacrifice. Then they will set up the abomination that causes desolation.

▭ ░░░░░░░ REASONS TO BELIEVE ░░░░░░░ ↩

11:36
The Amazing Bible

Even though this prophecy can be closely tied to a particular ancient tyrant (Antiochus V), the twentieth century is littered with stories of leaders who have followed this king's path to destruction. Although leaders like Stalin and Hitler have held "godlike" positions of power in their particular countries, they have all experienced the reality of verse 45: "He will come to his end, and no one will help him."

Amid all the strange images that you discover in this and other chapters in Daniel, one theme comes through loud and clear. No matter how powerful a political, religious, or any other type of leader becomes, God still has the last word on what happens to them on earth.

This world's power and possessions fade as time passes, but individuals who follow God's path receive a reward that will never end.

³²With flattery he will corrupt those who have violated the covenant, but the people who know their God will firmly resist him.

³³"Those who are wise will instruct many, though for a time they will fall by the sword

ᵃ17 Or *but she*   ᵇ30 Hebrew *of Kittim*

or be burned or captured or plundered. ³⁴When they fall, they will receive a little help, and many who are not sincere will join them. ³⁵Some of the wise will stumble, so that they may be refined, purified and made spotless until the time of the end, for it will still come at the appointed time.

The King Who Exalts Himself

³⁶"The king will do as he pleases. He will exalt and magnify himself above every god and will say unheard-of things against the God of gods. He will be successful until the time of wrath is completed, for what has been determined must take place. ³⁷He will show no regard for the gods of his fathers or for the one desired by women, nor will he regard any god, but will exalt himself above them all. ³⁸Instead of them, he will honor a god of fortresses; a god unknown to his fathers he will honor with gold and silver, with precious stones and costly gifts. ³⁹He will attack the mightiest fortresses with the help of a foreign god and will greatly honor those who acknowledge him. He will make them rulers over many people and will distribute the land at a price.ᵃ

⁴⁰"At the time of the end the king of the South will engage him in battle, and the king of the North will storm out against him with chariots and cavalry and a great fleet of ships. He will invade many countries and sweep through them like a flood. ⁴¹He will also invade the Beautiful Land. Many countries will fall, but Edom, Moab and the leaders of Ammon will be delivered from his hand. ⁴²He will extend his power over many countries; Egypt will not escape. ⁴³He will gain control of the treasures of gold and silver and all the riches of Egypt, with the Libyans and Nubians in submission. ⁴⁴But reports from the east and the north will alarm him, and he will set out in a great rage to destroy and annihilate many. ⁴⁵He will pitch his royal tents between the seas atᵇ the beautiful holy mountain. Yet he will come to his end, and no one will help him.

The End Times

12 "At that time Michael, the great prince who protects your people, will arise. There will be a time of distress such as has not happened from the beginning of nations until then. But at that time your people—everyone whose name is found written in the book—will be delivered. ²Multitudes who sleep in the dust of the earth will awake: some to everlasting life, others to shame and everlasting contempt. ³Those who are wiseᶜ will shine like the brightness of the heavens, and those who lead many to righteousness, like the stars for ever and ever. ⁴But you, Daniel, close up and seal the words of the scroll until the time of the end. Many will go here and there to increase knowledge."

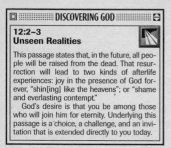

◻ ▦▦▦▦ DISCOVERING GOD ▦▦▦▦ ▣

12:2–3
Unseen Realities

This passage states that, in the future, all people will be raised from the dead. That resurrection will lead to two kinds of afterlife experiences: joy in the presence of God forever, "shin[ing] like the heavens"; or "shame and everlasting contempt."

God's desire is that you be among those who will join him for eternity. Underlying this passage is a choice, a challenge, and an invitation that is extended directly to you today.

⁵Then I, Daniel, looked, and there before me stood two others, one on this bank of the river and one on the opposite bank. ⁶One of them said to the man clothed in linen, who was above the waters of the river, "How long will it be before these astonishing things are fulfilled?"

⁷The man clothed in linen, who was above the waters of the river, lifted his right hand and his left hand toward heaven, and I heard him swear by him who lives forever,

ᵃ39 Or land for a reward   ᵇ45 Or the sea and   ᶜ3 Or who impart wisdom

saying, "It will be for a time, times and half a time.ᵃ When the power of the holy people has been finally broken, all these things will be completed."

⁸I heard, but I did not understand. So I asked, "My lord, what will the outcome of all this be?"

⁹He replied, "Go your way, Daniel, because the words are closed up and sealed until the time of the end. ¹⁰Many will be purified, made spotless and refined, but the wicked will continue to be wicked. None of the wicked will understand, but those who are wise will understand.

¹¹"From the time that the daily sacrifice is abolished and the abomination that causes desolation is set up, there will be 1,290 days. ¹²Blessed is the one who waits for and reaches the end of the 1,335 days.

¹³"As for you, go your way till the end. You will rest, and then at the end of the days you will rise to receive your allotted inheritance."

ᵃ7 Or a year, two years and half a year

THE MINOR PROPHETS

Introduction

THE BOTTOM LINE **T**welve Angry Men. That was the title of a popular courtroom-drama film in the 1950s, but the same title would also be appropriate for the 12 prophets of God whose messages you'll read in this section. The Bible's Old Testament ends with the booming voices of these sometimes reluctant prophets, each of whom calls people to turn from their wicked ways and to follow God. Each prophet wrote from his own circumstances and fits into his own place in Israel's history (see time line below). But a common theme runs through their message: As long as we trust in God and live by his directives, we will experience God's blessing on our lives—no matter what our situation.

CENTRAL IDEAS

- God calls messengers to bring his word to people—even when the messengers are reluctant to do so (see Jonah chapter 1 [p. 1205]).
- God wants all people to trust in him.
- God's requirements for us are simple—do justice, be merciful to others, and trust in him (see Micah chapter 6, verse 8 [p. 1215]).
- God will one day visibly restore his rule over this troubled earth (see Zechariah chapter 14, verse 9 [p. 1248]).

TITLES

Although these books are grouped together under the name "The Minor Prophets," there is nothing minor about the message each one of them presents; these books have received that title because of their relative brevity. Each of these 12 books is named after its author, who wrote out of his own particular context.

AUTHORS AND READERS

See above and the timeline below.

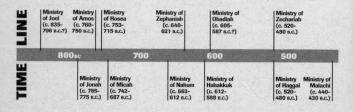

TIME LINE

| Ministry of Joel (c. 835–796 B.C.?) | Ministry of Amos (c. 760–750 B.C.) | Ministry of Hosea (c. 753–715 B.C.) | Ministry of Zephaniah (c. 640–621 B.C.) | Ministry of Obadiah (c. 605–587 B.C.?) | Ministry of Zechariah (c. 520–480 B.C.) |

800 B.C.   700   600   500

| Ministry of Jonah (c. 785–775 B.C.) | Ministry of Micah (c. 742–687 B.C.) | Ministry of Nahum (c. 663–612 B.C.) | Ministry of Habakkuk (c. 612–588 B.C.) | Ministry of Haggai (c. 520–480 B.C.) | Ministry of Malachi (c. 440–430 B.C.) |

On a sunny spring day in 1937, a boy begged his mother to let him go to a Brooklyn Dodgers' game. Instead, she made him go shopping with her. Years later, he was glad that he missed that game, because he learned one of the greatest lessons of his life that day.

While shopping in Macy's Department Store, his mother spotted a pair of gloves on a shelf above a glass counter. A short distance away, two sales clerks were chatting with each other.

The boy's mother cleared her throat to get their attention. The two women looked in her direction, but continued talking. Irritated, she took a large set of keys out of her purse and banged them on the glass counter. Immediately a clerk rushed over to the shopper.

The angry woman barked at the clerk, "Do you know who I am?"

Confused, the clerk said, "No, I'm afraid I don't."

"Well, do you know who you are?"

The clerk gazed at the woman for a moment and said, "I work here."

"Wrong answer! You work for me. I'm the customer."

"Wrong answer!" the boy's mother said. "You work for me. I'm the customer."*

In that moment the inexperienced clerk was reminded of her purpose for being at Macy's. And the boy learned a lesson that served him well during his career in business. Instead of serving the customer, those preoccupied clerks almost prevented a sale that day!

Sometimes people who represent God have the same effect on seekers. The Bible teaches that all God-followers are also supposed to be his ambassadors to people around them. If you've met someone who has "turned you off" to God, you may be interested to know that throughout history God has had a hard time getting his people to act appropriately toward those outside the church.

In one well-known story, God told a prophet named Jonah to travel to the non–Jewish city of Nineveh and warn the inhabitants to stop their immoral behavior. Instead, Jonah disobeyed God and fled on a ship in the opposite direction. Thrown overboard by frightened sailors, he was swallowed by a great fish. At God's command the creature burped up a repentant Jonah on the beach near Nineveh. Jonah walked to the city and delivered God's message. It was received with open arms, and the whole city straightened out its act virtually overnight.

If Jonah had worked at Macy's, he probably would have seen customers as a nuisance. God's people can sometimes make that mistake. When that happens and one of them lets you down, consider the real issue: What does *God* think about you? To see what God said about the people in Nineveh, turn to Jonah chapter 4 (page 1207).

*Used by permission of *Bob Farrell's Pickle Production, Inc.*

HOSEA

1 The word of the LORD that came to Hosea son of Beeri during the reigns of Uzziah, Jotham, Ahaz and Hezekiah, kings of Judah, and during the reign of Jeroboam son of Jehoash[a] king of Israel:

Hosea's Wife and Children

²When the LORD began to speak through Hosea, the LORD said to him, "Go, take to yourself an adulterous wife and children of unfaithfulness, because the land is guilty of the vilest adultery in departing from the LORD." ³So he married Gomer daughter of Diblaim, and she conceived and bore him a son.

⁴Then the LORD said to Hosea, "Call him Jezreel, because I will soon punish the house of Jehu for the massacre at Jezreel, and I will put an end to the kingdom of Israel. ⁵In that day I will break Israel's bow in the Valley of Jezreel."

⁶Gomer conceived again and gave birth to a daughter. Then the LORD said to Hosea, "Call her Lo-Ruhamah,[b] for I will no longer show love to the house of Israel, that I should at all forgive them. ⁷Yet I will show love to the house of Judah; and I will save them—not by bow, sword or battle, or by horses and horsemen, but by the LORD their God."

⁸After she had weaned Lo-Ruhamah, Gomer had another son. ⁹Then the LORD said, "Call him Lo-Ammi,[c] for you are not my people, and I am not your God.

¹⁰"Yet the Israelites will be like the sand on the seashore, which cannot be measured or counted. In the place where it was said to them, 'You are not my people,' they will be called 'sons of the living God.' ¹¹The people of Judah and the people of Israel will be reunited, and they will appoint one leader and will come up out of the land, for great will be the day of Jezreel.

2 "Say of your brothers, 'My people,' and of your sisters, 'My loved one.'

Israel Punished and Restored

²"Rebuke your mother, rebuke her,
    for she is not my wife,
    and I am not her husband.
Let her remove the adulterous look from her face
    and the unfaithfulness from between her breasts.
³Otherwise I will strip her naked
    and make her as bare as on the day she was born;
I will make her like a desert,
    turn her into a parched land,
    and slay her with thirst.
⁴I will not show my love to her children,
    because they are the children of adultery.
⁵Their mother has been unfaithful
    and has conceived them in disgrace.
She said, 'I will go after my lovers,

---

[a] 1 Hebrew *Joash*, a variant of *Jehoash*   [b] 6 *Lo-Ruhamah* means *not loved*.   [c] 9 *Lo-Ammi* means *not my people*.

who give me my food and my water,
my wool and my linen, my oil and my drink.'
⁶Therefore I will block her path with thornbushes;
I will wall her in so that she cannot find her way.
⁷She will chase after her lovers but not catch them;
she will look for them but not find them.
Then she will say,
'I will go back to my husband as at first,
for then I was better off than now.'
⁸She has not acknowledged that I was the one
who gave her the grain, the new wine and oil,
who lavished on her the silver and gold—
which they used for Baal.

⁹"Therefore I will take away my grain when it ripens,
and my new wine when it is ready.
I will take back my wool and my linen,
intended to cover her nakedness.
¹⁰So now I will expose her lewdness
before the eyes of her lovers;
no one will take her out of my hands.
¹¹I will stop all her celebrations:
her yearly festivals, her New Moons,
her Sabbath days—all her appointed feasts.
¹²I will ruin her vines and her fig trees,
which she said were her pay from her lovers;
I will make them a thicket,
and wild animals will devour them.
¹³I will punish her for the days
she burned incense to the Baals;
she decked herself with rings and jewelry,
and went after her lovers,
but me she forgot,"

declares the Lord.

¹⁴"Therefore I am now going to allure her;
I will lead her into the desert
and speak tenderly to her.
¹⁵There I will give her back her vineyards,
and will make the Valley of Achor*ᵃ* a door of hope.
There she will sing*ᵇ* as in the days of her youth,
as in the day she came up out of Egypt.

¹⁶"In that day," declares the Lord,
"you will call me 'my husband';
you will no longer call me 'my master.'*ᶜ*'
¹⁷I will remove the names of the Baals from her lips;
no longer will their names be invoked.
¹⁸In that day I will make a covenant for them
with the beasts of the field and the birds of the air
and the creatures that move along the ground.
Bow and sword and battle

ᵃ15 Achor means trouble.   *ᵇ15* Or respond   *ᶜ16* Hebrew baal

I will abolish from the land,
   so that all may lie down in safety.
¹⁹I will betroth you to me forever;
   I will betroth you in ᵃ righteousness and justice,
      in ᵇ love and compassion.
²⁰I will betroth you in faithfulness,
   and you will acknowledge the Lord.

²¹"In that day I will respond,"
   declares the Lord—
   "I will respond to the skies,
      and they will respond to the earth;
²²and the earth will respond to the grain,
   the new wine and oil,
      and they will respond to Jezreel. ᶜ
²³I will plant her for myself in the land;
   I will show my love to the one I called 'Not my loved one.' ᵈ
   I will say to those called 'Not my people, ᵉ' 'You are my people';
      and they will say, 'You are my God.'"

Hosea's Reconciliation With His Wife

3 The Lord said to me, "Go, show your love to your wife again, though she is loved by another and is an adulteress. Love her as the Lord loves the Israelites, though they turn to other gods and love the sacred raisin cakes."

²So I bought her for fifteen shekels ᶠ of silver and about a homer and a lethek ᵍ of barley. ³Then I told her, "You are to live with ʰ me many days; you must not be a prostitute or be intimate with any man, and I will live with ʰ you."

⁴For the Israelites will live many days without king or prince, without sacrifice or sacred stones, without ephod or idol. ⁵Afterward the Israelites will return and seek the Lord their God and David their king. They will come trembling to the Lord and to his blessings in the last days.

ᵃ19 Or with; also in verse 20   ᵇ19 Or with   ᶜ22 Jezreel means God plants.   ᵈ23 Hebrew Lo-Ruhamah
ᵉ23 Hebrew Lo-Ammi   ᶠ2 That is, about 6 ounces (about 170 grams)   ᵍ2 That is, probably about 10 bushels (about 330 liters)   ʰ3 Or wait for

---

┌──┐
│ ▣ :::::::::::::::::::::::::::: **DISCOVERING GOD** :::::::::::::::::::::::::::: ⬒ │

3:1
The God Who Is There

God asked the prophet Hosea to do the unthinkable—forgive and restore his relationship with his unfaithful wife, who was acting like a prostitute. This chapter details how Hosea actually bought his wife back. In doing so, this prophet gave the Israelites a picture of God's love for his unfaithful people.

If we are unfaithful and refuse to acknowledge God, he has a perfect right to do what, in effect, we have requested: leave us alone. No one would accuse God of being unfair if he honored the demand of people to go their own way. But God is merciful and doesn't exercise that right. Instead, he pursues us. His offer of acceptance is open for as long as we live.

As a seeker, you may think God has been hiding from you. But a more truthful statement may be that *you've been hiding from him!* If the life you've lived so far has excluded God from his rightful place at the center of your life, don't leave God out for even one more day. All he asks is that you recognize that you've pushed him away and accept his invitation to live in relationship with him. He has already paid the price to buy you back. Go to him by talking to him as best you know how, and he will welcome you with open arms.
└──┘

The Charge Against Israel

4 Hear the word of the LORD, you Israelites,
because the LORD has a charge to bring
against you who live in the land:
"There is no faithfulness, no love,
no acknowledgment of God in the land.
² There is only cursing,ᵃ lying and murder,
stealing and adultery;
they break all bounds,
and bloodshed follows bloodshed.
³ Because of this the land mourns,ᵇ
and all who live in it waste away;
the beasts of the field and the birds of the air
and the fish of the sea are dying.

⁴ "But let no man bring a charge,
let no man accuse another,
for your people are like those
who bring charges against a priest.
⁵ You stumble day and night,
and the prophets stumble with you.
So I will destroy your mother—
⁶ my people are destroyed from lack of knowledge.

"Because you have rejected knowledge,
I also reject you as my priests;
because you have ignored the law of your God,
I also will ignore your children.
⁷ The more the priests increased,
the more they sinned against me;
they exchangedᶜ theirᵈ Glory for something disgraceful.
⁸ They feed on the sins of my people
and relish their wickedness.
⁹ And it will be: Like people, like priests.
I will punish both of them for their ways
and repay them for their deeds.

¹⁰ "They will eat but not have enough;
they will engage in prostitution but not increase,
because they have deserted the LORD
to give themselves ¹¹to prostitution,
to old wine and new,
which take away the understanding ¹²of my people.
They consult a wooden idol
and are answered by a stick of wood.
A spirit of prostitution leads them astray;
they are unfaithful to their God.
¹³ They sacrifice on the mountaintops
and burn offerings on the hills,
under oak, poplar and terebinth,
where the shade is pleasant.

ᵃ2 That is, to pronounce a curse upon   ᵇ3 Or *dries up*   ᶜ7 Syriac and an ancient Hebrew scribal tradition; Masoretic
Text *I will exchange*   ᵈ7 Masoretic Text; an ancient Hebrew scribal tradition *my*

Therefore your daughters turn to prostitution
  and your daughters-in-law to adultery.

¹⁴"I will not punish your daughters
    when they turn to prostitution,
  nor your daughters-in-law
    when they commit adultery,
  because the men themselves consort with harlots
    and sacrifice with shrine prostitutes—
  a people without understanding will come to ruin!

¹⁵"Though you commit adultery, O Israel,
    let not Judah become guilty.

"Do not go to Gilgal;
    do not go up to Beth Aven.ᵃ
  And do not swear, 'As surely as the LORD lives!'
¹⁶The Israelites are stubborn,
    like a stubborn heifer.
  How then can the LORD pasture them
    like lambs in a meadow?
¹⁷Ephraim is joined to idols;
    leave him alone!
¹⁸Even when their drinks are gone,
    they continue their prostitution;
  their rulers dearly love shameful ways.
¹⁹A whirlwind will sweep them away,
    and their sacrifices will bring them shame.

Judgment Against Israel

5 "Hear this, you priests!
    Pay attention, you Israelites!
  Listen, O royal house!
    This judgment is against you:
  You have been a snare at Mizpah,
    a net spread out on Tabor.
²The rebels are deep in slaughter.
    I will discipline all of them.
³I know all about Ephraim;
    Israel is not hidden from me.
  Ephraim, you have now turned to prostitution;
    Israel is corrupt.

⁴"Their deeds do not permit them
    to return to their God.
  A spirit of prostitution is in their heart;
    they do not acknowledge the LORD.
⁵Israel's arrogance testifies against them;
    the Israelites, even Ephraim, stumble in their sin;
    Judah also stumbles with them.
⁶When they go with their flocks and herds
    to seek the LORD,
  they will not find him;
    he has withdrawn himself from them.

ᵃ 15 *Beth Aven* means *house of wickedness* (a name for Bethel, which means *house of God*).

⁷They are unfaithful to the LORD;
    they give birth to illegitimate children.
Now their New Moon festivals
    will devour them and their fields.

⁸"Sound the trumpet in Gibeah,
    the horn in Ramah.
Raise the battle cry in Beth Aven ᵃ;
    lead on, O Benjamin.
⁹Ephraim will be laid waste
    on the day of reckoning.
Among the tribes of Israel
    I proclaim what is certain.
¹⁰Judah's leaders are like those
    who move boundary stones.
I will pour out my wrath on them
    like a flood of water.
¹¹Ephraim is oppressed,
    trampled in judgment,
    intent on pursuing idols. ᵇ
¹²I am like a moth to Ephraim,
    like rot to the people of Judah.

¹³"When Ephraim saw his sickness,
    and Judah his sores,
then Ephraim turned to Assyria,
    and sent to the great king for help.
But he is not able to cure you,
    not able to heal your sores.
¹⁴For I will be like a lion to Ephraim,
    like a great lion to Judah.
I will tear them to pieces and go away;
    I will carry them off, with no one to rescue them.
¹⁵Then I will go back to my place
    until they admit their guilt.
And they will seek my face;
    in their misery they will earnestly seek me."

Israel Unrepentant

6 "Come, let us return to the LORD.
He has torn us to pieces
    but he will heal us;
he has injured us
    but he will bind up our wounds.
²After two days he will revive us;
    on the third day he will restore us,
    that we may live in his presence.
³Let us acknowledge the LORD;
    let us press on to acknowledge him.
As surely as the sun rises,
    he will appear;

ᵃ8 *Beth Aven* means *house of wickedness* (a name for Bethel, which means *house of God*).   ᵇ11 The meaning of the
Hebrew for this word is uncertain.

he will come to us like the winter rains,
   like the spring rains that water the earth."

4"What can I do with you, Ephraim?
   What can I do with you, Judah?
 Your love is like the morning mist,
   like the early dew that disappears.
5Therefore I cut you in pieces with my prophets,
   I killed you with the words of my mouth;
   my judgments flashed like lightning upon you.
6For I desire mercy, not sacrifice,
   and acknowledgment of God rather than burnt offerings.
7Like Adam,ᵃ they have broken the covenant—
   they were unfaithful to me there.
8Gilead is a city of wicked men,
   stained with footprints of blood.
9As marauders lie in ambush for a man,
   so do bands of priests;
 they murder on the road to Shechem,
   committing shameful crimes.
10I have seen a horrible thing
   in the house of Israel.
 There Ephraim is given to prostitution
   and Israel is defiled.

11"Also for you, Judah,
   a harvest is appointed.

"Whenever I would restore the fortunes of my people,
   1whenever I would heal Israel,
   the sins of Ephraim are exposed
   and the crimes of Samaria revealed.
 They practice deceit,
   thieves break into houses,
   bandits rob in the streets;
2but they do not realize
   that I remember all their evil deeds.
 Their sins engulf them;
   they are always before me.

3"They delight the king with their wickedness,
   the princes with their lies.
4They are all adulterers,
   burning like an oven
 whose fire the baker need not stir
   from the kneading of the dough till it rises.
5On the day of the festival of our king
   the princes become inflamed with wine,
   and he joins hands with the mockers.
6Their hearts are like an oven;
   they approach him with intrigue.
 Their passion smolders all night;
   in the morning it blazes like a flaming fire.
7All of them are hot as an oven;

ᵃ7 Or As at Adam; or Like men

they devour their rulers.
All their kings fall,
    and none of them calls on me.

8"Ephraim mixes with the nations;
    Ephraim is a flat cake not turned over.
9Foreigners sap his strength,
    but he does not realize it.
His hair is sprinkled with gray,
    but he does not notice.
10Israel's arrogance testifies against him,
    but despite all this
he does not return to the LORD his God
    or search for him.

11"Ephraim is like a dove,
    easily deceived and senseless—
now calling to Egypt,
    now turning to Assyria.
12When they go, I will throw my net over them;
    I will pull them down like birds of the air.
When I hear them flocking together,
    I will catch them.
13Woe to them,
    because they have strayed from me!
Destruction to them,
    because they have rebelled against me!
I long to redeem them
    but they speak lies against me.
14They do not cry out to me from their hearts
    but wail upon their beds.
They gather together*a* for grain and new wine
    but turn away from me.
15I trained them and strengthened them,
    but they plot evil against me.
16They do not turn to the Most High;
    they are like a faulty bow.
Their leaders will fall by the sword
    because of their insolent words.
For this they will be ridiculed
    in the land of Egypt.

Israel to Reap the Whirlwind

8 "Put the trumpet to your lips!
    An eagle is over the house of the LORD
because the people have broken my covenant
    and rebelled against my law.
2Israel cries out to me,
    'O our God, we acknowledge you!'
3But Israel has rejected what is good;
    an enemy will pursue him.
4They set up kings without my consent;
    they choose princes without my approval.

a 14 Most Hebrew manuscripts; some Hebrew manuscripts and Septuagint *They slash themselves*

With their silver and gold
    they make idols for themselves
        to their own destruction.
5Throw out your calf-idol, O Samaria!
    My anger burns against them.
How long will they be incapable of purity?
6   They are from Israel!
This calf—a craftsman has made it;
    it is not God.
It will be broken in pieces,
    that calf of Samaria.

7"They sow the wind
    and reap the whirlwind.
The stalk has no head;
    it will produce no flour.
Were it to yield grain,
    foreigners would swallow it up.
8Israel is swallowed up;
    now she is among the nations
    like a worthless thing.
9For they have gone up to Assyria
    like a wild donkey wandering alone.
    Ephraim has sold herself to lovers.
10Although they have sold themselves among the nations,
    I will now gather them together.
They will begin to waste away
    under the oppression of the mighty king.

11"Though Ephraim built many altars for sin offerings,
    these have become altars for sinning.
12I wrote for them the many things of my law,
    but they regarded them as something alien.
13They offer sacrifices given to me
    and they eat the meat,
    but the LORD is not pleased with them.
Now he will remember their wickedness
    and punish their sins:
    They will return to Egypt.
14Israel has forgotten his Maker
    and built palaces;
Judah has fortified many towns.
But I will send fire upon their cities
    that will consume their fortresses."

Punishment for Israel

9 Do not rejoice, O Israel;
    do not be jubilant like the other nations.
For you have been unfaithful to your God;
    you love the wages of a prostitute
    at every threshing floor.
2Threshing floors and winepresses will not feed the people;
    the new wine will fail them.
3They will not remain in the LORD's land;

Ephraim will return to Egypt
and eat unclean*a* food in Assyria.
[4]They will not pour out wine offerings to the LORD,
nor will their sacrifices please him.
Such sacrifices will be to them like the bread of mourners;
all who eat them will be unclean.
This food will be for themselves;
it will not come into the temple of the LORD.

[5]What will you do on the day of your appointed feasts,
on the festival days of the LORD?
[6]Even if they escape from destruction,
Egypt will gather them,
and Memphis will bury them.
Their treasures of silver will be taken over by briers,
and thorns will overrun their tents.
[7]The days of punishment are coming,
the days of reckoning are at hand.
Let Israel know this.
Because your sins are so many
and your hostility so great,
the prophet is considered a fool,
the inspired man a maniac.
[8]The prophet, along with my God,
is the watchman over Ephraim,*b*
yet snares await him on all his paths,
and hostility in the house of his God.
[9]They have sunk deep into corruption,
as in the days of Gibeah.
God will remember their wickedness
and punish them for their sins.

[10]"When I found Israel,
it was like finding grapes in the desert;
when I saw your fathers,
it was like seeing the early fruit on the fig tree.
But when they came to Baal Peor,
they consecrated themselves to that shameful idol
and became as vile as the thing they loved.
[11]Ephraim's glory will fly away like a bird—
no birth, no pregnancy, no conception.
[12]Even if they rear children,
I will bereave them of every one.
Woe to them
when I turn away from them!
[13]I have seen Ephraim, like Tyre,
planted in a pleasant place.
But Ephraim will bring out
their children to the slayer."

[14]Give them, O LORD—
what will you give them?

a3 That is, ceremonially unclean   *b8* Or *The prophet is the watchman over Ephraim, / the people of my God*

Give them wombs that miscarry
and breasts that are dry.

15"Because of all their wickedness in Gilgal,
I hated them there.
Because of their sinful deeds,
I will drive them out of my house.
I will no longer love them;
all their leaders are rebellious.
16Ephraim is blighted,
their root is withered,
they yield no fruit.
Even if they bear children,
I will slay their cherished offspring."

17My God will reject them
because they have not obeyed him;
they will be wanderers among the nations.

10   Israel was a spreading vine;
he brought forth fruit for himself.
As his fruit increased,
he built more altars;
as his land prospered,
he adorned his sacred stones.
2Their heart is deceitful,
and now they must bear their guilt.
The Lord will demolish their altars
and destroy their sacred stones.

3Then they will say, "We have no king
because we did not revere the Lord.
But even if we had a king,
what could he do for us?"
4They make many promises,
take false oaths
and make agreements;
therefore lawsuits spring up
like poisonous weeds in a plowed field.
5The people who live in Samaria fear
for the calf-idol of Beth Aven.*a*
Its people will mourn over it,
and so will its idolatrous priests,
those who had rejoiced over its splendor,
because it is taken from them into exile.
6It will be carried to Assyria
as tribute for the great king.
Ephraim will be disgraced;
Israel will be ashamed of its wooden idols.*b*
7Samaria and its king will float away
like a twig on the surface of the waters.
8The high places of wickedness*c* will be destroyed—
it is the sin of Israel.

---

a 5 Beth Aven means house of wickedness (a name for Bethel, which means *house of God*).   *b 6 Or its counsel*
c 8 Hebrew aven, a reference to Beth Aven (a derogatory name for Bethel)

Thorns and thistles will grow up
  and cover their altars.
Then they will say to the mountains, "Cover us!"
  and to the hills, "Fall on us!"

⁹"Since the days of Gibeah, you have sinned, O Israel,
  and there you have remained.ᵃ
Did not war overtake
  the evildoers in Gibeah?
¹⁰When I please, I will punish them;
  nations will be gathered against them
to put them in bonds for their double sin.
¹¹Ephraim is a trained heifer
  that loves to thresh;
so I will put a yoke
  on her fair neck.
I will drive Ephraim,
  Judah must plow,
  and Jacob must break up the ground.
¹²Sow for yourselves righteousness,
  reap the fruit of unfailing love,
and break up your unplowed ground;
  for it is time to seek the LORD,
until he comes
  and showers righteousness on you.
¹³But you have planted wickedness,
  you have reaped evil,
  you have eaten the fruit of deception.
Because you have depended on your own strength
  and on your many warriors,
¹⁴the roar of battle will rise against your people,
  so that all your fortresses will be devastated—
as Shalman devastated Beth Arbel on the day of battle,
  when mothers were dashed to the ground with their children.
¹⁵Thus will it happen to you, O Bethel,
  because your wickedness is great.
When that day dawns,
  the king of Israel will be completely destroyed.

God's Love for Israel

11 "When Israel was a child, I loved him,
  and out of Egypt I called my son.
²But the more Iᵇ called Israel,
  the further they went from me.ᶜ
They sacrificed to the Baals
  and they burned incense to images.
³It was I who taught Ephraim to walk,
  taking them by the arms;
but they did not realize
  it was I who healed them.
⁴I led them with cords of human kindness,
  with ties of love;

ᵃ9 Or *there a stand was taken*   ᵇ2 Some Septuagint manuscripts; Hebrew *they*   ᶜ2 Septuagint; Hebrew *them*

I lifted the yoke from their neck
  and bent down to feed them.

⁵"Will they not return to Egypt
  and will not Assyria rule over them
    because they refuse to repent?
⁶Swords will flash in their cities,
    will destroy the bars of their gates
    and put an end to their plans.
⁷My people are determined to turn from me.
    Even if they call to the Most High,
    he will by no means exalt them.

⁸"How can I give you up, Ephraim?
    How can I hand you over, Israel?
  How can I treat you like Admah?
    How can I make you like Zeboiim?
  My heart is changed within me;
    all my compassion is aroused.
⁹I will not carry out my fierce anger,
    nor will I turn and devastate Ephraim.
  For I am God, and not man—
    the Holy One among you.
  I will not come in wrath.*ᵃ*
¹⁰They will follow the LORD;
    he will roar like a lion.
  When he roars,
    his children will come trembling from the west.
¹¹They will come trembling
    like birds from Egypt,
    like doves from Assyria.
  I will settle them in their homes,"
    declares the LORD.

Israel's Sin

¹²Ephraim has surrounded me with lies,
    the house of Israel with deceit.
  And Judah is unruly against God,
    even against the faithful Holy One.

12 ¹Ephraim feeds on the wind;
    he pursues the east wind all day
    and multiplies lies and violence.
  He makes a treaty with Assyria
    and sends olive oil to Egypt.
²The LORD has a charge to bring against Judah;
    he will punish Jacobᵇ according to his ways
    and repay him according to his deeds.
³In the womb he grasped his brother's heel;
    as a man he struggled with God.
⁴He struggled with the angel and overcame him;
    he wept and begged for his favor.
  He found him at Bethel
    and talked with him there—

ᵃ9 Or come against any city   *ᵇ2 Jacob means he grasps the heel (figuratively, he deceives).*

⁵the Lord God Almighty,
    the Lord is his name of renown!
⁶But you must return to your God;
    maintain love and justice,
    and wait for your God always.

⁷The merchant uses dishonest scales;
    he loves to defraud.
⁸Ephraim boasts,
    "I am very rich; I have become wealthy.
With all my wealth they will not find in me
    any iniquity or sin."

⁹"I am the Lord your God,
    ˎwho brought youˏ out of^a Egypt;
I will make you live in tents again,
    as in the days of your appointed feasts.
¹⁰I spoke to the prophets,
    gave them many visions
    and told parables through them."

¹¹Is Gilead wicked?
    Its people are worthless!
Do they sacrifice bulls in Gilgal?
    Their altars will be like piles of stones
    on a plowed field.
¹²Jacob fled to the country of Aram^b;
    Israel served to get a wife,
    and to pay for her he tended sheep.
¹³The Lord used a prophet to bring Israel up from Egypt,
    by a prophet he cared for him.
¹⁴But Ephraim has bitterly provoked him to anger;
    his Lord will leave upon him the guilt of his bloodshed
    and will repay him for his contempt.

The Lord's Anger Against Israel

13 When Ephraim spoke, men trembled;
    he was exalted in Israel.
    But he became guilty of Baal worship and died.
²Now they sin more and more;
    they make idols for themselves from their silver,
cleverly fashioned images,
    all of them the work of craftsmen.
It is said of these people,
    "They offer human sacrifice
    and kiss^c the calf-idols."
³Therefore they will be like the morning mist,
    like the early dew that disappears,
    like chaff swirling from a threshing floor,
    like smoke escaping through a window.

⁴"But I am the Lord your God,
    ˎwho brought youˏ out of^a Egypt.
You shall acknowledge no God but me,

---

^a 9,4 Or God / ever since you were in   ^b 12 That is, Northwest Mesopotamia   ^c 2 Or "Men who sacrifice / kiss

no Savior except me.
⁵I cared for you in the desert,
  in the land of burning heat.
⁶When I fed them, they were satisfied;
  when they were satisfied, they became proud;
    then they forgot me.
⁷So I will come upon them like a lion,
  like a leopard I will lurk by the path.
⁸Like a bear robbed of her cubs,
  I will attack them and rip them open.
Like a lion I will devour them;
  a wild animal will tear them apart.

⁹"You are destroyed, O Israel,
  because you are against me, against your helper.
¹⁰Where is your king, that he may save you?
  Where are your rulers in all your towns,
of whom you said,
  'Give me a king and princes'?
¹¹So in my anger I gave you a king,
  and in my wrath I took him away.
¹²The guilt of Ephraim is stored up,
  his sins are kept on record.
¹³Pains as of a woman in childbirth come to him,
  but he is a child without wisdom;
when the time arrives,
  he does not come to the opening of the womb.

¹⁴"I will ransom them from the power of the grave*ᵃ*;
  I will redeem them from death.
Where, O death, are your plagues?
  Where, O grave,*ᵃ* is your destruction?

"I will have no compassion,
¹⁵   even though he thrives among his brothers.
An east wind from the LORD will come,
  blowing in from the desert;
his spring will fail
  and his well dry up.
His storehouse will be plundered
  of all its treasures.
¹⁶The people of Samaria must bear their guilt,
  because they have rebelled against their God.
They will fall by the sword;
  their little ones will be dashed to the ground,
    their pregnant women ripped open."

Repentance to Bring Blessing

Return, O Israel, to the LORD your God.
Your sins have been your downfall!
²Take words with you
  and return to the LORD.
Say to him:

"Forgive all our sins
and receive us graciously,
that we may offer the fruit of our lips.^a
³Assyria cannot save us;
we will not mount war-horses.
We will never again say 'Our gods'
to what our own hands have made,
for in you the fatherless find compassion."

⁴"I will heal their waywardness
and love them freely,
for my anger has turned away from them.
⁵I will be like the dew to Israel;
he will blossom like a lily.
Like a cedar of Lebanon
he will send down his roots;
⁶ his young shoots will grow.
His splendor will be like an olive tree,
his fragrance like a cedar of Lebanon.
⁷Men will dwell again in his shade.
He will flourish like the grain.
He will blossom like a vine,
and his fame will be like the wine from Lebanon.
⁸O Ephraim, what more have I^b to do with idols?
I will answer him and care for him.
I am like a green pine tree;
your fruitfulness comes from me."

⁹Who is wise? He will realize these things.
Who is discerning? He will understand them.
The ways of the LORD are right;
the righteous walk in them,
but the rebellious stumble in them.

---

^a2 Or offer our lips as sacrifices of bulls   ^b8 Or What more has Ephraim

1

The word of the LORD that came to Joel son of Pethuel.

An Invasion of Locusts

²Hear this, you elders;
  listen, all who live in the land.
Has anything like this ever happened in your days
  or in the days of your forefathers?
³Tell it to your children,
  and let your children tell it to their children,
  and their children to the next generation.
⁴What the locust swarm has left
  the great locusts have eaten;
what the great locusts have left
  the young locusts have eaten;
what the young locusts have left
  other locusts*ᵃ* have eaten.

⁵Wake up, you drunkards, and weep!
  Wail, all you drinkers of wine;
wail because of the new wine,
  for it has been snatched from your lips.
⁶A nation has invaded my land,
  powerful and without number;
it has the teeth of a lion,
  the fangs of a lioness.
⁷It has laid waste my vines
  and ruined my fig trees.
It has stripped off their bark
  and thrown it away,
  leaving their branches white.

⁸Mourn like a virgin*ᵇ* in sackcloth
  grieving for the husband*ᶜ* of her youth.
⁹Grain offerings and drink offerings
  are cut off from the house of the LORD.
The priests are in mourning,
  those who minister before the LORD.
¹⁰The fields are ruined,
  the ground is dried up*ᵈ*;
the grain is destroyed,
  the new wine is dried up,
  the oil fails.
¹¹Despair, you farmers,
  wail, you vine growers;

ᵃ 4 The precise meaning of the four Hebrew words used here for locusts is uncertain.   *ᵇ 8 Or young woman*   *ᶜ 8 Or betrothed*   *ᵈ 10 Or ground mourns*

grieve for the wheat and the barley,
   because the harvest of the field is destroyed.
¹²The vine is dried up
   and the fig tree is withered;
the pomegranate, the palm and the apple tree—
   all the trees of the field—are dried up.
Surely the joy of mankind
   is withered away.

A Call to Repentance

¹³Put on sackcloth, O priests, and mourn;
   wail, you who minister before the altar.
Come, spend the night in sackcloth,
   you who minister before my God;
for the grain offerings and drink offerings
   are withheld from the house of your God.
¹⁴Declare a holy fast;
   call a sacred assembly.
Summon the elders
   and all who live in the land
to the house of the LORD your God,
   and cry out to the LORD.

¹⁵Alas for that day!
   For the day of the LORD is near;
it will come like destruction from the Almighty. ᵃ

¹⁶Has not the food been cut off
   before our very eyes—
joy and gladness
   from the house of our God?
¹⁷The seeds are shriveled
   beneath the clods. ᵇ
The storehouses are in ruins,
   the granaries have been broken down,
   for the grain has dried up.
¹⁸How the cattle moan!
   The herds mill about
because they have no pasture;
   even the flocks of sheep are suffering.

¹⁹To you, O LORD, I call,
   for fire has devoured the open pastures
   and flames have burned up all the trees of the field.
²⁰Even the wild animals pant for you;
   the streams of water have dried up
   and fire has devoured the open pastures.

An Army of Locusts

2 Blow the trumpet in Zion;
   sound the alarm on my holy hill.
Let all who live in the land tremble,
   for the day of the LORD is coming.

ᵃ15 Hebrew Shaddai   ᵇ17 The meaning of the Hebrew for this word is uncertain.

It is close at hand—
² a day of darkness and gloom,
  a day of clouds and blackness.
Like dawn spreading across the mountains
  a large and mighty army comes,
such as never was of old
  nor ever will be in ages to come.

³Before them fire devours,
  behind them a flame blazes.
Before them the land is like the garden of Eden,
  behind them, a desert waste—
  nothing escapes them.
⁴They have the appearance of horses;
  they gallop along like cavalry.
⁵With a noise like that of chariots
  they leap over the mountaintops,
like a crackling fire consuming stubble,
  like a mighty army drawn up for battle.

⁶At the sight of them, nations are in anguish;
  every face turns pale.
⁷They charge like warriors;
  they scale walls like soldiers.
They all march in line,
  not swerving from their course.
⁸They do not jostle each other;
  each marches straight ahead.
They plunge through defenses
  without breaking ranks.
⁹They rush upon the city;
  they run along the wall.
They climb into the houses;
  like thieves they enter through the windows.

¹⁰Before them the earth shakes,
  the sky trembles,
the sun and moon are darkened,
  and the stars no longer shine.
¹¹The Lord thunders
  at the head of his army;
his forces are beyond number,
  and mighty are those who obey his command.
The day of the Lord is great;
  it is dreadful.
  Who can endure it?

Rend Your Heart

¹²"Even now," declares the Lord,
  "return to me with all your heart,
  with fasting and weeping and mourning."

¹³Rend your heart
  and not your garments.
Return to the Lord your God,

for he is gracious and compassionate,
  slow to anger and abounding in love,
    and he relents from sending calamity.
¹⁴Who knows? He may turn and have pity
    and leave behind a blessing—
  grain offerings and drink offerings
    for the LORD your God.

¹⁵Blow the trumpet in Zion,
    declare a holy fast,
    call a sacred assembly.
¹⁶Gather the people,
    consecrate the assembly;
  bring together the elders,
    gather the children,
    those nursing at the breast.
  Let the bridegroom leave his room
    and the bride her chamber.
¹⁷Let the priests, who minister before the LORD,
    weep between the temple porch and the altar.
  Let them say, "Spare your people, O LORD.
    Do not make your inheritance an object of scorn,
    a byword among the nations.
  Why should they say among the peoples,
    'Where is their God?'"

The LORD's Answer

¹⁸Then the LORD will be jealous for his land
    and take pity on his people.

¹⁹The LORD will reply*ᵃ* to them:

"I am sending you grain, new wine and oil,
    enough to satisfy you fully;
  never again will I make you
    an object of scorn to the nations.

²⁰"I will drive the northern army far from you,
    pushing it into a parched and barren land,
  with its front columns going into the eastern sea*ᵇ*
    and those in the rear into the western sea.*ᶜ*
  And its stench will go up;
    its smell will rise."

Surely he has done great things.*ᵈ*
²¹ Be not afraid, O land;
    be glad and rejoice.
  Surely the LORD has done great things.
²² Be not afraid, O wild animals,
    for the open pastures are becoming green.
  The trees are bearing their fruit;
    the fig tree and the vine yield their riches.
²³Be glad, O people of Zion,

ᵃ18,19 Or *LORD was jealous . . . / and took pity . . . / ¹⁹The LORD replied*   *ᵇ20* That is, the Dead Sea   *ᶜ20* That is, the Mediterranean   *ᵈ20* Or *rise. / Surely it has done great things."*

rejoice in the Lord your God,
   for he has given you
      the autumn rains in righteousness.[a]
He sends you abundant showers,
   both autumn and spring rains, as before.
24The threshing floors will be filled with grain;
   the vats will overflow with new wine and oil.

25"I will repay you for the years the locusts have eaten—
   the great locust and the young locust,
   the other locusts and the locust swarm[b]—
my great army that I sent among you.
26You will have plenty to eat, until you are full,
   and you will praise the name of the Lord your God,
      who has worked wonders for you;
never again will my people be shamed.
27Then you will know that I am in Israel,
   that I am the Lord your God,
      and that there is no other;
never again will my people be shamed.

The Day of the Lord

28"And afterward,
   I will pour out my Spirit on all people.
Your sons and daughters will prophesy,
   your old men will dream dreams,
   your young men will see visions.
29Even on my servants, both men and women,
   I will pour out my Spirit in those days.
30I will show wonders in the heavens
      and on the earth,
   blood and fire and billows of smoke.

---

[a]23 Or / the teacher for righteousness: [b]25 The precise meaning of the four Hebrew words used here for locusts is
uncertain.

::::::::::::::::::::: **DISCOVERING GOD** :::::::::::::::::::::

2:28–32
The Holy Spirit

In the Bible there are three personal manifestations of God: God the Father, God the Son (Jesus) and God the Holy Spirit (or just "the Spirit"). All three persons equally share being God. The Bible doesn't say that there are three Gods, but rather that there are three persons who share one divine nature (see 1 Peter chapter 1, verse 2 for an idea of the different characteristics of this three-personed God [page 1610]).

The prediction here by Joel about what the Spirit would do "in the last days" literally began to be fulfilled soon after Jesus rose from the dead (see the story in Acts chapter 2, verses 1–21 [page 1425]). While his followers were gathered together, they suddenly experienced an unusual and powerful work of God in them. God's Spirit came to dwell inside of them permanently—24 hours a day, seven days a week.

If you're a seeker, you should know that God loves you so much that he is not content just to have a relationship with you. His plan for all of his followers is to live inside them through the person of the Holy Spirit. This wonderful privilege, foretold centuries ago, is available to you today!

³¹The sun will be turned to darkness
    and the moon to blood
    before the coming of the great and dreadful day of the Lord.
³²And everyone who calls
    on the name of the Lord will be saved;
for on Mount Zion and in Jerusalem
    there will be deliverance,
    as the Lord has said,
among the survivors
    whom the Lord calls.

The Nations Judged

3   "In those days and at that time,
    when I restore the fortunes of Judah and Jerusalem,
²I will gather all nations
    and bring them down to the Valley of Jehoshaphat.ᵃ
There I will enter into judgment against them
    concerning my inheritance, my people Israel,
for they scattered my people among the nations
    and divided up my land.
³They cast lots for my people
    and traded boys for prostitutes;
they sold girls for wine
    that they might drink.

⁴"Now what have you against me, O Tyre and Sidon and all you regions of Philistia? Are you repaying me for something I have done? If you are paying me back, I will swiftly and speedily return on your own heads what you have done. ⁵For you took my silver and my gold and carried off my finest treasures to your temples. ⁶You sold the people of Judah and Jerusalem to the Greeks, that you might send them far from their homeland.

⁷"See, I am going to rouse them out of the places to which you sold them, and I will return on your own heads what you have done. ⁸I will sell your sons and daughters to the people of Judah, and they will sell them to the Sabeans, a nation far away." The Lord has spoken.

⁹Proclaim this among the nations:
    Prepare for war!
    Rouse the warriors!
    Let all the fighting men draw near and attack.
¹⁰Beat your plowshares into swords
    and your pruning hooks into spears.
Let the weakling say,
    "I am strong!"
¹¹Come quickly, all you nations from every side,
    and assemble there.

    Bring down your warriors, O Lord!

¹²"Let the nations be roused;
    let them advance into the Valley of Jehoshaphat,
for there I will sit
    to judge all the nations on every side.
¹³Swing the sickle,
    for the harvest is ripe.

ᵃ2 *Jehoshaphat* means *the Lord judges*; also in verse 12.

Come, trample the grapes,
   for the winepress is full
   and the vats overflow—
so great is their wickedness!"

¹⁴Multitudes, multitudes
   in the valley of decision!
For the day of the LORD is near
   in the valley of decision.
¹⁵The sun and moon will be darkened,
   and the stars no longer shine.
¹⁶The LORD will roar from Zion
   and thunder from Jerusalem;
   the earth and the sky will tremble.
But the LORD will be a refuge for his people,
   a stronghold for the people of Israel.

Blessings for God's People

¹⁷"Then you will know that I, the LORD your God,
   dwell in Zion, my holy hill.
Jerusalem will be holy;
   never again will foreigners invade her.

¹⁸"In that day the mountains will drip new wine,
   and the hills will flow with milk;
all the ravines of Judah will run with water.
A fountain will flow out of the LORD's house
   and will water the valley of acacias.ᵃ
¹⁹But Egypt will be desolate,
   Edom a desert waste,
because of violence done to the people of Judah,
   in whose land they shed innocent blood.
²⁰Judah will be inhabited forever
   and Jerusalem through all generations.
²¹Their bloodguilt, which I have not pardoned,
   I will pardon."

The LORD dwells in Zion!

ᵃ 18 Or Valley of Shittim

AMOS

1 The words of Amos, one of the shepherds of Tekoa—what he saw concerning Israel two years before the earthquake, when Uzziah was king of Judah and Jeroboam son of Jehoash*ᵃ* was king of Israel.

²He said:

> "The LORD roars from Zion
>   and thunders from Jerusalem;
> the pastures of the shepherds dry up,*ᵇ*
>   and the top of Carmel withers."

Judgment on Israel's Neighbors

³This is what the LORD says:

> "For three sins of Damascus,
>   even for four, I will not turn back ˻my wrath˼.
> Because she threshed Gilead
>   with sledges having iron teeth,
> ⁴I will send fire upon the house of Hazael
>   that will consume the fortresses of Ben-Hadad.
> ⁵I will break down the gate of Damascus;
>   I will destroy the king who is in*ᶜ* the Valley of Aven*ᵈ*
> and the one who holds the scepter in Beth Eden.
>   The people of Aram will go into exile to Kir,"

says the LORD.

⁶This is what the LORD says:

> "For three sins of Gaza,
>   even for four, I will not turn back ˻my wrath˼.
> Because she took captive whole communities
>   and sold them to Edom,
> ⁷I will send fire upon the walls of Gaza
>   that will consume her fortresses.
> ⁸I will destroy the king*ᵉ* of Ashdod
>   and the one who holds the scepter in Ashkelon.
> I will turn my hand against Ekron,
>   till the last of the Philistines is dead,"

says the Sovereign LORD.

⁹This is what the LORD says:

> "For three sins of Tyre,
>   even for four, I will not turn back ˻my wrath˼.
> Because she sold whole communities of captives to Edom,
>   disregarding a treaty of brotherhood,
> ¹⁰I will send fire upon the walls of Tyre
>   that will consume her fortresses."

ᵃ1 Hebrew *Joash,* a variant of *Jehoash*   *ᵇ2* Or *shepherds mourn*   *ᶜ5* Or *the inhabitants of*   *ᵈ5* *Aven means wickedness.*   *ᵉ8* Or *inhabitants*

¹¹This is what the LORD says:

"For three sins of Edom,
　　even for four, I will not turn back ˩my wrath˩.
Because he pursued his brother with a sword,
　　stifling all compassion,ᵃ
because his anger raged continually
　　and his fury flamed unchecked,
¹²I will send fire upon Teman
　　that will consume the fortresses of Bozrah."

¹³This is what the LORD says:

"For three sins of Ammon,
　　even for four, I will not turn back ˩my wrath˩.
Because he ripped open the pregnant women of Gilead
　　in order to extend his borders,
¹⁴I will set fire to the walls of Rabbah
　　that will consume her fortresses
amid war cries on the day of battle,
　　amid violent winds on a stormy day.
¹⁵Her kingᵇ will go into exile,
　　he and his officials together,"

　　　　　　　　　　　　　　　　　　　　　　says the LORD.

2 This is what the LORD says:

"For three sins of Moab,
　　even for four, I will not turn back ˩my wrath˩.
Because he burned, as if to lime,
　　the bones of Edom's king,
²I will send fire upon Moab
　　that will consume the fortresses of Kerioth.ᶜ
Moab will go down in great tumult
　　amid war cries and the blast of the trumpet.
³I will destroy her ruler
　　and kill all her officials with him,"

　　　　　　　　　　　　　　　　　　　　　　says the LORD.

⁴This is what the LORD says:

"For three sins of Judah,
　　even for four, I will not turn back ˩my wrath˩.
Because they have rejected the law of the LORD
　　and have not kept his decrees,
because they have been led astray by false gods,ᵈ
　　the godsᵉ their ancestors followed,
⁵I will send fire upon Judah
　　that will consume the fortresses of Jerusalem."

Judgment on Israel

⁶This is what the LORD says:

"For three sins of Israel,

ᵃ11 Or sword / and destroyed his allies　　ᵇ15 Or / Molech; Hebrew malcam　　ᶜ2 Or of her cities　　ᵈ4 Or by lies
ᵉ4 Or lies

even for four, I will not turn back ˌmy wrathˌ.
They sell the righteous for silver,
   and the needy for a pair of sandals.
⁷They trample on the heads of the poor
   as upon the dust of the ground
   and deny justice to the oppressed.
Father and son use the same girl
   and so profane my holy name.
⁸They lie down beside every altar
   on garments taken in pledge.
In the house of their god
   they drink wine taken as fines.

⁹"I destroyed the Amorite before them,
   though he was tall as the cedars
   and strong as the oaks.
I destroyed his fruit above
   and his roots below.

¹⁰"I brought you up out of Egypt,
   and I led you forty years in the desert
   to give you the land of the Amorites.
¹¹I also raised up prophets from among your sons
   and Nazirites from among your young men.
 Is this not true, people of Israel?"

                        declares the LORD.

¹²"But you made the Nazirites drink wine
   and commanded the prophets not to prophesy.

¹³"Now then, I will crush you
   as a cart crushes when loaded with grain.
¹⁴The swift will not escape,
   the strong will not muster their strength,
   and the warrior will not save his life.
¹⁵The archer will not stand his ground,
   the fleet-footed soldier will not get away,
   and the horseman will not save his life.
¹⁶Even the bravest warriors
   will flee naked on that day,"

                        declares the LORD.

Witnesses Summoned Against Israel

3 Hear this word the LORD has spoken against you, O people of Israel—against the whole family I brought up out of Egypt:

²"You only have I chosen
   of all the families of the earth;
therefore I will punish you
   for all your sins."

³Do two walk together
   unless they have agreed to do so?
⁴Does a lion roar in the thicket
   when he has no prey?
Does he growl in his den
   when he has caught nothing?

⁵Does a bird fall into a trap on the ground
    where no snare has been set?
Does a trap spring up from the earth
    when there is nothing to catch?
⁶When a trumpet sounds in a city,
    do not the people tremble?
When disaster comes to a city,
    has not the Lᴏʀᴅ caused it?

⁷Surely the Sovereign Lᴏʀᴅ does nothing
    without revealing his plan
    to his servants the prophets.

⁸The lion has roared—
    who will not fear?
The Sovereign Lᴏʀᴅ has spoken—
    who can but prophesy?

⁹Proclaim to the fortresses of Ashdod
    and to the fortresses of Egypt:
"Assemble yourselves on the mountains of Samaria;
    see the great unrest within her
    and the oppression among her people."

¹⁰"They do not know how to do right," declares the Lᴏʀᴅ,
    "who hoard plunder and loot in their fortresses."

¹¹Therefore this is what the Sovereign Lᴏʀᴅ says:

"An enemy will overrun the land;
    he will pull down your strongholds
    and plunder your fortresses."

¹²This is what the Lᴏʀᴅ says:

"As a shepherd saves from the lion's mouth
    only two leg bones or a piece of an ear,
so will the Israelites be saved,
    those who sit in Samaria
    on the edge of their beds
    and in Damascus on their couches. ᵃ"

¹³"Hear this and testify against the house of Jacob," declares the Lord, the Lᴏʀᴅ God Almighty.

¹⁴"On the day I punish Israel for her sins,
    I will destroy the altars of Bethel;
the horns of the altar will be cut off
    and fall to the ground.
¹⁵I will tear down the winter house
    along with the summer house;
the houses adorned with ivory will be destroyed
    and the mansions will be demolished."

                                     declares the Lᴏʀᴅ.

ᵃ 12 The meaning of the Hebrew for this line is uncertain.

Israel Has Not Returned to God

4 Hear this word, you cows of Bashan on Mount Samaria,
   you women who oppress the poor and crush the needy
   and say to your husbands, "Bring us some drinks!"
²The Sovereign LORD has sworn by his holiness:
   "The time will surely come
when you will be taken away with hooks,
   the last of you with fishhooks.
³You will each go straight out
   through breaks in the wall,
   and you will be cast out toward Harmon,ᵃ"

                             declares the LORD.

⁴"Go to Bethel and sin;
   go to Gilgal and sin yet more.
Bring your sacrifices every morning,
   your tithes every three years.ᵇ
⁵Burn leavened bread as a thank offering
   and brag about your freewill offerings—
boast about them, you Israelites,
   for this is what you love to do,"

                        declares the Sovereign LORD.

⁶"I gave you empty stomachsᶜ in every city
   and lack of bread in every town,
   yet you have not returned to me,"

                             declares the LORD.

⁷"I also withheld rain from you
   when the harvest was still three months away.
I sent rain on one town,
   but withheld it from another.
One field had rain;
   another had none and dried up.
⁸People staggered from town to town for water
   but did not get enough to drink,
   yet you have not returned to me,"

                             declares the LORD.

⁹"Many times I struck your gardens and vineyards,
   I struck them with blight and mildew.
Locusts devoured your fig and olive trees,
   yet you have not returned to me,"

                             declares the LORD.

¹⁰"I sent plagues among you
   as I did to Egypt.
I killed your young men with the sword,
   along with your captured horses.
I filled your nostrils with the stench of your camps,
   yet you have not returned to me,"

                             declares the LORD.

¹¹"I overthrew some of you

ᵃ3 Masoretic Text; with a different word division of the Hebrew (see Septuagint) *out, O mountain of oppression*   ᵇ4 Or *tithes on the third day*   ᶜ6 Hebrew *you cleanness of teeth*

as I*ᵃ* overthrew Sodom and Gomorrah.
You were like a burning stick snatched from the fire,
　yet you have not returned to me,"

declares the LORD.

¹²"Therefore this is what I will do to you, Israel,
　and because I will do this to you,
　prepare to meet your God, O Israel."

¹³He who forms the mountains,
　creates the wind,
　and reveals his thoughts to man,
he who turns dawn to darkness,
　and treads the high places of the earth—
　the LORD God Almighty is his name.

A Lament and Call to Repentance

5 Hear this word, O house of Israel, this lament I take up concerning you:

²"Fallen is Virgin Israel,
　never to rise again,
deserted in her own land,
　with no one to lift her up."

³This is what the Sovereign LORD says:

"The city that marches out a thousand strong for Israel
　will have only a hundred left;
the town that marches out a hundred strong
　will have only ten left."

⁴This is what the LORD says to the house of Israel:

"Seek me and live;
5 　do not seek Bethel,
do not go to Gilgal,
　do not journey to Beersheba.
For Gilgal will surely go into exile,
　and Bethel will be reduced to nothing.*ᵇ*"
⁶Seek the LORD and live,
　or he will sweep through the house of Joseph like a fire;
it will devour,
　and Bethel will have no one to quench it.

⁷You who turn justice into bitterness
　and cast righteousness to the ground
⁸(he who made the Pleiades and Orion,
　who turns blackness into dawn
　and darkens day into night,
who calls for the waters of the sea
　and pours them out over the face of the land—
　the LORD is his name—
⁹he flashes destruction on the stronghold
　and brings the fortified city to ruin),

ᵃ11 Hebrew *God*　　*ᵇ5* Or *grief;* or *wickedness;* Hebrew *aven,* a reference to Beth Aven (a derogatory name for Bethel)

¹⁰you hate the one who reproves in court
  and despise him who tells the truth.

¹¹You trample on the poor
  and force him to give you grain.
Therefore, though you have built stone mansions,
  you will not live in them;
though you have planted lush vineyards,
  you will not drink their wine.
¹²For I know how many are your offenses
  and how great your sins.

You oppress the righteous and take bribes
  and you deprive the poor of justice in the courts.
¹³Therefore the prudent man keeps quiet in such times,
  for the times are evil.

¹⁴Seek good, not evil,
  that you may live.
Then the LORD God Almighty will be with you,
  just as you say he is.
¹⁵Hate evil, love good;
  maintain justice in the courts.
Perhaps the LORD God Almighty will have mercy
  on the remnant of Joseph.

¹⁶Therefore this is what the Lord, the LORD God Almighty, says:

  "There will be wailing in all the streets
    and cries of anguish in every public square.
  The farmers will be summoned to weep
    and the mourners to wail.
¹⁷There will be wailing in all the vineyards,
  for I will pass through your midst,"

                                              says the LORD.

The Day of the LORD

¹⁸Woe to you who long
  for the day of the LORD!

▦▦▦▦ KNOWING YOURSELF ▦▦▦▦

5:14–15
A New Identity

In Amos's time, the people of Israel were prosperous. But with that prosperity they lost their spiritual edge. God was furious with them for compromising his principles in order to make a buck. In this passage Amos tells the people to "straighten out their act" and seek good, not evil.

Being familiar with Biblical truths and failing to live by them is extremely dangerous. That's the line Amos's contemporaries had crossed. The same thing happened in Jesus' day; the "religious types" knew the Bible thoroughly, yet failed to recognize God when he walked in their midst. And the same thing happens today as well. That being the case, sometimes seekers are closer to God than "religious" people!

If you're a seeker, realize that God desires for you to follow him in *every* area of your life. Don't be like those people who let God affect some areas of their lives but close him out of others.

Why do you long for the day of the LORD?
  That day will be darkness, not light.
¹⁹It will be as though a man fled from a lion
  only to meet a bear,
as though he entered his house
  and rested his hand on the wall
  only to have a snake bite him.
²⁰Will not the day of the LORD be darkness, not light—
  pitch-dark, without a ray of brightness?

²¹"I hate, I despise your religious feasts;
  I cannot stand your assemblies.
²²Even though you bring me burnt offerings and grain offerings,
  I will not accept them.
Though you bring choice fellowship offerings,ᵃ
  I will have no regard for them.
²³Away with the noise of your songs!
  I will not listen to the music of your harps.
²⁴But let justice roll on like a river,
  righteousness like a never-failing stream!

²⁵"Did you bring me sacrifices and offerings
  forty years in the desert, O house of Israel?
²⁶You have lifted up the shrine of your king,
  the pedestal of your idols,
  the star of your godᵇ—
  which you made for yourselves.
²⁷Therefore I will send you into exile beyond Damascus,"
  says the LORD, whose name is God Almighty.

Woe to the Complacent

6 Woe to you who are complacent in Zion,
  and to you who feel secure on Mount Samaria,
you notable men of the foremost nation,
  to whom the people of Israel come!
²Go to Calneh and look at it;
  go from there to great Hamath,
  and then go down to Gath in Philistia.
Are they better off than your two kingdoms?
  Is their land larger than yours?
³You put off the evil day
  and bring near a reign of terror.
⁴You lie on beds inlaid with ivory
  and lounge on your couches.
You dine on choice lambs
  and fattened calves.
⁵You strum away on your harps like David
  and improvise on musical instruments.
⁶You drink wine by the bowlful
  and use the finest lotions,
  but you do not grieve over the ruin of Joseph.

ᵃ22 Traditionally *peace offerings*   ᵇ26 Or *lifted up Sakkuth your king / and Kaiwan your idols, / your star-gods;* Septuagint
lifted up the shrine of Molech / and the star of your god Rephan. / their idols

⁷Therefore you will be among the first to go into exile;
    your feasting and lounging will end.

The Lord Abhors the Pride of Israel

⁸The Sovereign Lord has sworn by himself—the Lord God Almighty declares:

"I abhor the pride of Jacob
    and detest his fortresses;
I will deliver up the city
    and everything in it."

⁹If ten men are left in one house, they too will die. ¹⁰And if a relative who is to burn the bodies comes to carry them out of the house and asks anyone still hiding there, "Is anyone with you?" and he says, "No," then he will say, "Hush! We must not mention the name of the Lord."

¹¹For the Lord has given the command,
    and he will smash the great house into pieces
    and the small house into bits.

¹²Do horses run on the rocky crags?
    Does one plow there with oxen?
But you have turned justice into poison
    and the fruit of righteousness into bitterness—
¹³you who rejoice in the conquest of Lo Debar ᵃ
    and say, "Did we not take Karnaim ᵇ by our own strength?"

¹⁴For the Lord God Almighty declares,
    "I will stir up a nation against you, O house of Israel,
that will oppress you all the way
    from Lebo ᶜ Hamath to the valley of the Arabah."

Locusts, Fire and a Plumb Line

7 This is what the Sovereign Lord showed me: He was preparing swarms of locusts after the king's share had been harvested and just as the second crop was coming up. ²When they had stripped the land clean, I cried out, "Sovereign Lord, forgive! How can Jacob survive? He is so small!"

³So the Lord relented.

"This will not happen," the Lord said.

⁴This is what the Sovereign Lord showed me: The Sovereign Lord was calling for judgment by fire; it dried up the great deep and devoured the land. ⁵Then I cried out, "Sovereign Lord, I beg you, stop! How can Jacob survive? He is so small!"

⁶So the Lord relented.

"This will not happen either," the Sovereign Lord said.

⁷This is what he showed me: The Lord was standing by a wall that had been built true to plumb, with a plumb line in his hand. ⁸And the Lord asked me, "What do you see, Amos?"

"A plumb line," I replied.

Then the Lord said, "Look, I am setting a plumb line among my people Israel; I will spare them no longer.

⁹"The high places of Isaac will be destroyed

ᵃ13 Lo Debar means nothing.   ᵇ13 Karnaim means horns; horn here symbolizes strength.   ᶜ14 Or from the entrance to

> and the sanctuaries of Israel will be ruined;
> with my sword I will rise against the house of Jeroboam."

Amos and Amaziah

¹⁰Then Amaziah the priest of Bethel sent a message to Jeroboam king of Israel: "Amo
is raising a conspiracy against you in the very heart of Israel. The land cannot bear all hi
words. ¹¹For this is what Amos is saying:

> "'Jeroboam will die by the sword,
> and Israel will surely go into exile,
> away from their native land.'"

¹²Then Amaziah said to Amos, "Get out, you seer! Go back to the land of Judah. Ear
your bread there and do your prophesying there. ¹³Don't prophesy anymore at Bethe
because this is the king's sanctuary and the temple of the kingdom."

¹⁴Amos answered Amaziah, "I was neither a prophet nor a prophet's son, but I was
shepherd, and I also took care of sycamore-fig trees. ¹⁵But the LORD took me from tendin
the flock and said to me, 'Go, prophesy to my people Israel.' ¹⁶Now then, hear the wor
of the LORD. You say,

> "'Do not prophesy against Israel,
> and stop preaching against the house of Isaac.'

¹⁷"Therefore this is what the LORD says:

> "'Your wife will become a prostitute in the city,
> and your sons and daughters will fall by the sword.
> Your land will be measured and divided up,
> and you yourself will die in a pagan*ᵃ* country.
> And Israel will certainly go into exile,
> away from their native land.'"

A Basket of Ripe Fruit

8 This is what the Sovereign LORD showed me: a basket of ripe fruit. ²"What d
you see, Amos?" he asked.

"A basket of ripe fruit," I answered.

Then the LORD said to me, "The time is ripe for my people Israel; I will spare them n
longer.

³"In that day," declares the Sovereign LORD, "the songs in the temple will turn t
wailing.*ᵇ* Many, many bodies—flung everywhere! Silence!"

> ⁴Hear this, you who trample the needy
> and do away with the poor of the land,

⁵saying,

> "When will the New Moon be over
> that we may sell grain,
> and the Sabbath be ended
> that we may market wheat?"—
> skimping the measure,
> boosting the price
> and cheating with dishonest scales,
> ⁶buying the poor with silver
> and the needy for a pair of sandals,
> selling even the sweepings with the wheat.

ᵃ 17 Hebrew *an unclean*   *ᵇ 3* Or *'the temple singers will wail*

⁷The LORD has sworn by the Pride of Jacob: "I will never forget anything they have done.

⁸"Will not the land tremble for this,
    and all who live in it mourn?
The whole land will rise like the Nile;
    it will be stirred up and then sink
    like the river of Egypt.

⁹"In that day," declares the Sovereign LORD,

"I will make the sun go down at noon
    and darken the earth in broad daylight.
¹⁰I will turn your religious feasts into mourning
    and all your singing into weeping.
I will make all of you wear sackcloth
    and shave your heads.
I will make that time like mourning for an only son
    and the end of it like a bitter day.

¹¹"The days are coming," declares the Sovereign LORD,
    "when I will send a famine through the land—
not a famine of food or a thirst for water,
    but a famine of hearing the words of the LORD.
¹²Men will stagger from sea to sea
    and wander from north to east,
searching for the word of the LORD,
    but they will not find it.

¹³"In that day

"the lovely young women and strong young men
    will faint because of thirst.
¹⁴They who swear by the shame^a of Samaria,
    or say, 'As surely as your god lives, O Dan,'
    or, 'As surely as the god^b of Beersheba lives'—
they will fall,
    never to rise again."

Israel to Be Destroyed

9   I saw the Lord standing by the altar, and he said:

"Strike the tops of the pillars
    so that the thresholds shake.
Bring them down on the heads of all the people;
    those who are left I will kill with the sword.
Not one will get away,
    none will escape.
²Though they dig down to the depths of the grave,^{c}
    from there my hand will take them.
Though they climb up to the heavens,
    from there I will bring them down.
³Though they hide themselves on the top of Carmel,
    there I will hunt them down and seize them.

---

^{a} 14 Or by Ashima; or by the idol ^{b} 14 Or power ^{c} 2 Hebrew to Sheol

Though they hide from me at the bottom of the sea,
    there I will command the serpent to bite them.
[4]Though they are driven into exile by their enemies,
    there I will command the sword to slay them.
I will fix my eyes upon them
    for evil and not for good."

[5]The Lord, the LORD Almighty,
    he who touches the earth and it melts,
    and all who live in it mourn—
the whole land rises like the Nile,
    then sinks like the river of Egypt—
[6]he who builds his lofty palace[a] in the heavens
    and sets its foundation[b] on the earth,
who calls for the waters of the sea
    and pours them out over the face of the land—
    the LORD is his name.

[7]"Are not you Israelites
    the same to me as the Cushites[c]?"

                   declares the LORD.

"Did I not bring Israel up from Egypt,
    the Philistines from Caphtor[d]
    and the Arameans from Kir?

[8]"Surely the eyes of the Sovereign LORD
    are on the sinful kingdom.
I will destroy it
    from the face of the earth—
yet I will not totally destroy
    the house of Jacob,"

                   declares the LORD.

[9]"For I will give the command,
    and I will shake the house of Israel
    among all the nations
as grain is shaken in a sieve,
    and not a pebble will reach the ground.
[10]All the sinners among my people
    will die by the sword,
all those who say,
    'Disaster will not overtake or meet us.'

Israel's Restoration

[11]"In that day I will restore
    David's fallen tent.
I will repair its broken places,
    restore its ruins,
    and build it as it used to be,
[12]so that they may possess the remnant of Edom
    and all the nations that bear my name,[e]"
             declares the LORD, who will do these things.

---

[a]6 The meaning of the Hebrew for this phrase is uncertain.   [b]6 The meaning of the Hebrew for this word is uncertain.
[c]7 That is, people from the upper Nile region   [d]7 That is, Crete   [e]12 Hebrew; Septuagint *so that the remnant of men / and all the nations that bear my name may seek the Lord,*

¹³"The days are coming," declares the LORD,

> "when the reaper will be overtaken by the plowman,
> and the planter by the one treading grapes.
> New wine will drip from the mountains
> and flow from all the hills.
> ¹⁴I will bring back my exiled ᵃ people Israel;
> they will rebuild the ruined cities and live in them.
> They will plant vineyards and drink their wine;
> they will make gardens and eat their fruit.
> ¹⁵I will plant Israel in their own land,
> never again to be uprooted
> from the land I have given them,"

says the LORD your God.

ᵃ 14 Or will restore the fortunes of my

OBADIAH

¹The vision of Obadiah.

This is what the Sovereign LORD says about Edom—

> We have heard a message from the LORD:
>> An envoy was sent to the nations to say,
>> "Rise, and let us go against her for battle"—

²"See, I will make you small among the nations;
> you will be utterly despised.
³The pride of your heart has deceived you,
> you who live in the clefts of the rocks[a]
> and make your home on the heights,
you who say to yourself,
> 'Who can bring me down to the ground?'
⁴Though you soar like the eagle
> and make your nest among the stars,
> from there I will bring you down,"

declares the LORD.

⁵"If thieves came to you,
> if robbers in the night—
Oh, what a disaster awaits you—
> would they not steal only as much as they wanted?
If grape pickers came to you,
> would they not leave a few grapes?
⁶But how Esau will be ransacked,
> his hidden treasures pillaged!
⁷All your allies will force you to the border;
> your friends will deceive and overpower you;
those who eat your bread will set a trap for you,[b]
> but you will not detect it.

⁸"In that day," declares the LORD,
> "will I not destroy the wise men of Edom,
> men of understanding in the mountains of Esau?
⁹Your warriors, O Teman, will be terrified,
> and everyone in Esau's mountains
> will be cut down in the slaughter.
¹⁰Because of the violence against your brother Jacob,
> you will be covered with shame;
> you will be destroyed forever.
¹¹On the day you stood aloof
> while strangers carried off his wealth
and foreigners entered his gates
> and cast lots for Jerusalem,
> you were like one of them.

---

a 3 Or *of Sela*   *b 7* The meaning of the Hebrew for this clause is uncertain.

¹²You should not look down on your brother
in the day of his misfortune,
nor rejoice over the people of Judah
in the day of their destruction,
nor boast so much
in the day of their trouble.
¹³You should not march through the gates of my people
in the day of their disaster,
nor look down on them in their calamity
in the day of their disaster,
nor seize their wealth
in the day of their disaster.
¹⁴You should not wait at the crossroads
to cut down their fugitives,
nor hand over their survivors
in the day of their trouble.

¹⁵"The day of the LORD is near
for all nations.
As you have done, it will be done to you;
your deeds will return upon your own head.
¹⁶Just as you drank on my holy hill,
so all the nations will drink continually;
they will drink and drink
and be as if they had never been.
¹⁷But on Mount Zion will be deliverance;
it will be holy,
and the house of Jacob
will possess its inheritance.
¹⁸The house of Jacob will be a fire
and the house of Joseph a flame;
the house of Esau will be stubble,

▦▦▦ ADDRESSING QUESTIONS ▦▦▦

15
God

Q

The Bible acknowledges that our world is broken. Inequities exist, and no matter how hard we try, injustice plagues everyone at one time or another. Truly, life is not fair. But "life" is not God. This passage tells us that, at some point in the future, God will carry out his justice and fairness universally.

If that thought comes as a relief to you, think about it for a second: If everybody gets what they deserve, that means *you're going to get what you deserve!* That's probably not a comforting notion—not if you're completely honest with yourself.

Obadiah said that the scope of God's justice encompasses the whole world. In his letter he addressed the descendants of Esau, the Edomites, who had harassed Israel. Through this prophet, God warned these people that their future was in his hands.

Likewise, your future is in God's hands. How well will you fare if "your deeds . . . return upon your own head"? No doubt you've experienced some injustice—and yes, those people will have to give account for their actions. But what about you?

Give yourself to God, and humbly ask for his mercy. He wants to make all things right, but to do that, he has to make *you* right. He can do it, but only if you'll let him.

Will you?

and they will set it on fire and consume it.
There will be no survivors
    from the house of Esau."

The LORD has spoken.

¹⁹People from the Negev will occupy
    the mountains of Esau,
and people from the foothills will possess
    the land of the Philistines.
They will occupy the fields of Ephraim and Samaria,
    and Benjamin will possess Gilead.
²⁰This company of Israelite exiles who are in Canaan
    will possess ˻the land˼ as far as Zarephath;
the exiles from Jerusalem who are in Sepharad
    will possess the towns of the Negev.
²¹Deliverers will go up on[a] Mount Zion
    to govern the mountains of Esau.
    And the kingdom will be the LORD's.

---

a21 Or from

JONAH

Jonah Flees From the LORD

1 The word of the LORD came to Jonah son of Amittai: ²"Go to the great city of Nineveh and preach against it, because its wickedness has come up before me."

³But Jonah ran away from the LORD and headed for Tarshish. He went down to Joppa, where he found a ship bound for that port. After paying the fare, he went aboard and sailed for Tarshish to flee from the LORD.

⁴Then the LORD sent a great wind on the sea, and such a violent storm arose that the ship threatened to break up. ⁵All the sailors were afraid and each cried out to his own god. And they threw the cargo into the sea to lighten the ship.

But Jonah had gone below deck, where he lay down and fell into a deep sleep. ⁶The captain went to him and said, "How can you sleep? Get up and call on your god! Maybe he will take notice of us, and we will not perish."

⁷Then the sailors said to each other, "Come, let us cast lots to find out who is responsible for this calamity." They cast lots and the lot fell on Jonah.

⁸So they asked him, "Tell us, who is responsible for making all this trouble for us? What do you do? Where do you come from? What is your country? From what people are you?"

⁹He answered, "I am a Hebrew and I worship the LORD, the God of heaven, who made the sea and the land."

¹⁰This terrified them and they asked, "What have you done?" (They knew he was running away from the LORD, because he had already told them so.)

¹¹The sea was getting rougher and rougher. So they asked him, "What should we do to you to make the sea calm down for us?"

¹²"Pick me up and throw me into the sea," he replied, "and it will become calm. I know that it is my fault that this great storm has come upon you."

¹³Instead, the men did their best to row back to land. But they could not, for the sea grew even wilder than before. ¹⁴Then they cried to the LORD, "O LORD, please do not let us die for taking this man's life. Do not hold us accountable for killing an innocent man, for you, O LORD, have done as you pleased." ¹⁵Then they took Jonah and threw him overboard, and the raging sea grew calm. ¹⁶At this the men greatly feared the LORD, and they offered a sacrifice to the LORD and made vows to him.

¹⁷But the LORD provided a great fish to swallow Jonah, and Jonah was inside the fish three days and three nights.

Jonah's Prayer

2 From inside the fish Jonah prayed to the LORD his God. ²He said:

"In my distress I called to the LORD,
    and he answered me.
From the depths of the grave*a* I called for help,
    and you listened to my cry.
³You hurled me into the deep,
    into the very heart of the seas,

---

a2 Hebrew *Sheol*

and the currents swirled about me;
all your waves and breakers
    swept over me.
⁴I said, 'I have been banished
    from your sight;
yet I will look again
    toward your holy temple.'
⁵The engulfing waters threatened me,ᵃ
    the deep surrounded me;
    seaweed was wrapped around my head.
⁶To the roots of the mountains I sank down;
    the earth beneath barred me in forever.
But you brought my life up from the pit,
    O Lᴏʀᴅ my God.

⁷"When my life was ebbing away,
    I remembered you, Lᴏʀᴅ,
and my prayer rose to you,
    to your holy temple.

⁸"Those who cling to worthless idols
    forfeit the grace that could be theirs.
⁹But I, with a song of thanksgiving,
    will sacrifice to you.
What I have vowed I will make good.
    Salvation comes from the Lᴏʀᴅ."

¹⁰And the Lᴏʀᴅ commanded the fish, and it vomited Jonah onto dry land.

Jonah Goes to Nineveh

3 Then the word of the Lᴏʀᴅ came to Jonah a second time: ²"Go to the great city of Nineveh and proclaim to it the message I give you."

³Jonah obeyed the word of the Lᴏʀᴅ and went to Nineveh. Now Nineveh was a very important city—a visit required three days. ⁴On the first day, Jonah started into the city. He proclaimed: "Forty more days and Nineveh will be overturned." ⁵The Ninevites believed God. They declared a fast, and all of them, from the greatest to the least, put on sackcloth.

⁶When the news reached the king of Nineveh, he rose from his throne, took off his royal robes, covered himself with sackcloth and sat down in the dust. ⁷Then he issued a proclamation in Nineveh:

"By the decree of the king and his nobles:

Do not let any man or beast, herd or flock, taste anything; do not let them eat or drink. ⁸But let man and beast be covered with sackcloth. Let everyone call urgently on God. Let them give up their evil ways and their violence. ⁹Who knows? God may yet relent and with compassion turn from his fierce anger so that we will not perish."

¹⁰When God saw what they did and how they turned from their evil ways, he had compassion and did not bring upon them the destruction he had threatened.

ᵃ5 Or waters were at my throat

Jonah's Anger at the Lord's Compassion

4 But Jonah was greatly displeased and became angry. ²He prayed to the Lord, "O Lord, is this not what I said when I was still at home? That is why I was so quick to flee to Tarshish. I knew that you are a gracious and compassionate God, slow to anger and abounding in love, a God who relents from sending calamity. ³Now, O Lord, take away my life, for it is better for me to die than to live."

⁴But the Lord replied, "Have you any right to be angry?"

⁵Jonah went out and sat down at a place east of the city. There he made himself a shelter, sat in its shade and waited to see what would happen to the city. ⁶Then the Lord God provided a vine and made it grow up over Jonah to give shade for his head to ease his discomfort, and Jonah was very happy about the vine. ⁷But at dawn the next day God provided a worm, which chewed the vine so that it withered. ⁸When the sun rose, God provided a scorching east wind, and the sun blazed on Jonah's head so that he grew faint. He wanted to die, and said, "It would be better for me to die than to live."

⁹But God said to Jonah, "Do you have a right to be angry about the vine?"

"I do," he said. "I am angry enough to die."

¹⁰But the Lord said, "You have been concerned about this vine, though you did not tend it or make it grow. It sprang up overnight and died overnight. ¹¹But Nineveh has more than a hundred and twenty thousand people who cannot tell their right hand from their left, and many cattle as well. Should I not be concerned about that great city?"

▣ ▦▦▦▦▦▦▦▦▦ ADDRESSING QUESTIONS ▦▦▦▦▦▦▦▦▦ ▣

4:10–11
Life with God
Q

People matter to God.

That simple statement sums up the Bible's central message and gives us insight into God's heart. If you're a seeker, this concept is vitally important to your search for the God of the Bible. The whole reason why God sent messengers—prophets—was to win back wayward sons and daughters.

Jonah was one of those prophets. Yet in this book we find a curious situation—this "successful" prophet became angry that his hard work had paid off! God had sent Jonah to Nineveh to warn the people to repent, and they did (see chapter 3, verses 8–9). Yet this prophet was more agitated over a dead plant than he was excited by the incredible turnaround of a huge city full of people now eager to follow God.

Sad to say, many dedicated followers of God become calloused to the people around them. They don't appreciate it when a seeker takes a step toward God or when someone crosses the line of faith and becomes a believer. Sometimes the very people who know God—and should know better—get in the way of other people who are honestly trying to become followers of God. That's not the way it's supposed to be, but that's the way it is at times.

Perhaps you've run across some of these people in your own spiritual journey. But rest assured that God loves you and wants to have you as part of his family in spite of how the "Jonahs" in your life act!

MICAH

1 The word of the LORD that came to Micah of Moresheth during the reigns of Jotham, Ahaz and Hezekiah, kings of Judah—the vision he saw concerning Samaria and Jerusalem.

²Hear, O peoples, all of you,
   listen, O earth and all who are in it,
that the Sovereign LORD may witness against you,
   the Lord from his holy temple.

Judgment Against Samaria and Jerusalem

³Look! The LORD is coming from his dwelling place;
   he comes down and treads the high places of the earth.
⁴The mountains melt beneath him
   and the valleys split apart,
like wax before the fire,
   like water rushing down a slope.
⁵All this is because of Jacob's transgression,
   because of the sins of the house of Israel.
What is Jacob's transgression?
   Is it not Samaria?
What is Judah's high place?
   Is it not Jerusalem?

⁶"Therefore I will make Samaria a heap of rubble,
   a place for planting vineyards.
I will pour her stones into the valley
   and lay bare her foundations.
⁷All her idols will be broken to pieces;
   all her temple gifts will be burned with fire;
   I will destroy all her images.
Since she gathered her gifts from the wages of prostitutes,
   as the wages of prostitutes they will again be used."

Weeping and Mourning

⁸Because of this I will weep and wail;
   I will go about barefoot and naked.
I will howl like a jackal
   and moan like an owl.
⁹For her wound is incurable;
   it has come to Judah.
It*a* has reached the very gate of my people,
   even to Jerusalem itself.
¹⁰Tell it not in Gath*b*;
   weep not at all.*c*
In Beth Ophrah*d*

---

a9 Or *He*   *b10* *Gath* sounds like the Hebrew for *tell.*   *c10* Hebrew; Septuagint may suggest *not in Acco.* The Hebrew for *in Acco* sounds like the Hebrew for *weep.*   *d10* *Beth Ophrah* means *house of dust.*

roll in the dust.
¹¹Pass on in nakedness and shame,
    you who live in Shaphir.ᵃ
Those who live in Zaananᵇ
    will not come out.
Beth Ezel is in mourning;
    its protection is taken from you.
¹²Those who live in Marothᶜ writhe in pain,
    waiting for relief,
because disaster has come from the LORD,
    even to the gate of Jerusalem.
¹³You who live in Lachish,ᵈ
    harness the team to the chariot.
You were the beginning of sin
    to the Daughter of Zion,
for the transgressions of Israel
    were found in you.
¹⁴Therefore you will give parting gifts
    to Moresheth Gath.
The town of Aczibᵉ will prove deceptive
    to the kings of Israel.
¹⁵I will bring a conqueror against you
    who live in Mareshah.ᶠ
He who is the glory of Israel
    will come to Adullam.
¹⁶Shave your heads in mourning
    for the children in whom you delight;
make yourselves as bald as the vulture,
    for they will go from you into exile.

Man's Plans and God's

2 Woe to those who plan iniquity,
    to those who plot evil on their beds!
At morning's light they carry it out
    because it is in their power to do it.
²They covet fields and seize them,
    and houses, and take them.
They defraud a man of his home,
    a fellowman of his inheritance.

³Therefore, the LORD says:

"I am planning disaster against this people,
    from which you cannot save yourselves.
You will no longer walk proudly,
    for it will be a time of calamity.
⁴In that day men will ridicule you;
    they will taunt you with this mournful song:
'We are utterly ruined;

ᵃ11 *Shaphir* means *pleasant.*   ᵇ11 *Zaanan* sounds like the Hebrew for *come out.*   ᶜ12 *Maroth* sounds like the Hebrew for *bitter.*   ᵈ13 *Lachish* sounds like the Hebrew for *team.*   ᵉ14 *Aczib* means *deception.*   ᶠ15 *Mareshah* sounds like the Hebrew for *conqueror.*

> my people's possession is divided up.
> He takes it from me!
>> He assigns our fields to traitors.'"

⁵Therefore you will have no one in the assembly of the Lᴏʀᴅ
> to divide the land by lot.

False Prophets

> ⁶"Do not prophesy," their prophets say.
>> "Do not prophesy about these things;
>> disgrace will not overtake us."
> ⁷Should it be said, O house of Jacob:
>> "Is the Spirit of the Lᴏʀᴅ angry?
>> Does he do such things?"

>> "Do not my words do good
>> to him whose ways are upright?
> ⁸Lately my people have risen up
>> like an enemy.
> You strip off the rich robe
>> from those who pass by without a care,
>> like men returning from battle.
> ⁹You drive the women of my people
>> from their pleasant homes.
> You take away my blessing
>> from their children forever.
> ¹⁰Get up, go away!
>> For this is not your resting place,
> because it is defiled,
>> it is ruined, beyond all remedy.
> ¹¹If a liar and deceiver comes and says,
>> 'I will prophesy for you plenty of wine and beer,'
>> he would be just the prophet for this people!

Deliverance Promised

> ¹²"I will surely gather all of you, O Jacob;
>> I will surely bring together the remnant of Israel.
> I will bring them together like sheep in a pen,
>> like a flock in its pasture;
>> the place will throng with people.
> ¹³One who breaks open the way will go up before them;
>> they will break through the gate and go out.
> Their king will pass through before them,
>> the Lᴏʀᴅ at their head."

Leaders and Prophets Rebuked

3   Then I said,

> "Listen, you leaders of Jacob,
>> you rulers of the house of Israel.
> Should you not know justice,
> ²   you who hate good and love evil;

who tear the skin from my people
and the flesh from their bones;
³who eat my people's flesh,
strip off their skin
and break their bones in pieces;
who chop them up like meat for the pan,
like flesh for the pot?"

⁴Then they will cry out to the LORD,
but he will not answer them.
At that time he will hide his face from them
because of the evil they have done.

⁵This is what the LORD says:

"As for the prophets
who lead my people astray,
if one feeds them,
they proclaim 'peace';
if he does not,
they prepare to wage war against him.
⁶Therefore night will come over you, without visions,
and darkness, without divination.
The sun will set for the prophets,
and the day will go dark for them.
⁷The seers will be ashamed
and the diviners disgraced.
They will all cover their faces
because there is no answer from God."

⁸But as for me, I am filled with power,
with the Spirit of the LORD,
and with justice and might,
to declare to Jacob his transgression,
to Israel his sin.
⁹Hear this, you leaders of the house of Jacob,
you rulers of the house of Israel,
who despise justice
and distort all that is right;
¹⁰who build Zion with bloodshed,
and Jerusalem with wickedness.
¹¹Her leaders judge for a bribe,
her priests teach for a price,
and her prophets tell fortunes for money.
Yet they lean upon the LORD and say,
"Is not the LORD among us?
No disaster will come upon us."
¹²Therefore because of you,
Zion will be plowed like a field,
Jerusalem will become a heap of rubble,
the temple hill a mound overgrown with thickets.

The Mountain of the LORD

4 In the last days

the mountain of the LORD's temple will be established
as chief among the mountains;
it will be raised above the hills,
and peoples will stream to it.

²Many nations will come and say,

"Come, let us go up to the mountain of the LORD,
to the house of the God of Jacob.
He will teach us his ways,
so that we may walk in his paths."
The law will go out from Zion,
the word of the LORD from Jerusalem.
³He will judge between many peoples
and will settle disputes for strong nations far and wide.
They will beat their swords into plowshares
and their spears into pruning hooks.
Nation will not take up sword against nation,
nor will they train for war anymore.
⁴Every man will sit under his own vine
and under his own fig tree,
and no one will make them afraid,
for the LORD Almighty has spoken.
⁵All the nations may walk
in the name of their gods;
we will walk in the name of the LORD
our God for ever and ever.

The LORD's Plan

⁶"In that day," declares the LORD,

"I will gather the lame;
I will assemble the exiles
and those I have brought to grief.
⁷I will make the lame a remnant,
those driven away a strong nation.
The LORD will rule over them in Mount Zion
from that day and forever.
⁸As for you, O watchtower of the flock,
O stronghold *a* of the Daughter of Zion,
the former dominion will be restored to you;
kingship will come to the Daughter of Jerusalem."

⁹Why do you now cry aloud—
have you no king?
Has your counselor perished,
that pain seizes you like that of a woman in labor?

a 8 Or hill

¹⁰Writhe in agony, O Daughter of Zion,
  like a woman in labor,
for now you must leave the city
  to camp in the open field.
You will go to Babylon;
  there you will be rescued.
There the LORD will redeem you
  out of the hand of your enemies.

¹¹But now many nations
  are gathered against you.
They say, "Let her be defiled,
  let our eyes gloat over Zion!"
¹²But they do not know
  the thoughts of the LORD;
they do not understand his plan,
  he who gathers them like
    sheaves to the threshing
      floor.

¹³"Rise and thresh, O Daughter
    of Zion,
  for I will give you horns of
    iron;
I will give you hoofs of bronze
  and you will break to pieces
    many nations."

You will devote their ill-gotten
    gains to the LORD,
  their wealth to the Lord of all
    the earth.

▣ ▦▦▦▦▦▦ REASONS TO BELIEVE ▦▦▦▦▦▦ ➲

5:2–5
The Amazing Bible

Every skeptic should pause to thoughtfully
consider this passage.

Centuries before Jesus' time, this prophet
mentioned the city of Jesus' birth *by name.* Not
only were the scholars of Jesus' day aware of
this prediction, they pointed it out to the famous "wise men," or magi, who came from
the East seeking the newborn king (see
Matthew chapter 2, verses 5–6 [page 1259]).

Notice also the character of this coming
ruler. According to verses 4–5, he will be a
shepherd. And he will not just bring peace, he
will *be* peace. This fits with other descriptions
of the Messiah, who was said to be the great
Shepherd (Hebrews chapter 13, verse 20
[page 1601]) and the Prince of Peace (Isaiah
chapter 9, verse 6 [page 894]).

No other religious text can claim the clear
marks of supernatural origin that the Bible
can, with its wealth of precisely fulfilled prophetic statements.

A Promised Ruler From Bethlehem

5 Marshal your troops, O city of troops,ᵃ
      for a siege is laid against us.
They will strike Israel's ruler
  on the cheek with a rod.

²"But you, Bethlehem Ephrathah,
  though you are small among the clansᵇ of Judah,
out of you will come for me
  one who will be ruler over Israel,
whose originsᶜ are from of old,
  from ancient times.ᵈ"

³Therefore Israel will be abandoned
  until the time when she who is in labor gives birth
and the rest of his brothers return
  to join the Israelites.

ᵃ1 Or *Strengthen your walls, O walled city*   ᵇ2 Or *rulers*   ᶜ2 Hebrew *goings out*   ᵈ2 Or *from days of eternity*

4He will stand and shepherd his flock
   in the strength of the LORD,
   in the majesty of the name of the LORD his God.
And they will live securely, for then his greatness
   will reach to the ends of the earth.
5 And he will be their peace.

Deliverance and Destruction

When the Assyrian invades our land
   and marches through our fortresses,
we will raise against him seven shepherds,
   even eight leaders of men.
6They will rule*a* the land of Assyria with the sword,
   the land of Nimrod with drawn sword.*b*
He will deliver us from the Assyrian
   when he invades our land
   and marches into our borders.

7The remnant of Jacob will be
   in the midst of many peoples
like dew from the LORD,
   like showers on the grass,
which do not wait for man
   or linger for mankind.
8The remnant of Jacob will be among the nations,
   in the midst of many peoples,
like a lion among the beasts of the forest,
   like a young lion among flocks of sheep,
which mauls and mangles as it goes,
   and no one can rescue.
9Your hand will be lifted up in triumph over your enemies,
   and all your foes will be destroyed.

10"In that day," declares the LORD,

"I will destroy your horses from among you
   and demolish your chariots.
11I will destroy the cities of your land
   and tear down all your strongholds.
12I will destroy your witchcraft
   and you will no longer cast spells.
13I will destroy your carved images
   and your sacred stones from among you;
you will no longer bow down
   to the work of your hands.
14I will uproot from among you your Asherah poles*c*
   and demolish your cities.
15I will take vengeance in anger and wrath
   upon the nations that have not obeyed me."

a6 Or *crush*   *b6* Or *Nimrod in its gates*   *c14* That is, symbols of the goddess Asherah

The LORD's Case Against Israel

6 Listen to what the LORD says:

"Stand up, plead your case before the mountains;
  let the hills hear what you have to say.
²Hear, O mountains, the LORD's accusation;
  listen, you everlasting foundations of the earth.
For the LORD has a case against his people;
  he is lodging a charge against Israel.

³"My people, what have I done to you?
  How have I burdened you? Answer me.
⁴I brought you up out of Egypt
  and redeemed you from the land of slavery.
I sent Moses to lead you,
  also Aaron and Miriam.
⁵My people, remember
  what Balak king of Moab counseled
  and what Balaam son of Beor answered.
Remember ˪your journey˼ from Shittim to Gilgal,
  that you may know the righteous acts of the LORD."

⁶With what shall I come before the LORD
  and bow down before the exalted God?
Shall I come before him with burnt offerings,
  with calves a year old?
⁷Will the LORD be pleased with thousands of rams,
  with ten thousand rivers of oil?
Shall I offer my firstborn for my transgression,
  the fruit of my body for the sin of my soul?
⁸He has showed you, O man, what is good.
  And what does the LORD require of you?
To act justly and to love mercy
  and to walk humbly with your God.

================ DISCOVERING GOD ================

6:8
Life with God

This verse is a two-edged sword. It comforts in its simplicity, but it cuts deeply as well.

The positive side of these words is that they reduce our spiritual duty to basic terms: Walk with God and treat people fairly and mercifully. Jesus said something similar when he summed up the whole Old Testament code with two commandments: love God, and love your neighbor as yourself (Matthew chapter 22, verses 37–40 [page 1290]).

But the down side of this scriptural instruction is that *no one other than Jesus has ever perfectly fulfilled these commands.* So is God just looking for better-than-average performance from us? If we get a B and God grades on a curve, can we hope to measure up?

The fact is, God is completely righteous, and his standard is perfection. He really does want us to live a righteous life, but since we don't, our only hope is that he will forgive us. Micah points out that God is ready to do just that. He ends his prophecy on a high note, celebrating God's forgiveness for those who turn to him (chapter 7, verses 18–19).

Israel's Guilt and Punishment

⁹Listen! The Lᴏʀᴅ is calling to the city—
   and to fear your name is wisdom—
   "Heed the rod and the One who appointed it. *ᵃ*
¹⁰Am I still to forget, O wicked house,
   your ill-gotten treasures
   and the short ephah, *ᵇ* which is accursed?
¹¹Shall I acquit a man with dishonest scales,
   with a bag of false weights?
¹²Her rich men are violent;
   her people are liars
   and their tongues speak deceitfully.
¹³Therefore, I have begun to destroy you,
   to ruin you because of your sins.
¹⁴You will eat but not be satisfied;
   your stomach will still be empty. *ᶜ*
You will store up but save nothing,
   because what you save I will give to the sword.
¹⁵You will plant but not harvest;
   you will press olives but not use the oil on yourselves,
   you will crush grapes but not drink the wine.
¹⁶You have observed the statutes of Omri
   and all the practices of Ahab's house,
   and you have followed their traditions.
Therefore I will give you over to ruin
   and your people to derision;
   you will bear the scorn of the nations. *ᵈ*"

Israel's Misery

7   What misery is mine!
   I am like one who gathers summer fruit
   at the gleaning of the vineyard;
there is no cluster of grapes to eat,
   none of the early figs that I crave.
²The godly have been swept from the land;
   not one upright man remains.
All men lie in wait to shed blood;
   each hunts his brother with a net.
³Both hands are skilled in doing evil;
   the ruler demands gifts,
the judge accepts bribes,
   the powerful dictate what they desire—
   they all conspire together.
⁴The best of them is like a brier,
   the most upright worse than a thorn hedge.
The day of your watchmen has come,
   the day God visits you.
Now is the time of their confusion.
⁵Do not trust a neighbor;
   put no confidence in a friend.
Even with her who lies in your embrace

ᵃ9 The meaning of the Hebrew for this line is uncertain.   *ᵇ10* An ephah was a dry measure.   *ᶜ14* The meaning of the Hebrew for this word is uncertain.   *ᵈ16* Septuagint; Hebrew *scorn due my people*

be careful of your words.
⁶For a son dishonors his father,
    a daughter rises up against her mother,
a daughter-in-law against her mother-in-law—
    a man's enemies are the members of his own household.

⁷But as for me, I watch in hope for the LORD,
    I wait for God my Savior;
    my God will hear me.

Israel Will Rise

⁸Do not gloat over me, my enemy!
    Though I have fallen, I will rise.
Though I sit in darkness,
    the LORD will be my light.
⁹Because I have sinned against him,
    I will bear the LORD's wrath,
until he pleads my case
    and establishes my right.
He will bring me out into the light;
    I will see his righteousness.
¹⁰Then my enemy will see it
    and will be covered with shame,
she who said to me,
    "Where is the LORD your God?"
My eyes will see her downfall;
    even now she will be trampled underfoot
    like mire in the streets.

¹¹The day for building your walls will come,
    the day for extending your boundaries.
¹²In that day people will come to you
    from Assyria and the cities of Egypt,
even from Egypt to the Euphrates
    and from sea to sea
    and from mountain to mountain.
¹³The earth will become desolate because of its inhabitants,
    as the result of their deeds.

Prayer and Praise

¹⁴Shepherd your people with your staff,
    the flock of your inheritance,
which lives by itself in a forest,
    in fertile pasturelands. ᵃ
Let them feed in Bashan and Gilead
    as in days long ago.

¹⁵"As in the days when you came out of Egypt,
    I will show them my wonders."

¹⁶Nations will see and be ashamed,
    deprived of all their power.
They will lay their hands on their mouths
    and their ears will become deaf.

ᵃ 14 Or in the middle of Carmel

¹⁷They will lick dust like a snake,
    like creatures that crawl on the ground.
They will come trembling out of their dens;
    they will turn in fear to the Lord our God
    and will be afraid of you.
¹⁸Who is a God like you,
    who pardons sin and forgives the transgression
    of the remnant of his inheritance?
You do not stay angry forever
    but delight to show mercy.
¹⁹You will again have compassion on us;
    you will tread our sins underfoot
    and hurl all our iniquities into the depths of the sea.
²⁰You will be true to Jacob,
    and show mercy to Abraham,
  as you pledged on oath to our fathers
    in days long ago.

NAHUM

1 An oracle concerning Nineveh. The book of the vision of Nahum the Elkoshite.

The LORD's Anger Against Nineveh

²The LORD is a jealous and avenging God;
  the LORD takes vengeance and is filled with wrath.
The LORD takes vengeance on his foes
  and maintains his wrath against his enemies.
³The LORD is slow to anger and great in power;
  the LORD will not leave the guilty unpunished.
His way is in the whirlwind and the storm,
  and clouds are the dust of his feet.
⁴He rebukes the sea and dries it up;
  he makes all the rivers run dry.
Bashan and Carmel wither
  and the blossoms of Lebanon fade.
⁵The mountains quake before him
  and the hills melt away.
The earth trembles at his presence,
  the world and all who live in it.
⁶Who can withstand his indignation?
  Who can endure his fierce anger?
His wrath is poured out like fire;
  the rocks are shattered before him.

⁷The LORD is good,
  a refuge in times of trouble.

::::::::::::::::::::::::::: DISCOVERING GOD :::::::::::::::::::::::::::

1:6–7
Life with God

Within the space of two verses, Nahum describes God as both a fierce, rock-shattering fire and a refuge who tenderly cares for his own. Is this prophet having trouble making up his mind?

Actually, the Bible teaches that God's nature is perfectly consistent. The mystery can be explained by observing *us. Our* contrasting behaviors make God appear dual-natured. Look at it this way: When the sun shines on clay, the clay hardens. When the sun shines on wax, the wax softens. The same sun creates totally opposite effects because of the properties of the substances with which it interacts.

In the same way, people who reject God are likely to see him as an interference—or worse, a tyrant. But people who welcome him and live openly before him see his presence as a comfort and a help.

What is your view of God? Is he someone who you think exists primarily to spoil all your fun? Or is he the source of a joy that's impossible to capture in words? Whatever answer you give will probably depend more on where you stand than on where he stands.

He cares for those who trust in him,
⁸ but with an overwhelming flood
he will make an end of ⌞Nineveh⌟;
he will pursue his foes into darkness.

⁹Whatever they plot against the LORD
he^a will bring to an end;
trouble will not come a second time.
¹⁰They will be entangled among thorns
and drunk from their wine;
they will be consumed like dry stubble.^b
¹¹From you, ⌞O Nineveh,⌟ has one come forth
who plots evil against the LORD
and counsels wickedness.

¹²This is what the LORD says:

"Although they have allies and are numerous,
they will be cut off and pass away.
Although I have afflicted you, ⌞O Judah,⌟
I will afflict you no more.
¹³Now I will break their yoke from your neck
and tear your shackles away."

¹⁴The LORD has given a command concerning you, ⌞Nineveh⌟:
"You will have no descendants to bear your name.
I will destroy the carved images and cast idols
that are in the temple of your gods.
I will prepare your grave,
for you are vile."

¹⁵Look, there on the mountains,
the feet of one who brings good news,
who proclaims peace!
Celebrate your festivals, O Judah,
and fulfill your vows.
No more will the wicked invade you;
they will be completely destroyed.

Nineveh to Fall

2 An attacker advances against you, ⌞Nineveh⌟.
Guard the fortress,
watch the road,
brace yourselves,
marshal all your strength!

²The LORD will restore the splendor of Jacob
like the splendor of Israel,
though destroyers have laid them waste
and have ruined their vines.

³The shields of his soldiers are red;
the warriors are clad in scarlet.
The metal on the chariots flashes
on the day they are made ready;

---

^a9 Or *What do you foes plot against the LORD? / He*   ^b10 The meaning of the Hebrew for this verse is uncertain.

the spears of pine are brandished.[a]
⁴The chariots storm through the streets,
    rushing back and forth through the squares.
They look like flaming torches;
    they dart about like lightning.

⁵He summons his picked troops,
    yet they stumble on their way.
They dash to the city wall;
    the protective shield is put in place.
⁶The river gates are thrown open
    and the palace collapses.
⁷It is decreed[b] that ⌊the city⌋
    be exiled and carried away.
Its slave girls moan like doves
    and beat upon their breasts.
⁸Nineveh is like a pool,
    and its water is draining away.
"Stop! Stop!" they cry,
    but no one turns back.
⁹Plunder the silver!
    Plunder the gold!
The supply is endless,
    the wealth from all its treasures!
¹⁰She is pillaged, plundered, stripped!
    Hearts melt, knees give way,
    bodies tremble, every face grows pale.

¹¹Where now is the lions' den,
    the place where they fed their young,
where the lion and lioness went,
    and the cubs, with nothing to fear?
¹²The lion killed enough for his cubs
    and strangled the prey for his mate,
filling his lairs with the kill
    and his dens with the prey.

¹³"I am against you,"
    declares the LORD Almighty.
"I will burn up your chariots in smoke,
    and the sword will devour your young lions.
I will leave you no prey on the earth.
The voices of your messengers
    will no longer be heard."

Woe to Nineveh

3 Woe to the city of blood,
    full of lies,
full of plunder,
    never without victims!
²The crack of whips,
    the clatter of wheels,

---

a 3 Hebrew; Septuagint and Syriac / *the horsemen rush to and fro* uncertain.   b 7 The meaning of the Hebrew for this word is

galloping horses
  and jolting chariots!
³Charging cavalry,
  flashing swords
  and glittering spears!
Many casualties,
  piles of dead,
bodies without number,
  people stumbling over the corpses—
⁴all because of the wanton lust of a harlot,
  alluring, the mistress of sorceries,
who enslaved nations by her prostitution
  and peoples by her witchcraft.

⁵"I am against you," declares the LORD Almighty.
  "I will lift your skirts over your face.
I will show the nations your nakedness
  and the kingdoms your shame.
⁶I will pelt you with filth,
  I will treat you with contempt
  and make you a spectacle.
⁷All who see you will flee from you and say,
  'Nineveh is in ruins—who will mourn for her?'
  Where can I find anyone to comfort you?"

⁸Are you better than Thebes,ᵃ
  situated on the Nile,
  with water around her?
The river was her defense,
  the waters her wall.
⁹Cushᵇ and Egypt were her boundless strength;
  Put and Libya were among her allies.
¹⁰Yet she was taken captive
  and went into exile.
Her infants were dashed to pieces
  at the head of every street.
Lots were cast for her nobles,
  and all her great men were put in chains.
¹¹You too will become drunk;
  you will go into hiding
  and seek refuge from the enemy.

¹²All your fortresses are like fig trees
  with their first ripe fruit;
when they are shaken,
  the figs fall into the mouth of the eater.
¹³Look at your troops—
  they are all women!
The gates of your land
  are wide open to your enemies;
  fire has consumed their bars.

¹⁴Draw water for the siege,
  strengthen your defenses!

ᵃ8 Hebrew *No Amon*   ᵇ9 That is, the upper Nile region

Work the clay,
  tread the mortar,
  repair the brickwork!
¹⁵There the fire will devour you;
  the sword will cut you down
  and, like grasshoppers, consume you.
  Multiply like grasshoppers,
  multiply like locusts!
¹⁶You have increased the number of your merchants
  till they are more than the stars of the sky,
  but like locusts they strip the land
  and then fly away.
¹⁷Your guards are like locusts,
  your officials like swarms of locusts
  that settle in the walls on a cold day—
  but when the sun appears they fly away,
  and no one knows where.

¹⁸O king of Assyria, your shepherds[a] slumber;
  your nobles lie down to rest.
  Your people are scattered on the mountains
  with no one to gather them.
¹⁹Nothing can heal your wound;
  your injury is fatal.
  Everyone who hears the news about you
  claps his hands at your fall,
  for who has not felt
  your endless cruelty?

ᵃ18 Or rulers

HABAKKUK

 The oracle that Habakkuk the prophet received.

Habakkuk's Complaint

²How long, O LORD, must I call for help,
  but you do not listen?
Or cry out to you, "Violence!"
  but you do not save?
³Why do you make me look at injustice?
  Why do you tolerate wrong?
Destruction and violence are before me;
  there is strife, and conflict abounds.
⁴Therefore the law is paralyzed,
  and justice never prevails.
The wicked hem in the righteous,
  so that justice is perverted.

The LORD's Answer

⁵"Look at the nations and watch—
  and be utterly amazed.
For I am going to do something in your days
  that you would not believe,
  even if you were told.
⁶I am raising up the Babylonians,ᵃ
  that ruthless and impetuous people,
who sweep across the whole earth
  to seize dwelling places not their own.
⁷They are a feared and dreaded people;
  they are a law to themselves
  and promote their own honor.
⁸Their horses are swifter than leopards,
  fiercer than wolves at dusk.
Their cavalry gallops headlong;
  their horsemen come from afar.
They fly like a vulture swooping to devour;
⁹ they all come bent on violence.
Their hordesᵇ advance like a desert wind
  and gather prisoners like sand.
¹⁰They deride kings
  and scoff at rulers.
They laugh at all fortified cities;
  they build earthen ramps and capture them.
¹¹Then they sweep past like the wind and go on—
  guilty men, whose own strength is their god."

ᵃ6 Or Chaldeans   ᵇ9 The meaning of the Hebrew for this word is uncertain.

Habakkuk's Second Complaint

12O Lord, are you not from everlasting?
My God, my Holy One, we will not die.
O Lord, you have appointed them to execute judgment;
O Rock, you have ordained them to punish.
13Your eyes are too pure to look on evil;
you cannot tolerate wrong.
Why then do you tolerate the treacherous?
Why are you silent while the wicked
swallow up those more righteous than themselves?
14You have made men like fish in the sea,
like sea creatures that have no ruler.
15The wicked foe pulls all of them up with hooks,
he catches them in his net,
he gathers them up in his dragnet;
and so he rejoices and is glad.
16Therefore he sacrifices to his net
and burns incense to his dragnet,
for by his net he lives in luxury
and enjoys the choicest food.
17Is he to keep on emptying his net,
destroying nations without mercy?

2 I will stand at my watch
and station myself on the ramparts;
I will look to see what he will say to me,
and what answer I am to give to this complaint.*a*

The Lord's Answer

2Then the Lord replied:

"Write down the revelation
and make it plain on tablets
so that a herald*b* may run with it.
3For the revelation awaits an appointed time;
it speaks of the end
and will not prove false.
Though it linger, wait for it;
it*c* will certainly come and will not delay.

4"See, he is puffed up;
his desires are not upright—
but the righteous will live by his faith*d*—
5indeed, wine betrays him;
he is arrogant and never at rest.
Because he is as greedy as the grave*e*
and like death is never satisfied,
he gathers to himself all the nations
and takes captive all the peoples.

6"Will not all of them taunt him with ridicule and scorn, saying,

"'Woe to him who piles up stolen goods

a1 Or *and what to answer when I am rebuked*   *b2* Or *so that whoever reads it*   *c3* Or *Though he linger, wait for him;*
/ he   *d4* Or *faithfulness*   *e5* Hebrew *Sheol*

and makes himself wealthy by extortion!
How long must this go on?'
7Will not your debtors*a* suddenly arise?
Will they not wake up and make you tremble?
Then you will become their victim.
8Because you have plundered many nations,
the peoples who are left will plunder you.
For you have shed man's blood;
you have destroyed lands and cities and everyone in them.

9"Woe to him who builds his realm by unjust gain
to set his nest on high,
to escape the clutches of ruin!
10You have plotted the ruin of many peoples,
shaming your own house and forfeiting your life.
11The stones of the wall will cry out,
and the beams of the woodwork will echo it.

12"Woe to him who builds a city with bloodshed
and establishes a town by crime!
13Has not the LORD Almighty determined
that the people's labor is only fuel for the fire,
that the nations exhaust themselves for nothing?
14For the earth will be filled with the knowledge of the glory of the
LORD,
as the waters cover the sea.

15"Woe to him who gives drink to his neighbors,
pouring it from the wineskin till they are drunk,
so that he can gaze on their naked bodies.
16You will be filled with shame instead of glory.
Now it is your turn! Drink and be exposed*b*!
The cup from the LORD's right hand is coming around to you,

a 7 Or creditors   b 16 Masoretic Text; Dead Sea Scrolls, Aquila, Vulgate and Syriac (see also Septuagint) and stagger

---

☐ ▦▦▦▦▦▦▦▦▦▦▦ **DISCOVERING GOD** ▦▦▦▦▦▦▦▦▦▦▦ ◪

2:4
Life with God

This verse demonstrates the strong continuity that exists between the Old Testament and the New.
The emphasis in both is on a relationship with God based on trust (faith).

The Old Testament contains rules for relating to God that the people of ancient Israel followed. New Testament Christians broke with those practices and began a type of worship that is
more familiar to us today. But the timelessness of God's desire that we relate to him through faith
still runs strong through both parts of the Bible.

People who trust God obey him because they love him. People who don't trust God, if they
obey him, do so in the hope that their obedience will make God love them. Such attempts to win
God's approval have the opposite effect, for "without faith it is impossible to please God" (Hebrews
chapter 11, verse 6 [page 1596]).

The phrase "the righteous will live by faith" means that people who trust God have faith that
their salvation is complete through the work of Jesus. The good works that such people do are
done out of gratitude to God for that wonderful gift, not as an attempt to earn salvation on their
own terms. Now *that's* real freedom!

and disgrace will cover your glory.
¹⁷The violence you have done to Lebanon will overwhelm you,
    and your destruction of animals will terrify you.
For you have shed man's blood;
    you have destroyed lands and cities and everyone in them.

¹⁸"Of what value is an idol, since a man has carved it?
    Or an image that teaches lies?
For he who makes it trusts in his own creation;
    he makes idols that cannot speak.
¹⁹Woe to him who says to wood, 'Come to life!'
    Or to lifeless stone, 'Wake up!'
Can it give guidance?
    It is covered with gold and silver;
    there is no breath in it.
²⁰But the LORD is in his holy temple;
    let all the earth be silent before him."

Habakkuk's Prayer

3   A prayer of Habakkuk the prophet. On *shigionoth.* ͣ

²LORD, I have heard of your fame;
    I stand in awe of your deeds, O LORD.
Renew them in our day,
    in our time make them known;
    in wrath remember mercy.

³God came from Teman,
    the Holy One from Mount Paran.   *Selah* ᵇ
His glory covered the heavens
    and his praise filled the earth.
⁴His splendor was like the sunrise;
    rays flashed from his hand,
    where his power was hidden.
⁵Plague went before him;
    pestilence followed his steps.
⁶He stood, and shook the earth;
    he looked, and made the nations tremble.
The ancient mountains crumbled
    and the age-old hills collapsed.
    His ways are eternal.
⁷I saw the tents of Cushan in distress,
    the dwellings of Midian in anguish.

⁸Were you angry with the rivers, O LORD?
    Was your wrath against the streams?
Did you rage against the sea
    when you rode with your horses
    and your victorious chariots?
⁹You uncovered your bow,
    you called for many arrows.   *Selah*
You split the earth with rivers;
¹⁰   the mountains saw you and writhed.

ͣ *1 Probably a literary or musical term*   ᵇ *3 A word of uncertain meaning; possibly a musical term; also in verses 9 and 13*

Torrents of water swept by;
  the deep roared
  and lifted its waves on high.

¹¹Sun and moon stood still in the heavens
  at the glint of your flying arrows,
  at the lightning of your flashing spear.
¹²In wrath you strode through the earth
  and in anger you threshed the nations.
¹³You came out to deliver your people,
  to save your anointed one.
You crushed the leader of the land of wickedness,
  you stripped him from head to foot.   *Selah*
¹⁴With his own spear you pierced his head
  when his warriors stormed out to scatter us,
gloating as though about to devour
  the wretched who were in hiding.
¹⁵You trampled the sea with your horses,
  churning the great waters.

¹⁶I heard and my heart pounded,
  my lips quivered at the sound;
decay crept into my bones,
  and my legs trembled.
Yet I will wait patiently for the day of calamity
  to come on the nation invading us.
¹⁷Though the fig tree does not bud
  and there are no grapes on the vines,
though the olive crop fails
  and the fields produce no food,
though there are no sheep in the pen
  and no cattle in the stalls,
¹⁸yet I will rejoice in the LORD,
  I will be joyful in God my Savior.

¹⁹The Sovereign LORD is my strength;
  he makes my feet like the feet of a deer,
  he enables me to go on the heights.

For the director of music. On my stringed instruments.

ZEPHANIAH

1 The word of the LORD that came to Zephaniah son of Cushi, the son of Gedaliah, the son of Amariah, the son of Hezekiah, during the reign of Josiah son of Amon king of Judah:

Warning of Coming Destruction

²"I will sweep away everything
  from the face of the earth,"

                          declares the LORD.

³"I will sweep away both men and animals;
  I will sweep away the birds of the air
    and the fish of the sea.
The wicked will have only heaps of rubble[a]
  when I cut off man from the face of the earth,"

                          declares the LORD.

Against Judah

⁴"I will stretch out my hand against Judah
  and against all who live in Jerusalem.
I will cut off from this place every remnant of Baal,
  the names of the pagan and the idolatrous priests—
⁵those who bow down on the roofs
  to worship the starry host,
those who bow down and swear by the LORD
  and who also swear by Molech,[b]
⁶those who turn back from following the LORD
  and neither seek the LORD nor inquire of him.
⁷Be silent before the Sovereign LORD,
  for the day of the LORD is near.
The LORD has prepared a sacrifice;
  he has consecrated those he has invited.
⁸On the day of the LORD's sacrifice
  I will punish the princes
  and the king's sons
and all those clad
  in foreign clothes.
⁹On that day I will punish
  all who avoid stepping on the threshold,[c]
who fill the temple of their gods
  with violence and deceit.

¹⁰"On that day," declares the LORD,
  "a cry will go up from the Fish Gate,
  wailing from the New Quarter,
  and a loud crash from the hills.

---

a3 The meaning of the Hebrew for this line is uncertain.   *b5* Hebrew *Malcam*, that is, Milcom   *c9* See 1 Samuel 5:5.

¹¹Wail, you who live in the market district*ª*;
all your merchants will be wiped out,
all who trade with*ᵇ* silver will be ruined.
¹²At that time I will search Jerusalem with lamps
and punish those who are complacent,
who are like wine left on its dregs,
who think, 'The LORD will do nothing,
either good or bad.'
¹³Their wealth will be plundered,
their houses demolished.
They will build houses
but not live in them;
they will plant vineyards
but not drink the wine.

The Great Day of the LORD

¹⁴"The great day of the LORD is near—
near and coming quickly.
Listen! The cry on the day of the LORD will be bitter,
the shouting of the warrior there.
¹⁵That day will be a day of wrath,
a day of distress and anguish,
a day of trouble and ruin,
a day of darkness and gloom,
a day of clouds and blackness,
¹⁶a day of trumpet and battle cry
against the fortified cities
and against the corner towers.
¹⁷I will bring distress on the people
and they will walk like blind men,
because they have sinned against the LORD.
Their blood will be poured out like dust
and their entrails like filth.
¹⁸Neither their silver nor their gold
will be able to save them
on the day of the LORD's wrath.
In the fire of his jealousy
the whole world will be consumed,
for he will make a sudden end
of all who live in the earth."

2 Gather together, gather together,
O shameful nation,
²before the appointed time arrives
and that day sweeps on like chaff,
before the fierce anger of the LORD comes upon you,
before the day of the LORD's wrath comes upon you.
³Seek the LORD, all you humble of the land,
you who do what he commands.
Seek righteousness, seek humility;
perhaps you will be sheltered
on the day of the LORD's anger.

ª 11 Or the Mortar   *ᵇ 11 Or in*

Against Philistia

⁴Gaza will be abandoned
  and Ashkelon left in ruins.
 At midday Ashdod will be emptied
  and Ekron uprooted.
⁵Woe to you who live by the sea,
  O Kerethite people;
 the word of the LORD is against you,
  O Canaan, land of the Philistines.

 "I will destroy you,
  and none will be left."

⁶The land by the sea, where the Kerethites *a* dwell,
  will be a place for shepherds and sheep pens.
⁷It will belong to the remnant of the house of Judah;
  there they will find pasture.
 In the evening they will lie down
  in the houses of Ashkelon.
 The LORD their God will care for them;
  he will restore their fortunes. *b*

Against Moab and Ammon

⁸"I have heard the insults of Moab
  and the taunts of the Ammonites,
 who insulted my people
  and made threats against their land.
⁹Therefore, as surely as I live,"
  declares the LORD Almighty, the God of Israel,
 "surely Moab will become like Sodom,
  the Ammonites like Gomorrah—
 a place of weeds and salt pits,
  a wasteland forever.
 The remnant of my people will plunder them;
  the survivors of my nation will inherit their land."

¹⁰This is what they will get in return for their pride,
  for insulting and mocking the people of the LORD Almighty.
¹¹The LORD will be awesome to them
  when he destroys all the gods of the land.
 The nations on every shore will worship him,
  every one in its own land.

Against Cush

¹²"You too, O Cushites, *c*
  will be slain by my sword."

Against Assyria

¹³He will stretch out his hand against the north
  and destroy Assyria,
 leaving Nineveh utterly desolate
  and dry as the desert.

a 6 The meaning of the Hebrew for this word is uncertain.   *b 7* Or *will bring back their captives*   *c 12* That is, people
from the upper Nile region

14Flocks and herds will lie down there,
    creatures of every kind.
The desert owl and the screech owl
    will roost on her columns.
Their calls will echo through the windows,
    rubble will be in the doorways,
    the beams of cedar will be exposed.
15This is the carefree city
    that lived in safety.
She said to herself,
    "I am, and there is none besides me."
What a ruin she has become,
    a lair for wild beasts!
All who pass by her scoff
    and shake their fists.

The Future of Jerusalem

3 Woe to the city of oppressors,
    rebellious and defiled!
2She obeys no one,
    she accepts no correction.
She does not trust in the LORD,
    she does not draw near to her God.
3Her officials are roaring lions,
    her rulers are evening wolves,
    who leave nothing for the morning.
4Her prophets are arrogant;
    they are treacherous men.
Her priests profane the sanctuary
    and do violence to the law.
5The LORD within her is righteous;
    he does no wrong.
Morning by morning he dispenses his justice,
    and every new day he does not fail,
    yet the unrighteous know no shame.

6"I have cut off nations;

DISCOVERING GOD

3:1–17
Life with God

The prophet Zephaniah rebuked the Israelites for their sin in this chapter. These were God's people, but their actions certainly didn't show it! Then as now, some people chose to abuse their religious position for personal gain (verse 3). Their corruption was a symbol for the sin of God's people. And God was angry.

But in the midst of his anger against those who did not "trust in the LORD" (verse 2), Zephaniah spoke tenderly about those who did not "rejoice in their pride" (verse 11) and choose their own way over God's way. Of those people he said that God "take[s] great delight" in them, is their protector, and gives them peace through his love (verse 17).

As a seeker, you need to know that God wants to have a relationship with you characterized by these qualities. While that prospect may be difficult to grasp, take it on the authority of God's prophet that it's true.

their strongholds are demolished.
I have left their streets deserted,
  with no one passing through.
. Their cities are destroyed;
  no one will be left—no one at all.
⁷I said to the city,
  'Surely you will fear me
  and accept correction!'
Then her dwelling would not be cut off,
  nor all my punishments come upon her.
But they were still eager
  to act corruptly in all they did.
⁸Therefore wait for me," declares the LORD,
  "for the day I will stand up to testify.ᵃ
I have decided to assemble the nations,
  to gather the kingdoms
and to pour out my wrath on them—
  all my fierce anger.
The whole world will be consumed
  by the fire of my jealous anger.

⁹"Then will I purify the lips of the peoples,
  that all of them may call on the name of the LORD
  and serve him shoulder to shoulder.
¹⁰From beyond the rivers of Cushᵇ
  my worshipers, my scattered people,
  will bring me offerings.
¹¹On that day you will not be put to shame
  for all the wrongs you have done to me,
because I will remove from this city
  those who rejoice in their pride.
Never again will you be haughty
  on my holy hill.
¹²But I will leave within you
  the meek and humble,
  who trust in the name of the LORD.
¹³The remnant of Israel will do no wrong;
  they will speak no lies,
  nor will deceit be found in their mouths.
They will eat and lie down
  and no one will make them afraid."

¹⁴Sing, O Daughter of Zion;
  shout aloud, O Israel!
Be glad and rejoice with all your heart,
  O Daughter of Jerusalem!
¹⁵The LORD has taken away your punishment,
  he has turned back your enemy.
The LORD, the King of Israel, is with you;
  never again will you fear any harm.
¹⁶On that day they will say to Jerusalem,
  "Do not fear, O Zion;
  do not let your hands hang limp.

ᵃ8 Septuagint and Syriac; Hebrew *will rise up to plunder*   ᵇ10 That is, the upper Nile region

¹⁷The Lord your God is with you,
　　he is mighty to save.
He will take great delight in you,
　　he will quiet you with his love,
　　he will rejoice over you with singing."

¹⁸"The sorrows for the appointed feasts
　　I will remove from you;
　　they are a burden and a reproach to you.^a
¹⁹At that time I will deal
　　with all who oppressed you;
I will rescue the lame
　　and gather those who have been scattered.
I will give them praise and honor
　　in every land where they were put to shame.
²⁰At that time I will gather you;
　　at that time I will bring you home.
I will give you honor and praise
　　among all the peoples of the earth
when I restore your fortunes^b
　　before your very eyes,"

says the Lord.

a 18 Or *"I will gather you who mourn for the appointed feasts; / your reproach is a burden to you*　　*b 20* Or *I bring back your captives*

HAGGAI

A Call to Build the House of the LORD

1 In the second year of King Darius, on the first day of the sixth month, the word of the LORD came through the prophet Haggai to Zerubbabel son of Shealtiel, governor of Judah, and to Joshua*ᵃ* son of Jehozadak, the high priest:

²This is what the LORD Almighty says: "These people say, 'The time has not yet come for the LORD's house to be built.'"

³Then the word of the LORD came through the prophet Haggai: ⁴"Is it a time for you yourselves to be living in your paneled houses, while this house remains a ruin?"

⁵Now this is what the LORD Almighty says: "Give careful thought to your ways. ⁶You have planted much, but have harvested little. You eat, but never have enough. You drink, but never have your fill. You put on clothes, but are not warm. You earn wages, only to put them in a purse with holes in it."

⁷This is what the LORD Almighty says: "Give careful thought to your ways. ⁸Go up into the mountains and bring down timber and build the house, so that I may take pleasure in it and be honored," says the LORD. ⁹"You expected much, but see, it turned out to be little. What you brought home, I blew away. Why?" declares the LORD Almighty. "Because of my house, which remains a ruin, while each of you is busy with his own house. ¹⁰Therefore, because of you the heavens have withheld their dew and the earth its crops. ¹¹I called for a drought on the fields and the mountains, on the grain, the new wine, the oil and whatever the ground produces, on men and cattle, and on the labor of your hands."

¹²Then Zerubbabel son of Shealtiel, Joshua son of Jehozadak, the high priest, and the whole remnant of the people obeyed the voice of the LORD their God and the message of the prophet Haggai, because the LORD their God had sent him. And the people feared the LORD.

¹³Then Haggai, the LORD's messenger, gave this message of the LORD to the people: "I am with you," declares the LORD. ¹⁴So the LORD stirred up the spirit of Zerubbabel son of Shealtiel, governor of Judah, and the spirit of Joshua son of Jehozadak, the high priest, and the spirit of the whole remnant of the people. They came and began to work on the house of the LORD Almighty, their God, ¹⁵on the twenty-fourth day of the sixth month in the second year of King Darius.

The Promised Glory of the New House

2 On the twenty-first day of the seventh month, the word of the LORD came through the prophet Haggai: ²"Speak to Zerubbabel son of Shealtiel, governor of Judah, to Joshua son of Jehozadak, the high priest, and to the remnant of the people. Ask them, ³'Who of you is left who saw this house in its former glory? How does it look to you now? Does it not seem to you like nothing? ⁴But now be strong, O Zerubbabel,' declares the LORD. 'Be strong, O Joshua son of Jehozadak, the high priest. Be strong, all you people of the land,' declares the LORD, 'and work. For I am with you,' declares the LORD Almighty. ⁵'This is what I covenanted with you when you came out of Egypt. And my Spirit remains among you. Do not fear.'

⁶"This is what the LORD Almighty says: 'In a little while I will once more shake the heavens and the earth, the sea and the dry land. ⁷I will shake all nations, and the

---

ᵃ 1 A variant of Jeshua; here and elsewhere in Haggai

desired of all nations will come, and I will fill this house with glory,' says the LORD Almighty. ⁸'The silver is mine and the gold is mine,' declares the LORD Almighty. ⁹'The glory of this present house will be greater than the glory of the former house,' says the LORD Almighty. 'And in this place I will grant peace,' declares the LORD Almighty."

Blessings for a Defiled People

¹⁰On the twenty-fourth day of the ninth month, in the second year of Darius, the word of the LORD came to the prophet Haggai: ¹¹"This is what the LORD Almighty says: 'Ask the priests what the law says: ¹²If a person carries consecrated meat in the fold of his garment, and that fold touches some bread or stew, some wine, oil or other food, does it become consecrated?'"

The priests answered, "No."

¹³Then Haggai said, "If a person defiled by contact with a dead body touches one of these things, does it become defiled?"

"Yes," the priests replied, "it becomes defiled."

¹⁴Then Haggai said, "'So it is with this people and this nation in my sight,' declares the LORD. 'Whatever they do and whatever they offer there is defiled.

¹⁵'Now give careful thought to this from this day on*ᵃ*—consider how things were before one stone was laid on another in the LORD's temple. ¹⁶When anyone came to a

ᵃ 15 Or to the days past

╔══╗

▦ KNOWING YOURSELF ▦

2:13–14
Sin

Some people think that they can become "good" simply by attending church or by hanging around other "good" people, as if following God's way is as easy as catching a flu virus. But the prophet Haggai points out that holiness is not "contagious." In fact, the opposite sometimes happens: People who don't trust God can be a negative influence on others who are doing their best to live God's way.

When Haggai wrote this letter his concerns were quite specific. The Hebrews who had returned to Jerusalem from exile had neglected to rebuild God's temple. The foundation of the temple had been laid years before but, due to various circumstances, the structure had not been completed. Haggai reminded these people of the reason why they had been allowed to return to Jerusalem, and encouraged them to get back to the work at hand. By leaving the temple in disrepair and still trying to offer sacrifices to God, their worship was tainted. What the people needed, Haggai said, was to be internally purified before they came to participate in outward religious acts.

Jesus picked up on this same theme during his ministry. He told people not to waste their time offering God something when there was strife between them and someone else. Instead, they were told to reconcile with that person—*then* bring their offering. Otherwise, their remorseless hearts would contaminate the offering, *and* the whole ceremony would become hypocritical (Matthew chapter 5, verses 23–24 [page 1264]).

If Haggai were still alive, his message would be the same to us today. He would, for example, discourage two people from getting married in a church if the main reason for doing so was to make a basically godless relationship acceptable. He'd say that the couple must first surrender their individual lives to God. Or Haggai might question why a couple would present their child to God (through baptism) when they hadn't first committed themselves to him. Such actions make God appear foolish, as if by performing the right ritual we can trick God into blessing us when in real life we have no interest in his leadership.

And Haggai's message to you today is similar. Don't be fooled into believing that a religious ceremony can bestow on you some spiritual benefit when everything else you do indicates that you don't want God to be in charge. If you've decided that you want to pursue a relationship with God, make sure that the intentions of your heart match your outward actions.

╚══╝

heap of twenty measures, there were only ten. When anyone went to a wine vat to draw fifty measures, there were only twenty. ¹⁷I struck all the work of your hands with blight, mildew and hail, yet you did not turn to me,' declares the LORD. ¹⁸'From this day on, from this twenty-fourth day of the ninth month, give careful thought to the day when the foundation of the LORD's temple was laid. Give careful thought: ¹⁹Is there yet any seed left in the barn? Until now, the vine and the fig tree, the pomegranate and the olive tree have not borne fruit.

" 'From this day on I will bless you.' "

Zerubbabel the LORD's Signet Ring

²⁰The word of the LORD came to Haggai a second time on the twenty-fourth day of the month: ²¹"Tell Zerubbabel governor of Judah that I will shake the heavens and the earth. ²²I will overturn royal thrones and shatter the power of the foreign kingdoms. I will overthrow chariots and their drivers; horses and their riders will fall, each by the sword of his brother.

²³" 'On that day,' declares the LORD Almighty, 'I will take you, my servant Zerubbabel son of Shealtiel,' declares the LORD, 'and I will make you like my signet ring, for I have chosen you,' declares the LORD Almighty."

ZECHARIAH

A Call to Return to the LORD

1 In the eighth month of the second year of Darius, the word of the LORD came to the prophet Zechariah son of Berekiah, the son of Iddo:

²"The LORD was very angry with your forefathers. ³Therefore tell the people: This is what the LORD Almighty says: 'Return to me,' declares the LORD Almighty, 'and I will return to you,' says the LORD Almighty. ⁴Do not be like your forefathers, to whom the earlier prophets proclaimed: This is what the LORD Almighty says: 'Turn from your evil ways and your evil practices.' But they would not listen or pay attention to me, declares the LORD. ⁵Where are your forefathers now? And the prophets, do they live forever? ⁶But did not my words and my decrees, which I commanded my servants the prophets, overtake your forefathers?

"Then they repented and said, 'The LORD Almighty has done to us what our ways and practices deserve, just as he determined to do.'"

The Man Among the Myrtle Trees

⁷On the twenty-fourth day of the eleventh month, the month of Shebat, in the second year of Darius, the word of the LORD came to the prophet Zechariah son of Berekiah, the son of Iddo.

⁸During the night I had a vision—and there before me was a man riding a red horse! He was standing among the myrtle trees in a ravine. Behind him were red, brown and white horses.

⁹I asked, "What are these, my lord?"

The angel who was talking with me answered, "I will show you what they are."

¹⁰Then the man standing among the myrtle trees explained, "They are the ones the LORD has sent to go throughout the earth."

¹¹And they reported to the angel of the LORD, who was standing among the myrtle trees, "We have gone throughout the earth and found the whole world at rest and in peace."

¹²Then the angel of the LORD said, "LORD Almighty, how long will you withhold mercy from Jerusalem and from the towns of Judah, which you have been angry with these seventy years?" ¹³So the LORD spoke kind and comforting words to the angel who talked with me.

¹⁴Then the angel who was speaking to me said, "Proclaim this word: This is what the LORD Almighty says: 'I am very jealous for Jerusalem and Zion, ¹⁵but I am very angry with the nations that feel secure. I was only a little angry, but they added to the calamity.'

¹⁶"Therefore, this is what the LORD says: 'I will return to Jerusalem with mercy, and there my house will be rebuilt. And the measuring line will be stretched out over Jerusalem,' declares the LORD Almighty.

¹⁷"Proclaim further: This is what the LORD Almighty says: 'My towns will again overflow with prosperity, and the LORD will again comfort Zion and choose Jerusalem.'"

Four Horns and Four Craftsmen

¹⁸Then I looked up—and there before me were four horns! ¹⁹I asked the angel who was speaking to me, "What are these?"

He answered me, "These are the horns that scattered Judah, Israel and Jerusalem."

²⁰Then the LORD showed me four craftsmen. ²¹I asked, "What are these coming to do?"

He answered, "These are the horns that scattered Judah so that no one could raise his head, but the craftsmen have come to terrify them and throw down these horns of the nations who lifted up their horns against the land of Judah to scatter its people."

A Man With a Measuring Line

2 Then I looked up—and there before me was a man with a measuring line in his hand! ²I asked, "Where are you going?"

He answered me, "To measure Jerusalem, to find out how wide and how long it is."

³Then the angel who was speaking to me left, and another angel came to meet him ⁴and said to him: "Run, tell that young man, 'Jerusalem will be a city without walls because of the great number of men and livestock in it. ⁵And I myself will be a wall of fire around it,' declares the LORD, 'and I will be its glory within.'

⁶"Come! Come! Flee from the land of the north," declares the LORD, "for I have scattered you to the four winds of heaven," declares the LORD.

⁷"Come, O Zion! Escape, you who live in the Daughter of Babylon!" ⁸For this is what the LORD Almighty says: "After he has honored me and has sent me against the nations that have plundered you—for whoever touches you touches the apple of his eye— ⁹I will surely raise my hand against them so that their slaves will plunder them.ᵃ Then you will know that the LORD Almighty has sent me.

¹⁰"Shout and be glad, O Daughter of Zion. For I am coming, and I will live among you," declares the LORD. ¹¹"Many nations will be joined with the LORD in that day and will become my people. I will live among you and you will know that the LORD Almighty has sent me to you. ¹²The LORD will inherit Judah as his portion in the holy land and will again choose Jerusalem. ¹³Be still before the LORD, all mankind, because he has roused himself from his holy dwelling."

Clean Garments for the High Priest

3 Then he showed me Joshuaᵇ the high priest standing before the angel of the LORD, and Satanᶜ standing at his right side to accuse him. ²The LORD said to Satan, "The LORD rebuke you, Satan! The LORD, who has chosen Jerusalem, rebuke you! Is not this man a burning stick snatched from the fire?"

³Now Joshua was dressed in filthy clothes as he stood before the angel. ⁴The angel said to those who were standing before him, "Take off his filthy clothes."

Then he said to Joshua, "See, I have taken away your sin, and I will put rich garments on you."

⁵Then I said, "Put a clean turban on his head." So they put a clean turban on his head and clothed him, while the angel of the LORD stood by.

⁶The angel of the LORD gave this charge to Joshua: ⁷"This is what the LORD Almighty says: 'If you will walk in my ways and keep my requirements, then you will govern my house and have charge of my courts, and I will give you a place among these standing here.

⁸"'Listen, O high priest Joshua and your associates seated before you, who are men symbolic of things to come: I am going to bring my servant, the Branch. ⁹See, the stone I have set in front of Joshua! There are seven eyesᵈ on that one stone, and I will engrave an inscription on it,' says the LORD Almighty, 'and I will remove the sin of this land in a single day.

¹⁰"'In that day each of you will invite his neighbor to sit under his vine and fig tree,' declares the LORD Almighty."

ᵃ 8,9 Or says after . . . eye: ⁹"I . . . plunder them."   ᵇ 1 A variant of Jeshua; here and elsewhere in Zechariah   ᶜ 1 Satan
means accuser.   ᵈ 9 Or facets

The Gold Lampstand and the Two Olive Trees

4 Then the angel who talked with me returned and wakened me, as a man is wakened from his sleep. ²He asked me, "What do you see?"

I answered, "I see a solid gold lampstand with a bowl at the top and seven lights on it, with seven channels to the lights. ³Also there are two olive trees by it, one on the right of the bowl and the other on its left."

⁴I asked the angel who talked with me, "What are these, my lord?"

⁵He answered, "Do you not know what these are?"

"No, my lord," I replied.

⁶So he said to me, "This is the word of the Lord to Zerubbabel: 'Not by might nor by power, but by my Spirit,' says the Lord Almighty.

⁷"What *a* are you, O mighty mountain? Before Zerubbabel you will become level ground. Then he will bring out the capstone to shouts of 'God bless it! God bless it!'"

⁸Then the word of the Lord came to me: ⁹"The hands of Zerubbabel have laid the foundation of this temple; his hands will also complete it. Then you will know that the Lord Almighty has sent me to you.

¹⁰"Who despises the day of small things? Men will rejoice when they see the plumb line in the hand of Zerubbabel.

"(These seven are the eyes of the Lord, which range throughout the earth.)"

¹¹Then I asked the angel, "What are these two olive trees on the right and the left of the lampstand?"

¹²Again I asked him, "What are these two olive branches beside the two gold pipes that pour out golden oil?"

¹³He replied, "Do you not know what these are?"

"No, my lord," I said.

¹⁴So he said, "These are the two who are anointed to *b* serve the Lord of all the earth."

> **REASONS TO BELIEVE**
>
> **3:8–9**
> **The Amazing Bible**
>
> In this passage Zechariah predicts that the Branch, God's chosen Servant, will come some time in the future. When he does, God will take away all sin *in a single day*.
>
> On the day Jesus Christ died, this verse was literally fulfilled. God put on him all of the punishment for our sin and, in so doing, took away the world's sin *in a single day*. (For a complete description of this day, see Matthew chapter 27 [page 1298]. And don't miss the good news of Matthew chapter 28!)

The Flying Scroll

5 I looked again—and there before me was a flying scroll! ²He asked me, "What do you see?"

I answered, "I see a flying scroll, thirty feet long and fifteen feet wide. *c*"

³And he said to me, "This is the curse that is going out over the whole land; for according to what it says on one side, every thief will be banished, and according to what it says on the other, everyone who swears falsely will be banished. ⁴The Lord Almighty declares, 'I will send it out, and it will enter the house of the thief and the house of him who swears falsely by my name. It will remain in his house and destroy it, both its timbers and its stones.'"

The Woman in a Basket

⁵Then the angel who was speaking to me came forward and said to me, "Look up and see what this is that is appearing."

⁶I asked, "What is it?"

<hr />

a 7 Or *Who*   *b 14* Or *two who bring oil and*   *c 2* Hebrew *twenty cubits long and ten cubits wide* (about 9 meters long and 4.5 meters wide)

He replied, "It is a measuring basket.ᵃ" And he added, "This is the iniquityᵇ of the people throughout the land."

⁷Then the cover of lead was raised, and there in the basket sat a woman! ⁸He said, "This is wickedness," and he pushed her back into the basket and pushed the lead cover down over its mouth.

⁹Then I looked up—and there before me were two women, with the wind in their wings! They had wings like those of a stork, and they lifted up the basket between heaven and earth.

¹⁰"Where are they taking the basket?" I asked the angel who was speaking to me.

¹¹He replied, "To the country of Babyloniaᶜ to build a house for it. When it is ready, the basket will be set there in its place."

Four Chariots

6 I looked up again—and there before me were four chariots coming out from between two mountains—mountains of bronze! ²The first chariot had red horses, the second black, ³the third white, and the fourth dappled—all of them powerful. ⁴I asked the angel who was speaking to me, "What are these, my lord?"

⁵The angel answered me, "These are the four spiritsᵈ of heaven, going out from standing in the presence of the Lord of the whole world. ⁶The one with the black horses is going toward the north country, the one with the white horses toward the west,ᵉ and the one with the dappled horses toward the south."

⁷When the powerful horses went out, they were straining to go throughout the earth. And he said, "Go throughout the earth!" So they went throughout the earth.

⁸Then he called to me, "Look, those going toward the north country have given my Spiritᶠ rest in the land of the north."

A Crown for Joshua

⁹The word of the Lord came to me: ¹⁰"Take ⌊silver and gold⌋ from the exiles Heldai, Tobijah and Jedaiah, who have arrived from Babylon. Go the same day to the house of Josiah son of Zephaniah. ¹¹Take the silver and gold and make a crown, and set it on the head of the high priest, Joshua son of Jehozadak. ¹²Tell him this is what the Lord Almighty says: 'Here is the man whose name is the Branch, and he will branch out from his place and build the temple of the Lord. ¹³It is he who will build the temple of the Lord, and he will be clothed with majesty and will sit and rule on his throne. And he will be a priest on his throne. And there will be harmony between the two.' ¹⁴The crown will be given to Heldai,ᵍ Tobijah, Jedaiah and Henʰ son of Zephaniah as a memorial in the temple of the Lord. ¹⁵Those who are far away will come and help to build the temple of the Lord, and you will know that the Lord Almighty has sent me to you. This will happen if you diligently obey the Lord your God."

Justice and Mercy, Not Fasting

7 In the fourth year of King Darius, the word of the Lord came to Zechariah on the fourth day of the ninth month, the month of Kislev. ²The people of Bethel had sent Sharezer and Regem-Melech, together with their men, to entreat the Lord ³by asking the priests of the house of the Lord Almighty and the prophets, "Should I mourn and fast in the fifth month, as I have done for so many years?"

⁴Then the word of the Lord Almighty came to me: ⁵"Ask all the people of the land and the priests, 'When you fasted and mourned in the fifth and seventh months for the past seventy years, was it really for me that you fasted? ⁶And when you were eating and drinking, were you not just feasting for yourselves? ⁷Are these not the words the Lord

---

ᵃ6 Hebrew an ephah; also in verses 7-11   ᵇ6 Or appearance   ᶜ11 Hebrew Shinar   ᵈ5 Or winds   ᵉ6 Or horses after them   ᶠ8 Or spirit   ᵍ14 Syriac; Hebrew Helem   ʰ14 Or and the gracious one, the

proclaimed through the earlier prophets when Jerusalem and its surrounding towns were at rest and prosperous, and the Negev and the western foothills were settled?'"

⁸And the word of the LORD came again to Zechariah: ⁹"This is what the LORD Almighty says: 'Administer true justice; show mercy and compassion to one another. ¹⁰Do not oppress the widow or the fatherless, the alien or the poor. In your hearts do not think evil of each other.'

¹¹"But they refused to pay attention; stubbornly they turned their backs and stopped up their ears. ¹²They made their hearts as hard as flint and would not listen to the law or to the words that the LORD Almighty had sent by his Spirit through the earlier prophets. So the LORD Almighty was very angry.

¹³"When I called, they did not listen; so when they called, I would not listen,' says the LORD Almighty. ¹⁴'I scattered them with a whirlwind among all the nations, where they were strangers. The land was left so desolate behind them that no one could come or go. This is how they made the pleasant land desolate.'"

The LORD Promises to Bless Jerusalem

8 Again the word of the LORD Almighty came to me. ²This is what the LORD Almighty says: "I am very jealous for Zion; I am burning with jealousy for her."

³This is what the LORD says: "I will return to Zion and dwell in Jerusalem. Then Jerusalem will be called the City of Truth, and the mountain of the LORD Almighty will be called the Holy Mountain."

⁴This is what the LORD Almighty says: "Once again men and women of ripe old age will sit in the streets of Jerusalem, each with cane in hand because of his age. ⁵The city streets will be filled with boys and girls playing there."

⁶This is what the LORD Almighty says: "It may seem marvelous to the remnant of this people at that time, but will it seem marvelous to me?" declares the LORD Almighty.

⁷This is what the LORD Almighty says: "I will save my people from the countries of the east and the west. ⁸I will bring them back to live in Jerusalem; they will be my people, and I will be faithful and righteous to them as their God."

⁹This is what the LORD Almighty says: "You who now hear these words spoken by the prophets who were there when the foundation was laid for the house of the LORD Almighty, let your hands be strong so that the temple may be built. ¹⁰Before that time there were no wages for man or beast. No one could go about his business safely because of his enemy, for I had turned every man against his neighbor. ¹¹But now I will not deal with the remnant of this people as I did in the past," declares the LORD Almighty.

¹²"The seed will grow well, the vine will yield its fruit, the ground will produce its crops, and the heavens will drop their dew. I will give all these things as an inheritance to the remnant of this people. ¹³As you have been an object of cursing among the nations, O Judah and Israel, so will I save you, and you will be a blessing. Do not be afraid, but let your hands be strong."

¹⁴This is what the LORD Almighty says: "Just as I had determined to bring disaster upon you and showed no pity when your fathers angered me," says the LORD Almighty, ¹⁵"so now I have determined to do good again to Jerusalem and Judah. Do not be afraid. ¹⁶These are the things you are to do: Speak the truth to each other, and render true and sound judgment in your courts; ¹⁷do not plot evil against your neighbor, and do not love to swear falsely. I hate all this," declares the LORD.

¹⁸Again the word of the LORD Almighty came to me. ¹⁹This is what the LORD Almighty says: "The fasts of the fourth, fifth, seventh and tenth months will become joyful and glad occasions and happy festivals for Judah. Therefore love truth and peace."

²⁰This is what the LORD Almighty says: "Many peoples and the inhabitants of many cities will yet come, ²¹and the inhabitants of one city will go to another and say, 'Let us

go at once to entreat the Lord and seek the Lord Almighty. I myself am going.' ²²And many peoples and powerful nations will come to Jerusalem to seek the Lord Almighty and to entreat him."

²³This is what the Lord Almighty says: "In those days ten men from all languages and nations will take firm hold of one Jew by the hem of his robe and say, 'Let us go with you, because we have heard that God is with you.' "

Judgment on Israel's Enemies

An Oracle

9 The word of the Lord is against the land of Hadrach
and will rest upon Damascus—
for the eyes of men and all the tribes of Israel
are on the Lord—ᵃ
²and upon Hamath too, which borders on it,
and upon Tyre and Sidon, though they are very skillful.
³Tyre has built herself a stronghold;
she has heaped up silver like dust,
and gold like the dirt of the streets.
⁴But the Lord will take away her possessions
and destroy her power on the sea,
and she will be consumed by fire.
⁵Ashkelon will see it and fear;
Gaza will writhe in agony,
and Ekron too, for her hope will wither.
Gaza will lose her king
and Ashkelon will be deserted.
⁶Foreigners will occupy Ashdod,
and I will cut off the pride of the Philistines.
⁷I will take the blood from their mouths,
the forbidden food from between their teeth.
Those who are left will belong to our God
and become leaders in Judah,
and Ekron will be like the Jebusites.
⁸But I will defend my house against marauding forces.
Never again will an oppressor overrun my people,
for now I am keeping watch.

The Coming of Zion's King

⁹Rejoice greatly, O Daughter of Zion!
Shout, Daughter of Jerusalem!
See, your kingᵇ comes to you,
righteous and having salvation,
gentle and riding on a donkey,
on a colt, the foal of a donkey.

▣ ░░░░░░░ REASONS TO BELIEVE ░░░░░░░ ⇨

**9:9
The Amazing Bible**

In Zechariah's time, great leaders customarily rode in procession on powerful war horses or in splendidly decorated chariots. Yet this verse says that the coming king of Israel, the one who would save all of God's people, would enter Jerusalem on a *donkey*.

Jesus entered Jerusalem in exactly this manner shortly before his death. (You can read about it in Luke chapter 19, verses 28–40 [page 1370]). Once again, Jesus perfectly fulfilled the prophecies made about the Messiah.

ᵃ 1 Or *Damascus. / For the eye of the Lord is on all mankind, / as well as on the tribes of Israel,*   ᵇ 9 Or *King*

¹⁰I will take away the chariots from Ephraim
and the war-horses from Jerusalem,
and the battle bow will be broken.
He will proclaim peace to the nations.
His rule will extend from sea to sea
and from the River^a to the ends of the earth.^b
¹¹As for you, because of the blood of my covenant with you,
I will free your prisoners from the waterless pit.
¹²Return to your fortress, O prisoners of hope;
even now I announce that I will restore twice as much to you.
¹³I will bend Judah as I bend my bow
and fill it with Ephraim.
I will rouse your sons, O Zion,
against your sons, O Greece,
and make you like a warrior's sword.

The Lord Will Appear

¹⁴Then the Lord will appear over them;
his arrow will flash like lightning.
The Sovereign Lord will sound the trumpet;
he will march in the storms of the south,
¹⁵   and the Lord Almighty will shield them.
They will destroy
and overcome with slingstones.
They will drink and roar as with wine;
they will be full like a bowl
used for sprinkling^c the corners of the altar.
¹⁶The Lord their God will save them on that day
as the flock of his people.
They will sparkle in his land
like jewels in a crown.
¹⁷How attractive and beautiful they will be!
Grain will make the young men thrive,
and new wine the young women.

The Lord Will Care for Judah

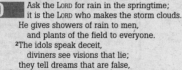

10 Ask the Lord for rain in the springtime;
it is the Lord who makes the storm clouds.
He gives showers of rain to men,
and plants of the field to everyone.
²The idols speak deceit,
diviners see visions that lie;
they tell dreams that are false,
they give comfort in vain.
Therefore the people wander like sheep
oppressed for lack of a shepherd.

³"My anger burns against the shepherds,
and I will punish the leaders;
for the Lord Almighty will care

^a10 That is, the Euphrates   ^b10 Or the end of the land   ^c15 Or bowl, / like

for his flock, the house of Judah,
and make them like a proud horse in battle.
⁴From Judah will come the cornerstone,
from him the tent peg,
from him the battle bow,
from him every ruler.
⁵Together they*ᵃ* will be like mighty men
trampling the muddy streets in battle.
Because the LORD is with them,
they will fight and overthrow the horsemen.

⁶"I will strengthen the house of Judah
and save the house of Joseph.
I will restore them
because I have compassion on them.
They will be as though
I had not rejected them,
for I am the LORD their God
and I will answer them.
⁷The Ephraimites will become like mighty men,
and their hearts will be glad as with wine.
Their children will see it and be joyful;
their hearts will rejoice in the LORD.
⁸I will signal for them
and gather them in.
Surely I will redeem them;
they will be as numerous as before.
⁹Though I scatter them among the peoples,
yet in distant lands they will remember me.
They and their children will survive,
and they will return.
¹⁰I will bring them back from Egypt
and gather them from Assyria.
I will bring them to Gilead and Lebanon,
and there will not be room enough for them.
¹¹They will pass through the sea of trouble;
the surging sea will be subdued
and all the depths of the Nile will dry up.
Assyria's pride will be brought down
and Egypt's scepter will pass away.
¹²I will strengthen them in the LORD
and in his name they will walk,"

declares the LORD.

11 Open your doors, O Lebanon,
so that fire may devour your cedars!
²Wail, O pine tree, for the cedar has fallen;
the stately trees are ruined!
Wail, oaks of Bashan;
the dense forest has been cut down!
³Listen to the wail of the shepherds;
their rich pastures are destroyed!

ᵃ 4,5 Or ruler, all of them together. / ⁵They

> Listen to the roar of the lions;
>> the lush thicket of the Jordan is ruined!

Two Shepherds

4This is what the LORD my God says: "Pasture the flock marked for slaughter. **5**Their buyers slaughter them and go unpunished. Those who sell them say, 'Praise the LORD, I am rich!' Their own shepherds do not spare them. **6**For I will no longer have pity on the people of the land," declares the LORD. "I will hand everyone over to his neighbor and his king. They will oppress the land, and I will not rescue them from their hands."

7So I pastured the flock marked for slaughter, particularly the oppressed of the flock. Then I took two staffs and called one Favor and the other Union, and I pastured the flock. **8**In one month I got rid of the three shepherds.

The flock detested me, and I grew weary of them **9**and said, "I will not be your shepherd. Let the dying die, and the perishing perish. Let those who are left eat one another's flesh."

10Then I took my staff called Favor and broke it, revoking the covenant I·had made with all the nations. **11**It was revoked on that day, and so the afflicted of the flock who were watching me knew it was the word of the LORD.

12I told them, "If you think it best, give me my pay; but if not, keep it." So they paid me thirty pieces of silver.

13And the LORD said to me, "Throw it to the potter"—the handsome price at which they priced me! So I took the thirty pieces of silver and threw them into the house of the LORD to the potter.

14Then I broke my second staff called Union, breaking the brotherhood between Judah and Israel.

15Then the LORD said to me, "Take again the equipment of a foolish shepherd. **16**For I am going to raise up a shepherd over the land who will not care for the lost, or seek the young, or heal the injured, or feed the healthy, but will eat the meat of the choice sheep, tearing off their hoofs.

> **17**"Woe to the worthless shepherd,
>> who deserts the flock!
> May the sword strike his arm and his
>> right eye!
>> May his arm be completely withered,
>> his right eye totally blinded!"

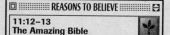

◧ ⦂⦂⦂⦂⦂⦂ REASONS TO BELIEVE ⦂⦂⦂⦂⦂⦂ ◨

11:12–13
The Amazing Bible

When Zechariah asked his listeners to pay him what they thought the word of God was worth, they gave him thirty shekels of silver—the price of a slave (Exodus chapter 21, verse 32 [page 98]). God mocked them for being so cheap and told Zechariah to throw the money back to the potter in the temple.

This act parallels what happened in Jesus' day when Judas betrayed Jesus. This time thirty shekels of silver was the meager price the people paid for the *Son* of God. As with Zechariah, Judas returned the money to the temple and it was given to a potter in return for a field in which to bury foreigners (this amazing fulfillment is recounted in Matthew chapter 27, verses 3–10 [page 1298]).

The early Christians were well aware of the parallels in these two stories, especially how God was undervalued for the exact same amount in both instances. Many such parallels point to the unique ministry of Jesus as the fulfillment of the Old Testament hope for a Messiah.

Jerusalem's Enemies to Be Destroyed

An Oracle

12 This is the word of the LORD concerning Israel. The LORD, who stretches out the heavens, who lays the foundation of the earth, and who forms the spirit of man within him, declares: **2**"I am going to make Jerusalem a cup that sends all the surrounding peoples reeling. Judah will be besieged as well as Jerusalem. **3**On that day, when all the nations of the earth are gathered against her, I will make Jerusalem an immovable rock for all the nations. All who try to move it will injure themselves. ⁴On that day I will strike every horse with panic and its rider with madness," declares the LORD. "I will keep a watchful eye over the house of Judah, but I will blind all the horses of the nations. ⁵Then the leaders of Judah will say in their hearts, 'The people of Jerusalem are strong, because the LORD Almighty is their God.'

⁶"On that day I will make the leaders of Judah like a firepot in a woodpile, like a flaming torch among sheaves. They will consume right and left all the surrounding peoples, but Jerusalem will remain intact in her place.

⁷"The LORD will save the dwellings of Judah first, so that the honor of the house of David and of Jerusalem's inhabitants may not be greater than that of Judah. ⁸On that day the LORD will shield those who live in Jerusalem, so that the feeblest among them will be like David, and the house of David will be like God, like the Angel of the LORD going before them. ⁹On that day I will set out to destroy all the nations that attack Jerusalem.

Mourning for the One They Pierced

¹⁰"And I will pour out on the house of David and the inhabitants of Jerusalem a spirit*ᵃ* of grace and supplication. They will look on*ᵇ* me, the one they have pierced, and they will mourn for him as one mourns for an only child, and grieve bitterly for him as one grieves for a firstborn son. ¹¹On that day the weeping in Jerusalem will be great, like the weeping of Hadad Rimmon in the plain of Megiddo. ¹²The land will mourn, each clan by itself, with their wives by themselves: the clan of the house of David and their wives, the clan of the house of Nathan and their wives, ¹³the clan of the house of Levi and their wives, the clan of Shimei and their wives, ¹⁴and all the rest of the clans and their wives.

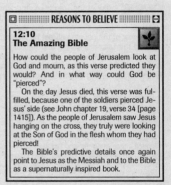

⫿⫿⫿⫿⫿ **REASONS TO BELIEVE** ⫿⫿⫿⫿⫿ ⏎

12:10
The Amazing Bible

How could the people of Jerusalem look at God and mourn, as this verse predicted they would? And in what way could God be "pierced"?

On the day Jesus died, this verse was fulfilled, because one of the soldiers pierced Jesus' side (see John chapter 19, verse 34 [page 1415]). As the people of Jerusalem saw Jesus hanging on the cross, they truly were looking at the Son of God in the flesh whom they had pierced!

The Bible's predictive details once again point to Jesus as the Messiah and to the Bible as a supernaturally inspired book.

Cleansing From Sin

13 "On that day a fountain will be opened to the house of David and the inhabitants of Jerusalem, to cleanse them from sin and impurity.

²"On that day, I will banish the names of the idols from the land, and they will be remembered no more," declares the LORD Almighty. "I will remove both the prophets and the spirit of impurity from the land. ³And if anyone still prophesies, his father and mother, to whom he was born, will say to him, 'You must die, because you have told lies in the LORD's name.' When he prophesies, his own parents will stab him.

⁴"On that day every prophet will be ashamed of his prophetic vision. He will not put on a prophet's garment of hair in order to deceive. ⁵He will say, 'I am not a prophet. I am a farmer; the land has been my livelihood since my youth.*ᶜ* ⁶If someone asks him, 'What are these wounds on your body*ᵈ*?' he will answer, 'The wounds I was given at the house of my friends.'

The Shepherd Struck, the Sheep Scattered

⁷"Awake, O sword, against my shepherd,
 against the man who is close to me!"
 declares the LORD Almighty.
"Strike the shepherd,

ᵃ10 Or *the Spirit* *ᵇ10* Or *to* *ᶜ5* Or *farmer; a man sold me in my youth* *ᵈ6* Or *wounds between your hands*

and the sheep will be scattered,
and I will turn my hand against the little ones.
⁸In the whole land," declares the LORD,
"two-thirds will be struck down and perish;
yet one-third will be left in it.
⁹This third I will bring into the fire;
I will refine them like silver
and test them like gold.
They will call on my name
and I will answer them;
I will say, 'They are my people,'
and they will say, 'The LORD is our God.'"

The LORD Comes and Reigns

14 A day of the LORD is coming when your plunder will be divided among you. ²I will gather all the nations to Jerusalem to fight against it; the city will be captured, the houses ransacked, and the women raped. Half of the city will go into exile, but the rest of the people will not be taken from the city.

³Then the LORD will go out and fight against those nations, as he fights in the day of battle. ⁴On that day his feet will stand on the Mount of Olives, east of Jerusalem, and the Mount of Olives will be split in two from east to west, forming a great valley, with half of the mountain moving north and half moving south. ⁵You will flee by my mountain valley,

for it will extend to Azel. You will flee as you fled from the earthquake[a] in the days of Uzziah king of Judah. Then the LORD my God will come, and all the holy ones with him.

⁶On that day there will be no light, no cold or frost. ⁷It will be a unique day, without daytime or nighttime—a day known to the LORD. When evening comes, there will be light.

⁸On that day living water will flow out from Jerusalem, half to the eastern sea[b] and half to the western sea,[c] in summer and in winter.

⁹The LORD will be king over the whole earth. On that day there will be one LORD, and his name the only name.

¹⁰The whole land, from Geba to Rimmon, south of Jerusalem, will become like the Arabah. But Jerusalem will be raised up and remain in its place, from the Benjamin Gate to the site of the First Gate, to the Corner Gate, and from the Tower of Hana-

nel to the royal winepresses. ¹¹It will be inhabited; never again will it be destroyed. Jerusalem will be secure.

¹²This is the plague with which the LORD will strike all the nations that fought against Jerusalem: Their flesh will rot while they are still standing on their feet, their eyes will rot in their sockets, and their tongues will rot in their mouths. ¹³On that day men will be stricken by the LORD with great panic. Each man will seize the hand of another, and they

---

DISCOVERING GOD

14:9
Life with God

This is one of many verses in the Bible that foretell a time when the world as we know it will be radically changed. Although many people resist God, he will someday be King over the whole earth, as this verse predicts. He will not be one among many gods; he will clearly be the *only* God.

As a seeker, this is an important claim with which to reckon. The God of the Bible will eventually rule in power and will run things as they were intended to run from the beginning. At that time, God will no longer tolerate evil.

Are you prepared for that new era? You can be, simply by putting your trust in God to make you ready. Ask Jesus Christ to come into your life and forgive your sin, and then take steps to keep growing in that relationship.

---

a5 Or ⁵My mountain valley will be blocked and will extend to Azel. It will be blocked as it was blocked because of the earthquake   *b8 That is, the Dead Sea*   *c8 That is, the Mediterranean*

will attack each other. ¹⁴Judah too will fight at Jerusalem. The wealth of all the surrounding nations will be collected—great quantities of gold and silver and clothing. ¹⁵A similar plague will strike the horses and mules, the camels and donkeys, and all the animals in those camps.

¹⁶Then the survivors from all the nations that have attacked Jerusalem will go up year after year to worship the King, the LORD Almighty, and to celebrate the Feast of Tabernacles. ¹⁷If any of the peoples of the earth do not go up to Jerusalem to worship the King, the LORD Almighty, they will have no rain. ¹⁸If the Egyptian people do not go up and take part, they will have no rain. The LORD*ᵃ* will bring on them the plague he inflicts on the nations that do not go up to celebrate the Feast of Tabernacles. ¹⁹This will be the punishment of Egypt and the punishment of all the nations that do not go up to celebrate the Feast of Tabernacles.

²⁰On that day HOLY TO THE LORD will be inscribed on the bells of the horses, and the cooking pots in the LORD's house will be like the sacred bowls in front of the altar. ²¹Every pot in Jerusalem and Judah will be holy to the LORD Almighty, and all who come to sacrifice will take some of the pots and cook in them. And on that day there will no longer be a Canaanite*ᵇ* in the house of the LORD Almighty.

ᵃ18 Or part, then the LORD   *ᵇ21* Or merchant

MALACHI

1 An oracle: The word of the LORD to Israel through Malachi. [a]

Jacob Loved, Esau Hated

²"I have loved you," says the LORD.

"But you ask, 'How have you loved us?'

"Was not Esau Jacob's brother?" the LORD says. "Yet I have loved Jacob, ³but Esau I have hated, and I have turned his mountains into a wasteland and left his inheritance to the desert jackals."

⁴Edom may say, "Though we have been crushed, we will rebuild the ruins."

But this is what the LORD Almighty says: "They may build, but I will demolish. They will be called the Wicked Land, a people always under the wrath of the LORD. ⁵You will see it with your own eyes and say, 'Great is the LORD—even beyond the borders of Israel!'

Blemished Sacrifices

⁶"A son honors his father, and a servant his master. If I am a father, where is the honor due me? If I am a master, where is the respect due me?" says the LORD Almighty. "It is you, O priests, who show contempt for my name.

"But you ask, 'How have we shown contempt for your name?'

⁷"You place defiled food on my altar.

"But you ask, 'How have we defiled you?'

"By saying that the LORD's table is contemptible. ⁸When you bring blind animals for sacrifice, is that not wrong? When you sacrifice crippled or diseased animals, is that not wrong? Try offering them to your governor! Would he be pleased with you? Would he accept you?" says the LORD Almighty.

⁹"Now implore God to be gracious to us. With such offerings from your hands, will he accept you?"—says the LORD Almighty.

¹⁰"Oh, that one of you would shut the temple doors, so that you would not light useless fires on my altar! I am not pleased with you," says the LORD Almighty, "and I will accept no offering from your hands. ¹¹My name will be great among the nations, from the rising to the setting of the sun. In every place incense and pure offerings will be brought to my name, because my name will be great among the nations," says the LORD Almighty.

¹²"But you profane it by saying of the Lord's table, 'It is defiled,' and of its food, 'It is contemptible.' ¹³And you say, 'What a burden!' and you sniff at it contemptuously," says the LORD Almighty.

"When you bring injured, crippled or diseased animals and offer them as sacrifices, should I accept them from your hands?" says the LORD. ¹⁴"Cursed is the cheat who has an acceptable male in his flock and vows to give it, but then sacrifices a blemished animal to the Lord. For I am a great king," says the LORD Almighty, "and my name is to be feared among the nations.

ᵃ 1 Malachi means my messenger.

Admonition for the Priests

2 "And now this admonition is for you, O priests. ²If you do not listen, and if you do not set your heart to honor my name," says the LORD Almighty, "I will send a curse upon you, and I will curse your blessings. Yes, I have already cursed them, because you have not set your heart to honor me.

³"Because of you I will rebuke[a] your descendants[b]; I will spread on your faces the offal from your festival sacrifices, and you will be carried off with it. ⁴And you will know that I have sent you this admonition so that my covenant with Levi may continue," says the LORD Almighty. ⁵"My covenant was with him, a covenant of life and peace, and I gave them to him; this called for reverence and he revered me and stood in awe of my name. ⁶True instruction was in his mouth and nothing false was found on his lips. He walked with me in peace and uprightness, and turned many from sin.

⁷"For the lips of a priest ought to preserve knowledge, and from his mouth men should seek instruction—because he is the messenger of the LORD Almighty. ⁸But you have turned from the way and by your teaching have caused many to stumble; you have violated the covenant with Levi," says the LORD Almighty. ⁹"So I have caused you to be despised and humiliated before all the people, because you have not followed my ways but have shown partiality in matters of the law."

Judah Unfaithful

¹⁰Have we not all one Father[c]? Did not one God create us? Why do we profane the covenant of our fathers by breaking faith with one another?

¹¹Judah has broken faith. A detestable thing has been committed in Israel and in Jerusalem: Judah has desecrated the sanctuary the LORD loves, by marrying the daughter of a foreign god. ¹²As for the man who does this, whoever he may be, may the LORD cut him off from the tents of Jacob[d]—even though he brings offerings to the LORD Almighty.

¹³Another thing you do: You flood the LORD's altar with tears. You weep and wail because he no longer pays attention to your offerings or accepts them with pleasure from your hands. ¹⁴You ask, "Why?" It is because the LORD is acting as the witness between you and the wife of your youth, because you have broken faith with her, though she is your partner, the wife of your marriage covenant.

¹⁵Has not ˌthe LORDˌ made them one? In flesh and spirit they are his. And why one? Because he was seeking godly offspring.[e] So guard yourself in your spirit, and do not break faith with the wife of your youth.

¹⁶"I hate divorce," says the LORD God of Israel, "and I hate a man's covering himself[f] with violence as well as with his garment," says the LORD Almighty.

So guard yourself in your spirit, and do not break faith.

▣ ▦STRENGTHENING RELATIONSHIPS▦ ↩

2:15–16
Marriage

Ever wonder what God thinks about divorce? Here it is in black and white!

Why is God so adamant about the permanence of the marriage relationship? For one thing, he doesn't want us to suffer the pain of separation that divorce produces in families. If two people are committed to their marriage, they will do whatever it takes to make their bad marriage good. Only when two people rule out divorce as an option will they work hard to make it last—and to be fulfilling.

Another reason why God hates divorce, mentioned in the New Testament, is because marriage mirrors our relationship with God (Ephesians chapter 5, verses 22–33 [page 1538]). Because God's commitment to us is permanent, the earthly counterpart of that commitment should also be permanent. God loves us for better or for worse. And those who pledge themselves to each other in marriage should do the same.

---

a 3 Or cut off (see Septuagint)   b 3 Or will blight your grain   c 10 Or father   d 12 Or ¹²May the LORD cut him off from the tents of Jacob anyone who gives testimony in behalf of the man who does this   e 15 Or ¹⁵But the one ˌwho is our father, did not do this, not as long as life remained in him. And what was he seeking? An offspring from God   f 16 Or his wife

The Day of Judgment

¹⁷You have wearied the LORD with your words.

"How have we wearied him?" you ask.

By saying, "All who do evil are good in the eyes of the LORD, and he is pleased with them" or "Where is the God of justice?"

3 "See, I will send my messenger, who will prepare the way before me. Then suddenly the Lord you are seeking will come to his temple; the messenger of the covenant, whom you desire, will come," says the LORD Almighty.

²But who can endure the day of his coming? Who can stand when he appears? For he will be like a refiner's fire or a launderer's soap. ³He will sit as a refiner and purifier of silver; he will purify the Levites and refine them like gold and silver. Then the LORD will have men who will bring offerings in righteousness, ⁴and the offerings of Judah and Jerusalem will be acceptable to the LORD, as in days gone by, as in former years.

⁵"So I will come near to you for judgment. I will be quick to testify against sorcerers, adulterers and perjurers, against those who defraud laborers of their wages, who oppress the widows and the fatherless, and deprive aliens of justice, but do not fear me," says the LORD Almighty.

REASONS TO BELIEVE

4:5-6
The Amazing Bible

According to this prophecy, Elijah is to come before the "day of the LORD." Even today Orthodox Jews set a place at the table for Elijah when they observe the Passover, because they think he still hasn't come.

Jesus claimed that this prediction was fulfilled through John the Baptist. Even though we read about him in the New Testament, John was the last of the Old Testament prophets. Why? Because his ministry came before the new covenant instituted when Christ came (for more information on this "new covenant," see Jeremiah chapter 31, verses 31-34 and note [page 1037]). According to Jesus, John the Baptist was the greatest of all the prophets—although Jesus went on to say that all of his followers are even greater than John because of the superiority of the new covenant over the old (Matthew chapter 11, verses 11-15 [page 1272]).

Robbing God

⁶"I the LORD do not change. So you, O descendants of Jacob, are not destroyed. ⁷Ever since the time of your forefathers you have turned away from my decrees and have not kept them. Return to me, and I will return to you," says the LORD Almighty.

"But you ask, 'How are we to return?'

⁸"Will a man rob God? Yet you rob me.

"But you ask, 'How do we rob you?'

"In tithes and offerings. ⁹You are under a curse—the whole nation of you—because you are robbing me. ¹⁰Bring the whole tithe into the storehouse, that there may be food in my house. Test me in this," says the LORD Almighty, "and see if I will not throw open the floodgates of heaven and pour out so much blessing that you will not have room enough for it. ¹¹I will prevent pests from devouring your crops, and the vines in your fields will not cast their fruit," says the LORD Almighty. ¹²"Then all the nations will call you blessed, for yours will be a delightful land," says the LORD Almighty.

¹³"You have said harsh things against me," says the LORD.

"Yet you ask, 'What have we said against you?'

¹⁴"You have said, 'It is futile to serve God. What did we gain by carrying out his requirements and going about like mourners before the LORD Almighty? ¹⁵But now we call the arrogant blessed. Certainly the evildoers prosper, and even those who challenge God escape.'"

¹⁶Then those who feared the LORD talked with each other, and the LORD listened and heard. A scroll of remembrance was written in his presence concerning those who feared the LORD and honored his name.

¹⁷"They will be mine," says the LORD Almighty, "in the day when I make up my trea-

sured possession. *a* I will spare them, just as in compassion a man spares his son who serves him. ¹⁸And you will again see the distinction between the righteous and the wicked, between those who serve God and those who do not.

The Day of the LORD

4 "Surely the day is coming; it will burn like a furnace. All the arrogant and every evildoer will be stubble, and that day that is coming will set them on fire,". says the LORD Almighty. "Not a root or a branch will be left to them. ²But for you who revere my name, the sun of righteousness will rise with healing in its wings. And you will go out and leap like calves released from the stall. ³Then you will trample down the wicked; they will be ashes under the soles of your feet on the day when I do these things," says the LORD Almighty.

⁴"Remember the law of my servant Moses, the decrees and laws I gave him at Horeb for all Israel.

⁵"See, I will send you the prophet Elijah before that great and dreadful day of the LORD comes. ⁶He will turn the hearts of the fathers to their children, and the hearts of the children to their fathers; or else I will come and strike the land with a curse."

a 17 Or Almighty, "my treasured possession, in the day when I act

NEW
Testament

MATTHEW

Introduction

THE BOTTOM LINE

This book begins the second part of the Bible. It is one of four different accounts of the life and teachings of Jesus called "the Gospels" (which means "good news"). Each gospel (Matthew, Mark, Luke, and John) contains similar teachings about Jesus, but each also has its own slant.

Matthew was a social outcast. Because he worked for the Roman government, he was wealthy but disliked. Yet one day he met Jesus, and his life was never the same (see chapter 9, verse 9 [page 1270]). This book shows that Jesus wants all people — even "successful losers" — to become his followers. Matthew points out the many connections between Jesus' teaching and the Old Testament. He shows us that Jesus is the fulfillment of all the promises made concerning the Jewish Messiah, the Savior of the world. This book serves as a great bridge between the two parts of the Bible, showing the same God at work but in a fresh way — he has come down to earth and become a man.

CENTRAL IDEAS

- Jesus is the one who fulfills all of God's promises to humanity—he's the Messiah, the Savior of the world.
- Jesus, who walked this earth, was God in the flesh.
- Jesus turned the wisdom of this world upside down (see chapter 5 [page 1262]).
- "Religiosity" is one of the biggest threats to a sincere relationship with God (see chapter 23 [page 1291]).

OUTLINE

1. Jesus' birth and early years (chs. 1—2)
2. Beginnings of Jesus' ministry (3:1—4:11)
3. Jesus' ministry in Galilee (4:12—14:12)
4. Jesus withdraws from Galilee (14:13—18:35)
5. Jesus' ministry in Judea and Perea (chs. 19—20)
6. Jesus' last week (chs. 21—27)
7. Jesus' resurrection from the dead and ascension into heaven (ch. 28)

TITLE

This book is titled after its author, a tax collector who became one of Jesus' disciples.

AUTHOR AND READERS

Matthew wrote this book to Jewish people who were looking for the fulfillment of God's promise to send them a king. He showed his readers how Jesus was a different kind of leader than they'd expected.

S tress. It's as American as baseball and apple pie. But it's a lot more fatal.

Every seven days more than 8,000 Americans die suddenly of heart attacks. Strangely, the highest number of these deaths occur on Mondays. Why Monday? Because that's the day most of us go back to work.

The thousands of people who succumb to fatal heart attacks are but a handful compared to the hordes of Americans who suffer daily discomfort, inconvenience or disability as the result of stress. Every year Americans consume 100 million prescriptions for tranquilizing drugs. Stress has become the most common cause of job dissatisfaction, reduced productivity in the workplace, family conflict and divorce.*

For many people, religion is just one more source of stress. "I feel bad if I don't attend a church," some may say, "but if I go, I often end up just feeling more guilty. On top of that, every time I think about the hereafter, I worry whether I've done enough. I don't want to go to hell, but how can I be sure I'm going to heaven?"

In contrast to what so many of us feel, Jesus promised rest, not stress. So why is our experience so different?

Every year Americans consume 100 million prescriptions for tranquilizing drugs.

Our spiritual stress takes root in the fertile soil of a fundamental misunderstanding about what God wants. If we picture God demanding more from us all the time, then we'll never reach a point where we can know he's satisfied. It's like being caught on a performance treadmill that has no "off" switch.

But what if God provided the very thing he wanted from us? What if, without changing his righteous demands, he somehow paid for all our spiritual shortcomings and foul-ups? And on top of that, what if God gave us his goodness so that we didn't have to worry about coming up with our own?

Jesus, the promised King of Israel and Savior of the world, claimed to do just that. Turn to Matthew chapter 11, verse 28 (page 1273), where you'll begin to find out more about his invitation to give you rest.

*Richard E. Ecker, *The Stress Myth* (Downers Grove, Ill.: InterVarsity Press, [1985]), pp. 9–10). Used by Permission.

TIME LINE

World's population estimated at about 250 million (7 B.C.)	Jesus, Mary and Joseph flee to Egypt (c. 5/4 B.C.)	Matthew becomes a disciple (c. A.D. 26)	Rome, under Nero, is partially destroyed by fire (A.D. 64)

| 20 | 10 B.C. | A.D. 1 | 10 | 20 | 30 | 40 | 50 | 60 | 70 | 80 | 90 |

Jesus is born (6/5 B.C.)	Beginning of Jesus' ministry (c. A.D. 26)	Jesus' death, resurrection, and ascension (c. A.D. 30)	Book of Matthew written (c. A.D. 70–80)

The Genealogy of Jesus

1 A record of the genealogy of Jesus Christ the son of David, the son of Abraham:

²Abraham was the father of Isaac,
  Isaac the father of Jacob,
  Jacob the father of Judah and his brothers,

³Judah the father of Perez and Zerah,
  whose mother was Tamar,
  Perez the father of Hezron,
  Hezron the father of Ram,
⁴Ram the father of Amminadab,
  Amminadab the father of Nahshon,
  Nahshon the father of Salmon,
⁵Salmon the father of Boaz, whose
  mother was Rahab,
  Boaz the father of Obed, whose
  mother was Ruth,
  Obed the father of Jesse,
⁶and Jesse the father of King David.

David was the father of Solomon, whose
  mother had been Uriah's wife,
⁷Solomon the father of Rehoboam,
  Rehoboam the father of Abijah,
  Abijah the father of Asa,
⁸Asa the father of Jehoshaphat,
  Jehoshaphat the father of Jehoram,
  Jehoram the father of Uzziah,
⁹Uzziah the father of Jotham,

◻ ▦▦▦▦▦ DISCOVERING GOD ▦▦▦▦▦ ↕

1:1–16
Jesus, the God-Man

To modern readers, this listing of names may not seem like the most scintillating way to start a book. But this genealogy emphasizes an important fact: Jesus walked this earth as a real person. He had ancestors who were Jewish and some (such as Tamar, Rahab, and Ruth) who were actually non-Jewish "seekers" at one time.

Jesus was a full member of the human race. He was also the Son of God, and lived a perfect life. In that sense he was *unlike* any other human—you'll find out more about that as you keep reading.

In spite of Matthew's somewhat "slow" start in these first few verses, the reality of Jesus' divinity and humanity makes for very interesting reading in the rest of this book!

Jotham the father of Ahaz,
  Ahaz the father of Hezekiah,
¹⁰Hezekiah the father of Manasseh,
  Manasseh the father of Amon,
  Amon the father of Josiah,
¹¹and Josiah the father of Jeconiah*a* and his brothers at the time of the exile to Babylon.

¹²After the exile to Babylon:
  Jeconiah was the father of Shealtiel,
  Shealtiel the father of Zerubbabel,
¹³Zerubbabel the father of Abiud,
  Abiud the father of Eliakim,
  Eliakim the father of Azor,
¹⁴Azor the father of Zadok,

a 11 That is, Jehoiachin; also in verse 12

Zadok the father of Akim,
Akim the father of Eliud,
¹⁵Eliud the father of Eleazar,
Eleazar the father of Matthan,
Matthan the father of Jacob,
¹⁶and Jacob the father of Joseph, the husband of Mary, of whom was born Jesus, who is called Christ.

¹⁷Thus there were fourteen generations in all from Abraham to David, fourteen from David to the exile to Babylon, and fourteen from the exile to the Christ.ᵃ

The Birth of Jesus Christ

¹⁸This is how the birth of Jesus Christ came about: His mother Mary was pledged to be married to Joseph, but before they came together, she was found to be with child through the Holy Spirit. ¹⁹Because Joseph her husband was a righteous man and did not want to expose her to public disgrace, he had in mind to divorce her quietly.

²⁰But after he had considered this, an angel of the Lord appeared to him in a dream and said, "Joseph son of David, do not be afraid to take Mary home as your wife, because what is conceived in her is from the Holy Spirit. ²¹She will give birth to a son, and you are to give him the name Jesus,ᵇ because he will save his people from their sins."

²²All this took place to fulfill what the Lord had said through the prophet: ²³"The virgin will be with child and will give birth to a son, and they will call him Immanuel"ᶜ— which means, "God with us."

²⁴When Joseph woke up, he did what the angel of the Lord had commanded him and took Mary home as his wife. ²⁵But he had no union with her until she gave birth to a son. And he gave him the name Jesus.

The Visit of the Magi

2 After Jesus was born in Bethlehem in Judea, during the time of King Herod, Magiᵈ from the east came to Jerusalem ²and asked, "Where is the one who has been born king of the Jews? We saw his star in the eastᵉ and have come to worship him."

³When King Herod heard this he was disturbed, and all Jerusalem with him. ⁴When he had called together all the people's chief priests and teachers of the law, he asked them where the Christᶠ was to be born. ⁵"In Bethlehem in Judea," they replied, "for this is what the prophet has written:

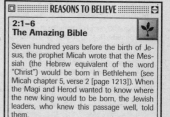

▣ ▒▒▒▒▒▒▒ **REASONS TO BELIEVE** ▒▒▒▒▒▒▒ ↻

2:1–6
The Amazing Bible

Seven hundred years before the birth of Jesus, the prophet Micah wrote that the Messiah (the Hebrew equivalent of the word "Christ") would be born in Bethlehem (see Micah chapter 5, verse 2 [page 1213]). When the Magi and Herod wanted to know where the new king would to be born, the Jewish leaders, who knew this passage well, told them.

Detailed predictions such as these show that the Bible is unlike any other religious book in the world. Jesus is the only founder of a major world religion whose birthplace was prophesied hundreds of years in advance of his birth.

Such unique evidence spurs "wise" men and women to seek him still!

⁶"'But you, Bethlehem, in the land of Judah,
are by no means least among the rulers of Judah;
for out of you will come a ruler
who will be the shepherd of my people Israel.'ᵍ"

⁷Then Herod called the Magi secretly and found out from them the exact time the star

---

ᵃ17 Or Messiah. "The Christ" (Greek) and "the Messiah" (Hebrew) both mean "the Anointed One."   ᵇ21 Jesus is the Greek form of Joshua, which means the LORD saves.   ᶜ23 Isaiah 7:14   ᵈ1 Traditionally Wise Men   ᵉ2 Or star when it rose   ᶠ4 Or Messiah   ᵍ6 Micah 5:2

had appeared. 8He sent them to Bethlehem and said, "Go and make a careful search for the child. As soon as you find him, report to me, so that I too may go and worship him."

9After they had heard the king, they went on their way, and the star they had seen in the east[a] went ahead of them until it stopped over the place where the child was. 10When they saw the star, they were overjoyed. 11On coming to the house, they saw the child with his mother Mary, and they bowed down and worshiped him. Then they opened their treasures and presented him with gifts of gold and of incense and of myrrh. 12And having been warned in a dream not to go back to Herod, they returned to their country by another route.

The Escape to Egypt

13When they had gone, an angel of the Lord appeared to Joseph in a dream. "Get up," he said, "take the child and his mother and escape to Egypt. Stay there until I tell you, for Herod is going to search for the child to kill him."

14So he got up, took the child and his mother during the night and left for Egypt, 15where he stayed until the death of Herod. And so was fulfilled what the Lord had said through the prophet: "Out of Egypt I called my son."[b]

16When Herod realized that he had been outwitted by the Magi, he was furious, and he gave orders to kill all the boys in Bethlehem and its vicinity who were two years old and under, in accordance with the time he had learned from the Magi. 17Then what was said through the prophet Jeremiah was fulfilled:

18"A voice is heard in Ramah,
    weeping and great mourning,
  Rachel weeping for her children
    and refusing to be comforted,
  because they are no more."[c]

The Return to Nazareth

19After Herod died, an angel of the Lord appeared in a dream to Joseph in Egypt 20and said, "Get up, take the child and his mother and go to the land of Israel, for those who were trying to take the child's life are dead."

21So he got up, took the child and his mother and went to the land of Israel. 22But when he heard that Archelaus was reigning in Judea in place of his father Herod, he was afraid to go there. Having been warned in a dream, he withdrew to the district of Galilee, 23and he went and lived in a town called Nazareth. So was fulfilled what was said through the prophets: "He will be called a Nazarene."

John the Baptist Prepares the Way

3 In those days John the Baptist came, preaching in the Desert of Judea 2and saying, "Repent, for the kingdom of heaven is near." 3This is he who was spoken of through the prophet Isaiah:

---

a9 Or seen when it rose   b15 Hosea 11:1   c18 Jer. 31:15

"A voice of one calling in the desert,
'Prepare the way for the Lord,
make straight paths for him.' " *a*

⁴John's clothes were made of camel's hair, and he had a leather belt around his waist. His food was locusts and wild honey. ⁵People went out to him from Jerusalem and all Judea and the whole region of the Jordan. ⁶Confessing their sins, they were baptized by him in the Jordan River.

⁷But when he saw many of the Pharisees and Sadducees coming to where he was baptizing, he said to them: "You brood of vipers! Who warned you to flee from the coming wrath? ⁸Produce fruit in keeping with repentance. ⁹And do not think you can say to yourselves, 'We have Abraham as our father.' I tell you that out of these stones God can raise up children for Abraham. ¹⁰The ax is already at the root of the trees, and every tree that does not produce good fruit will be cut down and thrown into the fire.

¹¹"I baptize you with *b* water for repentance. But after me will come one who is more powerful than I, whose sandals I am not fit to carry. He will baptize you with the Holy Spirit and with fire. ¹²His winnowing fork is in his hand, and he will clear his threshing floor, gathering his wheat into the barn and burning up the chaff with unquenchable fire."

The Baptism of Jesus

¹³Then Jesus came from Galilee to the Jordan to be baptized by John. ¹⁴But John tried to deter him, saying, "I need to be baptized by you, and do you come to me?"

¹⁵Jesus replied, "Let it be so now; it is proper for us to do this to fulfill all righteousness." Then John consented.

¹⁶As soon as Jesus was baptized, he went up out of the water. At that moment heaven was opened, and he saw the Spirit of God descending like a dove and lighting on him. ¹⁷And a voice from heaven said, "This is my Son, whom I love; with him I am well pleased."

The Temptation of Jesus

4 Then Jesus was led by the Spirit into the desert to be tempted by the devil. ²After fasting forty days and forty nights, he was hungry. ³The tempter came to him and said, "If you are the Son of God, tell these stones to become bread."

⁴Jesus answered, "It is written: 'Man does not live on bread alone, but on every word that comes from the mouth of God.' *c*"

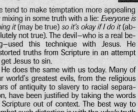

□ ▓▓▓ ADDRESSING QUESTIONS ▓▓▓ ⏎

4:1–11
Unseen Realities   **Q**

We tend to make temptation more appealing by mixing in some truth with a lie: *Everyone is doing it* (may be true) *so it's okay if I do it* (absolutely not true). The devil—who is a real being—used this technique with Jesus. He distorted truths from Scripture in an attempt to get Jesus to sin.

He does the same with us today. Many of our world's greatest evils, from the religious wars of antiquity to slavery to racial separation, have been justified by taking the words of Scripture out of context. The best way to combat such distortion is with the *whole* truth of the Bible. Jesus did that in this instance by quoting from other passages of the Bible to expose the devil's lies in the light of God's truth.

⁵Then the devil took him to the holy city and had him stand on the highest point of the temple. ⁶"If you are the Son of God," he said, "throw yourself down. For it is written:

" 'He will command his angels concerning you,
and they will lift you up in their hands,
so that you will not strike your foot against a stone.' *d*"

⁷Jesus answered him, "It is also written: 'Do not put the Lord your God to the test.' *e*"

a3 Isaiah 40:3   *b11* Or *in*   *c4* Deut. 8:3   *d6* Psalm 91:11,12   *e7* Deut. 6:16

⁸Again, the devil took him to a very high mountain and showed him all the kingdoms of the world and their splendor. ⁹"All this I will give you," he said, "if you will bow down and worship me."

¹⁰Jesus said to him, "Away from me, Satan! For it is written: 'Worship the Lord your God, and serve him only.'ᵃ"

¹¹Then the devil left him, and angels came and attended him.

Jesus Begins to Preach

¹²When Jesus heard that John had been put in prison, he returned to Galilee. ¹³Leaving Nazareth, he went and lived in Capernaum, which was by the lake in the area of Zebulun and Naphtali— ¹⁴to fulfill what was said through the prophet Isaiah:

> ¹⁵"Land of Zebulun and land of Naphtali,
>   the way to the sea, along the Jordan,
>   Galilee of the Gentiles—
> ¹⁶the people living in darkness
>   have seen a great light;
> on those living in the land of the shadow of death
>   a light has dawned."ᵇ

¹⁷From that time on Jesus began to preach, "Repent, for the kingdom of heaven is near."

The Calling of the First Disciples

¹⁸As Jesus was walking beside the Sea of Galilee, he saw two brothers, Simon called Peter and his brother Andrew. They were casting a net into the lake, for they were fishermen. ¹⁹"Come, follow me," Jesus said, "and I will make you fishers of men." ²⁰At once they left their nets and followed him.

²¹Going on from there, he saw two other brothers, James son of Zebedee and his brother John. They were in a boat with their father Zebedee, preparing their nets. Jesus called them, ²²and immediately they left the boat and their father and followed him.

Jesus Heals the Sick

²³Jesus went throughout Galilee, teaching in their synagogues, preaching the good news of the kingdom, and healing every disease and sickness among the people. ²⁴News about him spread all over Syria, and people brought to him all who were ill with various diseases, those suffering severe pain, the demon-possessed, those having seizures, and the paralyzed, and he healed them. ²⁵Large crowds from Galilee, the Decapolis,ᶜ Jerusalem, Judea and the region across the Jordan followed him.

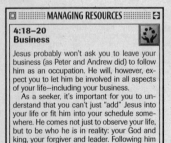

MANAGING RESOURCES

**4:18–20
Business**

Jesus probably won't ask you to leave your business (as Peter and Andrew did) to follow him as an occupation. He will, however, expect you to let him be involved in all aspects of your life—including your business.

As a seeker, it's important for you to understand that you can't just "add" Jesus into your life or fit him into your schedule somewhere. He comes not just to observe your life, but to be who he is in reality: your God and king, your forgiver and leader. Following him involves complete life commitment.

The Beatitudes

5 Now when he saw the crowds, he went up on a mountainside and sat down. His disciples came to him, ²and he began to teach them, saying:

ᵃ10 Deut. 6:13   ᵇ16 Isaiah 9:1,2   ᶜ25 That is, the Ten Cities

³"Blessed are the poor in spirit,
  for theirs is the kingdom of heaven.
⁴Blessed are those who mourn,
  for they will be comforted.
⁵Blessed are the meek,
  for they will inherit the earth.
⁶Blessed are those who hunger and thirst for righteousness,
  for they will be filled.
⁷Blessed are the merciful,
  for they will be shown mercy.
⁸Blessed are the pure in heart,
  for they will see God.
⁹Blessed are the peacemakers,
  for they will be called sons of
    God.
¹⁰Blessed are those who are
    persecuted because of
    righteousness,
  for theirs is the kingdom of
    heaven.

¹¹"Blessed are you when people insult you, persecute you and falsely say all kinds of evil against you because of me. ¹²Rejoice and be glad, because great is your reward in heaven, for in the same way they persecuted the prophets who were before you.

Salt and Light

¹³"You are the salt of the earth. But if the salt loses its saltiness, how can it be made salty again? It is no longer good for anything, except to be thrown out and trampled by men.

¹⁴"You are the light of the world. A city on a hill cannot be hidden. ¹⁵Neither do people light a lamp and put it under a bowl. Instead they put it on its stand, and it gives light to everyone in the house. ¹⁶In the same way, let your light shine before men, that they may see your good deeds and praise your Father in heaven.

▣ ∷∷∷∷∷∷ **KNOWING YOURSELF** ∷∷∷∷∷∷ ↔

Chapters 5–7
A New Identity

These chapters contain the most famous of Jesus' words, the "Sermon on the Mount" (so called because Jesus delivered it from a mountainside). It spells out the epitome of righteous behavior and outlines human life as God intended it.

As you read through these chapters, however, you'll discover how far short of this ideal we all fall. No person other than Jesus has ever lived it out perfectly. We've rejected this "divine manifesto," and have experienced painful and destructive consequences as a result.

So what are we supposed to do—try harder? Is that why Jesus came—to tell us to "bear down and do the best we can"?

Not even close. Since he knew that we could never attain God's standard for our lives, Jesus went beyond giving us a command we could never live up to. He gave us *himself,* literally sacrificing his life on the cross so that we could find forgiveness.

As you read these wonderful but convicting phrases in Jesus' most famous sermon, take heart. However distant you are from fulfilling them, you are not far from the One who fulfilled them perfectly—Jesus himself. And he has come, not just to show you how to live, but *to give you life!*

The Fulfillment of the Law

¹⁷"Do not think that I have come to abolish the Law or the Prophets; I have not come to abolish them but to fulfill them. ¹⁸I tell you the truth, until heaven and earth disappear, not the smallest letter, not the least stroke of a pen, will by any means disappear from the Law until everything is accomplished. ¹⁹Anyone who breaks one of the least of these commandments and teaches others to do the same will be called least in the kingdom of heaven, but whoever practices and teaches these commands will be called great in the kingdom of heaven. ²⁰For I tell you that unless your righteousness surpasses that of the

Pharisees and the teachers of the law, you will certainly not enter the kingdom of heaven.

Murder

21"You have heard that it was said to the people long ago, 'Do not murder,*a* and anyone who murders will be subject to judgment.' **22**But I tell you that anyone who is angry with his brother*b* will be subject to judgment. Again, anyone who says to his brother, 'Raca,*c*' is answerable to the Sanhedrin. But anyone who says, 'You fool!' will be in danger of the fire of hell.

23"Therefore, if you are offering your gift at the altar and there remember that your brother has something against you, **24**leave your gift there in front of the altar. First go and be reconciled to your brother; then come and offer your gift.

25"Settle matters quickly with your adversary who is taking you to court. Do it while you are still with him on the way, or he may hand you over to the judge, and the judge may hand you over to the officer, and you may be thrown into prison. **26**I tell you the truth, you will not get out until you have paid the last penny.*d*

Adultery

27"You have heard that it was said, 'Do not commit adultery.'*e* **28**But I tell you that anyone who looks at a woman lustfully has already committed adultery with her in his heart. **29**If your right eye causes you to sin, gouge it out and throw it away. It is better for you to lose one part of your body than for your whole body to be thrown into hell. **30**And if your right hand causes you to sin, cut it off and throw it away. It is better for you to lose one part of your body than for your whole body to go into hell.

Divorce

31"It has been said, 'Anyone who divorces his wife must give her a certificate of divorce.'*f* **32**But I tell you that anyone who divorces his wife, except for marital unfaithfulness, causes her to become an adulteress, and anyone who marries the divorced woman commits adultery.

Oaths

33"Again, you have heard that it was said to the people long ago, 'Do not break your oath, but keep the oaths you have made to the Lord.' **34**But I tell you, Do not swear at all: either by heaven, for it is God's throne; **35**or by the earth, for it is his footstool; or by Jerusalem, for it is the city of the Great King. **36**And do not swear by your head, for you cannot make even one hair white or black. **37**Simply let your 'Yes' be 'Yes,' and your 'No,' 'No'; anything beyond this comes from the evil one.

An Eye for an Eye

38"You have heard that it was said, 'Eye for eye, and tooth for tooth.'*g* **39**But I tell you, Do not resist an evil person. If someone strikes you on the right cheek, turn to him the other also. **40**And if someone wants to sue you and take your tunic, let him have your cloak as well. **41**If someone forces you to go one mile, go with him two miles. **42**Give to the one who asks you, and do not turn away from the one who wants to borrow from you.

Love for Enemies

43"You have heard that it was said, 'Love your neighbor*h* and hate your enemy.' **44**But I tell you: Love your enemies*i* and pray for those who persecute you, **45**that you may be

a21 Exodus 20:13   *b22* Some manuscripts *brother without cause*   *c22* An Aramaic term of contempt   *d26* Greek *kodrantes*   *e27* Exodus 20:14   *f31* Deut. 24:1   *g38* Exodus 21:24; Lev. 24:20; Deut. 19:21   *h43* Lev. 19:18   *i44* Some late manuscripts *enemies, bless those who curse you, do good to those who hate you*

sons of your Father in heaven. He causes his sun to rise on the evil and the good, and sends rain on the righteous and the unrighteous. ⁴⁶If you love those who love you, what reward will you get? Are not even the tax collectors doing that? ⁴⁷And if you greet only your brothers, what are you doing more than others? Do not even pagans do that? ⁴⁸Be perfect, therefore, as your heavenly Father is perfect.

Giving to the Needy

6 "Be careful not to do your 'acts of righteousness' before men, to be seen by them. If you do, you will have no reward from your Father in heaven.

²"So when you give to the needy, do not announce it with trumpets, as the hypocrites do in the synagogues and on the streets, to be honored by men. I tell you the truth, they have received their reward in full. ³But when you give to the needy, do not let your left hand know what your right hand is doing, ⁴so that your giving may be in secret. Then your Father, who sees what is done in secret, will reward you.

Prayer

⁵"And when you pray, do not be like the hypocrites, for they love to pray standing in the synagogues and on the street corners to be seen by men. I tell you the truth, they have received their reward in full. ⁶But when you pray, go into your room, close the door and pray to your Father, who is unseen. Then your Father, who sees what is done in secret, will reward you. ⁷And when you pray, do not keep on babbling like pagans, for they think they will be heard because of their many words. ⁸Do not be like them, for your Father knows what you need before you ask him.

⁹"This, then, is how you should pray:

📖 ::::::::::::::::::::::::::::::::: **ADDRESSING QUESTIONS** ::::::::::::::::::::::::::::::::: ↩

6:5–15
Human Experience **Q**

Have you ever wondered how to pray? Most of us have. The "Lord's Prayer," as this prayer is often called, wasn't originally intended as a prayer to be recited over and over (see verse 7). Instead, it shows us how to talk to our heavenly Father. Let's take a look at Jesus' instruction about prayer.

Prayer begins by setting the right framework. When we engage in conversation with God, we need to remember who we're talking to—the Creator of the universe who cares for each one of us deeply. In that sense, we need to recognize that God should be set apart and revered ("hallowed be your name").

Next we need to recognize that God wants to be intimately involved in each part of our lives. Even though we may sometimes feel that our needs are insignificant, especially in view of all the suffering in the world, God is certainly big enough to run the universe and care for each one of us at the same time. That's why we pray that his plans will be worked out in our lives ("your will be done"), which includes the request that he enable us to yield to his will in our lives and follow his commands. That's also why we bring before God even the most mundane matters of everyday living ("give us today our daily bread").

Next we need to look at the sin in our lives. Because sin creates a barrier between us and God and between us and others, God wants us to admit our wrongdoing ("forgive us our debts") and to forgive those who have wronged us ("as we also have forgiven our debtors"). Verses 14 and 15 underscore the importance of this aspect of prayer.

Finally, God wants us to live free from the painful consequences of sinful choices. We pray "lead us not into temptation" not because God tempts people to sin, but because we need his help to manage the effects of temptation. Someone once prayed, "God, protect me from the opportunity to sin when I have the inclination, and from the inclination when I have the opportunity!" That is very much in keeping with Jesus' pattern here.

Like a loving father, God cares about us and will listen to what we have to say. As our *heavenly* Father, he occupies a place of great power, which means that he is able to answer our prayers.

" 'Our Father in heaven,
hallowed be your name,
¹⁰your kingdom come,
your will be done
on earth as it is in heaven.
¹¹Give us today our daily bread.
¹²Forgive us our debts,
as we also have forgiven our debtors.
¹³And lead us not into temptation,
but deliver us from the evil one.ᵃ'

¹⁴For if you forgive men when they sin against you, your heavenly Father will also forgive you. ¹⁵But if you do not forgive men their sins, your Father will not forgive your sins.

Fasting

¹⁶"When you fast, do not look somber as the hypocrites do, for they disfigure their faces to show men they are fasting. I tell you the truth, they have received their reward in full. ¹⁷But when you fast, put oil on your head and wash your face, ¹⁸so that it will not be obvious to men that you are fasting, but only to your Father, who is unseen; and your Father, who sees what is done in secret, will reward you.

Treasures in Heaven

¹⁹"Do not store up for yourselves treasures on earth, where moth and rust destroy, and where thieves break in and steal. ²⁰But store up for yourselves treasures in heaven, where moth and rust do not destroy, and where thieves do not break in and steal. ²¹For where your treasure is, there your heart will be also.

²²"The eye is the lamp of the body. If your eyes are good, your whole body will be full of light. ²³But if your eyes are bad, your whole body will be full of darkness. If then the light within you is darkness, how great is that darkness!

²⁴"No one can serve two masters. Either he will hate the one and love the other, or he will be devoted to the one and despise the other. You cannot serve both God and Money.

Do Not Worry

²⁵"Therefore I tell you, do not worry about your life, what you will eat or drink; or about your body, what you will wear. Is not life more important than food, and the body more important than clothes? ²⁶Look at the birds of the air; they do not sow or reap or store away in barns, and yet your heavenly Father feeds them. Are you not much more valuable than they? ²⁷Who of you by worrying can add a single hour to his lifeᵇ?

²⁸"And why do you worry about clothes? See how the lilies of the field grow. They do not labor or spin. ²⁹Yet I tell you that not even Solomon in all his splendor was dressed like one of these. ³⁰If that is how God clothes the grass of the field, which is here today and tomorrow is thrown into the fire, will he not much more clothe you, O you of little faith? ³¹So do not worry, saying, 'What shall we eat?' or 'What shall we drink?' or 'What shall we wear?' ³²For the pagans run after all these things, and your heavenly Father knows that you need them. ³³But seek first his kingdom and his righteousness, and all these things will be given to you as well. ³⁴Therefore do not worry about tomorrow, for tomorrow will worry about itself. Each day has enough trouble of its own.

ᵃ13 Or from evil; some late manuscripts one, / for yours is the kingdom and the power and the glory forever. Amen.
ᵇ27 Or single cubit to his height

Judging Others

7 "Do not judge, or you too will be judged. ²For in the same way you judge others, you will be judged, and with the measure you use, it will be measured to you.

³"Why do you look at the speck of sawdust in your brother's eye and pay no attention to the plank in your own eye? ⁴How can you say to your brother, 'Let me take the speck out of your eye,' when all the time there is a plank in your own eye? ⁵You hypocrite, first take the plank out of your own eye, and then you will see clearly to remove the speck from your brother's eye.

⁶"Do not give dogs what is sacred; do not throw your pearls to pigs. If you do, they may trample them under their feet, and then turn and tear you to pieces.

Ask, Seek, Knock

⁷"Ask and it will be given to you; seek and you will find; knock and the door will be opened to you. ⁸For everyone who asks receives; he who seeks finds; and to him who knocks, the door will be opened.

⁹"Which of you, if his son asks for bread, will give him a stone? ¹⁰Or if he asks for a fish, will give him a snake? ¹¹If you, then, though you are evil, know how to give good gifts to your children, how much more will your Father in heaven give good gifts to those who ask him! ¹²So in everything, do to others what you would have them do to you, for this sums up the Law and the Prophets.

The Narrow and Wide Gates

¹³"Enter through the narrow gate. For wide is the gate and broad is the road that leads to destruction, and many enter through it. ¹⁴But small is the gate and narrow the road that leads to life, and only a few find it.

▨▨▨▨ DISCOVERING GOD ▨▨▨▨

6:25–34
Life with God

A man said to his friend, an incessant worrier, "I'll bet 90 percent of what you worry about never happens."

"You're right," the friend replied. "See how much it helps?"

In order to aid his followers in combating anxiety, Jesus explained six reasons why worrying is useless.

First, *worry ignores the logic of life* (verse 28). If God has given you life, the greater gift, doesn't it make sense that he'll give you adequate food and clothing, the lesser gift?

Second, *worry ignores the value of life* (verse 26). You are of far greater worth to God than birds, yet God takes care of them. How much more, then, will he watch over the affairs of your life?

Third, *worry ignores its own limitations* (verse 27). Do you think that if you sit and worry about something for several hours, you'll change the outcome? Of course not. Since worry can't change anything, why worry?

Fourth, *worry ignores God's faithfulness* (verses 28–30). The same God who faithfully clothes the flowers of the field is responsible for taking care of you.

Fifth, *worry ignores God's love* (verses 31–33). Those who know God have entered into a family relationship with him. God doesn't treat his children like orphans who must take care of themselves.

Finally, *worry ignores the present* (verse 34). When we worry about tomorrow we're missing out on today. Yes, some difficult situations may arise, but any problem can be managed if it is handled with God's help, one day at a time.

A Tree and Its Fruit

¹⁵"Watch out for false prophets. They come to you in sheep's clothing, but inwardly they are ferocious wolves. ¹⁶By their fruit you will recognize them. Do people pick grapes from thornbushes, or figs from thistles? ¹⁷Likewise every good tree bears good fruit, but a bad tree bears bad fruit. ¹⁸A good tree cannot bear bad fruit, and a bad tree cannot bear good fruit. ¹⁹Every tree that does not bear good fruit is cut down and thrown into the fire. ²⁰Thus, by their fruit you will recognize them.

²¹"Not everyone who says to me, 'Lord, Lord,' will enter the kingdom of heaven, but only he who does the will of my Father who is in heaven. ²²Many will say to me on that day, 'Lord, Lord, did we not prophesy in your name, and in your name drive out demons and perform many miracles?' ²³Then I will tell them plainly, 'I never knew you. Away from me, you evildoers!'

The Wise and Foolish Builders

²⁴"Therefore everyone who hears these words of mine and puts them into practice is like a wise man who built his house on the rock. ²⁵The rain came down, the streams rose, and the winds blew and beat against that house; yet it did not fall, because it had its foundation on the rock. ²⁶But everyone who hears these words of mine and does not put them into practice is like a foolish man who built his house on sand. ²⁷The rain came down, the streams rose, and the winds blew and beat against that house, and it fell with a great crash."

²⁸When Jesus had finished saying these things, the crowds were amazed at his teaching, ²⁹because he taught as one who had authority, and not as their teachers of the law.

The Man With Leprosy

8 When he came down from the mountainside, large crowds followed him. ²A man with leprosy[a] came and knelt before him and said, "Lord, if you are willing, you can make me clean."

³Jesus reached out his hand and touched the man. "I am willing," he said. "Be clean!" Immediately he was cured[b] of his leprosy. ⁴Then Jesus said to him, "See that you don't tell anyone. But go, show yourself to the priest and offer the gift Moses commanded, as a testimony to them."

The Faith of the Centurion

⁵When Jesus had entered Capernaum, a centurion came to him, asking for help. ⁶"Lord," he said, "my servant lies at home paralyzed and in terrible suffering."

⁷Jesus said to him, "I will go and heal him."

⁸The centurion replied, "Lord, I do not deserve to have you come under my roof. But just say the word, and my servant will be healed. ⁹For I myself am a man under authority, with soldiers under me. I tell this one, 'Go,' and he goes; and that one, 'Come,' and he comes. I say to my servant, 'Do this,' and he does it."

¹⁰When Jesus heard this, he was astonished and said to those following him, "I tell you the truth, I have not found anyone in Israel with such great faith. ¹¹I say to you that many will come from the east and the west, and will take their places at the feast with Abraham, Isaac and Jacob in the kingdom of heaven. ¹²But the subjects of the kingdom will be thrown outside, into the darkness, where there will be weeping and gnashing of teeth."

¹³Then Jesus said to the centurion, "Go! It will be done just as you believed it would." And his servant was healed at that very hour.

---

a 2 The Greek word was used for various diseases affecting the skin—not necessarily leprosy.   *b 3* Greek *made clean*

Jesus Heals Many

¹⁴When Jesus came into Peter's house, he saw Peter's mother-in-law lying in bed with a fever. ¹⁵He touched her hand and the fever left her, and she got up and began to wait on him.

¹⁶When evening came, many who were demon-possessed were brought to him, and he drove out the spirits with a word and healed all the sick. ¹⁷This was to fulfill what was spoken through the prophet Isaiah:

> "He took up our infirmities
> and carried our diseases."[a]

The Cost of Following Jesus

¹⁸When Jesus saw the crowd around him, he gave orders to cross to the other side of the lake. ¹⁹Then a teacher of the law came to him and said, "Teacher, I will follow you wherever you go."

²⁰Jesus replied, "Foxes have holes and birds of the air have nests, but the Son of Man has no place to lay his head."

²¹Another disciple said to him, "Lord, first let me go and bury my father."

²²But Jesus told him, "Follow me, and let the dead bury their own dead."

Jesus Calms the Storm

²³Then he got into the boat and his disciples followed him. ²⁴Without warning, a furious storm came up on the lake, so that the waves swept over the boat. But Jesus was sleeping. ²⁵The disciples went and woke him, saying, "Lord, save us! We're going to drown!"

²⁶He replied, "You of little faith, why are you so afraid?" Then he got up and rebuked the winds and the waves, and it was completely calm.

²⁷The men were amazed and asked, "What kind of man is this? Even the winds and the waves obey him!"

The Healing of Two Demon-possessed Men

²⁸When he arrived at the other side in the region of the Gadarenes,[b] two demon-possessed men coming from the tombs met him. They were so violent that no one could pass that way. ²⁹"What do you want with us, Son of God?" they shouted. "Have you come here to torture us before the appointed time?"

³⁰Some distance from them a large herd of pigs was feeding. ³¹The demons begged Jesus, "If you drive us out, send us into the herd of pigs."

³²He said to them, "Go!" So they came out and went into the pigs, and the whole herd rushed down the steep bank into the lake and died in the water. ³³Those tending the pigs ran off, went into the town and reported all this, including what had happened to the demon-possessed men. ³⁴Then the whole town went out to meet Jesus. And when they saw him, they pleaded with him to leave their region.

Jesus Heals a Paralytic

9 Jesus stepped into a boat, crossed over and came to his own town. ²Some men brought to him a paralytic, lying on a mat. When Jesus saw their faith, he said to the paralytic, "Take heart, son; your sins are forgiven."

³At this, some of the teachers of the law said to themselves, "This fellow is blaspheming!"

⁴Knowing their thoughts, Jesus said, "Why do you entertain evil thoughts in your hearts? ⁵Which is easier: to say, 'Your sins are forgiven,' or to say, 'Get up and walk'? ⁶But so that you may know that the Son of Man has authority on earth to forgive sins . . ."

---

a 17 Isaiah 53:4   *b 28* Some manuscripts *Gergesenes*; others *Gerasenes*

Then he said to the paralytic, "Get up, take your mat and go home." ⁷And the man got up and went home. ⁸When the crowd saw this, they were filled with awe; and they praised God, who had given such authority to men.

The Calling of Matthew

⁹As Jesus went on from there, he saw a man named Matthew sitting at the tax collector's booth. "Follow me," he told him, and Matthew got up and followed him.

¹⁰While Jesus was having dinner at Matthew's house, many tax collectors and "sinners" came and ate with him and his disciples. ¹¹When the Pharisees saw this, they asked his disciples, "Why does your teacher eat with tax collectors and 'sinners'?"

◨ ▦▦▦▦ DISCOVERING GOD ▦▦▦▦ ⬗

9:9–13
Jesus, the God-Man

Have you ever felt unworthy to follow Jesus? If so, you're not alone. Yet Jesus never refused anyone because of his or her past. Matthew provides an excellent example of that fact. As a tax collector, he was part of a despised profession. He fleeced his own countrymen and then turned around and lied to the Roman government.

When Jesus said to Matthew, "Follow me," he reached out to someone who was considered bad company by virtually everyone in town. Why did he do it? Because, like a good doctor, Jesus came to help the sick, not the healthy. After meeting Jesus, Matthew's life was never the same again. He became a dedicated disciple, and wrote the account of Jesus' life that you're looking at now.

If you're at all like Matthew, this is good news! Jesus specializes in finding seekers— even the ones who don't know they are seekers.

---

¹²On hearing this, Jesus said, "It is not the healthy who need a doctor, but the sick. ¹³But go and learn what this means: 'I desire mercy, not sacrifice.'ᵃ For I have not come to call the righteous, but sinners."

Jesus Questioned About Fasting

¹⁴Then John's disciples came and asked him, "How is it that we and the Pharisees fast, but your disciples do not fast?"

¹⁵Jesus answered, "How can the guests of the bridegroom mourn while he is with them? The time will come when the bridegroom will be taken from them; then they will fast.

¹⁶"No one sews a patch of unshrunk cloth on an old garment, for the patch will pull away from the garment, making the tear worse. ¹⁷Neither do men pour new wine into old wineskins. If they do, the skins will burst, the wine will run out and the wineskins will be ruined. No, they pour new wine into new wineskins, and both are preserved."

A Dead Girl and a Sick Woman

¹⁸While he was saying this, a ruler came and knelt before him and said, "My daughter has just died. But come and put your hand on her, and she will live." ¹⁹Jesus got up and went with him, and so did his disciples.

²⁰Just then a woman who had been subject to bleeding for twelve years came up behind him and touched the edge of his cloak. ²¹She said to herself, "If I only touch his cloak, I will be healed."

²²Jesus turned and saw her. "Take heart, daughter," he said, "your faith has healed you." And the woman was healed from that moment.

²³When Jesus entered the ruler's house and saw the flute players and the noisy crowd, ²⁴he said, "Go away. The girl is not dead but asleep." But they laughed at him. ²⁵After the crowd had been put outside, he went in and took the girl by the hand, and she got up. ²⁶News of this spread through all that region.

Jesus Heals the Blind and Mute

²⁷As Jesus went on from there, two blind men followed him, calling out, "Have mercy on us, Son of David!"

ᵃ13 Hosea 6:6

²⁸When he had gone indoors, the blind men came to him, and he asked them, "Do you believe that I am able to do this?"

"Yes, Lord," they replied.

²⁹Then he touched their eyes and said, "According to your faith will it be done to you"; ³⁰and their sight was restored. Jesus warned them sternly, "See that no one knows about this." ³¹But they went out and spread the news about him all over that region.

³²While they were going out, a man who was demon-possessed and could not talk was brought to Jesus. ³³And when the demon was driven out, the man who had been mute spoke. The crowd was amazed and said, "Nothing like this has ever been seen in Israel."

³⁴But the Pharisees said, "It is by the prince of demons that he drives out demons."

The Workers Are Few

³⁵Jesus went through all the towns and villages, teaching in their synagogues, preaching the good news of the kingdom and healing every disease and sickness. ³⁶When he saw the crowds, he had compassion on them, because they were harassed and helpless, like sheep without a shepherd. ³⁷Then he said to his disciples, "The harvest is plentiful but the workers are few. ³⁸Ask the Lord of the harvest, therefore, to send out workers into his harvest field."

Jesus Sends Out the Twelve

10 He called his twelve disciples to him and gave them authority to drive out evil*ᵃ* spirits and to heal every disease and sickness.

²These are the names of the twelve apostles: first, Simon (who is called Peter) and his brother Andrew; James son of Zebedee, and his brother John; ³Philip and Bartholomew; Thomas and Matthew the tax collector; James son of Alphaeus, and Thaddaeus; ⁴Simon the Zealot and Judas Iscariot, who betrayed him.

⁵These twelve Jesus sent out with the following instructions: "Do not go among the Gentiles or enter any town of the Samaritans. ⁶Go rather to the lost sheep of Israel. ⁷As you go, preach this message: 'The kingdom of heaven is near.' ⁸Heal the sick, raise the dead, cleanse those who have leprosy,*ᵇ* drive out demons. Freely you have received, freely give. ⁹Do not take along any gold or silver or copper in your belts; ¹⁰take no bag for the journey, or extra tunic, or sandals or a staff; for the worker is worth his keep.

¹¹"Whatever town or village you enter, search for some worthy person there and stay at his house until you leave. ¹²As you enter the home, give it your greeting. ¹³If the home is deserving, let your peace rest on it; if it is not, let your peace return to you. ¹⁴If anyone will not welcome you or listen to your words, shake the dust off your feet when you leave that home or town. ¹⁵I tell you the truth, it will be more bearable for Sodom and Gomorrah on the day of judgment than for that town. ¹⁶I am sending you out like sheep among wolves. Therefore be as shrewd as snakes and as innocent as doves.

¹⁷"Be on your guard against men; they will hand you over to the local councils and flog you in their synagogues. ¹⁸On my account you will be brought before governors and kings as witnesses to them and to the Gentiles. ¹⁹But when they arrest you, do not worry about what to say or how to say it. At that time you will be given what to say, ²⁰for it will not be you speaking, but the Spirit of your Father speaking through you.

²¹"Brother will betray brother to death, and a father his child; children will rebel against their parents and have them put to death. ²²All men will hate you because of me, but he who stands firm to the end will be saved. ²³When you are persecuted in one place, flee to another. I tell you the truth, you will not finish going through the cities of Israel before the Son of Man comes.

²⁴"A student is not above his teacher, nor a servant above his master. ²⁵It is enough for

---

ᵃ 1 Greek *unclean*   *ᵇ 8* The Greek word was used for various diseases affecting the skin—not necessarily leprosy.

the student to be like his teacher, and the servant like his master. If the head of the house has been called Beelzebub,^a how much more the members of his household!

²⁶"So do not be afraid of them. There is nothing concealed that will not be disclosed, or hidden that will not be made known. ²⁷What I tell you in the dark, speak in the daylight; what is whispered in your ear, proclaim from the roofs. ²⁸Do not be afraid of those who kill the body but cannot kill the soul. Rather, be afraid of the One who can destroy both soul and body in hell. ²⁹Are not two sparrows sold for a penny^b? Yet not one of them will fall to the ground apart from the will of your Father. ³⁰And even the very hairs of your head are all numbered. ³¹So don't be afraid; you are worth more than many sparrows.

³²"Whoever acknowledges me before men, I will also acknowledge him before my Father in heaven. ³³But whoever disowns me before men, I will disown him before my Father in heaven.

³⁴"Do not suppose that I have come to bring peace to the earth. I did not come to bring peace, but a sword. ³⁵For I have come to turn

> " 'a man against his father,
>   a daughter against her mother,
>   a daughter-in-law against her mother-in-law—
> 36   a man's enemies will be the members of his own household.'^c

³⁷"Anyone who loves his father or mother more than me is not worthy of me; anyone who loves his son or daughter more than me is not worthy of me; ³⁸and anyone who does not take his cross and follow me is not worthy of me. ³⁹Whoever finds his life will lose it, and whoever loses his life for my sake will find it.

⁴⁰"He who receives you receives me, and he who receives me receives the one who sent me. ⁴¹Anyone who receives a prophet because he is a prophet will receive a prophet's reward, and anyone who receives a righteous man because he is a righteous man will receive a righteous man's reward. ⁴²And if anyone gives even a cup of cold water to one of these little ones because he is my disciple, I tell you the truth, he will certainly not lose his reward."

Jesus and John the Baptist

11 After Jesus had finished instructing his twelve disciples, he went on from there to teach and preach in the towns of Galilee.^d

²When John heard in prison what Christ was doing, he sent his disciples ³to ask him, "Are you the one who was to come, or should we expect someone else?"

⁴Jesus replied, "Go back and report to John what you hear and see: ⁵The blind receive sight, the lame walk, those who have leprosy^e are cured, the deaf hear, the dead are raised, and the good news is preached to the poor. ⁶Blessed is the man who does not fall away on account of me."

⁷As John's disciples were leaving, Jesus began to speak to the crowd about John: "What did you go out into the desert to see? A reed swayed by the wind? ⁸If not, what did you go out to see? A man dressed in fine clothes? No, those who wear fine clothes are in kings' palaces. ⁹Then what did you go out to see? A prophet? Yes, I tell you, and more than a prophet. ¹⁰This is the one about whom it is written:

> " 'I will send my messenger ahead of you,
>   who will prepare your way before you.'^f

¹¹I tell you the truth: Among those born of women there has not risen anyone greater than John the Baptist; yet he who is least in the kingdom of heaven is greater than he. ¹²From the days of John the Baptist until now, the kingdom of heaven has been forcefully

advancing, and forceful men lay hold of it. ¹³For all the Prophets and the Law prophesied until John. ¹⁴And if you are willing to accept it, he is the Elijah who was to come. ¹⁵He who has ears, let him hear.

¹⁶"To what can I compare this generation? They are like children sitting in the marketplaces and calling out to others:

¹⁷"'We played the flute for you,
    and you did not dance;
we sang a dirge,
    and you did not mourn.'

¹⁸For John came neither eating nor drinking, and they say, 'He has a demon.' ¹⁹The Son of Man came eating and drinking, and they say, 'Here is a glutton and a drunkard, a friend of tax collectors and "sinners." ' But wisdom is proved right by her actions."

Woe on Unrepentant Cities

²⁰Then Jesus began to denounce the cities in which most of his miracles had been performed, because they did not repent. ²¹"Woe to you, Korazin! Woe to you, Bethsaida! If the miracles that were performed in you had been performed in Tyre and Sidon, they would have repented long ago in sackcloth and ashes. ²²But I tell you, it will be more bearable for Tyre and Sidon on the day of judgment than for you. ²³And you, Capernaum, will you be lifted up to the skies? No, you will go down to the depths.ᵃ If the miracles that were performed in you had been performed in Sodom, it would have remained to this day. ²⁴But I tell you that it will be more bearable for Sodom on the day of judgment than for you."

Rest for the Weary

²⁵At that time Jesus said, "I praise you, Father, Lord of heaven and earth, because you have hidden these things from the wise and learned, and revealed them to little children. ²⁶Yes, Father, for this was your good pleasure.

²⁷"All things have been committed to me by my Father. No one knows the Son except the Father, and no one knows the Father except the Son and those to whom the Son chooses to reveal him.

▦ ∷∷∷∷∷∷ REASONS TO BELIEVE ∷∷∷∷∷∷ ↩

11:28–30
The Christian Experience

What an invitation! Jesus says that everyone who is weary and burdened can come to him for rest. In the face of our fast-paced, hectic society, such a promise may seem too good to be true. What's the catch?

First, let's look at what Jesus is really offering here. He's not saying that we can look to him for an all-expenses-paid Caribbean holiday or for a week of snuggling up in front of a fire in a mountain cabin. Jesus invites us to come to *him*. He's offering *himself* in the midst of whatever is going on in our lives. He urges us to take his "yoke" upon ourselves and says that it is easy and that his burden is light. But what does that mean?

In ancient Israel, ox yokes were made of wood. Each was customized for a particular animal. If a yoke fit well, it wouldn't irritate the animal's neck. Pulling a wagon would be easy—almost effortless if the wagon also carried a light load. Jesus used this image to help us see that following him won't be a source of irritation and stress. He assures us that his yoke will fit and that pulling his "load" (he trades his for ours) will be easy.

Can Jesus really keep such promises? There's only one way to find out. You must put his offer to the test. Take Jesus' challenge, and find out what Christians have consistently experienced for nearly 2000 years: Jesus is unlike any other and is totally true to his word.

---

²⁸"Come to me, all you who are weary and burdened, and I will give you rest. ²⁹Take my yoke upon you and learn from me, for I am gentle and humble in heart, and you will find rest for your souls. ³⁰For my yoke is easy and my burden is light."

ᵃ23 Greek *Hades*

Lord of the Sabbath

12 At that time Jesus went through the grainfields on the Sabbath. His disciples were hungry and began to pick some heads of grain and eat them. ²When the Pharisees saw this, they said to him, "Look! Your disciples are doing what is unlawful on the Sabbath."

³He answered, "Haven't you read what David did when he and his companions were hungry? ⁴He entered the house of God, and he and his companions ate the consecrated bread—which was not lawful for them to do, but only for the priests? ⁵Or haven't you read in the Law that on the Sabbath the priests in the temple desecrate the day and yet are innocent? ⁶I tell you that one*a* greater than the temple is here. ⁷If you had known what these words mean, 'I desire mercy, not sacrifice,'*b* you would not have condemned the innocent. ⁸For the Son of Man is Lord of the Sabbath."

⁹Going on from that place, he went into their synagogue, ¹⁰and a man with a shriveled hand was there. Looking for a reason to accuse Jesus, they asked him, "Is it lawful to heal on the Sabbath?"

¹¹He said to them, "If any of you has a sheep and it falls into a pit on the Sabbath, will you not take hold of it and lift it out? ¹²How much more valuable is a man than a sheep! Therefore it is lawful to do good on the Sabbath."

¹³Then he said to the man, "Stretch out your hand." So he stretched it out and it was completely restored, just as sound as the other. ¹⁴But the Pharisees went out and plotted how they might kill Jesus.

God's Chosen Servant

¹⁵Aware of this, Jesus withdrew from that place. Many followed him, and he healed all their sick, ¹⁶warning them not to tell who he was. ¹⁷This was to fulfill what was spoken through the prophet Isaiah:

¹⁸"Here is my servant whom I have chosen,
    the one I love, in whom I delight;
  I will put my Spirit on him,
    and he will proclaim justice to the nations.
¹⁹He will not quarrel or cry out;
    no one will hear his voice in the streets.
²⁰A bruised reed he will not break,
    and a smoldering wick he will not snuff out,
  till he leads justice to victory.
²¹ In his name the nations will put their hope."*c*

Jesus and Beelzebub

²²Then they brought him a demon-possessed man who was blind and mute, and Jesus healed him, so that he could both talk and see. ²³All the people were astonished and said, "Could this be the Son of David?"

²⁴But when the Pharisees heard this, they said, "It is only by Beelzebub,*d* the prince of demons, that this fellow drives out demons."

²⁵Jesus knew their thoughts and said to them, "Every kingdom divided against itself will be ruined, and every city or household divided against itself will not stand. ²⁶If Satan drives out Satan, he is divided against himself. How then can his kingdom stand? ²⁷And if I drive out demons by Beelzebub, by whom do your people drive them out? So then, they will be your judges. ²⁸But if I drive out demons by the Spirit of God, then the kingdom of God has come upon you.

---

a6 Or *something;* also in verses 41 and 42   *b7* Hosea 6:6   *c21* Isaiah 42:1–4   *d24* Greek *Beezeboul* or *Beelzeboul;* also in verse 27

29"Or again, how can anyone enter a strong man's house and carry off his possessions unless he first ties up the strong man? Then he can rob his house.

30"He who is not with me is against me, and he who does not gather with me scatters. 31And so I tell you, every sin and blasphemy will be forgiven men, but the blasphemy against the Spirit will not be forgiven. 32Anyone who speaks a word against the Son of Man will be forgiven, but anyone who speaks against the Holy Spirit will not be forgiven, either in this age or in the age to come.

33"Make a tree good and its fruit will be good, or make a tree bad and its fruit will be bad, for a tree is recognized by its fruit. 34You brood of vipers, how can you who are evil say anything good? For out of the overflow of the heart the mouth speaks. 35The good man brings good things out of the good stored up in him, and the evil man brings evil things out of the evil stored up in him. 36But I tell you that men will have to give account on the day of judgment for every careless word they have spoken. 37For by your words you will be acquitted, and by your words you will be condemned."

The Sign of Jonah

38Then some of the Pharisees and teachers of the law said to him, "Teacher, we want to see a miraculous sign from you."

39He answered, "A wicked and adulterous generation asks for a miraculous sign! But none will be given it except the sign of the prophet Jonah. 40For as Jonah was three days and three nights in the belly of a huge fish, so the Son of Man will be three days and three nights in the heart of the earth. 41The men of Nineveh will stand up at the judgment with this generation and condemn it; for they repented at the preaching of Jonah, and now one[a] greater than Jonah is here. 42The Queen of the South will rise at the judgment with this generation and condemn it; for she came from the ends of the earth to listen to Solomon's wisdom, and now one greater than Solomon is here.

43"When an evil[b] spirit comes out of a man, it goes through arid places seeking rest and does not find it. 44Then it says, 'I will return to the house I left.' When it arrives, it finds the house unoccupied, swept clean and put in order. 45Then it goes and takes with it seven other spirits more wicked than itself, and they go in and live there. And the final condition of that man is worse than the first. That is how it will be with this wicked generation."

Jesus' Mother and Brothers

46While Jesus was still talking to the crowd, his mother and brothers stood outside, wanting to speak to him. 47Someone told him, "Your mother and brothers are standing outside, wanting to speak to you."[c]

48He replied to him, "Who is my mother, and who are my brothers?" 49Pointing to his disciples, he said, "Here are my mother and my brothers. 50For whoever does the will of my Father in heaven is my brother and sister and mother."

The Parable of the Sower

13 That same day Jesus went out of the house and sat by the lake. 2Such large crowds gathered around him that he got into a boat and sat in it, while all the people stood on the shore. 3Then he told them many things in parables, saying: "A farmer went out to sow his seed. 4As he was scattering the seed, some fell along the path, and the birds came and ate it up. 5Some fell on rocky places, where it did not have much soil. It sprang up quickly, because the soil was shallow. 6But when the sun came up, the plants were scorched, and they withered because they had no root. 7Other seed fell among thorns, which grew up and choked the plants. 8Still other seed fell on good soil, where it produced a crop—a hundred, sixty or thirty times what was sown. 9He who has ears, let him hear."

a41 Or something; also in verse 42   b43 Greek unclean   c47 Some manuscripts do not have verse 47.

¹⁰The disciples came to him and asked, "Why do you speak to the people in parables?"
¹¹He replied, "The knowledge of the secrets of the kingdom of heaven has been given to you, but not to them. ¹²Whoever has will be given more, and he will have an abundance. Whoever does not have, even what he has will be taken from him. ¹³This is why I speak to them in parables:

> "Though seeing, they do not see;
> though hearing, they do not hear or understand.

¹⁴In them is fulfilled the prophecy of Isaiah:

> " 'You will be ever hearing but never understanding;
> you will be ever seeing but never perceiving.
> ¹⁵For this people's heart has become calloused;
> they hardly hear with their ears,
> and they have closed their eyes.
> Otherwise they might see with their eyes,
> hear with their ears,
> understand with their hearts
> and turn, and I would heal them.' ᵃ

¹⁶But blessed are your eyes because they see, and your ears because they hear. ¹⁷For I tell you the truth, many prophets and righteous men longed to see what you see but did not see it, and to hear what you hear but did not hear it.

¹⁸"Listen then to what the parable of the sower means: ¹⁹When anyone hears the message about the kingdom and does not understand it, the evil one comes and snatches away what was sown in his heart. This is the seed sown along the path. ²⁰The one who received the seed that fell on rocky places is the man who hears the word and at once receives it with joy. ²¹But since he has no root, he lasts only a short time. When trouble or persecution comes because of the word, he quickly falls away. ²²The one who received the seed that fell among the thorns is the man who hears the word, but the worries of this life and the deceitfulness of wealth choke it, making it unfruitful. ²³But the one who received the seed that fell on good soil is the man who hears the word and understands it. He produces a crop, yielding a hundred, sixty or thirty times what was sown."

The Parable of the Weeds

²⁴Jesus told them another parable: "The kingdom of heaven is like a man who sowed good seed in his field. ²⁵But while everyone was sleeping, his enemy came and sowed weeds among the wheat, and went away. ²⁶When the wheat sprouted and formed heads, then the weeds also appeared.

²⁷"The owner's servants came to him and said, 'Sir, didn't you sow good seed in your field? Where then did the weeds come from?'

²⁸" 'An enemy did this,' he replied.

▣▦ ADDRESSING QUESTIONS ▦ ⬌

13:24–30
Human Experience   **Q**

In this short story, Jesus mentions one of the reasons why God allows evil to continue in the world. According to Jesus, if God uprooted all evil people (the weeds) now, others (the wheat) would suffer in the process.

For the moment, God is patient with evil, but that doesn't mean he condones it. Rather, God is giving people a chance to turn to him and accept his leadership in their lives. After all, if tonight at midnight God wiped out all the people who hadn't yet trusted in him, where would *you* be in the morning?

Verse 30 gives us an image of the separation that God will initiate at the end of time. God wants to gather you, as one of his people, into his heaven on that day. Won't you accept that gracious offer?

ᵃ *15* Isaiah 6:9,10

"The servants asked him, 'Do you want us to go and pull them up?'

²⁹"'No,' he answered, 'because while you are pulling the weeds, you may root up the wheat with them. ³⁰Let both grow together until the harvest. At that time I will tell the harvesters: First collect the weeds and tie them in bundles to be burned; then gather the wheat and bring it into my barn.'"

The Parables of the Mustard Seed and the Yeast

³¹He told them another parable: "The kingdom of heaven is like a mustard seed, which a man took and planted in his field. ³²Though it is the smallest of all your seeds, yet when it grows, it is the largest of garden plants and becomes a tree, so that the birds of the air come and perch in its branches."

³³He told them still another parable: "The kingdom of heaven is like yeast that a woman took and mixed into a large amount*ᵃ* of flour until it worked all through the dough."

³⁴Jesus spoke all these things to the crowd in parables; he did not say anything to them without using a parable. ³⁵So was fulfilled what was spoken through the prophet:

> "I will open my mouth in parables,
> I will utter things hidden since the creation of the world."*ᵇ*

The Parable of the Weeds Explained

³⁶Then he left the crowd and went into the house. His disciples came to him and said, "Explain to us the parable of the weeds in the field."

³⁷He answered, "The one who sowed the good seed is the Son of Man. ³⁸The field is the world, and the good seed stands for the sons of the kingdom. The weeds are the sons of the evil one, ³⁹and the enemy who sows them is the devil. The harvest is the end of the age, and the harvesters are angels.

⁴⁰"As the weeds are pulled up and burned in the fire, so it will be at the end of the age. ⁴¹The Son of Man will send out his angels, and they will weed out of his kingdom everything that causes sin and all who do evil. ⁴²They will throw them into the fiery furnace, where there will be weeping and gnashing of teeth. ⁴³Then the righteous will shine like the sun in the kingdom of their Father. He who has ears, let him hear.

The Parables of the Hidden Treasure and the Pearl

⁴⁴"The kingdom of heaven is like treasure hidden in a field. When a man found it, he hid it again, and then in his joy went and sold all he had and bought that field.

⁴⁵"Again, the kingdom of heaven is like a merchant looking for fine pearls. ⁴⁶When he found one of great value, he went away and sold everything he had and bought it.

The Parable of the Net

⁴⁷"Once again, the kingdom of heaven is like a net that was let down into the lake and caught all kinds of fish. ⁴⁸When it was full, the fishermen pulled it up on the shore. Then they sat down and collected the good fish in baskets, but threw the bad away. ⁴⁹This is how it will be at the end of the age. The angels will come and separate the wicked from the righteous ⁵⁰and throw them into the fiery furnace, where there will be weeping and gnashing of teeth.

⁵¹"Have you understood all these things?" Jesus asked.

"Yes," they replied.

⁵²He said to them, "Therefore every teacher of the law who has been instructed about the kingdom of heaven is like the owner of a house who brings out of his storeroom new treasures as well as old."

ᵃ33 Greek *three satas* (probably about 1/2 bushel or 22 liters)   *ᵇ35* Psalm 78:2

A Prophet Without Honor

⁵³When Jesus had finished these parables, he moved on from there. ⁵⁴Coming to his hometown, he began teaching the people in their synagogue, and they were amazed. "Where did this man get this wisdom and these miraculous powers?" they asked. ⁵⁵"Isn't this the carpenter's son? Isn't his mother's name Mary, and aren't his brothers James, Joseph, Simon and Judas? ⁵⁶Aren't all his sisters with us? Where then did this man get all these things?" ⁵⁷And they took offense at him.

But Jesus said to them, "Only in his hometown and in his own house is a prophet without honor."

⁵⁸And he did not do many miracles there because of their lack of faith.

John the Baptist Beheaded

14 At that time Herod the tetrarch heard the reports about Jesus, ²and he said to his attendants, "This is John the Baptist; he has risen from the dead! That is why miraculous powers are at work in him."

³Now Herod had arrested John and bound him and put him in prison because of Herodias, his brother Philip's wife, ⁴for John had been saying to him: "It is not lawful for you to have her." ⁵Herod wanted to kill John, but he was afraid of the people, because they considered him a prophet.

⁶On Herod's birthday the daughter of Herodias danced for them and pleased Herod so much ⁷that he promised with an oath to give her whatever she asked. ⁸Prompted by her mother, she said, "Give me here on a platter the head of John the Baptist." ⁹The king was distressed, but because of his oaths and his dinner guests, he ordered that her request be granted ¹⁰and had John beheaded in the prison. ¹¹His head was brought in on a platter and given to the girl, who carried it to her mother. ¹²John's disciples came and took his body and buried it. Then they went and told Jesus.

Jesus Feeds the Five Thousand

¹³When Jesus heard what had happened, he withdrew by boat privately to a solitary place. Hearing of this, the crowds followed him on foot from the towns. ¹⁴When Jesus landed and saw a large crowd, he had compassion on them and healed their sick.

¹⁵As evening approached, the disciples came to him and said, "This is a remote place, and it's already getting late. Send the crowds away, so they can go to the villages and buy themselves some food."

¹⁶Jesus replied, "They do not need to go away. You give them something to eat."

¹⁷"We have here only five loaves of bread and two fish," they answered.

¹⁸"Bring them here to me," he said. ¹⁹And he directed the people to sit down on the grass. Taking the five loaves and the two fish and looking up to heaven, he gave thanks and broke the loaves. Then he gave them to the disciples, and the disciples gave them to the people. ²⁰They all ate and were satisfied, and the disciples picked up twelve basketfuls of broken pieces that were left over. ²¹The number of those who ate was about five thousand men, besides women and children.

Jesus Walks on the Water

²²Immediately Jesus made the disciples get into the boat and go on ahead of him to the other side, while he dismissed the crowd. ²³After he had dismissed them, he went up on a mountainside by himself to pray. When evening came, he was there alone, ²⁴but the boat was already a considerable distance*ᵃ* from land, buffeted by the waves because the wind was against it. ²⁵During the fourth watch of the night Jesus went out to them, walking on the lake.

ᵃ24 Greek *many stadia*

²⁶When the disciples saw him walking on the lake, they were terrified. "It's a ghost," they said, and cried out in fear.

²⁷But Jesus immediately said to them: "Take courage! It is I. Don't be afraid."

²⁸"Lord, if it's you," Peter replied, "tell me to come to you on the water."

²⁹"Come," he said.

Then Peter got down out of the boat, walked on the water and came toward Jesus. ³⁰But when he saw the wind, he was afraid and, beginning to sink, cried out, "Lord, save me!"

³¹Immediately Jesus reached out his hand and caught him. "You of little faith," he said, "why did you doubt?"

³²And when they climbed into the boat, the wind died down. ³³Then those who were in the boat worshiped him, saying, "Truly you are the Son of God."

³⁴When they had crossed over, they landed at Gennesaret. ³⁵And when the men of that place recognized Jesus, they sent word to all the surrounding country. People brought all their sick to him ³⁶and begged him to let the sick just touch the edge of his cloak, and all who touched him were healed.

Clean and Unclean

15 Then some Pharisees and teachers of the law came to Jesus from Jerusalem and asked, ²"Why do your disciples break the tradition of the elders? They don't wash their hands before they eat!"

³Jesus replied, "And why do you break the command of God for the sake of your tradition? ⁴For God said, 'Honor your father and mother'ᵃ and 'Anyone who curses his father or mother must be put to death.'ᵇ ⁵But you say that if a man says to his father or mother, 'Whatever help you might otherwise have received from me is a gift devoted to God,' ⁶he is not to 'honor his fatherᶜ' with it. Thus you nullify the word of God for the sake of your tradition. ⁷You hypocrites! Isaiah was right when he prophesied about you:

⁸" 'These people honor me with their lips,
    but their hearts are far from me.
⁹They worship me in vain;
    their teachings are but rules taught by men.'ᵈ"

¹⁰Jesus called the crowd to him and said, "Listen and understand. ¹¹What goes into a

---

ᵃ4 Exodus 20:12; Deut. 5:16   ᵇ4 Exodus 21:17; Lev. 20:9   ᶜ6 Some manuscripts *father or his mother*   ᵈ9 Isaiah 29:13

man's mouth does not make him 'unclean,' but what comes out of his mouth, that is what makes him 'unclean.'"

¹²Then the disciples came to him and asked, "Do you know that the Pharisees were offended when they heard this?"

¹³He replied, "Every plant that my heavenly Father has not planted will be pulled up by the roots. ¹⁴Leave them; they are blind guides.ᵃ If a blind man leads a blind man, both will fall into a pit."

¹⁵Peter said, "Explain the parable to us."

¹⁶"Are you still so dull?" Jesus asked them. ¹⁷"Don't you see that whatever enters the mouth goes into the stomach and then out of the body? ¹⁸But the things that come out of the mouth come from the heart, and these make a man 'unclean.' ¹⁹For out of the heart come evil thoughts, murder, adultery, sexual immorality, theft, false testimony, slander. ²⁰These are what make a man 'unclean'; but eating with unwashed hands does not make him 'unclean.'"

The Faith of the Canaanite Woman

²¹Leaving that place, Jesus withdrew to the region of Tyre and Sidon. ²²A Canaanite woman from that vicinity came to him, crying out, "Lord, Son of David, have mercy on me! My daughter is suffering terribly from demon-possession."

²³Jesus did not answer a word. So his disciples came to him and urged him, "Send her away, for she keeps crying out after us."

²⁴He answered, "I was sent only to the lost sheep of Israel."

²⁵The woman came and knelt before him. "Lord, help me!" she said.

²⁶He replied, "It is not right to take the children's bread and toss it to their dogs."

²⁷"Yes, Lord," she said, "but even the dogs eat the crumbs that fall from their masters' table."

²⁸Then Jesus answered, "Woman, you have great faith! Your request is granted." And her daughter was healed from that very hour.

Jesus Feeds the Four Thousand

²⁹Jesus left there and went along the Sea of Galilee. Then he went up on a mountainside and sat down. ³⁰Great crowds came to him, bringing the lame, the blind, the crippled, the mute and many others, and laid them at his feet; and he healed them. ³¹The people were amazed when they saw the mute speaking, the crippled made well, the lame walking and the blind seeing. And they praised the God of Israel.

³²Jesus called his disciples to him and said, "I have compassion for these people; they have already been with me three days and have nothing to eat. I do not want to send them away hungry, or they may collapse on the way."

³³His disciples answered, "Where could we get enough bread in this remote place to feed such a crowd?"

³⁴"How many loaves do you have?" Jesus asked.

"Seven," they replied, "and a few small fish."

³⁵He told the crowd to sit down on the ground. ³⁶Then he took the seven loaves and the fish, and when he had given thanks, he broke them and gave them to the disciples, and they in turn to the people. ³⁷They all ate and were satisfied. Afterward the disciples picked up seven basketfuls of broken pieces that were left over. ³⁸The number of those who ate was four thousand, besides women and children. ³⁹After Jesus had sent the crowd away, he got into the boat and went to the vicinity of Magadan.

ᵃ 14 Some manuscripts *guides of the blind*

The Demand for a Sign

16 The Pharisees and Sadducees came to Jesus and tested him by asking him to show them a sign from heaven.

[2]He replied,[a] "When evening comes, you say, 'It will be fair weather, for the sky is red,' [3]and in the morning, 'Today it will be stormy, for the sky is red and overcast.' You know how to interpret the appearance of the sky, but you cannot interpret the signs of the times. [4]A wicked and adulterous generation looks for a miraculous sign, but none will be given it except the sign of Jonah." Jesus then left them and went away.

The Yeast of the Pharisees and Sadducees

[5]When they went across the lake, the disciples forgot to take bread. [6]"Be careful," Jesus said to them. "Be on your guard against the yeast of the Pharisees and Sadducees."

[7]They discussed this among themselves and said, "It is because we didn't bring any bread."

[8]Aware of their discussion, Jesus asked, "You of little faith, why are you talking among yourselves about having no bread? [9]Do you still not understand? Don't you remember the five loaves for the five thousand, and how many basketfuls you gathered? [10]Or the seven loaves for the four thousand, and how many basketfuls you gathered? [11]How is it you don't understand that I was not talking to you about bread? But be on your guard against the yeast of the Pharisees and Sadducees." [12]Then they understood that he was not telling them to guard against the yeast used in bread, but against the teaching of the Pharisees and Sadducees.

Peter's Confession of Christ

[13]When Jesus came to the region of Caesarea Philippi, he asked his disciples, "Who do people say the Son of Man is?"

[14]They replied, "Some say John the Baptist; others say Elijah; and still others, Jeremiah or one of the prophets."

[15]"But what about you?" he asked. "Who do you say I am?"

[16]Simon Peter answered, "You are the Christ,[b] the Son of the living God."

[17]Jesus replied, "Blessed are you, Simon son of Jonah, for this was not revealed to you by man, but by my Father in heaven. [18]And I tell you that you are Peter,[c] and on this rock I will build my church, and the gates of Hades[d] will not overcome it.[e] [19]I will give you the keys of the kingdom of heaven; whatever you bind on earth will be[f] bound in heaven, and whatever you loose on earth will be[f] loosed in heaven." [20]Then he warned his disciples not to tell anyone that he was the Christ.

🔲 ▓▓▓▓▓▓▓ **DISCOVERING GOD** ▓▓▓▓▓▓▓ 🔁

16:13–17
Jesus, the God-Man

Who do people say Jesus is? If you want to have some fun, take an informal survey around your workplace. You'll probably hear a variety of answers. Oddly enough, most everybody—in spite of probably not doing much research—will have a strong opinion.

This question is not an academic exercise. It is a very significant personal matter. When all the scholarly opinions are in, Jesus turns to you—as he did to Peter—and asks, "But what about *you*? . . . Who do you say I am?"

Before giving your answer, consider what is at stake. According to Jesus, God must do a work in your soul (verse 17) for you to be able to know that he is the Christ, the Son of the living God. That requires an open mind and a willingness to be influenced by God's Spirit. All of Jesus' true followers down through the ages have echoed Peter's bold claim (verse 16). Can you?

It's okay to say that you don't know, if that's the truth. But don't pretend it isn't important. According to Jesus himself, your eternal destiny depends on how you answer this question (see John chapter 8, verse 24 [page 1396]).

---

[a]2 Some early manuscripts do not have the rest of verse 2 and all of verse 3.   [b]16 Or *Messiah*; also in verse 20
[c]18 Peter means rock.   [d]18 Or hell   [e]18 Or not prove stronger than it   [f]19 Or have been

Jesus Predicts His Death

²¹From that time on Jesus began to explain to his disciples that he must go to Jerusalem and suffer many things at the hands of the elders, chief priests and teachers of the law, and that he must be killed and on the third day be raised to life.

²²Peter took him aside and began to rebuke him. "Never, Lord!" he said. "This shall never happen to you!"

²³Jesus turned and said to Peter, "Get behind me, Satan! You are a stumbling block to me; you do not have in mind the things of God, but the things of men."

²⁴Then Jesus said to his disciples, "If anyone would come after me, he must deny himself and take up his cross and follow me. ²⁵For whoever wants to save his life*ᵃ* will lose it, but whoever loses his life for me will find it. ²⁶What good will it be for a man if he gains the whole world, yet forfeits his soul? Or what can a man give in exchange for his soul? ²⁷For the Son of Man is going to come in his Father's glory with his angels, and then he will reward each person according to what he has done. ²⁸I tell you the truth, some who are standing here will not taste death before they see the Son of Man coming in his kingdom."

The Transfiguration

17 After six days Jesus took with him Peter, James and John the brother of James, and led them up a high mountain by themselves. ²There he was transfigured before them. His face shone like the sun, and his clothes became as white as the light. ³Just then there appeared before them Moses and Elijah, talking with Jesus.

⁴Peter said to Jesus, "Lord, it is good for us to be here. If you wish, I will put up three shelters—one for you, one for Moses and one for Elijah."

⁵While he was still speaking, a bright cloud enveloped them, and a voice from the cloud said, "This is my Son, whom I love; with him I am well pleased. Listen to him!"

⁶When the disciples heard this, they fell facedown to the ground, terrified. ⁷But Jesus came and touched them. "Get up," he said. "Don't be afraid." ⁸When they looked up, they saw no one except Jesus.

⁹As they were coming down the mountain, Jesus instructed them, "Don't tell anyone what you have seen, until the Son of Man has been raised from the dead."

¹⁰The disciples asked him, "Why then do the teachers of the law say that Elijah must come first?"

¹¹Jesus replied, "To be sure, Elijah comes and will restore all things. ¹²But I tell you, Elijah has already come, and they did not recognize him, but have done to him everything they wished. In the same way the Son of Man is going to suffer at their hands." ¹³Then the disciples understood that he was talking to them about John the Baptist.

The Healing of a Boy With a Demon

¹⁴When they came to the crowd, a man approached Jesus and knelt before him. ¹⁵"Lord, have mercy on my son," he said. "He has seizures and is suffering greatly. He often falls into the fire or into the water. ¹⁶I brought him to your disciples, but they could not heal him."

¹⁷"O unbelieving and perverse generation," Jesus replied, "how long shall I stay with you? How long shall I put up with you? Bring the boy here to me." ¹⁸Jesus rebuked the demon, and it came out of the boy, and he was healed from that moment.

¹⁹Then the disciples came to Jesus in private and asked, "Why couldn't we drive it out?"

²⁰He replied, "Because you have so little faith. I tell you the truth, if you have faith as small as a mustard seed, you can say to this mountain, 'Move from here to there' and it will move. Nothing will be impossible for you.*ᵇ*"

ᵃ25 The Greek word means either *life* or *soul*; also in verse 26. *ᵇ20* Some manuscripts *you. ²¹But this kind does not go out except by prayer and fasting.*

²²When they came together in Galilee, he said to them, "The Son of Man is going to be betrayed into the hands of men. ²³They will kill him, and on the third day he will be raised to life." And the disciples were filled with grief.

The Temple Tax

²⁴After Jesus and his disciples arrived in Capernaum, the collectors of the two-drachma tax came to Peter and asked, "Doesn't your teacher pay the temple tax*a*?"

²⁵"Yes, he does," he replied.

When Peter came into the house, Jesus was the first to speak. "What do you think, Simon?" he asked. "From whom do the kings of the earth collect duty and taxes—from their own sons or from others?"

²⁶"From others," Peter answered.

"Then the sons are exempt," Jesus said to him. ²⁷"But so that we may not offend them, go to the lake and throw out your line. Take the first fish you catch; open its mouth and you will find a four-drachma coin. Take it and give it to them for my tax and yours."

The Greatest in the Kingdom of Heaven

18 At that time the disciples came to Jesus and asked, "Who is the greatest in the kingdom of heaven?"

²He called a little child and had him stand among them. ³And he said: "I tell you the truth, unless you change and become like little children, you will never enter the kingdom of heaven. ⁴Therefore, whoever humbles himself like this child is the greatest in the kingdom of heaven.

⁵"And whoever welcomes a little child like this in my name welcomes me. ⁶But if anyone causes one of these little ones who believe in me to sin, it would be better for him to have a large millstone hung around his neck and to be drowned in the depths of the sea.

⁷"Woe to the world because of the things that cause people to sin! Such things must come, but woe to the man through whom they come! ⁸If your hand or your foot causes you to sin, cut it off and throw it away. It is better for you to enter life maimed or crippled than to have two hands or two feet and be thrown into eternal fire. ⁹And if your eye causes you to sin, gouge it out and throw it away. It is better for you to enter life with one eye than to have two eyes and be thrown into the fire of hell.

The Parable of the Lost Sheep

¹⁰"See that you do not look down on one of these little ones. For I tell you that their angels in heaven always see the face of my Father in heaven.*b*

¹²"What do you think? If a man owns a hundred sheep, and one of them wanders away, will he not leave the ninety-nine on

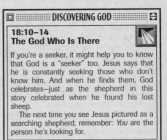

DISCOVERING GOD

18:10–14
The God Who Is There

If you're a seeker, it might help you to know that God is a "seeker" too. Jesus says that he is constantly seeking those who don't know him. And when he finds them, God celebrates—just as the shepherd in this story celebrated when he found his lost sheep.

The next time you see Jesus pictured as a searching shepherd, remember: *You* are the person he's looking for.

the hills and go to look for the one that wandered off? ¹³And if he finds it, I tell you the truth, he is happier about that one sheep than about the ninety-nine that did not wander off. ¹⁴In the same way your Father in heaven is not willing that any of these little ones should be lost.

a24 Greek *the two drachmas*   *b10* Some manuscripts *heaven.* ¹¹*The Son of Man came to save what was lost.*

A Brother Who Sins Against You

15"If your brother sins against you,*a* go and show him his fault, just between the two of you. If he listens to you, you have won your brother over. **16**But if he will not listen, take one or two others along, so that 'every matter may be established by the testimony of two or three witnesses.'*b* **17**If he refuses to listen to them, tell it to the church; and if he refuses to listen even to the church, treat him as you would a pagan or a tax collector.

18"I tell you the truth, whatever you bind on earth will be*c* bound in heaven, and whatever you loose on earth will be*c* loosed in heaven.

19"Again, I tell you that if two of you on earth agree about anything you ask for, it will be done for you by my Father in heaven. **20**For where two or three come together in my name, there am I with them."

The Parable of the Unmerciful Servant

21Then Peter came to Jesus and asked, "Lord, how many times shall I forgive my brother when he sins against me? Up to seven times?"

22Jesus answered, "I tell you, not seven times, but seventy-seven times.*d*

23"Therefore, the kingdom of heaven is like a king who wanted to settle accounts with his servants. **24**As he began the settlement, a man who owed him ten thousand talents*e* was brought to him. **25**Since he was not able to pay, the master ordered that he and his wife and his children and all that he had be sold to repay the debt.

26"The servant fell on his knees before him. 'Be patient with me,' he begged, 'and I will pay back everything.' **27**The servant's master took pity on him, canceled the debt and let him go.

28"But when that servant went out, he found one of his fellow servants who owed him a hundred denarii.*f* He grabbed him and began to choke him. 'Pay back what you owe me!' he demanded.

29"His fellow servant fell to his knees and begged him, 'Be patient with me, and I will pay you back.'

30"But he refused. Instead, he went off and had the man thrown into prison until he could pay the debt. **31**When the other servants saw what had happened, they were greatly distressed and went and told their master everything that had happened.

32"Then the master called the servant in. 'You wicked servant,' he said, 'I canceled all that debt of yours because you begged me to. **33**Shouldn't you have had mercy on your fellow servant just as I had on you?' **34**In anger his master turned him over to the jailers to be tortured, until he should pay back all he owed.

35"This is how my heavenly Father will treat each of you unless you forgive your brother from your heart."

Divorce

19 When Jesus had finished saying these things, he left Galilee and went into the region of Judea to the other side of the Jordan. **2**Large crowds followed him, and he healed them there.

3Some Pharisees came to him to test him. They asked, "Is it lawful for a man to divorce his wife for any and every reason?"

4"Haven't you read," he replied, "that at the beginning the Creator 'made them male and female,'*g* **5**and said, 'For this reason a man will leave his father and mother and be united to his wife, and the two will become one flesh'*h*? **6**So they are no longer two, but one. Therefore what God has joined together, let man not separate."

7"Why then," they asked, "did Moses command that a man give his wife a certificate of divorce and send her away?"

8Jesus replied, "Moses permitted you to divorce your wives because your hearts were

a15 Some manuscripts do not have *against you*.   *b16* Deut. 19:15   *c18* Or *have been seven*   *d22* Or *seventy times*   *e24* That is, millions of dollars   *f28* That is, a few dollars   *g4* Gen. 1:27   *h5* Gen. 2:24

hard. But it was not this way from the beginning. ⁹I tell you that anyone who divorces his wife, except for marital unfaithfulness, and marries another woman commits adultery."

¹⁰The disciples said to him, "If this is the situation between a husband and wife, it is better not to marry."

¹¹Jesus replied, "Not everyone can accept this word, but only those to whom it has been given. ¹²For some are eunuchs because they were born that way; others were made that way by men; and others have renounced marriage*ᵃ* because of the kingdom of heaven. The one who can accept this should accept it."

The Little Children and Jesus

¹³Then little children were brought to Jesus for him to place his hands on them and pray for them. But the disciples rebuked those who brought them.

¹⁴Jesus said, "Let the little children come to me, and do not hinder them, for the kingdom of heaven belongs to such as these." ¹⁵When he had placed his hands on them, he went on from there.

The Rich Young Man

¹⁶Now a man came up to Jesus and asked, "Teacher, what good thing must I do to get eternal life?"

¹⁷"Why do you ask me about what is good?" Jesus replied. "There is only One who is good. If you want to enter life, obey the commandments."

¹⁸"Which ones?" the man inquired.

Jesus replied, "'Do not murder, do not commit adultery, do not steal, do not give false testimony, ¹⁹honor your father and mother,'ᵇ and 'love your neighbor as yourself.'ᶜ"

²⁰"All these I have kept," the young man said. "What do I still lack?"

²¹Jesus answered, "If you want to be perfect, go, sell your possessions and give to the poor, and you will have treasure in heaven. Then come, follow me."

²²When the young man heard this, he went away sad, because he had great wealth.

²³Then Jesus said to his disciples, "I tell you the truth, it is hard for a rich man to enter the kingdom of heaven. ²⁴Again I tell you, it is easier for a camel to go through the eye of a needle than for a rich man to enter the kingdom of God."

²⁵When the disciples heard this, they were greatly astonished and asked, "Who then can be saved?"

²⁶Jesus looked at them and said, "With man this is impossible, but with God all things are possible."

▣ ⋮⋮⋮⋮⋮⋮ KNOWING YOURSELF ⋮⋮⋮⋮⋮⋮ ◪

19:16–26
Sin

What does it mean to be "good"? Do you consider yourself a good person? Or do you at least feel that you're good enough?

Look at the exchange between Jesus and this rich young man. Some of you reading these words are in exactly the same condition as he was. He was a "nice" guy—a real pillar of the community.

But Jesus says that this young man doesn't understand what it means to be "good" ("There is only One who is good" [verse 17]). If we compare this man to other people, he looks superior to most. But if we compare him to God – the ultimate "goodness" standard – he doesn't measure up. And neither do we.

This man's flaw, we assume, was that he trusted too much in his own wealth. Jesus sought to remove that invisible tumor in his soul. But rather than face his need for spiritual "surgery," rather than give up his security and surrender his life to Jesus, the young man walked away from the Doctor.

Perhaps you're a bit like this young man, searching for God on the outside but harboring some unseen resistance to following him. Maybe you've been asking God to show himself to you. But have you thought about what you'll do when he does? This story reinforces the important spiritual truth that everyone who seeks finds, *but not everyone who finds follows.*

ᵃ12 Or *have made themselves eunuchs*   *ᵇ19* Exodus 20:12-16; Deut. 5:16-20   *ᶜ19* Lev. 19:18

²⁷Peter answered him, "We have left everything to follow you! What then will there be for us?"

²⁸Jesus said to them, "I tell you the truth, at the renewal of all things, when the Son of Man sits on his glorious throne, you who have followed me will also sit on twelve thrones, judging the twelve tribes of Israel. ²⁹And everyone who has left houses or brothers or sisters or father or mother*ᵃ* or children or fields for my sake will receive a hundred times as much and will inherit eternal life. ³⁰But many who are first will be last, and many who are last will be first.

The Parable of the Workers in the Vineyard

20 "For the kingdom of heaven is like a landowner who went out early in the morning to hire men to work in his vineyard. ²He agreed to pay them a denarius for the day and sent them into his vineyard.

³"About the third hour he went out and saw others standing in the marketplace doing nothing. ⁴He told them, 'You also go and work in my vineyard, and I will pay you whatever is right.' ⁵So they went.

"He went out again about the sixth hour and the ninth hour and did the same thing. ⁶About the eleventh hour he went out and found still others standing around. He asked them, 'Why have you been standing here all day long doing nothing?'

⁷" 'Because no one has hired us,' they answered.

"He said to them, 'You also go and work in my vineyard.'

⁸"When evening came, the owner of the vineyard said to his foreman, 'Call the workers and pay them their wages, beginning with the last ones hired and going on to the first.'

⁹"The workers who were hired about the eleventh hour came and each received a denarius. ¹⁰So when those came who were hired first, they expected to receive more. But each one of them also received a denarius. ¹¹When they received it, they began to grumble against the landowner. ¹²'These men who were hired last worked only one hour,' they said, 'and you have made them equal to us who have borne the burden of the work and the heat of the day.'

¹³"But he answered one of them, 'Friend, I am not being unfair to you. Didn't you agree to work for a denarius? ¹⁴Take your pay and go. I want to give the man who was hired last the same as I gave you. ¹⁵Don't I have the right to do what I want with my own money? Or are you envious because I am generous?'

¹⁶"So the last will be first, and the first will be last."

Jesus Again Predicts His Death

¹⁷Now as Jesus was going up to Jerusalem, he took the twelve disciples aside and said to them, ¹⁸"We are going up to Jerusalem, and the Son of Man will be betrayed to the chief priests and the teachers of the law. They will condemn him to death ¹⁹and will turn him over to the Gentiles to be mocked and flogged and crucified. On the third day he will be raised to life!"

A Mother's Request

²⁰Then the mother of Zebedee's sons came to Jesus with her sons and, kneeling down, asked a favor of him.

²¹"What is it you want?" he asked.

She said, "Grant that one of these two sons of mine may sit at your right and the other at your left in your kingdom."

²²"You don't know what you are asking," Jesus said to them. "Can you drink the cup I am going to drink?"

"We can," they answered.

²³Jesus said to them, "You will indeed drink from my cup, but to sit at my right or left

ᵃ29 Some manuscripts mother or wife

s not for me to grant. These places belong to those for whom they have been prepared
by my Father."

²⁴When the ten heard about this, they were indignant with the two brothers. ²⁵Jesus
called them together and said, "You know that the rulers of the Gentiles lord it over them,
and their high officials exercise authority over them. ²⁶Not so with you. Instead, whoever
wants to become great among you must be your servant, ²⁷and whoever wants to be first
must be your slave— ²⁸just as the Son of Man did not come to be served, but to serve, and
to give his life as a ransom for many."

Two Blind Men Receive Sight

²⁹As Jesus and his disciples were leaving Jericho, a large crowd followed him. ³⁰Two
blind men were sitting by the roadside, and when they heard that Jesus was going by,
they shouted, "Lord, Son of David, have mercy on us!"

³¹The crowd rebuked them and told them to be quiet, but they shouted all the louder,
"Lord, Son of David, have mercy on us!"

³²Jesus stopped and called them. "What do you want me to do for you?" he asked.

³³"Lord," they answered, "we want our sight."

³⁴Jesus had compassion on them and touched their eyes. Immediately they received
their sight and followed him.

The Triumphal Entry

21 As they approached Jerusalem and came to Bethphage on the Mount of
Olives, Jesus sent two disciples, ²saying to them, "Go to the village ahead of
you, and at once you will find a donkey tied there, with her colt by her. Untie them and
bring them to me. ³If anyone says anything to you, tell him that the Lord needs them, and
he will send them right away."

⁴This took place to fulfill what was spoken through the prophet:

⁵"Say to the Daughter of Zion,
    'See, your king comes to you,
    gentle and riding on a donkey,
    on a colt, the foal of a donkey.' " ᵃ

⁶The disciples went and did as Jesus had instructed them. ⁷They brought the donkey
and the colt, placed their cloaks on them, and Jesus sat on them. ⁸A very large crowd
spread their cloaks on the road, while others cut branches from the trees and spread
them on the road. ⁹The crowds that went ahead of him and those that followed shouted,

"Hosanna ᵇ to the Son of David!"

"Blessed is he who comes in the name of the Lord!" ᶜ

"Hosanna ᵇ in the highest!"

¹⁰When Jesus entered Jerusalem, the whole city was stirred and asked, "Who is this?"
¹¹The crowds answered, "This is Jesus, the prophet from Nazareth in Galilee."

Jesus at the Temple

¹²Jesus entered the temple area and drove out all who were buying and selling there.
He overturned the tables of the money changers and the benches of those selling doves.
¹³"It is written," he said to them, " 'My house will be called a house of prayer,' ᵈ but you
are making it a 'den of robbers.' ᵉ"

¹⁴The blind and the lame came to him at the temple, and he healed them. ¹⁵But when
the chief priests and the teachers of the law saw the wonderful things he did and the

---

ᵃ5 Zech. 9:9   ᵇ9 A Hebrew expression meaning "Save!" which became an exclamation of praise; also in verse 15
ᶜ9 Psalm 118:26   ᵈ13 Isaiah 56:7   ᵉ13 Jer. 7:11

children shouting in the temple area, "Hosanna to the Son of David," they were indignant.

¹⁶"Do you hear what these children are saying?" they asked him.

"Yes," replied Jesus, "have you never read,

> "'From the lips of children and infants
>   you have ordained praise'ᵃ?"

¹⁷And he left them and went out of the city to Bethany, where he spent the night.

The Fig Tree Withers

¹⁸Early in the morning, as he was on his way back to the city, he was hungry. ¹⁹Seeing a fig tree by the road, he went up to it but found nothing on it except leaves. Then he said to it, "May you never bear fruit again!" Immediately the tree withered.

²⁰When the disciples saw this, they were amazed. "How did the fig tree wither so quickly?" they asked.

²¹Jesus replied, "I tell you the truth, if you have faith and do not doubt, not only can you do what was done to the fig tree, but also you can say to this mountain, 'Go, throw yourself into the sea,' and it will be done. ²²If you believe, you will receive whatever you ask for in prayer."

The Authority of Jesus Questioned

²³Jesus entered the temple courts, and, while he was teaching, the chief priests and the elders of the people came to him. "By what authority are you doing these things?" they asked. "And who gave you this authority?"

²⁴Jesus replied, "I will also ask you one question. If you answer me, I will tell you by what authority I am doing these things. ²⁵John's baptism—where did it come from? Was it from heaven, or from men?"

They discussed it among themselves and said, "If we say, 'From heaven,' he will ask, 'Then why didn't you believe him?' ²⁶But if we say, 'From men'—we are afraid of the people, for they all hold that John was a prophet."

²⁷So they answered Jesus, "We don't know."

Then he said, "Neither will I tell you by what authority I am doing these things.

The Parable of the Two Sons

²⁸"What do you think? There was a man who had two sons. He went to the first and said, 'Son, go and work today in the vineyard.'

²⁹"'I will not,' he answered, but later he changed his mind and went.

³⁰"Then the father went to the other son and said the same thing. He answered, 'I will, sir,' but he did not go.

³¹"Which of the two did what his father wanted?"

"The first," they answered.

Jesus said to them, "I tell you the truth, the tax collectors and the prostitutes are entering the kingdom of God ahead of you. ³²For John came to you to show you the way of righteousness, and you did not believe him, but the tax collectors and the prostitutes did. And even after you saw this, you did not repent and believe him.

The Parable of the Tenants

³³"Listen to another parable: There was a landowner who planted a vineyard. He put a wall around it, dug a winepress in it and built a watchtower. Then he rented the vineyard to some farmers and went away on a journey. ³⁴When the harvest time approached, he sent his servants to the tenants to collect his fruit.

³⁵"The tenants seized his servants; they beat one, killed another, and stoned a third.

ᵃ16 Psalm 8:2

36"Then he sent other servants to them, more than the first time, and the tenants treated them the same way. 37Last of all, he sent his son to them. 'They will respect my son,' he said.

38"But when the tenants saw the son, they said to each other, 'This is the heir. Come, let's kill him and take his inheritance.' 39So they took him and threw him out of the vineyard and killed him.

40"Therefore, when the owner of the vineyard comes, what will he do to those tenants?"

41"He will bring those wretches to a wretched end," they replied, "and he will rent the vineyard to other tenants, who will give him his share of the crop at harvest time."

42Jesus said to them, "Have you never read in the Scriptures:

> " 'The stone the builders rejected
> has become the capstone*a*;
> the Lord has done this,
> and it is marvelous in our eyes'*b*?

43"Therefore I tell you that the kingdom of God will be taken away from you and given to a people who will produce its fruit. 44He who falls on this stone will be broken to pieces, but he on whom it falls will be crushed."*c*

45When the chief priests and the Pharisees heard Jesus' parables, they knew he was talking about them. 46They looked for a way to arrest him, but they were afraid of the crowd because the people held that he was a prophet.

The Parable of the Wedding Banquet

22 Jesus spoke to them again in parables, saying: 2"The kingdom of heaven is like a king who prepared a wedding banquet for his son. 3He sent his servants to those who had been invited to the banquet to tell them to come, but they refused to come.

4"Then he sent some more servants and said, 'Tell those who have been invited that I have prepared my dinner: My oxen and fattened cattle have been butchered, and everything is ready. Come to the wedding banquet.'

5"But they paid no attention and went off—one to his field, another to his business. 6The rest seized his servants, mistreated them and killed them. 7The king was enraged. He sent his army and destroyed those murderers and burned their city.

8"Then he said to his servants, 'The wedding banquet is ready, but those I invited did not deserve to come. 9Go to the street corners and invite to the banquet anyone you find.' 10So the servants went out into the

▣ ▦▦▦▦▦▦ DISCOVERING GOD ▦▦▦▦▦▦ ◨

22:1–14
Life with God

This story holds both good news and bad news for seekers. The good news is that it shows God as a "seeking" God, going out like this king did to invite people in to his party. But it is bad news for those who don't follow God's call and put on the right spiritual "clothes."

Notice that both good and bad people get to stay for the feast (verse 10); relative "goodness" isn't the criterion for acceptance in heaven. What matters is whether each guest has put on the clothes the king has provided (verses 11–13; compare this with Isaiah chapter 61, verse 10 [page 974]). Those who want to join God's feast have to have *his* righteousness covering them, not their own.

God wants you to come to his big, eternal celebration, and he will give you the appropriate attire—the gift of salvation through his Son, Jesus Christ. Whatever you do, don't presume to stand in his presence in your own "clothes," trying to earn your own salvation. According to the Bible, our righteous deeds are "filthy rags" (Isaiah chapter 64, verse 6 [page 978]). Exchange your tattered fragments of goodness for his perfect—and free—"black tie." Then get ready to celebrate!

---

*a*42 Or cornerstone　　*b*42 Psalm 118:22,23　　*c*44 Some manuscripts do not have verse 44.

streets and gathered all the people they could find, both good and bad, and the wedding hall was filled with guests.

¹¹"But when the king came in to see the guests, he noticed a man there who was not wearing wedding clothes. ¹²'Friend,' he asked, 'how did you get in here without wedding clothes?' The man was speechless.

¹³"Then the king told the attendants, 'Tie him hand and foot, and throw him outside, into the darkness, where there will be weeping and gnashing of teeth.'

¹⁴"For many are invited, but few are chosen."

Paying Taxes to Caesar

¹⁵Then the Pharisees went out and laid plans to trap him in his words. ¹⁶They sent their disciples to him along with the Herodians. "Teacher," they said, "we know you are a man of integrity and that you teach the way of God in accordance with the truth. You aren't swayed by men, because you pay no attention to who they are. ¹⁷Tell us then, what is your opinion? Is it right to pay taxes to Caesar or not?"

¹⁸But Jesus, knowing their evil intent, said, "You hypocrites, why are you trying to trap me? ¹⁹Show me the coin used for paying the tax." They brought him a denarius, ²⁰and he asked them, "Whose portrait is this? And whose inscription?"

²¹"Caesar's," they replied.

Then he said to them, "Give to Caesar what is Caesar's, and to God what is God's."

²²When they heard this, they were amazed. So they left him and went away.

Marriage at the Resurrection

²³That same day the Sadducees, who say there is no resurrection, came to him with a question. ²⁴"Teacher," they said, "Moses told us that if a man dies without having children, his brother must marry the widow and have children for him. ²⁵Now there were seven brothers among us. The first one married and died, and since he had no children, he left his wife to his brother. ²⁶The same thing happened to the second and third brother, right on down to the seventh. ²⁷Finally, the woman died. ²⁸Now then, at the resurrection, whose wife will she be of the seven, since all of them were married to her?"

²⁹Jesus replied, "You are in error because you do not know the Scriptures or the power of God. ³⁰At the resurrection people will neither marry nor be given in marriage; they will be like the angels in heaven. ³¹But about the resurrection of the dead—have you not read what God said to you, ³²'I am the God of Abraham, the God of Isaac, and the God of Jacob'ᵃ? He is not the God of the dead but of the living."

³³When the crowds heard this, they were astonished at his teaching.

The Greatest Commandment

³⁴Hearing that Jesus had silenced the Sadducees, the Pharisees got together. ³⁵One of them, an expert in the law, tested him with this question: ³⁶"Teacher, which is the greatest commandment in the Law?"

³⁷Jesus replied: " 'Love the Lord your God with all your heart and with all your soul and with all your mind.'ᵇ ³⁸This is the first and greatest commandment. ³⁹And the second is like it: 'Love your neighbor as yourself.'ᶜ ⁴⁰All the Law and the Prophets hang on these two commandments."

Whose Son Is the Christ?

⁴¹While the Pharisees were gathered together, Jesus asked them, ⁴²"What do you think about the Christᵈ? Whose son is he?"

"The son of David," they replied.

⁴³He said to them, "How is it then that David, speaking by the Spirit, calls him 'Lord'? For he says,

ᵃ32 Exodus 3:6   ᵇ37 Deut. 6:5   ᶜ39 Lev. 19:18   ᵈ42 Or Messiah

⁴⁴"'The Lord said to my Lord:
"Sit at my right hand
until I put your enemies
under your feet." ' ᵃ

⁴⁵If then David calls him 'Lord,' how can he be his son?" ⁴⁶No one could say a word in reply, and from that day on no one dared to ask him any more questions.

Seven Woes

23 Then Jesus said to the crowds and to his disciples: ²"The teachers of the law and the Pharisees sit in Moses' seat. ³So you must obey them and do everything they tell you. But do not do what they do, for they do not practice what they preach. ⁴They tie up heavy loads and put them on men's shoulders, but they themselves are not willing to lift a finger to move them.

⁵"Everything they do is done for men to see: They make their phylacteries ᵇ wide and the tassels on their garments long; ⁶they love the place of honor at banquets and the most important seats in the synagogues; ⁷they love to be greeted in the marketplaces and to have men call them 'Rabbi.'

⁸"But you are not to be called 'Rabbi,' for you have only one Master and you are all brothers. ⁹And do not call anyone on earth 'father,' for you have one Father, and he is in heaven. ¹⁰Nor are you to be called 'teacher,' for you have one Teacher, the Christ.ᶜ ¹¹The greatest among you will be your servant. ¹²For whoever exalts himself will be humbled, and whoever humbles himself will be exalted.

¹³"Woe to you, teachers of the law and Pharisees, you hypocrites! You shut the kingdom of heaven in men's faces. You yourselves do not enter, nor will you let those enter who are trying to.ᵈ

¹⁵"Woe to you, teachers of the law and Pharisees, you hypocrites! You travel over land and sea to win a single convert, and when he becomes one, you make him twice as much a son of hell as you are.

¹⁶"Woe to you, blind guides! You say, 'If anyone swears by the temple, it means nothing; but if anyone swears by the gold of the temple, he is bound by his oath.' ¹⁷You blind fools! Which is greater: the gold, or the temple that makes the gold sacred? ¹⁸You also say, 'If anyone swears by the altar, it means nothing; but if anyone swears by the gift on it, he is bound by his oath.' ¹⁹You blind men! Which is greater: the gift, or the altar that makes the gift sacred? ²⁰Therefore, he who swears by the altar swears by it and by everything on it. ²¹And he who swears by the temple swears by it and by the one who dwells in it. ²²And he who swears by heaven swears by God's throne and by the one who sits on it.

²³"Woe to you, teachers of the law and Pharisees, you hypocrites! You give a tenth of your spices—mint, dill and cummin. But you have neglected the more important matters of the law—justice, mercy and faithfulness. You should have practiced the latter, without neglecting the former. ²⁴You blind guides! You strain out a gnat but swallow a camel.

²⁵"Woe to you, teachers of the law and Pharisees, you hypocrites! You clean the outside of the cup and dish, but inside they are full of greed and self-indulgence. ²⁶Blind Pharisee! First clean the inside of the cup and dish, and then the outside also will be clean.

²⁷"Woe to you, teachers of the law and Pharisees, you hypocrites! You are like whitewashed tombs, which look beautiful on the outside but on the inside are full of dead men's bones and everything unclean. ²⁸In the same way, on the outside you appear to people as righteous but on the inside you are full of hypocrisy and wickedness.

²⁹"Woe to you, teachers of the law and Pharisees, you hypocrites! You build tombs for the prophets and decorate the graves of the righteous. ³⁰And you say, 'If we had lived in

ᵃ44 Psalm 110:1   ᵇ5 That is, boxes containing Scripture verses, worn on forehead and arm   ᶜ10 Or Messiah
ᵈ13 Some manuscripts to. ¹⁴Woe to you, teachers of the law and Pharisees, you hypocrites! You devour widows' houses and for a show make lengthy prayers. Therefore you will be punished more severely.

the days of our forefathers, we would not have taken part with them in shedding the blood of the prophets.' ³¹So you testify against yourselves that you are the descendants of those who murdered the prophets. ³²Fill up, then, the measure of the sin of your forefathers!

³³"You snakes! You brood of vipers! How will you escape being condemned to hell? ³⁴Therefore I am sending you prophets and wise men and teachers. Some of them you will kill and crucify; others you will flog in your synagogues and pursue from town to town. ³⁵And so upon you will come all the righteous blood that has been shed on earth, from the blood of righteous Abel to the blood of Zechariah son of Berekiah, whom you murdered between the temple and the altar. ³⁶I tell you the truth, all this will come upon this generation.

³⁷"O Jerusalem, Jerusalem, you who kill the prophets and stone those sent to you, how often I have longed to gather your children together, as a hen gathers her chicks under her wings, but you were not willing. ³⁸Look, your house is left to you desolate. ³⁹For I tell you, you will not see me again until you say, 'Blessed is he who comes in the name of the Lord.' ᵃ"

Signs of the End of the Age

24 Jesus left the temple and was walking away when his disciples came up to him to call his attention to its buildings. ²"Do you see all these things?" he asked. "I tell you the truth, not one stone here will be left on another; every one will be thrown down."

³As Jesus was sitting on the Mount of Olives, the disciples came to him privately. "Tell us," they said, "when will this happen, and what will be the sign of your coming and of the end of the age?"

⁴Jesus answered: "Watch out that no one deceives you. ⁵For many will come in my name, claiming, 'I am the Christ,ᵇ' and will deceive many. ⁶You will hear of wars and rumors of wars, but see to it that you are not alarmed. Such things must happen, but the end is still to come. ⁷Nation will rise against nation, and kingdom against kingdom. There will be famines and earthquakes in various places. ⁸All these are the beginning of birth pains.

⁹"Then you will be handed over to be persecuted and put to death, and you will be hated by all nations because of me. ¹⁰At that time many will turn away from the faith and will betray and hate each other, ¹¹and many false prophets will appear and deceive many people. ¹²Because of the increase of wickedness, the love of most will grow cold, ¹³but he who stands firm to the end will be saved. ¹⁴And this gospel of the kingdom will be preached in the whole world as a testimony to all nations, and then the end will come.

¹⁵"So when you see standing in the holy place 'the abomination that causes desolation,'ᶜ spoken of through the prophet Daniel—let the reader understand— ¹⁶then let those who are in Judea flee to the mountains. ¹⁷Let no one on the roof of his house go down to take anything out of the house. ¹⁸Let no one in the field go back to get his cloak. ¹⁹How dreadful it will be in those days for pregnant women and nursing mothers! ²⁰Pray that your flight will not take place in winter or on the Sabbath. ²¹For then there will be great distress, unequaled from the beginning of the world until now—and never to be equaled again. ²²If those days had not been cut short, no one would survive, but for the sake of the elect those days will be shortened. ²³At that time if anyone says to you, 'Look, here is the Christ!' or, 'There he is!' do not believe it. ²⁴For false Christs and false prophets will appear and perform great signs and miracles to deceive even the elect—if that were possible. ²⁵See, I have told you ahead of time.

²⁶"So if anyone tells you, 'There he is, out in the desert,' do not go out; or, 'Here he is, in the inner rooms,' do not believe it. ²⁷For as lightning that comes from the east is visible

ᵃ39 Psalm 118:26   ᵇ5 Or Messiah; also in verse 23   ᶜ15 Daniel 9:27; 11:31; 12:11

en in the west, so will be the coming of the Son of Man. ²⁸Wherever there is a carcass, ⋯re the vultures will gather.

²⁹"Immediately after the distress of those days

" 'the sun will be darkened,
    and the moon will not give its light;
the stars will fall from the sky,
    and the heavenly bodies will be shaken.' ᵃ

³⁰"At that time the sign of the Son of Man will appear in the sky, and all the nations ⋯the earth will mourn. They will see the Son of Man coming on the clouds of the ⋯, with power and great glory. ³¹And he will send his angels with a loud trumpet call, ⋯ they will gather his elect from the four ⋯nds, from one end of the heavens to the ⋯er.

³²"Now learn this lesson from the fig ⋯e: As soon as its twigs get tender and its ⋯ves come out, you know that summer is ⋯ar. ³³Even so, when you see all these ⋯ngs, you know that it ᵇ is near, right at ⋯ door. ³⁴I tell you the truth, this genera-⋯nᶜ will certainly not pass away until all ⋯se things have happened. ³⁵Heaven and ⋯th will pass away, but my words will ⋯ver pass away.

⋯e Day and Hour Unknown

³⁶"No one knows about that day or hour, ⋯ even the angels in heaven, nor the Son, ᵈ ⋯ only the Father. ³⁷As it was in the days ⋯Noah, so it will be at the coming of the ⋯ of Man.

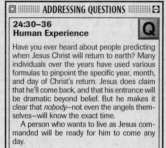

▣ ⦙⦙⦙⦙⦙⦙ ADDRESSING QUESTIONS ⦙⦙⦙⦙⦙⦙ ↴

24:30–36
Human Experience

Ⓠ

Have you ever heard about people predicting when Jesus Christ will return to earth? Many individuals over the years have used various formulas to pinpoint the specific year, month, and day of Christ's return. Jesus does claim that he'll come back, and that his entrance will be dramatic beyond belief. But he makes it clear that *nobody*—not even the angels them-selves—will know the exact time.

A person who wants to live as Jesus com-manded will be ready for him to come any day.

³⁸For in the days before the flood, people were eating and drinking, marrying ⋯d giving in marriage, up to the day Noah entered the ark; ³⁹and they knew nothing ⋯ut what would happen until the flood came and took them all away. That is how it ⋯l be at the coming of the Son of Man. ⁴⁰Two men will be in the field; one will be taken ⋯d the other left. ⁴¹Two women will be grinding with a hand mill; one will be taken and ⋯ other left.

⁴²"Therefore keep watch, because you do not know on what day your Lord will come. ⋯ut understand this: If the owner of the house had known at what time of night the ⋯ef was coming, he would have kept watch and would not have let his house be broken ⋯o. ⁴⁴So you also must be ready, because the Son of Man will come at an hour when ⋯ do not expect him.

⁴⁵"Who then is the faithful and wise servant, whom the master has put in charge of the ⋯vants in his household to give them their food at the proper time? ⁴⁶It will be good for ⋯t servant whose master finds him doing so when he returns. ⁴⁷I tell you the truth, he ⋯l put him in charge of all his possessions. ⁴⁸But suppose that servant is wicked and ⋯s to himself, 'My master is staying away a long time,' ⁴⁹and he then begins to beat his ⋯ow servants and to eat and drink with drunkards. ⁵⁰The master of that servant will ⋯ne on a day when he does not expect him and at an hour he is not aware of. ⁵¹He will ⋯ him to pieces and assign him a place with the hypocrites, where there will be ⋯eping and gnashing of teeth.

Isaiah 13:10; 34:4   ᵇ33 Or he   ᶜ34 Or race   ᵈ36 Some manuscripts do not have *nor the Son.*

The Parable of the Ten Virgins

25 "At that time the kingdom of heaven will be like ten virgins who took the lamps and went out to meet the bridegroom. ²Five of them were foolish an five were wise. ³The foolish ones took their lamps but did not take any oil with the ⁴The wise, however, took oil in jars along with their lamps. ⁵The bridegroom was a lo time in coming, and they all became drowsy and fell asleep.

⁶"At midnight the cry rang out: 'Here's the bridegroom! Come out to meet him!'

⁷Then all the virgins woke up and trimmed their lamps. ⁸The foolish ones said to th wise, 'Give us some of your oil; our lamps are going out.'

⁹"'No,' they replied, 'there may not be enough for both us and you. Instead, go to tho who sell oil and buy some for yourselves.'

¹⁰"But while they were on their way to buy the oil, the bridegroom arrived. The virgi who were ready went in with him to the wedding banquet. And the door was shut.

¹¹"Later the others also came. 'Sir! Sir!' they said. 'Open the door for us!'

¹²"But he replied, 'I tell you the truth, I don't know you.'

¹³"Therefore keep watch, because you do not know the day or the hour.

The Parable of the Talents

¹⁴"Again, it will be like a man going on a journey, who called his servants and entrus ed his property to them. ¹⁵To one he gave five talents*ᵃ* of money, to another two talen and to another one talent, each according to his ability. Then he went on his journe ¹⁶The man who had received the five talents went at once and put his money to wo and gained five more. ¹⁷So also, the one with the two talents gained two more. ¹⁸But th man who had received the one talent went off, dug a hole in the ground and hid h master's money.

¹⁹"After a long time the master of those servants returned and settled accounts wi them. ²⁰The man who had received the five talents brought the other five. 'Master,' l said, 'you entrusted me with five talents. See, I have gained five more.'

²¹"His master replied, 'Well done, good and faithful servant! You have been faithi with a few things; I will put you in charge of many things. Come and share your maste happiness!'

²²"The man with the two talents also came. 'Master,' he said, 'you entrusted me wi two talents; see, I have gained two more.'

²³"His master replied, 'Well done, good and faithful servant! You have been faithi with a few things; I will put you in charge of many things. Come and share your maste happiness!'

²⁴"Then the man who had received the one talent came. 'Master,' he said, 'I knew th you are a hard man, harvesting where you have not sown and gathering where you ha not scattered seed. ²⁵So I was afraid and went out and hid your talent in the ground. Se here is what belongs to you.'

²⁶"His master replied, 'You wicked, lazy servant! So you knew that I harvest where have not sown and gather where I have not scattered seed? ²⁷Well then, you shou have put my money on deposit with the bankers, so that when I returned I would ha received it back with interest.

²⁸"'Take the talent from him and give it to the one who has the ten talents. ²⁹F everyone who has will be given more, and he will have an abundance. Whoever do not have, even what he has will be taken from him. ³⁰And throw that worthless serva outside, into the darkness, where there will be weeping and gnashing of teeth.'

ᵃ 15 A talent was worth more than a thousand dollars.

e Sheep and the Goats

³¹"When the Son of Man comes in his glory, and all the angels with him, he will sit on
s throne in heavenly glory. ³²All the nations will be gathered before him, and he will
parate the people one from another as a shepherd separates the sheep from the goats.
He will put the sheep on his right and the goats on his left.

³⁴"Then the King will say to those on his right, 'Come, you who are blessed by my
ther; take your inheritance, the kingdom prepared for you since the creation of the
orld. ³⁵For I was hungry and you gave me something to eat, I was thirsty and you gave
e something to drink, I was a stranger and you invited me in, ³⁶I needed clothes and
u clothed me, I was sick and you looked after me, I was in prison and you came to
sit me.'

³⁷"Then the righteous will answer him, 'Lord, when did we see you hungry and feed
u, or thirsty and give you something to drink? ³⁸When did we see you a stranger and
vite you in, or needing clothes and clothe
u? ³⁹When did we see you sick or in
ison and go to visit you?'

⁴⁰"The King will reply, 'I tell you the
uth, whatever you did for one of the least
these brothers of mine, you did for me.'

⁴¹"Then he will say to those on his left,
epart from me, you who are cursed, into
e eternal fire prepared for the devil and
s angels. ⁴²For I was hungry and you
ve me nothing to eat, I was thirsty and
u gave me nothing to drink, ⁴³I was a
ranger and you did not invite me in, I
eeded clothes and you did not clothe me,
was sick and in prison and you did not
ok after me.'

⁴⁴"They also will answer, 'Lord, when
d we see you hungry or thirsty or a
ranger or needing clothes or sick or in
ison, and did not help you?'

⁴⁵"He will reply, 'I tell you the truth,
hatever you did not do for one of the
ast of these, you did not do for me.'

⁴⁶"Then they will go away to eternal
nishment, but the righteous to eternal
e."

ADDRESSING QUESTIONS

25:31–46
Unseen Realities

You might be surprised to learn that Jesus spoke more than anyone in the Bible about the reality of hell. It's a real place, and real people go there.

God does not enjoy it when people choose hell ("As surely as I live, declares the Sovereign Lord, I take no pleasure in the death of the wicked, but rather that they turn from their ways and live" [Ezekiel chapter 33, verse 11 (page 1127)]). If people repeatedly resist God's influence in their lives, he simply gives them what they want: lots of distance from him—for eternity.

None of us gets a second chance after we die—a decision for or against Christ while we're alive settles our eternity. Invite Jesus Christ to be involved in every aspect of your life. Ask him to be your forgiver and to lead you from this day forward. He doesn't want you to go away from him. That's why he came—to call you home and to be your "shepherd."

e Plot Against Jesus

26 When Jesus had finished saying all these things, he said to his disciples,
²"As you know, the Passover is two days away—and the Son of Man will be
nded over to be crucified."

³Then the chief priests and the elders of the people assembled in the palace of the
gh priest, whose name was Caiaphas, ⁴and they plotted to arrest Jesus in some sly way
d kill him. ⁵"But not during the Feast," they said, "or there may be a riot among the
ople."

sus Anointed at Bethany

⁶While Jesus was in Bethany in the home of a man known as Simon the Leper, ⁷a
oman came to him with an alabaster jar of very expensive perfume, which she poured
 his head as he was reclining at the table.

8When the disciples saw this, they were indignant. "Why this waste?" they aske 9"This perfume could have been sold at a high price and the money given to the poor

10Aware of this, Jesus said to them, "Why are you bothering this woman? She has dor a beautiful thing to me. 11The poor you will always have with you, but you will no always have me. 12When she poured this perfume on my body, she did it to prepare m for burial. 13I tell you the truth, wherever this gospel is preached throughout the worl what she has done will also be told, in memory of her."

Judas Agrees to Betray Jesus

14Then one of the Twelve—the one called Judas Iscariot—went to the chief pries 15and asked, "What are you willing to give me if I hand him over to you?" So the counted out for him thirty silver coins. 16From then on Judas watched for an opportuni to hand him over.

The Lord's Supper

17On the first day of the Feast of Unleavened Bread, the disciples came to Jesus an asked, "Where do you want us to make preparations for you to eat the Passover?"

18He replied, "Go into the city to a certain man and tell him, 'The Teacher says: M appointed time is near. I am going to celebrate the Passover with my disciples at you house.'" 19So the disciples did as Jesus had directed them and prepared the Passover.

20When evening came, Jesus was reclining at the table with the Twelve. 21And whil they were eating, he said, "I tell you the truth, one of you will betray me."

22They were very sad and began to say to him one after the other, "Surely not I, Lord? 23Jesus replied, "The one who has dipped his hand into the bowl with me will betra me. 24The Son of Man will go just as it is written about him. But woe to that man wh betrays the Son of Man! It would be better for him if he had not been born."

25Then Judas, the one who would betray him, said, "Surely not I, Rabbi?"

Jesus answered, "Yes, it is you."[a]

26While they were eating, Jesus took bread, gave thanks and broke it, and gave it t his disciples, saying, "Take and eat; this is my body."

27Then he took the cup, gave thanks and offered it to them, saying, "Drink from it, all c you. 28This is my blood of the[b] covenant, which is poured out for many for the forgive ness of sins. 29I tell you, I will not drink of this fruit of the vine from now on until that da when I drink it anew with you in my Father's kingdom."

30When they had sung a hymn, they went out to the Mount of Olives.

Jesus Predicts Peter's Denial

31Then Jesus told them, "This very night you will all fall away on account of me, for is written:

> "'I will strike the shepherd,
> and the sheep of the flock will be scattered.'[c]

32But after I have risen, I will go ahead of you into Galilee."

33Peter replied, "Even if all fall away on account of you, I never will."

34"I tell you the truth," Jesus answered, "this very night, before the rooster crows, yo will disown me three times."

35But Peter declared, "Even if I have to die with you, I will never disown you." And a the other disciples said the same.

Gethsemane

36Then Jesus went with his disciples to a place called Gethsemane, and he said t them, "Sit here while I go over there and pray." 37He took Peter and the two sons o

---

a25 Or "You yourself have said it"　　b28 Some manuscripts the new　　c31 Zech. 13:7

ebedee along with him, and he began to be sorrowful and troubled. **38**Then he said to em, "My soul is overwhelmed with sorrow to the point of death. Stay here and keep atch with me."

39Going a little farther, he fell with his face to the ground and prayed, "My Father, if it possible, may this cup be taken from me. Yet not as I will, but as you will."

40Then he returned to his disciples and found them sleeping. "Could you men not keep atch with me for one hour?" he asked Peter. **41**"Watch and pray so that you will not fall to temptation. The spirit is willing, but the body is weak."

42He went away a second time and prayed, "My Father, if it is not possible for this cup be taken away unless I drink it, may your will be done."

43When he came back, he again found them sleeping, because their eyes were heavy. So he left them and went away once ore and prayed the third time, saying me thing.

45Then he returned to the disciples and id to them, "Are you still sleeping and sting? Look, the hour is near, and the Son Man is betrayed into the hands of sin-rs. **46**Rise, let us go! Here comes my be-ayer!"

esus Arrested

47While he was still speaking, Judas, one the Twelve, arrived. With him was a rge crowd armed with swords and clubs, nt from the chief priests and the elders the people. **48**Now the betrayer had ar-nged a signal with them: "The one I kiss the man; arrest him." **49**Going at once to sus, Judas said, "Greetings, Rabbi!" and ssed him.

50Jesus replied, "Friend, do what you me for."*a*

Then the men stepped forward, seized sus and arrested him. **51**With that, one of sus' companions reached for his sword, ew it out and struck the servant of the gh priest, cutting off his ear.

> ### ▣ ▦▦▦▦▦ DISCOVERING GOD ▦▦▦▦▦ ⬒
>
> #### 26:36–46
> #### Life with God
>
> Jesus was in agony the night before his cru-cifixion. He prayed fervently, dreading the cross but submitting himself to his heavenly Father's higher purposes.
>
> You will face deep anguish in your life—everyone does. When that happens, you can do what Jesus did: *pray*. Pray hard, pray deep, pray honestly, pray out all your feelings—not a formula. Pray until you sweat and cry and fall down in exhaustion. Pray with others. Pray alone. Pray as long as it takes, and then pray longer. Pray because nothing else works, and keep praying when it doesn't seem to work. Pray because Jesus prayed, pray because you want to pray, pray because you don't want to pray. Pray out loud, pray quietly. Pray when-ever you think about it, pray instead of just thinking about it. Pray when you walk and when you drive and when you wake up and when you go to sleep. Pray before you forget. Pray right now.

52"Put your sword back in its place," Jesus said to him, "for all who draw the sword will e by the sword. **53**Do you think I cannot call on my Father, and he will at once put at my sposal more than twelve legions of angels? **54**But how then would the Scriptures be filled that say it must happen in this way?"

55At that time Jesus said to the crowd, "Am I leading a rebellion, that you have come t with swords and clubs to capture me? Every day I sat in the temple courts teaching, d you did not arrest me. **56**But this has all taken place that the writings of the prophets ight be fulfilled." Then all the disciples deserted him and fled.

efore the Sanhedrin

57Those who had arrested Jesus took him to Caiaphas, the high priest, where the achers of the law and the elders had assembled. **58**But Peter followed him at a distance, ght up to the courtyard of the high priest. He entered and sat down with the guards to e the outcome.

) Or *"Friend, why have you come?"*

⁵⁹The chief priests and the whole Sanhedrin were looking for false evidence again Jesus so that they could put him to death. ⁶⁰But they did not find any, though many fals witnesses came forward.

Finally two came forward ⁶¹and declared, "This fellow said, 'I am able to destroy th temple of God and rebuild it in three days.'"

⁶²Then the high priest stood up and sa to Jesus, "Are you not going to answer? Wh is this testimony that these men are bringir against you?" ⁶³But Jesus remained siler

The high priest said to him, "I charge yc under oath by the living God: Tell us if yc are the Christ,ᵃ the Son of God."

⁶⁴"Yes, it is as you say," Jesus replie "But I say to all of you: In the future yc will see the Son of Man sitting at the rigl hand of the Mighty One and coming on th clouds of heaven."

⁶⁵Then the high priest tore his cloth: and said, "He has spoken blasphemy! Wł do we need any more witnesses? Loc now you have heard the blasphem ⁶⁶What do you think?"

"He is worthy of death," they answere ⁶⁷Then they spit in his face and struck him with their fists. Others slapped hi ⁶⁸and said, "Prophesy to us, Christ. Who hit you?"

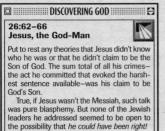

☐ ⬛ DISCOVERING GOD ⬛ ⏩

26:62–66
Jesus, the God-Man

Put to rest any theories that Jesus didn't know who he was or that he didn't claim to be the Son of God. The sum total of all his crimes— the act he committed that evoked the harshest sentence available—was his claim to be God's Son.

True, if Jesus wasn't the Messiah, such talk was pure blasphemy. But none of the Jewish leaders he addressed seemed to be open to the possibility that *he could have been right!* Don't make the same mistake.

Peter Disowns Jesus

⁶⁹Now Peter was sitting out in the courtyard, and a servant girl came to him. "You als were with Jesus of Galilee," she said.

⁷⁰But he denied it before them all. "I don't know what you're talking about," he sai ⁷¹Then he went out to the gateway, where another girl saw him and said to the peop there, "This fellow was with Jesus of Nazareth."

⁷²He denied it again, with an oath: "I don't know the man!"

⁷³After a little while, those standing there went up to Peter and said, "Surely you a one of them, for your accent gives you away."

⁷⁴Then he began to call down curses on himself and he swore to them, "I don't kno the man!"

Immediately a rooster crowed. ⁷⁵Then Peter remembered the word Jesus had spoke "Before the rooster crows, you will disown me three times." And he went outside ar wept bitterly.

Judas Hangs Himself

27 Early in the morning, all the chief priests and the elders of the people car to the decision to put Jesus to death. ²They bound him, led him away ar handed him over to Pilate, the governor.

³When Judas, who had betrayed him, saw that Jesus was condemned, he was seize with remorse and returned the thirty silver coins to the chief priests and the elders. ⁴ have sinned," he said, "for I have betrayed innocent blood."

"What is that to us?" they replied. "That's your responsibility."

⁵So Judas threw the money into the temple and left. Then he went away and hange himself.

ᵃ63 Or Messiah; also in verse 68

⁶The chief priests picked up the coins and said, "It is against the law to put this into the treasury, since it is blood money." ⁷So they decided to use the money to buy the potter's field as a burial place for foreigners. ⁸That is why it has been called the Field of Blood to this day. ⁹Then what was spoken by Jeremiah the prophet was fulfilled: "They took the thirty silver coins, the price set on him by the people of Israel, ¹⁰and they used them to buy the potter's field, as the Lord commanded me."ᵃ

Jesus Before Pilate

¹¹Meanwhile Jesus stood before the governor, and the governor asked him, "Are you the king of the Jews?"

"Yes, it is as you say," Jesus replied.

¹²When he was accused by the chief priests and the elders, he gave no answer. ¹³Then Pilate asked him, "Don't you hear the testimony they are bringing against you?" ¹⁴But Jesus made no reply, not even to a single charge—to the great amazement of the governor.

¹⁵Now it was the governor's custom at the Feast to release a prisoner chosen by the crowd. ¹⁶At that time they had a notorious prisoner, called Barabbas. ¹⁷So when the crowd had gathered, Pilate asked them, "Which one do you want me to release to you: Barabbas, or Jesus who is called Christ?" ¹⁸For he knew it was out of envy that they had handed Jesus over to him.

¹⁹While Pilate was sitting on the judge's seat, his wife sent him this message: "Don't have anything to do with that innocent man, for I have suffered a great deal today in a dream because of him."

²⁰But the chief priests and the elders persuaded the crowd to ask for Barabbas and to have Jesus executed.

²¹"Which of the two do you want me to release to you?" asked the governor.

"Barabbas," they answered.

²²"What shall I do, then, with Jesus who is called Christ?" Pilate asked.

They all answered, "Crucify him!"

²³"Why? What crime has he committed?" asked Pilate.

But they shouted all the louder, "Crucify him!"

²⁴When Pilate saw that he was getting nowhere, but that instead an uproar was starting, he took water and washed his hands in front of the crowd. "I am innocent of this man's blood," he said. "It is your responsibility!"

²⁵All the people answered, "Let his blood be on us and on our children!"

²⁶Then he released Barabbas to them. But he had Jesus flogged, and handed him over to be crucified.

The Soldiers Mock Jesus

²⁷Then the governor's soldiers took Jesus into the Praetorium and gathered the whole company of soldiers around him. ²⁸They stripped him and put a scarlet robe on him, ²⁹and then twisted together a crown of thorns and set it on his head. They put a staff in his right hand and knelt in front of him and mocked him. "Hail, king of the Jews!" they said. ³⁰They spit on him, and took the staff and struck him on the head again and again. ³¹After they had mocked him, they took off the robe and put his own clothes on him. Then they led him away to crucify him.

The Crucifixion

³²As they were going out, they met a man from Cyrene, named Simon, and they forced him to carry the cross. ³³They came to a place called Golgotha (which means The Place of

ᵃ10 See Zech. 11:12,13; Jer. 19:1-13; 32:6-9.

the Skull). ³⁴There they offered Jesus wine to drink, mixed with gall; but after tasting it, he refused to drink it. ³⁵When they had crucified him, they divided up his clothes by casting lots.ᵃ ³⁶And sitting down, they kept watch over him there. ³⁷Above his head they placed the written charge against him: THIS IS JESUS, THE KING OF THE JEWS. ³⁸Two robbers were crucified with him, one on his right and one on his left. ³⁹Those who passed by hurled insults at him, shaking their heads ⁴⁰and saying, "You who are going to destroy the temple and build it in three days, save yourself! Come down from the cross, if you are the Son of God!"

⁴¹In the same way the chief priests, the teachers of the law and the elders mocked him. ⁴²"He saved others," they said, "but he can't save himself! He's the King of Israel! Let him come down now from the cross, and we will believe in him. ⁴³He trusts in God. Let God rescue him now if he wants him, for he said, 'I am the Son of God.'" ⁴⁴In the same way the robbers who were crucified with him also heaped insults on him.

The Death of Jesus

⁴⁵From the sixth hour until the ninth hour darkness came over all the land. ⁴⁶About the ninth hour Jesus cried out in a loud voice, "*Eloi, Eloi,*ᵇ *lama sabachthani?*"—which means, "My God, my God, why have you forsaken me?"ᶜ

⁴⁷When some of those standing there heard this, they said, "He's calling Elijah."

⁴⁸Immediately one of them ran and got a sponge. He filled it with wine vinegar, put it on a stick, and offered it to Jesus to drink. ⁴⁹The rest said, "Now leave him alone. Let's see if Elijah comes to save him."

⁵⁰And when Jesus had cried out again in a loud voice, he gave up his spirit.

⁵¹At that moment the curtain of the temple was torn in two from top to bottom. The earth shook and the rocks split. ⁵²The tombs broke open and the bodies of many holy people who had died were raised to life. ⁵³They came out of the tombs, and after Jesus' resurrection they went into the holy city and appeared to many people.

⊡ ▓▓▓▓ ADDRESSING QUESTIONS ▓▓▓▓ ⇄

27:50–51
Unseen Realities   **Q**

The instant Jesus died, the curtain in the temple was miraculously torn. This curtain had separated the innermost part of the temple from all people except the high priest, and he could enter only once a year. But in tearing this curtain, God signified that Jesus' sacrificial death removed the barrier and opened the way to give people direct access to him.

Anyone can come into the presence of God if he or she comes in the name and with the merits of Jesus Christ. Direct access to God is a free gift for anyone who asks.

⁵⁴When the centurion and those with him who were guarding Jesus saw the earthquake and all that had happened, they were terrified, and exclaimed, "Surely he was the Sonᵈ of God!"

⁵⁵Many women were there, watching from a distance. They had followed Jesus from Galilee to care for his needs. ⁵⁶Among them were Mary Magdalene, Mary the mother of James and Joses, and the mother of Zebedee's sons.

The Burial of Jesus

⁵⁷As evening approached, there came a rich man from Arimathea, named Joseph, who had himself become a disciple of Jesus. ⁵⁸Going to Pilate, he asked for Jesus' body, and Pilate ordered that it be given to him. ⁵⁹Joseph took the body, wrapped it in a clean linen cloth, ⁶⁰and placed it in his own new tomb that he had cut out of the rock. He rolled a big

---

ᵃ35 A few late manuscripts *lots that the word spoken by the prophet might be fulfilled: "They divided my garments among themselves and cast lots for my clothing"* (Psalm 22:18)   ᵇ46 Some manuscripts *Eli, Eli*   ᶜ46 Psalm 22:1   ᵈ54 Or *a son*

stone in front of the entrance to the tomb and went away. ⁶¹Mary Magdalene and the other Mary were sitting there opposite the tomb.

The Guard at the Tomb

⁶²The next day, the one after Preparation Day, the chief priests and the Pharisees went to Pilate. ⁶³"Sir," they said, "we remember that while he was still alive that deceiver said, 'After three days I will rise again.' ⁶⁴So give the order for the tomb to be made secure until the third day. Otherwise, his disciples may come and steal the body and tell the people that he has been raised from the dead. This last deception will be worse than the first."

⁶⁵"Take a guard," Pilate answered. "Go, make the tomb as secure as you know how." ⁶⁶So they went and made the tomb secure by putting a seal on the stone and posting the guard.

The Resurrection

28 After the Sabbath, at dawn on the first day of the week, Mary Magdalene and the other Mary went to look at the tomb.

²There was a violent earthquake, for an angel of the Lord came down from heaven and, going to the tomb, rolled back the stone and sat on it. ³His appearance was like lightning, and his clothes were white as snow. ⁴The guards were so afraid of him that they shook and became like dead men.

⁵The angel said to the women, "Do not be afraid, for I know that you are looking for Jesus, who was crucified. ⁶He is not here; he has risen, just as he said. Come and see the place where he lay. ⁷Then go quickly and tell his disciples: 'He has risen from the dead and is going ahead of you into Galilee. There you will see him.' Now I have told you."

⁸So the women hurried away from the tomb, afraid yet filled with joy, and ran to tell his disciples. ⁹Suddenly Jesus met them. "Greetings," he said. They came to him, clasped his feet and worshiped him. ¹⁰Then Jesus said to them, "Do not be afraid. Go and tell my brothers to go to Galilee; there they will see me."

The Guards' Report

¹¹While the women were on their way, some of the guards went into the city and reported to the chief priests everything that had happened. ¹²When the chief priests had met with the elders and devised a plan, they gave the soldiers a large sum of money, ¹³telling them, "You are to say, 'His disciples came during the night and stole him away while we were asleep.' ¹⁴If this report gets to the governor, we will satisfy him and keep you out of trouble." ¹⁵So the soldiers took the money and did as they were instructed. And this story has been widely circulated among the Jews to this very day.

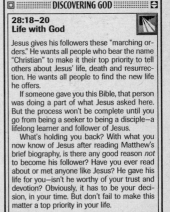

DISCOVERING GOD

28:18–20
Life with God

Jesus gives his followers these "marching orders." He wants all people who bear the name "Christian" to make it their top priority to tell others about Jesus' life, death and resurrection. He wants all people to find the new life he offers.

If someone gave you this Bible, that person was doing a part of what Jesus asked here. But the process won't be complete until you go from being a seeker to being a disciple—a lifelong learner and follower of Jesus.

What's holding you back? With what you now know of Jesus after reading Matthew's brief biography, is there any good reason *not* to become his follower? Have you ever read about or met anyone like Jesus? He gave his life for you—isn't he worthy of your trust and devotion? Obviously, it has to be your decision, in your time. But don't fail to make this matter a top priority in your life.

The Great Commission

¹⁶Then the eleven disciples went to Galilee, to the mountain where Jesus had told them to go. ¹⁷When they saw him, they worshiped him; but some doubted. ¹⁸Then Jesus came to them and said, "All authority in heaven and on earth has been given to me. ¹⁹Therefore go and make disciples of all nations, baptizing them in^a the name of the Father and of the Son and of the Holy Spirit, ²⁰and teaching them to obey everything I have commanded you. And surely I am with you always, to the very end of the age."

a 19 Or *into*; see Acts 8:16; 19:5; Romans 6:3; 1 Cor. 1:13; 10:2 and Gal. 3:27.

My life before I came to Christ was one of selfishness, uncontrolled sexual immorality, and total disregard for God's Word. I did what I wanted when I wanted, not caring about anyone else. My marriage crumbled as repeated adultery took me farther from God. Eventually I left my wife for another woman—a relationship that only lasted a few months.

During this time my ex-wife experienced extreme emotional and physical pain as information about my extramarital affairs unfolded. Seeing her in this state made the results of my actions crystal clear. Pain and guilt gripped my heart because of what I had done to her, an innocent victim of my selfishness. This realization brought me to my knees, asking God for forgiveness and affirming my faith in Jesus Christ as my Savior.

With God pouring his grace upon me, I have begun a new life in Christ—praying, studying and working every day to become more Christ-like. I know I am saved by God's grace and now try my best to walk in the path that God has chosen for me. My new life in Christ has changed me more than I could ever imagine, and that change is evident to people who know me well. I am like a sponge, absorbing God's Word daily while trying to live a loving and righteous life.

God, through his Holy Spirit, has moved me to reconcile with my ex-wife and ask for her forgiveness. We have begun the long road to remarriage and hope, through the power of God's working in our lives, to leave the past behind and embark on a new future. "Yea God" for being gracious!

I was raised to believe in God. I've always known that Jesus died for my sins and that God loves me. God's plan of salvation was presented to me on several occasions. However, I never fully understood what a personal relationship with Christ was or why I needed to commit my life to him.

After joining a Bible study in high school I began to see that the Christian life does not consist of just being a "good" person. There I learned that trust in Jesus' victory over sin through his death and resurrection is the key to salvation.

After an incident in which I nearly drowned, I realized that Jesus was and is actively involved in my life, not just a passive observer (as I had previously believed). Four months after that incident a friend challenged me to commit my life to Christ, and I did.

I now take time every day to read God's Word and look for his leading in my life. I'm making my life's goal one of seeking God and pleasing him in whatever I do instead of looking out for my own interests.

MARK

Introduction

THE BOTTOM LINE

In this book, the most succinct of all the stories about Jesus' life, Mark provides his readers with highlights of Christ's work on earth. Mark also reports reactions of people who watched Jesus in action. As with a modern newspaper reporter, Mark wanted his readers to believe in and feel the human element of his subject. As you read this book, however, you'll come to realize that Jesus was more than just human—he was also God, who came to earth as one of us.

CENTRAL IDEAS

- Understanding Jesus' mission requires careful study of his final week on earth—his death and resurrection from the dead.
- Jesus' divine power was brilliantly displayed in the miracles he performed.
- Christ gives us the ultimate example of leading by serving.
- Jesus is not just the Jewish Messiah—he came to be the Savior of the whole world.

OUTLINE

1. Beginnings of Jesus' ministry (1:1–13)
2. Jesus' ministry in Galilee (1:14–6:29)
3. Jesus withdraws from Galilee (6:30–9:50)
4. Jesus' ministry in Judea and Perea (ch. 10)
5. Jesus' final week (chs. 11–15)
6. Jesus' resurrection from the dead (ch. 16)

TITLE

This book is named after its author, Mark, who was a companion of Jesus' disciple Peter.

AUTHOR AND READERS

Mark wrote his gospel based on interviews with Peter, one of Jesus' most outspoken and colorful disciples. The book's distinctly non-Jewish flavor makes it likely that Mark wrote this book to believers in Rome.

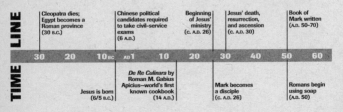

TIME LINE

Cleopatra dies; Egypt becomes a Roman province (30 B.C.)	Chinese political candidates required to take civil-service exams (6 A.D.)	Beginning of Jesus' ministry (c. A.D. 26)	Jesus' death, resurrection, and ascension (c. A.D. 30)	Book of Mark written (A.D. 50–70)
30 20 10 B.C. AD 1 10	20	30 40	50 60	
	De Re Culinara by Roman M. Gabius Apicius—world's first known cookbook (14 A.D.)			
Jesus is born (6/5 B.C.)		Mark becomes a disciple (c. A.D. 26)	Romans begin using soap (A.D. 50)	

In the 1930s and '40s Howard Hughes cut a dashing figure—as a white-scarfed aviator, as a tuxedoed film producer escorting beautiful screen stars, and as an aggressive industrialist. Hughes was a man who seemed to have it all.

After achieving success as a businessman and movie producer, he formed the Hughes Aircraft Company and test-piloted his own planes. By 1930 he was a national hero, having set three new speed records.

But as Hughes's wealth grew, his personal world slowly unraveled. After a series of mental breakdowns in the 1950s, he insulated himself from outsiders and conducted all his business through intermediaries. Visitors were required to perform odd cleansing procedures and wear white cotton gloves. He even quit wearing clothes for what he called "sanitary reasons."

Eventually, the billionaire became an inmate in his own asylum—a Las Vegas hotel that he owned. The man who had once been the toast of the town lay naked in a darkened penthouse. His straggly beard hung down to his waist, and his matted hair reached the middle of his back. His fingernails grew two inches long, and his toenails hadn't been trimmed for so long that they resembled corkscrews. When the 6'4" Texan died at the age of 70, he weighed a scant 90 pounds.

> **Eventually, the billionaire became an inmate in his own asylum.**

Howard Hughes had everything most of us would ever want—power, beauty, wealth, and fame. But why—with virtually unlimited wealth, hundreds of assistants, and countless beautiful women available to him—was he so lonely and unloved?

The answer is almost too simple. He mistook "the good life" for the endless pursuit of "life's goods." He starved his soul to feed his cravings. *Howard Hughes chose a life of consumption and in the end was consumed by it.*

Jesus warned about the danger of misdirected ambition. He explained how we can harness our energy for accomplishments that last. Because Mark wrote for readers outside the traditional Jewish religion of his day, his snapshots of Jesus have appealed to seekers throughout the centuries. If you're searching for real fulfillment, turn to Mark chapter 8, verses 34–36 (page 1317). In those three verses Jesus points to a quality of life that all the money in the world can't buy.

MARK

John the Baptist Prepares the Way

1 The beginning of the gospel about Jesus Christ, the Son of God.[a]

²It is written in Isaiah the prophet:

> "I will send my messenger ahead of you,
>   who will prepare your way"[b]—
> ³"a voice of one calling in the desert,
>   'Prepare the way for the Lord,
>   make straight paths for him.'"[c]

⁴And so John came, baptizing in the desert region and preaching a baptism of repentance for the forgiveness of sins. ⁵The whole Judean countryside and all the people of Jerusalem went out to him. Confessing their sins, they were baptized by him in the Jordan River. ⁶John wore clothing made of camel's hair, with a leather belt around his waist, and he ate locusts and wild honey. ⁷And this was his message: "After me will come one more powerful than I, the thongs of whose sandals I am not worthy to stoop down and untie. ⁸I baptize you with[d] water, but he will baptize you with the Holy Spirit."

The Baptism and Temptation of Jesus

⁹At that time Jesus came from Nazareth in Galilee and was baptized by John in the Jordan. ¹⁰As Jesus was coming up out of the water, he saw heaven being torn open and the Spirit descending on him like a dove. ¹¹And a voice came from heaven: "You are my Son, whom I love; with you I am well pleased."

¹²At once the Spirit sent him out into the desert, ¹³and he was in the desert forty days, being tempted by Satan. He was with the wild animals, and angels attended him.

The Calling of the First Disciples

¹⁴After John was put in prison, Jesus went into Galilee, proclaiming the good news of God. ¹⁵"The time has come," he said. "The kingdom of God is near. Repent and believe the good news!"

¹⁶As Jesus walked beside the Sea of Galilee, he saw Simon and his brother Andrew casting a net into the lake, for they were fishermen. ¹⁷"Come, follow me," Jesus said, "and I will make you fishers of men." ¹⁸At once they left their nets and followed him.

¹⁹When he had gone a little farther, he saw James son of Zebedee and his brother John in a boat, preparing their nets. ²⁰Without delay he called them, and they left their father Zebedee in the boat with the hired men and followed him.

Jesus Drives Out an Evil Spirit

²¹They went to Capernaum, and when the Sabbath came, Jesus went into the synagogue and began to teach. ²²The people were amazed at his teaching, because he taught them as one who had authority, not as the teachers of the law. ²³Just then a man in their synagogue who was possessed by an evil[e] spirit cried out, ²⁴"What do you want with

---

a1 Some manuscripts do not have *the Son of God.*   *b2* Mal. 3:1   *c3* Isaiah 40:3   *d8* Or *in*   *e23* Greek *unclean; also in verses 26 and 27*

us, Jesus of Nazareth? Have you come to destroy us? I know who you are—the Holy One of God!"

²⁵"Be quiet!" said Jesus sternly. "Come out of him!" ²⁶The evil spirit shook the man violently and came out of him with a shriek.

²⁷The people were all so amazed that they asked each other, "What is this? A new teaching—and with authority! He even gives orders to evil spirits and they obey him." ²⁸News about him spread quickly over the whole region of Galilee.

Jesus Heals Many

²⁹As soon as they left the synagogue, they went with James and John to the home of Simon and Andrew. ³⁰Simon's mother-in-law was in bed with a fever, and they told Jesus about her. ³¹So he went to her, took her hand and helped her up. The fever left her and she began to wait on them.

³²That evening after sunset the people brought to Jesus all the sick and demon-possessed. ³³The whole town gathered at the door, ³⁴and Jesus healed many who had various diseases. He also drove out many demons, but he would not let the demons speak because they knew who he was.

Jesus Prays in a Solitary Place

³⁵Very early in the morning, while it was still dark, Jesus got up, left the house and went off to a solitary place, where he prayed. ³⁶Simon and his companions went to look for him, ³⁷and when they found him, they exclaimed: "Everyone is looking for you!"

³⁸Jesus replied, "Let us go somewhere else—to the nearby villages—so I can preach there also. That is why I have come." ³⁹So he traveled throughout Galilee, preaching in their synagogues and driving out demons.

A Man With Leprosy

⁴⁰A man with leprosy*ᵃ* came to him and begged him on his knees, "If you are willing, you can make me clean."

⁴¹Filled with compassion, Jesus reached out his hand and touched the man. "I am willing," he said. "Be clean!" ⁴²Immediately the leprosy left him and he was cured.

⁴³Jesus sent him away at once with a strong warning: ⁴⁴"See that you don't tell this to

---

ᵃ40 The Greek word was used for various diseases affecting the skin—not necessarily leprosy.

◫ ▦▦▦▦▦▦▦▦▦▦▦▦ **DISCOVERING GOD** ▦▦▦▦▦▦▦▦▦▦▦▦ ⬒

1:40–45
Life with God

Loneliness is a horrible feeling. It's one of the most terrifying experiences we can undergo, and people will do almost anything to get relief from it.

The leper Jesus encountered was well acquainted with loneliness. Jewish law forced him to live apart from others. He had to wear a covering over his mouth and give warning of his approach by crying, "Unclean! Unclean!" When Jesus saw this man (who had sores on his skin and may have had fingers, toes or entire limbs missing), he felt compassion.

Then Jesus did an amazing thing: He touched the leper—sores and all. Jesus connected with this man in his desperate condition and healed him.

Even if we had that kind of power, most of us would have done the opposite. We would have first healed the man and *then* touched him. Not Jesus. He saw that he had to address this man's loneliness before he addressed his physical ailment.

If you're seeking God and feel that you need to clean up your life before he'll accept you, you've got it backwards. God wants to reach out to you just where you are, no matter what your spiritual condition. Then *he'll* do the miracle of cleaning you up!

anyone. But go, show yourself to the priest and offer the sacrifices that Moses command-ed for your cleansing, as a testimony to them." ⁴⁵Instead he went out and began to talk freely, spreading the news. As a result, Jesus could no longer enter a town openly but stayed outside in lonely places. Yet the people still came to him from everywhere.

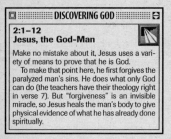

DISCOVERING GOD

2:1–12
Jesus, the God-Man

Make no mistake about it, Jesus uses a variety of means to prove that he is God.

To make that point here, he first forgives the paralyzed man's sins. He does what only God can do (the teachers have their theology right in verse 7). But "forgiveness" is an invisible miracle, so Jesus heals the man's body to give physical evidence of what he has already done spiritually.

Jesus Heals a Paralytic

2 A few days later, when Jesus again entered Capernaum, the people heard that he had come home. ²So many gathered that there was no room left, not even outside the door, and he preached the word to them. ³Some men came, bringing to him a paralytic, carried by four of them. ⁴Since they could not get him to Jesus because of the crowd, they made an opening in the roof above Jesus and, after digging through it, lowered the mat the paralyzed man was lying on. ⁵When Jesus saw their faith, he said to the paralytic, "Son, your sins are forgiven."

⁶Now some teachers of the law were sitting there, thinking to themselves, ⁷"Why does this fellow talk like that? He's blaspheming! Who can forgive sins but God alone?"

⁸Immediately Jesus knew in his spirit that this was what they were thinking in their hearts, and he said to them, "Why are you thinking these things? ⁹Which is easier: to say to the paralytic, 'Your sins are forgiven,' or to say, 'Get up, take your mat and walk'? ¹⁰But that you may know that the Son of Man has authority on earth to forgive sins . . ." He said to the paralytic, ¹¹"I tell you, get up, take your mat and go home." ¹²He got up, took his mat and walked out in full view of them all. This amazed everyone and they praised God, saying, "We have never seen anything like this!"

The Calling of Levi

¹³Once again Jesus went out beside the lake. A large crowd came to him, and he began to teach them. ¹⁴As he walked along, he saw Levi son of Alphaeus sitting at the tax collector's booth. "Follow me," Jesus told him, and Levi got up and followed him.

¹⁵While Jesus was having dinner at Levi's house, many tax collectors and "sinners" were eating with him and his disciples, for there were many who followed him. ¹⁶When the teachers of the law who were Pharisees saw him eating with the "sinners" and tax collectors, they asked his disciples: "Why does he eat with tax collectors and 'sinners'?"

¹⁷On hearing this, Jesus said to them, "It is not the healthy who need a doctor, but the sick. I have not come to call the righteous, but sinners."

Jesus Questioned About Fasting

¹⁸Now John's disciples and the Pharisees were fasting. Some people came and asked Jesus, "How is it that John's disciples and the disciples of the Pharisees are fasting, but yours are not?"

¹⁹Jesus answered, "How can the guests of the bridegroom fast while he is with them? They cannot, so long as they have him with them. ²⁰But the time will come when the bridegroom will be taken from them, and on that day they will fast.

²¹"No one sews a patch of unshrunk cloth on an old garment. If he does, the new piece will pull away from the old, making the tear worse. ²²And no one pours new wine into old wineskins. If he does, the wine will burst the skins, and both the wine and the wineskins will be ruined. No, he pours new wine into new wineskins."

Lord of the Sabbath

²³One Sabbath Jesus was going through the grainfields, and as his disciples walked along, they began to pick some heads of grain. ²⁴The Pharisees said to him, "Look, why are they doing what is unlawful on the Sabbath?"

²⁵He answered, "Have you never read what David did when he and his companions were hungry and in need? ²⁶In the days of Abiathar the high priest, he entered the house of God and ate the consecrated bread, which is lawful only for priests to eat. And he also gave some to his companions."

²⁷Then he said to them, "The Sabbath was made for man, not man for the Sabbath. ²⁸So the Son of Man is Lord even of the Sabbath."

3 Another time he went into the synagogue, and a man with a shriveled hand was there. ²Some of them were looking for a reason to accuse Jesus, so they watched him closely to see if he would heal him on the Sabbath. ³Jesus said to the man with the shriveled hand, "Stand up in front of everyone."

⁴Then Jesus asked them, "Which is lawful on the Sabbath: to do good or to do evil, to save life or to kill?" But they remained silent.

⁵He looked around at them in anger and, deeply distressed at their stubborn hearts, said to the man, "Stretch out your hand." He stretched it out, and his hand was completely restored. ⁶Then the Pharisees went out and began to plot with the Herodians how they might kill Jesus.

Crowds Follow Jesus

⁷Jesus withdrew with his disciples to the lake, and a large crowd from Galilee followed. ⁸When they heard all he was doing, many people came to him from Judea, Jerusalem, Idumea, and the regions across the Jordan and around Tyre and Sidon. ⁹Because of the crowd he told his disciples to have a small boat ready for him, to keep the people from crowding him. ¹⁰For he had healed many, so that those with diseases were pushing forward to touch him. ¹¹Whenever the evil*ᵃ* spirits saw him, they fell down before him and cried out, "You are the Son of God." ¹²But he gave them strict orders not to tell who he was.

The Appointing of the Twelve Apostles

¹³Jesus went up on a mountainside and called to him those he wanted, and they came to him. ¹⁴He appointed twelve—designating them apostles*ᵇ*—that they might be with him and that he might send them out to preach ¹⁵and to have authority to drive out demons. ¹⁶These are the twelve he appointed: Simon (to whom he gave the name Peter); ¹⁷James son of Zebedee and his brother John (to them he gave the name Boanerges, which means Sons of Thunder); ¹⁸Andrew, Philip, Bartholomew, Matthew, Thomas, James son of Alphaeus, Thaddaeus, Simon the Zealot ¹⁹and Judas Iscariot, who betrayed him.

Jesus and Beelzebub

²⁰Then Jesus entered a house, and again a crowd gathered, so that he and his disciples were not even able to eat. ²¹When his family heard about this, they went to take charge of him, for they said, "He is out of his mind."

²²And the teachers of the law who came down from Jerusalem said, "He is possessed by Beelzebub*ᶜ*! By the prince of demons he is driving out demons."

²³So Jesus called them and spoke to them in parables: "How can Satan drive out Satan? ²⁴If a kingdom is divided against itself, that kingdom cannot stand. ²⁵If a house is divided against itself, that house cannot stand. ²⁶And if Satan opposes himself and is divided, he cannot stand; his end has come. ²⁷In fact, no one can enter a strong man's

---

ᵃ11 Greek *unclean;* also in verse 30   *ᵇ14* Some manuscripts do not have *designating them apostles.*   *ᶜ22* Greek
Beezeboul or *Beelzeboul*

house and carry off his possessions unless he first ties up the strong man. Then he can rob his house. ²⁸I tell you the truth, all the sins and blasphemies of men will be forgiven them. ²⁹But whoever blasphemes against the Holy Spirit will never be forgiven; he is guilty of an eternal sin."

³⁰He said this because they were saying, "He has an evil spirit."

ADDRESSING QUESTIONS

3:29–30
Human Experience

Some people read this statement about an "unforgivable sin" and panic. They think, "What if I've already committed this sin without knowing it? Am I beyond hope?" But this statement's context shows us the only unforgivable sin: rejecting Christ in an ultimate and irrevocable fashion.

The religious leaders here attributed Jesus' miraculous powers to Satan. They viewed Jesus with such contempt that they explained away his miracles by saying the devil was behind those deeds. These men rejected the only One who could forgive them. In effect, they called God Satan. There is no remedy for such an irrational hatred of Jesus and such an upside-down view of the Holy Spirit's power.

If you're worried that you may have committed the unforgivable sin sometime in the past, take heart! The fact that you're concerned about it shows that you haven't committed it. Your sins are fully forgivable if you'll just come to Christ and receive the free gift of his salvation.

Jesus' Mother and Brothers

³¹Then Jesus' mother and brothers arrived. Standing outside, they sent someone in to call him. ³²A crowd was sitting around him, and they told him, "Your mother and brothers are outside looking for you."

³³"Who are my mother and my brothers?" he asked.

³⁴Then he looked at those seated in a circle around him and said, "Here are my mother and my brothers! ³⁵Whoever does God's will is my brother and sister and mother."

The Parable of the Sower

4 Again Jesus began to teach by the lake. The crowd that gathered around him was so large that he got into a boat and sat in it out on the lake, while all the people were along the shore at the water's edge. ²He taught them many things by parables, and in his teaching said: ³"Listen! A farmer went out to sow his seed. ⁴As he was scattering the seed, some fell along the path, and the birds came and ate it up. ⁵Some fell on rocky places, where it did not have much soil. It sprang up quickly, because the soil was shallow. ⁶But when the sun came up, the plants were scorched, and they withered because they had no root. ⁷Other seed fell among thorns, which grew up and choked the plants, so that they did not bear grain. ⁸Still other seed fell on good soil. It came up, grew and produced a crop, multiplying thirty, sixty, or even a hundred times."

⁹Then Jesus said, "He who has ears to hear, let him hear."

¹⁰When he was alone, the Twelve and the others around him asked him about the parables. ¹¹He told them, "The secret of the kingdom of God has been given to you. But to those on the outside everything is said in parables ¹²so that,

" 'they may be ever seeing but never perceiving,
    and ever hearing but never understanding;
otherwise they might turn and be forgiven!' ª "

¹³Then Jesus said to them, "Don't you understand this parable? How then will you understand any parable? ¹⁴The farmer sows the word. ¹⁵Some people are like seed along the path, where the word is sown. As soon as they hear it, Satan comes and takes away the word that was sown in them. ¹⁶Others, like seed sown on rocky places, hear the word and at once receive it with joy. ¹⁷But since they have no root, they last only a short time. When trouble or persecution comes because of the word, they quickly fall away. ¹⁸Still others, like seed sown among thorns, hear the word; ¹⁹but the worries of this life,

ª 12 Isaiah 6:9,10

the deceitfulness of wealth and the desires for other things come in and choke the word, making it unfruitful. ²⁰Others, like seed sown on good soil, hear the word, accept it, and produce a crop—thirty, sixty or even a hundred times what was sown."

A Lamp on a Stand

²¹He said to them, "Do you bring in a lamp to put it under a bowl or a bed? Instead, don't you put it on its stand? ²²For whatever is hidden is meant to be disclosed, and whatever is concealed is meant to be brought out into the open. ²³If anyone has ears to hear, let him hear."

²⁴"Consider carefully what you hear," he continued. "With the measure you use, it will be measured to you—and even more. ²⁵Whoever has will be given more; whoever does not have, even what he has will be taken from him."

The Parable of the Growing Seed

²⁶He also said, "This is what the kingdom of God is like. A man scatters seed on the ground. ²⁷Night and day, whether he sleeps or gets up, the seed sprouts and grows, though he does not know how. ²⁸All by itself the soil produces grain—first the stalk, then the head, then the full kernel in the head. ²⁹As soon as the grain is ripe, he puts the sickle to it, because the harvest has come."

The Parable of the Mustard Seed

³⁰Again he said, "What shall we say the kingdom of God is like, or what parable shall we use to describe it? ³¹It is like a mustard seed, which is the smallest seed you plant in the ground. ³²Yet when planted, it grows and becomes the largest of all garden plants, with such big branches that the birds of the air can perch in its shade."

³³With many similar parables Jesus spoke the word to them, as much as they could understand. ³⁴He did not say anything to them without using a parable. But when he was alone with his own disciples, he explained everything.

Jesus Calms the Storm

³⁵That day when evening came, he said to his disciples, "Let us go over to the other side." ³⁶Leaving the crowd behind, they took him along, just as he was, in the boat. There were also other boats with him. ³⁷A furious squall came up, and the waves broke over the boat, so that it was nearly swamped. ³⁸Jesus was in the stern, sleeping on a cushion. The disciples woke him and said to him, "Teacher, don't you care if we drown?"

³⁹He got up, rebuked the wind and said to the waves, "Quiet! Be still!" Then the wind died down and it was completely calm.

⁴⁰He said to his disciples, "Why are you so afraid? Do you still have no faith?"

⁴¹They were terrified and asked each other, "Who is this? Even the wind and the waves obey him!"

The Healing of a Demon-possessed Man

5 They went across the lake to the region of the Gerasenes.ᵃ ²When Jesus got out of the boat, a man with an evilᵇ spirit came from the tombs to meet him. ³This man lived in the tombs, and no one could bind him any more, not even with a chain. ⁴For he had often been chained hand and foot, but he tore the chains apart and broke the irons on his feet. No one was strong enough to subdue him. ⁵Night and day among the tombs and in the hills he would cry out and cut himself with stones.

⁶When he saw Jesus from a distance, he ran and fell on his knees in front of him. ⁷He shouted at the top of his voice, "What do you want with me, Jesus, Son of the Most High God? Swear to God that you won't torture me!" ⁸For Jesus had said to him, "Come out of this man, you evil spirit!"

ᵃ 1 Some manuscripts *Gadarenes*; other manuscripts *Gergesenes*   ᵇ 2 Greek *unclean*; also in verses 8 and 13

⁹Then Jesus asked him, "What is your name?"

"My name is Legion," he replied, "for we are many." ¹⁰And he begged Jesus again and again not to send them out of the area.

¹¹A large herd of pigs was feeding on the nearby hillside. ¹²The demons begged Jesus, "Send us among the pigs; allow us to go into them." ¹³He gave them permission, and the evil spirits came out and went into the pigs. The herd, about two thousand in number, rushed down the steep bank into the lake and were drowned.

¹⁴Those tending the pigs ran off and reported this in the town and countryside, and the people went out to see what had happened. ¹⁵When they came to Jesus, they saw the man who had been possessed by the legion of demons, sitting there, dressed and in his right mind; and they were afraid. ¹⁶Those who had seen it told the people what had happened to the demon-possessed man—and told about the pigs as well. ¹⁷Then the people began to plead with Jesus to leave their region.

¹⁸As Jesus was getting into the boat, the man who had been demon-possessed begged to go with him. ¹⁹Jesus did not let him, but said, "Go home to your family and tell them how much the Lord has done for you, and how he has had mercy on you." ²⁰So the man went away and began to tell in the Decapolis*ᵃ* how much Jesus had done for him. And all the people were amazed.

A Dead Girl and a Sick Woman

²¹When Jesus had again crossed over by boat to the other side of the lake, a large crowd gathered around him while he was by the lake. ²²Then one of the synagogue rulers, named Jairus, came there. Seeing Jesus, he fell at his feet ²³and pleaded earnestly with him, "My little daughter is dying. Please come and put your hands on her so that she will be healed and live." ²⁴So Jesus went with him.

A large crowd followed and pressed around him.

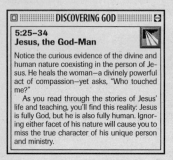

²⁵And a woman was there who had been subject to bleeding for twelve years. ²⁶She had suffered a great deal under the care of many doctors and had spent all she had, yet instead of getting better she grew worse. ²⁷When she heard about Jesus, she came up behind him in the crowd and touched his cloak, ²⁸because she thought, "If I just touch his clothes, I will be healed." ²⁹Immediately her bleeding stopped and she felt in her body that she was freed from her suffering.

³⁰At once Jesus realized that power had gone out from him. He turned around in the crowd and asked, "Who touched my clothes?"

³¹"You see the people crowding against you," his disciples answered, "and yet you can ask, 'Who touched me?' "

³²But Jesus kept looking around to see who had done it. ³³Then the woman, knowing what had happened to her, came and fell at his feet and, trembling with fear, told him the whole truth. ³⁴He said to her, "Daughter, your faith has healed you. Go in peace and be freed from your suffering."

³⁵While Jesus was still speaking, some men came from the house of Jairus, the synagogue ruler. "Your daughter is dead," they said. "Why bother the teacher any more?"

³⁶Ignoring what they said, Jesus told the synagogue ruler, "Don't be afraid; just believe."

ᵃ20 That is, the Ten Cities

37He did not let anyone follow him except Peter, James and John the brother of James. 38When they came to the home of the synagogue ruler, Jesus saw a commotion, with people crying and wailing loudly. 39He went in and said to them, "Why all this commotion and wailing? The child is not dead but asleep." 40But they laughed at him.

After he put them all out, he took the child's father and mother and the disciples who were with him, and went in where the child was. 41He took her by the hand and said to her, *"Talitha koum!"* (which means, "Little girl, I say to you, get up!"). 42Immediately the girl stood up and walked around (she was twelve years old). At this they were completely astonished. 43He gave strict orders not to let anyone know about this, and told them to give her something to eat.

A Prophet Without Honor

6 Jesus left there and went to his hometown, accompanied by his disciples. 2When the Sabbath came, he began to teach in the synagogue, and many who heard him were amazed.

"Where did this man get these things?" they asked. "What's this wisdom that has been given him, that he even does miracles! 3Isn't this the carpenter? Isn't this Mary's son and the brother of James, Joseph,*a* Judas and Simon? Aren't his sisters here with us?" And they took offense at him.

4Jesus said to them, "Only in his hometown, among his relatives and in his own house is a prophet without honor." 5He could not do any miracles there, except lay his hands on a few sick people and heal them. 6And he was amazed at their lack of faith.

Jesus Sends Out the Twelve

Then Jesus went around teaching from village to village. 7Calling the Twelve to him, he sent them out two by two and gave them authority over evil*b* spirits.

8These were his instructions: "Take nothing for the journey except a staff—no bread, no bag, no money in your belts. 9Wear sandals but not an extra tunic. 10Whenever you enter a house, stay there until you leave that town. 11And if any place will not welcome you or listen to you, shake the dust off your feet when you leave, as a testimony against them."

12They went out and preached that people should repent. 13They drove out many demons and anointed many sick people with oil and healed them.

John the Baptist Beheaded

14King Herod heard about this, for Jesus' name had become well known. Some were saying,*c* "John the Baptist has been raised from the dead, and that is why miraculous powers are at work in him."

15Others said, "He is Elijah."

And still others claimed, "He is a prophet, like one of the prophets of long ago."

16But when Herod heard this, he said, "John, the man I beheaded, has been raised from the dead!"

17For Herod himself had given orders to have John arrested, and he had him bound and put in prison. He did this because of Herodias, his brother Philip's wife, whom he had married. 18For John had been saying to Herod, "It is not lawful for you to have your brother's wife." 19So Herodias nursed a grudge against John and wanted to kill him. But she was not able to, 20because Herod feared John and protected him, knowing him to be a righteous and holy man. When Herod heard John, he was greatly puzzled*d*; yet he liked to listen to him.

21Finally the opportune time came. On his birthday Herod gave a banquet for his high

a3 Greek *Joses,* a variant of *Joseph*   *b7* Greek *unclean*   *c14* Some early manuscripts *He was saying*   *d20* Some early manuscripts *he did many things*

officials and military commanders and the leading men of Galilee. ²²When the daughter of Herodias came in and danced, she pleased Herod and his dinner guests.

The king said to the girl, "Ask me for anything you want, and I'll give it to you." ²³And he promised her with an oath, "Whatever you ask I will give you, up to half my kingdom."

²⁴She went out and said to her mother, "What shall I ask for?"

"The head of John the Baptist," she answered.

²⁵At once the girl hurried in to the king with the request: "I want you to give me right now the head of John the Baptist on a platter."

²⁶The king was greatly distressed, but because of his oaths and his dinner guests, he did not want to refuse her. ²⁷So he immediately sent an executioner with orders to bring John's head. The man went, beheaded John in the prison, ²⁸and brought back his head on a platter. He presented it to the girl, and she gave it to her mother. ²⁹On hearing this, John's disciples came and took his body and laid it in a tomb.

KNOWING YOURSELF

6:19–20
Character

Herod was an "armchair seeker." He loved to listen to John the Baptist's message, but he refused to reckon with its implications for his life and take appropriate action. It seems as if Herod used spiritual matters as a diversion to entertain him when other conversation became boring.

Have you ever slipped into the "Herod Syndrome"? Have you engaged Christians in spirited dialog with no intention of making any changes in your life, even if what they say turned out to be true? Be careful—God is not merely an interesting theory to be tossed around by people who love to play intellectual badminton. He is a *reality*, the Creator of the universe and giver of all life.

Though thoughtful discussion is an important part of the seeking process, Herod's refusal to take truth seriously shows us where to draw the line.

Jesus Feeds the Five Thousand

³⁰The apostles gathered around Jesus and reported to him all they had done and taught. ³¹Then, because so many people were coming and going that they did not even have a chance to eat, he said to them, "Come with me by yourselves to a quiet place and get some rest."

³²So they went away by themselves in a boat to a solitary place. ³³But many who saw them leaving recognized them and ran on foot from all the towns and got there ahead of them. ³⁴When Jesus landed and saw a large crowd, he had compassion on them, because they were like sheep without a shepherd. So he began teaching them many things.

³⁵By this time it was late in the day, so his disciples came to him. "This is a remote place," they said, "and it's already very late. ³⁶Send the people away so they can go to the surrounding countryside and villages and buy themselves something to eat."

³⁷But he answered, "You give them something to eat."

They said to him, "That would take eight months of a man's wages[a]! Are we to go and spend that much on bread and give it to them to eat?"

³⁸"How many loaves do you have?" he asked. "Go and see."

When they found out, they said, "Five—and two fish."

³⁹Then Jesus directed them to have all the people sit down in groups on the green grass. ⁴⁰So they sat down in groups of hundreds and fifties. ⁴¹Taking the five loaves and the two fish and looking up to heaven, he gave thanks and broke the loaves. Then he gave them to his disciples to set before the people. He also divided the two fish among them all. ⁴²They all ate and were satisfied, ⁴³and the disciples picked up twelve basketfuls of broken pieces of bread and fish. ⁴⁴The number of the men who had eaten was five thousand.

a 37 Greek take two hundred denarii

Jesus Walks on the Water

⁴⁵Immediately Jesus made his disciples get into the boat and go on ahead of him to Bethsaida, while he dismissed the crowd. ⁴⁶After leaving them, he went up on a mountainside to pray.

⁴⁷When evening came, the boat was in the middle of the lake, and he was alone on land. ⁴⁸He saw the disciples straining at the oars, because the wind was against them. About the fourth watch of the night he went out to them, walking on the lake. He was about to pass by them, ⁴⁹but when they saw him walking on the lake, they thought he was a ghost. They cried out, ⁵⁰because they all saw him and were terrified.

Immediately he spoke to them and said, "Take courage! It is I. Don't be afraid." ⁵¹Then he climbed into the boat with them, and the wind died down. They were completely amazed, ⁵²for they had not understood about the loaves; their hearts were hardened.

⁵³When they had crossed over, they landed at Gennesaret and anchored there. ⁵⁴As soon as they got out of the boat, people recognized Jesus. ⁵⁵They ran throughout that whole region and carried the sick on mats to wherever they heard he was. ⁵⁶And wherever he went—into villages, towns or countryside—they placed the sick in the marketplaces. They begged him to let them touch even the edge of his cloak, and all who touched him were healed.

Clean and Unclean

7 The Pharisees and some of the teachers of the law who had come from Jerusalem gathered around Jesus and ²saw some of his disciples eating food with hands that were "unclean," that is, unwashed. ³(The Pharisees and all the Jews do not eat unless they give their hands a ceremonial washing, holding to the tradition of the elders. ⁴When they come from the marketplace they do not eat unless they wash. And they observe many other traditions, such as the washing of cups, pitchers and kettles.ᵃ)

⁵So the Pharisees and teachers of the law asked Jesus, "Why don't your disciples live according to the tradition of the elders instead of eating their food with 'unclean' hands?"

⁶He replied, "Isaiah was right when he prophesied about you hypocrites; as it is written:

> "'These people honor me with their lips,
>   but their hearts are far from me.
> ⁷They worship me in vain;
>   their teachings are but rules taught by men.'ᵇ

⁸You have let go of the commands of God and are holding on to the traditions of men."

⁹And he said to them: "You have a fine way of setting aside the commands of God in order to observeᶜ your own traditions! ¹⁰For Moses said, 'Honor your father and your mother,'ᵈ and, 'Anyone who curses his father or mother must be put to death.'ᵉ ¹¹But you say that if a man says to his father or mother: 'Whatever help you might otherwise have received from me is Corban' (that is, a gift devoted to God), ¹²then you no longer let him do anything for his father or mother. ¹³Thus you nullify the word of God by your tradition that you have handed down. And you do many things like that."

¹⁴Again Jesus called the crowd to him and said, "Listen to me, everyone, and understand this. ¹⁵Nothing outside a man can make him 'unclean' by going into him. Rather, it is what comes out of a man that makes him 'unclean.'ᶠ"

¹⁷After he had left the crowd and entered the house, his disciples asked him about this parable. ¹⁸"Are you so dull?" he asked. "Don't you see that nothing that enters a man from the outside can make him 'unclean'? ¹⁹For it doesn't go into his heart but into his stomach, and then out of his body." (In saying this, Jesus declared all foods "clean.")

ᵃ4 Some early manuscripts *pitchers, kettles and dining couches*   ᵇ6,7 Isaiah 29:13   ᶜ9 Some manuscripts *set up*
ᵈ10 Exodus 20:12; Deut. 5:16   ᵉ10 Exodus 21:17; Lev. 20:9   ᶠ15 Some early manuscripts *'unclean.'* ¹⁶*If anyone has ears to hear, let him hear.*

20He went on: "What comes out of a man is what makes him 'unclean.' 21For from within, out of men's hearts, come evil thoughts, sexual immorality, theft, murder, adultery, 22greed, malice, deceit, lewdness, envy, slander, arrogance and folly. 23All these evils come from inside and make a man 'unclean.'"

The Faith of a Syrophoenician Woman

24Jesus left that place and went to the vicinity of Tyre.*a* He entered a house and did not want anyone to know it; yet he could not keep his presence secret. 25In fact, as soon as she heard about him, a woman whose little daughter was possessed by an evil*b* spirit came and fell at his feet. 26The woman was a Greek, born in Syrian Phoenicia. She begged Jesus to drive the demon out of her daughter.

27"First let the children eat all they want," he told her, "for it is not right to take the children's bread and toss it to their dogs."

28"Yes, Lord," she replied, "but even the dogs under the table eat the children's crumbs."

29Then he told her, "For such a reply, you may go; the demon has left your daughter."

30She went home and found her child lying on the bed, and the demon gone.

The Healing of a Deaf and Mute Man

31Then Jesus left the vicinity of Tyre and went through Sidon, down to the Sea of Galilee and into the region of the Decapolis.*c* 32There some people brought to him a man who was deaf and could hardly talk, and they begged him to place his hand on the man.

33After he took him aside, away from the crowd, Jesus put his fingers into the man's ears. Then he spit and touched the man's tongue. 34He looked up to heaven and with a deep sigh said to him, *"Ephphatha!"* (which means, "Be opened!"). 35At this, the man's ears were opened, his tongue was loosened and he began to speak plainly.

36Jesus commanded them not to tell anyone. But the more he did so, the more they kept talking about it. 37People were overwhelmed with amazement. "He has done everything well," they said. "He even makes the deaf hear and the mute speak."

Jesus Feeds the Four Thousand

8 During those days another large crowd gathered. Since they had nothing to eat, Jesus called his disciples to him and said, 2"I have compassion for these people; they have already been with me three days and have nothing to eat. 3If I send them home hungry, they will collapse on the way, because some of them have come a long distance."

4His disciples answered, "But where in this remote place can anyone get enough bread to feed them?"

5"How many loaves do you have?" Jesus asked.

"Seven," they replied.

6He told the crowd to sit down on the ground. When he had taken the seven loaves and given thanks, he broke them and gave them to his disciples to set before the people, and they did so. 7They had a few small fish as well; he gave thanks for them also and told the disciples to distribute them. 8The people ate and were satisfied. Afterward the disciples picked up seven basketfuls of broken pieces that were left over. 9About four thousand men were present. And having sent them away, 10he got into the boat with his disciples and went to the region of Dalmanutha.

11The Pharisees came and began to question Jesus. To test him, they asked him for a sign from heaven. 12He sighed deeply and said, "Why does this generation ask for a miraculous sign? I tell you the truth, no sign will be given to it." 13Then he left them, got back into the boat and crossed to the other side.

---

a24 Many early manuscripts *Tyre and Sidon*   *b25* Greek *unclean*   *c31* That is, the Ten Cities

The Yeast of the Pharisees and Herod

¹⁴The disciples had forgotten to bring bread, except for one loaf they had with them in the boat. ¹⁵"Be careful," Jesus warned them. "Watch out for the yeast of the Pharisees and that of Herod."

¹⁶They discussed this with one another and said, "It is because we have no bread."

¹⁷Aware of their discussion, Jesus asked them: "Why are you talking about having no bread? Do you still not see or understand? Are your hearts hardened? ¹⁸Do you have eyes but fail to see, and ears but fail to hear? And don't you remember? ¹⁹When I broke the five loaves for the five thousand, how many basketfuls of pieces did you pick up?"

"Twelve," they replied.

²⁰"And when I broke the seven loaves for the four thousand, how many basketfuls of pieces did you pick up?"

They answered, "Seven."

²¹He said to them, "Do you still not understand?"

The Healing of a Blind Man at Bethsaida

²²They came to Bethsaida, and some people brought a blind man and begged Jesus to touch him. ²³He took the blind man by the hand and led him outside the village. When he had spit on the man's eyes and put his hands on him, Jesus asked, "Do you see anything?"

²⁴He looked up and said, "I see people; they look like trees walking around."

²⁵Once more Jesus put his hands on the man's eyes. Then his eyes were opened, his sight was restored, and he saw everything clearly. ²⁶Jesus sent him home, saying, "Don't go into the village.ᵃ"

Peter's Confession of Christ

²⁷Jesus and his disciples went on to the villages around Caesarea Philippi. On the way he asked them, "Who do people say I am?"

²⁸They replied, "Some say John the Baptist; others say Elijah; and still others, one of the prophets."

²⁹"But what about you?" he asked. "Who do you say I am?"

Peter answered, "You are the Christ.ᵇ"

³⁰Jesus warned them not to tell anyone about him.

Jesus Predicts His Death

³¹He then began to teach them that the Son of Man must suffer many things and be rejected by the elders, chief priests and teachers of the law, and that he must be killed and after three days rise again. ³²He spoke plainly about this, and Peter took him aside and began to rebuke him.

³³But when Jesus turned and looked at his disciples, he rebuked Peter. "Get behind me, Satan!" he said. "You do not have in mind the things of God, but the things of men."

³⁴Then he called the crowd to him along with his disciples and said: "If anyone would come after me, he must deny himself and take up his cross and follow me. ³⁵For whoever wants to save his lifeᶜ will lose it, but whoever loses his life for me and for the gospel will save it. ³⁶What good is it for a man to gain the whole world, yet forfeit his soul? ³⁷Or what can a man give in exchange for his soul? ³⁸If anyone is ashamed of me and my words in this adulterous and sinful generation, the Son of Man will be ashamed of him when he comes in his Father's glory with the holy angels."

ᵃ26 Some manuscripts *Don't go and tell anyone in the village*   ᵇ29 Or *Messiah*. "The Christ" (Greek) and "the Messiah" (Hebrew) both mean "the Anointed One."   ᶜ35 The Greek word means either *life* or *soul*; also in verse 36.

9 And he said to them, "I tell you the truth, some who are standing here wi‍ not taste death before they see the kingdom of God come with power."

The Transfiguration

²After six days Jesus took Peter, James and John with him and led them up a high mountain, where they were all alone. There he was transfigured before them. ³Hi‍ clothes became dazzling white, whiter than anyone in the world could bleach them‍ ⁴And there appeared before them Elijah and Moses, who were talking with Jesus.

⁵Peter said to Jesus, "Rabbi, it is good for us to be here. Let us put up three shelters‍ one for you, one for Moses and one for Elijah." ⁶(He did not know what to say, they wer‍ so frightened.)

⁷Then a cloud appeared and enveloped them, and a voice came from the cloud: "This i‍ my Son, whom I love. Listen to him!"

⁸Suddenly, when they looked around, they no longer saw anyone with them excep‍ Jesus.

⁹As they were coming down the mountain, Jesus gave them orders not to tell anyone‍ what they had seen until the Son of Man had risen from the dead. ¹⁰They kept the matte‍ to themselves, discussing what "rising from the dead" meant.

¹¹And they asked him, "Why do the teachers of the law say that Elijah must come‍ first?"

¹²Jesus replied, "To be sure, Elijah does come first, and restores all things. Why then i‍ it written that the Son of Man must suffer much and be rejected? ¹³But I tell you, Elija‍ has come, and they have done to him everything they wished, just as it is written abou‍ him."

⬚ ▓▓▓▓▓▓▓▓▓▓▓▓▓ DISCOVERING GOD ▓▓▓▓▓▓▓▓▓▓▓▓▓ ◨

8:34–36
Life with God

We've all heard the adage, "Finders keepers, losers weepers." As children most of us uttered those words when we found a coin on the sidewalk, a ball in the grass, or piece of candy misplaced by a sibling. We felt that we had the *right* to take what we had found—too bad for the poor loser who misplaced it.

As adults we still occasionally think that way to justify our lack of concern for others. But ultimately we lose a bit of ourselves when we take from someone else. Jesus knew that, so he turned the old adage upside down. He said in effect, "Finders weepers, losers keepers."

Jesus demonstrated this reality in his own life. His ministry was totally devoted to helping others. He also literally lost his life for the sake of others, then was raised to new life after three days (see verse 31).

The person who selfishly protects himself (or herself) at the expense of others and clutches his possessions will lose his life. His soul will become empty even though his portfolio expands (remember the story of Ebenezer Scrooge?). One day, realizing that he has damaged his relationships with others in the pursuit of wealth, he will weep at the wasteland his life has become (verse 36). But the person who gives up ownership of his life, releases his possessions, and gives himself generously to God and to others will find true happiness and fulfillment. Not only will he keep eternal life, but he'll also know what it means to truly live while he's here on earth.

It doesn't matter whether you're young or old, rich or poor, weak or powerful; you will have a hard time letting go of what you have. Jesus has a message for you: When you give up those earthly attachments, you'll find that doing so is eternally worthwhile. "Whoever loses his life for me and for the gospel will save it."

If you're looking for true fulfillment, stop trying to find meaning in yourself, your friends, your possessions or your status. Take Jesus' advice and follow *him*. If you do, you'll discover firsthand that "losers" really are "keepers."

The Healing of a Boy With an Evil Spirit

¹⁴When they came to the other disciples, they saw a large crowd around them and the teachers of the law arguing with them. ¹⁵As soon as all the people saw Jesus, they were overwhelmed with wonder and ran to greet him.

¹⁶"What are you arguing with them about?" he asked.

¹⁷A man in the crowd answered, "Teacher, I brought you my son, who is possessed by a spirit that has robbed him of speech. ¹⁸Whenever it seizes him, it throws him to the ground. He foams at the mouth, gnashes his teeth and becomes rigid. I asked your disciples to drive out the spirit, but they could not."

¹⁹"O unbelieving generation," Jesus replied, "how long shall I stay with you? How long shall I put up with you? Bring the boy to me."

²⁰So they brought him. When the spirit saw Jesus, it immediately threw the boy into a convulsion. He fell to the ground and rolled around, foaming at the mouth.

²¹Jesus asked the boy's father, "How long has he been like this?"

"From childhood," he answered. ²²"It has often thrown him into fire or water to kill him. But if you can do anything, take pity on us and help us."

²³"'If you can'?" said Jesus. "Everything is possible for him who believes."

²⁴Immediately the boy's father exclaimed, "I do believe; help me overcome my unbelief!"

²⁵When Jesus saw that a crowd was running to the scene, he rebuked the evil *a* spirit. "You deaf and mute spirit," he said, "I command you, come out of him and never enter him again."

²⁶The spirit shrieked, convulsed him violently and came out. The boy looked so much like a corpse that many said, "He's dead." ²⁷But Jesus took him by the hand and lifted him to his feet, and he stood up.

²⁸After Jesus had gone indoors, his disciples asked him privately, "Why couldn't we drive it out?"

²⁹He replied, "This kind can come out only by prayer. *b*"

³⁰They left that place and passed through Galilee. Jesus did not want anyone to know where they were, ³¹because he was teaching his disciples. He said to them, "The Son of Man is going to be betrayed into the hands of men. They will kill him, and after three days he will rise." ³²But they did not understand what he meant and were afraid to ask him about it.

Who Is the Greatest?

³³They came to Capernaum. When he was in the house, he asked them, "What were you arguing about on the road?" ³⁴But they kept quiet because on the way they had argued about who was the greatest.

³⁵Sitting down, Jesus called the Twelve and said, "If anyone wants to be first, he must be the very last, and the servant of all."

³⁶He took a little child and had him stand among them. Taking him in his arms, he said to them, ³⁷"Whoever welcomes one of these little children in my name welcomes me; and whoever welcomes me does not welcome me but the one who sent me."

Whoever Is Not Against Us Is for Us

³⁸"Teacher," said John, "we saw a man driving out demons in your name and we told him to stop, because he was not one of us."

³⁹"Do not stop him," Jesus said. "No one who does a miracle in my name can in the next moment say anything bad about me, ⁴⁰for whoever is not against us is for us. ⁴¹I tell you the truth, anyone who gives you a cup of water in my name because you belong to Christ will certainly not lose his reward.

25 Greek *unclean*   *b29* Some manuscripts *prayer and fasting*

Causing to Sin

42"And if anyone causes one of these little ones who believe in me to sin, it would be better for him to be thrown into the sea with a large millstone tied around his neck. **43**If your hand causes you to sin, cut it off. It is better for you to enter life maimed than with two hands to go into hell, where the fire never goes out.*a* **45**And if your foot causes you to sin, cut it off. It is better for you to enter life crippled than to have two feet and be thrown into hell.*b* **47**And if your eye causes you to sin, pluck it out. It is better for you to enter the kingdom of God with one eye than to have two eyes and be thrown into hell, **48**where

> "'their worm does not die,
>   and the fire is not quenched.'*c*

49Everyone will be salted with fire.

50"Salt is good, but if it loses its saltiness, how can you make it salty again? Have salt in yourselves, and be at peace with each other."

Divorce

10 Jesus then left that place and went into the region of Judea and across the Jordan. Again crowds of people came to him, and as was his custom, he taught them.

2Some Pharisees came and tested him by asking, "Is it lawful for a man to divorce his wife?"

3"What did Moses command you?" he replied.

4They said, "Moses permitted a man to write a certificate of divorce and send her away."

5"It was because your hearts were hard that Moses wrote you this law," Jesus replied. **6**"But at the beginning of creation God 'made them male and female.'*d* **7**'For this reason a man will leave his father and mother and be united to his wife,*e* **8**and the two will become one flesh.'*f* So they are no longer two, but one. **9**Therefore what God has joined together, let man not separate."

10When they were in the house again the disciples asked Jesus about this. **11**He answered, "Anyone who divorces his wife and marries another woman commits adultery against her. **12**And if she divorces her husband and marries another man, she commits adultery."

▣ ▥▥▥STRENGTHENING RELATIONSHIPS▥▥▥ ⊟

10:2–9
Marriage

Some people are very interested in how to divorce "properly." Yet when these religious leaders threw thorny questions about divorce at Jesus, he redirected the conversation to the subject of marriage. He called attention to God's original design, implying that marriage was intended as a divine union based on commitment and unconditional love, not on romance or convenience.

If you want a fulfilling marriage, you must reject the thinking that divorce is an option. When you accept the fact that the only way *out* of problems is *through* them, you'll have the framework in which to build a solid and rewarding relationship with your spouse.

The Little Children and Jesus

13People were bringing little children to Jesus to have him touch them, but the disciples rebuked them. **14**When Jesus saw this, he was indignant. He said to them, "Let the little children come to me, and do not hinder them, for the kingdom of God belongs to such as these. **15**I tell you the truth, anyone who will not receive the kingdom of God like

*a 43 Some manuscripts out, 44where / "'their worm does not die, / and the fire is not quenched.'   b 45 Some manuscripts
hell, 46where / "'their worm does not die, / and the fire is not quenched.'   c 48 Isaiah 66:24   d 6 Gen. 1:27
e 7 Some early manuscripts do not have and be united to his wife.   f 8 Gen. 2:24*

little child will never enter it." ¹⁶And he took the children in his arms, put his hands on them and blessed them.

The Rich Young Man

¹⁷As Jesus started on his way, a man ran up to him and fell on his knees before him. "Good teacher," he asked, "what must I do to inherit eternal life?"

¹⁸"Why do you call me good?" Jesus answered. "No one is good—except God alone. ¹⁹You know the commandments: 'Do not murder, do not commit adultery, do not steal, do not give false testimony, do not defraud, honor your father and mother.'ᵃ"

²⁰"Teacher," he declared, "all these I have kept since I was a boy."

²¹Jesus looked at him and loved him. "One thing you lack," he said. "Go, sell everything you have and give to the poor, and you will have treasure in heaven. Then come, follow me."

²²At this the man's face fell. He went away sad, because he had great wealth.

²³Jesus looked around and said to his disciples, "How hard it is for the rich to enter the kingdom of God!"

²⁴The disciples were amazed at his words. But Jesus said again, "Children, how hard it ᵇ to enter the kingdom of God! ²⁵It is easier for a camel to go through the eye of a needle than for a rich man to enter the kingdom of God."

²⁶The disciples were even more amazed, and said to each other, "Who then can be saved?"

²⁷Jesus looked at them and said, "With man this is impossible, but not with God; all things are possible with God."

²⁸Peter said to him, "We have left everything to follow you!"

²⁹"I tell you the truth," Jesus replied, "no one who has left home or brothers or sisters or mother or father or children or fields for me and the gospel ³⁰will fail to receive a hundred times as much in this present age (homes, brothers, sisters, mothers, children and fields—and with them, persecutions) and in the age to come, eternal life. ³¹But many who are first will be last, and the last first."

Jesus Again Predicts His Death

³²They were on their way up to Jerusalem, with Jesus leading the way, and the disciples were astonished, while those who followed were afraid. Again he took the twelve aside and told them what was going to happen to him. ³³"We are going up to Jerusalem," he said, "and the Son of Man will be betrayed to the chief priests and teachers of the law. They will condemn him to death and will hand him over to the Gentiles, ³⁴who will mock him and spit on him, flog him and kill him. Three days later he will rise."

The Request of James and John

³⁵Then James and John, the sons of Zebedee, came to him. "Teacher," they said, "we want you to do for us whatever we ask."

³⁶"What do you want me to do for you?" he asked.

³⁷They replied, "Let one of us sit at your right and the other at your left in your glory."

³⁸"You don't know what you are asking," Jesus said. "Can you drink the cup I drink or be baptized with the baptism I am baptized with?"

³⁹"We can," they answered.

Jesus said to them, "You will drink the cup I drink and be baptized with the baptism I am baptized with, ⁴⁰but to sit at my right or left is not for me to grant. These places belong to those for whom they have been prepared."

⁴¹When the ten heard about this, they became indignant with James and John. ⁴²Jesus called them together and said, "You know that those who are regarded as rulers of the

ᵃ 19 Exodus 20:12-16; Deut. 5:16-20   ᵇ 24 Some manuscripts *is for those who trust in riches*

Gentiles lord it over them, and their high officials exercise authority over them. [43]Not s with you. Instead, whoever wants to become great among you must be your servan [44]and whoever wants to be first must be slave of all. [45]For even the Son of Man did n come to be served, but to serve, and to give his life as a ransom for many."

Blind Bartimaeus Receives His Sight

[46]Then they came to Jericho. As Jesus and his disciples, together with a large crowd were leaving the city, a blind man, Bartimaeus (that is, the Son of Timaeus), was sittin by the roadside begging. [47]When he heard that it was Jesus of Nazareth, he began t shout, "Jesus, Son of David, have mercy on me!"

[48]Many rebuked him and told him to be quiet, but he shouted all the more, "Son c David, have mercy on me!"

[49]Jesus stopped and said, "Call him."

So they called to the blind man, "Cheer up! On your feet! He's calling you." [50]Throwin his cloak aside, he jumped to his feet and came to Jesus.

[51]"What do you want me to do for you?" Jesus asked him.

The blind man said, "Rabbi, I want to see."

[52]"Go," said Jesus, "your faith has healed you." Immediately he received his sight an followed Jesus along the road.

The Triumphal Entry

11 As they approached Jerusalem and came to Bethphage and Bethany at th Mount of Olives, Jesus sent two of his disciples, [2]saying to them, "Go to th village ahead of you, and just as you enter it, you will find a colt tied there, which no on has ever ridden. Untie it and bring it here. [3]If anyone asks you, 'Why are you doing this? tell him, 'The Lord needs it and will send it back here shortly.'"

[4]They went and found a colt outside in the street, tied at a doorway. As they untied i [5]some people standing there asked, "What are you doing, untying that colt?" [6]The answered as Jesus had told them to, and the people let them go. [7]When they brought th colt to Jesus and threw their cloaks over it, he sat on it. [8]Many people spread their cloak on the road, while others spread branches they had cut in the fields. [9]Those who wer ahead and those who followed shouted,

"Hosanna![a]"

"Blessed is he who comes in the name of the Lord!"[b]

[10]"Blessed is the coming kingdom of our father David!"

"Hosanna in the highest!"

[11]Jesus entered Jerusalem and went to the temple. He looked around at everything, bu since it was already late, he went out to Bethany with the Twelve.

Jesus Clears the Temple

[12]The next day as they were leaving Bethany, Jesus was hungry. [13]Seeing in th distance a fig tree in leaf, he went to find out if it had any fruit. When he reached it, h found nothing but leaves, because it was not the season for figs. [14]Then he said to th tree, "May no one ever eat fruit from you again." And his disciples heard him say it.

[15]On reaching Jerusalem, Jesus entered the temple area and began driving out thos who were buying and selling there. He overturned the tables of the money changers an the benches of those selling doves, [16]and would not allow anyone to carry merchandis through the temple courts. [17]And as he taught them, he said, "Is it not written:

a9 A Hebrew expression meaning "Save!" which became an exclamation of praise; also in verse 10   *b9* Psalm 118:25,26

> " 'My house will be called
>   a house of prayer for all nations'ᵃ?
>
> But you have made it 'a den of robbers.'ᵇ"

¹⁸The chief priests and the teachers of the law heard this and began looking for a way to kill him, for they feared him, because the whole crowd was amazed at his teaching. ¹⁹When evening came, theyᶜ went out of the city.

The Withered Fig Tree

²⁰In the morning, as they went along, they saw the fig tree withered from the roots. ²¹Peter remembered and said to Jesus, "Rabbi, look! The fig tree you cursed has withered!"

²²"Haveᵈ faith in God," Jesus answered. ²³"I tell you the truth, if anyone says to this mountain, 'Go, throw yourself into the sea,' and does not doubt in his heart but believes that what he says will happen, it will be done for him. ²⁴Therefore I tell you, whatever you ask for in prayer, believe that you have received it, and it will be yours. ²⁵And when you stand praying, if you hold anything against anyone, forgive him, so that your Father in heaven may forgive you your sins. ᵉ"

The Authority of Jesus Questioned

²⁷They arrived again in Jerusalem, and while Jesus was walking in the temple courts, the chief priests, the teachers of the law and the elders came to him. ²⁸"By what authority are you doing these things?" they asked. "And who gave you authority to do this?"

²⁹Jesus replied, "I will ask you one question. Answer me, and I will tell you by what authority I am doing these things. ³⁰John's baptism—was it from heaven, or from men? Tell me!"

³¹They discussed it among themselves and said, "If we say, 'From heaven,' he will ask, 'Then why didn't you believe him?' ³²But if we say, 'From men' . . . ." (They feared the people, for everyone held that John really was a prophet.)

³³So they answered Jesus, "We don't know."

Jesus said, "Neither will I tell you by what authority I am doing these things."

▨▨▨▨▨ KNOWING YOURSELF ▨▨▨▨▨

11:1–11
Sin

Winston Churchill had no illusions about the fickle nature of people. Once a friend asked him, "Aren't you impressed to see thousands of people gather to hear you speak?"

Churchill replied, "No, because ten times as many would come to see me hanged!"

As the Jerusalem crowd gathered to greet Jesus, he knew that within a week most of them would be demanding his death. Yet Jesus still rode into Jerusalem and allowed the people to proclaim him the Messiah. By entering on a donkey, Jesus fulfilled the prophecy of Zechariah chapter 9, verse 9 (page 1243), announcing how the Messiah would present himself.

Imagine that you are one of the people in the crowd. Can you see yourself cheering for the One you believe will bring you a better life? He is offering himself to you now. But are you ready to reckon with the fact that, because of the sin in your life, Jesus had to die on a cross? Can you place your eternal destiny in Jesus' hands, trusting that he is who he says he is?

As you seek the truth about Jesus, remember that it's not the strength of your own commitment that will make a relationship with him work. Like the members of that Jerusalem crowd, you are fickle—at times, your commitment to Jesus will waver. Only because Jesus is strong, loving and forgiving can you (or any other person) call yourself his follower.

ᵃ17 Isaiah 56:7   ᵇ17 Jer. 7:11   ᶜ19 Some early manuscripts he   ᵈ22 Some early manuscripts If you have
ᵉ25 Some manuscripts sins. ²⁶But if you do not forgive, neither will your Father who is in heaven forgive your sins.

The Parable of the Tenants

12 He then began to speak to them in parables: "A man planted a vineyard. He put a wall around it, dug a pit for the winepress and built a watchtower. Then he rented the vineyard to some farmers and went away on a journey. ²At harvest time he sent a servant to the tenants to collect from them some of the fruit of the vineyard. ³But they seized him, beat him and sent him away empty-handed. ⁴Then he sent another servant to them; they struck this man on the head and treated him shamefully. ⁵He sent still another, and that one they killed. He sent many others; some of them they beat, others they killed.

⁶"He had one left to send, a son, whom he loved. He sent him last of all, saying, 'They will respect my son.'

⁷"But the tenants said to one another, 'This is the heir. Come, let's kill him, and the inheritance will be ours.' ⁸So they took him and killed him, and threw him out of the vineyard.

⁹"What then will the owner of the vineyard do? He will come and kill those tenants and give the vineyard to others. ¹⁰Haven't you read this scripture:

"'The stone the builders rejected
　has become the capstone*a*;
¹¹the Lord has done this,
　and it is marvelous in our eyes'*b*?"

¹²Then they looked for a way to arrest him because they knew he had spoken the parable against them. But they were afraid of the crowd; so they left him and went away.

Paying Taxes to Caesar

¹³Later they sent some of the Pharisees and Herodians to Jesus to catch him in his words. ¹⁴They came to him and said, "Teacher, we know you are a man of integrity. You aren't swayed by men, because you pay no attention to who they are; but you teach the way of God in accordance with the truth. Is it right to pay taxes to Caesar or not? ¹⁵Should we pay or shouldn't we?"

But Jesus knew their hypocrisy. "Why are you trying to trap me?" he asked. "Bring me a denarius and let me look at it." ¹⁶They brought the coin, and he asked them, "Whose portrait is this? And whose inscription?"

"Caesar's," they replied.

¹⁷Then Jesus said to them, "Give to Caesar what is Caesar's and to God what is God's."

And they were amazed at him.

Marriage at the Resurrection

¹⁸Then the Sadducees, who say there is no resurrection, came to him with a question. ¹⁹"Teacher," they said, "Moses wrote for us that if a man's brother dies and leaves a wife but no children, the man must marry the widow and have children for his brother. ²⁰Now there were seven brothers. The first one married and died without leaving any children. ²¹The second one married the widow, but he also died, leaving no child. It was the same with the third. ²²In fact, none of the seven left any children. Last of all, the woman died too. ²³At the resurrection*c* whose wife will she be, since the seven were married to her?"

²⁴Jesus replied, "Are you not in error because you do not know the Scriptures or the power of God? ²⁵When the dead rise, they will neither marry nor be given in marriage; they will be like the angels in heaven. ²⁶Now about the dead rising—have you not read in the book of Moses, in the account of the bush, how God said to him, 'I am the God of

---

a 10 Or *cornerstone*　　*b 11* Psalm 118:22,23　　*c 23* Some manuscripts *resurrection, when men rise from the dead.*

Abraham, the God of Isaac, and the God of Jacob'ª? ²⁷He is not the God of the dead, but of the living. You are badly mistaken!"

The Greatest Commandment

²⁸One of the teachers of the law came and heard them debating. Noticing that Jesus had given them a good answer, he asked him, "Of all the commandments, which is the most important?"

²⁹"The most important one," answered Jesus, "is this: 'Hear, O Israel, the Lord our God, the Lord is one.ᵇ ³⁰Love the Lord your God with all your heart and with all your soul and with all your mind and with all your strength.'ᶜ ³¹The second is this: 'Love your neighbor as yourself.'ᵈ There is no commandment greater than these."

³²"Well said, teacher," the man replied. "You are right in saying that God is one and there is no other but him. ³³To love him with all your heart, with all your understanding and with all your strength, and to love your neighbor as yourself is more important than all burnt offerings and sacrifices."

³⁴When Jesus saw that he had answered wisely, he said to him, "You are not far from the kingdom of God." And from then on no one dared ask him any more questions.

Whose Son Is the Christ?

³⁵While Jesus was teaching in the temple courts, he asked, "How is it that the teachers of the law say that the Christᵉ is the son of David? ³⁶David himself, speaking by the Holy Spirit, declared:

> " 'The Lord said to my Lord:
>   "Sit at my right hand
>   until I put your enemies
>   under your feet." 'ᶠ

³⁷David himself calls him 'Lord.' How then can he be his son?"

The large crowd listened to him with delight.

³⁸As he taught, Jesus said, "Watch out for the teachers of the law. They like to walk around in flowing robes and be greeted in the marketplaces, ³⁹and have the most important seats in the synagogues and the places of honor at banquets. ⁴⁰They devour widows' houses and for a show make lengthy prayers. Such men will be punished most severely."

The Widow's Offering

⁴¹Jesus sat down opposite the place where the offerings were put and watched the crowd putting their money into the temple treasury. Many rich people threw in large amounts. ⁴²But a poor widow came and put in two very small copper coins,ᵍ worth only a fraction of a penny.ʰ

⁴³Calling his disciples to him, Jesus said, "I tell you the truth, this poor widow has put more into the treasury than all the others. ⁴⁴They all gave out of their wealth; but she, out of her poverty, put in everything—all she had to live on."

Signs of the End of the Age

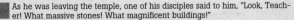

13 As he was leaving the temple, one of his disciples said to him, "Look, Teacher! What massive stones! What magnificent buildings!"

²"Do you see all these great buildings?" replied Jesus. "Not one stone here will be left on another; every one will be thrown down."

³As Jesus was sitting on the Mount of Olives opposite the temple, Peter, James, John and Andrew asked him privately, ⁴"Tell us, when will these things happen? And what will be the sign that they are all about to be fulfilled?"

ª26 Exodus 3:6   ᵇ29 Or the Lord our God is one Lord   ᶜ30 Deut. 6:4,5   ᵈ31 Lev. 19:18   ᵉ35 Or Messiah   ᶠ36 Psalm 110:1   ᵍ42 Greek two lepta   ʰ42 Greek kodrantes

⁵Jesus said to them: "Watch out that no one deceives you. ⁶Many will come in my name, claiming, 'I am he,' and will deceive many. ⁷When you hear of wars and rumors of wars, do not be alarmed. Such things must happen, but the end is still to come. ⁸Nation will rise against nation, and kingdom against kingdom. There will be earthquakes in various places, and famines. These are the beginning of birth pains.

⁹"You must be on your guard. You will be handed over to the local councils and flogged in the synagogues. On account of me you will stand before governors and kings as witnesses to them. ¹⁰And the gospel must first be preached to all nations. ¹¹Whenever you are arrested and brought to trial, do not worry beforehand about what to say. Just say whatever is given you at the time, for it is not you speaking, but the Holy Spirit.

¹²"Brother will betray brother to death, and a father his child. Children will rebel against their parents and have them put to death. ¹³All men will hate you because of me, but he who stands firm to the end will be saved.

¹⁴"When you see 'the abomination that causes desolation'ᵃ standing where itᵇ does not belong—let the reader understand—then let those who are in Judea flee to the mountains. ¹⁵Let no one on the roof of his house go down or enter the house to take anything out. ¹⁶Let no one in the field go back to get his cloak. ¹⁷How dreadful it will be in those days for pregnant women and nursing mothers! ¹⁸Pray that this will not take place in winter, ¹⁹because those will be days of distress unequaled from the beginning, when God created the world, until now—and never to be equaled again. ²⁰If the Lord had not cut short those days, no one would survive. But for the sake of the elect, whom he has chosen, he has shortened them. ²¹At that time if anyone says to you, 'Look, here is the Christ ᶜ!' or, 'Look, there he is!' do not believe it. ²²For false Christs and false prophets will appear and perform signs and miracles to deceive the elect—if that were possible. ²³So be on your guard; I have told you everything ahead of time.

▣ ⋮⋮⋮⋮⋮⋮⋮ DISCOVERING GOD ⋮⋮⋮⋮⋮⋮⋮ ⬅

13:21–23
Spiritual Fraud

Most of us think we could spot a spiritual fraud a mile away. But Jesus warns us that the clues are not that obvious. Even "signs and miracles"—extraordinary acts that seem to carry the stamp of God's approval—are no guarantee that God is at work. Even if the horoscope turns out to be right; even if the psychic says something that appears to be supernaturally revealed; even if the channeler seems to be relaying Jesus' new teaching; even if the spiritual leader claims to have seen an angel and heard the voice of God, Jesus says these things don't prove that the message or the messenger is from God.

So what's the test? Look at verse 31. If Jesus' words will never pass away, all we have to do is make sure the person's teaching is in harmony with Jesus' teachings. Any truthsource that disclaims or adds to the Bible in favor of a "better" or "more accurate" revelation cannot originate from God. Even occasionally quoting the Bible isn't enough—even the devil does that! To pass the test, any teaching that you hear must conform to Scripture in its totality, not just reference a verse here and there out of context. (See Matthew chapter 4, verses 1–11 [page 1261]) and note for more information on this subject.)

---

²⁴"But in those days, following that distress,

> " 'the sun will be darkened,
>   and the moon will not give its light;
> ²⁵the stars will fall from the sky,
>   and the heavenly bodies will be shaken.'ᵈ

²⁶"At that time men will see the Son of Man coming in clouds with great power and glory. ²⁷And he will send his angels and gather his elect from the four winds, from the ends of the earth to the ends of the heavens.

ᵃ14 Daniel 9:27; 11:31; 12:11   ᵇ14 Or he; also in verse 29   ᶜ21 Or Messiah   ᵈ25 Isaiah 13:10; 34:4

28"Now learn this lesson from the fig tree: As soon as its twigs get tender and its leaves come out, you know that summer is near. 29Even so, when you see these things happening, you know that it is near, right at the door. 30I tell you the truth, this generation*a* will certainly not pass away until all these things have happened. 31Heaven and earth will pass away, but my words will never pass away.

The Day and Hour Unknown

32"No one knows about that day or hour, not even the angels in heaven, nor the Son, but only the Father. 33Be on guard! Be alert*b*! You do not know when that time will come. 34It's like a man going away: He leaves his house and puts his servants in charge, each with his assigned task, and tells the one at the door to keep watch.

35"Therefore keep watch because you do not know when the owner of the house will come back—whether in the evening, or at midnight, or when the rooster crows, or at dawn. 36If he comes suddenly, do not let him find you sleeping. 37What I say to you, I say to everyone: 'Watch!'"

Jesus Anointed at Bethany

14 Now the Passover and the Feast of Unleavened Bread were only two days away, and the chief priests and the teachers of the law were looking for some sly way to arrest Jesus and kill him. 2"But not during the Feast," they said, "or the people may riot."

3While he was in Bethany, reclining at the table in the home of a man known as Simon the Leper, a woman came with an alabaster jar of very expensive perfume, made of pure nard. She broke the jar and poured the perfume on his head.

4Some of those present were saying indignantly to one another, "Why this waste of perfume? 5It could have been sold for more than a year's wages*c* and the money given to the poor." And they rebuked her harshly.

6"Leave her alone," said Jesus. "Why are you bothering her? She has done a beautiful thing to me. 7The poor you will always have with you, and you can help them any time you want. But you will not always have me. 8She did what she could. She poured perfume on my body beforehand to prepare for my burial. 9I tell you the truth, wherever the gospel is preached throughout the world, what she has done will also be told, in memory of her."

10Then Judas Iscariot, one of the Twelve, went to the chief priests to betray Jesus to them. 11They were delighted to hear this and promised to give him money. So he watched for an opportunity to hand him over.

The Lord's Supper

12On the first day of the Feast of Unleavened Bread, when it was customary to sacrifice the Passover lamb, Jesus' disciples asked him, "Where do you want us to go and make preparations for you to eat the Passover?"

13So he sent two of his disciples, telling them, "Go into the city, and a man carrying a jar of water will meet you. Follow him. 14Say to the owner of the house he enters, 'The Teacher asks: Where is my guest room, where I may eat the Passover with my disciples?' 15He will show you a large upper room, furnished and ready. Make preparations for us there."

16The disciples left, went into the city and found things just as Jesus had told them. So they prepared the Passover.

17When evening came, Jesus arrived with the Twelve. 18While they were reclining at the table eating, he said, "I tell you the truth, one of you will betray me—one who is eating with me."

19They were saddened, and one by one they said to him, "Surely not I?"

---

a30 Or race   *b33* Some manuscripts *alert and pray*   *c5* Greek *than three hundred denarii*

²⁰"It is one of the Twelve," he replied, "one who dips bread into the bowl with me. ²¹The Son of Man will go just as it is written about him. But woe to that man who betrays the Son of Man! It would be better for him if he had not been born."

²²While they were eating, Jesus took bread, gave thanks and broke it, and gave it to his disciples, saying, "Take it; this is my body."

²³Then he took the cup, gave thanks and offered it to them, and they all drank from it. ²⁴"This is my blood of theᵃ covenant, which is poured out for many," he said to them. ²⁵"I tell you the truth, I will not drink again of the fruit of the vine until that day when I drink it anew in the kingdom of God."

²⁶When they had sung a hymn, they went out to the Mount of Olives.

Jesus Predicts Peter's Denial

²⁷"You will all fall away," Jesus told them, "for it is written:

" 'I will strike the shepherd,
    and the sheep will be scattered.'ᵇ

²⁸But after I have risen, I will go ahead of you into Galilee."

²⁹Peter declared, "Even if all fall away, I will not."

³⁰"I tell you the truth," Jesus answered, "today—yes, tonight—before the rooster crows twiceᶜ you yourself will disown me three times."

³¹But Peter insisted emphatically, "Even if I have to die with you, I will never disown you." And all the others said the same.

Gethsemane

³²They went to a place called Gethsemane, and Jesus said to his disciples, "Sit here while I pray." ³³He took Peter, James and John along with him, and he began to be deeply distressed and troubled. ³⁴"My soul is overwhelmed with sorrow to the point of death," he said to them. "Stay here and keep watch."

³⁵Going a little farther, he fell to the ground and prayed that if possible the hour might pass from him. ³⁶"Abba,ᵈ Father," he said, "everything is possible for you. Take this cup from me. Yet not what I will, but what you will."

³⁷Then he returned to his disciples and found them sleeping. "Simon," he said to Peter, "are you asleep? Could you not keep watch for one hour? ³⁸Watch and pray so that you will not fall into temptation. The spirit is willing, but the body is weak."

³⁹Once more he went away and prayed the same thing. ⁴⁰When he came back, he again found them sleeping, because their eyes were heavy. They did not know what to say to him.

⁴¹Returning the third time, he said to them, "Are you still sleeping and resting? Enough! The hour has come. Look, the Son of Man is betrayed into the hands of sinners. ⁴²Rise! Let us go! Here comes my betrayer!"

Jesus Arrested

⁴³Just as he was speaking, Judas, one of the Twelve, appeared. With him was a crowd armed with swords and clubs, sent from the chief priests, the teachers of the law, and the elders. ⁴⁴Now the betrayer had arranged a signal with them: "The one I kiss is the man; arrest him and lead him away under guard." ⁴⁵Going at once to Jesus, Judas said, "Rabbi!" and kissed him. ⁴⁶The men seized Jesus and arrested him. ⁴⁷Then one of those standing near drew his sword and struck the servant of the high priest, cutting off his ear.

⁴⁸"Am I leading a rebellion," said Jesus, "that you have come out with swords and clubs to capture me? ⁴⁹Every day I was with you, teaching in the temple courts, and you

---

ᵃ24 Some manuscripts *the new*   ᵇ27 Zech. 13:7   ᶜ30 Some early manuscripts do not have *twice*.   ᵈ36 Aramaic for *Father*

did not arrest me. But the Scriptures must be fulfilled." ⁵⁰Then everyone deserted him and fled.

⁵¹A young man, wearing nothing but a linen garment, was following Jesus. When they seized him, ⁵²he fled naked, leaving his garment behind.

Before the Sanhedrin

⁵³They took Jesus to the high priest, and all the chief priests, elders and teachers of the law came together. ⁵⁴Peter followed him at a distance, right into the courtyard of the high priest. There he sat with the guards and warmed himself at the fire.

⁵⁵The chief priests and the whole Sanhedrin were looking for evidence against Jesus so that they could put him to death, but they did not find any. ⁵⁶Many testified falsely against him, but their statements did not agree.

⁵⁷Then some stood up and gave this false testimony against him: ⁵⁸"We heard him say, 'I will destroy this man-made temple and in three days will build another, not made by man.'" ⁵⁹Yet even then their testimony did not agree.

⁶⁰Then the high priest stood up before them and asked Jesus, "Are you not going to answer? What is this testimony that these men are bringing against you?" ⁶¹But Jesus remained silent and gave no answer.

Again the high priest asked him, "Are you the Christ,ᵃ the Son of the Blessed One?"

⁶²"I am," said Jesus. "And you will see the Son of Man sitting at the right hand of the Mighty One and coming on the clouds of heaven."

⁶³The high priest tore his clothes. "Why do we need any more witnesses?" he asked. ⁶⁴"You have heard the blasphemy. What do you think?"

They all condemned him as worthy of death. ⁶⁵Then some began to spit at him; they blindfolded him, struck him with their fists, and said, "Prophesy!" And the guards took him and beat him.

Peter Disowns Jesus

⁶⁶While Peter was below in the courtyard, one of the servant girls of the high priest came by. ⁶⁷When she saw Peter warming himself, she looked closely at him.

"You also were with that Nazarene, Jesus," she said.

⁶⁸But he denied it. "I don't know or understand what you're talking about," he said, and went out into the entryway.ᵇ

⁶⁹When the servant girl saw him there, she said again to those standing around, "This fellow is one of them." ⁷⁰Again he denied it.

After a little while, those standing near said to Peter, "Surely you are one of them, for you are a Galilean."

⁷¹He began to call down curses on himself, and he swore to them, "I don't know this man you're talking about."

⁷²Immediately the rooster crowed the second time.ᶜ Then Peter remembered the word Jesus had spoken to him: "Before the rooster crows twiceᵈ you will disown me three times." And he broke down and wept.

Jesus Before Pilate

15 Very early in the morning, the chief priests, with the elders, the teachers of the law and the whole Sanhedrin, reached a decision. They bound Jesus, led him away and handed him over to Pilate.

²"Are you the king of the Jews?" asked Pilate.

"Yes, it is as you say," Jesus replied.

³The chief priests accused him of many things. ⁴So again Pilate asked him, "Aren't you going to answer? See how many things they are accusing you of."

ᵃ61 Or Messiah   ᵇ68 Some early manuscripts entryway and the rooster crowed   ᶜ72 Some early manuscripts do not have the second time.   ᵈ72 Some early manuscripts do not have twice.

[5]But Jesus still made no reply, and Pilate was amazed.

[6]Now it was the custom at the Feast to release a prisoner whom the people requested. [7]A man called Barabbas was in prison with the insurrectionists who had committed murder in the uprising. [8]The crowd came up and asked Pilate to do for them what he usually did.

[9]"Do you want me to release to you the king of the Jews?" asked Pilate, [10]knowing it was out of envy that the chief priests had handed Jesus over to him. [11]But the chief priests stirred up the crowd to have Pilate release Barabbas instead.

[12]"What shall I do, then, with the one you call the king of the Jews?" Pilate asked them.

[13]"Crucify him!" they shouted.

[14]"Why? What crime has he committed?" asked Pilate.

But they shouted all the louder, "Crucify him!"

[15]Wanting to satisfy the crowd, Pilate released Barabbas to them. He had Jesus flogged, and handed him over to be crucified.

DISCOVERING GOD

15:1–15
Life with God

Imagine Barabbas sitting in his jail cell, wondering what's going on outside. He listens to the crowd yelling his name one moment, then changing to the horrifying chant, "Crucify him! Crucify him!" The guards unlock the door of his filthy cell and grab him roughly by the arms. As they drag him up the stairs and into the light, Barabbas thinks to himself, "This is it—now I die."

But instead of being led to a place of torture and death, Barabbas is released! Someone named Jesus has been condemned to death in his place! His knees buckle at the overwhelming sense of joy and relief that he feels at this moment.

If you've been searching for truth, know this: *You are Barabbas!*

Whatever cell you sit in today, whatever holds you as its prisoner, Jesus has provided an escape. He has paid the eternal penalty that you deserve by dying for you on the cross. All you need to do is receive what he has done for you. Walk out of your cell—the door stands open. Accept his gift. And then live the rest of your life in gratitude for the gift you've received.

The Soldiers Mock Jesus

[16]The soldiers led Jesus away into the palace (that is, the Praetorium) and called together the whole company of soldiers. [17]They put a purple robe on him, then twisted together a crown of thorns and set it on him. [18]And they began to call out to him, "Hail, king of the Jews!" [19]Again and again they struck him on the head with a staff and spit on him. Falling on their knees, they paid homage to him. [20]And when they had mocked him, they took off the purple robe and put his own clothes on him. Then they led him out to crucify him.

The Crucifixion

[21]A certain man from Cyrene, Simon, the father of Alexander and Rufus, was passing by on his way in from the country, and they forced him to carry the cross. [22]They brought Jesus to the place called Golgotha (which means The Place of the Skull). [23]Then they offered him wine mixed with myrrh, but he did not take it. [24]And they crucified him. Dividing up his clothes, they cast lots to see what each would get.

[25]It was the third hour when they crucified him. [26]The written notice of the charge against him read: THE KING OF THE JEWS. [27]They crucified two robbers with him, one on his right and one on his left.[a] [29]Those who passed by hurled insults at him, shaking their heads and saying, "So! You who are going to destroy the temple and build it in three days, [30]come down from the cross and save yourself!"

[31]In the same way the chief priests and the teachers of the law mocked him among themselves. "He saved others," they said, "but he can't save himself! [32]Let this Christ,[b]

[a]27 Some manuscripts left, [28]and the scripture was fulfilled which says, "He was counted with the lawless ones" (Isaiah 53:12)
[b]32 Or Messiah

this King of Israel, come down now from the cross, that we may see and believe." Those crucified with him also heaped insults on him.

The Death of Jesus

³³At the sixth hour darkness came over the whole land until the ninth hour. ³⁴And at the ninth hour Jesus cried out in a loud voice, *"Eloi, Eloi, lama sabachthani?"*—which means, "My God, my God, why have you forsaken me?"[a]

³⁵When some of those standing near heard this, they said, "Listen, he's calling Elijah."

³⁶One man ran, filled a sponge with wine vinegar, put it on a stick, and offered it to Jesus to drink. "Now leave him alone. Let's see if Elijah comes to take him down," he said.

³⁷With a loud cry, Jesus breathed his last.

³⁸The curtain of the temple was torn in two from top to bottom. ³⁹And when the centurion, who stood there in front of Jesus, heard his cry and[b] saw how he died, he said, "Surely this man was the Son[c] of God!"

⁴⁰Some women were watching from a distance. Among them were Mary Magdalene, Mary the mother of James the younger and of Joses, and Salome. ⁴¹In Galilee these women had followed him and cared for his needs. Many other women who had come up with him to Jerusalem were also there.

The Burial of Jesus

⁴²It was Preparation Day (that is, the day before the Sabbath). So as evening approached, ⁴³Joseph of Arimathea, a prominent member of the Council, who was himself waiting for the kingdom of God, went boldly to Pilate and asked for Jesus' body. ⁴⁴Pilate was surprised to hear that he was already dead. Summoning the centurion, he asked him if Jesus had already died. ⁴⁵When he learned from the centurion that it was so, he gave the body to Joseph. ⁴⁶So Joseph bought some linen cloth, took down the body, wrapped it in the linen, and placed it in a tomb cut out of rock. Then he rolled a stone against the entrance of the tomb. ⁴⁷Mary Magdalene and Mary the mother of Joses saw where he was laid.

The Resurrection

16 When the Sabbath was over, Mary Magdalene, Mary the mother of James, and Salome bought spices so that they might go to anoint Jesus' body. ²Very early on the first day of the week, just after sunrise, they were on their way to the tomb ³and they asked each other, "Who will roll the stone away from the entrance of the tomb?"

⁴But when they looked up, they saw that the stone, which was very large, had been rolled away. ⁵As they entered the tomb, they saw a young man dressed in a white robe sitting on the right side, and they were alarmed.

⁶"Don't be alarmed," he said. "You are looking for Jesus the Nazarene, who was crucified. He has risen! He is not here. See the place where they laid him. ⁷But go, tell his disciples and Peter, 'He is going ahead of you into Galilee. There you will see him, just as he told you.'"

⁸Trembling and bewildered, the women went out and fled from the tomb. They said nothing to anyone, because they were afraid.

[The earliest manuscripts and some other ancient witnesses do not have
Mark 16:9–20.]

⁹When Jesus rose early on the first day of the week, he appeared first to Mary Magdalene, out of whom he had driven seven demons. ¹⁰She went and told those who had

a34 Psalm 22:1   b39 Some manuscripts do not have *heard his cry and*   c39 Or *a son* been with him and who were mourning and weeping. [11]When they heard that Jesus was alive and that she had seen him, they did not believe it.

[12]Afterward Jesus appeared in a different form to two of them while they were walking in the country. [13]These returned and reported it to the rest; but they did not believe them either.

[14]Later Jesus appeared to the Eleven as they were eating; he rebuked them for their lack of faith and their stubborn refusal to believe those who had seen him after he had risen.

[15]He said to them, "Go into all the world and preach the good news to all creation. [16]Whoever believes and is baptized will be saved, but whoever does not believe will be condemned. [17]And these signs will accompany those who believe: In my name they will drive out demons; they will speak in new tongues; [18]they will pick up snakes with their hands; and when they drink deadly poison, it will not hurt them at all; they will place their hands on sick people, and they will get well."

[19]After the Lord Jesus had spoken to them, he was taken up into heaven and he sat at the right hand of God. [20]Then the disciples went out and preached everywhere, and the Lord worked with them and confirmed his word by the signs that accompanied it.

Before I trusted Jesus for my salvation, I was a workaholic—anxious, fearful, restless, and driven, 24 hours a day.

In 1988, a friend of mine invited me to her church. I found the message challenging; even though I had been educated in parochial schools, the concept of having a personal relationship with Jesus was new to me. I found the idea exciting.

Still, my work was my world. In the summer of 1989, that world shattered when a group of coworkers slandered me. Adding to my devastation was that I was denied an opportunity to challenge my accusers and clear my name.

My friend saw my distress. She encouraged me, through her words and deeds, to trust in Jesus for my salvation and for my immediate protection. When I asked Jesus to be my Savior that same summer, I felt an incredible sense of peace. Even though my career had derailed, I felt that my life was definitely on the right track.

Since that day, God has held me in his hands. I have been through good times and bad times, but through all of them I have been at peace. Jesus has shown himself to be faithful. He has guided me, protected me, taught me, comforted me, and walked with me each and every day since I committed myself to him.

When I look at my life, I see clearly the truth of Romans 8:28: "And we know that in all things God works for the good of those who love him, who have been called according to his purpose." God took what others planned for my destruction and used it for my eternal salvation and true happiness in this life! I now know that I will live eternally, and that eternity begins *right now*. I praise Jesus for giving me the assurance that my future is secure.

Eight years ago, my life was in chaos. My marriage was breaking up, my children were hanging out with the wrong crowd, and I didn't know which way was up.

Then I joined the self-help program at my church and discovered the 12 steps, the first three of which make a person come face-to-face with his or her spirituality. I was angry at God, so these steps were difficult for me. I thought if I was good and took care of others, that God would be good to me. It took 18 months for me to work through these steps. One night as I meditated and asked God to show me the way, I felt as if Jesus himself came and hugged me.

My life has changed dramatically since then. I'm now divorced and out of an abusive relationship, I have a new job that uses my gifts, and I'm allowing Christ to use me to make a difference in the lives of others. My daughters have seen the change in my life. They have recently shown interest in spiritual matters and are asking questions about Christ.

Introduction

THE BOTTOM LINE

Luke, the author of this gospel, was a doctor. It's not surprising, then, that we'd see an emphasis in this book on Jesus as the Great Physician—reaching out his hand of compassion to help those most in need of his assistance. As the perfect doctor, Jesus has the capability to listen closely to our problems; to heal our wounds, both physical and emotional; and to reach out to us in compassion and concern. A second benefit of Luke's writing is his attention to historical detail. He was very careful to connect the life of Jesus to people and events in world history—you'll notice that concern, for example, at the beginning of chapter 2 (page 1339). This kind of verifiable detail gives us confidence in the accuracy of the recorded events.

CENTRAL IDEAS

- Jesus was a perfect example of God-honoring human behavior.
- Jesus' miraculous ministry of healing proved his divine power.
- Jesus' life was not a myth or a made-up story, but real history.
- Jesus reaches out to poor, sick, and rejected individuals in society.

OUTLINE

1 Preface (1:1–4)
2 The coming of Jesus (1:5–2:52)
3 Preparation for Jesus' public ministry (3:1–4:13)
4 Jesus' ministry in Galilee (4:14–9:9)
5 Jesus' withdrawal from Galilee (9:10–50)
6 Jesus' ministry in Judea and Perea (9:51–19:27)
7 Jesus' last days: sacrifice and triumph (19:28–24:53)

TITLE

This book is named after Luke, the writer of this gospel.

AUTHOR AND READERS

Luke was a companion of the apostle Paul. He addressed this letter and the book of Acts to "Theophilus," which means "lover of God." This could have been an actual individual, or Luke's personification of all people who took an active interest in Jesus.

Bill Lishman was concerned about his friends. An experienced outdoorsman, he knew what it would take to survive the harsh Canadian winter. In spite of their inexperience and lack of appropriate provisions, however, his friends seemed determined to stay with him.

The Canadian sculptor decided he would convince them to leave by leaving with them. A 350-mile journey lay ahead of them, full of grave danger. He knew his friends might not even agree to go with him. But if they stayed behind, they probably wouldn't last the winter on their own.

Bill had to get through to them somehow. But despite his great concern for them, communicating with his friends was not easy. You see, Bill's friends were Canada geese. He had raised them himself. The only way he could lead them south would be to fly with them.

It took months of training for the geese to learn to join Bill as he flew in his ultralight aircraft. But eventually the geese began to follow him in the air as readily as they had waddled after him on land.

One crisp fall day Bill Lishman went airborne at the head of a wedge of 18 Canada geese. Behind the flock was photographer Joe Duff in an identical aircraft. He captured the whole journey on film. Six days later the geese reached their destination—a pond in Virginia.

A 350-mile journey lay ahead of them, full of grave danger.

One question remained—would the geese return to Canada in the spring? The following April the birds left Virginia on their own accord and arrived right back at Bill's doorstep.

The story of Bill Lishman's geese is entertaining and touching. But this story contains spiritual parallels to what God has done for us that are even more remarkable. We are like those geese—spiritual orphans lost in a dangerous world. To rescue us, God became a man himself, in Jesus Christ. He came down to our level to lead us to safety. Doing so required not only teaching us and serving as our example, but also paying the ultimate price for humanity. If we follow him, we will not just "survive"—we will live forever in heaven.

As a historian writing about Jesus for non-Jewish readers, Luke emphasized stories that show how Jesus became fully human, coming down to our level and empathizing with our human condition.

If the Canada geese could somehow grasp what had happened, they would probably be overwhelmed by Bill Lishman's dedication. But God's love for you is infinitely greater. If you want to learn more about "seeking God," turn to Luke chapter 15 (page 1363). There you will find three stories that Jesus told to help us see how desperately God wants to find lost people and bring them home again.

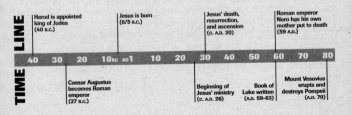

TIME LINE

Herod is appointed king of Judea (40 B.C.)

Jesus is born (6/5 B.C.)

Jesus' death, resurrection, and ascension (c. A.D. 30)

Roman emperor Nero has his own mother put to death (59 A.D.)

40   30   20   10 BC   AD 1   10   20   30   40   50   60   70   80

Caesar Augustus becomes Roman emperor (27 B.C.)

Beginning of Jesus' ministry (c. A.D. 26)

Book of Luke written (A.D. 59-63)

Mount Vesuvius erupts and destroys Pompeii (A.D. 79)

LUKE

Introduction

1 Many have undertaken to draw up an account of the things that have been fulfilled[a] among us, ²just as they were handed down to us by those who from the first were eyewitnesses and servants of the word. ³Therefore, since I myself have carefully investigated everything from the beginning, it seemed good also to me to write an orderly account for you, most excellent Theophilus, ⁴so that you may know the certainty of the things you have been taught.

The Birth of John the Baptist Foretold

⁵In the time of Herod king of Judea there was a priest named Zechariah, who belonged to the priestly division of Abijah; his wife Elizabeth was also a descendant of Aaron. ⁶Both of them were upright in the sight of God, observing all the Lord's commandments and regulations blamelessly. ⁷But they had no children, because Elizabeth was barren; and they were both well along in years.

⁸Once when Zechariah's division was on duty and he was serving as priest before God, ⁹he was chosen by lot, according to the custom of the priesthood, to go into the temple of the Lord and burn incense. ¹⁰And when the time for the burning of incense came, all the assembled worshipers were praying outside.

¹¹Then an angel of the Lord appeared to him, standing at the right side of the altar of incense. ¹²When Zechariah saw him, he was startled and was gripped with fear. ¹³But the angel said to him: "Do not be afraid, Zechariah; your prayer has been heard. Your wife Elizabeth will bear you a son, and you are to give him the name John. ¹⁴He will be a joy and delight to you, and many will rejoice because of his birth, ¹⁵for he will be great in the sight of the Lord. He is never to take wine or other fermented drink, and he will be filled with the Holy Spirit even from birth.[b] ¹⁶Many of the people of Israel will he bring back to the Lord their God. ¹⁷And he will go on before the Lord, in the spirit and power of Elijah, to turn the hearts of the fathers to their children and the disobedient to the wisdom of the righteous—to make ready a people prepared for the Lord."

¹⁸Zechariah asked the angel, "How can I be sure of this? I am an old man and my wife is well along in years."

¹⁹The angel answered, "I am Gabriel. I stand in the presence of God, and I have been

---

a 1 Or *been surely believed*   *b 15* Or *from his mother's womb* sent to speak to you and to tell you this good news. ²⁰And now you will be silent and not able to speak until the day this happens, because you did not believe my words, which will come true at their proper time."

²¹Meanwhile, the people were waiting for Zechariah and wondering why he stayed so long in the temple. ²²When he came out, he could not speak to them. They realized he had seen a vision in the temple, for he kept making signs to them but remained unable to speak.

²³When his time of service was completed, he returned home. ²⁴After this his wife Elizabeth became pregnant and for five months remained in seclusion. ²⁵"The Lord has done this for me," she said. "In these days he has shown his favor and taken away my disgrace among the people."

The Birth of Jesus Foretold

²⁶In the sixth month, God sent the angel Gabriel to Nazareth, a town in Galilee, ²⁷to a virgin pledged to be married to a man named Joseph, a descendant of David. The virgin's name was Mary. ²⁸The angel went to her and said, "Greetings, you who are highly favored! The Lord is with you."

²⁹Mary was greatly troubled at his words and wondered what kind of greeting this might be. ³⁰But the angel said to her, "Do not be afraid, Mary, you have found favor with God. ³¹You will be with child and give birth to a son, and you are to give him the name Jesus. ³²He will be great and will be called the Son of the Most High. The Lord God will give him the throne of his father David, ³³and he will reign over the house of Jacob forever; his kingdom will never end."

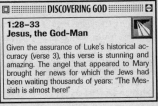

DISCOVERING GOD

1:28–33
Jesus, the God-Man

Given the assurance of Luke's historical accuracy (verse 3), this verse is stunning and amazing. The angel that appeared to Mary brought her news for which the Jews had been waiting thousands of years: "The Messiah is almost here!"

³⁴"How will this be," Mary asked the angel, "since I am a virgin?"

³⁵The angel answered, "The Holy Spirit will come upon you, and the power of the Most High will overshadow you. So the holy one to be born will be called ᵃ the Son of God. ³⁶Even Elizabeth your relative is going to have a child in her old age, and she who was said to be barren is in her sixth month. ³⁷For nothing is impossible with God."

³⁸"I am the Lord's servant," Mary answered. "May it be to me as you have said." Then the angel left her.

Mary Visits Elizabeth

³⁹At that time Mary got ready and hurried to a town in the hill country of Judea, ⁴⁰where she entered Zechariah's home and greeted Elizabeth. ⁴¹When Elizabeth heard Mary's greeting, the baby leaped in her womb, and Elizabeth was filled with the Holy Spirit. ⁴²In a loud voice she exclaimed: "Blessed are you among women, and blessed is the child you will bear! ⁴³But why am I so favored, that the mother of my Lord should come to me? ⁴⁴As soon as the sound of your greeting reached my ears, the baby in my womb leaped for joy. ⁴⁵Blessed is she who has believed that what the Lord has said to her will be accomplished!"

Mary's Song

⁴⁶And Mary said:

> "My soul glorifies the Lord
> ⁴⁷   and my spirit rejoices in God my Savior,

ᵃ35 Or So the child to be born will be called holy,

48for he has been mindful
    of the humble state of his servant.
From now on all generations will call me blessed,
49   for the Mighty One has done great things for me—
        holy is his name.
50His mercy extends to those who fear him,
    from generation to generation.
51He has performed mighty deeds with his arm;
    he has scattered those who are proud in their inmost thoughts.
52He has brought down rulers from their thrones
    but has lifted up the humble.
53He has filled the hungry with good things
    but has sent the rich away empty.
54He has helped his servant Israel,
    remembering to be merciful
55to Abraham and his descendants forever,
    even as he said to our fathers."

56Mary stayed with Elizabeth for about three months and then returned home.

The Birth of John the Baptist

57When it was time for Elizabeth to have her baby, she gave birth to a son. 58Her neighbors and relatives heard that the Lord had shown her great mercy, and they shared her joy.

59On the eighth day they came to circumcise the child, and they were going to name him after his father Zechariah, 60but his mother spoke up and said, "No! He is to be called John."

61They said to her, "There is no one among your relatives who has that name."

62Then they made signs to his father, to find out what he would like to name the child. 63He asked for a writing tablet, and to everyone's astonishment he wrote, "His name is John." 64Immediately his mouth was opened and his tongue was loosed, and he began to speak, praising God. 65The neighbors were all filled with awe, and throughout the hill country of Judea people were talking about all these things. 66Everyone who heard this wondered about it, asking, "What then is this child going to be?" For the Lord's hand was with him.

ADDRESSING QUESTIONS

1:46–56
Human Experience

Q

Mary, the mother of Jesus, is rightfully regarded as one of the great spiritual women of all time. Her attitude in verse 38 is one that people of all ages should emulate. Yet she was probably only a teenager when she became pregnant!

How did she respond to being chosen to give birth to the Son of God? She rejoiced in "God my Savior" (verse 47). Even though Mary was the earthly mother of Jesus, she recognized that her status as God's instrument wouldn't earn her salvation. She knew that she, like everyone else, needed to have a forgiver—a savior. She thanked God that he had promised to provide his Son, Jesus—the Savior of the world, and of herself as well.

Zechariah's Song

67His father Zechariah was filled with the Holy Spirit and prophesied:

68"Praise be to the Lord, the God of Israel,
    because he has come and has redeemed his people.
69He has raised up a horn*a* of salvation for us
    in the house of his servant David

a 69 Horn here symbolizes strength.

70(as he said through his holy prophets of long ago),
71salvation from our enemies
and from the hand of all who hate us—
72to show mercy to our fathers
and to remember his holy covenant,
73   the oath he swore to our father Abraham:
74to rescue us from the hand of our enemies,
and to enable us to serve him without fear
75   in holiness and righteousness before him all our days.

76And you, my child, will be called a prophet of the Most High;
for you will go on before the Lord to prepare the way for him,
77to give his people the knowledge of salvation
through the forgiveness of their sins,
78because of the tender mercy of our God,
by which the rising sun will come to us from heaven
79to shine on those living in darkness
and in the shadow of death,
to guide our feet into the path of peace."

80And the child grew and became strong in spirit; and he lived in the desert until he appeared publicly to Israel.

The Birth of Jesus

2 In those days Caesar Augustus issued a decree that a census should be taken of the entire Roman world. 2(This was the first census that took place while Quirinius was governor of Syria.) 3And everyone went to his own town to register.

4So Joseph also went up from the town of Nazareth in Galilee to Judea, to Bethlehem the town of David, because he belonged to the house and line of David. 5He went there to register with Mary, who was pledged to be married to him and was expecting a child. 6While they were there, the time came for the baby to be born, 7and she gave birth to her firstborn, a son. She wrapped him in cloths and placed him in a manger, because there was no room for them in the inn.

The Shepherds and the Angels

8And there were shepherds living out in the fields nearby, keeping watch over their flocks at night. 9An angel of the Lord appeared to them, and the glory of the Lord shone around them, and they were terrified. 10But the angel said to them, "Do not be afraid. I bring you good news of great joy that will be for all the people. 11Today in the town of David a Savior has been born to you; he is Christ a the Lord. 12This will be a sign to you: You will find a baby wrapped in cloths and lying in a manger."

13Suddenly a great company of the heavenly host appeared with the angel, praising God and saying,

14"Glory to God in the highest,
and on earth peace to men on whom his favor rests."

15When the angels had left them and gone into heaven, the shepherds said to one another, "Let's go to Bethlehem and see this thing that has happened, which the Lord has told us about."

16So they hurried off and found Mary and Joseph, and the baby, who was lying in the manger. 17When they had seen him, they spread the word concerning what had been told them about this child, 18and all who heard it were amazed at what the shepherds

---

a 11 Or Messiah. "The Christ" (Greek) and "the Messiah" (Hebrew) both mean "the Anointed One"; also in verse 26.

said to them. [19]But Mary treasured up all these things and pondered them in her heart. [20]The shepherds returned, glorifying and praising God for all the things they had heard and seen, which were just as they had been told.

Jesus Presented in the Temple

[21]On the eighth day, when it was time to circumcise him, he was named Jesus, the name the angel had given him before he had been conceived.

[22]When the time of their purification according to the Law of Moses had been completed, Joseph and Mary took him to Jerusalem to present him to the Lord [23](as it is written in the Law of the Lord, "Every firstborn male is to be consecrated to the Lord"[a], [24]and to offer a sacrifice in keeping with what is said in the Law of the Lord: "a pair of doves or two young pigeons."[b]

[25]Now there was a man in Jerusalem called Simeon, who was righteous and devout. He was waiting for the consolation of Israel, and the Holy Spirit was upon him. [26]It had been revealed to him by the Holy Spirit that he would not die before he had seen the Lord's Christ. [27]Moved by the Spirit, he went into the temple courts. When the parents brought in the child Jesus to do for him what the custom of the Law required, [28]Simeon took him in his arms and praised God, saying:

□ ::::::::::: DISCOVERING GOD ::::::::::: ⬁

2:25–35
Life with God

Simeon was a seeker of sorts. For years he had waited for the comfort Israel would know when the Messiah came. He was seeking the Jewish Savior, and God had promised Simeon that he would not die until he had seen "the Lord's Christ."

One day God told Simeon that today would be the day. Not only did Simeon see the baby Jesus, he took him in his arms and praised God—a fitting response for a seeker who had found the One for whom he had been seeking!

---

[29]"Sovereign Lord, as you have promised,
 you now dismiss[c] your
  servant in peace.
[30]For my eyes have seen your
  salvation,
[31] which you have prepared in the sight of all people,
[32]a light for revelation to the Gentiles
  and for glory to your people Israel."

[33]The child's father and mother marveled at what was said about him. [34]Then Simeon blessed them and said to Mary, his mother: "This child is destined to cause the falling and rising of many in Israel, and to be a sign that will be spoken against, [35]so that the thoughts of many hearts will be revealed. And a sword will pierce your own soul too."

[36]There was also a prophetess, Anna, the daughter of Phanuel, of the tribe of Asher. She was very old; she had lived with her husband seven years after her marriage, [37]and then was a widow until she was eighty-four.[d] She never left the temple but worshiped night and day, fasting and praying. [38]Coming up to them at that very moment, she gave thanks to God and spoke about the child to all who were looking forward to the redemption of Jerusalem.

[39]When Joseph and Mary had done everything required by the Law of the Lord, they returned to Galilee to their own town of Nazareth. [40]And the child grew and became strong; he was filled with wisdom, and the grace of God was upon him.

The Boy Jesus at the Temple

[41]Every year his parents went to Jerusalem for the Feast of the Passover. [42]When he was twelve years old, they went up to the Feast, according to the custom. [43]After the

[a]23 Exodus 13:2,12   [b]24 Lev. 12:8   [c]29 Or promised, / now dismiss   [d]37 Or widow for eighty-four years

Feast was over, while his parents were returning home, the boy Jesus stayed behind in Jerusalem, but they were unaware of it. ⁴⁴Thinking he was in their company, they traveled on for a day. Then they began looking for him among their relatives and friends. ⁴⁵When they did not find him, they went back to Jerusalem to look for him. ⁴⁶After three days they found him in the temple courts, sitting among the teachers, listening to them and asking them questions. ⁴⁷Everyone who heard him was amazed at his understanding and his answers. ⁴⁸When his parents saw him, they were astonished. His mother said to him, "Son, why have you treated us like this? Your father and I have been anxiously searching for you."

⁴⁹"Why were you searching for me?" he asked. "Didn't you know I had to be in my Father's house?" ⁵⁰But they did not understand what he was saying to them.

⁵¹Then he went down to Nazareth with them and was obedient to them. But his mother treasured all these things in her heart. ⁵²And Jesus grew in wisdom and stature, and in favor with God and men.

John the Baptist Prepares the Way

3 In the fifteenth year of the reign of Tiberius Caesar— when Pontius Pilate was governor of Judea, Herod tetrarch of Galilee, his brother Philip tetrarch of Iturea and Traconitis, and Lysanias tetrarch of Abilene— ²during the high priesthood of Annas and Caiaphas, the word of God came to John son of Zechariah in the desert. ³He went into all the country around the Jordan, preaching a baptism of repentance for the forgiveness of sins. ⁴As is written in the book of the words of Isaiah the prophet:

> "A voice of one calling in the
> desert,
> 'Prepare the way for the Lord,
>   make straight paths for him.
> ⁵Every valley shall be filled in,
>   every mountain and hill made
>   low.
> The crooked roads shall become
>   straight,
>   the rough ways smooth.
> ⁶And all mankind will see God's
>   salvation.' " ᵃ

MANAGING RESOURCES

**3:1–9
Position**

Here Luke records an impressive list of Roman dignitaries: Tiberius Caesar, Pontius Pilate, Herod, Philip and Lysanias were some of the most powerful men in the ancient world at the time Luke wrote his gospel. In addition, he records the names of the high priests Annas and Caiaphas, who were Israel's most influential religious figures at the time.

What's the point of the list? For one thing this list gives the reader a historical framework and reinforces the validity of Luke's narrative. But this list also highlights a contrast: Instead of giving his word to one of these high-powered political or religious leaders, God chose to speak to John, an unrefined desert-dweller.

Many people think that their rank in society guarantees a spot on God's VIP list. Surely God is impressed with their position in a church or some other religious group—right? This passage cautions those who think they have a special status before God: "Don't take pride in an office you hold. God may be doing something quite unexpected in an obscure place, and you'll miss it unless you humbly admit that God is no respecter of position."

---

⁷John said to the crowds coming out to be baptized by him, "You brood of vipers! Who warned you to flee from the coming wrath? ⁸Produce fruit in keeping with repentance. And do not begin to say to yourselves, 'We have Abraham as our father.' For I tell you that out of these stones God can raise up children for Abraham. ⁹The ax is already at the root of the trees, and every tree that does not produce good fruit will be cut down and thrown into the fire."

¹⁰"What should we do then?" the crowd asked.

¹¹John answered, "The man with two tunics should share with him who has none, and the one who has food should do the same."

ᵃ6 Isaiah 40:3-5

¹²Tax collectors also came to be baptized. "Teacher," they asked, "what should we do?" ¹³"Don't collect any more than you are required to," he told them.

¹⁴Then some soldiers asked him, "And what should we do?"

He replied, "Don't extort money and don't accuse people falsely—be content with your pay."

¹⁵The people were waiting expectantly and were all wondering in their hearts if John might possibly be the Christ.[a] ¹⁶John answered them all, "I baptize you with[b] water. But one more powerful than I will come, the thongs of whose sandals I am not worthy to untie. He will baptize you with the Holy Spirit and with fire. ¹⁷His winnowing fork is in his hand to clear his threshing floor and to gather the wheat into his barn, but he will burn up the chaff with unquenchable fire." ¹⁸And with many other words John exhorted the people and preached the good news to them.

¹⁹But when John rebuked Herod the tetrarch because of Herodias, his brother's wife, and all the other evil things he had done, ²⁰Herod added this to them all: He locked John up in prison.

The Baptism and Genealogy of Jesus

²¹When all the people were being baptized, Jesus was baptized too. And as he was praying, heaven was opened ²²and the Holy Spirit descended on him in bodily form like a dove. And a voice came from heaven: "You are my Son, whom I love; with you I am well pleased."

²³Now Jesus himself was about thirty years old when he began his ministry. He was the son, so it was thought, of Joseph,

the son of Heli, ²⁴the son of Matthat,
the son of Levi, the son of Melki,
the son of Jannai, the son of Joseph,
²⁵the son of Mattathias, the son of Amos,
the son of Nahum, the son of Esli,
the son of Naggai, ²⁶the son of Maath,
the son of Mattathias, the son of Semein,
the son of Josech, the son of Joda,
²⁷the son of Joanan, the son of Rhesa,
the son of Zerubbabel, the son of Shealtiel,
the son of Neri, ²⁸the son of Melki,
the son of Addi, the son of Cosam,
the son of Elmadam, the son of Er,
²⁹the son of Joshua, the son of Eliezer,
the son of Jorim, the son of Matthat,
the son of Levi, ³⁰the son of Simeon,
the son of Judah, the son of Joseph,
the son of Jonam, the son of Eliakim,
³¹the son of Melea, the son of Menna,
the son of Mattatha, the son of Nathan,
the son of David, ³²the son of Jesse,
the son of Obed, the son of Boaz,
the son of Salmon,[c] the son of Nahshon,
³³the son of Amminadab, the son of Ram,[d]
the son of Hezron, the son of Perez,
the son of Judah, ³⁴the son of Jacob,

---

[a]15 Or Messiah　　[b]16 Or in　　[c]32 Some early manuscripts Sala　　[d]33 Some manuscripts Amminadab, the son of Admin, the son of Arni; other manuscripts vary widely.

the son of Isaac, the son of Abraham,
the son of Terah, the son of Nahor,
35the son of Serug, the son of Reu,
the son of Peleg, the son of Eber,
the son of Shelah, 36the son of Cainan,
the son of Arphaxad, the son of Shem,
the son of Noah, the son of Lamech,
37the son of Methuselah, the son of Enoch,
the son of Jared, the son of Mahalalel,
the son of Kenan, 38the son of Enosh,
the son of Seth, the son of Adam,
the son of God.

The Temptation of Jesus

4 Jesus, full of the Holy Spirit, returned from the Jordan and was led by the Spirit in the desert, 2where for forty days he was tempted by the devil. He ate nothing during those days, and at the end of them he was hungry.

3The devil said to him, "If you are the Son of God, tell this stone to become bread."

4Jesus answered, "It is written: 'Man does not live on bread alone.'[a]"

5The devil led him up to a high place and showed him in an instant all the kingdoms of the world. 6And he said to him, "I will give you all their authority and splendor, for it has been given to me, and I can give it to anyone I want to. 7So if you worship me, it will all be yours."

8Jesus answered, "It is written: 'Worship the Lord your God and serve him only.'[b]"

9The devil led him to Jerusalem and had him stand on the highest point of the temple. "If you are the Son of God," he said, "throw yourself down from here. 10For it is written:

> "'He will command his angels concerning you
>   to guard you carefully;
> 11they will lift you up in their hands,
>   so that you will not strike your foot against a stone.'[c]"

12Jesus answered, "It says: 'Do not put the Lord your God to the test.'[d]"

13When the devil had finished all this tempting, he left him until an opportune time.

Jesus Rejected at Nazareth

14Jesus returned to Galilee in the power of the Spirit, and news about him spread through the whole countryside. 15He taught in their synagogues, and everyone praised him.

16He went to Nazareth, where he had been brought up, and on the Sabbath day he went into the synagogue, as was his custom. And he stood up to read. 17The scroll of the prophet Isaiah was handed to him. Unrolling it, he found the place where it is written:

> 18"The Spirit of the Lord is on me,
>   because he has anointed me
>   to preach good news to the poor.
> He has sent me to proclaim freedom for the prisoners
>   and recovery of sight for the blind,
>   to release the oppressed,
> 19   to proclaim the year of the Lord's favor."[e]

20Then he rolled up the scroll, gave it back to the attendant and sat down. The eyes of

a4 Deut. 8:3   b8 Deut. 6:13   c11 Psalm 91:11,12   d12 Deut. 6:16   e19 Isaiah 61:1,2

everyone in the synagogue were fastened on him, ²¹and he began by saying to them, "Today this scripture is fulfilled in your hearing."

²²All spoke well of him and were amazed at the gracious words that came from his lips. "Isn't this Joseph's son?" they asked.

²³Jesus said to them, "Surely you will quote this proverb to me: 'Physician, heal yourself! Do here in your hometown what we have heard that you did in Capernaum.'"

²⁴"I tell you the truth," he continued, "no prophet is accepted in his hometown. ²⁵I assure you that there were many widows in Israel in Elijah's time, when the sky was shut for three and a half years and there was a severe famine throughout the land. ²⁶Yet Elijah was not sent to any of them, but to a widow in Zarephath in the region of Sidon. ²⁷And there were many in Israel with leprosy*a* in the time of Elisha the prophet, yet not one of them was cleansed—only Naaman the Syrian."

²⁸All the people in the synagogue were furious when they heard this. ²⁹They got up, drove him out of the town, and took him to the brow of the hill on which the town was built, in order to throw him down the cliff. ³⁰But he walked right through the crowd and went on his way.

Jesus Drives Out an Evil Spirit

³¹Then he went down to Capernaum, a town in Galilee, and on the Sabbath began to teach the people. ³²They were amazed at his teaching, because his message had authority.

³³In the synagogue there was a man possessed by a demon, an evil*b* spirit. He cried out at the top of his voice, ³⁴"Ha! What do you want with us, Jesus of Nazareth? Have you come to destroy us? I know who you are—the Holy One of God!"

³⁵"Be quiet!" Jesus said sternly. "Come out of him!" Then the demon threw the man down before them all and came out without injuring him.

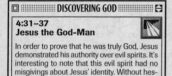

DISCOVERING GOD

4:31–37
Jesus the God-Man

In order to prove that he was truly God, Jesus demonstrated his authority over evil spirits. It's interesting to note that this evil spirit had no misgivings about Jesus' identity. Without hesitation the spirit called Jesus the "Holy One of God."

As a seeker, keep in mind that whatever you conclude about Jesus, it shouldn't be less reverent than what this demon said of him!

³⁶All the people were amazed and said to each other, "What is this teaching? With authority and power he gives orders to evil spirits and they come out!" ³⁷And the news about him spread throughout the surrounding area.

Jesus Heals Many

³⁸Jesus left the synagogue and went to the home of Simon. Now Simon's mother-in-law was suffering from a high fever, and they asked Jesus to help her. ³⁹So he bent over her and rebuked the fever, and it left her. She got up at once and began to wait on them.

⁴⁰When the sun was setting, the people brought to Jesus all who had various kinds of sickness, and laying his hands on each one, he healed them. ⁴¹Moreover, demons came out of many people, shouting, "You are the Son of God!" But he rebuked them and would not allow them to speak, because they knew he was the Christ.*c*

⁴²At daybreak Jesus went out to a solitary place. The people were looking for him and when they came to where he was, they tried to keep him from leaving them. ⁴³But he said, "I must preach the good news of the kingdom of God to the other towns also, because that is why I was sent." ⁴⁴And he kept on preaching in the synagogues of Judea.*d*

---

a 27 The Greek word was used for various diseases affecting the skin—not necessarily leprosy.   *b 33* Greek *unclean;* also in verse 36   *c 41* Or *Messiah*   *d 44* Or *the land of the Jews;* some manuscripts *Galilee*

The Calling of the First Disciples

5 One day as Jesus was standing by the Lake of Gennesaret,[a] with the people crowding around him and listening to the word of God, [2]he saw at the water's edge two boats, left there by the fishermen, who were washing their nets. [3]He got into one of the boats, the one belonging to Simon, and asked him to put out a little from shore. Then he sat down and taught the people from the boat.

[4]When he had finished speaking, he said to Simon, "Put out into deep water, and let down[b] the nets for a catch."

[5]Simon answered, "Master, we've worked hard all night and haven't caught anything. But because you say so, I will let down the nets."

[6]When they had done so, they caught such a large number of fish that their nets began to break. [7]So they signaled their partners in the other boat to come and help them, and they came and filled both boats so full that they began to sink.

[8]When Simon Peter saw this, he fell at Jesus' knees and said, "Go away from me, Lord; I am a sinful man!" [9]For he and all his companions were astonished at the catch of fish they had taken, [10]and so were James and John, the sons of Zebedee, Simon's partners.

Then Jesus said to Simon, "Don't be afraid; from now on you will catch men." [11]So they pulled their boats up on shore, left everything and followed him.

The Man With Leprosy

[12]While Jesus was in one of the towns, a man came along who was covered with leprosy.[c] When he saw Jesus, he fell with his face to the ground and begged him, "Lord, if you are willing, you can make me clean."

[13]Jesus reached out his hand and touched the man. "I am willing," he said. "Be clean!" And immediately the leprosy left him.

[14]Then Jesus ordered him, "Don't tell anyone, but go, show yourself to the priest and offer the sacrifices that Moses commanded for your cleansing, as a testimony to them."

[15]Yet the news about him spread all the more, so that crowds of people came to hear him and to be healed of their sicknesses. [16]But Jesus often withdrew to lonely places and prayed.

Jesus Heals a Paralytic

[17]One day as he was teaching, Pharisees and teachers of the law, who had come from every village of Galilee and from Judea and Jerusalem, were sitting there. And the power of the Lord was present for him to heal the sick. [18]Some men came carrying a paralytic on a mat and tried to take him into the house to lay him before Jesus. [19]When they could not find a way to do this because of the crowd, they went up on the roof and lowered him on his mat through the tiles into the middle of the crowd, right in front of Jesus.

[20]When Jesus saw their faith, he said, "Friend, your sins are forgiven."

[21]The Pharisees and the teachers of the law began thinking to themselves, "Who is this fellow who speaks blasphemy? Who can forgive sins but God alone?"

[22]Jesus knew what they were thinking and asked, "Why are you thinking these things in your hearts? [23]Which is easier: to say, 'Your sins are forgiven,' or to say, 'Get up and walk'? [24]But that you may know that the Son of Man has authority on earth to forgive sins . . ." He said to the paralyzed man, "I tell you, get up, take your mat and go home." [25]Immediately he stood up in front of them, took what he had been lying on and went home praising God. [26]Everyone was amazed and gave praise to God. They were filled with awe and said, "We have seen remarkable things today."

---

a 1 That is, Sea of Galilee   *b 4* The Greek verb is plural.   *c 12* The Greek word was used for various diseases affecting the skin—not necessarily leprosy.

The Calling of Levi

²⁷After this, Jesus went out and saw a tax collector by the name of Levi sitting at his tax booth. "Follow me," Jesus said to him, ²⁸and Levi got up, left everything and followed him.

²⁹Then Levi held a great banquet for Jesus at his house, and a large crowd of tax collectors and others were eating with them. ³⁰But the Pharisees and the teachers of the law who belonged to their sect complained to his disciples, "Why do you eat and drink with tax collectors and 'sinners'?"

³¹Jesus answered them, "It is not the healthy who need a doctor, but the sick. ³²I have not come to call the righteous, but sinners to repentance."

Jesus Questioned About Fasting

³³They said to him, "John's disciples often fast and pray, and so do the disciples of the Pharisees, but yours go on eating and drinking."

³⁴Jesus answered, "Can you make the guests of the bridegroom fast while he is with them? ³⁵But the time will come when the bridegroom will be taken from them; in those days they will fast."

³⁶He told them this parable: "No one tears a patch from a new garment and sews it on an old one. If he does, he will have torn the new garment, and the patch from the new will not match the old. ³⁷And no one pours new wine into old wineskins. If he does, the new wine will burst the skins, the wine will run out and the wineskins will be ruined. ³⁸No, new wine must be poured into new wineskins. ³⁹And no one after drinking old wine wants the new, for he says, 'The old is better.'"

Lord of the Sabbath

6 One Sabbath Jesus was going through the grainfields, and his disciples began to pick some heads of grain, rub them in their hands and eat the kernels. ²Some of the Pharisees asked, "Why are you doing what is unlawful on the Sabbath?"

³Jesus answered them, "Have you never read what David did when he and his companions were hungry? ⁴He entered the house of God, and taking the consecrated bread, he ate what is lawful only for priests to eat. And he also gave some to his companions." ⁵Then Jesus said to them, "The Son of Man is Lord of the Sabbath."

⁶On another Sabbath he went into the synagogue and was teaching, and a man was there whose right hand was shriveled. ⁷The Pharisees and the teachers of the law were looking for a reason to accuse Jesus, so they watched him closely to see if he would heal on the Sabbath. ⁸But Jesus knew what they were thinking and said to the man with the shriveled hand, "Get up and stand in front of everyone." So he got up and stood there.

⁹Then Jesus said to them, "I ask you, which is lawful on the Sabbath: to do good or to do evil, to save life or to destroy it?"

¹⁰He looked around at them all, and then said to the man, "Stretch out your hand." He did so, and his hand was completely restored. ¹¹But they were furious and began to discuss with one another what they might do to Jesus.

The Twelve Apostles

¹²One of those days Jesus went out to a mountainside to pray, and spent the night praying to God. ¹³When morning came, he called his disciples to him and chose twelve of them, whom he also designated apostles: ¹⁴Simon (whom he named Peter), his brother Andrew, James, John, Philip, Bartholomew, ¹⁵Matthew, Thomas, James son of Alphaeus, Simon who was called the Zealot, ¹⁶Judas son of James, and Judas Iscariot, who became a traitor.

Blessings and Woes

17He went down with them and stood on a level place. A large crowd of his disciples was there and a great number of people from all over Judea, from Jerusalem, and from the coast of Tyre and Sidon, **18**who had come to hear him and to be healed of their diseases. Those troubled by evil*ᵃ* spirits were cured, **19**and the people all tried to touch him, because power was coming from him and healing them all.

20Looking at his disciples, he said:

> "Blessed are you who are poor,
>   for yours is the kingdom of God.
> **21**Blessed are you who hunger now,
>   for you will be satisfied.
> Blessed are you who weep now,
>   for you will laugh.
> **22**Blessed are you when men hate you,
>   when they exclude you and insult you
>   and reject your name as evil,
>   because of the Son of Man.

23"Rejoice in that day and leap for joy, because great is your reward in heaven. For that is how their fathers treated the prophets.

> **24**"But woe to you who are rich,
>   for you have already received your comfort.
> **25**Woe to you who are well fed now,
>   for you will go hungry.
> Woe to you who laugh now,
>   for you will mourn and weep.
> **26**Woe to you when all men speak well of you,
>   for that is how their fathers treated the false prophets.

Love for Enemies

27"But I tell you who hear me: Love your enemies, do good to those who hate you, **28**bless those who curse you, pray for those who mistreat you. **29**If someone strikes you on one cheek, turn to him the other also. If someone takes your cloak, do not stop him from taking your tunic. **30**Give to everyone who asks you, and if anyone takes what belongs to you, do not demand it back. **31**Do to others as you would have them do to you.

32"If you love those who love you, what credit is that to you? Even 'sinners' love those who love them. **33**And if you do good to those who are good to you, what credit is that to you? Even 'sinners' do that. **34**And if you lend to those from whom you expect repayment, what credit is that to you? Even 'sinners' lend to 'sinners,' expecting to be repaid in full. **35**But love your enemies, do good to them, and lend to them without expecting to get anything back. Then your reward will be great, and you will be sons of the Most High, because he is kind to the ungrateful and wicked. **36**Be merciful, just as your Father is merciful.

▣ ▥▥▥ STRENGTHENING RELATIONSHIPS ▥▥▥ ⬆

6:27–36
Social

With these familiar words, Jesus continually calls his followers to a higher level of living. They are to love not only their friends, but their enemies as well. That's a tall order! Yet it's the very way Jesus loves all of us. Where would we be if he waited to love us until we loved him in return?

ᵃ 18 Greek *unclean*

Judging Others

37"Do not judge, and you will not be judged. Do not condemn, and you will not be condemned. Forgive, and you will be forgiven. **38**Give, and it will be given to you. A good measure, pressed down, shaken together and running over, will be poured into your lap. For with the measure you use, it will be measured to you."

39He also told them this parable: "Can a blind man lead a blind man? Will they not both fall into a pit? **40**A student is not above his teacher, but everyone who is fully trained will be like his teacher.

41"Why do you look at the speck of sawdust in your brother's eye and pay no attention to the plank in your own eye? **42**How can you say to your brother, 'Brother, let me take the speck out of your eye,' when you yourself fail to see the plank in your own eye? You hypocrite, first take the plank out of your own eye, and then you will see clearly to remove the speck from your brother's eye.

A Tree and Its Fruit

43"No good tree bears bad fruit, nor does a bad tree bear good fruit. **44**Each tree is recognized by its own fruit. People do not pick figs from thornbushes, or grapes from briers. **45**The good man brings good things out of the good stored up in his heart, and the evil man brings evil things out of the evil stored up in his heart. For out of the overflow of his heart his mouth speaks.

The Wise and Foolish Builders

46"Why do you call me, 'Lord, Lord,' and do not do what I say? **47**I will show you what he is like who comes to me and hears my words and puts them into practice. **48**He is like a man building a house, who dug down deep and laid the foundation on rock. When a flood came, the torrent struck that house but could not shake it, because it was well built. **49**But the one who hears my words and does not put them into practice is like a man who built a house on the ground without a foundation. The moment the torrent struck that house, it collapsed and its destruction was complete."

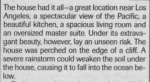

REASONS TO BELIEVE

6:46–49
The Christian Experience

The house had it all—a great location near Los Angeles, a spectacular view of the Pacific, a beautiful kitchen, a spacious living room and an oversized master suite. Under its extravagant beauty, however, lay an unseen risk. The house was perched on the edge of a cliff. A severe rainstorm could weaken the soil under the house, causing it to fall into the ocean below.

During one winter rainstorm, the unthinkable happened. Newspapers across the country carried pictures of the multimillion-dollar house hanging precariously over the cliff.

Why would anyone build a house in a place where it could slip into the sea? Better yet, why would anyone *buy* such a house? Maybe the owners hadn't been warned. Or maybe they had simply refused to heed whatever warning they'd received.

Jesus uses this analogy to warn us against building our lives on a foundation that isn't rock-solid. Will your current belief system stand up to the tests of life? Jesus promised that those who ground their lives upon a relationship with him and in line with his words will be able to withstand any storm.

The Faith of the Centurion

7 When Jesus had finished saying all this in the hearing of the people, he entered Capernaum. **2**There a centurion's servant, whom his master valued highly, was sick and about to die. **3**The centurion heard of Jesus and sent some elders of the Jews to him, asking him to come and heal his servant. **4**When they came to Jesus, they pleaded earnestly with him, "This man deserves to have you do this, **5**because he loves our nation and has built us our synagogue." **6**So Jesus went with them.

He was not far from the house when the centurion sent friends to say to him: "Lord, don't trouble yourself, for I do not deserve to have you come under my roof. **7**That is why I did not even consider myself worthy to come to you. But say the word, and my servant will be healed. ⁸For I myself am a man under authority, with soldiers under me. I tell this one, 'Go,' and he goes; and that one, 'Come,' and he comes. I say to my servant, 'Do this,' and he does it."

⁹When Jesus heard this, he was amazed at him, and turning to the crowd following him, he said, "I tell you, I have not found such great faith even in Israel." ¹⁰Then the men who had been sent returned to the house and found the servant well.

Jesus Raises a Widow's Son

¹¹Soon afterward, Jesus went to a town called Nain, and his disciples and a large crowd went along with him. ¹²As he approached the town gate, a dead person was being carried out—the only son of his mother, and she was a widow. And a large crowd from the town was with her. ¹³When the Lord saw her, his heart went out to her and he said, "Don't cry."

¹⁴Then he went up and touched the coffin, and those carrying it stood still. He said, "Young man, I say to you, get up!" ¹⁵The dead man sat up and began to talk, and Jesus gave him back to his mother.

¹⁶They were all filled with awe and praised God. "A great prophet has appeared among us," they said. "God has come to help his people." ¹⁷This news about Jesus spread throughout Judea*a* and the surrounding country.

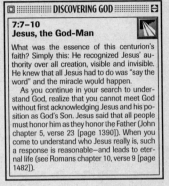

▓▓▓▓ DISCOVERING GOD ▓▓▓▓

7:7–10
Jesus, the God-Man

What was the essence of this centurion's faith? Simply this: He recognized Jesus' authority over all creation, visible and invisible. He knew that all Jesus had to do was "say the word" and the miracle would happen.

As you continue in your search to understand God, realize that you cannot meet God without first acknowledging Jesus and his position as God's Son. Jesus said that all people must honor him as they honor the Father (John chapter 5, verse 23 [page 1390]). When you come to understand who Jesus really is, such a response is reasonable—and leads to eternal life (see Romans chapter 10, verse 9 [page 1482]).

Jesus and John the Baptist

¹⁸John's disciples told him about all these things. Calling two of them, ¹⁹he sent them to the Lord to ask, "Are you the one who was to come, or should we expect someone else?"

²⁰When the men came to Jesus, they said, "John the Baptist sent us to you to ask, 'Are you the one who was to come, or should we expect someone else?'"

²¹At that very time Jesus cured many who had diseases, sicknesses and evil spirits, and gave sight to many who were blind. ²²So he replied to the messengers, "Go back and report to John what you have seen and heard: The blind receive sight, the lame walk, those who have leprosy*b* are cured, the deaf hear, the dead are raised, and the good news is preached to the poor. ²³Blessed is the man who does not fall away on account of me."

²⁴After John's messengers left, Jesus began to speak to the crowd about John: "What did you go out into the desert to see? A reed swayed by the wind? ²⁵If not, what did you go out to see? A man dressed in fine clothes? No, those who wear expensive clothes and indulge in luxury are in palaces. ²⁶But what did you go out to see? A prophet? Yes, I tell you, and more than a prophet. ²⁷This is the one about whom it is written:

> "'I will send my messenger ahead of you,
>   who will prepare your way before you.'*c*

²⁸I tell you, among those born of women there is no one greater than John; yet the one who is least in the kingdom of God is greater than he."

²⁹(All the people, even the tax collectors, when they heard Jesus' words, acknowl-

a 17 Or *the land of the Jews*   *b 22* The Greek word was used for various diseases affecting the skin—not necessarily leprosy.
c 27 Mal. 3:1

edged that God's way was right, because they had been baptized by John. ³⁰But the Pharisees and experts in the law rejected God's purpose for themselves, because they had not been baptized by John.)

³¹"To what, then, can I compare the people of this generation? What are they like? ³²They are like children sitting in the marketplace and calling out to each other:

> " 'We played the flute for you,
>   and you did not dance;
> we sang a dirge,
>   and you did not cry.'

³³For John the Baptist came neither eating bread nor drinking wine, and you say, 'He has a demon.' ³⁴The Son of Man came eating and drinking, and you say, 'Here is a glutton and a drunkard, a friend of tax collectors and "sinners." ' ³⁵But wisdom is proved right by all her children."

Jesus Anointed by a Sinful Woman

³⁶Now one of the Pharisees invited Jesus to have dinner with him, so he went to the Pharisee's house and reclined at the table. ³⁷When a woman who had lived a sinful life in that town learned that Jesus was eating at the Pharisee's house, she brought an alabaster jar of perfume, ³⁸and as she stood behind him at his feet weeping, she began to wet his feet with her tears. Then she wiped them with her hair, kissed them and poured perfume on them.

³⁹When the Pharisee who had invited him saw this, he said to himself, "If this man were a prophet, he would know who is touching him and what kind of woman she is—that she is a sinner."

⁴⁰Jesus answered him, "Simon, I have something to tell you."

"Tell me, teacher," he said.

⁴¹"Two men owed money to a certain moneylender. One owed him five hundred denarii,ᵃ and the other fifty. ⁴²Neither of them had the money to pay him back, so he canceled the debts of both. Now which of them will love him more?"

⁴³Simon replied, "I suppose the one who had the bigger debt canceled."

"You have judged correctly," Jesus said.

⁴⁴Then he turned toward the woman and said to Simon, "Do you see this woman? I came into your house. You did not give me any water for my feet, but she wet my feet with her tears and wiped them with her hair. ⁴⁵You did not give me a kiss, but this woman, from the time I entered, has not stopped kissing my feet. ⁴⁶You did not put oil on my head, but she has poured perfume on my feet. ⁴⁷Therefore, I tell you, her many sins have been forgiven—for she loved much. But he who has been forgiven little loves little."

⁴⁸Then Jesus said to her, "Your sins are forgiven."

⁴⁹The other guests began to say among themselves, "Who is this who even forgives sins?"

⁵⁰Jesus said to the woman, "Your faith has saved you; go in peace."

The Parable of the Sower

8 After this, Jesus traveled about from one town and village to another, proclaiming the good news of the kingdom of God. The Twelve were with him, ²and also some women who had been cured of evil spirits and diseases: Mary (called Magdalene) from whom seven demons had come out; ³Joanna the wife of Cuza, the manager of Herod's household; Susanna; and many others. These women were helping to support them out of their own means.

⁴While a large crowd was gathering and people were coming to Jesus from town after town, he told this parable: ⁵"A farmer went out to sow his seed. As he was scattering the

ᵃ41 A denarius was a coin worth about a day's wages.

seed, some fell along the path; it was trampled on, and the birds of the air ate it up. 6Some fell on rock, and when it came up, the plants withered because they had no moisture. 7Other seed fell among thorns, which grew up with it and choked the plants. 8Still other seed fell on good soil. It came up and yielded a crop, a hundred times more than was sown."

When he said this, he called out, "He who has ears to hear, let him hear."

9His disciples asked him what this parable meant. 10He said, "The knowledge of the secrets of the kingdom of God has been given to you, but to others I speak in parables, so that,

" 'though seeing, they may not see;
    though hearing, they may not understand.'ᵃ

11"This is the meaning of the parable: The seed is the word of God. 12Those along the path are the ones who hear, and then the devil comes and takes away the word from their hearts, so that they may not believe and be saved. 13Those on the rock are the ones who receive the word with joy when they hear it, but they have no root. They believe for a while, but in the time of testing they fall away. 14The seed that fell among thorns stands for those who hear, but as they go on their way they are choked by life's worries, riches and pleasures, and they do not mature. 15But the seed on good soil stands for those with a noble and good heart, who hear the word, retain it, and by persevering produce a crop.

A Lamp on a Stand

16"No one lights a lamp and hides it in a jar or puts it under a bed. Instead, he puts it on a stand, so that those who come in can see the light. 17For there is nothing hidden that will not be disclosed, and nothing concealed that will not be known or brought out into the open. 18Therefore consider carefully how you listen. Whoever has will be given more; whoever does not have, even what he thinks he has will be taken from him."

Jesus' Mother and Brothers

19Now Jesus' mother and brothers came to see him, but they were not able to get near him because of the crowd. 20Someone told him, "Your mother and brothers are standing outside, wanting to see you."

21He replied, "My mother and brothers are those who hear God's word and put it into practice."

Jesus Calms the Storm

22One day Jesus said to his disciples, "Let's go over to the other side of the lake." So they got into a boat and set out. 23As they sailed, he fell asleep. A squall came down on the lake, so that the boat was being swamped, and they were in great danger.

24The disciples went and woke him, saying, "Master, Master, we're going to drown!"

He got up and rebuked the wind and the raging waters; the storm subsided, and all was calm. 25"Where is your faith?" he asked his disciples.

In fear and amazement they asked one another, "Who is this? He commands even the winds and the water, and they obey him."

The Healing of a Demon-possessed Man

26They sailed to the region of the Gerasenes,ᵇ which is across the lake from Galilee. 27When Jesus stepped ashore, he was met by a demon-possessed man from the town. For a long time this man had not worn clothes or lived in a house, but had lived in the tombs. 28When he saw Jesus, he cried out and fell at his feet, shouting at the top of his voice, "What do you want with me, Jesus, Son of the Most High God? I beg you, don't

ᵃ 10 Isaiah 6:9   ᵇ 26 Some manuscripts Gadarenes; other manuscripts Gergesenes; also in verse 37 torture me!" ²⁹For Jesus had commanded the evil*ª* spirit to come out of the man. Many times it had seized him, and though he was chained hand and foot and kept under guard, he had broken his chains and had been driven by the demon into solitary places.

³⁰Jesus asked him, "What is your name?"

"Legion," he replied, because many demons had gone into him. ³¹And they begged him repeatedly not to order them to go into the Abyss.

³²A large herd of pigs was feeding there on the hillside. The demons begged Jesus to let them go into them, and he gave them permission. ³³When the demons came out of the man, they went into the pigs, and the herd rushed down the steep bank into the lake and was drowned.

³⁴When those tending the pigs saw what had happened, they ran off and reported this in the town and countryside, ³⁵and the people went out to see what had happened. When they came to Jesus, they found the man from whom the demons had gone out, sitting at Jesus' feet, dressed and in his right mind; and they were afraid. ³⁶Those who had seen it told the people how the demon-possessed man had been cured. ³⁷Then all the people of the region of the Gerasenes asked Jesus to leave them, because they were overcome with fear. So he got into the boat and left.

³⁸The man from whom the demons had gone out begged to go with him, but Jesus sent him away, saying, ³⁹"Return home and tell how much God has done for you." So the man went away and told all over town how much Jesus had done for him.

A Dead Girl and a Sick Woman

⁴⁰Now when Jesus returned, a crowd welcomed him, for they were all expecting him. ⁴¹Then a man named Jairus, a ruler of the synagogue, came and fell at Jesus' feet, pleading with him to come to his house ⁴²because his only daughter, a girl of about twelve, was dying.

As Jesus was on his way, the crowds almost crushed him. ⁴³And a woman was there who had been subject to bleeding for twelve years,*ᵇ* but no one could heal her. ⁴⁴She came up behind him and touched the edge of his cloak, and immediately her bleeding stopped.

⁴⁵"Who touched me?" Jesus asked.

When they all denied it, Peter said, "Master, the people are crowding and pressing against you."

⁴⁶But Jesus said, "Someone touched me; I know that power has gone out from me."

⁴⁷Then the woman, seeing that she could not go unnoticed, came trembling and fell at his feet. In the presence of all the people, she told why she had touched him and how she had been instantly healed. ⁴⁸Then he said to her, "Daughter, your faith has healed you. Go in peace."

⁴⁹While Jesus was still speaking, someone came from the house of Jairus, the synagogue ruler. "Your daughter is dead," he said. "Don't bother the teacher any more."

⁵⁰Hearing this, Jesus said to Jairus, "Don't be afraid; just believe, and she will be healed."

⁵¹When he arrived at the house of Jairus, he did not let anyone go in with him except Peter, John and James, and the child's father and mother. ⁵²Meanwhile, all the people were wailing and mourning for her. "Stop wailing," Jesus said. "She is not dead but asleep."

⁵³They laughed at him, knowing that she was dead. ⁵⁴But he took her by the hand and said, "My child, get up!" ⁵⁵Her spirit returned, and at once she stood up. Then Jesus told them to give her something to eat. ⁵⁶Her parents were astonished, but he ordered them not to tell anyone what had happened.

ª29 Greek *unclean*   *ᵇ43* Many manuscripts *years, and she had spent all she had on doctors*

Jesus Sends Out the Twelve

9 When Jesus had called the Twelve together, he gave them power and authority to drive out all demons and to cure diseases, ²and he sent them out to preach the kingdom of God and to heal the sick. ³He told them: "Take nothing for the journey—no staff, no bag, no bread, no money, no extra tunic. ⁴Whatever house you enter, stay there until you leave that town. ⁵If people do not welcome you, shake the dust off your feet when you leave their town, as a testimony against them." ⁶So they set out and went from village to village, preaching the gospel and healing people everywhere.

⁷Now Herod the tetrarch heard about all that was going on. And he was perplexed, because some were saying that John had been raised from the dead, ⁸others that Elijah had appeared, and still others that one of the prophets of long ago had come back to life. ⁹But Herod said, "I beheaded John. Who, then, is this I hear such things about?" And he tried to see him.

Jesus Feeds the Five Thousand

¹⁰When the apostles returned, they reported to Jesus what they had done. Then he took them with him and they withdrew by themselves to a town called Bethsaida, ¹¹but the crowds learned about it and followed him. He welcomed them and spoke to them about the kingdom of God, and healed those who needed healing.

¹²Late in the afternoon the Twelve came to him and said, "Send the crowd away so they can go to the surrounding villages and countryside and find food and lodging, because we are in a remote place here."

¹³He replied, "You give them something to eat."

They answered, "We have only five loaves of bread and two fish—unless we go and buy food for all this crowd." ¹⁴(About five thousand men were there.)

But he said to his disciples, "Have them sit down in groups of about fifty each." ¹⁵The disciples did so, and everybody sat down. ¹⁶Taking the five loaves and the two fish and looking up to heaven, he gave thanks and broke them. Then he gave them to the disciples to set before the people. ¹⁷They all ate and were satisfied, and the disciples picked up twelve basketfuls of broken pieces that were left over.

Peter's Confession of Christ

¹⁸Once when Jesus was praying in private and his disciples were with him, he asked them, "Who do the crowds say I am?"

¹⁹They replied, "Some say John the Baptist; others say Elijah; and still others, that one of the prophets of long ago has come back to life."

²⁰"But what about you?" he asked. "Who do you say I am?"

Peter answered, "The Christ[a] of God."

²¹Jesus strictly warned them not to tell this to anyone. ²²And he said, "The Son of Man must suffer many things and be rejected by the elders, chief priests and teachers of the law, and he must be killed and on the third day be raised to life."

²³Then he said to them all: "If anyone would come after me, he must deny himself and take up his cross daily and follow me. ²⁴For whoever wants to save his life will lose it, but whoever loses his life for me will save it. ²⁵What good is it for a man to gain the whole world, and yet lose or forfeit his very self? ²⁶If anyone is ashamed of me and my words, the Son of Man will be ashamed of him when he comes in his glory and in the glory of the Father and of the holy angels. ²⁷I tell you the truth, some who are standing here will not taste death before they see the kingdom of God."

ª 20 Or *Messiah*

The Transfiguration

28About eight days after Jesus said this, he took Peter, John and James with him and went up onto a mountain to pray. **29**As he was praying, the appearance of his face changed, and his clothes became as bright as a flash of lightning. **30**Two men, Moses and Elijah, **31**appeared in glorious splendor, talking with Jesus. They spoke about his departure, which he was about to bring to fulfillment at Jerusalem. **32**Peter and his companions were very sleepy, but when they became fully awake, they saw his glory and the two men standing with him. **33**As the men were leaving Jesus, Peter said to him, "Master, it is good for us to be here. Let us put up three shelters—one for you, one for Moses and one for Elijah." (He did not know what he was saying.)

34While he was speaking, a cloud appeared and enveloped them, and they were afraid as they entered the cloud. **35**A voice came from the cloud, saying, "This is my Son, whom I have chosen; listen to him." **36**When the voice had spoken, they found that Jesus was alone. The disciples kept this to themselves, and told no one at that time what they had seen.

The Healing of a Boy With an Evil Spirit

37The next day, when they came down from the mountain, a large crowd met him. **38**A man in the crowd called out, "Teacher, I beg you to look at my son, for he is my only child. **39**A spirit seizes him and he suddenly screams; it throws him into convulsions so that he foams at the mouth. It scarcely ever leaves him and is destroying him. **40**I begged your disciples to drive it out, but they could not."

41"O unbelieving and perverse generation," Jesus replied, "how long shall I stay with you and put up with you? Bring your son here."

42Even while the boy was coming, the demon threw him to the ground in a convulsion. But Jesus rebuked the evil*a* spirit, healed the boy and gave him back to his father. **43**And they were all amazed at the greatness of God.

While everyone was marveling at all that Jesus did, he said to his disciples, **44**"Listen carefully to what I am about to tell you: The Son of Man is going to be betrayed into the hands of men." **45**But they did not understand what this meant. It was hidden from them, so that they did not grasp it, and they were afraid to ask him about it.

Who Will Be the Greatest?

46An argument started among the disciples as to which of them would be the greatest. **47**Jesus, knowing their thoughts, took a little child and had him stand beside him. **48**Then he said to them, "Whoever welcomes this little child in my name welcomes me; and whoever welcomes me welcomes the one who sent me. For he who is least among you all—he is the greatest."

49"Master," said John, "we saw a man driving out demons in your name and we tried to stop him, because he is not one of us."

50"Do not stop him," Jesus said, "for whoever is not against you is for you."

Samaritan Opposition

51As the time approached for him to be taken up to heaven, Jesus resolutely set out for Jerusalem. **52**And he sent messengers on ahead, who went into a Samaritan village to get things ready for him; **53**but the people there did not welcome him, because he was heading for Jerusalem. **54**When the disciples James and John saw this, they asked, "Lord, do you want us to call fire down from heaven to destroy them*b*?" **55**But Jesus turned and rebuked them, **56**and*c* they went to another village.

---

a 42 Greek *unclean*   *b 54* Some manuscripts *them, even as Elijah did*   *c 55,56* Some manuscripts *them. And he said,
"You do not know what kind of spirit you are of, for the Son of Man did not come to destroy men's lives, but to save them." 56And*

The Cost of Following Jesus

57As they were walking along the road, a man said to him, "I will follow you wherever you go."

58Jesus replied, "Foxes have holes and birds of the air have nests, but the Son of Man has no place to lay his head."

59He said to another man, "Follow me."

But the man replied, "Lord, first let me go and bury my father."

60Jesus said to him, "Let the dead bury their own dead, but you go and proclaim the kingdom of God."

61Still another said, "I will follow you, Lord; but first let me go back and say good-by to my family."

62Jesus replied, "No one who puts his hand to the plow and looks back is fit for service in the kingdom of God."

Jesus Sends Out the Seventy-two

10 After this the Lord appointed seventy-two[a] others and sent them two by two ahead of him to every town and place where he was about to go. **2**He told them, "The harvest is plentiful, but the workers are few. Ask the Lord of the harvest, therefore, to send out workers into his harvest field. **3**Go! I am sending you out like lambs among wolves. **4**Do not take a purse or bag or sandals; and do not greet anyone on the road.

5"When you enter a house, first say, 'Peace to this house.' **6**If a man of peace is there, your peace will rest on him; if not, it will return to you. **7**Stay in that house, eating and drinking whatever they give you, for the worker deserves his wages. Do not move around from house to house.

8"When you enter a town and are welcomed, eat what is set before you. **9**Heal the sick who are there and tell them, 'The kingdom of God is near you.' **10**But when you enter a town and are not welcomed, go into its streets and say, **11**'Even the dust of your town that sticks to our feet we wipe off against you. Yet be sure of this: The kingdom of God is near.' **12**I tell you, it will be more bearable on that day for Sodom than for that town.

13"Woe to you, Korazin! Woe to you, Bethsaida! For if the miracles that were performed in you had been performed in Tyre and Sidon, they would have repented long ago, sitting in sackcloth and ashes. **14**But it will be more bearable for Tyre and Sidon at the judgment than for you. **15**And you, Capernaum, will you be lifted up to the skies? No, you will go down to the depths.[b]

16"He who listens to you listens to me; he who rejects you rejects me; but he who rejects me rejects him who sent me."

17The seventy-two returned with joy and said, "Lord, even the demons submit to us in your name."

18He replied, "I saw Satan fall like lightning from heaven. **19**I have given you authority to trample on snakes and scorpions and to overcome all the power of the enemy; nothing will harm you. **20**However, do not rejoice that the spirits submit to you, but rejoice that your names are written in heaven."

21At that time Jesus, full of joy through the Holy Spirit, said, "I praise you, Father, Lord of heaven and earth, because you have hidden these things from the wise and learned, and revealed them to little children. Yes, Father, for this was your good pleasure.

22"All things have been committed to me by my Father. No one knows who the Son is except the Father, and no one knows who the Father is except the Son and those to whom the Son chooses to reveal him."

23Then he turned to his disciples and said privately, "Blessed are the eyes that see

a 1 Some manuscripts *seventy;* also in verse 17   *b 15* Greek *Hades*

what you see. ²⁴For I tell you that many prophets and kings wanted to see what you see but did not see it, and to hear what you hear but did not hear it."

The Parable of the Good Samaritan

²⁵On one occasion an expert in the law stood up to test Jesus. "Teacher," he asked, "what must I do to inherit eternal life?"

²⁶"What is written in the Law?" he replied. "How do you read it?"

²⁷He answered: "'Love the Lord your God with all your heart and with all your soul and with all your strength and with all your mind'ᵃ; and, 'Love your neighbor as yourself.'ᵇ"

²⁸"You have answered correctly," Jesus replied. "Do this and you will live."

²⁹But he wanted to justify himself, so he asked Jesus, "And who is my neighbor?"

³⁰In reply Jesus said: "A man was going down from Jerusalem to Jericho, when he fell into the hands of robbers. They stripped him of his clothes, beat him and went away, leaving him half dead. ³¹A priest happened to be going down the same road, and when he saw the man, he passed by on the other side. ³²So too, a Levite, when he came to the place and saw him, passed by on the other side. ³³But a Samaritan, as he traveled, came where the man was; and when he saw him, he took pity on him. ³⁴He went to him and bandaged his wounds, pouring on oil and wine. Then he put the man on his own donkey, took him to an inn and took care of him. ³⁵The next day he took out two silver coinsᶜ and gave them to the innkeeper. 'Look after him,' he said, 'and when I return, I will reimburse you for any extra expense you may have.'

³⁶"Which of these three do you think was a neighbor to the man who fell into the hands of robbers?"

³⁷The expert in the law replied, "The one who had mercy on him."

Jesus told him, "Go and do likewise."

◫ ▒▒▒▒▒▒▒ KNOWING YOURSELF ▒▒▒▒▒▒▒ ⊟

10:25–37
Sin

Some people are more interested in making themselves look good than in facing reality. That was true of this "expert in the law." When Jesus told him to love both God and his neighbor, the man claimed he didn't know who his neighbor was. In response, Jesus told one of the most loved stories in the Bible—the parable of the good Samaritan. This story showed this religious leader that his "neighbor" was anyone he saw who had a need.

Of course, by that rule not one of us has completely loved our neighbor as ourselves. This story is intended both to encourage us in our daily walk and to help us see that we don't live up to God's standard and therefore need his forgiveness and help to do so.

At the Home of Martha and Mary

³⁸As Jesus and his disciples were on their way, he came to a village where a woman named Martha opened her home to him. ³⁹She had a sister called Mary, who sat at the Lord's feet listening to what he said. ⁴⁰But Martha was distracted by all the preparations that had to be made. She came to him and asked, "Lord, don't you care that my sister has left me to do the work by myself? Tell her to help me!"

⁴¹"Martha, Martha," the Lord answered, "you are worried and upset about many things, ⁴²but only one thing is needed.ᵈ Mary has chosen what is better, and it will not be taken away from her."

ᵃ27 Deut. 6:5   ᵇ27 Lev. 19:18   ᶜ35 Greek *two denarii*   ᵈ42 Some manuscripts *but few things are needed—or only one*

Jesus' Teaching on Prayer

11 One day Jesus was praying in a certain place. When he finished, one of his disciples said to him, "Lord, teach us to pray, just as John taught his disciples."

²He said to them, "When you pray, say:

" 'Father,ᵃ
hallowed be your name,
your kingdom come.ᵇ
³Give us each day our daily bread.
⁴Forgive us our sins,
for we also forgive everyone who sins against us.ᶜ
And lead us not into temptation.ᵈ' "

⁵Then he said to them, "Suppose one of you has a friend, and he goes to him at midnight and says, 'Friend, lend me three loaves of bread, ⁶because a friend of mine on a journey has come to me, and I have nothing to set before him.'

⁷"Then the one inside answers, 'Don't bother me. The door is already locked, and my children are with me in bed. I can't get up and give you anything.' ⁸I tell you, though he will not get up and give him the bread because he is his friend, yet because of the man's boldnessᵉ he will get up and give him as much as he needs.

⁹"So I say to you: Ask and it will be given to you; seek and you will find; knock and the door will be opened to you. ¹⁰For everyone who asks receives; he who seeks finds; and to him who knocks, the door will be opened.

¹¹"Which of you fathers, if your son asks forᶠ a fish, will give him a snake instead? ¹²Or if he asks for an egg, will give him a scorpion? ¹³If you then, though you are evil, know how to give good gifts to your children, how much more will your Father in heaven give the Holy Spirit to those who ask him!"

Jesus and Beelzebub

¹⁴Jesus was driving out a demon that was mute. When the demon left, the man who had been mute spoke, and the crowd was amazed. ¹⁵But some of them said, "By Beelzebub,ᵍ the prince of demons, he is driving out demons." ¹⁶Others tested him by asking for a sign from heaven.

¹⁷Jesus knew their thoughts and said to them: "Any kingdom divided against itself will be ruined, and a house divided against itself will fall. ¹⁸If Satan is divided against himself, how can his kingdom stand? I say this because you claim that I drive out demons by Beelzebub. ¹⁹Now if I drive out demons by Beelzebub, by whom do your followers drive them out? So then, they will be your judges. ²⁰But if I drive out demons by the finger of God, then the kingdom of God has come to you.

²¹"When a strong man, fully armed, guards his own house, his possessions are safe. ²²But when someone stronger attacks and overpowers him, he takes away the armor in which the man trusted and divides up the spoils.

²³"He who is not with me is against me, and he who does not gather with me, scatters.

²⁴"When an evilʰ spirit comes out of a man, it goes through arid places seeking rest and does not find it. Then it says, 'I will return to the house I left.' ²⁵When it arrives, it finds the house swept clean and put in order. ²⁶Then it goes and takes seven other spirits more wicked than itself, and they go in and live there. And the final condition of that man is worse than the first."

ᵃ2 *Some manuscripts* Our Father in heaven   ᵇ2 *Some manuscripts* come. May your will be done on earth as it is in heaven.
ᶜ4 *Greek* everyone who is indebted to us   ᵈ4 *Some manuscripts* temptation but deliver us from the evil one   ᵉ8 *Or*
persistence   ᶠ11 *Some manuscripts* for bread, will give him a stone; or if he asks for   ᵍ15 *Greek* Beezeboul *or*
Beelzeboul; also in verses 18 and 19   ʰ24 *Greek* unclean

²⁷As Jesus was saying these things, a woman in the crowd called out, "Blessed is the mother who gave you birth and nursed you."

²⁸He replied, "Blessed rather are those who hear the word of God and obey it."

The Sign of Jonah

²⁹As the crowds increased, Jesus said, "This is a wicked generation. It asks for a miraculous sign, but none will be given it except the sign of Jonah. ³⁰For as Jonah was a sign to the Ninevites, so also will the Son of Man be to this generation. ³¹The Queen of the South will rise at the judgment with the men of this generation and condemn them; for she came from the ends of the earth to listen to Solomon's wisdom, and now one^a greater than Solomon is here. ³²The men of Nineveh will stand up at the judgment with this generation and condemn it; for they repented at the preaching of Jonah, and now one greater than Jonah is here.

The Lamp of the Body

³³"No one lights a lamp and puts it in a place where it will be hidden, or under a bowl. Instead he puts it on its stand, so that those who come in may see the light. ³⁴Your eye is the lamp of your body. When your eyes are good, your whole body also is full of light. But when they are bad, your body also is full of darkness. ³⁵See to it, then, that the light within you is not darkness. ³⁶Therefore, if your whole body is full of light, and no part of it dark, it will be completely lighted, as when the light of a lamp shines on you."

Six Woes

³⁷When Jesus had finished speaking, a Pharisee invited him to eat with him; so he went in and reclined at the table. ³⁸But the Pharisee, noticing that Jesus did not first wash before the meal, was surprised.

³⁹Then the Lord said to him, "Now then, you Pharisees clean the outside of the cup and dish, but inside you are full of greed and wickedness. ⁴⁰You foolish people! Did not the one who made the outside make the inside also? ⁴¹But give what is inside ₍the dish₎^{b} to the poor, and everything will be clean for you.

⁴²"Woe to you Pharisees, because you give God a tenth of your mint, rue and all other kinds of garden herbs, but you neglect justice and the love of God. You should have practiced the latter without leaving the former undone.

⁴³"Woe to you Pharisees, because you love the most important seats in the synagogues and greetings in the marketplaces.

⁴⁴"Woe to you, because you are like unmarked graves, which men walk over without knowing it."

⁴⁵One of the experts in the law answered him, "Teacher, when you say these things, you insult us also."

⁴⁶Jesus replied, "And you experts in the law, woe to you, because you load people down with burdens they can hardly carry, and you yourselves will not lift one finger to help them.

⁴⁷"Woe to you, because you build tombs for the prophets, and it was your forefathers who killed them. ⁴⁸So you testify that you approve of what your forefathers did; they killed the prophets, and you build their tombs. ⁴⁹Because of this, God in his wisdom said, 'I will send them prophets and apostles, some of whom they will kill and others they will persecute.' ⁵⁰Therefore this generation will be held responsible for the blood of all the prophets that has been shed since the beginning of the world, ⁵¹from the blood of Abel to the blood of Zechariah, who was killed between the altar and the sanctuary. Yes, I tell you, this generation will be held responsible for it all.

⁵²"Woe to you experts in the law, because you have taken away the key to knowledge. You yourselves have not entered, and you have hindered those who were entering."

---

^{a}31 Or something; also in verse 32 ^{b}41 Or what you have

⁵³When Jesus left there, the Pharisees and the teachers of the law began to oppose him fiercely and to besiege him with questions, ⁵⁴waiting to catch him in something he might say.

Warnings and Encouragements

12 Meanwhile, when a crowd of many thousands had gathered, so that they were trampling on one another, Jesus began to speak first to his disciples, saying: "Be on your guard against the yeast of the Pharisees, which is hypocrisy. ²There is nothing concealed that will not be disclosed, or hidden that will not be made known. ³What you have said in the dark will be heard in the daylight, and what you have whispered in the ear in the inner rooms will be proclaimed from the roofs.

⁴"I tell you, my friends, do not be afraid of those who kill the body and after that can do no more. ⁵But I will show you whom you should fear: Fear him who, after the killing of the body, has power to throw you into hell. Yes, I tell you, fear him. ⁶Are not five sparrows sold for two pennies*ᵃ*? Yet not one of them is forgotten by God. ⁷Indeed, the very hairs of your head are all numbered. Don't be afraid; you are worth more than many sparrows.

⁸"I tell you, whoever acknowledges me before men, the Son of Man will also acknowledge him before the angels of God. ⁹But he who disowns me before men will be disowned before the angels of God. ¹⁰And everyone who speaks a word against the Son of Man will be forgiven, but anyone who blasphemes against the Holy Spirit will not be forgiven.

¹¹"When you are brought before synagogues, rulers and authorities, do not worry about how you will defend yourselves or what you will say, ¹²for the Holy Spirit will teach you at that time what you should say."

The Parable of the Rich Fool

¹³Someone in the crowd said to him, "Teacher, tell my brother to divide the inheritance with me."

¹⁴Jesus replied, "Man, who appointed me a judge or an arbiter between you?" ¹⁵Then he said to them, "Watch out! Be on your guard against all kinds of greed; a man's life does not consist in the abundance of his possessions."

¹⁶And he told them this parable: "The ground of a certain rich man produced a good crop. ¹⁷He thought to himself, 'What shall I do? I have no place to store my crops.'

¹⁸"Then he said, 'This is what I'll do. I will tear down my barns and build bigger ones, and there I will store all my grain and my goods. ¹⁹And I'll say to myself, "You have plenty of good things laid up for many years. Take life easy; eat, drink and be merry." '

²⁰"But God said to him, 'You fool! This very night your life will be demanded from you. Then who will get what you have prepared for yourself?'

²¹"This is how it will be with anyone who stores up things for himself but is not rich toward God."

Do Not Worry

²²Then Jesus said to his disciples: "Therefore I tell you, do not worry about your life, what you will eat; or about your body, what you will wear. ²³Life is more than food, and the body more than clothes. ²⁴Consider the ravens: They do not sow or reap, they have no storeroom or barn; yet God feeds them. And how much more valuable you are than birds! ²⁵Who of you by worrying can add a single hour to his life*ᵇ*? ²⁶Since you cannot do this very little thing, why do you worry about the rest?

²⁷"Consider how the lilies grow. They do not labor or spin. Yet I tell you, not even Solomon in all his splendor was dressed like one of these. ²⁸If that is how God clothes the grass of the field, which is here today, and tomorrow is thrown into the fire, how much

---

ᵃ6 Greek two assaria   *ᵇ25 Or single cubit to his height* more will he clothe you, O you of little faith! ²⁹And do not set your heart on what you will eat or drink; do not worry about it. ³⁰For the pagan world runs after all such things, and your Father knows that you need them. ³¹But seek his kingdom, and these things will be given to you as well.

³²"Do not be afraid, little flock, for your Father has been pleased to give you the kingdom. ³³Sell your possessions and give to the poor. Provide purses for yourselves that will not wear out, a treasure in heaven that will not be exhausted, where no thief comes near and no moth destroys. ³⁴For where your treasure is, there your heart will be also.

Watchfulness

³⁵"Be dressed ready for service and keep your lamps burning, ³⁶like men waiting for their master to return from a wedding banquet, so that when he comes and knocks they can immediately open the door for him. ³⁷It will be good for those servants whose master finds them watching when he comes. I tell you the truth, he will dress himself to serve, will have them recline at the table and will come and wait on them. ³⁸It will be good for those servants whose master finds them ready, even if he comes in the second or third watch of the night. ³⁹But understand this: If the owner of the house had known at what hour the thief was coming, he would not have let his house be broken into. ⁴⁰You also must be ready, because the Son of Man will come at an hour when you do not expect him."

⁴¹Peter asked, "Lord, are you telling this parable to us, or to everyone?"

⁴²The Lord answered, "Who then is the faithful and wise manager, whom the master puts in charge of his servants to give them their food allowance at the proper time? ⁴³It will be good for that servant whom the master finds doing so when he returns. ⁴⁴I tell you the truth, he will put him in charge of all his possessions. ⁴⁵But suppose the servant says to himself, 'My master is taking a long time in coming,' and he then begins to beat the menservants and maidservants and to eat and drink and get drunk. ⁴⁶The master of that servant will come on a day when he does not expect him and at an hour he is not aware of. He will cut him to pieces and assign him a place with the unbelievers.

⁴⁷"That servant who knows his master's will and does not get ready or does not do what his master wants will be beaten with many blows. ⁴⁸But the one who does not know and does things deserving punishment will be beaten with few blows. From everyone who has been given much, much will be demanded; and from the one who has been entrusted with much, much more will be asked.

Not Peace but Division

⁴⁹"I have come to bring fire on the earth, and how I wish it were already kindled! ⁵⁰But I have a baptism to undergo, and how distressed I am until it is completed! ⁵¹Do you think I came to bring peace on earth? No, I tell you, but division. ⁵²From now on there will be five in one family divided against each other, three against two and two against three. ⁵³They will be divided, father against son and son against father, mother against daughter and daughter against mother, mother-in-law against daughter-in-law and daughter-in-law against mother-in-law."

Interpreting the Times

⁵⁴He said to the crowd: "When you see a cloud rising in the west, immediately you say, 'It's going to rain,' and it does. ⁵⁵And when the south wind blows, you say, 'It's going to be hot,' and it is. ⁵⁶Hypocrites! You know how to interpret the appearance of the earth and the sky. How is it that you don't know how to interpret this present time?

⁵⁷"Why don't you judge for yourselves what is right? ⁵⁸As you are going with your adversary to the magistrate, try hard to be reconciled to him on the way, or he may drag

you off to the judge, and the judge turn you over to the officer, and the officer throw you into prison. [59]I tell you, you will not get out until you have paid the last penny.[a]"

Repent or Perish

13 Now there were some present at that time who told Jesus about the Galileans whose blood Pilate had mixed with their sacrifices. [2]Jesus answered, "Do you think that these Galileans were worse sinners than all the other Galileans because they suffered this way? [3]I tell you, no! But unless you repent, you too will all perish. [4]Or those eighteen who died when the tower in Siloam fell on them—do you think they were more guilty than all the others living in Jerusalem? [5]I tell you, no! But unless you repent, you too will all perish."

[6]Then he told this parable: "A man had a fig tree, planted in his vineyard, and he went to look for fruit on it, but did not find any. [7]So he said to the man who took care of the vineyard, 'For three years now I've been coming to look for fruit on this fig tree and haven't found any. Cut it down! Why should it use up the soil?'

[8]"'Sir,' the man replied, 'leave it alone for one more year, and I'll dig around it and fertilize it. [9]If it bears fruit next year, fine! If not, then cut it down.'"

A Crippled Woman Healed on the Sabbath

[10]On a Sabbath Jesus was teaching in one of the synagogues, [11]and a woman was there who had been crippled by a spirit for eighteen years. She was bent over and could not straighten up at all. [12]When Jesus saw her, he called her forward and said to her, "Woman, you are set free from your infirmity." [13]Then he put his hands on her, and immediately she straightened up and praised God.

[14]Indignant because Jesus had healed on the Sabbath, the synagogue ruler said to the people, "There are six days for work. So come and be healed on those days, not on the Sabbath."

[15]The Lord answered him, "You hypocrites! Doesn't each of you on the Sabbath untie his ox or donkey from the stall and lead it out to give it water? [16]Then should not this woman, a daughter of Abraham, whom Satan has kept bound for eighteen long years, be set free on the Sabbath day from what bound her?"

[17]When he said this, all his opponents were humiliated, but the people were delighted with all the wonderful things he was doing.

The Parables of the Mustard Seed and the Yeast

[18]Then Jesus asked, "What is the kingdom of God like? What shall I compare it to? [19]It is like a mustard seed, which a man took and planted in his garden. It grew and became a tree, and the birds of the air perched in its branches."

[20]Again he asked, "What shall I compare the kingdom of God to? [21]It is like yeast that a woman took and mixed into a large amount[b] of flour until it worked all through the dough."

The Narrow Door

[22]Then Jesus went through the towns and villages, teaching as he made his way to Jerusalem. [23]Someone asked him, "Lord, are only a few people going to be saved?"

He said to them, [24]"Make every effort to enter through the narrow door, because many, I tell you, will try to enter and will not be able to. [25]Once the owner of the house gets up and closes the door, you will stand outside knocking and pleading, 'Sir, open the door for us.'

"But he will answer, 'I don't know you or where you come from.'

[26]"Then you will say, 'We ate and drank with you, and you taught in our streets.'

---

[a]59 Greek lepton   [b]21 Greek three satas (probably about 1/2 bushel or 22 liters)

²⁷"But he will reply, 'I don't know you or where you come from. Away from me, all you evildoers!'

²⁸"There will be weeping there, and gnashing of teeth, when you see Abraham, Isaac and Jacob and all the prophets in the kingdom of God, but you yourselves thrown out. ²⁹People will come from east and west and north and south, and will take their places at the feast in the kingdom of God. ³⁰Indeed there are those who are last who will be first, and first who will be last."

ADDRESSING QUESTIONS

13:22–30
Human Experience

Sometimes people say, "It doesn't matter what you believe as long as you're sincere." The implication is that there are many ways to God and that sincerity guarantees that he'll be found. Yet Jesus himself taught that the way to God has only one path—through himself alone. Some people think this makes Christianity implausible. But truth is often very restrictive, such as "2 + 2 = 4" and "Drinking gasoline could kill you."

Jesus claimed to be the only way to God because he alone paid the penalty for our sins. As such, he alone can impart eternal life. If you're a seeker, don't be afraid to follow Jesus just because he offers a path to God that has boundaries. Instead, examine whether or not he speaks the truth. And be glad he has made a way, even if it does seem narrow.

Jesus' Sorrow for Jerusalem

³¹At that time some Pharisees came to Jesus and said to him, "Leave this place and go somewhere else. Herod wants to kill you."

³²He replied, "Go tell that fox, 'I will drive out demons and heal people today and tomorrow, and on the third day I will reach my goal.' ³³In any case, I must keep going today and tomorrow and the next day—for surely no prophet can die outside Jerusalem!

³⁴"O Jerusalem, Jerusalem, you who kill the prophets and stone those sent to you, how often I have longed to gather your children together, as a hen gathers her chicks under her wings, but you were not willing! ³⁵Look, your house is left to you desolate. I tell you, you will not see me again until you say, 'Blessed is he who comes in the name of the Lord.'ᵃ"

Jesus at a Pharisee's House

14 One Sabbath, when Jesus went to eat in the house of a prominent Pharisee, he was being carefully watched. ²There in front of him was a man suffering from dropsy. ³Jesus asked the Pharisees and experts in the law, "Is it lawful to heal on the Sabbath or not?" ⁴But they remained silent. So taking hold of the man, he healed him and sent him away.

⁵Then he asked them, "If one of you has a sonᵇ or an ox that falls into a well on the Sabbath day, will you not immediately pull him out?" ⁶And they had nothing to say.

⁷When he noticed how the guests picked the places of honor at the table, he told them this parable: ⁸"When someone invites you to a wedding feast, do not take the place of honor, for a person more distinguished than you may have been invited. ⁹If so, the host who invited both of you will come and say to you, 'Give this man your seat.' Then, humiliated, you will have to take the least important place. ¹⁰But when you are invited, take the lowest place, so that when your host comes, he will say to you, 'Friend, move up to a better place.' Then you will be honored in the presence of all your fellow guests. ¹¹For everyone who exalts himself will be humbled, and he who humbles himself will be exalted."

¹²Then Jesus said to his host, "When you give a luncheon or dinner, do not invite your friends, your brothers or relatives, or your rich neighbors; if you do, they may invite you back and so you will be repaid. ¹³But when you give a banquet, invite the poor, the

ᵃ35 Psalm 118:26   *ᵇ5* Some manuscripts *donkey*

crippled, the lame, the blind, ¹⁴and you will be blessed. Although they cannot repay you, you will be repaid at the resurrection of the righteous."

The Parable of the Great Banquet

¹⁵When one of those at the table with him heard this, he said to Jesus, "Blessed is the man who will eat at the feast in the kingdom of God."

¹⁶Jesus replied: "A certain man was preparing a great banquet and invited many guests. ¹⁷At the time of the banquet he sent his servant to tell those who had been invited, 'Come, for everything is now ready.'

¹⁸"But they all alike began to make excuses. The first said, 'I have just bought a field, and I must go and see it. Please excuse me.'

¹⁹"Another said, 'I have just bought five yoke of oxen, and I'm on my way to try them out. Please excuse me.'

²⁰"Still another said, 'I just got married, so I can't come.'

²¹"The servant came back and reported this to his master. Then the owner of the house became angry and ordered his servant, 'Go out quickly into the streets and alleys of the town and bring in the poor, the crippled, the blind and the lame.'

²²"'Sir,' the servant said, 'what you ordered has been done, but there is still room.'

²³"Then the master told his servant, 'Go out to the roads and country lanes and make them come in, so that my house will be full. ²⁴I tell you, not one of those men who were invited will get a taste of my banquet.'"

The Cost of Being a Disciple

²⁵Large crowds were traveling with Jesus, and turning to them he said: ²⁶"If anyone comes to me and does not hate his father and mother, his wife and children, his brothers and sisters—yes, even his own life—he cannot be my disciple. ²⁷And anyone who does not carry his cross and follow me cannot be my disciple.

²⁸"Suppose one of you wants to build a tower. Will he not first sit down and estimate the cost to see if he has enough money to complete it? ²⁹For if he lays the foundation and is not able to finish it, everyone who sees it will ridicule him, ³⁰saying, 'This fellow began to build and was not able to finish.'

³¹"Or suppose a king is about to go to war against another king. Will he not first sit down and consider whether he is able with ten thousand men to oppose the one coming against him with twenty thousand? ³²If he is not able, he will send a delegation while the other is still a long way off and will ask for terms of peace. ³³In the same way, any of you who does not give up everything he has cannot be my disciple.

³⁴"Salt is good, but if it loses its saltiness, how can it be made salty again? ³⁵It is fit neither for the soil nor for the manure pile; it is thrown out.

"He who has ears to hear, let him hear."

The Parable of the Lost Sheep

15 Now the tax collectors and "sinners" were all gathering around to hear him. ²But the Pharisees and the teachers of the law muttered, "This man welcomes sinners and eats with them."

³Then Jesus told them this parable: ⁴"Suppose one of you has a hundred sheep and loses one of them. Does he not leave the ninety-nine in the open country and go after the lost sheep until he finds it? ⁵And when he finds it, he joyfully puts it on his shoulders ⁶and goes home. Then he calls his friends and neighbors together and says, 'Rejoice with me; I have found my lost sheep.' ⁷I tell you that in the same way there will be more rejoicing in heaven over one sinner who repents than over ninety-nine righteous persons who do not need to repent.

The Parable of the Lost Coin

⁸"Or suppose a woman has ten silver coins*a* and loses one. Does she not light a lamp, sweep the house and search carefully until she finds it? ⁹And when she finds it, she calls her friends and neighbors together and says, 'Rejoice with me; I have found my lost coin.' ¹⁰In the same way, I tell you, there is rejoicing in the presence of the angels of God over one sinner who repents."

The Parable of the Lost Son

¹¹Jesus continued: "There was a man who had two sons. ¹²The younger one said to his father, 'Father, give me my share of the estate.' So he divided his property between them.

¹³"Not long after that, the younger son got together all he had, set off for a distant country and there squandered his wealth in wild living. ¹⁴After he had spent everything, there was a severe famine in that whole country, and he began to be in need. ¹⁵So he went and hired himself out to a citizen of that country, who sent him to his fields to feed pigs. ¹⁶He longed to fill his stomach with the pods that the pigs were eating, but no one gave him anything.

¹⁷"When he came to his senses, he said, 'How many of my father's hired men have food to spare, and here I am starving to death! ¹⁸I will set out and go back to my father and say to him: Father, I have sinned against heaven and against you. ¹⁹I am no longer worthy to be called your son; make me like one of your hired men.' ²⁰So he got up and went to his father.

"But while he was still a long way off, his father saw him and was filled with compassion for him; he ran to his son, threw his arms around him and kissed him.

---

a8 Greek *ten drachmas,* each worth about a day's wages

::::::::::::::::::::::::::::::::: **DISCOVERING GOD** :::::::::::::::::::::::::::::::::

15:1–32
The God Who Is There

Most people find it hard to identify with lost sheep. But a lost dog? Now that's a different story. If Jesus were to tell the parable of the lost sheep today, he might make it the parable of the lost dog. The idea is the same. If your dog runs off, you search for it until you find it. And when you bring it home your family celebrates.

The next story deserves a bit of historical illumination. Palestinian women traditionally received a set of 10 coins as a wedding gift. These coins were either carried around in a purse or on a chain, and held similar significance to a modern-day wedding ring. As such, these coins held sentimental value that went well beyond their monetary value. No wonder this woman would search so fervently to find the lost coin, and no wonder she would want to celebrate upon finding it!

We don't have to stretch too far to understand the third story. Imagine that you're a parent and that your son leaves home with as much money as he can pull together. He departs for a big city like New York, Los Angeles or San Francisco. After he blows every cent he has on drugs, sex and alcohol, he ends up on the street.

As his parent you wait for the day he'll come home. Every time the phone rings or you hear a car outside, you hope it's him. One day you open the front door, and there he stands! Instantly you throw your arms around him. Words can't express the joy you feel. Your son who was lost is home!

These three stories express how God feels about every seeker. And it's how he feels about you. He's looking for you because he loves you. God is eager to forgive you, and all of heaven is ready to celebrate your return. But, like the son in the third story, you must decide to come home to his waiting arms.

²¹"The son said to him, 'Father, I have sinned against heaven and against you. I am no longer worthy to be called your son.ᵃ'

²²"But the father said to his servants, 'Quick! Bring the best robe and put it on him. Put a ring on his finger and sandals on his feet. ²³Bring the fattened calf and kill it. Let's have a feast and celebrate. ²⁴For this son of mine was dead and is alive again; he was lost and is found.' So they began to celebrate.

²⁵"Meanwhile, the older son was in the field. When he came near the house, he heard music and dancing. ²⁶So he called one of the servants and asked him what was going on. ²⁷'Your brother has come,' he replied, 'and your father has killed the fattened calf because he has him back safe and sound.'

²⁸"The older brother became angry and refused to go in. So his father went out and pleaded with him. ²⁹But he answered his father, 'Look! All these years I've been slaving for you and never disobeyed your orders. Yet you never gave me even a young goat so I could celebrate with my friends. ³⁰But when this son of yours who has squandered your property with prostitutes comes home, you kill the fattened calf for him!'

³¹"'My son,' the father said, 'you are always with me, and everything I have is yours. ³²But we had to celebrate and be glad, because this brother of yours was dead and is alive again; he was lost and is found.'"

The Parable of the Shrewd Manager

16 Jesus told his disciples: "There was a rich man whose manager was accused of wasting his possessions. ²So he called him in and asked him, 'What is this I hear about you? Give an account of your management, because you cannot be manager any longer.'

³"The manager said to himself, 'What shall I do now? My master is taking away my job. I'm not strong enough to dig, and I'm ashamed to beg— ⁴I know what I'll do so that, when I lose my job here, people will welcome me into their houses.'

⁵"So he called in each one of his master's debtors. He asked the first, 'How much do you owe my master?'

⁶"'Eight hundred gallonsᵇ of olive oil,' he replied.

"The manager told him, 'Take your bill, sit down quickly, and make it four hundred.'

⁷"Then he asked the second, 'And how much do you owe?'

"'A thousand bushelsᶜ of wheat,' he replied.

"He told him, 'Take your bill and make it eight hundred.'

⁸"The master commended the dishonest manager because he had acted shrewdly. For the people of this world are more shrewd in dealing with their own kind than are the people of the light. ⁹I tell you, use worldly wealth to gain friends for yourselves, so that when it is gone, you will be welcomed into eternal dwellings.

¹⁰"Whoever can be trusted with very little can also be trusted with much, and whoever is dishonest with very little will also be dishonest with much. ¹¹So if you have not been trustworthy in handling worldly wealth, who will trust you with true riches? ¹²And if you have not been trustworthy with someone else's property, who will give you property of your own?

¹³"No servant can serve two masters. Either he will hate the one and love the other, or he will be devoted to the one and despise the other. You cannot serve both God and Money."

¹⁴The Pharisees, who loved money, heard all this and were sneering at Jesus. ¹⁵He said to them, "You are the ones who justify yourselves in the eyes of men, but God knows your hearts. What is highly valued among men is detestable in God's sight.

ᵃ21 Some early manuscripts son. Make me like one of your hired men.   ᵇ6 Greek one hundred batous (probably about 3 kiloliters)   ᶜ7 Greek one hundred korous (probably about 35 kiloliters)

Additional Teachings

¹⁶"The Law and the Prophets were proclaimed until John. Since that time, the good news of the kingdom of God is being preached, and everyone is forcing his way into it. ¹⁷It is easier for heaven and earth to disappear than for the least stroke of a pen to drop out of the Law.

¹⁸"Anyone who divorces his wife and marries another woman commits adultery, and the man who marries a divorced woman commits adultery.

The Rich Man and Lazarus

¹⁹"There was a rich man who was dressed in purple and fine linen and lived in luxury every day. ²⁰At his gate was laid a beggar named Lazarus, covered with sores ²¹and longing to eat what fell from the rich man's table. Even the dogs came and licked his sores.

²²"The time came when the beggar died and the angels carried him to Abraham's side. The rich man also died and was buried. ²³In hell,ᵃ where he was in torment, he looked up and saw Abraham far away, with Lazarus by his side. ²⁴So he called to him, 'Father Abraham, have pity on me and send Lazarus to dip the tip of his finger in water and cool my tongue, because I am in agony in this fire.'

²⁵"But Abraham replied, 'Son, remember that in your lifetime you received your good things, while Lazarus received bad things, but now he is comforted here and you are in agony. ²⁶And besides all this, between us and you a great chasm has been fixed, so that those who want to go from here to you cannot, nor can anyone cross over from there to us.'

²⁷"He answered, 'Then I beg you, father, send Lazarus to my father's house, ²⁸for I have five brothers. Let him warn them, so that they will not also come to this place of torment.'

²⁹"Abraham replied, 'They have Moses and the Prophets; let them listen to them.'

³⁰"'No, father Abraham,' he said, 'but if someone from the dead goes to them, they will repent.'

³¹"He said to him, 'If they do not listen to Moses and the Prophets, they will not be convinced even if someone rises from the dead.' "

Sin, Faith, Duty

17 Jesus said to his disciples: "Things that cause people to sin are bound to come, but woe to that person through whom they come. ²It would be better for him to be thrown into the sea with a millstone tied around his neck than for him to cause one of these little ones to sin. ³So watch yourselves.

"If your brother sins, rebuke him, and if he repents, forgive him. ⁴If he sins against you seven times in a day, and seven times comes back to you and says, 'I repent,' forgive him."

⁵The apostles said to the Lord, "Increase our faith!"

⁶He replied, "If you have faith as small as a mustard seed, you can say to this mulberry tree, 'Be uprooted and planted in the sea,' and it will obey you.

⁷"Suppose one of you had a servant plowing or looking after the sheep. Would he say to the servant when he comes in from the field, 'Come along now and sit down to eat'? ⁸Would he not rather say, 'Prepare my supper, get yourself ready and wait on me while I eat and drink; after that you may eat and drink'? ⁹Would he thank the servant because he did what he was told to do? ¹⁰So you also, when you have done everything you were told to do, should say, 'We are unworthy servants; we have only done our duty.' "

ᵃ23 Greek *Hades*

Ten Healed of Leprosy

¹¹Now on his way to Jerusalem, Jesus traveled along the border between Samaria and Galilee. ¹²As he was going into a village, ten men who had leprosy*a* met him. They stood at a distance ¹³and called out in a loud voice, "Jesus, Master, have pity on us!"

¹⁴When he saw them, he said, "Go, show yourselves to the priests." And as they went, they were cleansed.

¹⁵One of them, when he saw he was healed, came back, praising God in a loud voice. ¹⁶He threw himself at Jesus' feet and thanked him—and he was a Samaritan.

¹⁷Jesus asked, "Were not all ten cleansed? Where are the other nine? ¹⁸Was no one found to return and give praise to God except this foreigner?" ¹⁹Then he said to him, "Rise and go; your faith has made you well."

The Coming of the Kingdom of God

²⁰Once, having been asked by the Pharisees when the kingdom of God would come, Jesus replied, "The kingdom of God does not come with your careful observation, ²¹nor will people say, 'Here it is,' or 'There it is,' because the kingdom of God is within*b* you."

²²Then he said to his disciples, "The time is coming when you will long to see one of the days of the Son of Man, but you will not see it. ²³Men will tell you, 'There he is!' or 'Here he is!' Do not go running off after them. ²⁴For the Son of Man in his day*c* will be like the lightning, which flashes and lights up the sky from one end to the other. ²⁵But first he must suffer many things and be rejected by this generation.

²⁶"Just as it was in the days of Noah, so also will it be in the days of the Son of Man. ²⁷People were eating, drinking, marrying and being given in marriage up to the day Noah entered the ark. Then the flood came and destroyed them all.

²⁸"It was the same in the days of Lot. People were eating and drinking, buying and selling, planting and building. ²⁹But the day Lot left Sodom, fire and sulfur rained down from heaven and destroyed them all.

³⁰"It will be just like this on the day the Son of Man is revealed. ³¹On that day no one who is on the roof of his house, with his goods inside, should go down to get them. Likewise, no one in the field should go back for anything. ³²Remember Lot's wife! ³³Whoever tries to keep his life will lose it, and whoever loses his life will preserve it. ³⁴I tell you, on that night two people will be in one bed; one will be taken and the other left. ³⁵Two women will be grinding grain together; one will be taken and the other left.*d*"

³⁷"Where, Lord?" they asked.

He replied, "Where there is a dead body, there the vultures will gather."

The Parable of the Persistent Widow

18 Then Jesus told his disciples a parable to show them that they should always pray and not give up. ²He said: "In a certain town there was a judge who neither feared God nor cared about men. ³And there was a widow in that town who kept coming to him with the plea, 'Grant me justice against my adversary.'

⁴"For some time he refused. But finally he said to himself, 'Even though I don't fear God

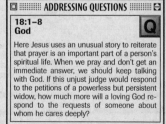

ADDRESSING QUESTIONS ❓

18:1–8
God

Here Jesus uses an unusual story to reiterate that prayer is an important part of a person's spiritual life. When we pray and don't get an immediate answer, we should keep talking with God. If this unjust judge would respond to the petitions of a powerless but persistent widow, how much more will a loving God respond to the requests of someone about whom he cares deeply?

---

a12 The Greek word was used for various diseases affecting the skin—not necessarily leprosy.   *b21* Or *among*
c24 Some manuscripts do not have *in his day.*   *d35* Some manuscripts *left.* ³⁶*Two men will be in the field; one will be taken and the other left.*

or care about men, ⁵yet because this widow keeps bothering me, I will see that she gets justice, so that she won't eventually wear me out with her coming!'"

⁶And the Lord said, "Listen to what the unjust judge says. ⁷And will not God bring about justice for his chosen ones, who cry out to him day and night? Will he keep putting them off? ⁸I tell you, he will see that they get justice, and quickly. However, when the Son of Man comes, will he find faith on the earth?"

The Parable of the Pharisee and the Tax Collector

⁹To some who were confident of their own righteousness and looked down on everybody else, Jesus told this parable: ¹⁰"Two men went up to the temple to pray, one a Pharisee and the other a tax collector. ¹¹The Pharisee stood up and prayed about[a] himself: 'God, I thank you that I am not like other men—robbers, evildoers, adulterers—or even like this tax collector. ¹²I fast twice a week and give a tenth of all I get.'

¹³"But the tax collector stood at a distance. He would not even look up to heaven, but beat his breast and said, 'God, have mercy on me, a sinner.'

¹⁴"I tell you that this man, rather than the other, went home justified before God. For everyone who exalts himself will be humbled, and he who humbles himself will be exalted."

The Little Children and Jesus

¹⁵People were also bringing babies to Jesus to have him touch them. When the disciples saw this, they rebuked them. ¹⁶But Jesus called the children to him and said, "Let the little children come to me, and do not hinder them, for the kingdom of God belongs to such as these. ¹⁷I tell you the truth, anyone who will not receive the kingdom of God like a little child will never enter it."

The Rich Ruler

¹⁸A certain ruler asked him, "Good teacher, what must I do to inherit eternal life?"

¹⁹"Why do you call me good?" Jesus answered. "No one is good—except God alone. ²⁰You know the commandments: 'Do not commit adultery, do not murder, do not steal, do not give false testimony, honor your father and mother.'[b]"

²¹"All these I have kept since I was a boy," he said.

²²When Jesus heard this, he said to him, "You still lack one thing. Sell everything you have and give to the poor, and you will have treasure in heaven. Then come, follow me."

²³When he heard this, he became very sad, because he was a man of great wealth. ²⁴Jesus looked at him and said, "How hard it is for the rich to enter the kingdom of God! ²⁵Indeed, it is easier for a camel to go through the eye of a needle than for a rich man to enter the kingdom of God."

²⁶Those who heard this asked, "Who then can be saved?"

²⁷Jesus replied, "What is impossible with men is possible with God."

²⁸Peter said to him, "We have left all we had to follow you!"

²⁹"I tell you the truth," Jesus said to them, "no one who has left home or wife or brothers or parents or children for the sake of the kingdom of God ³⁰will fail to receive many times as much in this age and, in the age to come, eternal life."

Jesus Again Predicts His Death

³¹Jesus took the Twelve aside and told them, "We are going up to Jerusalem, and everything that is written by the prophets about the Son of Man will be fulfilled. ³²He will be handed over to the Gentiles. They will mock him, insult him, spit on him, flog him and kill him. ³³On the third day he will rise again."

³⁴The disciples did not understand any of this. Its meaning was hidden from them, and they did not know what he was talking about.

a 11 Or *to*   *b 20* Exodus 20:12-16; Deut. 5:16-20

A Blind Beggar Receives His Sight

³⁵As Jesus approached Jericho, a blind man was sitting by the roadside begging. ³⁶When he heard the crowd going by, he asked what was happening. ³⁷They told him, "Jesus of Nazareth is passing by."

³⁸He called out, "Jesus, Son of David, have mercy on me!"

³⁹Those who led the way rebuked him and told him to be quiet, but he shouted all the more, "Son of David, have mercy on me!"

⁴⁰Jesus stopped and ordered the man to be brought to him. When he came near, Jesus asked him, ⁴¹"What do you want me to do for you?"

"Lord, I want to see," he replied.

⁴²Jesus said to him, "Receive your sight; your faith has healed you." ⁴³Immediately he received his sight and followed Jesus, praising God. When all the people saw it, they also praised God.

Zacchaeus the Tax Collector

19 Jesus entered Jericho and was passing through. ²A man was there by the name of Zacchaeus; he was a chief tax collector and was wealthy. ³He wanted to see who Jesus was, but being a short man he could not, because of the crowd. ⁴So he ran ahead and climbed a sycamore-fig tree to see him, since Jesus was coming that way.

⁵When Jesus reached the spot, he looked up and said to him, "Zacchaeus, come down immediately. I must stay at your house today." ⁶So he came down at once and welcomed him gladly.

⁷All the people saw this and began to mutter, "He has gone to be the guest of a 'sinner.'"

⁸But Zacchaeus stood up and said to the Lord, "Look, Lord! Here and now I give half of my possessions to the poor, and if I have cheated anybody out of anything, I will pay back four times the amount."

> ### ▣ ▦ DISCOVERING GOD ▦
>
> #### 19:1–10
> #### Life with God
>
> Nobody thought Jesus would want to meet with Zacchaeus. As a tax collector, he got rich by swindling his fellow countrymen. He collected what the Romans demanded and kept anything more he could get. He was undoubtedly one of the most unpopular men in town.
>
> But Zacchaeus was a seeker. So Jesus invited himself to Zacchaeus's home for dinner. That night the least-liked man in town, along with his family, received eternal life—a fact demonstrated both by Jesus' words and by Zacchaeus's change in lifestyle.
>
> Zacchaeus and the rest of Jericho discovered that the greatest seeker of all is Jesus. Verse 10 states in a nutshell the main purpose of Jesus' mission: "To seek and to save [the] lost."

⁹Jesus said to him, "Today salvation has come to this house, because this man, too, is a son of Abraham. ¹⁰For the Son of Man came to seek and to save what was lost."

The Parable of the Ten Minas

¹¹While they were listening to this, he went on to tell them a parable, because he was near Jerusalem and the people thought that the kingdom of God was going to appear at once. ¹²He said: "A man of noble birth went to a distant country to have himself appointed king and then to return. ¹³So he called ten of his servants and gave them ten minas.ᵃ 'Put this money to work,' he said, 'until I come back.'

¹⁴"But his subjects hated him and sent a delegation after him to say, 'We don't want this man to be our king.'

¹⁵"He was made king, however, and returned home. Then he sent for the servants to whom he had given the money, in order to find out what they had gained with it.

¹⁶"The first one came and said, 'Sir, your mina has earned ten more.'

ᵃ 13 A mina was about three months' wages.

¹⁷"'Well done, my good servant!' his master replied. 'Because you have been trustworthy in a very small matter, take charge of ten cities.'

¹⁸"The second came and said, 'Sir, your mina has earned five more.'

¹⁹"His master answered, 'You take charge of five cities.'

²⁰"Then another servant came and said, 'Sir, here is your mina; I have kept it laid away in a piece of cloth. ²¹I was afraid of you, because you are a hard man. You take out what you did not put in and reap what you did not sow.'

²²"His master replied, 'I will judge you by your own words, you wicked servant! You knew, did you, that I am a hard man, taking out what I did not put in, and reaping what I did not sow? ²³Why then didn't you put my money on deposit, so that when I came back, I could have collected it with interest?'

²⁴"Then he said to those standing by, 'Take his mina away from him and give it to the one who has ten minas.'

²⁵"'Sir,' they said, 'he already has ten!'

²⁶"He replied, 'I tell you that to everyone who has, more will be given, but as for the one who has nothing, even what he has will be taken away. ²⁷But those enemies of mine who did not want me to be king over them—bring them here and kill them in front of me.'"

The Triumphal Entry

²⁸After Jesus had said this, he went on ahead, going up to Jerusalem. ²⁹As he approached Bethphage and Bethany at the hill called the Mount of Olives, he sent two of his disciples, saying to them, ³⁰"Go to the village ahead of you, and as you enter it, you will find a colt tied there, which no one has ever ridden. Untie it and bring it here. ³¹If anyone asks you, 'Why are you untying it?' tell him, 'The Lord needs it.'"

³²Those who were sent ahead went and found it just as he had told them. ³³As they were untying the colt, its owners asked them, "Why are you untying the colt?"

³⁴They replied, "The Lord needs it."

³⁵They brought it to Jesus, threw their cloaks on the colt and put Jesus on it. ³⁶As he went along, people spread their cloaks on the road.

³⁷When he came near the place where the road goes down the Mount of Olives, the whole crowd of disciples began joyfully to praise God in loud voices for all the miracles they had seen:

³⁸"Blessed is the king who comes in the name of the Lord!"ᵃ

"Peace in heaven and glory in the highest!"

³⁹Some of the Pharisees in the crowd said to Jesus, "Teacher, rebuke your disciples!"

⁴⁰"I tell you," he replied, "if they keep quiet, the stones will cry out."

⁴¹As he approached Jerusalem and saw the city, he wept over it ⁴²and said, "If you, even you, had only known on this day what would bring you peace—but now it is hidden from your eyes. ⁴³The days will come upon you when your enemies will build an embankment against you and encircle you and hem you in on every side. ⁴⁴They will dash you to the ground, you and the children within your walls. They will not leave one stone on another, because you did not recognize the time of God's coming to you."

Jesus at the Temple

⁴⁵Then he entered the temple area and began driving out those who were selling. ⁴⁶"It is written," he said to them, "'My house will be a house of prayer'ᵇ; but you have made it 'a den of robbers.'ᶜ"

⁴⁷Every day he was teaching at the temple. But the chief priests, the teachers of the

ᵃ38 Psalm 118:26   ᵇ46 Isaiah 56:7   ᶜ46 Jer. 7:11

law and the leaders among the people were trying to kill him. ⁴⁸Yet they could not find any way to do it, because all the people hung on his words.

The Authority of Jesus Questioned

20 One day as he was teaching the people in the temple courts and preaching the gospel, the chief priests and the teachers of the law, together with the elders, came up to him. ²"Tell us by what authority you are doing these things," they said. "Who gave you this authority?"

³He replied, "I will also ask you a question. Tell me, ⁴John's baptism—was it from heaven, or from men?"

⁵They discussed it among themselves and said, "If we say, 'From heaven,' he will ask, 'Why didn't you believe him?' ⁶But if we say, 'From men,' all the people will stone us, because they are persuaded that John was a prophet."

⁷So they answered, "We don't know where it was from."

⁸Jesus said, "Neither will I tell you by what authority I am doing these things."

The Parable of the Tenants

⁹He went on to tell the people this parable: "A man planted a vineyard, rented it to some farmers and went away for a long time. ¹⁰At harvest time he sent a servant to the tenants so they would give him some of the fruit of the vineyard. But the tenants beat him and sent him away empty-handed. ¹¹He sent another servant, but that one also they beat and treated shamefully and sent away empty-handed. ¹²He sent still a third, and they wounded him and threw him out.

¹³"Then the owner of the vineyard said, 'What shall I do? I will send my son, whom I love; perhaps they will respect him.'

¹⁴"But when the tenants saw him, they talked the matter over. 'This is the heir,' they said. 'Let's kill him, and the inheritance will be ours.' ¹⁵So they threw him out of the vineyard and killed him.

"What then will the owner of the vineyard do to them? ¹⁶He will come and kill those tenants and give the vineyard to others."

When the people heard this, they said, "May this never be!"

¹⁷Jesus looked directly at them and asked, "Then what is the meaning of that which is written:

> "'The stone the builders rejected
>   has become the capstone$^{a\,'\,b}$?

¹⁸Everyone who falls on that stone will be broken to pieces, but he on whom it falls will be crushed."

¹⁹The teachers of the law and the chief priests looked for a way to arrest him immediately, because they knew he had spoken this parable against them. But they were afraid of the people.

Paying Taxes to Caesar

²⁰Keeping a close watch on him, they sent spies, who pretended to be honest. They hoped to catch Jesus in something he said so that they might hand him over to the power and authority of the governor. ²¹So the spies questioned him: "Teacher, we know that you speak and teach what is right, and that you do not show partiality but teach the way of God in accordance with the truth. ²²Is it right for us to pay taxes to Caesar or not?"

²³He saw through their duplicity and said to them, ²⁴"Show me a denarius. Whose portrait and inscription are on it?"

²⁵"Caesar's," they replied.

He said to them, "Then give to Caesar what is Caesar's, and to God what is God's."

a 17 Or cornerstone   b 17 Psalm 118:22

²⁶They were unable to trap him in what he had said there in public. And astonished by his answer, they became silent.

The Resurrection and Marriage

²⁷Some of the Sadducees, who say there is no resurrection, came to Jesus with a question. ²⁸"Teacher," they said, "Moses wrote for us that if a man's brother dies and leaves a wife but no children, the man must marry the widow and have children for his brother. ²⁹Now there were seven brothers. The first one married a woman and died childless. ³⁰The second ³¹and then the third married her, and in the same way the seven died, leaving no children. ³²Finally, the woman died too. ³³Now then, at the resurrection whose wife will she be, since the seven were married to her?"

³⁴Jesus replied, "The people of this age marry and are given in marriage. ³⁵But those who are considered worthy of taking part in that age and in the resurrection from the dead will neither marry nor be given in marriage, ³⁶and they can no longer die; for they are like the angels. They are God's children, since they are children of the resurrection. ³⁷But in the account of the bush, even Moses showed that the dead rise, for he calls the Lord 'the God of Abraham, and the God of Isaac, and the God of Jacob.'ᵃ ³⁸He is not the God of the dead, but of the living, for to him all are alive."

³⁹Some of the teachers of the law responded, "Well said, teacher!" ⁴⁰And no one dared to ask him any more questions.

Whose Son Is the Christ?

⁴¹Then Jesus said to them, "How is it that they say the Christᵇ is the Son of David? ⁴²David himself declares in the Book of Psalms:

"'The Lord said to my Lord:
"Sit at my right hand
⁴³until I make your enemies
a footstool for your feet."'ᶜ

⁴⁴David calls him 'Lord.' How then can he be his son?"

⁴⁵While all the people were listening, Jesus said to his disciples, ⁴⁶"Beware of the teachers of the law. They like to walk around in flowing robes and love to be greeted in the marketplaces and have the most important seats in the synagogues and the places of honor at banquets. ⁴⁷They devour widows' houses and for a show make lengthy prayers. Such men will be punished most severely."

The Widow's Offering

21 As he looked up, Jesus saw the rich putting their gifts into the temple treasury. ²He also saw a poor widow put in two very small copper coins.ᵈ ³"I tell you the truth," he said, "this poor widow has put in more than all the others. ⁴All these people gave their gifts out of their wealth; but she out of her poverty put in all she had to live on."

Signs of the End of the Age

⁵Some of his disciples were remarking about how the temple was adorned with beautiful stones and with gifts dedicated to God. But Jesus said, ⁶"As for what you see here, the time will come when not one stone will be left on another; every one of them will be thrown down."

⁷"Teacher," they asked, "when will these things happen? And what will be the sign that they are about to take place?"

⁸He replied: "Watch out that you are not deceived. For many will come in my name, claiming, 'I am he,' and, 'The time is near.' Do not follow them. ⁹When you hear of wars

ᵃ 37 Exodus 3:6   ᵇ 41 Or Messiah   ᶜ 43 Psalm 110:1   ᵈ 2 Greek two lepta

and revolutions, do not be frightened. These things must happen first, but the end will not come right away."

¹⁰Then he said to them: "Nation will rise against nation, and kingdom against kingdom. ¹¹There will be great earthquakes, famines and pestilences in various places, and fearful events and great signs from heaven.

¹²"But before all this, they will lay hands on you and persecute you. They will deliver you to synagogues and prisons, and you will be brought before kings and governors, and all on account of my name. ¹³This will result in your being witnesses to them. ¹⁴But make up your mind not to worry beforehand how you will defend yourselves. ¹⁵For I will give you words and wisdom that none of your adversaries will be able to resist or contradict. ¹⁶You will be betrayed even by parents, brothers, relatives and friends, and they will put some of you to death. ¹⁷All men will hate you because of me. ¹⁸But not a hair of your head will perish. ¹⁹By standing firm you will gain life.

²⁰"When you see Jerusalem being surrounded by armies, you will know that its desolation is near. ²¹Then let those who are in Judea flee to the mountains, let those in the city get out, and let those in the country not enter the city. ²²For this is the time of punishment in fulfillment of all that has been written. ²³How dreadful it will be in those days for pregnant women and nursing mothers! There will be great distress in the land and wrath against this people. ²⁴They will fall by the sword and will be taken as prisoners to all the nations. Jerusalem will be trampled on by the Gentiles until the times of the Gentiles are fulfilled.

²⁵"There will be signs in the sun, moon and stars. On the earth, nations will be in anguish and perplexity at the roaring and tossing of the sea. ²⁶Men will faint from terror, apprehensive of what is coming on the world, for the heavenly bodies will be shaken. ²⁷At that time they will see the Son of Man coming in a cloud with power and great glory. ²⁸When these things begin to take place, stand up and lift up your heads, because your redemption is drawing near."

²⁹He told them this parable: "Look at the fig tree and all the trees. ³⁰When they sprout leaves, you can see for yourselves and know that summer is near. ³¹Even so, when you see these things happening, you know that the kingdom of God is near.

³²"I tell you the truth, this generation*ᵃ* will certainly not pass away until all these things have happened. ³³Heaven and earth will pass away, but my words will never pass away.

³⁴"Be careful, or your hearts will be weighed down with dissipation, drunkenness and the anxieties of life, and that day will close on you unexpectedly like a trap. ³⁵For it will come upon all those who live on the face of the whole earth. ³⁶Be always on the watch, and pray that you may be able to escape all that is about to happen, and that you may be able to stand before the Son of Man."

³⁷Each day Jesus was teaching at the temple, and each evening he went out to spend the night on the hill called the Mount of Olives, ³⁸and all the people came early in the morning to hear him at the temple.

Judas Agrees to Betray Jesus

22 Now the Feast of Unleavened Bread, called the Passover, was approaching, ²and the chief priests and the teachers of the law were looking for some way to get rid of Jesus, for they were afraid of the people. ³Then Satan entered Judas, called Iscariot, one of the Twelve. ⁴And Judas went to the chief priests and the officers of the temple guard and discussed with them how he might betray Jesus. ⁵They were delighted and agreed to give him money. ⁶He consented, and watched for an opportunity to hand Jesus over to them when no crowd was present.

ᵃ32 Or race

The Last Supper

⁷Then came the day of Unleavened Bread on which the Passover lamb had to be sacrificed. ⁸Jesus sent Peter and John, saying, "Go and make preparations for us to eat the Passover."

⁹"Where do you want us to prepare for it?" they asked.

¹⁰He replied, "As you enter the city, a man carrying a jar of water will meet you. Follow him to the house that he enters, ¹¹and say to the owner of the house, 'The Teacher asks: Where is the guest room, where I may eat the Passover with my disciples?' ¹²He will show you a large upper room, all furnished. Make preparations there."

¹³They left and found things just as Jesus had told them. So they prepared the Passover.

¹⁴When the hour came, Jesus and his apostles reclined at the table. ¹⁵And he said to them, "I have eagerly desired to eat this Passover with you before I suffer. ¹⁶For I tell you, I will not eat it again until it finds fulfillment in the kingdom of God."

¹⁷After taking the cup, he gave thanks and said, "Take this and divide it among you. ¹⁸For I tell you I will not drink again of the fruit of the vine until the kingdom of God comes."

¹⁹And he took bread, gave thanks and broke it, and gave it to them, saying, "This is my body given for you; do this in remembrance of me."

²⁰In the same way, after the supper he took the cup, saying, "This cup is the new covenant in my blood, which is poured out for you. ²¹But the hand of him who is going to betray me is with mine on the table. ²²The Son of Man will go as it has been decreed, but woe to that man who betrays him." ²³They began to question among themselves which of them it might be who would do this.

²⁴Also a dispute arose among them as to which of them was considered to be greatest. ²⁵Jesus said to them, "The kings of the Gentiles lord it over them; and those who exercise authority over them call themselves Benefactors. ²⁶But you are not to be like that. Instead, the greatest among you should be like the youngest, and the one who rules like the one who serves. ²⁷For who is greater, the one who is at the table or the one who serves? Is it not the one who is at the table? But I am among you as one who serves. ²⁸You are those who have stood by me in my trials. ²⁹And I confer on you a kingdom, just as my Father conferred one on me, ³⁰so that you may eat and drink at my table in my kingdom and sit on thrones, judging the twelve tribes of Israel.

³¹"Simon, Simon, Satan has asked to sift you[a] as wheat. ³²But I have prayed for you, Simon, that your faith may not fail. And when you have turned back, strengthen your brothers."

³³But he replied, "Lord, I am ready to go with you to prison and to death."

³⁴Jesus answered, "I tell you, Peter, before the rooster crows today, you will deny three times that you know me."

³⁵Then Jesus asked them, "When I sent you without purse, bag or sandals, did you lack anything?"

"Nothing," they answered.

³⁶He said to them, "But now if you have a purse, take it, and also a bag; and if you don't have a sword, sell your cloak and buy one. ³⁷It is written: 'And he was numbered with the transgressors'[b]; and I tell you that this must be fulfilled in me. Yes, what is written about me is reaching its fulfillment."

³⁸The disciples said, "See, Lord, here are two swords."

"That is enough," he replied.

---

a 31 The Greek is plural.   b 37 Isaiah 53:12

Jesus Prays on the Mount of Olives

39Jesus went out as usual to the Mount of Olives, and his disciples followed him. **40**On reaching the place, he said to them, "Pray that you will not fall into temptation." **41**He withdrew about a stone's throw beyond them, knelt down and prayed, **42**"Father, if you are willing, take this cup from me; yet not my will, but yours be done." **43**An angel from heaven appeared to him and strengthened him. **44**And being in anguish, he prayed more earnestly, and his sweat was like drops of blood falling to the ground. *a*

45When he rose from prayer and went back to the disciples, he found them asleep, exhausted from sorrow. **46**"Why are you sleeping?" he asked them. "Get up and pray so that you will not fall into temptation."

Jesus Arrested

47While he was still speaking a crowd came up, and the man who was called Judas, one of the Twelve, was leading them. He approached Jesus to kiss him, **48**but Jesus asked him, "Judas, are you betraying the Son of Man with a kiss?"

49When Jesus' followers saw what was going to happen, they said, "Lord, should we strike with our swords?" **50**And one of them struck the servant of the high priest, cutting off his right ear.

51But Jesus answered, "No more of this!" And he touched the man's ear and healed him.

52Then Jesus said to the chief priests, the officers of the temple guard, and the elders, who had come for him, "Am I leading a rebellion, that you have come with swords and clubs? **53**Every day I was with you in the temple courts, and you did not lay a hand on me. But this is your hour—when darkness reigns."

Peter Disowns Jesus

54Then seizing him, they led him away and took him into the house of the high priest. Peter followed at a distance. **55**But when they had kindled a fire in the middle of the courtyard and had sat down together, Peter sat down with them. **56**A servant girl saw him seated there in the firelight. She looked closely at him and said, "This man was with him."

57But he denied it. "Woman, I don't know him," he said.

58A little later someone else saw him and said, "You also are one of them."

"Man, I am not!" Peter replied.

59About an hour later another asserted, "Certainly this fellow was with him, for he is a Galilean."

60Peter replied, "Man, I don't know what you're talking about!" Just as he was speaking, the rooster crowed. **61**The Lord turned and looked straight at Peter. Then Peter remembered the word the Lord had spoken to him: "Before the rooster crows today, you will disown me three times." **62**And he went outside and wept bitterly.

The Guards Mock Jesus

63The men who were guarding Jesus began mocking and beating him. **64**They blindfolded him and demanded, "Prophesy! Who hit you?" **65**And they said many other insulting things to him.

Jesus Before Pilate and Herod

66At daybreak the council of the elders of the people, both the chief priests and teachers of the law, met together, and Jesus was led before them. **67**"If you are the Christ, *b*" they said, "tell us."

Jesus answered, "If I tell you, you will not believe me, **68**and if I asked you, you would

a 44 Some early manuscripts do not have verses 43 and 44.   *b 67 Or Messiah* not answer. [69]But from now on, the Son of Man will be seated at the right hand of the mighty God."

[70]They all asked, "Are you then the Son of God?"

He replied, "You are right in saying I am."

[71]Then they said, "Why do we need any more testimony? We have heard it from his own lips."

23 Then the whole assembly rose and led him off to Pilate. [2]And they began to accuse him, saying, "We have found this man subverting our nation. He opposes payment of taxes to Caesar and claims to be Christ,[a] a king."

[3]So Pilate asked Jesus, "Are you the king of the Jews?"

"Yes, it is as you say," Jesus replied.

[4]Then Pilate announced to the chief priests and the crowd, "I find no basis for a charge against this man."

[5]But they insisted, "He stirs up the people all over Judea[b] by his teaching. He started in Galilee and has come all the way here."

[6]On hearing this, Pilate asked if the man was a Galilean. [7]When he learned that Jesus was under Herod's jurisdiction, he sent him to Herod, who was also in Jerusalem at that time.

[8]When Herod saw Jesus, he was greatly pleased, because for a long time he had been wanting to see him. From what he had heard about him, he hoped to see him perform some miracle. [9]He plied him with many questions, but Jesus gave him no answer. [10]The chief priests and the teachers of the law were standing there, vehemently accusing him. [11]Then Herod and his soldiers ridiculed and mocked him. Dressing him in an elegant robe, they sent him back to Pilate. [12]That day Herod and Pilate became friends—before this they had been enemies.

[13]Pilate called together the chief priests, the rulers and the people, [14]and said to them, "You brought me this man as one who was inciting the people to rebellion. I have examined him in your presence and have found no basis for your charges against him. [15]Neither has Herod, for he sent him back to us; as you can see, he has done nothing to deserve death. [16]Therefore, I will punish him and then release him.[c]"

[18]With one voice they cried out, "Away with this man! Release Barabbas to us!" [19](Barabbas had been thrown into prison for an insurrection in the city, and for murder.)

[20]Wanting to release Jesus, Pilate appealed to them again. [21]But they kept shouting, "Crucify him! Crucify him!"

[22]For the third time he spoke to them: "Why? What crime has this man committed? I have found in him no grounds for the death penalty. Therefore I will have him punished and then release him."

[23]But with loud shouts they insistently demanded that he be crucified, and their shouts prevailed. [24]So Pilate decided to grant their demand. [25]He released the man who had been thrown into prison for insurrection and murder, the one they asked for, and surrendered Jesus to their will.

The Crucifixion

[26]As they led him away, they seized Simon from Cyrene, who was on his way in from the country, and put the cross on him and made him carry it behind Jesus. [27]A large number of people followed him, including women who mourned and wailed for him. [28]Jesus turned and said to them, "Daughters of Jerusalem, do not weep for me; weep for yourselves and for your children. [29]For the time will come when you will say, 'Blessed are the barren women, the wombs that never bore and the breasts that never nursed!' [30]Then

---

a 2 Or Messiah; also in verses 35 and 39   b 5 Or over the land of the Jews   c 16 Some manuscripts him." 17Now he was obliged to release one man to them at the Feast.

" 'they will say to the mountains, "Fall on us!"
   and to the hills, "Cover us!" ' ᵃ

³¹For if men do these things when the tree is green, what will happen when it is dry?"

³²Two other men, both criminals, were also led out with him to be executed. ³³When they came to the place called the Skull, there they crucified him, along with the criminals—one on his right, the other on his left. ³⁴Jesus said, "Father, forgive them, for they do not know what they are doing." ᵇ And they divided up his clothes by casting lots.

³⁵The people stood watching, and the rulers even sneered at him. They said, "He saved others; let him save himself if he is the Christ of God, the Chosen One."

³⁶The soldiers also came up and mocked him. They offered him wine vinegar ³⁷and said, "If you are the king of the Jews, save yourself."

³⁸There was a written notice above him, which read: THIS IS THE KING OF THE JEWS.

³⁹One of the criminals who hung there hurled insults at him: "Aren't you the Christ? Save yourself and us!"

⁴⁰But the other criminal rebuked him. "Don't you fear God," he said, "since you are under the same sentence? ⁴¹We are punished justly, for we are getting what our deeds deserve. But this man has done nothing wrong."

⁴²Then he said, "Jesus, remember me when you come into your kingdom.ᶜ"

⁴³Jesus answered him, "I tell you the truth, today you will be with me in paradise."

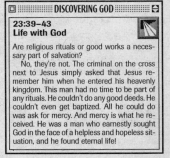

DISCOVERING GOD

23:39–43
Life with God

Are religious rituals or good works a necessary part of salvation?

No, they're not. The criminal on the cross next to Jesus simply asked that Jesus remember him when he entered his heavenly kingdom. This man had no time to be part of any rituals. He couldn't do any good deeds. He couldn't even get baptized. All he could do was ask for mercy. And mercy is what he received. He was a man who earnestly sought God in the face of a helpless and hopeless situation, and he found eternal life!

Jesus' Death

⁴⁴It was now about the sixth hour, and darkness came over the whole land until the ninth hour, ⁴⁵for the sun stopped shining. And the curtain of the temple was torn in two. ⁴⁶Jesus called out with a loud voice, "Father, into your hands I commit my spirit." When he had said this, he breathed his last.

⁴⁷The centurion, seeing what had happened, praised God and said, "Surely this was a righteous man." ⁴⁸When all the people who had gathered to witness this sight saw what took place, they beat their breasts and went away. ⁴⁹But all those who knew him, including the women who had followed him from Galilee, stood at a distance, watching these things.

Jesus' Burial

⁵⁰Now there was a man named Joseph, a member of the Council, a good and upright man, ⁵¹who had not consented to their decision and action. He came from the Judean town of Arimathea and he was waiting for the kingdom of God. ⁵²Going to Pilate, he asked for Jesus' body. ⁵³Then he took it down, wrapped it in linen cloth and placed it in a tomb cut in the rock, one in which no one had yet been laid. ⁵⁴It was Preparation Day, and the Sabbath was about to begin.

⁵⁵The women who had come with Jesus from Galilee followed Joseph and saw the tomb and how his body was laid in it. ⁵⁶Then they went home and prepared spices and perfumes. But they rested on the Sabbath in obedience to the commandment.

ᵃ30 Hosea 10:8   ᵇ34 Some early manuscripts do not have this sentence.   ᶜ42 Some manuscripts come with your kingly power

The Resurrection

24 On the first day of the week, very early in the morning, the women took the spices they had prepared and went to the tomb. [2]They found the stone rolled away from the tomb, [3]but when they entered, they did not find the body of the Lord Jesus. [4]While they were wondering about this, suddenly two men in clothes that gleamed like lightning stood beside them. [5]In their fright the women bowed down with their faces to the ground, but the men said to them, "Why do you look for the living among the dead? [6]He is not here; he has risen! Remember how he told you, while he was still with you in Galilee: [7]'The Son of Man must be delivered into the hands of sinful men, be crucified and on the third day be raised again.' " [8]Then they remembered his words.

[9]When they came back from the tomb, they told all these things to the Eleven and to all the others. [10]It was Mary Magdalene, Joanna, Mary the mother of James, and the others with them who told this to the apostles. [11]But they did not believe the women, because their words seemed to them like nonsense. [12]Peter, however, got up and ran to the tomb. Bending over, he saw the strips of linen lying by themselves, and he went away, wondering to himself what had happened.

On the Road to Emmaus

[13]Now that same day two of them were going to a village called Emmaus, about seven miles[a] from Jerusalem. [14]They were talking with each other about everything that had happened. [15]As they talked and discussed these things with each other, Jesus himself came up and walked along with them; [16]but they were kept from recognizing him.

[17]He asked them, "What are you discussing together as you walk along?"

They stood still, their faces downcast. [18]One of them, named Cleopas, asked him, "Are you only a visitor to Jerusalem and do not know the things that have happened there in these days?"

[19]"What things?" he asked.

"About Jesus of Nazareth," they replied. "He was a prophet, powerful in word and deed before God and all the people. [20]The chief priests and our rulers handed him over to be sentenced to death, and they crucified him; [21]but we had hoped that he was the one who was going to redeem Israel. And what is more, it is the third day since all this took place. [22]In addition, some of our women amazed us. They went to the tomb early this morning [23]but didn't find his body. They came and told us that they had seen a vision of angels, who said he was alive. [24]Then some of our companions went to the tomb and found it just as the women had said, but him they did not see."

[25]He said to them, "How foolish you are, and how slow of heart to believe all that the prophets have spoken! [26]Did not the Christ[b] have to suffer these things and then enter his glory?" [27]And beginning with Moses and all the Prophets, he explained to them what was said in all the Scriptures concerning himself.

[28]As they approached the village to which they were going, Jesus acted as if he were

REASONS TO BELIEVE

24:25–27
The Amazing Bible

The resurrected Jesus wanted his followers to know that his life, death, and resurrection were all foretold in the Hebrew Scriptures. All of the promises about the Messiah relate to him. Of course, that would be sheer arrogance for any of us to claim, but it was true of Jesus—and he had the credentials to prove it.

Notice that the disciples had a *physical* reaction as Jesus was talking to them (verse 32). When we realize that Jesus is the Son of God and that the Bible really does predict and validate him, the impression that knowledge leaves on us can be physical. But that's not the proof that Jesus is who he says he is. The proof of Jesus' identity lies in his character and in the sure word of God—the Bible.

a 13 Greek *sixty stadia* (about 11 kilometers)   b 26 Or *Messiah*; also in verse 46

going farther. ²⁹But they urged him strongly, "Stay with us, for it is nearly evening; the day is almost over." So he went in to stay with them.

³⁰When he was at the table with them, he took bread, gave thanks, broke it and began to give it to them. ³¹Then their eyes were opened and they recognized him, and he disappeared from their sight. ³²They asked each other, "Were not our hearts burning within us while he talked with us on the road and opened the Scriptures to us?"

³³They got up and returned at once to Jerusalem. There they found the Eleven and those with them, assembled together ³⁴and saying, "It is true! The Lord has risen and has appeared to Simon." ³⁵Then the two told what had happened on the way, and how Jesus was recognized by them when he broke the bread.

Jesus Appears to the Disciples

³⁶While they were still talking about this, Jesus himself stood among them and said to them, "Peace be with you."

³⁷They were startled and frightened, thinking they saw a ghost. ³⁸He said to them, "Why are you troubled, and why do doubts rise in your minds? ³⁹Look at my hands and my feet. It is I myself! Touch me and see; a ghost does not have flesh and bones, as you see I have."

⁴⁰When he had said this, he showed them his hands and feet. ⁴¹And while they still did not believe it because of joy and amazement, he asked them, "Do you have anything here to eat?" ⁴²They gave him a piece of broiled fish, ⁴³and he took it and ate it in their presence.

⁴⁴He said to them, "This is what I told you while I was still with you: Everything must be fulfilled that is written about me in the Law of Moses, the Prophets and the Psalms."

⁴⁵Then he opened their minds so they could understand the Scriptures. ⁴⁶He told them, "This is what is written: The Christ will suffer and rise from the dead on the third day, ⁴⁷and repentance and forgiveness of sins will be preached in his name to all nations, beginning at Jerusalem. ⁴⁸You are witnesses of these things. ⁴⁹I am going to send you what my Father has promised; but stay in the city until you have been clothed with power from on high."

▣ ▦▦▦▦▦ DISCOVERING GOD ▦▦▦▦▦ ⬒

24:37–43
Jesus, the God-Man

Was the resurrection of Jesus just a spiritual event? Jesus answers with a resounding, No!

The disciples actually saw Jesus' physical body—the one that had been nailed to a cross. That body had been changed in his resurrection, but it still bore the marks of his sacrifice. If his was not a physical resurrection, he could not have had his disciples touch him. He would not have claimed to have "flesh and bones." And he would not have been able to eat a piece of fish.

Some people claim that Jesus rose spiritually and not bodily. Besides ignoring the fact of Jesus' empty tomb, this claim undercuts one of the most important doctrines of Christianity and denies a belief that is essential to our salvation. Romans chapter 10, verse 9 says that "If you confess with your mouth, 'Jesus is Lord,' and believe in your heart that God raised him from the dead, you will be saved" (page 1482).

The Ascension

⁵⁰When he had led them out to the vicinity of Bethany, he lifted up his hands and blessed them. ⁵¹While he was blessing them, he left them and was taken up into heaven. ⁵²Then they worshiped him and returned to Jerusalem with great joy. ⁵³And they stayed continually at the temple, praising God.

JOHN

Introduction

THE BOTTOM LINE

This book will help you see Jesus as the divine Son of God. He may have been an ordinary man in appearance, but no other religious leader ever did the things he did, or claimed to be God in human form as he did. After he died, he did what was only possible for God to do—he came back to life and appeared to many witnesses. If you want to know God personally, only Jesus can "introduce" you to him (see chapter 14, verse 6 [page 1407]).

CENTRAL IDEAS

- Jesus was at the same time both totally human and totally divine.
- Jesus showed his power through miracles.
- Most of the disagreements people had with Jesus were not about his teaching, but about his claims to be God.
- We must get to know the real Jesus because only he has the power to forgive us and lead us to God.

OUTLINE

1 Prologue (1:1–18)
2 Beginnings of Jesus' ministry (1:19–51)
3 Jesus' public ministry: signs and discourses (chs. 2–11)
4 Jesus' final week (chs. 12–19)
5 Jesus' resurrection (20:1–29)
6 Statement of purpose (20:30–31)
7 Epilogue (ch. 21)

TITLE

This book is named after John, the disciple of Jesus who wrote this gospel.

AUTHOR AND READERS

John was one of Jesus' youngest followers; he lived the longest of any of Jesus' close associates after Jesus ascended to heaven. The original readers of John's book were mostly non-Jewish people who were being confused by Greek philosophies that contradicted the fact of Christ's divine and human nature. John tells us exactly why he wrote this book in chapter 20, verse 31 (page 1419): "These are written so that you may believe that Jesus is the Christ, the Son of God, and that by believing you may have life in his name."

TIME LINE

Jesus is born (6/5 B.C.)	Jesus begins his ministry (A.D. 26)	John becomes a disciple (c. A.D. 26)

John the apostle writes his Gospel (c. A.D. 80-95)

20	10 B.C.	AD 1	10	20	30	40	50	60	70	80	90

Sumo wrestling begins in Japan (23 B.C.)

Saddles first used in Europe (A.D. 1)

Jesus' death, resurrection, and ascension (c. A.D. 30)

John's exile on Patmos (c. A.D. 90-95)

When Jean Francois Gravelot first saw Niagara Falls he *knew* he had to cross it—on a rope. The year was 1858, and the French aerialist was touring America with P. T. Barnum. A year later he returned and stretched a 1,300-foot length of rope between the steep cliffs above the falls.

While 10,000 spectators held their breath, the 35-year-old "Great Blondin"—as he was called—stepped onto the rope. Stopping midway, he lowered a line to a waiting steamboat 190 feet below, drew up a bottle of wine, drank it, and continued to the other side.

For two summers Gravelot performed above Niagara Falls. He crossed over on a bicycle, on stilts, and at night. He swung by one arm, turned somersaults, and stood on his head on a chair. Once he pushed a stove in a wheelbarrow and cooked an omelet as he walked above the rushing water. But Gravelot's greatest feat was to carry a man across on his back. With his passenger secured by a harness with foot hooks, Gravelot grasped his 35-foot balancing pole and ventured down the steep incline. A gust of wind caused them to sway, and spectators gasped with terror. According to reporters, Gravelot sprinted the last few yards and plunged with his human cargo headlong into the crowd.

Gravelot plunged with his human cargo head-long into the crowd.

It's easy to be impressed with the courage and skill of the Great Blondin, but would you have had enough faith in him to put your life in his hands? In 1860 the Prince of Wales was given the opportunity—and turned down the invitation. He "believed" the Great Blondin could do what he claimed, but he refused to stake his life on it.

When some people say they believe in God, what they mean is that they intellectually acknowledge that he exists, yet their belief makes little or no difference in how they live. When it comes "down to the wire," they watch others step out in faith while they remain on the sidelines. If such people acknowledge the reality of God but go on living without relating to him, they actually have more in common with someone who denies his existence than with a true Christ-follower. As a matter of fact, that kind of "belief" is exactly what the devil himself has (see James chapter 2, verse 19 [page 1603])!

Fortunately, many people go beyond mere intellectual assent when they say they believe. They're like the man who climbed on the Great Blondin's back. Their belief involves trust. Yes, such belief includes an element of risk, *but they experience the benefit of belief because the one they trust in has time and again proven himself trustworthy.*

God wants this kind of faith from us. He asks us to consider the extraordinary claims of Jesus and, after we've examined his credentials, to cast ourselves unreservedly on the back of Christ, trusting in *his* merits to bring us across the chasm of sin so that we can know God.

The gospel of John is a great book for seekers because it was written to help people trust Christ with their lives. Within its pages Jesus invites those he meets to consider his claim to be "God with us"—all the while providing solid reasons to trust in and follow him. As you weigh out your decision whether to do just that, understand that questions and concerns will naturally arise. The same was true in Jesus' day. To read about one famous encounter between Jesus and a doubter, turn to John chapter 20, verses 24–31 (page 1417).

Strange Stories, Amazing Facts of America's Past, Jim Dwyer, ed. (Pleasantville, N.Y.: Reader's Digest Association, 1989), p. 27.

JOHN

God Became One of Us

1 In the beginning was the Word, and the Word was with God, and the Word was God. ²He was with God in the beginning.

³Through him all things were made; without him nothing was made that has been made. ⁴In him was life, and that life was the light of men. ⁵The light shines in the darkness, but the darkness has not understood*ᵃ* it.

⁶There came a man who was sent from God; his name was John. ⁷He came as a witness to testify concerning that light, so that through him all men might believe. ⁸He himself was not the light; he came only as a witness to the light. ⁹The true light that gives light to every man was coming into the world.*ᵇ*

¹⁰He was in the world, and though the world was made through him, the world did not recognize him. ¹¹He came to that which was his own, but his own did not receive him. ¹²Yet to all who received him, to those who believed in his name, he gave the right to become children of God— ¹³children born not of natural descent,*ᶜ* nor of human decision or a husband's will, but born of God.

¹⁴The Word became flesh and made his dwelling among us. We have seen his glory, the glory of the One and Only,*ᵈ* who came from the Father, full of grace and truth.

¹⁵John testifies concerning him. He cries out, saying, "This was he of whom I said, 'He who comes after me has surpassed me because he was before me.'" ¹⁶From the fullness of his grace we have all received one blessing after another. ¹⁷For the law was given through Moses; grace and truth came through Jesus Christ. ¹⁸No one has ever

---

ᵃ5 Or darkness, and the darkness has not overcome   *ᵇ9 Or This was the true light that gives light to every man who comes into the world*   *ᶜ13 Greek of bloods*   *ᵈ14 Or the Only Begotten*

DISCOVERING GOD

1:1–3
Jesus, the God-Man

John wrote this book to help his readers understand that Jesus is more than just a good man—he's the "God-Man."

John begins his collection of stories about Jesus by echoing the first sentence of the Bible. Genesis reads, "In the beginning, *God . . .*" John writes, "In the beginning *was the Word.*" This phrase, combined with the images of creation in verse 3, makes John's identification of Jesus as God unmistakable (see also verse 14). Jesus is the sum total of all God wants to say to us. He is the "flesh and bones" message of God—in short, God's *Word* to the world.

The basis of Christianity is not the moral teachings of Jesus, as important as those are. The true basis of Christianity is Jesus himself. As a seeker, you can dismiss Christianity if you can discredit the person of Jesus Christ. If he isn't who he said he was—namely, the eternal God (the second person of the trinity) who became one of us—then you're correct in saying that Christians are tragically deluded and that Christianity is just another human-made religion.

As you read this book, carefully consider the evidence about Jesus' identity. A seeker can answer no question more important than the one Jesus himself asked: *"Who do you say I am?"* (Matthew chapter 16, verse 15 [page 1281]; see also John chapter 8, verses 23–24 [page 1396], where Jesus further clarified his identity).

...een God, but God the One and Only,^{a,b} who is at the Father's side, has made him known.

John the Baptist Denies Being the Christ

¹⁹Now this was John's testimony when the Jews of Jerusalem sent priests and Levites to ask him who he was. ²⁰He did not fail to confess, but confessed freely, "I am not the Christ.^{c}"

²¹They asked him, "Then who are you? Are you Elijah?"

He said, "I am not."

"Are you the Prophet?"

He answered, "No."

²²Finally they said, "Who are you? Give us an answer to take back to those who sent us. What do you say about yourself?"

²³John replied in the words of Isaiah the prophet, "I am the voice of one calling in the desert, 'Make straight the way for the Lord.'"^{d}

²⁴Now some Pharisees who had been sent ²⁵questioned him, "Why then do you baptize if you are not the Christ, nor Elijah, nor the Prophet?"

²⁶"I baptize with^{e} water," John replied, "but among you stands one you do not know. ²⁷He is the one who comes after me, the thongs of whose sandals I am not worthy to untie."

²⁸This all happened at Bethany on the other side of the Jordan, where John was baptizing.

⬛ ▓▓▓▓▓ DISCOVERING GOD ▓▓▓▓▓ ↻

1:12–13
Life with God

Though we're all God's creatures, we don't become his children until we receive the forgiveness and leadership of Christ. This new beginning is described here as being "born of God" (in contrast to being born naturally from human parents). Jesus expands on this concept in his conversation with a man named Nicodemus in chapter 3 (page 1385).

Jesus the Lamb of God

²⁹The next day John saw Jesus coming toward him and said, "Look, the Lamb of God, who takes away the sin of the world! ³⁰This is the one I meant when I said, 'A man who comes after me has surpassed me because he was before me.' ³¹I myself did not know him, but the reason I came baptizing with water was that he might be revealed to Israel."

³²Then John gave this testimony: "I saw the Spirit come down from heaven as a dove and remain on him. ³³I would not have known him, except that the one who sent me to baptize with water told me, 'The man on whom you see the Spirit come down and remain is he who will baptize with the Holy Spirit.' ³⁴I have seen and I testify that this is the Son of God."

Jesus' First Disciples

³⁵The next day John was there again with two of his disciples. ³⁶When he saw Jesus passing by, he said, "Look, the Lamb of God!"

³⁷When the two disciples heard him say this, they followed Jesus. ³⁸Turning around, Jesus saw them following and asked, "What do you want?"

They said, "Rabbi" (which means Teacher), "where are you staying?"

³⁹"Come," he replied, "and you will see."

So they went and saw where he was staying, and spent that day with him. It was about the tenth hour.

⁴⁰Andrew, Simon Peter's brother, was one of the two who heard what John had said and who had followed Jesus. ⁴¹The first thing Andrew did was to find his brother Simon

and tell him, "We have found the Messiah" (that is, the Christ). ⁴²And he brought him to Jesus.

Jesus looked at him and said, "You are Simon son of John. You will be called Cephas" (which, when translated, is Peter*ᵃ*).

Jesus Calls Philip and Nathanael

⁴³The next day Jesus decided to leave for Galilee. Finding Philip, he said to him, "Follow me."

⁴⁴Philip, like Andrew and Peter, was from the town of Bethsaida. ⁴⁵Philip found Nathanael and told him, "We have found the one Moses wrote about in the Law, and about whom the prophets also wrote—Jesus of Nazareth, the son of Joseph."

⁴⁶"Nazareth! Can anything good come from there?" Nathanael asked.

"Come and see," said Philip.

⁴⁷When Jesus saw Nathanael approaching, he said of him, "Here is a true Israelite, in whom there is nothing false."

⁴⁸"How do you know me?" Nathanael asked.

Jesus answered, "I saw you while you were still under the fig tree before Philip called you."

⁴⁹Then Nathanael declared, "Rabbi, you are the Son of God; you are the King of Israel."

⁵⁰Jesus said, "You believeᵇ because I told you I saw you under the fig tree. You shall see greater things than that." ⁵¹He then added, "I tell youᶜ the truth, youᶜ shall see heaven open, and the angels of God ascending and descending on the Son of Man."

Jesus Changes Water to Wine

2 On the third day a wedding took place at Cana in Galilee. Jesus' mother was there, ²and Jesus and his disciples had also been invited to the wedding. ³When the wine was gone, Jesus' mother said to him, "They have no more wine."

⁴"Dear woman, why do you involve me?" Jesus replied. "My time has not yet come."

⁵His mother said to the servants, "Do whatever he tells you."

⁶Nearby stood six stone water jars, the kind used by the Jews for ceremonial washing, each holding from twenty to thirty gallons.ᵈ

⁷Jesus said to the servants, "Fill the jars with water"; so they filled them to the brim.

⁸Then he told them, "Now draw some out and take it to the master of the banquet."

They did so, ⁹and the master of the banquet tasted the water that had been turned into wine. He did not realize where it had come from, though the servants who had drawn the water knew. Then he called the bridegroom aside ¹⁰and said, "Everyone brings out the choice wine first and then the cheaper wine after the guests have had too much to drink; but you have saved the best till now."

REASONS TO BELIEVE

2:1–11
The Incomparable Jesus

Like all of Jesus' supernatural activities, this first miracle had obvious practical benefits—in this case, providing for this wedding's festivities and protecting the host from embarrassment.

But the main reason Jesus did miracles—and the primary reason John records them—is because of their value as "signposts" that point to Jesus as the Son of God. Jesus used his supernatural abilities to draw people to his person, not to his power. He desires that we do what the disciples did—put our faith (trust) in him.

---

¹¹This, the first of his miraculous signs, Jesus performed at Cana in Galilee. He thus revealed his glory, and his disciples put their faith in him.

ᵃ42 Both *Cephas* (Aramaic) and *Peter* (Greek) mean *rock.*   *ᵇ50* Or *Do you believe . . . ?*   *ᶜ51* The Greek is plural.
ᵈ6 Greek *two to three metretes* (probably about 75 to 115 liters)

Jesus Clears the Temple

¹²After this he went down to Capernaum with his mother and brothers and his disciples. There they stayed for a few days.

¹³When it was almost time for the Jewish Passover, Jesus went up to Jerusalem. ¹⁴In the temple courts he found men selling cattle, sheep and doves, and others sitting at tables exchanging money. ¹⁵So he made a whip out of cords, and drove all from the temple area, both sheep and cattle; he scattered the coins of the money changers and overturned their tables. ¹⁶To those who sold doves he said, "Get these out of here! How dare you turn my Father's house into a market!"

¹⁷His disciples remembered that it is written: "Zeal for your house will consume me."ᵃ ¹⁸Then the Jews demanded of him, "What miraculous sign can you show us to prove your authority to do all this?"

¹⁹Jesus answered them, "Destroy this temple, and I will raise it again in three days." ²⁰The Jews replied, "It has taken forty-six years to build this temple, and you are going to raise it in three days?" ²¹But the temple he had spoken of was his body. ²²After he was raised from the dead, his disciples recalled what he had said. Then they believed the Scripture and the words that Jesus had spoken.

²³Now while he was in Jerusalem at the Passover Feast, many people saw the miraculous signs he was doing and believed in his name.ᵇ ²⁴But Jesus would not entrust himself to them, for he knew all men. ²⁵He did not need man's testimony about man, for he knew what was in a man.

Jesus Teaches Nicodemus

3 Now there was a man of the Pharisees named Nicodemus, a member of the Jewish ruling council. ²He came to Jesus at night and said, "Rabbi, we know you are a teacher who has come from God. For no one could perform the miraculous signs you are doing if God were not with him."

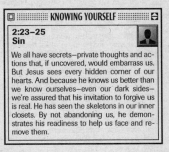

KNOWING YOURSELF

2:23–25
Sin

We all have secrets—private thoughts and actions that, if uncovered, would embarrass us. But Jesus sees every hidden corner of our hearts. And because he knows us better than we know ourselves—even our dark sides—we're assured that his invitation to forgive us is real. He has seen the skeletons in our inner closets. By not abandoning us, he demonstrates his readiness to help us face and remove them.

³In reply Jesus declared, "I tell you the truth, no one can see the kingdom of God unless he is born again.ᶜ"

⁴"How can a man be born when he is old?" Nicodemus asked. "Surely he cannot enter a second time into his mother's womb to be born!"

⁵Jesus answered, "I tell you the truth, no one can enter the kingdom of God unless he is born of water and the Spirit. ⁶Flesh gives birth to flesh, but the Spiritᵈ gives birth to spirit. ⁷You should not be surprised at my saying, 'Youᵉ must be born again.' ⁸The wind blows wherever it pleases. You hear its sound, but you cannot tell where it comes from or where it is going. So it is with everyone born of the Spirit."

⁹"How can this be?" Nicodemus asked.

¹⁰"You are Israel's teacher," said Jesus, "and do you not understand these things? ¹¹I tell you the truth, we speak of what we know, and we testify to what we have seen, but still you people do not accept our testimony. ¹²I have spoken to you of earthly things and you do not believe; how then will you believe if I speak of heavenly things? ¹³No one has ever gone into heaven except the one who came from heaven—the Son of Man.ᶠ ¹⁴Just as Moses lifted up the snake in the desert, so the Son of Man must be lifted up, ¹⁵that everyone who believes in him may have eternal life.ᵍ

ᵃ17 Psalm 69:9   ᵇ23 Or and believed in him   ᶜ3 Or born from above; also in verse 7   ᵈ6 Or but spirit
ᵉ7 The Greek is plural.   ᶠ13 Some manuscripts Man, who is in heaven   ᵍ15 Or believes may have eternal life in him

3:1–21
A New Identity

Jesus had an uncanny knack for cutting through "small talk."

Nicodemus, an important member of the religious ruling class, came to Jesus late one night. Was he afraid to be seen with Jesus? Did he want to avoid the crowds? We don't know for sure. But when he began his conversation with a few polite remarks, Jesus cut right to the chase. His statement in verse 3 can be loosely paraphrased, "Nicodemus, you're right about my spiritual position, but you're dead wrong about yours."

Jesus knew that Nicodemus didn't need a lot of tact—he needed truth.

Nicodemus's robes, his title, and his degrees impressed everyone in his religious circle. But Jesus saw right through those outer trappings. He knew that a human heart beat under all that finery—a struggling heart that was tired of carrying the weight, the responsibilities and the endless need to appear "in control" of his religious condition. So before Nicodemus could even formulate his question, Jesus gave the answer, telling him in effect, "What you need is a new start, Nicodemus. It's not too late."

If you, like Nicodemus, are counting on your accomplishments to lead to some sort of ultimate fulfillment or spiritual security, Jesus says the same thing to you.

Accomplishments can't be happy. Titles have no feelings. Degrees don't laugh. Even religion can get in the way of knowing God, because religion is mostly what *we* do. That's what was happening to Nicodemus, and what Jesus tried to address in their conversation. Life with God means becoming a "faith-follower," not trying to be a "do-gooder." Jesus knew that Nicodemus, a religious leader and teacher, didn't understand this basic truth.

Nicodemus needed to make a break with his religiously legalistic past, and to make a new spiritual start in his life, one that centered on a relationship with God. Jesus called this new start being "born again."

Then Jesus made mention of something that happened centuries before, in Moses' day (verse 14; see Numbers chapter 21, verses 4–9 [page 188] to read the story). When a plague of poisonous snakes killed many Israelites, Moses followed God's command to make a bronze snake and attach it to a pole. People who had been bitten didn't have to pray, go to the temple, try to drain the poison, or do any kind of "religious" act. They were simply told to take God at his word, look at the snake, and believe. Those who did were miraculously healed. Those who didn't died. (By the way, this biblical event is the origin of the snake on the pole in medical insignias.) By using this well-known story as a metaphor for his own crucifixion, Jesus knew that Nicodemus would get the point—God sent Jesus to earth so that people could believe in him, trust him, and have eternal life.

He further explained this principle in verse 16, one of the most famous verses in the Bible. This one sentence contains the greatest message, from the greatest source, describing the greatest love, demonstrated by the greatest sacrifice ever given. It contains important news for everyone, especially those who think they have to "be religious" to get God's approval.

The bad news is that we can't *do* enough to gain God's approval. The good news is that God has already *done* it on our behalf.

What would prevent you from accepting Jesus' invitation to Nicodemus (verse 3)? Being born again isn't complicated. Simply agree with Jesus that you have a spiritual need that you'll never be able to fill through your own efforts. Then recognize that Jesus didn't come to condemn you, but to pay for your sins, forgive you, and to begin to remake you from the inside. Finally, come to him as your rescuer and leader and ask him to do what he said he was dying to do—give you eternal life. This is not a cheap gift; Jesus gave his very lifeblood to obtain it. But it is a *free* gift. And it's yours for the asking.

Note: Later in Jesus' ministry, Nicodemus defended Jesus when the religious leaders of his day condemned him unfairly (see chapter 7, verses 50–51 [page 1395]). Nicodemus also showed up at Jesus' death, where he and another influential leader, Joseph of Arimathea, prepared Jesus' body for burial (chapter 19, verses 38–42 [page 1416]). Beyond that, we don't know anything about Nicodemus or his response to Jesus' invitation.

¹⁶"For God so loved the world that he gave his one and only Son,ᵃ that whoever believes in him shall not perish but have eternal life. ¹⁷For God did not send his Son into the world to condemn the world, but to save the world through him. ¹⁸Whoever believes in him is not condemned, but whoever does not believe stands condemned already because he has not believed in the name of God's one and only Son.ᵇ ¹⁹This is the verdict: Light has come into the world, but men loved darkness instead of light because their deeds were evil. ²⁰Everyone who does evil hates the light, and will not come into the light for fear that his deeds will be exposed. ²¹But whoever lives by the truth comes into the light, so that it may be seen plainly that what he has done has been done through God."ᶜ

John the Baptist's Testimony About Jesus

²²After this, Jesus and his disciples went out into the Judean countryside, where he spent some time with them, and baptized. ²³Now John also was baptizing at Aenon near Salim, because there was plenty of water, and people were constantly coming to be baptized. ²⁴(This was before John was put in prison.) ²⁵An argument developed between some of John's disciples and a certain Jewᵈ over the matter of ceremonial washing. ²⁶They came to John and said to him, "Rabbi, that man who was with you on the other side of the Jordan—the one you testified about—well, he is baptizing, and everyone is going to him."

²⁷To this John replied, "A man can receive only what is given him from heaven. ²⁸You yourselves can testify that I said, 'I am not the Christᵉ but am sent ahead of him.' ²⁹The bride belongs to the bridegroom. The friend who attends the bridegroom waits and listens for him, and is full of joy when he hears the bridegroom's voice. That joy is mine, and it is now complete. ³⁰He must become greater; I must become less.

³¹"The one who comes from above is above all; the one who is from the earth belongs to the earth, and speaks as one from the earth. The one who comes from heaven is above all. ³²He testifies to what he has seen and heard, but no one accepts his testimony. ³³The man who has accepted it has certified that God is truthful. ³⁴For the one whom God has sent speaks the words of God, for Godᶠ gives the Spirit without limit. ³⁵The Father loves the Son and has placed everything in his hands. ³⁶Whoever believes in the Son has eternal life, but whoever rejects the Son will not see life, for God's wrath remains on him."ᵍ

Jesus Talks With a Samaritan Woman

4 The Pharisees heard that Jesus was gaining and baptizing more disciples than John, ²although in fact it was not Jesus who baptized, but his disciples. ³When the Lord learned of this, he left Judea and went back once more to Galilee.

⁴Now he had to go through Samaria. ⁵So he came to a town in Samaria called Sychar, near the plot of ground Jacob had given to his son Joseph. ⁶Jacob's well was there, and Jesus, tired as he was from the journey, sat down by the well. It was about the sixth hour.

⁷When a Samaritan woman came to draw water, Jesus said to her, "Will you give me a drink?" ⁸(His disciples had gone into the town to buy food.)

⁹The Samaritan woman said to him, "You are a Jew and I am a Samaritan woman. How can you ask me for a drink?" (For Jews do not associate with Samaritans.ʰ)

¹⁰Jesus answered her, "If you knew the gift of God and who it is that asks you for a drink, you would have asked him and he would have given you living water."

¹¹"Sir," the woman said, "you have nothing to draw with and the well is deep. Where

ᵃ16 Or his only begotten Son   ᵇ18 Or God's only begotten Son   ᶜ21 Some interpreters end the quotation after verse 15.   ᵈ25 Some manuscripts and certain Jews   ᵉ28 Or Messiah   ᶠ34 Greek he   ᵍ36 Some interpreters end the quotation after verse 30.   ʰ9 Or do not use dishes Samaritans have used

can you get this living water? ¹²Are you greater than our father Jacob, who gave us the well and drank from it himself, as did also his sons and his flocks and herds?"

¹³Jesus answered, "Everyone who drinks this water will be thirsty again, ¹⁴but whoever drinks the water I give him will never thirst. Indeed, the water I give him will become in him a spring of water welling up to eternal life."

¹⁵The woman said to him, "Sir, give me this water so that I won't get thirsty and have to keep coming here to draw water."

¹⁶He told her, "Go, call your husband and come back."

¹⁷"I have no husband," she replied.

Jesus said to her, "You are right when you say you have no husband. ¹⁸The fact is, you have had five husbands, and the man you now have is not your husband. What you have just said is quite true."

DISCOVERING GOD

4:4–42
Jesus, the God-Man

Here is a classic encounter between Jesus and a seeker—in this case, an admittedly sinful woman who thought for sure that God would never bother with her.

This woman was an outcast, as evidenced by her coming to the well in the heat of the day to avoid others. Yet there she met a man who told her "everything [she] ever did." At first, she could hardly believe Jesus would take the time to speak to her. Then Jesus amazed her further by outlining the details of her immoral lifestyle!

Here Jesus demonstrated both tender compassion and supernatural insight. He overcame huge racial, gender, and positional barriers to reach into this woman's world. In reality, Jesus was a "seeker" in this situation too. And he still seeks out those who need him today.

The woman brought almost the whole town out to see Jesus, and they too discovered that he was unlike any person they had ever met. The townspeople said what people down through the ages have said after they have investigated the claims of Christ—"We have heard for ourselves, and we know that this man really is the Savior of the world" (verse 42).

---

¹⁹"Sir," the woman said, "I can see that you are a prophet. ²⁰Our fathers worshiped on this mountain, but you Jews claim that the place where we must worship is in Jerusalem."

²¹Jesus declared, "Believe me, woman, a time is coming when you will worship the Father neither on this mountain nor in Jerusalem. ²²You Samaritans worship what you do not know; we worship what we do know, for salvation is from the Jews. ²³Yet a time is coming and has now come when the true worshipers will worship the Father in spirit and truth, for they are the kind of worshipers the Father seeks. ²⁴God is spirit, and his worshipers must worship in spirit and in truth."

²⁵The woman said, "I know that Messiah" (called Christ) "is coming. When he comes, he will explain everything to us."

²⁶Then Jesus declared, "I who speak to you am he."

The Disciples Rejoin Jesus

²⁷Just then his disciples returned and were surprised to find him talking with a woman. But no one asked, "What do you want?" or "Why are you talking with her?"

²⁸Then, leaving her water jar, the woman went back to the town and said to the people, ²⁹"Come, see a man who told me everything I ever did. Could this be the Christ*ᵃ*?" ³⁰They came out of the town and made their way toward him.

³¹Meanwhile his disciples urged him, "Rabbi, eat something."

³²But he said to them, "I have food to eat that you know nothing about."

³³Then his disciples said to each other, "Could someone have brought him food?"

³⁴"My food," said Jesus, "is to do the will of him who sent me and to finish his work. ³⁵Do you not say, 'Four months more and then the harvest'? I tell you, open your eyes and look at the fields! They are ripe for harvest. ³⁶Even now the reaper draws his wages,

ven now he harvests the crop for eternal life, so that the sower and the reaper may be
glad together. ³⁷Thus the saying 'One sows and another reaps' is true. ³⁸I sent you to
reap what you have not worked for. Others have done the hard work, and you have
reaped the benefits of their labor."

Many Samaritans Believe

³⁹Many of the Samaritans from that town believed in him because of the woman's
testimony, "He told me everything I ever did." ⁴⁰So when the Samaritans came to him,
they urged him to stay with them, and he stayed two days. ⁴¹And because of his words
many more became believers.

⁴²They said to the woman, "We no longer believe just because of what you said; now
we have heard for ourselves, and we know that this man really is the Savior of the
world."

Jesus Heals the Official's Son

⁴³After the two days he left for Galilee. ⁴⁴(Now Jesus himself had pointed out that a
prophet has no honor in his own country.) ⁴⁵When he arrived in Galilee, the Galileans
welcomed him. They had seen all that he had done in Jerusalem at the Passover Feast,
for they also had been there.

⁴⁶Once more he visited Cana in Galilee, where he had turned the water into wine. And
there was a certain royal official whose son lay sick at Capernaum. ⁴⁷When this man
heard that Jesus had arrived in Galilee from Judea, he went to him and begged him to
come and heal his son, who was close to death.

⁴⁸"Unless you people see miraculous signs and wonders," Jesus told him, "you will
never believe."

⁴⁹The royal official said, "Sir, come down before my child dies."

⁵⁰Jesus replied, "You may go. Your son will live."

The man took Jesus at his word and departed. ⁵¹While he was still on the way, his
servants met him with the news that his boy was living. ⁵²When he inquired as to the
time when his son got better, they said to him, "The fever left him yesterday at the
seventh hour."

⁵³Then the father realized that this was the exact time at which Jesus had said to him,
"Your son will live." So he and all his household believed.

⁵⁴This was the second miraculous sign that Jesus performed, having come from Judea
to Galilee.

The Healing at the Pool

5 Some time later, Jesus went up to Jerusalem for a feast of the Jews. ²Now
there is in Jerusalem near the Sheep Gate a pool, which in Aramaic is called
Bethesda*a* and which is surrounded by five covered colonnades. ³Here a great number
of disabled people used to lie—the blind, the lame, the paralyzed.*b* ⁵One who was there
had been an invalid for thirty-eight years. ⁶When Jesus saw him lying there and learned
that he had been in this condition for a long time, he asked him, "Do you want to get
well?"

⁷"Sir," the invalid replied, "I have no one to help me into the pool when the water is
stirred. While I am trying to get in, someone else goes down ahead of me."

⁸Then Jesus said to him, "Get up! Pick up your mat and walk." ⁹At once the man was
cured; he picked up his mat and walked.

The day·on which this took place was a Sabbath, ¹⁰and so the Jews said to the man
who had been healed, "It is the Sabbath; the law forbids you to carry your mat."

*a2 Some manuscripts Bethzatha; other manuscripts Bethsaida   b3 Some less important manuscripts paralyzed—and they
waited for the moving of the waters. 4From time to time an angel of the Lord would come down and stir up the waters. The first
one into the pool after each such disturbance would be cured of whatever disease he had.*

[11]But he replied, "The man who made me well said to me, 'Pick up your mat an[d] walk.' "

[12]So they asked him, "Who is this fellow who told you to pick it up and walk?"

[13]The man who was healed had no idea who it was, for Jesus had slipped away int[o] the crowd that was there.

[14]Later Jesus found him at the temple and said to him, "See, you are well again. Sto[p] sinning or something worse may happen to you." [15]The man went away and told th[e] Jews that it was Jesus who had made him well.

Life Through the Son

[16]So, because Jesus was doing these things on the Sabbath, the Jews persecuted him[.] [17]Jesus said to them, "My Father is always at his work to this very day, and I, too, a[m] working." [18]For this reason the Jews tried all the harder to kill him; not only was h[e] breaking the Sabbath, but he was eve[n] calling God his own Father, making himsel[f] equal with God.

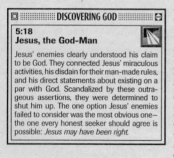

DISCOVERING GOD

5:18
Jesus, the God-Man

Jesus' enemies clearly understood his claim to be God. They connected Jesus' miraculous activities, his disdain for their man-made rules, and his direct statements about existing on a par with God. Scandalized by these outrageous assertions, they were determined to shut him up. The one option Jesus' enemies failed to consider was the most obvious one—the one every honest seeker should agree is possible: *Jesus may have been right.*

[19]Jesus gave them this answer: "I tell yo[u] the truth, the Son can do nothing by himself; he can do only what he sees his Father doing, because whatever the Father does the Son also does. [20]For the Father loves the Son and shows him all he does[.] Yes, to your amazement he will show hi[m] even greater things than these. [21]For jus[t] as the Father raises the dead and give[s] them life, even so the Son gives life t[o] whom he is pleased to give it. [22]Moreover[,] the Father judges no one, but has entruste[d] all judgment to the Son, [23]that all may hon[or] or the Son just as they honor the Father. H[e] who does not honor the Son does not honor the Father, who sent him.

[24]"I tell you the truth, whoever hears my word and believes him who sent me ha[s] eternal life and will not be condemned; he has crossed over from death to life. [25]I tell yo[u] the truth, a time is coming and has now come when the dead will hear the voice of th[e] Son of God and those who hear will live. [26]For as the Father has life in himself, so he ha[s] granted the Son to have life in himself. [27]And he has given him authority to judg[e] because he is the Son of Man.

[28]"Do not be amazed at this, for a time is coming when all who are in their graves wil[l] hear his voice [29]and come out—those who have done good will rise to live, and thos[e] who have done evil will rise to be condemned. [30]By myself I can do nothing; I judge onl[y] as I hear, and my judgment is just, for I seek not to please myself but him who sent m[e.]

Testimonies About Jesus

[31]"If I testify about myself, my testimony is not valid. [32]There is another who testifies i[n] my favor, and I know that his testimony about me is valid.

[33]"You have sent to John and he has testified to the truth. [34]Not that I accept huma[n] testimony; but I mention it that you may be saved. [35]John was a lamp that burned an[d] gave light, and you chose for a time to enjoy his light.

[36]"I have testimony weightier than that of John. For the very work that the Father ha[s] given me to finish, and which I am doing, testifies that the Father has sent me. [37]And th[e] Father who sent me has himself testified concerning me. You have never heard his voic[e] nor seen his form, [38]nor does his word dwell in you, for you do not believe the one h[e]

...nt. ³⁹You diligently study*ᵃ* the Scriptures because you think that by them you possess ...ternal life. These are the Scriptures that testify about me, ⁴⁰yet you refuse to come to me ...o have life.

⁴¹"I do not accept praise from men, ⁴²but I know you. I know that you do not have the ...ove of God in your hearts. ⁴³I have come in my Father's name, and you do not accept me; ...ut if someone else comes in his own name, you will accept him. ⁴⁴How can you believe ...f you accept praise from one another, yet make no effort to obtain the praise that comes ...om the only God*ᵇ*?

⁴⁵"But do not think I will accuse you before the Father. Your accuser is Moses, on whom ...our hopes are set. ⁴⁶If you believed Moses, you would believe me, for he wrote about ...e. ⁴⁷But since you do not believe what he ...rote, how are you going to believe what I ...ay?"

Jesus Feeds the Five Thousand

Some time after this, Jesus crossed to the far shore of the ...ea of Galilee (that is, the Sea of Tiberias), ...and a great crowd of people followed him ...ecause they saw the miraculous signs he ...ad performed on the sick. ³Then Jesus ...vent up on a mountainside and sat down ...vith his disciples. ⁴The Jewish Passover ...east was near.

⁵When Jesus looked up and saw a great ...rowd coming toward him, he said to Phil-...p, "Where shall we buy bread for these ...eople to eat?" ⁶He asked this only to test ...im, for he already had in mind what he ...vas going to do.

⁷Philip answered him, "Eight months' ...vages*ᶜ* would not buy enough bread for ...each one to have a bite!"

⁸Another of his disciples, Andrew, Simon ...eter's brother, spoke up, ⁹"Here is a boy ...vith five small barley loaves and two small ...ish, but how far will they go among so ...many?"

¹⁰Jesus said, "Have the people sit down." ...There was plenty of grass in that place, ...and the men sat down, about five thousand ...of them. ¹¹Jesus then took the loaves, gave ...thanks, and distributed to those who were ...seated as much as they wanted. He did the ...same with the fish.

¹²When they had all had enough to eat, ...he said to his disciples, "Gather the pieces that are left over. Let nothing be wasted." ¹³So ...they gathered them and filled twelve baskets with the pieces of the five barley loaves left ...over by those who had eaten.

¹⁴After the people saw the miraculous sign that Jesus did, they began to say, "Surely ...this is the Prophet who is to come into the world." ¹⁵Jesus, knowing that they intended to ...come and make him king by force, withdrew again to a mountain by himself.

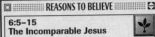

REASONS TO BELIEVE

6:5–15
The Incomparable Jesus

When Jesus gave a picnic, it was an event to remember!

This passage shows how Jesus' miraculous power convinced a crowd that someone great was in their midst. You may wonder why God doesn't do more miracles today—surely that would convince all doubters, right?

Not necessarily. And this story illustrates the problem with human belief that is based on miracles, as was the case with this crowd. These people were impressed with Jesus' power, but they wanted to use it for their own ends. After benefiting directly from Jesus' miracle, they wanted to make him king so he could use his miraculous power to defeat the oppression of their Roman rulers. But Jesus had no intention of ruling over an earthly kingdom. He wanted their loyalty for reasons other than his ability to influence the elements.

Notice how these fickle fans cheered Jesus at first, but gave up on him after the razzle-dazzle stopped (see verse 66). That's why Jesus used miracles sparingly, and why on many occasions he told people who had benefited directly from his power to keep it to themselves (see, for example, Mark chapter 5, verses 35–43 [page 1312]).

Ultimately, people need a relationship with Jesus that is based on love, forgiveness and trust. When the crowds left, Jesus' person and his words—not his wonders—secured his followers' lasting devotion (see verses 67–69).

ᵃ39 Or Study diligently (the imperative)   *ᵇ44 Some early manuscripts the Only One*   *ᶜ7 Greek two hundred denarii*

Jesus Walks on the Water

[16]When evening came, his disciples went down to the lake, [17]where they got into boat and set off across the lake for Capernaum. By now it was dark, and Jesus had n yet joined them. [18]A strong wind was blowing and the waters grew rough. [19]When the had rowed three or three and a half miles,[a] they saw Jesus approaching the boa walking on the water; and they were terrified. [20]But he said to them, "It is I; don't I afraid." [21]Then they were willing to take him into the boat, and immediately the bo reached the shore where they were heading.

[22]The next day the crowd that had stayed on the opposite shore of the lake realize that only one boat had been there, and that Jesus had not entered it with his disciple but that they had gone away alone. [23]Then some boats from Tiberias landed near th place where the people had eaten the bread after the Lord had given thanks. [24]Once th crowd realized that neither Jesus nor his disciples were there, they got into the boats an went to Capernaum in search of Jesus.

Jesus the Bread of Life

[25]When they found him on the other side of the lake, they asked him, "Rabbi, whe did you get here?"

[26]Jesus answered, "I tell you the truth, you are looking for me, not because you sa miraculous signs but because you ate the loaves and had your fill. [27]Do not work for foc that spoils, but for food that endures to eternal life, which the Son of Man will give yo On him God the Father has placed his seal of approval."

[28]Then they asked him, "What must we do to do the works God requires?"

[29]Jesus answered, "The work of God is this: to believe in the one he has sent."

[30]So they asked him, "What miraculous sign then will you give that we may see it an believe you? What will you do? [31]Our forefathers ate the manna in the desert; as it written: 'He gave them bread from heaven to eat.'[b]"

[32]Jesus said to them, "I tell you the truth, it is not Moses who has given you the brea from heaven, but it is my Father who gives you the true bread from heaven. [33]For th bread of God is he who comes down from heaven and gives life to the world."

[34]"Sir," they said, "from now on give us this bread."

[35]Then Jesus declared, "I am the bread of life. He who comes to me will never g hungry, and he who believes in me will never be thirsty. [36]But as I told you, you hav seen me and still you do not believe. [37]All that the Father gives me will come to me, an whoever comes to me I will never drive away. [38]For I have come down from heaven n to do my will but to do the will of him who sent me. [39]And this is the will of him wh sent me, that I shall lose none of all that he has given me, but raise them up at the la day. [40]For my Father's will is that everyone who looks to the Son and believes in hi shall have eternal life, and I will raise him up at the last day."

[41]At this the Jews began to grumble about him because he said, "I am the bread tha came down from heaven." [42]They said, "Is this not Jesus, the son of Joseph, whose fathe and mother we know? How can he now say, 'I came down from heaven'?"

[43]"Stop grumbling among yourselves," Jesus answered. [44]"No one can come to m unless the Father who sent me draws him, and I will raise him up at the last day. [45]It written in the Prophets: 'They will all be taught by God.'[c] Everyone who listens to th Father and learns from him comes to me. [46]No one has seen the Father except the on who is from God; only he has seen the Father. [47]I tell you the truth, he who believes ha everlasting life. [48]I am the bread of life. [49]Your forefathers ate the manna in the deser yet they died. [50]But here is the bread that comes down from heaven, which a man ma eat and not die. [51]I am the living bread that came down from heaven. If anyone eats

[a]19 Greek *rowed twenty-five or thirty stadia* (about 5 or 6 kilometers)   [b]31 Exodus 16:4; Neh. 9:15; Psalm 78:24,25   [c]45 Isaiah 54:13

his bread, he will live forever. This bread is my flesh, which I will give for the life of the world."

⁵²Then the Jews began to argue sharply among themselves, "How can this man give us his flesh to eat?"

⁵³Jesus said to them, "I tell you the truth, unless you eat the flesh of the Son of Man and drink his blood, you have no life in you. ⁵⁴Whoever eats my flesh and drinks my blood has eternal life, and I will raise him up at the last day. ⁵⁵For my flesh is real food and my blood is real drink. ⁵⁶Whoever eats my flesh and drinks my blood remains in me, and I in him. ⁵⁷Just as the living Father sent me and I live because of the Father, so the one who feeds on me will live because of me. ⁵⁸This is the bread that came down from heaven. Your forefathers ate manna and died, but he who feeds on this bread will live forever." ⁵⁹He said this while teaching in the synagogue in Capernaum.

Many Disciples Desert Jesus

⁶⁰On hearing it, many of his disciples said, "This is a hard teaching. Who can accept it?"

⁶¹Aware that his disciples were grumbling about this, Jesus said to them, "Does this offend you? ⁶²What if you see the Son of Man ascend to where he was before! ⁶³The Spirit gives life; the flesh counts for nothing. The words I have spoken to you are spiritᵃ and they are life. ⁶⁴Yet there are some of you who do not believe." For Jesus had known from the beginning which of them did not believe and who would betray him. ⁶⁵He went on to say, "This is why I told you that no one can come to me unless the Father has enabled him."

⁶⁶From this time many of his disciples turned back and no longer followed him.

⁶⁷"You do not want to leave too, do you?" Jesus asked the Twelve.

⁶⁸Simon Peter answered him, "Lord, to whom shall we go? You have the words of eternal life. ⁶⁹We believe and know that you are the Holy One of God."

⁷⁰Then Jesus replied, "Have I not chosen you, the Twelve? Yet one of you is a devil!" ⁷¹(He meant Judas, the son of Simon Iscariot, who, though one of the Twelve, was later to betray him.)

Jesus Goes to the Feast of Tabernacles

7 After this, Jesus went around in Galilee, purposely staying away from Judea because the Jews there were waiting to take his life. ²But when the Jewish Feast of Tabernacles was near, ³Jesus' brothers said to him, "You ought to leave here and go to Judea, so that your disciples may see the miracles you do. ⁴No one who wants to become a public figure acts in secret. Since you are doing these things, show yourself to the world." ⁵For even his own brothers did not believe in him.

⁶Therefore Jesus told them, "The right time for me has not yet come; for you any time is right. ⁷The world cannot hate you, but it hates me because I testify that what it does is evil. ⁸You go to the Feast. I am not yetᵇ going up to this Feast, because for me the right time has not yet come." ⁹Having said this, he stayed in Galilee.

¹⁰However, after his brothers had left for the Feast, he went also, not publicly, but in secret. ¹¹Now at the Feast the Jews were watching for him and asking, "Where is that man?"

¹²Among the crowds there was widespread whispering about him. Some said, "He is a good man."

Others replied, "No, he deceives the people." ¹³But no one would say anything publicly about him for fear of the Jews.

63 Or Spirit   b 8 Some early manuscripts do not have yet

Jesus Teaches at the Feast

¹⁴Not until halfway through the Feast did Jesus go up to the temple courts and begin to teach. ¹⁵The Jews were amazed and asked, "How did this man get such learning without having studied?"

¹⁶Jesus answered, "My teaching is not my own. It comes from him who sent me. ¹⁷If anyone chooses to do God's will, he will find out whether my teaching comes from God or whether I speak on my own. ¹⁸He who speaks on his own does so to gain honor for himself, but he who works for the honor of the one who sent him is a man of truth; there is nothing false about him. ¹⁹Has not Moses given you the law? Yet not one of you keeps the law. Why are you trying to kill me?"

²⁰"You are demon-possessed," the crowd answered. "Who is trying to kill you?"

²¹Jesus said to them, "I did one miracle, and you are all astonished. ²²Yet, because Moses gave you circumcision (though actually it did not come from Moses, but from the patriarchs), you circumcise a child on the Sabbath. ²³Now if a child can be circumcised on the Sabbath so that the law of Moses may not be broken, why are you angry with me for healing the whole man on the Sabbath? ²⁴Stop judging by mere appearances, and make a right judgment."

Is Jesus the Christ?

²⁵At that point some of the people of Jerusalem began to ask, "Isn't this the man they are trying to kill? ²⁶Here he is, speaking publicly, and they are not saying a word to him. Have the authorities really concluded that he is the Christᵃ? ²⁷But we know where this man is from; when the Christ comes, no one will know where he is from."

²⁸Then Jesus, still teaching in the temple courts, cried out, "Yes, you know me, and you know where I am from. I am not here on my own, but he who sent me is true. You do not know him, ²⁹but I know him because I am from him and he sent me."

³⁰At this they tried to seize him, but no one laid a hand on him, because his time had not yet come. ³¹Still, many in the crowd put their faith in him. They said, "When the Christ comes, will he do more miraculous signs than this man?"

³²The Pharisees heard the crowd whispering such things about him. Then the chief priests and the Pharisees sent temple guards to arrest him.

³³Jesus said, "I am with you for only a short time, and then I go to the one who sent me. ³⁴You will look for me, but you will not find me; and where I am, you cannot come."

³⁵The Jews said to one another, "Where does this man intend to go that we cannot find him? Will he go where our people live scattered among the Greeks, and teach the Greeks? ³⁶What did he mean when he said, 'You will look for me, but you will not find me,' and 'Where I am, you cannot come'?"

▣ ▦▦▦▦▦ DISCOVERING GOD ▦▦▦▦▦ ▤

7:37–39
The Holy Spirit

Friends of Jesus not only enjoy a close relationship with God, they also have the assurance that God's Spirit will come to dwell inside them. With Jesus' earthly appearance, something new happened in the ongoing saga of God's relationship to humankind (see also Genesis chapter 3 [page 7] and chapter 12, verses 1–3 [page 19]). God has always been available to people relationally, but through Jesus he has established the way to reside in his followers permanently. This individual indwelling of God is accomplished through the divine person here called "the Spirit" (elsewhere, the "Holy Spirit").

Jesus promised that after his resurrection from the dead, God would unite with his people in this new way. The result would be an internal, inexhaustible fountain of "living water"—a refreshing, spiritual power that would continually sustain believers in their relationship with him. (For more on the Holy Spirit, see chapters 14 and 16 [pages 1407 and 1409].)

That same Spirit and his power is available to you today!

ᵃ26 Or Messiah; also in verses 27, 31, 41 and 42

³⁷On the last and greatest day of the Feast, Jesus stood and said in a loud voice, "If anyone is thirsty, let him come to me and drink. ³⁸Whoever believes in me, as*ᵃ* the Scripture has said, streams of living water will flow from within him." ³⁹By this he meant the Spirit, whom those who believed in him were later to receive. Up to that time the Spirit had not been given, since Jesus had not yet been glorified.

⁴⁰On hearing his words, some of the people said, "Surely this man is the Prophet."

⁴¹Others said, "He is the Christ."

Still others asked, "How can the Christ come from Galilee? ⁴²Does not the Scripture say that the Christ will come from David's family*ᵇ* and from Bethlehem, the town where David lived?" ⁴³Thus the people were divided because of Jesus. ⁴⁴Some wanted to seize him, but no one laid a hand on him.

Unbelief of the Jewish Leaders

⁴⁵Finally the temple guards went back to the chief priests and Pharisees, who asked them, "Why didn't you bring him in?"

⁴⁶"No one ever spoke the way this man does," the guards declared.

⁴⁷"You mean he has deceived you also?" the Pharisees retorted. ⁴⁸"Has any of the rulers or of the Pharisees believed in him? ⁴⁹No! But this mob that knows nothing of the law—there is a curse on them."

⁵⁰Nicodemus, who had gone to Jesus earlier and who was one of their own number, asked, ⁵¹"Does our law condemn anyone without first hearing him to find out what he is doing?"

⁵²They replied, "Are you from Galilee, too? Look into it, and you will find that a proph-et*ᶜ* does not come out of Galilee."

[The earliest manuscripts and many other ancient witnesses do not have John 7:53–8:11.]

---

⁵³Then each went to his own home.

8 But Jesus went to the Mount of Olives. ²At dawn he appeared again in the temple courts, where all the people gathered around him, and he sat down to teach them. ³The teachers of the law and the Pharisees brought in a woman caught in adultery. They made her stand before the group ⁴and said to Jesus, "Teacher, this woman was caught in the act of adultery. ⁵In the Law Moses commanded us to stone such women. Now what do you say?" ⁶They were using this question as a trap, in order to have a basis for accusing him.

But Jesus bent down and started to write on the ground with his finger. ⁷When they kept on questioning him, he straightened up and said to them, "If any one of you is without sin, let him be the first to throw a stone at her." ⁸Again he stooped down and wrote on the ground.

⁹At this, those who heard began to go away one at a time, the older ones first, until only Jesus was left, with the woman still standing there. ¹⁰Jesus straightened up and asked her, "Woman, where are they? Has no one condemned you?"

¹¹"No one, sir," she said.

"Then neither do I condemn you," Jesus declared. "Go now and leave your life of sin."

ᵃ37,38 Or / If anyone is thirsty, let him come to me. / And let him drink. *38who believes in me. / As*   *ᵇ42* Greek seed
ᶜ52 Two early manuscripts the Prophet

The Validity of Jesus' Testimony

¹²When Jesus spoke again to the people, he said, "I am the light of the world. Whoever follows me will never walk in darkness, but will have the light of life."

¹³The Pharisees challenged him, "Here you are, appearing as your own witness; your testimony is not valid."

¹⁴Jesus answered, "Even if I testify on my own behalf, my testimony is valid, for I know where I came from and where I am going. But you have no idea where I come from or where I am going. ¹⁵You judge by human standards; I pass judgment on no one. ¹⁶But if I do judge, my decisions are right, because I am not alone. I stand with the Father, who sent me. ¹⁷In your own Law it is written that the testimony of two men is valid. ¹⁸I am one who testifies for myself; my other witness is the Father, who sent me."

¹⁹Then they asked him, "Where is your father?"

"You do not know me or my Father," Jesus replied. "If you knew me, you would know my Father also." ²⁰He spoke these words while teaching in the temple area near the place where the offerings were put. Yet no one seized him, because his time had not yet come.

²¹Once more Jesus said to them, "I am going away, and you will look for me, and you will die in your sin. Where I go, you cannot come."

²²This made the Jews ask, "Will he kill himself? Is that why he says, 'Where I go, you cannot come'?"

²³But he continued, "You are from below; I am from above. You are of this world; I am not of this world. ²⁴I told you that you would die in your sins; if you do not believe that I am ⌊the one I claim to be⌋,ᵃ you will indeed die in your sins."

²⁵"Who are you?" they asked.

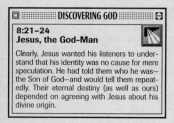

⊡ DISCOVERING GOD ⬒

8:21–24
Jesus, the God-Man

Clearly, Jesus wanted his listeners to understand that his identity was no cause for mere speculation. He had told them who he was—the Son of God—and would tell them repeatedly. Their eternal destiny (as well as ours) depended on agreeing with Jesus about his divine origin.

"Just what I have been claiming all along," Jesus replied. ²⁶"I have much to say in judgment of you. But he who sent me is reliable, and what I have heard from him I tell the world."

²⁷They did not understand that he was telling them about his Father. ²⁸So Jesus said, "When you have lifted up the Son of Man, then you will know that I am ⌊the one I claim to be⌋ and that I do nothing on my own but speak just what the Father has taught me. ²⁹The one who sent me is with me; he has not left me alone, for I always do what pleases him." ³⁰Even as he spoke, many put their faith in him.

The Children of Abraham

³¹To the Jews who had believed him, Jesus said, "If you hold to my teaching, you are really my disciples. ³²Then you will know the truth, and the truth will set you free."

³³They answered him, "We are Abraham's descendantsᵇ and have never been slaves of anyone. How can you say that we shall be set free?"

³⁴Jesus replied, "I tell you the truth, everyone who sins is a slave to sin. ³⁵Now a slave has no permanent place in the family, but a son belongs to it forever. ³⁶So if the Son sets you free, you will be free indeed. ³⁷I know you are Abraham's descendants. Yet you are ready to kill me, because you have no room for my word. ³⁸I am telling you what I have seen in the Father's presence, and you do what you have heard from your father.ᶜ"

³⁹"Abraham is our father," they answered.

"If you were Abraham's children," said Jesus, "then you wouldᵈ do the things Abra-

ᵃ24 Or I am he; also in verse 28   ᵇ33 Greek seed; also in verse 37   ᶜ38 Or presence. Therefore do what you have heard from the Father.   ᵈ39 Some early manuscripts "If you are Abraham's children," said Jesus, "then

ham did. ⁴⁰As it is, you are determined to kill me, a man who has told you the truth that I heard from God. Abraham did not do such things. ⁴¹You are doing the things your own father does."

"We are not illegitimate children," they protested. "The only Father we have is God himself."

The Children of the Devil

⁴²Jesus said to them, "If God were your Father, you would love me, for I came from God and now am here. I have not come on my own; but he sent me. ⁴³Why is my language not clear to you? Because you are unable to hear what I say. ⁴⁴You belong to your father, the devil, and you want to carry out your father's desire. He was a murderer from the beginning, not holding to the truth, for there is no truth in him. When he lies, he speaks his native language, for he is a liar and the father of lies. ⁴⁵Yet because I tell the truth, you do not believe me! ⁴⁶Can any of you prove me guilty of sin? If I am telling the truth, why don't you believe me? ⁴⁷He who belongs to God hears what God says. The reason you do not hear is that you do not belong to God."

The Claims of Jesus About Himself

⁴⁸The Jews answered him, "Aren't we right in saying that you are a Samaritan and demon-possessed?"

⁴⁹"I am not possessed by a demon," said Jesus, "but I honor my Father and you dishonor me. ⁵⁰I am not seeking glory for myself; but there is one who seeks it, and he is the judge. ⁵¹I tell you the truth, if anyone keeps my word, he will never see death."

⁵²At this the Jews exclaimed, "Now we know that you are demon-possessed! Abraham died and so did the prophets, yet you say that if anyone keeps your word, he will never taste death. ⁵³Are you greater than our father Abraham? He died, and so did the prophets. Who do you think you are?"

⁵⁴Jesus replied, "If I glorify myself, my glory means nothing. My Father, whom you claim as your God, is the one who glorifies me. ⁵⁵Though you do not know him, I know him. If I said I did not, I would be a liar like you, but I do know him and keep his word. ⁵⁶Your father Abraham rejoiced at the thought of seeing my day; he saw it and was glad."

⁵⁷"You are not yet fifty years old," the Jews said to him, "and you have seen Abraham!"

⁵⁸"I tell you the truth," Jesus answered, "before Abraham was born, I am!" ⁵⁹At this, they picked up stones to stone him, but Jesus hid himself, slipping away from the temple grounds.

Jesus Heals a Man Born Blind

9 As he went along, he saw a man blind from birth. ²His disciples asked him, "Rabbi, who sinned, this man or his parents, that he was born blind?"

³"Neither this man nor his parents sinned," said Jesus, "but this happened so that the work of God might be displayed in his life. ⁴As long as it is day, we must do the work of

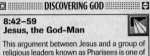

DISCOVERING GOD

8:42–59
Jesus, the God-Man

This argument between Jesus and a group of religious leaders known as Pharisees is one of the clearest examples in the New Testament of Jesus' claim to be God. Here Jesus asserts that he was alive in Abraham's day (some 1800 years earlier) by using the present tense—"I am," not the expected "I was." With that turn of a phrase, he takes on the very title of the one true God.

When God first appeared to Moses he called himself, "I AM WHO I AM" (Exodus chapter 3, verse 14 [page 76]). God also referred to himself similarly in the book of Isaiah with the phrase "I am he" (chapter 41, verse 4 [page 940], and chapter 48, verse 12 [page 954]). In this discussion, Jesus leaves absolutely no doubt about what he is claiming.

The crowd he is speaking to gets the point. In the face of such a statement, there are only two options: bow down and worship, or try to destroy this impostor who is pretending to be God. They chose the latter.

What will be your response?

him who sent me. Night is coming, when no one can work. ⁵While I am in the world, I am the light of the world."

⁶Having said this, he spit on the ground, made some mud with the saliva, and put it on the man's eyes. ⁷"Go," he told him, "wash in the Pool of Siloam" (this word means Sent). So the man went and washed, and came home seeing.

⁸His neighbors and those who had formerly seen him begging asked, "Isn't this the same man who used to sit and beg?" ⁹Some claimed that he was.

Others said, "No, he only looks like him."

But he himself insisted, "I am the man."

¹⁰"How then were your eyes opened?" they demanded.

¹¹He replied, "The man they call Jesus made some mud and put it on my eyes. He told me to go to Siloam and wash. So I went and washed, and then I could see."

¹²"Where is this man?" they asked him.

"I don't know," he said.

The Pharisees Investigate the Healing

¹³They brought to the Pharisees the man who had been blind. ¹⁴Now the day on which Jesus had made the mud and opened the man's eyes was a Sabbath. ¹⁵Therefore the Pharisees also asked him how he had received his sight. "He put mud on my eyes," the man replied, "and I washed, and now I see."

¹⁶Some of the Pharisees said, "This man is not from God, for he does not keep the Sabbath."

But others asked, "How can a sinner do such miraculous signs?" So they were divided.

¹⁷Finally they turned again to the blind man, "What have you to say about him? It was your eyes he opened."

The man replied, "He is a prophet."

¹⁸The Jews still did not believe that he had been blind and had received his sight until they sent for the man's parents. ¹⁹"Is this your son?" they asked. "Is this the one you say was born blind? How is it that now he can see?"

²⁰"We know he is our son," the parents answered, "and we know he was born blind. ²¹But how he can see now, or who opened his eyes, we don't know. Ask him. He is of age; he will speak for himself." ²²His parents said this because they were afraid of the Jews, for already the Jews had decided that anyone who acknowledged that Jesus was the Christ*a* would be put out of the synagogue. ²³That was why his parents said, "He is of age; ask him."

²⁴A second time they summoned the man who had been blind. "Give glory to God,*b*" they said. "We know this man is a sinner."

---

a 22 Or *Messiah*   *b 24* A solemn charge to tell the truth (see Joshua 7:19)

---

²⁵He replied, "Whether he is a sinner or not, I don't know. One thing I do know. I was blind but now I see!"

²⁶Then they asked him, "What did he do to you? How did he open your eyes?"

²⁷He answered, "I have told you already and you did not listen. Why do you want to hear it again? Do you want to become his disciples, too?"

²⁸Then they hurled insults at him and said, "You are this fellow's disciple! We are disciples of Moses! ²⁹We know that God spoke to Moses, but as for this fellow, we don't even know where he comes from."

³⁰The man answered, "Now that is remarkable! You don't know where he comes from, yet he opened my eyes. ³¹We know that God does not listen to sinners. He listens to the godly man who does his will. ³²Nobody has ever heard of opening the eyes of a man born blind. ³³If this man were not from God, he could do nothing."

³⁴To this they replied, "You were steeped in sin at birth; how dare you lecture us!" And they threw him out.

Spiritual Blindness

³⁵Jesus heard that they had thrown him out, and when he found him, he said, "Do you believe in the Son of Man?"

³⁶"Who is he, sir?" the man asked. "Tell me so that I may believe in him."

³⁷Jesus said, "You have now seen him; in fact, he is the one speaking with you."

³⁸Then the man said, "Lord, I believe," and he worshiped him.

³⁹Jesus said, "For judgment I have come into this world, so that the blind will see and those who see will become blind."

⁴⁰Some Pharisees who were with him heard him say this and asked, "What? Are we blind too?"

⁴¹Jesus said, "If you were blind, you would not be guilty of sin; but now that you claim you can see, your guilt remains.

The Shepherd and His Flock

10 "I tell you the truth, the man who does not enter the sheep pen by the gate, but climbs in by some other way, is a thief and a robber. ²The man who enters by the gate is the shepherd of his sheep. ³The watchman opens the gate for him, and the sheep listen to his voice. He calls his own sheep by name and leads them out. ⁴When he has brought out all his own, he goes on ahead of them, and his sheep follow him because they know his voice. ⁵But they will never follow a

---

□ ▓▓▓▓▓ REASONS TO BELIEVE ▓▓▓▓▓ ⤵

9:34–41
The Incomparable Jesus

The man whom Jesus heals in this chapter faces harsh treatment by the religious leaders for his unwillingness to renounce Jesus. Alone and rejected, this man ponders how he could have received such a wonderful gift, yet be so misunderstood by people who are supposed to know God. Jesus speaks to the confused man, asking him the most important question a seeker can hear: "Do you believe in [trust and rely on] the Son of Man?" (verse 35). In other words, do you believe in the One who came from God and who healed you? The man responds with belief and worship.

Notice the two-way seeking. Jesus is the original seeker. He finds people in need even before they can do any looking themselves. His activity precedes any human effort to reach out.

Is it too much to think that, as you read this story, God is attempting to let you know that he desires to reach you? Is he, right now, "touching your eyes" and opening them to see in new ways? If so, do as this man did—just say thanks for how he has brought you this far (in spite of how others around you may misunderstand what is happening). And don't shy away from putting your complete trust in Jesus for all of what life—and death—may hold. He has proven himself trustworthy.

---

stranger; in fact, they will run away from him because they do not recognize a stranger's voice." ⁶Jesus used this figure of speech, but they did not understand what he was telling them.

⁷Therefore Jesus said again, "I tell you the truth, I am the gate for the sheep. ⁸All who ever came before me were thieves and robbers, but the sheep did not listen to them. ⁹I

am the gate; whoever enters through me will be saved.[a] He will come in and go out, and find pasture. [10]The thief comes only to steal and kill and destroy; I have come that they may have life, and have it to the full.

[11]"I am the good shepherd. The good shepherd lays down his life for the sheep. [12]The hired hand is not the shepherd who owns the sheep. So when he sees the wolf coming, he abandons the sheep and runs away. Then the wolf attacks the flock and scatters it. [13]The man runs away because he is a hired hand and cares nothing for the sheep.

[14]"I am the good shepherd; I know my sheep and my sheep know me— [15]just as the Father knows me and I know the Father—and I lay down my life for the sheep. [16]I have other sheep that are not of this sheep pen. I must bring them also. They too will listen to my voice, and there shall be one flock and one shepherd. [17]The reason my Father loves me is that I lay down my life—only to take it up again. [18]No one takes it from me, but I lay it down of my own accord. I have authority to lay it down and authority to take it up again. This command I received from my Father."

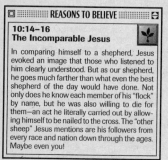

REASONS TO BELIEVE

10:14–16
The Incomparable Jesus

In comparing himself to a shepherd, Jesus evoked an image that those who listened to him clearly understood. But as our shepherd, he goes much farther than what even the best shepherd of the day would have done. Not only does he know each member of his "flock" by name, but he was also willing to die for them—an act he literally carried out by allowing himself to be nailed to the cross. The "other sheep" Jesus mentions are his followers from every race and nation down through the ages. Maybe even you!

[19]At these words the Jews were again divided. [20]Many of them said, "He is demon-possessed and raving mad. Why listen to him?" [21]But others said, "These are not the sayings of a man possessed by a demon. Can a demon open the eyes of the blind?"

The Unbelief of the Jews

[22]Then came the Feast of Dedication[b] at Jerusalem. It was winter, [23]and Jesus was in the temple area walking in Solomon's Colonnade. [24]The Jews gathered around him, saying, "How long will you keep us in suspense? If you are the Christ,[c] tell us plainly." [25]Jesus answered, "I did tell you, but you do not believe. The miracles I do in my Father's name speak for me, [26]but you do not believe because you are not my sheep. [27]My sheep listen to my voice; I know them, and they follow me. [28]I give them eternal life, and they shall never perish; no one can snatch them out of my hand. [29]My Father, who has given them to me, is greater than all[d]; no one can snatch them out of my Father's hand. [30]I and the Father are one."

[31]Again the Jews picked up stones to stone him, [32]but Jesus said to them, "I have shown you many great miracles from the Father. For which of these do you stone me?" [33]"We are not stoning you for any of these," replied the Jews, "but for blasphemy, because you, a mere man, claim to be God."

[34]Jesus answered them, "Is it not written in your Law, 'I have said you are gods'[e]? [35]If he called them 'gods,' to whom the word of God came—and the Scripture cannot be broken— [36]what about the one whom the Father set apart as his very own and sent into the world? Why then do you accuse me of blasphemy because I said, 'I am God's Son'? [37]Do not believe me unless I do what my Father does. [38]But if I do it, even though you do not believe me, believe the miracles, that you may know and understand that the Father is in me, and I in the Father." [39]Again they tried to seize him, but he escaped their grasp.

[40]Then Jesus went back across the Jordan to the place where John had been baptizing in the early days. Here he stayed [41]and many people came to him. They said, "Though

---

[a]9 Or kept safe   [b]22 That is, Hanukkah   [c]24 Or Messiah   [d]29 Many early manuscripts What my Father has given me is greater than all   [e]34 Psalm 82:6

John never performed a miraculous sign, all that John said about this man was true." ⁴²And in that place many believed in Jesus.

The Death of Lazarus

11 Now a man named Lazarus was sick. He was from Bethany, the village of Mary and her sister Martha. ²This Mary, whose brother Lazarus now lay sick, was the same one who poured perfume on the Lord and wiped his feet with her hair. ³So the sisters sent word to Jesus, "Lord, the one you love is sick."

⁴When he heard this, Jesus said, "This sickness will not end in death. No, it is for God's glory so that God's Son may be glorified through it." ⁵Jesus loved Martha and her sister and Lazarus. ⁶Yet when he heard that Lazarus was sick, he stayed where he was two more days.

⁷Then he said to his disciples, "Let us go back to Judea."

⁸"But Rabbi," they said, "a short while ago the Jews tried to stone you, and yet you are going back there?"

⁹Jesus answered, "Are there not twelve hours of daylight? A man who walks by day will not stumble, for he sees by this world's light. ¹⁰It is when he walks by night that he stumbles, for he has no light."

¹¹After he had said this, he went on to tell them, "Our friend Lazarus has fallen asleep; but I am going there to wake him up."

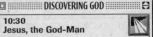

DISCOVERING GOD

10:30
Jesus, the God-Man

In this verse, Jesus again asserts his equality with God the Father.

Some interpreters have tried to soften the impact of these words by suggesting that maybe Jesus only claimed a "unity of purpose" with God. But Jesus' enemies knew exactly what he was claiming—and they were furious. They didn't even bother to deny his miracles; they just decided, based on an irrational bias, that he was a blasphemer who was worthy of death (verses 31–33).

Jesus' presence doesn't quell all doubts. Spectators who are determined to contradict him will be allowed to do so. Of course, they will have to discount important facts and react emotionally instead of rationally. But turning away—even from the miracle-working power of God—can be done. All it takes is a closed mind and a hard heart.

¹²His disciples replied, "Lord, if he sleeps, he will get better." ¹³Jesus had been speaking of his death, but his disciples thought he meant natural sleep.

¹⁴So then he told them plainly, "Lazarus is dead, ¹⁵and for your sake I am glad I was not there, so that you may believe. But let us go to him."

¹⁶Then Thomas (called Didymus) said to the rest of the disciples, "Let us also go, that we may die with him."

Jesus Comforts the Sisters

¹⁷On his arrival, Jesus found that Lazarus had already been in the tomb for four days. ¹⁸Bethany was less than two miles^a from Jerusalem, ¹⁹and many Jews had come to Martha and Mary to comfort them in the loss of their brother. ²⁰When Martha heard that Jesus was coming, she went out to meet him, but Mary stayed at home.

²¹"Lord," Martha said to Jesus, "if you had been here, my brother would not have died. ²²But I know that even now God will give you whatever you ask."

²³Jesus said to her, "Your brother will rise again."

²⁴Martha answered, "I know he will rise again in the resurrection at the last day."

²⁵Jesus said to her, "I am the resurrection and the life. He who believes in me will live, even though he dies; ²⁶and whoever lives and believes in me will never die. Do you believe this?"

²⁷"Yes, Lord," she told him, "I believe that you are the Christ,^b the Son of God, who was to come into the world."

^a18 Greek fifteen stadia (about 3 kilometers)   ^b27 Or Messiah

²⁸And after she had said this, she went back and called her sister Mary aside. "The Teacher is here," she said, "and is asking for you." ²⁹When Mary heard this, she got up quickly and went to him. ³⁰Now Jesus had not yet entered the village, but was still at the place where Martha had met him. ³¹When the Jews who had been with Mary in the house, comforting her, noticed how quickly she got up and went out, they followed her, supposing she was going to the tomb to mourn there.

³²When Mary reached the place where Jesus was and saw him, she fell at his feet and said, "Lord, if you had been here, my brother would not have died."

³³When Jesus saw her weeping, and the Jews who had come along with her also weeping, he was deeply moved in spirit and troubled. ³⁴"Where have you laid him?" he asked.

"Come and see, Lord," they replied.

³⁵Jesus wept.

³⁶Then the Jews said, "See how he loved him!"

³⁷But some of them said, "Could not he who opened the eyes of the blind man have kept this man from dying?"

Jesus Raises Lazarus From the Dead

³⁸Jesus, once more deeply moved, came to the tomb. It was a cave with a stone laid across the entrance. ³⁹"Take away the stone," he said.

"But, Lord," said Martha, the sister of the dead man, "by this time there is a bad odor, for he has been there four days."

⁴⁰Then Jesus said, "Did I not tell you that if you believed, you would see the glory of God?"

⁴¹So they took away the stone. Then Jesus looked up and said, "Father, I thank you that you have heard me. ⁴²I knew that you always hear me, but I said this for the benefit of the people standing here, that they may believe that you sent me."

⁴³When he had said this, Jesus called in a loud voice, "Lazarus, come out!" ⁴⁴The dead man came out, his hands and feet wrapped with strips of linen, and a cloth around his face.

Jesus said to them, "Take off the grave clothes and let him go."

The Plot to Kill Jesus

⁴⁵Therefore many of the Jews who had come to visit Mary, and had seen what Jesus did, put their faith in him. ⁴⁶But some of them went to the Pharisees and told them what Jesus had done. ⁴⁷Then the chief priests and the Pharisees called a meeting of the Sanhedrin.

"What are we accomplishing?" they asked. "Here is this man performing many miraculous signs. ⁴⁸If we let him go on like this, everyone will believe in him, and then the Romans will come and take away both our place ᵃ and our nation."

⁴⁹Then one of them, named Caiaphas, who was high priest that year, spoke up, "You

---

□ ▦▦▦▦ KNOWING YOURSELF ▦▦▦▦ ⊟

11:47–50
Sin

Sometimes people keep their distance from Jesus because they don't want him meddling in their lives.

Many of Jesus' contemporaries opposed him for that reason. Their security was wrapped up in a fragile political alliance with the Roman government that protected their land rights and place of worship. Jesus' appeal to the masses threatened that source of security. These Jewish leaders weren't willing to risk losing what they had—at best, a temporary security—for the promise of new life and eternal safe-keeping that Jesus had to offer.

Jesus knows that anything that takes the place of God in our lives will lead to disappointment. Humans simply aren't wired to function without a vital connection to our Creator. If we "hot wire" our lives to some other source of security, we'll self-destruct—as these religious leaders would soon learn.

---

know nothing at all! ⁵⁰You do not realize that it is better for you that one man die for the people than that the whole nation perish."

⁵¹He did not say this on his own, but as high priest that year he prophesied that Jesus would die for the Jewish nation, ⁵²and not only for that nation but also for the scattered children of God, to bring them together and make them one. ⁵³So from that day on they plotted to take his life.

⁵⁴Therefore Jesus no longer moved about publicly among the Jews. Instead he withdrew to a region near the desert, to a village called Ephraim, where he stayed with his disciples.

⁵⁵When it was almost time for the Jewish Passover, many went up from the country to Jerusalem for their ceremonial cleansing before the Passover. ⁵⁶They kept looking for Jesus, and as they stood in the temple area they asked one another, "What do you think? Isn't he coming to the Feast at all?" ⁵⁷But the chief priests and Pharisees had given orders that if anyone found out where Jesus was, he should report it so that they might arrest him.

Jesus Anointed at Bethany

12 Six days before the Passover, Jesus arrived at Bethany, where Lazarus lived, whom Jesus had raised from the dead. ²Here a dinner was given in Jesus' honor. Martha served, while Lazarus was among those reclining at the table with him. ³Then Mary took about a pint*ᵃ* of pure nard, an expensive perfume; she poured it on Jesus' feet and wiped his feet with her hair. And the house was filled with the fragrance of the perfume.

⁴But one of his disciples, Judas Iscariot, who was later to betray him, objected, ⁵"Why wasn't this perfume sold and the money given to the poor? It was worth a year's wages.*ᵇ* ⁶He did not say this because he cared about the poor but because he was a thief; as keeper of the money bag, he used to help himself to what was put into it.

⁷"Leave her alone," Jesus replied. "It was intended that she should save this perfume for the day of my burial. ⁸You will always have the poor among you, but you will not always have me."

⁹Meanwhile a large crowd of Jews found out that Jesus was there and came, not only because of him but also to see Lazarus, whom he had raised from the dead. ¹⁰So the chief priests made plans to kill Lazarus as well, ¹¹for on account of him many of the Jews were going over to Jesus and putting their faith in him.

The Triumphal Entry

¹²The next day the great crowd that had come for the Feast heard that Jesus was on his way to Jerusalem. ¹³They took palm branches and went out to meet him, shouting,

---

ᵃ3 Greek *a litra* (probably about 0.5 liter)   *ᵇ5* Greek *three hundred denarii*

"Hosanna!ᵃ"

"Blessed is he who comes in the name of the Lord!"ᵇ

"Blessed is the King of Israel!"

¹⁴Jesus found a young donkey and sat upon it, as it is written,

¹⁵"Do not be afraid, O Daughter of Zion;
    see, your king is coming,
    seated on a donkey's colt."ᶜ

¹⁶At first his disciples did not understand all this. Only after Jesus was glorified did they realize that these things had been written about him and that they had done these things to him.

¹⁷Now the crowd that was with him when he called Lazarus from the tomb and raised him from the dead continued to spread the word. ¹⁸Many people, because they had heard that he had given this miraculous sign, went out to meet him. ¹⁹So the Pharisees said to one another, "See, this is getting us nowhere. Look how the whole world has gone after him!"

Jesus Predicts His Death

²⁰Now there were some Greeks among those who went up to worship at the Feast. ²¹They came to Philip, who was from Bethsaida in Galilee, with a request. "Sir," they said, "we would like to see Jesus." ²²Philip went to tell Andrew; Andrew and Philip in turn told Jesus.

²³Jesus replied, "The hour has come for the Son of Man to be glorified. ²⁴I tell you the truth, unless a kernel of wheat falls to the ground and dies, it remains only a single seed. But if it dies, it produces many seeds. ²⁵The man who loves his life will lose it, while the man who hates his life in this world will keep it for eternal life. ²⁶Whoever serves me must follow me; and where I am, my servant also will be. My Father will honor the one who serves me.

²⁷"Now my heart is troubled, and what shall I say? 'Father, save me from this hour'? No, it was for this very reason I came to this hour. ²⁸Father, glorify your name!"

Then a voice came from heaven, "I have glorified it, and will glorify it again." ²⁹The crowd that was there and heard it said it had thundered; others said an angel had spoken to him.

³⁰Jesus said, "This voice was for your benefit, not mine. ³¹Now is the time for judgment on this world; now the prince of this world will be driven out. ³²But I, when I am lifted up from the earth, will draw all men to myself." ³³He said this to show the kind of death he was going to die.

³⁴The crowd spoke up, "We have heard from the Law that the Christᵈ will remain forever, so how can you say, 'The Son of Man must be lifted up'? Who is this 'Son of Man'?"

³⁵Then Jesus told them, "You are going to have the light just a little while longer. Walk while you have the light, before darkness overtakes you. The man who walks in the dark does not know where he is going. ³⁶Put your trust in the light while you have it, so that you may become sons of light." When he had finished speaking, Jesus left and hid himself from them.

The Jews Continue in Their Unbelief

³⁷Even after Jesus had done all these miraculous signs in their presence, they still would not believe in him. ³⁸This was to fulfill the word of Isaiah the prophet:

ᵃ13 A Hebrew expression meaning "Save!" which became an exclamation of praise   ᵇ13 Psalm 118:25, 26   ᶜ15 Zech. 9:9   ᵈ34 Or *Messiah*

"Lord, who has believed our message
and to whom has the arm of the Lord been revealed?"[a]

39For this reason they could not believe, because, as Isaiah says elsewhere:

40"He has blinded their eyes
and deadened their hearts,
so they can neither see with their eyes,
nor understand with their hearts,
nor turn—and I would heal them."[b]

41Isaiah said this because he saw Jesus' glory and spoke about him.

42Yet at the same time many even among the leaders believed in him. But because of the Pharisees they would not confess their faith for fear they would be put out of the synagogue; 43for they loved praise from men more than praise from God.

44Then Jesus cried out, "When a man believes in me, he does not believe in me only, but in the one who sent me. 45When he looks at me, he sees the one who sent me. 46I have come into the world as a light, so that no one who believes in me should stay in darkness.

47"As for the person who hears my words but does not keep them, I do not judge him. For I did not come to judge the world, but to save it. 48There is a judge for the one who rejects me and does not accept my words; that very word which I spoke will condemn him at the last day. 49For I did not speak of my own accord, but the Father who sent me commanded me what to say and how to say it. 50I know that his command leads to eternal life. So whatever I say is just what the Father has told me to say."

Jesus Washes His Disciples' Feet

13 It was just before the Passover Feast. Jesus knew that the time had come for him to leave this world and go to the Father. Having loved his own who were in the world, he now showed them the full extent of his love.[c]

2The evening meal was being served, and the devil had already prompted Judas Iscariot, son of Simon, to betray Jesus. 3Jesus knew that the Father had put all things under his power, and that he had come from God and was returning to God; 4so he got up from the meal, took off his outer clothing, and wrapped a towel around his waist. 5After that, he poured water into a basin and began to wash his disciples' feet, drying them with the towel that was wrapped around him.

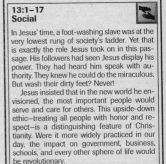

STRENGTHENING RELATIONSHIPS

13:1–17
Social

In Jesus' time, a foot-washing slave was at the very lowest rung of society's ladder. Yet that is exactly the role Jesus took on in this passage. His followers had seen Jesus display his power. They had heard him speak with authority. They knew he could do the miraculous. But wash their dirty feet? Never!

Jesus insisted that in the new world he envisioned, the most important people would serve and care for others. This upside-down ethic—treating all people with honor and respect—is a distinguishing feature of Christianity. Were it more widely practiced in our day, the impact on government, business, schools, and every other sphere of life would be revolutionary.

Many individuals spend time voluntarily serving other people. Those who do so in the name of God, in whose image we are all created, show the world not only that Jesus is who he says he is, but that his followers are who they say they are.

6He came to Simon Peter, who said to him, "Lord, are you going to wash my feet?" 7Jesus replied, "You do not realize now what I am doing, but later you will understand." 8"No," said Peter, "you shall never wash my feet."

Jesus answered, "Unless I wash you, you have no part with me."

a38 Isaiah 53:1   b40 Isaiah 6:10   c1 Or he loved them to the last

⁹"Then, Lord," Simon Peter replied, "not just my feet but my hands and my head as well!"

¹⁰Jesus answered, "A person who has had a bath needs only to wash his feet; his whole body is clean. And you are clean, though not every one of you." ¹¹For he knew who was going to betray him, and that was why he said not every one was clean.

¹²When he had finished washing their feet, he put on his clothes and returned to his place. "Do you understand what I have done for you?" he asked them. ¹³"You call me 'Teacher' and 'Lord,' and rightly so, for that is what I am. ¹⁴Now that I, your Lord and Teacher, have washed your feet, you also should wash one another's feet. ¹⁵I have set you an example that you should do as I have done for you. ¹⁶I tell you the truth, no servant is greater than his master, nor is a messenger greater than the one who sent him. ¹⁷Now that you know these things, you will be blessed if you do them.

▣ ▦ ADDRESSING QUESTIONS ▦ ⬌

**13:21–27
Unseen Realities** **Q**

No one knows for sure exactly why Judas handed Jesus over to the authorities. Whatever the reason, he received supernatural assistance from an evil angel called Satan (or the devil) to carry out his plan.

Notice that the devil did not force Judas to do anything. The devil's tools were (and still are today) human desires and decisions—he merely amplified and empowered the direction that Judas had already chosen. Judas later realized what he had done, and took his own life as a result (see Matthew chapter 27, verses 3–5 [page 1298]).

Dabbling in anything satanic leads a person into powerful spiritual bondage. Satan is like a caged lion. Get in the cage with him, and you will be in grave danger. Pretend he doesn't exist, and you leave the door of the cage open—he will get out and do harm. Only if you stay close to God are you safe (see James chapter 4, verses 7–10 [page 1605]). The devil may "roar" and try to scare you, but he is no match for God.

Jesus *always* won when he and the devil went toe-to-toe. That victory is still available to those who live in union with Jesus today.

Jesus Predicts His Betrayal

¹⁸"I am not referring to all of you; I know those I have chosen. But this is to fulfill the scripture: 'He who shares my bread has lifted up his heel against me.' ᵃ

¹⁹"I am telling you now before it happens, so that when it does happen you will believe that I am He. ²⁰I tell you the truth, whoever accepts anyone I send accepts me; and whoever accepts me accepts the one who sent me."

²¹After he had said this, Jesus was troubled in spirit and testified, "I tell you the truth, one of you is going to betray me."

²²His disciples stared at one another, at a loss to know which of them he meant. ²³One of them, the disciple whom Jesus loved, was reclining next to him. ²⁴Simon Peter motioned to this disciple and said, "Ask him which one he means."

²⁵Leaning back against Jesus, he asked him, "Lord, who is it?"

²⁶Jesus answered, "It is the one to whom I will give this piece of bread when I have dipped it in the dish." Then, dipping the piece of bread, he gave it to Judas Iscariot, son of Simon. ²⁷As soon as Judas took the bread, Satan entered into him.

"What you are about to do, do quickly," Jesus told him, ²⁸but no one at the meal understood why Jesus said this to him. ²⁹Since Judas had charge of the money, some thought Jesus was telling him to buy what was needed for the Feast, or to give something to the poor. ³⁰As soon as Judas had taken the bread, he went out. And it was night.

Jesus Predicts Peter's Denial

³¹When he was gone, Jesus said, "Now is the Son of Man glorified and God is glorified in him. ³²If God is glorified in him,ᵇ God will glorify the Son in himself, and will glorify him at once.

ᵃ 18 Psalm 41:9 ᵇ 32 Many early manuscripts do not have *If God is glorified in him.*

³³"My children, I will be with you only a little longer. You will look for me, and just as I told the Jews, so I tell you now: Where I am going, you cannot come.

³⁴"A new command I give you: Love one another. As I have loved you, so you must love one another. ³⁵By this all men will know that you are my disciples, if you love one another."

³⁶Simon Peter asked him, "Lord, where are you going?"

Jesus replied, "Where I am going, you cannot follow now, but you will follow later."

³⁷Peter asked, "Lord, why can't I follow you now? I will lay down my life for you."

³⁸Then Jesus answered, "Will you really lay down your life for me? I tell you the truth, before the rooster crows, you will disown me three times!

Jesus Comforts His Disciples

14 "Do not let your hearts be troubled. Trust in God*a*; trust also in me. ²In my Father's house are many rooms; if it were not so, I would have told you. I am going there to prepare a place for you. ³And if I go and prepare a place for you, I will come back and take you to be with me that you also may be where I am. ⁴You know the way to the place where I am going."

Jesus the Way to the Father

⁵Thomas said to him, "Lord, we don't know where you are going, so how can we know the way?"

⁶Jesus answered, "I am the way and the truth and the life. No one comes to the Father except through me. ⁷If you really knew me, you would know*b* my Father as well. From now on, you do know him and have seen him."

⁸Philip said, "Lord, show us the Father and that will be enough for us."

⁹Jesus answered: "Don't you know me, Philip, even after I have been among you such

---

a 1 Or *You trust in God*   *b 7* Some early manuscripts *If you really have known me, you will know*

ADDRESSING QUESTIONS

14:6
God   **Q**

Is belief in Jesus Christ the *one and only* way to find salvation?

Jesus' answer is clear from this passage. Many Christians have been accused of being narrow-minded (sometimes with good reason!); but when it comes to the claim that Jesus is the only way to God, Christians are narrow-minded because *Jesus* is. And every seeker must reckon with Jesus' claim. As British theologian and writer C.S. Lewis once pointed out, if Jesus isn't a liar or a lunatic, then he must be *Lord.*

Perhaps an illustration will shed some light on this idea. From the air an airport runway looks "narrow." A pilot who insists on landing there may well be considered narrow-minded. But a runway is the only safe place for a jet to land. Say, for example, that a well-intentioned passenger recommends that the pilot land on a local expressway instead of the runway. It looks safe, after all, and would be much more convenient than circling the city waiting for the runway to clear. The pilot, resisting the appeals of the uniformed passenger who proposes an unsafe alternative, will be credited with courage for saving the life of every passenger—even the one who complained about the inconvenience of it all.

Jesus is like that pilot, trying to tell us that it's not safe to put down anywhere else. He's not limiting our options—he's protecting us from a crash.

If this concept troubles you, you're not alone. It's a common criticism of Christianity in our pluralistic, relativistic culture. But realize that, as a seeker, you're ultimately going to have to take up this claim—not with Christians, but with Jesus Christ himself. Pit your arguments, your credentials, your character and your insight against his. But don't enter the debate unless you're willing to yield to the winner.

a long time? Anyone who has seen me has seen the Father. How can you say, 'Show us the Father'? ¹⁰Don't you believe that I am in the Father, and that the Father is in me? The words I say to you are not just my own. Rather, it is the Father, living in me, who is doing his work. ¹¹Believe me when I say that I am in the Father and the Father is in me; or at least believe on the evidence of the miracles themselves. ¹²I tell you the truth, anyone who has faith in me will do what I have been doing. He will do even greater things than these, because I am going to the Father. ¹³And I will do whatever you ask in my name, so that the Son may bring glory to the Father. ¹⁴You may ask me for anything in my name, and I will do it.

DISCOVERING GOD

14:14
Jesus, the God-Man

Jesus is the only person in the Bible who invites prayer *to* him, in *his* name, and who then says that *he* will grant those requests. Jesus clearly affirms his divine identity by claiming prerogatives belonging to God alone.

Jesus Promises the Holy Spirit

¹⁵"If you love me, you will obey what I command. ¹⁶And I will ask the Father, and he will give you another Counselor to be with you forever— ¹⁷the Spirit of truth. The world cannot accept him, because it neither sees him nor knows him. But you know him, for he lives with you and will be[a] in you. ¹⁸I will not leave you as orphans; I will come to you. ¹⁹Before long, the world will not see me anymore, but you will see me. Because I live, you also will live. ²⁰On that day you will realize that I am in my Father, and you are in me, and I am in you. ²¹Whoever has my commands and obeys them, he is the one who loves me. He who loves me will be loved by my Father, and I too will love him and show myself to him."

²²Then Judas (not Judas Iscariot) said, "But, Lord, why do you intend to show yourself to us and not to the world?"

²³Jesus replied, "If anyone loves me, he will obey my teaching. My Father will love him, and we will come to him and make our home with him. ²⁴He who does not love me will not obey my teaching. These words you hear are not my own; they belong to the Father who sent me.

²⁵"All this I have spoken while still with you. ²⁶But the Counselor, the Holy Spirit, whom the Father will send in my name, will teach you all things and will remind you of everything I have said to you. ²⁷Peace I leave with you; my peace I give you. I do not give to you as the world gives. Do not let your hearts be troubled and do not be afraid.

²⁸"You heard me say, 'I am going away and I am coming back to you.' If you loved me, you would be glad that I am going to the Father, for the Father is greater than I. ²⁹I have told you now before it happens, so that when it does happen you will believe. ³⁰I will not speak with you much longer, for the prince of this world is coming. He has no hold on me, ³¹but the world must learn that I love the Father and that I do exactly what my Father has commanded me.

"Come now; let us leave.

The Vine and the Branches

15 "I am the true vine, and my Father is the gardener. ²He cuts off every branch in me that bears no fruit, while every branch that does bear fruit he prunes[b] so that it will be even more fruitful. ³You are already clean because of the word I have spoken to you. ⁴Remain in me, and I will remain in you. No branch can bear fruit by itself; it must remain in the vine. Neither can you bear fruit unless you remain in me.

⁵"I am the vine; you are the branches. If a man remains in me and I in him, he will bear much fruit; apart from me you can do nothing. ⁶If anyone does not remain in me, he is like a branch that is thrown away and withers; such branches are picked up, thrown into the fire and burned. ⁷If you remain in me and my words remain in you, ask whatever you

---

a 17 Some early manuscripts *and is*   b 2 The Greek for *prunes* also means *cleans.*

wish, and it will be given you. ⁸This is to my Father's glory, that you bear much fruit, showing yourselves to be my disciples.

⁹"As the Father has loved me, so have I loved you. Now remain in my love. ¹⁰If you obey my commands, you will remain in my love, just as I have obeyed my Father's commands and remain in his love. ¹¹I have told you this so that my joy may be in you and that your joy may be complete. ¹²My command is this: Love each other as I have loved you. ¹³Greater love has no one than this, that he lay down his life for his friends. ¹⁴You are my friends if you do what I command. ¹⁵I no longer call you servants, because a servant does not know his master's business. Instead, I have called you friends, for everything that I learned from my Father I have made known to you. ¹⁶You did not choose me, but I chose you and appointed you to go and bear fruit—fruit that will last. Then the Father will give you whatever you ask in my name. ¹⁷This is my command: Love each other.

The World Hates the Disciples

¹⁸"If the world hates you, keep in mind that it hated me first. ¹⁹If you belonged to the world, it would love you as its own. As it is, you do not belong to the world, but I have chosen you out of the world. That is why the world hates you. ²⁰Remember the words I spoke to you: 'No servant is greater than his master.'ᵃ If they persecuted me, they will persecute you also. If they obeyed my teaching, they will obey yours also. ²¹They will treat you this way because of my name, for they do not know the One who sent me. ²²If I had not come and spoken to them, they would not be guilty of

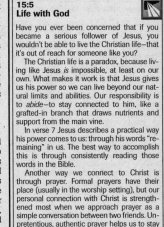

15:5
Life with God

Have you ever been concerned that if you became a serious follower of Jesus, you wouldn't be able to live the Christian life—that it's out of reach for someone like you?

The Christian life is a paradox, because living like Jesus *is* impossible, at least on our own. What makes it work is that Jesus gives us his power so we can live beyond our natural limits and abilities. Our responsibility is to *abide*—to stay connected to him, like a grafted-in branch that draws nutrients and support from the main vine.

In verse 7 Jesus describes a practical way his power comes to us: through his words "remaining" in us. The best way to accomplish this is through consistently reading those words in the Bible.

Another way we connect to Christ is through prayer. Formal prayers have their place (usually in the worship setting), but our personal connection with Christ is strengthened most when we approach prayer as a simple conversation between two friends. Unpretentious, authentic prayer helps us to stay closely connected—in other words, to *abide*—with Jesus.

sin. Now, however, they have no excuse for their sin. ²³He who hates me hates my Father as well. ²⁴If I had not done among them what no one else did, they would not be guilty of sin. But now they have seen these miracles, and yet they have hated both me and my Father. ²⁵But this is to fulfill what is written in their Law: 'They hated me without reason.'ᵇ

²⁶"When the Counselor comes, whom I will send to you from the Father, the Spirit of truth who goes out from the Father, he will testify about me. ²⁷And you also must testify, for you have been with me from the beginning.

16 "All this I have told you so that you will not go astray. ²They will put you out of the synagogue; in fact, a time is coming when anyone who kills you will think he is offering a service to God. ³They will do such things because they have not known the Father or me. ⁴I have told you this, so that when the time comes you will remember that I warned you. I did not tell you this at first because I was with you.

ᵃ20 John 13:16   ᵇ25 Psalms 35:19; 69:4

The Work of the Holy Spirit

⁵"Now I am going to him who sent me, yet none of you asks me, 'Where are you going?' ⁶Because I have said these things, you are filled with grief. ⁷But I tell you the truth: It is for your good that I am going away. Unless I go away, the Counselor will not come to you; but if I go, I will send him to you. ⁸When he comes, he will convict the world of guilt[a] in regard to sin and righteousness and judgment: ⁹in regard to sin, because men do not believe in me; ¹⁰in regard to righteousness, because I am going to the Father, where you can see me no longer; ¹¹and in regard to judgment, because the prince of this world now stands condemned.

¹²"I have much more to say to you, more than you can now bear. ¹³But when he, the Spirit of truth, comes, he will guide you into all truth. He will not speak on his own; he will speak only what he hears, and he will tell you what is yet to come. ¹⁴He will bring glory to me by taking from what is mine and making it known to you. ¹⁵All that belongs to the Father is mine. That is why I said the Spirit will take from what is mine and make it known to you.

¹⁶"In a little while you will see me no more, and then after a little while you will see me."

▣ ⫿⫿⫿⫿ DISCOVERING GOD ⫿⫿⫿⫿ ⮀

15:26–27
The Holy Spirit

Jesus refers to the Holy Spirit here as "the Counselor." The term literally means "one called alongside to help."

Perhaps you've felt the Spirit's ministry while reading this Bible or when a Christian friend or coworker was talking to you. Have you ever experienced a breakthrough during such times—a point at which "a light turned on" and the discussion began to make sense? That might well have been God working in you to help you grasp his message and apply it to your life. During such moments "the Counselor" does his work, just as Jesus promised he would 2000 years ago.

The Disciples' Grief Will Turn to Joy

¹⁷Some of his disciples said to one another, "What does he mean by saying, 'In a little while you will see me no more, and then after a little while you will see me,' and 'Because I am going to the Father'?" ¹⁸They kept asking, "What does he mean by 'a little while'? We don't understand what he is saying."

¹⁹Jesus saw that they wanted to ask him about this, so he said to them, "Are you asking one another what I meant when I said, 'In a little while you will see me no more, and then after a little while you will see me'? ²⁰I tell you the truth, you will weep and mourn while the world rejoices. You will grieve, but your grief will turn to joy. ²¹A woman giving birth to a child has pain because her time has come; but when her baby is born she forgets the anguish because of her joy that a child is born into the world. ²²So with you: Now is your time of grief, but I will see you again and you will rejoice, and no one will take away your joy. ²³In that day you will no longer ask me anything. I tell you the truth, my Father will give you whatever you ask in my name. ²⁴Until now you have not asked for anything in my name. Ask and you will receive, and your joy will be complete.

²⁵"Though I have been speaking figuratively, a time is coming when I will no longer use this kind of language but will tell you plainly about my Father. ²⁶In that day you will ask in my name. I am not saying that I will ask the Father on your behalf. ²⁷No, the Father himself loves you because you have loved me and have believed that I came from God. ²⁸I came from the Father and entered the world; now I am leaving the world and going back to the Father."

²⁹Then Jesus' disciples said, "Now you are speaking clearly and without figures of speech. ³⁰Now we can see that you know all things and that you do not even need to have anyone ask you questions. This makes us believe that you came from God."

³¹"You believe at last!"[b] Jesus answered. ³²"But a time is coming, and has come, when

---

a 8 Or will expose the guilt of the world   *b 31 Or "Do you now believe?"*

you will be scattered, each to his own home. You will leave me all alone. Yet I am not alone, for my Father is with me.

³³"I have told you these things, so that in me you may have peace. In this world you will have trouble. But take heart! I have overcome the world."

Jesus Prays for Himself

17 After Jesus said this, he looked toward heaven and prayed:

"Father, the time has come. Glorify your Son, that your Son may glorify you. ²For you granted him authority over all people that he might give eternal life to all those you have given him. ³Now this is eternal life: that they may know you, the only true God, and Jesus Christ, whom you have sent. ⁴I have brought you glory on earth by completing the work you gave me to do. ⁵And now, Father, glorify me in your presence with the glory I had with you before the world began.

Jesus Prays for His Disciples

⁶"I have revealed you*ᵃ* to those whom you gave me out of the world. They were yours; you gave them to me and they have obeyed your word. ⁷Now they know that everything you have given me comes from you. ⁸For I gave them the words you gave me and they accepted them. They knew with certainty that I came from you, and they believed that you sent me. ⁹I pray for them. I am not praying for the world, but for those you have given me, for they are yours. ¹⁰All I have is yours, and all you have is mine. And glory has come to me through them. ¹¹I will remain in the world no longer, but they are still in the world, and I am coming to you. Holy Father, protect them by the power of your name—the name you gave me—so that they may be one as we are one. ¹²While I was with them, I protected them and kept them safe by that name you gave me. None has been lost except the one doomed to destruction so that Scripture would be fulfilled.

>
> ## ▣ ▦▦▦▦ DISCOVERING GOD ▦▦▦▦ ◨
>
> **16:33**
> ### Life with God
>
> Jesus never promised his followers that their lives would be trouble-free. In fact, he promised just the opposite. But what did he mean when he said that he had "overcome the world"?
>
> Jesus was talking here about the final victory he would claim when God would raise him from the dead (you'll read more about this as you continue reading through this book). Jesus submitted to death on the cross out of his own will. After three days, as he predicted (see Mark chapter 8, verse 31 [page 1317]), God brought him back to life. In breaking the power of death, Jesus demolished the power of sin in this world. Individuals who place their trust in Jesus are personally connected to him and his victory.
>
> So, while life as a Christian may have its bleak periods, Jesus' resurrection gives believers hope that no defeat on earth is permanent. Jesus' troops may lose some battles, but his victory assures them that they'll win the war.

¹³"I am coming to you now, but I say these things while I am still in the world, so that they may have the full measure of my joy within them. ¹⁴I have given them your word and the world has hated them, for they are not of the world any more than I am of the world. ¹⁵My prayer is not that you take them out of the world but that you protect them from the evil one. ¹⁶They are not of the world, even as I am not of it. ¹⁷Sanctify*ᵇ* them by the truth; your word is truth. ¹⁸As you sent me into the world, I have sent them into the world. ¹⁹For them I sanctify myself, that they too may be truly sanctified.

ᵃ6 Greek *your name;* also in verse 26   *ᵇ17* Greek *hagiazo (set apart for sacred use or make holy);* also in verse 19

Jesus Prays for All Believers

20"My prayer is not for them alone. I pray also for those who will believe in me through their message, 21that all of them may be one, Father, just as you are in me and I am in you. May they also be in us so that the world may believe that you have sent me. 22I have given them the glory that you gave me, that they may be one as we are one: 23I in them and you in me. May they be brought to complete unity to let the world know that you sent me and have loved them even as you have loved me.

24"Father, I want those you have given me to be with me where I am, and to see my glory, the glory you have given me because you loved me before the creation of the world.

25"Righteous Father, though the world does not know you, I know you, and they know that you have sent me. 26I have made you known to them, and will continue to make you known in order that the love you have for me may be in them and that I myself may be in them."

Jesus Arrested

18 When he had finished praying, Jesus left with his disciples and crossed the Kidron Valley. On the other side there was an olive grove, and he and his disciples went into it.

2Now Judas, who betrayed him, knew the place, because Jesus had often met there with his disciples. 3So Judas came to the grove, guiding a detachment of soldiers and some officials from the chief priests and Pharisees. They were carrying torches, lanterns and weapons.

4Jesus, knowing all that was going to happen to him, went out and asked them, "Who is it you want?"

5"Jesus of Nazareth," they replied.

"I am he," Jesus said. (And Judas the traitor was standing there with them.) 6When Jesus said, "I am he," they drew back and fell to the ground.

7Again he asked them, "Who is it you want?"

And they said, "Jesus of Nazareth."

8"I told you that I am he," Jesus answered. "If you are looking for me, then let these men go." 9This happened so that the words he had spoken would be fulfilled: "I have not lost one of those you gave me."*a*

10Then Simon Peter, who had a sword, drew it and struck the high priest's servant, cutting off his right ear. (The servant's name was Malchus.)

11Jesus commanded Peter, "Put your sword away! Shall I not drink the cup the Father has given me?"

KNOWING YOURSELF

17:3
A New Identity

What does it mean to have "eternal life"?

According to Jesus, eternal life begins *right here on earth*—the very moment we invite Christ to be our forgiver and leader. We have a choice whether to live with him now or apart from him now. After physical death we continue experiencing the kind of spiritual life we had here: Either we live in heaven with Christ or in hell without him. But we continue to exist somewhere eternally.

So how do we receive eternal life with him? By doing the right rituals? Living a clean life? Appearing to be religious? None of these options open the way to eternal life. Jesus gives this simple answer: *we need to know him.* This goes beyond mere knowledge, however, because even the devil "knows him" in the sense of having accurate theology. Jesus calls us into a *relationship* with him. We have the chance to "know him" now and to be with him after we die.

That's the meaning of eternal life. It's a *quality* of life—both now and later—not just a *quantity* of life.

---

*a9 John 6:39

Jesus Taken to Annas

12Then the detachment of soldiers with its commander and the Jewish officials arrested Jesus. They bound him **13**and brought him first to Annas, who was the father-in-law of Caiaphas, the high priest that year. **14**Caiaphas was the one who had advised the Jews that it would be good if one man died for the people.

Peter's First Denial

15Simon Peter and another disciple were following Jesus. Because this disciple was known to the high priest, he went with Jesus into the high priest's courtyard, **16**but Peter had to wait outside at the door. The other disciple, who was known to the high priest, came back, spoke to the girl on duty there and brought Peter in.

17"You are not one of his disciples, are you?" the girl at the door asked Peter.

He replied, "I am not."

18It was cold, and the servants and officials stood around a fire they had made to keep warm. Peter also was standing with them, warming himself.

The High Priest Questions Jesus

19Meanwhile, the high priest questioned Jesus about his disciples and his teaching.

20"I have spoken openly to the world," Jesus replied. "I always taught in synagogues or at the temple, where all the Jews come together. I said nothing in secret. **21**Why question me? Ask those who heard me. Surely they know what I said."

22When Jesus said this, one of the officials nearby struck him in the face. "Is this the way you answer the high priest?" he demanded.

23"If I said something wrong," Jesus replied, "testify as to what is wrong. But if I spoke the truth, why did you strike me?" **24**Then Annas sent him, still bound, to Caiaphas the high priest. *a*

Peter's Second and Third Denials

25As Simon Peter stood warming himself, he was asked, "You are not one of his disciples, are you?"

He denied it, saying, "I am not."

26One of the high priest's servants, a relative of the man whose ear Peter had cut off, challenged him, "Didn't I see you with him in the olive grove?" **27**Again Peter denied it, and at that moment a rooster began to crow.

Jesus Before Pilate

28Then the Jews led Jesus from Caiaphas to the palace of the Roman governor. By now it was early morning, and to avoid ceremonial uncleanness the Jews did not enter the palace; they wanted to be able to eat the Passover. **29**So Pilate came out to them and asked, "What charges are you bringing against this man?"

30"If he were not a criminal," they replied, "we would not have handed him over to you."

31Pilate said, "Take him yourselves and judge him by your own law."

"But we have no right to execute anyone," the Jews objected. **32**This happened so that the words Jesus had spoken indicating the kind of death he was going to die would be fulfilled.

33Pilate then went back inside the palace, summoned Jesus and asked him, "Are you the king of the Jews?"

34"Is that your own idea," Jesus asked, "or did others talk to you about me?"

35"Am I a Jew?" Pilate replied. "It was your people and your chief priests who handed you over to me. What is it you have done?"

a24 Or (Now Annas had sent him, still bound, to Caiaphas the high priest.)

³⁶Jesus said, "My kingdom is not of this world. If it were, my servants would fight to prevent my arrest by the Jews. But now my kingdom is from another place."

³⁷"You are a king, then!" said Pilate.

Jesus answered, "You are right in saying I am a king. In fact, for this reason I was born, and for this I came into the world, to testify to the truth. Everyone on the side of truth listens to me."

³⁸"What is truth?" Pilate asked. With this he went out again to the Jews and said, "I find no basis for a charge against him. ³⁹But it is your custom for me to release to you one prisoner at the time of the Passover. Do you want me to release 'the king of the Jews'?"

⁴⁰They shouted back, "No, not him! Give us Barabbas!" Now Barabbas had taken part in a rebellion.

ADDRESSING QUESTIONS

18:39–40
Unseen Realities

Barabbas was guilty of a crime and deserving of death. Jesus was innocent and should have been released. But Jesus ended up dying—literally in Barabbas's place.

This exchange parallels a powerful spiritual transaction that occurred on the day Christ died. While hanging on the cross, Jesus took upon himself the sins of the world. God gave to his own Son the death sentence we owed for our rebellion. In that sense, Jesus died in our place that day. Because of his sacrifice, we, like Barabbas, can walk right out of our spiritual prison—if we simply receive the forgiveness and leadership of Christ.

Jesus Sentenced to be Crucified

19 Then Pilate took Jesus and had him flogged. ²The soldiers twisted together a crown of thorns and put it on his head. They clothed him in a purple robe ³and went up to him again and again, saying, "Hail, king of the Jews!" And they struck him in the face.

⁴Once more Pilate came out and said to the Jews, "Look, I am bringing him out to you to let you know that I find no basis for a charge against him." ⁵When Jesus came out wearing the crown of thorns and the purple robe, Pilate said to them, "Here is the man!"

⁶As soon as the chief priests and their officials saw him, they shouted, "Crucify! Crucify!"

But Pilate answered, "You take him and crucify him. As for me, I find no basis for a charge against him."

⁷The Jews insisted, "We have a law, and according to that law he must die, because he claimed to be the Son of God."

⁸When Pilate heard this, he was even more afraid, ⁹and he went back inside the palace. "Where do you come from?" he asked Jesus, but Jesus gave him no answer. ¹⁰"Do you refuse to speak to me?" Pilate said. "Don't you realize I have power either to free you or to crucify you?"

¹¹Jesus answered, "You would have no power over me if it were not given to you from above. Therefore the one who handed me over to you is guilty of a greater sin."

¹²From then on, Pilate tried to set Jesus free, but the Jews kept shouting, "If you let this man go, you are no friend of Caesar. Anyone who claims to be a king opposes Caesar."

¹³When Pilate heard this, he brought Jesus out and sat down on the judge's seat at a place known as the Stone Pavement (which in Aramaic is Gabbatha). ¹⁴It was the day of Preparation of Passover Week, about the sixth hour.

"Here is your king," Pilate said to the Jews.

¹⁵But they shouted, "Take him away! Take him away! Crucify him!"

"Shall I crucify your king?" Pilate asked.

"We have no king but Caesar," the chief priests answered.

¹⁶Finally Pilate handed him over to them to be crucified.

The Crucifixion

So the soldiers took charge of Jesus. ¹⁷Carrying his own cross, he went out to the place of the Skull (which in Aramaic is called Golgotha). ¹⁸Here they crucified him, and with him two others—one on each side and Jesus in the middle.

¹⁹Pilate had a notice prepared and fastened to the cross. It read: JESUS OF NAZARETH, THE KING OF THE JEWS. ²⁰Many of the Jews read this sign, for the place where Jesus was crucified was near the city, and the sign was written in Aramaic, Latin and Greek. ²¹The chief priests of the Jews protested to Pilate, "Do not write 'The King of the Jews,' but that this man claimed to be king of the Jews."

²²Pilate answered, "What I have written, I have written."

²³When the soldiers crucified Jesus, they took his clothes, dividing them into four shares, one for each of them, with the undergarment remaining. This garment was seamless, woven in one piece from top to bottom.

²⁴"Let's not tear it," they said to one another. "Let's decide by lot who will get it."

This happened that the scripture might be fulfilled which said,

> "They divided my garments among them
>   and cast lots for my clothing."[a]

So this is what the soldiers did.

²⁵Near the cross of Jesus stood his mother, his mother's sister, Mary the wife of Clopas, and Mary Magdalene. ²⁶When Jesus saw his mother there, and the disciple whom he loved standing nearby, he said to his mother, "Dear woman, here is your son," ²⁷and to the disciple, "Here is your mother." From that time on, this disciple took her into his home.

The Death of Jesus

²⁸Later, knowing that all was now completed, and so that the Scripture would be fulfilled, Jesus said, "I am thirsty." ²⁹A jar of wine vinegar was there, so they soaked a sponge in it, put the sponge on a stalk of the hyssop plant, and lifted it to Jesus' lips. ³⁰When he had received the drink, Jesus said, "It is finished." With that, he bowed his head and gave up his spirit.

³¹Now it was the day of Preparation, and the next day was to be a special Sabbath. Because the Jews did not want the bodies left on the crosses during the Sabbath, they asked Pilate to have the legs broken and the bodies taken down. ³²The soldiers therefore came and broke the legs of the first man who had been crucified with Jesus, and then those of the other. ³³But when they came to Jesus and found that he was already dead, they did not break his legs. ³⁴Instead, one of the soldiers pierced Jesus' side with a spear, bringing a sudden flow of blood and water. ³⁵The man who saw it has given testimony, and his testimony is true. He knows that he tells the truth, and he testifies so that you also may believe.

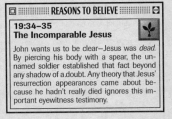

REASONS TO BELIEVE

19:34–35
The Incomparable Jesus

John wants us to be clear—Jesus was *dead*. By piercing his body with a spear, the unnamed soldier established that fact beyond any shadow of a doubt. Any theory that Jesus' resurrection appearances came about because he hadn't really died ignores this important eyewitness testimony.

³⁶These things happened so that the scripture would be fulfilled: "Not one of his bones will be broken,"[b] ³⁷and, as another scripture says, "They will look on the one they have pierced."[c]

a 24 Psalm 22:18   b 36 Exodus 12:46; Num. 9:12; Psalm 34:20   c 37 Zech. 12:10

The Burial of Jesus

38Later, Joseph of Arimathea asked Pilate for the body of Jesus. Now Joseph was a disciple of Jesus, but secretly because he feared the Jews. With Pilate's permission, he came and took the body away. **39**He was accompanied by Nicodemus, the man who earlier had visited Jesus at night. Nicodemus brought a mixture of myrrh and aloes, about seventy-five pounds.*a* **40**Taking Jesus' body, the two of them wrapped it, with the spices, in strips of linen. This was in accordance with Jewish burial customs. **41**At the

a39 Greek a hundred litrai (about 34 kilograms)

REASONS TO BELIEVE

19:23–24
The Amazing Bible

One of the distinguishing features of the Bible is its prophetic element. Centuries before Jesus' birth, a prophet named Isaiah penned several songs about a coming Servant. Though chosen by God, this Servant would be rejected by the very people he came to reach. Isaiah included incredible detail in his writings that is strikingly fulfilled in the life, death, and resurrection of Jesus.

Other Old Testament writers also made predictions about this coming Messiah. The events in this passage, for example, fulfill a prophecy written down some 1000 years earlier by Israel's King David (see Psalm chapter 22, verses 16–18 [page 672]).

The following chart shows some other amazing predictions that were fulfilled in Jesus' life. If Jesus had been a mere man, he couldn't have controlled many of these occurrences. The fact that they happened exactly as predicted proves that he is the fulfillment of these prophecies.

Event in Jesus' Life	Prophetic Passage
• Born in Bethlehem	Micah 5:2 (page 1213); fulfilled in Luke 2:4 – 7 (page 1339)
• Sold for 30 pieces of silver	Zechariah 11:13 (page 1246); fulfilled in Matthew 26:15 (page 1296)
• Betrayal money given to buy a potter's field	Zechariah 11:13 (page 1246); fulfilled in Matthew 27:6 (page 1299)
• Forsaken at the end of his life	Psalm 22:1 (page 670); fulfilled in Matthew 26:56 (page 1297)
• Silent when accused	Isaiah 53:7 (page 963); fulfilled in Matthew 27:12 – 14 (page 1299)
• Condemned with criminals	Isaiah 53:12 (page 963); fulfilled in Luke 23:32 – 33 (page 1377)
• Crucified (hands and feet pierced)	Psalm 22:16 (page 672); fulfilled in John 19:18 (page 1415)
• Mocked while he died	Psalm 22:7 – 8 (page 671); fulfilled in Luke 23:39 (page 1377)
• Raging thirst when dying	Psalm 22:15 (page 672); fulfilled in John 19:28 (page 1415)
• Died for our sins	Isaiah 53:4 – 6, 12 (page 962); fulfilled in John 19:30 (page 1415)
• Pierced after death	Isaiah 53:5 (page 962), Zechariah 12:10 (page 1247); fulfilled in Luke 23:46 (page 1377)
• Buried by a rich man	Isaiah 53:9 (page 963); fulfilled in Matthew 27:57 – 60 (page 1300)
• Suffering not the end (resurrection)	Isaiah 53:11 (page 963), Psalm 16:9 – 11 (page 664); fulfilled in Luke 24:1 – 8 (page 1378)

No other major world religion has prophetic writings that describe its leader in this kind of detail centuries before the leader appeared. Such prophecies give readers good reason to trust the Bible and recognize its divine origin.

place where Jesus was crucified, there was a garden, and in the garden a new tomb, in which no one had ever been laid. ⁴²Because it was the Jewish day of Preparation and since the tomb was nearby, they laid Jesus there.

The Empty Tomb

20 Early on the first day of the week, while it was still dark, Mary Magdalene went to the tomb and saw that the stone had been removed from the entrance. ²So she came running to Simon Peter and the other disciple, the one Jesus loved, and said, "They have taken the Lord out of the tomb, and we don't know where they have put him!"

³So Peter and the other disciple started for the tomb. ⁴Both were running, but the other disciple outran Peter and reached the tomb first. ⁵He bent over and looked in at the strips of linen lying there but did not go in. ⁶Then Simon Peter, who was behind him, arrived and went into the tomb. He saw the strips of linen lying there, ⁷as well as the burial cloth that had been around Jesus' head. The cloth was folded up by itself, separate from the linen. ⁸Finally the other disciple, who had reached the tomb first, also went inside. He saw and believed. ⁹(They still did not understand from Scripture that Jesus had to rise from the dead.)

Jesus Appears to Mary Magdalene

¹⁰Then the disciples went back to their homes, ¹¹but Mary stood outside the tomb crying. As she wept, she bent over to look into the tomb ¹²and saw two angels in white, seated where Jesus' body had been, one at the head and the other at the foot.

¹³They asked her, "Woman, why are you crying?"

"They have taken my Lord away," she said, "and I don't know where they have put him." ¹⁴At this, she turned around and saw Jesus standing there, but she did not realize that it was Jesus.

¹⁵"Woman," he said, "why are you crying? Who is it you are looking for?"

Thinking he was the gardener, she said, "Sir, if you have carried him away, tell me where you have put him, and I will get him."

¹⁶Jesus said to her, "Mary."

She turned toward him and cried out in Aramaic, "Rabboni!" (which means Teacher).

¹⁷Jesus said, "Do not hold on to me, for I have not yet returned to the Father. Go instead to my brothers and tell them, 'I am returning to my Father and your Father, to my God and your God.'"

¹⁸Mary Magdalene went to the disciples with the news: "I have seen the Lord!" And she told them that he had said these things to her.

Jesus Appears to His Disciples

¹⁹On the evening of that first day of the week, when the disciples were together, with the doors locked for fear of the Jews, Jesus came and stood among them and said, "Peace be with you!" ²⁰After he said this, he showed them his hands and side. The disciples were overjoyed when they saw the Lord.

²¹Again Jesus said, "Peace be with you! As the Father has sent me, I am sending you." ²²And with that he breathed on them and said, "Receive the Holy Spirit. ²³If you forgive anyone his sins, they are forgiven; if you do not forgive them, they are not forgiven."

Jesus Appears to Thomas

²⁴Now Thomas (called Didymus), one of the Twelve, was not with the disciples when Jesus came. ²⁵So the other disciples told him, "We have seen the Lord!"

But he said to them, "Unless I see the nail marks in his hands and put my finger where the nails were, and put my hand into his side, I will not believe it."

²⁶A week later his disciples were in the house again, and Thomas was with them.

20:1–31
The Incomparable Jesus

The resurrection of Jesus is the most fantastic event Christianity has ever asked the world to take seriously. If it isn't true, all of the claims of Jesus are irrelevant. If it is true, it substantiates all of Jesus' claims, and no other event in history has more significance. Establish the authenticity of the resurrection, and no other "son of God" need apply–the human race has its Savior.

As you read the account of the resurrection, notice that skeptics were everywhere. Jesus' disciples–especially Thomas–didn't expect to see him. Jesus' enemies didn't want to see him, and offered alternate–though easily refuted–explanations for the empty tomb. Let's look at two of those explanations.

Jesus' resurrection was just wishful thinking on the part of his disciples. They developed this myth to substantiate their claims.

Some modern critics speculate that the resurrection appearances were the disciples' hallucinations, which occurred because they worked themselves into a hysteria hoping that Jesus would come back from the dead. But that explanation doesn't take into account the disciples' overall misunderstanding of Jesus' resurrection predictions (see John chapter 16, verses 17–18).

After Jesus' death, the disciples didn't sit in anticipation of the resurrection. When Jesus appeared to most of them, they were hiding out in fear of the authorities (verses 19–20), not boldly proclaiming that their leader would return from the dead. Basically, the disciples didn't "get it" until after the fact. So lack of belief–not hysterical fantasizing–emerges as their state of mind before the resurrection.

But, for the sake of argument, let's say the disciples hallucinated. To refute their claim, their critics would only have had to go to the tomb and show everyone the body. The tomb, however, was empty. (*Note:* All of the world's religions have places of honor commemorating their dead founders. Only Christianity has an empty tomb.) Given the uncontested fact of a bodiless grave, another explanation surfaced.

Jesus' resurrection is an elaborate hoax. While the guards slept, the disciples came and stole the body, then told everyone that their leader was alive. (See Matthew chapter 28, verses 11–15 [page 1301].)

Many problems arise with this theory. For starters, the Jewish leaders of the day had taken great pains to ensure that the tomb could not be robbed (see Matthew chapter 27, verses 62–66 [page 1301]). Pilate himself placed those guards on special duty. And even if they had dozed off, how could the guards have known who robbed the tomb? They were supposedly sleeping!

This argument also ignores the disciples' fear of being caught and prosecuted by the Jewish leaders of the day. Verse 19 shows them all locked in a room together, hidden away in fear. These men weren't about to leave the building, let alone go up against armed guards to steal a body.

And what else but Jesus' resurrection could have transformed these disciples from timid cowards to bold advocates, preaching that Jesus was alive in the very city in which his murderers still held power? (See Acts chapter 2, verses 22–47 [page 1427].) Eventually, almost all of these men died martyrs' deaths. If this had been a hoax, wouldn't they have admitted to that fact when faced with the prospect of dying for it?

As a seeker trying to understand the most controversial claim of Christianity–that Jesus Christ, the Son of God, rose bodily from the grave–be sure to recognize its crucial importance in the context of world events. Explore all the theories you want; many more than these two have been posited over the centuries. But realize that in the 2000 years since Jesus' death, not one person has convincingly refuted the claims of the Bible on this score. Also realize that this event, the basis of Christianity, has changed millions upon millions of lives throughout the centuries.

Thomas, the disciple whose reputation as "the doubter" has dogged him for centuries, saw Jesus and believed. As you seek out the truth behind Christ's claims, remember his promise: "Blessed are those who have not seen and yet have believed" (verse 29).

Though the doors were locked, Jesus came and stood among them and said, "Peace be with you!" ²⁷Then he said to Thomas, "Put your finger here; see my hands. Reach out your hand and put it into my side. Stop doubting and believe."

²⁸Thomas said to him, "My Lord and my God!"

²⁹Then Jesus told him, "Because you have seen me, you have believed; blessed are those who have not seen and yet have believed."

³⁰Jesus did many other miraculous signs in the presence of his disciples, which are not recorded in this book. ³¹But these are written that you may *a* believe that Jesus is the Christ, the Son of God, and that by believing you may have life in his name.

Jesus and the Miraculous Catch of Fish

21 Afterward Jesus appeared again to his disciples, by the Sea of Tiberias.*b* It happened this way: ²Simon Peter, Thomas (called Didymus), Nathanael from Cana in Galilee, the sons of Zebedee, and two other disciples were together. ³"I'm going out to fish," Simon Peter told them, and they said, "We'll go with you." So they went out and got into the boat, but that night they caught nothing.

⁴Early in the morning, Jesus stood on the shore, but the disciples did not realize that it was Jesus.

⁵He called out to them, "Friends, haven't you any fish?"

"No," they answered.

⁶He said, "Throw your net on the right side of the boat and you will find some." When they did, they were unable to haul the net in because of the large number of fish.

⁷Then the disciple whom Jesus loved said to Peter, "It is the Lord!" As soon as Simon Peter heard him say, "It is the Lord," he wrapped his outer garment around him (for he had taken it off) and jumped into the water. ⁸The other disciples followed in the boat, towing the net full of fish, for they were not far from shore, about a hundred yards.*c* ⁹When they landed, they saw a fire of burning coals there with fish on it, and some bread.

¹⁰Jesus said to them, "Bring some of the fish you have just caught."

▒▒▒▒▒▒▒▒▒▒▒▒▒▒▒▒ REASONS TO BELIEVE ▒▒▒▒▒▒▒▒▒▒▒▒▒▒▒▒

21:12–19
The Incomparable Jesus

Ever wonder if you might push Jesus' patience to the limit and never get another chance? Peter's experience is instructive for those of us who are frightened that we've committed too great a sin to warrant Jesus' forgiveness.

Jesus—the champion of the second chance—sets the stage for Peter's restoration by preparing a breakfast of fish and bread. Perhaps the meal reminded Peter of Jesus' feeding the masses, and maybe the smell of the coals reminded him of the night he denied he knew Jesus while warming himself by a fire. Jesus reminds Peter not only of his failure, but also of their long and well-established relationship—one that has been sorely strained, but not destroyed.

Three times Jesus asks Peter to affirm his love, and three times Peter does so. Then Jesus gives Peter the charge to get back into the ministry. Jesus, the good shepherd, has finally turned Peter the fisherman into a shepherd himself. Peter's restoration is complete.

Jesus will do the same for you if you'll let him. He wants to make you his lifetime follower—his disciple. He'll even *remake* you as many times as is necessary.

Jesus is unlike any other person you'll ever meet. He will not—he *cannot*—let you down. He is, as John described him in the introduction of this book, "full of grace and truth" (chapter 1, verse 14). If you put your trust in him, you will not be disappointed.

---

a 31 Some manuscripts *may continue to*   *b 1* That is, Sea of Galilee   *c 8* Greek *about two hundred cubits* (about 90 meters)

¹¹Simon Peter climbed aboard and dragged the net ashore. It was full of large fish, 153, but even with so many the net was not torn. ¹²Jesus said to them, "Come and have breakfast." None of the disciples dared ask him, "Who are you?" They knew it was the Lord. ¹³Jesus came, took the bread and gave it to them, and did the same with the fish. ¹⁴This was now the third time Jesus appeared to his disciples after he was raised from the dead.

Jesus Reinstates Peter

¹⁵When they had finished eating, Jesus said to Simon Peter, "Simon son of John, do you truly love me more than these?"

"Yes, Lord," he said, "you know that I love you."

Jesus said, "Feed my lambs."

¹⁶Again Jesus said, "Simon son of John, do you truly love me?"

He answered, "Yes, Lord, you know that I love you."

Jesus said, "Take care of my sheep."

¹⁷The third time he said to him, "Simon son of John, do you love me?"

Peter was hurt because Jesus asked him the third time, "Do you love me?" He said, "Lord, you know all things; you know that I love you."

Jesus said, "Feed my sheep. ¹⁸I tell you the truth, when you were younger you dressed yourself and went where you wanted; but when you are old you will stretch out your hands, and someone else will dress you and lead you where you do not want to go." ¹⁹Jesus said this to indicate the kind of death by which Peter would glorify God. Then he said to him, "Follow me!"

²⁰Peter turned and saw that the disciple whom Jesus loved was following them. (This was the one who had leaned back against Jesus at the supper and had said, "Lord, who is going to betray you?") ²¹When Peter saw him, he asked, "Lord, what about him?"

²²Jesus answered, "If I want him to remain alive until I return, what is that to you? You must follow me." ²³Because of this, the rumor spread among the brothers that this disciple would not die. But Jesus did not say that he would not die; he only said, "If I want him to remain alive until I return, what is that to you?"

²⁴This is the disciple who testifies to these things and who wrote them down. We know that his testimony is true.

²⁵Jesus did many other things as well. If every one of them were written down, I suppose that even the whole world would not have room for the books that would be written.

EPILOGUE

The book you've just read is probably the most important book in the Bible. The most important person in the Bible is the one you've just read about. And the person God wants to affect through all this is the one reading these words right now—you!

Take a moment to turn back to chapter 3, verse 16 (page 1387). After reading through this book, you should know a lot more about Jesus, the Son of God. Will you accept his forgiveness and leadership in your life?

Whoever said "Your school years are the best years of your life" certainly didn't know me.

By the time I was in seventh grade, I was drinking heavily. Looking back I can see the beginnings of alcoholism in my life, even though I never would have admitted it. During my freshman year of high school I started smoking pot. I became involved in an unhealthy relationship with a fellow alcoholic who also had a drug problem. And before my sophomore year began, my parents' relationship ended in divorce. Between the substance abuse and the relationship problems I experienced, life was difficult. Shortly after my eighteenth birthday, I left a good job and began working in the adult entertainment industry.

My only philosophy on life and death was to do as much as I could of whatever I wanted and get the most out of life. I see now that those two statements contradict each other. As is the case with many people, I didn't realize that what I did had a direct effect on other people around me. By doing whatever I wanted, I was definitely not getting the most out of life.

By the end of my eighteenth year my best friend—my mom—had become seriously ill. Within the course of one month she was misdiagnosed with multiple sclerosis, mistreated, and was lying in a coma. After further testing the doctors determined that she had cancer, which had originated in her lungs (even though she was not a smoker) and spread throughout her body. She died about a month before my nineteenth birthday.

When Mom became ill, the seriousness of life and death finally dawned on me. The night before she died I asked Christ to come into my life and forgive me of all of my sins. It was amazing! The very next day my sister, her husband and I were able to comfort each other with God's love.

Unfortunately, I didn't give up any of my old ways. It wasn't long before I put God up on a shelf—a convenient distance away from the rest of my life.

It's incredible the way God works. One night after work, the girls and I went out drinking as usual. I was my normal self—swearing and drunk and looking for beautiful men. When I saw one, I went up to him and demanded his number. He gave it to me and added some Scripture at the bottom, along with a note saying "I am a Christian." Little did I know that God would use that stranger to get to me. I ran back to God and took him off that shelf.

I've been a devoted follower of Christ for about eight months now. I know I'm not where I want to be in my relationship with God, but I'm sure it's better than where I was. With God's help, I've been able to give up many of my former ways, including drinking, drugs, and unhealthy relationships. I've also traded my career in adult entertainment for a management position in a retail store.

My life has never been better! I've never known security or love like this. I have so much to be thankful for. I can't believe God has forgiven me for all that I've done, but he has. He walks with me day by day, providing me with everything I need to survive and picking me up when I fall along the way.

"Father, I'm so grateful I have you. Thank you so much, and please know that I love you!"

Introduction

THE BOTTOM LINE

The movie is over. As the credits roll and the lights slowly come up, you sit almost motionless, still captivated by the story. What happens next? Is there a sequel in the works? People who read the story of Jesus have the same reaction. *And this book is the sequel!*

Acts follows the trail of Jesus' disciples as they perform amazing miracles and preach to multitudes of people. It introduces you to Paul, a missionary who once viciously persecuted Jesus' followers. The story of Paul's conversion — including a flash of light from the sky and Jesus' own voice — is one of the most dramatic stories in the whole Bible. In the Gospels, Jesus promised his disciples that he would never leave them, even though he would no longer be with them physically. In this book, that promise is fulfilled. The Holy Spirit comes to dwell inside the disciples, as he does all of Jesus' followers today.

CENTRAL IDEAS

- The Holy Spirit has amazing power to change people's lives.
- The church spread as incredible numbers of new converts responded to the challenge of the gospel.
- The disciples faithfully followed Jesus' directives, even though doing so brought suffering.
- The gospel of Christ is for all people.

OUTLINE

1 Peter and the beginnings of the Jerusalem church (chs. 1–12)
2 Paul and the expansion of the church (chs. 13–28)

TITLE

The title of this book is short for "The Acts of the Apostles," the events that this book describes.

AUTHOR AND READERS

Luke, the gospel writer, also penned these words to chronicle the events of the early church.

While walking along a deserted beach one morning, a man spotted a little boy off in the distance throwing objects into the ocean. As the hiker got closer, he noticed that the boy was picking up starfish. The waves had washed up literally hundreds of thousands of them the night before.

Puzzled, he approached the boy. "Hello there. I was wondering what you're doing."

"I'm throwing starfish back into the ocean," answered the lad. "Otherwise, they'll die."

"Yes that's true," the hiker replied, "but look around you. There are so many of them on this beach. You can't help even a tiny fraction of them. What difference will it make?"

The boy smiled, bent down, and picked up another starfish. As he threw it back into the sea, he replied, "I bet it'll make a difference to that one!"

Making a difference—one person at a time. That's a picture of what God wants to do for all of us, and it's also a picture of what he wants all of us to do.

"I bet it'll make a difference to that one!"

After his resurrection, Jesus appeared to his disciples and gave them a mission that every Christ-follower must accept: to tell every human being on earth—one at a time—that he or she matters to God and that he or she can be forgiven and come to know him personally.

At first, such a mission seems unachievable. *How could I possibly make any difference when it comes to reaching the whole world with the message of Jesus?* It's like trying to.... well, like trying to rescue thousands of starfish washed up on a beach.

But remember this: You wouldn't even be in a position to consider your part in fulfilling God's purposes if someone hadn't talked to you. And if someone hadn't told that person. And if someone else hadn't told the person before, and so on. An unbroken chain of people sharing this message stretches from the first century right up to *you*.

Want a better picture of how Jesus set in motion a force that has gathered enough steam to propel the truth across the ages straight to you? Turn to Acts chapter 1, verse 8 (page 1425). Jesus' words might even inspire you to get in on the action and help spread his message to a whole new generation of seekers.

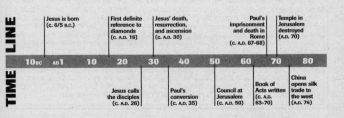

TIME LINE

10 BC	AD 1	10	20	30	40	50	60	70	80

Jesus is born (c. 6/5 B.C.)

First definite reference to diamonds (c. A.D. 16)

Jesus' death, resurrection, and ascension (c. A.D. 30)

Paul's imprisonment and death in Rome (c. A.D. 67–68)

Temple in Jerusalem destroyed (A.D. 70)

Jesus calls the disciples (c. A.D. 26)

Paul's conversion (c. A.D. 35)

Council at Jerusalem (c. A.D. 50)

Book of Acts written (c. A.D. 63–70)

China opens silk trade to the west (A.D. 74)

ACTS

Jesus Taken Up Into Heaven

1 In my former book, Theophilus, I wrote about all that Jesus began to do and to teach ²until the day he was taken up to heaven, after giving instructions through the Holy Spirit to the apostles he had chosen. ³After his suffering, he showed himself to these men and gave many convincing proofs that he was alive. He appeared to them over a period of forty days and spoke about the kingdom of God. ⁴On one occasion, while he was eating with them, he gave them this command: "Do not leave Jerusalem, but wait for the gift my Father promised, which you have heard me speak about. ⁵For John baptized with*ᵃ* water, but in a few days you will be baptized with the Holy Spirit."

⁶So when they met together, they asked him, "Lord, are you at this time going to restore the kingdom to Israel?"

ᵃ5 Or in

□ ⸬⸬⸬⸬⸬⸬⸬⸬⸬⸬⸬⸬⸬ **ADDRESSING QUESTIONS** ⸬⸬⸬⸬⸬⸬⸬⸬⸬⸬⸬⸬⸬ **↔**

1:8
Human Experience

Q

"Why am I here?"

The answer to that question—even if a person says "I don't know"—leads to the creation of a powerful mental map that his or her life's journey will inevitably follow.

After Jesus' resurrection his followers must have asked this same question. They probably wondered what was going to happen next. It's not hard to imagine them thinking, *If you're leaving, Jesus, why are we staying? What is our purpose here on earth?*

Jesus had a plan for his disciples—a plan to take over the world. But instead of overthrowing the Roman Empire militarily, he would conquer the hearts of men and women—one by one. His "army" would be those who knew him. Their "weapon" would be the message of forgiveness and new life offered by Christ himself. These "commandos" would relay God's commands and take captives with God's compassion—first their neighbors, then individuals across town, and finally people in other countries. Eventually they would tell the whole world about Jesus.

The words of verse 8, a variation on what is often called Jesus' "Great Commission," provide a purpose and direction for all of Jesus' followers. In light of the value that God's followers place on knowing him, what could be more important than helping others know him? Introducing someone else to God would bring that person into a relationship that would have eternal benefits.

And what about you? Consider for a moment the Bible you're now holding. Perhaps someone gave it to you, or perhaps you bought it out of your own spiritual curiosity. Either way, people who care about you and value Jesus' message passed it on to you in this written form. Yet before they could tell you about Jesus, someone else explained his story to them. And before those people became believers, there were others who in turn were taught by Jesus' followers before them. *An unbroken line of people relaying Jesus' truth goes all the way back to Jesus standing with his disciples on that hillside two thousand years ago—and it ends right here, in this moment, with you reading these words!*

If you accept this message as truth to trust, you'll begin an extraordinary adventure. You will fulfill your main purpose for living by experiencing all that Jesus has in mind for you—especially by sharing that reality with others. You'll be joining a continuous succession of believers who are serious about taking their leader's message "to the ends of the earth." That's why Jesus left those early followers on earth, and that's why he's eager to begin his work through you.

⁷He said to them: "It is not for you to know the times or dates the Father has set by his own authority. ⁸But you will receive power when the Holy Spirit comes on you; and you will be my witnesses in Jerusalem, and in all Judea and Samaria, and to the ends of the earth."

⁹After he said this, he was taken up before their very eyes, and a cloud hid him from their sight.

¹⁰They were looking intently up into the sky as he was going, when suddenly two men dressed in white stood beside them. ¹¹"Men of Galilee," they said, "why do you stand here looking into the sky? This same Jesus, who has been taken from you into heaven, will come back in the same way you have seen him go into heaven."

Matthias Chosen to Replace Judas

¹²Then they returned to Jerusalem from the hill called the Mount of Olives, a Sabbath day's walk*a* from the city. ¹³When they arrived, they went upstairs to the room where they were staying. Those present were Peter, John, James and Andrew; Philip and Thomas, Bartholomew and Matthew; James son of Alphaeus and Simon the Zealot, and Judas son of James. ¹⁴They all joined together constantly in prayer, along with the women and Mary the mother of Jesus, and with his brothers.

¹⁵In those days Peter stood up among the believers*b* (a group numbering about a hundred and twenty) ¹⁶and said, "Brothers, the Scripture had to be fulfilled which the Holy Spirit spoke long ago through the mouth of David concerning Judas, who served as guide for those who arrested Jesus— ¹⁷he was one of our number and shared in this ministry."

¹⁸(With the reward he got for his wickedness, Judas bought a field; there he fell headlong, his body burst open and all his intestines spilled out. ¹⁹Everyone in Jerusalem heard about this, so they called that field in their language Akeldama, that is, Field of Blood.)

²⁰"For," said Peter, "it is written in the book of Psalms,

> " 'May his place be deserted;
>   let there be no one to dwell in it,'*c*

and,

> " 'May another take his place of leadership.'*d*

¹Therefore it is necessary to choose one of the men who have been with us the whole time the Lord Jesus went in and out among us, ²²beginning from John's baptism to the time when Jesus was taken up from us. For one of these must become a witness with us of his resurrection."

²³So they proposed two men: Joseph called Barsabbas (also known as Justus) and Matthias. ²⁴Then they prayed, "Lord, you know everyone's heart. Show us which of these two you have chosen ²⁵to take over this apostolic ministry, which Judas left to go where he belongs." ²⁶Then they cast lots, and the lot fell to Matthias; so he was added to the eleven apostles.

The Holy Spirit Comes at Pentecost

2 When the day of Pentecost came, they were all together in one place. ²Suddenly a sound like the blowing of a violent wind came from heaven and filled the whole house where they were sitting. ³They saw what seemed to be tongues of fire that separated and came to rest on each of them. ⁴All of them were filled with the Holy Spirit and began to speak in other tongues*e* as the Spirit enabled them.

⁵Now there were staying in Jerusalem God-fearing Jews from every nation under

12 That is, about 3/4 mile (about 1,100 meters)   *b 15* Greek *brothers*   *c 20* Psalm 69:25   *d 20* Psalm 109:8
4 Or *languages;* also in verse 11

heaven. ⁶When they heard this sound, a crowd came together in bewilderment, because each one heard them speaking in his own language. ⁷Utterly amazed, they asked: "Are not all these men who are speaking Galileans? ⁸Then how is it that each of us hears them in his own native language? ⁹Parthians, Medes and Elamites; residents of Mesopotamia, Judea and Cappadocia, Pontus and Asia, ¹⁰Phrygia and Pamphylia, Egypt and the parts of Libya near Cyrene; visitors from Rome ¹¹(both Jews and converts to Judaism); Cretans and Arabs—we hear them declaring the wonders of God in our own tongues!" ¹²Amazed and perplexed, they asked one another, "What does this mean?"

¹³Some, however, made fun of them and said, "They have had too much wine.ᵃ"

Peter Addresses the Crowd

¹⁴Then Peter stood up with the Eleven, raised his voice and addressed the crowd: "Fellow Jews and all of you who live in Jerusalem, let me explain this to you; listen carefully to what I say. ¹⁵These men are not drunk, as you suppose. It's only nine in the morning! ¹⁶No, this is what was spoken by the prophet Joel:

> ¹⁷ 'In the last days, God says,
>   I will pour out my Spirit on all people.
> Your sons and daughters will prophesy,
>   your young men will see visions,
>   your old men will dream dreams.
> ¹⁸Even on my servants, both men and women,
>   I will pour out my Spirit in those days,
>   and they will prophesy.
> ¹⁹I will show wonders in the heaven above
>   and signs on the earth below,
>   blood and fire and billows of smoke.
> ²⁰The sun will be turned to darkness
>   and the moon to blood
>   before the coming of the great and glorious day of the Lord.

ᵃ13 Or sweet wine

▢ ▦▦▦▦▦▦▦▦▦▦▦▦ DISCOVERING GOD ▦▦▦▦▦▦▦▦▦▦▦▦ ▣

2:14–40
Jesus, the God-Man

This "sermon" is the first by one of Jesus' followers to be recorded in the Bible. It is of particular interest to seekers because in it, Peter succinctly touches on virtually every important aspect of Christianity. Grasp this message, and you'll have a good handle on what the Christian faith is all about. Among the points Peter mentions:

- Jesus did miracles and was unlike any other person who has ever lived (verse 22).
- Jesus was a real, historical person. He suffered, died, and was raised from death (verses 23–24). As such, the Christian message fulfills the plan that God began long before Jesus' life on earth.
- The Jewish prophets made specific prophecies about Jesus before he was born, giving proof that the Bible is God's Word (verses 16–21 and 25–28).
- Jesus is Lord (Ruler of all, God in a human body) and Christ (Messiah, the promised Deliverer of Israel [verse 36]).
- Trust in Jesus—not yourself—for salvation (verse 38).
- God wants to dwell in you through the Holy Spirit (verses 38–39).
- The rest of the world is headed for disaster apart from God. Don't get entangled by its corruption (verse 40).

²¹And everyone who calls
    on the name of the Lord will be saved.'ᵃ

²²"Men of Israel, listen to this: Jesus of Nazareth was a man accredited by God to you by miracles, wonders and signs, which God did among you through him, as you yourselves know. ²³This man was handed over to you by God's set purpose and foreknowledge; and you, with the help of wicked men,ᵇ put him to death by nailing him to the cross. ²⁴But God raised him from the dead, freeing him from the agony of death, because it was impossible for death to keep its hold on him. ²⁵David said about him:

    " 'I saw the Lord always before me.
        Because he is at my right hand,
        I will not be shaken.
²⁶Therefore my heart is glad and my tongue rejoices;
        my body also will live in hope,
²⁷because you will not abandon me to the grave,
        nor will you let your Holy One see decay.
²⁸You have made known to me the paths of life;
        you will fill me with joy in your presence.'ᶜ

²⁹"Brothers, I can tell you confidently that the patriarch David died and was buried, and his tomb is here to this day. ³⁰But he was a prophet and knew that God had promised him on oath that he would place one of his descendants on his throne. ³¹Seeing what was ahead, he spoke of the resurrection of the Christ,ᵈ that he was not abandoned to the grave, nor did his body see decay. ³²God has raised this Jesus to life, and we are all witnesses of the fact. ³³Exalted to the right hand of God, he has received from the Father the promised Holy Spirit and has poured out what you now see and hear. ³⁴For David did not ascend to heaven, and yet he said,

    " 'The Lord said to my Lord:
        "Sit at my right hand
³⁵until I make your enemies
        a footstool for your feet." 'ᵉ

³⁶"Therefore let all Israel be assured of this: God has made this Jesus, whom you crucified, both Lord and Christ."

³⁷When the people heard this, they were cut to the heart and said to Peter and the other apostles, "Brothers, what shall we do?"

³⁸Peter replied, "Repent and be baptized, every one of you, in the name of Jesus Christ for the forgiveness of your sins. And you will receive the gift of the Holy Spirit. ³⁹The promise is for you and your children and for all who are far off—for all whom the Lord our God will call."

⁴⁰With many other words he warned them; and he pleaded with them, "Save yourselves from this corrupt generation." ⁴¹Those who accepted his message were baptized, and about three thousand were added to their number that day.

The Fellowship of the Believers

⁴²They devoted themselves to the apostles' teaching and to the fellowship, to the breaking of bread and to prayer. ⁴³Everyone was filled with awe, and many wonders and miraculous signs were done by the apostles. ⁴⁴All the believers were together and had everything in common. ⁴⁵Selling their possessions and goods, they gave to anyone as he had need. ⁴⁶Every day they continued to meet together in the temple courts. They broke bread in their homes and ate together with glad and sincere hearts, ⁴⁷praising God and

---

ᵃ21 Joel 2:28-32   ᵇ23 Or of those not having the law (that is, Gentiles)   ᶜ28 Psalm 16:8-11   ᵈ31 Or Messiah.
"The Christ" (Greek) and "the Messiah" (Hebrew) both mean "the Anointed One"; also in verse 36.   ᵉ35 Psalm 110:1

enjoying the favor of all the people. And the Lord added to their number daily those who were being saved.

Peter Heals the Crippled Beggar

3 One day Peter and John were going up to the temple at the time of prayer—at three in the afternoon. ²Now a man crippled from birth was being carried to the temple gate called Beautiful, where he was put every day to beg from those going into the temple courts. ³When he saw Peter and John about to enter, he asked them for money. ⁴Peter looked straight at him, as did John. Then Peter said, "Look at us!" ⁵So the man gave them his attention, expecting to get something from them.

⁶Then Peter said, "Silver or gold I do not have, but what I have I give you. In the name of Jesus Christ of Nazareth, walk." ⁷Taking him by the right hand, he helped him up, and instantly the man's feet and ankles became strong. ⁸He jumped to his feet and began to walk. Then he went with them into the temple courts, walking and jumping, and praising God. ⁹When all the people saw him walking and praising God, ¹⁰they recognized him as the same man who used to sit begging at the temple gate called Beautiful, and they were filled with wonder and amazement at what had happened to him.

Peter Speaks to the Onlookers

¹¹While the beggar held on to Peter and John, all the people were astonished and came running to them in the place called Solomon's Colonnade. ¹²When Peter saw this, he said to them: "Men of Israel, why does this surprise you? Why do you stare at us as if by our own power or godliness we had made this man walk? ¹³The God of Abraham, Isaac and Jacob, the God of our fathers, has glorified his servant Jesus. You handed him over to be killed, and you disowned him before Pilate, though he had decided to let him go. ¹⁴You disowned the Holy and Righteous One and asked that a murderer be released to you. ¹⁵You killed the author of life, but God raised him from the dead. We are witnesses of this. ¹⁶By faith in the name of Jesus, this man whom you see and know was made strong. It is Jesus' name and the faith that comes through him that has given this complete healing to him, as you can all see.

¹⁷"Now, brothers, I know that you acted in ignorance, as did your leaders. ¹⁸But this is how God fulfilled what he had foretold through all the prophets, saying that his Christ[a] would suffer. ¹⁹Repent, then, and turn to God, so that your sins may be wiped out, that times of refreshing may come from the Lord, ²⁰and that he may send the Christ, who has been appointed for you—even Jesus. ²¹He must remain in heaven until the time comes for God to restore everything, as he promised long ago through his holy prophets. ²²For Moses said, 'The Lord your God will raise up for you a prophet like me from among your own people; you must listen to everything he tells you. ²³Anyone who does not listen to him will be completely cut off from among his people.'[b]

²⁴"Indeed, all the prophets from Samuel on, as many as have spoken, have foretold these days. ²⁵And you are heirs of the prophets and of the covenant God made with your fathers. He said to Abraham, 'Through your offspring all peoples on earth will be blessed.'[c] ²⁶When God raised up his servant, he sent him first to you to bless you by turning each of you from your wicked ways."

Peter and John Before the Sanhedrin

4 The priests and the captain of the temple guard and the Sadducees came up to Peter and John while they were speaking to the people. ²They were greatly disturbed because the apostles were teaching the people and proclaiming in Jesus the resurrection of the dead. ³They seized Peter and John, and because it was evening, they put them in jail until the next day. ⁴But many who heard the message believed, and the number of men grew to about five thousand.

---

a 18 Or *Messiah*; also in verse 20   *b 23* Deut. 18:15,18,19   *c 25* Gen. 22:18; 26:4

⁵The next day the rulers, elders and teachers of the law met in Jerusalem. ⁶Annas the high priest was there, and so were Caiaphas, John, Alexander and the other men of the high priest's family. ⁷They had Peter and John brought before them and began to question them: "By what power or what name did you do this?"

⁸Then Peter, filled with the Holy Spirit, said to them: "Rulers and elders of the people! ⁹If we are being called to account today for an act of kindness shown to a cripple and are asked how he was healed, ¹⁰then know this, you and all the people of Israel: It is by the name of Jesus Christ of Nazareth, whom you crucified but whom God raised from the dead, that this man stands before you healed. ¹¹He is

> " 'the stone you builders rejected,
>   which has become the capstone.ᵃ ' ᵇ

¹²Salvation is found in no one else, for there is no other name under heaven given to men by which we must be saved."

¹³When they saw the courage of Peter and John and realized that they were unschooled, ordinary men, they were astonished and they took note that these men had been with Jesus. ¹⁴But since they could see the man who had been healed standing there with them, there was nothing they could say. ¹⁵So they ordered them to withdraw from the Sanhedrin and then conferred together. ¹⁶"What are we going to do with these men?" they asked. "Everybody living in Jerusalem knows they have done an outstanding miracle, and we cannot deny it. ¹⁷But to stop this thing from spreading any further among the people, we must warn these men to speak no longer to anyone in this name."

¹⁸Then they called them in again and commanded them not to speak or teach at all in the name of Jesus. ¹⁹But Peter and John replied, "Judge for yourselves whether it is right in God's sight to obey us rather than God. ²⁰For we cannot help speaking about what we have seen and heard."

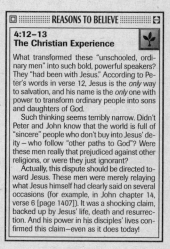

REASONS TO BELIEVE

4:12–13
The Christian Experience

What transformed these "unschooled, ordinary men" into such bold, powerful speakers? They "had been with Jesus." According to Peter's words in verse 12, Jesus is the *only* way to salvation, and his name is the *only* one with power to transform ordinary people into sons and daughters of God.

Such thinking seems terribly narrow. Didn't Peter and John know that the world is full of "sincere" people who don't buy into Jesus' deity – who follow "other paths to God"? Were these men really that prejudiced against other religions, or were they just ignorant?

Actually, this dispute should be directed toward Jesus. These men were merely relaying what Jesus himself had clearly said on several occasions (for example, in John chapter 14, verse 6 [page 1407]). It was a shocking claim, backed up by Jesus' life, death and resurrection. And his power in his disciples' lives confirmed this claim—even as it does today!

²¹After further threats they let them go. They could not decide how to punish them, because all the people were praising God for what had happened. ²²For the man who was miraculously healed was over forty years old.

The Believers' Prayer

²³On their release, Peter and John went back to their own people and reported all that the chief priests and elders had said to them. ²⁴When they heard this, they raised their voices together in prayer to God. "Sovereign Lord," they said, "you made the heaven and the earth and the sea, and everything in them. ²⁵You spoke by the Holy Spirit through the mouth of your servant, our father David:

ᵃ11 Or cornerstone   ᵇ11 Psalm 118:22

" 'Why do the nations rage
    and the peoples plot in vain?
²⁶The kings of the earth take their stand
    and the rulers gather together
  against the Lord
    and against his Anointed One.ᵃᵇ

²⁷Indeed Herod and Pontius Pilate met together with the Gentiles and the peopleᶜ of Israel in this city to conspire against your holy servant Jesus, whom you anointed. ²⁸They did what your power and will had decided beforehand should happen. ²⁹Now, Lord, consider their threats and enable your servants to speak your word with great boldness. ³⁰Stretch out your hand to heal and perform miraculous signs and wonders through the name of your holy servant Jesus."

³¹After they prayed, the place where they were meeting was shaken. And they were all filled with the Holy Spirit and spoke the word of God boldly.

The Believers Share Their Possessions

³²All the believers were one in heart and mind. No one claimed that any of his possessions was his own, but they shared everything they had. ³³With great power the apostles continued to testify to the resurrection of the Lord Jesus, and much grace was upon them all. ³⁴There were no needy persons among them. For from time to time those who owned lands or houses sold them, brought the money from the sales ³⁵and put it at the apostles' feet, and it was distributed to anyone as he had need.

³⁶Joseph, a Levite from Cyprus, whom the apostles called Barnabas (which means Son of Encouragement), ³⁷sold a field he owned and brought the money and put it at the apostles' feet.

Ananias and Sapphira

5 Now a man named Ananias, together with his wife Sapphira, also sold a piece of property. ²With his wife's full knowledge he kept back part of the money for himself, but brought the rest and put it at the apostles' feet.

³Then Peter said, "Ananias, how is it that Satan has so filled your heart that you have lied to the Holy Spirit and have kept for yourself some of the money you received for the land? ⁴Didn't it belong to you before it was sold? And after it was sold, wasn't the money at your disposal? What made you think of doing such a thing? You have not lied to men but to God."

⁵When Ananias heard this, he fell down and died. And great fear seized all who heard what had happened. ⁶Then the young men came forward, wrapped up his body, and carried him out and buried him.

⁷About three hours later his wife came in, not knowing what had happened. ⁸Peter asked her, "Tell me, is this the price you and Ananias got for the land?"

"Yes," she said, "that is the price."

⁹Peter said to her, "How could you agree to test the Spirit of the Lord? Look! The feet of the men who buried your husband are at the door, and they will carry you out also."

¹⁰At that moment she fell down at his feet and died. Then the young men came in and, finding her dead, carried her out and buried her beside her husband. ¹¹Great fear seized the whole church and all who heard about these events.

The Apostles Heal Many

¹²The apostles performed many miraculous signs and wonders among the people. And all the believers used to meet together in Solomon's Colonnade. ¹³No one else dared join

---

ᵃ26 That is, Christ or Messiah   ᵇ26 Psalm 2:1,2   ᶜ27 The Greek is plural

them, even though they were highly regarded by the people. ¹⁴Nevertheless, more and more men and women believed in the Lord and were added to their number. ¹⁵As a result, people brought the sick into the streets and laid them on beds and mats so that at least Peter's shadow might fall on some of them as he passed by. ¹⁶Crowds gathered also from the towns around Jerusalem, bringing their sick and those tormented by evil*ᵃ* spirits, and all of them were healed.

The Apostles Persecuted

¹⁷Then the high priest and all his associates, who were members of the party of the Sadducees, were filled with jealousy. ¹⁸They arrested the apostles and put them in the public jail. ¹⁹But during the night an angel of the Lord opened the doors of the jail and brought them out. ²⁰"Go, stand in the temple courts," he said, "and tell the people the full message of this new life."

²¹At daybreak they entered the temple courts, as they had been told, and began to teach the people.

When the high priest and his associates arrived, they called together the Sanhedrin— the full assembly of the elders of Israel—and sent to the jail for the apostles. ²²But on arriving at the jail, the officers did not find them there. So they went back and reported, ²³"We found the jail securely locked, with the guards standing at the doors; but when we opened them, we found no one inside." ²⁴On hearing this report, the captain of the temple guard and the chief priests were puzzled, wondering what would come of this.

²⁵Then someone came and said, "Look! The men you put in jail are standing in the temple courts teaching the people." ²⁶At that, the captain went with his officers and brought the apostles. They did not use force, because they feared that the people would stone them.

²⁷Having brought the apostles, they made them appear before the Sanhedrin to be questioned by the high priest. ²⁸"We gave you strict orders not to teach in this name," he said. "Yet you have filled Jerusalem with your teaching and are determined to make us guilty of this man's blood."

²⁹Peter and the other apostles replied: "We must obey God rather than men! ³⁰The God of our fathers raised Jesus from the dead—whom you had killed by hanging him on a tree. ³¹God exalted him to his own right hand as Prince and Savior that he might give repentance and forgiveness of sins to Israel. ³²We are witnesses of these things, and so is the Holy Spirit, whom God has given to those who obey him."

³³When they heard this, they were furious and wanted to put them to death. ³⁴But a Pharisee named Gamaliel, a teacher of the law, who was honored by all the people, stood up in the Sanhedrin and ordered that the men be put outside for a little while. ³⁵Then he addressed them: "Men of Israel, consider carefully what you intend to do to these men. ³⁶Some time ago Theudas appeared, claiming to be somebody, and about four hundred men rallied to him. He was killed, all his followers were dispersed, and it all came to nothing. ³⁷After him, Judas the Galilean appeared in the days of the census and led a band of people in revolt. He too was killed, and all his followers were scattered. ³⁸Therefore, in the present case I advise you: Leave these men alone! Let them go! For if their purpose or activity is of human origin, it will fail. ³⁹But if it is from God, you will not be able to stop these men; you will only find yourselves fighting against God."

⁴⁰His speech persuaded them. They called the apostles in and had them flogged. Then they ordered them not to speak in the name of Jesus, and let them go.

⁴¹The apostles left the Sanhedrin, rejoicing because they had been counted worthy of suffering disgrace for the Name. ⁴²Day after day, in the temple courts and from house to

ᵃ16 Greek *unclean*

house, they never stopped teaching and proclaiming the good news that Jesus is the Christ.*a*

The Choosing of the Seven

6 In those days when the number of disciples was increasing, the Grecian Jews among them complained against the Hebraic Jews because their widows were being overlooked in the daily distribution of food. ²So the Twelve gathered all the disciples together and said, "It would not be right for us to neglect the ministry of the word of God in order to wait on tables. ³Brothers, choose seven men from among you who are known to be full of the Spirit and wisdom. We will turn this responsibility over to them ⁴and will give our attention to prayer and the ministry of the word."

⁵This proposal pleased the whole group. They chose Stephen, a man full of faith and of the Holy Spirit; also Philip, Procorus, Nicanor, Timon, Parmenas, and Nicolas from Antioch, a convert to Judaism. ⁶They presented these men to the apostles, who prayed and laid their hands on them.

⁷So the word of God spread. The number of disciples in Jerusalem increased rapidly, and a large number of priests became obedient to the faith.

Stephen Seized

⁸Now Stephen, a man full of God's grace and power, did great wonders and miraculous signs among the people. ⁹Opposition arose, however, from members of the Synagogue of the Freedmen (as it was called)—Jews of Cyrene and Alexandria as well as the provinces of Cilicia and Asia. These men began to argue with Stephen, ¹⁰but they could not stand up against his wisdom or the Spirit by whom he spoke.

¹¹Then they secretly persuaded some men to say, "We have heard Stephen speak words of blasphemy against Moses and against God."

¹²So they stirred up the people and the elders and the teachers of the law. They seized Stephen and brought him before the Sanhedrin. ¹³They produced false witnesses, who testified, "This fellow never stops speaking against this holy place and against the law. ¹⁴For we have heard him say that this Jesus of Nazareth will destroy this place and change the customs Moses handed down to us."

¹⁵All who were sitting in the Sanhedrin looked intently at Stephen, and they saw that his face was like the face of an angel.

▣ ▦▦▦▦ REASONS TO BELIEVE ▦▦▦▦ ⬌

5:41–42
The Christian Experience

If the original purpose of Christianity had been to make life easier, Peter and the other apostles would probably have been checking the "fine print" for an escape clause! But they knew, after following Jesus and watching his example, that suffering is part of our human experience. They also knew that following Christ could at times make life more difficult.

So why did they go on? Because there is no one like Jesus and there is no adventure like following him. Jesus' followers take the bad with the good, much as a loving spouse stays faithful "for better or for worse."

The early Christians frequently faced severe persecution. This book and other early records abound with moving accounts of people who preferred to be punished or even killed rather than deny Jesus (see chapter 7, verses 54–60 [page 1434], for a story of a man forgiving his murderers even as they stone him to death).

In our own day, when some people are embarrassed to even mention spiritual matters among peers, such stories of courage serve as powerful evidence that Christianity is true. Jesus' message has radically transformed lives for thousands of years. Those who have accepted his message and have lived in the hope that it provides find that it is worth much more than anything this world has to offer—even life itself.

---

a 42 Or Messiah

Stephen's Speech to the Sanhedrin

7 Then the high priest asked him, "Are these charges true?" ²To this he replied: "Brothers and fathers, listen to me! The God of glory appeared to our father Abraham while he was still in Mesopotamia, before he lived in Haran. ³'Leave your country and your people,' God said, 'and go to the land I will show you.'ᵃ

⁴"So he left the land of the Chaldeans and settled in Haran. After the death of his father, God sent him to this land where you are now living. ⁵He gave him no inheritance here, not even a foot of ground. But God promised him that he and his descendants after him would possess the land, even though at that time Abraham had no child. ⁶God spoke to him in this way: 'Your descendants will be strangers in a country not their own, and they will be enslaved and mistreated four hundred years. ⁷But I will punish the nation they serve as slaves,' God said, 'and afterward they will come out of that country and worship me in this place.'ᵇ ⁸Then he gave Abraham the covenant of circumcision. And Abraham became the father of Isaac and circumcised him eight days after his birth. Later Isaac became the father of Jacob, and Jacob became the father of the twelve patriarchs.

⁹"Because the patriarchs were jealous of Joseph, they sold him as a slave into Egypt. But God was with him ¹⁰and rescued him from all his troubles. He gave Joseph wisdom and enabled him to gain the goodwill of Pharaoh king of Egypt; so he made him ruler over Egypt and all his palace.

¹¹"Then a famine struck all Egypt and Canaan, bringing great suffering, and our fathers could not find food. ¹²When Jacob heard that there was grain in Egypt, he sent our fathers on their first visit. ¹³On their second visit, Joseph told his brothers who he was, and Pharaoh learned about Joseph's family. ¹⁴After this, Joseph sent for his father Jacob and his whole family, seventy-five in all. ¹⁵Then Jacob went down to Egypt, where he and our fathers died. ¹⁶Their bodies were brought back to Shechem and placed in the tomb that Abraham had bought from the sons of Hamor at Shechem for a certain sum of money.

¹⁷"As the time drew near for God to fulfill his promise to Abraham, the number of our people in Egypt greatly increased. ¹⁸Then another king, who knew nothing about Joseph, became ruler of Egypt. ¹⁹He dealt treacherously with our people and oppressed our forefathers by forcing them to throw out their newborn babies so that they would die.

²⁰"At that time Moses was born, and he was no ordinary child.ᶜ For three months he was cared for in his father's house. ²¹When he was placed outside, Pharaoh's daughter took him and brought him up as her own son. ²²Moses was educated in all the wisdom of the Egyptians and was powerful in speech and action.

²³"When Moses was forty years old, he decided to visit his fellow Israelites. ²⁴He saw one of them being mistreated by an Egyptian, so he went to his defense and avenged him by killing the Egyptian. ²⁵Moses thought that his own people would realize that God was using him to rescue them, but they did not. ²⁶The next day Moses came upon two Israelites who were fighting. He tried to reconcile them by saying, 'Men, you are brothers; why do you want to hurt each other?'

²⁷"But the man who was mistreating the other pushed Moses aside and said, 'Who made you ruler and judge over us? ²⁸Do you want to kill me as you killed the Egyptian yesterday?'ᵈ ²⁹When Moses heard this, he fled to Midian, where he settled as a foreigner and had two sons.

³⁰"After forty years had passed, an angel appeared to Moses in the flames of a burning bush in the desert near Mount Sinai. ³¹When he saw this, he was amazed at the sight. As he went over to look more closely, he heard the Lord's voice: ³²'I am the God of your fathers, the God of Abraham, Isaac and Jacob.'ᵉ Moses trembled with fear and did not dare to look.

ᵃ3 Gen. 12:1   ᵇ7 Gen. 15:13,14   ᶜ20 Or *was fair in the sight of God*   ᵈ28 Exodus 2:14   ᵉ32 Exodus 3:6

³³"Then the Lord said to him, 'Take off your sandals; the place where you are standing is holy ground. ³⁴I have indeed seen the oppression of my people in Egypt. I have heard their groaning and have come down to set them free. Now come, I will send you back to Egypt.'ᵃ

³⁵"This is the same Moses whom they had rejected with the words, 'Who made you ruler and judge?' He was sent to be their ruler and deliverer by God himself, through the angel who appeared to him in the bush. ³⁶He led them out of Egypt and did wonders and miraculous signs in Egypt, at the Red Seaᵇ and for forty years in the desert.

³⁷"This is that Moses who told the Israelites, 'God will send you a prophet like me from your own people.'ᶜ ³⁸He was in the assembly in the desert, with the angel who spoke to him on Mount Sinai, and with our fathers; and he received living words to pass on to us.

³⁹"But our fathers refused to obey him. Instead, they rejected him and in their hearts turned back to Egypt. ⁴⁰They told Aaron, 'Make us gods who will go before us. As for this fellow Moses who led us out of Egypt—we don't know what has happened to him!'ᵈ ⁴¹That was the time they made an idol in the form of a calf. They brought sacrifices to it and held a celebration in honor of what their hands had made. ⁴²But God turned away and gave them over to the worship of the heavenly bodies. This agrees with what is written in the book of the prophets:

" 'Did you bring me sacrifices and offerings
    forty years in the desert, O house of Israel?
⁴³You have lifted up the shrine of Molech
    and the star of your god Rephan,
    the idols you made to worship.
Therefore I will send you into exile'ᵉ beyond Babylon.

⁴⁴"Our forefathers had the tabernacle of the Testimony with them in the desert. It had been made as God directed Moses, according to the pattern he had seen. ⁴⁵Having received the tabernacle, our fathers under Joshua brought it with them when they took the land from the nations God drove out before them. It remained in the land until the time of David, ⁴⁶who enjoyed God's favor and asked that he might provide a dwelling place for the God of Jacob.ᶠ ⁴⁷But it was Solomon who built the house for him.

⁴⁸"However, the Most High does not live in houses made by men. As the prophet says:

⁴⁹" 'Heaven is my throne,
    and the earth is my footstool.
What kind of house will you build for me?

says the Lord.

Or where will my resting place be?
⁵⁰Has not my hand made all these things?'ᵍ

⁵¹"You stiff-necked people, with uncircumcised hearts and ears! You are just like your fathers: You always resist the Holy Spirit! ⁵²Was there ever a prophet your fathers did not persecute? They even killed those who predicted the coming of the Righteous One. And now you have betrayed and murdered him— ⁵³you who have received the law that was put into effect through angels but have not obeyed it."

The Stoning of Stephen

⁵⁴When they heard this, they were furious and gnashed their teeth at him. ⁵⁵But Stephen, full of the Holy Spirit, looked up to heaven and saw the glory of God, and Jesus standing at the right hand of God. ⁵⁶"Look," he said, "I see heaven open and the Son of Man standing at the right hand of God."

⁵⁷At this they covered their ears and, yelling at the top of their voices, they all rushed

---

ᵃ34 Exodus 3:5,7,8,10   ᵇ36 That is, Sea of Reeds   ᶜ37 Deut. 18:15   ᵈ40 Exodus 32:1   ᵉ43 Amos 5:25-27
ᶠ46 Some early manuscripts *the house of Jacob*   ᵍ50 Isaiah 66:1,2

at him, [58]dragged him out of the city and began to stone him. Meanwhile, the witnesses laid their clothes at the feet of a young man named Saul.

[59]While they were stoning him, Stephen prayed, "Lord Jesus, receive my spirit." [60]Then he fell on his knees and cried out, "Lord, do not hold this sin against them." When he had said this, he fell asleep.

 And Saul was there, giving approval to his death.

The Church Persecuted and Scattered

On that day a great persecution broke out against the church at Jerusalem, and all except the apostles were scattered throughout Judea and Samaria. [2]Godly men buried Stephen and mourned deeply for him. [3]But Saul began to destroy the church. Going from house to house, he dragged off men and women and put them in prison.

Philip in Samaria

[4]Those who had been scattered preached the word wherever they went. [5]Philip went down to a city in Samaria and proclaimed the Christ[a] there. [6]When the crowds heard Philip and saw the miraculous signs he did, they all paid close attention to what he said. [7]With shrieks, evil[b] spirits came out of many, and many paralytics and cripples were healed. [8]So there was great joy in that city.

Simon the Sorcerer

[9]Now for some time a man named Simon had practiced sorcery in the city and amazed all the people of Samaria. He boasted that he was someone great, [10]and all the people, both high and low, gave him their attention and exclaimed, "This man is the divine power known as the Great Power." [11]They followed him because he had

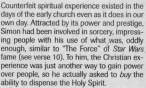

☐ ⠿⠿⠿⠿⠿⠿⠿⠿ DISCOVERING GOD ⠿⠿⠿⠿⠿⠿⠿⠿ ⬍

8:18–19
Spiritual Fraud

Counterfeit spiritual experience existed in the days of the early church even as it does in our own day. Attracted by its power and prestige, Simon had been involved in sorcery, impressing people with his use of what was, oddly enough, similar to "The Force" of *Star Wars* fame (see verse 10). To him, the Christian experience was just another way to gain power over people, so he actually asked to *buy* the ability to dispense the Holy Spirit.

Fundamental to all occult practices (astrology, divination, fortune-telling, channeling, Wicca, etc.) is the belief that one can manipulate the physical and spiritual environment by using the correct ritual, practice, knowledge or incantation. In contrast, Christianity says that we must *yield* our lives to be in a relationship with God. Christians don't control God, and certainly don't "use" him, but rather submit to and follow him.

Occult practices will never be compatible with Christianity, because they are fundamentally at odds with how God wants us to relate to him and our world. (See chapter 13, verses 6–12 [page 1442] for another confrontation between the Christian message and the occult. Also see Deuteronomy chapter 18, verses 9–13 [page 236], for further warnings from God concerning these practices.)

amazed them for a long time with his magic. [12]But when they believed Philip as he preached the good news of the kingdom of God and the name of Jesus Christ, they were baptized, both men and women. [13]Simon himself believed and was baptized. And he followed Philip everywhere, astonished by the great signs and miracles he saw.

[14]When the apostles in Jerusalem heard that Samaria had accepted the word of God, they sent Peter and John to them. [15]When they arrived, they prayed for them that they might receive the Holy Spirit, [16]because the Holy Spirit had not yet come upon any of them; they had simply been baptized into[c] the name of the Lord Jesus. [17]Then Peter and John placed their hands on them, and they received the Holy Spirit.

[18]When Simon saw that the Spirit was given at the laying on of the apostles' hands, he offered them money [19]and said, "Give me also this ability so that everyone on whom I lay my hands may receive the Holy Spirit."

[a]5 Or Messiah   [b]7 Greek unclean   [c]16 Or in

²⁰Peter answered: "May your money perish with you, because you thought you could buy the gift of God with money! ²¹You have no part or share in this ministry, because your heart is not right before God. ²²Repent of this wickedness and pray to the Lord. Perhaps he will forgive you for having such a thought in your heart. ²³For I see that you are full of bitterness and captive to sin."

²⁴Then Simon answered, "Pray to the Lord for me so that nothing you have said may happen to me."

²⁵When they had testified and proclaimed the word of the Lord, Peter and John returned to Jerusalem, preaching the gospel in many Samaritan villages.

Philip and the Ethiopian

²⁶Now an angel of the Lord said to Philip, "Go south to the road—the desert road—that goes down from Jerusalem to Gaza." ²⁷So he started out, and on his way he met an Ethiopian[a] eunuch, an important official in charge of all the treasury of Candace, queen of the Ethiopians. This man had gone to Jerusalem to worship, ²⁸and on his way home was sitting in his chariot reading the book of Isaiah the prophet. ²⁹The Spirit told Philip, "Go to that chariot and stay near it."

³⁰Then Philip ran up to the chariot and heard the man reading Isaiah the prophet. "Do you understand what you are reading?" Philip asked.

³¹"How can I," he said, "unless someone explains it to me?" So he invited Philip to come up and sit with him.

³²The eunuch was reading this passage of Scripture:

"He was led like a sheep to the slaughter,
    and as a lamb before the shearer is silent,
    so he did not open his mouth.
³³In his humiliation he was deprived of justice.
    Who can speak of his descendants?
    For his life was taken from the earth."[b]

³⁴The eunuch asked Philip, "Tell me, please, who is the prophet talking about, himself or someone else?" ³⁵Then Philip began with that very passage of Scripture and told him the good news about Jesus.

³⁶As they traveled along the road, they came to some water and the eunuch said, "Look, here is water. Why shouldn't I be baptized?"[c] ³⁸And he gave orders to stop the chariot. Then both Philip and the eunuch went down into the water and Philip baptized him. ³⁹When they came up out of the water, the Spirit of the Lord suddenly took Philip away, and the eunuch did not see him again, but went on his way rejoicing. ⁴⁰Philip, however, appeared at Azotus and traveled about, preaching the gospel in all the towns until he reached Caesarea.

Saul's Conversion

9 Meanwhile, Saul was still breathing out murderous threats against the Lord's disciples. He went to the high priest ²and asked him for letters to the synagogues in Damascus, so that if he found any there who belonged to the Way, whether men or women, he might take them as prisoners to Jerusalem. ³As he neared Damascus on his journey, suddenly a light from heaven flashed around him. ⁴He fell to the ground and heard a voice say to him, "Saul, Saul, why do you persecute me?"

⁵"Who are you, Lord?" Saul asked.

"I am Jesus, whom you are persecuting," he replied. ⁶"Now get up and go into the city, and you will be told what you must do."

---

a 27 That is, from the upper Nile region   *b 33* Isaiah 53:7,8   *c 36* Some late manuscripts *baptized?"* ³⁷*Philip said, "If you believe with all your heart, you may." The eunuch answered, "I believe that Jesus Christ is the Son of God."*

⁷The men traveling with Saul stood there speechless; they heard the sound but did not see anyone. ⁸Saul got up from the ground, but when he opened his eyes he could see nothing. So they led him by the hand into Damascus. ⁹For three days he was blind, and did not eat or drink anything.

¹⁰In Damascus there was a disciple named Ananias. The Lord called to him in a vision, "Ananias!"

"Yes, Lord," he answered.

¹¹The Lord told him, "Go to the house of Judas on Straight Street and ask for a man from Tarsus named Saul, for he is praying. ¹²In a vision he has seen a man named Ananias come and place his hands on him to restore his sight."

¹³"Lord," Ananias answered, "I have heard many reports about this man and all the harm he has done to your saints in Jerusalem. ¹⁴And he has come here with authority from the chief priests to arrest all who call on your name."

¹⁵But the Lord said to Ananias, "Go! This man is my chosen instrument to carry my name before the Gentiles and their kings and before the people of Israel. ¹⁶I will show him how much he must suffer for my name."

¹⁷Then Ananias went to the house and entered it. Placing his hands on Saul, he said, "Brother Saul, the Lord—Jesus, who appeared to you on the road as you were coming here—has sent me so that you may see again and be filled with the Holy Spirit." ¹⁸Immediately, something like scales fell from Saul's eyes, and he could see again. He got up and was baptized, ¹⁹and after taking some food, he regained his strength.

Saul in Damascus and Jerusalem

Saul spent several days with the disciples in Damascus. ²⁰At once he began to preach in the synagogues that Jesus is the Son of God. ²¹All those who heard him were astonished and asked, "Isn't he the man who raised havoc in Jerusalem among those who call on this name? And hasn't he come here to take them as prisoners to the chief priests?" ²²Yet Saul grew more and more powerful and baffled the Jews living in Damascus by proving that Jesus is the Christ.ᵃ

²³After many days had gone by, the Jews conspired to kill him, ²⁴but Saul learned of their plan. Day and night they kept close watch on the city gates in order to kill him. ²⁵But his followers took him by night and lowered him in a basket through an opening in the wall.

²⁶When he came to Jerusalem, he tried to join the disciples, but they were all afraid of him, not believing that he really was a disciple. ²⁷But Barnabas took him and brought him to the apostles. He told

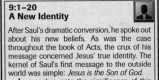

▒▒▒▒▒ KNOWING YOURSELF ▒▒▒▒▒

9:1–20
A New Identity

After Saul's dramatic conversion, he spoke out about his new beliefs. As was the case throughout the book of Acts, the crux of his message concerned Jesus' true identity. The kernel of Saul's first message to the outside world was simple: *Jesus is the Son of God.*

As a seeker, note the significance of this transformation. Saul became a new person, and his encounter with Jesus was at the heart of that change. Saul had known about Jesus and was convinced that he existed. What was at issue—and what radically changed—was Saul's belief about who Jesus is.

A personal encounter with Jesus will also be at the heart of any change that occurs in your life. Merely knowing about Jesus won't save you. But when you look to him for salvation and make the same confession as Saul did, you will most certainly find eternal life (see John chapter 3, verse 18 [page 1387]).

them how Saul on his journey had seen the Lord and that the Lord had spoken to him, and how in Damascus he had preached fearlessly in the name of Jesus. ²⁸So Saul stayed with them and moved about freely in Jerusalem, speaking boldly in the name of the Lord. ²⁹He talked and debated with the Grecian Jews, but they tried to kill him. ³⁰When the brothers learned of this, they took him down to Caesarea and sent him off to Tarsus.

ᵃ22 Or Messiah

³¹Then the church throughout Judea, Galilee and Samaria enjoyed a time of peace. It was strengthened; and encouraged by the Holy Spirit, it grew in numbers, living in the fear of the Lord.

Aeneas and Dorcas

³²As Peter traveled about the country, he went to visit the saints in Lydda. ³³There he found a man named Aeneas, a paralytic who had been bedridden for eight years. ³⁴"Aeneas," Peter said to him, "Jesus Christ heals you. Get up and take care of your mat." Immediately Aeneas got up. ³⁵All those who lived in Lydda and Sharon saw him and turned to the Lord.

³⁶In Joppa there was a disciple named Tabitha (which, when translated, is Dorcas[a]), who was always doing good and helping the poor. ³⁷About that time she became sick and died, and her body was washed and placed in an upstairs room. ³⁸Lydda was near Joppa; so when the disciples heard that Peter was in Lydda, they sent two men to him and urged him, "Please come at once!"

³⁹Peter went with them, and when he arrived he was taken upstairs to the room. All the widows stood around him, crying and showing him the robes and other clothing that Dorcas had made while she was still with them.

⁴⁰Peter sent them all out of the room; then he got down on his knees and prayed. Turning toward the dead woman, he said, "Tabitha, get up." She opened her eyes, and seeing Peter she sat up. ⁴¹He took her by the hand and helped her to her feet. Then he called the believers and the widows and presented her to them alive. ⁴²This became known all over Joppa, and many people believed in the Lord. ⁴³Peter stayed in Joppa for some time with a tanner named Simon.

Cornelius Calls for Peter

10 At Caesarea there was a man named Cornelius, a centurion in what was known as the Italian Regiment. ²He and all his family were devout and God-fearing; he gave generously to those in need and prayed to God regularly. ³One day at about three in the afternoon he had a vision. He distinctly saw an angel of God, who came to him and said, "Cornelius!"

⁴Cornelius stared at him in fear. "What is it, Lord?" he asked.

The angel answered, "Your prayers and gifts to the poor have come up as a memorial offering before God. ⁵Now send men to Joppa to bring back a man named Simon who is called Peter. ⁶He is staying with Simon the tanner, whose house is by the sea."

⁷When the angel who spoke to him had gone, Cornelius called two of his servants and a devout soldier who was one of his attendants. ⁸He told them everything that had happened and sent them to Joppa.

Peter's Vision

⁹About noon the following day as they were on their journey and approaching the city, Peter went up on the roof to pray. ¹⁰He became hungry and wanted something to eat, and while the meal was being prepared, he fell into a trance. ¹¹He saw heaven opened and something like a large sheet being let down to earth by its four corners. ¹²It contained all kinds of four-footed animals, as well as reptiles of the earth and birds of the air. ¹³Then a voice told him, "Get up, Peter. Kill and eat."

¹⁴"Surely not, Lord!" Peter replied. "I have never eaten anything impure or unclean."

¹⁵The voice spoke to him a second time, "Do not call anything impure that God has made clean."

¹⁶This happened three times, and immediately the sheet was taken back to heaven.

¹⁷While Peter was wondering about the meaning of the vision, the men sent by Cor-

---

a 36 Both Tabitha (Aramaic) and Dorcas (Greek) mean gazelle.

¹elius found out where Simon's house was and stopped at the gate. ¹⁸They called out, ₃sking if Simon who was known as Peter was staying there.

¹⁹While Peter was still thinking about the vision, the Spirit said to him, "Simon, three*ᵃ* ₃en are looking for you. ²⁰So get up and go downstairs. Do not hesitate to go with them, ₃r I have sent them."

²¹Peter went down and said to the men, "I'm the one you're looking for. Why have you ₃ome?"

²²The men replied, "We have come from Cornelius the centurion. He is a righteous and ₃od-fearing man, who is respected by all the Jewish people. A holy angel told him to ₃ave you come to his house so that he could hear what you have to say." ²³Then Peter ₃vited the men into the house to be his guests.

₃eter at Cornelius' House

The next day Peter started out with them, and some of the brothers from Joppa went ₃long. ²⁴The following day he arrived in Caesarea. Cornelius was expecting them and ₃ad called together his relatives and close ₃riends. ²⁵As Peter entered the house, Cor-₃elius met him and fell at his feet in rever-₃nce. ²⁶But Peter made him get up. "Stand ₃p," he said, "I am only a man myself."

²⁷Talking with him, Peter went inside ₃nd found a large gathering of people. ²⁸He ₃aid to them: "You are well aware that it is ₃gainst our law for a Jew to associate with ₃ Gentile or visit him. But God has shown ₃e that I should not call any man impure or ₃nclean. ²⁹So when I was sent for, I came ₃ithout raising any objection. May I ask ₃hy you sent for me?"

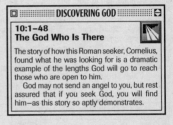

³⁰Cornelius answered: "Four days ago I was in my house praying at this hour, at three ₃n the afternoon. Suddenly a man in shining clothes stood before me ³¹and said, 'Corneli-₃s, God has heard your prayer and remembered your gifts to the poor. ³²Send to Joppa for ₃imon who is called Peter. He is a guest in the home of Simon the tanner, who lives by ₃he sea.' ³³So I sent for you immediately, and it was good of you to come. Now we are all ₃ere in the presence of God to listen to everything the Lord has commanded you to ₃ell us."

³⁴Then Peter began to speak: "I now realize how true it is that God does not show ₃avoritism ³⁵but accepts men from every nation who fear him and do what is right. ³⁶You ₃now the message God sent to the people of Israel, telling the good news of peace ₃hrough Jesus Christ, who is Lord of all. ³⁷You know what has happened throughout ₃udea, beginning in Galilee after the baptism that John preached— ³⁸how God anointed ₃esus of Nazareth with the Holy Spirit and power, and how he went around doing good ₃nd healing all who were under the power of the devil, because God was with him.

³⁹"We are witnesses of everything he did in the country of the Jews and in Jerusalem. ₃hey killed him by hanging him on a tree, ⁴⁰but God raised him from the dead on the ₃hird day and caused him to be seen. ⁴¹He was not seen by all the people, but by ₃vitnesses whom God had already chosen—by us who ate and drank with him after he ₃ose from the dead. ⁴²He commanded us to preach to the people and to testify that he is ₃he one whom God appointed as judge of the living and the dead. ⁴³All the prophets ₃estify about him that everyone who believes in him receives forgiveness of sins through ₃is name."

⁴⁴While Peter was still speaking these words, the Holy Spirit came on all who heard

the message. ⁴⁵The circumcised believers who had come with Peter were astonished that the gift of the Holy Spirit had been poured out even on the Gentiles. ⁴⁶For they heard them speaking in tongues*a* and praising God.

Then Peter said, ⁴⁷"Can anyone keep these people from being baptized with water? They have received the Holy Spirit just as we have." ⁴⁸So he ordered that they be baptized in the name of Jesus Christ. Then they asked Peter to stay with them for a few days.

Peter Explains His Actions

11 The apostles and the brothers throughout Judea heard that the Gentiles also had received the word of God. ²So when Peter went up to Jerusalem, the circumcised believers criticized him ³and said, "You went into the house of uncircumcised men and ate with them."

⁴Peter began and explained everything to them precisely as it had happened: ⁵"I was in the city of Joppa praying, and in a trance I saw a vision. I saw something like a large sheet being let down from heaven by its four corners, and it came down to where I was. ⁶I looked into it and saw four-footed animals of the earth, wild beasts, reptiles, and birds of the air. ⁷Then I heard a voice telling me, 'Get up, Peter. Kill and eat.'

⁸"I replied, 'Surely not, Lord! Nothing impure or unclean has ever entered my mouth.'

⁹"The voice spoke from heaven a second time, 'Do not call anything impure that God has made clean.' ¹⁰This happened three times, and then it was all pulled up to heaven again.

¹¹"Right then three men who had been sent to me from Caesarea stopped at the house where I was staying. ¹²The Spirit told me to have no hesitation about going with them. These six brothers also went with me, and we entered the man's house. ¹³He told us how he had seen an angel appear in his house and say, 'Send to Joppa for Simon who is called Peter. ¹⁴He will bring you a message through which you and all your household will be saved.'

¹⁵"As I began to speak, the Holy Spirit came on them as he had come on us at the beginning. ¹⁶Then I remembered what the Lord had said: 'John baptized with*b* water, but you will be baptized with the Holy Spirit.' ¹⁷So if God gave them the same gift as he gave us, who believed in the Lord Jesus Christ, who was I to think that I could oppose God?"

¹⁸When they heard this, they had no further objections and praised God, saying, "So then, God has granted even the Gentiles repentance unto life."

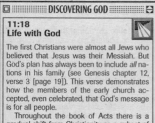

DISCOVERING GOD

11:18
Life with God

The first Christians were almost all Jews who believed that Jesus was their Messiah. But God's plan has always been to include *all* nations in his family (see Genesis chapter 12, verse 3 [page 19]). This verse demonstrates how the members of the early church accepted, even celebrated, that God's message is for all people.

Throughout the book of Acts there is a gradual shift from Christianity as a subset of Judaism to a faith that increasingly draws in people from non-Jewish backgrounds. Twenty centuries later, Jesus is still the promised Messiah to the Jews. But he is much more than that—he is truly the Savior of the *world.*

The Church in Antioch

¹⁹Now those who had been scattered by the persecution in connection with Stephen traveled as far as Phoenicia, Cyprus and Antioch, telling the message only to Jews. ²⁰Some of them, however, men from Cyprus and Cyrene, went to Antioch and began to speak to Greeks also, telling them the good news about the Lord Jesus. ²¹The Lord's hand was with them, and a great number of people believed and turned to the Lord.

²²News of this reached the ears of the church at Jerusalem, and they sent Barnabas to

a 46 Or other languages   *b 16 Or in*

Antioch. ²³When he arrived and saw the evidence of the grace of God, he was glad and encouraged them all to remain true to the Lord with all their hearts. ²⁴He was a good man, full of the Holy Spirit and faith, and a great number of people were brought to the Lord.

²⁵Then Barnabas went to Tarsus to look for Saul, ²⁶and when he found him, he brought him to Antioch. So for a whole year Barnabas and Saul met with the church and taught great numbers of people. The disciples were called Christians first at Antioch.

²⁷During this time some prophets came down from Jerusalem to Antioch. ²⁸One of them, named Agabus, stood up and through the Spirit predicted that a severe famine would spread over the entire Roman world. (This happened during the reign of Claudius.) ²⁹The disciples, each according to his ability, decided to provide help for the brothers living in Judea. ³⁰This they did, sending their gift to the elders by Barnabas and Saul.

Peter's Miraculous Escape From Prison

12 It was about this time that King Herod arrested some who belonged to the church, intending to persecute them. ²He had James, the brother of John, put to death with the sword. ³When he saw that this pleased the Jews, he proceeded to seize Peter also. This happened during the Feast of Unleavened Bread. ⁴After arresting him, he put him in prison, handing him over to be guarded by four squads of four soldiers each. Herod intended to bring him out for public trial after the Passover.

⁵So Peter was kept in prison, but the church was earnestly praying to God for him.

⁶The night before Herod was to bring him to trial, Peter was sleeping between two soldiers, bound with two chains, and sentries stood guard at the entrance. ⁷Suddenly an angel of the Lord appeared and a light shone in the cell. He struck Peter on the side and woke him up. "Quick, get up!" he said, and the chains fell off Peter's wrists.

⁸Then the angel said to him, "Put on your clothes and sandals." And Peter did so. "Wrap your cloak around you and follow me," the angel told him. ⁹Peter followed him out of the prison, but he had no idea that what the angel was doing was really happening; he thought he was seeing a vision. ¹⁰They passed the first and second guards and came to the iron gate leading to the city. It opened for them by itself, and they went through it. When they had walked the length of one street, suddenly the angel left him.

¹¹Then Peter came to himself and said, "Now I know without a doubt that the Lord sent his angel and rescued me from Herod's clutches and from everything the Jewish people were anticipating."

¹²When this had dawned on him, he went to the house of Mary the mother of John, also called Mark, where many people had gathered and were praying. ¹³Peter knocked at the outer entrance, and a servant girl named Rhoda came to answer the door. ¹⁴When she recognized Peter's voice, she was so overjoyed she ran back without opening it and exclaimed, "Peter is at the door!"

¹⁵"You're out of your mind," they told her. When she kept insisting that it was so, they said, "It must be his angel."

¹⁶But Peter kept on knocking, and when they opened the door and saw him, they were astonished. ¹⁷Peter motioned with his hand for them to be quiet and described how the Lord had brought him out of prison. "Tell James and the brothers about this," he said, and then he left for another place.

¹⁸In the morning, there was no small commotion among the soldiers as to what had become of Peter. ¹⁹After Herod had a thorough search made for him and did not find him, he cross-examined the guards and ordered that they be executed.

Herod's Death

Then Herod went from Judea to Caesarea and stayed there a while. ²⁰He had been quarreling with the people of Tyre and Sidon; they now joined together and sought an audience with him. Having secured the support of Blastus, a trusted personal servant of the king, they asked for peace, because they depended on the king's country for their food supply.

²¹On the appointed day Herod, wearing his royal robes, sat on his throne and delivered a public address to the people. ²²They shouted, "This is the voice of a god, not of a man." ²³Immediately, because Herod did not give praise to God, an angel of the Lord struck him down, and he was eaten by worms and died.

²⁴But the word of God continued to increase and spread.

²⁵When Barnabas and Saul had finished their mission, they returned from*a* Jerusalem, taking with them John, also called Mark.

Barnabas and Saul Sent Off

13 In the church at Antioch there were prophets and teachers: Barnabas, Simeon called Niger, Lucius of Cyrene, Manaen (who had been brought up with Herod the tetrarch) and Saul. ²While they were worshiping the Lord and fasting, the Holy Spirit said, "Set apart for me Barnabas and Saul for the work to which I have called them." ³So after they had fasted and prayed, they placed their hands on them and sent them off.

On Cyprus

⁴The two of them, sent on their way by the Holy Spirit, went down to Seleucia and sailed from there to Cyprus. ⁵When they arrived at Salamis, they proclaimed the word of God in the Jewish synagogues. John was with them as their helper.

⁶They traveled through the whole island until they came to Paphos. There they met a Jewish sorcerer and false prophet named Bar-Jesus, ⁷who was an attendant of the proconsul, Sergius Paulus. The proconsul, an intelligent man, sent for Barnabas and Saul because he wanted to hear the word of God. ⁸But Elymas the sorcerer (for that is what his name means) opposed them and tried to turn the proconsul from the faith. ⁹Then Saul, who was also called Paul, filled with the Holy Spirit, looked straight at Elymas and said, ¹⁰"You are a child of the devil and an enemy of everything that is right! You are full of all kinds of deceit and trickery. Will you never stop perverting the right ways of the Lord? ¹¹Now the hand of the Lord is against you. You are going to be blind, and for a time you will be unable to see the light of the sun."

Immediately mist and darkness came over him, and he groped about, seeking someone to lead him by the hand. ¹²When the proconsul saw what had happened, he believed, for he was amazed at the teaching about the Lord.

In Pisidian Antioch

¹³From Paphos, Paul and his companions sailed to Perga in Pamphylia, where John left them to return to Jerusalem. ¹⁴From Perga they went on to Pisidian Antioch. On the Sabbath they entered the synagogue and sat down. ¹⁵After the reading from the Law and the Prophets, the synagogue rulers sent word to them, saying, "Brothers, if you have a message of encouragement for the people, please speak."

¹⁶Standing up, Paul motioned with his hand and said: "Men of Israel and you Gentiles who worship God, listen to me! ¹⁷The God of the people of Israel chose our fathers; he made the people prosper during their stay in Egypt, with mighty power he led them out of that country, ¹⁸he endured their conduct*b* for about forty years in the desert, ¹⁹he overthrew seven nations in Canaan and gave their land to his people as their inheritance. ²⁰All this took about 450 years.

"After this, God gave them judges until the time of Samuel the prophet. ²¹Then the people asked for a king, and he gave them Saul son of Kish, of the tribe of Benjamin, who ruled forty years. ²²After removing Saul, he made David their king. He testified concern-

---

*a*25 Some manuscripts *to*   *b*18 Some manuscripts *and cared for them* ing him: 'I have found David son of Jesse a man after my own heart; he will do everything I want him to do.'

²³"From this man's descendants God has brought to Israel the Savior Jesus, as he promised. ²⁴Before the coming of Jesus, John preached repentance and baptism to all the people of Israel. ²⁵As John was completing his work, he said: 'Who do you think I am? I am not that one. No, but he is coming after me, whose sandals I am not worthy to untie.'

²⁶"Brothers, children of Abraham, and you God-fearing Gentiles, it is to us that this message of salvation has been sent. ²⁷The people of Jerusalem and their rulers did not recognize Jesus, yet in condemning him they fulfilled the words of the prophets that are read every Sabbath. ²⁸Though they found no proper ground for a death sentence, they asked Pilate to have him executed. ²⁹When they had carried out all that was written about him, they took him down from the tree and laid him in a tomb. ³⁰But God raised him from the dead, ³¹and for many days he was seen by those who had traveled with him from Galilee to Jerusalem. They are now his witnesses to our people.

³²"We tell you the good news: What God promised our fathers ³³he has fulfilled for us, their children, by raising up Jesus. As it is written in the second Psalm:

    " 'You are my Son;
        today I have become your
            Father.'*ᵃ*ᵇ

³⁴The fact that God raised him from the dead, never to decay, is stated in these words:

    " 'I will give you the holy and
        sure blessings promised
            to David.'ᶜ

³⁵So it is stated elsewhere:

    " 'You will not let your Holy One
        see decay.'ᵈ

³⁶"For when David had served God's purpose in his own generation, he fell asleep; he was buried with his fathers and his body decayed. ³⁷But the one whom God raised from the dead did not see decay.

³⁸"Therefore, my brothers, I want you to know that through Jesus the forgiveness of sins is proclaimed to you. ³⁹Through him everyone who believes is justified from everything you could not be justified from by the law of Moses. ⁴⁰Take care that what the prophets have said does not happen to you:

    ⁴¹" 'Look, you scoffers,
        wonder and perish,
    for I am going to do something in your days
        that you would never believe,
            even if someone told you.'ᵉ"

⁴²As Paul and Barnabas were leaving the synagogue, the people invited them to speak

---

| REASONS TO BELIEVE |

13:38–41
The Incomparable Jesus

Notice how Paul sums up his message: Jesus is the source of God's forgiveness. Jesus can give us what no amount of religious rule-keeping can—forgiveness and relief from sin.

As a seeker, you may be looking for a way to salve your troubled conscience. You may regret past actions that have hurt other people. You may have even adopted religious rules and regulations to try to change your behavior. But change begins when you accept God's forgiveness first.

God's plan is hard to accept because it goes against our human inclination to try to earn our way back to God. But here's the good news: Jesus has come and is prepared to give you what you can't gain for yourself. If you are ready to respond, why not ask Jesus, even right now, to be your forgiver and leader? And when you do, tell someone about your decision and do what Paul advised in verse 43: "Continue in the grace of God" for the rest of your life. It's a decision you'll never regret!

ᵃ33 Or have begotten you   ᵇ33 Psalm 2:7   ᶜ34 Isaiah 55:3   ᵈ35 Psalm 16:10   ᵉ41 Hab. 1:5

further about these things on the next Sabbath. ⁴³When the congregation was dismissed, many of the Jews and devout converts to Judaism followed Paul and Barnabas, who talked with them and urged them to continue in the grace of God.

⁴⁴On the next Sabbath almost the whole city gathered to hear the word of the Lord. ⁴⁵When the Jews saw the crowds, they were filled with jealousy and talked abusively against what Paul was saying.

⁴⁶Then Paul and Barnabas answered them boldly: "We had to speak the word of God to you first. Since you reject it and do not consider yourselves worthy of eternal life, we now turn to the Gentiles. ⁴⁷For this is what the Lord has commanded us:

"'I have made you[a] a light for the Gentiles,
    that you[a] may bring salvation to the ends of the earth.'[b]"

⁴⁸When the Gentiles heard this, they were glad and honored the word of the Lord; and all who were appointed for eternal life believed.

⁴⁹The word of the Lord spread through the whole region. ⁵⁰But the Jews incited the God-fearing women of high standing and the leading men of the city. They stirred up persecution against Paul and Barnabas, and expelled them from their region. ⁵¹So they shook the dust from their feet in protest against them and went to Iconium. ⁵²And the disciples were filled with joy and with the Holy Spirit.

In Iconium

14 At Iconium Paul and Barnabas went as usual into the Jewish synagogue. There they spoke so effectively that a great number of Jews and Gentiles believed. ²But the Jews who refused to believe stirred up the Gentiles and poisoned their minds against the brothers. ³So Paul and Barnabas spent considerable time there, speaking boldly for the Lord, who confirmed the message of his grace by enabling them to do miraculous signs and wonders. ⁴The people of the city were divided; some sided with the Jews, others with the apostles. ⁵There was a plot afoot among the Gentiles and Jews, together with their leaders, to mistreat them and stone them. ⁶But they found out about it and fled to the Lycaonian cities of Lystra and Derbe and to the surrounding country, ⁷where they continued to preach the good news.

In Lystra and Derbe

⁸In Lystra there sat a man crippled in his feet, who was lame from birth and had never walked. ⁹He listened to Paul as he was speaking. Paul looked directly at him, saw that he had faith to be healed ¹⁰and called out, "Stand up on your feet!" At that, the man jumped up and began to walk.

¹¹When the crowd saw what Paul had done, they shouted in the Lycaonian language, "The gods have come down to us in human form!" ¹²Barnabas they called Zeus, and Paul they called Hermes because he was the chief speaker. ¹³The priest of Zeus, whose temple was just outside the city, brought bulls and wreaths to the city gates because he and the crowd wanted to offer sacrifices to them.

¹⁴But when the apostles Barnabas and Paul heard of this, they tore their clothes and rushed out into the crowd, shouting: ¹⁵"Men, why are you doing this? We too are only men, human like you. We are bringing you good news, telling you to turn from these worthless things to the living God, who made heaven and earth and sea and everything in them. ¹⁶In the past, he let all nations go their own way. ¹⁷Yet he has not left himself without testimony: He has shown kindness by giving you rain from heaven and crops in their seasons; he provides you with plenty of food and fills your hearts with joy." ¹⁸Even with these words, they had difficulty keeping the crowd from sacrificing to them.

¹⁹Then some Jews came from Antioch and Iconium and won the crowd over. They stoned Paul and dragged him outside the city, thinking he was dead. ²⁰But after the

a 47 The Greek is singular.   b 47 Isaiah 49:6

disciples had gathered around him, he got up and went back into the city. The next day he and Barnabas left for Derbe.

The Return to Antioch in Syria

²¹They preached the good news in that city and won a large number of disciples. Then they returned to Lystra, Iconium and Antioch, ²²strengthening the disciples and encouraging them to remain true to the faith. "We must go through many hardships to enter the kingdom of God," they said. ²³Paul and Barnabas appointed elders*a* for them in each church and, with prayer and fasting, committed them to the Lord, in whom they had put their trust. ²⁴After going through Pisidia, they came into Pamphylia, ²⁵and when they had preached the word in Perga, they went down to Attalia.

²⁶From Attalia they sailed back to Antioch, where they had been committed to the grace of God for the work they had now completed. ²⁷On arriving there, they gathered the church together and reported all that God had done through them and how he had opened the door of faith to the Gentiles. ²⁸And they stayed there a long time with the disciples.

The Council at Jerusalem

15 Some men came down from Judea to Antioch and were teaching the brothers: "Unless you are circumcised, according to the custom taught by Moses, you cannot be saved." ²This brought Paul and Barnabas into sharp dispute and debate with them. So Paul and Barnabas were appointed, along with some other believers, to go up to Jerusalem to see the apostles and elders about this question. ³The church sent them on their way, and as they traveled through Phoenicia and Samaria, they told how the Gentiles had been converted. This news made all the brothers very glad. ⁴When they came to Jerusalem, they were welcomed by the church and the apostles and elders, to whom they reported everything God had done through them.

⁵Then some of the believers who belonged to the party of the Pharisees stood up and said, "The Gentiles must be circumcised and required to obey the law of Moses."

⁶The apostles and elders met to consider this question. ⁷After much discussion, Peter got up and addressed them: "Brothers, you know that some time ago God made a choice among you that the Gentiles might hear from my lips the message of the gospel and believe. ⁸God, who knows the heart, showed that he accepted them by giving the Holy Spirit to them, just as he did to us. ⁹He made no distinction between us and them, for he purified their hearts by faith. ¹⁰Now then, why do you try to test God by putting on the necks of the disciples a yoke that neither we nor our fathers have been able to bear? ¹¹No! We believe it is through the grace of our Lord Jesus that we are saved, just as they are."

¹²The whole assembly became silent as they listened to Barnabas and Paul telling

DISCOVERING GOD

14:15
Spiritual Fraud

People are incurably religious. The problem is, they tend to worship the wrong things. Here the crowd, after witnessing a healing miracle, wanted to worship Paul and Barnabas instead of God. These two missionaries sternly rebuked the crowd for their misdirected praise. True believers direct glory and attention to God, not themselves.

It's not enough to be "religious." Paul said that we must turn from "worthless things" (here Zeus; in our own day—well, you fill in the blank!) and instead put our trust in the living God who made everything. Christianity is incompatible with other religions—it claims that we must leave them behind as a false hope and instead put all our faith in Christ.

Christianity is also incompatible with a lifestyle that makes anything more important than God. Someone once lamented, "We worship our work, work at our play, and play at our worship." Only through embracing true Christianity can we rearrange our scrambled priorities!

*a*23 Or *Barnabas ordained elders;* or *Barnabas had elders elected*

about the miraculous signs and wonders God had done among the Gentiles through them. [13]When they finished, James spoke up: "Brothers, listen to me. [14]Simon[a] has described to us how God at first showed his concern by taking from the Gentiles a people for himself. [15]The words of the prophets are in agreement with this, as it is written:

> [16]" 'After this I will return
>   and rebuild David's fallen tent.
>   Its ruins I will rebuild,
>   and I will restore it,
> [17]that the remnant of men may seek the Lord,
>   and all the Gentiles who bear my name,
>   says the Lord, who does these things'[b]
> [18]   that have been known for ages.[c]

[19]"It is my judgment, therefore, that we should not make it difficult for the Gentiles who are turning to God. [20]Instead we should write to them, telling them to abstain from food polluted by idols, from sexual immorality, from the meat of strangled animals and from blood. [21]For Moses has been preached in every city from the earliest times and is read in the synagogues on every Sabbath."

The Council's Letter to Gentile Believers

[22]Then the apostles and elders, with the whole church, decided to choose some of their own men and send them to Antioch with Paul and Barnabas. They chose Judas (called Barsabbas) and Silas, two men who were leaders among the brothers. [23]With them they sent the following letter:

The apostles and elders, your brothers,

To the Gentile believers in Antioch, Syria and Cilicia:

Greetings.

[24]We have heard that some went out from us without our authorization and disturbed you, troubling your minds by what they said. [25]So we all agreed to choose some men and send them to you with our dear friends Barnabas and Paul— [26]men who have risked their lives for the name of our Lord Jesus Christ. [27]Therefore we are sending Judas and Silas to confirm by word of mouth what we are writing. [28]It seemed good to the Holy Spirit and to us not to burden you with anything beyond the following requirements: [29]You are to abstain from food sacrificed to idols, from blood, from the meat of strangled animals and from sexual immorality. You will do well to avoid these things.

Farewell.

[30]The men were sent off and went down to Antioch, where they gathered the church together and delivered the letter. [31]The people read it and were glad for its encouraging message. [32]Judas and Silas, who themselves were prophets, said much to encourage and strengthen the brothers. [33]After spending some time there, they were sent off by the brothers with the blessing of peace to return to those who had sent them.[d] [35]But Paul and Barnabas remained in Antioch, where they and many others taught and preached the word of the Lord.

---

[a]14 Greek *Simeon,* a variant of *Simon;* that is, Peter   [b]17 Amos 9:11,12   [c]17,18 Some manuscripts *things'—/* [18]*known to the Lord for ages is his work*   [d]33 Some manuscripts *them,* [34]*but Silas decided to remain there*

Disagreement Between Paul and Barnabas

36Some time later Paul said to Barnabas, "Let us go back and visit the brothers in all the towns where we preached the word of the Lord and see how they are doing." 37Barnabas wanted to take John, also called Mark, with them, 38but Paul did not think it wise to take him, because he had deserted them in Pamphylia and had not continued with them in the work. 39They had such a sharp disagreement that they parted company. Barnabas took Mark and sailed for Cyprus, 40but Paul chose Silas and left, commended by the brothers to the grace of the Lord. 41He went through Syria and Cilicia, strengthening the churches.

Timothy Joins Paul and Silas

16 He came to Derbe and then to Lystra, where a disciple named Timothy lived, whose mother was a Jewess and a believer, but whose father was a Greek. The brothers at Lystra and Iconium spoke well of him. 3Paul wanted to take him along on the journey, so he circumcised him because of the Jews who lived in that area, for they all knew that his father was a Greek. 4As they traveled from town to town, they delivered the decisions reached by the apostles and elders in Jerusalem for the people to obey. 5So the churches were strengthened in the faith and grew daily in numbers.

Paul's Vision of the Man of Macedonia

6Paul and his companions traveled throughout the region of Phrygia and Galatia, having been kept by the Holy Spirit from preaching the word in the province of Asia. 7When they came to the border of Mysia, they tried to enter Bithynia, but the Spirit of Jesus would not allow them to. 8So they passed by Mysia and went down to Troas. 9During the night Paul had a vision of a man of Macedonia standing and begging him, "Come over to Macedonia and help us." 10After Paul had seen the vision, we got ready at once to leave for Macedonia, concluding that God had called us to preach the gospel to them.

Lydia's Conversion in Philippi

11From Troas we put out to sea and sailed straight for Samothrace, and the next day on to Neapolis. 12From there we traveled to Philippi, a Roman colony and the leading city of that district of Macedonia. And we stayed there several days.

13On the Sabbath we went outside the city gate to the river, where we expected to find a place of prayer. We sat down and began to speak to the women who had gathered there. 14One of those listening was a woman named Lydia, a dealer in purple cloth from the city of Thyatira, who was a worshiper of God. The Lord opened her heart to respond to Paul's message. 15When she and the members of her household were baptized, she invited us to her home. "If you consider me a believer in the Lord," she said, "come and stay at my house." And she persuaded us.

Paul and Silas in Prison

16Once when we were going to the place of prayer, we were met by a slave girl who had a spirit by which she predicted the future. She earned a great deal of money for her owners by fortune-telling. 17This girl followed Paul and the rest of us, shouting, "These men are servants of the Most High God, who are telling you the way to be saved." 18She kept this up for many days. Finally Paul became so troubled that he turned around and said to the spirit, "In the name of Jesus Christ I command you to come out of her!" At that moment the spirit left her.

19When the owners of the slave girl realized that their hope of making money was gone, they seized Paul and Silas and dragged them into the marketplace to face the authorities. 20They brought them before the magistrates and said, "These men are Jews, and are throwing our city into an uproar 21by advocating customs unlawful for us Romans to accept or practice."

²²The crowd joined in the attack against Paul and Silas, and the magistrates ordered them to be stripped and beaten. ²³After they had been severely flogged, they were thrown into prison, and the jailer was commanded to guard them carefully. ²⁴Upon receiving such orders, he put them in the inner cell and fastened their feet in the stocks.

²⁵About midnight Paul and Silas were praying and singing hymns to God, and the other prisoners were listening to them. ²⁶Suddenly there was such a violent earthquake that the foundations of the prison were shaken. At once all the prison doors flew open, and everybody's chains came loose. ²⁷The jailer woke up, and when he saw the prison doors open, he drew his sword and was about to kill himself because he thought the prisoners had escaped. ²⁸But Paul shouted, "Don't harm yourself! We are all here!"

²⁹The jailer called for lights, rushed in and fell trembling before Paul and Silas. ³⁰He then brought them out and asked, "Sirs, what must I do to be saved?"

³¹They replied, "Believe in the Lord Jesus, and you will be saved—you and your household." ³²Then they spoke the word of the Lord to him and to all the others in his house. ³³At that hour of the night the jailer took them and washed their wounds; then immediately he and all his family were baptized. ³⁴The jailer brought them into his house and set a meal before them; he was filled with joy because he had come to believe in God—he and his whole family.

³⁵When it was daylight, the magistrates sent their officers to the jailer with the order: "Release those men." ³⁶The jailer told Paul, "The magistrates have ordered that you and Silas be released. Now you can leave. Go in peace."

▣ ▓▓▓▓▓ DISCOVERING GOD ▓▓▓▓▓ ⬒

16:25–31
The God Who Is There

This man, who had just moments before nearly committed suicide, fell before Paul and Silas. His brush with death shook him out of his complacency – he was ready to start life all over again. Earnestly – desperately – he begged: "What must I do to be saved?"

What would you have told him? Paul had a ready answer, saying in effect: "Go to Jesus. Believe in him; trust him; depend on him. He will give you a new start. And not just you— your family can have it too."

The Christian message is simple. God may use a crisis to help you get to the point where you just want the bottom line, and want it *now*, as this jailer did. When that happens, the answer will be the same today as back then: "Believe in the Lord Jesus, and you will be saved."

Why wait for a crisis when you can know and experience him now?

---

³⁷But Paul said to the officers: "They beat us publicly without a trial, even though we are Roman citizens, and threw us into prison. And now do they want to get rid of us quietly? No! Let them come themselves and escort us out."

³⁸The officers reported this to the magistrates, and when they heard that Paul and Silas were Roman citizens, they were alarmed. ³⁹They came to appease them and escorted them from the prison, requesting them to leave the city. ⁴⁰After Paul and Silas came out of the prison, they went to Lydia's house, where they met with the brothers and encouraged them. Then they left.

In Thessalonica

17 When they had passed through Amphipolis and Apollonia, they came to Thessalonica, where there was a Jewish synagogue. ²As his custom was, Paul went into the synagogue, and on three Sabbath days he reasoned with them from the Scriptures, ³explaining and proving that the Christ*ᵃ* had to suffer and rise from the dead. "This Jesus I am proclaiming to you is the Christ,*ᵃ*" he said. ⁴Some of the Jews were persuaded and joined Paul and Silas, as did a large number of God-fearing Greeks and not a few prominent women.

⁵But the Jews were jealous; so they rounded up some bad characters from the market-

ᵃ3 Or Messiah

place, formed a mob and started a riot in the city. They rushed to Jason's house in search of Paul and Silas in order to bring them out to the crowd.[a] [6]But when they did not find them, they dragged Jason and some other brothers before the city officials, shouting: "These men who have caused trouble all over the world have now come here, [7]and Jason has welcomed them into his house. They are all defying Caesar's decrees, saying that there is another king, one called Jesus." [8]When they heard this, the crowd and the city officials were thrown into turmoil. [9]Then they made Jason and the others post bond and let them go.

In Berea

[10]As soon as it was night, the brothers sent Paul and Silas away to Berea. On arriving there, they went to the Jewish synagogue. [11]Now the Bereans were of more noble character than the Thessalonians, for they received the message with great eagerness and examined the Scriptures every day to see if what Paul said was true. [12]Many of the Jews believed, as did also a number of prominent Greek women and many Greek men.

[13]When the Jews in Thessalonica learned that Paul was preaching the word of God at Berea, they went there too, agitating the crowds and stirring them up. [14]The brothers immediately sent Paul to the coast, but Silas and Timothy stayed at Berea. [15]The men who escorted Paul brought him to Athens and then left with instructions for Silas and Timothy to join him as soon as possible.

In Athens

[16]While Paul was waiting for them in Athens, he was greatly distressed to see that the city was full of idols. [17]So he reasoned in the synagogue with the Jews and the God-fearing Greeks, as well as in the marketplace day by day with those who happened to be there. [18]A group of Epicurean and Stoic philosophers began to dispute with him. Some of them asked, "What is this babbler trying to say?" Others remarked, "He seems to be advocating foreign gods." They said this because Paul was preaching the good news about Jesus and the resurrection. [19]Then they took him and brought him to a meeting of the Areopagus, where they said to him, "May we know what this new teaching is that you are presenting? [20]You are bringing some strange ideas to our ears, and we want to know what they mean." [21](All the Athenians and the foreigners who lived there spent their time doing nothing but talking about and listening to the latest ideas.)

[22]Paul then stood up in the meeting of the Areopagus and said: "Men of Athens! I see that in every way you are very religious. [23]For as I walked around and looked carefully at your objects of worship, I even found an altar with this inscription: TO AN UNKNOWN GOD. Now what you worship as something unknown I am going to proclaim to you.

[24]"The God who made the world and everything in it is the Lord of heaven and earth and does not live in temples built by hands. [25]And he is not served by human hands, as if he needed anything, because he himself gives all men life and breath and everything else. [26]From one man he made every nation of men, that they should inhabit the whole earth; and he determined the times set for them and the exact places where they should live. [27]God did this so that men would seek him and perhaps reach out for him and find him, though he is not far from each one of us. [28]'For in him we live and move and have our being.' As some of your own poets have said, 'We are his offspring.'

[29]"Therefore since we are God's offspring, we should not think that the divine being is like gold or silver or stone—an image made by man's design and skill. [30]In the past God overlooked such ignorance, but now he commands all people everywhere to repent. [31]For he has set a day when he will judge the world with justice by the man he has appointed. He has given proof of this to all men by raising him from the dead."

[32]When they heard about the resurrection of the dead, some of them sneered, but others said, "We want to hear you again on this subject." [33]At that, Paul left the Council.

---

[a] 5 Or the assembly of the people

³⁴A few men became followers of Paul and believed. Among them was Dionysius, a member of the Areopagus, also a woman named Damaris, and a number of others.

In Corinth

18 After this, Paul left Athens and went to Corinth. ²There he met a Jew named Aquila, a native of Pontus, who had recently come from Italy with his wife Priscilla, because Claudius had ordered all the Jews to leave Rome. Paul went to see them, ³and because he was a tentmaker as they were, he stayed and worked with them. ⁴Every Sabbath he reasoned in the synagogue, trying to persuade Jews and Greeks.

⁵When Silas and Timothy came from Macedonia, Paul devoted himself exclusively to preaching, testifying to the Jews that Jesus was the Christ.ᵃ ⁶But when the Jews opposed Paul and became abusive, he shook out his clothes in protest and said to them, "Your blood be on your own heads! I am clear of my responsibility. From now on I will go to the Gentiles."

⁷Then Paul left the synagogue and went next door to the house of Titius Justus, a worshiper of God. ⁸Crispus, the synagogue ruler, and his entire household believed in the Lord; and many of the Corinthians who heard him believed and were baptized.

⁹One night the Lord spoke to Paul in a vision: "Do not be afraid; keep on speaking, do not be silent. ¹⁰For I am with you, and no one is going to attack and harm you, because I have many people in this city." ¹¹So Paul stayed for a year and a half, teaching them the word of God.

¹²While Gallio was proconsul of Achaia, the Jews made a united attack on Paul and brought him into court. ¹³"This man," they charged, "is persuading the people to worship God in ways contrary to the law."

¹⁴Just as Paul was about to speak, Gallio said to the Jews, "If you Jews were making a complaint about some misdemeanor or serious crime, it would be reasonable for me to listen to you. ¹⁵But since it involves questions about words and names and your own law—settle the matter yourselves. I will not be a judge of such things." ¹⁶So he had them ejected from the court. ¹⁷Then they all turned on Sosthenes the synagogue ruler and beat him in front of the court. But Gallio showed no concern whatever.

Priscilla, Aquila and Apollos

¹⁸Paul stayed on in Corinth for some time. Then he left the brothers and sailed for Syria, accompanied by Priscilla and Aquila. Before he sailed, he had his hair cut off at Cenchrea because of a vow he had taken. ¹⁹They arrived at Ephesus, where Paul left Priscilla and Aquila. He himself went into the synagogue and reasoned with the Jews. ²⁰When they asked him to spend more time with them, he declined. ²¹But as he left, he promised, "I will come back if it is God's will." Then he set sail from Ephesus. ²²When he landed at Caesarea, he went up and greeted the church and then went down to Antioch.

²³After spending some time in Antioch, Paul set out from there and traveled from place to place throughout the region of Galatia and Phrygia, strengthening all the disciples.

²⁴Meanwhile a Jew named Apollos, a native of Alexandria, came to Ephesus. He was a learned man, with a thorough knowledge of the Scriptures. ²⁵He had been instructed in the way of the Lord, and he spoke with great fervorᵇ and taught about Jesus accurately, though he knew only the baptism of John. ²⁶He began to speak boldly in the synagogue. When Priscilla and Aquila heard him, they invited him to their home and explained to him the way of God more adequately.

²⁷When Apollos wanted to go to Achaia, the brothers encouraged him and wrote to the disciples there to welcome him. On arriving, he was a great help to those who by grace had believed. ²⁸For he vigorously refuted the Jews in public debate, proving from the Scriptures that Jesus was the Christ.

ᵃ5 Or Messiah; also in verse 28   ᵇ25 Or with fervor in the Spirit

Paul in Ephesus

19 While Apollos was at Corinth, Paul took the road through the interior and arrived at Ephesus. There he found some disciples ²and asked them, "Did you receive the Holy Spirit when*ᵃ* you believed?"

They answered, "No, we have not even heard that there is a Holy Spirit."

³So Paul asked, "Then what baptism did you receive?"

"John's baptism," they replied.

⁴Paul said, "John's baptism was a baptism of repentance. He told the people to believe in the one coming after him, that is, in Jesus." ⁵On hearing this, they were baptized into*ᵇ* the name of the Lord Jesus. ⁶When Paul placed his hands on them, the Holy Spirit came on them, and they spoke in tongues*ᶜ* and prophesied. ⁷There were about twelve men in all.

⁸Paul entered the synagogue and spoke boldly there for three months, arguing persuasively about the kingdom of God. ⁹But some of them became obstinate; they refused to believe and publicly maligned the Way. So Paul left them. He took the disciples with him and had discussions daily in the lecture hall of Tyrannus. ¹⁰This went on for two years, so that all the Jews and Greeks who lived in the province of Asia heard the word of the Lord.

¹¹God did extraordinary miracles through Paul, ¹²so that even handkerchiefs and aprons that had touched him were taken to the sick, and their illnesses were cured and the evil spirits left them.

¹³Some Jews who went around driving out evil spirits tried to invoke the name of the Lord Jesus over those who were demon-possessed. They would say, "In the name of Jesus, whom Paul preaches, I command you to come out." ¹⁴Seven sons of Sceva, a Jewish chief priest, were doing this. ¹⁵One day, the evil spirit answered them, "Jesus I know, and I know about Paul, but who are you?" ¹⁶Then the man who had the evil spirit jumped on them and overpowered them all. He gave them such a beating that they ran out of the house naked and bleeding.

¹⁷When this became known to the Jews and Greeks living in Ephesus, they were all seized with fear, and the name of the Lord Jesus was held in high honor. ¹⁸Many of those who believed now came and openly confessed their evil deeds. ¹⁹A number who had practiced sorcery brought their scrolls together and burned them publicly. When they calculated the value of the scrolls, the total came to fifty thousand drachmas.*ᵈ* ²⁰In this way the word of the Lord spread widely and grew in power.

²¹After all this had happened, Paul decided to go to Jerusalem, passing through Macedonia and Achaia. "After I have been there," he said, "I must visit Rome also." ²²He sent two of his helpers, Timothy and Erastus, to Macedonia, while he stayed in the province of Asia a little longer.

▣ ▦▦▦ REASONS TO BELIEVE ▦▦▦ ▣

18:27–28
The Christian Experience

The practice of giving evidence to support the claims of the gospel message has a long history in the Christian tradition.

Apollos was a powerful public spokesman for Jesus. He didn't promise favors from God in exchange for financial support, as some shady televangelists do today. Rather, he "vigorously" debated Christ's claims with thoughtful opponents and effectively showed how Scripture verified Jesus' role as the Messiah. Paul did the same thing in chapter 19, verse 8.

If you're a seeker, it's okay to ask questions about the validity of Christianity. There are plenty of reference materials and Christian people who can help you find the answers you need. The evidence is there, and you will find it if you keep seeking.

---

*ᵃ*2 Or *after*   *ᵇ*5 Or *in*   *ᶜ*6 Or *other languages*   *ᵈ*19 A drachma was a silver coin worth about a day's wages.

The Riot in Ephesus

²³About that time there arose a great disturbance about the Way. ²⁴A silversmith named Demetrius, who made silver shrines of Artemis, brought in no little business for the craftsmen. ²⁵He called them together, along with the workmen in related trades, and said: "Men, you know we receive a good income from this business. ²⁶And you see and hear how this fellow Paul has convinced and led astray large numbers of people here in Ephesus and in practically the whole province of Asia. He says that man-made gods are no gods at all. ²⁷There is danger not only that our trade will lose its good name, but also that the temple of the great goddess Artemis will be discredited, and the goddess herself, who is worshiped throughout the province of Asia and the world, will be robbed of her divine majesty."

²⁸When they heard this, they were furious and began shouting: "Great is Artemis of the Ephesians!" ²⁹Soon the whole city was in an uproar. The people seized Gaius and Aristarchus, Paul's traveling companions from Macedonia, and rushed as one man into the theater. ³⁰Paul wanted to appear before the crowd, but the disciples would not let him. ³¹Even some of the officials of the province, friends of Paul, sent him a message begging him not to venture into the theater.

³²The assembly was in confusion: Some were shouting one thing, some another. Most of the people did not even know why they were there. ³³The Jews pushed Alexander to the front, and some of the crowd shouted instructions to him. He motioned for silence in order to make a defense before the people. ³⁴But when they realized he was a Jew, they all shouted in unison for about two hours: "Great is Artemis of the Ephesians!"

³⁵The city clerk quieted the crowd and said: "Men of Ephesus, doesn't all the world know that the city of Ephesus is the guardian of the temple of the great Artemis and of her image, which fell from heaven? ³⁶Therefore, since these facts are undeniable, you ought to be quiet and not do anything rash. ³⁷You have brought these men here, though they have neither robbed temples nor blasphemed our goddess. ³⁸If, then, Demetrius and his fellow craftsmen have a grievance against anybody, the courts are open and there are proconsuls. They can press charges. ³⁹If there is anything further you want to bring up, it must be settled in a legal assembly. ⁴⁰As it is, we are in danger of being charged with rioting because of today's events. In that case we would not be able to account for this commotion, since there is no reason for it." ⁴¹After he had said this, he dismissed the assembly.

Through Macedonia and Greece

20 When the uproar had ended, Paul sent for the disciples and, after encouraging them, said good-by and set out for Macedonia. ²He traveled through that area, speaking many words of encouragement to the people, and finally arrived in Greece, ³where he stayed three months. Because the Jews made a plot against him just as he was about to sail for Syria, he decided to go back through Macedonia. ⁴He was accompanied by Sopater son of Pyrrhus from Berea, Aristarchus and Secundus from Thessalonica, Gaius from Derbe, Timothy also, and Tychicus and Trophimus from the province of Asia. ⁵These men went on ahead and waited for us at Troas. ⁶But we sailed from Philippi after the Feast of Unleavened Bread, and five days later joined the others at Troas, where we stayed seven days.

Eutychus Raised From the Dead at Troas

⁷On the first day of the week we came together to break bread. Paul spoke to the people and, because he intended to leave the next day, kept on talking until midnight. ⁸There were many lamps in the upstairs room where we were meeting. ⁹Seated in a window was a young man named Eutychus, who was sinking into a deep sleep as Paul talked on and on. When he was sound asleep, he fell to the ground from the third story and was picked up dead. ¹⁰Paul went down, threw himself on the young man and put his

arms around him. "Don't be alarmed," he said. "He's alive!" ¹¹Then he went upstairs again and broke bread and ate. After talking until daylight, he left. ¹²The people took the young man home alive and were greatly comforted.

Paul's Farewell to the Ephesian Elders

¹³We went on ahead to the ship and sailed for Assos, where we were going to take Paul aboard. He had made this arrangement because he was going there on foot. ¹⁴When he met us at Assos, we took him aboard and went on to Mitylene. ¹⁵The next day we set sail from there and arrived off Kios. The day after that we crossed over to Samos, and on the following day arrived at Miletus. ¹⁶Paul had decided to sail past Ephesus to avoid spending time in the province of Asia, for he was in a hurry to reach Jerusalem, if possible, by the day of Pentecost.

¹⁷From Miletus, Paul sent to Ephesus for the elders of the church. ¹⁸When they arrived, he said to them: "You know how I lived the whole time I was with you, from the first day I came into the province of Asia. ¹⁹I served the Lord with great humility and with tears, although I was severely tested by the plots of the Jews. ²⁰You know that I have not hesitated to preach anything that would be helpful to you but have taught you publicly and from house to house. ²¹I have declared to both Jews and Greeks that they must turn to God in repentance and have faith in our Lord Jesus.

²²"And now, compelled by the Spirit, I am going to Jerusalem, not knowing what will happen to me there. ²³I only know that in every city the Holy Spirit warns me that prison and hardships are facing me. ²⁴However, I consider my life worth nothing to me, if only I may finish the race and complete the task the Lord Jesus has given me—the task of testifying to the gospel of God's grace.

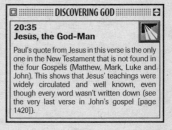

DISCOVERING GOD

**20:35
Jesus, the God-Man**

Paul's quote from Jesus in this verse is the only one in the New Testament that is not found in the four Gospels (Matthew, Mark, Luke and John). This shows that Jesus' teachings were widely circulated and well known, even though every word wasn't written down (see the very last verse in John's gospel [page 1420]).

²⁵"Now I know that none of you among whom I have gone about preaching the kingdom will ever see me again. ²⁶Therefore, I declare to you today that I am innocent of the blood of all men. ²⁷For I have not hesitated to proclaim to you the whole will of God. ²⁸Keep watch over yourselves and all the flock of which the Holy Spirit has made you overseers.ᵃ Be shepherds of the church of God,ᵇ which he bought with his own blood. ²⁹I know that after I leave, savage wolves will come in among you and will not spare the flock. ³⁰Even from your own number men will arise and distort the truth in order to draw away disciples after them. ³¹So be on your guard! Remember that for three years I never stopped warning each of you night and day with tears.

³²"Now I commit you to God and to the word of his grace, which can build you up and give you an inheritance among all those who are sanctified. ³³I have not coveted anyone's silver or gold or clothing. ³⁴You yourselves know that these hands of mine have supplied my own needs and the needs of my companions. ³⁵In everything I did, I showed you that by this kind of hard work we must help the weak, remembering the words the Lord Jesus himself said: 'It is more blessed to give than to receive.'"

³⁶When he had said this, he knelt down with all of them and prayed. ³⁷They all wept as they embraced him and kissed him. ³⁸What grieved them most was his statement that they would never see his face again. Then they accompanied him to the ship.

ᵃ28 Traditionally *bishops*   ᵇ28 Many manuscripts *of the Lord*

On to Jerusalem

21 After we had torn ourselves away from them, we put out to sea and sailed straight to Cos. The next day we went to Rhodes and from there to Patara. ²We found a ship crossing over to Phoenicia, went on board and set sail. ³After sighting Cyprus and passing to the south of it, we sailed on to Syria. We landed at Tyre, where our ship was to unload its cargo. ⁴Finding the disciples there, we stayed with them seven days. Through the Spirit they urged Paul not to go on to Jerusalem. ⁵But when our time was up, we left and continued on our way. All the disciples and their wives and children accompanied us out of the city, and there on the beach we knelt to pray. ⁶After saying good-by to each other, we went aboard the ship, and they returned home.

⁷We continued our voyage from Tyre and landed at Ptolemais, where we greeted the brothers and stayed with them for a day. ⁸Leaving the next day, we reached Caesarea and stayed at the house of Philip the evangelist, one of the Seven. ⁹He had four unmarried daughters who prophesied.

¹⁰After we had been there a number of days, a prophet named Agabus came down from Judea. ¹¹Coming over to us, he took Paul's belt, tied his own hands and feet with it and said, "The Holy Spirit says, 'In this way the Jews of Jerusalem will bind the owner of this belt and will hand him over to the Gentiles.'"

¹²When we heard this, we and the people there pleaded with Paul not to go up to Jerusalem. ¹³Then Paul answered, "Why are you weeping and breaking my heart? I am ready not only to be bound, but also to die in Jerusalem for the name of the Lord Jesus." ¹⁴When he would not be dissuaded, we gave up and said, "The Lord's will be done."

¹⁵After this, we got ready and went up to Jerusalem. ¹⁶Some of the disciples from Caesarea accompanied us and brought us to the home of Mnason, where we were to stay. He was a man from Cyprus and one of the early disciples.

Paul's Arrival at Jerusalem

¹⁷When we arrived at Jerusalem, the brothers received us warmly. ¹⁸The next day Paul and the rest of us went to see James, and all the elders were present. ¹⁹Paul greeted them and reported in detail what God had done among the Gentiles through his ministry.

²⁰When they heard this, they praised God. Then they said to Paul: "You see, brother, how many thousands of Jews have believed, and all of them are zealous for the law. ²¹They have been informed that you teach all the Jews who live among the Gentiles to turn away from Moses, telling them not to circumcise their children or live according to our customs. ²²What shall we do? They will certainly hear that you have come, ²³so do what we tell you. There are four men with us who have made a vow. ²⁴Take these men, join in their purification rites and pay their expenses, so that they can have their heads shaved. Then everybody will know there is no truth in these reports about you, but that you yourself are living in obedience to the law. ²⁵As for the Gentile believers, we have written to them our decision that they should abstain from food sacrificed to idols, from blood, from the meat of strangled animals and from sexual immorality."

²⁶The next day Paul took the men and purified himself along with them. Then he went to the temple to give notice of the date when the days of purification would end and the offering would be made for each of them.

Paul Arrested

²⁷When the seven days were nearly over, some Jews from the province of Asia saw Paul at the temple. They stirred up the whole crowd and seized him, ²⁸shouting, "Men of Israel, help us! This is the man who teaches all men everywhere against our people and our law and this place. And besides, he has brought Greeks into the temple area and defiled this holy place." ²⁹(They had previously seen Trophimus the Ephesian in the city with Paul and assumed that Paul had brought him into the temple area.)

³⁰The whole city was aroused, and the people came running from all directions. Seiz-

ing Paul, they dragged him from the temple, and immediately the gates were shut. [31]While they were trying to kill him, news reached the commander of the Roman troops that the whole city of Jerusalem was in an uproar. [32]He at once took some officers and soldiers and ran down to the crowd. When the rioters saw the commander and his soldiers, they stopped beating Paul.

[33]The commander came up and arrested him and ordered him to be bound with two chains. Then he asked who he was and what he had done. [34]Some in the crowd shouted one thing and some another, and since the commander could not get at the truth because of the uproar, he ordered that Paul be taken into the barracks. [35]When Paul reached the steps, the violence of the mob was so great he had to be carried by the soldiers. [36]The crowd that followed kept shouting, "Away with him!"

Paul Speaks to the Crowd

[37]As the soldiers were about to take Paul into the barracks, he asked the commander, "May I say something to you?"

"Do you speak Greek?" he replied. [38]"Aren't you the Egyptian who started a revolt and led four thousand terrorists out into the desert some time ago?"

[39]Paul answered, "I am a Jew, from Tarsus in Cilicia, a citizen of no ordinary city. Please let me speak to the people."

[40]Having received the commander's permission, Paul stood on the steps and motioned to the crowd. When they were all silent, he said to them in Aramaic[a]:

22 [1]"Brothers and fathers, listen now to my defense."

[2]When they heard him speak to them in Aramaic, they became very quiet.

Then Paul said: [3]"I am a Jew, born in Tarsus of Cilicia, but brought up in this city. Under Gamaliel I was thoroughly trained in the law of our fathers and was just as zealous for God as any of you are today. [4]I persecuted the followers of this Way to their death, arresting both men and women and throwing them into prison, [5]as also the high priest and all the Council can testify. I even obtained letters from them to their brothers in Damascus, and went there to bring these people as prisoners to Jerusalem to be punished.

[6]"About noon as I came near Damascus, suddenly a bright light from heaven flashed around me. [7]I fell to the ground and heard a voice say to me, 'Saul! Saul! Why do you persecute me?'

[8]"'Who are you, Lord?' I asked.

"'I am Jesus of Nazareth, whom you are persecuting,' he replied. [9]My companions saw the light, but they did not understand the voice of him who was speaking to me.

[10]"'What shall I do, Lord?' I asked.

"'Get up,' the Lord said, 'and go into Damascus. There you will be told all that you have been assigned to do.' [11]My companions led me by the hand into Damascus, because the brilliance of the light had blinded me.

[12]"A man named Ananias came to see me. He was a devout observer of the law and highly respected by all the Jews living there. [13]He stood beside me and said, 'Brother Saul, receive your sight!' And at that very moment I was able to see him.

[14]"Then he said: 'The God of our fathers has chosen you to know his will and to see the Righteous One and to hear words from his mouth. [15]You will be his witness to all men of what you have seen and heard. [16]And now what are you waiting for? Get up, be baptized and wash your sins away, calling on his name.'

[17]"When I returned to Jerusalem and was praying at the temple, I fell into a trance [18]and saw the Lord speaking. 'Quick!' he said to me. 'Leave Jerusalem immediately, because they will not accept your testimony about me.'

[19]"'Lord,' I replied, 'these men know that I went from one synagogue to another to imprison and beat those who believe in you. [20]And when the blood of your martyr[b]

---

[a]40 Or possibly *Hebrew*; also in 22:2   [b]20 Or *witness*

Stephen was shed, I stood there giving my approval and guarding the clothes of those who were killing him.'

²¹"Then the Lord said to me, 'Go; I will send you far away to the Gentiles.' "

Paul the Roman Citizen

²²The crowd listened to Paul until he said this. Then they raised their voices and shouted, "Rid the earth of him! He's not fit to live!"

ADDRESSING QUESTIONS

22:21–22
Human Experience

Paul's testimony about his conversion in this chapter highlights a central theme that made Christianity controversial in the first century—its claim that it was the one religion for all the people of the world. The Jewish people who heard Paul speak felt that taking Jesus' story to non-Jews diluted the faith and compromised their practices. But reaching spiritual outsiders was Jesus' priority; he never intended that his message be strictly for the Jews. People who were distressed that Christ's message was also for those who were not like them were putting faith in the wrong thing.

Oddly enough, sometimes people who are most familiar with Jesus' teaching act like the Jews of Paul's day—they have a hard time reaching out to nonbelievers. But to be a consistent follower of Jesus is to value what he valued, and Jesus said he "came to seek and to save what was lost" (Luke chapter 19, verse 10 [page 1369]).

Perhaps you've run into some Christians in your spiritual journey that haven't been too enthused about your questions. If so, realize that God is seeking you out even though his earthly followers might fail from time to time. Keep looking and asking questions—you'll find what you're after!

²³As they were shouting and throwing off their cloaks and flinging dust into the air, ²⁴the commander ordered Paul to be taken into the barracks. He directed that he be flogged and questioned in order to find out why the people were shouting at him like this. ²⁵As they stretched him out to flog him, Paul said to the centurion standing there, "Is it legal for you to flog a Roman citizen who hasn't even been found guilty?"

²⁶When the centurion heard this, he went to the commander and reported it. "What are you going to do?" he asked. "This man is a Roman citizen."

²⁷The commander went to Paul and asked, "Tell me, are you a Roman citizen?"

"Yes, I am," he answered.

²⁸Then the commander said, "I had to pay a big price for my citizenship."

"But I was born a citizen," Paul replied.

²⁹Those who were about to question him withdrew immediately. The commander himself was alarmed when he realized that he had put Paul, a Roman citizen, in chains.

Before the Sanhedrin

³⁰The next day, since the commander wanted to find out exactly why Paul was being accused by the Jews, he released him and ordered the chief priests and all the Sanhedrin to assemble. Then he brought Paul and had him stand before them.

23 Paul looked straight at the Sanhedrin and said, "My brothers, I have fulfilled my duty to God in all good conscience to this day." ²At this the high priest Ananias ordered those standing near Paul to strike him on the mouth. ³Then Paul said to him, "God will strike you, you whitewashed wall! You sit there to judge me according to the law, yet you yourself violate the law by commanding that I be struck!"

⁴Those who were standing near Paul said, "You dare to insult God's high priest?"

⁵Paul replied, "Brothers, I did not realize that he was the high priest; for it is written: 'Do not speak evil about the ruler of your people.'ᵃ"

⁶Then Paul, knowing that some of them were Sadducees and the others Pharisees, called out in the Sanhedrin, "My brothers, I am a Pharisee, the son of a Pharisee. I stand on trial because of my hope in the resurrection of the dead." ⁷When he said this, a

ᵃ5 Exodus 22:28

dispute broke out between the Pharisees and the Sadducees, and the assembly was divided. ⁸(The Sadducees say that there is no resurrection, and that there are neither angels nor spirits, but the Pharisees acknowledge them all.)

⁹There was a great uproar, and some of the teachers of the law who were Pharisees stood up and argued vigorously. "We find nothing wrong with this man," they said. "What if a spirit or an angel has spoken to him?" ¹⁰The dispute became so violent that the commander was afraid Paul would be torn to pieces by them. He ordered the troops to go down and take him away from them by force and bring him into the barracks.

¹¹The following night the Lord stood near Paul and said, "Take courage! As you have testified about me in Jerusalem, so you must also testify in Rome."

The Plot to Kill Paul

¹²The next morning the Jews formed a conspiracy and bound themselves with an oath not to eat or drink until they had killed Paul. ¹³More than forty men were involved in this plot. ¹⁴They went to the chief priests and elders and said, "We have taken a solemn oath not to eat anything until we have killed Paul. ¹⁵Now then, you and the Sanhedrin petition the commander to bring him before you on the pretext of wanting more accurate information about his case. We are ready to kill him before he gets here."

¹⁶But when the son of Paul's sister heard of this plot, he went into the barracks and told Paul.

¹⁷Then Paul called one of the centurions and said, "Take this young man to the commander; he has something to tell him." ¹⁸So he took him to the commander.

The centurion said, "Paul, the prisoner, sent for me and asked me to bring this young man to you because he has something to tell you."

¹⁹The commander took the young man by the hand, drew him aside and asked, "What is it you want to tell me?"

²⁰He said: "The Jews have agreed to ask you to bring Paul before the Sanhedrin tomorrow on the pretext of wanting more accurate information about him. ²¹Don't give in to them, because more than forty of them are waiting in ambush for him. They have taken an oath not to eat or drink until they have killed him. They are ready now, waiting for your consent to their request."

²²The commander dismissed the young man and cautioned him, "Don't tell anyone that you have reported this to me."

Paul Transferred to Caesarea

²³Then he called two of his centurions and ordered them, "Get ready a detachment of two hundred soldiers, seventy horsemen and two hundred spearmenᵃ to go to Caesarea at nine tonight. ²⁴Provide mounts for Paul so that he may be taken safely to Governor Felix."

²⁵He wrote a letter as follows:

²⁶Claudius Lysias,

To His Excellency, Governor Felix:

Greetings.

²⁷This man was seized by the Jews and they were about to kill him, but I came with my troops and rescued him, for I had learned that he is a Roman citizen. ²⁸I wanted to know why they were accusing him, so I brought him to their Sanhedrin. ²⁹I found that the accusation had to do with questions about their law, but there was no charge against him that deserved death or imprisonment. ³⁰When I was informed

<hr>

ᵃ23 The meaning of the Greek for this word is uncertain.

of a plot to be carried out against the man, I sent him to you at once. I also ordered his accusers to present to you their case against him.

³¹So the soldiers, carrying out their orders, took Paul with them during the night and brought him as far as Antipatris. ³²The next day they let the cavalry go on with him, while they returned to the barracks. ³³When the cavalry arrived in Caesarea, they delivered the letter to the governor and handed Paul over to him. ³⁴The governor read the letter and asked what province he was from. Learning that he was from Cilicia, ³⁵he said, "I will hear your case when your accusers get here." Then he ordered that Paul be kept under guard in Herod's palace.

The Trial Before Felix

24 Five days later the high priest Ananias went down to Caesarea with some of the elders and a lawyer named Tertullus, and they brought their charges against Paul before the governor. ²When Paul was called in, Tertullus presented his case before Felix: "We have enjoyed a long period of peace under you, and your foresight has brought about reforms in this nation. ³Everywhere and in every way, most excellent Felix, we acknowledge this with profound gratitude. ⁴But in order not to weary you further, I would request that you be kind enough to hear us briefly.

⁵"We have found this man to be a troublemaker, stirring up riots among the Jews all over the world. He is a ringleader of the Nazarene sect ⁶and even tried to desecrate the temple; so we seized him. ⁸By*ᵃ* examining him yourself you will be able to learn the truth about all these charges we are bringing against him."

⁹The Jews joined in the accusation, asserting that these things were true.

¹⁰When the governor motioned for him to speak, Paul replied: "I know that for a number of years you have been a judge over this nation; so I gladly make my defense. ¹¹You can easily verify that no more than twelve days ago I went up to Jerusalem to worship. ¹²My accusers did not find me arguing with anyone at the temple, or stirring up a crowd in the synagogues or anywhere else in the city. ¹³And they cannot prove to you the charges they are now making against me. ¹⁴However, I admit that I worship the God of our fathers as a follower of the Way, which they call a sect. I believe everything that agrees with the Law and that is written in the Prophets, ¹⁵and I have the same hope in God as these men, that there will be a resurrection of both the righteous and the wicked. ¹⁶So I strive always to keep my conscience clear before God and man.

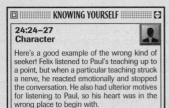

¹⁷"After an absence of several years, I came to Jerusalem to bring my people gifts for the poor and to present offerings. ¹⁸I was ceremonially clean when they found me in the temple courts doing this. There was no crowd with me, nor was I involved in any disturbance. ¹⁹But there are some Jews from the province of Asia, who ought to be here before you and bring charges if they have anything against me. ²⁰Or these who are here should state what crime they found in me when I stood before the Sanhedrin— ²¹unless

---

ᵃ6–8 Some manuscripts him and wanted to judge him according to our law. ⁷But the commander, Lysias, came and with the use of much force snatched him from our hands ⁸and ordered his accusers to come before you. By

it was this one thing I shouted as I stood in their presence: 'It is concerning the resurrection of the dead that I am on trial before you today.'"

²²Then Felix, who was well acquainted with the Way, adjourned the proceedings. "When Lysias the commander comes," he said, "I will decide your case." ²³He ordered the centurion to keep Paul under guard but to give him some freedom and permit his friends to take care of his needs.

²⁴Several days later Felix came with his wife Drusilla, who was a Jewess. He sent for Paul and listened to him as he spoke about faith in Christ Jesus. ²⁵As Paul discoursed on righteousness, self-control and the judgment to come, Felix was afraid and said, "That's enough for now! You may leave. When I find it convenient, I will send for you." ²⁶At the same time he was hoping that Paul would offer him a bribe, so he sent for him frequently and talked with him.

²⁷When two years had passed, Felix was succeeded by Porcius Festus, but because Felix wanted to grant a favor to the Jews, he left Paul in prison.

The Trial Before Festus

25 Three days after arriving in the province, Festus went up from Caesarea to Jerusalem, ²where the chief priests and Jewish leaders appeared before him and presented the charges against Paul. ³They urgently requested Festus, as a favor to them, to have Paul transferred to Jerusalem, for they were preparing an ambush to kill him along the way. ⁴Festus answered, "Paul is being held at Caesarea, and I myself am going there soon. ⁵Let some of your leaders come with me and press charges against the man there, if he has done anything wrong."

⁶After spending eight or ten days with them, he went down to Caesarea, and the next day he convened the court and ordered that Paul be brought before him. ⁷When Paul appeared, the Jews who had come down from Jerusalem stood around him, bringing many serious charges against him, which they could not prove.

⁸Then Paul made his defense: "I have done nothing wrong against the law of the Jews or against the temple or against Caesar."

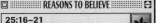

REASONS TO BELIEVE

25:16–21
The Incomparable Jesus

Although Festus didn't believe that Jesus' resurrection had taken place, he understood that it was at the very center of Christianity.

Paul once wrote, "If you confess with your mouth, 'Jesus is Lord,' and believe in your heart that God raised him from the dead, you will be saved" (Romans chapter 10, verse 9 [page 1482]). Christianity without Christ is a virtual impossibility; but Christianity without a *risen* Christ is just as invalid and cannot lead to a saving, transforming relationship with him.

⁹Festus, wishing to do the Jews a favor, said to Paul, "Are you willing to go up to Jerusalem and stand trial before me there on these charges?"

¹⁰Paul answered: "I am now standing before Caesar's court, where I ought to be tried. I have not done any wrong to the Jews, as you yourself know very well. ¹¹If, however, I am guilty of doing anything deserving death, I do not refuse to die. But if the charges brought against me by these Jews are not true, no one has the right to hand me over to them. I appeal to Caesar!"

¹²After Festus had conferred with his council, he declared: "You have appealed to Caesar. To Caesar you will go!"

Festus Consults King Agrippa

¹³A few days later King Agrippa and Bernice arrived at Caesarea to pay their respects to Festus. ¹⁴Since they were spending many days there, Festus discussed Paul's case with the king. He said: "There is a man here whom Felix left as a prisoner. ¹⁵When I went

to Jerusalem, the chief priests and elders of the Jews brought charges against him and asked that he be condemned.

¹⁶"I told them that it is not the Roman custom to hand over any man before he has faced his accusers and has had an opportunity to defend himself against their charges. ¹⁷When they came here with me, I did not delay the case, but convened the court the next day and ordered the man to be brought in. ¹⁸When his accusers got up to speak, they did not charge him with any of the crimes I had expected. ¹⁹Instead, they had some points of dispute with him about their own religion and about a dead man named Jesus who Paul claimed was alive. ²⁰I was at a loss how to investigate such matters; so I asked if he would be willing to go to Jerusalem and stand trial there on these charges. ²¹When Paul made his appeal to be held over for the Emperor's decision, I ordered him held until I could send him to Caesar."

²²Then Agrippa said to Festus, "I would like to hear this man myself."

He replied, "Tomorrow you will hear him."

Paul Before Agrippa

²³The next day Agrippa and Bernice came with great pomp and entered the audience room with the high ranking officers and the leading men of the city. At the command of Festus, Paul was brought in. ²⁴Festus said: "King Agrippa, and all who are present with us, you see this man! The whole Jewish community has petitioned me about him in Jerusalem and here in Caesarea, shouting that he ought not to live any longer. ²⁵I found he had done nothing deserving of death, but because he made his appeal to the Emperor I decided to send him to Rome. ²⁶But I have nothing definite to write to His Majesty about him. Therefore I have brought him before all of you, and especially before you, King Agrippa, so that as a result of this investigation I may have something to write. ²⁷For I think it is unreasonable to send on a prisoner without specifying the charges against him."

26 Then Agrippa said to Paul, "You have permission to speak for yourself."

So Paul motioned with his hand and began his defense: ²"King Agrippa, I consider myself fortunate to stand before you today as I make my defense against all the accusations of the Jews, ³and especially so because you are well acquainted with all the Jewish customs and controversies. Therefore, I beg you to listen to me patiently.

⁴"The Jews all know the way I have lived ever since I was a child, from the beginning of my life in my own country, and also in Jerusalem. ⁵They have known me for a long time and can testify, if they are willing, that according to the strictest sect of our religion, I lived as a Pharisee. ⁶And now it is because of my hope in what God has promised our fathers that I am on trial today. ⁷This is the promise our twelve tribes are hoping to see fulfilled as they earnestly serve God day and night. O king, it is because of this hope that the Jews are accusing me. ⁸Why should any of you consider it incredible that God raises the dead?

⁹"I too was convinced that I ought to do all that was possible to oppose the name of Jesus of Nazareth. ¹⁰And that is just what I did in Jerusalem. On the authority of the chief priests I put many of the saints in prison, and when they were put to death, I cast my vote against them. ¹¹Many a time I went from one synagogue to another to have them punished, and I tried to force them to blaspheme. In my obsession against them, I even went to foreign cities to persecute them.

¹²"On one of these journeys I was going to Damascus with the authority and commission of the chief priests. ¹³About noon, O king, as I was on the road, I saw a light from heaven, brighter than the sun, blazing around me and my companions. ¹⁴We all fell to the ground, and I heard a voice saying to me in Aramaic,ᵃ 'Saul, Saul, why do you persecute me? It is hard for you to kick against the goads.'

¹⁵"Then I asked, 'Who are you, Lord?'

" 'I am Jesus, whom you are persecuting,' the Lord replied. ¹⁶'Now get up and stand on your feet. I have appeared to you to appoint you as a servant and as a witness of what you have seen of me and what I will show you. ¹⁷I will rescue you from your own people and from the Gentiles. I am sending you to them ¹⁸to open their eyes and turn them from darkness to light, and from the power of Satan to God, so that they may receive forgiveness of sins and a place among those who are sanctified by faith in me.'

¹⁹"So then, King Agrippa, I was not disobedient to the vision from heaven. ²⁰First to those in Damascus, then to those in Jerusalem and in all Judea, and to the Gentiles also, I preached that they should repent and turn to God and prove their repentance by their deeds. ²¹That is why the Jews seized me in the temple courts and tried to kill me. ²²But I have had God's help to this very day, and so I stand here and testify to small and great alike. I am saying nothing beyond what the prophets and Moses said would happen— ²³that the Christᵇ would suffer and, as the first to rise from the dead, would proclaim light to his own people and to the Gentiles."

²⁴At this point Festus interrupted Paul's defense. "You are out of your mind, Paul!" he shouted. "Your great learning is driving you insane."

²⁵"I am not insane, most excellent Festus," Paul replied. "What I am saying is true and reasonable. ²⁶The king is familiar with these things, and I can speak freely to him. I am convinced that none of this has escaped his notice, because it was not done in a corner. ²⁷King Agrippa, do you believe the prophets? I know you do."

²⁸Then Agrippa said to Paul, "Do you think that in such a short time you can persuade me to be a Christian?"

²⁹Paul replied, "Short time or long—I pray God that not only you but all who are listening to me today may become what I am, except for these chains."

³⁰The king rose, and with him the governor and Bernice and those sitting with them. ³¹They left the room, and while talking with one another, they said, "This man is not doing anything that deserves death or imprisonment."

³²Agrippa said to Festus, "This man could have been set free if he had not appealed to Caesar."

Paul Sails for Rome

27 When it was decided that we would sail for Italy, Paul and some other prisoners were handed over to a centurion named Julius, who belonged to the Imperial Regiment. ²We boarded a ship from Adramyttium about to sail for ports along the coast of the province of Asia, and we put out to sea. Aristarchus, a Macedonian from Thessalonica, was with us.

³The next day we landed at Sidon; and Julius, in kindness to Paul, allowed him to go to his friends so they might provide for his needs. ⁴From there we put out to sea again and passed to the lee of Cyprus because the winds were against us. ⁵When we had sailed

ᵃ14 Or Hebrew   ᵇ23 Or Messiah

across the open sea off the coast of Cilicia and Pamphylia, we landed at Myra in Lycia. 6There the centurion found an Alexandrian ship sailing for Italy and put us on board. 7We made slow headway for many days and had difficulty arriving off Cnidus. When the wind did not allow us to hold our course, we sailed to the lee of Crete, opposite Salmone. 8We moved along the coast with difficulty and came to a place called Fair Havens, near the town of Lasea.

9Much time had been lost, and sailing had already become dangerous because by now it was after the Fast.ᵃ So Paul warned them, 10"Men, I can see that our voyage is going to be disastrous and bring great loss to ship and cargo, and to our own lives also." 11But the centurion, instead of listening to what Paul said, followed the advice of the pilot and of the owner of the ship. 12Since the harbor was unsuitable to winter in, the majority decided that we should sail on, hoping to reach Phoenix and winter there. This was a harbor in Crete, facing both southwest and northwest.

The Storm

13When a gentle south wind began to blow, they thought they had obtained what they wanted; so they weighed anchor and sailed along the shore of Crete. 14Before very long, a wind of hurricane force, called the "northeaster," swept down from the island. 15The ship was caught by the storm and could not head into the wind; so we gave way to it and were driven along. 16As we passed to the lee of a small island called Cauda, we were hardly able to make the lifeboat secure. 17When the men had hoisted it aboard, they passed ropes under the ship itself to hold it together. Fearing that they would run aground on the sandbars of Syrtis, they lowered the sea anchor and let the ship be driven along. 18We took such a violent battering from the storm that the next day they began to throw the cargo overboard. 19On the third day, they threw the ship's tackle overboard with their own hands. 20When neither sun nor stars appeared for many days and the storm continued raging, we finally gave up all hope of being saved.

21After the men had gone a long time without food, Paul stood up before them and said: "Men, you should have taken my advice not to sail from Crete; then you would have spared yourselves this damage and loss. 22But now I urge you to keep up your courage, because not one of you will be lost; only the ship will be destroyed. 23Last night an angel of the God whose I am and whom I serve stood beside me 24and said, 'Do not be afraid, Paul. You must stand trial before Caesar; and God has graciously given you the lives of all who sail with you.' 25So keep up your courage, men, for I have faith in God that it will happen just as he told me. 26Nevertheless, we must run aground on some island."

The Shipwreck

27On the fourteenth night we were still being driven across the Adriaticᵇ Sea, when about midnight the sailors sensed they were approaching land. 28They took soundings and found that the water was a hundred and twenty feetᶜ deep. A short time later they took soundings again and found it was ninety feetᵈ deep. 29Fearing that we would be dashed against the rocks, they dropped four anchors from the stern and prayed for daylight. 30In an attempt to escape from the ship, the sailors let the lifeboat down into the sea, pretending they were going to lower some anchors from the bow. 31Then Paul said to the centurion and the soldiers, "Unless these men stay with the ship, you cannot be saved." 32So the soldiers cut the ropes that held the lifeboat and let it fall away.

33Just before dawn Paul urged them all to eat. "For the last fourteen days," he said, "you have been in constant suspense and have gone without food—you haven't eaten anything. 34Now I urge you to take some food. You need it to survive. Not one of you will lose a single hair from his head." 35After he said this, he took some bread and gave

---

ᵃ9 That is, the Day of Atonement (Yom Kippur)   ᵇ27 In ancient times the name referred to an area extending well south of Italy.   ᶜ28 Greek twenty orguias (about 37 meters)   ᵈ28 Greek fifteen orguias (about 27 meters)

hanks to God in front of them all. Then he broke it and began to eat. ³⁶They were all
ncouraged and ate some food themselves. ³⁷Altogether there were 276 of us on board.
³⁸When they had eaten as much as they wanted, they lightened the ship by throwing
ne grain into the sea.

³⁹When daylight came, they did not recognize the land, but they saw a bay with a
andy beach, where they decided to run the ship aground if they could. ⁴⁰Cutting loose
he anchors, they left them in the sea and at the same time untied the ropes that held the
udders. Then they hoisted the foresail to the wind and made for the beach. ⁴¹But the
hip struck a sandbar and ran aground. The bow stuck fast and would not move, and
he stern was broken to pieces by the pounding of the surf.

⁴²The soldiers planned to kill the prisoners to prevent any of them from swimming
way and escaping. ⁴³But the centurion wanted to spare Paul's life and kept them from
arrying out their plan. He ordered those who could swim to jump overboard first and get
o land. ⁴⁴The rest were to get there on planks or on pieces of the ship. In this way
veryone reached land in safety.

Ashore on Malta

28 Once safely on shore, we found out that the island was called Malta. ²The
islanders showed us unusual kindness. They built a fire and welcomed us all
because it was raining and cold. ³Paul gathered a pile of brushwood and, as he put it on
he fire, a viper, driven out by the heat, fastened itself on his hand. ⁴When the islanders
saw the snake hanging from his hand, they said to each other, "This man must be a
murderer; for though he escaped from the sea, Justice has not allowed him to live." ⁵But
Paul shook the snake off into the fire and suffered no ill effects. ⁶The people expected
him to swell up or suddenly fall dead, but after waiting a long time and seeing nothing
unusual happen to him, they changed their minds and said he was a god.

⁷There was an estate nearby that belonged to Publius, the chief official of the island.
He welcomed us to his home and for three days entertained us hospitably. ⁸His father
was sick in bed, suffering from fever and dysentery. Paul went in to see him and, after
prayer, placed his hands on him and healed him. ⁹When this had happened, the rest of
the sick on the island came and were cured. ¹⁰They honored us in many ways and when
we were ready to sail, they furnished us with the supplies we needed.

Arrival at Rome

¹¹After three months we put out to sea in a ship that had wintered in the island. It was
an Alexandrian ship with the figurehead of the twin gods Castor and Pollux. ¹²We put in
at Syracuse and stayed there three days. ¹³From there we set sail and arrived at Rhegi-
um. The next day the south wind came up, and on the following day we reached Puteoli.
¹⁴There we found some brothers who invited us to spend a week with them. And so we
came to Rome. ¹⁵The brothers there had heard that we were coming, and they traveled
as far as the Forum of Appius and the Three Taverns to meet us. At the sight of these men
Paul thanked God and was encouraged. ¹⁶When we got to Rome, Paul was allowed to
live by himself, with a soldier to guard him.

Paul Preaches at Rome Under Guard

¹⁷Three days later he called together the leaders of the Jews. When they had assembled, Paul said to them: "My brothers, although I have done nothing against our people or
against the customs of our ancestors, I was arrested in Jerusalem and handed over to the
Romans. ¹⁸They examined me and wanted to release me, because I was not guilty of any
crime deserving death. ¹⁹But when the Jews objected, I was compelled to appeal to
Caesar—not that I had any charge to bring against my own people. ²⁰For this reason I

have asked to see you and talk with you. It is because of the hope of Israel that I am bound with this chain."

²¹They replied, "We have not received any letters from Judea concerning you, and none of the brothers who have come from there has reported or said anything bad about you. ²²But we want to hear what your views are, for we know that people everywhere are talking against this sect."

²³They arranged to meet Paul on a certain day, and came in even larger numbers to the place where he was staying. From morning till evening he explained and declared to them the kingdom of God and tried to convince them about Jesus from the Law of Moses and from the Prophets. ²⁴Some were convinced by what he said, but others would not believe. ²⁵They disagreed among themselves and began to leave after Paul had made this final statement: "The Holy Spirit spoke the truth to your forefathers when he said through Isaiah the prophet:

²⁶"'Go to this people and say,
  "You will be ever hearing but never understanding;
  you will be ever seeing but never perceiving."
²⁷For this people's heart has become calloused;
  they hardly hear with their ears,
  and they have closed their eyes.
Otherwise they might see with their eyes,
  hear with their ears,
  understand with their hearts
and turn, and I would heal them.'ᵃ

²⁸"Therefore I want you to know that God's salvation has been sent to the Gentiles, and they will listen!"ᵇ

³⁰For two whole years Paul stayed there in his own rented house and welcomed all who came to see him. ³¹Boldly and without hindrance he preached the kingdom of God and taught about the Lord Jesus Christ.

REASONS TO BELIEVE

28:23–28
The Christian Experience

By the end of the book of Acts, Paul had spent many years teaching about Jesus. Here, in prison, he patiently encountered yet another mixture of belief and rejection on the part of his listeners.

Yet this time Paul's words had an ominous finality (see verse 28). The early church had been almost exclusively Jewish. But the work of Paul and the other apostles had flung open the church's doors to the whole world. Paul had decided to minister primarily to non-Jews, and was determined to pull as many as he could into that wonderful new order called the kingdom of God.

Paul's work in taking Jesus' message to the Gentiles is part of the reason Christianity became a *world* religion. Today anyone—you too!—can be included in God's family regardless of any religious or ethnic background.

ᵃ27 Isaiah 6:9,10   ᵇ28 Some manuscripts listen!" ²⁹After he said this, the Jews left, arguing vigorously among themselves.

EPILOGUE

The story of the spread of Christianity makes for fascinating reading. The reasons behind this explosive first-century reaction are complex, but clearly something about the Christian message was very compelling.

The "Five Alive" reading plan is designed to help you comprehend that powerful message by reading five books. The final book on the list is Romans. It is a logical masterpiece that reads like a well-argued lawyer's explanation and defense of Christianity. Take your time with it. You will want to read that book slowly and with careful attention to the flow of thought. But reading it will be well worth the effort, because it is the apostle Paul's *magnum opus*, containing the best and most thorough articulation of the Christian message in the Bible.

Turn to page 1468 to begin reading Romans.

My parents divorced when I was seven. After living for three years with an aunt and uncle, I moved to Chicago to live with my dad and stepmother, where I stayed through high school. Those years were difficult for me; my father and his wife were alcoholics, my brother was (and still is) a homosexual, and my sisters left home at age 17. It helped that my dad was a choir director for our church. Although I hadn't given my life to Christ, I often found peace in Christian music.

I overcame all of my childhood traumas by being a superachiever and a caretaker. I thought to myself, "*I* will try harder; *I* will make everyone happy; *I* will succeed on my own! Through sheer effort and self-will, everything will be fine." From the ages of 21 to 38 I built my world on my good deeds, all the while ignoring my relationship with God. I had a good job where I was well-respected; I had a solid, 10-year marriage and two kids; I had a nice house, two cars and a cat. In retrospect, however, I can see that I was building my life on a foundation of stacked cards.

In October of 1989, my "house of cards" completely collapsed. My wife revealed to me that she had been having an affair with a neighbor for two years, and that she now wanted to marry him. I was devastated, and fear of being abandoned by my wife and children dominated both my waking and sleeping hours.

After the divorce, my ex-wife's sister gave me a call. When we talked about the affair, she explained that she felt my ex-wife's problem was that she had taken God out of his rightful place at the center of her world. At the end of our conversation, she invited me to go with her to a "Seeker service" at her church, and I agreed.

As I sat at church that night, I realized that I had the exact same problem! I had been ignoring God for years. That realization was a real turning point, and the following two years were a time of healing and growing for me. During that time I learned to take responsibility for all the pain I had caused others by not being a "truth-seeking" husband. I decided to commit my life to Christ, realizing that true joy would begin in my life only when I opened the door of my heart to God and became a fully devoted follower of Christ.

God's grace is truly amazing! The fact that he'd still want me after I had turned my back on him for so many years still leaves me speechless. Although some days are still shaky and challenging, my faith has given my life a new and solid foundation, along with many new opportunities and friends. I still have a long way to go; growth in Christ seems to be a slow and gradual process, and listening to God's will is a difficult task (especially since I'd rather do my own will!). But my life is much more at peace now—more authentic, more honest, and more enjoyable! I'm just beginning to realize what it means to be free!

Introduction

THE BOTTOM LINE

Well, nobody's perfect." That's a common idiom all people—regardless of their religious beliefs—seem to agree upon. It's also the starting point of this book. In it Paul explains that, no matter how good we think we are, we still fall short of God's plan for our lives. But the good news of Romans is that God still wants to have a relationship with us in spite of our imperfections. Jesus' work on our behalf makes us acceptable in God's eyes. In chapter 8, one of the Bible's most powerful passages, Paul takes this concept a step further by describing the immense benefits of living a life directed by faith in Christ (see page 1478). This book explains more clearly than perhaps any other book in the Bible how you can have that kind of life.

CENTRAL IDEAS

- Paul reveals the universality of the problem of sin.
- This book explains the message of Christ's salvation and how we can accept it by faith.
- Paul responds to persecution with patience and frankly discusses his own inner struggles.
- Paul explains the benefits of living life in the power of the Holy Spirit.
- Paul gives practical guidance on living out the Christian faith.

OUTLINE

1 Introduction (1:1–15)
2 God is sinless and perfect (1:16–17)
3 People are imperfect (1:18–3:20)
4 Jesus offers us salvation (3:21–5:21)
5 People can have Christ's power (chs. 6–8)
6 Why God rejects evil (chs. 9–11)
7 The practice of the Christian life (12:1–15:13)
8 Conclusion (15:14–33)
9 Final greetings (ch. 16)

TITLE
This book is titled after its original recipients—Christians in Rome.

AUTHOR AND READERS
Paul, the author of this book, wrote this especially to the non-Jewish believers in Rome. He was preparing the way for his eventual visit, reminding them of the basics of salvation. He also wanted to outline to his readers the relationship between the Jew and the non-Jew in the early church.

Every religion tries to answer a fundamental question, phrased in a multitude of ways, that essentially boils down to this: "What must a person do to gain eternal life?"

Every world religion—except Christianity—says that eternal life must be earned.

In Buddhism the ultimate goal is enlightenment. It is called "Nirvana," or the blissful extinction of all desires. According to the Buddha's teaching, all pain and suffering originate in human desire. If desire itself can be overcome by following the Eightfold Path, one can achieve "Nirvana," which is total nothingness.

The Hindu's ultimate destiny is to discover that the individual soul is really part of the bigger world soul, which includes everything else that exists. Hindus say that people are repeatedly reborn in endless cycles of reincarnation to try to work out their "karma" (the law of reaping what you sow) so that they can eventually reach this highest state. Achieving this Hindu goal is like being a drop of water that is returned to the ocean. Individuality is lost as the self is absorbed into the world soul.

"What must a person do to gain eternal life?"

The afterlife to which followers of Islam aspire is called "Paradise"—a spiritual wonderland of sensual delights. Muslims achieve paradise by staying away from earthly sensual delights in anticipation of their heavenly reward. In addition, a Muslim must follow the Five Pillars of Islam: repeating the Islamic creed, making a pilgrimage to Mecca, giving alms to the poor, praying five times a day, and keeping the fast of the month of Ramadan. Failure to fulfill these commands jeopardizes one's chances that Allah, the Muslim god, will allow the individual into Paradise.

Note the common teaching in all of these world religions that one can achieve the afterlife through human effort. Based on such a system, people can never know for sure where they will end up after they die. It's like taking a test in school, but never knowing if you have a passing score.

Unlike other world religions, Christianity teaches that people can know for sure that they have eternal life. The Bible teaches that Jesus took God's test in our place—and passed it. Now Jesus offers to write our names on that perfect exam, so that his "A" is applied to us. In other words, we can have eternal life based on the merits of what Jesus has done for us.

The highest goal of God's highest creation—you and me—is not to be absorbed into God, but to have a relationship with him and to enjoy him forever. The apostle Paul explains in the book of Romans how a person can know God. This book, more than any other in the Bible, discusses the basis and benefits of a relationship with God. If you're interested in knowing what you must do to have eternal life, turn to Romans chapter 10, verses 9–13 (page 1482).

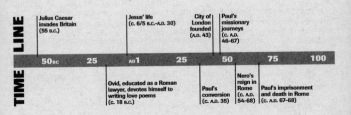

TIME LINE

Julius Caesar invades Britain (55 B.C.)		Jesus' life (c. 6/5 B.C.–A.D. 30)		City of London founded (A.D. 43)	Paul's missionary journeys (c. A.D. 46–67)		
50 BC	**25**	**AD 1**	**25**	**50**	**75**	**100**
	Ovid, educated as a Roman lawyer, devotes himself to writing love poems (c. 18 B.C.)			Paul's conversion (c. A.D. 35)	Nero's reign in Rome (c. A.D. 54–68)	Paul's imprisonment and death in Rome (c. A.D. 67–68)

ROMANS

1 Paul, a servant of Christ Jesus, called to be an apostle and set apart for the gospel of God— ²the gospel he promised beforehand through his prophets in the Holy Scriptures ³regarding his Son, who as to his human nature was a descendant of David, ⁴and who through the Spirit*ᵃ* of holiness was declared with power*ᵇ* to be the Son of God by his resurrection from the dead: Jesus Christ our Lord. ⁵Through him and for his name's sake, we received grace and apostleship to call people from among all the Gentiles to the obedience that comes from faith. ⁶And you also are among those who are called to belong to Jesus Christ.

⁷To all in Rome who are loved by God and called to be saints:

Grace and peace to you from God our Father and from the Lord Jesus Christ.

Paul's Longing to Visit Rome

⁸First, I thank my God through Jesus Christ for all of you, because your faith is being reported all over the world. ⁹God, whom I serve with my whole heart in preaching the gospel of his Son, is my witness how constantly I remember you ¹⁰in my prayers at all times; and I pray that now at last by God's will the way may be opened for me to come to you.

¹¹I long to see you so that I may impart to you some spiritual gift to make you strong— ¹²that is, that you and I may be mutually encouraged by each other's faith. ¹³I do not want you to be unaware, brothers, that I planned many times to come to you (but have been prevented from doing so until now) in order that I might have a harvest among you, just as I have had among the other Gentiles.

¹⁴I am obligated both to Greeks and non-Greeks, both to the wise and the foolish. ¹⁵That is why I am so eager to preach the gospel also to you who are at Rome.

¹⁶I am not ashamed of the gospel, because it is the power of God for the salvation of everyone who believes: first for the Jew, then for the Gentile. ¹⁷For in the gospel a

ᵃ4 Or who as to his spirit   ᵇ4 Or was appointed to be the Son of God with power

righteousness from God is revealed, a righteousness that is by faith from first to last,[a] just as it is written: "The righteous will live by faith."[b]

God's Wrath Against Mankind

[18]The wrath of God is being revealed from heaven against all the godlessness and wickedness of men who suppress the truth by their wickedness, [19]since what may be known about God is plain to them, because God has made it plain to them. [20]For since the creation of the world God's invisible qualities—his eternal power and divine nature—have been clearly seen, being understood from what has been made, so that men are without excuse.

[21]For although they knew God, they neither glorified him as God nor gave thanks to him, but their thinking became futile and their foolish hearts were darkened. [22]Although they claimed to be wise, they became fools [23]and exchanged the glory of the immortal God for images made to look like mortal man and birds and animals and reptiles.

[24]Therefore God gave them over in the sinful desires of their hearts to sexual impurity for the degrading of their bodies with one another. [25]They exchanged the truth of God for a lie, and worshiped and served created things rather than the Creator—who is forever praised. Amen.

[26]Because of this, God gave them over to shameful lusts. Even their women exchanged natural relations for unnatural ones. [27]In the same way the men also abandoned natural relations with women and were inflamed with lust for one another. Men committed indecent acts with other men, and received in themselves the due penalty for their perversion.

[28]Furthermore, since they did not think it worthwhile to retain the knowledge of God, he gave them over to a depraved mind, to do what ought not to be done. [29]They have become filled with every kind of wickedness, evil, greed and depravity. They are full of envy, murder, strife, deceit and malice. They are gossips, [30]slanderers, God-haters, insolent, arrogant and boastful; they invent ways of doing evil; they disobey their parents; [31]they are senseless, faithless, heartless, ruthless. [32]Although they know God's righteous decree that those who do such things deserve death, they not only continue to do these very things but also approve of those who practice them.

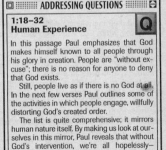

▣ :::::::::: **DISCOVERING GOD** :::::::::: ⬦

1:16–17
Life with God

Paul states the theme of Romans in these two verses: God will rescue women and men who turn to him in faith from the consequences of sin, regardless of their ethnic or religious background. That freedom will transform their lives here on earth and assure them of life after death.

　Note especially Paul's explanation of how salvation is obtained: by trusting Jesus Christ. Paul declared that people who are right with God get that way *by faith*. He challenged the popular religious assumption that God bases admission into heaven on a person's good deeds. Instead, Paul proclaimed that Jesus Christ has already done the work of saving people, and that the proper response is to receive that gift and live in the reality of Jesus' forgiveness.

▣ :::::::::: **ADDRESSING QUESTIONS** :::::::::: ⬦

1:18–32
Human Experience

In this passage Paul emphasizes that God makes himself known to all people through his glory in creation. People are "without excuse"; there is no reason for anyone to deny that God exists.

　Still, people live as if there is no God at all. In the next few verses Paul outlines some of the activities in which people engage, willfully distorting God's created order.

　The list is quite comprehensive; it mirrors human nature itself. By making us look at ourselves in this mirror, Paul reveals that without God's intervention, we're all hopelessly—though justifiably—lost. But keep reading . . . there's good news coming.

---

[a]17 Or *is from faith to faith*　　[b]17 Hab. 2:4

God's Righteous Judgment

2 You, therefore, have no excuse, you who pass judgment on someone else, for at whatever point you judge the other, you are condemning yourself, because you who pass judgment do the same things. ²Now we know that God's judgment against those who do such things is based on truth. ³So when you, a mere man, pass judgment on them and yet do the same things, do you think you will escape God's judgment? ⁴Or do you show contempt for the riches of his kindness, tolerance and patience, not realizing that God's kindness leads you toward repentance?

⁵But because of your stubbornness and your unrepentant heart, you are storing up wrath against yourself for the day of God's wrath, when his righteous judgment will be revealed. ⁶God "will give to each person according to what he has done."[a] ⁷To those who by persistence in doing good seek glory, honor and immortality, he will give eternal life. ⁸But for those who are self-seeking and who reject the truth and follow evil, there will be wrath and anger. ⁹There will be trouble and distress for every human being who does evil: first for the Jew, then for the Gentile; ¹⁰but glory, honor and peace for everyone who does good: first for the Jew, then for the Gentile. ¹¹For God does not show favoritism.

¹²All who sin apart from the law will also perish apart from the law, and all who sin under the law will be judged by the law. ¹³For it is not those who hear the law who are righteous in God's sight, but it is those who obey the law who will be declared righteous. ¹⁴(Indeed, when Gentiles, who do not have the law, do by nature things required by the law, they are a law for themselves, even though they do not have the law, ¹⁵since they show that the requirements of the law are written on their hearts, their consciences also bearing witness, and their thoughts now accusing, now even defending them.) ¹⁶This will take place on the day when God will judge men's secrets through Jesus Christ, as my gospel declares.

◫ ▦▦▦ KNOWING YOURSELF ▦▦▦ ⊟

2:1–16
Sin

Black sheep. Bad seed. Rebel. Criminal.

Have any of these labels ever been applied to you? If so, perhaps you feel like God is farther away from you than from other people. If not, perhaps you feel closer to God because you try to live right. Whatever your response, Paul has news for you: *In God's eyes, we're all the same.*

There's not a person on earth who can live up to God's perfect moral code. Those who look down their noses and accuse others of being hopelessly corrupt need to start looking in the mirror at some of their own thoughts, desires, and motives. Paul says that no matter what kind of evil we've done or how good we've tried to be in our lives, we all stand under God's judgment and in need of his forgiveness.

The Jews and the Law

¹⁷Now you, if you call yourself a Jew; if you rely on the law and brag about your relationship to God; ¹⁸if you know his will and approve of what is superior because you are instructed by the law; ¹⁹if you are convinced that you are a guide for the blind, a light for those who are in the dark, ²⁰an instructor of the foolish, a teacher of infants, because you have in the law the embodiment of knowledge and truth— ²¹you, then, who teach others, do you not teach yourself? You who preach against stealing, do you steal? ²²You who say that people should not commit adultery, do you commit adultery? You who abhor idols, do you rob temples? ²³You who brag about the law, do you dishonor God by breaking the law? ²⁴As it is written: "God's name is blasphemed among the Gentiles because of you."[b]

²⁵Circumcision has value if you observe the law, but if you break the law, you have

---

a6 Psalm 62:12; Prov. 24:12   *b24* Isaiah 52:5; Ezek. 36:22

become as though you had not been circumcised. ²⁶If those who are not circumcised keep the law's requirements, will they not be regarded as though they were circumcised? ²⁷The one who is not circumcised physically and yet obeys the law will condemn you who, even though you have the *ᵃ* written code and circumcision, are a lawbreaker.

²⁸A man is not a Jew if he is only one outwardly, nor is circumcision merely outward and physical. ²⁹No, a man is a Jew if he is one inwardly; and circumcision is circumcision of the heart, by the Spirit, not by the written code. Such a man's praise is not from men, but from God.

God's Faithfulness

3 What advantage, then, is there in being a Jew, or what value is there in circumcision? ²Much in every way! First of all, they have been entrusted with the very words of God.

³What if some did not have faith? Will their lack of faith nullify God's faithfulness? ⁴Not at all! Let God be true, and every man a liar. As it is written:

"So that you may be proved
    right when you speak
and prevail when you
    judge."*ᵇ*

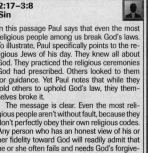

☐ ▒▒▒▒▒▒ KNOWING YOURSELF ▒▒▒▒▒▒ ⊟

2:17–3:8
Sin

In this passage Paul says that even the most religious people among us break God's laws. To illustrate, Paul specifically points to the religious Jews of his day. They knew all about God. They practiced the religious ceremonies God had prescribed. Others looked to them for guidance. Yet Paul notes that while they told others to uphold God's law, they themselves broke it.

The message is clear. Even the most religious people aren't without fault, because they don't perfectly obey their own religious codes. Any person who has an honest view of his or her fidelity toward God will readily admit that he or she often fails and needs God's forgiveness.

⁵But if our unrighteousness brings out God's righteousness more clearly, what shall we say? That God is unjust in bringing his wrath on us? (I am using a human argument.) ⁶Certainly not! If that were so, how could God judge the world? ⁷Someone might argue, "If my falsehood enhances God's truthfulness and so increases his glory, why am I still condemned as a sinner?" ⁸Why not say—as we are being slanderously reported as saying and as some claim that we say—"Let us do evil that good may result"? Their condemnation is deserved.

No One Is Righteous

⁹What shall we conclude then? Are we any better*ᶜ*? Not at all! We have already made the charge that Jews and Gentiles alike are all under sin. ¹⁰As it is written:

"There is no one righteous, not even one;
¹¹   there is no one who understands,
        no one who seeks God.
¹²All have turned away,
        they have together become worthless;
    there is no one who does good,
        not even one."*ᵈ*
¹³"Their throats are open graves;
        their tongues practice deceit."*ᵉ*
    "The poison of vipers is on their lips."*ᶠ*
¹⁴   "Their mouths are full of cursing and bitterness."*ᵍ*
¹⁵"Their feet are swift to shed blood;

ᵃ27 Or who, by means of a   *ᵇ4 Psalm 51:4*   *ᶜ9 Or worse*   *ᵈ12 Psalms 14:1-3; 53:1-3; Eccles. 7:20*
ᵉ13 Psalm 5:9   *ᶠ13 Psalm 140:3*   *ᵍ14 Psalm 10:7*

16   ruin and misery mark their ways,
17and the way of peace they do not know."*a*
18   "There is no fear of God before their eyes."*b*

19Now we know that whatever the law says, it says to those who are under the law, so that every mouth may be silenced and the whole world held accountable to God. 20Therefore no one will be declared righteous in his sight by observing the law; rather, through the law we become conscious of sin.

DISCOVERING GOD

3:21–31
Life with God

As Paul has demonstrated, we're all sinful and deserving of God's judgment (chapter 1, verse 18 through chapter 3, verse 21). But since we can't earn God's favor, is life just a cruel joke? Is Paul holding up a goal that's impossible for any of us to achieve?

No. Paul's discussion is meant to drive us to the realization that we need a gift from God, not an opportunity to earn a spiritual merit badge.

Paul says in verse 24 that we are justified by God's grace. The word "justified" refers to the act by which God, the righteous Judge, declares sinful people righteous, or "right" with him.

Consider this illustration: Sin is like a speeding ticket that we receive after breaking the law (as we all do). God is the judge who recognizes that the speeding ticket is valid (fair and justly given), but then declares it "paid in full"—and takes care of the payment himself.

In past ages, the payment for wrongdoing was the blood of animals (see the note on Leviticus chapter 1, verses 3–5 [page 124]). At one point in history, however, Jesus died as the once-and-for-all sin sacrifice *par excellence*. Now, because Jesus' blood has paid for our sin, God can declare us righteous. Those who put their trust in Jesus will never say, "I know God because I've lived a good life." On the contrary, they'll say, "I deserve God's judgment, but he has forgiven me on the basis of Jesus' blood."

Righteousness Through Faith

21But now a righteousness from God, apart from law, has been made known, to which the Law and the Prophets testify. 22This righteousness from God comes through faith in Jesus Christ to all who believe. There is no difference, 23for all have sinned and fall short of the glory of God, 24and are justified freely by his grace through the redemption that came by Christ Jesus. 25God presented him as a sacrifice of atonement,*c* through faith in his blood. He did this to demonstrate his justice, because in his forbearance he had left the sins committed beforehand unpunished— 26he did it to demonstrate his justice at the present time, so as to be just and the one who justifies those who have faith in Jesus.

27Where, then, is boasting? It is excluded. On what principle? On that of observing the law? No, but on that of faith. 28For we maintain that a man is justified by faith apart from observing the law. 29Is God the God of Jews only? Is he not the God of Gentiles too? Yes, of Gentiles too, 30since there is only one God, who will justify the circumcised by faith and the uncircumcised through that same faith. 31Do we, then, nullify the law by this faith? Not at all! Rather, we uphold the law.

Abraham Justified by Faith

4 What then shall we say that Abraham, our forefather, discovered in this matter? 2If, in fact, Abraham was justified by works, he had something to boast about—but not before God. 3What does the Scripture say? "Abraham believed God, and it was credited to him as righteousness."*d*

4Now when a man works, his wages are not credited to him as a gift, but as an obligation. 5However, to the man who does not work but trusts God who justifies the wicked, his faith is credited as righteousness. 6David says the same thing when he

a 17 Isaiah 59:7,8   *b 18* Psalm 36:1   *c 25* Or *as the one who would turn aside his wrath, taking away sin*
d 3 Gen. 15:6; also in verse 22

peaks of the blessedness of the man to whom God credits righteousness apart from works:

> [7]"Blessed are they
>   whose transgressions are forgiven,
>   whose sins are covered.
> [8]Blessed is the man
>   whose sin the Lord will never count against him."[a]

[9]Is this blessedness only for the circumcised, or also for the uncircumcised? We have been saying that Abraham's faith was credited to him as righteousness. [10]Under what circumstances was it credited? Was it after he was circumcised, or before? It was not after, but before! [11]And he received the sign of circumcision, a seal of the righteousness that he had by faith while he was still uncircumcised. So then, he is the father of all who believe but have not been circumcised, in order that righteousness might be credited to them. [12]And he is also the father of the circumcised who not only are circumcised but who also walk in the footsteps of the faith that our father Abraham had before he was circumcised.

[13]It was not through law that Abraham and his offspring received the promise that he would be heir of the world, but through the righteousness that comes by faith. [14]For if those who live by law are heirs, faith has no value and the promise is worthless, [15]because law brings wrath. And where there is no law there is no transgression.

[16]Therefore, the promise comes by faith, so that it may be by grace and may be guaranteed to all Abraham's offspring—not only to those who are of the law but also to those who are of the faith of Abraham. He is the father of us all. [17]As it is written: "I have made you a father of many nations."[b] He is our father in the sight of God, in whom he believed—the God who gives life to the dead and calls things that are not as though they were.

[18]Against all hope, Abraham in hope believed and so became the father of many nations, just as it had been said to him, "So shall your offspring be."[c] [19]Without weakening in his faith, he faced the fact that his body was as good as dead—since he was about

a 8 Psalm 32:1,2   b 17 Gen. 17:5   c 18 Gen. 15:5

::::::::::::::::: **DISCOVERING GOD** :::::::::::::::::

4:1–25
Life with God

To validate his statement that faith is the link that connects us with God, Paul uses an illustration that his Jewish readers readily understood. Almost 2000 years before Christ, a man named Abraham became the father of a new nation later named Israel. He had a very close relationship with God that Jewish people desired to imitate.

Paul discusses how this relationship between Abraham and God began, pointing out that Abraham was connected to God through simple belief (faith) before he received the rite of circumcision, and long before God gave people the law of Moses (verses 13–22). Abraham's faith, not his good works or participation in religious rituals, cemented his relationship with God. To the Jewish person of Paul's day, this was probably a startling realization. Circumcision and the law were the cornerstones of Jewish religious practice, yet here Paul asserts that neither of those saved Abraham, nor can they save anybody else!

If you're a seeker, Paul's point is good news for you. Salvation isn't based on something you must do for God. Religious rituals don't impress him. Good deeds won't win his favor. Rather, he wants you to believe (trust) in what he has already done for you through his Son, Jesus Christ. Then, as a forgiven son or daughter of God, you'll naturally want to serve him and others around you—not to earn anything, but out of a heart filled with gratitude for what God has done.

a hundred years old—and that Sarah's womb was also dead. [20]Yet he did not waver through unbelief regarding the promise of God, but was strengthened in his faith and gave glory to God, [21]being fully persuaded that God had power to do what he had promised. [22]This is why "it was credited to him as righteousness." [23]The words "it was credited to him" were written not for him alone, [24]but also for us, to whom God will credit righteousness—for us who believe in him who raised Jesus our Lord from the dead. [25]He was delivered over to death for our sins and was raised to life for our justification.

Peace and Joy

5 Therefore, since we have been justified through faith, we[a] have peace with God through our Lord Jesus Christ, [2]through whom we have gained access by faith into this grace in which we now stand. And we[a] rejoice in the hope of the glory of God. [3]Not only so, but we[a] also rejoice in our sufferings, because we know that suffering produces perseverance; [4]perseverance, character; and character, hope. [5]And hope does not disappoint us, because God has poured out his love into our hearts by the Holy Spirit, whom he has given us.

[6]You see, at just the right time, when we were still powerless, Christ died for the ungodly. [7]Very rarely will anyone die for a righteous man, though for a good man someone might possibly dare to die. [8]But God demonstrates his own love for us in this: While we were still sinners, Christ died for us.

[9]Since we have now been justified by his blood, how much more shall we be saved from God's wrath through him! [10]For if, when we were God's enemies, we were reconciled to him through the death of his Son, how much more, having been reconciled, shall we be saved through his life! [11]Not only is this so, but we also rejoice in God through our Lord Jesus Christ, through whom we have now received reconciliation.

◼ ▦▦▦▦▦ REASONS TO BELIEVE ▦▦▦▦▦ ▣

5:1-11
The Christian Experience

Are there any practical benefits to following Christ?

Paul lists three in these verses: peace with God, hope in affliction, and love that's unconditional.

When Jesus said, "Whoever loses his life for me will find it" (Matthew chapter 16, verse 25 [page 1282]), he didn't mean that our lives would become empty when we made the trade. Paul helps us see some of the wonderful blessings that fill our lives when we make that exchange.

Life is full of peaks and valleys. Christ-followers make it through both the good times and the tough times by clinging to promises such as these that God has made.

Death Through Adam, Life Through Christ

[12]Therefore, just as sin entered the world through one man, and death through sin, and in this way death came to all men, because all sinned— [13]for before the law was given, sin was in the world. But sin is not taken into account when there is no law. [14]Nevertheless, death reigned from the time of Adam to the time of Moses, even over those who did not sin by breaking a command, as did Adam, who was a pattern of the one to come.

[15]But the gift is not like the trespass. For if the many died by the trespass of the one man, how much more did God's grace and the gift that came by the grace of the one man, Jesus Christ, overflow to the many! [16]Again, the gift of God is not like the result of the one man's sin: The judgment followed one sin and brought condemnation, but the gift followed many trespasses and brought justification. [17]For if, by the trespass of the one man, death reigned through that one man, how much more will those who receive God's abundant provision of grace and of the gift of righteousness reign in life through the one man, Jesus Christ.

[a]1,2,3 Or let us

¹⁸Consequently, just as the result of one trespass was condemnation for all men, so also the result of one act of righteousness was justification that brings life for all men. ¹⁹For just as through the disobedience of the one man the many were made sinners, so also through the obedience of the one man the many will be made righteous.

²⁰The law was added so that the trespass might increase. But where sin increased, grace increased all the more, ²¹so that, just as sin reigned in death, so also grace might reign through righteousness to bring eternal life through Jesus Christ our Lord.

Dead to Sin, Alive in Christ

6 What shall we say, then? Shall we go on sinning so that grace may increase? ²By no means! We died to sin; how can we live in it any longer? ³Or don't you know that all of us who were baptized into Christ Jesus were baptized into his death? ⁴We were therefore buried with him through baptism into death in order that, just as Christ was raised from the dead through the glory of the Father, we too may live a new life.

⁵If we have been united with him like this in his death, we will certainly also be united with him in his resurrection. ⁶For we know that our old self was crucified with him so that the body of sin might be done away with,ᵃ that we should no longer be slaves to sin— ⁷because anyone who has died has been freed from sin.

⁸Now if we died with Christ, we believe that we will also live with him. ⁹For we know that since Christ was raised from the dead, he cannot die again; death no longer has mastery over him. ¹⁰The death he died, he died to sin once for all; but the life he lives, he lives to God.

¹¹In the same way, count yourselves dead to sin but alive to God in Christ Jesus. ¹²Therefore do not let sin reign in your mortal body so that you obey its evil desires. ¹³Do not offer the parts of your body to sin, as instruments of wickedness, but rather offer yourselves to God, as those who have been brought from death to life; and offer the parts of your body to him as instruments of righteousness. ¹⁴For sin shall not be your master, because you are not under law, but under grace.

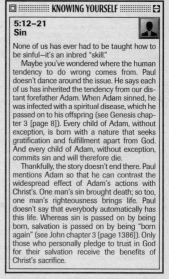

::::::::::: KNOWING YOURSELF :::::::::::

5:12-21
Sin

None of us has ever had to be taught how to be sinful—it's an inbred "skill."

Maybe you've wondered where the human tendency to do wrong comes from. Paul doesn't dance around the issue. He says each of us has inherited the tendency from our distant forefather Adam. When Adam sinned, he was infected with a spiritual disease, which he passed on to his offspring (see Genesis chapter 3 [page 8]). Every child of Adam, without exception, is born with a nature that seeks gratification and fulfillment apart from God. And every child of Adam, without exception, commits sin and will therefore die.

Thankfully, the story doesn't end there. Paul mentions Adam so that he can contrast the widespread effect of Adam's actions with Christ's. One man's sin brought death; so too, one man's righteousness brings life. Paul doesn't say that everybody automatically has this life. Whereas sin is passed on by being born, salvation is passed on by being "born again" (see John chapter 3 [page 1386]). Only those who personally pledge to trust in God for their salvation receive the benefits of Christ's sacrifice.

Slaves to Righteousness

¹⁵What then? Shall we sin because we are not under law but under grace? By no means! ¹⁶Don't you know that when you offer yourselves to someone to obey him as slaves, you are slaves to the one whom you obey—whether you are slaves to sin, which leads to death, or to obedience, which leads to righteousness? ¹⁷But thanks be to God that, though you used to be slaves to sin, you wholeheartedly obeyed the form of teach-

ᵃ6 Or be rendered powerless

ing to which you were entrusted. ¹⁸You have been set free from sin and have become slaves to righteousness.

¹⁹I put this in human terms because you are weak in your natural selves. Just as you used to offer the parts of your body in slavery to impurity and to ever-increasing wickedness, so now offer them in slavery to righteousness leading to holiness. ²⁰When you were slaves to sin, you were free from the control of righteousness. ²¹What benefit did you reap at that time from the things you are now ashamed of? Those things result in death! ²²But now that you have been set free from sin and have become slaves to God, the benefit you reap leads to holiness, and the result is eternal life. ²³For the wages of sin is death, but the gift of God is eternal life in^a Christ Jesus our Lord.

ADDRESSING QUESTIONS

**6:1–14
Human Experience**

The idea that salvation is a free gift may have raised this question in your mind: *If I don't have to do anything to win God's favor, what's to keep me from living a wild life after I accept Christ?*

Paul anticipated that question and gave a profound answer. When people trust Jesus to rescue them from their sin, an amazing transaction occurs: They are spiritually identified—tied together—with Christ. Since sin has no power over Christ, those who are united with Christ have also been delivered from the power of sin.

Paul also points out that it doesn't make sense to come to Jesus with the intention of disobeying him. That's like getting married with the intention of regularly committing adultery—possible, but utterly foolish and completely at odds with the purpose of the relationship.

Imagine a ceiling fan with blades driven by a belt connected to an electric motor. If someone disconnects the belt, the electric motor will still operate, but it won't be able to turn the blades. Similarly, when we come to Christ, the belt on the motor that drives us to sin gets disconnected. It's still there, and we unfortunately choose to reengage it at times, but we don't have to sin the way we did before we became Christ-followers.

The more we realize that we've been liberated from the power of sin, the more we want to live free from its destructive effects. Jesus' gift of salvation sets us free *from* sin, not free *to* sin!

An Illustration From Marriage

7 Do you not know, brothers—for I am speaking to men who know the law—that the law has authority over a man only as long as he lives? ²For example, by law a married woman is bound to her husband as long as he is alive, but if her husband dies, she is released from the law of marriage. ³So then, if she marries another man while her husband is still alive, she is called an adulteress. But if her husband dies, she is released from that law and is not an adulteress, even though she marries another man.

⁴So, my brothers, you also died to the law through the body of Christ, that you might belong to another, to him who was raised from the dead, in order that we might bear fruit to God. ⁵For when we were controlled by the sinful nature,^b the sinful passions aroused by the law were at work in our bodies, so that we bore fruit for death. ⁶But now, by dying to what once bound us, we have been released from the law so that we serve in the new way of the Spirit, and not in the old way of the written code.

Struggling With Sin

⁷What shall we say, then? Is the law sin? Certainly not! Indeed I would not have known what sin was except through the law. For I would not have known what coveting really was if the law had not said, "Do not covet."^c ⁸But sin, seizing the opportunity afforded by the commandment, produced in me every kind of covetous desire. For apart from law, sin is dead. ⁹Once I was alive apart from law; but when the commandment came, sin sprang to life and I died. ¹⁰I found that the very commandment that was intended to bring life actually brought death. ¹¹For sin, seizing the opportunity afforded

^a23 Or *through*   ^b5 Or *the flesh*; also in verse 25   ^c7 Exodus 20:17; Deut. 5:21

by the commandment, deceived me, and through the commandment put me to death. ¹²So then, the law is holy, and the commandment is holy, righteous and good.

¹³Did that which is good, then, become death to me? By no means! But in order that sin might be recognized as sin, it produced death in me through what was good, so that through the commandment sin might become utterly sinful.

¹⁴We know that the law is spiritual; but I am unspiritual, sold as a slave to sin. ¹⁵I do not understand what I do. For what I want to do I do not do, but what I hate I do. ¹⁶And if I do what I do not want to do, I agree that the law is good. ¹⁷As it is, it is no longer I myself who do it, but it is sin living in me. ¹⁸I know that nothing good lives in me, that is, in my sinful nature.ᵃ For I have the desire to do what is good, but I cannot carry it out. ¹⁹For what I do is not the good I want to do; no, the evil I do not want to do—this I keep on doing. ²⁰Now if I do what I do not want to do, it is no longer I who do it, but it is sin living in me that does it.

²¹So I find this law at work: When I want to do good, evil is right there with me. ²²For in my inner being I delight in God's law; ²³but I see another law at work in the members of my body, waging war against the law of my mind and making me a prisoner of the law of sin at work within my members. ²⁴What a wretched man I am! Who will rescue me from this body of death? ²⁵Thanks be to God—through Jesus Christ our Lord!

So then, I myself in my mind am a slave to God's law, but in the sinful nature a slave to the law of sin.

ᵃ18 Or my flesh

■ **REASONS TO BELIEVE** ■

7:1–25
The Incomparable Jesus

Perhaps one thing that has kept you from following Christ is your belief that you could never live up to God's expectations. You don't want to be a hypocrite, so you don't even bother trying to live up to standards that you know you'll never achieve.

In a way, you're right. Only one person has ever lived the Christian life perfectly—Jesus. So you're not alone in your belief that you can't hack it. God's commands are impossible to follow—not because he is unreasonable, but because we're so sinful. In fact, Paul says that one of the reasons why God gave us his commandments is so we'll stop believing that we're "good." Through the law we see that we can't fully obey God. That's why we need to rely on Jesus for forgiveness.

Paul notes three purposes for the law. First, *it reveals sin* (verse 7). A driver doesn't know he's speeding until he passes a speed-limit sign and compares it with his speedometer. Similarly, we don't know that some things are wrong until God points them out.

Second, *God's law provokes sin so that it comes into full view* (verses 8–13). To illustrate: What's your first response to a sign that says "Wet Paint—Do Not Touch"? Making something off limits actually increases our desire to disobey. That doesn't make God's law evil. It just points out how evil we are—how ready we are to do wrong.

Third, *God's law spells out the consequences of sin* (verse 13). If we're caught speeding, we get a ticket—that's the law. If we continually refuse to admit our sins to God and ask for his forgiveness, we pay the penalty and die spiritually.

Even the apostle Paul, as spiritually mature as he was, despaired that he ended up doing the very things he didn't want to (verses 15–23). His cry in verse 25 and his immediate response in verse 26 demonstrate the principle that he discusses in this chapter: Even though we live in a sinful world and experience sin's effects, we can look to Jesus for release from our bondage to sin. When we give our lives to Christ, we trust him to change us from the inside as we mature spiritually. It's a matter of growing into obedience—*training* to be like Jesus over time instead of *trying* to be like him in our own power.

Life Through the Spirit

8 Therefore, there is now no condemnation for those who are in Christ Jesus,[a] [2]because through Christ Jesus the law of the Spirit of life set me free from the law of sin and death. [3]For what the law was powerless to do in that it was weakened by the sinful nature,[b] God did by sending his own Son in the likeness of sinful man to be a sin offering.[c] And so he condemned sin in sinful man,[d] [4]in order that the righteous requirements of the law might be fully met in us, who do not live according to the sinful nature but according to the Spirit.

[5]Those who live according to the sinful nature have their minds set on what that nature desires; but those who live in accordance with the Spirit have their minds set on what the Spirit desires. [6]The mind of sinful man[e] is death, but the mind controlled by the Spirit is life and peace; [7]the sinful mind[f] is hostile to God. It does not submit to God's law, nor can it do so. [8]Those controlled by the sinful nature cannot please God.

[9]You, however, are controlled not by the sinful nature but by the Spirit, if the Spirit of God lives in you. And if anyone does not have the Spirit of Christ, he does not belong to Christ. [10]But if Christ is in you, your body is dead because of sin, yet your spirit is alive because of righteousness. [11]And if the Spirit of him who raised Jesus from the dead is living in you, he who raised Christ from the dead will also give life to your mortal bodies through his Spirit, who lives in you.

[12]Therefore, brothers, we have an obligation—but it is not to the sinful nature, to live according to it. [13]For if you live according to the sinful nature, you will die; but if by the Spirit you put to death the misdeeds of the body, you will live, [14]because those who are led by the Spirit of God are sons of God. [15]For you did not receive a spirit that makes you a slave again to fear, but you received the Spirit of sonship.[g] And by him we cry, *"Abba,[h] Father."* [16]The Spirit himself testifies with our spirit that we are God's children. [17]Now if we are children, then we are heirs—heirs of God and co-heirs with Christ, if indeed we share in his sufferings in order that we may also share in his glory.

▣ ▦▦▦▦▦▦ DISCOVERING GOD ▦▦▦▦▦▦ ▨

8:1–11
Life with God

Trying harder. It's a well-worn path. Tired, frustrated people take it when they resolve to live their lives differently. Unfortunately, that uphill path is just as worn with footprints moving in the opposite direction. People who resolve to "pull themselves up by the bootstraps" and change their lives for the better often find themselves in the same predicament within a few days, weeks, or months.

But it doesn't have to be that way. In this chapter, Paul spells out God's plan for us to experience the inner transformation that results in a changed lifestyle.

First, he says that we must *recognize that God will accept us completely in Christ* (verse 1). Even though repeated sin might make us feel guilty, God's condemnation becomes a thing of the past when we receive Christ as our forgiver and leader.

Second, we need to *recognize the freedom we have available in Christ* (verses 2–4). Through his Spirit, Jesus wants to liberate us from the downward spiral of sin. Just as aerodynamics, when properly applied, overcome the effects of gravity, so the Spirit frees us from the "gravity" of sin, allowing us to soar above the limitations of our sinful appetites and to please God.

Third, we must *remember that we now have a choice whether to be controlled by our sinful desires or by God's Spirit* (verses 5–11). Controlled by sin, we're rebellious and obsessed with gratifying our own self-seeking agendas. But when we're directed by God's Spirit, we're empowered by a new impulse to please him.

---

[a]1 Some later manuscripts *Jesus, who do not live according to the sinful nature but according to the Spirit*.   [b]3 Or *the flesh*; also in verses 4, 5, 8, 9, 12 and 13   [c]3 Or *man, for sin*   [d]3 Or *in the flesh*   [e]6 Or *mind set on the flesh*   [f]7 Or *The mind set on the flesh*   [g]15 Or *adoption*   [h]15 Aramaic for *Father*

uture Glory

18I consider that our present sufferings are not worth comparing with the glory that vill be revealed in us. **19**The creation waits in eager expectation for the sons of God to be evealed. **20**For the creation was subjected to frustration, not by its own choice, but by the ill of the one who subjected it, in hope **21**that*ᵃ* the creation itself will be liberated from s bondage to decay and brought into the glorious freedom of the children of God.

22We know that the whole creation has been groaning as in the pains of childbirth ght up to the present time. **23**Not only so, but we ourselves, who have the firstfruits of ie Spirit, groan inwardly as we wait ea-erly for our adoption as sons, the redemp-on of our bodies. **24**For in this hope we vere saved. But hope that is seen is no ope at all. Who hopes for what he already as? **25**But if we hope for what we do not et have, we wait for it patiently.

26In the same way, the Spirit helps us in ur weakness. We do not know what we ught to pray for, but the Spirit himself in-ercedes for us with groans that words can-ot express. **27**And he who searches our earts knows the mind of the Spirit, be-ause the Spirit intercedes for the saints in ccordance with God's will.

More Than Conquerors

28And we know that in all things God vorks for the good of those who love im,*ᵇ* who*ᶜ* have been called according o his purpose. **29**For those God foreknew ie also predestined to be conformed to the keness of his Son, that he might be the irstborn among many brothers. **30**And hose he predestined, he also called; those e called, he also justified; those he justi-ied, he also glorified.

31What, then, shall we say in response to his? If God is for us, who can be against is? **32**He who did not spare his own Son, ut gave him up for us all—how will he not lso, along with him, graciously give us all hings? **33**Who will bring any charge gainst those whom God has chosen? It is God who justifies. **34**Who is he that condemns? hrist Jesus, who died—more than that, who was raised to life—is at the right hand of iod and is also interceding for us. **35**Who shall separate us from the love of Christ? Shall rouble or hardship or persecution or famine or nakedness or danger or sword? **36**As it is vritten:

> "For your sake we face death all day long;
> we are considered as sheep to be slaughtered."*ᵈ*

7No, in all these things we are more than conquerors through him who loved us. **38**For I

■ ▓▓▓▓▓ **DISCOVERING GOD** ▓▓▓▓▓ ◨

8:28–30
Life with God

Imagine putting together a large puzzle with-out being able to look at the picture on the cover of the box. It would be next to impossi-ble, wouldn't it? You might successfully get the edges together. You might even make some progress on small sections. But your work would be painfully slow and frustrating as you held up each piece and wondered, *Where does this fit in?*

The same is true in life. Some pieces of the puzzle don't make sense when seen by them-selves. We wonder where our disappoint-ments, failures, and losses fit in. We want the box top—the "big picture" that assures us that all our experiences have a purpose.

God doesn't provide a box-top view of our lives, but he does give his followers a promise: Every experience in life's puzzle will be used for some good. While that doesn't mean that everything that happens to us will be good in and of itself, it does mean that, in the end, there will be no missing or useless pieces. God promises that he'll work to fit our expe-riences together, making even the painful and confusing times into a beautiful picture that has purpose and makes sense. That's a promise that "those who love him" can count on (verse 28).

20,21 Or *subjected it in hope.* **21**For   *ᵇ***28** *Some manuscripts* And we know that all things work together for good to those *ho love God*   *ᶜ***28** Or *works together with those who love him to bring about what is good—with those who*
36 *Psalm 44:22*

am convinced that neither death nor life, neither angels nor demons,[a] neither the present nor the future, nor any powers, **39**neither height nor depth, nor anything else in all creation, will be able to separate us from the love of God that is in Christ Jesus our Lord.

God's Sovereign Choice

9 I speak the truth in Christ—I am not lying, my conscience confirms it in the Holy Spirit— **2**I have great sorrow and unceasing anguish in my heart. **3**For I could wish that I myself were cursed and cut off from Christ for the sake of my brothers, those of my own race, **4**the people of Israel. Theirs is the adoption as sons; theirs the divine glory, the covenants, the receiving of the law, the temple worship and the promises. **5**Theirs are the patriarchs, and from them is traced the human ancestry of Christ, who is God over all, forever praised![b] Amen.

6It is not as though God's word had failed. For not all who are descended from Israel are Israel. **7**Nor because they are his descendants are they all Abraham's children. On the contrary, "It is through Isaac that your offspring will be reckoned."[c] **8**In other words, it is not the natural children who are God's children, but it is the children of the promise who are regarded as Abraham's offspring. **9**For this was how the promise was stated: "At the appointed time I will return, and Sarah will have a son."[d]

10Not only that, but Rebekah's children had one and the same father, our father Isaac.

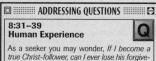

⬛ ADDRESSING QUESTIONS ↩

8:31–39
Human Experience **Q**

As a seeker you may wonder, *If I become a true Christ-follower, can I ever lose his forgiveness and the eternal life he gives me?*

According to this passage, if you choose to trust Christ, you'll receive a salvation that can never be taken from you. Paul goes so far as to say that *nothing in all creation* can separate you from the love of God in Christ.

Whenever you sin, Jesus Christ is your defense attorney (verse 34). He died for your sins—released you from them—and his resurrection proves you've been acquitted. When you're united with Jesus, the outcome of your case is not pending—it's *over.* If anyone—even you—tries to reopen the case against you, Jesus tells than you've already been forgiven. That is true freedom!

11Yet, before the twins were born or had done anything good or bad—in order that God's purpose in election might stand: **12**not by works but by him who calls—she was told, "The older will serve the younger."[e] **13**Just as it is written: "Jacob I loved, but Esau I hated."[f]

14What then shall we say? Is God unjust? Not at all! **15**For he says to Moses,

"I will have mercy on whom I have
    mercy,
and I will have compassion on
    whom I have compassion."[g]

16It does not, therefore, depend on man's desire or effort, but on God's mercy. **17**For the Scripture says to Pharaoh: "I raised you up for this very purpose, that I might display my power in you and that my name might be proclaimed in all the earth."[h] **18**Therefore God has mercy on whom he wants to have mercy, and he hardens whom he wants to harden.

19One of you will say to me: "Then why does God still blame us? For who resists his will?" **20**But who are you, O man, to talk back to God? "Shall what is formed say to him who formed it, 'Why did you make me like this?'"[i] **21**Does not the potter have the right to make out of the same lump of clay some pottery for noble purposes and some for common use?

22What if God, choosing to show his wrath and make his power known, bore with great patience the objects of his wrath—prepared for destruction? **23**What if he did this to

[a]38 Or *nor heavenly rulers*   [b]5 Or *Christ, who is over all. God be forever praised!* Or *Christ. God who is over all be forever praised!*   [c]7 Gen. 21:12   [d]9 Gen. 18:10,14   [e]12 Gen. 25:23   [f]13 Mal. 1:2,3   [g]15 Exodus 33:19   [h]17 Exodus 9:16   [i]20 Isaiah 29:16; 45:9

make the riches of his glory known to the objects of his mercy, whom he prepared in advance for glory— ²⁴even us, whom he also called, not only from the Jews but also from the Gentiles? ²⁵As he says in Hosea:

> "I will call them 'my people'
>   who are not my people;
> and I will call her 'my loved
>   one' who is not my
>   loved one,"ᵃ

²⁶and,

> "It will happen that in the very
>   place where it was said
>   to them,
>   'You are not my people,'
> they will be called 'sons of the
>   living God.'"ᵇ

²⁷Isaiah cries out concerning Israel:

> "Though the number of the
>   Israelites be like the
>   sand by the sea,
> only the remnant will be
>   saved.
> ²⁸For the Lord will carry out
>   his sentence on earth with speed and finality."ᶜ

²⁹It is just as Isaiah said previously:

> "Unless the Lord Almighty
>   had left us descendants,
> we would have become like Sodom,
>   we would have been like Gomorrah."ᵈ

Israel's Unbelief

³⁰What then shall we say? That the Gentiles, who did not pursue righteousness, have obtained it, a righteousness that is by faith; ³¹but Israel, who pursued a law of righteousness, has not attained it. ³²Why not? Because they pursued it not by faith but as if it were by works. They stumbled over the "stumbling stone." ³³As it is written:

> "See, I lay in Zion a stone that causes men to stumble
>   and a rock that makes them fall,
> and the one who trusts in him will never be put to shame."ᵉ

10 Brothers, my heart's desire and prayer to God for the Israelites is that they may be saved. ²For I can testify about them that they are zealous for God, but their zeal is not based on knowledge. ³Since they did not know the righteousness that comes from God and sought to establish their own, they did not submit to God's righteousness. ⁴Christ is the end of the law so that there may be righteousness for everyone who believes.

⁵Moses describes in this way the righteousness that is by the law: "The man who does these things will live by them."ᶠ ⁶But the righteousness that is by faith says: "Do not say

---

ADDRESSING QUESTIONS

9:1–8
God

Q

Paul grieved that the Jewish people had turned from their Messiah, Jesus Christ (the word "Christ" means "Messiah"). Even though historically Israel had a special relationship with God, most of the Israelites rejected Christ. Paul therefore focused his ministry on non-Jews who were willing to believe in Jesus as the Jewish Messiah and receive the benefits of that belief.

Paul argued that the true Israel consists of all people who share Abraham's faith, rather than his direct ancestry. That includes both Jews and non-Jews, and it can include *you* if you respond to God in faith, as Abraham did.

ᵃ25 Hosea 2:23   ᵇ26 Hosea 1:10   ᶜ28 Isaiah 10:22,23   ᵈ29 Isaiah 1:9   ᵉ33 Isaiah 8:14; 28:16
ᶠ5 Lev. 18:5

in your heart, 'Who will ascend into heaven?'ᵃ" (that is, to bring Christ down) ⁷"or 'Who will descend into the deep?'ᵇ" (that is, to bring Christ up from the dead). ⁸But what does it say? "The word is near you; it is in your mouth and in your heart,"ᶜ that is, the word of faith we are proclaiming: ⁹That if you confess with your mouth, "Jesus is Lord," and believe in your heart that God raised him from the dead, you will be saved. ¹⁰For it is with your heart that you believe and are justified, and it is with your mouth that you confess and are saved. ¹¹As the Scripture says, "Anyone who trusts in him will never be put to shame."ᵈ ¹²For there is no difference between Jew and Gentile—the same Lord is Lord of all and richly blesses all who call on him, ¹³for, "Everyone who calls on the name of the Lord will be saved."ᵉ

¹⁴How, then, can they call on the one they have not believed in? And how can they believe in the one of whom they have not heard? And how can they hear without someone preaching to them? ¹⁵And how can they preach unless they are sent? As it is written, "How beautiful are the feet of those who bring good news!"ᶠ

¹⁶But not all the Israelites accepted the good news. For Isaiah says, "Lord, who has believed our message?"ᵍ ¹⁷Consequently, faith comes from hearing the message, and the message is heard through the word of Christ. ¹⁸But I ask: Did they not hear? Of course they did:

> "Their voice has gone out into all the earth,
>   their words to the ends of the world."ʰ

¹⁹Again I ask: Did Israel not understand? First, Moses says,

> "I will make you envious by those who are not a nation;
>   I will make you angry by a nation that has no understanding."ⁱ

²⁰And Isaiah boldly says,

> "I was found by those who did not seek me;
>   I revealed myself to those who did not ask for me."ʲ

²¹But concerning Israel he says,

---

a6 Deut. 30:12   *b7* Deut. 30:13   *c8* Deut. 30:14   *d11* Isaiah 28:16   *e13* Joel 2:32
f15 Isaiah 52:7   *g16* Isaiah 53:1   *h18* Psalm 19:4   *i19* Deut. 32:21   *j20* Isaiah 65:1

≡ DISCOVERING GOD ≡

10:9–13
Life with God

The smartly dressed couple stands in front of family and friends, nervous but excited. Although an invisible attraction has brought them to this moment, their unseen love is about to become a matter of public record. The words and phrases that accompany this public ceremony are simple, yet the commitment behind those words is profoundly deep and life-changing.

Starting a new life with God is not all that different from beginning a marriage. According to Paul's words in this passage, that commitment is expressed by affirming the name that is higher and more important than all others. Like a bride uniting with her husband, we unite with Jesus, and his riches become ours through that marriage.

If you're a seeker, this is the place to come when you're ready to say, "I want to live forever with Jesus." You must acknowledge who Jesus is (Lord, Master, Leader) and be convinced that he rose from the dead and is alive right now. God's promise to you is that when you forsake all others and give yourself to him who conquered death for you, *you will be rescued*. Not maybe. Not possibly. But *absolutely*.

This is the "gospel" that Paul devoted his life to telling others about. This is the core assurance of Christianity. It can be yours too—if you just say, "I do."

"All day long I have held out my hands
to a disobedient and obstinate people."[a]

The Remnant of Israel

11 I ask then: Did God reject his people? By no means! I am an Israelite myself, a descendant of Abraham, from the tribe of Benjamin. [2]God did not reject his people, whom he foreknew. Don't you know what the Scripture says in the passage about Elijah—how he appealed to God against Israel: [3]"Lord, they have killed your prophets and torn down your altars; I am the only one left, and they are trying to kill me"[b]? [4]And what was God's answer to him? "I have reserved for myself seven thousand who have not bowed the knee to Baal."[c] [5]So too, at the present time there is a remnant chosen by grace. [6]And if by grace, then it is no longer by works; if it were, grace would no longer be grace.[d]

[7]What then? What Israel sought so earnestly it did not obtain, but the elect did. The others were hardened, [8]as it is written:

"God gave them a spirit of
stupor,
eyes so that they could not
see
and ears so that they could
not hear,
to this very day."[e]

[9]And David says:

"May their table become a
snare and a trap,
a stumbling block and a
retribution for them.
[10]May their eyes be darkened so
they cannot see,
and their backs be bent
forever."[f]

Ingrafted Branches

[11]Again I ask: Did they stumble so as to fall beyond recovery? Not at all! Rather, because of their transgression, salvation has come to the Gentiles to make Israel envious. [12]But if their transgression means riches for the world, and their loss means riches for the Gentiles, how much greater riches will their fullness bring!

[13]I am talking to you Gentiles. Inasmuch as I am the apostle to the Gentiles, I make much of my ministry [14]in the hope that I may somehow arouse my own people to envy and save some of them. [15]For if their rejection is the reconciliation of the world, what will their acceptance be but life from the dead? [16]If the part of the dough offered as firstfruits is holy, then the whole batch is holy; if the root is holy, so are the branches.

[17]If some of the branches have been broken off, and you, though a wild olive shoot, have been grafted in among the others and now share in the nourishing sap from the olive root, [18]do not boast over those branches. If you do, consider this: You do not support the root, but the root supports you. [19]You will say then, "Branches were broken off so that

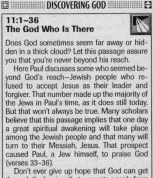

▣ ▦▦▦ DISCOVERING GOD ▦▦▦ ⬧

**11:1–36
The God Who Is There**

Does God sometimes seem far away or hidden in a thick cloud? Let this passage assure you that you're never beyond his reach.

Here Paul discusses some who seemed beyond God's reach—Jewish people who refused to accept Jesus as their leader and forgiver. That number made up the majority of the Jews in Paul's time, as it does still today. But that won't always be true. Many scholars believe that this passage implies that one day a great spiritual awakening will take place among the Jewish people and that many will turn to their Messiah, Jesus. That prospect caused Paul, a Jew himself, to praise God (verses 33–36).

Don't ever give up hope that God can get through the barriers that separate people from him. He can do it for individuals, groups of people and even nations. But, more specifically, he can do it for *you!*

---

[a]21 Isaiah 65:2   [b]3 1 Kings 19:10,14   [c]4 1 Kings 19:18   [d]6 Some manuscripts by grace. But if by works, then it is no longer grace; if it were, work would no longer be work.   [e]8 Deut. 29:4; Isaiah 29:10   [f]10 Psalm 69:22,23

I could be grafted in." ²⁰Granted. But they were broken off because of unbelief, and you stand by faith. Do not be arrogant, but be afraid. ²¹For if God did not spare the natural branches, he will not spare you either.

²²Consider therefore the kindness and sternness of God: sternness to those who fell, but kindness to you, provided that you continue in his kindness. Otherwise, you also will be cut off. ²³And if they do not persist in unbelief, they will be grafted in, for God is able to graft them in again. ²⁴After all, if you were cut out of an olive tree that is wild by nature, and contrary to nature were grafted into a cultivated olive tree, how much more readily will these, the natural branches, be grafted into their own olive tree!

All Israel Will Be Saved

²⁵I do not want you to be ignorant of this mystery, brothers, so that you may not be conceited: Israel has experienced a hardening in part until the full number of the Gentiles has come in. ²⁶And so all Israel will be saved, as it is written:

> "The deliverer will come from Zion;
>   he will turn godlessness away from Jacob.
> ²⁷And this is[a] my covenant with them
>   when I take away their sins."[b]

²⁸As far as the gospel is concerned, they are enemies on your account; but as far as election is concerned, they are loved on account of the patriarchs, ²⁹for God's gifts and his call are irrevocable. ³⁰Just as you who were at one time disobedient to God have now received mercy as a result of their disobedience, ³¹so they too have now become disobedient in order that they too may now[c] receive mercy as a result of God's mercy to you. ³²For God has bound all men over to disobedience so that he may have mercy on them all.

Doxology

³³Oh, the depth of the riches of the
        wisdom and[d] knowledge of
        God!
    How unsearchable his judgments,
        and his paths beyond tracing out!
³⁴"Who has known the mind of the
        Lord?
    Or who has been his counselor?"[e]
³⁵"Who has ever given to God,
        that God should repay him?"[f]
³⁶For from him and through him and to him are all things.
    To him be the glory forever! Amen.

:::::::::: DISCOVERING GOD ::::::::::

12:1–8
Life with God

What difference does being a Christ-follower make in our day-to-day lives? A huge one! Paul takes the rest of the book of Romans (chapters 12–16) to tell us about it.

When we accept Christ's leadership in our lives, we experience an entire change in life focus. To use Paul's illustration, an animal lying on an altar has basically one purpose, and very few earthly concerns. In the same way our lives, once given to God, are now totally at his disposal; our talents and our selfish former agenda are now surrendered to his purpose. And the more we give of ourselves to him, the more he will empower, bless and use us.

Living Sacrifices

12 Therefore, I urge you, brothers, in view of God's mercy, to offer your bodies as living sacrifices, holy and pleasing to God—this is your spiritual[g] act of worship. ²Do not conform any longer to the pattern of this world, but be transformed by the renewing of your mind. Then you will be able to test and approve what God's will is—his good, pleasing and perfect will.

---

[a]27 Or will be　[b]27 Isaiah 59:20,21; 27:9; Jer. 31:33,34　[c]31 Some manuscripts do not have now.　[d]33 Or riches and the wisdom and the　[e]34 Isaiah 40:13　[f]35 Job 41:11　[g]1 Or reasonable

³For by the grace given me I say to every one of you: Do not think of yourself more ᵢighly than you ought, but rather think of yourself with sober judgment, in accordance ᵥith the measure of faith God has given you. ⁴Just as each of us has one body with many ᵐembers, and these members do not all have the same function, ⁵so in Christ we who ᵣe many form one body, and each member belongs to all the others. ⁶We have different ᵢifts, according to the grace given us. If a man's gift is prophesying, let him use it in ᵖroportion to his*ᵃ* faith. ⁷If it is serving, let him serve; if it is teaching, let him teach; ⁸if ᵗ is encouraging, let him encourage; if it is contributing to the needs of others, let him ᵍive generously; if it is leadership, let him govern diligently; if it is showing mercy, let ᵢm do it cheerfully.

ₒove

⁹Love must be sincere. Hate what is evil; cling to what is good. ¹⁰Be devoted to one ₐnother in brotherly love. Honor one another above yourselves. ¹¹Never be lacking in ₑal, but keep your spiritual fervor, serving the Lord. ¹²Be joyful in hope, patient in ᶠfliction, faithful in prayer. ¹³Share with God's people who are in need. Practice hospi-ₐlity.

¹⁴Bless those who persecute you; bless and do not curse. ¹⁵Rejoice with those who ₑjoice; mourn with those who mourn. ¹⁶Live in harmony with one another. Do not be ᵣoud, but be willing to associate with people of low position.*ᵇ* Do not be conceited.

¹⁷Do not repay anyone evil for evil. Be ₐreful to do what is right in the eyes of ₑverybody. ¹⁸If it is possible, as far as it ₑepends on you, live at peace with every-ₙe. ¹⁹Do not take revenge, my friends, but ₑave room for God's wrath, for it is written: It is mine to avenge; I will repay,"*ᶜ* says ₕe Lord. ²⁰On the contrary:

> "If your enemy is hungry, feed
>   him;
> if he is thirsty, give him
>   something to drink.
> In doing this, you will heap
>   burning coals on his
>   head."*ᵈ*

¹Do not be overcome by evil, but overcome ᵥil with good.

ₛubmission to the Authorities

13 Everyone must submit himself to the governing authorities,

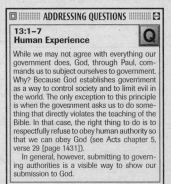

□ ▒▒▒▒ **ADDRESSING QUESTIONS** ▒▒▒▒ ⧉

13:1–7
Human Experience Q

While we may not agree with everything our government does, God, through Paul, commands us to subject ourselves to government. Why? Because God establishes government as a way to control society and to limit evil in the world. The only exception to this principle is when the government asks us to do something that directly violates the teaching of the Bible. In that case, the right thing to do is to respectfully refuse to obey human authority so that we can obey God (see Acts chapter 5, verse 29 [page 1431]).

In general, however, submitting to governing authorities is a visible way to show our submission to God.

ₒr there is no authority except that which God has established. The authorities that exist ᵃave been established by God. ²Consequently, he who rebels against the authority is ₑbelling against what God has instituted, and those who do so will bring judgment on ᵗhemselves. ³For rulers hold no terror for those who do right, but for those who do wrong. ᴰo you want to be free from fear of the one in authority? Then do what is right and he ᵥill commend you. ⁴For he is God's servant to do you good. But if you do wrong, be ᵃfraid, for he does not bear the sword for nothing. He is God's servant, an agent of wrath ₒ bring punishment on the wrongdoer. ⁵Therefore, it is necessary to submit to the ₐuthorities, not only because of possible punishment but also because of conscience.

⁶This is also why you pay taxes, for the authorities are God's servants, who give their

⁶ Or in agreement with the   *ᵇ16* Or willing to do menial work   *ᶜ19* Deut. 32:35   *ᵈ20* Prov. 25:21,22

full time to governing. ⁷Give everyone what you owe him: If you owe taxes, pay taxes; if revenue, then revenue; if respect, then respect; if honor, then honor.

Love, for the Day Is Near

⁸Let no debt remain outstanding, except the continuing debt to love one another, for he who loves his fellowman has fulfilled the law. ⁹The commandments, "Do not commit adultery," "Do not murder," "Do not steal," "Do not covet,"[a] and whatever other commandment there may be, are summed up in this one rule: "Love your neighbor as yourself."[b] ¹⁰Love does no harm to its neighbor. Therefore love is the fulfillment of the law.

> **□ STRENGTHENING RELATIONSHIPS**
>
> **13:8–14**
> **Social**
>
> The kind of love that Paul talks about here doesn't always come easily. How can we express Christ's love when our emotions are running high or when we're faced with some sort of injustice? One approach is to clench our fists, grit our teeth, and say, "I'll love you in spite of what a louse you are!" But that act doesn't fool anybody.
>
> A better way is to admit our "love limits" and ask God for his help. Ask yourself, "What would a truly loving person do in such a situation?" Then rely on Jesus to clothe you with his love (verse 14), so that you can show it to others.

¹¹And do this, understanding the present time. The hour has come for you to wake up from your slumber, because our salvation is nearer now than when we first believed. ¹²The night is nearly over; the day is almost here. So let us put aside the deeds of darkness and put on the armor of light. ¹³Let us behave decently, as in the daytime, not in orgies and drunkenness, not in sexual immorality and debauchery, not in dissension and jealousy. ¹⁴Rather, clothe yourselves with the Lord Jesus Christ, and do not think about how to gratify the desires of the sinful nature.[c]

The Weak and the Strong

14 Accept him whose faith is weak, without passing judgment on disputable matters. ²One man's faith allows him to eat everything, but another man, whose faith is weak, eats only vegetables. ³The man who eats everything must not look down on him who does not, and the man who does not eat everything must not condemn the man who does, for God has accepted him. ⁴Who are you to judge someone else's servant? To his own master he stands or falls. And he will stand, for the Lord is able to make him stand.

⁵One man considers one day more sacred than another; another man considers every day alike. Each one should be fully convinced in his own mind. ⁶He who regards one day as special, does so to the Lord. He who eats meat, eats to the Lord, for he gives thanks to God; and he who abstains, does so to the Lord and gives thanks to God. ⁷For none of us lives to himself alone and none of us dies to himself alone. ⁸If we live, we live to the Lord; and if we die, we die to the Lord. So, whether we live or die, we belong to the Lord.

⁹For this very reason, Christ died and returned to life so that he might be the Lord of both the dead and the living. ¹⁰You, then, why do you judge your brother? Or why do you look down on your brother? For we will all stand before God's judgment seat. ¹¹It is written:

> "'As surely as I live,' says the Lord,
> 'every knee will bow before me;
> every tongue will confess to God.'"[d]

¹²So then, each of us will give an account of himself to God.

¹³Therefore let us stop passing judgment on one another. Instead, make up your mind

---

[a]9 Exodus 20:13-15,17; Deut. 5:17-19,21   [b]9 Lev. 19:18   [c]14 Or *the flesh*   [d]11 Isaiah 45:23

ot to put any stumbling block or obstacle in your brother's way. **14**As one who is in the ord Jesus, I am fully convinced that no food*ᵃ* is unclean in itself. But if anyone regards omething as unclean, then for him it is unclean. **15**If your brother is distressed because of vhat you eat, you are no longer acting in love. Do not by your eating destroy your rother for whom Christ died. **16**Do not allow what you consider good to be spoken of as vil. **17**For the kingdom of God is not a matter of eating and drinking, but of righteous- ess, peace and joy in the Holy Spirit, **18**because anyone who serves Christ in this way is leasing to God and approved by men.

19Let us therefore make every effort to do what leads to peace and to mutual edifica- on. **20**Do not destroy the work of God for the sake of food. All food is clean, but it is vrong for a man to eat anything that causes someone else to stumble. **21**It is better not to at meat or drink wine or to do anything else that will cause your brother to fall.

22So whatever you believe about these things keep between yourself and God. Blessed the man who does not condemn himself by what he approves. **23**But the man who has oubts is condemned if he eats, because his eating is not from faith; and everything that oes not come from faith is sin.

15 We who are strong ought to bear with the failings of the weak and not to please ourselves. **2**Each of us should please his neighbor for his good, to uild him up. **3**For even Christ did not please himself but, as it is written: "The insults of nose who insult you have fallen on me."*ᵇ* **4**For everything that was written in the past vas written to teach us, so that through endurance and the encouragement of the Scrip- ures we might have hope.

5May the God who gives endurance and encouragement give you a spirit of unity mong yourselves as you follow Christ Jesus, **6**so that with one heart and mouth you may lorify the God and Father of our Lord Jesus Christ.

7Accept one another, then, just as Christ accepted you, in order to bring praise to God. For I tell you that Christ has become a servant of the Jews*ᶜ* on behalf of God's truth, to

14 Or *that nothing*   *b3* Psalm 69:9   *c8* Greek *circumcision*

⊡ :::::::::::::::::::::::::::::::::: **STRENGTHENING RELATIONSHIPS** :::::::::::::::::::::::::::::::::: ⬅

14:1–12
Social

If you're a seeker, perhaps one thing that has kept you from Christ is the fear that the Bible's rules will take away your freedom. Actually, Paul says just the opposite: We have so much freedom as Christians, we need to be careful how we handle it.

In this passage, Paul talks about two kinds of Christ-followers. Some believers feel that cer- tain issues (in this case, eating meat that had been sacrificed to idols) don't affect a person's re- lationship with God. Others, because of their backgrounds (Jews were specifically forbidden to eat such meat), believe certain things are off-limits.

Paul's discussion is specifically tied to the cultural situation in which he wrote. In our day, and even in your own community, these issues are different. For example, one family may feel strongly that drinking alcoholic beverages should be strictly off-limits to Christians. The family next door may not subscribe to such restrictions. Paul's advice in such situations is straightforward: Be careful not to criticize, and don't be condescending. Ultimately, each of us must answer to God, not to each other.

What's the practical implication of Paul's advice? When the two families get together for din- ner, the one family shouldn't offer wine with the meal, and the other family shouldn't write their neighbors off as "sinners" when they see a full wine rack in the kitchen. Believers need to exer- cise their Christian freedom in a way that builds others up. The freest people are those who act compassionately, not compulsively, toward other people, seeking to build them up and encourage them in their walk with God.

confirm the promises made to the patriarchs ⁹so that the Gentiles may glorify God for hi mercy, as it is written:

> "Therefore I will praise you among the Gentiles;
>> I will sing hymns to your name."ᵃ

¹⁰Again, it says,

> "Rejoice, O Gentiles, with his people."ᵇ

¹¹And again,

> "Praise the Lord, all you Gentiles,
>> and sing praises to him, all you peoples."ᶜ

¹²And again, Isaiah says,

> "The Root of Jesse will spring up,
>> one who will arise to rule over the nations;
>> the Gentiles will hope in him."ᵈ

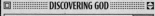

DISCOVERING GOD

15:1–13
Life with God

Followers of Christ don't measure success by how much money they make or how much power they acquire. A Christian's goal is simply to clearly reflect the life of Jesus—to do what Jesus would do if he were in our body.

In this passage, Paul outlines some specific ways his readers can reflect the life of Jesus: Be considerate of others who are at different points in their spiritual journey; diligently seek to please others instead of yourself; accept people who are different from you.

This is a tall order, since only Christ himself is strong enough to live this way. But people who follow Christ live in his strength, and the Spirit that lives within them gives them the power to treat others as Jesus would.

---

¹³May the God of hope fill you with al joy and peace as you trust in him, so tha you may overflow with hope by the powe of the Holy Spirit.

Paul the Minister to the Gentiles

¹⁴I myself am convinced, my brothers that you yourselves are full of goodness complete in knowledge and competent t instruct one another. ¹⁵I have written yo quite boldly on some points, as if to remin you of them again, because of the grac God gave me ¹⁶to be a minister of Chris Jesus to the Gentiles with the priestly dut of proclaiming the gospel of God, so tha the Gentiles might become an offering ac ceptable to God, sanctified by the Hol Spirit.

¹⁷Therefore I glory in Christ Jesus in m service to God. ¹⁸I will not venture to spea of anything except what Christ has accom plished through me in leading the Gentile to obey God by what I have said and done— ¹⁹by the power of signs and miracles through the power of the Spirit. So from Jerusalem all the way around to Illyricum, I hav fully proclaimed the gospel of Christ. ²⁰It has always been my ambition to preach th gospel where Christ was not known, so that I would not be building on someone else' foundation. ²¹Rather, as it is written:

> "Those who were not told about him will see,
>> and those who have not heard will understand."ᵉ

²²This is why I have often been hindered from coming to you.

Paul's Plan to Visit Rome

²³But now that there is no more place for me to work in these regions, and since I hav been longing for many years to see you, ²⁴I plan to do so when I go to Spain. I hope t

---

ᵃ9 2 Samuel 22:50; Psalm 18:49   ᵇ10 Deut. 32:43   ᶜ11 Psalm 117:1   ᵈ12 Isaiah 11:10   ᵉ21 Isaiah 52:15

sit you while passing through and to have you assist me on my journey there, after I ave enjoyed your company for a while. ²⁵Now, however, I am on my way to Jerusalem the service of the saints there. ²⁶For Macedonia and Achaia were pleased to make a ontribution for the poor among the saints in Jerusalem. ²⁷They were pleased to do it, nd indeed they owe it to them. For if the Gentiles have shared in the Jews' spiritual essings, they owe it to the Jews to share with them their material blessings. ²⁸So after

have completed this task and have made
ure that they have received this fruit, I will
to Spain and visit you on the way. ²⁹I
now that when I come to you, I will come
the full measure of the blessing of Christ.

³⁰I urge you, brothers, by our Lord Jesus
hrist and by the love of the Spirit, to join
e in my struggle by praying to God for
e. ³¹Pray that I may be rescued from the
nbelievers in Judea and that my service in
erusalem may be acceptable to the saints
here, ³²so that by God's will I may come to
ou with joy and together with you be re-
reshed. ³³The God of peace be with you
ll. Amen.

ersonal Greetings

16 I commend to you our sister
Phoebe, a servant*ᵃ* of the
hurch in Cenchrea. ²I ask you to receive
er in the Lord in a way worthy of the
aints and to give her any help she may
eed from you, for she has been a great
elp to many people, including me.

³Greet Priscilla*ᵇ* and Aquila, my fellow
    workers in Christ Jesus. ⁴They risked
    their lives for me. Not only I but all
    the churches of the Gentiles are
    grateful to them.
⁵Greet also the church that meets at their
    house.

Greet my dear friend Epenetus, who was the first convert to Christ in the province of
    Asia.
⁶Greet Mary, who worked very hard for you.
⁷Greet Andronicus and Junias, my relatives who have been in prison with me. They are
    outstanding among the apostles, and they were in Christ before I was.
⁸Greet Ampliatus, whom I love in the Lord.
⁹Greet Urbanus, our fellow worker in Christ, and my dear friend Stachys.
¹⁰Greet Apelles, tested and approved in Christ.
Greet those who belong to the household of Aristobulus.
¹¹Greet Herodion, my relative.
Greet those in the household of Narcissus who are in the Lord.
¹²Greet Tryphena and Tryphosa, those women who work hard in the Lord.
Greet my dear friend Persis, another woman who has worked very hard in the Lord.
¹³Greet Rufus, chosen in the Lord, and his mother, who has been a mother to me, too.

n *1* Or *deaconess*   *b3* Greek *Prisca,* a variant of *Priscilla*

¹⁴Greet Asyncritus, Phlegon, Hermes, Patrobas, Hermas and the brothers with them. ¹⁵Greet Philologus, Julia, Nereus and his sister, and Olympas and all the saints with the ¹⁶Greet one another with a holy kiss.

All the churches of Christ send greetings.

¹⁷I urge you, brothers, to watch out for those who cause divisions and put obstacles your way that are contrary to the teaching you have learned. Keep away from them. ¹⁸ such people are not serving our Lord Chri but their own appetites. By smooth ta and flattery they deceive the minds of r ive people. ¹⁹Everyone has heard abc your obedience, so I am full of joy over yc but I want you to be wise about what good, and innocent about what is evil.

²⁰The God of peace will soon crush Sat under your feet.

The grace of our Lord Jesus be with yc

²¹Timothy, my fellow worker, sends N greetings to you, as do Lucius, Jason a Sosipater, my relatives.

²²I, Tertius, who wrote down this lett greet you in the Lord.

²³Gaius, whose hospitality I and t whole church here enjoy, sends you N greetings.

Erastus, who is the city's director of public works, and our brother Quartus send y their greetings. ᵃ

²⁵Now to him who is able to establish you by my gospel and the proclamation of Jes Christ, according to the revelation of the mystery hidden for long ages past, ²⁶but nc revealed and made known through the prophetic writings by the command of the eterr God, so that all nations might believe and obey him— ²⁷to the only wise God be glc forever through Jesus Christ! Amen.

ᵃ 23 Some manuscripts *their greetings.* ²⁴*May the grace of our Lord Jesus Christ be with all of you. Amen.*

▣ ⫶⫶⫶ ADDRESSING QUESTIONS ⫶⫶⫶ ↔

**16:1–24
Human Experience** **Q**

Paul's personal connection with his readers is evident in that he greets 35 people by name at the end of this letter. This great theological treatise is *personal*. It was written to individuals.

Don't miss an important implication. If you're a seeker, you're not just a face in the crowd. Nothing would delight God more than including your name on the list of his children. He already knows your name. All you have to do is say yes to his invitation.

▣ ⫶⫶⫶⫶⫶⫶⫶⫶⫶⫶⫶⫶ EPILOGUE ⫶⫶⫶⫶⫶⫶⫶⫶⫶⫶⫶⫶ E

The book of Romans is the last one in the "Five Alive" series. If you've read all of these books, you have a good bird's-eye view of the Bible's main themes.

By now you probably have a sense of what aspects you agree with and what questions still remain. The next step is to keep reading—just turn a few pages and continue with the book called 1 Corinthians. When you're ready for a break, go back and check out the other three books that recount the life of Jesus: Matthew, Mark and Luke. In the Old Testament, the Psalms contain rich reflections on life with God; and the practical, down-to-earth wisdom of the Proverbs is a favorite among beginners as well as Bible-study veterans.

If you haven't done so already, find a small group of Christians who you can talk to about your questions and who can guide you into a greater understanding of the Bible's truths. Learning is both an individual and a collective process, and you'll make better progress if you have others around who you can learn from, and vice-versa.

Whatever roadblocks you experience, Christ promises that you'll find your way around them if you keep seeking. He earnestly desires to have a saving, life-transforming relationship with you. He wants to show himself to you as the unique Son of God, the One who died to give you new life.

Before I decided to trust Christ, my life was focused on earthly matters. I was very materialistic. To feed that craving I devoted most of my energy to my career rather than to my marriage. My marriage fell apart as a result, and the cumulative financial rewards from my successful career were consumed entirely by the legal process of divorce.

I decided to trust Christ alone for my salvation when I participated in a support group for divorced persons. Prior to my divorce I believed that I could handle anything on my own, without God's help. The divorce brought me to my knees, and I learned that I needed to place my faith in Christ in order to survive.

The decision to trust Christ has transformed my life. I am much happier now that I've changed the focus of my life to following Christ on a daily basis. I've turned away from my past ways, and am trying to conduct my life in a way that pleases God.

Although I was raised as a "good little Christian boy" from birth, it was a far different kind of Christianity than I now know. I was baptized at age seven in our fear-based church, and when my mother remarried, I was baptized again at age 15 in a church that was even more "shame and punishment" focused.

Ten years in a 12-step recovery group and more than three years at my current church have brought me along a journey of faith and surrender, a journey from pride to greater humility. The world tells me that "there is no free lunch," but the Holy Spirit tells me that grace and forgiveness are not only free, but that they delight and honor the Giver.

Along this journey there have been many times when I have committed myself to Jesus, God's Son, on a deeper and deeper level. I am sure that he will call me closer and closer to him in the future. Now the reality of God's grace and unconditional love overwhelms the "logic" of the world that tells me I need to earn my salvation. And while my life hasn't gotten any easier, it now has definite purpose and direction.

1 CORINTHIANS/2 CORINTHIANS

Introduction

THE BOTTOM LINE

As long as I'm already forgiven, I can do anything I want, right?" The new Christians in Corinth were in desperate need of some straight talk about living the way Jesus wanted them to live. They were enthusiastic about their relationship with him but thoroughly confused about how it should affect their lifestyle. They also lived in a society that was distinctly anti-Christian. Sexual immorality, greed, excess, and self-interest were characteristic of life all around them, and the church itself felt the prevailing culture's effects. The letters that the apostle Paul wrote to these Christians, therefore, are applicable to us today. As you read through these two books, consider your own situation—are there areas of your lifestyle that don't yet match the example set by Jesus? How can you put into practice some of Paul's advice *this week*?

CENTRAL IDEAS

- Paul warns against sexual immorality in the strongest possible terms (1 Corinthians chapter 6, verses 9–20 [p. 1498]).
- We all need to learn to live together without petty quarreling.
- There is hope for the future—eternal life (2 Corinthians chapter 5, verses 1–10 [p. 1514]).
- Jesus' resurrection from the dead foreshadows our own (1 Corinthians chapter 15, verses 12–58 [p. 1508]).
- Paul sets an example of love and concern for others.

TITLES

These books are titled after their intended audience—Christians in the city of Corinth, an important commercial city in Greece.

AUTHOR AND READERS

Paul authored these letters to the Corinthian Christians. They are among his earliest writings. The church at Corinth had, from its beginning, struggled with immorality and misunderstandings about proper worship and Christian conduct. Paul wrote to challenge these Christians to make an immediate lifestyle change.

Focus. It can be the difference between reaching a goal or falling short, hitting a target or missing, winning a race or losing.

Professional golfer Arnold Palmer learned that lesson in a way he has never forgotten. On the final hole of the 1961 Masters' Tournament, Palmer held a one-stroke lead and had just hit a very satisfying tee shot. He felt that he was in good shape to win. As he approached his ball, he saw an old friend standing at the edge of the gallery. The man motioned Palmer over, stuck out his hand and said, "Congratulations!"

Palmer took the time to walk over and shake his friend's hand. An innocent gesture, to be sure, but in that moment he lost his focus. On his next three respective shots he hit the ball into a sand trap, put it over the edge of the green, and missed a putt. As a result, victory slipped through his hands. Many years later Palmer said, "You don't forget a mistake like that; you just learn from it and become determined that you will never do that again. I haven't in the 30 years since."

> *Anybody who has ever gone on a diet, begun an exercise routine, or taken on a new responsibility knows just how easy it is to lose focus.*

Focus isn't important only on the golf course; it's crucial in all of life. Anybody who has ever gone on a diet, begun an exercise routine, or taken on a new responsibility knows just how easy it is to lose focus. And he or she also knows what happens if they don't regain it—defeat lies just around the corner.

Christians can't grow spiritually without focus, either. Living like Christ demands intense focus, since it involves bridling some of our strongest passions and redirecting many of our greatest strengths. But it's worth it! If we commit our lives to Christ and maintain our focus in the spiritual arena, we'll be on our way to becoming all that God wants us to be.

When the apostle Paul wrote to the members of the church at Corinth he knew that they had lost their focus. They had started their Christian lives well; but since Paul had left, the church had been sidetracked by immoral behavior and internal fighting. Paul dealt lovingly but firmly with the Corinthians' waywardness. He insisted that they regain their focus and told them how to do just that. Turn to 1 Corinthians chapter 9, verses 24–27 (page 1502) for an analogy designed to help them—and those of us who have become Christ-followers—maintain our spiritual focus.

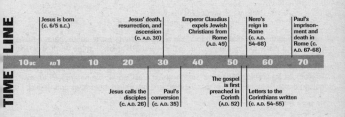

TIME LINE

	Jesus is born (c. 6/5 B.C.)		Jesus' death, resurrection, and ascension (c. A.D. 30)	Emperor Claudius expels Jewish Christians from Rome (A.D. 49)		Nero's reign in Rome (c. A.D. 54–68)	Paul's imprisonment and death in Rome (c. A.D. 67–68)
10 B.C. **A.D. 1**	**10**	**20**	**30**	**40**	**50**	**60**	**70**
		Jesus calls the disciples (c. A.D. 26)	Paul's conversion (c. A.D. 35)	The gospel is first preached in Corinth (A.D. 52)	Letters to the Corinthians written (c. A.D. 54–55)		

1 CORINTHIANS

1 Paul, called to be an apostle of Christ Jesus by the will of God, and our brother Sosthenes,

²To the church of God in Corinth, to those sanctified in Christ Jesus and called to be holy, together with all those everywhere who call on the name of our Lord Jesus Christ—their Lord and ours:

³Grace and peace to you from God our Father and the Lord Jesus Christ.

Thanksgiving

⁴I always thank God for you because of his grace given you in Christ Jesus. ⁵For in him you have been enriched in every way—in all your speaking and in all your knowledge—⁶because our testimony about Christ was confirmed in you. ⁷Therefore you do not lack any spiritual gift as you eagerly wait for our Lord Jesus Christ to be revealed. ⁸He will keep you strong to the end, so that you will be blameless on the day of our Lord Jesus Christ. ⁹God, who has called you into fellowship with his Son Jesus Christ our Lord, is faithful.

Divisions in the Church

¹⁰I appeal to you, brothers, in the name of our Lord Jesus Christ, that all of you agree with one another so that there may be no divisions among you and that you may be perfectly united in mind and thought. ¹¹My brothers, some from Chloe's household have informed me that there are quarrels among you. ¹²What I mean is this: One of you says, "I follow Paul"; another, "I follow Apollos"; another, "I follow Cephas*a*"; still another, "I follow Christ."

¹³Is Christ divided? Was Paul crucified for you? Were you baptized into*b* the name of Paul? ¹⁴I am thankful that I did not baptize any of you except Crispus and Gaius, ¹⁵so no one can say that you were baptized into my name. ¹⁶(Yes, I also baptized the household of Stephanas; beyond that, I don't remember if I baptized anyone else.) ¹⁷For Christ did not send me to baptize, but to preach the gospel—not with words of human wisdom, lest the cross of Christ be emptied of its power.

Christ the Wisdom and Power of God

¹⁸For the message of the cross is foolishness to those who are perishing, but to us who are being saved it is the power of God. ¹⁹For it is written:

> "I will destroy the wisdom of the wise;
>   the intelligence of the intelligent I will frustrate."*c*

²⁰Where is the wise man? Where is the scholar? Where is the philosopher of this age? Has not God made foolish the wisdom of the world? ²¹For since in the wisdom of God the world through its wisdom did not know him, God was pleased through the foolishness of what was preached to save those who believe. ²²Jews demand miraculous signs and Greeks look for wisdom, ²³but we preach Christ crucified: a stumbling block to Jews and foolishness to Gentiles, ²⁴but to those whom God has called, both Jews and Greeks, Christ

a 12 That is, Peter   *b 13* Or *in;* also in verse 15   *c 19* Isaiah 29:14

the power of God and the wisdom of God. 25For the foolishness of God is wiser than man's wisdom, and the weakness of God is stronger than man's strength.

26Brothers, think of what you were when you were called. Not many of you were wise by human standards; not many were influential; not many were of noble birth. 27But God chose the foolish things of the world to shame the wise; God chose the weak things of the world to shame the strong. 28He chose the lowly things of this world and the de-spised things—and the things that are not—to nullify the things that are, 29so that no one may boast before him. 30It is because of him that you are in Christ Jesus, who has become for us wisdom from God—that is, our righteousness, holiness and redemp-tion. 31Therefore, as it is written: "Let him who boasts boast in the Lord."a

2 When I came to you, brothers, I did not come with eloquence or superior wisdom as I proclaimed to you the testimony about God.b 2For I resolved to know nothing while I was with you ex-cept Jesus Christ and him crucified. 3I came to you in weakness and fear, and with much trembling. 4My message and my preaching were not with wise and persua-sive words, but with a demonstration of the Spirit's power, 5so that your faith might not rest on men's wisdom, but on God's power.

Wisdom From the Spirit

6We do, however, speak a message of wisdom among the mature, but not the wisdom of this age or of the rulers of this age, who are coming to nothing. 7No, we speak of God's secret wisdom, a wisdom that has been hidden and that God des-tined for our glory before time began. 8None of the rulers of this age understood it, for if they had, they would not have cru-cified the Lord of glory. 9However, as it is written:

> "No eye has seen,
>   no ear has heard,
> no mind has conceived
>   what God has prepared for those who love him"c—

10but God has revealed it to us by his Spirit.

The Spirit searches all things, even the deep things of God. 11For who among men knows the thoughts of a man except the man's spirit within him? In the same way no one knows the thoughts of God except the Spirit of God. 12We have not received the spirit of the world but the Spirit who is from God, that we may understand what God has freely given us. 13This is what we speak, not in words taught us by human wisdom but in words taught by the Spirit, expressing spiritual truths in spiritual words.d 14The man

DISCOVERING GOD

1:18–25
Jesus, the God-Man

Some people want to see supernatural signs before they'll believe in God. Others demand irrefutable proof of his existence. God under-stands our need for evidence, but offers us a picture of himself that most people don't ex-pect.

God's sign to us comes in the form of a Sav-ior who was nailed to a cross, but that sign leaves many people unconvinced. People looking for a demonstration of God's power see that and ask, "Why should I follow some-one who couldn't save himself from his ene-mies?" People who want to sound intelligent say, "That seems so irrational—God in human form giving himself as a sacrifice for sin."

Paul's point in this passage is that Jesus' crucifixion is a tremendous illustration of power and wisdom—if you look at it in the right way. God submitting to human need—con-trolling his urge to save himself so that he can save others—truly demonstrates power of an-other magnitude.

Look at Jesus' crucifixion from this view-point, and you'll see that it is the most amaz-ing and profound demonstration of God's strength and love ever. While it may be "fool-ishness to those who are perishing," it is the "power of God" to those who believe in Christ's saving ability (verse 18).

---

a31 Jer. 9:24   b1 Some manuscripts as I proclaimed to you God's mystery   c9 Isaiah 64:4   d13 Or Spirit, interpreting spiritual truths to spiritual men

without the Spirit does not accept the things that come from the Spirit of God, for they are foolishness to him, and he cannot understand them, because they are spiritually discerned. ¹⁵The spiritual man makes judgments about all things, but he himself is not subject to any man's judgment:

> ¹⁶"For who has known the mind of the Lord
> that he may instruct him?"ᵃ

But we have the mind of Christ.

On Divisions in the Church

3 Brothers, I could not address you as spiritual but as worldly—mere infants in Christ. ²I gave you milk, not solid food, for you were not yet ready for it. Indeed, you are still not ready. ³You are still worldly. For since there is jealousy and quarreling among you, are you not worldly? Are you not acting like mere men? ⁴For when one says, "I follow Paul," and another, "I follow Apollos," are you not mere men?

⁵What, after all, is Apollos? And what is Paul? Only servants, through whom you came to believe—as the Lord has assigned to each his task. ⁶I planted the seed, Apollos watered it, but God made it grow. ⁷So neither he who plants nor he who waters is anything, but only God, who makes things grow. ⁸The man who plants and the man who waters have one purpose, and each will be rewarded according to his own labor. ⁹For we are God's fellow workers; you are God's field, God's building.

¹⁰By the grace God has given me, I laid a foundation as an expert builder, and someone else is building on it. But each one should be careful how he builds. ¹¹For no one can lay any foundation other than the one already laid, which is Jesus Christ. ¹²If any man builds on this foundation using gold, silver, costly stones, wood, hay or straw, ¹³his work will be shown for what it is, because the Day will bring it to light. It will be revealed with fire, and the fire will test the quality of each man's work. ¹⁴If what he has built survives, he will receive his reward. ¹⁵If it is burned up, he will suffer loss; he himself will be saved, but only as one escaping through the flames.

¹⁶Don't you know that you yourselves are God's temple and that God's Spirit lives in you? ¹⁷If anyone destroys God's temple, God will destroy him; for God's temple is sacred, and you are that temple.

¹⁸Do not deceive yourselves. If any one of you thinks he is wise by the standards of this age, he should become a "fool" so that he may become wise. ¹⁹For the wisdom of this world is foolishness in God's sight. As it is written: "He catches the wise in their craftiness"ᵇ; ²⁰and again, "The Lord knows that the thoughts of the wise are futile."ᶜ ²¹So then, no more boasting about men! All things are yours, ²²whether Paul or Apollos or Cephasᵈ or the world or life or death or the present or the future—all are yours, ²³and you are of Christ, and Christ is of God.

Apostles of Christ

4 So then, men ought to regard us as servants of Christ and as those entrusted with the secret things of God. ²Now it is required that those who have been given a trust must prove faithful. ³I care very little if I am judged by you or by any human court; indeed, I do not even judge myself. ⁴My conscience is clear, but that does not make me innocent. It is the Lord who judges me. ⁵Therefore judge nothing before the appointed time; wait till the Lord comes. He will bring to light what is hidden in darkness and will expose the motives of men's hearts. At that time each will receive his praise from God.

⁶Now, brothers, I have applied these things to myself and Apollos for your benefit, so that you may learn from us the meaning of the saying, "Do not go beyond what is written." Then you will not take pride in one man over against another. ⁷For who make

---

ᵃ16 Isaiah 40:13   ᵇ19 Job 5:13   ᶜ20 Psalm 94:11   ᵈ22 That is, Peter

you different from anyone else? What do you have that you did not receive? And if you did receive it, why do you boast as though you did not?

⁸Already you have all you want! Already you have become rich! You have become kings—and that without us! How I wish that you really had become kings so that we might be kings with you! ⁹For it seems to me that God has put us apostles on display at the end of the procession, like men condemned to die in the arena. We have been made a spectacle to the whole universe, to angels as well as to men. ¹⁰We are fools for Christ, but you are so wise in Christ! We are weak, but you are strong! You are honored, we are dishonored! ¹¹To this very hour we go hungry and thirsty, we are in rags, we are brutally treated, we are homeless. ¹²We work hard with our own hands. When we are cursed, we bless; when we are persecuted, we endure it; ¹³when we are slandered, we answer kindly. Up to this moment we have become the scum of the earth, the refuse of the world.

¹⁴I am not writing this to shame you, but to warn you, as my dear children. ¹⁵Even though you have ten thousand guardians in Christ, you do not have many fathers, for in Christ Jesus I became your father through the gospel. ¹⁶Therefore I urge you to imitate me. ¹⁷For this reason I am sending to you Timothy, my son whom I love, who is faithful in the Lord. He will remind you of my way of life in Christ Jesus, which agrees with what I teach everywhere in every church.

¹⁸Some of you have become arrogant, as if I were not coming to you. ¹⁹But I will come to you very soon, if the Lord is willing, and then I will find out not only how these arrogant people are talking, but what power they have. ²⁰For the kingdom of God is not a matter of talk but of power. ²¹What do you prefer? Shall I come to you with a whip, or in love and with a gentle spirit?

Expel the Immoral Brother!

5 It is actually reported that there is sexual immorality among you, and of a kind that does not occur even among pagans: A man has his father's wife. ²And you are proud! Shouldn't you rather have been filled with grief and have put out of your fellowship the man who did this? ³Even though I am not physically present, I am with you in spirit. And I have already passed judgment on the one who did this, just as if I were present. ⁴When you are assembled in the name of our Lord Jesus and I am with you in spirit, and the power of our Lord Jesus is present, ⁵hand this man over to Satan, so that the sinful nature[a] may be destroyed and his spirit saved on the day of the Lord.

⁶Your boasting is not good. Don't you know that a little yeast works through the whole batch of dough? ⁷Get rid of the old yeast that you may be a new batch without yeast—as you really are. For Christ, our Passover lamb, has been sacrificed. ⁸Therefore let us keep the Festival, not with the old yeast, the yeast of malice and wickedness, but with bread without yeast, the bread of sincerity and truth.

⁹I have written you in my letter not to associate with sexually immoral people— ¹⁰not at all meaning the people of this world who are immoral, or the greedy and swindlers, or idolaters. In that case you would have to leave this world. ¹¹But now I am writing you that you must not associate with anyone who calls himself a brother but is sexually immoral or greedy, an idolater or a slanderer, a drunkard or a swindler. With such a man do not even eat.

¹²What business is it of mine to judge those outside the church? Are you not to judge those inside? ¹³God will judge those outside. "Expel the wicked man from among you."[b]

Lawsuits Among Believers

6 If any of you has a dispute with another, dare he take it before the ungodly for judgment instead of before the saints? ²Do you not know that the saints will judge the world? And if you are to judge the world, are you not competent to judge trivial cases? ³Do you not know that we will judge angels? How much more the things of

---

a5 Or that his body; or that the flesh   b13 Deut. 17:7; 19:19; 21:21; 22:21,24; 24:7

this life! [4]Therefore, if you have disputes about such matters, appoint as judges even men of little account in the church![a] [5]I say this to shame you. Is it possible that there is nobody among you wise enough to judge a dispute between believers? [6]But instead, one brother goes to law against another—and this in front of unbelievers!

[7]The very fact that you have lawsuits among you means you have been completely defeated already. Why not rather be wronged? Why not rather be cheated? [8]Instead, you yourselves cheat and do wrong, and you do this to your brothers.

[9]Do you not know that the wicked will not inherit the kingdom of God? Do not be deceived: Neither the sexually immoral nor idolaters nor adulterers nor male prostitutes nor homosexual offenders [10]nor thieves nor the greedy nor drunkards nor slanderers nor swindlers will inherit the kingdom of God. [11]And that is what some of you were. But you were washed, you were sanctified, you were justified in the name of the Lord Jesus Christ and by the Spirit of our God.

□□ ::::::::::: KNOWING YOURSELF :::::::::: ⬍

6:9–11
Sin

Do you find any of your behaviors on this list? If you've ever thought that God would never accept you because of your sin, consider the implication of verse 11: All of these were former habits of individuals who had been accepted into the Corinthian church's fellowship. Nothing you've ever done will disqualify you for eternal life *if you will let Jesus forgive and cleanse you.* The same God who accepted these people and gave them a new start in life is alive today. Through Paul's words in this passage he extends the very same offer to you right now.

Sexual Immorality

[12]"Everything is permissible for me"—but not everything is beneficial. "Everything is permissible for me"—but I will not be mastered by anything. [13]"Food for the stomach and the stomach for food"—but God will destroy them both. The body is not meant for sexual immorality, but for the Lord, and the Lord for the body. [14]By his power God raised the Lord from the dead, and he will raise us also. [15]Do you not know that your bodies are members of Christ himself? Shall I then take the members of Christ and unite them with a prostitute? Never! [16]Do you not know that he who unites himself with a prostitute is one with her in body? For it is said, "The two will become one flesh."[b] [17]But he who unites himself with the Lord is one with him in spirit.

[18]Flee from sexual immorality. All other sins a man commits are outside his body, but he who sins sexually sins against his own body. [19]Do you not know that your body is a temple of the Holy Spirit, who is in you, whom you have received from God? You are not your own; [20]you were bought at a price. Therefore honor God with your body.

Marriage

7 Now for the matters you wrote about: It is good for a man not to marry.[c] [2]But since there is so much immorality, each man should have his own wife, and each woman her own husband. [3]The husband should fulfill his marital duty to his wife, and likewise the wife to her husband. [4]The wife's body does not belong to her alone but also to her husband. In the same way, the husband's body does not belong to him alone but also to his wife. [5]Do not deprive each other except by mutual consent and for a time, so that you may devote yourselves to prayer. Then come together again so that Satan will not tempt you because of your lack of self-control. [6]I say this as a concession, not as a command. [7]I wish that all men were as I am. But each man has his own gift from God; one has this gift, another has that.

[8]Now to the unmarried and the widows I say: It is good for them to stay unmarried, as

---

[a]4 Or *matters, do you appoint as judges men of little account in the church?*   [b]16 Gen. 2:24   [c]1 Or *"It is good for a man not to have sexual relations with a woman."*

I am. ⁹But if they cannot control themselves, they should marry, for it is better to marry than to burn with passion.

¹⁰To the married I give this command (not I, but the Lord): A wife must not separate from her husband. ¹¹But if she does, she must remain unmarried or else be reconciled to her husband. And a husband must not divorce his wife.

¹²To the rest I say this (I, not the Lord): If any brother has a wife who is not a believer and she is willing to live with him, he must not divorce her. ¹³And if a woman has a husband who is not a believer and he is willing to live with her, she must not divorce him. ¹⁴For the unbelieving husband has been sanctified through his wife, and the unbelieving wife has been sanctified through her believing husband. Otherwise your children would be unclean, but as it is, they are holy.

¹⁵But if the unbeliever leaves, let him do so. A believing man or woman is not bound in such circumstances; God has called us to live in peace. ¹⁶How do you know, wife, whether you will save your husband? Or, how do you know, husband, whether you will save your wife?

¹⁷Nevertheless, each one should retain the place in life that the Lord assigned to him and to which God has called him. This

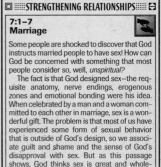

STRENGTHENING RELATIONSHIPS

7:1–7
Marriage

Some people are shocked to discover that God instructs married people to have sex! How can God be concerned with something that most people consider so, well, *unspiritual?*

The fact is that God designed sex—the requisite anatomy, nerve endings, erogenous zones and emotional bonding were his idea. When celebrated by a man and a woman committed to each other in marriage, sex is a wonderful gift. The problem is that most of us have experienced some form of sexual behavior that is outside of God's design, so we associate guilt and shame and the sense of God's disapproval with sex. But as this passage shows, God thinks sex is great and wholeheartedly endorses it in marriage—even to the point of instructing couples not to be so "spiritual" that they don't get "physical" too!

is the rule I lay down in all the churches. ¹⁸Was a man already circumcised when he was called? He should not become uncircumcised. Was a man uncircumcised when he was called? He should not be circumcised. ¹⁹Circumcision is nothing and uncircumcision is nothing. Keeping God's commands is what counts. ²⁰Each one should remain in the situation which he was in when God called him. ²¹Were you a slave when you were called? Don't let it trouble you—although if you can gain your freedom, do so. ²²For he who was a slave when he was called by the Lord is the Lord's freedman; similarly, he who was a free man when he was called is Christ's slave. ²³You were bought at a price; do not become slaves of men. ²⁴Brothers, each man, as responsible to God, should remain in the situation God called him to.

²⁵Now about virgins: I have no command from the Lord, but I give a judgment as one who by the Lord's mercy is trustworthy. ²⁶Because of the present crisis, I think that it is good for you to remain as you are. ²⁷Are you married? Do not seek a divorce. Are you unmarried? Do not look for a wife. ²⁸But if you do marry, you have not sinned; and if a virgin marries, she has not sinned. But those who marry will face many troubles in this life, and I want to spare you this.

²⁹What I mean, brothers, is that the time is short. From now on those who have wives should live as if they had none; ³⁰those who mourn, as if they did not; those who are happy, as if they were not; those who buy something, as if it were not theirs to keep; ³¹those who use the things of the world, as if not engrossed in them. For this world in its present form is passing away.

³²I would like you to be free from concern. An unmarried man is concerned about the Lord's affairs—how he can please the Lord. ³³But a married man is concerned about the affairs of this world—how he can please his wife— ³⁴and his interests are divided. An unmarried woman or virgin is concerned about the Lord's affairs: Her aim is to be devoted

to the Lord in both body and spirit. But a married woman is concerned about the affairs of this world—how she can please her husband. ³⁵I am saying this for your own good, not to restrict you, but that you may live in a right way in undivided devotion to the Lord.

³⁶If anyone thinks he is acting improperly toward the virgin he is engaged to, and if she is getting along in years and he feels he ought to marry, he should do as he wants. He is not sinning. They should get married. ³⁷But the man who has settled the matter in his own mind, who is under no compulsion but has control over his own will, and who has made up his mind not to marry the virgin—this man also does the right thing. ³⁸So then, he who marries the virgin does right, but he who does not marry her does even better.ᵃ

³⁹A woman is bound to her husband as long as he lives. But if her husband dies, she is free to marry anyone she wishes, but he must belong to the Lord. ⁴⁰In my judgment, she is happier if she stays as she is—and I think that I too have the Spirit of God.

Food Sacrificed to Idols

8 Now about food sacrificed to idols: We know that we all possess knowledge.ᵇ Knowledge puffs up, but love builds up. ²The man who thinks he knows something does not yet know as he ought to know. ³But the man who loves God is known by God.

⁴So then, about eating food sacrificed to idols: We know that an idol is nothing at all in the world and that there is no God but one. ⁵For even if there are so-called gods, whether in heaven or on earth (as indeed there are many "gods" and many "lords"), ⁶yet for us there is but one God, the Father, from whom all things came and for whom we live; and there is but one Lord, Jesus Christ, through whom all things came and through whom we live.

⁷But not everyone knows this. Some people are still so accustomed to idols that when they eat such food they think of it as having been sacrificed to an idol, and since their conscience is weak, it is defiled. ⁸But food does not bring us near to God; we are no worse if we do not eat, and no better if we do.

⁹Be careful, however, that the exercise of your freedom does not become a stumbling block to the weak. ¹⁰For if anyone with a weak conscience sees you who have this knowledge eating in an idol's temple, won't he be emboldened to eat what has been sacrificed to idols? ¹¹So this weak brother, for whom Christ died, is destroyed by your knowledge. ¹²When you sin against your brothers in this way and wound their weak conscience, you sin against Christ. ¹³Therefore, if what I eat causes my brother to fall into sin, I will never eat meat again, so that I will not cause him to fall.

The Rights of an Apostle

9 Am I not free? Am I not an apostle? Have I not seen Jesus our Lord? Are you not the result of my work in the Lord? ²Even though I may not be an apostle to others, surely I am to you! For you are the seal of my apostleship in the Lord.

³This is my defense to those who sit in judgment on me. ⁴Don't we have the right to food and drink? ⁵Don't we have the right to take a believing wife along with us, as do the other apostles and the Lord's brothers and Cephasᶜ? ⁶Or is it only I and Barnabas who must work for a living?

⁷Who serves as a soldier at his own expense? Who plants a vineyard and does not eat of its grapes? Who tends a flock and does not drink of the milk? ⁸Do I say this merely from a human point of view? Doesn't the Law say the same thing? ⁹For it is written in the

---

ᵃ*36-38 Or ³⁶If anyone thinks he is not treating his daughter properly, and if she is getting along in years, and he feels she ought to marry, he should do as he wants. He is not sinning. He should let her get married. ³⁷But the man who has settled the matter in his own mind, who is under no compulsion but has control over his own will, and who has made up his mind to keep the virgin unmarried—this man also does the right thing. ³⁸So then, he who gives his virgin in marriage does right, but he who does not give her in marriage does even better.*   ᵇ*1 Or "We all possess knowledge," as you say*   ᶜ*5 That is, Peter*

Law of Moses: "Do not muzzle an ox while it is treading out the grain."*ᵃ* Is it about oxen that God is concerned? ¹⁰Surely he says this for us, doesn't he? Yes, this was written for us, because when the plowman plows and the thresher threshes, they ought to do so in the hope of sharing in the harvest. ¹¹If we have sown spiritual seed among you, is it too much if we reap a material harvest from you? ¹²If others have this right of support from you, shouldn't we have it all the more?

But we did not use this right. On the contrary, we put up with anything rather than hinder the gospel of Christ. ¹³Don't you know that those who work in the temple get their food from the temple, and those who serve at the altar share in what is offered on the altar? ¹⁴In the same way, the Lord has commanded that those who preach the gospel should receive their living from the gospel.

¹⁵But I have not used any of these rights. And I am not writing this in the hope that you will do such things for me. I would rather die than have anyone deprive me of this boast. ¹⁶Yet when I preach the gospel, I cannot boast, for I am compelled to preach. Woe to me if I do not preach the gospel! ¹⁷If I preach voluntarily, I have a reward; if not voluntarily, I am simply discharging the trust committed to me. ¹⁸What then is my reward? Just this: that in preaching the gospel I may offer it free of charge, and so not make use of my rights in preaching it.

¹⁹Though I am free and belong to no man, I make myself a slave to everyone, to win as

ᵃ9 Deut. 25:4

═══════════ ▦ DISCOVERING GOD ▦ ═══════════

9:24–27
Life with God

At age 44, Nolan Ryan pitched a no-hitter. Amazing!

"There's no secret to what I do," he said. "God gave me a great right arm, but it's up to me to do the hard training it takes to keep on playing. If that sounds boring—and that's the way most major leaguers feel about it—that may be the reason most quit in their thirties.

"But I'm not bored; I like work, especially when it pays off, as it did that spring night when a guy who felt old did a young man's job."

Athletes like Nolan Ryan must undergo strict training to win the prize. They must control their appetites and schedules. They have to say no to some things they would enjoy doing. If you've ever watched the Olympics and seen interviews of the athletes, you have a good picture of the kind of intensity and dedication needed to perform at that level.

The apostle Paul isn't calling on you to don a sweat suit. Instead, he's challenging you to pursue something of greater value than a no-hitter, something worth more than an Olympic gold medal. After all, the glory of a no-hitter will fade. A gold medal will lose its luster. But God wants to give you an eternal prize—a reward in heaven for a life that pleases him.

Heaven itself is not a reward for a good life; it's a gift of grace to all who simply receive it. But if you've settled the matter of your salvation through trusting Christ alone, following through on that commitment requires a new discipline and a renewed spiritual focus.

Paul says that he lived his Christian life like a runner and a boxer. He didn't run all over the track from one lane to another; he focused on the finish line and ran hard toward it. He disciplined himself and trained spiritually so that he could give and take the powerful blows that his life as a traveling church leader required. Paul trained like a top-flight athlete because he wanted to have the self-control to finish the race of life without being disqualified. In doing so, he made sure that he "walked the talk" so those who listened to him could see the benefits of belief in Christ.

How can you sharpen your spiritual focus? One way is to spend time in prayer. Another way is to carve out a little time each day to read your Bible. As you read it, ask God to help you discover how you can know and follow him better. With that knowledge will come a life that will please him as you put into practice what you learn. And as you serve God, he'll reserve rewards for you beyond your wildest imagination.

many as possible. ²⁰To the Jews I became like a Jew, to win the Jews. To those under the law I became like one under the law (though I myself am not under the law), so as to win those under the law. ²¹To those not having the law I became like one not having the law (though I am not free from God's law but am under Christ's law), so as to win those not having the law. ²²To the weak I became weak, to win the weak. I have become all things to all men so that by all possible means I might save some. ²³I do all this for the sake of the gospel, that I may share in its blessings.

²⁴Do you not know that in a race all the runners run, but only one gets the prize? Run in such a way as to get the prize. ²⁵Everyone who competes in the games goes into strict training. They do it to get a crown that will not last; but we do it to get a crown that will last forever. ²⁶Therefore I do not run like a man running aimlessly; I do not fight like a man beating the air. ²⁷No, I beat my body and make it my slave so that after I have preached to others, I myself will not be disqualified for the prize.

Warnings From Israel's History

10 For I do not want you to be ignorant of the fact, brothers, that our forefathers were all under the cloud and that they all passed through the sea. ²They were all baptized into Moses in the cloud and in the sea. ³They all ate the same spiritual food ⁴and drank the same spiritual drink; for they drank from the spiritual rock that accompanied them, and that rock was Christ. ⁵Nevertheless, God was not pleased with most of them; their bodies were scattered over the desert.

⁶Now these things occurred as examples*ᵃ* to keep us from setting our hearts on evil things as they did. ⁷Do not be idolaters, as some of them were; as it is written: "The people sat down to eat and drink and got up to indulge in pagan revelry."*ᵇ* ⁸We should not commit sexual immorality, as some of them did—and in one day twenty-three thousand of them died. ⁹We should not test the Lord, as some of them did—and were killed by snakes. ¹⁰And do not grumble, as some of them did—and were killed by the destroying angel.

¹¹These things happened to them as examples and were written down as warnings for us, on whom the fulfillment of the ages has come. ¹²So, if you think you are standing firm, be careful that you don't fall! ¹³No temptation has seized you except what is common to man. And God is faithful; he will not let you be tempted beyond what you can bear. But when you are tempted, he will also provide a way out so that you can stand up under it.

◻ ▦▦▦▦▦ KNOWING YOURSELF ▦▦▦▦▦ ↔

10:13
A New Identity

If you become a Christian, you ought to know this wonderful piece of news: You never *have* *to* sin again. According to what Paul says here, every temptation that comes to a Christian is also accompanied by a way out—an "escape hatch," if you will.

Most sins can be avoided by using two parts of our bodies: eyelids and feet! Not looking and walking away can stop a lot of sin before it ever really gets going.

If getting away from sin is so simple, why do people—including Christians—still sin so much? Paul doesn't promise that people *won't* sin. He promises that God will be available to help people escape from every sinful circumstance if they choose to look to him for help. That's good news!

Idol Feasts and the Lord's Supper

¹⁴Therefore, my dear friends, flee from idolatry. ¹⁵I speak to sensible people; judge for yourselves what I say. ¹⁶Is not the cup of thanksgiving for which we give thanks a participation in the blood of Christ? And is not the bread that we break a participation in the body of Christ? ¹⁷Because there is one loaf, we, who are many, are one body, for we all partake of the one loaf.

ᵃ6 Or types; also in verse 11   *ᵇ7 Exodus 32:6*

[18]Consider the people of Israel: Do not those who eat the sacrifices participate in the altar? [19]Do I mean then that a sacrifice offered to an idol is anything, or that an idol is anything? [20]No, but the sacrifices of pagans are offered to demons, not to God, and I do not want you to be participants with demons. [21]You cannot drink the cup of the Lord and the cup of demons too; you cannot have a part in both the Lord's table and the table of demons. [22]Are we trying to arouse the Lord's jealousy? Are we stronger than he?

The Believer's Freedom

[23]"Everything is permissible"—but not everything is beneficial. "Everything is permissible"—but not everything is constructive. [24]Nobody should seek his own good, but the good of others.

[25]Eat anything sold in the meat market without raising questions of conscience, [26]for, "The earth is the Lord's, and everything in it." [a]

[27]If some unbeliever invites you to a meal and you want to go, eat whatever is put before you without raising questions of conscience. [28]But if anyone says to you, "This has been offered in sacrifice," then do not eat it, both for the sake of the man who told you and for conscience' sake [b]— [29]the other man's conscience, I mean, not yours. For why should my freedom be judged by another's conscience? [30]If I take part in the meal with thankfulness, why am I denounced because of something I thank God for?

[31]So whether you eat or drink or whatever you do, do it all for the glory of God. [32]Do not cause anyone to stumble, whether Jews, Greeks or the church of God— [33]even as I try to please everybody in every way. For I am not seeking my own good but the good of many, so that they may be saved. [1]Follow my example, as I follow the example of Christ.

Propriety in Worship

[2]I praise you for remembering me in everything and for holding to the teachings, [c] just as I passed them on to you.

[3]Now I want you to realize that the head of every man is Christ, and the head of the woman is man, and the head of Christ is God. [4]Every man who prays or prophesies with his head covered dishonors his head. [5]And every woman who prays or prophesies with her head uncovered dishonors her head—it is just as though her head were shaved. [6]If a woman does not cover her head, she should have her hair cut off; and if it is a disgrace for a woman to have her hair cut or shaved off, she should cover her head. [7]A man ought not to cover his head, [d] since he is the image and glory of God; but the woman is the glory of man. [8]For man did not come from woman, but woman from man; [9]neither was man created for woman, but woman for man. [10]For this reason, and because of the angels, the woman ought to have a sign of authority on her head.

[11]In the Lord, however, woman is not independent of man, nor is man independent of woman. [12]For as woman came from man, so also man is born of woman. But everything comes from God. [13]Judge for yourselves: Is it proper for a woman to pray to God with her head uncovered? [14]Does not the very nature of things teach you that if a man has long hair, it is a disgrace to him, [15]but that if a woman has long hair, it is her glory? For long hair is given to her as a covering. [16]If anyone wants to be contentious about this, we have no other practice—nor do the churches of God.

The Lord's Supper

[17]In the following directives I have no praise for you, for your meetings do more harm than good. [18]In the first place, I hear that when you come together as a church, there are

---

a26 Psalm 24:1   *b28* Some manuscripts conscience' sake, for "the earth is the Lord's and everything in it"   *c2* Or traditions   *d4–7* Or *4Every man who prays or prophesies with long hair dishonors his head. 5And every woman who prays or prophesies with no covering of hair, on her head dishonors her head—she is just like one of the "shorn women." 6If a woman has no covering, let her be for now with short hair, but since it is a disgrace for a woman to have her hair shorn or shaved, she should grow it again. 7A man ought not to have long hair*

divisions among you, and to some extent I believe it. ¹⁹No doubt there have to be differences among you to show which of you have God's approval. ²⁰When you come together, it is not the Lord's Supper you eat, ²¹for as you eat, each of you goes ahead without waiting for anybody else. One remains hungry, another gets drunk. ²²Don't you have homes to eat and drink in? Or do you despise the church of God and humiliate those who have nothing? What shall I say to you? Shall I praise you for this? Certainly not!

²³For I received from the Lord what I also passed on to you: The Lord Jesus, on the night he was betrayed, took bread, ²⁴and when he had given thanks, he broke it and said, "This is my body, which is for you; do this in remembrance of me." ²⁵In the same way, after supper he took the cup, saying, "This cup is the new covenant in my blood; do this, whenever you drink it, in remembrance of me." ²⁶For whenever you eat this bread and drink this cup, you proclaim the Lord's death until he comes.

²⁷Therefore, whoever eats the bread or drinks the cup of the Lord in an unworthy manner will be guilty of sinning against the body and blood of the Lord. ²⁸A man ought to examine himself before he eats of the bread and drinks of the cup. ²⁹For anyone who eats and drinks without recognizing the body of the Lord eats and drinks judgment on himself. ³⁰That is why many among you are weak and sick, and a number of you have fallen asleep. ³¹But if we judged ourselves, we would not come under judgment. ³²When we are judged by the Lord, we are being disciplined so that we will not be condemned with the world.

³³So then, my brothers, when you come together to eat, wait for each other. ³⁴If anyone is hungry, he should eat at home, so that when you meet together it may not result in judgment.

And when I come I will give further directions.

> ## ◨ ▓▓▓▓▓ ADDRESSING QUESTIONS ▓▓▓▓▓ ◧
>
> ### 11:23–26
> ### Human Experience
>
>
>
> Jesus intended that the practice of Communion be a profoundly enriching spiritual experience. To this day, the ceremony unites Christians all over the world as they remember Jesus' sacrifice of his own body and blood for their salvation.
>
> Paul goes on to outline the prerequisites for participating in this sacrament (verses 27–29). He makes it clear that this act is not to be taken lightly. It is reserved for those who have received Christ and accepted his forgiveness.
>
> If you're a seeker, there's no reason you can't share in this fellowship. Perhaps the next time you are with a group of Christians who are taking Communion, you can make the decision to apply Jesus' payment to your life and be included in God's family. That service will be one of the most memorable in your life as you eat the bread and drink from the cup for the first time, knowing that you are now genuinely trusting in what Christ did for you on the cross.

Spiritual Gifts

12 Now about spiritual gifts, brothers, I do not want you to be ignorant. ²You know that when you were pagans, somehow or other you were influenced and led astray to mute idols. ³Therefore I tell you that no one who is speaking by the Spirit of God says, "Jesus be cursed," and no one can say, "Jesus is Lord," except by the Holy Spirit.

⁴There are different kinds of gifts, but the same Spirit. ⁵There are different kinds of service, but the same Lord. ⁶There are different kinds of working, but the same God works all of them in all men.

⁷Now to each one the manifestation of the Spirit is given for the common good. ⁸To one there is given through the Spirit the message of wisdom, to another the message of knowledge by means of the same Spirit, ⁹to another faith by the same Spirit, to another gifts of healing by that one Spirit, ¹⁰to another miraculous powers, to another prophecy, to another distinguishing between spirits, to another speaking in different kinds of

tongues,*a* and to still another the interpretation of tongues.*a* ¹¹All these are the work of one and the same Spirit, and he gives them to each one, just as he determines.

One Body, Many Parts

¹²The body is a unit, though it is made up of many parts; and though all its parts are many, they form one body. So it is with Christ. ¹³For we were all baptized by*b* one Spirit into one body—whether Jews or Greeks, slave or free—and we were all given the one Spirit to drink.

¹⁴Now the body is not made up of one part but of many. ¹⁵If the foot should say, "Because I am not a hand, I do not belong to the body," it would not for that reason cease to be part of the body. ¹⁶And if the ear should say, "Because I am not an eye, I do not belong to the body," it would not for that reason cease to be part of the body. ¹⁷If the whole body were an eye, where would the sense of hearing be? If the whole body were an ear, where would the sense of smell be? ¹⁸But in fact God has arranged the parts in the body, every one of them, just as he wanted them to be. ¹⁹If they were all one part, where would the body be? ²⁰As it is, there are many parts, but one body.

²¹The eye cannot say to the hand, "I don't need you!" And the head cannot say to the feet, "I don't need you!" ²²On the contrary, those parts of the body that seem to be weaker are indispensable, ²³and the parts that we think are less honorable we treat with special honor. And the parts that are unpresentable are treated with special modesty, ²⁴while our presentable parts need no special treatment. But God has combined the members of the body and has given greater honor to the parts that lacked it, ²⁵so that there should be no division in the body, but that its parts should have equal concern for each other. ²⁶If one part suffers, every part suffers with it; if one part is honored, every part rejoices with it.

²⁷Now you are the body of Christ, and each one of you is a part of it. ²⁸And in the church God has appointed first of all apostles, second prophets, third teachers, then workers of miracles, also those having gifts of healing, those able to help others, those with gifts of administration, and those speaking in different kinds of tongues. ²⁹Are all apostles? Are all prophets? Are all teachers? Do all work miracles? ³⁰Do all have gifts of healing? Do all speak in tongues*c*? Do all interpret? ³¹But eagerly desire*d* the greater gifts.

Love

And now I will show you the most excellent way.

13 If I speak in the tongues*e* of men and of angels, but have not love, I am only a resounding gong or a clanging cymbal. ²If I have the gift of prophecy and can fathom all mysteries and all knowledge, and if I have a faith that can move mountains, but have not love, I am nothing. ³If I give all I possess to the poor and surrender my body to the flames,*f* but have not love, I gain nothing.

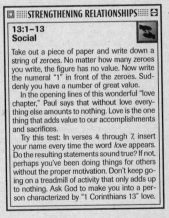

▓▓▓ STRENGTHENING RELATIONSHIPS ▓▓▓

13:1–13
Social

Take out a piece of paper and write down a string of zeroes. No matter how many zeroes you write, the figure has no value. Now write the numeral "1" in front of the zeroes. Suddenly you have a number of great value.

In the opening lines of this wonderful "love chapter," Paul says that without love everything else amounts to nothing. Love is the one thing that adds value to our accomplishments and sacrifices.

Try this test: In verses 4 through 7, insert your name every time the word *love* appears. Do the resulting statements sound true? If not, perhaps you've been doing things for others without the proper motivation. Don't keep going on a treadmill of activity that only adds up to nothing. Ask God to make you into a person characterized by "1 Corinthians 13" love.

---

a 10 Or *languages; also in verse 28*   *b 13* Or *with; or in*   *c 30* Or *other languages*   *d 31* Or *But you are eagerly desiring*   *e 1* Or *languages*   *f 3* Some early manuscripts *body that I may boast*

⁴Love is patient, love is kind. It does not envy, it does not boast, it is not proud. ⁵It is not rude, it is not self-seeking, it is not easily angered, it keeps no record of wrongs. ⁶Love does not delight in evil but rejoices with the truth. ⁷It always protects, always trusts, always hopes, always perseveres.

⁸Love never fails. But where there are prophecies, they will cease; where there are tongues, they will be stilled; where there is knowledge, it will pass away. ⁹For we know in part and we prophesy in part, ¹⁰but when perfection comes, the imperfect disappears. ¹¹When I was a child, I talked like a child, I thought like a child, I reasoned like a child. When I became a man, I put childish ways behind me. ¹²Now we see but a poor reflection as in a mirror; then we shall see face to face. Now I know in part; then I shall know fully, even as I am fully known.

¹³And now these three remain: faith, hope and love. But the greatest of these is love.

Gifts of Prophecy and Tongues

14 Follow the way of love and eagerly desire spiritual gifts, especially the gift of prophecy. ²For anyone who speaks in a tongue*ᵃ* does not speak to men but to God. Indeed, no one understands him; he utters mysteries with his spirit.*ᵇ* ³But everyone who prophesies speaks to men for their strengthening, encouragement and comfort. ⁴He who speaks in a tongue edifies himself, but he who prophesies edifies the church. ⁵I would like every one of you to speak in tongues,*ᶜ* but I would rather have you prophesy. He who prophesies is greater than one who speaks in tongues,*ᶜ* unless he interprets, so that the church may be edified.

⁶Now, brothers, if I come to you and speak in tongues, what good will I be to you, unless I bring you some revelation or knowledge or prophecy or word of instruction? ⁷Even in the case of lifeless things that make sounds, such as the flute or harp, how will anyone know what tune is being played unless there is a distinction in the notes? ⁸Again, if the trumpet does not sound a clear call, who will get ready for battle? ⁹So it is with you. Unless you speak intelligible words with your tongue, how will anyone know what you are saying? You will just be speaking into the air. ¹⁰Undoubtedly there are all sorts of languages in the world, yet none of them is without meaning. ¹¹If then I do not grasp the meaning of what someone is saying, I am a foreigner to the speaker, and he is a foreigner to me. ¹²So it is with you. Since you are eager to have spiritual gifts, try to excel in gifts that build up the church.

¹³For this reason anyone who speaks in a tongue should pray that he may interpret what he says. ¹⁴For if I pray in a tongue, my spirit prays, but my mind is unfruitful. ¹⁵So what shall I do? I will pray with my spirit, but I will also pray with my mind; I will sing with my spirit, but I will also sing with my mind. ¹⁶If you are praising God with your spirit, how can one who finds himself among those who do not understand*ᵈ* say "Amen" to your thanksgiving, since he does not know what you are saying? ¹⁷You may be giving thanks well enough, but the other man is not edified.

¹⁸I thank God that I speak in tongues more than all of you. ¹⁹But in the church I would rather speak five intelligible words to instruct others than ten thousand words in a tongue.

²⁰Brothers, stop thinking like children. In regard to evil be infants, but in your thinking be adults. ²¹In the Law it is written:

> "Through men of strange tongues
>   and through the lips of foreigners
> I will speak to this people,
>   but even then they will not listen to me,"*ᵉ*

says the Lord.

ᵃ2 Or another language; also in verses 4, 13, 14, 19, 26 and 27   *ᵇ2 Or by the Spirit*   *ᶜ5 Or other languages; also in verses 6, 18, 22, 23 and 39*   *ᵈ16 Or among the inquirers*   *ᵉ21 Isaiah 28:11,12*

²²Tongues, then, are a sign, not for believers but for unbelievers; prophecy, however, is for believers, not for unbelievers. ²³So if the whole church comes together and everyone speaks in tongues, and some who do not understand*ᵃ* or some unbelievers come in, will they not say that you are out of your mind? ²⁴But if an unbeliever or someone who does not understand*ᵇ* comes in while everybody is prophesying, he will be convinced by all that he is a sinner and will be judged by all, ²⁵and the secrets of his heart will be laid bare. So he will fall down and worship God, exclaiming, "God is really among you!"

Orderly Worship

²⁶What then shall we say, brothers? When you come together, everyone has a hymn, or a word of instruction, a revelation, a tongue or an interpretation. All of these must be done for the strengthening of the church. ²⁷If anyone speaks in a tongue, two—or at the most three—should speak, one at a time, and someone must interpret. ²⁸If there is no interpreter, the speaker should keep quiet in the church and speak to himself and God.

²⁹Two or three prophets should speak, and the others should weigh carefully what is said. ³⁰And if a revelation comes to someone who is sitting down, the first speaker should stop. ³¹For you can all prophesy in turn so that everyone may be instructed and encouraged. ³²The spirits of prophets are subject to the control of prophets. ³³For God is not a God of disorder but of peace.

As in all the congregations of the saints, ³⁴women should remain silent in the churches. They are not allowed to speak, but must be in submission, as the Law says. ³⁵If they want to inquire about something, they should ask their own husbands at home; for it is disgraceful for a woman to speak in the church.

³⁶Did the word of God originate with you? Or are you the only people it has reached? ³⁷If anybody thinks he is a prophet or spiritually gifted, let him acknowledge that what I am writing to you is the Lord's command. ³⁸If he ignores this, he himself will be ignored.*ᶜ*

³⁹Therefore, my brothers, be eager to prophesy, and do not forbid speaking in tongues. ⁴⁰But everything should be done in a fitting and orderly way.

The Resurrection of Christ

15 Now, brothers, I want to remind you of the gospel I preached to you, which you received and on which you have taken your stand. ²By this gospel you are saved, if you hold firmly to the word I preached to you. Otherwise, you have believed in vain.

³For what I received I passed on to you as of first importance*ᵈ*: that Christ died for our sins according to the Scriptures, ⁴that he was buried, that he was raised on the third day according to the Scriptures, ⁵and that he appeared to Peter,*ᵉ* and then to the Twelve. ⁶After that, he appeared to

░░░░░░░ **REASONS TO BELIEVE** ░░░░░░░
15:3–8
The Incomparable Jesus
Eyewitness testimony is one of the most reliable proofs that an event has occurred. When Paul wanted to remind the Corinthians that the resurrection of Jesus really happened, he didn't rely on hearsay. Besides giving a personal account, he referred to more than 500 eyewitnesses who saw the risen Jesus simultaneously.
Since most of those eyewitnesses were still living at the time Paul wrote (along with many others who would have loved to prove them wrong), this reference adds significant weight to his argument that the resurrection of Jesus is historical fact.

more than five hundred of the brothers at the same time, most of whom are still living, though some have fallen asleep. ⁷Then he appeared to James, then to all the apostles, ⁸and last of all he appeared to me also, as to one abnormally born.

⁹For I am the least of the apostles and do not even deserve to be called an apostle,

ᵃ23 Or some inquirers   *ᵇ24 Or or some inquirer*   *ᶜ38 Some manuscripts If he is ignorant of this, let him be ignorant*   *ᵈ3 Or you at the first*   *ᵉ5 Greek Cephas*

because I persecuted the church of God. ¹⁰But by the grace of God I am what I am, and his grace to me was not without effect. No, I worked harder than all of them—yet not I, but the grace of God that was with me. ¹¹Whether, then, it was I or they, this is what we preach, and this is what you believed.

The Resurrection of the Dead

¹²But if it is preached that Christ has been raised from the dead, how can some of you say that there is no resurrection of the dead? ¹³If there is no resurrection of the dead, then not even Christ has been raised. ¹⁴And if Christ has not been raised, our preaching is useless and so is your faith. ¹⁵More than that, we are then found to be false witnesses about God, for we have testified about God that he raised Christ from the dead. But he did not raise him if in fact the dead are not raised. ¹⁶For if the dead are not raised, then Christ has not been raised either. ¹⁷And if Christ has not been raised, your faith is futile; you are still in your sins. ¹⁸Then those also who have fallen asleep in Christ are lost. ¹⁹If only for this life we have hope in Christ, we are to be pitied more than all men.

²⁰But Christ has indeed been raised from the dead, the firstfruits of those who have fallen asleep. ²¹For since death came through a man, the resurrection of the dead comes also through a man. ²²For as in Adam all die, so in Christ all will be made alive. ²³But each in his own turn: Christ, the firstfruits; then, when he comes, those who belong to him. ²⁴Then the end will come, when he hands over the kingdom to God the Father after he has destroyed all dominion, authority and power. ²⁵For he must reign until he has put all his enemies under his feet. ²⁶The last enemy to be destroyed is death. ²⁷For he "has put everything under his feet."ᵃ Now when it says that "everything" has been put under him, it is clear that this does not include God himself, who put everything under Christ. ²⁸When he has done this, then the Son himself will be made subject to him who put everything under him, so that God may be all in all.

²⁹Now if there is no resurrection, what will those do who are baptized for the dead? If the dead are not raised at all, why are people baptized for them? ³⁰And as for us, why do we endanger ourselves every hour? ³¹I die every day—I mean that, brothers—just as surely as I glory over you in Christ Jesus our Lord. ³²If I fought wild beasts in Ephesus for merely human reasons, what have I gained? If the dead are not raised,

> "Let us eat and drink,
>   for tomorrow we die."ᵇ

³³Do not be misled: "Bad company corrupts good character." ³⁴Come back to your senses as you ought, and stop sinning; for there are some who are ignorant of God—I say this to your shame.

The Resurrection Body

³⁵But someone may ask, "How are the dead raised? With what kind of body will they come?" ³⁶How foolish! What you sow does not come to life unless it dies. ³⁷When you sow, you do not plant the body that will be, but just a seed, perhaps of wheat or of something else. ³⁸But God gives it a body as he has determined, and to each kind of seed he gives its own body. ³⁹All flesh is not the same: Men have one kind of flesh, animals have another, birds another and fish another. ⁴⁰There are also heavenly bodies and there are earthly bodies; but the splendor of the heavenly bodies is one kind, and the splendor of the earthly bodies is another. ⁴¹The sun has one kind of splendor, the moon another and the stars another; and star differs from star in splendor.

⁴²So will it be with the resurrection of the dead. The body that is sown is perishable, it is raised imperishable; ⁴³it is sown in dishonor, it is raised in glory; it is sown in weakness, it is raised in power; ⁴⁴it is sown a natural body, it is raised a spiritual body.

If there is a natural body, there is also a spiritual body. ⁴⁵So it is written: "The first man

---

ᵃ27 Psalm 8:6   ᵇ32 Isaiah 22:13

Adam became a living being"[a]; the last Adam, a life-giving spirit. [46]The spiritual did not come first, but the natural, and after that the spiritual. [47]The first man was of the dust of the earth, the second man from heaven. [48]As was the earthly man, so are those who are of the earth; and as is the man from heaven, so also are those who are of heaven. [49]And just as we have borne the likeness of the earthly man, so shall we[b] bear the likeness of the man from heaven.

[50]I declare to you, brothers, that flesh and blood cannot inherit the kingdom of God, nor does the perishable inherit the imperishable. [51]Listen, I tell you a mystery: We will not all sleep, but we will all be changed— [52]in a flash, in the twinkling of an eye, at the last trumpet. For the trumpet will sound, the dead will be raised imperishable, and we will be changed. [53]For the perishable must clothe itself with the imperishable, and the mortal with immortality. [54]When the perishable has been clothed with the imperishable, and the mortal with immortality, then the saying that is written will come true: "Death has been swallowed up in victory."[c]

> [55]"Where, O death, is your victory?
> Where, O death, is your sting?"[d]

[56]The sting of death is sin, and the power of sin is the law. [57]But thanks be to God! He gives us the victory through our Lord Jesus Christ.

[58]Therefore, my dear brothers, stand firm. Let nothing move you. Always give yourselves fully to the work of the Lord, because you know that your labor in the Lord is not in vain.

The Collection for God's People

16 Now about the collection for God's people: Do what I told the Galatian churches to do. [2]On the first day of every week, each one of you should set aside a sum of money in keeping with his income, saving it up, so that when I come no collections will have to be made.

◻ ▦▦▦ ADDRESSING QUESTIONS ▦▦▦ ⮀

15:55–57
Unseen Realities **Q**

Death is humankind's greatest enemy. Yet it is an enemy that Christ has defeated. In a sense, when Jesus died for our sins, death left its "stinger" in him—the same way a bee leaves its stinger in its victim and can't hurt anyone else. When Jesus rose from the dead he defeated the power of sin and death. Everyone who trusts Christ for forgiveness will eventually be raised from the dead to be with him, sharing his victory over death and sin.

The certainty that death is not the end—that what we do in life truly matters—can radically alter our everyday living. Such a hope gives us the ability to stand firm and not be shaken by the difficulties of life. It infuses us with the confidence that, when we choose to follow Jesus, we will be remembered and rewarded at the appropriate time.

---

[3]Then, when I arrive, I will give letters of introduction to the men you approve and send them with your gift to Jerusalem. [4]If it seems advisable for me to go also, they will accompany me.

Personal Requests

[5]After I go through Macedonia, I will come to you—for I will be going through Macedonia. [6]Perhaps I will stay with you awhile, or even spend the winter, so that you can help me on my journey, wherever I go. [7]I do not want to see you now and make only a passing visit; I hope to spend some time with you, if the Lord permits. [8]But I will stay on at Ephesus until Pentecost, [9]because a great door for effective work has opened to me, and there are many who oppose me.

[10]If Timothy comes, see to it that he has nothing to fear while he is with you, for he is carrying on the work of the Lord, just as I am. [11]No one, then, should refuse to accept him. Send him on his way in peace so that he may return to me. I am expecting him along with the brothers.

---

a45 Gen. 2:7   *b49* Some early manuscripts *so let us*   *c54* Isaiah 25:8   *d55* Hosea 13:14

¹²Now about our brother Apollos: I strongly urged him to go to you with the brothers. He was quite unwilling to go now, but he will go when he has the opportunity.

¹³Be on your guard; stand firm in the faith; be men of courage; be strong. ¹⁴Do everything in love.

¹⁵You know that the household of Stephanas were the first converts in Achaia, and they have devoted themselves to the service of the saints. I urge you, brothers, ¹⁶to submit to such as these and to everyone who joins in the work, and labors at it. ¹⁷I was glad when Stephanas, Fortunatus and Achaicus arrived, because they have supplied what was lacking from you. ¹⁸For they refreshed my spirit and yours also. Such men deserve recognition.

Final Greetings

¹⁹The churches in the province of Asia send you greetings. Aquila and Priscilla*ᵃ* greet you warmly in the Lord, and so does the church that meets at their house. ²⁰All the brothers here send you greetings. Greet one another with a holy kiss.

²¹I, Paul, write this greeting in my own hand.

²²If anyone does not love the Lord—a curse be on him. Come, O Lord*ᵇ*!

²³The grace of the Lord Jesus be with you.

²⁴My love to all of you in Christ Jesus. Amen.*ᶜ*

ᵃ19 Greek *Prisca*, a variant of *Priscilla*   *ᵇ22* In Aramaic the expression *Come, O Lord* is *Marana tha*.   *ᶜ24* Some manuscripts do not have *Amen*.

2 CORINTHIANS

1 Paul, an apostle of Christ Jesus by the will of God, and Timothy our brother,

To the church of God in Corinth, together with all the saints throughout Achaia:

²Grace and peace to you from God our Father and the Lord Jesus Christ.

The God of All Comfort

³Praise be to the God and Father of our Lord Jesus Christ, the Father of compassion and the God of all comfort, ⁴who comforts us in all our troubles, so that we can comfort those in any trouble with the comfort we ourselves have received from God. ⁵For just as the sufferings of Christ flow over into our lives, so also through Christ our comfort overflows. ⁶If we are distressed, it is for your comfort and salvation; if we are comforted, it is for your comfort, which produces in you patient endurance of the same sufferings we suffer. ⁷And our hope for you is firm, because we know that just as you share in our sufferings, so also you share in our comfort.

⁸We do not want you to be uninformed, brothers, about the hardships we suffered in the province of Asia. We were under great pressure, far beyond our ability to endure, so that we despaired even of life. ⁹Indeed, in our hearts we felt the sentence of death. But this happened that we might not rely on ourselves but on God, who raises the dead. ¹⁰He has delivered us from such a deadly peril, and he will deliver us. On him we have set our hope that he will continue to deliver us, ¹¹as you help us by your prayers. Then many will give thanks on our*a* behalf for the gracious favor granted us in answer to the prayers of many.

Paul's Change of Plans

¹²Now this is our boast: Our conscience testifies that we have conducted ourselves in the world, and especially in our relations with you, in the holiness and sincerity that are from God. We have done so not according to worldly wisdom but according to God's

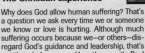

□ :::::::::::::: **REASONS TO BELIEVE** :::::::::::::: ⊡

1:3–11
The Christian Experience

Why does God allow human suffering? That's a question we ask every time we or someone we know or love is hurting. Although much suffering occurs because we—or others—disregard God's guidance and leadership, that's not the whole answer. Here the apostle Paul gives some reasons why believers are allowed to suffer.

First, *God allows us to suffer so we can learn to treat others compassionately* (verses 3–7). When those we know are hurting, we need to wrap them in the blanket of God's care and comfort. Nobody can identify with hurting people like those who have suffered themselves.

Second, *sometimes we suffer so we will learn not to be overconfident in ourselves* (verses 8–9). Nothing strips away arrogance and pride like hard times or physical difficulties. When such times come, even if we reach the brink of death, God wants us to turn to him and rely on his strength, not our own.

Third, *God allows us to suffer so we can see his power at work in practical ways* (verses 10–11). When we support others going through difficulties—and when we ourselves experience others rallying to support us—believers discover an aspect of God's care unknown to those who do not live in a relationship with him.

The compassion of the Christian community and the individual's hope in the face of suffering are two aspects of Christianity that give God-followers good reason to believe.

grace. ¹³For we do not write you anything you cannot read or understand. And I hop
that, ¹⁴as you have understood us in part, you will come to understand fully that you ca
boast of us just as we will boast of you in the day of the Lord Jesus.

¹⁵Because I was confident of this, I planned to visit you first so that you might benef
twice. ¹⁶I planned to visit you on my way to Macedonia and to come back to you fron
Macedonia, and then to have you send me on my way to Judea. ¹⁷When I planned this
did I do it lightly? Or do I make my plans in a worldly manner so that in the same breath
I say, "Yes, yes" and "No, no"?

¹⁸But as surely as God is faithful, our message to you is not "Yes" and "No." ¹⁹For th
Son of God, Jesus Christ, who was preached among you by me and Silas ᵃ and Timothy
was not "Yes" and "No," but in him it has always been "Yes." ²⁰For no matter how man
promises God has made, they are "Yes" in Christ. And so through him the "Amen" i
spoken by us to the glory of God. ²¹Now it is God who makes both us and you stand firm
in Christ. He anointed us, ²²set his seal of ownership on us, and put his Spirit in ou
hearts as a deposit, guaranteeing what is to come.

²³I call God as my witness that it was in order to spare you that I did not return to
Corinth. ²⁴Not that we lord it over your faith, but we work with you for your joy, becaus
2 it is by faith you stand firm. ¹So I made up my mind that I would not make
another painful visit to you. ²For if I grieve you, who is left to make me glad bu
you whom I have grieved? ³I wrote as I did so that when I came I should not be
distressed by those who ought to make me rejoice. I had confidence in all of you, that you
would all share my joy. ⁴For I wrote you out of great distress and anguish of heart and
with many tears, not to grieve you but to let you know the depth of my love for you.

Forgiveness for the Sinner

⁵If anyone has caused grief, he has not so much grieved me as he has grieved all c
you, to some extent—not to put it too severely. ⁶The punishment inflicted on him by th
majority is sufficient for him. ⁷Now instead, you ought to forgive and comfort him, so tha
he will not be overwhelmed by excessive sorrow. ⁸I urge you, therefore, to reaffirm you
love for him. ⁹The reason I wrote you was to see if you would stand the test and be
obedient in everything. ¹⁰If you forgive anyone, I also forgive him. And what I have
forgiven—if there was anything to forgive—I have forgiven in the sight of Christ for you
sake, ¹¹in order that Satan might not outwit us. For we are not unaware of his schemes

Ministers of the New Covenant

¹²Now when I went to Troas to preach the gospel of Christ and found that the Lord had
opened a door for me, ¹³I still had no peace of mind, because I did not find my brothe
Titus there. So I said good-by to them and went on to Macedonia.

¹⁴But thanks be to God, who always leads us in triumphal procession in Christ and
through us spreads everywhere the fragrance of the knowledge of him. ¹⁵For we are to
God the aroma of Christ among those who are being saved and those who are perishing
¹⁶To the one we are the smell of death; to the other, the fragrance of life. And who i
equal to such a task? ¹⁷Unlike so many, we do not peddle the word of God for profit. Or
the contrary, in Christ we speak before God with sincerity, like men sent from God.

3 Are we beginning to commend ourselves again? Or do we need, like som
people, letters of recommendation to you or from you? ²You yourselves are
our letter, written on our hearts, known and read by everybody. ³You show that you are
a letter from Christ, the result of our ministry, written not with ink but with the Spirit o
the living God, not on tablets of stone but on tablets of human hearts.

⁴Such confidence as this is ours through Christ before God. ⁵Not that we are competen
in ourselves to claim anything for ourselves, but our competence comes from God. ⁶He

---

ᵃ 19 Greek Silvanus, a variant of Silas

as made us competent as ministers of a new covenant—not of the letter but of the Spirit; r the letter kills, but the Spirit gives life.

he Glory of the New Covenant

[7]Now if the ministry that brought death, which was engraved in letters on stone, came ith glory, so that the Israelites could not look steadily at the face of Moses because of its ory, fading though it was, [8]will not the ministry of the Spirit be even more glorious? [9]If e ministry that condemns men is glorious, how much more glorious is the ministry that rings righteousness! [10]For what was glorious has no glory now in comparison with the rpassing glory. [11]And if what was fading away came with glory, how much greater is e glory of that which lasts!

[12]Therefore, since we have such a hope, we are very bold. [13]We are not like Moses, ho would put a veil over his face to keep the Israelites from gazing at it while the diance was fading away. [14]But their minds were made dull, for to this day the same eil remains when the old covenant is read. It has not been removed, because only in hrist is it taken away. [15]Even to this day when Moses is read, a veil covers their hearts. But whenever anyone turns to the Lord, the veil is taken away. [17]Now the Lord is the pirit, and where the Spirit of the Lord is, there is freedom. [18]And we, who with unveiled ces all reflect[a] the Lord's glory, are being transformed into his likeness with ever-in-reasing glory, which comes from the Lord, who is the Spirit.

reasures in Jars of Clay

4　Therefore, since through God's mercy we have this ministry, we do not lose heart. [2]Rather, we have renounced secret and shameful ways; we do not use eception, nor do we distort the word of God. On the contrary, by setting forth the truth ainly we commend ourselves to every man's conscience in the sight of God. [3]And even our gospel is veiled, it is veiled to those who are perishing. [4]The god of this age has linded the minds of unbelievers, so that they cannot see the light of the gospel of the ory of Christ, who is the image of God. [5]For we do not preach ourselves, but Jesus Christ s Lord, and ourselves as your servants for Jesus' sake. [6]For God, who said, "Let light hine out of darkness,"[b] made his light shine in our hearts to give us the light of the nowledge of the glory of God in the face of Christ.

[7]But we have this treasure in jars of clay to show that this all-surpassing power is from od and not from us. [8]We are hard pressed on every side, but not crushed; perplexed, but ot in despair; [9]persecuted, but not abandoned; struck down, but not destroyed. [10]We lways carry around in our body the death of Jesus, so that the life of Jesus may also be evealed in our body. [11]For we who are alive are always being given over to death for esus' sake, so that his life may be revealed in our mortal body. [12]So then, death is at vork in us, but life is at work in you.

[13]It is written: "I believed; therefore I have spoken."[c] With that same spirit of faith we lso believe and therefore speak, [14]because we know that the one who raised the Lord esus from the dead will also raise us with Jesus and present us with you in his presence. [15]All this is for your benefit, so that the grace that is reaching more and more people may ause thanksgiving to overflow to the glory of God.

[16]Therefore we do not lose heart. Though outwardly we are wasting away, yet in-vardly we are being renewed day by day. [17]For our light and momentary troubles are chieving for us an eternal glory that far outweighs them all. [18]So we fix our eyes not on vhat is seen, but on what is unseen. For what is seen is temporary, but what is unseen s eternal.

18 Or contemplate　　[b]6 Gen. 1:3　　[c]13 Psalm 116:10

Our Heavenly Dwelling

5 Now we know that if the earthly tent we live in is destroyed, we have a building from God, an eternal house in heaven, not built by human hand. [2]Meanwhile we groan, longing to be clothed with our heavenly dwelling, [3]because when we are clothed, we will not be found naked. [4]For while we are in this tent, we groan and are burdened, because we do not wish to be unclothed but to be clothed with our heavenly dwelling, so that what is mortal may be swallowed up by life. [5]Now it is God who has made us for this very purpose and has given us the Spirit as a deposit, guaranteeing what is to come.

[6]Therefore we are always confident and know that as long as we are at home in the body we are away from the Lord. [7]We live by faith, not by sight. [8]We are confident, I say, and would prefer to be away from the body and at home with the Lord. [9]So we make it our goal to please him, whether we are at home in the body or away from it. [10]For we must all appear before the judgment seat of Christ, that each one may receive what is due him for the things done while in the body, whether good or bad.

The Ministry of Reconciliation

[11]Since, then, we know what it is to fear the Lord, we try to persuade men. What we are is plain to God, and I hope it is also plain to your conscience. [12]We are not trying to commend ourselves to you again, but are giving you an opportunity to take pride in us, so that you can answer those who take pride in what is seen rather than in what is in the heart. [13]If we are out of our mind, it is for the sake of God; if we are in our right mind, it is for you. [14]For Christ's love compels us, because we are convinced that one died for all, and therefore all died. [15]And he died for all, that those who live should no longer live for themselves but for him who died for them and was raised again.

[16]So from now on we regard no one from a worldly point of view. Though we once regarded Christ in this way, we do so no longer. [17]Therefore, if anyone is in Christ, he is a new creation; the old has gone, the new has come! [18]All this is from God, who reconciled us to himself through Christ and gave us the ministry of reconciliation: [19]that God was reconciling the world to himself in Christ, not counting men's sins against them. And he has committed to us the message of reconciliation. [20]We are therefore Christ's ambassadors, as though God were making his appeal through us. We implore you on Christ's behalf: Be reconciled to God. [21]God made him who had no sin to be sin[a] for us, so that in him we might become the righteousness of God.

6 As God's fellow workers we urge you not to receive God's grace in vain. [2]For he says,

---

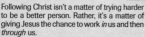

KNOWING YOURSELF

5:17–21
A New Identity

Following Christ isn't a matter of trying harder to be a better person. Rather, it's a matter of giving Jesus the chance to work *in* us and then *through* us.

Two spiritual realities help us do that. First, Jesus died in our place—God punished him instead of us so we could experience eternal life. Becoming a follower of Christ involves believing that truth and trusting in Jesus for salvation. That's what it means to be "reconciled to God" (verse 20)—we break our old patterns of behavior that excluded God and invite him to be our forgiver and leader.

Second, when we become Christ-followers, we become a "new creation" (verse 17). Since this is true, we recognize that spiritual living isn't a matter of "getting better." Our old self never can or will improve. Only through Christ's rejuvenating power can we live our lives as God wants.

If you are now a Christian you can live out of the richness and vigor of your new identity—the real you that has been remade through the power of Christ. Strengthen that new self through prayer, reading the Bible, and developing relationships with other Christians.

---

[a] 21 Or *be a sin offering*

"In the time of my favor I heard you,
and in the day of salvation I helped you."[a]

I tell you, now is the time of God's favor, now is the day of salvation.

Paul's Hardships

[3]We put no stumbling block in anyone's path, so that our ministry will not be discredited. [4]Rather, as servants of God we commend ourselves in every way: in great endurance; in troubles, hardships and distresses; [5]in beatings, imprisonments and riots; in hard work, sleepless nights and hunger; [6]in purity, understanding, patience and kindness; in the Holy Spirit and in sincere love; [7]in truthful speech and in the power of God; with weapons of righteousness in the right hand and in the left; [8]through glory and dishonor, bad report and good report; genuine, yet regarded as impostors; [9]known, yet regarded as unknown; dying, and yet we live on; beaten, and yet not killed; [10]sorrowful, yet always rejoicing; poor, yet making many rich; having nothing, and yet possessing everything.

[11]We have spoken freely to you, Corinthians, and opened wide our hearts to you. [12]We are not withholding our affection from you, but you are withholding yours from us. [13]As a fair exchange—I speak as to my children—open wide your hearts also.

Do Not Be Yoked With Unbelievers

[14]Do not be yoked together with unbelievers. For what do righteousness and wickedness have in common? Or what fellowship can light have with darkness? [15]What harmony is there between Christ and Belial[b]? What does a believer have in common with an unbeliever? [16]What agreement is there between the temple of God and idols? For we are the temple of the living God. As God has said: "I will live with them and walk among them, and I will be their God, and they will be my people."[c]

[17]"Therefore come out from them
and be separate,

says the Lord.

Touch no unclean thing,
and I will receive you."[d]
[18]"I will be a Father to you,
and you will be my sons and daughters,

says the Lord Almighty."[e]

7 Since we have these promises, dear friends, let us purify ourselves from everything that contaminates body and spirit, perfecting holiness out of reverence for God.

Paul's Joy

[2]Make room for us in your hearts. We have wronged no one, we have corrupted no one, we have exploited no one. [3]I do not say this to condemn you; I have said before that you have such a place in our hearts that we would live or die with you. [4]I have great confidence in you; I take great pride in you. I am greatly encouraged; in all our troubles my joy knows no bounds.

[5]For when we came into Macedonia, this body of ours had no rest, but we were harassed at every turn—conflicts on the outside, fears within. [6]But God, who comforts the downcast, comforted us by the coming of Titus, [7]and not only by his coming but also by the comfort you had given him. He told us about your longing for me, your deep sorrow, your ardent concern for me, so that my joy was greater than ever.

[8]Even if I caused you sorrow by my letter, I do not regret it. Though I did regret it—I see

[a]2 Isaiah 49:8 Ezek. 20:34,41   [b]15 Greek *Beliar*, a variant of *Belial*   [c]16 Lev. 26:12; Jer. 32:38; Ezek. 37:27   [d]17 Isaiah 52:11; [e]18 2 Samuel 7:14; 7:8

that my letter hurt you, but only for a little while— [9]yet now I am happy, not because you were made sorry, but because your sorrow led you to repentance. For you became sorrowful as God intended and so were not harmed in any way by us. [10]Godly sorrow brings repentance that leads to salvation and leaves no regret, but worldly sorrow brings death. [11]See what this godly sorrow has produced in you: what earnestness, what eagerness to clear yourselves, what indignation, what alarm, what longing, what concern, what readiness to see justice done. At every point you have proved yourselves to be innocent in this matter. [12]So even though I wrote to you, it was not on account of the one who did the wrong or of the injured party, but rather that before God you could see for yourselves how devoted to us you are. [13]By all this we are encouraged.

In addition to our own encouragement, we were especially delighted to see how happy Titus was, because his spirit has been refreshed by all of you. [14]I had boasted to him about you, and you have not embarrassed me. But just as everything we said to you was true, so our boasting about you to Titus has proved to be true as well. [15]And his affection for you is all the greater when he remembers that you were all obedient, receiving him with fear and trembling. [16]I am glad I can have complete confidence in you.

Generosity Encouraged

8 And now, brothers, we want you to know about the grace that God has given the Macedonian churches. [2]Out of the most severe trial, their overflowing joy and their extreme poverty welled up in rich generosity. [3]For I testify that they gave as much as they were able, and even beyond their ability. Entirely on their own, [4]they urgently pleaded with us for the privilege of sharing in this service to the saints. [5]And they did not do as we expected, but they gave themselves first to the Lord and then to us in keeping with God's will. [6]So we urged Titus, since he had earlier made a beginning, to bring also to completion this act of grace on your part. [7]But just as you excel in everything—in faith, in speech, in knowledge, in complete earnestness and in your love for us[a]—see that you also excel in this grace of giving.

[8]I am not commanding you, but I want to test the sincerity of your love by comparing it with the earnestness of others. [9]For you know the grace of our Lord Jesus Christ, that though he was rich, yet for your sakes he became poor, so that you through his poverty might become rich.

[10]And here is my advice about what is best for you in this matter: Last year you were the first not only to give but also to have the desire to do so. [11]Now finish the work, so that your eager willingness to do it may be matched by your completion of it, according to your means. [12]For if the willingness is there, the gift is acceptable according to what one has, not according to what he does not have.

[13]Our desire is not that others might be relieved while you are hard pressed, but that there might be equality. [14]At the present time your plenty will supply what they need, so that in turn their plenty will supply what you need. Then there will be equality, [15]as it is written: "He who gathered much did not have too much, and he who gathered little did not have too little."[b]

Titus Sent to Corinth

[16]I thank God, who put into the heart of Titus the same concern I have for you. [17]For Titus not only welcomed our appeal, but he is coming to you with much enthusiasm and on his own initiative. [18]And we are sending along with him the brother who is praised by all the churches for his service to the gospel. [19]What is more, he was chosen by the churches to accompany us as we carry the offering, which we administer in order to honor the Lord himself and to show our eagerness to help. [20]We want to avoid any

---

a 7 Some manuscripts *in our love for you*   *b 15* Exodus 16:18

criticism of the way we administer this liberal gift. ²¹For we are taking pains to do what is right, not only in the eyes of the Lord but also in the eyes of men.

²²In addition, we are sending with them our brother who has often proved to us in many ways that he is zealous, and now even more so because of his great confidence in you. ²³As for Titus, he is my partner and fellow worker among you; as for our brothers, they are representatives of the churches and an honor to Christ. ²⁴Therefore show these men the proof of your love and the reason for our pride in you, so that the churches can see it.

9 There is no need for me to write to you about this service to the saints. ²For I know your eagerness to help, and I have been boasting about it to the Macedonians, telling them that since last year you in Achaia were ready to give; and your enthusiasm has stirred most of them to action. ³But I am sending the brothers in order that our boasting about you in this matter should not prove hollow, but that you may be ready, as I said you would be. ⁴For if any Macedonians come with me and find you unprepared, we—not to say anything about you—would be ashamed of having been so confident. ⁵So I thought it necessary to urge the brothers to visit you in advance and finish the arrangements for the generous gift you had promised. Then it will be ready as a generous gift, not as one grudgingly given.

Sowing Generously

⁶Remember this: Whoever sows sparingly will also reap sparingly, and whoever sows generously will also reap generously. ⁷Each man should give what he has decided in his heart to give, not reluctantly or under compulsion, for God loves a cheerful giver. ⁸And God is able to make all grace abound to you, so that in all things at all times, having all that you need, you will abound in every good work. ⁹As it is written:

> "He has scattered abroad his
>   gifts to the poor;
> his righteousness endures
>   forever." ^a

¹⁰Now he who supplies seed to the sower and bread for food will also supply and increase your store of seed and will enlarge the harvest of your righteousness. ¹¹You will be made rich in every way so that you can be generous on every occasion, and through us your generosity will result in thanksgiving to God.

::::::::: MANAGING RESOURCES :::::::::

9:6–11
Possessions

As a seeker, it is helpful to know God's attitude toward money. Since God created the world and owns everything in it, he certainly doesn't need money. He does, however, use it to teach important spiritual lessons.

Notice here that God promises to multiply the gifts of generous people (verse 10). In the same way a farmer "gives away" seed to his field which is then multiplied back to him at harvest time, God promises to take what his children offer in his name and multiply it back to them in new ways.

Does that mean if a person gives $1000 to a church, he or she will get a $20,000 bonus at some later date? No, that sort of crass exchange is not what Paul is talking about here. God is not some sort of celestial slot machine that always pays 20 to 1 odds!

Paul focuses on attitude and says that cheerful giving has its reward. It's enough to know that God will provide for us no matter how the financial specifics work out in life. And when God entrusts us with more wealth, it's so we can be even more generous, not so we can hoard our money. The point of giving is to learn to trust God and be generous toward others, not to become independently wealthy.

---

¹²This service that you perform is not only supplying the needs of God's people but is also overflowing in many expressions of thanks to God. ¹³Because of the service by which you have proved yourselves, men will praise God for the obedience that accompanies your confession of the gospel of Christ, and for your generosity in sharing with them and

^a9 Psalm 112:9

with everyone else. ¹⁴And in their prayers for you their hearts will go out to you, because of the surpassing grace God has given you. ¹⁵Thanks be to God for his indescribable gift!

Paul's Defense of His Ministry

10 By the meekness and gentleness of Christ, I appeal to you—I, Paul, who am "timid" when face to face with you, but "bold" when away! ²I beg you that when I come I may not have to be as bold as I expect to be toward some people who think that we live by the standards of this world. ³For though we live in the world, we do not wage war as the world does. ⁴The weapons we fight with are not the weapons of the world. On the contrary, they have divine power to demolish strongholds. ⁵We demolish arguments and every pretension that sets itself up against the knowledge of God, and we take captive every thought to make it obedient to Christ. ⁶And we will be ready to punish every act of disobedience, once your obedience is complete.

⁷You are looking only on the surface of things.ᵃ If anyone is confident that he belongs to Christ, he should consider again that we belong to Christ just as much as he. ⁸For even if I boast somewhat freely about the authority the Lord gave us for building you up rather than pulling you down, I will not be ashamed of it. ⁹I do not want to seem to be trying to frighten you with my letters. ¹⁰For some say, "His letters are weighty and forceful, but in person he is unimpressive and his speaking amounts to nothing." ¹¹Such people should realize that what we are in our letters when we are absent, we will be in our actions when we are present.

¹²We do not dare to classify or compare ourselves with some who commend themselves. When they measure themselves by themselves and compare themselves with themselves, they are not wise. ¹³We, however, will not boast beyond proper limits, but will confine our boasting to the field God has assigned to us, a field that reaches even to you. ¹⁴We are not going too far in our boasting, as would be the case if we had not come to you, for we did get as far as you with the gospel of Christ. ¹⁵Neither do we go beyond our limits by boasting of work done by others.ᵇ Our hope is that, as your faith continues to grow, our area of activity among you will greatly expand, ¹⁶so that we can preach the gospel in the regions beyond you. For we do not want to boast about work already done in another man's territory. ¹⁷But, "Let him who boasts boast in the Lord."ᶜ ¹⁸For it is not the one who commends himself who is approved, but the one whom the Lord commends.

Paul and the False Apostles

11 I hope you will put up with a little of my foolishness; but you are already doing that. ²I am jealous for you with a godly jealousy. I promised you to one husband, to Christ, so that I might present you as a pure virgin to him. ³But I am afraid that just as Eve was deceived by the serpent's cunning, your minds may somehow be led astray from your sincere and pure devotion to Christ. ⁴For if someone comes to you and preaches a Jesus other than the Jesus we preached, or if you receive a different spirit from the one you received, or a different gospel from the one you accepted, you put up with it easily enough. ⁵But I do not think I am in the least inferior to those "super-apostles." ⁶I may not be a trained speaker, but I do have knowledge. We have made this perfectly clear to you in every way.

⁷Was it a sin for me to lower myself in order to elevate you by preaching the gospel of God to you free of charge? ⁸I robbed other churches by receiving support from them so as to serve you. ⁹And when I was with you and needed something, I was not a burden to anyone, for the brothers who came from Macedonia supplied what I needed. I have kept myself from being a burden to you in any way, and will continue to do so. ¹⁰As surely as the truth of Christ is in me, nobody in the regions of Achaia will stop this boasting of

ᵃ7 Or Look at the obvious facts   ᵇ13-15 Or ¹³We, however, will not boast about things that cannot be measured, but we will boast according to the standard of measurement that the God of measure has assigned us—a measurement that relates even to you. ¹⁴ . . . . ¹⁵Neither do we boast about things that cannot be measured in regard to the work done by others.   ᶜ17 Jer. 9:24

mine. ¹¹Why? Because I do not love you? God knows I do! ¹²And I will keep on doing what I am doing in order to cut the ground from under those who want an opportunity to be considered equal with us in the things they boast about.

¹³For such men are false apostles, deceitful workmen, masquerading as apostles of Christ. ¹⁴And no wonder, for Satan himself masquerades as an angel of light. ¹⁵It is not surprising, then, if his servants masquerade as servants of righteousness. Their end will be what their actions deserve.

Paul Boasts About His Sufferings

¹⁶I repeat: Let no one take me for a fool. But if you do, then receive me just as you would a fool, so that I may do a little boasting. ¹⁷In this self-confident boasting I am not talking as the Lord would, but as a fool. ¹⁸Since many are boasting in the way the world does, I too will boast. ¹⁹You gladly put up with fools since you are so wise! ²⁰In fact, you even put up with anyone who enslaves you or exploits you or takes advantage of you or pushes himself forward or slaps you in the face. ²¹To my shame I admit that we were too weak for that!

What anyone else dares to boast about—I am speaking as a fool—I also dare to boast about. ²²Are they Hebrews? So am I. Are they Israelites? So am I. Are they Abraham's descendants? So am I. ²³Are they servants of Christ? (I am out of my mind to talk like this.) I am more. I have worked much harder, been in prison more frequently, been flogged more severely, and been exposed to death again and again. ²⁴Five times I received from the Jews the forty lashes minus one. ²⁵Three times I was beaten with rods, once I was stoned, three times I was shipwrecked, I spent a night

DISCOVERING GOD

11:13–15
Spiritual Fraud

"I don't understand it. There was so much love within our group. We felt like we were the few God had chosen. How could I have been so deceived?"

People who leave cult groups are often emotionally devastated. Usually they have a difficult time dealing with the sense that everything about the group seemed so good. How could something so good have gone so wrong? But events in the last few decades have shown us just how twisted and destructive such cults can be. Many individuals have become so convinced that a certain gifted leader was a messenger from God they have willingly followed that person to the point of death.

Paul points out that Satan, the devil, appears as an angel of light. That means that spiritual evil can appear to be beautiful. To say that some experience or group must be from God because good comes out of it is to misunderstand the nature of spiritual deception. Mixing 10 parts truth with 1 part error produces a spiritually deadly potion. That's what many cult leaders have done since the church began.

False teachers may use the name of Christ, preach a "gospel," quote Bible verses, and have a persuasive spiritual power (see verses 3–4). But if any of their teachings are at odds with the Bible, that person is a deceiver and should not be listened to or followed.

and a day in the open sea, ²⁶I have been constantly on the move. I have been in danger from rivers, in danger from bandits, in danger from my own countrymen, in danger from Gentiles; in danger in the city, in danger in the country, in danger at sea; and in danger from false brothers. ²⁷I have labored and toiled and have often gone without sleep; I have known hunger and thirst and have often gone without food; I have been cold and naked. ²⁸Besides everything else, I face daily the pressure of my concern for all the churches. ²⁹Who is weak, and I do not feel weak? Who is led into sin, and I do not inwardly burn?

³⁰If I must boast, I will boast of the things that show my weakness. ³¹The God and Father of the Lord Jesus, who is to be praised forever, knows that I am not lying. ³²In Damascus the governor under King Aretas had the city of the Damascenes guarded in order to arrest me. ³³But I was lowered in a basket from a window in the wall and slipped through his hands.

Paul's Vision and His Thorn

12 I must go on boasting. Although there is nothing to be gained, I will go on to visions and revelations from the Lord. ²I know a man in Christ who fourteen years ago was caught up to the third heaven. Whether it was in the body or out of the body I do not know—God knows. ³And I know that this man—whether in the body or apart from the body I do not know, but God knows— ⁴was caught up to paradise. He heard inexpressible things, things that man is not permitted to tell. ⁵I will boast about a man like that, but I will not boast about myself, except about my weaknesses. ⁶Even if I should choose to boast, I would not be a fool, because I would be speaking the truth. But I refrain, so no one will think more of me than is warranted by what I do or say.

⁷To keep me from becoming conceited because of these surpassingly great revelations, there was given me a thorn in my flesh, a messenger of Satan, to torment me. ⁸Three times I pleaded with the Lord to take it away from me. ⁹But he said to me, "My grace is sufficient for you, for my power is made perfect in weakness." Therefore I will boast all the more gladly about my weaknesses, so that Christ's power may rest on me. ¹⁰That is why, for Christ's sake, I delight in weaknesses, in insults, in hardships, in persecutions, in difficulties. For when I am weak, then I am strong.

Paul's Concern for the Corinthians

¹¹I have made a fool of myself, but you drove me to it. I ought to have been commended by you, for I am not in the least inferior to the "super-apostles," even though I am nothing. ¹²The things that mark an apostle—signs, wonders and miracles—were done among you with great perseverance. ¹³How were you inferior to the other churches, except that I was never a burden to you? Forgive me this wrong!

¹⁴Now I am ready to visit you for the third time, and I will not be a burden to you,

---

ADDRESSING QUESTIONS

12:1–10
Human Experience

Q

On May 18, 1980, at 8:30 A.M., Washington's Mount St. Helens erupted with an incredible explosion of rock and hot gases. For five minutes the volcano roared at 680 degrees Fahrenheit, spreading devastation over a 200-square-mile area. Whole forests were leveled in minutes; 100-foot trees were strewn about like soda straws. The surrounding areas were covered in a blizzard of ash, and the armed forces were called in to help residents dig out.

Scientists said it might take 50 years for life to return to the scene. But since the eruption, birds, animals and wind updrafts have carried seeds into the devastated areas. The mountain is changing from total gray to gray-green much quicker than anyone predicted, and tiny flowers pierce the ash.

Occasionally we experience a traumatic event that feels like a volcano erupting in our lives. During such times we may feel as if our bodies, spirits and emotions are covered with a thick blanket of dark soot. But the Bible assures us that even when we seem completely surrounded by loss and pain, God's comfort and power are available.

Paul writes about a time when a "thorn" pierced his own life. We don't know what it was, but it caused him pain. Three times he pleaded with God to remove it, and three times God refused. But God did give Paul what he needed—*power to manage anyway.*

Like a tiny seedling pushing aside the gray ash, God's grace broke through Paul's limitations and weaknesses and grew to mighty proportions. In fact, Paul reported that he actually "delighted" in his hardships because of the spiritual benefits that kept coming his way (verse 10).

If you're a seeker, you need to know that with God, hardships can take on a new significance. When difficulties arise, something occurs in the believer's life that is hard to explain but wonderful to experience. It's the amazing paradox of God being most real and most at work when devastating circumstances arise.

ecause what I want is not your possessions but you. After all, children should not have o save up for their parents, but parents for their children. 15So I will very gladly spend or you everything I have and expend myself as well. If I love you more, will you love me ess? 16Be that as it may, I have not been a burden to you. Yet, crafty fellow that I am, I aught you by trickery! 17Did I exploit you through any of the men I sent you? 18I urged Titus to go to you and I sent our brother with him. Titus did not exploit you, did he? Did we not act in the same spirit and follow the same course?

19Have you been thinking all along that we have been defending ourselves to you? We have been speaking in the sight of God as those in Christ; and everything we do, dear friends, is for your strengthening. 20For I am afraid that when I come I may not find you as I want you to be, and you may not find me as you want me to be. I fear that there may be quarreling, jealousy, outbursts of anger, factions, slander, gossip, arrogance and disorder. 21I am afraid that when I come again my God will humble me before you, and I will be grieved over many who have sinned earlier and have not repented of the impurity, sexual sin and debauchery in which they have indulged.

Final Warnings

13 This will be my third visit to you. "Every matter must be established by the testimony of two or three witnesses."*a* 2I already gave you a warning when I was with you the second time. I now repeat it while absent: On my return I will not spare those who sinned earlier or any of the others, 3since you are demanding proof that Christ is speaking through me. He is not weak in dealing with you, but is powerful among you. 4For to be sure, he was crucified in weakness, yet he lives by God's power. Likewise, we are weak in him, yet by God's power we will live with him to serve you.

5Examine yourselves to see whether you are in the faith; test yourselves. Do you not realize that Christ Jesus is in you—unless, of course, you fail the test? 6And I trust that you will discover that we have not failed the test. 7Now we pray to God that you will not do anything wrong. Not that people will see that we have stood the test but that you will do what is right even though we may seem to have failed. 8For we cannot do anything against the truth, but only for the truth. 9We are glad whenever we are weak but you are strong; and our prayer is for your perfection. 10This is why I write these things when I am absent, that when I come I may not have to be harsh in my use of authority—the authority the Lord gave me for building you up, not for tearing you down.

Final Greetings

11Finally, brothers, good-by. Aim for perfection, listen to my appeal, be of one mind, live in peace. And the God of love and peace will be with you.

12Greet one another with a holy kiss. 13All the saints send their greetings.

14May the grace of the Lord Jesus Christ, and the love of God, and the fellowship of the Holy Spirit be with you all.

a 1 Deut. 19:15

GALATIANS

Introduction

THE BOTTOM LINE

Freedom isn't just the absence of restraint—it's the presence of something too. In this book, Paul talks about the freedom that those who follow Christ's teachings have from the weight of evil in their lives. But he goes on to explain that freedom is the power to do what you *choose* to do, not just the right to do anything you feel like doing. People whose lives have been changed by Christ, who have accepted his work on their behalf, live as free people in the sight of God. Read on to learn how you can be liberated as well.

CENTRAL IDEAS

- Paul clearly outlines the good news of Christ's work and how to apply it to life.
- New life doesn't come by doing good things, but by trusting in Jesus.
- Religious legalism stems from a misunderstanding of God's grace.
- Freedom in Christ means living a life of love toward God and others.

OUTLINE

1. Introduction (1:1–9)
2. Paul defends his credentials as an apostle (1:10–2:21)
3. Our freedom in Christ (chs. 3–4)
4. The practice of Christian liberty (5:1–6:10)
5. Conclusion (6:11–18)

TITLE

This letter is titled after its recipients—Christians in the region of Galatia, a Roman province in the central part of modern-day Turkey.

AUTHOR AND READERS

Paul wrote this letter to squelch some of the false teachings that had infiltrated this church, and to encourage the believers in their freedom in Christ.

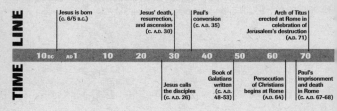

TIME LINE

| | Jesus is born (c. 6/5 B.C.) | Jesus' death, resurrection, and ascension (c. A.D. 30) | Paul's conversion (c. A.D. 35) | | Arch of Titus erected at Rome in celebration of Jerusalem's destruction (A.D. 71) |

10 BC AD 1 10 20 30 40 50 60 70

| | Jesus calls the disciples (c. A.D. 26) | Book of Galatians written (c. A.D. 48–53) | Persecution of Christians begins at Rome (A.D. 64) | Paul's imprisonment and death in Rome (c. A.D. 67-68) |

With tears streaming down her cheeks, Sherry expressed years of hurt and disappointment. "I'm tired of never knowing where I stand. No matter what I do, it's never enough for Bob."

Sherry and Bob had been dating for more than five years and had been engaged for three of those years. Sherry shared their story: "When we first started dating, Bob wanted me to lose weight and get in shape. We joined a health club, and I worked hard. Within a few months I had shed my extra weight and was feeling great. Bob praised my appearance. But it wasn't long before he started talking about my clothes. He wanted me to 'update' my wardrobe—which I did. Then he wanted me to get a new car and move into a nicer apartment. This has been going on for five years. Just about the time I make one change, he wants me to do something else."

It's easy to see why Sherry would be frustrated. Most of us would tell her to get rid of the guy!

God is willing to accept you apart from anything you ever have done or ever will do.

Why is it then that some people cast God in the same role as Bob? These people make God seem extremely demanding, telling us that we need to live by various rules and regulations. If this is what we have to do to be in relationship with God, how can we ever be sure we've done enough? Will he ever accept us? Or will he raise the bar just as we're about to clear it?

Many years ago, the members of the Galatian churches struggled with these same questions. They bought into the false teaching that they had to perform all kinds of religious rituals to win God's favor. The apostle Paul had an important message for them—and for you, if you're a seeker. Quite simply, God is willing to accept you apart from anything you ever have done or ever will do. If you let Christ justify you—instead of trying to justify yourself—you will have a new life both now and forever.

And there's more. Through Jesus, God's Spirit will actually live in you and enable you to live a life that pleases him. If you'd like to see these promises from God in writing, turn to Galatians chapter 2, verses 16–20 (page 1525).

GALATIANS

1 Paul, an apostle—sent not from men nor by man, but by Jesus Christ and God the Father, who raised him from the dead— [2]and all the brothers with me,

To the churches in Galatia:

[3]Grace and peace to you from God our Father and the Lord Jesus Christ, [4]who gave himself for our sins to rescue us from the present evil age, according to the will of our God and Father, [5]to whom be glory for ever and ever. Amen.

No Other Gospel

[6]I am astonished that you are so quickly deserting the one who called you by the grace of Christ and are turning to a different gospel— [7]which is really no gospel at all. Evidently some people are throwing you into confusion and are trying to pervert the gospel of Christ. [8]But even if we or an angel from heaven should preach a gospel other than the one we preached to you, let him be eternally condemned! [9]As we have already said, so now I say again: If anybody is preaching to you a gospel other than what you accepted, let him be eternally condemned!

[10]Am I now trying to win the approval of men, or of God? Or am I trying to please men? If I were still trying to please men, I would not be a servant of Christ.

▒▒ DISCOVERING GOD ▒▒

1:8–9
Spiritual Fraud

If an angel came to you, would you be confident that it was God trying to talk to you?

The point Paul makes here is that we must test any spiritual experience—including even an angelic visit—by comparing that experience with previously established truth from God. In other words, if what you hear from someone doesn't match the message Jesus taught in the Bible, reject the message as a counterfeit—even if the one speaking has wings!

Paul Called by God

[11]I want you to know, brothers, that the gospel I preached is not something that man made up. [12]I did not receive it from any man, nor was I taught it; rather, I received it by revelation from Jesus Christ.

[13]For you have heard of my previous way of life in Judaism, how intensely I persecuted the church of God and tried to destroy it. [14]I was advancing in Judaism beyond many Jews of my own age and was extremely zealous for the traditions of my fathers. [15]But when God, who set me apart from birth[a] and called me by his grace, was pleased [16]to reveal his Son in me so that I might preach him among the Gentiles, I did not consult any man, [17]nor did I go up to Jerusalem to see those who were apostles before I was, but I went immediately into Arabia and later returned to Damascus.

[18]Then after three years, I went up to Jerusalem to get acquainted with Peter[b] and stayed with him fifteen days. [19]I saw none of the other apostles—only James, the Lord's brother. [20]I assure you before God that what I am writing you is no lie. [21]Later I went to Syria and Cilicia. [22]I was personally unknown to the churches of Judea that are in Christ. [23]They only heard the report: "The man who formerly persecuted us is now preaching the faith he once tried to destroy." [24]And they praised God because of me.

a 15 Or from my mother's womb   *b 18 Greek Cephas*

Paul Accepted by the Apostles

2 Fourteen years later I went up again to Jerusalem, this time with Barnabas. I took Titus along also. ²I went in response to a revelation and set before them the gospel that I preach among the Gentiles. But I did this privately to those who seemed to be leaders, for fear that I was running or had run my race in vain. ³Yet not even Titus, who was with me, was compelled to be circumcised, even though he was a Greek. ⁴This matter arose, because some false brothers had infiltrated our ranks to spy on the freedom we have in Christ Jesus and to make us slaves. ⁵We did not give in to them for a moment, so that the truth of the gospel might remain with you.

⁶As for those who seemed to be important—whatever they were makes no difference to me; God does not judge by external appearance—those men added nothing to my message. ⁷On the contrary, they saw that I had been entrusted with the task of preaching the gospel to the Gentiles,ᵃ just as Peter had been to the Jews.ᵇ ⁸For God, who was at work in the ministry of Peter as an apostle to the Jews, was also at work in my ministry as an apostle to the Gentiles. ⁹James, Peterᶜ and John, those reputed to be pillars, gave me and Barnabas the right hand of fellowship when they recognized the grace given to me. They agreed that we should go to the Gentiles, and they to the Jews. ¹⁰All they asked was that we should continue to remember the poor, the very thing I was eager to do.

Paul Opposes Peter

¹¹When Peter came to Antioch, I opposed him to his face, because he was clearly in the wrong. ¹²Before certain men came from James, he used to eat with the Gentiles. But when they arrived, he began to draw back and separate himself from the Gentiles because he was afraid of those who belonged to the circumcision group. ¹³The other Jews joined him in his hypocrisy, so that by their hypocrisy even Barnabas was led astray.

¹⁴When I saw that they were not acting in line with the truth of the gospel, I said to Peter in front of them all, "You are a Jew, yet you live like a Gentile and not like a Jew. How is it, then, that you force Gentiles to follow Jewish customs?

¹⁵"We who are Jews by birth and not 'Gentile sinners' ¹⁶know that a man is not justified by observing the law, but by faith in Jesus Christ. So we, too, have put our faith

---

▣ ▦ ADDRESSING QUESTIONS ▦ ◪

2:11–21
Human Experience **Q**

What do you do when a friend who is a recognized spiritual authority makes a serious mistake?

That's the question the apostle Paul wrestled with here. Peter, another apostle and a disciple of Jesus, had fallen in with a group of Jewish Christians who taught that becoming a follower of Christ demanded not only faith, but also the observance of Jewish rituals. In doing so, Peter deviated from his former teaching and practice of nondiscrimination. The message he delivered to the Antioch believers through his actions was, "Unless you observe Jewish religious rituals—like us—you're not a first-class Christian."

Paul dealt with Peter's hypocrisy head-on, reminding his friend that nobody can be made right with God by observing religious rituals. Christians live by faith in Christ, knowing that they can't do anything to earn a new life or improve on what Christ has done. "For if righteousness could be gained through the law, Christ died for nothing!" (verse 21).

Does that mean that followers of Jesus have no moral responsibility? No, Christians try to obey God. But they do so not to win his approval; they obey God because they already *have* his approval.

If you decide to accept Christ, God will accept you because of what Jesus has done for you on the cross. Furthermore, Christ will actually dwell in you. His Spirit will enable you to live a life that pleases God. And you'll be motivated to live that way as an expression of gratitude, not out of a feeling of obligation.

ᵃ7 Greek *uncircumcised*   ᵇ7 Greek *circumcised*; also in verses 8 and 9   ᶜ9 Greek *Cephas*; also in verses 11 and 14

in Christ Jesus that we may be justified by faith in Christ and not by observing the law, because by observing the law no one will be justified.

17"If, while we seek to be justified in Christ, it becomes evident that we ourselves are sinners, does that mean that Christ promotes sin? Absolutely not! **18**If I rebuild what I destroyed, I prove that I am a lawbreaker. **19**For through the law I died to the law so that I might live for God. **20**I have been crucified with Christ and I no longer live, but Christ lives in me. The life I live in the body, I live by faith in the Son of God, who loved me and gave himself for me. **21**I do not set aside the grace of God, for if righteousness could be gained through the law, Christ died for nothing!"*a*

Faith or Observance of the Law

3 You foolish Galatians! Who has bewitched you? Before your very eyes Jesus Christ was clearly portrayed as crucified. **2**I would like to learn just one thing from you: Did you receive the Spirit by observing the law, or by believing what you heard? **3**Are you so foolish? After beginning with the Spirit, are you now trying to attain your goal by human effort? **4**Have you suffered so much for nothing—if it really was for nothing? **5**Does God give you his Spirit and work miracles among you because you observe the law, or because you believe what you heard?

6Consider Abraham: "He believed God, and it was credited to him as righteousness."*b* **7**Understand, then, that those who believe are children of Abraham. **8**The Scripture foresaw that God would justify the Gentiles by faith, and announced the gospel in advance to Abraham: "All nations will be blessed through you."*c* **9**So those who have faith are blessed along with Abraham, the man of faith.

10All who rely on observing the law are under a curse, for it is written: "Cursed is everyone who does not continue to do everything written in the Book of the Law."*d* **11**Clearly no one is justified before God by the law, because, "The righteous will live by faith."*e* **12**The law is not based on faith; on the contrary, "The man who does these things will live by them."*f* **13**Christ redeemed us from the curse of the law by becoming a curse for us, for it is written: "Cursed is everyone who is hung on a tree."*g* **14**He redeemed us in order that the blessing given to Abraham might come to the Gentiles through Christ Jesus, so that by faith we might receive the promise of the Spirit.

The Law and the Promise

15Brothers, let me take an example from everyday life. Just as no one can set aside or add to a human covenant that has been duly established, so it is in this case. **16**The promises were spoken to Abraham and to his seed. The Scripture does not say "and to seeds," meaning many people, but "and to your seed,"*h* meaning one person, who is Christ. **17**What I mean is this: The law, introduced 430 years later, does not set aside the covenant previously established by God and thus do away with the promise. **18**For if the inheritance depends on the law, then it no longer depends on a promise; but God in his grace gave it to Abraham through a promise.

19What, then, was the purpose of the law? It was added because of transgressions until the Seed to whom the promise referred had come. The law was put into effect through angels by a mediator. **20**A mediator, however, does not represent just one party; but God is one.

21Is the law, therefore, opposed to the promises of God? Absolutely not! For if a law had been given that could impart life, then righteousness would certainly have come by the law. **22**But the Scripture declares that the whole world is a prisoner of sin, so that what was promised, being given through faith in Jesus Christ, might be given to those who believe.

23Before this faith came, we were held prisoners by the law, locked up until faith

---

a 21 Some interpreters end the quotation after verse 14.   *b 6* Gen. 15:6   *c 8* Gen. 12:3; 18:18; 22:18   *d 10* Deut. 27:26   *e 11* Hab. 2:4   *f 12* Lev. 18:5   *g 13* Deut. 21:23   *h 16* Gen. 12:7; 13:15; 24:7

should be revealed. 24So the law was put in charge to lead us to Christ*a* that we might be justified by faith. 25Now that faith has come, we are no longer under the supervision of the law.

Sons of God

26You are all sons of God through faith in Christ Jesus, 27for all of you who were baptized into Christ have clothed yourselves with Christ. 28There is neither Jew nor Greek, slave nor free, male nor female, for you are all one in Christ Jesus. 29If you belong to Christ, then you are Abraham's seed, and heirs according to the promise.

4 What I am saying is that as long as the heir is a child, he is no different from a slave, although he owns the whole estate. 2He is subject to guardians and trustees until the time set by his father. 3So also, when we were children, we were in slavery under the basic principles of the world. 4But when the time had fully come, God sent his Son, born of a woman, born under law, 5to redeem those under law, that we might receive the full rights of sons. 6Because you are sons, God sent the Spirit of his Son into our hearts, the Spirit who calls out, "Abba,*b* Father." 7So you are no longer a slave, but a son; and since you are a son, God has made you also an heir.

Paul's Concern for the Galatians

8Formerly, when you did not know God, you were slaves to those who by nature are not gods. 9But now that you know God—or rather are known by God—how is it that you are turning back to those weak and miserable principles? Do you wish to be enslaved by them all over again? 10You are observing special days and months and seasons and years! 11I fear for you, that somehow I have wasted my efforts on you.

12I plead with you, brothers, become like me, for I became like you. You have done me no wrong. 13As you know, it was because of an illness that I first preached the gospel to you. 14Even though my illness was a trial to you, you did not treat me with contempt or scorn. Instead, you welcomed me as if I were an angel of God, as if I were Christ Jesus himself. 15What has happened to all your joy? I can testify that, if you could have done so, you would have torn out your eyes and given them to me. 16Have I now become your enemy by telling you the truth?

17Those people are zealous to win you over, but for no good. What they want is to alienate you ˌfrom us˳, so that you may be zealous for them. 18It is fine to be zealous, provided the purpose is good, and to be so always and not just when I am with you. 19My dear children, for whom I am again in the pains of childbirth until Christ is formed in you, 20how I wish I could be with you now and change my tone, because I am perplexed about you!

🔲 ▓▓▓▓▓▓ ADDRESSING QUESTIONS ▓▓▓▓▓▓ 🔁

3:23—4:5
Human Experience **Q**

Seekers are often confused about why God gave the Old Testament law. Paul says here that God gave us the law to show us our need for Christ.

To illustrate this point, Paul borrows from a familiar cultural situation in New Testament times. In many Roman and Greek homes, well-educated and trusted servants were responsible to take the children to and from school and supervise them. They weren't qualified to instruct, nor were they given total authority to control the children. Instead, the servants were appointed to watch over and protect the children until they didn't need such close supervision.

Today the Ten Commandments act as our guardians and prepare us for a mature spiritual relationship with Christ. God's holy law shows us that we need rescuing—though it has no power to actually do the rescuing. Since obedience won't gain God's favor (because we can't consistently obey), we need to have faith in God and in his provision through Christ's death on our behalf.

---

a24 Or charge until Christ came   *b6 Aramaic for Father*

Hagar and Sarah

²¹Tell me, you who want to be under the law, are you not aware of what the law says? ²²For it is written that Abraham had two sons, one by the slave woman and the other by the free woman. ²³His son by the slave woman was born in the ordinary way; but his son by the free woman was born as the result of a promise.

²⁴These things may be taken figuratively, for the women represent two covenants. One covenant is from Mount Sinai and bears children who are to be slaves: This is Hagar. ²⁵Now Hagar stands for Mount Sinai in Arabia and corresponds to the present city of Jerusalem, because she is in slavery with her children. ²⁶But the Jerusalem that is above is free, and she is our mother. ²⁷For it is written:

> "Be glad, O barren woman,
>   who bears no children;
> break forth and cry aloud,
>   you who have no labor pains;
> because more are the children of the desolate woman
>   than of her who has a husband."ᵃ

²⁸Now you, brothers, like Isaac, are children of promise. ²⁹At that time the son born in the ordinary way persecuted the son born by the power of the Spirit. It is the same now. ³⁰But what does the Scripture say? "Get rid of the slave woman and her son, for the slave woman's son will never share in the inheritance with the free woman's son."ᵇ ³¹Therefore, brothers, we are not children of the slave woman, but of the free woman.

Freedom in Christ

5 It is for freedom that Christ has set us free. Stand firm, then, and do not let yourselves be burdened again by a yoke of slavery.

²Mark my words! I, Paul, tell you that if you let yourselves be circumcised, Christ will be of no value to you at all. ³Again I declare to every man who lets himself be circumcised that he is obligated to obey the whole law. ⁴You who are trying to be justified by law have been alienated from Christ; you have fallen away from grace. ⁵But by faith we eagerly await through the Spirit the righteousness for which we hope. ⁶For in Christ Jesus neither circumcision nor uncircumcision has any value. The only thing that counts is faith expressing itself through love.

⁷You were running a good race. Who cut in on you and kept you from obeying the truth? ⁸That kind of persuasion does not come from the one who calls you. ⁹"A little yeast works through the whole batch of dough." ¹⁰I am confident in the Lord that you will take no other view. The one who is throwing you into confusion will pay the penalty, whoever he may be. ¹¹Brothers, if I am still preaching circumcision, why am I still being persecuted? In that case the offense of the cross has been abolished. ¹²As for those agitators, I wish they would go the whole way and emasculate themselves!

¹³You, my brothers, were called to be free. But do not use your freedom to indulge the sinful natureᶜ; rather, serve one another in love. ¹⁴The entire law is summed up in a single command: "Love your neighbor as yourself."ᵈ ¹⁵If you keep on biting and devouring each other, watch out or you will be destroyed by each other.

Life by the Spirit

¹⁶So I say, live by the Spirit, and you will not gratify the desires of the sinful nature. ¹⁷For the sinful nature desires what is contrary to the Spirit, and the Spirit what is contrary to the sinful nature. They are in conflict with each other, so that you do not do what you want. ¹⁸But if you are led by the Spirit, you are not under law.

¹⁹The acts of the sinful nature are obvious: sexual immorality, impurity and debauch-

---

ᵃ27 Isaiah 54:1   ᵇ30 Gen. 21:10   ᶜ13 Or the flesh; also in verses 16, 17, 19 and 24   ᵈ14 Lev. 19:18

ery; ²⁰idolatry and witchcraft; hatred, discord, jealousy, fits of rage, selfish ambition, dissensions, factions ²¹and envy; drunkenness, orgies, and the like. I warn you, as I did before, that those who live like this will not inherit the kingdom of God.

²²But the fruit of the Spirit is love, joy, peace, patience, kindness, goodness, faithfulness, ²³gentleness and self-control. Against such things there is no law. ²⁴Those who belong to Christ Jesus have crucified the sinful nature with its passions and desires. ²⁵Since we live by the Spirit, let us keep in step with the Spirit. ²⁶Let us not become conceited, provoking and envying each other.

Doing Good to All

6 Brothers, if someone is caught in a sin, you who are spiritual should restore him gently. But watch yourself, or you also may be tempted. ²Carry each other's burdens, and in this way you will fulfill the law of Christ. ³If anyone thinks he is something when he is nothing, he deceives himself. ⁴Each one should test his own actions. Then he can take pride in himself, without comparing himself to somebody else, ⁵for each one should carry his own load.

⁶Anyone who receives instruction in the word must share all good things with his instructor.

⁷Do not be deceived: God cannot be mocked. A man reaps what he sows. ⁸The one who sows to please his sinful nature, from that nature*ᵃ* will reap destruction; the one who sows to please the Spirit, from the Spirit will reap eternal life. ⁹Let us not become weary in doing good, for at the proper time we will reap a harvest if we do not give up. ¹⁰Therefore, as we have opportunity, let us do good to all people, especially to those who belong to the family of believers.

Not Circumcision but a New Creation

¹¹See what large letters I use as I write to you with my own hand!

¹²Those who want to make a good impression outwardly are trying to compel you to be circumcised. The only reason they do this is to avoid being persecuted for the cross of Christ. ¹³Not even those who are circumcised obey the law, yet they want you to be circumcised that they may boast about your flesh. ¹⁴May I never boast except in the cross

---

KNOWING YOURSELF

5:16–26
A New Identity

Here Paul says that followers of Christ possess two natures: sinful and spiritual. The key to living the Christian life is setting aside the sinful nature and learning to live spiritually "in step" with the Holy Spirit. While followers of Christ can't make this transition on their own, the Spirit who lives in all Christ-followers helps them resist the temptations produced by the sinful nature.

STRENGTHENING RELATIONSHIPS

6:1–5
Social

How are Christians supposed to help other people who are caught in destructive patterns?

According to Paul, first, Christians must be strong and secure in their walk with God. Second, they must speak with gentleness. Third, they must exercise humility. Believers who try to help people engaged in destructive behaviors must be aware that they are also vulnerable to temptation. They must imitate Christ by coming alongside those who are having trouble with the goal of restoring their relationship with God and with other people.

If you're a seeker, think of this as a standard that all Christians are given—a prescription for helping others. Unfortunately, not all Christians live up to this standard. But if someone in your life has helped you or is trying to help you break a destructive life-pattern, recognize that that person is trying to follow Paul's instructions here. God is concerned that you break the negative patterns in your life, and has charged his followers with the responsibility of helping you do just that.

ᵃ 8 Or his flesh, from the flesh

of our Lord Jesus Christ, through which^a the world has been crucified to me, and I to the world. ¹⁵Neither circumcision nor uncircumcision means anything; what counts is a new creation. ¹⁶Peace and mercy to all who follow this rule, even to the Israel of God.

¹⁷Finally, let no one cause me trouble, for I bear on my body the marks of Jesus.

¹⁸The grace of our Lord Jesus Christ be with your spirit, brothers. Amen.

---

^{a} 14 Or whom

Six years ago I turned to my wife at the dinner table and said, "There must be more to life than this." I was referring to the nice house, the nice car, and all that we had acquired. I was a busy, successful professional with a happy marriage, but something was missing. There seemed to be no meaning to life. God did not factor into my life at that time.

My wife, who had been attending a local church, dragged me to a Sunday church service. I dug my heels in all the way. After that first Sunday, however, I began attending services regularly with my wife. While attending a small group, I found what I had been searching for and asked Christ into my life as my Lord and Savior.

Since that time I have cut back on my work so that I can devote more time to my family and to church. My view of the world has been forever changed since asking Christ into my life.

Before I trusted Christ alone for my salvation, I tried my best to be a good person. I always knew, however, that I could never be good enough to earn a relationship with God or a place in his heaven. Through a relationship with a Christian friend and instruction at her church, I finally accepted God's love for me. Only then could I take the next step—accepting Christ's sacrifice for my sin.

The decision to trust Christ alone for my salvation has broken down the barriers of shame, guilt and inadequacy that had prevented me from having a relationship with God. Although I am now even more aware of my sinfulness, I know without a doubt that God accepts me as I am and welcomes me with open arms. I have so much to learn and so many ways to grow, but that's OK. I know that God is always there walking with me, loving me, teaching me and allowing me to be close to him.

EPHESIANS

Introduction

THE BOTTOM LINE Sometimes, when you're sitting in the middle of a traffic jam on a broiling hot summer day, do you ever wonder why you do what you do? What's the point of your daily activity? A sense of purpose isn't something you can learn in a college class. It isn't something you'll earn with your next promotion. And it isn't something someone else can magically bestow on you. Purpose is something you have when you're working toward a worthy and compelling goal.

In this book, Paul outlines God's intention to sum up everything in Christ and his church. He points out that we all have a place in that grand scheme—if we are "in Christ." His plans for us don't necessarily involve a big house, a hefty stock portfolio or private schools for our kids. They will, however, provide a sense of permanent—even eternal—direction in life.

CENTRAL IDEAS

- God has included you in the "big picture."
- God's purpose for your life supersedes—and is much more satisfying than—any personal goals you may have.
- Becoming a Christian means being a functioning part of a larger "body" of believers called the church.
- Paul outlines how people can live in unity with one another.

OUTLINE

1 Doctrine (chs. 1—3)
2 Practical living (chs. 4—6)
3 Conclusion (6:21—24)

TITLE

This book is titled after its recipients—Christians in the city of Ephesus, which was at the time the most important city in Asia Minor (modern Turkey).

AUTHOR AND READERS

Paul wrote this letter to encourage unity among the believers in the church in Ephesus. He intended to instill in them a higher purpose—God's purpose—and to help them learn to relate to one another as parts of the same body.

What's that?" a friend asked, pointing at a one-pound rock sitting on my bookshelf.

"It's a piece of the Berlin Wall. I got it last year while I was in Germany," I replied.

What a chunk of history. That rock is a fragment of a wall that divided a city and a nation. It barricaded parents from their children. It divided brothers and sisters.

For decades the Western world watched television news reports showing desperate people trying to scale that wall. Guards chased down some people and threw them to the ground. They shot and killed other people. To the watching world, the Berlin wall seemed like a fixture—a permanent symbol of strife and division.

That's why the world was so surprised when that wall came down in 1989. Television screens showed celebrating masses beating down the wall with sledgehammers and picks. As it crumbled, mothers wept and embraced children they hadn't held in decades. Siblings and friends who thought they would never meet again threw their arms around

To the watching world, the Berlin wall seemed like a fixture.

each other. The world celebrated. And a rock from that wall became a priceless reminder to me that insurmountable barriers can be destroyed. People who are divided can be reunited.

Many people feel that religion is just another force that creates walls between us. Don't religious people see themselves as a cut above those who aren't religious? Aren't some of society's greatest tensions centered around various religious groups?

The apostle Paul recognized religion's power to create barriers. That's why he made it clear to the Christ-followers in the city of Ephesus that Jesus wants to destroy man-made divisions and unify everyone under God's loving leadership. True, some people are outside the walls of the kingdom of God (the condition in which we all start out). Some have responded to God's call and now live within those walls. *But no one has to stay outside, and certainly no barriers should exist within God's family.*

If you're frustrated by the feeling that you're on the outside looking in, recognize that God has torn down the barriers between you and him. He invites you to join him. When you do, you'll discover a new order of humanity made up of people who've been bought by Christ himself. To discover the picture of how God's new community of believers is supposed to work, turn to Ephesians chapter 2, verses 13–18 (page 1535).

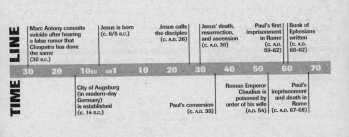

TIME LINE

Marc Antony commits suicide after hearing a false rumor that Cleopatra has done the same (30 B.C.)	Jesus is born (c. 6/5 B.C.)	Jesus calls the disciples (c. A.D. 26)	Jesus' death, resurrection, and ascension (c. A.D. 30)	Paul's first imprisonment in Rome (c. A.D. 59–62)	Book of Ephesians written (c. A.D. 60–62)

30   20   10 BC   AD 1   10   20   30   40   50   60   70

City of Augsburg (in modern-day Germany) is established (c. 14 B.C.)	Paul's conversion (c. A.D. 35)	Roman Emperor Claudius is poisoned by order of his wife (A.D. 54)	Paul's imprisonment and death in Rome (c. A.D. 67–68)

EPHESIANS

1 Paul, an apostle of Christ Jesus by the will of God,

To the saints in Ephesus,[a] the faithful[b] in Christ Jesus:

[2]Grace and peace to you from God our Father and the Lord Jesus Christ.

Spiritual Blessings in Christ

[3]Praise be to the God and Father of our Lord Jesus Christ, who has blessed us in the heavenly realms with every spiritual blessing in Christ. [4]For he chose us in him before the creation of the world to be holy and blameless in his sight. In love [5]he[c] predestined us to be adopted as his sons through Jesus Christ, in accordance with his pleasure and will— [6]to the praise of his glorious grace, which he has freely given us in the One he loves. [7]In him we have redemption through his blood, the forgiveness of sins, in accordance with the riches of God's grace [8]that he lavished on us with all wisdom and understanding. [9]And he[d] made known to us the mystery of his will according to his good pleasure, which he purposed in Christ, [10]to be put into effect when the times will have reached their fulfillment—to bring all things in heaven and on earth together under one head, even Christ.

[11]In him we were also chosen,[e] having been predestined according to the plan of him who works out everything in conformity with the purpose of his will, [12]in order that we, who were the first to hope in Christ, might be for the praise of his glory. [13]And you also were included in Christ when you heard the word of truth, the gospel of your salvation. Having believed, you were marked in him with a seal, the promised Holy Spirit, [14]who is a deposit guaranteeing our inheritance until the redemption of those who are God's possession—to the praise of his glory.

Thanksgiving and Prayer

[15]For this reason, ever since I heard about your faith in the Lord Jesus and your love for all the saints, [16]I have not stopped giving thanks for you, remembering you in my prayers. [17]I keep asking that the God of our Lord Jesus Christ, the glorious Father, may give you the Spirit[f] of wisdom and revelation, so that you may know him better. [18]I pray also that the eyes of your heart may be enlightened in order that you may know the hope to which he has called you, the riches of his glorious inheritance in the saints, [19]and his incomparably great power for us who believe. That power is like the working of his mighty strength, [20]which he exerted in Christ when he raised him from the dead and seated him at his right hand in the heavenly realms, [21]far above all rule and authority, power and dominion, and every title that can be given, not only in the present age but also in the one to come. [22]And God placed all things under his feet and appointed him to be head over everything for the church, [23]which is his body, the fullness of him who fills everything in every way.

---

a 1 Some early manuscripts do not have *in Ephesus.*   *b 1* Or *believers who are*   *c 4,5* Or *sight in love.* 5He   *d 8,9* Or *us. With all wisdom and understanding, 9he*   *e 11* Or *were made heirs*   *f 17* Or *a spirit*

Made Alive in Christ

2 As for you, you were dead in your transgressions and sins, ²in which you used to live when you followed the ways of this world and of the ruler of the kingdom of the air, the spirit who is now at work in those who are disobedient. ³All of us also lived among them at one time, gratifying the cravings of our sinful nature*a* and following its desires and thoughts. Like the rest, we were by nature objects of wrath. ⁴But because of his great love for us, God, who is rich in mercy, ⁵made us alive with Christ even when we were dead in transgressions—it is by grace you have been saved. ⁶And God raised us up with Christ and seated us with him in the heavenly realms in Christ Jesus, ⁷in order that in the coming ages he might show the incomparable riches of his grace, expressed in his kindness to us in Christ Jesus. ⁸For it is by grace you have been saved, through faith—and this not from yourselves, it is the gift of God— ⁹not by works, so that no one can boast. ¹⁰For we are God's workmanship, created in Christ Jesus to do good works, which God prepared in advance for us to do.

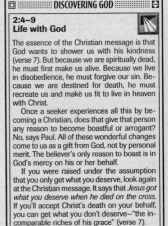

One in Christ

¹¹Therefore, remember that formerly you who are Gentiles by birth and called "uncircumcised" by those who call themselves "the circumcision" (that done in the body by the hands of men)— ¹²remember that at that time you were separate from Christ, excluded from citizenship in Israel and foreigners to the covenants of the promise, without hope and without God in the world. ¹³But now in Christ Jesus you who once were far away have been brought near through the blood of Christ.

¹⁴For he himself is our peace, who has made the two one and has destroyed the barrier, the dividing wall of hostility, ¹⁵by abolishing in his flesh the law with its commandments and regulations. His purpose was to create in himself one new man out of the two, thus making peace, ¹⁶and in this one body to reconcile both of them to God through the cross, by which he put to death their hostility. ¹⁷He came and preached peace to you who were far away and peace to those who were near. ¹⁸For through him we both have access to the Father by one Spirit.

¹⁹Consequently, you are no longer foreigners and aliens, but fellow citizens with God's people and members of God's household, ²⁰built on the foundation of the apostles and prophets, with Christ Jesus himself as the chief cornerstone. ²¹In him the whole building is joined together and rises to become a holy temple in the Lord. ²²And in him you too are being built together to become a dwelling in which God lives by his Spirit.

*3 Or our flesh

Paul the Preacher to the Gentiles

3 For this reason I, Paul, the prisoner of Christ Jesus for the sake of you Gentiles—

²Surely you have heard about the administration of God's grace that was given to me for you, ³that is, the mystery made known to me by revelation, as I have already written briefly. ⁴In reading this, then, you will be able to understand my insight into the mystery of Christ, ⁵which was not made known to men in other generations as it has now been revealed by the Spirit to God's holy apostles and prophets. ⁶This mystery is that through the gospel the Gentiles are heirs together with Israel, members together of one body, and sharers together in the promise in Christ Jesus.

⁷I became a servant of this gospel by the gift of God's grace given me through the working of his power. ⁸Although I am less than the least of all God's people, this grace was given me: to preach to the Gentiles the unsearchable riches of Christ, ⁹and to make plain to everyone the administration of this mystery, which for ages past was kept hidden in God, who created all things. ¹⁰His intent was that now, through the church, the manifold wisdom of God should be made known to the rulers and authorities in the heavenly realms, ¹¹according to his eternal purpose which he accomplished in Christ Jesus our Lord. ¹²In him and through faith in him we may approach God with freedom and confidence. ¹³I ask you, therefore, not to be discouraged because of my sufferings for you, which are your glory.

A Prayer for the Ephesians

¹⁴For this reason I kneel before the Father, ¹⁵from whom his whole family*a* in heaven and on earth derives its name. ¹⁶I pray that out of his glorious riches he may strengthen you with power through his Spirit in your inner being, ¹⁷so that Christ may dwell in your hearts through faith. And I pray that you, being rooted and established in love, ¹⁸may have power, together with all the saints, to grasp how wide and long and high and deep is the love of Christ, ¹⁹and to know this love that surpasses knowledge—that you may be filled to the measure of all the fullness of God.

²⁰Now to him who is able to do immeasurably more than all we ask or imagine, according to his power that is at work within us, ²¹to him be glory in the church and in Christ Jesus throughout all generations, for ever and ever! Amen.

a 15 Or whom all fatherhood

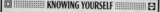

▣ ▦▦▦▦▦ KNOWING YOURSELF ▦▦▦▦▦ ⬌

2:11–13, 19–22
A New Identity

Prejudice isn't new. It existed in biblical times just as it does today. Ancient Gentiles were separated from the Jews by nationality and religion. But the most vivid symbol of that separation was a wall in the Jewish temple beyond which non-Jews could never walk.

Jesus changed all that forever. When he died on the cross he paid the penalty for the sins of everyone—Jew and Gentile alike. Whoever accepts his payment for sin approaches God on an equal footing with everyone else. Paul told the Ephesians that, in Jesus, the whole human race can stand together in unity. Jesus has torn down the walls that divide individuals.

Perhaps when you enter a church you feel out of place—like the whole affair is meant for someone else, not you. The people there probably mean well, but too often churches unknowingly make seekers feel uncomfortable. Try to be patient with the process of finding a church that will help you grow. And remember that God isn't a wall-builder. He wants you to be included, to be part of the family. He wants you to experience peace—with him, with yourself, and with his "new community" on earth, called the church.

Unity in the Body of Christ

4 As a prisoner for the Lord, then, I urge you to live a life worthy of the calling you have received. ²Be completely humble and gentle; be patient, bearing with one another in love. ³Make every effort to keep the unity of the Spirit through the bond of peace. ⁴There is one body and one Spirit— just as you were called to one hope when you were called— ⁵one Lord, one faith, one baptism; ⁶one God and Father of all, who is over all and through all and in all.

⁷But to each one of us grace has been given as Christ apportioned it. ⁸This is why it[a] says:

> "When he ascended on high,
> he led captives in his train
> and gave gifts to men."[b]

⁹(What does "he ascended" mean except that he also descended to the lower, earthly regions[c]? ¹⁰He who descended is the very one who ascended higher than all the heavens, in order to fill the whole universe.) ¹¹It was he who gave some to be apostles, some to be prophets, some to be evangelists, and some to be pastors and teachers, ¹²to prepare God's people for works of service, so that the body of Christ may be built up ¹³until we all reach unity in the faith and in the knowledge of the Son of God and become mature, attaining to the whole measure of the fullness of Christ.

¹⁴Then we will no longer be infants, tossed back and forth by the waves, and blown here and there by every wind of teaching and by the cunning and craftiness of men in their deceitful scheming. ¹⁵Instead, speaking the truth in love, we will in all things grow up into him who is the Head, that is, Christ. ¹⁶From him the whole body, joined and held together by every supporting ligament, grows and builds itself up in love, as each part does its work.

Living as Children of Light

¹⁷So I tell you this, and insist on it in the Lord, that you must no longer live as the Gentiles do, in the futility of their thinking. ¹⁸They are darkened in their understanding and separated from the life of God because of the ignorance that is in them due to the hardening of their hearts. ¹⁹Having lost all sensitivity, they have given themselves over to sensuality so as to indulge in every kind of impurity, with a continual lust for more.

²⁰You, however, did not come to know Christ that way. ²¹Surely you heard of him and were taught in him in accordance with the truth that is in Jesus. ²²You were taught, with

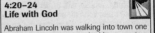

> **⌂ DISCOVERING GOD ⌂**
>
> **4:20–24**
> ### Life with God
>
> Abraham Lincoln was walking into town one day when he was approached by a man in a horse-drawn wagon going in the same direction. Lincoln hailed him and asked, "Will you have the goodness to take my overcoat to town for me?"
>
> "With pleasure," responded the stranger, "but how will you get it again?"
>
> "Oh, very easily. I intend to remain in it!"
>
> This clever story of Lincoln's idea for a ride parallels what happens when a seeker trusts Christ as his or her Savior. Becoming a Christian means "putting off the old self" and "putting on the new self,"—that is, being "clothed" in Jesus' righteousness. Because Christians are "wearing Jesus," Jesus goes with them wherever they are.
>
> The good news of Christianity is that Christ is prepared to take you where you can't get on your own (heaven). How can you receive that great offer? By trusting Christ. Believe that he died in your place and was raised from the dead, and then trust him to forgive you and give you eternal life. The moment you do that, Jesus will become your "spiritual overcoat." Not only will God accept you, but Christ will live in you and empower you to live a life that pleases God.

---

a8 Or God   b8 Psalm 68:18   c9 Or the depths of the earth

regard to your former way of life, to put off your old self, which is being corrupted by its deceitful desires; ²³to be made new in the attitude of your minds; ²⁴and to put on the new self, created to be like God in true righteousness and holiness.

²⁵Therefore each of you must put off falsehood and speak truthfully to his neighbor, for we are all members of one body. ²⁶"In your anger do not sin"ᵃ: Do not let the sun go down while you are still angry, ²⁷and do not give the devil a foothold. ²⁸He who has been stealing must steal no longer, but must work, doing something useful with his own hands, that he may have something to share with those in need.

²⁹Do not let any unwholesome talk come out of your mouths, but only what is helpful for building others up according to their needs, that it may benefit those who listen. ³⁰And do not grieve the Holy Spirit of God, with whom you were sealed for the day of redemption. ³¹Get rid of all bitterness, rage and anger, brawling and slander, along with every form of malice. ³²Be kind and compassionate to one another, forgiving each other, just as in Christ God forgave you.

5 Be imitators of God, therefore, as dearly loved children ²and live a life of love, just as Christ loved us and gave himself up for us as a fragrant offering and sacrifice to God.

³But among you there must not be even a hint of sexual immorality, or of any kind of impurity, or of greed, because these are improper for God's holy people. ⁴Nor should there be obscenity, foolish talk or coarse joking, which are out of place, but rather thanksgiving. ⁵For of this you can be sure: No immoral, impure or greedy person—such a man is an idolater—has any inheritance in the kingdom of Christ and of God.ᵇ ⁶Let no one deceive you with empty words, for because of such things God's wrath comes on those who are disobedient. ⁷Therefore do not be partners with them.

⁸For you were once darkness, but now you are light in the Lord. Live as children of light ⁹(for the fruit of the light consists in all goodness, righteousness and truth) ¹⁰and find out what pleases the Lord. ¹¹Have nothing to do with the fruitless deeds of darkness, but rather expose them. ¹²For it is shameful even to mention what the disobedient do in secret. ¹³But everything exposed by the light becomes visible, ¹⁴for it is light that makes everything visible. This is why it is said:

> "Wake up, O sleeper,
>   rise from the dead,
> and Christ will shine on you."

¹⁵Be very careful, then, how you live—not as unwise but as wise, ¹⁶making the most of every opportunity, because the days are evil. ¹⁷Therefore do not be foolish, but understand what the Lord's will is. ¹⁸Do not get drunk on wine, which leads to debauchery. Instead, be filled with the Spirit. ¹⁹Speak to one another with psalms, hymns and spiritual songs. Sing and make music in your heart to the Lord, ²⁰always giving thanks to God the Father for everything, in the name of our Lord Jesus Christ.

²¹Submit to one another out of reverence for Christ.

Wives and Husbands

²²Wives, submit to your husbands as to the Lord. ²³For the husband is the head of the wife as Christ is the head of the church, his body, of which he is the Savior. ²⁴Now as the church submits to Christ, so also wives should submit to their husbands in everything.

²⁵Husbands, love your wives, just as Christ loved the church and gave himself up for her ²⁶to make her holy, cleansingᶜ her by the washing with water through the word, ²⁷and to present her to himself as a radiant church, without stain or wrinkle or any other blemish, but holy and blameless. ²⁸In this same way, husbands ought to love their wives as their own bodies. He who loves his wife loves himself. ²⁹After all, no one ever hated his own body, but he feeds and cares for it, just as Christ does the church— ³⁰for we are

ᵃ26 Psalm 4:4   ᵇ5 Or kingdom of the Christ and God   ᶜ26 Or having cleansed members of his body. ³¹"For this reason a man will leave his father and mother and be united to his wife, and the two will become one flesh."ᵃ ³²This is a profound mystery—but I am talking about Christ and the church. ³³However, each one of you also must love his wife as he loves himself, and the wife must respect her husband.

Children and Parents

6 Children, obey your parents in the Lord, for this is right. ²"Honor your father and mother"—which is the first commandment with a promise—³"that it may go well with you and that you may enjoy long life on the earth."ᵇ

⁴Fathers, do not exasperate your children; instead, bring them up in the training and instruction of the Lord.

Slaves and Masters

⁵Slaves, obey your earthly masters with respect and fear, and with sincerity of heart, just as you would obey Christ. ⁶Obey them not only to win their favor when their eye is on you, but like slaves of Christ, doing the will of God from your heart. ⁷Serve wholeheartedly, as if you were serving the Lord, not men, ⁸because you know that the Lord will reward everyone for whatever good he does, whether he is slave or free.

⁹And masters, treat your slaves in the same way. Do not threaten them, since you know that he who is both their Master and yours is in heaven, and there is no favoritism with him.

▣ ▤▤▤ STRENGTHENING RELATIONSHIPS ▤▤▤ ⬕

5:21–33
Marriage

For many modern couples this passage may seem hopelessly out of date, a paternalistic flashback to the dark ages. Verse 22 especially jumps out at most readers as a troublesome directive—how can Paul, much less God himself, endorse such a chauvenistic attitude?

But notice verse 21. It contains a pivotal command that sets the tone for the discussion that follows. *Both* husband and wife must submit to each other. In other words, they must both be willing to give and take in order to make a marriage work. Later verses in this passage talk about husbands loving their wives "as their own bodies"—in other words, caring for them as if the two were "one flesh." That's the kind of teamwork—and *mutual* deference—Paul is talking about here.

Having a Christlike marriage doesn't mean that one spouse commands while the other one cowers. It means that both spouses choose to give of themselves for the well-being of the other. That kind of love powerfully demonstrates Christ's own character, and is the responsibility and privilege of both marriage partners.

The Armor of God

¹⁰Finally, be strong in the Lord and in his mighty power. ¹¹Put on the full armor of God so that you can take your stand against the devil's schemes. ¹²For our struggle is not against flesh and blood, but against the rulers, against the authorities, against the powers of this dark world and against the spiritual forces of evil in the heavenly realms. ¹³Therefore put on the full armor of God, so that when the day of evil comes, you may be able to stand your ground, and after you have done everything, to stand. ¹⁴Stand firm then, with the belt of truth buckled around your waist, with the breastplate of righteousness in place, ¹⁵and with your feet fitted with the readiness that comes from the gospel of peace. ¹⁶In addition to all this, take up the shield of faith, with which you can extinguish all the flaming arrows of the evil one. ¹⁷Take the helmet of salvation and the sword of the Spirit, which is the word of God. ¹⁸And pray in the Spirit on all occasions with all kinds of prayers and requests. With this in mind, be alert and always keep on praying for all the saints.

¹⁹Pray also for me, that whenever I open my mouth, words may be given me so that I will fearlessly make known the mystery of the gospel, ²⁰for which I am an ambassador in chains. Pray that I may declare it fearlessly, as I should.

ᵃ31 Gen. 2:24   ᵇ3 Deut. 5:16

Final Greetings

²¹Tychicus, the dear brother and faithful servant in the Lord, will tell you everything, so that you also may know how I am and what I am doing. ²²I am sending him to you for this very purpose, that you may know how we are, and that he may encourage you.

²³Peace to the brothers, and love with faith from God the Father and the Lord Jesus Christ. ²⁴Grace to all who love our Lord Jesus Christ with an undying love.

Before I understood what the decision to follow Christ was about, I was looking for something to make me truly happy. I had an unfillable void in my heart, and I didn't understand that only Christ could make my heart and life complete.

My husband and I began attending church services on Mother's Day one year and continued to attend each week in spite of the 40- to 60-minute commute each way. Shortly after that Mother's Day we began to come to midweek services as well. During our commute we began listening to tapes that the church provided, and I was crushed by the reality that if I accepted the Bible as truth, I had broken all of the Ten Commandments. I had approached salvation with the hope of "getting in on the curve," as if God would say, "She's not as bad as the worst, better than many, and tries hard."

The following Wednesday I attended my first communion service at the church. As I walked through the door my brother-in-law greeted me. I said to him, "I don't deserve God's grace." He simply answered, "None of us do. That's why it's called amazing grace." I was astounded by the truth of that statement. As if someone had lifted a veil from my eyes, *I finally understood.* That knowledge affected me so powerfully that I cried through the whole service. Soon after, I committed my heart and soul to Jesus Christ.

That decision has turned my life downside up. My husband and I have put our house on the market in an effort to move closer to our church. We want to join a small group and become more involved in the church community.

I simply want my life and my family's lives to be centered around Christ. While that goal often gets lost in the business of everyday living, that is my heart's core desire. That has not changed since I have dedicated my life to Christ.

I was a recently divorced mom with two children and no family in the area to help me out. The children's father had moved out of state, and I felt alone, unlovable and worthless. One Sunday I walked into a local church where I heard about a God in heaven who knew my name and everything else about me, yet still loved me despite my past. I entered the church's hospitality room where I spoke with a gentleman who encouraged me to pray and to ask Christ to come into my life.

That was a life-changing experience. I now have God with me, I am loved, and I have worth because I am a child of God. I will never have to be alone again.

Introduction

THE BOTTOM LINE

Is there a difference between "joy" and "happiness"? Perhaps you've never thought about it, but "happiness" depends on *happenings*. It can fade when an experience is over, such as at the end of a family reunion or a relaxing vacation. "Joy," on the other hand, is the kind of enduring contentedness that gets us through the tough times. In this letter, Paul talks about the joy that we can experience as believers in Jesus. The good news of this book is that we needn't rely on passing experience—always a shaky commodity at best—to maintain our positive attitude toward life. We can tap into a divine source that will help us maintain joy in any situation.

CENTRAL IDEAS

- People who have hope in God can be joyful no matter what their situation.
- Christ is our ultimate role model; imitating him will produce lifelong joy.
- Death has no power over those who trust in Christ.

OUTLINE

1 Greetings (1:1–11)
2 Paul's personal story (1:12–26)
3 Encouragement to live a life worthy of Christ (1:27–2:30)
4 Warnings against false teachers (3:1–4:1)
5 Conclusion (4:2–23)

TITLE

This letter was written to believers in the city of Philippi, an important Roman colony in Greece. The city itself was originally named after Philip II, father of Alexander the Great.

AUTHOR AND READERS

Paul wrote this letter to the Philippian believers while imprisoned under Roman guard. His challenge to his readers to rejoice in all situations is, therefore, both amazing and inspiring at the same time. The practical advice that Paul gives for living a joyful life has direct application to our lives today.

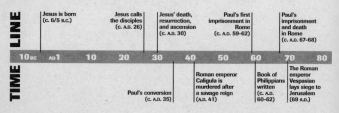

TIME LINE

Jesus is born (c. 6/5 B.C.)

Jesus calls the disciples (c. A.D. 26)

Jesus' death, resurrection, and ascension (c. A.D. 30)

Paul's first imprisonment in Rome (c. A.D. 59–62)

Paul's imprisonment and death in Rome (c. A.D. 67–68)

10 BC   AD 1   10   20   30   40   50   60   70   80

Paul's conversion (c. A.D. 35)

Roman emperor Caligula is murdered after a savage reign (A.D. 41)

Book of Philippians written (c. A.D. 60–62)

The Roman emperor Vespasian lays siege to Jerusalem (69 A.D.)

Worry jumps out at us from behind a multitude of circumstances. A teenager who is late getting home. Our company announcement of major cutbacks. A small lump and a doctor who says, "I think we should do a biopsy."

And it isn't easy to get rid of worry. Once it sinks its fangs into us, we tend to carry it around like a parasite. Just ask someone with an ulcer what worry is capable of doing to our insides—it can eat us alive.

One man who recognized the destructive power of anxiety was Amadeo Peter Giannini. Although you may have never heard of him, you've probably heard of the business he created—the Bank of America. He believed that the world's most precious commodity was people, not money. With that in mind, he built a bank with the intention of protecting his customers from unnecessary worry.

Giannini organized his first bank in 1904. Then he did what no other banker had ever done—he advertised his services. He convinced people that their money was safer in his bank than hidden under their mattresses. He recycled this newfound capital back into the community by giving personal loans to individuals whose wages were their only collateral. And when he saw that smaller local banks could distribute money more efficiently, Giannini became the pioneer of branch banking.

> **God knows how destructive worry can be.**

Giannini made sure his customers had nothing to worry about. When an earthquake struck San Francisco in 1906, he removed all the bank's cash and hid it from looters. The day after the disaster, his was the only bank in town open for business. In 1907, when unbridled financial speculation ruined many banks, Giannini again displayed his foresight. In his tellers' windows he placed stacks of the gold he had hoarded—a display of confidence that convinced his customers they had no need to worry.*

God knows how destructive worry can be. So he has taken steps to assure us that the "big issues" in life can be secured. Through the pen of the apostle Paul, God stacked up golden truths about the riches and power that Jesus extends to us. He inspired these and other writings so that you and I would know, regardless of the problems we face, that God can help us through our most troubling times.

If you're worried about money, health, a broken relationship or any other circumstance of life, turn to Philippians chapter 4, verses 4–7 (page 1547). God cares for you infinitely more than any banker ever cared for any of his customers. And he wants to give you the kind of peace that will help you deal with anxiety and its effects.

Strange Stories, Amazing Facts of America's Past, Jim Dwyer, ed. (Pleasantville, N.Y.: The Reader's Digest Association, 1989), p. 149.

PHILIPPIANS

1 Paul and Timothy, servants of Christ Jesus,

To all the saints in Christ Jesus at Philippi, together with the overseers[a] and deacons

²Grace and peace to you from God our Father and the Lord Jesus Christ.

Thanksgiving and Prayer

³I thank my God every time I remember you. ⁴In all my prayers for all of you, I always pray with joy ⁵because of your partnership in the gospel from the first day until now, ⁶being confident of this, that he who began a good work in you will carry it on to completion until the day of Christ Jesus.

⁷It is right for me to feel this way about all of you, since I have you in my heart; for whether I am in chains or defending and confirming the gospel, all of you share in God's grace with me. ⁸God can testify how I long for all of you with the affection of Christ Jesus.

⁹And this is my prayer: that your love may abound more and more in knowledge and depth of insight, ¹⁰so that you may be able to discern what is best and may be pure and blameless until the day of Christ, ¹¹filled with the fruit of righteousness that comes through Jesus Christ—to the glory and praise of God.

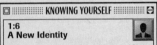

KNOWING YOURSELF

1:6
A New Identity

If there is one characteristic a follower of Christ should have, it's confidence concerning the future. The apostle Paul said that every believer possesses the transforming power of Christ. And the One who started the "good work" in the believer—God himself—won't stop until he's finished.

Like acorns that over time grow into giant oak trees, Christians are meant to grow continually in their knowledge of God and of his mercy in their lives. God initiates salvation, and promises to help his followers grow until "the day of Christ Jesus," when all believers will receive their reward. (See Revelation chapter 21, verses 1–4 [page 1653] for a vivid word-picture of that day.)

Paul's Chains Advance the Gospel

¹²Now I want you to know, brothers, that what has happened to me has really served to advance the gospel. ¹³As a result, it has become clear throughout the whole palace guard[b] and to everyone else that I am in chains for Christ. ¹⁴Because of my chains, most of the brothers in the Lord have been encouraged to speak the word of God more courageously and fearlessly.

¹⁵It is true that some preach Christ out of envy and rivalry, but others out of goodwill. ¹⁶The latter do so in love, knowing that I am put here for the defense of the gospel. ¹⁷The former preach Christ out of selfish ambition, not sincerely, supposing that they can stir up trouble for me while I am in chains.[c] ¹⁸But what does it matter? The important thing is that in every way, whether from false motives or true, Christ is preached. And because of this I rejoice.

Yes, and I will continue to rejoice, ¹⁹for I know that through your prayers and the help

---

a 1 Traditionally *bishops*   *b 13* Or *whole palace*   *c 16,17* Some late manuscripts have verses 16 and 17 in reverse order.

given by the Spirit of Jesus Christ, what has happened to me will turn out for my deliverance.[a] [20]I eagerly expect and hope that I will in no way be ashamed, but will have sufficient courage so that now as always Christ will be exalted in my body, whether by life or by death. [21]For to me, to live is Christ and to die is gain. [22]If I am to go on living in the body, this will mean fruitful labor for me. Yet what shall I choose? I do not know! [23]I am torn between the two: I desire to depart and be with Christ, which is better by far; [24]but it is more necessary for you that I remain in the body. [25]Convinced of this, I know that I will remain, and I will continue with all of you for your progress and joy in the faith, [26]so that through my being with you again your joy in Christ Jesus will overflow on account of me.

[27]Whatever happens, conduct yourselves in a manner worthy of the gospel of Christ. Then, whether I come and see you or only hear about you in my absence, I will know that you stand firm in one spirit, contending as one man for the faith of the gospel [28]without being frightened in any way by those who oppose you. This is a sign to them that they will be destroyed, but that you will be saved—and that by God. [29]For it has been granted to you on behalf of Christ not only to believe on him, but also to suffer for him, [30]since you are going through the same struggle you saw I had, and now hear that I still have.

Imitating Christ's Humility

2 If you have any encouragement from being united with Christ, if any comfort from his love, if any fellowship with the Spirit, if any tenderness and compassion, [2]then make my joy complete by being like-minded, having the same love, being one in spirit and purpose. [3]Do nothing out of selfish ambition or vain conceit, but in humility consider others better than yourselves. [4]Each of you should look not only to your own interests, but also to the interests of others.

[5]Your attitude should be the same as that of Christ Jesus:

[6]Who, being in very nature[b] God,
did not consider equality with
God something to be
grasped,
[7]but made himself nothing,
taking the very nature[c] of a
servant,
being made in human likeness.
[8]And being found in appearance as a man,
he humbled himself
and became obedient to death—
even death on a cross!
[9]Therefore God exalted him to the highest place
and gave him the name that is above every name,
[10]that at the name of Jesus every knee should bow,

in heaven and on earth and under the earth,
¹¹and every tongue confess that Jesus Christ is Lord,
to the glory of God the Father.

Shining as Stars

¹²Therefore, my dear friends, as you have always obeyed—not only in my presence, but now much more in my absence—continue to work out your salvation with fear and trembling, ¹³for it is God who works in you to will and to act according to his good purpose.

¹⁴Do everything without complaining or arguing, ¹⁵so that you may become blameless and pure, children of God without fault in a crooked and depraved generation, in which you shine like stars in the universe ¹⁶as you hold out*a* the word of life—in order that I may boast on the day of Christ that I did not run or labor for nothing. ¹⁷But even if I am being poured out like a drink offering on the sacrifice and service coming from your faith, I am glad and rejoice with all of you. ¹⁸So you too should be glad and rejoice with me.

Timothy and Epaphroditus

¹⁹I hope in the Lord Jesus to send Timothy to you soon, that I also may be cheered when I receive news about you. ²⁰I have no one else like him, who takes a genuine interest in your welfare. ²¹For everyone looks out for his own interests, not those of Jesus Christ. ²²But you know that Timothy has proved himself, because as a son with his father he has served with me in the work of the gospel. ²³I hope, therefore, to send him as soon as I see how things go with me. ²⁴And I am confident in the Lord that I myself will come soon.

²⁵But I think it is necessary to send back to you Epaphroditus, my brother, fellow worker and fellow soldier, who is also your messenger, whom you sent to take care of my needs. ²⁶For he longs for all of you and is distressed because you heard he was ill. ²⁷Indeed he was ill, and almost died. But God had mercy on him, and not on him only but also on me, to spare me sorrow upon sorrow. ²⁸Therefore I am all the more eager to send him, so that when you see him again you may be glad and I may have less anxiety. ²⁹Welcome him in the Lord with great joy, and honor men like him, ³⁰because he almost died for the work of Christ, risking his life to make up for the help you could not give me.

No Confidence in the Flesh

3 Finally, my brothers, rejoice in the Lord! It is no trouble for me to write the same things to you again, and it is a safeguard for you.

²Watch out for those dogs, those men who do evil, those mutilators of the flesh. ³For it is we who are the circumcision, we who worship by the Spirit of God, who glory in Christ Jesus, and who put no confidence in the flesh— ⁴though I myself have reasons for such confidence.

If anyone else thinks he has reasons to put confidence in the flesh, I have more: ⁵circumcised on the eighth day, of the people of Israel, of the tribe of Benjamin, a Hebrew of Hebrews; in regard to the law, a Pharisee; ⁶as for zeal, persecuting the church; as for legalistic righteousness, faultless.

⁷But whatever was to my profit I now consider loss for the sake of Christ. ⁸What is more, I consider everything a loss compared to the surpassing greatness of knowing Christ Jesus my Lord, for whose sake I have lost all things. I consider them rubbish, that I may gain Christ ⁹and be found in him, not having a righteousness of my own that comes from the law, but that which is through faith in Christ—the righteousness that comes from God and is by faith. ¹⁰I want to know Christ and the power of his resurrection and the fellowship of sharing in his sufferings, becoming like him in his death, ¹¹and so, somehow, to attain to the resurrection from the dead.

a 16 Or hold on to

Pressing on Toward the Goal

¹²Not that I have already obtained all this, or have already been made perfect, but I press on to take hold of that for which Christ Jesus took hold of me. ¹³Brothers, I do not consider myself yet to have taken hold of it. But one thing I do: Forgetting what is behind and straining toward what is ahead, ¹⁴I press on toward the goal to win the prize for which God has called me heavenward in Christ Jesus.

¹⁵All of us who are mature should take such a view of things. And if on some point you think differently, that too God will make clear to you. ¹⁶Only let us live up to what we have already attained.

¹⁷Join with others in following my example, brothers, and take note of those who live according to the pattern we gave you. ¹⁸For, as I have often told you before and now say again even with tears, many live as enemies of the cross of Christ. ¹⁹Their destiny is destruction, their god is their stomach, and their glory is in their shame. Their mind is on earthly things. ²⁰But our citizenship is in heaven. And we eagerly await a Savior from there, the Lord Jesus Christ, ²¹who, by the power that enables him to bring everything under his control, will transform our lowly bodies so that they will be like his glorious body.

4 Therefore, my brothers, you whom I love and long for, my joy and crown, that is how you should stand firm in the Lord, dear friends!

Exhortations

²I plead with Euodia and I plead with Syntyche to agree with each other in the Lord. ³Yes, and I ask you, loyal yokefellow,[a] help these women who have contended at my side in the cause of the gospel, along with Clement and the rest of my fellow workers, whose names are in the book of life.

⁴Rejoice in the Lord always. I will say it again: Rejoice! ⁵Let your gentleness be evident to all. The Lord is near. ⁶Do not be anxious about anything, but in everything, by prayer and petition, with thanksgiving, present your requests to God. ⁷And the peace of God, which transcends all understanding, will guard your hearts and your minds in Christ Jesus.

⁸Finally, brothers, whatever is true, whatever is noble, whatever is right, whatever is pure, whatever is lovely, whatever is admirable—if anything is excellent or praiseworthy—think about such things. ⁹Whatever you have learned or received or heard from me, or seen in me—put it into practice. And the God of peace will be with you.

⬛ ▨▨▨▨▨▨ DISCOVERING GOD ▨▨▨▨▨▨ ⬛

4:4–7
Life with God

As he ended his letter to the Philippians, Paul described the strength and joy he found in Christ. As a Roman prisoner, Paul had plenty to worry about. But in spite of his hardships, he drew near to God and found indescribable peace. Paul wanted his readers to do the same, and this passage is as applicable to us today as it was to the Philippians.

How can we experience such peace? First, Paul tells us to replace worry with prayer (verse 6). We tend to worry when the demands of our everyday lives seem to get the best of us. Our anxiety levels rise when we perceive that we're running out of money, time, good health, or emotional stamina. When we surrender our anxiety to God through prayer, however, our focus shifts away from our own limited resources and toward God's provision.

After we present our requests to God, Paul says, we will experience peace (verse 7). This will not be a superficial peace resulting from a change of fortune, but rather a deep sense of calm resulting from the confidence that God will care for us.

If you're struggling with anxiety today, spend some time alone with God. Talk to him about your problems. While he may not take them away immediately, he wants you to depend on his resources so you can find the same peace that Paul experienced.

---

a 3 Or loyal Syzygus

Thanks for Their Gifts

[10]I rejoice greatly in the Lord that at last you have renewed your concern for me. Indeed, you have been concerned, but you had no opportunity to show it. [11]I am not saying this because I am in need, for I have learned to be content whatever the circumstances. [12]I know what it is to be in need, and I know what it is to have plenty. I have learned the secret of being content in any and every situation, whether well fed or hungry, whether living in plenty or in want. [13]I can do everything through him who gives me strength.

[14]Yet it was good of you to share in my troubles. [15]Moreover, as you Philippians know, in the early days of your acquaintance with the gospel, when I set out from Macedonia, not one church shared with me in the matter of giving and receiving, except you only; [16]for even when I was in Thessalonica, you sent me aid again and again when I was in need. [17]Not that I am looking for a gift, but I am looking for what may be credited to your account. [18]I have received full payment and even more; I am amply supplied, now that I have received from Epaphroditus the gifts you sent. They are a fragrant offering, an acceptable sacrifice, pleasing to God. [19]And my God will meet all your needs according to his glorious riches in Christ Jesus.

[20]To our God and Father be glory for ever and ever. Amen.

Final Greetings

[21]Greet all the saints in Christ Jesus. The brothers who are with me send greetings. [22]All the saints send you greetings, especially those who belong to Caesar's household. [23]The grace of the Lord Jesus Christ be with your spirit. Amen.[a]

[a]23 Some manuscripts do not have Amen.

Before I decided to trust Christ I was a very confused woman. Though I was born and raised in a religious tradition, God wasn't important to me in the least. I can honestly say that I never opened a Bible for the first 32 years of my life. Life was good, and everything came easy. Then, around the time I turned 30, everything changed. To quote a psychiatrist I visited, "I was kicked out of Disneyland."

During this time my life was in turmoil and my emotions were frayed. One day I was visited by a Jehovah's Witness; I was ready to hear her message about "Jehovah's Kingdom," and was certainly ready to learn about the Bible. My husband and I began to study with this woman and her husband, buying into their message more and more as time went on.

The only way I can explain how we got out of the Watchtower organization is by saying that the Holy Spirit led us out. My husband and I prayed constantly for God to show us the truth. And though he didn't show us the truth right away, he did show us that the religion of the Witnesses is false.

Leaving the Witnesses was difficult. Though I knew they were wrong, my mind was brainwashed to the point that I wondered if I had set my family up for destruction by rejecting their version of truth.

About this time we began attending a local nondenominational church. What struck me most about the church was the joy that spread throughout the congregation at the praise time during the worship service. That was so unlike worship at the kingdom hall!

I have to admit it took me at least six months to reject all the false doctrines I had been taught and to accept the true teachings of Christianity. I was able to accept Christ as the source of my salvation when I learned the truth about God's grace. As soon as I understood salvation as a free gift, I couldn't believe how blind I had been all those years. I took the first step of accepting Christ as my Savior, and now I strive each day to grow more in my understanding of God and his plans for me.

Introduction

THE BOTTOM LINE

Our culture's appetite for self-improvement is voracious. Many different venues—from Eastern religions to infomercials—offer programs that either guide you to discover your inner self or help you to drastically alter it. The apostle Paul says in this book that there's only one way to rise above the chaos in our world and fully realize our potential as individuals. It's through following Christ, "who is head over every power and authority" (chapter 2, verse 10 [p. 1553]).

CENTRAL IDEAS

- Jesus Christ is God, and he rules over the universe.
- Don't let man-made philosophies confuse you—hold fast to Jesus.
- Some kinds of "religious" behavior actually interfere with true spiritual living.

OUTLINE

1. Introduction (1:1–14)
2. Christ is supreme (1:15–23)
3. Paul's work for the church (1:24–2:7)
4. Freedom through Christ (2:8–23)
5. Guidelines for Christ-like living (3:1–4:6)
6. Final greetings (4:7–18)

TITLE

This book is named after the people of the church at Colosse, to whom it was addressed.

AUTHOR AND READERS

Paul wrote this letter to the believers in Colosse during a time when first-century religions threatened to undermine the Christian faith. His discussion of the supremacy of Jesus Christ was meant to keep these believers faithful to Christ and his saving work.

TIME LINE

	Jesus is born (c. 6/5 B.C.)			Jesus' death, resurrection, and ascension (c. A.D. 30)			Book of Colossians written (c. A.D. 60–62)	
10 B.C.	A.D. 1	10	20	30	40	50	60	70
				Jesus calls the disciples (c. A.D. 26)	Paul's conversion (c. A.D. 35)	Emperor Claudius fortifies the city of Cologne (modern-day France) (50 A.D.)		Paul's imprisonment and death in Rome (c. A.D. 67–68)

Did you ever get the feeling that the experts aren't really all that expert? For instance, the managing director of the World Monetary Fund in 1959 concluded, "In all likelihood, world inflation is over."

Or, how about the MGM executive who warned Louis B. Mayer regarding *Gone with the Wind,* "Forget it Louis, no Civil War movie ever made a nickel."

The fields of business and technology are crowded with similarly error-prone experts. One such authority was a former president of Digital Equipment Corporation. He declared in 1977 that "there is no reason for any individual to have a computer in the home."

Another high-tech expert who missed is the *Business Week* pro who in 1968 judged, "With over fifty foreign cars already on sale here in America, the Japanese auto industry isn't likely to carve out a big share of the market for itself." Oops!

And finally, this prediction made by Henry Ford III in 1955: "The Edsel is here to stay."

"The Edsel is here to stay."

If there's one lesson these bold declarations teach us, it's that experts can be wrong. That's also the message Paul wanted to communicate to the Colossian people. Some so-called spiritual experts had infiltrated their church and were telling them that there were certain foods they couldn't eat, certain days they needed to regard as holy, certain religious rituals they had to observe, and certain things they couldn't touch. Since these people sounded knowledgeable, many of the Colossian Christians followed their advice.

But these teachers ignored what Jesus had accomplished through his death and resurrection. One of the main reasons the apostle Paul wrote this letter was to correct the misinformation these teachers were spreading.

Maybe you've encountered similar "religious experts." They intimidate people with Bible knowledge and try to convince them that other experts are wrong. They teach people that their own list of specific do's and dont's are necessary steps toward getting in line with God. Virtually every cult today smothers God's grace by choking it with some performance-based behavior or procedure without which, they claim, a person cannot be in a right relationship with God.

If you've ever been frustrated and confused by the "experts," you'll find the words of Paul helpful. Turn to Colossians chapter 2, verses 8–10 (page 1553), where you'll discover God's response to such teaching.

COLOSSIANS

1 Paul, an apostle of Christ Jesus by the will of God, and Timothy our brother,

²To the holy and faithful*ᵃ* brothers in Christ at Colosse:

Grace and peace to you from God our Father.*ᵇ*

Thanksgiving and Prayer

³We always thank God, the Father of our Lord Jesus Christ, when we pray for you, ⁴because we have heard of your faith in Christ Jesus and of the love you have for all the saints— ⁵the faith and love that spring from the hope that is stored up for you in heaven and that you have already heard about in the word of truth, the gospel ⁶that has come to you. All over the world this gospel is bearing fruit and growing, just as it has been doing among you since the day you heard it and understood God's grace in all its truth. ⁷You learned it from Epaphras, our dear fellow servant, who is a faithful minister of Christ on our*ᶜ* behalf, ⁸and who also told us of your love in the Spirit.

⁹For this reason, since the day we heard about you, we have not stopped praying for you and asking God to fill you with the knowledge of his will through all spiritual wisdom and understanding. ¹⁰And we pray this in order that you may live a life worthy of the Lord and may please him in every way: bearing fruit in every good work, growing in the knowledge of God, ¹¹being strengthened with all power according to his glorious might so that you may have great endurance and patience, and joyfully ¹²giving thanks to the Father, who has qualified you*ᵈ* to share in the inheritance of the saints in the kingdom of light. ¹³For he has rescued us from the dominion of darkness and brought us into the kingdom of the Son he loves, ¹⁴in whom we have redemption,*ᵉ* the forgiveness of sins.

The Supremacy of Christ

¹⁵He is the image of the invisible God, the firstborn over all creation. ¹⁶For by him all things were created: things in heaven and on earth, visible and invisible, whether thrones or powers or rulers or authorities; all things were created by him and for him. ¹⁷He is before all things, and in him all things hold together. ¹⁸And he is the head of the body, the church; he is the beginning and the firstborn from among the dead, so that in everything he might have the supremacy. ¹⁹For God was pleased to have all his fullness dwell in him, ²⁰and through him to

---

□ ▓▓▓▓▓▓▓ **DISCOVERING GOD** ▓▓▓▓▓▓▓ ⇄

1:15–16
Jesus, the God-Man

Here Paul describes Christ in language that can only be applied to deity—"the image of the invisible God." In the original language the word for "image" means "likeness," just as the image on a coin bears the likeness of the die from which it was made. But Jesus Christ doesn't just bear a resemblance to God—he is marked by the very character and nature of God.

At first glance, the phrase "firstborn over all creation" might sound like Jesus is the first of all created beings. But Paul uses a well-known figure of speech to indicate that Christ is first in rank, not in sequence. Jesus holds the pre-eminent position in all the universe, which he, as God, created (verse 16).

ᵃ2 Or believing manuscripts us ᵇ2 Some manuscripts *Father and the Lord Jesus Christ* ᶜ7 Some manuscripts *your* ᵈ12 Some ᵉ14 A few late manuscripts *redemption through his blood*

reconcile to himself all things, whether things on earth or things in heaven, by making peace through his blood, shed on the cross.

²¹Once you were alienated from God and were enemies in your minds because of^a your evil behavior. ²²But now he has reconciled you by Christ's physical body through death to present you holy in his sight, without blemish and free from accusation— ²³if you continue in your faith, established and firm, not moved from the hope held out in the gospel. This is the gospel that you heard and that has been proclaimed to every creature under heaven, and of which I, Paul, have become a servant.

Paul's Labor for the Church

²⁴Now I rejoice in what was suffered for you, and I fill up in my flesh what is still lacking in regard to Christ's afflictions, for the sake of his body, which is the church. ²⁵I have become its servant by the commission God gave me to present to you the word of God in its fullness— ²⁶the mystery that has been kept hidden for ages and generations, but is now disclosed to the saints. ²⁷To them God has chosen to make known among the Gentiles the glorious riches of this mystery, which is Christ in you, the hope of glory.

²⁸We proclaim him, admonishing and teaching everyone with all wisdom, so that we may present everyone perfect in Christ. ²⁹To this end I labor, struggling with all his energy, which so powerfully works in me.

2 I want you to know how much I am struggling for you and for those at Laodicea, and for all who have not met me personally. ²My purpose is that they may be encouraged in heart and united in love, so that they may have the full riches of complete understanding, in order that they may know the mystery of God, namely, Christ, ³in whom are hidden all the treasures of wisdom and knowledge. ⁴I tell you this so that no one may deceive you by fine-sounding arguments. ⁵For though I am absent from you in body, I am present with you in spirit and delight to see how orderly you are and how firm your faith in Christ is.

Freedom From Human Regulations Through Life With Christ

⁶So then, just as you received Christ Jesus as Lord, continue to live in him, ⁷rooted and built up in him, strengthened in the faith as you were taught, and overflowing with thankfulness.

⁸See to it that no one takes you captive through hollow and deceptive philosophy, which depends on human tradition and the basic principles of this world rather than on Christ.

▦▦▦ DISCOVERING GOD ▦▦▦

2:8–10
Spiritual Fraud

The best way to spot a counterfeit is to become familiar with the real thing. That was Paul's recommendation for dealing with the false teachers he referred to in this letter.

Paul noted that these false teachers based their philosophy on "human tradition" (verse 8). Certain religious groups of Paul's day had long lists of rules and regulations. They urged people to neglect or abuse their bodies. They also promoted angel worship. Even today some teachers encourage similar practices. They captivate others with their religious zeal and mystical "other-worldliness," focusing attention on themselves as the ones who hold "real truth" or some sort of supernatural connectedness.

Paul said that real faith doesn't come from different religious practices or philosophies, but only from Jesus Christ. He is the only source that will meet our spiritual need. Since Jesus is God, he is the head "over every power and authority" (verse 10). There is therefore no need to show allegiance or submission to any other spiritual—or earthly—being.

Keep studying the Bible. Learn all you can about Jesus. The more you learn about him, the more you'll find that he alone is worthy of your trust, and the only teacher worth following.

---

⁹For in Christ all the fullness of the Deity lives in bodily form, ¹⁰and you have been given fullness in Christ, who is the head over every power and authority. ¹¹In him you

^a 21 Or minds, as shown by

were also circumcised, in the putting off of the sinful nature,[a] not with a circumcision done by the hands of men but with the circumcision done by Christ, [12]having been buried with him in baptism and raised with him through your faith in the power of God, who raised him from the dead.

[13]When you were dead in your sins and in the uncircumcision of your sinful nature,[b] God made you[c] alive with Christ. He forgave us all our sins; [14]having canceled the written code, with its regulations, that was against us and that stood opposed to us; he took it away, nailing it to the cross. [15]And having disarmed the powers and authorities, he made a public spectacle of them, triumphing over them by the cross.[d]

[16]Therefore do not let anyone judge you by what you eat or drink, or with regard to a religious festival, a New Moon celebration or a Sabbath day. [17]These are a shadow of the things that were to come; the reality, however, is found in Christ. [18]Do not let anyone who delights in false humility and the worship of angels disqualify you for the prize. Such a person goes into great detail about what he has seen, and his unspiritual mind puffs him up with idle notions. [19]He has lost connection with the Head, from whom the whole body, supported and held together by its ligaments and sinews, grows as God causes it to grow.

[20]Since you died with Christ to the basic principles of this world, why, as though you still belonged to it, do you submit to its rules: [21]"Do not handle! Do not taste! Do not touch!"? [22]These are all destined to perish with use, because they are based on human commands and teachings. [23]Such regulations indeed have an appearance of wisdom, with their self-imposed worship, their false humility and their harsh treatment of the body, but they lack any value in restraining sensual indulgence.

◻ ▦▦▦ **DISCOVERING GOD** ▦▦▦ ⬔

2:18–19
Spiritual Fraud

History is full of people who claim to have had supernatural visions and revelations. Even today you'll find people who are eager to talk about how they've communicated with unseen spirits or have an inside track with the divine. The apostle Paul said such people *think* they're spiritually superior to others, but in fact they are disconnected from Christ (verse 19).

As you continue your search for God's truth, you may run across such people—those who turn your attention away from Jesus and toward themselves. Be careful of such people. They may claim they're serving Christ, but according to Paul, they're void of that lifegiving connection with him.

Rules for Holy Living

3 Since, then, you have been raised with Christ, set your hearts on things above, where Christ is seated at the right hand of God. [2]Set your minds on things above, not on earthly things. [3]For you died, and your life is now hidden with Christ in God. [4]When Christ, who is your[e] life, appears, then you also will appear with him in glory.

[5]Put to death, therefore, whatever belongs to your earthly nature: sexual immorality, impurity, lust, evil desires and greed, which is idolatry. [6]Because of these, the wrath of God is coming.[f] [7]You used to walk in these ways, in the life you once lived. [8]But now you must rid yourselves of all such things as these: anger, rage, malice, slander, and filthy language from your lips. [9]Do not lie to each other, since you have taken off your old self with its practices [10]and have put on the new self, which is being renewed in knowledge in the image of its Creator. [11]Here there is no Greek or Jew, circumcised or uncircumcised, barbarian, Scythian, slave or free, but Christ is all, and is in all.

[12]Therefore, as God's chosen people, holy and dearly loved, clothe yourselves with compassion, kindness, humility, gentleness and patience. [13]Bear with each other and forgive whatever grievances you may have against one another. Forgive as the Lord

---

[a]11 Or *the flesh*   [b]13 Or *your flesh*   [c]13 Some manuscripts *us*   [d]15 Or *them in him*   [e]4 Some manuscripts *our*   [f]6 Some early manuscripts *coming on those who are disobedient*

forgave you. ¹⁴And over all these virtues put on love, which binds them all together in perfect unity.

¹⁵Let the peace of Christ rule in your hearts, since as members of one body you were called to peace. And be thankful. ¹⁶Let the word of Christ dwell in you richly as you teach and admonish one another with all wisdom, and as you sing psalms, hymns and spiritual songs with gratitude in your hearts to God. ¹⁷And whatever you do, whether in word or deed, do it all in the name of the Lord Jesus, giving thanks to God the Father through him.

Rules for Christian Households

¹⁸Wives, submit to your husbands, as is fitting in the Lord.

¹⁹Husbands, love your wives and do not be harsh with them.

²⁰Children, obey your parents in everything, for this pleases the Lord.

²¹Fathers, do not embitter your children, or they will become discouraged.

²²Slaves, obey your earthly masters in everything; and do it, not only when their eye is on you and to win their favor, but with sincerity of heart and reverence for the Lord. ²³Whatever you do, work at it with all your heart, as working for the Lord, not for men, ²⁴since you know that you will receive an inheritance from the Lord as a reward. It is the Lord Christ you are serving. ²⁵Anyone who does wrong will be repaid for his wrong, and there is no favoritism.

4 Masters, provide your slaves with what is right and fair, because you know that you also have a Master in heaven.

Further Instructions

²Devote yourselves to prayer, being watchful and thankful. ³And pray for us, too, that God may open a door for our message, so that we may proclaim the mystery of Christ, for which I am in chains. ⁴Pray that I may proclaim it clearly, as I should. ⁵Be wise in the way you act toward outsiders; make the most of every opportunity. ⁶Let your conversation be always full of grace, seasoned with salt, so that you may know how to answer everyone.

Final Greetings

⁷Tychicus will tell you all the news about me. He is a dear brother, a faithful minister and fellow servant in the Lord. ⁸I am sending him to you for the express purpose that you may know about our*a* circumstances and that he may encourage your hearts. ⁹He is coming with Onesimus, our faithful and dear brother, who is one of you. They will tell you everything that is happening here.

a 8 Some manuscripts that he may know about your

> **▣ ∷∷∷∷∷∷ KNOWING YOURSELF ∷∷∷∷∷∷ ▣**
>
> **3:1–10**
> **A New Identity**
>
> When you come to the point of trusting Christ to be your forgiver and leader, a miraculous occurrence takes place. You become invisibly united with Jesus in his death, burial, and resurrection (verse 3). You become a new creation.
>
> Even so, you still possess a sinful nature with all of its appetites. Paul outlines some of the old practices that cater to those appetites, and says that you must choose daily to put off—like an old coat—your earthly nature, and put on your new self in Christ. One simple way to accomplish this is to remind yourself throughout each day, "I'm a new person in Jesus Christ. Right now I'm choosing to do what Jesus would do if he were in my body."

> **▣ ∷∷∷∷∷∷ DISCOVERING GOD ∷∷∷∷∷∷ ▣**
>
> **3:17**
> **Life with God**
>
> This verse sums up an important section of this letter. It also outlines the goal of every person who has decided to place his or her trust in Christ. This is the pervasive mindset that people who have experienced God's forgiveness strive to maintain out of gratitude to him.

┌─────────────────────────────────┐
│ ▣ ░░░░░░░░ DISCOVERING GOD ░░░░░░░░ ▣ │
│   │
│ **4:2**   │
│ **Life with God**   │

Prayer, as an exercise, isn't easy. Even devoted followers of Christ can find their minds wandering at times during prayer. And as the mind drifts, so can our spiritual lives. That's why Paul urges us to be "watchful" when we talk to God.

When you come to God in prayer, realize that God is listening and is eager to hear what you have to say to him. One practical suggestion is to write down your requests, or at least your general ideas, to help you focus and to keep you on track as you pray. Remember that God is more than a heavenly Santa Clause. He is aware of what you need before you ask, so you're not telling him anything he doesn't know already.

Prayer should include more than just a list of things you want— it should be communication between two friends who enjoy spending time with each other and who love to talk about everything.

---

¹⁰My fellow prisoner Aristarchus sends you his greetings, as does Mark, the cousin of Barnabas. (You have received instructions about him; if he comes to you, welcome him.) ¹¹Jesus, who is called Justus, also sends greetings. These are the only Jews among my fellow workers for the kingdom of God, and they have proved a comfort to me. ¹²Epaphras, who is one of you and a servant of Christ Jesus, sends greetings. He is always wrestling in prayer for you, that you may stand firm in all the will of God, mature and fully assured. ¹³I vouch for him that he is working hard for you and for those at Laodicea and Hierapolis. ¹⁴Our dear friend Luke, the doctor, and Demas send greetings. ¹⁵Give my greetings to the brothers at Laodicea, and to Nympha and the church in her house.

¹⁶After this letter has been read to you, see that it is also read in the church of the Laodiceans and that you in turn read the letter from Laodicea.

¹⁷Tell Archippus: "See to it that you complete the work you have received in the Lord."

¹⁸I, Paul, write this greeting in my own hand. Remember my chains. Grace be with you.

I became a sexaholic at a very early age and developed a secret life. As the years went by, my addiction became worse and worse until evil was almost totally in command of my life. Pornography ruled me. I knew its power and recognized its hold on me, but I could not act; I was powerless over the evil that gripped me. I could see that my marriage of 28 years was fast coming to an end. Still, I could not change my course.

Then one day, four and a half years ago, at the urging of my daughter and wife, I went to a "Seeker service" at my wife's church. This experience ignited a spark—the beginning of my salvation. Although my secret was still hidden at the time, God began to slowly and gently open my heart. Finally my secret became known.

My coming to know Christ has been slow. Approximately ten months ago, after three and a half years of Christian counseling, 12-step programs, and church involvement, I began praying directly to Jesus to take my hand and lead me out of my despair and hopelessness. That was when my life really started to change.

Today I am beginning to feel like a human being again. God has worked miracles; my lifestyle and attitudes have changed. The power of prayer is real. I asked God to hold my marriage together and he did. It's on the mend. Can you believe it? Yea God! Yea God!

Even though more than half of my life is behind me, I am very grateful now for the opportunity God has given me through Jesus Christ to be born again. What a tremendous gift to a guy who for such a long time traveled down some very dark roads.

1 THESSALONIANS/2 THESSALONIANS

Introduction

THE BOTTOM LINE

A modern-day preacher observed, "Whenever the apostle Paul entered a city, the residents started a riot; when I visit one, they serve tea." Why would this man admire a "troublemaker" like Paul? Simply because the message of Jesus Christ should never be considered "safe." When properly understood, it is life-changing and demands total commitment. The people in the metropolis of Thessalonica understood the radical nature of Jesus' claim. Those who accepted it were transformed—those who didn't turned hostile. (You can read about the riot they started in Acts chapter 17, verses 5–10 [p. 1448]). Obviously, there's a time for quiet reflection when you read the Bible. But if you've never felt stirred deep in your soul when you consider what is at stake, you haven't understood how "outrageous" Christianity truly is.

CENTRAL IDEAS

- Christ's spirit helps believers to remain strong in the midst of cultural opposition.
- Paul gives his readers guidelines for living Christ-centered lives.
- Christ will one day return to earth.
- If we trust in Christ, we will live with him forever.

TITLE

These letters are named after the believers they were sent to at Thessalonica, an important trade route and communications hub in the northern Mediterranean region. It had a population of about 200,000, making it the largest city in Macedonia.

AUTHOR AND READERS

Paul wrote these letters to believers who were faithfully living Christ-centered lives in the midst of incredible cultural pressure to do otherwise. Thessalonica was flush with wealth—and with the corruption and excess that tend to go with it. Paul wrote to encourage these believers and to correct a few misunderstandings.

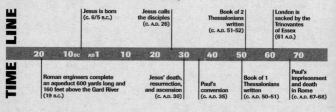

TIME LINE

| | Jesus is born (c. 6/5 B.C.) | Jesus calls the disciples (c. A.D. 26) | | Book of 2 Thessalonians written (c. A.D. 51–52) | London is sacked by the Trinovantes of Essex (61 A.D.) |

| 20 | 10 B.C. | A.D. 1 | 10 | 20 | 30 | 40 | 50 | 60 | 70 |

| | Roman engineers complete an aqueduct 600 yards long and 160 feet above the Gard River (19 B.C.) | | Jesus' death, resurrection, and ascension (c. A.D. 30) | Paul's conversion (c. A.D. 35) | Book of 1 Thessalonians written (c. A.D. 50–51) | Paul's imprisonment and death in Rome (c. A.D. 67–68) |

My cousin Jim and I were having a blast. We were also making a lot of noise.

"You boys get to sleep!" my dad yelled from the living room.

Jim and I froze.

"We'd better be quiet," he whispered to me.

"Right," I said as I hit him in the head with a pillow.

"Watch out!" he yelled as he retaliated with a pillow across my face.

We heard my dad walking quickly down the hall. Instantly we both jumped back into our beds and pretended to be sleeping.

Dad opened the door and turned on the light. "If I hear you boys again," he said, "you'll be in big trouble." He then turned off the light and shut the door.

No sooner were the lights out than we both started giggling—as quietly as possible, of course. Being the master of stealth, I climbed out of bed and tiptoed over to Jim's bed undetected. As I stood over Jim with my pillow raised high, the bedroom light suddenly came back on. There stood my dad by the closed door. He had never left the room!

> **"If I hear you boys again," he said, "you'll be in big trouble."**

Had I known my dad was right there, I would have obeyed him. But our human nature makes us think we can get away with things we'd never try if an authority figure were present.

When Paul wrote to the ancient Thessalonians, he praised them for eagerly anticipating the return of Jesus Christ. They embraced the promise Jesus made that he would literally and triumphantly come back to earth someday—and their lives reflected that hope.

If you're a seeker, such an idea may be new to you. Perhaps it's even a bit frightening. What if you're in the same kind of situation I was in when my dad unexpectedly turned on the lights?

You don't have to be caught by surprise. Paul summarized what we need to do to please God and to be confident when Christ returns. Look at 1 Thessalonians chapter 1, verses 9–10 (page 1560), to see how you can gain that kind of confidence.

1 THESSALONIANS

1 Paul, Silas[a] and Timothy,

To the church of the Thessalonians in God the Father and the Lord Jesus Christ:

Grace and peace to you.[b]

Thanksgiving for the Thessalonians' Faith

[2]We always thank God for all of you, mentioning you in our prayers. [3]We continually remember before our God and Father your work produced by faith, your labor prompted by love, and your endurance inspired by hope in our Lord Jesus Christ.

[4]For we know, brothers loved by God, that he has chosen you, [5]because our gospel came to you not simply with words, but also with power, with the Holy Spirit and with deep conviction. You know how we lived among you for your sake. [6]You became imitators of us and of the Lord; in spite of severe suffering, you welcomed the message with the joy given by the Holy Spirit. [7]And so you became a model to all the believers in Macedonia and Achaia. [8]The Lord's message rang out from you not only in Macedonia and Achaia—your faith in God has become known everywhere. Therefore we do not need to say anything about it, [9]for they themselves report what kind of reception you gave us. They tell how you turned to God from idols to serve the living and true God, [10]and to wait

---

[a] 1 Greek *Silvanus*, a variant of *Silas*   [b] 1 Some early manuscripts *you from God our Father and the Lord Jesus Christ*

⬛ ▦▦▦▦▦▦▦▦▦▦▦▦▦▦ ADDRESSING QUESTIONS ▦▦▦▦▦▦▦▦▦▦▦▦▦▦ ▣

1:9–10
Human Experience **Q**

In this short passage, Paul outlines the three marks of true conversion: first, turning from idols; second, serving God; third, waiting for Christ to return.

What about that first item on the list? What does it mean to turn from idols? If "worshiping an object of wood or stone" was the definition of idolatry, then most of us wouldn't consider ourselves idolaters. But *worship* isn't just a matter of bowing down in a temple, and an *idol* isn't just a carved image. Idolatry is the practice of allowing something other than God to occupy the number-one position in our lives.

For instance, money can become an idol if we trust it to give us security or significance. Alcohol, drugs, sex, food, even another person—anything other than God that we allow to dominate our lives—can be considered an idol. Just as the Thessalonians had to turn from their idols to embrace God, so do we.

Unlike an idol, the "living and true God" (verse 9) wants to have a relationship with us. He wants us to dedicate our lives to his service, anticipating the day when he will interrupt history and come for his followers (see Matthew chapter 24, verses 30–31 [page 1293]).

Jesus' first coming was the occasion for splitting time into B.C. (before Christ) and A.D. (*Anno Domine*, or "the year of our Lord"). His second coming will create a whole new era of time. On that day Jesus will fulfill every aspect of his kingly role, and this world will function according to his original design.

Do you want to be part of that new world? The invitation is still open. Turn from your "idols" and put your trust in God. Let Jesus come into your life as your forgiver and leader.

or his Son from heaven, whom he raised from the dead—Jesus, who rescues us from the coming wrath.

Paul's Ministry in Thessalonica

2 You know, brothers, that our visit to you was not a failure. [2]We had previously suffered and been insulted in Philippi, as you know, but with the help of our God we dared to tell you his gospel in spite of strong opposition. [3]For the appeal we make does not spring from error or impure motives, nor are we trying to trick you. [4]On the contrary, we speak as men approved by God to be entrusted with the gospel. We are not trying to please men but God, who tests our hearts. [5]You know we never used flattery, nor did we put on a mask to cover up greed—God is our witness. [6]We were not looking for praise from men, not from you or anyone else.

As apostles of Christ we could have been a burden to you, [7]but we were gentle among you, like a mother caring for her little children. [8]We loved you so much that we were delighted to share with you not only the gospel of God but our lives as well, because you had become so dear to us. [9]Surely you remember, brothers, our toil and hardship; we worked night and day in order not to be a burden to anyone while we preached the gospel of God to you.

[10]You are witnesses, and so is God, of how holy, righteous and blameless we were among you who believed. [11]For you know that we dealt with each of you as a father deals with his own children, [12]encouraging, comforting and urging you to live lives worthy of God, who calls you into his kingdom and glory.

[13]And we also thank God continually because, when you received the word of God, which you heard from us, you accepted it not as the word of men, but as it actually is,

> ◻ ▦ **STRENGTHENING RELATIONSHIPS** ▦ ↩
>
> **2:6–9**
> **Social**
>
> The problem with loving other people is that we become vulnerable. In expressing love, we open ourselves to the possibility that we could be hurt.
>
> While that reality can be frightening, the apostle Paul felt such care for others was worth it. In fact, he dedicated his life to serving the people he met and spoke to. In light of the hardships he described in this passage, do you sense any regret from him?
>
> God designed humans as social beings with the deep need to give themselves away—to be in relationship with other people. If you allow yourself to be guided by God's Spirit, you too will find the fulfillment that Paul found. Even though you may open yourself to heartache, you'll find that touching others' lives with the love of God is well worth taking that risk.

the word of God, which is at work in you who believe. [14]For you, brothers, became imitators of God's churches in Judea, which are in Christ Jesus: You suffered from your own countrymen the same things those churches suffered from the Jews, [15]who killed the Lord Jesus and the prophets and also drove us out. They displease God and are hostile to all men [16]in their effort to keep us from speaking to the Gentiles so that they may be saved. In this way they always heap up their sins to the limit. The wrath of God has come upon them at last. [a]

Paul's Longing to See the Thessalonians

[17]But, brothers, when we were torn away from you for a short time (in person, not in thought), out of our intense longing we made every effort to see you. [18]For we wanted to come to you—certainly I, Paul, did, again and again—but Satan stopped us. [19]For what is our hope, our joy, or the crown in which we will glory in the presence of our Lord Jesus when he comes? Is it not you? [20]Indeed, you are our glory and joy.

a 16 Or them fully

3 So when we could stand it no longer, we thought it best to be left by ourselves in Athens. ²We sent Timothy, who is our brother and God's fellow worker[a] in spreading the gospel of Christ, to strengthen and encourage you in your faith, ³so that no one would be unsettled by these trials. You know quite well that we were destined for them. ⁴In fact, when we were with you, we kept telling you that we would be persecuted. And it turned out that way, as you well know. ⁵For this reason, when I could stand it no longer, I sent to find out about your faith. I was afraid that in some way the tempter might have tempted you and our efforts might have been useless.

Timothy's Encouraging Report

⁶But Timothy has just now come to us from you and has brought good news about your faith and love. He has told us that you always have pleasant memories of us and that you long to see us, just as we also long to see you. ⁷Therefore, brothers, in all our distress and persecution we were encouraged about you because of your faith. ⁸For now we really live, since you are standing firm in the Lord. ⁹How can we thank God enough for you in return for all the joy we have in the presence of our God because of you? ¹⁰Night and day we pray most earnestly that we may see you again and supply what is lacking in your faith.

¹¹Now may our God and Father himself and our Lord Jesus clear the way for us to come to you. ¹²May the Lord make your love increase and overflow for each other and for everyone else, just as ours does for you. ¹³May he strengthen your hearts so that you will be blameless and holy in the presence of our God and Father when our Lord Jesus comes with all his holy ones.

▣ ▦▦▦▦▦ REASONS TO BELIEVE ▦▦▦▦▦ ↔

4:13–18
The Christian Experience

For a Christian, death can be called "sleep" because it's not permanent. Paul's words reiterate the promise that, when Jesus comes back to earth from heaven, an incredible transformation will take place. Living people will be changed in an instant, and dead people will be raised from the grave. All believers will then be with Christ and with each other for eternity.

Christ-followers grieve when a fellow believer dies, but it's not a hopeless sadness—it's the pain of a temporary separation. Because they trust in Jesus, they rely on God's promise that one day all people who have accepted Christ's salvation will reunited. This wonderful truth provides a source of great encouragement that "our present sufferings are not worth comparing with the glory that will be revealed in us" (Romans chapter 8, verse 18 [page 1479]). That assurance permeates this life and gives Christians bright hope for the next.

Living to Please God

4 Finally, brothers, we instructed you how to live in order to please God, as in fact you are living. Now we ask you and urge you in the Lord Jesus to do this more and more. ²For you know what instructions we gave you by the authority of the Lord Jesus.

³It is God's will that you should be sanctified: that you should avoid sexual immorality; ⁴that each of you should learn to control his own body[b] in a way that is holy and honorable, ⁵not in passionate lust like the heathen, who do not know God; ⁶and that in this matter no one should wrong his brother or take advantage of him. The Lord will punish men for all such sins, as we have already told you and warned you. ⁷For God did not call us to be impure, but to live a holy life. ⁸Therefore, he who rejects this instruction does not reject man but God, who gives you his Holy Spirit.

⁹Now about brotherly love we do not need to write to you, for you yourselves have been taught by God to love each other. ¹⁰And in fact, you do love all the brothers throughout Macedonia. Yet we urge you, brothers, to do so more and more.

¹¹Make it your ambition to lead a quiet life, to mind your own business and to work with your hands, just as we told you, ¹²so that your daily life may win the respect of outsiders and so that you will not be dependent on anybody.

The Coming of the Lord

¹³Brothers, we do not want you to be ignorant about those who fall asleep, or to grieve like the rest of men, who have no hope. ¹⁴We believe that Jesus died and rose again and so we believe that God will bring with Jesus those who have fallen asleep in him. ¹⁵According to the Lord's own word, we tell you that we who are still alive, who are left till the coming of the Lord, will certainly not precede those who have fallen asleep. ¹⁶For the Lord himself will come down from heaven, with a loud command, with the voice of the archangel and with the trumpet call of God, and the dead in Christ will rise first. ¹⁷After that, we who are still alive and are left will be caught up together with them in the clouds to meet the Lord in the air. And so we will be with the Lord forever. ¹⁸Therefore encourage each other with these words.

5 Now, brothers, about times and dates we do not need to write to you, ²for you know very well that the day of the Lord will come like a thief in the night. ³While people are saying, "Peace and safety," destruction will come on them suddenly, as labor pains on a pregnant woman, and they will not escape.

⁴But you, brothers, are not in darkness so that this day should surprise you like a thief. ⁵You are all sons of the light and sons of the day. We do not belong to the night or to the darkness. ⁶So then, let us not be like others, who are asleep, but let us be alert and self-controlled. ⁷For those who sleep, sleep at night, and those who get drunk, get drunk at night. ⁸But since we belong to the day, let us be self-controlled, putting on faith and love as a breastplate, and the hope of salvation as a helmet. ⁹For God did not appoint us to suffer wrath but to receive salvation through our Lord Jesus Christ. ¹⁰He died for us so that, whether we are awake or asleep, we may live together with him. ¹¹Therefore encourage one another and build each other up, just as in fact you are doing.

Final Instructions

¹²Now we ask you, brothers, to respect those who work hard among you, who are over you in the Lord and who admonish you. ¹³Hold them in the highest regard in love because of their work. Live in peace with each other. ¹⁴And we urge you, brothers, warn those who are idle, encourage the timid, help the weak, be patient with everyone. ¹⁵Make sure that nobody pays back wrong for wrong, but always try to be kind to each other and to everyone else.

¹⁶Be joyful always; ¹⁷pray continually; ¹⁸give thanks in all circumstances, for this is God's will for you in Christ Jesus.

¹⁹Do not put out the Spirit's fire; ²⁰do not treat prophecies with contempt. ²¹Test everything. Hold on to the good. ²²Avoid every kind of evil.

::::::::::::::: DISCOVERING GOD :::::::::::::::

5:21
Spiritual Fraud

Having the desire to be sure about the things we believe is not evidence of a lack of faith. As a matter of fact, Paul commands us to test everything. We can't be too quick to assume that everything we hear is God's truth. In that sense, he encourages all people—from first-time seekers to veteran Christ-followers—to continually search for truth.

We live in a world full of deception and spiritual counterfeits. Many new ideas and fraudulent philosophies have come and gone over the centuries, but God's revelation in the Bible doesn't change. Then as now, God's word is the ultimate test of the validity of any new teaching.

²³May God himself, the God of peace, sanctify you through and through. May you whole spirit, soul and body be kept blameless at the coming of our Lord Jesus Christ ²⁴The one who calls you is faithful and he will do it.

²⁵Brothers, pray for us. ²⁶Greet all the brothers with a holy kiss. ²⁷I charge you before the Lord to have this letter read to all the brothers.

²⁸The grace of our Lord Jesus Christ be with you.

2 THESSALONIANS

1 Paul, Silas[a] and Timothy,

To the church of the Thessalonians in God our Father and the Lord Jesus Christ:

²Grace and peace to you from God the Father and the Lord Jesus Christ.

Thanksgiving and Prayer

³We ought always to thank God for you, brothers, and rightly so, because your faith is growing more and more, and the love every one of you has for each other is increasing. ⁴Therefore, among God's churches we boast about your perseverance and faith in all the persecutions and trials you are enduring.

⁵All this is evidence that God's judgment is right, and as a result you will be counted worthy of the kingdom of God, for which you are suffering. ⁶God is just: He will pay back trouble to those who trouble you ⁷and give relief to you who are troubled, and to us as well. This will happen when the Lord Jesus is revealed from heaven in blazing fire with his powerful angels. ⁸He will punish those who do not know God and do not obey the gospel of our Lord Jesus. ⁹They will be punished with everlasting destruction and shut out from the presence of the Lord and from the majesty of his power ¹⁰on the day he comes to be glorified in his holy people and to be marveled at among all those who have believed. This includes you, because you believed our testimony to you.

¹¹With this in mind, we constantly pray for you, that our God may count you worthy of his calling, and that by his power he may fulfill every good purpose of yours and every act prompted by your faith. ¹²We pray this so that the name of our Lord Jesus may be glorified in you, and you in him, according to the grace of our God and the Lord Jesus Christ.[b]

The Man of Lawlessness

2 Concerning the coming of our Lord Jesus Christ and our being gathered to him, we ask you, brothers, ²not to become easily unsettled or alarmed by some prophecy, report or letter supposed to have come from us, saying that the day of the Lord has already come. ³Don't let anyone deceive you in any way, for ₍that day will not come₎ until the rebellion occurs and the man of lawlessness[c] is revealed, the man doomed to destruction. ⁴He will oppose and will exalt himself over everything that is

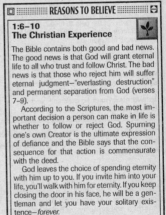

▣ ▦▦▦▦▦▦▦ REASONS TO BELIEVE ▦▦▦▦▦▦▦ ↻

1:6–10
The Christian Experience

The Bible contains both good and bad news. The good news is that God will grant eternal life to all who trust and follow Christ. The bad news is that those who reject him will suffer eternal judgment—"everlasting destruction" and permanent separation from God (verses 7–9).

According to the Scriptures, the most important decision a person can make in life is whether to follow or reject God. Spurning one's own Creator is the ultimate expression of defiance and the Bible says that the consequence for that action is commensurate with the deed.

God leaves the choice of spending eternity with him up to you. If you invite him into your life, you'll walk with him for eternity. If you keep closing the door in his face, he will be a gentleman and let you have your solitary existence—forever.

---

a 1 Greek Silvanus, a variant of Silas   *b 12 Or God and Lord, Jesus Christ*   *c 3 Some manuscripts sin*

called God or is worshiped, so that he sets himself up in God's temple, proclaiming himself to be God.

⁵Don't you remember that when I was with you I used to tell you these things? ⁶And now you know what is holding him back, so that he may be revealed at the proper time. ⁷For the secret power of lawlessness is already at work; but the one who now holds it back will continue to do so till he is taken out of the way. ⁸And then the lawless one will be revealed, whom the Lord Jesus will overthrow with the breath of his mouth and destroy by the splendor of his coming. ⁹The coming of the lawless one will be in accordance with the work of Satan displayed in all kinds of counterfeit miracles, signs and wonders, ¹⁰and in every sort of evil that deceives those who are perishing. They perish because they refused to love the truth and so be saved. ¹¹For this reason God sends them a powerful delusion so that they will believe the lie ¹²and so that all will be condemned who have not believed the truth but have delighted in wickedness.

> ### ☐ ▒▒▒▒▒ DISCOVERING GOD ▒▒▒▒▒ ⬒
>
>
> ### 2:9–12
> ### Spiritual Fraud
>
> God would never deceive anyone, but if someone persists in following error, God may work mercifully to make sure other people aren't caught up in that lie.
>
> According to verse 10, people who abandon love of the truth open themselves up to the consequences of their actions. In the same way certain diseases show external symptoms that warn others to avoid contamination, God allows some spiritual diseases to evidence symptoms so that others can keep from embracing the same error. By God's mercy, people's persistently poor spiritual decisions have consequences that lead them even farther off the track, sending a clear signal to onlookers that theirs is not the path to follow. (See Romans chapter 1, verses 24–28 [page 1469] for an example of this truth.)
>
> The only safeguard against such contamination mentioned in this passage is to "love the truth and so be saved" (verse 10). Don't love human opinions; don't love charming spiritual leaders; don't love power; don't love emotional experiences—love only truth. True spiritual reality must be constantly and vigilantly pursued.

Stand Firm

¹³But we ought always to thank God for you, brothers loved by the Lord, because from the beginning God chose you*ᵃ* to be saved through the sanctifying work of the Spirit and through belief in the truth. ¹⁴He called you to this through our gospel, that you might share in the glory of our Lord Jesus Christ. ¹⁵So then, brothers, stand firm and hold to the teachings*ᵇ* we passed on to you, whether by word of mouth or by letter.

¹⁶May our Lord Jesus Christ himself and God our Father, who loved us and by his grace gave us eternal encouragement and good hope, ¹⁷encourage your hearts and strengthen you in every good deed and word.

Request for Prayer

3 Finally, brothers, pray for us that the message of the Lord may spread rapidly and be honored, just as it was with you. ²And pray that we may be delivered from wicked and evil men, for not everyone has faith. ³But the Lord is faithful, and he will strengthen and protect you from the evil one. ⁴We have confidence in the Lord that you are doing and will continue to do the things we command. ⁵May the Lord direct your hearts into God's love and Christ's perseverance.

Warning Against Idleness

⁶In the name of the Lord Jesus Christ, we command you, brothers, to keep away from every brother who is idle and does not live according to the teaching*ᶜ* you received from us. ⁷For you yourselves know how you ought to follow our example. We were not idle when we were with you, ⁸nor did we eat anyone's food without paying for it. On the

---

ᵃ13 Some manuscripts *because God chose you as his firstfruits*   *ᵇ15* Or *traditions*   *ᶜ6* Or *tradition*

contrary, we worked night and day, laboring and toiling so that we would not be a burden to any of you. 9We did this, not because we do not have the right to such help, but in order to make ourselves a model for you to follow. 10For even when we were with you, we gave you this rule: "If a man will not work, he shall not eat."

11We hear that some among you are idle. They are not busy; they are busybodies. 12Such people we command and urge in the Lord Jesus Christ to settle down and earn the bread they eat. 13And as for you, brothers, never tire of doing what is right.

14If anyone does not obey our instruction in this letter, take special note of him. Do not associate with him, in order that he may feel ashamed. 15Yet do not regard him as an enemy, but warn him as a brother.

Final Greetings

16Now may the Lord of peace himself give you peace at all times and in every way. The Lord be with all of you.

17I, Paul, write this greeting in my own hand, which is the distinguishing mark in all my letters. This is how I write.

18The grace of our Lord Jesus Christ be with you all.

Introduction

THE BOTTOM LINE

et's think about the early church in terms of athletic teams. Paul was like a first-century franchise manager. He had expanded the organization into several different cities, leaving the newly formed and growing teams in the hands of two very capable coaches, Timothy and Titus. In the books of the Bible that bear their names, Paul gives these men tips for more effective coaching, advice on managing intersquad disputes, some winning strategies and encouragement that they are playing for the right team. Philemon, on the other hand, was embroiled in a labor dispute. Paul was the mediator assigned to resolve the situation, urging Philemon to be gentle with his former "employee" (i.e., slave) on the grounds that Onesimus—since his escape—had been recruited and now wore the same "uniform" as his former master. If you want to be a "player" in God's kingdom, take a little time to get familiar with the instructions given in these books. They are Jesus' game plan for his churches in Paul's day—and our own.

CENTRAL IDEAS

- "Christ Jesus came into the world to save sinners" (1 Tim. chapter 1, verse 15 [p.1570]).
- Leadership requires lifestyle modification and, above all, strong character.
- Paul discusses the decaying condition of a society in which God has been rejected.
- The church, in spite of its flaws, does the work of Jesus on earth.

TITLES

The names of these books are taken from the names of the people to whom Paul wrote them.

AUTHOR AND READERS

Paul wrote these letters to leaders who were in need of his advice and direction. Timothy was the leader of the church at Ephesus. Titus had a hand in planting many churches but accepted this letter while on the island of Crete. Philemon was a member of the church at Colosse.

You can tell a lot about a person from his or her gravestone.

For instance, film star Clark Gable has these words inscribed on his gravestone: "Back to silents."

Author Ernest Hemingway's tombstone reads, "Pardon me for not getting up."

The tombstone of comedian W. C. Fields reads, "On the whole I'd rather be in Philadelphia."

And this from a gravestone in Edinburgh: "Stranger, tread this ground with gravity; Dentist Brown is filling his last cavity."

Many tombstones carry a more serious message. Sentiments from broken hearts, stories of interrupted lives, and hopes for reunion are frequent graveyard themes.

One thing common to all gravestones is the way they measure time. Each one has the person's date of birth, a dash, and the date of death. To the casual observer, that tiny dash sums up that person's life, regardless of its length or quality.

Of course, as our own lives draw to a close, we'll look back and see more than a dash.

Do you want the dash on your tombstone to represent something significant?

We'll see our years of childhood and growing up, recall the development of skills, our first job, perhaps marriage and children, and think back on our careers. We'll see some opportunities we missed and some we seized. We'll see disappointments and joys.

Paul wrote the books of 1 and 2 Timothy, Titus, and Philemon from the perspective of a life that was near it's end. Second Timothy may have been completed only weeks before Paul was executed, when he knew his death was imminent. These letters contain Paul's look back on his life—reflections on his "dash"—and an evaluation of how he had lived. The letters of 1 and 2 Timothy and Titus are sometimes called the "pastoral epistles." Paul wrote these letters to instruct two young Christian ministers concerning the various leadership challenges they were facing. He wrote the letter of Philemon to the owner of a newly converted runaway slave.

Do you want the dash on your tombstone to represent something significant? To read the words of one man who had a deep sense of purpose, turn to 2 Timothy chapter 4, verses 7–8 (page 1577). You'll get an idea of how you can make a lasting difference, too.

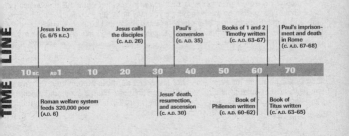

TIME LINE

Jesus is born (c. 6/5 B.C.)	Jesus calls the disciples (c. A.D. 26)	Paul's conversion (c. A.D. 35)	Books of 1 and 2 Timothy written (c. A.D. 63–67)	Paul's imprisonment and death in Rome (c. A.D. 67–68)	

10 B.C.   AD 1   10   20   30   40   50   60   70

Roman welfare system feeds 320,000 poor (A.D. 6)	Jesus' death, resurrection, and ascension (c. A.D. 30)	Book of Philemon written (c. A.D. 60–62)	Book of Titus written (c. A.D. 63–65)

1 TIMOTHY

1 Paul, an apostle of Christ Jesus by the command of God our Savior and ⌐ Christ Jesus our hope,

²To Timothy my true son in the faith:

Grace, mercy and peace from God the Father and Christ Jesus our Lord.

Warning Against False Teachers of the Law

³As I urged you when I went into Macedonia, stay there in Ephesus so that you ma⌐ command certain men not to teach false doctrines any longer ⁴nor to devote themselve⌐ to myths and endless genealogies. These promote controversies rather than God's work⌐ which is by faith. ⁵The goal of this command is love, which comes from a pure heart an⌐ a good conscience and a sincere faith. ⁶Some have wandered away from these an⌐ turned to meaningless talk. ⁷They want to be teachers of the law, but they do not kno⌐ what they are talking about or what they so confidently affirm.

⁸We know that the law is good if one uses it properly. ⁹We also know that law*ᵃ* ⌐ made not for the righteous but for lawbreakers and rebels, the ungodly and sinful, th⌐ unholy and irreligious; for those who kill their fathers or mothers, for murderers, ¹⁰fc⌐ adulterers and perverts, for slave traders and liars and perjurers—and for whatever else ⌐ contrary to the sound doctrine ¹¹that conforms to the glorious gospel of the blessed Goc⌐ which he entrusted to me.

The Lord's Grace to Paul

¹²I thank Christ Jesus our Lord, who has given me strength, that he considered m⌐ faithful, appointing me to his service. ¹³Even though I was once a blasphemer and ⌐ persecutor and a violent man, I was shown mercy because I acted in ignorance an⌐ unbelief. ¹⁴The grace of our Lord was poured out on me abundantly, along with the fait⌐ and love that are in Christ Jesus.

¹⁵Here is a trustworthy saying that deserves full acceptance: Christ Jesus came into th⌐ world to save sinners—of whom I am the worst. ¹⁶But for that very reason I was show⌐ mercy so that in me, the worst of sinners, Christ Jesus might display his unlimite⌐ patience as an example for those who would believe on him and receive eternal life⌐ ¹⁷Now to the King eternal, immortal, invisible, the only God, be honor and glory for eve⌐ and ever. Amen.

¹⁸Timothy, my son, I give you this instruction in keeping with the prophecies onc⌐ made about you, so that by following them you may fight the good fight, ¹⁹holding on t⌐ faith and a good conscience. Some have rejected these and so have shipwrecked the⌐ faith. ²⁰Among them are Hymenaeus and Alexander, whom I have handed over to Sata⌐ to be taught not to blaspheme.

Instructions on Worship

2 I urge, then, first of all, that requests, prayers, intercession and thanksgivin⌐ be made for everyone— ²for kings and all those in authority, that we ma⌐ live peaceful and quiet lives in all godliness and holiness. ³This is good, and pleases Goc⌐ our Savior, ⁴who wants all men to be saved and to come to a knowledge of the truth. ⁵Fc⌐

ᵃ9 Or that the law

there is one God and one mediator between God and men, the man Christ Jesus, ⁶who gave himself as a ransom for all men—the testimony given in its proper time. ⁷And for this purpose I was appointed a herald and an apostle—I am telling the truth, I am not lying—and a teacher of the true faith to the Gentiles.

⁸I want men everywhere to lift up holy hands in prayer, without anger or disputing.

⁹I also want women to dress modestly, with decency and propriety, not with braided hair or gold or pearls or expensive clothes, ¹⁰but with good deeds, appropriate for women who profess to worship God.

¹¹A woman should learn in quietness and full submission. ¹²I do not permit a woman to teach or to have authority over a man; she must be silent. ¹³For Adam was formed first, then Eve. ¹⁴And Adam was not the one deceived; it was the woman who was deceived and became a sinner. ¹⁵But women*a* will be saved*b* through childbearing—if they continue in faith, love and holiness with propriety.

Overseers and Deacons

3 Here is a trustworthy saying: If anyone sets his heart on being an overseer,*c* he desires a noble task. ²Now the overseer must be above reproach, the husband of but one wife, temperate, self-controlled, respectable, hospitable, able to teach, ³not given to drunkenness, not violent but gentle, not quarrelsome, not a lover of money. ⁴He must manage his own family well and see that his children obey him with proper respect. ⁵(If anyone does not know how to manage his own family, how can he take care of God's church?) ⁶He must not be a recent convert, or he may become conceited and fall under the same judgment as the devil. ⁷He must also have a good reputation with outsiders, so that he will not fall into disgrace and into the devil's trap.

⁸Deacons, likewise, are to be men worthy of respect, sincere, not indulging in much wine, and not pursuing dishonest gain. ⁹They must keep hold of the deep truths of the

a15 Greek *she*   *b15* Or *restored*   *c1* Traditionally *bishop;* also in verse 2

1:15–17
Life with God

A few years ago newspapers ran a story about two men, Nathan Carriker and James Bixby, who were joy-riding in their single-engine plane above the rugged mountains east of Los Angeles, California one December. As they entered a canyon, they soon found that they didn't have enough room to turn around at the end of it. And without the power to gain the necessary altitude, they crashed into the canyon wall.

Carriker, the pilot, was trapped in the wreckage. Even though Bixby had broken bones in his back, face, and foot, he managed to hike five miles over treacherous terrain—boulders, rocks and ravines—in total darkness. It took him seven and a half hours to reach help, but because of Bixby's heroic effort, Carriker was rescued.

This remarkable story provides us with an illustration of what Jesus did for us. He left heaven and came into the world to save those who couldn't save themselves. Broken and bruised on the cross, he "went the distance" for our salvation. Jesus, however, submitted to this sacrifice for the very people who were persecuting him. Unlike the friend in the illustration, he took his journey amid taunts and mistreatment by the very people he was seeking to save.

The apostle Paul was keenly aware of how he had fought against Christ earlier in his life. That's why he called himself "the worst of sinners." Using himself as an illustration, Paul suggested that if Jesus could forgive *him,* Jesus can forgive anybody. That, of course, means that Jesus can forgive you.

Do you want to receive Jesus' forgiveness? Paul tells you what to do in verse 16: "Believe on him [Jesus] and receive eternal life."

faith with a clear conscience. ¹⁰They must first be tested; and then if there is nothing against them, let them serve as deacons.

¹¹In the same way, their wives[a] are to be women worthy of respect, not malicious talkers but temperate and trustworthy in everything.

¹²A deacon must be the husband of but one wife and must manage his children and his household well. ¹³Those who have served well gain an excellent standing and great assurance in their faith in Christ Jesus.

¹⁴Although I hope to come to you soon, I am writing you these instructions so that, ¹⁵if I am delayed, you will know how people ought to conduct themselves in God's household, which is the church of the living God, the pillar and foundation of the truth. ¹⁶Beyond all question, the mystery of godliness is great:

> He[b] appeared in a body,[c]
> was vindicated by the Spirit,
> was seen by angels,
> was preached among the nations,
> was believed on in the world,
> was taken up in glory.

Instructions to Timothy

 The Spirit clearly says that in later times some will abandon the faith and follow deceiving spirits and things taught by demons. ²Such teachings come through hypocritical liars, whose consciences have been seared as with a hot iron. ³They forbid people to marry and order them to abstain from certain foods, which God created to be received with thanksgiving by those who believe and who know the truth. ⁴For everything God created is good, and nothing is to be rejected if it is received with thanksgiving, ⁵because it is consecrated by the word of God and prayer.

⁶If you point these things out to the brothers, you will be a good minister of Christ Jesus, brought up in the truths of the faith and of the good teaching that you have followed. ⁷Have nothing to do with godless myths and old wives' tales; rather, train yourself to be godly. ⁸For physical training is of some value, but godliness has value for all things, holding promise for both the present life and the life to come.

⁹This is a trustworthy saying that deserves full acceptance ¹⁰(and for this we labor and strive), that we have put our hope in the living God, who is the Savior of all men, and especially of those who believe.

¹¹Command and teach these things. ¹²Don't let anyone look down on you because you are young, but set an example for the believers in speech, in life, in love, in faith and in purity. ¹³Until I come, devote yourself to the public reading of Scripture, to preaching and

---

████ ▒▒▒▒▒▒ DISCOVERING GOD ▒▒▒▒▒▒ ⬛

4:1–5
Spiritual Fraud

One of the most remarkable things about cults is their intricate, persuasive, and often Christian-sounding belief systems. Many cult teachings are so close to Biblical truth that their members can't tell the difference.

Paul wanted his readers to know what hostile spiritual forces lie behind such teachings (verse 1). Even the leaders of cult groups are deceived by powers they barely understand. Deceptive spiritual "sales techniques" can trap even the most perceptive and rational people into believing false doctrines and devoting themselves to a useless system of religion.

In Paul's day, teachers who promoted an ascetic way of life as a way to reach God exemplified such cult-like activity. "Deny yourself marriage and certain foods," they told their followers, "and you'll be able to earn your way to heaven." Doesn't that sound "spiritual"?

Nonsense! The Bible says that nothing we do can earn us eternal life. Beware of anyone who says you can find salvation by any other method than simply trusting in what Christ has already done for you.

---

[a] 11 Or *way, deaconesses*   [b] 16 Some manuscripts *God*   [c] 16 Or *in the flesh*

teaching. [14]Do not neglect your gift, which was given you through a prophetic message when the body of elders laid their hands on you.

[15]Be diligent in these matters; give yourself wholly to them, so that everyone may see our progress. [16]Watch your life and doctrine closely. Persevere in them, because if you do, you will save both yourself and your hearers.

Advice About Widows, Elders and Slaves

5 Do not rebuke an older man harshly, but exhort him as if he were your father. Treat younger men as brothers, [2]older women as mothers, and younger women as sisters, with absolute purity.

[3]Give proper recognition to those widows who are really in need. [4]But if a widow has children or grandchildren, these should learn first of all to put their religion into practice by caring for their own family and so repaying their parents and grandparents, for this is pleasing to God. [5]The widow who is really in need and left all alone puts her hope in God and continues night and day to pray and to ask God for help. [6]But the widow who lives for pleasure is dead even while she lives. [7]Give the people these instructions, too, so that no one may be open to blame. [8]If anyone does not provide for his relatives, and especially for his immediate family, he has denied the faith and is worse than an unbeliever.

[9]No widow may be put on the list of widows unless she is over sixty, has been faithful to her husband,[a] [10]and is well known for her good deeds, such as bringing up children, showing hospitality, washing the feet of the saints, helping those in trouble and devoting herself to all kinds of good deeds.

[11]As for younger widows, do not put them on such a list. For when their sensual desires overcome their dedication to Christ, they want to marry. [12]Thus they bring judgment on themselves, because they have broken their first pledge. [13]Besides, they get into the habit of being idle and going about from house to house. And not only do they become idlers, but also gossips and busybodies, saying things they ought not to. [14]So I counsel younger widows to marry, to have children, to manage their homes and to give the enemy no opportunity for slander. [15]Some have in fact already turned away to follow Satan.

[16]If any woman who is a believer has widows in her family, she should help them and not let the church be burdened with them, so that the church can help those widows who are really in need.

[17]The elders who direct the affairs of the church well are worthy of double honor, especially those whose work is preaching and teaching. [18]For the Scripture says, "Do not muzzle the ox while it is treading out the grain,"[b] and "The worker deserves his wages."[c] [19]Do not entertain an accusation against an elder unless it is brought by two or three witnesses. [20]Those who sin are to be rebuked publicly, so that the others may take warning.

[21]I charge you, in the sight of God and Christ Jesus and the elect angels, to keep these instructions without partiality, and to do nothing out of favoritism.

[22]Do not be hasty in the laying on of hands, and do not share in the sins of others. Keep yourself pure.

[23]Stop drinking only water, and use a little wine because of your stomach and your frequent illnesses.

[24]The sins of some men are obvious, reaching the place of judgment ahead of them; the sins of others trail behind them. [25]In the same way, good deeds are obvious, and even those that are not cannot be hidden.

---

a 9 Or has had but one husband   *b 18 Deut. 25:4*   *c 18 Luke 10:7*

6 All who are under the yoke of slavery should consider their masters worthy of full respect, so that God's name and our teaching may not be slandered. ²Those who have believing masters are not to show less respect for them because they are brothers. Instead, they are to serve them even better, because those who benefit from their service are believers, and dear to them. These are the things you are to teach and urge on them.

Love of Money

³If anyone teaches false doctrines and does not agree to the sound instruction of our Lord Jesus Christ and to godly teaching, ⁴he is conceited and understands nothing. He has an unhealthy interest in controversies and quarrels about words that result in envy, strife, malicious talk, evil suspicions ⁵and constant friction between men of corrupt mind, who have been robbed of the truth and who think that godliness is a means to financial gain.

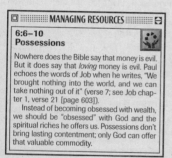

MANAGING RESOURCES

6:6–10
Possessions

Nowhere does the Bible say that money is evil. But it does say that *loving* money is evil. Paul echoes the words of Job when he writes, "We brought nothing into the world, and we can take nothing out of it" (verse 7; see Job chapter 1, verse 21 [page 603]).

Instead of becoming obsessed with wealth, we should be "obsessed" with God and the spiritual riches he offers us. Possessions don't bring lasting contentment; only God can offer that valuable commodity.

⁶But godliness with contentment is great gain. ⁷For we brought nothing into the world, and we can take nothing out of it. ⁸But if we have food and clothing, we will be content with that. ⁹People who want to get rich fall into temptation and a trap and into many foolish and harmful desires that plunge men into ruin and destruction. ¹⁰For the love of money is a root of all kinds of evil. Some people, eager for money, have wandered from the faith and pierced themselves with many griefs.

Paul's Charge to Timothy

¹¹But you, man of God, flee from all this, and pursue righteousness, godliness, faith, love, endurance and gentleness. ¹²Fight the good fight of the faith. Take hold of the eternal life to which you were called when you made your good confession in the presence of many witnesses. ¹³In the sight of God, who gives life to everything, and of Christ Jesus, who while testifying before Pontius Pilate made the good confession, I charge you ¹⁴to keep this command without spot or blame until the appearing of our Lord Jesus Christ, ¹⁵which God will bring about in his own time—God, the blessed and only Ruler, the King of kings and Lord of lords, ¹⁶who alone is immortal and who lives in unapproachable light, whom no one has seen or can see. To him be honor and might forever. Amen.

¹⁷Command those who are rich in this present world not to be arrogant nor to put their hope in wealth, which is so uncertain, but to put their hope in God, who richly provides us with everything for our enjoyment. ¹⁸Command them to do good, to be rich in good deeds, and to be generous and willing to share. ¹⁹In this way they will lay up treasure for themselves as a firm foundation for the coming age, so that they may take hold of the life that is truly life.

²⁰Timothy, guard what has been entrusted to your care. Turn away from godless chatter and the opposing ideas of what is falsely called knowledge, ²¹which some have professed and in so doing have wandered from the faith.

Grace be with you.

2 TIMOTHY

1 Paul, an apostle of Christ Jesus by the will of God, according to the promise of life that is in Christ Jesus,

²To Timothy, my dear son:

Grace, mercy and peace from God the Father and Christ Jesus our Lord.

Encouragement to Be Faithful

³I thank God, whom I serve, as my forefathers did, with a clear conscience, as night and day I constantly remember you in my prayers. ⁴Recalling your tears, I long to see you, so that I may be filled with joy. ⁵I have been reminded of your sincere faith, which first lived in your grandmother Lois and in your mother Eunice and, I am persuaded, now lives in you also. ⁶For this reason I remind you to fan into flame the gift of God, which is in you through the laying on of my hands. ⁷For God did not give us a spirit of timidity, but a spirit of power, of love and of self-discipline.

⁸So do not be ashamed to testify about our Lord, or ashamed of me his prisoner. But join with me in suffering for the gospel, by the power of God, ⁹who has saved us and called us to a holy life—not because of anything we have done but because of his own purpose and grace. This grace was given us in Christ Jesus before the beginning of time, ¹⁰but it has now been revealed through the appearing of our Savior, Christ Jesus, who has destroyed death and has brought life and immortality to light through the gospel. ¹¹And of this gospel I was appointed a herald and an apostle and a teacher. ¹²That is why I am suffering as I am. Yet I am not ashamed, because I know whom I have believed, and am convinced that he is able to guard what I have entrusted to him for that day.

¹³What you heard from me, keep as the pattern of sound teaching, with faith and love in Christ Jesus. ¹⁴Guard the good deposit that was entrusted to you—guard it with the help of the Holy Spirit who lives in us.

¹⁵You know that everyone in the province of Asia has deserted me, including Phygelus and Hermogenes.

¹⁶May the Lord show mercy to the household of Onesiphorus, because he often refreshed me and was not ashamed of my chains. ¹⁷On the contrary, when he was in Rome, he searched hard for me until he found me. ¹⁸May the Lord grant that he will find mercy from the Lord on that day! You know very well in how many ways he helped me in Ephesus.

2 You then, my son, be strong in the grace that is in Christ Jesus. ²And the things you have heard me say in the presence of many witnesses entrust to reliable men who will also be qualified to teach others. ³Endure hardship with us like a good soldier of Christ Jesus. ⁴No one serving as a soldier gets involved in civilian affairs—he wants to please his commanding officer. ⁵Similarly, if anyone competes as an athlete, he does not receive the victor's crown unless he competes according to the rules. ⁶The hardworking farmer should be the first to receive a share of the crops. ⁷Reflect on what I am saying, for the Lord will give you insight into all this.

⁸Remember Jesus Christ, raised from the dead, descended from David. This is my gospel, ⁹for which I am suffering even to the point of being chained like a criminal. But God's word is not chained. ¹⁰Therefore I endure everything for the sake of the elect, that they too may obtain the salvation that is in Christ Jesus, with eternal glory.

¹¹Here is a trustworthy saying:

> If we died with him,
>   we will also live with him;
> [12]if we endure,
>   we will also reign with him.
> If we disown him,
>   he will also disown us;
> [13]if we are faithless,
>   he will remain faithful,
>   for he cannot disown himself.

A Workman Approved by God

[14]Keep reminding them of these things. Warn them before God against quarreling about words; it is of no value, and only ruins those who listen. [15]Do your best to present yourself to God as one approved, a workman who does not need to be ashamed and who correctly handles the word of truth. [16]Avoid godless chatter, because those who indulge in it will become more and more ungodly. [17]Their teaching will spread like gangrene. Among them are Hymenaeus and Philetus, [18]who have wandered away from the truth. They say that the resurrection has already taken place, and they destroy the faith of some. [19]Nevertheless, God's solid foundation stands firm, sealed with this inscription: "The Lord knows those who are his,"[a] and, "Everyone who confesses the name of the Lord must turn away from wickedness."

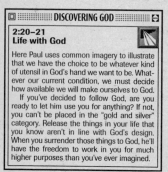

DISCOVERING GOD

2:20–21
Life with God

Here Paul uses common imagery to illustrate that we have the choice to be whatever kind of utensil in God's hand we want to be. Whatever our current condition, we must decide how available we will make ourselves to God.

If you've decided to follow God, are you ready to let him use you for anything? If not, you can't be placed in the "gold and silver" category. Release the things in your life that you know aren't in line with God's design. When you surrender those things to God, he'll have the freedom to work in you for much higher purposes than you've ever imagined.

[20]In a large house there are articles not only of gold and silver, but also of wood and clay; some are for noble purposes and some for ignoble. [21]If a man cleanses himself from the latter, he will be an instrument for noble purposes, made holy, useful to the Master and prepared to do any good work.

[22]Flee the evil desires of youth, and pursue righteousness, faith, love and peace, along with those who call on the Lord out of a pure heart. [23]Don't have anything to do with foolish and stupid arguments, because you know they produce quarrels. [24]And the Lord's servant must not quarrel; instead, he must be kind to everyone, able to teach, not resentful. [25]Those who oppose him he must gently instruct, in the hope that God will grant them repentance leading them to a knowledge of the truth, [26]and that they will come to their senses and escape from the trap of the devil, who has taken them captive to do his will.

Godlessness in the Last Days

3 But mark this: There will be terrible times in the last days. [2]People will be lovers of themselves, lovers of money, boastful, proud, abusive, disobedient to their parents, ungrateful, unholy, [3]without love, unforgiving, slanderous, without self-control, brutal, not lovers of the good, [4]treacherous, rash, conceited, lovers of pleasure rather than lovers of God— [5]having a form of godliness but denying its power. Have nothing to do with them.

[6]They are the kind who worm their way into homes and gain control over weak-willed women, who are loaded down with sins and are swayed by all kinds of evil desires,

[7]always learning but never able to acknowledge the truth. [8]Just as Jannes and Jambres opposed Moses, so also these men oppose the truth—men of depraved minds, who, as far as the faith is concerned, are rejected. [9]But they will not get very far because, as in the case of those men, their folly will be clear to everyone.

Paul's Charge to Timothy

[10]You, however, know all about my teaching, my way of life, my purpose, faith, patience, love, endurance, [11]persecutions, sufferings—what kinds of things happened to me in Antioch, Iconium and Lystra, the persecutions I endured. Yet the Lord rescued me from all of them. [12]In fact, everyone who wants to live a godly life in Christ Jesus will be persecuted, [13]while evil men and impostors will go from bad to worse, deceiving and being deceived. [14]But as for you, continue in what you have learned and have become convinced of, because you know those from whom you learned it, [15]and how from infancy you have known the holy Scriptures, which are able to make you wise for salvation through faith in Christ Jesus. [16]All Scripture is God-breathed and is useful for teaching, rebuking, correcting and training in righteousness, [17]so that the man of God may be thoroughly equipped for every good work.

4 In the presence of God and of Christ Jesus, who will judge the living and the dead, and in view of his appearing and his kingdom, I give you this charge: [2]Preach the Word; be prepared in season and out of season; correct, rebuke and encourage—with great patience and careful instruction. [3]For the time will come when men will not put up with sound doctrine. Instead, to suit their own desires, they will gather around them a great number of teachers to say what their itching ears want to hear. [4]They will turn their ears away from the truth and turn aside to myths. [5]But you, keep your head in all situations, endure hardship, do the work of an evangelist, discharge all the duties of your ministry.

[6]For I am already being poured out like a drink offering, and the time has come for my departure. [7]I have fought the good fight, I have finished the race, I have kept the faith. [8]Now there is in store for me the crown of righteousness, which the Lord, the righteous Judge, will award to me on that day—and not only to me, but also to all who have longed for his appearing.

▦ MANAGING RESOURCES ⬙

4:7–8
Time

We all want our lives to count for something significant. Like a runner, we want to find a trophy at the finish line—something that leaves a mark on this world and that gives our lives meaning.

The apostle Paul was in a Roman prison facing death when he gave Timothy this honest appraisal of his own life and ministry. Like a prize-fighter, he had made it to the last round. Like a distance runner, he was right at the finish line and still in full stride. He expressed great joy in knowing that he had lived his life without compromising his faith in God.

One thing God wants from each of us is faithfulness. He wants us to remain true to him. If you're a seeker, such a life begins by taking the first step: Trusting Christ to forgive you and give you direction. Once you do that, Christ will come to live in you. Through his Spirit, Jesus will enable you to faithfully complete your life's race.

A life marked by faithfully walking with God is a life that truly counts. Whatever else you think you'll be able to look back on at the end of your life—interests, accomplishments, acquisitions—nothing will compare with the satisfaction of knowing that you invested your life in things that really last. Better to face God confident that you lived your life *his* way than any other way.

Personal Remarks

[9]Do your best to come to me quickly, [10]for Demas, because he loved this world, has deserted me and has gone to Thessalonica. Crescens has gone to Galatia, and Titus to Dalmatia. [11]Only Luke is with me. Get Mark and bring him with you, because he is helpful

to me in my ministry. 12I sent Tychicus to Ephesus. 13When you come, bring the cloak that I left with Carpus at Troas, and my scrolls, especially the parchments.

14Alexander the metalworker did me a great deal of harm. The Lord will repay him for what he has done. 15You too should be on your guard against him, because he strongly opposed our message.

16At my first defense, no one came to my support, but everyone deserted me. May it not be held against them. 17But the Lord stood at my side and gave me strength, so that through me the message might be fully proclaimed and all the Gentiles might hear it. And I was delivered from the lion's mouth. 18The Lord will rescue me from every evil attack and will bring me safely to his heavenly kingdom. To him be glory for ever and ever. Amen.

Final Greetings

19Greet Priscilla[a] and Aquila and the household of Onesiphorus. 20Erastus stayed in Corinth, and I left Trophimus sick in Miletus. 21Do your best to get here before winter. Eubulus greets you, and so do Pudens, Linus, Claudia and all the brothers.

22The Lord be with your spirit. Grace be with you.

---

a 19 Greek Prisca, a variant of Priscilla

TITUS

1 Paul, a servant of God and an apostle of Jesus Christ for the faith of God's elect and the knowledge of the truth that leads to godliness— ²a faith and knowledge resting on the hope of eternal life, which God, who does not lie, promised before the beginning of time, ³and at his appointed season he brought his word to light through the preaching entrusted to me by the command of God our Savior,

⁴To Titus, my true son in our common faith:

Grace and peace from God the Father and Christ Jesus our Savior.

Titus' Task on Crete

⁵The reason I left you in Crete was that you might straighten out what was left unfinished and appoint*ᵃ* elders in every town, as I directed you. ⁶An elder must be blameless, the husband of but one wife, a man whose children believe and are not open to the charge of being wild and disobedient. ⁷Since an overseer*ᵇ* is entrusted with God's work, he must be blameless—not overbearing, not quick-tempered, not given to drunkenness, not violent, not pursuing dishonest gain. ⁸Rather he must be hospitable, one who loves what is good, who is self-controlled, upright, holy and disciplined. ⁹He must hold firmly to the trustworthy message as it has been taught, so that he can encourage others by sound doctrine and refute those who oppose it.

¹⁰For there are many rebellious people, mere talkers and deceivers, especially those of the circumcision group. ¹¹They must be silenced, because they are ruining whole households by teaching things they ought not to teach—and that for the sake of dishonest gain. ¹²Even one of their own prophets has said, "Cretans are always liars, evil brutes, lazy gluttons." ¹³This testimony is true. Therefore, rebuke them sharply, so that they will be sound in the faith ¹⁴and will pay no attention to Jewish myths or to the commands of those who reject the truth. ¹⁵To the pure, all things are pure, but to those who are corrupted and do not believe, nothing is pure. In fact, both their minds and consciences are corrupted. ¹⁶They claim to know God, but by their actions they deny him. They are detestable, disobedient and unfit for doing anything good.

DISCOVERING GOD

1:11
Spiritual Fraud

False teachers are dangerous. That's why Paul wrote that they need to be "silenced," or more literally, "muzzled."

The false teachers that Paul spoke about here were people who insisted that new Christians not only accept Christ, but also keep the Jewish ceremonial law. These people were disrupting entire households and leading people astray. Their motivation for doing so is clear from this verse.

The best defense against false teachers is a thorough knowledge of the truth. If you're a seeker, examine the Bible carefully. It contains the information you'll need to know to distinguish between the unstable teaching of deceptive individuals and the sure foundation of God's truth.

ᵃ5 Or *ordain*   *ᵇ7* Traditionally *bishop*

What Must Be Taught to Various Groups

2 You must teach what is in accord with sound doctrine. ²Teach the older men to be temperate, worthy of respect, self-controlled, and sound in faith, in love and in endurance.

³Likewise, teach the older women to be reverent in the way they live, not to be slanderers or addicted to much wine, but to teach what is good. ⁴Then they can train the younger women to love their husbands and children, ⁵to be self-controlled and pure, to be busy at home, to be kind, and to be subject to their husbands, so that no one will malign the word of God.

⁶Similarly, encourage the young men to be self-controlled. ⁷In everything set them an example by doing what is good. In your teaching show integrity, seriousness ⁸and soundness of speech that cannot be condemned, so that those who oppose you may be ashamed because they have nothing bad to say about us.

⁹Teach slaves to be subject to their masters in everything, to try to please them, not to talk back to them, ¹⁰and not to steal from them, but to show that they can be fully trusted, so that in every way they will make the teaching about God our Savior attractive.

¹¹For the grace of God that brings salvation has appeared to all men. ¹²It teaches us to say "No" to ungodliness and worldly passions, and to live self-controlled, upright and godly lives in this present age, ¹³while we wait for the blessed hope—the glorious appearing of our great God and Savior, Jesus Christ, ¹⁴who gave himself for us to redeem us from all wickedness and to purify for himself a people that are his very own, eager to do what is good.

¹⁵These, then, are the things you should teach. Encourage and rebuke with all authority. Do not let anyone despise you.

Doing What Is Good

3 Remind the people to be subject to rulers and authorities, to be obedient, to be ready to do whatever is good, ²to slander no one, to be peaceable and considerate, and to show true humility toward all men.

³At one time we too were foolish, disobedient, deceived and enslaved by all kinds of passions and pleasures. We lived in malice and envy, being hated and hating one another. ⁴But when the kindness and love of God our Savior appeared, ⁵he saved us, not because of righteous things we had done, but because of his mercy. He saved us through the washing of rebirth and renewal by the Holy Spirit, ⁶whom he poured out on us generously through Jesus Christ our Savior, ⁷so that, having been justified by his grace, we might become heirs having the hope of eternal life. ⁸This is a trustworthy saying. And I want you to stress these things, so

---

◻ DISCOVERING GOD ◳

**3:3–7
Life with God**

She sat alone in the orphanage—no parents, no siblings. She was without connection in the world, powerless and headed for a life of anonymity.

Then one day two visitors came to the orphanage. They were financially prepared and eager to provide a safe and nurturing environment in which a child could grow. "That's the one," the wife said, looking at the little girl. The father scooped up the child and said, "Little one, you are now our daughter. Soon you will come to live in the place we've been preparing for you."

What did the orphan do to deserve the kindness of that couple? Nothing. Why did they choose her? We don't know. But they did, and it had nothing to do with any action on her part. They simply had love to give, and set their affections on this child.

Do you know that's how God feels about you? You are like that orphan. God comes to you today with the invitation to grow up in his home, live with his guidance, and enjoy his provisions. That's what these verses mean when they say that you can become God's "heir." You can be adopted into God's family simply by being "reborn" through the power of the Holy Spirit. It isn't necessarily an emotional experience, but it's one that has eternal significance.

God's arms are open, and he's saying, "Come live with me." Why not accept his invitation today?

that those who have trusted in God may be careful to devote themselves to doing what is good. These things are excellent and profitable for everyone.

⁹But avoid foolish controversies and genealogies and arguments and quarrels about the law, because these are unprofitable and useless. ¹⁰Warn a divisive person once, and then warn him a second time. After that, have nothing to do with him. ¹¹You may be sure that such a man is warped and sinful; he is self-condemned.

Final Remarks

¹²As soon as I send Artemas or Tychicus to you, do your best to come to me at Nicopolis, because I have decided to winter there. ¹³Do everything you can to help Zenas the lawyer and Apollos on their way and see that they have everything they need. ¹⁴Our people must learn to devote themselves to doing what is good, in order that they may provide for daily necessities and not live unproductive lives.

¹⁵Everyone with me sends you greetings. Greet those who love us in the faith.

Grace be with you all.

PHILEMON

¹Paul, a prisoner of Christ Jesus, and Timothy our brother,

To Philemon our dear friend and fellow worker, ²to Apphia our sister, to Archippus our fellow soldier and to the church that meets in your home:

³Grace to you and peace from God our Father and the Lord Jesus Christ.

Thanksgiving and Prayer

⁴I always thank my God as I remember you in my prayers, ⁵because I hear about your faith in the Lord Jesus and your love for all the saints. ⁶I pray that you may be active in sharing your faith, so that you will have a full understanding of every good thing we have in Christ. ⁷Your love has given me great joy and encouragement, because you, brother, have refreshed the hearts of the saints.

Paul's Plea for Onesimus

⁸Therefore, although in Christ I could be bold and order you to do what you ought to do, ⁹yet I appeal to you on the basis of love. I then, as Paul—an old man and now also a prisoner of Christ Jesus— ¹⁰I appeal to you for my son Onesimus,^a who became my son while I was in chains. ¹¹Formerly he was useless to you, but now he has become useful both to you and to me.

¹²I am sending him—who is my very heart—back to you. ¹³I would have liked to keep him with me so that he could take your place in helping me while I am in chains for the gospel. ¹⁴But I did not want to do anything without your consent, so that any favor you do will be spontaneous and not forced. ¹⁵Perhaps the reason he was separated from you for a little while was that you might have him back for good— ¹⁶no longer as a slave, but better than a slave, as a dear brother. He is very dear to me but even dearer to you, both as a man and as a brother in the Lord.

¹⁷So if you consider me a partner, welcome him as you would welcome me. ¹⁸If he has done you any wrong or owes you

---

▣ ▥▥▥▥▥ DISCOVERING GOD ▥▥▥▥▥ ⬀

15–16
Life with God

Slavery was at one time the most divisive issue in American politics. It took a civil war to finally eradicate this evil from our nation.

While some Christians used the Bible to justify their pro-slavery stance (even the devil knows how to quote from this book!), the overwhelming majority of anti-slavery activists found their inspiration to fight slavery by what they read in the Bible.

This short letter deals with that very issue. Here Paul returns a runaway slave to his friend Philemon. But something wonderful has happened to that slave since his escape—he has become a Christ-follower. Due to this transformation Paul gently admonishes Philemon to accept this man back as a brother in Christ, not as an escaped slave.

Don't miss the radical nature of Paul's request. In Paul's culture a slave was considered property, and now Paul asks Philemon to "welcome him as you would welcome me" (verse 17). Paul offers to repay any losses (verse 18), and expresses his confidence that Philemon will do what he asks (verse 21).

Wherever true Christianity goes, it champions the rights and needs of disadvantaged individuals. Slaves, children, women, minorities—even the unborn—all people are precious in God's sight and are to be valued and treated with justice and fairness. That's one of the Bible's main themes, and one of the main goals of a true Christ-follower.

---

^a 10 *Onesimus* means *useful.*

nything, charge it to me. [19]I, Paul, am writing this with my own hand. I will pay it ack—not to mention that you owe me your very self. [20]I do wish, brother, that I may ave some benefit from you in the Lord; refresh my heart in Christ. [21]Confident of your bedience, I write to you, knowing that you will do even more than I ask.

[22]And one thing more: Prepare a guest room for me, because I hope to be restored to ou in answer to your prayers.

[23]Epaphras, my fellow prisoner in Christ Jesus, sends you greetings. [24]And so do Mark, ristarchus, Demas and Luke, my fellow workers.

[25]The grace of the Lord Jesus Christ be with your spirit.

HEBREWS

Introduction

THE BOTTOM LINE

What is your definition of "the good life?" Perhaps it involves more education, more money, a bigger house or a newer car. There's no doubt that these things *can* provide you with a better way of life. But if you would rather have *a way to a better life,* Christianity has the only answer. The book of Hebrews forcefully challenges its readers to compare a "religious" experience based on the old Jewish traditions and the new life that Jesus Christ offers. Through that comparison, the superiority of following Jesus emerges unequaled. That challenge is now presented to you. Get ready to see how good life can be when Jesus is allowed to take his rightful place in your life.

CENTRAL IDEAS

- Jesus Christ sacrificed his life so that we could be forgiven of our wrongdoings.
- Jesus Christ has no equal—he is superior to all.
- We have examples of others who have lived by faith that can inspire us.
- Willfully rejecting the teachings of Christ is an act that has dire consequences.

OUTLINE

1 God's new revelation in Christ is superior to anything (1:1–4)
2 Christ is superior to Old Testament religious leaders (1:5–7:28)
3 Christ's sacrificial work explained (chs. 8–10)
4 Encouragement for believers to stay strong in their faith (chs. 11–12)
5 Conclusion (ch. 13)

TITLE

This letter is named after an unknown group of Jewish converts to Christianity—the Hebrews whom the author addressed.

AUTHOR AND READERS

An unknown author penned this book to first-century seekers and believers. In the process of laying out his argument, the author reviewed in detail how Jesus fulfills Jewish prophecy and refuted the need for the old Jewish worship practices. For that reason, chapters 5 through 10 contain many details familiar to the people addressed but less so to modern readers; still, these chapters contain truths that make this book well worth reading.

Explorer John Wesley Powell, a self-taught geologist and naturalist, led a nine-person climbing expedition along the cliffs of the Colorado River and its tributaries.

As Powell inched along a treacherous rock face 800 feet above the Green River in Utah, he saw a promising foothold, made a short leap—and found himself trapped. He was "rimmed"—he clutched the cliff wall, but was unable to move without risking a fall.

Powell shouted to his companion, George Bradley, who was able to climb to a ledge above him. Still too far away, Bradley searched for a branch to let down. When he couldn't find one he tried the case of the barometer they carried for scientific observations. But the case was too thick for Powell to grasp securely.

By this time Powell's legs were close to giving out. But Bradley had an idea. He quickly stripped off his long underwear and dangled one of the legs down toward Powell.

The risk of grabbing the article of clothing was made even more challenging by the fact that Powell clung to the cliff *with his one and only arm.* He was an amputee, wounded in the Battle of Shiloh during the Civil War. With only one arm, Powell would have to completely let go of the rock to grab the waving cloth. And there was nothing else to secure him if he missed his target.

Powell let go of the rock. As he started to fall, he lunged for the cloth . . .

With his heart in his throat, Powell let go of the rock. As he started to fall, he lunged for the cloth—and snagged it. The material held, and Powell made it to safety.

Powell went on to chart the Grand Canyon and later to head both the U.S. Geological Survey and the Bureau of American Ethnology. In his day he was America's most important scientific administrator.*

Had he not made the decision to let go of one thing in order to take hold of another, Powell would have fallen to his death. In a similar way, God asks you to let go of whatever you're holding on to for security—such as wealth, education, or ability—and put your trust in him. Taking such a step requires risk, but without doing so you'll never be able to experience God's deliverance. And you'll never learn what he can do in and through you.

Biblical faith is all about trust. It's simple, but it's not easy. Turn to Hebrews chapter 11, verses 1–2 (page 1596), for the clearest definition of faith found in the Bible. These words were a timely reminder to the original readers of this book. In the face of extreme adversity, these Jewish believers were tempted to give up on God. The author of Hebrews urged them to stand strong in their relationship with God, citing their ancestors as examples of a faith that would carry them through even the most difficult of circumstances. The same can be true for us today.

* *Strange Stories, Amazing Facts of America's Past,* Jim Dwyer, ed. (Pleasantville, N.Y.: The Reader's Digest Association, 1989), p. 288.

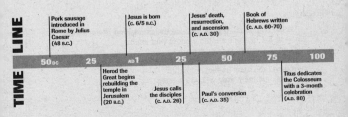

HEBREWS

The Son Superior to Angels

1 In the past God spoke to our forefathers through the prophets at many times and in various ways, ²but in these last days he has spoken to us by his Son, whom he appointed heir of all things, and through whom he made the universe. ³The Son is the radiance of God's glory and the exact representation of his being, sustaining all things by his powerful word. After he had provided purification for sins, he sat down at the right hand of the Majesty in heaven. ⁴So he became as much superior to the angels as the name he has inherited is superior to theirs.

⁵For to which of the angels did God ever say,

> "You are my Son;
> today I have become your
> Father*ᵃ*"*ᵇ*?

Or again,

> "I will be his Father,
> and he will be my Son"*ᶜ*?

⁶And again, when God brings his firstborn into the world, he says,

> "Let all God's angels worship him."*ᵈ*

⁷In speaking of the angels he says,

> "He makes his angels winds,
> his servants flames of fire."*ᵉ*

◫ ▒▒▒▒▒ DISCOVERING GOD ▒▒▒▒▒ ⮌

1:1–8
Jesus, the God-Man

These verses spell out the theme of the whole book of Hebrews. In these first few verses, the unnamed writer wants us to know that Jesus is superior to any other spiritual power or being. He echoes the words of other Biblical writers who describe Christ as being equal with God (see John chapter 1, verse 1 [page 1382]) and the Creator and Sustainer of this world (see Colossians chapter 1, verses 16–17 [page 1552]).

Whatever any religion can offer, Jesus offers more. That's not just the message of the book of Hebrews, that's the message of the entire New Testament, as well as of the prophecies of the Old Testament.

---

⁸But about the Son he says,

> "Your throne, O God, will last for ever and ever,
> and righteousness will be the scepter of your kingdom.
> ⁹You have loved righteousness and hated wickedness;
> therefore God, your God, has set you above your companions
> by anointing you with the oil of joy."*ᶠ*

¹⁰He also says,

> "In the beginning, O Lord, you laid the foundations of the earth,
> and the heavens are the work of your hands.
> ¹¹They will perish, but you remain;
> they will all wear out like a garment.
> ¹²You will roll them up like a robe;
> like a garment they will be changed.

ᵃ5 Or *have begotten you*   *ᵇ5* Psalm 2:7   *ᶜ5* 2 Samuel 7:14; 1 Chron. 17:13   *ᵈ6* Deut. 32:43 (see Dead Sea Scrolls and Septuagint)   *ᵉ7* Psalm 104:4   *ᶠ9* Psalm 45:6,7

> But you remain the same,
> and your years will never end."[a]

To which of the angels did God ever say,

> "Sit at my right hand
> until I make your enemies
> a footstool for your feet"[b]?

Are not all angels ministering spirits sent to serve those who will inherit salvation?

Warning to Pay Attention

2 We must pay more careful attention, therefore, to what we have heard, so that we do not drift away. [2]For if the message spoken by angels was binding, and every violation and disobedience received its just punishment, [3]how shall we escape if we ignore such a great salvation? This salvation, which was first announced by the Lord, was confirmed to us by those who heard him. [4]God also testified to it by signs, wonders and various miracles, and gifts of the Holy Spirit distributed according to his will.

Jesus Made Like His Brothers

[5]It is not to angels that he has subjected the world to come, about which we are speaking. [6]But there is a place where someone has testified:

> "What is man that you are mindful of him,
> the son of man that you care for him?
> [7]You made him a little[c] lower than the angels;
> you crowned him with glory and honor
> [8]   and put everything under his feet."[d]

In putting everything under him, God left nothing that is not subject to him. Yet at present we do not see everything subject to him. [9]But we see Jesus, who was made a little lower than the angels, now crowned with glory and honor because he suffered death, so that by the grace of God he might taste death for everyone.

[10]In bringing many sons to glory, it was fitting that God, for whom and through whom everything exists, should make the author of their salvation perfect through suffering. [11]Both the one who makes men holy and those who are made holy are of the same family. So Jesus is not ashamed to call them brothers. [12]He says,

> "I will declare your name to my brothers;
> in the presence of the congregation I will sing your praises."[e]

And again,

> "I will put my trust in him."[f]

And again he says,

> "Here am I, and the children God has given me."[g]

[14]Since the children have flesh and blood, he too shared in their humanity so that by his death he might destroy him who holds the power of death—that is, the devil— [15]and free those who all their lives were held in slavery by their fear of death. [16]For surely it is not angels he helps, but Abraham's descendants. [17]For this reason he had to be made like his brothers in every way, in order that he might become a merciful and faithful high priest in service to God, and that he might make atonement for[h] the sins of the people.

---

a 12 Psalm 102:25-27   *b* 13 Psalm 110:1   *c* 7 Or *him for a little while; also in verse 9*   *d* 8 Psalm 8:4-6
e 12 Psalm 22:22   *f* 13 Isaiah 8:17   *g* 13 Isaiah 8:18   *h* 17 Or *and that he might turn aside God's wrath, taking away*

[18]Because he himself suffered when he was tempted, he is able to help those who a[r]e being tempted.

Jesus Greater Than Moses

3 Therefore, holy brothers, who share in the heavenly calling, fix you[r] thoughts on Jesus, the apostle and high priest whom we confess. [2]He wa[s] faithful to the one who appointed him, just as Moses was faithful in all God's hous[e]. [3]Jesus has been found worthy of greater honor than Moses, just as the builder of a house has greater honor than the house i[t]self. [4]For every house is built by someone, but God is the builder of everything. [5]Mo[s]es was faithful as a servant in all God's house, testifying to what would be said i[n] the future. [6]But Christ is faithful as a so[n] over God's house. And we are his house, we hold on to our courage and the hope [of] which we boast.

> **DISCOVERING GOD**
>
> **2:18**
> **Jesus, the God-Man**
>
> Jesus is eminently qualified to become our helper when we're tempted. Why? Because when he walked the earth he was subjected to the same kinds of temptations that we experience every day. As a result, Jesus can identify with us at every level.
>
> The next time you're struggling to take the right path, think of Jesus struggling there with you. Listen for his words of encouragement and direction—not audibly, of course, but in your spirit as you remember his teachings in the Bible.

Warning Against Unbelief

[7]So, as the Holy Spirit says:

> "Today, if you hear his voice,
> [8] do not harden your hearts
>   as you did in the rebellion,
>   during the time of testing in the dese[rt,]
> [9]where your fathers tested and tried me
>   and for forty years saw what I did.
> [10]That is why I was angry with that generation,
>   and I said, 'Their hearts are always going
>   astray,
>   and they have not known my ways.'
> [11]So I declared on oath in my anger,
>   'They shall never enter my rest.' " [a]

[12]See to it, brothers, that none of you has a sinful, unbelieving heart that turns awa[y] from the living God. [13]But encourage one another daily, as long as it is called Toda[y,] so that none of you may be hardened by sin's deceitfulness. [14]We have come to sha[re] in Christ if we hold firmly till the end the confidence we had at first. [15]As has just bee[n] said:

> "Today, if you hear his voice,
>   do not harden your hearts
>   as you did in the rebellion." [b]

[16]Who were they who heard and rebelled? Were they not all those Moses led out [of] Egypt? [17]And with whom was he angry for forty years? Was it not with those wh[o] sinned, whose bodies fell in the desert? [18]And to whom did God swear that they wou[ld] never enter his rest if not to those who disobeyed[c]? [19]So we see that they were n[ot] able to enter, because of their unbelief.

[a]11 Psalm 95:7-11   [b]15 Psalm 95:7,8   [c]18 Or disbelieved

A Sabbath-Rest for the People of God

4 Therefore, since the promise of entering his rest still stands, let us be careful that none of you be found to have fallen short of it. ²For we also have had the gospel preached to us, just as they did; but the message they heard was of no value to them, because those who heard did not combine it with faith.ᵃ ³Now we who have believed enter that rest, just as God has said,

> "So I declared on oath in my anger,
> 'They shall never enter my rest.'"ᵇ

And yet his work has been finished since the creation of the world. ⁴For somewhere he has spoken about the seventh day in these words: "And on the seventh day God rested from all his work."ᶜ ⁵And again in the passage above he says, "They shall never enter my rest."

⁶It still remains that some will enter that rest, and those who formerly had the gospel preached to them did not go in, because of their disobedience. ⁷Therefore God again set a certain day, calling it Today, when a long time later he spoke through David, as was said before:

> "Today, if you hear his voice,
> do not harden your hearts."ᵈ

⁸For if Joshua had given them rest, God would not have spoken later about another day. ⁹There remains, then, a Sabbath-rest for the people of God; ¹⁰for anyone who enters God's rest also rests from his own work, just as God did from his. ¹¹Let us, therefore, make every effort to enter that rest, so that no one will fall by following their example of disobedience.

¹²For the word of God is living and active. Sharper than any double-edged sword, it penetrates even to dividing soul and spirit, joints and marrow; it judges the thoughts and attitudes of the heart. ¹³Nothing in all creation is hidden from God's sight. Everything is uncovered and laid bare before the eyes of him to whom we must give account.

Jesus the Great High Priest

¹⁴Therefore, since we have a great high priest who has gone through the heavens,ᵉ Jesus the Son of God, let us hold firmly to the faith we profess. ¹⁵For we do not have a high priest who is unable to sympathize with our weaknesses, but we have one who has been tempted in every way, just as we are—yet was without sin. ¹⁶Let us then approach the throne of grace with confidence, so that we may receive mercy and find grace to help us in our time of need.

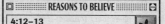

REASONS TO BELIEVE

4:12–13
The Amazing Bible

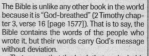

The Bible is unlike any other book in the world because it is "God-breathed" (2 Timothy chapter 3, verse 16 [page 1577]). That is to say, the Bible contains the words of the people who wrote it, but their words carry God's message without deviation.

That means that the book that you're holding is backed by the power of the Creator of the universe. The author of Hebrews compares God's word to a sword that cuts and pierces deeply into our souls. It allows individuals to see inside themselves and exposes all the hidden intentions of the human heart. In so doing, the writer implies that the Bible's activity and God's activity are in effect the same.

As you read and study this book you'll discover the razor edge of God's truth. Sometimes you'll find out more about yourself than you'd like to know. You may even be tempted to pull back and stop reading, but don't do it! Open yourself to what God shows you in these pages, and then act on what you learn. It may not be easy, but the benefits of that discipline will be immeasurable.

ᵃ *2 Many manuscripts because they did not share in the faith of those who obeyed*   ᵇ *3 Psalm 95:11; also in verse 5*
ᶜ *4 Gen. 2:2*   ᵈ *7 Psalm 95:7,8*   ᵉ *14 Or gone into heaven*

5 Every high priest is selected from among men and is appointed to represent them in matters related to God, to offer gifts and sacrifices for sins. ²He is able to deal gently with those who are ignorant and are going astray, since he himself is subject to weakness. ³This is why he has to offer sacrifices for his own sins, as well as for the sins of the people.

⁴No one takes this honor upon himself; he must be called by God, just as Aaron was. ⁵So Christ also did not take upon himself the glory of becoming a high priest. But God said to him,

> "You are my Son;
>   today I have become your Father.ᵃ"ᵇ

⁶And he says in another place,

> "You are a priest forever,
>   in the order of Melchizedek."ᶜ

⁷During the days of Jesus' life on earth, he offered up prayers and petitions with loud cries and tears to the one who could save him from death, and he was heard because of his reverent submission. ⁸Although he was a son, he learned obedience from what he suffered ⁹and, once made perfect, he became the source of eternal salvation for all who obey him ¹⁰and was designated by God to be high priest in the order of Melchizedek.

Warning Against Falling Away

¹¹We have much to say about this, but it is hard to explain because you are slow to learn. ¹²In fact, though by this time you ought to be teachers, you need someone to teach you the elementary truths of God's word all over again. You need milk, not solid food! ¹³Anyone who lives on milk, being still an infant, is not acquainted with the teaching about righteousness. ¹⁴But solid food is for the mature, who by constant use have trained themselves to distinguish good from evil.

6 Therefore let us leave the elementary teachings about Christ and go on to maturity, not laying again the foundation of repentance from acts that lead to death,ᵈ and of faith in God, ²instruction about baptisms, the laying on of hands, the resurrection of the dead, and eternal judgment. ³And God permitting, we will do so.

⁴It is impossible for those who have once been enlightened, who have tasted the heavenly gift, who have shared in the Holy Spirit, ⁵who have tasted the goodness of the word of God and the powers of the coming age, ⁶if they fall away, to be brought back to repentance, becauseᵉ to their loss they are crucifying the Son of God all over again and subjecting him to public disgrace.

⁷Land that drinks in the rain often falling on it and that produces a crop useful to those for whom it is farmed receives the blessing of God. ⁸But land that produces thorns and thistles is worthless and is in danger of being cursed. In the end it will be burned.

⁹Even though we speak like this, dear friends, we are confident of better things in your case—things that accompany salvation. ¹⁰God is not unjust; he will not forget your work and the love you have shown him as you have helped his people and continue to help them. ¹¹We want each of you to show this same diligence to the very end, in order to make your hope sure. ¹²We do not want you to become lazy, but to imitate those who through faith and patience inherit what has been promised.

The Certainty of God's Promise

¹³When God made his promise to Abraham, since there was no one greater for him to swear by, he swore by himself, ¹⁴saying, "I will surely bless you and give you many descendants."ᶠ ¹⁵And so after waiting patiently, Abraham received what was promised.

ᵃ5 Or have begotten you   ᵇ5 Psalm 2:7   ᶜ6 Psalm 110:4   ᵈ1 Or from useless rituals   ᵉ6 Or repentance
while   ᶠ14 Gen. 22:17

¹⁶Men swear by someone greater than themselves, and the oath confirms what is said and puts an end to all argument. ¹⁷Because God wanted to make the unchanging nature of his purpose very clear to the heirs of what was promised, he confirmed it with an oath. ¹⁸God did this so that, by two unchangeable things in which it is impossible for God to lie, we who have fled to take hold of the hope offered to us may be greatly encouraged. ¹⁹We have this hope as an anchor for the soul, firm and secure. It enters the inner sanctuary behind the curtain, ²⁰where Jesus, who went before us, has entered on our behalf. He has become a high priest forever, in the order of Melchizedek.

Melchizedek the Priest

7 This Melchizedek was king of Salem and priest of God Most High. He met Abraham returning from the defeat of the kings and blessed him, ²and Abraham gave him a tenth of everything. First, his name means "king of righteousness"; then also, "king of Salem" means "king of peace." ³Without father or mother, without genealogy, without beginning of days or end of life, like the Son of God he remains a priest forever.

⁴Just think how great he was: Even the patriarch Abraham gave him a tenth of the plunder! ⁵Now the law requires the descendants of Levi who become priests to collect a tenth from the people—that is, their brothers—even though their brothers are descended from Abraham. ⁶This man, however, did not trace his descent from Levi, yet he collected a tenth from Abraham and blessed him who had the promises. ⁷And without doubt the lesser person is blessed by the greater. ⁸In the one case, the tenth is collected by men who die; but in the other case, by him who is declared to be living. ⁹One might even say that Levi, who collects the tenth, paid the tenth through Abraham, ¹⁰because when Melchizedek met Abraham, Levi was still in the body of his ancestor.

Jesus Like Melchizedek

¹¹If perfection could have been attained through the Levitical priesthood (for on the basis of it the law was given to the people), why was there still need for another priest to come—one in the order of Melchizedek, not in the order of Aaron? ¹²For when there is a change of the priesthood, there must also be a change of the law. ¹³He of whom these things are said belonged to a different tribe, and no one from that tribe has ever served at the altar. ¹⁴For it is clear that our Lord descended from Judah, and in regard to that tribe Moses said nothing about priests. ¹⁵And what we have said is even more clear if another priest like Melchizedek appears, ¹⁶one who has become a priest not on the basis of a regulation as to his ancestry but on the basis of the power of an indestructible life. ¹⁷For it is declared:

> "You are a priest forever,
>   in the order of Melchizedek."^a

¹⁸The former regulation is set aside because it was weak and useless ¹⁹(for the law made nothing perfect), and a better hope is introduced, by which we draw near to God. ²⁰And it was not without an oath! Others became priests without any oath, ²¹but he became a priest with an oath when God said to him:

> "The Lord has sworn
>   and will not change his mind:
> 'You are a priest forever.'"^a

²²Because of this oath, Jesus has become the guarantee of a better covenant. ²³Now there have been many of those priests, since death prevented them from continuing in office; ²⁴but because Jesus lives forever, he has a permanent priesthood.

7,21 Psalm 110:4

²⁵Therefore he is able to save completely[a] those who come to God through him, becaus(e) he always lives to intercede for them.

²⁶Such a high priest meets our need—one who is holy, blameless, pure, set apart from sinners, exalted above the heavens. ²⁷Unlike the other high priests, he does not need t(o) offer sacrifices day after day, first for his own sins, and then for the sins of the people. H(e) sacrificed for their sins once for all when he offered himself. ²⁸For the law appoints a(s) high priests men who are weak; but the oath, which came after the law, appointed th(e) Son, who has been made perfect forever.

The High Priest of a New Covenant

8 The point of what we are saying is this: We do have such a high priest, wh(o) sat down at the right hand of the throne of the Majesty in heaven, ²and wh(o) serves in the sanctuary, the true tabernacle set up by the Lord, not by man.

³Every high priest is appointed to offer both gifts and sacrifices, and so it was neces(sary) for this one also to have something to offer. ⁴If he were on earth, he would not be a priest, for there are already men who offer the gifts prescribed by the law. ⁵They serve a(t) a sanctuary that is a copy and shadow of what is in heaven. This is why Moses wa(s) warned when he was about to build the tabernacle: "See to it that you make everything according to the pattern shown you on the mountain."[b] ⁶But the ministry Jesus ha(s) received is as superior to theirs as the covenant of which he is mediator is superior to th(e) old one, and it is founded on better promises.

⁷For if there had been nothing wrong with that first covenant, no place would have been sought for another. ⁸But God found fault with the people and said[c]:

> "The time is coming, declares the Lord,
>   when I will make a new covenant
> with the house of Israel
>   and with the house of Judah.
> ⁹It will not be like the covenant
>   I made with their forefathers
> when I took them by the hand
>   to lead them out of Egypt,
> because they did not remain faithful to my covenant,
>   and I turned away from them,
>
>   declares the Lord.
> ¹⁰This is the covenant I will make with the house of Israel
>   after that time, declares the Lord.
> I will put my laws in their minds
>   and write them on their hearts.
> I will be their God,
>   and they will be my people.
> ¹¹No longer will a man teach his neighbor,
>   or a man his brother, saying, 'Know the Lord,'
> because they will all know me,
>   from the least of them to the greatest.
> ¹²For I will forgive their wickedness
>   and will remember their sins no more."[d]

¹³By calling this covenant "new," he has made the first one obsolete; and what is obsolete and aging will soon disappear.

---

[a]25 Or *forever*   [b]5 Exodus 25:40   [c]8 Some manuscripts may be translated *fault and said to the people.*
[d]12 Jer. 31:31-34

Worship in the Earthly Tabernacle

9 Now the first covenant had regulations for worship and also an earthly sanctuary. ²A tabernacle was set up. In its first room were the lampstand, the table and the consecrated bread; this was called the Holy Place. ³Behind the second curtain was a room called the Most Holy Place, ⁴which had the golden altar of incense and the gold-covered ark of the covenant. This ark contained the gold jar of manna, Aaron's staff that had budded, and the stone tablets of the covenant. ⁵Above the ark were the cherubim of the Glory, overshadowing the atonement cover.ᵃ But we cannot discuss these things in detail now.

⁶When everything had been arranged like this, the priests entered regularly into the outer room to carry on their ministry. ⁷But only the high priest entered the inner room, and that only once a year, and never without blood, which he offered for himself and for the sins the people had committed in ignorance. ⁸The Holy Spirit was showing by this that the way into the Most Holy Place had not yet been disclosed as long as the first tabernacle was still standing. ⁹This is an illustration for the present time, indicating that the gifts and sacrifices being offered were not able to clear the conscience of the worshiper. ¹⁰They are only a matter of food and drink and various ceremonial washings—external regulations applying until the time of the new order.

The Blood of Christ

¹¹When Christ came as high priest of the good things that are already here,ᵇ he went through the greater and more perfect tabernacle that is not man-made, that is to say, not a part of this creation. ¹²He did not enter by means of the blood of goats and calves; but he entered the Most Holy Place once for all by his own blood, having obtained eternal redemption. ¹³The blood of goats and bulls and the ashes of a heifer sprinkled on those who are ceremonially unclean sanctify them so that they are outwardly clean. ¹⁴How much more, then, will the blood of Christ, who through the eternal Spirit offered himself unblemished to God, cleanse our consciences from acts that lead to death,ᶜ so that we may serve the living God!

¹⁵For this reason Christ is the mediator of a new covenant, that those who are called may receive the promised eternal inheritance—now that he has died as a ransom to set them free from the sins committed under the first covenant.

¹⁶In the case of a will,ᵈ it is necessary to prove the death of the one who made it, ¹⁷because a will is in force only when somebody has died; it never takes effect while the one who made it is living. ¹⁸This is why even the first covenant was not put into effect without blood. ¹⁹When Moses had proclaimed every commandment of the law to all the people, he took the blood of calves, together with water, scarlet wool and branches of

---

⊡ ∷∷∷∷∷∷ **REASONS TO BELIEVE** ∷∷∷∷∷∷ ⊠

9:1–14
The Incomparable Jesus

This passage is educational for seekers in that it provides a brief essay on the mechanics of the Jewish sacrificial system. The writer uses these images, which were very familiar to his original readers, to describe why Jesus' sacrifice for sin on the cross eliminates the need for such sacrifices.

The old Jewish sacrificial system was unable to cleanse the human conscience (verses 8–10). For one thing, under that system the way into God's presence was barred to his people. Only the high priest could enter the Most Holy Place in the temple, and then only once a year. Something more than ritual was required to unite people with their God.

That something was the blood of Christ. Jesus entered the Most Holy Place and offered his own blood as the sacrifice for sin (verse 12). When we accept Jesus' actions on our behalf, our sins are washed away and our consciences are clear. When we've experienced such true forgiveness, we're free from the weight of guilt in our lives and ready to serve God with our whole selves.

---

a 5 Traditionally the mercy seat   b 11 Some early manuscripts are to come   c 14 Or from useless rituals   d 16 Same Greek word as covenant; also in verse 17 hyssop, and sprinkled the scroll and all the people. ²⁰He said, "This is the blood of the covenant, which God has commanded you to keep."ᵃ ²¹In the same way, he sprinkled with the blood both the tabernacle and everything used in its ceremonies. ²²In fact, the law requires that nearly everything be cleansed with blood, and without the shedding of blood there is no forgiveness.

²³It was necessary, then, for the copies of the heavenly things to be purified with these sacrifices, but the heavenly things themselves with better sacrifices than these. ²⁴For Christ did not enter a man-made sanctuary that was only a copy of the true one; he entered heaven itself, now to appear for us in God's presence. ²⁵Nor did he enter heaven to offer himself again and again, the way the high priest enters the Most Holy Place every year with blood that is not his own. ²⁶Then Christ would have had to suffer many times since the creation of the world. But now he has appeared once for all at the end of the ages to do away with sin by the sacrifice of himself. ²⁷Just as man is destined to die once, and after that to face judgment, ²⁸so Christ was sacrificed once to take away the sins of many people; and he will appear a second time, not to bear sin, but to bring salvation to those who are waiting for him.

Christ's Sacrifice Once for All

10 The law is only a shadow of the good things that are coming—not the realities themselves. For this reason it can never, by the same sacrifices repeated endlessly year after year, make perfect those who draw near to worship. ²If it could, would they not have stopped being offered? For the worshipers would have been cleansed once for all, and would no longer have felt guilty for their sins. ³But those sacrifices are an annual reminder of sins, ⁴because it is impossible for the blood of bulls and goats to take away sins.

⁵Therefore, when Christ came into the world, he said:

> "Sacrifice and offering you did not desire,
>   but a body you prepared for me;
> ⁶with burnt offerings and sin offerings
>   you were not pleased.
> ⁷Then I said, 'Here I am—it is written about me in the scroll—
>   I have come to do your will, O God.'"ᵇ

⁸First he said, "Sacrifices and offerings, burnt offerings and sin offerings you did not desire, nor were you pleased with them" (although the law required them to be made). ⁹Then he said, "Here I am, I have come to do your will." He sets aside the first to establish the second. ¹⁰And by that will, we have been made holy through the sacrifice of the body of Jesus Christ once for all.

¹¹Day after day every priest stands and performs his religious duties; again and again he offers the same sacrifices, which can never take away sins. ¹²But when this priest had offered for all time one sacrifice for sins, he sat down at the right hand of God. ¹³Since that time he waits for his enemies to be made his footstool, ¹⁴because by one sacrifice he has made perfect forever those who are being made holy.

¹⁵The Holy Spirit also testifies to us about this. First he says:

> ¹⁶"This is the covenant I will make with them
>   after that time, says the Lord.
> I will put my laws in their hearts,
>   and I will write them on their minds."ᶜ

¹⁷Then he adds:

ᵃ20 Exodus 24:8   ᵇ7 Psalm 40:6-8 (see Septuagint)   ᶜ16 Jer. 31:33

> "Their sins and lawless acts
> I will remember no more."[a]

[18]And where these have been forgiven, there is no longer any sacrifice for sin.

A Call to Persevere

[19]Therefore, brothers, since we have confidence to enter the Most Holy Place by the blood of Jesus, [20]by a new and living way opened for us through the curtain, that is, his body, [21]and since we have a great priest over the house of God, [22]let us draw near to God with a sincere heart in full assurance of faith, having our hearts sprinkled to cleanse us from a guilty conscience and having our bodies washed with pure water. [23]Let us hold unswervingly to the hope we profess, for he who promised is faithful. [24]And let us consider how we may spur one another on toward love and good deeds. [25]Let us not give up meeting together, as some are in the habit of doing, but let us encourage one another—and all the more as you see the Day approaching.

[26]If we deliberately keep on sinning after we have received the knowledge of the truth, no sacrifice for sins is left, [27]but only a fearful expectation of judgment and of raging fire that will consume the enemies of God. [28]Anyone who rejected the law of Moses died without mercy on the testimony of two or three witnesses. [29]How much more severely do you think a man deserves to be punished who has trampled the Son of God under foot, who has treated as an unholy thing the blood of the covenant that sanctified him, and who has insulted the Spirit of grace? [30]For we know him who said, "It is mine to avenge; I will repay,"[b] and again, "The Lord will judge his people."[c] [31]It is a dreadful thing to fall into the hands of the living God.

[32]Remember those earlier days after you had received the light, when you stood your ground in a great contest in the face of suffering. [33]Sometimes you were publicly exposed to insult and persecution; at other times you stood side by side with those who were so treated. [34]You sympathized with those in prison and joyfully accepted the confiscation of your property, because you knew that you yourselves had better and lasting possessions.

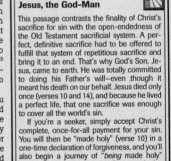

▣ ▦▦▦▦▦ DISCOVERING GOD ▦▦▦▦▦ ⬒

10:10–14
Jesus, the God-Man

This passage contrasts the finality of Christ's sacrifice for sin with the open-endedness of the Old Testament sacrificial system. A perfect, definitive sacrifice had to be offered to fulfill that system of repetitious sacrifice and bring it to an end. That's why God's Son, Jesus, came to earth. He was totally committed to doing his Father's will—even though it meant his death on our behalf. Jesus died only once (verses 10 and 14), and because he lived a perfect life, that one sacrifice was enough to cover all the world's sin.

If you're a seeker, simply accept Christ's complete, once-for-all payment for your sin. You will then be "made holy" (verse 10) in a one-time declaration of forgiveness, and you'll also begin a journey of "*being* made holy" (verse 14) as you walk with Christ each day and grow to increasingly mirror his character.

[35]So do not throw away your confidence; it will be richly rewarded. [36]You need to persevere so that when you have done the will of God, you will receive what he has promised. [37]For in just a very little while,

> "He who is coming will come and will not delay.
> [38] But my righteous one[d] will live by faith.
> And if he shrinks back,
> I will not be pleased with him."[e]

---

[a]17 Jer. 31:34   [b]30 Deut. 32:35   [c]30 Deut. 32:36; Psalm 135:14   [d]38 One early manuscript *But the righteous*
[e]38 Hab. 2:3,4

³⁹But we are not of those who shrink back and are destroyed, but of those who believe and are saved.

By Faith

11 Now faith is being sure of what we hope for and certain of what we do not see. ²This is what the ancients were commended for.

³By faith we understand that the universe was formed at God's command, so that what is seen was not made out of what was visible.

⁴By faith Abel offered God a better sacrifice than Cain did. By faith he was commended as a righteous man, when God spoke well of his offerings. And by faith he still speaks, even though he is dead.

⁵By faith Enoch was taken from this life, so that he did not experience death; he could not be found, because God had taken him away. For before he was taken, he was commended as one who pleased God. ⁶And without faith it is impossible to please God, because anyone who comes to him must believe that he exists and that he rewards those who earnestly seek him.

⁷By faith Noah, when warned about things not yet seen, in holy fear built an ark to save his family. By his faith he condemned the world and became heir of the righteousness that comes by faith.

⁸By faith Abraham, when called to go to a place he would later receive as his inheritance, obeyed and went, even though he did not know where he was going. ⁹By faith he made his home in the promised land like a stranger in a foreign country; he lived in tents, as did Isaac and Jacob, who were heirs with him of the same promise. ¹⁰For he was looking forward to the city with foundations, whose architect and builder is God.

¹¹By faith Abraham, even though he was past age—and Sarah herself was barren—was enabled to become a father because he ᵃ considered him faithful who had made the promise. ¹²And so from this one man, and he as good as dead, came descendants as numerous as the stars in the sky and as countless as the sand on the seashore.

¹³All these people were still living by faith when they died. They did not receive the things promised; they only saw them and welcomed them from a distance. And they admitted that they were aliens and strangers on earth. ¹⁴People who say such things show that they are looking for a country of their own. ¹⁵If they had been thinking of the

ADDRESSING QUESTIONS

11:1–2
Human Experience

Did you know that you're a person of great faith?

It's true—you are, and so is everyone else. Not a day passes without each of us exercising considerable faith. For example, you did it when you showered this morning. You trusted that the soap manufacturer didn't put some caustic substance in the soap that would burn your skin. When you drove to work, you trusted that the drivers of the oncoming cars wouldn't suddenly pull in front of you. When you got to work and flipped on the light switch, you believed that the light would come on, didn't you?

The author of Hebrews tells us that faith is like that. It's being sure of things you hope for without having them yet; it's being certain that unseen things are very real.

Notice that faith is not just positive thinking. And it's more than mere intuition. Faith is only as good as its object; it must have a worthy focus or else it's just a blind hunch. When God asks you to trust him, he isn't asking you to take a blind leap. Faith in God is built on the evidence he has supplied, which includes fulfilled prophecy, eyewitness reports, historical and archaeological confirmations of the Bible's trustworthiness, God's divine insight into human nature as seen in the pages of Scripture, Jesus' resurrection from the dead (which confirmed his supernatural credentials), and the changed lives of believers down through history—to name just a few examples.

Seeing as you already live by faith in many areas of your life, why not put your full confidence in God instead of in all the other less-reliable things that you depend on daily?

ᵃ 11 Or *By faith even Sarah, who was past age, was enabled to bear children because she*

country they had left, they would have had opportunity to return. ¹⁶Instead, they were longing for a better country—a heavenly one. Therefore God is not ashamed to be called their God, for he has prepared a city for them.

¹⁷By faith Abraham, when God tested him, offered Isaac as a sacrifice. He who had received the promises was about to sacrifice his one and only son, ¹⁸even though God had said to him, "It is through Isaac that your offspring*ᵃ* will be reckoned."*ᵇ* ¹⁹Abraham reasoned that God could raise the dead, and figuratively speaking, he did receive Isaac back from death.

²⁰By faith Isaac blessed Jacob and Esau in regard to their future.

²¹By faith Jacob, when he was dying, blessed each of Joseph's sons, and worshiped as he leaned on the top of his staff.

²²By faith Joseph, when his end was near, spoke about the exodus of the Israelites from Egypt and gave instructions about his bones.

²³By faith Moses' parents hid him for three months after he was born, because they saw he was no ordinary child, and they were not afraid of the king's edict.

²⁴By faith Moses, when he had grown up, refused to be known as the son of Pharaoh's daughter. ²⁵He chose to be mistreated along with the people of God rather than to enjoy the pleasures of sin for a short time. ²⁶He regarded disgrace for the sake of Christ as of greater value than the treasures of Egypt, because he was looking ahead to his reward. ²⁷By faith he left Egypt, not fearing the king's anger; he persevered because he saw him who is invisible. ²⁸By faith he kept the Passover and the sprinkling of blood, so that the destroyer of the firstborn would not touch the firstborn of Israel.

²⁹By faith the people passed through the Red Sea*ᶜ* as on dry land; but when the Egyptians tried to do so, they were drowned.

³⁰By faith the walls of Jericho fell, after the people had marched around them for seven days.

³¹By faith the prostitute Rahab, because she welcomed the spies, was not killed with those who were disobedient.*ᵈ*

³²And what more shall I say? I do not have time to tell about Gideon, Barak, Samson, Jephthah, David, Samuel and the prophets, ³³who through faith conquered kingdoms, administered justice, and gained what was promised; who shut the mouths of lions, ³⁴quenched the fury of the flames, and escaped the edge of the sword; whose weakness was turned to strength; and who became powerful in battle and routed foreign armies. ³⁵Women received back their dead, raised to life again. Others were tortured and refused to be released, so that they might gain a better resurrection. ³⁶Some faced jeers and flogging, while still others were chained and put in prison. ³⁷They were stoned*ᵉ*; they were sawed in two; they were put to death by the sword. They went about in sheepskins and goatskins, destitute, persecuted and mistreated— ³⁸the world was not worthy of them. They wandered in deserts and mountains, and in caves and holes in the ground.

³⁹These were all commended for their faith, yet none of them received what had been promised. ⁴⁰God had planned something better for us so that only together with us would they be made perfect.

God Disciplines His Sons

12 Therefore, since we are surrounded by such a great cloud of witnesses, let us throw off everything that hinders and the sin that so easily entangles, and let us run with perseverance the race marked out for us. ²Let us fix our eyes on Jesus, the author and perfecter of our faith, who for the joy set before him endured the cross, scorning its shame, and sat down at the right hand of the throne of God. ³Consider him who endured such opposition from sinful men, so that you will not grow weary and lose heart.

18 Greek seed　*ᵇ18* Gen. 21:12　*ᶜ29* That is, Sea of Reeds　*ᵈ31* Or unbelieving　*ᵉ37* Some early manuscripts stoned; they were put to the test;

[4]In your struggle against sin, you have not yet resisted to the point of shedding your blood. [5]And you have forgotten that word of encouragement that addresses you as sons:

> "My son, do not make light of the Lord's discipline,
>   and do not lose heart when he rebukes you,
> [6]because the Lord disciplines those he loves,
>   and he punishes everyone he accepts as a son."[a]

[7]Endure hardship as discipline; God is treating you as sons. For what son is not disciplined by his father? [8]If you are not disciplined (and everyone undergoes discipline), then you are illegitimate children and not true sons. [9]Moreover, we have all had human fathers who disciplined us and we respected them for it. How much more should we submit to the Father of our spirits and live! [10]Our fathers disciplined us for a little while as they thought best; but God disciplines us for our good, that we may share in his holiness. [11]No discipline seems pleasant at the time, but painful. Later on, however, it produces a harvest of righteousness and peace for those who have been trained by it.

[12]Therefore, strengthen your feeble arms and weak knees. [13]"Make level paths for your feet,"[b] so that the lame may not be disabled, but rather healed.

Warning Against Refusing God

[14]Make every effort to live in peace with all men and to be holy; without holiness no one will see the Lord. [15]See to it that no one misses the grace of God and that no bitter root grows up to cause trouble and defile many. [16]See that no one is sexually immoral, or is godless like Esau, who for a single meal sold his inheritance rights as the oldest son. [17]Afterward, as you know, when he wanted to inherit this blessing, he was rejected. He could bring about no change of mind, though he sought the blessing with tears.

[18]You have not come to a mountain that can be touched and that is burning with fire; to darkness, gloom and storm; [19]to a trumpet blast or to such a voice speaking words that those who heard it begged that no further word be spoken to them, [20]because they could not bear what was commanded: "If even an animal touches the mountain, it must be stoned."[c] [21]The sight was so terrifying that Moses said, "I am trembling with fear."[d]

[22]But you have come to Mount Zion, to the heavenly Jerusalem, the city of the living God. You have come to thousands upon thousands of angels in joyful assembly, [23]to the church of the firstborn, whose names are written in heaven. You have come to God, the judge of all men, to the spirits of righteous men made perfect, [24]to Jesus the mediator of a new covenant, and to the sprinkled blood that speaks a better word than the blood of Abel.

[25]See to it that you do not refuse him who speaks. If they did not escape when they refused him who warned them on earth, how much less will we, if we turn away from him who warns us from heaven? [26]At that time his voice shook the earth, but now he has promised, "Once more I will shake not only the earth but also the heavens."[e] [27]The words "once more" indicate the removing of what can be shaken—that is, created things—so that what cannot be shaken may remain.

[28]Therefore, since we are receiving a kingdom that cannot be shaken, let us be thankful, and so worship God acceptably with reverence and awe, [29]for our "God is a consuming fire."[f]

Concluding Exhortations

13 Keep on loving each other as brothers. [2]Do not forget to entertain strangers, for by so doing some people have entertained angels without knowing it. [3]Remember those in prison as if you were their fellow prisoners, and those who are mistreated as if you yourselves were suffering.

a6 Prov. 3:11,12   *b13* Prov. 4:26   *c20* Exodus 19:12,13   *d21* Deut. 9:19   *e26* Haggai 2:6
f29 Deut. 4:24

⁴Marriage should be honored by all, and the marriage bed kept pure, for God will judge the adulterer and all the sexually immoral. ⁵Keep your lives free from the love of money and be content with what you have, because God has said,

> "Never will I leave you;
> never will I forsake you."ᵃ

⁶So we say with confidence,

> "The Lord is my helper; I will not
> be afraid.
> What can man do to me?"ᵇ

⁷Remember your leaders, who spoke the word of God to you. Consider the outcome of their way of life and imitate their faith. ⁸Jesus Christ is the same yesterday and today and forever.

⁹Do not be carried away by all kinds of strange teachings. It is good for our hearts to be strengthened by grace, not by ceremonial foods, which are of no value to those who eat them. ¹⁰We have an altar from which those who minister at the tabernacle have no right to eat.

¹¹The high priest carries the blood of animals into the Most Holy Place as a sin offering, but the bodies are burned outside the camp. ¹²And so Jesus also suffered outside the city gate to make the people holy through his own blood. ¹³Let us, then, go to him outside the camp, bearing the disgrace he bore. ¹⁴For here we do not have an enduring city, but we are looking for the city that is to come.

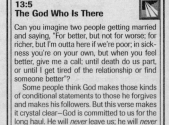

DISCOVERING GOD

13:5
The God Who Is There

Can you imagine two people getting married and saying, "For better, but not for worse; for richer, but I'm outta here if we're poor; in sickness you're on your own, but when you feel better, give me a call; until death do us part, or until I get tired of the relationship or find someone better"?

Some people think God makes those kinds of conditional statements to those he forgives and makes his followers. But this verse makes it crystal clear—God is committed to us for the long haul. He will *never* leave us; he will *never* forsake us.

If you're a seeker, this is the promise God offers if you will give yourself to him. With love like that extended to you, what could possibly stand in the way of you saying "I do"?

¹⁵Through Jesus, therefore, let us continually offer to God a sacrifice of praise—the fruit of lips that confess his name. ¹⁶And do not forget to do good and to share with others, for with such sacrifices God is pleased.

¹⁷Obey your leaders and submit to their authority. They keep watch over you as men who must give an account. Obey them so that their work will be a joy, not a burden, for that would be of no advantage to you.

¹⁸Pray for us. We are sure that we have a clear conscience and desire to live honorably in every way. ¹⁹I particularly urge you to pray so that I may be restored to you soon.

²⁰May the God of peace, who through the blood of the eternal covenant brought back from the dead our Lord Jesus, that great Shepherd of the sheep, ²¹equip you with everything good for doing his will, and may he work in us what is pleasing to him, through Jesus Christ, to whom be glory for ever and ever. Amen.

²²Brothers, I urge you to bear with my word of exhortation, for I have written you only a short letter.

²³I want you to know that our brother Timothy has been released. If he arrives soon, I will come with him to see you.

²⁴Greet all your leaders and all God's people. Those from Italy send you their greetings. ²⁵Grace be with you all.

ᵃ5 Deut. 31:6   ᵇ6 Psalm 118:6,7

JAMES

Introduction

THE BOTTOM LINE

What would you think of a person who lectured you on the dangers of smoking while lighting up a cigarette from her third pack that day? You might say that such a person has a credibility problem. She might be right about smoking—but it's pretty hard to hear it from *her.* In the same way, the book of James cautions people who have decided to follow Jesus to take that commitment seriously—to put their faith into action. James says that a faith that is not demonstrated by loving acts is one that stands on shaky ground. So if you're ready to trust in Jesus—or if you already do—be ready to let it show in the way you live.

CENTRAL IDEAS

■ Do not merely listen to truth—do what it says.
■ The tongue can be a dangerous weapon.
■ Trust in God for all of your tomorrows.
■ Pray, because God listens.

OUTLINE

1 Greetings (1:1)
2 How to handle tough times (1:2–18)
3 Listening and doing (1:19–27)
4 Favoritism forbidden (2:1–13)
5 Faith and deeds (2:14–26)
6 Taming your tongue (3:1–12)
7 Two kinds of wisdom (3:13–18)
8 Warnings against worldliness and oppression (4:1—5:20)

TITLE

This book is titled after its author—James, a half-brother of Jesus himself.

AUTHOR AND READERS

James, the brother of Jesus, penned this book to a general audience: "To the twelve tribes scattered among the nations"—a figurative reference to believers worldwide. That general address includes Christians of all times and places, including today. Given its early date, this could have been the first New Testament book written.

Exactly what do you want?" the trainer asked.

I looked at him, puzzled. Here I was, standing in a weight room talking to a weight trainer. What did he think I wanted—dance lessons?

"I want to get in shape," I said.

"How much time are you willing to spend?"

"Fifteen minutes a day," I replied.

He smiled. "Okay, we'll see what we can do."

During the next hour he introduced me to 13 exercises that worked every major muscle group in my body. After the session I stumbled out of the weight room with my legs shaking and my arms trembling. The next day I felt pain in muscles I didn't even know I had.

Eventually (although not soon enough!) the pain went away. And the 15-minute workout expanded to an hour. Thirteen years later, I'm still working out and pushing myself.

One of the lessons I've learned from lifting weights is that the adage "No pain, no gain" is right. The main idea behind weight training is to tear down muscle fibers so that they grow back stronger. Since pain is involved, few men and women who work out with weights would say that it's fun. But they will say it's worth it.

I felt pain in muscles I didn't even know I had.

In a similar way, God wants you—if you've chosen to follow and serve him—to be spiritually strong. To facilitate your growth, God will take you through a personalized routine that will increase your moral fibers. You might call it "*wait*" training." While the benefits are great, the process involves pain, disappointment, failure, and even some suffering. God doesn't spare his children life's difficulties. He just uses those trials for gain.

Such a routine may sound like something you'd rather avoid. But unlike weight training, *wait* training isn't optional—at least not for those who desire to get into Christlike spiritual shape.

Since you're going to experience your share of pain anyway, doesn't it make sense to gain as much from it as you can? James wrote his letter to a group of people who were undergoing great hardship. Not only did James tell them how to endure suffering, he actually told them to find joy in the midst of it.

If you're hurting or know someone who is, James's words may provide you with a beneficial perspective. This little book can give you a reason to rejoice in the face of suffering. Your first wait training station is James chapter 1, verses 2–4 (page 1602). It's not the whole workout routine, but it's a great place to start. And if you stay with the program, you'll become a spiritual heavyweight before you know it!

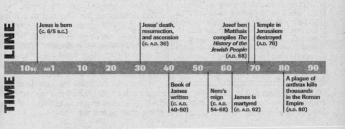

TIME LINE

| | Jesus is born (c. 6/5 B.C.) | | | Jesus' death, resurrection, and ascension (c. A.D. 30) | | | Josef ben Matthais compiles *The History of the Jewish People* (A.D. 68) | Temple in Jerusalem destroyed (A.D. 70) |

10BC AD1 10 20 30 40 50 60 70 80 90

| | | | | Book of James written (c. A.D. 40–50) | | Nero's reign (c. A.D. 54–68) | James is martyred (c. A.D. 62) | | A plague of anthrax kills thousands in the Roman Empire (A.D. 80) |

JAMES

1 James, a servant of God and of the Lord Jesus Christ,

To the twelve tribes scattered among the nations:

Greetings.

Trials and Temptations

²Consider it pure joy, my brothers, whenever you face trials of many kinds, ³because you know that the testing of your faith develops perseverance. ⁴Perseverance must finish its work so that you may be mature and complete, not lacking anything. ⁵If any of you lacks wisdom, he should ask God, who gives generously to all without finding fault, and it will be given to him. ⁶But when he asks, he must believe and not doubt, because he who doubts is like a wave of the sea, blown and tossed by the wind. ⁷That man should not think he will receive anything from the Lord; ⁸he is a double-minded man, unstable in all he does.

⁹The brother in humble circumstances ought to take pride in his high position. ¹⁰But the one who is rich should take pride in his low position, because he will pass away like a wild flower. ¹¹For the sun rises with scorching heat and withers the plant; its blossom falls and its beauty is destroyed. In the same way, the rich man will fade away even while he goes about his business.

¹²Blessed is the man who perseveres under trial, because when he has stood the test, he will receive the crown of life that God has promised to those who love him.

¹³When tempted, no one should say, "God is tempting me." For God cannot be tempted by evil, nor does he tempt anyone; ¹⁴but each one is tempted when, by his own evil desire, he is dragged away and enticed. ¹⁵Then, after desire has conceived, it gives birth to sin; and sin, when it is full-grown, gives birth to death.

¹⁶Don't be deceived, my dear brothers. ¹⁷Every good and perfect gift is from above, coming down from the Father of the heavenly lights, who does not change like shifting shadows. ¹⁸He chose to give us birth through the word of truth, that we might be a kind of firstfruits of all he created.

▣ ▥▥▥▥ KNOWING YOURSELF ▥▥▥▥ ⤢

1:2–4
Character

James' opening words may have startled his readers—people who were experiencing unparalleled hardship because they were Christ-followers. Yet he exhorted them to consider their trials a source of joy. His words almost sound like a greeting card that reads, "Rejoice in your cancer," or "Be happy that you're unemployed."

James didn't tell them to be glad because they were in pain, but because of the benefit coming their way as a result of the pain. Joy was possible because such trials would produce spiritual character ("perseverance") in their lives.

The original word James used for *testing* (verse 3) refers to the way gold is processed, and illustrates what he meant. When gold is liquefied by fire, the impurities come to the surface and are skimmed off. The result is purified gold. Similarly, adversity brings spiritual impurities to the surface so the believer can get rid of them and mature in his or her faith.

God uses adversity to purify his followers. But what if you're not his follower yet? Then God offers to turn the pain you experience into something positive. Without him, the Bible offers no assurance that your pain will serve any good purpose. But when you accept God's leading in your life, he promises to use everything—even hard times—to further your development and bring you closer to him.

Listening and Doing

¹⁹My dear brothers, take note of this: Everyone should be quick to listen, slow to speak and slow to become angry, ²⁰for man's anger does not bring about the righteous life that God desires. ²¹Therefore, get rid of all moral filth and the evil that is so prevalent and humbly accept the word planted in you, which can save you.

²²Do not merely listen to the word, and so deceive yourselves. Do what it says. ²³Anyone who listens to the word but does not do what it says is like a man who looks at his face in a mirror ²⁴and, after looking at himself, goes away and immediately forgets what he looks like. ²⁵But the man who looks intently into the perfect law that gives freedom, and continues to do this, not forgetting what he has heard, but doing it—he will be blessed in what he does.

²⁶If anyone considers himself religious and yet does not keep a tight rein on his tongue, he deceives himself and his religion is worthless. ²⁷Religion that God our Father accepts as pure and faultless is this: to look after orphans and widows in their distress and to keep oneself from being polluted by the world.

Favoritism Forbidden

2 My brothers, as believers in our glorious Lord Jesus Christ, don't show favoritism. ²Suppose a man comes into your meeting wearing a gold ring and fine clothes, and a poor man in shabby clothes also comes in. ³If you show special attention to the man wearing fine clothes and say, "Here's a good seat for you," but say to the poor man, "You stand there" or "Sit on the floor by my feet," ⁴have you not discriminated among yourselves and become judges with evil thoughts?

⁵Listen, my dear brothers: Has not God chosen those who are poor in the eyes of the world to be rich in faith and to inherit the kingdom he promised those who love him? ⁶But you have insulted the poor. Is it not the rich who are exploiting you? Are they not the ones who are dragging you into court? ⁷Are they not the ones who are slandering the noble name of him to whom you belong?

⁸If you really keep the royal law found in Scripture, "Love your neighbor as yourself,"ᵃ you are doing right. ⁹But if you show favoritism, you sin and are convicted by the law as lawbreakers. ¹⁰For whoever keeps the whole law and yet stumbles at just one point is guilty of breaking all of it. ¹¹For he who said, "Do not commit adultery,"ᵇ also said, "Do not murder."ᶜ If you do not commit adultery but do commit murder, you have become a lawbreaker.

¹²Speak and act as those who are going to be judged by the law that gives freedom, ¹³because judgment without mercy will be shown to anyone who has not been merciful. Mercy triumphs over judgment!

Faith and Deeds

¹⁴What good is it, my brothers, if a man claims to have faith but has no deeds? Can such faith save him? ¹⁵Suppose a brother or sister is without clothes and daily food. ¹⁶If one of you says to him, "Go, I wish you well; keep warm and well fed," but does nothing about his physical needs, what good is it? ¹⁷In the same way, faith by itself, if it is not accompanied by action, is dead.

¹⁸But someone will say, "You have faith; I have deeds."

Show me your faith without deeds, and I will show you my faith by what I do. ¹⁹You believe that there is one God. Good! Even the demons believe that—and shudder. ²⁰You foolish man, do you want evidence that faith without deeds is uselessᵈ? ²¹Was not our ancestor Abraham considered righteous for what he did when he offered his son

---

ᵃ8 Lev. 19:18   ᵇ11 Exodus 20:14; Deut. 5:18   ᶜ11 Exodus 20:13; Deut. 5:17   ᵈ20 Some early manuscripts dead

Isaac on the altar? ²²You see that his faith and his actions were working together, and his faith was made complete by what he did. ²³And the scripture was fulfilled that says, "Abraham believed God, and it was credited to him as righteousness,"ᵃ and he was called God's friend. ²⁴You see that a person is justified by what he does and not by faith alone.

²⁵In the same way, was not even Rahab the prostitute considered righteous for what she did when she gave lodging to the spies and sent them off in a different direction? ²⁶As the body without the spirit is dead, so faith without deeds is dead.

Taming the Tongue

3 Not many of you should presume to be teachers, my brothers, because you know that we who teach will be judged more strictly. ²We all stumble in many ways. If anyone is never at fault in what he says, he is a perfect man, able to keep his whole body in check.

³When we put bits into the mouths of horses to make them obey us, we can turn the whole animal. ⁴Or take ships as an example. Although they are so large and are driven by strong winds, they are steered by a very small rudder wherever the pilot wants to go. ⁵Likewise the tongue is a small part of the body, but it makes great boasts. Consider what a great forest is set on fire by a small spark. ⁶The tongue also is a fire, a world of evil among the parts of the body. It corrupts the whole person, sets the whole course of his life on fire, and is itself set on fire by hell.

ᵃ23 Gen. 15:6

☐ ░░░░░░░░░░░ **ADDRESSING QUESTIONS** ░░░░░░░░░░░ ◀

2:14–26
Human Experience

Q

Is a relationship with God something you have to earn, or is it a free gift?

Through the centuries the book of James has stirred controversy over this question. On the surface, James seemed to contradict what Paul taught (such as in Romans 3:28 [page 1472]). Many people have held the mistaken belief that James was debating whether a person is made right with God by performing good works or by having faith. But a careful look discloses that James intended rather to draw the contrast between a *living* faith and a *dead* faith—between an empty profession of belief and a life that demonstrates a dynamic trust in God.

When James spoke of "deeds" he wasn't referring to actions that are done to win God's approval. Instead, he was speaking of spontaneous acts that flow out of a genuine faith in Christ. A faith that doesn't produce acts of kindness is useless (verse 14). True faith involves more than believing proper doctrine (verses 18-19). Even demons, the spiritual beings who work against God, believe that he exists. However, they don't allow that knowledge to change their behavior. James says that people whose faith is alive will allow their faith to so permeate their lives that acts of mercy and care for others become a natural function of daily life.

To demonstrate his point further, James referred to two examples from Israel's history (verses 20-25): Abraham, the father of the faith, and Rahab, a woman who had protected Israelite spies. (You can read their stories in Genesis chapter 22 [page 29] and Joshua chapter 2 [page 263], respectively.) Both demonstrated the genuineness of their faith by deeds, so that their "faith was made complete" by what they did.

The apparent contradiction between Paul and James can easily be resolved by noting how they used the same word with different meanings. Paul used the word "justified" in the sense that God declares guilty people right with him, while James spoke of being "justified" in the eyes of others—having a faith that's so real that others can see it in action.

To provide a final example of such a faith, James drew from the nature of human life itself (verse 26). Just as a body without breath, brain waves and functioning organs is dead, so faith without works is dead.

7All kinds of animals, birds, reptiles and creatures of the sea are being tamed and have been tamed by man, 8but no man can tame the tongue. It is a restless evil, full of deadly poison.

9With the tongue we praise our Lord and Father, and with it we curse men, who have been made in God's likeness. 10Out of the same mouth come praise and cursing. My brothers, this should not be. 11Can both fresh water and salt*a* water flow from the same spring? 12My brothers, can a fig tree bear olives, or a grapevine bear figs? Neither can a salt spring produce fresh water.

Two Kinds of Wisdom

13Who is wise and understanding among you? Let him show it by his good life, by deeds done in the humility that comes from wisdom. 14But if you harbor bitter envy and selfish ambition in your hearts, do not boast about it or deny the truth. 15Such "wisdom" does not come down from heaven but is earthly, unspiritual, of the devil. 16For where you have envy and selfish ambition, there you find disorder and every evil practice.

17But the wisdom that comes from heaven is first of all pure; then peace-loving, considerate, submissive, full of mercy and good fruit, impartial and sincere. 18Peacemakers who sow in peace raise a harvest of righteousness.

Submit Yourselves to God

4 What causes fights and quarrels among you? Don't they come from your desires that battle within you? 2You want something but don't get it. You kill and covet, but you cannot have what you want. You quarrel and fight. You do not have, because you do not ask God. 3When you ask, you do not receive, because you ask with wrong motives, that you may spend what you get on your pleasures.

4You adulterous people, don't you know that friendship with the world is hatred toward God? Anyone who chooses to be a friend of the world becomes an enemy of God. 5Or do you think Scripture says without reason that the spirit he caused to live in us envies intensely?*b* 6But he gives us more grace. That is why Scripture says:

> "God opposes the proud
> but gives grace to the humble."*c*

7Submit yourselves, then, to God. Resist the devil, and he will flee from you. 8Come near to God and he will come near to you. Wash your hands, you sinners, and purify your hearts, you double-minded. 9Grieve, mourn and wail. Change your laughter to mourning and your joy to gloom. 10Humble yourselves before the Lord, and he will lift you up.

11Brothers, do not slander one another. Anyone who speaks against his brother or judges him speaks against the law and judges it. When you judge the law, you are not keeping it, but sitting in judgment on it. 12There is only one Lawgiver and Judge, the one who is able to save and destroy. But you—who are you to judge your neighbor?

Boasting About Tomorrow

13Now listen, you who say, "Today or tomorrow we will go to this or that city, spend a year there, carry on business and make money." 14Why, you do not even know what will happen tomorrow. What is your life? You are a mist that appears for a little while and then vanishes. 15Instead, you ought to say, "If it is the Lord's will, we will live and do this or that." 16As it is, you boast and brag. All such boasting is evil. 17Anyone, then, who knows the good he ought to do and doesn't do it, sins.

---

a 11 Greek bitter (see also verse 14)   *b 5* Or that God jealously longs for the spirit that he made to live in us; or that the Spirit he caused to live in us longs jealously   *c 6* Prov. 3:34

Warning to Rich Oppressors

5 Now listen, you rich people, weep and wail because of the misery that is coming upon you. ²Your wealth has rotted, and moths have eaten your clothes. ³Your gold and silver are corroded. Their corrosion will testify against you and eat your flesh like fire. You have hoarded wealth in the last days. ⁴Look! The wages you failed to pay the workmen who mowed your fields are crying out against you. The cries of the harvesters have reached the ears of the Lord Almighty. ⁵You have lived on earth in luxury and self-indulgence. You have fattened yourselves in the day of slaughter.ᵃ ⁶You have condemned and murdered innocent men, who were not opposing you.

Patience in Suffering

⁷Be patient, then, brothers, until the Lord's coming. See how the farmer waits for the land to yield its valuable crop and how patient he is for the autumn and spring rains. ⁸You too, be patient and stand firm, because the Lord's coming is near. ⁹Don't grumble against each other, brothers, or you will be judged. The Judge is standing at the door!

¹⁰Brothers, as an example of patience in the face of suffering, take the prophets who spoke in the name of the Lord. ¹¹As you know, we consider blessed those who have persevered. You have heard of Job's perseverance and have seen what the Lord finally brought about. The Lord is full of compassion and mercy.

¹²Above all, my brothers, do not swear—not by heaven or by earth or by anything else. Let your "Yes" be yes, and your "No," no, or you will be condemned.

▣ ::::::::::: DISCOVERING GOD ::::::::::: ⬆⬇

5:13–16
Life with God

In this last section of his letter, James reiterates the power of prayer in the life of a Christ-follower. Whether one experiences good or bad events in life, prayer is always the appropriate response.

If you're a seeker, take this passage as James's message to you that God listens to and answers prayer. Whatever your state of mind, God wants to hear from you. Don't worry about what you're feeling or whether you have the "right" attitude—just come to him as you are. He's ready to listen to you.

The Prayer of Faith

¹³Is any one of you in trouble? He should pray. Is anyone happy? Let him sing songs of praise. ¹⁴Is any one of you sick? He should call the elders of the church to pray over him and anoint him with oil in the name of the Lord. ¹⁵And the prayer offered in faith will make the sick person well; the Lord will raise him up. If he has sinned, he will be forgiven. ¹⁶Therefore confess your sins to each other and pray for each other so that you may be healed. The prayer of a righteous man is powerful and effective.

¹⁷Elijah was a man just like us. He prayed earnestly that it would not rain, and it did not rain on the land for three and a half years. ¹⁸Again he prayed, and the heavens gave rain, and the earth produced its crops.

¹⁹My brothers, if one of you should wander from the truth and someone should bring him back, ²⁰remember this: Whoever turns a sinner from the error of his way will save him from death and cover over a multitude of sins.

ᵃ5 Or *yourselves as in a day of feasting*

Prior to becoming a Christian, I adhered to a vague and comfortable notion that we all get to heaven by basically being good, that God surely sends only truly evil people to hell, and that there are many acceptable paths to salvation among the world's religions. My notion of world religions (I later realized) was wrapped more in a warm fuzzy sense of global peace and brotherly love than in any concrete study of their tenets. Unfortunately, I never read the Bible or learned about Jesus.

My path to Christ began when my wife returned from a church-sponsored conference full of energy and hope and with the desire to put her trust in God alone. I later realized that this conference was truly a "defining moment" for her. As a Mother's Day request, she asked if I'd go with her to a church service. I did, and began a very short seeker phase during which time we attended services and talked often to my older sister and her husband (who are long-time Christians).

My defining moment came on Father's Day in 1994. As the father of three wonderful children, I was deeply touched by the pastor's message that day. After the service my brother-in-law introduced me to the pastor, who said something to me that I'll never forget: "Keep on growing." At that point I realized that many signs and impressions had opened my heart to accept God's truth. I didn't experience a Paul-like conversion. Rather, I had the wonderful sense of Jesus patiently knocking and waiting for me to finally open the door. That night my wife and I prayed together, and I felt a peace that I know is only possible through God's touch.

Although I'm not free of life's routine trials and tasks, as a believer I strive to take time every day to pray and center myself before God. The ultimate decision is already made! Now I seek to learn and follow God's plan for the rest of my earthly life. My desire is to serve God and please him in all that I do. My goal is still to "Keep on growing."

Introduction

THE BOTTOM LINE

There isn't a person in the world who doesn't need a shot of encouragement. Whether you're struggling to reach the top of a hill or struggling with a bout of depression, it's great to hear another person say, "Keep going! You can make it!" In the first of these two books, Christians will find the encouragement to keep going forward spiritually even in the midst of struggles. In the second book, the author gives his readers guidelines for discerning false teachings from true ones. The main goal of these two books is to keep those who have decided to be Christ-followers on the right path, and to give them the motivation to keep going when times get tough. Through these books God tells his followers, "Keep going, I'll help you make it!"

CENTRAL IDEAS

■ Salvation is a gracious gift from God that is more valuable than anything on earth.

■ Even though a life of trusting God can be tough, God will give us the strength to press on.

■ We need to discern what is true and what is false teaching, and resist anything that turns us away from God's truth.

■ Christ will one day return and make all things right.

TITLES

These books are titled after their author, Peter, who was one of Jesus' disciples.

AUTHOR AND READERS

Peter wrote these books to Christians in Rome who were suffering intense persecution for their new-found faith. By the time the second letter was written, the Emperor Nero had begun to crack down on Christians, accusing them of subversion and torturing them mercilessly. It was in this context that Peter wrote his words of encouragement, keeping his readers' eyes on the goal of eternal life beyond the grave.

TIME LINE

	Jesus is born (6/5 B.C.)			Jesus' death, resurrection, and ascension (c. A.D. 30)			Books of 1 and 2 Peter written (c. A.D. 60-68)		Peter's death (c. A.D. 67-68)
10 B.C.	**A.D. 1**	**10**	**20**	**30**	**40**	**50**	**60**	**70**	
				Peter becomes a disciple (c. A.D. 26)			Nero's reign (c. A.D. 54-68)	Paul's imprisonment and death in Rome (c. A.D. 67-68)	

Joseph was a thief.

He was tried and convicted without a word of defense. What could he say? He and everyone else knew he was guilty.

One day while serving his term in a Berlin prison, he received an unexpected visitor. Touring the prison that day was Frederick the Great, the man who reigned over Prussia from 1740 to 1786.

"Why are you here?" he asked one man.

"I'm innocent," the man insisted. "They convicted the wrong guy!"

"And what about you?" the king inquired of another inmate.

"I couldn't have committed the crime," he said. "I was with a friend."

Man after man fell on his knees and begged the king for a pardon. Each insisted on his innocence.

Then Frederick addressed Joseph. "Why are you here?" the king asked.

"Armed robbery, Your Majesty."

"And are you guilty?"

"Yes, indeed, Your Majesty. I entirely deserve my punishment." Joseph lowered his eyes as the shame of his crime poured over him.

> **"Warden!" the king barked. "Have a guard release this guilty wretch at once."**

"Warden!" the king barked. "Have a guard release this guilty wretch at once. I will not have him kept in this prison where he will corrupt all the fine innocent people who occupy it."*

Joseph was released because he humbled himself in the presence of the king. He discovered that the first step to being rid of his guilt was to honestly *own up to it.*

What Frederick did for Joseph, God wants to do for you. But his forgiveness isn't something you can demand, and you won't get it by feigning innocence. Instead, God asks you to first own up to your sin. Stop blaming others, and for now set aside the bad things people have done to you.

The path of humility begins with a low doorway, one that you'll have to get on your knees to pass through. But on the other side is a wonderful hall full of beauty and truth—and most importantly, full of grace.

If you want to experience the goodness of God personally, turn to 1 Peter chapter 5, verses 6–7 (page 1615). Then, as best you know how, do what it says.

---

* *The Little Brown Book of Anecdotes,* Clifton Fadiman, ed. (Boston, Little, Brown & Co., 1985), p. 221.

1 PETER

1 Peter, an apostle of Jesus Christ,

To God's elect, strangers in the world, scattered throughout Pontus, Galatia, Cappadocia, Asia and Bithynia, ²who have been chosen according to the foreknowledge of God the Father, through the sanctifying work of the Spirit, for obedience to Jesus Christ and sprinkling by his blood:

Grace and peace be yours in abundance.

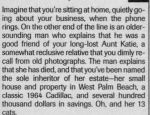

▣ ░░░░░░ REASONS TO BELIEVE ░░░░░░ ↹
1:3-5
The Christian Experience

Imagine that you're sitting at home, quietly going about your business, when the phone rings. On the other end of the line is an older-sounding man who explains that he was a good friend of your long-lost Aunt Katie, a somewhat reclusive relative that you dimly recall from old photographs. The man explains that she has died, and that you've been named the sole inheritor of her estate—her small house and property in West Palm Beach, a classic 1964 Cadillac, and several hundred thousand dollars in savings. Oh, and her 13 cats.

Almost everybody has dreamed, at one time or another, of inheriting a large estate. But for those who have received new birth through Christ, a spiritual fortune is a certainty.

Because of Christ's resurrection and victory over death, his followers share in his undying life. People who put their trust in Jesus and spiritually unite with him can be sure of victory over the grave and eternal life with him in heaven. And while the inheritance that Christ-followers anticipate is a deferred gift, it is inestimably more valuable than any earthly possession. In heaven, that inheritance can't "perish, spoil or fade." (Or shed!) Which is more than can be said for Aunt Katie's fortune!

Praise to God for a Living Hope

³Praise be to the God and Father of our Lord Jesus Christ! In his great mercy he has given us new birth into a living hope through the resurrection of Jesus Christ from the dead, ⁴and into an inheritance that can never perish, spoil or fade—kept in heaven for you, ⁵who through faith are shielded by God's power until the coming of the salvation that is ready to be revealed in the last time. ⁶In this you greatly rejoice, though now for a little while you may have had to suffer grief in all kinds of trials. ⁷These have come so that your faith—of greater worth than gold, which perishes even though refined by fire—may be proved genuine and may result in praise, glory and honor when Jesus Christ is revealed. ⁸Though you have not seen him, you love him; and even though you do not see him now, you believe in him and are filled with an inexpressible and glorious joy, ⁹for you are receiving the goal of your faith, the salvation of your souls.

¹⁰Concerning this salvation, the prophets, who spoke of the grace that was to come to you, searched intently and with the greatest care, ¹¹trying to find out the time and circumstances to which the Spirit of Christ in them was pointing when he predicted the sufferings of Christ and the glories that would follow. ¹²It was revealed to them that they were not serving themselves but you, when they spoke of the things that have now been told you by those who have preached the gospel to you by the Holy Spirit sent from heaven. Even angels long to look into these things.

Be Holy

¹³Therefore, prepare your minds for action; be self-controlled; set your hope fully on the grace to be given you when Jesus Christ is revealed. ¹⁴As obedient children, do not conform to the evil desires you had when you lived in ignorance. ¹⁵But just as he who called you is holy, so be holy in all you do; ¹⁶for it is written: "Be holy, because I am holy."ᵃ

¹⁷Since you call on a Father who judges each man's work impartially, live your lives as strangers here in reverent fear. ¹⁸For you know that it was not with perishable things such as silver or gold that you were redeemed from the empty way of life handed down to you from your forefathers, ¹⁹but with the precious blood of Christ, a lamb without blemish or defect. ²⁰He was chosen before the creation of the world, but was revealed in these last times for your sake. ²¹Through him you believe in God, who raised him from the dead and glorified him, and so your faith and hope are in God.

²²Now that you have purified yourselves by obeying the truth so that you have sincere love for your brothers, love one another deeply, from the heart.ᵇ ²³For you have been born again, not of perishable seed, but of imperishable, through the living and enduring word of God. ²⁴For,

> "All men are like grass,
>   and all their glory is like the flowers of the field;
> the grass withers and the flowers fall,
> 25   but the word of the Lord stands forever."ᶜ

And this is the word that was preached to you.

2 Therefore, rid yourselves of all malice and all deceit, hypocrisy, envy, and slander of every kind. ²Like newborn babies, crave pure spiritual milk, so that by it you may grow up in your salvation, ³now that you have tasted that the Lord is good.

The Living Stone and a Chosen People

⁴As you come to him, the living Stone—rejected by men but chosen by God and precious to him— ⁵you also, like living stones, are being built into a spiritual house to be a holy priesthood, offering spiritual sacrifices acceptable to God through Jesus Christ. ⁶For in Scripture it says:

> "See, I lay a stone in Zion,
>   a chosen and precious cornerstone,
> and the one who trusts in him
>   will never be put to shame."ᵈ

⁷Now to you who believe, this stone is precious. But to those who do not believe,

> "The stone the builders rejected
>   has become the capstone,"ᵉ·ᶠ

⁸and,

> "A stone that causes men to stumble
>   and a rock that makes them fall."ᵍ

They stumble because they disobey the message—which is also what they were destined for.

⁹But you are a chosen people, a royal priesthood, a holy nation, a people belonging to God, that you may declare the praises of him who called you out of darkness into his

---

ᵃ16 Lev. 11:44,45; 19:2; 20:7   ᵇ22 Some early manuscripts *from a pure heart*   ᶜ25 Isaiah 40:6-8
ᵈ6 Isaiah 28:16   ᵉ7 Or *cornerstone*   ᶠ7 Psalm 118:22   ᵍ8 Isaiah 8:14

wonderful light. ¹⁰Once you were not a people, but now you are the people of God; once you had not received mercy, but now you have received mercy.

¹¹Dear friends, I urge you, as aliens and strangers in the world, to abstain from sinful desires, which war against your soul. ¹²Live such good lives among the pagans that, though they accuse you of doing wrong, they may see your good deeds and glorify God on the day he visits us.

Submission to Rulers and Masters

¹³Submit yourselves for the Lord's sake to every authority instituted among men: whether to the king, as the supreme authority, ¹⁴or to governors, who are sent by him to punish those who do wrong and to commend those who do right. ¹⁵For it is God's will that by doing good you should silence the ignorant talk of foolish men. ¹⁶Live as free men, but do not use your freedom as a cover-up for evil; live as servants of God. ¹⁷Show proper respect to everyone: Love the brotherhood of believers, fear God, honor the king.

¹⁸Slaves, submit yourselves to your masters with all respect, not only to those who are good and considerate, but also to those who are harsh. ¹⁹For it is commendable if a man bears up under the pain of unjust suffering because he is conscious of God. ²⁰But how is it to your credit if you receive a beating for doing wrong and endure it? But if you suffer for doing good and you endure it, this is commendable before God. ²¹To this you were called, because Christ suffered for you, leaving you an example, that you should follow in his steps.

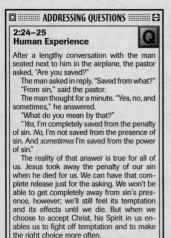

ADDRESSING QUESTIONS

2:24–25
Human Experience

After a lengthy conversation with the man seated next to him in the airplane, the pastor asked, "Are you saved?"

The man asked in reply, "Saved from what?"

"From sin," said the pastor.

The man thought for a minute. "Yes, no, and sometimes," he answered.

"What do you mean by that?"

"*Yes,* I'm completely saved from the penalty of sin. *No,* I'm not saved from the presence of sin. And *sometimes* I'm saved from the power of sin."

The reality of that answer is true for all of us. Jesus took away the penalty of our sin when he died for us. We can have that complete release just for the asking. We won't be able to get completely away from sin's presence, however; we'll still feel its temptation and its effects until we die. But when we choose to accept Christ, his Spirit in us enables us to fight off temptation and to make the right choice more often.

People who choose to follow Christ don't automatically become sinless. They do, however, become forgiven—and sin less.

²²"He committed no sin,
    and no deceit was found in his
        mouth." ᵃ

²³When they hurled their insults at him, he did not retaliate; when he suffered, he made no threats. Instead, he entrusted himself to him who judges justly. ²⁴He himself bore our sins in his body on the tree, so that we might die to sins and live for righteousness; by his wounds you have been healed. ²⁵For you were like sheep going astray, but now you have returned to the Shepherd and Overseer of your souls.

Wives and Husbands

3 Wives, in the same way be submissive to your husbands so that, if any of them do not believe the word, they may be won over without words by the behavior of their wives, ²when they see the purity and reverence of your lives. ³Your beauty should not come from outward adornment, such as braided hair and the wearing of gold jewelry and fine clothes. ⁴Instead, it should be that of your inner self, the unfading beauty of a gentle and quiet spirit, which is of great worth in God's sight. ⁵For this is the way the holy women of the past who put their hope in God used to make themselves

ᵃ 22 Isaiah 53:9

beautiful. They were submissive to their own husbands, ⁶like Sarah, who obeyed Abraham and called him her master. You are her daughters if you do what is right and do not give way to fear.

⁷Husbands, in the same way be considerate as you live with your wives, and treat them with respect as the weaker partner and as heirs with you of the gracious gift of life, so that nothing will hinder your prayers.

Suffering for Doing Good

⁸Finally, all of you, live in harmony with one another; be sympathetic, love as brothers, be compassionate and humble. ⁹Do not repay evil with evil or insult with insult, but with blessing, because to this you were called so that you may inherit a blessing. ¹⁰For,

> "Whoever would love life
>   and see good days
> must keep his tongue from evil
>   and his lips from deceitful speech.
> ¹¹He must turn from evil and do good;
>   he must seek peace and pursue it.
> ¹²For the eyes of the Lord are on the righteous
>   and his ears are attentive to their prayer,
> but the face of the Lord is against those who do evil."ᵃ

¹³Who is going to harm you if you are eager to do good? ¹⁴But even if you should suffer for what is right, you are blessed. "Do not fear what they fearᵇ; do not be frightened."ᶜ ¹⁵But in your hearts set apart Christ as Lord. Always be prepared to give an answer to everyone who asks you to give the reason for the hope that you have. But do this with gentleness and respect, ¹⁶keeping a clear conscience, so that those who speak maliciously against your good behavior in Christ may be ashamed of their slander. ¹⁷It is better, if it is God's will, to suffer for doing good than for doing evil. ¹⁸For Christ died for sins once for all, the righteous for the unrighteous, to bring you to God. He was put to death in the body but made alive by the Spirit, ¹⁹through whomᵈ also he went and preached to the spirits in prison ²⁰who disobeyed long ago when God waited patiently in the days of Noah while the ark was being built. In it only a few people, eight in all, were saved through water, ²¹and this water symbolizes baptism that now saves you also—not the removal of dirt from the body but the pledgeᵉ of a good conscience toward God. It saves you by the resurrection of Jesus Christ, ²²who has gone into heaven and is at God's right hand—with angels, authorities and powers in submission to him.

Living for God

4 Therefore, since Christ suffered in his body, arm yourselves also with the same attitude, because he who has suffered in his body is done with sin. ²As a result, he does not live the rest of his earthly life for evil human desires, but rather for the will of God. ³For you have spent enough time in the past doing what pagans choose to do—living in debauchery, lust, drunkenness, orgies, carousing and detestable idolatry. ⁴They think it strange that you do not plunge with them into the same flood of dissipation, and they heap abuse on you. ⁵But they will have to give account to him who is ready to judge the living and the dead. ⁶For this is the reason the gospel was preached even to those who are now dead, so that they might be judged according to men in regard to the body, but live according to God in regard to the spirit.

⁷The end of all things is near. Therefore be clear minded and self-controlled so that you can pray. ⁸Above all, love each other deeply, because love covers over a multitude of sins. ⁹Offer hospitality to one another without grumbling. ¹⁰Each one should use what-

a 12 Psalm 34:12-16   *b 14* Or *not fear their threats*   *c 14* Isaiah 8:12   *d 18,19* Or *alive in the spirit,* ¹⁹*through which*   *e 21* Or *response*

ever gift he has received to serve others, faithfully administering God's grace in it various forms. ¹¹If anyone speaks, he should do it as one speaking the very words of God If anyone serves, he should do it with the strength God provides, so that in all things Go may be praised through Jesus Christ. To him be the glory and the power for ever an ever. Amen.

Suffering for Being a Christian

¹²Dear friends, do not be surprised at the painful trial you are suffering, as thoug something strange were happening to you. ¹³But rejoice that you participate in the suf ferings of Christ, so that you may be overjoyed when his glory is revealed. ¹⁴If you ar insulted because of the name of Christ, you are blessed, for the Spirit of glory and of Go rests on you. ¹⁵If you suffer, it should not be as a murderer or thief or any other kind o criminal, or even as a meddler. ¹⁶However, if you suffer as a Christian, do not b ashamed, but praise God that you bear that name. ¹⁷For it is time for judgment to begi with the family of God; and if it begins with us, what will the outcome be for those wh do not obey the gospel of God? ¹⁸And,

> "If it is hard for the righteous to be saved,
>   what will become of the ungodly and the sinner?"ᵃ

¹⁹So then, those who suffer according to God's will should commit themselves to the faithful Creator and continue to do good.

To Elders and Young Men

5 To the elders among you, I appeal as a fellow elder, a witness of Christ' sufferings and one who also will share in the glory to be revealed: ²B shepherds of God's flock that is under your care, serving as overseers—not because yo must, but because you are willing, as God wants you to be; not greedy for money, bu eager to serve; ³not lording it over those entrusted to you, but being examples to th

ᵃ18 Prov. 11:31

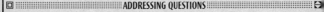

ADDRESSING QUESTIONS

5:8–9
Unseen Realities

Q

Peter personifies the devil in this passage as a vicious lion who prowls the earth in search of prey. Other Bible writers picture the devil, or Satan, as a snake (Genesis chapter 3 [page 7]) and a dragon (Revelation chapter 12 [page 1644]). And a story in Matthew chapter 4 (page 1261) demonstrates how Satan even tried to lure Jesus, the Son of God, into his trap.

The Bible consistently describes Satan as the enemy of God; a real being who continually works against God's purposes on earth. Every day we're alive, we feel the hot breath of this "lion" on our necks. Peter's advice for taming this cat? "Resist him, standing firm in the faith." This advice echoes the words of James, who wrote, "Resist the devil, and he will flee from you" (James chapter 4, verse 7 [page 1605]).

There are certain earlier steps to such resistance, however. In order to avoid the devil's grasp, we must first acknowledge that he exists; second, we must be aware of his activities (see 2 Corinthians chapter 2, verse 11 [page 1512]); third, we must accept Christ, without whose power we will be unable to stand firm against the devil's attacks.

Those who choose to live in the power of Christ's Spirit can also claim power over the devil in their lives. Yes, believers will still feel the effects of his activities (that's the "suffering" Peter mentions in verses 9 and 10). But, since Jesus has defeated Satan's greatest weapon—death itself—people who are in Christ will ultimately survive the devil's attacks. The same will not be true for those who choose to reject Jesus in this life.

flock. ⁴And when the Chief Shepherd appears, you will receive the crown of glory that will never fade away.

⁵Young men, in the same way be submissive to those who are older. All of you, clothe yourselves with humility toward one another, because,

> "God opposes the proud
>   but gives grace to the humble."ᵃ

⁶Humble yourselves, therefore, under God's mighty hand, that he may lift you up in due time. ⁷Cast all your anxiety on him because he cares for you.

⁸Be self-controlled and alert. Your enemy the devil prowls around like a roaring lion looking for someone to devour. ⁹Resist him, standing firm in the faith, because you know that your brothers throughout the world are undergoing the same kind of sufferings.

¹⁰And the God of all grace, who called you to his eternal glory in Christ, after you have suffered a little while, will himself restore you and make you strong, firm and steadfast. ¹¹To him be the power for ever and ever. Amen.

Final Greetings

¹²With the help of Silas,ᵇ whom I regard as a faithful brother, I have written to you briefly, encouraging you and testifying that this is the true grace of God. Stand fast in it. ¹³She who is in Babylon, chosen together with you, sends you her greetings, and so does my son Mark. ¹⁴Greet one another with a kiss of love.

Peace to all of you who are in Christ.

ᵃ5 Prov. 3:34   ᵇ12 Greek Silvanus, a variant of Silas

2 PETER

1 Simon Peter, a servant and apostle of Jesus Christ,

To those who through the righteousness of our God and Savior Jesus Christ have received a faith as precious as ours:

²Grace and peace be yours in abundance through the knowledge of God and of Jesus our Lord.

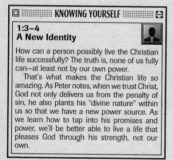

KNOWING YOURSELF

1:3–4
A New Identity

How can a person possibly live the Christian life successfully? The truth is, none of us fully can—at least not by our own power.

That's what makes the Christian life so amazing. As Peter notes, when we trust Christ, God not only delivers us from the penalty of sin, he also plants his "divine nature" within us so that we have a new power source. As we learn how to tap into his promises and power, we'll be better able to live a life that pleases God through his strength, not our own.

Making One's Calling and Election Sure

³His divine power has given us everything we need for life and godliness through our knowledge of him who called us by his own glory and goodness. ⁴Through these he has given us his very great and precious promises, so that through them you may participate in the divine nature and escape the corruption in the world caused by evil desires.

⁵For this very reason, make every effort to add to your faith goodness; and to goodness, knowledge; ⁶and to knowledge, self-control; and to self-control, perseverance; and to perseverance, godliness; ⁷and to godliness, brotherly kindness; and to brotherly kindness, love. ⁸For if you possess these qualities in increasing measure, they will keep you from being ineffective and unproductive in your knowledge of our Lord Jesus Christ. ⁹But if anyone does not have them, he is nearsighted and blind, and has forgotten that he has been cleansed from his past sins.

¹⁰Therefore, my brothers, be all the more eager to make your calling and election sure. For if you do these things, you will never fall, ¹¹and you will receive a rich welcome into the eternal kingdom of our Lord and Savior Jesus Christ.

Prophecy of Scripture

¹²So I will always remind you of these things, even though you know them and are firmly established in the truth you now have. ¹³I think it is right to refresh your memory as long as I live in the tent of this body, ¹⁴because I know that I will soon put it aside, as our Lord Jesus Christ has made clear to me. ¹⁵And I will make every effort to see that after my departure you will always be able to remember these things.

¹⁶We did not follow cleverly invented stories when we told you about the power and coming of our Lord Jesus Christ, but we were eyewitnesses of his majesty. ¹⁷For he received honor and glory from God the Father when the voice came to him from the Majestic Glory, saying, "This is my Son, whom I love; with him I am well pleased."ᵃ ¹⁸We ourselves heard this voice that came from heaven when we were with him on the sacred mountain.

ᵃ17 Matt. 17:5; Mark 9:7; Luke 9:35

¹⁹And we have the word of the prophets made more certain, and you will do well to pay attention to it, as to a light shining in a dark place, until the day dawns and the morning star rises in your hearts. ²⁰Above all, you must understand that no prophecy of scripture came about by the prophet's own interpretation. ²¹For prophecy never had its origin in the will of man, but men spoke from God as they were carried along by the Holy Spirit.

False Teachers and Their Destruction

2 But there were also false prophets among the people, just as there will be false teachers among you. They will secretly introduce destructive heresies, even denying the sovereign Lord who bought them—bringing swift destruction on themselves. ²Many will follow their shameful ways and will bring the way of truth into disrepute. ³In their greed these teachers will exploit you with stories they have made up. Their condemnation has long been hanging over them, and their destruction has not been sleeping.

⁴For if God did not spare angels when they sinned, but sent them to hell,ᵃ putting them into gloomy dungeonsᵇ to be held for judgment; ⁵if he did not spare the ancient world when he brought the flood on its ungodly people, but protected Noah, a preacher of righteousness, and seven others; ⁶if he condemned the cities of Sodom and Gomorrah by burning them to ashes, and made them an example of what is going to happen to the ungodly; ⁷and if he rescued Lot, a righteous man, who was distressed by the filthy lives of lawless men ⁸(for that righteous man, living among them day after day, was tormented in his righteous soul by the lawless deeds he saw and heard)— ⁹if this is so, then the Lord knows how to rescue godly men from trials and to hold the unrighteous for the day of judgment, while continuing their punishment.ᶜ ¹⁰This is especially true of those who follow the corrupt desire of the sinful natureᵈ and despise authority.

Bold and arrogant, these men are not afraid to slander celestial beings; ¹¹yet even angels, although they are stronger and more powerful, do not bring slanderous accusations against such beings in the presence of the Lord. ¹²But these men blaspheme in matters they do not understand. They are like brute beasts, creatures of instinct, born only to be caught and destroyed, and like beasts they too will perish.

¹³They will be paid back with harm for the harm they have done. Their idea of pleasure is to carouse in broad daylight. They are blots and blemishes, reveling in their pleasures while they feast with you.ᵉ ¹⁴With eyes full of adultery, they never stop sinning; they seduce the unstable; they are experts in greed—an accursed brood! ¹⁵They have left the straight way and wandered off to follow the way of Balaam son of Beor, who loved the wages of wickedness. ¹⁶But he was rebuked for his wrongdoing by a donkey—a beast without speech—who spoke with a man's voice and restrained the prophet's madness.

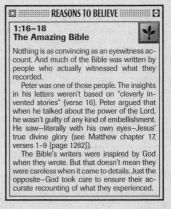

⧉ ▦▦▦▦▦ REASONS TO BELIEVE ▦▦▦▦▦ ⊟

1:16–18
The Amazing Bible

Nothing is as convincing as an eyewitness account. And much of the Bible was written by people who actually witnessed what they recorded.

Peter was one of those people. The insights in his letters weren't based on "cleverly invented stories" (verse 16). Peter argued that when he talked about the power of the Lord, he wasn't guilty of any kind of embellishment. He saw—literally with his own eyes—Jesus' true divine glory (see Matthew chapter 17, verses 1–9 [page 1282]).

The Bible's writers were inspired by God when they wrote. But that doesn't mean they were careless when it came to details. Just the opposite—God took care to ensure their accurate recounting of what they experienced.

ᵃ4 Greek *Tartarus*   ᵇ4 Some manuscripts *into chains of darkness*   ᶜ9 Or *unrighteous for punishment until the day of judgment*   ᵈ10 Or *the flesh*   ᵉ13 Some manuscripts *in their love feasts*

¹⁷These men are springs without water and mists driven by a storm. Blackest darkness is reserved for them. ¹⁸For they mouth empty, boastful words and, by appealing to the lustful desires of sinful human nature, they entice people who are just escaping from those who live in error. ¹⁹They promise them freedom, while they themselves are slaves of depravity—for a man is a slave to whatever has mastered him. ²⁰If they have escaped the corruption of the world by knowing our Lord and Savior Jesus Christ and are again entangled in it and overcome, they are worse off at the end than they were at the beginning. ²¹It would have been better for them not to have known the way of righteousness, than to have known it and then to turn their backs on the sacred command that was passed on to them. ²²Of them the proverbs are true: "A dog returns to its vomit,"ᵃ and, "A sow that is washed goes back to her wallowing in the mud."

The Day of the Lord

3 Dear friends, this is now my second letter to you. I have written both of them as reminders to stimulate you to wholesome thinking. ²I want you to recall the words spoken in the past by the holy prophets and the command given by our Lord and Savior through your apostles.

³First of all, you must understand that in the last days scoffers will come, scoffing and following their own evil desires. ⁴They will say, "Where is this 'coming' he promised? Ever since our fathers died, everything goes on as it has since the beginning of creation." ⁵But they deliberately forget that long ago by God's word the heavens existed and the earth was formed out of water and by water. ⁶By these waters also the world of that time was deluged and destroyed. ⁷By the same word the present heavens and earth are reserved for fire, being kept for the day of judgment and destruction of ungodly men.

⁸But do not forget this one thing, dear friends: With the Lord a day is like a thousand years, and a thousand years are like a day. ⁹The Lord is not slow in keeping his promise as some understand slowness. He is patient with you, not wanting anyone to perish, but everyone to come to repentance.

¹⁰But the day of the Lord will come like a thief. The heavens will disappear with a roar; the elements will be destroyed by fire, and the earth and everything in it will be laid bare.ᵇ

¹¹Since everything will be destroyed in this way, what kind of people ought you to be? You ought to live holy and godly lives ¹²as you look forward to the day of God and speed its coming.ᶜ That day will bring about the destruction of the heavens by fire, and the elements will melt in the heat. ¹³But in keeping with his promise we are looking forward to a new heaven and a new earth, the home of righteousness.

¹⁴So then, dear friends, since you are looking forward to this, make every effort to be found spotless, blameless and at peace with him. ¹⁵Bear in mind that our Lord's patience means salvation, just as our dear brother Paul also wrote you with the wisdom that God gave him. ¹⁶He writes the same way in all his letters, speaking in them of these matters. His letters contain some things

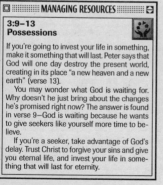

ᵃ22 Prov. 26:11   ᵇ10 Some manuscripts be burned up   ᶜ12 Or as you wait eagerly for the day of God to come

hat are hard to understand, which ignorant and unstable people distort, as they do the
ther Scriptures, to their own destruction.

[17]Therefore, dear friends, since you already know this, be on your guard so that you
may not be carried away by the error of lawless men and fall from your secure position.
[8]But grow in the grace and knowledge of our Lord and Savior Jesus Christ. To him be
glory both now and forever! Amen.

Introduction

THE BOTTOM LINE

The phone rings. "Not now!" you say to yourself, swamped under a stack of paperwork. You reluctantly pick up the phone. Instantly you recognize the voice—it's a friend from whom you haven't heard in a long time. Your conversation, though brief, is refreshing and encouraging. As you hang up the phone, you continue your work with a different attitude.

That's what these four short books are like—brief messages from people who can encourage believers as they try to live a life of faithfully trusting in God. First John gives practical advice on living in relationship with God. Second John and Jude warn believers about false teaching and help them to stay on track. Third John is a brief message reminding God-followers to be open to showing hospitality. All of these are meant to provide a "pick-me-up" that will help believers stay on the task at hand—cultivating a growing relationship with God.

CENTRAL IDEAS

- Jesus is our ultimate role model.
- We can know for sure that we have a relationship with God, the creator of the universe.
- Christ's greatest command is to love one another.
- We need to be on our guard against people who distort God's teachings in the Bible.

TITLES

These books are titled after their authors: John, a follower of Jesus; and Jude, Jesus' half-brother and full brother of James, another New Testament writer.

AUTHORS AND READERS

John wrote his letters to encourage believers in the region of Ephesus, the site of modern-day Turkey. Third John is written specifically to John's friend, Gaius. Jude wrote his letter to sound an alarm among his readers about false teachers.

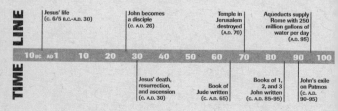

TIME LINE

Jesus' life (c. 6/5 B.C.–A.D. 30)

John becomes a disciple (c. A.D. 26)

Temple in Jerusalem destroyed (A.D. 70)

Aqueducts supply Rome with 250 million gallons of water per day (A.D. 95)

10 BC · AD 1 · 10 · 20 · 30 · 40 · 50 · 60 · 70 · 80 · 90 · 100

Jesus' death, resurrection, and ascension (c. A.D. 30)

Book of Jude written (c. A.D. 65)

Books of 1, 2, and 3 John written (c. A.D. 85–95)

John's exile on Patmos (c. A.D. 90–95)

Abbes Tehami lost the 1991 Brussels marathon by a mustache.

When Tehami, wearing number 62, started the race, he was quite sure he would win. The mustached runner kept fairly close to the front of the pack. By the seven-and-a-half-mile mark he was trailing the leader by 400 yards. Three miles later, however, he was inexplicably reinvigorated and stormed back on a tough climb. By the end of the race, Tehami had won easily. But there was one small problem. When Tehami tried to pick up the first-place check of $7,150, somebody noticed that he no longer had his mustache.

As it turned out, Tehami never did have a mustache. Yet Bensalem Hamiani, his coach, did. The two men looked so much alike that they figured they could outsmart the race organizers. Hamiani started the race, and Tehami finished it. The only thing they overlooked was the mustache. It was the subtle difference that, once noticed, exposed the deceit.

The difference between a fraud and the real thing is rarely obvious. Counterfeiters don't print $100 bills on pink paper. They make them look as much like the real thing as possible. Only by knowing *in detail* what a real bill looks like can a trained observer spot a counterfeit.

The difference between a fraud and the real thing is rarely obvious.

The same is true in the spiritual realm. People who appear to be "Christian" may show up at your door and even quote the Bible. But these "nice" people can still be passing out a counterfeit gospel and teaching a view of Jesus that is contrary to the truth about him as taught in the Bible. Don't think you can't be fooled. Under the right circumstances, any of us can be taken in.

The Bible's writers recognized the possibility of fraud and warned that not everyone who appears to be "spiritual" is from God. This is a hard message to hear in a society that seems to accept everybody's opinions as equally valid. But keep this detail in mind if you don't want to be deceived: At a crucial point, spiritual counterfeits give themselves away— *they all distort Jesus' identity and message.*

The books of 1, 2, 3 John and Jude warn us about spiritual counterfeits, and give advice on how to spot a deceiver. Turn to 1 John chapter 4, verses 1–3 (page 1625), to see what test to apply.

1 JOHN

The Word of Life

1 That which was from the beginning, which we have heard, which we have seen with our eyes, which we have looked at and our hands have touched— this we proclaim concerning the Word of life. ²The life appeared; we have seen it and testify to it, and we proclaim to you the eternal life, which was with the Father and has appeared to us. ³We proclaim to you what we have seen and heard, so that you also may have fellowship with us. And our fellowship is with the Father and with his Son, Jesus Christ. ⁴We write this to make our^a joy complete.

▣ ▦ DISCOVERING GOD ▦ ▣

1:1–4
Jesus, the God-Man

The Jesus whom John proclaimed wasn't a mythological figure or a ghostlike phantom. He was God in a real human body. John knew this to be true because he saw, heard, and *touched* him (verses 1–3).

When John explained how God had clothed himself with flesh, he also included an invitation for each of us. He wanted his readers to enjoy "fellowship" with the "Father and with his Son, Jesus Christ." The word *fellowship* speaks of partnership. It refers to people who share something in common. John didn't just want us to know *about* Jesus; he wanted us to experience him as a friend.

If you're a seeker, John invites you to enter into relationship with God the Father through his Son, Jesus Christ, as well as with other Christ-followers around the world. Just ask to be included. And if you do—welcome to the family!

Walking in the Light

⁵This is the message we have heard from him and declare to you: God is light; in him there is no darkness at all. ⁶If we claim to have fellowship with him yet walk in the darkness, we lie and do not live by the truth. ⁷But if we walk in the light, as he is in the light, we have fellowship with one another, and the blood of Jesus, his Son, purifies us from all^b sin.

⁸If we claim to be without sin, we deceive ourselves and the truth is not in us. ⁹If we confess our sins, he is faithful and just and will forgive us our sins and purify us from all unrighteousness. ¹⁰If we claim we have not sinned, we make him out to be a liar and his word has no place in our lives.

2 My dear children, I write this to you so that you will not sin. But if anybody does sin, we have one who speaks to the Father in our defense—Jesus Christ, the Righteous One. ²He is the atoning sacrifice for our sins, and not only for ours but also for^c the sins of the whole world.

³We know that we have come to know him if we obey his commands. ⁴The man who says, "I know him," but does not do what he commands is a liar, and the truth is not in him. ⁵But if anyone obeys his word, God's love^d is truly made complete in him. This is how we know we are in him: ⁶Whoever claims to live in him must walk as Jesus did.

⁷Dear friends, I am not writing you a new command but an old one, which you have had since the beginning. This old command is the message you have heard. ⁸Yet I am writing you a new command; its truth is seen in him and you, because the darkness is passing and the true light is already shining.

⁹Anyone who claims to be in the light but hates his brother is still in the darkness.

---

^a4 Some manuscripts your   ^b7 Or every   ^c2 Or He is the one who turns aside God's wrath, taking away our sins, and not only ours but also   ^d5 Or word, love for God

¹⁰Whoever loves his brother lives in the light, and there is nothing in him*a* to make him stumble. ¹¹But whoever hates his brother is in the darkness and walks around in the darkness; he does not know where he is going, because the darkness has blinded him.

> ¹²I write to you, dear children,
> because your sins have been forgiven on account of his name.
> ¹³I write to you, fathers,
> because you have known him who is from the beginning.
> I write to you, young men,
> because you have overcome the evil one.
> I write to you, dear children,
> because you have known the Father.
> ¹⁴I write to you, fathers,
> because you have known him who is from the beginning.
> I write to you, young men,
> because you are strong,
> and the word of God lives in you,
> and you have overcome the evil one.

Do Not Love the World

¹⁵Do not love the world or anything in the world. If anyone loves the world, the love of the Father is not in him. ¹⁶For everything in the world—the cravings of sinful man, the lust of his eyes and the boasting of what he has and does—comes not from the Father but from the world. ¹⁷The world and its desires pass away, but the man who does the will of God lives forever.

Warning Against Antichrists

¹⁸Dear children, this is the last hour; and as you have heard that the antichrist is coming, even now many antichrists have come. This is how we know it is the last hour. ¹⁹They went out from us, but they did not really belong to us. For if they had belonged to us, they would have remained with us; but their going showed that none of them belonged to us.

²⁰But you have an anointing from the Holy One, and all of you know the truth.*b* ²¹I do not write to you because you do not know the truth, but because you do know it and because no lie comes from the truth. ²²Who is the liar? It is the man who denies that Jesus is the Christ. Such a man is the antichrist—he denies the Father and the Son. ²³No one who denies the Son has the Father; whoever acknowledges the Son has the Father also.

²⁴See that what you have heard from the beginning remains in you. If it does, you also will remain in the Son and in the Father. ²⁵And this is what he promised us—even eternal life.

²⁶I am writing these things to you about those who are trying to lead you astray. ²⁷As

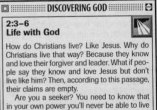

⣿⣿ DISCOVERING GOD ⣿⣿

2:3–6
Life with God

How do Christians live? Like Jesus. Why do Christians live that way? Because they know and love their forgiver and leader. What if people say they know and love Jesus but don't live like him? Then, according to this passage, their claims are empty.

Are you a seeker? You need to know that in your own power you'll never be able to live like Jesus—don't even try. But if you do become his follower, *follow him.* In other words, *live like him.*

With God's power at work in you, such a lifestyle is possible. When you accept his help, the changes you'll observe will be a powerful testimony that something supernatural has happened in your life.

a 10 Or it   *b 20 Some manuscripts and you know all things*

for you, the anointing you received from him remains in you, and you do not need anyone to teach you. But as his anointing teaches you about all things and as that anointing is real, not counterfeit—just as it has taught you, remain in him.

Children of God

²⁸And now, dear children, continue in him, so that when he appears we may be confident and unashamed before him at his coming.

²⁹If you know that he is righteous, you know that everyone who does what is right has been born of him.

3 How great is the love the Father has lavished on us, that we should be called children of God! And that is what we are! The reason the world does not know us is that it did not know him. ²Dear friends, now we are children of God, and what we will be has not yet been made known. But we know that when he appears,ᵃ we shall be like him, for we shall see him as he is. ³Everyone who has this hope in him purifies himself, just as he is pure.

⁴Everyone who sins breaks the law; in fact, sin is lawlessness. ⁵But you know that he appeared so that he might take away our sins. And in him is no sin. ⁶No one who lives in him keeps on sinning. No one who continues to sin has either seen him or known him.

⁷Dear children, do not let anyone lead you astray. He who does what is right is righteous, just as he is righteous. ⁸He who does what is sinful is of the devil, because the devil has been sinning from the beginning. The reason the Son of God appeared was to destroy the devil's work. ⁹No one who is born of God will continue to sin, because God's seed remains in him; he cannot go on sinning, because he has been born of God. ¹⁰This is how we know who the children of God are and who the children of the devil are: Anyone who does not do what is right is not a child of God; nor is anyone who does not love his brother.

Love One Another

¹¹This is the message you heard from the beginning: We should love one another. ¹²Do not be like Cain, who belonged to the evil one and murdered his brother. And why did he murder him? Because his own actions were evil and his brother's were righteous. ¹³Do not be surprised, my brothers, if the world hates you. ¹⁴We know that we have passed from death to life, because we love our brothers. Anyone who does not love remains in death. ¹⁵Anyone who hates his brother is a murderer, and you know that no murderer has eternal life in him.

¹⁶This is how we know what love is: Jesus Christ laid down his life for us. And we ought to lay down our lives for our brothers. ¹⁷If anyone has material possessions and sees his brother in need but has no pity on him, how can the love of God be in him? ¹⁸Dear children, let us not love with words or tongue but with actions and in truth. ¹⁹This then is how we know that we belong to the truth, and how we set our hearts at rest in his presence ²⁰whenever our hearts condemn us. For God is greater than our hearts, and he knows everything.

²¹Dear friends, if our hearts do not condemn us, we have confidence before God ²²and receive from him anything we ask, because we obey his commands and do what pleases him. ²³And this is his command: to believe in the name of his Son, Jesus Christ, and to love one another as he commanded us. ²⁴Those who obey his commands live in him, and he in them. And this is how we know that he lives in us: We know it by the Spirit he gave us.

ᵃ2 Or when it is made known

Test the Spirits

4 Dear friends, do not believe every spirit, but test the spirits to see whether they are from God, because many false prophets have gone out into the world. ²This is how you can recognize the Spirit of God: Every spirit that acknowledges that Jesus Christ has come in the flesh is from God, ³but every spirit that does not acknowledge Jesus is not from God. This is the spirit of the antichrist, which you have heard is coming and even now is already in the world.

⁴You, dear children, are from God and have overcome them, because the one who is in you is greater than the one who is in the world. ⁵They are from the world and therefore speak from the viewpoint of the world, and the world listens to them. ⁶We are from God, and whoever knows God listens to us; but whoever is not from God does not listen to us. This is how we recognize the Spirit*a* of truth and the spirit of falsehood.

God's Love and Ours

⁷Dear friends, let us love one another, for love comes from God. Everyone who loves has been born of God and knows God. ⁸Whoever does not love does not know God, because God is love. ⁹This is how God showed his love among us: He sent his one and only Son*b* into the world that we might live through him. ¹⁰This is love: not that we loved God, but that he loved us and sent his Son as an atoning sacrifice for*c* our sins. ¹¹Dear friends, since God so loved us, we also ought to love one another. ¹²No one has ever seen God; but if we love one another, God lives in us and his love is made complete in us.

¹³We know that we live in him and he in us, because he has given us of his Spirit. ¹⁴And we have seen and testify that the Father has sent his Son to be the Savior of the world. ¹⁵If anyone acknowledges that Jesus is the Son of God, God lives in him and he in God. ¹⁶And so we know and rely on the love God has for us.

▒▒▒▒▒ DISCOVERING GOD ▒▒▒▒▒

4:1–6
Spiritual Fraud

John knows that telling a counterfeit from the real thing can be difficult. Here John tells his readers how to test the authenticity of a teacher and his or her message.

First, a person has to believe that counterfeit religion actually exists. If you think all religions are just different paths up the same mountain which all lead to God, then you won't be suspicious of any of them. But such a belief, while sounding "open-minded," flies in the face of clear and overwhelming evidence that charlatans exist and that religions teach radically different and contradictory things. In other words, "Many false prophets have gone out into the world" (verse 1).

Even if you agree with John and acknowledge that false teachers exist, you still may not be able to identify one unless you discover how he or she interprets the identity of Jesus Christ. False teachers will say that Jesus was a good man, a prophet, an archangel—anything but the eternal God. John says that a true teacher will acknowledge that Jesus is God in human flesh. He or she will recognize that Jesus is fully God and fully man (verse 2; John echoes this idea again in 2 John, verse 7 [page 1627]).

The next time you hear someone teach about Jesus and you're not sure where he or she stands, ask a few questions. While the teacher may say flattering things about Jesus, find out if he or she thinks Jesus is both God and man, or something less. Only by preaching the genuine Christ of the Bible can a teacher bring life-giving truth.

God is love. Whoever lives in love lives in God, and God in him. ¹⁷In this way, love is made complete among us so that we will have confidence on the day of judgment, because in this world we are like him. ¹⁸There is no fear in love. But perfect love drives out fear, because fear has to do with punishment. The one who fears is not made perfect in love.

¹⁹We love because he first loved us. ²⁰If anyone says, "I love God," yet hates his

a6 Or *spirit*   *b9* Or *his only begotten Son*   *c10* Or *as the one who would turn aside his wrath, taking away*

brother, he is a liar. For anyone who does not love his brother, whom he has seen, cannot love God, whom he has not seen. ²¹And he has given us this command: Whoever loves God must also love his brother.

Faith in the Son of God

5 Everyone who believes that Jesus is the Christ is born of God, and everyone who loves the father loves his child as well. ²This is how we know that we love the children of God: by loving God and carrying out his commands. ³This is love for God: to obey his commands. And his commands are not burdensome, ⁴for everyone born of God overcomes the world. This is the victory that has overcome the world, even our faith. ⁵Who is it that overcomes the world? Only he who believes that Jesus is the Son of God.

⁶This is the one who came by water and blood—Jesus Christ. He did not come by water only, but by water and blood. And it is the Spirit who testifies, because the Spirit is the truth. ⁷For there are three that testify: ⁸the ᵃ Spirit, the water and the blood; and the three are in agreement. ⁹We accept man's testimony, but God's testimony is greater because it is the testimony of God, which he has given about his Son. ¹⁰Anyone who believes in the Son of God has this testimony in his heart. Anyone who does not believe God has made him out to be a liar, because he has not believed the testimony God has given about his Son. ¹¹And this is the testimony: God has given us eternal life, and this life is in his Son. ¹²He who has the Son has life; he who does not have the Son of God does not have life.

▣ DISCOVERING GOD ▣

5:11–13
Life with God

Is it possible for people to know for sure that they possess eternal life?

John's answer is a definite Yes! He states this truth positively and then negatively (verses 11–12). Because Jesus is himself God, he is an eternal being (see John chapter 8, verse 58 [page 1397], for example). Since that's true, John says, all who receive Jesus also receive his eternal life. On the other hand, those who don't share in Christ's life have only their own human life, which cannot enter into the kingdom of God.

Then John says something astonishing. He wants those who believe to "know" that they have eternal life. That statement would be extremely presumptuous if eternal life was something we earned by doing good deeds. In that case, no one could ever be sure that they'd done enough. But Jesus said, "Whoever believes in [me] shall not perish but have eternal life" (John chapter 3, verse 16 [page 1387]). So if you trust in him, you can know for certain that you have eternal life!

Concluding Remarks

¹³I write these things to you who believe in the name of the Son of God so that you may know that you have eternal life. ¹⁴This is the confidence we have in approaching God: that if we ask anything according to his will, he hears us. ¹⁵And if we know that he hears us—whatever we ask—we know that we have what we asked of him.

¹⁶If anyone sees his brother commit a sin that does not lead to death, he should pray and God will give him life. I refer to those whose sin does not lead to death. There is a sin that leads to death. I am not saying that he should pray about that. ¹⁷All wrongdoing is sin, and there is sin that does not lead to death.

¹⁸We know that anyone born of God does not continue to sin; the one who was born of God keeps him safe, and the evil one cannot harm him. ¹⁹We know that we are children of God, and that the whole world is under the control of the evil one. ²⁰We know also that the Son of God has come and has given us understanding, so that we may know him who is true. And we are in him who is true—even in his Son Jesus Christ. He is the true God and eternal life.

²¹Dear children, keep yourselves from idols.

ᵃ 7,8 Late manuscripts of the Vulgate *testify in heaven: the Father, the Word and the Holy Spirit, and these three are one.* ⁸*And there are three that testify on earth: the* (not found in any Greek manuscript before the sixteenth century)

2 JOHN

¹The elder,

To the chosen lady and her children, whom I love in the truth—and not I only, but also all who know the truth— ²because of the truth, which lives in us and will be with us forever:

³Grace, mercy and peace from God the Father and from Jesus Christ, the Father's Son, will be with us in truth and love.

⁴It has given me great joy to find some of your children walking in the truth, just as the Father commanded us. ⁵And now, dear lady, I am not writing you a new command but one we have had from the beginning. I ask that we love one another. ⁶And this is love: that we walk in obedience to his commands. As you have heard from the beginning, his command is that you walk in love.

⁷Many deceivers, who do not acknowledge Jesus Christ as coming in the flesh, have gone out into the world. Any such person is the deceiver and the antichrist. ⁸Watch out that you do not lose what you have worked for, but that you may be rewarded fully. ⁹Anyone who runs ahead and does not continue in the teaching of Christ does not have God; whoever continues in the teaching has both the Father and the Son. ¹⁰If anyone comes to you and does not bring this teaching, do not take him into your house or welcome him. ¹¹Anyone who welcomes him shares in his wicked work.

¹²I have much to write to you, but I do not want to use paper and ink. Instead, I hope to visit you and talk with you face to face, so that our joy may be complete.

¹³The children of your chosen sister send their greetings.

▦ DISCOVERING GOD ▦

7–11
Spiritual Fraud

Throughout the ages deceivers have attempted to mislead gullible people. At the time John wrote this letter, many deceivers refused to believe or teach that Jesus was God in a human body. If there's one common trait of false teachers, it's that they distort the person of Christ.

False teachers also add to the teachings of Christ. They "[run] ahead and [do] not continue in the teaching of Christ" (verse 9). Sometimes this will take the form of some "new revelation," a document or teaching that is supposedly necessary to understanding the Bible. Teachers who advocate the use of such material usually claim direct inspiration and may assert that there are no contradictions between their doctrines and the Bible. In that case a person will need to ask a few penetrating questions to spot the inconsistencies. At other times deceivers claim outright prophetic superiority to Scripture—boldfaced evidence that they've strayed from Biblical truth.

The only safe place to ground oneself spiritually is in the Scriptures. John admonishes both seekers and believers to reject the idea that clear understanding of Christ's teachings comes only through some revelation or prophet other than what is found in the Bible.

3 JOHN

¹The elder,

To my dear friend Gaius, whom I love in the truth.

²Dear friend, I pray that you may enjoy good health and that all may go well with you, even as your soul is getting along well. ³It gave me great joy to have some brothers come and tell about your faithfulness to the truth and how you continue to walk in the truth. ⁴I have no greater joy than to hear that my children are walking in the truth.

⁵Dear friend, you are faithful in what you are doing for the brothers, even though they are strangers to you. ⁶They have told the church about your love. You will do well to send them on their way in a manner worthy of God. ⁷It was for the sake of the Name that they went out, receiving no help from the pagans. ⁸We ought therefore to show hospitality to such men so that we may work together for the truth.

⁹I wrote to the church, but Diotrephes, who loves to be first, will have nothing to do with us. ¹⁰So if I come, I will call attention to what he is doing, gossiping maliciously about us. Not satisfied with that, he refuses to welcome the brothers. He also stops those who want to do so and puts them out of the church.

¹¹Dear friend, do not imitate what is evil but what is good. Anyone who does what is good is from God. Anyone who does what is evil has not seen God. ¹²Demetrius is well spoken of by everyone—and even by the truth itself. We also speak well of him, and you know that our testimony is true.

¹³I have much to write you, but I do not want to do so with pen and ink. ¹⁴I hope to see you soon, and we will talk face to face.

Peace to you. The friends here send their greetings. Greet the friends there by name.

▦ MANAGING RESOURCES ⮂

5–8
Possessions

In this passage the apostle John commends his friend Gaius for his gracious hospitality. The word *hospitality* in the original language literally meant "a love for strangers" (see verse 5).

John writes that devoted followers of Christ should show kindness not only to people they know, but also to people they don't know. Christ-followers must realize that all God has given them, including their homes, is to be available for God's use.

When is the last time you had someone over for a meal? Why not show someone hospitality—especially a person who has no way of paying you back? John's exhortation is that such behavior is to be characteristic of all Christ-followers.

JUDE

¹Jude, a servant of Jesus Christ and a brother of James,

To those who have been called, who are loved by God the Father and kept by^a Jesus Christ:

²Mercy, peace and love be yours in abundance.

The Sin and Doom of Godless Men

³Dear friends, although I was very eager to write to you about the salvation we share, I felt I had to write and urge you to contend for the faith that was once for all entrusted to the saints. ⁴For certain men whose condemnation was written about^b long ago have secretly slipped in among you. They are godless men, who change the grace of our God into a license for immorality and deny Jesus Christ our only Sovereign and Lord.

⁵Though you already know all this, I want to remind you that the Lord^c delivered his people out of Egypt, but later destroyed those who did not believe. ⁶And the angels who did not keep their positions of authority but abandoned their own home—these he has kept in darkness, bound with everlasting chains for judgment on the great Day. ⁷In a similar way, Sodom and Gomorrah and the surrounding towns gave themselves up to sexual immorality and perversion. They serve as an example of those who suffer the punishment of eternal fire.

⁸In the very same way, these dreamers pollute their own bodies, reject authority and slander celestial beings. ⁹But even the archangel Michael, when he was disputing with the devil about the body of Moses, did not dare to bring a slanderous accusation against him, but said, "The Lord rebuke you!"

▦ DISCOVERING GOD ▦

3–4
Spiritual Fraud

Some arguments are pointless, but others are worth engaging in. Jude says one discussion that is worth some "heat" is one that centers around a challenge to Christianity's truthfulness. John tells those who follow Christ to "contend for the faith." That doesn't mean that believers are to endlessly badger people for disagreeing with the Bible. But there are good answers for the questions skeptics ask and solid reasons for the beliefs that constitute the Christian faith.

Notice also what Jude claims here. "The faith" we contend for is a set body of truth. It has been "once for all entrusted to the saints" (the word *saint*, as it is used here, is another word for a Christian, not a special class of superbelievers). Where is this faith found? In the Bible, which contains the sum total of Christian truth that believers need to defend.

¹⁰Yet these men speak abusively against whatever they do not understand; and what things they do understand by instinct, like unreasoning animals—these are the very things that destroy them.

¹¹Woe to them! They have taken the way of Cain; they have rushed for profit into Balaam's error; they have been destroyed in Korah's rebellion.

¹²These men are blemishes at your love feasts, eating with you without the slightest qualm—shepherds who feed only themselves. They are clouds without rain, blown along by the wind; autumn trees, without fruit and uprooted—twice dead. ¹³They are wild

^a 1 Or for; or in   ^b 4 Or men who were marked out for condemnation   ^c 5 Some early manuscripts Jesus

waves of the sea, foaming up their shame; wandering stars, for whom blackest darkness has been reserved forever.

[14]Enoch, the seventh from Adam, prophesied about these men: "See, the Lord is coming with thousands upon thousands of his holy ones [15]to judge everyone, and to convict all the ungodly of all the ungodly acts they have done in the ungodly way, and of all the harsh words ungodly sinners have spoken against him." [16]These men are grumblers and faultfinders; they follow their own evil desires; they boast about themselves and flatter others for their own advantage.

A Call to Persevere

[17]But, dear friends, remember what the apostles of our Lord Jesus Christ foretold. [18]They said to you, "In the last times there will be scoffers who will follow their own ungodly desires." [19]These are the men who divide you, who follow mere natural instinct and do not have the Spirit.

[20]But you, dear friends, build yourselves up in your most holy faith and pray in the Holy Spirit. [21]Keep yourselves in God's love as you wait for the mercy of our Lord Jesus Christ to bring you to eternal life.

[22]Be merciful to those who doubt; [23]snatch others from the fire and save them; to others show mercy, mixed with fear—hating even the clothing stained by corrupted flesh.

Doxology

[24]To him who is able to keep you from falling and to present you before his glorious presence without fault and with great joy— [25]to the only God our Savior be glory, majesty, power and authority, through Jesus Christ our Lord, before all ages, now and forevermore! Amen.

I knew about God and Jesus from my childhood and my church upbringing. I knew God was good and holy and righteous. I knew Jesus was sent to die for all humanity, making it possible for people to get to heaven. I loved God with all my heart and understanding, and wanted to be with him forever in heaven. I tried to be good for God's sake, to try to please him. But I knew that as wonderful and pure and holy as God is, I wasn't good enough to be fully accepted by him.

So here I was, not good enough for heaven, but not bad enough (so I thought) for hell. The stress of not knowing was a continual part of my life. I knew that if I died and someone in heaven told me, "Sorry, you missed out on step number six," it would be too late to make any changes. I thought I had to have everything in order here in this life.

When I asked people in my church, "How can I be sure if I'm going to heaven?" I didn't get answers that I could understand. They usually said something like, "It depends on your state of grace," without explaining exactly what that meant. Furthermore, they seemed to think that no one could really know that they were going to heaven, and that those who claimed they did know were either arrogant or naive. They told me to keep trying to do everything I could to stay morally upright and honest. That would be enough; surely God would honor my good efforts.

But that advice didn't ease my fear that I might be on my way to hell forever. That, combined with the exhaustion of "trying harder" to work my way to heaven and the feeling that I wasn't working hard enough, was robbing me of the peace and joy that I had felt as a child.

Several years later I went to a Christian businessperson's dinner meeting. The speaker told us that, as Christians, we could know *for sure* that we were saved. I stepped forward for counseling and was shown 1 John 5:13: "I write these things to you who believe in the name of the Son of God so that you may know that you have eternal life." The counselor repeated what I had heard in the main session, that Jesus paid the price for my sin out of his great love for me, and that he wanted to take *me* into heaven, not my basket full of good works. I learned that if I accepted Jesus' completed work on the cross, I would be clothed in his robe of righteousness and that God would see me, through his Son, as sinless.

That Scripture verse and the counselor's words rang true in my soul. I thanked Jesus right then and there for paying the price to get this little insignificant someone off this dusty planet. I praised him for taking me away from the hell that I deserved and into his glorious kingdom. I accepted him as my Savior.

The peace I have now is beautiful. I have no more fear about what is to become of me after death. My life has become more joy filled, and my good works are now done solely out of love for others and out of thanksgiving for what Jesus has done for me. My hunger and love for God's Word has grown, and I feel that God guides, instructs and comforts me through his promises in Scripture. I have a relationship with God, one that didn't exist before when I was trying so hard to fill my life with good works.

I know exactly what I want to say to God when I see him face to face on that glorious day when he calls me home: "Nothing in my hand I bring, only to the cross I cling." I'm trusting Jesus 100 percent for my salvation, and not relying on the good works that I had been trying to amass for myself.

REVELATION

Introduction

THE BOTTOM LINE

The Cuban Missile Crisis of 1962 was a dark period in human history. For a period of several weeks, United States president John F. Kennedy and Soviet premier Nikita Khrushchev faced off in the most dangerous nuclear showdown the world has ever seen. Though it wasn't the end of the world, it got a lot of people thinking about it! Historians say that it's the closest we've ever come to ending human life on earth. This book tells the story of how human history as we know it is *really* going to end—with Jesus Christ's return to earth in victory. Through the unusual messages and mostly symbolic images in this book, one theme rings true: God—not human political figures—is ultimately in control of the events of this world. And a time will come when Christ will return to destroy evil forever and to visibly rule over his kingdom.

CENTRAL IDEAS

- The world as we know it will come to an end.
- Jesus Christ will return to earth to make all things right.
- At the end of human history, evil will be judged and contained forever.
- Those who trust in Christ for their salvation will enjoy eternal life with him.

OUTLINE

1. Introduction (ch. 1)
2. Letters to the seven churches (chs. 2–3)
3. The throne, the scroll, and the lamb (chs. 4–5)
4. Three sets of seven judgments (6:1–16:21)
5. Babylon (17:1–19:5)
6. The wedding of the lamb (19:6–10)
7. Events surrounding Christ's return (19:11–22:5)
8. Conclusion (22:6–21)

TITLE

The title of this book is a shortened version of "The Revelation of God to John the Apostle."

AUTHOR AND READERS

John, the writer of several other New Testament books and a follower of Jesus, is the author of this last book of the Bible. He wrote this book to Christians in Rome who were experiencing intense persecution; he himself wrote from exile in a Roman penal colony as the result of his missionary activity. This letter of ultimate victory serves to encourage believers of all ages—Christ *will* have the ultimate victory over evil!

If there's one spiritual truth to which most people doggedly cling, it's their belief in an afterlife. Year after year, surveys indicate that the vast majority of people, regardless of religious persuasion, believe in heaven. Where people differ is in their ideas of what heaven will be like, who will be there, and how one enters. Listen to the answers some children gave when asked about heaven:

- Steve, an eight-year-old, said, "When you die, God takes care of you like your mother did when you were alive, only God doesn't yell at you all the time."
- Jimmy, another eight-year-old, noted, "When you die, they bury you in the ground and your soul goes to heaven, but your body can't go to heaven, because it's too crowded up there already."
- Marsha, a nine-year-old, said, "When you die, you don't have to do homework in heaven, unless your teacher is there too."
- Diane, a ten-year-old, summed up how most people feel about life after death: "Heaven is a nice place to go, but nobody is in a hurry to get there."

Most of us are curious as to what heaven will be like and who will be there. While the Bible doesn't give us a lot of detail about heaven, it does say enough for us to be certain of its beauty. No, it's not boring—like the image some people have of everybody sitting on a clouds and playing harps. Heaven is full of color, variety, and activity. Most importantly, it's devoid of anything that is evil, harmful, or out of character with the holy, loving God who made it.

"You don't have to do homework in heaven, unless your teacher is there too."

The book of Revelation is the apostle John's record of a vision given to him by God. It speaks of the past, present, and future (see Revelation chapter 1, verse 19 [page 1635]). It also says a lot about heaven. The images John writes about are highly symbolic; wild and speculative interpretations come easy. As such, familiarity with the rest of the Bible will help you as you try to understand this book.

Even if you can't nail down all the specifics, this book inspires awe. This is one of the few books you can enjoy in spite of not knowing exactly what it means! While you'll need to exercise caution when trying to figure out whether a passage refers to some modern-day event or space-age technology, you'll find some magnificent pictures of God's ultimate triumph in human history. And for a dazzling description of heaven, read Revelation chapter 21 through chapter 22, verse 5 (page 1653). While you read, keep in mind that the God who has proven trustworthy throughout the pages of this Bible promises to welcome those of us who trust and follow Christ to this fantastic place for all of eternity!

									Temple in Jerusalem destroyed (A.D. 70)			John's exile on Patmos (c. A.D. 90-95)	Book of Revelation written (c. A.D. 90-96)

Jesus' life (c. 6/5 B.C.–A.D. 30)

10 B.C. **AD 1** **10** **20** **30** **40** **50** **60** **70** **80** **90** **100**

John becomes a disciple (c. A.D. 26)

Nero's reign in Rome (c. A.D. 54-68)

Eruption of Mt. Vesuvius (A.D. 79)

Catacomb walls display Christian art (c. A.D.101)

REVELATION

Prologue

1 The revelation of Jesus Christ, which God gave him to show his servants what must soon take place. He made it known by sending his angel to his servant John, ²who testifies to everything he saw—that is, the word of God and the testimony of Jesus Christ. ³Blessed is the one who reads the words of this prophecy, and blessed are those who hear it and take to heart what is written in it, because the time is near.

□ ⠿⠿⠿⠿ ADDRESSING QUESTIONS ⠿⠿⠿⠿ ⬒

1:1–3
Unseen Realities   **Q**

God's timeless view is that the prophecies in this book will be fulfilled "soon," that "the time is near." The point is not to nail down how soon these things will happen, but to emphasize that they *will* happen and that we need to be ready.

Since John wrote this letter, Bible scholars have debated how much of this material applied to a first-century audience and how much pointed to events that would happen later. The notes in this Bible book don't try to definitively answer questions that have stumped great scholarly minds for centuries. Instead, they take a "seeker-friendly" approach, looking at areas of wide agreement rather than getting too specific about interpreting difficult symbolic passages. With that in mind, prepare yourself to experience some of the wildest and most vivid images in the whole Bible!

Greetings and Doxology

⁴John,

To the seven churches in the province of Asia:

Grace and peace to you from him who is, and who was, and who is to come, and from the seven spirits*ᵃ* before his throne, ⁵and from Jesus Christ, who is the faithful witness, the firstborn from the dead, and the ruler of the kings of the earth.

To him who loves us and has freed us from our sins by his blood, ⁶and has made us to be a kingdom and priests to serve his God and Father—to him be glory and power for ever and ever! Amen.

⁷Look, he is coming with the clouds,
   and every eye will see him,
   even those who pierced him;
and all the peoples of the earth will mourn because of him.
                                 So shall it be! Amen.

⁸"I am the Alpha and the Omega," says the Lord God, "who is, and who was, and who is to come, the Almighty."

One Like a Son of Man

⁹I, John, your brother and companion in the suffering and kingdom and patient endurance that are ours in Jesus, was on the island of Patmos because of the word of God and the testimony of Jesus. ¹⁰On the Lord's Day I was in the Spirit, and I heard behind me a loud voice like a trumpet, ¹¹which said: "Write on a scroll what you see and send it to the

---

ᵃ 4 Or the sevenfold Spirit

seven churches: to Ephesus, Smyrna, Pergamum, Thyatira, Sardis, Philadelphia and Laodicea."

¹²I turned around to see the voice that was speaking to me. And when I turned I saw seven golden lampstands, ¹³and among the lampstands was someone "like a son of man,"*ᵃ* dressed in a robe reaching down to his feet and with a golden sash around his chest. ¹⁴His head and hair were white like wool, as white as snow, and his eyes were like blazing fire. ¹⁵His feet were like bronze glowing in a furnace, and his voice was like the sound of rushing waters. ¹⁶In his right hand he held seven stars, and out of his mouth came a sharp double-edged sword. His face was like the sun shining in all its brilliance.

¹⁷When I saw him, I fell at his feet as though dead. Then he placed his right hand on me and said: "Do not be afraid. I am the First and the Last. ¹⁸I am the Living One; I was dead, and behold I am alive for ever and ever! And I hold the keys of death and Hades.

¹⁹"Write, therefore, what you have seen, what is now and what will take place later. ²⁰The mystery of the seven stars that you saw in my right hand and of the seven golden lampstands is this: The seven stars are the angels*ᵇ* of the seven churches, and the seven lampstands are the seven churches.

To the Church in Ephesus

2 "To the angel*ᶜ* of the church in Ephesus write:

These are the words of him who holds the seven stars in his right hand and walks among the seven golden lampstands: ²I know your deeds, your hard work and your perseverance. I know that you cannot tolerate wicked men, that you have tested those who claim to be apostles but are not, and have found them false. ³You have persevered and have endured hardships for my name, and have not grown weary.

⁴Yet I hold this against you: You have forsaken your first love. ⁵Remember the height from which you have fallen! Repent and do the things you did at first. If you do not repent, I will come to you and remove your lampstand from its place. ⁶But you have this in your favor: You hate the practices of the Nicolaitans, which I also hate.

⁷He who has an ear, let him hear what the Spirit says to the churches. To him who overcomes, I will give the right to eat from the tree of life, which is in the paradise of God.

To the Church in Smyrna

⁸"To the angel of the church in Smyrna write:

These are the words of him who is the First and the Last, who died and came to life again. ⁹I know your afflictions and your poverty—yet you are rich! I know the slander of those who say they are Jews and are not, but are a synagogue of Satan.

▣ ═══════ DISCOVERING GOD ═══════ ⮂

1:9–18
Jesus, the God-Man

A voice like the blast of a trumpet captured John's attention and told him to write down what he saw. When he turned to see who spoke, he saw the Lord Jesus, dressed as a priest and judge, standing in the middle of seven golden lampstands.

How did John respond when the saw the Lord? He fell at Jesus' feet in humility and worship. If Jesus were not God, such a reaction would have been pure blasphemy (John did this later to an angel and was rebuked; see Revelation chapter 22, verses 8 and 9 [page 1655]). The Jesus of the Bible is more than a prophet and more than an angel—he is God, and he is worthy to receive worship.

John's vivid descriptions will give you an idea of the awesome character of the risen Christ, the One who is God and who offers you salvation through his death on the cross. Keep that in mind as you continue reading through this book.

ᵃ 13 Daniel 7:13   *ᵇ 20* Or *messengers*   *ᶜ 1* Or *messenger;* also in verses 8, 12 and 18

¹⁰Do not be afraid of what you are about to suffer. I tell you, the devil will put some of you in prison to test you, and you will suffer persecution for ten days. Be faithful, even to the point of death, and I will give you the crown of life.

¹¹He who has an ear, let him hear what the Spirit says to the churches. He who overcomes will not be hurt at all by the second death.

To the Church in Pergamum

¹²"To the angel of the church in Pergamum write:

These are the words of him who has the sharp, double-edged sword. ¹³I know where you live—where Satan has his throne. Yet you remain true to my name. You did not renounce your faith in me, even in the days of Antipas, my faithful witness, who was put to death in your city—where Satan lives.

¹⁴Nevertheless, I have a few things against you: You have people there who hold to the teaching of Balaam, who taught Balak to entice the Israelites to sin by eating food sacrificed to idols and by committing sexual immorality. ¹⁵Likewise you also have those who hold to the teaching of the Nicolaitans. ¹⁶Repent therefore! Otherwise, I will soon come to you and will fight against them with the sword of my mouth.

¹⁷He who has an ear, let him hear what the Spirit says to the churches. To him who overcomes, I will give some of the hidden manna. I will also give him a white stone with a new name written on it, known only to him who receives it.

ADDRESSING QUESTIONS

2:1–3:22
Human Experience

Jesus gave John individual messages to seven churches that existed at the time John wrote. The Lord found something to commend in all the churches, with the exception of Laodicea (chapter 3, verses 14–22).

In spite of their imperfections, churches are the representation of Jesus on earth, and he wants them to be pure. That's why he strongly urged believers in these churches to pursue more Christlike behavior.

As you read through this passage, try to identify behaviors that Jesus commends and those he wants his followers to change. That will give you a glimpse of what he expects of those who choose to follow him.

To the Church in Thyatira

¹⁸"To the angel of the church in Thyatira write:

These are the words of the Son of God, whose eyes are like blazing fire and whose feet are like burnished bronze. ¹⁹I know your deeds, your love and faith, your service and perseverance, and that you are now doing more than you did at first.

²⁰Nevertheless, I have this against you: You tolerate that woman Jezebel, who calls herself a prophetess. By her teaching she misleads my servants into sexual immorality and the eating of food sacrificed to idols. ²¹I have given her time to repent of her immorality, but she is unwilling. ²²So I will cast her on a bed of suffering, and I will make those who commit adultery with her suffer intensely, unless they repent of her ways. ²³I will strike her children dead. Then all the churches will know that I am he who searches hearts and minds, and I will repay each of you according to your deeds. ²⁴Now I say to the rest of you in Thyatira, to you who do not hold to her teaching and have not learned Satan's so-called deep secrets (I will not impose any other burden on you): ²⁵Only hold on to what you have until I come.

²⁶To him who overcomes and does my will to the end, I will give authority over the nations—

> 27'He will rule them with an iron scepter;
> he will dash them to pieces like pottery'^{a}—

just as I have received authority from my Father. 28I will also give him the morning star. 29He who has an ear, let him hear what the Spirit says to the churches.

To the Church in Sardis

3 "To the angel^b of the church in Sardis write:

These are the words of him who holds the seven spirits^c of God and the seven stars. I know your deeds; you have a reputation of being alive, but you are dead. 2Wake up! Strengthen what remains and is about to die, for I have not found your deeds complete in the sight of my God. 3Remember, therefore, what you have received and heard; obey it, and repent. But if you do not wake up, I will come like a thief, and you will not know at what time I will come to you.

4Yet you have a few people in Sardis who have not soiled their clothes. They will walk with me, dressed in white, for they are worthy. 5He who overcomes will, like them, be dressed in white. I will never blot out his name from the book of life, but will acknowledge his name before my Father and his angels. 6He who has an ear, let him hear what the Spirit says to the churches.

To the Church in Philadelphia

7"To the angel of the church in Philadelphia write:

These are the words of him who is holy and true, who holds the key of David. What he opens no one can shut, and what he shuts no one can open. 8I know your deeds. See, I have placed before you an open door that no one can shut. I know that you have little strength, yet you have kept my word and have not denied my name. 9I will make those who are of the synagogue of Satan, who claim to be Jews though they are not, but are liars—I will make them come and fall down at your feet and acknowledge that I have loved you. 10Since you have kept my command to endure patiently, I will also keep you from the hour of trial that is going to come upon the whole world to test those who live on the earth.

11I am coming soon. Hold on to what you have, so that no one will take your crown. 12Him who overcomes I will make a pillar in the temple of my God. Never again will he leave it. I will write on him the name of my God and the name of the city of my God, the new Jerusalem, which is coming down out of heaven from my God; and I will also write on him my new name. 13He who has an ear, let him hear what the Spirit says to the churches.

To the Church in Laodicea

14"To the angel of the church in Laodicea write:

These are the words of the Amen, the faithful and true witness, the ruler of God's creation. 15I know your deeds, that you are neither cold nor hot. I wish you were either one or the other! 16So, because you are lukewarm—neither hot nor cold—I am about to spit you out of my mouth. 17You say, 'I am rich; I have acquired wealth and do not need a thing.' But you do not realize that you are wretched, pitiful, poor, blind and naked. 18I counsel you to buy from me gold refined in the fire, so you can become rich; and white clothes to wear, so you can cover your shameful nakedness; and salve to put on your eyes, so you can see.

19Those whom I love I rebuke and discipline. So be earnest, and repent. 20Here I

^{a}27 Psalm 2:9 ^{b}1 Or *messenger*; also in verses 7 and 14 ^{c}1 Or *the sevenfold Spirit*

am! I stand at the door and knock. If anyone hears my voice and opens the door, I will come in and eat with him, and he with me.

²¹To him who overcomes, I will give the right to sit with me on my throne, just as I overcame and sat down with my Father on his throne. ²²He who has an ear, let him hear what the Spirit says to the churches."

The Throne in Heaven

4 After this I looked, and there before me was a door standing open in heaven. And the voice I had first heard speaking to me like a trumpet said, "Come up here, and I will show you what must take place after this." ²At once I was in the Spirit, and there before me was a throne in heaven with someone sitting on it. ³And the one who sat there had the appearance of jasper and carnelian. A rainbow, resembling an emerald, encircled the throne. ⁴Surrounding the throne were twenty-four other thrones, and seated on them were twenty-four elders. They were dressed in white and had crowns of gold on their heads. ⁵From the throne came flashes of lightning, rumblings and peals of thunder. Before the throne, seven lamps were blazing. These are the seven spirits⁰ of God. ⁶Also before the throne there was what looked like a sea of glass, clear as crystal.

In the center, around the throne, were four living creatures, and they were covered with eyes, in front and in back. ⁷The first living creature was like a lion, the second was like an ox, the third had a face like a man, the fourth was like a flying eagle. ⁸Each of the four living creatures had six wings and was covered with eyes all around, even under his wings. Day and night they never stop saying:

> "Holy, holy, holy
> is the Lord God Almighty,
> who was, and is, and is to come."

⁹Whenever the living creatures give glory, honor and thanks to him who sits on the throne and who lives for ever and ever, ¹⁰the twenty-four elders fall down before him who sits on the throne, and worship him who lives for ever and ever. They lay their crowns before the throne and say:

> ¹¹"You are worthy, our Lord and God,
>   to receive glory and honor and power,
> for you created all things,
>   and by your will they were created
>   and have their being."

The Scroll and the Lamb

5 Then I saw in the right hand of him who sat on the throne a scroll with writing on both sides and sealed with seven seals. ²And I saw a mighty angel proclaiming in a loud voice, "Who is worthy to break the seals and open the scroll?" ³But no one in heaven or on earth or under the earth could open the scroll or even look inside it. ⁴I wept and wept because no one was found who was worthy to open the scroll or look inside. ⁵Then one of the elders said to me, "Do not weep! See, the Lion of the tribe of Judah, the Root of David, has triumphed. He is able to open the scroll and its seven seals."

⁶Then I saw a Lamb, looking as if it had been slain, standing in the center of the throne, encircled by the four living creatures and the elders. He had seven horns and seven eyes, which are the seven spirits⁰ of God sent out into all the earth. ⁷He came an

⁰5,6 Or *the sevenfold Spirit*

took the scroll from the right hand of him who sat on the throne. 8And when he had taken it, the four living creatures and the twenty-four elders fell down before the Lamb. Each one had a harp and they were holding golden bowls full of incense, which are the prayers of the saints. 9And they sang a new song:

> "You are worthy to take the scroll
>   and to open its seals,
> because you were slain,
>   and with your blood you purchased men for God
>   from every tribe and language and people and nation.
> 10You have made them to be a kingdom and priests to serve our God,
>   and they will reign on the earth."

11Then I looked and heard the voice of many angels, numbering thousands upon thousands, and ten thousand times ten thousand. They encircled the throne and the living creatures and the elders. 12In a loud voice they sang:

> "Worthy is the Lamb, who was slain,
> to receive power and wealth and wisdom and strength
> and honor and glory and praise!"

13Then I heard every creature in heaven and on earth and under the earth and on the sea, and all that is in them, singing:

> "To him who sits on the throne and to the Lamb
> be praise and honor and glory and power,
>   for ever and ever!"

14The four living creatures said, "Amen," and the elders fell down and worshiped.

The Seals

6 I watched as the Lamb opened the first of the seven seals. Then I heard one of the four living creatures say in a voice like thunder, "Come!" 2I looked, and there before me was a white horse! Its rider held a bow, and he was given a crown, and he rode out as a conqueror bent on conquest.

3When the Lamb opened the second seal, I heard the second living creature say, "Come!" 4Then another horse came out, a fiery red one. Its rider was given power to take peace from the earth and to make men slay each other. To him was given a large sword.

5When the Lamb opened the third seal, I heard the third living creature say, "Come!" I looked, and there before me was a black horse! Its rider was holding a pair of scales in his hand. 6Then I heard what sounded like a voice among the four living creatures, saying, "A quart*a* of wheat for a day's wages,*b* and three quarts of barley for a day's wages,*b* and do not damage the oil and the wine!"

7When the Lamb opened the fourth seal, I heard the voice of the fourth living creature say, "Come!" 8I looked, and there before me was a pale horse! Its rider was named Death, and Hades was following close behind him. They were given power over a fourth of the earth to kill by sword, famine and plague, and by the wild beasts of the earth.

9When he opened the fifth seal, I saw under the altar the souls of those who had been slain because of the word of God and the testimony they had maintained. 10They called out in a loud voice, "How long, Sovereign Lord, holy and true, until you judge the inhabitants of the earth and avenge our blood?" 11Then each of them was given a white robe, and they were told to wait a little longer, until the number of their fellow servants and brothers who were to be killed as they had been was completed.

---

a 6 Greek *a choinix* (probably about a liter)   *b* 6 Greek *a denarius*

¹²I watched as he opened the sixth seal. There was a great earthquake. The sun turned black like sackcloth made of goat hair, the whole moon turned blood red, ¹³and the stars in the sky fell to earth, as late figs drop from a fig tree when shaken by a strong wind. ¹⁴The sky receded like a scroll, rolling up, and every mountain and island was removed from its place.

DISCOVERING GOD

6:1–17
The God Who Is There

Chapter 6 begins a series of pronouncements on the earth called the "seal judgments." Scrolls in John's day were closed with a small amount of melted wax. To break the seal, then, is to open the scroll. These judgments and the ones that follow (seven trumpets and seven bowls—through chapter 16) unfold in a chronological pattern, and each successive set of seven judgments is more severe than the preceding one.

Why are all these judgments recorded? The persecuted first-century Christians found comfort in these descriptions of One more powerful than the tyrants who overwhelmed them. These arresting images of God's forces crashing down on those who stubbornly resist him (see chapter 9, verses 20–21) assured the believers that a time was coming when widespread human rebellion against God would be corrected.

The God of the Bible is all-powerful. His apparent silence in the face of human evil is not evidence that he can't or won't act. He chooses not to act because he is waiting for more seekers to "open the door" (Revelation chapter 3, verse 20 [page 1637]) and find him. In other words, he's waiting for *you*. Rest assured, however, that a time is coming when he *will* act!

---

¹⁵Then the kings of the earth, the princes, the generals, the rich, the mighty, and every slave and every free man hid in caves and among the rocks of the mountains. ¹⁶They called to the mountains and the rocks, "Fall on us and hide us from the face of him who sits on the throne and from the wrath of the Lamb! ¹⁷For the great day of their wrath has come, and who can stand?"

144,000 Sealed

7 After this I saw four angels standing at the four corners of the earth, holding back the four winds of the earth to prevent any wind from blowing on the land or on the sea or on any tree. ²Then I saw another angel coming up from the east, having the seal of the living God. He called out in a loud voice to the four angels who had been given power to harm the land and the sea: ³"Do not harm the land or the sea or the trees until we put a seal on the foreheads of the servants of our God." ⁴Then I heard the number of those who were sealed: 144,000 from all the tribes of Israel.

⁵From the tribe of Judah 12,000 were sealed,
   from the tribe of Reuben 12,000,
   from the tribe of Gad 12,000,
   ⁶from the tribe of Asher 12,000,

from the tribe of Naphtali 12,000,
   from the tribe of Manasseh 12,000,
   ⁷from the tribe of Simeon 12,000,
   from the tribe of Levi 12,000,
   from the tribe of Issachar 12,000,
   ⁸from the tribe of Zebulun 12,000,
   from the tribe of Joseph 12,000,
   from the tribe of Benjamin 12,000.

The Great Multitude in White Robes

⁹After this I looked and there before me was a great multitude that no one could count, from every nation, tribe, people and language, standing before the throne and in front of the Lamb. They were wearing white robes and were holding palm branches in their hands. ¹⁰And they cried out in a loud voice:

> "Salvation belongs to our God,
> who sits on the throne,
> and to the Lamb."

¹¹All the angels were standing around the throne and around the elders and the four living creatures. They fell down on their faces before the throne and worshiped God, ¹²saying:

> "Amen!
> Praise and glory
> and wisdom and thanks and
> honor
> and power and strength
> be to our God for ever and ever.
> Amen!"

¹³Then one of the elders asked me, "These in white robes—who are they, and where did they come from?"

¹⁴I answered, "Sir, you know."

And he said, "These are they who have come out of the great tribulation; they have washed their robes and made them white in the blood of the Lamb. ¹⁵Therefore,

> "they are before the throne of
> God
> and serve him day and night
> in his temple;
> and he who sits on the throne
> will spread his tent over
> them.
> ¹⁶Never again will they hunger;
> never again will they thirst.
> The sun will not beat upon them,
> nor any scorching heat.
> ¹⁷For the Lamb at the center of the
> throne will be their
> shepherd;
> he will lead them to springs
> of living water.
> And God will wipe away every
> tear from their eyes."

REASONS TO BELIEVE

7:1–17
The Incomparable Jesus

In contrast to chapter 6, which gives a chronological sequence of events, chapter 7 doesn't advance Revelation's narrative. Instead, it directs the reader's attention to two major groups of believers during this period of judgment. The opening part of the chapter describes 144,000 representatives of the godly remnant of Israel. The latter part of the chapter describes a great multitude of martyred people in heaven from every race, nation and language on earth. These people died rather than deny their faith.

Persecution of Christians continues today in many forms. But not many Western Christians feel the kind of persecution that first-century Christians experienced. Back then, seekers who came to believe in Christ risked their lives when they made that decision. Under those conditions, we can assume, new believers were completely committed to the truth they had heard.

What made those believers so sure and so committed? The only explanation that makes sense is that these men and women were convinced—by the very eyewitnesses who saw him—that Jesus Christ had overcome death and had risen from the tomb alive. For these Christians, even persecution to the point of death was endurable. They knew that Christ had likewise suffered and had promised to care for and be with them whether they lived or died.

The Seventh Seal and the Golden Censer

8 When he opened the seventh seal, there was silence in heaven for about half an hour.

²And I saw the seven angels who stand before God, and to them were given seven trumpets.

³Another angel, who had a golden censer, came and stood at the altar. He was given much incense to offer, with the prayers of all the saints, on the golden altar before the throne. ⁴The smoke of the incense, together with the prayers of the saints, went up before God from the angel's hand. ⁵Then the angel took the censer, filled it with fire from the altar, and hurled it on the earth; and there came peals of thunder, rumblings, flashes of lightning and an earthquake.

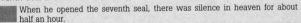

The Trumpets

⁶Then the seven angels who had the seven trumpets prepared to sound them.

⁷The first angel sounded his trumpet, and there came hail and fire mixed with blood, and it was hurled down upon the earth. A third of the earth was burned up, a third of the trees were burned up, and all the green grass was burned up.

⁸The second angel sounded his trumpet, and something like a huge mountain, all ablaze, was thrown into the sea. A third of the sea turned into blood, ⁹a third of the living creatures in the sea died, and a third of the ships were destroyed.

¹⁰The third angel sounded his trumpet, and a great star, blazing like a torch, fell from the sky on a third of the rivers and on the springs of water— ¹¹the name of the star is Wormwood.ᵃ A third of the waters turned bitter, and many people died from the waters that had become bitter.

¹²The fourth angel sounded his trumpet, and a third of the sun was struck, a third of the moon, and a third of the stars, so that a third of them turned dark. A third of the day was without light, and also a third of the night.

¹³As I watched, I heard an eagle that was flying in midair call out in a loud voice: "Woe! Woe! Woe to the inhabitants of the earth, because of the trumpet blasts about to be sounded by the other three angels!"

9 The fifth angel sounded his trumpet, and I saw a star that had fallen from the sky to the earth. The star was given the key to the shaft of the Abyss. ²When he opened the Abyss, smoke rose from it like the smoke from a gigantic furnace. The sun and sky were darkened by the smoke from the Abyss. ³And out of the smoke locusts came down upon the earth and were given power like that of scorpions of the earth. ⁴They were told not to harm the grass of the earth or any plant or tree, but only those people who did not have the seal of God on their foreheads. ⁵They were not given power to kill them, but only to torture them for five months. And the agony they suffered was like that of the sting of a scorpion when it strikes a man. ⁶During those days men will seek death, but will not find it; they will long to die, but death will elude them.

⁷The locusts looked like horses prepared for battle. On their heads they wore something like crowns of gold, and their faces resembled human faces. ⁸Their hair was like women's hair, and their teeth were like lions' teeth. ⁹They had breastplates like breastplates of iron, and the sound of their wings was like the thundering of many horses and chariots rushing into battle. ¹⁰They had tails and stings like scorpions, and in their tails they had power to torment people for five months. ¹¹They had as king over them the angel of the Abyss, whose name in Hebrew is Abaddon, and in Greek, Apollyon.ᵇ

¹²The first woe is past; two other woes are yet to come.

¹³The sixth angel sounded his trumpet, and I heard a voice coming from the hornsᶜ of the golden altar that is before God. ¹⁴It said to the sixth angel who had the trumpet, "Release the four angels who are bound at the great river Euphrates." ¹⁵And the four angels who had been kept ready for this very hour and day and month and year were released to kill a third of mankind. ¹⁶The number of the mounted troops was two hundred million. I heard their number.

¹⁷The horses and riders I saw in my vision looked like this: Their breastplates were fiery red, dark blue, and yellow as sulfur. The heads of the horses resembled the heads of lions, and out of their mouths came fire, smoke and sulfur. ¹⁸A third of mankind was killed by the three plagues of fire, smoke and sulfur that came out of their mouths. ¹⁹The power of the horses was in their mouths and in their tails; for their tails were like snakes, having heads with which they inflict injury.

ᵃ *11* That is, Bitterness   ᵇ *11* *Abaddon* and *Apollyon* mean *Destroyer*.   ᶜ *13* That is, projections

20The rest of mankind that were not killed by these plagues still did not repent of the work of their hands; they did not stop worshiping demons, and idols of gold, silver, bronze, stone and wood—idols that cannot see or hear or walk. 21Nor did they repent of their murders, their magic arts, their sexual immorality or their thefts.

The Angel and the Little Scroll

10 Then I saw another mighty angel coming down from heaven. He was robed in a cloud, with a rainbow above his head; his face was like the sun, and his legs were like fiery pillars. 2He was holding a little scroll, which lay open in his hand. He planted his right foot on the sea and his left foot on the land, 3and he gave a loud shout like the roar of a lion. When he shouted, the voices of the seven thunders spoke. 4And when the seven thunders spoke, I was about to write; but I heard a voice from heaven say, "Seal up what the seven thunders have said and do not write it down."

5Then the angel I had seen standing on the sea and on the land raised his right hand to heaven. 6And he swore by him who lives for ever and ever, who created the heavens and all that is in them, the earth and all that is in it, and the sea and all that is in it, and said, "There will be no more delay! 7But in the days when the seventh angel is about to sound his trumpet, the mystery of God will be accomplished, just as he announced to his servants the prophets."

8Then the voice that I had heard from heaven spoke to me once more: "Go, take the scroll that lies open in the hand of the angel who is standing on the sea and on the land."

9So I went to the angel and asked him to give me the little scroll. He said to me, "Take it and eat it. It will turn your stomach sour, but in your mouth it will be as sweet as honey." 10I took the little scroll from the angel's hand and ate it. It tasted as sweet as honey in my mouth, but when I had eaten it, my stomach turned sour. 11Then I was told, "You must prophesy again about many peoples, nations, languages and kings."

The Two Witnesses

11 I was given a reed like a measuring rod and was told, "Go and measure the temple of God and the altar, and count the worshipers there. 2But exclude the outer court; do not measure it, because it has been given to the Gentiles. They will trample on the holy city for 42 months. 3And I will give power to my two witnesses, and they will prophesy for 1,260 days, clothed in sackcloth." 4These are the two olive trees and the two lampstands that stand before the Lord of the earth. 5If anyone tries to harm them, fire comes from their mouths and devours their enemies. This is how anyone who wants to harm them must die. 6These men have power to shut up the sky so that it will not rain during the time they are prophesying; and they have power to turn the waters into blood and to strike the earth with every kind of plague as often as they want.

7Now when they have finished their testimony, the beast that comes up from the Abyss will attack them, and overpower and kill them. 8Their bodies will lie in the street of the great city, which is figuratively called Sodom and Egypt, where also their Lord was crucified. 9For three and a half days men from every people, tribe, language and nation will gaze on their bodies and refuse them burial. 10The inhabitants of the earth will gloat over them and will celebrate by sending each other gifts, because these two prophets had tormented those who live on the earth.

11But after the three and a half days a breath of life from God entered them, and they stood on their feet, and terror struck those who saw them. 12Then they heard a loud voice from heaven saying to them, "Come up here." And they went up to heaven in a cloud, while their enemies looked on.

13At that very hour there was a severe earthquake and a tenth of the city collapsed.

Seven thousand people were killed in the earthquake, and the survivors were terrified and gave glory to the God of heaven.

¹⁴The second woe has passed; the third woe is coming soon.

The Seventh Trumpet

¹⁵The seventh angel sounded his trumpet, and there were loud voices in heaven, which said:

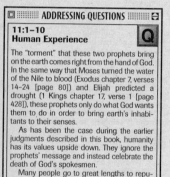

> ☐ ▦▦▦▦ **ADDRESSING QUESTIONS** ▦▦▦▦ ⬆
>
> **11:1–10**
> **Human Experience**   **Q**
>
> The "torment" that these two prophets bring on the earth comes right from the hand of God. In the same way that Moses turned the water of the Nile to blood (Exodus chapter 7, verses 14–24 [page 80]) and Elijah predicted a drought (1 Kings chapter 17, verse 1 [page 428]), these prophets only do what God wants them to do in order to bring earth's inhabitants to their senses.
>
> As has been the case during the earlier judgments described in this book, humanity has its values upside down. They ignore the prophets' message and instead celebrate the death of God's spokesmen.
>
> Many people go to great lengths to repudiate God's ultimate rule over their lives. But God wants all people to turn to him and experience his salvation. Regardless of what anyone else does, what will *you* do with God's invitation?

> "The kingdom of the world has become
>   the kingdom of our Lord and of
>   his Christ,
>   and he will reign for ever and ever."

¹⁶And the twenty-four elders, who were seated on their thrones before God, fell on their faces and worshiped God, ¹⁷saying:

> "We give thanks to you, Lord God
>   Almighty,
>   the One who is and who was,
> because you have taken your great
>   power
>   and have begun to reign.
> ¹⁸The nations were angry;
>   and your wrath has come.
> The time has come for judging the
>   dead,
>   and for rewarding your servants
>   the prophets
> and your saints and those who
>   reverence your name,
>   both small and great—
> and for destroying those who destroy
>   the earth."

¹⁹Then God's temple in heaven was opened, and within his temple was seen the ark of his covenant. And there came flashes of lightning, rumblings, peals of thunder, an earthquake and a great hailstorm.

The Woman and the Dragon

12 A great and wondrous sign appeared in heaven: a woman clothed with the sun, with the moon under her feet and a crown of twelve stars on her head. ²She was pregnant and cried out in pain as she was about to give birth. ³Then another sign appeared in heaven: an enormous red dragon with seven heads and ten horns and seven crowns on his heads. ⁴His tail swept a third of the stars out of the sky and flung them to the earth. The dragon stood in front of the woman who was about to give birth, so that he might devour her child the moment it was born. ⁵She gave birth to a son, a male child, who will rule all the nations with an iron scepter. And her child was snatched up to God and to his throne. ⁶The woman fled into the desert to a place prepared for her by God, where she might be taken care of for 1,260 days.

⁷And there was war in heaven. Michael and his angels fought against the dragon, and the dragon and his angels fought back. ⁸But he was not strong enough, and they lost their place in heaven. ⁹The great dragon was hurled down—that ancient serpent called

the devil, or Satan, who leads the whole world astray. He was hurled to the earth, and his angels with him.

10Then I heard a loud voice in heaven say:

"Now have come the salvation and the power and the kingdom of our God,
  and the authority of his Christ.
For the accuser of our brothers,
  who accuses them before our
    God day and night,
  has been hurled down.
11They overcame him
  by the blood of the Lamb
  and by the word of their
    testimony;
they did not love their lives so
    much
  as to shrink from death.
12Therefore rejoice, you heavens
  and you who dwell in them!
But woe to the earth and the
    sea,
  because the devil has gone
    down to you!
He is filled with fury,
  because he knows that his
    time is short."

13When the dragon saw that he had been hurled to the earth, he pursued the woman who had given birth to the male child. 14The woman was given the two wings of a great eagle, so that she might fly to the place prepared for her in the desert, where she would be taken care of for a time, times and half a time, out of the serpent's reach. 15Then from his mouth the serpent spewed water like a river, to overtake the woman and sweep her away with the torrent. 16But the earth helped the woman by opening its mouth and swallowing the river that the dragon had spewed out of his mouth. 17Then the dragon was enraged at the woman and went off to make war against the rest of her offspring—those who obey God's commandments and hold to the testimony of Jesus. 1And the dragon*a* stood on the shore of the sea.

13

The Beast out of the Sea

And I saw a beast coming out of the sea. He had ten horns and seven heads, with ten crowns on his horns, and on each head a blasphemous name. 2The beast I saw resembled a leopard, but had feet like those of a bear and a mouth like that of a lion. The

---

> ☐ ▓▓▓▓▓▓▓ **DISCOVERING GOD** ▓▓▓▓▓▓▓ ⬆
>
> ### Chapters 12—14
> ### Spiritual Fraud
>
> Chapters 12–14 introduce another parenthetical section that brims with puzzling images and numbers. These have been creatively interpreted over the years by many people who look to calculate when Jesus will return (a futile exercise, based on Jesus' words in chapter 16, verse 15 [page 1649]).
>
> Revelation 12 describes the spiritual war that spills over from the earth (verses 1–6) into heaven (verses 7–12) and back to earth again (verses 13–17).
>
> Chapter 13 contains a description of the beast, or Antichrist, and his false prophet, who gain great power during the final days leading up to Christ's return.
>
> In chapter 14, the 144,000 are commended for remaining true in their devotion to the Lord (verses 1–5). The remainder of the chapter contains various angelic announcements concerning "Beast" worshipers, and the symbolic harvesting of the earth.
>
> One theme to follow through all these strange images is that, once again, God's people find themselves at odds with the world's system. That system has power and prestige and lures people away from worshiping the one true God. Throughout the ages, forces that oppose God have tried to win people over to their side. As a seeker, that means your spiritual search is not conducted on neutral ground. Exercise caution as you continue your search so that you're not deceived.

---

a 1 Some late manuscripts *And I*

dragon gave the beast his power and his throne and great authority. ³One of the heads of the beast seemed to have had a fatal wound, but the fatal wound had been healed. The whole world was astonished and followed the beast. ⁴Men worshiped the dragon because he had given authority to the beast, and they also worshiped the beast and asked, "Who is like the beast? Who can make war against him?"

⁵The beast was given a mouth to utter proud words and blasphemies and to exercise his authority for forty-two months. ⁶He opened his mouth to blaspheme God, and to slander his name and his dwelling place and those who live in heaven. ⁷He was given power to make war against the saints and to conquer them. And he was given authority over every tribe, people, language and nation. ⁸All inhabitants of the earth will worship the beast—all whose names have not been written in the book of life belonging to the Lamb that was slain from the creation of the world.ᵃ

⁹He who has an ear, let him hear.

> ¹⁰If anyone is to go into captivity,
>   into captivity he will go.
> If anyone is to be killedᵇ with the sword,
>   with the sword he will be killed.

This calls for patient endurance and faithfulness on the part of the saints.

The Beast out of the Earth

¹¹Then I saw another beast, coming out of the earth. He had two horns like a lamb, but he spoke like a dragon. ¹²He exercised all the authority of the first beast on his behalf, and made the earth and its inhabitants worship the first beast, whose fatal wound had been healed. ¹³And he performed great and miraculous signs, even causing fire to come down from heaven to earth in full view of men. ¹⁴Because of the signs he was given power to do on behalf of the first beast, he deceived the inhabitants of the earth. He ordered them to set up an image in honor of the beast who was wounded by the sword and yet lived. ¹⁵He was given power to give breath to the image of the first beast, so that it could speak and cause all who refused to worship the image to be killed. ¹⁶He also forced everyone, small and great, rich and poor, free and slave, to receive a mark on his right hand or on his forehead, ¹⁷so that no one could buy or sell unless he had the mark, which is the name of the beast or the number of his name.

¹⁸This calls for wisdom. If anyone has insight, let him calculate the number of the beast, for it is man's number. His number is 666.

The Lamb and the 144,000

14 Then I looked, and there before me was the Lamb, standing on Mount Zion, and with him 144,000 who had his name and his Father's name written on their foreheads. ²And I heard a sound from heaven like the roar of rushing waters and like a loud peal of thunder. The sound I heard was like that of harpists playing their harps. ³And they sang a new song before the throne and before the four living creatures and the elders. No one could learn the song except the 144,000 who had been redeemed from the earth. ⁴These are those who did not defile themselves with women, for they kept themselves pure. They follow the Lamb wherever he goes. They were purchased from among men and offered as firstfruits to God and the Lamb. ⁵No lie was found in their mouths; they are blameless.

The Three Angels

⁶Then I saw another angel flying in midair, and he had the eternal gospel to proclaim to those who live on the earth—to every nation, tribe, language and people. ⁷He said in a

---

ᵃ8 Or *written from the creation of the world in the book of life belonging to the Lamb that was slain*   ᵇ10 Some manuscripts *anyone kills*

loud voice, "Fear God and give him glory, because the hour of his judgment has come. Worship him who made the heavens, the earth, the sea and the springs of water."

⁸A second angel followed and said, "Fallen! Fallen is Babylon the Great, which made all the nations drink the maddening wine of her adulteries."

⁹A third angel followed them and said in a loud voice: "If anyone worships the beast and his image and receives his mark on the forehead or on the hand, ¹⁰he, too, will drink of the wine of God's fury, which has been poured full strength into the cup of his wrath. He will be tormented with burning sulfur in the presence of the holy angels and of the Lamb. ¹¹And the smoke of their torment rises for ever and ever. There is no rest day or night for those who worship the beast and his image, or for anyone who receives the mark of his name." ¹²This calls for patient endurance on the part of the saints who obey God's commandments and remain faithful to Jesus.

¹³Then I heard a voice from heaven say, "Write: Blessed are the dead who die in the Lord from now on."

"Yes," says the Spirit, "they will rest from their labor, for their deeds will follow them."

The Harvest of the Earth

¹⁴I looked, and there before me was a white cloud, and seated on the cloud was one "like a son of man"ᵃ with a crown of gold on his head and a sharp sickle in his hand. ¹⁵Then another angel came out of the temple and called in a loud voice to him who was sitting on the cloud, "Take your sickle and reap, because the time to reap has come, for the harvest of the earth is ripe." ¹⁶So he who was seated on the cloud swung his sickle over the earth, and the earth was harvested.

¹⁷Another angel came out of the temple in heaven, and he too had a sharp sickle. ¹⁸Still another angel, who had charge of the fire, came from the altar and called in a loud voice to him who had the sharp sickle, "Take your sharp sickle and gather the clusters of grapes from the earth's vine, because its grapes are ripe." ¹⁹The angel swung his sickle on the earth, gathered its grapes and threw them into the great winepress of God's wrath. ²⁰They were trampled in the winepress outside the city, and blood flowed out of the press, rising as high as the horses' bridles for a distance of 1,600 stadia.ᵇ

Seven Angels With Seven Plagues

15 I saw in heaven another great and marvelous sign: seven angels with the seven last plagues—last, because with them God's wrath is completed. ²And I saw what looked like a sea of glass mixed with fire and, standing beside the sea, those who had been victorious over the beast and his image and over the number of his name. They held harps given them by God ³and sang the song of Moses the servant of God and the song of the Lamb:

> "Great and marvelous are your deeds,
>   Lord God Almighty.
> Just and true are your ways,
>   King of the ages.
> ⁴Who will not fear you, O Lord,
>   and bring glory to your name?
> For you alone are holy.
> All nations will come
>   and worship before you,
> for your righteous acts have been revealed."

⁵After this I looked and in heaven the temple, that is, the tabernacle of the Testimony, was opened. ⁶Out of the temple came the seven angels with the seven plagues. They were dressed in clean, shining linen and wore golden sashes around their chests. ⁷Then

ᵃ14 Daniel 7:13   ᵇ20 That is, about 180 miles (about 300 kilometers) one of the four living creatures gave to the seven angels seven golden bowls filled with the wrath of God, who lives for ever and ever. **8**And the temple was filled with smoke from the glory of God and from his power, and no one could enter the temple until the seven plagues of the seven angels were completed.

▣ ▤▤▤▤ ADDRESSING QUESTIONS ▤▤▤▤ ⮂

16:1–21
Human Experience

The bowl judgments complete what the other judgments began. The second trumpet, for instance, killed one-third of the sea creatures (chapter 8, verse 9); the sea's destruction is complete in the second bowl. Note also that the sixth bowl clears the way for the climactic Battle of Armageddon, and the seventh literally levels the earth. Most intriguing—and saddest of all—is that rather than turning to God, earth dwellers shake a fist in God's face and curse his name as these bowls are poured out (verses 9–11 and 21).

Pain is not a good thing, but God uses it for good. It is, in the words of one writer, "God's megaphone to rouse a sleeping world." Whether you're a seeker or a dedicated believer, God may allow pain in your life. He doesn't want you to be miserable, but rather wants to bring you to an awareness of your finite nature and of your need of a Savior—his Son, Jesus Christ.

The Seven Bowls of God's Wrath

16 Then I heard a loud voice from the temple saying to the seven angels, "Go, pour out the seven bowls of God's wrath on the earth."

2The first angel went and poured out his bowl on the land, and ugly and painful sores broke out on the people who had the mark of the beast and worshiped his image.

3The second angel poured out his bowl on the sea, and it turned into blood like that of a dead man, and every living thing in the sea died.

4The third angel poured out his bowl on the rivers and springs of water, and they became blood. **5**Then I heard the angel in charge of the waters say:

"You are just in these judgments,
    you who are and who were, the Holy
        One,
    because you have so judged;
6for they have shed the blood of your saints and prophets,
    and you have given them blood to drink as they deserve."

7And I heard the altar respond:

"Yes, Lord God Almighty,
    true and just are your judgments."

8The fourth angel poured out his bowl on the sun, and the sun was given power to scorch people with fire. **9**They were seared by the intense heat and they cursed the name of God, who had control over these plagues, but they refused to repent and glorify him.

10The fifth angel poured out his bowl on the throne of the beast, and his kingdom was plunged into darkness. Men gnawed their tongues in agony **11**and cursed the God of heaven because of their pains and their sores, but they refused to repent of what they had done.

12The sixth angel poured out his bowl on the great river Euphrates, and its water was dried up to prepare the way for the kings from the East. **13**Then I saw three evil*ᵃ* spirits that looked like frogs; they came out of the mouth of the dragon, out of the mouth of the beast and out of the mouth of the false prophet. **14**They are spirits of demons performing miraculous signs, and they go out to the kings of the whole world, to gather them for the battle on the great day of God Almighty.

ᵃ 13 Greek *unclean*

¹⁵"Behold, I come like a thief! Blessed is he who stays awake and keeps his clothes with him, so that he may not go naked and be shamefully exposed."

¹⁶Then they gathered the kings together to the place that in Hebrew is called Armageddon.

¹⁷The seventh angel poured out his bowl into the air, and out of the temple came a loud voice from the throne, saying, "It is done!" ¹⁸Then there came flashes of lightning, rumblings, peals of thunder and a severe earthquake. No earthquake like it has ever occurred since man has been on earth, so tremendous was the quake. ¹⁹The great city split into three parts, and the cities of the nations collapsed. God remembered Babylon the Great and gave her the cup filled with the wine of the fury of his wrath. ²⁰Every island fled away and the mountains could not be found. ²¹From the sky huge hailstones of about a hundred pounds each fell upon men. And they cursed God on account of the plague of hail, because the plague was so terrible.

The Woman on the Beast

17 One of the seven angels who had the seven bowls came and said to me, "Come, I will show you the punishment of the great prostitute, who sits on many waters. ²With her the kings of the earth committed adultery and the inhabitants of the earth were intoxicated with the wine of her adulteries."

³Then the angel carried me away in the Spirit into a desert. There I saw a woman sitting on a scarlet beast that was covered with blasphemous names and had seven heads and ten horns. ⁴The woman was dressed in purple and scarlet, and was glittering with gold, precious stones and pearls. She held a golden cup in her hand, filled with abominable things and the filth of her adulteries. ⁵This title was written on her forehead:

MYSTERY
BABYLON THE GREAT
THE MOTHER OF PROSTITUTES
AND OF THE ABOMINATIONS OF THE EARTH.

⁶I saw that the woman was drunk with the blood of the saints, the blood of those who bore testimony to Jesus.

When I saw her, I was greatly astonished. ⁷Then the angel said to me: "Why are you astonished? I will explain to you the mystery of the woman and of the beast she rides, which has the seven heads and ten horns. ⁸The beast, which you saw, once was, now is not, and will come up out of the Abyss and go to his destruction. The inhabitants of the earth whose names have not been written in the book of life from the creation of the world will be astonished when they see the beast, because he once was, now is not, and yet will come.

⁹"This calls for a mind with wisdom. The seven heads are seven hills on which the woman sits. ¹⁰They are also seven kings. Five have fallen, one is, the other has not yet come; but when he does come, he must remain for a little while. ¹¹The beast who once was, and now is not, is an eighth king. He belongs to the seven and is going to his destruction.

¹²"The ten horns you saw are ten kings who have not yet received a kingdom, but who for one hour will receive authority as kings along with the beast. ¹³They have one purpose and will give their power and authority to the beast. ¹⁴They will make war against the Lamb, but the Lamb will overcome them because he is Lord of lords and King of kings—and with him will be his called, chosen and faithful followers."

¹⁵Then the angel said to me, "The waters you saw, where the prostitute sits, are peoples, multitudes, nations and languages. ¹⁶The beast and the ten horns you saw will hate the prostitute. They will bring her to ruin and leave her naked; they will eat her flesh and burn her with fire. ¹⁷For God has put it into their hearts to accomplish his

purpose by agreeing to give the beast their power to rule, until God's words are fulfilled. ¹⁸The woman you saw is the great city that rules over the kings of the earth."

The Fall of Babylon

18 After this I saw another angel coming down from heaven. He had great authority, and the earth was illuminated by his splendor. ²With a mighty voice he shouted:

> "Fallen! Fallen is Babylon the Great!
> She has become a home for demons
> and a haunt for every evil[a] spirit,
> a haunt for every unclean and detestable bird.
> ³For all the nations have drunk
> the maddening wine of her adulteries.
> The kings of the earth committed adultery with her,
> and the merchants of the earth grew rich from her excessive
> luxuries."

⁴Then I heard another voice from heaven say:

> "Come out of her, my people,
> so that you will not share in her sins,
> so that you will not receive any of her plagues;
> ⁵for her sins are piled up to heaven,
> and God has remembered her crimes.
> ⁶Give back to her as she has given;
> pay her back double for what she has done.
> Mix her a double portion from her own cup.
> ⁷Give her as much torture and grief
> as the glory and luxury she gave herself.
> In her heart she boasts,
> 'I sit as queen; I am not a widow,
> and I will never mourn.'
> ⁸Therefore in one day her plagues will overtake her:
> death, mourning and famine.
> She will be consumed by fire,
> for mighty is the Lord God who judges her.

⁹"When the kings of the earth who committed adultery with her and shared her luxury see the smoke of her burning, they will weep and mourn over her. ¹⁰Terrified at her torment, they will stand far off and cry:

> "'Woe! Woe, O great city,
> O Babylon, city of power!
> In one hour your doom has come!'

¹¹"The merchants of the earth will weep and mourn over her because no one buys their cargoes any more— ¹²cargoes of gold, silver, precious stones and pearls; fine linen, purple, silk and scarlet cloth; every sort of citron wood, and articles of every kind made of ivory, costly wood, bronze, iron and marble; ¹³cargoes of cinnamon and spice, of incense, myrrh and frankincense, of wine and olive oil, of fine flour and wheat; cattle and sheep; horses and carriages; and bodies and souls of men.

¹⁴"They will say, 'The fruit you longed for is gone from you. All your riches and splendor have vanished, never to be recovered.' ¹⁵The merchants who sold these things and

---

a2 Greek *unclean*

gained their wealth from her will stand far off, terrified at her torment. They will weep and mourn ¹⁶and cry out:

> " 'Woe! Woe, O great city,
>   dressed in fine linen, purple and scarlet,
>   and glittering with gold, precious stones and pearls!
> ¹⁷In one hour such great wealth has been brought to ruin!'

"Every sea captain, and all who travel by ship, the sailors, and all who earn their living from the sea, will stand far off. ¹⁸When they see the smoke of her burning, they will exclaim, 'Was there ever a city like this great city?' ¹⁹They will throw dust on their heads, and with weeping and mourning cry out:

> " 'Woe! Woe, O great city,
>   where all who had ships on the sea
>   became rich through her wealth!
> In one hour she has been brought to ruin!
> ²⁰Rejoice over her, O heaven!
>   Rejoice, saints and apostles and prophets!
>   God has judged her for the way she treated you.' "

²¹Then a mighty angel picked up a boulder the size of a large millstone and threw it into the sea, and said:

> "With such violence
>   the great city of Babylon will be thrown down,
>   never to be found again.
> ²²The music of harpists and musicians, flute players and trumpeters,
>   will never be heard in you again.
> No workman of any trade
>   will ever be found in you again.
> The sound of a millstone
>   will never be heard in you again.
> ²³The light of a lamp
>   will never shine in you again.
> The voice of bridegroom and bride
>   will never be heard in you again.
> Your merchants were the world's great men.
>   By your magic spell all the nations were led astray.
> ²⁴In her was found the blood of prophets and of the saints,
>   and of all who have been killed on the earth."

Hallelujah!

19 After this I heard what sounded like the roar of a great multitude in heaven shouting:

> "Hallelujah!
> Salvation and glory and power belong to our God,
> ² for true and just are his judgments.
> He has condemned the great prostitute
>   who corrupted the earth by her adulteries.
> He has avenged on her the blood of his servants."

³And again they shouted:

> "Hallelujah!
> The smoke from her goes up for ever and ever."

⁴The twenty-four elders and the four living creatures fell down and worshiped God, who was seated on the throne. And they cried:

> "Amen, Hallelujah!"

⁵Then a voice came from the throne, saying:

> "Praise our God,
>   all you his servants,
> you who fear him,
>   both small and great!"

⁶Then I heard what sounded like a great multitude, like the roar of rushing waters and like loud peals of thunder, shouting:

> "Hallelujah!
>   For our Lord God Almighty reigns.
> ⁷Let us rejoice and be glad
>   and give him glory!
> For the wedding of the Lamb has come,
>   and his bride has made herself ready.
> ⁸Fine linen, bright and clean,
>   was given her to wear."

(Fine linen stands for the righteous acts of the saints.)

⁹Then the angel said to me, "Write: 'Blessed are those who are invited to the wedding supper of the Lamb!'" And he added, "These are the true words of God."

¹⁰At this I fell at his feet to worship him. But he said to me, "Do not do it! I am a fellow servant with you and with your brothers who hold to the testimony of Jesus. Worship God! For the testimony of Jesus is the spirit of prophecy."

The Rider on the White Horse

¹¹I saw heaven standing open and there before me was a white horse, whose rider is called Faithful and True. With justice he judges and makes war. ¹²His eyes are like blazing fire, and on his head are many crowns. He has a name written on him that no one knows but he himself. ¹³He is dressed in a robe dipped in blood, and his name is the Word of God. ¹⁴The armies of heaven were following him, riding on white horses and dressed in fine linen, white and clean. ¹⁵Out of his mouth comes a sharp sword with which to strike down the nations. "He will rule them with an iron scepter."ᵃ He treads the winepress of the fury of the wrath of God Almighty. ¹⁶On his robe and on his thigh he has this name written:

KING OF KINGS AND LORD OF LORDS.

¹⁷And I saw an angel standing in the sun, who cried in a loud voice to all the birds flying in midair, "Come, gather together for the great supper of God, ¹⁸so that you may eat the flesh of kings, generals, and mighty men, of horses and their riders, and the flesh of all people, free and slave, small and great."

¹⁹Then I saw the beast and the kings of the earth and their armies gathered together to make war against the rider on the horse and his army. ²⁰But the beast was captured, and with him the false prophet who had performed the miraculous signs on his behalf. With these signs he had deluded those who had received the mark of the beast and worshiped his image. The two of them were thrown alive into the fiery lake of burning sulfur. ²¹The rest of them were killed with the sword that came out of the mouth of the rider on the horse, and all the birds gorged themselves on their flesh.

ᵃ15 Psalm 2:9

The Thousand Years

20 And I saw an angel coming down out of heaven, having the key to the Abyss and holding in his hand a great chain. ²He seized the dragon, that ancient serpent, who is the devil, or Satan, and bound him for a thousand years. ³He threw him into the Abyss, and locked and sealed it over him, to keep him from deceiving the nations anymore until the thousand years were ended. After that, he must be set free for a short time.

⁴I saw thrones on which were seated those who had been given authority to judge. And I saw the souls of those who had been beheaded because of their testimony for Jesus and because of the word of God. They had not worshiped the beast or his image and had not received his mark on their foreheads or their hands. They came to life and reigned with Christ a thousand years. ⁵(The rest of the dead did not come to life until the thousand years were ended.) This is the first resurrection. ⁶Blessed and holy are those who have part in the first resurrection. The second death has no power over them, but they will be priests of God and of Christ and will reign with him for a thousand years.

REASONS TO BELIEVE

20:1–15
The Incomparable Jesus

One of the great chapters of the Bible, Revelation 20 presents a series of events, including Christ's reign over the earth, Satan's doom, and the judgment of the dead.

God-followers have known for centuries that the world is not functioning according to God's original design. Their prayer has been, "Your kingdom come, your will be done on earth as it is in heaven" since Jesus spoke those words (Matthew chapter 6, verse 10 [page 1266]). Here at last is the fulfillment of generations of yearning.

If you become a believer, you too can cling to this hope—the promise that Jesus Christ's will is going to be done on earth just as it is in heaven. That's a world worth being part of—and it's worth the wait!

Satan's Doom

⁷When the thousand years are over, Satan will be released from his prison ⁸and will go out to deceive the nations in the four corners of the earth—Gog and Magog—to gather them for battle. In number they are like the sand on the seashore. ⁹They marched across the breadth of the earth and surrounded the camp of God's people, the city he loves. But fire came down from heaven and devoured them. ¹⁰And the devil, who deceived them, was thrown into the lake of burning sulfur, where the beast and the false prophet had been thrown. They will be tormented day and night for ever and ever.

The Dead Are Judged

¹¹Then I saw a great white throne and him who was seated on it. Earth and sky fled from his presence, and there was no place for them. ¹²And I saw the dead, great and small, standing before the throne, and books were opened. Another book was opened, which is the book of life. The dead were judged according to what they had done as recorded in the books. ¹³The sea gave up the dead that were in it, and death and Hades gave up the dead that were in them, and each person was judged according to what he had done. ¹⁴Then death and Hades were thrown into the lake of fire. The lake of fire is the second death. ¹⁵If anyone's name was not found written in the book of life, he was thrown into the lake of fire.

The New Jerusalem

21 Then I saw a new heaven and a new earth, for the first heaven and the first earth had passed away, and there was no longer any sea. ²I saw the Holy City, the new Jerusalem, coming down out of heaven from God, prepared as a bride beautifully dressed for her husband. ³And I heard a loud voice from the throne saying, "Now the dwelling of God is with men, and he will live with them. They will be his people, and God himself will be with them and be their God. ⁴He will wipe every tear from their eyes. There will be no more death or mourning or crying or pain, for the old order of things has passed away."

⁵He who was seated on the throne said, "I am making everything new!" Then he said, "Write this down, for these words are trustworthy and true."

⁶He said to me: "It is done. I am the Alpha and the Omega, the Beginning and the End. To him who is thirsty I will give to drink without cost from the spring of the water of life. ⁷He who overcomes will inherit all this, and I will be his God and he will be my son. ⁸But the cowardly, the unbelieving, the vile, the murderers, the sexually immoral, those who practice magic arts, the idolaters and all liars—their place will be in the fiery lake of burning sulfur. This is the second death."

⁹One of the seven angels who had the seven bowls full of the seven last plagues came and said to me, "Come, I will show you the bride, the wife of the Lamb." ¹⁰And he carried me away in the Spirit to a mountain great and high, and showed me the Holy City, Jerusalem, coming down out of heaven from God. ¹¹It shone with the glory of God, and its brilliance was like that of a very precious jewel, like a jasper, clear as crystal. ¹²It had a great, high wall with twelve gates, and with twelve angels at the gates. On the gates were written the names of the twelve tribes of Israel. ¹³There were three gates on the east, three on the north, three on the south and three on the west. ¹⁴The wall of the city

---

██ ▒▒▒▒▒▒▒▒▒▒▒▒▒▒▒▒▒▒▒ **ADDRESSING QUESTIONS** ▒▒▒▒▒▒▒▒▒▒▒▒▒▒▒▒▒▒▒ ↕

21:1–27
Unseen Realities

Q

What will heaven be like?

To give us a glimpse of that glorious place, the Bible uses symbolic terminology rich with inviting images. The 200-foot-thick walls of this city will be adorned with precious and colorful metals and stones, and the city's main street will be paved with gold so pure that it's transparent (verses 16–21). The city won't require a temple or any other place of worship, because God and the Lamb (Jesus Christ) will be there. Likewise there will be no sun, for God's glory will light the city (verses 22–23).

In chapter 4, verses 2–6 (page 1638), John describes heaven as a place of great beauty and light. The apostle sees a rainbow and bright, almost blinding flashes of light around God's throne. Since God will be the only source of light, perhaps the differing colors will be refractions of his glory, just as a prism refracts the rays of the sun into different colors. Everywhere people look they will see the beauty of God in a spectacular array of colored light.

In heaven there will be no death, mourning, crying or pain (verse 4). Those who occupy heaven will have bodies like Jesus' resurrected body. After being raised from the dead, Jesus wasn't limited by space or time and had the ability to pass instantly from one dimension (visible) to another (invisible; see John chapter 20, verse 26 [page 1417], for example). Yet not only will people be like him in regard to their new bodies, they will also be free from all destructive and sinful appetites, actions, attitudes and words (see 1 John chapter 3, verse 2 [page 1624]).

What will Christ-followers do in heaven? One thing is certain, life won't be boring. The Bible indicates that they will reign with Christ (chapter 22, verse 5; also 1 Corinthians chapter 6, verses 2–3 [page 1497]) and enjoy their relationship with God and with other people from past ages. They'll be serving God without time demands, frustration, fear of failure or exhaustion (chapter 22, verse 3). And they'll enjoy the beauty of heaven for all eternity!

Who will be in heaven? Jesus said that those who "wash their robes" will enter through its gates (chapter 22, verse 14). He was referring to those who have cleansed their souls by being washed in Jesus' blood. While such a picture has some unusual aspects, it ties in with the message found in the earlier books of the Bible about the Jewish system of animal sacrifices and how Jesus fulfills that system. If we'll accept his payment for sin on our behalf, our sins will be forgiven and we will enter heaven upon death.

If you're a seeker, why not accept his offer today?

had twelve foundations, and on them were the names of the twelve apostles of the Lamb.

¹⁵The angel who talked with me had a measuring rod of gold to measure the city, its gates and its walls. ¹⁶The city was laid out like a square, as long as it was wide. He measured the city with the rod and found it to be 12,000 stadia *ᵃ* in length, and as wide and high as it is long. ¹⁷He measured its wall and it was 144 cubits *ᵇ* thick, *ᶜ* by man's measurement, which the angel was using. ¹⁸The wall was made of jasper, and the city of pure gold, as pure as glass. ¹⁹The foundations of the city walls were decorated with every kind of precious stone. The first foundation was jasper, the second sapphire, the third chalcedony, the fourth emerald, ²⁰the fifth sardonyx, the sixth carnelian, the seventh chrysolite, the eighth beryl, the ninth topaz, the tenth chrysoprase, the eleventh jacinth, and the twelfth amethyst. *ᵈ* ²¹The twelve gates were twelve pearls, each gate made of a single pearl. The great street of the city was of pure gold, like transparent glass.

²²I did not see a temple in the city, because the Lord God Almighty and the Lamb are its temple. ²³The city does not need the sun or the moon to shine on it, for the glory of God gives it light, and the Lamb is its lamp. ²⁴The nations will walk by its light, and the kings of the earth will bring their splendor into it. ²⁵On no day will its gates ever be shut, for there will be no night there. ²⁶The glory and honor of the nations will be brought into it. ²⁷Nothing impure will ever enter it, nor will anyone who does what is shameful or deceitful, but only those whose names are written in the Lamb's book of life.

The River of Life

22 Then the angel showed me the river of the water of life, as clear as crystal, flowing from the throne of God and of the Lamb ²down the middle of the great street of the city. On each side of the river stood the tree of life, bearing twelve crops of fruit, yielding its fruit every month. And the leaves of the tree are for the healing of the nations. ³No longer will there be any curse. The throne of God and of the Lamb will be in the city, and his servants will serve him. ⁴They will see his face, and his name will be on their foreheads. ⁵There will be no more night. They will not need the light of a lamp or the light of the sun, for the Lord God will give them light. And they will reign for ever and ever.

⁶The angel said to me, "These words are trustworthy and true. The Lord, the God of the spirits of the prophets, sent his angel to show his servants the things that must soon take place."

Jesus Is Coming

⁷"Behold, I am coming soon! Blessed is he who keeps the words of the prophecy in this book."

⁸I, John, am the one who heard and saw these things. And when I had heard and seen them, I fell down to worship at the feet of the angel who had been showing them to me. ⁹But he said to me, "Do not do it! I am a fellow servant with you and with your brothers the prophets and of all who keep the words of this book. Worship God!"

¹⁰Then he told me, "Do not seal up the words of the prophecy of this book, because the time is near. ¹¹Let him who does wrong continue to do wrong; let him who is vile continue to be vile; let him who does right continue to do right; and let him who is holy continue to be holy."

¹²"Behold, I am coming soon! My reward is with me, and I will give to everyone according to what he has done. ¹³I am the Alpha and the Omega, the First and the Last, the Beginning and the End.

ᵃ 16 That is, about 1,400 miles (about 2,200 kilometers)   *ᵇ 17* That is, about 200 feet (about 65 meters)   *ᶜ 17* Or *high*
ᵈ 20 The precise identification of some of these precious stones is uncertain.

¹⁴"Blessed are those who wash their robes, that they may have the right to the tree of life and may go through the gates into the city. ¹⁵Outside are the dogs, those who practice magic arts, the sexually immoral, the murderers, the idolaters and everyone who loves and practices falsehood.

¹⁶"I, Jesus, have sent my angel to give you*a* this testimony for the churches. I am the Root and the Offspring of David, and the bright Morning Star."

¹⁷The Spirit and the bride say, "Come!" And let him who hears say, "Come!" Whoever is thirsty, let him come; and whoever wishes, let him take the free gift of the water of life.

¹⁸I warn everyone who hears the words of the prophecy of this book: If anyone adds anything to them, God will add to him the plagues described in this book. ¹⁹And if anyone takes words away from this book of prophecy, God will take away from him his share in the tree of life and in the holy city, which are described in this book.

²⁰He who testifies to these things says, "Yes, I am coming soon."

Amen. Come, Lord Jesus.

²¹The grace of the Lord Jesus be with God's people. Amen.

a 16 The Greek is plural.

REASONS TO BELIEVE

22:12–21
The Incomparable Jesus

These are Jesus' final words to his followers. With these words, all the wisdom that God has chosen to reveal to his people is complete. No other writings can compare with the words in this Bible, written down by people under God's inspiration.

These last words comprise Jesus' final promises to his followers. And with John's "Amen" in verse 20, these words ring throughout the centuries as the anthem of Christians from all times and all places.

The book of Revelation leaves no doubt that the risen, glorified Jesus will come to earth again one day to establish his eternal kingdom. On that day all people will be judged, and those who have accepted his offer of eternal life and freedom from sin will live with him forever. No one knows when that day will come. It may happen before you close the cover of this book. That's why all people need to take Jesus' words in verse 20 very seriously.

The words of the Bible are trustworthy and true; millions who have looked to Jesus for salvation have found peace and hope for their lives that is beyond description. If you're a seeker who hasn't yet decided to place his or her trust in Christ, don't put off Jesus' invitation for one more day. As best you know how, ask him to forgive you of your sin and take away your guilt. It's a decision that will affect the rest of your life—both now, and through all eternity.

TABLE OF WEIGHTS AND MEASURES

The figures of the table are calculated on the basis of a shekel equaling 11.5 grams, a cubit equaling 18 inches and an ephah equaling 22 liters. The quart referred to is either a dry quart (slightly larger than a liter) or a liquid quart (slightly smaller than a liter), whichever is applicable. The ton referred to in the footnotes is the American ton of 2,000 pounds.

This table is based upon the best available information, but it is not intended to be mathematically precise; like the measurement equivalents in the footnotes, it merely gives the approximate amounts and distances. Weights and measures differed somewhat at various times and places in the ancient world. There is uncertainty particularly about the ephah and the bath; further discoveries may give more light on these units of capacity.

		Biblical Unit	Approximate American Equivalent	Approximate Metric Equivalent
WEIGHTS	talent	(60 minas)	75 pounds	34 kilograms
	mina	(50 shekels)	1 1/4 pounds	0.6 kilogram
	hekel	(2 bekas)	2/5 ounce	11.5 grams
	pim	(2/3 shekel)	1/3 ounce	7.6 grams
	beka	(10 gerahs)	1/5 ounce	5.5 grams
	gerah		1/50 ounce	0.6 gram
LENGTH	cubit		18 inches	0.5 meter
	span		9 inches	23 centimeters
	handbreadth		3 inches	8 centimeters
CAPACITY **Dry Measure**				
	cor [homer]	(10 ephahs)	6 bushels	220 liters
	lethek	(5 ephahs)	3 bushels	110 liters
	ephah	(10 omers)	3/5 bushel	22 liters
	seah	(1/3 ephah)	7 quarts	7.3 liters
	omer	(1/10 ephah)	2 quarts	2 liters
Liquid Measure	cab	(1/18 ephah)	1 quart	1 liter
	bath	(1 ephah)	6 gallons	22 liters
	hin	(1/6 bath)	4 quarts	4 liters
	log	(1/72 bath)	1/3 quart	0.3 liter

THE NEW INTERNATIONAL VERSION is a completely new translation of the Holy Bible made by over a hundred scholars working directly from the best available Hebrew, Aramaic and Greek texts. It had its beginning in 1965 when, after several years of exploratory study by committees from the Christian Reformed Church and the National Association of Evangelicals, a group of scholars met at Palos Heights, Illinois, and concurred in the need for a new translation of the Bible in contemporary English. This group, though not made up of official church representatives, was transdenominational. Its conclusion was endorsed by a large number of leaders from many denominations who met in Chicago in 1966.

Responsibility for the new version was delegated by the Palos Heights group to a self-governing body of fifteen, the Committee on Bible Translation, composed for the most part of biblical scholars from colleges, universities and seminaries. In 1967 the New York Bible Society (now the International Bible Society) generously undertook the financial sponsorship of the project—a sponsorship that made it possible to enlist the help of many distinguished scholars. The fact that participants from the United States, Great Britain, Canada, Australia and New Zealand worked together gave the project its international scope. That they were from many denominations—including Anglican, Assemblies of God, Baptist, Brethren, Christian Reformed, Church of Christ, Evangelical Free, Lutheran, Mennonite, Methodist, Nazarene, Presbyterian, Wesleyan and other churches—helped to safeguard the translation from sectarian bias.

How it was made helps to give the New International Version its distinctiveness. The translation of each book was assigned to a team of scholars. Next, one of the Intermediate Editorial Committees revised the initial translation, with constant reference to the Hebrew, Aramaic or Greek. Their work then went to one of the General Editorial Committees, which checked it in detail and made another thorough revision. This revision in turn was carefully reviewed by the Committee on Bible Translation, which made further changes and then released the final version for publication. In this way the entire Bible underwent three revisions, during each of which the translation was examined for its faithfulness to the original languages and for its English style.

All this involved many thousands of hours of research and discussion regarding the meaning of the texts and the precise way of putting them into English. It may well be that no other translation has been made by a more thorough process of review and revision from committee to committee than this one.

From the beginning of the project, the Committee on Bible Translation held to certain goals for the New International Version: that it would be an accurate translation and one that would have clarity and literary quality and so prove suitable for public and private reading, teaching, preaching, memorizing and liturgical use. The Committee also sought to preserve some measure of continuity with the long tradition of translating the Scriptures into English.

In working toward these goals, the translators were united in their commitment to the authority and infallibility of the Bible as God's Word in written form. They believe that it contains the divine answer to the deepest needs of humanity, that it sheds unique light on our path in a dark world, and that it sets forth the way to our eternal well-being.

The first concern of the translators has been the accuracy of the translation and its fidelity to the thought of the biblical writers. They have weighed the significance of the lexical and grammatical details of the Hebrew, Aramaic and Greek texts. At the same time, they have striven for more than a word-for-word translation. Because thought patterns and syntax differ from language to language, faithful communication of the meaning of the writers of the

Bible demands frequent modifications in sentence structure and constant regard for the contextual meanings of words.

A sensitive feeling for style does not always accompany scholarship. Accordingly the Committee on Bible Translation submitted the developing version to a number of stylistic consultants. Two of them read every book of both Old and New Testaments twice—once before and once after the last major revision—and made invaluable suggestions. Samples of the translation were tested for clarity and ease of reading by various kinds of people—young and old, highly educated and less well educated, ministers and laymen.

Concern for clear and natural English—that the New International Version should be idiomatic but not idiosyncratic, contemporary but not dated—motivated the translators and consultants. At the same time, they tried to reflect the differing styles of the biblical writers. In view of the international use of English, the translators sought to avoid obvious Americanisms on the one hand and obvious Anglicisms on the other. A British edition reflects the comparatively few differences of significant idiom and of spelling.

As for the traditional pronouns "thou," "thee" and "thine" in reference to the Deity, the translators judged that to use these archaisms (along with the old verb forms such as "doest," "wouldest" and "hadst") would violate accuracy in translation. Neither Hebrew, Aramaic nor Greek uses special pronouns for the persons of the Godhead. A present-day translation is not enhanced by forms that in the time of the King James Version were used in everyday speech, whether referring to God or man.

For the Old Testament the standard Hebrew text, the Masoretic Text as published in the latest editions of *Biblia Hebraica*, was used throughout. The Dead Sea Scrolls contain material bearing on an earlier stage of the Hebrew text. They were consulted, as were the Samaritan Pentateuch and the ancient scribal traditions relating to textual changes. Sometimes a variant Hebrew reading in the margin of the Masoretic Text was followed instead of the text itself. Such instances, being variants within the Masoretic tradition, are not specified by footnotes. In rare cases, words in the consonantal text were divided differently from the way they appear in the Masoretic Text. Footnotes indicate this. The translators also consulted the more important early versions—the Septuagint; Aquila, Symmachus and Theodotion; the Vulgate; the Syriac Peshitta; the Targums; and for the Psalms the *Juxta Hebraica* of Jerome. Readings from these versions were occasionally followed where the Masoretic Text seemed doubtful and where accepted principles of textual criticism showed that one or more of these textual witnesses appeared to provide the correct reading. Such instances are footnoted. Sometimes vowel letters and vowel signs did not, in the judgment of the translators, represent the correct vowels for the original consonantal text. Accordingly some words were read with a different set of vowels. These instances are usually not indicated by footnotes.

The Greek text used in translating the New Testament was an eclectic one. No other piece of ancient literature has such an abundance of manuscript witnesses as does the New Testament. Where existing manuscripts differ, the translators made their choice of readings according to accepted principles of New Testament textual criticism. Footnotes call attention to places where there was uncertainty about what the original text was. The best current printed texts of the Greek New Testament were used.

There is a sense in which the work of translation is never wholly finished. This applies to all great literature and uniquely so to the Bible. In 1973 the New Testament in the New International Version was published. Since then, suggestions for corrections and revisions have been received from various sources. The Committee on Bible Translation carefully considered the suggestions and adopted a number of them. These were incorporated in the first printing of the entire Bible in 1978. Additional revisions were made by the Committee on Bible Translation in 1983 and appear in printings after that date.

As in other ancient documents, the precise meaning of the biblical texts is sometimes uncertain. This is more often the case with the Hebrew and Aramaic texts than with the Greek text. Although archaeological and linguistic discoveries in this century aid in understanding difficult passages, some uncertainties remain. The more significant of these have been called to the reader's attention in the footnotes.

In regard to the divine name *YHWH*, commonly referred to as the *Tetragrammaton,* the translators adopted the device used in most English versions of rendering that name as "LORD" in capital letters to distinguish it from *Adonai,* another Hebrew word rendered "Lord," for which small letters are used. Wherever the two names stand together in the Old Testament as a compound name of God, they are rendered "Sovereign LORD."

Because for most readers today the phrases "the LORD of hosts" and "God of hosts" have little meaning, this version renders them "the LORD Almighty" and "God Almighty." These renderings convey the sense of the Hebrew, namely, "he who is sovereign over all the 'hosts' (powers) in heaven and on earth, especially over the "hosts" (armies) of Israel." For readers unacquainted with Hebrew this does not make clear the distinction between *Sabaoth* ("hosts" or "Almighty") and *Shaddai* (which can also be translated "Almighty"), but the latter occurs infrequently and is always footnoted. When *Adonai* and *YHWH Sabaoth* occur together, they are rendered "the Lord, the LORD Almighty."

As for other proper nouns, the familiar spellings of the King James Version are generally retained. Names traditionally spelled with "ch," except where it is final, are usually spelled in this translation with "k" or "c," since the biblical languages do not have the sound that "ch" frequently indicates in English—for example, in *chant.* For well-known names such as Zechariah, however, the traditional spelling has been retained. Variation in the spelling of names in the original languages has usually not been indicated. Where a person or place has two or more different names in the Hebrew, Aramaic or Greek texts, the more familiar one has generally been used, with footnotes where needed.

To achieve clarity the translators sometimes supplied words not in the original texts but required by the context. If there was uncertainty about such material, it is enclosed in brackets. Also for the sake of clarity or style, nouns, including some proper nouns, are sometimes substituted for pronouns, and vice versa. And though the Hebrew writers often shifted back and forth between first, second and third personal pronouns without change of antecedent, this translation often makes them uniform, in accordance with English style and without the use of footnotes.

Poetical passages are printed as poetry, that is, with indentation of lines with separate stanzas. These are generally designed to reflect the structure of Hebrew poetry. This poetry is normally characterized by parallelism in balanced lines. Most of the poetry in the Bible is in the Old Testament, and scholars differ regarding the scansion of Hebrew lines. The translators determined the stanza divisions for the most part by analysis of the subject matter. The stanzas therefore serve as poetic paragraphs.

As an aid to the reader, italicized sectional headings are inserted in most of the books. They are not to be regarded as part of the NIV text, are not for oral reading, and are not intended to dictate the interpretation of the sections they head.

The footnotes in this version are of several kinds, most of which need no explanation. Those giving alternative translations begin with "Or" and generally introduce the alternative with the last word preceding it in the text, except when it is a single-word alternative; in poetry quoted in a footnote a slant mark indicates a line division. Footnotes introduced by "Or" do not have uniform significance. In some cases two possible translations were considered to have about equal validity. In other cases, though the translators were convinced that the translation in the text was correct, they judged that another interpretation was possible and of sufficient importance to be represented in a footnote.

In the New Testament, footnotes that refer to uncertainty regarding the original text are introduced by "Some manuscripts" or similar expressions. In the Old Testament, evidence for the reading chosen is given first and evidence for the alternative is added after a semicolon (for example: Septuagint; Hebrew *father*). In such notes the term "Hebrew" refers to the Masoretic Text.

It should be noted that minerals, flora and fauna, architectural details, articles of clothing and jewelry, musical instruments and other articles cannot always be identified with precision. Also measures of capacity in the biblical period are particularly uncertain (see the table of weights and measures following the text).

Like all translations of the Bible, made as they are by imperfect man, this one undoubtedly falls short of its goals. Yet we are grateful to God for the extent to which he has enabled us to realize these goals and for the strength he has given us and our colleagues to complete our task. We offer this version of the Bible to him in whose name and for whose glory it has been made. We pray that it will lead many into a better understanding of the Holy Scriptures and a fuller knowledge of Jesus Christ the incarnate Word, of whom the Scriptures so faithfully testify.

The Committee on Bible Translation
June 1978 (Revised August 1983)

Names of the translators and editors may be secured
from the International Bible Society,
translation sponsors of the New International Version,
1820 Jet Stream Drive, Colorado Springs, Colorado
80923–3696 U.S.A.

This subject index is intended to help you target your study. It shows the Scripture location and page number of every information "window" on a particular topic.

Spiritual Fraud

REASONS TO BELIEVE

The Incomparable Jesus

KNOWING YOURSELF

Character

Emotions

Sin

A New Identity

STRENGTHENING RELATIONSHIPS

MANAGING RESOURCES

This tool has been designed to help define unfamiliar names, places, or terms that you find as you read the Bible. Some familiar terms that call for an expanded definition are also included. Many of the entries have book, chapter, and verse references that help place the term in its Biblical context. If the term you're questioning isn't included here, or if you'd like to look into a particular subject more thoroughly, see the *NIV Complete Concordance* or consult a smaller concordance such as the one included in the *NIV Study Bible*.

AARON—the brother of Moses; he served as Moses' spokesman before Pharaoh (Ex 4:14–16,27–31; 7:1–2); he was Israel's first high priest (Ex 28:1; Nu 17; Heb 5:1–4).

ABBA—the word for *father* in Aramaic, one of the three languages Jesus spoke.

| Ro | 8: 15 | And by him we cry "*A*, Father." |
| Gal | 4: 6 | the Spirit who calls out, "*A*, Father." |

ABEL—the second son of Adam (Ge 4:2); he offered the proper sacrifice to God (Ge 4:4; Heb 11:4), but was murdered by his brother Cain (Ge 4:8; Mt 23:35; 1Jn 3:12).

ABIGAIL—the wife of Nabal; she helped save David's life (1Sa 25:14–35) and later became his wife (1Sa 25:36–42).

ABOMINATION—a thing to be hated.

ABOUND—to be more than enough; to overflow.

| Ex | 34: 6 | slow to anger, *a* in love |
| Php | 1: 9 | that your love may *a* more |

ABRAHAM—the father of the Jewish nation and of all believers. God promised that he would make a mighty nation of Abraham's children and would give them the land of Canaan (Ge 15; 17; 22; Ro 4; Heb 6:13–15). As a test, God told him to offer his son Isaac as a sacrifice (Ge 22; Heb 11:17–19) but withdrew this command when Abraham showed that he would trust the Lord even in this matter.

ABSALOM—a son of David (2Sa 3:3); he plotted to take David's throne. He met death when his long hair became entangled in an oak tree

and Joab, David's commander, thrust javelins into his heart (2Sa 14–18).

ABYSS—the place of the dead; the place where evil spirits live.

ACHAN—an Israelite who kept spoil from the conquest of Jericho for himself; as a result of Achan's stealing what belonged to God, the Israelites were defeated at Ai and he and his family were stoned to death (Jos 7; 22:20).

ACKNOWLEDGE—to know and to say that something is true; to recognize.

| Mt | 10: 32 | *a* him before my Father in heaven. |
| 2Ti | 3: 7 | but never able to *a* the truth. |

ADAM—the first man God created (Ge 1:26–2:25); he sinned by disobeying God (Ge 3) thereby bringing all people under the curse of sin (Ro 5:12–21).

ADMONISH—to give warning or advice in a caring way.

ADULTERY—having sexual relations with someone other than one's husband or wife. Spiritual adultery means being unfaithful to God (Jer 3).

| Ex | 20: 14 | You shall not commit *a*. |
| Mt | 5: 28 | lustfully has already committed *a* |

ADVOCATE—1. (*v.*) to speak in favor of. 2. (*n.*) someone who speaks in another person's defense. Jesus is our advocate.

AFFLICTION—trouble or pain that lasts a long time.

| Ro | 12: 12 | patient in *a*, faithful in prayer. |

AHAB—a wicked king of Israel; the husband of Jezebel (1Ki 16:31). He caused Israel to worship Baal rather than God (1Ki 16:31-33) and was opposed by God's prophet Elijah (1Ki 17:1; 18; 21).

ALABASTER—a hard marblelike material that can be made into jars, vases or sculptures.

ALIEN—a foreigner or stranger.

Ex 22: 21 "Do not mistreat an *a*
Eph 2: 19 no longer foreigners and *a*, but
            fellow citizens
1Pe 2: 11 as *a* and strangers in the world,

ALMIGHTY—a name used to show how strong and powerful God is.

Ge 17: 1 "I am God *A*; walk before me
Isa 6: 3 "Holy, holy, holy is the LORD *A*;

ALTAR—a raised platform, made of stones, metal, dirt or wood, on which sacrifices were made.

AMEN—Hebrew words that means "so be it" or "let it become true."

AMOS—a prophet of Israel who ministered about the same time as Hosea and Jonah; he spoke about God's justice and righteousness.

ANANIAS—1. the husband of Sapphira; he was struck dead for lying to God (Ac 5:1-11); 2. the disciple who baptized Saul (Ac 9:10-19); 3. the high priest before whom Paul was tried in Jerusalem (Ac 22:30-24:1).

ANDREW—one of the twelve apostles; the brother of Peter (Mt 4:18; 10:2; Ac 1:13).

ANGEL—a heavenly being.

Ps 34: 7 The *a* of the LORD encamps
Heb 1: 14 Are not all *a* ministering spirits
Heb 2: 7 made him a little lower than
            the *a*;
1Pe 1: 12 Even *a* long to look

ANNIHILATE—to destroy completely.

ANOINT—to pour oil on a person's head, either for a physical benefit (Jas 5:14) or in order to set apart someone for service to God (Ex 28:41).

ANTICHRIST—a person who is against Christ.

1Jn 2: 18 have heard that the *a* is coming,
1Jn 2: 22 a man is the *a*—he denies

APOLLOS—a Christian from Alexandria who knew the Scriptures well (Ac 18:24-28) and helped Paul to minister in Corinth (Ac 19:1; 1Co 1:12).

APOSTLE—1. any of the twelve men Jesus chose to work with him during his earthly ministry; after being equipped by the Holy Spirit, they were sent out to preach about Jesus; 2. later, someone who had been with Jesus, had seen his miracles and then taught others about him.

Mk 3: 14 twelve—designating them *a*—
1Co 12: 28 God has appointed first of all *a*,
1Co 15: 9 For I am the least of the *a*

AQUILA—the husband of Priscilla; Aquila and Priscilla were co-workers with Paul in Corinth (Ac 18; Ro 16:3).

ARAMAIC—the language that was commonly spoken in the countries east of the Mediterranean Sea during Jesus' earthly ministry.

ARK OF THE TESTIMONY—also called the ark of the covenant; a large gold-covered box, which contained the Ten Commandments (Tablets of Testimony), a jar of manna and Aaron's staff, and was kept inside the Most Holy Place in the tabernacle (Tent of Meeting). It was a reminder to the Israelites of God's presence with them.

ASCEND—to go up. Jesus ascended to heaven to return to God the Father.

ASCRIBE—to think of as caused by, coming from or belonging to.

1Ch 16: 28 *a* to the LORD glory and strength,

ASSYRIA—one of the powerful nations of Biblical times; it often attacked the Israelites; its capital was Nineveh.

ATONE—to make right, by paying the penalty, the relationship between God and humans that was broken through sin. In the Old Testament people atoned symbolically for their sins by offering sacrifices to God. In the New Testament Jesus corrected the relationship between God and people once and for all by dying to take away sins.

ATONEMENT—the payment that corrects the relationship between God and humans that was broken through sin.

ev 17: 11	it is the blood that makes *a*	
ev 23: 27	this seventh month is the Day of *A.*	
to 3: 25	presented him as a sacrifice of *a,*	
Heb 2: 17	that he might make *a* for the sins	

AUTHORITY—the right and power to give rders.

Mt 9: 6	the Son of Man has *a* on earth	
Mt 28: 18	"All *a* in heaven and on earth has	
Ro 13: 1	for there is no *a* except that which	
Heb 13: 17	your leaders and submit to their *a.*	

AVENGE—to get back at or punish someone who has done wrong.

Dt 32: 35	It is mine to *a;* I will repay.	

AWE—respect and wonder; a holy fear of God because of his great power.

Ecc 5: 7	Therefore stand in *a* of God.	

BAAL—the name of many false gods in Canaan.

1Ki 18: 25	Elijah said to the prophets of *B,*	

BABEL—a tower built soon after the flood; the builders were attempting to reach up to God, but God confused their language so that the building was discontinued.

BABYLON—the beautiful capital of Babylonia; it was a powerful and influential city in the Near East from the eighteenth to the sixth centuries B.C. In the New Testament, Babylon represents the godless city.

Ps 137: 1	By the rivers of *B* we sat and wept	
Rev 14: 8	Fallen is *B* the Great,	

BALAAM—a seer who tried to curse Israel during their journey to the promised land, but God would not allow it (Nu 22–24).

BALM—a skin cream used to heal sores and relieve pain.

Jer 8: 22	Is there no *b* in Gilead?	

BANISH—to force a person away from a place.

BAPTIZE—a religious ceremony in which water is used as a symbol of cleansing from sin. Churches today baptize by sprinkling or pouring or immersing in water. Baptism is a sign that sin is washed away.

Mk 1: 9	and was *b* by John in the Jordan.	
Mk 16: 16	believes and is *b* will be saved,	
Ac 1: 5	but in a few days you will be *b*	
Ac 2: 38	"Repent and be *b,* every one of you,	

BARABBAS—the Jews chose this criminal, rather than Jesus, to be released by Pilate (Mt 27:26).

BARNABAS—an apostle; he was a co-worker with Paul on his first missionary journey (Ac 9:27; Ac 13–15).

BARREN—1. unable to have children; 2. unable to produce crops.

BARTHOLOMEW—one of the twelve apostles (Mt 10:3; Ac 1:13). He was also probably known as Nathanael (Jn 1:45–49; 21:2).

BATHSHEBA—the wife of Uriah; she committed adultery with David and later became his wife (2Sa 11); she was the mother of Solomon (2Sa 12:24).

BEELZEBUB—the prince of demons; Satan. Lk 11:15 "By *B,* the prince of demons,

BEERSHEBA—an important town that marked the southern boundary of Judah.

BELIEVE—to accept as true; to trust; to have faith.

Mk 1: 15	Repent and *b* the good news!"	
Mk 9: 24	"I do *b;* help me overcome my	
Jn 1: 7	that through him all men might *b.*	
Jn 3: 18	does not *b* stands condemned	
Jn 20: 27	Stop doubting and *b."*	
Ac 16: 31	They replied,"*B* in the Lord Jesus,	
Ro 3: 22	faith in Jesus Christ to all who *b.*	
1Th 4: 14	We *b* that Jesus died and rose again	

BENJAMIN—the twelfth son of Jacob. Rachel was his mother and he was the younger brother of Joseph (Ge 35:16–24; Ge 42–45).

BESIEGE—to surround a city or town completely with an army, so that nothing can go in or out.

BESTOW—to give.

BETHLEHEM—the city in Judea where Jesus was born (Mt 2:1).

BETRAY—to turn a friend over to his or her enemies; to be unfaithful to.

| Mt | 27: | 3 | When Judas, who had *b* him, |
| 1Co | 11: | 23 | on the night he was *b*, took bread, |

BETROTH—to promise to marry.

BIRTHRIGHT—the special rights of the first-born son. In the Old Testament, after the father died the oldest son received the father's power and right to make decisions for the entire family. He also got twice as much money and property as each of his brothers.

BLASPHEME—to speak carelessly, falsely or insultingly about God or holy things.

| Mk | 3: | 29 | whoever *b* against the Holy Spirit |

BLEMISH—a spot or mark that makes something imperfect.

| 1Pe | 1: | 19 | a lamb without *b* or defect. |

BLESS—1. to make holy; 2. to show favor to; 3. to ask God to show favor to.

Ge	2:	3	And God *b* the seventh day
Ge	12:	3	I will *b* those who *b* you,
Mt	5:	3	"'*B* are the poor in spirit
Ro	12:	14	*b* those who persecute you; *b*

BLIGHT—a disease in plants that makes them shrivel up and die.

BLIND—unable to see. Spiritual blindness is an inability to understand the things of God.

| Mt | 11: | 5 | The *b* receive sight, the lame walk, |
| Jn | 9: | 25 | I was *b* but now I see!" |

BLOOD—as the life-giving fluid in the body, it represents life itself. In the Old Testament the blood of sacrifices was symbolized the giving of life for life. Through the blood of Jesus on the cross, believers are saved from death for their sins.

Ex	12:	13	and when I see the *b*, I will pass
Lev	17:	11	For the life of a creature is in the *b*,
Mt	26:	28	This is my *b* of the covenant,
Eph	1:	7	we have redemption through his *b*,
Heb	9:	12	once for all by his own *b*,

BLOT—to erase or get rid of.

| Ex | 32: | 32 | then *b* me out of the book you have |

| Ps | 51: | 1 | *b* out my transgressions. |

BOAZ—a wealthy man who lived in Bethlehem in the days of the judges; he married Ruth (Ru 2; 4).

BODY—1. physical part of a person; 2. a group working as a unit.

Ro	6:	13	Do not offer the parts of your *b*
Ro	12:	1	to offer your *b* as living sacrifices,
1Co	6:	19	not know that your *b* is a temple
Eph	5:	30	for we are members of his *b*.

BORN AGAIN—refers to the experience of salvation; entering God's family through faith in Christ.

| Jn | 3: | 3 | no on can see the kingdom of God unless he is *b* again. |
| 1Pe | 1: | 23 | For you have been *b* again, |

BRANCH—an extension of another body or system.

| Jer | 33: | 15 | I will make a righteous *B* sprout |
| Jn | 15: | 5 | "I am the vine; you are the *b*. |

BREASTPIECE—a decorated square of linen cloth worn by the high priest when he entered the Holy Place.

BREASTPLATE—a chest-covering made of metal or leather, worn by soldiers for protection.

BRIBE—money or favor given to influence judgment or conduct.

| Ex | 23: | 8 | "Do not accept a *b*, |

BURNT OFFERING—in the Old Testament a sacrifice to the Lord that expressed devotion and complete surrender (Ge 8:20; Ex 29:18).

CAESAR—the title of many Roman emperors.

| Lk | 2: | 1 | In those days *C* Augustus |
| Mt | 22: | 21 | "Give to *C* what is Caesar's, |

CAIN—Adam and Eve's firstborn son; he murdered his brother Abel (Ge 4:1–16).

CALAMITY—a disaster, usually causing great loss and suffering.

CALEB—one of the twelve men who spied out Canaan. He came back with a positive report and encouraged the Israelites to take possession of Canaan (Nu 13:6–14:38; Dt 1:36).

CALL—1. (v.) to ask to come; 2. to give a name to; 3 (n.) a summons for a particular purpose or job.

2Ch	7: 14	if my people, who are c
Ps	145: 18	near to all who c on him,
Mt	9: 13	come to c the righteous,
Ro	8: 30	And those he predestined, he also c,
Ro	11: 29	gifts and his c are irrevocable.
1Pe	2: 9	of him who c you out of darkness

CANAAN—1. the land God promised to the nation of Israel; 2. the promised land.

CAPSTONE—the stone that holds two walls together; the stone that finishes a wall.

| 1Pe | 2: 7 | has become the c," |

CENSER—a bowl or dish used for carrying hot coals or for burning incense.

CENTURION—a Roman army officer in charge of one hundred soldiers.

CHAFF—the seed covering of a grain such as wheat. In Bible times the grain and chaff were separated by tossing the grain into the air so the wind could blow the chaff away.

| Ps | 1: 4 | They are like c |
| Mt | 3: 12 | up the c with unquenchable fire." |

CHARIOT—a two-wheeled vehicle pulled by horses.

| 2Ki | 6: 17 | and c of fire all around Elisha. |

CHERUB (pl. cherubim)—an angel, with an appearance something like a human being.

CHRIST—the official title of Jesus, meaning "the Anointed One." It is a Greek word, and it means the same as the Hebrew word *Messiah.*

Mt	1: 16	was born Jesus, who is called C.
Jn	20: 31	you may believe that Jesus is the C,
Ro	5: 8	While we were still sinners, C died
Eph	5: 23	as C is the head of the church,
Php	1: 21	to live is C and to die is gain.

CHRISTIAN—a believer in or follower of Christ.

| Ac | 11: 26 | The disciples were called C first |
| 1Pe | 4: 16 | as a C, do not be ashamed, |

CHRONICLES—a history of events in the order in which they took place.

CHURCH—the entire group of people who believe in Christ.

Mt	16: 18	and on this rock I will build my c,
Eph	5: 23	as Christ is the head of the c,
Col	1: 24	the sake of his body, which is the c.

CIRCUMCISION—the cutting off of the loose fold of skin at the end of the penis; it symbolized the agreement God made with the Israelites, and they came to be known as "the circumcision" (Eph 2:11).

| Ge | 17: 10 | Every male among you shall be c. |

CISTERN—a pit dug into the ground for storing rainwater.

CITADEL—a tower or building, especially in a city, equipped for war.

CITY OF REFUGE—one of six cities set aside by Moses and Joshua for those who had accidentally killed someone. Such people were safe there until a fair trial could be held (Nu 35:9–15).

CLAN—a group of people belonging to the same extended family.

| Ge | 24: 38 | to my father's family and to my own c, |
| Zec | 12: 12 | The land will mourn, each c by itself, |

CLEAN ANIMALS—animals God allowed the Israelites to sacrifice and eat.

COMMANDMENT—an order given by God. God gave the Ten Commandments to the Israelites while they were encamped in the area of Mount Sinai.

Ex	20: 6	who love me and keep my c.
Mt	22: 38	This is the first and greatest c.
Jn	13: 34	"A new c I give you: Love one

COMMEND—1. to praise; 2. to hand over to someone for safekeeping.

| Ps | 145: 4 | One generation will c your works |

COMPASSION (COMPASSIONATE)—sympathy; pity.

Ne	9: 17	gracious and c, slow to anger
Ps	103: 4	and crowns you with love and c,
Mt	9: 36	When he saw the crowds, he had c

Ro   9: 15   and I will have *c* on whom I have *c.*"
Col 3: 12   clothe yourselves with *c,* kindness,

CONCUBINE—in Bible times, a woman who belonged to a man but did not have the rights of a wife. She was often one of the spoils of war, and her primary purpose was to bear children for the man.

CONDEMN (CONDEMNATION)—to give out punishment to; to pronounce guilty.

Jn   3: 17   Son into the world to *c* the world,
Ro   8: 1   there is now no *c* for those who are

CONFESS—1. to say what you believe; 2. to tell your sins to someone.

Ro   10: 9   That if you *c* with your mouth,
Php 2: 11   every tongue *c* that Jesus Christ is
1Jn 1: 9   If we *c* our sins, he is faithful

CONSCIENCE—the sense of knowing if something is good or bad; a sense of right and wrong.

Ro   2: 15   their *c* also bearing witness,
Tit 1: 15   their minds and *c* are corrupted.
Heb 9: 14   cleanse our *c* from acts that lead

CONSECRATE—to set aside or dedicate for God's use.

Ex   13: 2   "*C* to me every firstborn male.
Lev 20: 7   "*C* yourselves and be holy,

CONTEMPT—lack of respect; looking down on someone or something as being worthless.

Pr   14: 31 He who oppresses the poor shows *c*
1Th 5: 20   do not treat prophecies with *c.*

CONTRITE—to feel sorry for one's sins; to feel repentant.

Ps   51: 17 a broken and *c* heart,
Isa 66: 2   he who is humble and *c* in spirit,

CONVERT—a person who has changed from one belief to another.

1Ti 3: 6   He must not be a recent *c*

CORNELIUS—a Roman to whom Peter preached the gospel; he became the first Gentile Christian (Ac 10).

CORNERSTONE—the first or most important stone laid when constructing a building.

Eph 2: 20   with Christ Jesus himself as the chief *c.*

COUNSELOR—another name for the Holy Spirit.

Jn   14: 26 But the *C,* the Holy Spirit,
Jn   15: 26 "When the *C* comes, whom I will

COVENANT—1. an agreement between two people or two groups of people, in which both usually make specific promises; 2. the promises of God for salvation.

Ge   9: 9   "I now establish my *c* with you
Ex   19: 5   if you obey me fully and keep my *c,*
Jer 31: 31 "when I will make a new *c*
1Co 11: 25 "This cup is the new *c* in my blood;
Heb 9: 15   Christ is the mediator of a new *c,*

COVET—to want for oneself something that belongs to another person.

Ex   20: 17 "You shall not *c* your neighbor's

CROSS—a horrible means by which criminals were put to death in Roman times.

Mt   10: 38 and anyone who does not take his *c*
Gal 6: 14   in the *c* of our Lord Jesus Christ,
Php 2: 8   even death on a *c!*
Col 2: 14   he took it away, nailing it to the *c.*
Heb 12: 2   set before him endured the *c,*

CROWN—a headpiece worn to symbolize glory, honor and victory.

1Co 9: 25   it to get a *c* that will last forever.
2Ti 4: 8   store for me the *c* of righteousness,
Rev 2: 10   and I will give you the *c* of life.

CRUCIFY—to put to death by nailing or tying a person's body to a cross.

Mt   27: 22 They all answered, "*C* him!"
1Co 1: 23   but we preach Christ *c:* a stumbling
Gal 2: 20   I have been *c* with Christ

CUBIT—a measure of length in Bible times; about 18 inches.

CUPBEARER—an officer of considerable responsibility who tasted the king's food and wine before serving them to him (Ne 1:11).

CURSE—1. (v.) to ask God to bring evil or injury to; 2. (n.) a prayer or desire that evil or injury come upon someone.

Lev	20: 9	"If anyone c his father or mother,
Lk	6: 28	bless those who c you, pray
Gal	3: 13	"C is everyone who is hung on a tree."

CYPRESS—an evergreen tree of the pine family.

DANIEL—a young Jewish exile; he lived in Babylon during the reign of several kings, including Nebuchadnezzar. For praying to God, contrary to an edict prohibiting prayer to anyone except the king, he was thrown into a lion's den (Da 1–6).

DAVID—the son of Jesse; anointed by Samuel to become king of Israel (1Sa 16:1–13); killed the giant Goliath (1Sa 17); during his reign Israel's place in the land of Canaan was made secure.

DEACON—a church officer whose qualifications are given in 1 Ti 3:8–13.

DEATH—the end of physical life; also the penalty for sin (Ro 6:23).

Ps	23: 4	the valley of the shadow of d,
Ecc	7: 1	for d is the destiny of every man;
Isa	25: 8	he will swallow up d forever.
1Co	15: 21	For since d came through a man,
1Co	15: 55	"Where, O d, is your sting?"
Rev	21: 4	There will be no more d

DEBAUCHERY—living an immoral life or a life without religion; living to please only oneself.

DEBORAH—a prophetess who led Israel to victory over the Canaanites (Jdg 4–5).

DEFILE—to make something that is good and pure into something impure or unclean.

DEFRAUD—to cheat someone by trickery.

DEITY—God.

| Col | 2: 9 | of the D lives in bodily form, |

DEMON—evil spirit. A demon-possessed person is one who is controlled by evil spirits.

| Mk | 5: 15 | possessed by the legion of d, |
| Jas | 2: 19 | Good! Even the d believe that |

DENARIUS—a small Roman coin made of silver. During Jesus' earthly ministry, one denarius was the payment for about one day's work.

DENOUNCE—to say a person or thing is evil.

DEPRAVED (DEPRAVITY)—evil or sinful.

| Php | 2: 15 | fault in a crooked and d generation, |
| 2Pe | 2: 19 | they themselves are slaves of d |

DEPRIVE—to take something away from.

| Am | 5: 12 | d the poor of justice |

DEPTHS—the deepest part of a thing.

| Ps | 130: 1 | Out of the d I cry |
| La | 3: 55 | from the d of the pit. |

DESECRATE—to treat without respect or reverence.

DESTINY—(v.) a predetermined course of events.

| Php | 3: 19 | Their d is destruction, |

DESTITUTE—not having necessary things such as money and food.

DEVIL—the great enemy of God and tempter of people.

Lk	4: 2	forty days he was tempted by the d.
Eph	6: 11	stand against the d schemes.
2Ti	2: 26	and escape from the trap of the d,
Jas	4: 7	Resist the d, and he will flee
1Pe	5: 8	Your enemy the d prowls

DEVOTE—to set apart for a special person or for a special reason; to set apart for God's use.

DEVOUT—religious; giving much time to prayer and worship.

DIE—1. to become lifeless; 2. to become insensitive to, as to die to, the law (Gal 2:19).

Ge	2: 17	when you eat of it you will surely d."
Ecc	3: 2	a time to be born and a time to d,
Eze	18: 4	soul who sins is the one who will d.
Jn	11: 26	and believes in me will never d.
1Co	15: 22	in Adam all d, so in Christ all will
Php	1: 21	to live is Christ and to d is gain.

DISCERN—to understand; to come to know the difference between two or more things.

| Php | 1: 10 | you may be able to d what is best |

DISCIPLE—a follower or student, especially one who believes what the leader teaches. Anyone who believes in Jesus is his disciple.

Lk 14: 27 and follow me cannot be my *d.*
Jn 13: 35 men will know that you are my *d.*

DISCIPLINE—1. (*v.*) to correct; to teach what is right; 2. (*n.*) training that corrects, molds or perfects moral character.

Pr 29: 17 *D* your son, and he will give you
Heb 12: 6 the Lord *d* those he loves,
Rev 3: 19 Those whom I love I rebuke and *d.*

DISOWN—to reject someone or something so completely that it no longer belongs to you.

Mt 26: 34 you will *d* me three times."
2Ti 2: 12 If we *d* him,

DISSENSION—disagreement; quarreling.

DIVINATION—seeing into the future by magic.

Lev 19: 26 "Do not practice *d* or sorcery.

DIVINE—given by God; belonging to God.

Ro 1: 20 his eternal power and *d* nature

DIVORCE—to legally dissolve a marriage.

Mal 2: 16 "I hate *d,*" says the LORD God
Mt 19: 3 for a man to *d* his wife for any
1Co 7: 11 And a husband must not *d* his wife.

DOCTRINE—teachings or beliefs about God.

1Ti 4: 16 Watch your life and *d* closely.
Tit 2: 1 is in accord with sound *d.*

DOMINION—power; rule.

Ps 22: 28 for *d* belongs to the LORD
Eph 1: 21 far above all rule and authority, power and *d,*

DOOM—1. (*v.*) to make certain something will fail or be destroyed; 2. (*n.*) fate; condemnation; ruin.

DOOR—a barrier that can be opened and closed; Christians open the doors of their hearts to Jesus.

Mt 7: 7 and the *d* will be opened to you.
Rev 3: 20 I stand at the *d* and knock.

DROSS—the impure scum that floats on the surface of molten metals; sometimes used as a picture of the wicked.

DWELLING—place in which people live; house; in Scripture usually refers to the place where God lives.

1Ki 8: 30 Hear from heaven, your *d* place,
Ps 84: 1 How lovely is your *d* place,

EARTH—the place that God created for human beings to live.

Ge 1: 1 God created the heavens and the *e.*
Ps 24: 1 *e* is the LORD's and everything
Mt 6: 10 done on *e* as it is in heaven.
Mt 24: 35 Heaven and *e* will pass away,
Lk 2: 14 on *e* peace to men
Php 2: 10 in heaven and on *e* and under the *e,*
2Pe 3: 13 to a new heaven and a new *e,*

EDEN—the location of the beautiful garden God planted for Adam and Eve.

EDICT—an order or law made by a person who has the power to enforce it.

EDIFY—to teach someone to live a godly life, or to help someone to live in such a way.

1Co 14: 4 but he who prophesies *e* the church.

EGYPT—one of the most powerful nations of ancient times, located in the northeast corner of Africa; the Israelites were captives in Egypt at the beginning of the book of Exodus.

ELDERS—1. the older men of a town or nation; they were the leaders of their community and made all the important decisions; 2. the leaders of the church.

1Ti 5: 17 The *e* who direct the affairs
Tit 1: 5 and appoint *e* in every town,

ELECTION—the choosing of Christians by God, as people who belong to him. Christians are called "the elect" (2Ti 2:10).

Ro 9: 11 God's purpose in *e* might stand:
2Pe 1: 10 to make your calling and *e* sure.

ELI—the high priest with whom Samuel spent the early years of his life (1Sa 2:11–26).

ELIJAH—a prophet of the Lord who predicted a famine in Israel (1Ki 17:1) and defeated the prophets of Baal in the test of whose God would set fire to the altar (1Ki 18:16–46).

ELISHA—the prophet who succeeded Elijah. He was present when God took Elijah to heaven,

d he took his place as prophet to Israel (2Ki
-18).

IZABETH—the mother of John the Baptist.
ary went to visit her when she found out she,
, was pregnant (Lk 1:5–58).

ICHANTER – a   magician   or   snake
armer.

ICOURAGE—to inspire with courage or
pe.

| a | 19: 7 | Now go out and e your men. |
| h | 4: 18 | Therefore e each other with these words. |

IDURE—to continue; to keep on going; to
ar something that is difficult or painful.

	136: 1	His love e forever.
al	3: 2	who can e the day of his coming?
	2: 3	E hardship with us like a good

IOCH—a man who "walked with God." Later
life, God "took him away" (Ge 5:18–24).

ITICE—to tempt or lure.

IVOY—a person who represents one government in its dealings with another.

PHOD—a linen apron worn by a priest over
robe. It was decorated with gold, blue, purand scarlet yarns.

PHRAIM—1. one of Joseph's sons; 2. the
be of Israel whose members were descennts of Ephraim; 3. a name for the northern
gdom of Israel after the ten tribes of Israel
d the two tribes of Judah separated from each
er.

SAU—the firstborn son of Isaac and twin of
st 2:7) and became queen (Est 2:8–18). He sold his birthright to
cob for a pot of stew (Ge 25:29–34) and was
cked out of his blessing by this same brother
e 27).

STHER—a Jewish woman who lived in Persia
st 2:7) and became queen (Est 2:8–18). Upon
ing told of a plot to kill the Jews, she went to
e king and pleaded for the Jewish people and
us saved them (Est 3–4; 7–9).

ERNAL—without beginning or end; forever;
neless.

| | 33: 27 | The e God is your refuge, |

EUNUCH—a man whose sex organs have
been removed so that he cannot produce children. Often in Bible times these men were
important officials in royal palaces.

Jn	3: 16	him shall not perish but have e life.
Ro	6: 23	but the gift of God is e life
1Jn	5: 13	you may know that you have e life.

EVE—the first woman God created (Ge
2:20–24). Her name means "mother of all the living" (Ge 3:20).

EVERLASTING—forever; without end.

Ps	90: 2	from e to e you are God.
Isa	9: 6	E Father, Prince of Peace.
Isa	55: 3	I will make an e covenant with you,
Jn	6: 47	the truth, he who believes has e life.

EVIL—wicked; doing things against God's will.

Ge	2: 9	of the knowledge of good and e.
Ps	23: 4	I will fear no e.
Mt	6: 13	but deliver us from the e one."
Ro	12: 9	Hate what is e; cling
Ro	12: 17	Do not repay anyone e for e.
Eph	6: 16	all the flaming arrows of the e one.

EXALT—to praise; to raise to an important position.

Ps	118: 28	you are my God, and I will e you.
Ps	148: 13	for his name alone is e;
Pr	14: 34	Righteousness e a nation,
Mt	23: 12	For whoever e himself will be

EXILE—1. (v.) to force someone to leave his or
her country or home; 2. (n.) forced removal from
one's country or home.

EXODUS—the departure of a large group of
people from one place to go to another. The
book of Exodus is the story of the Israelites' journey from Egypt to Canaan.

EXPANSE—the atmosphere or sky as seen
from the earth.

| Ge | 1: 8 | God called the e "sky." |

EXTOL—to praise.

| Ps | 34: 1 | I will e the LORD at all times; |
| Ps | 95: 2 | and e him with music and song. |

EXTORTION—something gotten from a person by force or by using other illegal means.

EZEKIEL—a priest who was called to be a prophet to the Jewish people when they were in exile in Babylon (Eze 1-3). He had many visions from the Lord (Eze 37; 40).

EZRA—a priest and teacher of the Law; he led a group of Jewish exiles back to Israel and helped them reestablish the temple of God and restore proper worship (Ezr 7-8).

FAINT—1. (adj.) lacking courage; 2. (v.) to lose courage.

Ps 142: 3   When my spirit grows f within me;
Lk 21: 26   Men will f from terror,

FAITH—belief and trust in God; knowing that God is real, even though one can't see him.

Hab 2: 4   but the righteous will live by his f
Mt 17: 20   if you have f as small as a mustard
Lk   7: 9   I have not found such great f
Ro 1: 17   "The righteous will live by f."
Ro 3: 22   comes through f in Jesus Christ
1Co 13: 2   and if I have a f that can move
2Co 5: 7   We live by f, not by sight.
Eph 6: 16 to all this, take up the shield of f,
1Ti 6: 12 Fight the good fight of the f.
Heb 11: 1   f is being sure of what we hope for
Heb 11: 8   By f Abraham, when called to go
Heb 12: 2   the author and perfecter of our f
Jas 2: 26 so f without deeds is dead.

FAITHFUL (FAITHFULNESS)—trust-worthy; loyal.

Ps 145: 13 The Lord is f to all his promises
La   3: 23 great is your f.
Mt 25: 21   "Well done, good and f servant!"
Ro 12: 12   patient in affliction, f in prayer.
1Co 10: 13 And God is f; he will not let you
1Jn 1: 9   he is f and just and will forgive us
Rev 1: 5   who is the f witness, the firstborn

FAST—1. (adj.) firmly fixed; not movable; 2. (v.) to go without food for a period of time.

Ps 139: 10 your right hand will hold me f.
Mt   6: 16 "When you f, do not look somber

FATHER—a male parent; God is also known as one's father.

Ge   2: 24 this reason a man will leave his f

Ge 17: 4   You will be the f of many nations.
Ex 20: 12 "Honor your f and your mother,
Mt   6: 9   "Our F in heaven,
Lk 11: 11 "Which of you f, if your son ask
Jn 10: 30 I and the F are one."
Jn 14: 6   No one comes to the F

FEAR—(v.) 1. to respect highly; to feel reverence and awe for; to be afraid of; (n.) 1. profound reverence toward God; 2. anticipation or awareness of danger.

Dt   6: 13 F the Lord your God, serve him
Ps 91: 5   You will not f the terror of night
Ps 111: 10 f of the Lord is the beginning
Isa 41: 10 So do not f, for I am with you
Php 2: 12 to work out your salvation with f

FEAST—a special celebration that was part of the Jewish religion.

Ezr 6: 22 with joy the F of Unleavened Bread,
Jn   4: 45 in Jerusalem at the Passover F,

FELLOWSHIP—companionship or friendship.

1Jn 1: 6   claim to have f with him yet walk
1Jn 1: 7   we have f with one another,

FESTIVAL—a religious celebration.

Nu 29: 12 Celebrate a f to the Lord

FIG—1. a brownish pear-shaped fruit that grows in countries near the Mediterranean Sea; 2. the tree that grows this fruit.

FIRSTBORN—a family's first child. The first born son in an Israelite family became the head of the family when his father died, and he received twice as much money and property as each of his brothers.

Ex 11: 5   Every f son in Egypt will die,

FIRSTFRUITS—the first vegetables, fruits and grains harvested from the field.

Ex 23: 19 "Bring the best of the f of your soil

FLESH—1. the soft parts of the bodies of humans and animals; 2. the believer's sinful nature.

Job 6: 12 Is my f bronze?
Php 3: 3   put no confidence in the f

FLOG—to beat with a stick or a whip.

FOE—an enemy.

Ps 61: 3   a strong tower against the f.

ᴼLLY—foolishness; the lack of wisdom.

| 26: | 5 | Answer a fool according to his *f,* |
| | 3: | 9 | their *f* will be clear to everyone. |

ᴼOL—a person who is not wise.

| 14: | 1 | The *f* says in his heart, |
| 12: | 20 | "But God said to him, 'You *f!* |

ᴼRGIVE—to pardon or excuse; to no longer ᴀme or be angry with someone who has done ᴜ wrong.

6:	14	For if you *f* men when they sin
23:	34	Jesus said, "Father, *f* them,
3:	13	*F* as the Lord forgave you.
1:	9	and just and will *f* us our sins

ᴼRSAKE—to leave another completely alone, ᴛh no hope that you will ever return.

1:	5	I will never leave you nor *f* you.
55:	7	Let the wicked *f* his way
27:	46	my God, why have you *f* me?"

ᴿEE (FREEDOM)—not bound; liberated.

8:	32	and the truth will set you *f.*"
6:	18	You have been set *f* from sin
3:	17	the Spirit of the Lord is, there is *f.*

ᴿUITFUL—productive; yielding much fruit.

| 1: | 22 | "Be *f* and increase in number |
| 15: | 2 | cleans so that it will be even more *f.* |

ᴸLFILL (FULFILLMENT)—to complete a ᴏmise or project.

116:	14	I will *f* my vows to the Lᴏʀᴅ
14:	49	But the Scriptures must be *f.*"
13:	10	Therefore love is the *f* of the law.

ᴿY—intense anger.

| 34: | 7 | They were filled with grief and *f,* |

ᴀBRIEL—the angel who announced the ᴛhs of John the Baptist and Jesus (Lk 1:11–20, –38).

ᴀLILEE—the northern part of Palestine. Jesus ᴇw up, preached and did most of his miracles ᴇre. Today this area is in northern Israel.

ᴀLL—1. a plant with an extremely bitter-tast-ᴪ fruit; 2. the liquid made by the liver.

| 27: | 34 | mixed with *g;* but after tasting it, |

ᴇNEALOGY—a list of a person's ancestors descendants; a family tree.

ᴇNTILE—anyone who is not a Jew.

Ro 3: 9 and *G* alike are all under sin.
Ro 11: 13 as I am the apostle to the *G,*

GIDEON—a judge who freed Israel from the rule and terror of the Midianites (Jdg 6–8). He asked for a sign from God, and God showed him his will by means of dew and a fleece (Jdg 6:36–40).

GIFT—1. a present; 2. a talent or ability.

Ro	6:	23	but the *g* of God is eternal life
1Co	12:	4	There are different kinds of *g,*
2Co	9:	15	be to God for his indescribable *g!*

GLEAN—to pick up the grain or fruit left behind after harvesting; usually a way for the poor to get food.

GLORIFY—to praise and honor in worship.

| Ps | 34: | 3 | *G* the Lᴏʀᴅ with me; |
| Jn | 17: | 1 | *G* your Son, that your Son may |

GLORY—1. honor; praise; 2. a source of pride or worthiness.

Ps	8:	5	and crowned him with *g* and honor.
Ps	19:	1	The heavens declare the *g* of God;
Lk	2:	14	"*G* to God in the highest,
Jn	1:	14	We have seen his *g,* the *g* of the One
1Co	10:	31	whatever you do, do it all for the *g*
Rev	4:	11	to receive *g* and honor and power

GOD—the supreme creator and the powerful force of the universe; the one who is to be wor-shiped.

Ge	1:	1	In the beginning *G* created
Ex	20:	5	the Lᴏʀᴅ your *G,* am a jealous *G,*
Nu	23:	19	*G* is not a man, that he should lie,
Dt	6:	4	Lᴏʀᴅ our *G,* the Lᴏʀᴅ is one.
Dt	6:	5	Love the Lᴏʀᴅ your *G*
Ps	46:	1	*G* is our refuge and strength,
Jn	1:	18	ever seen *G,* but *G* the One
Jn	3:	16	"For *G* so loved the world that he
Jn	4:	24	*G* is spirit, and his worshipers must
1Jn	4:	16	*G* is love.
Rev	4:	8	holy is the Lord *G* Almighty,

GODLY—to be devoted and loving toward God, wanting to do his will.

| 1Ti | 4: | 7 | train yourself to be *g.* |

2Pe   3: 11   live holy and *g* lives

GOLGOTHA—the hill outside Jerusalem where Jesus was hung on a cross.

GOLIATH—the Philistine giant who was killed by David (1Sa 17; 21:9).

GOSPEL—1. the good news that Jesus died for sins and rose again; 2. any of the first four books of the New Testament.
Ro   1: 16   I am not ashamed of the *g*,
1Co   9: 16   Woe to me if I do not preach the *g*!
1Co 15: 2   By this *g* you are saved,

GRACE—an undeserved favor or gift; the undeserved forgiveness, kindness and mercy that God gives us.
Ro   3: 24   and are justified freely by his *g*
Ro   5: 20   where sin increased, *g* increased all
2Co 12: 9   "My *g* is sufficient for you,
Eph   2: 5   it is by *g* you have been saved.
Tit   3: 7   having been justified by his *g*,

GUILTY—deserving punishment for having broken a law or commandment.
Ex   34: 7   does not leave the *g* unpunished;
Heb 10: 22   to cleanse us from a *g* conscience
Jas   2: 10   at just one point is *g* of breaking all

HADES—the grave or place of the dead.
Mt   16: 18   the gates of *H* will not overcome it.

HAGAR—a servant of Sarah and one of Abraham's wives; the mother of Ishmael (Ge 16:1–6; 25:12).

HAGGAI—a prophet who encouraged the Israelites returning from exile in Babylon to rebuild the temple (Ezr 5:1; Hag 1–2).

HALLELUJAH—praise the Lord; a song of praise.
Rev 19: 1   "*H*! Salvation and glory and power

HALLOWED—holy; sacred.
Mt   6: 9   *h* be your name,

HAM—the youngest of Noah's three sons (Ge 5:32).

HANNAH—she prayed for a son and God ga her Samuel. She dedicated him to God and F lived in the temple as a boy and became prophet and judge (1Sa 1–2).
Mk 13: 13   All men will *h* you because of me,

HAUGHTY—proud.
Pr   16: 18   a *h* spirit before a fall.

HEART—the center of a person's life, includin the mind, the will and the emotions.
Dt   6: 5   LORD your God with all your *h*
1Sa 16: 7   but the LORD looks at the *h*."
Ps   51: 10   Create in me a pure *h*, O God,
Ps 119: 11   I have hidden your word in my *h*
Ps 139: 23   Search me, O God, and know my *h*;
Eze 36: 26   I will give you a new *h*
Mt   5: 8   Blessed are the pure in *h*,

HEAVEN—1. the place where God lives; 2. th sky.
Ge   14: 19   Creator of *h* and earth.
Mt   19: 23   man to enter the kingdom of *h*.
Mk 16: 19   he was taken up into *h*
Php   3: 20   But our citizenship is in *h*.
Rev 21: 1   Then I saw a new *h* and a new earth,

HEBREW—1. another name for an Israelite; descendant of Abraham; 2. the language spo ken by the Jews. The Old Testament was writ ten in Hebrew.

HEIR—someone who receives the property o blessings of a person who has died.
Ro   8: 17   then we are *h–h* of God
Eph   3: 6   gospel the Gentiles are *h* together

HEROD—the family name of five kings whc ruled Palestine under the Roman emperor Herod the Great (Mt 2:16); Herod Antipas (Mk 6:14–29); Herod Philip (Mt 14:3; Mk 6:17); Herod Agrippa I (Ac 12:1–4,19–23); Herod Agrippa I (Ac 23:35; 25:13–26:32).

HERODIAS—the wife of Herod Antipas; she persuaded her daughter to ask Antipas for the head of John the Baptist (Mk 6:17).

HEZEKIAH—a king of Judah; he restored the temple, reinstituted proper worship and sought the Lord's help against the Assyrians.

IGH PRIEST—the chief religious official in
e Jewish religion. In the Old Testament he
fered the most important sacrifices to God in
ehalf of the people.
eb 4: 14   have a great high *p* who has
            gone
eb 7: 26   Such a high *p* meets our need

OLY—set apart for God; belonging to God;
ure; godly.
    20: 8   the Sabbath day by keeping it *h.*
ev 11: 44   and be *h,* because I am *h.*
a   6: 3   "*H, h, h* is the LORD Almighty,
) 12: 1   as living sacrifices, *h* and pleas-
            ing
ev 4: 8   "*H, h, h* is the Lord God
            Almighty,

OLY SPIRIT—the third person of the Trinity;
e lives and works in the hearts and minds of
elievers; he came at Pentecost in a powerful
ay (Ac 2). Other names are: the Spirit, Coun-
lor and Comforter.
   51: 11   or take your Holy *S* from me.
   14: 26   But the Counselor, the Holy *S,*
   20: 22   and said, "Receive the Holy *S.*
   2: 4   of them were filled with the Holy
            S
al 5: 22   But the fruit of the *S* is love, joy,

OPE—the anticipation of something good.
   42: 5   Put your *h* in God,
   40: 31   but those who *h* in the LORD
)   8: 24   But *h* that is seen is no *h* at all.
Co 15: 19   for this life we have *h* in Christ,
eb 11: 1   faith is being sure of what we *h*
            for

OSANNA—a Hebrew word of praise mean-
g "save."
t 21: 9   "*H* in the highest!"

UMBLE—1. (*v.*) to make lower; 2. (*adj.*) not
oud; not pretending to be important.
  147: 6   The LORD sustains the *h*
t 23: 12   whoever exalts himself will be *h,*
s   4: 10   *H* yourselves before the Lord,

YMN—a song of praise to God.
h   5: 19   to one another with psalms, *h*

YPOCRITE—a person who pretends to be
etter than he or she is.
t   6: 5   when you pray, do not be like
            the *h,*
t   7: 5   You *h,* first take the plank out

HYSSOP—a plant used to sprinkle water or
blood for religious cleansing.
Ps 51: 7   with *h,* and I will be clean;

IDLE—1. lacking worth or basis; 2. lazy.
Dt 32: 47   They are not just *i* words
1Th 5: 14   warn those who are *i,*

IDOL—a statue made by people and worshiped
as if it had the power of a god; anything that
takes the place of God in a person's life. Worshiping idols is called idolatry.
1Co 8: 4   We know that an *i* is nothing at
             all
Col 3: 5   evil desires and greed, which is *i.*

IMAGE—likeness.
Ge 1: 27   So God created man in his own
            i,
Da 3: 12   nor worship the *i* of gold you
            have set up."

IMMANUEL—a name for Jesus meaning
"God with us."
Mt 1: 23   and they will call him *I*'

IMMORTAL (IMMORTALITY)—free from
death; not able to die.
1Co 15: 53   and the mortal with *i.*
1Ti 1: 17   Now to the King eternal, *i,*

IMPERISHABLE—not able to die or to be
destroyed.
1Pe 1: 23   not of perishable seed, but of *i,*

IMPURE—not pure; not clean.
Ac 10: 15   not call anything *i* that God has
1Th 4: 7   For God did not call us to be *i,*

INCENSE—1. spices burned to make a sweet-
smelling smoke, as a way of worshiping God;
2. the sweet smell or the smoke of burning
spices.
Ps 141: 2   my prayer be set before you
             like *i;*
Mt   2: 11   him with gifts of gold and of *i*

INHERIT—to receive money, property or keep-
sakes from a person after his or her death.
Mt   5: 5   for they will *i* the earth.
Mk 10: 17   "what must I do to *i* eternal life?"

INIQUITY—sin; wickedness.
Ps 51: 2   Wash away all my *i*
Ps 103: 10   or repay us according to our *i.*
Isa 53: 6   the *i* of us all.

INJUSTICE—unfairness.

INSURRECTION—revolt or rebellion against a government.

INTERCEDE—to beg or plead for another person.
Ro   8: 26   but the Spirit himself *i* for us

INTERCESSION—the plea made on behalf of another person.
Isa 53: 12   and made *i* for the transgressors.

INVOKE—to call for help or support.
Ac 19: 13   to *i* the name of the Lord Jesus

ISAAC—the promised son of Abraham and Sarah (Ge 17:19; 21:1-7); offered as a sacrifice by Abraham (Ge 22); married Rebekah (Ge 24) and was the father of Esau and Jacob (Ge 25).

ISAIAH—prophet called by God (Isa 6) to prophesy to Judah (Isa 1:1). Some of his prophesies are about the coming Messiah (Isa 53).

ISHMAEL—the son of Abraham and Hagar (Ge 16); he was not to be the son of the covenant (Ge 17:18-21).

ISRAEL—1. the new name God gave to Jacob (Ge 32:28); 2. the nation made up of descendants of the twelve sons of Jacob; 3. the northern ten tribes after they separated from Judah and Benjamin.
Dt   6: 4   Hear, O *I*: The LORD our God,
Lk 22: 30   judging the twelve tribes of *I*.
Eph 3: 6   Gentiles are heirs together with *I*,

ISRAELITES—the people of Israel.
Ex 14: 22   and the *I* went through the sea
Ro   9: 27   the number of the *I* be like the sand

JACOB—the son of Isaac and Rebekah; he was the twin brother of Esau (Ge 25:21-26); he bought Esau's birthright for a pot of stew (Ge 25:29-34); he wrestled with God, and his name was changed to Israel (Ge 32:22-32); the descendants of his twelve sons became the nation of Israel.

JAMES—1. one of the twelve apostles; the brother of John (Mt 4:21-22); 2. one of the twelve apostles; the son of Alphaeus (Mt 10:3); 3. the brother of Jesus (Mk 6:30); the author of the letter of James (Jas 1:1).

JAPHETH—one of the sons of Noah (Ge 5:32); he was blessed because he covered his father's nakedness (Ge 9:18-28).

JEALOUS (JEALOUSY)—1. afraid of losing someone's love or affection; 2. angry or unhappy because of what someone else has; 3. careful to guard or keep what one has.
Joel 2: 18   the LORD will be *j* for his land
2Co 11: 2   I am *j* for you with a godly *j*.
Gal   5: 20   hatred, discord, *j*, fits of rage,

JEREMIAH—a prophet called by God to prophesy to Judah (Jer 1:1-3). He is often referred to as the prophet of gloom, because he prophesied about the destruction of Judah.

JERICHO—the ancient city destroyed by Joshua as the Hebrews entered Canaan (Jos 6).

JEROBOAM—an official in Solomon's court; he rebelled and became the first king of the northern ten tribes of Israel (1Ki 11:26-40; 12:1-20).

JERUSALEM—the political and religious center of the Jews; it was the site of many important events in the Biblical accounts; also called "Zion" and "the City of David."
2Ki 23: 27   and I will reject *J*, the city I chose,
Ne   2: 17   Come, let us rebuild the wall of *J*.
Ps 137: 5   If I forget you, O *J*,
Jn   4: 20   where we must worship is in *J*."
Rev 21: 2   I saw the Holy City, the new *J*,

JESSE—the father of David, king of Israel (1Sa 16:10-13).

JESUS—The Son of God; the Savior of the world; the Messiah; the only One through whom people can be saved.
Mt   1: 21   you are to give him the name *J*,
Php 2: 10   name of *J* every knee should bow,

JEW—an Israelite; one of the chosen people of God; a descendant of Abraham through Jacob.
Mt   2: 2   who has been born king of the *J*?
Ro   3: 29   Is God the God of *J* only?
Gal   3: 28   There is neither *J* nor Greek,

JEZEBEL—the wife of King Ahab (1Ki 16:31). She promoted Baal worship in Israel (1Ki 16:32-33), had many prophets of God killed (1Ki

18:4,13) and opposed the prophet Elijah (1Ki 19:1-2).

JOAB—the commander of the armies of King David.

JOASH—the boy-king of Judah; he repaired the temple (2Ki 12).

JOB—a wealthy man from the land of Uz who feared God (Job 1:1-5). His righteousness was tested by disaster (Job 1:6-22) and personal affliction (Job 2), but in the end God restored wealth and honor to him (Job 42).

JOHN—1. the Baptist (Mk 1:2-8); the son of Zechariah and Elizabeth (Lk 1). He preached in the desert, preparing the people for Jesus (Mt 3:11-12); baptized Jesus in the Jordan River (Mt 3:13-17); executed by Herod (Mk 6:14-29); 2. one of the twelve apostles; brother of the apostle James (Lk 5:1-10); wrote the Gospel of John, the letters of John (2Jn 1; 3Jn 1) and the book of Revelation (Rev 1:1; 22:8).

JOHN MARK (see Mark, John).

JONAH—a prophet who was called to preach to Nineveh but instead fled to Tarshish (Jnh 1:1-3). While at sea a great storm arose because of his disobedience; he was thrown into the sea and was swallowed by a large fish (Jnh 1:4-17). He then repented and went to Nineveh and preached, telling the people to repent (Jnh 3).

JONATHAN—a son of King Saul (1Sa 13:16) who had a special friendship with David (1Sa 18:1-4; 19-20; 23:16-18). When he was killed (1Sa 31) David mourned greatly for him (2Sa 1).

JOPPA—an ancient walled town on the coast of Palestine.

JORDAN—a river in Palestine that flows between the Sea of Galilee and the Dead Sea.

Jos 4: 22 "Israel crossed the *J* on dry ground."
Mt 3: 6 baptized by him in the *J* River.

JOSEPH—1. the son of Jacob and Rachel (Ge 30:24), who was favored by his father but hated by his brothers (Ge 37:3-4). He was sold into slavery (Ge 37:12-36), taken to Egypt and eventually given a high position under Pharaoh (Ge 41:41-57); 2. the husband of Mary and childhood father of Jesus (Mt 1:16-24; 2:13-19); 3. a disciple of Jesus from Arimathea; he gave his

tomb for Jesus' burial (Mt 27:57-61); 4. the original name of Barnabas (Ac 4:36).

JOSHUA—1. the son of Nun (Nu 13:8); Moses' aide and later his successor (Dt 31:1-18); he led the Israelites across the Jordan River into Canaan (Jos 3-4); was the commander in the conquest of Jericho (Jos 6), Ai (Jos 7-8), and a large part of Canaan (Jos 10-12); oversaw the dividing up of the promised land among the twelve tribes of Israel (Jos 13-22); 2. the high priest in Israel during the rebuilding of both the temple (Hag 1-2) and the altar (Ezr 3:2,8); also called Jeshua.

JOSIAH—king of Judah for thirty-one years shortly before the destruction of Jerusalem.

JUDAH—1. Jacob's fourth son; 2. the tribe of Israel whose members were descendants of Judah; 3. a name for the southern kingdom after Judah and Benjamin separated from the northern ten tribes.

Zec 10: 4 From *J* will come the cornerstone,
Mt 2: 6 Bethlehem, in the land of *J*,
Rev 5: 5 See, the Lion of the tribe of *J*,

JUDAISM—the teachings of the Jewish religion.

JUDAS—1. one of the twelve apostles (Lk 6:16; Ac 1:13); was probably also called Thaddaeus (Mt 10:3); 2. one of the brothers of Jesus (Mt 13:55); author of the last letter in the New Testament (Jude 1); 3. one of the twelve apostles, also called Iscariot; he betrayed Jesus (Mk 3:19; 14:10-50) and then hung himself (Mt 27:3-5).

JUDEA—the area of Palestine where the tribe of Judah lived after the exile.

Mk 10: 1 into the region of *J* and across the Jordan.
Gal 1: 22 to the churches of *J* that are in Christ.

JUDGMENT—1. a decision or opinion; 2. a decision of guilt or innocence made by a judge in a court of law; punishment decided on by a court; 3. a decision from God, especially the final judgment when God will reward those who believe in him and condemn all others to hell.

Dt 1: 17 of any man, for *j* belongs to God.
Ps 119: 66 Teach me knowledge and good *j*,
Isa 66: 16 the LORD will execute *j*
Mt 5: 21 who murders will be subject to *j*'

Mt	12: 36	have to give account on the day of *j*
Jn	5: 22	but has entrusted all *j* to the Son,
Ro	14: 10	stand before God's *j* seat.
2Co	5: 10	appear before the *j* seat of Christ,

JUSTICE—fairness.

Isa	61: 8	"For I, the LORD, love *j*,
Lk	11: 42	you neglect *j* and the love of God.

JUSTIFY (JUSTIFICATION)—to erase someone's sins; to declare righteous.

Ac	13: 39	him everyone who believes is *j*
Ro	3: 24	and are *j* freely by his grace
Ro	4: 25	and was raised to life for our *j*.
Ro	5: 1	since we have been *j* through faith,
Gal	3: 24	to Christ that we might be *j* by faith.

KING—ruler over a country or kingdom; Christ is often referred to as the King of kings.

1Ki	22: 3	The *k* of Israel had said
Rev	19: 16	he has this name written: *K* of *k*

KINGDOM—a realm headed by a king; God's kingdom, or the kingdom of heaven, is made up of all believers.

Ex	19: 6	you will be for me a *k* of priests
Mt	3: 2	"Repent, for the *k* of heaven is near."
Mt	5: 3	for theirs is the *k* of heaven.
Mt	6: 33	But seek first his *k* and his
Mt	16: 19	the keys of the *k* of heaven;
Jn	18: 36	"My *k* is not of this world.
1Co	15: 24	hands over the *k* to God the Father
Rev	11: 15	of the world has become the *k*

KINSMAN-REDEEMER—in Old Testament times a close male relative who had the responsibility to marry a widow and buy ("redeem") her husband's property (Dt 25:5–6).

Ruth	3: 9	over me, since you are a *k*."

KISH—the father of King Saul, the first king of Israel.

KNOWLEDGE—possessing the facts, understanding.

Pr	1: 7	of the LORD is the beginning of *k*,
Hos	4: 6	are destroyed from lack of *k*.
1Co	8: 1	*K* puffs up, but love builds up.

LABAN—the brother of Rebekah (Ge 24:29–51) and father of Rachel and Leah (Ge 29–31).

LAMB—a principal sacrificial animal in the Old Testament; since Jesus is the supreme sacrifice of God, he is called the "Lamb of God."

Isa	53: 7	he was led like a *l* to the slaughter,
Jn	1: 29	*L* of God, who takes away the sin
1Co	5: 7	our Passover *l*, has been sacrificed.
Rev	5: 6	Then I saw a *L*, looking

LAMENT, LAMENTATION—a cry of grief.

LAW—1. God's rules, which help his people know what is right and wrong (the Ten Commandments are part of God's law); 2. (cap.) the first five books of the Bible, written by Moses.

Ps	1: 2	and on his *l* he meditates day
Ps	19: 7	The *l* of the LORD is perfect,
Ps	119: 97	Oh, how I love your *l*!
Mt	22: 40	All the *L* and the Prophets hang
Ro	8: 3	For what the *l* was powerless to do
Ro	13: 10	love is the fulfillment of the *l*.
Gal	3: 24	So the *l* was put in charge to lead us

LAZARUS—1. the poor man in one of Jesus' parables (Lk 16:19–31); 2. the brother of Mary and Martha; Jesus raised him from the dead (Jn 11:1–12:19).

LEAH—the wife of Jacob; she had six sons and one daughter (Ge 29:16–30:21).

LEPROSY—a word used in the Bible for many different skin diseases and infections.

LEVITE—a member of the tribe of Levi. The Levites took care of the temple. Only Levites could become priests, but not all Levites were priests.

LIFE—the total substance of a person's existence; can refer to both physical and spiritual existence.

Ge	2: 7	into his nostrils the breath of *l*,
Jn	3: 16	shall not perish but have eternal *l*.
Jn	11: 25	"I am the resurrection and the *l*.
Jn	14: 6	am the way and the truth and the *l*.
Ro	6: 23	but the gift of God is eternal *l*

LIGHT—the form of energy that allows a person to see; in the Old Testament it symbolized life and blessing.

Ge	1: 3	"Let there be l," and there was l.
Ps	27: 1	LORD is my l and my salvation
Ps	119:105	and a l for my path.
Isa	9: 2	have seen a great l,
Mt	5: 16	let your l shine before men,
Jn	8: 12	he said, "I am the l of the world.
1Jn	1: 5	God is l; in him there is no

LINEN—cloth made from the fiber of flax plants.

LIVE—to be alive; may refer to both physical and spiritual existence.

Ex	20: 12	so that you may l long
Ro	1: 17	"The righteous will l by faith."
2Co	5: 7	We l by faith, not by sight.
Php	1: 21	to l is Christ and to die is gain.

LOCUSTS—a type of grasshopper. When they settle in a grain field, orchard or other cultivated area, they can devastate the crop.

LORD—refers to God as the master. (See also LORD.)

Mt	3: 3	'Prepare the way for the L,
Lk	2: 9	glory of the L shone around them,
Ac	16: 31	replied, "Believe in the L Jesus,
Ro	10: 13	on the name of the L will be saved."
Php	2: 11	confess that Jesus Christ is L,
2Pe	1: 16	and coming of our L Jesus Christ,
Rev	17: 14	he is L of lords and King of kings
Rev	22: 20	Come, L Jesus.

LORD (Yahweh)—the intimate and personal name of God; it emphasizes his role as Israel's Redeemer and covenant Lord. (See also Lord.)

Ge	2: 4	When the L God made the earth
Ex	20: 2	"I am the L your God, who
Ps	23: 1	The L is my shepherd, I shall lack
Ps	103: 1	Praise the L, O my soul
Pr	1: 7	The fear of the L is the beginning
Isa	6: 3	"Holy, holy, holy is the L Almighty,
Isa	55: 6	Seek the L while he may be found;

LOT—the nephew of Abraham (Ge 12:5). He chose to live in Sodom (Ge 13); Abraham pleaded with God for Lot's life when God was about to destroy Sodom (Ge 19:1–29).

LOT—one of the ways used in Bible times to find out God's will about a matter. It is something like drawing straws.

Mt	27: 35	divided up his clothes by casting l.
Ac	1: 26	Then they cast l, and the l fell

LOVE—wanting good to come to another person; being concerned and willing to work for another person's benefit.

Ex	20: 6	showing l to thousands of those who l me
Ps	23: 6	Surely goodness and l will follow
Ps	136:1–26	His l endures forever.
Mt	3: 17	"This is my Son, whom I l,
Mt	5: 44	L your enemies and pray
Mt	19: 19	and "'IT'l your neighbor as yourself.' "
Jn	13: 34	I give you: L one another.
Jn	15: 13	Greater l has no one than this,
Ro	13: 10	Therefore l is the fulfillment
Gal	5: 22	But the fruit of the Spirit is l, joy,
Eph	1: 4	In l he predestined us
1Jn	3: 10	anyone who does not l his brother.
1Jn	3: 16	This is how we know what l is:
1Jn	4: 7	for l comes from God.
1Jn	4: 10	This is l: not that we loved God,
1Jn	4: 16	God is l.

LUKE—a co-worker with Paul; he wrote the books of Luke and Acts (Col 4:14).

LUST—a strong desire for something wrong.

Pr	6: 25	Do not l in your heart
Ro	1: 26	God gave them over to shameful l.

LYRE—a small lap harp with three to twelve strings.

MACEDONIA—a Roman province; the first part of Europe to receive Christianity.

MAGI—men of Arabia and Persia who studied the stars. People thought they had the power to tell the meaning of dreams.

Mt	2: 1	M from the east came to Jerusalem

MAJESTIC (MAJESTY)—great and powerful.

Ex	15: 6	was m in power.
Ps	8: 1	how m is your name in all the earth!
Ps	111: 3	Glorious and m are his deeds,

MANASSEH—1. the older son of Joseph and the tribe descended from him (Ge 41:51; Nu 1:34); 2. one of the kings of Judah (2Ki 21:1).

MANGER—a feed box for cows or other animals.

| Lk | 2: 7 | placed him in a *m*, because there |

MANNA—the special food God gave daily to the Israelites until they reached the promised land.

| Ex | 16: 31 | people of Israel called the bread *m*. |
| Jn | 6: 49 | Your forefathers ate the *m* |

MARK, JOHN—the cousin of Barnabas (Col 4:10); a helper to Paul and Barnabas (Ac 13:5); later a co-worker with Paul (Phm 24); author of the second Gospel, according to early church tradition.

MARTHA—the sister of Mary and Lazarus, the man whom Jesus raised from the dead (Jn 11; 12:2).

MARY—1. the mother of Jesus (Mt 1:16–25); 2. Mary Magdalene—a woman whom Jesus freed from demons (Lk 8:2), who was present at the cross (Mk 15:40) and who came on Easter morning to the tomb (Mt 27:61); 3. the sister of Martha and Lazarus; she washed Jesus' feet with expensive perfume (Jn 12:1–8).

MATTHEW—a tax collector who became one of the twelve apostles (Mt 9:9–13); also called Levi (Mk 2:14–17).

MEDIATOR—one who makes peace between two people or two groups who are displeased and/or angry with each other. Jesus is the mediator between us and God.

| 1Ti | 2: 5 | and one *m* between God and men, |
| Heb | 9: 15 | For this reason Christ is the *m* |

MEDITATE—to think seriously and carefully.

| Ps | 1: 2 | and on his law he *m* day and night. |
| Ps | 119: 15 | I *m* on your precepts |

MEDIUM—a person who can supposedly talk with the spirits of people who have died.

MEEK—patient; mild; gentle.

| Mt | 5: 5 | Blessed are the *m*, |

MELCHIZEDEK—a priest and king of early Salem (Jerusalem); Jesus was said to be a priest like Melchizedek (Heb 5:6).

MEPHIBOSHETH—son of Jonathan and grandson of Saul; he lived out his life under King David's protection (2Sa 9:11).

MERCY—kindness and forgiveness, especially when given to a person who doesn't deserve it.

Mic	6: 8	To act justly and to love *m*
Ro	9: 15	"I will have *m* on whom I have *m*,
1Pe	1: 3	In his great *m* he has given us new

MESSIAH—the "Anointed One"; Christ; the one the Jews expected to come and be their king.

| Jn | 1: 41 | "We have found the *M*" |

METHUSELAH—a man in early Bible times who lived 969 years (Ge 5:27).

MICHAL—daughter of Saul, wife of David, both of whom were kings of Israel.

MIDWIFE—a woman who helped with the birth of a baby.

MILLSTONE—one of a pair of stones used to crush grain for flour.

| Lk | 17: 2 | sea with a *m* tied around his neck |

MINISTER—1. (*v.*) to serve; to give care or attention to; 2. (*n.*) one who serves others as God directs.

| 2Co | 3: 6 | as *m* of a new covenant |
| 1Ti | 4: 6 | you will be a good *m* |

MIRACLE—an unusual happening, one that goes against the normal laws of nature. Miracles are done by the power of God.

Ps	77: 14	You are the God who performs *m*;
Jn	14: 11	the evidence of the *m* themselves.
Ac	2: 22	accredited by God to you by *m*,
Heb	2: 4	it by signs, wonders and various *m*,

MIRIAM—the sister of Moses and Aaron (Nu 26:59); led the Israelites in praising God in dance and song after he had parted the waters of the Red Sea (Ex 15:20–21); later temporarily struck with leprosy because she criticized Moses (Nu 12).

MOAB—1. a son of Lot whose descendants became bitter enemies of the Israelites; 2. the land occupied by the Moabites, to the east of the Dead Sea.

MORDECAI—cousin of Esther, queen of Persia; he and Esther saved the Jews from a plot to put them all to death.

MORTAL—human; able to die.
1Co 15: 53   and the *m* with immortality,

MOSES—the leader of Israel in the exodus out of Egypt, culminating in their passing through the Red Sea (Ex 1-14). He received the law of God at Sinai (Ex 19-23) and gave it to the people of Israel. Moses was allowed to view the land of Canaan from the top of Mount Nebo, but died without entering it (Nu 20:1-13; Dt 34:5-12).

MYRRH—the sweet-smelling sap of the myrrh bush. It was used to make the sacred anointing oil.
Mt   2: 11   of gold and of incense and of *m*.

NABAL—a rich sheepherder in Judah who insulted David; when David planned to take revenge, Nabal's wife Abigail brought gifts to calm David; Nabal died shortly thereafter and Abigail married David (1Sa 25:1-42).

NABOTH—owner of a vineyard that King Ahab wanted and gained by having Naboth accused of blasphemy and stoned (1Ki 21:1-29).

NAOMI—the mother-in-law of Ruth (Ru 1); she advised Ruth to seek marriage with Boaz (Ru 2-4).

NAPHTALI—a son of Jacob and father of the tribe of Naphtali (Nu 1:42-43).

NARD—an expensive, pleasant-smelling oil from the spikenard, a plant that grew in India.

NATHAN—the prophet of God who exposed David's sin with Bathsheba, causing David to repent (2Sa 12:1-25).

NATHANAEL—one of the twelve apostles (Jn 1:45-49); was probably also called Bartholomew (Mt 10:3).

NAZARENE—a person who lived in or came from the town of Nazareth in Galilee.
Mk 16: 6   looking for Jesus the *N*,

NAZIRITE—a person who separated himself or herself by taking a vow to do special work for God. This included a promise not to cut one's hair and not to drink wine.

NEBUCHADNEZZAR—king of Babylon who took Judah into captivity.

NEGEV—the desert region south of Judea.
Ge 24: 62   for he was living in the *N*.

NEHEMIAH—the Jewish "cupbearer" of King Artaxerxes of Persia (Ne 2:1); while in Jerusalem rebuilt the walls of the city (Ne 2-6) and with Ezra reestablished the worship of God there after the Babylonian exile (Ne 8).

NICODEMUS—a Pharisee who visited Jesus at night (Jn 3) and learned about being born again.

NILE—the primary river in Egypt.

NINEVEH—the city to which Jonah was sent to preach (Jnh 1:2); the ancient capital of Assyria.

NOAH—"a righteous man" in early Bible times; he built an ark, as God commanded him (Ge 6-8). God made a covenant with him never again to cover the entire earth with a flood (Ge 9).

OATH—a promise in which one asks God to witness that something is true.

OFFERING—1. something given to God as an act of worship; 2. the sacrifice of an animal to make the relationship between God and man right again. In the Old Testament, animals and grains were regularly used as offerings in an attempt to bring the people closer to God.
Ge 22: 8   provide the lamb for the burnt *o*,
Isa 53: 10   the LORD makes his life a guilt *o*,
Mk 12: 33   is more important than all burnt *o*
Eph 5: 2   as a fragrant *o* and sacrifice to God.

OIL—almost always refers to olive oil; used to anoint someone for a physical benefit or to set someone apart for service.
2Ki 9: 6   the prophet poured *o* on Jehu's head
Lk   7: 46   You did not pour *o* on my head

ORACLE—1. a saying or answer; 2. the word of the Lord.

ORDAIN—1. to set apart for a specific office or duty; 2. to order or command.

ORDINANCE—1. an official law; 2. a law made or commanded by God.

OVERSEER—one of the terms used for leaders in the early church.

| Ac | 20: 28 | the Holy Spirit has made you *o*. |
| 1Ti | 3: 2 | Now the *o* must be above reproach, |

PAGAN—a person who does not worship God, especially someone who worships idols.

| 1Pe | 2: 12 | such good lives among the *p* that, |

PAPYRUS—1. a large water plant, similar to the reed, which grows in marshes and lakes. Moses' mother put him in a basket made from papyrus (Ex 2:3); 2. a paper made from this plant.

PARABLE—a story that tells a special lesson or truth. Jesus told many parables.

PASSOVER—an annual Jewish holiday that yet today reminds the Jewish people of how God freed them from slavery in Egypt. The Lord "passed over" the homes marked with the blood of a lamb on their doorframes, but he killed all the other firstborn in Egypt.

| Ex | 12: 11 | Eat it in haste; it is the LORD's *P.* |

PASSOVER LAMB—the lamb killed on the Passover as a sacrifice. Jesus is our Passover lamb, because he was sacrificed for our deliverance from sin, in the same way a lamb was sacrificed when the Israelites were delivered from Egypt.

| 1Co | 5: 7 | our *P* lamb, has been sacrificed. |

PATRIARCH—the father and ruler of a family; the head of a tribe.

PAUL—a Pharisee from Tarsus (Ac 9:11); named Saul at birth (Ac 13:9). Jesus appeared to him on the road to Damascus (Ac 9:4–9), and he became an powerful apostle (Gal 1). His writings make up a significant portion of the New Testament, ranging from intricate theology to passionate letters to struggling churches.

PEACE—freedom from disturbance; calm.

Isa	9: 6	Everlasting Father, Prince of *P.*
Lk	2: 14	on earth *p* to men on whom his
Jn	14: 27	*P* I leave with you; my *p*

| Ro | 5: 1 | we have *p* with God |
| Gal | 5: 22 | joy, *p*, patience, kindness, |

PENTECOST—a Jewish feast celebrated fifty days after the Passover. Today the Christian church celebrates Pentecost because it was the day the Holy Spirit came to dwell with Christ's followers (Ac 2:1–4).

PERSECUTE (PERSECUTION)—to continually treat someone cruelly and unfairly, even though that person has done nothing wrong. The early Christians were persecuted for believing in Jesus as the Son of God.

Jn	15: 20	they *p* me, they will *p* you
Ac	26: 14	'Saul, Saul, why do you *p* me?
Ro	12: 14	Bless those who *p* you; bless

PERSEVERE   (PERSEVERANCE)—to refuse to give up; to keep on trying; to continue in one's actions or beliefs in spite of problems.

Ro	5: 3	we know that suffering produces *p*;
Ro	5: 4	*p*, character; and character, hope.
Heb	10: 36	You need to *p* so that

PERSIA—ancient geographical area and kingdom located north of the Persian Gulf.

PESTILENCE—a plague; a disease that spreads quickly and kills many people.

PETER—one of the twelve apostles; the brother of Andrew; also called Simon (Lk 6:14) and Cephas (Jn 1:42); he denied Jesus three times (Mk 14:66–72) but became a bold evangelist. He wrote the books of 1 and 2 Peter.

PHARAOH—the title given to the ruler of Egypt.

PHARISEES—a group of Jews who obeyed very strictly both God's laws and all their own rules about God's laws.

| Mt | 5: 20 | surpasses that of the *P* |

PHILIP—1. one of the twelve apostles (Mt 10:3); 2. a deacon (Ac 6:1–7) and evangelist in Samaria; he witnessed to an Ethiopian (Ac 8:4–40).

PHILISTINES—enemies of the Israelites throughout much of Old Testament history; they were especially powerful during the reigns of Saul and David.

PILATE—the governor of Judea who questioned Jesus (Lk 22:66–23:25) and then sent him to Herod (Lk 23:6–12). Pilate finally consented to Jesus' crucifixion when the crowds chose Barabbas rather than Jesus to be released (Lk 23:13–25).

PLAGUE—1. a disease that kills many people, such as the plague of boils; 2. an event that causes much suffering or loss, especially a trouble in which there is a great number of offending agents, such as the plague of locusts.

PLOWSHARE—the pointed part of the plow; it cuts into the soil to make rows.

PLUNDER—1. (v.) to loot or rob during a war; 2. (n.) property taken by plundering.

POMEGRANATE—a reddish fruit about the size of an orange. It has many seeds and a juicy pulp.

POOR—those who have little money.

Dt	15: 4	there should be no p among you,
Isa	61: 1	me to preach good news to the p.
Mt	26: 11	The p you will always have
1Co	13: 3	If I give all I possess to the p
2Co	8: 9	yet for your sakes he became p,

PORTICO—a porch, usually at the front of a building.

| 2Ch | 3: 4 | The p at the front of the temple |

PRAISE—1. (v.) to glorify; to say good things about someone or something; 2. (n.) approval; worship.

Ex	15: 2	He is my God, and I will p him,
Ps	119:175	Let me live that I may p you,
Eph	1: 12	might be for the p of his glory.

PRAY—to talk with God.

2Ch	7: 14	will humble themselves and p
Mt	6: 5	"And when you p, do not be like
Ro	8: 26	do not know what we ought to p
1Th	5:16,17	Be joyful always; p continually;

PRECEPT—command; law; rule.

| Ps | 19: 8 | The p of the LORD are right, |
| Ps | 119: 69 | I keep your p with all my heart. |

PREDESTINE—to decide or decree ahead of time.

| Ro | 8: 30 | And those he p, he also called; |
| Eph | 1: 5 | he p us to be adopted |

PRIEST (PRIESTHOOD)—a Levite who offered sacrifices and prayers to God for the people.

| 1Pe | 2: 9 | you are a chosen people, a royal p, |

PROFANE—to make a holy thing impure by treating it with disrespect or irreverence.

| Lev | 22: 32 | Do not p my holy name. |

PROPHECY—a message from God that a prophet brings to the people.

| 1Co | 13: 8 | where there are p, they will cease; |
| 2Pe | 1: 20 | you must understand that no p |

PROPHESY—to give the message of God to the people.

| Joel | 2: 28 | Your sons and daughters will p, |
| 1Co | 14: 39 | my brothers, be eager to p, |

PROPHET—a person who receives messages from God to tell to his people. A prophet is called by God to speak for him.

Dt	18: 18	up for them a p like you
Lk	24: 25	believe all that the p have spoken!
Ac	10: 43	All the p testify about him that
2Pe	1: 19	word of the p made more certain,

PROSTRATE—lying face down on the ground.

PROVERBS—1. wise sayings; 2. (cap) a book of the Bible that contains many wise sayings.

PSALMS—1. poetry written to praise God; 2. (cap) a book of the Bible that contains many psalms.

| Eph | 5: 19 | Speak to one another with p, |

PURE—perfectly free from fault or blemish.

| Ps | 51: 10 | Create in me a p heart, O God, |

PURIM—an annual Jewish holiday celebrating Queen Esther's rescue of the Jews when Haman plotted to destroy them.

RABBI—a teacher of Jewish law.

RACHEL—the daughter of Laban (Ge 29:16); she became Jacob's wife (Ge 29:28) and bore him two sons, Joseph and Benjamin (Ge 30:22–24; 35:16–24).

RANSOM—the price paid to get back a person who is held as a slave. Because people are slaves of sin, a ransom has to be paid, which was the death of the sinless one, Jesus.

Mt 20: 28   and to give his life as a *r* for many."
Heb 9: 15   as a *r* to set them free

REAP—1. to cut down grain at harvest time; to gather a crop together; 2. to get as a result or reward.

Gal 6: 7   A man *r* what he sows.

REBEKAH—Isaac's wife (Ge 24); the mother of Esau and Jacob (Ge 25:19–26). With her encouragement Jacob tricked his father into giving him the blessing that belonged to Esau (Ge 27:1–17).

REBUKE—to scold sharply.

2Ti 4: 2   correct, *r* and encourage
Rev 3: 19   Those whom I love I *r*

RECONCILE (RECONCILIATION)—to return to friendship after a quarrel; human beings are 'reconciled' to God through Christ.

Mt 5: 24   First go and be *r* to your brother;
Ro 5: 10   we were *r* to him through the death
2Co 5: 18   and gave us the ministry of *r*.

REDEEM (REDEMPTION)—1. to free from evil by paying a price (Gal 3:13); 2. to buy back.

Gal 3: 13   Christ *r* us from the curse
Eph 1: 7   In him we have *r* through his blood,
Col 1: 14   in whom we have *r*, the forgiveness

RED SEA—the body of water the Israelites crossed in a miraculous way when they were running from slavery in Egypt.

REHOBOAM—the son of Solomon; he became king after his father's death (1Ki 11:43). Because of his harsh treatment of the people, Israel was divided into two kingdoms (1Ki 12:1–24; 14:21–31).

REIGN—the time during which a king or other official rules.

REJOICE—to express joy or gladness.

Ps 118: 24   let us *r* and be glad in it.
Lk 1: 47   and my spirit *r* in God my Savior,
Php 4: 4   *R* in the Lord always.

REMNANT—a small part remaining; a small surviving group.

REPENT (REPENTANCE)—to turn away from sin; to be sorry for what one has done and to promise not to do it again.

Mt 4: 17   "*R*, for the kingdom of heaven is
Lk 3: 8   Produce fruit in keeping with *r*.
Ac 2: 38   Peter replied, "*R* and be baptized,

REPROACH—1. (*v.*) to blame or accuse; 2. (*n.*) something for which one can be blamed or criticized.

RESURRECTION—the act of coming back to life after being dead.

Jn 11: 25   Jesus said to her, "I am the *r*
Ro 1: 4   Son of God by his *r* from the dead:
1Co 15: 12   some of you say that there is no *r*

RETRIBUTION—punishment for doing wrong.

Jer 51: 56   For the LORD is a God of *r*;

REUBEN—oldest son of Jacob and founder of the tribe of the same name.

REVELATION—the act of making known or telling about.

Gal 1: 12   I received it by *r* from Jesus Christ.
Rev 1: 1   *r* of Jesus Christ, which God gave

REVERENCE (REVERE)—a deep respect, honor and awe.

Ps 5: 7   in *r* will I bow down
Col 3: 22   of heart and *r* for the Lord.

RIGHTEOUS (RIGHTEOUSNESS)—being "in the right" in relation to God; "not guilty" before God.

Isa 64: 6   and all our *r* acts are like filthy rags;
Ro 3: 10   "There is no one *r*, not even one;

ROME—1. the empire that controlled much of the known world at the time of Christ; 2. the capital city of the Roman Empire, located in Italy.

RUTH—a Moabite widow who went with her mother-in-law Naomi to Bethlehem (Ru 1). There she gathered the gleanings from the field of Boaz (Ru 2), whom she later married (Ru 3–4:12). She was an ancestor of David (Ru 4:13–22) and of Jesus (Mt 1:5).

RUTHLESS—merciless; cruel.

Hab 1: 6 that *r* and impetuous people,
Ro 1: 31 they are senseless, faithless, heartless, *r*

SABBATH—the seventh day of the week; the Jewish day of rest and worship. It extended from Friday sunset until Saturday sunset.
Ex 20: 8 "Remember the *S* day

SACKCLOTH—a rough cloth, usually woven from goats' hair. Clothing made of sackcloth was worn as a sign of mourning for the dead or as a sign that a person was sorry for his or her sins.

SACRED—holy; set apart for God in a special way.

SACRIFICE—1. (*v.*) to offer something as a gift to God; 2. (*n.*) an offering given to God. In the Old Testament God commanded the people to pay for their sins by sacrificing the blood of cattle, lambs, goats, doves or pigeons. These sacrifices were pictures of Jesus' coming as a once-for-all sacrifice for sinners.
Ex 12: 27 'It is the Passover *s* to the LORD,
1Sa 15: 22 to obey is better than *s*,
Ro 12: 1 to offer your bodies as living *s*,
Heb 9: 28 so Christ was *s* once
1Jn 2: 2 He is the atoning *s* for our sins,

SADDUCEES—a group of Jewish leaders, many of them priests. Unlike the Pharisees, the Sadducees did not believe in a resurrection of the dead, but they agreed with the Pharisees in their hatred of Jesus.
Mk 12: 18 *S*, who say there is no resurrection,

SAINTS—Christians; people whom God has made holy. A saint can be either a Christian who is alive on earth or one who is already in heaven.
Ro 8: 27 intercedes for the *s* in accordance
Eph 1: 1 To the *s* in Ephesus,

SALVATION—deliverance from the guilt and power of sin. By his death and resurrection, Jesus brings salvation to people who believe in him.
Ps 27: 1 The LORD is my light and my *s*
Lk 2: 30 For my eyes have seen your *s*,
Ac 4: 12 *S* is found in no one else,
2Co 7: 10 brings repentance that leads to *s*
Php 2: 12 to work out your *s* with fear

Heb 2: 3 escape if we ignore such a great *s*?

SAMARITAN—a person who lived in or came from Samaria. Because the Samaritans were only partly Jewish and worshiped God differently from the Jews, Jews from Judea and Galilee hated the Samaritans. They would go out of their way to travel around Samaria (Lk 10:30–37).

SAMSON—an Israelite judge who was known for his great strength. He was betrayed by Delilah but in the end was used by God to punish the Philistines (Jdg 16).

SAMUEL—often called the last of Israel's judges and the first of her prophets (see also Heb 11:32). His birth was earnestly prayed for by his mother Hannah (1Sa 1:10–18), and when he was old enough she brought him to the temple and he was dedicated to the Lord (1Sa 1:21–28). There he was raised by Eli (1Sa 2:11; 18–26) and was called to be a prophet (1Sa 3).

SANCTIFY (SANCTIFICATION)—to make holy; sanctification is the ongoing work of the Holy Spirit in the hearts of believers.
Ro 15: 16 to God, *s* by the Holy Spirit.
1Th 5: 23 *s* you through and through.
2Th 2: 13 through the *s* work of the Spirit

SANCTUARY—a place where God is worshiped; a holy place.

SANHEDRIN—the ruling council of the Jews in Jesus' time. It was made up of seventy men, and the leader was the high priest. The Sanhedrin could decide whether someone was innocent or guilty of breaking a Jewish law, but it could not put anyone to death without the permission of the Roman governor.
Mk 14: 55 the whole *S* were looking for evidence

SARAH—the wife of Abraham and mother of Isaac; first called Sarai (Ge 11:29–31). God promised her that, though she had been barren throughout her life, she would give birth to a son in her old age (Ge 17:15–21; 18:10–15).

SATAN—the devil; the leader of the fallen spirits; the most powerful enemy of God and humans.
Mk 4: 15 *S* comes and takes away the word

2Co 11: 14   for *S* himself masquerades
Rev 12: 9   serpent called the devil, or *S,*

SATRAP—the governor of a province in ancient Persia.

SAUL—1. the first king of Israel (1Sa 9–10). He was anointed by Samuel but was later rejected by God because of disobedience; David was chosen to be his successor; 2. see Paul.

SAVED—1. (*v.*) rescued from danger; 2. (*n.*) people who acknowledge that by Jesus' death they have been rescued from the punishment of death that their sins deserve.

Ro 10: 13   on the name of the Lord will be
             s."
Eph 2: 8   For it is by grace you have been

SAVIOR—a name for Jesus that means he saves his people from sin.

Lk 1: 47   and my spirit rejoices in God
             my *S,*
1Ti 4: 10   who is the *S* of all men,
1Jn 4: 14   Son to be the *S* of the world.

SCOURGE—to whip.

2Ch 10: 11   My father *s* you with whips;

SCRIBE—a person with the important task of copying letters, books and legal papers.

SCRIPTURE—all or part of the Bible. When the Bible uses this word it means the Old Testament, since the New Testament had not yet been written. Today we call the Old and New Testaments the Bible or Scripture.

Jn 10: 35   and the *S* cannot be broken
2Ti 3: 16   All *S* is God-breathed
2Pe 1: 20   that no prophecy of *S* came
             about

SCROLL—a book made of a long piece of leather or paper that was rolled around a stick at both ends.

Eze 3: 1   eat what is before you, eat this *s;*

SEAL—1. a tool with a design raised on it or cut into it; 2. the mark made by pressing this tool onto wax, paper or other soft material. A seal was used to close a letter or legal paper or to prove the authority of the paper.

2Co 1: 22   set his *s* of ownership on us,
Rev 5: 2   "Who is worthy to break the *s*

SECT—a group of people who hold one or more beliefs in common; especially, a small religious group that has separated from a larger group.

SEER—a prophet; a person who, with God's help, can see what will happen in the future.

SELFISH—centered on oneself; not interested in others.

Php 2: 3   Do nothing out of *s* ambition

SENNACHERIB—an Assyrian king who raided Judah during the time of Hezekiah.

SEXUAL IMMORALITY—using sex in ways God says are wrong.

1Co 6: 13   body is not meant for *s* immoral-
             ity,
1Th 4: 3   that you should avoid *s* immoral-
             ity,

SHEKEL—a specific weight of silver, used as money.

SHEM—one of the three sons of Noah (Ge 5:32). He, along with his brother Japheth, covered his father when he was naked (Ge 9:21–31). Abraham was one of his descendants (Ge 11:10–32).

SHEPHERD—someone who takes care of a flock of sheep. It is often used in the Bible as a figure of speech for anyone who cares for a group of people.

Ps 23: 1   LORD is my *s,* I shall not be in
             want.
Jer 31: 10   will watch over his flock like a *s.'*
Jn 10: 11   The good *s* lays down his life
Ac 20: 28   Be *s* of the church of God,

SICKLE—a tool with a long, curved blade and a short handle, used for cutting grain.

SIGNET—a ring with a design on it. The design was stamped in wax to seal a letter or legal paper. Signet rings were usually worn by people in authority.

SILAS—a member of the church in Jerusalem; he traveled with Paul.

SIMON—1. see Peter; 2. one of the twelve apostles; also called the Zealot (Mt 10:4; Ac 1:13); 3. a sorcerer in Samaria who had great influence on the Samaritan people during the early days of the church; he was severely rebuked by Peter (Ac 8:9–24) for attempting to buy the power of the Holy Spirit.

SIN—1. (v.) to break the law of God; 2. (n.) the act of not doing what God wants.

Nu	32: 23	be sure that your *s* will find you
Ps	51: 2	and cleanse me from my *s.*
Ps	119: 11	that I might not *s* against you.
Isa	1: 18	"Though your *s* are like scarlet,
Mt	1: 21	he will save his people from their *s.*"
Lk	11: 4	Forgive us our *s,*
Jn	1: 29	who takes away the *s* of the world!
Ro	3: 23	for all have *s* and fall short
Ro	6: 23	For the wages of *s* is death,
2Co	5: 21	God made him who had no *s* to be *s*
1Jn	1: 9	If we confess our *s,* he is faithful

SINAI, MOUNT—the mountain where Moses received the Ten Commandments (Ex 19–20).

SINNER—a person who breaks the law of God.

Ps	1: 1	or stand in the way of *s*
Mt	9: 13	come to call the righteous, but *s.*"
Lk	15: 7	in heaven over one *s* who repents
Lk	18: 13	'God, have mercy on me, a *s.*'
Ro	5: 8	While we were still *s,* Christ died

SLAVE—1. a person who is owned by another; 2. a person who is dominated or controlled by an outside force.

| Ro | 7: 14 | I am unspiritual, sold as a *s* to sin. |
| Gal | 3: 28 | *s* nor free, male nor female, |

SLUGGARD—a lazy person.

SNARE—a trap; something risky that tempts or endangers a person.

SODOM AND GOMORRAH—the two cities destroyed by God because the people were so wicked.

| Ge | 19: 24 | rained down burning sulfur on *S* |

SOLOMON—the son of David and Bathsheba (2Sa 12:24). He became king of Israel after David died (1Ki 1). He asked God for wisdom and was given it (1Ki 3), and he built the temple (1Ki 5–7). His many foreign wives turned his heart away from God (1Ki 11:1–13).

SON OF MAN—a title Jesus used for himself to show his humanity as distinct from his divinity. It was also a reference to the Messiah prophesied about in Daniel 7:13.

Mt	20: 18	and the *S* of Man will be betrayed
Mk	14: 62	you will see the *S* of Man sitting
Lk	19: 10	For the *S* of Man came to seek
Jn	3: 14	so the *S* of Man must be lifted up,

SOUL—the spiritual part of a person.

Dt	6: 5	with all your *s* and with all your
Ps	23: 3	he restores my *s.*
Mt	10: 28	kill the body but cannot kill the *s.*
Mt	11: 29	and you will find rest for your *s.*
Mt	16: 26	yet forfeits his *s?* Or what can
Mt	22: 37	with all your *s* and with all your

SOVEREIGN—having authority over everything; often used in Scripture as a descriptive title for God, "Sovereign LORD."

SOW—to plant seeds. In Jesus' time seeds were sown by scattering them by hand over the ground.

Job	4: 8	and those who *s* trouble reap it.
Mk	4: 3	A farmer went out to *s* his seed.
Gal	6: 7	A man reaps what he *s.*

SPIRIT—1. the part of a person that is not the body; the soul; 2. a being who does not have a body; 3. (cap.) see Holy Spirit.

Ps	31: 5	Into your hands I commit my *s;*
Eze	36: 26	you a new heart and put a new *s*
Mt	5: 3	"Blessed are the poor in *s,*
Mt	26: 41	*s* is willing, but the body is weak."
1Jn	4: 1	Dear friends, do not believe every *s,*

SPOILS—booty or plunder taken from an enemy in war.

SPRINGS—a source of water coming up from the ground.

| Dt | 8: 7 | with *s* flowing in the valleys |
| Rev | 7: 17 | lead them to *s* of living water. |

STAFF—a stick used to lean on; a rod used by a shepherd.

| Ps | 23: 4 | your rod and your *s,* |

STATUTES—established rules or laws.

| Ps | 19: 7 | *s* of the LORD are trustworthy, |

STEADFAST—settled; not changing or wavering.

Ps 51: 10   and renew a *s* spirit within me.

STEPHEN—one of the first seven men to serve the Jerusalem church (Ac 6:5); he became the first Christian martyr (Ac 7:60).

STIFF-NECKED—stubborn.

STONE—to kill or to try to kill someone by throwing rocks or stones.

STRENGTH—power; forcefulness.

Ex 15: 2   The LORD is my *s* and my song;
Dt   6: 5   all your soul and with all your *s*.
Ps 46: 1   God is our refuge and *s*,
Isa 40: 31   will renew their *s*.
Php 4: 13   through him who gives me *s*.

STRONGHOLD—a fortified place; a place of security.

1Sa 24: 22   David and his men went up to the *s*.
Ps 27: 1   The LORD is the *s* of my life—

SUBMISSION—humbleness; obedience.

1Co 14: 34   but must be in *s*, as the Law says.
1Ti   2: 11   learn in quietness and full *s*.

SUBMIT—to willingly yield to another.

Ro 13: 1   Everyone must *s* himself
Eph 5: 21   *S* to one another out of reverence
Jas   4: 7   *S* yourselves, then, to God.

SUFFER—to bear or endure something painful.

Mk   8: 31   the Son of Man must *s* many things
1Co 12: 26   If one part *s*, every part *s* with it;

SUFFERING—the experience of enduring pain.

Isa 53: 3   of sorrows, and familiar with *s*.
Ac   5: 41   worthy of *s* disgrace for the Name.

SWEAR—to promise emphatically or earnestly.

1Sa 30: 15   "*S* to me before God that you will

SYMBOL—an object or action that stands for or suggests something else. The cross is a symbol of Jesus' death.

SYNAGOGUE—the Jewish place of worship and religious teaching.

Lk   4: 16   the Sabbath day he went into the *s*,
Ac 17: 2   custom was, Paul went into the *s*,

TABERNACLE—the tent used by the Israelites for meeting with God; the place where God chose to show his presence. The tabernacle was made by God's command and according to his plans. It is described in detail in Exodus 26.

Ex 40: 34   the glory of the LORD filled the *t*

TALENT—a large amount of silver or gold, worth very much money.

Mt 25: 15   to another one *t*, each according

TEMPLE—1. the place where the Jewish people worshiped and sacrificed in Jerusalem; the first temple was built by King Solomon as a house for God; 2. any place of worship. In this sense, the human body is referred to as a temple (1Co 6:19).

1Ki   8: 27   How much less this *t* I have built!
Ac 17: 24   does not live in *t* built by hands.
2Co   6: 16   For we are the *t* of the living God.

TEMPTATION—trying to get someone to do wrong.

Mt   4: 1   into the desert to be *t* by the devil.
1Co 10: 13   No *t* has seized you except what

TENANT—one who rents land or a house from a landlord.

TETRARCH—a ruler over one-fourth of a kingdom.

THADDAEUS—one of the twelve apostles (Mk 3:18); son of James and probably also known as Judas (Lk 6:16; Ac 1:13).

THANKS—the expression of gratitude.

1Ch 16: 8   Give *t* to the LORD, call
Ps 100: 4   give *t* to him and praise his name.
1Co 15: 57   *t* be to God! He gives us the victory
2Co   9: 15   *T* be to God for his indescribable
1Th   5: 18   give *t* in all circumstances,

THOMAS—one of the twelve apostles (Lk 6:15; Ac 1:13); he doubted Jesus' resurrection but, upon seeing Jesus, he believed (Jn 20:24–28).

THUMMIM—see Urim.

THRESHING FLOOR—the place where grain was trampled by oxen or beaten with a stick to separate it from the stalk.

TIMOTHY—fellow-traveler and official representative of the apostle Paul. He joined Paul on his second missionary journey (Ac 16–20), and at one point in this journey Paul sent him to minister to the church at Corinth (1Co 4:17; 16:10). He was the leader of the church at Ephesus (1Ti 1:3) and a co-writer with Paul (1Th 1:1; 2Ti 1:1; Phm 1).

TITHE—the giving to God of one-tenth of what one earns.
Lev 27: 30 " 'A *t* of everything from the land,
Mal 3: 10 the whole *t* into the storehouse,

TITUS—a Gentile co-worker with Paul (Gal 2:1–3; 2Ti 4:10). Paul sent him to Corinth to aid in solving some of the problems there (2Co 2:13; 7–8; 12:18).

TOMB—a burial place. In Bible times, a tomb was often either a cave or a cavity dug into a stone cliff, with a large stone rolled in front to close it.
Mt 27: 65 make the *t* as secure as you know
Lk 24: 2 the stone rolled away from the *t*,

TORMENT—extreme pain or anguish; agony.
2Co 12: 7 a messenger of Satan, to *t* me.

TRANSFIGURE—to change the appearance of; to make bright and glorious.
Mt 17: 2 There he was *t* before them.

TRANSGRESSION—sin; disobeying the law of God.
Ps 32: 1 whose *t* are forgiven,
Isa 53: 5 But he was pierced for our *t*,
Eph 2: 1 you were dead in your *t* and sins,

TRESPASS—sin; wrongdoing.
Ro 5: 17 For if, by the *t* of the one man,

TRIBUTE—payment by one ruler or nation to another as an act of submission or in order to guarantee protection.

TRUE—certain; exactly right.
Ps 119:160 All your words are *t*,
Jn 17: 3 the only *t* God, and Jesus Christ,
Ro 3: 4 Let God be *t*, and every man a liar.
Php 4: 8 whatever is *t*, whatever is noble,

TRUST—firm belief or faith in another.
Ps 37: 3 *T* in the LORD and do good;
Pr 3: 5 *T* in the LORD with all your heart
Isa 30: 15 in quietness and *t* is your strength,
Jn 14: 1 *T* in God; *t* also in me.
1Co 4: 2 been given a *t* must prove faithful.

TRUTH—that which conforms to the facts.
Ps 51: 6 Surely you desire *t*
Zec 8: 16 are to do: Speak the *t* to each other,
Jn 8: 32 know the *t* and the *t*
Jn 14: 6 I am the way and the *t* and the life.
Ro 1: 25 They exchanged the *t* of God
1Co 13: 6 in evil but rejoices with the *t*.
Eph 4: 15 Instead, speaking the *t* in love,
Heb 10: 26 received the knowledge of the *t*,
1Jn 1: 6 we lie and do not live by the *t*.
1Jn 1: 8 deceive ourselves and the *t* is not

TUNIC—a long shirt worn by men in Bible times.
Lk 6: 29 do not stop him from taking your *t*.

TURBAN—a head-covering made by winding a cloth around the head.

UNBELIEF—doubt.
Mk 9: 24 help me overcome my *u*!"

UNBELIEVER—one who does not believe in Jesus.

UNCLEAN—morally or spiritually impure; unclean animals were those which the Israelites were not allowed to sacrifice or to eat.

UNITY—being one.
Ps 133: 1 when brothers live together in *u*
Col 3: 14 them all together in perfect *u*.

UNLEAVENED BREAD—bread made without yeast. It is usually flat, like a pancake or cracker.
Ex 12: 17 "Celebrate the Feast of *U* Bread,

UPRIGHT—honest; doing what is right and good.

URIM AND THUMMIM—objects that were placed on the vest of the high priest; used to determine God's will for the nation of Israel.

USURY—very high and unfair interest charged on a loan.

Ne   5: 10   But let the exacting of *u* stop!

VAIN—worthless; unsuccessful; foolish. "In vain" means without success or result.

VENGEANCE—hurt or punishment done to another person who has done something wrong against another.

Isa 34: 8   For the LORD has a day of *v,*

VILE—disgusting, evil.

VIPER—1. a venomous snake; 2. a treacherous or vicious person.

VIRGIN—a woman or girl who has never had sexual intercourse.

Isa   · 7: 14   The *v* will be with child
Mt   1: 23   "The *v* will be with child

VISION—a dream from God.

Nu   12: 6   I reveal myself to him in *v,*
Joel 2: 28   your young men will see *v.*
Ac   26: 19   disobedient to the *v* from heaven.

VOW—a solemn promise made before God or to God.

Jdg 11: 30   Jephthah made a *v* to the LORD:
Ps 116: 14   I will fulfill my *v* to the LORD

WAGES—payment received for work completed.

WALK—to follow a certain course.

Ps   1: 1   who does not *w* in the counsel
Isa   2: 5   let us *w* in the light of the LORD.
Mic   6: 8   and to *w* humbly with your God.
2Jn 6 his command is that you *w* in love.

WAY—the means of getting somewhere; the path.

2Sa 22: 31   "As for God, his *w* is perfect;
Ps   1: 1   or stand in the *w* of sinners
Ps   37: 5   Commit your *w* to the LORD;
Isa 53: 6   each of us has turned to his own *w;*
Jn   14: 6   "I am the *w* and the truth
1Co 12: 31   will show you the most excellent *w.*

WEANED—to help a child or animal begin to eat solid food rather than his or her mother's milk.

WHOLEHEARTED—sincere; devoted without holding anything back.

WILL—desire; seeking God's will means looking for what God wants to be done.

Ps 143: 10   Teach me to do your *w,*
Mt   6: 10   your *w* be done
Mt   26: 39   Yet not as I *w,* but as you *w."*
Ro   12: 2   and approve what God's *w* is
Rev   4: 11   and by your *w* they were created

WINEPRESS—a vat or tub in which the juice of grapes is pressed out. Used in the Bible as a symbol for the anger of God against wickedness.

Rev 14: 19   into the great *w* of God's wrath.

WISDOM—the understanding that comes from God.

Lk   2: 52   And Jesus grew in *w* and stature,
Jas   1: 5   of you lack, *w,* he should ask God,

WITNESS—one who personally sees an event take place.

Ac   22: 15   You will be his *w* to all men

WOE—'great misery; distress.

Isa   6: 5   "*W* to me!" I cried.
Lk   11: 42   "*W* to you Pharisees, because you

WORD—1. the means of expressing oneself through language; 2. the Bible, as God's written message to people; 3. (cap.) Jesus is the Word sent from God because his life on earth told the message of God.

Jn   1: 14   The *W* became flesh and made his
Heb   4: 12   For the *w* of God is living

WORLD—1. the earth and those who live in it; 2. the secular, as opposed to the spiritual or religious.

Mt   5: 14   "You are the light of the *w.*
Jn   1: 29   who takes away the sin of the *w!*
Jn   3: 16   so loved the *w* that he gave his one
Jn   8: 12   he said, "I am the light of the *w.*

WORLDLY—loving the things of the world more than the things of God.

Tit   2: 12   to ungodliness and *w* passions,

WORSHIP—1. (v.) to give praise, honor and respect to God; 2. (n.) reverence given to God.

| Ps | 95: 6 | Come, let us bow down in w, |
| Jn | 4:24 | and his worshipers must w in spirit |

WORTHY—having value; honorable; deserving.

1Ch 16: 25	For great is the LORD and most w
Eph	4: 1	to live a life w of the calling you
Rev	5: 2	"Who is w to break the seals

WRATH—great anger; the strong anger of God.

| Pr | 15: 1 | A gentle answer turns away w, |
| Ro | 5: 9 | saved from God's w through him! |

XERXES—king of Persia; he made Esther, a young Jewess, his queen (Est 2:15–18).

YEAST—the ingredient that makes dough rise; sometimes a figure of speech for the influence someone has over others.

| Mt | 16: 6 | guard against the y of the Pharisees |
| Gal | 5: 9 | little y works through the whole |

YIELD—1. to submit; 2. to grow or produce fruit.

| Ps | 67: 6 | Then the land will y its harvest, |
| Isa | 48: 11 | I will not y my glory to another. |

YOKE—1. (v.) to join together; 2. (n.) a wooden bar that goes over the necks of two animals, usually oxen. The yoke holds the animals together as they pull an object, such as a plow or a cart.

| Mt | 11: 29 | Take my y upon you and learn |
| 2Co | 6: 14 | Do not be y together |

ZACCHAEUS—a tax collector who climbed a tree in order to see Jesus.

ZEAL—eagerness; strong desire.

| Ro | 12: 11 | Never be lacking in z, |

ZEALOT—a member of the Jewish group that wanted to fight against and overthrow the Roman government.

ZECHARIAH—a prophet and priest who returned to Jerusalem from the Babylonian captivity; he encouraged the Jews to rebuild the temple (Ezr 5:1; 6:14; Zec 1:1).

ZERUBBABEL—a descendant of David (1Ch 3:19); he led the return of the Jews from the Babylonian captivity (Ezr 1–3; Ne 7:7; Hag 1–2; Zec 4).

ZION—1. the hill on which the city of Jerusalem first stood; David's royal palace and the temple were both built on Mount Zion; 2. the entire city of Jerusalem.

| Jer | 50: 5 | They will ask the way to Z |
| Ro | 11: 26 | "The deliverer will come from Z; |

Peter's escape from prison: Acts chapter 12, verses 1–19, *1441*
Paul and Silas in prison: Acts chapter 16, verses 16–40, *1447*

MIRACLES OF JESUS
(in Biblical order)

Healing of individuals
Man with leprosy: Matthew chapter 8, verses 1–4, *1268*; Mark chapter 1, verses 40–44, *1307*; Luke chapter 5, verses 12–14, *1345*
Roman centurion's servant: Matthew chapter 8, verses 5–13, *1268*; Luke chapter 7, verses 1–10, *1348*
Peter's mother-in-law: Matthew chapter 8, verses 14–17, *1269*; Mark chapter 1, verses 29–31, *1307*; Luke chapter 4, verses 38–39, *1344*
Two demon-possessed men from Gadara: Matthew chapter 8, verses 28–34, *1269*
Paralyzed man: Matthew chapter 9, verses 1–8, *1269*; Mark chapter 2, verses 1–12, *1308*; Luke chapter 5, verses 17–26, *1345*
Two blind men: Matthew chapter 9, verses 27–31, *1270*
Man mute and possessed: Matthew chapter 9, verses 32–33, *1271*
Man blind, mute and possessed: Matthew chapter 12, verse 22, *1274*
Canaanite woman's daughter: Matthew chapter 15, verses 21–28, *1280*
Boy with epilepsy: Matthew chapter 17, verses 14–18, *1282*
Two blind men: Matthew chapter 20, verses 29–34, *1287*
Man with a shriveled hand: Matthew chapter 12, verses 9–13, *1274*; Mark chapter 3, verses 1–5, *1309*; Luke chapter 6, verses 6–11, *1346*
Man with an evil spirit: Mark chapter 1, verses 23–26, *1306*; Luke chapter 4, verses 33–36, *1344*
Deaf mute: Mark chapter 7, verses 31–37, *1316*
Blind man: Mark chapter 8, verses 22–26, *1317*
Bartimaeus, or one blind man: Mark chapter 10, verses 46–52, *1322*; Luke chapter 18, verses 35–43, *1369*
Woman with bleeding: Luke chapter 8, verses 43–48, *1352*
Crippled woman: Luke chapter 13, verses 11–13, *1361*
Man with dropsy: Luke chapter 14, verses 1–4, *1362*
Ten men with leprosy: Luke chapter 17, verses 11–19, *1367*
The high priest's servant: Luke chapter 22, verses 50–51, *1375*
Royal official's son: John chapter 4, verses 46–54, *1389*
Man at the pool of Bethesda: John chapter 5, verses 1–9, *1389*

Control of nature
Calming the storm: Matthew chapter 8, verses 23–27, *1269*; Mark chapter 4, verses 35–41, *1311*; Luke chapter 8, verses 22–25, *1351*
Feeding of 5,000: Matthew chapter 14, verses 1–21, *1278*; Mark chapter 6, verses 35–44, *1314*; Luke chapter 9, verses 12–17, *1353*; John chapter 6, verses 5–15, *1391*
Walking on water: Matthew chapter 14, verses 22–23, *1278*; Mark chapter 6, verses 45–52, *1315*; John chapter 6, verses 16–21, *1392*
Feeding of 4,000: Matthew chapter 15, verses 29 – 39, *1280*; Mark chapter 8, verses 1 – 9, *1316*
Fish with coin: Matthew chapter 17, verses 24–27, *1283*
Fig tree withers: Matthew chapter 21, verses 18–22, *1288*; Mark chapter 11, verses 12–14, 20–25, *1322*
Huge catch of fish: Luke chapter 5, verses 1 – 11, *1345*; John chapter 21 verses 1 – 11, *1419*
Water into wine: John chapter 2, verses 1–11, *1384*

Raising the dead
Jairus's daughter: Mark chapter 5, verses 22–42, *1312*
Widow at Nain's son: Luke chapter 7, verses 11–15, *1349*
Lazarus: John chapter 11, verses 1–44, *1401*

PARABLES OF JESUS
(in alphabetical order)

TEACHINGS OF JESUS
(in alphabetical order)